Collins
Thesaurus
A–Z

fourth edition 2001

latest reprint 2004

HarperCollins Publishers
Westerhill Road, Bishopbriggs, Glasgow G64 2QT
Great Britain

www.collins.co.uk

Collins® and Bank of English® are registered trademarks
of HarperCollins Publishers Limited

ISBN 0-00-719588-5

A catalogue record for this book is available from the British Library

Corpus Acknowledgements
We would like to thank those authors and publishers who
kindly gave permission for copyright material to be used
in the Bank of English. We would also like to thank
Times Newspapers Ltd for providing valuable data.

Typeset by Ann Rautenbach

Printed and bound in Great Britain by
Clays Ltd, St Ives plc

EDITORIAL STAFF

FOREWORD

Collins Paperback Thesaurus, which was first published in 1986, has proved itself to be an immensely popular language resource. It allows you to look up a word and find a wide selection of alternatives that can replace it. It is, therefore, tremendously helpful when you are trying to find different ways of expressing yourself, as well as being an invaluable aid for crosswords and puzzles.

Collins thesauruses have always been designed to give the user as much help as possible in finding the right word for any occasion. Collins pioneered the A-Z arrangement of main entry words. This lets you go straight to any word without having to resort to an index, just as if you were looking up a word in a dictionary. This arrangement is continued in the new **Paperback Thesaurus**, but the number of main entry words has been increased, thus giving you an even greater chance of finding the word you want. At the same time, the list of alternative words (synonyms) for each main entry word has been not only increased but reviewed so that the widest possible choice of the most helpful alternatives are included in each case. The new edition also takes account of recent changes in the language, with new terms like *gridlock, nerd* and *Internet* included as main entry words, and words and idioms like *gut-wrenching, in the loop, big hitter* and *go pear-shaped* being found among the synonyms.

The **Collins Paperback Thesaurus** also includes lists of antonyms at many of the main entry words. These lists give a range of opposites which provide you with another way of expressing yourself. For instance, if you want to say that something is *difficult*, it can sometimes be effective to use a negative construction and, taking a word from the antonym list, you may think of a phrase such as "*by no means straightforward.*"

This new edition further demonstrates Collins' commitment to helping the user. As part of an innovative design, key synonyms have been highlighted in bold type and placed first in each list. This layout enables you to see immediately which sense of the word is referred to. This is particularly helpful when a main entry word has a number of different senses. It also gives you an idea of which synonym is the closest alternative to the word you have looked up. Where helpful, the key synonym is also given in bold type at the start of the appropriate list of antonyms in the entry, allowing you to identify at once the particular sense for which these can be used as opposites.

These innovations mean that the **Collins Paperback Thesaurus** continues to provide the user with a treasury of useful words arranged in the most helpful format possible.

FEATURES OF THE THESAURUS

Synonyms
words, listed in alphabetical order, that can be used in place of the headword

Foreign words and phrases

Most helpful synonym
given first and highlighted

Sense numbers
synonyms divided according to meaning to help you find the sense you want

Parts of speech

Antonyms
words, listed in alphabetical order, that mean the opposite of the headword

Labels
show context of use

converge *verb* **= come together**, coincide, combine, concentrate, focus, gather, join, meet, merge, mingle

conversant *adjective* **conversant with = experienced in**, acquainted with, *au fait with*, familiar with, knowledgeable about, practised in, proficient in, skilled in, versed in, well-informed about, well up in (*informal*)

conversation *noun* **= talk**, chat, chinwag (*Brit. informal*), colloquy, communication, communion, confab (*informal*), confabulation, conference, converse, dialogue, discourse, discussion, exchange, gossip, intercourse, powwow, tête-à-tête

conversational *adjective* **= chatty**, colloquial, communicative, informal

converse[1] *verb* **= talk**, chat, commune, confer, discourse, exchange views

converse[2] *noun* **1 = opposite**, antithesis, contrary, obverse, other side of the coin, reverse ♦ *adjective* **2 = opposite**, contrary, counter, reverse, reversed, transposed

conversion *noun* **1 = change**, metamorphosis, transfiguration, transformation, transmogrification (*jocular*), transmutation **2 = adaptation**, alteration, modification, reconstruction, remodelling, reorganization **3 = reformation**, change of heart, proselytization, rebirth, regeneration

convert *verb* **1 = change**, alter, interchange metamorphose, transform, transmogrify (*jocular*), transmute, transpose, turn **2 = adapt**, apply, appropriate, customize, modify, remodel, reorganize, restyle, revise **3 = reform**, baptize, bring to God, convince, proselytize, regenerate, save ♦ *noun* **4 = neophyte**, catechumen, disciple, proselyte

convex *adjective* **= rounded**, bulging, gibbous, outcurved, protuberant
➤ **Antonyms**
concave, cupped, depressed, excavated, hollowed, indented, sunken

convey *verb* **1 = communicate**, disclose, impart, make known, relate, reveal, tell **2 = carry**, bear, bring, conduct, fetch, forward grant, guide, move, send, support, transmit, transport **3** *Law* **= transfer**, bequeath, cede, deliver, demise, devolve, grant, lease, will

conveyance *noun* **1** *Old-fashioned* **= vehicle**, transport **2 = transportation**, carriage, movement, transfer, transference, transmission, transport

convict *verb* **1 = find guilty**, condemn, imprison, pronounce guilty, sentence ♦ *noun* **2 = prisoner**, con (*slang*), criminal, culprit, felon, jailbird, lag (*slang*), malefactor, villain

conviction *noun* **1 = belief**, creed, faith, opinion, persuasion, principle, tenet, view **2**

FEATURES OF THE THESAURUS

= **confidence**, assurance, certainty, certitude, earnestness, fervour, firmness, reliance

convince *verb* = **persuade**, assure, bring round, gain the confidence of, prevail upon, prove to, satisfy, sway, win over

Phrases and idioms

convincing *adjective* = **persuasive**, cogent, conclusive, credible, impressive, incontrovertible, likely, plausible, powerful, probable, telling, verisimilar
➤ **Antonyms**
beyond belief, cock-and-bull (*informal*), dubious, far-fetched, implausible, improbable, inconclusive, incredible, unconvincing, unlikely

convoy *noun* **1** = **escort**, armed guard, attendance, attendant, guard, protection
♦ *verb* **2** = **escort**, accompany, attend, guard, pilot, protect, shepherd, usher

Labels
a label in brackets applies only to the word preceding it

convulse *verb* = **shake**, agitate, churn up, derange, disorder, disturb, shatter, twist, work

convulsion *noun* **1** = **spasm**, contortion, contraction, cramp, fit, paroxysm, seizure, throe (*rare*), tremor **2** = **upheaval**, agitation, commotion, disturbance, furore, shaking, tumult, turbulence

cook up *verb* *Informal* = **invent**, concoct, contrive, devise, dream up, fabricate, improvise, manufacture, plot, prepare, scheme, trump up

a label which is not in brackets relates to the whole of that particular sense

cool *adjective* **1** = **cold**, chilled, chilling, chilly, coldish, nippy, refreshing **2** = **calm**, collected, composed, deliberate, dispassionate, imperturbable, laid-back (*informal*), level-headed, placid, quiet, relaxed, sedate, self-controlled, self-possessed, serene, together (*slang*), unemotional, unexcited, unfazed (*informal*), unruffled **3** = **unfriendly**, aloof, apathetic, distant, frigid, incurious, indifferent, lukewarm, offhand, reserved, standoffish, uncommunicative, unconcerned, unenthusiastic, uninterested, unresponsive, unwelcoming **4** = **impudent**, audacious, bold, brazen, cheeky, impertinent, presumptuous, shameless **5** *Informal* = **sophisticated**, cosmopolitan, elegant, urbane ♦ *verb* **6** = **chill**, cool off, freeze, lose heat, refrigerate **7** = **calm (down)**, abate, allay, assuage, dampen, lessen, moderate, quiet, temper ♦ *noun* **8** *Slang* = **calmness**, composure, control, poise, self-control, self-discipline, self-possession, temper
➤ **Antonyms**
adjective ≠**cold:** lukewarm, moderately hot, sunny, tepid, warm ≠**calm:** agitated, antsy (*informal*), delirious, excited, impassioned, nervous, overwrought, perturbed, tense, troubled, twitchy (*informal*) ≠**unfriendly:** amiable, chummy (*informal*), cordial, friendly, outgoing, receptive, responsive,

Antonym senses
where there is more than one synonym sense, its corresponding antonym list is introduced by the key synonym with a ≠ sign to show which sense the antonym list refers to

A a

abaft *adverb, adjective Nautical* = **behind**, aft, astern

abandon *verb* **1** = **leave**, desert, forsake, jilt, leave behind, leave in the lurch, let (someone) stew in their own juice, strand **2** = **evacuate**, quit, vacate, withdraw from **3** = **give up**, abdicate, cede, relinquish, renounce, resign, surrender, waive, yield **4** = **stop**, desist, discontinue, drop, forgo, kick (*informal*) ♦ *noun* **5** = **wildness**, careless freedom, dash, recklessness, unrestraint, wantonness, wild impulse
➤ **Antonyms**
verb ≠**evacuate:** defend, maintain, uphold ≠**give up:** claim, hold, keep, take ≠**stop:** continue ♦ *noun* ≠**wildness:** control, moderation, restraint

abandoned *adjective* **1** = **left**, cast aside, cast away, cast out, derelict, deserted, discarded, ditched, dropped, forlorn, forsaken, jilted, neglected, outcast, out of the window, rejected, relinquished, stranded **2** = **unoccupied**, vacant **3** = **depraved**, corrupt, debauched, dissipated, dissolute, profligate, reprobate, sinful, wanton, wicked **4** = **uninhibited**, uncontrolled, unrestrained, wild
➤ **Antonyms**
≠**unoccupied:** claimed, kept, maintained, occupied ≠**depraved:** good, high-principled, honest, moral, pure, reputable, righteous, upright, virtuous, worthy ≠**uninhibited:** conscious, inhibited, restrained

abandonment *noun* **1** = **leaving**, dereliction, desertion, forsaking, jilting **2** = **evacuation**, quitting, withdrawal from **3** = **giving up**, abdication, cession, relinquishment, renunciation, resignation, surrender, waiver **4** = **stopping**, desistance, discontinuation, dropping

abase *verb* = **humble**, belittle, bring low, cast down, debase, degrade, demean, demote, denigrate, depress, disgrace, dishonour, downgrade, humiliate, lower, mortify, put in one's place, reduce
➤ **Antonyms**
advance, aggrandize, dignify, elevate, exalt, glorify, honour, prefer, promote, raise, upgrade

abasement *noun* = **humbling**, belittlement, debasement, degradation, demotion, depression, disgrace, dishonour,

downgrading, humiliation, lowering, mortification, reduction, shame

abashed *adjective* = **embarrassed**, affronted, ashamed, astounded, bewildered, chagrined, confounded, confused, discomfited, discomposed, disconcerted, discountenanced, dismayed, humbled, humiliated, mortified, perturbed, shamefaced, taken aback
➤ **Antonyms**
at ease, blatant, bold, brazen, composed, confident, unabashed, unashamed, undaunted, undismayed, unperturbed

abate *verb* = **decrease**, alleviate, appease, attenuate, decline, diminish, dull, dwindle, ease, ebb, fade, lessen, let up, mitigate, moderate, quell, reduce, relax, relieve, sink, slacken, slake, slow, subside, taper off, wane, weaken
➤ **Antonyms**
add to, amplify, augment, boost, enhance, escalate, increase, intensify, magnify, multiply, strengthen

abatement *noun* = **decrease**, alleviation, allowance, attenuation, cessation, decline, diminution, dulling, dwindling, easing, extenuation, fading, lessening, let-up (*informal*), mitigation, moderation, quelling, reduction, relief, remission, slackening, slaking, slowing, tapering off, waning, weakening

abbey *noun* = **monastery**, cloister, convent, friary, nunnery, priory

abbreviate *verb* = **shorten**, abridge, abstract, clip, compress, condense, contract, curtail, cut, epitomize, précis, reduce, summarize, trim, truncate
➤ **Antonyms**
amplify, draw out, elongate, expand, extend, increase, lengthen, prolong, protract, spin out, stretch out

abbreviation *noun* = **shortening**, abridgment, abstract, clipping, compendium, compression, condensation, conspectus, contraction, curtailment, digest, epitome, précis, reduction, résumé, summary, synopsis, trimming, truncation

abdicate *verb* = **give up**, abandon, abjure, abnegate, cede, forgo, quit, relinquish, renounce, resign, retire, step down (*informal*), surrender, vacate, waive, yield

abdication *noun* = **giving up**,

abandonment, abjuration, abnegation, cession, quitting, relinquishment, renunciation, resignation, retiral (*especially Scot.*), retirement, surrender, waiver, yielding

abdominal *adjective* = **gastric**, intestinal, stomachic, stomachical, visceral

abduct *verb* = **kidnap**, carry off, make off with, run away with, run off with, seize, snatch (*slang*)

abduction *noun* = **kidnapping**, carrying off, seizure

aberration *noun* = **oddity**, aberrancy, abnormality, anomaly, defect, deviation, divergence, eccentricity, irregularity, lapse, peculiarity, quirk, rambling, straying, wandering

abet *verb* **1** = **help**, aid, assist, back, condone, connive at, promote, sanction, second, succour, support, sustain, uphold **2** = **encourage**, egg on, incite, prompt, spur, urge

abeyance *noun* **in abeyance** = **shelved**, hanging fire, in cold storage (*informal*), on ice (*informal*), pending, suspended

abhor *verb* = **hate**, abominate, detest, execrate, loathe, recoil from, regard with repugnance *or* horror, shrink from, shudder at
➤ **Antonyms**
admire, adore, cherish, delight in, desire, enjoy, like, love, relish

abhorrent *adjective* = **hateful**, abominable, detestable, disgusting, distasteful, execrable, hated, heinous, horrible, horrid, loathsome, obnoxious, obscene, odious, offensive, repellent, repugnant, repulsive, revolting, yucky *or* yukky (*slang*)

abide *verb* **1** = **tolerate**, accept, bear, brook, endure, hack (*slang*), put up with, stand, stomach, submit to, suffer **2** = **last**, continue, endure, persist, remain, survive **3** = **stay**, dwell, linger, live, lodge, reside, rest, sojourn, stop, tarry, wait

abide by *verb* **1** = **obey**, acknowledge, agree to, comply with, conform to, follow, observe, submit to, toe the line **2** = **carry out**, adhere to, discharge, fulfil, hold to, keep to, persist in, stand by

abiding *adjective* = **everlasting**, constant, continuing, durable, enduring, eternal, fast, firm, immortal, immutable, indissoluble, lasting, permanent, persistent, persisting, steadfast, surviving, tenacious, unchanging, unending
➤ **Antonyms**
brief, ephemeral, evanescent, fleeting, momentary, passing, short, short-lived, temporary, transient, transitory

ability *noun* = **skill**, adeptness, aptitude, capability, capacity, competence, competency, craft, dexterity, endowment, energy, expertise, expertness, facility, faculty, flair, force, gift, knack, know-how (*informal*), potentiality, power, proficiency, qualification, talent
➤ **Antonyms**
inability, incapability, incapacity, incompetence, powerlessness, weakness

abject *adjective* **1** = **miserable**, deplorable, forlorn, hopeless, outcast, pitiable, wretched **2** = **servile**, base, contemptible, cringing, debased, degraded, despicable, dishonourable, fawning, grovelling, humiliating, ignoble, ignominious, low, mean, slavish, sordid, submissive, vile, worthless
➤ **Antonyms**
≠**servile:** august, dignified, distinguished, elevated, eminent, exalted, grand, great, high, lofty, noble, patrician, worthy

abjectness *noun* **1** = **misery**, destitution, forlornness, hopelessness, pitiableness, pitifulness, squalor, wretchedness **2** = **degradation**, abjection, baseness, contemptibleness, debasement, dishonour, humbleness, humiliation, ignominy, lowness, meanness, servility, slavishness, sordidness, submissiveness, vileness, worthlessness

ablaze *adjective* **1** = **on fire**, afire, aflame, alight, blazing, burning, fiery, flaming, ignited, lighted **2** = **glowing**, aglow, brilliant, flashing, gleaming, illuminated, incandescent, luminous, radiant, sparkling **3** = **furious**, angry, fit to be tied (*slang*), foaming at the mouth, fuming, incandescent, incensed, on the warpath, raging **4** = **aroused**, enthusiastic, excited, fervent, frenzied, impassioned, passionate, stimulated

able *adjective* = **capable**, accomplished, adept, adequate, adroit, clever, competent, effective, efficient, experienced, expert, fit, fitted, gifted, highly endowed, masterful, masterly, powerful, practised, proficient, qualified, skilful, skilled, strong, talented
➤ **Antonyms**
amateurish, inadequate, incapable, incompetent, ineffective, inefficient, inept, mediocre, no great shakes (*informal*), unfit, unskilful, weak

able-bodied *adjective* = **strong**, firm, fit, hale, hardy, healthy, hearty, lusty, powerful, right as rain (*Brit. informal*), robust, sound, staunch, stout, strapping, sturdy, vigorous
➤ **Antonyms**
ailing, debilitated, feeble, frail, sickly, weak

ablutions *plural noun* = **washing**, bath, bathing, cleansing, lavation, purification, shower, wash

abnegation *noun* = **giving up**, abandonment, abjuration, abstinence,

continence, disallowance, eschewal,
forbearance, refusal, rejection,
relinquishment, renunciation, sacrifice,
self-denial, surrender, temperance

abnormal *adjective* = **unusual**, aberrant,
anomalous, atypical, curious, deviant,
eccentric, erratic, exceptional, extraordinary,
irregular, monstrous, odd, oddball
(*informal*), off-the-wall (*slang*), outré,
peculiar, queer, singular, strange,
uncommon, unexpected, unnatural,
untypical, wacko (*slang*), weird
➤ **Antonyms**
common, conventional, customary, familiar,
natural, normal, ordinary, regular,
unexceptional, usual

abnormality *noun* = **oddity**, aberration,
anomaly, atypicalness, bizarreness,
deformity, deviation, eccentricity, exception,
extraordinariness, flaw, irregularity,
monstrosity, peculiarity, queerness,
singularity, strangeness, uncommonness,
unexpectedness, unnaturalness,
untypicalness, unusualness, weirdness

abode *noun* = **home**, domicile, dwelling,
dwelling-place, habitat, habitation, house,
lodging, pad (*slang*), quarters, residence

abolish *verb* = **do away with**, abrogate,
annihilate, annul, axe (*informal*), blot out,
cancel, destroy, eliminate, end, eradicate,
expunge, exterminate, extinguish, extirpate,
invalidate, nullify, obliterate, overthrow,
overturn, put an end to, quash, repeal,
repudiate, rescind, revoke, stamp out,
subvert, suppress, terminate, vitiate, void,
wipe out
➤ **Antonyms**
authorize, continue, create, establish, found,
institute, introduce, legalize, promote,
reinstate, reintroduce, restore, revive, sustain

abolition *noun* = **ending**, abrogation,
annihilation, annulment, blotting out,
cancellation, destruction, elimination, end,
eradication, expunction, extermination,
extinction, extirpation, invalidation,
nullification, obliteration, overthrow,
overturning, quashing, repeal, repudiation,
rescission, revocation, stamping out,
subversion, suppression, termination,
vitiation, voiding, wiping out, withdrawal

abominable *adjective* = **terrible**,
abhorrent, accursed, atrocious, base,
contemptible, despicable, detestable,
disgusting, execrable, foul, godawful
(*slang*), hateful, heinous, hellish, horrible,
horrid, loathsome, nauseous, obnoxious,
obscene, odious, repellent, reprehensible,
repugnant, repulsive, revolting, vile,
villainous, wretched, yucky or yukky (*slang*)
➤ **Antonyms**
admirable, agreeable, charming,

commendable, delightful, desirable, good,
laudable, likable or likeable, lovable,
pleasant, pleasing, wonderful

abominate *verb* = **hate**, abhor, detest,
execrate, loathe, recoil from, regard with
repugnance, shudder at
➤ **Antonyms**
admire, adore, cherish, dote on, esteem,
idolize, love, revere, treasure, worship

abomination *noun* **1** = **hatred**,
abhorrence, antipathy, aversion, detestation,
disgust, distaste, execration, hate, horror,
loathing, odium, repugnance, revulsion **2**
= **evil**, anathema, bête noire, bugbear, curse,
disgrace, horror, plague, shame, torment

aboriginal *adjective* = **native**, ancient,
autochthonous, earliest, first, indigenous,
original, primary, primeval, primitive,
primordial, pristine

abort *verb* **1** = **terminate** (*a pregnancy*),
miscarry **2** = **stop**, arrest, axe (*informal*), call
off, check, end, fail, halt, terminate

abortion *noun* **1** = **termination**, aborticide,
deliberate miscarriage, feticide, miscarriage **2**
= **failure**, disappointment, fiasco,
misadventure, monstrosity, vain effort

abortive *adjective* **1** = **failed**, bootless,
failing, fruitless, futile, idle, ineffectual,
miscarried, unavailing, unsuccessful, useless,
vain **2** *Biology* = **imperfectly developed**,
incomplete, rudimentary, stunted

abound *verb* = **be plentiful**, be jammed
with, be packed with, crowd, flourish,
increase, infest, luxuriate, overflow,
proliferate, superabound, swarm, swell,
teem, thrive

abounding *adjective* = **plentiful**, abundant,
bountiful, copious, filled, flourishing,
flowing, flush, full, lavish, luxuriant,
overflowing, plenteous, profuse, prolific,
rank, replete, rich, superabundant, teeming,
thick on the ground, two a penny

about *preposition* **1** = **regarding**, anent
(*Scot.*), as regards, concerned with,
concerning, connected with, dealing with,
on, re, referring to, relating to, relative to,
respecting, touching, with respect to **2**
= **near**, adjacent to, beside, circa (*used with
dates*), close to, nearby **3** = **around**,
encircling, on all sides, round, surrounding **4**
= **throughout**, all over, over, through
♦ *adverb* **5** = **nearly**, almost, approaching,
approximately, around, close to, more or
less, nearing, roughly **6** = **here and there**,
from place to place, hither and thither, to
and fro ♦ *adjective* **7** = **around**, active, astir,
in motion, present, stirring

about to *adverb* = **on the point of**,
intending to, on the verge or brink of, ready
to

above *preposition* **1** = **over**, atop, beyond, exceeding, higher than, on top of, upon **2** = **superior to**, before, beyond, exceeding, surpassing ♦ *adverb* **3** = **overhead**, aloft, atop, in heaven, on high ♦ *adjective* **4** = **preceding**, aforementioned, aforesaid, earlier, foregoing, previous, prior
➤ **Antonyms**
preposition ≠**over**: below, beneath, under, underneath ≠**superior to**: inferior, lesser, less than, lower than, subordinate

above board *adjective* **1** = **honest**, candid, fair and square, forthright, frank, guileless, honourable, kosher (*informal*), legitimate, on the up and up, open, overt, square, straight, straightforward, true, trustworthy, truthful, upfront (*informal*), upright, veracious ♦ *adverb* **2** = **honestly**, candidly, forthrightly, frankly, honourably, openly, overtly, straightforwardly, truly, truthfully, uprightly, veraciously, without guile
➤ **Antonyms**
adjective ≠**honest**: clandestine, crooked, deceitful, deceptive, devious, dishonest, fraudulent, furtive, secret, secretive, shady, sly, sneaky, underhand

abracadabra *noun* = **spell**, chant, charm, conjuration, hocus-pocus, incantation, invocation, magic, mumbo jumbo, sorcery, voodoo, witchcraft

abrade *verb* = **scrape**, erase, erode, file, grind, rub off, scour, scrape away, scrape out, wear away, wear down, wear off

abrasion *noun* **1** *Medical* = **graze**, chafe, scrape, scratch, scuff, surface injury, trauma (*Pathology*) **2** = **scraping**, abrading, chafing, erosion, friction, grating, rubbing, scouring, scratching, scuffing, wearing away, wearing down

abrasive *adjective* **1** = **unpleasant**, annoying, biting, caustic, cutting, galling, grating, hurtful, irritating, nasty, rough, sharp, vitriolic **2** = **rough**, chafing, erosive, frictional, grating, scraping, scratching, scratchy, scuffing ♦ *adjective, noun* **3** = **scourer**, abradant, burnisher, grinder, scarifier

abreast *adjective* **1** = **alongside**, beside, level, neck and neck, shoulder to shoulder, side by side **2 abreast of** = **informed about**, acquainted with, *au courant* with, *au fait* with, conversant with, familiar with, in the picture about, in touch with, keeping one's finger on the pulse of, knowledgeable about, up to date with, up to speed with

abridge *verb* = **shorten**, abbreviate, abstract, clip, compress, concentrate, condense, contract, curtail, cut, cut down, decrease, digest, diminish, downsize, epitomize, lessen, précis, reduce, summarize, synopsize (*U.S.*), trim

➤ **Antonyms**
amplify, augment, enlarge, expand, extend, go into detail, lengthen, prolong, protract, spin out, stretch out

abridgment *noun* = **shortening**, abbreviation, abstract, compendium, condensation, conspectus, contraction, curtailment, cutting, decrease, digest, diminishing, diminution, epitome, lessening, limitation, outline, précis, reduction, restraint, restriction, résumé, summary, synopsis

abroad *adverb* **1** = **overseas**, beyond the sea, in foreign lands, out of the country **2** = **about**, at large, away, circulating, current, elsewhere, extensively, far, far and wide, forth, in circulation, out, out-of-doors, outside, publicly, widely, without

abrupt *adjective* **1** = **sudden**, hasty, headlong, hurried, precipitate, quick, surprising, swift, unanticipated, unexpected, unforeseen **2** = **steep**, precipitous, sharp, sheer, sudden **3** = **uneven**, broken, disconnected, discontinuous, irregular, jerky **4** = **curt**, blunt, brisk, brusque, clipped, direct, discourteous, gruff, impatient, impolite, monosyllabic, rough, rude, short, snappish, snappy, terse, unceremonious, uncivil, ungracious
➤ **Antonyms**
≠**sudden**: easy, leisurely, slow, thoughtful, unhurried ≠**steep**: gradual ≠**curt**: civil, courteous, gracious, polite

abscond *verb* = **flee**, bolt, clear out, decamp, disappear, do a bunk (*Brit. slang*), do a runner (*slang*), escape, flit (*informal*), fly, fly the coop (*U.S. & Canad. informal*), make off, run off, skedaddle (*informal*), slip away, sneak away, steal away, take a powder (*U.S. & Canad. slang*), take it on the lam (*U.S. & Canad. slang*)

absence *noun* **1** = **nonattendance**, absenteeism, nonappearance, truancy **2** = **lack**, default, defect, deficiency, need, nonexistence, omission, privation, unavailability, want

absent *adjective* **1** = **missing**, away, elsewhere, gone, lacking, nonattendant, nonexistent, not present, out, truant, unavailable, wanting **2** = **absent-minded**, absorbed, abstracted, bemused, blank, daydreaming, distracted, dreamy, empty, faraway, heedless, inattentive, musing, oblivious, preoccupied, unaware, unconscious, unheeding, unthinking, vacant, vague ♦ *verb* **3 absent oneself** = **stay away**, abscond, bunk off (*slang*), depart, keep away, play truant, remove, slope off (*informal*), truant, withdraw
➤ **Antonyms**
adjective ≠**missing**: attendant, in

attendance, present ≠**absent-minded**: alert, attentive, aware, conscious, thoughtful
◆ *verb* ≠**stay away**: attend, show up (*informal*)

absently *adverb* = absent-mindedly, abstractedly, bemusedly, blankly, distractedly, dreamily, emptily, heedlessly, inattentively, obliviously, on automatic pilot, unconsciously, unheedingly, vacantly, vaguely

absent-minded *adjective* = vague, absent, absorbed, abstracted, bemused, distracted, ditzy *or* ditsy (*slang*), dreaming, dreamy, engrossed, faraway, forgetful, heedless, in a brown study, inattentive, musing, oblivious, preoccupied, unaware, unconscious, unheeding, unthinking
➤ Antonyms
alert, awake, observant, on one's toes, on the ball, perceptive, quick, vigilant, wary, wide-awake

absolute *adjective* 1 = total, arrant, complete, consummate, deep-dyed (*usually derogatory*), downright, entire, full-on (*informal*), out-and-out, outright, perfect, pure, sheer, thorough, unadulterated, unalloyed, unmitigated, unmixed, unqualified, utter 2 = supreme, absolutist, arbitrary, autarchical, autocratic, autonomous, despotic, dictatorial, full, peremptory, sovereign, tyrannical, unbounded, unconditional, unlimited, unqualified, unquestionable, unrestrained, unrestricted 3 = definite, actual, categorical, certain, conclusive, decided, decisive, exact, genuine, infallible, positive, precise, sure, unambiguous, unequivocal, unquestionable

absolutely *adverb* 1 = totally, completely, consummately, entirely, every inch, fully, lock, stock and barrel, one hundred per cent, perfectly, purely, thoroughly, to the hilt, unmitigatedly, utterly, wholly 2 = supremely, arbitrarily, autocratically, autonomously, despotically, dictatorially, fully, peremptorily, sovereignly, tyrannically, unconditionally, unquestionably, unrestrainedly, without qualification 3 = definitely, actually, categorically, certainly, conclusively, decidedly, decisively, exactly, genuinely, infallibly, positively, precisely, surely, truly, unambiguously, unequivocally, unquestionably
➤ Antonyms
≠**totally**: fairly, probably, reasonably, somewhat

absoluteness *noun* 1 = totality, consummateness, entirety, perfection, purity, thoroughness, unmitigatedness, wholeness 2 = supremacy, arbitrariness, autonomy, despotism, dictatorialness, fullness, peremptoriness, tyranny, unboundedness, unquestionability, unrestrainedness,

unrestrictedness 3 = certainty, assuredness, certitude, conclusiveness, correctness, decidedness, decisiveness, definiteness, exactitude, genuineness, infallibility, positiveness, precision, sureness, surety, truth, unambiguousness, unequivocalness

absolution *noun* = forgiveness, acquittal, amnesty, deliverance, discharge, dispensation, exculpation, exemption, exoneration, freeing, indulgence, liberation, mercy, pardon, release, remission, setting free, shriving, vindication

absolutism *noun* = dictatorship, absoluteness, arbitrariness, autarchy, authoritarianism, autocracy, despotism, totalitarianism, tyranny

absolutist *noun* = dictator, arbiter, authoritarian, autocrat, despot, totalitarian, tyrant

absolve *verb* = forgive, acquit, clear, deliver, discharge, exculpate, excuse, exempt, exonerate, free, let off, liberate, loose, pardon, release, remit, set free, shrive, vindicate
➤ Antonyms
blame, censure, charge, condemn, convict, damn, denounce, excoriate, pass sentence on, reprehend, reproach, reprove, sentence, upbraid

absorb *verb* 1 = soak up, assimilate, consume, devour, digest, drink in, exhaust, imbibe, incorporate, ingest, osmose, receive, suck up, take in 2 = preoccupy, captivate, engage, engross, enwrap, fascinate, fill, fill up, fix, hold, immerse, monopolize, occupy, rivet

absorbed *adjective* 1 = preoccupied, captivated, concentrating, engaged, engrossed, fascinated, fixed, held, immersed, involved, lost, occupied, rapt, riveted, up to one's ears, wrapped up 2 = digested, assimilated, consumed, devoured, exhausted, imbibed, incorporated, received, soaked up

absorbent *adjective* = permeable, porous, receptive, spongy

absorbing *adjective* = fascinating, arresting, captivating, engrossing, gripping, interesting, intriguing, preoccupying, riveting, spellbinding
➤ Antonyms
boring, dreary, dull, humdrum, mind-numbing, monotonous, tedious, tiresome, unexciting

absorption *noun* 1 = soaking up, assimilation, consumption, digestion, exhaustion, incorporation, osmosis, sucking up 2 = concentration, captivation, engagement, fascination, holding, immersion, intentness, involvement, occupation, preoccupation, raptness

abstain *verb* = **refrain**, avoid, cease, decline, deny (oneself), desist, fast, forbear, forgo, give up, keep from, kick (*informal*), refuse, renounce, shun, stop, withhold
➤ **Antonyms**
abandon oneself, give in, indulge, partake, yield

abstemious *adjective* = **self-denying**, abstinent, ascetic, austere, continent, frugal, moderate, sober, sparing, temperate
➤ **Antonyms**
gluttonous, greedy, immoderate, incontinent, intemperate, self-indulgent

abstention *noun* = **refusal**, abstaining, abstinence, avoidance, desistance, eschewal, forbearance, nonindulgence, refraining, self-control, self-denial, self-restraint

abstinence *noun* = **self-denial**, abstemiousness, asceticism, avoidance, continence, forbearance, moderation, refraining, self-restraint, soberness, sobriety, teetotalism, temperance
➤ **Antonyms**
abandon, acquisitiveness, covetousness, excess, gluttony, greediness, indulgence, self-indulgence, wantonness

abstinent *adjective* = **self-denying**, abstaining, abstemious, continent, forbearing, moderate, self-controlled, self-restraining, sober, temperate

abstract *adjective* 1 = **theoretical**, abstruse, arcane, complex, conceptual, deep, general, generalized, hypothetical, indefinite, intellectual, nonconcrete, notional, occult, philosophical, profound, recondite, separate, subtle, theoretic, unpractical, unrealistic ♦ *noun* 2 = **summary**, abridgment, compendium, condensation, digest, epitome, essence, outline, précis, recapitulation, résumé, synopsis ♦ *verb* 3 = **summarize**, abbreviate, abridge, condense, digest, epitomize, outline, précis, shorten, synopsize (*U.S.*) 4 = **remove**, detach, dissociate, extract, isolate, separate, steal, take away, take out, withdraw
➤ **Antonyms**
adjective actual ≠**theoretical**: concrete, definite, factual, material, real, specific
♦ *noun* ≠**summary**: enlargement, expansion
♦ *verb* ≠**remove**: add, combine, inject

abstracted *adjective* = **preoccupied**, absent, absent-minded, bemused, daydreaming, dreamy, faraway, inattentive, remote, withdrawn, woolgathering

abstraction *noun* 1 = **idea**, concept, formula, generality, generalization, hypothesis, notion, theorem, theory, thought 2 = **absent-mindedness**, absence, bemusedness, dreaminess, inattention,

pensiveness, preoccupation, remoteness, woolgathering

abstruse *adjective* = **obscure**, abstract, arcane, complex, dark, deep, Delphic, enigmatic, esoteric, hidden, incomprehensible, mysterious, mystical, occult, perplexing, profound, puzzling, recondite, subtle, unfathomable, vague
➤ **Antonyms**
apparent, bold, clear, conspicuous, evident, manifest, open, overt, patent, perceptible, plain, self-evident, transparent, unsubtle

absurd *adjective* = **ridiculous**, crazy (*informal*), daft (*informal*), dumb-ass (*slang*), farcical, foolish, idiotic, illogical, inane, incongruous, irrational, laughable, ludicrous, meaningless, nonsensical, preposterous, senseless, silly, stupid, unreasonable
➤ **Antonyms**
intelligent, logical, prudent, rational, reasonable, sagacious, sensible, smart, wise

absurdity *noun* = **ridiculousness**, bêtise (*rare*), craziness (*informal*), daftness (*informal*), farce, farcicality, farcicalness, folly, foolishness, idiocy, illogicality, illogicalness, incongruity, irrationality, joke, ludicrousness, meaninglessness, nonsense, preposterousness, senselessness, silliness, stupidity, unreasonableness

abundance *noun* 1 = **plenty**, affluence, ampleness, bounty, copiousness, exuberance, fullness, heap (*informal*), plenitude, plenteousness, profusion 2 = **wealth**, affluence, big bucks (*informal, chiefly U.S.*), big money, fortune, megabucks (*U.S. & Canad. slang*), opulence, pretty penny (*informal*), riches, tidy sum (*informal*), wad (*U.S. & Canad. slang*)
➤ **Antonyms**
≠**plenty**: dearth, deficiency, lack, need, paucity, scantiness, scarcity, sparseness

abundant *adjective* = **plentiful**, ample, bounteous, bountiful, copious, exuberant, filled, full, lavish, luxuriant, overflowing, plenteous, profuse, rank, rich, teeming, thick on the ground, two a penny, well-provided, well-supplied
➤ **Antonyms**
deficient, few, few and far between, inadequate, in short supply, insufficient, lacking, rare, scant, scanty, scarce, short, sparse, thin on the ground

abuse *noun* 1 = **ill-treatment**, damage, exploitation, harm, hurt, imposition, injury, maltreatment, manhandling, oppression, spoiling, wrong 2 = **insults**, blame, calumniation, castigation, censure, character assassination, contumely, curses, cursing, defamation, derision, disparagement,

invective, libel, opprobrium, reproach,
revilement, scolding, slander, swearing,
tirade, traducement, upbraiding, vilification,
vituperation **3** = **misuse**, misapplication
♦ *verb* **4** = **ill-treat**, damage, dump on
(*slang, chiefly U.S.*), exploit, harm, hurt,
impose upon, injure, maltreat, manhandle,
mar, misapply, misuse, oppress, shit on
(*taboo slang*), spoil, take advantage of,
wrong **5** = **insult**, calumniate, castigate,
curse, defame, disparage, inveigh against,
libel, malign, revile, scold, slander, slate
(*informal, chiefly Brit.*), smear, swear at,
traduce, upbraid, vilify, vituperate
➤ **Antonyms**
verb ≠**ill-treat:** care for, protect ≠**insult:**
acclaim, commend, compliment, extol,
flatter, praise, respect

abusive *adjective* **1** = **insulting**,
calumniating, castigating, censorious,
contumelious, defamatory, derisive,
disparaging, invective, libellous, maligning,
offensive, opprobrious, reproachful, reviling,
rude, scathing, scolding, slanderous,
traducing, upbraiding, vilifying, vituperative
2 = **harmful**, brutal, cruel, destructive,
hurtful, injurious, rough
➤ **Antonyms**
≠**insulting:** approving, complimentary,
eulogistic, flattering, laudatory, panegyrical,
praising

abysmal *adjective* = **terrible**, appalling,
awful, bad, dire, dreadful, godawful
(*informal*)

abyss *noun* = **pit**, abysm, bottomless depth,
chasm, crevasse, fissure, gorge, gulf, void

academic *adjective* **1** = **scholarly**, bookish,
campus, college, collegiate, erudite,
highbrow, learned, lettered, literary,
scholastic, school, studious, university **2**
= **hypothetical**, abstract, conjectural,
impractical, notional, speculative, theoretical
♦ *noun* **3** = **scholar**, academician, don,
fellow, lecturer, master, professor, pupil,
scholastic, schoolman, student, tutor

accede *verb* **1** = **agree**, accept, acquiesce,
admit, assent, comply, concede, concur,
consent, endorse, grant, own, yield **2**
= **inherit**, assume, attain, come to, enter
upon, succeed, succeed to (*as heir*)

accelerate *verb* = **speed up**, advance,
expedite, forward, further, hasten, hurry,
pick up speed, precipitate, quicken, speed,
spur, step up (*informal*), stimulate
➤ **Antonyms**
decelerate, delay, hinder, impede, obstruct,
slow down

acceleration *noun* = **speeding up**,
expedition, hastening, hurrying, quickening,
spurring, stepping up (*informal*), stimulation

accent *noun* **1** = **pronunciation**,
articulation, brogue, enunciation, inflection,
intonation, modulation, tone **2** = **emphasis**,
beat, cadence, force, ictus, pitch, rhythm,
stress, timbre, tonality ♦ *verb* **3**
= **emphasize**, accentuate, stress, underline,
underscore

accentuate *verb* = **emphasize**, accent,
draw attention to, foreground, highlight,
stress, underline, underscore
➤ **Antonyms**
gloss over, make light *or* little of, minimize,
play down, soft-pedal (*informal*), underplay

accept *verb* **1** = **receive**, acquire, gain, get,
have, obtain, secure, take **2** = **agree to**,
accede, acknowledge, acquiesce, admit,
adopt, affirm, approve, believe, buy (*slang*),
buy into (*slang*), concur with, consent to,
cooperate with, recognize, swallow
(*informal*), take on board **3** = **stand**, bear,
bow to, brook, defer to, like it or lump it
(*informal*), put up with, submit to, suffer,
take, tolerate, yield to **4** = **take on**,
acknowledge, admit, assume, avow, bear,
undertake
➤ **Antonyms**
≠**agree to:** decline, deny, disown, rebut,
refuse, reject, repudiate, spurn

acceptable *adjective* **1** = **satisfactory**,
adequate, admissible, all right, fair,
moderate, passable, so-so (*informal*),
standard, suitable, tolerable, up to scratch
(*informal*) **2** = **pleasant**, agreeable,
delightful, grateful, gratifying, pleasing,
welcome
➤ **Antonyms**
≠**satisfactory:** unacceptable, unsatisfactory,
unsuitable

acceptance *noun* **1** = **accepting**, acquiring,
gaining, getting, having, obtaining, receipt,
securing, taking **2** = **agreement**, accedence,
accession, acknowledgment, acquiescence,
admission, adoption, affirmation,
approbation, approval, assent, belief,
compliance, concession, concurrence,
consensus, consent, cooperation, credence,
O.K. *or* okay (*informal*), permission,
recognition, stamp *or* seal of approval **3**
= **submission**, deference, standing, taking,
yielding **4** = **taking on**, acknowledgment,
admission, assumption, avowal,
undertaking

accepted *adjective* = **agreed**, acceptable,
acknowledged, admitted, agreed upon,
approved, authorized, common, confirmed,
conventional, customary, established,
normal, received, recognized, regular,
sanctioned, standard, time-honoured,
traditional, universal, usual
➤ **Antonyms**
abnormal, irregular, strange, unconventional,

uncustomary, unorthodox, unusual, unwonted

access *noun* **1** = **entrance**, admission, admittance, approach, avenue, course, door, entering, entrée, entry, gateway, key, passage, passageway, path, road, way in **2** *Medical* = **attack**, fit, onset, outburst, paroxysm

accessibility *noun* **1** = **handiness**, approachability, attainability, availability, nearness, obtainability, possibility, readiness **2** = **approachability**, affability, conversableness, cordiality, friendliness, informality **3** = **openness**, exposedness, susceptibility

accessible *adjective* **1** = **handy**, achievable, a hop, skip and a jump away, at hand, at one's fingertips, attainable, available, get-at-able (*informal*), near, nearby, obtainable, on hand, possible, reachable, ready **2** = **approachable**, affable, available, cordial, friendly, informal **3** = **open**, exposed, liable, subject, susceptible, vulnerable, wide-open
➤ **Antonyms**
≠**handy**: far-off, inaccessible, unavailable, unobtainable, unreachable

accession *noun* **1** = **taking up**, assumption, attaining to, attainment of, entering upon, succession (*to a throne, dignity, or office*), taking on, taking over **2** = **agreement**, accedence, acceptance, acquiescence, assent, concurrence, consent **3** = **increase**, addition, augmentation, enlargement, extension

accessory *noun* **1** = **addition**, accent, accompaniment, add-on, adjunct, adornment, aid, appendage, attachment, component, convenience, decoration, extension, extra, frill, help, supplement, trim, trimming **2** = **accomplice**, abettor, assistant, associate (*in crime*), colleague, confederate, helper, partner ◆ *adjective* **3** = **additional**, abetting, aiding, ancillary, assisting in, auxiliary, contributory, extra, secondary, subordinate, supplemental, supplementary

accident *noun* **1** = **misfortune**, blow, calamity, casualty, chance, collision, crash, disaster, misadventure, mischance, mishap, pile-up (*informal*) **2** = **chance**, fate, fluke, fortuity, fortune, hazard, luck

accidental *adjective* = **unintentional**, adventitious, casual, chance, contingent, fortuitous, haphazard, inadvertent, incidental, inessential, nonessential, random, uncalculated, uncertain, unessential, unexpected, unforeseen, unintended, unlooked-for, unplanned, unpremeditated, unwitting
➤ **Antonyms**
calculated, designed, expected, foreseen,

intended, intentional, planned, prepared

accidentally *adverb* = **unintentionally**, adventitiously, by accident, by chance, by mistake, casually, fortuitously, haphazardly, inadvertently, incidentally, randomly, unconsciously, undesignedly, unexpectedly, unwittingly
➤ **Antonyms**
by design, consciously, deliberately, designedly, on purpose, wilfully

acclaim *verb* **1** = **praise**, applaud, approve, celebrate, cheer, clap, commend, crack up (*informal*), eulogize, exalt, extol, hail, honour, laud, salute, welcome ◆ *noun* **2** = **praise**, acclamation, applause, approbation, approval, celebration, cheering, clapping, commendation, eulogizing, exaltation, honour, kudos, laudation, plaudits, welcome
➤ **Antonyms**
noun ≠**praise**: bad press, brickbats, censure, criticism, denigration, disparagement, fault-finding, flak (*informal*), panning (*informal*), stick (*slang*), vituperation

acclamation *noun* = **praise**, acclaim, adulation, approbation, approval, cheer, cheering, cheers, enthusiasm, kudos, laudation, loud homage, ovation, plaudit, salutation, shouting, tribute

acclimatization *noun* = **adaptation**, acclimation, accommodation, acculturation, adjustment, habituation, inurement, naturalization

acclimatize *verb* = **adapt**, accommodate, acculturate, acculture, accustom, adjust, become seasoned to, get used to, habituate, inure, naturalize

accolade *noun* = **praise**, acclaim, applause, approval, commendation, compliment, ovation, recognition, tribute

accommodate *verb* **1** = **house**, billet, board, cater for, entertain, harbour, lodge, put up, quarter, shelter **2** = **help**, afford, aid, assist, furnish, oblige, provide, purvey, serve, supply **3** = **adapt**, accustom, adjust, comply, compose, conform, fit, harmonize, modify, reconcile, settle

accommodating *adjective* = **helpful**, complaisant, considerate, cooperative, friendly, hospitable, kind, obliging, polite, unselfish, willing
➤ **Antonyms**
disobliging, inconsiderate, rude, uncooperative, unhelpful

accommodation *noun* **1** = **housing**, board, digs (*Brit. informal*), harbouring, house, lodging(s), quartering, quarters, shelter, sheltering **2** = **help**, aid, assistance, provision, service, supply **3** = **adaptation**, adjustment, compliance, composition, compromise, conformity, fitting, harmony, modification, reconciliation, settlement

accompaniment *noun* 1 = supplement, accessory, companion, complement 2 = backing music, backing

accompany *verb* 1 = go with, attend, chaperon, conduct, convoy, escort, hold (someone's) hand, squire, usher 2 = occur with, belong to, coexist with, coincide with, come with, follow, go cheek by jowl, go together with, join with, supplement

accompanying *adjective* = additional, accessory, added, appended, associate, associated, attached, attendant, complementary, concomitant, concurrent, connected, fellow, joint, related, supplemental, supplementary

accomplice *noun* = helper, abettor, accessory, ally, assistant, associate, coadjutor, collaborator, colleague, confederate, henchman, partner

accomplish *verb* = do, achieve, attain, bring about, bring off (*informal*), carry out, complete, conclude, consummate, effect, effectuate, execute, finish, fulfil, manage, perform, produce, put the tin lid on, realize
➤ **Antonyms**
fail, fall short, forsake, give up

accomplished *adjective* 1 = skilled, adept, consummate, cultivated, expert, gifted, masterly, polished, practised, proficient, skilful, talented 2 = done, achieved, attained, brought about, carried out, completed, concluded, consummated, effected, executed, finished, fulfilled, in the can (*informal*), managed, performed, produced, realized
➤ **Antonyms**
≠skilled: amateurish, incapable, incompetent, inexpert, unestablished, unproven, unrealized, unskilled, untalented

accomplishment *noun* 1 = completion, achievement, attainment, bringing about, carrying out, conclusion, consummation, doing, effecting, execution, finishing, fulfilment, management, performance, production, realization 2 = achievement, act, attainment, coup, deed, exploit, feat, stroke, triumph 3 *often plural* = skill, ability, achievement, art, attainment, capability, craft, gift, proficiency, talent

accord *noun* 1 = agreement, accordance, assent, concert, concurrence, conformity, congruence, correspondence, harmony, rapport, sympathy, unanimity, unison ♦ *verb* 2 = grant, allow, bestow, concede, confer, endow, give, present, render, tender, vouchsafe 3 = agree, assent, be in tune (*informal*), concur, conform, correspond, fit, harmonize, match, suit, tally

➤ **Antonyms**
noun ≠agreement: conflict, contention, disagreement, discord ♦ *verb* ≠grant: hold back, refuse, withhold ≠agree: conflict, contrast, differ, disagree, discord

accordance *noun* As in **in accordance with** = agreement, accord, assent, concert, concurrence, conformity, congruence, correspondence, harmony, rapport, sympathy, unanimity

accordingly *adverb* 1 = appropriately, correspondingly, fitly, properly, suitably 2 = consequently, as a result, ergo, hence, in consequence, so, therefore, thus

according to *adverb* 1 = as stated by, as believed by, as maintained by, in the light of, on the authority of, on the report of 2 = in keeping with, after, after the manner of, consistent with, in accordance with, in compliance with, in conformity with, in harmony with, in line with, in obedience to, in step with, in the manner of, obedient to 3 = in relation, commensurate with, in proportion

accost *verb* = approach, buttonhole, confront, greet, hail

account *noun* 1 = description, chronicle, detail, explanation, history, narration, narrative, recital, record, relation, report, statement, story, tale, version 2 *Commerce* = statement, balance, bill, book, books, charge, computation, inventory, invoice, ledger, reckoning, register, score, tally 3 = importance, advantage, benefit, consequence, distinction, esteem, honour, import, merit, note, profit, rank, repute, significance, standing, use, value, worth 4 = reason, basis, cause, consideration, ground, grounds, interest, motive, regard, sake, score ♦ *verb* 5 = consider, appraise, assess, believe, calculate, compute, count, deem, esteem, estimate, explain, gauge, hold, judge, rate, reckon, regard, think, value, weigh

accountability *noun* = responsibility, answerability, chargeability, culpability, liability

accountable *adjective* = responsible, amenable, answerable, charged with, liable, obligated, obliged

accountant *noun* = auditor, bean counter (*informal*), book-keeper

account for *verb* 1 = explain, answer for, clarify, clear up, elucidate, illuminate, justify, rationalize 2 = put out of action, destroy, incapacitate, kill, put paid to

accredit *verb* 1 = authorize, appoint, certify, commission, depute, empower, endorse, entrust, guarantee, license, recognize, sanction, vouch for 2 = attribute, ascribe, assign, credit

accredited *adjective* = **authorized**, appointed, certified, commissioned, deputed, deputized, empowered, endorsed, guaranteed, licensed, official, recognized, sanctioned, vouched for

accrue *verb* = **increase**, accumulate, amass, arise, be added, build up, collect, enlarge, ensue, flow, follow, grow, issue, spring up

accumulate *verb* = **collect**, accrue, amass, build up, cumulate, gather, grow, hoard, increase, pile up, stockpile, store
➤ **Antonyms**
diffuse, disperse, disseminate, dissipate, distribute, propagate, scatter

accumulation *noun* = **collection**, aggregation, augmentation, build-up, conglomeration, gathering, growth, heap, hoard, increase, mass, pile, rick, stack, stock, stockpile, store

accuracy *noun* = **exactness**, accurateness, authenticity, carefulness, closeness, correctness, exactitude, faithfulness, faultlessness, fidelity, meticulousness, niceness, nicety, precision, strictness, truth, truthfulness, veracity, verity
➤ **Antonyms**
carelessness, erroneousness, imprecision, inaccuracy, incorrectness, inexactitude, laxity, laxness

accurate *adjective* = **exact**, authentic, careful, close, correct, faithful, faultless, just, meticulous, nice, on the money (*U.S.*), precise, proper, regular, right, scrupulous, spot-on (*Brit. informal*), strict, true, truthful, unerring, veracious
➤ **Antonyms**
careless, defective, faulty, imperfect, imprecise, inaccurate, incorrect, inexact, wrong

accurately *adverb* = **exactly**, authentically, carefully, closely, correctly, faithfully, faultlessly, justly, meticulously, nicely, precisely, properly, regularly, rightly, scrupulously, strictly, to the letter, truly, truthfully, unerringly, veraciously

accursed *adjective* **1** = **cursed**, bedevilled, bewitched, condemned, damned, doomed, hopeless, ill-fated, ill-omened, jinxed, luckless, ruined, undone, unfortunate, unlucky, wretched **2** = **hateful**, abominable, despicable, detestable, execrable, hellish, horrible
➤ **Antonyms**
≠**cursed:** blessed, charmed, favoured, fortunate, lucky

accusation *noun* = **charge**, allegation, arraignment, attribution, citation, complaint, denunciation, impeachment, imputation, incrimination, indictment, recrimination

accuse *verb* = **charge**, allege, arraign, attribute, blame, censure, cite, denounce, impeach, impute, incriminate, indict, point a *or* the finger at, recriminate, tax
➤ **Antonyms**
absolve, defend, exonerate, vindicate

accustom *verb* = **adapt**, acclimatize, acquaint, discipline, exercise, familiarize, habituate, inure, season, train

accustomed *adjective* **1** = **usual**, common, conventional, customary, established, everyday, expected, fixed, general, habitual, normal, ordinary, regular, routine, set, traditional, wonted **2** = **used**, acclimatized, acquainted, adapted, disciplined, exercised, familiar, familiarized, given to, habituated, in the habit of, inured, seasoned, trained
➤ **Antonyms**
≠**usual:** abnormal, infrequent, occasional, odd, peculiar, rare, strange, unaccustomed, uncommon, unfamiliar, unusual ≠**used:** unaccustomed, unfamiliar, unused

ace *noun* **1** *Cards, dice, etc.* = **one**, single point **2** *Informal* = **expert**, adept, buff (*informal*), champion, dab hand (*Brit. informal*), genius, hotshot (*informal*), master, maven (*U.S.*), star, virtuoso, whizz (*informal*), winner, wizard (*informal*)
♦ *adjective* **3** *Informal* = **excellent**, awesome (*slang*), brilliant, champion, expert, fine, great, masterly, outstanding, superb, virtuoso

ache *verb* **1** = **hurt**, pain, pound, smart, suffer, throb, twinge **2** = **suffer**, agonize, eat one's heart out, grieve, mourn, sorrow **3** = **long**, covet, crave, desire, eat one's heart out over, hanker, hope, hunger, need, pine, set one's heart on, thirst, yearn ♦ *noun* **4** = **pain**, hurt, pang, pounding, smart, smarting, soreness, suffering, throb, throbbing **5** = **suffering**, anguish, grief, mourning, sorrow **6** = **longing**, craving, desire, hankering, hope, hunger, need, pining, thirst, yearning

achievable *adjective* = **attainable**, accessible, accomplishable, acquirable, feasible, obtainable, possible, practicable, reachable, realizable, winnable, within one's grasp

achieve *verb* = **attain**, accomplish, acquire, bring about, carry out, complete, consummate, do, earn, effect, execute, finish, fulfil, gain, get, obtain, perform, procure, put the tin lid on, reach, realize, win

achievement *noun* **1** = **accomplishment**, act, deed, effort, exploit, feat, feather in one's cap, stroke **2** accomplishment, = **fulfilment**, acquirement, attainment, completion, execution, performance, production, realization

acid *adjective* **1** = **sour**, acerb, acerbic,

acetic, acidulous, acrid, biting, pungent, sharp, tart, vinegarish, vinegary **2 = sharp**, acerbic, biting, bitter, caustic, cutting, harsh, hurtful, mordacious, mordant, pungent, stinging, trenchant, vitriolic
➤ **Antonyms**
≠**sour**: alkaline, bland, mild, pleasant, sweet
≠**sharp**: benign, bland, gentle, kindly, mild, pleasant, sweet

acidity *noun* **1 = sourness**, acerbity, acidulousness, acridity, acridness, bitterness, pungency, sharpness, tartness, vinegariness, vinegarishness **2 = sharpness**, acerbity, acridity, acridness, bitterness, causticity, causticness, harshness, hurtfulness, mordancy, pungency, trenchancy

acknowledge *verb* **1 = accept**, accede, acquiesce, admit, allow, concede, confess, declare, grant, own, profess, recognize, yield **2 = greet**, address, hail, notice, recognize, salute **3 = reply to**, answer, notice, react to, recognize, respond to, return
➤ **Antonyms**
≠**accept**: contradict, deny, disclaim, discount, reject, renounce, repudiate
≠**greet**: disdain, disregard, ignore, reject, snub, spurn ≠**reply to**: deny, disavow, disregard, ignore, rebut

acknowledged *adjective* **= accepted**, accredited, admitted, answered, approved, conceded, confessed, declared, professed, recognized, returned

acknowledgment *noun* **1 = acceptance**, accession, acquiescence, admission, allowing, confession, declaration, profession, realization, yielding **2 = greeting**, addressing, hail, hailing, notice, recognition, salutation, salute **3 = appreciation**, answer, credit, gratitude, reaction, recognition, reply, response, return, thanks

acme *noun* **= high point**, apex, climax, crest, crown, culmination, height, optimum, peak, pinnacle, summit, top, vertex, zenith
➤ **Antonyms**
bottom, depths, low point, minimum, nadir, rock bottom, zero

acquaint *verb* **= tell**, advise, announce, apprise, disclose, divulge, enlighten, familiarize, inform, let (someone) know, notify, reveal

acquaintance *noun* **1 = associate**, colleague, contact **2 = knowledge**, association, awareness, cognizance, companionship, conversance, conversancy, experience, familiarity, fellowship, intimacy, relationship, social contact, understanding
➤ **Antonyms**
≠**associate**: buddy, good friend, intimate
≠**knowledge**: ignorance, unfamiliarity

acquainted with *adjective* **= familiar**

with, alive to, apprised of, *au fait* with, aware of, cognizant of, conscious of, conversant with, experienced in, informed of, in on, knowledgeable about, privy to, up to speed with, versed in

acquiesce *verb* **= agree**, accede, accept, allow, approve, assent, bow to, comply, concur, conform, consent, give in, go along with, play ball (*informal*), submit, yield
➤ **Antonyms**
balk at, contest, demur, disagree, dissent, fight, object, protest, refuse, resist, veto

acquiescence *noun* **= agreement**, acceptance, accession, approval, assent, compliance, concurrence, conformity, consent, giving in, obedience, submission, yielding

acquiescent *adjective* **= agreeing**, acceding, accepting, agreeable, approving, assenting, compliant, concurrent, conforming, consenting, obedient, submissive, yielding

acquire *verb* **= get**, achieve, amass, attain, buy, collect, earn, gain, gather, land, obtain, pick up, procure, realize, receive, score (*slang*), secure, win
➤ **Antonyms**
be deprived of, forfeit, forgo, give up, lose, relinquish, renounce, surrender, waive

acquirement *noun* **1 = acquisition**, accomplishment, achievement, attainment, gathering, grip **2 = skill**, knowledge, learning, mastery, qualification

acquisition *noun* **1 = possession**, buy, gain, prize, property, purchase **2 = acquiring**, achievement, acquirement, attainment, gaining, obtainment, procurement, pursuit

acquisitive *adjective* **= greedy**, avaricious, avid, covetous, grabbing, grasping, predatory, rapacious
➤ **Antonyms**
bounteous, bountiful, generous, lavish, liberal, munificent, open-handed, unselfish, unstinting

acquisitiveness *noun* **= greed**, avarice, avidity, avidness, covetousness, graspingness, predatoriness, rapaciousness, rapacity

acquit *verb* **1 = clear**, absolve, deliver, discharge, exculpate, exonerate, free, fulfil, liberate, release, relieve, vindicate **2 = pay off**, discharge, pay, repay, satisfy, settle **3 = behave**, bear, comport, conduct, perform
➤ **Antonyms**
≠**clear**: blame, charge, condemn, convict, damn, find guilty, sentence

acquittal *noun* **= clearance**, absolution, deliverance, discharge, exculpation, exoneration, freeing, liberation, release, relief, vindication

acrid *adjective* **1** = **pungent**, acerb, acid, astringent, biting, bitter, burning, caustic, harsh, irritating, sharp, stinging, vitriolic **2** = **sharp**, acrimonious, biting, bitter, caustic, cutting, harsh, mordacious, mordant, nasty, sarcastic, trenchant, vitriolic

acrimonious *adjective* = **bitter**, acerbic, astringent, biting, caustic, censorious, churlish, crabbed, cutting, irascible, mordacious, mordant, peevish, petulant, pungent, rancorous, sarcastic, severe, sharp, spiteful, splenetic, tart, testy, trenchant, vitriolic
➤ **Antonyms**
affable, benign, forgiving, good-tempered

acrimony *noun* = **bitterness**, acerbity, asperity, astringency, churlishness, harshness, ill will, irascibility, mordancy, peevishness, pungency, rancour, sarcasm, spleen, tartness, trenchancy, virulence
➤ **Antonyms**
amity, friendliness, friendship, good feelings, goodwill, liking, warmth

act *noun* **1** = **deed**, accomplishment, achievement, action, blow, doing, execution, exertion, exploit, feat, move, operation, performance, step, stroke, undertaking **2** = **law**, bill, decree, edict, enactment, measure, ordinance, resolution, statute **3** = **performance**, routine, show, sketch, turn **4** = **pretence**, affectation, attitude, counterfeit, dissimulation, fake, feigning, front, performance, pose, posture, sham, show, stance ♦ *verb* **5** = **do**, acquit, bear, behave, carry, carry out, comport, conduct, enact, execute, exert, function, go about, make, move, operate, perform, react, serve, strike, take effect, undertake, work **6** = **perform**, act out, characterize, enact, impersonate, mime, mimic, personate, personify, play, play *or* take the part of, portray, represent **7** = **pretend**, affect, assume, counterfeit, dissimulate, feign, imitate, perform, pose, posture, put on, seem, sham

act for *verb* = **stand in for**, cover for, deputize for, fill in for, function in place of, replace, represent, serve, substitute for, take the place of

acting *noun* **1** = **performance**, characterization, dramatics, enacting, impersonation, performing, playing, portrayal, portraying, stagecraft, theatre ♦ *adjective* **2** = **temporary**, interim, pro tem, provisional, substitute, surrogate

action *noun* **1** = **deed**, accomplishment, achievement, act, blow, exercise, exertion, exploit, feat, move, operation, performance, step, stroke, undertaking **2** = **lawsuit**, case, cause, litigation, proceeding, prosecution,

suit **3** = **energy**, activity, force, liveliness, spirit, vigour, vim, vitality **4** = **movement**, activity, effect, effort, exertion, force, functioning, influence, motion, operation, power, process, work, working **5** = **battle**, affray, clash, combat, conflict, contest, encounter, engagement, fight, fighting, fray, skirmish, sortie, warfare

actions *plural noun* = **behaviour**, bearing, comportment, conduct, demeanour, deportment, manners, ways

activate *verb* = **start**, actuate, animate, arouse, energize, galvanize, get going, impel, initiate, kick-start (*informal*), mobilize, motivate, move, prod, prompt, propel, rouse, set going, set in motion, set off, stimulate, stir, switch on, trigger (off), turn on
➤ **Antonyms**
arrest, check, deactivate, halt, impede, stall, stop, terminate, turn off

active *adjective* **1** = **busy**, bustling, engaged, full, hard-working, involved, occupied, on the go (*informal*), on the move, strenuous **2** = **energetic**, alert, alive and kicking, animated, diligent, industrious, lively, nimble, on the go (*informal*), quick, spirited, sprightly, spry, vibrant, vigorous, vital, vivacious **3** = **enthusiastic**, activist, aggressive, ambitious, assertive, committed, devoted, energetic, engaged, enterprising, forceful, forward, hard-working, industrious, militant, zealous **4** = **in operation**, acting, astir, at work, doing, effectual, functioning, in action, in business, in force, live, moving, operative, running, stirring, working
➤ **Antonyms**
dormant, dull, idle, inactive, inoperative, lazy, sedentary, slow, sluggish, torpid, unimaginative, unoccupied

activist *noun* = **militant**, organizer, partisan

activity *noun* **1** = **action**, activeness, animation, bustle, enterprise, exercise, exertion, hurly-burly, hustle, labour, life, liveliness, motion, movement, stir, work **2** = **pursuit**, act, avocation, deed, endeavour, enterprise, hobby, interest, job, labour, occupation, pastime, project, scheme, task, undertaking, venture, work
➤ **Antonyms**
≠ **action:** dullness, idleness, immobility, inaction, inactivity, indolence, inertia, lethargy, passivity, sluggishness, torpor

act on, act upon *verb* **1** = **obey**, act in accordance with, carry out, comply with, conform to, follow, heed, yield to **2** = **affect**, alter, change, impact, influence, modify, sway, transform

actor *noun* = **performer**, actress, dramatic artist, leading man, luvvie (*informal*), play-actor, player, thesp (*informal*),

= **confess**, acknowledge,
concede, cough (*slang*),
ose, divulge, 'fess up (*U.S.*
profess, reveal **2** = **allow**,
let, permit, recognize **3** = **let**
llow, allow to enter, give access,
oduce, receive, take in

ny, dismiss, forbid, negate,
ect ≠**let in**: exclude, keep out

e *noun* = **letting in**, acceptance,
itting, allowing, entrance, entry,
ception

verb = **reprimand**, advise, bawl
al), berate, carpet (*informal*),
nsure, check, chew out (*U.S. &*
ormal), chide, counsel, enjoin,
ewarn, give a rocket (*Brit. & N.Z.*
rap over the knuckles, read the
ebuke, reprove, scold, slap on the
into (*informal*), tear (someone)
(*Brit. informal*), tell off (*informal*),
warn
yms
commend, compliment,
ate, praise

tion *noun* = **reprimand**, advice,
caution, chiding, counsel, rebuke,
ance, reproach, reproof, scolding,
f (*informal*), upbraiding, warning

tory *adjective* = **reprimanding**,
hing, advisory, cautionary, rebuking,
ful, reproving, scolding, warning

n = **fuss**, agitation, bother, bustle,
tion, confusion, delay, disturbance,
ent, flurry, pother, stir, to-do, trouble

ence *noun* **1** = **youth**, boyhood,
, juvenescence, minority, teens **2**
fulness, boyishness, childishness,
ess, immaturity, juvenility, puerility

cent *adjective* **1** = **young**, boyish,
growing, immature, juvenile, puerile,
e, youthful ♦ *noun* **2** = **youth**,
, minor, teenager, youngster

verb **1** = **foster**, take in **2** = **choose**,
appropriate, approve, assume,
ce, endorse, espouse, follow, maintain,
select, support, take on, take over,
p

tonyms
ose: abandon, abnegate, cast aside,
ff, disavow, disclaim, disown, forswear,
up, reject, renounce, repudiate, spurn,
one's hands of

tion *noun* **1** = **fostering**, adopting,
rage, taking in **2** = **choice**, acceptance,
obation, appropriation, approval,
mption, embracing, endorsement,
usal, following, maintenance,
cation, selection, support, taking on,

taking over, taking up

adorable *adjective* = **lovable**, appealing,
attractive, captivating, charming, cute,
darling, dear, delightful, fetching, pleasing,
precious, sweet
➤ **Antonyms**
despicable, displeasing, hateful, unlikable *or*
unlikeable, unlovable

adoration *noun* = **love**, admiration, esteem,
estimation, exaltation, glorification, honour,
idolatry, idolization, reverence, veneration,
worship, worshipping

adore *verb* = **love**, admire, bow to, cherish,
dote on, esteem, exalt, glorify, honour,
idolize, revere, reverence, venerate, worship
➤ **Antonyms**
abhor, abominate, despise, detest, execrate,
hate, loathe

adoring *adjective* = **loving**, admiring,
affectionate, devoted, doting, fond
➤ **Antonyms**
despising, detesting, hating, loathing

adorn *verb* = **decorate**, array, beautify,
bedeck, deck, embellish, emblazon,
engarland, enhance, enrich, festoon, garnish
gild the lily, grace, ornament, trim

adornment *noun* **1** = **decoration**,
accessory, embellishment, festoon, frill,
frippery, ornament, supplement, trimming **2**
= **ornamentation**, beautification,
decorating, decoration, embellishment,
trimming

adrift *adjective* **1** = **drifting**, afloat,
unanchored, unmoored **2** = **aimless**,
directionless, goalless, purposeless ♦ *adverb*
3 = **wrong**, amiss, astray, off course

adroit *adjective* = **skilful**, able, adept, apt,
artful, bright (*informal*), clever, cunning,
deft, dexterous, expert, ingenious, masterful,
neat, nimble, proficient, quick-witted, skilled
➤ **Antonyms**
awkward, blundering, bungling,
cack-handed (*informal*), clumsy, ham-fisted
or ham-handed (*informal*), inept, inexpert,
maladroit, uncoordinated, unhandy, unskilful

adroitness *noun* = **skill**, ability, ableness,
address, adeptness, aptness, artfulness,
cleverness, craft, cunning, deftness,
dexterity, expertise, ingeniousness,
ingenuity, knack, masterfulness, mastery,
nimbleness, proficiency, quick-wittedness,
skilfulness

adulation *noun* = **worship**, blandishment,
bootlicking (*informal*), extravagant flattery,
fawning, fulsome praise, servile flattery,
sycophancy
➤ **Antonyms**
abuse, calumniation, censure,
condemnation, disparagement, revilement,
ridicule, vilification, vituperation

Thespian, tragedian, trouper

actress *noun* = **performer**, actor, dramatic
artist, leading lady, play-actor, player, starlet,
Thespian, tragedienne, trouper

actual *adjective* **1** = **definite**, absolute,
categorical, certain, concrete, corporeal,
factual, indisputable, indubitable, physical,
positive, real, substantial, tangible,
undeniable, unquestionable **2** = **real**,
authentic, confirmed, genuine, realistic, true,
truthful, verified
➤ **Antonyms**
fictitious, hypothetical, made-up, probable,
supposed, theoretical, unreal, untrue

actually *adverb* = **really**, absolutely, as a
matter of fact, de facto, essentially, indeed,
in fact, in point of fact, in reality, in truth,
literally, truly, veritably

actuate *verb* = **motivate**, animate, arouse,
cause, dispose, drive, excite, get going,
impel, incite, induce, influence, inspire,
instigate, move, prompt, quicken, rouse,
spur, stimulate, stir, urge

act up *verb* = **misbehave**, be naughty, carry
on, cause trouble, give bother, give trouble,
horse around (*informal*), malfunction, mess
about, piss about (*taboo slang*), piss around
(*taboo slang*), play up (*Brit. informal*), raise
Cain

act upon *see* ACT ON

acumen *noun* = **judgment**, acuteness,
astuteness, cleverness, discernment,
ingenuity, insight, intelligence, keenness,
penetration, perception, perspicacity,
perspicuity, sagacity, sharpness, shrewdness,
smartness, smarts (*slang, chiefly U.S.*),
wisdom, wit

acute *adjective* **1** = **serious**, critical, crucial,
dangerous, decisive, essential, grave,
important, severe, sudden, urgent, vital **2**
= **sharp**, cutting, distressing, excruciating,
exquisite, fierce, harrowing, intense,
overpowering, overwhelming, piercing,
poignant, powerful, racking, severe,
shooting, shrill, stabbing, sudden, violent **3**
= **perceptive**, astute, canny, clever,
discerning, discriminating, incisive,
ingenious, insightful, intuitive, keen,
observant, on the ball (*informal*),
penetrating, perspicacious, piercing,
sensitive, sharp, smart, subtle
➤ **Antonyms**
≠**perceptive**: dense, dim, dim-witted, dull,
obtuse, slow, stupid, unintelligent

acuteness *noun* **1** = **seriousness**, criticality,
criticalness, cruciality, danger,
dangerousness, decisiveness, essentiality,
gravity, importance, severity, suddenness,
urgency, vitalness **2** = **sharpness**,
distressingness, exquisiteness, fierceness,

intenseness, intensity, poignancy,
powerfulness, severity, shrillness,
suddenness, violence **3** = **perceptiveness**,
acuity, astuteness, canniness, cleverness,
discernment, discrimination, ingenuity,
insight, intuition, intuitiveness, keenness,
perception, perspicacity, sensitivity,
sharpness, smartness, subtleness, subtlety, wit

adage *noun* = **saying**, aphorism,
apophthegm, axiom, by-word, dictum,
maxim, motto, precept, proverb, saw

adamant *adjective* = **determined**, firm,
fixed, immovable, inexorable, inflexible,
insistent, intransigent, obdurate, relentless,
resolute, rigid, set, stiff, stubborn,
unbending, uncompromising, unrelenting,
unshakable, unyielding
➤ **Antonyms**
compliant, compromising, easy-going,
flexible, lax, pliant, receptive, responsive,
susceptible, tractable, yielding

adapt *verb* = **adjust**, acclimatize,
accommodate, alter, apply, change, comply,
conform, convert, customize, familiarize,
fashion, fit, habituate, harmonize, make,
match, modify, prepare, qualify, remodel,
shape, suit, tailor, tweak (*informal*)

adaptability *noun* = **flexibility**,
adaptableness, adjustability, alterability,
changeability, compliancy, convertibility,
malleability, modifiability, plasticity, pliability,
pliancy, resilience, variability, versatility

adaptable *adjective* = **flexible**, adjustable,
alterable, changeable, compliant,
conformable, convertible, easy-going,
easy-oasy (*slang*), malleable, modifiable,
plastic, pliant, resilient, variable, versatile

adaptation *noun* **1** = **acclimatization**,
accustomedness, familiarization, habituation,
naturalization **2** = **conversion**, adjustment,
alteration, change, modification, refitting,
remodelling, reworking, shift,
transformation, variation, version

add *verb* **1** = **count up**, add up, compute,
reckon, sum up, total, tot up **2** = **include**,
adjoin, affix, amplify, annex, append, attach,
augment, enlarge by, increase by,
supplement
➤ **Antonyms**
deduct, diminish, lessen, reduce, remove,
subtract, take away, take from

addendum *noun* = **addition**, adjunct, affix,
appendage, appendix, attachment,
augmentation, codicil, extension, extra,
postscript, supplement

addict *noun* **1** = **junkie** (*informal*),
dope-fiend (*slang*), fiend (*informal*), freak
(*informal*), head (*slang*), pill-popper
(*informal*), user (*informal*) **2** = **fan**,
adherent, buff (*informal*), devotee,

enthusiast, follower, freak (*informal*), nut (*slang*)

addicted *adjective* = **hooked** (*slang*), absorbed, accustomed, dedicated, dependent, devoted, disposed, fond, habituated, inclined, obsessed, prone

addiction *noun* = **dependence**, craving, enslavement, habit, obsession

addition *noun* **1** = **inclusion**, accession, adding, adjoining, affixing, amplification, annexation, attachment, augmentation, enlargement, extension, increasing **2** = **extra**, addendum, additive, adjunct, affix, appendage, appendix, extension, gain, increase, increment, supplement **3** = **counting up**, adding up, computation, reckoning, summation, summing up, totalling, totting up **4 in addition (to)** = **as well (as)**, additionally, also, besides, into the bargain, moreover, over and above, to boot, too, withal
➤ **Antonyms**
≠**inclusion**, **counting up**: deduction, detachment, diminution, lessening, reduction, removal, subtraction

additional *adjective* = **extra**, added, add-on, affixed, appended, fresh, further, increased, more, new, other, over-and-above, spare, supplementary

address *noun* **1** = **location**, abode, domicile, dwelling, home, house, lodging, pad (*slang*), place, residence, situation, whereabouts **2** = **direction**, inscription, superscription **3** = **speech**, discourse, disquisition, dissertation, harangue, lecture, oration, sermon, talk ◆ *verb* **4** = **speak to**, accost, apostrophize, approach, greet, hail, invoke, salute, talk to **5** = **give a speech**, discourse, give a talk, harangue, lecture, orate, sermonize, speak, spout, talk **6 address (oneself) to** = **concentrate on**, apply (oneself) to, attend to, devote (oneself) to, engage in, focus on, knuckle down to, look to, take care of, take up, turn to, undertake

adduce *verb* = **mention**, advance, allege, cite, designate, name, offer, present, quote

add up *verb* **1** = **count up**, add, compute, count, reckon, sum up, total, tot up **2** = **mean**, amount, come to, imply, indicate, reveal, signify **3** = **make sense**, be plausible, be reasonable, hold water, ring true, stand to reason

adept *adjective* **1** = **skilful**, able, accomplished, adroit, dexterous, expert, masterful, masterly, practised, proficient, skilled, versed ◆ *noun* **2** = **expert**, buff (*informal*), dab hand (*Brit. informal*), genius, hotshot (*informal*), master, maven (*U.S.*), whizz (*informal*)

➤ **Antonyms**
adjective ≠**skilful**: amateurish, awkward, clumsy, inept, unskilled

adequacy *noun* = **sufficiency**, capability, commensurateness, competence, fairness, requisiteness, satisfactoriness, suitability, tolerability

adequate *adjective* = **enough**, capable, commensurate, competent, fair, passable, requisite, satisfactory, sufficient, suitable, tolerable, up to scratch (*informal*)
➤ **Antonyms**
deficient, inadequate, insufficient, lacking, meagre, scant, short, unsatisfactory, unsuitable

adhere *verb* **1** = **stick**, attach, cement, cleave, cling, cohere, fasten, fix, glue, glue on, hold fast, paste, stick fast, unite **2** = **support**, abide by, be attached, be constant, be devoted, be faithful, be loyal, be true, cleave to, cling, follow, fulfil, heed, keep, keep to, maintain, mind, obey, observe, respect, stand by

adherent *noun* **1** = **supporter**, admirer, advocate, devotee, disciple, fan, follower, hanger-on, henchman, partisan, protagonist, sectary, upholder, votary ◆ *adjective* **2** = **sticky**, adhering, adhesive, clinging, gluey, glutinous, gummy, holding, mucilaginous, sticking, tacky, tenacious
➤ **Antonyms**
noun ≠**supporter**: adversary, antagonist, disputant, enemy, foe, opponent, opposer, opposition, rival

adhesive *adjective* **1** = **sticky**, adhering, attaching, clinging, cohesive, gluey, glutinous, gummy, holding, mucilaginous, sticking, tacky, tenacious ◆ *noun* **2** = **glue**, cement, gum, mucilage, paste

adieu *noun* = **goodbye**, congé, farewell, leave-taking, parting, valediction

adipose *adjective* = **fatty**, fat, greasy, obese, oily, oleaginous, sebaceous

adjacent *adjective* = **next**, abutting, adjoining, alongside, beside, bordering, cheek by jowl, close, contiguous, near, neighbouring, next door, proximate, touching, within sniffing distance (*informal*)
➤ **Antonyms**
distant, far away, remote, separated

adjoin *verb* = **connect**, abut, add, affix, annex, append, approximate, attach, border, combine, communicate with, couple, impinge, interconnect, join, link, neighbour, touch, unite, verge

adjoining *adjective* = **connecting**, abutting, adjacent, bordering, contiguous, interconnecting, joined, joining, near, neighbouring, next door, touching, verging

adjourn *verb* = **postpone**, defer, delay,

discontinue, interrupt, prorogue, put off, put on the back burner (*informal*), recess, stay, suspend, take a rain check on (*U.S. & Canad. informal*)
➤ **Antonyms**
assemble, continue, convene, gather, open, remain, reopen, stay

adjournment *noun* = **postponement**, deferment, deferral, delay, discontinuation, interruption, prorogation, putting off, recess, stay, suspension

adjudge *verb* = **judge**, adjudicate, allot, apportion, assign, award, decide, declare, decree, determine, distribute, order, pronounce

adjudicate *verb* = **judge**, adjudge, arbitrate, decide, determine, mediate, referee, settle, umpire

adjudication *noun* = **judgment**, adjudgment, arbitration, conclusion, decision, determination, finding, pronouncement, ruling, settlement, verdict

adjunct *noun* = **addition**, accessory, addendum, add-on, appendage, appurtenance, auxiliary, complement, supplement

adjure *verb* **1** = **beg**, appeal to, beseech, entreat, implore, invoke, pray, supplicate **2** = **order**, charge, command, direct, enjoin

adjust *verb* = **alter**, acclimatize, accommodate, accustom, adapt, arrange, compose, convert, customize, dispose, fit, fix, harmonize, make conform, measure, modify, order, reconcile, rectify, redress, regulate, remodel, set, settle, suit, tune (up), tweak (*informal*)

adjustable *adjective* = **alterable**, adaptable, flexible, malleable, modifiable, mouldable, movable, tractable

adjustment *noun* **1** = **alteration**, adaptation, arrangement, arranging, fitting, fixing, modification, ordering, rectification, redress, regulation, remodelling, setting, tuning **2** = **acclimatization**, harmonization, orientation, reconciliation, settlement, settling in

ad-lib *verb* **1** = **improvise**, busk, extemporize, make up, speak extemporaneously, speak impromptu, speak off the cuff, vamp, wing it (*informal*) ◆ *adjective* **2** = **improvised**, extemporaneous, extempore, extemporized, impromptu, made up, off-the-cuff (*informal*), off the top of one's head, unprepared, unrehearsed ◆ *adverb* **3 ad lib** = **off the cuff**, extemporaneously, extempore, impromptu, off the top of one's head (*informal*), spontaneously, without preparation, without rehearsal

administer *verb* **1** = **manage**, conduct,

control, di... superinten... contribute, impose, me...

administra...
administerin... direction, dis... execution, g... overseeing, p... superintenden... = **government**... management, ...

administrati...
directorial, exe... gubernatorial (... organizational, ...

administrator...
bureaucrat, exe... supervisor

admirable *adje...*
commendable, e... laudable, merito... sterling, superior, ... worthy
➤ **Antonyms**
bad, commonplac... disappointing, disp... great shakes (*infor...*)

admiration *noun*...
affection, amazeme... approbation, approv... delight, esteem, plea... surprise, veneration, ...

admire *verb* **1** = **resp...**
approve, esteem, ido... prize, take one's hat ... value, venerate, wors... appreciate, delight in, ... wonder at
➤ **Antonyms**
contemn, deride, desp... look down one's nose a... misprize, scorn, sneer a...

admirer *noun* **1** = **suito...**
lover, sweetheart, wooe... buff (*informal*), devotee... follower, partisan, protag... votary, worshipper

admissible *adjective* = ...
acceptable, allowable, allo... permitted, tolerable, toler...
➤ **A...**
≠**ch...**
cast give was...

admission *noun* **1** = **entra...**
access, admittance, entrée, ... initiation, introduction **2** = ... acknowledgment, admitting, ... allowance, avowal, concessio... disclosure, divulgence, profes...

admit *verb*...
affirm, avow... declare, disc... slang), ow... agree, gran... in, accept, ... initiate, int...
➤ **Anton...**
≠**allow**: de... prohibit, re...

admittanc...
access, adm... passage, r...

admonish...
out (*infor...*) caution, c... Canad. in... exhort, fo... informal) riot act, ... wrist, tea... off a strip... upbraid, r...
➤ **Anto...**
applaud, ... congratu...

admonit...
berating... remonst... telling o...

admoni...
admonit... reproac...

ado *nou...*
comm... exciten...

adoles...
girlhoo... = you... girlish...

adoles...
girlish... teena... juven...

adopt...
acce... embr... ratify... take ...
➤ **A...**
≠**ch...**
cast give was...

adop...
fost... app... ass... esp... rati...

adulatory *adjective* = **worshipping**, blandishing, bootlicking (*informal*), fawning, flattering, obsequious, praising, servile, slavish, sycophantic

adult *noun* 1 = **grown-up**, grown *or* grown-up person (man *or* woman), person of mature age ♦ *adjective* 2 = **fully grown**, full grown, fully developed, grown-up, mature, of age, ripe

adulterate *verb* 1 = **debase**, attenuate, bastardize, contaminate, corrupt, depreciate, deteriorate, devalue, make impure, mix with, thin, vitiate, water down, weaken ♦ *adjective* 2 = **debased**, adulterated, attenuated, bastardized, contaminated, corrupt, depreciated, deteriorated, devalued, mixed, thinned, vitiated, watered down, weakened

adumbrate *verb* = **foreshadow**, augur, forecast, foretell, portend, predict, prefigure, presage, prognosticate, prophesy

adumbration *noun* = **foretelling**, augury, forecast, foreshadowing, omen, portent, prediction, prefiguration, prefigurement, presage, prognostication, prophecy, sign

advance *verb* 1 = **progress**, accelerate, come forward, go ahead, go forward, go on, make inroads, move onward, move up, press on, proceed 2 = **promote**, accelerate, bring forward, bring up, elevate, hasten, send forward, send up, speed, upgrade 3 = **benefit**, further, grow, improve, multiply, prosper, thrive 4 = **suggest**, adduce, allege, cite, offer, present, proffer, put forward, submit 5 = **lend**, pay beforehand, supply on credit ♦ *noun* 6 = **progress**, advancement, development, forward movement, headway, inroads, onward movement 7 = **improvement**, advancement, amelioration, betterment, breakthrough, furtherance, gain, growth, progress, promotion, step 8 = **loan**, credit, deposit, down payment, increase (*in price*), prepayment, retainer, rise (*in price*) 9 **advances** = **overtures**, approach, approaches, moves, proposals, proposition ♦ *adjective* 10 = **prior**, beforehand, early, foremost, forward, in front, leading 11 **in advance** = **beforehand**, ahead, earlier, in the forefront, in the lead, in the van, on the barrelhead, previously
➤ **Antonyms**
verb ≠**progress**: decrease, diminish, lessen, move back, regress, retreat, weaken ≠**promote**: demote, hold back, impede, retard, set back ≠**suggest**: hide, hold back, suppress, withhold ≠**lend**: defer payment, withhold payment

advanced *adjective* = **foremost**, ahead, avant-garde, extreme, forward, higher, leading, precocious, progressive

➤ **Antonyms**
backward, behind, late, retarded, underdeveloped, undeveloped

advancement *noun* 1 = **promotion**, advance, amelioration, betterment, gain, growth, improvement, preferment, progress, rise 2 = **progress**, advance, forward movement, headway, onward movement

advantage *noun* = **benefit**, ace in the hole, ace up one's sleeve, aid, ascendancy, asset, assistance, avail, blessing, boon, boot (*obsolete*), convenience, dominance, edge, gain, good, help, inside track, interest, lead, mileage (*informal*), precedence, pre-eminence, profit, service, start, superiority, sway, upper hand, use, utility, welfare
➤ **Antonyms**
curse, difficulty, disadvantage, downside, drawback, handicap, hindrance, inconvenience, snag

advantageous *adjective* 1 = **beneficial**, convenient, expedient, helpful, of service, profitable, useful, valuable, worthwhile 2 = **superior**, dominant, dominating, favourable
➤ **Antonyms**
≠**beneficial**: detrimental, unfavourable, unfortunate, unhelpful, useless

advent *noun* = **coming**, appearance, approach, arrival, entrance, occurrence, onset, visitation

adventitious *adjective* = **accidental**, casual, chance, extraneous, foreign, fortuitous, incidental, nonessential, unexpected

adventure *noun* = **escapade**, chance, contingency, enterprise, experience, exploit, hazard, incident, occurrence, risk, speculation, undertaking, venture

adventurer *noun* 1 = **mercenary**, charlatan, fortune-hunter, gambler, opportunist, rogue, speculator 2 = **hero**, daredevil, heroine, knight-errant, soldier of fortune, swashbuckler, traveller, venturer, voyager, wanderer

adventurous *adjective* = **daring**, adventuresome, audacious, bold, dangerous, daredevil, enterprising, foolhardy, have-a-go (*informal*), hazardous, headstrong, intrepid, rash, reckless, risky, temerarious (*rare*), venturesome
➤ **Antonyms**
careful, cautious, chary, circumspect, hesitant, prudent, safe, tentative, timid, timorous, unadventurous, wary

adversary *noun* = **opponent**, antagonist, competitor, contestant, enemy, foe, opposer, rival
➤ **Antonyms**
accomplice, ally, associate, collaborator,

colleague, confederate, co-worker, friend, helper, partner, supporter

adverse *adjective* = **unfavourable**, antagonistic, conflicting, contrary, detrimental, disadvantageous, hostile, inexpedient, inimical, injurious, inopportune, negative, opposing, opposite, reluctant, repugnant, unfortunate, unfriendly, unlucky, unpropitious, unwilling
➤ **Antonyms**
advantageous, auspicious, beneficial, favourable, fortunate, helpful, lucky, opportune, promising, propitious, suitable

adversity *noun* = **hardship**, affliction, bad luck, calamity, catastrophe, deep water, disaster, distress, hard times, ill-fortune, ill-luck, misery, misfortune, mishap, reverse, sorrow, suffering, trial, trouble, woe, wretchedness

advert *noun Brit. informal* = **advertisement**, ad (*informal*), announcement, bill, blurb, circular, commercial, display, notice, placard, plug (*informal*), poster, promotion, publicity, puff

advertise *verb* = **publicize**, advise, announce, apprise, blazon, crack up (*informal*), declare, display, flaunt, inform, make known, notify, plug (*informal*), praise, proclaim, promote, promulgate, publish, puff, push (*informal*), tout

advertisement *noun* = **advert** (*Brit. informal*), ad (*informal*), announcement, bill, blurb, circular, commercial, display, notice, placard, plug (*informal*), poster, promotion, publicity, puff

advice *noun* **1** = **guidance**, admonition, caution, counsel, help, injunction, opinion, recommendation, suggestion, view **2** = **notification**, information, instruction, intelligence, notice, warning, word

advisability *noun* = **wisdom**, appropriateness, aptness, desirability, expediency, fitness, judiciousness, profitability, propriety, prudence, seemliness, soundness, suitability

advisable *adjective* = **wise**, appropriate, apt, desirable, expedient, fit, fitting, judicious, politic, profitable, proper, prudent, recommended, seemly, sensible, sound, suggested, suitable
➤ **Antonyms**
ill-advised, impolitic, improper, imprudent, inappropriate, inexpedient, injudicious, silly, stupid, undesirable, unfitting, unprofitable, unseemly, unsound, unsuitable, unwise

advise *verb* **1** = **recommend**, admonish, caution, commend, counsel, enjoin, prescribe, suggest, urge **2** = **notify**, acquaint, apprise, inform, let (someone) know, make known, report, tell, warn

adviser *noun* = **guide**, aide, authority, coach, confidant, consultant, counsel, counsellor, guru, helper, lawyer, mentor, right-hand man, solicitor, teacher, tutor

advisory *adjective* = **advising**, consultative, counselling, helping, recommending

advocacy *noun* = **recommendation**, advancement, argument for, backing, campaigning for, championing, defence, encouragement, espousal, justification, pleading for, promotion, promulgation, propagation, proposal, spokesmanship, support, upholding, urging

advocate *verb* **1** = **recommend**, advise, argue for, campaign for, champion, commend, countenance, defend, encourage, espouse, favour, hold a brief for (*informal*), justify, plead for, prescribe, press for, promote, propose, speak for, support, uphold, urge ♦ *noun* **2** = **supporter**, apologist, apostle, backer, campaigner, champion, counsellor, defender, pleader, promoter, proponent, proposer, speaker, spokesman, upholder **3** *Law* = **lawyer**, attorney, barrister, counsel, solicitor
➤ **Antonyms**
verb ≠**recommend**: contradict, oppose, resist, speak against, take a stand against, take issue with

aegis *noun As in* **under the aegis of** = **protection**, advocacy, auspices, backing, favour, guardianship, patronage, shelter, sponsorship, support, wing

affability *noun* = **friendliness**, amiability, amicability, approachability, benevolence, benignity, civility, congeniality, cordiality, courtesy, geniality, good humour, good nature, graciousness, kindliness, mildness, obligingness, pleasantness, sociability, urbanity, warmth

affable *adjective* = **friendly**, amiable, amicable, approachable, benevolent, benign, civil, congenial, cordial, courteous, genial, good-humoured, good-natured, gracious, kindly, mild, obliging, pleasant, sociable, urbane, warm
➤ **Antonyms**
brusque, cold, discourteous, distant, haughty, rude, stand-offish, surly, unapproachable, uncivil, unfriendly, ungracious, unpleasant, unsociable

affair *noun* **1** = **event**, activity, business, circumstance, concern, episode, happening, incident, interest, matter, occurrence, proceeding, project, question, subject, transaction, undertaking **2** = **relationship**, amour, intrigue, liaison, romance

affect[1] *verb* **1** = **influence**, act on, alter, bear upon, change, concern, impact, impinge upon, interest, involve, modify, prevail over, regard, relate to, sway, transform **2 = move,** disturb, impress, overcome, perturb, stir, touch, tug at (someone's) heartstrings (*often facetious*), upset

affect² *verb* = **put on**, adopt, aspire to, assume, contrive, counterfeit, feign, imitate, pretend, sham, simulate

affectation *noun* = **pretence**, act, affectedness, appearance, artificiality, assumed manners, façade, fakery, false display, insincerity, mannerism, pose, pretension, pretentiousness, sham, show, simulation, unnatural imitation

affected *adjective* **1 = influenced**, afflicted, altered, changed, concerned, damaged, deeply moved, distressed, hurt, impaired, impressed, injured, melted, stimulated, stirred, touched, troubled, upset **2 = pretended**, artificial, arty-farty (*informal*), assumed, camp (*informal*), conceited, contrived, counterfeit, feigned, insincere, la-di-da (*informal*), mannered, mincing, phoney *or* phony (*informal*), pompous, precious, pretentious, put-on, sham, simulated, spurious, stiff, studied, unnatural
➤ Antonyms
≠**influenced:** cured, unaffected, unconcerned, unharmed, uninjured, unmoved, untouched ≠**pretended:** genuine, natural, real, unaffected

affecting *adjective* = **moving**, pathetic, piteous, pitiable, pitiful, poignant, sad, saddening, touching

affection *noun* = **fondness**, amity, attachment, care, desire, feeling, friendliness, goodwill, inclination, kindness, liking, love, passion, propensity, tenderness, warmth

affectionate *adjective* = **fond**, attached, caring, devoted, doting, friendly, kind, loving, tender, warm, warm-hearted
➤ Antonyms
cold, cool, glacial, indifferent, stony, uncaring, undemonstrative, unfeeling, unresponsive

affiliate *verb* = **join**, ally, amalgamate, annex, associate, band together, combine, confederate, connect, incorporate, link, unite

affiliation *noun* = **connection**, alliance, amalgamation, association, banding together, coalition, combination, confederation, incorporation, joining, league, merging, relationship, union

affinity *noun* **1 = attraction**, fondness, inclination, leaning, liking, partiality, rapport, sympathy **2 = similarity**, alliance, analogy, closeness, compatibility, connection, correspondence, kinship, likeness, relation, relationship, resemblance
➤ Antonyms
≠**attraction:** abhorrence, animosity,

antipathy, aversion, dislike, hatred, hostility, loathing, repugnance, revulsion ≠**similarity:** difference, disparity, dissimilarity

affirm *verb* = **declare**, assert, asseverate, attest, aver, avouch, avow, certify, confirm, maintain, pronounce, ratify, state, swear, testify
➤ Antonyms
deny, disallow, rebut, refute, reject, renounce, repudiate, rescind, retract

affirmation *noun* = **declaration**, assertion, asseveration, attestation, averment, avouchment, avowal, certification, confirmation, oath, pronouncement, ratification, statement, testimony

affirmative *adjective* = **agreeing**, approving, assenting, concurring, confirming, consenting, corroborative, favourable, positive
➤ Antonyms
denying, disagreeing, disapproving, dissenting, negating, negative

affix *verb* = **attach**, add, annex, append, bind, fasten, glue, join, paste, put on, stick, subjoin, tack, tag
➤ Antonyms
detach, disconnect, remove, take off, unfasten, unglue

afflict *verb* = **torment**, ail, beset, burden, distress, grieve, harass, hurt, oppress, pain, plague, rack, smite, trouble, try, wound

affliction *noun* = **suffering**, adversity, calamity, cross, curse, depression, disease, distress, grief, hardship, misery, misfortune, ordeal, pain, plague, scourge, sickness, sorrow, torment, trial, tribulation, trouble, woe, wretchedness

affluence *noun* = **wealth**, abundance, big bucks (*informal, chiefly U.S.*), big money, exuberance, fortune, megabucks (*U.S. & Canad. slang*), opulence, plenty, pretty penny (*informal*), profusion, prosperity, riches, tidy sum (*informal*), wad (*U.S. & Canad. slang*)

affluent *adjective* **1 = wealthy**, loaded (*slang*), moneyed, opulent, prosperous, rich, rolling in money (*slang*), well-heeled (*informal*), well-off, well-to-do **2 = plentiful**, abundant, copious, exuberant, plenteous
➤ Antonyms
≠**wealthy:** broke (*informal*), destitute, down at heel, hard-up (*informal*), impecunious, impoverished, indigent, on the breadline, penniless, penurious, poor, poverty-stricken, skint (*Brit. slang*), stony-broke (*Brit. slang*)

afford *verb* **1** *As in* **can afford** = **spare**, bear, manage, stand, sustain **2 = give**, bestow, furnish, grant, impart, offer, produce, provide, render, supply, yield

affordable *adjective* = **inexpensive**, cheap, economical, low-cost, moderate, modest, reasonable
➤ **Antonyms**
beyond one's means, costly, dear, exorbitant, expensive, unaffordable, uneconomical

affray *noun* = **fight**, *bagarre,* brawl, contest, disturbance, dogfight, encounter, feud, fracas, free-for-all (*informal*), mêlée, outbreak, quarrel, scrap, scrimmage, scuffle, set-to (*informal*), shindig (*informal*), shindy (*informal*), skirmish, tumult

affront *noun* 1 = **insult**, abuse, indignity, injury, offence, outrage, provocation, slap in the face (*informal*), slight, slur, vexation, wrong ♦ *verb* 2 = **offend**, abuse, anger, annoy, displease, insult, outrage, pique, provoke, put *or* get one's back up, slight, vex

afire *adjective* 1 = **burning**, ablaze, aflame, alight, blazing, fiery, flaming, ignited, lighted, lit, on fire 2 = **passionate**, aglow, aroused, excited, fervent, impassioned, stimulated

aflame *adjective* 1 = **burning**, ablaze, afire, alight, blazing, fiery, flaming, ignited, lighted, lit, on fire 2 = **passionate**, afire, aroused, excited, fervent, impassioned, stimulated 3 = **red**, aglow, flushed, inflamed, ruddy

afoot *adjective* = **going on**, about, abroad, afloat, astir, brewing, circulating, current, happening, hatching, in preparation, in progress, in the wind, on the go (*informal*), operating, up (*informal*)

afraid *adjective* 1 = **scared**, alarmed, anxious, apprehensive, cowardly, faint-hearted, fearful, frightened, intimidated, nervous, reluctant, suspicious, timid, timorous 2 = **sorry**, regretful, unhappy
➤ **Antonyms**
≠scared: audacious, bold, fearless, inapprehensive, indifferent, unafraid ≠sorry: happy, pleased

afresh *adverb* = **again**, anew, newly, once again, once more, over again

after *adverb* = **following**, afterwards, behind, below, later, subsequently, succeeding, thereafter
➤ **Antonyms**
before, earlier, in advance, in front, previously, prior to, sooner

aftermath *noun* = **effects**, aftereffects, consequences, end, end result, outcome, results, sequel, upshot, wake

again *adverb* 1 = **once more**, afresh, anew, another time 2 = **also**, besides, furthermore, in addition, moreover 3 = **on the other hand**, on the contrary

against *preposition* 1 = **beside**, abutting, close up to, facing, fronting, in contact with, on, opposite to, touching, upon 2 = **opposed to**, anti (*informal*), averse to, contra (*informal*), counter, hostile to, in defiance of, in opposition to, in the face of, opposing, resisting, versus 3 = **in preparation for**, in anticipation of, in expectation of, in provision for

age *noun* 1 = **time**, date, day(s), duration, epoch, era, generation, lifetime, period, span 2 = **old age**, advancing years, decline (*of life*), majority, maturity, senescence, senility, seniority ♦ *verb* 3 = **grow old**, decline, deteriorate, mature, mellow, ripen
➤ **Antonyms**
noun ≠old age: adolescence, boyhood *or* girlhood, childhood, immaturity, salad days, young days, youth

aged *adjective* = **old**, age-old, ancient, antiquated, antique, cobwebby, elderly, getting on, grey, hoary, past it (*informal*), senescent, superannuated
➤ **Antonyms**
adolescent, boyish *or* girlish, childish, immature, juvenile, young, youthful

agency *noun* 1 = **business**, bureau, department, office, organization 2 *Old-fashioned* = **medium**, action, activity, auspices, efficiency, force, influence, instrumentality, intercession, intervention, means, mechanism, mediation, operation, power, work

agenda *noun* = **list**, calendar, diary, plan, programme, schedule, timetable

agent *noun* 1 = **representative**, advocate, deputy, emissary, envoy, factor, go-between, negotiator, rep (*informal*), substitute, surrogate 2 = **worker**, actor, author, doer, executor, mover, officer, operative, operator, performer 3 = **force**, agency, cause, instrument, means, power, vehicle

aggravate *verb* 1 = **make worse**, add insult to injury, exacerbate, exaggerate, fan the flames of, heighten, increase, inflame, intensify, magnify, worsen 2 *Informal* = **annoy**, be on one's back (*slang*), bother, exasperate, gall, get in one's hair (*informal*), get on one's nerves (*informal*), get on one's wick (*Brit. slang*), get under one's skin (*informal*), get up one's nose (*informal*), hassle (*informal*), irk, irritate, nark (*Brit., Austral., & N.Z. slang*), needle (*informal*), nettle, pester, piss one off (*taboo slang*), provoke, rub (someone) up the wrong way (*informal*), tease, vex
➤ **Antonyms**
≠make worse: alleviate, assuage, calm, diminish, ease, improve, lessen, mitigate, smooth ≠annoy: assuage, calm, pacify, please

aggravation *noun* 1 = **worsening**, exacerbation, exaggeration, heightening, increase, inflaming, intensification, magnification 2 *Informal* = **annoyance**, exasperation, gall, grief (*informal*), hassle (*informal*), irksomeness, irritation, provocation, teasing, vexation

aggregate *noun* 1 = **total**, accumulation, agglomeration, amount, assemblage, body, bulk, collection, combination, heap, lump, mass, mixture, pile, sum, whole ♦ *adjective* 2 = **total**, accumulated, added, assembled, collected, collective, combined, composite, corporate, cumulative, mixed ♦ *verb* 3 = **combine**, accumulate, amass, assemble, collect, heap, mix, pile

aggression *noun* 1 = **hostility**, aggressiveness, antagonism, belligerence, destructiveness, pugnacity 2 = **attack**, assault, encroachment, injury, invasion, offence, offensive, onslaught, raid

aggressive *adjective* 1 = **hostile**, belligerent, destructive, offensive, pugnacious, quarrelsome 2 = **forceful**, assertive, bold, dynamic, energetic, enterprising, in-your-face (*slang*), militant, pushing, pushy (*informal*), vigorous, zealous
➤ **Antonyms**
≠**hostile**: friendly, peaceful ≠**forceful**: mild, quiet, retiring, submissive

aggressor *noun* = **attacker**, assailant, assaulter, invader

aggrieved *adjective* = **hurt**, afflicted, distressed, disturbed, harmed, ill-used, injured, peeved (*informal*), saddened, unhappy, woeful, wronged

aghast *adjective* = **horrified**, afraid, amazed, appalled, astonished, astounded, awestruck, confounded, frightened, horror-struck, shocked, startled, stunned, thunder-struck

agile *adjective* 1 = **nimble**, active, brisk, limber, lissom(e), lithe, lively, quick, sprightly, spry, supple, swift 2 = **acute**, alert, bright (*informal*), clever, lively, nimble, prompt, quick, quick-witted, sharp
➤ **Antonyms**
≠**nimble**: awkward, clumsy, heavy, lumbering, ponderous, slow, slow-moving, stiff, ungainly, unsupple

agility *noun* 1 = **nimbleness**, activity, briskness, litheness, liveliness, quickness, sprightliness, spryness, suppleness, swiftness 2 = **acuteness**, alertness, cleverness, liveliness, promptitude, promptness, quickness, quick-wittedness, sharpness

agitate *verb* 1 = **upset**, alarm, arouse, confuse, disconcert, disquiet, distract, disturb, excite, faze, ferment, fluster, incite, inflame, perturb, rouse, ruffle, stimulate, trouble, unnerve, work up, worry 2 = **stir**, beat, churn, convulse, disturb, rock, rouse, shake, toss
➤ **Antonyms**
≠**upset**: appease, assuage, calm, calm down, mollify, pacify, placate, quiet, quieten, soothe, still, tranquillize

agitation *noun* 1 = **turmoil**, alarm, arousal, clamour, commotion, confusion, discomposure, disquiet, distraction, disturbance, excitement, ferment, flurry, fluster, incitement, lather (*informal*), outcry, stimulation, tizzy, tizz *or* tiz-woz (*informal*), trouble, tumult, upheaval, upset, worry 2 = **turbulence**, churning, convulsion, disturbance, rocking, shake, shaking, stir, stirring, tossing, upheaval

agitator *noun* = **troublemaker**, agent provocateur, demagogue, firebrand, inciter, instigator, rabble-rouser, revolutionary, stirrer (*informal*)

agog *adjective* = **eager**, avid, curious, enthralled, enthusiastic, excited, expectant, impatient, in suspense, keen
➤ **Antonyms**
apathetic, incurious, indifferent, unconcerned, uninterested

agonize *verb* = **suffer**, be distressed, be in agony, be in anguish, go through the mill, labour, strain, strive, struggle, worry, writhe

agony *noun* = **suffering**, affliction, anguish, distress, misery, pain, pangs, throes, torment, torture, woe

agree *verb* 1 = **concur**, accede, acquiesce, admit, allow, assent, be of the same mind, be of the same opinion, comply, concede, consent, engage, grant, permit, see eye to eye, settle, shake hands 2 = **get on (together)**, accord, answer, chime, coincide, conform, correspond, fit, harmonize, match, square, suit, tally
➤ **Antonyms**
≠**concur**: contradict, deny, differ, disagree, dispute, dissent, rebut, refute, retract

agreeable *adjective* 1 = **pleasant**, acceptable, congenial, delightful, enjoyable, gratifying, likable *or* likeable, pleasing, pleasurable, satisfying, to one's liking, to one's taste 2 = **consenting**, acquiescent, agreeing, amenable, approving, complying, concurring, in accord, onside (*informal*), responsive, sympathetic, well-disposed, willing
➤ **Antonyms**
≠**pleasant**: disagreeable, displeasing, horrid, offensive, unlikable *or* unlikeable, unpleasant

agreement *noun* 1 = **concurrence**, agreeing, assent, compliance, concord, consent, harmony, union, unison 2 = **correspondence**, accord, accordance, affinity, agreeing, analogy, compatibility,

conformity, congruity, consistency, similarity, suitableness **3 = contract**, arrangement, bargain, compact, covenant, deal (*informal*), pact, settlement, treaty, understanding
➤ **Antonyms**
≠ **concurrence**: altercation, argument, clash, conflict, discord, dispute, dissent, division, falling-out, quarrel, row, squabble, strife, tiff, wrangle ≠ **correspondence**: difference, discrepancy, disparity, dissimilarity, diversity, incompatibility, incongruity

agricultural *adjective* = **farming**, agrarian, country, rural, rustic

agriculture *noun* = **farming**, agronomics, agronomy, cultivation, culture, husbandry, tillage

aground *adverb* = **beached**, ashore, foundered, grounded, high and dry, on the rocks, stranded, stuck

ahead *adverb* = **in front**, along, at an advantage, at the head, before, forwards, in advance, in the foreground, in the lead, in the vanguard, leading, on, onwards, to the fore, winning

aid *noun* **1 = help**, assistance, benefit, encouragement, favour, promotion, relief, service, succour, support **2 = helper**, abettor, adjutant, aide, aide-de-camp, assistant, second, supporter ♦ *verb* **3 = help**, abet, assist, befriend, encourage, favour, give a leg up (*informal*), promote, relieve, second, serve, subsidize, succour, support, sustain
➤ **Antonyms**
noun ≠ **help**: hindrance ♦ *verb* ≠ **help**: detract from, harm, hinder, hurt, impede, obstruct, oppose, thwart

aide *noun* = **assistant**, attendant, helper, right-hand man, second, supporter

ailing *adjective* = **ill**, indisposed, infirm, poorly, sick, under the weather (*informal*), unwell, weak

ailment *noun* = **illness**, affliction, complaint, disease, disorder, infirmity, malady, sickness

aim *verb* **1 = intend**, aspire, attempt, design, direct, draw a bead (on), endeavour, level, mean, plan, point, propose, purpose, resolve, seek, set one's sights on, sight, strive, take aim (at), train, try, want, wish ♦ *noun* **2 = intention**, ambition, aspiration, course, design, desire, direction, end, goal, Holy Grail (*informal*), intent, mark, object, objective, plan, purpose, scheme, target, wish

aimless *adjective* = **purposeless**, chance, directionless, erratic, frivolous, goalless, haphazard, pointless, random, stray, undirected, unguided, unpredictable, vagrant, wayward
➤ **Antonyms**
decided, deliberate, determined, firm, fixed,

positive, purposeful, resolute, resolved, settled, single-minded

air *noun* **1 = atmosphere**, heavens, sky **2 = wind**, blast, breath, breeze, draught, puff, waft, whiff, zephyr **3 = manner**, ambience, appearance, atmosphere, aura, bearing, character, demeanour, effect, feeling, flavour, impression, look, mood, quality, style, tone, vibes (*slang*) **4 = tune**, aria, lay, melody, song **5 = circulation**, display, dissemination, exposure, expression, publicity, utterance, vent, ventilation ♦ *verb* **6 = publicize**, circulate, communicate, declare, disclose, display, disseminate, divulge, exhibit, expose, express, give vent to, make known, make public, proclaim, reveal, take the wraps off, tell, utter, ventilate, voice **7 = ventilate**, aerate, expose, freshen

airborne *adjective* = **flying**, floating, gliding, hovering, in flight, in the air, on the wing

airily *adverb* = **light-heartedly**, animatedly, blithely, breezily, buoyantly, gaily, happily, high-spiritedly, jauntily

airiness *noun* **1 = freshness**, breeziness, draughtiness, gustiness, lightness, openness, windiness **2 = light-heartedness**, animation, blitheness, breeziness, buoyancy, gaiety, happiness, high spirits, jauntiness, lightness of heart

airing *noun* **1 = ventilation**, aeration, drying, freshening **2 = exposure**, circulation, display, dissemination, expression, publicity, utterance, vent, ventilation

airless *adjective* = **stuffy**, breathless, close, heavy, muggy, oppressive, stale, stifling, suffocating, sultry, unventilated
➤ **Antonyms**
airy, blowy, breezy, draughty, fresh, gusty, light, open, spacious, well-ventilated

airs *plural noun* = **affectation**, affectedness, arrogance, haughtiness, hauteur, pomposity, pretensions, superciliousness, swank (*informal*)

airy *adjective* **1 = well-ventilated**, blowy, breezy, draughty, fresh, gusty, light, lofty, open, spacious, uncluttered, windy **2 = light-hearted**, animated, blithe, buoyant, cheerful, cheery, chirpy (*informal*), debonair, frolicsome, gay, genial, graceful, happy, high-spirited, jaunty, light, lively, merry, nonchalant, sprightly, upbeat (*informal*) **3 = insubstantial**, aerial, delicate, ethereal, fanciful, flimsy, illusory, imaginary, immaterial, incorporeal, light, vaporous, visionary, weightless, wispy
➤ **Antonyms**
≠ **well-ventilated**: airless, close, heavy, muggy, oppressive, stale, stifling, stuffy,

suffocating, unventilated ≠**light-hearted:**
cheerless, dismal, gloomy, glum,
melancholy, miserable, morose, sad
≠**insubstantial:** concrete, corporeal,
material, real, realistic, substantial, tangible

aisle *noun* = **passageway**, alley, corridor,
gangway, lane, passage, path

alacrity *noun* = **eagerness**, alertness,
avidity, briskness, cheerfulness, dispatch,
enthusiasm, gaiety, hilarity, joyousness,
liveliness, promptness, quickness, readiness,
speed, sprightliness, willingness, zeal
➤ **Antonyms**
apathy, dullness, inertia, lethargy, reluctance,
slowness, sluggishness, unconcern,
unwillingness

alarm *noun* **1** = **fear**, anxiety, apprehension,
consternation, dismay, distress, fright,
nervousness, panic, scare, terror, trepidation,
unease, uneasiness **2** = **danger signal**, alarm
bell, alert, bell, distress signal, hooter, siren,
tocsin, warning ♦ *verb* **3** = **frighten**, daunt,
dismay, distress, give (someone) a turn
(*informal*), make (someone's) hair stand on
end, panic, put the wind up (someone)
(*informal*), scare, startle, terrify, unnerve
➤ **Antonyms**
noun ≠**fear:** calm, calmness, composure,
sang-froid, serenity ♦ *verb* ≠**frighten:**
assure, calm, comfort, reassure, relieve,
soothe

alarming *adjective* = **frightening**, daunting,
dismaying, distressing, disturbing, dreadful,
scaring, shocking, startling, terrifying,
unnerving

alcoholic *noun* **1** = **drunkard**, bibber,
boozer (*informal*), dipsomaniac, drinker,
drunk, hard drinker, inebriate, soak (*slang*),
sot, sponge (*informal*), tippler, toper,
tosspot (*informal*), wino (*informal*)
♦ *adjective* **2** = **intoxicating**, brewed,
distilled, fermented, hard, inebriant,
inebriating, spirituous, strong, vinous

alcove *noun* = **recess**, bay, bower,
compartment, corner, cubbyhole, cubicle,
niche, nook

alert *adjective* **1** = **watchful**, active, agile,
attentive, awake, bright-eyed and
bushy-tailed (*informal*), brisk, careful,
circumspect, heedful, keeping a weather eye
on, lively, nimble, observant, on guard, on
one's toes, on the ball (*informal*), on the
lookout, on the watch, perceptive, quick,
ready, spirited, sprightly, vigilant, wary,
wide-awake ♦ *noun* **2** = **warning**, alarm,
signal, siren ♦ *verb* **3** = **warn**, alarm,
forewarn, inform, notify, signal
➤ **Antonyms**
adjective ≠**watchful:** careless, heedless,
inactive, languid, lethargic, listless, oblivious,
slow, unaware, unconcerned, unwary

♦ *noun* ≠**warning:** all clear ♦ *verb* ≠**warn:**
lull

alertness *noun* = **watchfulness**, activeness,
agility, attentiveness, briskness, carefulness,
circumspection, heedfulness, liveliness,
nimbleness, perceptiveness, promptitude,
quickness, readiness, spiritedness,
sprightliness, vigilance, wariness

alias *adverb* **1** = **also known as**, also called,
otherwise, otherwise known as ♦ *noun* **2**
= **pseudonym**, assumed name, nom de
guerre, nom de plume, pen name, stage
name

alibi *noun* = **excuse**, defence, explanation,
justification, plea, pretext, reason

alien *adjective* **1** = **strange**, adverse, beyond
one's ken, conflicting, contrary, estranged,
exotic, foreign, inappropriate, incompatible,
incongruous, not native, not naturalized,
opposed, outlandish, remote, repugnant,
separated, unfamiliar ♦ *noun* **2** = **foreigner**,
newcomer, outsider, stranger
➤ **Antonyms**
adjective ≠**strange:** affiliated, akin, alike,
allied, analogous, cognate, connected,
corresponding, kindred, like, parallel, related,
similar ♦ *noun* ≠**foreigner:** citizen,
countryman, dweller, inhabitant, national,
resident

alienate *verb* **1** = **set against**, break off,
disaffect, divert, divorce, estrange, make
unfriendly, separate, turn away, withdraw **2**
Law = **transfer**, abalienate, convey

alienation *noun* **1** = **setting against**,
breaking off, disaffection, diversion, divorce,
estrangement, indifference, remoteness,
rupture, separation, turning away,
withdrawal **2** *Law* = **transfer**, abalienation,
conveyance

alight¹ *verb* **1** = **get off**, descend, disembark,
dismount, get down **2** = **land**, come down,
come to rest, descend, light, perch, settle,
touch down
➤ **Antonyms**
≠**land:** ascend, climb, float up, fly up, go
up, lift off, mount, move up, rise, scale, soar,
take off

alight² *adjective* **1** = **on fire**, ablaze, aflame,
blazing, burning, fiery, flaming, flaring,
ignited, lighted, lit **2** = **lit up**, bright,
brilliant, illuminated, shining

align *verb* **1** = **ally**, affiliate, agree, associate,
cooperate, join, side, sympathize **2** = **line
up**, arrange in line, coordinate, even, even
up, make parallel, order, range, regulate,
sequence, straighten

alignment *noun* **1** = **alliance**, affiliation,
agreement, association, cooperation,
sympathy, union **2** = **lining up**, adjustment,
arrangement, coordination, evening, evening

up, line, order, ranging, regulating, sequence, straightening up

alike *adjective* 1 = **similar**, akin, analogous, corresponding, cut from the same cloth, duplicate, equal, equivalent, even, identical, like two peas in a pod, of a piece, parallel, resembling, the same, uniform ♦ *adverb* 2 = **similarly**, analogously, correspondingly, equally, evenly, identically, uniformly
➤ Antonyms
adjective ≠ **similar**: different, dissimilar, diverse, separate, unlike ♦ *adverb* ≠ **similarly**: differently, distinctly, unequally

alive *adjective* 1 = **living**, animate, breathing, having life, in the land of the living (*informal*), subsisting 2 = **in existence**, active, existent, existing, extant, functioning, in force, operative, unquenched 3 = **lively**, active, alert, animated, awake, brisk, cheerful, chirpy (*informal*), eager, energetic, full of beans (*informal*), full of life, quick, spirited, sprightly, spry, vigorous, vital, vivacious, zestful
➤ Antonyms
≠ **living**: dead, deceased, departed, expired, extinct, gone, inanimate, lifeless ≠ **in existence**: extinct, inactive, inoperative, lost ≠ **lively**: apathetic, dull, inactive, lifeless, spiritless

alive to *adjective* = **aware of**, alert to, awake to, cognizant of, eager for, sensible of, sensitive to, susceptible to

alive with *adjective* = **swarming with**, abounding in, bristling with, bustling with, buzzing with, crawling with, hopping with, infested with, jumping with, lousy with (*slang*), overrun by, packed with, teeming with, thronged with

all *adjective* 1 = **the whole of**, every bit of, the complete, the entire, the sum of, the totality of, the total of 2 = **every**, each, each and every, every one of, every single 3 = **complete**, entire, full, greatest, perfect, total, utter ♦ *adverb* 4 = **completely**, altogether, entirely, fully, totally, utterly, wholly ♦ *noun* 5 = **whole amount**, aggregate, entirety, everything, sum, sum total, total, total amount, totality, utmost, whole

allegation *noun* = **claim**, accusation, affirmation, assertion, asseveration, averment, avowal, charge, declaration, deposition, plea, profession, statement

allege *verb* = **claim**, advance, affirm, assert, asseverate, aver, avow, charge, declare, depose, maintain, plead, profess, put forward, state
➤ Antonyms
abjure, contradict, deny, disagree with, disavow, disclaim, gainsay (*archaic or literary*), oppose, refute, renounce, repudiate

alleged *adjective* 1 = **stated**, affirmed, asserted, averred, declared, described, designated 2 = **supposed**, doubtful, dubious, ostensible, professed, purported, so-called, suspect, suspicious, unproved

allegiance *noun* = **loyalty**, adherence, constancy, devotion, duty, faithfulness, fealty, fidelity, homage, obedience, obligation, troth (*archaic*)
➤ Antonyms
disloyalty, faithlessness, falseness, inconstancy, infidelity, perfidy, treachery, treason, unfaithfulness

allegorical *adjective* = **symbolic**, emblematic, figurative, parabolic, symbolizing

allegory *noun* = **symbol**, apologue, emblem, fable, myth, parable, story, symbolism, tale

allergic *adjective* 1 = **sensitive**, affected by, hypersensitive, sensitized, susceptible 2 *Informal* = **averse**, antipathetic, disinclined, hostile, loath, opposed

allergy *noun* 1 = **sensitivity**, antipathy, hypersensitivity, susceptibility 2 *Informal* = **dislike**, antipathy, aversion, disinclination, hostility, loathing, opposition

alleviate *verb* = **ease**, allay, lessen, lighten, moderate, reduce, relieve, soothe

alley *noun* = **passage**, alleyway, backstreet, lane, passageway, pathway, walk

alliance *noun* = **union**, affiliation, affinity, agreement, association, coalition, combination, compact, concordat, confederacy, confederation, connection, federation, league, marriage, pact, partnership, treaty
➤ Antonyms
alienation, breach, break, disaffection, dissociation, disunion, disunity, division, rupture, separation, severance, split, split-up

allied *adjective* = **united**, affiliated, amalgamated, associated, bound, combined, confederate, connected, hand in glove (*informal*), in cahoots (*U.S. informal*), in league, joined, joint, kindred, leagued, linked, married, related, unified, wed

allocate *verb* = **assign**, allot, allow, apportion, appropriate, budget, designate, earmark, mete, set aside, share out

allocation *noun* = **assignment**, allotment, allowance, apportionment, appropriation, grant, lot, measure, portion, quota, ration, share, stint, stipend

allot *verb* = **assign**, allocate, apportion, appropriate, budget, designate, earmark, mete, set aside, share out

allotment *noun* 1 = **plot**, kitchen garden, patch, tract 2 = **assignment**, allocation, allowance, apportionment, appropriation, grant, lot, measure, portion, quota, ration, share, stint, stipend

all-out *adjective* = **total**, complete, determined, exhaustive, full, full-on (*informal*), full-scale, maximum, optimum, outright, resolute, supreme, thorough, thoroughgoing, undivided, unlimited, unremitting, unrestrained, unstinted, utmost
➤ **Antonyms**
careless, cursory, half-hearted, negligent, off-hand, perfunctory, unenthusiastic

allow *verb* **1** = **permit**, approve, authorize, bear, brook, enable, endure, give leave, let, put up with (*informal*), sanction, stand, suffer, tolerate **2** = **give**, allocate, allot, assign, deduct, grant, provide, remit, set aside, spare **3** = **acknowledge**, acquiesce, admit, concede, confess, grant, own
➤ **Antonyms**
≠**permit**: ban, disallow, forbid, prohibit, proscribe, refuse ≠**give**: deny, forbid, refuse ≠**acknowledge**: contradict, deny, disagree with, gainsay (*archaic or literary*), oppose

allowable *adjective* = **permissible**, acceptable, admissible, all right, appropriate, approved, sanctionable, sufferable, suitable, tolerable

allowance *noun* **1** = **portion**, allocation, allotment, amount, annuity, apportionment, grant, lot, measure, pension, quota, ration, remittance, share, stint, stipend, subsidy **2** = **concession**, deduction, discount, rebate, reduction

allow for *verb* = **take into account**, arrange for, consider, foresee, keep in mind, make allowances for, make concessions for, make provision for, plan for, provide for, set (something) aside for, take into consideration

alloy *noun* **1** = **mixture**, admixture, amalgam, blend, combination, composite, compound, hybrid, meld ◆ *verb* **2** = **mix**, admix, amalgamate, blend, combine, compound, fuse, meld

all right *adjective* **1** = **satisfactory**, acceptable, adequate, average, fair, O.K. *or* okay (*informal*), passable, so-so (*informal*), standard, unobjectionable, up to scratch (*informal*) **2** = **well**, hale, healthy, O.K. *or* okay (*informal*), out of the woods, safe, sound, unharmed, unimpaired, uninjured, whole ◆ *adverb* **3** = **satisfactorily**, acceptably, adequately, O.K. *or* okay (*informal*), passably, unobjectionably, well enough
➤ **Antonyms**
adjective ≠**satisfactory**: bad, inadequate, not good enough, not up to scratch (*informal*), objectionable, poor, unacceptable, unsatisfactory ≠**well**: ailing, bad, ill, injured, off colour, out of sorts, poorly, sick, sickly, unhealthy, unwell

allude *verb* = **refer**, hint, imply, intimate, mention, suggest, touch upon

allure *noun* **1** = **attractiveness**, appeal, attraction, charm, enchantment, enticement, glamour, lure, persuasion, seductiveness, temptation ◆ *verb* **2** = **attract**, beguile, cajole, captivate, charm, coax, decoy, enchant, entice, inveigle, lead on, lure, persuade, seduce, tempt, win over

alluring *adjective* = **attractive**, beguiling, bewitching, captivating, come-hither, enchanting, fascinating, fetching, glamorous, intriguing, seductive, sexy, tempting
➤ **Antonyms**
abhorrent, off-putting (*Brit. informal*), repellent, repugnant, repulsive, unattractive

allusion *noun* = **reference**, casual remark, glance, hint, implication, indirect reference, innuendo, insinuation, intimation, mention, suggestion

ally *noun* **1** = **partner**, abettor, accessory, accomplice, associate, coadjutor, collaborator, colleague, confederate, co-worker, friend, helper ◆ *verb* **2** = **unite**, affiliate, associate, band together, collaborate, combine, confederate, connect, join, join battle with, join forces, league, marry, unify
➤ **Antonyms**
noun ≠**partner**: adversary, antagonist, competitor, enemy, foe, opponent, rival
◆ *verb* ≠**unite**: alienate, disaffect, disunite, divide, drive apart, separate, set at odds

almighty *adjective* **1** = **all-powerful**, absolute, invincible, omnipotent, supreme, unlimited **2** *Informal* = **great**, awful, desperate, enormous, excessive, intense, loud, severe, terrible
➤ **Antonyms**
≠**all-powerful**: helpless, impotent, powerless, weak ≠**great**: feeble, insignificant, paltry, poor, slight, tame, weak

almost *adverb* = **nearly**, about, all but, approximately, as good as, close to, just about, not far from, not quite, on the brink of, practically, so near (and) yet so far, virtually, well-nigh

alone *adjective* = **by oneself**, abandoned, apart, by itself, deserted, desolate, detached, forlorn, forsaken, isolated, lonely, lonesome, only, on one's tod (*slang*), out on a limb, separate, single, single-handed, sole, solitary, unaccompanied, unaided, unassisted, unattended, uncombined, unconnected, under one's own steam, unescorted
➤ **Antonyms**
accompanied, aided, among others, assisted, escorted, helped, joint, together

aloof *adjective* = **distant**, chilly, cold, cool, detached, forbidding, formal, haughty,

indifferent, remote, reserved, standoffish, supercilious, unapproachable, unfriendly, uninterested, unresponsive, unsociable, unsympathetic
➤ Antonyms
friendly, gregarious, neighbourly, open, sociable, sympathetic, warm

aloud *adverb* = **out loud**, audibly, clearly, distinctly, intelligibly, plainly

already *adverb* = **before now**, as of now, at present, before, by now, by that time, by then, by this time, even now, heretofore, just now, previously

also *adverb* = **too**, additionally, along with, and, as well, as well as, besides, further, furthermore, in addition, including, into the bargain, moreover, on top of that, plus, to boot

alter *verb* = **change**, adapt, adjust, amend, convert, diversify, metamorphose, modify, recast, reform, remodel, reshape, revise, shift, transform, transmute, turn, tweak (*informal*), vary

alteration *noun* = **change**, adaptation, adjustment, amendment, conversion, difference, diversification, metamorphosis, modification, reformation, remodelling, reshaping, revision, shift, transformation, transmutation, variance, variation

alternate *verb* 1 = **change**, act reciprocally, alter, fluctuate, follow in turn, follow one another, interchange, intersperse, oscillate, rotate, substitute, take turns ◆ *adjective* 2 = **every other**, alternating, every second, interchanging, rotating 3 = **second**, alternative, another, different, substitute

alternative *noun* 1 = **choice**, option, other (*of two*), preference, recourse, selection, substitute ◆ *adjective* 2 = **different**, alternate, another, other, second, substitute

alternatively *adverb* = **or**, as an alternative, by way of alternative, if not, instead, on the other hand, otherwise

although *conjunction* = **though**, albeit, despite the fact that, even if, even supposing, even though, notwithstanding, tho' (*U.S. or poetic*), while

altitude *noun* = **height**, elevation, loftiness, peak, summit

altogether *adverb* 1 = **completely**, absolutely, every inch, fully, lock, stock and barrel, perfectly, quite, thoroughly, totally, utterly, wholly 2 = **on the whole**, all in all, all things considered, as a whole, collectively, generally, in general, *in toto* 3 = **in total**, all told, everything included, in all, in sum, *in toto*, taken together
➤ Antonyms
≠**completely**: halfway, incompletely, in part, in some measure, not fully, partially,

relatively, slightly, somewhat, to a certain degree *or* extent, up to a certain point

altruistic *adjective* = **selfless**, benevolent, charitable, considerate, generous, humanitarian, philanthropic, public-spirited, self-sacrificing, unselfish
➤ Antonyms
egoistic(al), egotistic(al), greedy, looking out for number one (*informal*), mean, self-centred, self-interested, selfish, self-seeking, ungenerous

always *adverb* = **continually**, aye (*Scot.*), consistently, constantly, eternally, ever, everlastingly, evermore, every time, forever, *in perpetuum*, invariably, perpetually, repeatedly, unceasingly, without exception
➤ Antonyms
hardly, hardly ever, infrequently, once in a blue moon, once in a while, only now and then, on rare occasions, rarely, scarcely ever, seldom

amalgamate *verb* = **combine**, alloy, ally, blend, coalesce, commingle, compound, fuse, incorporate, integrate, intermix, meld, merge, mingle, unite
➤ Antonyms
disunite, divide, part, separate, split, split up

amalgamation *noun* = **combination**, admixture, alliance, alloy, amalgam, amalgamating, blend, coalition, commingling, composite, compound, fusion, incorporation, integration, joining, meld, merger, mingling, mixing, mixture, union

amass *verb* = **collect**, accumulate, aggregate, assemble, compile, garner, gather, heap up, hoard, pile up, rake up, scrape together

amateur *noun* = **nonprofessional**, dabbler, dilettante, layman

amateurish *adjective* = **unprofessional**, amateur, bungling, clumsy, crude, inexpert, unaccomplished, unskilful
➤ Antonyms
experienced, expert, practised, professional, skilled

amaze *verb* = **astonish**, alarm, astound, bewilder, boggle the mind, bowl over (*informal*), confound, daze, dumbfound, electrify, flabbergast, shock, stagger, startle, stun, stupefy, surprise

amazement *noun* = **astonishment**, admiration, bewilderment, confusion, marvel, perplexity, shock, stupefaction, surprise, wonder

amazing *adjective* = **astonishing**, astounding, breathtaking, eye-opening, jaw-dropping, overwhelming, staggering, startling, stunning, surprising

ambassador *noun* = **representative**, agent, consul, deputy, diplomat, emissary, envoy, legate, minister, plenipotentiary

ambiguity *noun* = **vagueness**, doubt, doubtfulness, dubiety, dubiousness, enigma, equivocacy, equivocality, equivocation, inconclusiveness, indefiniteness, indeterminateness, obscurity, puzzle, tergiversation, uncertainty

ambiguous *adjective* = **unclear**, clear as mud (*informal*), cryptic, Delphic, doubtful, dubious, enigmatic, enigmatical, equivocal, inconclusive, indefinite, indeterminate, obscure, oracular, puzzling, uncertain, vague
> **Antonyms**
clear, definite, explicit, obvious, plain, simple, specific, unequivocal, unmistakable, unquestionable

ambition *noun* 1 = **enterprise**, aspiration, avidity, desire, drive, eagerness, get-up-and-go (*informal*), hankering, longing, striving, yearning, zeal 2 = **goal**, aim, aspiration, desire, dream, end, Holy Grail (*informal*), hope, intent, objective, purpose, wish

ambitious *adjective* 1 = **enterprising**, aspiring, avid, desirous, driving, eager, hopeful, intent, purposeful, striving, zealous 2 = **demanding**, arduous, bold, challenging, difficult, elaborate, energetic, exacting, formidable, grandiose, hard, impressive, industrious, pretentious, severe, strenuous
> **Antonyms**
≠**enterprising**: apathetic, good-for-nothing, lazy, unambitious, unaspiring ≠**demanding**: easy, modest, simple, unambitious

ambivalence *noun* = **indecision**, clash, conflict, contradiction, doubt, equivocation, fluctuation, hesitancy, irresolution, opposition, uncertainty, vacillation, wavering

ambivalent *adjective* = **undecided**, clashing, conflicting, contradictory, debatable, doubtful, equivocal, fluctuating, hesitant, inconclusive, in two minds, irresolute, mixed, opposed, uncertain, unresolved, unsure, vacillating, warring, wavering
> **Antonyms**
certain, clear, conclusive, convinced, decided, definite, free from doubt, positive, sure, unwavering

amble *verb* = **stroll**, dawdle, meander, mosey (*informal*), ramble, saunter, walk, wander

ambush *noun* 1 = **trap**, ambuscade, attack, concealment, cover, hiding, hiding place, lying in wait, retreat, shelter, waylaying
♦ *verb* 2 = **trap**, ambuscade, attack, bushwhack (*U.S.*), ensnare, surprise, waylay

amenable *adjective* = **receptive**, able to be influenced, acquiescent, agreeable, compliant, open, persuadable, responsive, susceptible, tractable
> **Antonyms**
inflexible, intractable, mulish, obdurate, obstinate, pig-headed, recalcitrant, stiff-necked, stubborn, unbending, unyielding

amend *verb* = **change**, alter, ameliorate, better, correct, enhance, fix, improve, mend, modify, rectify, reform, remedy, repair, revise, tweak (*informal*)

amendment *noun* 1 = **change**, alteration, amelioration, betterment, correction, emendation, enhancement, improvement, mending, modification, rectification, reform, remedy, repair, revision 2 = **alteration**, addendum, addition, adjunct, attachment, clarification

amends *plural noun* As in **make amends for** = **compensation**, apology, atonement, expiation, indemnity, recompense, redress, reparation, requital, restitution, restoration, satisfaction

amenity *noun* 1 = **facility**, advantage, comfort, convenience, service 2 = **courtesy**, affability, agreeableness, amiability, complaisance, mildness, pleasantness, politeness, refinement, suavity
> **Antonyms**
≠**courtesy**: bad manners, discourtesy, impoliteness, incivility, rudeness, ungraciousness

amiability *noun* = **pleasantness**, affability, agreeableness, amiableness, attractiveness, benignity, charm, cheerfulness, delightfulness, engagingness, friendliness, friendship, geniality, good humour, good nature, kindliness, kindness, lovableness, pleasingness, sociability, sweetness, sweetness and light (*informal*), sweet temper, winsomeness

amiable *adjective* = **pleasant**, affable, agreeable, attractive, benign, charming, cheerful, congenial, delightful, engaging, friendly, genial, good-humoured, good-natured, kind, kindly, likable or likeable, lovable, obliging, pleasing, sociable, sweet-tempered, winning, winsome
> **Antonyms**
disagreeable, displeasing, hostile, ill-natured, loathsome, repellent, sour, unfriendly, unpleasant

amicable *adjective* = **friendly**, amiable, brotherly, civil, cordial, courteous, fraternal, good-humoured, harmonious, kind, kindly, neighbourly, peaceable, peaceful, polite, sociable
> **Antonyms**
antagonistic, bellicose, belligerent, disagreeable, hostile, ill-disposed, impolite, inimical, pugnacious, quarrelsome, uncivil, unfriendly, unkind, unsociable

amid, amidst *preposition* = **in the middle of**, among, amongst, in the midst of, in the thick of, surrounded by

amiss *adverb* **1** = **wrongly**, erroneously, faultily, improperly, inappropriately, incorrectly, mistakenly, unsuitably **2** *As in* **take (something) amiss** = **as an insult**, as offensive, out of turn, wrongly ♦ *adjective* **3** = **wrong**, awry, confused, defective, erroneous, fallacious, false, faulty, improper, inaccurate, inappropriate, incorrect, mistaken, out of order, unsuitable, untoward ➤ **Antonyms**
adverb ≠**wrongly**: appropriately, correctly, properly, rightly, suitably, well ♦ *adjective* ≠**wrong**: accurate, appropriate, correct, in order, O.K. or okay (*informal*), perfect, proper, right, suitable, true

ammunition *noun* = **munitions**, armaments, cartridges, explosives, materiel, powder, rounds, shells, shot, shot and shell

amnesty *noun* = **general pardon**, absolution, condonation, dispensation, forgiveness, immunity, oblivion, remission (*of penalty*), reprieve

amok, amuck *adverb* *As in* **run amok** = **madly**, berserk, destructively, ferociously, frenziedly, in a frenzy, insanely, maniacally, murderously, savagely, uncontrollably, violently, wildly

among, amongst *preposition* **1** = **in the midst of**, amid, amidst, in association with, in the middle of, in the thick of, midst, surrounded by, together with, with **2** = **in the group of**, in the class of, in the company of, in the number of, out of **3** = **to each of**, between ♦ *adverb* **4** = **with one another**, by all of, by the joint action of, by the whole of, mutually

amorous *adjective* = **loving**, affectionate, amatory, ardent, attached, doting, enamoured, erotic, fond, impassioned, in love, lovesick, lustful, passionate, tender ➤ **Antonyms**
aloof, cold, distant, frigid, frosty, indifferent, passionless, stand-offish, undemonstrative, unfeeling, unloving

amorphous *adjective* = **shapeless**, characterless, formless, inchoate, indeterminate, irregular, nebulous, nondescript, unformed, unshaped, unshapen, unstructured, vague ➤ **Antonyms**
definite, distinct, regular, shaped, structured

amount *noun* **1** = **quantity**, bulk, expanse, extent, lot, magnitude, mass, measure, number, supply, volume **2** = **total**, addition, aggregate, entirety, extent, lot, sum, sum total, whole

amount to *verb* = **add up to**, aggregate, become, come to, develop into, equal, grow, mean, purport, total

ample *adjective* = **plenty**, abounding, abundant, big, bountiful, broad, capacious, commodious, copious, enough and to spare, expansive, extensive, full, generous, great, large, lavish, liberal, plenteous, plentiful, profuse, rich, roomy, spacious, substantial, two a penny, unrestricted, voluminous, wide ➤ **Antonyms**
inadequate, insufficient, little, meagre, restricted, scant, skimpy, small, sparse, unsatisfactory

amplification *noun* **1** = **explanation**, augmentation, development, elaboration, expansion, expatiation, fleshing out, rounding out, supplementing **2** = **increase**, augmentation, boosting, deepening, dilation, enlargement, expansion, extension, heightening, intensification, lengthening, magnification, raising, strengthening, stretching, widening

amplify *verb* **1** = **go into detail**, augment, develop, elaborate, enlarge, expand, expatiate, explain, flesh out, round out, supplement **2** = **expand**, augment, boost, deepen, dilate, enlarge, extend, heighten, increase, intensify, lengthen, magnify, raise, strengthen, stretch, widen ➤ **Antonyms**
≠**go into detail**: abbreviate, abridge, simplify ≠**expand**: boil down, condense, curtail, cut down, decrease, reduce

amply *adverb* = **fully**, abundantly, bountifully, capaciously, completely, copiously, extensively, generously, greatly, lavishly, liberally, plenteously, plentifully, profusely, richly, substantially, thoroughly, unstintingly, well, with a blank cheque, with a free hand, without stinting ➤ **Antonyms**
inadequately, insufficiently, meagrely, poorly, scantily, skimpily, sparsely, thinly

amputate *verb* = **cut off**, curtail, lop, remove, separate, sever, truncate

amuck *see* AMOK

amuse *verb* = **entertain**, beguile, charm, cheer, delight, divert, enliven, gladden, gratify, interest, occupy, please, recreate, regale, tickle ➤ **Antonyms**
be tedious, bore, jade, pall on, send to sleep, tire, weary

amusement *noun* **1** = **entertainment**, beguilement, cheer, delight, diversion, enjoyment, fun, gladdening, gratification, hilarity, interest, jollies (*slang*), laughter, merriment, mirth, pleasing, pleasure, recreation, regalement, sport **2** = **pastime**, distraction, diversion, entertainment, game,

hobby, joke, lark, prank, recreation, sport
➤ **Antonyms**
≠**entertainment**: boredom, displeasure,
monotony, sadness, tedium

amusing *adjective* = **funny**, charming,
cheerful, cheering, comical, delightful,
diverting, droll, enjoyable, entertaining,
facetious, gladdening, gratifying, humorous,
interesting, jocular, laughable, lively, merry,
pleasant, pleasing, rib-tickling, waggish,
witty
➤ **Antonyms**
boring, dead, dull, flat, humdrum,
monotonous, stale, tedious, tiresome,
unamusing, unexciting, unfunny,
uninteresting, wearisome

anaemic *adjective* = **pale**, ashen, bloodless,
characterless, colourless, dull, enervated,
feeble, frail, infirm, like death warmed up
(*informal*), pallid, sickly, wan, weak
➤ **Antonyms**
blooming, florid, full-blooded, glowing,
hearty, radiant, rosy, rosy-cheeked, rubicund,
ruddy, sanguine

anaesthetic *noun* **1** = **painkiller**, analgesic,
anodyne, narcotic, opiate, sedative, soporific,
stupefacient, stupefactive ♦ *adjective* **2**
= **pain-killing**, analgesic, anodyne,
deadening, dulling, narcotic, numbing,
opiate, sedative, sleep-inducing, soporific,
stupefacient, stupefactive

analogous *adjective* = **similar**, agreeing,
akin, alike, comparable, corresponding,
equivalent, homologous, like, of a piece,
parallel, related, resembling
➤ **Antonyms**
contrasting, different, discrepant, disparate,
dissimilar, diverse, unlike

analogy *noun* = **similarity**, agreement,
comparison, correlation, correspondence,
equivalence, homology, likeness, parallel,
relation, resemblance, similitude

analyse *verb* **1** = **examine**, assay, estimate,
evaluate, interpret, investigate, judge,
research, test, work over **2** = **break down**,
anatomize, consider, dissect, dissolve, divide,
resolve, separate, study, think through

analysis *noun* **1** = **examination**,
anatomization, anatomy, assay, breakdown,
dissection, dissolution, division, inquiry,
investigation, perusal, resolution, scrutiny,
separation, sifting, test **2** = **finding**,
estimation, evaluation, interpretation,
judgment, opinion, reasoning, study

analytic, analytical *adjective* = **rational**,
detailed, diagnostic, discrete, dissecting,
explanatory, expository, inquiring,
inquisitive, interpretative, interpretive,
investigative, logical, organized,
problem-solving, questioning, searching,

studious, systematic, testing

anarchic *adjective* = **lawless**, chaotic,
confused, disordered, disorganized,
misgoverned, misruled, off the rails,
rebellious, revolutionary, rioting, riotous,
ungoverned
➤ **Antonyms**
controlled, decorous, disciplined,
law-abiding, ordered, peaceable, peaceful,
quiet, restrained, well-behaved

anarchist *noun* = **revolutionary**, insurgent,
nihilist, rebel, terrorist

anarchy *noun* = **lawlessness**, chaos,
confusion, disorder, disorganization,
misgovernment, misrule, rebellion,
revolution, riot
➤ **Antonyms**
control, discipline, government, law, law and
order, order, peace, rule

anathema *noun* = **abomination**, bane,
bête noire, bugbear, enemy, pariah

anathematize *verb* = **curse**, abominate,
ban, condemn, damn, denounce,
excommunicate, execrate, imprecate,
proscribe

anatomize *verb* = **examine**, analyse, break
down, dissect, dissolve, divide, resolve,
scrutinize, separate, study

anatomy *noun* **1** = **examination**, analysis,
dismemberment, dissection, division, inquiry,
investigation, study **2** = **structure**, build,
composition, frame, framework, make-up

ancestor *noun* = **forefather**, forebear,
forerunner, precursor, predecessor,
progenitor
➤ **Antonyms**
descendant, inheritor, issue, offspring,
progeny, successor

ancestry *noun* = **origin**, ancestors,
antecedents, blood, derivation, descent,
extraction, family, forebears, forefathers,
genealogy, house, line, lineage, parentage,
pedigree, progenitors, race, stock

ancient *adjective* = **old**, aged, age-old,
antediluvian, antiquated, antique, archaic,
bygone, cobwebby, early, hoary, obsolete,
old as the hills, olden, old-fashioned,
outmoded, out-of-date, primeval, primordial,
superannuated, timeworn
➤ **Antonyms**
current, fresh, in vogue, late, modern,
modish, new, newfangled, new-fashioned,
novel, recent, state-of-the-art, up-to-date,
with it (*informal*), young

ancillary *adjective* = **supplementary**,
accessory, additional, auxiliary, contributory,
extra, secondary, subordinate, subsidiary,
supporting
➤ **Antonyms**
cardinal, chief, main, major, premier,

primary, prime, principal

and *conjunction* = **also**, along with, as well as, furthermore, in addition to, including, moreover, plus, together with

anecdote *noun* = **story**, reminiscence, short story, sketch, tale, urban legend, urban myth, yarn

anew *adverb* = **again**, afresh, another time, from scratch, from the beginning, once again, once more, over again

angel *noun* **1** = **divine messenger**, archangel, cherub, guardian spirit, seraph, spiritual being **2** *Informal* = **dear**, beauty, darling, dream, gem, ideal, jewel, paragon, saint, treasure

angelic *adjective* **1** = **pure**, adorable, beatific, beautiful, entrancing, innocent, lovely, saintly, virtuous **2** = **heavenly**, celestial, cherubic, ethereal, seraphic
➤ **Antonyms**
≠**heavenly:** demonic, devilish, diabolic, diabolical, fiendish, hellish, infernal, satanic

anger *noun* **1** = **rage**, annoyance, antagonism, choler, displeasure, exasperation, fury, ill humour, ill temper, indignation, ire, irritability, irritation, outrage, passion, pique, resentment, seeing red, spleen, temper, vexation, wrath ♦ *verb* **2** = **enrage**, affront, aggravate (*informal*), annoy, antagonize, be on one's back (*slang*), displease, exasperate, excite, fret, gall, get in one's hair (*informal*), get one's back up, get one's dander up (*informal*), get on one's nerves (*informal*), hassle (*informal*), incense, infuriate, irritate, madden, make one's blood boil, nark (*Brit., Austral., & N.Z. slang*), nettle, offend, outrage, pique, piss one off (*taboo slang*), provoke, put one's back up, rile, vex
➤ **Antonyms**
noun ≠**rage:** acceptance, amiability, approval, calmness, forgiveness, goodwill, gratification, liking, patience, peace, pleasure ♦ *verb* ≠**enrage:** appease, calm, pacify, placate, please, soothe

angle[1] *noun* **1** = **intersection**, bend, corner, crook, crotch, cusp, edge, elbow, knee, nook, point **2** = **point of view**, approach, aspect, outlook, perspective, position, side, slant, standpoint, take (*informal*), viewpoint

angle[2] *verb* = **fish**, cast

angle for *verb* = **be after** (*informal*), aim for, cast about *or* around for, contrive, fish for, hunt, invite, look for, scheme, seek, set one's sights on, solicit, try for

angry *adjective* = **furious**, annoyed, antagonized, as black as thunder, at daggers drawn, choked, choleric, cross, displeased, enraged, exasperated, fit to be tied (*slang*), foaming at the mouth, hacked (off) (*U.S.*

slang), heated, hot, hot under the collar (*informal*), ill-tempered, incandescent, incensed, indignant, infuriated, in high dudgeon, irascible, irate, ireful, irritable, irritated, mad (*informal*), nettled, on the warpath, outraged, passionate, piqued, pissed (*taboo slang*), pissed off (*taboo slang*), provoked, raging, resentful, riled, splenetic, tumultuous, up in arms, uptight (*informal*), wrathful
➤ **Antonyms**
agreeable, amiable, calm, congenial, friendly, gratified, happy, loving, mild, peaceful, pleasant, pleased

angst *noun* = **anxiety**, apprehension, unease, worry
➤ **Antonyms**
calmness, composure, contentment, ease, nonchalance, peace of mind, satisfaction

anguish *noun* = **suffering**, agony, distress, grief, heartache, heartbreak, misery, pain, pang, sorrow, throe, torment, torture, woe

anguished *adjective* = **suffering**, afflicted, agonized, brokenhearted, distressed, grief-stricken, tormented, tortured, wounded, wretched

angular *adjective* = **skinny**, bony, gaunt, lank, lanky, lean, macilent (*rare*), rangy, rawboned, scrawny, spare

animal *noun* **1** = **creature**, beast, brute **2** *Applied to a person* = **brute**, barbarian, beast, monster, savage, wild man ♦ *adjective* **3** = **physical**, bestial, bodily, brutish, carnal, fleshly, gross, sensual

animate *verb* **1** = **enliven**, activate, breathe life into, embolden, encourage, energize, excite, fire, gee up, gladden, impel, incite, inspire, inspirit, instigate, invigorate, kick-start (*informal*), kindle, liven up, move, prod, quicken, revive, rouse, spark, spur, stimulate, stir, urge, vitalize, vivify ♦ *adjective* **2** = **living**, alive, alive and kicking, breathing, live, moving
➤ **Antonyms**
verb ≠**enliven:** check, curb, deaden, deter, devitalize, discourage, dull, inhibit, kill, make lifeless, put a damper on, restrain

animated *adjective* = **lively**, active, airy, alive and kicking, ardent, brisk, buoyant, dynamic, ebullient, elated, energetic, enthusiastic, excited, fervent, full of beans (*informal*), gay, passionate, quick, sparky, spirited, sprightly, vibrant, vigorous, vital, vivacious, vivid, zealous, zestful
➤ **Antonyms**
apathetic, boring, dejected, depressed, dull, inactive, lethargic, lifeless, listless, monotonous, passive

animation *noun* = **liveliness**, action, activity, airiness, ardour, brio, briskness, buoyancy, dynamism, ebullience, elation, energy, enthusiasm, excitement, exhilaration, fervour, gaiety, high spirits, life, passion, pep, pizzazz *or* pizazz (*informal*), sparkle, spirit, sprightliness, verve, vibrancy, vigour, vitality, vivacity, zeal, zest, zing (*informal*)

animosity *noun* = **hostility**, acrimony, animus, antagonism, antipathy, bad blood, bitterness, enmity, hate, hatred, ill will, malevolence, malice, malignity, rancour, resentment, virulence
➤ **Antonyms**
amity, benevolence, congeniality, friendliness, friendship, goodwill, harmony, kindness, love, rapport, sympathy

annals *plural noun* = **records**, accounts, archives, chronicles, history, journals, memorials, registers

annex *verb* **1** = **seize**, acquire, appropriate, arrogate, conquer, expropriate, occupy, take over **2** = **join**, add, adjoin, affix, append, attach, connect, fasten, subjoin, tack, unite
➤ **Antonyms**
≠**join**: detach, disconnect, disengage, disjoin, disunite, remove, separate, unfasten

annexation *noun* = **seizure**, annexing, appropriation, arrogation, conquest, expropriation, occupation, takeover

annexe *noun* **1** = **extension**, ell, supplementary building, wing **2** = **addition**, addendum, adjunct, affix, appendix, attachment, supplement

annihilate *verb* = **destroy**, abolish, eradicate, erase, exterminate, extinguish, extirpate, liquidate, nullify, obliterate, root out, wipe from the face of the earth, wipe out

annihilation *noun* = **destruction**, abolition, eradication, erasure, extermination, extinction, extinguishing, extirpation, liquidation, nullification, obliteration, rooting out, wiping out

annotate *verb* = **make notes**, commentate, comment on, elucidate, explain, footnote, gloss, illustrate, interpret, make observations, note

annotation *noun* = **note**, comment, commentary, elucidation, exegesis, explanation, explication, footnote, gloss, illustration, interpretation, observation

announce *verb* **1** = **make known**, advertise, blow wide open (*slang*), broadcast, declare, disclose, divulge, give out, intimate, proclaim, promulgate, propound, publish, report, reveal, shout from the rooftops (*informal*), tell **2** = **be a sign of**, augur, betoken, foretell, harbinger, herald, portend, presage, signal, signify

➤ **Antonyms**
≠**make known**: bury, conceal, cover up, hide, hold back, hush (up), keep back, keep quiet, keep secret, suppress, withhold

announcement *noun* = **statement**, advertisement, broadcast, bulletin, communiqué, declaration, disclosure, divulgence, intimation, proclamation, promulgation, publication, report, revelation

announcer *noun* = **presenter**, anchor man, broadcaster, commentator, master of ceremonies, newscaster, newsreader, reporter

annoy *verb* = **irritate**, aggravate (*informal*), anger, badger, bedevil, be on one's back (*slang*), bore, bother, bug (*informal*), displease, disturb, exasperate, gall, get (*informal*), get in one's hair (*informal*), get one's back up, get one's dander up (*informal*), get one's goat (*slang*), get on one's nerves (*informal*), get on one's wick (*Brit. slang*), get under one's skin (*informal*), get up one's nose (*informal*), harass, harry, hassle (*informal*), incommode, irk, madden, make one's blood boil, molest, nark (*Brit., Austral., & N.Z. slang*), needle (*informal*), nettle, peeve, pester, piss one off (*taboo slang*), plague, provoke, put one's back up, rile, rub (someone) up the wrong way (*informal*), ruffle, tease, trouble, vex
➤ **Antonyms**
appease, calm, comfort, console, mollify, solace, soothe

annoyance *noun* **1** = **irritation**, aggravation, anger, bedevilment, bother, displeasure, disturbance, exasperation, grief (*informal*), harassment, hassle (*informal*), nuisance, provocation, trouble, vexation **2** = **nuisance**, bind (*informal*), bore, bother, drag (*informal*), gall, pain (*informal*), pain in the arse (*taboo informal*), pain in the neck (*informal*), pest, plague, tease

annoying *adjective* = **irritating**, aggravating, bedevilling, boring, bothersome, displeasing, disturbing, exasperating, galling, harassing, irksome, maddening, peeving (*informal*), provoking, teasing, troublesome, vexatious
➤ **Antonyms**
agreeable, amusing, charming, delightful, diverting, enjoyable, entertaining, gratifying, pleasant

annual *adjective* = **yearly**, once a year, yearlong

annually *adverb* = **yearly**, by the year, each year, every year, once a year, per annum, per year, year after year

annul *verb* = **invalidate**, abolish, abrogate, cancel, countermand, declare *or* render null and void, negate, nullify, obviate, recall, repeal, rescind, retract, reverse, revoke, void

➤ **Antonyms**
bring back, re-enforce, re-establish, reimpose, reinstate, reintroduce, restore

annulment *noun* = **invalidation**, abolition, abrogation, cancellation, countermanding, negation, nullification, recall, repeal, rescindment, rescission, retraction, reversal, revocation, voiding

anodyne *noun* 1 = **painkiller**, analgesic, narcotic, pain reliever, palliative ♦ *adjective* 2 = **pain-killing**, analgesic, deadening, dulling, narcotic, numbing, pain-relieving, palliative

anoint *verb* 1 = **smear**, daub, embrocate, grease, oil, rub, spread over 2 = **consecrate**, anele (*archaic*), bless, hallow, sanctify

anomalous *adjective* = **unusual**, aberrant, abnormal, atypical, bizarre, deviating, eccentric, exceptional, incongruous, inconsistent, irregular, odd, oddball (*informal*), off-the-wall (*slang*), outré, peculiar, rare
➤ **Antonyms**
common, customary, familiar, natural, normal, ordinary, regular, typical, usual

anomaly *noun* = **irregularity**, aberration, abnormality, departure, deviation, eccentricity, exception, incongruity, inconsistency, oddity, peculiarity, rarity

anon *adverb* Old-fashioned or informal = **soon**, before long, betimes (*archaic*), erelong (*archaic or poetic*), forthwith, in a couple of shakes (*informal*), presently, promptly, shortly

anonymous *adjective* 1 = **unnamed**, incognito, innominate, nameless, unacknowledged, unattested, unauthenticated, uncredited, unidentified, unknown, unsigned 2 = **nondescript**, characterless, undistinguished, unexceptional
➤ **Antonyms**
≠unnamed: accredited, acknowledged, attested, authenticated, credited, identified, known, named, signed

answer *verb* 1 = **reply**, acknowledge, explain, react, refute, rejoin, resolve, respond, retort, return, solve 2 = **do**, conform, correlate, correspond, fill, fit, fulfil, measure up, meet, pass, qualify, satisfy, serve, suffice, suit, work ♦ *noun* 3 = **reply**, acknowledgment, comeback, counterattack, defence, explanation, plea, reaction, refutation, rejoinder, report, resolution, response, retort, return, riposte, solution, vindication
➤ **Antonyms**
verb ≠**reply**: ask, inquire, interrogate, query, question ♦ *noun* ≠**reply**: inquiry, interrogation, query, question

answerable *adjective*, usually with **for** or

to = **responsible**, accountable, amenable, chargeable, liable, subject, to blame

answer back *verb* = **be impertinent**, argue, be cheeky, cheek (*informal*), contradict, disagree, dispute, rebut, retort, talk back

answer for *verb* 1 = **be responsible for**, be accountable for, be answerable for, be chargeable for, be liable for, be to blame for, take the rap for (*slang*) 2 = **pay for**, atone for, make amends for, suffer for

answer to *verb* 1 = **be responsible to**, be accountable to, be answerable to, be ruled by, obey 2 = **fit**, agree, confirm, correspond, match, meet

antagonism *noun* = **hostility**, antipathy, competition, conflict, contention, discord, dissension, friction, opposition, rivalry
➤ **Antonyms**
accord, agreement, amity, friendship, harmony, love, peacefulness, sympathy

antagonist *noun* = **opponent**, adversary, competitor, contender, enemy, foe, opposer, rival

antagonistic *adjective* = **hostile**, adverse, antipathetic, at odds, at variance, averse, conflicting, contentious, ill-disposed, incompatible, in dispute, inimical, opposed, unfriendly

antagonize *verb* = **annoy**, aggravate (*informal*), alienate, anger, be on one's back (*slang*), disaffect, estrange, gall, get in one's hair (*informal*), get on one's nerves (*informal*), get on one's wick (*Brit. slang*), get under one's skin (*informal*), get up one's nose (*informal*), hassle (*informal*), insult, irritate, nark (*Brit., Austral., & N.Z. slang*), offend, piss one off (*taboo slang*), repel, rub (someone) up the wrong way (*informal*)
➤ **Antonyms**
appease, calm, conciliate, disarm, mollify, pacify, placate, propitiate, soothe, win over

antecedent *adjective* = **preceding**, anterior, earlier, foregoing, former, precursory, preliminary, previous, prior
➤ **Antonyms**
after, coming, consequent, ensuing, following, later, posterior, subsequent, succeeding, successive

antecedents *plural noun* 1 = **ancestors**, ancestry, blood, descent, extraction, family, forebears, forefathers, genealogy, line, progenitors, stock 2 = **past**, background, history

antediluvian *adjective* 1 = **prehistoric**, primeval, primitive, primordial 2 = **old-fashioned**, ancient, antiquated, antique, archaic, obsolete, old as the hills, out-of-date, out of the ark (*informal*), passé

anteroom *noun* = **outer room**, antechamber, foyer, lobby, reception room, vestibule, waiting room

anthem *noun* **1** = **hymn**, canticle, carol, chant, chorale, psalm **2** = **song of praise**, paean

anthology *noun* = **collection**, analects, choice, compendium, compilation, digest, garland, miscellany, selection, treasury

anticipate *verb* **1** = **expect**, apprehend, await, count upon, forecast, foresee, foretell, hope for, look for, look forward to, predict, prepare for **2** = **forestall**, antedate, beat (someone) to it (*informal*), intercept, prevent

anticipation *noun* = **expectation**, apprehension, awaiting, expectancy, foresight, foretaste, forethought, hope, preconception, premonition, prescience, presentiment

anticlimax *noun* = **disappointment**, bathos, comedown (*informal*), letdown
➤ Antonyms
climax, culmination, height, highlight, high point, peak, summit, top, zenith

antics *plural noun* = **clowning**, buffoonery, capers, escapades, foolishness, frolics, horseplay, larks, mischief, monkey tricks, playfulness, pranks, silliness, skylarking, stunts, tomfoolery, tricks

antidote *noun* = **cure**, antitoxin, antivenin, corrective, counteragent, countermeasure, neutralizer, nostrum, preventive, remedy, specific

antipathetic *adjective* = **hostile**, abhorrent, antagonistic, averse, disgusting, distasteful, hateful, incompatible, invidious, loathsome, obnoxious, odious, offensive, repellent, repugnant, repulsive, revolting, yucky *or* yukky (*slang*)

antipathy *noun* = **hostility**, abhorrence, animosity, animus, antagonism, aversion, bad blood, contrariety, disgust, dislike, distaste, enmity, hatred, ill will, incompatibility, loathing, odium, opposition, rancour, repugnance, repulsion
➤ Antonyms
affection, affinity, attraction, bond, empathy, fellow-feeling, goodwill, harmony, partiality, rapport, sympathy, tie

antiquated *adjective* **1** = **obsolete**, antediluvian, antique, archaic, dated, old-fashioned, old hat, outmoded, out-of-date, outworn, passé, past it (*informal*), superannuated **2** = **old**, aged, ancient, cobwebby, elderly, hoary, old as the hills
➤ Antonyms
≠**obsolete:** all-singing, all-dancing, current, fashionable, fresh, modern, modish, new, state-of-the-art, stylish, up-to-date, young

antique *noun* **1** = **period piece**, bygone, heirloom, object of virtu, relic ♦ *adjective* **2** = **vintage**, antiquarian, classic, olden **3** = **old**, aged, ancient, elderly, superannuated **4** = **old-fashioned**, archaic, obsolete, outdated

antiquity *noun* **1** = **old age**, age, ancientness, elderliness, oldness **2** = **distant past**, ancient times, olden days, time immemorial **3** = **antique**, relic, ruin

antiseptic *adjective* **1** = **hygienic**, aseptic, clean, germ-free, pure, sanitary, sterile, uncontaminated, unpolluted ♦ *noun* **2** = **disinfectant**, bactericide, germicide, purifier
➤ Antonyms
adjective ≠**hygienic:** contaminated, dirty, impure, infected, insanitary, polluted, septic, unhygienic

antisocial *adjective* **1** = **unsociable**, alienated, asocial, misanthropic, reserved, retiring, uncommunicative, unfriendly, withdrawn **2** = **disruptive**, antagonistic, belligerent, disorderly, hostile, menacing, rebellious, uncooperative
➤ Antonyms
≠**unsociable:** companionable, friendly, gregarious, philanthropic, sociable, social

antithesis *noun* **1** = **opposite**, antipode, contrary, contrast, converse, inverse, reverse **2** = **contrast**, contradiction, contraposition, contrariety, inversion, opposition, reversal

anxiety *noun* = **uneasiness**, angst, apprehension, care, concern, disquiet, disquietude, distress, foreboding, fretfulness, misgiving, nervousness, restlessness, solicitude, suspense, tension, trepidation, unease, watchfulness, worry
➤ Antonyms
assurance, calmness, confidence, contentment, relief, security, serenity

anxious *adjective* **1** = **uneasy**, angsty, antsy (*informal*), apprehensive, careful, concerned, disquieted, distressed, disturbed, fearful, fretful, hot and bothered, in suspense, nervous, neurotic, on pins and needles, on tenterhooks, overwrought, restless, solicitous, taut, tense, troubled, twitchy (*informal*), unquiet (*chiefly literary*), watchful, wired (*slang*), worried **2** = **eager**, ardent, avid, desirous, expectant, impatient, intent, itching, keen, yearning
➤ Antonyms
≠**uneasy:** assured, calm, certain, collected, composed, confident, cool, nonchalant, unfazed (*informal*), unperturbed ≠**eager:** disinclined, hesitant, loath, nonchalant, reluctant

apart *adverb* **1** = **to pieces**, asunder, in bits, in pieces, into parts, to bits **2** = **separate**, afar, alone, aloof, aside, away, by itself, by oneself, cut off, distant, distinct, divorced, excluded, independent, independently, isolated, out on a limb, piecemeal, separated, separately, singly, to itself, to oneself, to one side **3 apart from = except for**, aside from, besides, but, excluding, not counting, other than, save

apartment *noun* = **room**, accommodation, chambers, compartment, flat, living quarters, penthouse, quarters, rooms, suite

apathetic *adjective* = **uninterested**, cold, cool, emotionless, impassive, indifferent, insensible, listless, passive, phlegmatic, sluggish, stoic, stoical, torpid, unconcerned, unemotional, unfeeling, unmoved, unresponsive
➤ **Antonyms**
active, anxious, aroused, bothered, caring, committed, concerned, emotional, enthusiastic, excited, interested, moved, passionate, responsive, troubled, worried, zealous

apathy *noun* = **lack of interest**, coldness, coolness, emotionlessness, impassibility, impassivity, indifference, inertia, insensibility, listlessness, nonchalance, passiveness, passivity, phlegm, sluggishness, stoicism, torpor, unconcern, unfeelingness, uninterestedness, unresponsiveness
➤ **Antonyms**
anxiety, attention, concern, emotion, enthusiasm, feeling, interest, zeal

ape *verb* = **imitate**, affect, caricature, copy, counterfeit, echo, mimic, mirror, mock, parody, parrot

aperture *noun* = **opening**, breach, chink, cleft, crack, eye, eyelet, fissure, gap, hole, interstice, orifice, passage, perforation, rent, rift, slit, slot, space, vent

apex *noun* = **highest point**, acme, apogee, climax, crest, crown, culmination, height, peak, pinnacle, point, summit, tip, top, vertex, zenith
➤ **Antonyms**
base, bottom, depths, lowest point, nadir, perigee, rock bottom

aphorism *noun* = **saying**, adage, apothegm, axiom, dictum, gnome, maxim, precept, proverb, saw

apiece *adverb* = **each**, for each, from each, individually, respectively, separately, severally, to each
➤ **Antonyms**
all together, as a group, collectively, en masse, overall, together

aplomb *noun* = **self-possession**, balance, calmness, composure, confidence, coolness, equanimity, level-headedness, poise, sang-froid, self-assurance, self-confidence, stability

➤ **Antonyms**
awkwardness, chagrin, confusion, discomfiture, discomposure, embarrassment, self-consciousness

apocryphal *adjective* = **dubious**, doubtful, equivocal, fictitious, legendary, mythical, questionable, spurious, unauthenticated, uncanonical, unsubstantiated, unverified
➤ **Antonyms**
attested, authentic, authenticated, authorized, canonical, credible, factual, substantiated, true, undisputed, unquestionable, verified

apologetic *adjective* = **regretful**, contrite, penitent, remorseful, rueful, sorry

apologist *noun* = **defender**, advocate, arguer, champion, justifier, maintainer, pleader, spokesman, supporter, vindicator

apologize *verb* = **say sorry**, ask forgiveness, beg pardon, express regret, say one is sorry

apology *noun* **1** = **defence**, acknowledgment, confession, excuse, explanation, extenuation, justification, plea, vindication **2** *As in* **an apology for** = **mockery**, caricature, excuse, imitation, travesty

apostate *noun* **1** = **deserter**, backslider, defector, heretic, recreant (*archaic*), renegade, traitor, turncoat ◆ *adjective* **2** = **disloyal**, backsliding, faithless, false, heretical, perfidious, recreant, traitorous, treacherous, unfaithful, untrue

apostle *noun* **1** = **evangelist**, herald, messenger, missionary, preacher, proselytizer **2** = **supporter**, advocate, champion, pioneer, propagandist, propagator, proponent

apotheosis *noun* = **deification**, elevation, exaltation, glorification, idealization, idolization

appal *verb* = **horrify**, alarm, astound, daunt, dishearten, dismay, frighten, harrow, intimidate, make one's hair stand on end (*informal*), outrage, petrify, scare, shock, terrify, unnerve

appalling *adjective* = **horrifying**, alarming, astounding, awful, daunting, dire, disheartening, dismaying, dreadful, fearful, frightening, frightful, from hell (*informal*), ghastly, godawful (*slang*), grim, harrowing, hellacious (*U.S. slang*), hideous, horrible, horrid, horrific, intimidating, petrifying, scaring, shocking, terrible, terrifying, unnerving
➤ **Antonyms**
comforting, consolatory, consoling, encouraging, heartening, reassuring

apparatus *noun* **1** = **equipment**, appliance, contraption (*informal*), device, gear, implements, machine, machinery, materials,

means, mechanism, outfit, tackle, tools,
utensils **2 = organization**, bureaucracy,
chain of command, hierarchy, network,
setup (*informal*), structure, system

apparel *noun Old-fashioned* = **clothing**,
accoutrements, array (*poetic*), attire, clothes,
costume, dress, equipment, garb, garments,
gear (*informal*), habiliments, habit, outfit,
raiment (*archaic or poetic*), robes, threads
(*slang*), trappings, vestments

apparent *adjective* **1 = obvious**, blatant,
bold, clear, conspicuous, discernible, distinct,
evident, indubitable, manifest, marked,
open, overt, patent, plain, plain as the nose
on your face, salient, understandable,
unmistakable, visible **2 = seeming**,
ostensible, outward, specious, superficial
➤ **Antonyms**
≠**obvious**: ambiguous, doubtful, dubious,
hazy, indefinite, indistinct, obscure,
uncertain, unclear, vague ≠**seeming**: actual,
authentic, bona fide, genuine, honest,
intrinsic, real, sincere, true

apparently *adverb* = **it appears that**, it
seems that, on the face of it, ostensibly,
outwardly, seemingly, speciously, superficially

apparition *noun* = **ghost**, chimera, eidolon,
phantom, revenant, shade (*literary*), spectre,
spirit, spook (*informal*), visitant, wraith

appeal *verb* **1 = plead**, adjure, apply, ask,
beg, beseech, call, call upon, entreat,
implore, petition, pray, refer, request, resort
to, solicit, sue, supplicate **2 = attract**, allure,
charm, engage, entice, fascinate, interest,
invite, please, tempt ♦ *noun* **3 = plea**,
adjuration, application, entreaty, invocation,
petition, prayer, request, solicitation, suit,
supplication **4 = attraction**, allure,
attractiveness, beauty, charm, engagingness,
fascination, interestingness, pleasingness
➤ **Antonyms**
verb ≠**plead**: deny, refuse, reject, repudiate,
repulse ≠**attract**: alienate, bore, repulse,
revolt ♦ *noun* ≠**plea**: denial, refusal,
rejection, repudiation ≠**attraction**:
repulsiveness

appealing *adjective* = **attractive**, alluring,
charming, desirable, engaging, winsome
➤ **Antonyms**
disgusting, forbidding, loathsome,
objectionable, obnoxious, odious, offensive,
repellent, repugnant, repulsive, revolting,
sickening, unalluring, unappealing,
unattractive, undesirable

appear *verb* **1 = come into view**, arise,
arrive, attend, be present, come forth, come
into sight, come out, come to light, crop up
(*informal*), develop, emerge, issue, loom,
materialize, occur, show (*informal*), show
one's face, show up (*informal*), surface, turn
out, turn up **2 = look (like** *or* **as if)**, occur,

seem, strike one as **3 = be obvious**, be
apparent, be clear, be evident, be manifest,
be patent, be plain **4 = perform**, act, be
exhibited, come on, come onstage, enter,
play, play a part, take part **5 = come into
being**, become available, be created, be
developed, be invented, be published, come
into existence, come out
➤ **Antonyms**
≠**come into view**: disappear, vanish ≠**be
obvious**: be doubtful, be unclear

appearance *noun* **1 = arrival**, advent,
appearing, coming, debut, emergence,
introduction, presence, showing up
(*informal*), turning up **2 = look**, air, aspect,
bearing, demeanour, expression, face, figure,
form, image, looks, manner, mien (*literary*)
3 = impression, front, guise, illusion, image,
outward show, pretence, semblance

appease *verb* **1 = pacify**, calm, conciliate,
mollify, placate, pour oil on troubled waters,
quiet, satisfy, soothe **2 = ease**, allay,
alleviate, assuage, blunt, calm, compose,
diminish, lessen, lull, mitigate, quell, quench,
quiet, relieve, satisfy, soothe, subdue,
tranquillize
➤ **Antonyms**
≠**pacify**: aggravate (*informal*), anger,
annoy, antagonize, arouse, be on one's back
(*slang*), disturb, enrage, get in one's hair
(*informal*), get on one's nerves (*informal*),
hassle (*informal*), incense, inflame, infuriate,
irritate, madden, nark (*Brit., Austral., & N.Z.
slang*), piss one off (*taboo slang*), provoke,
rile, upset

appeasement *noun* **1 = pacification**,
acceding, accommodation, compromise,
concession, conciliation, mollification,
placation, propitiation **2 = easing**,
abatement, alleviation, assuagement,
blunting, lessening, lulling, mitigation,
quelling, quenching, quieting, relieving,
satisfaction, softening, solace, soothing,
tranquillization

appellation *noun Formal* = **name**, address,
description, designation, epithet, sobriquet,
style, term, title

append *verb Formal* = **add**, adjoin, affix,
annex, attach, fasten, hang, join, subjoin,
tack on, tag on
➤ **Antonyms**
detach, disconnect, disengage, remove,
separate, take off

appendage *noun* **1 = attachment**,
accessory, addendum, addition, adjunct,
affix, ancillary, annexe, appendix,
appurtenance, auxiliary, supplement **2**
Zoology = **limb**, extremity, member,
projection, protuberance

appendix *noun* = **supplement**, addendum,
addition, add-on, adjunct, appendage,

codicil, postscript

appertain *verb* **appertain to = relate to**, apply to, bear upon, be characteristic of, be connected to, belong to, be part of, be pertinent to, be proper to, be relevant to, have to do with, inhere in, pertain to, refer to, touch upon

appetence, appetency *noun* **1 = desire**, ache, appetite, craving, hankering, hunger, longing, need, yearning **2 = inclination**, bent, drive, instinct, leaning, penchant, propensity **3 = liking**, affection, affinity, allurement, attraction, fondness, partiality

appetite *noun* **= desire**, appetence, appetency, craving, demand, hankering, hunger, inclination, liking, longing, passion, proclivity, propensity, relish, stomach, taste, willingness, yearning, zeal, zest
➤ **Antonyms**
abhorrence, aversion, disgust, disinclination, dislike, distaste, loathing, repugnance, repulsion, revulsion

appetizer *noun* **1 = hors d'oeuvre**, antipasto, canapé, titbit **2 = apéritif**, cocktail

appetizing *adjective* **= delicious**, appealing, inviting, mouthwatering, palatable, savoury, scrumptious (*informal*), succulent, tasty, tempting
➤ **Antonyms**
distasteful, nauseating, unappetizing, unpalatable, unsavoury

applaud *verb* **= praise**, acclaim, approve, cheer, clap, commend, compliment, crack up (*informal*), encourage, eulogize, extol, give (someone) a big hand, laud, magnify (*archaic*)
➤ **Antonyms**
blast, boo, censure, condemn, criticize, decry, deprecate, deride, disparage, excoriate, hiss, lambast(e), pan (*informal*), put down, ridicule, run down, slag (off) (*slang*), tear into (*informal*), vilify

applause *noun* **= ovation**, acclaim, acclamation, accolade, approbation, approval, big hand, cheering, cheers, clapping, commendation, eulogizing, hand, hand-clapping, laudation, plaudit, praise

appliance *noun* **= device**, apparatus, gadget, implement, instrument, machine, mechanism, tool, waldo

applicable *adjective* **= appropriate**, apposite, apropos, apt, befitting, fit, fitting, germane, pertinent, relevant, suitable, suited, to the point, to the purpose, useful
➤ **Antonyms**
inapplicable, inappropriate, irrelevant, unsuitable, wrong

applicant *noun* **= candidate**, aspirant, claimant, inquirer, petitioner, postulant, suitor, suppliant

application *noun* **1 = request**, appeal, claim, inquiry, petition, requisition, solicitation, suit **2 = relevance**, appositeness, appropriateness, exercise, function, germaneness, pertinence, practice, purpose, use, value **3 = effort**, assiduity, attention, attentiveness, commitment, dedication, diligence, hard work, industry, perseverance, study **4 = lotion**, balm, cream, dressing, emollient, ointment, poultice, salve, unguent

apply *verb* **1 = request**, appeal, claim, inquire, make application, petition, put in, requisition, solicit, sue **2 = use**, administer, assign, bring into play, bring to bear, carry out, employ, engage, execute, exercise, exert, implement, practise, put to use, utilize **3 = put on**, anoint, bring into contact with, cover with, lay on, paint, place, smear, spread on, touch to **4 = be relevant**, appertain, be applicable, be appropriate, bear upon, be fitting, fit, pertain, refer, relate, suit **5 apply oneself = try**, address oneself, be assiduous, be diligent, be industrious, buckle down (*informal*), commit oneself, concentrate, dedicate oneself, devote oneself, make an effort, pay attention, persevere, study, work hard

appoint *verb* **1 = assign**, choose, commission, delegate, elect, install, name, nominate, select **2 = decide**, allot, arrange, assign, choose, designate, determine, establish, fix, set, settle **3 = equip**, fit out, furnish, provide, supply
➤ **Antonyms**
≠**assign**: discharge, dismiss, fire, give the sack (*informal*), sack (*informal*) ≠**decide**: cancel ≠**equip**: dismantle, divest, strip

appointed *adjective* **1 = assigned**, chosen, commissioned, delegated, elected, installed, named, nominated, selected **2 = decided**, allotted, arranged, assigned, chosen, designated, determined, established, fixed, set, settled **3 = equipped**, fitted out, furnished, provided, supplied

appointment *noun* **1 = meeting**, arrangement, assignation, consultation, date, engagement, interview, rendezvous, session, tryst (*archaic*) **2 = selection**, allotment, assignment, choice, choosing, commissioning, delegation, designation, election, installation, naming, nomination **3 = appointee**, candidate, delegate, nominee, office-holder, representative **4 = job**, assignment, berth (*informal*), office, place, position, post, situation, station **5 appointments = fittings**, accoutrements, appurtenances, equipage, fixtures, furnishings, gear, outfit, paraphernalia, trappings

apportion *verb* **= divide**, allocate, allot, assign, deal, dispense, distribute, dole out, give out, measure out, mete out, parcel out, ration out, share

apportionment noun = division, allocation, allotment, assignment, dealing out, dispensing, distribution, doling out, measuring out, meting out, parcelling out, rationing out, sharing

apposite adjective = appropriate, appertaining, applicable, apropos, apt, befitting, fitting, germane, pertinent, proper, relevant, suitable, suited, to the point, to the purpose
➤ Antonyms
inapplicable, inappropriate, inapt, irrelevant, unsuitable, unsuited

appraisal noun 1 = assessment, estimate, estimation, evaluation, judgment, opinion, recce (slang), sizing up (informal) 2 = valuation, assay, pricing, rating, reckoning, survey

appraise verb = assess, assay, estimate, evaluate, eye up, gauge, inspect, judge, price, rate, recce (slang), review, size up (informal), survey, value

appreciable adjective = significant, ascertainable, clear-cut, considerable, definite, detectable, discernible, distinguishable, evident, marked, material, measurable, noticeable, obvious, perceivable, perceptible, pronounced, recognizable, substantial, visible
➤ Antonyms
immaterial, imperceptible, inappreciable, indiscernible, indistinguishable, insignificant, invisible, minor, minute, negligible, small, trivial, undetectable, unnoticeable, unsubstantial

appreciate verb 1 = value, admire, cherish, enjoy, esteem, like, prize, rate highly, regard, relish, respect, savour, treasure 2 = be aware of, acknowledge, be alive to, be cognizant of, be conscious of, comprehend, estimate, know, perceive, realize, recognize, sympathize with, take account of, understand 3 = be grateful for, be appreciative, be indebted, be obliged, be thankful for, give thanks for 4 = increase, enhance, gain, grow, improve, inflate, raise the value of, rise
➤ Antonyms
≠value: belittle, denigrate, disdain, disparage, scorn ≠be aware of: be unaware of, misunderstand, underrate ≠be grateful for: be ungrateful for ≠increase: deflate, depreciate, devaluate, fall

appreciation noun 1 = gratitude, acknowledgment, gratefulness, indebtedness, obligation, thankfulness, thanks 2 = awareness, admiration, appraisal, assessment, cognizance, comprehension, enjoyment, esteem, estimation, knowledge,

liking, perception, realization, recognition, regard, relish, respect, responsiveness, sensitivity, sympathy, understanding, valuation 3 = praise, acclamation, criticism, critique, notice, recognition, review, tribute 4 = increase, enhancement, gain, growth, improvement, inflation, rise
➤ Antonyms
≠gratitude: ingratitude ≠awareness: ignorance, incomprehension ≠increase: decline, depreciation, devaluation, fall

appreciative adjective 1 = grateful, beholden, indebted, obliged, thankful 2 = aware, admiring, cognizant, conscious, enthusiastic, in the know (informal), knowledgeable, mindful, perceptive, pleased, regardful, respectful, responsive, sensitive, supportive, sympathetic, understanding

apprehend verb 1 = arrest, bust (informal), capture, catch, collar (informal), feel one's collar (slang), lift (slang), nab (informal), nail (informal), nick (slang, chiefly Brit.), pinch (informal), run in (slang), seize, take, take prisoner 2 = understand, appreciate, believe, comprehend, conceive, get the message, get the picture, grasp, imagine, know, perceive, realize, recognize, think
➤ Antonyms
≠arrest: discharge, free, let go, liberate, release ≠understand: be at cross-purposes, be unaware of, be unconscious of, get one's lines crossed, misapprehend, misconceive, miss, misunderstand

apprehension noun 1 = anxiety, alarm, apprehensiveness, concern, disquiet, doubt, dread, fear, foreboding, misgiving, mistrust, pins and needles, premonition, suspicion, trepidation, unease, uneasiness, worry 2 = arrest, capture, catching, seizure, taking 3 = awareness, comprehension, grasp, intellect, intelligence, ken, knowledge, perception, understanding 4 = idea, belief, concept, conception, conjecture, impression, notion, opinion, sentiment, thought, view
➤ Antonyms
≠anxiety: assurance, composure, confidence, nonchalance, serenity, unconcern ≠arrest: discharge, liberation, release ≠awareness: incomprehension

apprehensive adjective = anxious, afraid, alarmed, antsy (informal), concerned, disquieted, doubtful, fearful, foreboding, mistrustful, nervous, neurotic, suspicious, twitchy (informal), uneasy, worried
➤ Antonyms
assured, at ease, composed, confident, nonchalant, unafraid

apprentice noun = trainee, beginner, learner, neophyte, novice, probationer, pupil, student, tyro

➤ **Antonyms**
ace (*informal*), adept, dab hand (*Brit. informal*), expert, master, past master, pro

approach *verb* **1** = **move towards**, advance, catch up, come close, come near, come to, draw near, gain on, meet, near, push forward, reach **2** = **be like**, approximate, be comparable to, come close to, come near to, compare with, resemble **3** = **make a proposal to**, appeal to, apply to, broach the matter with, make advances to, make overtures to, sound out **4** = **set about**, begin work on, commence, embark on, enter upon, make a start, undertake ♦ *noun* **5** = **coming**, advance, advent, arrival, drawing near, nearing **6** *often plural* = **proposal**, advance, appeal, application, invitation, offer, overture, proposition **7** = **access**, avenue, entrance, passage, road, way **8** = **way**, attitude, course, manner, means, method, mode, modus operandi, procedure, style, technique **9** = **likeness**, approximation, semblance

approachable *adjective* **1** = **friendly**, affable, congenial, cordial, open, sociable **2** = **accessible**, attainable, come-at-able (*informal*), get-at-able (*informal*), reachable
➤ **Antonyms**
≠**friendly**: aloof, chilly, cold as ice, cool, distant, frigid, remote, reserved, standoffish, unfriendly, unsociable, withdrawn ≠**accessible**: inaccessible, out of reach, out-of-the-way, remote, un-get-at-able (*informal*), unreachable

approbation *noun* = **approval**, acceptance, acclaim, applause, assent, commendation, congratulation, encouragement, endorsement, favour, laudation, praise, ratification, recognition, sanction, support
➤ **Antonyms**
blame, censure, condemnation, disapprobation, disapproval, disfavour, dislike, displeasure, dissatisfaction, reproof, stricture

appropriate *adjective* **1** = **suitable**, adapted, applicable, apposite, appurtenant, apropos, apt, becoming, befitting, belonging, congruous, correct, felicitous, fit, fitting, germane, meet (*archaic*), opportune, pertinent, proper, relevant, right, seemly, to the point, to the purpose, well-suited, well-timed ♦ *verb* **2** = **seize**, annex, arrogate, assume, commandeer, confiscate, expropriate, impound, pre-empt, take, take over, take possession of, usurp **3** = **steal**, embezzle, filch, misappropriate, pilfer, pocket **4** = **allocate**, allot, apportion, assign, devote, earmark, set aside
➤ **Antonyms**
adjective ≠**suitable**: improper,

inappropriate, incompatible, incorrect, inopportune, irrelevant, unfitting, unsuitable, untimely ♦ *verb* ≠**seize**: cede, donate, give, relinquish ≠**allocate**: withhold

appropriateness *noun* = **suitability**, applicability, appositeness, aptness, becomingness, congruousness, correctness, felicitousness, felicity, fitness, fittingness, germaneness, opportuneness, pertinence, properness, relevance, rightness, seemliness, timeliness, well-suitedness

appropriation *noun* **1** = **setting aside**, allocation, allotment, apportionment, assignment, earmarking **2** = **seizure**, annexation, arrogation, assumption, commandeering, confiscation, expropriation, impoundment, pre-emption, takeover, taking, usurpation

approval *noun* **1** = **consent**, acquiescence, agreement, assent, authorization, blessing, compliance, concurrence, confirmation, countenance, endorsement, imprimatur, leave, licence, mandate, O.K. *or* okay (*informal*), permission, ratification, recommendation, sanction, the go-ahead (*informal*), the green light, validation **2** = **favour**, acclaim, admiration, applause, appreciation, approbation, Brownie points, commendation, esteem, good opinion, liking, praise, regard, respect
➤ **Antonyms**
≠**favour**: denigration, disapproval, dislike, disparagement, displeasure, dissatisfaction

approve *verb* **1** = **favour**, acclaim, admire, applaud, appreciate, be pleased with, commend, esteem, have a good opinion of, like, praise, regard highly, respect, think highly of **2** = **agree to**, accede to, accept, advocate, allow, assent to, authorize, bless, buy into (*informal*), concur in, confirm, consent to, countenance, endorse, give the go-ahead (*informal*), give the green light, go along with, mandate, O.K. *or* okay (*informal*), pass, permit, ratify, recommend, sanction, second, subscribe to, uphold, validate
➤ **Antonyms**
≠**favour**: blame, censure, condemn, deplore, deprecate, disapprove, dislike, find unacceptable, frown on, look down one's nose at (*informal*), object to, take exception to ≠**agree to**: disallow, discountenance, veto

approximate *adjective* **1** = **close**, almost accurate, almost exact, near **2** = **rough**, estimated, inexact, loose **3** = **like**, analogous, close, comparable, near, relative, similar, verging on ♦ *verb* **4** = **come close**, approach, border on, come near, reach, resemble, touch, verge on
➤ **Antonyms**
adjective ≠**close**, **rough**: accurate, correct, definite, exact, precise, specific

approximately *adverb* = **almost**, about, around, circa (*used with dates*), close to, generally, in the neighbourhood of, in the region of, in the vicinity of, just about, loosely, more or less, nearly, not far off, relatively, roughly

approximation *noun* 1 = **guess**, ballpark estimate (*informal*), ballpark figure (*informal*), conjecture, estimate, estimation, guesswork, rough calculation, rough idea 2 = **likeness**, approach, correspondence, resemblance, semblance

appurtenances *plural noun* = **accompaniments**, accessories, accoutrements, appendages, equipment, impedimenta, paraphernalia, trappings

a priori *adjective* = **deduced**, deductive, from cause to effect, inferential

apron *noun* = **pinny** (*informal*), pinafore

apropos *adjective* 1 = **appropriate**, applicable, apposite, apt, befitting, belonging, correct, fit, fitting, germane, meet (*archaic*), opportune, pertinent, proper, related, relevant, right, seemly, suitable, to the point, to the purpose ♦ *adverb* 2 = **appropriately**, aptly, opportunely, pertinently, relevantly, suitably, timely, to the point, to the purpose 3 = **incidentally**, by the bye, by the way, in passing, parenthetically, while on the subject

apropos of *preposition* = **regarding**, in respect of, on the subject of, re, respecting, with reference to, with regard to, with respect to

apt *adjective* 1 = **inclined**, disposed, given, liable, likely, of a mind, prone, ready 2 = **appropriate**, applicable, apposite, apropos, befitting, correct, fit, fitting, germane, meet (*archaic*), pertinent, proper, relevant, seemly, suitable, timely, to the point, to the purpose 3 = **gifted**, astute, bright, clever, expert, ingenious, intelligent, prompt, quick, sharp, skilful, smart, talented, teachable
➤ **Antonyms**
≠**appropriate**: ill-fitted, ill-suited, ill-timed, improper, inapplicable, inapposite, inappropriate, infelicitous, inopportune, irrelevant, unsuitable, untimely ≠**gifted**: awkward, clumsy, dull, gauche, incompetent, inept, inexpert, maladroit, slow, stupid

aptitude *noun* 1 = **tendency**, bent, disposition, inclination, leaning, predilection, proclivity, proneness, propensity 2 = **gift**, ability, aptness, capability, capacity, cleverness, faculty, flair, giftedness, intelligence, knack, proficiency, quickness, talent

aptness *noun* 1 = **tendency**, aptitude, bent, disposition, inclination, leaning, liability,

likelihood, likeliness, predilection, proclivity, proneness, propensity, readiness 2 = **appropriateness**, applicability, appositeness, becomingness, congruousness, correctness, felicitousness, felicity, fitness, fittingness, germaneness, opportuneness, pertinence, properness, relevance, rightness, seemliness, suitability, timeliness, well-suitedness 3 = **gift**, ability, capability, capacity, cleverness, faculty, fitness, flair, giftedness, intelligence, knack, proficiency, quickness, suitability, talent

arable *adjective* = **productive**, cultivable, farmable, fecund, fertile, fruitful, ploughable, tillable

arbiter *noun* 1 = **judge**, adjudicator, arbitrator, referee, umpire 2 = **authority**, controller, dictator, expert, governor, lord, master, pundit, ruler

arbitrariness *noun* 1 = **randomness**, capriciousness, fancifulness, inconsistency, subjectivity, unreasonableness, whimsicality, wilfulness 2 = **dictatorialness**, absoluteness, despotism, dogmatism, domineeringness, high-handedness, imperiousness, magisterialness, overbearingness, peremptoriness, summariness, tyrannicalness, tyrannousness, tyranny, uncontrolledness, unlimitedness, unrestrainedness

arbitrary *adjective* 1 = **random**, capricious, chance, discretionary, erratic, fanciful, inconsistent, optional, personal, subjective, unreasonable, whimsical, wilful 2 = **dictatorial**, absolute, autocratic, despotic, dogmatic, domineering, high-handed, imperious, magisterial, overbearing, peremptory, summary, tyrannical, tyrannous, uncontrolled, unlimited, unrestrained
➤ **Antonyms**
≠**random**: consistent, judicious, logical, objective, rational, reasonable, reasoned, sensible, sound

arbitrate *verb* = **settle**, adjudge, adjudicate, decide, determine, judge, mediate, pass judgment, referee, sit in judgment, umpire

arbitration *noun* = **settlement**, adjudication, arbitrament, decision, determination, judgment

arbitrator *noun* = **judge**, adjudicator, arbiter, referee, umpire

arc *noun* = **curve**, arch, bend, bow, crescent, half-moon

arcade *noun* = **gallery**, cloister, colonnade, covered walk, mall, portico

arcane *adjective* = **mysterious**, cabbalistic, esoteric, hidden, occult, recondite, secret

arch¹ *noun* 1 = **archway**, curve, dome, span, vault 2 = **curve**, arc, bend, bow, curvature, hump, semicircle ♦ *verb* 3 = **curve**, arc, bend, bow, bridge, span

arch[2] *adjective* = **playful**, frolicsome, mischievous, pert, roguish, saucy, sly, waggish

arch- *adjective* = **chief**, accomplished, consummate, expert, finished, first, foremost, greatest, head, highest, lead, leading, main, major, master, pre-eminent, primary, principal, top

archaic *adjective* **1** = **old**, ancient, antique, bygone, olden (*archaic*), primitive **2** = **old-fashioned**, antiquated, behind the times, obsolete, old hat, outmoded, out of date, passé, superannuated
➤ **Antonyms**
≠**old**: contemporary, current, modern, new, present, recent ≠**old-fashioned**: fresh, latest, modern, modish, new, newfangled, novel, state-of-the-art, up-to-date, up-to-the-minute, with it (*informal*)

arched *adjective* = **curved**, domed, embowed, vaulted

archer *noun* = **bowman** (*archaic*), toxophilite (*formal*)

archetypal *adjective* **1** = **typical**, classic, ideal, model, standard **2** = **original**, prototypic *or* prototypical

archetype *noun* **1** = **standard**, classic, exemplar, form, ideal, model, norm, paradigm, pattern, prime example **2** = **original**, prototype

architect *noun* **1** = **designer**, master builder, planner **2** = **creator**, author, contriver, deviser, engineer, founder, instigator, inventor, maker, originator, planner, prime mover, shaper

architecture *noun* **1** = **design**, architectonics, building, construction, planning **2** = **structure**, construction, design, framework, make-up, style

archive *noun* **1** = **record office**, museum, registry, repository **2 archives** = **records**, annals, chronicles, documents, papers, registers, rolls

arctic *adjective Informal* = **freezing**, chilly, cold, cold as ice, frigid, frost-bound, frosty, frozen, gelid, glacial, icy

Arctic *adjective* = **polar**, far-northern, hyperborean

ardent *adjective* **1** = **passionate**, ablaze, amorous, fervent, fervid, fierce, fiery, flaming, hot, hot-blooded, impassioned, intense, lusty, spirited, vehement, warm, warm-blooded **2** = **enthusiastic**, avid, eager, keen, keen as mustard, zealous
➤ **Antonyms**
≠**passionate**: cold, cool, frigid, impassive ≠**enthusiastic**: apathetic, indifferent, lukewarm, unenthusiastic

ardour *noun* **1** = **passion**, devotion, feeling, fervour, fierceness, fire, heat, intensity, spirit, vehemence, warmth **2** = **enthusiasm**, avidity, eagerness, earnestness, keenness, zeal

arduous *adjective* = **difficult**, backbreaking, burdensome, exhausting, fatiguing, formidable, gruelling, hard, harsh, heavy, laborious, onerous, painful, punishing, rigorous, severe, steep, strenuous, taxing, tiring, toilsome, tough, troublesome, trying
➤ **Antonyms**
child's play (*informal*), easy, easy-peasy (*slang*), effortless, facile, light, no bother, no trouble, painless, simple, undemanding

area *noun* **1** = **region**, district, domain, locality, neck of the woods (*informal*), neighbourhood, patch, plot, realm, sector, sphere, stretch, territory, tract, turf (*U.S. slang*), zone **2** = **part**, portion, section, sector **3** = **field**, arena, department, domain, province, realm, sphere, territory **4** = **sunken space**, yard **5** = **range**, ambit, breadth, compass, expanse, extent, scope, size, width

arena *noun* **1** = **ring**, amphitheatre, bowl, coliseum, enclosure, field, ground, park (*U.S. & Canad.*), stadium, stage **2** = **sphere**, area, domain, field, province, realm, scene, scope, sector, territory, theatre

argot *noun* = **jargon**, cant, dialect, idiom, lingo (*informal*), parlance, patois, patter, slang, vernacular

argue *verb* **1** = **discuss**, assert, claim, contend, controvert, debate, dispute, expostulate, hold, maintain, plead, question, reason, remonstrate **2** = **quarrel**, altercate, bandy words, be at sixes and sevens, bicker, cross swords, disagree, dispute, fall out (*informal*), feud, fight, fight like cat and dog, go at it hammer and tongs, have an argument, squabble, wrangle **3** = **persuade**, convince, prevail upon, talk into, talk round **4** = **suggest**, demonstrate, denote, display, evince, exhibit, imply, indicate, manifest, point to, show

argument *noun* **1** = **quarrel**, altercation, barney (*informal*), bickering, clash, controversy, difference of opinion, disagreement, dispute, falling out (*informal*), feud, fight, row, squabble, wrangle **2** = **discussion**, assertion, claim, contention, debate, dispute, expostulation, plea, pleading, questioning, remonstrance, remonstration **3** = **reason**, argumentation, case, defence, dialectic, ground(s), line of reasoning, logic, polemic, reasoning
➤ **Antonyms**
≠**quarrel**: accord, agreement, concurrence

argumentative *adjective* = **quarrelsome**, belligerent, combative, contentious, contrary, disputatious, litigious, opinionated
➤ **Antonyms**
accommodating, amenable, complaisant,

compliant, conciliatory, easy-going, obliging

arid *adjective* **1** = **dry**, barren, desert, dried up, moistureless, parched, sterile, torrid, waterless **2** = **boring**, as dry as dust, colourless, dreary, dry, dull, flat, jejune, lifeless, spiritless, tedious, tiresome, uninspired, uninteresting, vapid
➤ **Antonyms**
≠**dry**: fertile, fruitful, lush, rich, verdant
≠**boring**: exciting, interesting, lively, sexy (*informal*), spirited, stimulating, vivacious

aridity, aridness *noun* **1** = **dryness**, barrenness, moisturelessness, parchedness, sterility, waterlessness **2** = **boredom**, colourlessness, dreariness, dryness, dullness, flatness, jejuneness, jejunity, lifelessness, spiritlessness, tediousness, tedium, uninspiredness, uninterestingness, vapidity, vapidness

aright *adverb* = **correctly**, accurately, appropriately, aptly, duly, exactly, fitly, in due order, justly, properly, rightly, suitably, truly, without error

arise *verb* **1** = **happen**, appear, begin, come into being, come to light, commence, crop up (*informal*), emanate, emerge, ensue, follow, issue, occur, originate, proceed, result, set in, spring, start, stem **2** *Old-fashioned* = **get up**, get to one's feet, go up, rise, stand up, wake up **3** = **ascend**, climb, lift, mount, move upward, rise, soar, tower

aristocracy *noun* = **upper class**, body of nobles, elite, gentry, *haut monde*, nobility, noblesse (*literary*), patricians, patriciate, peerage, ruling class, upper crust (*informal*)
➤ **Antonyms**
commoners, common people, hoi polloi, lower classes, masses, plebeians, plebs, proles (*derogatory slang, chiefly Brit.*), proletariat, working classes

aristocrat *noun* = **noble**, aristo (*informal*), childe (*archaic*), grandee, lady, lord, nobleman, noblewoman, patrician, peer, peeress

aristocratic *adjective* **1** = **upper-class**, blue-blooded, elite, gentle (*archaic*), gentlemanly, highborn, lordly, noble, patrician, titled, well-born **2** = **refined**, courtly, dignified, elegant, fine, haughty, polished, snobbish, stylish, well-bred
➤ **Antonyms**
≠**upper-class**: common, lower-class, plebeian, proletarian, working-class
≠**refined**: boorish, coarse, common, crass, crude, ill-bred, uncouth, unrefined, vulgar

arm[1] *noun* **1** = **upper limb**, appendage, limb **2** = **section**, bough, branch, department, detachment, division, extension, offshoot, projection, sector **3** = **power**, authority, command, force, might, potency, strength, sway

arm[2] *verb* **1** *Especially with weapons* = **equip**, accoutre, array, deck out, furnish, issue with, outfit, provide, rig, supply **2** = **mobilize**, muster forces, prepare for war, take up arms **3** = **provide**, brace, equip, forearm, fortify, gird one's loins, guard, make ready, outfit, prepare, prime, protect, strengthen

armada *noun* = **fleet**, flotilla, navy, squadron

armaments *plural noun* = **weapons**, ammunition, arms, guns, materiel, munitions, ordnance, weaponry

armed *adjective* = **carrying weapons**, accoutred, arrayed, equipped, fitted out, forearmed, fortified, furnished, girded, guarded, in arms, prepared, primed, protected, provided, ready, rigged out, strengthened, supplied, tooled up (*slang*), under arms

armistice *noun* = **truce**, ceasefire, peace, suspension of hostilities

armour *noun* = **protection**, armour plate, covering, sheathing, shield

armoured *adjective* = **protected**, armour-plated, bombproof, bulletproof, ironclad, mailed, steel-plated

armoury *noun* = **arsenal**, ammunition dump, arms depot, magazine, ordnance depot

arms *plural noun* **1** = **weapons**, armaments, firearms, guns, instruments of war, ordnance, weaponry **2** = **heraldry**, blazonry, crest, escutcheon, insignia

army *noun* **1** = **soldiers**, armed force, host (*archaic*), land forces, legions, military, military force, soldiery, troops **2** = **vast number**, array, horde, host, multitude, pack, swarm, throng

aroma *noun* = **scent**, bouquet, fragrance, odour, perfume, redolence, savour, smell

aromatic *adjective* = **fragrant**, balmy, odoriferous, perfumed, pungent, redolent, savoury, spicy, sweet-scented, sweet-smelling
➤ **Antonyms**
acrid, bad-smelling, fetid, foul, foul-smelling, malodorous, niffy (*Brit. slang*), noisome, offensive, olid, rank, reeking, smelly, stinking, whiffy (*Brit. slang*)

around *preposition* **1** = **surrounding**, about, encircling, enclosing, encompassing, environing, on all sides of, on every side of **2** = **approximately**, about, circa (*used with dates*), roughly ◆ *adverb* **3** = **everywhere**, about, all over, here and there, in all directions, on all sides, throughout, to and fro **4** = **near**, at hand, close, close at hand, close by, nearby, nigh (*archaic or dialect*)

arouse *verb* 1 = **stimulate**, agitate, animate, call forth, enliven, excite, foment, foster, goad, incite, inflame, instigate, kindle, move, prod, provoke, quicken, sharpen, spark, spur, stir up, summon up, warm, whet, whip up 2 = **awaken**, rouse, waken, wake up
➤ **Antonyms**
≠**stimulate**: allay, alleviate, assuage, calm, dampen, dull, end, lull, pacify, quell, quench, still

arrange *verb* 1 = **plan**, construct, contrive, devise, fix up, organize, prepare, project, schedule 2 = **agree**, adjust, come to terms, compromise, determine, settle 3 = **put in order**, align, array, class, classify, dispose, file, form, group, line up, marshal, order, organize, position, range, rank, sequence, set out, sort, sort out (*informal*), systematize, tidy 4 = **adapt**, instrument, orchestrate, score
➤ **Antonyms**
≠**put in order**: disarrange, disorganize, disturb, mess up, scatter

arrangement *noun* 1 *often plural* = **plan**, construction, devising, organization, planning, preparation, provision, schedule 2 = **agreement**, adjustment, compact, compromise, deal, settlement, terms 3 = **order**, alignment, array, classification, design, display, disposition, form, grouping, line-up, marshalling, ordering, organization, ranging, rank, setup (*informal*), structure, system 4 = **adaptation**, instrumentation, interpretation, orchestration, score, version

arrant *adjective* = **total**, absolute, atrocious, blatant, complete, deep-dyed (*usually derogatory*), downright, egregious, extreme, flagrant, gross, infamous, monstrous, notorious, out-and-out, outright, rank, thorough, thoroughgoing, undisguised, unmitigated, utter, vile

array *noun* 1 = **arrangement**, collection, display, disposition, exhibition, formation, line-up, marshalling, muster, order, parade, show, supply 2 *Poetic* = **clothing**, apparel, attire, clothes, dress, finery, garb, garments, raiment (*archaic or poetic*), regalia, schmutter (*slang*), threads (*slang*) ♦ *verb* 3 = **arrange**, align, display, dispose, draw up, exhibit, form up, group, line up, marshal, muster, order, parade, place in order, range, sequence, set in line (*Military*), show 4 = **dress**, accoutre, adorn, apparel (*archaic*), attire, bedeck, caparison, clothe, deck, decorate, equip, festoon, fit out, garb, get ready, outfit, robe, supply, wrap

arrest *verb* 1 = **capture**, apprehend, bust (*informal*), catch, collar (*informal*), detain, feel one's collar (*slang*), lay hold of, lift (*slang*), nab (*informal*), nail (*informal*), nick

(*slang, chiefly Brit.*), pinch (*informal*), run in (*slang*), seize, take, take into custody, take prisoner 2 = **stop**, block, check, delay, end, halt, hinder, hold, inhibit, interrupt, obstruct, restrain, retard, slow, stall, stay, suppress 3 = **grip**, absorb, catch, engage, engross, fascinate, hold, intrigue, occupy ♦ *noun* 4 = **capture**, apprehension, bust (*informal*), cop (*slang*), detention, seizure 5 = **stopping**, blockage, check, delay, end, halt, hindrance, inhibition, interruption, obstruction, restraint, stalling, stay, suppression
➤ **Antonyms**
verb ≠**capture**: free, let go, release, set free ≠**stop**: accelerate, encourage, precipitate, promote, quicken, speed up ♦ *noun* ≠**capture**: freeing, release ≠**stopping**: acceleration, encouragement, precipitation, promotion, quickening

arresting *adjective* = **striking**, conspicuous, dramatic, engaging, extraordinary, impressive, jaw-dropping, noticeable, outstanding, remarkable, salient, stunning, surprising
➤ **Antonyms**
inconspicuous, unimpressive, unnoticeable, unremarkable

arrival *noun* 1 = **coming**, advent, appearance, arriving, entrance, happening, occurrence, taking place 2 = **newcomer**, arriver, caller, comer, entrant, incomer, visitant, visitor

arrive *verb* 1 = **come**, appear, attain, befall, enter, get to, happen, occur, reach, show up (*informal*), take place, turn up 2 *Informal* = **succeed**, achieve recognition, become famous, make good, make it (*informal*), make one's mark (*informal*), make the grade (*informal*), reach the top
➤ **Antonyms**
≠**come**: depart, disappear, exit, go, go away, leave, pack one's bags (*informal*), retire, take (one's) leave, vanish, withdraw

arrogance *noun* = **conceit**, bluster, conceitedness, contemptuousness, disdainfulness, haughtiness, hauteur, high-handedness, hubris, imperiousness, insolence, loftiness, lordliness, overweeningness, pomposity, pompousness, presumption, pretension, pretentiousness, pride, scornfulness, superciliousness, swagger, uppishness (*Brit. informal*)
➤ **Antonyms**
bashfulness, diffidence, humility, meekness, modesty, politeness, shyness

arrogant *adjective* = **conceited**, assuming, blustering, contemptuous, disdainful, haughty, high and mighty (*informal*), high-handed, imperious, insolent, looking down one's nose at, lordly, overbearing,

overweening, pompous, presumptuous, pretentious, proud, scornful, supercilious, swaggering, too big for one's boots *or* breeches, turning up one's nose at, uppish (*Brit. informal*)
➤ **Antonyms**
bashful, deferential, diffident, humble, modest, polite, servile, shy, unassuming

arrogate *verb* = **seize**, appropriate, assume, claim unduly, commandeer, demand, expropriate, presume, usurp

arrogation *noun* = **seizure**, appropriation, assumption, commandeering, demand, expropriation, presumption, usurpation

arrow *noun* **1** = **dart**, bolt, flight, quarrel, reed (*archaic*), shaft (*archaic*) **2** = **pointer**, indicator

arsenal *noun* = **armoury**, ammunition dump, arms depot, magazine, ordnance depot, stock, stockpile, store, storehouse, supply

art *noun* **1** = **skill**, adroitness, aptitude, artifice (*archaic*), artistry, craft, craftsmanship, dexterity, expertise, facility, ingenuity, knack, knowledge, mastery, method, profession, trade, virtuosity **2** = **cunning**, artfulness, artifice, astuteness, craftiness, deceit, duplicity, guile, trickery, wiliness

artful *adjective* **1** = **cunning**, clever, crafty, deceitful, designing, foxy, intriguing, politic, scheming, sharp, shrewd, sly, smart, subtle, tricky, wily **2** = **skilful**, adept, adroit, clever, dexterous, ingenious, masterly, proficient, resourceful, smart, subtle
➤ **Antonyms**
≠**cunning**: artless, frank, ingenuous, open, simple, straightforward ≠**skilful**: artless, clumsy, unadept, unskilled, untalented

article *noun* **1** = **piece**, composition, discourse, essay, feature, item, paper, story, treatise **2** = **thing**, commodity, item, object, piece, substance, unit **3** = **clause**, branch, count, detail, division, head, heading, item, matter, paragraph, part, particular, passage, piece, point, portion, section

articulate *adjective* **1** = **expressive**, clear, coherent, comprehensible, eloquent, fluent, intelligible, lucid, meaningful, understandable, vocal, well-spoken ♦ *verb* **2** = **express**, enounce, enunciate, pronounce, say, speak, state, talk, utter, verbalize, vocalize, voice
➤ **Antonyms**
adjective ≠**expressive**: dumb, faltering, halting, hesitant, incoherent, incomprehensible, indistinct, mumbled, mute, poorly-spoken, silent, speechless, stammering, stuttering, tongue-tied, unclear, unintelligible, voiceless

articulation *noun* **1** = **expression**, delivery, diction, enunciation, pronunciation, saying, speaking, statement, talking, utterance, verbalization, vocalization, voicing **2** = **joint**, connection, coupling, hinge, jointing, juncture

artifice *noun* **1** = **trick**, contrivance, device, dodge, expedient, hoax, machination, manoeuvre, ruse, stratagem, subterfuge, tactic, wile **2** = **cunning**, artfulness, chicanery, craft, craftiness, deception, duplicity, guile, scheming, slyness, trickery **3** = **cleverness**, adroitness, deftness, facility, finesse, ingenuity, invention, inventiveness, skill

artificer *noun* = **craftsman**, artisan, mechanic

artificial *adjective* **1** = **synthetic**, man-made, manufactured, non-natural, plastic **2** = **fake**, bogus, counterfeit, ersatz, imitation, mock, phoney *or* phony (*informal*), pseudo (*informal*), sham, simulated, specious, spurious **3** = **insincere**, affected, assumed, contrived, false, feigned, forced, hollow, meretricious, phoney *or* phony (*informal*), pretended, spurious, unnatural
➤ **Antonyms**
≠**fake**: authentic ≠**insincere**: frank, genuine, honest, natural, sincere, true, unaffected

artillery *noun* = **big guns**, battery, cannon, cannonry, gunnery, ordnance

artisan *noun* = **craftsman**, artificer, handicraftsman, journeyman, mechanic, skilled workman, technician

artistic *adjective* = **creative**, aesthetic, beautiful, cultivated, cultured, decorative, elegant, exquisite, graceful, imaginative, ornamental, refined, sensitive, sophisticated, stylish, tasteful
➤ **Antonyms**
inartistic, inelegant, tasteless, unattractive, untalented

artistry *noun* = **skill**, accomplishment, art, artistic ability, brilliance, craft, craftsmanship, creativity, finesse, flair, genius, mastery, proficiency, sensibility, style, talent, taste, touch, virtuosity, workmanship

artless *adjective* **1** = **straightforward**, candid, direct, fair, frank, genuine, guileless, honest, open, plain, round, sincere, true, undesigning, upfront (*informal*) **2** = **natural**, humble, plain, pure, simple, unadorned, unaffected, uncontrived, unpretentious **3** = **unskilled**, awkward, bungling, clumsy, crude, incompetent, inept, maladroit, primitive, rude, untalented
➤ **Antonyms**
≠**straightforward**: artful, crafty, cunning,

designing, dishonest, false, insincere
≠**natural**: affected, artificial, unnatural
≠**unskilled**: aesthetic, artful, artistic, crafty,
cunning, sophisticated

as *conjunction* **1** = **when**, at the time that,
during the time that, just as, while **2** = **in
the way that**, in the manner that, like **3**
= **what**, that which **4** = **since**, because,
considering that, seeing that **5** = **for
instance**, like, such as ♦ *preposition* **6**
= **being**, in the character of, in the role of,
under the name of **7** **as for** = **with regard
to**, as regards, in reference to, on the subject
of, with reference to, with respect to **8** **as it
were** = **in a way**, in a manner of speaking,
so to say, so to speak

ascend *verb* = **move up**, climb, float up, fly
up, go up, lift off, mount, rise, scale, slope
upwards, soar, take off, tower
➤ **Antonyms**
alight, descend, dip, drop, fall, go down,
incline, move down, plummet, plunge, sink,
slant, slope, subside, tumble

ascendancy, ascendence *noun*
= **influence**, authority, command, control,
dominance, domination, dominion, mastery,
power, predominance, pre-eminence,
prevalence, reign, rule, sovereignty,
superiority, supremacy, sway, upper hand
➤ **Antonyms**
inferiority, servility, subjection,
subordination, weakness

ascendant, ascendent *adjective* **1**
= **influential**, authoritative, commanding,
controlling, dominant, powerful,
predominant, pre-eminent, prevailing,
ruling, superior, supreme, uppermost
♦ *noun* **2** **in the ascendant** = **rising**,
ascending, climbing, commanding,
dominant, dominating, flourishing, growing,
increasing, influential, mounting, on the rise,
on the way up, powerful, prevailing,
supreme, up-and-coming, uppermost,
winning

ascent *noun* **1** = **rise**, ascending, ascension,
clambering, climb, climbing, mounting,
rising, scaling, upward movement **2**
= **upward slope**, acclivity, gradient, incline,
ramp, rise, rising ground

ascertain *verb* = **find out**, confirm,
determine, discover, establish, ferret out, fix,
identify, learn, make certain, settle, suss
(out) (*slang*), verify

ascetic *noun* **1** = **monk**, abstainer,
anchorite, hermit, nun, recluse, self-denier
♦ *adjective* **2** = **self-denying**, abstemious,
abstinent, austere, celibate, frugal, harsh,
plain, puritanical, rigorous, self-disciplined,
severe, Spartan, stern
➤ **Antonyms**
noun ≠**monk**: hedonist, sensualist,

voluptuary ♦ *adjective* ≠**self-denying**:
abandoned, comfortable, luxurious,
self-indulgent, sensuous, voluptuous

asceticism *noun* = **self-denial**,
abstemiousness, abstinence, austerity,
celibacy, frugality, harshness, mortification of
the flesh, plainness, puritanism, rigorousness,
rigour, self-abnegation, self-discipline,
self-mortification

ascribe *verb* = **attribute**, assign, charge,
credit, impute, put down, refer, set down

ashamed *adjective* = **embarrassed**,
abashed, bashful, blushing, chagrined,
conscience-stricken, crestfallen, discomfited,
distressed, guilty, humbled, humiliated,
mortified, prudish, reluctant, remorseful,
shamefaced, sheepish, shy, sorry
➤ **Antonyms**
gratified, honoured, pleased, proud,
satisfied, unashamed, vain

ashen *adjective* = **pale**, anaemic, ashy,
colourless, grey, leaden, like death warmed
up (*informal*), livid, pallid, pasty, wan,
white
➤ **Antonyms**
blooming, blushing, florid, flushed, glowing,
radiant, red, reddish, rosy, rosy-cheeked,
rubicund, ruddy

ashore *adverb* = **on land**, aground,
landwards, on dry land, on the beach, on
the shore, shorewards, to the shore

aside *adverb* **1** = **to one side**, alone,
alongside, apart, away, beside, in isolation,
in reserve, on one side, out of mind, out of
the way, privately, separately, to the side
♦ *noun* **2** = **interpolation**, interposition,
parenthesis **3** = **digression**, departure,
excursion, excursus, tangent

asinine *adjective* = **stupid**, braindead
(*informal*), brainless, daft (*informal*), dead
from the neck up (*informal*), dumb-ass
(*slang*), dunderheaded, fatuous, foolish,
goofy (*informal*), gormless (*Brit. informal*),
halfwitted, idiotic, imbecile, imbecilic, inane,
moronic, senseless, silly, thickheaded,
thick-witted
➤ **Antonyms**
brainy (*informal*), bright, clever, intelligent,
quick-witted, sage, sane, sensible, sharp,
smart, wise

ask *verb* **1** = **inquire**, interrogate, query,
question, quiz **2** = **request**, appeal, apply,
beg, beseech, claim, crave, demand,
entreat, implore, petition, plead, pray, seek,
solicit, sue, supplicate **3** = **invite**, bid,
summon
➤ **Antonyms**
≠**inquire**: answer, reply, respond

askance *adverb* As in **look askance at 1**
= **out of the corner of one's eye**, awry,

indirectly, obliquely, sideways, with a side glance **2 = suspiciously**, disapprovingly, distrustfully, doubtfully, dubiously, mistrustfully, sceptically

askew *adverb* **1 = crookedly**, aslant, awry, obliquely, off-centre, to one side ♦ *adjective* **2 = crooked**, awry, cockeyed (*informal*), lopsided, oblique, off-centre, skewwhiff (*Brit. informal*)
➤ **Antonyms**
adverb ≠ **crookedly:** aligned, evenly, in line, level, right, squarely, straight, true ♦ *adjective* ≠ **crooked:** aligned, even, in line, level, right, square, straight, true

asleep *adjective* **= sleeping**, crashed out (*slang*), dead to the world (*informal*), dormant, dozing, fast asleep, napping, out for the count, slumbering, snoozing (*informal*), sound asleep

aspect *noun* **1 = feature**, angle, facet, side **2 = position**, bearing, direction, exposure, outlook, point of view, prospect, scene, situation, view **3 = appearance**, air, attitude, bearing, condition, countenance, demeanour, expression, look, manner, mien (*literary*)

asperity *noun* **= sharpness**, acerbity, acrimony, bitterness, churlishness, crabbedness, crossness, harshness, irascibility, irritability, moroseness, peevishness, roughness, ruggedness, severity, sourness, sullenness

asphyxiate *verb* **= suffocate**, choke, smother, stifle, strangle, strangulate, throttle

aspirant *noun* **1 = candidate**, applicant, aspirer, hopeful, postulant, seeker, suitor ♦ *adjective* **2 = hopeful**, ambitious, aspiring, eager, endeavouring, longing, striving, wishful

aspiration *noun* **= aim**, ambition, craving, desire, dream, eagerness, endeavour, goal, hankering, Holy Grail (*informal*), hope, longing, object, objective, wish, yearning

aspire *verb* **= aim**, be ambitious, be eager, crave, desire, dream, hanker, hope, long, pursue, seek, set one's heart on, wish, yearn

aspiring *adjective* **= hopeful**, ambitious, aspirant, eager, endeavouring, longing, striving, wannabe (*informal*), wishful, would-be

ass *noun* **1 = donkey**, jennet, moke (*slang*) **2 = fool**, airhead (*slang*), berk (*Brit. slang*), blockhead, bonehead (*slang*), charlie (*Brit. informal*), coot, daftie (*informal*), dickhead (*slang*), dickwit (*slang*), dipstick (*Brit. slang*), divvy (*Brit. slang*), dolt, dope (*informal*), dork (*slang*), dumb-ass (*slang*), dunce, dweeb (*U.S. slang*), fathead (*informal*), fuckwit (*taboo slang*), geek (*slang*), gobshite (*Irish taboo slang*), gonzo

(*slang*), halfwit, idiot, jackass, jerk (*slang, chiefly U.S. & Canad.*), nerd *or* nurd (*slang*), nincompoop, ninny, nitwit (*informal*), numbskull *or* numskull, numpty (*Scot. informal*), oaf, pillock (*Brit. slang*), plank (*Brit. slang*), plonker (*slang*), prat (*slang*), prick (*slang*), schmuck (*U.S. slang*), simpleton, twerp *or* twirp (*informal*), twit (*informal, chiefly Brit.*), wally (*slang*), weenie (*U.S. informal*)

assail *verb* **1 = attack**, assault, belabour, beset, charge, encounter, fall upon, invade, lay into (*informal*), maltreat, set about, set upon **2 = criticize**, abuse, berate, blast, go for the jugular, impugn, lambast(e), malign, put down, revile, tear into (*informal*), vilify

assailant *noun* **= attacker**, aggressor, assailer, assaulter, invader

assassin *noun* **= murderer**, eliminator (*slang*), executioner, hatchet man (*slang*), hit man (*slang*), killer, liquidator, slayer

assassinate *verb* **= murder**, blow away (*slang, chiefly U.S.*), eliminate (*slang*), hit (*slang*), kill, liquidate, slay, take out (*slang*)

assault *noun* **1 = attack**, aggression, campaign, charge, incursion, inroad, invasion, offensive, onset, onslaught, storm, storming, strike ♦ *verb* **2 = attack**, assail, belabour, beset, charge, fall upon, invade, lay into (*informal*), set about, set upon, storm, strike at
➤ **Antonyms**
noun ≠ **attack:** defence, protection, resistance ♦ *verb* ≠ **attack:** defend, protect, resist

assay *verb* **1 = analyse**, appraise, assess, evaluate, examine, inspect, investigate, prove, test, try, weigh ♦ *noun* **2 = analysis**, examination, inspection, investigation, test, trial

assemble *verb* **1 = gather**, accumulate, amass, bring together, call together, collect, come together, congregate, convene, convoke, flock, foregather, marshal, meet, muster, rally, round up, summon **2 = put together**, build up, connect, construct, erect, fabricate, fit together, join, make, manufacture, piece together, set up
➤ **Antonyms**
≠ **gather:** adjourn, break up (*informal*), disband, dismiss, disperse, distribute, scatter ≠ **put together:** disassemble, divide, take apart

assembly *noun* **1 = gathering**, accumulation, aggregation, assemblage, body, collection, company, conclave, conference, congregation, congress, convention, convocation, council, crowd, diet, flock, group, house, mass, meeting, multitude, rally, synod, throng **2 = putting**

together, building up, connecting, construction, erection, fabrication, fitting together, joining, manufacture, piecing together, setting up

assent noun 1 = **agreement**, acceptance, accession, accord, acquiescence, approval, compliance, concurrence, consent, permission, sanction ♦ verb 2 = **agree**, accede, accept, acquiesce, allow, approve, comply, concur, consent, fall in with, go along with, grant, permit, sanction, subscribe
➤ **Antonyms**
noun ≠**agreement**: denial, disagreement, disapproval, dissension, dissent, objection, refusal ♦ verb ≠**agree**: deny, differ, disagree, dissent, object, protest, rebut, reject, retract

assert verb 1 = **state**, affirm, allege, asseverate, attest, aver, avouch (archaic), avow, contend, declare, maintain, predicate, profess, pronounce, swear 2 = **insist upon**, claim, defend, press, put forward, stand up for, stress, uphold, vindicate 3 **assert oneself** = **be forceful**, exert one's influence, make one's presence felt, put oneself forward, put one's foot down (informal)
➤ **Antonyms**
≠**state**, **insist upon**: deny, disavow, disclaim, rebut, refute, retract

assertion noun 1 = **statement**, affirmation, allegation, asseveration, attestation, avowal, claim, contention, declaration, predication, profession, pronouncement 2 = **insistence**, defence, maintenance, stressing, vindication

assertive adjective = **confident**, aggressive, can-do (informal), decided, decisive, demanding, dogmatic, domineering, emphatic, feisty (informal, chiefly U.S. & Canad.), firm, forceful, forward, insistent, in-your-face (Brit. slang), overbearing, positive, pushy (informal), self-assured, strong-willed
➤ **Antonyms**
backward, bashful, diffident, hesitant, insecure, meek, modest, reserved, retiring, self-conscious, self-effacing, sheepish, shrinking, shy, timid, timorous, unassertive, unobtrusive

assess verb 1 = **judge**, appraise, compute, determine, estimate, evaluate, eye up, fix, gauge, rate, size up (informal), value, weigh 2 = **evaluate**, demand, fix, impose, levy, rate, tax, value

assessment noun 1 = **judgment**, appraisal, computation, determination, estimate, estimation, evaluation, rating, valuation 2 = **evaluation**, charge, demand, duty, fee, impost, levy, rate, rating, tariff, tax, taxation, toll, valuation

asset noun 1 = **benefit**, ace in the hole, ace up one's sleeve, advantage, aid, blessing,

boon, feather in one's cap, help, resource, service 2 **assets** = **property**, capital, estate, funds, goods, holdings, means, money, possessions, reserves, resources, valuables, wealth
➤ **Antonyms**
≠**benefit**: albatross, burden, disadvantage, drag, drawback, encumbrance, handicap, hindrance, impediment, liability, millstone, minus (informal), nuisance

assiduous adjective = **diligent**, attentive, constant, hard-working, indefatigable, industrious, laborious, persevering, persistent, sedulous, steady, studious, unflagging, untiring, unwearied
➤ **Antonyms**
careless, idle, inattentive, indolent, lax, lazy, negligent, slack

assign verb 1 = **select**, appoint, choose, delegate, designate, name, nominate 2 = **give**, allocate, allot, apportion, consign, distribute, give out, grant, make over 3 = **attribute**, accredit, ascribe, put down 4 = **fix**, appoint, appropriate, determine, set apart, stipulate

assignation noun 1 = **secret meeting**, clandestine meeting, illicit meeting, rendezvous, tryst (archaic) 2 = **selection**, appointment, assignment, choice, delegation, designation, nomination 3 = **giving**, allocation, allotment, apportionment, consignment, distribution, grant 4 = **attribution**, accrediting, ascription 5 = **fixing**, appointment, appropriation, determination, specification, stipulation

assignment noun 1 = **task**, appointment, charge, commission, duty, job, mission, position, post, responsibility 2 = **selection**, appointment, choice, delegation, designation, nomination 3 = **giving**, allocation, allotment, apportionment, assignation (Law, chiefly Scot.), consignment, distribution, grant 4 = **attribution**, accrediting, ascription 5 = **fixing**, appointment, appropriation, determination, specification, stipulation

assimilate verb 1 = **learn**, absorb, digest, imbibe (literary), incorporate, ingest, take in 2 = **adjust**, acclimatize, accommodate, acculturate, accustom, adapt, become like, become similar, blend in, conform, fit, homogenize, intermix, mingle

assist verb = **help**, abet, aid, back, benefit, boost, collaborate, cooperate, encourage, expedite, facilitate, further, give a leg up (informal), lend a helping hand, promote, reinforce, relieve, second, serve, succour, support, sustain, work for, work with
➤ **Antonyms**
frustrate, hamper, handicap, hinder, hold back, hold up, impede, obstruct, resist,

thwart, work against

assistance *noun* = **help**, abetment, aid, backing, benefit, boost, collaboration, cooperation, encouragement, furtherance, helping hand, promotion, reinforcement, relief, service, succour, support, sustenance
➤ **Antonyms**
hindrance, obstruction, opposition, resistance

assistant *noun* = **helper**, abettor, accessory, accomplice, aide, aider, ally, associate, auxiliary, backer, coadjutor (*rare*), collaborator, colleague, confederate, cooperator, helpmate, henchman, partner, protagonist, right-hand man, second, supporter

associate *verb* **1** = **connect**, affiliate, ally, combine, confederate, conjoin, correlate, couple, identify, join, league, link, lump together, mention in the same breath, mix, pair, relate, think of together, unite, yoke **2** = **mix**, accompany, befriend, be friends, consort, fraternize, hang (*informal, chiefly U.S.*), hang about, hang out (*informal*), hobnob, mingle, run around (*informal*), socialize ◆ *noun* **3** = **partner**, collaborator, colleague, confederate, co-worker **4** = **friend**, ally, companion, compeer, comrade, confrère, mate (*informal*)
➤ **Antonyms**
verb ≠**connect**: detach, disconnect, dissociate, distance, distinguish, divorce, isolate, segregate, separate, set apart ≠**mix**: avoid, be alienated, be estranged, break off, part company

association *noun* **1** = **group**, affiliation, alliance, band, clique, club, coalition, combine, company, confederacy, confederation, cooperative, corporation, federation, fraternity, league, order, organization, partnership, society, syndicate, union **2** = **connection**, blend, bond, combination, concomitance, correlation, identification, joining, juxtaposition, linkage, linking, lumping together, mixing, mixture, pairing, relation, tie, union, yoking **3** = **friendship**, affinity, companionship, comradeship, familiarity, fellowship, fraternization, intimacy, liaison, partnership, relations, relationship

assort *verb* = **group**, arrange, array, categorize, classify, dispose, distribute, file, grade, range, rank, sort, type

assorted *adjective* **1** = **various**, different, diverse, diversified, heterogeneous, manifold, miscellaneous, mixed, motley, sundry, varied, variegated **2** = **grouped**, arranged, arrayed, categorized, classified, disposed, filed, graded, matched, ranged, ranked, sorted, typed
➤ **Antonyms**
≠**various**: alike, homogeneous, identical, like, same, similar, uniform, unvaried

assortment *noun* **1** = **variety**, array, choice, collection, diversity, farrago, hotchpotch, jumble, medley, *mélange*, miscellany, mishmash, mixed bag (*informal*), mixture, pick 'n' mix, potpourri, salmagundi, selection **2** = **sorting**, arrangement, categorizing, classification, disposition, distribution, filing, grading, grouping, ranging, ranking, typing

assuage *verb* **1** = **relieve**, allay, alleviate, calm, ease, lessen, lighten, mitigate, moderate, palliate, quench, soothe, temper **2** = **calm**, appease, lull, mollify, pacify, pour oil on troubled waters, quiet, relax, satisfy, soften, soothe, still, tranquillize
➤ **Antonyms**
≠**relieve**: aggravate, exacerbate, heighten, increase, intensify, worsen ≠**calm**: aggravate, embitter, enrage, infuriate, madden, provoke

assume *verb* **1** = **take for granted**, accept, believe, expect, fancy, guess (*informal, chiefly U.S. & Canad.*), imagine, infer, presume, presuppose, suppose, surmise, suspect, think **2** = **take on**, accept, acquire, attend to, begin, don, embark upon, embrace, enter upon, put on, set about, shoulder, take over, take responsibility for, take up, undertake **3** = **put on**, adopt, affect, counterfeit, feign, imitate, impersonate, mimic, pretend to, sham, simulate **4** = **take over**, acquire, appropriate, arrogate, commandeer, expropriate, pre-empt, seize, take, usurp
➤ **Antonyms**
≠**take for granted**: know, prove ≠**take on**, **take over**: give up, hand over, leave, put aside, relinquish

assumed *adjective* **1** = **false**, affected, bogus, counterfeit, fake, feigned, fictitious, imitation, made-up, make-believe, phoney or phony (*informal*), pretended, pseudonymous, sham, simulated, spurious **2** = **taken for granted**, accepted, expected, hypothetical, presumed, presupposed, supposed, surmised
➤ **Antonyms**
≠**false**: actual, authentic, natural, real ≠**taken for granted**: known, positive, stated, true

assumption *noun* **1** = **presumption**, acceptance, belief, conjecture, expectation, fancy, guess, hypothesis, inference, postulate, postulation, premise, premiss, presupposition, supposition, surmise, suspicion, theory **2** = **taking on**, acceptance, acquisition, adoption, embracing, entering upon, putting on, shouldering, takeover, taking up, undertaking **3** = **taking**, acquisition, appropriation, arrogation,

expropriation, pre-empting, seizure,
takeover, usurpation **4 = presumptuousness,**
arrogance, conceit, imperiousness, pride,
self-importance

assurance *noun* **1 = assertion,** affirmation,
declaration, guarantee, oath, pledge,
profession, promise, protestation, statement,
vow, word, word of honour **2 = confidence,**
assertiveness, assuredness, boldness,
certainty, certitude, conviction, coolness,
courage, faith, firmness, nerve, poise,
positiveness, security, self-confidence,
self-reliance, sureness
➤ **Antonyms**
≠**assertion:** falsehood, lie ≠**confidence:**
apprehension, diffidence, distrust, doubt,
self-doubt, self-effacement, shyness, timidity,
uncertainty

assure *verb* **1 = promise,** affirm, attest,
certify, confirm, declare confidently, give
one's word to, guarantee, pledge, swear,
vow **2 = convince,** comfort, embolden,
encourage, hearten, persuade, reassure,
soothe **3 = make certain,** clinch, complete,
confirm, ensure, guarantee, make sure, seal,
secure

assured *adjective* **1 = confident,** assertive,
audacious, bold, brazen, certain,
complacent, overconfident, poised, positive,
pushy (*informal*), resting on one's laurels,
self-assured, self-confident, self-possessed,
sure of oneself **2 = certain,** beyond doubt,
clinched, confirmed, dependable, ensured,
fixed, guaranteed, indubitable, in the bag
(*slang*), irrefutable, made certain, sealed,
secure, settled, sure, unquestionable
➤ **Antonyms**
≠**confident:** bashful, diffident, hesitant,
retiring, self-conscious, self-effacing, timid
≠**certain:** ambiguous, doubtful, indefinite,
questionable, uncertain, unconfirmed,
unsettled, unsure

astonish *verb* **= amaze,** astound, bewilder,
boggle the mind, confound, daze,
dumbfound, flabbergast (*informal*), stagger,
stun, stupefy, surprise

astonishing *adjective* **= amazing,**
astounding, bewildering, breathtaking,
brilliant, impressive, jaw-dropping,
sensational (*informal*), staggering, striking,
stunning, stupefying, surprising, wondrous
(*archaic or literary*)

astonishment *noun* **= amazement,** awe,
bewilderment, confusion, consternation,
stupefaction, surprise, wonder, wonderment

astound *verb* **= amaze,** astonish, bewilder,
boggle the mind, confound, daze,
dumbfound, flabbergast (*informal*),
overwhelm, stagger, stun, stupefy, surprise,
take one's breath away

astounding *adjective* **= amazing,**
astonishing, bewildering, breathtaking,
brilliant, impressive, jaw-dropping,
sensational (*informal*), staggering, striking,
stunning, stupefying, surprising, wondrous
(*archaic or literary*)

astray *adjective, adverb* **1 = off the right
track,** adrift, afield, amiss, lost, off, off
course, off the mark, off the subject
♦ *adverb* **2 = into sin,** into error, to the bad,
wrong

astronaut *noun* **= space traveller,**
cosmonaut, spaceman, space pilot,
spacewoman

astute *adjective* **= intelligent,** adroit, artful,
bright, calculating, canny, clever, crafty,
cunning, discerning, foxy, insightful, keen,
knowing, on the ball (*informal*),
penetrating, perceptive, politic, sagacious,
sharp, shrewd, sly, subtle, wily
➤ **Antonyms**
dull, ingenuous, naive, slow, straightforward,
stupid, unintelligent, unknowing

astuteness *noun* **= intelligence,** acumen,
adroitness, artfulness, brightness, canniness,
cleverness, craftiness, cunning, discernment,
foxiness, insight, keenness, knowledge,
penetration, perceptiveness, sagacity,
sharpness, shrewdness, slyness, smarts
(*slang, chiefly U.S.*), subtlety, suss (*slang*),
wiliness

asylum *noun* **1 = refuge,** harbour, haven,
preserve, retreat, safety, sanctuary, shelter **2**
Old-fashioned **= mental hospital,** funny
farm (*facetious*), hospital, institution,
laughing academy (*U.S. slang*), loony bin
(*slang*), madhouse (*informal*), nuthouse
(*slang*), psychiatric hospital, rubber room
(*U.S. slang*)

atheism *noun* **= nonbelief,** disbelief,
freethinking, godlessness, heathenism,
infidelity, irreligion, paganism, scepticism,
unbelief

atheist *noun* **= nonbeliever,** disbeliever,
freethinker, heathen, infidel, irreligionist,
pagan, sceptic, unbeliever

athlete *noun* **= sportsperson,** competitor,
contender, contestant, games player,
gymnast, player, runner, sportsman,
sportswoman

athletic *adjective* **= fit,** able-bodied, active,
brawny, energetic, herculean, husky
(*informal*), lusty, muscular, powerful, robust,
sinewy, strapping, strong, sturdy, vigorous,
well-proportioned
➤ **Antonyms**
delicate, feeble, frail, puny, sickly, weedy
(*informal*)

athletics *plural noun* **= sports,** contests,
exercises, games of strength, gymnastics,

races, track and field events

atmosphere *noun* 1 = **air**, aerosphere, heavens, sky 2 = **feeling**, air, ambience, aura, character, climate, environment, feel, flavour, mood, quality, spirit, surroundings, tone, vibes (*slang*)

atom *noun* = **particle**, bit, crumb, dot, fragment, grain, iota, jot, mite, molecule, morsel, mote, scintilla (*rare*), scrap, shred, speck, spot, tittle, trace, whit

atone *verb, usually with* **for** = **make amends**, answer for, compensate, do penance, make redress, make reparation, make up for, pay for, recompense, redress

atonement *noun* = **amends**, compensation, expiation, payment, penance, propitiation, recompense, redress, reparation, restitution, satisfaction

atrocious *adjective* 1 = **cruel**, barbaric, brutal, diabolical, fiendish, flagrant, godawful (*slang*), heinous, hellacious (*U.S. slang*), infamous, infernal, inhuman, monstrous, nefarious, ruthless, savage, vicious, villainous, wicked 2 *Informal* = **shocking**, appalling, detestable, execrable, grievous, horrible, horrifying, terrible
➤ **Antonyms**
≠**cruel**: civilized, generous, gentle, good, honourable, humane, kind, merciful
≠**shocking**: admirable, fine, tasteful

atrocity *noun* 1 = **cruelty**, atrociousness, barbarity, barbarousness, brutality, enormity, fiendishness, grievousness, heinousness, horror, infamy, inhumanity, monstrousness, nefariousness, ruthlessness, savagery, shockingness, viciousness, villainousness, wickedness 2 = **act of cruelty**, abomination, barbarity, brutality, crime, cruelty, enormity, evil, horror, monstrosity, outrage, villainy

attach *verb* 1 = **connect**, add, adhere, affix, annex, append, bind, couple, fasten, fix, join, link, make fast, secure, stick, subjoin, tie, unite 2 = **put**, ascribe, assign, associate, attribute, connect, impute, invest with, lay, place 3 **attach oneself** *or* **be attached to** = **join**, accompany, affiliate oneself with, associate with, become associated with, combine with, join forces with, latch on to, sign on with, sign up with, unite with
➤ **Antonyms**
≠**connect**: detach, disconnect, dissociate, loosen, remove, retire, separate, untie, withdraw

attached *adjective* 1 = **spoken for**, accompanied, engaged, married, partnered 2 **attached to** = **fond of**, affectionate towards, devoted to, full of regard for

attachment *noun* 1 = **fondness**, affection, affinity, attraction, bond, devotion, fidelity, friendship, liking, love, loyalty, partiality,

possessiveness, predilection, regard, tenderness 2 = **accessory**, accoutrement, adaptor *or* adapter, addition, add-on, adjunct, appendage, appurtenance, auxiliary, extension, extra, fitting, fixture, supplement, supplementary part 3 = **connector**, adaptor *or* adapter, bond, clamp, connection, coupling, fastener, fastening, joint, junction, link, tie
➤ **Antonyms**
≠**fondness**: animosity, antipathy, aversion, disinclination, distaste, hatred, hostility, loathing

attack *verb* 1 = **assault**, assail, charge, fall upon, invade, lay into (*informal*), raid, rush, set about, set upon, storm, strike (at) 2 = **criticize**, abuse, berate, bite someone's head off, blame, blast, censure, excoriate, go for the jugular, have a go (at) (*informal*), impugn, lambast(e), malign, put down, revile, snap someone's head off, tear into (*informal*), vilify ◆ *noun* 3 = **assault**, aggression, campaign, charge, foray, incursion, inroad, invasion, offensive, onset, onslaught, raid, rush, strike 4 = **criticism**, abuse, blame, calumny, censure, character assassination, denigration, impugnment, stick (*slang*), vilification 5 = **bout**, access, convulsion, fit, paroxysm, seizure, spasm, spell, stroke
➤ **Antonyms**
verb ≠**assault**: defend, guard, protect, retreat, support, sustain, withdraw ◆ *noun* ≠**assault**: defence, retreat, support, withdrawal

attacker *noun* = **assailant**, aggressor, assaulter, intruder, invader, raider

attain *verb* = **achieve**, accomplish, acquire, arrive at, bring off, complete, earn, effect, fulfil, gain, get, grasp, land, obtain, procure, reach, realize, reap, score (*slang*), secure, win

attainable *adjective* = **achievable**, accessible, accomplishable, at hand, feasible, gettable, graspable, likely, obtainable, possible, potential, practicable, probable, procurable, reachable, realizable, within reach
➤ **Antonyms**
impossible, impracticable, improbable, inaccessible, out of reach, unattainable, unfeasible, unlikely, unobtainable, unprocurable, unreachable

attainment *noun* 1 = **achievement**, accomplishment, acquirement, acquisition, arrival at, completion, feat, fulfilment, gaining, getting, obtaining, procurement, reaching, realization, reaping, winning 2 = **skill**, ability, accomplishment, achievement, art, capability, competence, gift, mastery, proficiency, talent

attempt *verb* 1 = **try**, endeavour, essay,

experiment, have a crack, have a go (*informal*), have a shot (*informal*), have a stab (*informal*), jump through hoops (*informal*), seek, strive, tackle, take on, take the bit between one's teeth, try one's hand at, undertake, venture ♦ *noun* **2 = try**, assault, attack, bid, crack (*informal*), effort, endeavour, essay, experiment, go (*informal*), shot (*informal*), stab (*informal*), trial, undertaking, venture

attend *verb* **1 = be present**, appear, be at, be here, be there, frequent, go to, haunt, make one (*archaic*), put in an appearance, show oneself, show up (*informal*), turn up, visit **2 = look after**, care for, mind, minister to, nurse, take care of, tend **3 = pay attention**, follow, hear, hearken (*archaic*), heed, listen, look on, mark, mind, note, notice, observe, pay heed, regard, take to heart, watch **4 = escort**, accompany, chaperon, companion, convoy, guard, squire, usher **5 = accompany**, arise from, be associated with, be connected with, be consequent on, follow, go hand in hand with, issue from, occur with, result from **6 = serve**, be in the service of, wait upon, work for **7 attend to = apply oneself to**, concentrate on, devote oneself to, get to work on, look after, occupy oneself with, see to, take care of
➤ **Antonyms**
≠**be present**: be absent, miss, play truant ≠**look after, apply oneself to**: neglect ≠**pay attention**: discount, disregard, ignore, neglect ≠**accompany**: dissociate

attendance *noun* **1 = presence**, appearance, attending, being there **2 = turnout**, audience, crowd, gate, house, number present

attendant *noun* **1 = assistant**, aide, auxiliary, chaperon, companion, custodian, escort, flunky, follower, guard, guide, helper, lackey, menial, page, servant, steward, underling, usher, waiter ♦ *adjective* **2 = accompanying**, accessory, associated, concomitant, consequent, related

attention *noun* **1 = concentration**, consideration, contemplation, deliberation, heed, heedfulness, intentness, mind, scrutiny, thinking, thought, thoughtfulness **2 = notice**, awareness, consciousness, consideration, observation, recognition, regard **3 = care**, concern, looking after, ministration, treatment **4 attentions = courtesy**, assiduities, care, civility, compliment, consideration, deference, gallantry, mindfulness, politeness, regard, respect, service
➤ **Antonyms**
≠**concentration, notice**: carelessness, disregard, disrespect, distraction, inattention,

laxity, laxness, thoughtlessness, unconcern ≠**care**: negligence ≠**courtesy**: discourtesy, impoliteness

attentive *adjective* **1 = intent**, alert, awake, careful, concentrating, heedful, listening, mindful, observant, on one's toes, regardful, studious, watchful **2 = considerate**, accommodating, civil, conscientious, courteous, devoted, gallant, gracious, helpful, kind, obliging, polite, respectful, thoughtful
➤ **Antonyms**
≠**intent**: absent-minded, careless, distracted, dreamy, heedless, inattentive, preoccupied, unheeding, unmindful ≠**considerate**: neglectful, negligent, remiss, thoughtless

attest *verb* **= testify**, adjure, affirm, assert, authenticate, aver, bear out, bear witness, certify, confirm, corroborate, declare, demonstrate, display, evince, exhibit, give evidence, invoke, manifest, prove, ratify, seal, show, substantiate, swear, verify, vouch for, warrant, witness
➤ **Antonyms**
contradict, controvert, deny, disprove, gainsay (*archaic or literary*), give the lie to, make a nonsense of, prove false, rebut, refute

attic *noun* **= loft**, garret

attire *noun* **1 = clothes**, accoutrements, apparel, array (*poetic*), clothing, costume, dress, garb, garments, gear (*informal*), habiliments, habit, outfit, raiment (*archaic or poetic*), robes, threads (*slang*), uniform, vestment, wear ♦ *verb* **2 = dress**, accoutre, apparel (*archaic*), array, clothe, costume, deck out, equip, fit out, garb, get ready, rig out, robe, turn out

attitude *noun* **1 = disposition**, approach, frame of mind, mood, opinion, outlook, perspective, point of view, position, stance, view **2 = manner**, air, aspect, bearing, carriage, condition, demeanour, mien (*literary*) **3 = position**, pose, posture, stance

attract *verb* **= appeal to**, allure, bewitch, captivate, catch (someone's) eye, charm, decoy, draw, enchant, endear, engage, entice, fascinate, incline, induce, interest, invite, lure, pull (*informal*), tempt
➤ **Antonyms**
disgust, give one the creeps (*informal*), put one off, repel, repulse, revolt, turn one off (*informal*)

attraction *noun* **= appeal**, allure, attractiveness, bait, captivation, charm, come-on (*informal*), draw, enchantment, endearment, enticement, fascination, incentive, inducement, interest, invitation, lure, magnetism, pull (*informal*), temptation, temptingness

attractive *adjective* **= appealing**, agreeable,

alluring, beautiful, bonny, captivating, charming, comely, cute, engaging, enticing, fair, fascinating, fetching, glamorous, good-looking, gorgeous, handsome, interesting, inviting, likable or likeable, lovely, magnetic, pleasant, pleasing, prepossessing, pretty, seductive, tempting, winning, winsome
➤ Antonyms
disagreeable, displeasing, distasteful, offensive, repulsive, ugly, unappealing, unbecoming, uninviting, unlikable or unlikeable, unpleasant, unsightly

attribute verb 1 = ascribe, apply, assign, blame, charge, credit, impute, lay at the door of, put down to, refer, set down to, trace to ♦ noun 2 = quality, aspect, character, characteristic, facet, feature, idiosyncrasy, indication, mark, note, peculiarity, point, property, quirk, sign, symbol, trait, virtue

attrition noun = wearing down, attenuation, debilitation, harassment, harrying, thinning out, weakening

attune verb = accustom, acclimatize, accord, adapt, adjust, coordinate, familiarize, harmonize, modulate, regulate, set, tune

auburn adjective = reddish-brown, chestnut-coloured, copper-coloured, henna, nutbrown, russet, rust-coloured, tawny, Titian red

audacious adjective 1 = daring, adventurous, bold, brave, courageous, daredevil, dauntless, death-defying, enterprising, fearless, intrepid, rash, reckless, risky, valiant, venturesome 2 = cheeky, assuming, brazen, defiant, disrespectful, forward, fresh (informal), impertinent, impudent, insolent, in-your-face (Brit. slang), pert, presumptuous, rude, sassy (U.S. informal), shameless
➤ Antonyms
≠daring: careful, cautious, cowardly, frightened, guarded, prudent, timid, unadventurous, unenterprising ≠cheeky: deferential, gracious, tactful, unassuming

audacity noun 1 = daring, adventurousness, audaciousness, boldness, bravery, courage, dauntlessness, enterprise, face (informal), fearlessness, front, guts (informal), intrepidity, nerve, rashness, recklessness, valour, venturesomeness 2 = cheek, audaciousness, brass neck (Brit. informal), chutzpah (U.S. & Canad. informal), defiance, disrespectfulness, effrontery, forwardness, gall (informal), impertinence, impudence, insolence, neck (informal), nerve, pertness, presumption, rudeness, sassiness (U.S. informal), shamelessness

audible adjective = clear, detectable,

discernible, distinct, hearable, perceptible
➤ Antonyms
faint, imperceptible, inaudible, indistinct, low, out of earshot

audience noun 1 = spectators, assemblage, assembly, congregation, crowd, gallery, gathering, house, listeners, onlookers, turnout, viewers 2 = public, devotees, fans, following, market 3 = interview, consultation, hearing, meeting, reception

audit Accounting ♦ noun 1 = inspection, balancing, check, checking, examination, investigation, review, scrutiny, verification ♦ verb 2 = inspect, balance, check, examine, go over, go through, investigate, review, scrutinize, verify

au fait adjective = fully informed, abreast of, au courant, clued-up (informal), conversant, expert, familiar, in the know, in the loop, in touch, knowledgeable, on the ball (informal), up to speed, well-acquainted, well up

augment verb = increase, add to, amplify, boost, build up, dilate, enhance, enlarge, expand, extend, grow, heighten, inflate, intensify, magnify, multiply, raise, reinforce, strengthen, swell
➤ Antonyms
contract, curtail, cut down, decrease, diminish, lessen, lower, reduce, shrink

augmentation noun = increase, accession, addition, amplification, boost, build-up, dilation, enhancement, enlargement, expansion, extension, growth, heightening, inflation, intensification, magnification, multiplication, reinforcement, rise, strengthening, swelling

augur verb = bode, be an omen of, bespeak (archaic), betoken, foreshadow, harbinger, herald, portend, predict, prefigure, presage, promise, prophesy, signify

augury noun 1 = prediction, divination, prophecy, soothsaying, sortilege 2 = omen, auspice, forerunner, forewarning, harbinger, herald, portent, precursor, presage, prognostication, promise, prophecy, sign, token, warning

august adjective = noble, dignified, exalted, glorious, grand, high-ranking, imposing, impressive, kingly, lofty, magnificent, majestic, monumental, regal, solemn, stately, superb

aura noun = air, ambience, aroma, atmosphere, emanation, feel, feeling, mood, odour, quality, scent, suggestion, tone, vibes (slang), vibrations (slang)

auspice noun As in under the auspices of = support, advocacy, aegis, authority, backing, care, championship, charge, control, countenance, guidance, influence, patronage, protection, sponsorship, supervision

auspicious *adjective* = **favourable**, bright, encouraging, felicitous, fortunate, happy, hopeful, lucky, opportune, promising, propitious, prosperous, rosy, timely
➤ Antonyms
bad, black, discouraging, ill-omened, inauspicious, infelicitous, ominous, unfavourable, unfortunate, unlucky, unpromising, unpropitious

austere *adjective* 1 = **stern**, cold, exacting, forbidding, formal, grave, grim, hard, harsh, inflexible, rigorous, serious, severe, solemn, stiff, strict, stringent, unfeeling, unrelenting 2 = **ascetic**, abstemious, abstinent, chaste, continent, economical, exacting, puritanical, rigid, self-denying, self-disciplined, sober, solemn, Spartan, strait-laced, strict, unrelenting 3 = **plain**, bleak, economical, harsh, severe, simple, spare, Spartan, stark, subdued, unadorned, unornamented
➤ Antonyms
≠stern: affable, cheerful, convivial, flexible, free-and-easy, genial, indulgent, jovial, kindly, permissive, sweet ≠ascetic: abandoned, free-and-easy, immoral, indulgent, loose, permissive ≠plain: comfortable, indulgent, luxurious

austerity *noun* 1 = **sternness**, coldness, exactingness, forbiddingness, formality, gravity, grimness, hardness, harshness, inflexibility, rigour, seriousness, severity, solemnity, stiffness, strictness 2 = **asceticism**, abstemiousness, abstinence, chasteness, chastity, continence, economy, exactingness, puritanism, rigidity, self-denial, self-discipline, sobriety, solemnity, Spartanism, strictness 3 = **plainness**, economy, severity, simplicity, spareness, Spartanism, starkness

authentic *adjective* = **genuine**, accurate, actual, authoritative, bona fide, certain, dependable, factual, faithful, legitimate, on the level (*informal*), original, pure, real, reliable, simon-pure (*rare*), the real McCoy, true, true-to-life, trustworthy, valid, veritable
➤ Antonyms
counterfeit, fake, false, fictitious, fraudulent, hypothetical, imitation, misleading, mock, pseudo (*informal*), spurious, supposed, synthetic, unfaithful, unreal, untrue

authenticate *verb* = **verify**, attest, authorize, avouch, certify, confirm, endorse, guarantee, validate, vouch for, warrant
➤ Antonyms
annul, invalidate, render null and void

authenticity *noun* = **genuineness**, accuracy, actuality, authoritativeness, certainty, dependability, factualness, faithfulness, legitimacy, purity, realness, reliability, trustworthiness, truth, truthfulness,

validity, veritableness, verity

author *noun* 1 = **writer**, composer, creator 2 = **creator**, architect, designer, doer, fabricator, father, founder, framer, initiator, inventor, maker, mover, originator, parent, planner, prime mover, producer

authoritarian *adjective* 1 = **strict**, absolute, autocratic, despotic, dictatorial, disciplinarian, doctrinaire, dogmatic, domineering, harsh, imperious, rigid, severe, tyrannical, unyielding ◆ *noun* 2 = **disciplinarian**, absolutist, autocrat, despot, dictator, tyrant
➤ Antonyms
adjective ≠strict: broad-minded, democratic, flexible, indulgent, lenient, liberal, permissive, tolerant

authoritative *adjective* 1 = **reliable**, accurate, authentic, definitive, dependable, factual, faithful, learned, scholarly, sound, true, trustworthy, truthful, valid, veritable 2 = **official**, approved, authorized, commanding, legitimate, sanctioned, sovereign 3 = **commanding**, assertive, autocratic, confident, decisive, dictatorial, dogmatic, dominating, imperative, imperious, imposing, lordly, masterly, peremptory, self-assured
➤ Antonyms
≠reliable: deceptive, undependable, unreliable ≠official: unauthorized, unofficial, unsanctioned ≠commanding: humble, subservient, timid, weak

authority *noun* 1 = **power**, ascendancy, charge, command, control, direction, domination, dominion, force, government, influence, jurisdiction, might, prerogative, right, rule, say-so, strength, supremacy, sway, weight 2 *usually plural* = **powers that be**, administration, government, management, officialdom, police, the Establishment 3 = **expert**, arbiter, bible, connoisseur, guru, judge, master, professional, scholar, specialist, textbook 4 = **permission**, a blank cheque, authorization, justification, licence, permit, sanction, say-so, warrant

authorization *noun* 1 = **power**, ability, authority, right, say-so, strength 2 = **permission**, a blank cheque, approval, credentials, leave, licence, permit, sanction, say-so, warrant

authorize *verb* 1 = **empower**, accredit, commission, enable, entitle, give authority 2 = **permit**, accredit, allow, approve, confirm, countenance, give a blank cheque to, give authority for, give leave, give the green light for, license, ratify, sanction, vouch for, warrant
➤ Antonyms
ban, debar, disallow, exclude, forbid, outlaw,

preclude, prohibit, proscribe, rule out, veto

autocracy *noun* = **dictatorship**, absolutism, despotism, tyranny

autocrat *noun* = **dictator**, absolutist, despot, tyrant

autocratic *adjective* = **dictatorial**, absolute, all-powerful, despotic, domineering, imperious, tyrannical, tyrannous, unlimited

automatic *adjective* 1 = **mechanical**, automated, mechanized, push-button, robot, self-acting, self-activating, self-moving, self-propelling, self-regulating 2 = **involuntary**, instinctive, instinctual, mechanical, natural, reflex, spontaneous, unconscious, unwilled 3 = **inevitable**, assured, certain, inescapable, necessary, routine, unavoidable
➤ **Antonyms**
≠**mechanical**: done by hand, hand-operated, human, manual, physical ≠**involuntary**: conscious, deliberate, intentional, voluntary

autonomous *adjective* = **self-ruling**, free, independent, self-determining, self-governing, sovereign

autonomy *noun* = **independence**, freedom, home rule, self-determination, self-government, self-rule, sovereignty
➤ **Antonyms**
dependency, foreign rule, subjection

autopsy *noun* = **postmortem**, dissection, necropsy, postmortem examination

auxiliary *adjective* 1 = **supplementary**, back-up, emergency, fall-back, reserve, secondary, subsidiary, substitute 2 = **supporting**, accessory, aiding, ancillary, assisting, helping ♦ *noun* 3 = **backup**, reserve 4 = **helper**, accessory, accomplice, ally, assistant, associate, companion, confederate, henchman, partner, protagonist, subordinate, supporter
➤ **Antonyms**
adjective ≠**supplementary**, **supporting**: cardinal, chief, essential, first, leading, main, primary, prime, principal

avail *verb* 1 = **benefit**, aid, assist, be of advantage, be useful, help, profit ♦ *noun* 2 = **benefit**, advantage, aid, good, help, profit, use

availability *noun* = **accessibility**, attainability, handiness, readiness

available *adjective* = **accessible**, applicable, at hand, at one's disposal, at one's fingertips, attainable, convenient, free, handy, obtainable, on hand, on tap, ready, ready for use, to hand, vacant
➤ **Antonyms**
busy, engaged, inaccessible, in use, occupied, spoken for, taken, unattainable, unavailable, unobtainable

avalanche *noun* 1 = **snow-slide**, landslide, landslip, snow-slip 2 = **flood**, barrage, deluge, inundation, torrent

avant-garde *adjective* = **progressive**, experimental, far-out (*slang*), ground-breaking, innovative, innovatory, pioneering, unconventional, way-out (*informal*)
➤ **Antonyms**
conservative, conventional, hidebound, reactionary, traditional

avarice *noun* = **greed**, acquisitiveness, close-fistedness, covetousness, cupidity, graspingness, greediness, meanness, miserliness, niggardliness, parsimony, penny-pinching, penuriousness, rapacity, stinginess
➤ **Antonyms**
benevolence, bountifulness, extravagance, generosity, largesse *or* largess, liberality, unselfishness

avaricious *adjective* = **grasping**, acquisitive, close-fisted, covetous, greedy, mean, miserable, miserly, niggardly, parsimonious, penny-pinching, penurious, rapacious, snoep (*S. Afr. informal*), stingy, tight-arsed (*taboo slang*), tight as a duck's arse (*taboo slang*), tight-assed (*U.S. taboo slang*)

avenge *verb* = **get revenge for**, even the score for, get even for (*informal*), get one's own back, hit back, pay (someone) back for, pay (someone) back in his *or* her own coin, punish, repay, requite, retaliate, revenge, take revenge for, take satisfaction for, take vengeance

avenue *noun* = **street**, access, alley, approach, boulevard, channel, course, drive, driveway, entrance, entry, pass, passage, path, pathway, road, route, thoroughfare, way

aver *verb* = **state**, affirm, allege, assert, asseverate, avouch, avow, declare, maintain, proclaim, profess, pronounce, protest, say, swear

average *noun* 1 = **usual**, common run, mean, medium, midpoint, norm, normal, par, rule, run, run of the mill, standard 2 **on average** = **usually**, as a rule, for the most part, generally, normally, typically ♦ *adjective* 3 = **usual**, common, commonplace, fair, general, normal, ordinary, regular, standard, typical 4 = **mean**, intermediate, median, medium, middle 5 = **mediocre**, banal, bog-standard (*Brit. & Irish slang*), indifferent, middle-of-the-road, middling, moderate, no great shakes (*informal*), not bad, passable, run-of-the-mill, so-so (*informal*), tolerable, undistinguished, unexceptional, vanilla (*slang*) ♦ *verb* 6 = **make on average**,

balance out to, be on average, do on average, even out to
➤ Antonyms
adjective ≠**usual:** abnormal, awful, bad, different, exceptional, great, memorable, notable, outstanding, remarkable, special, terrible, unusual ≠**mean:** maximum, minimum

averse *adjective* = **opposed**, antipathetic, backward, disinclined, hostile, ill-disposed, indisposed, inimical, loath, reluctant, unfavourable, unwilling
➤ Antonyms
agreeable, amenable, disposed, eager, favourable, inclined, keen, sympathetic, willing

aversion *noun* = **hatred**, abhorrence, animosity, antipathy, detestation, disgust, disinclination, dislike, distaste, hate, horror, hostility, indisposition, loathing, odium, opposition, reluctance, repugnance, repulsion, revulsion, unwillingness
➤ Antonyms
desire, inclination, liking, love, willingness

avert *verb* **1** = **turn away**, turn, turn aside **2** = **ward off**, avoid, fend off, forestall, frustrate, preclude, prevent, stave off

aviation *noun* = **flying**, aeronautics, flight, powered flight

aviator *noun* = **pilot**, aeronaut, airman, flyer

avid *adjective* **1** = **enthusiastic**, ardent, devoted, eager, fanatical, fervent, intense, keen, keen as mustard, passionate, zealous **2** = **insatiable**, acquisitive, athirst, avaricious, covetous, grasping, greedy, hungry, rapacious, ravenous, thirsty, voracious
➤ Antonyms
≠**enthusiastic:** apathetic, impassive, indifferent, lukewarm, unenthusiastic

avidity *noun* **1** = **enthusiasm**, ardour, devotion, eagerness, fervour, keenness, zeal **2** = **insatiability**, acquisitiveness, avarice, covetousness, cupidity, desire, graspingness, greediness, hankering, hunger, longing, rapacity, ravenousness, thirst, voracity

avocation *noun* *Old-fashioned* **1** = **job**, business, calling, employment, occupation, profession, pursuit, trade, vocation, work **2** = **hobby**, diversion, occupation, pastime, recreation

avoid *verb* **1** = **refrain from**, dodge, duck (out of) (*informal*), eschew, fight shy of, shirk **2** = **prevent**, avert **3** = **keep away from**, body-swerve (*Scot.*), bypass, circumvent, dodge, elude, escape, evade, give a wide berth to, keep aloof from, shun, sidestep, slip through the net, steer clear of
➤ Antonyms
≠**keep away from:** approach, confront, contact, face, face up to, find, invite, pursue,

seek out, solicit

avoidance *noun* **1** = **refraining**, dodging, eschewal, shirking **2** = **prevention 3** = **evasion**, body swerve (*Scot.*), circumvention, dodging, eluding, escape, keeping away, shunning, steering clear

avowed *adjective* **1** = **declared**, open, professed, self-proclaimed, sworn **2** = **confessed**, acknowledged, admitted

await *verb* **1** = **wait for**, abide, anticipate, expect, look for, look forward to, stay for **2** = **be in store for**, attend, be in readiness for, be prepared for, be ready for, wait for

awake *adjective* **1** = **not sleeping**, aroused, awakened, aware, bright-eyed and bushy-tailed, conscious, wakeful, waking, wide-awake **2** = **alert**, alive, attentive, aware, heedful, observant, on guard, on one's toes, on the alert, on the lookout, vigilant, watchful ◆ *verb* **3** = **wake up**, awaken, rouse, wake **4** = **alert**, activate, animate, arouse, awaken, breathe life into, call forth, enliven, excite, fan, incite, kick-start (*informal*), kindle, provoke, revive, stimulate, stir up, vivify
➤ Antonyms
adjective ≠**not sleeping:** asleep, crashed out (*slang*), dead to the world (*informal*), dormant, dozing, napping, sleeping, unconscious ≠**alert:** inattentive, unaware

awaken *verb* **1** = **awake**, arouse, revive, rouse, wake **2** = **alert**, activate, animate, breathe life into, call forth, enliven, excite, fan, incite, kick-start (*informal*), kindle, provoke, stimulate, stir up, vivify

awakening *noun* = **waking up**, activation, animating, arousal, awaking, birth, enlivening, incitement, kindling, provocation, revival, rousing, stimulation, stirring up, vivification, waking

award *verb* **1** = **give**, accord, adjudge, allot, apportion, assign, bestow, confer, decree, distribute, endow, gift, grant, hand out, present, render ◆ *noun* **2** = **prize**, bonsela (*S. Afr.*), decoration, gift, grant, trophy, verdict **3** = **giving**, allotment, bestowal, conferment, conferral, endowment, hand-out, order, presentation, stipend **4** *Law* = **decision**, adjudication, decree

aware *adjective* **1** **aware of** = **knowing about**, acquainted with, alive to, appreciative of, apprised of, attentive to, cognizant of, conscious of, conversant with, familiar with, hip to (*slang*), mindful of, sensible of, wise to (*slang*) **2** = **informed**, *au courant*, clued-up (*informal*), enlightened, in the loop, in the picture, keeping one's finger on the pulse, knowledgeable
➤ Antonyms
ignorant, insensible, oblivious, unaware,

unfamiliar with, unknowledgeable

awareness *noun* = **knowledge**, acquaintance, appreciation, attention, cognizance, consciousness, enlightenment, familiarity, mindfulness, perception, realization, recognition, sensibility, sentience, understanding

away *adverb* **1** = **off**, abroad, elsewhere, from here, from home, hence **2** = **at a distance**, apart, far, remote **3** = **aside**, out of the way, to one side **4** = **continuously**, incessantly, interminably, relentlessly, repeatedly, uninterruptedly, unremittingly ♦ *adjective* **5** = **not present**, abroad, absent, elsewhere, gone, not at home, not here, not there, out ♦ *interjection* **6** = **go away**, beat it (*slang*), begone, be off, bugger off (*taboo slang*), fuck off (*offensive taboo slang*), get lost (*informal*), get out, go, on your bike (*slang*), on your way

awe *noun* **1** = **wonder**, admiration, amazement, astonishment, dread, fear, horror, respect, reverence, terror, veneration ♦ *verb* **2** = **impress**, amaze, astonish, cow, daunt, frighten, horrify, intimidate, put the wind up (*informal*), stun, terrify
➤ **Antonyms**
noun ≠**wonder**: arrogance, boldness, contempt, disrespect, fearlessness, irreverence, scorn

awe-inspiring *adjective* = **impressive**, amazing, astonishing, awesome, breathtaking, daunting, fearsome, intimidating, jaw-dropping, magnificent, striking, stunning (*informal*), wonderful, wondrous (*archaic or literary*)
➤ **Antonyms**
bland, boring, dull, flat, humdrum, insipid, prosaic, tame, tedious, unimpressive, uninspiring, vapid

awesome *adjective* = **awe-inspiring**, alarming, amazing, astonishing, awful, breathtaking, daunting, dreadful, fearful, fearsome, formidable, frightening, horrible, horrifying, imposing, impressive, intimidating, jaw-dropping, magnificent, majestic, overwhelming, redoubtable, shocking, solemn, striking, stunning, stupefying, terrible, terrifying, wonderful, wondrous (*archaic or literary*)

awestruck *or* **awe-stricken** *adjective* = **impressed**, afraid, amazed, astonished, awed, awe-inspired, cowed, daunted, dumbfounded, fearful, frightened, horrified, intimidated, shocked, struck dumb, stunned, terrified, wonder-stricken, wonder-struck

awful *adjective* **1** = **terrible**, abysmal, alarming, appalling, deplorable, dire, distressing, dreadful, fearful, frightful, from hell (*informal*), ghastly, godawful (*slang*), gruesome, harrowing, hellacious (*U.S.*

slang), hideous, horrendous, horrible, horrid, horrific, horrifying, nasty, shocking, tremendous, ugly, unpleasant, unsightly **2** *Obsolete* = **awe-inspiring**, amazing, awesome, dread, fearsome, majestic, portentous, solemn
➤ **Antonyms**
≠**terrible**: amazing, brilliant, excellent, fabulous (*informal*), fantastic, great (*informal*), magnificent, marvellous, miraculous, sensational (*informal*), smashing (*informal*), super (*informal*), superb, terrific, tremendous, wonderful

awfully *adverb* **1** = **badly**, disgracefully, disreputably, dreadfully, inadequately, reprehensibly, shoddily, unforgivably, unpleasantly, wickedly, woefully, wretchedly **2** *Informal* = **very**, badly, dreadfully, exceedingly, exceptionally, excessively, extremely, greatly, immensely, quite, seriously (*informal*), terribly, very much

awhile *adverb* = **for a while**, briefly, for a little while, for a moment, for a short time

awkward *adjective* **1** = **clumsy**, all thumbs, artless, blundering, bungling, clownish, coarse, gauche, gawky, graceless, ham-fisted *or* ham-handed (*informal*), ill-bred, inelegant, inept, inexpert, lumbering, maladroit, oafish, rude, skill-less, stiff, uncoordinated, uncouth, ungainly, ungraceful, unpolished, unrefined, unskilful, unskilled **2** = **uncooperative**, annoying, bloody-minded (*Brit. informal*), difficult, disobliging, exasperating, hard to handle, intractable, irritable, perverse, prickly, stubborn, touchy, troublesome, trying, unhelpful, unpredictable, vexatious, vexing **3** = **risky**, chancy (*informal*), dangerous, difficult, hazardous, perilous **4** = **inconvenient**, clunky (*informal*), cumbersome, difficult, troublesome, unhandy, unmanageable, unwieldy **5** = **embarrassing**, compromising, cringe-making (*Brit. informal*), cringeworthy (*Brit. informal*), delicate, difficult, embarrassed, ill at ease, inconvenient, inopportune, painful, perplexing, sticky (*informal*), thorny, ticklish, toe-curling (*slang*), troublesome, trying, uncomfortable, unpleasant, untimely
➤ **Antonyms**
≠**clumsy**: adept, adroit, dexterous, graceful, skilful ≠**inconvenient**: convenient, easy, handy ≠**embarrassing**: comfortable, pleasant

awkwardness *noun* **1** = **clumsiness**, artlessness, clownishness, coarseness, gaucheness, gaucherie, gawkiness, gracelessness, ill-breeding, inelegance, ineptness, inexpertness, maladroitness, oafishness, rudeness, stiffness, uncoordination, uncouthness, ungainliness, unskilfulness, unskilledness **2** = **uncooperativeness**, bloody-mindedness (*Brit. informal*), difficulty, disobligingness, intractability, irritability, perversity, prickliness, stubbornness, touchiness, unhelpfulness, unpredictability ♦ *adjective* **3** = **difficulty**, chanciness (*informal*), danger, hazardousness, peril, perilousness, risk, riskiness **4** = **unwieldiness**, cumbersomeness, difficulty, inconvenience, troublesomeness, unhandiness, unmanageability **5** = **embarrassment**, delicacy, difficulty, discomfort, inconvenience, inopportuneness, painfulness, perplexingness, stickiness (*informal*), thorniness, ticklishness, unpleasantness, untimeliness

axe *noun* **1** = **hatchet**, adze, chopper **2 an axe to grind** = **pet subject**, grievance, personal consideration, private ends, private purpose, ulterior motive **3 the axe** *Informal* = **the sack** (*informal*), cancellation, cutback, discharge, dismissal, termination, the boot (*slang*), the chop (*slang*), the (old) heave-ho (*informal*), the order of the boot (*slang*), wind-up ♦ *verb* **4** = **cut down**,

chop, fell, hew **5** *Informal* = **cut back**, cancel, discharge, dismiss, dispense with, eliminate, fire (*informal*), get rid of, give (someone) their marching orders, give the boot to (*slang*), give the bullet to (*Brit. slang*), give the push, oust, pull, pull the plug on, relegate, remove, sack (*informal*), terminate, throw out, turn off (*informal*), wind up

axiom *noun* = **principle**, adage, aphorism, apophthegm, dictum, fundamental, gnome, maxim, postulate, precept, truism

axiomatic *adjective* **1** = **epigrammatic**, aphoristic, apophthegmatic, gnomic, pithy, terse **2** = **self-evident**, absolute, accepted, apodictic *or* apodeictic, assumed, certain, fundamental, given, granted, indubitable, manifest, presupposed, understood, unquestioned

axis *noun* = **pivot**, axle, centre line, shaft, spindle

axle *noun* = **shaft**, arbor, axis, mandrel, pin, pivot, rod, spindle

azure *adjective* = **sky-blue**, blue, cerulean, clear blue, sky-coloured, ultramarine

B b

babble *verb* **1** = **gabble**, burble, chatter, jabber, prate, prattle, rabbit (on) (*Brit. informal*), waffle (*informal, chiefly Brit.*) **2** = **gibber**, gurgle **3** = **blab**, run off at the mouth (*slang*) ♦ *noun* **4** = **gabble**, burble, drivel, gibberish, waffle (*informal, chiefly Brit.*)

babe *noun* **1** = **baby**, ankle-biter (*Austral. slang*), bairn (*Scot.*), child, infant, nursling, rug rat (*slang*), sprog (*slang*), suckling **2** = **innocent**, babe in arms, ingénue *or* (*masc.*) ingénu

baby *noun* **1** = **infant**, ankle-biter (*Austral. slang*), babe, babe in arms, bairn (*Scot.*), child, newborn child, rug rat (*slang*), sprog (*slang*) ♦ *adjective* **2** = **small**, diminutive, dwarf, little, midget, mini, miniature, minute, pygmy *or* pigmy, teensy-weensy, teeny-weeny, tiny, wee ♦ *verb* **3** = **mollycoddle**, coddle, cosset, humour, indulge, overindulge, pamper, pet, spoil, spoon-feed

babyish *adjective* = **childish**, baby, foolish, immature, infantile, juvenile, namby-pamby, puerile, silly, sissy, soft (*informal*), spoiled
➤ **Antonyms**
adult, grown-up, mature, of age

back *noun* **1** = **rear**, backside, end, far end, hind part, hindquarters, posterior, reverse, stern, tail end **2 behind one's back** = **secretly**, covertly, deceitfully, sneakily, surreptitiously ♦ *verb* **3** = **move back**, back off, backtrack, go back, regress, retire, retreat, reverse, turn tail, withdraw **4** = **support**, abet, advocate, assist, champion, countenance, encourage, endorse, espouse, favour, finance, promote, sanction, second, side with, sponsor, subsidize, sustain, underwrite ♦ *adjective* **5** = **rear**, end, hind, hindmost, posterior, tail **6** = **previous**, delayed, earlier, elapsed, former, overdue, past
➤ **Antonyms**
noun ≠**rear**: face, fore, front, head ♦ *verb* ≠**move back**: advance, approach, move forward, progress ≠**support**: attack, combat, hinder, thwart, undermine, weaken ♦ *adjective* ≠**rear**: advance, fore, front ≠**previous**: future, late

backbiting *noun* = **slander**, abuse, aspersion, bitchiness (*slang*), calumniation, calumny, cattiness (*informal*), defamation, denigration, detraction, disparagement, gossip, malice, maligning, scandalmongering, spite, spitefulness, vilification, vituperation

backbone *noun* **1** *Medical* = **spinal column**, spine, vertebrae, vertebral column **2** = **strength of character**, bottle (*Brit. slang*), character, courage, determination, firmness, fortitude, grit, hardihood, mettle, moral fibre, nerve, pluck, resolution, resolve, stamina, steadfastness, tenacity, toughness, will, willpower **3** = **foundation**, basis, mainstay, support

backbreaking *adjective* = **exhausting**, arduous, crushing, gruelling, hard, killing, laborious, punishing, strenuous, toilsome, wearing, wearying

back down *verb* = **give in**, accede, admit defeat, back-pedal, cave in (*informal*), concede, surrender, withdraw, yield

backer *noun* = **supporter**, advocate, angel (*informal*), benefactor, patron, promoter, second, sponsor, subscriber, underwriter, well-wisher

backfire *verb* = **fail**, boomerang, disappoint, flop (*informal*), miscarry, rebound, recoil

background *noun* = **history**, breeding, circumstances, credentials, culture, education, environment, experience, grounding, milieu, preparation, qualifications, tradition, upbringing

backhanded *adjective* = **ambiguous**, double-edged, equivocal, indirect, ironic, oblique, sarcastic, sardonic, two-edged, with tongue in cheek

backing *noun* = **support**, abetment, accompaniment, advocacy, aid, assistance, championing, encouragement, endorsement, espousal, funds, grant, moral support, patronage, promotion, sanction, seconding, sponsorship, subsidy

backlash *noun* = **reaction**, backfire, boomerang, counteraction, counterblast, kickback, recoil, repercussion, resentment, resistance, response, retaliation, retroaction

backlog *noun* = **build-up**, accumulation, excess, hoard, reserve, reserves, resources, stock, supply

back out *verb, often with* **of** = **withdraw**, abandon, cancel, chicken out (*informal*), cop out (*slang*), give up, go back on, recant, renege, resign, retreat

backslide *verb* = **relapse**, fall from grace,

go astray, go wrong, lapse, regress, renege, retrogress, revert, sin, slip, stray, weaken

backslider *noun* = **relapser**, apostate, deserter, recidivist, recreant, renegade, reneger, turncoat

back up *verb* = **support**, aid, assist, bolster, confirm, corroborate, reinforce, second, stand by, substantiate

backward *adjective* **1** = **slow**, behind, behindhand, braindead (*informal*), dead from the neck up (*informal*), dense, dozy (*Brit. informal*), dull, obtuse, retarded, stupid, subnormal, underdeveloped, undeveloped **2** = **shy**, bashful, diffident, hesitating, late, reluctant, sluggish, tardy, unwilling, wavering ♦ *adverb* **3** = **towards the rear**, behind, in reverse, rearward
➤ **Antonyms**
adjective ≠**shy**: bold, brash, eager, forward, pushy (*informal*), willing ♦ *adverb*
≠**towards the rear**: forward, frontward

backwards, backward *adverb*
= **towards the rear**, behind, in reverse, rearward

backwoods *plural noun* = **sticks** (*informal*), back country (*U.S.*), backlands (*U.S.*), back of beyond, middle of nowhere, outback

bacteria *plural noun* = **microorganisms**, bacilli, bugs (*slang*), germs, microbes, pathogens, viruses

bad *adjective* **1** = **inferior**, chickenshit (*U.S. slang*), defective, deficient, duff (*Brit. informal*), erroneous, fallacious, faulty, imperfect, inadequate, incorrect, low-rent (*informal, chiefly U.S.*), of a sort *or* of sorts, pants (*informal*), pathetic, poor, poxy (*slang*), substandard, unsatisfactory **2** = **harmful**, damaging, dangerous, deleterious, detrimental, hurtful, injurious, ruinous, unhealthy **3** = **wicked**, base, corrupt, criminal, delinquent, evil, immoral, mean, sinful, vile, villainous, wrong **4** = **naughty**, disobedient, mischievous, unruly **5** = **rotten**, decayed, mouldy, off, putrid, rancid, sour, spoiled **6** = **severe**, disastrous, distressing, grave, harsh, painful, serious, terrible **7** = **sorry**, apologetic, conscience-stricken, contrite, guilty, regretful, remorseful, sad, upset **8** = **unfavourable**, adverse, discouraged, discouraging, distressed, distressing, gloomy, grim, low, melancholy, troubled, troubling, unfortunate, unpleasant **9** = **ill**, ailing, diseased, sick, unwell **10 not bad** *Informal* = **O.K.** *or* **okay** (*informal*), all right, average, fair, fair to middling (*informal*), moderate, passable, respectable, so-so (*informal*), tolerable
➤ **Antonyms**
≠**inferior**: adequate, fair, satisfactory

≠**harmful**: agreeable, beneficial, good, healthful, safe, sound, wholesome ≠**wicked**: ethical, fine, first-rate, good, moral, righteous, virtuous ≠**naughty**: biddable, docile, good, obedient, well-behaved

bad blood *noun* = **ill feeling**, acrimony, anger, animosity, antagonism, dislike, enmity, feud, hatred, ill will, malevolence, malice, rancour, resentment, seeing red

badge *noun* = **mark**, brand, device, emblem, identification, insignia, sign, stamp, token

badger *verb* = **pester**, bend someone's ear (*informal*), bully, chivvy, goad, harass, harry, hound, importune, nag, plague, torment

badinage *noun* = **wordplay**, banter, chaff, drollery, mockery, persiflage, pleasantry, raillery, repartee, teasing, waggery

badly *adverb* **1** = **poorly**, carelessly, defectively, erroneously, faultily, imperfectly, inadequately, incorrectly, ineptly, shoddily, wrong, wrongly **2** = **unfavourably**, unfortunately, unsuccessfully **3** = **severely**, acutely, deeply, desperately, exceedingly, extremely, gravely, greatly, intensely, painfully, seriously
➤ **Antonyms**
≠**poorly**: ably, competently, correctly, properly, rightly, satisfactorily, splendidly, well

bad manners *plural noun* = **rudeness**, boorishness, churlishness, coarseness, discourtesy, disrespect, impoliteness, incivility, inconsideration, indelicacy, unmannerliness
➤ **Antonyms**
civility, cordiality, courteousness, courtesy, good manners, graciousness, politeness, urbanity

baffle *verb* **1** = **puzzle**, amaze, astound, bewilder, boggle the mind, confound, confuse, daze, disconcert, dumbfound, elude, flummox, mystify, nonplus, perplex, stump, stun **2** = **frustrate**, balk, check, defeat, foil, hinder, thwart, upset
➤ **Antonyms**
≠**puzzle**: clarify, clear up, elucidate, explain, explicate, interpret, make plain, shed *or* throw light upon, spell out

bag *noun* **1** = **container**, poke (*Scot.*), receptacle, sac, sack ♦ *verb* **2** = **bulge**, balloon, droop, sag, swell **3** = **catch**, capture, gain, get, kill, land, shoot, take, trap

baggage *noun* = **luggage**, accoutrements, bags, belongings, equipment, gear, impedimenta, paraphernalia, suitcases, things

baggy *adjective* = **loose**, billowing, bulging, droopy, floppy, ill-fitting, oversize, roomy, sagging, seated, slack
➤ **Antonyms**
close, close-fitting, constricted, cramped,

narrow, snug, stretched, taut, tight, tight-fitting

bail[1], **bale** verb = **scoop**, dip, drain off, ladle

bail[2] noun Law = **security**, bond, guarantee, guaranty, pledge, surety, warranty

bail out see BALE OUT

bait noun 1 = **lure**, allurement, attraction, bribe, carrot and stick, decoy, enticement, incentive, inducement, snare, temptation ◆ verb 2 = **tease**, aggravate (informal), annoy, be on one's back (slang), bother, gall, get in one's hair (informal), get one's back up, get on one's nerves (informal), get or take a rise out of, harass, hassle (informal), hound, irk, irritate, nark (Brit., Austral., & N.Z. slang), needle (informal), persecute, piss one off (taboo slang), provoke, put one's back up, torment, wind up (Brit. slang) 3 = **lure**, allure, beguile, entice, seduce, tempt

baked adjective = **dry**, arid, desiccated, parched, scorched, seared, sun-baked, torrid

balance noun 1 = **stability**, composure, equanimity, poise, self-control, self-possession, steadiness 2 = **equilibrium**, correspondence, equipoise, equity, equivalence, evenness, parity, symmetry 3 = **remainder**, difference, residue, rest, surplus ◆ verb 4 = **stabilize**, level, match, parallel, poise, steady 5 = **compare**, assess, consider, deliberate, estimate, evaluate, weigh 6 = **equalize**, adjust, compensate for, counteract, counterbalance, counterpoise, equate, make up for, neutralize, offset 7 Accounting = **calculate**, compute, settle, square, tally, total
➤ **Antonyms**
noun ≠**equilibrium**: disproportion, instability, unbalance ◆ verb ≠**stabilize**: outweigh, overbalance, upset

balanced adjective = **unbiased**, disinterested, equitable, even-handed, fair, impartial, just, unprejudiced
➤ **Antonyms**
biased, distorted, jaundiced, lopsided, one-sided, partial, predisposed, prejudiced, slanted, unfair, warped, weighted

balance sheet noun = **statement**, account, budget, credits and debits, ledger, report

balcony noun 1 = **terrace**, veranda 2 = **upper circle**, gallery, gods

bald adjective 1 = **hairless**, baldheaded, baldpated, depilated, glabrous (Biology) 2 = **barren**, bleak, exposed, naked, stark, treeless, uncovered 3 = **plain**, bare, blunt, direct, downright, forthright, outright, severe, simple, straight, straightforward, unadorned, unvarnished, upfront (informal)

balderdash noun = **nonsense**, balls (taboo slang), bilge (informal), bosh (informal), bull (slang), bullshit (taboo slang), bunk (informal), bunkum or buncombe (chiefly U.S.), claptrap (informal), cobblers (Brit. taboo slang), crap (slang), drivel, eyewash (informal), garbage (informal), gibberish, guff (slang), hogwash, hokum (slang, chiefly U.S. & Canad.), horsefeathers (U.S. slang), hot air (informal), kak (S. Afr. slang), moonshine, pap, piffle (informal), poppycock (informal), rot, rubbish, shit (taboo slang), tommyrot, tosh (slang, chiefly Brit.), trash, tripe (informal), twaddle, waffle

baldness noun 1 = **hairlessness**, alopecia (Pathology), baldheadedness, baldpatedness, glabrousness (Biology) 2 = **barrenness**, bleakness, nakedness, sparseness, starkness, treelessness 3 = **plainness**, austerity, bluntness, severity, simplicity

bale see BAIL[1]

baleful adjective = **menacing**, calamitous, deadly, evil, harmful, hurtful, injurious, maleficent, malevolent, malignant, mournful, noxious, ominous, pernicious, ruinous, sinister, venomous, vindictive, woeful
➤ **Antonyms**
beneficial, benevolent, benign, friendly, good, healthy, salubrious

bale out, bail out verb 1 Informal = **help**, aid, relieve, rescue, save (someone's) bacon (informal, chiefly Brit.) 2 = **escape**, quit, retreat, withdraw

balk, baulk verb 1 = **recoil**, demur, dodge, evade, flinch, hesitate, jib, refuse, resist, shirk, shrink from 2 = **foil**, baffle, bar, check, counteract, defeat, disconcert, forestall, frustrate, hinder, obstruct, prevent, thwart
➤ **Antonyms**
≠**recoil**: accede, accept, acquiesce, comply, relent, submit, yield ≠**foil**: abet, advance, aid, assist, further, help, promote, support, sustain

ball noun 1 = **sphere**, drop, globe, globule, orb, pellet, spheroid 2 = **shot**, ammunition, bullet, grapeshot, pellet, slug

ballast noun = **counterbalance**, balance, counterweight, equilibrium, sandbag, stability, stabilizer, weight

balloon verb = **swell**, belly, billow, bloat, blow up, dilate, distend, enlarge, expand, grow rapidly, inflate, puff out

ballot noun = **vote**, election, poll, polling, voting

ballyhoo noun Informal 1 = **fuss**, babble, commotion, hubbub, hue and cry, hullabaloo, noise, racket, to-do 2 = **publicity**, advertising, build-up, hype, PR, promotion, propaganda

balm noun 1 = ointment, balsam, cream, embrocation, emollient, lotion, salve, unguent 2 = comfort, anodyne, consolation, curative, palliative, restorative, solace

balmy adjective 1 = mild, clement, pleasant, summery, temperate 2 see BARMY
➤ Antonyms
annoying, discomforting, harsh, inclement, intense, irksome, rough, stormy

bamboozle verb Informal 1 = cheat, con (informal), deceive, defraud, delude, dupe, fool, hoax, hoodwink, pull a fast one on (informal), skin (slang), swindle, trick 2 = puzzle, baffle, befuddle, confound, confuse, mystify, perplex, stump

ban verb 1 = prohibit, banish, bar, black, blackball, block, boycott, debar, disallow, disqualify, exclude, forbid, interdict, outlaw, proscribe, restrict, suppress ♦ noun 2 = prohibition, block, boycott, censorship, disqualification, embargo, interdict, interdiction, proscription, restriction, stoppage, suppression, taboo
➤ Antonyms
verb ≠prohibit: allow, approve, authorize, enable, let, permit, sanction ♦ noun ≠prohibition: allowance, approval, permission, sanction

banal adjective = unoriginal, clichéd, cliché-ridden, commonplace, everyday, hackneyed, humdrum, mundane, old hat, ordinary, pedestrian, platitudinous, stale, stereotyped, stock, threadbare, tired, trite, unimaginative, vanilla (slang), vapid
➤ Antonyms
challenging, distinctive, fresh, ground-breaking, imaginative, interesting, new, novel, original, stimulating, unique, unusual

banality noun = unoriginality, bromide (informal), cliché, commonplace, platitude, triteness, trite phrase, triviality, truism, vapidity

band[1] noun 1 = ensemble, combo, group, orchestra 2 = gang, assembly, association, bevy, body, camp, clique, club, company, coterie, crew (informal), group, horde, party, posse (informal), society, troop ♦ verb 3 = unite, affiliate, ally, consolidate, federate, gather, group, join, merge
➤ Antonyms
verb ≠unite: cleave, disperse, disunite, divide, part, segregate, separate, split, sunder

band[2] noun = strip, bandage, belt, binding, bond, chain, cord, fetter, fillet, ligature, manacle, ribbon, shackle, strap, tie

bandage noun 1 = dressing, compress, gauze, plaster ♦ verb 2 = dress, bind, cover, swathe

bandit noun = robber, brigand, crook, desperado, footpad, freebooter, gangster, gunman, highwayman, hijacker, marauder, outlaw, pirate, racketeer, thief

bandy adjective 1 = bow-legged, bandy-legged, bent, bowed, crooked, curved ♦ verb 2 = exchange, barter, interchange, pass, shuffle, swap, throw, toss, trade

bane noun = plague, affliction, bête noire, blight, burden, calamity, curse, despair, destruction, disaster, downfall, misery, nuisance, pest, ruin, scourge, torment, trial, trouble, woe
➤ Antonyms
blessing, comfort, consolation, joy, pleasure, relief, solace, support

baneful adjective = harmful, baleful, calamitous, deadly, deleterious, destructive, disastrous, fatal, hurtful, injurious, maleficent, noxious, pernicious, pestilential, ruinous, venomous

bang noun 1 = explosion, boom, burst, clang, clap, clash, detonation, peal, pop, report, shot, slam, thud, thump 2 = blow, belt (informal), box, bump, cuff, hit, knock, punch, smack, stroke, wallop (informal), whack ♦ verb 3 = hit, bash (informal), beat, belt (informal), bump, clatter, crash, hammer, knock, pound, pummel, rap, slam, strike, thump, tonk (informal) 4 = explode, boom, burst, clang, detonate, drum, echo, peal, resound, thump, thunder ♦ adverb 5 = hard, abruptly, headlong, noisily, suddenly 6 = straight, precisely, slap, smack

banish verb 1 = expel, deport, drive away, eject, evict, exclude, excommunicate, exile, expatriate, ostracize, outlaw, shut out, transport 2 = get rid of, ban, cast out, discard, dislodge, dismiss, dispel, eliminate, eradicate, oust, remove, shake off
➤ Antonyms
≠expel: accept, admit, embrace, hail, invite, offer hospitality to, receive, welcome

banishment noun = expulsion, deportation, exile, expatriation, proscription, transportation

banisters plural noun = railing, balusters, balustrade, handrail, rail

bank[1] noun 1 = storehouse, depository, repository 2 = store, accumulation, fund, hoard, reserve, reservoir, savings, stock, stockpile ♦ verb 3 = save, deposit, keep 4 = deal with, transact business with

bank[2] noun 1 = mound, banking, embankment, heap, mass, pile, ridge 2 = side, brink, edge, margin, shore ♦ verb 3 = pile, amass, heap, mass, mound, stack 4 = tilt, camber, cant, heel, incline, pitch, slant, slope, tip

bank[3] *noun* = **row**, arrangement, array, file, group, line, rank, sequence, series, succession, tier, train

bank on *verb* = **rely on**, assume, believe in, count on, depend on, lean on, look to, trust

bankrupt *adjective* = **insolvent**, beggared, broke (*informal*), depleted, destitute, exhausted, failed, impoverished, in queer street, in the red, lacking, on one's uppers, on the rocks, ruined, spent, wiped out (*informal*)
➤ **Antonyms**
in the money (*informal*), on the up and up, prosperous, solvent, sound, wealthy

bankruptcy *noun* = **insolvency**, crash, disaster, exhaustion, failure, indebtedness, lack, liquidation, ruin

banner *noun* = **flag**, banderole, burgee, colours, ensign, fanion, gonfalon, pennant, pennon, placard, standard, streamer

banquet *noun* = **feast**, dinner, meal, repast, revel, treat

banter *verb* 1 = **joke**, chaff, deride, jeer, jest, josh (*slang, chiefly U.S. & Canad.*), kid (*informal*), make fun of, rib (*informal*), ridicule, take the mickey (*informal*), taunt, tease, twit ◆ *noun* 2 = **joking**, badinage, chaff, chaffing, derision, jeering, jesting, kidding (*informal*), mockery, persiflage, pleasantry, raillery, repartee, ribbing (*informal*), ridicule, teasing, wordplay

baptism *noun* 1 *Christianity* = **christening**, immersion, purification, sprinkling 2 = **initiation**, beginning, debut, dedication, introduction, launching, rite of passage

baptize *verb* 1 *Christianity* = **purify**, besprinkle, cleanse, immerse 2 = **initiate**, admit, enrol, recruit 3 = **name**, call, christen, dub, title

bar *noun* 1 = **rod**, batten, crosspiece, paling, palisade, pole, rail, shaft, stake, stick 2 = **obstacle**, barricade, barrier, block, deterrent, hindrance, impediment, interdict, obstruction, rail, railing, stop 3 = **public house**, boozer (*Brit., Austral. & N.Z. informal*), canteen, counter, hostelry (*archaic or facetious*), inn, lounge, pub (*informal, chiefly Brit.*), saloon, taproom, tavern, watering hole (*facetious slang*) 4 = **dock**, bench, court, courtroom, law court ◆ *verb* 5 = **fasten**, barricade, bolt, latch, lock, secure 6 = **obstruct**, hinder, prevent, restrain 7 = **exclude**, ban, black, blackball, forbid, keep out, prohibit
➤ **Antonyms**
noun ≠**obstacle**: aid, benefit, help ◆ *verb* ≠**exclude**: accept, admit, allow, let, permit, receive

Bar *noun* **the Bar** *Law* = **barristers**, body of lawyers, counsel, court, judgment, tribunal

barb *noun* 1 = **dig**, affront, cut, gibe, insult, rebuff, sarcasm, scoff, sneer 2 = **point**, bristle, prickle, prong, quill, spike, spur, thorn

barbarian *noun* 1 = **savage**, brute, yahoo 2 = **lout**, bigot, boor, hooligan, ignoramus, illiterate, lowbrow, ned (*slang*), philistine, ruffian, vandal ◆ *adjective* 3 = **uncivilized**, boorish, crude, lowbrow, philistine, primitive, rough, uncouth, uncultivated, uncultured, unsophisticated, vulgar, wild
➤ **Antonyms**
adjective ≠**uncivilized**: civil, civilized, cultured, genteel, highbrow, refined, sophisticated, urbane, well-mannered

barbaric *adjective* 1 = **uncivilized**, primitive, rude, wild 2 = **brutal**, barbarous, boorish, coarse, crude, cruel, fierce, inhuman, savage, uncouth, vulgar
➤ **Antonyms**
civilized, cultivated, cultured, gentlemanly, gracious, humane, refined, sophisticated, urbane

barbarism *noun* 1 = **atrocity**, barbarity, enormity, outrage 2 = **savagery**, coarseness, crudity, uncivilizedness 3 = **misuse**, corruption, misusage, solecism, vulgarism

barbarity *noun* = **viciousness**, brutality, cruelty, inhumanity, ruthlessness, savagery

barbarous *adjective* 1 = **uncivilized**, barbarian, brutish, primitive, rough, rude, savage, uncouth, wild 2 = **brutal**, barbaric, cruel, ferocious, heartless, inhuman, monstrous, ruthless, vicious 3 = **ignorant**, coarse, crude, uncultured, unlettered, unrefined, vulgar

barbed *adjective* 1 = **cutting**, critical, hostile, hurtful, nasty, pointed, scathing, unkind 2 = **spiked**, hooked, jagged, prickly, spiny, thorny

bare *adjective* 1 = **naked**, buck naked (*slang*), denuded, exposed, in the bare scud (*slang*), in the raw (*informal*), naked as the day one was born (*informal*), nude, peeled, scuddy (*slang*), shorn, stripped, unclad, unclothed, uncovered, undressed, without a stitch on (*informal*) 2 = **empty**, barren, lacking, mean, open, poor, scanty, scarce, unfurnished, vacant, void, wanting 3 = **plain**, bald, basic, cold, essential, hard, literal, sheer, simple, stark, unembellished 4 = **simple**, austere, basic, severe, spare, spartan, unadorned, unembellished, unfussy, unvarnished
➤ **Antonyms**
≠**naked**: attired, clad, clothed, concealed, covered, dressed, hidden ≠**empty**: abundant, full, plentiful, profuse, well-stocked ≠**simple**: adorned

barefaced *adjective* 1 = **obvious**, bald, blatant, flagrant, glaring, manifest, naked,

open, palpable, patent, transparent, unconcealed 2 = **shameless**, audacious, bold, brash, brazen, impudent, insolent
➤ **Antonyms**
≠**obvious:** concealed, covered, hidden, inconspicuous, masked, obscured, secret, tucked away, unseen

barely adverb = **only just**, almost, at a push, by the skin of one's teeth, hardly, just, scarcely
➤ **Antonyms**
amply, completely, fully, profusely

bargain noun 1 = **agreement**, arrangement, business, compact, contract, convention, engagement, negotiation, pact, pledge, promise, stipulation, transaction, treaty, understanding 2 = **good buy**, (cheap) purchase, discount, giveaway, good deal, good value, reduction, snip (informal), steal (informal) ♦ verb 3 = **negotiate**, agree, contract, covenant, cut a deal, promise, stipulate, transact 4 = **haggle**, barter, buy, deal, sell, trade, traffic

bargain for verb = **anticipate**, contemplate, expect, foresee, imagine, look for, plan for

bargain on verb = **depend on**, assume, bank on, count on, plan on, rely on

barge noun = **canal boat**, flatboat, lighter, narrow boat, scow

barge in verb Informal = **interrupt**, break in, burst in, butt in, infringe, intrude, muscle in (informal)

barge into verb Informal = **bump into**, cannon into, collide with, hit, push, shove

bark[1] noun, verb 1 = **yap**, bay, growl, howl, snarl, woof, yelp ♦ verb 2 = **shout**, bawl, bawl at, berate, bluster, growl, snap, snarl, yell

bark[2] noun 1 = **covering**, casing, cortex (Anatomy, botany), crust, husk, rind, skin ♦ verb 2 = **scrape**, abrade, flay, rub, shave, skin, strip

barmy adjective Also **balmy** Slang = **insane**, crackpot (informal), crazy, daft (informal), dippy, doolally, dumb-ass (slang) (slang), foolish, gonzo (slang), goofy (informal), idiotic, loony (slang), loopy (informal), nuts (slang), nutty (slang), odd, off one's rocker (slang), off one's trolley (slang), out of one's mind, out to lunch (informal), round the twist (Brit. slang), silly, stupid, up the pole (informal), wacko or whacko (informal)
➤ **Antonyms**
all there (informal), in one's right mind, of sound mind, rational, reasonable, sane, sensible

baroque adjective = **ornate**, bizarre, convoluted, elaborate, extravagant, flamboyant, florid, grotesque,

overdecorated, rococo

barracks plural noun = **camp**, billet, cantonment, casern, encampment, garrison, quarters

barrage noun 1 = **torrent**, assault, attack, burst, deluge, hail, mass, onslaught, plethora, profusion, rain, storm, stream 2 Military = **bombardment**, battery, cannonade, curtain of fire, fusillade, gunfire, salvo, shelling, volley

barred adjective 1 = **striped**, banded, crosshatched, lined, marked, ribbed, ridged, streaked, veined 2 = **excluded**, banned, forbidden, off limits, outlawed, prohibited, proscribed, taboo

barren adjective 1 = **infertile**, childless, infecund, sterile, unprolific 2 = **unproductive**, arid, desert, desolate, dry, empty, unfruitful, waste 3 = **unprofitable**, fruitless, unsuccessful, useless 4 = **dull**, boring, flat, lacklustre, stale, uninformative, uninspiring, uninstructive, uninteresting, unrewarding, vapid
➤ **Antonyms**
≠**unproductive:** fecund, fertile, fruitful, lush, productive, profitable, rich, useful
≠**unprofitable:** productive, profitable, useful
≠**dull:** instructive, interesting

barricade noun 1 = **barrier**, blockade, bulwark, fence, obstruction, palisade, rampart, stockade ♦ verb 2 = **bar**, block, blockade, defend, fortify, obstruct, protect, shut in

barrier noun 1 = **barricade**, bar, block, blockade, boundary, ditch, fence, fortification, obstacle, obstruction, pale, railing, rampart, stop, wall 2 = **hindrance**, check, difficulty, drawback, handicap, hazard, hurdle, impediment, limitation, obstacle, restriction, stumbling block

barter verb = **trade**, bargain, drive a hard bargain, exchange, haggle, sell, swap, traffic

base[1] noun 1 = **bottom**, bed, foot, foundation, groundwork, pedestal, rest, stand, support 2 = **basis**, core, essence, essential, fundamental, heart, key, origin, principle, root, source 3 = **centre**, camp, headquarters, home, post, settlement, starting point, station ♦ verb 4 = **found**, build, construct, depend, derive, establish, ground, hinge 5 = **place**, locate, post, station
➤ **Antonyms**
noun ≠**bottom:** apex, crest, crown, peak, summit, top, vertex

base[2] adjective 1 = **dishonourable**, abject, contemptible, corrupt, depraved, despicable, disreputable, evil, ignoble, immoral, infamous, scandalous, shameful, sordid, vile, villainous, vulgar, wicked 2 = **inferior**,

downtrodden, grovelling, low, lowly, mean, menial, miserable, paltry, pitiful, poor, servile, slavish, sorry, subservient, worthless, wretched **3** = **counterfeit**, adulterated, alloyed, debased, fake, forged, fraudulent, impure, pinchbeck, spurious
➤ **Antonyms**
≠ **dishonourable**: admirable, good, honest, honourable, just, moral, noble, pure, rare, righteous, upright, valuable, virtuous
≠ **inferior**: lofty, noble ≠ **counterfeit**: pure, unalloyed

baseless *adjective* = **unfounded**, groundless, unconfirmed, uncorroborated, ungrounded, unjustifiable, unjustified, unsubstantiated, unsupported
➤ **Antonyms**
authenticated, confirmed, corroborated, proven, substantiated, supported, validated, verified, well-founded

baseness *noun* **1** = **depravity**, contemptibility, degradation, depravation, despicability, disgrace, ignominy, infamy, notoriety, obloquy, turpitude **2** = **inferiority**, lowliness, meanness, misery, poverty, servility, slavishness, subservience, worthlessness, wretchedness

bash *verb* **1** *Informal* = **hit**, belt (*informal*), biff (*slang*), break, chin (*slang*), crash, crush, deck (*slang*), lay one on (*slang*), punch, slosh (*Brit. slang*), smash, sock (*slang*), strike, tonk (*informal*), wallop (*informal*) ♦ *noun* **2** *Informal* = **attempt**, crack (*informal*), go (*informal*), shot (*informal*), stab (*informal*), try

bashful *adjective* = **shy**, abashed, blushing, confused, constrained, coy, diffident, easily embarrassed, nervous, overmodest, reserved, reticent, retiring, self-conscious, self-effacing, shamefaced, sheepish, shrinking, timid, timorous
➤ **Antonyms**
aggressive, arrogant, bold, brash, conceited, confident, egoistic, fearless, forward, immodest, impudent, intrepid, pushy (*informal*), self-assured

bashfulness *noun* = **shyness**, constraint, coyness, diffidence, embarrassment, hesitation, modesty, reserve, self-consciousness, sheepishness, timidity, timorousness

basic *adjective* = **essential**, bog-standard (*informal*), central, elementary, fundamental, immanent, indispensable, inherent, intrinsic, key, necessary, primary, radical, underlying, vital
➤ **Antonyms**
complementary, minor, peripheral, secondary, supplementary, supporting, trivial, unessential

basically *adverb* = **essentially**, at bottom, at heart, *au fond*, firstly, fundamentally, inherently, in substance, intrinsically, mostly, primarily, radically

basics *plural noun* = **essentials**, brass tacks (*informal*), core, facts, fundamentals, hard facts, necessaries, nitty-gritty (*informal*), nuts and bolts (*informal*), practicalities, principles, rudiments

basis *noun* **1** = **foundation**, base, bottom, footing, ground, groundwork, support **2** = **principle**, chief ingredient, core, essential, fundamental, heart, premise, principal element, theory

bask *verb* **1** = **lie in**, laze, loll, lounge, relax, sunbathe, swim in, toast oneself, warm oneself **2** = **enjoy**, delight in, indulge oneself, luxuriate, relish, revel, savour, take pleasure, wallow

bass *adjective* = **deep**, deep-toned, grave, low, low-pitched, resonant, sonorous

bastard *noun* **1** *Informal, offensive* = **rogue**, blackguard, caitiff (*archaic*), criminal, evildoer, knave (*archaic*), libertine, malefactor, miscreant, profligate, rapscallion, reprobate, scoundrel, villain, wretch **2** = **illegitimate child**, by-blow (*archaic*), love child, natural child, whoreson (*archaic*)
♦ *adjective* **3** = **illegitimate**, baseborn, misbegotten **4** = **false**, adulterated, counterfeit, illegitimate, imperfect, impure, inferior, irregular, sham, spurious

bastion *noun* = **stronghold**, bulwark, citadel, defence, fastness, fortress, mainstay, prop, rock, support, tower of strength

bat *noun, verb* = **hit**, bang, punch, rap, smack, strike, swat, thump, wallop (*informal*), whack

batch *noun* = **group**, accumulation, aggregation, amount, assemblage, bunch, collection, crowd, lot, pack, quantity, set

bath *noun* **1** = **wash**, ablution, cleansing, douche, douse, scrubbing, shower, soak, soaping, sponging, tub, washing ♦ *verb* **2** = **wash**, bathe, clean, douse, lave (*archaic*), scrub down, shower, soak, soap, sponge, tub

bathe *verb* **1** = **swim 2** = **wash**, cleanse, rinse **3** = **cover**, flood, immerse, steep, suffuse ♦ *noun* **4** *Brit.* = **swim**, dip, dook (*Scot.*)

bathing costume *noun* = **swimming costume**, bathing suit, bikini, swimsuit, trunks

bathos *noun* = **anticlimax**, false pathos, letdown, mawkishness, sentimentality

baton *noun* = **stick**, club, crook, mace, rod, sceptre, staff, truncheon, wand

battalion *noun* = **army**, brigade, company, contingent, division, force, horde, host, legion, multitude, regiment, squadron, team, throng, troop

batten[1] *verb, usually with* **down** = **fasten**, board up, clamp down, cover up, fasten down, fix, nail down, secure, tighten

batten[2] *verb, usually with* **on** = **thrive**, fatten, flourish, gain, grow, increase, prosper

batter *verb* **1** = **beat**, assault, bash (*informal*), beat the living daylights out of, belabour, break, buffet, clobber (*slang*), dash against, lambast(e), lash, pelt, pound, pummel, smash, smite, thrash, wallop (*informal*) **2** = **damage**, bruise, crush, deface, demolish, destroy, disfigure, hurt, injure, mangle, mar, maul, ruin, shatter, shiver, total (*slang*), trash (*slang*)

battered *adjective* **1** = **beaten**, beat-up (*informal*), black-and-blue, bruised, crushed, injured, squashed **2** = **damaged**, beat-up (*informal*), broken-down, dilapidated, ramshackle

battery *noun* **1** = **series**, chain, ring, sequence, set, suite **2** *Criminal law* = **beating**, assault, attack, mayhem, onslaught, physical violence, thumping **3** = **artillery**, cannon, cannonry, gun emplacements, guns

battle *noun* **1** = **fight**, action, attack, combat, encounter, engagement, fray, hostilities, skirmish, war, warfare **2** = **conflict**, agitation, campaign, clash, contest, controversy, crusade, debate, disagreement, dispute, head-to-head, strife, struggle ◆ *verb* **3** = **struggle**, agitate, argue, clamour, combat, contend, contest, dispute, feud, fight, lock horns, strive, war
➤ **Antonyms**
noun ≠**fight**, **conflict:** accord, agreement, armistice, ceasefire, concord, entente, peace, suspension of hostilities, truce

battle-axe *noun* = **harridan**, ballbreaker (*slang*), disciplinarian, fury, scold, shrew, tartar, termagant, virago, vixen

battle cry *noun* **1** = **slogan**, catchword, motto, watchword **2** = **war cry**, war whoop

battlefield *noun* = **battleground**, combat zone, field, field of battle, front

battlement *noun* = **rampart**, barbican, bartizan, bastion, breastwork, bulwark, crenellation, fortification, parapet

battleship *noun* = **warship**, capital ship, gunboat, man-of-war, ship of the line

batty *adjective* = **crazy**, as daft as a brush (*informal, chiefly Brit.*), barking (*slang*), barking mad (*slang*), barmy (*slang*), bats (*slang*), bonkers (*slang, chiefly Brit.*), cracked (*slang*), crackers (*Brit. slang*), crackpot (*informal*), cranky (*informal*), daft (*informal*), doolally (*slang*), dotty (*slang, chiefly Brit.*), eccentric, gonzo (*slang*), insane, loony (*slang*), loopy (*informal*),

lunatic, mad, not the full shilling (*informal*), nuts (*slang*), nutty (*slang*), odd, oddball (*informal*), off one's rocker (*slang*), off one's trolley (*slang*), off the rails, off-the-wall (*slang*), out of one's mind, outré, out to lunch (*informal*), peculiar, potty (*Brit. informal*), queer (*informal*), round the twist (*Brit. slang*), screwy (*informal*), touched, up the pole (*informal*), wacko *or* whacko (*slang*)

bauble *noun* = **trinket**, bagatelle, gewgaw, gimcrack, kickshaw, knick-knack, plaything, toy, trifle

baulk *see* BALK

bawd *noun* = **madam**, brothel-keeper, pimp, procuress, prostitute, whore, working girl (*facetious slang*)

bawdy *adjective* = **rude**, blue, coarse, dirty, erotic, gross, indecent, indecorous, indelicate, lascivious, lecherous, lewd, libidinous, licentious, lustful, near the knuckle (*informal*), obscene, prurient, ribald, risqué, salacious, smutty, steamy (*informal*), suggestive, vulgar, X-rated (*informal*)
➤ **Antonyms**
chaste, clean, decent, good, modest, moral, respectable, seemly, undefiled, upright, virtuous

bawl *verb* **1** = **cry**, blubber, sob, squall, wail, weep **2** = **shout**, bellow, call, clamour, halloo, howl, roar, vociferate, yell

bay[1] *noun* = **inlet**, bight, cove, gulf, natural harbour, sound

bay[2] *noun* = **recess**, alcove, compartment, embrasure, niche, nook, opening

bay[3] *verb, noun* **1** = **howl**, bark, bell, clamour, cry, growl, yelp ◆ *noun* **2 at bay** = **cornered**, caught, trapped

bayonet *verb* = **stab**, impale, knife, run through, spear, stick, transfix

bays *plural noun* = **garland**, chaplet, glory, laurel crown, praise, prize, renown, trophy, wreath

bazaar *noun* **1** = **fair**, bring-and-buy, fête, sale of work **2** = **market**, exchange, marketplace, mart

be *verb* **1** = **exist**, be alive, breathe, inhabit, live **2** = **take place**, befall, come about, come to pass, happen, occur, transpire (*informal*) **3** = **remain**, abide, continue, endure, last, obtain, persist, prevail, stand, stay, survive

beach *noun* = **shore**, coast, lido, littoral, margin, plage, sands, seaboard (*chiefly U.S.*), seashore, seaside, shingle, strand, water's edge

beachcomber *noun* = **scavenger**, forager, loafer, scrounger, tramp, vagabond, vagrant, wanderer

beached *adjective* = **stranded**, abandoned, aground, ashore, deserted, grounded, high and dry, marooned, wrecked

beacon *noun* = **signal**, beam, bonfire, flare, lighthouse, pharos, rocket, sign, signal fire, smoke signal, watchtower

bead *noun* = **drop**, blob, bubble, dot, droplet, globule, pellet, pill, spherule

beads *plural noun* = **necklace**, chaplet, choker, necklet, pearls, pendant

beady *adjective* = **bright**, gleaming, glinting, glittering, sharp, shining

beak *noun* **1** = **bill**, mandible, neb (*archaic or dialect*), nib **2** *Slang* = **nose**, proboscis, snout

beam *noun* **1** = **smile**, grin **2** = **ray**, bar, emission, gleam, glimmer, glint, glow, radiation, shaft, streak, stream **3** = **rafter**, girder, joist, plank, spar, support, timber ♦ *verb* **4** = **smile**, grin **5** = **radiate**, emit, glare, gleam, glitter, glow, shine **6** = **send out**, broadcast, emit, transmit

beaming *adjective* **1** = **smiling**, cheerful, grinning, happy, joyful, sunny **2** = **radiating**, beautiful, bright, brilliant, flashing, gleaming, glistening, glittering, radiant, scintillating, shining, sparkling

bear *verb* **1** = **support**, cherish, entertain, exhibit, harbour, have, hold, maintain, possess, shoulder, sustain, uphold, weigh upon **2** = **carry**, bring, convey, hump (*Brit. slang*), move, take, tote (*informal*), transport **3** = **produce**, beget, breed, bring forth, develop, engender, generate, give birth to, yield **4** = **tolerate**, abide, admit, allow, brook, endure, hack (*slang*), permit, put up with (*informal*), stomach, suffer, undergo
➤ **Antonyms**
≠**support**: abandon, cease, desert, discontinue, drop, give up, leave, quit, relinquish ≠**carry**: drop, put down, shed

bearable *adjective* = **tolerable**, admissible, endurable, manageable, passable, sufferable, supportable, sustainable
➤ **Antonyms**
insufferable, insupportable, intolerable, oppressive, too much (*informal*), unacceptable, unbearable, unendurable

beard *noun* **1** = **whiskers**, bristles, five-o'clock shadow, stubble ♦ *verb* **2** = **confront**, brave, dare, defy, face, oppose, tackle

bearded *adjective* = **unshaven**, bewhiskered, bristly, bushy, hairy, hirsute, shaggy, stubbly, whiskered

beardless *adjective* = **clean-shaven**, barefaced, hairless, smooth, smooth-faced

bear down *verb* **1** = **press down**, burden, compress, encumber, push, strain, weigh down **2** = **approach**, advance on, attack, close in, converge on, move in

bearer *noun* **1** = **carrier**, agent, conveyor, messenger, porter, runner, servant **2** = **payee**, beneficiary, consignee

bearing *noun* **1** *usually with* **on** *or* **upon** = **relevance**, application, connection, import, pertinence, reference, relation, significance **2** = **manner**, air, aspect, attitude, behaviour, carriage, demeanour, deportment, mien, posture **3** *Nautical* = **position**, course, direction, point of compass
➤ **Antonyms**
≠**relevance**: inappositeness, inappropriateness, inaptness, inconsequence, irrelevance, irrelevancy, non sequitur

bearings *plural noun* = **position**, aim, course, direction, location, orientation, situation, track, way, whereabouts

bear on *verb* = **be relevant to**, affect, appertain to, belong to, concern, involve, pertain to, refer to, relate to, touch upon

bear out *verb* = **support**, confirm, corroborate, endorse, justify, prove, substantiate, uphold, vindicate

bear up *verb* = **cope**, bear the brunt, carry on, endure, go through the mill, grin and bear it (*informal*), keep one's chin up, persevere, suffer, take it on the chin (*informal*), withstand

bear with *verb* = **be patient with**, make allowances for, put up with (*informal*), suffer, tolerate, wait for

beast *noun* **1** = **animal**, brute, creature **2** = **brute**, barbarian, fiend, ghoul, monster, ogre, sadist, savage, swine

beastly *adjective* **1** *Informal* = **brutal**, animal, barbarous, bestial, brutish, coarse, cruel, depraved, inhuman, monstrous, repulsive, sadistic, savage **2** = **unpleasant**, awful, disagreeable, foul, horrid, mean, nasty, rotten, shitty (*taboo slang*), terrible
➤ **Antonyms**
≠**brutal**: humane, sensitive ≠**unpleasant**: agreeable, fine, good, pleasant

beat *verb* **1** = **hit**, bang, batter, belt (*informal*), break, bruise, buffet, cane, chin (*slang*), clobber (*slang*), cudgel, deck (*slang*), drub, flog, knock, lambast(e), lash, lay one on (*slang*), lick (*informal*), maul, pelt, pound, punch, strike, thrash, thwack, tonk (*informal*), whip **2** = **flap**, flutter **3** = **throb**, palpitate, pound, pulsate, pulse, quake, quiver, shake, thump, tremble, vibrate **4** = **shape**, fashion, forge, form, hammer, model, work **5** = **defeat**, best, blow out of the water (*slang*), bring to their knees, clobber (*slang*), conquer, excel, knock spots off (*informal*), lick (*informal*), make mincemeat of (*informal*), master, outdo, outrun, outstrip, overcome, overwhelm, pip at the post, put in the shade (*informal*), run rings around (*informal*), stuff (*slang*), subdue, surpass, tank (*slang*), undo, vanquish, wipe the floor with (*informal*) **6 beat it** *Slang* = **go away**, bugger off (*taboo slang*), depart, exit, fuck off (*offensive taboo slang*), get lost (*informal*), get on one's bike (*Brit. slang*), go to hell (*informal*), hook it (*slang*), hop it (*slang*), leave, make tracks, pack one's bags (*informal*), piss off (*taboo slang*), scarper (*Brit. slang*), scram (*informal*), shoo, skedaddle (*informal*), sling one's hook (*Brit. slang*), vamoose (*slang, chiefly U.S.*) ♦ *noun* **7 = blow**, belt (*informal*), hit, lash, punch, shake, slap, strike, swing, thump **8 = throb**, palpitation, pulsation, pulse **9 = route**, circuit, course, path, rounds, way **10 = rhythm**, accent, cadence, ictus, measure (*Prosody*), metre, stress, time ♦ *adjective* **11** *Slang* = **exhausted**, clapped out (*Austral. & N.Z. informal*), fatigued, on one's last legs, shagged out (*Brit. slang*), tired, wearied, wiped out (*informal*), worn out, zonked (*slang*)

beaten *adjective* **1 = stirred**, blended, foamy, frothy, mixed, whipped, whisked **2 = shaped**, forged, formed, hammered, stamped, worked **3 = defeated**, baffled, cowed, disappointed, disheartened, frustrated, overcome, overwhelmed, thwarted, vanquished **4 = well-trodden**, much travelled, trampled, trodden, well-used, worn

beating *noun* **1 = thrashing**, belting (*informal*), caning, chastisement, corporal punishment, flogging, pasting (*slang*), slapping, smacking, whipping **2 = defeat**, conquest, downfall, overthrow, pasting (*slang*), rout, ruin

beatitude *noun* = **blessedness**, beatification, bliss, ecstasy, exaltation, felicity, happiness, holy joy, saintliness

beat up *verb* *Informal* = **assault**, attack, batter, beat the living daylights out of (*informal*), clobber (*slang*), do over (*Brit., Austral. & N.Z. slang*), duff up (*Brit. slang*), fill in (*Brit. slang*), knock about *or* around, lambast(e), put the boot in (*slang*), thrash, work over (*slang*)

beau *noun* **1** *Chiefly U.S.* = **boyfriend**, admirer, escort, fancy man (*slang*), fiancé, guy (*informal*), leman (*archaic*), lover, suitor, swain, sweetheart **2 = dandy**, cavalier, coxcomb, fop, gallant, ladies' man, popinjay, swell (*informal*)

beautiful *adjective* = **attractive**, alluring, appealing, charming, comely, delightful,

drop-dead (*slang*), exquisite, fair, fine, glamorous, good-looking, gorgeous, graceful, handsome, lovely, pleasing, radiant, ravishing, stunning (*informal*)
➤ **Antonyms**
awful, bad, hideous, repulsive, terrible, ugly, unattractive, unpleasant, unsightly

beautify *verb* = **make beautiful**, adorn, array, bedeck, deck, decorate, embellish, enhance, festoon, garnish, gild, glamorize, grace, ornament

beauty *noun* **1 = attractiveness**, allure, bloom, charm, comeliness, elegance, exquisiteness, fairness, glamour, grace, handsomeness, loveliness, pulchritude, seemliness, symmetry **2 = belle**, charmer, cracker (*slang*), goddess, good-looker, humdinger (*slang*), lovely (*slang*), stunner (*informal*), Venus **3** *Informal* = **advantage**, asset, attraction, benefit, blessing, boon, excellence, feature, good thing
➤ **Antonyms**
≠**attractiveness**: repulsiveness, ugliness, unpleasantness, unseemliness ≠**advantage**: detraction, disadvantage, flaw

beaver away *verb* = **work**, exert oneself, graft (*informal*), hammer away, keep one's nose to the grindstone, peg away, persevere, persist, plug away (*informal*), slog

becalmed *adjective* = **still**, motionless, settled, stranded, stuck

because *conjunction* = **since**, as, by reason of, in that, on account of, owing to, thanks to

beckon *verb* **1 = gesture**, bid, gesticulate, motion, nod, signal, summon, wave at **2 = lure**, allure, attract, call, coax, draw, entice, invite, pull, tempt

become *verb* **1 = come to be**, alter to, be transformed into, change into, develop into, evolve into, grow into, mature into, metamorphose into, ripen into **2 = suit**, embellish, enhance, fit, flatter, grace, harmonize, ornament, set off

becoming *adjective* **1 = appropriate**, befitting, *comme il faut*, compatible, congruous, decent, decorous, fit, fitting, in keeping, meet (*archaic*), proper, seemly, suitable, worthy **2 = flattering**, attractive, comely, enhancing, graceful, neat, pretty, tasteful
➤ **Antonyms**
≠**appropriate**: improper, inappropriate, unfit, unsuitable, unworthy ≠**flattering**: ugly, unattractive, unbecoming, unflattering

bed *noun* **1 = bedstead**, berth, bunk, cot, couch, divan, pallet **2 = plot**, area, border, garden, patch, row, strip **3 = bottom**, base, foundation, groundwork, substratum ♦ *verb* **4 = fix**, base, embed, establish, found, implant, insert, plant, settle, set up

bedaub *verb* = **smear**, besmear, smirch, soil, spatter, splash, stain

bedazzle *verb* = **dazzle**, amaze, astound, bewilder, blind, captivate, confuse, daze, dumbfound, enchant, overwhelm, stagger, stun, sweep off one's feet

bedclothes *plural noun* = **bedding**, bed linen, blankets, coverlets, covers, duvets, eiderdowns, pillowcases, pillows, quilts, sheets

bed down *verb* = **sleep**, hit the hay (*slang*), lie, retire, settle down, turn in (*informal*)

bedeck *verb* = **decorate**, adorn, array, bedight (*archaic*), bedizen (*archaic*), embellish, engarland, festoon, garnish, ornament, trim

bedevil *verb* **1** = **torment**, afflict, aggravate (*informal*), annoy, be on one's back (*slang*), breathe down someone's neck, distress, frustrate, get in one's hair (*informal*), get on one's nerves (*informal*), get on one's wick (*Brit. slang*), get under one's skin (*informal*), get up one's nose (*informal*), harass, hassle (*informal*), irk, irritate, pester, plague, torture, trouble, vex, worry **2** = **confuse**, confound

bedlam *noun* = **pandemonium**, chaos, clamour, commotion, confusion, furore, hubbub, hullabaloo, madhouse (*informal*), noise, tumult, turmoil, uproar

bedraggled *adjective* = **messy**, dirty, dishevelled, disordered, drenched, dripping, muddied, muddy, sodden, soiled, stained, sullied, unkempt, untidy

bedridden *adjective* = **confined to bed**, confined, flat on one's back, incapacitated, laid up (*informal*)

bedrock *noun* **1** = **bottom**, bed, foundation, rock bottom, substratum, substructure **2** = **basics**, basis, core, essentials, fundamentals, nuts and bolts (*informal*), roots

beef *noun* **1** *Informal* = **flesh**, brawn, heftiness, muscle, physique, robustness, sinew, strength **2** *Slang* = **complaint**, criticism, dispute, grievance, gripe (*informal*), grouch (*informal*), grouse, grumble, objection, protest, protestation

beefy *adjective Informal* = **brawny**, bulky, burly, hulking, muscular, stalwart, stocky, strapping, sturdy, thickset
> **Antonyms**
feeble, frail, puny, scrawny, skinny, weak

beetling *adjective* = **overhanging**, hanging over, jutting, leaning over, pendent, projecting, prominent, protruding, sticking out, swelling over

befall *verb Archaic or literary* = **happen**, bechance, betide, chance, come to pass, ensue, fall, follow, materialize, occur, supervene, take place, transpire (*informal*)

befitting *adjective* = **appropriate**, apposite, becoming, fit, fitting, meet (*archaic*), proper, right, seemly, suitable
> **Antonyms**
improper, inappropriate, irrelevant, unbecoming, unfit, unsuitable, wrong

before *preposition* **1** = **ahead of**, in advance of, in front of **2** = **earlier than**, in advance of, prior to **3** = **in the presence of**, in front of ◆ *adverb* **4** = **previously**, ahead, earlier, formerly, in advance, sooner **5** = **in front**, ahead
> **Antonyms**
preposition ≠**ahead of**, **earlier than**: after, behind, following, succeeding ◆ *adverb* ≠**previously**, **in front**: after, afterwards, behind, later, subsequently, thereafter

beforehand *adverb* = **in advance**, ahead of time, already, before, before now, earlier, early, in anticipation, previously, sooner

befriend *verb* = **help**, advise, aid, assist, back, benefit, encourage, favour, patronize, side with, stand by, succour, support, sustain, uphold, welcome

befuddle *verb* = **confuse**, baffle, bewilder, daze, disorient, intoxicate, muddle, puzzle, stupefy
> **Antonyms**
clarify, clear up, elucidate, explicate, illuminate, interpret, make clear, make plain, resolve, simplify, throw *or* shed light on

befuddled *adjective* = **confused**, at sea, dazed, fuddled, groggy (*informal*), inebriated, intoxicated, muddled, woozy (*informal*)

beg *verb* **1** = **scrounge**, blag (*slang*), cadge, call for alms, mooch (*slang*), seek charity, solicit charity, sponge on, touch (someone) for (*slang*) **2** = **implore**, beseech, crave, desire, entreat, importune, petition, plead, pray, request, solicit, supplicate **3** *As in beg the question* = **dodge**, avoid, duck (*informal*), equivocate, eschew, evade, fend off, flannel (*Brit. informal*), hedge, parry, shirk, shun, sidestep
> **Antonyms**
≠**scrounge**: claim, demand, exact, extort, insist on ≠**implore**: apportion, award, bestow, commit, confer, contribute, donate, give, grant, impart, present

beget *verb Old-fashioned* **1** = **cause**, bring, bring about, create, effect, engender, give rise to, occasion, produce, result in **2** = **father**, breed, generate, get, procreate, propagate, sire

beggar *noun* **1** = **scrounger** (*informal*),

cadger, mendicant, sponger (*informal*), supplicant **2** = **tramp**, bag lady (*chiefly U.S.*), bankrupt, bum (*informal*), down-and-out, pauper, starveling, vagrant ♦ *verb* **3** *As in* **beggar description** = **defy**, baffle, challenge, surpass

beggarly *adjective* **1** = **poor**, abject, base, contemptible, despicable, destitute, impoverished, indigent, needy, pathetic, pitiful, poverty-stricken, vile, wretched **2** = **mean**, inadequate, low, meagre, miserly, niggardly, stingy

beggary *noun* = **poverty**, bankruptcy, destitution, indigence, need, pauperism, vagrancy, want, wretchedness

begin *verb* **1** = **start**, commence, embark on, get the show on the road (*informal*), inaugurate, initiate, instigate, institute, prepare, set about, set on foot **2** = **happen**, appear, arise, be born, come into being, come into existence, commence, crop up (*informal*), dawn, emerge, originate, spring, start
➤ **Antonyms**
cease, complete, end, finish, stop, terminate

beginner *noun* = **novice**, amateur, apprentice, cub, fledgling, freshman, greenhorn (*informal*), initiate, learner, neophyte, recruit, starter, student, tenderfoot, trainee, tyro
➤ **Antonyms**
authority, expert, master, old hand, old stager, old-timer, past master *or* past mistress, pro (*informal*), professional, trouper, veteran

beginning *noun* **1** = **start**, birth, commencement, inauguration, inception, initiation, onset, opening, opening move, origin, outset, overture, preface, prelude, rise, rudiments, source, starting point **2** = **seed**, embryo, fount, fountainhead, germ, root
➤ **Antonyms**
≠**start**: closing, completion, conclusion, end, ending, finish, termination

begrudge *verb* = **resent**, be jealous, be reluctant, be stingy, envy, grudge

beguile *verb* **1** = **fool**, befool, cheat, deceive, delude, dupe, hoodwink, impose on, mislead, take for a ride (*informal*), trick **2** = **charm**, amuse, cheer, delight, distract, divert, engross, entertain, occupy, solace, tickle the fancy of
➤ **Antonyms**
≠**fool**: alarm, alert, enlighten, put right

beguiling *adjective* = **charming**, alluring, attractive, bewitching, captivating, diverting, enchanting, entertaining, enthralling, interesting, intriguing

behalf *noun* = **benefit**, account, advantage, defence, good, interest, part, profit, sake, side, support

behave *verb* **1** = **act**, function, operate, perform, run, work **2** = **conduct oneself properly**, act correctly, keep one's nose clean, mind one's manners
➤ **Antonyms**
≠**conduct oneself properly**: act up (*informal*), be bad, be insubordinate, be naughty, carry on (*informal*), get up to mischief (*informal*), misbehave, muck about (*Brit. slang*)

behaviour *noun* **1** = **conduct**, actions, bearing, carriage, comportment, demeanour, deportment, manner, manners, ways **2** = **action**, functioning, operation, performance

behest *noun* = **command**, bidding, canon, charge, commandment, decree, dictate, direction, expressed desire, injunction, instruction, mandate, order, precept, wish

behind *preposition* **1** = **after**, at the back of, at the heels of, at the rear of, following, later than **2** = **causing**, at the bottom of, initiating, instigating, responsible for **3** = **supporting**, backing, for, in agreement, on the side of ♦ *adverb* **4** = **after**, afterwards, following, in the wake (of), next, subsequently **5** = **overdue**, behindhand, in arrears, in debt ♦ *noun* **6** *Informal* = **bottom**, arse (*taboo slang*), ass (*U.S. & Canad. taboo slang*), bum (*Brit. slang*), buns (*U.S. slang*), butt (*U.S. & Canad. informal*), buttocks, derrière (*euphemistic*), jacksy (*Brit. slang*), posterior, rump, seat, tail (*informal*), tush (*U.S. slang*)
➤ **Antonyms**
adverb ≠**after**: earlier than, in advance of, in front of, in the presence of, prior to
≠**overdue**: ahead, earlier, formerly, in advance, previously, sooner

behindhand *adjective* = **late**, behind time, dilatory, remiss, slow, tardy

behind the times *adjective* = **out of the ark** (*informal*), antiquated, dated, démodé, obsolete, old-fashioned, old hat, outmoded, out of date, passé
➤ **Antonyms**
advanced, avant-garde, experimental, far-out (*slang*), ground-breaking, innovative, pioneering, progressive, trendy (*Brit. informal*), unconventional, way-out (*informal*)

behold *verb* *Archaic or literary* = **look at**, check, check out (*informal*), clock (*Brit. slang*), consider, contemplate, discern, eye, eyeball (*slang*), get a load of (*informal*), observe, perceive, recce (*slang*), regard, scan, survey, take a dekko at (*Brit. slang*), view, watch, witness

beholden *adjective* = **indebted**, bound, grateful, obligated, obliged, owing, under obligation

beige *adjective, noun* = **fawn**, biscuit, buff, *café au lait*, camel, cinnamon, coffee, cream, ecru, khaki, mushroom, neutral, oatmeal, sand, tan

being *noun* 1 = **existence**, actuality, animation, life, living, reality 2 = **nature**, entity, essence, soul, spirit, substance 3 = **creature**, animal, beast, body, human being, individual, living thing, mortal, thing
➤ **Antonyms**
≠**existence**: nonbeing, nonexistence, nothingness, nullity, oblivion

belabour *verb* 1 = **beat**, batter, clobber (*slang*), flog, lambast(e), thrash, whip 2 = **attack**, berate, blast, castigate, censure, criticize, excoriate, flay, go for the jugular, lambast(e), lay into (*informal*), put down, tear into (*informal*)

belated *adjective* = **late**, behindhand, behind time, delayed, late in the day, overdue, tardy

belch *verb* 1 = **burp** (*informal*), eruct, eructate, hiccup 2 = **emit**, discharge, disgorge, erupt, give off, gush, spew forth, vent, vomit

beleaguered *adjective* 1 = **harassed**, aggravated (*informal*), annoyed, badgered, hassled (*informal*), persecuted, pestered, plagued, put upon, vexed 2 = **besieged**, assailed, beset, blockaded, encompassed, environed, hemmed in, surrounded

belie *verb* 1 = **disprove**, confute, contradict, deny, gainsay (*archaic or literary*), give the lie to, make a nonsense of, negate, rebut, repudiate 2 = **misrepresent**, conceal, deceive, disguise, falsify, gloss over, mislead

belief *noun* 1 = **trust**, admission, assent, assurance, confidence, conviction, credit, feeling, impression, judgment, notion, opinion, persuasion, presumption, reliance, theory, view 2 = **faith**, credence, credo, creed, doctrine, dogma, ideology, principles, tenet
➤ **Antonyms**
≠**trust**: disbelief, distrust, doubt, dubiety, incredulity, mistrust, scepticism

believable *adjective* = **credible**, acceptable, authentic, creditable, imaginable, likely, plausible, possible, probable, reliable, trustworthy, verisimilar
➤ **Antonyms**
cock-and-bull (*informal*), doubtful, dubious, fabulous, implausible, incredible, questionable, unacceptable, unbelievable

believe *verb* 1 = **accept**, be certain of, be convinced of, buy (*slang*), count on, credit, depend on, have faith in, hold, place

confidence in, presume true, rely on, swallow (*informal*), swear by, take as gospel, take on board, trust 2 = **think**, assume, conjecture, consider, gather, guess (*informal, chiefly U.S. & Canad.*), imagine, judge, maintain, postulate, presume, reckon, speculate, suppose
➤ **Antonyms**
disbelieve, distrust, doubt, know, question

believer *noun* = **follower**, adherent, convert, devotee, disciple, proselyte, protagonist, supporter, upholder, zealot
➤ **Antonyms**
agnostic, atheist, disbeliever, doubting Thomas, infidel, sceptic, unbeliever

belittle *verb* = **disparage**, decry, denigrate, deprecate, depreciate, deride, derogate, detract, diminish, downgrade, minimize, scoff at, scorn, sneer at, underestimate, underrate, undervalue
➤ **Antonyms**
boast about, elevate, exalt, magnify, praise, vaunt

belligerent *adjective* 1 = **aggressive**, antagonistic, argumentative, bellicose, combative, contentious, hostile, litigious, pugnacious, quarrelsome, unfriendly, warlike, warring ◆ *noun* 2 = **fighter**, combatant, warring nation
➤ **Antonyms**
adjective ≠**aggressive**: amicable, benign, conciliatory, friendly, harmonious, nonviolent, without hostility

bellow *noun, verb* = **shout**, bawl, bell, call, clamour, cry, howl, roar, scream, shriek, yell

belly *noun* 1 = **stomach**, abdomen, breadbasket (*slang*), corporation (*informal*), gut, insides (*informal*), paunch, potbelly, tummy, vitals ◆ *verb* 2 = **swell out**, billow, bulge, fill, spread, swell

bellyful *noun* = **surfeit**, enough, excess, glut, plateful, plenty, satiety, superabundance, too much

belonging *noun* = **relationship**, acceptance, affiliation, affinity, association, attachment, fellowship, inclusion, kinship, loyalty, rapport

belongings *plural noun* = **possessions**, accoutrements, chattels, effects, gear, goods, paraphernalia, personal property, stuff, things

belong to *verb* 1 = **be the property of**, be at the disposal of, be held by, be owned by 2 = **be a member of**, be affiliated to, be allied to, be associated with, be included in 3 = **go with**, attach to, be connected with, be fitting, be part of, fit, have as a proper place, pertain to, relate to

beloved *adjective* = **dear**, admired, adored, cherished, darling, dearest, loved, pet, precious, prized, revered, sweet, treasured, valued, worshipped

below *preposition* 1 = **lesser**, inferior, subject, subordinate 2 = **less than**, lower than 3 = **unworthy of**, beneath 4 **below par** = **poor**, below average, imperfect, inferior, off colour, off form, second-rate, unfit ♦ *adverb* 5 = **lower**, beneath, down, under, underneath

belt *noun* 1 = **waistband**, band, cincture, cummerbund, girdle, girth, sash 2 *Geography* = **zone**, area, district, layer, region, stretch, strip, tract 3 **below the belt** *Informal* = **unfair**, cowardly, foul, not playing the game (*informal*), unjust, unscrupulous, unsporting, unsportsmanlike

bemoan *verb* = **lament**, bewail, cry over spilt milk, deplore, express sorrow, grieve for, moan over, mourn, regret, rue, weep for

bemuse *verb* = **puzzle**, amaze, bewilder, confuse, daze, flummox, muddle, nonplus, overwhelm, perplex, stun

bemused *adjective* = **puzzled**, absent-minded, at sea, bewildered, confused, dazed, engrossed, flummoxed, fuddled, half-drunk, muddled, nonplussed, perplexed, preoccupied, stunned, stupefied, tipsy

bench *noun* 1 = **seat**, form, pew, settle, stall 2 = **worktable**, board, counter, table, trestle table, workbench 3 **the bench** = **court**, courtroom, judge, judges, judiciary, magistrate, magistrates, tribunal

benchmark *noun* = **reference point**, criterion, example, gauge, level, measure, model, norm, par, reference, standard, touchstone, yardstick

bend *verb* 1 = **curve**, arc, arch, bow, buckle, contort, crouch, deflect, diverge, flex, incline, incurvate, lean, stoop, swerve, turn, twist, veer, warp 2 = **submit**, yield 3 = **force**, compel, direct, influence, mould, persuade, shape, subdue, sway ♦ *noun* 4 = **curve**, angle, arc, arch, bow, corner, crook, hook, loop, turn, twist, zigzag

beneath *preposition* 1 = **under**, below, lower than, underneath 2 = **inferior to**, below, less than 3 = **unworthy of**, unbefitting ♦ *adverb* 4 = **underneath**, below, in a lower place
➤ **Antonyms**
preposition ≠**under**: above, atop, higher than, on top of, over, upon ≠**inferior to**: higher than, over

benediction *noun* = **benison**, beatitude, *benedictus*, blessing, consecration, favour, grace, gratitude, invocation, orison, prayer, thankfulness, thanksgiving

benefactor *noun* = **supporter**, angel (*informal*), backer, contributor, donor, helper, patron, philanthropist, promoter,

sponsor, subscriber, subsidizer, well-wisher

beneficial *adjective* = **helpful**, advantageous, benign, expedient, favourable, gainful, healthful, profitable, salubrious, salutary, serviceable, useful, valuable, wholesome
➤ **Antonyms**
detrimental, disadvantageous, harmful, pernicious, useless

beneficiary *noun* = **recipient**, assignee, heir, inheritor, legatee, payee, receiver, successor

benefit *noun* 1 = **help**, advantage, aid, asset, assistance, avail, betterment, blessing, boon, boot (*obsolete*), favour, gain, good, inside track (*informal*), interest, mileage (*informal*), profit, use, utility ♦ *verb* 2 = **help**, advance, advantage, aid, ameliorate, assist, avail, better, enhance, further, improve, profit, promote, serve
➤ **Antonyms**
noun ≠**help**: damage, detriment, disadvantage, downside, harm, impairment, injury, loss ♦ *verb* ≠**help**: damage, deprive, detract from, harm, impair, injure, worsen

benevolence *noun* = **kindness**, altruism, charity, compassion, fellow feeling, generosity, goodness, goodwill, humanity, kind-heartedness, sympathy
➤ **Antonyms**
ill will, malevolence, selfishness, stinginess, unkindness

benevolent *adjective* = **kind**, affable, altruistic, beneficent, benign, bounteous, bountiful, caring, charitable, compassionate, considerate, generous, humane, humanitarian, kind-hearted, liberal, philanthropic, tender-hearted, warm-hearted, well-disposed

benighted *adjective* = **uncivilized**, backward, crude, ignorant, illiterate, primitive, uncultivated, unenlightened

benign *adjective* 1 = **kindly**, affable, amiable, complaisant, friendly, generous, genial, gracious, kind, liberal, obliging, sympathetic 2 = **favourable**, advantageous, auspicious, beneficial, encouraging, good, lucky, propitious, salutary 3 *Medical* = **harmless**, curable, limited, remediable, slight, superficial
➤ **Antonyms**
≠**kindly**: bad, disobliging, harsh, hateful, inhumane, malicious, malign, severe, stern, unfavourable, unkind, unpleasant, unsympathetic ≠**favourable**: bad, unfavourable, unlucky ≠**harmless**: malignant

bent *adjective* 1 = **curved**, angled, arched, bowed, crooked, hunched, stooped, twisted 2 **bent on** = **determined to**, disposed to, fixed on, inclined to, insistent on, predisposed to, resolved on, set on ♦ *noun* **3** = **inclination**, ability, aptitude, bag (*slang*), cup of tea (*informal*), facility, faculty, flair, forte, knack, leaning, penchant, preference, proclivity, propensity, talent, tendency

➤ **Antonyms**

adjective ≠ **curved:** aligned, erect, even, horizontal, in line, level, perpendicular, plumb, smooth, square, straight, true, upright, vertical

bequeath *verb* = **leave**, bestow, commit, endow, entrust, give, grant, hand down, impart, leave to by will, pass on, transmit, will

bequest *noun* = **legacy**, bequeathal, bestowal, dower, endowment, estate, gift, heritage, inheritance, settlement, trust

berate *verb* = **scold**, bawl out (*informal*), blast, carpet (*informal*), castigate, censure, chew out (*U.S. & Canad. informal*), chide, criticize, excoriate, give a rocket (*Brit. & N.Z. informal*), harangue, lambast(e), put down, rail at, rap over the knuckles, read the riot act, rebuke, reprimand, reproach, reprove, revile, slap on the wrist, slate (*informal, chiefly Brit.*), tear into (*informal*), tear (someone) off a strip (*Brit. informal*), tell off (*informal*), upbraid, vituperate

➤ **Antonyms**

acclaim, admire, applaud, approve, cheer, commend, compliment, congratulate, extol, laud, praise, take one's hat off to

bereavement *noun* = **loss**, affliction, death, deprivation, misfortune, tribulation

bereft *adjective* = **deprived**, cut off, destitute, devoid, lacking, minus, parted from, robbed of, shorn, wanting

berserk *adverb* = **crazy**, amok, ape (*slang*), apeshit (*slang*), enraged, frantic, frenzied, insane, mad, maniacal, manic, rabid, raging, uncontrollable, violent, wild

berth *noun* **1** = **bunk**, bed, billet, cot (*Nautical*), hammock **2** *Nautical* = **anchorage**, dock, harbour, haven, pier, port, quay, slip, wharf **3** = **job**, appointment, employment, living, position, post, situation ♦ *verb* **4** *Nautical* = **anchor**, dock, drop anchor, land, moor, tie up

beseech *verb* = **beg**, adjure, ask, call upon, crave, entreat, implore, importune, petition, plead, pray, solicit, sue, supplicate

beset *verb* **1** = **plague**, badger, bedevil, embarrass, entangle, harass, perplex, pester, trouble **2** = **attack**, assail, besiege, encircle, enclose, encompass, environ, hem in, surround

besetting *adjective* = **troublesome**, habitual, harassing, inveterate, persistent, prevalent

beside *preposition* **1** = **next to**, abreast of, adjacent to, alongside, at the side of, cheek by jowl, close to, near, nearby, neighbouring, next door to, overlooking **2** **beside oneself** = **distraught**, apoplectic, at the end of one's tether, berserk, crazed, delirious, demented, deranged, desperate, frantic, frenzied, insane, mad, out of one's mind, unbalanced, uncontrolled, unhinged

besides *adverb* **1** = **too**, also, as well, further, furthermore, in addition, into the bargain, moreover, otherwise, what's more ♦ *preposition* **2** = **apart from**, barring, excepting, excluding, in addition to, other than, over and above, without

beside the point *adjective* = **irrelevant**, extraneous, immaterial, inapplicable, inapposite, inappropriate, inconsequent, neither here nor there, unconnected

➤ **Antonyms**

admissible, applicable, apposite, appropriate, appurtenant, apt, fitting, germane, pertinent, relevant, significant, to the point

besiege *verb* **1** = **surround**, beleaguer, beset, blockade, confine, encircle, encompass, environ, hedge in, hem in, invest (*rare*), lay siege to, shut in **2** = **harass**, badger, bend someone's ear (*informal*), bother, harry, hassle (*informal*), hound, importune, nag, pester, plague, trouble

besotted *adjective* **1** = **infatuated**, doting, hypnotized, smitten, spellbound **2** = **drunk**, befuddled, bevvied (*dialect*), bladdered (*slang*), blitzed (*slang*), blotto (*slang*), bombed (*slang*), Brahms and Liszt (*slang*), intoxicated, legless (*informal*), lit up (*slang*), out of it (*slang*), out to it (*Austral. & N.Z. slang*), paralytic (*informal*), pissed (*taboo slang*), rat-arsed (*taboo slang*), smashed (*slang*), steamboats (*Scot. slang*), steaming (*slang*), stupefied, wasted (*slang*), wrecked (*slang*), zonked (*slang*) **3** = **foolish**, confused, muddled, witless

bespatter *verb* **1** = **splatter**, bedaub, befoul, begrime, besprinkle, muddy, smear, spatter **2** = **slander**, besmirch, dishonour, sully

best *adjective* **1** = **finest**, chief, first, first-class, first-rate, foremost, highest, leading, most excellent, outstanding, perfect, pre-eminent, principal, superlative, supreme, unsurpassed **2** = **most fitting**, advantageous, apt, correct, golden, most desirable, right **3** = **greatest**, largest, most ♦ *adverb* **4** = **most highly**, extremely, greatly, most deeply, most fully **5** = **excellently**, advantageously, attractively, most fortunately ♦ *noun* **6** = **finest**, choice, cream, *crème de la crème*, elite, favourite, first, flower, pick, prime, top **7** = **utmost**, hardest, highest endeavour ♦ *verb* **8**

= **defeat**, beat, blow out of the water (*slang*), conquer, get the better of, lick (*informal*), master, outclass, outdo, put in the shade (*informal*), stuff (*slang*), surpass, tank (*slang*), thrash, triumph over, trounce, undo, wipe the floor with (*informal*)

bestial *adjective* = **brutal**, animal, barbaric, barbarous, beastlike, beastly, brutish, carnal, degraded, depraved, gross, inhuman, low, savage, sensual, sordid, vile

bestow *verb* = **present**, accord, allot, apportion, award, commit, confer, donate, endow, entrust, give, grant, hand out, honour with, impart, lavish, render to
➤ **Antonyms**
acquire, attain, come by, earn, gain, get, land, make, net, obtain, procure, secure

bestride *verb* = **straddle**, bestraddle, bridge, dominate, extend, mount, span, step over, tower over

bet *noun* 1 = **gamble**, ante, hazard, long shot, pledge, risk, speculation, stake, venture, wager ♦ *verb* 2 = **gamble**, chance, hazard, pledge, punt (*chiefly Brit.*), put money on, put one's shirt on, risk, speculate, stake, venture, wager

betide *verb* = **happen**, bechance, befall, chance, come to pass, crop up (*informal*), ensue, occur, overtake, supervene, take place, transpire (*informal*)

betimes *adverb* = **early**, anon, beforehand, before long, erelong (*archaic or poetic*), first thing, in good time, punctually, seasonably, soon

betoken *verb* = **indicate**, augur, bespeak, bode, declare, denote, evidence, manifest, mark, portend, presage, prognosticate, promise, represent, signify, suggest, typify

betray *verb* 1 = **be disloyal**, be treacherous, be unfaithful, break one's promise, break with, double-cross (*informal*), grass (*Brit. slang*), grass up (*slang*), inform on *or* against, put the finger on (*informal*), sell down the river (*informal*), sell out (*informal*), sell the pass (*informal*), shop (*slang, chiefly Brit.*), stab in the back 2 = **give away**, blurt out, disclose, divulge, evince, expose, lay bare, let slip, manifest, reveal, show, tell, tell on, uncover, unmask 3 = **abandon**, desert, forsake, jilt, walk out on

betrayal *noun* 1 = **disloyalty**, deception, double-cross (*informal*), double-dealing, duplicity, falseness, perfidy, sell-out (*informal*), treachery, treason, trickery, unfaithfulness 2 = **giving away**, blurting out, disclosure, divulgence, revelation, telling
➤ **Antonyms**
≠**disloyalty**: allegiance, constancy, devotion, faithfulness, fealty, fidelity, loyalty,

steadfastness, trustiness, trustworthiness ≠**giving away**: guarding, keeping, keeping secret, preserving, safeguarding

betrayer *noun* = **traitor**, apostate, conspirator, deceiver, renegade, snake in the grass

betrothal *noun* Old-fashioned = **engagement**, affiancing, betrothing, espousal (*archaic*), marriage compact, plight, promise, troth, vow

better *adjective* 1 = **superior**, bigger, excelling, finer, fitter, greater, higher-quality, larger, more appropriate, more desirable, more expert, more fitting, more suitable, more useful, more valuable, preferable, streets ahead, surpassing, worthier 2 = **well**, cured, fitter, fully recovered, healthier, improving, less ill, mending, more healthy, on the mend (*informal*), progressing, recovering, stronger 3 = **greater**, bigger, larger, longer ♦ *adverb* 4 = **in a more excellent manner**, in a superior way, more advantageously, more attractively, more competently, more effectively 5 = **to a greater degree**, more completely, more thoroughly ♦ *noun* 6 **get the better of** = **defeat**, beat, best, get the upper hand, outdo, outsmart (*informal*), outwit, prevail over, score off, surpass, triumph over, worst ♦ *verb* 7 = **improve**, advance, ameliorate, amend, correct, enhance, forward, further, meliorate, mend, promote, raise, rectify, reform 8 = **beat**, cap (*informal*), clobber (*slang*), exceed, excel, improve on *or* upon, knock spots off (*informal*), lick (*informal*), outdo, outstrip, put in the shade (*informal*), run rings around (*informal*), surpass, top
➤ **Antonyms**
adjective ≠**superior**: inferior, lesser, smaller, substandard, worse ≠**well**: worse ♦ *adverb* ≠**in a more excellent manner**: worse ♦ *verb* ≠**improve**: depress, devaluate, go downhill, impoverish, lessen, lower, weaken, worsen

between *preposition* = **amidst**, among, betwixt, in the middle of, mid

beverage *noun* = **drink**, bevvy (*dialect*), draught, libation (*facetious*), liquid, liquor, potable, potation, refreshment

bevy *noun* 1 = **group**, band, bunch (*informal*), collection, company, crowd, gathering, pack, troupe 2 = **flock**, covey, flight

bewail *verb* = **lament**, bemoan, cry over, deplore, express sorrow, grieve for, keen, moan, mourn, regret, repent, rue, wail, weep over

beware *verb* = **be careful**, avoid, be cautious, be wary, guard against, heed, look out, mind, refrain from, shun, steer clear of, take heed, watch out

bewilder *verb* = **confound**, baffle, befuddle, bemuse, confuse, daze, flummox, mix up, mystify, nonplus, perplex, puzzle, stun, stupefy

bewildered *adjective* = **confused**, at a loss, at sea, awed, baffled, bamboozled (*informal*), disconcerted, dizzy, flummoxed, giddy, mystified, nonplussed, perplexed, puzzled, speechless, startled, stunned, surprised, taken aback, uncertain

bewitch *verb* = **enchant**, absorb, allure, attract, beguile, captivate, charm, enrapture, entrance, fascinate, hypnotize, ravish, spellbind

➤ **Antonyms**
disgust, give one the creeps (*informal*), make one sick, offend, repel, repulse, sicken, turn off (*informal*)

bewitched *adjective* = **enchanted**, charmed, entranced, fascinated, mesmerized, possessed, spellbound, transformed, under a spell, unrecognizable

beyond *preposition* 1 = **past**, above, apart from, at a distance, away from, outwith (*Scot.*), over 2 = **exceeding**, out of reach of, superior to, surpassing

bias *noun* 1 = **prejudice**, bent, bigotry, favouritism, inclination, intolerance, jobs for the boys (*informal*), leaning, narrow-mindedness, nepotism, one-sidedness, partiality, penchant, predilection, predisposition, proclivity, proneness, propensity, tendency, turn, unfairness 2 = **slant**, angle, cross, diagonal line ♦ *verb* 3 = **prejudice**, distort, influence, predispose, slant, sway, twist, warp, weight

➤ **Antonyms**
noun ≠**prejudice**: equality, equity, fairness, impartiality, neutrality, objectivity, open-mindedness

biased *adjective* = **prejudiced**, distorted, embittered, jaundiced, one-sided, partial, predisposed, slanted, swayed, twisted, warped, weighted

bicker *verb* = **quarrel**, argue, cross swords, disagree, dispute, fight, fight like cat and dog, go at it hammer and tongs, row (*informal*), scrap (*informal*), spar, squabble, wrangle

➤ **Antonyms**
accord, acquiesce, agree, assent, concur, cooperate, get on, harmonize

bid *verb* 1 = **offer**, proffer, propose, submit, tender 2 = **say**, call, greet, tell, wish 3 = **tell**, ask, call, charge, command, desire, direct, enjoin, instruct, invite, order, require, solicit, summon ♦ *noun* 4 = **offer**, advance, amount, price, proposal, proposition, submission, sum, tender 5 = **attempt**, crack

(*informal*), effort, endeavour, go (*informal*), stab (*informal*), try, venture

biddable *adjective* = **obedient**, amenable, complaisant, cooperative, docile, teachable, tractable

➤ **Antonyms**
awkward, difficult, disobedient, intractable, petulant, querulous, refractory, unruly

bidding *noun* 1 = **order**, beck, beck and call, behest, call, canon, charge, command, demand, direction, injunction, instruction, invitation, request, summons 2 = **offers**, auction, offer, proposal, tender

big *adjective* 1 = **large**, bulky, burly, colossal, considerable, elephantine, enormous, extensive, gigantic, great, huge, hulking, humongous *or* humungous (*U.S. slang*), immense, mammoth, massive, ponderous, prodigious, sizable *or* sizeable, spacious, stellar (*informal*), substantial, vast, voluminous 2 = **important**, big-time (*informal*), eminent, influential, leading, main, major league (*informal*), momentous, paramount, powerful, prime, principal, prominent, serious, significant, valuable, weighty 3 = **grown-up**, adult, elder, grown, mature 4 = **generous**, altruistic, benevolent, gracious, heroic, magnanimous, noble, princely, unselfish 5 = **boastful**, arrogant, bragging, conceited, haughty, inflated, pompous, pretentious, proud

➤ **Antonyms**
≠**large**: diminutive, insignificant, little, mini, miniature, petite, pint-sized (*informal*), pocket-sized, pygmy *or* pigmy, small, tiny, wee ≠**important**: humble, ignoble, insignificant, minor, modest, ordinary, unimportant, unknown ≠**grown-up**: immature, young

bighead *noun Informal* = **boaster**, braggart, know-all (*informal*)

bigheaded *adjective* = **boastful**, arrogant, bumptious, cocky, conceited, egotistic, full of oneself, immodest, overconfident, swollen-headed, too big for one's boots *or* breeches

bigot *noun* = **fanatic**, dogmatist, persecutor, racist, sectarian, zealot

bigoted *adjective* = **intolerant**, biased, dogmatic, illiberal, narrow-minded, obstinate, opinionated, prejudiced, sectarian, twisted, warped

➤ **Antonyms**
broad-minded, equitable, open-minded, tolerant, unbiased, unbigoted, unprejudiced

bigotry *noun* = **intolerance**, bias, discrimination, dogmatism, fanaticism, ignorance, injustice, mindlessness, narrow-mindedness, pig-ignorance (*slang*), prejudice, provincialism, racialism, racism,

sectarianism, sexism, unfairness
> **Antonyms**
broad-mindedness, forbearance,
open-mindedness, permissiveness, tolerance

bigwig *noun Informal* = **important person,**
big cheese (*slang, old-fashioned*), big gun
(*informal*), big hitter (*informal*), big name,
big noise (*informal*), big shot (*informal*),
celeb (*informal*), celebrity, dignitary, heavy
hitter (*informal*), heavyweight (*informal*),
mogul, nob (*slang*), notability, notable,
panjandrum, personage, somebody, V.I.P.
> **Antonyms**
cipher, lightweight (*informal*), nobody,
nonentity, nothing, zero

bile *noun* = **bitterness,** anger, churlishness, ill
humour, irascibility, irritability, nastiness,
peevishness, rancour, spleen

bilious *adjective* **1** = **sick,** liverish, nauseated,
nauseous, out of sorts, queasy **2** *Informal*
= **bad-tempered,** cantankerous, crabby,
cross, crotchety, edgy, grouchy (*informal*),
grumpy, ill-humoured, ill-tempered, irritable,
like a bear with a sore head, nasty, peevish,
ratty (*Brit. & N.Z. informal*),
short-tempered, testy, tetchy, touchy

bilk *verb* = **cheat,** bamboozle (*informal*), con
(*informal*), cozen, deceive, defraud, do
(*slang*), fleece, pull a fast one on (*informal*),
rook (*slang*), sell a pup, skin (*slang*), stiff
(*slang*), swindle, trick

bill[1] *noun* **1** = **charges,** account, invoice, note
of charge, reckoning, score, statement, tally
2 = **proposal,** measure, piece of legislation,
projected law **3** = **advertisement,**
broadsheet, bulletin, circular, handbill,
handout, leaflet, notice, placard, playbill,
poster **4** = **list,** agenda, card, catalogue,
inventory, listing, programme, roster,
schedule, syllabus ♦ *verb* **5** = **charge,** debit,
figure, invoice, reckon, record **6** = **advertise,**
announce, give advance notice of, post

bill[2] *noun* = **beak,** mandible, neb (*archaic or
dialect*), nib

billet *verb* **1** = **quarter,** accommodate, berth,
station ♦ *noun* **2** = **quarters,**
accommodation, barracks, lodging

billow *noun* **1** = **wave,** breaker, crest, roller,
surge, swell, tide **2** = **surge,** cloud, deluge,
flood, outpouring, rush, wave ♦ *verb* **3**
= **surge,** balloon, belly, puff up, rise up, roll,
swell

billowy *adjective* **1** = **wavy,** rippling,
undulating, waving **2** = **surging,** heaving,
rolling, swelling, swirling

bind *verb* **1** = **tie,** attach, fasten, glue, hitch,
lash, paste, rope, secure, stick, strap, tie up,
truss, wrap **2** = **oblige,** compel, constrain,
engage, force, necessitate, obligate,
prescribe, require **3** = **restrict,** confine,

detain, hamper, hinder, restrain **4** = **edge,**
border, finish, hem, trim **5** = **bandage,**
cover, dress, encase, swathe, wrap ♦ *noun* **6**
Informal = **nuisance,** bore, difficulty,
dilemma, drag (*informal*), hot water
(*informal*), pain in the arse (*taboo
informal*), pain in the neck (*informal*),
predicament, quandary, spot (*informal*),
tight spot
> **Antonyms**
verb ≠**tie:** free, loosen, release, unbind,
undo, unfasten, untie

binding *adjective* = **compulsory,** conclusive,
imperative, indissoluble, irrevocable,
mandatory, necessary, obligatory,
unalterable
> **Antonyms**
discretionary, free, noncompulsory, optional,
uncompelled, unconstrained, unforced,
voluntary

binge *noun Informal* = **bout,** beano (*Brit.
slang*), bender (*informal*), blind (*slang*),
feast, fling, jag (*slang*), orgy, spree

biography *noun* = **life story,** account,
curriculum vitae, CV, life, life history,
memoir, memoirs, profile, record

birth *noun* **1** = **childbirth,** delivery, nativity,
parturition **2** = **beginning,** emergence,
fountainhead, genesis, origin, rise, source **3**
= **ancestry,** background, blood, breeding,
derivation, descent, extraction, forebears,
genealogy, line, lineage, nobility, noble
extraction, parentage, pedigree, race, stock,
strain
> **Antonyms**
≠**childbirth:** death, demise, end, extinction,
passing, passing away or on

bisect *verb* = **cut in two,** bifurcate, cross,
cut across, cut in half, divide in two, halve,
intersect, separate, split, split down the
middle

bisexual *adjective* **1** = **bi** (*slang*), AC/DC
(*slang*), ambidextrous (*slang*), swinging
both ways (*slang*) **2** = **hermaphrodite,**
androgyne, androgynous, epicene,
gynandromorphic *or* gynandromorphous
(*Entomology*), gynandrous, hermaphroditic,
monoclinous (*Botany*)

bishopric *noun* = **diocese,** episcopacy,
episcopate, primacy, see

bit[1] *noun* **1** = **piece,** atom, chip, crumb,
fragment, grain, iota, jot, mite, morsel,
mouthful, part, remnant, scrap, segment,
slice, small piece, speck, tittle, whit **2** = **little
while,** instant, jiffy (*informal*), minute,
moment, period, second, spell, tick (*Brit.
informal*), time

bit[2] *noun* **1** = **curb,** brake, check, restraint,
snaffle **2 take the bit in** *or* **between one's
teeth** = **get to grips with,** get stuck into

(*informal*), set about

bitchy *adjective Informal* = **spiteful**, backbiting, catty (*informal*), cruel, malicious, mean, nasty, rancorous, shrewish, snide, venomous, vicious, vindictive, vixenish
➤ **Antonyms**
charitable, generous, gracious, kindly, magnanimous, nice

bite *verb* 1 = **cut**, champ, chew, clamp, crunch, crush, gnaw, grip, hold, masticate, nibble, nip, pierce, pinch, rend, seize, snap, tear, wound 2 = **eat into**, burn, corrode, eat away, erode, smart, sting, tingle, wear away ♦ *noun* 3 = **wound**, itch, nip, pinch, prick, smarting, sting, tooth marks 4 = **snack**, food, light meal, morsel, mouthful, piece, refreshment, taste 5 = **kick** (*informal*), edge, piquancy, punch (*informal*), pungency, spice

biting *adjective* 1 = **piercing**, bitter, blighting, cold, cold as ice, cutting, freezing, harsh, nipping, penetrating, sharp 2 = **sarcastic**, caustic, cutting, incisive, mordacious, mordant, scathing, severe, sharp, stinging, trenchant, vitriolic, withering

bitter *adjective* 1 = **sour**, acerb, acid, acrid, astringent, harsh, sharp, tart, unsweetened, vinegary 2 = **resentful**, acrimonious, begrudging, crabbed, embittered, hostile, morose, rancorous, sore, sour, sullen, with a chip on one's shoulder 3 = **grievous**, calamitous, cruel, dire, distressing, galling, gut-wrenching, harsh, heartbreaking, merciless, painful, poignant, ruthless, savage, vexatious 4 = **freezing**, biting, fierce, intense, severe, stinging
➤ **Antonyms**
≠**sour**: bland, mellow, mild, pleasant, sugary, sweet ≠**resentful**: appreciative, friendly, gentle, grateful, happy, mellow, mild, pleasant, sweet, thankful ≠**grievous**: fortunate, happy, pleasant ≠**freezing**: balmy, gentle, mild, pleasant

bitterness *noun* 1 = **sourness**, acerbity, acidity, sharpness, tartness, vinegariness 2 = **resentment**, acrimony, animosity, asperity, chip on one's shoulder (*informal*), grudge, hostility, pique, rancour, sarcasm, venom, virulence

bizarre *adjective* = **strange**, abnormal, comical, curious, eccentric, extraordinary, fantastic, freakish, grotesque, left-field (*informal*), ludicrous, odd, oddball (*informal*), off-beat, off the rails, off-the-wall (*slang*), outlandish, outré, peculiar, queer, ridiculous, rum (*Brit. slang*), unusual, wacko (*slang*), way-out (*informal*), weird, zany
➤ **Antonyms**
common, customary, normal, ordinary, regular, routine, standard, typical

blab *verb* = **tell**, blow the gaff (*Brit. slang*), blow wide open (*slang*), blurt out, disclose,

divulge, give away, gossip, let slip, let the cat out of the bag, open one's mouth, reveal, shop (*slang, chiefly Brit.*), sing (*slang, chiefly U.S.*), spill one's guts (*slang*), spill the beans (*informal*), tattle, tell all, tell on

blabber *noun* 1 = **gossip**, busybody, informer, rumour-monger, scandalmonger, talebearer, tattler, telltale ♦ *verb* 2 = **prattle**, blather, blether (*Scot.*), chatter, gab (*informal*), jabber, run off at the mouth

black *adjective* 1 = **dark**, coal-black, dusky, ebony, inky, jet, murky, pitch-black, pitchy, raven, sable, starless, stygian, swarthy 2 = **gloomy**, atrocious, depressing, dismal, distressing, doleful, foreboding, funereal, hopeless, horrible, lugubrious, mournful, ominous, sad, sombre 3 = **dirty**, dingy, filthy, grimy, grubby, soiled, sooty, stained 4 = **angry**, furious, hostile, menacing, resentful, sullen, threatening 5 = **wicked**, bad, evil, iniquitous, nefarious, villainous ♦ *noun* 6 **in the black** = **in credit**, in funds, solvent, without debt ♦ *verb* 7 = **boycott**, ban, bar, blacklist
➤ **Antonyms**
adjective ≠**dark**: bright, illuminated, light, lighted, lit, moonlit, sunny ≠**gloomy**: cheerful, happy, warm ≠**dirty**: clean, pure, white ≠**angry**: amicable, cheerful, friendly, happy, pleased, warm ≠**wicked**: good, honourable, moral, pure

blackball *verb* = **exclude**, ban, bar, blacklist, debar, drum out, expel, ostracize, oust, repudiate, snub, vote against

blacken *verb* 1 = **darken**, befoul, begrime, cloud, dirty, grow black, make black, smudge, soil 2 = **discredit**, bad-mouth (*slang, chiefly U.S. & Canad.*), calumniate, decry, defame, defile, denigrate, dishonour, knock (*informal*), malign, rubbish (*informal*), slag (off) (*slang*), slander, smear, smirch, stain, sully, taint, tarnish, traduce, vilify

blackguard *noun* = **scoundrel**, bad egg (*old-fashioned informal*), bastard (*offensive*), blighter (*Brit. informal*), bounder (*old-fashioned Brit. slang*), bugger (*taboo slang*), miscreant, rascal, rogue, scumbag (*slang*), shit (*taboo slang*), skelm (*S. Afr.*), son-of-a-bitch (*slang, chiefly U.S. & Canad.*), swine, villain, wretch

blacklist *verb* = **exclude**, ban, bar, blackball, boycott, debar, expel, ostracize, preclude, proscribe, reject, repudiate, snub, vote against

black magic *noun* = **witchcraft**, black art, diabolism, necromancy, sorcery, voodoo, wizardry

blackmail *noun* 1 = **threat**, exaction,

extortion, hush money (*slang*), intimidation, milking, pay-off (*informal*), protection (*informal*), ransom, shakedown ◆ *verb* **2** = **threaten**, bleed (*informal*), coerce, compel, demand, exact, extort, force, hold to ransom, intimidate, milk, squeeze

blackness *noun* = **darkness**, duskiness, gloom, inkiness, melanism, murkiness, nigrescence, nigritude (*rare*), swarthiness
➤ Antonyms
brightness, brilliance, effulgence, incandescence, lambency, light, lightness, luminescence, luminosity, phosphorescence, radiance

blackout *noun* **1** = **unconsciousness**, coma, faint, loss of consciousness, oblivion, swoon, syncope (*Pathology*) **2** = **power cut**, power failure **3** = **noncommunication**, censorship, radio silence, secrecy, suppression, withholding news

black out *verb* **1** = **darken**, conceal, cover, eclipse, obfuscate, shade **2** = **pass out**, collapse, faint, flake out (*informal*), lose consciousness, swoon

black sheep *noun* = **disgrace**, bad egg (*old-fashioned informal*), dropout, ne'er-do-well, outcast, prodigal, renegade, reprobate, wastrel

blame *verb* **1** = **hold responsible**, accuse, point a *or* the finger at **2** = **criticize**, admonish, blast, censure, charge, chide, condemn, disapprove, express disapprobation, find fault with, lambast(e), put down, reprehend, reproach, reprove, tax, tear into (*informal*), upbraid ◆ *noun* **3** = **responsibility**, accountability, accusation, culpability, fault, guilt, incrimination, liability, onus, rap (*slang*) **4** = **condemnation**, castigation, censure, charge, complaint, criticism, recrimination, reproach, reproof, stick (*slang*)
➤ Antonyms
verb ≠**hold responsible**: absolve, acquit, clear, excuse, exonerate, forgive, vindicate ≠**criticize**: acclaim, approve of, commend, compliment, praise ◆ *noun* ≠**responsibility**: absolution, alibi, excuse, exoneration, vindication ≠**condemnation**: acclaim, Brownie points, commendation, credit, honour, praise, tribute

blameless *adjective* = **innocent**, above suspicion, clean, faultless, guiltless, immaculate, impeccable, in the clear, irreproachable, perfect, squeaky-clean, stainless, unblemished, unimpeachable, unoffending, unspotted, unsullied, untarnished, upright, virtuous
➤ Antonyms
at fault, censurable, culpable, guilty, reprovable, responsible, to blame

blameworthy *adjective* = **reprehensible**, discreditable, disreputable, indefensible, inexcusable, iniquitous, reproachable, shameful

bland *adjective* **1** = **dull**, boring, flat, humdrum, insipid, monotonous, tasteless, tedious, tiresome, undistinctive, unexciting, uninspiring, uninteresting, unstimulating, vanilla (*informal*), vapid, weak **2** = **smooth**, affable, amiable, congenial, courteous, debonair, friendly, gentle, gracious, suave, unemotional, urbane
➤ Antonyms
≠**dull**: distinctive, exciting, inspiring, interesting, rousing, stimulating, turbulent, volatile

blandishments *plural noun* = **flattery**, blarney, cajolery, coaxing, compliments, fawning, ingratiation, inveiglement, soft soap (*informal*), soft words, sweet talk (*informal*), wheedling, winning caresses

blank *adjective* **1** = **unmarked**, bare, clean, clear, empty, plain, spotless, uncompleted, unfilled, void, white **2** = **expressionless**, deadpan, dull, empty, hollow, impassive, inane, lifeless, poker-faced (*informal*), vacant, vacuous, vague **3** = **puzzled**, at a loss, at sea, bewildered, confounded, confused, disconcerted, dumbfounded, flummoxed, muddled, nonplussed, uncomprehending **4** = **absolute**, complete, out and out, outright, thorough, total, unqualified, utter ◆ *noun* **5** = **empty space**, emptiness, gap, nothingness, space, tabula rasa, vacancy, vacuity, vacuum, void
➤ Antonyms
adjective ≠**unmarked**: busy, completed, filled in, full, marked ≠**expressionless**: alert, expressive, intelligent, interested, lively, thoughtful

blanket *noun* **1** = **cover**, afghan, coverlet, rug **2** = **covering**, carpet, cloak, coat, coating, envelope, film, layer, mantle, sheet, wrapper, wrapping ◆ *adjective* **3** = **comprehensive**, across-the-board, all-inclusive, overall, sweeping, wide-ranging ◆ *verb* **4** = **cover**, cloak, cloud, coat, conceal, eclipse, hide, mask, obscure, suppress, surround

blankness *noun* = **vacancy**, abstraction, fatuity, inanity, indifference, obliviousness, vacuity

blare *verb* = **sound out**, blast, boom, clamour, clang, honk, hoot, peal, resound, roar, scream, toot, trumpet

blarney *noun* = **flattery**, blandishment, cajolery, coaxing, exaggeration, honeyed words, overpraise, soft soap (*informal*), spiel, sweet talk (*informal*), wheedling

blasé *adjective* = **indifferent**, apathetic, bored, cloyed, glutted, jaded, lukewarm,

nonchalant, offhand, satiated, surfeited, unconcerned, unexcited, uninterested, unmoved, weary, world-weary
➤ **Antonyms**
affected, caring, enthusiastic, excited, interested, responsive, stimulated

blaspheme *verb* = **curse**, abuse, anathematize, damn, desecrate, execrate, profane, revile, swear

blasphemous *adjective* = **irreverent**, godless, impious, irreligious, profane, sacrilegious, ungodly
➤ **Antonyms**
devout, God-fearing, godly, pious, religious, respectful, reverent, reverential

blasphemy *noun* = **irreverence**, cursing, desecration, execration, impiety, impiousness, indignity (*to God*), profanation, profaneness, profanity, sacrilege, swearing

blast *noun* **1** = **explosion**, bang, blow-up, burst, crash, detonation, discharge, eruption, outburst, salvo, volley **2** = **gust**, gale, squall, storm, strong breeze, tempest **3** = **blare**, blow, clang, honk, peal, scream, toot, wail ◆ *verb* **4** = **blow up**, blow sky-high, break up, burst, demolish, destroy, explode, put paid to, ruin, shatter **5** = **blight**, kill, shrivel, wither **6** = **criticize**, attack, castigate, flay, lambast(e), put down, rail at, tear into (*informal*)

blasted *adjective* = **ruined**, blighted, desolated, destroyed, devastated, ravaged, shattered, spoiled, wasted, withered

blastoff *noun* = **launch**, discharge, expulsion, firing, launching, liftoff, projection, shot

blatant *adjective* = **obvious**, bald, brazen, conspicuous, flagrant, flaunting, glaring, naked, obtrusive, ostentatious, outright, overt, prominent, pronounced, sheer, unmitigated
➤ **Antonyms**
hidden, inconspicuous, quiet, soft, subtle, tasteful, unnoticeable, unobtrusive

blather *noun* = **jabbering**, blether (*Scot.*), claptrap (*informal*), drivel, gibberish, gobbledegook, jabber, moonshine, pap, twaddle

blaze *noun* **1** = **fire**, bonfire, conflagration, flame, flames **2** = **glare**, beam, brilliance, flare, flash, gleam, glitter, glow, light, radiance **3** = **outburst**, blast, burst, eruption, flare-up, fury, outbreak, rush, storm, torrent ◆ *verb* **4** = **burn**, fire, flame **5** = **shine**, beam, flare, flash, glare, gleam, glow **6** = **flare up**, boil, explode, fume, seethe

blazon *verb* = **proclaim**, broadcast, celebrate, flourish, make known, renown, trumpet

bleach *verb* = **whiten**, blanch, etiolate, fade, grow pale, lighten, peroxide, wash out

bleached *adjective* = **whiten**, achromatic, etiolated, faded, lightened, peroxided, stone-washed, washed-out

bleak *adjective* **1** = **exposed**, bare, barren, chilly, cold, desolate, gaunt, open, raw, stark, unsheltered, weather-beaten, windswept, windy **2** = **dismal**, cheerless, comfortless, depressing, discouraging, disheartening, dreary, gloomy, grim, hopeless, joyless, sombre, unpromising
➤ **Antonyms**
≠**exposed**: protected, sheltered, shielded
≠**dismal**: cheerful, cosy, encouraging, promising

bleary *adjective* = **dim**, blurred, blurry, fogged, foggy, fuzzy, hazy, indistinct, misty, murky, rheumy, watery

bleed *verb* **1** = **lose blood**, exude, flow, gush, ooze, run, seep, shed blood, spurt, trickle, weep **2** = **draw** *or* **take blood**, extract, leech, phlebotomize (*Medical*) **3** *Informal* = **extort**, drain, exhaust, fleece, milk, squeeze **4** = **drain**, extract

blemish *noun* **1** = **mark**, blot, blotch, blot on one's escutcheon, blur, defect, demerit, disfigurement, disgrace, dishonour, fault, flaw, imperfection, scar, smirch, smudge, speck, spot, stain, taint ◆ *verb* **2** = **mark**, blot, blotch, blur, damage, deface, disfigure, flaw, impair, injure, mar, smirch, smudge, spoil, spot, stain, sully, taint, tarnish
➤ **Antonyms**
noun ≠**mark**: enhancement, improvement, ornament, perfection, purity, refinement ◆ *verb* ≠**mark**: correct, enhance, improve, perfect, purify, refine, restore

blend *verb* **1** = **mix**, amalgamate, coalesce, combine, compound, fuse, intermix, meld, merge, mingle, synthesize, unite **2** = **go well**, complement, fit, go with, harmonize, suit ◆ *noun* **3** = **mixture**, alloy, amalgam, amalgamation, combination, composite, compound, concoction, fusion, meld, mix, synthesis, union

bless *verb* **1** = **sanctify**, anoint, consecrate, dedicate, exalt, hallow, invoke happiness on, ordain **2** = **praise**, extol, give thanks to, glorify, magnify, thank **3** = **endow**, bestow, favour, give, grace, grant, provide
➤ **Antonyms**
≠**sanctify**: anathematize, curse, damn, excommunicate, execrate, fulminate, imprecate ≠**endow**: afflict, blight, burden, curse, destroy, doom, plague, scourge, torment, trouble, vex

blessed *adjective* **1** = **holy**, adored, beatified, divine, hallowed, revered, sacred, sanctified **2** = **endowed**, favoured, fortunate,

granted, jammy (*Brit. slang*), lucky **3**
= **happy**, blissful, contented, glad, joyful,
joyous

blessedness *noun* **1** = **sanctity**, beatitude,
heavenly joy, state of grace, *summum
bonum* **2** = **happiness**, bliss, blissfulness,
content, felicity, pleasure

blessing *noun* **1** = **benediction**, benison,
commendation, consecration, dedication,
grace, invocation, thanksgiving **2**
= **approval**, approbation, backing,
concurrence, consent, favour, good wishes,
leave, permission, regard, sanction, support
3 = **benefit**, advantage, boon, boot
(*obsolete*), bounty, favour, gain, gift,
godsend, good fortune, help, kindness,
manna from heaven, profit, service, windfall
➤ **Antonyms**
≠**benediction**: condemnation, curse,
malediction ≠**approval**: disapproval,
disfavour, objection, reproof ≠**benefit**:
damage, deprivation, disadvantage,
drawback, harm, misfortune

blether *noun Scot.* = **jabbering**, blather,
claptrap (*informal*), drivel, gibberish,
gobbledegook, jabber, moonshine, pap,
twaddle

blight *noun* **1** = **curse**, affliction, bane,
contamination, corruption, evil, plague,
pollution, scourge, woe **2** = **disease**, canker,
decay, fungus, infestation, mildew, pest,
pestilence, rot ♦ *verb* **3** = **destroy**, blast,
injure, nip in the bud, ruin, shrivel, taint with
mildew, wither **4** = **frustrate**, annihilate,
crush, dash, disappoint, mar, nullify, put a
damper on, ruin, spoil, undo, wreck
➤ **Antonyms**
noun ≠**curse**: benefaction, blessing, boon,
bounty, favour, godsend, help, service

blind *adjective* **1** = **sightless**, destitute of
vision, eyeless, stone-blind, unseeing,
unsighted, visionless **2** = **unaware of**,
careless, heedless, ignorant, inattentive,
inconsiderate, indifferent, injudicious,
insensitive, neglectful, oblivious, thoughtless,
unconscious of, uncritical, undiscerning,
unmindful of, unobservant **3** = **unreasoning**,
indiscriminate, prejudiced **4** = **unthinking**,
hasty, impetuous, irrational, mindless, rash,
reckless, senseless, uncontrollable,
uncontrolled, violent, wild **5** = **hidden**,
concealed, dim, obscured **6** = **dead-end**,
closed, dark, leading nowhere, obstructed,
without exit ♦ *noun* **7** = **cover**, camouflage,
cloak, façade, feint, front, mask,
masquerade, screen, smoke screen
➤ **Antonyms**
adjective ≠**sightless**: seeing, sighted
≠**unaware of**: alive to, attentive, aware,
concerned, conscious, discerning, heedful,
knowledgeable, noticeable, observant

≠**hidden**: obvious, open

blindly *adverb* **1** = **thoughtlessly**, carelessly,
heedlessly, impulsively, inconsiderately,
passionately, recklessly, regardlessly,
senselessly, unreasonably, wilfully **2**
= **aimlessly**, at random, confusedly,
frantically, indiscriminately, instinctively,
madly, purposelessly, wildly

blink *verb* **1** = **wink**, bat, flutter, glimpse,
nictate, nictitate, peer, squint **2** = **flicker**,
flash, gleam, glimmer, scintillate, shine,
sparkle, twinkle, wink **3** = **turn a blind eye
to**, condone, connive at, disregard, ignore,
overlook, pass by ♦ *noun* **4 on the blink**
Slang = **not working (properly)**, faulty,
malfunctioning, on the fritz (*U.S. slang*), out
of action, out of order, playing up

bliss *noun* = **joy**, beatitude, blessedness,
blissfulness, ecstasy, euphoria, felicity,
gladness, happiness, heaven, nirvana,
paradise, rapture
➤ **Antonyms**
affliction, anguish, distress, grief, heartbreak,
misery, mourning, regret, sadness, sorrow,
unhappiness, woe, wretchedness

blissful *adjective* = **joyful**, cock-a-hoop,
delighted, ecstatic, elated, enchanted,
enraptured, euphoric, happy, heavenly
(*informal*), in ecstasies, joyous, over the
moon (*informal*), rapt, rapturous

blister *noun* = **sore**, abscess, blain, bleb,
boil, bubble, canker, carbuncle, cyst,
furuncle (*Pathology*), pimple, pustule,
swelling, ulcer, welt, wen

blithe *adjective* **1** = **heedless**, careless,
casual, indifferent, nonchalant, thoughtless,
unconcerned, untroubled **2** = **happy**,
animated, buoyant, carefree, cheerful,
cheery, chirpy (*informal*), debonair, gay,
genial, gladsome (*archaic*), jaunty,
light-hearted, merry, mirthful, sprightly,
sunny, upbeat (*informal*), vivacious
➤ **Antonyms**
≠**heedless**: concerned, preoccupied,
thoughtful ≠**happy**: dejected, depressed,
gloomy, melancholy, morose, sad, unhappy

blitz *noun* = **attack**, assault, blitzkrieg,
bombardment, campaign, offensive,
onslaught, raid, strike

blizzard *noun* = **snowstorm**, blast, gale,
squall, storm, tempest

bloat *verb* = **puff up**, balloon, blow up,
dilate, distend, enlarge, expand, inflate, swell
➤ **Antonyms**
contract, deflate, shrink, shrivel, wither,
wrinkle

blob *noun* = **drop**, ball, bead, bubble, dab,
dewdrop, droplet, glob, globule, lump,
mass, pearl, pellet, pill

bloc *noun* = **group**, alliance, axis, cabal,

clique, coalition, combine, entente, faction, league, ring, schism, union, wing

block *noun* 1 = **piece**, bar, brick, cake, chunk, cube, hunk, ingot, lump, mass, nugget, square 2 = **obstruction**, bar, barrier, blockage, hindrance, impediment, jam, obstacle, occlusion, stoppage ♦ *verb* 3 = **obstruct**, bung up (*informal*), choke, clog, close, plug, stem the flow, stop up 4 = **stop**, arrest, bar, check, deter, halt, hinder, hobble, impede, obstruct, put a spoke in someone's wheel, throw a spanner in the works, thwart
➤ **Antonyms**
verb ≠**obstruct**: clear, open, unblock, unclog ≠**stop**: advance, aid, expedite, facilitate, foster, further, lend support to, promote, push, support

blockade *noun* = **stoppage**, barricade, barrier, block, closure, encirclement, hindrance, impediment, obstacle, obstruction, restriction, siege

blockage *noun* = **obstruction**, block, blocking, impediment, occlusion, stoppage, stopping up

blockhead *noun* = **idiot**, berk (*Brit. slang*), bimbo (*slang*), bonehead (*slang*), charlie (*Brit. informal*), chump (*informal*), coot, dickhead (*slang*), dimwit (*informal*), dipstick (*Brit. slang*), divvy (*Brit. slang*), dolt, dork (*slang*), dullard, dumb-ass (*slang*), dunce, dweeb (*U.S. slang*), fathead (*informal*), fool, fuckwit (*taboo slang*), geek (*slang*), gobshite (*Irish taboo slang*), gonzo (*slang*), ignoramus, jerk (*slang, chiefly U.S. & Canad.*), nerd *or* nurd (*slang*), nitwit, noodle, numbskull *or* numskull, numpty (*Scot. informal*), pillock (*Brit. slang*), plank (*Brit. slang*), plonker (*slang*), prat (*slang*), prick (*slang*), schmuck (*U.S. slang*), thickhead, twit (*informal, chiefly Brit.*), wally (*slang*)

block out *verb* = **outline**, chart, map out, plan, sketch

bloke *noun Informal* = **man**, bastard (*informal*), bod (*informal*), body, boy, bugger (*slang*), chap, character (*informal*), customer (*informal*), fellow, guy (*informal*), individual, person, punter (*informal*)

blond, blonde *adjective* = **fair**, fair-haired, fair-skinned, flaxen, golden-haired, light, light-coloured, light-complexioned, tow-headed

blood *noun* 1 = **lifeblood**, gore, vital fluid 2 = **family**, ancestry, birth, consanguinity, descendants, descent, extraction, kindred, kinship, lineage, noble extraction, relations 3 = **feeling**, anger, disposition, passion, spirit, temper

bloodcurdling *adjective* = **terrifying**,

appalling, chilling, dreadful, fearful, frightening, hair-raising, horrendous, horrifying, scaring, spine-chilling

bloodless *adjective* 1 = **pale**, anaemic, ashen, chalky, colourless, like death warmed up (*informal*), pallid, pasty, sallow, sickly, wan 2 = **listless**, cold, languid, lifeless, passionless, spiritless, torpid, unemotional, unfeeling

bloodshed *noun* = **killing**, blood bath, blood-letting, butchery, carnage, gore, massacre, murder, slaughter, slaying

bloodthirsty *adjective* = **cruel**, barbarous, brutal, cut-throat, ferocious, gory, inhuman, murderous, ruthless, savage, vicious, warlike

bloody *adjective* 1 = **bloodstained**, bleeding, blood-soaked, blood-spattered, gaping, raw, unstaunched 2 = **cruel**, ferocious, fierce, sanguinary, savage

bloom *noun* 1 = **flower**, blossom, blossoming, bud, efflorescence, opening (*of flowers*) 2 = **prime**, beauty, flourishing, health, heyday, perfection, vigour 3 = **glow**, blush, flush, freshness, lustre, radiance, rosiness ♦ *verb* 4 = **blossom**, blow, bud, burgeon, open, sprout 5 = **flourish**, develop, fare well, grow, prosper, succeed, thrive, wax
➤ **Antonyms**
noun ≠**glow**: bloodlessness, paleness, pallor, wanness, whiteness ♦ *verb* ≠**blossom**, **flourish**: decay, decline, die, droop, fade, fail, languish, perish, shrink, shrivel, wane, waste, wilt, wither

blossom *noun* 1 = **flower**, bloom, bud, floret, flowers ♦ *verb* 2 = **flower**, bloom, burgeon 3 = **grow**, bloom, develop, flourish, mature, progress, prosper, thrive

blot *noun* 1 = **spot**, blotch, mark, patch, smear, smudge, speck, splodge 2 = **stain**, blemish, blot on one's escutcheon, blur, defect, demerit, disgrace, fault, flaw, scar, smirch, spot, taint ♦ *verb* 3 = **stain**, bespatter, disfigure, disgrace, mark, smirch, smudge, spoil, spot, sully, tarnish 4 = **soak up**, absorb, dry, take up 5 **blot out**: a = **obliterate**, darken, destroy, eclipse, efface, obscure, shadow b = **erase**, cancel, expunge

blotch *noun, verb* = **mark**, blemish, blot, patch, scar, smirch, smudge, smutch, splash, splodge, spot, stain

blotchy *adjective* = **spotty**, blemished, macular, patchy, reddened, scurvy, uneven

blow[1] *verb* 1 = **carry**, bear, buffet, drive, fling, flutter, move, sweep, waft, whirl, whisk 2 = **exhale**, breathe, pant, puff 3 = **play**, blare, mouth, pipe, sound, toot, trumpet, vibrate 4 **blow one's top** *Informal* = **lose one's temper**, blow up (*informal*), do one's nut (*Brit. slang*), explode, flip one's lid (*slang*), fly into a temper, fly off the handle (*informal*), go spare (*Brit. slang*), have a fit (*informal*), lose it (*informal*), lose the plot (*informal*), see red (*informal*), throw a tantrum ◆ *noun* **5** = **gust**, blast, draught, flurry, gale, puff, strong breeze, tempest, wind

blow² *noun* **1** = **knock**, bang, bash (*informal*), belt (*informal*), buffet, clomp (*slang*), clout (*informal*), clump (*slang*), punch, rap, slosh (*Brit. slang*), smack, sock (*slang*), stroke, thump, tonk (*informal*), wallop (*informal*), whack **2** = **setback**, affliction, bolt from the blue, bombshell, bummer (*slang*), calamity, catastrophe, choker (*informal*), comedown (*informal*), disappointment, disaster, jolt, misfortune, reverse, shock, sucker punch, upset, whammy (*informal, chiefly U.S.*)

blowout *noun* **1** = **burst**, break, flat, flat tyre, leak, puncture, rupture, tear **2** = **explosion**, blast, detonation, eruption **3** *Slang* = **binge** (*informal*), beano (*Brit. slang*), carousal, carouse, feast, hooley *or* hoolie (*chiefly Irish & N.Z.*), party, rave (*Brit. slang*), rave-up (*Brit. slang*), spree

blow out *verb* **1** = **put out**, extinguish, snuff **2** = **burst**, erupt, explode, rupture, shatter

blow over *verb* = **die down**, be forgotten, cease, disappear, end, finish, pass, pass away, subside, vanish

blowsy, blowzy *adjective* **1** = **slovenly**, bedraggled, dishevelled, frowzy, slatternly, slipshod, sloppy, sluttish, tousled, unkempt, untidy **2** = **red-faced**, florid, ruddy

blow up *verb* **1** = **explode**, blast, blow sky-high, bomb, burst, detonate, dynamite, go off, rupture, shatter **2** = **inflate**, bloat, distend, enlarge, expand, fill, puff up, pump up, swell **3** = **exaggerate**, blow out of (all) proportion, enlarge, enlarge on, heighten, magnify, make a mountain out of a molehill, make a production out of, overstate **4** *Informal* = **lose one's temper**, become angry, become enraged, blow a fuse (*slang, chiefly U.S.*), crack up (*informal*), erupt, flip one's lid (*slang*), fly off the handle (*informal*), go ballistic (*slang, chiefly U.S.*), go off the deep end (*informal*), go up the wall (*slang*), hit the roof (*informal*), lose it (*informal*), lose the plot (*informal*), rage, see red (*informal*), wig out (*slang*)

bludgeon *noun* **1** = **club**, cosh (*Brit.*), cudgel, shillelagh, truncheon ◆ *verb* **2** = **club**, beat, beat up, cosh (*Brit.*), cudgel, knock down, strike **3** = **bully**, browbeat, bulldoze (*informal*), coerce, dragoon, force, hector, put the screws on, railroad (*informal*), steamroller

blue *adjective* **1** = **azure**, cerulean, cobalt, cyan, navy, sapphire, sky-coloured, ultramarine **2** = **depressed**, dejected, despondent, dismal, downcast, down-hearted, down in the dumps (*informal*), down in the mouth, fed up, gloomy, glum, low, melancholy, sad, unhappy **3** = **smutty**, bawdy, dirty, indecent, lewd, naughty, near the knuckle (*informal*), obscene, risqué, vulgar, X-rated (*informal*)
➤ **Antonyms**
≠**depressed:** blithe, cheerful, cheery, chirpy (*informal*), elated, genial, happy, jolly, merry, optimistic, sunny ≠**smutty:** decent, respectable

blueprint *noun* = **plan**, design, draft, layout, norm, outline, pattern, pilot scheme, project, prototype, scheme, sketch

blues *plural noun* = **depression**, dejection, despondency, doldrums, dumps (*informal*), gloom, gloominess, glumness, low spirits, melancholy, moodiness, the hump (*Brit. informal*), unhappiness

bluff¹ *verb* **1** = **deceive**, con, defraud, delude, fake, feign, humbug, lie, mislead, pretend, pull the wool over someone's eyes, sham ◆ *noun* **2** = **deception**, bluster, boast, braggadocio, bragging, bravado, deceit, fake, feint, fraud, humbug, idle boast, lie, mere show, pretence, sham, show, subterfuge

bluff² *noun* **1** = **precipice**, bank, cliff, crag, escarpment, headland, peak, promontory, ridge, scarp ◆ *adjective* **2** = **hearty**, abrupt, blunt, blustering, downright, frank, genial, good-natured, open, outspoken, plain-spoken **3** = **steep**, abrupt, perpendicular, precipitous, sheer, towering
➤ **Antonyms**
adjective ≠**hearty:** delicate, diplomatic, discreet, judicious, sensitive, tactful, thoughtful

blunder *noun* **1** = **mistake**, bloomer (*Brit. informal*), boob (*Brit. slang*), boo-boo (*informal*), clanger (*informal*), faux pas, gaffe, gaucherie, howler (*informal*), impropriety, indiscretion **2** = **error**, fault, inaccuracy, mistake, oversight, slip, slip-up (*informal*) ◆ *verb* **3** = **make a mistake**, bodge (*informal*), botch, bungle, drop a brick (*Brit. informal*), drop a clanger (*informal*), err, flub (*U.S. slang*), put one's foot in it (*informal*), slip up (*informal*) **4** = **stumble**, bumble, confuse, flounder, misjudge
➤ **Antonyms**
noun ≠**error:** accuracy, correctness ◆ *verb* ≠**make a mistake:** be correct, be exact, get it right

blunt *adjective* **1** = **dull**, dulled, edgeless, pointless, rounded, unsharpened **2**

= **forthright**, bluff, brusque, discourteous, downright, explicit, frank, impolite, outspoken, plain-spoken, rude, straightforward, straight from the shoulder, tactless, trenchant, uncivil, unpolished, upfront (*informal*) ♦ *verb* 3 = **dull**, dampen, deaden, numb, soften, take the edge off, water down, weaken
➤ Antonyms
adjective ≠**dull**: keen, pointed, sharp ≠**forthright**: acute, courteous, diplomatic, keen, pointed, sensitive, sharp, subtle, tactful ♦ *verb* ≠**dull**: animate, put an edge on, sharpen, stimulate, vitalize

blur *verb* 1 = **make indistinct**, becloud, bedim, befog, blear, cloud, darken, dim, fog, make hazy, make vague, mask, obscure, soften 2 = **smudge**, blot, smear, spot, stain ♦ *noun* 3 = **indistinctness**, blear, blurredness, cloudiness, confusion, dimness, fog, haze, obscurity 4 = **smudge**, blot, smear, spot, stain

blurred *adjective* = **indistinct**, bleary, blurry, dim, faint, foggy, fuzzy, hazy, ill-defined, lacking definition, misty, nebulous, out of focus, unclear, vague

blurt out *verb* = **exclaim**, babble, blab, blow the gaff (*Brit. slang*), cry, disclose, gush, let the cat out of the bag, reveal, run off at the mouth (*slang*), spill, spill one's guts (*slang*), spill the beans (*informal*), spout (*informal*), sputter, tattle, tell all, utter suddenly

blush *verb* 1 = **turn red**, colour, crimson, flush, go red (as a beetroot), redden, turn scarlet ♦ *noun* 2 = **reddening**, colour, flush, glow, pink tinge, rosiness, rosy tint, ruddiness
➤ Antonyms
verb ≠**turn red**: blanch, blench, drain, fade, pale, turn pale, whiten

bluster *verb* 1 = **roar**, bulldoze, bully, domineer, hector, rant, roister, storm 2 = **boast**, blow one's own horn (*U.S. & Canad.*), blow one's own trumpet, brag, swagger, swell, vaunt ♦ *noun* 3 = **hot air** (*informal*), bluff, boasting, boisterousness, bombast, bragging, bravado, crowing, swagger, swaggering

blustery *adjective* = **gusty**, blusterous, boisterous, inclement, squally, stormy, tempestuous, violent, wild, windy

board *noun* 1 = **plank**, panel, piece of timber, slat, timber 2 = **directors**, advisers, advisory group, committee, conclave, council, directorate, panel, quango, trustees 3 = **meals**, daily meals, provisions, victuals ♦ *verb* 4 = **get on**, embark, embus, enplane, enter, entrain, mount 5 = **lodge**, accommodate, feed, house, put up, quarter, room

➤ Antonyms
verb ≠**get on**: alight, arrive, disembark, dismount, get off, go ashore, land

boast *verb* 1 = **brag**, blow one's own trumpet, bluster, crow, exaggerate, puff, strut, swagger, talk big (*slang*), vaunt 2 = **possess**, be proud of, congratulate oneself on, exhibit, flatter oneself, pride oneself on, show off ♦ *noun* 3 = **brag**, avowal, gasconade (*rare*), rodomontade (*literary*), swank (*informal*), vaunt 4 = **source of pride**, gem, joy, pride, pride and joy, treasure
➤ Antonyms
verb ≠**brag**: cover up, depreciate, disavow, disclaim ♦ *noun* ≠**brag**: disavowal, disclaimer

boastful *adjective* = **bragging**, cocky, conceited, crowing, egotistical, full of oneself, puffed-up, swaggering, swanky (*informal*), swollen-headed, vainglorious, vaunting
➤ Antonyms
deprecating, humble, modest, self-belittling, self-effacing, unassuming

bob *verb* = **duck**, bounce, hop, jerk, leap, nod, oscillate, quiver, skip, waggle, weave, wobble

bode *verb* = **portend**, augur, be an omen of, betoken, forebode, foreshadow, foretell, forewarn, omen, predict, presage, prophesy, signify, threaten

bodily *adjective* = **physical**, actual, carnal, corporal, corporeal, fleshly, material, substantial, tangible

body *noun* 1 = **physique**, build, figure, form, frame, shape 2 = **torso**, trunk 3 = **corpse**, cadaver, carcass, dead body, relics, remains, stiff (*slang*) 4 = **organization**, association, band, bloc, collection, company, confederation, congress, corporation, society 5 = **mass**, crowd, horde, majority, mob, multitude, throng 6 = **main part**, bulk, essence, mass, material, matter, substance 7 = **consistency**, density, firmness, richness, solidity, substance 8 *Informal* = **person**, being, creature, human, human being, individual, mortal

boffin *noun Brit. informal* = **expert**, authority, bluestocking (*usually disparaging*), brain(s) (*informal*), brainbox, egghead, genius, guru, intellect, intellectual, inventor, mastermind, maven (*U.S.*), planner, thinker, virtuoso, wizard

bog *noun* = **marsh**, fen, marshland, mire, morass, moss (*Scot. & Northern English dialect*), peat bog, quagmire, slough, swamp, wetlands

bog down *verb* = **hold up**, delay, halt, impede, sink, slow down, slow up, stall, stick

bogey *noun* 1 = **spirit**, apparition,

bogeyman, goblin, hobgoblin, imp, spectre, spook (*informal*), sprite **2 = bugbear**, bête noire, bugaboo, nightmare

boggle *verb* **1 = be confused**, be alarmed, be surprised, be taken aback, shy, stagger, startle, take fright **2 = hesitate**, demur, dither (*chiefly Brit.*), doubt, equivocate, falter, hang back, hover, jib, shillyshally (*informal*), shrink from, vacillate, waver

boggy *adjective* **= marshy**, fenny, miry, muddy, oozy, quaggy, soft, spongy, swampy, waterlogged, yielding

bogus *adjective* **= fake**, artificial, counterfeit, dummy, ersatz, false, forged, fraudulent, imitation, phoney *or* phony (*informal*), pseudo (*informal*), sham, spurious
➤ Antonyms
actual, authentic, genuine, real, true

bohemian *adjective* **1 = unconventional**, alternative, artistic, arty (*informal*), avant-garde, eccentric, exotic, left bank, nonconformist, oddball (*informal*), offbeat, off-the-wall (*slang*), outré, unorthodox, way-out (*informal*) ♦ *noun* **2 = nonconformist**, beatnik, dropout, hippy, iconoclast
➤ Antonyms
adjective ≠**unconventional**: bourgeois, conservative, conventional, Pooterish, square (*informal*), straight (*slang*), straight-laced, stuffy

boil[1] *verb* **1 = bubble**, agitate, churn, effervesce, fizz, foam, froth, seethe **2 = be furious**, be angry, be indignant, blow a fuse (*slang, chiefly U.S.*), crack up (*informal*), fly off the handle (*informal*), foam at the mouth (*informal*), fulminate, fume, go ballistic (*slang, chiefly U.S.*), go off the deep end (*informal*), go up the wall (*slang*), rage, rave, see red (*informal*), storm, wig out (*slang*)

boil[2] *noun* **= pustule**, blain, blister, carbuncle, furuncle (*Pathology*), gathering, swelling, tumour, ulcer

boil down *verb* **= reduce**, come down, condense, decrease

boiling *adjective* **1 = very hot**, baking, blistering, hot, roasting, scorching, tropical **2 = furious**, angry, choked, cross, enraged, foaming at the mouth, fuming, incandescent, incensed, indignant, infuriated, on the warpath

boisterous *adjective* **1 = unruly**, bouncy, clamorous, disorderly, impetuous, loud, noisy, obstreperous, riotous, rollicking, rowdy, rumbustious, unrestrained, uproarious, vociferous, wild **2 = stormy**, blustery, gusty, raging, rough, squally, tempestuous, tumultuous, turbulent
➤ Antonyms
≠**unruly**: calm, controlled, peaceful, quiet, restrained, self-controlled, subdued ≠**stormy**: calm, peaceful, quiet

bold *adjective* **1 = fearless**, adventurous, audacious, brave, courageous, daring, dauntless, enterprising, gallant, gritty, heroic, intrepid, lion-hearted, valiant, valorous **2 = impudent**, barefaced, brash, brazen, cheeky, confident, feisty (*informal, chiefly U.S. & Canad.*), forward, fresh (*informal*), insolent, in-your-face (*Brit. slang*), pert, pushy (*informal*), rude, sassy (*U.S. informal*), saucy, shameless **3 = conspicuous**, bright, colourful, eye-catching, flashy, forceful, lively, loud, prominent, pronounced, salient, showy, spirited, striking, strong, vivid
➤ Antonyms
≠**fearless**: cowardly, faint-hearted, fearful, timid, timorous ≠**impudent**: conservative, cool, courteous, meek, modest, polite, retiring, shy, tactful ≠**conspicuous**: dull, ordinary, pale, soft

bolster *verb* **= support**, aid, assist, augment, boost, brace, buoy up, buttress, cushion, give a leg up (*informal*), help, hold up, maintain, pillow, prop, reinforce, shore up, stay, strengthen

bolt *noun* **1 = bar**, catch, fastener, latch, lock, sliding bar **2 = pin**, peg, rivet, rod **3 = dash**, bound, dart, escape, flight, rush, spring, sprint **4 = arrow**, dart, missile, projectile, shaft, thunderbolt ♦ *verb* **5 = run away**, abscond, bound, dash, decamp, do a runner (*slang*), escape, flee, fly, fly the coop (*U.S. & Canad. informal*), hurtle, jump, leap, make a break (for it), run, run for it, rush, skedaddle (*informal*), spring, sprint, take a powder (*U.S. & Canad. slang*), take it on the lam (*U.S. & Canad. slang*) **6 = lock**, bar, fasten, latch, secure **7 = gobble**, cram, devour, gorge, gulp, guzzle, stuff, swallow whole, wolf

bomb *noun* **1 = explosive**, bombshell, charge, device, grenade, mine, missile, projectile, rocket, shell, torpedo ♦ *verb* **2 = blow up**, attack, blow sky-high, bombard, destroy, shell, strafe, torpedo

bombard *verb* **1 = bomb**, assault, blast, blitz, cannonade, fire upon, open fire, pound, shell, strafe **2 = attack**, assail, barrage, batter, beset, besiege, harass, hound, pester

bombardment *noun* **= bombing**, assault, attack, barrage, blitz, cannonade, fire, flak, fusillade, shelling, strafe

bombast *noun* **= grandiloquence**, bluster, brag, braggadocio, extravagant boasting, fustian, gasconade (*rare*), grandiosity, hot air (*informal*), magniloquence, pomposity, rant, rodomontade (*literary*)

bombastic *adjective* = **grandiloquent**, declamatory, fustian, grandiose, high-flown, histrionic, inflated, magniloquent, pompous, ranting, turgid, verbose, windy, wordy

bona fide *adjective* = **genuine**, actual, authentic, honest, kosher (*informal*), lawful, legal, legitimate, on the level (*informal*), real, the real McCoy, true
➤ **Antonyms**
bogus, counterfeit, ersatz, fake, false, imitation, phoney *or* phony (*informal*), sham

bond *noun* **1** = **fastening**, band, binding, chain, cord, fetter, ligature, link, manacle, shackle, tie **2** = **tie**, affiliation, affinity, attachment, connection, link, relation, union **3** = **agreement**, compact, contract, covenant, guarantee, obligation, pledge, promise, word ♦ *verb* **4** = **hold together**, bind, connect, fasten, fix together, fuse, glue, gum, paste

bondage *noun* = **slavery**, captivity, confinement, enslavement, imprisonment, subjugation

bonny *adjective Scot. & N English dialect* = **beautiful**, comely, fair, handsome, lovely, pretty, sweet

bonus *noun* = **extra**, benefit, bounty, commission, dividend, gift, gratuity, hand-out, honorarium, icing on the cake, perk (*Brit. informal*), plus, premium, prize, reward

bon vivant *noun* = **gourmet**, bon viveur, epicure, epicurean, foodie, gastronome, hedonist, luxurist, pleasure-seeker, voluptuary
➤ **Antonyms**
abstainer, ascetic, celibate, self-denier

bony *adjective* = **thin**, angular, emaciated, gangling, gaunt, lanky, lean, macilent (*rare*), rawboned, scrawny, skin and bone, skinny

book *noun* **1** = **work**, hardback, manual, paperback, publication, roll, scroll, textbook, title, tome, tract, volume **2** = **notebook**, album, diary, exercise book, jotter, pad ♦ *verb* **3** = **reserve**, arrange for, bill, charter, engage, line up, make reservations, organize, procure, programme, schedule **4** = **note**, enrol, enter, insert, list, log, mark down, post, put down, record, register, write down

bookish *adjective* = **studious**, academic, donnish, erudite, intellectual, learned, literary, pedantic, scholarly, well-read

booklet *noun* = **brochure**, leaflet, pamphlet

boom *verb* **1** = **bang**, blast, crash, explode, resound, reverberate, roar, roll, rumble, thunder **2** = **flourish**, develop, expand, gain, grow, increase, intensify, prosper, spurt, strengthen, succeed, swell, thrive ♦ *noun* **3** = **bang**, blast, burst, clap, crash, explosion, roar, rumble, thunder **4** = **expansion**,

advance, boost, development, gain, growth, improvement, increase, jump, push, spurt, upsurge, upswing, upturn
➤ **Antonyms**
verb ≠**flourish**: crash, fail, fall, slump ♦ *noun* ≠**expansion**: bust (*informal*), collapse, crash, decline, depression, downturn, failure, hard times, recession, slump

boomerang *verb* = **rebound**, backfire, come back, come home to roost, recoil, return, reverse, ricochet

boon[1] *noun* = **benefit**, advantage, benefaction, blessing, donation, favour, gift, godsend, grant, gratuity, hand-out, manna from heaven, present, windfall

boon[2] *adjective* = **intimate**, close, special

boor *noun* = **lout**, barbarian, brute, bumpkin, churl, clodhopper (*informal*), clodpole, hayseed (*U.S. & Canad. informal*), hick (*informal, chiefly U.S. & Canad.*), oaf, peasant, philistine, redneck (*U.S. slang*), vulgarian

boorish *adjective* = **loutish**, awkward, barbaric, bearish, churlish, clownish, coarse, crude, gross, gruff, hick (*informal, chiefly U.S. & Canad.*), ill-bred, lubberly, oafish, rude, rustic, uncivilized, uncouth, uneducated, unrefined, vulgar
➤ **Antonyms**
cultured, gallant, genteel, polite, refined, sophisticated, urbane

boost *noun* **1** = **help**, encouragement, gee-up, hype, improvement, praise, promotion **2** = **push**, heave, hoist, lift, raise, shove, thrust **3** = **rise**, addition, expansion, improvement, increase, increment, jump ♦ *verb* **4** = **increase**, add to, amplify, develop, enlarge, expand, heighten, hoick, jack up, magnify, raise **5** = **promote**, advance, advertise, assist, crack up (*informal*), encourage, foster, further, gee up, hype, improve, inspire, plug (*informal*), praise, support, sustain **6** = **raise**, elevate, heave, hoist, lift, push, shove, thrust
➤ **Antonyms**
noun ≠**help**: condemnation, criticism, knock (*informal*) ≠**rise**: cut-back, decline, decrease, deterioration, fall, reduction ♦ *verb* ≠**increase**: cut, decrease, diminish, drop, lessen, lower, moderate, pare, reduce, scale down ≠**promote**: condemn, criticize, hinder, hold back, knock (*informal*) ≠**raise**: drop, let down, lower

boot *verb* = **kick**, drive, drop-kick, knock, punt, put the boot in(to) (*slang*), shove

bootless *adjective* = **useless**, fruitless, futile, ineffective, profitless, to no avail, unavailing, unsuccessful, vain

boot out *verb Informal* **1** = **throw out**,

eject, give the bum's rush (*slang*), kick out, show one the door, throw out on one's ear (*informal*) **2** = **sack** (*informal*), dismiss, expel, give (someone) their marching orders, give the boot (*slang*), give the bullet (*Brit. slang*), give the heave *or* push (*informal*), kick out, kiss off (*slang, chiefly U.S. & Canad.*), oust, relegate

booty *noun* = **plunder**, boodle (*slang, chiefly U.S.*), gains, haul, loot, pillage, prey, spoil, spoils, swag (*slang*), takings, winnings

border *noun* **1** = **frontier**, borderline, boundary, line, march **2** = **edge**, bound, boundary, bounds, brim, brink, confine, confines, flange, hem, limit, limits, lip, margin, pale, rim, skirt, verge ♦ *verb* **3** = **edge**, bind, decorate, fringe, hem, rim, trim

borderline *adjective* = **marginal**, ambivalent, doubtful, equivocal, indecisive, indefinite, indeterminate, inexact, unclassifiable

border on *verb* **1** = **adjoin**, abut, connect, contact, impinge, join, march, neighbour, touch, verge on **2** = **come close to**, approach, approximate, be like, be similar to, come near, echo, match, parallel, resemble

bore[1] *verb* **1** = **drill**, burrow, gouge out, mine, penetrate, perforate, pierce, sink, tunnel ♦ *noun* **2** = **hole**, borehole, calibre, drill hole, shaft, tunnel

bore[2] *verb* **1** = **tire**, annoy, be tedious, bother, exhaust, fatigue, jade, pall on, pester, send to sleep, trouble, vex, wear out, weary, worry ♦ *noun* **2** = **nuisance**, anorak (*informal*), bother, drag (*informal*), dullard, dull person, headache (*informal*), pain (*informal*), pain in the arse (*taboo informal*), pain in the neck (*informal*), pest, tiresome person, wearisome talker, yawn (*informal*)
➤ **Antonyms**
verb ≠ **tire**: amuse, divert, engross, excite, fascinate, hold the attention of, interest, stimulate

bored *adjective* = **fed up**, listless, tired, uninterested, wearied

boredom *noun* = **tedium**, apathy, doldrums, dullness, ennui, flatness, irksomeness, monotony, sameness, tediousness, weariness, world-weariness
➤ **Antonyms**
amusement, entertainment, excitement, interest, stimulation

boring *adjective* = **uninteresting**, dead, dull, flat, ho-hum (*informal*), humdrum, insipid, mind-numbing, monotonous, old, repetitious, routine, stale, tedious, tiresome, tiring, unexciting, unvaried, wearisome

borrow *verb* **1** = **take on loan**, blag (*slang*), cadge, mooch (*slang*), scrounge (*informal*), take and return, touch (someone) for (*slang*), use temporarily **2** = **steal**, acquire, adopt, appropriate, copy, filch, imitate, obtain, pilfer, pirate, plagiarize, simulate, take, use, usurp
➤ **Antonyms**
≠ **take on loan**: advance, give, lend, loan, provide, return, supply

bosom *noun* **1** = **breast**, bust, chest **2** = **feelings**, affections, emotions, heart, sentiments, soul, spirit, sympathies **3** = **midst**, centre, circle, core, protection, shelter ♦ *adjective* **4** = **intimate**, boon, cherished, close, confidential, dear, very dear

boss[1] *noun* **1** = **head**, administrator, big cheese (*slang, old-fashioned*), chief, director, employer, executive, foreman, gaffer (*informal, chiefly Brit.*), governor (*informal*), kingpin, leader, manager, master, Mister Big (*slang, chiefly U.S.*), numero uno (*informal*), overseer, owner, superintendent, supervisor, torchbearer ♦ *verb* **2** = **be in charge**, administrate, call the shots, call the tune, command, control, direct, employ, manage, oversee, run, superintend, supervise, take charge

boss[2] *noun* = **stud**, knob, nub, nubble, point, protuberance, tip

boss around *verb Informal* = **domineer**, bully, dominate, oppress, order, overbear, push around (*slang*), put upon, ride roughshod over, tyrannize

bossy *adjective Informal* = **domineering**, arrogant, authoritarian, autocratic, despotic, dictatorial, hectoring, high-handed, imperious, lordly, overbearing, tyrannical

botch *verb* **1** = **spoil**, balls up (*taboo slang*), blunder, bodge (*informal*), bungle, butcher, cobble, cock up (*Brit. slang*), flub (*U.S. slang*), fuck up (*offensive taboo slang*), fumble, make a nonsense of (*informal*), make a pig's ear of (*informal*), mar, mend, mess up, mismanage, muff, patch, screw up (*informal*) ♦ *noun* **2** = **mess**, balls-up (*taboo slang*), blunder, bungle, bungling, cock-up (*Brit. slang*), failure, fuck-up (*offensive taboo slang*), fumble, hash, miscarriage, pig's breakfast (*informal*), pig's ear (*informal*)

bother *verb* **1** = **trouble**, alarm, annoy, bend someone's ear (*informal*), breathe down someone's neck, concern, dismay, distress, disturb, gall, get on one's nerves (*informal*), get on one's wick (*Brit. slang*), harass, hassle (*informal*), inconvenience, irritate, molest, nag, nark (*Brit., Austral. & N.Z. slang*), pester, plague, put out, upset, vex, worry ♦ *noun* **2** = **trouble**, aggravation, annoyance, bustle, difficulty, flurry, fuss, gall,

grief (*informal*), hassle (*informal*), inconvenience, irritation, molestation, nuisance, perplexity, pest, problem, strain, vexation, worry
➤ **Antonyms**
verb ≠**trouble**: aid, assist, facilitate, further, help, relieve, succour, support ♦ *noun* ≠**trouble**: advantage, aid, benefit, comfort, convenience, help, service, use

bothersome *adjective* = **troublesome**, aggravating, annoying, distressing, exasperating, inconvenient, irritating, tiresome, vexatious, vexing
➤ **Antonyms**
appropriate, beneficial, commodious, convenient, handy, helpful, serviceable, useful

bottleneck *noun* = **hold-up**, block, blockage, congestion, impediment, jam, obstacle, obstruction, snarl-up (*informal, chiefly Brit.*)

bottle up *verb* = **suppress**, check, contain, curb, keep back, restrict, shut in, trap

bottom *noun* 1 = **lowest part**, base, basis, bed, deepest part, depths, floor, foot, foundation, groundwork, pedestal, support 2 = **underside**, lower side, sole, underneath 3 = **buttocks**, arse (*taboo slang*), ass (*U.S. & Canad. taboo slang*), backside, behind (*informal*), bum (*Brit. slang*), buns (*U.S. slang*), butt (*U.S. & Canad. informal*), derrière (*euphemistic*), fundament, jacksy (*Brit. slang*), posterior, rear, rear end, rump, seat, tail (*informal*), tush (*U.S. slang*) 4 = **basis**, base, cause, core, essence, ground, heart, mainspring, origin, principle, root, source, substance ♦ *adjective* 5 = **lowest**, base, basement, basic, ground, last, undermost
➤ **Antonyms**
noun ≠**lowest part**: cover, crown, height, lid, peak, summit, surface, top ♦ *adjective* ≠**lowest**: higher, highest, top, upper

bottomless *adjective* = **unlimited**, boundless, deep, fathomless, immeasurable, inexhaustible, infinite, unfathomable

bounce *verb* 1 = **rebound**, bob, bound, bump, jounce, jump, leap, recoil, resile, ricochet, spring, thump 2 *Slang* = **throw out**, boot out (*informal*), eject, fire (*informal*), kick out (*informal*), oust, relegate ♦ *noun* 3 *Informal* = **life**, animation, brio, dynamism, energy, go (*informal*), liveliness, pep, vigour, vitality, vivacity, zip (*informal*) 4 = **springiness**, bound, elasticity, give, rebound, recoil, resilience, spring

bouncing *adjective* = **lively**, alive and kicking, blooming, bonny, fighting fit, fit as a fiddle (*informal*), healthy, robust, thriving, vigorous

bound[1] *adjective* 1 = **tied**, cased, fastened, fixed, pinioned, secured, tied up 2 = **certain**, destined, doomed, fated, sure 3 = **obliged**, beholden, committed, compelled, constrained, duty-bound, forced, obligated, pledged, required

bound[2] *verb* = **limit**, circumscribe, confine, define, delimit, demarcate, encircle, enclose, hem in, restrain, restrict, surround, terminate

bound[3] *verb, noun* = **leap**, bob, bounce, caper, frisk, gambol, hurdle, jump, lope, pounce, prance, skip, spring, vault

boundary *noun* = **limits**, barrier, border, borderline, bounds, brink, confines, edge, extremity, fringe, frontier, march, margin, pale, precinct, termination, verge

boundless *adjective* = **unlimited**, endless, illimitable, immeasurable, immense, incalculable, inexhaustible, infinite, limitless, measureless, the sky's the limit, unbounded, unconfined, unending, untold, vast
➤ **Antonyms**
bounded, confined, limited, little, restricted, small

bounds *plural noun* 1 = **boundary**, border, confine, edge, extremity, fringe, limit, line, march, margin, pale, periphery, rim, termination, verge 2 **out of bounds** = **forbidden**, banned, barred, off-limits (*chiefly U.S. military*), prohibited, taboo

bountiful *adjective Literary* 1 = **plentiful**, abundant, ample, bounteous, copious, exuberant, lavish, luxuriant, plenteous, prolific 2 = **generous**, beneficent, bounteous, liberal, magnanimous, munificent, open-handed, princely, prodigal, unstinting

bounty *noun Literary* 1 = **generosity**, benevolence, charity, kindness, largesse *or* largess, liberality, philanthropy 2 = **reward**, bonus, gift, present

bouquet *noun* 1 = **bunch of flowers**, boutonniere, buttonhole, corsage, garland, nosegay, posy, spray, wreath 2 = **aroma**, fragrance, perfume, redolence, savour, scent

bourgeois *adjective* = **middle-class**, conventional, hidebound, materialistic, Pooterish, traditional

bout *noun* 1 = **period**, course, fit, round, run, session, spell, spree, stint, stretch, term, time, turn 2 = **fight**, battle, boxing match, competition, contest, encounter, engagement, head-to-head, match, set-to, struggle

bovine *adjective* = **dull**, dense, dozy (*Brit. informal*), slow, sluggish, stolid, stupid, thick

bow[1] *verb* 1 = **bend**, bob, droop, genuflect, incline, make obeisance, nod, stoop 2 = **give in**, accept, acquiesce, comply, concede, defer, kowtow, relent, submit, succumb, surrender, yield ♦ *noun* **3** = **bending**, bob, genuflexion, inclination, kowtow, nod, obeisance, salaam

bow[2] *noun Nautical* = **prow**, beak, fore, head, stem

bowdlerize *verb* = **censor**, blue-pencil, clean up, expurgate, mutilate, sanitize

bowels *plural noun* **1** = **guts**, entrails, innards (*informal*), insides (*informal*), intestines, viscera, vitals **2** = **depths**, belly, core, deep, hold, inside, interior

bower *noun* = **arbour**, alcove, grotto, leafy shelter, shady recess, summerhouse

bowl[1] *noun* = **basin**, dish, vessel

bowl[2] *verb* **1** = **roll**, revolve, rotate, spin, trundle, whirl **2** = **throw**, fling, hurl, pitch

bowl over *verb* **1** *Informal* = **surprise**, amaze, astonish, astound, dumbfound, stagger, startle, stun, sweep off one's feet **2** = **knock down**, bring down, deck (*slang*), fell, floor, overthrow, overturn

bow out *verb* = **give up**, abandon, back out, call it a day *or* night, cop out (*slang*), get out, pull out, quit, resign, retire, step down (*informal*), throw in the sponge, throw in the towel, withdraw

box[1] *noun* **1** = **container**, ark (*dialect*), carton, case, casket, chest, coffret, kist (*Scot. & Northern English dialect*), pack, package, portmanteau, receptacle, trunk ♦ *verb* **2** = **pack**, package, wrap

box[2] *verb* **1** = **fight**, exchange blows, spar **2** = **punch**, belt (*informal*), buffet, butt, chin (*slang*), clout (*informal*), cuff, deck (*slang*), hit, lay one on (*slang*), slap, sock (*slang*), strike, thwack, tonk (*informal*), wallop (*informal*), whack ♦ *noun* **3** = **punch**, belt (*informal*), blow, buffet, clout (*informal*), cuff, slap, stroke, thumping, wallop (*informal*)

boxer *noun* = **fighter**, prizefighter, pugilist, sparrer, sparring partner

box in *verb* = **confine**, cage, contain, coop up, enclose, hem in, isolate, shut in, surround, trap

boxing *noun* = **prizefighting**, fisticuffs, pugilism, sparring, the fight game (*informal*), the ring

boy *noun* = **lad**, fellow, junior, schoolboy, stripling, youngster, youth

boycott *verb* = **embargo**, ban, bar, black, blackball, blacklist, exclude, ostracize, outlaw, prohibit, proscribe, refrain from, refuse, reject, spurn
➤ **Antonyms**
accept, advocate, back, champion, defend, espouse, help, patronize, promote, support, welcome

boyfriend *noun* = **sweetheart**, admirer,

beau, date, follower, leman (*archaic*), lover, man, steady, suitor, swain, toy boy, young man

boyish *adjective* = **youthful**, adolescent, childish, immature, innocent, juvenile, puerile, young

brace *noun* **1** = **support**, bolster, bracer, bracket, buttress, prop, reinforcement, stanchion, stay, strut, truss ♦ *verb* **2** = **support**, bandage, bind, bolster, buttress, fasten, fortify, hold up, prop, reinforce, shove, shove up, steady, strap, strengthen, tie, tighten

bracing *adjective* = **refreshing**, brisk, chilly, cool, crisp, energizing, exhilarating, fortifying, fresh, invigorating, lively, restorative, reviving, rousing, stimulating, tonic, vigorous
➤ **Antonyms**
debilitating, draining, enervating, exhausting, fatiguing, sapping, soporific, taxing, tiring, weakening

brackish *adjective* = **salty**, bitter, brak (*S. Afr.*), briny, saline, salt, undrinkable
➤ **Antonyms**
clean, clear, fresh, pure, sweet, unpolluted

brag *verb* = **boast**, blow one's own horn (*U.S. & Canad.*), blow one's own trumpet, bluster, crow, swagger, talk big (*slang*), vaunt

braggart *noun* = **boaster**, bigmouth (*slang*), bluffer, blusterer, brag, braggadocio, bragger, hot dog (*chiefly U.S.*), show-off (*informal*), swaggerer, swashbuckler

braid *verb* = **interweave**, entwine, interlace, intertwine, lace, plait, ravel, twine, weave

brain *noun Informal* = **intellectual**, bluestocking (*usually disparaging*), brainbox, egghead (*informal*), genius, highbrow, intellect, mastermind, prodigy, pundit, sage, scholar

brainless *adjective* = **stupid**, braindead (*informal*), dead from the neck up (*informal*), dumb-ass (*slang*), foolish, idiotic, inane, inept, mindless, senseless, thoughtless, unintelligent, witless

brains *plural noun* = **intelligence**, capacity, intellect, mind, nous (*Brit. slang*), reason, sagacity, savvy (*slang*), sense, shrewdness, smarts (*slang, chiefly U.S.*), suss (*slang*), understanding, wit

brainwashing *noun* = **indoctrination**, alteration, conditioning, persuasion, re-education

brainwave *noun* = **idea**, bright idea, stroke of genius, thought

brainy *adjective Informal* = **intelligent**, bright, brilliant, clever, smart

brake noun **1** = **control**, check, constraint, curb, rein, restraint ◆ verb **2** = **slow**, check, decelerate, halt, moderate, reduce speed, slacken, stop

branch noun **1** = **bough**, arm, limb, offshoot, prong, ramification, shoot, spray, sprig **2** = **division**, chapter, department, local office, office, part, section, subdivision, subsection, wing

branch out verb = **expand**, add to, develop, diversify, enlarge, extend, have a finger in every pie, increase, multiply, proliferate, ramify, spread out

brand noun **1** = **label**, emblem, hallmark, logo, mark, marker, sign, stamp, symbol, trademark **2** = **kind**, cast, class, grade, make, quality, sort, species, type, variety **3** = **stigma**, blot, disgrace, infamy, mark, reproach, slur, smirch, stain, taint ◆ verb **4** = **mark**, burn, burn in, label, scar, stamp **5** = **stigmatize**, censure, denounce, discredit, disgrace, expose, mark

brandish verb = **wave**, display, exhibit, flaunt, flourish, parade, raise, shake, swing, wield

brash adjective = **bold**, brazen, cocky, forward, heedless, impertinent, impudent, insolent, pushy (informal), rude
➤ Antonyms
careful, cautious, polite, prudent, reserved, respectful, thoughtful, timid, uncertain

brass noun Informal = **nerve** (informal), audacity, brass neck (Brit. informal), cheek, chutzpah (U.S. & Canad. informal), effrontery, face (informal), front, gall, impertinence, impudence, insolence, neck (informal), presumption, rudeness, sassiness (U.S. informal)

brassy adjective **1** = **brazen**, barefaced, bold, brash, forward, impudent, insolent, loud-mouthed, pert, pushy (informal), saucy **2** = **flashy**, blatant, garish, gaudy, hard, jazzy (informal), loud, obtrusive, showy, vulgar **3** = **strident**, blaring, cacophonous, dissonant, grating, harsh, jangling, jarring, loud, noisy, piercing, raucous, shrill
➤ Antonyms
≠flashy: discreet, low-key, modest, played down, quiet, restrained, subdued, toned down, understated

bravado noun = **swagger**, bluster, boast, boastfulness, boasting, bombast, brag, braggadocio, fanfaronade (rare), swaggering, swashbuckling, vaunting

brave adjective **1** = **courageous**, ballsy (taboo slang), bold, daring, dauntless, fearless, gallant, gritty, heroic, intrepid, plucky, resolute, undaunted, valiant, valorous ◆ verb **2** = **confront**, bear, beard, challenge, dare, defy, endure, face, face the music, go

through the mill, stand up to, suffer, tackle, walk into the lion's den, withstand
➤ Antonyms
adjective ≠**courageous**: afraid, cowardly, craven, faint-hearted, fearful, frightened, scared, shrinking, timid ◆ verb ≠**confront**: give in to, retreat from, surrender to

bravery noun = **courage**, balls (taboo slang), ballsiness (taboo slang), boldness, bravura, daring, dauntlessness, doughtiness, fearlessness, fortitude, gallantry, grit, guts (informal), hardihood, hardiness, heroism, indomitability, intrepidity, mettle, pluck, pluckiness, spirit, spunk (informal), valour
➤ Antonyms
cowardice, faint-heartedness, fearfulness, fright, timidity

bravo noun = **hired killer**, assassin, bandit, brigand, cut-throat, desperado, murderer, villain

bravura noun = **brilliance**, animation, audacity, boldness, brio, daring, dash, display, élan, energy, exhibitionism, ostentation, panache, punch (informal), spirit, verve, vigour, virtuosity

brawl noun **1** = **fight**, affray (Law), altercation, argument, bagarre, battle, broil, clash, disorder, dispute, donnybrook, fracas, fray, free-for-all (informal), melee or mêlée, punch-up (Brit. informal), quarrel, row (informal), ruckus (informal), rumpus, scrap (informal), scrimmage, scuffle, shindig (informal), shindy (informal), skirmish, squabble, tumult, uproar, wrangle ◆ verb **2** = **fight**, altercate, argue, battle, dispute, fight like Kilkenny cats, go at it hammer and tongs, quarrel, row (informal), scrap (informal), scuffle, tussle, wrangle, wrestle

brawn noun = **muscle**, beef (informal), beefiness (informal), brawniness, flesh, might, muscles, muscularity, power, robustness, strength, vigour

brawny adjective = **muscular**, athletic, beefy (informal), bulky, burly, fleshy, hardy, hefty (informal), herculean, husky (informal), lusty, powerful, robust, sinewy, stalwart, strapping, strong, sturdy, thewy, thickset, vigorous, well-built, well-knit
➤ Antonyms
frail, scrawny, skinny, thin, undeveloped, weak, weakly, weedy (informal), wimpish or wimpy (informal), wussy (slang)

bray verb **1** = **heehaw**, bell, bellow, blare, hoot, roar, screech, trumpet ◆ noun **2** = **heehaw**, bawl, bell, bellow, blare, cry, harsh sound, hoot, roar, screech, shout

brazen adjective **1** = **bold**, audacious, barefaced, brash, brassy (informal), defiant, forward, immodest, impudent, insolent, pert, pushy (informal), saucy, shameless,

unabashed, unashamed **2** = **brassy**, brass, bronze, metallic ♦ *verb* **3 brazen it out** = be unashamed, be impenitent, confront, defy, outface, outstare, persevere
➤ **Antonyms**
adjective ≠**bold**: cautious, decorous, diffident, mannerly, modest, reserved, respectful, reticent, secret, shy, stealthy, timid

breach *noun* **1** = **nonobservance**, contravention, disobedience, infraction, infringement, noncompliance, offence, transgression, trespass, violation **2** = **disagreement**, alienation, difference, disaffection, dissension, division, estrangement, falling-out (*informal*), parting of the ways, quarrel, schism, separation, severance, variance **3** = **crack**, aperture, break, chasm, cleft, fissure, gap, hole, opening, rent, rift, rupture, split
➤ **Antonyms**
≠**nonobservance**: adherence to, attention, compliance, discharge, fulfilment, heeding, honouring, observation, performance

bread *noun* **1** = **food**, aliment, diet, fare, necessities, nourishment, nutriment, provisions, subsistence, sustenance, viands, victuals **2** *Slang* = **money**, ackers (*slang*), brass (*Northern English dialect*), cash, dibs (*slang*), dosh (*Brit. & Austral. slang*), dough (*slang*), finance, funds, necessary (*informal*), needful (*informal*), rhino (*Brit. slang*), shekels (*informal*), silver, spondulicks (*slang*), tin (*slang*)

breadth *noun* **1** = **width**, beam (*of a ship*), broadness, latitude, span, spread, wideness **2** = **extent**, amplitude, area, compass, comprehensiveness, dimension, expanse, extensiveness, magnitude, measure, range, reach, scale, scope, size, space, spread, sweep, vastness **3** = **broad-mindedness**, freedom, latitude, liberality, open-mindedness, openness, permissiveness

break *verb* **1** = **separate**, batter, burst, crack, crash, demolish, destroy, disintegrate, divide, fracture, fragment, part, rend, sever, shatter, shiver, smash, snap, splinter, split, tear, total (*slang*), trash (*slang*) **2** = **disobey**, breach, contravene, disregard, infract (*Law*), infringe, renege on, transgress, violate **3** = **reveal**, announce, come out, come out in the wash, disclose, divulge, impart, inform, let out, make public, proclaim, tell **4** = **stop**, abandon, cut, discontinue, give up, interrupt, pause, rest, suspend **5** = **weaken**, cow, cripple, demoralize, dispirit, enervate, enfeeble, impair, incapacitate, subdue, tame, undermine **6** *Of a record, etc.* = **beat**, better, cap (*informal*), exceed, excel, go beyond, outdo, outstrip, surpass, top **7** = **reduce**, cushion, diminish, lessen, lighten, moderate, soften, weaken **8** = **ruin**,

bankrupt, bust (*informal*), degrade, demote, discharge, dismiss, humiliate, impoverish, make bankrupt, reduce **9** = **happen**, appear, burst out, come forth suddenly, emerge, erupt, occur ♦ *noun* **10** = **division**, breach, cleft, crack, fissure, fracture, gap, gash, hole, opening, rent, rift, rupture, split, tear **11** = **breach**, alienation, disaffection, dispute, divergence, estrangement, rift, rupture, schism, separation, split **12** = **rest**, breather (*informal*), breathing space, entr'acte, halt, hiatus, interlude, intermission, interruption, interval, let-up (*informal*), lull, pause, recess, respite, suspension **13** *Informal* = **stroke of luck**, advantage, chance, fortune, opening, opportunity
➤ **Antonyms**
verb ≠**separate**: attach, bind, connect, fasten, join, repair, unite ≠**disobey**: abide by, adhere to, conform, discharge, follow, obey, observe

breakable *adjective* = **fragile**, brittle, crumbly, delicate, flimsy, frail, frangible, friable
➤ **Antonyms**
durable, indestructible, lasting, nonbreakable, resistant, rugged, shatterproof, solid, strong, toughened, unbreakable

break away *verb* **1** = **flee**, decamp, escape, fly, hook it (*slang*), make a break for it, make a run for it (*informal*), make off, run away **2** = **break with**, detach, part company, secede, separate

breakdown *noun* **1** = **collapse**, crackup (*informal*), disintegration, disruption, failure, mishap, stoppage **2** = **analysis**, categorization, classification, detailed list, diagnosis, dissection, itemization

break down *verb* **1** = **collapse**, come unstuck, conk out (*informal*), fail, go kaput (*informal*), go phut, seize up, stop, stop working **2** = **be overcome**, crack up (*informal*), go to pieces

breaker *noun* = **wave**, billow, comber, roller, whitecap, white horse

break-in *noun* = **burglary**, breaking and entering, invasion, robbery

break in *verb* **1** = **burgle**, break and enter, invade, rob **2** = **interrupt**, barge in, burst in, butt in, interfere, interject, interpose, intervene, intrude, put one's oar in, put one's two cents in (*U.S. slang*) **3** = **get used to**, accustom, condition, habituate, initiate, prepare, tame, train

break into *verb* = **begin**, burst into, burst out, commence, dissolve into, give way to, launch into

break off *verb* **1** = **detach**, divide, part, pull off, separate, sever, snap off, splinter **2**

= **stop**, belay (*Nautical*), cease, desist, discontinue, end, finish, halt, pause, pull the plug on, suspend, terminate

break out *verb* **1** = **begin**, appear, arise, commence, emerge, happen, occur, set in, spring up, start **2** = **escape**, abscond, bolt, break loose, burst out, flee, get free **3** = **erupt**, burst out

breakthrough *noun* = **development**, advance, discovery, find, finding, gain, improvement, invention, leap, progress, quantum leap, step forward

break-up *noun* = **separation**, breakdown, breaking, crackup (*informal*), disintegration, dispersal, dissolution, divorce, ending, parting, rift, split, splitting, termination, wind-up

break up *verb* **1** = **separate**, dissolve, divide, divorce, end, part, scatter, sever, split **2** = **stop**, adjourn, disband, dismantle, disperse, disrupt, end, suspend, terminate

breakwater *noun* = **sea wall**, groyne, jetty, mole, spur

breast *noun* **1** = **bosom**, boob (*slang*), bust, chest, front, teat, thorax, tit (*slang*), udder **2** = **heart**, being, conscience, core, emotions, feelings, seat of the affections, sentiments, soul, thoughts

breath *noun* **1** = **respiration**, air, animation, breathing, exhalation, gasp, gulp, inhalation, pant, wheeze **2** = **odour**, aroma, niff (*Brit. slang*), smell, vapour, whiff **3** = **gust**, faint breeze, flutter, puff, sigh, slight movement, waft, zephyr **4** = **rest**, break, breather, breathing-space, instant, moment, pause, respite, second **5** = **suggestion**, hint, murmur, suspicion, undertone, whisper **6** = **life**, animation, energy, existence, lifeblood, life force, vitality

breathe *verb* **1** = **inhale and exhale**, draw in, gasp, gulp, pant, puff, respire, wheeze **2** = **instil**, imbue, impart, infuse, inject, inspire, transfuse **3** = **whisper**, articulate, express, murmur, say, sigh, utter, voice

breather *noun Informal* = **rest**, break, breathing space, breath of air, halt, pause, recess, respite

breathless *adjective* **1** = **out of breath**, choking, exhausted, gasping, gulping, out of whack (*informal*), panting, short-winded, spent, wheezing, winded **2** = **excited**, agog, anxious, astounded, avid, eager, flabbergasted (*informal*), gobsmacked (*Brit. slang*), on tenterhooks, open-mouthed, thunderstruck, with bated breath

breathtaking *adjective* = **amazing**, astonishing, awe-inspiring, awesome, brilliant, dramatic, exciting, heart-stirring, impressive, jaw-dropping, magnificent, moving, overwhelming, sensational, striking,

stunning (*informal*), thrilling, wondrous (*archaic or literary*)

breed *verb* **1** = **reproduce**, bear, beget, bring forth, engender, generate, hatch, multiply, originate, procreate, produce, propagate **2** = **bring up**, cultivate, develop, discipline, educate, foster, instruct, nourish, nurture, raise, rear **3** = **produce**, arouse, bring about, cause, create, generate, give rise to, induce, make, occasion, originate, stir up ◆ *noun* **4** = **variety**, pedigree, race, species, stock, strain, type **5** = **kind**, brand, sort, stamp, type, variety **6** = **lineage**, class, extraction, family, ilk, line, pedigree, race, stock

breeding *noun* **1** = **upbringing**, ancestry, cultivation, development, lineage, nurture, raising, rearing, reproduction, training **2** = **refinement**, civility, conduct, courtesy, cultivation, culture, gentility, manners, polish, sophistication, urbanity

breeze *noun* **1** = **light wind**, air, breath of wind, capful of wind, current of air, draught, flurry, gust, puff of air, waft, whiff, zephyr ◆ *verb* **2** = **move briskly**, flit, glide, hurry, pass, sail, sally, sweep, trip

breezy *adjective* **1** = **windy**, airy, blowing, blowy, blusterous, blustery, fresh, gusty, squally **2** = **carefree**, airy, animated, blithe, buoyant, casual, cheerful, chirpy (*informal*), debonair, easy-going, free and easy, full of beans (*informal*), genial, informal, jaunty, light, light-hearted, lively, sparkling, sparky, spirited, sprightly, sunny, upbeat (*informal*), vivacious
➤ **Antonyms**
≠**windy**: calm, heavy, oppressive, windless
≠**carefree**: calm, depressed, dull, heavy, lifeless, mournful, sad, serious

brevity *noun* **1** = **shortness**, briefness, ephemerality, impermanence, transience, transitoriness **2** = **conciseness**, concision, condensation, crispness, curtness, economy, pithiness, succinctness, terseness
➤ **Antonyms**
≠**conciseness**: diffuseness, discursiveness, long-windedness, prolixity, rambling, redundancy, tautology, tediousness, verbiage, verboseness, verbosity, wordiness

brew *verb* **1** = **make** (*beer*), boil, ferment, infuse (*tea*), prepare by fermentation, seethe, soak, steep, stew **2** = **develop**, breed, concoct, contrive, devise, excite, foment, form, gather, hatch, plan, plot, project, scheme, start, stir up ◆ *noun* **3** = **drink**, beverage, blend, concoction, distillation, fermentation, infusion, liquor, mixture, preparation

bribe *verb* **1** = **buy off**, corrupt, get at, grease the palm or hand of (*slang*), influence by gifts, lure, oil the palm of (*informal*), pay off (*informal*), reward, square, suborn ♦ *noun* **2 = inducement**, allurement, backhander (*slang*), boodle (*slang, chiefly U.S.*), corrupting gift, enticement, graft (*informal*), hush money (*slang*), incentive, kickback (*U.S.*), pay-off (*informal*), payola (*informal*), reward for treachery, sop, sweetener (*slang*)

bribery *noun* **= buying off**, corruption, graft (*informal*), inducement, palm-greasing (*slang*), payola (*informal*), protection, subornation

bric-a-brac *noun* **= knick-knacks**, baubles, bibelots, curios, gewgaws, kickshaws, objects of virtu, *objets d'art*, ornaments, trinkets

bridal *adjective* **= matrimonial**, bride's, conjugal, connubial, hymeneal, marital, marriage, nuptial, spousal, wedding

bridge *noun* **1 = arch**, flyover, overpass, span, viaduct **2 = link**, band, bond, connection, tie ♦ *verb* **3 = connect**, arch over, attach, bind, couple, cross, cross over, extend across, go over, join, link, reach across, span, traverse, unite
➤ **Antonyms**
verb ≠**connect**: cleave, come apart, disjoin, divide, keep apart, separate, sever, split, sunder, widen

bridle *noun* **1 = curb**, check, control, rein, restraint, trammels ♦ *verb* **2 = curb**, check, constrain, control, govern, have in one's pocket, keep a tight rein on, keep in check, keep on a string, master, moderate, rein, repress, restrain, subdue **3 = get angry**, be indignant, bristle, draw (oneself) up, get one's back up, raise one's hackles, rear up

brief *adjective* **1 = short**, ephemeral, fast, fleeting, hasty, little, momentary, quick, quickie (*informal*), short-lived, swift, temporary, transitory **2 = curt**, abrupt, blunt, brusque, sharp, short, surly **3 = concise**, clipped, compendious, compressed, crisp, curt, laconic, limited, monosyllabic, pithy, short, succinct, terse, thumbnail, to the point ♦ *noun* **4 = summary**, abridgment, abstract, digest, epitome, outline, précis, sketch, synopsis **5 = case**, argument, contention, data, defence, demonstration ♦ *verb* **6 = inform**, advise, clue in (*informal*), explain, fill in (*informal*), gen up (*Brit. informal*), give (someone) a rundown, give (someone) the gen (*Brit. informal*), instruct, keep posted, prepare, prime, put (someone) in the picture (*informal*)
➤ **Antonyms**
adjective ≠**short**: extensive, lengthy, long, protracted ≠**concise**: circuitous, detailed, diffuse, lengthy, long, long-drawn-out, long-winded

briefing *noun* **= instructions**, conference, directions, guidance, information,

instruction, meeting, preamble, preparation, priming, rundown

briefly *adverb* **= shortly**, abruptly, briskly, casually, concisely, cursorily, curtly, fleetingly, hastily, hurriedly, in a few words, in a nutshell, in brief, in outline, in passing, momentarily, precisely, quickly, temporarily

brigade *noun* **= group**, band, body, camp, company, contingent, corps, crew, force, organization, outfit, party, squad, team, troop, unit

brigand *noun* **= bandit**, desperado, footpad (*archaic*), freebooter, gangster, highwayman, marauder, outlaw, plunderer, robber, ruffian

bright *adjective* **1 = shining**, beaming, blazing, brilliant, dazzling, effulgent, flashing, gleaming, glistening, glittering, glowing, illuminated, intense, lambent, luminous, lustrous, radiant, resplendent, scintillating, shimmering, sparkling, twinkling, vivid **2 = promising**, auspicious, encouraging, excellent, favourable, golden, good, hopeful, optimistic, palmy, propitious, prosperous, rosy **3 = cheerful**, chirpy (*informal*), full of beans (*informal*), gay, genial, glad, happy, jolly, joyful, joyous, light-hearted, lively, merry, sparky, upbeat (*informal*), vivacious **4 = intelligent**, acute, astute, aware, brainy, brilliant, clear-headed, clever, ingenious, inventive, keen, quick, quick-witted, sharp, smart, wide-awake **5 = sunny**, clear, clement, cloudless, fair, limpid, lucid, pellucid, pleasant, translucent, transparent, unclouded
➤ **Antonyms**
≠**intelligent**: dense, dim, dim-witted (*informal*), dull, dumb (*informal*), dumb-ass (*slang*), foolish, idiotic, ignorant, retarded, simple, slow, stupid, thick, unintelligent, witless ≠**sunny**: cloudy, dark, dim, dusky, gloomy, grey, overcast, poorly lit

brighten *verb* **1 = light up**, clear up, enliven, gleam, glow, illuminate, lighten, make brighter, shine **2 = cheer up**, become cheerful, buck up (*informal*), buoy up, encourage, enliven, gladden, hearten, make happy, perk up
➤ **Antonyms**
≠**light up**: becloud, blacken, cloud over *or* up, dim, dull, obscure, overshadow, shade, shadow ≠**cheer up**: become angry, become gloomy, blacken, cloud, deject, depress, dispirit, look black, sadden

brightness *noun* **1 = shine**, brilliance, glare, incandescence, intensity, light, luminosity, radiance, vividness **2 = intelligence**, acuity, cleverness, quickness, sharpness, smartness
➤ **Antonyms**
≠**shine**: dimness, dullness

brilliance, brilliancy *noun* **1**
= **brightness**, blaze, dazzle, effulgence,
gleam, glitter, intensity, luminosity, lustre,
radiance, refulgence, resplendence, sheen,
sparkle, vividness **2** = **cleverness**, acuity,
aptitude, braininess, distinction, excellence,
genius, giftedness, greatness, inventiveness,
talent, wisdom **3** = **splendour**, éclat, gilt,
glamour, gorgeousness, grandeur,
illustriousness, magnificence, pizzazz *or*
pizazz (*informal*)
➤ Antonyms
≠**brightness**: darkness, dimness, dullness,
paleness ≠**cleverness**: folly, idiocy, inanity,
incompetence, ineptitude, silliness,
simple-mindedness, stupidity

brilliant *adjective* **1** = **shining**, ablaze,
bright, coruscating, dazzling, glittering,
glossy, intense, luminous, lustrous, radiant,
refulgent, resplendent, scintillating,
sparkling, vivid **2** = **splendid**, celebrated,
eminent, exceptional, famous, glorious,
illustrious, magnificent, notable, outstanding,
superb **3** = **intelligent**, accomplished, acute,
astute, brainy, clever, discerning, expert,
gifted, intellectual, inventive, masterly,
penetrating, profound, quick, talented
➤ Antonyms
≠**shining**: dark, dim, dull, gloomy
≠**splendid**: dull, ordinary, run-of-the-mill,
unaccomplished, unexceptional, untalented
≠**intelligent**: dim, simple, slow, stupid

brim *noun* **1** = **rim**, border, brink,
circumference, edge, flange, lip, margin,
skirt, verge ♦ *verb* **2** = **be full**, fill, fill up,
hold no more, overflow, run over, spill, well
over

brimful *adjective* = **full**, brimming, filled,
flush, level with, overflowing, overfull,
packed, running over

bring *verb* **1** = **take**, accompany, bear, carry,
conduct, convey, deliver, escort, fetch,
gather, guide, import, lead, transfer,
transport, usher **2** = **cause**, contribute to,
create, effect, engender, inflict, occasion,
produce, result in, wreak **3** = **make**, compel,
convince, dispose, force, induce, influence,
move, persuade, prevail on *or* upon,
prompt, sway **4** = **sell for**, command, earn,
fetch, gross, net, produce, return, yield

bring about *verb* = **cause**, accomplish,
achieve, bring to pass, compass, create,
effect, effectuate, generate, give rise to,
make happen, manage, occasion, produce,
realize

bring down *verb* **1** = **lower**, cut down,
drop, fell, floor, lay low, level, pull down,
shoot down, upset **2** = **overthrow**, abase,
overturn, reduce, undermine

bring in *verb* = **produce**, accrue, bear, be
worth, fetch, generate, gross, net, profit,

realize, return, yield

bring off *verb* = **accomplish**, achieve, bring
home the bacon (*informal*), bring to pass,
carry off, carry out, crack it (*informal*), cut it
(*informal*), discharge, execute, perform, pull
off, succeed

bring up *verb* **1** = **rear**, breed, develop,
educate, form, nurture, raise, support, teach,
train **2** = **mention**, advance, allude to,
broach, introduce, move, propose, put
forward, raise, submit

brink *noun* = **edge**, border, boundary, brim,
fringe, frontier, limit, lip, margin, point, rim,
skirt, threshold, verge

brisk *adjective* **1** = **lively**, active, agile, alert,
animated, bustling, busy, energetic, nimble,
no-nonsense, quick, sparky, speedy,
sprightly, spry, vigorous, vivacious **2**
= **invigorating**, biting, bracing, crisp,
exhilarating, fresh, keen, nippy, refreshing,
sharp, snappy, stimulating
➤ Antonyms
≠**lively**: heavy, lazy, lethargic, slow, sluggish,
unenergetic ≠**invigorating**: boring, dull,
enervating, tiring, wearisome

briskly *adverb* = **quickly**, actively, apace,
brusquely, coolly, decisively, efficiently,
energetically, firmly, incisively, nimbly, pdq
(*slang*), posthaste, promptly, pronto
(*informal*), rapidly, readily, smartly,
vigorously

bristle *noun* **1** = **hair**, barb, prickle, spine,
stubble, thorn, whisker ♦ *verb* **2** = **stand up**,
horripilate, prickle, rise, stand on end **3** = **be
angry**, be infuriated, be maddened, bridle,
flare up, get one's dander up (*slang*), go
ballistic (*slang, chiefly U.S.*), rage, see red,
seethe, spit (*informal*), wig out (*slang*) **4**
= **be thick**, abound, be alive, crawl, hum,
swarm, teem

bristly *adjective* = **hairy**, bearded,
bewhiskered, prickly, rough, stubbly,
unshaven, whiskered

brittle *adjective* **1** = **fragile**, breakable, crisp,
crumbling, crumbly, delicate, frail, frangible,
friable, shatterable, shivery **2** = **tense**, curt,
edgy, irritable, nervous, prim, stiff, stilted,
wired (*slang*)
➤ Antonyms
≠**fragile**: durable, elastic, flexible,
infrangible, nonbreakable, resistant, rugged,
shatterproof, strong, sturdy, toughened

broach *verb* **1** = **bring up**, approach, hint
at, introduce, mention, open up, propose,
raise the subject, speak of, suggest, talk of,
touch on **2** = **open**, crack, draw off, pierce,
puncture, start, tap, uncork

broad *adjective* **1** = **wide**, ample, beamy (*of
a ship*), capacious, expansive, extensive,
generous, large, roomy, spacious, vast,

voluminous, widespread **2 = general**, all-embracing, catholic, comprehensive, encyclopedic, far-reaching, global, inclusive, nonspecific, overarching, sweeping, undetailed, universal, unlimited, wide, wide-ranging **3** As in **broad daylight = clear**, full, obvious, open, plain, straightforward, undisguised **4 = tolerant**, broad-minded, liberal, open, open-minded, permissive, progressive, unbiased **5 = vulgar**, blue, coarse, gross, improper, indecent, indelicate, near the knuckle (*informal*), unrefined
➤ **Antonyms**
≠**wide**: close, confined, constricted, cramped, limited, meagre, narrow, restricted, tight

broadcast *noun* **1 = transmission**, programme, show, telecast ◆ *verb* **2 = transmit**, air, beam, cable, put on the air, radio, relay, show, televise **3 = make public**, advertise, announce, circulate, disseminate, proclaim, promulgate, publish, report, shout from the rooftops (*informal*), spread

broaden *verb* **= expand**, augment, develop, enlarge, extend, fatten, increase, open up, spread, stretch, supplement, swell, widen
➤ **Antonyms**
circumscribe, constrain, diminish, narrow, reduce, restrict, tighten

broad-minded *adjective* **= tolerant**, catholic, cosmopolitan, dispassionate, flexible, free-thinking, indulgent, liberal, open-minded, permissive, responsive, unbiased, unbigoted, undogmatic, unprejudiced
➤ **Antonyms**
biased, bigoted, closed-minded, dogmatic, inflexible, intolerant, narrow-minded, prejudiced, uncharitable

broadside *noun* **= attack**, abuse, assault, battering, bombardment, censure, criticism, denunciation, diatribe, philippic, stick (*slang*), swipe

brochure *noun* **= booklet**, advertisement, circular, folder, handbill, hand-out, leaflet, mailshot, pamphlet

broke *adjective Informal* **= penniless**, bankrupt, bust (*informal*), cleaned out (*slang*), dirt-poor (*informal*), down and out, flat broke (*informal*), impoverished, in queer street, insolvent, in the red, on one's uppers, penurious, ruined, short, skint (*Brit. slang*), stony-broke (*Brit. slang*), strapped for cash (*informal*), without a penny to one's name, without two pennies to rub together (*informal*)
➤ **Antonyms**
affluent, comfortable, flush (*informal*), in the money (*informal*), prosperous, rich, solvent, wealthy, well-to-do

broken *adjective* **1 = smashed**, burst, demolished, destroyed, fractured, fragmented, rent, ruptured, separated, severed, shattered, shivered **2 = interrupted**, disconnected, discontinuous, disturbed, erratic, fragmentary, incomplete, intermittent, spasmodic **3 = not working**, defective, imperfect, kaput (*informal*), not functioning, on its last legs, on the blink (*slang*), out of order, ruined **4 = violated**, dishonoured, disobeyed, disregarded, forgotten, ignored, infringed, isolated, not kept, retracted, traduced, transgressed **5 = imperfect**, disjointed, halting, hesitating, stammering **6 = defeated**, beaten, browbeaten, crippled, crushed, demoralized, humbled, oppressed, overpowered, subdued, tamed, vanquished

broken-down *adjective* **= not in working order**, collapsed, dilapidated, in disrepair, inoperative, kaput (*informal*), not functioning, old, on the blink (*slang*), on the fritz (*U.S. slang*), out of commission, out of order, worn out

brokenhearted *adjective* **= heartbroken**, choked, crestfallen, desolate, despairing, devastated, disappointed, disconsolate, down in the dumps (*informal*), grief-stricken, heart-sick, inconsolable, miserable, mournful, prostrated, sorrowful, wretched

broker *noun* **= dealer**, agent, factor, go-between, intermediary, middleman, negotiator

bronze *adjective* **= reddish-brown**, brownish, chestnut, copper, copper-coloured, metallic brown, reddish-tan, rust, tan, yellowish-brown

brood *noun* **1 = offspring**, breed, chicks, children, clutch, family, hatch, infants, issue, litter, progeny, young ◆ *verb* **2 = incubate**, cover, hatch, set, sit upon **3 = think upon**, agonize, dwell upon, eat one's heart out, fret, have a long face, meditate, mope, mull over, muse, obsess, ponder, repine, ruminate

brook *noun* **= stream**, beck, burn, gill (*dialect*), rill, rivulet, runnel (*literary*), streamlet, watercourse

brothel *noun* **= whorehouse**, bagnio, bawdy house (*archaic*), bordello, cathouse (*U.S. slang*), house of ill fame, house of ill repute, house of prostitution, knocking shop (*slang*), red-light district, stews (*archaic*)

brother *noun* **1 = sibling**, blood brother, kin, kinsman, relation, relative **2 = comrade**, associate, chum (*informal*), cock (*Brit. informal*), colleague, companion, compeer, confrère, fellow member, mate, pal (*informal*), partner **3 = monk**, cleric, friar, regular, religious

brotherhood *noun* **1** = **fellowship**, brotherliness, camaraderie, companionship, comradeship, friendliness, kinship **2** = **association**, alliance, clan, clique, community, coterie, fraternity, guild, league, order, society, union

brotherly *adjective* = **kind**, affectionate, altruistic, amicable, benevolent, cordial, fraternal, friendly, neighbourly, philanthropic, sympathetic

brow *noun* **1** = **forehead**, air, appearance, aspect, bearing, countenance, eyebrow, face, front, mien, temple **2** = **top**, brim, brink, crest, crown, edge, peak, rim, summit, tip, verge

browbeat *verb* = **bully**, badger, bulldoze (*informal*), coerce, cow, domineer, dragoon, hector, intimidate, lord it over, oppress, overawe, overbear, ride roughshod over, threaten, tyrannize
➤ **Antonyms**
beguile, cajole, coax, entice, flatter, inveigle, lure, manoeuvre, seduce, sweet-talk (*informal*), tempt, wheedle

brown *adjective* **1** = **brunette**, auburn, bay, brick, bronze, bronzed, browned, chestnut, chocolate, coffee, dark, donkey brown, dun, dusky, fuscous, ginger, hazel, rust, sunburnt, tan, tanned, tawny, toasted, umber ♦ *verb* **2** = **fry**, cook, grill, sauté, seal, sear

browned off *adjective* = **fed up**, cheesed off (*Brit. slang*), discontented, discouraged, disgruntled, disheartened, pissed off (*taboo slang*), sick as a parrot (*informal*), weary

brown study *noun* = **preoccupation**, absorption, abstractedness, abstraction, contemplation, meditation, musing, reflection, reverie, rumination

browse *verb* **1** = **skim**, dip into, examine cursorily, flip through, glance at, leaf through, look round, look through, peruse, scan, survey **2** = **graze**, crop, eat, feed, nibble, pasture

bruise *verb* **1** = **discolour**, blacken, blemish, contuse, crush, damage, deface, injure, mar, mark, pound, pulverize **2** = **hurt**, displease, grieve, injure, insult, offend, pain, sting, wound ♦ *noun* **3** = **discoloration**, black-and-blue mark, black mark, blemish, contusion, injury, mark, swelling, trauma (*Pathology*)

brunt *noun* = **full force**, burden, force, impact, pressure, shock, strain, stress, thrust, violence

brush[1] *noun* **1** = **broom**, besom, sweeper **2** = **encounter**, clash, conflict, confrontation, fight, fracas, scrap (*informal*), set-to (*informal*), skirmish, slight engagement, spot of bother (*informal*), tussle ♦ *verb* **3** = **clean**, buff, paint, polish, sweep, wash **4**

= **touch**, caress, contact, flick, glance, graze, kiss, scrape, stroke, sweep

brush[2] *noun* = **shrubs**, brushwood, bushes, copse, scrub, thicket, undergrowth, underwood

brush aside *verb* = **dismiss**, discount, disregard, have no time for, ignore, kiss off (*slang, chiefly U.S. & Canad.*), override, sweep aside

brush-off *noun Slang* = **snub**, bum's rush (*slang*), cold shoulder, cut, dismissal, go-by (*slang*), kick in the teeth (*slang*), kiss-off (*slang, chiefly U.S. & Canad.*), knock-back (*slang*), rebuff, refusal, rejection, repudiation, repulse, slight, the (old) heave-ho (*informal*)

brush off *verb Slang* = **ignore**, blank (*slang*), cold-shoulder, cut, deny, disdain, dismiss, disown, disregard, kiss off (*slang, chiefly U.S. & Canad.*), put down, rebuff, refuse, reject, repudiate, scorn, send to Coventry, slight, snub, spurn

brush up *verb* = **revise**, bone up (*informal*), cram, go over, polish up, read up, refresh one's memory, relearn, study

brusque *adjective* = **curt**, abrupt, blunt, discourteous, gruff, hasty, impolite, monosyllabic, sharp, short, surly, tart, terse, unmannerly
➤ **Antonyms**
accommodating, civil, courteous, gentle, patient, polite, well-mannered

brutal *adjective* **1** = **cruel**, barbarous, bloodthirsty, ferocious, heartless, inhuman, merciless, pitiless, remorseless, ruthless, savage, uncivilized, vicious **2** = **harsh**, bearish, callous, gruff, impolite, insensitive, rough, rude, severe, uncivil, unfeeling, unmannerly **3** = **bestial**, animal, beastly, brute, brutish, carnal, coarse, crude, sensual
➤ **Antonyms**
≠**cruel**: civilized, gentle, humane, kind, merciful, soft-hearted ≠**harsh**: polite, refined, sensitive

brutality *noun* = **cruelty**, atrocity, barbarism, bloodthirstiness, ferocity, inhumanity, ruthlessness, savagery, viciousness

brutally *adverb* = **cruelly**, barbarically, barbarously, brutishly, callously, ferociously, fiercely, hardheartedly, heartlessly, in cold blood, inhumanly, meanly, mercilessly, murderously, pitilessly, remorselessly, ruthlessly, savagely, unkindly, viciously

brute *noun* **1** = **savage**, barbarian, beast, devil, fiend, ghoul, monster, ogre, sadist, swine **2** = **animal**, beast, creature, wild animal ♦ *adjective* **3** = **mindless**, bodily, carnal, fleshly, instinctive, physical, senseless, unthinking **4** = **coarse**, animal, bestial, depraved, gross, sensual

bubble noun 1 = air ball, bead, blister, blob, drop, droplet, globule, vesicle ♦ verb 2 = foam, boil, effervesce, fizz, froth, percolate, seethe, sparkle 3 = gurgle, babble, burble, murmur, purl, ripple, trickle, trill

bubbly adjective 1 = lively, alive and kicking, animated, bouncy, elated, excited, full of beans (informal), happy, merry, sparky 2 = frothy, carbonated, curly, effervescent, fizzy, foamy, lathery, sparkling, sudsy

buccaneer noun = pirate, corsair, freebooter, privateer, sea-rover

buckle noun 1 = fastener, catch, clasp, clip, hasp 2 = distortion, bulge, contortion, kink, warp ♦ verb 3 = fasten, catch, clasp, close, hook, secure 4 = distort, bend, bulge, cave in, collapse, contort, crumple, fold, twist, warp

buckle down verb Informal = apply oneself, exert oneself, launch into, pitch in, put one's shoulder to the wheel, set to

buck up verb 1 = cheer up, brighten, encourage, hearten, inspirit, perk up, rally, take heart 2 Informal = hurry up, get a move on, hasten, shake a leg, speed up

bucolic adjective = rustic, agrarian, agrestic, agricultural, country, pastoral, rural

bud noun 1 = shoot, embryo, germ, sprout ♦ verb 2 = develop, burgeon, burst forth, grow, pullulate, shoot, sprout

budding adjective = developing, beginning, burgeoning, embryonic, fledgling, flowering, germinal, growing, incipient, nascent, potential, promising

budge verb 1 = move, dislodge, give way, inch, propel, push, remove, roll, shift, slide, stir 2 = change, bend, convince, give way, influence, persuade, sway, yield

budget noun 1 = allowance, allocation, cost, finances, financial statement, fiscal estimate, funds, means, resources ♦ verb 2 = plan, allocate, apportion, cost, cost out, estimate, ration

buff[1] adjective 1 = yellowish-brown, sandy, straw, tan, yellowish ♦ noun 2 in the buff = naked, bare, buck naked (slang), in one's birthday suit (informal), in the altogether (informal), in the bare scud (slang), in the raw (informal), nude, scuddy (slang), unclad, unclothed, with bare skin, without a stitch on (informal) ♦ verb 3 = polish, brush, burnish, rub, shine, smooth

buff[2] noun Informal = expert, addict, admirer, aficionado, connoisseur, devotee, enthusiast, fan, fiend (informal), freak (informal), grandmaster, hotshot (informal),

maven (U.S.), whizz (informal)

buffer noun = safeguard, bulwark, bumper, cushion, fender, intermediary, screen, shield, shock absorber

buffet[1] noun = snack bar, brasserie, café, cafeteria, cold table, counter, cupboard, refreshment counter, salad bar, sideboard, smorgasbord

buffet[2] verb 1 = batter, bang, beat, box, bump, clobber (slang), cuff, flail, knock, lambast(e), pound, pummel, punch, push, rap, shove, slap, strike, thump, wallop (informal) ♦ noun 2 = blow, bang, box, bump, cuff, jolt, knock, push, rap, shove, slap, smack, thump, wallop (informal)

buffoon noun = clown, comedian, comic, droll, fool, harlequin, jester, joculator or (fem.) joculatrix, joker, merry-andrew, silly billy (informal), wag

bug noun 1 Informal = illness, disease, infection, lurgy (informal), virus 2 Informal = mania, craze, fad, obsession, rage 3 = fault, blemish, catch, defect, error, failing, flaw, glitch, gremlin, imperfection, snarl-up (informal, chiefly Brit.), virus ♦ verb 4 Informal = annoy, aggravate (informal), badger, be on one's back (slang), bother, disturb, gall, get in one's hair (informal), get on one's nerves (informal), get on one's wick (Brit. slang), get under one's skin (informal), get up one's nose (informal), harass, hassle (informal), irk, irritate, nark (Brit., Austral. & N.Z. slang), needle (informal), nettle, pester, piss one off (taboo slang), plague, vex 5 = tap, eavesdrop, listen in, spy, wiretap

bugbear noun = pet hate, anathema, bane, bête noire, bogey, bogeyman, bugaboo, devil, dread, fiend, horror, nightmare

build verb 1 = construct, assemble, erect, fabricate, form, make, put up, raise 2 = establish, base, begin, constitute, formulate, found, inaugurate, initiate, institute, originate, set up, start 3 = increase, accelerate, amplify, augment, develop, enlarge, escalate, extend, improve, intensify, strengthen ♦ noun 4 = physique, body, figure, form, frame, shape, structure
➤ **Antonyms**
verb ≠construct: demolish, dismantle, tear down ≠establish: end, finish, relinquish, suspend ≠increase: decline, decrease, impair, lower, reduce, weaken

building noun 1 = structure, domicile, dwelling, edifice, fabric, house, pile 2 = construction, architecture, erection, fabricating, raising

build-up noun 1 = increase, accumulation, development, enlargement, escalation, expansion, gain, growth 2 = accumulation, accretion, heap, load, mass, rick, stack, stockpile, store **3** = **hype**, ballyhoo (*informal*), plug (*informal*), promotion, publicity, puff

built-in *adjective* = **integral**, essential, immanent, implicit, in-built, included, incorporated, inherent, inseparable, part and parcel of

bulbous *adjective* = **bulging**, bloated, convex, rounded, swelling, swollen

bulge *noun* **1** = **swelling**, bump, hump, lump, projection, protrusion, protuberance **2** = **increase**, boost, intensification, rise, surge ♦ *verb* **3** = **swell out**, bag, dilate, distend, enlarge, expand, project, protrude, puff out, sag, stand out, stick out, swell
➤ **Antonyms**
noun ≠ **swelling**: bowl, cave, cavity, concavity, crater, dent, depression, hole, hollow, indentation, pit, trough

bulk *noun* **1** = **size**, amplitude, bigness, dimensions, immensity, largeness, magnitude, massiveness, substance, volume, weight **2** = **main part**, better part, body, generality, lion's share, majority, major part, mass, most, nearly all, plurality, preponderance ♦ *verb* **3 bulk large** = **be important**, carry weight, dominate, loom, loom large, preponderate, stand out, threaten

bulky *adjective* = **large**, big, colossal, cumbersome, elephantine, enormous, ginormous (*informal*), heavy, huge, hulking, humongous *or* humungous (*U.S. slang*), immense, mammoth, massive, massy, mega (*slang*), ponderous, substantial, unmanageable, unwieldy, very large, voluminous, weighty
➤ **Antonyms**
convenient, handy, manageable, neat, slim, small

bulldoze *verb* **1** = **demolish**, flatten, level, raze **2** *Informal* = **force**, browbeat, bully, coerce, cow, dragoon, hector, intimidate, put the screws on, railroad (*informal*) **3** = **push**, drive, force, propel, shove, thrust

bullet *noun* = **projectile**, ball, missile, pellet, shot, slug

bulletin *noun* = **announcement**, account, communication, communiqué, dispatch, message, news flash, notification, report, statement

bull-headed *adjective* = **stubborn**, headstrong, inflexible, mulish, obstinate, pig-headed, stiff-necked, stupid, tenacious, uncompromising, unyielding, wilful

bully *noun* **1** = **persecutor**, big bully, browbeater, bully boy, coercer, intimidator, oppressor, ruffian, tormentor, tough ♦ *verb* **2** = **persecute**, bluster, browbeat, bulldoze

(*informal*), bullyrag, coerce, cow, domineer, hector, intimidate, oppress, overbear, push around (*slang*), ride roughshod over, swagger, terrorize, tyrannize ♦ *interjection* **3** As in **bully for you, him,** *etc.* = **well done**, bravo, capital, good, grand, great

bulwark *noun* **1** = **fortification**, bastion, buttress, defence, embankment, outwork, partition, rampart, redoubt **2** = **defence**, buffer, guard, mainstay, safeguard, security, support

bumbling *adjective* = **clumsy**, awkward, blundering, botching, bungling, incompetent, inefficient, inept, lumbering, maladroit, muddled
➤ **Antonyms**
able, capable, competent, efficient, fit

bump *verb* **1** = **knock**, bang, collide (with), crash, hit, slam, smash into, strike **2** = **jerk**, bounce, jar, jolt, jostle, jounce, rattle, shake **3** = **move**, budge, dislodge, displace, remove, shift ♦ *noun* **4** = **knock**, bang, blow, collision, crash, hit, impact, jar, jolt, rap, shock, smash, thud, thump **5** = **lump**, bulge, contusion, hump, knob, knot, node, nodule, protuberance, swelling

bumper *adjective* = **exceptional**, abundant, bountiful, excellent, jumbo (*informal*), massive, mega (*slang*), prodigal, spanking (*informal*), teeming, unusual, whacking (*informal, chiefly Brit.*), whopping (*informal*)

bump into *verb* *Informal* = **meet**, chance upon, come across, encounter, happen upon, light upon, meet up with, run across, run into

bumpkin *noun* = **yokel**, boor, clodhopper, clown, country bumpkin, hayseed (*U.S. & Canad. informal*), hick (*informal, chiefly U.S. & Canad.*), hillbilly, lout, lubber, oaf, peasant, rustic

bump off *verb* *Slang* = **murder**, assassinate, blow away (*slang, chiefly U.S.*), dispatch, do away with, do in (*slang*), eliminate, finish off, kill, knock off (*slang*), liquidate, remove, rub out (*U.S. slang*), take out (*slang*), wipe out (*informal*)

bumptious *adjective* = **cocky**, arrogant, boastful, brash, conceited, egotistic, forward, full of oneself, impudent, overbearing, overconfident, presumptuous, pushy (*informal*), self-assertive, showy, swaggering, vainglorious, vaunting

bumpy *adjective* = **rough**, bone-breaking, bouncy, choppy, irregular, jarring, jerky, jolting, jolty, knobby, lumpy, pitted, potholed, rutted, uneven

bunch *noun* **1** = **number**, assortment, batch, bouquet, bundle, clump, cluster, collection, heap, lot, mass, parcel, pile, quantity, rick, sheaf, spray, stack, tuft **2** = **group**, band, bevy, crew (*informal*), crowd, flock, gang, gathering, knot, mob, multitude, party, posse (*informal*), swarm, team, troop ♦ *verb* **3 = group**, assemble, bundle, cluster, collect, congregate, cram together, crowd, flock, herd, huddle, mass, pack

bundle *noun* **1 = bunch**, accumulation, assortment, batch, collection, group, heap, mass, pile, quantity, rick, stack **2 = package**, bag, bale, box, carton, crate, pack, packet, pallet, parcel, roll ♦ *verb* **3 = package**, bale, bind, fasten, pack, palletize, tie, tie together, tie up, truss, wrap **4** *with* **out, off, into,** *etc.* **= push**, hurry, hustle, rush, shove, throw, thrust

bundle up *verb* **= wrap up**, clothe warmly, muffle up, swathe

bungle *verb* **= mess up**, blow (*slang*), blunder, bodge (*informal*), botch, butcher, cock up (*Brit. slang*), drop a brick *or* clanger (*informal*), flub (*U.S. slang*), foul up, fuck up (*offensive taboo slang*), fudge, louse up (*slang*), make a mess of, make a nonsense of (*informal*), make a pig's ear of (*informal*), mar, miscalculate, mismanage, muff, ruin, screw up (*informal*), spoil
➤ **Antonyms**
accomplish, achieve, carry off, effect, fulfil, succeed, triumph

bungling *adjective* **= incompetent**, awkward, blundering, botching, cack-handed (*informal*), clumsy, ham-fisted (*informal*), ham-handed (*informal*), inept, maladroit, unskilful

bunk, bunkum *noun Informal* **= nonsense**, balderdash, balls (*taboo slang*), baloney (*informal*), bilge (*informal*), bosh (*informal*), bullshit (*taboo slang*), cobblers (*Brit. taboo slang*), crap (*slang*), eyewash (*informal*), garbage (*informal*), guff (*slang*), havers (*Scot.*), hogwash, hokum (*slang, chiefly U.S. & Canad.*), hooey (*slang*), horsefeathers (*U.S. slang*), hot air (*informal*), kak (*S. Afr. slang*), moonshine, piffle (*informal*), poppycock (*informal*), rot, rubbish, shit (*taboo slang*), stuff and nonsense, tarradiddle, tomfoolery, tommyrot, tosh (*slang, chiefly Brit.*), trash, tripe (*informal*), truck (*informal*), twaddle

buoy *noun* **1 = marker**, beacon, float, guide, signal ♦ *verb* **2 buoy up = encourage**, boost, cheer, cheer up, gee up, hearten, keep afloat, lift, raise, support, sustain

buoyancy *noun* **1 = lightness**, floatability, weightlessness **2 = cheerfulness**, animation, bounce (*informal*), cheeriness, good humour, high spirits, liveliness, pep, spiritedness, sunniness, zing (*informal*)

buoyant *adjective* **1 = floating**, afloat, floatable, light, weightless **2 = cheerful**,

animated, blithe, bouncy, breezy, bright, carefree, chirpy (*informal*), debonair, full of beans (*informal*), genial, happy, jaunty, joyful, light-hearted, lively, peppy (*informal*), sparky, sunny, upbeat (*informal*), vivacious
➤ **Antonyms**
≠**cheerful:** cheerless, depressed, despairing, dull, forlorn, gloomy, glum, hopeless, melancholy, moody, morose, pessimistic, sad, sullen, unhappy

burden *noun* **1 = load**, encumbrance, weight **2 = trouble**, affliction, albatross, anxiety, care, clog, encumbrance, grievance, millstone, obstruction, onus, pigeon (*informal*), responsibility, sorrow, strain, stress, trial, weight, worry **3** *Nautical* **= tonnage**, cargo, freight, lading ♦ *verb* **4 = weigh down**, bother, encumber, handicap, load, oppress, overload, overwhelm, saddle with, strain, tax, worry

bureau *noun* **1 = office**, agency, branch, department, division, service **2 = desk**, writing desk

bureaucracy *noun* **1 = government**, administration, authorities, civil service, corridors of power, directorate, ministry, officialdom, officials, the system **2 = red tape**, bumbledom, officialdom, officialese, regulations

bureaucrat *noun* **= official**, administrator, apparatchik, civil servant, functionary, mandarin, minister, office-holder, officer, public servant

burglar *noun* **= housebreaker**, cat burglar, filcher, picklock, pilferer, robber, sneak thief, thief

burglary *noun* **= breaking and entering**, break-in, filching, housebreaking, larceny, pilferage, robbery, stealing, theft, thieving

burial *noun* **= interment**, burying, entombment, exequies, funeral, inhumation, obsequies, sepulture

buried *adjective* **1 = interred**, coffined, consigned to the grave, entombed, laid to rest **2 = hidden**, cloistered, concealed, private, sequestered, tucked away **3 = engrossed**, caught up, committed, concentrating, devoted, immersed, intent, lost, occupied, preoccupied, rapt **4 = forgotten**, covered, hidden, repressed, sunk in oblivion, suppressed

burlesque *noun* **1 = parody**, caricature, mock, mockery, satire, send-up (*Brit. informal*), spoof (*informal*), takeoff (*informal*), travesty ♦ *adjective* **2 = satirical**, caricatural, comic, farcical, hudibrastic, ironical, ludicrous, mock, mock-heroic, mocking, parodic, travestying ♦ *verb* **3 = satirize**, ape, caricature, exaggerate, imitate, lampoon, make a monkey out of, make fun of, mock, parody, ridicule, send up (*Brit. informal*), spoof (*informal*), take off (*informal*), take the piss out of (*taboo slang*), travesty

burly *adjective* = **brawny**, beefy (*informal*), big, bulky, hefty, hulking, muscular, powerful, stocky, stout, strapping, strong, sturdy, thickset, well-built
➤ Antonyms
lean, puny, scraggy, scrawny, slight, spare, thin, weak, weedy (*informal*), wimpish *or* wimpy (*informal*), wussy (*slang*)

burn *verb* 1 = **be on fire**, be ablaze, blaze, flame, flare, flash, flicker, glow, go up in flames, smoke 2 = **set on fire**, brand, calcine, char, ignite, incinerate, kindle, light, parch, reduce to ashes, scorch, sear, shrivel, singe, toast, wither 3 = **sting**, bite, hurt, pain, smart, tingle 4 = **be passionate**, be angry, be aroused, be excited, be inflamed, blaze, desire, fume, seethe, simmer, smoulder, yearn

burning *adjective* 1 = **intense**, ablaze, afire, all-consuming, ardent, eager, earnest, fervent, fervid, flaming, frantic, frenzied, impassioned, passionate, vehement, zealous 2 = **crucial**, acute, compelling, critical, essential, important, now or never, pressing, significant, urgent, vital 3 = **blazing**, fiery, flaming, flashing, gleaming, glowing, hot, illuminated, scorching, smouldering 4 = **stinging**, acrid, biting, caustic, irritating, painful, piercing, prickling, pungent, reeking, smarting, tingling
➤ Antonyms
≠intense: apathetic, calm, cool, faint, indifferent, mild, passive ≠stinging: cooling, mild, numbing, soothing

burnish *verb* 1 = **polish**, brighten, buff, furbish, glaze, rub up, shine, smooth ♦ *noun* 2 = **shine**, gloss, lustre, patina, polish, sheen
➤ Antonyms
verb ≠polish: abrade, graze, scratch, scuff

burrow *noun* 1 = **hole**, den, lair, retreat, shelter, tunnel ♦ *verb* 2 = **dig**, delve, excavate, hollow out, scoop out, tunnel

burst *verb* 1 = **explode**, blow up, break, crack, disintegrate, fly open, fragment, puncture, rend asunder, rupture, shatter, shiver, split, tear apart 2 = **rush**, barge, break, break out, erupt, gush forth, run, spout ♦ *noun* 3 = **explosion**, bang, blast, blasting, blowout, blow-up, breach, break, crack, discharge, rupture, split 4 = **rush**, eruption, fit, gush, gust, outbreak, outburst, outpouring, spate, spurt, surge, torrent ♦ *adjective* 5 = **ruptured**, flat, punctured, rent, split

bury *verb* 1 = **inter**, consign to the grave, entomb, inearth, inhume, lay to rest, sepulchre 2 = **embed**, drive in, engulf,

implant, sink, submerge 3 = **hide**, conceal, cover, cover up, draw a veil over, enshroud, secrete, shroud, stash (*informal*), stow away 4 = **engross**, absorb, engage, immerse, interest, occupy
➤ Antonyms
≠inter, hide: bring to light, dig up, discover, disinter, dredge up, exhume, expose, find, reveal, turn up, uncover, unearth

bush *noun* 1 = **shrub**, hedge, plant, shrubbery, thicket 2 **the bush** = **the wild**, back country (*U.S.*), backlands (*U.S.*), backwoods, brush, scrub, scrubland, woodland

bushy *adjective* = **thick**, bristling, bristly, fluffy, fuzzy, luxuriant, rough, shaggy, spreading, stiff, unruly, wiry

busily *adverb* = **actively**, assiduously, briskly, carefully, diligently, earnestly, energetically, industriously, intently, purposefully, speedily, strenuously

business *noun* 1 = **trade**, bargaining, commerce, dealings, industry, manufacturing, merchandising, selling, trading, transaction 2 = **establishment**, company, concern, corporation, enterprise, firm, organization, venture 3 = **profession**, calling, career, craft, employment, function, job, line, métier, occupation, pursuit, trade, vocation, work 4 = **concern**, affair, assignment, duty, function, issue, matter, pigeon (*informal*), point, problem, question, responsibility, subject, task, topic

businesslike *adjective* = **efficient**, correct, matter-of-fact, methodical, orderly, organized, practical, professional, regular, routine, systematic, thorough, well-ordered, workaday
➤ Antonyms
careless, disorderly, disorganized, frivolous, impractical, inefficient, irregular, sloppy, unprofessional, unsystematic, untidy

businessman, businesswoman *noun* = **executive**, capitalist, employer, entrepreneur, financier, *homme d'affaires*, industrialist, merchant, tradesman, tycoon

bust¹ *noun* = **bosom**, breast, chest, front, torso

bust² *Informal* ♦ *verb* 1 = **break**, burst, fracture, rupture 2 = **arrest**, catch, collar (*informal*), cop (*slang*), feel one's collar (*slang*), lift (*slang*), nab (*informal*), nail (*informal*), raid, search ♦ *adjective* 3 **go bust** = **go bankrupt**, become insolvent, be ruined, break, fail ♦ *noun* 4 = **arrest**, capture, cop (*slang*), raid, search, seizure

bustle *verb* 1 = **hurry**, beetle, bestir, dash, flutter, fuss, hasten, rush, scamper, scramble, scurry, scuttle, stir, tear ♦ *noun* 2 = **activity**,

ado, agitation, commotion, excitement, flurry, fuss, haste, hurly-burly, hurry, pother, stir, to-do, tumult
➤ Antonyms
verb ≠ **hurry**: be indolent, idle, laze, lie around, loaf, loiter, loll, relax, rest, take it easy ◆ noun ≠ **activity**: inaction, inactivity, quiet, quietness, stillness, tranquillity

bustling adjective = **busy**, active, buzzing, crowded, full, humming, lively, swarming, teeming

busy adjective 1 = **occupied**, active, assiduous, brisk, diligent, employed, engaged, engrossed, hard at work, industrious, in harness, on active service, on duty, persevering, rushed off one's feet, slaving, working 2 = **lively**, active, energetic, exacting, full, hectic, hustling, on the go (informal), restless, strenuous, tireless, tiring ◆ verb 3 = **occupy**, absorb, employ, engage, engross, immerse, interest
➤ Antonyms
adjective ≠ **occupied, lively**: idle, inactive, indolent, lackadaisical, lazy, off duty, relaxed, slothful, unoccupied

busybody noun = **nosy parker** (informal), eavesdropper, gossip, intriguer, intruder, meddler, pry, scandalmonger, snoop, snooper, stirrer (informal), troublemaker

but conjunction 1 = **however**, further, moreover, nevertheless, on the contrary, on the other hand, still, yet ◆ preposition 2 = **except**, bar, barring, excepting, excluding, notwithstanding, save, with the exception of ◆ adverb 3 = **only**, just, merely, simply, singly, solely

butcher noun 1 = **murderer**, destroyer, killer, slaughterer, slayer ◆ verb 2 = **slaughter**, carve, clean, cut, cut up, dress, joint, prepare 3 = **kill**, assassinate, cut down, destroy, exterminate, liquidate, massacre, put to the sword, slaughter, slay 4 = **mess up**, bodge (informal), botch, destroy, mutilate, ruin, spoil, wreck

butchery noun = **slaughter**, blood bath, blood-letting, bloodshed, carnage, killing, massacre, mass murder, murder

butt[1] noun 1 = **end**, haft, handle, hilt, shaft, shank, stock 2 = **stub**, base, end, fag end (informal), foot, leftover, tail, tip

butt[2] noun = **target**, Aunt Sally, dupe, laughing stock, mark, object, point, subject, victim

butt[3] verb, noun 1 With or of the head or horns ≠ **knock**, buck, buffet, bump, bunt, jab, poke, prod, punch, push, ram, shove, thrust ◆ verb 2 butt in = **interfere**, chip in (informal), cut in, interrupt, intrude, meddle, put one's oar in, put one's two cents in (U.S. slang), stick one's nose in

butt[4] noun = **cask**, barrel, pipe

buttonhole verb = **detain**, accost, bore, catch, grab, importune, persuade importunately, take aside, waylay

buttress noun 1 = **support**, abutment, brace, mainstay, pier, prop, reinforcement, shore, stanchion, stay, strut ◆ verb 2 = **support**, augment, back up, bolster, brace, prop, prop up, reinforce, shore, shore up, strengthen, sustain, uphold

buxom adjective = **plump**, ample, bosomy, busty, comely, curvaceous, debonair, fresh-looking, full-bosomed, healthy, hearty, jocund, jolly, lively, lusty, merry, robust, sprightly, voluptuous, well-rounded, winsome
➤ Antonyms
delicate, frail, slender, slight, slim, svelte, sylphlike, thin, trim

buy verb 1 = **purchase**, acquire, get, invest in, obtain, pay for, procure, score (slang), shop for 2 buy off = **bribe**, corrupt, fix (informal), grease someone's palm (slang), square, suborn ◆ noun 3 = **purchase**, acquisition, bargain, deal
➤ Antonyms
verb ≠ **purchase**: auction, barter, retail, sell, vend

buzz noun 1 = **hum**, bombilation or bombination (literary), buzzing, drone, hiss, murmur, purr, ring, ringing, sibilation, susurration or susurrus (literary), whir, whisper 2 Informal = **gossip**, dirt (U.S. slang), gen (Brit. informal), hearsay, latest (informal), news, report, rumour, scandal, scuttlebutt (U.S. slang), whisper, word ◆ verb 3 = **hum**, bombilate or bombinate (literary), drone, fizzle, murmur, reverberate, ring, sibilate, susurrate (literary), whir, whisper, whizz 4 = **gossip**, chatter, natter, rumour, tattle

by preposition 1 = **via**, by way of, over 2 = **through**, through the agency of, under the aegis of 3 = **near**, along, beside, close to, next to, past ◆ adverb 4 = **near**, at hand, close, handy, in reach 5 = **past**, aside, away, to one side

by and by adverb = **presently**, anon, before long, erelong (archaic or poetic), eventually, in a while, in the course of time, one day, shortly, soon

bygone adjective = **past**, ancient, antiquated, departed, erstwhile, extinct, forgotten, former, gone by, lost, of old, of yore, olden, one-time, past recall, previous, sunk in oblivion
➤ Antonyms
coming, forthcoming, future, prospective, to be, to come

bypass verb = **go round**, avoid,

body-swerve (*Scot.*), circumvent, depart from, detour round, deviate from, get round, give a wide berth to, pass round
➤ **Antonyms**
abut, adjoin, come together, connect, converge, cross, intersect, join, link, meet, touch, unite

bystander *noun* = **onlooker**, eyewitness, looker-on, observer, passer-by, spectator, viewer, watcher, witness
➤ **Antonyms**
contributor, partaker, participant, party

byword *noun* = **saying**, adage, maxim, motto, precept, proverb, slogan

C c

cab *noun* = **taxi**, hackney, hackney carriage, minicab, taxicab

cabal *noun* 1 = **clique**, caucus, conclave, faction, league, party, set 2 = **plot**, conspiracy, intrigue, machination, scheme

cabin *noun* 1 = **room**, berth, compartment, deckhouse, quarters 2 = **hut**, berth, bothy, chalet, cot, cottage, crib, hovel, lodge, shack, shanty, shed

cabinet *noun* = **cupboard**, case, chiffonier, closet, commode, dresser, escritoire, locker

Cabinet *noun* = **council**, administration, assembly, counsellors, ministry

cackle *verb* 1 = **laugh**, chuckle, giggle, snicker, snigger, titter 2 = **squawk**, babble, chatter, cluck, crow, gabble, gibber, jabber, prattle

cad *noun Old-fashioned, informal* = **scoundrel**, bounder (*old-fashioned Brit. slang*), churl, cur, dastard (*archaic*), heel (*slang*), knave, rat (*informal*), rotter (*slang, chiefly Brit.*), scumbag (*slang*)

cadaverous *adjective* = **deathly**, ashen, blanched, bloodless, corpse-like, deathlike, emaciated, exsanguinous, gaunt, ghastly, haggard, hollow-eyed, like death warmed up (*informal*), pale, pallid, wan

caddish *adjective* = **ungentlemanly**, despicable, ill-bred, low, unmannerly
➤ **Antonyms**
gentlemanly, honourable, mannerly

cadence *noun* 1 = **rhythm**, beat, lilt, measure (*Prosody*), metre, pulse, swing, tempo, throb 2 = **intonation**, accent, inflection, modulation

café *noun* = **snack bar**, brasserie, cafeteria, coffee bar, coffee shop, eatery *or* eaterie, lunchroom, restaurant, tearoom

cage *noun* 1 = **enclosure**, corral (*U.S.*), pen, pound ♦ *verb* 2 = **shut up**, confine, coop up, fence in, immure, impound, imprison, incarcerate, lock up, mew, pound, restrain

cagey, cagy *adjective Informal* = **wary**, careful, cautious, chary, discreet, guarded, noncommittal, shrewd, wily
➤ **Antonyms**
careless, imprudent, indiscreet, reckless, unthinking, unwary

cajole *verb* = **persuade**, beguile, coax, decoy, dupe, entice, entrap, flatter, inveigle, lure, manoeuvre, mislead, seduce, sweet-talk (*informal*), tempt, wheedle

cake *noun* 1 = **block**, bar, cube, loaf, lump, mass, slab ♦ *verb* 2 = **encrust**, bake, cement, coagulate, congeal, consolidate, dry, harden, inspissate (*archaic*), ossify, solidify, thicken

calamitous *adjective* = **disastrous**, blighting, cataclysmic, catastrophic, deadly, devastating, dire, fatal, pernicious, ruinous, tragic, woeful
➤ **Antonyms**
advantageous, beneficial, favourable, fortunate, good, helpful

calamity *noun* = **disaster**, adversity, affliction, cataclysm, catastrophe, distress, downfall, hardship, misadventure, mischance, misfortune, mishap, reverse, ruin, scourge, tragedy, trial, tribulation, woe, wretchedness
➤ **Antonyms**
advantage, benefit, blessing, boon, good fortune, good luck, help

calculate *verb* 1 = **work out**, adjust, compute, consider, count, determine, enumerate, estimate, figure, gauge, judge, rate, reckon, value, weigh 2 = **plan**, aim, design, intend

calculated *adjective* = **deliberate**, considered, intended, intentional, planned, premeditated, purposeful
➤ **Antonyms**
haphazard, hasty, heedless, hurried, impetuous, impulsive, rash, spontaneous, unintentional, unplanned, unpremeditated

calculating *adjective* = **scheming**, canny, cautious, contriving, crafty, cunning, designing, devious, Machiavellian, manipulative, politic, sharp, shrewd, sly
➤ **Antonyms**
blunt, direct, downright, frank, guileless, honest, open, outspoken, sincere, undesigning

calculation *noun* 1 = **working out**, answer, computation, estimate, estimation, figuring, forecast, judgment, reckoning, result 2 = **planning**, caution, circumspection, contrivance, deliberation, discretion, foresight, forethought, precaution

calibre *noun* 1 = **worth**, ability, capacity, distinction, endowment, faculty, force, gifts, merit, parts, quality, scope, stature, strength, talent 2 = **diameter**, bore, gauge, measure

call *verb* **1** = **name**, christen, denominate, describe as, designate, dub, entitle, label, style, term **2** = **consider**, estimate, judge, regard, think **3** = **cry**, announce, arouse, awaken, cry out, hail, halloo, proclaim, rouse, shout, waken, yell **4** = **phone**, give (someone) a bell (*Brit. slang*), ring up (*informal, chiefly Brit.*), telephone **5** = **summon**, assemble, bid, collect, contact, convene, convoke, gather, invite, muster, rally ♦ *noun* **6** = **cry**, hail, scream, shout, signal, whoop, yell **7** = **summons**, announcement, appeal, command, demand, invitation, notice, order, plea, request, supplication, visit **8** = **need**, cause, claim, excuse, grounds, justification, occasion, reason, right, urge
➤ **Antonyms**
verb ≠**cry**: be quiet, be silent, murmur, mutter, speak softly, whisper ≠**summon**: call off, cancel, dismiss, disperse, excuse, release ♦ *noun* ≠**cry**: murmur, mutter, whisper ≠**summons**: dismissal, release

call for *verb* **1** = **require**, demand, entail, involve, necessitate, need, occasion, suggest **2** = **fetch**, collect, pick up, uplift (*Scot.*)

calling *noun* = **profession**, business, career, employment, life's work, line, métier, mission, occupation, province, pursuit, trade, vocation, walk of life, work

call on *verb* **1** = **visit**, drop in on, look in on, look up, see **2** = **request**, appeal to, ask, bid, call upon, entreat, invite, invoke, summon, supplicate

callous *adjective* = **heartless**, affectless, apathetic, case-hardened, cold, hard-bitten, hard-boiled (*informal*), hardened, hardhearted, harsh, indifferent, indurated (*rare*), insensate, insensible, insensitive, inured, obdurate, soulless, thick-skinned, torpid, uncaring, unfeeling, unresponsive, unsusceptible, unsympathetic
➤ **Antonyms**
caring, compassionate, considerate, gentle, sensitive, soft, sympathetic, tender, understanding

callow *adjective* = **inexperienced**, green, guileless, immature, naive, raw, unsophisticated

calm *adjective* **1** = **cool**, as cool as a cucumber, collected, composed, dispassionate, equable, impassive, imperturbable, keeping one's cool, relaxed, sedate, self-possessed, undisturbed, unemotional, unexcitable, unexcited, unfazed (*informal*), unflappable (*informal*), unmoved, unruffled **2** = **still**, balmy, halcyon, mild, pacific, peaceful, placid, quiet, restful, serene, smooth, tranquil, windless ♦ *noun* **3** = **peacefulness**, calmness, hush, peace, quiet, repose, serenity, stillness

♦ *verb* **4** = **quieten**, hush, mollify, placate, relax, soothe
➤ **Antonyms**
adjective ≠**cool**: agitated, aroused, discomposed, disturbed, emotional, excited, fierce, frantic, heated, perturbed, shaken, troubled, worried ≠**still**: rough, stormy, wild ♦ *noun* ≠**peacefulness**: agitation, disturbance, wildness ♦ *verb* ≠**quieten**: aggravate, agitate, arouse, disturb, excite, irritate, stir

calmness *noun* **1** = **coolness**, composure, cool (*slang*), dispassion, equanimity, impassivity, imperturbability, poise, sang-froid, self-possession **2** = **peacefulness**, calm, hush, motionlessness, peace, placidity, quiet, repose, restfulness, serenity, smoothness, stillness, tranquillity

calumny *noun* = **slander**, abuse, aspersion, backbiting, calumniation, defamation, denigration, derogation, detraction, evil-speaking, insult, libel, lying, misrepresentation, obloquy, revilement, smear, stigma, vilification, vituperation

camouflage *noun* **1** = **disguise**, blind, cloak, concealment, cover, deceptive markings, false appearance, front, guise, mask, masquerade, mimicry, protective colouring, screen, subterfuge ♦ *verb* **2** = **disguise**, cloak, conceal, cover, hide, mask, obfuscate, obscure, screen, veil
➤ **Antonyms**
verb ≠**disguise**: bare, display, exhibit, expose, reveal, show, uncover, unmask, unveil

camp[1] *noun* = **camp site**, bivouac, camping ground, cantonment (*Military*), encampment, tents

camp[2] *adjective Informal* = **effeminate**, affected, artificial, camped up (*informal*), campy (*informal*), mannered, ostentatious, poncy (*slang*), posturing

campaign *noun* = **operation**, attack, crusade, drive, expedition, jihad (*rare*), movement, offensive, push

canal *noun* = **waterway**, channel, conduit, duct, passage, watercourse

cancel *verb* **1** = **call off**, abolish, abort, abrogate, annul, blot out, countermand, cross out, delete, do away with, efface, eliminate, erase, expunge, obliterate, obviate, quash, repeal, repudiate, rescind, revoke **2 cancel out** = **make up for**, balance out, compensate for, counterbalance, neutralize, nullify, obviate, offset, redeem

cancellation *noun* = **abandonment**, abandoning, abolition, annulment, deletion, elimination, quashing, repeal, revocation

cancer *noun* = **growth**, blight, canker, carcinoma (*Pathology*), corruption, evil, malignancy, pestilence, rot, sickness, tumour

candid *adjective* **1** = **honest**, blunt, downright, fair, forthright, frank, free, guileless, impartial, ingenuous, just, open, outspoken, plain, round, sincere, straightforward, truthful, unbiased, unequivocal, unprejudiced, upfront (*informal*) **2** = **informal**, impromptu, uncontrived, unposed
➤ **Antonyms**
≠**honest**: biased, complimentary, diplomatic, flattering, kind, subtle

candidate *noun* = **contender**, applicant, aspirant, claimant, competitor, contestant, entrant, nominee, possibility, runner, solicitant, suitor

candour *noun* = **honesty**, artlessness, directness, fairness, forthrightness, frankness, guilelessness, impartiality, ingenuousness, naïveté, openness, outspokenness, simplicity, sincerity, straightforwardness, truthfulness, unequivocalness
➤ **Antonyms**
bias, cunning, deceit, diplomacy, dishonesty, flattery, insincerity, prejudice, subtlety

canker *noun* **1** = **disease**, bane, blight, blister, cancer, corrosion, corruption, infection, lesion, rot, scourge, sore, ulcer ♦ *verb* **2** = **rot**, blight, consume, corrode, corrupt, embitter, envenom, inflict, poison, pollute, rust, waste away

cannon *noun* = **gun**, artillery piece, big gun, field gun, mortar

cannonade *noun* = **bombardment**, barrage, battery, broadside, gunfire, pounding, salvo, shelling, volley

canny *adjective* = **shrewd**, acute, artful, astute, careful, cautious, circumspect, clever, judicious, knowing, on the ball (*informal*), perspicacious, prudent, sagacious, sharp, subtle, wise, worldly-wise
➤ **Antonyms**
bumbling, inept, obtuse, unskilled

canon *noun* **1** = **rule**, criterion, dictate, formula, precept, principle, regulation, standard, statute, yardstick **2** = **list**, catalogue, roll

canopy *noun* = **awning**, baldachin, covering, shade, sunshade, tester

cant[1] *noun* **1** = **hypocrisy**, affected piety, humbug, insincerity, lip service, pious platitudes, pretence, pretentiousness, sanctimoniousness, sham holiness **2** = **jargon**, argot, lingo, patter, slang, vernacular

cant[2] *verb* = **tilt**, angle, bevel, incline, rise, slant, slope

cantankerous *adjective* = **bad-tempered**, captious, choleric, contrary, crabby, cranky (*U.S., Canad., & Irish informal*), crotchety

(*informal*), crusty, difficult, disagreeable, grouchy (*informal*), grumpy, ill-humoured, irascible, irritable, liverish, peevish, perverse, quarrelsome, ratty (*Brit. & N.Z. informal*), testy, tetchy, waspish
➤ **Antonyms**
agreeable, amiable, breezy, cheerful, complaisant, congenial, genial, good-natured, happy, kindly, merry, placid, pleasant, vivacious

canter *noun* **1** = **jog**, amble, dogtrot, easy gait, lope ♦ *verb* **2** = **jog**, amble, lope

canting *adjective* = **hypocritical**, insincere, Janus-faced, sanctimonious, two-faced

canvass *verb* **1** = **campaign**, electioneer, solicit, solicit votes **2** = **poll**, analyse, examine, fly a kite, inspect, investigate, scan, scrutinize, sift, study, ventilate ♦ *noun* **3** = **poll**, examination, investigation, scrutiny, survey, tally

canyon *noun* = **gorge**, coulee (*U.S.*), gulch (*U.S.*), gulf, gully, ravine, valley

cap *verb Informal* = **beat**, better, clobber (*slang*), complete, cover, crown, eclipse, exceed, excel, finish, lick (*informal*), outdo, outstrip, overtop, put in the shade, run rings around (*informal*), surpass, top, transcend

capability *noun* = **ability**, capacity, competence, facility, faculty, means, potential, potentiality, power, proficiency, qualification(s), wherewithal
➤ **Antonyms**
inability, incompetence, inefficiency, ineptitude, powerlessness

capable *adjective* = **able**, accomplished, adapted, adept, adequate, apt, clever, competent, efficient, experienced, fitted, gifted, intelligent, masterly, proficient, qualified, skilful, suited, susceptible, talented
➤ **Antonyms**
incapable, incompetent, ineffective, inept, inexpert, unqualified, unskilled

capacious *adjective* = **spacious**, ample, broad, comfortable, commodious, comprehensive, expansive, extended, extensive, generous, liberal, roomy, sizable *or* sizeable, substantial, vast, voluminous, wide
➤ **Antonyms**
confined, constricted, cramped, enclosed, incommodious, insubstantial, limited, narrow, poky, restricted, small, tight, tiny, uncomfortable, ungenerous

capacity *noun* **1** = **size**, amplitude, compass, dimensions, extent, magnitude, range, room, scope, space, volume **2** = **ability**, aptitude, aptness, brains, capability, cleverness, competence, competency, efficiency, facility, faculty, forte, genius, gift, intelligence, power, readiness, strength 3 = **function**, appointment, office, position, post, province, role, service, sphere

cape noun = **headland**, chersonese (poetic), head, ness (archaic), peninsula, point, promontory

caper noun 1 = **escapade**, antic, dido (informal), gambol, high jinks, hop, jape, jest, jump, lark (informal), leap, mischief, practical joke, prank, revel, shenanigan (informal), sport, stunt ♦ verb 2 = **dance**, bounce, bound, cavort, cut a rug (informal), frisk, frolic, gambol, hop, jump, leap, romp, skip, spring, trip

capital noun 1 = **money**, assets, cash, finance, finances, financing, funds, investment(s), means, principal, property, resources, stock, wealth, wherewithal ♦ adjective 2 = **principal**, cardinal, central, chief, controlling, essential, foremost, important, leading, main, major, overruling, paramount, pre-eminent, primary, prime, prominent, vital 3 Old-fashioned = **first-rate**, excellent, fine, first, prime, splendid, sterling, superb, world-class

capitalism noun = **private enterprise**, free enterprise, laissez faire or laisser faire, private ownership

capitalize on verb = **take advantage of**, benefit from, cash in on (informal), exploit, gain from, make the most of, profit from

capitulate verb = **give in**, cave in (informal), come to terms, give up, relent, submit, succumb, surrender, yield
➤ **Antonyms**
beat, conquer, crush, defeat, get the better of, lick (informal), overcome, overpower, subdue, subjugate, vanquish

capitulation noun = **surrender**, accedence, cave-in (informal), submission, yielding

caprice noun = **whim**, changeableness, fad, fancy, fickleness, fitfulness, freak, humour, impulse, inconstancy, notion, quirk, vagary, whimsy

capricious adjective = **unpredictable**, changeful, crotchety (informal), erratic, fanciful, fickle, fitful, freakish, impulsive, inconsistent, inconstant, mercurial, odd, queer, quirky, variable, wayward, whimsical
➤ **Antonyms**
certain, consistent, constant, decisive, determined, firm, immovable, resolute, responsible, stable, unchangeable, unwavering

capsize verb = **overturn**, invert, keel over, tip over, turn over, turn turtle, upset

capsule noun 1 = **pill**, bolus, lozenge, tablet, troche (Medical) 2 Botany = **pod**, case, pericarp (Botany), receptacle, seed case, sheath, shell, vessel

captain noun = **leader**, boss, chief, chieftain, commander, head, master, number one (informal), officer, (senior) pilot, skipper, torchbearer

captivate verb = **charm**, absorb, allure, attract, beguile, bewitch, dazzle, enamour, enchant, enrapture, enslave, ensnare, enthral, entrance, fascinate, hypnotize, infatuate, lure, mesmerize, ravish, seduce, sweep off one's feet, win
➤ **Antonyms**
alienate, disenchant, disgust, repel, repulse

captive noun 1 = **prisoner**, bondservant, convict, detainee, hostage, internee, prisoner of war, slave ♦ adjective 2 = **confined**, caged, enslaved, ensnared, imprisoned, incarcerated, locked up, penned, restricted, subjugated

captivity noun = **confinement**, bondage, custody, detention, durance (archaic), duress, enthralment, imprisonment, incarceration, internment, restraint, servitude, slavery, thraldom, vassalage

capture verb 1 = **catch**, apprehend, arrest, bag, collar (informal), feel one's collar (slang), lift (slang), nab (informal), nail (informal), secure, seize, take, take into custody, take prisoner ♦ noun 2 = **catching**, apprehension, arrest, imprisonment, seizure, taking, taking captive, trapping
➤ **Antonyms**
verb ≠catch: free, let go, let out, liberate, release, set free, turn loose

car noun 1 = **vehicle**, auto (U.S.), automobile, jalopy (informal), machine, motor, motorcar, wheels (informal) 2 U.S. & Canad. = **(railway) carriage**, buffet car, cable car, coach, dining car, sleeping car, van

carafe noun = **jug**, decanter, flagon, flask, pitcher

carcass noun = **body**, cadaver (Medical), corpse, corse (archaic), dead body, framework, hulk, remains, shell, skeleton

cardinal adjective = **principal**, capital, central, chief, essential, first, foremost, fundamental, greatest, highest, important, key, leading, main, paramount, pre-eminent, primary, prime
➤ **Antonyms**
dispensable, inessential, least important, lowest, secondary, subordinate

care verb 1 = **be concerned**, be bothered, be interested, mind ♦ noun 2 = **caution**, attention, carefulness, circumspection, consideration, direction, forethought, heed, management, meticulousness, pains, prudence, regard, vigilance, watchfulness 3 = **protection**, charge, control, custody, guardianship, keeping, management, ministration, supervision, ward 4 = **worry**, affliction, anxiety, burden, concern, disquiet,

hardship, interest, perplexity, pressure, responsibility, solicitude, stress, tribulation, trouble, vexation, woe
> **Antonyms**
noun ≠ **caution**: abandon, carelessness, heedlessness, inattention, indifference, laxity, laxness, neglect, negligence, unconcern ≠ **worry**: pleasure, relaxation

career *noun* 1 = **occupation**, calling, employment, life's work, livelihood, pursuit, vocation 2 = **progress**, course, passage, path, procedure, race, walk ♦ *verb* 3 = **rush**, barrel (along) (*informal, chiefly U.S. & Canad.*), bolt, burn rubber (*informal*), dash, hurtle, race, speed, tear

care for *verb* 1 = **look after**, attend, foster, mind, minister to, nurse, protect, provide for, tend, watch over 2 = **like**, be fond of, desire, enjoy, find congenial, love, prize, take to, want

carefree *adjective* = **untroubled**, airy, blithe, breezy, buoyant, careless, cheerful, cheery, chirpy (*informal*), easy-going, halcyon, happy, happy-go-lucky, insouciant, jaunty, light-hearted, lightsome (*archaic*), radiant, sunny
> **Antonyms**
blue, careworn, cheerless, dejected, depressed, desolate, despondent, down, down in the dumps (*informal*), gloomy, low, melancholy, miserable, sad, unhappy, worried

careful *adjective* 1 = **cautious**, accurate, attentive, chary, circumspect, conscientious, discreet, fastidious, heedful, painstaking, precise, prudent, punctilious, scrupulous, thoughtful, thrifty 2 = **thorough**, conscientious, meticulous, painstaking, particular, precise
> **Antonyms**
abandoned, careless, casual, inaccurate, inattentive, inexact, neglectful, negligent, reckless, remiss, slovenly, thoughtless, unconcerned, untroubled

careless *adjective* 1 = **slapdash**, cavalier, inaccurate, irresponsible, lackadaisical, neglectful, offhand, slipshod, sloppy (*informal*) 2 = **negligent**, absent-minded, cursory, forgetful, hasty, heedless, incautious, inconsiderate, indiscreet, perfunctory, regardless, remiss, thoughtless, unconcerned, unguarded, unmindful, unthinking 3 = **nonchalant**, artless, casual, unstudied
> **Antonyms**
≠ **slapdash**: accurate, careful, neat, orderly, painstaking, tidy ≠ **negligent**: alert, anxious, attentive, careful, cautious, concerned, correct, on the ball (*informal*), wary, watchful

carelessness *noun* = **negligence**,

inaccuracy, inattention, inconsiderateness, indiscretion, irresponsibility, laxity, laxness, neglect, omission, remissness, slackness, sloppiness (*informal*), thoughtlessness

caress *verb* 1 = **stroke**, cuddle, embrace, fondle, hug, kiss, neck (*informal*), nuzzle, pet ♦ *noun* 2 = **stroke**, cuddle, embrace, fondling, hug, kiss, pat

caretaker *noun* 1 = **warden**, concierge, curator, custodian, janitor, keeper, porter, superintendent, watchman ♦ *adjective* 2 = **temporary**, holding, interim, short-term

cargo *noun* = **load**, baggage, consignment, contents, freight, goods, lading, merchandise, shipment, tonnage, ware

caricature *noun* 1 = **parody**, burlesque, cartoon, distortion, farce, lampoon, mimicry, pasquinade, satire, send-up (*Brit. informal*), takeoff (*informal*), travesty ♦ *verb* 2 = **parody**, burlesque, distort, lampoon, mimic, mock, ridicule, satirize, send up (*Brit. informal*), take off (*informal*)

carnage *noun* = **slaughter**, blood bath, bloodshed, butchery, havoc, holocaust, massacre, mass murder, murder, shambles

carnal *adjective* = **sexual**, amorous, animal, erotic, fleshly, impure, lascivious, lecherous, lewd, libidinous, licentious, lustful, prurient, randy (*informal, chiefly Brit.*), raunchy (*slang*), salacious, sensual, sensuous, sexy (*informal*), steamy (*informal*), unchaste, voluptuous, wanton

carnival *noun* = **festival**, celebration, fair, fête, fiesta, gala, holiday, jamboree, jubilee, Mardi Gras, merrymaking, revelry

carol *noun* = **song**, canticle, canzonet, chorus, ditty, hymn, lay, noel, strain

carouse *verb* = **drink**, bend the elbow (*informal*), bevvy (*dialect*), booze (*informal*), imbibe, make merry, quaff, roister, wassail

carp *verb* = **find fault**, beef (*slang*), cavil, censure, complain, criticize, hypercriticize, knock (*informal*), kvetch (*U.S. slang*), nag, pick holes, quibble, reproach
> **Antonyms**
admire, applaud, approve, commend, compliment, extol, laud (*literary*), pay tribute to, praise, sing the praises of, speak highly of

carpenter *noun* = **joiner**, cabinet-maker, woodworker

carping *adjective* = **fault-finding**, captious, cavilling, critical, grouchy (*informal*), hard to please, hypercritical, nagging, nit-picking (*informal*), on someone's back (*informal*), picky (*informal*), reproachful

carriage *noun* 1 = **vehicle**, cab, coach, conveyance 2 = **bearing**, air, behaviour, comportment, conduct, demeanour, deportment, gait, manner, mien, posture, presence **3 = transportation**, carrying, conveyance, conveying, delivery, freight, transport

carry *verb* **1 = transport**, bear, bring, conduct, convey, fetch, haul, hump (*Brit. slang*), lift, lug, move, relay, take, tote (*informal*), transfer, transmit **2 = support**, bear, bolster, hold up, maintain, shoulder, stand, suffer, sustain, underpin, uphold **3 = include**, broadcast, communicate, display, disseminate, give, offer, publish, release, stock **4 = win**, accomplish, capture, effect, gain, secure

carry on *verb* **1 = continue**, endure, keep going, last, maintain, perpetuate, persevere, persist **2 = run**, administer, manage, operate **3** *Informal* **= make a fuss**, create (*slang*), misbehave, raise Cain

carry out *verb* **= perform**, accomplish, achieve, carry through, consummate, discharge, effect, execute, fulfil, implement, realize

carton *noun* **= box**, case, container, pack, package, packet

cartoon *noun* **1 = drawing**, caricature, comic strip, lampoon, parody, satire, sketch, takeoff (*informal*) **2 = animation**, animated cartoon, animated film

cartridge *noun* **1 = shell**, charge, round **2 = container**, capsule, case, cassette, cylinder, magazine

carve *verb* **= cut**, chip, chisel, divide, engrave, etch, fashion, form, grave (*archaic*), hack, hew, incise, inscribe, mould, sculpt, sculpture, slash, slice, whittle

cascade *noun* **1 = waterfall**, avalanche, cataract, deluge, downpour, falls, flood, fountain, outpouring, shower, torrent ♦ *verb* **2 = flow**, descend, fall, flood, gush, overflow, pitch, plunge, pour, spill, surge, teem, tumble

case[1] *noun* **1 = instance**, example, illustration, occasion, occurrence, specimen **2 = situation**, circumstance(s), condition, context, contingency, dilemma, event, plight, position, predicament, state **3** *Law* **= lawsuit**, action, cause, dispute, proceedings, process, suit, trial

case[2] *noun* **1 = container**, box, cabinet, canister, capsule, carton, cartridge, casket, chest, coffret, compact, crate, holder, receptacle, suitcase, tray, trunk **2 = covering**, capsule, casing, cover, envelope, folder, integument, jacket, sheath, shell, wrapper, wrapping

cash *noun* **= money**, ackers (*slang*), banknotes, brass (*Northern English dialect*), bread (*slang*), bullion, change, coin,

coinage, currency, dibs (*slang*), dosh (*Brit. & Austral. slang*), dough (*slang*), funds, necessary (*informal*), needful (*informal*), notes, payment, ready (*informal*), ready money, resources, rhino (*Brit. slang*), shekels (*informal*), silver, specie, spondulicks (*slang*), tin (*slang*), wherewithal

cashier[1] *noun* **= teller**, accountant, bank clerk, banker, bursar, clerk, purser, treasurer

cashier[2] *verb* **= dismiss**, break, cast off, discard, discharge, drum out, expel, give the boot to (*slang*)

casket *noun* **= box**, ark (*dialect*), case, chest, coffer, coffret, jewel box, kist (*Scot. & Northern English dialect*)

cast *noun* **1 = actors**, characters, company, dramatis personae, players, troupe **2 = type**, air, appearance, complexion, demeanour, look, manner, mien, semblance, shade, stamp, style, tinge, tone, turn **3 = throw**, fling, lob, thrust, toss ♦ *verb* **4 = choose**, allot, appoint, assign, name, pick, select **5 = give out**, bestow, deposit, diffuse, distribute, emit, radiate, scatter, shed, spread **6 = form**, found, model, mould, set, shape **7 = throw**, chuck (*informal*), drive, drop, fling, hurl, impel, launch, lob, pitch, project, shed, shy, sling, thrust, toss

cast down *verb* **= discourage**, deject, depress, desolate, dishearten, dispirit

caste *noun* **= class**, estate, grade, lineage, order, race, rank, social order, species, station, status, stratum

castigate *verb* **= reprimand**, bawl out (*informal*), beat, berate, blast, cane, carpet (*informal*), censure, chasten, chastise, chew out (*U.S. & Canad. informal*), correct, criticize, discipline, dress down (*informal*), excoriate, flail, flay, flog, give a rocket (*Brit. & N.Z. informal*), haul over the coals (*informal*), lambast(e), lash, put down, rap over the knuckles, read the riot act, rebuke, scold, scourge, slap on the wrist, slate (*informal, chiefly Brit.*), tear into (*informal*), tear (someone) off a strip (*Brit. informal*), whip

cast-iron *adjective* **= certain**, copper-bottomed, definite, established, fixed, guaranteed, settled

castle *noun* **= fortress**, chateau, citadel, donjon, fastness, keep, mansion, palace, peel, stronghold, tower

cast-off *adjective* **1 = unwanted**, discarded, rejected, scrapped, surplus to requirements, unneeded, useless ♦ *noun* **2 = reject**, discard, failure, outcast, second

castrate *verb* **= neuter**, emasculate, geld

casual *adjective* **1 = careless**, apathetic, blasé, cursory, indifferent, informal, insouciant, lackadaisical, nonchalant, offhand, perfunctory, relaxed, unconcerned **2 = chance**, accidental, contingent, fortuitous, hit-and-miss *or* hit-or-miss (*informal*), incidental, irregular, occasional, random, serendipitous, uncertain, unexpected, unforeseen, unintentional, unpremeditated **3 = informal**, non-dressy, sporty ➤ **Antonyms** ≠**careless**: committed, concerned, direct, enthusiastic, passionate, serious ≠**chance**: arranged, deliberate, expected, fixed, foreseen, intentional, planned, premeditated ≠**informal**: ceremonial, dressy, formal

casualty *noun* **1 = victim**, death, fatality, loss, sufferer, wounded **2 = accident**, calamity, catastrophe, disaster, misadventure, misfortune, mishap

cat *noun* **= feline**, gib, grimalkin, kitty (*informal*), malkin (*archaic*), moggy (*slang*), mouser, puss (*informal*), pussy (*informal*), tabby

catacombs *plural noun* **= vault**, crypt, tomb

catalogue *noun* **1 = list**, directory, gazetteer, index, inventory, record, register, roll, roster, schedule ♦ *verb* **2 = list**, accession, alphabetize, classify, file, index, inventory, register, tabulate

catapult *noun* **1 = sling**, ballista, slingshot (*U.S.*), trebuchet ♦ *verb* **2 = shoot**, heave, hurl, hurtle, pitch, plunge, propel, toss

cataract *noun* **1** *Medical* **= opacity** (*of the eye*) **2 = waterfall**, cascade, deluge, downpour, falls, Niagara, rapids, torrent

catastrophe *noun* **= disaster**, adversity, affliction, blow, bummer (*slang*), calamity, cataclysm, deep water, devastation, failure, fiasco, ill, meltdown (*informal*), mischance, misfortune, mishap, reverse, tragedy, trial, trouble, whammy (*informal, chiefly U.S.*)

catcall *noun* **1 = jeer**, boo, gibe, hiss, raspberry, whistle ♦ *verb* **2 = jeer**, boo, deride, gibe, give the bird to (*informal*), hiss, whistle

catch *verb* **1 = seize**, clutch, get, grab, grasp, grip, lay hold of, snatch, take **2 = capture**, apprehend, arrest, ensnare, entangle, entrap, feel one's collar (*slang*), lift (*slang*), nab (*informal*), nail (*informal*), snare, trap **3 = discover**, catch in the act, detect, expose, find out, surprise, take unawares, unmask **4 = contract**, develop, get, go down with, incur, succumb to, suffer from **5 = attract**, bewitch, captivate, capture, charm, delight, enchant, enrapture, fascinate **6 = make out**, apprehend, comprehend, discern, feel, follow, get, grasp, hear, perceive, recognize, sense, take in, twig (*Brit. informal*) ♦ *noun* **7**

= fastener, bolt, clasp, clip, hasp, hook, hook and eye, latch, sneck (*dialect, chiefly Scot. & N. English*), snib (*Scot.*) **8** *Informal* **= drawback**, disadvantage, fly in the ointment, hitch, snag, stumbling block, trap, trick ➤ **Antonyms** *verb* ≠**seize**: drop, free, give up, liberate, loose, release ≠**contract**: avert, avoid, escape, ward off ≠**attract**: alienate, bore, disenchant, disgust, fail to interest, repel ♦ *noun* ≠**drawback**: advantage, benefit, bonus, boon, reward

catching *adjective* **= infectious**, communicable, contagious, infective, transferable, transmittable ➤ **Antonyms** incommunicable, non-catching, non-contagious, non-infectious, non-transmittable

catch on *verb Informal* **= understand**, comprehend, find out, get the picture, grasp, see, see the light of day, see through, twig (*Brit. informal*)

catchword *noun* **= slogan**, byword, motto, password, refrain, watchword

catchy *adjective* **= memorable**, captivating, haunting, popular

catechize *verb* **= question**, cross-examine, drill, examine, grill (*informal*), interrogate

categorical *adjective* **= absolute**, direct, downright, emphatic, explicit, express, positive, unambiguous, unconditional, unequivocal, unqualified, unreserved ➤ **Antonyms** conditional, hesitant, indefinite, qualified, questionable, uncertain, vague

category *noun* **= class**, classification, department, division, grade, grouping, head, heading, list, order, rank, section, sort, type

cater *verb* **= provide**, furnish, outfit, provision, purvey, supply, victual

catharsis *noun* **= release**, abreaction, cleansing, lustration, purgation, purging, purification

catholic *adjective* **= wide**, all-embracing, all-inclusive, broad-minded, charitable, comprehensive, eclectic, ecumenical, general, global, liberal, tolerant, unbigoted, universal, unsectarian, whole, world-wide ➤ **Antonyms** bigoted, exclusive, illiberal, limited, narrow-minded, parochial, sectarian

cattle *plural noun* **= cows**, beasts, bovines, kine (*archaic*), livestock, neat (*archaic*), stock

catty *adjective* **= spiteful**, backbiting, bitchy (*informal*), ill-natured, malevolent, malicious, mean, rancorous, shrewish, snide, venomous ➤ **Antonyms** benevolent, charitable, compassionate, considerate, generous, kind, pleasant

caucus *noun* = **meeting**, assembly, conclave, congress, convention, get-together (*informal*), parley, session

cause *noun* **1** = **origin**, agent, beginning, creator, genesis, mainspring, maker, originator, prime mover, producer, root, source, spring **2** = **reason**, account, agency, aim, basis, consideration, end, grounds, incentive, inducement, justification, motivation, motive, object, purpose, the why and wherefore **3** = **aim**, attempt, belief, conviction, enterprise, ideal, movement, principle, purpose, undertaking ♦ *verb* **4** = **produce**, begin, bring about, compel, create, effect, engender, generate, give rise to, incite, induce, lead to, motivate, occasion, precipitate, provoke, result in
➤ **Antonyms**
noun ≠**origin**: consequence, effect, end, outcome, result ♦ *verb* ≠**produce**: deter, foil, inhibit, prevent, stop

caustic *adjective* **1** = **burning**, acrid, astringent, biting, corroding, corrosive, keen, mordant, vitriolic **2** = **sarcastic**, acrimonious, cutting, mordacious, pungent, scathing, severe, stinging, trenchant, virulent, vitriolic
➤ **Antonyms**
≠**sarcastic**: agreeable, bland, gentle, kind, loving, mild, pleasant, soft, soothing, sweet

caution *noun* **1** = **care**, alertness, belt and braces, carefulness, circumspection, deliberation, discretion, forethought, heed, heedfulness, prudence, vigilance, watchfulness **2** = **warning**, admonition, advice, counsel, injunction ♦ *verb* **3** = **warn**, admonish, advise, tip off, urge
➤ **Antonyms**
noun ≠**care**: carelessness, daring, imprudence, rashness, recklessness ♦ *verb* ≠**warn**: dare

cautious *adjective* = **careful**, alert, belt-and-braces, cagey (*informal*), chary, circumspect, discreet, guarded, heedful, judicious, keeping a weather eye on, on one's toes, prudent, tentative, vigilant, wary, watchful
➤ **Antonyms**
adventurous, bold, careless, daring, foolhardy, heedless, impetuous, inattentive, incautious, indiscreet, madcap, rash, reckless, unguarded, unheedful, venturesome, venturous

cavalcade *noun* = **parade**, array, march-past, procession, spectacle, train

cavalier *adjective* **1** = **haughty**, arrogant, condescending, curt, disdainful, insolent, lofty, lordly, offhand, scornful, supercilious ♦ *noun* **2** = **gentleman**, beau, blade (*archaic*), escort, gallant **3** = **knight**, chevalier, equestrian, horseman

cavalry *noun* = **horsemen**, horse, mounted troops
➤ **Antonyms**
foot soldiers, infantrymen

cave *noun* = **hollow**, cavern, cavity, den, grotto

caveat *noun* = **warning**, admonition, caution

cavern *noun* = **cave**, hollow, pothole

cavernous *adjective* **1** = **deep**, concave, hollow, sunken, yawning **2** = **resonant**, echoing, reverberant, sepulchral

cavil *verb* = **find fault**, beef (*slang*), carp, censure, complain, hypercriticize, kvetch (*U.S. slang*), object, quibble

cavity *noun* = **hollow**, crater, dent, gap, hole, pit

cease *verb* = **stop**, belay (*Nautical*), break off, bring *or* come to an end, conclude, culminate, desist, die away, discontinue, end, fail, finish, halt, leave off, refrain, stay, terminate
➤ **Antonyms**
begin, commence, continue, initiate, start

ceaseless *adjective* = **continual**, constant, continuous, endless, eternal, everlasting, incessant, indefatigable, interminable, never-ending, nonstop, perennial, perpetual, unending, unremitting, untiring
➤ **Antonyms**
broken, erratic, intermittent, irregular, occasional, periodic, spasmodic, sporadic

cede *verb* = **surrender**, abandon, abdicate, allow, concede, convey, grant, hand over, make over, relinquish, renounce, resign, step down (*informal*), transfer, yield

celebrate *verb* **1** = **rejoice**, commemorate, drink to, keep, kill the fatted calf, observe, put the flags out, toast **2** = **perform**, bless, honour, reverence, solemnize **3** = **praise**, commend, crack up (*informal*), eulogize, exalt, extol, glorify, honour, laud, proclaim, publicize

celebrated *adjective* = **well-known**, acclaimed, distinguished, eminent, famed, famous, glorious, illustrious, lionized, notable, outstanding, popular, pre-eminent, prominent, renowned, revered
➤ **Antonyms**
dishonoured, forgotten, insignificant, obscure, trivial, unacclaimed, undistinguished, unknown, unnotable, unpopular

celebration *noun* **1** = **party**, beano (*Brit. slang*), carousal, -fest (*in combination*), festival, festivity, gala, hooley *or* hoolie (*chiefly Irish & N.Z.*), jollification, jubilee, junketing, merrymaking, rave (*Brit. slang*), rave-up (*Brit. slang*), red-letter day, revelry **2** = **performance**, anniversary, commemoration, honouring, observance, remembrance, solemnization

celebrity noun 1 = **personality**, big name, big shot (*informal*), bigwig (*informal*), celeb (*informal*), dignitary, face (*informal*), lion, luminary, megastar (*informal*), name, personage, star, superstar, V.I.P. 2 = **fame**, distinction, éclat, glory, honour, notability, popularity, pre-eminence, prestige, prominence, renown, reputation, repute, stardom
➤ **Antonyms**
≠ **personality**: has-been, nobody, unknown ≠ **fame**: obscurity

celerity noun Formal = **speed**, dispatch, expedition, fleetness, haste, promptness, quickness, rapidity, swiftness, velocity

celestial adjective = **heavenly**, angelic, astral, divine, elysian, empyrean (*poetic*), eternal, ethereal, godlike, immortal, seraphic, spiritual, sublime, supernatural

celibacy noun = **chastity**, continence, purity, singleness, virginity

cell noun 1 = **room**, cavity, chamber, compartment, cubicle, dungeon, stall 2 = **unit**, caucus, core, coterie, group, nucleus

cement noun 1 = **mortar**, adhesive, binder, glue, gum, paste, plaster, sealant ◆ verb 2 = **stick together**, attach, bind, bond, cohere, combine, glue, gum, join, plaster, seal, solder, unite, weld

cemetery noun = **graveyard**, burial ground, churchyard, God's acre, necropolis

censor verb = **cut**, blue-pencil, bowdlerize, expurgate

censorious adjective = **critical**, captious, carping, cavilling, condemnatory, disapproving, disparaging, fault-finding, hypercritical, scathing, severe

censure noun 1 = **disapproval**, blame, castigation, condemnation, criticism, dressing down (*informal*), obloquy, rebuke, remonstrance, reprehension, reprimand, reproach, reproof, stick (*slang*), stricture ◆ verb 2 = **criticize**, abuse, bawl out (*informal*), berate, blame, blast, carpet (*informal*), castigate, chew out (*U.S. & Canad. informal*), chide, condemn, denounce, excoriate, give (someone) a rocket (*Brit. & N.Z. informal*), lambast(e), put down, rap over the knuckles, read the riot act, rebuke, reprehend, reprimand, reproach, reprove, scold, slap on the wrist, slate (*informal, chiefly U.S.*), tear into (*informal*), tear (someone) off a strip (*Brit. informal*), upbraid
➤ **Antonyms**
noun ≠ **disapproval**: approval, commendation, compliment, encouragement ◆ verb ≠ **criticize**: applaud,

commend, compliment

central adjective 1 = **middle**, inner, interior, mean, median, mid 2 = **main**, chief, essential, focal, fundamental, key, primary, principal
➤ **Antonyms**
≠ **middle**: exterior, outer, outermost ≠ **main**: minor, secondary, subordinate, subsidiary

centralize verb = **unify**, amalgamate, compact, concentrate, concentre, condense, converge, incorporate, rationalize, streamline

centre noun 1 = **middle**, bull's-eye, core, crux, focus, heart, hub, kernel, mid (*archaic*), midpoint, nucleus, pivot ◆ verb 2 = **focus**, cluster, concentrate, converge, revolve
➤ **Antonyms**
noun ≠ **middle**: border, boundary, brim, circumference, edge, fringe, limit, lip, margin, perimeter, periphery, rim

centrepiece noun = **focus**, cynosure, epergne, highlight, hub, star

ceremonial adjective 1 = **ritual**, formal, liturgical, ritualistic, solemn, stately ◆ noun 2 = **ritual**, ceremony, formality, rite, solemnity
➤ **Antonyms**
adjective ≠ **ritual**: casual, informal, relaxed, simple

ceremonious adjective = **formal**, civil, courteous, courtly, deferential, dignified, exact, precise, punctilious, ritual, solemn, starchy (*informal*), stately, stiff

ceremony noun 1 = **ritual**, commemoration, function, observance, parade, rite, service, show, solemnities 2 = **formality**, ceremonial, decorum, etiquette, form, formal courtesy, niceties, pomp, propriety, protocol

certain adjective 1 = **sure**, assured, confident, convinced, positive, satisfied 2 = **known**, ascertained, conclusive, incontrovertible, indubitable, irrefutable, plain, true, undeniable, undoubted, unequivocal, unmistakable, valid 3 = **inevitable**, bound, definite, destined, fated, ineluctable, inescapable, inexorable, sure 4 = **fixed**, decided, definite, established, settled 5 = **particular**, express, individual, precise, special, specific
➤ **Antonyms**
disputable, doubtful, dubious, equivocal, fallible, indefinite, questionable, uncertain, unconvinced, undecided, unlikely, unreliable, unsettled, unsure

certainly adverb = **definitely**, assuredly, indisputably, indubitably, surely, truly, undeniably, undoubtedly, without doubt

certainty noun 1 = **sureness**, assurance, authoritativeness, certitude, confidence,

conviction, faith, indubitableness, inevitability, positiveness, trust, validity **2** = **fact**, banker, reality, sure thing (*informal*), surety, truth
➤ **Antonyms**
≠**sureness**: disbelief, doubt, indecision, qualm, scepticism, uncertainty, unsureness

certificate *noun* = **document**, authorization, credential(s), diploma, licence, testimonial, voucher, warrant

certify *verb* = **confirm**, ascertain, assure, attest, authenticate, aver, avow, corroborate, declare, endorse, guarantee, notify, show, testify, validate, verify, vouch, witness

chafe *verb* **1** = **rub**, abrade, rasp, scrape, scratch **2** = **be annoyed**, be angry, be exasperated, be impatient, be incensed, be inflamed, be irritated, be narked (*Brit., Austral., & N.Z. slang*), be offended, be ruffled, be vexed, fret, fume, rage, worry

chaff[1] *noun* = **waste**, dregs, glumes, hulls, husks, refuse, remains, rubbish, trash

chaff[2] *verb* **1** = **tease**, banter, deride, jeer, josh (*slang, chiefly U.S. & Canad.*), mock, rib (*informal*), ridicule, scoff, take the piss out of (*taboo slang*), taunt ◆ *noun* **2** = **teasing**, badinage, banter, joking, josh (*slang, chiefly U.S. & Canad.*), persiflage, raillery

chagrin *noun* **1** = **annoyance**, discomfiture, discomposure, displeasure, disquiet, dissatisfaction, embarrassment, fretfulness, humiliation, ill-humour, irritation, mortification, peevishness, spleen, vexation ◆ *verb* **2** = **annoy**, discomfit, discompose, displease, disquiet, dissatisfy, embarrass, humiliate, irk, irritate, mortify, peeve, vex

chain *noun* **1** = **link**, bond, coupling, fetter, manacle, shackle, union **2** = **series**, concatenation, progression, sequence, set, string, succession, train ◆ *verb* **3** = **bind**, confine, enslave, fetter, gyve (*archaic*), handcuff, manacle, restrain, shackle, tether, trammel, unite

chairman *noun* = **director**, chairperson, chairwoman, master of ceremonies, president, presider, speaker, spokesman, toastmaster

chalk up *verb Informal* = **score**, accumulate, achieve, attain, credit, enter, gain, log, mark, record, register, tally, win

challenge *noun* **1** = **test**, confrontation, dare, defiance, face-off (*slang*), interrogation, provocation, question, summons to contest, trial, ultimatum ◆ *verb* **2** = **test**, accost, arouse, beard, brave, call out, call (someone's) bluff, claim, confront, dare, defy, demand, dispute, face off (*slang*), impugn, investigate, object to, provoke, question, require, stimulate,

summon, tackle, tax, throw down the gauntlet, try

chamber *noun* **1** = **room**, apartment, bedroom, cavity, compartment, cubicle, enclosure, hall, hollow **2** = **council**, assembly, legislative body, legislature

champion *noun* **1** = **winner**, challenger, conqueror, hero, nonpareil, title holder, victor, warrior **2** = **defender**, backer, guardian, patron, protector, upholder, vindicator ◆ *verb* **3** = **support**, advocate, back, commend, defend, encourage, espouse, fight for, promote, stick up for (*informal*), uphold

chance *noun* **1** = **probability**, liability, likelihood, odds, possibility, prospect **2** = **opportunity**, occasion, opening, scope, time, window **3** = **luck**, accident, casualty, coincidence, contingency, destiny, fate, fortuity, fortune, misfortune, peril, providence **4** = **risk**, gamble, hazard, jeopardy, speculation, uncertainty ◆ *verb* **5** = **risk**, endanger, gamble, go out on a limb, hazard, jeopardize, skate on thin ice, stake, try, venture, wager **6** = **happen**, befall, betide, come about, come to pass, fall out, occur ◆ *adjective* **7** = **accidental**, casual, contingent, fortuitous, inadvertent, incidental, random, serendipitous, unforeseeable, unforeseen, unintentional, unlooked-for
➤ **Antonyms**
noun ≠**probability**: certainty, design, impossibility, improbability, intention, surety, unlikelihood ◆ *adjective* ≠**accidental**: arranged, deliberate, designed, expected, foreseen, intentional, planned

chancy *adjective Informal* = **risky**, dangerous, dicey (*informal, chiefly Brit.*), dodgy (*Brit., Austral., & N.Z. slang*), hazardous, perilous, problematical, speculative, uncertain
➤ **Antonyms**
certain, reliable, safe, secure, sound, stable, sure

change *noun* **1** = **alteration**, difference, innovation, metamorphosis, modification, mutation, permutation, revolution, transformation, transition, transmutation, vicissitude **2** = **variety**, break (*informal*), departure, diversion, novelty, variation, whole new ball game (*informal*) **3** = **exchange**, conversion, interchange, substitution, swap, trade ◆ *verb* **4** = **alter**, convert, diversify, fluctuate, metamorphose, moderate, modify, mutate, reform, remodel, reorganize, restyle, shift, transform, transmute, vacillate, vary, veer **5** = **exchange**, alternate, barter, convert, displace, interchange, remove, replace, substitute, swap, trade, transmit

➤ **Antonyms**
noun ≠**alteration, variety:** constancy, invariability, monotony, permanence, stability, uniformity ♦ *verb* ≠**alter:** hold, keep, remain, stay

changeable *adjective* = **variable,** capricious, changeful, chequered, erratic, fickle, fitful, fluid, inconstant, irregular, kaleidoscopic, labile (*Chemistry*), mercurial, mobile, mutable, protean, shifting, temperamental, uncertain, uneven, unpredictable, unreliable, unsettled, unstable, unsteady, vacillating, versatile, volatile, wavering, whimsical
➤ **Antonyms**
constant, invariable, irreversible, regular, reliable, stable, steady, unchangeable

changeless *adjective* = **unchanging,** abiding, consistent, constant, eternal, everlasting, fixed, immovable, immutable, permanent, perpetual, regular, reliable, resolute, settled, stationary, steadfast, steady, unalterable, uniform, unvarying

channel *noun* **1** = **route,** approach, artery, avenue, course, means, medium, path, way **2** = **passage,** canal, chamber, conduit, duct, fluting, furrow, groove, gutter, main, route, strait ♦ *verb* **3** = **direct,** conduct, convey, guide, transmit

chant *verb* **1** = **sing,** carol, chorus, croon, descant, intone, recite, warble ♦ *noun* **2** = **song,** carol, chorus, melody, psalm

chaos *noun* = **disorder,** anarchy, bedlam, confusion, disorganization, entropy, lawlessness, mayhem, pandemonium, tumult
➤ **Antonyms**
neatness, orderliness, organization, tidiness

chaotic *adjective* = **disordered,** anarchic, confused, deranged, disorganized, lawless, purposeless, rampageous, riotous, topsy-turvy, tumultuous, uncontrolled

chap *noun Informal* = **fellow,** bloke (*Brit. informal*), character, cove (*slang*), customer (*informal*), dude (*U.S. & Canad. informal*), guy (*informal*), individual, man, person, sort, type

chaperone *noun* **1** = **escort,** companion, duenna, governess ♦ *verb* **2** = **escort,** accompany, attend, protect, safeguard, shepherd, watch over

chapter *noun* = **section,** clause, division, episode, part, period, phase, stage, topic

char *verb* = **scorch,** carbonize, cauterize, sear, singe

character *noun* **1** = **nature,** attributes, bent, calibre, cast, complexion, constitution, disposition, individuality, kidney, make-up, marked traits, personality, quality, temper, temperament, type **2** = **reputation,** honour, integrity, rectitude, strength, uprightness **3**

= **role,** part, persona, portrayal **4** = **eccentric,** card (*informal*), nut (*slang*), oddball (*informal*), odd bod (*informal*), oddity, original, queer fish (*Brit. informal*), wacko *or* whacko (*informal*) **5** *Informal* = **person,** fellow, guy (*informal*), individual, sort, type **6** = **symbol,** cipher, device, emblem, figure, hieroglyph, letter, logo, mark, rune, sign, type

characteristic *noun* **1** = **feature,** attribute, faculty, idiosyncrasy, mark, peculiarity, property, quality, quirk, trait ♦ *adjective* **2** = **typical,** distinctive, distinguishing, idiosyncratic, individual, peculiar, representative, singular, special, specific, symbolic, symptomatic
➤ **Antonyms**
adjective ≠**typical:** rare, uncharacteristic, unrepresentative, unusual

characterize *verb* = **identify,** brand, distinguish, indicate, inform, mark, represent, stamp, typify

charade *noun* = **pretence,** fake, farce, pantomime, parody, travesty

charge *verb* **1** = **accuse,** arraign, blame, impeach, incriminate, indict, involve **2** = **attack,** assail, assault, rush, stampede, storm **3** = **fill,** instil, lade, load, suffuse **4** *Formal* = **command,** bid, commit, demand, enjoin, entrust, exhort, instruct, order, require ♦ *noun* **5** = **price,** amount, cost, damage (*informal*), expenditure, expense, outlay, payment, rate, toll **6** = **accusation,** allegation, imputation, indictment **7** = **attack,** assault, onset, onslaught, rush, sortie, stampede **8** = **care,** custody, duty, office, responsibility, safekeeping, trust **9** = **ward,** burden, concern **10** = **instruction,** canon, command, demand, dictate, direction, exhortation, injunction, mandate, order, precept
➤ **Antonyms**
verb ≠**accuse:** absolve, acquit, clear, exonerate, pardon ≠**attack:** back off, retreat, withdraw ♦ *noun* ≠**accusation:** absolution, acquittal, clearance, exoneration, pardon, reprieve ≠**attack:** retreat, withdrawal

charisma *noun* = **charm,** allure, attraction, lure, magnetism, personality

charismatic *adjective* = **charming,** alluring, attractive, enticing, influential, magnetic

charitable *adjective* **1** = **kind,** broad-minded, considerate, favourable, forgiving, gracious, humane, indulgent, lenient, magnanimous, sympathetic, tolerant, understanding **2** = **generous,** beneficent, benevolent, bountiful, eleemosynary, kind, lavish, liberal, philanthropic

> **Antonyms**
≠**kind**: inconsiderate, mean, strict, uncharitable, unforgiving, unkind, unsympathetic ≠**generous**: mean, stingy, ungenerous

charity *noun* **1** = **donations**, alms-giving, assistance, benefaction, contributions, endowment, fund, gift, hand-out, help, largesse *or* largess, philanthropy, relief **2** = **kindness**, affection, Agape, altruism, benevolence, benignity, bountifulness, bounty, compassion, fellow feeling, generosity, goodness, goodwill, humanity, indulgence, love, pity, tenderheartedness
> **Antonyms**
≠**donations**: meanness, miserliness, selfishness, stinginess ≠**kindness**: hatred, ill will, intolerance, malice

charlatan *noun* = **fraud**, cheat, con man (*informal*), fake, fraudster, grifter (*slang, chiefly U.S. & Canad.*), impostor, mountebank, phoney *or* phony (*informal*), pretender, quack, sham, swindler

charm *noun* **1** = **attraction**, allure, allurement, appeal, desirability, fascination, magnetism **2** = **spell**, enchantment, magic, sorcery **3** = **talisman**, amulet, fetish, good-luck piece, lucky piece, periapt (*rare*), trinket ◆ *verb* **4** = **attract**, absorb, allure, beguile, bewitch, cajole, captivate, delight, enamour, enchant, enrapture, entrance, fascinate, mesmerize, please, ravish, win, win over
> **Antonyms**
noun ≠**attraction**: repulsiveness, unattractiveness ◆ *verb* ≠**attract**: alienate, repel, repulse

charming *adjective* = **attractive**, appealing, bewitching, captivating, cute, delectable, delightful, engaging, eye-catching, fetching, irresistible, likable *or* likeable, lovely, pleasant, pleasing, seductive, winning, winsome
> **Antonyms**
disgusting, horrid, repulsive, unappealing, unattractive, unlikable *or* unlikeable, unpleasant, unpleasing

chart *noun* **1** = **table**, blueprint, diagram, graph, map, plan, tabulation ◆ *verb* **2** = **plot**, delineate, draft, graph, map out, outline, shape, sketch

charter *noun* **1** = **document**, bond, concession, contract, deed, franchise, indenture, licence, permit, prerogative, privilege, right ◆ *verb* **2** = **hire**, commission, employ, lease, rent **3** = **authorize**, sanction

chase *verb* **1** = **pursue**, course, follow, hunt, run after, track **2** = **drive away**, drive, expel, hound, put to flight ◆ *noun* **3** = **pursuit**, hunt, hunting, race, venery (*archaic*)

chasm *noun* = **gulf**, abyss, alienation, breach, cavity, cleft, crack, crater, crevasse, fissure, gap, gorge, hiatus, hollow, opening, ravine, rent, rift, split, void

chassis *noun* = **frame**, anatomy, bodywork, framework, fuselage, skeleton, substructure

chaste *adjective* = **pure**, austere, decent, decorous, elegant, immaculate, incorrupt, innocent, modest, moral, neat, quiet, refined, restrained, simple, unaffected, uncontaminated, undefiled, unsullied, vestal, virginal, virtuous, wholesome
> **Antonyms**
corrupt, dirty, dishonourable, immoral, impure, promiscuous, self-indulgent, tainted, unchaste, unclean, unrestrained, wanton

chasten *verb* = **subdue**, afflict, castigate, chastise, correct, cow, curb, discipline, humble, humiliate, put in one's place, repress, soften, tame

chastise *verb* **1** = **scold**, berate, castigate, censure, correct, discipline, upbraid **2** *Old-fashioned* = **beat**, flog, lash, lick (*informal*), punish, scourge, whip
> **Antonyms**
≠**scold**: commend, compliment, congratulate, praise, reward ≠**beat**: caress, cuddle, embrace, fondle, hug

chastity *noun* = **purity**, celibacy, continence, innocence, maidenhood, modesty, virginity, virtue
> **Antonyms**
debauchery, immorality, lewdness, licentiousness, profligacy, promiscuity, wantonness

chat *noun* **1** = **talk**, chatter, chinwag (*Brit. informal*), confab (*informal*), conversation, gossip, heart-to-heart, natter, schmooze (*slang*), tête-à-tête ◆ *verb* **2** = **talk**, chatter, chew the rag *or* fat (*slang*), gossip, jaw (*slang*), natter, rabbit (on) (*Brit. informal*), run off at the mouth (*U.S. slang*), schmooze (*slang*), shoot the breeze (*U.S. slang*)

chatter *noun* **1** = **prattle**, babble, blather, chat, gab (*informal*), gossip, jabber, natter, rabbit (*Brit. informal*), tattle, twaddle ◆ *verb* **2** = **prattle**, babble, blather, chat, gab (*informal*), gossip, jabber, natter, prate, rabbit (on) (*Brit. informal*), run off at the mouth (*U.S. slang*), schmooze (*slang*), tattle

chatty *adjective* = **talkative**, colloquial, familiar, friendly, gossipy, informal, newsy (*informal*)
> **Antonyms**
aloof, cold, distant, formal, hostile, quiet, reserved, shy, silent, standoffish, taciturn, timid, unfriendly, unsociable

cheap *adjective* **1** = **inexpensive**, bargain, cheapo (*informal*), cut-price, economical, economy, keen, low-cost, low-priced,

reasonable, reduced, sale **2** = **inferior**, bush-league (*Austral. & N.Z. informal*), chickenshit (*U.S. slang*), common, crappy (*slang*), dime-a-dozen (*informal*), low-rent (*informal, chiefly U.S.*), paltry, piss-poor (*U.S. taboo slang*), poor, poxy (*slang*), second-rate, shoddy, tatty, tawdry, tinhorn (*U.S. slang*), two a penny, two-bit (*U.S. & Canad. slang*), worthless **3** *Informal* = **despicable**, base, contemptible, low, mean, scurvy, sordid, vulgar
➤ **Antonyms**
≠**inexpensive**: costly, dear, expensive, pricey (*informal*), steep ≠**inferior**: admirable, decent, elegant, good, high-class, superior, tasteful, valuable ≠**despicable**: admirable, decent, generous, good, honourable

cheapen *verb* = **degrade**, belittle, debase, demean, denigrate, depreciate, derogate, devalue, discredit, disparage, lower

cheat *verb* **1** = **deceive**, bamboozle (*informal*), beguile, bilk, con (*informal*), cozen, defraud, diddle (*informal*), do (*informal*), do the dirty on (*Brit. informal*), double-cross (*informal*), dupe, finagle (*informal*), fleece, fool, gull (*archaic*), hoax, hoodwink, kid (*informal*), mislead, pull a fast one on (*informal*), rip off (*slang*), skin (*slang*), stiff (*slang*), sting (*informal*), stitch up (*slang*), swindle, take for a ride (*informal*), take in (*informal*), thwart, trick, victimize **2** = **foil**, baffle, check, defeat, deprive, frustrate, prevent, thwart ◆ *noun* **3** = **deceiver**, charlatan, cheater, chiseller (*informal*), con man (*informal*), dodger, double-crosser (*informal*), fraudster, grifter (*slang, chiefly U.S. & Canad.*), impostor, knave (*archaic*), rogue, shark, sharper, swindler, trickster **4** = **deception**, artifice, deceit, fraud, imposture, rip-off (*slang*), scam (*slang*), sting (*informal*), swindle, trickery

check *verb* **1** = **examine**, check out (*informal*), compare, confirm, inquire into, inspect, investigate, look at, look over, make sure, monitor, note, probe, research, scrutinize, study, take a dekko at (*Brit. slang*), test, tick, verify, vet, work over **2** = **stop**, arrest, bar, bridle, control, curb, delay, halt, hinder, hobble, impede, inhibit, limit, nip in the bud, obstruct, pause, put a spoke in someone's wheel, rein, repress, restrain, retard, stem the flow, thwart ◆ *noun* **3** = **examination**, inspection, investigation, once-over (*informal*), research, scrutiny, test **4** = **stoppage**, constraint, control, curb, damper, hindrance, impediment, inhibition, limitation, obstacle, obstruction, rein, restraint **5** = **setback**, blow, disappointment, frustration, rejection, reverse, whammy (*informal, chiefly U.S.*)

➤ **Antonyms**
verb ≠**examine**: disregard, ignore, neglect, overlook, pass over, pay no attention to ≠**stop**: accelerate, advance, begin, encourage, further, give free rein, help, release, start

cheek *noun Informal* = **impudence**, audacity, brass neck (*Brit. informal*), brazenness, chutzpah (*U.S. & Canad. informal*), disrespect, effrontery, face (*informal*), front, gall (*informal*), impertinence, insolence, lip (*slang*), neck (*informal*), nerve, sassiness (*U.S. informal*), sauce (*informal*), temerity

cheeky *adjective* = **impudent**, audacious, disrespectful, forward, fresh (*informal*), impertinent, insolent, insulting, lippy (*U.S. & Canad. slang*), pert, sassy (*U.S. informal*), saucy
➤ **Antonyms**
civil, complaisant, courteous, decorous, deferential, mannerly, polite, respectful, well-behaved, well-mannered

cheer *verb* **1** = **applaud**, acclaim, clap, hail, hurrah **2** = **cheer up**, animate, brighten, buoy up, comfort, console, elate, elevate, encourage, enliven, exhilarate, gladden, hearten, incite, inspirit, solace, uplift, warm ◆ *noun* **3** = **applause**, acclamation, ovation, plaudits **4** = **cheerfulness**, animation, buoyancy, comfort, gaiety, gladness, glee, hopefulness, joy, liveliness, merriment, merry-making, mirth, optimism, solace
➤ **Antonyms**
verb ≠**applaud**: blow a raspberry, boo, hiss, jeer, ridicule ≠**cheer up**: darken, depress, discourage, dishearten, sadden

cheerful *adjective* = **happy**, animated, blithe, bright, bucked (*informal*), buoyant, cheery, chirpy (*informal*), contented, enlivening, enthusiastic, gay, genial, glad, gladsome (*archaic*), hearty, jaunty, jolly, joyful, light-hearted, lightsome (*archaic*), merry, optimistic, pleasant, sparkling, sprightly, sunny, upbeat (*informal*)
➤ **Antonyms**
cheerless, dejected, depressed, depressing, despondent, dismal, down, downcast, down in the dumps (*informal*), dull, gloomy, low, melancholy, miserable, morose, pensive, sad, unhappy, unpleasant

cheerfulness *noun* = **happiness**, buoyancy, exuberance, gaiety, geniality, gladness, good cheer, good humour, high spirits, jauntiness, joyousness, light-heartedness

cheering *adjective* = **encouraging**, auspicious, bright, comforting, heartening, promising, propitious

cheerless *adjective* = **gloomy**, austere, bleak, comfortless, dark, dejected, depressed,

desolate, despondent, disconsolate, dismal, dolorous, drab, dreary, dull, forlorn, funereal, grim, joyless, melancholy, miserable, mournful, sad, sombre, sorrowful, sullen, unhappy, woebegone, woeful
➤ **Antonyms**
cheerful, cheery, elated, happy, jolly, joyful, light-hearted, merry

cheer up *verb* **1** = **comfort**, brighten, encourage, enliven, gee up, gladden, hearten, jolly along (*informal*) **2** = **take heart**, buck up (*informal*), perk up, rally

cheery *adjective* = **cheerful**, breezy, carefree, chirpy (*informal*), full of beans (*informal*), genial, good-humoured, happy, jovial, lively, pleasant, sunny, upbeat (*informal*)

chemical *noun* = **compound**, drug, potion, substance, synthetic

chemist *noun* = **pharmacist**, apothecary (*obsolete*), dispenser, pharmacologist

cherish *verb* **1** = **cling to**, cleave to, encourage, entertain, foster, harbour, hold dear, nurture, prize, sustain, treasure **2** = **care for**, comfort, cosset, hold dear, love, nourish, nurse, shelter, support, treasure
➤ **Antonyms**
abandon, desert, despise, disdain, dislike, forsake, hate, neglect

cherubic *adjective* = **angelic**, adorable, heavenly, innocent, lovable, seraphic, sweet

chest *noun* = **box**, ark (*dialect*), case, casket, coffer, crate, kist (*Scot. & Northern English dialect*), strongbox, trunk

chew *verb* **1** = **bite**, champ, chomp, crunch, gnaw, grind, masticate, munch **2 chew over** = **consider**, deliberate upon, meditate, mull (over), muse on, ponder, reflect upon, ruminate, weigh

chewy *adjective* = **tough**, as tough as old boots, fibrous, leathery

chic *adjective* = **stylish**, elegant, fashionable, modish, sexy (*informal*), smart, trendy (*Brit. informal*), up-to-date, urbane
➤ **Antonyms**
dinosaur, inelegant, naff (*Brit. slang*), old-fashioned, outmoded, out-of-date, passé, shabby, unfashionable

chide *verb* *Old-fashioned* = **scold**, admonish, bawl out (*informal*), berate, blame, blast, carpet (*informal*), censure, check, chew out (*U.S. & Canad. informal*), criticize, find fault, give (someone) a rocket (*Brit. & N.Z. informal*), give (someone) a row (*Scot. informal*), lambast(e), lecture, put down, rap over the knuckles, read the riot act, rebuke, reprehend, reprimand, reproach, reprove, slap on the wrist, slate (*informal, chiefly Brit.*), tear into (*informal*), tear (someone) off a strip (*Brit. informal*), tell off (*informal*),

tick off (*informal*), upbraid

chief *noun* **1** = **head**, boss (*informal*), captain, chieftain, commander, director, governor, leader, lord, manager, master, principal, ringleader, ruler, superintendent, superior, suzerain, torchbearer ♦ *adjective* **2** = **primary**, big-time (*informal*), capital, cardinal, central, especial, essential, foremost, grand, highest, key, leading, main, major league (*informal*), most important, outstanding, paramount, predominant, pre-eminent, premier, prevailing, prime, principal, superior, supreme, uppermost, vital
➤ **Antonyms**
noun ≠**head**: follower, subject, subordinate ♦ *adjective* ≠**primary**: least, minor, subordinate, subsidiary

chiefly *adverb* **1** = **especially**, above all, essentially, primarily, principally **2** = **mainly**, in general, in the main, largely, mostly, on the whole, predominantly, usually

child *noun* = **youngster**, ankle-biter (*Austral. slang*), babe, babe in arms (*informal*), baby, bairn (*Scot.*), brat, chit, descendant, infant, issue, juvenile, kid (*informal*), little one, minor, nipper (*informal*), nursling, offspring, progeny, rug rat (*slang*), sprog (*slang*), suckling, toddler, tot, wean (*Scot.*)

childbirth *noun* = **child-bearing**, accouchement, confinement, delivery, labour, lying-in, parturition, travail

childhood *noun* = **youth**, boyhood *or* girlhood, immaturity, infancy, minority, schooldays

childish *adjective* = **immature**, boyish *or* girlish, foolish, frivolous, infantile, juvenile, puerile, silly, simple, trifling, weak, young
➤ **Antonyms**
adult, grown-up, manly *or* womanly, mature, sensible, sophisticated

childlike *adjective* = **innocent**, artless, credulous, guileless, ingenuous, naive, simple, trustful, trusting, unfeigned

chill *noun* **1** = **cold**, bite, coldness, coolness, crispness, frigidity, nip, rawness, sharpness ♦ *verb* **2** = **cool**, congeal, freeze, refrigerate **3** = **dishearten**, dampen, deject, depress, discourage, dismay ♦ *adjective* **4** = **cold**, biting, bleak, chilly, freezing, frigid, parky (*Brit. informal*), raw, sharp, wintry **5** = **unfriendly**, aloof, cool, depressing, distant, frigid, hostile, stony, ungenial, unresponsive, unwelcoming

chilly *adjective* **1** = **cool**, blowy, breezy, brisk, crisp, draughty, fresh, nippy, parky (*Brit. informal*), penetrating, sharp **2** = **unfriendly**, cold as ice, frigid, hostile, unresponsive, unsympathetic, unwelcoming

> **Antonyms**
≠ **cool:** balmy, hot, mild, scorching, sunny, sweltering, warm ≠ **unfriendly:** affable, chummy (*informal*), congenial, cordial, friendly, responsive, sociable, sympathetic, warm, welcoming

chime *verb, noun* = **ring**, boom, clang, dong, jingle, peal, sound, tinkle, toll

china *noun* = **pottery**, ceramics, crockery, porcelain, service, tableware, ware

chink *noun* = **opening**, aperture, cleft, crack, cranny, crevice, cut, fissure, flaw, gap, rift

chip *noun* 1 = **scratch**, dent, flake, flaw, fragment, nick, notch, paring, scrap, shard, shaving, sliver, wafer ♦ *verb* 2 = **nick**, chisel, damage, gash, whittle

chip in *verb Informal* = **contribute**, donate, go Dutch (*informal*), interpose, interrupt, pay, subscribe

chirp *verb* = **chirrup**, cheep, peep, pipe, tweet, twitter, warble

chivalrous *adjective* = **courteous**, bold, brave, courageous, courtly, gallant, gentlemanly, heroic, high-minded, honourable, intrepid, knightly, magnanimous, true, valiant
> **Antonyms**
boorish, cowardly, dishonourable, disloyal, rude, uncourtly, ungallant, unmannerly

chivalry *noun* = **courtesy**, courage, courtliness, gallantry, gentlemanliness, knight-errantry, knighthood, politeness

chivvy *verb Brit.* = **nag**, annoy, badger, bend someone's ear (*informal*), breathe down someone's neck (*informal*), bug (*informal*), harass, hassle (*informal*), hound, pester, plague, pressure (*informal*), prod, torment

choice *noun* 1 = **option**, alternative, discrimination, election, pick, preference, say 2 = **selection**, range, variety ♦ *adjective* 3 = **best**, bad (*slang*), crucial (*slang*), dainty, def (*slang*), elect, elite, excellent, exclusive, exquisite, hand-picked, nice, precious, prime, prize, rare, select, special, superior, uncommon, unusual, valuable

choke *verb* 1 = **strangle**, asphyxiate, gag, overpower, smother, stifle, suffocate, suppress, throttle 2 = **block**, bar, bung, clog, close, congest, constrict, dam, obstruct, occlude, stop

choleric *adjective* = **bad-tempered**, angry, cross, fiery, hasty, hot, hot-tempered, ill-tempered, irascible, irritable, passionate, petulant, quick-tempered, ratty (*Brit. & N.Z. informal*), testy, tetchy, touchy

choose *verb* = **pick**, adopt, cherry-pick, cull, designate, desire, elect, espouse, fix on, opt for, predestine, prefer, see fit, select, settle

upon, single out, take, wish
> **Antonyms**
decline, dismiss, exclude, forgo, leave, refuse, reject, throw aside

choosy *adjective Informal* = **fussy**, discriminating, exacting, faddy, fastidious, finicky, particular, picky (*informal*), selective
> **Antonyms**
easy (*informal*), easy to please, indiscriminate, undemanding, unselective

chop *verb* 1 = **cut**, axe, cleave, fell, hack, hew, lop, sever, shear, slash, truncate
♦ *noun* 2 **the chop** *Slang, chiefly Brit.* = **the sack** (*informal*), dismissal, one's cards, sacking (*informal*), termination, the axe (*informal*), the boot (*slang*), the (old) heave-ho (*informal*), the order of the boot (*slang*)

choppy *adjective* = **rough**, blustery, broken, ruffled, squally, tempestuous
> **Antonyms**
calm, smooth, windless

chop up *verb* = **cut up**, cube, dice, divide, fragment, mince

chore *noun* = **task**, burden, duty, errand, fag (*informal*), job, no picnic

chortle *verb, noun* = **chuckle**, cackle, crow, guffaw

chorus *noun* 1 = **choir**, choristers, ensemble, singers, vocalists 2 = **refrain**, burden, response, strain 3 = **unison**, accord, concert, harmony

christen *verb* 1 = **baptize** 2 = **name**, call, designate, dub, style, term, title

Christmas *noun* = **festive season**, Noel, Xmas (*informal*), Yule (*archaic*), Yuletide (*archaic*)

chronic *adjective* 1 = **habitual**, confirmed, deep-rooted, deep-seated, incessant, incurable, ineradicable, ingrained, inveterate, persistent 2 *Informal* = **dreadful**, abysmal, appalling, atrocious, awful
> **Antonyms**
≠ **habitual:** infrequent, occasional, temporary

chronicle *noun* 1 = **record**, account, annals, diary, history, journal, narrative, register, story ♦ *verb* 2 = **record**, enter, narrate, put on record, recount, register, relate, report, set down, tell

chronicler *noun* = **recorder**, annalist, diarist, historian, historiographer, narrator, reporter, scribe

chronological *adjective* = **in order**, consecutive, historical, in sequence, ordered, progressive, sequential
> **Antonyms**
haphazard, intermittent, irregular, out-of-order, random

chubby *adjective* = **plump**, buxom, flabby,

fleshy, podgy, portly, roly-poly, rotund, round, stout, tubby

➤ Antonyms

lean, skinny, slender, slight, slim, sylphlike, thin

chuck verb Informal = **throw**, cast, discard, fling, heave, hurl, pitch, shy, sling, toss

chuckle verb = **laugh**, chortle, crow, exult, giggle, snigger, titter

chum noun Informal = **friend**, cock (Brit. informal), companion, comrade, crony, mate (informal), pal (informal)

chunk noun = **piece**, block, dollop (informal), hunk, lump, mass, nugget, portion, slab, wad, wodge (Brit. informal)

chunky adjective = **thickset**, beefy (informal), dumpy, stocky, stubby

churl noun 1 = **boor**, lout, oaf 2 Archaic = **peasant**, bumpkin, clodhopper (informal), clown, hayseed (U.S. & Canad. informal), hick (informal, chiefly U.S. & Canad.), hillbilly, rustic, yokel

churlish adjective 1 = **boorish**, loutish, oafish, uncouth, unmannerly, vulgar 2 = **rude**, brusque, crabbed, harsh, ill-tempered, impolite, morose, sullen, surly, uncivil

➤ Antonyms

≠boorish: cultivated, mannerly, noble, well-bred ≠rude: agreeable, amiable, civil, courteous, good-tempered, pleasant, polite

churlishness noun 1 = **boorishness**, crassness, crudeness, loutishness, oafishness, uncouthness 2 = **rudeness**, surliness

churn verb = **stir up**, agitate, beat, boil, convulse, foam, froth, seethe, swirl, toss

cigarette noun = **fag** (Brit. slang), cancer stick (slang), ciggy (informal), coffin nail (slang), gasper (slang), smoke

cinema noun = **films**, big screen (informal), flicks (slang), motion pictures, movies, pictures

cipher noun 1 = **code**, cryptograph 2 = **symbol**, character, digit, figure, number, numeral 3 = **monogram**, device, logo, mark 4 = **nobody**, nonentity 5 Obsolete = **zero**, nil, nothing, nought

circle noun 1 = **ring**, band, circumference, coil, cordon, cycle, disc, globe, lap, loop, orb, perimeter, periphery, revolution, round, sphere, turn 2 = **area**, bounds, circuit, compass, domain, enclosure, field, orbit, province, range, realm, region, scene, sphere 3 = **group**, assembly, class, clique, club, company, coterie, crowd, fellowship, fraternity, order, school, set, society ♦ verb 4 = **go round**, belt, circumnavigate, circumscribe, coil, compass, curve, encircle, enclose, encompass, envelop, enwreath,

gird, hem in, pivot, revolve, ring, rotate, surround, tour, wheel, whirl

circuit noun 1 = **course**, area, compass, journey, lap, orbit, perambulation, revolution, round, route, tour, track 2 = **range**, boundary, bounding line, bounds, circumference, compass, district, limit, pale, region, tract

circuitous adjective = **indirect**, ambagious (archaic), devious, labyrinthine, meandering, oblique, rambling, roundabout, tortuous, winding

➤ Antonyms

as the crow flies, direct, straight, undeviating, unswerving

circular adjective 1 = **round**, ring-shaped, rotund, spherical 2 = **orbital**, circuitous, cyclical ♦ noun 3 = **advertisement**, notice

circulate verb 1 = **spread**, broadcast, diffuse, disseminate, distribute, issue, make known, promulgate, propagate, publicize, publish 2 = **flow**, gyrate, radiate, revolve, rotate

circulation noun 1 = **bloodstream** 2 = **flow**, circling, motion, rotation 3 = **distribution**, currency, dissemination, spread, transmission, vogue

circumference noun = **boundary**, ambit, border, bounds, circuit, edge, extremity, fringe, limits, outline, pale, perimeter, periphery, rim, verge

circumscribe verb Formal = **restrict**, bound, confine, define, delimit, delineate, demarcate, encircle, enclose, encompass, environ, hem in, limit, mark off, restrain, straiten, surround

circumspect adjective = **cautious**, attentive, canny, careful, deliberate, discreet, discriminating, guarded, heedful, judicious, observant, politic, prudent, sagacious, sage, vigilant, wary, watchful

➤ Antonyms

bold, careless, daring, foolhardy, heedless, imprudent, rash, venturous

circumstance noun = **event**, accident, condition, contingency, detail, element, fact, factor, happening, incident, item, occurrence, particular, position, respect, situation

circumstances plural noun = **situation**, lie of the land, lifestyle, means, position, resources, state, state of affairs, station, status, times

circumstantial adjective 1 = **conjectural**, contingent, founded on circumstances, hearsay, incidental, indirect, inferential, presumptive, provisional 2 = **detailed**, particular, specific

cistern noun = **tank**, basin, reservoir, sink, vat

citadel noun = fortress, bastion, fastness, fortification, keep, stronghold, tower

citation noun 1 = commendation, award, mention 2 = quotation, commendation, excerpt, illustration, passage, quote, reference, source

cite verb 1 = quote, adduce, advance, allude to, enumerate, evidence, extract, mention, name, specify 2 Law = summon, call, subpoena

citizen noun = inhabitant, burgess, burgher, denizen, dweller, freeman, ratepayer, resident, subject, townsman

city noun 1 = town, conurbation, megalopolis, metropolis, municipality ♦ adjective 2 = urban, civic, metropolitan, municipal

civic adjective = public, borough, communal, community, local, municipal

civil adjective 1 = civic, domestic, home, interior, municipal, political 2 = polite, accommodating, affable, civilized, complaisant, courteous, courtly, obliging, polished, refined, urbane, well-bred, well-mannered
➤ **Antonyms**
≠civic: military, religious, state ≠polite: discourteous, ill-mannered, impolite, rude, uncivil, unfriendly, ungracious, unpleasant

civility noun = politeness, affability, amiability, breeding, complaisance, cordiality, courteousness, courtesy, good manners, graciousness, politesse, tact, urbanity

civilization noun 1 = culture, advancement, cultivation, development, education, enlightenment, progress, refinement, sophistication 2 = society, community, nation, people, polity 3 = customs, mores, way of life

civilize verb = cultivate, educate, enlighten, humanize, improve, polish, refine, sophisticate, tame

civilized adjective = cultured, educated, enlightened, humane, polite, sophisticated, tolerant, urbane
➤ **Antonyms**
ignorant, naive, primitive, simple, uncivilized, uncultivated, uncultured, undeveloped, unenlightened, unsophisticated, wild

claim verb 1 = assert, allege, challenge, exact, hold, insist, maintain, profess, uphold 2 = demand, ask, call for, insist, need, require 3 = take, collect, pick up ♦ noun 4 = assertion, affirmation, allegation, pretension, privilege, protestation 5 = demand, application, call, petition, request, requirement 6 = right, title

clairvoyant noun 1 = psychic, diviner, fortune-teller, visionary ♦ adjective 2

= psychic, extrasensory, second-sighted, telepathic, visionary

clamber verb = climb, claw, scale, scrabble, scramble, shin

clammy adjective = moist, close, damp, dank, sticky, sweaty

clamorous adjective = noisy, blaring, deafening, insistent, loud, lusty, riotous, strident, tumultuous, uproarious, vehement, vociferous

clamour noun = noise, agitation, babel, blare, brouhaha, commotion, din, exclamation, hubbub, hullabaloo, outcry, racket, shout, shouting, uproar, vociferation

clamp noun 1 = vice, bracket, fastener, grip, press ♦ verb 2 = fasten, brace, clinch, fix, impose, make fast, secure

clan noun = family, band, brotherhood, clique, coterie, faction, fraternity, gens, group, house, order, race, schism, sect, sept, set, society, sodality, tribe

clandestine adjective = secret, cloak-and-dagger, concealed, covert, furtive, private, stealthy, surreptitious, underground

clang verb 1 = ring, bong, chime, clank, clash, jangle, resound, reverberate, toll ♦ noun 2 = ringing, clangour, ding-dong, knell, reverberation

clap verb 1 = applaud, acclaim, cheer, give (someone) a big hand 2 = strike, bang, pat, punch, slap, thrust, thwack, wallop (informal), whack
➤ **Antonyms**
≠applaud: blow a raspberry, boo, catcall, hiss, jeer

claptrap noun Informal = nonsense, affectation, balls (taboo slang), bilge (informal), blarney, bombast, bosh (informal), bull (informal), bullshit (taboo slang), bunk (informal), bunkum or buncombe (chiefly U.S.), cobblers (Brit. taboo slang), crap (slang), drivel, eyewash (informal), flannel (Brit. informal), garbage (informal), guff (slang), hogwash, hokum (slang, chiefly U.S. & Canad.), horsefeathers (U.S. slang), hot air (informal), humbug, insincerity, moonshine, pap, piffle (informal), poppycock (informal), rodomontade (literary), rot, rubbish, shit (taboo slang), tommyrot, tosh (slang, chiefly Brit.), trash, tripe (informal), twaddle

clarification noun = explanation, elucidation, exposition, illumination, interpretation, simplification

clarify verb 1 = explain, clear the air, clear up, elucidate, explicate, illuminate, interpret, make plain, resolve, simplify, throw or shed light on 2 = refine, cleanse, purify

clarity noun = clearness, comprehensibility,

definition, explicitness, intelligibility,
limpidity, lucidity, obviousness, precision,
simplicity, transparency
➤ **Antonyms**
cloudiness, complexity, complication,
dullness, haziness, imprecision, intricacy,
murkiness, obscurity

clash verb 1 = **conflict**, cross swords, feud,
grapple, lock horns, quarrel, war, wrangle 2
= **crash**, bang, clang, clank, clatter, jangle,
jar, rattle ♦ noun 3 = **conflict**, brush,
collision, confrontation, difference of
opinion, disagreement, fight, showdown
(informal)

clasp noun 1 = **fastening**, brooch, buckle,
catch, clip, fastener, grip, hasp, hook, pin,
press stud, snap 2 = **grasp**, embrace, grip,
hold, hug ♦ verb 3 = **grasp**, attack, clutch,
embrace, enfold, grapple, grip, hold, hug,
press, seize, squeeze 4 = **fasten**,
concatenate, connect

class noun 1 = **group**, caste, category,
classification, collection, denomination,
department, division, genre, genus, grade,
grouping, kind, league, order, rank, set, sort,
species, sphere, stamp, status, type, value
♦ verb 2 = **classify**, brand, categorize,
codify, designate, grade, group, label, rank,
rate

classic adjective 1 = **definitive**, archetypal,
exemplary, ideal, master, model,
paradigmatic, quintessential, standard 2
= **typical**, characteristic, regular, standard,
time-honoured, usual 3 = **best**,
consummate, finest, first-rate, masterly,
world-class 4 = **lasting**, abiding, ageless,
deathless, enduring, immortal, undying
♦ noun 5 = **standard**, exemplar,
masterpiece, masterwork, model, paradigm,
prototype
➤ **Antonyms**
adjective ≠**best**: inferior, modern, poor,
second-rate, terrible

classical adjective 1 = **pure**, chaste,
elegant, harmonious, refined, restrained,
symmetrical, understated, well-proportioned
2 = **Greek**, Attic, Augustan, Grecian,
Hellenic, Latin, Roman

classification noun = **categorization**,
analysis, arrangement, cataloguing,
codification, grading, sorting, taxonomy

classify verb = **categorize**, arrange,
catalogue, codify, dispose, distribute, file,
grade, pigeonhole, rank, sort, systematize,
tabulate

classy adjective Informal = **high-class**,
elegant, exclusive, posh (informal, chiefly
Brit.), stylish, superior, top-drawer, up-market

clause noun 1 = **section**, article, chapter,
condition, paragraph, part, passage 2

= **point**, heading, item, provision, proviso,
rider, specification, stipulation

claw noun 1 = **nail**, nipper, pincer, talon,
tentacle, unguis ♦ verb 2 = **scratch**, dig,
graze, lacerate, mangle, maul, rip, scrabble,
scrape, tear

clean adjective 1 = **pure**, faultless, flawless,
fresh, hygienic, immaculate, impeccable,
laundered, sanitary, spotless, squeaky-clean,
unblemished, unsoiled, unspotted,
unstained, unsullied, washed 2 = **hygienic**,
antiseptic, clarified, decontaminated, natural,
purified, sterile, sterilized, unadulterated,
uncontaminated, unpolluted 3 = **moral**,
chaste, decent, exemplary, good,
honourable, impeccable, innocent, pure,
respectable, undefiled, upright, virtuous 4
= **complete**, conclusive, decisive, entire,
final, perfect, thorough, total, unimpaired,
whole 5 = **neat**, delicate, elegant, graceful,
simple, tidy, trim, uncluttered ♦ verb 6
= **cleanse**, bath, deodorize, disinfect, do up,
dust, launder, lave, mop, purge, purify,
rinse, sanitize, scour, scrub, sponge, swab,
sweep, vacuum, wash, wipe
➤ **Antonyms**
adjective ≠**pure**: dirty, filthy, mucky, scuzzy
(slang, chiefly U.S.), soiled, sullied,
unwashed ≠**hygienic**: adulterated,
contaminated, infected, polluted ≠**moral**:
dishonourable, immoral, impure, indecent,
unchaste ≠**neat**: chaotic, disorderly,
disorganized, higgledy-piggledy (informal),
shambolic (informal), untidy ♦ verb
≠**cleanse**: adulterate, defile, dirty, infect,
mess up, pollute, soil, stain

clean-cut adjective = **clear**, chiselled,
definite, etched, neat, outlined, sharp, trim,
well-defined

cleanse verb = **clean**, absolve, clear,
lustrate, purge, purify, rinse, scour, scrub,
wash

cleanser noun = **detergent**, disinfectant,
purifier, scourer, soap, soap powder, solvent

clear adjective 1 = **certain**, convinced,
decided, definite, positive, resolved, satisfied,
sure 2 = **obvious**, apparent, articulate,
audible, blatant, bold, coherent,
comprehensible, conspicuous, cut-and-dried
(informal), definite, distinct, evident,
explicit, express, incontrovertible, intelligible,
lucid, manifest, palpable, patent, perceptible,
plain, pronounced, recognizable,
unambiguous, unequivocal, unmistakable,
unquestionable 3 = **transparent**, crystalline,
glassy, limpid, pellucid, see-through,
translucent 4 = **bright**, cloudless, fair, fine,
halcyon, light, luminous, shining, sunny,
unclouded, undimmed 5 = **unobstructed**,
empty, free, open, smooth, unhampered,
unhindered, unimpeded, unlimited 6

= **unblemished**, clean, guiltless, immaculate, innocent, pure, sinless, stainless, undefiled, untarnished, untroubled ♦ *verb* **7** = **unblock**, disengage, disentangle, extricate, free, loosen, open, rid, unclog, unload, unpack **8** = **pass over**, jump, leap, miss, vault **9** = **brighten**, break up, clarify, lighten **10** = **clean**, cleanse, erase, purify, refine, sweep away, tidy (up), wipe **11** = **absolve**, acquit, excuse, exonerate, justify, vindicate **12** = **gain**, acquire, earn, make, reap, secure
➤ **Antonyms**
adjective ≠**obvious**: ambiguous, confused, doubtful, equivocal, hidden, inarticulate, inaudible, incoherent, indistinct, inexplicit, obscured, unrecognizable ≠**transparent**: cloudy, muddy, non-translucent, non-transparent, opaque, turbid ≠**bright**: cloudy, dark, dull, foggy, hazy, misty, murky, overcast, stormy ≠**unobstructed**: barricaded, blocked, closed, hampered, impeded, obstructed ♦ *verb* ≠**absolve**: accuse, blame, charge, condemn, convict, find guilty

clearance *noun* **1** = **evacuation**, depopulation, emptying, eviction, removal, unpeopling, withdrawal **2** = **permission**, authorization, blank cheque, consent, endorsement, go-ahead (*informal*), green light, leave, O.K. *or* okay (*informal*), sanction **3** = **space**, allowance, gap, headroom, margin

clear-cut *adjective* = **straightforward**, black-and-white, cut-and-dried (*informal*), definite, explicit, plain, precise, specific, unambiguous, unequivocal

clearly *adverb* = **obviously**, beyond doubt, distinctly, evidently, incontestably, incontrovertibly, markedly, openly, overtly, undeniably, undoubtedly

clear out *verb* **1** = **get rid of**, empty, exhaust, sort, tidy up **2** *Informal* = **go away**, beat it (*slang*), decamp, depart, hook it (*slang*), leave, make oneself scarce, make tracks, pack one's bags (*informal*), retire, slope off, take oneself off, withdraw

clear up *verb* **1** = **tidy (up)**, order, rearrange **2** = **solve**, answer, clarify, elucidate, explain, resolve, straighten out, unravel

cleave[1] *verb* = **split**, crack, dissever, disunite, divide, hew, open, part, rend, rive, sever, slice, sunder, tear asunder

cleave[2] *verb* = **stick**, abide by, adhere, agree, attach, be devoted to, be true, cling, cohere, hold, remain, stand by

clergy *noun* = **priesthood**, churchmen, clergymen, clerics, ecclesiastics, first estate, holy orders, ministry, the cloth

clergyman *noun* = **minister**, chaplain, churchman, cleric, curate, divine, father,

man of God, man of the cloth, padre, parson, pastor, priest, rabbi, rector, reverend (*informal*), vicar

clerical *adjective* **1** = **office**, book-keeping, clerkish, clerkly, secretarial, stenographic **2** = **ecclesiastical**, pastoral, priestly, sacerdotal

clever *adjective* = **intelligent**, able, adroit, apt, astute, brainy (*informal*), bright, canny, capable, cunning, deep, dexterous, discerning, expert, gifted, ingenious, inventive, keen, knowing, knowledgeable, quick, quick-witted, rational, resourceful, sagacious, sensible, shrewd, skilful, smart, talented, witty
➤ **Antonyms**
awkward, clumsy, dense, dull, dumb (*informal*), ham-fisted (*informal*), inept, inexpert, maladroit, slow, stupid, thick, unaccomplished, unimaginative, witless

cleverness *noun* = **intelligence**, ability, adroitness, astuteness, brains, brightness, canniness, dexterity, flair, gift, gumption (*Brit. informal*), ingenuity, nous (*Brit. slang*), quickness, quick wits, resourcefulness, sagacity, sense, sharpness, shrewdness, smartness, smarts (*slang, chiefly U.S.*), suss (*slang*), talent, wit

cliché *noun* = **platitude**, banality, bromide, chestnut (*informal*), commonplace, hackneyed phrase, old saw, stereotype, truism

click *noun, verb* **1** = **snap**, beat, clack, tick ♦ *verb* **2** *Informal* = **become clear**, come home (to), fall into place, make sense **3** *Slang* = **get on**, be compatible, be on the same wavelength, feel a rapport, get on like a house on fire (*informal*), go over, hit it off (*informal*), make a hit, succeed, take to each other

client *noun* = **customer**, applicant, buyer, consumer, dependant, habitué, patient, patron, protégé, shopper

clientele *noun* = **customers**, business, clients, following, market, patronage, regulars, trade

cliff *noun* = **rock face**, bluff, crag, escarpment, face, overhang, precipice, scar, scarp

climactic *adjective* = **crucial**, climactical, critical, decisive, paramount, peak

climate *noun* **1** = **weather**, clime, country, region, temperature **2** = **trend**, ambience, disposition, feeling, mood, temper, tendency

climax *noun* **1** = **culmination**, acme, apogee, crest, head, height, highlight, high point, high spot (*informal*), *ne plus ultra*, pay-off (*informal*), peak, summit, top, zenith ♦ *verb* **2** = **culminate**, come to a head, peak

climb *verb* = **ascend**, clamber, mount, rise, scale, shin up, soar, top

climb down verb 1 = **descend**, dismount 2
= **back down**, eat crow (U.S. informal), eat
one's words, retract, retreat

clinch verb 1 = **settle**, assure, cap, conclude,
confirm, decide, determine, seal, secure, set
the seal on, sew up (informal), tip the
balance, verify 2 = **secure**, bolt, clamp,
fasten, fix, make fast, nail, rivet 3 = **grasp**,
clutch, cuddle, embrace, hug, squeeze

cling verb = **stick**, adhere, attach to, be true
to, clasp, cleave to, clutch, embrace, fasten,
grasp, grip, hug, twine round

clinical adjective = **unemotional**, analytic,
cold, detached, dispassionate, impersonal,
objective, scientific

clip[1] verb 1 = **trim**, crop, curtail, cut, cut
short, dock, pare, prune, shear, shorten, snip
♦ noun, verb 2 Informal = **smack**, belt
(informal), box, clout (informal), cuff,
knock, punch, skelp (dialect), strike, thump,
wallop (informal), whack ♦ noun 3 Informal
= **speed**, gallop, lick (informal), rate, velocity

clip[2] verb = **attach**, fasten, fix, hold, pin,
staple

clique noun = **group**, cabal, circle, clan,
coterie, crew (informal), crowd, faction,
gang, mob, pack, posse (informal), schism,
set

cloak noun 1 = **cape**, coat, mantle, wrap 2
= **cover**, blind, front, mask, pretext, shield
♦ verb 3 = **cover**, camouflage, conceal,
disguise, hide, mask, obscure, screen, veil

clodhopper noun Informal = **oaf**, booby,
boor, bumpkin, clown, galoot (slang, chiefly
U.S.), loon (informal), lout, yokel

clog verb = **obstruct**, block, bung, burden,
congest, dam up, hamper, hinder, impede,
jam, occlude, shackle, stop up

cloistered adjective = **sheltered**, cloistral,
confined, hermitic, insulated, protected,
reclusive, restricted, secluded, sequestered,
shielded, shut off, withdrawn
➤ Antonyms
extrovert, genial, gregarious, outgoing,
public, sociable, social

close[1] verb 1 = **shut**, bar, block, bung,
choke, clog, confine, cork, fill, lock, obstruct,
plug, seal, secure, shut up, stop up 2 = **end**,
axe (informal), cease, complete, conclude,
culminate, discontinue, finish, mothball, shut
down, terminate, wind up 3 = **connect**,
come together, couple, fuse, grapple, join,
unite ♦ noun 4 = **end**, cessation,
completion, conclusion, culmination,
denouement, ending, finale, finish, run-in,
termination
➤ Antonyms
verb ≠**shut**: clear, free, open, release,
unblock, unclog, uncork, unstop, widen
≠**end**: begin, commence, initiate, open,

start ≠**connect**: disconnect, disjoin,
disunite, divide, part, separate, split,
uncouple

close[2] adjective 1 = **near**, adjacent,
adjoining, a hop, skip and a jump away,
approaching, at hand, cheek by jowl, handy,
hard by, imminent, impending, just round
the corner, nearby, neighbouring, nigh,
proximate, upcoming, within sniffing
distance, within spitting distance (informal),
within striking distance (informal) 2
= **intimate**, attached, confidential, dear,
devoted, familiar, inseparable, loving 3
= **careful**, alert, assiduous, attentive,
concentrated, detailed, dogged, earnest,
fixed, intense, intent, keen, minute,
painstaking, rigorous, searching, thorough 4
= **compact**, congested, cramped, cropped,
crowded, dense, impenetrable, jam-packed,
packed, short, solid, thick, tight 5
= **accurate**, conscientious, exact, faithful,
literal, precise, strict 6 = **stifling**, airless,
confined, frowsty, fuggy, heavy, humid,
muggy, oppressive, stale, stuffy, suffocating,
sweltering, thick, unventilated 7 = **secretive**,
hidden, private, reticent, retired, secluded,
secret, taciturn, uncommunicative,
unforthcoming 8 = **mean**, illiberal, mingy
(Brit. informal), miserly, near, niggardly,
parsimonious, penurious, stingy, tight as a
duck's arse (taboo slang), tight-fisted,
ungenerous
➤ Antonyms
≠**near**: distant, far, far away, far off, future,
outlying, remote ≠**intimate**: alienated,
aloof, chilly, cold, cool, distant, indifferent,
standoffish, unfriendly ≠**compact**:
dispersed, empty, free, loose, penetrable,
porous, uncongested, uncrowded ≠**stifling**:
airy, fresh, refreshing, roomy, spacious
≠**mean**: charitable, extravagant, generous,
lavish, liberal, magnanimous, unstinting

closed adjective 1 = **shut**, fastened, locked,
out of business, out of service, sealed 2
= **exclusive**, restricted 3 = **finished**,
concluded, decided, ended, over, resolved,
settled, terminated
➤ Antonyms
≠**shut**: ajar, open, unclosed, unfastened,
unlocked, unsealed

cloth noun = **fabric**, dry goods, material,
stuff, textiles

clothe verb = **dress**, accoutre, apparel, array,
attire, bedizen (archaic), caparison, cover,
deck, doll up (slang), drape, endow,
enwrap, equip, fit out, garb, get ready,
habit, invest, outfit, rig, robe, swathe
➤ Antonyms
disrobe, divest, expose, strip, strip off,
unclothe, uncover, undress

clothes plural noun = **clothing**, apparel,

attire, clobber (*Brit. slang*), costume, dress, duds (*informal*), ensemble, garb, garments, gear (*informal*), get-up (*informal*), glad rags (*informal*), habits, outfit, raiment (*archaic or poetic*), rigout (*informal*), schmutter (*slang*), threads (*slang*), togs (*informal*), vestments, vesture, wardrobe, wear

clothing *noun* = **clothes**, apparel, attire, clobber (*Brit. slang*), costume, dress, duds (*informal*), ensemble, garb, garments, gear (*informal*), get-up (*informal*), glad rags (*informal*), habits, outfit, raiment (*archaic or poetic*), rigout (*informal*), schmutter (*slang*), threads (*slang*), togs (*informal*), vestments, vesture, wardrobe, wear

cloud *noun* 1 = **mist**, billow, darkness, fog, gloom, haze, murk, nebula, nebulosity, obscurity, vapour 2 = **dense mass**, crowd, flock, horde, host, multitude, shower, swarm, throng ♦ *verb* 3 = **obscure**, becloud, darken, dim, eclipse, obfuscate, overcast, overshadow, shade, shadow, veil 4 = **confuse**, disorient, distort, impair, muddle, muddy the waters

cloudy *adjective* 1 = **dull**, dark, dim, dismal, dusky, gloomy, leaden, louring *or* lowering, nebulous, obscure, overcast, sombre, sullen, sunless 2 = **opaque**, emulsified, muddy, murky 3 = **confused**, blurred, hazy, indistinct, unclear
➤ Antonyms
≠**dull**: bright, clear, fair, sunny, unclouded ≠**confused**: clear, distinct, obvious, plain

clout *Informal* ♦ *noun* 1 = **influence**, authority, bottom, power, prestige, pull, standing, weight ♦ *verb* 2 = **hit**, box, chin (*slang*), clobber (*slang*), cuff, deck (*slang*), lay one on (*slang*), punch, skelp (*dialect*), sock (*slang*), strike, thump, tonk (*informal*), wallop (*informal*), wham

clown *noun* 1 = **comedian**, buffoon, comic, dolt, fool, harlequin, jester, joculator *or* (*fem.*) joculatrix, joker, merry-andrew, mountebank, pierrot, prankster, punchinello 2 = **boor**, clodhopper (*informal*), hind (*obsolete*), peasant, swain (*archaic*), yahoo, yokel ♦ *verb* 3 = **play the fool**, act the fool, act the goat, jest, mess about, piss about *or* around (*taboo slang*), play the goat

club *noun* 1 = **association**, circle, clique, company, fraternity, group, guild, lodge, order, set, society, sodality, union 2 = **stick**, bat, bludgeon, cosh (*Brit.*), cudgel, truncheon ♦ *verb* 3 = **beat**, bash, baste, batter, bludgeon, clobber (*slang*), clout (*informal*), cosh (*Brit.*), hammer, pommel (*rare*), pummel, strike

clue *noun* = **indication**, evidence, hint, inkling, intimation, lead, pointer, sign, suggestion, suspicion, tip, tip-off, trace

clueless *adjective* = **stupid**, dense, dim, dopey (*informal*), dozy (*Brit. informal*), dull, dumb (*informal*), half-witted, moronic, naive, simple, simple-minded, slow, slow on the uptake (*informal*), thick, unintelligent, witless

clump *noun* 1 = **cluster**, bunch, bundle, group, mass, shock ♦ *verb* 2 = **stomp**, bumble, clomp, lumber, plod, stamp, stump, thud, thump, tramp

clumsy *adjective* = **awkward**, accident-prone, blundering, bumbling, bungling, butterfingered (*informal*), cack-handed (*informal*), clunky (*informal*), gauche, gawky, ham-fisted (*informal*), ham-handed (*informal*), heavy, ill-shaped, inept, inexpert, klutzy (*U.S. & Canad. slang*), like a bull in a china shop, lumbering, maladroit, ponderous, uncoordinated, uncouth, ungainly, unhandy, unskilful, unwieldy
➤ Antonyms
adept, adroit, competent, deft, dexterous, expert, graceful, handy, proficient, skilful

cluster *noun* 1 = **gathering**, assemblage, batch, bunch, clump, collection, group, knot ♦ *verb* 2 = **gather**, assemble, bunch, collect, flock, group

clutch *verb* = **seize**, catch, clasp, cling to, embrace, fasten, grab, grapple, grasp, grip, snatch

clutches *plural noun* = **power**, claws, control, custody, grasp, grip, hands, keeping, possession, sway

clutter *verb* 1 = **litter**, scatter, strew ♦ *noun* 2 = **untidiness**, confusion, disarray, disorder, hotchpotch, jumble, litter, mess, muddle
➤ Antonyms
verb ≠**litter**: arrange, order, organize, straighten, tidy ♦ *noun* ≠**untidiness**: neatness, order, organization, tidiness

coach *noun* 1 = **bus**, car, carriage, charabanc, vehicle 2 = **instructor**, handler, teacher, trainer, tutor ♦ *verb* 3 = **instruct**, cram, drill, exercise, prepare, train, tutor

coalesce *verb* = **blend**, amalgamate, cohere, combine, come together, commingle, commix, consolidate, fraternize, fuse, incorporate, integrate, meld, merge, mix, unite

coalition *noun* = **alliance**, affiliation, amalgam, amalgamation, association, bloc, combination, compact, confederacy, confederation, conjunction, fusion, integration, league, merger, union

coarse *adjective* 1 = **rough**, coarse-grained, crude, homespun, impure, rough-hewn, unfinished, unpolished, unprocessed, unpurified, unrefined 2 = **loutish**, boorish, brutish, coarse-grained, foul-mouthed, gruff,

rough, rude, uncivil **3 = vulgar,** bawdy, earthy, immodest, impolite, improper, impure, indecent, indelicate, mean, offensive, raunchy (*slang*), ribald, rude, smutty
➤ **Antonyms**
≠**rough:** fine-grained, polished, purified, refined, smooth, soft ≠**loutish:** civilized, cultured, fine, genteel, refined, sophisticated, urbane, well-bred, well-mannered ≠**vulgar:** inoffensive, polite, proper

coarsen *verb* = **roughen,** anaesthetize, blunt, callous, deaden, desensitize, dull, harden, indurate

coarseness *noun* **1 = roughness,** crudity, unevenness **2 = vulgarity,** bawdiness, boorishness, crudity, earthiness, indelicacy, offensiveness, poor taste, ribaldry, roughness, smut, smuttiness, uncouthness

coast *noun* **1 = shore,** beach, border, coastline, littoral, seaboard, seaside, strand ◆ *verb* **2 = cruise,** drift, freewheel, get by, glide, sail, taxi

coat *noun* **1 = fur,** fleece, hair, hide, pelt, skin, wool **2 = layer,** coating, covering, overlay ◆ *verb* **3 = cover,** apply, Artex (*Trademark*), plaster, smear, spread

coating *noun* = **layer,** blanket, coat, covering, dusting, film, finish, glaze, lamination, membrane, patina, sheet, skin, varnish, veneer

coax *verb* = **persuade,** allure, beguile, cajole, decoy, entice, flatter, inveigle, prevail upon, soft-soap (*informal*), soothe, sweet-talk (*informal*), talk into, twist (someone's) arm, wheedle
➤ **Antonyms**
browbeat, bully, coerce, force, harass, intimidate, pressurize, threaten

cock *noun* **1 = cockerel,** chanticleer, rooster ◆ *verb* **2 = raise,** perk up, prick, stand up

cockeyed *adjective Informal* **1 = crooked,** askew, asymmetrical, awry, lopsided, skewwhiff (*Brit. informal*), squint (*informal*) **2 = absurd,** crazy, ludicrous, nonsensical, preposterous

cocktail *noun* = **mixture,** amalgamation, blend, combination, mix

cocky *adjective* = **overconfident,** arrogant, brash, cocksure, conceited, egotistical, full of oneself, lordly, swaggering, swollen-headed, vain
➤ **Antonyms**
hesitant, lacking confidence, modest, self-effacing, uncertain, unsure

coddle *verb* = **pamper,** baby, cosset, humour, indulge, mollycoddle, nurse, pet, spoil, wet-nurse (*informal*)

code *noun* **1 = cipher,** cryptograph **2 = principles,** canon, convention, custom,

ethics, etiquette, manners, maxim, regulations, rules, system

cogency *noun* = **conviction,** force, potency, power, strength

cogent *adjective* = **convincing,** compelling, compulsive, conclusive, effective, forceful, forcible, influential, irresistible, potent, powerful, strong, urgent, weighty

cogitate *verb* = **think,** consider, contemplate, deliberate, meditate, mull over, muse, ponder, reflect, ruminate

cogitation *noun* = **thought,** consideration, contemplation, deliberation, meditation, reflection, rumination

cognate *adjective* = **related,** affiliated, akin, alike, allied, analogous, associated, connected, kindred, similar

cognition *noun Formal* = **perception,** apprehension, awareness, comprehension, discernment, insight, intelligence, reasoning, understanding

coherent *adjective* **1 = consistent,** logical, lucid, meaningful, orderly, organized, rational, reasoned, systematic **2 = intelligible,** articulate, comprehensible
➤ **Antonyms**
≠**consistent:** confusing, disjointed, illogical, inconsistent, meaningless, rambling, vague ≠**intelligible:** incomprehensible, unintelligible

coil *verb* = **wind,** convolute, curl, entwine, loop, snake, spiral, twine, twist, wreathe, writhe

coin *noun* **1 = money,** cash, change, copper, dosh (*Brit. & Austral. slang*), silver, specie ◆ *verb* **2 = invent,** conceive, create, fabricate, forge, formulate, frame, make up, mint, mould, originate, think up

coincide *verb* **1 = occur simultaneously,** be concurrent, coexist, synchronize **2 = agree,** accord, concur, correspond, harmonize, match, square, tally
➤ **Antonyms**
≠**agree:** be inconsistent, be unlike, contradict, differ, disagree, diverge, divide, part, separate

coincidence *noun* **1 = chance,** accident, eventuality, fluke, fortuity, happy accident, luck, stroke of luck **2 = coinciding,** concomitance, concurrence, conjunction, correlation, correspondence, synchronism

coincident *adjective* = **coinciding,** concomitant, concurring, consonant, contemporaneous, coordinate, correspondent, synchronous

coincidental *adjective* **1 = chance,** accidental, casual, fluky (*informal*), fortuitous, unintentional, unplanned **2 = coinciding,** coincident, concomitant, concurrent, simultaneous, synchronous

➤ **Antonyms**
≠**chance:** calculated, deliberate, done on purpose, intentional, planned, prearranged

cold *adjective* **1 = chilly,** arctic, biting, bitter, bleak, brumal, chill, cool, freezing, frigid, frosty, frozen, gelid, harsh, icy, inclement, parky (*Brit. informal*), raw, wintry **2 = numb,** benumbed, chilled, chilly, freezing, frozen to the marrow, shivery **3 = unfriendly,** affectless, aloof, apathetic, cold-blooded, dead, distant, frigid, glacial, indifferent, inhospitable, lukewarm, passionless, phlegmatic, reserved, spiritless, standoffish, stony, undemonstrative, unfeeling, unmoved, unresponsive, unsympathetic **4 give (someone) the cold shoulder = snub,** cut (*informal*), ignore, ostracize, put down, rebuff, send (someone) to Coventry, shun ◆ *noun* **5 = coldness,** chill, chilliness, frigidity, frostiness, iciness, inclemency

➤ **Antonyms**
adjective ≠**chilly:** balmy, heated, hot, mild, sunny, warm ≠**unfriendly:** alive, animated, caring, compassionate, demonstrative, emotional, friendly, loving, open, passionate, responsive, spirited, sympathetic, warm

cold-blooded *adjective* **= callous,** barbarous, brutal, cruel, dispassionate, heartless, inhuman, merciless, pitiless, ruthless, savage, steely, stony-hearted, unemotional, unfeeling, unmoved

➤ **Antonyms**
caring, charitable, civilized, concerned, emotional, feeling, friendly, humane, involved, kind, kind-hearted, merciful, open, passionate, sensitive, warm

cold-hearted *adjective* **= heartless,** callous, detached, frigid, hardhearted, harsh, indifferent, inhuman, insensitive, stony-hearted, uncaring, unfeeling, unkind, unsympathetic

collaborate *verb* **1 = work together,** cooperate, coproduce, join forces, participate, play ball (*informal*), team up **2 = conspire,** collude, cooperate, fraternize

collaboration *noun* **= teamwork,** alliance, association, concert, cooperation, partnership

collaborator *noun* **1 = co-worker,** associate, colleague, confederate, partner, team-mate **2 = traitor,** collaborationist, fraternizer, quisling, turncoat

collapse *verb* **1 = fall down,** cave in, crumple, fall, fall apart at the seams, give way, subside **2 = fail,** come to nothing, fold, founder, go belly-up (*informal*) **3 = faint,** break down, crack up (*informal*) ◆ *noun* **4 = falling down,** cave-in, disintegration, falling apart, ruin, subsidence **5 = failure,** downfall, flop, slump **6 = faint,** breakdown, exhaustion, prostration

collar *verb Informal* **= seize,** apprehend, appropriate, arrest, capture, catch, catch in the act, grab, lay hands on, nab (*informal*), nail (*informal*)

colleague *noun* **= fellow worker,** aider, ally, assistant, associate, auxiliary, coadjutor (*rare*), collaborator, companion, comrade, confederate, confrère, helper, partner, team-mate, workmate

collect *verb* **1 = assemble,** cluster, congregate, convene, converge, flock together, rally **2 = gather,** accumulate, aggregate, amass, assemble, heap, hoard, save, stockpile **3 = obtain,** acquire, muster, raise, secure, solicit

➤ **Antonyms**
≠**gather:** disperse, distribute, scatter, spread, strew

collected *adjective* **= calm,** as cool as a cucumber, composed, confident, cool, keeping one's cool, placid, poised, sedate, self-controlled, self-possessed, serene, together (*slang*), unfazed (*informal*), unperturbable, unperturbed, unruffled

➤ **Antonyms**
agitated, antsy (*informal*), distressed, emotional, excitable, irritable, nervous, perturbed, ruffled, shaky, troubled, twitchy (*informal*)

collection *noun* **1 = accumulation,** anthology, compilation, congeries, heap, hoard, mass, pile, set, stockpile, store **2 = group,** assemblage, assembly, assortment, cluster, company, congregation, convocation, crowd, gathering **3 = contribution,** alms, offering, offertory

collective *adjective* **= combined,** aggregate, common, composite, concerted, cooperative, corporate, cumulative, joint, shared, unified, united

➤ **Antonyms**
divided, individual, piecemeal, split, uncombined, uncooperative

collide *verb* **1 = crash,** clash, come into collision, meet head-on **2 = conflict,** clash

collision *noun* **1 = crash,** accident, bump, impact, pile-up (*informal*), prang (*informal*), smash **2 = conflict,** clash, clashing, confrontation, encounter, opposition, skirmish

colloquial *adjective* **= informal,** conversational, demotic, everyday, familiar, idiomatic, vernacular

collusion *noun* **= conspiracy,** cahoots (*informal*), complicity, connivance, craft, deceit, fraudulent artifice, intrigue, secret understanding

colonist *noun* **= settler,** colonial, colonizer, frontiersman, homesteader (*U.S.*), immigrant, pioneer, planter

colonize verb = **settle**, open up, people, pioneer, populate, put down roots

colonnade noun = **cloisters**, arcade, covered walk, peristyle, portico

colony noun = **settlement**, community, dependency, dominion, outpost, possession, province, satellite state, territory

colossal adjective = **huge**, Brobdingnagian, elephantine, enormous, gargantuan, gigantic, ginormous (informal), herculean, humongous or humungous (U.S. slang), immense, mammoth, massive, monstrous, monumental, mountainous, prodigious, stellar (informal), titanic, vast
➤ Antonyms
average, diminutive, little, miniature, minute, ordinary, pygmy or pigmy, slight, small, tiny, weak, wee

colour noun 1 = **hue**, colorant, coloration, complexion, dye, paint, pigment, pigmentation, shade, tincture, tinge, tint 2 = **rosiness**, animation, bloom, blush, brilliance, flush, glow, liveliness, ruddiness, vividness 3 = **pretext**, appearance, disguise, excuse, façade, false show, guise, plea, pretence, semblance ◆ verb 4 = **paint**, colourwash, dye, stain, tinge, tint 5 = **blush**, burn, crimson, flush, go as red as a beetroot, go crimson, redden 6 = **misrepresent**, disguise, distort, embroider, exaggerate, falsify, garble, gloss over, pervert, prejudice, slant, taint

colourful adjective 1 = **bright**, brilliant, Day-glo (Trademark), intense, jazzy (informal), kaleidoscopic, motley, multicoloured, psychedelic, rich, variegated, vibrant, vivid 2 = **interesting**, characterful, distinctive, graphic, lively, picturesque, rich, stimulating, unusual, vivid
➤ Antonyms
≠**bright**: colourless, dark, drab, dreary, dull, faded, pale, washed out ≠**interesting**: boring, characterless, dull, flat, lifeless, monotonous, unexciting, uninteresting, unvaried

colourless adjective 1 = **drab**, achromatic, achromic, anaemic, ashen, bleached, faded, neutral, sickly, wan, washed out 2 = **uninteresting**, characterless, dreary, dull, insipid, lacklustre, tame, unmemorable, vacuous, vapid
➤ Antonyms
≠**drab**: blooming, flushed, glowing, healthy, radiant, robust, ruddy ≠**uninteresting**: animated, bright, colourful, compelling, distinctive, exciting, interesting, unusual

colours plural noun 1 = **flag**, banner, emblem, ensign, standard 2 As in **show one's true colours** = **nature**, aspect, breed, character, identity, stamp, strain

column noun 1 = **pillar**, caryatid, obelisk, pilaster, post, shaft, support, upright 2 = **line**, cavalcade, file, list, procession, queue, rank, row, string, train

columnist noun = **journalist**, correspondent, critic, editor, gossip columnist, journo (slang), reporter, reviewer

coma noun = **unconsciousness**, insensibility, lethargy, oblivion, somnolence, stupor, torpor, trance

comatose adjective = **unconscious**, drugged, insensible, lethargic, somnolent, stupefied, torpid

comb verb 1 = **untangle**, arrange, curry, dress, groom 2 Of flax, wool, etc. = **card**, tease, teasel, teazle 3 = **search**, forage, go through with a fine-tooth comb, hunt, rake, ransack, rummage, scour, screen, sift, sweep

combat noun 1 = **fight**, action, battle, conflict, contest, encounter, engagement, skirmish, struggle, war, warfare ◆ verb 2 = **fight**, battle, contend, contest, cope, defy, do battle with, engage, oppose, resist, strive, struggle, withstand
➤ Antonyms
noun ≠**fight**: agreement, armistice, peace, surrender, truce ◆ verb ≠**fight**: accept, acquiesce, declare a truce, give up, make peace, support, surrender

combatant noun 1 = **fighter**, adversary, antagonist, belligerent, contender, enemy, fighting man, gladiator, opponent, serviceman, soldier, warrior ◆ adjective 2 = **fighting**, battling, belligerent, combative, conflicting, contending, opposing, warring

combative adjective = **aggressive**, antagonistic, bellicose, belligerent, contentious, militant, pugnacious, quarrelsome, truculent, warlike
➤ Antonyms
nonaggressive, nonbelligerent, nonviolent, pacific, pacifist, peaceable, peaceful, peace-loving

combination noun 1 = **mixture**, amalgam, amalgamation, blend, coalescence, composite, connection, meld, mix 2 = **association**, alliance, cabal, cartel, coalition, combine, compound, confederacy, confederation, consortium, conspiracy, federation, merger, syndicate, unification, union

combine verb = **join together**, amalgamate, associate, bind, blend, bond, compound, connect, cooperate, fuse, incorporate, integrate, link, marry, meld, merge, mix, pool, put together, synthesize, unify, unite
➤ Antonyms
detach, dissociate, dissolve, disunite, divide, part, separate, sever

combustible *adjective* = **flammable**, explosive, incendiary, inflammable

come *verb* 1 = **move towards**, advance, appear, approach, arrive, become, draw near, enter, happen, materialize, move, near, occur, originate, show up (*informal*), turn out, turn up (*informal*) 2 = **arrive**, appear, attain, enter, materialize, reach, show up (*informal*), turn up (*informal*) 3 = **happen**, fall, occur, take place 4 = **result**, arise, emanate, emerge, end up, flow, issue, originate, turn out 5 = **reach**, extend 6 = **be available**, be made, be offered, be on offer, be produced

come about *verb* = **happen**, arise, befall, come to pass, occur, result, take place, transpire (*informal*)

come across *verb* = **find**, bump into (*informal*), chance upon, discover, encounter, happen upon, hit upon, light upon, meet, notice, stumble upon, unearth

come along *verb* = **improve**, develop, mend, perk up, pick up, progress, rally, recover, recuperate

come apart *verb* = **fall to pieces**, break, come unstuck, crumble, disintegrate, give way, separate, split, tear

come at *verb* = **attack**, assail, assault, charge, fall upon, fly at, go for, light into, rush, rush at

comeback *noun* 1 *Informal* = **return**, rally, rebound, recovery, resurgence, revival, triumph 2 = **response**, rejoinder, reply, retaliation, retort, riposte

come back *verb* = **return**, reappear, recur, re-enter

come between *verb* = **separate**, alienate, divide, estrange, interfere, meddle, part, set at odds

come by *verb* = **get**, acquire, land, lay hold of, obtain, procure, score (*slang*), secure, take possession of, win

come clean *verb Informal* = **confess**, acknowledge, admit, come out of the closet, cough up (*slang*), get (something) off one's chest (*informal*), make a clean breast of, own up, reveal, sing (*slang, chiefly U.S.*), spill one's guts (*slang*)

comedian *noun* = **comic**, card (*informal*), clown, funny man, humorist, jester, joculator *or (fem.)* joculatrix, joker, laugh (*informal*), wag, wit

comedown *noun* 1 = **decline**, deflation, demotion, reverse 2 *Informal* = **disappointment**, anticlimax, blow, humiliation, letdown, whammy (*informal, chiefly U.S.*)

come down *verb* 1 = **descend**, go downhill 2 = **decline**, degenerate,

deteriorate, fall, go to pot (*informal*), reduce, worsen 3 = **decide**, choose, favour, recommend

come down on *verb* = **reprimand**, bawl out (*informal*), blast, carpet (*informal*), chew out (*U.S. & Canad. informal*), criticize, dress down (*informal*), give (someone) a rocket (*Brit. & N.Z. informal*), jump on (*informal*), lambast(e), put down, rap over the knuckles, read the riot act, rebuke, tear into (*informal*), tear (someone) off a strip (*Brit. informal*)

come down to *verb* = **amount to**, boil down to, end up as, result in

come down with *verb* = **catch**, ail, be stricken with, contract, fall ill, fall victim to, get, sicken, take, take sick

comedy *noun* = **humour**, chaffing, drollery, facetiousness, farce, fun, hilarity, jesting, joking, light entertainment, sitcom (*informal*), slapstick, wisecracking, witticisms
➤ **Antonyms**
high drama, melancholy, melodrama, sadness, seriousness, serious play, soap opera, solemnity, tragedy

come forward *verb* = **volunteer**, offer one's services, present *or* proffer oneself

come in *verb* 1 = **enter**, appear, arrive, cross the threshold, show up (*informal*) 2 = **finish**, reach

come in for *verb* = **receive**, acquire, bear the brunt of, endure, get, suffer

comely *adjective* 1 *Old-fashioned* = **good-looking**, attractive, beautiful, becoming, blooming, bonny, buxom, cute, fair, graceful, handsome, lovely, pleasing, pretty, wholesome, winsome 2 *Archaic* = **proper**, decent, decorous, fit, fitting, seemly, suitable
➤ **Antonyms**
≠**good-looking**: disagreeable, distasteful, faded, homely, mumsy, plain, repulsive, ugly, unattractive, unpleasant ≠**proper**: improper, indecorous, unbecoming, unfitting, unnatural, unseemly

come off *verb Informal* = **happen**, go off, occur, succeed, take place, transpire (*informal*)

come on *verb* 1 = **progress**, advance, develop, improve, make headway, proceed 2 = **begin**, appear, take place

come out *verb* 1 = **be revealed**, appear, be announced, be divulged, be issued, be published, be released, be reported 2 = **end up**, result, turn out

come out with *verb* = **say**, acknowledge, come clean, declare, disclose, divulge, lay open, own, own up

come round *verb* 1 = **regain**

consciousness, come to, rally, recover, revive **2 = change one's opinion**, accede, acquiesce, allow, concede, grant, mellow, relent, yield **3 = call**, drop in, pop in, stop by, visit

come through *verb* **1 = survive**, endure, weather the storm, withstand **2 = accomplish**, achieve, make the grade (*informal*), prevail, succeed, triumph

come up *verb* **= happen**, arise, crop up, occur, rise, spring up, turn up

comeuppance *noun Informal* **= punishment**, chastening, deserts, due reward, dues, merit, recompense, requital, retribution

come up to *verb* **= compare with**, admit of comparison with, approach, equal, match, measure up to, meet, resemble, rival, stand *or* bear comparison with

come up with *verb* **= produce**, advance, create, discover, furnish, offer, present, propose, provide, submit, suggest

comfort *noun* **1 = luxury**, cosiness, creature comforts, ease, opulence, snugness, wellbeing **2 = relief**, aid, alleviation, cheer, compensation, consolation, ease, encouragement, enjoyment, help, satisfaction, succour, support ◆ *verb* **3 = console**, alleviate, assuage, cheer, commiserate with, ease, encourage, enliven, gladden, hearten, inspirit, invigorate, reassure, refresh, relieve, solace, soothe, strengthen
➤ **Antonyms**
noun ≠**relief**: aggravation, annoyance, discouragement, displeasure, hassle (*informal*), inconvenience, irritation ◆ *verb* ≠**console**: aggravate (*informal*), agitate, annoy, bother, depress, discomfort, distress, excite, hassle (*informal*), irk, irritate, rile, ruffle, sadden, trouble

comfortable *adjective* **1 = pleasant**, agreeable, convenient, cosy, delightful, easy, enjoyable, homely, relaxing, restful **2 = happy**, at ease, at home, contented, gratified, relaxed, serene **3** *Informal* **= well-off**, affluent, in clover (*informal*), prosperous, well-to-do
➤ **Antonyms**
≠**pleasant**: inadequate, uncomfortable, unpleasant ≠**happy**: distressed, disturbed, ill at ease, like a fish out of water, miserable, nervous, on tenterhooks, tense, troubled, uncomfortable, uneasy

comforting *adjective* **= consoling**, cheering, consolatory, encouraging, heart-warming, inspiriting, reassuring, soothing
➤ **Antonyms**
alarming, dismaying, disturbing, perplexing,

upsetting, worrying

comic *adjective* **1 = funny**, amusing, comical, droll, facetious, farcical, humorous, jocular, joking, light, rich, waggish, witty ◆ *noun* **2 = comedian**, buffoon, clown, funny man, humorist, jester, joculator *or* (*fem.*) joculatrix, wag, wit
➤ **Antonyms**
adjective ≠**funny**: depressing, melancholy, pathetic, sad, serious, solemn, touching, tragic

comical *adjective* **= funny**, absurd, amusing, comic, diverting, droll, entertaining, farcical, hilarious, humorous, laughable, ludicrous, priceless, ridiculous, risible, side-splitting, silly, whimsical, zany

coming *adjective* **1 = approaching**, at hand, due, en route, forthcoming, future, imminent, impending, in store, in the wind, just round the corner, near, next, nigh, on the cards, upcoming **2 = up-and-coming**, aspiring, future, promising ◆ *noun* **3 = arrival**, accession, advent, approach

command *verb* **1 = order**, bid, charge, compel, demand, direct, enjoin, require **2 = have authority over**, administer, call the shots, call the tune, control, dominate, govern, handle, head, lead, manage, reign over, rule, supervise, sway ◆ *noun* **3 = order**, behest, bidding, canon, commandment, decree, demand, direction, directive, edict, fiat, injunction, instruction, mandate, precept, requirement, ultimatum **4 = authority**, charge, control, direction, domination, dominion, government, grasp, management, mastery, power, rule, supervision, sway, upper hand
➤ **Antonyms**
verb ≠**order**: appeal (to), ask, beg, beseech, plead, request, supplicate ≠**have authority over**: be inferior, be subordinate, follow

commandeer *verb* **= seize**, appropriate, confiscate, expropriate, hijack, requisition, sequester, sequestrate, usurp

commander *noun* **= officer**, boss, captain, chief, C in C, C.O., commander-in-chief, commanding officer, director, head, leader, ruler

commanding *adjective* **1 = controlling**, advantageous, decisive, dominant, dominating, superior **2 = authoritative**, assertive, autocratic, compelling, forceful, imposing, impressive, peremptory
➤ **Antonyms**
≠**authoritative**: retiring, shrinking, shy, submissive, timid, unassertive, unimposing, weak

commemorate *verb* **= remember**, celebrate, honour, immortalize, keep, memorialize, observe, pay tribute to,

recognize, salute, solemnize
➤ **Antonyms**
disregard, forget, ignore, omit, overlook,
pass over, take no notice of
commemoration *noun* = **remembrance**,
ceremony, honouring, memorial service,
observance, tribute
commemorative *adjective* = **memorial**,
celebratory, dedicatory, in honour, in
memory, in remembrance
commence *verb* = **begin**, embark on, enter
upon, get the show on the road (*informal*),
inaugurate, initiate, open, originate, start
➤ **Antonyms**
bring *or* come to an end, cease, complete,
conclude, desist, end, finish, halt, stop,
terminate, wind up
commend *verb* **1** = **praise**, acclaim,
applaud, approve, compliment, crack up
(*informal*), eulogize, extol, recommend,
speak highly of **2** = **entrust**, commit,
confide, consign, deliver, hand over, yield
➤ **Antonyms**
≠**praise**: attack, blast, censure, condemn,
criticize, denounce, disapprove, knock
(*informal*), lambast(e), put down, slam, tear
into (*informal*) ≠**entrust**: hold back, keep,
keep back, retain, withdraw, withhold
commendable *adjective* = **praiseworthy**,
admirable, creditable, deserving, estimable,
exemplary, laudable, meritorious, worthy
commendation *noun* = **praise**, acclaim,
acclamation, approbation, approval, Brownie
points, credit, encomium, encouragement,
good opinion, panegyric, recommendation
commensurate *adjective*
= **proportionate**, adequate, appropriate,
coextensive, comparable, compatible,
consistent, corresponding, due, equivalent,
fit, fitting, in accord, sufficient
comment *noun* **1** = **remark**,
animadversion, observation, statement **2**
= **note**, annotation, commentary, criticism,
elucidation, explanation, exposition,
illustration ♦ *verb* **3** = **remark**, animadvert,
interpose, mention, note, observe, opine,
point out, say, utter **4** = **annotate**, criticize,
elucidate, explain, interpret
commentary *noun* **1** = **narration**,
description, voice-over **2** = **notes**, analysis,
critique, exegesis, explanation, review,
treatise
commentator *noun* **1** = **reporter**,
commenter, special correspondent,
sportscaster **2** = **critic**, annotator, expositor,
interpreter, scholiast
commerce *noun* **1** = **trade**, business,
dealing, exchange, merchandising, traffic **2**
Literary = **relations**, communication,
dealings, intercourse, socializing

commercial *adjective* **1** = **mercantile**,
business, profit-making, sales, trade, trading
2 = **profitable**, in demand, marketable,
popular, saleable **3** = **materialistic**,
exploited, mercenary, monetary, pecuniary,
profit-making, venal
commingle *verb* = **mix**, amalgamate,
blend, combine, commix, intermingle,
intermix, join, meld, mingle, unite
commiserate *verb* = **sympathize**, console,
feel for, pity
commission *noun* **1** = **duty**, appointment,
authority, charge, employment, errand,
function, mandate, mission, task, trust,
warrant **2** = **fee**, allowance, brokerage,
compensation, cut, percentage, rake-off
(*slang*), royalties **3** = **committee**, board,
body of commissioners, commissioners,
delegation, deputation, representatives
♦ *verb* **4** = **appoint**, authorize, contract,
delegate, depute, empower, engage,
nominate, order, select, send
commit *verb* **1** = **do**, carry out, enact,
execute, perform, perpetrate **2** = **give**,
commend, confide, consign, deliver, deposit,
engage, entrust, hand over **3** = **pledge**,
align, bind, compromise, endanger, make
liable, obligate, rank **4** = **put in custody**,
confine, imprison
➤ **Antonyms**
≠**do**: omit ≠**give**: receive, withhold
≠**pledge**: disavow, vacillate, waver ≠**put in
custody**: free, let out, release, set free
commitment *noun* **1** = **dedication**,
adherence, devotion, involvement, loyalty **2**
= **responsibility**, duty, engagement, liability,
obligation, tie **3** = **pledge**, assurance,
guarantee, promise, undertaking, vow, word
➤ **Antonyms**
≠**dedication**: indecisiveness, vacillation,
wavering ≠**pledge**: disavowal, negation
common *adjective* **1** = **average**, a dime a
dozen, bog-standard (*Brit. & Irish slang*),
commonplace, conventional, customary,
daily, everyday, familiar, frequent, general,
habitual, humdrum, obscure, ordinary, plain,
regular, routine, run-of-the-mill, simple,
standard, stock, usual, vanilla (*slang*),
workaday **2** = **popular**, accepted, general,
prevailing, prevalent, universal, widespread **3**
= **collective**, communal, community,
popular, public, social **4** = **vulgar**, coarse,
hackneyed, inferior, low, pedestrian,
plebeian, stale, trite, undistinguished
➤ **Antonyms**
≠**average**: abnormal, famous, formal,
important, infrequent, noble, outstanding,
rare, scarce, sophisticated, strange, superior,
uncommon, unknown, unusual ≠**collective**:
personal, private ≠**vulgar**: cultured,
distinguished, gentle, refined, sensitive

commonplace *adjective* **1** = everyday, banal, common, customary, dime-a-dozen (*informal*), humdrum, mundane, obvious, ordinary, pedestrian, run-of-the-mill, stale, threadbare, trite, uninteresting, vanilla (*slang*), widespread, worn out ♦ *noun* **2** = cliché, banality, platitude, truism
➤ **Antonyms**
adjective ≠ everyday: exciting, extraordinary, ground-breaking, infrequent, interesting, left-field (*informal*), new, novel, original, rare, strange, uncommon, unfamiliar, unique, unusual

common-sense, common-sensical *adjective* = sensible, astute, down-to-earth, hard-headed, judicious, level-headed, matter-of-fact, practical, realistic, reasonable, sane, shrewd, sound
➤ **Antonyms**
airy-fairy (*informal*), daft (*informal*), foolish, impractical, irrational, unrealistic, unreasonable, unthinking, unwise

common sense *noun* = good sense, gumption (*Brit. informal*), horse sense, level-headedness, mother wit, native intelligence, nous (*Brit. slang*), practicality, prudence, reasonableness, smarts (*slang, chiefly U.S.*), sound judgment, soundness, wit

commotion *noun* = disturbance, ado, agitation, brouhaha, bustle, disorder, excitement, ferment, furore, fuss, hubbub, hue and cry, hullabaloo, hurly-burly, perturbation, racket, riot, rumpus, to-do, tumult, turmoil, upheaval, uproar

communal *adjective* = public, collective, communistic, community, general, joint, neighbourhood, shared
➤ **Antonyms**
exclusive, individual, personal, private, single, unshared

commune *noun* = community, collective, cooperative, kibbutz

commune with *verb* **1** = contemplate, meditate on, muse on, ponder, reflect on **2** = talk to, communicate with, confer with, confide in, converse with, discourse with, discuss with, parley with

communicable *adjective* = infectious, catching, contagious, taking, transferable, transmittable

communicate *verb* = make known, acquaint, announce, be in contact, be in touch, connect, convey, correspond, declare, disclose, disseminate, divulge, impart, inform, pass on, phone, proclaim, publish, report, reveal, ring up (*informal, chiefly Brit.*), signify, spread, transmit, unfold
➤ **Antonyms**
conceal, cover up, hold back, hush up, keep

back, keep secret, keep under wraps, repress, sit on (*informal*), suppress, whitewash (*informal*), withhold

communication *noun* **1** = passing on, connection, contact, conversation, correspondence, dissemination, intercourse, link, transmission **2** = message, announcement, disclosure, dispatch, information, intelligence, news, report, statement, word

communications *plural noun* **1** = transport, routes, travel **2** = information technology, media, publicity, public relations, telecommunications

communicative *adjective* = talkative, candid, chatty, conversable, expansive, forthcoming, frank, informative, loquacious, open, outgoing, unreserved, voluble
➤ **Antonyms**
quiet, reserved, reticent, secretive, taciturn, uncommunicative, uninformative, untalkative

communion *noun* = closeness, accord, affinity, agreement, communing, concord, consensus, converse, fellowship, harmony, intercourse, participation, rapport, sympathy, togetherness, unity

Communion *noun Church* = Eucharist, Lord's Supper, Mass, Sacrament

communiqué *noun* = announcement, bulletin, dispatch, news flash, official communication, report

Communism *noun* = socialism, Bolshevism, collectivism, Eurocommunism, Maoism, Marxism, Marxism-Leninism, Stalinism, state socialism, Titoism, Trotskyism

Communist *noun* = socialist, Bolshevik, collectivist, Marxist, Red (*informal*)

community *noun* = society, association, body politic, brotherhood, commonwealth, company, district, general public, locality, people, populace, population, public, residents, state

commute *verb* **1** *Law: of penalties, etc.* = reduce, alleviate, curtail, mitigate, modify, remit, shorten, soften **2** = substitute, barter, exchange, interchange, switch, trade

commuter *noun* = daily traveller, straphanger (*informal*), suburbanite

compact[1] *adjective* **1** = closely packed, compressed, condensed, dense, firm, impenetrable, impermeable, pressed together, solid, thick **2** = brief, compendious, concise, epigrammatic, laconic, pithy, pointed, succinct, terse, to the point ♦ *verb* **3** = pack closely, compress, condense, cram, stuff, tamp
➤ **Antonyms**
adjective ≠ closely packed: dispersed, large, loose, roomy, scattered, spacious, sprawling ≠ brief: circumlocutory, garrulous, lengthy,

long-winded, prolix, rambling, verbose, wordy ♦ verb ≠**pack closely**: disperse, loosen, separate

compact² noun = **agreement**, alliance, arrangement, bargain, bond, concordat, contract, covenant, deal, entente, pact, stipulation, treaty, understanding

companion noun **1** = **friend**, accomplice, ally, associate, buddy (informal), colleague, comrade, confederate, consort, crony, gossip (archaic), homeboy (slang, chiefly U.S.), mate (informal), partner **2** = **escort**, aide, assistant, attendant, chaperon, duenna, squire **3** = **mate**, complement, counterpart, fellow, match, twin

companionable adjective = **friendly**, affable, congenial, conversable, convivial, cordial, familiar, genial, gregarious, neighbourly, outgoing, sociable

companionship noun = **fellowship**, amity, camaraderie, company, comradeship, conviviality, esprit de corps, fraternity, friendship, rapport, togetherness

company noun **1** = **business**, association, concern, corporation, establishment, firm, house, partnership, syndicate **2** = **group**, assemblage, assembly, band, bevy, body, camp, circle, collection, community, concourse, convention, coterie, crew, crowd, ensemble, gathering, league, party, set, throng, troop, troupe, turnout **3** = **companionship**, fellowship, presence, society **4** = **guests**, callers, party, visitors

comparable adjective **1** = **on a par**, a match for, as good as, commensurate, equal, equivalent, in a class with, proportionate, tantamount **2** = **similar**, akin, alike, analogous, cognate, corresponding, cut from the same cloth, of a piece, related
➤ **Antonyms**
different, dissimilar, incommensurable, incomparable, unequal

comparative adjective = **relative**, approximate, by comparison, qualified

compare verb **1** = **weigh**, balance, collate, contrast, juxtapose, set against **2** usually with **with** = **be on a par with**, approach, approximate to, bear comparison, be in the same class as, be the equal of, come up to, compete with, equal, hold a candle to, match, vie **3 compare to** = **liken to**, correlate to, equate to, identify with, mention in the same breath as, parallel, resemble

comparison noun **1** = **contrast**, collation, distinction, juxtaposition **2** = **similarity**, analogy, comparability, correlation, likeness, resemblance

compartment noun **1** = **section**, alcove, bay, berth, booth, carrel, carriage, cell,

chamber, cubbyhole, cubicle, locker, niche, pigeonhole **2** = **category**, area, department, division, section, subdivision

compass noun **1** = **range**, area, bound, boundary, circle, circuit, circumference, enclosure, extent, field, limit, reach, realm, round, scope, sphere, stretch, zone ♦ verb **2** = **surround**, beset, besiege, blockade, circumscribe, encircle, enclose, encompass, environ, hem in, invest (rare)

compassion noun = **sympathy**, charity, clemency, commiseration, compunction, condolence, fellow feeling, heart, humanity, kindness, mercy, pity, quarter, ruth (archaic), soft-heartedness, sorrow, tender-heartedness, tenderness, understanding
➤ **Antonyms**
apathy, cold-heartedness, indifference, mercilessness, unconcern

compassionate adjective = **sympathetic**, benevolent, charitable, humane, humanitarian, indulgent, kind-hearted, kindly, lenient, merciful, pitying, tender, tender-hearted, understanding
➤ **Antonyms**
callous, harsh, heartless, inhumane, pitiless, uncaring, unfeeling, unmerciful, unsympathetic

compatibility noun = **harmony**, affinity, agreement, amity, concord, congeniality, empathy, like-mindedness, rapport, single-mindedness, sympathy

compatible adjective = **harmonious**, accordant, adaptable, agreeable, congenial, congruent, congruous, consistent, consonant, in harmony, in keeping, like-minded, reconcilable, suitable
➤ **Antonyms**
contradictory, inappropriate, inapt, incompatible, unfitting, unharmonious, unsuitable

compatriot noun = **fellow countryman**, countryman, fellow citizen

compel verb = **force**, bulldoze (informal), coerce, constrain, dragoon, drive, enforce, exact, hustle (slang), impel, make, necessitate, oblige, railroad (informal), restrain, squeeze, urge

compelling adjective **1** = **fascinating**, enchanting, enthralling, gripping, hypnotic, irresistible, mesmeric, spellbinding **2** = **pressing**, binding, coercive, imperative, overriding, peremptory, unavoidable, urgent **3** = **convincing**, cogent, conclusive, forceful, irrefutable, powerful, telling, weighty
➤ **Antonyms**
≠**fascinating**: boring, dull, humdrum, monotonous, ordinary, repetitious, tiresome, uneventful, uninteresting, wearisome

compensate *verb* **1** = **recompense**, atone, indemnify, make amends, make good, make restitution, refund, reimburse, remunerate, repay, requite, reward, satisfy **2** = **cancel (out)**, balance, counteract, counterbalance, countervail, make up for, offset, redress

compensation *noun* = **recompense**, amends, atonement, damages, indemnification, indemnity, meed (*archaic*), offset, payment, reimbursement, remuneration, reparation, requital, restitution, reward, satisfaction

compete *verb* = **contend**, be in the running, challenge, contest, emulate, fight, pit oneself against, rival, strive, struggle, vie

competence *noun* = **ability**, adequacy, appropriateness, capability, capacity, competency, craft, expertise, fitness, proficiency, skill, suitability
➤ **Antonyms**
inability, inadequacy, incompetence

competent *adjective* = **able**, adapted, adequate, appropriate, capable, clever, endowed, equal, fit, pertinent, proficient, qualified, sufficient, suitable
➤ **Antonyms**
inadequate, incapable, incompetent, inexperienced, inexpert, unqualified, unskilled

competition *noun* **1** = **rivalry**, contention, contest, emulation, one-upmanship (*Informal*), opposition, strife, struggle **2** = **contest**, championship, event, head-to-head, puzzle, quiz, tournament **3** = **opposition**, challengers, field, rivals

competitive *adjective* **1** = **cut-throat**, aggressive, antagonistic, at odds, dog-eat-dog, opposing, rival, vying **2** = **ambitious**, combative

competitor *noun* = **contestant**, adversary, antagonist, challenger, competition, emulator, opponent, opposition, rival

compilation *noun* = **collection**, accumulation, anthology, assemblage, assortment, treasury

compile *verb* = **put together**, accumulate, amass, anthologize, collect, cull, garner, gather, marshal, organize

complacency *noun* = **self-satisfaction**, contentment, gratification, pleasure, satisfaction, smugness

complacent *adjective* = **self-satisfied**, contented, gratified, pleased, pleased with oneself, resting on one's laurels, satisfied, self-assured, self-contented, self-righteous, serene, smug, unconcerned
➤ **Antonyms**
discontent, dissatisfied, insecure, troubled, uneasy, unsatisfied

complain *verb* = **find fault**, beef (*slang*), bellyache (*slang*), bemoan, bewail, bitch

(*slang*), bleat, carp, deplore, fuss, grieve, gripe (*informal*), groan, grouch (*informal*), grouse, growl, grumble, kick up a fuss (*informal*), kvetch (*U.S. slang*), lament, moan, put the boot in (*slang*), whine, whinge (*informal*)

complaint *noun* **1** = **criticism**, accusation, annoyance, beef (*slang*), bitch (*slang*), charge, dissatisfaction, fault-finding, grievance, gripe (*informal*), grouch (*informal*), grouse, grumble, lament, moan, plaint, protest, remonstrance, trouble, wail **2** = **illness**, affliction, ailment, disease, disorder, indisposition, malady, sickness, upset

complement *noun* **1** = **completion**, companion, consummation, correlative, counterpart, finishing touch, rounding-off, supplement **2** = **total**, aggregate, capacity, entirety, quota, totality, wholeness ◆ *verb* **3** = **complete**, cap (*informal*), crown, round off, set off

complementary *adjective* = **completing**, companion, correlative, corresponding, fellow, interdependent, interrelating, matched, reciprocal
➤ **Antonyms**
contradictory, different, incompatible, incongruous, uncomplementary

complete *adjective* **1** = **total**, absolute, consummate, deep-dyed (*usually derogatory*), dyed-in-the-wool, outright, perfect, thorough, thoroughgoing, utter **2** = **finished**, accomplished, achieved, concluded, ended **3** = **entire**, all, faultless, full, intact, integral, plenary, unabridged, unbroken, undivided, unimpaired, whole ◆ *verb* **4** = **finish**, accomplish, achieve, cap, close, conclude, crown, discharge, do, end, execute, fill in, finalize, fulfil, perfect, perform, put the tin lid on, realize, round off, settle, terminate, wrap up (*informal*)
➤ **Antonyms**
adjective ≠**total**: partial ≠**finished**: inconclusive, unaccomplished, unfinished, unsettled ≠**entire**: deficient, imperfect, incomplete, spoilt ◆ *verb* ≠**finish**: begin, commence, initiate, mar, spoil, start

completely *adverb* = **totally**, absolutely, a hundred per cent, altogether, down to the ground, en masse, entirely, every inch, from A to Z, from beginning to end, fully, heart and soul, hook, line and sinker, in full, *in toto*, lock, stock and barrel, one hundred per cent, perfectly, quite, root and branch, solidly, thoroughly, utterly, wholly

completion *noun* = **finishing**, accomplishment, attainment, bitter end, close, conclusion, consummation, culmination, end, expiration, finalization, fruition, fulfilment, realization

complex *adjective* **1** = **compound**, composite, compounded, heterogeneous, manifold, multifarious, multiple **2** = **complicated**, circuitous, convoluted, Daedalian (*literary*), elaborate, intricate, involved, knotty, labyrinthine, mingled, mixed, tangled, tortuous ♦ *noun* **3** = **structure**, aggregate, composite, network, organization, scheme, synthesis, system **4** *Informal* = **obsession**, fixation, fixed idea, *idée fixe*, phobia, preoccupation
➤ **Antonyms**
adjective ≠**complicated**: clear, easy, easy-peasy (*slang*), elementary, obvious, simple, straightforward, uncomplicated

complexion *noun* **1** = **skin**, colour, colouring, hue, pigmentation, skin tone **2** = **nature**, appearance, aspect, cast, character, countenance, disposition, guise, light, look, make-up, stamp

complexity *noun* = **complication**, convolution, elaboration, entanglement, intricacy, involvement, multiplicity, ramification

compliance *noun* = **obedience**, acquiescence, agreement, assent, complaisance, concession, concurrence, conformity, consent, deference, observance, passivity, submission, submissiveness, yielding
➤ **Antonyms**
defiance, disobedience, non-compliance, nonconformity, opposition, refusal, resistance, revolt

complicate *verb* = **make difficult**, confuse, embroil, entangle, interweave, involve, make intricate, muddle, ravel, snarl up
➤ **Antonyms**
clarify, clear up, disentangle, elucidate, explain, facilitate, simplify, spell out, unsnarl

complicated *adjective* **1** = **difficult**, involved, perplexing, problematic, puzzling, troublesome **2** = **involved**, Byzantine (*of attitudes, etc.*), complex, convoluted, elaborate, interlaced, intricate, labyrinthine
➤ **Antonyms**
≠**difficult**: clear, easy, easy-peasy (*slang*), undemanding, understandable, user-friendly ≠**involved**: simple, straightforward, uncomplicated, uninvolved

complication *noun* **1** = **complexity**, combination, confusion, entanglement, intricacy, mixture, web **2** = **problem**, aggravation, difficulty, drawback, embarrassment, factor, obstacle, snag

complicity *noun* = **collusion**, abetment, collaboration, concurrence, connivance

compliment *noun* **1** = **praise**, admiration, bouquet, commendation, congratulations, courtesy, eulogy, favour, flattery, honour,
tribute ♦ *verb* **2** = **praise**, commend, congratulate, crack up (*informal*), extol, felicitate, flatter, laud, pat on the back, pay tribute to, salute, sing the praises of, speak highly of, wish joy to
➤ **Antonyms**
noun ≠**praise**: complaint, condemnation, criticism, disparagement, insult, reproach ♦ *verb* ≠**praise**: blast, condemn, criticize, decry, disparage, insult, lambast(e), put down, reprehend, reproach, tear into (*informal*)

complimentary *adjective* **1** = **flattering**, appreciative, approving, commendatory, congratulatory, eulogistic, laudatory, panegyrical **2** = **free**, courtesy, donated, free of charge, gratis, gratuitous, honorary, on the house
➤ **Antonyms**
≠**flattering**: abusive, critical, disparaging, fault-finding, insulting, scathing, uncomplimentary, unflattering

compliments *plural noun* = **greetings**, good wishes, regards, remembrances, respects, salutation

comply *verb* = **obey**, abide by, accede, accord, acquiesce, adhere to, agree to, conform to, consent to, defer, discharge, follow, fulfil, observe, perform, play ball (*informal*), respect, satisfy, submit, toe the line, yield
➤ **Antonyms**
break, defy, disobey, disregard, fight, ignore, oppose, refuse to obey, reject, repudiate, resist, spurn, violate

component *noun* **1** = **part**, constituent, element, ingredient, item, piece, unit ♦ *adjective* **2** = **constituent**, composing, inherent, intrinsic

compose *verb* **1** = **put together**, build, compound, comprise, constitute, construct, fashion, form, make, make up **2** = **create**, contrive, devise, frame, imagine, indite, invent, produce, write **3** = **calm**, appease, assuage, collect, control, pacify, placate, quell, quiet, soothe, still, tranquillize **4** = **arrange**, adjust, reconcile, regulate, resolve, settle
➤ **Antonyms**
≠**put together**: bulldoze, demolish, destroy, dismantle, obliterate, raze ≠**calm**: agitate, disturb, excite, perturb, trouble, unsettle, upset

composed *adjective* = **calm**, as cool as a cucumber, at ease, collected, confident, cool, imperturbable, keeping one's cool, laid-back (*informal*), level-headed, poised, relaxed, sedate, self-controlled, self-possessed, serene, together (*slang*), tranquil, unfazed (*informal*), unflappable, unruffled, unworried

➤ **Antonyms**
agitated, antsy (*informal*), anxious, disturbed,
excited, hot and bothered (*informal*),
nervous, ruffled, twitchy (*informal*),
uncontrolled, uneasy, unpoised, upset

composite *adjective* 1 = **compound**,
blended, combined, complex, conglomerate,
mixed, synthesized ♦ *noun* 2 = **compound**,
amalgam, blend, conglomerate, fusion,
meld, synthesis

composition *noun* 1 = **creation**,
compilation, fashioning, formation,
formulation, invention, making, mixture,
production, putting together 2 = **design**,
arrangement, configuration, constitution,
form, formation, layout, make-up,
organization, structure 3 = **arrangement**,
balance, concord, consonance, harmony,
placing, proportion, symmetry 4 = **essay**,
creation, exercise, literary work, opus, piece,
study, treatise, work, writing

compost *noun* = **organic fertilizer**, humus,
mulch

composure *noun* = **calmness**, aplomb,
calm, collectedness, cool (*slang*), coolness,
dignity, ease, equanimity, imperturbability,
placidity, poise, sang-froid, sedateness,
self-assurance, self-possession, serenity,
tranquillity
➤ **Antonyms**
agitation, discomposure, excitability,
impatience, nervousness, perturbation,
uneasiness

compound *noun* 1 = **combination**, alloy,
amalgam, blend, composite, composition,
conglomerate, fusion, medley, meld,
mixture, synthesis ♦ *verb* 2 = **combine**,
amalgamate, blend, coalesce, concoct, fuse,
intermingle, meld, mingle, mix, synthesize,
unite 3 = **intensify**, add insult to injury, add
to, aggravate, augment, complicate,
exacerbate, heighten, magnify, worsen 4
Used of a dispute, difference, etc. = **settle**,
adjust, arrange, compose ♦ *adjective* 5
= **complex**, composite, conglomerate,
intricate, multiple, not simple
➤ **Antonyms**
noun ≠**combination**: element ♦ *verb*
≠**combine**: divide, part, segregate
≠**intensify**: decrease, lessen, minimize,
moderate, modify ♦ *adjective* ≠**complex**:
pure, simple, single, unmixed

comprehend *verb* 1 = **understand**,
apprehend, assimilate, conceive, discern,
fathom, get the hang of (*informal*), get the
picture, grasp, know, make out, perceive,
see, see the light of day, take in 2 = **include**,
comprise, contain, embody, embrace,
enclose, encompass, involve, take in
➤ **Antonyms**
≠**understand**: be at cross-purposes, get (it)

wrong, get one's lines crossed, get the
wrong end of the stick, misapprehend,
misconceive, misconstrue, misinterpret, miss
the point of, mistake, misunderstand, pervert

comprehensible *adjective*
= **understandable**, clear, coherent,
conceivable, explicit, graspable, intelligible,
plain, user-friendly

comprehension *noun* 1
= **understanding**, conception, discernment,
grasp, intelligence, judgment, knowledge,
perception, realization, sense 2 = **inclusion**,
compass, domain, field, limits, province,
range, reach, scope
➤ **Antonyms**
≠**understanding**: incomprehension,
misapprehension, misunderstanding,
unawareness

comprehensive *adjective* = **broad**,
all-embracing, all-inclusive, blanket, catholic,
complete, encyclopedic, exhaustive,
extensive, full, inclusive, overarching,
sweeping, thorough, umbrella, wide
➤ **Antonyms**
incomplete, limited, narrow, restricted,
specialized, specific

compress *verb* = **squeeze**, abbreviate,
compact, concentrate, condense, constrict,
contract, cram, crowd, crush, knit, press,
pucker, shorten, squash, summarize, wedge

compressed *adjective* = **squeezed**,
abridged, compact, compacted,
concentrated, concise, consolidated,
constricted, flattened, reduced, shortened,
squashed

compression *noun* = **squeezing**,
condensation, consolidation, constriction,
crushing, pressure, wedging

comprise *verb* 1 = **be composed of**,
comprehend, consist of, contain, embrace,
encompass, include, take in 2 = **make up**,
compose, constitute, form

compromise *noun* 1 = **give-and-take**,
accommodation, accord, adjustment,
agreement, concession, half measures,
middle ground, settlement, trade-off ♦ *verb*
2 = **meet halfway**, adjust, agree, arbitrate,
compose, compound, concede, give and
take, go fifty-fifty (*informal*), settle, strike a
balance 3 = **weaken**, discredit, dishonour,
embarrass, endanger, expose, hazard,
imperil, implicate, jeopardize, prejudice
➤ **Antonyms**
noun ≠**give-and-take**: contention,
controversy, difference, disagreement,
dispute, quarrel ♦ *verb* ≠**meet halfway**:
argue, contest, differ, disagree ≠**weaken**:
assure, boost, enhance, support

compulsion *noun* 1 = **urge**, drive,
necessity, need, obsession, preoccupation 2

= **force**, coercion, constraint, demand, duress, obligation, pressure, urgency

compulsive *adjective* = **irresistible**, besetting, compelling, driving, neurotic, obsessive, overwhelming, uncontrollable, urgent

compulsory *adjective* = **obligatory**, binding, *de rigueur*, forced, imperative, mandatory, required, requisite
➤ **Antonyms**
discretionary, elective, non-obligatory, non-requisite, optional, unimperative, unnecessary, voluntary

compute *verb* = **calculate**, add up, cast up, cipher, count, enumerate, estimate, figure, figure out, measure, rate, reckon, sum, tally, total

comrade *noun* = **companion**, ally, associate, buddy (*informal*), cock (*Brit. informal*), colleague, compatriot, compeer, confederate, co-worker, crony, fellow, friend, homeboy (*slang, chiefly U.S.*), mate (*informal*), pal (*informal*), partner

con *Informal* ◆ *noun* 1 = **swindle**, deception, fraud, scam (*slang*), sting (*informal*), trick ◆ *verb* 2 = **swindle**, cheat, deceive, defraud, double-cross (*informal*), dupe, hoodwink, rip off (*slang*), trick

concave *adjective* = **hollow**, cupped, depressed, excavated, hollowed, incurved, indented, scooped, sunken
➤ **Antonyms**
bulging, convex, curving, protuberant, rounded

conceal *verb* = **hide**, bury, camouflage, cover, disguise, dissemble, draw a veil over, keep dark, keep secret, keep under one's hat, mask, obscure, screen, secrete, shelter, stash (*informal*)
➤ **Antonyms**
disclose, display, divulge, expose, lay bare, reveal, show, uncover, unmask, unveil

concealed *adjective* = **hidden**, covered, covert, inconspicuous, masked, obscured, screened, secret, secreted, tucked away, under wraps, unseen

concealment *noun* = **hiding**, camouflage, cover, disguise, hideaway, hide-out, secrecy
➤ **Antonyms**
disclosure, display, exposure, give-away, leak, revelation, showing, uncovering

concede *verb* 1 = **admit**, accept, acknowledge, allow, confess, grant, own 2 = **give up**, cede, hand over, relinquish, surrender, yield
➤ **Antonyms**
≠**admit**: contest, deny, disclaim, dispute, protest, refute, reject ≠**give up**: beat, conquer, defeat, fight to the bitter end, make a stand

conceit *noun* 1 = **self-importance**, amour-propre, arrogance, complacency, egotism, narcissism, pride, self-love, swagger, vainglory, vanity 2 *Archaic* = **fancy**, belief, fantasy, idea, image, imagination, judgment, notion, opinion, quip, thought, vagary, whim, whimsy

conceited *adjective* = **self-important**, arrogant, bigheaded (*informal*), cocky, egotistical, full of oneself, immodest, narcissistic, overweening, puffed up, stuck up (*informal*), swollen-headed, too big for one's boots *or* breeches, vain, vainglorious
➤ **Antonyms**
humble, modest, self-effacing, unassuming

conceivable *adjective* = **imaginable**, believable, credible, possible, thinkable
➤ **Antonyms**
inconceivable, incredible, unbelievable, unimaginable, unthinkable

conceive *verb* 1 = **imagine**, appreciate, apprehend, believe, comprehend, envisage, fancy, get the picture, grasp, realize, suppose, think, understand 2 = **think up**, contrive, create, design, develop, devise, form, formulate, produce, project, purpose 3 = **become pregnant**, become impregnated

concentrate *verb* 1 = **focus one's attention on**, be engrossed in, consider closely, give all one's attention to, put one's mind to, rack one's brains 2 = **focus**, bring to bear, centre, cluster, converge 3 = **gather**, accumulate, cluster, collect, congregate, huddle
➤ **Antonyms**
≠**focus one's attention on**: disregard, let one's mind wander, lose concentration, pay no attention to, pay no heed to ≠**focus, gather**: diffuse, disperse, dissipate, scatter, spread out

concentrated *adjective* 1 = **intense**, all-out (*informal*), deep, hard, intensive 2 = **condensed**, boiled down, evaporated, reduced, rich, thickened, undiluted

concentration *noun* 1 = **single-mindedness**, absorption, application, heed 2 = **focusing**, bringing to bear, centralization, centring, combination, compression, consolidation, convergence, intensification 3 = **convergence**, accumulation, aggregation, cluster, collection, horde, mass
➤ **Antonyms**
≠**single-mindedness**: absent-mindedness, disregard, distraction, inattention ≠**focusing, convergence**: diffusion, dispersal, scattering, spreading-out

concept *noun* = **idea**, abstraction, conception, conceptualization, hypothesis, image, impression, notion, theory, view

conception noun 1 = **idea**, concept, design, image, notion, plan 2 = **understanding**, appreciation, clue, comprehension, impression, inkling, perception, picture 3 = **impregnation**, fertilization, germination, insemination 4 = **origin**, beginning, birth, formation, inception, initiation, invention, launching, outset

concern noun 1 = **worry**, anxiety, apprehension, attention, burden, care, consideration, disquiet, disquietude, distress, heed, responsibility, solicitude 2 = **importance**, bearing, interest, reference, relation, relevance 3 = **business**, affair, charge, department, field, interest, involvement, job, matter, mission, occupation, pigeon (informal), responsibility, task, transaction 4 = **business**, company, corporation, enterprise, establishment, firm, house, organization ◆ verb 5 = **worry**, bother, disquiet, distress, disturb, make anxious, make uneasy, perturb, trouble 6 = **be relevant to**, affect, apply to, bear on, interest, involve, pertain to, regard, touch

concerned adjective 1 = **involved**, active, implicated, interested, mixed up, privy to 2 = **worried**, anxious, bothered, distressed, disturbed, exercised, troubled, uneasy, upset 3 = **caring**, attentive, interested, solicitous
➤ Antonyms
aloof, carefree, detached, indifferent, neglectful, unconcerned, uninterested, untroubled, without a care

concerning preposition = **regarding**, about, anent (Scot.), apropos of, as regards, as to, in the matter of, on the subject of, re, relating to, respecting, touching, with reference to

concert noun 1 = **agreement**, accord, concord, concordance, harmony, unanimity, union, unison 2 **in concert** = **together**, concertedly, in collaboration, in league, in unison, jointly, shoulder to shoulder, unanimously

concerted adjective = **coordinated**, agreed upon, collaborative, combined, joint, planned, prearranged, united
➤ Antonyms
disunited, separate, uncontrived, uncooperative, unplanned

concession noun 1 = **grant**, adjustment, allowance, boon, compromise, indulgence, permit, privilege, sop 2 = **conceding**, acknowledgment, admission, assent, confession, surrender, yielding

conciliate verb = **pacify**, appease, clear the air, disarm, mediate, mollify, placate, pour

oil on troubled waters, propitiate, reconcile, restore harmony, soothe, win over

conciliation noun = **pacification**, appeasement, disarming, mollification, placation, propitiation, reconciliation, soothing

conciliatory adjective = **pacifying**, appeasing, disarming, irenic, mollifying, pacific, peaceable, placatory, propitiative

concise adjective = **brief**, compact, compendious, compressed, condensed, epigrammatic, in a nutshell, laconic, pithy, short, succinct, summary, synoptic, terse, to the point
➤ Antonyms
diffuse, discursive, garrulous, lengthy, long-winded, prolix, rambling, verbose, wordy

conclave noun = **secret** or **private meeting**, assembly, cabinet, conference, congress, council, parley, session

conclude verb 1 = **decide**, assume, clinch, deduce, determine, establish, fix, gather, infer, judge, reckon (informal), resolve, settle, sum up, suppose, surmise, work out 2 = **end**, bring down the curtain, cease, close, come to an end, complete, draw to a close, finish, round off, terminate, wind up 3 = **accomplish**, bring about, carry out, effect, pull off
➤ Antonyms
≠end: begin, commence, initiate, open, start

conclusion noun 1 = **decision**, agreement, conviction, deduction, inference, judgment, opinion, resolution, settlement, verdict 2 = **end**, bitter end, close, completion, ending, finale, finish, result, termination 3 = **outcome**, consequence, culmination, end result, issue, result, sequel, upshot 4 **in conclusion** = **finally**, in closing, lastly, to sum up

conclusive adjective = **decisive**, clinching, convincing, definite, definitive, final, irrefutable, ultimate, unanswerable, unarguable
➤ Antonyms
contestable, disputable, doubtful, dubious, inconclusive, indecisive, indefinite, questionable, refutable, unconvincing, vague

concoct verb = **make up**, brew, contrive, cook up (informal), design, devise, fabricate, formulate, hatch, invent, manufacture, mature, plot, prepare, project, think up, trump up

concoction noun = **mixture**, blend, brew, combination, compound, contrivance, creation, preparation

concrete noun 1 = **cement** (not in technical usage), concretion ◆ adjective 2 = **specific**, definite, explicit 3 = **real**, actual,

factual, material, sensible, substantial, tangible
➤ **Antonyms**
adjective ≠ **specific**: indefinite, unspecified, vague ≠ **real**: abstract, immaterial, insubstantial, intangible, notional, theoretical

concubine *noun Old-fashioned* = **mistress**, courtesan, kept woman, leman (*archaic*), odalisque, paramour

concupiscence *noun Formal* = **lust**, appetite, desire, horniness (*slang*), lasciviousness, lechery, libidinousness, libido, lickerishness (*archaic*), lustfulness, randiness (*informal, chiefly Brit.*)

concur *verb* = **agree**, accede, accord, acquiesce, approve, assent, buy into (*informal*), coincide, combine, consent, cooperate, harmonize, join

concurrent *adjective* **1** = **simultaneous**, coexisting, coincident, concerted, concomitant, contemporaneous, synchronous **2** = **converging**, confluent, convergent, uniting **3** = **in agreement**, agreeing, at one, compatible, consentient, consistent, cooperating, harmonious, in rapport, like-minded, of the same mind

concussion *noun* = **shaking**, clash, collision, crash, impact, jarring, jolt, jolting, shock

condemn *verb* **1** = **disapprove**, blame, censure, criticize, damn, denounce, excoriate, reprehend, reproach, reprobate, reprove, upbraid **2** = **sentence**, convict, damn, doom, pass sentence on, proscribe
➤ **Antonyms**
≠ **disapprove**: acclaim, applaud, approve, commend, compliment, condone, praise ≠ **sentence**: acquit, free, liberate

condemnation *noun* **1** = **disapproval**, blame, censure, denouncement, denunciation, reproach, reprobation, reproof, stricture **2** = **sentence**, conviction, damnation, doom, judgment, proscription

condensation *noun* **1** = **distillation**, condensate, deliquescence, liquefaction, precipitate, precipitation **2** = **abridgment**, contraction, digest, précis, synopsis **3** = **concentration**, compression, consolidation, crystallization, curtailment, reduction

condense *verb* **1** = **abridge**, abbreviate, compact, compress, concentrate, contract, curtail, encapsulate, epitomize, précis, shorten, summarize **2** = **concentrate**, boil down, coagulate, decoct, precipitate (*Chemistry*), reduce, solidify, thicken
➤ **Antonyms**
≠ **abridge**: elaborate, enlarge, expand, expatiate, increase, lengthen, pad out, spin out ≠ **concentrate**: dilute, make thinner,

thin (out), water down, weaken

condensed *adjective* **1** = **abridged**, compressed, concentrated, curtailed, shortened, shrunken, slimmed-down, summarized **2** = **concentrated**, boiled down, clotted, coagulated, precipitated (*Chemistry*), reduced, thickened

condescend *verb* **1** = **patronize**, talk down to **2** = **lower oneself**, be courteous, bend, come down off one's high horse (*informal*), deign, humble *or* demean oneself, see fit, stoop, submit, unbend (*informal*), vouchsafe

condescending *adjective* = **patronizing**, disdainful, lofty, lordly, on one's high horse (*informal*), snobbish, snooty (*informal*), supercilious, superior, toffee-nosed (*slang, chiefly Brit.*)

condition *noun* **1** = **state**, case, circumstances, lie of the land, plight, position, predicament, shape, situation, state of affairs, status quo **2** = **requirement**, arrangement, article, demand, limitation, modification, prerequisite, provision, proviso, qualification, requisite, restriction, rider, rule, stipulation, terms **3** = **health**, fettle, fitness, kilter, order, shape, state of health, trim **4** = **ailment**, complaint, infirmity, malady, problem, weakness ◆ *verb* **5** = **accustom**, adapt, educate, equip, habituate, inure, make ready, prepare, ready, tone up, train, work out

conditional *adjective* = **dependent**, contingent, limited, provisional, qualified, subject to, with reservations
➤ **Antonyms**
absolute, categorical, unconditional, unrestricted

conditioned *adjective* = **accustomed**, acclimatized, adapted, adjusted, familiarized, habituated, inured, made ready, prepared, seasoned, trained, used

conditioning *noun* **1** = **accustoming**, familiarization, grooming, hardening, inurement, preparation, readying, reorientation, seasoning, training ◆ *adjective* **2** = **toning**, astringent

conditions *plural noun* = **circumstances**, environment, milieu, situation, surroundings, way of life

condom *noun* = **sheath**, French letter (*slang*), French tickler (*slang*), rubber (*U.S. slang*), rubber johnny (*Brit. slang*), safe (*U.S. & Canad. slang*)

condone *verb* = **overlook**, disregard, excuse, forgive, let pass, look the other way, make allowance for, pardon, turn a blind eye to, wink at
➤ **Antonyms**
censure, condemn, denounce, disapprove, punish

conduct *noun* 1 = **behaviour**, attitude, bearing, carriage, comportment, demeanour, deportment, manners, mien (*literary*), ways 2 = **management**, administration, control, direction, guidance, handling, leadership, organization, running, supervision ♦ *verb* 3 = **carry out**, administer, control, direct, govern, handle, manage, organize, preside over, regulate, run, supervise 4 = **behave**, acquit, act, carry, comport, deport 5 = **accompany**, attend, chair, convey, escort, guide, lead, pilot, steer, usher

confederacy *noun* = **union**, alliance, bund, coalition, compact, confederation, conspiracy, covenant, federation, league

confederate *noun* 1 = **associate**, abettor, accessory, accomplice, ally, colleague, partner ♦ *adjective* 2 = **allied**, associated, combined, federal, federated, in alliance ♦ *verb* 3 = **unite**, ally, amalgamate, associate, band together, combine, federate, merge

confer *verb* 1 = **discuss**, consult, converse, deliberate, discourse, parley, talk 2 = **grant**, accord, award, bestow, give, hand out, present, vouchsafe

conference *noun* = **meeting**, colloquium, congress, consultation, convention, convocation, discussion, forum, seminar, symposium, teach-in

confess *verb* 1 = **admit**, acknowledge, allow, blurt out, come clean (*informal*), come out of the closet, concede, confide, disclose, divulge, 'fess up (*U.S.*), get (something) off one's chest (*informal*), grant, make a clean breast of, own, own up, recognize, sing (*slang, chiefly U.S.*), spill one's guts (*slang*) 2 = **declare**, affirm, assert, attest, aver, confirm, evince, manifest, profess, prove, reveal
➤ **Antonyms**
≠**admit**: button one's lips, conceal, cover, deny, hide, hush up, keep mum, keep secret, keep under wraps, repudiate, suppress, withhold

confession *noun* = **admission**, acknowledgment, avowal, disclosure, divulgence, exposure, revelation, unbosoming

confidant, confidante *noun* = **close friend**, alter ego, bosom friend, crony, familiar, intimate

confide *verb* 1 = **tell**, admit, breathe, confess, disclose, divulge, impart, reveal, whisper 2 *Formal* = **entrust**, commend, commit, consign

confidence *noun* 1 = **trust**, belief, credence, dependence, faith, reliance 2 = **self-assurance**, aplomb, assurance, boldness, courage, firmness, nerve, self-possession, self-reliance 3 **in confidence** = **in secrecy**, between you and me (and the gatepost), confidentially, privately
➤ **Antonyms**
≠**trust**: disbelief, distrust, doubt, misgiving, mistrust ≠**self-assurance**: apprehension, fear, self-doubt, shyness, uncertainty

confident *adjective* 1 = **certain**, convinced, counting on, positive, satisfied, secure, sure 2 = **self-assured**, assured, bold, can-do (*informal*), dauntless, fearless, self-reliant
➤ **Antonyms**
≠**certain**: doubtful, dubious, not sure, tentative, uncertain, unconvinced, unsure ≠**self-assured**: afraid, hesitant, insecure, jittery, lacking confidence, mousy, nervous, scared, self-doubting, unsure

confidential *adjective* 1 = **secret**, classified, hush-hush (*informal*), intimate, off the record, private, privy 2 = **trusted**, faithful, familiar, trustworthy, trusty

confidentially *adverb* = **in secret**, behind closed doors, between ourselves, in camera, in confidence, personally, privately, sub rosa

confine *verb* = **restrict**, bind, bound, cage, circumscribe, clip someone's wings, enclose, hem in, hold back, immure, imprison, incarcerate, intern, keep, limit, repress, restrain, shut up, straiten

confined *adjective* 1 = **restricted**, enclosed, limited 2 = **in childbirth**, in childbed, lying-in

confinement *noun* 1 = **imprisonment**, custody, detention, incarceration, internment, porridge (*slang*) 2 = **childbirth**, accouchement, childbed, labour, lying-in, parturition, time, travail

confines *plural noun* = **limits**, boundaries, bounds, circumference, edge, pale, precincts

confirm *verb* 1 = **prove**, approve, authenticate, bear out, corroborate, endorse, ratify, sanction, substantiate, validate, verify 2 = **strengthen**, assure, buttress, clinch, establish, fix, fortify, reinforce, settle

confirmation *noun* 1 = **proof**, authentication, corroboration, evidence, substantiation, testimony, validation, verification 2 = **sanction**, acceptance, agreement, approval, assent, endorsement, ratification
➤ **Antonyms**
≠**proof**: contradiction, denial, disavowal, repudiation ≠**sanction**: annulment, cancellation, disapproval, refusal, rejection

confirmed *adjective* = **long-established**, chronic, dyed-in-the-wool, habitual, hardened, ingrained, inured, inveterate, rooted, seasoned

confiscate *verb* = **seize**, appropriate, commandeer, expropriate, impound,

sequester, sequestrate
➤ **Antonyms**
free, give, give back, hand back, release, restore, return

confiscation *noun* = **seizure**, appropriation, expropriation, forfeiture, impounding, sequestration, takeover

conflict *noun* **1** = **opposition**, antagonism, bad blood, difference, disagreement, discord, dissension, divided loyalties, friction, hostility, interference, strife, variance **2** = **battle**, clash, collision, combat, contention, contest, encounter, engagement, fight, fracas, head-to-head, set-to (*informal*), strife, war, warfare ◆ *verb* **3** = **be incompatible**, be at variance, clash, collide, combat, contend, contest, differ, disagree, fight, interfere, strive, struggle
➤ **Antonyms**
noun ≠ **opposition**, **battle**: accord, agreement, harmony, peace, treaty, truce
◆ *verb* ≠ **be incompatible**: agree, coincide, harmonize, reconcile

conflicting *adjective* = **incompatible**, antagonistic, clashing, contradictory, contrary, discordant, inconsistent, opposed, opposing, paradoxical
➤ **Antonyms**
accordant, agreeing, compatible, congruous, consistent, harmonious, similar, unopposing

conform *verb* **1** = **comply**, adapt, adjust, fall in with, follow, follow the crowd, obey, run with the pack, toe the line, yield **2** = **agree**, accord, assimilate, correspond, harmonize, match, square, suit, tally

conformation *noun* = **shape**, anatomy, arrangement, build, configuration, form, framework, outline, structure

conformist *noun* = **traditionalist**, Babbitt (*U.S.*), conventionalist, stick-in-the-mud (*informal*), yes man

conformity *noun* **1** = **compliance**, allegiance, Babbittry (*U.S.*), conventionality, observance, orthodoxy, traditionalism **2** = **likeness**, affinity, agreement, conformance, congruity, consonance, correspondence, harmony, resemblance, similarity

confound *verb* **1** = **bewilder**, amaze, astonish, astound, baffle, be all Greek to (*informal*), boggle the mind, confuse, dumbfound, flabbergast (*informal*), flummox, mix up, mystify, nonplus, perplex, startle, surprise **2** = **destroy**, annihilate, contradict, demolish, explode, make a nonsense of, overthrow, overwhelm, refute, ruin

confront *verb* = **face**, accost, beard, brave, bring face to face with, call out, challenge, defy, encounter, face off (*slang*), face the

music, face up to, oppose, stand up to, tackle, walk into the lion's den
➤ **Antonyms**
avoid, body-swerve (*Scot.*), circumvent, dodge, evade, flee, give a wide berth to, keep *or* steer clear of, sidestep

confrontation *noun* = **conflict**, contest, crisis, encounter, face-off (*slang*), fight, head-to-head, set-to (*informal*), showdown (*informal*)

confuse *verb* **1** = **mix up**, blend, confound, disarrange, disorder, intermingle, involve, jumble, mingle, mistake, muddle, ravel, snarl up (*informal*), tangle **2** = **bewilder**, baffle, be all Greek to (*informal*), bemuse, darken, faze, flummox, muddy the waters, mystify, nonplus, obscure, perplex, puzzle **3** = **disconcert**, abash, addle, demoralize, discomfit, discompose, discountenance, disorient, embarrass, fluster, mortify, nonplus, rattle (*informal*), shame, throw into disorder, throw off balance, unnerve, upset

confused *adjective* **1** = **bewildered**, at a loss, at sea, at sixes and sevens, baffled, dazed, discombobulated (*informal, chiefly U.S. & Canad.*), disorganized, disoriented, flummoxed, muddled, muzzy (*U.S. informal*), nonplussed, not knowing if one is coming or going, not with it (*informal*), perplexed, puzzled, taken aback, thrown off balance, upset **2** = **disordered**, at sixes and sevens, chaotic, disarranged, disarrayed, disorderly, disorganized, higgledy-piggledy (*informal*), hugger-mugger (*archaic*), in disarray, jumbled, mistaken, misunderstood, mixed up, out of order, topsy-turvy, untidy
➤ **Antonyms**
≠ **bewildered**: aware, enlightened, informed, on the ball (*informal*), with it (*informal*)
≠ **disordered**: arranged, in order, ordered, orderly, organized, tidy

confusing *adjective* = **bewildering**, ambiguous, baffling, clear as mud (*informal*), complicated, contradictory, disconcerting, inconsistent, misleading, muddling, perplexing, puzzling, unclear
➤ **Antonyms**
clear, definite, explicit, plain, simple, straightforward, uncomplicated, understandable

confusion *noun* **1** = **bewilderment**, befuddlement, bemusement, disorientation, mystification, perplexity, puzzlement **2** = **disconcertion**, abashment, chagrin, demoralization, discomfiture, distraction, embarrassment, fluster, mind-fuck (*taboo slang*), perturbation **3** = **disorder**, bustle, chaos, clutter, commotion, disarrangement, disarray, disorganization, hodgepodge (*U.S.*), hotchpotch, jumble, mess, muddle, pig's breakfast (*informal*), shambles, state,

tangle, turmoil, untidiness, upheaval
➤ **Antonyms**
≠**bewilderment**: clarification,
enlightenment, explanation, solution
≠**disorder**: arrangement, neatness, order,
organization, tidiness
congenial *adjective* **1** = **pleasant**, affable,
agreeable, companionable, complaisant,
favourable, friendly, genial, kindly, pleasing **2**
= **compatible**, adapted, fit, kindred,
like-minded, suitable, sympathetic, well-suited
congenital *adjective* **1** = **inborn**,
constitutional, immanent, inbred, inherent,
innate, natural **2** *Informal* = **complete**,
deep-dyed (*usually derogatory*), inveterate,
thorough, utter
congested *adjective* **1** = **overcrowded**,
crowded, teeming **2** = **clogged**, blocked-up,
crammed, jammed, overfilled, overflowing,
packed, stuffed, stuffed-up
➤ **Antonyms**
≠**overcrowded**: empty, half-full, uncrowded
≠**clogged**: clear, free, uncongested,
unhampered, unhindered, unimpeded,
unobstructed
congestion *noun* **1** = **overcrowding**,
crowding **2** = **clogging**, bottleneck, jam,
mass, snarl-up (*informal, chiefly Brit.*), surfeit
conglomerate *noun* **1** = **corporation**,
agglomerate, aggregate, multinational
♦ *verb* **2** = **amass**, accumulate, agglomerate,
aggregate, cluster, coalesce, snowball
♦ *adjective* **3** = **amassed**, clustered,
composite, heterogeneous, massed
conglomeration *noun* = **mass**,
accumulation, aggregation, assortment,
combination, composite, hotchpotch,
medley, miscellany, mishmash, potpourri
congratulate *verb* = **compliment**,
felicitate, pat on the back, wish joy to
congratulations *plural noun, interjection*
= **good wishes**, best wishes, compliments,
felicitations, greetings, pat on the back
congregate *verb* = **come together**,
assemble, collect, concentrate, convene,
converge, convoke, flock, forgather, gather,
mass, meet, muster, rally, rendezvous,
throng
➤ **Antonyms**
break up, dispel, disperse, dissipate, part,
scatter, separate, split up
congregation *noun* = **assembly**, brethren,
crowd, fellowship, flock, host, laity,
multitude, parish, parishioners, throng
congress *noun* = **meeting**, assembly,
chamber of deputies, conclave, conference,
convention, convocation, council, delegates,
diet, house, legislative assembly, legislature,
parliament, quango, representatives
conic, conical *adjective* = **cone-shaped**,

conoid, funnel-shaped, pointed, pyramidal,
tapered, tapering
conjecture *noun* **1** = **guess**, assumption,
conclusion, fancy, guesstimate (*informal*),
guesswork, hypothesis, inference, notion,
presumption, shot in the dark, speculation,
supposition, surmise, theorizing, theory
♦ *verb* **2** = **guess**, assume, fancy,
hypothesize, imagine, infer, speculate,
suppose, surmise, suspect, theorize
conjugal *adjective* = **marital**, bridal,
connubial, hymeneal, married, matrimonial,
nuptial, spousal, wedded
conjunction *noun* = **joining**, association,
coincidence, combination, concurrence,
juxtaposition, union
conjure *verb* **1** = **perform tricks**, juggle **2**
= **summon up**, bewitch, call upon, cast a
spell, charm, enchant, invoke, raise, rouse **3**
Formal = **appeal to**, adjure, beg, beseech,
crave, entreat, implore, importune, pray,
supplicate
conjure up *verb* = **bring to mind**, contrive,
create, evoke, produce as if by magic, recall,
recollect
conjuror, conjurer *noun* = **magician**,
illusionist, miracle-worker, sorcerer,
thaumaturge (*rare*), wizard
connect *verb* = **link**, affix, ally, associate,
attach, cohere, combine, couple, fasten, join,
relate, unite
➤ **Antonyms**
detach, disconnect, dissociate, divide, part,
separate, sever, unfasten
connected *adjective* **1** = **linked**, affiliated,
akin, allied, associated, banded together,
bracketed, combined, coupled, joined,
related, united **2** *Of speech* = **coherent**,
comprehensible, consecutive, intelligible
connection *noun* **1** = **association**,
affiliation, affinity, bond, commerce,
communication, correlation,
correspondence, intercourse, interrelation,
liaison, link, marriage, nexus, relation,
relationship, relevance, tie-in **2** = **link**,
alliance, association, attachment, coupling,
fastening, junction, tie, union **3** = **contact**,
acquaintance, ally, associate, friend, sponsor
4 = **relative**, kin, kindred, kinsman, kith,
relation **5** = **context**, frame of reference,
reference
connivance *noun* = **collusion**, abetment,
abetting, complicity, conspiring, tacit consent
connive *verb* **1** = **conspire**, cabal, collude,
cook up (*informal*), intrigue, plot, scheme **2**
connive at = **turn a blind eye to**, abet, aid,
be an accessory to, be a party to, be in
collusion with, blink at, disregard, lend
oneself to, let pass, look the other way,
overlook, pass by, shut one's eyes to, wink at

connoisseur *noun* = **expert**, aficionado, appreciator, arbiter, authority, buff (*informal*), cognoscente, devotee, judge, maven (*U.S.*), savant, specialist, whiz (*informal*)

conquer *verb* **1** = **defeat**, beat, blow out of the water (*slang*), bring to their knees, checkmate, clobber (*slang*), crush, discomfit, get the better of, humble, lick (*informal*), make mincemeat of (*informal*), master, overcome, overpower, overthrow, prevail, put in their place, quell, rout, run rings around (*informal*), stuff (*slang*), subdue, subjugate, succeed, surmount, tank (*slang*), triumph, undo, vanquish, wipe the floor with (*informal*) **2** = **seize**, acquire, annex, obtain, occupy, overrun, win
> **Antonyms**
≠**defeat**: be defeated, capitulate, give in, give up, lose, quit, submit, surrender, throw in the towel, yield

conqueror *noun* = **winner**, champion, conquistador, defeater, hero, lord, master, subjugator, vanquisher, victor

conquest *noun* **1** = **defeat**, discomfiture, mastery, overthrow, pasting (*slang*), rout, triumph, vanquishment, victory **2** = **takeover**, acquisition, annexation, appropriation, coup, invasion, occupation, subjection, subjugation **3** = **captivation**, enchantment, enthralment, enticement, seduction **4** = **catch**, acquisition, adherent, admirer, fan, feather in one's cap, follower, prize, supporter, worshipper

conscience *noun* **1** = **principles**, moral sense, scruples, sense of right and wrong, still small voice **2 in all conscience** = **in fairness**, assuredly, certainly, fairly, honestly, in truth, rightly, truly

conscience-stricken *adjective* = **guilty**, ashamed, compunctious, contrite, disturbed, penitent, remorseful, repentant, sorry, troubled

conscientious *adjective* **1** = **thorough**, careful, diligent, exact, faithful, having one's nose to the grindstone, meticulous, painstaking, particular, punctilious **2** = **honourable**, high-minded, high-principled, honest, incorruptible, just, moral, responsible, scrupulous, straightforward, strict, upright
> **Antonyms**
≠**thorough**: careless, irresponsible, negligent, remiss, slack, thoughtless, unconscientious, unreliable, untrustworthy
≠**honourable**: unprincipled, unscrupulous

conscious *adjective* **1** = **aware**, alert, alive to, awake, clued-up (*informal*), cognizant, percipient, responsive, sensible, sentient, wise to (*slang*) **2** = **deliberate**, calculated, intentional, knowing, premeditated, rational, reasoning, reflective, responsible, self-conscious, studied, wilful
> **Antonyms**
≠**aware**: ignorant, insensible, oblivious, unaware, unconscious ≠**deliberate**: accidental, uncalculated, unintended, unintentional, unplanned, unpremeditated, unwitting

consciousness *noun* = **awareness**, apprehension, knowledge, realization, recognition, sensibility

consecrate *verb* = **sanctify**, dedicate, devote, exalt, hallow, ordain, set apart, venerate

consecutive *adjective* = **successive**, chronological, following, in sequence, in turn, running, sequential, seriatim, succeeding, uninterrupted

consensus *noun* = **agreement**, assent, common consent, concord, concurrence, general agreement, harmony, unanimity, unity

consent *noun* **1** = **agreement**, acquiescence, approval, assent, compliance, concession, concurrence, go-ahead (*informal*), green light, O.K. *or* okay (*informal*), permission, sanction ♦ *verb* **2** = **agree**, accede, acquiesce, allow, approve, assent, comply, concede, concur, permit, play ball (*informal*), yield
> **Antonyms**
noun ≠**agreement**: disagreement, disapproval, dissent, refusal, unwillingness
♦ *verb* ≠**agree**: decline, demur, disagree, disapprove, dissent, refuse, resist

consequence *noun* **1** = **result**, effect, end, end result, event, issue, outcome, repercussion, sequel, upshot **2** = **importance**, account, concern, import, interest, moment, note, portent, significance, value, weight **3** = **status**, bottom, distinction, eminence, notability, rank, repute, standing **4 in consequence** = **as a result**, because, following

consequent *adjective* = **following**, ensuing, resultant, resulting, sequential, subsequent, successive

consequently *adverb* = **as a result**, accordingly, ergo, hence, necessarily, subsequently, therefore, thus

conservation *noun* = **protection**, custody, economy, guardianship, husbandry, maintenance, preservation, safeguarding, safekeeping, saving, upkeep

conservative *adjective* **1** = **traditional**, cautious, conventional, die-hard, guarded, hidebound, middle-of-the-road, moderate, quiet, reactionary, sober ♦ *noun* **2** = **traditionalist**, die-hard, middle-of-the-roader, moderate, reactionary,

stick-in-the-mud (*informal*)
➤ **Antonyms**
adjective ≠**traditional**: imaginative, innovative, liberal, progressive, radical ♦ *noun* ≠**traditionalist**: changer, innovator, progressive, radical

Conservative *adjective* **1** = **Tory**, right-wing ♦ *noun* **2** = **Tory**, right-winger

conservatory *noun* = **greenhouse**, glasshouse, hothouse

conserve *verb* = **protect**, go easy on, hoard, husband, keep, nurse, preserve, save, store up, take care of, use sparingly
➤ **Antonyms**
be extravagant, blow (*slang*), dissipate, fritter away, misspend, misuse, spend, spend like water, squander, use up, waste

consider *verb* **1** = **think**, believe, deem, hold to be, judge, rate, regard as **2** = **think about**, chew over, cogitate, consult, contemplate, deliberate, discuss, examine, eye up, meditate, mull over, muse, ponder, reflect, revolve, ruminate, study, turn over in one's mind, weigh, work over **3** = **bear in mind**, care for, keep in view, make allowance for, reckon with, regard, remember, respect, take into account

considerable *adjective* **1** = **large**, abundant, ample, appreciable, comfortable, goodly, great, lavish, marked, much, noticeable, plentiful, reasonable, sizable *or* sizeable, substantial, tidy, tolerable **2** = **important**, distinguished, influential, notable, noteworthy, renowned, significant, venerable
➤ **Antonyms**
≠**large**: insignificant, insubstantial, meagre, paltry, small ≠**important**: insignificant, ordinary, unimportant, unremarkable

considerably *adverb* = **greatly**, appreciably, markedly, noticeably, remarkably, seriously (*informal*), significantly, substantially, very much

considerate *adjective* = **thoughtful**, attentive, charitable, circumspect, concerned, discreet, forbearing, kind, kindly, mindful, obliging, patient, tactful, unselfish
➤ **Antonyms**
heedless, inconsiderate, selfish, thoughtless

consideration *noun* **1** = **thought**, analysis, attention, cogitation, contemplation, deliberation, discussion, examination, perusal, reflection, regard, review, scrutiny, study **2** = **factor**, concern, issue, point **3** = **thoughtfulness**, concern, considerateness, friendliness, kindliness, kindness, respect, solicitude, tact **4** = **payment**, fee, perquisite, recompense, remuneration, reward, tip **5 take into consideration** = **bear in mind**, make allowance for, take into account, weigh

considering *preposition* **1** = **taking into account**, in the light of, in view of ♦ *adverb* **2** *Informal* = **all things considered**, all in all

consignment *noun* **1** = **shipment**, batch, delivery, goods **2** = **handing over**, assignment, committal, entrusting, relegation **3** = **sending**, dispatch, distribution, shipment, transmittal

consist *verb* **1 consist of** = **be made up of**, amount to, be composed of, comprise, contain, embody, include, incorporate, involve **2 consist in** = **lie in**, be expressed by, be found *or* contained in, inhere in, reside in

consistency *noun* **1** = **texture**, compactness, density, firmness, thickness, viscosity **2** = **constancy**, evenness, regularity, steadfastness, steadiness, uniformity

consistent *adjective* **1** = **unchanging**, constant, dependable, persistent, regular, steady, true to type, undeviating **2** = **agreeing**, accordant, all of a piece, coherent, compatible, congruous, consonant, harmonious, logical
➤ **Antonyms**
≠**unchanging**: changing, deviating, erratic, inconsistent, irregular ≠**agreeing**: contradictory, contrary, discordant, incompatible, incongruous, inconsistent, inharmonious

consolation *noun* = **comfort**, alleviation, assuagement, cheer, ease, easement, encouragement, help, relief, solace, succour, support

console *verb* = **comfort**, assuage, calm, cheer, encourage, express sympathy for, relieve, solace, soothe
➤ **Antonyms**
aggravate (*informal*), agitate, annoy, discomfort, distress, hassle (*informal*), hurt, sadden, torment, trouble, upset

consolidate *verb* **1** = **strengthen**, fortify, reinforce, secure, stabilize **2** = **combine**, amalgamate, cement, compact, condense, conjoin, federate, fuse, harden, join, solidify, thicken, unite

consolidation *noun* **1** = **strengthening**, fortification, reinforcement **2** = **combination**, alliance, amalgamation, association, compression, condensation, federation, fusion

consort *verb* **1** = **associate**, fraternize, go around with, hang about, around *or* out with, hang with (*informal, chiefly U.S.*), keep company, mingle, mix **2** = **agree**, accord, be consistent, correspond, harmonize, square, tally ♦ *noun* **3** = **spouse**, associate, companion, fellow, husband, partner, significant other (*U.S. informal*), wife

conspicuous *adjective* **1** = **obvious**,

apparent, blatant, clear, discernible, easily seen, evident, manifest, noticeable, patent, perceptible, salient, visible 2 = **noteworthy**, celebrated, distinguished, eminent, famous, illustrious, notable, outstanding, prominent, remarkable, salient, signal, striking
> **Antonyms**
≠**obvious**: concealed, hidden, imperceptible, inconspicuous, indiscernible, invisible, obscure, unnoticeable ≠**noteworthy**: humble, inconspicuous, insignificant, ordinary, unacclaimed, undistinguished, unmemorable, unnotable

conspiracy noun = **plot**, cabal, collusion, confederacy, frame-up (slang), intrigue, league, machination, scheme, treason

conspirator noun = **plotter**, cabalist, conspirer, intriguer, schemer, traitor

conspire verb 1 = **plot**, cabal, confederate, contrive, devise, hatch treason, intrigue, machinate, manoeuvre, plan, scheme 2 = **work together**, combine, concur, conduce, contribute, cooperate, tend

constancy noun 1 = **steadiness**, firmness, fixedness, permanence, perseverance, regularity, stability, steadfastness, tenacity, uniformity 2 = **faithfulness**, devotion, fidelity

constant adjective 1 = **continuous**, ceaseless, continual, endless, eternal, everlasting, incessant, interminable, never-ending, nonstop, perpetual, persistent, relentless, sustained, uninterrupted, unrelenting, unremitting 2 = **unchanging**, continual, even, firm, fixed, habitual, immovable, immutable, invariable, permanent, perpetual, regular, stable, steadfast, steady, unalterable, unbroken, uniform, unvarying 3 = **faithful**, attached, dependable, devoted, loyal, stalwart, staunch, tried-and-true, true, trustworthy, trusty, unfailing
> **Antonyms**
≠**continuous**: erratic, inconstant, intermittent, irregular, occasional, random, unsustained ≠**unchanging**: changeable, changing, deviating, uneven, unstable, variable ≠**faithful**: disloyal, fickle, irresolute, undependable

constantly adverb = **continuously**, all the time, always, aye (Scot.), continually, endlessly, everlastingly, incessantly, interminably, invariably, morning, noon and night, night and day, nonstop, perpetually, persistently, relentlessly
> **Antonyms**
(every) now and then, every so often, from time to time, intermittently, irregularly, now and again, occasionally, off and on, periodically, sometimes

consternation noun = **dismay**, alarm, amazement, anxiety, awe, bewilderment,

confusion, distress, dread, fear, fright, horror, panic, shock, terror, trepidation

constituent noun 1 = **voter**, elector 2 = **component**, element, essential, factor, ingredient, part, principle, unit ♦ adjective 3 = **component**, basic, elemental, essential, integral

constitute verb 1 = **make up**, compose, comprise, create, enact, establish, fix, form, found, make, set up 2 = **set up**, appoint, authorize, commission, delegate, depute, empower, name, nominate, ordain

constitution noun 1 = **health**, build, character, disposition, physique, temper, temperament 2 = **structure**, composition, form, make-up, nature 3 = **establishment**, composition, formation, organization

constitutional adjective 1 = **statutory**, chartered, vested 2 = **inherent**, congenital, immanent, inborn, intrinsic, organic ♦ noun 3 = **walk**, airing, stroll, turn

constrain verb 1 = **force**, bind, coerce, compel, drive, impel, necessitate, oblige, pressure, pressurize, urge 2 = **restrict**, chain, check, confine, constrict, curb, hem in, rein, restrain, straiten

constrained adjective = **forced**, embarrassed, guarded, inhibited, reserved, reticent, subdued, unnatural

constraint noun 1 = **restriction**, check, curb, damper, deterrent, hindrance, limitation, rein 2 = **force**, coercion, compulsion, necessity, pressure, restraint 3 = **repression**, bashfulness, diffidence, embarrassment, inhibition, reservation, restraint, timidity

construct verb = **build**, assemble, compose, create, design, elevate, engineer, erect, establish, fabricate, fashion, form, formulate, found, frame, make, manufacture, organize, put together, put up, raise, set up, shape
> **Antonyms**
bulldoze, demolish, destroy, devastate, dismantle, flatten, knock down, level, pull down, raze, tear down

construction noun 1 = **building**, assembly, composition, creation, edifice, erection, fabrication, formation 2 = **structure**, composition, fabric, figure, form, shape 3 Formal = **interpretation**, explanation, inference, reading, rendering, take (informal, chiefly U.S.)

constructive adjective = **helpful**, positive, practical, productive, useful, valuable
> **Antonyms**
destructive, futile, ineffective, limp-wristed, negative, unhelpful, unproductive, useless, vain, worthless

consult verb 1 = **ask**, ask advice of, commune, compare notes, confer, consider, debate, deliberate, interrogate, pick (someone's) brains, question, refer to, take counsel, turn to **2** = **consider**, have regard for, regard, respect, take account of, take into consideration

consultant *noun* = **specialist**, adviser, authority

consultation *noun* = **seminar**, appointment, conference, council, deliberation, dialogue, discussion, examination, hearing, interview, meeting, session

consume *verb* **1** = **eat**, devour, eat up, gobble (up), guzzle, polish off (*informal*), put away, swallow **2** = **use up**, absorb, deplete, dissipate, drain, eat up, employ, exhaust, expend, finish up, fritter away, lavish, lessen, spend, squander, use, utilize, vanish, waste, wear out **3** = **destroy**, annihilate, decay, demolish, devastate, lay waste, ravage **4** *often passive* = **obsess**, absorb, devour, dominate, eat up, engross, monopolize, preoccupy

consumer *noun* = **buyer**, customer, purchaser, shopper, user

consuming *adjective* = **overwhelming**, absorbing, compelling, devouring, engrossing, excruciating, gripping, immoderate, tormenting

consummate *verb* **1** = **complete**, accomplish, achieve, carry out, compass, conclude, crown, effectuate, end, finish, fulfil, perfect, perform, put the tin lid on ♦ *adjective* **2** = **skilled**, accomplished, matchless, perfect, polished, practised, superb, supreme **3** = **complete**, absolute, conspicuous, deep-dyed (*usually derogatory*), extreme, supreme, total, transcendent, ultimate, unqualified, utter
➤ **Antonyms**
verb ≠**complete**: begin, commence, conceive, get under way, inaugurate, initiate, originate, start

consumption *noun* **1** = **using up**, consuming, decay, decrease, depletion, destruction, diminution, dissipation, drain, exhaustion, expenditure, loss, use, utilization, waste **2** *Old-fashioned* = **tuberculosis**, atrophy, emaciation, phthisis, T.B.

contact *noun* **1** = **communication**, association, connection **2** = **touch**, approximation, contiguity, junction, juxtaposition, union **3** = **acquaintance**, connection ♦ *verb* **4** = **get** or **be in touch with**, approach, call, communicate with, get hold of, phone, reach, ring (up) (*informal, chiefly Brit.*), speak to, touch base with (*U.S. & Canad. informal*), write to

contagious *adjective* = **infectious**,

catching, communicable, epidemic, epizootic (*Veterinary medicine*), pestiferous, pestilential, spreading, taking (*informal*), transmissible

contain *verb* **1** = **hold**, accommodate, enclose, have capacity for, incorporate, seat **2** = **include**, comprehend, comprise, consist of, embody, embrace, involve **3** = **restrain**, control, curb, hold back, hold in, keep a tight rein on, repress, stifle

container *noun* = **holder**, receptacle, repository, vessel

contaminate *verb* = **pollute**, adulterate, befoul, corrupt, defile, deprave, infect, radioactivate, smirch, soil, stain, sully, taint, tarnish, vitiate
➤ **Antonyms**
clean, cleanse, decontaminate, deodorize, disinfect, fumigate, purify, sanitize, sterilize

contamination *noun* = **pollution**, adulteration, contagion, corruption, decay, defilement, dirtying, filth, foulness, impurity, infection, poisoning, radioactivation, rottenness, taint

contemplate *verb* **1** = **think about**, brood over, consider, deliberate, meditate, meditate on, mull over, muse over, observe, ponder, reflect upon, revolve or turn over in one's mind, ruminate (upon) **2** = **consider**, aspire to, design, envisage, expect, foresee, have in view or in mind, intend, mean, plan, propose, think of **3** = **look at**, behold, check out (*informal*), examine, eye, eye up, gaze at, inspect, recce (*slang*), regard, scrutinize, stare at, study, survey, view, weigh

contemplation *noun* **1** = **thought**, cogitation, consideration, deliberation, meditation, musing, pondering, reflection, reverie, rumination **2** = **looking at**, examination, gazing at, inspection, observation, recce (*slang*), scrutiny, survey, viewing

contemplative *adjective* = **thoughtful**, deep or lost in thought, in a brown study, intent, introspective, meditative, musing, pensive, rapt, reflective, ruminative

contemporary *adjective* **1** = **coexisting**, coetaneous (*rare*), coeval, coexistent, concurrent, contemporaneous, synchronous **2** = **modern**, à la mode, current, happening (*informal*), in fashion, latest, newfangled, present, present-day, recent, trendy (*Brit. informal*), ultramodern, up-to-date, up-to-the-minute, with it (*informal*) ♦ *noun* **3** = **peer**, compeer, fellow
➤ **Antonyms**
adjective ≠**modern**: antecedent, antique, early, obsolete, old, old-fashioned, out-of-date, passé

contempt *noun* = **scorn**, condescension,

contumely, derision, despite (*archaic*), disdain, disregard, disrespect, mockery, neglect, slight
➤ **Antonyms**
admiration, esteem, honour, liking, regard, respect

contemptible *adjective* = **despicable**, abject, base, cheap, degenerate, detestable, ignominious, low, low-down (*informal*), mean, measly, paltry, pitiful, scurvy, shabby, shameful, vile, worthless
➤ **Antonyms**
admirable, attractive, honourable, laudable, pleasant, praiseworthy

contemptuous *adjective* = **scornful**, arrogant, cavalier, condescending, derisive, disdainful, haughty, high and mighty, insolent, insulting, on one's high horse (*informal*), sneering, supercilious, withering
➤ **Antonyms**
civil, courteous, deferential, gracious, humble, mannerly, obsequious, polite, respectful

contend *verb* 1 = **compete**, clash, contest, cope, emulate, fight, grapple, jostle, litigate, skirmish, strive, struggle, vie 2 = **argue**, affirm, allege, assert, aver, avow, debate, dispute, hold, maintain

content[1] *noun* 1 = **meaning**, burden, essence, gist, ideas, matter, significance, substance, text, thoughts 2 = **amount**, capacity, load, measure, size, volume

content[2] *adjective* 1 = **satisfied**, agreeable, at ease, comfortable, contented, fulfilled, willing to accept ♦ *verb* 2 = **satisfy**, appease, delight, gladden, gratify, humour, indulge, mollify, placate, please, reconcile, sate, suffice ♦ *noun* 3 = **satisfaction**, comfort, contentment, ease, gratification, peace, peace of mind, pleasure

contented *adjective* = **satisfied**, at ease, at peace, cheerful, comfortable, complacent, content, glad, gratified, happy, pleased, serene, thankful
➤ **Antonyms**
annoyed, discontented, displeased, dissatisfied, pissed off (*taboo slang*), troubled, uncomfortable, uneasy

contention *noun* 1 = **dispute**, bone of contention, competition, contest, disagreement, discord, dissension, enmity, feuding, hostility, rivalry, row, strife, struggle, wrangling 2 = **assertion**, affirmation, allegation, argument, asseveration, belief, claim, declaration, ground, idea, maintaining, opinion, position, profession, stand, thesis, view

contentious *adjective* = **argumentative**, bickering, cantankerous, captious, cavilling, combative, cross, disputatious, factious,

litigious, peevish, perverse, pugnacious, quarrelsome, querulous, wrangling

contentment *noun* = **satisfaction**, comfort, complacency, content, contentedness, ease, equanimity, fulfilment, gladness, gratification, happiness, peace, pleasure, repletion, serenity
➤ **Antonyms**
discomfort, discontent, discontentment, displeasure, dissatisfaction, uneasiness, unhappiness

contents *plural noun* 1 = **constituents**, elements, ingredients, load 2 = **chapters**, divisions, subject matter, subjects, themes, topics

contest *noun* 1 = **competition**, game, head-to-head, match, tournament, trial 2 = **struggle**, affray, altercation, battle, combat, conflict, controversy, debate, discord, dispute, encounter, fight, shock ♦ *verb* 3 = **dispute**, argue, call in or into question, challenge, debate, doubt, litigate, object to, oppose, question 4 = **compete**, contend, fight, fight over, strive, vie

contestant *noun* = **competitor**, aspirant, candidate, contender, entrant, participant, player

context *noun* 1 = **circumstances**, ambience, conditions, situation 2 = **frame of reference**, background, connection, framework, relation

continent *adjective* = **self-restrained**, abstemious, abstinent, ascetic, austere, celibate, chaste, sober

contingency *noun* = **possibility**, accident, chance, emergency, event, eventuality, fortuity, happening, incident, juncture, uncertainty

contingent *noun* 1 = **group**, batch, body, bunch (*informal*), deputation, detachment, mission, quota, section, set ♦ *adjective* 2 = **chance**, accidental, casual, fortuitous, haphazard, random, uncertain 3 **contingent on** or **upon** = **dependent on**, conditional on, controlled by, subject to

continual *adjective* = **constant**, continuous, endless, eternal, everlasting, frequent, incessant, interminable, oft-repeated, perpetual, recurrent, regular, repeated, repetitive, unceasing, uninterrupted, unremitting
➤ **Antonyms**
broken, ceasing, erratic, fluctuating, fragmentary, infrequent, intermittent, interrupted, irregular, occasional, periodic, spasmodic, sporadic

continually *adverb* = **constantly**, all the time, always, aye (*Scot.*), endlessly, eternally, everlastingly, forever, incessantly, interminably, nonstop, persistently, repeatedly

continuance *noun* = duration, continuation, period, protraction, term

continuation *noun* 1 = continuing, maintenance, perpetuation, prolongation, resumption 2 = addition, extension, furtherance, postscript, sequel, supplement

continue *verb* 1 = remain, abide, carry on, endure, last, live on, persist, rest, stay, stay on, survive 2 = keep on, carry on, go on, keep at, keep one's hand in, keep the ball rolling, keep up, maintain, persevere, persist in, prolong, pursue, stick at, stick to, sustain 3 = resume, carry on, pick up where one left off, proceed, recommence, return to, take up 4 = go on, draw out, extend, lengthen, project, prolong, reach
> Antonyms
≠remain: abdicate, leave, quit, resign, retire, step down ≠keep on, resume: break off, call it a day, cease, discontinue, give up, leave off, pack in (*Brit. informal*), quit, stop

continuing *adjective* = lasting, enduring, in progress, ongoing, sustained

continuity *noun* = sequence, cohesion, connection, flow, interrelationship, progression, succession, whole

continuous *adjective* = constant, connected, continued, extended, prolonged, unbroken, unceasing, undivided, uninterrupted
> Antonyms
broken, disconnected, ending, inconstant, intermittent, interrupted, occasional, passing, spasmodic

contour *noun* = outline, curve, figure, form, lines, profile, relief, shape, silhouette

contraband *noun* 1 = smuggling, black-marketing, bootlegging, moonshine (*U.S.*), rum-running, trafficking ♦ *adjective* 2 = smuggled, banned, black-market, bootleg, bootlegged, forbidden, hot (*informal*), illegal, illicit, interdicted, prohibited, unlawful

contract *noun* 1 = agreement, arrangement, bargain, bond, commission, commitment, compact, concordat, convention, covenant, deal (*informal*), engagement, pact, settlement, stipulation, treaty, understanding ♦ *verb* 2 = agree, arrange, bargain, clinch, close, come to terms, commit oneself, covenant, engage, enter into, negotiate, pledge, shake hands, stipulate 3 = shorten, abbreviate, abridge, compress, condense, confine, constrict, curtail, diminish, dwindle, epitomize, knit, lessen, narrow, pucker, purse, reduce, shrink, shrivel, tighten, wither, wrinkle 4 = catch, acquire, be afflicted with, develop, get, go down with, incur
> Antonyms
verb ≠agree: decline, disagree, refuse, turn

down ≠shorten: broaden, develop, distend, enlarge, expand, grow, increase, inflate, multiply, spread, stretch, swell, widen ≠catch: avert, avoid, escape, ward off

contraction *noun* = shortening, abbreviation, compression, constriction, diminution, drawing in, elision, narrowing, reduction, shrinkage, shrivelling, tensing, tightening

contradict *verb* = deny, be at variance with, belie, challenge, contravene, controvert, counter, counteract, dispute, fly in the face of, gainsay (*archaic or literary*), impugn, make a nonsense of, negate, oppose, rebut
> Antonyms
affirm, agree, authenticate, confirm, defend, endorse, support, verify

contradiction *noun* = denial, conflict, confutation, contravention, incongruity, inconsistency, negation, opposite

contradictory *adjective* = inconsistent, antagonistic, antithetical, conflicting, contrary, discrepant, incompatible, irreconcilable, opposed, opposite, paradoxical, repugnant

contraption *noun Informal* = device, apparatus, contrivance, gadget, instrument, mechanism, rig, waldo

contrary *noun* 1 = opposite, antithesis, converse, reverse 2 on the contrary = quite the opposite *or* reverse, conversely, in contrast, not at all, on the other hand ♦ *adjective* 3 = opposed, adverse, antagonistic, clashing, contradictory, counter, discordant, hostile, inconsistent, inimical, opposite, paradoxical 4 = perverse, awkward, balky, cantankerous, cussed (*informal*), difficult, disobliging, froward (*archaic*), intractable, obstinate, stroppy (*Brit. slang*), thrawn (*Northern English dialect*), unaccommodating, wayward, wilful
> Antonyms
adjective ≠opposed: accordant, congruous, consistent, harmonious, in agreement, parallel, unopposed ≠perverse: accommodating, agreeable, amiable, cooperative, eager to please, helpful, obliging, tractable, willing

contrast *noun* 1 = difference, comparison, contrariety, differentiation, disparity, dissimilarity, distinction, divergence, foil, opposition ♦ *verb* 2 = differentiate, compare, differ, distinguish, oppose, set in opposition, set off

contribute *verb* 1 = give, add, afford, bestow, chip in (*informal*), donate, furnish, provide, subscribe, supply 2 contribute to = be partly responsible for, be conducive to, be instrumental in, conduce to, help, lead to, tend to

contribution *noun* = **gift**, addition, bestowal, donation, grant, input, offering, stipend, subscription

contributor *noun* **1** = **giver**, backer, bestower, conferrer, donor, patron, subscriber, supporter **2** = **writer**, correspondent, freelance, freelancer, journalist, journo (*slang*), reporter

contrite *adjective* = **sorry**, chastened, conscience-stricken, humble, in sackcloth and ashes, penitent, regretful, remorseful, repentant, sorrowful

contrivance *noun* **1** = **device**, apparatus, appliance, contraption, equipment, gadget, gear, implement, instrument, invention, machine, mechanism **2** = **plan**, artifice, design, dodge, expedient, fabrication, formation, intrigue, inventiveness, machination, measure, plot, project, ruse, scheme, stratagem, trick

contrive *verb* **1** = **bring about**, arrange, effect, hit upon, manage, manoeuvre, plan, plot, scheme, succeed **2** = **devise**, concoct, construct, create, design, engineer, fabricate, frame, improvise, invent, manufacture, wangle (*informal*)

contrived *adjective* = **forced**, artificial, elaborate, laboured, overdone, planned, recherché, strained, unnatural
➤ **Antonyms**
genuine, natural, relaxed, spontaneous, unaffected, unconstrained, unfeigned, unforced, unpretentious

control *noun* **1** = **power**, authority, charge, command, direction, discipline, government, guidance, jurisdiction, management, mastery, oversight, rule, superintendence, supervision, supremacy **2** = **restraint**, brake, check, curb, limitation, regulation ◆ *verb* **3** = **have power over**, administer, boss (*informal*), call the shots, call the tune, command, conduct, direct, dominate, govern, handle, have charge of, have (someone) in one's pocket, hold the purse strings, keep a tight rein on, keep on a string, lead, manage, manipulate, oversee, pilot, reign over, rule, steer, superintend, supervise **4** = **restrain**, bridle, check, constrain, contain, curb, hold back, limit, master, rein in, repress, subdue

controls *plural noun* = **instruments**, console, control panel, dash, dashboard, dials

controversial *adjective* = **disputed**, at issue, contended, contentious, controvertible, debatable, disputable, open to question, polemic, under discussion

controversy *noun* = **argument**, altercation, contention, debate, discussion, dispute, dissension, polemic, quarrel, row,

squabble, strife, wrangle, wrangling

convalescence *noun* = **recovery**, improvement, recuperation, rehabilitation, return to health

convalescent *adjective* = **recovering**, getting better, improving, mending, on the mend, recuperating

convene *verb* = **gather**, assemble, bring together, call, come together, congregate, convoke, meet, muster, rally, summon

convenience *noun* **1** = **usefulness**, accessibility, advantage, appropriateness, availability, benefit, fitness, handiness, opportuneness, serviceability, suitability, utility **2** = **suitable time**, chance, leisure, opportunity, spare moment, spare time **3** = **appliance**, amenity, comfort, facility, help, labour-saving device
➤ **Antonyms**
≠**usefulness**: inconvenience, uselessness

convenient *adjective* **1** = **useful**, adapted, appropriate, beneficial, commodious, fit, fitted, handy, helpful, labour-saving, opportune, seasonable, serviceable, suitable, suited, timely, well-timed **2** = **nearby**, accessible, at hand, available, close at hand, handy, just round the corner, within reach
➤ **Antonyms**
≠**useful**: awkward, inconvenient, unsuitable, useless ≠**nearby**: distant, inaccessible, inconvenient, out-of-the-way

convent *noun* = **nunnery**, convent school, religious community

convention *noun* **1** = **custom**, code, etiquette, formality, practice, propriety, protocol, tradition, usage **2** = **agreement**, bargain, compact, concordat, contract, pact, protocol, stipulation, treaty **3** = **assembly**, conference, congress, convocation, council, delegates, meeting, representatives

conventional *adjective* **1** = **ordinary**, accepted, bog-standard (*Brit. & Irish slang*), common, correct, customary, decorous, expected, formal, habitual, normal, orthodox, prevailing, prevalent, proper, regular, ritual, standard, traditional, usual, wonted **2** = **unoriginal**, banal, bourgeois, commonplace, hackneyed, hidebound, pedestrian, Pooterish, prosaic, routine, run-of-the-mill, stereotyped, vanilla (*slang*)
➤ **Antonyms**
abnormal, left-field (*informal*), off-the-wall (*slang*), uncommon, unconventional, unorthodox

converge *verb* = **come together**, coincide, combine, concentrate, focus, gather, join, meet, merge, mingle

conversant *adjective* **conversant with** = **experienced in**, acquainted with, *au fait* with, familiar with, knowledgeable about, practised in, proficient in, skilled in, versed in, well-informed about, well up in (*informal*)

conversation *noun* = **talk**, chat, chinwag (*Brit. informal*), colloquy, communication, communion, confab (*informal*), confabulation, conference, converse, dialogue, discourse, discussion, exchange, gossip, intercourse, powwow, tête-à-tête

conversational *adjective* = **chatty**, colloquial, communicative, informal

converse¹ *verb* = **talk**, chat, commune, confer, discourse, exchange views

converse² *noun* **1** = **opposite**, antithesis, contrary, obverse, other side of the coin, reverse ♦ *adjective* **2** = **opposite**, contrary, counter, reverse, reversed, transposed

conversion *noun* **1** = **change**, metamorphosis, transfiguration, transformation, transmogrification (*jocular*), transmutation **2** = **adaptation**, alteration, modification, reconstruction, remodelling, reorganization **3** = **reformation**, change of heart, proselytization, rebirth, regeneration

convert *verb* **1** = **change**, alter, interchange, metamorphose, transform, transmogrify (*jocular*), transmute, transpose, turn **2** = **adapt**, apply, appropriate, customize, modify, remodel, reorganize, restyle, revise **3** = **reform**, baptize, bring to God, convince, proselytize, regenerate, save ♦ *noun* **4** = **neophyte**, catechumen, disciple, proselyte

convex *adjective* = **rounded**, bulging, gibbous, outcurved, protuberant
➤ **Antonyms**
concave, cupped, depressed, excavated, hollowed, indented, sunken

convey *verb* **1** = **communicate**, disclose, impart, make known, relate, reveal, tell **2** = **carry**, bear, bring, conduct, fetch, forward, grant, guide, move, send, support, transmit, transport **3** *Law* = **transfer**, bequeath, cede, deliver, demise, devolve, grant, lease, will

conveyance *noun* **1** *Old-fashioned* = **vehicle**, transport **2** = **transportation**, carriage, movement, transfer, transference, transmission, transport

convict *verb* **1** = **find guilty**, condemn, imprison, pronounce guilty, sentence ♦ *noun* **2** = **prisoner**, con (*slang*), criminal, culprit, felon, jailbird, lag (*slang*), malefactor, villain

conviction *noun* **1** = **belief**, creed, faith, opinion, persuasion, principle, tenet, view **2** = **confidence**, assurance, certainty, certitude, earnestness, fervour, firmness, reliance

convince *verb* = **persuade**, assure, bring round, gain the confidence of, prevail upon, prove to, satisfy, sway, win over

convincing *adjective* = **persuasive**, cogent,

conclusive, credible, impressive, incontrovertible, likely, plausible, powerful, probable, telling, verisimilar
➤ **Antonyms**
beyond belief, cock-and-bull (*informal*), dubious, far-fetched, implausible, improbable, inconclusive, incredible, unconvincing, unlikely

convoy *noun* **1** = **escort**, armed guard, attendance, attendant, guard, protection ♦ *verb* **2** = **escort**, accompany, attend, guard, pilot, protect, shepherd, usher

convulse *verb* = **shake**, agitate, churn up, derange, disorder, disturb, shatter, twist, work

convulsion *noun* **1** = **spasm**, contortion, contraction, cramp, fit, paroxysm, seizure, throe (*rare*), tremor **2** = **upheaval**, agitation, commotion, disturbance, furore, shaking, tumult, turbulence

cook up *verb Informal* = **invent**, concoct, contrive, devise, dream up, fabricate, improvise, manufacture, plot, prepare, scheme, trump up

cool *adjective* **1** = **cold**, chilled, chilling, chilly, coldish, nippy, refreshing **2** = **calm**, collected, composed, deliberate, dispassionate, imperturbable, laid-back (*informal*), level-headed, placid, quiet, relaxed, sedate, self-controlled, self-possessed, serene, together (*slang*), unemotional, unexcited, unfazed (*informal*), unruffled **3** = **unfriendly**, aloof, apathetic, distant, frigid, incurious, indifferent, lukewarm, offhand, reserved, standoffish, uncommunicative, unconcerned, unenthusiastic, uninterested, unresponsive, unwelcoming **4** = **impudent**, audacious, bold, brazen, cheeky, impertinent, presumptuous, shameless **5** *Informal* = **sophisticated**, cosmopolitan, elegant, urbane ♦ *verb* **6** = **chill**, cool off, freeze, lose heat, refrigerate **7** = **calm (down)**, abate, allay, assuage, dampen, lessen, moderate, quiet, temper ♦ *noun* **8** *Slang* = **calmness**, composure, control, poise, self-control, self-discipline, self-possession, temper
➤ **Antonyms**
adjective ≠**cold**: lukewarm, moderately hot, sunny, tepid, warm ≠**calm**: agitated, antsy (*informal*), delirious, excited, impassioned, nervous, overwrought, perturbed, tense, troubled, twitchy (*informal*) ≠**unfriendly**: amiable, chummy (*informal*), cordial, friendly, outgoing, receptive, responsive, sociable, warm ♦ *verb* ≠**chill**: heat, reheat, take the chill off, thaw, warm (up)

coop *noun* **1** = **pen**, box, cage, corral (*chiefly U.S. & Canad.*), enclosure, hutch, pound ♦ *verb* **2 coop up** = **confine**, cage, immure, impound, imprison, pen, pound, shut up

cooperate *verb* 1 = **work together**, collaborate, combine, concur, conduce, conspire, coordinate, join forces, pool resources, pull together 2 = **help**, abet, aid, assist, contribute, go along with, lend a helping hand, pitch in, play ball (*informal*)
➤ **Antonyms**
conflict, contend with, fight, hamper, hamstring, hinder, impede, obstruct, oppose, prevent, put the mockers on (*informal*), resist, struggle against, stymie, thwart

cooperation *noun* 1 = **teamwork**, collaboration, combined effort, concert, concurrence, esprit de corps, give-and-take, unity 2 = **help**, assistance, helpfulness, participation, responsiveness
➤ **Antonyms**
discord, dissension, hindrance, opposition, rivalry

cooperative *adjective* 1 = **helpful**, accommodating, obliging, onside (*informal*), responsive, supportive 2 = **shared**, coactive, collective, combined, concerted, coordinated, joint, unified, united

coordinate *verb* 1 = **bring together**, correlate, harmonize, integrate, match, mesh, organize, relate, synchronize, systematize ◆ *adjective* 2 = **equivalent**, coequal, correlative, correspondent, equal, parallel, tantamount

cope *verb* 1 = **manage**, carry on, get by (*informal*), hold one's own, make out (*informal*), make the grade, rise to the occasion, struggle through, survive 2 **cope with** = **deal with**, contend with, dispatch, encounter, grapple with, handle, struggle with, tangle with, tussle with, weather, wrestle with

copious *adjective* = **abundant**, ample, bounteous, bountiful, extensive, exuberant, full, generous, lavish, liberal, luxuriant, overflowing, plenteous, plentiful, profuse, rich, superabundant

copulate *verb* = **have intercourse**, ball (*taboo slang, chiefly U.S.*), bonk (*informal*), fuck (*taboo slang*), have sex, hump (*taboo slang*), screw (*taboo slang*), shag (*taboo slang, chiefly Brit.*)

copy *noun* 1 = **reproduction**, archetype, carbon copy, counterfeit, duplicate, facsimile, fake, fax, forgery, image, imitation, likeness, model, pattern, photocopy, Photostat (*Trademark*), print, replica, replication, representation, transcription, Xerox (*Trademark*) ◆ *verb* 2 = **reproduce**, counterfeit, duplicate, photocopy, Photostat (*Trademark*), replicate, transcribe, Xerox (*Trademark*) 3 = **imitate**, act like, ape, behave like, echo, emulate, follow, follow suit, follow the example of, mimic, mirror,

parrot, repeat, simulate
➤ **Antonyms**
noun ≠**reproduction**: model, original, pattern, prototype, the real thing ◆ *verb* ≠**reproduce**: create, originate

cord *noun* = **rope**, line, string, twine

cordial *adjective* = **warm**, affable, affectionate, agreeable, cheerful, congenial, earnest, friendly, genial, heartfelt, hearty, invigorating, sociable, warm-hearted, welcoming, wholehearted
➤ **Antonyms**
aloof, cold, distant, formal, frigid, reserved, unfriendly, ungracious

cordiality *noun* = **warmth**, affability, amiability, friendliness, geniality, heartiness, sincerity, wholeheartedness

cordon *noun* 1 = **chain**, barrier, line, ring ◆ *verb* 2 **cordon off** = **surround**, close off, encircle, enclose, fence off, isolate, picket, separate

core *noun* = **centre**, crux, essence, gist, heart, kernel, nub, nucleus, pith

corner *noun* 1 = **angle**, bend, crook, joint 2 = **space**, cavity, cranny, hideaway, hide-out, hidey-hole (*informal*), hole, niche, nook, recess, retreat 3 = **tight spot**, hole (*informal*), hot water (*informal*), pickle (*informal*), predicament, spot (*informal*) ◆ *verb* 4 = **trap**, bring to bay, run to earth 5 *As in* **corner the market** = **monopolize**, dominate, engross, hog (*slang*)

cornerstone *noun* 1 = **basis**, bedrock, key, premise, starting point 2 = **quoin**

corny *adjective Slang* = **unoriginal**, banal, commonplace, dull, feeble, hackneyed, maudlin, mawkish, old-fashioned, old hat, sentimental, stale, stereotyped, trite

corporal *adjective* = **bodily**, anatomical, carnal, corporeal (*archaic*), fleshly, material, physical, somatic

corporate *adjective* = **collective**, allied, collaborative, combined, communal, joint, merged, pooled, shared, united

corporation *noun* 1 = **business**, association, corporate body, society 2 = **town council**, civic authorities, council, municipal authorities 3 *Informal* = **paunch**, beer belly (*informal*), middle-age spread (*informal*), pod, pot, potbelly, spare tyre (*Brit. slang*), spread (*informal*)

corps *noun* = **team**, band, body, company, contingent, crew, detachment, division, regiment, squad, squadron, troop, unit

corpse *noun* = **body**, cadaver, carcass, remains, stiff (*slang*)

corpulent *adjective* = **fat**, beefy (*informal*), bulky, burly, fattish, fleshy, large, lusty, obese, overweight, plump, portly, roly-poly,

rotund, stout, tubby, well-padded
➤ **Antonyms**
anorexic, bony, emaciated, gaunt, scrawny, skin and bones (*informal*), skinny, slim, thin, thin as a rake, underweight

correct *adjective* 1 = **true**, accurate, equitable, exact, faultless, flawless, just, O.K. or okay (*informal*), on the right lines, precise, regular, right, strict 2 = **proper**, acceptable, appropriate, diplomatic, fitting, kosher (*informal*), O.K. or okay (*informal*), seemly, standard ◆ *verb* 3 = **rectify**, adjust, amend, cure, emend, improve, redress, reform, regulate, remedy, right, set the record straight 4 = **punish**, admonish, chasten, chastise, chide, discipline, rebuke, reprimand, reprove
➤ **Antonyms**
adjective ≠**true**: false, inaccurate, incorrect, untrue, wrong ≠**proper**: improper, inappropriate, unacceptable, unfitting, unsuitable ◆ *verb* ≠**rectify**: damage, harm, impair, ruin, spoil ≠**punish**: compliment, excuse, praise

correction *noun* 1 = **rectification**, adjustment, alteration, amendment, emendation, improvement, modification, righting 2 = **punishment**, admonition, castigation, chastisement, discipline, reformation, reproof

corrective *adjective* 1 = **remedial**, palliative, rehabilitative, restorative, therapeutic 2 = **disciplinary**, penal, punitive, reformatory

correctly *adverb* = **rightly**, accurately, aright, perfectly, precisely, properly, right

correctness *noun* 1 = **truth**, accuracy, exactitude, exactness, faultlessness, fidelity, preciseness, precision, regularity 2 = **decorum**, bon ton, civility, good breeding, propriety, seemliness

correlate *verb* = **correspond**, associate, compare, connect, coordinate, equate, interact, parallel, tie in

correlation *noun* = **correspondence**, alternation, equivalence, interaction, interchange, interdependence, interrelationship, reciprocity

correspond *verb* 1 = **be consistent**, accord, agree, be related, coincide, complement, conform, correlate, dovetail, fit, harmonize, match, square, tally 2 = **communicate**, exchange letters, keep in touch, write
➤ **Antonyms**
≠**be consistent**: be at variance, be dissimilar, be inconsistent, belie, be unlike, differ, disagree, diverge, vary

correspondence *noun* 1 = **letters**, communication, mail, post, writing 2

= **relation**, agreement, analogy, coincidence, comparability, comparison, concurrence, conformity, congruity, correlation, fitness, harmony, match, similarity

correspondent *noun* 1 = **letter writer**, pen friend *or* pal 2 = **reporter**, contributor, gazetteer (*archaic*), journalist, journo (*slang*), special correspondent ◆ *adjective* 3 = **corresponding**, analogous, comparable, like, of a piece, parallel, reciprocal, similar

corresponding *adjective* = **related**, analogous, answering, complementary, correlative, correspondent, equivalent, identical, interrelated, matching, reciprocal, similar, synonymous

corridor *noun* = **passage**, aisle, alley, hallway, passageway

corroborate *verb* = **support**, authenticate, back up, bear out, confirm, document, endorse, establish, ratify, substantiate, sustain, validate
➤ **Antonyms**
contradict, disprove, invalidate, negate, rebut, refute

corrode *verb* = **eat away**, canker, consume, corrupt, deteriorate, erode, gnaw, impair, oxidize, rust, waste, wear away

corrosive *adjective* 1 = **corroding**, acrid, biting, caustic, consuming, erosive, virulent, vitriolic, wasting, wearing 2 = **cutting**, caustic, incisive, mordant, sarcastic, trenchant, venomous, vitriolic

corrugated *adjective* = **furrowed**, channelled, creased, crinkled, fluted, grooved, puckered, ridged, rumpled, wrinkled

corrupt *adjective* 1 = **dishonest**, bent (*slang*), bribable, crooked (*informal*), fraudulent, rotten, shady (*informal*), unethical, unprincipled, unscrupulous, venal 2 = **depraved**, abandoned, debased, defiled, degenerate, demoralized, dishonoured, dissolute, profligate, vicious 3 = **contaminated**, adulterated, decayed, defiled, infected, polluted, putrescent, putrid, rotten, tainted 4 = **distorted**, altered, doctored, falsified ◆ *verb* 5 = **bribe**, buy off, entice, fix (*informal*), grease (someone's) palm (*slang*), lure, square, suborn 6 = **deprave**, debauch, demoralize, pervert, subvert 7 = **contaminate**, adulterate, debase, defile, infect, putrefy, spoil, taint, vitiate 8 = **distort**, doctor, tamper with
➤ **Antonyms**
adjective ≠**dishonest, depraved**: ethical, honest, honourable, moral, noble, principled, righteous, scrupulous, straight, upright, virtuous ◆ *verb* ≠**deprave**: correct, reform ≠**contaminate**: purify

corruption *noun* 1 = **dishonesty**, breach of

trust, bribery, bribing, crookedness (*informal*), demoralization, extortion, fiddling (*informal*), fraud, fraudulency, graft (*informal*), jobbery, profiteering, shadiness, shady dealings (*informal*), unscrupulousness, venality **2 = depravity**, baseness, decadence, degeneration, degradation, evil, immorality, impurity, iniquity, perversion, profligacy, sinfulness, turpitude, vice, viciousness, wickedness **3 = rotting**, adulteration, debasement, decay, defilement, foulness, infection, pollution, putrefaction, putrescence, rot, rottenness **4 = distortion**, doctoring, falsification

corset *noun* = **girdle**, belt, bodice, corselet, foundation garment, panty girdle, stays (*rare*)

cosmetic *adjective* = **beautifying**, nonessential, superficial, surface, touching-up

cosmic *adjective* **1 = universal**, stellar **2 = vast**, grandiose, huge, immense, infinite, limitless, measureless

cosmonaut *noun* = **astronaut**, spaceman, space pilot

cosmopolitan *adjective* **1 = sophisticated**, broad-minded, catholic, open-minded, universal, urbane, well-travelled, worldly, worldly-wise ♦ *noun* **2 = man** or **woman of the world**, cosmopolite, jet-setter, sophisticate
➤ **Antonyms**
adjective ≠ **sophisticated**: hidebound, illiberal, insular, limited, narrow-minded, parochial, provincial, restricted, rustic, unsophisticated

cost *noun* **1 = price**, amount, charge, damage (*informal*), expenditure, expense, figure, outlay, payment, rate, worth **2 = loss**, damage, deprivation, detriment, expense, harm, hurt, injury, penalty, sacrifice, suffering ♦ *verb* **3 = sell at**, come to, command a price of, set (someone) back (*informal*) **4 = lose**, do disservice to, harm, hurt, injure, necessitate

costly *adjective* **1 = splendid**, gorgeous, lavish, luxurious, opulent, precious, priceless, rich, sumptuous **2 = expensive**, dear, excessive, exorbitant, extortionate, highly-priced, steep (*informal*), stiff, valuable **3 = damaging**, catastrophic, deleterious, disastrous, harmful, loss-making, ruinous, sacrificial
➤ **Antonyms**
≠ **expensive**: cheap, cheapo (*informal*), dirt-cheap, economical, fair, inexpensive, low-priced, reasonable, reduced

costs *plural noun* **1 = expenses**, budget, outgoings, overheads **2 at all costs = no matter what**, at any price, regardless, without fail

costume *noun* = **outfit**, apparel, attire, clothing, dress, ensemble, garb, get-up (*informal*), livery, national dress, robes, uniform

cosy *adjective* = **snug**, comfortable, comfy (*informal*), cuddled up, homely, intimate, secure, sheltered, snuggled down, tucked up, warm

cottage *noun* = **cabin**, but-and-ben (*Scot.*), chalet, cot, hut, lodge, shack

couch *noun* **1 = sofa**, bed, chaise longue, chesterfield, day bed, divan, ottoman, settee ♦ *verb* **2 = express**, frame, phrase, set forth, utter, word

cough *noun* **1 = frog** or **tickle in one's throat**, bark, hack ♦ *verb* **2 = clear one's throat**, bark, hack, hawk, hem

cough up *verb Informal* = **give up**, ante up (*informal, chiefly U.S.*), come across, deliver, fork out (*slang*), hand over, shell out (*informal*), surrender

council *noun* = **governing body**, assembly, board, cabinet, chamber, committee, conclave, conference, congress, convention, convocation, diet, house, ministry, panel, parliament, quango, synod

counsel *noun* **1 = advice**, admonition, caution, consideration, consultation, deliberation, direction, forethought, guidance, information, recommendation, suggestion, warning **2 = legal adviser**, advocate, attorney, barrister, lawyer, solicitor ♦ *verb* **3 = advise**, admonish, advocate, caution, exhort, instruct, prescribe, recommend, urge, warn

count *verb* **1 = add (up)**, calculate, cast up, check, compute, enumerate, estimate, number, reckon, score, tally, tot up **2 = matter**, be important, carry weight, cut any ice (*informal*), enter into consideration, rate, signify, tell, weigh **3 = consider**, deem, esteem, impute, judge, look upon, rate, regard, think **4 = take into account** or **consideration**, include, number among ♦ *noun* **5 = calculation**, computation, enumeration, numbering, poll, reckoning, sum, tally

countenance *noun* **1** *Literary* = **face**, appearance, aspect, expression, features, look, mien, physiognomy, visage **2 = support**, aid, approval, assistance, backing, endorsement, favour, sanction ♦ *verb* **3 = support**, abet, aid, approve, back, champion, commend, condone, encourage, endorse, help, sanction **4 = tolerate**, brook, endure, hack (*slang*), put up with (*informal*), stand for (*informal*)

counter *verb* **1 = retaliate**, answer, hit back, meet, obviate, offset, oppose, parry, resist, respond, return, ward off ♦ *adverb* **2**

= **opposite to**, against, at variance with, contrarily, contrariwise, conversely, in defiance of, versus ♦ *adjective* **3** = **opposing**, adverse, against, conflicting, contradictory, contrary, contrasting, obverse, opposed, opposite
➤ **Antonyms**
verb ≠**retaliate**: accept, cave in (*informal*), give in, surrender, take, yield ♦ *adverb* ≠**opposite to**: in agreement, parallel
♦ *adjective* ≠**opposing**: accordant, parallel, similar

counteract *verb* = **act against**, annul, check, contravene, counterbalance, countervail, cross, defeat, foil, frustrate, hinder, invalidate, negate, neutralize, obviate, offset, oppose, resist, thwart

counterbalance *verb* = **offset**, balance, compensate, counterpoise, countervail, make up for, set off

counterfeit *adjective* **1** = **fake**, bogus, copied, ersatz, false, feigned, forged, fraudulent, imitation, phoney *or* phony (*informal*), pseud *or* pseudo (*informal*), sham, simulated, spurious, supposititious
♦ *noun* **2** = **fake**, copy, forgery, fraud, imitation, phoney *or* phony (*informal*), reproduction, sham ♦ *verb* **3** = **fake**, copy, fabricate, feign, forge, imitate, impersonate, pretend, sham, simulate
➤ **Antonyms**
adjective ≠**fake**: authentic, genuine, good, original, real, the real thing

countermand *verb* = **cancel**, annul, override, repeal, rescind, retract, reverse, revoke

counterpart *noun* **1** = **opposite number**, complement, correlative, equal, fellow, match, mate, supplement, tally, twin **2** = **copy**, duplicate

countless *adjective* = **innumerable**, endless, immeasurable, incalculable, infinite, legion, limitless, measureless, multitudinous, myriad, numberless, uncounted, untold
➤ **Antonyms**
finite, limited, restricted

count on *or* **upon** *verb* = **depend on**, bank on, believe (in), lean on, pin one's faith on, reckon on, rely on, take for granted, take on trust, trust

count out *verb Informal* = **leave out**, disregard, except, exclude, leave out of account, pass over

country *noun* **1** = **nation**, commonwealth, kingdom, people, realm, sovereign state, state **2** = **territory**, land, part, region, terrain **3** = **people**, citizenry, citizens, community, electors, grass roots, inhabitants, nation, populace, public, society, voters **4** = **countryside**, back country (*U.S.*),

backlands (*U.S.*), backwoods, boondocks (*U.S. slang*), farmland, green belt, outback (*Austral. & N.Z.*), outdoors, provinces, rural areas, sticks (*informal*), the back of beyond, the middle of nowhere, wide open spaces (*Informal*) **5** = **native land**, fatherland, homeland, motherland, nationality, *patria* ♦ *adjective* **6** = **rural**, agrarian, agrestic, Arcadian, bucolic, georgic (*literary*), landed, pastoral, provincial, rustic
➤ **Antonyms**
noun ≠**countryside**: city, metropolis, town
♦ *adjective* ≠**rural**: city, cosmopolitan, sophisticated, urban, urbane

countryman *noun* **1** = **compatriot**, fellow citizen **2** = **yokel**, bumpkin, cockie (*N.Z.*), country dweller, farmer, hayseed (*U.S. & Canad. informal*), hick (*informal, chiefly U.S. & Canad.*), hind (*obsolete*), husbandman, peasant, provincial, rustic, swain

countryside *noun* = **country**, farmland, green belt, outback (*Austral. & N.Z.*), outdoors, panorama, sticks (*informal*), view, wide open spaces (*informal*)

count up *verb* = **add**, reckon up, sum, tally, total

county *noun* **1** = **province**, shire ♦ *adjective* **2** *Informal* = **upper-class**, green-wellie, huntin', shootin', and fishin' (*informal*), plummy (*informal*), tweedy, upper-crust (*informal*)

coup *noun* = **masterstroke**, accomplishment, action, deed, exploit, feat, manoeuvre, stratagem, stroke, stroke of genius, stunt, *tour de force*

couple *noun* **1** = **pair**, brace, duo, item, span (*of horses or oxen*), twain (*archaic*), two, twosome ♦ *verb* **2** = **link**, buckle, clasp, conjoin, connect, hitch, join, marry, pair, unite, wed, yoke

coupon *noun* = **slip**, card, certificate, detachable portion, ticket, token, voucher

courage *noun* = **bravery**, balls (*taboo slang*), ballsiness (*taboo slang*), boldness, bottle (*Brit. slang*), daring, dauntlessness, fearlessness, firmness, fortitude, gallantry, grit, guts (*informal*), hardihood, heroism, intrepidity, lion-heartedness, mettle, nerve, pluck, resolution, spunk (*informal*), valour
➤ **Antonyms**
cowardice, cravenness, faint-heartedness, fear, timidity

courageous *adjective* = **brave**, audacious, ballsy (*taboo slang*), bold, daring, dauntless, fearless, gallant, gritty, hardy, heroic, indomitable, intrepid, lion-hearted, plucky, resolute, stalwart, stouthearted, valiant, valorous

➤ **Antonyms**
chicken (*slang*), chicken-hearted, chickenshit
(*U.S. slang*), cowardly, craven, dastardly,
faint-hearted, gutless (*informal*), lily-livered,
pusillanimous, scared, spineless, timid,
timorous, yellow (*informal*)

courier *noun* 1 = **guide**, representative 2
= **messenger**, bearer, carrier, emissary,
envoy, herald, runner

course *noun* 1 = **classes**, course of study,
curriculum, lectures, programme, schedule,
studies 2 = **progression**, advance,
advancement, continuity, development,
flow, furtherance, march, movement, order,
progress, sequence, succession, tenor,
unfolding 3 = **route**, channel, direction, line,
orbit, passage, path, road, tack, track, trail,
trajectory, way 4 = **racecourse**, cinder track,
circuit, lap, race, round 5 = **procedure**,
behaviour, conduct, manner, method,
mode, plan, policy, programme, regimen 6
= **period**, duration, lapse, passage, passing,
sweep, term, time 7 **in due course** = **in
time**, eventually, finally, in the course of
time, in the end, sooner or later 8 **of course**
= **naturally**, certainly, definitely, indubitably,
needless to say, obviously, undoubtedly,
without a doubt ♦ *verb* 9 = **run**, dash, flow,
gush, move apace, race, scud, scurry, speed,
stream, surge, tumble 10 = **hunt**, chase,
follow, pursue

court *noun* 1 = **law court**, bar, bench, court
of justice, seat of judgment, tribunal 2
= **courtyard**, cloister, piazza, plaza, quad
(*informal*), quadrangle, square, yard 3
= **palace**, hall, manor 4 = **royal household**,
attendants, cortege, entourage, retinue,
suite, train ♦ *verb* 5 = **woo**, chase, date, go
(out) with, go steady with (*informal*), keep
company with, make love to, pay court to,
pay one's addresses to, pursue, run after,
serenade, set one's cap at, sue (*archaic*),
take out, walk out with 6 = **cultivate**, curry
favour with, fawn upon, flatter, pander to,
seek, solicit 7 = **invite**, attract, bring about,
incite, prompt, provoke, seek

courteous *adjective* = **polite**, affable,
attentive, ceremonious, civil, courtly,
elegant, gallant, gracious, mannerly,
polished, refined, respectful, urbane,
well-bred, well-mannered
➤ **Antonyms**
discourteous, disrespectful, ill-mannered,
impolite, insolent, rude, uncivil, ungracious,
unkind

courtesy *noun* 1 = **politeness**, affability,
civility, courteousness, courtliness, elegance,
gallantness, gallantry, good breeding, good
manners, grace, graciousness, polish, urbanity
2 = **favour**, benevolence, consent,
consideration, generosity, indulgence, kindness

courtier *noun* = **attendant**, follower,
henchman, liegeman, pursuivant
(*Historical*), squire, train-bearer

courtly *adjective* = **ceremonious**, affable,
aristocratic, chivalrous, civil, decorous,
dignified, elegant, flattering, formal, gallant,
highbred, lordly, obliging, polished, refined,
stately, urbane

courtship *noun* = **wooing**, courting,
engagement, keeping company, pursuit,
romance, suit

courtyard *noun* = **yard**, area, enclosure,
peristyle, playground, quad, quadrangle

cove *noun* = **bay**, anchorage, bayou, creek,
firth *or* frith (*Scot.*), inlet, sound

covenant *noun* 1 = **promise**, agreement,
arrangement, bargain, commitment,
compact, concordat, contract, convention,
pact, pledge, stipulation, treaty, trust 2 *Law*
= **deed**, bond ♦ *verb* 3 = **promise**, agree,
bargain, contract, engage, pledge, shake
hands, stipulate, undertake

cover *verb* 1 = **clothe**, dress, envelop, invest,
put on, wrap 2 = **overlay**, canopy, coat,
daub, encase, envelop, layer, mantle,
overspread 3 = **submerge**, engulf, flood,
overrun, wash over 4 = **conceal**, camouflage,
cloak, cover up, curtain, disguise, eclipse,
enshroud, hide, hood, house, mask, obscure,
screen, secrete, shade, shroud, veil 5
= **travel over**, cross, pass through *or* over,
range, traverse 6 = **protect**, defend, guard,
reinforce, shelter, shield, watch over 7
= **report**, describe, detail, investigate,
narrate, recount, relate, tell of, write up 8
= **make up for**, balance, compensate,
counterbalance, insure, make good, offset 9
= **deal with**, comprehend, comprise,
consider, contain, embody, embrace,
encompass, examine, include, incorporate,
involve, provide for, refer to, survey, take
account of 10 **cover for** = **stand in for**,
double for, fill in for, hold the fort
(*informal*), relieve, substitute, take over, take
the rap for (*slang*) ♦ *noun* 11 = **covering**,
awning, binding, canopy, cap, case,
clothing, coating, dress, envelope, jacket, lid,
sheath, top, wrapper 12 = **disguise**, cloak,
cover-up, façade, front, mask, pretence,
pretext, screen, smoke screen, veil,
window-dressing 13 = **protection**,
camouflage, concealment, defence, guard,
hiding place, refuge, sanctuary, shelter,
shield, undergrowth, woods 14 = **insurance**,
compensation, indemnity, payment,
protection, reimbursement
➤ **Antonyms**
verb ≠**conceal:** exhibit, expose, reveal,
show, unclothe, uncover, unmask, unwrap
≠**deal with:** exclude, omit ♦ *noun*
≠**covering:** base, bottom

covering *adjective* **1** = **explanatory**, accompanying, descriptive, introductory ♦ *noun* **2** = **cover**, blanket, casing, clothing, coating, housing, layer, overlay, protection, shelter, top, wrap, wrapper, wrapping

cover-up *noun* = **concealment**, complicity, conspiracy, front, smoke screen, whitewash (*informal*)

cover up *verb* = **conceal**, cover one's tracks, draw a veil over, feign ignorance, hide, hush up, keep dark, keep secret, keep silent about, keep under one's hat (*informal*), repress, stonewall, suppress, sweep under the carpet, whitewash (*informal*)

covet *verb* = **long for**, aspire to, begrudge, crave, desire, envy, fancy (*informal*), hanker after, have one's eye on, lust after, set one's heart on, thirst for, would give one's eyeteeth for, yearn for

covetous *adjective* = **envious**, acquisitive, avaricious, close-fisted, grasping, greedy, jealous, mercenary, rapacious, yearning

cow *verb* = **intimidate**, awe, browbeat, bully, daunt, dishearten, dismay, frighten, overawe, psych out (*informal*), scare, subdue, terrorize, unnerve

coward *noun* = **wimp** (*informal*), caitiff (*archaic*), chicken (*slang*), craven, dastard (*archaic*), faint-heart, funk (*informal*), poltroon, recreant (*archaic*), renegade, scaredy-cat (*informal*), skulker, sneak, yellow-belly (*slang*)

cowardice *noun* = **faint-heartedness**, fearfulness, spinelessness, weakness

cowardly *adjective* = **faint-hearted**, abject, base, boneless, caitiff (*archaic*), chicken (*slang*), chicken-hearted, chickenshit (*U.S. slang*), craven, dastardly, fearful, gutless (*informal*), lily-livered, pusillanimous, recreant (*archaic*), scared, shrinking, soft, spineless, timorous, weak, weak-kneed (*informal*), white-livered, yellow (*informal*)
➤ **Antonyms**
audacious, bold, brave, courageous, daring, dauntless, doughty, intrepid, plucky, valiant

cowboy *noun* = **cowhand**, broncobuster (*U.S.*), buckaroo (*U.S.*), cattleman, cowpuncher (*U.S. informal*), drover, gaucho (*S. American*), herder, herdsman, rancher, ranchero (*U.S.*), stockman, wrangler (*U.S.*)

cower *verb* = **cringe**, crouch, draw back, fawn, flinch, grovel, quail, shrink, skulk, sneak, tremble, truckle

coy *adjective* = **shy**, arch, backward, bashful, coquettish, demure, evasive, flirtatious, kittenish, modest, overmodest, prudish, reserved, retiring, self-effacing, shrinking, skittish, timid
➤ **Antonyms**
bold, brash, brass-necked (*Brit. informal*),

brassy (*informal*), brazen, flip (*informal*), forward, impertinent, impudent, pert, pushy (*informal*), saucy, shameless

crabbed *adjective* **1** = **unreadable**, awkward, cramped, hieroglyphical, illegible, indecipherable, laboured, squeezed **2** = **bad-tempered**, acrid, acrimonious, captious, churlish, cross, cynical, difficult, fretful, harsh, ill-tempered, irritable, morose, perverse, petulant, prickly, ratty (*Brit. & N.Z. informal*), sour, splenetic, surly, tart, testy, tetchy, tough, trying

crack *verb* **1** = **break**, burst, chip, chop, cleave, crackle, craze, fracture, rive, snap, splinter, split **2** = **snap**, burst, crash, detonate, explode, pop, ring **3** = **give in**, break down, collapse, give way, go to pieces, lose control, succumb, yield **4** *Informal* = **hit**, buffet, clip (*informal*), clout (*informal*), cuff, slap, smack, thump, wallop (*informal*), whack **5** = **solve**, decipher, fathom, get the answer to, work out ♦ *noun* **6** = **snap**, burst, clap, crash, explosion, pop, report **7** = **break**, breach, chink, chip, cleft, cranny, crevice, fissure, fracture, gap, interstice, rift **8** *Informal* = **blow**, buffet, clip (*informal*), clout (*informal*), cuff, slap, smack, thump, wallop (*informal*), whack **9** *Informal* = **attempt**, go (*informal*), opportunity, shot, stab (*informal*), try **10** *Informal* = **joke**, dig, funny remark, gag (*informal*), insult, jibe, quip, smart-alecky remark, wisecrack, witticism ♦ *adjective* **11** *Slang* = **first-class**, ace, choice, elite, excellent, first-rate, hand-picked, superior, world-class

crackdown *noun* = **suppression**, clampdown, crushing, repression

cracked *adjective* **1** = **broken**, chipped, crazed, damaged, defective, faulty, fissured, flawed, imperfect, split **2** *Informal* = **crazy** (*informal*), bats (*slang*), batty (*slang*), crackbrained, crackpot (*informal*), daft (*informal*), doolally (*slang*), eccentric, gonzo (*slang*), insane, loony (*slang*), loopy (*informal*), nuts (*slang*), nutty (*slang*), oddball (*informal*), off one's head *or* nut (*slang*), off one's rocker (*slang*), off one's trolley (*slang*), off-the-wall (*slang*), out of one's mind, outré, out to lunch (*informal*), round the bend (*slang*), round the twist (*Brit. slang*), touched, up the pole (*informal*), wacko *or* whacko (*informal*)

cracked up *adjective* As in **not all it is cracked up to be** = **overrated**, blown up, exaggerated, hyped (up), overpraised, puffed up

crack up *verb Informal* = **have a breakdown**, break down, collapse, come apart at the seams (*informal*), flip one's lid (*slang*), fly off the handle (*informal*), freak out (*informal*), go ape (*slang*), go apeshit (*slang*), go berserk, go crazy (*informal*), go off one's head (*slang*), go off one's rocker (*slang*), go off the deep end (*informal*), go out of one's mind, go to pieces, throw a wobbly (*slang*)

cradle *noun* 1 = **crib**, bassinet, cot, Moses basket 2 = **birthplace**, beginning, fount, fountainhead, origin, source, spring, wellspring ♦ *verb* 3 = **hold**, lull, nestle, nurse, rock, support

craft *noun* 1 = **occupation**, business, calling, employment, handicraft, handiwork, line, pursuit, trade, vocation, work 2 = **skill**, ability, aptitude, art, artistry, cleverness, dexterity, expertise, expertness, ingenuity, knack, know-how (*informal*), technique, workmanship 3 = **cunning**, artfulness, artifice, contrivance, craftiness, deceit, duplicity, guile, ruse, scheme, shrewdness, stratagem, subterfuge, subtlety, trickery, wiles 4 = **vessel**, aircraft, barque, boat, plane, ship, spacecraft

craftiness *noun* = **cunning**, artfulness, astuteness, canniness, deviousness, duplicity, foxiness, guile, shrewdness, slyness, subtlety, trickiness, wiliness

craftsman *noun* = **skilled worker**, artificer, artisan, maker, master, smith, technician, wright

craftsmanship *noun* = **workmanship**, artistry, expertise, mastery, technique

crafty *adjective* = **cunning**, artful, astute, calculating, canny, deceitful, designing, devious, duplicitous, foxy, fraudulent, guileful, insidious, knowing, scheming, sharp, shrewd, sly, subtle, tricksy, tricky, wily
> **Antonyms**
as green as grass, candid, ethical, frank, honest, ingenuous, innocent, naive, open, simple, wet behind the ears

crag *noun* = **rock**, aiguille, bluff, peak, pinnacle, tor

cram *verb* 1 = **stuff**, compact, compress, crowd, crush, fill to overflowing, force, jam, overcrowd, overfill, pack, pack in, press, ram, shove, squeeze 2 = **overeat**, glut, gorge, gormandize, guzzle, overfeed, pig out (*slang*), put *or* pack away, satiate, stuff 3 = **study**, bone up (*informal*), con, grind, mug up (*slang*), revise, swot, swot up

cramp[1] *noun* = **spasm**, ache, contraction, convulsion, crick, pain, pang, shooting pain, stiffness, stitch, twinge

cramp[2] *verb* = **restrict**, check, circumscribe, clip someone's wings, clog, confine, constrain, encumber, hamper, hamstring, handicap, hinder, impede, inhibit, obstruct, shackle, stymie, thwart

cramped *adjective* 1 = **closed in**, awkward,

circumscribed, confined, congested, crowded, hemmed in, jammed in, narrow, overcrowded, packed, restricted, squeezed, uncomfortable 2 = **small**, crabbed, indecipherable, irregular
> **Antonyms**
≠**closed in:** capacious, commodious, large, open, roomy, sizable *or* sizeable, spacious, uncongested, uncrowded

crank *noun Informal* = **eccentric**, case (*informal*), character (*informal*), freak (*informal*), kook (*U.S. & Canad. informal*), nut (*slang*), oddball (*informal*), odd fish (*informal*), queer fish (*Brit. informal*), rum customer (*Brit. slang*), screwball (*slang, chiefly U.S. & Canad.*), wacko *or* whacko (*informal*), weirdo *or* weirdie (*informal*)

cranky *adjective Informal* = **eccentric**, bizarre, capricious, erratic, freakish, freaky (*slang*), funny (*informal*), idiosyncratic, odd, oddball (*informal*), off-the-wall (*slang*), outré, peculiar, queer, quirky, rum (*Brit. slang*), strange, wacko *or* whacko (*informal*), wacky (*slang*)

cranny *noun* = **crevice**, breach, chink, cleft, crack, fissure, gap, hole, interstice, nook, opening, rift

crash *noun* 1 = **collision**, accident, bump, jar, jolt, pile-up (*informal*), prang (*informal*), smash, smash-up, thud, thump, wreck 2 = **smash**, bang, boom, clang, clash, clatter, clattering, din, racket, smashing, thunder 3 = **collapse**, bankruptcy, debacle, depression, downfall, failure, ruin, smash ♦ *verb* 4 = **collide**, bang, bump (into), crash-land (*an aircraft*), drive into, have an accident, hit, hurtle into, plough into, run together, wreck 5 = **smash**, break, break up, dash to pieces, disintegrate, fracture, fragment, shatter, shiver, splinter 6 = **collapse**, be ruined, fail, fold, fold up, go belly up (*informal*), go broke (*informal*), go bust (*informal*), go to the wall, go under, smash 7 = **hurtle**, come a cropper (*informal*), dash, fall, fall headlong, give way, lurch, overbalance, pitch, plunge, precipitate oneself, sprawl, topple ♦ *adjective* 8 = **intensive**, emergency, immediate, round-the-clock, speeded-up, telescoped, urgent

crass *adjective* = **insensitive**, asinine, blundering, boorish, bovine, coarse, dense, doltish, gross, indelicate, lumpish, oafish, obtuse, stupid, unrefined, witless
> **Antonyms**
brainy (*informal*), bright, clever, elegant, intelligent, polished, refined, sensitive, sharp, smart

crate *noun* 1 = **container**, box, case, packing case, tea chest ♦ *verb* 2 = **box**, case, encase, enclose, pack, pack up

crater noun = **hollow**, depression, dip, shell hole

crave verb **1** = **long for**, be dying for, cry out for (informal), desire, eat one's heart out over, fancy (informal), hanker after, hope for, hunger after, lust after, need, pant for, pine for, require, set one's heart on, sigh for, thirst for, want, would give one's eyeteeth for, yearn for **2** Informal = **beg**, ask, beseech, entreat, implore, petition, plead for, pray for, seek, solicit, supplicate

craven adjective **1** = **cowardly**, abject, caitiff (archaic), chicken-hearted, chickenshit (U.S. slang), dastardly, fearful, lily-livered, mean-spirited, niddering (archaic), pusillanimous, scared, timorous, weak, yellow (informal) ◆ noun **2** = **coward**, base fellow (archaic), caitiff (archaic), dastard (archaic), niddering (archaic), poltroon, recreant (archaic), renegade, wheyface, yellow-belly (slang)

craving noun = **longing**, ache, appetite, cacoethes, desire, hankering, hope, hunger, lust, thirst, urge, yearning, yen (informal)

crawl verb **1** = **creep**, advance slowly, drag, go on all fours, inch, move at a snail's pace, move on hands and knees, pull or drag oneself along, slither, worm one's way, wriggle, writhe **2** = **grovel**, abase oneself, brown-nose (taboo slang), creep, cringe, fawn, humble oneself, kiss ass (U.S. & Canad. taboo slang), lick someone's arse (taboo slang), lick someone's boots (slang), pander to, suck up to someone (slang), toady, truckle **3** = **be full of**, be alive, be lousy, be overrun (slang), swarm, teem
➤ Antonyms
≠**creep**: dart, dash, fly, hasten, hurry, race, run, rush, sprint, step on it (informal), walk

craze noun **1** = **fad**, enthusiasm, fashion, infatuation, mania, mode, novelty, passion, preoccupation, rage, the latest (informal), thing, trend, vogue ◆ verb **2** = **drive mad**, bewilder, confuse, dement, derange, distemper, enrage, infatuate, inflame, madden, make insane, send crazy or berserk, unbalance, unhinge, unsettle

crazy adjective **1** Informal = **ridiculous**, absurd, bird-brained (informal), cockeyed (informal), derisory, fatuous, foolhardy, foolish, half-baked (informal), idiotic, ill-conceived, impracticable, imprudent, inane, inappropriate, irresponsible, ludicrous, nonsensical, potty (Brit. informal), preposterous, puerile, quixotic, senseless, short-sighted, unrealistic, unwise, unworkable, wild **2** = **strange**, bizarre, eccentric, fantastic, odd, oddball (informal), outrageous, peculiar, ridiculous, rum (Brit. slang), silly, wacko or whacko (informal), weird **3** = **fanatical**, ablaze, ardent, devoted, eager, enamoured, enthusiastic, hysterical, infatuated, into (informal), mad, passionate, smitten, very keen, wild (informal), zealous **4** = **insane**, a bit lacking upstairs (informal), as daft as a brush (informal, chiefly Brit.), barking (slang), barking mad (slang), barmy (slang), batty (slang), berserk, bonkers (slang, chiefly Brit.), cracked (slang), crackpot (informal), crazed, cuckoo (informal), daft (informal), delirious, demented, deranged, doolally (slang), idiotic, loopy (informal), lunatic, mad, mad as a hatter, mad as a March hare, maniacal, mental (slang), not all there (informal), not right in the head, not the full shilling (informal), nuts (slang), nutty (slang), nutty as a fruitcake (slang), off one's head (slang), off one's rocker (slang), off one's trolley (slang), off-the-wall (slang), of unsound mind, out of one's mind, out to lunch (informal), potty (Brit. informal), round the bend (slang), round the twist (Brit. slang), touched, unbalanced, unhinged, up the pole (informal)
➤ Antonyms
≠**ridiculous**: appropriate, brilliant, feasible, possible, practicable, prudent, realistic, responsible, sensible, wise, workable ≠**strange**: common, conventional, normal, ordinary, orthodox, regular, usual ≠**fanatical**: cool, indifferent, uncaring, unenthusiastic, uninterested ≠**insane**: all there (informal), compos mentis, down-to-earth, in one's right mind, intelligent, mentally sound, practical, prudent, rational, reasonable, sane, sensible, smart, wise

creak verb = **squeak**, grate, grind, groan, rasp, scrape, scratch, screech, squeal

cream noun **1** = **lotion**, cosmetic, emulsion, essence, liniment, oil, ointment, paste, salve, unguent **2** = **best**, crème de la crème, elite, flower, pick, prime ◆ adjective **3** = **off-white**, yellowish-white

creamy adjective = **smooth**, buttery, creamed, lush, milky, oily, rich, soft, velvety

crease noun **1** = **line**, bulge, corrugation, fold, groove, overlap, pucker, ridge, ruck, tuck, wrinkle ◆ verb **2** = **wrinkle**, corrugate, crimp, crinkle, crumple, double up, fold, pucker, ridge, ruck up, rumple, screw up

create verb **1** = **make**, beget, bring into being or existence, coin, compose, concoct, design, develop, devise, dream up (informal), form, formulate, generate, give birth to, give life to, hatch, initiate, invent, originate, produce, spawn **2** = **cause**, bring about, lead to, occasion **3** = **appoint**, constitute, establish, found, install, invest, make, set up

➤ **Antonyms**

≠**make:** annihilate, demolish, destroy

creation *noun* **1 = making,** conception, formation, generation, genesis, procreation, siring **2 = setting up,** constitution, development, establishment, formation, foundation, inception, institution, laying down, origination, production **3 = invention,** achievement, brainchild (*informal*), chef-d'oeuvre, concept, concoction, handiwork, magnum opus, *pièce de résistance,* production **4 = universe,** all living things, cosmos, life, living world, natural world, nature, world

creative *adjective* **= imaginative,** artistic, clever, fertile, gifted, ingenious, inspired, inventive, original, productive, stimulating, visionary

creativity *noun* **= imagination,** cleverness, fecundity, fertility, imaginativeness, ingenuity, inspiration, inventiveness, originality, productivity, talent

creator *noun* **= maker,** architect, author, begetter, designer, father, framer, initiator, inventor, originator, prime mover

creature *noun* **1 = living thing,** animal, beast, being, brute, critter (*U.S. dialect*), dumb animal, lower animal, quadruped **2 = person,** body, character, fellow, human being, individual, man, mortal, soul, wight (*archaic*), woman **3 = minion,** cohort (*chiefly U.S.*), dependant, hanger-on, hireling, instrument (*informal*), lackey, puppet, retainer, tool, wretch

credentials *plural noun* **= certification,** attestation, authorization, card, deed, diploma, docket, document, letter of recommendation *or* introduction, letters of credence, licence, missive, papers, passport, recommendation, reference(s), testament, testimonial, title, voucher, warrant

credibility *noun* **= believability,** believableness, integrity, plausibility, reliability, tenability, trustworthiness

credible *adjective* **1 = believable,** conceivable, imaginable, likely, plausible, possible, probable, reasonable, supposable, tenable, thinkable, verisimilar **2 = reliable,** dependable, honest, sincere, trustworthy, trusty

➤ **Antonyms**

≠**believable:** doubtful, implausible, inconceivable, incredible, questionable, unbelievable, unlikely ≠**reliable:** dishonest, insincere, not dependable, unreliable, untrustworthy

credit *noun* **1 = praise,** acclaim, acknowledgment, approval, Brownie points, commendation, fame, glory, honour, kudos, merit, recognition, thanks, tribute **2** *As in* **be**

a credit to = source of satisfaction *or* **pride,** feather in one's cap, honour **3 = prestige,** character, clout (*informal*), esteem, estimation, good name, influence, position, regard, reputation, repute, standing, status **4 = belief,** confidence, credence, faith, reliance, trust **5 on credit = on account,** by deferred payment, by instalments, on hire-purchase, on (the) H.P., on the slate (*informal*), on tick (*informal*) ♦ *verb* **6 = believe,** accept, bank on, buy (*slang*), depend on, fall for, have faith in, rely on, swallow (*informal*), trust **7 credit with = attribute to,** accredit to, ascribe to, assign to, chalk up to (*informal*), impute to, refer to

creditable *adjective* **= praiseworthy,** admirable, commendable, deserving, estimable, exemplary, honourable, laudable, meritorious, reputable, respectable, worthy

credulity *noun* **= gullibility,** blind faith, credulousness, naïveté, silliness, simplicity, stupidity

credulous *adjective* **= gullible,** as green as grass, born yesterday (*informal*), dupable, green, naive, overtrusting, trustful, uncritical, unsuspecting, unsuspicious, wet behind the ears (*informal*)

➤ **Antonyms**

cynical, incredulous, sceptical, suspecting, unbelieving, wary

creed *noun* **= belief,** articles of faith, canon, catechism, confession, credo, doctrine, dogma, persuasion, principles, profession (*of faith*), tenet

creek *noun* **1 = inlet,** bay, bight, cove, firth *or* frith (*Scot.*) **2** *U.S., Canad., Austral., & N.Z.* **= stream,** bayou, brook, rivulet, runnel, streamlet, tributary, watercourse

creep *verb* **1 = sneak,** approach unnoticed, skulk, slink, steal, tiptoe **2 = crawl,** crawl on all fours, glide, insinuate, slither, squirm, worm, wriggle, writhe **3 = drag,** crawl, dawdle, edge, inch, proceed at a snail's pace **4 = grovel,** bootlick (*informal*), brown-nose (*taboo slang*), cower, cringe, fawn, kiss (someone's) ass (*U.S. & Canad. taboo slang*), kowtow, pander to, scrape, suck up to (*informal*), toady, truckle ♦ *noun* **5** *Slang* **= bootlicker** (*informal*), ass-kisser (*U.S. & Canad. taboo slang*), brown-noser (*taboo slang*), crawler (*slang*), sneak, sycophant, toady

creeper *noun* **= climbing plant,** climber, rambler, runner, trailing plant, vine (*chiefly U.S.*)

creeps *plural noun* **give one the creeps** *Informal* **= disgust,** frighten, horrify, make one flinch, make one quail, make one's hair stand on end, make one shrink, make one squirm, make one wince, repel, repulse, scare, terrify, terrorize

creepy *adjective Informal* = **disturbing**, awful, direful, disgusting, eerie, forbidding, frightening, ghoulish, goose-pimply (*informal*), gruesome, hair-raising, horrible, macabre, menacing, nightmarish, ominous, scary (*informal*), sinister, terrifying, threatening, unpleasant, weird

crescent *noun* 1 = **meniscus**, half-moon, new moon, old moon, sickle, sickle-shape ♦ *adjective* 2 = **sickle-shaped**, arched, bow-shaped, curved, falcate, semicircular 3 *Archaic* = **waxing**, growing, increasing

crest *noun* 1 = **top**, apex, crown, head, height, highest point, peak, pinnacle, ridge, summit 2 = **tuft**, aigrette, caruncle (*Zoology*), cockscomb, comb, crown, mane, panache, plume, tassel, topknot 3 = **emblem**, badge, bearings, charge, device, insignia, symbol

crestfallen *adjective* = **disappointed**, chapfallen, choked, dejected, depressed, despondent, disconsolate, discouraged, disheartened, downcast, downhearted, sick as a parrot (*informal*)
➤ Antonyms
cock-a-hoop, elated, encouraged, exuberant, happy, in seventh heaven, joyful, on cloud nine (*informal*), over the moon (*informal*)

crevice *noun* = **gap**, chink, cleft, crack, cranny, fissure, fracture, hole, interstice, opening, rent, rift, slit, split

crew *noun* 1 = **(ship's) company**, hands, (ship's) complement 2 = **team**, company, corps, gang, party, posse, squad, working party 3 *Informal* = **crowd**, assemblage, band, bunch (*informal*), camp, company, gang, herd, horde, lot, mob, pack, posse (*informal*), set, swarm, troop

crib *noun* 1 *Informal* = **translation**, key, trot (*U.S. slang*) 2 = **cradle**, bassinet, bed, cot 3 = **manger**, bin, box, bunker, rack, stall ♦ *verb* 4 *Informal* = **copy**, cheat, pass off as one's own work, pilfer, pirate, plagiarize, purloin, steal 5 = **confine**, box up, cage, coop, coop up, enclose, fence, imprison, limit, pen, rail, restrict, shut in

crime *noun* 1 = **offence**, atrocity, fault, felony, job (*informal*), malfeasance, misdeed, misdemeanour, outrage, transgression, trespass, unlawful act, violation, wrong 2 = **lawbreaking**, corruption, delinquency, guilt, illegality, iniquity, malefaction, misconduct, sin, unrighteousness, vice, villainy, wickedness, wrong, wrongdoing

criminal *noun* 1 = **lawbreaker**, con (*slang*), con man (*informal*), convict, crook (*informal*), culprit, delinquent, evildoer, felon, jailbird, lag (*slang*), malefactor, offender, sinner, skelm (*S. Afr.*), transgressor, villain ♦ *adjective* 2 = **unlawful**, bent (*slang*), corrupt, crooked (*informal*), culpable, felonious, illegal, illicit, immoral, indictable, iniquitous, lawless, nefarious, under-the-table, unrighteous, vicious, villainous, wicked, wrong 3 *Informal* = **disgraceful**, deplorable, foolish, preposterous, ridiculous, scandalous, senseless
➤ Antonyms
adjective ≠**unlawful**: commendable, honest, honourable, innocent, law-abiding, lawful, legal, right

criminality *noun* = **illegality**, corruption, culpability, delinquency, depravity, guiltiness, sinfulness, turpitude, villainy, wickedness

cringe *verb* 1 = **shrink**, blench, cower, dodge, draw back, duck, flinch, quail, quiver, recoil, shy, start, tremble, wince 2 = **grovel**, bend, bootlick (*informal*), bow, brown-nose (*taboo slang*), crawl, creep, crouch, fawn, kiss ass (*U.S. & Canad. taboo slang*), kneel, kowtow, pander to, sneak, stoop, toady, truckle

cripple *verb* 1 = **disable**, debilitate, enfeeble, hamstring, incapacitate, lame, maim, mutilate, paralyse, weaken 2 = **damage**, bring to a standstill, cramp, destroy, halt, impair, put out of action, put paid to, ruin, spoil, vitiate
➤ Antonyms
≠**damage**: advance, aid, assist, assist the progress of, ease, expedite, facilitate, further, help, promote

crippled *adjective* = **disabled**, bedridden, deformed, enfeebled, handicapped, housebound, incapacitated, laid up (*informal*), lame, paralysed

crisis *noun* 1 = **critical point**, climacteric, climax, confrontation, crunch (*informal*), crux, culmination, height, moment of truth, point of no return, turning point 2 = **emergency**, catastrophe, critical situation, deep water, dilemma, dire straits, disaster, exigency, extremity, meltdown (*informal*), mess, panic stations (*informal*), pass, plight, predicament, quandary, strait, trouble

crisp *adjective* 1 = **firm**, brittle, crispy, crumbly, crunchy, fresh, unwilted 2 = **clean**, clean-cut, neat, orderly, smart, snappy, spruce, tidy, trig (*archaic or dialect*), trim, well-groomed, well-pressed 3 = **bracing**, brisk, fresh, invigorating, refreshing 4 = **brief**, brusque, clear, incisive, pithy, short, succinct, tart, terse
➤ Antonyms
≠**firm**: drooping, droopy, flaccid, floppy, limp, soft, wilted, withered ≠**bracing**: balmy, clement, mild, pleasant, warm

criterion noun = standard, bench mark, canon, gauge, measure, norm, par, principle, proof, rule, test, touchstone, yardstick

critic noun 1 = judge, analyst, arbiter, authority, commentator, connoisseur, expert, expositor, pundit, reviewer 2 = fault-finder, attacker, carper, caviller, censor, censurer, detractor, knocker (informal), Momus, reviler, vilifier

critical adjective 1 = crucial, all-important, dangerous, deciding, decisive, grave, hairy (slang), high-priority, momentous, now or never, perilous, pivotal, precarious, pressing, psychological, risky, serious, urgent, vital 2 = disparaging, captious, carping, cavilling, censorious, derogatory, disapproving, fault-finding, nagging, niggling, nit-picking (informal), on someone's back (informal), scathing 3 = analytical, accurate, diagnostic, discerning, discriminating, fastidious, judicious, penetrating, perceptive, precise
➤ Antonyms
≠crucial: safe, secure, settled, unimportant ≠disparaging: appreciative, approving, complimentary, uncritical ≠analytical: undiscriminating

criticism noun 1 = fault-finding, animadversion, bad press, brickbats (informal), censure, character assassination, critical remarks, denigration, disapproval, disparagement, flak (informal), knocking (informal), panning (informal), slagging (slang), slam (slang), slating (informal), stick (slang), stricture 2 = analysis, appraisal, appreciation, assessment, comment, commentary, critique, elucidation, evaluation, judgment, notice, review

criticize verb 1 = find fault with, animadvert on or upon, blast, carp, censure, condemn, disapprove of, disparage, excoriate, give (someone or something) a bad press, have a go (at) (informal), knock (informal), lambast(e), nag at, pan (informal), pass strictures upon, pick holes in, pick to pieces, put down, slam (slang), slate (informal), tear into (informal) 2 = analyse, appraise, assess, comment upon, evaluate, give an opinion, judge, pass judgment on, review
➤ Antonyms
≠find fault with: commend, compliment, extol, laud (literary), praise

critique noun = essay, analysis, appraisal, assessment, commentary, examination, review, treatise

croak verb 1 = squawk, caw, gasp, grunt, utter or speak harshly, utter or speak huskily, utter or speak throatily, wheeze 2 Slang = die, buy it (U.S. slang), buy the farm

(U.S. slang), check out (U.S. slang), expire, go belly-up (slang), hop the twig (informal), kick it (slang), kick the bucket (informal), pass away, peg it (informal), peg out (informal), perish, pop one's clogs (informal)

crook noun 1 Informal = criminal, cheat, chiseller (informal), fraudster, grifter (slang, chiefly U.S. & Canad.), knave (archaic), lag (slang), racketeer, robber, rogue, shark, skelm (S. Afr.), swindler, thief, villain ◆ verb 2 = bend, angle, bow, curve, flex, hook

crooked adjective 1 = bent, anfractuous, bowed, crippled, curved, deformed, deviating, disfigured, distorted, hooked, irregular, meandering, misshapen, out of shape, tortuous, twisted, twisting, warped, winding, zigzag 2 = at an angle, angled, askew, asymmetric, awry, lopsided, off-centre, skewwhiff (Brit. informal), slanted, slanting, squint, tilted, to one side, uneven, unsymmetrical 3 Informal = dishonest, bent (slang), corrupt, crafty, criminal, deceitful, dishonourable, dubious, fraudulent, illegal, knavish, nefarious, questionable, shady (informal), shifty, treacherous, underhand, under-the-table, unlawful, unprincipled, unscrupulous
➤ Antonyms
≠bent: flat, straight ≠dishonest: ethical, fair, honest, honourable, lawful, legal, straight, upright

croon verb = sing, breathe, hum, purr, warble

crop noun 1 = produce, fruits, gathering, harvest, reaping, season's growth, vintage, yield ◆ verb 2 = cut, clip, curtail, dock, lop, mow, pare, prune, reduce, shear, shorten, snip, top, trim 3 = harvest, bring home, bring in, collect, garner, gather, mow, pick, reap 4 = graze, browse, nibble

crop up verb Informal = happen, appear, arise, emerge, occur, spring up, turn up

cross verb 1 = go across, bridge, cut across, extend over, ford, meet, move across, pass over, ply, span, traverse, zigzag 2 = intersect, crisscross, intertwine, lace, lie athwart of 3 = oppose, block, deny, foil, frustrate, hinder, impede, interfere, obstruct, resist, thwart 4 = interbreed, blend, crossbreed, cross-fertilize, cross-pollinate, hybridize, intercross, mix, mongrelize ◆ noun 5 = crucifix, rood 6 = crossroads, crossing, intersection, junction 7 = crossbreed, cur, hybrid, mongrel, mutt (slang) 8 = mixture, amalgam, blend, combination 9 = trouble, affliction, burden, grief, load, misery, misfortune, trial, tribulation, woe, worry ◆ adjective 10 = angry, annoyed, cantankerous, captious, choked, churlish, crotchety (informal), crusty, disagreeable, fractious, fretful, grouchy (*informal*), grumpy, hacked (off) (*U.S. slang*), ill-humoured, ill-tempered, impatient, in a bad mood, irascible, irritable, liverish, out of humour, peeved (*informal*), peevish, pettish, petulant, pissed (*taboo slang*), pissed off (*taboo slang*), put out, querulous, ratty (*Brit. & N.Z. informal*), shirty (*slang, chiefly Brit.*), short, snappish, snappy, splenetic, sullen, surly, testy, tetchy, vexed, waspish **11 = transverse**, crosswise, diagonal, intersecting, oblique **12 = opposing**, adverse, contrary, opposed, unfavourable **13 = reciprocal**, opposite

➤ Antonyms

adjective ≠ **angry**: affable, agreeable, calm, cheerful, civil, congenial, even-tempered, genial, good-humoured, good-natured, nice, placid, pleasant, sweet

cross-examine *verb* = **question**, catechize, grill (*informal*), interrogate, pump, quiz

cross out *or* **off** *verb* = **strike off** *or* **out**, blue-pencil, cancel, delete, eliminate, score off *or* out

crotch *noun* = **groin**, crutch

crotchety *adjective Informal* = **bad-tempered**, awkward, cantankerous, contrary, crabby, cross, crusty, curmudgeonly, difficult, disagreeable, fractious, grumpy, irritable, liverish, obstreperous, peevish, ratty (*Brit. & N.Z. informal*), surly, testy, tetchy

crouch *verb* = **bend down**, bow, duck, hunch, kneel, squat, stoop

crow *verb* = **gloat**, blow one's own trumpet, bluster, boast, brag, drool, exult, flourish, glory in, strut, swagger, triumph, vaunt

crowd *noun* **1 = multitude**, army, assembly, bevy, company, concourse, flock, herd, horde, host, mass, mob, pack, press, rabble, swarm, throng, troupe **2 = group**, bunch (*informal*), circle, clique, lot, set **3 = audience**, attendance, gate, house, spectators **4 the crowd = masses**, hoi polloi, mob, people, populace, proletariat, public, rabble, rank and file, riffraff, vulgar herd ♦ *verb* **5 = flock**, cluster, congregate, cram, foregather, gather, huddle, mass, muster, press, push, stream, surge, swarm, throng **6 = squeeze**, bundle, congest, cram, pack, pile **7** *Informal* = **jostle**, batter, butt, elbow, shove

crowded *adjective* = **packed**, busy, congested, cramped, crushed, full, huddled, jam-packed, mobbed, overflowing, populous, swarming, teeming, thronged

crown *noun* **1 = coronet**, chaplet, circlet, coronal (*poetic*), diadem, tiara **2 = laurel wreath**, bays, distinction, garland, honour,

kudos, laurels, prize, trophy, wreath **3 = high point**, acme, apex, crest, head, perfection, pinnacle, summit, tip, top, ultimate, zenith ♦ *verb* **4 = honour**, adorn, dignify, festoon, invest, reward **5 = cap**, be the climax *or* culmination of, complete, consummate, finish, fulfil, perfect, put the finishing touch to, put the tin lid on, round off, surmount, terminate, top **6** *Slang* = **strike**, belt (*informal*), biff (*slang*), box, cuff, hit over the head, punch

Crown *noun* **1 = monarchy**, royalty, sovereignty **2 = monarch**, emperor *or* empress, king *or* queen, *rex*, ruler, sovereign

crowning *adjective* = **supreme**, climactic, consummate, culminating, final, mother of all (*informal*), paramount, sovereign, ultimate

crucial *adjective* **1** *Informal* = **vital**, essential, high-priority, important, momentous, now or never, pressing, urgent **2 = critical**, central, decisive, pivotal, psychological, searching, testing, trying

crucify *verb* **1 = execute**, harrow, persecute, rack, torment, torture **2** *Slang* = **pan** (*informal*), lampoon, ridicule, tear to pieces, wipe the floor with (*informal*)

crude *adjective* **1 = primitive**, clumsy, makeshift, outline, rough, rough-and-ready, rough-hewn, rude, rudimentary, simple, sketchy, undeveloped, unfinished, unformed, unpolished **2 = vulgar**, boorish, coarse, crass, dirty, gross, indecent, lewd, obscene, smutty, tactless, tasteless, uncouth, X-rated (*informal*) **3 = unrefined**, natural, raw, unmilled, unpolished, unprepared, unprocessed

➤ Antonyms

≠ **vulgar**: genteel, polished, refined, subtle, tasteful *≠* **unrefined**: fine, fine-grained, polished, prepared, processed, refined

crudely *adverb* = **vulgarly**, bluntly, clumsily, coarsely, impolitely, indecently, pulling no punches (*informal*), roughly, rudely, sketchily, tastelessly

crudity *noun* **1 = roughness**, clumsiness, crudeness, primitiveness, rudeness **2 = vulgarity**, coarseness, crudeness, impropriety, indecency, indelicacy, lewdness, loudness, lowness, obscenity, obtrusiveness, smuttiness

cruel *adjective* **1 = brutal**, atrocious, barbarous, bitter, bloodthirsty, brutish, callous, cold-blooded, depraved, excruciating, fell (*archaic*), ferocious, fierce, flinty, grim, hard, hard-hearted, harsh, heartless, hellish, implacable, inclement, inexorable, inhuman, Inhumane, malevolent, murderous, painful, poignant, ravening, raw, relentless, remorseless, sadistic, sanguinary, savage, severe, spiteful, stony-hearted,

unfeeling, unkind, unnatural, vengeful, vicious 2 = **merciless**, pitiless, ruthless, unrelenting
➤ Antonyms
benevolent, caring, compassionate, gentle, humane, kind, merciful, sympathetic, warm-hearted

cruelly adverb 1 = **brutally**, barbarously, brutishly, callously, ferociously, fiercely, heartlessly, in cold blood, mercilessly, pitilessly, sadistically, savagely, spitefully, unmercifully, viciously 2 = **bitterly**, deeply, fearfully, grievously, monstrously, mortally, severely

cruelty noun = **brutality**, barbarity, bestiality, bloodthirstiness, brutishness, callousness, depravity, ferocity, fiendishness, hardheartedness, harshness, heartlessness, inhumanity, mercilessness, murderousness, ruthlessness, sadism, savagery, severity, spite, spitefulness, venom, viciousness

cruise noun 1 = **sail**, boat trip, sea trip, voyage ♦ verb 2 = **sail**, coast, voyage 3 = **travel along**, coast, drift, keep a steady pace

crumb noun = **bit**, atom, fragment, grain, mite, morsel, particle, scrap, shred, sliver, snippet, soupçon, speck

crumble verb 1 = **disintegrate**, break down, break up, collapse, come to dust, decay, decompose, degenerate, deteriorate, fall apart, go to pieces, go to wrack and ruin, moulder, perish, tumble down 2 = **crush**, bruise, crumb, fragment, granulate, grind, pound, powder, pulverize, triturate

crumple verb 1 = **crush**, crease, pucker, rumple, screw up, scrumple, wrinkle 2 = **collapse**, break down, cave in, fall, give way, go to pieces

crunch verb 1 = **chomp**, champ, chew noisily, grind, masticate, munch ♦ noun 2 Informal = **critical point**, crisis, crux, emergency, hour of decision, moment of truth, test

crusade noun = **campaign**, cause, drive, holy war, jihad, movement, push

crusader noun = **campaigner**, advocate, champion, reformer

crush verb 1 = **squash**, break, bruise, comminute, compress, contuse, crease, crumble, crumple, crunch, mash, pound, press, pulverize, rumple, scrumple, smash, squeeze, wrinkle 2 = **squeeze**, embrace, enfold, hug, press 3 = **overcome**, conquer, extinguish, overpower, overwhelm, put down, quell, stamp out, subdue, vanquish 4 = **humiliate**, abash, browbeat, chagrin, dispose of, mortify, put down (slang), quash, shame ♦ noun 5 = **crowd**, huddle, jam, party

crust noun = **layer**, caking, coat, coating, concretion, covering, film, incrustation, outside, scab, shell, skin, surface

crusty adjective 1 = **crispy**, brittle, crisp, friable, hard, short, well-baked, well-done 2 = **irritable**, brusque, cantankerous, captious, choleric, crabby, cross, curt, gruff, ill-humoured, peevish, prickly, ratty (Brit. & N.Z. informal), short, short-tempered, snappish, snarling, splenetic, surly, testy, tetchy, touchy

cry verb 1 = **weep**, bawl, bewail, blubber, boohoo, greet (Scot. or archaic), howl one's eyes out, keen, lament, mewl, pule, shed tears, snivel, sob, wail, whimper, whine, whinge (informal), yowl 2 = **shout**, bawl, bell, bellow, call, call out, ejaculate, exclaim, hail, halloo, holler (informal), howl, roar, scream, screech, shriek, sing out, vociferate, whoop, yell ♦ noun 3 = **weeping**, bawling, blubbering, crying, greet (Scot. or archaic), howl, keening, lament, lamentation, plaint (archaic), snivel, snivelling, sob, sobbing, sorrowing, wailing, weep 4 = **shout**, bawl, bell, bellow, call, ejaculation, exclamation, holler (informal), hoot, howl, outcry, roar, scream, screech, shriek, squawk, whoop, yell, yelp, yoo-hoo 5 = **appeal**, plea
➤ Antonyms
verb ≠weep: chortle, chuckle, giggle, laugh, snicker, snigger ≠shout: drone, mumble, murmur, mutter, speak in hushed tones, speak softly, utter indistinctly, whisper

cry down verb = **run down**, asperse, bad-mouth (slang, chiefly U.S. & Canad.), belittle, decry, denigrate, disparage, knock (informal), rubbish (informal), slag (off) (slang)

cry off verb Informal = **back out**, beg off, cop out (slang), excuse oneself, quit, withdraw, withdraw from

crypt noun = **vault**, catacomb, ossuary, tomb, undercroft

cub noun 1 = **young**, offspring, whelp 2 = **youngster**, babe (informal), beginner, fledgling, greenhorn (informal), lad, learner, puppy, recruit, tenderfoot, trainee, whippersnapper

cubbyhole noun 1 = **compartment**, niche, pigeonhole, recess, slot 2 = **hideaway**, den, hole, snug

cuddle verb = **hug**, bill and coo, canoodle (slang), clasp, cosset, embrace, fondle, nestle, pet, snuggle

cuddly adjective = **soft**, buxom, cuddlesome, curvaceous, huggable, lovable, plump, warm

cudgel noun 1 = **club**, bastinado, baton, bludgeon, cosh (Brit.), shillelagh, stick, truncheon ♦ verb 2 = **beat**, bang, baste, batter, bludgeon, cane, cosh (*Brit.*), drub, maul, pound, pummel, thrash, thump, thwack

cue *noun* = **signal**, catchword, hint, key, nod, prompting, reminder, sign, suggestion

cuff *noun* **off the cuff** *Informal* = **impromptu**, ad lib, extempore, improvised, offhand, off the top of one's head, on the spur of the moment, spontaneous, spontaneously, unrehearsed

cul-de-sac *noun* = **dead end**, blind alley

culminate *verb* = **end up**, climax, close, come to a climax, come to a head, conclude, end, finish, rise to a crescendo, terminate, wind up

culmination *noun* = **climax**, acme, apex, apogee, completion, conclusion, consummation, crown, crowning touch, finale, height, *ne plus ultra,* peak, perfection, pinnacle, punch line, summit, top, zenith

culpable *adjective* = **blameworthy**, answerable, at fault, blamable, censurable, found wanting, guilty, in the wrong, liable, reprehensible, sinful, to blame, wrong
➤ **Antonyms**
blameless, clean (*slang*), guiltless, innocent, in the clear, not guilty, squeaky-clean

culprit *noun* = **offender**, criminal, delinquent, evildoer, felon, guilty party, malefactor, miscreant, person responsible, rascal, sinner, transgressor, villain, wrongdoer

cult *noun* **1** = **sect**, body, church, clique, denomination, faction, faith, following, party, religion, school **2** = **devotion**, admiration, craze, idolization, reverence, veneration, worship

cultivate *verb* **1** = **farm**, bring under cultivation, fertilize, harvest, plant, plough, prepare, tend, till, work **2** = **develop**, ameliorate, better, bring on, cherish, civilize, discipline, elevate, enrich, foster, improve, polish, promote, refine, train **3** = **encourage**, aid, devote oneself to, forward, foster, further, help, patronize, promote, pursue, support **4** = **court**, associate with, butter up, consort with, dance attendance upon, run after, seek out, seek someone's company *or* friendship, take trouble *or* pains with

cultivation *noun* **1** = **farming**, agronomy, gardening, husbandry, planting, ploughing, tillage, tilling, working **2** = **development**, advancement, advocacy, encouragement, enhancement, fostering, furtherance, help, nurture, patronage, promotion, support **3** = **devotion to**, pursuit, study **4** = **refinement**, breeding, civility, civilization, culture, discernment, discrimination, education, enlightenment, gentility, good taste, learning, letters, manners, polish,

sophistication, taste

cultural *adjective* = **artistic**, broadening, civilizing, developmental, edifying, educational, educative, elevating, enlightening, enriching, humane, humanizing, liberal, liberalizing

culture *noun* **1** = **civilization**, customs, lifestyle, mores, society, stage of development, the arts, way of life **2** = **refinement**, accomplishment, breeding, education, elevation, enlightenment, erudition, gentility, good taste, improvement, polish, politeness, sophistication, urbanity **3** = **farming**, agriculture, agronomy, cultivation, husbandry

cultured *adjective* = **refined**, accomplished, advanced, educated, enlightened, erudite, genteel, highbrow, knowledgeable, polished, scholarly, sophisticated, urbane, versed, well-bred, well-informed, well-read
➤ **Antonyms**
coarse, common, inelegant, uncultivated, uneducated, unpolished, unrefined, vulgar

culvert *noun* = **drain**, channel, conduit, gutter, watercourse

cumbersome *adjective* = **awkward**, bulky, burdensome, clumsy, clunky (*informal*), cumbrous, embarrassing, heavy, hefty (*informal*), incommodious, inconvenient, oppressive, unmanageable, unwieldy, weighty
➤ **Antonyms**
compact, convenient, easy to use, handy, manageable, practical, serviceable, wieldy

cumulative *adjective* = **collective**, accruing, accumulative, aggregate, amassed, heaped, increasing, snowballing

cunning *adjective* **1** = **crafty**, artful, astute, canny, devious, foxy, guileful, knowing, Machiavellian, sharp, shifty, shrewd, sly, subtle, tricky, wily **2** = **skilful**, adroit, deft, dexterous, imaginative, ingenious ✦ *noun* **3** = **craftiness**, artfulness, astuteness, deceitfulness, deviousness, foxiness, guile, shrewdness, slyness, trickery, wiliness **4** = **skill**, ability, adroitness, art, artifice, cleverness, craft, deftness, dexterity, finesse, ingenuity, subtlety
➤ **Antonyms**
adjective ≠**crafty:** artless, dull, ethical, frank, honest, ingenuous ≠**skilful:** maladroit
✦ *noun* ≠**craftiness:** candour, ingenuousness, sincerity ≠**skill:** clumsiness

cup *noun* **1** = **mug**, beaker, bowl, cannikin, chalice, demitasse, goblet, teacup **2** = **trophy**

cupboard *noun* = **cabinet**, ambry (*obsolete*), closet, locker, press

Cupid *noun* = **god of love**, amoretto, Eros, love

curb *noun* **1** = **restraint**, brake, bridle, check, control, deterrent, limitation, rein ♦ *verb* **2** = **restrain**, bite back, bridle, check, constrain, contain, control, hinder, impede, inhibit, keep a tight rein on, moderate, muzzle, repress, restrict, retard, stem the flow, subdue, suppress

curdle *verb* = **congeal**, clot, coagulate, condense, curd, solidify, thicken, turn sour
➤ **Antonyms**
deliquesce, dissolve, liquefy, melt, soften, thaw

cure *verb* **1** = **make better**, alleviate, correct, ease, heal, help, mend, rehabilitate, relieve, remedy, restore, restore to health **2** = **preserve**, dry, kipper, pickle, salt, smoke ♦ *noun* **3** = **remedy**, alleviation, antidote, corrective, healing, medicine, nostrum, panacea, recovery, restorative, specific, treatment

cure-all *noun* = **panacea**, catholicon, elixir, *elixir vitae,* nostrum

curiosity *noun* **1** = **inquisitiveness**, interest, nosiness (*informal*), prying, snooping (*informal*) **2** = **oddity**, celebrity, freak, marvel, novelty, phenomenon, rarity, sight, spectacle, wonder **3** = **collector's item**, bibelot, bygone, curio, knick-knack, *objet d'art,* trinket

curious *adjective* **1** = **inquiring**, inquisitive, interested, puzzled, questioning, searching **2** = **inquisitive**, meddling, nosy (*informal*), peeping, peering, prying, snoopy (*informal*) **3** = **unusual**, bizarre, exotic, extraordinary, marvellous, mysterious, novel, odd, peculiar, puzzling, quaint, queer, rare, rum (*Brit. slang*), singular, strange, unconventional, unexpected, unique, unorthodox, wonderful
➤ **Antonyms**
≠**inquiring**: incurious, indifferent, uninquisitive, uninterested ≠**unusual**: common, everyday, familiar, ordinary

curl *verb* **1** = **twirl**, bend, coil, convolute, corkscrew, crimp, crinkle, crisp, curve, entwine, frizz, loop, meander, ripple, spiral, turn, twine, twist, wind, wreathe, writhe ♦ *noun* **2** = **twist**, coil, curlicue, kink, ringlet, spiral, whorl

curly *adjective* = **curling**, corkscrew, crimped, crimpy, crinkly, crisp, curled, frizzy, fuzzy, kinky, permed, spiralled, waved, wavy, winding

currency *noun* **1** = **money**, bills, coinage, coins, dosh (*Brit. & Austral. slang*), medium of exchange, notes **2** = **acceptance**, circulation, exposure, popularity, prevalence, publicity, transmission, vogue

current *adjective* **1** = **present**, contemporary, fashionable, happening (*informal*), in, in fashion, in vogue, now (*informal*), present-day, sexy (*informal*),

trendy (*Brit. informal*), up-to-date, up-to-the-minute **2** = **prevalent**, accepted, circulating, common, customary, general, going around, in circulation, in progress, in the air, in the news, ongoing, popular, prevailing, rife, topical, widespread ♦ *noun* **3** = **flow**, course, draught, jet, progression, river, stream, tide, tideway, undertow **4** = **mood**, atmosphere, drift, feeling, inclination, tendency, trend, undercurrent, vibes (*slang*)
➤ **Antonyms**
adjective ≠**present**: archaic, obsolete, old-fashioned, outmoded, out-of-date, passé, past

curse *verb* **1** = **swear**, be foul-mouthed, blaspheme, cuss (*informal*), take the Lord's name in vain, turn the air blue (*informal*), use bad language **2** = **damn**, accurse, anathematize, excommunicate, execrate, fulminate, imprecate **3** = **afflict**, blight, burden, destroy, doom, plague, scourge, torment, trouble, vex ♦ *noun* **4** = **oath**, blasphemy, expletive, obscenity, swearing, swearword **5** = **denunciation**, anathema, ban, evil eye, excommunication, execration, hoodoo (*informal*), imprecation, jinx, malediction, malison (*archaic*) **6** = **affliction**, bane, burden, calamity, cross, disaster, evil, hardship, misfortune, ordeal, plague, scourge, torment, tribulation, trouble, vexation

cursed *adjective* **1** = **damned**, accursed, bedevilled, blighted, cast out, confounded, doomed, excommunicate, execrable, fey (*Scot.*), foredoomed, ill-fated, star-crossed, unholy, unsanctified, villainous **2** = **hateful**, abominable, damnable, detestable, devilish, fell (*archaic*), fiendish, infamous, infernal, loathsome, odious, pernicious, pestilential, vile

curt *adjective* = **short**, abrupt, blunt, brief, brusque, concise, gruff, monosyllabic, offhand, pithy, rude, sharp, snappish, succinct, summary, tart, terse, unceremonious, uncivil, ungracious

curtail *verb* = **cut short**, abbreviate, abridge, contract, cut, cut back, decrease, diminish, dock, lessen, lop, pare down, reduce, retrench, shorten, trim, truncate

curtailment *noun* = **cutting short**, abbreviation, abridgment, contraction, cutback, cutting, docking, retrenchment, truncation

curtain *noun* **1** = **hanging**, drape (*chiefly U.S.*) ♦ *verb* **2** = **conceal**, drape, hide, screen, shroud, shut off, shutter, veil

curve *noun* **1** = **bend**, arc, camber, curvature, half-moon, loop, trajectory, turn ♦ *verb* **2** = **bend**, arc, arch, bow, coil, hook, inflect, spiral, swerve, turn, twist, wind

curved adjective = **bent**, arced, arched, bowed, crooked, humped, rounded, serpentine, sinuous, sweeping, turned, twisted, twisty

cushion noun 1 = **pillow**, beanbag, bolster, hassock, headrest, pad, scatter cushion, squab ♦ verb 2 = **soften**, bolster, buttress, cradle, dampen, deaden, muffle, pillow, protect, stifle, support, suppress

cushy adjective Informal = **easy**, comfortable, jammy (Brit. slang), soft, undemanding

custody noun 1 = **safekeeping**, aegis, auspices, care, charge, custodianship, guardianship, keeping, observation, preservation, protection, supervision, trusteeship, tutelage, ward, watch 2 = **imprisonment**, arrest, confinement, detention, durance (archaic), duress, incarceration

custom noun 1 = **tradition**, convention, etiquette, fashion, form, formality, matter of course, observance, observation, policy, practice, praxis, ritual, rule, style, unwritten law, usage, use 2 = **habit**, habitude (rare), manner, mode, practice, procedure, routine, way, wont 3 = **customers**, patronage, trade

customarily adverb = **usually**, as a rule, commonly, generally, habitually, in the ordinary way, normally, ordinarily, regularly, traditionally

customary adjective = **usual**, accepted, accustomed, acknowledged, bog-standard (Brit. & Irish slang), common, confirmed, conventional, established, everyday, familiar, fashionable, general, habitual, normal, ordinary, popular, regular, routine, traditional, wonted
➤ **Antonyms**
exceptional, infrequent, irregular, occasional, rare, uncommon, unusual

customer noun = **client**, buyer, consumer, habitué, patron, prospect, purchaser, regular (informal), shopper

customs plural noun = **duty**, import charges, tariff, tax, toll

cut verb 1 = **penetrate**, chop, cleave, divide, gash, incise, lacerate, lance, nick, notch, pierce, score, sever, slash, slice, slit, wound 2 = **divide**, bisect, carve, cleave, cross, dissect, interrupt, intersect, part, segment, sever, slice, split, sunder 3 = **trim**, clip, dock, fell, gather, hack, harvest, hew, lop, mow, pare, prune, reap, saw down, shave, snip 4 = **abridge**, abbreviate, condense, curtail, delete, edit out, excise, precis, shorten 5 = **reduce**, contract, cut back, decrease, diminish, downsize, ease up on, lower, rationalize, slash, slim (down) 6 = **shape**, carve, chip, chisel, chop, engrave, fashion, form, inscribe, saw, sculpt, sculpture, whittle 7 = **hurt**, grieve, insult, pain, put down, snub, sting, wound 8 Informal = **ignore**, avoid, cold-shoulder, freeze (someone) out (informal), look straight through (someone), send to Coventry, slight, spurn, turn one's back on ♦ noun 9 = **incision**, gash, graze, groove, laceration, nick, rent, rip, slash, slit, snip, stroke, wound 10 = **reduction**, cutback, decrease, decrement, diminution, economy, fall, lowering, saving 11 Informal = **share**, chop (slang), division, kickback (chiefly U.S.), percentage, piece, portion, rake-off (slang), section, slice 12 = **style**, configuration, fashion, form, look, mode, shape 13 a **cut above** Informal = **superior to**, better than, higher than, more capable than, more competent than, more efficient than, more reliable than, more trustworthy than, more useful than ♦ adjective 14 **cut and dried** Informal = **prearranged**, automatic, fixed, organized, predetermined, settled, sorted out (informal)
➤ **Antonyms**
verb ≠**abridge**, reduce: add to, augment, enlarge, expand, extend, fill out, increase ≠**ignore**: accept gladly, embrace, greet, hail, receive, welcome with open arms

cutback noun = **reduction**, cut, decrease, economy, lessening, retrenchment

cut back verb 1 = **trim**, prune, shorten 2 = **reduce**, check, curb, decrease, downsize, draw or pull in one's horns (informal), economize, lessen, lower, retrench, slash

cut down verb 1 = **fell**, hew, level, lop, raze 2 = **reduce**, decrease, lessen, lower 3 = **kill**, blow away (slang, chiefly U.S.), dispatch, massacre, mow down, slaughter, slay (archaic), take out (slang) 4 **cut (someone) down to size** = **make (someone) look small**, abash, humiliate, take the wind out of (someone's) sails

cute adjective = **appealing**, attractive, charming, delightful, engaging, lovable, sweet, winning, winsome

cut in verb = **interrupt**, break in, butt in, interpose, intervene, intrude, move in (informal)

cut off verb 1 = **separate**, isolate, sever 2 = **interrupt**, disconnect, intercept, intersect 3 = **halt**, bring to an end, discontinue, obstruct, suspend 4 = **disinherit**, disown, renounce

cut out verb 1 = **stop**, cease, delete, extract, give up, kick (informal), refrain from, remove, sever 2 Informal = **exclude**, displace, eliminate, oust, supersede, supplant

cut out for adjective = **suited**, adapted, adequate, competent, designed, eligible, equipped, fitted, qualified, suitable

cut-price *adjective* = **cheap**, bargain, cheapo (*informal*), cut-rate (*chiefly U.S.*), reduced, sale

cut short *verb* = **interrupt**, abort, break off, bring to an end, check, dock, halt, leave unfinished, postpone, pull the plug on, stop, terminate, truncate

cutthroat *adjective* **1** = **competitive**, dog-eat-dog, fierce, relentless, ruthless, unprincipled **2** = **murderous**, barbarous, bloodthirsty, bloody, cruel, death-dealing, ferocious, homicidal, savage, thuggish, violent ♦ *noun* **3** = **murderer**, assassin, bravo, butcher, executioner, heavy (*slang*), hit man (*slang*), homicide, killer, liquidator, slayer (*archaic*), thug

cutting *adjective* **1** = **hurtful**, acid, acrimonious, barbed, bitter, caustic, malicious, mordacious, pointed, sarcastic, sardonic, scathing, severe, trenchant, vitriolic, wounding **2** = **piercing**, biting, bitter, chilling, keen, numbing, penetrating, raw, sharp, stinging
➤ **Antonyms**
≠**hurtful**: consoling, flattering, kind, mild

≠**piercing**: balmy, pleasant, soothing

cut up *verb* **1** = **chop**, carve, dice, divide, mince, slice **2** = **slash**, injure, knife, lacerate, wound ♦ *adjective* **3** *Informal* = **upset**, agitated, dejected, desolated, distressed, disturbed, heartbroken, stricken, wretched

cycle *noun* = **era**, aeon, age, circle, period, phase, revolution, rotation, round (*of years*)

cynic *noun* = **sceptic**, doubter, misanthrope, misanthropist, pessimist, scoffer

cynical *adjective* = **sceptical**, contemptuous, derisive, distrustful, ironic, misanthropic, misanthropical, mocking, mordacious, pessimistic, sarcastic, sardonic, scoffing, scornful, sneering, unbelieving
➤ **Antonyms**
credulous, green, gullible, hopeful, optimistic, trustful, trusting, unsceptical, unsuspecting

cynicism *noun* = **scepticism**, disbelief, doubt, misanthropy, pessimism, sarcasm, sardonicism

D d

dab *verb* **1** = **pat**, daub, stipple, tap, touch ◆ *noun* **2** = **spot**, hit, drop, pat, smudge, speck **3** = **pat**, flick, stroke, tap, touch

dabble *verb* **1** = **play at**, dally, dip into, potter, tinker, trifle (with) **2** = **splash**, dip, guddle (*Scot.*), moisten, paddle, spatter, sprinkle, wet

dabbler *noun* = **amateur**, dilettante, potterer, tinkerer, trifler

dab hand *noun Brit. informal* = **expert**, ace (*informal*), adept, buff (*informal*), dabster (*dialect*), hotshot (*informal*), maven (*U.S.*), past master, whizz (*informal*), wizard

daft *adjective Informal, chiefly Brit.* **1** = **foolish**, absurd, asinine, crackpot (*informal*), crazy, doolally (*slang*), dopey (*informal*), dumb-ass (*slang*), giddy, gonzo (*slang*), goofy (*informal*), idiotic, inane, loopy (*informal*), off one's head (*informal*), off one's trolley (*slang*), out to lunch (*informal*), scatty (*Brit. informal*), silly, simple, stupid, up the pole (*informal*), wacko *or* whacko (*slang*), witless **2** = **crazy**, barking (*slang*), barking mad (*slang*), crackers (*Brit. slang*), demented, deranged, insane, lunatic, mental (*slang*), not right in the head, not the full shilling (*informal*), nuts (*slang*), nutty (*slang*), round the bend (*Brit. slang*), touched, unhinged **3 daft about** = **enthusiastic**, besotted, crazy (*informal*), doting, dotty (*slang, chiefly Brit.*), infatuated by, mad, nuts (*slang*), nutty (*informal*), potty (*Brit. informal*), sweet on

dagger *noun* **1** = **knife**, bayonet, dirk, poniard, skean, stiletto **2 at daggers drawn** = **on bad terms**, at enmity, at loggerheads, at odds, at war, up in arms **3 look daggers** = **glare**, frown, glower, look black, lour *or* lower, scowl

daily *adjective* **1** = **everyday**, circadian, diurnal, quotidian **2** = **day-to-day**, common, commonplace, everyday, ordinary, quotidian, regular, routine ◆ *adverb* **3** = **every day**, constantly, day after day, day by day, often, once a day, per diem, regularly

dainty *adjective* **1** = **delicate**, charming, elegant, exquisite, fine, graceful, neat, petite, pretty **2** = **delectable**, choice, delicious, palatable, savoury, tasty, tender, toothsome **3** = **particular**, choosy, fastidious, finical, finicky, fussy, mincing, nice, picky (*informal*), refined, scrupulous ◆ *noun* **4**

= **delicacy**, *bonne bouche*, fancy, sweetmeat, titbit
> **Antonyms**
adjective ≠**delicate**: awkward, clumsy, coarse, gauche, inelegant, maladroit, uncouth, ungainly

dale *noun* = **valley**, bottom, coomb, dell, dingle, glen, strath (*Scot.*), vale

dally *verb* **1** *Old-fashioned* = **waste time**, dawdle, delay, dilly-dally (*informal*), drag one's feet *or* heels, fool (about *or* around), fritter away, hang about, linger, loiter, procrastinate, tarry, while away **2 dally with** = **flirt**, caress, fondle, fool (about *or* around), frivol (*informal*), lead on, play, play fast and loose (*informal*), tamper, tease, toy, trifle
> **Antonyms**
≠**waste time**: hasten, hurry (up), make haste, push forward *or* on, run, step on it (*informal*)

dam *noun* **1** = **barrier**, barrage, embankment, hindrance, obstruction, wall ◆ *verb* **2** = **block up**, barricade, block, check, choke, confine, hold back, hold in, obstruct, restrict

damage *verb* **1** = **harm**, deface, hurt, impair, incapacitate, injure, mar, mutilate, play (merry) hell with (*informal*), ruin, spoil, tamper with, undo, weaken, wreck ◆ *noun* **2** = **harm**, destruction, detriment, devastation, hurt, impairment, injury, loss, mischief, mutilation, suffering **3** *Informal* = **cost**, bill, charge, expense, total
> **Antonyms**
verb ≠**harm**: better, fix, improve, mend, repair ◆ *noun* ≠**harm**: gain, improvement, reparation

damages *plural noun Law* = **compensation**, fine, indemnity, reimbursement, reparation, satisfaction

damaging *adjective* = **harmful**, deleterious, detrimental, disadvantageous, hurtful, injurious, prejudicial, ruinous
> **Antonyms**
advantageous, favourable, healthful, helpful, profitable, salutary, useful, valuable, wholesome

dame *noun* = **noblewoman**, baroness, dowager, *grande dame*, lady, matron (*archaic*), peeress

damn *verb* **1** = **criticize**, blast, castigate, censure, condemn, denounce, denunciate,

excoriate, inveigh against, lambast(e), pan (*informal*), put down, slam (*slang*), slate (*informal*), tear into (*informal*) **2** = **curse**, abuse, anathematize, blaspheme, execrate, imprecate, revile, swear **3** = **sentence**, condemn, doom ♦ *noun* **4 not give a damn** *Informal* = **not care**, be indifferent, not care a brass farthing, not care a jot, not care a whit, not give a hoot, not give a tinker's curse *or* damn (*slang*), not give two hoots, not mind
➤ **Antonyms**
verb ≠ **criticize**: acclaim, admire, applaud, approve, cheer, compliment, congratulate, extol, honour, laud, praise, take one's hat off to ≠ **curse**: adore, bless, exalt, glorify, pay homage to

damnable *adjective* = **detestable**, abominable, accursed, atrocious, culpable, cursed, despicable, execrable, hateful, horrible, offensive, wicked
➤ **Antonyms**
admirable, commendable, creditable, excellent, exemplary, fine, honourable, laudable, meritorious, praiseworthy, worthy

damnation *noun Theology* = **condemnation**, anathema, ban, consigning to perdition, damning, denunciation, doom, excommunication, objurgation, proscription, sending to hell

damned *adjective* **1** = **doomed**, accursed, anathematized, condemned, infernal, lost, reprobate, unhappy **2** *Slang* = **detestable**, confounded, despicable, hateful, infamous, infernal, loathsome, revolting

damning *adjective* = **incriminating**, accusatorial, condemnatory, damnatory, dooming, implicating, implicative

damp *adjective* **1** = **moist**, clammy, dank, dewy, dripping, drizzly, humid, misty, muggy, sodden, soggy, sopping, vaporous, wet ♦ *noun* **2** = **moisture**, clamminess, dampness, dankness, dew, drizzle, fog, humidity, mist, mugginess, vapour ♦ *verb* **3** = **moisten**, dampen, wet **4 damp down** = **curb**, allay, check, chill, cool, dash, deaden, deject, depress, diminish, discourage, dispirit, dull, inhibit, moderate, pour cold water on, reduce, restrain, stifle
➤ **Antonyms**
adjective ≠ **moist**: arid, dry, watertight ♦ *noun* ≠ **moisture**: aridity, dryness ♦ *verb* ≠ **curb**: encourage, gee up, hearten, inspire

dampen *verb* **1** = **reduce**, check, dull, lessen, moderate, restrain, stifle **2** = **moisten**, make damp, spray, wet

damper *noun As in* **put a damper on** = **discouragement**, chill, cloud, cold water (*informal*), curb, gloom, hindrance, killjoy, pall, restraint, wet blanket (*informal*)

dance *verb* **1** = **prance**, bob up and down, caper, cut a rug (*informal*), frolic, gambol, hop, jig, rock, skip, spin, sway, swing, trip, whirl ♦ *noun* **2** = **ball**, dancing party, disco, discotheque, hop (*informal*), knees-up (*Brit. informal*), social

dancer *noun* = **ballerina**, Terpsichorean

dandy *noun* **1** = **fop**, beau, blade (*archaic*), blood (*rare*), buck (*archaic*), coxcomb, dude (*U.S. & Canad. informal*), exquisite (*obsolete*), macaroni (*obsolete*), man about town, peacock, popinjay, swell (*informal*), toff (*Brit. slang*) ♦ *adjective* **2** *Informal* = **excellent**, capital, fine, first-rate, great, splendid

danger *noun* = **peril**, endangerment, hazard, insecurity, jeopardy, menace, pitfall, precariousness, risk, threat, venture, vulnerability

dangerous *adjective* = **perilous**, alarming, breakneck, chancy (*informal*), exposed, hairy (*slang*), hazardous, insecure, menacing, nasty, parlous (*archaic*), precarious, risky, threatening, treacherous, ugly, unchancy (*Scot.*), unsafe, vulnerable
➤ **Antonyms**
harmless, innocuous, O.K. *or* okay (*informal*), out of danger, out of harm's way, protected, safe, safe and sound, secure

dangerously *adverb* **1** = **perilously**, alarmingly, carelessly, daringly, desperately, harmfully, hazardously, precariously, recklessly, riskily, unsafely, unsecurely **2** = **seriously**, critically, gravely, severely

dangle *verb* **1** = **hang**, depend, flap, hang down, sway, swing, trail **2** = **wave**, brandish, entice, flaunt, flourish, lure, tantalize, tempt

dangling *adjective* = **hanging**, disconnected, drooping, loose, swaying, swinging, trailing, unconnected

dapper *adjective* = **neat**, active, brisk, chic, dainty, natty (*informal*), nice, nimble, smart, soigné *or* soignée, spruce, spry, stylish, trig (*archaic or dialect*), trim, well-groomed, well turned out
➤ **Antonyms**
blowsy, disarrayed, dishevelled, dowdy, frowzy, ill-groomed, rumpled, slobby (*informal*), sloppy (*informal*), slovenly, unkempt, untidy

dapple *verb* = **mottle**, bespeckle, dot, fleck, freckle, speckle, spot, stipple

dappled *adjective* = **mottled**, brindled, checkered, flecked, freckled, piebald, pied, speckled, spotted, stippled, variegated

dare *verb* **1** = **risk**, brave, endanger, gamble, hazard, make bold, presume, skate on thin ice, stake, venture **2** = **challenge**, defy, goad, provoke, taunt, throw down the gauntlet ♦ *noun* **3** = **challenge**, defiance, provocation, taunt

daredevil *noun* **1** = **adventurer**, adrenalin junky (*slang*), desperado, exhibitionist, hot dog (*chiefly U.S.*), madcap, show-off (*informal*), stunt man ♦ *adjective* **2** = **daring**, adventurous, audacious, bold, death-defying, madcap, reckless

daring *adjective* **1** = **brave**, adventurous, audacious, ballsy (*taboo slang*), bold, daredevil, fearless, game (*informal*), have-a-go (*informal*), impulsive, intrepid, plucky, rash, reckless, valiant, venturesome ♦ *noun* **2** = **bravery**, audacity, balls (*taboo slang*), ballsiness (*taboo slang*), boldness, bottle (*Brit. slang*), courage, derring-do (*archaic*), face (*informal*), fearlessness, grit, guts (*informal*), intrepidity, nerve (*informal*), pluck, rashness, spirit, spunk (*informal*), temerity
➤ **Antonyms**
adjective ≠**brave**: anxious, careful, cautious, cowardly, faint-hearted, fearful, timid, uncourageous, wary ♦ *noun* ≠**bravery**: anxiety, caution, cowardice, fear, timidity

dark *adjective* **1** = **dim**, cloudy, darksome (*literary*), dingy, indistinct, murky, overcast, pitch-black, pitchy, shadowy, shady, sunless, unlit **2** = **brunette**, black, dark-skinned, dusky, ebony, sable, swarthy **3** = **gloomy**, bleak, cheerless, dismal, doleful, drab, grim, joyless, morbid, morose, mournful, sad, sombre **4** = **evil**, atrocious, damnable, foul, hellish, horrible, infamous, infernal, nefarious, satanic, sinful, sinister, vile, wicked **5** = **secret**, abstruse, arcane, concealed, cryptic, deep, Delphic, enigmatic, hidden, mysterious, mystic, obscure, occult, puzzling, recondite **6** = **angry**, dour, forbidding, frowning, glowering, glum, ominous, scowling, sulky, sullen, threatening ♦ *noun* **7** = **darkness**, dimness, dusk, gloom, murk, murkiness, obscurity, semi-darkness **8** = **night**, evening, nightfall, night-time, twilight
➤ **Antonyms**
adjective ≠**brunette**: blond, blonde, fair, fair-haired, flaxen-haired, light, light-complexioned, towheaded ≠**gloomy**: bright, cheerful, clear, genial, glad, hopeful, pleasant, sunny

darken *verb* **1** = **make dark**, becloud, blacken, cloud up *or* over, deepen, dim, eclipse, make darker, make dim, obscure, overshadow, shade, shadow **2** = **become gloomy**, become angry, blacken, cast a pall over, cloud, deject, depress, dispirit, grow troubled, look black, sadden
➤ **Antonyms**
≠**make dark**: brighten, clear up, enliven, gleam, glow, illuminate, lighten, light up, make bright, shine ≠**become gloomy**:

become cheerful, cheer, encourage, gladden, hearten, make happy, perk up

darkness *noun* **1** = **dark**, blackness, dimness, dusk, duskiness, gloom, murk, murkiness, nightfall, obscurity, shade, shadiness, shadows **2** = **secrecy**, blindness, concealment, ignorance, mystery, privacy, unawareness

darling *noun* **1** = **beloved**, dear, dearest, love, sweetheart, truelove **2** = **favourite**, apple of one's eye, blue-eyed boy, fair-haired boy (*U.S.*), pet, spoilt child ♦ *adjective* **3** = **beloved**, adored, cherished, dear, precious, treasured **4** = **adorable**, attractive, captivating, charming, cute, enchanting, lovely, sweet

darn *verb* **1** = **mend**, cobble up, patch, repair, sew up, stitch ♦ *noun* **2** = **mend**, invisible repair, patch, reinforcement

dart *verb* **1** = **dash**, bound, flash, flit, fly, race, run, rush, scoot, shoot, spring, sprint, start, tear, whistle, whizz **2** = **throw**, cast, fling, hurl, launch, propel, send, shoot, sling

dash *verb* **1** = **rush**, barrel (along) (*informal, chiefly U.S. & Canad.*), bolt, bound, burn rubber (*informal*), dart, fly, haste, hasten, hurry, race, run, speed, spring, sprint, tear **2** = **throw**, cast, fling, hurl, slam, sling **3** = **crash**, break, destroy, shatter, shiver, smash, splinter **4** = **frustrate**, blight, foil, ruin, spoil, thwart, undo **5** = **disappoint**, abash, chagrin, confound, dampen, discomfort, discourage ♦ *noun* **6** = **rush**, bolt, dart, haste, onset, race, run, sortie, sprint, spurt **7** = **little**, bit, drop, flavour, hint, pinch, smack, soupçon, sprinkling, suggestion, tinge, touch **8** = **style**, brio, élan, flair, flourish, panache, spirit, verve, vigour, vivacity
➤ **Antonyms**
verb ≠**rush**: crawl, dawdle, walk ≠**frustrate**: enhance, improve ♦ *noun* ≠**little**: lot, much

dashing *adjective* **1** = **bold**, daring, debonair, exuberant, gallant, lively, plucky, spirited, swashbuckling **2** = **stylish**, dapper, dazzling, elegant, flamboyant, jaunty, showy, smart, sporty, swish (*informal, chiefly Brit.*), urbane
➤ **Antonyms**
≠**bold**: boring, dreary, dull, lacklustre, stolid, unexciting, uninteresting

data *noun* = **information**, details, documents, dope (*informal*), facts, figures, info (*informal*), input, materials, statistics

date *noun* **1** = **time**, age, epoch, era, period, stage **2** = **appointment**, assignation, engagement, meeting, rendezvous, tryst **3** = **partner**, escort, friend, steady (*informal*) **4** **out of date** = **old-fashioned**, antiquated, archaic, dated, obsolete, old, passé **5** **to date**

= **up to now**, now, so far, up to the present, up to this point, yet **6 up-to-date** = **modern**, à la mode, contemporary, current, fashionable, trendy (*Brit. informal*), up-to-the-minute ♦ *verb* **7** = **put a date on**, assign a date to, determine the date of, fix the period of **8** = **become old-fashioned**, be dated, obsolesce, show one's age **9 date from** *or* **date back to** = **come from**, bear a date of, belong to, exist from, originate in

dated *adjective* = **old-fashioned**, antiquated, archaic, *démodé*, obsolete, old hat, out, outdated, outmoded, out of date, out of the ark (*informal*), passé, unfashionable, untrendy (*Brit. informal*)
➤ **Antonyms**
à la mode, all the rage, chic, cool (*informal*), current, hip (*slang*), in vogue, latest, modern, modish, popular, stylish, trendy (*Brit. informal*), up-to-date

daub *verb* **1** = **smear**, coat, cover, paint, plaster, slap on (*informal*) **2** = **stain**, bedaub, begrime, besmear, blur, deface, dirty, grime, smirch, smudge, spatter, splatter, sully ♦ *noun* **3** = **smear**, blot, blotch, smirch, splodge, splotch, spot, stain

daunt *verb* **1** = **intimidate**, alarm, appal, cow, dismay, frighten, frighten off, overawe, scare, subdue, terrify **2** = **discourage**, deter, dishearten, dispirit, put off, shake
➤ **Antonyms**
cheer, comfort, encourage, hearten, inspire, reassure, spur, support

daunted *adjective* = **intimidated**, alarmed, cowed, demoralized, deterred, discouraged, disillusioned, dismayed, dispirited, downcast, frightened, hesitant, overcome, put off, unnerved

daunting *adjective* = **intimidating**, alarming, demoralizing, disconcerting, discouraging, disheartening, frightening, off-putting (*Brit. informal*), unnerving
➤ **Antonyms**
cheering, comforting, encouraging, heartening, reassuring

dauntless *adjective* = **fearless**, bold, brave, courageous, daring, doughty, gallant, gritty, heroic, indomitable, intrepid, lion-hearted, resolute, stouthearted, undaunted, unflinching, valiant, valorous

dawdle *verb* = **waste time**, dally, delay, dilly-dally (*informal*), drag one's feet *or* heels, fritter away, hang about, idle, lag, loaf, loiter, potter, trail
➤ **Antonyms**
fly, get a move on (*informal*), hasten, hurry, lose no time, make haste, rush, scoot, step on it (*informal*)

dawn *noun* **1** = **daybreak**, aurora (*poetic*), cockcrow, crack of dawn, dawning, daylight,

dayspring (*poetic*), morning, sunrise, sunup **2** = **beginning**, advent, birth, dawning, emergence, genesis, inception, onset, origin, outset, rise, start, unfolding ♦ *verb* **3** = **grow light**, break, brighten, gleam, glimmer, lighten **4** = **begin**, appear, develop, emerge, initiate, open, originate, rise, unfold **5 dawn on** *or* **upon** = **hit**, become apparent, come into one's head, come to mind, cross one's mind, flash across one's mind, occur, register (*informal*), strike

day *noun* **1** = **twenty-four hours**, daylight, daylight hours, daytime, working day **2** = **point in time**, date, particular day, set time, time **3** = **time**, age, ascendancy, cycle, epoch, era, generation, height, heyday, period, prime, zenith **4 call it a day** *Informal* = **stop**, end, finish, knock off (*informal*), leave off, pack it in (*slang*), pack up (*informal*), shut up shop **5 day after day** = **continually**, monotonously, persistently, regularly, relentlessly **6 day by day** = **gradually**, daily, progressively, steadily

daybreak *noun* = **dawn**, break of day, cockcrow, crack of dawn, dayspring (*poetic*), first light, morning, sunrise, sunup

daydream *noun* **1** = **fantasy**, castle in the air *or* in Spain, dream, fancy, figment of the imagination, fond hope, imagining, pipe dream, reverie, wish ♦ *verb* **2** = **fantasize**, dream, envision, fancy, hallucinate, imagine, muse, stargaze

daydreamer *noun* = **fantasizer**, castle-builder, dreamer, pipe dreamer, visionary, Walter Mitty, wishful thinker, woolgatherer

daylight *noun* **1** = **sunlight**, light of day, sunshine **2** = **daytime**, broad day, daylight hours **3** = **full view**, light of day, openness, public attention

daze *verb* **1** = **stun**, benumb, numb, paralyse, shock, stupefy **2** = **confuse**, amaze, astonish, astound, befog, bewilder, blind, dazzle, dumbfound, flabbergast (*informal*), flummox, nonplus, perplex, stagger, startle, surprise ♦ *noun* **3** = **shock**, bewilderment, confusion, distraction, mind-fuck (*taboo slang*), stupor, trance, trancelike state

dazed *adjective* = **shocked**, at sea, baffled, bemused, bewildered, confused, disorientated, dizzy, dopey (*slang*), flabbergasted (*informal*), flummoxed, fuddled, groggy (*informal*), light-headed, muddled, nonplussed, numbed, perplexed, punch-drunk, staggered, stunned, stupefied, woozy (*informal*)

dazzle *verb* **1** = **impress**, amaze, astonish, awe, bowl over (*informal*), fascinate, hypnotize, overawe, overpower, overwhelm, strike dumb, stupefy, take one's breath away

2 = **blind**, bedazzle, blur, confuse, daze
♦ *noun* 3 = **splendour**, brilliance, éclat, flash, glitter, magnificence, razzle-dazzle (*slang*), razzmatazz (*slang*), sparkle

dazzling *adjective* = **splendid**, brilliant, divine, drop-dead (*slang*), glittering, glorious, radiant, ravishing, scintillating, sensational (*informal*), shining, sparkling, stunning, sublime, superb, virtuoso
➤ Antonyms
dull, ordinary, tedious, unexceptional, unexciting, uninspiring, uninteresting, unmemorable, unremarkable, vanilla (*slang*)

dead *adjective* 1 = **deceased**, defunct, departed, extinct, gone, late, passed away, perished, pushing up (the) daisies 2 = **inanimate**, lifeless 3 = **not working**, barren, inactive, inoperative, obsolete, stagnant, sterile, still, unemployed, unprofitable, useless 4 = **spiritless**, apathetic, callous, cold, dull, frigid, glassy, glazed, indifferent, lukewarm, torpid, unresponsive, wooden 5 = **numb**, inert, paralysed 6 = **total**, absolute, complete, downright, entire, outright, thorough, unqualified, utter 7 *Informal* = **exhausted**, dead beat (*informal*), spent, tired, worn out 8 = **boring**, dead-and-alive, dull, flat, ho-hum (*informal*), insipid, stale, tasteless, uninteresting, vapid ♦ *noun* 9 = **middle**, depth, midst ♦ *adverb* 10 *Informal* = **exactly**, absolutely, completely, directly, entirely, totally
➤ Antonyms
adjective ≠**deceased**: alive, alive and kicking, animate, existing, living ≠**inanimate**: animated, lively, responsive ≠**not working**: active, alive, effective, in use, operative, productive, working ≠**spiritless**: active, alive, alive and kicking, animated, full of beans (*informal*), lively, vivacious

deaden *verb* = **reduce**, abate, alleviate, anaesthetize, benumb, blunt, check, cushion, damp, dampen, diminish, dull, hush, impair, lessen, muffle, mute, numb, paralyse, quieten, smother, stifle, suppress, weaken

deadline *noun* = **time limit**, cutoff point, limit, target date

deadlock *noun* = **impasse**, cessation, dead heat, draw, full stop, gridlock, halt, stalemate, standoff, standstill, tie

deadlocked *adjective* = **even**, equal, level, neck and neck

deadly *adjective* 1 = **lethal**, baleful, baneful, dangerous, death-dealing, deathly, destructive, fatal, malignant, mortal, noxious, pernicious, poisonous, venomous 2 *Informal* = **boring**, as dry as dust, dull, ho-hum (*informal*), mind-numbing, monotonous, tedious, tiresome,

uninteresting, wearisome 3 = **deathly**, ashen, deathlike, ghastly, ghostly, pallid, wan, white 4 = **ruthless**, cruel, grim, implacable, mortal, savage, unrelenting 5 = **accurate**, effective, exact, on target, precise, sure, true, unerring, unfailing

deadpan *adjective* = **expressionless**, blank, empty, impassive, inexpressive, inscrutable, poker-faced, straight-faced

deaf *adjective* 1 = **hard of hearing**, stone deaf, without hearing 2 = **oblivious**, indifferent, unconcerned, unhearing, unmoved

deafen *verb* = **make deaf**, din, drown out, split *or* burst the eardrums

deafening *adjective* = **ear-piercing**, booming, dinning, ear-splitting, intense, overpowering, piercing, resounding, ringing, thunderous

deal *noun* 1 *Informal* = **agreement**, arrangement, bargain, contract, pact, transaction, understanding 2 = **amount**, degree, distribution, extent, portion, quantity, share, transaction 3 = **hand**, cut and shuffle, distribution, round, single game ♦ *verb* 4 = **sell**, bargain, buy and sell, do business, negotiate, stock, trade, traffic

dealer *noun* = **trader**, chandler, marketer, merchandiser, merchant, purveyor, supplier, tradesman, wholesaler

dealings *plural noun* = **business**, business relations, commerce, trade, traffic, transactions, truck

deal out *verb* = **distribute**, allot, apportion, assign, bestow, dispense, divide, dole out, give, mete out, reward, share

deal with *verb* 1 = **handle**, attend to, come to grips with, cope with, get to grips with, manage, oversee, see to, take care of, treat 2 = **be concerned with**, consider, treat of 3 = **behave towards**, act towards, conduct oneself towards

dear *noun* 1 = **beloved**, angel, darling, loved one, precious, treasure ♦ *adjective* 2 = **beloved**, cherished, close, darling, esteemed, familiar, favourite, intimate, precious, prized, respected, treasured 3 = **expensive**, at a premium, costly, high-priced, overpriced, pricey (*informal*) ♦ *adverb* 4 = **dearly**, at a heavy cost, at a high price, at great cost
➤ Antonyms
adjective ≠**beloved**: disliked, hated ≠**expensive**: cheap, common, inexpensive, worthless

dearly *adverb* 1 = **very much**, extremely, greatly, profoundly 2 = **at great cost**, at a heavy cost, at a high price, dear

dearth *noun* = **scarcity**, deficiency, inadequacy, insufficiency, lack, paucity, poverty, shortage, want

death noun 1 = **dying**, bereavement, cessation, curtains (*informal*), decease, demise, departure, dissolution, end, exit, expiration, loss, passing, quietus, release 2 = **destruction**, annihilation, downfall, ending, eradication, extermination, extinction, finish, grave, obliteration, ruin, ruination, undoing 3 *sometimes capital* = **grim reaper**, Dark Angel
➤ Antonyms
≠ **dying**: birth ≠ **destruction**: beginning, emergence, genesis, growth, origin, rise, source

deathless adjective = **eternal**, everlasting, immortal, imperishable, incorruptible, timeless, undying
➤ Antonyms
corporeal, earthly, ephemeral, human, mortal, passing, temporal, transient, transitory

deathly adjective 1 = **deathlike**, cadaverous, gaunt, ghastly, grim, haggard, like death warmed up (*informal*), pale, pallid, wan 2 = **fatal**, deadly, extreme, intense, mortal, terrible

debacle noun = **disaster**, catastrophe, collapse, defeat, devastation, downfall, fiasco, havoc, overthrow, reversal, rout, ruin, ruination

debase verb 1 = **degrade**, abase, cheapen, demean, devalue, disgrace, dishonour, drag down, humble, humiliate, lower, reduce, shame 2 = **contaminate**, adulterate, bastardize, corrupt, defile, depreciate, impair, pollute, taint, vitiate
➤ Antonyms
≠ **degrade**: elevate, enhance, exalt, improve, uplift ≠ **contaminate**: purify

debased adjective 1 = **degraded**, abandoned, base, corrupt, debauched, depraved, devalued, fallen, low, perverted, sordid, vile 2 = **contaminated**, adulterated, depreciated, impure, lowered, mixed, polluted, reduced
➤ Antonyms
≠ **degraded**: chaste, decent, ethical, good, honourable, incorruptible, innocent, moral, pure, upright, virtuous ≠ **contaminated**: pure

debasement noun 1 = **degradation**, abasement, baseness, corruption, depravation, devaluation, perversion 2 = **contamination**, adulteration, depreciation, pollution, reduction

debatable adjective = **doubtful**, arguable, borderline, controversial, disputable, dubious, iffy (*informal*), in dispute, moot, open to question, problematical, questionable, uncertain, undecided, unsettled

debate noun 1 = **discussion**, altercation, argument, contention, controversy, disputation, dispute, polemic, row 2 = **consideration**, cogitation, deliberation, meditation, reflection ♦ verb 3 = **discuss**, argue, contend, contest, controvert, dispute, question, wrangle 4 = **consider**, cogitate, deliberate, meditate upon, mull over, ponder, reflect, revolve, ruminate, weigh

debauched adjective = **corrupt**, abandoned, debased, degenerate, degraded, depraved, dissipated, dissolute, immoral, licentious, perverted, pervy (*slang*), profligate, sleazy, wanton

debauchery noun = **depravity**, dissipation, dissoluteness, excess, indulgence, intemperance, lewdness, overindulgence

debilitate verb = **weaken**, devitalize, enervate, enfeeble, exhaust, incapacitate, prostrate, relax, sap, undermine, wear out
➤ Antonyms
animate, brighten, energize, enliven, excite, fire, invigorate, pep up, perk up, rouse, stimulate, vitalize

debility noun = **weakness**, decrepitude, enervation, enfeeblement, exhaustion, faintness, feebleness, frailty, incapacity, infirmity, languor, malaise, sickliness

debonair adjective = **elegant**, affable, buoyant, charming, cheerful, courteous, dashing, jaunty, light-hearted, refined, smooth, sprightly, suave, urbane, well-bred

debrief verb = **interrogate**, cross-examine, examine, probe, question, quiz

debris noun = **remains**, bits, brash, detritus, dross, fragments, litter, pieces, rubbish, rubble, ruins, waste, wreck, wreckage

debt noun 1 = **debit**, arrears, bill, claim, commitment, due, duty, liability, obligation, score 2 **in debt** = **owing**, accountable, beholden, in arrears, in hock (*informal, chiefly U.S.*), in the red (*informal*), liable, responsible

debtor noun = **borrower**, defaulter, insolvent, mortgagor

debunk verb *Informal* = **expose**, cut down to size, deflate, disparage, lampoon, mock, puncture, ridicule, show up

debut noun = **introduction**, beginning, bow, coming out, entrance, first appearance, inauguration, initiation, launching, presentation

decadence noun = **degeneration**, corruption, debasement, decay, decline, deterioration, dissipation, dissolution, fall, perversion, retrogression

decadent adjective = **degenerate**, abandoned, corrupt, debased, debauched, decaying, declining, degraded, depraved,

dissolute, immoral, self-indulgent
➤ **Antonyms**
decent, ethical, good, high-minded,
honourable, incorruptible, moral, principled,
proper, upright, upstanding, virtuous

decant verb = **pour out**, drain, draw off, tap

decapitate verb = **behead**, execute,
guillotine

decay verb **1** = **decline**, atrophy, break
down, crumble, degenerate, deteriorate,
disintegrate, dissolve, dwindle, moulder,
shrivel, sink, spoil, wane, waste away, wear
away, wither **2** = **rot**, corrode, decompose,
mortify, perish, putrefy ◆ noun **3** = **decline**,
atrophy, collapse, decadence, degeneracy,
degeneration, deterioration, dying, fading,
failing, wasting, withering **4** = **rot**, caries,
cariosity, decomposition, gangrene,
mortification, perishing, putrefaction,
putrescence, putridity, rotting
➤ **Antonyms**
verb ≠**decline**: expand, flourish, flower,
grow, increase ◆ noun ≠**decline**: growth

decayed adjective = **rotten**, bad, carious,
carrion, corroded, decomposed, perished,
putrefied, putrid, rank, spoiled, wasted,
withered

decaying adjective = **rotting**, crumbling,
deteriorating, disintegrating, gangrenous,
perishing, putrefacient, wasting away,
wearing away

decease noun Formal = **death**, demise,
departure, dissolution, dying, release

deceased adjective = **dead**, defunct,
departed, expired, finished, former, gone,
late, lifeless, lost, pushing up daisies

deceit noun **1** = **dishonesty**, artifice,
cheating, chicanery, craftiness, cunning,
deceitfulness, deception, dissimulation,
double-dealing, duplicity, fraud, fraudulence,
guile, hypocrisy, imposition, lying, pretence,
slyness, treachery, trickery, underhandedness
2 = **lie**, artifice, blind, cheat, chicanery,
deception, duplicity, fake, feint, fraud,
imposture, misrepresentation, pretence, ruse,
scam (slang), sham, shift, sting (informal),
stratagem, subterfuge, swindle, trick, wile
➤ **Antonyms**
≠**dishonesty**: candour, frankness, honesty,
openness, sincerity, truthfulness

deceitful adjective = **dishonest**, counterfeit,
crafty, deceiving, deceptive, designing,
disingenuous, double-dealing, duplicitous,
fallacious, false, fraudulent, guileful,
hypocritical, illusory, insincere, knavish
(archaic), sneaky, treacherous, tricky,
two-faced, underhand, untrustworthy

deceive verb **1** = **take in** (informal),
bamboozle (informal), beguile, betray,
cheat, con (informal), cozen, delude,

disappoint, double-cross (informal), dupe,
ensnare, entrap, fool, hoax, hoodwink,
impose upon, kid (informal), lead
(someone) on (informal), mislead, outwit,
pull a fast one (slang), pull the wool over
(someone's) eyes, stiff (slang), sting
(informal), swindle, take for a ride
(informal), trick **2 be deceived by** = **be
taken in (by)**, be made a fool of, be the
dupe of, bite, fall for, fall into a trap, swallow
(informal), swallow hook, line, and sinker
(informal), take the bait

deceiver noun = **liar**, cheat, con man
(informal), double-dealer, fraud, impostor,
swindler, trickster

decency noun = **respectability**,
appropriateness, civility, correctness,
courtesy, decorum, etiquette, fitness, good
form, good manners, modesty, propriety,
seemliness

decent adjective **1** = **satisfactory**,
acceptable, adequate, ample, average,
competent, fair, passable, reasonable,
sufficient, tolerable **2** = **respectable**, chaste,
decorous, delicate, modest, nice, polite,
presentable, proper, pure **3** = **proper**,
appropriate, becoming, befitting, comely,
comme il faut, fit, fitting, seemly, suitable **4**
Informal = **kind**, accommodating, courteous,
friendly, generous, gracious, helpful,
obliging, thoughtful
➤ **Antonyms**
≠**satisfactory**: clumsy, inept, unsatisfactory
≠**proper**: awkward, immodest, improper,
incorrect, indecent, unseemly, unsuitable
≠**kind**: awkward, discourteous

deception noun **1** = **trickery**, craftiness,
cunning, deceit, deceitfulness, deceptiveness,
dissimulation, duplicity, fraud, fraudulence,
guile, hypocrisy, imposition, insincerity,
legerdemain, treachery **2** = **trick**, artifice,
bluff, canard, cheat, decoy, feint, fraud,
hoax, hokum (slang, chiefly U.S. & Canad.),
illusion, imposture, leg-pull (Brit. informal),
lie, pork pie (Brit. slang), porky (Brit. slang),
ruse, sham, snare, snow job (slang, chiefly
U.S. & Canad.), stratagem, subterfuge, wile
➤ **Antonyms**
≠**trickery**: artlessness, candour, fidelity,
frankness, honesty, openness,
scrupulousness, straightforwardness,
trustworthiness, truthfulness

deceptive adjective = **misleading**,
ambiguous, deceitful, delusive, dishonest,
fake, fallacious, false, fraudulent, illusory,
mock, specious, spurious, unreliable

decide verb = **reach** or **come to a decision**,
adjudge, adjudicate, choose, come to a
conclusion, commit oneself, conclude,
decree, determine, elect, end, make a
decision, make up one's mind, purpose,

resolve, settle, tip the balance
➤ Antonyms
be indecisive, be unable to decide, blow hot
and cold (*informal*), dither (*chiefly Brit.*),
falter, fluctuate, hesitate, hum and haw,
seesaw, shillyshally (*informal*), swither
(*Scot.*), vacillate
decided *adjective* **1 = definite**, absolute,
categorical, certain, clear-cut, distinct,
express, indisputable, positive, pronounced,
unambiguous, undeniable, undisputed,
unequivocal, unquestionable **2
= determined**, assertive, decisive, deliberate,
emphatic, firm, resolute, strong-willed,
unfaltering, unhesitating
➤ Antonyms
≠**definite**: doubtful, dubious, questionable,
undetermined ≠**determined**: hesitant,
indecisive, irresolute, undetermined, weak
decidedly *adverb* **= definitely**, absolutely,
certainly, clearly, decisively, distinctly,
downright, positively, unequivocally,
unmistakably
deciding *adjective* **= determining**, chief,
conclusive, critical, crucial, decisive,
influential, prime, principal, significant
decimate *verb* **= devastate**, destroy, lay
waste, ravage, wreak havoc on
decipher *verb* **= figure out** (*informal*),
construe, crack, decode, deduce, explain,
interpret, make out, read, reveal, solve, suss
(out) (*slang*), understand, unfold, unravel
decision *noun* **1 = judgment**, arbitration,
conclusion, finding, outcome, resolution,
result, ruling, sentence, settlement, verdict **2
= decisiveness**, determination, firmness,
purpose, purposefulness, resoluteness,
resolution, resolve, strength of mind *or* will
decisive *adjective* **1 = crucial**, absolute,
conclusive, critical, definite, definitive,
fateful, final, influential, momentous,
positive, significant **2 = resolute**, decided,
determined, firm, forceful, incisive,
strong-minded, trenchant
➤ Antonyms
≠**crucial**: doubtful, indecisive, uncertain,
undecided ≠**resolute**: hesitant, hesitating,
indecisive, in two minds (*informal*),
irresolute, pussy-footing (*informal*),
uncertain, undecided, vacillating
deck *verb* **1 = decorate**, adorn, apparel
(*archaic*), array, attire, beautify, bedeck,
bedight (*archaic*), bedizen (*archaic*), clothe,
dress, embellish, engarland, festoon,
garland, grace, ornament, trim **2 deck up** *or*
out = dress up, doll up (*slang*), get ready,
prettify, pretty up, prink, rig out, tog up *or*
out, trick out
declaim *verb* **1 = orate**, harangue, hold
forth, lecture, perorate, proclaim, rant,

recite, speak, spiel (*informal*) **2 = declaim
against = protest against**, attack, decry,
denounce, inveigh, rail
declamation *noun* **= oration**, address,
harangue, lecture, rant, recitation, speech,
tirade
declaration *noun* **1 = statement**,
acknowledgment, affirmation, assertion,
attestation, averment, avowal, deposition,
disclosure, protestation, revelation, testimony
2 = announcement, edict, manifesto,
notification, proclamation, profession,
promulgation, pronouncement,
pronunciamento
declaratory, declarative *adjective*
= affirmative, definite, demonstrative,
enunciatory, explanatory, expository,
expressive, positive
declare *verb* **1 = state**, affirm, announce,
assert, asseverate, attest, aver, avow, certify,
claim, confirm, maintain, notify, proclaim,
profess, pronounce, swear, testify, utter,
validate **2 = make known**, confess, convey,
disclose, manifest, reveal, show
decline *verb* **1 = lessen**, decrease, diminish,
drop, dwindle, ebb, fade, fail, fall, fall off,
flag, shrink, sink, wane **2 = deteriorate**,
decay, degenerate, droop, languish, pine,
weaken, worsen **3 = refuse**, abstain, avoid,
deny, forgo, reject, say 'no', send one's
regrets, turn down **4 = slope**, descend, dip,
sink, slant ♦ *noun* **5 = lessening**, abatement,
diminution, downturn, drop, dwindling,
falling off, recession, slump **6
= deterioration**, decay, decrepitude,
degeneration, enfeeblement, failing, senility,
weakening, worsening **7 = consumption**,
phthisis, tuberculosis **8 = slope**, declivity, hill,
incline
➤ Antonyms
verb ≠**lessen**: increase, rise ≠**deteriorate**:
improve ≠**refuse**: accept, agree, consent
♦ *noun* ≠**lessening**: rise, upswing
≠**deterioration**: improvement
decode *verb* **= decipher**, crack, decrypt,
interpret, solve, unscramble, work out
➤ Antonyms
encipher, encode, encrypt, scramble
decompose *verb* **1 = rot**, break up,
crumble, decay, fall apart, fester, putrefy,
spoil **2 = break down**, analyse, atomize,
break up, decompound, disintegrate, dissect,
dissolve, distil, separate
decomposition *noun* **1 = rot**, corruption,
decay, putrefaction, putrescence, putridity **2
= breakdown**, atomization, disintegration,
dissolution, division
decor *noun* **= decoration**, colour scheme,
furnishing style, ornamentation
decorate *verb* **1 = adorn**, beautify, bedeck,

deck, embellish, engarland, enrich, festoon, grace, ornament, trim **2 = do up** (*informal*), colour, furbish, paint, paper, renovate, wallpaper **3 = pin a medal on**, cite, confer an honour on *or* upon

decoration *noun* **1 = adornment**, beautification, elaboration, embellishment, enrichment, garnishing, ornamentation, trimming **2 = ornament**, arabesque, bauble, cartouch(e), curlicue, falderal, festoon, flounce, flourish, frill, furbelow, garnish, scroll, spangle, trimmings, trinket **3 = medal**, award, badge, colours, emblem, garter, order, ribbon, star

decorative *adjective* **= ornamental**, adorning, arty-crafty, beautifying, enhancing, fancy, nonfunctional, pretty

decorous *adjective* **= proper**, appropriate, becoming, befitting, comely, *comme il faut*, correct, decent, dignified, fit, fitting, mannerly, polite, refined, sedate, seemly, staid, suitable, well-behaved
➤ **Antonyms**
inapposite, inappropriate, malapropos, out of keeping, unbefitting, undignified, unseemly

decorum *noun* **= propriety**, behaviour, breeding, courtliness, decency, deportment, dignity, etiquette, gentility, good grace, good manners, gravity, politeness, politesse, protocol, punctilio, respectability, seemliness
➤ **Antonyms**
bad manners, churlishness, impoliteness, impropriety, indecorum, rudeness, unseemliness

decoy *noun* **1 = lure**, attraction, bait, ensnarement, enticement, inducement, pretence, trap ◆ *verb* **2 = lure**, allure, bait, deceive, ensnare, entice, entrap, inveigle, seduce, tempt

decrease *verb* **1 = lessen**, abate, contract, curtail, cut down, decline, diminish, drop, dwindle, ease, fall off, lower, peter out, reduce, shrink, slacken, subside, wane ◆ *noun* **2 = lessening**, abatement, contraction, cutback, decline, diminution, downturn, dwindling, ebb, falling off, loss, reduction, shrinkage, subsidence
➤ **Antonyms**
verb ≠**lessen**: enlarge, expand, extend, increase ◆ *noun* ≠**lessening**: expansion, extension, growth

decree *noun* **1 = law**, act, canon, command, demand, dictum, edict, enactment, mandate, order, ordinance, precept, proclamation, regulation, ruling, statute ◆ *verb* **2 = order**, command, decide, demand, determine, dictate, enact, establish, lay down, ordain, prescribe, proclaim, pronounce, rule

decrepit *adjective* **1 = weak**, aged, crippled, debilitated, doddering, effete, feeble, frail, incapacitated, infirm, past it, superannuated, wasted **2 = worn-out**, antiquated, battered, beat-up (*informal*), broken-down, deteriorated, dilapidated, ramshackle, rickety, run-down, tumbledown, weather-beaten

decry *verb* **= condemn**, abuse, asperse, belittle, blame, blast, censure, criticize, cry down, denigrate, denounce, depreciate, derogate, detract, devalue, discredit, disparage, excoriate, lambast(e), put down, rail against, run down, tear into (*informal*), traduce, underestimate, underrate, undervalue

dedicate *verb* **1 = devote**, commit, give over to, pledge, surrender **2 = inscribe**, address, assign, offer **3 = consecrate**, bless, hallow, sanctify, set apart

dedicated *adjective* **= devoted**, committed, enthusiastic, given over to, purposeful, single-minded, sworn, wholehearted, zealous
➤ **Antonyms**
indifferent, uncaring, uncommitted, unconcerned, uninterested

dedication *noun* **1 = devotion**, adherence, allegiance, commitment, devotedness, faithfulness, loyalty, single-mindedness, wholeheartedness **2 = inscription**, address, message **3 = consecration**, hallowing, sanctification
➤ **Antonyms**
≠**devotion**: apathy, coolness, indifference, insensibility, torpor, unconcern, uninterestedness

deduce *verb* **= conclude**, derive, draw, gather, glean, infer, put two and two together, read between the lines, reason, take to mean, understand

deduct *verb* **= subtract**, decrease by, knock off (*informal*), reduce by, remove, take away, take from, take off, take out, withdraw
➤ **Antonyms**
add, add to, enlarge

deduction *noun* **1 = subtraction**, abatement, allowance, decrease, diminution, discount, reduction, withdrawal **2 = conclusion**, assumption, consequence, corollary, finding, inference, reasoning, result

deed *noun* **1 = action**, achievement, act, exploit, fact, feat, performance, reality, truth **2** *Law* **= document**, contract, indenture, instrument, title, title deed, transaction

deem *verb* **= consider**, account, believe, conceive, esteem, estimate, hold, imagine, judge, reckon, regard, suppose, think

deep *adjective* **1 = wide**, abyssal, bottomless, broad, far, profound, unfathomable, yawning **2 = mysterious**, abstract, abstruse,

arcane, esoteric, hidden, obscure, recondite, secret **3 = intense**, extreme, grave, great, profound, serious (*informal*), unqualified **4 = wise**, acute, discerning, learned, penetrating, sagacious **5 = cunning**, artful, astute, canny, designing, devious, insidious, knowing, scheming, shrewd **6 = absorbed**, engrossed, immersed, lost, preoccupied, rapt **7 = dark**, intense, rich, strong, vivid **8 = low**, bass, booming, full-toned, low-pitched, resonant, sonorous ◆ *noun* **9 = middle**, culmination, dead, mid point **10 the deep** *Poetic* **= ocean**, briny (*informal*), high seas, main, sea ◆ *adverb* **11 = far into**, deeply, far down, late
➤ **Antonyms**
adjective ≠**wide**: shallow ≠**mysterious**: shallow ≠**intense**: shallow, superficial ≠**wise**: simple ≠**cunning**: shallow, simple ≠**dark**: light, pale ≠**low**: high, sharp

deepen *verb* **1 = dig out**, dredge, excavate, hollow, scoop out, scrape out **2 = intensify**, grow, increase, magnify, reinforce, strengthen

deeply *adverb* **1 = thoroughly**, completely, gravely, profoundly, seriously, severely, to the core, to the heart, to the quick **2 = intensely**, acutely, affectingly, distressingly, feelingly, mournfully, movingly, passionately, sadly

deep-rooted *or* **deep-seated** *adjective* **= fixed**, confirmed, dyed-in-the-wool, entrenched, ineradicable, ingrained, inveterate, rooted, settled, subconscious, unconscious
➤ **Antonyms**
eradicable, exterior, external, on the surface, shallow, skin-deep, slight, superficial, surface

deface *verb* **= vandalize**, blemish, damage, deform, destroy, disfigure, impair, injure, mar, mutilate, obliterate, spoil, sully, tarnish, total (*slang*), trash (*slang*)

defacement *noun* **= vandalism**, blemish, damage, destruction, disfigurement, distortion, impairment, injury, mutilation

de facto *adverb* **1 = in fact**, actually, in effect, in reality, really ◆ *adjective* **2 = actual**, existing, real

defamation *noun* **= slander**, aspersion, calumny, character assassination, denigration, disparagement, libel, obloquy, opprobrium, scandal, slur, smear, traducement, vilification

defamatory *adjective* **= slanderous**, abusive, calumnious, contumelious, denigrating, derogatory, disparaging, injurious, insulting, libellous, vilifying, vituperative

defame *verb* **= slander**, asperse, bad-mouth (*slang, chiefly U.S. & Canad.*), belie,

besmirch, blacken, calumniate, cast a slur on, cast aspersions on, denigrate, detract, discredit, disgrace, dishonour, disparage, knock (*informal*), libel, malign, rubbish (*informal*), slag (off) (*slang*), smear, speak evil of, stigmatize, traduce, vilify, vituperate

default *noun* **1 = failure**, absence, defect, deficiency, dereliction, evasion, fault, lack, lapse, neglect, nonpayment, omission, want ◆ *verb* **2 = fail**, bilk, defraud, dodge, evade, levant (*Brit.*), neglect, rat (*informal*), swindle, welsh (*slang*)

defaulter *noun* **= nonpayer**, delinquent, embezzler, levanter (*Brit.*), offender, peculator, welsher (*slang*)

defeat *verb* **1 = beat**, blow out of the water (*slang*), clobber (*slang*), conquer, crush, lick (*informal*), make mincemeat of (*informal*), master, outplay, overpower, overthrow, overwhelm, pip at the post, quell, repulse, rout, run rings around (*informal*), stuff (*slang*), subdue, subjugate, tank (*slang*), trounce, undo, vanquish, wipe the floor with (*informal*), worst **2 = frustrate**, baffle, balk, confound, disappoint, discomfit, foil, get the better of, ruin, thwart ◆ *noun* **3 = conquest**, beating, debacle, overthrow, pasting (*slang*), repulse, rout, trouncing, vanquishment **4 = frustration**, disappointment, discomfiture, failure, rebuff, repulse, reverse, setback, thwarting
➤ **Antonyms**
verb ≠**beat**: bow, cave in (*informal*), lose, submit, succumb, surrender, yield ◆ *noun* ≠**conquest**: success, triumph, victory

defeated *adjective* **= beaten**, balked, bested, checkmated, conquered, crushed, licked (*informal*), overcome, overpowered, overwhelmed, routed, thrashed, thwarted, trounced, vanquished, worsted
➤ **Antonyms**
conquering, dominant, glorious, successful, triumphal, triumphant, undefeated, victorious, winning

defeatist *noun* **1 = pessimist**, prophet of doom, quitter, submitter, yielder ◆ *adjective* **2 = pessimistic**

defect *noun* **1 = imperfection**, blemish, blotch, error, failing, fault, flaw, foible, mistake, spot, taint, want **2 = deficiency**, absence, default, frailty, inadequacy, lack, shortcoming, weakness ◆ *verb* **3 = desert**, abandon, apostatize, break faith, change sides, go over, rebel, revolt, tergiversate, walk out on (*informal*)

defection *noun* **= desertion**, abandonment, apostasy, backsliding, dereliction, rebellion, revolt

defective *adjective* **1 = faulty**, broken, deficient, flawed, imperfect, inadequate,

incomplete, insufficient, not working, on the blink (*slang*), out of order, scant, short **2 = abnormal**, mentally deficient, retarded, subnormal
➤ **Antonyms**
≠**faulty**: adequate, intact, perfect, whole, working ≠**abnormal**: normal

defector *noun* = **deserter**, apostate, rat (*informal*), recreant (*archaic*), renegade, runagate (*archaic*), tergiversator, turncoat

defence *noun* **1 = protection**, armament, cover, deterrence, guard, immunity, resistance, safeguard, security, shelter **2 = shield**, barricade, bastion, buckler, bulwark, buttress, fastness, fortification, rampart **3 = argument**, apologia, apology, excuse, exoneration, explanation, extenuation, justification, plea, vindication **4** *Law* = **plea**, alibi, case, declaration, denial, pleading, rebuttal, testimony

defenceless *adjective* = **helpless**, endangered, exposed, naked, powerless, unarmed, unguarded, unprotected, vulnerable, wide open
➤ **Antonyms**
free from harm, guarded, out of harm's way, protected, safe, safe and sound, secure

defend *verb* **1 = protect**, cover, fortify, guard, keep safe, preserve, safeguard, screen, secure, shelter, shield, ward off, watch over **2 = support**, assert, champion, endorse, espouse, justify, maintain, plead, speak up for, stand by, stand up for, stick up for (*informal*), sustain, uphold, vindicate

defendant *noun* = **the accused**, appellant, defence, litigant, offender, prisoner at the bar, respondent

defender *noun* **1 = protector**, bodyguard, escort, guard **2 = supporter**, advocate, champion, patron, sponsor, vindicator

defensible *adjective* **1 = justifiable**, pardonable, permissible, plausible, tenable, valid, vindicable **2 = secure**, holdable, impregnable, safe, unassailable
➤ **Antonyms**
≠**justifiable**: inexcusable, insupportable, unforgivable, unjustifiable, unpardonable, untenable, wrong

defensive *adjective* = **on guard**, averting, defending, on the defensive, opposing, protective, safeguarding, uptight (*informal*), watchful, withstanding

defensively *adverb* = **in self-defence**, at bay, in defence, on guard, on the defensive, suspiciously

defer¹ *verb* = **postpone**, adjourn, delay, hold over, procrastinate, prorogue, protract, put off, put on ice (*informal*), put on the back burner (*informal*), set aside, shelve, suspend, table, take a rain check on (*U.S. & Canad. informal*)

defer² *verb* = **comply**, accede, bow, capitulate, give in, give way to, respect, submit, yield

deference *noun* **1 = respect**, attention, civility, consideration, courtesy, esteem, homage, honour, obeisance, politeness, regard, reverence, thoughtfulness, veneration **2 = obedience**, acquiescence, capitulation, complaisance, compliance, obeisance, submission, yielding
➤ **Antonyms**
≠**respect**: contempt, discourtesy, dishonour, disregard, disrespect, impertinence, impoliteness, impudence, incivility, insolence, irreverence, lack of respect, rudeness ≠**obedience**: disobedience, insubordination, noncompliance, nonobservance, revolt

deferential *adjective* = **respectful**, civil, complaisant, considerate, courteous, dutiful, ingratiating, obedient, obeisant, obsequious, polite, regardful, reverential, submissive

deferment, deferral *noun* = **postponement**, adjournment, delay, moratorium, putting off, stay, suspension

defiance *noun* = **resistance**, challenge, confrontation, contempt, contumacy, disobedience, disregard, insolence, insubordination, opposition, provocation, rebelliousness, recalcitrance, spite
➤ **Antonyms**
accordance, acquiescence, compliance, deference, obedience, observance, regard, respect, subservience

defiant *adjective* = **resisting**, aggressive, audacious, bold, challenging, contumacious, daring, disobedient, insolent, insubordinate, mutinous, provocative, rebellious, recalcitrant, refractory, truculent
➤ **Antonyms**
cowardly, meek, obedient, respectful, submissive

deficiency *noun* **1 = lack**, absence, dearth, deficit, inadequacy, insufficiency, scantiness, scarcity, shortage **2 = failing**, defect, demerit, fault, flaw, frailty, imperfection, shortcoming, weakness
➤ **Antonyms**
≠**lack**: abundance, adequacy, sufficiency, superfluity, surfeit

deficient *adjective* **1 = lacking**, exiguous, inadequate, insufficient, meagre, pathetic, scant, scanty, scarce, short, skimpy, wanting **2 = unsatisfactory**, defective, faulty, flawed, impaired, imperfect, incomplete, inferior, weak

deficit *noun* = **shortfall**, arrears, default, deficiency, loss, shortage

defiled *adjective* **1 = unclean**, besmirched,

dirtied, impure, polluted, spoilt, tainted **2** = **desecrated**, profaned **3** = **dishonoured**, ravished, violated
➤ **Antonyms**
≠**unclean**: clean, immaculate, spotless, uncontaminated, uncorrupted, undefiled, unstained, unsullied, untainted
≠**dishonoured**: chaste, innocent

define verb **1** = **describe**, characterize, designate, detail, determine, explain, expound, interpret, specify, spell out **2** = **mark out**, bound, circumscribe, delimit, delineate, demarcate, limit, outline

definite adjective **1** = **clear**, black-and-white, clear-cut, clearly defined, cut-and-dried (informal), determined, exact, explicit, express, fixed, marked, obvious, particular, precise, specific **2** = **certain**, assured, decided, guaranteed, positive, settled, sure
➤ **Antonyms**
≠**clear**: confused, fuzzy, general, hazy, ill-defined, imprecise, indefinite, indeterminate, indistinct, inexact, loose, obscure, unclear, undetermined, vague
≠**certain**: uncertain, undecided

definitely adverb = **certainly**, absolutely, beyond any doubt, categorically, clearly, come hell or high water (informal), decidedly, easily, far and away, finally, indubitably, needless to say, obviously, plainly, positively, surely, undeniably, unequivocally, unmistakably, unquestionably, without doubt, without fail, without question

definition noun **1** = **explanation**, clarification, elucidation, exposition, statement of meaning **2** = **description**, delimitation, delineation, demarcation, determination, fixing, outlining, settling **3** = **sharpness**, clarity, contrast, distinctness, focus, precision

definitive adjective **1** = **final**, absolute, complete, conclusive, decisive **2** = **authoritative**, exhaustive, mother of all (informal), perfect, reliable, ultimate

deflate verb **1** = **collapse**, contract, empty, exhaust, flatten, puncture, shrink, void **2** = **humiliate**, chasten, dash, debunk (informal), disconcert, dispirit, humble, mortify, put down (slang), squash, take the wind out of (someone's) sails **3** Economics = **reduce**, decrease, depreciate, depress, devalue, diminish
➤ **Antonyms**
≠**collapse**: balloon, bloat, blow up, dilate, distend, enlarge, expand, increase, inflate, puff up or out, pump up, swell ≠**humiliate**: boost, expand, increase, inflate

deflect verb = **turn aside**, bend, deviate, diverge, glance off, ricochet, shy, sidetrack, slew, swerve, turn, twist, veer, wind

deflection noun = **deviation**, aberration, bend, declination, divergence, drift, refraction, swerve, turning aside, veer

deform verb **1** = **distort**, buckle, contort, gnarl, malform, mangle, misshape, twist, warp **2** = **disfigure**, cripple, deface, injure, maim, mar, mutilate, ruin, spoil

deformed adjective **1** = **distorted**, bent, blemished, crooked, malformed, mangled, misshapen, twisted, warped **2** = **disfigured**, crippled, maimed, marred, misbegotten

deformity noun **1** = **abnormality**, defect, disfigurement, malformation **2** = **distortion**, irregularity, misproportion, misshapenness

defraud verb = **cheat**, beguile, bilk, con (informal), cozen, delude, diddle (informal), do (slang), dupe, embezzle, fleece, gull (archaic), gyp (slang), outwit, pilfer, pull a fast one on (informal), rip off (slang), rob, rook (slang), skin (slang), stiff (slang), stitch up (slang), swindle, trick

deft adjective = **skilful**, able, adept, adroit, agile, clever, dexterous, expert, handy, neat, nimble, proficient
➤ **Antonyms**
awkward, bumbling, cack-handed (informal), clumsy, gauche, inept, maladroit, unskilful

defunct adjective **1** = **dead**, deceased, departed, extinct, gone **2** = **obsolete**, a dead letter, bygone, expired, inoperative, invalid, nonexistent, not functioning, out of commission

defy verb **1** = **resist**, beard, brave, confront, contemn, despise, disobey, disregard, face, flout, hurl defiance at, scorn, slight, spurn **2** = **foil**, baffle, call (someone's) bluff, defeat, elude, frustrate, repel, repulse, thwart, withstand **3** Formal = **challenge**, dare, provoke

degenerate adjective **1** = **depraved**, base, corrupt, debased, debauched, decadent, degenerated, degraded, deteriorated, dissolute, fallen, immoral, low, mean, perverted, pervy (slang) ♦ verb **2** = **worsen**, decay, decline, decrease, deteriorate, fall off, go to pot, lapse, regress, retrogress, rot, sink, slip

degeneration noun = **deterioration**, debasement, decline, degeneracy, descent, dissipation, dissolution, regression

degradation noun **1** = **disgrace**, discredit, dishonour, humiliation, ignominy, mortification, shame **2** = **deterioration**, abasement, debasement, decadence, decline, degeneracy, degeneration, demotion, derogation, downgrading, perversion

degrade verb **1** = **demean**, cheapen, corrupt, debase, discredit, disgrace,

dishonour, humble, humiliate, impair, injure, pervert, shame, vitiate **2 = adulterate**, dilute, doctor, mix, thin, water, water down, weaken **3 = demote**, break, cashier, depose, downgrade, lower, reduce to inferior rank
➤ **Antonyms**
≠**demean**: dignify, enhance, ennoble, honour, improve ≠**demote**: elevate, promote, raise

degraded *adjective* = **disgraced**, abandoned, base, corrupt, debased, debauched, decadent, depraved, despicable, disreputable, dissolute, low, mean, profligate, sordid, vicious, vile

degrading *adjective* = **demeaning**, cheapening, contemptible, debasing, disgraceful, dishonourable, humiliating, infra dig (*informal*), lowering, shameful, undignified, unworthy

degree *noun* **1 = stage**, division, extent, gradation, grade, interval, limit, mark, measure, notch, point, rung, scale, step, unit **2 = rank**, class, grade, level, order, position, standing, station, status **3 = extent**, ambit, calibre, intensity, level, measure, proportion, quality, quantity, range, rate, ratio, scale, scope, severity, standard **4 by degrees = little by little**, bit by bit, gently, gradually, imperceptibly, inch by inch, slowly, step by step

deign *verb* = **condescend**, consent, deem worthy, lower oneself, see fit, stoop, think fit

deity *noun* = **god**, celestial being, divine being, divinity, goddess, godhead, idol, immortal, supreme being

dejected *adjective* = **downhearted**, blue, cast down, crestfallen, depressed, despondent, disconsolate, disheartened, dismal, doleful, down, downcast, down in the dumps (*informal*), gloomy, glum, low, low-spirited, melancholy, miserable, morose, sad, sick as a parrot (*informal*), woebegone, wretched
➤ **Antonyms**
blithe, cheerful, chirpy (*informal*), encouraged, genial, happy, joyous, light-hearted, upbeat (*informal*)

dejection *noun* = **low spirits**, blues, depression, despair, despondency, doldrums, downheartedness, dumps (*informal*), gloom, gloominess, heavy-heartedness, melancholy, sadness, sorrow, the hump (*Brit. informal*), unhappiness

de jure *adverb* = **legally**, according to the law, by right, rightfully

delay *verb* **1 = put off**, beat about the bush, defer, hold over, play for time, postpone, procrastinate, prolong, protract, put on the back burner (*informal*), shelve, stall, suspend, table, take a rain check on (*U.S. &*

Canad. informal), temporize **2 = hold up**, arrest, bog down, check, detain, halt, hinder, hold back, impede, obstruct, retard, set back, slow up, stop, throw a spanner in the works **3 = drag one's feet** *or* **heels** (*Informal*), dawdle, dilly-dally (*informal*), drag, lag, linger, loiter, tarry ♦ *noun* **4 = putting off**, deferment, postponement, procrastination, stay, suspension **5 = hold-up**, check, detention, hindrance, impediment, interruption, interval, obstruction, setback, stoppage, wait **6 = dawdling**, dilly-dallying (*informal*), lingering, loitering, tarrying
➤ **Antonyms**
verb ≠**hold up**: accelerate, advance, dispatch, expedite, facilitate, forward, hasten, hurry, precipitate, press, promote, quicken, rush, speed (up), urge

delectable *adjective* = **delicious**, adorable, agreeable, appetizing, charming, dainty, delightful, enjoyable, enticing, gratifying, inviting, luscious, lush, pleasant, pleasurable, satisfying, scrumptious (*informal*), tasty, toothsome, yummy (*slang*)
➤ **Antonyms**
awful, disagreeable, disgusting, distasteful, dreadful, horrible, horrid, nasty, offensive, terrible, unappetizing, unpleasant, yucky *or* yukky (*slang*)

delectation *noun* Formal = **enjoyment**, amusement, delight, diversion, entertainment, gratification, happiness, jollies (*slang*), pleasure, refreshment, relish, satisfaction

delegate *noun* **1 = representative**, agent, ambassador, commissioner, deputy, envoy, legate, vicar ♦ *verb* **2 = entrust**, assign, consign, devolve, give, hand over, pass on, relegate, transfer **3 = appoint**, accredit, authorize, commission, depute, designate, empower, mandate

delegation *noun* **1 = deputation**, commission, contingent, embassy, envoys, legation, mission **2 = devolution**, assignment, commissioning, committal, deputizing, entrustment, relegation

delete *verb* = **remove**, blot out, blue-pencil, cancel, cross out, cut out, dele, edit, edit out, efface, erase, excise, expunge, obliterate, rub out, strike out

deliberate *adjective* **1 = intentional**, calculated, conscious, considered, designed, planned, prearranged, premeditated, purposeful, studied, thoughtful, wilful **2 = unhurried**, careful, cautious, circumspect, heedful, measured, methodical, ponderous, prudent, slow, thoughtful, wary ♦ *verb* **3 = consider**, cogitate, consult, debate, discuss, meditate, mull over, ponder, reflect, think, weigh

➤ **Antonyms**

adjective ≠**intentional:** accidental, inadvertent, unconscious, unintended, unpremeditated, unthinking ≠**unhurried:** fast, haphazard, hasty, heedless, hurried, impetuous, impulsive, rash

deliberately *adverb* = **intentionally,** by design, calculatingly, consciously, determinedly, emphatically, in cold blood, knowingly, on purpose, pointedly, resolutely, studiously, wilfully, wittingly

deliberation *noun* **1** = **consideration,** calculation, care, carefulness, caution, circumspection, cogitation, coolness, forethought, meditation, prudence, purpose, reflection, speculation, study, thought, wariness **2** = **discussion,** conference, consultation, debate

delicacy *noun* **1** = **fineness,** accuracy, daintiness, elegance, exquisiteness, lightness, nicety, precision, subtlety **2** = **fragility,** debility, flimsiness, frailness, frailty, infirmity, slenderness, tenderness, weakness **3** = **treat,** bonne bouche, dainty, luxury, relish, savoury, titbit **4** = **fastidiousness,** discrimination, finesse, purity, refinement, sensibility, taste **5** = **sensitivity,** sensitiveness, tact

delicate *adjective* **1** = **fine,** accurate, deft, detailed, elegant, exquisite, graceful, minute, precise, skilled, subtle **2** = **subtle,** choice, dainty, delicious, fine, savoury, tender **3** = **soft,** faint, muted, pastel, subdued, subtle **4** = **fragile,** flimsy, frail, slender, slight, tender, weak **5** = **sickly,** ailing, debilitated, frail **6** = **difficult,** built on sand, critical, precarious, sensitive, sticky (*informal*), ticklish, touchy **7** = **considerate,** diplomatic, discreet, sensitive, tactful **8** = **fastidious,** careful, critical, discriminating, nice, prudish, pure, refined, scrupulous, squeamish

➤ **Antonyms**

≠**fine:** coarse, crude, indelicate, unrefined ≠**subtle:** harsh, strong ≠**soft:** bright, harsh, rough ≠**sickly:** healthy, strong ≠**considerate:** harsh, inconsiderate, indelicate, insensitive, rough ≠**fastidious:** careless, crude, rough

delicately *adverb* **1** = **finely,** carefully, daintily, deftly, elegantly, exquisitely, gracefully, lightly, precisely, skilfully, softly, subtly **2** = **tactfully,** diplomatically, sensitively

delicious *adjective* **1** = **delectable,** ambrosial, appetizing, choice, dainty, luscious, mouthwatering, nectareous, palatable, savoury, scrumptious (*informal*), tasty, toothsome, yummy (*slang*) **2** = **delightful,** agreeable, charming, enjoyable, entertaining, exquisite, pleasant, pleasing

➤ **Antonyms**

≠**delectable:** disagreeable, distasteful, unpleasant

delight *noun* **1** = **pleasure,** ecstasy, enjoyment, felicity, gladness, glee, gratification, happiness, jollies (*slang*), joy, rapture, transport ♦ *verb* **2** = **please,** amuse, charm, cheer, divert, enchant, gratify, ravish, rejoice, satisfy, thrill **3 delight in** = **take pleasure in,** appreciate, enjoy, feast on, glory in, indulge in, like, love, luxuriate in, relish, revel in, savour

➤ **Antonyms**

noun ≠**pleasure:** disapprobation, disfavour, dislike, displeasure, dissatisfaction, distaste ♦ *verb* ≠**please:** disgust, displease, dissatisfy, gall, irk, offend, upset, vex

delighted *adjective* = **pleased,** blissed out, captivated, charmed, cock-a-hoop, ecstatic, elated, enchanted, gladdened, happy, in seventh heaven, joyous, jubilant, overjoyed, over the moon (*informal*), rapt, sent, thrilled

delightful *adjective* = **pleasant,** agreeable, amusing, captivating, charming, congenial, delectable, enchanting, engaging, enjoyable, entertaining, fascinating, gratifying, heavenly, pleasing, pleasurable, rapturous, ravishing, thrilling

➤ **Antonyms**

disagreeable, displeasing, distasteful, horrid, nasty, unpleasant

delinquency *noun* = **crime,** fault, misbehaviour, misconduct, misdeed, misdemeanour, offence, wrongdoing

delinquent *noun* = **criminal,** culprit, defaulter, juvenile delinquent, lawbreaker, malefactor, miscreant, offender, villain, wrongdoer, young offender

delirious *adjective* **1** = **mad,** crazy, demented, deranged, gonzo (*slang*), incoherent, insane, light-headed, raving, unhinged **2** = **ecstatic,** beside oneself, blissed out, carried away, Corybantic, excited, frantic, frenzied, hysterical, sent, wild

➤ **Antonyms**

calm, clear-headed, coherent, *compos mentis,* in one's right mind, lucid, rational, sane, sensible

delirium *noun* **1** = **madness,** aberration, derangement, hallucination, insanity, lunacy, raving **2** = **frenzy,** ecstasy, fever, fury, hysteria, passion, rage

deliver *verb* **1** = **carry,** bear, bring, cart, convey, distribute, transport **2** = **hand over,** cede, commit, give up, grant, make over, relinquish, resign, surrender, transfer, turn over, yield **3** = **give,** announce, declare, give forth, present, proclaim, pronounce, publish, read, utter **4** = **release,** acquit, discharge, emancipate, free, liberate, loose, ransom, redeem, rescue, save **5** = **strike**, administer, aim, deal, direct, give, inflict, launch, throw **6** = **provide**, discharge, dispense, feed, give forth, purvey, release, supply

deliverance noun = **release**, emancipation, escape, liberation, ransom, redemption, rescue, salvation

delivery noun **1** = **handing over**, consignment, conveyance, dispatch, distribution, surrender, transfer, transmission, transmittal **2** = **speech**, articulation, elocution, enunciation, intonation, utterance **3** = **childbirth**, confinement, labour, parturition **4** = **release**, deliverance, escape, liberation, rescue

delude verb = **deceive**, bamboozle (informal), beguile, cheat, con (informal), cozen, dupe, fool, gull (archaic), hoax, hoodwink, impose on, kid (informal), lead up the garden path (informal), misguide, mislead, pull the wool over someone's eyes, take for a ride (informal), take in (informal), trick

deluge noun **1** = **flood**, cataclysm, downpour, inundation, overflowing, spate, torrent **2** = **rush**, avalanche, barrage, flood, spate, torrent ◆ verb **3** = **flood**, douse, drench, drown, inundate, soak, submerge, swamp **4** = **overwhelm**, engulf, inundate, overload, overrun, swamp

delusion noun = **misconception**, deception, error, fallacy, false impression, fancy, hallucination, illusion, misapprehension, misbelief, mistake, phantasm, self-deception

de luxe adjective = **luxurious**, choice, costly, elegant, exclusive, expensive, gorgeous, grand, opulent, palatial, plush (informal), rich, select, special, splendid, splendiferous (facetious), sumptuous, superior

delve verb = **research**, burrow, dig into, examine, explore, ferret out, forage, investigate, look into, probe, ransack, rummage, search, unearth

demagogue noun = **agitator**, firebrand, haranguer, rabble-rouser, soapbox orator

demand verb **1** = **request**, ask, challenge, inquire, interrogate, question **2** = **require**, call for, cry out for, entail, involve, necessitate, need, take, want **3** = **claim**, exact, expect, insist on, order ◆ noun **4** = **request**, bidding, charge, inquiry, interrogation, order, question, requisition **5** = **need**, call, claim, market, necessity, requirement, want **6 in demand** = **sought after**, fashionable, in vogue, like gold dust, needed, popular, requested
> **Antonyms**
verb ≠ **require**, **claim**: come up with, contribute, furnish, give, grant, produce, provide, supply, yield

demanding adjective **1** = **difficult**, challenging, exacting, exhausting, exigent, hard, taxing, tough, trying, wearing **2** = **insistent**, clamorous, imperious, importunate, nagging, pressing, urgent
> **Antonyms**
≠ **difficult**: a piece of cake (informal), child's play (informal), easy, easy-peasy (slang), effortless, facile, no bother, painless, simple, straightforward, uncomplicated, undemanding

demarcate verb = **delimit**, define, determine, differentiate, distinguish between, fix, mark, separate

demarcation noun **1** = **delimitation**, differentiation, distinction, division, separation **2** = **limit**, bound, boundary, confine, enclosure, margin, pale

demean verb = **lower**, abase, debase, degrade, descend, humble, stoop

demeanour noun = **behaviour**, air, bearing, carriage, comportment, conduct, deportment, manner, mien

demented adjective = **mad**, barking (slang), barking mad (slang), crackbrained, crackpot (informal), crazed, crazy, daft (informal), deranged, distraught, doolally (slang), dotty (slang, chiefly Brit.), foolish, frenzied, gonzo (slang), idiotic, insane, loopy (informal), lunatic, maniacal, manic, non compos mentis, not the full shilling (informal), off one's trolley (slang), out to lunch (informal), unbalanced, unhinged, up the pole (slang), wacko or whacko (slang)
> **Antonyms**
all there (informal), compos mentis, in one's right mind, lucid, mentally sound, normal, of sound mind, rational, reasonable, sensible, sound

demise noun **1** = **failure**, collapse, downfall, end, fall, ruin **2** Euphemistic = **death**, decease, departure

democracy noun = **self-government**, commonwealth, government by the people, representative government, republic

democratic adjective = **self-governing**, autonomous, egalitarian, popular, populist, representative, republican

demolish verb **1** = **knock down**, bulldoze, destroy, dismantle, flatten, level, overthrow, pulverize, raze, ruin, tear down, total (slang), trash (slang) **2** = **defeat**, annihilate, blow out of the water (slang), destroy, lick (informal), master, overthrow, overturn, stuff (slang), tank (slang), undo, wipe the floor with (informal), wreck **3** Facetious = **devour**, consume, eat, gobble up, put away

> ➤ Antonyms
> ≠**knock down:** build, construct, create, repair, restore, strengthen

demolition *noun* = **knocking down,** bulldozing, destruction, explosion, levelling, razing, tearing down, wrecking

demon *noun* **1** = **evil spirit,** devil, fiend, ghoul, goblin, malignant spirit **2** = **monster,** devil, fiend, ghoul, rogue, villain **3** = **wizard,** ace (*informal*), addict, fanatic, fiend, master

demonic, demoniac, demoniacal *adjective* **1** = **devilish,** diabolic, diabolical, fiendish, hellish, infernal, satanic **2** = **frenzied,** crazed, frantic, frenetic, furious, hectic, like one possessed, mad, maniacal, manic

demonstrable *adjective* = **provable,** attestable, axiomatic, certain, evident, evincible, incontrovertible, indubitable, irrefutable, obvious, palpable, positive, self-evident, undeniable, unmistakable, verifiable

demonstrate *verb* **1** = **prove,** display, establish, evidence, evince, exhibit, indicate, manifest, show, testify to **2** = **show how,** describe, explain, illustrate, make clear, teach **3** = **march,** parade, picket, protest, rally

demonstration *noun* **1** = **march,** mass lobby, parade, picket, protest, rally, sit-in **2** = **explanation,** description, exposition, presentation, test, trial **3** = **proof,** affirmation, confirmation, display, evidence, exhibition, expression, illustration, manifestation, substantiation, testimony, validation

demonstrative *adjective* **1** = **open,** affectionate, effusive, emotional, expansive, expressive, gushing, loving, unreserved, unrestrained **2** = **indicative,** evincive, explanatory, expository, illustrative, symptomatic
> ➤ Antonyms
> ≠**open:** aloof, cold, contained, distant, formal, impassive, reserved, restrained, stiff, unaffectionate, undemonstrative, unemotional, unresponsive

demoralize *verb* = **dishearten,** cripple, daunt, deject, depress, disconcert, discourage, dispirit, enfeeble, psych out (*informal*), rattle (*informal*), sap, shake, undermine, unnerve, weaken
> ➤ Antonyms
> boost, cheer, egg on, encourage, gee up, hearten, spur

demoralized *adjective* = **disheartened,** broken, crushed, depressed, discouraged, dispirited, downcast, sick as a parrot (*informal*), subdued, unmanned, unnerved, weakened

demote *verb* = **downgrade,** declass,

degrade, disrate (*Naval*), kick downstairs (*slang*), lower in rank, relegate
> ➤ Antonyms
> advance, elevate, kick upstairs (*informal*), prefer, promote, raise, upgrade

demur *verb* **1** = **object,** balk, cavil, disagree, dispute, doubt, hesitate, pause, protest, refuse, take exception, waver ♦ *noun* **2** *As in* **without demur** = **objection,** compunction, demurral, demurrer, dissent, hesitation, misgiving, protest, qualm, scruple

demure *adjective* **1** = **shy,** decorous, diffident, grave, modest, reserved, reticent, retiring, sedate, sober, staid, unassuming **2** = **coy,** affected, bashful, niminy-piminy, priggish, prim, prissy (*informal*), prudish, strait-laced
> ➤ Antonyms
> brash, brazen, forward, immodest, impudent, shameless

den *noun* **1** = **lair,** cave, cavern, haunt, hide-out, hole, shelter **2** *Chiefly U.S.* = **study,** cloister, cubbyhole, hideaway, retreat, sanctuary, sanctum, snuggery

denial *noun* **1** = **negation,** adjuration, contradiction, disavowal, disclaimer, dismissal, dissent, renunciation, repudiation, retraction **2** = **refusal,** prohibition, rebuff, rejection, repulse, veto
> ➤ Antonyms
> ≠**negation:** acknowledgment, admission, affirmation, avowal, confession, declaration, disclosure, divulgence, profession, revelation

denigrate *verb* = **disparage,** asperse, bad-mouth (*slang, chiefly U.S. & Canad.*), belittle, besmirch, blacken, calumniate, decry, defame, impugn, knock (*informal*), malign, revile, rubbish (*informal*), run down, slag (off) (*slang*), slander, vilify
> ➤ Antonyms
> acclaim, admire, approve, cheer, compliment, eulogize, extol, honour, laud, praise, take one's hat off to

denigration *noun* = **disparagement,** aspersion, backbiting, defamation, detraction, obloquy, scandal, scurrility, slander, vilification

denominate *verb* = **name,** call, christen, designate, dub, entitle, phrase, style, term

denomination *noun* **1** = **religious group,** belief, communion, creed, persuasion, school, sect **2** = **unit,** grade, size, value **3** = **name,** appellation, designation, label, style, term, title **4** = **classification,** body, category, class, group

denote *verb* = **indicate,** betoken, designate, express, imply, import, mark, mean, show, signify, typify

denounce *verb* = **condemn,** accuse, arraign, attack, brand, castigate, censure, declaim against, decry, denunciate, excoriate, impugn, point a or the finger at, proscribe, revile, stigmatize, vilify

dense adjective 1 = **thick**, close, close-knit, compact, compressed, condensed, heavy, impenetrable, opaque, solid, substantial, thickset 2 Informal = **stupid**, blockish, braindead (informal), crass, dead from the neck up (informal), dozy (Brit. informal), dull, dumb (informal), obtuse, slow, slow-witted, stolid, thick, thick-witted
➤ Antonyms
≠**thick**: light, scattered, sparse, thin, transparent ≠**stupid**: alert, bright, clever, intelligent, quick

density noun 1 = **tightness**, body, bulk, closeness, compactness, consistency, crowdedness, denseness, impenetrability, mass, solidity, thickness 2 Informal = **stupidity**, crassness, dullness, obtuseness, slowness, stolidity, thickness

dent noun 1 = **hollow**, chip, concavity, crater, depression, dimple, dip, impression, indentation, pit ♦ verb 2 = **make a dent in**, depress, dint, gouge, hollow, imprint, make concave, press in, push in

denude verb = **strip**, bare, divest, expose, lay bare, uncover

deny verb 1 = **contradict**, disagree with, disprove, gainsay (archaic or literary), oppose, rebuff, rebut, refute 2 = **refuse**, begrudge, decline, disallow, forbid, negate, reject, turn down, veto, withhold 3 = **renounce**, abjure, disavow, discard, disclaim, disown, recant, renege, repudiate, retract, revoke
➤ Antonyms
≠**contradict**: accept, acknowledge, admit, affirm, agree, allow, concede, confirm, recognize, take on board ≠**refuse**: accept, grant, let, permit, receive

deodorant noun = **antiperspirant**, air freshener, deodorizer, disinfectant, fumigant

depart verb 1 = **leave**, absent (oneself), decamp, disappear, escape, exit, go, go away, hook it (slang), make tracks, migrate, pack one's bags (informal), quit, remove, retire, retreat, set forth, slope off, start out, take (one's) leave, vanish, withdraw 2 = **deviate**, differ, digress, diverge, stray, swerve, turn aside, vary, veer
➤ Antonyms
≠**leave**: arrive, remain, show up (informal), stay, turn up

departed adjective Euphemistic = **dead**, deceased, expired, late

department noun 1 = **section**, branch, bureau, division, office, station, subdivision, unit 2 = **region**, district, division, province, sector 3 Informal = **speciality**, area, domain,

function, line, province, realm, responsibility, sphere

departure noun 1 = **leaving**, exit, exodus, going, going away, leave-taking, removal, retirement, withdrawal 2 = **divergence**, abandonment, branching off, deviation, digression, variation, veering 3 = **shift**, branching out, change, difference, innovation, novelty, whole new ball game (informal)
➤ Antonyms
≠**leaving**: advent, appearance, arrival, coming, entrance, return

depend verb 1 = **trust in**, bank on, build upon, calculate on, confide in, count on, lean on, reckon on, rely upon, turn to 2 = **be determined by**, be based on, be contingent on, be subject to, be subordinate to, hang on, hinge on, rest on, revolve around

dependable adjective = **reliable**, faithful, reputable, responsible, staunch, steady, sure, trustworthy, trusty, unfailing
➤ Antonyms
irresponsible, undependable, unreliable, unstable, untrustworthy

dependant noun = **relative**, child, client, cohort (chiefly U.S.), hanger-on, henchman, minion, minor, protégé, retainer, subordinate, vassal

dependent adjective 1 = **reliant**, counting on, defenceless, helpless, immature, relying on, vulnerable, weak 2 **dependent on** or **upon** = **determined by**, conditional on, contingent on, depending on, influenced by, liable to, relative to, subject to
➤ Antonyms
≠**reliant**: autarkic, autonomous, independent, self-determining, self-governing, self-reliant

depict verb 1 = **draw**, delineate, illustrate, limn, outline, paint, picture, portray, render, reproduce, sculpt, sketch 2 = **describe**, characterize, detail, narrate, outline, represent, sketch

depiction noun = **representation**, delineation, description, picture, portrayal, sketch

deplete verb = **use up**, bankrupt, consume, decrease, drain, empty, evacuate, exhaust, expend, impoverish, lessen, milk, reduce
➤ Antonyms
add to, augment, enhance, expand, increase, raise, step up (informal), swell

depleted adjective = **used (up)**, consumed, decreased, depreciated, devoid of, drained, effete, emptied, exhausted, lessened, out of, reduced, short of, spent, wasted, weakened, worn out

depletion noun = **using up**, attenuation, consumption, decrease, deficiency, diminution, drain, dwindling, exhaustion, expenditure, lessening, lowering, reduction

deplorable *adjective* 1 = **terrible**, calamitous, dire, disastrous, distressing, grievous, heartbreaking, lamentable, melancholy, miserable, pitiable, regrettable, sad, unfortunate, wretched 2 = **disgraceful**, blameworthy, dishonourable, disreputable, execrable, opprobrious, reprehensible, scandalous, shameful
➤ Antonyms
≠**terrible**: A1 *or* A-one (*informal*), bad (*slang*), bodacious (*slang, chiefly U.S.*), brilliant, excellent, fantastic, great (*informal*), marvellous, outstanding, super (*informal*), superb ≠**disgraceful**: admirable, laudable, notable, praiseworthy

deplore *verb* 1 = **disapprove of**, abhor, censure, condemn, denounce, deprecate, excoriate, object to, take a dim view of 2 = **lament**, bemoan, bewail, grieve for, mourn, regret, rue, sorrow over

deploy *verb* = **position**, arrange, dispose, extend, redistribute, set out, set up, spread out, station, use, utilize

deployment *noun* = **position**, arrangement, disposition, organization, setup, spread, stationing, use, utilization

deport *verb* 1 = **expel**, banish, exile, expatriate, extradite, oust 2 **deport oneself** = **behave**, acquit oneself, act, bear oneself, carry oneself, comport oneself, conduct oneself, hold oneself

deportation *noun* = **expulsion**, banishment, eviction, exile, expatriation, extradition, transportation

deportment *noun* = **bearing**, air, appearance, aspect, behaviour, carriage, cast, comportment, conduct, demeanour, manner, mien, posture, stance

depose *verb* 1 = **remove from office**, break, cashier, degrade, demote, dethrone, dismiss, displace, downgrade, oust 2 *Law* = **testify**, avouch, declare, make a deposition

deposit *verb* 1 = **put**, drop, lay, locate, place, precipitate, settle, sit down 2 = **store**, amass, bank, consign, entrust, hoard, lodge, save ◆ *noun* 3 = **down payment**, instalment, money (*in bank*), part payment, pledge, retainer, security, stake, warranty 4 = **sediment**, accumulation, alluvium, deposition, dregs, lees, precipitate, silt

deposition *noun* 1 *Law* = **sworn statement**, affidavit, declaration, evidence, testimony 2 = **removal**, dethronement, dismissal, displacement, ousting

depository *noun* = **storehouse**, depot, repository, safe-deposit box, store, warehouse

depot *noun* 1 = **storehouse**, depository, repository, warehouse 2 *Chiefly U.S. &*

Canad. = **bus station**, garage, terminus 3 *Military* = **arsenal**, dump

deprave *verb* = **corrupt**, brutalize, debase, debauch, degrade, demoralize, lead astray, pervert, seduce, subvert, vitiate

depraved *adjective* = **corrupt**, abandoned, debased, debauched, degenerate, degraded, dissolute, evil, immoral, lascivious, lewd, licentious, perverted, pervy (*slang*), profligate, shameless, sinful, vicious, vile, wicked
➤ Antonyms
chaste, decent, ethical, good, honourable, innocent, moral, principled, proper, pure, upright, virtuous, wholesome

depravity *noun* = **corruption**, baseness, contamination, criminality, debasement, debauchery, degeneracy, depravation, evil, immorality, iniquity, profligacy, sinfulness, turpitude, vice, viciousness, vitiation, wickedness

depreciate *verb* 1 = **decrease**, deflate, devaluate, devalue, lessen, lose value, lower, reduce 2 = **disparage**, belittle, decry, denigrate, deride, detract, look down on, ridicule, run down, scorn, sneer at, traduce, underestimate, underrate, undervalue
➤ Antonyms
≠**decrease**: add to, appreciate, augment, enhance, enlarge, expand, grow, increase, rise ≠**disparage**: admire, appreciate, cherish, esteem, like, prize, rate highly, regard, respect, value

depreciation *noun* 1 = **devaluation**, deflation, depression, drop, fall, slump 2 = **disparagement**, belittlement, denigration, deprecation, derogation, detraction, pejoration

depress *verb* 1 = **sadden**, cast down, chill, damp, daunt, deject, desolate, discourage, dishearten, dispirit, make despondent, oppress, weigh down 2 = **lower**, cheapen, depreciate, devaluate, devalue, diminish, downgrade, impair, lessen, reduce 3 = **press down**, flatten, level, lower, push down
➤ Antonyms
≠**sadden**: cheer, elate, hearten, heighten, increase, lift, raise, strengthen, uplift ≠**lower**: heighten, increase, raise, strengthen

depressed *adjective* 1 = **low-spirited**, blue, crestfallen, dejected, despondent, discouraged, dispirited, down, downcast, downhearted, down in the dumps (*informal*), fed up, glum, low, melancholy, moody, morose, pessimistic, sad, unhappy 2 = **poverty-stricken**, deprived, destitute, disadvantaged, distressed, grey, needy, poor, run-down 3 = **lowered**, cheapened, depreciated, devalued, impaired, weakened 4 = **sunken**, concave, hollow, indented, recessed, set back

depressing _adjective_ = **bleak**, black, daunting, dejecting, depressive, discouraging, disheartening, dismal, dispiriting, distressing, dreary, funereal, gloomy, harrowing, heartbreaking, hopeless, melancholy, sad, saddening, sombre

depression _noun_ 1 = **low spirits**, dejection, despair, despondency, dolefulness, downheartedness, dumps (_informal_), gloominess, hopelessness, melancholia, melancholy, sadness, the blues, the hump (_Brit. Informal_) 2 = **recession**, dullness, economic decline, hard or bad times, inactivity, lowness, slump, stagnation 3 = **hollow**, bowl, cavity, concavity, dent, dimple, dip, excavation, impression, indentation, pit, sag, sink, valley

deprivation _noun_ 1 = **withholding**, denial, deprival, dispossession, divestment, expropriation, removal, withdrawal 2 = **want**, destitution, detriment, disadvantage, distress, hardship, need, privation

deprive _verb_ = **withhold**, bereave, despoil, dispossess, divest, expropriate, rob, strip, wrest

deprived _adjective_ = **poor**, bereft, denuded, destitute, disadvantaged, down at heel, forlorn, in need, in want, lacking, necessitous, needy
➤ **Antonyms**
born with a silver spoon in one's mouth, favoured, fortunate, golden, happy, having a charmed life, lucky, prosperous, sitting pretty (_informal_), successful, well-off

depth _noun_ 1 = **deepness**, drop, extent, measure, profoundness, profundity 2 = **profoundness**, astuteness, discernment, insight, penetration, profundity, sagacity, wisdom 3 = **complexity**, abstruseness, obscurity, reconditeness 4 = **intensity**, richness, strength 5 **in depth** = **thoroughly**, comprehensively, extensively, intensively
➤ **Antonyms**
≠**deepness**: apex, apogee, crest, crown, height, peak, pinnacle, summit, top, vertex, zenith ≠**profoundness**: emptiness, lack of depth or substance, superficiality, triviality

depths _plural noun_ = **deepest part**, abyss, bowels of the earth, furthest part, innermost part, middle, midst, most intense part, remotest part

deputation _noun_ 1 = **delegation**, commission, delegates, deputies, embassy, envoys, legation 2 = **appointment**, assignment, commission, designation, nomination

deputize _verb_ 1 = **stand in for**, act for, take the place of, understudy 2 = **appoint**, commission, delegate, depute

deputy _noun_ 1 = **substitute**, agent, ambassador, commissioner, delegate, legate, lieutenant, number two, nuncio, proxy, representative, second-in-command, surrogate, vicegerent ◆ _adjective_ 2 = **assistant**, depute (_Scot._), subordinate

derange _verb_ 1 = **disorder**, confound, confuse, disarrange, disarray, discompose, disconcert, displace, disturb, ruffle, unsettle, upset 2 = **drive mad**, craze, dement (_rare_), madden, make insane, unbalance, unhinge

deranged _adjective_ = **mad**, barking (_slang_), barking mad (_slang_), berserk, crackpot (_informal_), crazed, crazy, delirious, demented, distracted, doolally (_slang_), frantic, frenzied, gonzo (_slang_), insane, irrational, loopy (_informal_), lunatic, maddened, not the full shilling (_informal_), off one's trolley (_slang_), out to lunch (_informal_), unbalanced, unhinged, up the pole (_informal_), wacko or whacko (_slang_)
➤ **Antonyms**
all there (_informal_), calm, _compos mentis_, in one's right mind, lucid, mentally sound, normal, of sound mind

derelict _adjective_ 1 = **abandoned**, deserted, dilapidated, discarded, forsaken, neglected, ruined 2 = **negligent**, careless, irresponsible, lax, remiss, slack ◆ _noun_ 3 = **tramp**, bag lady, bum (_informal_), down-and-out, good-for-nothing, ne'er-do-well, outcast, vagrant, wastrel

dereliction _noun_ 1 = **abandonment**, abdication, desertion, forsaking, relinquishment, renunciation 2 = **negligence**, delinquency, evasion, failure, faithlessness, fault, neglect, nonperformance, remissness

deride _verb_ = **mock**, chaff, contemn, detract, disdain, disparage, flout, gibe, insult, jeer, knock (_informal_), pooh-pooh, ridicule, scoff, scorn, sneer, take the piss out of (_taboo slang_), taunt

derision _noun_ = **mockery**, contempt, contumely, denigration, disdain, disparagement, disrespect, insult, laughter, raillery, ridicule, satire, scoffing, scorn, sneering

derisory _adjective_ = **ridiculous**, contemptible, insulting, laughable, ludicrous, outrageous, preposterous

derivation _noun_ 1 = **origin**, ancestry, basis, beginning, descent, etymology, foundation, genealogy, root, source 2 = **obtaining**, acquiring, deriving, extraction, getting

derivative _adjective_ 1 = **unoriginal**, copied, imitative, plagiaristic, plagiarized, rehashed, secondary, second-hand, uninventive ◆ _noun_ 2 = **by-product**, derivation, descendant, offshoot, outgrowth, spin-off

> ➤ **Antonyms**
> *adjective* ≠**unoriginal:** archetypal, authentic, first-hand, genuine, master, original, prototypical, seminal

derive *verb* = **obtain,** collect, deduce, draw, elicit, extract, follow, gain, gather, get, glean, infer, procure, receive, trace

derive from *verb* = **come from,** arise from, descend from, emanate from, flow from, issue from, originate from, proceed from, spring from, stem from

derogatory *adjective* = **disparaging,** belittling, damaging, defamatory, depreciative, detracting, discreditable, dishonouring, injurious, offensive, slighting, uncomplimentary, unfavourable, unflattering
> ➤ **Antonyms**
> appreciative, complimentary, flattering, fulsome

descend *verb* **1** = **move down,** alight, dismount, drop, fall, go down, plummet, plunge, sink, subside, tumble **2** = **slope,** dip, gravitate, incline, slant **3** = **lower oneself,** abase oneself, condescend, degenerate, deteriorate, stoop **4 be descended** = **originate,** be handed down, be passed down, derive, issue, proceed, spring **5 descend on** = **attack,** arrive, assail, assault, come in force, invade, pounce, raid, swoop
> ➤ **Antonyms**
> ≠**move down:** ascend, climb, go up, mount, rise, scale, soar

descent *noun* **1** = **coming down,** drop, fall, plunge, swoop **2** = **slope,** declination, declivity, dip, drop, incline, slant **3** = **ancestry,** extraction, family tree, genealogy, heredity, lineage, origin, parentage **4** = **decline,** debasement, decadence, degeneration, degradation, deterioration

describe *verb* **1** = **relate,** characterize, define, depict, detail, explain, express, illustrate, narrate, portray, recount, report, specify, tell **2** = **trace,** delineate, draw, mark out, outline

description *noun* **1** = **account,** characterization, delineation, depiction, detail, explanation, narration, narrative, portrayal, report, representation, sketch **2** = **kind,** brand, breed, category, class, genre, genus, ilk, kidney, order, sort, species, type, variety

descriptive *adjective* = **graphic,** circumstantial, depictive, detailed, explanatory, expressive, illustrative, pictorial, picturesque, vivid

desecrate *verb* = **commit sacrilege,** abuse, blaspheme, contaminate, defile, despoil, dishonour, pervert, pollute, profane, violate

> ➤ **Antonyms**
> esteem, exalt, glorify, hallow, prize, respect, revere, value, venerate, worship

desert[1] *noun* **1** = **wilderness,** solitude, waste, wasteland, wilds ♦ *adjective* **2** = **barren,** arid, bare, desolate, infertile, lonely, solitary, uncultivated, uninhabited, unproductive, untilled, waste, wild

desert[2] *verb* = **abandon,** abscond, betray, decamp, defect, forsake, give up, go over the hill (*Military slang*), jilt, leave, leave high and dry, leave (someone) in the lurch, leave stranded, maroon, quit, rat (on) (*informal*), relinquish, renounce, resign, run out on (*informal*), strand, throw over, vacate, walk out on (*informal*)
> ➤ **Antonyms**
> be a source of strength to, look after, maintain, provide for, succour, sustain, take care of

deserted *adjective* = **abandoned,** bereft, cast off, derelict, desolate, empty, forlorn, forsaken, godforsaken, isolated, left in the lurch, left stranded, lonely, neglected, solitary, unfriended, unoccupied, vacant

deserter *noun* = **defector,** absconder, apostate, escapee, fugitive, rat (*informal*), renegade, runaway, traitor, truant

desertion *noun* = **abandonment,** absconding, apostasy, betrayal, defection, departure, dereliction, escape, evasion, flight, forsaking, relinquishment, truancy

deserve *verb* = **merit,** be entitled to, be worthy of, earn, gain, justify, procure, rate, warrant, win

deserved *adjective* = **well-earned,** appropriate, condign, due, earned, fair, fitting, just, justifiable, justified, meet (*archaic*), merited, proper, right, rightful, suitable, warranted

deserving *adjective* = **worthy,** commendable, estimable, laudable, meritorious, praiseworthy, righteous
> ➤ **Antonyms**
> not deserving of, not good enough, not worth, undeserving, unworthy

design *verb* **1** = **plan,** delineate, describe, draft, draw, outline, sketch, trace **2** = **create,** conceive, fabricate, fashion, invent, originate, think up **3** = **intend,** aim, contrive, destine, devise, make, mean, plan, project, propose, purpose, scheme, tailor ♦ *noun* **4** = **plan,** blueprint, delineation, draft, drawing, model, outline, scheme, sketch **5** = **arrangement,** configuration, construction, figure, form, motif, organization, pattern, shape, style **6** = **intention,** aim, end, goal, intent, meaning, object, objective, point, purport, purpose, target, view

designate *verb* **1** = **name,** call, christen, dub, entitle, label, nominate, style, term **2**

= **appoint**, allot, assign, choose, delegate, depute, nominate, select **3** = **specify**, characterize, define, denote, describe, earmark, indicate, pinpoint, show, stipulate

designation *noun* **1** = **name**, denomination, description, epithet, label, mark, title **2** = **appointment**, classification, delegation, indication, selection, specification

designer *noun* = **creator**, architect, artificer, couturier, deviser, inventor, originator, planner, stylist

designing *adjective* = **scheming**, artful, astute, conniving, conspiring, crafty, crooked (*informal*), cunning, deceitful, devious, intriguing, Machiavellian, plotting, sharp, shrewd, sly, treacherous, tricky, unscrupulous, wily

desirability *noun* = **worth**, advantage, benefit, merit, profit, usefulness, value

desirable *adjective* **1** = **agreeable**, advantageous, advisable, beneficial, covetable, eligible, enviable, good, pleasing, preferable, profitable, to die for (*informal*), worthwhile **2** = **attractive**, adorable, alluring, fascinating, fetching, glamorous, seductive, sexy (*informal*)
➤ **Antonyms**
≠**agreeable:** disagreeable, distasteful, unacceptable, unappealing, unattractive, undesirable, unpleasant, unpopular ≠**attractive:** unappealing, unattractive, undesirable, unsexy (*informal*)

desire *verb* **1** = **want**, aspire to, covet, crave, desiderate, fancy, hanker after, hope for, long for, set one's heart on, thirst for, wish for, yearn for **2** *Formal* = **request**, ask, entreat, importune, petition, solicit ♦ *noun* **3** = **wish**, ache, appetite, aspiration, craving, hankering, hope, longing, need, thirst, want, yearning, yen (*informal*) **4** = **request**, appeal, entreaty, importunity, petition, solicitation, supplication **5** = **lust**, appetite, concupiscence, lasciviousness, lechery, libido, lustfulness, passion

desired *adjective* = **required**, accurate, appropriate, correct, exact, expected, express, fitting, necessary, particular, proper, right

desirous *adjective* = **wishing**, ambitious, anxious, aspiring, avid, craving, desiring, eager, hopeful, hoping, keen, longing, ready, willing, yearning
➤ **Antonyms**
averse, disinclined, grudging, indisposed, loath, opposed, reluctant, unenthusiastic, unwilling

desist *verb* = **stop**, abstain, belay (*Nautical*), break off, cease, discontinue, end, forbear, give over (*informal*), give up, have done with, kick (*informal*), leave off,

pause, refrain from, remit, suspend

desolate *adjective* **1** = **uninhabited**, bare, barren, bleak, desert, dreary, godforsaken, ruined, solitary, unfrequented, waste, wild **2** = **miserable**, abandoned, bereft, cheerless, comfortless, companionless, dejected, depressing, despondent, disconsolate, dismal, downcast, down in the dumps (*informal*), forlorn, forsaken, gloomy, lonely, melancholy, wretched ♦ *verb* **3** = **lay waste**, depopulate, despoil, destroy, devastate, lay low, pillage, plunder, ravage, ruin **4** = **deject**, daunt, depress, discourage, dishearten, dismay, distress, grieve
➤ **Antonyms**
adjective ≠**uninhabited:** inhabited, populous ≠**miserable:** cheerful, happy, joyous, light-hearted ♦ *verb* ≠**lay waste:** develop ≠**deject:** cheer, encourage, hearten

desolation *noun* **1** = **ruin**, destruction, devastation, havoc, ravages, ruination **2** = **bleakness**, barrenness, desolateness, forlornness, isolation, loneliness, solitariness, solitude, wildness **3** = **misery**, anguish, dejection, despair, distress, gloom, gloominess, melancholy, sadness, unhappiness, woe, wretchedness

despair *noun* **1** = **despondency**, anguish, dejection, depression, desperation, disheartenment, gloom, hopelessness, melancholy, misery, wretchedness **2** = **hardship**, burden, cross, ordeal, pain, trial, tribulation ♦ *verb* **3** = **lose hope**, despond, give up, lose heart

despairing *adjective* = **hopeless**, anxious, at the end of one's tether, broken-hearted, dejected, depressed, desperate, despondent, disconsolate, dismal, downcast, down in the dumps (*informal*), frantic, grief-stricken, inconsolable, melancholy, miserable, suicidal, wretched

despatch *see* DISPATCH

desperado *noun* = **criminal**, bandit, cut-throat, gangster, gunman, heavy (*slang*), hoodlum (*chiefly U.S.*), lawbreaker, mugger (*informal*), outlaw, ruffian, skelm (*S. African*), thug, villain

desperate *adjective* **1** = **reckless**, audacious, dangerous, daring, death-defying, determined, foolhardy, frantic, furious, hasty, hazardous, headstrong, impetuous, madcap, precipitate, rash, risky, violent, wild **2** = **grave**, acute, critical, dire, drastic, extreme, great, urgent, very grave **3** = **hopeless**, at the end of one's tether, despairing, despondent, forlorn, inconsolable, irrecoverable, irremediable, irretrievable, wretched

desperately *adverb* **1** = **gravely**, badly, dangerously, perilously, seriously, severely **2**

= **hopelessly**, appallingly, fearfully, frightfully, shockingly

desperation noun 1 = **recklessness**, defiance, foolhardiness, frenzy, heedlessness, impetuosity, madness, rashness 2 = **misery**, agony, anguish, anxiety, despair, despondency, distraction, heartache, hopelessness, pain, sorrow, torture, trouble, unhappiness, worry

despicable adjective = **contemptible**, abject, base, beyond contempt, cheap, degrading, detestable, disgraceful, disreputable, hateful, ignominious, infamous, low, mean, pitiful, reprehensible, scurvy, shameful, sordid, vile, worthless, wretched
➤ **Antonyms**
admirable, estimable, ethical, exemplary, good, honest, honourable, moral, noble, praiseworthy, righteous, upright, virtuous, worthy

despise verb = **look down on**, abhor, contemn, deride, detest, disdain, disregard, flout, have a down on (informal), loathe, neglect, revile, scorn, slight, spurn, undervalue
➤ **Antonyms**
admire, adore, be fond of, be keen on, cherish, dig (slang), esteem, fancy (informal), love, relish, revel in, take to

despite preposition = **in spite of**, against, even with, in contempt of, in defiance of, in the face of, in the teeth of, notwithstanding, regardless of, undeterred by

despoil verb Formal = **plunder**, denude, deprive, destroy, devastate, dispossess, divest, loot, pillage, ravage, rifle, rob, strip, total (slang), trash (slang), vandalize, wreak havoc upon, wreck

despondency noun = **dejection**, depression, despair, desperation, disconsolateness, discouragement, dispiritedness, downheartedness, gloom, hopelessness, low spirits, melancholy, misery, sadness, the hump (Brit. informal), wretchedness

despondent adjective = **dejected**, blue, depressed, despairing, disconsolate, discouraged, disheartened, dismal, dispirited, doleful, down, downcast, downhearted, down in the dumps (informal), gloomy, glum, hopeless, in despair, low, low-spirited, melancholy, miserable, morose, sad, sick as a parrot (informal), sorrowful, woebegone, wretched
➤ **Antonyms**
buoyant, cheerful, cheery, chirpy (informal), genial, glad, happy, hopeful, joyful, light-hearted, optimistic, upbeat (informal)

despot noun = **tyrant**, autocrat, dictator, monocrat, oppressor

despotic adjective = **tyrannical**, absolute, arbitrary, arrogant, authoritarian, autocratic, dictatorial, domineering, imperious, monocratic, oppressive, unconstitutional

despotism noun = **tyranny**, absolutism, autarchy, autocracy, dictatorship, monocracy, oppression, totalitarianism

destination noun 1 = **journey's end**, harbour, haven, landing-place, resting-place, station, stop, terminus 2 = **objective**, aim, ambition, design, end, goal, intention, object, purpose, target

destine verb = **fate**, allot, appoint, assign, consecrate, decree, design, devote, doom, earmark, intend, mark out, ordain, predetermine, preordain, purpose, reserve

destined adjective 1 = **fated**, bound, certain, designed, doomed, foreordained, ineluctable, inescapable, inevitable, intended, meant, ordained, predestined, unavoidable 2 = **bound for**, assigned, booked, directed, en route, heading for, on the road to, routed, scheduled

destiny noun = **fate**, cup, divine decree, doom, fortune, karma, kismet, lot, portion

destitute adjective 1 = **penniless**, dirt-poor (informal), distressed, down and out, flat broke (informal), impecunious, impoverished, indigent, in queer street (informal), insolvent, moneyless, necessitous, needy, on one's uppers, on the breadline (informal), on the rocks, penurious, poor, poverty-stricken, short, without two pennies to rub together (informal) 2 = **lacking**, bereft of, deficient in, depleted, deprived of, devoid of, drained, empty of, in need of, wanting, without

destitution noun = **pennilessness**, beggary, dire straits, distress, impecuniousness, indigence, neediness, pauperism, penury, privation, utter poverty, want
➤ **Antonyms**
affluence, fortune, good fortune, life of luxury, luxury, plenty, prosperity, riches, wealth

destroy verb = **ruin**, annihilate, blow sky-high, blow to bits, break down, crush, demolish, desolate, devastate, dismantle, dispatch, eradicate, extinguish, extirpate, gut, kill, put paid to, ravage, raze, shatter, slay, smash, torpedo, total (slang), trash (slang), waste, wipe out, wreck

destruction noun = **ruin**, annihilation, crushing, demolition, devastation, downfall, end, eradication, extermination, extinction, havoc, liquidation, massacre, overthrow, overwhelming, ruination, shattering, slaughter, undoing, wreckage, wrecking

destructive adjective 1 = **damaging**,

baleful, baneful, calamitous, cataclysmic, catastrophic, deadly, deleterious, detrimental, devastating, fatal, harmful, hurtful, injurious, lethal, maleficent, noxious, pernicious, ruinous 2 = **negative**, adverse, antagonistic, contrary, derogatory, discouraging, discrediting, disparaging, hostile, invalidating, opposed, undermining, vicious

detach verb = **separate**, cut off, disconnect, disengage, disentangle, disjoin, disunite, divide, free, isolate, loosen, remove, segregate, sever, tear off, unbridle, uncouple, unfasten, unhitch
➤ **Antonyms**
attach, bind, connect, fasten

detached adjective 1 = **separate**, disconnected, discrete, disjoined, divided, free, loosened, severed, unconnected 2 = **uninvolved**, aloof, disinterested, dispassionate, impartial, impersonal, neutral, objective, reserved, unbiased, uncommitted, unprejudiced
➤ **Antonyms**
≠**uninvolved**: biased, concerned, interested, involved, partisan, prejudiced

detachment noun 1 = **indifference**, aloofness, coolness, nonchalance, remoteness, unconcern 2 = **impartiality**, disinterestedness, fairness, neutrality, nonpartisanship, objectivity 3 Military = **unit**, body, detail, force, party, patrol, squad, task force 4 = **separation**, disconnection, disengagement, disjoining, severing

detail noun 1 = **point**, aspect, component, count, element, fact, factor, feature, item, particular, respect, specific, technicality 2 = **fine point**, minutiae, nicety, part, particular, triviality 3 Military = **party**, assignment, body, detachment, duty, fatigue, force, squad 4 **in detail** = **comprehensively**, exhaustively, inside out, item by item, point by point, thoroughly
♦ verb 5 = **list**, catalogue, delineate, depict, describe, enumerate, individualize, itemize, narrate, particularize, portray, recite, recount, rehearse, relate, specify, tabulate 6 = **appoint**, allocate, assign, charge, commission, delegate, detach, send

detailed adjective = **comprehensive**, blow-by-blow, circumstantial, elaborate, exact, exhaustive, full, intricate, itemized, meticulous, minute, particular, particularized, specific, thorough
➤ **Antonyms**
brief, compact, concise, condensed, limited, pithy, short, slight, succinct, summary, superficial, terse

detain verb 1 = **delay**, check, hinder, hold up, impede, keep, keep back, retard, slow

up (or down), stay, stop 2 = **hold**, arrest, confine, intern, restrain

detect verb 1 = **notice**, ascertain, catch, descry, distinguish, identify, note, observe, perceive, recognize, scent, spot 2 = **discover**, catch, disclose, expose, find, reveal, track down, uncover, unmask

detection noun = **discovery**, exposé, exposure, ferreting out, revelation, tracking down, uncovering, unearthing, unmasking

detective noun = **investigator**, bizzy (slang), C.I.D. man, constable, cop (slang), copper (slang), dick (slang, chiefly U.S.), gumshoe (U.S. slang), private eye, private investigator, sleuth (informal), tec (slang)

detention noun = **imprisonment**, confinement, custody, delay, hindrance, holding back, incarceration, keeping in, porridge (slang), quarantine, restraint, withholding
➤ **Antonyms**
acquittal, discharge, emancipation, freedom, liberation, liberty, release

deter verb = **discourage**, caution, check, damp, daunt, debar, dissuade, frighten, hinder, inhibit from, intimidate, prevent, prohibit, put off, restrain, stop, talk out of

detergent noun 1 = **cleaner**, cleanser
♦ adjective 2 = **cleansing**, abstergent, cleaning, detersive, purifying

deteriorate verb 1 = **decline**, corrupt, debase, degenerate, degrade, deprave, depreciate, go downhill (informal), go to pot, go to the dogs (informal), impair, injure, lower, slump, spoil, worsen 2 = **disintegrate**, be the worse for wear (informal), break down, crumble, decay, decline, decompose, ebb, fade, fall apart, lapse, retrogress, weaken, wear away
➤ **Antonyms**
≠**decline**: advance, ameliorate, get better, improve

deterioration noun 1 = **decline**, debasement, degeneration, degradation, dégringolade, depreciation, descent, downturn, drop, fall, retrogression, slump, vitiation, worsening 2 = **disintegration**, atrophy, corrosion, dilapidation, lapse, meltdown (informal)

determination noun 1 = **resolution**, backbone, constancy, conviction, dedication, doggedness, drive, firmness, fortitude, indomitability, perseverance, persistence, resoluteness, resolve, single-mindedness, steadfastness, tenacity, willpower 2 = **decision**, conclusion, judgment, purpose, resolve, result, settlement, solution, verdict
➤ **Antonyms**
≠**resolution**: doubt, hesitancy, hesitation, indecision, instability, irresolution, vacillation

determine verb **1** = **settle**, arbitrate, conclude, decide, end, finish, fix upon, ordain, regulate, terminate **2** = **find out**, ascertain, certify, check, detect, discover, establish, learn, verify, work out **3** = **affect**, condition, control, decide, dictate, direct, govern, impel, impose, incline, induce, influence, lead, modify, regulate, rule, shape **4** = **decide**, choose, elect, establish, fix, make up one's mind, purpose, resolve

determined adjective = **resolute**, bent on, constant, dogged, firm, fixed, immovable, intent, persevering, persistent, purposeful, set on, single-minded, stalwart, steadfast, strong-minded, strong-willed, tenacious, unflinching, unwavering

determining adjective = **deciding**, conclusive, critical, crucial, decisive, definitive, essential, final, important, settling

deterrent noun = **discouragement**, check, curb, defensive measures, determent, disincentive, hindrance, impediment, obstacle, restraint
➤ **Antonyms**
bait, carrot (informal), enticement, incentive, inducement, lure, motivation, spur, stimulus

detest verb = **hate**, abhor, abominate, despise, dislike intensely, execrate, feel aversion towards, feel disgust towards, feel hostility towards, feel repugnance towards, loathe, recoil from
➤ **Antonyms**
adore, cherish, dig (slang), dote on, love, relish

detonate verb = **explode**, blast, blow up, discharge, fulminate, set off, touch off, trigger

detonation noun = **explosion**, bang, blast, blow-up, boom, discharge, fulmination, report

detour noun = **diversion**, bypass, byway, circuitous route, deviation, indirect course, roundabout way

detract verb **1** = **lessen**, derogate, devaluate, diminish, lower, reduce, take away from **2** = **divert**, deflect, distract, shift
➤ **Antonyms**
≠**lessen:** add to, augment, boost, complement, enhance, improve, reinforce, strengthen

detraction noun = **disparagement**, abuse, aspersion, belittlement, calumny, defamation, denigration, deprecation, innuendo, insinuation, misrepresentation, muckraking, running down, scandalmongering, scurrility, slander, traducement, vituperation

detractor noun = **slanderer**, backbiter, belittler, defamer, denigrator, derogator

(rare), disparager, muckraker, scandalmonger, traducer

detriment noun = **damage**, disadvantage, disservice, harm, hurt, impairment, injury, loss, mischief, prejudice

detrimental adjective = **damaging**, adverse, baleful, deleterious, destructive, disadvantageous, harmful, inimical, injurious, mischievous, pernicious, prejudicial, unfavourable
➤ **Antonyms**
advantageous, beneficial, efficacious, favourable, good, helpful, salutary

devastate verb **1** = **destroy**, demolish, desolate, despoil, lay waste, level, pillage, plunder, ravage, raze, ruin, sack, spoil, total (slang), trash (slang), waste, wreck **2** Informal = **overwhelm**, chagrin, confound, discomfit, discompose, disconcert, floor (informal), nonplus, overpower, take aback

devastating adjective = **overwhelming**, caustic, cutting, effective, incisive, keen, mordant, overpowering, ravishing, sardonic, satirical, savage, stunning, trenchant, vitriolic, withering

devastation noun = **destruction**, demolition, depredation, desolation, havoc, pillage, plunder, ravages, ruin, ruination, spoliation

develop verb **1** = **advance**, blossom, cultivate, evolve, flourish, foster, grow, mature, progress, promote, prosper, ripen **2** = **form**, acquire, begin, breed, commence, contract, establish, generate, invent, originate, pick up, start **3** = **expand**, amplify, augment, broaden, dilate upon, elaborate, enlarge, unfold, work out **4** = **result**, be a direct result of, break out, come about, ensue, follow, happen

development noun **1** = **growth**, advance, advancement, evolution, expansion, improvement, increase, maturity, progress, progression, spread, unfolding, unravelling **2** = **event**, change, circumstance, happening, incident, issue, occurrence, outcome, phenomenon, result, situation, turn of events, upshot

deviant adjective **1** = **perverted**, aberrant, abnormal, bent (slang), deviate, devious, freaky (slang), heretical, kinky (slang), perverse, pervy (slang), queer (informal, derogatory), sick (informal), sicko (informal), twisted, warped, wayward
♦ noun **2** = **pervert**, deviate, freak, misfit, odd type, queer (informal, derogatory), sicko (informal)
➤ **Antonyms**
adjective ≠**perverted:** conventional, normal, orthodox, straight, straightforward

deviate verb = **differ**, avert, bend, deflect,

depart, digress, diverge, drift, err, meander, part, stray, swerve, turn, turn aside, vary, veer, wander

deviation noun = **departure**, aberration, alteration, change, deflection, digression, discrepancy, disparity, divergence, fluctuation, inconsistency, irregularity, shift, variance, variation

device noun **1** = **gadget**, apparatus, appliance, contraption, contrivance, gimmick, gizmo or gismo (slang, chiefly U.S. & Canad.), implement, instrument, invention, machine, tool, utensil, waldo **2** = **ploy**, artifice, design, dodge, expedient, gambit, improvisation, manoeuvre, plan, project, purpose, ruse, scheme, shift, stratagem, strategy, stunt, trick, wile **3** = **emblem**, badge, colophon, crest, design, figure, insignia, logo, motif, motto, symbol, token

devil noun **1 the Devil** = **Satan**, Abbadon, Apollyon, archfiend, Beelzebub, Belial, Clootie (Scot.), deil (Scot.), demon, Deuce, Evil One, fiend, Foul Fiend, Lord of the Flies, Lucifer, Mephisto, Mephistopheles, Old Gentleman (informal), Old Harry (informal), Old Hornie (informal), Old Nick (informal), Old One, Old Scratch (informal), Prince of Darkness, Tempter, Wicked One **2** = **brute**, beast, demon, fiend, ghoul, monster, ogre, rogue, savage, terror, villain **3** = **scamp**, imp, monkey (informal), pickle (Brit. informal), rascal, rogue, scoundrel **4** = **person**, beggar, creature, thing, unfortunate, wretch **5** = **enthusiast**, demon, fiend, go-getter (informal)

devilish adjective = **fiendish**, accursed, atrocious, damnable, detestable, diabolic, diabolical, execrable, hellish, infernal, satanic, wicked

devil-may-care adjective = **happy-go-lucky**, careless, casual, easy-going, flippant, heedless, insouciant, nonchalant, reckless, swaggering, swashbuckling, unconcerned

devilry noun **1** = **mischief**, devilment, jiggery-pokery (informal, chiefly Brit.), knavery, mischievousness, monkey-business (informal), rascality, roguery **2** = **wickedness**, cruelty, evil, malevolence, malice, vice, viciousness, villainy **3** = **sorcery**, black magic, diablerie, diabolism

devious adjective **1** = **sly**, calculating, crooked (informal), deceitful, dishonest, double-dealing, evasive, indirect, insidious, insincere, not straightforward, scheming, surreptitious, treacherous, tricky, underhand, wily **2** = **indirect**, circuitous, confusing, crooked, deviating, erratic, excursive, misleading, rambling, roundabout, tortuous, wandering

➤ **Antonyms**
≠**sly**: blunt, candid, direct, downright, forthright, frank, honest, straight, straightforward ≠**indirect**: blunt, direct, downright, forthright, straight, straightforward, undeviating, unswerving

devise verb = **work out**, arrange, conceive, concoct, construct, contrive, design, dream up, form, formulate, frame, imagine, invent, plan, plot, prepare, project, scheme, think up

devoid adjective = **lacking**, barren, bereft, deficient, denuded, destitute, empty, free from, sans (archaic), vacant, void, wanting, without

devolution noun = **decentralization**, delegation

devolve verb **1** = **fall upon** or **to**, be transferred, commission, consign, delegate, depute, entrust, rest with, transfer **2** Law = **be handed down**, alienate, convey

devote verb = **dedicate**, allot, apply, appropriate, assign, commit, concern oneself, consecrate, enshrine, give, occupy oneself, pledge, reserve, set apart

devoted adjective = **dedicated**, ardent, caring, committed, concerned, constant, devout, faithful, fond, loving, loyal, staunch, steadfast, true
➤ **Antonyms**
disloyal, inconstant, indifferent, uncommitted, undedicated, unfaithful

devotee noun = **enthusiast**, addict, adherent, admirer, aficionado, buff (informal), disciple, fan, fanatic, follower, supporter, votary

devotion noun **1** = **dedication**, adherence, allegiance, commitment, consecration, constancy, faithfulness, fidelity, loyalty **2** = **love**, affection, ardour, attachment, earnestness, fervour, fondness, intensity, passion, zeal **3** = **devoutness**, adoration, godliness, holiness, piety, prayer, religiousness, reverence, sanctity, spirituality, worship **4 devotions** = **prayers**, church service, divine office, religious observance
➤ **Antonyms**
≠**dedication**: carelessness, disregard, inattention, indifference, laxity, laxness, neglect, thoughtlessness ≠**devoutness**: derision, disrespect, impiety, irreverence

devour verb **1** = **eat**, bolt, consume, cram, dispatch, gobble, gorge, gulp, guzzle, pig out on (slang), polish off (informal), stuff, swallow, wolf **2** = **destroy**, annihilate, consume, ravage, spend, waste, wipe out **3** = **enjoy**, absorb, appreciate, be engrossed by, be preoccupied, delight in, drink in, feast on, go through, read compulsively or voraciously, relish, revel in, take in

devouring adjective = **overwhelming**,

consuming, excessive, flaming, insatiable, intense, passionate, powerful

devout adjective 1 = **religious**, godly, holy, orthodox, pious, prayerful, pure, reverent, saintly 2 = **sincere**, ardent, deep, devoted, earnest, fervent, genuine, heartfelt, intense, passionate, profound, serious, zealous
➤ Antonyms
≠**religious:** impious, irreligious, irreverent, sacrilegious ≠**sincere:** indifferent, passive

devoutly adverb = **with all one's heart**, fervently, heart and soul, profoundly, sincerely

dexterity noun 1 = **skill**, adroitness, artistry, craft, deftness, effortlessness, expertise, facility, finesse, handiness, knack, mastery, neatness, nimbleness, proficiency, smoothness, touch 2 = **cleverness**, ability, address, adroitness, aptitude, aptness, art, expertness, ingenuity, readiness, skilfulness, tact
➤ Antonyms
clumsiness, gaucheness, inability, incapacity, incompetence, ineptitude, uselessness

diabolical adjective Informal = **dreadful**, abysmal, appalling, atrocious, damnable, difficult, disastrous, excruciating, fiendish, from hell (informal), hellacious (U.S. slang), hellish, nasty, outrageous, shocking, terrible, tricky, unpleasant, vile

diagnose verb = **identify**, analyse, determine, distinguish, interpret, investigate, pinpoint, pronounce, put one's finger on, recognize

diagnosis noun 1 = **examination**, analysis, investigation, scrutiny 2 = **opinion**, conclusion, interpretation, pronouncement

diagonal adjective = **slanting**, angled, cater-cornered (U.S. informal), cornerways, cross, crossways, crosswise, oblique

diagonally adverb = **aslant**, at an angle, cornerwise, crosswise, obliquely, on the bias, on the cross

diagram noun = **plan**, chart, drawing, figure, graph, layout, outline, representation, sketch

dialect noun = **language**, accent, brogue, idiom, jargon, lingo (informal), localism, patois, pronunciation, provincialism, speech, tongue, vernacular

dialectic noun 1 = **debate**, argumentation, contention, discussion, disputation, logic, polemics, ratiocination, reasoning
♦ adjective 2 = **logical**, analytic, argumentative, dialectical, polemical, rational, ratiocinative

dialogue noun 1 = **conversation**, colloquy, communication, confabulation, conference, converse, discourse, discussion, duologue, exchange, interlocution 2 = **lines**,

conversation, script, spoken part

diametric, diametrical adjective = **opposed**, antipodal, antithetical, conflicting, contrary, contrasting, counter, opposite, poles apart

diametrically adverb = **completely**, absolutely, entirely, totally, utterly

diarrhoea noun = **the runs**, dysentery, gippy tummy, holiday tummy, looseness, Montezuma's revenge (informal), Spanish tummy, the skits (informal), the skitters (informal), the trots (informal)

diary noun = **journal**, appointment book, chronicle, daily record, day-to-day account, engagement book, Filofax (Trademark)

diatribe noun = **tirade**, abuse, castigation, criticism, denunciation, disputation, harangue, invective, philippic, reviling, stream of abuse, stricture, verbal onslaught, vituperation

dicey adjective Informal, chiefly Brit. = **dangerous**, chancy (informal), difficult, hairy (slang), risky, ticklish, tricky

dicky adjective Brit. informal = **weak**, fluttery, queer, shaky, unreliable, unsound, unsteady

dictate verb 1 = **speak**, read out, say, transmit, utter 2 = **order**, command, decree, demand, direct, enjoin, establish, impose, lay down, lay down the law, ordain, prescribe, pronounce ♦ noun 3 = **command**, behest, bidding, decree, demand, direction, edict, fiat, injunction, mandate, order, ordinance, requirement, statute, ultimatum, word 4 = **principle**, canon, code, dictum, law, precept, rule

dictator noun = **absolute ruler**, autocrat, despot, oppressor, tyrant

dictatorial adjective 1 = **absolute**, arbitrary, autocratic, despotic, totalitarian, tyrannical, unlimited, unrestricted 2 = **domineering**, authoritarian, bossy (informal), dogmatical, imperious, iron-handed, magisterial, oppressive, overbearing
➤ Antonyms
≠**absolute:** constitutional, democratic, egalitarian, restricted ≠**domineering:** humble, servile, suppliant, tolerant

dictatorship noun = **absolute rule**, absolutism, authoritarianism, autocracy, despotism, reign of terror, totalitarianism, tyranny

diction noun = **pronunciation**, articulation, delivery, elocution, enunciation, fluency, inflection, intonation, speech

dictionary noun = **wordbook**, concordance, encyclopedia, glossary, lexicon, vocabulary

didactic adjective = **instructive**, edifying,

educational, enlightening, homiletic, moral, moralizing, pedagogic, pedantic, preceptive

die *verb* **1** = **pass away**, breathe one's last, buy it (*U.S. slang*), buy the farm (*U.S. slang*), check out (*U.S. slang*), croak (*slang*), decease, depart, expire, finish, give up the ghost, go belly-up (*slang*), hop the twig (*slang*), kick it (*slang*), kick the bucket (*slang*), peg it (*informal*), peg out (*informal*), perish, pop one's clogs (*informal*), snuff it (*slang*) **2** = **dwindle**, decay, decline, disappear, ebb, end, fade, lapse, pass, sink, subside, vanish, wane, wilt, wither **3** = **stop**, break down, fade out *or* away, fail, fizzle out, halt, lose power, peter out, run down **4** **be dying for** = **long for**, ache for, be eager for, desire, hunger for, languish for, pine for, set one's heart on, swoon over, yearn for **5** **be dying of** *Informal* = **be overcome with**, collapse with, succumb to
➤ **Antonyms**
≠**pass away**: be born, begin, come to life, exist, live, survive ≠**dwindle**, **stop**: flourish, grow, increase

die-hard *noun* **1** = **reactionary**, fanatic, intransigent, old fogey, stick-in-the-mud (*informal*), ultraconservative, zealot
♦ *adjective* **2** = **reactionary**, dyed-in-the-wool, immovable, inflexible, intransigent, ultraconservative, uncompromising, unreconstructed (*chiefly U.S.*)

diet[1] *noun* **1** = **food**, aliment, comestibles, commons, edibles, fare, nourishment, nutriment, provisions, rations, subsistence, sustenance, viands, victuals **2** = **regime**, abstinence, dietary, fast, regimen ♦ *verb* **3** = **slim**, abstain, eat sparingly, fast, lose weight
➤ **Antonyms**
verb ≠**slim**: get fat, glut, gobble, gormandize, guzzle, indulge, overindulge, pig out (*slang*), stuff oneself

diet[2] *noun* = **council**, chamber, congress, convention, legislative assembly, legislature, meeting, parliament, sitting

differ *verb* **1** = **be dissimilar**, be distinct, contradict, contrast, depart from, diverge, run counter to, stand apart, vary **2** = **disagree**, clash, contend, debate, demur, dispute, dissent, oppose, take exception, take issue
➤ **Antonyms**
≠**be dissimilar**: accord, coincide, harmonize ≠**disagree**: accord, acquiesce, agree, assent, concur, cooperate

difference *noun* **1** = **dissimilarity**, alteration, change, contrast, deviation, differentiation, discrepancy, disparity, distinction, distinctness, divergence, diversity, unlikeness, variation, variety **2** = **distinction**, exception, idiosyncrasy, particularity, peculiarity, singularity **3** = **disagreement**, argument, clash, conflict, contention, contrariety, contretemps, controversy, debate, discordance, dispute, quarrel, row, set-to (*informal*), strife, tiff, wrangle **4** = **remainder**, balance, rest, result
➤ **Antonyms**
≠**dissimilarity**: affinity, comparability, conformity, congruence, likeness, relation, resemblance, sameness, similarity, similitude ≠**disagreement**: agreement, concordance

different *adjective* **1** = **unlike**, altered, at odds, at variance, changed, clashing, contrasting, deviating, discrepant, disparate, dissimilar, divergent, diverse, inconsistent, opposed, streets apart **2** = **various**, assorted, divers (*archaic*), diverse, manifold, many, miscellaneous, multifarious, numerous, several, some, sundry, varied **3** = **unusual**, another story, atypical, bizarre, distinctive, extraordinary, left-field (*informal*), out of the ordinary, peculiar, rare, singular, something else, special, strange, uncommon, unconventional, unique **4** = **other**, another, discrete, distinct, individual, separate

differential *adjective* **1** = **distinctive**, diacritical, discriminative, distinguishing ♦ *noun* **2** = **difference**, amount of difference, discrepancy, disparity

differentiate *verb* **1** = **distinguish**, contrast, discern, discriminate, make a distinction, mark off, separate, set off *or* apart, tell apart **2** = **make different**, adapt, alter, change, convert, modify, transform

difficult *adjective* **1** = **hard**, arduous, burdensome, demanding, formidable, laborious, like getting blood out of a stone, no picnic (*informal*), onerous, painful, strenuous, toilsome, uphill, wearisome **2** = **problematical**, abstract, abstruse, baffling, complex, complicated, delicate, enigmatical, intricate, involved, knotty, obscure, perplexing, thorny, ticklish **3** = **troublesome**, demanding, fastidious, fractious, fussy, hard to please, intractable, obstreperous, perverse, refractory, rigid, tiresome, trying, unaccommodating, unamenable, unmanageable **4** = **tough**, dark, full of hardship, grim, hard, straitened, trying
➤ **Antonyms**
≠**hard**: easy, easy-peasy (*slang*), light, manageable, obvious, plain, simple, straightforward, uncomplicated ≠**troublesome**: accommodating, amenable, cooperative, pleasant ≠**tough**: easy, pleasant

difficulty *noun* **1** = **laboriousness**, arduousness, awkwardness, hardship, labour, pain, painfulness, strain, strenuousness, tribulation **2** = **predicament**, deep water, dilemma, distress, embarrassment, fix (*informal*), hot water (*informal*), jam (*informal*), mess, perplexity, pickle (*informal*), plight, quandary, spot (*informal*), straits, tight spot, trial, trouble **3** = **problem**, complication, hassle (*informal*), hazard, hindrance, hurdle, impediment, objection, obstacle, opposition, pitfall, protest, snag, stumbling block

diffidence *noun* = **shyness**, backwardness, bashfulness, constraint, doubt, fear, hesitancy, hesitation, humility, insecurity, lack of self-confidence, meekness, modesty, reluctance, reserve, self-consciousness, sheepishness, timidity, timidness, timorousness, unassertiveness
➤ **Antonyms**
assurance, boldness, confidence, courage, firmness, self-confidence, self-possession

diffident *adjective* = **shy**, backward, bashful, constrained, distrustful, doubtful, hesitant, insecure, meek, modest, reluctant, reserved, self-conscious, self-effacing, sheepish, shrinking, suspicious, timid, timorous, unassertive, unassuming, unobtrusive, unsure, withdrawn

diffuse *verb* **1** = **spread**, circulate, dispel, dispense, disperse, disseminate, dissipate, distribute, propagate, scatter ♦ *adjective* **2** = **spread out**, dispersed, scattered, unconcentrated **3** = **rambling**, circumlocutory, copious, diffusive, digressive, discursive, long-winded, loose, maundering, meandering, prolix, vague, verbose, waffling (*informal*), wordy
➤ **Antonyms**
adjective ≠ **spread out**: concentrated ≠ **rambling**: apposite, brief, compendious, concise, succinct, terse, to the point

diffusion *noun* **1** = **spread**, circulation, dispersal, dispersion, dissemination, dissipation, distribution, expansion, propaganda, propagation, scattering **2** = **rambling**, circuitousness, diffuseness, digressiveness, discursiveness, long-windedness, prolixity, verbiage, verbosity, wandering, wordiness

dig *verb* **1** = **excavate**, break up, burrow, delve, gouge, grub, hoe, hollow out, mine, penetrate, pierce, quarry, scoop, till, tunnel, turn over **2** = **investigate**, delve, dig down, go into, probe, research, search **3** *with* **out** *or* **up** = **find**, bring to light, come across, come up with, discover, expose, extricate, retrieve, root (*informal*), rootle, uncover, unearth, uproot **4** *Informal* = **like**, appreciate, enjoy, follow, groove (*dated slang*), understand **5** = **poke**, drive, jab, prod, punch, thrust ♦ *noun* **6** = **poke**, jab, prod, punch, thrust **7** = **cutting remark**, barb, crack (*slang*), gibe, insult, jeer, quip,

sneer, taunt, wisecrack (*informal*)

digest *verb* **1** = **ingest**, absorb, assimilate, concoct, dissolve, incorporate, macerate **2** = **take in**, absorb, assimilate, con, consider, contemplate, grasp, master, meditate, ponder, study, understand ♦ *noun* **3** = **summary**, abridgment, abstract, compendium, condensation, epitome, précis, résumé, synopsis

digestion *noun* = **ingestion**, absorption, assimilation, conversion, incorporation, transformation

dig in *verb Informal* **1** = **start eating**, begin, fall to, set about, tuck in (*informal*) **2** = **entrench**, defend, establish, fortify, maintain

dignified *adjective* = **distinguished**, august, decorous, exalted, formal, grave, honourable, imposing, lofty, lordly, noble, reserved, solemn, stately, upright
➤ **Antonyms**
crass, inelegant, unbecoming, undignified, unseemly, vulgar

dignify *verb* = **distinguish**, adorn, advance, aggrandize, elevate, ennoble, exalt, glorify, grace, honour, promote, raise

dignitary *noun* = **public figure**, bigwig (*informal*), celeb (*informal*), high-up (*informal*), notability, notable, personage, pillar of society, pillar of the church, pillar of the state, V.I.P., worthy

dignity *noun* **1** = **decorum**, courtliness, grandeur, gravity, hauteur, loftiness, majesty, nobility, propriety, solemnity, stateliness **2** = **honour**, elevation, eminence, excellence, glory, greatness, importance, nobleness, rank, respectability, standing, station, status **3** = **self-importance**, amour-propre, pride, self-esteem, self-possession, self-regard, self-respect

digress *verb* = **wander**, be diffuse, depart, deviate, diverge, drift, expatiate, get off the point *or* subject, go off at a tangent, meander, ramble, stray, turn aside

digression *noun* = **departure**, apostrophe, aside, detour, deviation, divergence, diversion, footnote, obiter dictum, parenthesis, straying, wandering

dilapidated *adjective* = **ruined**, battered, beat-up (*informal*), broken-down, crumbling, decayed, decaying, decrepit, fallen in, falling apart, gone to rack and ruin, in ruins, neglected, ramshackle, rickety, ruinous, run-down, shabby, shaky, tumbledown, uncared for, worn-out

dilate *verb* **1** = **enlarge**, broaden, distend, expand, extend, puff out, stretch, swell, widen **2** = **expand**, amplify, be profuse, be prolix, descant, detail, develop, dwell on, enlarge, expatiate, expound, spin out

➤ **Antonyms**
≠**enlarge:** compress, constrict, contract, narrow, shrink

dilation noun = **enlargement**, broadening, dilatation, distension, expansion, extension, increase, spread

dilatory adjective = **time-wasting**, backward, behindhand, dallying, delaying, laggard, lingering, loitering, procrastinating, putting off, slack, slow, sluggish, snail-like, tardy, tarrying
➤ **Antonyms**
on-the-ball (informal), prompt, punctual, sharp (informal)

dilemma noun **1** = **predicament**, difficulty, embarrassment, fix (informal), how-do-you-do (informal), jam (informal), mess, perplexity, pickle (informal), plight, problem, puzzle, quandary, spot (informal), strait, tight corner or spot **2 on the horns of a dilemma** = **between the devil and the deep blue sea**, between a rock and a hard place (informal), between Scylla and Charybdis

dilettante noun = **amateur**, aesthete, dabbler, nonprofessional, trifler

diligence noun = **application**, activity, assiduity, assiduousness, attention, attentiveness, care, constancy, earnestness, heedfulness, industry, intentness, laboriousness, perseverance, sedulousness

diligent adjective = **hard-working**, active, assiduous, attentive, busy, careful, conscientious, constant, earnest, indefatigable, industrious, laborious, painstaking, persevering, persistent, sedulous, studious, tireless
➤ **Antonyms**
careless, dilatory, good-for-nothing, inconstant, indifferent, lazy

dilly-dally verb Informal = **dawdle**, dally, delay, dither (chiefly Brit.), falter, fluctuate, hesitate, hover, hum and haw, linger, loiter, potter, procrastinate, shillyshally (informal), trifle, vacillate, waver

dilute verb **1** = **water down**, adulterate, cut, make thinner, thin (out), weaken **2** = **reduce**, attenuate, decrease, diffuse, diminish, lessen, mitigate, temper, weaken
➤ **Antonyms**
≠**water down:** concentrate, condense, strengthen, thicken ≠**reduce:** Intensify, strengthen

dim adjective **1** = **poorly lit**, caliginous (archaic), cloudy, dark, darkish, dusky, grey, overcast, shadowy, tenebrous, unilluminated **2** = **unclear**, bleary, blurred, faint, fuzzy, ill-defined, indistinct, obscured, shadowy **3** Informal = **stupid**, braindead (informal), dense, doltish, dozy (Brit. informal), dull,

dumb (informal), obtuse, slow, slow on the uptake (informal), thick **4** = **obscure**, confused, hazy, imperfect, indistinct, intangible, remote, shadowy, vague **5** = **dull**, dingy, feeble, lacklustre, muted, opaque, pale, sullied, tarnished, weak **6** = **unfavourable**, depressing, discouraging, gloomy, sombre, unpromising **7 take a dim view** = **disapprove**, be displeased, be sceptical, look askance, reject, suspect, take exception, view with disfavour ◆ verb **8** = **dull**, bedim, blur, cloud, darken, fade, lower, obscure, tarnish, turn down
➤ **Antonyms**
adjective ≠**poorly lit:** bright, clear, cloudless, fair, limpid, pleasant, sunny, unclouded ≠**unclear:** bright, brilliant, clear, distinct, limpid ≠**stupid:** acute, astute, aware, brainy, bright, clever, intelligent, keen, quick-witted, sharp, smart

dimension noun, often plural = **measurement**, amplitude, bulk, capacity, extent, proportions, size, volume

dimensions plural noun = **extent**, bigness, greatness, importance, largeness, magnitude, measure, range, scale, scope

diminish verb **1** = **decrease**, abate, contract, curtail, cut, downsize, lessen, lower, reduce, retrench, shrink, taper, weaken **2** = **dwindle**, decline, die out, ebb, fade away, peter out, recede, shrivel, slacken, subside, wane **3** = **belittle**, cheapen, demean, depreciate, devalue
➤ **Antonyms**
≠**decrease:** amplify, augment, enhance, enlarge, expand, grow, heighten, increase

diminution noun = **decrease**, abatement, contraction, curtailment, cut, cutback, decay, decline, deduction, lessening, reduction, retrenchment, weakening

diminutive adjective = **small**, bantam, Lilliputian, little, midget, mini, miniature, minute, petite, pocket(-sized), pygmy or pigmy, teensy-weensy, teeny-weeny, tiny, undersized, wee
➤ **Antonyms**
big, colossal, enormous, giant, gigantic, great, immense, jumbo (informal), king-size, massive (informal)

din noun **1** = **noise**, babel, clamour, clangour, clash, clatter, commotion, crash, hubbub, hullabaloo, outcry, pandemonium, racket, row, shout, uproar ◆ verb **2 din (something) into (someone)** = **instil**, drum into, go on at, hammer into, inculcate, instruct, teach
➤ **Antonyms**
noun ≠**noise:** calm, calmness, hush, peace, quiet, quietness, silence, tranquillity

dine verb **1** = **eat**, banquet, chow down (slang), feast, lunch, sup **2 dine on** or **off**

= **eat**, consume, feed on

dingy *adjective* **1** = **dull**, bedimmed, colourless, dark, dim, drab, dreary, dusky, faded, gloomy, murky, obscure, sombre **2** = **discoloured**, dirty, grimy, seedy, shabby, soiled, tacky (*informal*)

dinky *adjective Brit. informal* = **cute**, dainty, mini, miniature, natty (*informal*), neat, petite, small, trim

dinner *noun* = **meal**, banquet, beanfeast (*Brit. informal*), blowout (*slang*), collation, feast, main meal, refection, repast, spread (*informal*)

dip *verb* **1** = **plunge**, bathe, douse, duck, dunk, immerse, rinse, souse **2** = **slope**, decline, descend, disappear, droop, drop (down), fade, fall, lower, sag, set, sink, slump, subside, tilt ♦ *noun* **3** = **plunge**, douche, drenching, ducking, immersion, soaking **4** = **bathe**, dive, plunge, swim **5** = **hollow**, basin, concavity, depression, hole, incline, slope **6** = **drop**, decline, fall, lowering, sag, slip, slump **7** = **mixture**, concoction, dilution, infusion, preparation, solution, suspension

dip into *verb* **1** = **draw upon**, reach into **2** = **sample**, browse, dabble, glance at, peruse, play at, run over, skim, try

diplomacy *noun* **1** = **statesmanship**, international negotiation, statecraft **2** = **tact**, artfulness, craft, delicacy, discretion, finesse, savoir-faire, skill, subtlety
➤ **Antonyms**
≠**tact**: awkwardness, clumsiness, ineptness, tactlessness, thoughtlessness

diplomat *noun* = **negotiator**, conciliator, go-between, mediator, moderator, politician, public relations expert, tactician

diplomatic *adjective* = **tactful**, adept, discreet, polite, politic, prudent, sensitive, subtle
➤ **Antonyms**
impolitic, insensitive, rude, tactless, thoughtless, undiplomatic, unsubtle

dire *adjective* **1** = **disastrous**, alarming, appalling, awful, calamitous, cataclysmic, catastrophic, cruel, godawful (*slang*), horrible, horrid, ruinous, terrible, woeful **2** = **desperate**, critical, crucial, crying, drastic, exigent, extreme, now or never, pressing, urgent **3** = **grim**, bodeful, dismal, dreadful, fearful, gloomy, ominous, portentous

direct *adjective* **1** = **straight**, nonstop, not crooked, shortest, through, unbroken, undeviating, uninterrupted **2** = **first-hand**, face-to-face, head-on, immediate, personal **3** = **straightforward**, candid, downright, frank, honest, man-to-man, matter-of-fact, open, outspoken, plain-spoken, round, sincere, straight, upfront (*informal*) **4**

= **explicit**, absolute, blunt, categorical, downright, express, plain, point-blank, unambiguous, unequivocal ♦ *verb* **5** = **control**, administer, advise, call the shots, call the tune, conduct, dispose, govern, guide, handle, lead, manage, mastermind, oversee, preside over, regulate, rule, run, superintend, supervise **6** = **order**, bid, charge, command, demand, dictate, enjoin, instruct **7** = **guide**, indicate, lead, point in the direction of, point the way, show **8** = **address**, label, mail, route, send, superscribe **9** = **aim**, address, cast, fix, focus, intend, level, mean, point, train, turn
➤ **Antonyms**
adjective ≠**straight**: circuitous, crooked, indirect ≠**first-hand**: indirect, mediated ≠**straightforward**: circuitous, crooked, devious, indirect, sly, subtle ≠**explicit**: ambiguous, circuitous, indirect

direction *noun* **1** = **way**, aim, bearing, course, line, path, road, route, track **2** = **tendency**, bent, bias, current, drift, end, leaning, orientation, proclivity, tack, tenor, trend **3** = **management**, administration, charge, command, control, government, guidance, leadership, order, oversight, superintendence, supervision

directions *plural noun* = **instructions**, briefing, guidance, guidelines, indication, plan, recommendation, regulations

directive *noun* = **order**, canon, charge, command, decree, dictate, edict, fiat, imperative, injunction, instruction, mandate, notice, ordinance, regulation, ruling

directly *adverb* **1** = **straight**, by the shortest route, exactly, in a beeline, precisely, unswervingly, without deviation **2** = **honestly**, candidly, face-to-face, in person, openly, overtly, personally, plainly, point-blank, straightforwardly, truthfully, unequivocally, without prevarication **3** = **at once**, as soon as possible, dead, due, forthwith, immediately, in a second, instantaneously, instantly, pdq (*slang*), posthaste, presently, promptly, pronto (*informal*), quickly, right away, soon, speedily, straightaway

director *noun* = **controller**, administrator, boss (*informal*), chairman, chief, executive, governor, head, leader, manager, organizer, principal, producer, supervisor

dirge *noun* = **lament**, coronach (*Scot. & Irish*), dead march, elegy, funeral song, requiem, threnody

dirt *noun* **1** = **filth**, crap (*slang*), crud (*slang*), dust, excrement, grime, grot (*slang*), impurity, kak (*S. African slang*), mire, muck, mud, shit (*taboo slang*), slime, slob (*Irish*), smudge, stain, tarnish **2** = **soil**, clay, earth, loam **3** = **obscenity**, indecency, pornography, sleaze, smut

dirty *adjective* 1 = **filthy**, begrimed, foul, grimy, grotty (*slang*), grubby, grungy (*slang, chiefly U.S.*), messy, mucky, muddy, nasty, polluted, scuzzy (*slang, chiefly U.S.*), soiled, sullied, unclean 2 = **dark**, clouded, dull, miry, muddy, not clear 3 = **dishonest**, corrupt, crooked, fraudulent, illegal, treacherous, unfair, unscrupulous, unsporting 4 = **despicable**, base, beggarly, contemptible, cowardly, ignominious, low, low-down (*informal*), mean, nasty, scurvy, shabby, sordid, squalid, vile 5 = **obscene**, blue, indecent, off-colour, pornographic, risqué, salacious, sleazy, smutty, vulgar, X-rated (*informal*) 6 *As in* **a dirty look** = **angry**, annoyed, bitter, choked, indignant, offended, resentful, scorching 7 = **stormy**, gusty, louring *or* lowering, rainy, squally ◆ *verb* 8 = **soil**, begrime, blacken, defile, foul, mess up, muddy, pollute, smear, smirch, smudge, spoil, stain, sully
➤ **Antonyms**
adjective ≠**filthy**: clean, pure ≠**dishonest**: decent, honest, moral, reputable, respectable, upright ≠**obscene**: clean, decent ≠**stormy**: pleasant ◆ *verb* ≠**soil**: clean, tidy up

disability *noun* 1 = **handicap**, affliction, ailment, complaint, defect, disablement, disorder, impairment, infirmity, malady 2 = **incapacity**, disqualification, impotency, inability, incompetency, unfitness, weakness

disable *verb* 1 = **handicap**, cripple, damage, debilitate, enfeeble, hamstring, immobilize, impair, incapacitate, paralyse, prostrate, put out of action, render *hors de combat*, render inoperative, unfit, unman, weaken 2 = **disqualify**, disenable, invalidate, render *or* declare incapable

disabled *adjective* = **handicapped**, bedridden, crippled, incapacitated, infirm, lame, maimed, mangled, mutilated, paralysed, weak, weakened, wrecked
➤ **Antonyms**
able-bodied, fit, hale, healthy, hearty, robust, sound, strong, sturdy

disadvantage *noun* 1 = **harm**, damage, detriment, disservice, hurt, injury, loss, prejudice 2 = **drawback**, burden, downside, flaw, fly in the ointment (*informal*), handicap, hardship, hindrance, impediment, inconvenience, liability, minus (*informal*), nuisance, privation, snag, trouble, weakness, weak point 3 **at a disadvantage** = **vulnerable**, boxed in, cornered, handicapped, in a corner, with one's hands tied behind one's back
➤ **Antonyms**
≠**harm**, **drawback**: advantage, aid, benefit, convenience, gain, help, merit, profit

disadvantageous *adjective* = **unfavourable**, adverse, damaging, deleterious, detrimental, harmful, hurtful, ill-timed, inconvenient, inexpedient, injurious, inopportune, prejudicial

disaffected *adjective* = **alienated**, antagonistic, discontented, disloyal, dissatisfied, estranged, hostile, mutinous, rebellious, seditious, uncompliant, unsubmissive

disaffection *noun* = **alienation**, animosity, antagonism, antipathy, aversion, breach, disagreement, discontent, dislike, disloyalty, dissatisfaction, estrangement, hostility, ill will, repugnance, resentment, unfriendliness

disagree *verb* 1 = **differ (in opinion)**, argue, be at sixes and sevens, bicker, clash, contend, contest, cross swords, debate, dispute, dissent, fall out (*informal*), have words (*informal*), object, oppose, quarrel, take issue with, wrangle 2 = **conflict**, be discordant, be dissimilar, contradict, counter, depart, deviate, differ, diverge, run counter to, vary 3 = **make ill**, be injurious, bother, discomfort, distress, hurt, nauseate, sicken, trouble, upset
➤ **Antonyms**
≠**differ (in opinion)**: agree, concur, get on (together) ≠**conflict**: accord, coincide, harmonize

disagreeable *adjective* 1 = **nasty**, disgusting, displeasing, distasteful, horrid, objectionable, obnoxious, offensive, repellent, repugnant, repulsive, uninviting, unpalatable, unpleasant, unsavoury, yucky *or* yukky (*slang*) 2 = **ill-natured**, bad-tempered, brusque, churlish, contrary, cross, difficult, disobliging, irritable, nasty, peevish, ratty (*Brit. & N.Z. informal*), rude, surly, tetchy, unfriendly, ungracious, unlikable *or* unlikeable, unpleasant
➤ **Antonyms**
≠**nasty**: agreeable, delightful, enjoyable, lovely, nice, pleasant ≠**ill-natured**: agreeable, congenial, delightful, friendly, good-natured, lovely, nice, pleasant

disagreement *noun* 1 = **incompatibility**, difference, discrepancy, disparity, dissimilarity, dissimilitude, divergence, diversity, incongruity, unlikeness, variance 2 = **argument**, altercation, clash, conflict, debate, difference, discord, dispute, dissent, division, falling out, misunderstanding, quarrel, row, squabble, strife, tiff, wrangle 3 **in disagreement** = **at odds**, at daggers drawn, at loggerheads, at variance, disunited, in conflict, in disharmony
➤ **Antonyms**
≠**incompatibility**: correspondence, harmony, similarity ≠**argument**: accord, agreement, assent, consensus, unison, unity

disallow *verb* 1 = **reject**, abjure, disavow, disclaim, dismiss, disown, rebuff, refuse, repudiate 2 = **cancel**, ban, boycott, embargo, forbid, prohibit, proscribe, veto

disappear *verb* 1 = **vanish**, be lost to view, drop out of sight, ebb, evanesce, fade away, pass, recede, vanish off the face of the earth, wane 2 = **flee**, abscond, depart, escape, fly, go, retire, withdraw 3 = **cease**, cease to be known, cease to exist, die out, dissolve, end, evaporate, expire, fade, leave no trace, melt away, pass away, perish, vanish
➤ Antonyms
appear, arrive, materialize, reappear

disappearance *noun* = **vanishing**, departure, desertion, disappearing, disappearing trick, eclipse, evanescence, evaporation, fading, flight, going, loss, melting, passing, vanishing point

disappoint *verb* 1 = **let down**, chagrin, dash, deceive, delude, disenchant, disgruntle, dishearten, disillusion, dismay, dissatisfy, fail, sadden, vex 2 = **frustrate**, baffle, balk, defeat, disconcert, foil, hamper, hinder, thwart

disappointed *adjective* = **let down**, balked, cast down, choked, depressed, despondent, discontented, discouraged, disenchanted, disgruntled, disillusioned, dissatisfied, distressed, downhearted, foiled, frustrated, saddened, thwarted, upset
➤ Antonyms
content, contented, fulfilled, happy, pleased, satisfied

disappointing *adjective* = **unsatisfactory**, depressing, disagreeable, disconcerting, discouraging, failing, inadequate, inferior, insufficient, lame, not much cop (*Brit. slang*), pathetic, sad, second-rate, sorry, unexpected, unhappy, unworthy, upsetting

disappointment *noun* 1 = **frustration**, chagrin, discontent, discouragement, disenchantment, disillusionment, displeasure, dissatisfaction, distress, failure, ill-success, mortification, regret, unfulfilment 2 = **letdown**, blow, calamity, choker (*informal*), disaster, failure, fiasco, miscarriage, misfortune, setback, washout (*informal*), whammy (*informal, chiefly U.S.*)

disapproval *noun* = **displeasure**, censure, condemnation, criticism, denunciation, deprecation, disapprobation, dissatisfaction, objection, reproach, stick (*slang*)

disapprove *verb* 1 = **condemn**, blame, censure, deplore, deprecate, discountenance, dislike, find unacceptable, frown on, have a down on (*informal*), look down one's nose at (*informal*), object to, raise an *or* one's eyebrow, reject, take a dim view of, take exception to 2 = **turn down**, disallow, reject,

set aside, spurn, veto
➤ Antonyms
≠condemn: applaud, approve, commend, compliment (*informal*), like ≠turn down: endorse, give the go-ahead (to), O.K. *or* okay (*informal*)

disarm *verb* 1 = **render defenceless**, disable 2 = **win over**, persuade, set at ease 3 = **demilitarize**, deactivate, demobilize, disband

disarmament *noun* = **arms reduction**, arms limitation, de-escalation, demilitarization, demobilization

disarming *adjective* = **charming**, irresistible, likable *or* likeable, persuasive, winning

disarrange *verb* = **disorder**, confuse, derange, discompose, disorganize, disturb, jumble (up), mess (up), scatter, shake (up), shuffle, unsettle, untidy

disarray *noun* 1 = **confusion**, discomposure, disharmony, dismay, disorder, disorderliness, disorganization, disunity, indiscipline, unruliness, upset 2 = **untidiness**, chaos, clutter, dishevelment, hodgepodge (*U.S.*), hotchpotch, jumble, mess, mix-up, muddle, pig's breakfast (*informal*), shambles, state, tangle
➤ Antonyms
arrangement, harmony, method, neatness, order, orderliness, organization, pattern, plan, regularity, symmetry, system, tidiness

disaster *noun* = **catastrophe**, accident, act of God, adversity, blow, bummer (*slang*), calamity, cataclysm, misadventure, mischance, misfortune, mishap, reverse, ruin, ruination, stroke, tragedy, trouble, whammy (*informal, chiefly U.S.*)

disastrous *adjective* = **terrible**, adverse, calamitous, cataclysmal, cataclysmic, catastrophic, destructive, detrimental, devastating, dire, dreadful, fatal, hapless, harmful, ill-fated, ill-starred, ruinous, tragic, unfortunate, unlucky, unpropitious, untoward

disbelief *noun* = **scepticism**, distrust, doubt, dubiety, incredulity, mistrust, unbelief
➤ Antonyms
belief, credence, credulity, faith, trust

disbelieve *verb* = **doubt**, discount, discredit, give no credence to, mistrust, not accept, not buy (*slang*), not credit, not swallow (*informal*), reject, repudiate, scoff at, suspect

disbeliever *noun* = **sceptic**, agnostic, atheist, doubter, doubting Thomas, questioner, scoffer
➤ Antonyms
adherent, believer, devotee, disciple, follower, supporter, upholder, zealot

disbelievingly *adverb* = **sceptically**,

askance, cynically, doubtingly, incredulously, mistrustfully, quizzically, suspiciously, with a pinch of salt

discard *verb* = **get rid of**, abandon, axe (*informal*), cast aside, chuck (*informal*), dispense with, dispose of, ditch (*slang*), drop, dump (*informal*), jettison, junk (*informal*), reject, relinquish, remove, repudiate, scrap, shed, throw away *or* out
➤ **Antonyms**
hang *or* hold on to, hold back, keep, reserve, retain, save

discerning *adjective* = **discriminating**, acute, astute, clear-sighted, critical, ingenious, intelligent, judicious, knowing, penetrating, perceptive, percipient, perspicacious, piercing, sagacious, sensitive, sharp, shrewd, subtle, wise

discharge *verb* **1** = **release**, absolve, acquit, allow to go, clear, exonerate, free, liberate, pardon, set free **2** = **dismiss**, cashier, discard, eject, expel, fire (*informal*), give (someone) the boot (*slang*), give (someone) the sack (*informal*), oust, remove, sack (*informal*) **3** = **fire**, detonate, explode, let loose (*informal*), let off, set off, shoot **4** = **pour forth**, disembogue, dispense, emit, empty, excrete, exude, give off, gush, leak, ooze, release, void **5** = **off-load**, disburden, lighten, remove, unburden, unload **6** = **carry out**, accomplish, do, execute, fulfil, observe, perform **7** = **pay**, clear, honour, meet, relieve, satisfy, settle, square up ♦ *noun* **8** = **release**, acquittal, clearance, exoneration, liberation, pardon, remittance **9** = **dismissal**, congé, demobilization, ejection, the boot (*slang*), the (old) heave-ho (*informal*), the order of the boot (*slang*), the sack (*informal*) **10** = **firing**, blast, burst, detonation, discharging, explosion, fusillade, report, salvo, shot, volley **11** = **emission**, emptying, excretion, flow, ooze, pus, secretion, seepage, suppuration, vent, voiding **12** = **unloading**, disburdening, emptying, unburdening **13** = **carrying out**, accomplishment, achievement, execution, fulfilment, observance, performance **14** = **payment**, satisfaction, settlement

disciple *noun* = **follower**, adherent, apostle, believer, catechumen, convert, devotee, learner, partisan, proselyte, pupil, student, supporter, votary
➤ **Antonyms**
guru, leader, master, swami, teacher

disciplinarian *noun* = **authoritarian**, despot, drill sergeant, hard master, martinet, stickler, strict teacher, taskmaster, tyrant

discipline *noun* **1** = **training**, drill, exercise, method, practice, regimen, regulation **2** = **punishment**, castigation, chastisement, correction **3** = **self-control**, conduct, control,

orderliness, regulation, restraint, strictness **4** = **field of study**, area, branch of knowledge, course, curriculum, speciality, subject ♦ *verb* **5** = **train**, break in, bring up, check, control, drill, educate, exercise, form, govern, instruct, inure, prepare, regulate, restrain **6** = **punish**, bring to book, castigate, chasten, chastise, correct, penalize, reprimand, reprove

disclaim *verb* = **deny**, abandon, abjure, abnegate, decline, disaffirm, disallow, disavow, disown, forswear, rebut, reject, renege, renounce, repudiate, retract

disclose *verb* **1** = **make known**, blow wide open (*slang*), broadcast, communicate, confess, divulge, get off one's chest (*informal*), impart, leak, let slip, make public, out (*informal*), publish, relate, reveal, spill one's guts about (*slang*), spill the beans about (*informal*), tell, unveil, utter **2** = **show**, bring to light, discover, exhibit, expose, lay bare, reveal, take the wraps off, uncover, unveil
➤ **Antonyms**
conceal, cover, dissemble, hide, keep dark, keep secret, mask, obscure, veil

disclosure *noun* = **revelation**, acknowledgment, admission, announcement, broadcast, confession, declaration, discovery, divulgence, exposé, exposure, leak, publication, uncovering

discolour *verb* = **stain**, fade, mar, mark, rust, soil, streak, tarnish, tinge

discomfort *noun* **1** = **pain**, ache, hurt, irritation, malaise, soreness **2** = **uneasiness**, annoyance, disquiet, distress, gall, hardship, inquietude, irritation, nuisance, trouble, unpleasantness, vexation ♦ *verb* **3** = **make uncomfortable**, discomfit, discompose, disquiet, distress, disturb, embarrass
➤ **Antonyms**
noun ≠**pain**: comfort, ease ≠**uneasiness**: ease, reassurance, solace ♦ *verb* ≠**make uncomfortable**: alleviate, assuage, comfort, ease, reassure, solace, soothe

discomposure *noun* = **disturbance**, agitation, anxiety, confusion, discomfiture, disquiet, disquietude, distraction, embarrassment, fluster, inquietude, malaise, nervousness, perturbation, trepidation, uneasiness

disconcert *verb* **1** = **disturb**, abash, agitate, bewilder, discompose, faze, flummox, flurry, fluster, nonplus, perplex, perturb, put out of countenance, rattle (*informal*), ruffle, shake up (*informal*), take aback, throw off balance, trouble, unbalance, unnerve, unsettle, upset, worry **2** = **frustrate**, baffle, balk, confuse, defeat, disarrange, hinder, put off, thwart, undo

disconcerted *adjective* = disturbed, annoyed, at sea, bewildered, caught off balance, confused, distracted, embarrassed, fazed, flummoxed, flurried, flustered, mixed-up, nonplussed, out of countenance, perturbed, rattled (*informal*), ruffled, shook up (*informal*), taken aback, thrown (*informal*), troubled, unsettled, upset, worried

disconcerting *adjective* = disturbing, alarming, awkward, baffling, bewildering, bothersome, confusing, dismaying, distracting, embarrassing, off-putting (*Brit. informal*), perplexing, upsetting

disconnect *verb* = cut off, detach, disengage, divide, part, separate, sever, take apart, uncouple

disconnected *adjective* = illogical, confused, disjointed, garbled, incoherent, irrational, jumbled, mixed-up, rambling, uncoordinated, unintelligible, wandering

disconnection *noun* = cutting off, cessation, cut-off, discontinuation, discontinuity, interruption, separation, severance, stoppage, suspension

disconsolate *adjective* = inconsolable, crushed, dejected, desolate, despairing, dismal, down in the dumps (*informal*), forlorn, gloomy, grief-stricken, heartbroken, hopeless, low, melancholy, miserable, sad, unhappy, woeful, wretched

discontent *noun* = dissatisfaction, discontentment, displeasure, envy, fretfulness, regret, restlessness, uneasiness, unhappiness, vexation

discontented *adjective* = dissatisfied, brassed off (*Brit. slang*), cheesed off (*Brit. slang*), complaining, disaffected, disgruntled, displeased, exasperated, fed up, fretful, miserable, pissed off (*taboo slang*), unhappy, vexed, with a chip on one's shoulder (*informal*)
➤ **Antonyms**
cheerful, content, contented, happy, pleased, satisfied

discontinue *verb* = stop, abandon, axe (*informal*), belay (*Nautical*), break off, cease, drop, end, finish, give up, halt, interrupt, kick (*informal*), leave off, pause, pull the plug on, put an end to, quit, refrain from, suspend, terminate, throw in the sponge, throw in the towel

discontinued *adjective* = stopped, abandoned, ended, finished, given up *or* over, halted, no longer made, terminated

discord *noun* 1 = disagreement, clashing, conflict, contention, difference, discordance, dispute, dissension, disunity, division, friction, incompatibility, lack of concord, opposition, row, rupture, strife, variance,

wrangling 2 = disharmony, cacophony, din, dissonance, harshness, jangle, jarring, racket, tumult
➤ **Antonyms**
≠disagreement: accord, agreement, concord, friendship, harmony, peace, understanding, unison, unity ≠disharmony: concord, euphony, harmony, melody, tunefulness, unison

discordant *adjective* 1 = disagreeing, at odds, clashing, conflicting, contradictory, contrary, different, divergent, incompatible, incongruous, inconsistent, opposite 2 = inharmonious, cacophonous, dissonant, grating, harsh, jangling, jarring, shrill, strident, unmelodious

discount *verb* 1 = leave out, brush off (*slang*), disbelieve, disregard, ignore, overlook, pass over 2 = deduct, lower, mark down, rebate, reduce, take off ♦ *noun* 3 = deduction, abatement, allowance, concession, cut, cut price, drawback, percentage (*informal*), rebate, reduction

discountenance *verb* 1 = embarrass, abash, chagrin, confuse, discompose, disconcert, humiliate, put down (*slang*), shame 2 = disapprove, condemn, discourage, disfavour, frown on, object to, oppose, resist, take exception to, veto

discourage *verb* 1 = dishearten, abash, awe, cast down, cow, damp, dampen, dash, daunt, deject, demoralize, depress, dismay, dispirit, frighten, intimidate, overawe, psych out (*informal*), put a damper on, scare, unman, unnerve 2 = put off, check, curb, deprecate, deter, discountenance, disfavour, dissuade, divert from, hinder, inhibit, prevent, restrain, talk out of, throw cold water on (*informal*) 3 = prevent, check, curb, deter, hinder, inhibit
➤ **Antonyms**
≠dishearten: embolden, encourage, gee up, hearten, inspire ≠put off: bid, countenance, encourage, urge

discouraged *adjective* = put off, crestfallen, dashed, daunted, deterred, disheartened, dismayed, dispirited, downcast, down in the mouth, glum, pessimistic, sick as a parrot (*informal*)

discouragement *noun* 1 = loss of confidence, cold feet (*informal*), dejection, depression, despair, despondency, disappointment, discomfiture, dismay, downheartedness, hopelessness, low spirits, pessimism 2 = deterrent, constraint, curb, damper, disincentive, hindrance, impediment, obstacle, opposition, rebuff, restraint, setback

discouraging *adjective* = disheartening, dampening, daunting, depressing, disappointing, dispiriting, off-putting (*Brit.*

informal), unfavourable, unpropitious

discourse *noun* **1** = **conversation**, chat, communication, converse, dialogue, discussion, seminar, speech, talk **2** = **speech**, address, disquisition, dissertation, essay, homily, lecture, oration, sermon, talk, treatise ♦ *verb* **3** = **hold forth**, confer, converse, debate, declaim, discuss, expatiate, speak, talk

discourteous *adjective* = **rude**, abrupt, bad-mannered, boorish, brusque, curt, disrespectful, ill-bred, ill-mannered, impolite, insolent, offhand, uncivil, uncourteous, ungentlemanly, ungracious, unmannerly
➤ **Antonyms**
civil, courteous, courtly, gracious, mannerly, polite, respectful, well-mannered

discourtesy *noun* **1** = **rudeness**, bad manners, disrespectfulness, ill-breeding, impertinence, impoliteness, incivility, insolence, ungraciousness, unmannerliness **2** = **insult**, affront, cold shoulder, kick in the teeth (*slang*), rebuff, slight, snub

discover *verb* **1** = **find**, bring to light, come across, come upon, dig up, light upon, locate, turn up, uncover, unearth **2** = **find out**, ascertain, descry, detect, determine, discern, disclose, espy, get wise to (*informal*), learn, notice, perceive, realize, recognize, reveal, see, spot, suss (out) (*slang*), turn up, uncover **3** = **invent**, conceive, contrive, design, devise, originate, pioneer

discoverer *noun* = **inventor**, author, explorer, founder, initiator, originator, pioneer

discovery *noun* **1** = **finding**, ascertainment, detection, disclosure, espial, exploration, introduction, locating, location, origination, revelation, uncovering **2** = **breakthrough**, bonanza, coup, find, findings, godsend, innovation, invention, secret

discredit *verb* **1** = **disgrace**, blame, bring into disrepute, censure, defame, degrade, detract from, dishonour, disparage, reproach, slander, slur, smear, vilify **2** = **doubt**, challenge, deny, disbelieve, discount, dispute, distrust, mistrust, question ♦ *noun* **3** = **disgrace**, aspersion, censure, dishonour, disrepute, ignominy, ill-repute, imputation, odium, reproach, scandal, shame, slur, smear, stigma **4** = **doubt**, distrust, mistrust, question, scepticism, suspicion
➤ **Antonyms**
verb ≠**disgrace**: acclaim, applaud, commend, honour, laud, pay tribute to, praise ♦ *noun* ≠**disgrace**: acclaim, acknowledgment, approval, commendation, credit, honour, merit, praise

discreditable *adjective* = **disgraceful**, blameworthy, degrading, dishonourable, humiliating, ignominious, improper, infamous, reprehensible, scandalous, shameful, unprincipled, unworthy

discredited *adjective* = **debunked**, discarded, exploded, exposed, obsolete, outworn, refuted, rejected

discreet *adjective* = **tactful**, careful, cautious, circumspect, considerate, diplomatic, discerning, guarded, judicious, politic, prudent, reserved, sagacious, sensible, wary
➤ **Antonyms**
incautious, indiscreet, injudicious, rash, tactless, undiplomatic, unthinking, unwise

discrepancy *noun* = **disagreement**, conflict, contradiction, contrariety, difference, discordance, disparity, dissimilarity, dissonance, divergence, incongruity, inconsistency, variance, variation

discretion *noun* **1** = **tact**, acumen, care, carefulness, caution, circumspection, consideration, diplomacy, discernment, good sense, heedfulness, judgment, judiciousness, maturity, prudence, sagacity, wariness **2** = **choice**, disposition, inclination, liking, mind, option, pleasure, predilection, preference, responsibility, volition, will, wish
➤ **Antonyms**
≠**tact**: carelessness, indiscretion, insensitivity, rashness, tactlessness, thoughtlessness

discretionary *adjective* = **optional**, arbitrary (*Law*), elective, nonmandatory, open, open to choice, unrestricted

discriminate *verb* **1** = **show prejudice**, disfavour, favour, show bias, single out, treat as inferior, treat differently, victimize **2** = **differentiate**, assess, discern, distinguish, draw a distinction, evaluate, segregate, separate, separate the wheat from the chaff, sift, tell the difference

discriminating *adjective* = **discerning**, acute, astute, critical, cultivated, fastidious, keen, particular, refined, selective, sensitive, tasteful
➤ **Antonyms**
careless, desultory, general, hit or miss (*informal*), indiscriminate, random, undiscriminating, unselective, unsystematic

discrimination *noun* **1** = **prejudice**, bias, bigotry, favouritism, inequity, intolerance, unfairness **2** = **discernment**, acumen, acuteness, clearness, insight, judgment, keenness, penetration, perception, refinement, sagacity, subtlety, taste

discriminatory *adjective* **1** = **prejudiced**, biased, favouring, inequitable, one-sided, partial, partisan, preferential, prejudicial, unjust, weighted **2** = **discerning**, analytical, astute, differentiating, discriminating, perceptive, perspicacious

discuss *verb* = **talk about**, argue, confer, consider, consult with, converse, debate, deliberate, examine, exchange views on, get together, go into, reason about, review, sift, thrash out, ventilate, weigh up the pros and cons

discussion *noun* = **talk**, analysis, argument, colloquy, confabulation, conference, consideration, consultation, conversation, debate, deliberation, dialogue, discourse, examination, exchange, review, scrutiny, seminar, symposium

disdain *noun* **1** = **contempt**, arrogance, contumely, derision, dislike, haughtiness, hauteur, indifference, scorn, sneering, snobbishness, superciliousness ♦ *verb* **2** = **scorn**, belittle, contemn, deride, despise, disregard, look down on, look down one's nose at (*informal*), misprize, pooh-pooh, reject, slight, sneer at, spurn, undervalue

disdainful *adjective* = **contemptuous**, aloof, arrogant, derisive, haughty, high and mighty (*informal*), hoity-toity (*informal*), insolent, looking down one's nose (at), on one's high horse (*informal*), proud, scornful, sneering, supercilious, superior, turning up one's nose (at)

disease *noun* **1** = **illness**, affliction, ailment, complaint, condition, disorder, ill health, indisposition, infection, infirmity, lurgy (*informal*), malady, sickness, upset **2** = **malady**, blight, cancer, canker, contagion, contamination, disorder, plague

diseased *adjective* = **sick**, ailing, infected, rotten, sickly, tainted, unhealthy, unsound, unwell, unwholesome

disembark *verb* = **land**, alight, arrive, get off, go ashore, step out of

disembodied *adjective* = **bodiless**, ghostly, immaterial, incorporeal, intangible, phantom, spectral, spiritual, unbodied

disembowel *verb* = **eviscerate**, draw, gut, paunch

disenchanted *adjective* = **disillusioned**, blasé, cynical, disappointed, indifferent, jaundiced, let down, out of love, sick of, soured, undeceived

disenchantment *noun* = **disillusionment**, disappointment, disillusion, revulsion, rude awakening

disengage *verb* **1** = **release**, disentangle, ease, extricate, free, liberate, loosen, set free, unbridle, unloose, untie **2** = **detach**, disconnect, disjoin, disunite, divide, separate, undo, withdraw

disengaged *adjective* **1** = **unconnected**, apart, detached, free, loose, out of gear,

released, separate, unattached, uncoupled **2** = **free**, at ease, at leisure, not busy, uncommitted, unoccupied, vacant

disengagement *noun* = **disconnection**, detachment, disentanglement, division, separation, withdrawal

disentangle *verb* **1** = **untangle**, detach, disconnect, disengage, extricate, free, loose, separate, sever, unfold, unravel, unsnarl, untwist **2** = **sort out**, clarify, clear (up), resolve, simplify, work out

disfavour *noun* **1** = **disapproval**, disapprobation, dislike, displeasure **2** *As in* **fall into disfavour** = **unpopularity**, bad books (*informal*), discredit, disesteem, disgrace, doghouse (*informal*), shame

disfigure *verb* = **damage**, blemish, deface, deform, disfeature, distort, injure, maim, make ugly, mar, mutilate, scar

disfigurement *noun* = **damage**, blemish, defacement, defect, deformity, distortion, impairment, injury, mutilation, scar, spot, stain, trauma (*Pathology*)

disgorge *verb* **1** = **vomit**, barf (*U.S. slang*), belch, blow lunch (*U.S. slang*), chuck (up) (*slang, chiefly U.S.*), chunder (*slang, chiefly Austral.*), discharge, do a technicolour yawn (*slang*), eject, empty, expel, lose one's lunch (*U.S. slang*), regurgitate, spew, spit up, spout, throw up, toss one's cookies (*U.S. slang*), upchuck (*U.S. slang*) **2** = **give up**, cede, relinquish, renounce, resign, surrender, yield

disgrace *noun* **1** = **shame**, baseness, degradation, dishonour, disrepute, ignominy, infamy, odium, opprobrium **2** = **stain**, aspersion, blemish, blot, blot on one's escutcheon, defamation, reproach, scandal, slur, stigma **3** = **discredit**, contempt, disesteem, disfavour, obloquy ♦ *verb* **4** = **bring shame upon**, abase, defame, degrade, discredit, disfavour, dishonour, disparage, humiliate, reproach, shame, slur, stain, stigmatize, sully, taint
➤ **Antonyms**
noun ≠**shame:** credit, esteem, favour, grace, honour, repute ♦ *verb* ≠**bring shame upon:** credit, grace, honour

disgraced *adjective* = **shamed**, branded, degraded, discredited, dishonoured, humiliated, in disgrace, in the doghouse (*informal*), mortified, stigmatized, under a cloud

disgraceful *adjective* = **shameful**, blameworthy, contemptible, degrading, detestable, discreditable, dishonourable, disreputable, ignominious, infamous, low, mean, opprobrious, scandalous, shocking, unworthy

disgruntled *adjective* = **discontented**,

annoyed, cheesed off (*Brit. slang*), displeased, dissatisfied, grumpy, hacked (off) (*U.S. slang*), huffy, irritated, malcontent, peeved, peevish, petulant, pissed off (*taboo slang*), put out, sulky, sullen, testy, vexed

disguise *verb* 1 = **hide**, camouflage, cloak, conceal, cover, mask, screen, secrete, shroud, veil 2 = **misrepresent**, deceive, dissemble, dissimulate, fake, falsify, fudge, gloss over ♦ *noun* 3 = **costume**, camouflage, cloak, cover, get-up (*informal*), mask, screen, veil 4 = **façade**, deception, dissimulation, front, pretence, semblance, trickery, veneer

disguised *adjective* = **in disguise**, camouflaged, cloaked, covert, fake, false, feigned, incognito, masked, pretend, undercover, unrecognizable

disgust *noun* 1 = **loathing**, abhorrence, abomination, antipathy, aversion, detestation, dislike, distaste, hatefulness, hatred, nausea, odium, repugnance, repulsion, revulsion ♦ *verb* 2 = **sicken**, cause aversion, displease, fill with loathing, gross out (*U.S. slang*), nauseate, offend, outrage, put off, repel, revolt, turn one's stomach
➤ **Antonyms**
noun ≠**loathing**: liking, love, pleasure, satisfaction, taste ♦ *verb* ≠**sicken**: delight, impress, please

disgusted *adjective* = **sickened**, appalled, nauseated, offended, outraged, repelled, repulsed, scandalized, sick and tired of (*informal*), sick of (*informal*)

disgusting *adjective* = **sickening**, abominable, cringe-making (*Brit. informal*), detestable, distasteful, foul, gross, grotty (*slang*), hateful, loathsome, nasty, nauseating, nauseous, noisome, objectionable, obnoxious, odious, offensive, repellent, repugnant, revolting, shameless, stinking, vile, vulgar, yucky *or* yukky (*slang*)

dish *noun* 1 = **bowl**, plate, platter, salver 2 = **food**, fare, recipe ♦ *verb* 3 *Slang* = **ruin**, finish, muck up (*slang*), spoil, torpedo, wreck

dishearten *verb* = **discourage**, cast down, crush, damp, dampen, dash, daunt, deject, depress, deter, dismay, dispirit, put a damper on
➤ **Antonyms**
buck up (*informal*), cheer up, encourage, gee up, hearten, lift, perk up, rally

disheartened *adjective* = **discouraged**, choked, crestfallen, crushed, daunted, dejected, depressed, disappointed, dismayed, dispirited, downcast, downhearted, sick as a parrot (*informal*)

dishevelled *adjective* = **untidy**, bedraggled, blowsy, disarranged, disarrayed, disordered, frowzy, hanging loose, messy, ruffled, rumpled, tousled, uncombed, unkempt
➤ **Antonyms**
chic, dapper, neat, smart, soigné *or* soignée, spick-and-span, spruce, tidy, trim, well-groomed

dishonest *adjective* = **deceitful**, bent (*slang*), cheating, corrupt, crafty, crooked (*informal*), deceiving, deceptive, designing, disreputable, double-dealing, false, fraudulent, guileful, knavish (*archaic*), lying, mendacious, perfidious, shady (*informal*), swindling, treacherous, unfair, unprincipled, unscrupulous, untrustworthy, untruthful
➤ **Antonyms**
honest, honourable, law-abiding, lawful, principled, true, trustworthy, upright

dishonesty *noun* = **deceit**, cheating, chicanery, corruption, craft, criminality, crookedness, duplicity, falsehood, falsity, fraud, fraudulence, graft (*informal*), improbity, mendacity, perfidy, sharp practice, stealing, treachery, trickery, unscrupulousness, wiliness

dishonour *verb* 1 = **disgrace**, abase, blacken, corrupt, debase, debauch, defame, degrade, discredit, shame, sully 2 = **seduce**, defile, deflower, pollute, rape, ravish ♦ *noun* 3 = **disgrace**, abasement, degradation, discredit, disfavour, disrepute, ignominy, infamy, obloquy, odium, opprobrium, reproach, scandal, shame 4 = **insult**, abuse, affront, discourtesy, indignity, offence, outrage, sacrilege, slight
➤ **Antonyms**
verb ≠**disgrace**: esteem, exalt, respect, revere, worship ♦ *noun* ≠**disgrace**: decency, goodness, honour, integrity, morality, principles, rectitude

dishonourable *adjective* 1 = **shameful**, base, contemptible, despicable, discreditable, disgraceful, ignoble, ignominious, infamous, not cricket (*informal*), scandalous 2 = **untrustworthy**, blackguardly, corrupt, disreputable, shameless, treacherous, unprincipled, unscrupulous

dish out *verb Informal* = **distribute**, allocate, dole out, hand out, inflict, mete out

dish up *verb* = **serve**, hand out, ladle, prepare, present, produce, scoop, spoon

disillusion *verb* = **shatter one's illusions**, break the spell, bring down to earth, disabuse, disenchant, open the eyes of, undeceive

disillusioned *adjective* = **disenchanted**, disabused, disappointed, enlightened, indifferent, out of love, sadder and wiser, undeceived

disincentive *noun* = **discouragement**,

damper, determent, deterrent, dissuasion, impediment

disinclination *noun* = **reluctance,** alienation, antipathy, aversion, demur, dislike, hesitance, lack of desire, lack of enthusiasm, loathness, objection, opposition, repugnance, resistance, unwillingness

disinclined *adjective* = **reluctant,** antipathetic, averse, balking, hesitating, indisposed, loath, not in the mood, opposed, resistant, unwilling

disinfect *verb* = **sterilize,** clean, cleanse, decontaminate, deodorize, fumigate, purify, sanitize
➤ **Antonyms**
contaminate, defile, infect, poison, pollute, taint

disinfectant *noun* = **antiseptic,** germicide, sanitizer, sterilizer

disingenuous *adjective* = **insincere,** artful, cunning, deceitful, designing, dishonest, duplicitous, feigned, guileful, insidious, shifty, sly, two-faced, uncandid, underhanded, unfair, wily

disinherit *verb* Law = **cut off,** cut off without a penny, disown, dispossess, oust, repudiate

disintegrate *verb* = **break up,** break apart, crumble, disunite, fall apart, fall to pieces, go to pieces, go to seed, reduce to fragments, separate, shatter, splinter

disinterest *noun* = **impartiality,** candidness, detachment, disinterestedness, dispassionateness, equity, fairness, justice, neutrality, unbiasedness

disinterested *adjective* = **impartial,** candid, detached, dispassionate, equitable, even-handed, free from self-interest, impersonal, neutral, objective, outside, unbiased, uninvolved, unprejudiced, unselfish
➤ **Antonyms**
biased, involved, partial, prejudiced, selfish

disjointed *adjective* **1** = **incoherent,** aimless, confused, disconnected, disordered, fitful, loose, rambling, spasmodic, unconnected **2** = **disconnected,** dislocated, displaced, disunited, divided, separated, split

dislike *verb* **1** = **be averse to,** abhor, abominate, despise, detest, disapprove, disfavour, disrelish, hate, have a down on (*informal*), have no taste *or* stomach for, loathe, not be able to bear *or* abide *or* stand, object to, scorn, shun, take a dim view of ◆ *noun* **2** = **aversion,** animosity, animus, antagonism, antipathy, detestation, disapprobation, disapproval, disgust, disinclination, displeasure, distaste, enmity, hatred, hostility, loathing, odium, repugnance

➤ **Antonyms**
verb ≠**be averse to:** esteem, favour, like
◆ *noun* ≠**aversion:** admiration, attraction, delight, esteem, inclination, liking

dislocate *verb* **1** = **put out of joint,** disarticulate, disconnect, disengage, disjoint, disunite, luxate (*Medical*), unhinge **2** = **shift,** disorder, displace, disrupt, disturb, misplace

dislocation *noun* **1** = **putting out of joint,** disarticulation, disconnection, disengagement, luxation (*Medical*), unhinging **2** = **shift,** disarray, disorder, disorganization, disruption, disturbance, misplacement

dislodge *verb* = **displace,** disturb, extricate, force out, knock loose, oust, remove, uproot

disloyal *adjective* = **treacherous,** apostate, disaffected, faithless, false, perfidious, seditious, subversive, traitorous, treasonable, two-faced, unfaithful, unpatriotic, untrustworthy
➤ **Antonyms**
constant, dependable, dutiful, faithful, loyal, steadfast, true, trustworthy, trusty

disloyalty *noun* = **treachery,** betrayal of trust, breach of trust, breaking of faith, deceitfulness, double-dealing, falseness, falsity, inconstancy, infidelity, perfidy, Punic faith, treason, unfaithfulness

dismal *adjective* = **gloomy,** black, bleak, cheerless, dark, depressing, despondent, discouraging, dolorous, dreary, forlorn, funereal, gruesome, lonesome, louring *or* lowering, lugubrious, melancholy, sad, sombre, sorrowful, wretched
➤ **Antonyms**
bright, cheerful, cheery, glad, happy, joyful, light-hearted, sunny

dismantle *verb* = **take apart,** demolish, disassemble, strip, take to pieces

dismay *verb* **1** = **alarm,** affright, appal, distress, fill with consternation, frighten, horrify, paralyse, scare, terrify, unnerve **2** = **disappoint,** daunt, discourage, dishearten, disillusion, dispirit, put off ◆ *noun* **3** = **alarm,** agitation, anxiety, apprehension, consternation, distress, dread, fear, fright, horror, panic, terror, trepidation **4** = **disappointment,** chagrin, discouragement, disillusionment, upset

dismember *verb* = **cut into pieces,** amputate, anatomize, disjoint, dislocate, dissect, divide, mutilate, rend, sever

dismiss *verb* **1** = **sack** (*informal*), axe (*informal*), cashier, discharge, fire (*informal*), give notice to, give (someone) their marching orders, give the boot to (*slang*), give the bullet to (*Brit. slang*), kiss off (*slang, chiefly U.S. & Canad.*), lay off, oust, remove, send packing (*informal*) **2**

= let go, disband, disperse, dissolve, free, release, send away **3 = put out of one's mind**, banish, discard, dispel, disregard, drop, lay aside, pooh-pooh, reject, relegate, repudiate, set aside, shelve, spurn

dismissal *noun* **1 = the sack** *(informal)*, discharge, expulsion, kiss-off *(slang, chiefly U.S. & Canad.)*, marching orders *(informal)*, notice, one's books *or* cards *(informal)*, removal, the boot *(slang)*, the bum's rush *(slang)*, the (old) heave-ho *(informal)*, the order of the boot *(slang)*, the push *(slang)* **2 = permission to go**, adjournment, congé, end, freedom to depart, release

disobedience *noun* **= defiance**, indiscipline, infraction, insubordination, mutiny, noncompliance, nonobservance, recalcitrance, revolt, unruliness, waywardness

disobedient *adjective* **= defiant**, contrary, contumacious, disorderly, froward *(archaic)*, insubordinate, intractable, mischievous, naughty, noncompliant, nonobservant, obstreperous, refractory, undisciplined, unruly, wayward, wilful
➤ **Antonyms**
biddable, compliant, dutiful, manageable, obedient, submissive, well-behaved

disobey *verb* **= refuse to obey**, contravene, defy, dig one's heels in *(informal)*, disregard, flout, go counter to, ignore, infringe, overstep, rebel, resist, transgress, violate

disorder *noun* **1 = untidiness**, chaos, clutter, confusion, disarray, jumble, mess, muddle, shambles **2 = disturbance**, commotion, riot, turmoil, unrest, unruliness, uproar **3 = illness**, affliction, ailment, complaint, disease, malady, sickness

disorderly *adjective* **1 = untidy**, chaotic, confused, disorganized, higgledy-piggledy *(informal)*, indiscriminate, irregular, jumbled, messy, shambolic *(informal)*, unsystematic **2 = unruly**, boisterous, disruptive, indisciplined, lawless, obstreperous, rebellious, refractory, riotous, rowdy, stormy, tumultuous, turbulent, ungovernable, unlawful, unmanageable
➤ **Antonyms**
≠ **untidy:** arranged, neat, orderly, organized, tidy

disorganize *verb* **= disrupt**, break up, confuse, convulse, derange, destroy, disarrange, discompose, disorder, disturb, jumble, make a shambles of, muddle, turn topsy-turvy, unsettle, upset

disorganized *adjective* **= muddled**, chaotic, confused, disordered, haphazard, jumbled, off the rails, shuffled, unmethodical, unorganized, unsystematic

disown *verb* **= deny**, abandon, abnegate, cast off, disallow, disavow, disclaim, rebut, refuse to acknowledge *or* recognize, reject, renounce, repudiate, retract

disparage *verb* **= run down**, asperse, bad-mouth *(slang, chiefly U.S. & Canad.)*, belittle, blast, criticize, decry, defame, degrade, denigrate, deprecate, depreciate, deride, derogate, detract from, discredit, disdain, dismiss, knock *(informal)*, lambast(e), malign, minimize, put down, ridicule, rubbish *(informal)*, scorn, slag (off) *(slang)*, slander, tear into *(informal)*, traduce, underestimate, underrate, undervalue, vilify

disparagement *noun* **= contempt**, aspersion, belittlement, condemnation, contumely, criticism, debasement, degradation, denigration, denunciation, depreciation, derision, derogation, detraction, discredit, disdain, impairment, lessening, prejudice, reproach, ridicule, scorn, slander, underestimation

dispassionate *adjective* **1 = unemotional**, calm, collected, composed, cool, imperturbable, moderate, quiet, serene, sober, temperate, unexcitable, unexcited, unfazed *(informal)*, unmoved, unruffled **2 = objective**, candid, detached, disinterested, fair, impartial, impersonal, indifferent, neutral, unbiased, uninvolved, unprejudiced
➤ **Antonyms**
≠ **unemotional:** ablaze, ardent, emotional, excited, fervent, impassioned, intense, passionate ≠ **objective:** biased, concerned, interested, involved, partial, prejudiced

dispatch, despatch *verb* **1 = send**, accelerate, consign, dismiss, express, forward, hasten, hurry, quicken, remit, transmit **2 = carry out**, conclude, discharge, dispose of, expedite, finish, make short work of *(informal)*, perform, settle **3 = murder**, assassinate, blow away *(slang, chiefly U.S.)*, bump off *(slang)*, butcher, eliminate *(slang)*, execute, finish off, kill, put an end to, slaughter, slay, take out *(slang)* ♦ *noun* **4 = message**, account, bulletin, communication, communiqué, document, instruction, item, letter, missive, news, piece, report, story **5** *As in* **with dispatch = promptness**, alacrity, celerity, expedition, haste, precipitateness, promptitude, quickness, rapidity, speed, swiftness

dispel *verb* **= drive away**, allay, banish, chase away, dismiss, disperse, dissipate, eliminate, expel, resolve, rout, scatter

dispensable *adjective* **= expendable**, disposable, inessential, needless, nonessential, superfluous, unnecessary, unrequired, useless

> **Antonyms**
crucial, essential, important, indispensable, necessary, requisite, vital

dispensation *noun* **1** = **distribution**, allotment, appointment, apportionment, bestowal, conferment, consignment, dealing out, disbursement, endowment, supplying **2** = **exemption**, exception, immunity, indulgence, licence, permission, privilege, relaxation, relief, remission, reprieve

dispense *verb* **1** = **distribute**, allocate, allot, apportion, assign, deal out, disburse, dole out, mete out, share **2** = **prepare**, measure, mix, supply **3** = **administer**, apply, carry out, direct, discharge, enforce, execute, implement, operate, undertake **4** = **exempt**, except, excuse, exonerate, let off (*informal*), release, relieve, reprieve **5 dispense with: a** = **do away with**, abolish, brush aside, cancel, dispose of, disregard, get rid of, ignore, pass over, render needless, shake off **b** = **do without**, abstain from, forgo, give up, omit, relinquish, waive

disperse *verb* **1** = **scatter**, broadcast, circulate, diffuse, disseminate, dissipate, distribute, spread, strew **2** = **break up**, disappear, disband, dismiss, dispel, dissolve, rout, scatter, send off, separate, vanish
> **Antonyms**
amass, assemble, collect, concentrate, congregate, convene, gather, muster, pool

dispirited *adjective* = **disheartened**, crestfallen, dejected, depressed, despondent, discouraged, down, downcast, gloomy, glum, in the doldrums, low, morose, sad, sick as a parrot (*informal*)

displace *verb* **1** = **move**, derange, disarrange, disturb, misplace, shift, transpose **2** = **dismiss**, cashier, depose, discard, discharge, fire (*informal*), remove, sack (*informal*) **3** = **replace**, crowd out, oust, succeed, supersede, supplant, take the place of **4** = **force out**, dislocate, dislodge, dispossess, eject, evict, unsettle

display *verb* **1** = **show**, betray, demonstrate, disclose, evidence, evince, exhibit, expose, manifest, open, open to view, present, reveal, take the wraps off, unveil **2** = **spread out**, expand, extend, model, open out, stretch out, unfold, unfurl **3** = **show off**, boast, flash (*informal*), flaunt, flourish, parade, vaunt ♦ *noun* **4** = **exhibition**, array, demonstration, exposition, exposure, manifestation, presentation, revelation, show **5** = **show**, flourish, ostentation, pageant, parade, pomp, spectacle
> **Antonyms**
verb ≠ **show**: conceal, cover, hide, keep dark, keep secret, mask, secrete, veil

displease *verb* = **annoy**, aggravate (*informal*), anger, disgust, dissatisfy, exasperate, gall, hassle (*informal*), incense, irk, irritate, nark (*Brit., Austral., & N.Z. slang*), nettle, offend, pique, piss one off (*taboo slang*), provoke, put one's back up, put out, rile, upset, vex

displeasure *noun* = **annoyance**, anger, disapprobation, disapproval, disfavour, disgruntlement, dislike, dissatisfaction, distaste, indignation, irritation, offence, pique, resentment, vexation, wrath
> **Antonyms**
approval, pleasure, satisfaction

disposable *adjective* **1** = **throwaway**, biodegradable, compostable, decomposable, nonreturnable, paper **2** = **available**, at one's service, consumable, expendable, free for use, spendable

disposal *noun* **1** = **throwing away**, clearance, discarding, dumping (*informal*), ejection, jettisoning, parting with, relinquishment, removal, riddance, scrapping **2** = **arrangement**, array, dispensation, disposition, distribution, grouping, placing, position **3** = **transfer**, assignment, bequest, bestowal, consignment, conveyance, dispensation, gift, settlement **4 at one's disposal** = **available**, at one's service, consumable, expendable, free for use, spendable

dispose *verb* **1** = **arrange**, adjust, array, determine, distribute, fix, group, marshal, order, place, put, range, rank, regulate, set, settle, stand **2** = **lead**, actuate, adapt, bias, condition, incline, induce, influence, motivate, move, predispose, prompt, tempt

disposed *adjective* = **inclined**, apt, given, liable, likely, of a mind to, predisposed, prone, ready, subject, tending towards

dispose of *verb* **1** = **get rid of**, bin (*informal*), chuck (*informal*), destroy, discard, dump (*informal*), get shot of, jettison, junk (*informal*), scrap, throw out *or* away, unload **2** = **give**, bestow, make over, part with, sell, transfer **3** = **deal with**, decide, determine, end, finish with, settle

disposition *noun* **1** = **character**, constitution, make-up, nature, spirit, temper, temperament **2** = **tendency**, bent, bias, habit, inclination, leaning, predisposition, proclivity, proneness, propensity, readiness **3** = **arrangement**, adjustment, classification, disposal, distribution, grouping, ordering, organization, placement **4** = **control**, direction, disposal, management, regulation

disproportion *noun* = **inequality**, asymmetry, discrepancy, disparity, imbalance, inadequacy, insufficiency, lopsidedness, unevenness, unsuitableness
> **Antonyms**
balance, congruity, harmony, proportion, symmetry

disproportionate *adjective* = **unequal**, excessive, incommensurate, inordinate, out of proportion, too much, unbalanced, uneven, unreasonable

disprove *verb* = **prove false**, blow out of the water (*slang*), confute, contradict, controvert, discredit, expose, give the lie to, invalidate, make a nonsense of, negate, rebut, refute
➤ **Antonyms**
ascertain, bear out, confirm, evince, prove, show, substantiate, verify

disputation *noun* = **dispute**, argumentation, controversy, debate, dissension, polemics

dispute *noun* 1 = **disagreement**, altercation, argument, *bagarre*, brawl, conflict, discord, disturbance, feud, friction, quarrel, shindig (*informal*), shindy (*informal*), strife, wrangle 2 = **argument**, contention, controversy, debate, discussion, dissension ♦ *verb* 3 = **doubt**, challenge, contest, contradict, controvert, deny, impugn, question, rebut 4 = **argue**, altercate, brawl, clash, contend, cross swords, debate, discuss, quarrel, row, spar, squabble, wrangle

disqualification *noun* 1 = **ban**, debarment, disenablement, disentitlement, elimination, exclusion, incompetence, ineligibility, rejection 2 = **unfitness**, disability, disablement, incapacitation, incapacity

disqualified *adjective* = **ineligible**, debarred, eliminated, knocked out, out of the running

disqualify *verb* 1 = **ban**, debar, declare ineligible, disentitle, preclude, prohibit, rule out 2 = **invalidate**, disable, incapacitate, unfit (*rare*)

disquiet *noun* 1 = **uneasiness**, alarm, angst, anxiety, concern, disquietude, distress, disturbance, fear, foreboding, fretfulness, nervousness, restlessness, trepidation, trouble, unrest, worry ♦ *verb* 2 = **make uneasy**, agitate, annoy, bother, concern, discompose, distress, disturb, fret, harass, hassle (*informal*), incommode, perturb, pester, plague, trouble, unsettle, upset, vex, worry

disquieting *adjective* = **worrying**, annoying, bothersome, disconcerting, distressing, disturbing, harrowing, irritating, perturbing, troubling, unnerving, unsettling, upsetting, vexing

disregard *verb* 1 = **ignore**, brush aside *or* away, discount, disobey, laugh off, leave out of account, make light of, neglect, overlook, pass over, pay no attention to, pay no heed to, take no notice of, turn a blind eye to 2

= **snub**, brush off (*slang*), cold-shoulder, contemn, despise, disdain, disparage, send to Coventry, slight ♦ *noun* 3 = **inattention**, brushoff (*slang*), contempt, disdain, disrespect, heedlessness, ignoring, indifference, neglect, negligence, oversight, slight, the cold shoulder
➤ **Antonyms**
verb ≠**ignore**: attend, heed, listen to, mind, note, pay attention to, regard, respect, take into consideration, take notice of

disrepair *noun* 1 = **dilapidation**, collapse, decay, deterioration, ruination 2 **in disrepair** = **out of order**, broken, bust (*informal*), decayed, decrepit, kaput (*informal*), not functioning, on the blink (*slang*), out of commission, worn-out

disreputable *adjective* 1 = **discreditable**, base, contemptible, derogatory, disgraceful, dishonourable, disorderly, ignominious, infamous, louche, low, mean, notorious, opprobrious, scandalous, shady (*informal*), shameful, shocking, unprincipled, vicious, vile 2 = **scruffy**, bedraggled, dilapidated, dingy, dishevelled, down at heel, seedy, shabby, threadbare, worn
➤ **Antonyms**
≠**discreditable**: decent, reputable, respectable, respected, upright, worthy

disrepute *noun* = **discredit**, disesteem, disfavour, disgrace, dishonour, ignominy, ill favour, ill repute, infamy, obloquy, shame, unpopularity

disrespect *noun* = **contempt**, cheek, discourtesy, dishonour, disregard, impertinence, impoliteness, impudence, incivility, insolence, irreverence, lack of respect, lese-majesty, rudeness, sauce, unmanderliness
➤ **Antonyms**
esteem, regard, respect

disrespectful *adjective* = **contemptuous**, bad-mannered, cheeky, discourteous, ill-bred, impertinent, impolite, impudent, insolent, insulting, irreverent, misbehaved, rude, uncivil

disrupt *verb* 1 = **disturb**, agitate, confuse, convulse, disorder, disorganize, spoil, throw into disorder, upset 2 = **interrupt**, break up *or* into, interfere with, intrude, obstruct, unsettle, upset

disruption *noun* = **disturbance**, confusion, disarray, disorder, disorderliness, interference, interruption, stoppage

disruptive *adjective* = **disturbing**, confusing, disorderly, distracting, obstreperous, troublemaking, troublesome, unruly, unsettling, upsetting
➤ **Antonyms**
biddable, compliant, cooperative, docile,

obedient, well-behaved

dissatisfaction *noun* = **discontent**, annoyance, chagrin, disappointment, discomfort, dislike, dismay, displeasure, distress, exasperation, frustration, irritation, regret, resentment, unhappiness

dissatisfied *adjective* = **discontented**, disappointed, disgruntled, displeased, fed up, frustrated, not satisfied, unfulfilled, ungratified, unhappy, unsatisfied
➤ **Antonyms**
content, contented, pleased, satisfied

dissect *verb* **1** = **cut up** *or* **apart**, anatomize, dismember, lay open **2** = **analyse**, break down, explore, inspect, investigate, research, scrutinize, study

dissection *noun* **1** = **cutting up**, anatomization, anatomy, autopsy, dismemberment, necropsy, postmortem (examination) **2** = **analysis**, breakdown, examination, inspection, investigation, research, scrutiny

disseminate *verb* = **spread**, broadcast, circulate, diffuse, disperse, dissipate, distribute, proclaim, promulgate, propagate, publicize, publish, scatter, sow

dissemination *noun* = **spread**, broadcasting, circulation, diffusion, distribution, promulgation, propagation, publication, publishing

dissension *noun* = **disagreement**, conflict, conflict of opinion, contention, difference, discord, discordance, dispute, dissent, friction, quarrel, row, strife, variance

dissent *verb* **1** = **disagree**, decline, differ, object, protest, refuse, withhold assent *or* approval ♦ *noun* **2** = **disagreement**, difference, discord, dissension, dissidence, nonconformity, objection, opposition, refusal, resistance
➤ **Antonyms**
verb ≠ **disagree**: agree, assent, concur
♦ *noun* ≠ **disagreement**: accord, agreement, assent, concurrence, consensus

dissenter *noun* = **objector**, disputant, dissident, nonconformist, protestant

dissenting *adjective* = **disagreeing**, conflicting, differing, dissident, opposing, protesting

dissertation *noun* = **thesis**, critique, discourse, disquisition, essay, exposition, treatise

disservice *noun* = **bad turn**, disfavour, harm, ill turn, injury, injustice, unkindness, wrong
➤ **Antonyms**
courtesy, good turn, indulgence, kindness, obligement (*Scot. or archaic*), service

dissident *adjective* **1** = **dissenting**,

differing, disagreeing, discordant, dissentient, heterodox, nonconformist, schismatic ♦ *noun* **2** = **protester**, agitator, dissenter, rebel, recusant

dissimilar *adjective* = **different**, disparate, divergent, diverse, heterogeneous, manifold, mismatched, not alike, not capable of comparison, not similar, unlike, unrelated, various
➤ **Antonyms**
alike, comparable, congruous, corresponding, in agreement, much the same, resembling, uniform

dissimilarity *noun* = **difference**, discrepancy, disparity, dissimilitude, distinction, divergence, heterogeneity, incomparability, nonuniformity, unlikeness, unrelatedness

dissipate *verb* **1** = **squander**, burn up, consume, deplete, expend, fritter away, indulge oneself, lavish, misspend, run through, spend, waste **2** = **disperse**, disappear, dispel, dissolve, drive away, evaporate, scatter, vanish

dissipated *adjective* **1** = **debauched**, abandoned, dissolute, intemperate, profligate, rakish, self-indulgent **2** = **squandered**, consumed, destroyed, exhausted, scattered, wasted

dissipation *noun* **1** = **dispersal**, disappearance, disintegration, dissemination, dissolution, scattering, vanishing **2** = **debauchery**, abandonment, dissoluteness, drunkenness, excess, extravagance, indulgence, intemperance, lavishness, prodigality, profligacy, squandering, wantonness, waste

dissociate *verb* **1** = **break away**, break off, disband, disrupt, part company, quit **2** = **separate**, detach, disconnect, distance, divorce, isolate, segregate, set apart

dissolute *adjective* = **immoral**, abandoned, corrupt, debauched, degenerate, depraved, dissipated, lax, lewd, libertine, licentious, loose, profligate, rakish, unrestrained, vicious, wanton, wild
➤ **Antonyms**
chaste, clean-living, good, moral, squeaky-clean, upright, virtuous, worthy

dissolution *noun* **1** = **breaking up**, disintegration, division, divorce, parting, resolution, separation **2** = **adjournment**, conclusion, disbandment, discontinuation, dismissal, end, ending, finish, suspension, termination **3** = **debauchery**, corruption, dissipation, intemperance, wantonness
➤ **Antonyms**
≠ **breaking up**: alliance, amalgamation, coalition, combination, unification, union

dissolve *verb* **1** = **melt**, deliquesce, flux,

fuse, liquefy, soften, thaw **2 = disappear,** break down, crumble, decompose, diffuse, disintegrate, disperse, dissipate, dwindle, evanesce, evaporate, fade, melt away, perish, vanish, waste away **3 = break up,** collapse, disorganize, disunite, divorce, loose, resolve into, separate, sever **4 = end,** axe (*Informal*), break up, destroy, discontinue, dismiss, overthrow, ruin, suspend, terminate, wind up

dissuade *verb* = **deter,** advise against, discourage, disincline, divert, expostulate, persuade not to, put off, remonstrate, talk out of, urge not to, warn
➤ **Antonyms**
bring round (*informal*), coax, convince, persuade, sway, talk into

distance *noun* **1 = space,** absence, extent, gap, interval, lapse, length, range, reach, remoteness, remove, separation, span, stretch, width **2 = reserve,** aloofness, coldness, coolness, frigidity, remoteness, restraint, stiffness **3 go the distance = finish,** bring to an end, complete, see through, stay the course **4 in the distance = far off,** afar, far away, on the horizon, yonder **5 keep one's distance = be reserved,** avoid, be aloof, be indifferent, keep (someone) at arm's length, shun
♦ *verb* **6 distance oneself = separate oneself,** be distanced from, dissociate oneself, put in proportion

distant *adjective* **1 = far-off,** abroad, afar, far, faraway, far-flung, outlying, out-of-the-way, remote, removed **2 = apart,** disparate, dispersed, distinct, scattered, separate **3 = reserved,** aloof, at arm's length, ceremonious, cold, cool, formal, haughty, restrained, reticent, standoffish, stiff, unapproachable, unfriendly, withdrawn **4 = faint,** indistinct, obscure, slight, uncertain
➤ **Antonyms**
≠**far-off:** adjacent, adjoining, at hand, close, handy, imminent, just round the corner, near, nearby, neighbouring, nigh, proximate, within sniffing distance (*informal*) ≠**reserved:** close, friendly, intimate, warm

distaste *noun* = **dislike,** abhorrence, antipathy, aversion, detestation, disfavour, disgust, disinclination, displeasure, disrelish, dissatisfaction, horror, loathing, odium, repugnance, revulsion

distasteful *adjective* = **unpleasant,** abhorrent, disagreeable, displeasing, loathsome, nauseous, objectionable, obnoxious, obscene, offensive, repugnant, repulsive, undesirable, uninviting, unpalatable, unsavoury
➤ **Antonyms**
agreeable, charming, enjoyable, pleasing, pleasurable

distend *verb* = **swell,** balloon, bloat, bulge, dilate, enlarge, expand, increase, inflate, puff, stretch, widen

distended *adjective* = **swollen,** bloated, dilated, enlarged, expanded, inflated, puffy, stretched, tumescent

distil *verb* = **extract,** condense, draw out, evaporate, express, press out, purify, rectify, refine, sublimate, vaporize

distillation *noun* = **essence,** elixir, extract, quintessence, spirit

distinct *adjective* **1 = different,** detached, discrete, dissimilar, individual, separate, unconnected **2 = definite,** apparent, black-and-white, blatant, bold, clear, clear-cut, decided, evident, lucid, manifest, marked, noticeable, obvious, palpable, patent, plain, recognizable, sharp, unambiguous, unmistakable, well-defined
➤ **Antonyms**
≠**different:** common, connected, identical, indistinct, similar ≠**definite:** fuzzy, indefinite, indistinct, obscure, unclear, vague

distinction *noun* **1 = differentiation,** discernment, discrimination, penetration, perception, separation **2 = feature,** characteristic, distinctiveness, individuality, mark, particularity, peculiarity, quality **3 = difference,** contrast, differential, division, fine line, separation **4 = excellence,** account, celebrity, consequence, credit, eminence, fame, greatness, honour, importance, merit, name, note, prominence, quality, rank, renown, reputation, repute, superiority, worth

distinctive *adjective* = **characteristic,** different, distinguishing, extraordinary, idiosyncratic, individual, original, peculiar, singular, special, typical, uncommon, unique
➤ **Antonyms**
common, ordinary, run-of-the-mill, typical

distinctly *adverb* = **definitely,** clearly, decidedly, evidently, manifestly, markedly, noticeably, obviously, palpably, patently, plainly, precisely, sharply, unmistakably

distinctness *noun* **1 = clearness,** clarity, lucidity, obviousness, plainness, sharpness, vividness **2 = difference,** detachment, discreteness, disparateness, dissimilarity, dissociation, distinctiveness, individuality, separation

distinguish *verb* **1 = differentiate,** ascertain, decide, determine, discriminate, judge, tell apart, tell between, tell the difference **2 = characterize,** categorize, classify, individualize, make distinctive, mark, separate, set apart, single out **3 = make out,** discern, know, perceive, pick out, recognize, see, tell 4 = **make famous**, celebrate, dignify, honour, immortalize, signalize

distinguishable *adjective* = **recognizable**, bold, clear, conspicuous, discernible, evident, manifest, noticeable, obvious, perceptible, plain, well-marked

distinguished *adjective* 1 = **eminent**, acclaimed, celebrated, conspicuous, famed, famous, illustrious, notable, noted, renowned, well-known 2 = **marked**, conspicuous, extraordinary, outstanding, signal, striking
➤ **Antonyms**
common, inferior, undistinguished, unknown

distinguishing *adjective* = **characteristic**, different, differentiating, distinctive, individualistic, marked, peculiar, typical

distort *verb* 1 = **misrepresent**, bias, colour, falsify, garble, pervert, slant, twist 2 = **deform**, bend, buckle, contort, disfigure, misshape, twist, warp, wrench, wrest

distortion *noun* 1 = **misrepresentation**, bias, colouring, falsification, perversion, slant 2 = **deformity**, bend, buckle, contortion, crookedness, malformation, twist, twistedness, warp

distract *verb* 1 = **divert**, draw away, sidetrack, turn aside 2 = **amuse**, beguile, engross, entertain, occupy 3 = **agitate**, bewilder, confound, confuse, derange, discompose, disconcert, disturb, harass, madden, perplex, puzzle, torment, trouble

distracted *adjective* 1 = **agitated**, at sea, bemused, bewildered, confounded, confused, flustered, harassed, in a flap (*informal*), perplexed, puzzled, troubled 2 = **frantic**, at the end of one's tether, crazy, deranged, desperate, distraught, frenzied, gonzo (*slang*), grief-stricken, insane, mad, overwrought, raving, wild

distracting *adjective* = **disturbing**, bewildering, bothering, confusing, disconcerting, dismaying, off-putting (*Brit. informal*), perturbing

distraction *noun* 1 = **diversion**, disturbance, interference, interruption 2 = **entertainment**, amusement, beguilement, diversion, divertissement, pastime, recreation 3 = **agitation**, abstraction, bewilderment, commotion, confusion, discord, disorder, disturbance 4 = **frenzy**, aberration, alienation, delirium, derangement, desperation, hallucination, incoherence, insanity, mania

distraught *adjective* = **frantic**, agitated, anxious, at the end of one's tether, beside oneself, crazed, desperate, distracted, distressed, hysterical, mad, out of one's mind, overwrought, raving, wild, worked-up, wrought-up

distress *noun* 1 = **worry**, affliction, agony, anguish, anxiety, desolation, discomfort, grief, heartache, misery, pain, sadness, sorrow, suffering, torment, torture, woe, wretchedness 2 = **need**, adversity, calamity, destitution, difficulties, hardship, indigence, misfortune, poverty, privation, straits, trial, trouble ♦ *verb* 3 = **upset**, afflict, agonize, bother, disturb, grieve, harass, harrow, pain, perplex, sadden, torment, trouble, worry, wound

distressed *adjective* 1 = **upset**, afflicted, agitated, anxious, distracted, distraught, saddened, tormented, troubled, worried, wretched 2 = **poverty-stricken**, destitute, down at heel, indigent, needy, poor, straitened

distressing *adjective* = **upsetting**, affecting, afflicting, distressful, disturbing, grievous, gut-wrenching, harrowing, heart-breaking, hurtful, lamentable, nerve-racking, painful, sad, worrying

distribute *verb* 1 = **hand out**, circulate, convey, deliver, pass round 2 = **spread**, diffuse, disperse, disseminate, scatter, strew 3 = **share**, administer, allocate, allot, apportion, assign, deal, dispense, dispose, divide, dole out, give, measure out, mete 4 = **classify**, arrange, assort, categorize, class, file, group

distribution *noun* 1 = **delivery**, dealing, handling, mailing, marketing, trading, transport, transportation 2 = **spreading**, circulation, diffusion, dispersal, dispersion, dissemination, propagation, scattering 3 = **sharing**, allocation, allotment, apportionment, dispensation, division, dole, partition 4 = **classification**, arrangement, assortment, disposition, grouping, location, organization, placement

district *noun* = **area**, community, locale, locality, neck of the woods (*informal*), neighbourhood, parish, quarter, region, sector, vicinity, ward

distrust *verb* 1 = **suspect**, be sceptical of, be suspicious of, be wary of, disbelieve, discredit, doubt, misbelieve, mistrust, question, smell a rat (*informal*), wonder about ♦ *noun* 2 = **suspicion**, disbelief, doubt, dubiety, lack of faith, misgiving, mistrust, qualm, question, scepticism, wariness
➤ **Antonyms**
verb ≠**suspect**: believe, depend, have confidence, have faith, trust ♦ *noun*
≠**suspicion**: confidence, faith, reliance, trust

disturb *verb* 1 = **interrupt**, bother, butt in on, disrupt, interfere with, intrude on, pester, rouse, startle 2 = **upset**, agitate, alarm, annoy, confound, discompose, distract, distress, excite, fluster, harass, hassle

(*informal*), perturb, ruffle, shake, trouble, unnerve, unsettle, worry **3 = muddle**, confuse, derange, disarrange, disorder, disorganize, unsettle
➤ **Antonyms**
≠**upset:** calm, compose, lull, pacify, quiet, quieten, reassure, relax, relieve, settle, soothe

disturbance *noun* **1 = interruption**, agitation, annoyance, bother, confusion, derangement, disorder, distraction, hindrance, intrusion, molestation, perturbation, upset **2 = disorder**, bother (*informal*), brawl, commotion, fracas, fray, hubbub, riot, ruckus (*informal*), ruction (*informal*), rumpus, shindig (*informal*), shindy (*informal*), tumult, turmoil, upheaval, uproar

disturbed *adjective* **1** *Psychiatry* **= unbalanced**, disordered, maladjusted, neurotic, troubled, upset **2 = worried**, agitated, angsty (*informal*), antsy (*informal*), anxious, apprehensive, bothered, concerned, disquieted, nervous, troubled, uneasy, upset
➤ **Antonyms**
≠**unbalanced:** balanced, untroubled
≠**worried:** calm, collected, self-possessed, unfazed (*informal*), untroubled

disturbing *adjective* **= worrying**, agitating, alarming, disconcerting, discouraging, dismaying, disquieting, distressing, frightening, harrowing, perturbing, startling, threatening, troubling, unsettling, upsetting

disuse *noun* **= neglect**, abandonment, decay, desuetude, discontinuance, idleness, non-employment, nonuse
➤ **Antonyms**
application, employment, practice, service, usage, use

ditch *noun* **1 = channel**, drain, dyke, furrow, gully, moat, trench, watercourse ♦ *verb* **2** *Slang* **= get rid of**, abandon, axe (*informal*), bin (*informal*), chuck (*informal*), discard, dispose of, drop, dump (*informal*), jettison, junk (*informal*), scrap, throw out *or* overboard

dither *verb* **1** *Chiefly Brit.* **= vacillate**, faff about (*Brit. informal*), falter, haver, hesitate, hum and haw, oscillate, shillyshally (*informal*), swither (*Scot.*), teeter, waver ♦ *noun* **2** *Chiefly Brit.* **= flutter**, bother, flap (*informal*), fluster, pother, stew (*informal*), tiz-woz (*informal*), tizzy (*informal*), twitter (*informal*)
➤ **Antonyms**
verb ≠**vacillate:** come to a conclusion, conclude, decide, make a decision, make up one's mind, reach *or* come to a decision, resolve, settle

dive *verb* **1 = plunge**, descend, dip, disappear, drop, duck, fall, go underwater,

jump, leap, nose-dive, pitch, plummet, submerge, swoop ♦ *noun* **2 = plunge**, dash, header (*informal*), jump, leap, lunge, nose dive, spring **3** *Slang* **= sleazy bar**, honky-tonk (*U.S. slang*), joint (*slang*)

diverge *verb* **1 = separate**, bifurcate, branch, divaricate, divide, fork, part, radiate, split, spread **2 = be at variance**, be at odds, conflict, differ, disagree, dissent **3 = deviate**, depart, digress, meander, stray, turn aside, wander

divergence *noun* **= separation**, branching out, deflection, departure, deviation, difference, digression, disparity, divagation, ramification, varying

divergent *adjective* **= separate**, conflicting, deviating, different, differing, disagreeing, dissimilar, diverging, diverse, variant

divers *adjective* *Archaic or literary* **= various**, different, manifold, many, multifarious, numerous, several, some, sundry, varied

diverse *adjective* **1 = various**, assorted, diversified, manifold, miscellaneous, of every description, several, sundry, varied **2 = different**, differing, discrete, disparate, dissimilar, distinct, divergent, separate, unlike, varying

diversify *verb* **= vary**, alter, assort, branch out, change, expand, have a finger in every pie, mix, modify, spread out, transform, variegate

diversion *noun* **1** *Chiefly Brit.* **= detour**, alteration, change, deflection, departure, deviation, digression, variation **2 = pastime**, amusement, beguilement, delight, distraction, divertissement, enjoyment, entertainment, game, gratification, jollies (*slang*), play, pleasure, recreation, relaxation, sport

diversity *noun* **= difference**, assortment, dissimilarity, distinctiveness, divergence, diverseness, diversification, heterogeneity, medley, multiplicity, range, unlikeness, variance, variegation, variety

divert *verb* **1 = redirect**, avert, deflect, switch, turn aside **2 = distract**, detract, draw *or* lead away from, lead astray, sidetrack **3 = entertain**, amuse, beguile, delight, gratify, recreate, regale

diverting *adjective* **= entertaining**, amusing, beguiling, enjoyable, fun, humorous, pleasant

divest *verb* **1 = strip**, denude, disrobe, doff, remove, take off, unclothe, undress **2 = deprive**, despoil, dispossess, strip

divide *verb* **1 = separate**, bisect, cleave, cut (up), detach, disconnect, part, partition, segregate, sever, shear, split, subdivide, sunder **2 = share**, allocate, allot, apportion,

deal out, dispense, distribute, divvy (up) (*informal*), dole out, measure out, portion **3** = **cause to disagree**, alienate, break up, come between, disunite, estrange, set at variance *or* odds, set *or* pit against one another, sow dissension, split **4** = **classify**, arrange, categorize, grade, group, put in order, separate, sort
➤ **Antonyms**
≠ **separate**: combine, come together, connect, join, knit, marry, splice, unite

dividend *noun* = **bonus**, cut (*informal*), divvy (*informal*), extra, gain, plus, portion, share, surplus

divine *adjective* **1** = **heavenly**, angelic, celestial, godlike, holy, spiritual, superhuman, supernatural **2** = **sacred**, consecrated, holy, religious, sanctified, spiritual **3** = **mystical**, beatific, blissful, exalted, rapturous, supreme, transcendent, transcendental, transmundane **4** *Informal* = **wonderful**, beautiful, excellent, glorious, marvellous, perfect, splendid, superlative
♦ *noun* **5** = **priest**, churchman, clergyman, cleric, ecclesiastic, minister, pastor, reverend
♦ *verb* **6** = **infer**, apprehend, conjecture, deduce, discern, foretell, guess, intuit, perceive, prognosticate, suppose, surmise, suspect, understand **7** *Of water or minerals* = **dowse**

diviner *noun* **1** = **seer**, astrologer, augur, oracle, prophet, sibyl, soothsayer **2** *Of water or minerals* = **dowser**

divinity *noun* **1** = **theology**, religion, religious studies **2** = **god** *or* **goddess**, daemon, deity, genius, guardian spirit, spirit **3** = **godliness**, deity, divine nature, godhead, godhood, holiness, sanctity

divisible *adjective* = **dividable**, fractional, separable, splittable

division *noun* **1** = **separation**, bisection, cutting up, detaching, dividing, partition, splitting up **2** = **sharing**, allotment, apportionment, distribution **3** = **dividing line**, border, boundary, demarcation, divide, divider, partition **4** = **part**, branch, category, class, compartment, department, group, head, portion, section, sector, segment **5** = **disagreement**, breach, difference of opinion, discord, disunion, estrangement, feud, rupture, split, variance
➤ **Antonyms**
≠ **disagreement**: accord, agreement, concord, harmony, peace, union, unity

divisive *adjective* = **disruptive**, alienating, damaging, detrimental, discordant, estranging, inharmonious, pernicious, troublesome, unsettling

divorce *noun* **1** = **separation**, annulment, breach, break, decree nisi, dissolution,

disunion, rupture, severance, split-up ♦ *verb* **2** = **separate**, annul, disconnect, dissociate, dissolve (*marriage*), disunite, divide, part, sever, split up, sunder

divulge *verb* = **make known**, betray, blow wide open (*slang*), communicate, confess, cough (*slang*), declare, disclose, exhibit, expose, get off one's chest (*informal*), impart, leak, let slip, out (*informal*), proclaim, promulgate, publish, reveal, spill (*informal*), spill one's guts about (*slang*), tell, uncover
➤ **Antonyms**
conceal, hide, keep secret

dizzy *adjective* **1** = **giddy**, faint, light-headed, off balance, reeling, shaky, staggering, swimming, vertiginous, weak at the knees, wobbly, woozy (*informal*) **2** = **confused**, at sea, befuddled, bemused, bewildered, dazed, dazzled, muddled **3** = **steep**, lofty, vertiginous **4** *Informal* = **scatterbrained**, capricious, ditzy *or* ditsy (*slang*), fickle, flighty, foolish, frivolous, giddy, light-headed, silly

do *verb* **1** = **perform**, accomplish, achieve, act, carry out, complete, conclude, discharge, end, execute, produce, transact, undertake, work **2** = **be adequate**, answer, be enough, be of use, be sufficient, cut the mustard, pass muster, satisfy, serve, suffice, suit **3** = **get ready**, arrange, be responsible for, fix, look after, make, make ready, organize, prepare, see to, take on **4** = **solve**, decipher, decode, figure out, puzzle out, resolve, work out **5** = **behave**, bear oneself, carry oneself, comport oneself, conduct oneself **6** = **cause**, bring about, create, effect, produce **7** = **get on**, fare, get along, make out, manage, proceed **8** *Informal* = **visit**, cover, explore, journey through *or* around, look at, stop in, tour, travel **9** *Informal* = **cheat**, con (*informal*), cozen, deceive, defraud, diddle (*informal*), dupe, fleece, hoax, pull a fast one on (*informal*), skin (*slang*), stiff (*slang*), swindle, take (someone) for a ride (*informal*), trick **10** = **perform**, act, give, present, produce, put on ♦ *noun* **11** *Informal, chiefly Brit. & N.Z.* = **event**, affair, function, gathering, occasion, party **12 do's and don'ts** *Informal* = **rules**, code, customs, etiquette, instructions, regulations, standards

do away with *verb* **1** = **kill**, blow away (*slang, chiefly U.S.*), bump off (*slang*), destroy, do in (*slang*), exterminate, liquidate, murder, slay, take out (*slang*) **2** = **get rid of**, abolish, axe (*informal*), chuck (*informal*), discard, discontinue, eliminate, junk (*informal*), pull, put an end to, put paid to, remove

docile *adjective* = **submissive**, amenable,

biddable, compliant, ductile, manageable, obedient, pliant, teachable (*rare*), tractable
➤ **Antonyms**
difficult, intractable, obstreperous, troublesome, trying, uncooperative, unmanageable

docility *noun* = **submissiveness**, amenability, biddableness, compliance, ductility, manageability, meekness, obedience, pliancy, tractability

dock[1] *noun* 1 = **wharf**, harbour, pier, quay, waterfront ♦ *verb* 2 = **moor**, anchor, berth, drop anchor, land, put in, tie up 3 *Of spacecraft* = **link up**, couple, hook up, join, rendezvous, unite

dock[2] *verb* 1 = **deduct**, decrease, diminish, lessen, reduce, subtract, withhold 2 = **cut off**, clip, crop, curtail, cut short, diminish, lessen, shorten
➤ **Antonyms**
≠**deduct**: augment, boost, increase, raise

docket *noun* 1 = **label**, bill, certificate, chit, chitty, counterfoil, receipt, tab, tag, tally, ticket, voucher ♦ *verb* 2 = **label**, catalogue, file, index, mark, register, tab, tag, ticket

doctor *noun* 1 = **G.P.**, general practitioner, medic (*informal*), medical practitioner, physician ♦ *verb* 2 = **change**, alter, disguise, falsify, fudge, misrepresent, pervert, tamper with 3 = **add to**, adulterate, cut, dilute, mix with, spike, water down

doctrinaire *adjective* 1 = **dogmatic**, biased, fanatical, inflexible, insistent, opinionated, rigid 2 = **impractical**, hypothetical, ideological, speculative, theoretical, unpragmatic, unrealistic

doctrine *noun* = **teaching**, article, article of faith, belief, canon, concept, conviction, creed, dogma, opinion, precept, principle, tenet

document *noun* 1 = **paper**, certificate, instrument, legal form, record, report ♦ *verb* 2 = **support**, authenticate, back up, certify, cite, corroborate, detail, give weight to, instance, particularize, substantiate, validate, verify

doddering *adjective* = **tottering**, aged, decrepit, doddery, faltering, feeble, floundering, infirm, senile, shaky, shambling, trembly, unsteady, weak

doddle *noun Brit. informal* = **piece of cake** (*informal*), cakewalk (*informal*), child's play (*informal*), cinch (*slang*), easy-peasy (*slang*), money for old rope, no sweat (*slang*), picnic (*informal*), pushover (*slang*)

dodge *verb* 1 = **duck**, body-swerve (*Scot.*), dart, shift, sidestep, swerve, turn aside 2 = **evade**, avoid, body-swerve (*Scot.*), deceive, elude, equivocate, fend off, flannel (*Brit. informal*), fudge, get out of, hedge,

parry, shirk, shuffle, trick ♦ *noun* 3 = **trick**, contrivance, device, feint, flannel (*Brit. informal*), machination, ploy, ruse, scheme, stratagem, subterfuge, wheeze (*Brit. slang*), wile

doer *noun* = **achiever**, active person, activist, bustler, dynamo, go-getter (*informal*), live wire (*slang*), organizer, powerhouse (*slang*), wheeler-dealer (*informal*)

doff *verb* 1 *Of a hat* = **tip**, lift, raise, remove, take off, touch 2 *Of clothing* = **take off**, cast off, discard, remove, shed, slip off, slip out of, throw off, undress

dog *noun* 1 = **hound**, bitch, canine, cur, kuri *or* goorie (*N.Z.*), man's best friend, mongrel, mutt (*slang*), pooch (*slang*), pup, puppy, tyke 2 *Informal* = **scoundrel**, beast, blackguard, cur, heel (*slang*), knave (*archaic*), villain 3 **dog-eat-dog** = **ruthless**, cut-throat, ferocious, fierce, vicious, with no holds barred 4 **go to the dogs** *Informal* = **go to ruin**, degenerate, deteriorate, go down the drain, go to pot ♦ *verb* 5 = **trouble**, follow, haunt, hound, plague, pursue, shadow, tail (*informal*), track, trail

dogged *adjective* = **determined**, firm, immovable, indefatigable, obstinate, persevering, persistent, pertinacious, resolute, single-minded, staunch, steadfast, steady, stiff-necked, stubborn, tenacious, unflagging, unshakable, unyielding
➤ **Antonyms**
doubtful, half-hearted, hesitant, irresolute, undetermined, unsteady

doggedness *noun* = **determination**, bulldog tenacity, endurance, obstinacy, perseverance, persistence, pertinacity, relentlessness, resolution, single-mindedness, steadfastness, steadiness, stubbornness, tenaciousness, tenacity

dogma *noun* = **doctrine**, article, article of faith, belief, credo, creed, opinion, precept, principle, teachings, tenet

dogmatic *adjective* 1 = **opinionated**, arbitrary, arrogant, assertive, categorical, dictatorial, doctrinaire, downright, emphatic, imperious, magisterial, obdurate, overbearing, peremptory 2 = **doctrinal**, authoritative, canonical, categorical, ex cathedra, oracular, positive

dogmatism *noun* = **opinionatedness**, arbitrariness, arrogance, dictatorialness, imperiousness, peremptoriness, positiveness, presumption

dogsbody *noun Informal* = **drudge**, general factotum, maid or man of all work, menial, skivvy (*chiefly Brit.*), slave

do in *verb Slang* 1 = **kill**, blow away (*slang, chiefly U.S.*), butcher, dispatch, eliminate (*slang*), execute, liquidate, murder, slaughter, slay, take out (*slang*) **2 = exhaust**, fag (*informal*), fatigue, knacker (*slang*), shatter (*informal*), tire, wear out, weary

doing *noun* **= carrying out** *or* **through**, achievement, act, action, deed, execution, exploit, handiwork, implementation, performance

doings *plural noun* **= deeds**, actions, affairs, concerns, dealings, events, exploits, goings-on (*informal*), handiwork, happenings, proceedings, transactions

doldrums *noun* **the doldrums = inactivity**, apathy, blues, boredom, depression, dullness, dumps (*informal*), ennui, gloom, inertia, lassitude, listlessness, malaise, stagnation, tedium, the hump (*Brit. informal*), torpor

dole *noun* **1** *Brit. & Austral. informal* **= benefit**, allowance, alms, donation, gift, grant, gratuity, handout, modicum, parcel, pittance, portion, quota, share ♦ *verb* **2 dole out = give out**, administer, allocate, allot, apportion, assign, deal, dispense, distribute, divide, hand out, mete, share

dollop *noun* **= lump**, helping, portion, scoop, serving

doll up *verb Slang* **= dress up**, deck out, get ready, gussy up (*slang*), preen, primp, prink, tart up (*slang*), titivate, trick out

dolt *noun* **= idiot**, ass, berk (*Brit. slang*), blockhead, booby, charlie (*Brit. informal*), chump (*informal*), clot (*Brit. informal*), coot, dickwit (*slang*), dimwit (*informal*), dipstick (*Brit. slang*), dope (*informal*), dork (*slang*), dullard, dumb-ass (*slang*), dunce, dweeb (*U.S. slang*), fathead (*informal*), fool, fuckwit (*taboo slang*), geek (*slang*), gobshite (*Irish taboo slang*), gonzo (*slang*), ignoramus, jerk (*slang, chiefly U.S. & Canad.*), lamebrain (*informal*), nerd *or* nurd (*slang*), nitwit (*informal*), numbskull *or* numskull, numpty (*Scot. informal*), oaf, plank (*Brit. slang*), plonker (*slang*), prat (*slang*), prick (*slang*), schmuck (*U.S. slang*), simpleton, thickhead, twit (*informal, chiefly Brit.*), wally (*slang*)

domestic *adjective* **1 = home**, domiciliary, family, household, private **2 = home-loving**, domesticated, homely, housewifely, stay-at-home **3 = domesticated**, house, house-trained, pet, tame, trained **4 = native**, indigenous, internal, not foreign ♦ *noun* **5 = servant**, char (*informal*), charwoman, daily, daily help, help, maid, woman (*informal*)

domesticate *verb* **1 = tame**, break, gentle, house-train, train **2 = accustom**, acclimatize, familiarize, habituate, naturalize

domesticated *adjective* **1** *Of plants or animals* **= tame**, broken (in), naturalized,

tamed **2 = home-loving**, domestic, homely, house-trained (*jocular*), housewifely
➤ **Antonyms**
≠**tame:** feral, ferocious, savage, unbroken, undomesticated, untamed, wild

dominant *adjective* **1 = controlling**, ascendant, assertive, authoritative, commanding, governing, leading, presiding, ruling, superior, supreme **2 = main**, chief, influential, outstanding, paramount, predominant, pre-eminent, prevailing, prevalent, primary, principal, prominent
➤ **Antonyms**
ancillary, auxiliary, inferior, junior, lesser, lower, minor, secondary, subservient, subsidiary

dominate *verb* **1 = control**, direct, domineer, govern, have the upper hand over, have the whip hand over, keep under one's thumb, lead, lead by the nose (*informal*), master, monopolize, overbear, rule, rule the roost, tyrannize **2 = tower above**, bestride, loom over, overlook, stand head and shoulders above, stand over, survey **3 = predominate**, detract from, eclipse, outshine, overrule, overshadow, prevail over

domination *noun* **1 = control**, ascendancy, authority, command, influence, mastery, power, rule, superiority, supremacy, sway **2 = dictatorship**, despotism, oppression, repression, subjection, subordination, suppression, tyranny

domineer *verb* **= boss around** *or* **about** (*informal*), bluster, browbeat, bully, hector, intimidate, lord it over, menace, overbear, ride roughshod over, swagger, threaten, tyrannize

domineering *adjective* **= overbearing**, arrogant, authoritarian, autocratic, bossy (*informal*), coercive, despotic, dictatorial, high-handed, imperious, iron-handed, magisterial, masterful, oppressive, tyrannical
➤ **Antonyms**
meek, obsequious, servile, shy, submissive, subservient

dominion *noun* **1 = control**, ascendancy, authority, command, domination, government, jurisdiction, mastery, power, rule, sovereignty, supremacy, sway **2 = kingdom**, country, domain, empire, patch, province, realm, region, territory, turf (*U.S. slang*)

don *verb* **= put on**, clothe oneself in, dress in, get into, pull on, slip on *or* into

donate *verb* **= give**, bequeath, bestow, chip in (*informal*), contribute, gift, hand out, make a gift of, present, subscribe

donation *noun* **= contribution**, alms, benefaction, boon, gift, grant, gratuity, hand-out, largesse or largess, offering, present, stipend, subscription

done interjection **1** = **agreed**, it's a bargain, O.K. or okay (informal) ♦ adjective **2** = **finished**, accomplished, completed, concluded, consummated, ended, executed, in the can (informal), over, perfected, realized, terminated, through **3** = **cooked enough**, cooked, cooked sufficiently, cooked to a turn, ready **4** = **used up**, depleted, exhausted, finished, spent **5** = **acceptable**, conventional, de rigueur, proper **6** Informal = **cheated**, conned (informal), duped, taken for a ride (informal), tricked **7 done for** Informal = **finished**, beaten, broken, dashed, defeated, destroyed, doomed, foiled, lost, ruined, undone, wrecked **8 done in** or **up** Informal = **exhausted**, all in (slang), bushed (informal), clapped out (Austral. & N.Z. informal), creamcrackered (Brit. slang), dead (informal), dead beat (informal), dog-tired (informal), fagged out (informal), knackered (slang), on one's last legs, ready to drop, tired out, worn out, worn to a frazzle (informal), zonked (slang) ♦ verb **9 have done with** = **be through with**, be finished with, desist, end relations with, give up, throw over, wash one's hands of

donnish adjective = **scholarly**, bookish, erudite, formalistic, pedagogic, pedantic, precise, scholastic

donor noun = **giver**, almsgiver, benefactor, contributor, donator, grantor (Law), philanthropist
➤ **Antonyms**
assignee, beneficiary, inheritor, legatee, payee, receiver, recipient

doom noun **1** = **destruction**, catastrophe, death, destiny, downfall, fate, fortune, lot, portion, ruin **2** = **sentence**, condemnation, decision, decree, judgment, verdict ♦ verb **3** = **condemn**, consign, damn, decree, destine, foreordain, judge, predestine, preordain, sentence, sound the death knell, threaten

doomed adjective = **condemned**, bedevilled, bewitched, cursed, fated, hopeless, ill-fated, ill-omened, luckless, star-crossed

door noun **1** = **opening**, doorway, egress, entrance, entry, exit, ingress **2 lay at the door of** = **blame**, censure, charge, hold responsible, impute to **3 out of doors** = **in the open air**, alfresco, out, outdoors, outside **4 show someone the door** = **throw out**, ask to leave, boot out (informal), bounce (slang), eject, oust, show out

do out of verb = **cheat**, balk, bilk, con (informal), cozen, deprive, diddle (informal), swindle, trick

dope noun **1** Slang = **drug**, narcotic, opiate **2** Informal = **idiot**, berk (Brit. slang), blockhead, charlie (Brit. informal), coot, dickhead (slang), dickwit (slang), dimwit (informal), dipstick (Brit. slang), divvy (Brit. slang), dull, dork (slang), dumb-ass (slang), dunce, dweeb (U.S. slang), fathead (informal), fool, fuckwit (taboo slang), geek (slang), gobshite (Irish taboo slang), gonzo (slang), jerk (slang, chiefly U.S. & Canad.), lamebrain (informal), nerd or nurd (slang), nitwit (informal), numbskull or numskull, numpty (Scot. informal), oaf, pillock (Brit. slang), plank (Brit. slang), plonker (slang), prat (slang), prick (slang), schmuck (U.S. slang), simpleton, twit (informal, chiefly Brit.), wally (slang) **3** = **information**, details, facts, gen (Brit. informal), info (informal), inside information, lowdown (informal), news, tip ♦ verb **4** = **drug**, anaesthetize, doctor, inject, knock out, narcotize, sedate, stupefy

dormant adjective = **inactive**, asleep, comatose, fallow, hibernating, inert, inoperative, latent, quiescent, sleeping, sluggish, slumbering, suspended, torpid
➤ **Antonyms**
active, alert, alive and kicking, aroused, awake, awakened, conscious, wakeful, wide-awake

dose noun = **quantity**, dosage, draught, drench, measure, portion, potion, prescription

dot noun **1** = **spot**, atom, circle, dab, fleck, full stop, iota, jot, mark, mite, mote, point, speck, speckle **2 on the dot** = **on time**, exactly, on the button (informal), precisely, promptly, punctually, to the minute ♦ verb **3** = **spot**, dab, dabble, fleck, speckle, sprinkle, stipple, stud

dotage noun = **senility**, decrepitude, eld (archaic), feebleness, imbecility, old age, second childhood, weakness

dote on or **upon** verb = **adore**, admire, hold dear, idolize, lavish affection on, prize, treasure

doting adjective = **adoring**, devoted, fond, foolish, indulgent, lovesick

double adjective **1** = **twice**, binate (Botany), coupled, doubled, dual, duplicate, in pairs, paired, twin, twofold **2** = **deceitful**, dishonest, false, hypocritical, insincere, Janus-faced, knavish (archaic), perfidious, treacherous, two-faced, vacillating ♦ verb **3** = **multiply**, duplicate, enlarge, fold, grow, increase, magnify, plait, repeat ♦ noun **4** = **twin**, clone, copy, counterpart, dead ringer (slang), Doppelgänger, duplicate, fellow, impersonator, lookalike, mate, replica, ringer (slang), spitting image (informal) **5 at** or **on the double** = **quickly**, at full speed, briskly, immediately, in double-quick time, pdq (*slang*), posthaste, without delay

double-cross *verb* = **betray**, cheat, cozen, defraud, hoodwink, mislead, sell down the river (*informal*), swindle, trick, two-time (*informal*)

double-dealer *noun* = **cheat**, betrayer, con man (*informal*), cozener, deceiver, dissembler, double-crosser (*informal*), fraud, fraudster, grifter (*slang, chiefly U.S. & Canad.*), hypocrite, rogue, snake in the grass (*informal*), swindler, traitor, two-timer (*informal*)

double-dealing *noun* 1 = **treachery**, bad faith, betrayal, cheating, deceit, deception, dishonesty, duplicity, foul play, hypocrisy, mendacity, perfidy, trickery, two-timing (*informal*) ♦ *adjective* 2 = **treacherous**, cheating, crooked (*informal*), deceitful, dishonest, duplicitous, fraudulent, hypocritical, lying, perfidious, sneaky, swindling, tricky, two-faced, two-timing (*informal*), underhanded, untrustworthy, wily

double entendre *noun* = **double meaning**, ambiguity, innuendo, play on words, pun

doubt *noun* 1 = **uncertainty**, dubiety, hesitancy, hesitation, indecision, irresolution, lack of conviction, suspense, vacillation 2 = **suspicion**, apprehension, disquiet, distrust, fear, incredulity, lack of faith, misgiving, mistrust, qualm, scepticism 3 = **difficulty**, ambiguity, can of worms (*informal*), confusion, dilemma, perplexity, problem, quandary 4 **no doubt** = **certainly**, admittedly, assuredly, doubtless, doubtlessly, probably, surely ♦ *verb* 5 = **be uncertain**, be dubious, demur, fluctuate, hesitate, scruple, vacillate, waver 6 = **suspect**, discredit, distrust, fear, lack confidence in, misgive, mistrust, query, question
➤ **Antonyms**
noun ≠**uncertainty**: belief, certainty, confidence, conviction ≠**suspicion**: confidence, trust ♦ *verb* ≠**suspect**: accept, believe, buy (*slang*), have faith in, swallow (*informal*), take on board, trust

doubter *noun* = **sceptic**, agnostic, disbeliever, doubting Thomas, questioner, unbeliever

doubtful *adjective* 1 = **unlikely**, ambiguous, debatable, dodgy (*Brit., Austral., & N.Z. informal*), dubious, equivocal, hazardous, iffy (*informal*), improbable, inconclusive, indefinite, indeterminate, inexact, obscure, precarious, problematic(al), questionable, unclear, unconfirmed, vague 2 = **unsure**, distrustful, hesitating, in two minds (*informal*), irresolute, leery (*slang*), perplexed, sceptical, suspicious, tentative,

uncertain, unconvinced, undecided, unresolved, unsettled, vacillating, wavering 3 = **questionable**, disreputable, dodgy (*Brit., Austral., & N.Z. informal*), dubious, shady (*informal*), suspect, suspicious
➤ **Antonyms**
≠**unlikely**: certain, definite, indubitable
≠**unsure**: certain, decided, positive, resolute

doubtless *adverb* 1 = **certainly**, assuredly, clearly, indisputably, of course, precisely, surely, truly, undoubtedly, unquestionably, without doubt 2 = **probably**, apparently, most likely, ostensibly, presumably, seemingly, supposedly

dour *adjective* = **gloomy**, dismal, dreary, forbidding, grim, morose, sour, sullen, unfriendly
➤ **Antonyms**
carefree, cheerful, cheery, chirpy (*informal*), genial, good-humoured, happy, jovial, pleasant, sunny

dovetail *verb* 1 = **fit together**, fit, interlock, join, link, mortise, tenon, unite 2 = **correspond**, accord, agree, coincide, conform, harmonize, match, tally

dowdy *adjective* = **frumpy**, dingy, drab, frowzy, frumpish, ill-dressed, old-fashioned, scrubby (*Brit. informal*), shabby, slovenly, tacky (*U.S. informal*), unfashionable
➤ **Antonyms**
chic, dressy, fashionable, neat, smart, spruce, trim, well-dressed

dower *noun* = **dowry**, inheritance, legacy, portion, provision, share

do without *verb* = **manage without**, abstain from, dispense with, forgo, get along without, give up, kick (*informal*)

down *adjective* 1 = **depressed**, blue, dejected, disheartened, dismal, downcast, down in the dumps (*informal*), low, miserable, sad, sick as a parrot (*informal*), unhappy ♦ *verb* 2 *Informal* = **swallow**, drain, drink (down), gulp, put away, toss off 3 = **bring down**, deck (*slang*), fell, floor, knock down, overthrow, prostrate, subdue, tackle, throw, trip ♦ *noun* 4 = **drop**, decline, descent, dropping, fall, falling, reverse 5 **have a down on** *Informal* = **be antagonistic** *or* **hostile to**, be anti (*informal*), bear a grudge towards, be contra (*informal*), be prejudiced against, be set against, feel ill will towards, have it in for (*slang*)

down-and-out *noun* 1 = **tramp**, bag lady, beggar, bum (*informal*), derelict, dosser (*Brit. slang*), loser, outcast, pauper, vagabond, vagrant ♦ *adjective* 2 = **destitute**, derelict, dirt-poor (*informal*), flat broke (*informal*), impoverished, on one's uppers (*informal*), penniless, ruined, short, without two pennies to rub together (*informal*)

downcast *adjective* = **dejected**, cheerless, choked, crestfallen, daunted, depressed, despondent, disappointed, disconsolate, discouraged, disheartened, dismal, dismayed, dispirited, down in the dumps (*informal*), miserable, sad, sick as a parrot (*informal*), unhappy
➤ **Antonyms**
cheerful, cheery, chirpy (*informal*), contented, elated, genial, happy, joyful, light-hearted, optimistic

downfall *noun* 1 = **ruin**, breakdown, collapse, comedown, comeuppance (*slang*), debacle, descent, destruction, disgrace, fall, overthrow, undoing 2 = **rainstorm**, cloudburst, deluge, downpour

downgrade *verb* 1 = **demote**, degrade, humble, lower *or* reduce in rank, take down a peg (*informal*) 2 = **run down**, decry, denigrate, detract from, disparage
➤ **Antonyms**
≠**demote:** advance, better, elevate, enhance, improve, promote, raise, upgrade

downhearted *adjective* = **dejected**, blue, chapfallen, crestfallen, depressed, despondent, discouraged, disheartened, dismayed, dispirited, downcast, low-spirited, sad, sick as a parrot (*informal*), sorrowful, unhappy

downpour *noun* = **rainstorm**, cloudburst, deluge, flood, inundation, torrential rain

downright *adjective* 1 = **complete**, absolute, arrant, blatant, categorical, clear, deep-dyed (*usually derogatory*), explicit, out-and-out, outright, plain, positive, simple, thoroughgoing, total, undisguised, unequivocal, unqualified, utter 2 = **blunt**, candid, forthright, frank, honest, open, outspoken, plain, sincere, straightforward, straight-from-the-shoulder, upfront (*informal*)

down-to-earth *adjective* = **sensible**, common-sense, hard-headed, matter-of-fact, mundane, no-nonsense, plain-spoken, practical, realistic, sane, unsentimental

downtrodden *adjective* = **oppressed**, abused, afflicted, distressed, exploited, helpless, subjugated, subservient, tyrannized

downward *adjective* = **descending**, declining, earthward, heading down, sliding, slipping

doze *verb* 1 = **nap**, catnap, drop off (*informal*), drowse, kip (*Brit. slang*), nod, nod off (*informal*), sleep, sleep lightly, slumber, snooze (*informal*), zizz (*Brit. informal*) ♦ *noun* 2 = **nap**, catnap, forty winks (*informal*), kip (*Brit. slang*), little sleep, shuteye (*slang*), siesta, snooze

(*informal*), zizz (*Brit. informal*)

drab *adjective* = **dull**, cheerless, colourless, dingy, dismal, dreary, flat, gloomy, grey, lacklustre, shabby, sombre, uninspired, vapid
➤ **Antonyms**
bright, cheerful, colourful, jazzy (*informal*), vibrant, vivid

draft *noun* 1 = **outline**, abstract, delineation, plan, preliminary form, rough, sketch, version 2 = **order**, bill (*of exchange*), cheque, postal order ♦ *verb* 3 = **outline**, compose, delineate, design, draw, draw up, formulate, plan, sketch

drag *verb* 1 = **pull**, draw, hale, haul, lug, tow, trail, tug, yank 2 = **go slowly**, crawl, creep, inch, limp along, shamble, shuffle 3 = **lag behind**, dawdle, draggle, linger, loiter, straggle, trail behind 4 **drag on** *or* **out** = **last**, draw out, extend, keep going, lengthen, persist, prolong, protract, spin out, stretch out 5 **drag one's feet** *Informal* = **stall**, block, hold back, obstruct, procrastinate ♦ *noun* 6 *Slang* = **nuisance**, annoyance, bore, bother, pain (*informal*), pain in the arse (*taboo informal*), pest

dragging *adjective* = **tedious**, boring, dull, going slowly, humdrum, mind-numbing, monotonous, tiresome, wearisome

dragoon *verb* = **force**, browbeat, bully, coerce, compel, constrain, drive, impel, intimidate, railroad (*informal*), strong-arm (*informal*)

drain *noun* 1 = **pipe**, channel, conduit, culvert, ditch, duct, outlet, sewer, sink, trench, watercourse 2 = **reduction**, depletion, drag, exhaustion, expenditure, sap, strain, withdrawal 3 **down the drain** = **wasted**, gone, gone for good, lost, ruined ♦ *verb* 4 = **remove**, bleed, draw off, dry, empty, evacuate, milk, pump off *or* out, tap, withdraw 5 = **flow out**, discharge, effuse, exude, leak, ooze, seep, trickle, well out 6 = **drink up**, finish, gulp down, quaff, swallow 7 = **exhaust**, consume, deplete, dissipate, empty, sap, strain, tax, use up, weary

drainage *noun* = **sewerage**, bilge (water), seepage, sewage, waste

dram *noun* = **shot** (*informal*), drop, glass, measure, slug, snifter (*informal*), snort (*slang*), tot

drama *noun* 1 = **play**, dramatization, show, stage play, stage show, theatrical piece 2 = **theatre**, acting, dramatic art, dramaturgy, stagecraft, Thespian art 3 = **excitement**, crisis, dramatics, histrionics, scene, spectacle, theatrics, turmoil

dramatic *adjective* 1 = **theatrical**, dramaturgic, dramaturgical, Thespian 2 = **powerful**, affecting, effective, expressive,

impressive, moving, striking, vivid **3** = **exciting**, breathtaking, climactic, electrifying, emotional, high-octane (*informal*), melodramatic, sensational, shock-horror (*facetious*), startling, sudden, suspenseful, tense, thrilling
➤ **Antonyms**
≠ **powerful**: ordinary, run-of-the-mill, undramatic, unexceptional, unmemorable

dramatist *noun* = **playwright**, dramaturge, screenwriter, scriptwriter

dramatize *verb* = **exaggerate**, act, lay it on (thick) (*slang*), make a performance of, overdo, overstate, play-act, play to the gallery

drape *verb* **1** = **cover**, adorn, array, cloak, fold, swathe, wrap **2** = **hang**, dangle, droop, drop, lean over, let fall, suspend

drastic *adjective* = **extreme**, desperate, dire, forceful, harsh, radical, severe, strong

draught *noun* **1** = **breeze**, current, flow, influx, movement, puff **2** = **drink**, cup, dose, drench, potion, quantity **3** = **pulling**, dragging, drawing, haulage, traction

draw *verb* **1** = **sketch**, delineate, depict, design, map out, mark out, outline, paint, portray, trace **2** = **pull**, drag, haul, tow, tug **3** = **take out**, extort, extract, pull out **4** = **attract**, allure, bring forth, call forth, elicit, engage, entice, evoke, induce, influence, invite, persuade **5** = **deduce**, derive, get, infer, make, take **6** = **choose**, pick, select, single out, take **7** = **stretch**, attenuate, elongate, extend, lengthen **8** = **inhale**, breathe in, drain, inspire, puff, pull, respire, suck **9** = **draft**, compose, formulate, frame, prepare, write ♦ *noun* **10** *Informal* = **attraction**, enticement, lure, pull (*informal*) **11** = **tie**, dead heat, deadlock, impasse, stalemate

drawback *noun* = **disadvantage**, defect, deficiency, detriment, difficulty, downside, fault, flaw, fly in the ointment (*informal*), handicap, hazard, hindrance, hitch, impediment, imperfection, nuisance, obstacle, snag, stumbling block, trouble
➤ **Antonyms**
advantage, asset, benefit, gain, help, service, use

draw back *verb* = **recoil**, back off, retract, retreat, shrink, start back, withdraw

drawing *noun* = **picture**, cartoon, delineation, depiction, illustration, outline, portrayal, representation, sketch, study

drawl *verb* = **draw out**, drag out, extend, lengthen, prolong, protract

drawling *adjective* = **droning**, dragging, drawly, dull, twanging, twangy

drawn *adjective* = **tense**, fatigued, fraught, haggard, harassed, harrowed, pinched, sapped, strained, stressed, taut, tired, worn

draw on *verb* = **make use of**, employ, exploit, extract, fall back on, have recourse to, rely on, take from, use

draw out *verb* = **extend**, drag out, lengthen, make longer, prolong, prolongate, protract, spin out, stretch, string out
➤ **Antonyms**
curtail, cut, cut short, dock, pare down, reduce, shorten, trim, truncate

draw up *verb* **1** = **draft**, compose, formulate, frame, prepare, write out **2** = **halt**, bring to a stop, pull up, run in, stop, stop short

dread *verb* **1** = **fear**, anticipate with horror, cringe at, have cold feet (*informal*), quail, shrink from, shudder, tremble ♦ *noun* **2** = **fear**, affright, alarm, apprehension, aversion, awe, dismay, fright, funk (*informal*), heebie-jeebies (*slang*), horror, terror, trepidation ♦ *adjective* **3** *Literary* = **frightening**, alarming, awe-inspiring, awful, dire, dreaded, dreadful, frightful, horrible, terrible, terrifying

dreadful *adjective* = **terrible**, abysmal, alarming, appalling, atrocious, awful, dire, distressing, fearful, formidable, frightful, from hell (*informal*), ghastly, godawful (*slang*), grievous, hellacious (*U.S. slang*), hideous, horrendous, horrible, monstrous, shocking, tragic, tremendous

dream *noun* **1** = **vision**, delusion, hallucination, illusion, imagination, reverie, speculation, trance, vagary **2** = **daydream**, fantasy, pipe dream **3** = **ambition**, aim, aspiration, design, desire, goal, Holy Grail (*informal*), hope, notion, thirst, wish **4** = **delight**, beauty, gem, joy, marvel, pleasure, treasure ♦ *verb* **5** = **have dreams**, conjure up, envisage, fancy, hallucinate, imagine, think, visualize **6** = **daydream**, build castles in the air *or* in Spain, fantasize, stargaze

dreamer *noun* = **idealist**, daydreamer, Don Quixote, escapist, fantasist, fantasizer, fantast, romancer, theorizer, utopian, visionary, Walter Mitty

dreamland *noun* = **land of make-believe**, cloud-cuckoo-land, cloudland, dream world, fairyland, fantasy, illusion, land of dreams, land of Nod, never-never land (*informal*)

dream up *verb* = **invent**, concoct, contrive, cook up (*informal*), create, devise, hatch, imagine, spin, think up

dreamy *adjective* **1** = **vague**, absent, abstracted, daydreaming, faraway, in a reverie, musing, pensive, preoccupied, with one's head in the clouds **2** = **impractical**, airy-fairy, dreamlike, fanciful, imaginary, quixotic, speculative, surreal, vague, visionary **3** = **unreal**, chimerical, dreamlike,

dreary

drip

fantastic, intangible, misty, phantasmagoric, phantasmagorical, shadowy **4 = relaxing,** calming, gentle, lulling, romantic, soothing
➤ Antonyms
≠**vague, impractical:** common-sense, down-to-earth, feet-on-the-ground, practical, pragmatic, realistic, unromantic

dreary *adjective* **1 = dull,** as dry as dust, boring, colourless, drab, ho-hum (*informal*), humdrum, lifeless, mind-numbing, monotonous, routine, tedious, tiresome, uneventful, uninteresting, wearisome **2 = dismal,** bleak, cheerless, comfortless, depressing, doleful, downcast, drear, forlorn, funereal, gloomy, glum, joyless, lonely, lonesome, melancholy, mournful, sad, solitary, sombre, sorrowful, wretched
➤ Antonyms
≠**dull:** bright, interesting ≠**dismal:** cheerful, happy, joyful

dregs *plural noun* **1 = sediment,** deposit, draff, dross, grounds, lees, residue, residuum, scourings, scum, trash, waste **2 = scum,** canaille, down-and-outs, good-for-nothings, outcasts, rabble, ragtag and bobtail, riffraff

drench *verb* **1 = soak,** drown, duck, flood, imbrue, inundate, saturate, souse, steep, swamp, wet ◆ *noun* **2** *Veterinary* **= dose,** physic, purge

dress *noun* **1 = frock,** costume, ensemble, garment, get-up (*informal*), gown, outfit, rigout (*informal*), robe, suit **2 = clothing,** apparel, attire, clothes, costume, garb, garments, gear (*informal*), guise, habiliment, raiment (*archaic or poetic*), schmutter (*slang*), threads (*slang*), togs, vestment ◆ *verb* **3 = put on,** attire, change, clothe, don, garb, robe, slip on *or* into **4 = decorate,** adorn, apparel (*archaic*), array, bedeck, deck, drape, embellish, festoon, furbish, ornament, rig, trim **5 = bandage,** bind up, plaster, treat **6 = arrange,** adjust, align, comb (out), dispose, do (up), fit, get ready, groom, prepare, set, straighten
➤ Antonyms
verb ≠**put on:** disrobe, divest oneself of, peel off (*slang*), shed, strip, take off one's clothes

dress down *verb Informal* **= reprimand,** bawl out (*informal*), berate, carpet (*informal*), castigate, chew out (*U.S. & Canad. informal*), give a rocket (*Brit. & N.Z. informal*), haul over the coals, rap over the knuckles, read the riot act, rebuke, reprove, scold, slap on the wrist, tear into (*informal*), tear (someone) off a strip (*Brit. informal*), tell off (*informal*), upbraid

dressmaker *noun* **= seamstress,** couturier, modiste, sewing woman, tailor

dress up *verb* **1 = dress formally,** doll up

(*slang*), dress for dinner, put on one's best bib and tucker (*informal*), put on one's glad rags (*informal*) **2 = put on fancy dress,** disguise, play-act, wear a costume

dribble *verb* **1 = run,** drip, drop, fall in drops, leak, ooze, seep, trickle **2 = drool,** drip saliva, drivel, slaver, slobber

drift *verb* **1 = float,** be carried along, coast, go (aimlessly), meander, stray, waft, wander **2 = pile up,** accumulate, amass, bank up, drive, gather ◆ *noun* **3 = accumulation,** bank, heap, mass, mound **4 = meaning,** aim, design, direction, gist, implication, import, intention, object, purport, scope, significance, tendency, tenor, thrust **5 = current,** course, direction, flow, impulse, movement, rush, sweep, trend

drifter *noun* **= wanderer,** beachcomber, bum (*informal*), hobo (*U.S.*), itinerant, rolling stone, vagrant

drill *noun* **1 = boring tool,** bit, borer, gimlet, rotary tool **2 = training,** discipline, exercise, instruction, practice, preparation, repetition ◆ *verb* **3 = bore,** penetrate, perforate, pierce, puncture, sink in **4 = train,** coach, discipline, exercise, instruct, practise, rehearse, teach

drink *verb* **1 = swallow,** absorb, drain, gulp, guzzle, imbibe, partake of, quaff, sip, suck, sup, swig (*informal*), swill, toss off, wash down, wet one's whistle (*informal*) **2 = booze** (*informal*), bend the elbow (*informal*), bevvy (*dialect*), carouse, go on a binge *or* bender (*informal*), hit the bottle (*informal*), indulge, pub-crawl (*informal, chiefly Brit.*), revel, tipple, tope, wassail ◆ *noun* **3 = beverage,** liquid, potion, refreshment, thirst quencher **4 = alcohol,** booze (*informal*), Dutch courage, hooch *or* hootch (*informal, chiefly U.S. & Canad.*), liquor, spirits, the bottle (*informal*) **5 = glass,** cup, draught, gulp, noggin, sip, snifter (*informal*), swallow, swig (*informal*), taste, tipple **6 the drink** *Informal* **= the sea,** the briny (*informal*), the deep, the main, the ocean

drinker *noun* **= alcoholic,** bibber, boozer (*informal*), dipsomaniac, drunk, drunkard, guzzler, inebriate, lush (*slang*), soak (*slang*), sot, sponge (*informal*), tippler, toper, wino (*informal*)

drink in *verb* **= pay attention,** absorb, assimilate, be all ears (*informal*), be fascinated by, be rapt, hang on (someone's) words, hang on the lips of

drink to *verb* **= toast,** pledge, pledge the health of, salute

drip *verb* **1 = drop,** dribble, drizzle, exude, filter, plop, splash, sprinkle, trickle ◆ *noun* **2 = drop,** dribble, dripping, leak, trickle **3**

Informal = **weakling**, milksop, mummy's boy (*informal*), namby-pamby, ninny, softie (*informal*), weed (*informal*), wet (*Brit. informal*)

drive *verb* 1 = **operate**, direct, go, guide, handle, manage, motor, ride, steer, travel 2 = **goad**, actuate, coerce, compel, constrain, dragoon, force, harass, impel, motivate, oblige, overburden, overwork, press, prick, prod, prompt, railroad (*informal*), rush, spur 3 = **push**, herd, hurl, impel, propel, send, urge 4 = **thrust**, dig, hammer, plunge, push, ram, sink, stab ♦ *noun* 5 = **run**, excursion, hurl (*Scot.*), jaunt, journey, outing, ride, spin (*informal*), trip, turn 6 = **campaign**, action, advance, appeal, crusade, effort, push (*informal*), surge 7 = **initiative**, ambition, effort, energy, enterprise, get-up-and-go (*informal*), motivation, pep, pressure, push (*informal*), vigour, zip (*informal*)

drive at *verb Informal* = **mean**, aim, allude to, get at, have in mind, hint at, imply, indicate, insinuate, intend, intimate, refer to, signify, suggest

drivel *noun* 1 = **nonsense**, balderdash, balls (*taboo slang*), bilge (*informal*), blah (*slang*), bosh (*informal*), bull (*slang*), bullshit (*taboo slang*), bunk (*informal*), bunkum *or* buncombe (*chiefly U.S.*), cobblers (*Brit. taboo slang*), crap (*slang*), dross, eyewash (*informal*), fatuity, garbage (*informal*), gibberish, guff (*slang*), hogwash, hokum (*slang, chiefly U.S. & Canad.*), horsefeathers (*U.S. slang*), hot air (*informal*), moonshine, pap, piffle (*informal*), poppycock (*informal*), prating, rot, rubbish, shit (*taboo slang*), stuff, tommyrot, tosh (*slang, chiefly Brit.*), trash, tripe (*informal*), twaddle, waffle (*informal, chiefly Brit.*) 2 = **saliva**, slaver, slobber ♦ *verb* 3 = **babble**, blether, gab (*informal*), gas (*informal*), maunder, prate, ramble, waffle (*informal, chiefly Brit.*) 4 = **dribble**, drool, slaver, slobber

driving *adjective* = **forceful**, compelling, dynamic, energetic, galvanic, storming (*informal*), sweeping, vigorous, violent

drizzle *noun* 1 = **fine rain**, Scotch mist, smir (*Scot.*) ♦ *verb* 2 = **rain**, mizzle (*dialect*), shower, spot *or* spit with rain, spray, sprinkle

droll *adjective* = **amusing**, clownish, comic, comical, diverting, eccentric, entertaining, farcical, funny, humorous, jocular, laughable, ludicrous, odd, oddball (*informal*), off-the-wall (*slang*), quaint, ridiculous, risible, waggish, whimsical

drone[1] *noun* = **parasite**, couch potato (*slang*), idler, leech, loafer, lounger, scrounger (*informal*), skiver (*Brit. slang*), sluggard, sponger (*informal*)

drone[2] *verb* 1 = **hum**, buzz, purr, thrum, vibrate, whirr 2 **drone on** = **speak monotonously**, be boring, chant, drawl, intone, prose about, spout, talk interminably ♦ *noun* 3 = **hum**, buzz, murmuring, purr, thrum, vibration, whirr, whirring

drool *verb* 1 = **dribble**, drivel, salivate, slaver, slobber, water at the mouth 2 **drool over** = **gloat over**, dote on, fondle, gush, make much of, pet, rave about (*informal*), slobber over, spoil

droop *verb* 1 = **sag**, bend, dangle, drop, fall down, hang (down), sink 2 = **flag**, decline, diminish, fade, faint, languish, slump, wilt, wither

drop *verb* 1 = **fall**, decline, depress, descend, diminish, dive, droop, lower, plummet, plunge, sink, tumble 2 = **drip**, dribble, fall in drops, trickle 3 = **set down**, deposit, leave, let off, unload 4 = **discontinue**, abandon, axe (*informal*), cease, desert, forsake, give up, kick (*informal*), leave, quit, relinquish, remit, terminate 5 *Informal* = **reject**, disown, ignore, jilt, renounce, repudiate, throw over ♦ *noun* 6 = **droplet**, bead, bubble, driblet, drip, globule, pearl, tear 7 = **dash**, dab, mouthful, nip, pinch, shot (*informal*), sip, spot, taste, tot, trace, trickle 8 = **decrease**, cut, decline, deterioration, downturn, fall-off, lowering, reduction, slump 9 = **fall**, abyss, chasm, declivity, descent, plunge, precipice, slope

drop in (on) *verb Informal* = **visit**, blow in (*informal*), call, call in, go and see, look in (on), look up, pop in (*informal*), roll up (*informal*), stop, turn up

drop off *verb* 1 = **set down**, allow to alight, deliver, leave, let off 2 *Informal* = **fall asleep**, catnap, doze (off), drowse, have forty winks (*informal*), nod (off), snooze (*informal*) 3 = **decrease**, decline, diminish, dwindle, fall off, lessen, slacken

drop out *verb* = **leave**, abandon, back out, cop out (*slang*), fall by the wayside, forsake, give up, quit, renege, stop, withdraw

drought *noun* 1 = **dry spell**, aridity, dehydration, drouth (*Scot.*), dryness, dry weather, parchedness 2 = **shortage**, dearth, deficiency, insufficiency, lack, need, scarcity, want
➤ **Antonyms**
≠**dry spell:** deluge, downpour, flood, flow, inundation, outpouring, rush, stream, torrent ≠**shortage:** abundance, profusion

drove *noun* = **herd**, collection, company, crowd, flock, gathering, horde, mob, multitude, press, swarm, throng

drown *verb* 1 = **drench**, deluge, engulf, flood, go down, go under, immerse, inundate, sink, submerge, swamp 2

= **overpower**, deaden, engulf, muffle, obliterate, overcome, overwhelm, stifle, swallow up, wipe out

drowse verb 1 = **be sleepy**, be drowsy, be lethargic, doze, drop off (informal), kip (Brit. slang), nap, nod, sleep, slumber, snooze (informal), zizz (Brit. informal) ◆ noun 2 = **sleep**, doze, forty winks (informal), kip (Brit. slang), nap, slumber, zizz (Brit. Informal)

drowsy adjective 1 = **sleepy**, comatose, dazed, dopey (slang), dozy, drugged, half asleep, heavy, lethargic, nodding, somnolent, tired, torpid 2 = **peaceful**, dreamy, lulling, quiet, restful, sleepy, soothing, soporific
➤ Antonyms
≠**sleepy**: alert, awake, bright-eyed and bushy-tailed, full of beans (informal), lively, perky

drubbing noun 1 = **beating**, clobbering (slang), flogging, hammering (informal), licking (informal), pasting (slang), pounding, pummelling, thrashing, walloping (informal), whipping 2 = **defeat**, clobbering (slang), hammering (informal), licking (informal), pasting (slang), thrashing, trouncing

drudge noun 1 = **menial**, dogsbody (informal), factotum, hack, maid or man of all work, plodder, scullion (archaic), servant, skivvy (chiefly Brit.), slave, toiler, worker ◆ verb 2 = **toil**, grind (informal), keep one's nose to the grindstone, labour, moil (archaic or dialect), plod, plug away (informal), slave, work

drudgery noun = **menial labour**, chore, donkey-work, fag (informal), grind (informal), hack work, hard work, labour, skivvying (Brit.), slavery, slog, sweat (informal), sweated labour, toil

drug noun 1 = **medication**, medicament, medicine, physic, poison, remedy 2 = **dope** (slang), narcotic, opiate, stimulant ◆ verb 3 = **dose**, administer a drug, dope (slang), medicate, treat 4 = **knock out**, anaesthetize, deaden, numb, poison, stupefy

drug addict noun = **junkie** (informal), acid head (informal), crack-head (informal), dope-fiend (slang), head (informal), hop-head (informal), tripper (informal)

drugged adjective = **stoned** (slang), bombed (slang), comatose, doped (slang), dopey (slang), flying (slang), high (informal), on a trip (informal), out of it (slang), out of one's mind (slang), out to it (Austral. & N.Z. slang), smashed (slang), spaced out (slang), stupefied, tripping (informal), turned on (slang), under the influence (informal), wasted (slang),

wrecked (slang), zonked (slang)

drum verb 1 = **beat**, pulsate, rap, reverberate, tap, tattoo, throb 2 **drum into** = **drive home**, din into, hammer away, harp on, instil into, reiterate

drum up verb = **canvass**, attract, bid for, obtain, petition, round up, solicit

drunk adjective 1 = **intoxicated**, babalas (S. African), bacchic, bevvied (dialect), bladdered (slang), blitzed (slang), blotto (slang), bombed (slang), Brahms and Liszt (slang), canned (slang), drunken, flying (slang), fu' (Scot.), fuddled, half seas over (informal), inebriated, legless (informal), lit up (slang), loaded (slang, chiefly U.S. & Canad.), maudlin, merry (Brit. informal), muddled, out of it (slang), out to it (Austral. & N.Z. slang), paralytic (informal), pickled (informal), pie-eyed (slang), pissed (taboo slang), plastered (slang), rat-arsed (taboo slang), sloshed (slang), smashed (slang), soaked (informal), steamboats (Scot. slang), steaming (slang), stewed (slang), stoned (slang), tanked up (slang), tiddly (slang, chiefly Brit.), tight (informal), tipsy, tired and emotional (euphemistic), under the influence (informal), wasted (slang), well-oiled (slang), wrecked (slang), zonked (slang) ◆ noun 2 = **drunkard**, alcoholic, boozer (informal), inebriate, lush (slang), soak (slang), sot, toper, wino (informal)

drunkard noun = **drinker**, alcoholic, carouser, dipsomaniac, drunk, lush (slang), soak (slang), sot, tippler, toper, wino (informal)

drunken adjective 1 = **intoxicated**, bevvied (dialect), bibulous, bladdered (slang), blitzed (slang), blotto (slang), bombed (slang), boozing (informal), Brahms and Liszt (slang), drunk, flying (slang), (gin-)sodden, inebriate, legless (informal), lit up (slang), out of it (slang), out to it (Austral. & N.Z. slang), paralytic (informal), pissed (taboo slang), rat-arsed (taboo slang), red-nosed, smashed (slang), sottish, steamboats (Scot. slang), steaming (slang), tippling, toping, under the influence (informal), wasted (slang), wrecked (slang), zonked (slang) 2 = **debauched**, bacchanalian, bacchic, boozy (informal), dionysian, dissipated, orgiastic, riotous, saturnalian

drunkenness noun = **intoxication**, alcoholism, bibulousness, dipsomania, inebriation, insobriety, intemperance, sottishness, tipsiness

dry adjective 1 = **dehydrated**, arid, barren, desiccated, dried up, juiceless, moistureless, parched, sapless, thirsty, torrid, waterless 2 = **dull**, boring, dreary, ho-hum (informal), monotonous, plain, tedious, tiresome,

uninteresting **3 = sarcastic**, cutting,
deadpan, droll, keen, low-key, quietly
humorous, sharp, sly ♦ *verb* **4 = dehydrate**,
dehumidify, desiccate, drain, make dry,
parch, sear
➤ **Antonyms**
adjective ≠**dehydrated**: damp, humid,
moist, wet ≠**dull**: entertaining, interesting,
lively ♦ *verb* ≠**dehydrate**: moisten, wet

dryness *noun* **= aridity**, aridness,
dehumidification, dehydration, drought,
thirst, thirstiness

dry out *or* **up** *verb* **= become dry**, become
unproductive, harden, mummify, shrivel up,
wilt, wither, wizen

dual *adjective* **= twofold**, binary, coupled,
double, duplex, duplicate, matched, paired,
twin

dubious *adjective* **1 = suspect**, dodgy (*Brit.*,
Austral., & *N.Z. informal*), fishy (*informal*),
questionable, shady (*informal*), suspicious,
undependable, unreliable, untrustworthy **2**
= doubtful, ambiguous, debatable, dodgy
(*Brit.*, *Austral.*, & *N.Z. informal*), equivocal
3 = unsure, doubtful, hesitant, iffy
(*informal*), leery (*slang*), sceptical,
uncertain, unconvinced, undecided,
wavering
➤ **Antonyms**
≠**suspect**: dependable, reliable, trustworthy
≠**unsure**: certain, definite, positive, sure

duck *verb* **1 = bob**, bend, bow, crouch,
dodge, drop, lower, stoop **2 = plunge**, dip,
dive, douse, dunk, immerse, souse,
submerge, wet **3** *Informal* **= dodge**, avoid,
body-swerve (*Scot.*), escape, evade, shirk,
shun, sidestep

duct *noun* **= pipe**, canal, channel, conduit,
funnel, passage, tube

dud *Informal* ♦ *noun* **1 = failure**, clinker
(*slang, chiefly U.S.*), clunker (*informal*), flop
(*informal*), washout (*informal*) ♦ *adjective* **2**
= useless, broken, bust (*informal*), duff (*Brit.
informal*), failed, inoperative, kaput
(*informal*), not functioning, valueless,
worthless

dudgeon *noun* **in high dudgeon**
= indignant, angry, choked, fuming,
offended, resentful, vexed

due *adjective* **1 = expected**, expected to
arrive, scheduled **2 = payable**, in arrears,
outstanding, owed, owing, unpaid **3**
= fitting, appropriate, becoming, bounden,
deserved, fit, just, justified, merited,
obligatory, proper, requisite, right, rightful,
suitable, well-earned ♦ *noun* **4 = right(s)**,
comeuppance (*slang*), deserts, merits,
prerogative, privilege ♦ *adverb* **5 = directly**,
dead, direct, exactly, straight, undeviatingly

duel *noun* **1 = single combat**, affair of

honour **2 = contest**, clash, competition,
encounter, engagement, fight,
head-to-head, rivalry ♦ *verb* **3 = fight**, clash,
compete, contend, contest, lock horns, rival,
struggle, vie with

dues *plural noun* **= membership fee**,
charge, charges, contribution, fee, levy

duffer *noun Informal* **= clot** (*Brit. informal*),
blunderer, booby, bungler, clod, galoot
(*slang, chiefly U.S.*), lubber, lummox
(*informal*), oaf

dulcet *adjective* **= sweet**, agreeable,
charming, delightful, euphonious,
harmonious, honeyed, mellifluent,
mellifluous, melodious, musical, pleasant,
pleasing, soothing

dull *adjective* **1 = boring**, as dry as dust,
commonplace, dozy, dreary, dry, flat,
ho-hum (*informal*), humdrum,
mind-numbing, monotonous, plain, prosaic,
run-of-the-mill, tedious, tiresome,
unimaginative, uninteresting, vapid **2**
= stupid, braindead (*informal*), daft, dense,
dim, dim-witted (*informal*), doltish, dozy
(*Brit. informal*), obtuse, slow, stolid, thick,
unintelligent **3 = cloudy**, dim, dismal,
gloomy, leaden, opaque, overcast, turbid **4**
= lifeless, apathetic, blank, callous, dead,
empty, heavy, indifferent, insensible,
insensitive, listless, passionless, slow,
sluggish, unresponsive, unsympathetic,
vacuous **5 = drab**, faded, feeble, murky,
muted, sombre, subdued, subfusc,
toned-down **6 = blunt**, blunted, dulled,
edgeless, not keen, not sharp, unsharpened
♦ *verb* **7 = dampen**, deject, depress,
discourage, dishearten, dispirit, sadden **8**
= relieve, allay, alleviate, assuage, blunt,
lessen, mitigate, moderate, palliate, paralyse,
soften, stupefy, take the edge off **9 = cloud**,
darken, dim, fade, obscure, stain, sully,
tarnish
➤ **Antonyms**
adjective ≠**boring**: exciting, interesting
≠**stupid**: bright, clever, intelligent, sharp
≠**cloudy**: bright ≠**lifeless**: active, full of
beans (*informal*), lively ≠**blunt**: sharp

duly *adverb* **1 = properly**, accordingly,
appropriately, befittingly, correctly,
decorously, deservedly, fittingly, rightfully,
suitably **2 = on time**, at the proper time,
punctually

dumb *adjective* **1 = mute**, at a loss for
words, inarticulate, mum, silent, soundless,
speechless, tongue-tied, voiceless, wordless **2**
Informal **= stupid**, asinine, braindead
(*informal*), dense, dim-witted (*informal*),
dozy (*Brit. informal*), dull, foolish, obtuse,
thick, unintelligent
➤ **Antonyms**
≠**mute**: articulate ≠**stupid**: bright, clever,

intelligent, quick-witted, smart

dumbfounded, dumfounded
adjective = **amazed**, astonished, astounded, at sea, bewildered, bowled over (*informal*), breathless, confounded, confused, dumb, flabbergasted (*informal*), flummoxed, gobsmacked (*Brit. slang*), knocked for six (*informal*), knocked sideways (*informal*), lost for words, nonplussed, overcome, overwhelmed, speechless, staggered, startled, stunned, taken aback, thrown, thunderstruck

dummy *noun* 1 = **model**, figure, form, lay figure, manikin, mannequin 2 = **copy**, counterfeit, duplicate, imitation, sham, substitute 3 *Slang* = **fool**, berk (*Brit. slang*), blockhead, charlie (*Brit. informal*), coot, dickhead (*slang*), dickwit (*slang*), dimwit (*informal*), dipstick (*Brit. slang*), divvy (*Brit. slang*), dolt, dork (*slang*), dullard, dumb-ass (*slang*), dunce, dweeb (*U.S. slang*), fathead (*informal*), fuckwit (*taboo slang*), geek (*slang*), gobshite (*Irish taboo slang*), gonzo (*slang*), idiot, jerk (*slang, chiefly U.S. & Canad.*), lamebrain (*informal*), nerd *or* nurd (*slang*), nitwit (*informal*), numbskull *or* numskull, numpty (*Scot. informal*), oaf, pillock (*Brit. slang*), plank (*Brit. slang*), plonker (*slang*), prat (*slang*), prick (*slang*), schmuck (*U.S. slang*), simpleton, wally (*slang*), weenie (*U.S. informal*) ◆ *adjective* 4 = **imitation**, artificial, bogus, fake, false, mock, phoney *or* phony (*informal*), sham, simulated 5 = **practice**, mock, simulated, trial

dump *verb* 1 = **drop**, deposit, fling down, let fall, throw down 2 = **get rid of**, coup (*Scot.*), discharge, dispose of, ditch (*slang*), empty out, jettison, scrap, throw away *or* out, tip, unload ◆ *noun* 3 = **rubbish tip**, junkyard, refuse heap, rubbish heap, tip 4 *Informal* = **pigsty**, hole (*informal*), hovel, joint (*slang*), mess, shack, shanty, slum

dumps *plural noun* As in **down in the dumps** = **low spirits**, blues, dejection, depression, despondency, dolour, gloom, gloominess, melancholy, mopes, sadness, the hump (*Brit. informal*), unhappiness, woe

dunce *noun* = **simpleton**, ass, blockhead, bonehead (*slang*), dimwit (*informal*), dolt, donkey, duffer (*informal*), dullard, dunderhead, fathead (*informal*), goose (*informal*), halfwit, ignoramus, lamebrain (*informal*), loon (*informal*), moron, nincompoop, nitwit (*informal*), numbskull *or* numskull, oaf, thickhead

dungeon *noun* = **prison**, cage, calaboose (*U.S. informal*), cell, donjon, lockup, oubliette, vault

duplicate *adjective* 1 = **identical**, corresponding, matched, matching, twin, twofold ◆ *noun* 2 = **copy**, carbon copy,

clone, dead ringer (*slang*), double, facsimile, fax, likeness, lookalike, match, mate, photocopy, Photostat (*Trademark*), replica, reproduction, ringer (*slang*), twin, Xerox (*Trademark*) ◆ *verb* 3 = **copy**, clone, double, echo, fax, photocopy, Photostat (*Trademark*), reinvent the wheel, repeat, replicate, reproduce, Xerox (*Trademark*)

duplicity *noun* = **deceit**, artifice, chicanery, deception, dishonesty, dissimulation, double-dealing, falsehood, fraud, guile, hypocrisy, perfidy
➤ **Antonyms**
candour, honesty, straightforwardness

durability *noun* = **durableness**, constancy, endurance, imperishability, lastingness, permanence, persistence

durable *adjective* = **long-lasting**, abiding, constant, dependable, enduring, fast, firm, fixed, hard-wearing, lasting, permanent, persistent, reliable, resistant, sound, stable, strong, sturdy, substantial, tough
➤ **Antonyms**
breakable, brittle, delicate, fragile, impermanent, perishable, weak

duration *noun* = **length**, extent, period, span, spell, stretch, term, time

duress *noun* 1 = **pressure**, coercion, compulsion, constraint, threat 2 = **imprisonment**, captivity, confinement, constraint, hardship, incarceration, restraint

dusk *noun* 1 = **twilight**, dark, evening, eventide, gloaming (*Scot. or poetic*), nightfall, sundown, sunset 2 *Poetic* = **shade**, darkness, gloom, murk, obscurity, shadowiness
➤ **Antonyms**
≠**twilight:** aurora (*poetic*), cockcrow, dawn, dawning, daybreak, daylight, morning, sunlight, sunup

dusky *adjective* 1 = **dark**, dark-complexioned, dark-hued, sable, swarthy 2 = **dim**, caliginous (*archaic*), cloudy, crepuscular, darkish, gloomy, murky, obscure, overcast, shadowy, shady, tenebrous, twilight, twilit, veiled

dust *noun* 1 = **grime**, fine fragments, grit, particles, powder, powdery dirt 2 = **earth**, dirt, ground, soil 3 **bite the dust** *Informal* = **die**, drop dead, expire, fall in battle, pass away, perish 4 **throw dust in the eyes of** = **mislead**, con (*slang*), confuse, deceive, fool, have (someone) on, hoodwink, take in (*informal*) ◆ *verb* 5 = **sprinkle**, cover, dredge, powder, scatter, sift, spray, spread

dusty *adjective* 1 = **dirty**, grubby, sooty, unclean, undusted, unswept 2 = **powdery**, chalky, crumbly, friable, granular, sandy

dutiful *adjective* = **conscientious**, compliant, deferential, devoted, docile, filial, obedient,

punctilious, respectful, reverential,
submissive
➤ **Antonyms**
disobedient, disrespectful, insubordinate,
remiss, uncaring
duty *noun* 1 = **responsibility**, assignment,
business, calling, charge, engagement,
function, job, mission, obligation, office,
onus, pigeon (*informal*), province, role,
service, task, work 2 = **loyalty**, allegiance,
deference, obedience, respect, reverence 3
= **tax**, customs, due, excise, impost, levy,
tariff, toll 4 **be the duty of** = **be up to**
(*informal*), behove (*archaic*), be incumbent
upon, belong to, be (someone's) pigeon
(*Brit. informal*), devolve upon, pertain to,
rest with 5 **off duty** = **off work**, at leisure,
free, off, on holiday 6 **on duty** = **at work**,
busy, engaged, on active service
dwarf *verb* 1 = **tower above** *or* **over**, dim,
diminish, dominate, minimize, overshadow 2
= **stunt**, check, cultivate by bonsai, lower,
retard ◆ *adjective* 3 = **miniature**, baby,
bonsai, diminutive, dwarfed, Lilliputian,
petite, pint-sized, pocket, small,
teensy-weensy, teeny-weeny, tiny,
undersized ◆ *noun* 4 = **midget**, bantam,
homunculus, hop-o'-my-thumb, Lilliputian,
manikin, munchkin (*informal, chiefly U.S.*),
pygmy *or* pigmy, Tom Thumb 5 = **gnome**,
goblin
dwell *verb Formal, literary* = **live**, abide,
establish oneself, hang out (*informal*),
inhabit, lodge, quarter, remain, reside, rest,
settle, sojourn, stay, stop
dwelling *noun Formal, literary* = **home**,
abode, domicile, dwelling house,
establishment, habitation, house, lodging,
pad (*slang*), quarters, residence
dwell on *or* **upon** *verb* = **go on about**

(*informal*), be engrossed in, continue,
elaborate, emphasize, expatiate, harp on,
linger over, tarry over
dwindle *verb* = **lessen**, abate, contract,
decay, decline, decrease, die away, die
down, die out, diminish, ebb, fade, fall,
grow less, peter out, pine, shrink, shrivel,
sink, subside, taper off, wane, waste away,
weaken, wither
➤ **Antonyms**
advance, amplify, develop, dilate, enlarge,
escalate, expand, grow, heighten, increase,
magnify, multiply, swell, wax
dye *noun* 1 = **colouring**, colorant, colour,
pigment, stain, tinge, tint ◆ *verb* 2 = **colour**,
pigment, stain, tincture, tinge, tint
dyed-in-the-wool *adjective* = **confirmed**,
complete, deep-dyed (*usually derogatory*),
deep-rooted, die-hard, entrenched,
established, inveterate, through-and-through
dying *adjective* = **expiring**, at death's door,
ebbing, fading, failing, final, going, *in
extremis*, moribund, mortal, not long for this
world, passing, perishing, sinking
dynamic *adjective* = **energetic**, active, alive
and kicking, driving, electric, forceful, full of
beans (*informal*), go-ahead, go-getting
(*informal*), high-octane (*informal*),
high-powered, lively, magnetic, powerful,
storming (*informal*), vigorous, vital, zippy
(*informal*)
➤ **Antonyms**
apathetic, couldn't-care-less (*informal*),
impassive, inactive, listless, sluggish, torpid,
undynamic, unenergetic
dynasty *noun* = **empire**, ascendancy,
dominion, government, house, regime, rule,
sovereignty, sway

E e

each *adjective* **1** = **every** ♦ *pronoun* **2**
= **every one**, each and every one, each one,
one and all ♦ *adverb* **3** = **apiece**, for each,
from each, individually, per capita, per head,
per person, respectively, singly, to each

eager *adjective* = **keen**, agog, anxious,
ardent, athirst, avid, bright-eyed and
bushy-tailed (*informal*), earnest, enthusiastic,
fervent, fervid, greedy, hot, hungry,
impatient, intent, keen as mustard, longing,
raring, up for it (*informal*), vehement,
yearning, zealous
➤ **Antonyms**
apathetic, blasé, impassive, indifferent, lazy,
nonchalant, opposed, unambitious,
unconcerned, unenthusiastic, unimpressed,
uninterested

eagerness *noun* = **keenness**, ardour,
avidity, earnestness, enthusiasm, fervour,
greediness, heartiness, hunger, impatience,
impetuosity, intentness, longing, thirst,
vehemence, yearning, zeal

ear *noun* **1** = **sensitivity**, appreciation,
discrimination, musical perception, taste **2**
= **attention**, consideration, hearing, heed,
notice, regard

early *adjective* **1** = **premature**, advanced,
forward, untimely **2** = **primitive**, primeval,
primordial, undeveloped, young ♦ *adverb* **3**
= **too soon**, ahead of time, beforehand,
betimes (*archaic*), in advance, in good time,
prematurely
➤ **Antonyms**
adjective ≠**primitive:** developed, mature,
ripe, seasoned ♦ *adverb* ≠**too soon:** behind,
belated, late, overdue, tardy

earmark *verb* = **set aside**, allocate,
designate, flag, label, mark out, reserve

earn *verb* **1** = **make**, bring in, collect, draw,
gain, get, gross, net, obtain, procure, realize,
reap, receive **2** = **deserve**, acquire, attain, be
entitled to, be worthy of, merit, rate,
warrant, win

earnest[1] *adjective* **1** = **serious**, close,
constant, determined, firm, fixed, grave,
intent, resolute, resolved, sincere, solemn,
stable, staid, steady, thoughtful **2**
= **heartfelt**, ablaze, ardent, devoted, eager,
enthusiastic, fervent, fervid, impassioned,
keen, keen as mustard, passionate,
purposeful, urgent, vehement, warm,
zealous ♦ *noun* **3** *As in* **in earnest**
= **seriousness**, determination, reality,
resolution, sincerity, truth
➤ **Antonyms**
adjective ≠**serious:** flippant, frivolous,
insincere, trifling ≠**heartfelt:** apathetic,
couldn't-care-less, half-hearted, indifferent,
unconcerned, unenthusiastic, uninterested
♦ *noun* ≠**seriousness:** apathy, indifference,
unconcern

earnest[2] *noun* *Old-fashioned* = **down
payment**, assurance, deposit, earnest money
(*Law*), foretaste, guarantee, pledge,
promise, security, token

earnings *plural noun* = **income**,
emolument, gain, pay, proceeds, profits,
receipts, remuneration, return, reward,
salary, stipend, takings, wages

earth *noun* **1** = **world**, globe, orb, planet,
sphere, terrestrial sphere **2** = **soil**, clay, clod,
dirt, ground, land, loam, mould, sod,
topsoil, turf

earthenware *noun* = **crockery**, ceramics,
crocks, pots, pottery, terracotta

earthly *adjective* **1** = **worldly**, human,
material, mortal, non-spiritual, profane,
secular, temporal **2** *Informal* = **possible**,
conceivable, feasible, imaginable, likely,
practical **3** = **terrestrial**, mundane,
sublunary, tellurian, telluric, terrene, worldly
4 = **carnal**, base, fleshly, gross, low,
materialistic, physical, sensual, sordid, vile
➤ **Antonyms**
≠**worldly:** ethereal, heavenly, immaterial,
immortal, otherworldly, spiritual,
supernatural, unearthly

earthy *adjective* = **crude**, bawdy, coarse,
raunchy (*slang*), ribald, robust, uninhibited,
unsophisticated

ease *noun* **1** = **effortlessness**, easiness,
facility, readiness, simplicity **2** = **peace of
mind**, calmness, comfort, content,
contentment, enjoyment, happiness, peace,
quiet, quietude, serenity, tranquillity **3**
= **leisure**, relaxation, repose, rest, restfulness
4 = **freedom**, flexibility, informality, liberty,
naturalness, unaffectedness, unconstraint,
unreservedness ♦ *verb* **5** = **relieve**, abate,
allay, alleviate, appease, assuage, calm,
comfort, disburden, lessen, lighten, mitigate,
moderate, mollify, pacify, palliate, quiet,
relax, relent, slacken, soothe, still, tranquillize
6 = **make easier**, aid, assist, expedite,
facilitate, forward, further, give a leg up
(*informal*), lessen the labour of, simplify,

smooth, speed up **7 = move carefully**, edge, guide, inch, manoeuvre, slide, slip, squeeze, steer

➤ Antonyms

≠**effortlessness**: arduousness, awkwardness, clumsiness, difficulty, effort, exertion, toil ≠**peace of mind**: agitation, awkwardness, clumsiness, discomfort, disturbance, tension *noun* ≠**leisure**: difficulty, discomfort, hardship, irritation, pain, poverty, tribulation ≠**freedom**: awkwardness, clumsiness, constraint, formality ◆ *verb* ≠**relieve**: aggravate, discomfort, exacerbate, irritate, worsen ≠**make easier**: hinder, retard

easily *adverb* **1 = without difficulty**, comfortably, effortlessly, facilely, like a knife through butter, readily, simply, smoothly, standing on one's head, with ease, with one hand tied behind one's back, with one's eyes closed *or* shut, without trouble **2 = without a doubt**, absolutely, beyond question, by far, certainly, clearly, definitely, doubtlessly, far and away, indisputably, indubitably, plainly, surely, undeniably, undoubtedly, unequivocally, unquestionably

easy *adjective* **1 = not difficult**, a bed of roses, a piece of cake (*informal*), a piece of piss (*taboo slang*), a pushover (*slang*), child's play (*informal*), clear, easy-peasy (*slang*), effortless, facile, light, no bother, no trouble, painless, plain sailing, simple, smooth, straightforward, uncomplicated, undemanding **2 = carefree**, calm, comfortable, contented, cushy (*informal*), easeful, leisurely, peaceful, pleasant, quiet, relaxed, satisfied, serene, tranquil, undisturbed, untroubled, unworried, well-to-do **3 = tolerant**, easy-going, flexible, indulgent, lenient, liberal, light, mild, permissive, unburdensome, unoppressive **4 = relaxed**, affable, casual, easy-going, friendly, gentle, graceful, gracious, informal, laid-back (*informal*), mild, natural, open, pleasant, smooth, tolerant, unaffected, unceremonious, unconstrained, undemanding, unforced, unpretentious **5** *Informal* = **accommodating**, amenable, biddable, compliant, docile, gullible, manageable, pliant, soft, submissive, suggestible, susceptible, tractable, trusting, yielding

➤ Antonyms

≠**not difficult**: arduous, complex, demanding, difficult, exacting, exhausting, formidable, hard, impossible, onerous, stiff ≠**carefree**: difficult, insecure, stressful, uncomfortable, worried ≠**tolerant**: demanding, dictatorial, difficult, exacting, hard, harsh, inflexible, intolerant, rigid, stern, strict, unyielding ≠**relaxed**: affected, anxious, forced, formal, self-conscious, stiff, uncomfortable, unnatural, worried

≠**accommodating**: difficult, impossible, unyielding

easy-going *adjective* = **relaxed**, amenable, calm, carefree, casual, complacent, easy, easy-oasy (*slang*), even-tempered, flexible, happy-go-lucky, indulgent, insouciant, laid-back (*informal*), lenient, liberal, mild, moderate, nonchalant, permissive, placid, serene, tolerant, unconcerned, uncritical, undemanding, unhurried

➤ Antonyms

anxious, edgy, fussy, hung-up (*slang*), intolerant, irritated, nervy (*Brit. informal*), neurotic, on edge, strict, tense, uptight (*informal*)

eat *verb* **1 = consume**, chew, devour, gobble, ingest, munch, scoff (*slang*), swallow **2 = have a meal**, break bread, chow down (*slang*), dine, feed, take food, take nourishment **3 = destroy**, corrode, crumble, decay, dissolve, erode, rot, waste away, wear away **4 eat one's words = retract**, abjure, recant, rescind, take (a statement) back

eavesdrop *verb* = **listen in**, bug (*informal*), earwig (*informal*), monitor, overhear, snoop (*informal*), spy, tap

ebb *verb* **1 = flow back**, abate, fall away, fall back, go out, recede, retire, retreat, retrocede, sink, subside, wane, withdraw **2 = decline**, decay, decrease, degenerate, deteriorate, diminish, drop, dwindle, fade away, fall away, flag, lessen, peter out, shrink, sink, slacken, weaken ◆ *noun* **3 = flowing back**, ebb tide, going out, low tide, low water, reflux, regression, retreat, retrocession, subsidence, wane, waning, withdrawal **4 = decline**, decay, decrease, degeneration, deterioration, diminution, drop, dwindling, fading away, flagging, lessening, petering out, shrinkage, sinking, slackening, weakening

eccentric *adjective* **1 = odd**, aberrant, abnormal, anomalous, bizarre, capricious, erratic, freakish, idiosyncratic, irregular, oddball (*informal*), off the rails, off-the-wall (*slang*), outlandish, outré, peculiar, queer (*informal*), quirky, rum (*Brit. slang*), singular, strange, uncommon, unconventional, wacko (*slang*), weird, whimsical ◆ *noun* **2 = crank** (*informal*), card (*informal*), case (*informal*), character (*informal*), freak (*informal*), kook (*U.S. & Canad. informal*), loose cannon, nonconformist, nut (*informal*), oddball (*informal*), odd fish (*informal*), oddity, queer fish (*Brit. informal*), rum customer (*Brit. slang*), screwball (*slang, chiefly U.S. & Canad.*), wacko (*slang*), weirdo *or* weirdie (*informal*)

➤ Antonyms

adjective ≠**odd**: average, conventional,

normal, ordinary, regular, run-of-the-mill, straightforward, typical

eccentricity *noun* = **oddity**, aberration, abnormality, anomaly, bizarreness, caprice, capriciousness, foible, freakishness, idiosyncrasy, irregularity, nonconformity, oddness, outlandishness, peculiarity, queerness (*informal*), quirk, singularity, strangeness, unconventionality, waywardness, weirdness, whimsicality, whimsicalness

ecclesiastic *noun* 1 = **clergyman**, churchman, cleric, divine, holy man, man of the cloth, minister, parson, pastor, priest ♦ *adjective* 2 *Also* **ecclesiastical** = **clerical**, church, churchly, divine, holy, pastoral, priestly, religious, spiritual

echo *noun* 1 = **repetition**, answer, reverberation 2 = **copy**, imitation, mirror image, parallel, reflection, reiteration, reproduction 3 = **reminder**, allusion, evocation, hint, intimation, memory, suggestion, trace 4 *often plural* = **repercussion**, aftereffect, aftermath, consequence ♦ *verb* 5 = **repeat**, resound, reverberate 6 = **copy**, ape, imitate, mirror, parallel, parrot, recall, reflect, reiterate, reproduce, resemble, ring, second

eclipse *noun* 1 = **obscuring**, darkening, dimming, extinction, occultation, shading 2 = **decline**, diminution, failure, fall, loss ♦ *verb* 3 = **surpass**, exceed, excel, outdo, outshine, put in the shade (*informal*), transcend 4 = **obscure**, blot out, cloud, darken, dim, extinguish, overshadow, shroud, veil

economic *adjective* 1 = **financial**, business, commercial, industrial, mercantile, trade 2 = **profitable**, money-making, productive, profit-making, remunerative, solvent, viable 3 = **monetary**, bread-and-butter (*informal*), budgetary, financial, fiscal, material, pecuniary 4 *Informal Also* **economical** = **inexpensive**, cheap, fair, low, low-priced, modest, reasonable

economical *adjective* 1 *Also* **economic** = **inexpensive**, cheap, fair, low, low-priced, modest, reasonable 2 = **thrifty**, careful, economizing, frugal, prudent, saving, scrimping, sparing 3 = **cost-effective**, efficient, money-saving, neat, sparing, time-saving, unwasteful, work-saving
➤ **Antonyms**
≠**inexpensive**: exorbitant, expensive, unprofitable ≠**thrifty**: extravagant, generous, imprudent, lavish, profligate, spendthrift, uneconomical, unthrifty, wasteful ≠**cost-effective**: loss-making, uneconomical, unprofitable, wasteful

economize *verb* = **cut back**, be economical, be frugal, be on a shoestring,

be sparing, draw in one's horns, husband, pull in one's horns, retrench, save, scrimp, tighten one's belt
➤ **Antonyms**
be extravagant, push the boat out (*informal*), spend, splurge, squander

economy *noun* = **thrift**, frugality, husbandry, parsimony, providence, prudence, restraint, retrenchment, saving, sparingness, thriftiness

ecstasy *noun* = **rapture**, bliss, delight, elation, enthusiasm, euphoria, exaltation, fervour, frenzy, joy, ravishment, rhapsody, seventh heaven, trance, transport
➤ **Antonyms**
affliction, agony, anguish, distress, hell, misery, pain, suffering, torment, torture

ecstatic *adjective* = **rapturous**, blissed out, blissful, cock-a-hoop, delirious, elated, enraptured, enthusiastic, entranced, euphoric, fervent, floating on air, frenzied, in exaltation, in seventh heaven, in transports of delight, joyful, joyous, on cloud nine (*informal*), overjoyed, over the moon (*informal*), rhapsodic, sent, transported, walking on air

eddy *noun* 1 = **swirl**, counter-current, counterflow, tideway, undertow, vortex, whirlpool ♦ *verb* 2 = **swirl**, whirl

edge *noun* 1 = **border**, bound, boundary, brim, brink, contour, flange, fringe, limit, line, lip, margin, outline, perimeter, periphery, rim, side, threshold, verge 2 = **sharpness**, acuteness, animation, bite, effectiveness, force, incisiveness, interest, keenness, point, pungency, sting, urgency, zest 3 *As in* **have the edge on** = **advantage**, ascendancy, dominance, lead, superiority, upper hand 4 *on edge* = **nervous**, antsy (*informal*), apprehensive, eager, edgy, excited, ill at ease, impatient, irritable, keyed up, on tenterhooks, tense, tetchy, twitchy (*informal*), uptight (*informal*), wired (*slang*) ♦ *verb* 5 = **border**, bind, fringe, hem, rim, shape, trim 6 = **inch**, creep, ease, sidle, steal, work, worm 7 = **sharpen**, hone, strop, whet

edgy *adjective* = **nervous**, antsy (*informal*), anxious, ill at ease, irascible, irritable, keyed up, nervy (*Brit. informal*), neurotic, on edge, on pins and needles, on tenterhooks, restive, tense, tetchy, touchy, twitchy (*informal*), uptight (*informal*), wired (*slang*)

edible *adjective* = **eatable**, comestible (*rare*), digestible, esculent, fit to eat, good, harmless, palatable, wholesome
➤ **Antonyms**
baneful, harmful, indigestible, inedible, noxious, pernicious, poisonous, uneatable

edict *noun* = **decree**, act, canon, command, demand, dictate, dictum, enactment, fiat, injunction, law, mandate, manifesto, order, ordinance, proclamation, pronouncement, pronunciamento, regulation, ruling, statute, ukase (*rare*)

edifice *noun* = **building**, construction, erection, fabric (*rare*), habitation, house, pile, structure

edify *verb* = **instruct**, educate, elevate, enlighten, guide, improve, inform, nurture, school, teach, uplift

edit *verb* 1 = **revise**, adapt, annotate, censor, check, condense, correct, emend, polish, redact, rephrase, rewrite 2 = **put together**, assemble, compose, rearrange, reorder, select

edition *noun* = **version**, copy, impression, issue, number, printing, programme (*TV, Radio*), volume

educate *verb* = **teach**, civilize, coach, cultivate, develop, discipline, drill, edify, enlighten, exercise, foster, improve, indoctrinate, inform, instruct, mature, rear, school, train, tutor

educated *adjective* 1 = **taught**, coached, informed, instructed, nurtured, schooled, tutored 2 = **cultured**, civilized, cultivated, enlightened, experienced, informed, knowledgeable, learned, lettered, literary, polished, refined, sophisticated, tasteful
➤ **Antonyms**
≠**taught**: ignorant, illiterate, uneducated, unlettered, unread, unschooled, untaught ≠**cultured**: benighted, lowbrow, philistine, uncultivated, uncultured, uneducated

education *noun* = **teaching**, breeding, civilization, coaching, cultivation, culture, development, discipline, drilling, edification, enlightenment, erudition, improvement, indoctrination, instruction, knowledge, nurture, scholarship, schooling, training, tuition, tutoring

educational *adjective* = **instructive**, cultural, didactic, edifying, educative, enlightening, heuristic, improving, informative

educative *adjective* = **instructive**, didactic, edifying, educational, enlightening, heuristic, improving, informative

eerie *adjective* = **frightening**, awesome, creepy (*informal*), eldritch (*poetic*), fearful, ghostly, mysterious, scary (*informal*), spectral, spooky (*informal*), strange, uncanny, unearthly, uneasy, weird

efface *verb* 1 = **obliterate**, annihilate, blot out, cancel, cross out, delete, destroy, dim, eradicate, erase, excise, expunge, extirpate, raze, rub out, wipe out 2 **efface oneself** = **make oneself inconspicuous**, be bashful, be diffident, be modest, be retiring, be timid, be unassertive, humble oneself, lower oneself, withdraw

effect *noun* 1 = **result**, aftermath, conclusion, consequence, end result, event, fruit, issue, outcome, upshot 2 = **power**, clout (*informal*), effectiveness, efficacy, efficiency, fact, force, influence, reality, strength, use, validity, vigour, weight 3 = **operation**, action, enforcement, execution, force, implementation 4 = **impression**, drift, essence, impact, import, meaning, purport, purpose, sense, significance, tenor 5 **in effect** = **in fact**, actually, effectively, essentially, for practical purposes, in actuality, in reality, in truth, really, to all intents and purposes, virtually 6 **take effect** = **produce results**, become operative, begin, come into force, work
♦ *verb* 7 = **bring about**, accomplish, achieve, actuate, carry out, cause, complete, consummate, create, effectuate, execute, fulfil, give rise to, initiate, make, perform, produce

effective *adjective* 1 = **efficient**, able, active, adequate, capable, competent, effectual, efficacious, energetic, operative, productive, serviceable, useful 2 = **in operation**, active, actual, current, in effect, in execution, in force, operative, real 3 = **powerful**, cogent, compelling, convincing, emphatic, forceful, forcible, impressive, moving, persuasive, potent, striking, telling
➤ **Antonyms**
≠**efficient**: futile, inadequate, incompetent, ineffective, inefficient, insufficient, otiose, unimpressive, unproductive, useless, vain, worthless ≠**in operation**: inactive, inoperative ≠**powerful**: feeble, ineffectual, pathetic, powerless, tame, weak

effectiveness *noun* = **power**, bottom, capability, clout (*informal*), cogency, effect, efficacy, efficiency, force, influence, potency, strength, success, use, validity, vigour, weight

effects *plural noun* = **belongings**, chattels, furniture, gear, goods, movables, paraphernalia, possessions, property, things, trappings

effeminacy *noun* = **womanliness**, delicacy, femininity, softness, tenderness, unmanliness, weakness, womanishness

effeminate *adjective* = **womanly**, camp (*informal*), delicate, feminine, poofy (*slang*), sissy, soft, tender, unmanly, weak, wimpish or wimpy (*informal*), womanish, womanlike, wussy (*slang*)
➤ **Antonyms**
butch (*slang*), he-man (*informal*), macho, manly, virile

effervesce *verb* = **bubble**, ferment, fizz, foam, froth, sparkle

effervescence *noun* 1 = **bubbling**, ferment, fermentation, fizz, foam, foaming, froth, frothing, sparkle 2 = **liveliness**, animation, brio, buoyancy, ebullience, enthusiasm, excitedness, excitement, exhilaration, exuberance, gaiety, high spirits, pizzazz or pizazz (*informal*), vim (*slang*), vitality, vivacity, zing (*informal*)

effervescent *adjective* 1 = **bubbling**, bubbly, carbonated, fermenting, fizzing, fizzy, foaming, foamy, frothing, frothy, sparkling 2 = **lively**, animated, bubbly, buoyant, ebullient, enthusiastic, excited, exhilarated, exuberant, gay, in high spirits, irrepressible, merry, vital, vivacious, zingy (*informal*)
➤ **Antonyms**
≠**bubbling:** flat, flavourless, insipid, stale, watery, weak ≠**lively:** boring, dull, flat, insipid, jejune, lacklustre, lifeless, spiritless, stale, unexciting, vapid

effete *adjective* 1 = **decadent**, corrupt, debased, decayed, decrepit, degenerate, dissipated, enervated, enfeebled, feeble, ineffectual, overrefined, spoiled, weak 2 = **worn out**, burnt out, drained, enervated, exhausted, played out, spent, used up, wasted 3 = **sterile**, barren, fruitless, infecund, infertile, unfruitful, unproductive, unprolific

efficacious *adjective* = **effective**, active, adequate, capable, competent, effectual, efficient, energetic, operative, potent, powerful, productive, serviceable, successful, useful
➤ **Antonyms**
abortive, futile, ineffective, ineffectual, inefficacious, unavailing, unproductive, unsuccessful, useless

efficacy *noun* = **effectiveness**, ability, capability, competence, effect, efficaciousness, efficiency, energy, force, influence, potency, power, strength, success, use, vigour, virtue, weight

efficiency *noun* = **competence**, ability, adeptness, capability, economy, effectiveness, efficacy, power, productivity, proficiency, readiness, skilfulness, skill

efficient *adjective* = **competent**, able, adept, businesslike, capable, economic, effective, effectual, organized, powerful, productive, proficient, ready, skilful, well-organized, workmanlike
➤ **Antonyms**
cowboy (*informal*), disorganized, incompetent, ineffectual, inefficient, inept, slipshod, sloppy, unbusinesslike, unproductive, wasteful

effigy *noun* = **likeness**, dummy, figure, guy, icon, idol, image, picture, portrait, representation, statue

effluent *noun* 1 = **waste**, effluvium, pollutant, sewage 2 = **outflow**, discharge,

effluence, efflux, emanation, emission, exhalation, flow, issue, outpouring
♦ *adjective* 3 = **outflowing**, discharged, emanating, emitted

effort *noun* 1 = **exertion**, application, blood, sweat, and tears (*informal*), elbow grease (*facetious*), endeavour, energy, force, labour, pains, power, strain, stress, stretch, striving, struggle, toil, travail (*literary*), trouble, work 2 = **attempt**, endeavour, essay, go (*informal*), shot (*informal*), stab (*informal*), try 3 = **creation**, accomplishment, achievement, act, deed, feat, job, product, production

effortless *adjective* = **easy**, easy-peasy (*slang*), facile, painless, plain sailing, simple, smooth, uncomplicated, undemanding, untroublesome
➤ **Antonyms**
demanding, difficult, formidable, hard, onerous, uphill

effrontery *noun* = **insolence**, arrogance, audacity, brazenness, cheek (*informal*), impertinence, impudence, nerve, presumption, temerity

effulgent *adjective* = **radiant**, beaming, blazing, bright, brilliant, Day-Glo, dazzling, flaming, fluorescent, fulgent (*poetic*), glowing, incandescent, lucent, luminous, lustrous, refulgent (*literary*), resplendent, shining, splendid, vivid

effusion *noun* 1 = **talk**, address, outpouring, speech, utterance, writing 2 = **outpouring**, discharge, effluence, efflux, emission, gush, issue, outflow, shedding, stream

effusive *adjective* = **demonstrative**, ebullient, enthusiastic, expansive, extravagant, exuberant, free-flowing, fulsome, gushing, lavish, overflowing, profuse, talkative, unreserved, unrestrained, wordy

egg on *verb* = **encourage**, exhort, goad, incite, prod, prompt, push, spur, urge
➤ **Antonyms**
deter, discourage, dissuade, hold back, put off, talk out of

egocentric *adjective* = **self-centred**, egoistic, egoistical, egotistic, egotistical, selfish

egotism, egoism *noun*
= **self-centredness**, conceitedness, egocentricity, egomania, narcissism, self-absorption, self-admiration, self-conceit, self-esteem, self-importance, self-interest, selfishness, self-love, self-praise, self-regard, self-seeking, superiority, vainglory, vanity

egotist, egoist *noun* = **egomaniac**, bighead (*informal*), blowhard (*informal*), boaster, braggadocio, braggart, narcissist, self-admirer, self-seeker, swaggerer

egotistic, egotistical, egoistic *or*
egoistical *adjective* = **self-centred**,
boasting, bragging, conceited, egocentric,
egomaniacal, full of oneself, narcissistic,
opinionated, self-absorbed, self-admiring,
self-important, self-seeking, superior, vain,
vainglorious

egress *noun Formal* = **exit**, departure,
emergence, escape, exodus, issue, outlet,
passage out, vent, way out, withdrawal

eject *verb* **1** = **emit**, cast out, discharge,
disgorge, expel, spew, spout, throw out,
vomit **2** = **throw out**, banish, boot out
(*informal*), bounce (*slang*), deport,
dispossess, drive out, evacuate, evict, exile,
expel, give the bum's rush (*slang*), oust,
relegate, remove, show one the door, throw
out on one's ear (*informal*), turn out **3**
= **dismiss**, discharge, dislodge, fire
(*informal*), get rid of, kick out (*informal*),
oust, sack (*informal*), throw out

ejection *noun* **1** = **emission**, casting out,
disgorgement, expulsion, spouting, throwing
out **2** = **expulsion**, banishment, deportation,
dispossession, evacuation, eviction, exile,
ouster (*Law*), removal, the bum's rush
(*slang*) **3** = **dismissal**, discharge,
dislodgement, firing (*informal*), sacking
(*informal*), the boot (*slang*), the sack
(*informal*)

eke out *verb* = **be sparing with**, be
economical with, be frugal with, economize
on, husband, stretch out

elaborate *adjective* **1** = **detailed**, careful,
exact, intricate, laboured, minute,
painstaking, perfected, precise, skilful,
studied, thorough **2** = **complicated**,
complex, decorated, detailed, extravagant,
fancy, fussy, involved, ornamented, ornate,
ostentatious, showy ◆ *verb* **3** = **expand**
(**upon**), add detail, amplify, complicate,
decorate, develop, devise, embellish,
enhance, enlarge, flesh out, garnish,
improve, ornament, polish, produce, refine,
work out
➤ **Antonyms**
adjective ≠**complicated**: basic, minimal,
modest, plain, severe, simple, unadorned,
unembellished, unfussy ◆ *verb* ≠**expand**
(**upon**): abbreviate, condense, put in a
nutshell, reduce to essentials, simplify,
streamline, summarize, truncate

elapse *verb* = **pass**, glide by, go, go by,
lapse, pass by, roll by, roll on, slip away, slip
by

elastic *adjective* **1** = **flexible**, ductile, plastic,
pliable, pliant, resilient, rubbery, springy,
stretchable, stretchy, supple, tensile, yielding
2 = **adaptable**, accommodating, adjustable,
complaisant, compliant, flexible, supple,
tolerant, variable, yielding

➤ **Antonyms**
≠**flexible**: firm, immovable, inflexible, rigid,
set, stiff, unyielding ≠**adaptable**: firm,
immovable, inflexible, intractable, obdurate,
resolute, rigid, set, stiff, strict, stringent,
unyielding

elated *adjective* = **joyful**, animated, blissed
out, blissful, cheered, cock-a-hoop,
delighted, ecstatic, elevated, euphoric,
excited, exhilarated, exultant, floating *or*
walking on air, gleeful, in high spirits, in
seventh heaven, joyous, jubilant, overjoyed,
over the moon (*informal*), proud, puffed up,
rapt, roused, sent
➤ **Antonyms**
dejected, depressed, discouraged, dispirited,
downcast, down in the dumps (*informal*),
miserable, sad, unhappy, woebegone

elation *noun* = **joy**, bliss, delight, ecstasy,
euphoria, exaltation, exhilaration, exultation,
glee, high spirits, joyfulness, joyousness,
jubilation, rapture

elbow *noun* **1** = **joint**, angle, bend, corner,
turn **2 at one's elbow** = **within reach**, at
hand, close by, handy, near, to hand **3 out
at elbow(s)** = **impoverished**, beggarly,
down at heel, in rags, ragged, seedy,
shabby, tattered **4 rub elbows with**
= **associate**, fraternize, hang out (*informal*),
hobnob, mingle, mix, socialize **5 up to the
elbows** = **occupied**, absorbed, busy,
engaged, engrossed, immersed, tied up, up
to the ears, wrapped up ◆ *verb* **6** = **push**,
bump, crowd, hustle, jostle, knock, nudge,
shoulder, shove

elbow room *noun* = **scope**, freedom,
latitude, leeway, play, room, space

elder *adjective* **1** = **older**, ancient, earlier
born, first-born, senior ◆ *noun* **2** = **older
person**, senior **3** *Presbyterianism* = **church
official**, office bearer, presbyter

elect *verb* **1** = **choose**, appoint, decide upon,
designate, determine, opt for, pick, pick out,
prefer, select, settle on, vote ◆ *adjective* **2**
= **selected**, choice, chosen, elite,
hand-picked, picked, preferred, select

election *noun* = **voting**, appointment,
choice, choosing, decision, determination,
judgment, preference, selection, vote

elector *noun* = **voter**, chooser, constituent,
selector

electric *adjective* = **charged**, dynamic,
exciting, high-octane (*informal*), rousing,
stimulating, stirring, tense, thrilling

electrify *verb* = **startle**, amaze, animate,
astonish, astound, excite, fire, galvanize,
invigorate, jolt, rouse, shock, stimulate, stir,
take one's breath away, thrill
➤ **Antonyms**
be tedious, bore, exhaust, fatigue, jade, send

to sleep, tire, weary

elegance *noun* = **style**, beauty, courtliness, dignity, exquisiteness, gentility, grace, gracefulness, grandeur, luxury, polish, politeness, refinement, sumptuousness, taste

elegant *adjective* 1 = **stylish**, à la mode, artistic, beautiful, chic, choice, comely, courtly, cultivated, delicate, exquisite, fashionable, fine, genteel, graceful, handsome, luxurious, modish, nice, polished, refined, sumptuous, tasteful, urbane 2 = **ingenious**, appropriate, apt, clever, effective, neat, simple
➤ **Antonyms**
≠**stylish**: awkward, clumsy, clunky (*informal*), coarse, gauche, graceless, inelegant, misshapen, plain, tasteless, tawdry, ugly, uncouth, undignified, ungraceful, unrefined

elegy *noun* = **lament**, coronach (*Scot. & Irish*), dirge, keen, plaint (*archaic*), requiem, threnody

element *noun* 1 = **component**, basis, constituent, essential factor, factor, feature, ingredient, member, part, section, subdivision, unit 2 *As in* **in one's element** = **environment**, domain, field, habitat, medium, milieu, sphere

elementary *adjective* 1 = **simple**, clear, easy, facile, plain, rudimentary, straightforward, uncomplicated 2 = **basic**, bog-standard (*informal*), elemental, fundamental, initial, introductory, original, primary, rudimentary
➤ **Antonyms**
≠**simple**: complex, complicated, sophisticated ≠**basic**: advanced, higher, highly-developed, progressive, secondary

elements *plural noun* 1 = **basics**, essentials, foundations, fundamentals, nuts and bolts (*informal*), principles, rudiments 2 = **weather conditions**, atmospheric conditions, atmospheric forces, powers of nature

elevate *verb* 1 = **raise**, heighten, hoist, lift, lift up, uplift, upraise 2 = **promote**, advance, aggrandize, exalt, prefer, upgrade 3 = **cheer**, animate, boost, brighten, buoy up, elate, excite, exhilarate, hearten, lift up, perk up, raise, rouse, uplift

elevated *adjective* 1 = **high-minded**, dignified, exalted, grand, high, high-flown, inflated, lofty, noble, sublime 2 = **in high spirits**, animated, bright, cheerful, cheery, elated, excited, exhilarated, gleeful, overjoyed
➤ **Antonyms**
≠**high-minded**: humble, lowly, modest, simple

elevation *noun* 1 = **promotion**, advancement, aggrandizement, exaltation, preferment, upgrading 2 = **altitude**, height 3 = **rise**, acclivity, eminence, height, hill, hillock, mountain, rising ground

elicit *verb* 1 = **bring about**, bring forth, bring out, bring to light, call forth, cause, derive, evolve, give rise to 2 = **obtain**, draw out, educe, evoke, exact, extort, extract, wrest

eligible *adjective* = **qualified**, acceptable, appropriate, desirable, fit, preferable, proper, suitable, suited, worthy
➤ **Antonyms**
inappropriate, ineligible, unacceptable, unqualified, unsuitable, unsuited

eliminate *verb* 1 = **get rid of**, cut out, dispose of, do away with, eradicate, exterminate, get shot of, remove, stamp out, take out, wipe from the face of the earth 2 = **drop**, axe (*informal*), dispense with, disregard, eject, exclude, expel, ignore, knock out, leave out, omit, put out, reject, throw out 3 *Slang* = **murder**, annihilate, blow away (*slang, chiefly U.S.*), bump off (*slang*), kill, liquidate, rub out (*U.S. slang*), slay, take out (*slang*), terminate, waste (*informal*)

elite *noun* 1 = **best**, aristocracy, cream, crème de la crème, elect, flower, gentry, high society, nobility, pick, upper class
♦ *adjective* 2 = **best**, aristocratic, choice, crack (*slang*), elect, exclusive, first-class, noble, pick, selected, upper-class
➤ **Antonyms**
noun ≠**best**: dregs, hoi polloi, rabble, riffraff

elitist *adjective* 1 = **snobbish**, exclusive, selective ♦ *noun* 2 = **snob**

elixir *noun* = **panacea**, nostrum

elocution *noun* = **diction**, articulation, declamation, delivery, enunciation, oratory, pronunciation, public speaking, rhetoric, speech, speechmaking, utterance, voice production

elongate *verb* = **make longer**, draw out, extend, lengthen, prolong, protract, stretch

elope *verb* = **run away**, abscond, bolt, decamp, disappear, escape, leave, run off, slip away, steal away

eloquence *noun* = **expressiveness**, expression, fluency, forcefulness, oratory, persuasiveness, rhetoric, way with words

eloquent *adjective* 1 = **silver-tongued**, articulate, fluent, forceful, graceful, moving, persuasive, stirring, well-expressed 2 = **expressive**, meaningful, pregnant, revealing, suggestive, telling, vivid
➤ **Antonyms**
≠**silver-tongued**: faltering, halting, hesitant, inarticulate, speechless, stumbling, tongue-tied, wordless

elsewhere *adverb* = **in** *or* **to another place**, abroad, away, hence (*archaic*), not here, somewhere else

elucidate *verb* = **clarify**, annotate, clear the air, clear up, explain, explicate, expound, gloss, illuminate, illustrate, interpret, make plain, shed *or* throw light upon, spell out, unfold

elucidation *noun* = **clarification**, annotation, comment, commentary, explanation, explication, exposition, gloss, illumination, illustration, interpretation

elude *verb* 1 = **escape**, avoid, body-swerve (*Scot.*), circumvent, dodge, duck (*informal*), evade, flee, get away from, outrun, shirk, shun, slip through one's fingers, slip through the net 2 = **baffle**, be beyond (someone), confound, escape, foil, frustrate, puzzle, stump, thwart

elusive *adjective* 1 = **difficult to catch**, shifty, slippery, tricky 2 = **indefinable**, baffling, fleeting, intangible, puzzling, subtle, transient, transitory 3 = **evasive**, ambiguous, deceitful, deceptive, elusory, equivocal, fallacious, fraudulent, illusory, misleading, oracular, unspecific

emaciated *adjective* = **skeletal**, atrophied, attenuate, attenuated, cadaverous, gaunt, haggard, lank, lean, macilent (*rare*), meagre, pinched, scrawny, thin, undernourished, wasted

emaciation *noun* = **thinness**, atrophy, attenuation, gauntness, haggardness, leanness, meagreness, scrawniness, wasting away

emanate *verb* 1 = **flow**, arise, come forth, derive, emerge, issue, originate, proceed, spring, stem 2 = **give out**, discharge, emit, exhale, give off, issue, radiate, send forth

emanation *noun* 1 = **flow**, arising, derivation, emergence, origination, proceeding 2 = **emission**, discharge, effluent, efflux, effusion, exhalation, radiation

emancipate *verb* = **free**, deliver, discharge, disencumber, disenthral, enfranchise, liberate, manumit, release, set free, unbridle, unchain, unfetter, unshackle
➤ **Antonyms**
bind, capture, enchain, enslave, enthral, fetter, shackle, subjugate, yoke

emancipation *noun* = **freedom**, deliverance, discharge, enfranchisement, liberation, liberty, manumission, release
➤ **Antonyms**
bondage, captivity, confinement, detention, enthralment, imprisonment, servitude, slavery, thraldom, vassalage

embalm *verb* 1 = **preserve**, mummify 2 = **enshrine**, cherish, consecrate, conserve, immortalize, store, treasure

embargo *noun* 1 = **ban**, bar, barrier, block, blockage, boycott, check, hindrance, impediment, interdict, interdiction, prohibition, proscription, restraint, restriction, stoppage ◆ *verb* 2 = **ban**, bar, block, boycott, check, impede, interdict, prohibit, proscribe, restrict, stop

embark *verb* 1 = **go aboard**, board ship, put on board, take on board, take ship 2 **embark on** *or* **upon** = **begin**, broach, commence, engage, enter, get the show on the road (*informal*), initiate, launch, plunge into, set about, set out, start, take up, undertake
➤ **Antonyms**
≠**go aboard**: alight, arrive, get off, go ashore, land, step out of

embarrass *verb* = **shame**, abash, chagrin, confuse, discomfit, discompose, disconcert, discountenance, distress, faze, fluster, humiliate, mortify, put out of countenance, show up (*informal*)

embarrassed *adjective* = **ashamed**, awkward, blushing, discomfited, disconcerted, humiliated, mortified, red-faced, self-conscious, sheepish

embarrassing *adjective* = **humiliating**, awkward, blush-making, compromising, cringe-making (*Brit. informal*), cringeworthy (*Brit. informal*), discomfiting, disconcerting, distressing, mortifying, sensitive, shameful, shaming, toe-curling (*slang*), touchy, tricky, uncomfortable

embarrassment *noun* 1 = **shame**, awkwardness, bashfulness, chagrin, confusion, discomfiture, discomposure, distress, humiliation, mortification, self-consciousness, showing up (*informal*) 2 = **predicament**, bind (*informal*), difficulty, mess, pickle (*informal*), scrape (*informal*)

embellish *verb* = **decorate**, adorn, beautify, bedeck, deck, dress up, elaborate, embroider, enhance, enrich, exaggerate, festoon, garnish, gild, gild the lily, grace, ornament, tart up (*slang*), varnish

embellishment *noun* = **decoration**, adornment, elaboration, embroidery, enhancement, enrichment, exaggeration, gilding, ornament, ornamentation, trimming

embezzle *verb* = **misappropriate**, abstract, appropriate, defalcate (*Law*), filch, have one's hand in the till (*informal*), misapply, misuse, peculate, pilfer, purloin, rip off (*slang*), steal

embezzlement *noun* = **misappropriation**, abstraction, appropriation, defalcation (*Law*), filching, fraud, larceny, misapplication, misuse, peculation, pilferage, pilfering, purloining, stealing, theft, thieving

embitter *verb* 1 = **make bitter** *or* **resentful**,

alienate, anger, disaffect, disillusion, envenom, poison, sour **2 = aggravate**, exacerbate, exasperate, worsen

embittered *adjective* = **resentful**, angry, bitter, disaffected, disillusioned, rancorous, soured, with a chip on one's shoulder (*informal*)

emblazon *verb* **1 = decorate**, adorn, blazon, colour, embellish, illuminate, ornament, paint **2 = publicize**, crack up (*informal*), extol, glorify, laud (*literary*), praise, proclaim, publish, trumpet

emblem *noun* = **symbol**, badge, crest, device, figure, image, insignia, mark, representation, sigil (*rare*), sign, token, type

embodiment *noun* **1 = personification**, bodying forth, epitome, example, exemplar, exemplification, expression, incarnation, incorporation, manifestation, realization, reification, representation, symbol, type **2 = incorporation**, bringing together, codification, collection, combination, comprehension, concentration, consolidation, inclusion, integration, organization, systematization

embody *verb* **1 = personify**, exemplify, manifest, represent, stand for, symbolize, typify **2 = incorporate**, collect, combine, comprise, contain, include

embolden *verb* = **encourage**, animate, cheer, fire, gee up, hearten, inflame, inspirit, invigorate, nerve, reassure, rouse, stimulate, stir, strengthen, vitalize

embrace *verb* **1 = hug**, clasp, cuddle, encircle, enfold, envelop, grasp, hold, neck (*informal*), seize, squeeze, take *or* hold in one's arms **2 = accept**, adopt, avail oneself of, espouse, grab, make use of, receive, seize, take on board, take up, welcome **3 = include**, comprehend, comprise, contain, cover, deal with, embody, enclose, encompass, involve, provide for, subsume, take in, take into account ♦ *noun* **4 = hug**, canoodle (*slang*), clasp, clinch (*slang*), cuddle, squeeze

embroil *verb* = **involve**, complicate, compromise, confound, confuse, disorder, disturb, encumber, enmesh, ensnare, entangle, implicate, incriminate, mire, mix up, muddle, perplex, stitch up (*slang*), trouble

embryo *noun* = **germ**, beginning, nucleus, root, rudiment

embryonic *adjective* = **early**, beginning, germinal, immature, inchoate, incipient, primary, rudimentary, seminal, undeveloped
➤ **Antonyms**
advanced, developed, progressive

emend *verb* = **revise**, amend, correct, edit, improve, rectify, redact

emendation *noun* = **revision**, amendment, correction, editing, improvement, rectification, redaction

emerge *verb* **1 = come into view**, appear, arise, become visible, come forth, come out, come up, emanate, issue, proceed, rise, spring up, surface **2 = become apparent**, become known, come out, come out in the wash, come to light, crop up, develop, materialize, transpire, turn up
➤ **Antonyms**
≠**come into view**: depart, disappear, fade, fall, recede, retreat, sink, submerge, vanish from sight, wane, withdraw

emergence *noun* = **coming**, advent, apparition, appearance, arrival, dawn, development, disclosure, emanation, issue, materialization, rise

emergency *noun* = **crisis**, danger, difficulty, exigency, extremity, necessity, panic stations (*informal*), pass, pinch, plight, predicament, quandary, scrape (*informal*), strait

emigrate *verb* = **move abroad**, migrate, move, remove

emigration *noun* = **departure**, exodus, migration, removal

eminence *noun* **1 = prominence**, celebrity, dignity, distinction, esteem, fame, greatness, illustriousness, importance, notability, note, pre-eminence, prestige, rank, renown, reputation, repute, superiority **2 = high ground**, elevation, height, hill, hillock, knoll, rise, summit

eminent *adjective* = **prominent**, big-time (*informal*), celebrated, conspicuous, distinguished, elevated, esteemed, exalted, famous, grand, great, high, high-ranking, illustrious, important, major league (*informal*), notable, noted, noteworthy, outstanding, paramount, pre-eminent, prestigious, renowned, signal, superior, well-known
➤ **Antonyms**
anonymous, commonplace, infamous, lowly, ordinary, undistinguished, unheard-of, unimportant, unknown, unremarkable, unsung

eminently *adverb* = **extremely**, conspicuously, exceedingly, exceptionally, greatly, highly, notably, outstandingly, prominently, remarkably, seriously (*informal*), signally, strikingly, surpassingly, well

emission *noun* = **giving off** *or* **out**, diffusion, discharge, ejaculation, ejection, emanation, exhalation, exudation, issuance, issue, radiation, shedding, transmission, utterance, venting

emit *verb* = **give off**, breathe forth, cast out,

diffuse, discharge, eject, emanate, exhale, exude, give out, give vent to, issue, radiate, send forth, send out, shed, throw out, transmit, utter, vent
➤ **Antonyms**
absorb, assimilate, consume, devour, digest, drink in, incorporate, ingest, receive, soak up, suck up, take in

emolument noun = **fee**, benefit, compensation, earnings, gain, hire, pay, payment, profits, recompense, remuneration, return, reward, salary, stipend, wages

emotion noun = **feeling**, agitation, ardour, excitement, fervour, passion, perturbation, sensation, sentiment, vehemence, warmth

emotional adjective **1** = **sensitive**, demonstrative, excitable, feeling, hot-blooded, passionate, responsive, sentimental, susceptible, temperamental, tender, touchy-feely (informal), warm **2** = **moving**, affecting, emotive, exciting, heart-warming, pathetic, poignant, sentimental, stirring, tear-jerking (informal), three-hankie (informal), thrilling, touching **3** = **passionate**, ablaze, ardent, enthusiastic, fervent, fervid, fiery, flaming, heated, impassioned, roused, stirred, zealous
➤ **Antonyms**
≠sensitive: apathetic, cold, detached, insensitive, phlegmatic, undemonstrative, unemotional, unfeeling, unmoved, unsentimental ≠passionate: dispassionate, unenthusiastic, unexcitable, unruffled

emotive adjective **1** = **sensitive**, argumentative, controversial, delicate, touchy **2** = **moving**, affecting, emotional, exciting, heart-warming, pathetic, poignant, sentimental, stirring, tear-jerking (informal), three-hankie (informal), thrilling, touching

emphasis noun = **stress**, accent, accentuation, attention, decidedness, force, importance, impressiveness, insistence, intensity, moment, positiveness, power, pre-eminence, priority, prominence, significance, strength, underscoring, weight

emphasize verb = **stress**, accent, accentuate, dwell on, foreground, give priority to, highlight, insist on, lay stress on, play up, press home, put the accent on, underline, underscore, weight
➤ **Antonyms**
gloss over, make light of, make little of, minimize, play down, soft-pedal (informal), underplay

emphatic adjective = **forceful**, absolute, categorical, certain, decided, definite, direct, distinct, earnest, energetic, forcible, important, impressive, insistent, in spades, marked, momentous, positive, powerful, pronounced, resounding, significant, storming (informal), striking, strong, telling,

unequivocal, unmistakable, vigorous
➤ **Antonyms**
commonplace, equivocal, hesitant, insignificant, tame, tentative, uncertain, undecided, unremarkable, unsure, weak

empire noun **1** = **kingdom**, commonwealth, domain, imperium (rare), realm **2** = **power**, authority, command, control, dominion, government, rule, sovereignty, supremacy, sway

empirical, empiric adjective = **first-hand**, experiential, experimental, observed, practical, pragmatic
➤ **Antonyms**
academic, assumed, conjectural, hypothetical, putative, speculative, theoretic(al)

emplacement noun **1** = **position**, location, lodgment, platform, site, situation, station **2** = **positioning**, placement, placing, putting in place, setting up, stationing

employ verb **1** = **hire**, commission, engage, enlist, retain, take on **2** = **keep busy**, engage, fill, make use of, occupy, spend, take up, use up **3** = **use**, apply, bring to bear, exercise, exert, make use of, ply, put to use, utilize ♦ noun **4** As in **in the employ of** = **service**, employment, engagement, hire

employed adjective = **working**, active, busy, engaged, in a job, in employment, in work, occupied
➤ **Antonyms**
idle, jobless, laid off, on the dole (Brit. informal), out of a job, out of work, redundant, unoccupied

employee noun = **worker**, hand, job-holder, staff member, wage-earner, workman

employer noun = **boss** (informal), business, company, establishment, firm, gaffer (informal, chiefly Brit.), organization, outfit (informal), owner, patron, proprietor

employment noun **1** = **taking on**, engagement, enlistment, hire, retaining **2** = **use**, application, exercise, exertion, utilization **3** = **job**, avocation (archaic), business, calling, craft, employ, line, métier, occupation, profession, pursuit, service, trade, vocation, work

emporium noun Old-fashioned = **shop**, bazaar, market, mart, store, warehouse

empower verb = **enable**, allow, authorize, commission, delegate, entitle, license, permit, qualify, sanction, warrant

emptiness noun **1** = **bareness**, blankness, desertedness, desolation, destitution, vacancy, vacantness, vacuum, void, waste **2** = **purposelessness**, aimlessness, banality, barrenness, frivolity, futility, hollowness, inanity, ineffectiveness, meaninglessness, senselessness, silliness, unreality, unsatisfactoriness, unsubstantiality, vainness, valuelessness, vanity, worthlessness **3** = **insincerity**, cheapness, hollowness, idleness, triviality, trivialness **4** = **blankness**, absentness, expressionlessness, unintelligence, vacancy, vacantness, vacuity, vacuousness

empty *adjective* **1** = **bare**, blank, clear, deserted, desolate, destitute, hollow, unfurnished, uninhabited, unoccupied, untenanted, vacant, void, waste **2** = **purposeless**, aimless, banal, bootless, frivolous, fruitless, futile, hollow, inane, ineffective, meaningless, otiose, senseless, silly, unreal, unsatisfactory, unsubstantial, vain, valueless, worthless **3** = **insincere**, cheap, hollow, idle, trivial **4** = **blank**, absent, expressionless, unintelligent, vacant, vacuous **5** *Informal* = **hungry**, esurient, famished, ravenous, starving (*informal*), unfed, unfilled ◆ *verb* **6** = **evacuate**, clear, consume, deplete, discharge, drain, dump, exhaust, gut, pour out, unburden, unload, use up, vacate, void
➤ **Antonyms**
adjective ≠**bare**: full, inhabited, occupied, packed, stuffed ≠**purposeless**: busy, fulfilled, full, interesting, meaningful, occupied, purposeful, satisfying, serious, significant, useful, valuable, worthwhile ◆ *verb* ≠**evacuate**: cram, fill, pack, replenish, stock, stuff

empty-headed *adjective* = **scatterbrained**, brainless, ditzy *or* ditsy (*slang*), dizzy (*informal*), featherbrained, flighty, frivolous, giddy, goofy (*informal*), harebrained, inane, silly, skittish, vacuous

emulate *verb* = **imitate**, challenge, compete with, contend with, copy, echo, follow, follow in the footsteps of, follow suit, follow the example of, mimic, rival, take after, take a leaf out of someone's book, vie with

enable *verb* = **allow**, authorize, capacitate, commission, empower, entitle, facilitate, fit, license, permit, prepare, qualify, sanction, warrant
➤ **Antonyms**
bar, block, hinder, impede, obstruct, prevent, stop, thwart

enact *verb* **1** = **establish**, authorize, command, decree, legislate, ordain, order, pass, proclaim, ratify, sanction **2** = **perform**, act, act out, appear as, depict, personate, play, play the part of, portray, represent

enactment *noun* **1** = **decree**, authorization, canon, command, commandment, dictate, edict, law, legislation, order, ordinance, proclamation, ratification, regulation, statute **2** = **portrayal**, acting, depiction, performance, personation, play-acting,

playing, representation

enamoured *adjective* = **in love**, bewitched, captivated, charmed, crazy about (*informal*), enchanted, enraptured, entranced, fascinated, fond, infatuated, nuts on *or* about (*slang*), smitten, swept off one's feet, taken, wild about (*informal*)

encampment *noun* = **camp**, base, bivouac, camping ground, campsite, cantonment, quarters, tents

encapsulate, incapsulate *verb* = **sum up**, abridge, compress, condense, digest, epitomize, précis, summarize

enchant *verb* = **fascinate**, beguile, bewitch, captivate, cast a spell on, charm, delight, enamour, enrapture, enthral, hypnotize, mesmerize, ravish, spellbind

enchanter *noun* = **sorcerer**, conjuror, magician, magus, necromancer, spellbinder, warlock, witch, wizard

enchanting *adjective* = **fascinating**, alluring, appealing, attractive, bewitching, captivating, charming, delightful, endearing, entrancing, lovely, Orphean, pleasant, ravishing, winsome

enchantment *noun* **1** = **fascination**, allure, allurement, beguilement, bliss, charm, delight, hypnotism, mesmerism, rapture, ravishment, transport **2** = **spell**, charm, conjuration, incantation, magic, necromancy, sorcery, witchcraft, wizardry

enchantress *noun* **1** = **sorceress**, conjuror, lamia, magician, necromancer, spellbinder, witch **2** = **seductress**, charmer, *femme fatale*, siren, vamp (*informal*)

enclose, inclose *verb* **1** = **surround**, bound, circumscribe, cover, encase, encircle, encompass, environ, fence, hedge, hem in, impound, pen, pound, shut in, wall in, wrap **2** = **send with**, include, insert, put in **3** = **include**, comprehend, contain, embrace, hold, incorporate

encompass *verb* **1** = **surround**, circle, circumscribe, encircle, enclose, envelop, environ, enwreath, girdle, hem in, ring **2** = **include**, admit, comprehend, comprise, contain, cover, embody, embrace, hold, incorporate, involve, subsume, take in

encounter *verb* **1** = **meet**, bump into (*informal*), chance upon, come upon, confront, experience, face, happen on *or* upon, run across, run into (*informal*) **2** = **battle with**, attack, clash with, combat, come into conflict with, contend, cross swords with, do battle with, engage, face off (*slang*), fight, grapple with, join battle with, strive, struggle ◆ *noun* **3** = **meeting**, brush, confrontation, rendezvous **4** = **battle**, action, clash, collision, combat, conflict, contest, dispute, engagement, face-off (*slang*), fight, head-to-head, run-in (*informal*), set to (*informal*), skirmish

encourage verb 1 = **inspire**, animate, buoy up, cheer, comfort, console, embolden, gee up, hearten, incite, inspirit, rally, reassure, rouse, stimulate 2 = **spur**, abet, advance, advocate, aid, boost, commend, egg on, favour, forward, foster, further, help, promote, prompt, strengthen, succour, support, urge
➤ Antonyms
daunt, depress, deter, discourage, dishearten, dispirit, dissuade, hinder, inhibit, intimidate, prevent, retard, scare, throw cold water on (*informal*)

encouragement noun = **inspiration**, advocacy, aid, boost, cheer, clarion call, consolation, favour, gee-up, help, incitement, inspiritment, promotion, reassurance, security blanket (*informal*), stimulation, stimulus, succour, support, urging

encouraging adjective = **promising**, bright, cheerful, cheering, comforting, good, heartening, hopeful, reassuring, rosy, satisfactory, stimulating
➤ Antonyms
daunting, depressing, disappointing, discouraging, disheartening, dispiriting, off-putting (*informal*), unfavourable, unpropitious

encroach verb = **intrude**, appropriate, arrogate, impinge, infringe, invade, make inroads, overstep, trench, trespass, usurp

encroachment noun = **intrusion**, appropriation, arrogation, impingement, incursion, infringement, inroad, invasion, trespass, usurpation, violation

encumber verb = **burden**, clog, cramp, embarrass, hamper, handicap, hinder, impede, incommode, inconvenience, make difficult, obstruct, oppress, overload, retard, saddle, slow down, trammel, weigh down

encumbrance noun = **burden**, albatross, clog, difficulty, drag, embarrassment, handicap, hindrance, impediment, inconvenience, liability, load, millstone, obstacle, obstruction

end noun 1 = **extremity**, bound, boundary, edge, extent, extreme, limit, point, terminus, tip 2 = **finish**, cessation, close, closure, ending, expiration, expiry, stop, termination, wind-up 3 = **conclusion**, attainment, completion, consequence, consummation, culmination, denouement, ending, end result, finale, issue, outcome, resolution, result, sequel, upshot 4 = **remnant**, bit, butt, fragment, leftover, oddment, remainder, scrap, stub, tag end, tail end 5 = **destruction**, annihilation, death, demise,

dissolution, doom, extermination, extinction, ruin, ruination 6 = **purpose**, aim, aspiration, design, drift, goal, intent, intention, object, objective, point, reason 7 **the end** *Slang* = **the worst**, beyond endurance, insufferable, intolerable, the final blow, the last straw, the limit (*informal*), too much (*informal*), unbearable, unendurable ◆ verb 8 = **finish**, axe (*informal*), belay (*Nautical*), bring to an end, cease, close, complete, conclude, culminate, dissolve, expire, nip in the bud, pull the plug on, put paid to, resolve, stop, terminate, wind up 9 = **destroy**, abolish, annihilate, exterminate, extinguish, kill, put to death, ruin
➤ Antonyms
noun ≠finish: beginning, birth, commencement, inception, launch, opening, origin, outset, prelude, source, start ◆ verb ≠finish: begin, come into being, commence, initiate, launch, originate, start

endanger verb = **put at risk**, compromise, hazard, imperil, jeopardize, put in danger, risk, threaten
➤ Antonyms
defend, guard, preserve, protect, safeguard, save, secure

endear verb = **attract**, attach, bind, captivate, charm, engage, win

endearing adjective = **attractive**, adorable, captivating, charming, cute, engaging, lovable, sweet, winning, winsome

endearment noun 1 = **loving word**, affectionate utterance, sweet nothing 2 = **affection**, attachment, fondness, love

endeavour *Formal* ◆ verb 1 = **try**, aim, aspire, attempt, bend over backwards (*informal*), break one's neck (*informal*), bust a gut (*informal*), do one's best, do one's damnedest (*informal*), essay, give it one's all (*informal*), give it one's best shot (*informal*), go for broke (*slang*), go for it (*informal*), have a crack (*informal*), have a go, have a shot (*informal*), have a stab (*informal*), jump through hoops (*informal*), knock oneself out (*informal*), labour, make an all-out effort (*informal*), make an effort, rupture oneself (*informal*), strive, struggle, take pains, undertake ◆ noun 2 = **effort**, aim, attempt, crack (*informal*), enterprise, essay, go (*informal*), shot (*informal*), stab (*informal*), trial, try, undertaking, venture

ending noun = **finish**, cessation, close, completion, conclusion, consummation, culmination, denouement, end, finale, resolution, termination, wind-up
➤ Antonyms
birth, commencement, inauguration, inception, onset, opening, origin, preface, source, start, starting point

endless adjective 1 = **eternal**, boundless,

ceaseless, constant, continual, everlasting, immortal, incessant, infinite, interminable, limitless, measureless, perpetual, unbounded, unbroken, undying, unending, uninterrupted, unlimited **2 = interminable**, monotonous, overlong **3 = continuous**, unbroken, undivided, whole
➤ **Antonyms**
≠ **eternal:** bounded, brief, circumscribed, finite, limited, passing, restricted, temporary, terminable, transient, transitory

endorse, indorse *verb* **1 = approve**, advocate, affirm, authorize, back, champion, confirm, espouse, favour, prescribe, promote, ratify, recommend, sanction, subscribe to, support, sustain, vouch for, warrant **2 = sign**, countersign, superscribe, undersign

endorsement, indorsement *noun* **1 = approval**, advocacy, affirmation, approbation, authorization, backing, championship, confirmation, espousal, favour, fiat, O.K. *or* okay (*informal*), promotion, ratification, recommendation, sanction, seal of approval, subscription to, support, warrant **2 = signature**, comment, countersignature, qualification, superscription

endow *verb* **= provide**, award, bequeath, bestow, confer, donate, endue, enrich, favour, finance, fund, furnish, give, grant, invest, leave, make over, purvey, settle on, supply, will

endowment *noun* **1 = provision**, award, benefaction, bequest, bestowal, boon, donation, fund, gift, grant, hand-out, income, largesse *or* largess, legacy, presentation, property, revenue, stipend **2** *often plural* **= talent**, ability, aptitude, attribute, capability, capacity, faculty, flair, genius, gift, power, qualification, quality

end up *verb* **1 = arrive**, come to a halt, fetch up (*informal*), finish up, stop, wind up **2 = turn out to be**, become eventually, finish as, finish up, pan out (*informal*)

endurable *adjective* **= bearable**, acceptable, sufferable, supportable, sustainable, tolerable
➤ **Antonyms**
insufferable, insupportable, intolerable, too much (*informal*), unbearable, unendurable

endurance *noun* **1 = staying power**, bearing, fortitude, patience, perseverance, persistence, pertinacity, resignation, resolution, stamina, strength, submission, sufferance, tenacity, toleration **2 = permanence**, continuation, continuity, durability, duration, immutability, lastingness, longevity, stability

endure *verb* **1 = bear**, brave, cope with, experience, go through, stand, stick it out

(*informal*), suffer, support, sustain, take it (*informal*), thole (*Scot.*), undergo, weather, withstand **2 = put up with**, abide, allow, bear, brook, countenance, hack (*slang*), permit, stand, stick (*slang*), stomach, submit to, suffer, swallow, take patiently, tolerate **3 = last**, abide, be durable, continue, have a good innings, hold, live, live on, persist, prevail, remain, stand, stay, survive, wear well

enduring *adjective* **= long-lasting**, abiding, continuing, durable, eternal, firm, immortal, immovable, imperishable, lasting, living, perennial, permanent, persistent, persisting, prevailing, remaining, steadfast, steady, surviving, unfaltering, unwavering
➤ **Antonyms**
brief, ephemeral, fleeting, momentary, passing, short, short-lived, temporary, transient, transitory

enemy *noun* **= foe**, adversary, antagonist, competitor, opponent, rival, the opposition, the other side
➤ **Antonyms**
ally, confederate, friend, supporter

energetic *adjective* **= vigorous**, active, alive and kicking, animated, bright-eyed and bushy-tailed (*informal*), brisk, dynamic, forceful, forcible, full of beans (*informal*), high-octane (*informal*), high-powered, indefatigable, lively, potent, powerful, spirited, storming (*informal*), strenuous, strong, tireless, zippy (*informal*)
➤ **Antonyms**
debilitated, dull, enervated, inactive, lazy, lethargic, lifeless, listless, slow, sluggish, torpid, weak

energy *noun* **= vigour**, activity, animation, ardour, brio, drive, efficiency, élan, elbow grease (*facetious*), exertion, fire, force, forcefulness, get-up-and-go (*informal*), go (*informal*), intensity, life, liveliness, pep, pluck, power, spirit, stamina, strength, strenuousness, verve, vim (*slang*), vitality, vivacity, zeal, zest, zip (*informal*)

enfold, infold *verb* **= wrap**, clasp, embrace, enclose, encompass, envelop, enwrap, fold, hold, hug, shroud, swathe, wrap up

enforce *verb* **= impose**, administer, apply, carry out, coerce, compel, constrain, exact, execute, implement, insist on, oblige, prosecute, put in force, put into effect, reinforce, require, urge

enforced *adjective* **= imposed**, compelled, compulsory, constrained, dictated, involuntary, necessary, ordained, prescribed, required, unavoidable, unwilling

enforcement *noun* **= imposition**, administration, application, carrying out, exaction, execution, implementation, prosecution, reinforcement

enfranchise *verb* **1** = **give the vote to**, grant suffrage to, grant the franchise to, grant voting rights to **2** = **free**, emancipate, liberate, manumit, release, set free

enfranchisement *noun* **1** = **giving the vote**, granting suffrage *or* the franchise, granting voting rights **2** = **freeing**, emancipation, freedom, liberating, liberation, manumission, release, setting free

engage *verb* **1** = **participate**, embark on, enter into, join, partake, practise, set about, take part, undertake **2** = **occupy**, absorb, busy, engross, grip, involve, preoccupy, tie up **3** = **captivate**, allure, arrest, attach, attract, catch, charm, draw, enamour, enchant, fascinate, fix, gain, win **4** = **employ**, appoint, commission, enlist, enrol, hire, retain, take on **5** = **book**, bespeak, charter, hire, lease, prearrange, rent, reserve, secure **6** = **promise**, affiance, agree, betroth (*archaic*), bind, commit, contract, covenant, guarantee, obligate, oblige, pledge, undertake, vouch, vow **7** *Military* = **begin battle with**, assail, attack, combat, come to close quarters with, encounter, face off (*slang*), fall on, fight with, give battle to, join battle with, meet, take on **8** = **set going**, activate, apply, bring into operation, energize, switch on **9** = **interlock**, dovetail, interact, interconnect, join, mesh
➤ **Antonyms**
≠**employ**: axe (*informal*), discharge, dismiss, fire (*informal*), give notice to, lay off, oust, remove, sack (*informal*)

engaged *adjective* **1** = **betrothed** (*archaic*), affianced, pledged, promised, spoken for **2** = **occupied**, absorbed, busy, committed, employed, engrossed, in use, involved, preoccupied, tied up, unavailable
➤ **Antonyms**
≠**betrothed**: available, fancy-free, free, unattached, uncommitted, unengaged
≠**occupied**: available, free, uncommitted, unengaged

engagement *noun* **1** = **appointment**, arrangement, commitment, date, meeting **2** = **betrothal**, troth (*archaic*) **3** = **promise**, assurance, bond, compact, contract, oath, obligation, pact, pledge, undertaking, vow, word **4** = **job**, commission, employment, gig (*informal*), post, situation, stint, work **5** = **battle**, action, combat, conflict, confrontation, contest, encounter, face-off (*slang*), fight

engaging *adjective* = **charming**, agreeable, appealing, attractive, captivating, cute, enchanting, fascinating, fetching (*informal*), likable *or* likeable, lovable, pleasant, pleasing, winning, winsome

➤ **Antonyms**
disagreeable, objectionable, obnoxious, offensive, repulsive, unattractive, unlikable *or* unlikeable, unlovely, unpleasant

engender *verb* = **produce**, beget, breed, bring about, cause, create, excite, foment, generate, give rise to, hatch, incite, induce, instigate, lead to, make, occasion, precipitate, provoke

engine *noun* = **machine**, mechanism, motor

engineer *verb* = **bring about**, cause, concoct, contrive, control, create, devise, effect, encompass, finagle (*informal*), manage, manoeuvre, mastermind, originate, plan, plot, scheme, wangle (*informal*)

engrave *verb* **1** = **carve**, chase, chisel, cut, enchase (*rare*), etch, grave (*archaic*), inscribe **2** = **imprint**, impress, print **3** = **fix**, embed, impress, imprint, infix, ingrain, lodge

engraving *noun* **1** = **cutting**, carving, chasing, chiselling, dry point, enchasing (*rare*), etching, inscribing, inscription **2** = **carving**, block, etching, inscription, plate, woodcut **3** = **print**, etching, impression

engross *verb* = **absorb**, arrest, engage, engulf, hold, immerse, involve, occupy, preoccupy

engrossed *adjective* = **absorbed**, captivated, caught up, deep, enthralled, fascinated, gripped, immersed, intent, intrigued, lost, preoccupied, rapt, riveted

engrossing *adjective* = **absorbing**, captivating, compelling, enthralling, fascinating, gripping, interesting, intriguing, riveting

engulf *verb* = **immerse**, envelop, inundate, overrun, overwhelm, submerge, swallow up, swamp

enhance *verb* = **improve**, add to, augment, boost, complement, elevate, embellish, exalt, heighten, increase, intensify, lift, magnify, raise, reinforce, strengthen, swell
➤ **Antonyms**
debase, decrease, depreciate, devalue, diminish, lower, minimize, reduce, spoil

enigma *noun* = **mystery**, conundrum, problem, puzzle, riddle, teaser

enigmatic, enigmatical *adjective* = **mysterious**, ambiguous, cryptic, Delphic, doubtful, equivocal, incomprehensible, indecipherable, inexplicable, inscrutable, obscure, oracular, perplexing, puzzling, recondite, sphinxlike, uncertain, unfathomable, unintelligible
➤ **Antonyms**
clear, comprehensible, simple, straightforward, uncomplicated

enjoin *verb* **1** = **order**, advise, bid, call upon, charge, command, counsel, demand, direct, instruct, prescribe, require, urge, warn **2** *Law* = **prohibit**, ban, bar, disallow, forbid, interdict, place an injunction on, preclude, proscribe, restrain

enjoy *verb* **1** = **take pleasure in** *or* **from**, appreciate, be entertained by, be pleased with, delight in, like, rejoice in, relish, revel in, take joy in **2** = **have**, be blessed *or* favoured with, experience, have the benefit of, have the use of, own, possess, reap the benefits of, use **3** **enjoy oneself** = **have a good time**, have a ball (*informal*), have a field day (*informal*), have fun, let one's hair down, make merry
➤ **Antonyms**
≠**take pleasure in** *or* **from**: abhor, despise, detest, dislike, hate, have no taste *or* stomach for, loathe

enjoyable *adjective* = **pleasurable**, agreeable, amusing, delectable, delicious, delightful, entertaining, gratifying, pleasant, pleasing, satisfying, to one's liking
➤ **Antonyms**
despicable, disagreeable, displeasing, hateful, loathsome, obnoxious, offensive, repugnant, unenjoyable, unpleasant, unsatisfying, unsavoury

enjoyment *noun* = **pleasure**, amusement, beer and skittles (*informal*), delectation, delight, diversion, entertainment, fun, gladness, gratification, gusto, happiness, indulgence, joy, recreation, relish, satisfaction, zest

enlarge *verb* **1** = **increase**, add to, amplify, augment, blow up (*informal*), broaden, diffuse, dilate, distend, elongate, expand, extend, grow, heighten, inflate, lengthen, magnify, make *or* grow larger, multiply, stretch, swell, wax, widen **2** **enlarge on** = **expand on**, descant on, develop, elaborate on, expatiate on, give further details about
➤ **Antonyms**
≠**increase**: compress, condense, curtail, decrease, diminish, lessen, narrow, reduce, shorten, shrink, trim, truncate ≠**expand on**: abbreviate, abridge, condense, shorten

enlighten *verb* = **inform**, advise, apprise, cause to understand, civilize, counsel, edify, educate, instruct, make aware, teach

enlightened *adjective* = **informed**, aware, broad-minded, civilized, cultivated, educated, knowledgeable, liberal, literate, open-minded, reasonable, refined, sophisticated
➤ **Antonyms**
ignorant, narrow-minded, short-sighted, small-minded, unaware, uneducated, unenlightened

enlightenment *noun* = **understanding**, awareness, broad-mindedness, civilization, comprehension, cultivation, edification, education, information, insight, instruction, knowledge, learning, literacy, open-mindedness, refinement, sophistication, teaching, wisdom

enlist *verb* **1** = **join up**, enrol, enter (into), gather, join, muster, register, secure, sign up, volunteer **2** = **obtain**, engage, procure, recruit

enliven *verb* = **cheer up**, animate, brighten, buoy up, cheer, excite, exhilarate, fire, gladden, hearten, inspire, inspirit, invigorate, pep up, perk up, quicken, rouse, spark, stimulate, vitalize, vivify, wake up
➤ **Antonyms**
chill, dampen, deaden, depress, put a damper on, repress, subdue

enmity *noun* = **hostility**, acrimony, animosity, animus, antagonism, antipathy, aversion, bad blood, bitterness, hate, hatred, ill will, malevolence, malice, malignity, rancour, spite, venom
➤ **Antonyms**
affection, amity, cordiality, friendliness, friendship, geniality, goodwill, harmony, love, warmth

ennoble *verb* = **dignify**, aggrandize, elevate, enhance, exalt, glorify, honour, magnify, raise

ennui *noun Literary* = **boredom**, dissatisfaction, lassitude, listlessness, tedium, the doldrums

enormity *noun* **1** = **wickedness**, atrociousness, atrocity, depravity, disgrace, evilness, heinousness, monstrousness, nefariousness, outrageousness, turpitude, viciousness, vileness, villainy **2** = **atrocity**, abomination, crime, disgrace, evil, horror, monstrosity, outrage, villainy **3** *Informal* = **hugeness**, enormousness, greatness, immensity, magnitude, massiveness, vastness

enormous *adjective* = **huge**, astronomic, Brobdingnagian, colossal, elephantine, excessive, gargantuan, gigantic, ginormous (*informal*), gross, humongous *or* humungous (*U.S. slang*), immense, jumbo (*informal*), mammoth, massive, monstrous, mountainous, prodigious, stellar (*informal*), titanic, tremendous, vast
➤ **Antonyms**
diminutive, dwarf, infinitesimal, insignificant, Lilliputian, little, meagre, microscopic, midget, minute, petite, pint-sized (*informal*), small, tiny, trivial, wee

enough *adjective* **1** = **sufficient**, abundant, adequate, ample, plenty ♦ *noun* **2** = **sufficiency**, abundance, adequacy, ample supply, plenty, right amount ♦ *adverb* **3** = **sufficiently**, abundantly, adequately, amply, fairly, moderately, passably, reasonably, satisfactorily, tolerably

enquire *see* INQUIRE

enquiry *see* INQUIRY

enrage *verb* = **anger**, aggravate (*informal*), exasperate, gall, get one's back up, incense, incite, inflame, infuriate, irritate, madden, make one's blood boil, make one see red (*informal*), nark (*Brit., Austral., & N.Z. slang*), provoke, put one's back up
➤ Antonyms
appease, assuage, calm, conciliate, mollify, pacify, placate, soothe

enraged *adjective* = **furious**, aggravated (*informal*), angered, angry, boiling mad, choked, cross, exasperated, fuming, incandescent, incensed, inflamed, infuriated, irate, irritated, livid (*informal*), mad (*informal*), on the warpath, pissed (*taboo slang*), pissed off (*taboo slang*), raging, raging mad, wild

enrich *verb* **1** = **enhance**, aggrandize, ameliorate, augment, cultivate, develop, endow, improve, refine, supplement **2** = **make rich**, make wealthy

enrol *verb* **1** = **enlist**, accept, admit, engage, join up, matriculate, recruit, register, sign up *or* on, take on **2** = **record**, chronicle, inscribe, list, note

enrolment *noun* = **enlistment**, acceptance, admission, engagement, matriculation, recruitment, registration

en route *adverb* = **on** *or* **along the way**, in transit, on the road

ensemble *noun* **1** = **whole**, aggregate, assemblage, collection, entirety, set, sum, total, totality, whole thing **2** = **outfit**, costume, get-up (*informal*), suit **3** = **group**, band, cast, chorus, company, supporting cast, troupe

enshrine *verb* = **preserve**, apotheosize, cherish, consecrate, dedicate, embalm, exalt, hallow, revere, sanctify, treasure

enshroud *verb* = **cover**, cloak, cloud, conceal, enclose, enfold, envelop, enwrap, hide, obscure, pall, shroud, veil, wrap

ensign *noun* = **flag**, badge, banner, colours, jack, pennant, pennon, standard, streamer

enslave *verb* = **subjugate**, bind, dominate, enchain, enthral, reduce to slavery, yoke

ensue *verb* = **follow**, arise, attend, be consequent on, befall, come after, come next, come to pass (*archaic*), derive, flow, issue, proceed, result, stem, succeed, supervene, turn out *or* up
➤ Antonyms
antecede, come first, forerun, go ahead of, go before, introduce, lead, pave the way, precede, usher

ensure, insure *verb* **1** = **make certain**, certify, confirm, effect, guarantee, make

sure, secure, warrant **2** = **protect**, guard, make safe, safeguard, secure

entail *verb* = **involve**, bring about, call for, cause, demand, encompass, give rise to, impose, lead to, necessitate, occasion, require, result in

entangle *verb* **1** = **tangle**, catch, compromise, embroil, enmesh, ensnare, entrap, foul, implicate, involve, knot, mat, mix up, ravel, snag, snare, trammel, trap **2** = **mix up**, bewilder, complicate, confuse, jumble, muddle, perplex, puzzle, snarl, twist
➤ Antonyms
≠tangle: detach, disconnect, disengage, disentangle, extricate, free, loose, separate, sever, unfold, unravel, unsnarl, untangle, untwist ≠mix up: clarify, clear (up), resolve, simplify, work out

entanglement *noun* **1** = **tangle**, complication, confusion, ensnarement, entrapment, imbroglio, involvement, jumble, knot, mesh, mess, mix-up, muddle, snare, snarl-up (*informal, chiefly Brit.*), toils, trap **2** = **difficulty**, embarrassment, imbroglio, involvement, liaison, predicament, tie

enter *verb* **1** = **come** *or* **go in** *or* **into**, arrive, insert, introduce, make an entrance, pass into, penetrate, pierce **2** = **join**, become a member of, begin, commence, commit oneself to, embark upon, enlist, enrol, participate in, set about, set out on, sign up, start, take part in, take up **3** = **record**, inscribe, list, log, note, register, set down, take down
➤ Antonyms
≠come *or* go in *or* into: depart, exit, go, issue from, leave, take one's leave, withdraw ≠join: drop out, go, leave, pull out, resign, retire, withdraw

enterprise *noun* **1** = **firm**, business, company, concern, establishment, operation **2** = **undertaking**, adventure, effort, endeavour, essay, operation, plan, programme, project, venture **3** = **initiative**, activity, adventurousness, alertness, audacity, boldness, daring, dash, drive, eagerness, energy, enthusiasm, get-up-and-go (*informal*), gumption (*informal*), pep, push (*informal*), readiness, resource, resourcefulness, spirit, vigour, zeal

enterprising *adjective* = **resourceful**, active, adventurous, alert, audacious, bold, daring, dashing, eager, energetic, enthusiastic, go-ahead, intrepid, keen, ready, spirited, stirring, up-and-coming, venturesome, vigorous, zealous

entertain *verb* **1** = **amuse**, charm, cheer, delight, divert, occupy, please, recreate (*rare*), regale **2** = **show hospitality to**, accommodate, be host to, harbour, have company, have guests *or* visitors, lodge, put up, treat **3 = consider**, cherish, cogitate on, conceive, contemplate, foster, harbour, hold, imagine, keep in mind, maintain, muse over, ponder, support, think about, think over

entertaining *adjective* **= enjoyable**, amusing, charming, cheering, delightful, diverting, funny, humorous, Interesting, pleasant, pleasing, pleasurable, recreative (*rare*), witty

entertainment *noun* **= enjoyment**, amusement, beer and skittles (*informal*), cheer, distraction, diversion, fun, good time, leisure activity, pastime, play, pleasure, recreation, satisfaction, sport, treat

enthral *verb* **= fascinate**, absorb, beguile, captivate, charm, enchant, enrapture, entrance, grip, hold spellbound, hypnotize, intrigue, mesmerize, ravish, rivet, spellbind

enthralling *adjective* **= fascinating**, beguiling, captivating, charming, compelling, compulsive, enchanting, entrancing, gripping, hypnotizing, intriguing, mesmerizing, riveting, spellbinding

enthusiasm *noun* **1 = keenness**, ardour, avidity, devotion, eagerness, earnestness, excitement, fervour, frenzy, interest, passion, relish, vehemence, warmth, zeal, zest, zing (*informal*) **2 = passion**, craze, fad (*informal*), hobby, hobbyhorse, interest, mania, rage

enthusiast *noun* **= lover**, admirer, aficionado, buff (*informal*), devotee, fan, fanatic, fiend (*informal*), follower, freak (*informal*), supporter, zealot

enthusiastic *adjective* **= keen**, ablaze, ardent, avid, bright-eyed and bushy-tailed (*informal*), devoted, eager, earnest, ebullient, excited, exuberant, fervent, fervid, forceful, full of beans (*informal*), hearty, keen as mustard, lively, passionate, spirited, unqualified, unstinting, vehement, vigorous, warm, wholehearted, zealous
➤ **Antonyms**
apathetic, blasé, bored, cool, dispassionate, half-hearted, indifferent, nonchalant, unconcerned, unenthusiastic, uninterested

entice *verb* **= attract**, allure, beguile, cajole, coax, dangle a carrot in front of (someone's) nose, decoy, draw, inveigle, lead on, lure, persuade, prevail on, seduce, tempt, wheedle

entire *adjective* **1 = whole**, complete, full, gross, total **2 = total**, absolute, full, outright, thorough, undiminished, unmitigated, unreserved, unrestricted **3 = intact**, perfect, sound, unbroken, undamaged, unmarked, unmarred, whole, without a scratch **4 = continuous**, integrated, unbroken, undivided, unified

entirely *adverb* **1 = completely**, absolutely, altogether, every inch, fully, in every respect, lock, stock and barrel, perfectly, thoroughly, totally, unreservedly, utterly, wholly, without exception, without reservation **2 = only**, exclusively, solely
➤ **Antonyms**
≠**completely**: incompletely, moderately, partially, partly, piecemeal, slightly, somewhat, to a certain extent *or* degree

entirety *noun* **1 = whole**, aggregate, sum, total, unity **2 = wholeness**, absoluteness, completeness, fullness, totality, undividedness, unity

entitle *verb* **1 = give the right to**, accredit, allow, authorize, empower, enable, enfranchise, fit for, license, make eligible, permit, qualify for, warrant **2 = call**, characterize, christen, denominate, designate, dub, label, name, style, term, title

entity *noun* **= thing**, being, body, creature, existence, individual, object, organism, presence, quantity, substance

entourage *noun* **= retinue**, associates, attendants, companions, company, cortege, court, escort, followers, following, retainers, staff, suite, train

entrails *plural noun* **= intestines**, bowels, guts, innards (*informal*), insides (*informal*), offal, viscera

entrance[1] *noun* **1 = way in**, access, avenue, door, doorway, entry, gate, ingress, inlet, opening, passage, portal **2 = appearance**, arrival, coming in, entry, ingress, introduction **3 = admission**, access, admittance, entrée, entry, ingress, permission to enter
➤ **Antonyms**
≠**way in**: exit, outlet, way out
≠**appearance**: departure, egress, exit, exodus, leave-taking

entrance[2] *verb* **1 = enchant**, absorb, bewitch, captivate, charm, delight, enrapture, enthral, fascinate, gladden, ravish, spellbind, transport **2 = mesmerize**, hypnotize, put in a trance
➤ **Antonyms**
≠**enchant**: bore, disenchant, irritate, offend, put off, turn off (*informal*)

entrant *noun* **1 = competitor**, candidate, contestant, entry, participant, player **2 = new member**, beginner, convert, initiate, neophyte, newcomer, novice, probationer, tyro

entreaty *noun* **= plea**, appeal, earnest request, exhortation, importunity, petition, prayer, request, solicitation, suit, supplication

entrench *verb* **1 = fix**, anchor, dig in, embed, ensconce, establish, implant, ingrain, install, lodge, plant, root, seat, set, settle **2** *Military* **= fortify**, construct defences, dig in, dig trenches

entrenched *adjective* = **fixed**, deep-rooted, deep-seated, firm, indelible, ineradicable, ingrained, rooted, set, unshakable, well-established

entrepreneur *noun* = **businessman** *or* **businesswoman**, contractor, director, financier, impresario, industrialist, magnate, tycoon

entrust *verb* = **give custody of**, assign, authorize, charge, commend, commit, confide, consign, delegate, deliver, hand over, invest, trust, turn over

entry *noun* **1** = **way in**, access, avenue, door, doorway, entrance, gate, ingress, inlet, opening, passage, passageway, portal **2** = **coming in**, appearance, entering, entrance, initiation, introduction **3** = **admission**, access, entrance, entrée, free passage, permission to enter **4** = **record**, account, item, jotting, listing, memo, memorandum, minute, note, registration **5** = **competitor**, attempt, candidate, contestant, effort, entrant, participant, player, submission
➤ **Antonyms**
≠**way in**: exit, way out ≠**coming in**: departure, egress, exit, leave, leave-taking, withdrawal

entwine *verb* = **twist**, braid, embrace, encircle, entwist (*archaic*), interlace, intertwine, interweave, knit, plait, ravel, surround, twine, weave, wind
➤ **Antonyms**
disentangle, extricate, free, separate, straighten out, undo, unravel, untangle, unwind

enumerate *verb* **1** = **list**, cite, detail, itemize, mention, name, quote, recapitulate, recite, recount, rehearse, relate, specify, spell out, tell **2** = **count**, add up, calculate, compute, number, reckon, sum up, tally, total

enunciate *verb* **1** = **pronounce**, articulate, enounce, say, sound, speak, utter, vocalize, voice **2** = **state**, declare, proclaim, promulgate, pronounce, propound, publish

envelop *verb* = **enclose**, blanket, cloak, conceal, cover, embrace, encase, encircle, encompass, enfold, engulf, enwrap, hide, obscure, sheathe, shroud, surround, swaddle, swathe, veil, wrap

envelope *noun* = **wrapping**, case, casing, coating, cover, covering, jacket, sheath, shell, skin, wrapper

enviable *adjective* = **desirable**, advantageous, blessed, covetable, favoured, fortunate, lucky, much to be desired, privileged, to die for (*informal*)
➤ **Antonyms**
disagreeable, painful, thankless,

uncomfortable, undesirable, unenviable, unpleasant

envious *adjective* = **covetous**, begrudging, green-eyed, green with envy, grudging, jaundiced, jealous, malicious, resentful, spiteful

environment *noun* = **surroundings**, atmosphere, background, conditions, context, domain, element, habitat, locale, medium, milieu, scene, setting, situation, territory

environmental *adjective* = **ecological**, green

environmentalist *noun* = **conservationist**, ecologist, friend of the earth, green

environs *plural noun* = **surrounding area**, district, locality, neighbourhood, outskirts, precincts, purlieus, suburbs, vicinity

envisage *verb* **1** = **imagine**, conceive (of), conceptualize, contemplate, fancy, picture, think up, visualize **2** = **foresee**, anticipate, envision, predict, see

envision *verb* = **conceive of**, anticipate, contemplate, envisage, foresee, predict, see, visualize

envoy *noun* = **messenger**, agent, ambassador, courier, delegate, deputy, diplomat, emissary, intermediary, legate, minister, plenipotentiary, representative

envy *noun* **1** = **covetousness**, enviousness, grudge, hatred, ill will, jealousy, malice, malignity, resentfulness, resentment, spite, the green-eyed monster (*informal*) ◆ *verb* **2** = **covet**, be envious (of), begrudge, be jealous (of), grudge, resent

ephemeral *adjective* = **brief**, evanescent, fleeting, flitting, fugacious, fugitive, impermanent, momentary, passing, short, short-lived, temporary, transient, transitory
➤ **Antonyms**
abiding, durable, enduring, eternal, immortal, lasting, long-lasting, persisting, steadfast

epicure *noun* **1** = **gourmet**, bon vivant, epicurean, foodie, gastronome **2** = **hedonist**, glutton, gourmand, sensualist, sybarite, voluptuary

epicurean *adjective* **1** = **hedonistic**, bacchanalian, gluttonous, gourmandizing, libertine, luscious, lush, luxurious, pleasure-seeking, self-indulgent, sensual, sybaritic, voluptuous ◆ *noun* **2** = **gourmet**, bon vivant, epicure, foodie, gastronome

epidemic *noun* **1** = **spread**, contagion, growth, outbreak, plague, rash, upsurge, wave ◆ *adjective* **2** = **widespread**, general, pandemic, prevailing, prevalent, rampant, rife, sweeping, wide-ranging

epigram *noun* = **witticism**, aphorism, bon mot, quip

epilogue *noun* = **conclusion**, afterword, coda, concluding speech, postscript
➤ **Antonyms**
exordium, foreword, introduction, preamble, preface, prelude, prologue

episode *noun* 1 = **event**, adventure, affair, business, circumstance, escapade, experience, happening, incident, matter, occurrence 2 = **part**, chapter, instalment, passage, scene, section

epistle *noun* = **letter**, communication, message, missive, note

epitaph *noun* = **monument**, inscription

epithet *noun* = **name**, appellation, description, designation, moniker *or* monicker (*slang*), nickname, sobriquet, tag, title

epitome *noun* 1 = **personification**, archetype, embodiment, essence, exemplar, norm, quintessence, representation, type, typical example 2 = **summary**, abbreviation, abridgment, abstract, compendium, condensation, conspectus, contraction, digest, précis, résumé, syllabus, synopsis

epitomize *verb* 1 = **typify**, embody, exemplify, illustrate, incarnate, personify, represent, symbolize 2 = **summarize**, abbreviate, abridge, abstract, condense, contract, curtail, cut, encapsulate, précis, reduce, shorten, synopsize

epoch *noun* = **era**, age, date, period, time

equable *adjective* 1 = **even-tempered**, agreeable, calm, composed, easy-going, imperturbable, level-headed, placid, serene, temperate, unexcitable, unfazed (*informal*), unflappable (*informal*), unruffled 2 = **constant**, consistent, even, on an even keel, regular, smooth, stable, steady, temperate, tranquil, unchanging, uniform, unvarying
➤ **Antonyms**
≠**even-tempered**: excitable, nervous, temperamental ≠**constant**: changeable, fitful, inconsistent, irregular, temperamental, uneven, unstable, volatile

equal *adjective* 1 = **identical**, alike, commensurate, corresponding, equivalent, like, matched, one and the same, proportionate, tantamount, the same, uniform 2 = **regular**, symmetrical, uniform, unvarying 3 = **even**, balanced, evenly balanced, evenly matched, evenly proportioned, fifty-fifty (*informal*), level pegging (*Brit. informal*) 4 = **fair**, egalitarian, equable, even-handed, impartial, just, unbiased 5 **equal to** = **capable of**, able to, adequate for, competent to, fit for, good

enough for, ready for, strong enough, suitable for, up to ♦ *noun* 6 = **match**, brother, compeer, counterpart, equivalent, fellow, mate, parallel, peer, rival, twin ♦ *verb* 7 = **match**, agree with, amount to, balance, be equal to, be even with, be level with, be tantamount to, come up to, correspond to, equalize, equate, even, level, parallel, rival, square with, tally with, tie with
➤ **Antonyms**
adjective ≠**identical**: different, disproportionate, dissimilar, diverse, unequal, unlike ≠**regular**: irregular ≠**even**: unbalanced, unequal, uneven, unmatched ≠**fair**: biased, inequitable, partial, unequal, unfair, unjust ≠**capable of**: inadequate, incapable, incompetent, not good enough, not up to, unequal, unfit ♦ *verb* ≠**match**: be different, be unequal, disagree

equality *noun* 1 = **sameness**, balance, coequality, correspondence, equatability, equivalence, evenness, identity, likeness, similarity, uniformity 2 = **fairness**, egalitarianism, equal opportunity, parity
➤ **Antonyms**
≠**sameness**: disparity, lack of balance, unevenness ≠**fairness**: bias, discrimination, imparity, inequality, prejudice, unfairness

equalize *verb* = **make equal**, balance, equal, equate, even up, level, match, regularize, smooth, square, standardize

equate *verb* = **make or be equal**, agree, balance, be commensurate, compare, correspond with *or* to, equalize, liken, match, mention in the same breath, offset, pair, parallel, square, tally, think of together

equation *noun* = **equating**, agreement, balancing, comparison, correspondence, equality, equalization, equivalence, likeness, match, pairing, parallel

equestrian *adjective* 1 = **on horseback**, in the saddle, mounted ♦ *noun* 2 = **rider**, cavalier (*archaic*), horseman, knight

equilibrium *noun* 1 = **stability**, balance, counterpoise, equipoise, evenness, rest, steadiness, symmetry 2 = **composure**, calm, calmness, collectedness, coolness, equanimity, poise, self-possession, serenity, stability, steadiness

equip *verb* = **supply**, accoutre, arm, array, attire, deck out, dress, endow, fit out, fit up, furnish, kit out, outfit, prepare, provide, rig, stock

equipment *noun* = **apparatus**, accoutrements, appurtenances, baggage, equipage, furnishings, furniture, gear, materiel, outfit, paraphernalia, rig, stuff, supplies, tackle, tools

equitable *adjective* = **fair**, candid, disinterested, dispassionate, due,

even-handed, honest, impartial, just,
nondiscriminatory, proper, proportionate,
reasonable, right, rightful, unbiased,
unprejudiced

equity *noun* = **fairness**, disinterestedness,
equitableness, even-handedness,
fair-mindedness, fair play, honesty,
impartiality, integrity, justice, reasonableness,
rectitude, righteousness, uprightness
➤ **Antonyms**
bias, discrimination, injustice, partiality,
preference, prejudice, unfairness

equivalence *noun* = **equality**, agreement,
alikeness, conformity, correspondence,
evenness, identity, interchangeableness,
likeness, match, parallel, parity, sameness,
similarity, synonymy

equivalent *noun* **1** = **equal**, correspondent,
counterpart, match, opposite number,
parallel, peer, twin ♦ *adjective* **2** = **equal**,
alike, commensurate, comparable,
correspondent, corresponding, even,
homologous, interchangeable, of a kind, of a
piece, same, similar, synonymous,
tantamount
➤ **Antonyms**
adjective ≠**equal**: different, dissimilar,
incomparable, unequal, unlike

equivocal *adjective* = **ambiguous**,
ambivalent, doubtful, dubious, evasive,
indefinite, indeterminate, misleading,
oblique, obscure, oracular, prevaricating,
questionable, suspicious, uncertain, vague
➤ **Antonyms**
absolute, certain, clear, clear-cut,
cut-and-dried (*informal*), decisive, definite,
evident, explicit, incontrovertible,
indubitable, manifest, plain, positive,
straight, unambiguous, unequivocal

equivocate *verb* = **be evasive**, avoid the
issue, beat about the bush (*informal*),
dodge, evade, fence, flannel (*Brit. informal*),
fudge, hedge, parry, prevaricate, pussyfoot
(*informal*), quibble, shuffle, sidestep,
tergiversate, waffle (*informal, chiefly Brit.*)

equivocation *noun* = **ambiguity**, double
talk, doubtfulness, evasion, hedging,
prevarication, quibbling, shuffling,
tergiversation, waffle (*informal, chiefly Brit.*),
weasel words (*informal, chiefly U.S.*)

era *noun* = **age**, aeon, cycle, date, day *or*
days, epoch, generation, period, stage, time

eradicate *verb* = **wipe out**, abolish,
annihilate, deracinate, destroy, efface,
eliminate, erase, expunge,
exterminate, extinguish, extirpate, get rid of,
obliterate, put paid to, remove, root out,
stamp out, uproot, weed out, wipe from the
face of the earth

eradication *noun* = **wiping out**, abolition,

annihilation, deracination, destruction,
effacement, elimination, erasure, expunction,
extermination, extinction, extirpation,
obliteration, removal

erase *verb* = **wipe out**, blot, cancel, delete,
efface, excise, expunge, obliterate, remove,
rub out, scratch out

erect *verb* **1** = **build**, construct, elevate, lift,
mount, pitch, put up, raise, rear, set up,
stand up **2** = **found**, create, establish, form,
initiate, institute, organize, set up
♦ *adjective* **3** = **upright**, elevated, firm,
perpendicular, pricked-up, raised, rigid,
standing, stiff, straight, vertical
➤ **Antonyms**
verb ≠**build**: demolish, destroy, dismantle,
raze, tear down ♦ *adjective* ≠**upright**: bent,
flaccid, horizontal, leaning, limp, prone,
recumbent, relaxed, supine

erection *noun* **1** = **building**, assembly,
construction, creation, elevation,
establishment, fabrication, manufacture **2**
= **structure**, building, construction, edifice,
pile

erode *verb* = **wear down** *or* **away**, abrade,
consume, corrode, destroy, deteriorate,
disintegrate, eat away, grind down, spoil

erosion *noun* = **deterioration**, abrasion,
attrition, consumption, corrasion, corrosion,
destruction, disintegration, eating away,
grinding down, spoiling, wear, wearing
down *or* away

erotic *adjective* = **sexual**, amatory,
aphrodisiac, carnal, erogenous, lustful,
rousing, seductive, sensual, sexy (*informal*),
steamy (*informal*), stimulating, suggestive,
titillating, voluptuous

err *verb* **1** = **make a mistake**, be inaccurate,
be incorrect, be in error, blot one's
copybook (*informal*), blunder, drop a brick
or clanger (*informal*), go astray, go wrong,
misapprehend, miscalculate, misjudge,
mistake, put one's foot in it (*informal*), slip
up (*informal*) **2** = **sin**, be out of order, blot
one's copybook (*informal*), deviate, do
wrong, fall, go astray, lapse, misbehave,
offend, transgress, trespass

errand *noun* = **job**, charge, commission,
message, mission, task

errant *adjective* **1** = **sinning**, aberrant,
deviant, erring, offending, straying,
wayward, wrong **2** *Old-fashioned or literary*
= **wandering**, itinerant, journeying,
nomadic, peripatetic, rambling, roaming,
roving

erratic *adjective* = **unpredictable**, aberrant,
abnormal, capricious, changeable, desultory,
eccentric, fitful, inconsistent, inconstant,
irregular, shifting, uneven, unreliable,
unstable, variable, wayward

➤ **Antonyms**
certain, consistent, constant, dependable, invariable, natural, normal, predictable, regular, reliable, stable, steady, straight, unchanging, undeviating

erroneous *adjective* = **incorrect**, amiss, fallacious, false, faulty, flawed, inaccurate, inexact, invalid, mistaken, spurious, unfounded, unsound, untrue, wide of the mark, wrong
➤ **Antonyms**
accurate, correct, factual, faultless, flawless, precise, right, true, veracious

error *noun* 1 = **mistake**, bloomer (*Brit. informal*), blunder, boner (*slang*), boob (*Brit. slang*), delusion, erratum, fallacy, fault, flaw, howler (*informal*), inaccuracy, misapprehension, miscalculation, misconception, oversight, slip, solecism 2 = **wrongdoing**, delinquency, deviation, fault, lapse, misdeed, offence, sin, transgression, trespass, wrong

erstwhile *adjective* = **former**, bygone, ex (*informal*), late, old, once, one-time, past, previous, quondam, sometime

erudite *adjective* = **learned**, cultivated, cultured, educated, knowledgeable, lettered, literate, scholarly, well-educated, well-read
➤ **Antonyms**
ignorant, illiterate, shallow, uneducated, uninformed, unlettered, unschooled, untaught, unthinking

erupt *verb* 1 = **explode**, be ejected, belch forth, blow up, break out, burst forth, burst into, burst out, discharge, flare up, gush, pour forth, spew forth *or* out, spit out, spout, throw off, vent, vomit 2 *Medical* = **break out**, appear

eruption *noun* 1 = **explosion**, discharge, ejection, flare-up, outbreak, outburst, sally, venting 2 *Medical* = **inflammation**, outbreak, rash

escalate *verb* = **increase**, amplify, ascend, be increased, enlarge, expand, extend, grow, heighten, intensify, magnify, mount, raise, rise, step up
➤ **Antonyms**
abate, contract, decrease, descend, diminish, fall, lessen, limit, lower, shrink, wane, wind down

escapade *noun* = **adventure**, antic, caper, fling, lark (*informal*), mischief, prank, romp, scrape (*informal*), spree, stunt, trick

escape *verb* 1 = **get away**, abscond, bolt, break free *or* out, decamp, do a bunk (*Brit. slang*), do a runner (*slang*), flee, fly, fly the coop (*U.S. & Canad. informal*), hook it (*slang*), make one's getaway, make *or* effect one's escape, run away *or* off, skedaddle (*informal*), skip, slip away, slip through

one's fingers, take a powder (*U.S. & Canad. slang*), take it on the lam (*U.S. & Canad. slang*) 2 = **avoid**, body-swerve (*Scot.*), circumvent, dodge, duck, elude, evade, pass, shun, slip 3 = **leak**, discharge, drain, emanate, exude, flow, gush, issue, pour forth, seep, spurt 4 = **be forgotten by**, baffle, be beyond (someone), elude, puzzle, stump ♦ *noun* 5 = **getaway**, bolt, break, break-out, decampment, flight 6 = **avoidance**, circumvention, elusion, evasion 7 = **relaxation**, distraction, diversion, pastime, recreation, relief 8 = **leak**, discharge, drain, effluence, efflux, emanation, emission, gush, leakage, outflow, outpour, seepage, spurt

eschew *verb* = **avoid**, abandon, abjure, abstain from, elude, fight shy of, forgo, forswear, give a wide berth to, give up, have nothing to do with, keep *or* steer clear of, kick (*informal*), refrain from, renounce, shun, swear off

escort *noun* 1 = **guard**, bodyguard, company, convoy, cortege, entourage, protection, retinue, safeguard, train 2 = **companion**, attendant, beau, chaperon, guide, partner, protector, squire (*rare*) ♦ *verb* 3 = **accompany**, chaperon, conduct, convoy, guard, guide, hold (someone's) hand, lead, partner, protect, shepherd, squire, usher

especial *adjective* 1 *Formal* = **exceptional**, chief, distinguished, extraordinary, marked, notable, noteworthy, outstanding, principal, signal, special, uncommon, unusual 2 = **particular**, exclusive, express, individual, peculiar, personal, private, singular, special, specific, unique

especially *adverb* 1 = **exceptionally**, chiefly, conspicuously, extraordinarily, largely, mainly, markedly, notably, outstandingly, principally, remarkably, seriously (*informal*), signally, specially, strikingly, supremely, uncommonly, unusually 2 = **particularly**, exclusively, expressly, peculiarly, singularly, specifically, uniquely

espionage *noun* = **spying**, counter-intelligence, intelligence, surveillance, undercover work

espousal *noun* 1 = **support**, adoption, advocacy, backing, championing, championship, defence, embracing, maintenance, promotion, taking up 2 *Old-fashioned* = **engagement**, affiancing, betrothal, betrothing (*archaic*), espousing (*archaic*), marriage, nuptials, plighting, wedding

espouse *verb* 1 = **support**, adopt, advocate, back, champion, defend, embrace, maintain, promote, stand up for, take up, uphold 2

Old-fashioned = **marry**, betroth (*archaic*), plight one's troth (*old-fashioned*), take as spouse, take to wife, wed

essay *noun* 1 = **composition**, article, discourse, disquisition, dissertation, paper, piece, tract, treatise ♦ *verb* 2 *Formal* = **attempt**, aim, endeavour, try, undertake

essence *noun* 1 = **fundamental nature**, being, bottom line, core, crux, entity, heart, kernel, life, lifeblood, meaning, nature, pith, principle, quiddity, quintessence, significance, soul, spirit, substance 2 = **concentrate**, distillate, elixir, extract, spirits, tincture 3 **in essence** = **essentially**, basically, fundamentally, in effect, in substance, in the main, materially, substantially, to all intents and purposes, virtually 4 **of the essence** = **vitally important**, crucial, essential, indispensable, of the utmost importance, vital

essential *adjective* 1 = **vital**, crucial, important, indispensable, necessary, needed, requisite 2 = **fundamental**, basic, cardinal, constitutional, elemental, elementary, immanent, inherent, innate, intrinsic, key, main, principal, radical 3 = **perfect**, absolute, complete, ideal, quintessential 4 = **concentrated**, distilled, extracted, rectified, refined, volatile ♦ *noun* 5 = **prerequisite**, basic, fundamental, must, necessity, principle, requisite, rudiment, *sine qua non*, vital part
➤ **Antonyms**
adjective ≠**vital**, **fundamental**: accessory, dispensable, expendable, extra, extraneous, incidental, inessential, lesser, minor, nonessential, optional, secondary, superfluous, surplus, trivial, unimportant, unnecessary

establish *verb* 1 = **create**, base, constitute, decree, enact, ensconce, entrench, fix, form, found, ground, implant, inaugurate, install, institute, organize, plant, put down roots, root, secure, settle, set up, sow the seeds, start 2 = **prove**, authenticate, certify, confirm, corroborate, demonstrate, ratify, show, substantiate, validate, verify

establishment *noun* 1 = **creation**, enactment, formation, foundation, founding, inauguration, installation, institution, organization, setting up 2 = **organization**, business, company, concern, corporation, enterprise, firm, house, institute, institution, outfit (*informal*), setup (*informal*), structure, system 3 = **office**, building, factory, house, plant, quarters 4 = **house**, abode, domicile, dwelling, home, household, pad (*slang*), residence 5 **the Establishment** = **the authorities**, established order, institutionalized authority, ruling class, the powers that be, the system

estate *noun* 1 = **lands**, area, demesne, domain, holdings, manor, property 2 *Law* = **property**, assets, belongings, effects, fortune, goods, possessions, wealth 3 *History* = **class**, caste, order, rank 4 = **status**, condition, lot, period, place, position, quality, rank, situation, standing, state, station

esteem *noun* 1 = **respect**, admiration, Brownie points, consideration, credit, estimation, good opinion, honour, regard, reverence, veneration ♦ *verb* 2 = **respect**, admire, be fond of, cherish, honour, like, love, prize, regard highly, revere, reverence, take off one's hat to, think highly of, treasure, value, venerate 3 *Formal* = **consider**, account, believe, calculate, deem, estimate, hold, judge, rate, reckon, regard, think, view

estimate *verb* 1 = **calculate roughly**, appraise, assess, evaluate, gauge, guess, judge, number, reckon, value 2 = **form an opinion**, assess, believe, conjecture, consider, guess, judge, rank, rate, reckon, surmise, think ♦ *noun* 3 = **approximate calculation**, appraisal, appraisement, assessment, ballpark estimate (*informal*), ballpark figure (*informal*), evaluation, guess, guesstimate (*informal*), judgment, reckoning, valuation 4 = **opinion**, appraisal, appraisement, assessment, belief, conjecture, educated guess, estimation, judgment, surmise, thought(s)

estimation *noun* 1 = **opinion**, appraisal, appreciation, assessment, belief, consideration, considered opinion, estimate, evaluation, judgment, view 2 = **respect**, admiration, Brownie points, credit, esteem, good opinion, honour, regard, reverence, veneration

estrange *verb* = **alienate**, antagonize, disaffect, disunite, divide, drive apart, lose *or* destroy the affection of, make hostile, part, separate, set at odds, withdraw, withhold
➤ **Antonyms**
ally, associate, couple, fuse, join, link, marry, unite

estrangement *noun* = **alienation**, antagonization, breach, break-up, disaffection, dissociation, disunity, division, hostility, parting, separation, split, withdrawal, withholding

estuary *noun* = **inlet**, creek, firth, fjord, mouth

et cetera *adverb* 1 = **and so on**, and so forth ♦ *noun* 2 = **and the rest**, and others, and the like, et al.

etch *verb* = **cut**, carve, corrode, eat into, engrave, furrow, impress, imprint, incise, ingrain, inscribe, stamp

etching *noun* = **print**, carving, engraving, impression, imprint, inscription

eternal *adjective* **1** = **everlasting**, abiding, ceaseless, constant, deathless, endless, immortal, infinite, interminable, never-ending, perennial, perpetual, sempiternal (*literary*), timeless, unceasing, undying, unending, unremitting, without end **2** = **permanent**, deathless, enduring, everlasting, immortal, immutable, imperishable, indestructible, lasting, unchanging
➤ Antonyms
≠everlasting: finite, fleeting, infrequent, irregular, mortal, occasional, random, rare, temporal ≠permanent: changing, ephemeral, evanescent, perishable, transient, transitory

eternity *noun* **1** = **infinity**, age, ages, endlessness, immortality, infinitude, perpetuity, timelessness, time without end **2** *Theology* = **the afterlife**, heaven, paradise, the hereafter, the next world

ethical *adjective* = **moral**, conscientious, correct, decent, fair, fitting, good, honest, honourable, just, principled, proper, right, righteous, upright, virtuous
➤ Antonyms
dishonourable, disreputable, immoral, improper, indecent, low-down (*informal*), not cricket (*informal*), underhand, unethical, unfair, unscrupulous, unseemly

ethics *plural noun* = **moral code**, conscience, morality, moral philosophy, moral values, principles, rules of conduct, standards

ethnic, ethnical *adjective* = **cultural**, folk, indigenous, national, native, racial, traditional

etiquette *noun* = **good** or **proper behaviour**, civility, code, convention, courtesy, customs, decorum, formalities, manners, politeness, politesse, propriety, protocol, p's and q's, rules, usage

eulogize *verb* = **praise**, acclaim, applaud, commend, compliment, crack up (*informal*), cry up, exalt, extol, glorify, laud, magnify (*archaic*), panegyrize, pay tribute to, sing or sound the praises of

eulogy *noun* = **praise**, acclaim, acclamation, accolade, applause, commendation, compliment, encomium, exaltation, glorification, laudation, paean, panegyric, plaudit, tribute

euphoria *noun* = **elation**, bliss, ecstasy, exaltation, exhilaration, exultation, glee, high spirits, intoxication, joy, joyousness, jubilation, rapture, transport
➤ Antonyms
depression, despair, despondency, dolefulness, downheartedness, dumps

(*informal*), gloominess, hopelessness, low spirits, melancholia, melancholy, sadness, the blues

evacuate *verb* **1** = **clear**, abandon, decamp, depart, desert, forsake, leave, move out, pull out, quit, relinquish, remove, vacate, withdraw **2** *Physiology* = **excrete**, crap (*taboo slang*), defecate, discharge, eject, eliminate, empty, expel, shit (*taboo slang*), void

evade *verb* **1** = **avoid**, body-swerve (*Scot.*), circumvent, decline, dodge, duck, elude, escape, escape the clutches of, eschew, get away from, shirk, shun, sidestep, slip through one's fingers, slip through the net, steer clear of **2** = **avoid answering**, balk, beat about the bush, circumvent, cop out (*slang*), equivocate, fence, fend off, flannel (*Brit. informal*), fudge, hedge, parry, prevaricate, quibble, waffle (*informal, chiefly Brit.*)
➤ Antonyms
≠avoid: brave, confront, encounter, face, meet, meet face to face

evaluate *verb* = **assess**, appraise, assay, calculate, estimate, gauge, judge, rank, rate, reckon, size up (*informal*), value, weigh

evaluation *noun* = **assessment**, appraisal, calculation, estimate, estimation, judgment, opinion, rating, valuation

evanescent *adjective Formal* = **ephemeral**, brief, fading, fleeting, fugacious, fugitive, impermanent, momentary, passing, short-lived, transient, transitory, vanishing

evangelical, evangelistic *adjective* = **crusading**, missionary, propagandizing, proselytizing, zealous

evaporate *verb* **1** = **dry up**, dehydrate, desiccate, dry, vaporize **2** = **disappear**, dematerialize, dispel, disperse, dissipate, dissolve, evanesce, fade, fade away, melt, melt away, vanish

evaporation *noun* **1** = **drying up**, dehydration, desiccation, drying, vaporization **2** = **disappearance**, dematerialization, dispelling, dispersal, dissipation, dissolution, evanescence, fading, fading away, melting, melting away, vanishing

evasion *noun* **1** = **avoidance**, circumvention, dodging, elusion, escape **2** = **deception**, artifice, cop-out (*slang*), cunning, equivocation, evasiveness, excuse, fudging, obliqueness, pretext, prevarication, ruse, shift, shirking, shuffling, sophism, sophistry, subterfuge, trickery, waffle (*informal, chiefly Brit.*)

evasive *adjective* = **deceptive**, cagey (*informal*), casuistic, casuistical, cunning, deceitful, devious, dissembling, equivocating, indirect, misleading, oblique, prevaricating, shifty, shuffling, slippery, sophistical, tricky

➤ **Antonyms**

candid, direct, frank, guileless, honest, open, straight, straightforward, truthful, unequivocating

eve *noun* **1** = **night before**, day before, vigil **2** = **brink**, edge, point, threshold, verge

even *adjective* **1** = **level**, flat, flush, horizontal, parallel, plane, plumb, smooth, steady, straight, true, uniform **2** = **regular**, constant, metrical, smooth, steady, unbroken, uniform, uninterrupted, unvarying, unwavering **3** = **equal**, coequal, commensurate, comparable, drawn, equalized, equally balanced, fifty-fifty (*informal*), identical, level, level pegging (*Brit. informal*), like, matching, neck and neck, on a par, parallel, similar, square, the same, tied, uniform **4** = **fair**, balanced, disinterested, dispassionate, equitable, fair and square, impartial, just, unbiased, unprejudiced **5** = **calm**, composed, cool, equable, equanimous, even-tempered, imperturbable, peaceful, placid, serene, stable, steady, tranquil, undisturbed, unexcitable, unruffled, well-balanced **6 get even (with)** *Informal* = **pay back**, be revenged *or* revenge oneself, even the score, get one's own back, give tit for tat, pay (someone) back in his *or* her own coin, reciprocate, repay, requite, return like for like, settle the score, take an eye for an eye, take vengeance ◆ *adverb* **7** = **despite**, disregarding, in spite of, notwithstanding **8** = **all the more**, much, still, yet **9 even as** = **while**, at the same time as, at the time that, during the time that, exactly as, just as, whilst **10 even so** = **nevertheless**, all the same, be that as it may, despite (that), however, in spite of (that), nonetheless, notwithstanding (that), still, yet ◆ *verb* **11 even out** = **make** *or* **become level**, align, flatten, level, regularize, smooth, square, stabilize, steady **12 even the score** = **pay (someone) back**, be revenged *or* revenge oneself, equalize, get even (*informal*), get one's own back, give tit for tat, reciprocate, repay, requite, return like for like, settle the score, take an eye for an eye, take vengeance **13 even up** = **equalize**, balance, equal, match

➤ **Antonyms**

adjective ≠**level**: asymmetrical, awry, bumpy, curving, rough, twisting, undulating, uneven, wavy ≠**regular**: broken, changeable, changing, different, fluctuating, irregular, odd, uneven, variable ≠**equal**: disproportionate, ill-matched, imbalanced, irregular, unequal, uneven ≠**fair**: biased, partial, prejudiced, unbalanced, unequal,

unfair ≠**calm**: agitated, changeable, emotional, excitable, quick-tempered, unpredictable

even-handed *adjective* = **fair**, balanced, disinterested, equitable, fair and square, impartial, just, unbiased, unprejudiced

evening *noun* = **dusk**, crepuscule, e'en (*archaic or poetic*), eve, even (*archaic*), eventide (*archaic or poetic*), gloaming (*Scot. or poetic*), twilight, vesper (*archaic*)

event *noun* **1** = **incident**, adventure, affair, business, circumstance, episode, escapade, experience, fact, happening, matter, milestone, occasion, occurrence **2** = **competition**, bout, contest, game, tournament **3** *As in* **in the event** = **outcome**, conclusion, consequence, effect, end, issue, result, termination, upshot **4 at all events** = **whatever happens**, at any rate, come what may, in any case, in any event, regardless

even-tempered *adjective* = **calm**, composed, cool, cool-headed, equable, imperturbable, level-headed, peaceful, placid, serene, steady, tranquil, unexcitable, unruffled

➤ **Antonyms**

emotional, excitable, hasty, highly-strung, hot-headed, hot-tempered, irascible, quick-tempered, temperamental, touchy, volatile

eventful *adjective* = **exciting**, active, busy, consequential, critical, crucial, decisive, dramatic, fateful, full, historic, important, lively, memorable, momentous, notable, noteworthy, remarkable, significant

➤ **Antonyms**

commonplace, dull, humdrum, insignificant, ordinary, trivial, uneventful, unexceptional, unexciting, unimportant, uninteresting, unremarkable

eventual *adjective* = **final**, concluding, consequent, ensuing, future, later, overall, prospective, resulting, ultimate

eventuality *noun* = **possibility**, case, chance, contingency, event, likelihood, probability

eventually *adverb* = **in the end**, after all, at the end of the day, finally, in the course of time, in the fullness of time, in the long run, one day, some day, some time, sooner or later, ultimately, when all is said and done

ever *adverb* **1** = **at any time**, at all, at any period, at any point, by any chance, in any case, on any occasion **2** = **always**, at all times, aye (*Scot.*), constantly, continually, endlessly, eternally, everlastingly, evermore, for ever, incessantly, perpetually, relentlessly, to the end of time, unceasingly, unendingly

everlasting *adjective* **1** = **eternal**, abiding,

deathless, endless, immortal, imperishable, indestructible, infinite, interminable, never-ending, perpetual, timeless, undying **2 = continual**, ceaseless, constant, continuous, endless, incessant, interminable, never-ending, unceasing, uninterrupted, unremitting
➤ Antonyms
≠**eternal:** brief, ephemeral, fleeting, impermanent, passing, short-lived, temporary, transient, transitory

evermore adverb **= for ever**, always, eternally, ever, in perpetuum, to the end of time

every adjective **= each**, all, each one, the whole number

everybody pronoun **= everyone**, all and sundry, each one, each person, every person, one and all, the whole world

everyday adjective **1 = ordinary**, accustomed, banal, bog-standard (Brit. & Irish slang), common, common or garden (informal), commonplace, conventional, customary, dime-a-dozen (informal), dull, familiar, frequent, habitual, informal, mundane, routine, run-of-the-mill, stock, unexceptional, unimaginative, usual, vanilla (slang), wonted, workaday **2 = daily**, quotidian
➤ Antonyms
≠**ordinary:** best, exceptional, exciting, extraordinary, incidental, individual, infrequent, interesting, irregular, now and then, occasional, original, outlandish, periodic, special, uncommon, unusual
≠**daily:** infrequent, irregular, now and then, occasional, periodic

everyone pronoun **= everybody**, all and sundry, each one, each person, every person, one and all, the whole world

everything pronoun **= all**, each thing, the aggregate, the entirety, the lot, the sum, the total, the whole, the whole caboodle (informal), the whole kit and caboodle (informal), the whole lot

everywhere adverb **= to or in every place**, all around, all over, far and wide or near, high and low, in each place, in every nook and cranny, omnipresent, the world over, ubiquitous, ubiquitously

evict verb **= expel**, boot out (informal), chuck out (informal), dislodge, dispossess, eject, kick out (informal), oust, put out, remove, show the door (to), throw on to the streets, throw out, turf out (informal), turn out

eviction noun **= expulsion**, clearance, dislodgement, dispossession, ejection, ouster (Law), removal

evidence noun **1 = proof**, affirmation,

attestation, averment, confirmation, corroboration, data, declaration, demonstration, deposition, grounds, indication, manifestation, mark, sign, substantiation, testimony, token, witness ♦ verb **2 = show**, demonstrate, denote, display, evince, exhibit, indicate, manifest, prove, reveal, signify, testify to, witness

evident adjective **= obvious**, apparent, blatant, bold, clear, conspicuous, incontestable, incontrovertible, indisputable, manifest, noticeable, palpable, patent, perceptible, plain, plain as the nose on your face, salient, tangible, unmistakable, visible
➤ Antonyms
ambiguous, concealed, doubtful, dubious, hidden, imperceptible, obscure, questionable, secret, uncertain, unclear, unknown, vague

evidently adverb **1 = obviously**, clearly, doubtless, doubtlessly, incontestably, incontrovertibly, indisputably, manifestly, patently, plainly, undoubtedly, unmistakably, without question **2 = apparently**, it seems, it would seem, ostensibly, outwardly, seemingly, to all appearances

evil noun **1 = wickedness**, badness, baseness, corruption, curse, depravity, heinousness, immorality, iniquity, maleficence, malignity, sin, sinfulness, turpitude, vice, viciousness, villainy, wrong, wrongdoing **2 = harm**, affliction, calamity, catastrophe, disaster, hurt, ill, injury, mischief, misery, misfortune, pain, ruin, sorrow, suffering, woe ♦ adjective **3 = wicked**, bad, base, corrupt, depraved, heinous, immoral, iniquitous, maleficent, malevolent, malicious, malignant, nefarious, reprobate, sinful, unholy, vicious, vile, villainous, wrong **4 = harmful**, baneful (archaic), calamitous, catastrophic, deleterious, destructive, detrimental, dire, disastrous, hurtful, inauspicious, injurious, mischievous, painful, pernicious, ruinous, sorrowful, unfortunate, unlucky, woeful **5 = offensive**, foul, mephitic, noxious, pestilential, putrid, unpleasant, vile

evoke verb **1 = arouse**, awaken, call, excite, give rise to, induce, recall, rekindle, stimulate, stir up, summon up **2 = provoke**, call forth, educe (rare), elicit, produce
➤ Antonyms
≠**arouse:** contain, hold in check, inhibit, muffle, repress, restrain, smother, stifle, suppress

evolution noun **= development**, enlargement, evolvement, expansion, growth, increase, maturation, progress, progression, unfolding, unrolling, working out

evolve verb **= develop**, disclose, educe, elaborate, enlarge, expand, grow, increase, mature, open, progress, unfold, unroll, work out

exact *adjective* **1** = **accurate**, careful, correct, definite, explicit, express, faithful, faultless, identical, literal, methodical, on the money (*U.S.*), orderly, particular, precise, right, specific, true, unequivocal, unerring, veracious, very **2** = **meticulous**, careful, exacting, painstaking, punctilious, rigorous, scrupulous, severe, strict ♦ *verb* **3** = **demand**, call for, claim, command, compel, extort, extract, force, impose, insist upon, require, squeeze, wrest, wring
➤ **Antonyms**
adjective ≠ **accurate**: approximate, careless, imprecise, inaccurate, incorrect, indefinite, inexact, loose, rough, slovenly

exacting *adjective* = **demanding**, difficult, hard, harsh, imperious, oppressive, painstaking, rigid, rigorous, severe, stern, strict, stringent, taxing, tough, unsparing
➤ **Antonyms**
easy, easy-peasy (*slang*), effortless, no bother, simple, undemanding

exactly *adverb* **1** = **precisely**, accurately, carefully, correctly, definitely, explicitly, faithfully, faultlessly, literally, methodically, rigorously, scrupulously, severely, strictly, truly, truthfully, unequivocally, unerringly, veraciously **2** = **in every respect**, absolutely, bang, explicitly, expressly, indeed, just, on the button (*informal*), particularly, precisely, prompt (*informal*), quite, specifically, to the letter **3** *not exactly Ironical* = **not at all**, by no means, certainly not, hardly, in no manner, in no way, not by any means, not quite, not really ♦ *interjection* **4** = **precisely**, absolutely, assuredly, as you say, certainly, indeed, just so, of course, quite, quite so, spot-on (*Brit. informal*), truly

exactness *noun* = **precision**, accuracy, carefulness, correctness, exactitude, faithfulness, faultlessness, nicety, orderliness, painstakingness, preciseness, promptitude, regularity, rigorousness, rigour, scrupulousness, strictness, truth, unequivocalness, veracity
➤ **Antonyms**
imprecision, inaccuracy, incorrectness, inexactness, unfaithfulness

exaggerate *verb* = **overstate**, amplify, blow out of all proportion, embellish, embroider, emphasize, enlarge, exalt, hyperbolize, inflate, lay it on thick (*informal*), magnify, make a federal case of (*U.S. informal*), make a mountain out of a molehill (*informal*), make a production (out) of (*informal*), overdo, overemphasize, overestimate

exaggerated *adjective* = **overstated**, amplified, exalted, excessive, extravagant,

fulsome, highly coloured, hyped, hyperbolic, inflated, overblown, overdone, overestimated, over the top (*informal*), pretentious, tall (*informal*)

exaggeration *noun* = **overstatement**, amplification, embellishment, emphasis, enlargement, exaltation, excess, extravagance, hyperbole, inflation, magnification, overemphasis, overestimation, pretension, pretentiousness
➤ **Antonyms**
litotes, restraint, underplaying, understatement

exalt *verb* **1** = **praise**, acclaim, apotheosize, applaud, bless, crack up (*informal*), extol, glorify, idolize, laud, magnify (*archaic*), pay homage to, pay tribute to, reverence, set on a pedestal, worship **2** = **raise**, advance, aggrandize, dignify, elevate, ennoble, honour, promote, upgrade **3** = **stimulate**, animate, arouse, electrify, elevate, excite, fire the imagination (of), heighten, inspire, inspirit, uplift **4** = **elate**, delight, exhilarate, fill with joy, thrill

exaltation *noun* **1** = **praise**, acclaim, acclamation, apotheosis, applause, blessing, extolment, glorification, glory, homage, idolization, laudation, lionization, magnification, panegyric, plaudits, reverence, tribute, worship **2** = **rise**, advancement, aggrandizement, dignity, elevation, eminence, ennoblement, grandeur, high rank, honour, loftiness, prestige, promotion, upgrading **3** = **stimulation**, animation, elevation, excitement, inspiration, uplift **4** = **elation**, bliss, delight, ecstasy, exhilaration, exultation, joy, joyousness, jubilation, rapture, transport

exalted *adjective* **1** = **high-ranking**, august, dignified, elevated, eminent, grand, high, honoured, lofty, prestigious **2** = **noble**, elevated, high-minded, ideal, intellectual, lofty, sublime, superior, uplifting **3** *Informal* = **inflated**, elevated, exaggerated, excessive, overblown, pretentious **4** = **elated**, animated, blissful, cock-a-hoop, ecstatic, elevated, excited, exhilarated, exultant, in high spirits, in seventh heaven, inspired, inspirited, joyous, jubilant, on cloud nine (*informal*), over the moon (*informal*), rapturous, stimulated, transported, uplifted

examination *noun* **1** = **inspection**, analysis, assay, checkup, exploration, interrogation, investigation, observation, once-over (*informal*), perusal, recce (*slang*), research, review, scrutiny, search, study, survey, test, trial **2** = **questioning**, catechism, inquiry, inquisition, probe, quiz, test

examine *verb* **1** = **inspect**, analyse,

example 247 **exceptional**

appraise, assay, check, check out, consider, explore, go over or through, investigate, look over, peruse, ponder, pore over, probe, recce (*slang*), research, review, scan, scrutinize, sift, study, survey, take stock of, test, vet, weigh, work over **2 = question**, catechize, cross-examine, grill (*informal*), inquire, interrogate, quiz, test

example *noun* **1 = specimen**, case, case in point, exemplification, illustration, instance, sample **2 = model**, archetype, exemplar, ideal, illustration, norm, paradigm, paragon, pattern, precedent, prototype, standard **3 = warning**, admonition, caution, lesson **4 for example = as an illustration**, by way of illustration, e.g., *exempli gratia*, for instance, to cite an instance, to illustrate

exasperate *verb* **= irritate**, aggravate (*informal*), anger, annoy, bug (*informal*), embitter, enrage, exacerbate, excite, gall, get (*informal*), get in one's hair (*informal*), get on one's nerves (*informal*), get on one's wick (*Brit. slang*), hassle (*informal*), incense, inflame, infuriate, irk, madden, nark (*Brit., Austral., & N.Z. slang*), needle (*informal*), nettle, peeve (*informal*), pique, piss one off (*taboo slang*), provoke, rankle, rile (*informal*), rouse, try the patience of, vex
➤ **Antonyms**
appease, assuage, calm, conciliate, mollify, pacify, placate, soothe

exasperation *noun* **= irritation**, aggravation (*informal*), anger, annoyance, exacerbation, fury, ire (*literary*), passion, pique, provocation, rage, vexation, wrath

excavate *verb* **= dig out**, burrow, cut, delve, dig, dig up, gouge, hollow, mine, quarry, scoop, trench, tunnel, uncover, unearth

excavation *noun* **= hole**, burrow, cavity, cut, cutting, dig, diggings, ditch, dugout, hollow, mine, pit, quarry, shaft, trench, trough

exceed *verb* **1 = surpass**, beat, be superior to, better, cap (*informal*), eclipse, excel, go beyond, knock spots off (*informal*), outdistance, outdo, outreach, outrun, outshine, outstrip, overtake, pass, put in the shade (*informal*), run rings around (*informal*), surmount, top, transcend **2 = go over the limit of**, go beyond the bounds of, go over the top, overstep

exceeding *adjective* **= extraordinary**, enormous, exceptional, excessive, great, huge, pre-eminent, streets ahead, superior, superlative, surpassing, vast

exceedingly *adverb* **= extremely**, enormously, especially, exceptionally, excessively, extraordinarily, greatly, highly, hugely, inordinately, seriously (*informal*),

superlatively, surpassingly, to a fault, to the nth degree, unusually, vastly, very

excel *verb* **1 = be superior**, beat, better, cap (*informal*), eclipse, exceed, go beyond, outdo, outrival, outshine, pass, put in the shade (*informal*), run rings around (*informal*), steal the show (*informal*), surmount, surpass, top, transcend **2 excel in** or **at = be good at**, be master of, be proficient in, be skilful at, be talented at, have (something) down to a fine art, predominate in, shine at, show talent in

excellence *noun* **= high quality**, distinction, eminence, fineness, goodness, greatness, merit, perfection, pre-eminence, purity, superiority, supremacy, transcendence, virtue, worth

excellent *adjective* **= outstanding**, A1 or A-one (*informal*), admirable, bitchin' (*U.S. slang*), bodacious (*slang, chiefly U.S.*), boffo (*slang*), brill (*informal*), brilliant, capital, champion, chillin' (*U.S. slang*), choice, cracking (*Brit. informal*), crucial (*slang*), def (*slang*), distinguished, dope (*slang*), estimable, exemplary, exquisite, fine, first-class, first-rate, good, great, jim-dandy (*slang*), mean (*slang*), mega (*slang*), meritorious, notable, noted, prime, select, sovereign, sterling, superb, superior, superlative, the dog's bollocks (*taboo slang*), tiptop, top-notch (*informal*), topping (*Brit. slang*), world-class, worthy
➤ **Antonyms**
abysmal, bad, dreadful, faulty, imperfect, incompetent, inexpert, inferior, lousy (*slang*), mediocre, no great shakes (*informal*), piss-poor (*taboo slang*), poor, rotten (*informal*), second-class, second-rate, substandard, terrible, unskilled

except *preposition* **1** Also **except for = apart from**, bar, barring, besides, but, excepting, excluding, exclusive of, omitting, other than, save (*archaic*), saving, with the exception of ♦ *verb* **2 = exclude**, ban, bar, disallow, leave out, omit, pass over, reject, rule out

exception *noun* **1 = special case**, anomaly, departure, deviation, freak, inconsistency, irregularity, oddity, peculiarity, quirk **2 = exclusion**, debarment, disallowment, excepting, leaving out, omission, passing over, rejection **3 take exception to = object to**, be offended at, be resentful of, demur at, disagree with, quibble at, take offence at, take umbrage at

exceptional *adjective* **1 = unusual**, aberrant, abnormal, anomalous, atypical, deviant, extraordinary, inconsistent, irregular, odd, peculiar, rare, singular, special, strange, uncommon **2 = remarkable**, bodacious (*slang, chiefly*

U.S.), excellent, extraordinary, marvellous, notable, one in a million, outstanding, phenomenal, prodigious, special, superior
➤ **Antonyms**
≠**unusual:** average, common, customary, familiar, normal, ordinary, regular, straightforward, typical, unexceptional, unremarkable, usual ≠**remarkable:** average, awful, bad, lousy (*slang*), mediocre, no great shakes (*informal*), second-rate

excerpt *noun* = **extract**, fragment, part, passage, piece, quotation, section, selection

excess *noun* 1 = **surfeit**, glut, leftover, overabundance, overdose, overflow, overload, plethora, remainder, superabundance, superfluity, surplus, too much 2 = **overindulgence**, debauchery, dissipation, dissoluteness, exorbitance, extravagance, immoderation, intemperance, prodigality, unrestraint ◆ *adjective* 3 = **spare**, extra, leftover, redundant, remaining, residual, superfluous, surplus
➤ **Antonyms**
noun ≠**surfeit:** dearth, deficiency, insufficiency, lack, shortage, want ≠**overindulgence:** moderation, restraint, self-control, self-discipline, self-restraint, temperance

excessive *adjective* = **immoderate**, disproportionate, enormous, exaggerated, exorbitant, extravagant, extreme, fulsome, inordinate, intemperate, needless, O.T.T. (*slang*), overdone, overmuch, over the odds, over the top (*slang*), prodigal, profligate, superfluous, too much, unconscionable, undue, unfair, unreasonable

exchange *verb* 1 = **interchange**, bandy, barter, change, commute, convert into, reciprocate, swap, switch, trade, truck ◆ *noun* 2 = **interchange**, barter, dealing, quid pro quo, reciprocity, substitution, swap, switch, tit for tat, trade, traffic, truck 3 = **market**, Bourse

excitable *adjective* = **nervous**, edgy, emotional, hasty, highly strung, hot-headed, hot-tempered, irascible, mercurial, passionate, quick-tempered, sensitive, susceptible, temperamental, testy, touchy, uptight (*informal*), violent, volatile
➤ **Antonyms**
calm, cool, cool-headed, even-tempered, imperturbable, laid-back (*informal*), placid, unexcitable, unruffled

excite *verb* 1 = **arouse**, agitate, animate, awaken, elicit, evoke, fire, foment, galvanize, incite, inflame, inspire, instigate, kindle, move, provoke, quicken, rouse, stimulate, stir up, waken, whet, work up 2 = **thrill**, electrify, titillate

excited *adjective* = **worked up**, aflame, agitated, animated, aroused, awakened,

discomposed, disturbed, enthusiastic, feverish, flurried, high (*informal*), hot and bothered (*informal*), moved, nervous, overwrought, roused, stimulated, stirred, thrilled, tumultuous, wild

excitement *noun* 1 = **agitation**, action, activity, ado, adventure, animation, commotion, discomposure, elation, enthusiasm, ferment, fever, flurry, furore, heat, kicks (*informal*), passion, perturbation, thrill, tumult, warmth 2 = **stimulus**, impulse, incitement, instigation, motivation, motive, provocation, stimulation, thrill, urge

exciting *adjective* = **stimulating**, dramatic, electrifying, exhilarating, inspiring, intoxicating, moving, provocative, rip-roaring (*informal*), rousing, sensational, sexy (*informal*), stirring, thrilling, titillating
➤ **Antonyms**
boring, dreary, dull, flat, humdrum, mind-numbing, monotonous, unexciting, uninspiring, uninteresting

exclaim *verb* = **cry out**, call, call out, cry, declare, ejaculate, proclaim, shout, utter, vociferate, yell

exclamation *noun* = **cry**, call, ejaculation, expletive, interjection, outcry, shout, utterance, vociferation, yell

exclude *verb* 1 = **keep out**, ban, bar, black, blackball, boycott, debar, disallow, embargo, forbid, interdict, ostracize, prohibit, proscribe, refuse, shut out, veto 2 = **remove**, bounce (*slang*), drive out, eject, evict, expel, force out, get rid of, oust, throw out 3 = **leave out**, count out, eliminate, except, ignore, not count, omit, pass over, preclude, reject, repudiate, rule out, set aside
➤ **Antonyms**
≠**keep out, remove:** accept, admit, allow, let in, permit, receive, welcome ≠**leave out:** accept, count, include

exclusion *noun* 1 = **ban**, bar, boycott, debarment, disqualification, embargo, forbiddance, interdict, nonadmission, preclusion, prohibition, proscription, refusal, veto 2 = **removal**, eviction, expulsion 3 = **elimination**, exception, omission, rejection, repudiation

exclusive *adjective* 1 = **sole**, absolute, complete, entire, full, only, private, single, total, undivided, unique, unshared, whole 2 = **limited**, confined, peculiar, restricted, unique 3 = **select**, aristocratic, chic, choice, clannish, classy (*slang*), cliquish, closed, discriminative, elegant, fashionable, high-toned, limited, narrow, posh (*informal, chiefly Brit.*), private, restricted, restrictive, ritzy (*slang*), selfish, snobbish, swish (*informal, chiefly Brit.*), top-drawer, up-market 4 **exclusive of** = **except for**, debarring, excepting, excluding, leaving

aside, not counting, omitting, restricting, ruling out
➤ **Antonyms**
≠**sole, limited**: inclusive, nonexclusive, partial, shared ≠**select**: common, communal, open, popular, public, unrestricted

excommunicate *verb* = **expel**, anathematize, ban, banish, cast out, denounce, eject, exclude, proscribe, remove, repudiate, unchurch

excruciating *adjective* = **agonizing**, acute, burning, exquisite, extreme, harrowing, insufferable, intense, piercing, racking, searing, severe, tormenting, torturous, unbearable, unendurable, violent

exculpate *verb* = **absolve**, acquit, clear, discharge, dismiss, excuse, exonerate, free, justify, pardon, release, vindicate

excursion *noun* **1** = **trip**, airing, day trip, expedition, jaunt, journey, outing, pleasure trip, ramble, tour **2** = **digression**, detour, deviation, episode, excursus, wandering

excusable *adjective* = **forgivable**, allowable, defensible, justifiable, minor, pardonable, permissible, slight, understandable, venial, warrantable

excuse *noun* **1** = **justification**, apology, defence, explanation, grounds, mitigation, plea, pretext, reason, vindication **2** = **pretext**, cop-out (*slang*), disguise, evasion, expedient, makeshift, pretence, semblance, shift, subterfuge **3** *Informal* = **poor substitute**, apology, makeshift, mockery, travesty ♦ *verb* **4** = **justify**, apologize for, condone, defend, explain, mitigate, vindicate **5** = **forgive**, absolve, acquit, bear with, exculpate, exonerate, extenuate, indulge, make allowances for, overlook, pardon, pass over, tolerate, turn a blind eye to, wink at **6** = **free**, absolve, discharge, exempt, let off, liberate, release, relieve, spare
➤ **Antonyms**
noun ≠**justification**: accusation, charge, imputation, indictment ♦ *verb* ≠**justify**: accuse, blame, censure, chasten, chastise, compel, condemn, correct, criticize, hold responsible, oblige, point a *or* the finger at, punish ≠**free**: arraign, charge, convict, indict, sentence

execrate *verb* **1** = **loathe**, abhor, abominate, condemn, denounce, deplore, despise, detest, excoriate, hate, revile, slam (*slang*), vilify **2** = **curse**, anathematize, damn, imprecate

execration *noun* **1** = **loathing**, abhorrence, abomination, condemnation, contempt, detestation, excoriation, hate, hatred, odium, vilification **2** = **curse**, anathema,

damnation, imprecation, malediction

execute *verb* **1** = **put to death**, behead, electrocute, guillotine, hang, kill, shoot **2** = **carry out**, accomplish, achieve, administer, bring off, complete, consummate, discharge, do, effect, enact, enforce, finish, fulfil, implement, perform, prosecute, put into effect, realize, render **3** *Law* = **validate**, deliver, seal, serve, sign

execution *noun* **1** = **carrying out**, accomplishment, achievement, administration, completion, consummation, discharge, effect, enactment, enforcement, implementation, operation, performance, prosecution, realization, rendering **2** = **killing**, capital punishment, hanging, necktie party (*informal*) **3** = **technique**, delivery, manner, mode, performance, rendition, style

executioner *noun* **1** = **hangman**, headsman **2** = **killer**, assassin, exterminator, hit man (*slang*), liquidator, murderer, slayer

executive *noun* **1** = **administrator**, director, manager, official **2** = **administration**, directorate, directors, government, hierarchy, leadership, management ♦ *adjective* **3** = **administrative**, controlling, decision-making, directing, governing, managerial

exemplary *adjective* **1** = **ideal**, admirable, commendable, correct, estimable, excellent, fine, good, honourable, laudable, meritorious, model, praiseworthy, punctilious, sterling **2** = **warning**, admonitory, cautionary, monitory **3** = **typical**, characteristic, illustrative, representative

exemplify *verb* = **show**, demonstrate, depict, display, embody, evidence, exhibit, illustrate, instance, manifest, represent, serve as an example of

exempt *adjective* **1** = **immune**, absolved, clear, discharged, excepted, excused, favoured, free, liberated, not liable, not subject, privileged, released, spared ♦ *verb* **2** = **grant immunity**, absolve, discharge, except, excuse, exonerate, free, let off, liberate, release, relieve, spare
➤ **Antonyms**
adjective ≠**immune**: accountable, answerable, chargeable, liable, obligated, responsible, subject

exemption *noun* = **immunity**, absolution, discharge, dispensation, exception, exoneration, freedom, privilege, release

exercise *noun* **1** = **exertion**, action, activity, discipline, drill, drilling, effort, labour, toil, training, work, work-out **2** = **task**, drill, lesson, practice, problem, schooling, schoolwork, work **3** = **use**, accomplishment, application, discharge, employment, enjoyment, exertion, fulfilment, implementation, practice, utilization ◆ *verb* **4** = **put to use**, apply, bring to bear, employ, enjoy, exert, practise, use, utilize, wield **5** = **train**, discipline, drill, habituate, inure, practise, work out **6** = **worry**, afflict, agitate, annoy, burden, distress, disturb, occupy, pain, perturb, preoccupy, trouble, try, vex

exert *verb* **1** = **use**, apply, bring into play, bring to bear, employ, exercise, expend, make use of, put forth, utilize, wield **2 exert oneself** = **make an effort**, apply oneself, bend over backwards (*informal*), break one's neck (*informal*), bust a gut (*informal*), do one's best, do one's damnedest (*informal*), endeavour, get one's finger out (*Brit. informal*), give it one's all (*informal*), give it one's best shot (*informal*), go for broke (*slang*), go for it (*informal*), knock oneself out (*informal*), labour, make an all-out effort (*informal*), pull one's finger out (*Brit. informal*), rupture oneself (*informal*), spare no effort, strain, strive, struggle, toil, try hard, work

exertion *noun* **1** = **effort**, action, attempt, elbow grease (*facetious*), endeavour, exercise, industry, labour, pains, strain, stretch, struggle, toil, travail (*literary*), trial **2** = **use**, application, employment, utilization

exhaust *verb* **1** = **tire out**, bankrupt, cripple, debilitate, disable, drain, enervate, enfeeble, fatigue, impoverish, prostrate, sap, tire, weaken, wear out **2** = **use up**, consume, deplete, dissipate, expend, finish, run through, spend, squander, waste **3** = **empty**, drain, dry, strain, void

exhausted *adjective* **1** = **worn out**, all in (*slang*), beat (*slang*), buggered (*slang*), clapped out (*Austral. & N.Z. informal*), creamcrackered (*Brit. slang*), crippled, dead (*informal*), dead beat (*informal*), dead tired, debilitated, disabled, dog-tired (*informal*), done in (*informal*), drained, effete, enervated, enfeebled, fatigued, jaded, knackered (*slang*), on one's last legs (*informal*), out on one's feet (*informal*), prostrated, ready to drop, sapped, shagged out (*Brit. slang*), spent, tired out, wasted, weak, wiped out (*informal*), worn to a frazzle (*informal*), zonked (*slang*) **2** = **used up**, at an end, consumed, depleted, dissipated, done, expended, finished, gone, spent, squandered, wasted **3** = **empty**, bare, drained, dry, void
➤ **Antonyms**
≠**worn out**: active, alive and kicking, animated, enlivened, invigorated, refreshed, rejuvenated, restored, revived, stimulated

≠**used up**: conserved, kept, preserved, replenished, restored

exhausting *adjective* = **tiring**, arduous, backbreaking, crippling, debilitating, difficult, draining, enervating, fatiguing, gruelling, hard, laborious, punishing, sapping, strenuous, taxing, testing

exhaustion *noun* **1** = **tiredness**, debilitation, enervation, fatigue, feebleness, lassitude, prostration, weariness **2** = **depletion**, consumption, emptying, using up

exhaustive *adjective* = **thorough**, all-embracing, all-inclusive, all-out (*informal*), complete, comprehensive, detailed, encyclopedic, extensive, far-reaching, full, full-scale, in-depth, intensive, sweeping, thoroughgoing, total
➤ **Antonyms**
casual, cursory, desultory, incomplete, perfunctory, sketchy, superficial

exhibit *verb* **1** = **display**, air, demonstrate, disclose, evidence, evince, expose, express, flaunt, indicate, make clear *or* plain, manifest, offer, parade, present, put on view, reveal, show ◆ *noun* **2** = **display**, exhibition, illustration, model, show

exhibition *noun* = **display**, airing, demonstration, exhibit, expo (*informal*), exposition, fair, manifestation, performance, presentation, representation, show, showing, spectacle

exhilarating *adjective* = **exciting**, breathtaking, cheering, enlivening, exalting, exhilarant, exhilarative, exhilaratory, gladdening, invigorating, stimulating, thrilling, vitalizing

exhilaration *noun* = **excitement**, animation, cheerfulness, delight, elation, exaltation, gaiety, gladness, gleefulness, high spirits, hilarity, joy, joyfulness, liveliness, mirth, sprightliness, vivacity
➤ **Antonyms**
dejection, depression, despondency, gloom, low spirits, melancholy, misery, sadness

exhort *verb Formal* = **urge**, admonish, advise, beseech, bid, call upon, caution, counsel, encourage, enjoin, entreat, goad, incite, persuade, press, prompt, spur, warn

exhortation *noun Formal* = **urging**, admonition, advice, beseeching, bidding, caution, clarion call, counsel, encouragement, enjoinder (*rare*), entreaty, goading, incitement, lecture, persuasion, sermon, warning

exhume *verb Formal* = **dig up**, disentomb, disinter, unbury, unearth
➤ **Antonyms**
bury, entomb, inter

exigency, exigence *noun* **1** = **need**,

constraint, demand, necessity, requirement, wont **2 = urgency**, acuteness, constraint, criticalness, demandingness, difficulty, distress, emergency, imperativeness, necessity, needfulness, pressingness, pressure, stress **3 = emergency**, crisis, difficulty, extremity, fix (*informal*), hardship, jam (*informal*), juncture, panic stations (*informal*), pass, pickle (*informal*), pinch, plight, predicament, quandary, scrape (*informal*), strait

exigent *adjective* Formal **1 = urgent**, acute, constraining, critical, crucial, imperative, importunate, insistent, necessary, needful, pressing **2 = demanding**, arduous, difficult, exacting, hard, harsh, rigorous, severe, stiff, strict, stringent, taxing, tough

exile *noun* **1 = banishment**, deportation, expatriation, expulsion, ostracism, proscription, separation **2 = expatriate**, deportee, émigré, outcast, refugee ◆ *verb* **3 = banish**, deport, drive out, eject, expatriate, expel, ostracize, oust, proscribe

exist *verb* **1 = be**, abide, be extant, be living, be present, breathe, continue, endure, happen, last, live, obtain, occur, prevail, remain, stand, survive **2 = survive**, eke out a living, get along *or* by, keep one's head above water, stay alive, subsist

existence *noun* **1 = being**, actuality, animation, breath, continuance, continuation, duration, endurance, life, subsistence, survival **2 = creature**, being, entity, thing **3 = creation**, life, reality, the world

existent *adjective* **= in existence**, abiding, alive, around, current, enduring, existing, extant, living, obtaining, present, prevailing, remaining, standing, surviving, to the fore (*Scot.*)

exit *noun* **1 = way out**, door, egress, gate, outlet, passage out, vent **2 = departure**, adieu, evacuation, exodus, farewell, going, goodbye, leave-taking, retirement, retreat, withdrawal ◆ *verb* **3 = depart**, bid farewell, go away, go offstage (*Theatre*), go out, issue, leave, make tracks, retire, retreat, say goodbye, take one's leave, withdraw
➤ **Antonyms**
noun ≠**way out**: entrance, entry, ingress, inlet, opening, way in ◆ *verb* ≠**depart**: arrive, come *or* go in *or* into, enter, make an entrance

exodus *noun* **= departure**, evacuation, exit, flight, going out, leaving, migration, retirement, retreat, withdrawal

exonerate *verb* **1 = clear**, absolve, acquit, discharge, dismiss, exculpate, excuse, justify, pardon, vindicate **2 = exempt**, discharge, dismiss, except, excuse, free, let off, liberate,

release, relieve

exorbitant *adjective* **= excessive**, enormous, extortionate, extravagant, extreme, immoderate, inordinate, outrageous, preposterous, ridiculous, unconscionable, undue, unreasonable, unwarranted
➤ **Antonyms**
cheap, fair, moderate, reasonable

exorcise *verb* **= drive out**, adjure, cast out, deliver (from), expel, purify

exorcism *noun* **= driving out**, adjuration, casting out, deliverance, expulsion, purification

exotic *adjective* **1 = unusual**, beyond one's ken, bizarre, colourful, curious, different, extraordinary, fascinating, glamorous, mysterious, outlandish, peculiar, strange, striking, unfamiliar **2 = foreign**, alien, external, extraneous, extrinsic, imported, introduced, naturalized, not native
➤ **Antonyms**
≠**unusual**: conventional, familiar, ordinary, pedestrian, plain, run-of-the-mill, unmemorable, unremarkable

expand *verb* **1 = increase**, amplify, augment, bloat, blow up, broaden, develop, dilate, distend, enlarge, extend, fatten, fill out, grow, heighten, inflate, lengthen, magnify, multiply, prolong, protract, swell, thicken, wax, widen **2 = spread (out)**, diffuse, open (out), outspread, stretch (out), unfold, unfurl, unravel, unroll **3 expand on = go into detail about**, amplify, develop, dilate, elaborate on, embellish, enlarge on, expatiate on, expound on, flesh out
➤ **Antonyms**
≠**increase**: condense, contract, decrease, reduce, shorten, shrink ≠**go into detail about**: abbreviate, condense, shorten

expanse *noun* **= area**, breadth, extent, field, plain, range, space, stretch, sweep, tract

expansion *noun* **= increase**, amplification, augmentation, development, diffusion, dilatation, distension, enlargement, expanse, growth, inflation, magnification, multiplication, opening out, spread, swelling, unfolding, unfurling

expansive *adjective* **1 = wide**, all-embracing, broad, comprehensive, extensive, far-reaching, inclusive, thorough, voluminous, wide-ranging, widespread **2 = talkative**, affable, communicative, easy, effusive, free, friendly, garrulous, genial, loquacious, open, outgoing, sociable, unreserved, warm **3 = expanding**, dilating, distending, elastic, enlargeable, extendable, inflatable, stretching, stretchy, swelling

expatiate *verb* Formal **= go into detail**, amplify, descant, develop, dilate, dwell on, elaborate, embellish, enlarge, expound

expatriate *adjective* **1** = **exiled**, banished, emigrant, émigré ♦ *noun* **2** = **exile**, emigrant, émigré, refugee ♦ *verb* **3** = **exile**, banish, expel, ostracize, proscribe

expect *verb* **1** = **think**, assume, believe, calculate, conjecture, forecast, foresee, imagine, presume, reckon, suppose, surmise, trust **2** = **look forward to**, anticipate, await, bargain for, contemplate, envisage, hope for, look ahead to, look for, predict, watch for **3** = **require**, call for, count on, demand, insist on, look for, rely upon, want, wish

expectancy *noun* **1** = **likelihood**, outlook, prospect **2** = **expectation**, anticipation, assumption, belief, conjecture, hope, looking forward, prediction, presumption, probability, supposition, surmise, suspense, waiting

expectant *adjective* **1** = **expecting**, anticipating, anxious, apprehensive, awaiting, eager, hopeful, in suspense, ready, watchful **2** = **pregnant**, enceinte, expecting (*informal*), gravid

expectation *noun* **1** = **probability**, assumption, assurance, belief, calculation, confidence, conjecture, forecast, likelihood, presumption, supposition, surmise, trust **2** = **anticipation**, apprehension, chance, expectancy, fear, hope, looking forward, outlook, possibility, prediction, promise, prospect, suspense **3** = **requirement**, demand, insistence, reliance, trust, want, wish

expecting *adjective* = **pregnant**, enceinte, expectant, gravid, in the club (*Brit. slang*), in the family way (*informal*), with child

expediency, expedience *noun* **1** = **means**, contrivance, device, expedient, makeshift, manoeuvre, measure, method, resort, resource, scheme, shift, stopgap, stratagem, substitute **2** = **suitability**, advantageousness, advisability, appropriateness, aptness, benefit, convenience, desirability, effectiveness, fitness, helpfulness, judiciousness, meetness, practicality, pragmatism, profitability, properness, propriety, prudence, usefulness, utilitarianism, utility

expedient *noun* **1** = **means**, contrivance, device, expediency, makeshift, manoeuvre, measure, method, resort, resource, scheme, shift, stopgap, stratagem, substitute ♦ *adjective* **2** = **advantageous**, advisable, appropriate, beneficial, convenient, desirable, effective, fit, helpful, judicious, meet, opportune, politic, practical, pragmatic, profitable, proper, prudent, suitable, useful, utilitarian, worthwhile
➤ Antonyms
adjective ≠**advantageous**: detrimental,

disadvantageous, futile, harmful, ill-advised, impractical, imprudent, inadvisable, inappropriate, ineffective, inexpedient, unwise, wrong

expedite *verb Formal* = **speed (up)**, accelerate, advance, assist, dispatch, facilitate, forward, hasten, hurry, precipitate, press, promote, quicken, rush, urge
➤ Antonyms
block, curb, decelerate, delay, handicap, hold up, obstruct, restrict, slow up *or* down

expedition *noun* **1** = **journey**, enterprise, excursion, exploration, mission, quest, safari, tour, trek, trip, undertaking, voyage **2** = **team**, company, crew, explorers, travellers, voyagers, wayfarers **3** = **speed**, alacrity, celerity, dispatch, expeditiousness, haste, hurry, promptness, quickness, rapidity, readiness, swiftness

expeditious *adjective* = **quick**, active, alert, brisk, diligent, efficient, fast, hasty, immediate, instant, nimble, prompt, rapid, ready, speedy, swift

expel *verb* **1** = **drive out**, belch, cast out, discharge, dislodge, eject, remove, spew, throw out **2** = **dismiss**, ban, banish, bar, black, blackball, discharge, drum out, evict, exclude, exile, expatriate, give the bum's rush (*slang*), oust, proscribe, relegate, send packing, show one the door, throw out, throw out on one's ear (*informal*), turf out (*informal*)
➤ Antonyms
≠**dismiss**: admit, allow to enter, give access, let in, receive, take in, welcome

expend *verb Formal* = **spend**, consume, disburse, dissipate, employ, exhaust, fork out (*slang*), go through, lay out (*informal*), pay out, shell out (*informal*), use (up)

expendable *adjective* = **dispensable**, inessential, nonessential, replaceable, unimportant, unnecessary
➤ Antonyms
crucial, essential, indispensable, key, necessary, vital

expenditure *noun* = **spending**, application, charge, consumption, cost, disbursement, expense, outgoings, outlay, output, payment, use

expense *noun* = **cost**, charge, consumption, disbursement, expenditure, loss, outlay, output, payment, sacrifice, spending, toll, use

expensive *adjective* = **dear**, costly, excessive, exorbitant, extravagant, high-priced, inordinate, lavish, overpriced, rich, steep (*informal*), stiff
➤ Antonyms
bargain, budget, cheap, cut-price, economical, inexpensive, low-cost,

low-priced, reasonable

experience *noun* **1** = **knowledge**, contact, doing, evidence, exposure, familiarity, involvement, know-how (*informal*), observation, participation, practice, proof, training, trial, understanding **2** = **event**, adventure, affair, encounter, episode, happening, incident, occurrence, ordeal, test, trial ♦ *verb* **3** = **undergo**, apprehend, become familiar with, behold, encounter, endure, face, feel, go through, have, know, live through, meet, observe, participate in, perceive, sample, sense, suffer, sustain, taste, try

experienced *adjective* **1** = **knowledgeable**, accomplished, adept, capable, competent, expert, familiar, master, practised, professional, qualified, seasoned, skilful, tested, trained, tried, veteran, well-versed **2** = **worldly-wise**, knowing, mature, sophisticated, wise, worldly
➤ **Antonyms**
≠**knowledgeable**: apprentice, green, incompetent, inexperienced, new, unqualified, unskilled, untrained, untried

experiment *noun* **1** = **test**, assay, attempt, examination, experimentation, investigation, procedure, proof, research, trial, trial and error, trial run, venture ♦ *verb* **2** = **test**, assay, examine, investigate, put to the test, research, sample, try, verify

experimental *adjective* = **test**, empirical, exploratory, pilot, preliminary, probationary, provisional, speculative, tentative, trial, trial-and-error

expert *noun* **1** = **master**, ace (*informal*), adept, authority, buff (*informal*), connoisseur, dab hand (*Brit. informal*), guru, hotshot (*informal*), maven (*U.S.*), past master, pro (*informal*), professional, specialist, virtuoso, whizz (*informal*), wizard ♦ *adjective* **2** = **skilful**, able, adept, adroit, apt, clever, deft, dexterous, experienced, facile, handy, knowledgeable, master, masterly, practised, professional, proficient, qualified, skilled, trained, virtuoso
➤ **Antonyms**
noun ≠**master**: amateur, dabbler, ham, layman, nonprofessional, novice ♦ *adjective* ≠**skilful**: amateurish, cack-handed (*informal*), clumsy, incompetent, inexperienced, unpractised, unqualified, unskilled, untrained

expertise *noun* = **skill**, ableness, adroitness, aptness, cleverness, command, craft, deftness, dexterity, expertness, facility, grasp, grip, judgment, knack, know-how (*informal*), knowing inside out, knowledge, masterliness, mastery, proficiency, skilfulness

expertness *noun* = **skill**, ableness, adroitness, aptness, command, craft,

deftness, dexterity, expertise, facility, grasp, grip, judgment, know-how (*informal*), knowing inside out, knowledge, masterliness, mastery, proficiency, skilfulness

expire *verb* **1** = **finish**, cease, close, come to an end, conclude, end, lapse, run out, stop, terminate **2** = **breathe out**, emit, exhale, expel **3** = **die**, buy it (*U.S. slang*), check out (*U.S. slang*), croak (*slang*), decease, depart, go belly-up (*slang*), kick it (*slang*), kick the bucket (*informal*), pass away or on, peg it (*informal*), peg out (*informal*), perish, pop one's clogs (*informal*), snuff it (*informal*)

explain *verb* **1** = **make clear** *or* **plain**, clarify, clear up, define, demonstrate, describe, disclose, elucidate, explicate (*formal*), expound, illustrate, interpret, resolve, solve, teach, unfold **2** = **account for**, excuse, give an explanation for, give a reason for, justify

explanation *noun* **1** = **reason**, account, answer, cause, excuse, justification, meaning, mitigation, motive, sense, significance, the why and wherefore, vindication **2** = **description**, clarification, definition, demonstration, elucidation, explication, exposition, illustration, interpretation, resolution

explanatory *adjective* = **descriptive**, demonstrative, elucidatory, explicative, expository, illuminative, illustrative, interpretive, justifying

explicit *adjective* = **clear**, absolute, categorical, certain, definite, direct, distinct, exact, express, frank, open, outspoken, patent, plain, positive, precise, specific, stated, straightforward, unambiguous, unequivocal, unqualified, unreserved, upfront (*informal*)
➤ **Antonyms**
ambiguous, cryptic, general, implicit, implied, indefinite, indirect, inexact, obscure, oracular, suggested, uncertain, vague

explode *verb* **1** = **blow up**, burst, detonate, discharge, erupt, go off, set off, shatter, shiver **2** = **disprove**, belie, blow out of the water (*slang*), debunk, discredit, give the lie to, invalidate, refute, repudiate

exploit *verb* **1** = **take advantage of**, abuse, dump on (*slang, chiefly U.S.*), impose upon, manipulate, milk, misuse, play on *or* upon, shit on (*taboo slang*) **2** = **make the best use of**, capitalize on, cash in on (*informal*), live off the backs of, make capital out of, profit by *or* from, put to use, turn to account, use, use to advantage, utilize ♦ *noun* **3** = **feat**, accomplishment, achievement, adventure, attainment, deed, escapade, stunt

exploitation *noun* = **misuse**, abuse,

manipulation, using

exploration noun 1 = investigation, analysis, examination, inquiry, inspection, once-over (informal), probe, research, scrutiny, search, study 2 = expedition, recce (slang), reconnaissance, survey, tour, travel, trip

exploratory adjective = investigative, analytic, experimental, fact-finding, probing, searching, trial

explore verb 1 = investigate, analyse, examine, inquire into, inspect, look into, probe, prospect, research, scrutinize, search, work over 2 = travel, case (slang), have or take a look around, range over, recce (slang), reconnoitre, scout, survey, tour, traverse

explosion noun 1 = bang, blast, burst, clap, crack, detonation, discharge, outburst, report 2 = outburst, eruption, fit, outbreak, paroxysm

explosive adjective 1 = unstable, volatile 2 = violent, fiery, stormy, touchy, vehement 3 = dangerous, charged, hazardous, overwrought, perilous, tense, ugly

exponent noun 1 = advocate, backer, champion, defender, promoter, propagandist, proponent, spokesman, spokeswoman, supporter, upholder 2 = performer, executant, interpreter, player, presenter 3 = interpreter, commentator, demonstrator, elucidator, expositor, expounder, illustrator

expose verb 1 = uncover, display, exhibit, manifest, present, put on view, reveal, show, take the wraps off, unveil 2 = reveal, air, betray, blow wide open (slang), bring to light, denounce, detect, disclose, divulge, lay bare, let out, make known, out (informal), show up, smoke out, uncover, unearth, unmask 3 = make vulnerable, endanger, hazard, imperil, jeopardize, lay open, leave open, risk, subject 4 expose (someone) to = Introduce to, acquaint with, bring into contact with, familiarize with, make conversant with
➤ Antonyms
≠uncover: conceal, cover, hide, mask, protect, screen, shelter, shield ≠reveal: conceal, cover, hide, keep secret

exposed adjective 1 = unconcealed, bare, exhibited, laid bare, made manifest, made public, on display, on show, on view, revealed, shown, uncovered, unveiled 2 = unsheltered, open, open to the elements, unprotected 3 = vulnerable, in danger, in peril, laid bare, laid open, left open, liable, open, susceptible, wide open

exposition noun 1 = explanation, account, commentary, critique, description,

elucidation, exegesis, explication, illustration, interpretation, presentation 2 = exhibition, demonstration, display, expo (informal), fair, presentation, show

expostulate verb = reason (with), argue (with), dissuade, protest, remonstrate (with)

exposure noun 1 = vulnerability, danger, hazard, jeopardy, risk 2 = revelation, airing, betrayal, denunciation, detection, disclosure, divulgence, divulging, exposé, unmasking 3 = publicity, baring, display, exhibition, manifestation, presentation, revelation, showing, uncovering, unveiling 4 = contact, acquaintance, conversancy, experience, familiarity, introduction, knowledge 5 = position, aspect, frontage, location, outlook, setting, view

expound verb = explain, describe, elucidate, explicate (formal), illustrate, interpret, set forth, spell out, unfold

express verb 1 = state, articulate, assert, asseverate, communicate, couch, declare, enunciate, phrase, pronounce, put, put across, put into words, say, speak, tell, utter, verbalize, voice, word 2 = show, bespeak, convey, denote, depict, designate, disclose, divulge, embody, evince, exhibit, indicate, intimate, make known, manifest, represent, reveal, signify, stand for, symbolize, testify 3 = squeeze out, extract, force out, press out ♦ adjective 4 = explicit, accurate, categorical, certain, clear, definite, direct, distinct, exact, outright, plain, pointed, precise, unambiguous 5 = specific, clear-cut, deliberate, especial, particular, singular, special 6 = fast, direct, high-speed, nonstop, quick, quickie (informal), rapid, speedy, swift

expression noun 1 = statement, announcement, assertion, asseveration, communication, declaration, enunciation, mention, pronouncement, speaking, utterance, verbalization, voicing 2 = indication, demonstration, embodiment, exhibition, manifestation, representation, show, sign, symbol, token 3 = look, air, appearance, aspect, countenance, face, mien (literary) 4 = phrase, idiom, locution, remark, set phrase, term, turn of phrase, word 5 = choice of words, delivery, diction, emphasis, execution, intonation, language, phraseology, phrasing, speech, style, wording

expressive adjective 1 = vivid, eloquent, emphatic, energetic, forcible, lively, mobile, moving, poignant, striking, strong, sympathetic, telling 2 = meaningful, allusive, demonstrative, indicative, pointed, pregnant, revealing, significant, suggestive, thoughtful
➤ Antonyms
≠vivid: blank, dead-pan, dull, empty, impassive, inscrutable, poker-faced

(*informal*), straight-faced, vacuous, wooden

expressly *adverb* **1** = **definitely**, absolutely, categorically, clearly, decidedly, distinctly, explicitly, in no uncertain terms, manifestly, outright, plainly, pointedly, positively, unambiguously, unequivocally, unmistakably **2** = **specifically**, deliberately, especially, exactly, intentionally, on purpose, particularly, precisely, purposely, specially

expropriate *verb Formal* = **seize**, appropriate, arrogate, assume, commandeer, confiscate, impound, requisition, take, take over

expulsion *noun* = **ejection**, banishment, debarment, discharge, dislodgment, dismissal, eviction, exclusion, exile, expatriation, extrusion, proscription, removal

expurgate *verb* = **censor**, blue-pencil, bowdlerize, clean up (*informal*), cut, purge, purify, sanitize

exquisite *adjective* **1** = **beautiful**, attractive, charming, comely, lovely, pleasing, striking **2** = **fine**, beautiful, dainty, delicate, elegant, lovely, precious **3** = **refined**, appreciative, consummate, cultivated, discerning, discriminating, fastidious, impeccable, meticulous, polished, selective, sensitive **4** = **intense**, acute, excruciating, keen, piercing, poignant, sharp **5** = **excellent**, admirable, choice, consummate, delicious, divine, fine, flawless, incomparable, matchless, outstanding, peerless, perfect, rare, select, splendid, superb, superlative
➤ **Antonyms**
≠**beautiful**: ill-favoured, ugly, unattractive, unlovely, unsightly ≠**excellent**: flawed, imperfect

extempore *adverb, adjective* = **impromptu**, ad lib, extemporaneous, extemporary, freely, improvised, offhand, off the cuff (*informal*), off the top of one's head, on the spot, spontaneously, unplanned, unpremeditated, unprepared

extemporize *verb* = **improvise**, ad-lib, busk, make up, play (it) by ear, vamp, wing it (*informal*)

extend *verb* **1** = **make longer**, carry on, continue, drag out, draw out, elongate, lengthen, prolong, protract, spin out, spread out, stretch, unfurl, unroll **2** = **reach**, amount to, attain, go as far as, spread **3** = **last**, carry on, continue, go on, take **4** = **widen**, add to, amplify, augment, broaden, develop, dilate, enhance, enlarge, expand, increase, spread, supplement **5** = **offer**, advance, bestow, confer, give, grant, hold out, impart, present, proffer, put forth, reach out, stretch out, yield
➤ **Antonyms**
≠**make longer**: condense, contract, curtail,

cut, decrease, limit, reduce, restrict, shorten, take back ≠**widen**: abbreviate, abridge, condense, contract, cut, decrease, reduce, restrict, shorten ≠**offer**: take back, withdraw

extended *adjective* **1** = **lengthened**, continued, drawn-out, elongated, enlarged, long, prolonged, protracted, spread (out), stretched out, unfolded, unfurled, unrolled **2** = **broad**, comprehensive, enlarged, expanded, extensive, far-reaching, large-scale, sweeping, thorough, wide, widespread **3** = **outstretched**, conferred, proffered, stretched out

extension *noun* **1** = **annexe**, addendum, addition, add-on, adjunct, appendage, appendix, branch, ell, supplement, wing **2** = **lengthening**, amplification, augmentation, broadening, continuation, delay, development, dilatation, distension, elongation, enlargement, expansion, extent, increase, postponement, prolongation, protraction, spread, stretching, widening

extensive *adjective* = **wide**, all-inclusive, broad, capacious, commodious, comprehensive, expanded, extended, far-flung, far-reaching, general, great, huge, humongous or humungous (*U.S. slang*), large, large-scale, lengthy, long, pervasive, prevalent, protracted, spacious, sweeping, thorough, universal, vast, voluminous, wholesale, widespread
➤ **Antonyms**
circumscribed, confined, constricted, limited, narrow, restricted, tight

extent *noun* **1** = **size**, amount, amplitude, area, breadth, bulk, degree, duration, expanse, expansion, length, magnitude, measure, quantity, stretch, term, time, volume, width **2** = **range**, ambit, bounds, compass, play, reach, scope, sphere, sweep

extenuating *adjective* = **mitigating**, justifying, moderating, qualifying, serving as an excuse

exterior *noun* **1** = **outside**, appearance, aspect, coating, covering, façade, face, finish, shell, skin, surface ◆ *adjective* **2** = **outside**, external, outer, outermost, outward, superficial, surface **3** = **external**, alien, exotic, extraneous, extrinsic, foreign, outside
➤ **Antonyms**
noun ≠**outside**: inner, inside, interior ◆ *adjective* ≠**outside**: inherent, inside, interior, internal, intrinsic ≠**external**: domestic, internal, intrinsic

exterminate *verb* = **destroy**, abolish, annihilate, eliminate, eradicate, extirpate

external *adjective* **1** = **outer**, apparent, exterior, outermost, outside, outward, superficial, surface, visible **2 = outside**, alien, exotic, exterior, extramural, extraneous, extrinsic, foreign, independent

> **Antonyms**

≠**outer:** inherent, inner, inside, interior, internal, intrinsic ≠**outside:** inside, interior, intrinsic

extinct *adjective* **1 = dead**, defunct, gone, lost, vanished **2 = obsolete**, abolished, defunct, ended, terminated, void **3 = inactive**, doused, extinguished, out, quenched, snuffed out

> **Antonyms**

≠**dead:** active, alive, existing, extant, flourishing, living, surviving, thriving

extinction *noun* **= dying out**, abolition, annihilation, death, destruction, eradication, excision, extermination, extirpation, obliteration, oblivion

extinguish *verb* **1 = put out**, blow out, douse, quench, smother, snuff out, stifle **2 = destroy**, abolish, annihilate, eliminate, end, eradicate, erase, expunge, exterminate, extirpate, kill, obscure, put paid to, remove, suppress, wipe out

extol *verb* **= praise**, acclaim, applaud, celebrate, commend, crack up (*informal*), cry up, eulogize, exalt, glorify, laud, magnify (*archaic*), panegyrize, pay tribute to, sing the praises of

extort *verb* **= force**, blackmail, bleed (*informal*), bully, coerce, exact, extract, squeeze, wrest, wring

extortion *noun* **1 = force**, blackmail, coercion, compulsion, demand, exaction, oppression, rapacity, shakedown (*U.S. slang*) **2 = overcharging**, enormity, exorbitance, expensiveness

extortionate *adjective* **= exorbitant**, excessive, extravagant, immoderate, inflated, inordinate, outrageous, preposterous, sky-high, unreasonable

> **Antonyms**

fair, inexpensive, moderate, modest, reasonable

extra *adjective* **1 = additional**, accessory, added, add-on, ancillary, auxiliary, fresh, further, more, new, other, supplemental, supplementary **2 = surplus**, excess, extraneous, inessential, leftover, needless, redundant, reserve, spare, supererogatory, superfluous, supernumerary, unnecessary, unneeded, unused ♦ *noun* **3 = addition**, accessory, addendum, add-on, adjunct, affix, appendage, appurtenance, attachment, bonus, complement, extension, supernumerary, supplement ♦ *adverb* **4 = exceptionally**, especially, extraordinarily, extremely, particularly, remarkably, uncommonly, unusually

> **Antonyms**

adjective ≠**additional:** compulsory, essential, mandatory, necessary, needed, obligatory, required, requisite, vital ♦ *noun* ≠**addition:** essential, must, necessity, precondition, prerequisite, requirement, requisite

extract *verb* **1 = pull out**, draw, extirpate, pluck out, pull, remove, take out, uproot, withdraw **2 = derive**, bring out, draw, elicit, evoke, exact, gather, get, glean, obtain, reap, wrest, wring **3 = obtain**, distil, draw out, express, press out, separate out, squeeze, take out **4 = copy out**, abstract, choose, cite, cull, cut out, quote, select **5 = develop**, deduce, derive, educe, elicit, evolve ♦ *noun* **6 = passage**, abstract, citation, clipping, cutting, excerpt, quotation, selection **7 = essence**, concentrate, decoction, distillate, distillation, juice

extraction *noun* **1 = taking out**, drawing, extirpation, pulling, removal, uprooting, withdrawal **2 = distillation**, derivation, separation **3 = origin**, ancestry, birth, blood, derivation, descent, family, lineage, parentage, pedigree, race, stock

extraneous *adjective* **1 = nonessential**, accidental, additional, adventitious, extra, incidental, inessential, needless, peripheral, redundant, superfluous, supplementary, unessential, unnecessary, unneeded **2 = irrelevant**, beside the point, immaterial, impertinent, inadmissible, inapplicable, inapposite, inappropriate, inapt, off the subject, unconnected, unrelated **3 = external**, adventitious, alien, exotic, extrinsic, foreign, out of place, strange

extraordinary *adjective* **= unusual**, amazing, beyond one's ken, bizarre, curious, exceptional, fantastic, marvellous, notable, odd, out of this world (*informal*), outstanding, particular, peculiar, phenomenal, rare, remarkable, serious (*informal*), singular, special, strange, surprising, uncommon, unfamiliar, unheard-of, unique, unprecedented, unwonted, weird, wonderful, wondrous (*archaic or literary*)

> **Antonyms**

banal, common, commonplace, customary, everyday, ordinary, unexceptional, unremarkable, usual

extravagance *noun* **1 = waste**, improvidence, lavishness, overspending, prodigality, profligacy, profusion, squandering, wastefulness **2 = excess**, absurdity, dissipation, exaggeration, exorbitance, folly, immoderation, outrageousness, preposterousness, recklessness, unreasonableness, unrestraint, wildness

extravagant *adjective* 1 = **wasteful**, excessive, having money to burn, improvident, imprudent, lavish, prodigal, profligate, spendthrift 2 = **overpriced**, costly, excessive, exorbitant, expensive, extortionate, inordinate, steep (*informal*), unreasonable 3 = **excessive**, absurd, exaggerated, exorbitant, fanciful, fantastic, foolish, immoderate, inordinate, O.T.T. (*slang*), outrageous, outré, over the top (*slang*), preposterous, reckless, unreasonable, unrestrained, wild 4 = **showy**, fancy, flamboyant, flashy, garish, gaudy, grandiose, ornate, ostentatious, pretentious
➤ Antonyms
≠**wasteful:** careful, close, economical, frugal, miserly, moderate, prudent, sensible, sparing, thrifty, tight-fisted (*informal*) ≠**overpriced:** economical, moderate, reasonable ≠**excessive:** conservative, down-to-earth, moderate, prudent, realistic, reasonable, restrained, sensible, sober ≠**showy:** conservative, moderate, restrained, sober

extreme *adjective* 1 = **maximum**, acute, great, greatest, high, highest, intense, mother of all (*informal*), severe, supreme, ultimate, utmost, uttermost, worst 2 = **severe**, dire, drastic, harsh, radical, rigid, stern, strict, unbending, uncompromising 3 = **excessive**, downright, egregious, exaggerated, exceptional, extraordinary, extravagant, fanatical, immoderate, inordinate, intemperate, O.T.T. (*slang*), out-and-out, outrageous, over the top (*slang*), radical, remarkable, sheer, uncommon, unconventional, unreasonable, unusual, utter, zealous 4 = **farthest**, faraway, far-off, final, last, most distant, outermost, remotest, terminal, ultimate, utmost, uttermost ♦ *noun* 5 = **limit**, acme, apex, apogee, boundary, climax, consummation, depth, edge, end, excess, extremity, height, maximum, minimum, nadir, pinnacle, pole, termination, top, ultimate, zenith
➤ Antonyms
adjective ≠**maximum:** average, common, mild, moderate, modest, ordinary, reasonable, traditional, unremarkable ≠**farthest:** nearest

extremely *adverb* = **very**, acutely, awfully (*informal*), exceedingly, exceptionally, excessively, extraordinarily, greatly, highly, inordinately, intensely, markedly, quite, severely, terribly, to a fault, to *or* in the extreme, to the nth degree, ultra, uncommonly, unusually, utterly

extremist *noun* = **fanatic**, die-hard, radical, ultra, zealot

extremity *noun* 1 = **limit**, acme, apex, apogee, border, bound, boundary, brim, brink, edge, end, extreme, farthest point, frontier, margin, maximum, minimum, nadir, pinnacle, pole, rim, terminal, termination, terminus, tip, top, ultimate, verge, zenith 2 = **crisis**, adversity, dire straits, disaster, emergency, exigency, hardship, pass, pinch, plight, setback, trouble 3 **extremities** = **hands and feet**, fingers and toes, limbs

extricate *verb* = **free**, clear, deliver, disembarrass, disengage, disentangle, get out, get (someone) off the hook (*slang*), liberate, release, relieve, remove, rescue, withdraw, wriggle out of

extrovert *adjective* = **outgoing**, amiable, exuberant, gregarious, hearty, sociable, social
➤ Antonyms
introspective, introverted, inward-looking, self-contained, withdrawn

exuberance *noun* 1 = **high spirits**, animation, brio, buoyancy, cheerfulness, eagerness, ebullience, effervescence, energy, enthusiasm, excitement, exhilaration, life, liveliness, pep, spirit, sprightliness, vigour, vitality, vivacity, zest 2 = **luxuriance**, abundance, copiousness, lavishness, lushness, plenitude, profusion, rankness, richness, superabundance, teemingness 3 = **fulsomeness**, effusiveness, exaggeration, excessiveness, lavishness, prodigality, superfluity

exuberant *adjective* 1 = **high-spirited**, animated, buoyant, cheerful, chirpy (*informal*), eager, ebullient, effervescent, elated, energetic, enthusiastic, excited, exhilarated, full of beans (*informal*), full of life, in high spirits, lively, sparkling, spirited, sprightly, upbeat (*informal*), vigorous, vivacious, zestful 2 = **luxuriant**, abundant, copious, lavish, lush, overflowing, plenteous, plentiful, profuse, rank, rich, superabundant, teeming 3 = **fulsome**, effusive, exaggerated, excessive, lavish, overdone, prodigal, superfluous
➤ Antonyms
≠**high-spirited:** apathetic, dull, lifeless, subdued, unenthusiastic

exult *verb* 1 = **be joyful**, be delighted, be elated, be in high spirits, be jubilant, be overjoyed, celebrate, jubilate, jump for joy, make merry, rejoice 2 = **triumph**, boast, brag, crow, drool, gloat, glory (in), revel, take delight in, taunt, vaunt

exultant *adjective* = **joyful**, cock-a-hoop, delighted, elated, exulting, flushed, gleeful, joyous, jubilant, overjoyed, over the moon (*informal*), rapt, rejoicing, revelling, transported, triumphant

exultation *noun* 1 = **joy**, celebration, delight, elation, glee, high spirits, joyousness, jubilation, merriness, rejoicing, transport **2** = **triumph**, boasting, bragging, crowing, gloating, glory, glorying, revelling

eye *noun* **1** = **eyeball**, optic (*informal*), orb (*poetic*), peeper (*slang*) **2** = **appreciation**, discernment, discrimination, judgment, perception, recognition, taste **3** *often plural* = **opinion**, belief, judgment, mind, point of view, viewpoint **4 an eye for an eye** = **retaliation**, justice, reprisal, requital, retribution, revenge, vengeance **5 clap, lay** *or* **set eyes on** = **see**, behold, come across, encounter, meet, notice, observe, run into **6 keep an** *or* **one's eye on** = **watch**, guard, keep in view, keep tabs on (*informal*), keep under surveillance, look after, look out for, monitor, observe, pay attention to, regard, scrutinize, supervise, survey, watch like a hawk, watch over **7 see eye to eye** = **agree**, accord, back, be in unison, coincide, concur, fall in, get on, go along, harmonize, jibe (*informal*), speak the same language, subscribe to **8 up to one's eyes** = **busy**, caught up, engaged, flooded out, fully occupied, inundated, overwhelmed, up to here, up to one's elbows, wrapped up in

♦ *verb* **9** = **look at**, behold (*archaic or literary*), check, check out (*informal*), clock (*Brit. slang*), contemplate, eyeball (*slang*), gaze at, get a load of (*informal*), glance at, have *or* take a look at, inspect, peruse, recce (*slang*), regard, scan, scrutinize, stare at, study, survey, take a dekko at (*Brit. slang*), view, watch **10** = **ogle**, eye up (*informal*), give (someone) the (glad) eye, leer at, make eyes at

eyeful *noun Slang* **1** = **look**, butcher's (*Brit. slang*), gander (*informal*), gaze, glance, shufti (*Brit. slang*), sight, view **2** = **spectacle**, beauty, dazzler, humdinger (*slang*), knockout (*informal*), show, sight, sight for sore eyes (*informal*), stunner (*informal*), vision

eyesight *noun* = **vision**, observation, perception, range of vision, sight

eyesore *noun* = **mess**, atrocity, blemish, blight, blot, disfigurement, disgrace, horror, monstrosity, sight (*informal*), ugliness

eyewitness *noun* = **observer**, bystander, looker-on, onlooker, passer-by, spectator, viewer, watcher, witness

F f

fable *noun* 1 = **story**, allegory, apologue, legend, myth, parable, tale 2 = **fiction**, fabrication, fairy story (*informal*), falsehood, fantasy, fib, figment, invention, lie, romance, tall story (*informal*), untruth, urban legend, urban myth, white lie, yarn (*informal*)
➤ **Antonyms**
actuality, certainty, fact, reality, truth, verity

fabled *adjective* = **legendary**, fabulous, famed, famous, fictional, mythical

fabric *noun* 1 = **cloth**, material, stuff, textile, web 2 = **framework**, constitution, construction, foundations, infrastructure, make-up, organization, structure

fabricate *verb* 1 = **make up**, coin, concoct, devise, fake, falsify, feign, forge, form, invent, trump up 2 = **build**, assemble, construct, erect, fashion, form, frame, make, manufacture, shape

fabrication *noun* 1 = **forgery**, cock-and-bull story (*informal*), concoction, fable, fairy story (*informal*), fake, falsehood, fiction, figment, invention, lie, myth, pork pie (*Brit. slang*), porky (*Brit. slang*), untruth 2 = **construction**, assemblage, assembly, building, erection, manufacture, production

fabulous *adjective* 1 *Informal* = **wonderful**, brilliant, fantastic (*informal*), magic (*informal*), marvellous, out-of-this-world (*informal*), sensational (*informal*), spectacular, superb 2 = **astounding**, amazing, breathtaking, fictitious, immense, inconceivable, incredible, legendary, phenomenal, unbelievable 3 = **legendary**, apocryphal, fantastic, fictitious, imaginary, invented, made-up, mythical, unreal
➤ **Antonyms**
actual, common, commonplace, credible, genuine, natural, ordinary, real

façade *noun* = **appearance**, exterior, face, front, frontage, guise, mask, pretence, semblance, show, veneer

face *noun* 1 = **countenance**, clock (*Brit. slang*), dial (*Brit. slang*), features, kisser (*slang*), lineaments, mug (*slang*), phiz or phizog (*slang*), physiognomy, visage 2 = **expression**, appearance, aspect, look 3 = **scowl**, frown, grimace, *moue*, pout, smirk 4 = **side**, aspect, cover, exterior, facet, front, outside, right side, surface 5 *As in* **save** or **lose face** = **self-respect**, authority, dignity, honour, image, prestige, reputation, standing, status 6 *As in* **put a good face on** = **façade**, air, appearance, disguise, display, exterior, front, mask, pretence, semblance, show 7 **on the face of it** = **to all appearances**, apparently, at first sight, seemingly, to the eye 8 **to one's face** = **directly**, in one's presence, openly, straight ◆ *verb* 9 = **look onto**, be opposite, front onto, give towards or onto, overlook 10 = **confront**, be confronted by, brave, come up against, cope with, deal with, defy, encounter, experience, face off (*slang*), meet, oppose, tackle 11 = **coat**, clad, cover, dress, finish, level, line, overlay, sheathe, surface, veneer

faceless *adjective* = **impersonal**, anonymous, remote, unidentified, unknown

face-lift *noun* 1 = **cosmetic surgery**, plastic surgery 2 = **renovation**, restoration

facer *noun Brit. old-fashioned* = **problem**, difficulty, dilemma, how-do-you-do (*informal*), poser, puzzle, teaser

facet *noun* = **aspect**, angle, face, part, phase, plane, side, slant, surface

facetious *adjective* = **funny**, amusing, comical, droll, flippant, frivolous, humorous, jesting, jocose, jocular, merry, playful, pleasant, tongue in cheek, unserious, waggish, witty
➤ **Antonyms**
earnest, genuine, grave, lugubrious, pensive, sedate, serious, sincere, sober, thoughtful

face up to *verb* = **accept**, acknowledge, come to terms with, confront, cope with, deal with, face the music, meet head-on, tackle

facile *adjective* 1 = **superficial**, cursory, glib, hasty, shallow, slick 2 = **easy**, adept, adroit, dexterous, effortless, fluent, light, proficient, quick, ready, simple, skilful, smooth, uncomplicated
➤ **Antonyms**
≠**easy**: awkward, careful, clumsy, difficult, maladroit, slow, unskilful

facilitate *verb* = **promote**, assist the progress of, ease, expedite, forward, further, help, make easy, oil the wheels, pave the way for, smooth the path of, speed up
➤ **Antonyms**
delay, encumber, frustrate, hamper, handicap, hinder, hold up or back, impede, obstruct, prevent, restrain, thwart

facility *noun* 1 *often plural* = **equipment**,

advantage, aid, amenity, appliance, convenience, means, opportunity, resource **2 = ease**, ability, adroitness, craft, dexterity, efficiency, effortlessness, expertness, fluency, gift, knack, proficiency, quickness, readiness, skilfulness, skill, smoothness, talent
➤ **Antonyms**
≠**ease**: awkwardness, clumsiness, difficulty, hardship, ineptness, maladroitness, pains

facing noun **1 = overlay**, cladding, coating, façade, false front, front, plaster, reinforcement, stucco, surface, trimming, veneer ◆ adjective **2 = opposite**, fronting, partnering

facsimile noun **= copy**, carbon, carbon copy, duplicate, fax, photocopy, Photostat (Trademark), print, replica, reproduction, transcript, Xerox (Trademark)

fact noun **1 = event**, act, deed, fait accompli, happening, incident, occurrence, performance **2 = truth**, actuality, certainty, gospel (truth), naked truth, reality **3 = detail**, circumstance, feature, item, particular, point, specific **4 in fact = actually**, indeed, in point of fact, in reality, in truth, really, truly
➤ **Antonyms**
≠**truth**: delusion, fable, fabrication, falsehood, fiction, invention, lie, tall story, untruth, yarn (informal)

faction noun **1 = group**, bloc, cabal, camp, caucus, clique, coalition, combination, confederacy, contingent, coterie, division, gang, ginger group, junta, lobby, minority, party, pressure group, schism, section, sector, set, splinter group **2 = dissension**, conflict, disagreement, discord, disharmony, disunity, division, divisiveness, friction, infighting, rebellion, sedition, strife, tumult, turbulence
➤ **Antonyms**
≠**dissension**: accord, agreement, amity, assent, concord, consensus, friendship, goodwill, harmony, peace, rapport, unanimity, unity

factitious adjective **= artificial**, affected, assumed, counterfeited, engineered, fabricated, fake, false, imitation, insincere, made-up, manufactured, mock, phoney or phony (informal), pinchbeck, pseudo (informal), put-on, sham, simulated, spurious, synthetic, unnatural, unreal

factor noun **1 = element**, aspect, cause, circumstance, component, consideration, determinant, influence, item, part, point, thing **2** Scot. **= agent**, deputy, estate manager, middleman, reeve, steward

factory noun **= works**, manufactory (obsolete), mill, plant

factotum noun **= Man Friday** or **Girl**

Friday, handyman, jack of all trades, man of all work, odd job man

facts plural noun **= information**, data, details, gen (Brit. informal), info (informal), ins and outs, the lowdown (informal), the score (informal), the whole story

factual adjective **= true**, accurate, authentic, circumstantial, close, correct, credible, exact, faithful, genuine, literal, matter-of-fact, objective, precise, real, sure, true-to-life, unadorned, unbiased, veritable
➤ **Antonyms**
embellished, fanciful, fictitious, fictive, figurative, imaginary, unreal

faculties plural noun **= powers**, capabilities, intelligence, reason, senses, wits

faculty noun **1 = ability**, adroitness, aptitude, bent, capability, capacity, cleverness, dexterity, facility, gift, knack, power, propensity, readiness, skill, talent, turn **2 = department**, branch of learning, discipline, profession, school, teaching staff (chiefly U.S.)
➤ **Antonyms**
≠**ability**: failing, inability, shortcoming, unskilfulness, weakness, weak point

fad noun **= craze**, affectation, fancy, fashion, mania, mode, rage, trend, vogue, whim

fade verb **1 = pale**, blanch, bleach, blench, dim, discolour, dull, grow dim, lose colour, lose lustre, wash out **2** As in **fade away** or **out = dwindle**, decline, die away, die out, dim, disappear, disperse, dissolve, droop, ebb, etiolate, evanesce, fail, fall, flag, languish, melt away, perish, shrivel, vanish, vanish into thin air, wane, waste away, wilt, wither

faded adjective **= discoloured**, bleached, dim, dull, etiolated, indistinct, lustreless, pale, washed out

fading adjective **= declining**, decreasing, disappearing, dying, on the decline, vanishing

faeces plural noun **= excrement**, bodily waste, droppings, dung, excreta, ordure, stools

fag[1] noun Informal **= chore**, bind (informal), bore, bother, drag (informal), inconvenience, irritation, nuisance, pain in the arse (taboo informal)

fag[2] noun Offensive slang **= homosexual**, bender (slang), catamite, fairy (slang), gay, homo (informal), nancy boy (slang), poof (slang), poofter (slang), queen (slang), queer (informal, derogatory), woofter (slang)

fagged out adjective Informal **= exhausted**, all in (slang), beat (slang), clapped out (Austral. & N.Z. informal), creamcrackered (Brit. informal), fatigued, jaded, jiggered (*informal*), knackered (*slang*), on one's last legs (*informal*), shagged out (*Brit. slang*), wasted, weary, wiped out (*informal*), worn out, zonked (*slang*)

fail *verb* **1** = **be unsuccessful**, be defeated, be found lacking *or* wanting, be in vain, bite the dust, break down, come a cropper (*informal*), come to grief, come to naught, come to nothing, come unstuck, fall, fall by the wayside, fall flat, fall flat on one's face, fall short, fall short of, fall through, fizzle out (*informal*), flop (*informal*), founder, go astray, go belly-up (*slang*), go by the board, go down, go down like a lead balloon (*informal*), go up in smoke, lay an egg (*slang, chiefly U.S. & Canad.*), meet with disaster, miscarry, misfire, miss, not make the grade (*informal*), run aground, turn out badly **2** = **give out**, be on one's last legs (*informal*), cease, conk out (*informal*), cut out, decline, die, disappear, droop, dwindle, fade, fall apart at the seams, give up, go phut, gutter, languish, peter out, sicken, sink, stop working, wane, weaken **3** = **disappoint**, abandon, break one's word, desert, forget, forsake, let down, neglect, omit, turn one's back on **4** = **go bankrupt**, become insolvent, close down, crash, fold (*informal*), go broke (*informal*), go bust (*informal*), go into receivership, go out of business, go to the wall, go under, smash ◆ *noun* **5 without fail** = **regularly**, conscientiously, constantly, dependably, like clockwork, punctually, religiously, without exception
➤ Antonyms
verb ≠**be unsuccessful**: bloom, flourish, grow, pass, prosper, strengthen, succeed, thrive, triumph

failing *noun* **1** = **weakness**, blemish, blind spot, defect, deficiency, drawback, error, failure, fault, flaw, foible, frailty, imperfection, lapse, miscarriage, misfortune, shortcoming ◆ *preposition* **2** = **in the absence of**, in default of, lacking
➤ Antonyms
noun ≠**weakness**: advantage, asset, forte, metier, speciality, strength, strong suit

failure *noun* **1** = **lack of success**, abortion, breakdown, collapse, defeat, downfall, fiasco, frustration, miscarriage, overthrow, wreck **2** = **shortcoming**, default, deficiency, dereliction, neglect, negligence, nonobservance, nonperformance, nonsuccess, omission, remissness, stoppage **3** = **loser**, black sheep, clinker (*slang, chiefly U.S.*), clunker (*informal*), dead duck (*slang*), disappointment, dud (*informal*), flop (*informal*), incompetent, ne'er-do-well, no-good, no-hoper (*chiefly Austral.*),

nonstarter, washout (*informal*) **4** = **breakdown**, decay, decline, deterioration, failing, loss **5** = **bankruptcy**, crash, downfall, folding (*informal*), insolvency, liquidation, ruin
➤ Antonyms
≠**lack of success**: effectiveness, success, triumph ≠**shortcoming**: care, observance ≠**bankruptcy**: fortune, prosperity

fain *adverb Old-fashioned* = **gladly**, as lief (*rare*), as soon, cheerfully, eagerly, willingly

faint *adjective* **1** = **dim**, bleached, delicate, distant, dull, faded, faltering, feeble, hazy, hushed, ill-defined, indistinct, light, low, muffled, muted, soft, subdued, thin, vague, whispered **2** = **dizzy**, drooping, enervated, exhausted, faltering, fatigued, giddy, languid, lethargic, light-headed, muzzy, vertiginous, weak, woozy (*informal*) **3** = **slight**, feeble, remote, unenthusiastic, weak ◆ *verb* **4** = **pass out**, black out, collapse, fade, fail, flake out (*informal*), keel over (*informal*), languish, lose consciousness, swoon (*literary*), weaken ◆ *noun* **5** = **blackout**, collapse, swoon (*literary*), syncope (*Pathology*), unconsciousness
➤ Antonyms
adjective ≠**dim**: bright, clear, conspicuous, distinct, loud, powerful, strong ≠**dizzy**: energetic, fresh, hearty, vigorous

faint-hearted *adjective* = **timid**, chickenshit (*U.S. slang*), cowardly, diffident, half-arsed (*Brit. slang*), half-assed (*U.S. & Canad. slang*), half-hearted, irresolute, spineless, timorous, weak, yellow
➤ Antonyms
audacious, bold, brave, courageous, daring, dauntless, fearless, game (*informal*), intrepid, plucky, stouthearted

faintly *adverb* **1** = **softly**, feebly, in a whisper, indistinctly, weakly **2** = **slightly**, a little, dimly, somewhat

fair[1] *adjective* **1** = **unbiased**, above board, according to the rules, clean, disinterested, dispassionate, equal, equitable, even-handed, honest, honourable, impartial, just, lawful, legitimate, objective, on the level (*informal*), proper, square, trustworthy, unprejudiced, upright **2** = **light**, blond, blonde, fair-haired, flaxen-haired, light-complexioned, tow-haired, towheaded **3** = **beautiful**, beauteous, bonny, comely, handsome, lovely, pretty, well-favoured **4** = **respectable**, adequate, all right, average, decent, mediocre, middling, moderate, not bad, O.K. *or* okay (*informal*), passable, reasonable, satisfactory, so-so (*informal*), tolerable **5** = **fine**, bright, clear, clement, cloudless, dry, favourable, sunny, sunshiny, unclouded

➤ **Antonyms**

≠**unbiased:** bad, biased, bigoted, discriminatory, dishonest, inequitable, one-sided, partial, partisan, prejudiced, unfair, unjust ≠**beautiful:** homely, plain, ugly

fair² *noun* = **carnival**, bazaar, expo (*informal*), exposition, festival, fête, gala, market, show

fair and square *adjective* = **just**, above board, correct, honest, kosher (*informal*), on the level (*informal*), straight

fairly *adverb* 1 = **moderately**, adequately, pretty well, quite, rather, reasonably, somewhat, tolerably 2 = **positively**, absolutely, in a manner of speaking, really, veritably 3 = **deservedly**, equitably, honestly, impartially, justly, objectively, properly, without fear or favour

fairness *noun* = **impartiality**, decency, disinterestedness, equitableness, equity, justice, legitimacy, rightfulness, uprightness

fairy *noun* = **sprite**, brownie, elf, hob, leprechaun, peri, pixie, Robin Goodfellow

fairy tale *or* **fairy story** *noun* 1 = **folk tale**, romance 2 = **lie**, cock-and-bull story (*informal*), fabrication, fantasy, fiction, invention, pork pie (*Brit. slang*), porky (*Brit. slang*), tall story, untruth, urban legend, urban myth

faith *noun* 1 = **confidence**, assurance, conviction, credence, credit, dependence, reliance, trust 2 = **religion**, belief, church, communion, creed, denomination, dogma, persuasion 3 = **allegiance**, constancy, faithfulness, fealty, fidelity, loyalty, troth (*archaic*), truth, truthfulness 4 *As in* **bad faith** *or* **good faith** = **honesty**, honour, pledge, promise, sincerity, vow, word, word of honour

➤ **Antonyms**

≠**confidence:** apprehension, denial, disbelief, distrust, doubt, incredulity, misgiving, mistrust, rejection, scepticism, suspicion, uncertainty ≠**religion:** agnosticism ≠**allegiance:** infidelity

faithful *adjective* 1 = **loyal**, attached, constant, dependable, devoted, immovable, reliable, staunch, steadfast, true, true-blue, trusty, truthful, unswerving, unwavering 2 = **accurate**, close, exact, just, precise, strict, true 3 **the faithful** = **believers**, adherents, brethren, communicants, congregation, followers, the elect

➤ **Antonyms**

≠**loyal:** disloyal, faithless, false, false-hearted, fickle, inconstant, perfidious, traitorous, treacherous, unfaithful, unreliable, untrue, untrustworthy

faithfulness *noun* 1 = **loyalty**, adherence,

constancy, dependability, devotion, fealty, fidelity, trustworthiness 2 = **accuracy**, closeness, exactness, justice, strictness, truth

faithless *adjective* = **disloyal**, doubting, false, false-hearted, fickle, inconstant, perfidious, recreant (*archaic*), traitorous, treacherous, unbelieving, unfaithful, unreliable, untrue, untrustworthy, untruthful

faithlessness *noun* = **disloyalty**, betrayal, fickleness, inconstancy, infidelity, perfidy, treachery, unfaithfulness

fake *verb* 1 = **sham**, affect, assume, copy, counterfeit, fabricate, feign, forge, pretend, put on, simulate ♦ *noun* 2 = **impostor**, charlatan, copy, forgery, fraud, hoax, imitation, mountebank, phoney *or* phony (*informal*), reproduction, sham ♦ *adjective* 3 = **artificial**, affected, assumed, counterfeit, false, forged, imitation, mock, phoney *or* phony (*informal*), pinchbeck, pseudo (*informal*), reproduction, sham

➤ **Antonyms**

adjective ≠**artificial:** actual, authentic, bona fide, faithful, genuine, honest, legitimate, real, true, veritable

fall *verb* 1 = **descend**, be precipitated, cascade, collapse, come a cropper (*informal*), crash, dive, drop, drop down, go head over heels, keel over, nose-dive, pitch, plummet, plunge, settle, sink, stumble, subside, topple, trip, trip over, tumble 2 = **decrease**, abate, become lower, decline, depreciate, diminish, drop, dwindle, ebb, fall off, flag, go down, lessen, slump, subside 3 = **slope**, fall away, incline, incline downwards 4 = **die**, be a casualty, be killed, be lost, be slain, meet one's end, perish 5 = **be overthrown**, be taken, capitulate, give in *or* up, give way, go out of office, pass into enemy hands, resign, succumb, surrender, yield 6 = **occur**, become, befall, chance, come about, come to pass, fall out, happen, take place 7 = **lapse**, backslide, err, go astray, offend, sin, transgress, trespass, yield to temptation 8 **fall short** = **be inadequate**, disappoint, fail, fall down on (*informal*), not come up to expectations *or* scratch (*informal*) ♦ *noun* 9 = **descent**, dive, drop, nose dive, plummet, plunge, slip, spill, tumble 10 = **decrease**, cut, decline, diminution, dip, drop, dwindling, falling off, lessening, lowering, reduction, slump 11 = **collapse**, capitulation, death, defeat, destruction, downfall, failure, overthrow, resignation, ruin, surrender 12 = **lapse**, degradation, failure, sin, slip, transgression

➤ **Antonyms**

verb ≠**descend:** ascend, climb, go up, increase, mount, rise, scale, soar ≠**decrease:** advance, appreciate, climb, escalate, extend, heighten, increase, wax ≠**die:** endure, hold out, survive ≠be overthrown: prevail, triumph

fallacious adjective = **incorrect**, deceptive, delusive, delusory, erroneous, false, fictitious, illogical, illusory, misleading, mistaken, sophistic, sophistical, spurious, untrue, wrong

fallacy noun = **error**, casuistry, deceit, deception, delusion, falsehood, faultiness, flaw, illusion, inconsistency, misapprehension, misconception, mistake, sophism, sophistry, untruth

fall apart verb = **break up**, come apart at the seams, crumble, disband, disintegrate, disperse, dissolve, fall to bits, go or come to pieces, go to seed, lose cohesion, shatter

fall asleep verb = **drop off** (informal), doze off, go out like a light, go to sleep, nod off (informal)

fall back verb = **retreat**, back off, draw back, recede, recoil, retire, withdraw

fall back on verb = **resort to**, call upon, employ, have recourse to, make use of, press into service

fall behind verb **1** = **lag**, drop back, get left behind, lose one's place, trail **2** = **be in arrears**

fall down verb = **fail**, disappoint, fail to make the grade, fall short, go wrong, prove unsuccessful

fallen adjective **1** = **collapsed**, decayed, flat, on the ground, ruinous, sunken **2** Old-fashioned = **dishonoured**, disgraced, immoral, loose, lost, ruined, shamed, sinful, unchaste **3** = **killed**, dead, lost, perished, slain, slaughtered

fall for verb **1** = **fall in love with**, become infatuated with, desire, lose one's head over, succumb to the charms of **2** = **be fooled by**, accept, be deceived by, be duped by, be taken in by, buy (slang), give credence to, swallow (informal), take on board

fallible adjective = **imperfect**, erring, frail, ignorant, mortal, prone to error, uncertain, weak
➤ **Antonyms**
divine, faultless, impeccable, infallible, omniscient, perfect, superhuman, unerring, unimpeachable

fall in verb = **collapse**, cave in, come down about one's ears, fall apart at the seams, sink

falling off noun = **decrease**, deceleration, decline, deterioration, downward trend, drop, slackening, slowing down, slump, waning, worsening

fall in with verb = **go along with**, accept, agree with, assent, buy into (informal), concur with, cooperate with, support, take on board

fall off verb **1** = **tumble**, be unseated, come

a cropper or purler (informal), plummet, take a fall or tumble, topple **2** = **decrease**, decline, diminish, drop, dwindle, ebb away, fade, fall away, go down or downhill, lessen, peter out, reduce, shrink, slacken, slump, subside, tail off (informal), wane, weaken
➤ **Antonyms**
≠decrease: improve, increase, pick up, rally, recover, revive

fall on or **fall upon** verb = **attack**, assail, assault, belabour, descend upon, lay into, pitch into (informal), set upon or about, snatch, tear into (informal)

fall out verb Informal = **argue**, altercate, clash, come to blows, differ, disagree, fight, quarrel, squabble

fallow adjective = **uncultivated**, dormant, idle, inactive, inert, resting, undeveloped, unplanted, untilled, unused

falls plural noun = **waterfall**, cascade, cataract, force (Northern English dialect), linn (Scot.), rapids

fall short verb = **be lacking**, be deficient, be wanting, fail, miss, prove inadequate

fall through verb = **fail**, come to nothing, fizzle out (informal), go by the board, miscarry

fall to verb **1** = **be the responsibility of**, be up to, come down to, devolve upon **2** = **begin**, apply oneself to, commence, set about, start

false adjective **1** = **incorrect**, concocted, erroneous, faulty, fictitious, improper, inaccurate, inexact, invalid, mistaken, unfounded, unreal, wrong **2** = **artificial**, bogus, counterfeit, ersatz, fake, feigned, forged, imitation, mock, pretended, pseudo (informal), sham, simulated, spurious, synthetic **3** = **untrue**, lying, mendacious, truthless, unreliable, unsound, untrustworthy, untruthful **4** = **deceptive**, deceitful, deceiving, delusive, fallacious, fraudulent, hypocritical, misleading, trumped up **5** = **treacherous**, dishonest, dishonourable, disloyal, double-dealing, duplicitous, faithless, false-hearted, hypocritical, perfidious, treasonable, two-faced, unfaithful, untrustworthy
➤ **Antonyms**
≠incorrect: correct, exact, right, sound, valid ≠artificial: authentic, bona fide, genuine, honest, kosher (informal), real, sincere ≠untrue: reliable, true ≠treacherous: faithful, loyal, trustworthy

falsehood noun **1** = **untruthfulness**, deceit, deception, dishonesty, dissimulation, inveracity (rare), mendacity, perjury, prevarication **2** = **lie**, fabrication, fib, fiction, misstatement, pork pie (Brit. slang), porky (Brit. slang), story, untruth

falsification *noun* = **misrepresentation**, adulteration, deceit, dissimulation, distortion, forgery, perversion, tampering with

falsify *verb* = **alter**, belie, cook (*slang*), counterfeit, distort, doctor, fake, forge, garble, misrepresent, misstate, pervert, tamper with

falsity *noun* 1 = **untruth**, deceit, deceptiveness, dishonesty, double-dealing, duplicity, fraudulence, hypocrisy, inaccuracy, mendacity, perfidy, treachery, unreality 2 = **lie**, cheating, deception, fraud, pork pie (*Brit. slang*), porky (*Brit. slang*)

falter *verb* = **hesitate**, break, shake, speak haltingly, stammer, stumble, stutter, totter, tremble, vacillate, waver
➤ **Antonyms**
continue, endure, keep going, last, persevere, persist, proceed, stand firm, stick at

faltering *adjective* = **hesitant**, broken, irresolute, stammering, tentative, timid, uncertain, weak

fame *noun* = **prominence**, celebrity, credit, eminence, glory, honour, illustriousness, name, public esteem, renown, reputation, repute, stardom
➤ **Antonyms**
disgrace, dishonour, disrepute, ignominy, infamy, oblivion, obscurity, shame

famed *adjective* = **renowned**, acclaimed, celebrated, recognized, widely-known

familiar *adjective* 1 = **well-known**, accustomed, common, common or garden (*informal*), conventional, customary, domestic, everyday, frequent, household, mundane, ordinary, recognizable, repeated, routine, stock 2 = **friendly**, amicable, buddy-buddy (*slang, chiefly U.S. & Canad.*), chummy (*informal*), close, confidential, cordial, easy, free, free-and-easy, hail-fellow-well-met, informal, intimate, near, open, palsy-walsy (*informal*), relaxed, unceremonious, unconstrained, unreserved 3 = **disrespectful**, bold, forward, impudent, intrusive, overfree, presuming, presumptuous 4 **familiar with** = **acquainted with**, abreast of, at home with, *au courant with, au fait with*, aware of, conscious of, conversant with, introduced to, knowledgeable about, no stranger to, on speaking terms with, versed in, well up in
➤ **Antonyms**
≠**well-known**: infrequent, unaccustomed, uncommon, unfamiliar, unknown, unusual ≠**friendly**: aloof, cold, detached, distant, formal, unfriendly ≠**acquainted with**: ignorant, unaccustomed, unacquainted, unfamiliar, uninformed, unskilled

familiarity *noun* 1 = **acquaintance**, acquaintanceship, awareness, experience, grasp, understanding 2 = **friendliness**, absence of reserve, closeness, ease, fellowship, freedom, friendship, informality, intimacy, naturalness, openness, sociability, unceremoniousness 3 = **disrespect**, boldness, forwardness, liberties, liberty, presumption
➤ **Antonyms**
≠**acquaintance**: ignorance, inexperience, unfamiliarity ≠**friendliness**: distance, formality, reserve ≠**disrespect**: constraint, decorum, propriety, respect

familiarize *verb* = **accustom**, bring into common use, coach, get to know (about), habituate, instruct, inure, make conversant, make used to, prime, school, season, train

family *noun* 1 = **relations**, brood, children, descendants, folk (*informal*), household, issue, kin, kindred, kinsfolk, kinsmen, kith and kin, ménage, offspring, one's nearest and dearest, one's own flesh and blood, people, progeny, relatives 2 = **clan**, ancestors, ancestry, birth, blood, descent, dynasty, extraction, forebears, forefathers, genealogy, house, line, lineage, parentage, pedigree, race, sept, stemma, stirps, strain, tribe 3 = **group**, class, classification, genre, kind, network, subdivision, system

family tree *noun* = **lineage**, ancestry, extraction, genealogy, line, line of descent, pedigree, stemma, stirps

famine *noun* = **hunger**, dearth, destitution, scarcity, starvation

famished *adjective* = **starving**, ravening, ravenous, ready to eat a horse (*informal*), starved, voracious

famous *adjective* = **well-known**, acclaimed, celebrated, conspicuous, distinguished, eminent, excellent, far-famed, glorious, honoured, illustrious, legendary, lionized, much-publicized, notable, noted, prominent, remarkable, renowned, signal
➤ **Antonyms**
forgotten, mediocre, obscure, uncelebrated, undistinguished, unexceptional, unknown, unremarkable

fan[1] *noun* 1 = **blower**, air conditioner, blade, propeller, punkah (*in India*), vane, ventilator ♦ *verb* 2 = **blow**, air-condition, air-cool, cool, refresh, ventilate, winnow (*rare*) 3 = **stimulate**, add fuel to the flames, agitate, arouse, enkindle, excite, impassion, increase, provoke, rouse, stir up, whip up, work up

fan[2] *noun* = **supporter**, addict, adherent, admirer, aficionado, buff (*informal*), devotee, enthusiast, fiend (*informal*), follower, freak (*informal*), groupie (*slang*), lover, rooter (*U.S.*), zealot

fanatic *noun* = **extremist**, activist, addict,

bigot, buff (*informal*), devotee, energumen, enthusiast, militant, visionary, zealot

fanatical *adjective* = **obsessive**, bigoted, burning, enthusiastic, extreme, fervent, frenzied, immoderate, mad, overenthusiastic, passionate, rabid, visionary, wild, zealous

fanaticism *noun* = **immoderation**, bigotry, dedication, devotion, enthusiasm, extremism, infatuation, madness, monomania, obsessiveness, overenthusiasm, single-mindedness, zeal, zealotry

fancier *noun* = **expert**, aficionado, amateur, breeder, connoisseur

fanciful *adjective* = **unreal**, capricious, chimerical, curious, extravagant, fabulous, fairy-tale, fantastic, ideal, imaginary, imaginative, mythical, poetic, romantic, visionary, whimsical, wild
➤ **Antonyms**
conventional, down-to-earth, dry, dull, literal, matter of fact, ordinary, pedestrian, predictable, routine, sensible, sober, unimaginative, uninspired

fancy *adjective* **1** = **elaborate**, baroque, decorated, decorative, elegant, embellished, extravagant, fanciful, intricate, ornamental, ornamented, ornate ♦ *noun* **2** = **whim**, caprice, desire, humour, idea, impulse, inclination, notion, thought, urge **3** = **partiality**, fondness, hankering, inclination, liking, predilection, preference, relish, thirst **4** *Old-fashioned or literary* = **imagination**, conception, image, impression **5** = **delusion**, chimera, daydream, dream, fantasy, nightmare, phantasm, vision ♦ *verb* **6** *Informal* = **be attracted to**, be captivated by, desire, favour, go for, have an eye for, like, lust after, prefer, take a liking to, take to **7** = **wish for**, be attracted to, crave, desire, dream of, hanker after, have a yen for, hope for, long for, relish, thirst for, would like, yearn for **8** = **suppose**, be inclined to think, believe, conceive, conjecture, guess (*informal, chiefly U.S. & Canad.*), imagine, infer, reckon, surmise, think, think likely
➤ **Antonyms**
adjective ≠**elaborate**: basic, cheap, common, inferior, ordinary, plain, simple, unadorned, undecorated, unfussy ♦ *noun* ≠**partiality**: aversion, disinclination, dislike

fanfare *noun* = **trumpet call**, flourish, trump (*archaic*)

fang *noun* = **tooth**, tusk

fan out *verb* = **spread out**, disperse, lay out, open out, space out, spread, unfurl

fantasize *verb* = **daydream**, dream, envision, imagine

fantastic *adjective* **1** *Informal* = **wonderful**, awesome (*slang*), bitchin' (*U.S. slang*), boffo (*slang*), brill (*informal*), chillin' (*U.S.*

slang), cracking (*Brit. informal*), crucial (*slang*), def (*slang*), dope (*slang*), excellent, first-rate, jim-dandy (*slang*), marvellous, mean (*slang*), mega (*slang*), out of this world (*informal*), sensational (*informal*), sovereign, superb, the dog's bollocks (*taboo slang*), topping (*Brit. slang*), world-class **2** *Informal* = **enormous**, extreme, great, overwhelming, severe, tremendous **3** = **strange**, comical, eccentric, exotic, fanciful, freakish, grotesque, imaginative, odd, oddball (*informal*), off-the-wall (*slang*), outlandish, outré, peculiar, phantasmagorical, quaint, queer, rococo, unreal, weird, whimsical, zany **4** = **unrealistic**, ambitious, chimerical, extravagant, far-fetched, grandiose, illusory, ludicrous, ridiculous, visionary, wild **5** = **implausible**, absurd, capricious, cock-and-bull (*informal*), incredible, irrational, mad, preposterous, unlikely
➤ **Antonyms**
≠**wonderful**: common, everyday, normal, ordinary, poor, typical ≠**unrealistic**, **implausible**: credible, moderate, rational, realistic, sensible

fantasy *noun* **1** = **imagination**, creativity, fancy, invention, originality **2** = **daydream**, apparition, delusion, dream, fancy, figment of the imagination, flight of fancy, hallucination, illusion, mirage, nightmare, pipe dream, reverie, vision

far *adverb* **1** = **a long way**, afar, a good way, a great distance, deep, miles **2** = **much**, considerably, decidedly, extremely, greatly, incomparably, very much **3 by far** = **very much**, by a long chalk (*informal*), by a long shot, by a long way, easily, far and away, immeasurably, incomparably, to a great degree **4 far and wide** = **extensively**, broadly, everywhere, far and near, here, there and everywhere, in every nook and cranny, widely, worldwide **5 so far** = **up to now**, thus far, to date, until now, up to the present ♦ *adjective* **6** = **remote**, distant, faraway, far-flung, far-off, far-removed, long, outlying, out-of-the-way, removed
➤ **Antonyms**
adjective ≠**remote**: adjacent, adjoining, alongside, at close quarters, beside, bordering, close, contiguous, just round the corner, near, nearby, neighbouring, proximate, within sniffing distance (*informal*)

faraway *adjective* **1** = **distant**, beyond the horizon, far, far-flung, far-off, far-removed, outlying, remote **2** = **dreamy**, absent, abstracted, distant, lost, vague

farce *noun* **1** = **comedy**, broad comedy, buffoonery, burlesque, satire, slapstick **2** = **mockery**, absurdity, joke, nonsense, parody, ridiculousness, sham, travesty

farcical *adjective* = **ludicrous**, absurd, amusing, comic, custard-pie, derisory, diverting, droll, funny, laughable, nonsensical, preposterous, ridiculous, risible, slapstick

fare *noun* 1 = **charge**, passage money, price, ticket money, transport cost 2 = **passenger**, pick-up (*informal*), traveller 3 = **food**, commons, diet, eatables, feed, meals, menu, nosebag (*slang*), provisions, rations, sustenance, table, tack (*informal*), victuals, vittles (*obsolete or dialect*) ♦ *verb* 4 = **get on**, do, get along, make out, manage, prosper

farewell *noun* = **goodbye**, adieu, adieux *or* adieus, departure, leave-taking, parting, sendoff (*informal*), valediction

far-fetched *adjective* = **unconvincing**, cock-and-bull (*informal*), doubtful, dubious, fantastic, hard to swallow (*informal*), implausible, improbable, incredible, preposterous, strained, unbelievable, unlikely, unnatural, unrealistic
➤ **Antonyms**
acceptable, authentic, believable, credible, feasible, imaginable, likely, plausible, possible, probable, realistic, reasonable

farm *noun* 1 = **smallholding**, acreage, acres, croft (*Scot.*), farmstead, grange, holding, homestead, land, plantation, ranch (*chiefly North American*), station (*Austral. & N.Z.*) ♦ *verb* 2 = **cultivate**, bring under cultivation, operate, plant, practise husbandry, till the soil, work

farmer *noun* = **agriculturist**, agronomist, cockie (*N.Z.*), husbandman, smallholder, yeoman

farming *noun* = **agriculture**, agronomy, husbandry

far-out *adjective* = **strange**, advanced, avant-garde, bizarre, off-the-wall (*slang*), outlandish, outré, unconventional, unusual, weird, wild

farrago *noun* = **hotchpotch**, gallimaufry, hash, hodgepodge, jumble, medley, *mélange*, miscellany, mishmash, mixed bag, mixture, potpourri, salmagundi

far-reaching *adjective* = **extensive**, broad, important, momentous, pervasive, significant, sweeping, widespread

far-sighted *adjective* = **prudent**, acute, canny, cautious, discerning, far-seeing, judicious, politic, prescient, provident, sage, shrewd, wise

fascinate *verb* = **entrance**, absorb, allure, beguile, bewitch, captivate, charm, delight, enamour, enchant, engross, enrapture, enthral, hold spellbound, hypnotize, infatuate, intrigue, mesmerize, ravish, rivet, spellbind, transfix

➤ **Antonyms**
alienate, bore, disenchant, disgust, irritate, jade, put one off, sicken, turn one off (*informal*)

fascinated *adjective* = **entranced**, absorbed, beguiled, bewitched, captivated, charmed, engrossed, enthralled, hooked on, hypnotized, infatuated, smitten, spellbound, under a spell

fascinating *adjective* = **captivating**, alluring, bewitching, compelling, enchanting, engaging, engrossing, enticing, gripping, intriguing, irresistible, ravishing, riveting, seductive
➤ **Antonyms**
boring, dull, mind-numbing, unexciting, uninteresting

fascination *noun* = **attraction**, allure, charm, enchantment, glamour, lure, magic, magnetism, pull, sorcery, spell

fascism *noun* = **authoritarianism**, absolutism, autocracy, dictatorship, Hitlerism, totalitarianism

fashion *noun* 1 = **style**, convention, craze, custom, fad, latest, latest style, look, mode, prevailing taste, rage, trend, usage, vogue 2 = **method**, attitude, demeanour, manner, mode, style, way 3 **after a fashion** = **to some extent**, in a manner of speaking, in a way, moderately, somehow, somehow or other, to a degree ♦ *verb* 4 = **make**, construct, contrive, create, design, forge, form, manufacture, mould, shape, work

fashionable *adjective* = **popular**, à la mode, all the go (*informal*), all the rage, chic, cool (*slang*), current, customary, genteel, happening (*informal*), hip (*slang*), in (*informal*), in vogue, latest, modern, modish, prevailing, smart, stylish, trendsetting, trendy (*Brit. informal*), up-to-date, up-to-the-minute, usual, voguish (*informal*), with it (*informal*)
➤ **Antonyms**
behind the times, dated, frumpy, obsolete, old-fashioned, old-hat, outmoded, out of date, out of the ark (*informal*), uncool (*slang*), unfashionable, unpopular, unstylish, untrendy (*Brit. informal*)

fast[1] *adjective* 1 = **quick**, accelerated, brisk, fleet, flying, hasty, hurried, mercurial, nippy (*Brit. informal*), quickie (*informal*), rapid, speedy, swift, winged 2 = **dissipated**, dissolute, extravagant, gadabout (*informal*), giddy, immoral, intemperate, licentious, loose, profligate, promiscuous, rakish, reckless, self-indulgent, wanton, wild 3 = **fixed**, close, constant, fastened, firm, fortified, immovable, impregnable, lasting, loyal, permanent, secure, sound, stalwart, staunch, steadfast, tight, unwavering 4 **pull a fast one** *Informal* = **trick**, bamboozle

(*informal*), cheat, con (*informal*), deceive, defraud, hoodwink, put one over on (*informal*), swindle, take advantage of, take for a ride (*informal*) ♦ *adverb* **5 = quickly**, apace, at a rate of knots, hastily, hell for leather (*informal*), hotfoot, hurriedly, in haste, like a bat out of hell (*slang*), like a flash, like a shot (*informal*), like greased lightning (*informal*), like lightning, like nobody's business (*informal*), like the clappers (*Brit. informal*), pdq (*slang*), posthaste, presto, rapidly, speedily, swiftly, with all haste **6 = soundly**, deeply, firmly, fixedly, securely, tightly
➤ **Antonyms**
adjective ≠**quick**: leisurely, plodding, slow, slow moving, unhurried ≠**fixed**: inconstant, irresolute, unfaithful, unreliable, unstable, wavering, weak ♦ *adverb* ≠**quickly**: at a snail's pace, at one's leisure, gradually, leisurely, slowly, steadily, unhurriedly

fast² *verb* **1 = go hungry**, abstain, deny oneself, go without food, practise abstention, refrain from food *or* eating ♦ *noun* **2 = fasting**, abstinence

fasten *verb* **1 = fix**, affix, anchor, attach, bind, bolt, chain, connect, grip, join, lace, link, lock, make fast, make firm, seal, secure, tie, unite **2 = direct**, aim, bend, concentrate, fix, focus, rivet

fastening *noun* **= tie**, affixation, attachment, binding, bond, concatenation, connection, coupling, fusion, joint, junction, ligature, link, linking, union

fastidious *adjective* **= particular**, choosy, critical, dainty, difficult, discriminating, finicky, fussy, hard to please, hypercritical, meticulous, nice, overdelicate, overnice, pernickety, picky (*informal*), punctilious, squeamish
➤ **Antonyms**
careless, casual, disorderly, easy-going, lenient, slack, slipshod, sloppy, slovenly, unsystematic

fat *adjective* **1 = overweight**, beefy (*informal*), broad in the beam (*informal*), corpulent, elephantine, fleshy, gross, heavy, obese, plump, podgy, portly, roly-poly, rotund, solid, stout, tubby **2 = fatty**, adipose, greasy, lipid, oily, oleaginous, suety **3 = profitable**, affluent, cushy (*slang*), fertile, flourishing, fruitful, jammy (*Brit. slang*), lucrative, lush, productive, prosperous, remunerative, rich, thriving ♦ *noun* **4 = fatness**, adipose tissue, beef (*informal*), blubber, bulk, cellulite, corpulence, flab, flesh, obesity, overweight, paunch, weight problem
➤ **Antonyms**
adjective ≠**overweight**: angular, bony, gaunt, lank, lean, scrawny, skinny, slender,

slight, slim, spare, thin ≠**fatty**: lean ≠**profitable**: barren, poor, scanty, scarce, unproductive, unprofitable, unrewarding

fatal *adjective* **1 = lethal**, deadly, destructive, final, incurable, killing, malignant, mortal, pernicious, terminal **2 = disastrous**, baleful, baneful, calamitous, catastrophic, lethal, ruinous
➤ **Antonyms**
≠**lethal**: beneficial, benign, harmless, innocuous, inoffensive, non-lethal, non-toxic, wholesome ≠**disastrous**: inconsequential, minor

fatalism *noun* **= resignation**, acceptance, determinism, necessitarianism, passivity, predestinarianism, stoicism

fatality *noun* **= death**, casualty, deadliness, disaster, fatal accident, lethalness, loss, mortality

fate *noun* **1 = destiny**, chance, divine will, fortune, kismet, nemesis, predestination, providence, weird (*archaic*) **2 = fortune**, cup, horoscope, lot, portion, stars **3 = downfall**, death, destruction, doom, end, ruin

fated *adjective* **= destined**, doomed, foreordained, ineluctable, inescapable, inevitable, marked down, predestined, pre-elected, preordained, sure, written

fateful *adjective* **1 = crucial**, critical, decisive, important, portentous, significant **2 = disastrous**, deadly, destructive, fatal, lethal, ominous, ruinous
➤ **Antonyms**
≠**crucial**: inconsequential, insignificant, nugatory, ordinary, unimportant

fathead *noun Informal* **= idiot**, ass, berk (*Brit. slang*), booby, charlie (*Brit. informal*), coot, dimwit (*informal*), divvy (*Brit. slang*), dope (*informal*), dumb-ass (*slang*), dunderhead, fool, goose, imbecile, jackass, jerk (*slang, chiefly U.S. & Canad.*), lamebrain (*informal*), nerd *or* nurd (*slang*), nincompoop, nitwit (*informal*), numbskull *or* numskull, pillock (*Brit. slang*), plonker (*slang*), prat (*slang*), prick (*derogatory slang*), schmuck (*U.S. slang*), twerp *or* twirp (*informal*), twit (*informal, chiefly Brit.*), wally (*slang*)

father *noun* **1 = daddy** (*informal*), begetter, dad (*informal*), governor (*informal*), old boy (*informal*), old man (*informal*), pa (*informal*), papa (*old-fashioned informal*), pater, paterfamilias, patriarch, pop (*informal*), sire **2 = forefather**, ancestor, forebear, predecessor, progenitor **3 = founder**, architect, author, creator, inventor, maker, originator, prime mover **4 = leader**, city father, elder, patriarch, patron, senator **5 = priest**, abbé, confessor, curé, padre (*informal*), pastor ♦ *verb* **6** = **sire**, beget, get, procreate

fatherland *noun* = **homeland**, land of one's birth, land of one's fathers, motherland, native land, old country

fatherly *adjective* = **paternal**, affectionate, benevolent, benign, forbearing, indulgent, kind, kindly, patriarchal, protective, supportive, tender

fathom *verb* = **understand**, comprehend, get to the bottom of, grasp, interpret

fathomless *adjective* = **profound**, abysmal, bottomless, deep, immeasurable, impenetrable, incomprehensible, unfathomable, unplumbed

fatigue *noun* **1** = **tiredness**, debility, ennui, heaviness, languor, lethargy, listlessness, overtiredness ♦ *verb* **2** = **tire**, drain, drain of energy, exhaust, fag (out) (*informal*), jade, knacker (*slang*), overtire, poop (*informal*), take it out of (*informal*), weaken, wear out, weary, whack (*Brit. informal*)
➤ **Antonyms**
noun ≠**tiredness**: alertness, animation, energy, freshness, get-up-and-go (*informal*), go, indefatigability, life, vigour, zest ♦ *verb* ≠**tire**: refresh, rejuvenate, relieve, rest, revive, stimulate

fatness *noun* = **obesity**, beef (*informal*), bulkiness, corpulence, *embonpoint*, flab, flesh, fleshiness, girth, grossness, heaviness, overweight, podginess, rotundity, size, stoutness, weight, weight problem

fatten *verb* **1** = **grow fat**, broaden, coarsen, expand, gain weight, put on weight, spread, swell, thicken, thrive **2** *often with* **up** = **feed up**, bloat, build up, cram, distend, feed, nourish, overfeed, stuff

fatty *adjective* = **greasy**, adipose, fat, oily, oleaginous, rich

fatuity *noun* = **foolishness**, absurdity, brainlessness, daftness (*informal*), denseness, fatuousness, folly, idiocy, imbecility, insanity, ludicrousness, lunacy, mindlessness, stupidity

fatuous *adjective* = **foolish**, absurd, asinine, brainless, dense, dull, dumb-ass (*slang*), idiotic, inane, ludicrous, lunatic, mindless, moronic, puerile, silly, stupid, vacuous, weak-minded, witless

fault *noun* **1** = **responsibility**, accountability, culpability, liability **2** = **mistake**, blunder, boob (*Brit. slang*), error, error of judgment, inaccuracy, indiscretion, lapse, negligence, offence, omission, oversight, slip, slip-up **3** = **flaw**, blemish, defect, deficiency, demerit, drawback, failing, imperfection, infirmity, lack, shortcoming, snag, weakness, weak point **4** **at fault** = **guilty**, answerable, blamable, culpable, in the wrong, responsible, to blame **5** **find fault with**

= **criticize**, carp at, complain, pick holes in, pull to pieces, quibble, take to task **6** **to a fault** = **excessively**, immoderately, in the extreme, needlessly, out of all proportion, overly (*U.S.*), overmuch, preposterously, ridiculously, unduly ♦ *verb* **7** = **criticize**, blame, call to account, censure, find fault with, find lacking, hold (someone) accountable, hold (someone) responsible, hold (someone) to blame, impugn
➤ **Antonyms**
noun ≠**flaw**: asset, attribute, credit, goodness, merit, perfection, strength, virtue

fault-finding *noun* = **criticism**, carping, hairsplitting, nagging, niggling, nit-picking (*informal*)

faultless *adjective* **1** = **flawless**, accurate, classic, correct, exemplary, faithful, foolproof, impeccable, model, perfect, unblemished **2** = **blameless**, above reproach, guiltless, immaculate, impeccable, innocent, irreproachable, pure, sinless, spotless, squeaky-clean, stainless, unblemished, unspotted, unsullied

faulty *adjective* = **defective**, bad, blemished, broken, damaged, erroneous, fallacious, flawed, impaired, imperfect, imprecise, inaccurate, incorrect, invalid, malfunctioning, not working, on the blink, out of order, unsound, weak, wrong

faux pas *noun* = **gaffe**, bloomer (*Brit. informal*), blunder, boob (*Brit. slang*), breach of etiquette, clanger (*informal*), gaucherie, impropriety, indiscretion, solecism

favour *noun* **1** = **approval**, approbation, backing, bias, championship, espousal, esteem, favouritism, friendliness, good opinion, goodwill, grace, kindness, kind regard, partiality, patronage, promotion, support **2** = **good turn**, benefit, boon, courtesy, indulgence, kindness, obligement (*Scot. or archaic*), service **3** **in favour of** = **for**, all for (*informal*), backing, on the side of, pro, supporting, to the benefit of ♦ *verb* **4** = **prefer**, incline towards, single out **5** = **indulge**, be partial to, esteem, have in one's good books, pamper, pull strings for (*informal*), reward, side with, smile upon, spoil, treat with partiality, value **6** = **support**, advocate, approve, back, be in favour of, champion, choose, commend, countenance, encourage, espouse, fancy, like, opt for, patronize
➤ **Antonyms**
noun ≠**approval**: animosity, antipathy, disapproval, disfavour, ill will, malevolence ≠**good turn**: disservice, harm, injury, wrong ♦ *verb* ≠**prefer**: disapprove, disdain, dislike, object to ≠**support**: oppose, thwart

favourable *adjective* **1** = **advantageous**, appropriate, auspicious, beneficial,

convenient, encouraging, fair, fit, good, helpful, hopeful, opportune, promising, propitious, suitable, timely **2 = positive**, affirmative, agreeable, amicable, approving, benign, encouraging, enthusiastic, friendly, kind, reassuring, sympathetic, understanding, welcoming, well-disposed
➤ **Antonyms**
≠**advantageous**: disadvantageous, inauspicious, unfavourable, unhelpful, unpromising, useless ≠**positive**: disapproving, ill-disposed, unfavourable, unfriendly, unsympathetic

favourably *adverb* **1 = advantageously**, auspiciously, conveniently, fortunately, opportunely, profitably, to one's advantage, well **2 = positively**, agreeably, approvingly, enthusiastically, genially, graciously, helpfully, in a kindly manner, with approbation, with approval, with cordiality, without prejudice

favourite *adjective* **1 = preferred**, best-loved, choice, dearest, esteemed, fave (*informal*), favoured ♦ *noun* **2 = darling**, beloved, blue-eyed boy (*informal*), choice, dear, fave (*informal*), idol, pet, pick, preference, teacher's pet, the apple of one's eye

favouritism *noun* **= preferential treatment**, bias, jobs for the boys (*informal*), nepotism, one-sidedness, partiality, partisanship, preference
➤ **Antonyms**
equality, equity, even-handedness, fairness, impartiality, neutrality, objectivity, open-mindedness

fawn[1] *verb, often with* **on** *or* **upon** **= ingratiate oneself**, be obsequious, be servile, bow and scrape, brown-nose (*taboo slang*), court, crawl, creep, cringe, curry favour, dance attendance, flatter, grovel, kiss ass (*U.S. & Canad. taboo slang*), kneel, kowtow, lick (someone's) arse (*taboo slang*), lick (someone's) boots, pander to, pay court, toady, truckle

fawn[2] *adjective* **= beige**, buff, greyish-brown, neutral

fawning *adjective* **= obsequious**, abject, bootlicking (*informal*), bowing and scraping, crawling, cringing, deferential, flattering, grovelling, prostrate, servile, slavish, sycophantic

fealty *noun* **= loyalty**, allegiance, devotion, faith, faithfulness, fidelity, homage, obeisance, submission, troth (*archaic*)

fear *noun* **1 = dread**, alarm, apprehensiveness, awe, blue funk (*informal*), consternation, cravenness, dismay, fright, horror, panic, qualms, terror, timidity, tremors, trepidation **2 = bugbear**, bête

noire, bogey, horror, nightmare, phobia, spectre ♦ *verb* **3 = be afraid**, apprehend, be apprehensive, be frightened, be in a blue funk (*informal*), be scared, dare not, dread, have a horror of, have a phobia about, have butterflies in one's stomach (*informal*), have qualms, live in dread of, shake in one's shoes, shudder at, take fright, tremble at **4 fear for = worry about**, be anxious about, be concerned about, be disquieted over, be distressed about, feel concern for, tremble for

fearful *adjective* **1 = scared**, afraid, alarmed, anxious, apprehensive, diffident, faint-hearted, frightened, hellacious (*U.S. slang*), hesitant, intimidated, jittery (*informal*), jumpy, nervous, nervy (*Brit. informal*), neurotic, panicky, pusillanimous, shrinking, tense, timid, timorous, uneasy, wired (*slang*) **2 = frightful**, appalling, atrocious, awful, dire, distressing, dreadful, ghastly, grievous, grim, gruesome, hair-raising, harrowing, hideous, horrendous, horrible, horrific, monstrous, shocking, terrible, unspeakable
➤ **Antonyms**
≠**scared**: ballsy (*taboo slang*), bold, brave, confident, courageous, daring, dauntless, doughty, gallant, game (*informal*), gutsy (*slang*), heroic, indomitable, intrepid, lion-hearted, plucky, unabashed, unafraid, undaunted, unflinching, valiant, valorous

fearfully *adverb* **1 = nervously**, apprehensively, diffidently, in fear and trembling, timidly, timorously, uneasily, with bated breath, with many misgivings *or* forebodings, with one's heart in one's mouth **2 = very**, awfully, exceedingly, excessively, frightfully, terribly, tremendously

fearless *adjective* **= brave**, ballsy (*taboo slang*), bold, confident, courageous, daring, dauntless, doughty, gallant, game (*informal*), gutsy (*slang*), heroic, indomitable, intrepid, lion-hearted, plucky, unabashed, unafraid, undaunted, unflinching, valiant, valorous

fearlessness *noun* **= bravery**, balls (*taboo slang*), ballsiness (*taboo slang*), boldness, confidence, courage, dauntlessness, guts (*informal*), indomitability, intrepidity, lion-heartedness, nerve, pluckiness

fearsome *adjective* **= terrifying**, alarming, appalling, awe-inspiring, awesome, awful, baleful, daunting, dismaying, formidable, frightening, hair-raising, hellacious (*U.S. slang*), horrendous, horrifying, menacing, unnerving

feasibility *noun* **= possibility**, expediency, practicability, usefulness, viability, workability

feasible *adjective* **= possible**, achievable, attainable, likely, practicable, realizable, reasonable, viable, workable

> ➤ **Antonyms**

impossible, impracticable, inconceivable, unreasonable, untenable, unviable, unworkable

feast *noun* 1 = **banquet**, barbecue, beanfeast (*Brit. informal*), beano (*Brit. slang*), blowout (*slang*), carousal, carouse, dinner, entertainment, festive board, jollification, junket, repast, revels, slap-up meal (*Brit. informal*), spread (*informal*), treat 2 = **treat**, delight, enjoyment, gratification, pleasure 3 = **festival**, celebration, -fest, fête, gala day, holiday, holy day, red-letter day, saint's day ◆ *verb* 4 = **eat one's fill**, eat to one's heart's content, fare sumptuously, gorge, gormandize, indulge, overindulge, pig out (*slang*), stuff, stuff one's face (*slang*), wine and dine 5 = **treat**, entertain, hold a reception for, kill the fatted calf for, regale, wine and dine

feat *noun* = **accomplishment**, achievement, act, attainment, deed, exploit, feather in one's cap, performance

feathers *plural noun* = **plumage**, down, plumes

feathery *adjective* = **downy**, feathered, fluffy, plumate *or* plumose (*Botany & Zoology*), plumed, plumy, wispy

feature *noun* 1 = **aspect**, attribute, characteristic, facet, factor, hallmark, mark, peculiarity, point, property, quality, trait 2 = **highlight**, attraction, crowd puller (*informal*), draw, innovation, main item, special, special attraction, speciality, specialty 3 = **article**, column, comment, item, piece, report, story ◆ *verb* 4 = **spotlight**, accentuate, call attention to, emphasize, foreground, give prominence to, give the full works (*slang*), headline, play up, present, promote, set off, star

features *plural noun* = **face**, countenance, lineaments, physiognomy

febrile *adjective Formal* = **feverish**, delirious, fevered, fiery, flushed, hot, inflamed, pyretic (*Medical*)

feckless *adjective* = **irresponsible**, aimless, feeble, futile, good-for-nothing, hopeless, incompetent, ineffectual, shiftless, useless, weak, worthless

fecund *adjective Literary* = **fertile**, fructiferous, fruitful, productive, prolific, teeming

fecundity *noun* = **fertility**, fruitfulness, productiveness

federate *verb* = **unite**, amalgamate, associate, combine, confederate, integrate, syndicate, unify

federation *noun* = **union**, alliance, amalgamation, association, *Bund*, coalition, combination, confederacy, copartnership,

entente, federacy, league, syndicate

fed up *adjective* = **dissatisfied**, annoyed, blue, bored, brassed off (*Brit. slang*), browned-off (*informal*), depressed, discontented, dismal, down, down in the mouth, gloomy, glum, hacked (off) (*U.S. slang*), pissed off (*taboo slang*), sick and tired (*informal*), tired, weary

fee *noun* = **charge**, account, bill, compensation, emolument, hire, honorarium, meed (*archaic*), pay, payment, recompense, remuneration, reward, toll

feeble *adjective* 1 = **weak**, debilitated, delicate, doddering, effete, enervated, enfeebled, etiolated, exhausted, failing, faint, frail, infirm, languid, powerless, puny, shilpit (*Scot.*), sickly, weakened, weedy (*informal*) 2 = **flimsy**, flat, inadequate, incompetent, indecisive, ineffective, ineffectual, inefficient, insignificant, insufficient, lame, paltry, pathetic, poor, slight, tame, thin, unconvincing, weak

> ➤ **Antonyms**

≠weak: energetic, hale, healthy, hearty, lusty, robust, stalwart, strong, sturdy, vigorous ≠flimsy: effective, forceful, successful

feeble-minded *adjective* = **half-witted**, addle-pated, bone-headed (*slang*), braindead (*informal*), deficient, dim-witted (*informal*), dozy (*Brit. informal*), dull, dumb (*informal*), dumb-ass (*slang*), idiotic, imbecilic, lacking, moronic, obtuse, retarded, simple, slow on the uptake, slow-witted, soft in the head (*informal*), stupid, vacant, weak-minded

> ➤ **Antonyms**

astute, aware, bright, clear-headed, clever, intelligent, keen, quick-witted, smart

feebleness *noun* 1 = **weakness**, debility, delicacy, effeteness, enervation, etiolation, exhaustion, frailness, frailty, incapacity, infirmity, lack of strength, languor, lassitude, sickliness 2 = **flimsiness**, inadequacy, incompetence, indecisiveness, ineffectualness, insignificance, insufficiency, lameness, weakness

feed *verb* 1 = **cater for**, nourish, provide for, provision, supply, sustain, victual, wine and dine 2 *sometimes with* **on** = **eat**, devour, exist on, fare, graze, live on, nurture, partake of, pasture, subsist, take nourishment 3 = **encourage**, augment, bolster, foster, fuel, minister to, strengthen, supply ◆ *noun* 4 = **food**, fodder, forage, pasturage, provender, silage 5 *Informal* = **meal**, feast, nosh (*slang*), nosh-up (*Brit. slang*), repast, spread (*informal*), tuck-in (*informal*)

feel *verb* 1 = **touch**, caress, finger, fondle, handle, manipulate, maul, paw, run one's hands over, stroke 2 = **experience**, be aware of, be sensible of, endure, enjoy, go through, have, have a sensation of, know, notice, observe, perceive, suffer, take to heart, undergo **3 = explore**, fumble, grope, sound, test, try **4 = sense**, be convinced, feel in one's bones, have a hunch, have the impression, intuit **5 = believe**, be of the opinion that, consider, deem, hold, judge, think **6** with **for = feel compassion for**, be moved by, be sorry for, bleed for, commiserate, condole with, empathize, pity, sympathize with **7 feel like = fancy**, could do with, desire, feel inclined, feel the need for, feel up to, have the inclination, want ◆ noun **8 = texture**, finish, surface, touch **9 = impression**, air, ambience, atmosphere, feeling, quality, sense, vibes (slang)

feeler noun **1 = antenna**, tentacle, whisker **2** As in **put out feelers = approach**, advance, probe

feeling noun **1 = emotion**, affection, ardour, fervour, fondness, heat, intensity, passion, sentiment, sentimentality, warmth **2 = impression**, apprehension, consciousness, hunch, idea, inkling, notion, presentiment, sense, suspicion **3 = opinion**, inclination, instinct, point of view, view **4 = sympathy**, appreciation, compassion, concern, empathy, pity, sensibility, sensitivity, understanding **5 = sense of touch**, feel, perception, sensation, sense, touch **6 = atmosphere**, air, ambience, aura, feel, mood, quality, vibes (slang) **7 bad feeling = hostility**, anger, dislike, distrust, enmity, upset

feelings plural noun **= emotions**, ego, self-esteem, sensitivities, susceptibilities

feign verb **= pretend**, act, affect, assume, counterfeit, fake, forge, give the appearance of, imitate, make a show of, put on, sham, simulate

feigned adjective **= pretended**, affected, artificial, assumed, counterfeit, ersatz, fake, false, imitation, insincere, pseudo (informal), sham, simulated

feint noun **= bluff**, artifice, blind, distraction, dodge, expedient, gambit, manoeuvre, mock attack, play, pretence, ruse, stratagem, subterfuge, wile

felicitous adjective **= fitting**, apposite, appropriate, apropos, apt, happy, inspired, neat, opportune, pat, propitious, suitable, timely, well-chosen, well-timed

felicity noun **1 = happiness**, blessedness, bliss, blissfulness, delectation, ecstasy, joy **2 = aptness**, applicability, appropriateness, becomingness, effectiveness, grace, propriety, suitability, suitableness

feline adjective **1 = catlike**, leonine **2 = graceful**, flowing, sinuous, sleek, slinky,

smooth, stealthy

fell verb **= cut down**, cut, deck (slang), demolish, flatten, floor, hew, knock down, level, prostrate, raze, strike down

fellow noun **1** Old-fashioned **= man**, bloke (Brit. informal), boy, chap (informal), character, customer (informal), guy (informal), individual, person, punter (informal) **2 = associate**, colleague, companion, compeer, comrade, co-worker, equal, friend, member, partner, peer ◆ adjective **3 = co-**, affiliated, akin, allied, associate, associated, like, related, similar

fellow feeling noun **= sympathy**, compassion, empathy, pity, understanding

fellowship noun **1 = camaraderie**, amity, brotherhood, communion, companionability, companionship, familiarity, fraternization, intercourse, intimacy, kindliness, sociability **2 = society**, association, brotherhood, club, fraternity, guild, league, order, sisterhood, sodality

feminine adjective **= womanly**, delicate, gentle, girlie, girlish, graceful, ladylike, modest, soft, tender
➤ **Antonyms**
Amazonian, butch, indelicate, manly, mannish, masculine, rough, unfeminine, unladylike, unwomanly, virile

femininity noun **= womanliness**, delicacy, feminineness, gentleness, girlishness, muliebrity, softness, womanhood

femme fatale noun **= seductress**, charmer, Circe, enchantress, siren, vamp (informal)

fen noun **= marsh**, bog, holm (dialect), morass, moss (Scot.), quagmire, slough, swamp

fence noun **1 = barrier**, barbed wire, barricade, defence, guard, hedge, paling, palisade, railings, rampart, shield, stockade, wall **2 on the fence = uncommitted**, between two stools, irresolute, uncertain, undecided, vacillating ◆ verb **3** often with **in** or **off = enclose**, bound, circumscribe, confine, coop, defend, encircle, fortify, guard, hedge, impound, pen, pound, protect, restrict, secure, separate, surround **4 = evade**, beat about the bush, cavil, dodge, equivocate, flannel (Brit. informal), hedge, parry, prevaricate, quibble, shift, stonewall, tergiversate

fend for verb **= look after**, make do, make provision for, provide for, shift for, support, sustain, take care of

fend off verb **= turn aside**, avert, beat off, deflect, drive back, hold or keep at bay, keep off, parry, repel, repulse, resist, stave off, ward off

feral adjective **1 = wild**, unbroken,

uncultivated, undomesticated, untamed **2** = **savage**, bestial, brutal, fell, ferocious, fierce, vicious

ferment noun **1** = **commotion**, agitation, brouhaha, disruption, excitement, fever, frenzy, furore, glow, heat, hubbub, imbroglio, state of unrest, stew, stir, tumult, turbulence, turmoil, unrest, uproar **2** = **yeast**, bacteria, barm, fermentation agent, leaven, leavening ◆ verb **3** = **brew**, boil, bubble, concoct, effervesce, foam, froth, heat, leaven, rise, seethe, work
➤ Antonyms
noun ≠ **commotion**: calmness, hush, peacefulness, quiet, restfulness, stillness, tranquillity

ferocious adjective **1** = **fierce**, feral, predatory, rapacious, ravening, savage, violent, wild **2** = **cruel**, barbaric, barbarous, bloodthirsty, brutal, brutish, merciless, pitiless, relentless, ruthless, tigerish, vicious
➤ Antonyms
≠ **fierce**: calm, docile, gentle, mild, subdued, submissive, tame

ferocity noun = **savagery**, barbarity, bloodthirstiness, brutality, cruelty, ferociousness, fierceness, inhumanity, rapacity, ruthlessness, savageness, viciousness, wildness

ferret out verb = **track down**, bring to light, dig up, disclose, discover, drive out, elicit, get at, nose out, root out, run to earth, search out, smell out, trace, unearth

ferry noun **1** = **ferry boat**, packet, packet boat ◆ verb **2** = **carry**, chauffeur, convey, run, ship, shuttle, transport

fertile adjective = **productive**, abundant, fat, fecund, flowering, flowing with milk and honey, fruit-bearing, fruitful, generative, luxuriant, plenteous, plentiful, prolific, rich, teeming, yielding
➤ Antonyms
barren, dry, impotent, infecund, infertile, poor, sterile, unfruitful, unproductive

fertility noun = **fruitfulness**, abundance, fecundity, luxuriance, productiveness, richness

fertilization noun **1** = **propagation**, implantation, impregnation, insemination, pollination, procreation **2** = **manuring**, dressing, mulching, top dressing

fertilize verb **1** = **make fruitful**, fecundate, fructify, impregnate, inseminate, make pregnant, pollinate **2** = **feed**, compost, dress, enrich, manure, mulch, top-dress

fertilizer noun = **compost**, dressing, dung, guano, manure, marl

fervent, fervid adjective = **intense**, animated, ardent, devout, eager, earnest, ecstatic, emotional, enthusiastic, excited, fiery, flaming, heartfelt, impassioned, passionate, perfervid (literary), vehement, warm, zealous
➤ Antonyms
apathetic, cold, cool, detached, dispassionate, frigid, impassive, unfeeling, unimpassioned

fervour noun = **intensity**, animation, ardour, eagerness, earnestness, enthusiasm, excitement, fervency, passion, vehemence, warmth, zeal

fester verb **1** = **intensify**, aggravate, chafe, gall, irk, rankle, smoulder **2** = **putrefy**, become inflamed, decay, gather, maturate, suppurate, ulcerate

festival noun **1** = **celebration**, carnival, entertainment, -fest, festivities, fête, field day, gala, jubilee, treat **2** = **holy day**, anniversary, commemoration, feast, fête, fiesta, holiday, red-letter day, saint's day

festive adjective = **celebratory**, back-slapping, carnival, cheery, Christmassy, convivial, festal, gala, gay, gleeful, happy, hearty, holiday, jolly, jovial, joyful, joyous, jubilant, light-hearted, merry, mirthful, sportive
➤ Antonyms
depressing, drab, dreary, funereal, gloomy, lugubrious, mournful, sad

festivity noun **1** = **merrymaking**, amusement, conviviality, fun, gaiety, jollification, joviality, joyfulness, merriment, mirth, pleasure, revelry, sport **2** often plural = **celebration**, beano (Brit. slang), carousal, entertainment, festival, festive event, festive proceedings, fun and games, hooley or hoolie (chiefly Irish & N.Z.), jollification, party, rave (Brit. slang), rave-up (Brit. slang)

festoon verb **1** = **decorate**, array, bedeck, beribbon, deck, drape, engarland, garland, hang, swathe, wreathe ◆ noun **2** = **decoration**, chaplet, garland, lei, swag, swathe, wreath

fetch verb **1** = **bring**, carry, conduct, convey, deliver, escort, get, go for, lead, obtain, retrieve, transport **2** = **sell for**, bring in, earn, go for, make, realize, yield

fetching adjective = **attractive**, alluring, captivating, charming, cute, enchanting, enticing, fascinating, intriguing, sweet, taking, winsome

fetch up verb = **end up**, arrive, come, finish up, halt, land, reach, stop, turn up

fête, fete noun **1** = **fair**, bazaar, festival, gala, garden party, sale of work ◆ verb **2** = **entertain**, bring out the red carpet for (someone), hold a reception for (someone), honour, kill the fatted calf for (someone), lionize, make much of, treat, wine and dine

fetid adjective = **stinking**, corrupt, foul,

malodorous, mephitic, noisome, noxious, offensive, olid, rancid, rank, reeking

fetish *noun* 1 = **fixation**, *idée fixe*, mania, obsession, thing (*informal*) 2 = **talisman**, amulet, cult object

fetter *verb* 1 = **restrict**, bind, clip someone's wings, confine, curb, encumber, hamper, hamstring, restrain, straiten 2 = **chain**, hobble, hold captive, manacle, put a straitjacket on, shackle, tie, tie up

fetters *plural noun* 1 = **restraint**, bondage, captivity, check, curb, hindrance, obstruction 2 = **chains**, bonds, irons, leg irons, manacles, shackles

feud *noun* 1 = **hostility**, argument, bad blood, bickering, broil, conflict, contention, disagreement, discord, dissension, enmity, estrangement, faction, falling out, grudge, quarrel, rivalry, row, strife, vendetta ◆ *verb* 2 = **quarrel**, be at daggers drawn, be at odds, bicker, brawl, clash, contend, dispute, duel, fall out, row, squabble, war

fever *noun* 1 = **ague**, pyrexia (*Medical*) 2 = **excitement**, agitation, delirium, ecstasy, ferment, fervour, flush, frenzy, heat, intensity, passion, restlessness, turmoil, unrest

feverish *or* **fevered** *adjective* 1 = **hot**, burning, febrile, fevered, flaming, flushed, hectic, inflamed, pyretic (*Medical*) 2 = **excited**, agitated, desperate, distracted, frantic, frenetic, frenzied, impatient, obsessive, overwrought, restless
➤ **Antonyms**
≠**excited**: calm, collected, composed, cool, dispassionate, nonchalant, offhand, serene, tranquil, unemotional, unexcitable, unfazed (*informal*), unruffled

few *adjective* 1 = **not many**, hardly any, inconsiderable, infrequent, insufficient, meagre, negligible, rare, scant, scanty, scarce, scarcely any, scattered, sparse, sporadic, thin 2 **few and far between** = **scarce**, at great intervals, hard to come by, infrequent, in short supply, irregular, rare, scattered, seldom met with, thin on the ground, uncommon, unusual, widely spaced ◆ *pronoun* 3 = **small number**, handful, scarcely any, scattering, some
➤ **Antonyms**
adjective ≠**not many**, scarce: abundant, bounteous, divers (*archaic*), inexhaustible, manifold, many, multifarious, plentiful, sundry

fiancé, fiancée *noun* = **husband-** *or* **wife-to-be**, betrothed, intended, prospective spouse

fiasco *noun* = **flop** (*informal*), balls-up (*taboo slang*), catastrophe, cock-up (*Brit. slang*), debacle, disaster, failure, fuck-up (*offensive taboo slang*), mess, rout, ruin,

washout (*informal*)

fiat *noun* 1 = **order**, command, decree, demand, dictate, dictum, edict, mandate, ordinance, proclamation 2 = **permission**, authorization, sanction, warrant

fib *noun* = **lie**, fiction, pork pie (*Brit. slang*), porky (*Brit. slang*), prevarication, story, untruth, white lie, whopper (*informal*)

fibre *noun* 1 = **thread**, fibril, filament, pile, staple, strand, texture, wisp 2 *As in* **moral fibre** = **strength of character**, resolution, stamina, strength, toughness 3 = **essence**, nature, quality, spirit, substance

fickle *adjective* = **changeable**, blowing hot and cold, capricious, faithless, fitful, flighty, inconstant, irresolute, mercurial, mutable, quicksilver, temperamental, unfaithful, unpredictable, unstable, unsteady, vacillating, variable, volatile
➤ **Antonyms**
changeless, constant, faithful, firm, invariable, loyal, reliable, resolute, settled, stable, staunch, steadfast, true, trustworthy

fickleness *noun* = **inconstancy**, capriciousness, fitfulness, flightiness, mutability, unfaithfulness, unpredictability, unsteadiness, volatility

fiction *noun* 1 = **tale**, fable, fantasy, legend, myth, novel, romance, story, storytelling, work of imagination, yarn (*informal*) 2 = **lie**, cock and bull story (*informal*), concoction, fabrication, falsehood, fancy, fantasy, figment of the imagination, imagination, improvisation, invention, pork pie (*Brit. slang*), porky (*Brit. slang*), tall story, untruth, urban legend, urban myth

fictional *adjective* = **imaginary**, invented, legendary, made-up, nonexistent, unreal

fictitious *adjective* = **false**, apocryphal, artificial, assumed, bogus, counterfeit, fabricated, fanciful, feigned, imaginary, imagined, improvised, invented, made-up, make-believe, mythical, spurious, unreal, untrue
➤ **Antonyms**
actual, authentic, genuine, legitimate, real, true, truthful, veracious, veritable

fiddle *noun* 1 = **violin** 2 *Brit. informal* = **fraud**, fix, graft (*informal*), piece of sharp practice, racket, scam (*slang*), sting (*informal*), swindle, wangle (*informal*) 3 **fit as a fiddle** *Informal* = **healthy**, blooming, hale and hearty, in fine fettle, in good form, in good shape, in rude health, in the pink, sound, strong ◆ *verb* 4 *Informal* = **cheat**, cook the books (*informal*), diddle (*informal*), finagle (*informal*), fix, gerrymander, graft (*informal*), manoeuvre, racketeer, sting (*informal*), swindle, wangle (*informal*) 5 = **fidget**, finger, interfere with, mess about or around, play, tamper with, tinker, toy, trifle

fiddling adjective = **trivial**, futile, insignificant, nickel-and-dime (U.S. slang), pettifogging, petty, trifling

fidelity noun 1 = **loyalty**, allegiance, constancy, dependability, devotedness, devotion, faith, faithfulness, fealty, integrity, lealty (archaic or Scot.), staunchness, troth (archaic), true-heartedness, trustworthiness 2 = **accuracy**, adherence, closeness, correspondence, exactitude, exactness, faithfulness, preciseness, precision, scrupulousness
➤ **Antonyms**
≠ **loyalty**: disloyalty, faithlessness, falseness, infidelity, perfidiousness, treachery, unfaithfulness, untruthfulness ≠ **accuracy**: inaccuracy, inexactness

fidget verb 1 = **move restlessly**, be like a cat on hot bricks (informal), bustle, chafe, fiddle (informal), fret, jiggle, jitter (informal), squirm, twitch, worry ♦ noun 2 **the fidgets** = **restlessness**, fidgetiness, jitters (informal), nervousness, unease, uneasiness

fidgety adjective = **restless**, antsy (informal), impatient, jerky, jittery (informal), jumpy, nervous, on edge, restive, twitchy (informal), uneasy

field noun 1 = **meadow**, grassland, green, greensward (archaic or literary), lea (poetic), mead (archaic), pasture 2 = **competitors**, applicants, candidates, competition, contestants, entrants, possibilities, runners 3 = **speciality**, bailiwick, bounds, confines, department, discipline, domain, environment, limits, line, metier, pale, province, purview, range, scope, specialty, sphere of activity, sphere of influence, sphere of interest, sphere of study, territory ♦ verb 4 Sport = **retrieve**, catch, pick up, return, stop 5 Informal = **deal with**, deflect, handle, turn aside

fiend noun 1 = **demon**, devil, evil spirit, hellhound 2 = **brute**, barbarian, beast, degenerate, ghoul, monster, ogre, savage 3 Informal = **enthusiast**, addict, energumen, fanatic, freak (informal), maniac

fiendish adjective = **wicked**, accursed, atrocious, black-hearted, cruel, demoniac, devilish, diabolical, hellish, implacable, infernal, inhuman, malevolent, malicious, malignant, monstrous, satanic, savage, ungodly, unspeakable

fierce adjective 1 = **wild**, baleful, barbarous, brutal, cruel, dangerous, fell (archaic), feral, ferocious, fiery, menacing, murderous, passionate, savage, threatening, tigerish, truculent, uncontrollable, untamed, vicious 2 = **stormy**, blustery, boisterous, furious,

howling, inclement, powerful, raging, strong, tempestuous, tumultuous, uncontrollable, violent 3 = **intense**, cut-throat, keen, relentless, strong
➤ **Antonyms**
≠ **wild**: affectionate, calm, civilized, cool, docile, domesticated, gentle, harmless, kind, mild, peaceful, submissive, tame ≠ **stormy**: temperate, tranquil

fiercely adverb = **ferociously**, frenziedly, furiously, in a frenzy, like cat and dog, menacingly, passionately, savagely, tempestuously, tigerishly, tooth and nail, uncontrolledly, viciously, with bared teeth, with no holds barred

fiery adjective 1 = **burning**, ablaze, afire, aflame, blazing, flaming, on fire 2 = **excitable**, fierce, hot-headed, impetuous, irascible, irritable, passionate

fiesta noun = **carnival**, celebration, fair, feast, festival, festivity, fête, gala, holiday, merrymaking, party, revel, revelry

fight verb 1 = **battle**, assault, bear arms against, box, brawl, carry on war, clash, close, combat, come to blows, conflict, contend, cross swords, do battle, engage, engage in hostilities, exchange blows, feud, fight like Kilkenny cats, go to war, grapple, joust, lock horns, row, scrap (informal), spar, struggle, take the field, take up arms against, tilt, tussle, wage war, war, wrestle 2 = **oppose**, contest, defy, dispute, make a stand against, resist, stand up to, strive, struggle, withstand 3 = **quarrel**, argue, bicker, dispute, fall out (informal), squabble, wrangle 4 = **engage in**, carry on, conduct, prosecute, wage 5 **fight shy of** = **avoid**, duck out of (informal), keep aloof from, keep at arm's length, shun, steer clear of ♦ noun 6 = **battle**, action, affray (Law), altercation, bagarre, bout, brawl, brush, clash, combat, conflict, contest, dispute, dissension, dogfight, duel, encounter, engagement, exchange of blows, fracas, fray, free-for-all (informal), head-to-head, hostilities, joust, melee or mêlée, passage of arms, riot, row, rumble (U.S. & N.Z. slang), scrap (informal), scrimmage, scuffle, set-to (informal), shindig (informal), shindy (informal), skirmish, sparring match, struggle, tussle, war 7 = **resistance**, belligerence, gameness, mettle, militancy, pluck, spirit, will to resist

fighter noun 1 = **boxer**, bruiser (informal), prize fighter, pugilist 2 = **soldier**, fighting man, man-at-arms, warrior 3 = **combatant**, antagonist, battler, belligerent, contender, contestant, disputant, militant

fighting noun = **battle**, bloodshed, blows struck, combat, conflict, hostilities, warfare

fight off verb = **repel**, beat off, drive away,

keep or hold at bay, repress, repulse, resist, stave off, ward off

figment noun As in **figment of one's imagination** = **invention**, creation, fable, fabrication, falsehood, fancy, fiction, improvisation, production

figurative adjective 1 = **symbolical**, allegorical, emblematical, metaphorical, representative, typical 2 = **poetical**, descriptive, fanciful, florid, flowery, ornate, pictorial
➤ Antonyms
≠**symbolical**: accurate, exact, factual, faithful, literal ≠**poetical**: prosaic, simple, true, unpoetical, unvarnished

figure noun 1 = **number**, character, cipher, digit, numeral, symbol 2 = **amount**, cost, price, sum, total, value 3 = **outline**, form, shadow, shape, silhouette 4 = **shape**, body, build, chassis (slang), frame, physique, proportions, torso 5 = **character**, big name, celebrity, dignitary, face (informal), force, leader, notability, notable, personage, personality, presence, somebody, worthy 6 = **diagram**, depiction, design, device, drawing, emblem, illustration, motif, pattern, representation, sketch ◆ verb 7 = **calculate**, add, compute, count, reckon, sum, tally, tot up, work out 8 usually with **in** = **feature**, act, appear, be conspicuous, be featured, be included, be mentioned, contribute to, have a place in, play a part 9 **it figures** = **it is to be expected**, it follows, it goes without saying

figured adjective = **decorated**, adorned, embellished, marked, ornamented, patterned, variegated

figurehead noun = **front man**, cipher, dummy, leader in name only, man of straw, mouthpiece, name, nonentity, puppet, straw man (chiefly U.S.), titular or nominal head, token

figure of speech noun = **expression**, conceit, image, trope, turn of phrase

figure out verb 1 = **calculate**, compute, reckon, work out 2 = **understand**, comprehend, decipher, fathom, make head or tail of (informal), make out, resolve, see, suss (out) (slang)

filament noun = **strand**, cilium (Biology & Zoology), fibre, fibril, pile, staple, string, thread, wire, wisp

filch verb = **steal**, abstract, cabbage (Brit. slang), crib (informal), embezzle, half-inch (old-fashioned slang), lift (informal), misappropriate, nick (slang, chiefly Brit.), pilfer, pinch (informal), purloin, rip off (slang), snaffle (Brit. informal), swipe (slang), take, thieve, walk off with

file¹ noun 1 = **folder**, case, data, documents,

dossier, information, portfolio 2 = **line**, column, list, queue, row, string ◆ verb 3 = **register**, document, enter, pigeonhole, put in place, record, slot in (informal) 4 = **march**, parade, troop

file² verb = **smooth**, abrade, burnish, furbish, polish, rasp, refine, rub, rub down, scrape, shape

filibuster noun 1 Chiefly U.S., with reference to legislation = **obstruction**, delay, hindrance, postponement, procrastination ◆ verb 2 Chiefly U.S., with reference to legislation = **obstruct**, delay, hinder, play for time, prevent, procrastinate, put off

filigree noun = **wirework**, lace, lacework, lattice, tracery

fill verb 1 = **stuff**, brim over, cram, crowd, furnish, glut, gorge, inflate, pack, pervade, replenish, sate, satiate, satisfy, stock, store, supply, swell 2 = **saturate**, charge, imbue, impregnate, overspread, pervade, suffuse 3 = **plug**, block, bung, close, cork, seal, stop 4 = **perform**, assign, carry out, discharge, engage, execute, fulfil, hold, occupy, officiate, take up ◆ noun 5 **one's fill** = **sufficient**, all one wants, ample, a sufficiency, enough, plenty
➤ Antonyms
verb ≠**stuff**: diminish, drain, empty, exhaust, shrink, subside, vacate, void

filler noun = **padding**, makeweight, stopgap

fill in verb 1 = **complete**, answer, fill out (U.S.), fill up 2 = **replace**, deputize, represent, stand in, sub, substitute, take the place of 3 Informal = **inform**, acquaint, apprise, bring up to date, give the facts or background, put wise (slang)

filling noun 1 = **stuffing**, contents, filler, innards (informal), inside, insides, padding, wadding ◆ adjective 2 = **satisfying**, ample, heavy, square, substantial

fillip noun = **stimulus**, goad, incentive, prod, push, spice, spur, zest

film noun 1 = **movie**, flick (slang), motion picture 2 = **layer**, coat, coating, covering, dusting, gauze, integument, membrane, pellicle, scum, skin, tissue ◆ verb 3 = **photograph**, shoot, take, video, videotape 4 **film over** = **cloud**, blear, blur, dull, haze, mist, veil

filmy adjective = **transparent**, chiffon, cobwebby, delicate, diaphanous, fine, finespun, flimsy, floaty, fragile, gauzy, gossamer, insubstantial, see-through, sheer

filter noun 1 = **sieve**, gauze, membrane, mesh, riddle, strainer ◆ verb 2 = **purify**, clarify, filtrate, refine, screen, sieve, sift, strain, winnow 3 = **trickle**, dribble, escape, exude, leach, leak, ooze, penetrate, percolate, seep, well

filth noun 1 = **dirt**, carrion, contamination, crap (*slang*), crud (*slang*), defilement, dung, excrement, excreta, faeces, filthiness, foul matter, foulness, garbage, grime, grot (*slang*), kak (*S. African slang*), muck, nastiness, ordure, pollution, putrefaction, putrescence, refuse, sewage, shit (*taboo slang*), slime, sludge, squalor, uncleanness 2 = **obscenity**, corruption, dirty-mindedness, impurity, indecency, pornography, smut, vileness, vulgarity

filthy adjective 1 = **dirty**, faecal, feculent, foul, nasty, polluted, putrid, scummy, scuzzy (*slang, chiefly U.S.*), slimy, squalid, unclean, vile 2 = **muddy**, begrimed, black, blackened, grimy, grubby, miry, mucky, mud-encrusted, scuzzy (*slang, chiefly U.S.*), smoky, sooty, unwashed 3 = **obscene**, bawdy, coarse, corrupt, depraved, dirty-minded, foul, foul-mouthed, impure, indecent, lewd, licentious, pornographic, smutty, suggestive, X-rated (*informal*)

final adjective 1 = **last**, closing, concluding, end, eventual, last-minute, latest, terminal, terminating, ultimate 2 = **conclusive**, absolute, decided, decisive, definite, definitive, determinate, finished, incontrovertible, irrevocable, settled
➤ **Antonyms**
≠**last**: earliest, first, initial, introductory, maiden, opening, original, precursory, prefatory, premier, preparatory

finale noun = **ending**, climax, close, conclusion, crowning glory, culmination, denouement, epilogue, finis, last act
➤ **Antonyms**
commencement, exordium, foreword, intro (*informal*), lead-in, opening, overture, preamble, preface, preliminaries, prelude, proem, prolegomenon, prologue

finality noun = **conclusiveness**, certitude, decidedness, decisiveness, definiteness, inevitableness, irrevocability, resolution, unavoidability

finalize verb = **complete**, agree, clinch, conclude, decide, settle, sew up (*informal*), shake hands, tie up, work out, wrap up (*informal*)

finally adverb 1 = **eventually**, at last, at length, at long last, at the end of the day, at the last, at the last moment, in the end, in the fullness of time, in the long run, lastly, ultimately, when all is said and done 2 = **in conclusion**, in summary, lastly, to conclude 3 = **conclusively**, beyond the shadow of a doubt, completely, convincingly, decisively, for all time, for ever, for good, inescapably, inexorably, irrevocably, once and for all, permanently

finance verb 1 = **fund**, back, bankroll (*U.S.*), float, guarantee, pay for, provide security for, set up in business, subsidize, support, underwrite ◆ noun 2 = **economics**, accounts, banking, business, commerce, financial affairs, investment, money, money management

finances plural noun = **resources**, affairs, assets, capital, cash, financial condition, funds, money, wherewithal

financial adjective = **economic**, budgeting, fiscal, monetary, money, pecuniary

find verb 1 = **discover**, catch sight of, chance upon, come across, come up with, descry, encounter, espy, expose, ferret out, hit upon, lay one's hand on, light upon, locate, meet, recognize, run to earth, run to ground, spot, stumble upon, track down, turn up, uncover, unearth 2 = **realise**, arrive at, ascertain, become aware, detect, discover, experience, learn, note, notice, observe, perceive, remark 3 = **get**, achieve, acquire, attain, earn, gain, obtain, procure, win 4 = **provide**, be responsible for, bring, contribute, cough up (*informal*), furnish, purvey, supply ◆ noun 5 = **discovery**, acquisition, asset, bargain, catch, good buy
➤ **Antonyms**
verb ≠**discover**: lose, mislay, misplace, miss, overlook

finding noun = **conclusion**, award, decision, decree, judgment, pronouncement, recommendation, verdict

find out verb 1 = **learn**, detect, discover, note, observe, perceive, realize 2 = **detect**, bring to light, catch, disclose, expose, reveal, rumble (*Brit. informal*), suss (out) (*slang*), uncover, unmask

fine[1] adjective 1 = **excellent**, accomplished, admirable, beautiful, choice, divine, exceptional, exquisite, first-class, first-rate, great, magnificent, masterly, ornate, outstanding, rare, select, showy, skilful, splendid, sterling, superior, supreme, world-class 2 = **sunny**, balmy, bright, clear, clement, cloudless, dry, fair, pleasant 3 = **satisfactory**, acceptable, agreeable, all right, convenient, good, hunky-dory (*informal*), O.K. or okay (*informal*), suitable 4 = **delicate**, dainty, elegant, expensive, exquisite, fragile, quality 5 = **subtle**, abstruse, acute, critical, discriminating, fastidious, hairsplitting, intelligent, keen, minute, nice, precise, quick, refined, sensitive, sharp, tasteful, tenuous 6 = **slender**, delicate, diaphanous, fine-grained, flimsy, gauzy, gossamer, light, lightweight, powdered, powdery, pulverized, sheer, small, thin 7 = **sharp**, brilliant, cutting, honed, keen, polished, razor-sharp 8 = **good-looking**, attractive, bonny, handsome, lovely, smart, striking, stylish, well-favoured

fine

277

fire

> **Antonyms**
≠**excellent:** indifferent, inferior, poor, second rate, substandard ≠**sunny:** cloudy, dull, overcast, unpleasant ≠**delicate:** blunt, coarse, crude, dull, heavy, rough

fine² *noun* **1** = **penalty**, amercement (*obsolete*), damages, forfeit, punishment ◆ *verb* **2** = **penalize**, amerce (*archaic*), mulct, punish

finery *noun* = **splendour**, best bib and tucker (*informal*), decorations, frippery, gear (*informal*), gewgaws, glad rags (*informal*), ornaments, showiness, Sunday best, trappings, trinkets

finesse *noun* **1** = **skill**, adeptness, adroitness, artfulness, cleverness, craft, delicacy, diplomacy, discretion, know-how (*informal*), polish, quickness, savoir-faire, sophistication, subtlety, tact ◆ *verb* **2** = **manoeuvre**, bluff, manipulate

finger *verb* **1** = **touch**, feel, fiddle with (*informal*), handle, manipulate, maul, meddle with, paw (*informal*), play about with, toy with ◆ *noun* **2 put one's finger on** = **identify**, bring to mind, discover, find out, hit the nail on the head, hit upon, indicate, locate, pin down, place, recall, remember

finicky *adjective* = **fussy**, choosy (*informal*), critical, dainty, difficult, fastidious, finicking, hard to please, nit-picking (*informal*), overnice, overparticular, particular, picky (*informal*), scrupulous, squeamish

finish *verb* **1** = **stop**, accomplish, achieve, bring to a close *or* conclusion, carry through, cease, close, complete, conclude, culminate, deal with, discharge, do, end, execute, finalize, fulfil, get done, get out of the way, make short work of, put the finishing touch(es) to, put the tin lid on, round off, settle, terminate, wind up, wrap up (*informal*) **2** = **consume**, deplete, devour, dispatch, dispose of, drain, drink, eat, empty, exhaust, expend, spend, use, use up **3** = **perfect**, elaborate, polish, refine **4** = **coat**, face, gild, lacquer, polish, smooth off, stain, texture, veneer, wax **5** = **destroy**, administer *or* give the coup de grâce, annihilate, best, bring down, defeat, dispose of, drive to the wall, exterminate, get rid of, kill, move in for the kill, overcome, overpower, put an end to, put paid to, rout, ruin, worst ◆ *noun* **6** = **end**, cessation, close, closing, completion, conclusion, culmination, denouement, ending, finale, last stage(s), run-in, termination, winding up (*informal*), wind-up **7** = **defeat**, annihilation, bankruptcy, curtains (*informal*), death, end, end of the road, liquidation, ruin **8** = **surface**, appearance, grain, lustre, patina, polish, shine, smoothness, texture **9** = **polish**, cultivation, culture, elaboration,

perfection, refinement, sophistication
> **Antonyms**
verb ≠**stop:** begin, commence, create, embark on, instigate, start, undertake ◆ *noun* ≠**end:** beginning, birth, commencement, conception, genesis, inauguration, inception, instigation, preamble, preface, prologue

finished *adjective* **1** = **over**, accomplished, achieved, closed, complete, completed, concluded, done, ended, entire, final, finalized, full, in the past, over and done with, sewed up (*informal*), shut, terminated, through, tied up, wrapped up (*informal*) **2** = **spent**, done, drained, empty, exhausted, gone, played out (*informal*), used up **3** = **polished**, accomplished, classic, consummate, cultivated, elegant, expert, flawless, impeccable, masterly, perfected, professional, proficient, refined, skilled, smooth, urbane **4** = **ruined**, bankrupt, defeated, devastated, done for (*informal*), doomed, gone, liquidated, lost, through, undone, washed up (*informal, chiefly U.S.*), wiped out, wound up, wrecked
> **Antonyms**
≠**over:** begun, incomplete ≠**polished:** basic, coarse, crude, imperfect, rough, unfinished, unrefined, unskilled, unsophisticated

finite *adjective* = **limited**, bounded, circumscribed, conditioned, delimited, demarcated, restricted, subject to limitations, terminable
> **Antonyms**
boundless, endless, eternal, everlasting, immeasurable, infinite, interminable, limitless, perpetual, unbounded

fire *noun* **1** = **flames**, blaze, combustion, conflagration, inferno **2** = **bombardment**, barrage, cannonade, flak, fusillade, hail, salvo, shelling, sniping, volley **3** = **passion**, animation, ardour, brio, burning passion, dash, eagerness, élan, enthusiasm, excitement, fervency, fervour, force, heat, impetuosity, intensity, life, light, lustre, pizzazz *or* pizazz (*informal*), radiance, scintillation, sparkle, spirit, splendour, verve, vigour, virtuosity, vivacity **4 on fire: a** = **burning**, ablaze, aflame, alight, blazing, fiery, flaming, in flames **b** = **ardent**, eager, enthusiastic, excited, inspired, passionate ◆ *verb* **5** = **shoot**, detonate, discharge, eject, explode, hurl, launch, let loose (*informal*), let off, loose, pull the trigger, set off, shell, touch off **6** *Informal* = **dismiss**, cashier, discharge, give marching orders, give the boot (*slang*), give the bullet (*Brit. slang*), give the push, kiss off (*slang, chiefly U.S. & Canad.*), make redundant, sack (*informal*), show the door **7** = **set fire to**, enkindle,

ignite, kindle, light, put a match to, set
ablaze, set aflame, set alight, set on fire,
torch **8** = **inspire**, animate, arouse, electrify,
enliven, excite, galvanize, impassion, incite,
inflame, inspirit, irritate, quicken, rouse, stir

firearm *noun* = **weapon**, gun, handgun,
piece (*slang*), pistol, revolver, shooter
(*slang*)

firebrand *noun* = **rabble-rouser**, agitator,
demagogue, fomenter, incendiary,
instigator, soapbox orator, tub-thumper

fireworks *plural noun* **1** = **pyrotechnics**,
illuminations **2** *Informal* = **trouble**, fit of
rage, hysterics, paroxysms, rage, row, storm,
temper, uproar

firm [1] *adjective* **1** = **hard**, close-grained,
compact, compressed, concentrated,
congealed, dense, inelastic, inflexible, jelled,
jellified, rigid, set, solid, solidified, stiff,
unyielding **2** = **secure**, anchored, braced,
cemented, embedded, fast, fastened, fixed,
immovable, motionless, riveted, robust,
rooted, secured, stable, stationary, steady,
strong, sturdy, taut, tight, unfluctuating,
unmoving, unshakable **3** = **determined**,
adamant, constant, definite, fixed,
immovable, inflexible, obdurate, resolute,
resolved, set on, settled, stalwart, staunch,
steadfast, strict, true, unalterable,
unbending, unfaltering, unflinching,
unshakable, unshaken, unswerving,
unwavering, unyielding
➤ **Antonyms**
≠**hard:** flabby, flaccid, limp, soft ≠**secure:**
flimsy, insecure, loose, shaky, unreliable,
unstable, unsteady ≠**determined:**
inconstant, irresolute, wavering

firm [2] *noun* = **company**, association, business,
concern, conglomerate, corporation,
enterprise, house, organization, outfit
(*informal*), partnership

firmament *noun Literary* = **sky**, heaven,
heavens, the blue, the skies, vault, vault of
heaven

firmly *adverb* **1** = **securely**, enduringly,
immovably, like a rock, motionlessly,
steadily, tightly, unflinchingly, unshakably **2**
= **resolutely**, determinedly, staunchly,
steadfastly, strictly, through thick and thin,
unchangeably, unwaveringly, with a rod of
iron, with decision

firmness *noun* **1** = **hardness**, compactness,
density, fixedness, inelasticity, inflexibility,
resistance, rigidity, solidity, stiffness **2**
= **steadiness**, immovability, soundness,
stability, strength, tautness, tensile strength,
tension, tightness **3** = **resolve**, constancy,
fixedness, fixity of purpose, inflexibility,
obduracy, resolution, staunchness,
steadfastness, strength of will, strictness

first *adjective* **1** = **earliest**, initial,
introductory, maiden, opening, original,
premier, primeval, primitive, primordial,
pristine **2** = **elementary**, basic, cardinal,
fundamental, key, primary, rudimentary **3**
= **foremost**, chief, head, highest, leading,
pre-eminent, prime, principal, ruling ♦ *noun*
4 *As in* **from the first** = **start**, beginning,
commencement, inception, introduction,
outset, starting point, word "go" (*informal*)
♦ *adverb* **5** = **to begin with**, at the
beginning, at the outset, before all else,
beforehand, firstly, initially, in the first place,
to start with

first-class *adjective* = **excellent**, A1 *or*
A-one (*informal*), ace (*informal*), bad
(*slang*), bitchin' (*U.S. slang*), boffo (*slang*),
brill (*informal*), brilliant, capital, champion,
choice, crack (*slang*), cracking (*Brit.
informal*), crucial (*slang*), dope (*slang*),
elite, exceptional, exemplary, first-rate,
five-star, great, jim-dandy (*slang*),
marvellous, matchless, mean (*slang*),
outstanding, premium, prime, second to
none, sovereign, superb, superlative, tiptop,
top, top-class, top-drawer, top-flight,
top-notch (*informal*), topping (*Brit. slang*),
tops (*slang*), twenty-four carat, very good,
world-class
➤ **Antonyms**
inferior, second-class, second-rate, shocking
(*informal*), terrible, third-rate

first-hand *adjective, adverb* = **direct**,
straight from the horse's mouth

first-rate *adjective* = **excellent**, A1 *or* A-one
(*informal*), admirable, bitchin' (*U.S. slang*),
bodacious (*slang, chiefly U.S.*), boffo
(*slang*), brill (*informal*), chillin' (*U.S. slang*),
crack (*slang*), cracking (*Brit. informal*),
crucial (*slang*), def (*slang*), dope (*slang*),
elite, exceptional, exclusive, first class,
jim-dandy (*slang*), mean (*slang*), mega
(*slang*), outstanding, prime, second to
none, sovereign, superb, superlative, the
dog's bollocks (*taboo slang*), tiptop, top,
top-notch (*informal*), topping (*Brit. slang*),
tops (*slang*), world-class

fiscal *adjective* = **financial**, budgetary,
economic, monetary, money, pecuniary

fish for *verb* = **seek**, angle for, elicit, hint at,
hope for, hunt for, invite, look for, search
for, solicit

fish out *verb* = **pull out**, extract, extricate,
find, haul out, produce

fishy *adjective* **1** *Informal* = **suspicious**,
cock-and-bull (*informal*), dodgy (*Brit.,
Austral., & N.Z. slang*), doubtful,
dubious, funny (*informal*), implausible,
improbable, odd, queer, questionable, rum
(*Brit. slang*), suspect, unlikely **2** = **fishlike**,
piscatorial, piscatory, piscine

fission *noun* = **splitting**, breaking, cleavage, division, parting, rending, rupture, schism, scission

fissure *noun* = **crack**, breach, break, chink, cleavage, cleft, cranny, crevice, fault, fracture, gap, hole, interstice, opening, rent, rift, rupture, slit, split

fit[1] *verb* **1** = **suit**, accord, agree, be consonant, belong, concur, conform, correspond, dovetail, go, interlock, join, match, meet, tally **2** = **adapt**, adjust, alter, arrange, customize, dispose, fashion, modify, place, position, shape, tweak (*informal*) **3** = **equip**, accommodate, accoutre, arm, fit out, kit out, outfit, prepare, provide, rig out ♦ *adjective* **4** = **appropriate**, able, adapted, adequate, apposite, apt, becoming, capable, competent, convenient, correct, deserving, equipped, expedient, fitted, fitting, good enough, meet (*archaic*), prepared, proper, qualified, ready, right, seemly, suitable, trained, well-suited, worthy **5** = **healthy**, able-bodied, as right as rain, hale, in good condition, in good shape, in good trim, robust, strapping, toned up, trim, well
➤ **Antonyms**
adjective ≠**appropriate:** amiss, ill-fitted, ill-suited, improper, inadequate, inappropriate, unfit, unprepared, unseemly, unsuitable, untimely ≠**healthy:** flabby, in poor condition, out of shape, out of trim, unfit, unhealthy

fit[2] *noun* **1** = **seizure**, attack, bout, convulsion, paroxysm, spasm **2** = **outbreak**, bout, burst, outburst, spell **3 by fits and starts** = **spasmodically**, erratically, fitfully, intermittently, irregularly, on and off, sporadically, unsystematically

fitful *adjective* = **irregular**, broken, desultory, disturbed, erratic, flickering, fluctuating, haphazard, impulsive, inconstant, intermittent, spasmodic, sporadic, uneven, unstable, variable
➤ **Antonyms**
constant, equable, even, orderly, predictable, regular, steady, systematic, unchanging, uniform

fitfully *adverb* = **irregularly**, by fits and starts, desultorily, erratically, in fits and starts, in snatches, intermittently, interruptedly, off and on, spasmodically, sporadically

fitness *noun* **1** = **appropriateness**, adaptation, applicability, aptness, competence, eligibility, pertinence, preparedness, propriety, qualifications, readiness, seemliness, suitability **2** = **health**, good condition, good health, robustness, strength, vigour, wellness

fitted *adjective* **1** *often with* **with** = **equipped**, accoutred, appointed, armed, furnished, outfitted, provided, rigged out, set up, supplied **2** = **built-in**, permanent

fitting *adjective* **1** = **appropriate**, apposite, becoming, *comme il faut*, correct, decent, decorous, desirable, meet (*archaic*), proper, right, seemly, suitable ♦ *noun* **2** = **accessory**, attachment, component, connection, part, piece, unit
➤ **Antonyms**
adjective ≠**appropriate:** ill-suited, improper, unfitting, unseemly, unsuitable

fittings *plural noun* = **furnishings**, accessories, accoutrements, appointments, appurtenances, bells and whistles, conveniences, equipment, extras, furniture, trimmings

fix *verb* **1** = **place**, anchor, embed, establish, implant, install, locate, plant, position, root, set, settle **2** = **repair**, adjust, correct, mend, patch up, put to rights, regulate, see to, sort **3** = **fasten**, attach, bind, cement, connect, couple, glue, link, make fast, pin, secure, stick, tie **4** = **decide**, agree on, appoint, arrange, arrive at, conclude, define, determine, establish, limit, name, resolve, set, settle, specify **5** = **focus**, direct, level at, rivet **6** *Informal* = **rig**, bribe, fiddle (*informal*), influence, manipulate, manoeuvre, pull strings (*informal*) **7** *Slang* = **sort (someone) out** (*informal*), cook (someone's) goose (*informal*), get even with (*informal*), get revenge on, pay back, settle (someone's) hash (*informal*), take retribution on, wreak vengeance on ♦ *noun* **8** *Informal* = **predicament**, difficult situation, difficulty, dilemma, embarrassment, hole (*slang*), hot water (*informal*), jam (*informal*), mess, pickle (*informal*), plight, quandary, spot (*informal*), ticklish situation, tight spot

fixated *adjective* = **obsessed**, absorbed, attached, besotted, captivated, caught up in, devoted, engrossed, fascinated, hung up on (*slang*), hypnotized, infatuated, mesmerized, preoccupied, single-minded, smitten, spellbound, taken up with, wrapped up in
➤ **Antonyms**
detached, disinterested, dispassionate, indifferent, open-minded, uncommitted, unconcerned, uninvolved

fixation *noun* = **obsession**, addiction, complex, hang-up (*informal*), *idée fixe*, infatuation, mania, preoccupation, thing (*informal*)

fixed *adjective* **1** = **immovable**, anchored, attached, established, made fast, permanent, rigid, rooted, secure, set **2** = **steady**, intent, level, resolute, unbending, unblinking, undeviating, unflinching, unwavering **3** = **agreed**, arranged, decided, definite, established, planned, resolved, settled **4** = **mended**, going, in working order, put

right, repaired, sorted **5** *Informal* = **rigged**, framed, manipulated, packed, put-up
➤ **Antonyms**
≠**immovable:** bending, mobile, motile, moving, pliant, unfixed ≠**steady:** inconstant, varying, wavering

fixity *noun* = **steadiness**, doggedness, intentness, perseverance, persistence, stability

fix up *verb* **1** = **arrange**, agree on, fix, organize, plan, settle, sort out **2** *often with* **with** = **provide**, accommodate, arrange for, bring about, furnish, lay on

fizz *verb* = **bubble**, effervesce, fizzle, froth, hiss, sparkle, sputter

fizzle out *verb Informal* = **die away**, abort, collapse, come to nothing, end in disappointment, fail, fall through, fold (*informal*), miss the mark, peter out

fizzy *adjective* = **bubbly**, bubbling, carbonated, effervescent, gassy, sparkling

flab *noun* = **fat**, beef (*informal*), flabbiness, flesh, fleshiness, heaviness, overweight, plumpness, slackness, weight

flabbergasted *adjective* = **astonished**, abashed, amazed, astounded, bowled over (*informal*), confounded, dazed, disconcerted, dumbfounded, gobsmacked (*Brit. slang*), lost for words, nonplussed, overcome, overwhelmed, rendered speechless, speechless, staggered, struck dumb, stunned

flabby *adjective* **1** = **limp**, baggy, drooping, flaccid, floppy, hanging, lax, loose, pendulous, sagging, slack, sloppy, toneless, unfit, yielding **2** = **weak**, effete, enervated, feeble, impotent, ineffective, ineffectual, nerveless, spineless, wimpish *or* wimpy (*informal*), wussy (*slang*)
➤ **Antonyms**
≠**limp:** firm, hard, solid, strong, taut, tense, tight, tough

flaccid *adjective* = **limp**, drooping, flabby, lax, loose, nerveless, slack, soft, weak

flaccidity *noun* = **limpness**, flabbiness, looseness, nervelessness, slackness, softness

flag¹ *noun* **1** = **banner**, banderole, colours, ensign, gonfalon, jack, pennant, pennon, standard, streamer ♦ *verb* **2** = **mark**, docket, indicate, label, note, tab **3** *sometimes with* **down** = **hail**, salute, signal, warn, wave

flag² *verb* = **weaken**, abate, decline, die, droop, ebb, fade, fail, faint, fall, fall off, feel the pace, languish, peter out, pine, sag, sink, slump, succumb, taper off, wane, weary, wilt

flagellate *verb* = **whip**, beat, castigate, chastise, flay, flog, lambast(e), lash, scourge, thrash

flagellation *noun* = **whipping**, beating, flogging, lashing, thrashing

flagging *adjective* = **weakening**, declining, decreasing, deteriorating, ebbing, fading, failing, faltering, giving up, sinking, slowing down, tiring, waning, wilting

flagrant *adjective* = **outrageous**, arrant, atrocious, awful, barefaced, blatant, bold, brazen, crying, dreadful, egregious, enormous, flagitious, flaunting, glaring, heinous, immodest, infamous, notorious, open, ostentatious, out-and-out, scandalous, shameless, undisguised
➤ **Antonyms**
delicate, faint, implied, indirect, insinuated, slight, subtle, understated

flagstone *noun* = **paving stone**, block, flag, slab

flail *verb* = **thrash**, beat, thresh, windmill

flair *noun* **1** = **ability**, accomplishment, aptitude, faculty, feel, genius, gift, knack, mastery, talent **2** = **style**, chic, dash, discernment, elegance, panache, stylishness, taste

flak *noun* = **criticism**, abuse, bad press, censure, complaints, condemnation, denigration, disapprobation, disapproval, disparagement, fault-finding, hostility, opposition, stick (*slang*)

flake *noun* **1** = **chip**, disk, lamina, layer, peeling, scale, shaving, sliver, squama (*Biology*), wafer ♦ *verb* **2** = **chip**, blister, desquamate, peel (off), scale (off)

flake out *verb* = **collapse**, faint, keel over, lose consciousness, pass out, swoon (*literary*)

flamboyance *noun* = **showiness**, bravura, brio, chic, dash, élan, exhibitionism, extravagance, flair, flamboyancy, flashiness, ostentation, panache, pizzazz *or* pizazz (*informal*), pomp, show, sparkle, style, stylishness, swagger, swank (*informal*), theatricality
➤ **Antonyms**
drabness, dullness, flatness, restraint, simplicity, unobtrusiveness

flamboyant *adjective* **1** = **showy**, actorly, baroque, camp (*informal*), dashing, elaborate, extravagant, florid, ornate, ostentatious, over the top (*informal*), rich, rococo, swashbuckling, theatrical **2** = **colourful**, brilliant, dazzling, exciting, glamorous, glitzy (*slang*)

flame *noun* **1** = **fire**, blaze, brightness, light **2** = **passion**, affection, ardour, enthusiasm, fervency, fervour, fire, intensity, keenness, warmth **3** *Informal* = **sweetheart**, beau, beloved, boyfriend, girlfriend, heart-throb (*Brit.*), ladylove, lover ♦ *verb* **4** = **burn**, blaze, flare, flash, glare, glow, shine

flaming *adjective* **1** = **burning**, ablaze, afire, blazing, brilliant, fiery, glowing, ignited, in flames, raging, red, red-hot **2** = **intense**, angry, ardent, aroused, frenzied, hot, impassioned, raging, scintillating, vehement, vivid

flammable *adjective* = **combustible**, ignitable, incendiary, inflammable

flank *noun* 1 = **side**, ham, haunch, hip, loin, quarter, thigh 2 = **wing**, side ◆ *verb* 3 = **border**, book-end, bound, edge, fringe, line, screen, skirt, wall

flannel *noun* 1 *Informal* = **prevarication**, baloney (*informal*), blarney, equivocation, flattery, hedging, soft soap (*informal*), sweet talk (*U.S. informal*), waffle (*informal, chiefly Brit.*), weasel words (*informal, chiefly U.S.*) ◆ *verb* 2 *Informal* = **prevaricate**, blarney, butter up, equivocate, flatter, hedge, pull the wool over (someone's) eyes, soft-soap (*informal*), sweet-talk (*informal*), waffle (*informal, chiefly Brit.*)

flap *verb* 1 = **flutter**, agitate, beat, flail, shake, swing, swish, thrash, thresh, vibrate, wag, wave ◆ *noun* 2 = **flutter**, bang, banging, beating, shaking, swinging, swish, waving 3 = **cover**, apron, fly, fold, lapel, lappet, overlap, skirt, tab, tail 4 *Informal* = **panic**, agitation, commotion, fluster, state (*informal*), stew (*informal*), sweat (*informal*), tizzy (*informal*), twitter (*informal*)

flare *verb* 1 = **blaze**, burn up, dazzle, flicker, flutter, glare, waver 2 = **widen**, broaden, spread out ◆ *noun* 3 = **flame**, blaze, burst, dazzle, flash, flicker, glare

flare up *verb* = **lose one's temper**, blaze, blow one's top (*informal*), boil over, break out, explode, fire up, fly off the handle (*informal*), lose control, lose it (*informal*), lose one's cool (*informal*), lose the plot (*informal*), throw a tantrum

flash *noun* 1 = **blaze**, burst, coruscation, dazzle, flare, flicker, gleam, ray, scintillation, shaft, shimmer, spark, sparkle, streak, twinkle 2 = **burst**, demonstration, display, manifestation, outburst, show, sign, touch 3 = **moment**, bat of an eye (*informal*), instant, jiffy (*informal*), second, shake, split second, trice, twinkling, twinkling of an eye, two shakes of a lamb's tail (*informal*) ◆ *adjective* 4 *Informal* = **ostentatious**, cheap, glamorous, naff (*Brit. slang*), tacky (*informal*), tasteless, vulgar ◆ *verb* 5 = **blaze**, coruscate, flare, flicker, glare, gleam, glint, glisten, glitter, light, scintillate, shimmer, sparkle, twinkle 6 = **speed**, barrel (along) (*informal, chiefly U.S. & Canad.*), bolt, burn rubber (*informal*), dart, dash, fly, race, shoot, sprint, streak, sweep, whistle, zoom 7 *Informal* = **show**, display, exhibit, expose, flaunt, flourish

flashy *adjective* = **showy**, brash, cheap,

cheap and nasty, flamboyant, flaunting, garish, gaudy, glittery, glitzy (*slang*), in poor taste, jazzy (*informal*), loud, meretricious, naff (*Brit. slang*), ostentatious, over the top (*informal*), snazzy (*informal*), tacky (*informal*), tasteless, lawdry, tinselly
➤ **Antonyms**
downbeat, low-key, modest, natural, plain, unaffected, understated

flat[1] *adjective* 1 = **even**, horizontal, level, levelled, low, planar, plane, smooth, unbroken 2 = **horizontal**, laid low, lying full length, outstretched, prone, prostrate, reclining, recumbent, supine 3 = **punctured**, blown out, burst, collapsed, deflated, empty 4 = **absolute**, categorical, direct, downright, explicit, final, fixed, out-and-out, peremptory, plain, positive, straight, unconditional, unequivocal, unmistakable, unqualified 5 = **dull**, boring, dead, flavourless, ho-hum (*informal*), insipid, jejune, lacklustre, lifeless, monotonous, pointless, prosaic, spiritless, stale, tedious, tiresome, uninteresting, vapid, watery, weak ◆ *adverb* 6 = **completely**, absolutely, categorically, exactly, point blank, precisely, utterly 7 **flat out** *Informal* = **at full speed**, all out, at full gallop, at full tilt, for all one is worth, hell for leather (*informal*), posthaste, under full steam ◆ *noun* 8 *often plural* = **plain**, lowland, marsh, mud flat, shallow, shoal, strand, swamp
➤ **Antonyms**
adjective ≠**even**: broken, hilly, irregular, rolling, rough, rugged, slanting, sloping, uneven, up and down ≠**horizontal**: on end, perpendicular, straight, upright, vertical ≠**dull**: bubbly, effervescent, exciting, fizzy, sparkling, zestful

flat[2] *noun* = **apartment**, rooms

flatly *adverb* = **absolutely**, categorically, completely, positively, unhesitatingly

flatness *noun* 1 = **evenness**, horizontality, levelness, smoothness, uniformity 2 = **dullness**, emptiness, insipidity, monotony, staleness, tedium, vapidity

flatten *verb* 1 = **level**, compress, even out, iron out, plaster, raze, roll, smooth off, squash, trample 2 *Informal* = **knock down**, bowl over, deck (*slang*), fell, floor, knock off one's feet, prostrate 3 *Informal* = **crush**, subdue

flatter *verb* 1 = **praise**, blandish, butter up, cajole, compliment, court, fawn, flannel (*Brit. informal*), humour, inveigle, lay it on (thick) (*slang*), pander to, puff, soft-soap (*informal*), sweet-talk (*informal*), wheedle 2 = **suit**, become, do something for, enhance, set off, show to advantage

flattering *adjective* 1 = **ingratiating**, adulatory, complimentary, fawning, fulsome,

gratifying, honeyed, honey-tongued, laudatory, sugary **2 = becoming**, effective, enhancing, kind, well-chosen
➤ **Antonyms**
≠**ingratiating**: blunt, candid, honest, straight, uncomplimentary ≠**becoming**: not shown in the best light, not shown to advantage, plain, unattractive, unbecoming, unflattering, warts and all

flattery *noun* **= obsequiousness**, adulation, blandishment, blarney, cajolery, false praise, fawning, flannel (*Brit. informal*), fulsomeness, honeyed words, servility, soft-soap (*informal*), sweet-talk (*informal*), sycophancy, toadyism

flatulence *noun* **= wind**, borborygmus (*Medical*), eructation

flaunt *verb* **= show off**, boast, brandish, display, disport, exhibit, flash about, flourish, make a (great) show of, make an exhibition of, parade, sport (*informal*), vaunt

flavour *noun* **1 = taste**, aroma, essence, extract, flavouring, odour, piquancy, relish, savour, seasoning, smack, tang, zest, zing (*informal*) **2 = quality**, aspect, character, essence, feel, feeling, property, soupçon, stamp, style, suggestion, tinge, tone, touch ♦ *verb* **3 = season**, ginger up, imbue, infuse, lace, leaven, spice
➤ **Antonyms**
noun ≠**taste**: blandness, flatness, insipidity, tastelessness

flavouring *noun* **= essence**, extract, spirit, tincture, zest

flaw *noun* **= weakness**, blemish, chink in one's armour, defect, disfigurement, failing, fault, imperfection, scar, speck, spot, weak spot

flawed *adjective* **= damaged**, blemished, broken, chipped, cracked, defective, erroneous, faulty, imperfect, unsound

flawless *adjective* **= perfect**, faultless, impeccable, spotless, unblemished, unsullied

flay *verb* **1 = skin**, excoriate **2 = upbraid**, castigate, excoriate, execrate, give a tongue-lashing, pull to pieces (*informal*), revile, slam (*slang*), tear a strip off, tear into (*informal*)

fleabite *noun* **= trifle**, drop in the ocean, nothing, piddling amount, pinprick

flea-bitten *adjective Informal* **= shabby**, crawling, decrepit, fetid, flea-ridden, frowsty, grotty (*slang*), grubby, infested, insalubrious, lousy, mean, mucky, pediculous (*Medical*), run-down, scabby, scruffy, scurfy, sleazy, slummy, sordid, squalid, tatty, unhygienic

fleck *noun* **1 = mark**, dot, pinpoint, speck, speckle, spot, streak ♦ *verb* **2 = speckle**, bespeckle, besprinkle, dapple, dot, dust,

mark, mottle, spot, stipple, streak, variegate

fledgling *noun* **= chick**, nestling

flee *verb* **= run away**, abscond, avoid, beat a hasty retreat, bolt, cut and run (*informal*), decamp, depart, do a runner (*slang*), escape, fly, fly the coop (*U.S. & Canad. informal*), get away, hook it (*slang*), leave, make a quick exit, make off, make oneself scarce (*informal*), make one's escape, make one's getaway, scarper (*Brit. slang*), shun, skedaddle (*informal*), slope off, split (*slang*), take a powder (*U.S. & Canad. slang*), take flight, take it on the lam (*U.S. & Canad. slang*), take off (*informal*), take to one's heels, turn tail, vanish

fleece *noun* **1 = wool** ♦ *verb* **2 = cheat**, bleed (*informal*), con (*informal*), cozen, defraud, despoil, diddle (*informal*), mulct, overcharge, plunder, rifle, rip off (*slang*), rob, rook (*slang*), sell a pup, skin (*slang*), soak (*U.S. & Canad. slang*), steal, stiff (*slang*), swindle, take for a ride (*informal*), take to the cleaners (*slang*) **3 = shear**, clip

fleecy *adjective* **= woolly**, downy, fluffy, shaggy, soft

fleet[1] *noun* **= navy**, argosy, armada, flotilla, naval force, sea power, squadron, task force, vessels, warships

fleet[2] *adjective* **= swift**, fast, flying, mercurial, meteoric, nimble, nimble-footed, quick, rapid, speedy, winged

fleeting *adjective* **= momentary**, brief, ephemeral, evanescent, flitting, flying, fugacious, fugitive, here today, gone tomorrow, passing, short, short-lived, temporary, transient, transitory
➤ **Antonyms**
abiding, continuing, durable, enduring, eternal, imperishable, lasting, long-lasting, long-lived, permanent

flesh *noun* **1 = meat**, beef (*informal*), body, brawn, fat, fatness, food, tissue, weight **2 = physical nature**, animality, body, carnality, flesh and blood, human nature, physicality, sensuality **3 one's own flesh and blood = family**, blood, kin, kindred, kinsfolk, kith and kin, relations, relatives

fleshly *adjective* **1 = carnal**, animal, bodily, erotic, lascivious, lecherous, lustful, sensual **2 = worldly**, corporal, corporeal, earthly, human, material, mundane, of this world, physical, secular, terrestrial

fleshy *adjective* **= plump**, ample, beefy (*informal*), brawny, chubby, chunky, corpulent, fat, hefty, meaty, obese, overweight, podgy, stout, tubby, well-padded

flex *verb* **= bend**, angle, contract, crook, curve, tighten

flexibility *noun* **1 = pliancy**, elasticity, give

(*informal*), pliability, resilience, springiness, tensility **2 = adaptability**, adjustability, complaisance

flexible *adjective* **1 = pliable**, bendable, ductile, elastic, limber, lissom(e), lithe, mouldable, plastic, pliant, springy, stretchy, supple, tensile, willowy, yielding **2 = adaptable**, adjustable, discretionary, open, variable
➤ **Antonyms**
≠**pliable**: fixed, immovable, inflexible, rigid, stiff, tough, unyielding ≠**adaptable**: absolute, inflexible

flick *verb* **1 = strike**, dab, fillip, flip, hit, jab, peck, rap, tap, touch **2 flick through = browse**, flip through, glance at, skim, skip, thumb ◆ *noun* **3 = tap**, fillip, flip, jab, peck, rap, touch

flicker *verb* **1 = twinkle**, flare, flash, glimmer, gutter, shimmer, sparkle **2 = flutter**, quiver, vibrate, waver ◆ *noun* **3 = glimmer**, flare, flash, gleam, spark **4 = trace**, atom, breath, drop, glimmer, iota, spark, vestige

flier *see* FLYER

flight[1] *noun* **1** *Of air travel* **= journey**, trip, voyage **2 = aviation**, aerial navigation, aeronautics, air transport, flying **3 = flying**, mounting, soaring, winging **4 = flock**, cloud, formation, squadron, swarm, unit, wing

flight[2] *noun* **1 = escape**, departure, exit, exodus, fleeing, getaway, retreat, running away **2 take (to) flight = run away** *or* **off**, abscond, beat a retreat, bolt, decamp, do a bunk (*Brit. slang*), do a runner (*slang*), flee, fly the coop (*U.S. & Canad. informal*), light out (*informal*), make a hasty retreat, skedaddle (*informal*), take a powder (*U.S. & Canad. slang*), take it on the lam (*U.S. & Canad. slang*), turn tail, withdraw hastily **3 put to flight = drive off**, chase off, disperse, rout, scare off, scatter, send packing, stampede

flightiness *noun* **= frivolity**, capriciousness, fickleness, flippancy, giddiness, irresponsibility, levity, lightness, mercurialness, volatility

flighty *adjective* **= frivolous**, capricious, changeable, ditzy *or* ditsy (*slang*), dizzy, fickle, giddy, harebrained, impetuous, impulsive, irresponsible, light-headed, mercurial, scatterbrained, skittish, thoughtless, unbalanced, unstable, unsteady, volatile, wild

flimsy *adjective* **1 = fragile**, delicate, frail, gimcrack, insubstantial, makeshift, rickety, shaky, shallow, slight, superficial, unsubstantial **2 = thin**, chiffon, gauzy, gossamer, light, sheer, transparent **3 = unconvincing**, feeble, frivolous,

implausible, inadequate, pathetic, poor, tenuous, thin, transparent, trivial, unsatisfactory, weak
➤ **Antonyms**
≠**fragile**: durable, heavy, robust, solid, sound, stout, strong, sturdy, substantial

flinch *verb* **= recoil**, back off, baulk, blench, cower, cringe, draw back, duck, flee, quail, retreat, shirk, shrink, shy away, start, swerve, wince, withdraw

fling *verb* **1 = throw**, cast, catapult, chuck (*informal*), heave, hurl, jerk, let fly, lob (*informal*), pitch, precipitate, propel, send, shy, sling, toss ◆ *noun* **2 = binge** (*informal*), bash, beano (*Brit. slang*), bit of fun, good time, hooley *or* hoolie (*chiefly Irish & N.Z.*), indulgence, party, rave (*Brit. slang*), rave-up (*Brit. slang*), spree **3 = try**, attempt, bash (*informal*), crack (*informal*), gamble, go (*informal*), shot (*informal*), stab (*informal*), trial, venture, whirl (*informal*)

flip *verb*, *noun* **= toss**, cast, flick, jerk, pitch, snap, spin, throw, twist

flippancy *noun* **= frivolity**, cheek (*informal*), cheekiness, disrespectfulness, impertinence, irreverence, levity, pertness, sauciness

flippant *adjective* **= frivolous**, cheeky, disrespectful, flip (*informal*), glib, impertinent, impudent, irreverent, offhand, pert, rude, saucy, superficial
➤ **Antonyms**
gracious, mannerly, polite, respectful, serious, sincere, solicitous, well-mannered

flirt *verb* **1 = chat up** (*informal*), coquet, dally, lead on, make advances, make eyes at, make sheep's eyes at, philander **2** *usually* **with = toy with**, consider, dabble in, entertain, expose oneself to, give a thought to, play with, trifle with ◆ *noun* **3 = tease**, coquette, heart-breaker, philanderer, trifler, wanton

flirtation *noun* **= teasing**, coquetry, dalliance, intrigue, philandering, toying, trifling

flirtatious *adjective* **= teasing**, amorous, arch, come-hither, come-on (*informal*), coquettish, coy, enticing, flirty, provocative, sportive

flit *verb* **= fly**, dart, flash, fleet, flutter, pass, skim, speed, whisk, wing

float *verb* **1 = be buoyant**, be *or* lie on the surface, displace water, hang, hover, poise, rest on water, stay afloat **2 = glide**, bob, drift, move gently, sail, slide, slip along **3 = launch**, get going, promote, push off, set up
➤ **Antonyms**
≠**be buoyant**: dip, drown, founder, go down, settle, sink, submerge ≠**launch**:

abolish, annul, cancel, dissolve, terminate

floating *adjective* = **free**, fluctuating, migratory, movable, unattached, uncommitted, unfixed, variable, wandering

flock *noun* **1** = **herd**, colony, drove, flight, gaggle, skein **2** = **crowd**, assembly, bevy, collection, company, congregation, convoy, gathering, group, herd, host, mass, multitude, throng ♦ *verb* **3** = **gather**, collect, congregate, converge, crowd, group, herd, huddle, mass, throng, troop

flog *verb* = **beat**, castigate, chastise, flagellate, flay, lambast(e), lash, scourge, thrash, trounce, whack, whip

flogging *noun* = **beating**, caning, flagellation, hiding (*informal*), horsewhipping, lashing, scourging, thrashing, trouncing, whipping

flood *noun* **1** = **deluge**, downpour, flash flood, freshet, inundation, overflow, spate, tide, torrent **2** = **torrent**, abundance, flow, glut, multitude, outpouring, profusion, rush, stream ♦ *verb* **3** = **immerse**, brim over, deluge, drown, inundate, overflow, pour over, submerge, swamp, teem **4** = **engulf**, flow, gush, overwhelm, rush, surge, swarm, sweep **5** = **oversupply**, choke, fill, glut, saturate

floor *noun* **1** = **tier**, level, stage, storey ♦ *verb* **2** = **knock down**, deck (*slang*), prostrate **3** *Informal* = **disconcert**, baffle, beat, bewilder, bowl over (*informal*), bring up short, confound, conquer, defeat, discomfit, dumbfound, faze, nonplus, overthrow, perplex, puzzle, stump, throw (*informal*)

flop *verb* **1** = **fall**, collapse, dangle, droop, drop, hang limply, sag, slump, topple, tumble **2** *Informal* = **fail**, bomb (*U.S. & Canad. slang*), close, come to nothing, come unstuck, fall flat, fall short, fold (*informal*), founder, go belly-up (*slang*), go down like a lead balloon (*informal*), misfire ♦ *noun* **3** *Informal* = **failure**, cockup (*Brit. slang*), debacle, disaster, fiasco, loser, nonstarter, washout (*informal*)
➤ **Antonyms**
verb ≠**fail**: flourish, make a hit, make it (*informal*), prosper, succeed, triumph, work ♦ *noun* ≠**failure**: hit, success, triumph

floppy *adjective* = **droopy**, baggy, flaccid, limp, loose, pendulous, sagging, soft

floral *adjective* = **flowery**, flower-patterned

florid *adjective* **1** = **flushed**, blowsy, high-coloured, high-complexioned, rubicund, ruddy **2** = **ornate**, baroque, busy, embellished, euphuistic, figurative, flamboyant, flowery, fussy, grandiloquent, high-flown, overelaborate

➤ **Antonyms**
≠**flushed**: anaemic, bloodless, pale, pallid, pasty, wan, washed out ≠**ornate**: bare, dull, plain, unadorned

flotsam *noun* = **debris**, detritus, jetsam, junk, odds and ends, sweepings, wreckage

flounce *verb* = **bounce**, fling, jerk, spring, stamp, storm, throw, toss

flounder *verb* = **struggle**, be in the dark, blunder, fumble, grope, muddle, plunge, stumble, thrash, toss, tumble, wallow

flourish *verb* **1** = **thrive**, bear fruit, be in one's prime, be successful, be vigorous, bloom, blossom, boom, burgeon, develop, do well, flower, get ahead, get on, go great guns (*slang*), go up in the world, grow, grow fat, increase, prosper, succeed **2** = **wave**, brandish, display, flaunt, flutter, shake, sweep, swing, swish, twirl, vaunt, wag, wield ♦ *noun* **3** = **wave**, brandishing, dash, display, fanfare, parade, shaking, show, showy gesture, twirling **4** = **ornamentation**, curlicue, decoration, embellishment, plume, sweep
➤ **Antonyms**
verb ≠**thrive**: decline, diminish, dwindle, fade, fail, grow less, pine, shrink, wane

flourishing *adjective* = **successful**, blooming, burgeoning, doing well, going places, going strong, in the pink, in top form, lush, luxuriant, mushrooming, on a roll, on the up and up (*informal*), prospering, rampant, thriving

flout *verb* = **defy**, deride, gibe at, insult, jeer at, laugh in the face of, mock, outrage, ridicule, scoff at, scorn, scout (*archaic*), show contempt for, sneer at, spurn, take the piss out of (*taboo slang*), taunt, treat with disdain
➤ **Antonyms**
esteem, heed, honour, mind, note, pay attention to, regard, respect, revere, value

flow *verb* **1** = **run**, circulate, course, glide, move, purl, ripple, roll, slide **2** = **pour**, cascade, deluge, flood, gush, inundate, issue, overflow, run, run out, rush, spew, spill, spurt, squirt, stream, surge, sweep, swirl, teem, well forth, whirl **3** = **issue**, arise, emanate, emerge, pour, proceed, result, spring ♦ *noun* **4** = **stream**, course, current, drift, flood, flux, gush, issue, outflow, outpouring, spate, tide, tideway, undertow **5** = **outpouring**, abundance, deluge, effusion, emanation, outflow, plenty, plethora, succession, train

flower *noun* **1** = **bloom**, blossom, efflorescence **2** = **elite**, best, choicest part, cream, *crème de la crème*, freshness, greatest *or* finest point, height, pick, vigour ♦ *verb* **3** = **bloom**, blossom, blow, burgeon, effloresce, flourish, mature, open, unfold

flowering *adjective* = **blooming**, abloom, blossoming, florescent, in bloom, in blossom, in flower, open, out, ready

flowery *adjective* = **ornate**, baroque, embellished, euphuistic, fancy, figurative, florid, high-flown, overwrought, rhetorical
➤ **Antonyms**
austere, bare, basic, modest, muted, plain, restrained, simple, spartan, unadorned, unembellished

flowing *adjective* **1** = **streaming**, falling, gushing, rolling, rushing, smooth, sweeping **2** = **fluent**, continuous, cursive, easy, smooth, unbroken, uninterrupted **3** = **abundant**, abounding, brimming over, flooded, full, overrun, prolific, rich, teeming

fluctuate *verb* = **change**, alter, alternate, ebb and flow, go up and down, hesitate, oscillate, rise and fall, seesaw, shift, swing, undulate, vacillate, vary, veer, waver

fluctuation *noun* = **change**, alternation, fickleness, inconstancy, instability, oscillation, shift, swing, unsteadiness, vacillation, variation, wavering

fluency *noun* = **ease**, articulateness, assurance, command, control, facility, glibness, readiness, slickness, smoothness, volubility

fluent *adjective* = **effortless**, articulate, easy, facile, flowing, glib, natural, ready, smooth, smooth-spoken, voluble, well-versed
➤ **Antonyms**
faltering, halting, hesitant, hesitating, inarticulate, stammering, stumbling, tongue-tied

fluff *noun* **1** = **fuzz**, down, dust, dustball, lint, nap, oose (*Scot.*), pile ♦ *verb* **2** *Informal* = **mess up** (*informal*), bungle, cock up (*Brit. slang*), foul up (*informal*), fuck up (*offensive taboo slang*), make a mess off, make a nonsense of, muddle, screw up (*informal*), spoil

fluffy *adjective* = **soft**, downy, feathery, fleecy, fuzzy

fluid *noun* **1** = **liquid**, liquor, solution ♦ *adjective* **2** = **liquid**, aqueous, flowing, in solution, liquefied, melted, molten, running, runny, watery **3** = **changeable**, adaptable, adjustable, flexible, floating, fluctuating, indefinite, mercurial, mobile, mutable, protean, shifting
➤ **Antonyms**
adjective ≠**liquid**: firm, hard, rigid, set, solid ≠**changeable**: definite, firm, fixed, immobile, immutable

fluke *noun* = **stroke of luck**, accident, blessing, break, chance, chance occurrence, coincidence, fortuity, freak, lucky break, quirk, quirk of fate, serendipity, stroke, windfall

flummox *verb* = **baffle**, bamboozle (*informal*), bewilder, bring up short, defeat, fox, mystify, nonplus, perplex, puzzle, stump, stymie

flummoxed *adjective* = **baffled**, at a loss, at sea, bewildered, foxed, mystified, nonplussed, puzzled, stumped, stymied

flunk *Informal verb* = **fail**, be found lacking, be unsuccessful, fall short, flop (*informal*), founder, miss, not come up to scratch, not come up to the mark (*informal*), not make the grade (*informal*), screw up (*informal*), underachieve, underperform
➤ **Antonyms**
be successful, get by *or* through, make it, pass

flunky *noun* **1** = **manservant**, footman, lackey, valet **2** = **minion**, assistant, cohort (*chiefly U.S.*), drudge, hanger-on, menial, slave, toady, tool, underling, yes man

flurry *noun* **1** = **commotion**, ado, agitation, bustle, disturbance, excitement, ferment, flap, fluster, flutter, furore, fuss, hurry, stir, to-do, tumult, whirl **2** = **burst**, outbreak, spell, spurt **3** = **gust**, flaw, squall ♦ *verb* **4** = **confuse**, agitate, bewilder, bother, disconcert, disturb, faze, fluster, flutter, fuss, hassle (*informal*), hurry, hustle, rattle (*informal*), ruffle, unnerve, unsettle, upset

flush¹ *verb* **1** = **blush**, burn, colour, colour up, crimson, flame, glow, go as red as a beetroot, go red, redden, suffuse **2** = **rinse out**, cleanse, douche, drench, eject, expel, flood, hose down, swab, syringe, wash out ♦ *noun* **3** = **blush**, bloom, colour, freshness, glow, redness, rosiness

flush² *adjective* **1** = **level**, even, flat, plane, square, true **2** *Informal* = **wealthy**, in funds, in the money (*informal*), moneyed, rich, rolling (*slang*), well-heeled (*informal*), well-off, well-supplied ♦ *adverb* **3** = **level with**, even with, hard against, in contact with, squarely, touching

flush³ *verb* = **drive out**, discover, disturb, put to flight, rouse, start, uncover

flushed *adjective* **1** = **blushing**, burning, crimson, embarrassed, feverish, glowing, hot, red, rosy, rubicund, ruddy **2** *often with* **with** = **exhilarated**, animated, aroused, elated, enthused, excited, high (*informal*), inspired, intoxicated, thrilled

fluster *verb* **1** = **upset**, agitate, bother, bustle, confound, confuse, disturb, excite, flurry, hassle (*informal*), heat, hurry, make nervous, perturb, rattle (*informal*), ruffle, throw off balance, unnerve ♦ *noun* **2** = **turmoil**, agitation, bustle, commotion, disturbance, dither (*chiefly Brit.*), flap (*informal*), flurry, flutter, furore, perturbation, ruffle, state (*informal*)

fluted *adjective* = **grooved**, channelled, corrugated, furrowed

flutter *verb* 1 = **beat**, agitate, bat, flap, flicker, flit, flitter, fluctuate, hover, palpitate, quiver, ripple, ruffle, shiver, tremble, vibrate, waver ◆ *noun* 2 = **vibration**, palpitation, quiver, quivering, shiver, shudder, tremble, tremor, twitching 3 = **agitation**, commotion, confusion, dither (*chiefly Brit.*), excitement, flurry, fluster, perturbation, state (*informal*), state of nervous excitement, tremble, tumult

flux *noun* 1 = **change**, alteration, fluctuation, instability, modification, mutability, mutation, transition, unrest 2 = **flow**, fluidity, motion

fly[1] *verb* 1 = **take wing**, flit, flutter, hover, mount, sail, soar, take to the air, wing 2 = **pilot**, aviate, be at the controls, control, manoeuvre, operate 3 = **display**, flap, float, flutter, show, wave 4 = **rush**, barrel (along) (*informal, chiefly U.S. & Canad.*), be off like a shot (*informal*), bolt, burn rubber (*informal*), career, dart, dash, hare (*Brit. informal*), hasten, hurry, race, scamper, scoot, shoot, speed, sprint, tear, whizz (*informal*), zoom 5 = **pass**, elapse, flit, glide, pass swiftly, roll on, run its course, slip away 6 = **flee**, abscond, avoid, beat a retreat, clear out (*informal*), cut and run (*informal*), decamp, disappear, do a runner (*slang*), escape, fly the coop (*U.S. & Canad. informal*), get away, hightail (*informal, chiefly U.S.*), light out (*informal*), make a getaway, make a quick exit, make one's escape, run, run for it, run from, show a clean pair of heels, skedaddle (*informal*), take a powder (*U.S. & Canad. slang*), take flight, take it on the lam (*U.S. & Canad. slang*), take off, take to one's heels 7 **let fly: a** *Informal* = **lose one's temper**, burst forth, give free reign, keep nothing back, lash out, let (someone) have it, tear into (*informal*), vent **b** = **throw**, cast, chuck (*informal*), fire, fling, heave, hurl, hurtle, launch, let off, lob (*informal*), shoot, sling

fly[2] *adjective Slang, chiefly Brit.* = **cunning**, astute, canny, careful, knowing, nobody's fool, not born yesterday, on the ball (*informal*), sharp, shrewd, smart, wide-awake

fly at *verb* = **attack**, assail, assault, belabour, fall upon, get stuck into (*informal*), go for, go for the jugular, have a go at (*informal*), lay about, pitch into (*informal*), rush at

fly-by-night *adjective Informal* = **unreliable**, cowboy (*informal*), dubious, questionable, shady, undependable, untrustworthy

flyer, flier *noun* 1 = **leaflet**, advert (*Brit. informal*), bill, booklet, circular, handbill, handout, leaf, literature (*informal*), notice, pamphlet, promotional material, publicity material, release 2 = **goer**, racer, runner, sprinter 3 *Old-fashioned* = **pilot**, aeronaut, airman *or* airwoman, aviator *or* aviatrix

flying *adjective* 1 = **hurried**, brief, fleeting, fugacious, hasty, rushed, short-lived, transitory 2 = **fast**, express, fleet, mercurial, mobile, rapid, speedy, winged 3 = **airborne**, flapping, floating, fluttering, gliding, hovering, in the air, soaring, streaming, waving, wind-borne

foam *noun* 1 = **froth**, bubbles, head, lather, spray, spume, suds ◆ *verb* 2 = **bubble**, boil, effervesce, fizz, froth, lather

foamy *adjective* = **bubbly**, foaming, frothy, lathery, spumescent, sudsy

fob off *verb* 1 = **put off**, appease, deceive, equivocate with, flannel (*Brit. informal*), give (someone) the run-around (*informal*), stall 2 = **pass off**, dump, foist, get rid of, inflict, palm off, unload

focus *verb* 1 = **concentrate**, aim, bring to bear, centre, converge, direct, fix, join, meet, pinpoint, rivet, spotlight, zero in (*informal*), zoom in ◆ *noun* 2 = **centre**, bull's eye, centre of activity, centre of attraction, core, cynosure, focal point, headquarters, heart, hub, meeting place, target 3 **in focus** = **clear**, distinct, sharp-edged, sharply defined 4 **out of focus** = **blurred**, fuzzy, ill-defined, indistinct, muzzy, unclear

fodder *noun* = **feed**, food, foodstuff, forage, provender, rations, tack (*informal*), victuals, vittles (*obsolete or dialect*)

foe *noun* = **enemy**, adversary, antagonist, foeman (*archaic*), opponent, rival
➤ **Antonyms**
ally, companion, comrade, confederate, friend, partner

fog *noun* 1 = **mist**, gloom, miasma, murk, murkiness, peasouper (*informal*), smog ◆ *verb* 2 = **mist over** *or* **up**, cloud, steam up 3 = **obscure**, becloud, bedim, befuddle, bewilder, blear, blind, cloud, confuse, darken, daze, dim, muddle, muddy the waters, obfuscate, perplex, stupefy

fogey, fogy *noun* = **fuddy-duddy** (*informal*), dinosaur, dodo (*informal*), fossil (*informal*), square (*informal*), stick-in-the-mud (*informal*)

foggy *adjective* 1 = **misty**, blurred, cloudy, dim, grey, hazy, indistinct, murky, nebulous, obscure, smoggy, soupy, vaporous 2 = **unclear**, befuddled, bewildered, clouded, cloudy, confused, dark, dazed, dim, indistinct, muddled, obscure, stupefied, stupid, vague
➤ **Antonyms**
≠**misty**: bright, clear ≠**unclear**: alert, awake, clear, distinct, lucid, sharp, undimmed

foible noun = **idiosyncrasy**, defect, failing, fault, imperfection, infirmity, peculiarity, quirk, weakness, weak point

foil[1] verb = **thwart**, baffle, balk, check, checkmate, circumvent, cook (someone's) goose (informal), counter, defeat, disappoint, elude, frustrate, nip in the bud, nullify, outwit, put a spoke in (someone's) wheel (Brit.), stop

foil[2] noun = **contrast**, antithesis, background, complement, setting

foist verb = **impose**, fob off, get rid of, insert, insinuate, interpolate, introduce, palm off, pass off, put over, sneak in, unload

fold verb 1 = **bend**, crease, crumple, dog-ear, double, double over, gather, intertwine, overlap, pleat, tuck, turn under 2 = **wrap**, do up, enclose, enfold, entwine, envelop, wrap up 3 Informal = **go bankrupt**, be ruined, close, collapse, crash, fail, go belly-up (slang), go bust (informal), go by the board, go down like a lead balloon (informal), go to the wall, go under, shut down ♦ noun 4 = **crease**, bend, double thickness, folded portion, furrow, knife-edge, layer, overlap, pleat, turn, wrinkle

folder noun = **file**, binder, envelope, portfolio

folk noun = **people**, clan, ethnic group, family, kin, kindred, race, tribe

follow verb 1 = **come after**, come next, step into the shoes of, succeed, supersede, supplant, take the place of 2 = **accompany**, attend, bring up the rear, come after, come or go with, escort, tag along, tread on the heels of 3 = **pursue**, chase, dog, hound, hunt, run after, shadow, stalk, tail (informal), track, trail 4 = **result**, arise, be consequent, develop, emanate, ensue, flow, issue, proceed, spring, supervene 5 = **obey**, act in accordance with, be guided by, comply, conform, give allegiance to, heed, mind, note, observe, regard, toe the line, watch 6 = **copy**, adopt, emulate, imitate, live up to, pattern oneself upon, take a leaf out of someone's book, take as example 7 = **understand**, appreciate, catch, catch on (informal), comprehend, fathom, get, get the hang of (informal), get the picture, grasp, keep up with, realize, see, take in 8 = **be interested in**, be a devotee or supporter of, be devoted to, cultivate, keep abreast of, support
➤ Antonyms
≠**come after:** guide, lead, precede ≠**pursue:** avoid, elude, escape ≠**obey:** abandon, desert, disobey, flout, forsake, give up, ignore, reject, renounce, shun

follower noun = **supporter**, adherent, admirer, apostle, backer, believer, cohort (chiefly U.S.), convert, devotee, disciple, fan, fancier, habitué, henchman, partisan, protagonist, pupil, representative, votary, worshipper
➤ Antonyms
guru, leader, mentor, svengali, swami, teacher, tutor

following adjective 1 = **next**, coming, consequent, consequential, ensuing, later, specified, subsequent, succeeding, successive ♦ noun 2 = **supporters**, audience, circle, clientele, coterie, entourage, fans, patronage, public, retinue, suite, support, train

follow through verb = **complete**, bring to a conclusion, conclude, consummate, pursue, see through

follow up verb 1 = **investigate**, check out, find out about, look into, make inquiries, pursue, research 2 = **continue**, consolidate, make sure, reinforce

folly noun = **foolishness**, absurdity, bêtise (rare), daftness (informal), desipience, fatuity, idiocy, imbecility, imprudence, indiscretion, irrationality, lunacy, madness, nonsense, preposterousness, rashness, recklessness, silliness, stupidity
➤ Antonyms
judgment, level-headedness, moderation, prudence, rationality, reason, sanity, sense, wisdom

foment verb = **stir up**, abet, agitate, arouse, brew, encourage, excite, fan the flames, foster, goad, incite, instigate, promote, provoke, quicken, raise, rouse, sow the seeds of, spur, stimulate, whip up

fond adjective 1 = **loving**, adoring, affectionate, amorous, caring, devoted, doting, indulgent, tender, warm 2 = **foolish**, absurd, credulous, deluded, delusive, delusory, empty, indiscreet, naive, overoptimistic, vain 3 **fond of** = **keen on**, addicted to, attached to, enamoured of, having a fancy for, having a liking for, having a soft spot for, having a taste for, hooked on, into (informal), partial to, predisposed towards
➤ Antonyms
≠**loving:** aloof, austere, averse, disinterested, indifferent, unaffectionate, unconcerned, undemonstrative ≠**foolish:** rational, sensible

fondle verb = **caress**, cuddle, dandle, pat, pet, stroke

fondly adverb 1 = **lovingly**, affectionately, dearly, indulgently, possessively, tenderly, with affection 2 = **foolishly**, credulously, naively, stupidly, vainly

fondness noun 1 = **liking**, attachment, fancy, love, partiality, penchant, predilection, preference, soft spot, susceptibility, taste, weakness 2 = **devotion**, affection,

attachment, kindness, love, tenderness
➤ **Antonyms**
abhorrence, animosity, animus, antagonism, antipathy, aversion, bad blood, coldness, contempt, detestation, dislike, enmity, harshness, hatred, hostility, ill will, loathing, malevolence, malice, repugnance, repulsion, resentment, unfriendliness

food *noun* **1** = **nourishment**, board, bread, chow (*informal*), comestibles, commons, cooking, cuisine, diet, eatables (*slang*), eats (*slang*), fare, feed, foodstuffs, grub (*slang*), meat, nosh (*slang*), nutriment, nutrition, provender, provisions, rations, refreshment, scoff (*slang*), stores, subsistence, survival rations, sustenance, tack (*informal*), tuck (*informal*), tucker (*Austral. & N.Z. informal*), viands, victuals, vittles (*obsolete or dialect*) **2** *Cattle, etc.* = **fodder**, feed, forage, provender

foodie *noun Informal* = **gourmet**, bon vivant, bon viveur, connoisseur, epicure, gastronome, gourmand

fool *noun* **1** = **simpleton**, ass, berk (*Brit. slang*), bird-brain (*informal*), blockhead, bonehead (*slang*), charlie (*Brit. informal*), chump (*informal*), clot (*Brit. informal*), coot, dickhead (*slang*), dickwit (*slang*), dimwit (*informal*), dipstick (*Brit. slang*), divvy (*Brit. slang*), dolt, dope (*informal*), dork (*slang*), dumb-ass (*slang*), dunce, dunderhead, fathead (*informal*), geek (*slang*), goose (*informal*), halfwit, idiot, ignoramus, illiterate, imbecile (*informal*), jackass, jerk (*slang, chiefly U.S. & Canad.*), lamebrain (*informal*), moron, nerd *or* nurd (*slang*), nincompoop, ninny, nit (*informal*), nitwit (*informal*), numbskull *or* numskull, numpty (*Scot. informal*), oaf, pillock (*Brit. slang*), prat (*slang*), prick (*derogatory slang*), sap (*slang*), schmuck (*U.S. slang*), silly, twerp *or* twirp (*informal*), twit (*informal, chiefly Brit.*), wally (*slang*) **2** = **dupe**, butt, chump (*informal*), easy mark (*informal*), fall guy (*informal*), greenhorn (*informal*), gull (*archaic*), laughing stock, mug (*Brit. slang*), stooge (*slang*), sucker (*slang*) **3** = **clown**, buffoon, comic, harlequin, jester, joculator *or* (*fem.*) joculatrix, merry-andrew, motley, pierrot, punchinello **4** *act or* **play the fool** = **clown**, act the goat, act up, be silly, frolic, lark about (*informal*), mess about, piss about (*taboo slang*), piss around (*taboo slang*), play (silly) games, play the goat, show off (*informal*) ♦ *verb* **5** = **deceive**, bamboozle, beguile, bluff, cheat, con (*informal*), delude, dupe, have (someone) on, hoax, hoodwink, kid (*informal*), make a fool of, mislead, play a trick on, pull a fast one on (*informal*), put one over on (*informal*), take for a ride

(*informal*), take in, trick **6** *with* **with**, **around with**, *or* **about with** *Informal* = **play**, fiddle (*informal*), meddle, mess, monkey, piss about (*taboo slang*), piss around (*taboo slang*), tamper, toy, trifle
➤ **Antonyms**
noun ≠ **simpleton**: expert, genius, master, sage, savant, scholar, wise man

fool around *or* **about** *verb Informal* = **mess about**, act the fool, dawdle, footle (*informal*), hang around, idle, kill time, lark, play about, play the fool, waste time

foolery *noun* = **nonsense**, antics, capers, carry-on (*informal, chiefly Brit.*), childishness, clowning, desipience, folly, fooling, horseplay, larks, mischief, monkey tricks (*informal*), practical jokes, pranks, shenanigans (*informal*), silliness, tomfoolery

foolhardy *adjective* = **rash**, adventurous, bold, hot-headed, impetuous, imprudent, incautious, irresponsible, madcap, precipitate, reckless, temerarious, venturesome, venturous
➤ **Antonyms**
alert, careful, cautious, chary, circumspect, heedful, judicious, prudent, shrewd, solicitous, thoughtful, wary, watchful

foolish *adjective* **1** = **unwise**, absurd, asinine, ill-advised, ill-considered, ill-judged, imprudent, inane, incautious, indiscreet, injudicious, nonsensical, senseless, short-sighted, silly, unintelligent, unreasonable **2** = **silly**, as daft as a brush (*informal, chiefly Brit.*), braindead (*informal*), brainless, crackpot (*informal*), crazy, daft (*informal*), doltish, dumb-ass (*slang*), fatuous, goofy (*informal*), half-baked (*informal*), half-witted, harebrained, idiotic, imbecilic, inane, loopy (*informal*), ludicrous, mad, moronic, off one's head (*informal*), potty (*Brit. informal*), ridiculous, senseless, simple, stupid, weak, witless
➤ **Antonyms**
bright, cautious, clever, commonsensical, intelligent, judicious, prudent, rational, sagacious, sane, sensible, sharp, smart, sound, thoughtful, wise

foolishly *adverb* = **unwisely**, absurdly, idiotically, ill-advisedly, imprudently, incautiously, indiscreetly, injudiciously, like a fool, mistakenly, short-sightedly, stupidly, without due consideration

foolishness *noun* **1** = **stupidity**, absurdity, bêtise (*rare*), folly, idiocy, imprudence, inanity, indiscretion, irresponsibility, silliness, weakness **2** = **nonsense**, bunk (*informal*), bunkum *or* buncombe (*chiefly U.S.*), carrying-on (*informal, chiefly Brit.*), claptrap (*informal*), foolery, rigmarole, rubbish, trash

foolproof *adjective* = **infallible**, certain,

guaranteed, never-failing, safe, sure-fire (*informal*), unassailable, unbreakable

footing *noun* **1** = **basis**, establishment, foot-hold, foundation, ground, groundwork, installation, settlement **2** = **relationship**, condition, grade, position, rank, relations, standing, state, status, terms

footling *adjective* = **trivial**, fiddling, fussy, hairsplitting, immaterial, insignificant, irrelevant, minor, nickel-and-dime (*U.S. slang*), niggly, petty, pointless, silly, time-wasting, trifling, unimportant

footstep *noun* **1** = **step**, footfall, tread **2** = **footprint**, footmark, trace, track

footwear *noun* = **footgear**

fop *noun* = **dandy**, beau, Beau Brummel, clotheshorse, coxcomb (*archaic*), peacock, popinjay, swell

foppish *adjective* = **dandyish**, dapper, dressy (*informal*), natty (*informal*), spruce

forage *verb* **1** = **search**, cast about, explore, hunt, look round, plunder, raid, ransack, rummage, scavenge, scour, scrounge (*informal*), seek ◆ *noun* **2** *Cattle, etc.* = **fodder**, feed, food, foodstuffs, provender

foray *noun* = **raid**, incursion, inroad, invasion, sally, sortie, swoop

forbear *verb* = **refrain**, abstain, avoid, cease, decline, desist, eschew, hold back, keep from, omit, pause, resist the temptation to, restrain oneself, stop, withhold

forbearance *noun* **1** = **patience**, indulgence, leniency, long-suffering, resignation, restraint, self-control, temperance, tolerance **2** = **abstinence**, avoidance, refraining
➤ **Antonyms**
≠**patience:** anger, impatience, impetuosity, intolerance, irritability, shortness

forbearing *adjective* = **patient**, clement, easy, forgiving, indulgent, lenient, long-suffering, merciful, mild, moderate, tolerant

forbid *verb* = **prohibit**, ban, debar, disallow, exclude, hinder, inhibit, interdict, outlaw, preclude, proscribe, rule out, veto
➤ **Antonyms**
allow, approve, authorize, bid, enable, endorse, grant, let, license, O.K. *or* okay (*informal*), order, permit, sanction

forbidden *adjective* = **prohibited**, banned, outlawed, out of bounds, proscribed, taboo, verboten, vetoed

forbidding *adjective* = **threatening**, baleful, bodeful, daunting, foreboding, frightening, grim, hostile, menacing, ominous, sinister, unfriendly
➤ **Antonyms**
alluring, attractive, beguiling, enticing,

inviting, magnetic, tempting, welcoming, winning

force *noun* **1** = **power**, dynamism, energy, impact, impulse, life, might, momentum, muscle, potency, pressure, stimulus, strength, stress, vigour **2** = **compulsion**, arm-twisting (*informal*), coercion, constraint, duress, enforcement, pressure, violence **3** = **influence**, bite, cogency, effect, effectiveness, efficacy, persuasiveness, power, punch (*informal*), strength, validity, weight **4** = **intensity**, drive, emphasis, fierceness, persistence, vehemence, vigour **5** = **army**, battalion, body, corps, detachment, division, host, legion, patrol, regiment, squad, squadron, troop, unit **6 in force: a** = **valid**, binding, current, effective, in operation, on the statute book, operative, working **b** = **in great numbers**, all together, in full strength ◆ *verb* **7** = **compel**, bring pressure to bear upon, coerce, constrain, dragoon, drive, impel, impose, make, necessitate, obligate, oblige, overcome, press, press-gang, pressure, pressurize, put the screws on (*informal*), put the squeeze on (*informal*), railroad (*informal*), strong-arm (*informal*), twist (someone's) arm, urge **8** = **extort**, drag, exact, wring **9** = **push**, propel, thrust **10** = **break open**, blast, prise, use violence on, wrench, wrest
➤ **Antonyms**
noun ≠**power:** debility, enervation, feebleness, fragility, frailty, impotence, ineffectiveness, irresolution, powerlessness, weakness ◆ *verb* ≠**extort:** coax, convince, induce, persuade, prevail, talk into

forced *adjective* **1** = **compulsory**, conscripted, enforced, involuntary, mandatory, obligatory, slave, unwilling **2** = **false**, affected, artificial, contrived, insincere, laboured, stiff, strained, unnatural, wooden
➤ **Antonyms**
≠**compulsory:** spontaneous, voluntary
≠**false:** easy, natural, simple, sincere, spontaneous, unforced, unpretending

forceful *adjective* = **powerful**, cogent, compelling, convincing, dynamic, effective, persuasive, pithy, potent, telling, vigorous, weighty
➤ **Antonyms**
enervated, exhausted, faint, feeble, frail, powerless, spent, weak

forcible *adjective* **1** = **violent**, aggressive, armed, coercive, compulsory, drastic **2** = **compelling**, active, cogent, effective, efficient, energetic, forceful, impressive, mighty, potent, powerful, strong, telling, valid, weighty

forcibly *adverb* = **by force**, against one's will, by main force, compulsorily, under compulsion, under protest, willy-nilly

forebear *noun* = **ancestor**, father, forefather, forerunner, predecessor, progenitor

foreboding *noun* = **dread**, anxiety, apprehension, apprehensiveness, chill, fear, misgiving, premonition, presentiment

forecast *verb* **1** = **predict**, anticipate, augur, calculate, call, divine, estimate, foresee, foretell, plan, prognosticate, prophesy ♦ *noun* **2** = **prediction**, anticipation, conjecture, foresight, forethought, guess, outlook, planning, prognosis, projection, prophecy

forefather *noun* = **ancestor**, father, forebear, forerunner, predecessor, primogenitor, procreator, progenitor

forefront *noun* = **lead**, centre, fore, foreground, front, prominence, spearhead, van, vanguard

forego *see* FORGO

foregoing *adjective* = **preceding**, above, antecedent, anterior, former, previous, prior

foreground *noun* = **front**, centre, forefront, limelight, prominence

foreign *adjective* **1** = **alien**, beyond one's ken, borrowed, distant, exotic, external, imported, outlandish, outside, overseas, remote, strange, unfamiliar, unknown **2** = **extraneous**, extrinsic, incongruous, irrelevant, unassimilable, uncharacteristic, unrelated
➤ **Antonyms**
≠**alien**: customary, domestic, familiar, native, well-known ≠**extraneous**: characteristic, intrinsic, relevant

foreigner *noun* = **alien**, immigrant, incomer, newcomer, outlander, stranger

foreknowledge *noun* = **prior knowledge**, clairvoyance, foresight, forewarning, precognition, prescience, prevision

foremost *adjective* = **leading**, chief, first, front, headmost, highest, inaugural, initial, paramount, pre-eminent, primary, prime, principal, supreme

foreordain *verb* = **predestine**, doom, fate, prearrange, predetermine, preordain

forerunner *noun* **1** = **precursor**, ancestor, announcer, forebear, foregoer, harbinger, herald, predecessor, progenitor, prototype **2** = **omen**, augury, foretoken, indication, portent, premonition, sign, token

foresee *verb* = **predict**, anticipate, divine, envisage, forebode, forecast, foretell, prophesy

foreshadow *verb* = **predict**, augur, betoken, bode, forebode, imply, indicate, portend, prefigure, presage, promise, prophesy, signal

foresight *noun* = **forethought**, anticipation, care, caution, circumspection, far-sightedness, precaution, premeditation, preparedness, prescience, provision, prudence
➤ **Antonyms**
carelessness, hindsight, imprudence, inconsideration, lack of foresight, neglect, thoughtlessness, unpreparedness

forestall *verb* = **prevent**, anticipate, balk, circumvent, frustrate, head off, hinder, intercept, nip in the bud, obviate, parry, preclude, provide against, thwart

forestry *noun* = **woodcraft**, arboriculture, woodmanship

foretaste *noun* = **sample**, example, foretoken, indication, prelude, preview, trailer, warning

foretell *verb* = **predict**, augur, bode, call, forebode, forecast, foreshadow, foreshow, forewarn, portend, presage, prognosticate, prophesy, signify

forethought *noun* = **anticipation**, far-sightedness, foresight, precaution, providence, provision, prudence
➤ **Antonyms**
carelessness, imprudence, impulsiveness, inconsideration, neglect, unpreparedness

forever *adverb* **1** = **evermore**, always, for all time, for good and all (*informal*), for keeps, in perpetuity, till Doomsday, till the cows come home (*informal*), till the end of time, world without end **2** = **constantly**, all the time, continually, endlessly, eternally, everlastingly, incessantly, interminably, perpetually, unremittingly

forewarn *verb* = **caution**, admonish, advise, alert, apprise, dissuade, give fair warning, put on guard, tip off

foreword *noun* = **introduction**, preamble, preface, preliminary, prolegomenon, prologue

forfeit *noun* **1** = **penalty**, amercement (*obsolete*), damages, fine, forfeiture, loss, mulct ♦ *verb* **2** = **lose**, be deprived of, be stripped of, give up, relinquish, renounce, say goodbye to, surrender

forfeiture *noun* = **loss**, confiscation, giving up, relinquishment, sequestration (*Law*), surrender

forge *verb* **1** = **create**, construct, contrive, devise, fabricate, fashion, form, frame, hammer out, invent, make, mould, shape, work **2** = **fake**, coin, copy, counterfeit, falsify, feign, imitate

forger *noun* = **counterfeiter**, coiner, falsifier

forgery *noun* **1** = **fake**, counterfeit, falsification, imitation, phoney *or* phony (*informal*), sham **2** = **falsification**, coining, counterfeiting, fraudulence, fraudulent imitation

forget verb 1 = **neglect**, leave behind, lose sight of, omit, overlook 2 = **dismiss from one's mind**, consign to oblivion, let bygones be bygones, let slip from the memory
➤ **Antonyms**
bring to mind, mind, recall, recollect, remember, retain

forgetful adjective = **absent-minded**, apt to forget, careless, dreamy, having a memory like a sieve, heedless, inattentive, lax, neglectful, negligent, oblivious, slapdash, slipshod, unmindful, vague
➤ **Antonyms**
attentive, careful, mindful, unforgetful, unforgetting

forgive verb = **excuse**, absolve, accept (someone's) apology, acquit, bear no malice, condone, exonerate, let bygones be bygones, let off (informal), pardon, remit
➤ **Antonyms**
blame, censure, charge, condemn, find fault with, reproach, reprove

forgiveness noun = **pardon**, absolution, acquittal, amnesty, condonation, exoneration, mercy, overlooking, remission

forgiving adjective = **lenient**, clement, compassionate, forbearing, humane, magnanimous, merciful, mild, soft-hearted, tolerant

forgo, forego verb = **give up**, abandon, abjure, cede, do without, kick (informal), leave alone or out, relinquish, renounce, resign, sacrifice, say goodbye to, surrender, waive, yield

forgotten adjective = **unremembered**, blotted out, buried, bygone, consigned to oblivion, gone (clean) out of one's mind, left behind, lost, obliterated, omitted, past, past recall

fork verb = **branch**, bifurcate, branch off, diverge, divide, go separate ways, part, split

forked adjective = **branching**, angled, bifurcate(d), branched, divided, pronged, split, tined, zigzag

forlorn adjective = **miserable**, abandoned, bereft, desolate, disconsolate, down in the dumps (informal), forgotten, forsaken, helpless, homeless, hopeless, lonely, lost, pathetic, pitiable, pitiful, unhappy, woebegone, wretched
➤ **Antonyms**
busy, cheerful, happy, hopeful, optimistic, thriving

form noun 1 = **shape**, appearance, cast, configuration, construction, cut, fashion, formation, model, mould, pattern, stamp, structure 2 = **build**, anatomy, being, body, figure, frame, outline, person, physique,

shape, silhouette 3 = **mode**, arrangement, character, design, guise, manifestation, semblance 4 = **type**, description, kind, manner, method, order, practice, sort, species, stamp, style, system, variety, way 5 = **condition**, fettle, fitness, good condition, good spirits, health, shape, trim 6 = **document**, application, paper, sheet 7 = **class**, grade, rank 8 = **procedure**, behaviour, ceremony, conduct, convention, custom, done thing, etiquette, formality, manners, protocol, ritual, rule 9 = **structure**, format, framework, harmony, order, orderliness, organization, plan, proportion, symmetry ♦ verb 10 = **make**, assemble, bring about, build, concoct, construct, contrive, create, devise, establish, fabricate, fashion, forge, found, invent, manufacture, model, mould, produce, put together, set up, shape, stamp 11 = **arrange**, combine, design, dispose, draw up, frame, organize, pattern, plan, think up 12 = **take shape**, accumulate, appear, become visible, come into being, crystallize, grow, materialize, rise, settle, show up (informal) 13 = **train**, bring up, discipline, educate, instruct, rear, school, teach 14 = **develop**, acquire, contract, cultivate, get into (informal), pick up 15 = **constitute**, compose, comprise, make, make up, serve as

formal adjective 1 = **official**, approved, ceremonial, fixed, lawful, legal, methodical, prescribed, pro forma, regular, rigid, ritualistic, set, solemn, strict 2 = **conventional**, affected, aloof, ceremonious, correct, exact, precise, prim, punctilious, reserved, starched, stiff, unbending
➤ **Antonyms**
casual, easy-going, informal, laid-back (informal), relaxed, unceremonious, unofficial

formality noun 1 = **convention**, ceremony, conventionality, custom, form, matter of form, procedure, red tape, rite, ritual 2 = **correctness**, ceremoniousness, decorum, etiquette, politesse, protocol, p's and q's, punctilio

format noun = **arrangement**, appearance, construction, form, layout, look, make-up, plan, style, type

formation noun 1 = **development**, accumulation, compilation, composition, constitution, crystallization, establishment, evolution, forming, generation, genesis, manufacture, organization, production 2 = **arrangement**, configuration, design, disposition, figure, grouping, pattern, rank, structure

formative adjective 1 = **impressionable**, malleable, mouldable, pliant, sensitive, susceptible 2 = **developmental**, determinative, influential, moulding, shaping

former *adjective* **1** = **previous**, antecedent, anterior, earlier, erstwhile, ex-, late, one-time, prior, quondam **2** = **past**, ancient, bygone, departed, long ago, long gone, of yore, old, old-time **3** = **aforementioned**, above, aforesaid, first mentioned, foregoing, preceding
➤ **Antonyms**
≠**previous**: coming, current, ensuing, following, future, latter, subsequent, succeeding ≠**past**: current, future, modern, present, present-day

formerly *adverb* = **previously**, already, at one time, before, heretofore, lately, once

formidable *adjective* **1** = **intimidating**, appalling, baleful, dangerous, daunting, dismaying, dreadful, fearful, frightful, horrible, menacing, shocking, terrifying, threatening **2** = **difficult**, arduous, challenging, colossal, mammoth, onerous, overwhelming, staggering **3** = **impressive**, awesome, great, indomitable, mighty, powerful, puissant, redoubtable, terrific, tremendous
➤ **Antonyms**
≠**intimidating**: cheering, comforting, encouraging, genial, heartening, pleasant, reassuring ≠**difficult**: easy

formless *adjective* = **shapeless**, amorphous, disorganized, inchoate, incoherent, indefinite, nebulous, unformed, vague

formula *noun* **1** = **method**, blueprint, modus operandi, precept, prescription, principle, procedure, recipe, rule, way **2** = **form of words**, rite, ritual, rubric

formulate *verb* **1** = **define**, codify, detail, express, frame, give form to, particularize, set down, specify, systematize **2** = **devise**, coin, develop, evolve, forge, invent, map out, originate, plan, work out

fornication *noun* = **adultery**, extra-curricular sex (*informal*), extra-marital congress *or* relations *or* sex, infidelity, living in sin, pre-marital congress *or* relations *or* sex, unfaithfulness

forsake *verb* **1** = **desert**, abandon, cast off, disown, jettison, jilt, leave, leave in the lurch, quit, repudiate, strand, throw over **2** = **give up**, abdicate, forgo, forswear, have done with, kick (*informal*), relinquish, renounce, set aside, surrender, turn one's back on, yield

forsaken *adjective* = **deserted**, abandoned, cast off, destitute, disowned, ditched, forlorn, friendless, ignored, isolated, jilted, left behind, left in the lurch, lonely, marooned, outcast, solitary, stranded

forswear *verb* **1** = **renounce**, abandon, abjure, drop (*informal*), forgo, forsake, give up, swear off **2** = **reject**, deny, disavow,

disclaim, disown, recant, repudiate, retract **3** = **lie**, perjure oneself, renege, swear falsely

fort *noun* **1** = **fortress**, blockhouse, camp, castle, citadel, fastness, fortification, garrison, station, stronghold **2 hold the fort** *Informal* = **carry on**, keep things moving, keep things on an even keel, maintain the status quo, stand in, take over the reins

forte *noun* = **speciality**, gift, long suit (*informal*), métier, strength, strong point, talent
➤ **Antonyms**
Achilles heel, chink in one's armour, defect, failing, imperfection, shortcoming, weak point

forth *adverb Formal or old-fashioned* = **forward**, ahead, away, into the open, onward, out, out of concealment, outward

forthcoming *adjective* **1** = **approaching**, coming, expected, future, imminent, impending, prospective, upcoming **2** = **available**, accessible, at hand, in evidence, obtainable, on tap (*informal*), ready **3** = **communicative**, chatty, expansive, free, informative, open, sociable, talkative, unreserved

forthright *adjective* = **outspoken**, above-board, blunt, candid, direct, downright, frank, open, plain-spoken, straightforward, straight from the shoulder (*informal*), upfront (*informal*)
➤ **Antonyms**
dishonest, furtive, secret, secretive, sneaky, underhand, untruthful

forthwith *adverb* = **at once**, directly, immediately, instantly, quickly, right away, straightaway, *tout de suite*, without delay

fortification *noun* **1** = **strengthening**, embattlement, reinforcement **2** = **defence**, bastion, bulwark, castle, citadel, fastness, fort, fortress, keep, protection, stronghold

fortify *verb* **1** = **protect**, augment, brace, buttress, embattle, garrison, reinforce, secure, shore up, strengthen, support **2** = **strengthen**, brace, cheer, confirm, embolden, encourage, hearten, invigorate, reassure, stiffen, sustain
➤ **Antonyms**
≠**strengthen**: debilitate, demoralize, dilute, dishearten, impair, reduce, sap the strength of, weaken

fortitude *noun* = **courage**, backbone, bravery, dauntlessness, determination, endurance, fearlessness, firmness, grit, guts (*informal*), hardihood, intrepidity, patience, perseverance, pluck, resolution, staying power, stoutheartedness, strength, strength of mind, valour

fortress *noun* = **castle**, citadel, fastness, fort, redoubt, stronghold

fortuitous *adjective* **1** = **chance**, accidental, arbitrary, casual, contingent, incidental, random, unforeseen, unplanned **2** = **lucky**, fluky (*informal*), fortunate, happy, providential, serendipitous

fortunate *adjective* **1** = **lucky**, born with a silver spoon in one's mouth, bright, favoured, golden, happy, having a charmed life, in luck, jammy (*Brit. slang*), on a roll, prosperous, rosy, sitting pretty (*informal*), successful, well-off **2** = **providential**, advantageous, auspicious, convenient, encouraging, expedient, favourable, felicitous, fortuitous, helpful, opportune, profitable, promising, propitious, timely
> **Antonyms**
hapless, ill-fated, ill-starred, miserable, poor, unfortunate, unhappy, unlucky, unsuccessful, wretched

fortunately *adverb* = **luckily**, by a happy chance, by good luck, happily, providentially

fortune *noun* **1** = **luck**, accident, chance, contingency, destiny, fate, hazard, kismet, providence **2 fortunes** = **destiny**, adventures, circumstances, doom, experiences, history, life, lot, portion, star, success **3** = **wealth**, affluence, an arm and a leg (*informal*), big bucks (*informal, chiefly U.S.*), big money, bomb (*Brit. slang*), bundle (*slang*), gold mine, king's ransom, megabucks (*U.S. & Canad. slang*), mint, opulence, packet (*slang*), pile (*informal*), possessions, pretty penny (*informal*), property, prosperity, riches, tidy sum (*informal*), treasure, wad (*U.S. & Canad. slang*)
> **Antonyms**
≠**wealth:** destitution, hardship, indigence, penury, poverty, privation

forum *noun* = **meeting**, assemblage, assembly, body, caucus (*chiefly U.S. & Canad.*), colloquium, conclave, conference, congregation, congress, convention, convergence, convocation, council, court, gathering, get-together (*informal*), parliament, rally, seminar, senate, symposium, synod, tribunal (*archaic or literary*)

forward *adjective* **1** = **leading**, advance, first, fore, foremost, front, head **2** = **presumptuous**, bare-faced, bold, brash, brass-necked (*Brit. informal*), brazen, brazen-faced, cheeky, confident, familiar, fresh (*informal*), impertinent, impudent, overassertive, overweening, pert, presuming, pushy (*informal*), sassy (*U.S. informal*) **3** = **well-developed**, advanced, advancing, early, forward-looking, onward, precocious, premature, progressive ♦ *adverb* **4** *Also* **forwards** = **forth**, ahead, on, onward **5** = **to the front**, into consideration, into

prominence, into the open, into view, out, to light, to the surface ♦ *verb* **6** = **send**, dispatch, post, route, send on, ship, transmit **7** = **promote**, advance, aid, assist, back, encourage, expedite, favour, foster, further, hasten, help, hurry, speed, support
> **Antonyms**
adjective ≠**presumptuous:** backward, diffident, modest, regressive, retiring, shy ♦ *adverb* ≠**forth:** backward(s) ♦ *verb* ≠**promote:** bar, block, hinder, hold up, impede, obstruct, retard, thwart

foster *verb* **1** = **bring up**, mother, nurse, raise, rear, take care of **2** = **promote**, cultivate, encourage, feed, foment, nurture, stimulate, support, uphold
> **Antonyms**
≠**promote:** combat, curb, curtail, hold out against, inhibit, oppose, resist, restrain, subdue, suppress, withstand

foul *adjective* **1** = **offensive**, abhorrent, abominable, base, despicable, detestable, disgraceful, dishonourable, egregious, hateful, heinous, infamous, iniquitous, nefarious, notorious, scandalous, shameful, shitty (*taboo slang*), vicious, vile, wicked **2** = **dirty**, contaminated, disgusting, fetid, filthy, grotty (*slang*), grungy (*slang, chiefly U.S.*), impure, loathsome, malodorous, mephitic, nasty, nauseating, noisome, offensive, polluted, putrid, rank, repulsive, revolting, rotten, scuzzy (*slang, chiefly U.S.*), squalid, stinking, sullied, tainted, unclean, yucky or yukky (*slang*) **3** = **obscene**, abusive, blasphemous, blue, coarse, dirty, filthy, foul-mouthed, gross, indecent, lewd, low, profane, scatological, scurrilous, smutty, vulgar **4** = **unfair**, crooked, dirty, dishonest, fraudulent, inequitable, shady (*informal*), underhand, unjust, unscrupulous, unsportsmanlike **5** = **stormy**, bad, blustery, disagreeable, foggy, murky, rainy, rough, wet, wild ♦ *verb* **6** = **dirty**, begrime, besmear, besmirch, contaminate, defile, pollute, smear, smirch, soil, stain, sully, taint **7** = **clog**, block, catch, choke, ensnare, entangle, jam, snarl, twist
> **Antonyms**
adjective ≠**offensive:** admirable, attractive, decent, pleasant, respectable ≠**dirty:** clean, clear, fair, fragrant, fresh, pure, spotless, undefiled ♦ *verb* ≠**dirty:** clean, cleanse, clear, purge, purify, sanitize

foul-mouthed *adjective* = **profane**, abusive, blasphemous, coarse, obscene, offensive

foul play *noun* = **crime**, chicanery, corruption, deception, dirty work, double-dealing, duplicity, fraud, perfidy, roguery, sharp practice, skulduggery, treachery, villainy

foul up *verb* = **bungle**, bodge (*informal*), botch, cock up (*Brit. slang*), make a mess of, make a nonsense of, make a pig's ear of (*informal*), mismanage, muck up (*slang*), put a spanner in the works (*Brit. informal*), spoil

found *verb* 1 = **establish**, bring into being, constitute, construct, create, endow, erect, fix, inaugurate, institute, organize, originate, plant, raise, settle, set up, start 2 = **base**, bottom, build, ground, rest, root, sustain

foundation *noun* 1 = **basis**, base, bedrock, bottom, footing, groundwork, substructure, underpinning 2 = **setting up**, endowment, establishment, inauguration, institution, organization, settlement

founder[1] *noun* = **initiator**, architect, author, beginner, benefactor, builder, constructor, designer, establisher, father, framer, generator, institutor, inventor, maker, organizer, originator, patriarch

founder[2] *verb* 1 = **fail**, abort, bite the dust, break down, collapse, come to grief, come to nothing, come unstuck, fall by the wayside, fall through, go belly-up (*slang*), go down like a lead balloon (*informal*), miscarry, misfire 2 = **sink**, be lost, go down, go to the bottom, submerge 3 = **stumble**, collapse, fall, go lame, lurch, sprawl, stagger, trip

foundling *noun* = **orphan**, outcast, stray, waif

fountain *noun* 1 = **jet**, font, fount, reservoir, spout, spray, spring, well 2 = **source**, beginning, cause, commencement, derivation, fount, fountainhead, genesis, origin, rise, wellhead, wellspring

fountainhead *noun* = **source**, fount, inspiration, mainspring, origin, spring, well, wellspring

foursquare *adverb* 1 = **squarely**, firmly, resolutely ♦ *adjective* 2 = **strong**, firm, firmly-based, immovable, resolute, solid, steady, unyielding

foxy *adjective* = **crafty**, artful, astute, canny, cunning, devious, guileful, knowing, sharp, shrewd, sly, tricky, wily

foyer *noun* = **entrance hall**, antechamber, anteroom, lobby, reception area, vestibule

fracas *noun* = **brawl**, affray (*Law*), aggro (*slang*), disturbance, fight, free-for-all (*informal*), melee *or* mêlée, quarrel, riot, row, rumpus, scrimmage, scuffle, shindig (*informal*), shindy (*informal*), skirmish, trouble, uproar

fraction *noun* 1 = **piece**, cut, division, moiety, part, percentage, portion, proportion, quota, ratio, section, sector, segment, share, slice, subdivision 2 = **fragment**, atom, bit, bite, chip, crumb, drop, flake, grain, granule, iota, jot, morsel, mote, particle, scrap, shard, shred, sliver, smithereen (*informal*), splinter, whit

fractious *adjective* = **irritable**, awkward, captious, crabby, cross, fretful, froward (*archaic*), grouchy (*informal*), peevish, pettish, petulant, querulous, ratty (*Brit. & N.Z. informal*), recalcitrant, refractory, testy, tetchy, touchy, unruly
➤ **Antonyms**
affable, agreeable, amiable, biddable, complaisant, genial, good-natured, good-tempered, tractable

fracture *noun* 1 = **break**, breach, cleft, crack, fissure, gap, opening, rent, rift, rupture, schism, split ♦ *verb* 2 = **break**, crack, rupture, splinter, split

fragile *adjective* = **delicate**, breakable, brittle, dainty, feeble, fine, flimsy, frail, frangible, infirm, slight, weak
➤ **Antonyms**
durable, elastic, flexible, hardy, lasting, reliable, resilient, robust, strong, sturdy, tough

fragility *noun* = **delicacy**, brittleness, feebleness, frailty, frangibility, infirmity, weakness

fragment *noun* 1 = **piece**, bit, chip, fraction, morsel, oddment, part, particle, portion, remnant, scrap, shiver, shred, sliver ♦ *verb* 2 = **break**, break up, come apart, come to pieces, crumble, disintegrate, disunite, divide, shatter, shiver, splinter, split, split up
➤ **Antonyms**
verb ≠**break:** bond, combine, compound, fuse, join together, link, marry, merge, synthesize, unify

fragmentary *adjective* = **incomplete**, bitty, broken, disconnected, disjointed, incoherent, partial, piecemeal, scattered, scrappy, sketchy, unsystematic

fragrance *noun* = **scent**, aroma, bouquet, perfume, redolence, smell, sweet odour
➤ **Antonyms**
effluvium, miasma, niff (*Brit. slang*), offensive smell, pong (*Brit. informal*), reek, smell, stink, whiff (*Brit. slang*)

fragrant *adjective* = **aromatic**, ambrosial, balmy, odoriferous, odorous, perfumed, redolent, sweet-scented, sweet-smelling
➤ **Antonyms**
fetid, foul-smelling, malodorous, niffy (*Brit. slang*), noisome, olid, pongy (*Brit. informal*), reeking, smelling, smelly, stinking

frail *adjective* = **weak**, breakable, brittle, decrepit, delicate, feeble, flimsy, fragile, frangible, infirm, insubstantial, puny, slight, tender, unsound, vulnerable, wispy
➤ **Antonyms**
hale, healthy, robust, sound, stalwart,

strong, sturdy, substantial, tough, vigorous

frailty *noun* 1 = **weakness**, fallibility, feebleness, frailness, infirmity, puniness, susceptibility 2 = **fault**, blemish, chink in one's armour, defect, deficiency, failing, flaw, foible, imperfection, shortcoming, vice, weak point
> **Antonyms**
≠**weakness:** fortitude, might, robustness, strength ≠**fault:** asset, strong point, virtue

frame *noun* 1 = **casing**, construction, fabric, form, framework, scheme, shell, structure, system 2 = **mounting**, mount, setting 3 = **physique**, anatomy, body, build, carcass, morphology, skeleton 4 **frame of mind** = **mood**, attitude, disposition, fettle, humour, outlook, spirit, state, temper ♦ *verb* 5 = **construct**, assemble, build, constitute, fabricate, fashion, forge, form, institute, invent, make, manufacture, model, mould, put together, set up 6 = **devise**, block out, compose, conceive, concoct, contrive, cook up, draft, draw up, form, formulate, hatch, map out, plan, shape, sketch 7 = **mount**, case, enclose, surround

frame-up *noun Slang* = **false charge**, fabrication, fit-up (*slang*), put-up job, trumped-up charge

framework *noun* = **structure**, core, fabric, foundation, frame, frame of reference, groundwork, plan, schema, shell, skeleton, the bare bones

franchise *noun* 1 = **vote**, suffrage 2 = **right**, authorization, charter, exemption, freedom, immunity, prerogative, privilege

frank *adjective* = **honest**, artless, blunt, candid, direct, downright, forthright, free, ingenuous, open, outright, outspoken, plain, plain-spoken, round, sincere, straightforward, straight from the shoulder (*informal*), transparent, truthful, unconcealed, undisguised, unreserved, unrestricted, upfront (*informal*)
> **Antonyms**
artful, crafty, cunning, evasive, indirect, inscrutable, reserved, reticent, secretive, shifty, shy, underhand

frankly *adverb* 1 = **honestly**, candidly, in truth, to be honest 2 = **openly**, bluntly, directly, freely, overtly, plainly, straight, straight from the shoulder, without reserve

frankness *noun* = **outspokenness**, absence of reserve, bluntness, candour, forthrightness, ingenuousness, laying it on the line, openness, plain speaking, truthfulness

frantic *adjective* 1 = **distraught**, at one's wits' end, at the end of one's tether, berserk, beside oneself, distracted, furious, mad, overwrought, raging, raving, uptight

(*informal*), wild 2 = **hectic**, desperate, fraught (*informal*), frenetic, frenzied
> **Antonyms**
calm, collected, composed, cool, laid-back, poised, self-possessed, together (*slang*), unfazed (*informal*), unruffled

fraternity *noun* 1 = **association**, brotherhood, circle, clan, club, company, guild, league, order, set, sodality, union 2 = **companionship**, brotherhood, camaraderie, comradeship, fellowship, kinship

fraternize *verb* = **associate**, concur, consort, cooperate, go around with, hang out (*informal*), hang with (*informal, chiefly U.S.*), hobnob, keep company, mingle, mix, socialize, sympathize, unite
> **Antonyms**
avoid, eschew, keep away from, shun, steer clear of

fraud *noun* 1 = **deception**, cheat, chicanery, deceit, double-dealing, duplicity, guile, hoax, humbug, imposture, scam (*slang*), sharp practice, spuriousness, sting (*informal*), stratagems, swindling, treachery, trickery 2 *Informal* = **impostor**, bluffer, charlatan, cheat, counterfeit, double-dealer, fake, forgery, fraudster, grifter (*slang, chiefly U.S. & Canad.*), hoax, hoaxer, phoney *or* phony (*informal*), pretender, quack, sham, swindler
> **Antonyms**
≠**deception:** fairness, good faith, honesty, integrity, probity, rectitude, trustworthiness, virtue

fraudulent *adjective* = **deceitful**, counterfeit, crafty, criminal, crooked (*informal*), deceptive, dishonest, double-dealing, duplicitous, false, phoney *or* phony (*informal*), sham, spurious, swindling, treacherous
> **Antonyms**
above board, genuine, honest, honourable, lawful, principled, reputable, true, trustworthy, upright

fraught *adjective* 1 *with* **with** = **filled**, abounding, accompanied, attended, bristling, charged, full, heavy, laden, stuffed 2 *Informal* = **tense**, agitated, anxious, difficult, distracted, distressed, distressing, emotionally charged, emotive, on tenterhooks, strung-up, tricky, trying, uptight (*informal*), wired (*slang*)

fray[1] *noun* = **fight**, battle, brawl, broil, clash, combat, conflict, disturbance, melee *or* mêlée, quarrel, riot, row, ruckus (*informal*), rumpus, scrimmage, scuffle, set-to (*informal*), shindig (*informal*), shindy (*informal*), skirmish

fray[2] *verb* = **wear thin**, become threadbare, chafe, fret, rub, wear, wear away

frayed *adjective* = **worn**, frazzled, out at elbows, ragged, tattered, threadbare

freak *noun* **1** = **oddity**, aberration, abnormality, abortion, anomaly, grotesque, malformation, monster, monstrosity, mutant, queer fish (*Brit. informal*), weirdo *or* weirdie (*informal*) **2** *Informal* = **enthusiast**, addict, aficionado, buff (*informal*), devotee, fan, fanatic, fiend (*informal*), nut (*slang*) ♦ *adjective* **3** = **abnormal**, aberrant, atypical, bizarre, erratic, exceptional, fluky (*informal*), fortuitous, odd, queer, unaccountable, unexpected, unforeseen, unparalleled, unpredictable, unusual

freakish *adjective* = **odd**, aberrant, abnormal, fantastic, freaky (*slang*), grotesque, malformed, monstrous, outlandish, outré, preternatural, strange, unconventional, weird

freaky *adjective* = **weird**, abnormal, bizarre, crazy, far-out (*slang*), freakish, odd, queer, rum (*Brit. slang*), strange, unconventional, wild

free *adjective* **1** = **at liberty**, at large, footloose, independent, liberated, loose, off the hook (*slang*), on the loose, uncommitted, unconstrained, unengaged, unfettered, unrestrained **2** = **allowed**, able, clear, disengaged, loose, open, permitted, unattached, unengaged, unhampered, unimpeded, unobstructed, unregulated, unrestricted, untrammelled **3** *with* **of** = **unaffected by**, above, beyond, deficient in, devoid of, exempt from, immune to, lacking (in), not liable to, safe from, unencumbered by, untouched by, without **4** = **independent**, autarchic, autonomous, democratic, emancipated, self-governing, self-ruling, sovereign **5** = **complimentary**, for free (*informal*), for nothing, free of charge, gratis, gratuitous, on the house, unpaid, without charge **6** = **available**, at leisure, empty, extra, idle, not tied down, spare, unemployed, uninhabited, unoccupied, unused, vacant **7** = **generous**, big (*informal*), bounteous, bountiful, charitable, eager, hospitable, lavish, liberal, munificent, open-handed, prodigal, unsparing, unstinting, willing **8 free and easy** = **relaxed**, casual, easy-going, informal, laid-back (*informal*), lax, lenient, liberal, tolerant, unceremonious ♦ *adverb* **9** = **freely**, abundantly, copiously, idly, loosely **10** = **without charge**, at no cost, for love, gratis ♦ *verb* **11** = **release**, deliver, discharge, emancipate, let go, let out, liberate, loose, set at liberty, set free, turn loose, unbridle, uncage, unchain, unfetter, unleash, untie **12** = **clear**, cut loose, disengage, disentangle, extricate, relieve, rescue, rid, unburden, undo

➤ **Antonyms**
adjective ≠ **at liberty**: bound, captive, confined, dependent, fettered, immured, incarcerated, restrained, restricted, secured ≠ **generous**: close, mean, mingy (*informal*), stingy, tight, ungenerous ♦ *verb* ≠ **release**: confine, imprison, incarcerate, inhibit, limit, restrain, restrict, straiten

freebooter *noun* = **pirate**, bandit, brigand, buccaneer, looter, marauder, pillager, plunderer, raider, reiver (*dialect*), robber

freedom *noun* **1** = **liberty**, autonomy, deliverance, emancipation, home rule, independence, manumission, release, self-government **2** = **exemption**, immunity, impunity, privilege **3** = **licence**, ability, a free hand, blank cheque, carte blanche, discretion, elbowroom, facility, flexibility, free rein, latitude, leeway, opportunity, play, power, range, scope **4** = **openness**, abandon, candour, directness, ease, familiarity, frankness, informality, ingenuousness, lack of restraint *or* reserve, unconstraint **5** = **overfamiliarity**, boldness, brazenness, disrespect, forwardness, impertinence, laxity, licence, presumption

➤ **Antonyms**
≠ **liberty**: bondage, captivity, dependence, imprisonment, servitude, slavery, thraldom ≠ **licence**: limitation, restriction ≠ **openness**: caution, restraint ≠ **overfamiliarity**: respectfulness

free-for-all *noun Informal* = **fight**, brawl, dust-up (*informal*), fracas, melee *or* mêlée, riot, row, scrimmage, shindig (*informal*), shindy (*informal*)

free hand *noun* = **freedom**, authority, blank cheque, carte blanche, discretion, latitude, liberty, scope

freely *adverb* **1** = **willingly**, of one's own accord, of one's own free will, spontaneously, voluntarily, without prompting **2** = **openly**, candidly, frankly, plainly, unreservedly, without reserve **3** = **without restraint**, as you please, unchallenged, without let or hindrance **4** = **abundantly**, amply, bountifully, copiously, extravagantly, lavishly, liberally, like water, open-handedly, unstintingly, with a free hand **5** = **easily**, cleanly, loosely, readily, smoothly

freethinker *noun* = **unbeliever**, agnostic, doubter, sceptic

freewheel *verb* = **coast**, drift, float, glide

freeze *verb* **1** = **chill**, benumb, congeal, glaciate, harden, ice over *or* up, stiffen **2** = **suspend**, fix, hold up, inhibit, peg, stop

freezing *adjective* = **icy**, arctic, biting, bitter, chill, chilled, cold as ice, cutting, frost-bound, frosty, glacial, numbing, parky

(*Brit. informal*), penetrating, polar, raw, Siberian, wintry

freight *noun* 1 = **transportation**, carriage, conveyance, shipment 2 = **cargo**, bales, bulk, burden, consignment, contents, goods, haul, lading, load, merchandise, payload, tonnage

French *adjective* = **Gallic**

frenetic *adjective* = **wild**, demented, distraught, excited, fanatical, frantic, frenzied, hyped up (*slang*), insane, mad, maniacal, obsessive, overwrought, unbalanced

frenzied *adjective* = **uncontrolled**, agitated, all het up (*informal*), berserk, convulsive, distracted, distraught, excited, feverish, frantic, frenetic, furious, hysterical, mad, maniacal, rabid, wild

frenzy *noun* 1 = **fury**, aberration, agitation, delirium, derangement, distraction, hysteria, insanity, lunacy, madness, mania, paroxysm, passion, rage, seizure, transport, turmoil 2 = **fit**, bout, burst, convulsion, outburst, paroxysm, spasm
➤ **Antonyms**
≠**fury:** calm, collectedness, composure, coolness, sanity

frequency *noun* = **recurrence**, constancy, frequentness, periodicity, prevalence, repetition

frequent *adjective* 1 = **common**, constant, continual, customary, everyday, familiar, habitual, incessant, numerous, persistent, recurrent, recurring, reiterated, repeated, usual ◆ *verb* 2 = **visit**, attend, be a regular customer of, be found at, hang out at (*informal*), haunt, patronize, resort
➤ **Antonyms**
adjective ≠**common:** few, few and far between, infrequent, occasional, rare, scanty, sporadic ◆ *verb* ≠**visit:** avoid, keep away, shun, spurn

frequently *adverb* = **often**, commonly, customarily, habitually, many a time, many times, much, not infrequently, over and over again, repeatedly, thick and fast, very often
➤ **Antonyms**
hardly ever, infrequently, occasionally, once in a blue moon (*informal*), rarely, seldom

fresh *adjective* 1 = **new**, different, ground-breaking, latest, left-field (*informal*), modern, modernistic, new-fangled, novel, original, recent, unconventional, unusual, up-to-date 2 = **additional**, added, auxiliary, extra, further, more, other, renewed, supplementary 3 = **natural**, crude, green, raw, uncured, undried, unprocessed, unsalted 4 = **invigorating**, bracing, bright, brisk, clean, clear, cool, crisp, pure, refreshing, sparkling, stiff, sweet, unpolluted

5 = **lively**, alert, bouncing, bright, bright-eyed and bushy-tailed (*informal*), chipper (*informal*), energetic, full of beans (*informal*), full of vim and vigour (*informal*), invigorated, keen, like a new man, refreshed, rested, restored, revived, sprightly, spry, vigorous, vital 6 = **vivid**, dewy, undimmed, unfaded, unwearied, unwithered, verdant 7 = **rosy**, blooming, clear, fair, florid, glowing, good, hardy, healthy, ruddy, wholesome 8 = **inexperienced**, artless, callow, green, natural, new, raw, uncultivated, untrained, untried, youthful 9 *Informal* = **cheeky**, bold, brazen, disrespectful, familiar, flip (*informal*), forward, impudent, insolent, pert, presumptuous, sassy (*U.S. informal*), saucy, smart-alecky (*informal*)
➤ **Antonyms**
≠**new:** dull, old, ordinary, stereotyped, trite ≠**natural:** frozen, pickled, preserved, salted, tinned ≠**invigorating:** impure, musty, stale, warm ≠**lively:** exhausted, weary ≠**vivid:** old, weary ≠**rosy:** pallid, sickly ≠**inexperienced:** experienced, old ≠**cheeky:** well-mannered

freshen *verb* = **refresh**, enliven, freshen up, liven up, restore, revitalize, rouse, spruce up, titivate

freshness *noun* 1 = **novelty**, innovativeness, inventiveness, newness, originality 2 = **cleanness**, bloom, brightness, clearness, dewiness, glow, shine, sparkle, vigour, wholesomeness

fret *verb* 1 = **worry**, agonize, anguish, brood, lose sleep over, obsess about, upset *or* distress oneself 2 = **rub**, abrade, chafe, erode, fray, gall, wear, wear away 3 = **annoy**, agitate, bother, distress, disturb, gall, goad, grieve, harass, irk, irritate, nag, nettle, peeve (*informal*), pique, provoke, rankle with, rile, ruffle, torment, trouble, vex

fretful *adjective* = **irritable**, captious, complaining, cross, crotchety (*informal*), edgy, fractious, out of sorts, peevish, petulant, querulous, ratty (*Brit. & N.Z. informal*), short-tempered, splenetic, testy, tetchy, touchy, uneasy

friable *adjective* = **crumbly**, brittle, crisp, powdery, pulverizable

friction *noun* 1 = **rubbing**, abrasion, attrition, chafing, erosion, fretting, grating, irritation, rasping, resistance, scraping, wearing away 2 = **hostility**, animosity, antagonism, bad blood, bad feeling, bickering, conflict, disagreement, discontent, discord, disharmony, dispute, dissension, incompatibility, opposition, resentment, rivalry, wrangling

friend *noun* 1 = **companion**, alter ego, boon companion, bosom friend, buddy (*informal*), china (*Brit. slang*), chum

(*informal*), comrade, confidant, crony, intimate, mate (*informal*), pal, partner, playmate, soul mate **2** = **supporter**, adherent, advocate, ally, associate, backer, benefactor, partisan, patron, protagonist, well-wisher
➤ **Antonyms**
adversary, antagonist, competitor, enemy, foe, opponent, rival

friendless *adjective* = **alone**, abandoned, alienated, all alone, cut off, deserted, estranged, forlorn, forsaken, isolated, lonely, lonesome, ostracized, shunned, solitary, unattached, with no one to turn to, without a friend in the world, without ties

friendliness *noun* = **amiability**, affability, companionability, congeniality, conviviality, geniality, kindliness, mateyness *or* matiness (*Brit. informal*), neighbourliness, open arms, sociability, warmth

friendly *adjective* = **amiable**, affable, affectionate, amicable, attached, attentive, auspicious, beneficial, benevolent, benign, chummy (*informal*), close, companionable, comradely, conciliatory, confiding, convivial, cordial, familiar, favourable, fond, fraternal, genial, good, helpful, intimate, kind, kindly, matey *or* maty (*Brit. informal*), neighbourly, on good terms, on visiting terms, outgoing, pally (*informal*), peaceable, propitious, receptive, sociable, sympathetic, thick (*informal*), welcoming, well-disposed
➤ **Antonyms**
antagonistic, belligerent, cold, contentious, distant, inauspicious, sinister, uncongenial, unfriendly

friendship *noun* = **friendliness**, affection, affinity, alliance, amity, attachment, benevolence, closeness, concord, familiarity, fondness, good-fellowship, goodwill, harmony, intimacy, love, rapport, regard
➤ **Antonyms**
animosity, antagonism, antipathy, aversion, bad blood, conflict, enmity, hatred, hostility, resentment, strife, unfriendliness

fright *noun* **1** = **fear**, alarm, apprehension, (blue) funk (*informal*), cold sweat, consternation, dismay, dread, fear and trembling, horror, panic, quaking, scare, shock, terror, the shivers, trepidation **2** *Informal* = **sight** (*informal*), eyesore, frump, mess (*informal*), scarecrow
➤ **Antonyms**
≠**fear**: boldness, bravery, courage, pluck, valor

frighten *verb* = **scare**, alarm, appal, cow, daunt, dismay, freeze one's blood, get the wind up, intimidate, make one's blood run cold, make one's hair stand on end (*informal*), make (someone) jump out of his skin (*informal*), petrify, put the wind up

(someone) (*informal*), scare (someone) stiff, scare the living daylights out of (someone) (*informal*), shock, startle, terrify, terrorize, throw into a fright, throw into a panic, unnerve
➤ **Antonyms**
allay, assuage, calm, comfort, encourage, hearten, reassure, soothe

frightened *adjective* = **afraid**, abashed, alarmed, cowed, dismayed, frozen, in a cold sweat, in a panic, in fear and trepidation, numb with fear, panicky, petrified, scared, scared shitless (*taboo slang*), scared stiff, shit-scared (*taboo slang*), startled, terrified, terrorized, terror-stricken, unnerved

frightening *adjective* = **terrifying**, alarming, appalling, baleful, bloodcurdling, daunting, dismaying, dreadful, fearful, fearsome, hair-raising, horrifying, intimidating, menacing, scary (*informal*), shocking, spooky (*informal*), unnerving

frightful *adjective* **1** = **terrifying**, alarming, appalling, awful, dire, dread, dreadful, fearful, from hell (*informal*), ghastly, godawful (*slang*), grim, grisly, gruesome, harrowing, hellacious (*U.S. slang*), hideous, horrendous, horrible, horrid, lurid, macabre, petrifying, shocking, terrible, traumatic, unnerving, unspeakable **2** = **dreadful**, annoying, awful, disagreeable, extreme, great, insufferable, terrible, terrific, unpleasant
➤ **Antonyms**
≠**terrifying**: attractive, beautiful, calming, lovely, nice, pleasant, soothing ≠**dreadful**: moderate, pleasant, slight

frigid *adjective* **1** = **unresponsive**, aloof, austere, cold as ice, cold-hearted, forbidding, formal, icy, lifeless, passionless, passive, repellent, rigid, stiff, unapproachable, unbending, unfeeling, unloving **2** = **cold**, arctic, chill, cool, frost-bound, frosty, frozen, gelid, glacial, hyperboreal, icy, Siberian, wintry
➤ **Antonyms**
≠**unresponsive**: ardent, cordial, friendly, hospitable, hot, impassioned, passionate, responsive, sensual, warm ≠**cold**: hot, stifling, sweltering, warm

frigidity *noun* = **unresponsiveness**, aloofness, austerity, chill, cold-heartedness, coldness, frostiness, iciness, impassivity, lack of response, lifelessness, passivity, touch-me-not attitude, unapproachability, wintriness

frill *noun* = **ruffle**, flounce, gathering, ruche, ruching, ruff, tuck

frills *plural noun* = **trimmings**, additions, bells and whistles, bits and pieces, decoration(s), dressing up, embellishments, extras, fanciness, finery, frilliness, frippery, fuss, gewgaws, icing on the cake, jazz (*slang*), mannerisms, nonsense, ornamentation, ostentation

frilly *adjective* = **ruffled**, fancy, flouncy, frothy, lacy, ruched

fringe *noun* 1 ■ **border**, binding, edging, hem, tassel, trimming 2 = **edge**, borderline, limits, march, marches, margin, outskirts, perimeter, periphery ♦ *adjective* 3 = **unofficial**, unconventional, unorthodox ♦ *verb* 4 = **border**, edge, enclose, skirt, surround, trim

fringed *adjective* = **edged**, befringed, bordered, margined, outlined, overhung

frippery *noun* 1 = **frills**, fanciness, finery, flashiness, frilliness, fussiness, gaudiness, glad rags (*informal*), nonsense, ostentation, showiness 2 = **decoration**, adornment, bauble, fandangle, gewgaw, icing on the cake, knick-knack, ornament, toy, trinket

frisk *verb* 1 = **frolic**, bounce, caper, cavort, curvet, dance, gambol, hop, jump, play, prance, rollick, romp, skip, sport, trip 2 *Informal* = **search**, check, inspect, run over, shake down (*U.S. slang*)

frisky *adjective* = **lively**, bouncy, coltish, frolicsome, full of beans (*informal*), full of joie de vivre, high-spirited, in high spirits, kittenish, playful, rollicking, romping, spirited, sportive
➤ **Antonyms**
demure, dull, lacklustre, pensive, sedate, stodgy, stolid, wooden

fritter away *verb* = **waste**, dally away, dissipate, idle away, misspend, run through, spend like water, squander

frivolity *noun* = **flippancy**, childishness, desipience, flightiness, flummery, folly, frivolousness, fun, gaiety, giddiness, jest, levity, light-heartedness, lightness, nonsense, puerility, shallowness, silliness, superficiality, trifling, triviality
➤ **Antonyms**
earnestness, gravity, humourlessness, importance, sedateness, seriousness, significance, soberness, sobriety

frivolous *adjective* 1 = **flippant**, childish, ditzy or ditsy (*slang*), dizzy, empty-headed, flighty, flip (*informal*), foolish, giddy, idle, ill-considered, juvenile, light-minded, nonserious, pucrile, silly, superficial 2 = **trivial**, footling (*informal*), impractical, light, minor, nickel-and-dime (*U.S. slang*), niggling, paltry, peripheral, petty, pointless, shallow, trifling, unimportant
➤ **Antonyms**
≠**flippant**: earnest, mature, practical, responsible, sensible, serious, solemn
≠**trivial**: important, serious, vital

frizzle *verb* = **crisp**, fry, hiss, roast, scorch,

sizzle, sputter

frolic *verb* 1 = **play**, caper, cavort, cut capers, frisk, gambol, lark, make merry, romp, sport ♦ *noun* 2 = **merriment**, amusement, drollery, fun, fun and games, gaiety, high jinks, skylarking (*informal*), sport 3 = **revel**, antic, escapade, gambol, game, lark, prank, romp, spree

frolicsome *adjective* = **playful**, coltish, frisky, full of beans (*informal*), gay, kittenish, lively, merry, rollicking, sportive, sprightly

front *noun* 1 = **exterior**, anterior, façade, face, facing, foreground, forepart, frontage, obverse 2 = **forefront**, beginning, fore, front line, head, lead, top, van, vanguard 3 = **appearance**, air, aspect, bearing, countenance, demeanour, expression, exterior, face, manner, mien, show 4 *Informal* = **disguise**, blind, cover, cover-up, façade, mask, pretext, show 5 **in front** = **in advance**, ahead, before, first, in the lead, in the van, leading, preceding, to the fore ♦ *adjective* 6 = **foremost**, first, head, headmost, lead, leading, topmost ♦ *verb* 7 = **face onto**, look over or onto, overlook
➤ **Antonyms**
adjective ≠**foremost**: aft, back, back end, behind, hindmost, nethermost, rear

frontier *noun* = **boundary**, borderland, borderline, bound, confines, edge, limit, marches, perimeter, verge

frost *noun* = **hoarfrost**, freeze, freeze-up, Jack Frost, rime

frosty *adjective* 1 = **cold**, chilly, frozen, ice-capped, icicled, icy, parky (*Brit. informal*), wintry 2 = **unfriendly**, cold as ice, discouraging, frigid, off-putting (*Brit. informal*), standoffish, unenthusiastic, unwelcoming

froth *noun* 1 = **foam**, bubbles, effervescence, head, lather, scum, spume, suds ♦ *verb* 2 = **fizz**, bubble over, come to a head, effervesce, foam, lather

frothy *adjective* 1 = **foamy**, foaming, spumescent, spumous, spumy, sudsy 2 = **trivial**, empty, frilly, frivolous, light, petty, slight, trifling, unnecessary, unsubstantial, vain

frown *verb* 1 = **scowl**, give a dirty look, glare, glower, knit one's brows, look daggers, lour or lower 2 **frown on** = **disapprove of**, discountenance, discourage, dislike, look askance at, not take kindly to, show disapproval or displeasure, take a dim view of, view with disfavour

frowsty *adjective* = **stale**, close, fuggy, fusty, ill-smelling, musty, stuffy

frowzy *adjective* = **slovenly**, blowsy, dirty, frumpy, messy, slatternly, sloppy, sluttish, ungroomed, unkempt, untidy, unwashed

frozen *adjective* 1 = **icy**, arctic, chilled, chilled to the marrow, frigid, frosted, icebound, ice-cold, ice-covered, numb 2 = **fixed**, pegged (*of prices*), stopped, suspended 3 = **motionless**, petrified, rooted, stock-still, turned to stone

frugal *adjective* = **thrifty**, abstemious, careful, cheeseparing, economical, meagre, niggardly, parsimonious, penny-wise, provident, prudent, saving, sparing
➤ **Antonyms**
excessive, extravagant, imprudent, lavish, luxurious, prodigal, profligate, spendthrift, wasteful

frugality *noun* = **thrift**, carefulness, conservation, economizing, economy, good management, husbandry, moderation, providence, thriftiness

fruit *noun* 1 = **produce**, crop, harvest, product, yield 2 *plural* = **result**, advantage, benefit, consequence, effect, end result, outcome, profit, return, reward

fruitful *adjective* 1 = **useful**, advantageous, beneficial, effective, gainful, productive, profitable, rewarding, successful, well-spent, worthwhile 2 = **fertile**, fecund 3 = **plentiful**, abundant, copious, flush, plenteous, productive, profuse, prolific, rich, spawning
➤ **Antonyms**
≠**useful**: fruitless, futile, ineffectual, pointless, unfruitful, unproductive, useless, vain ≠**fertile**: barren, fruitless, infertile, sterile, unfruitful, unproductive ≠**plentiful**: scarce

fruition *noun* = **fulfilment**, actualization, attainment, completion, consummation, enjoyment, materialization, maturation, maturity, perfection, realization, ripeness

fruitless *adjective* 1 = **useless**, abortive, bootless, futile, idle, ineffectual, in vain, pointless, profitless, to no avail, to no effect, unavailing, unfruitful, unproductive, unprofitable, unsuccessful, vain 2 = **barren**, unfruitful, unproductive, unprolific
➤ **Antonyms**
≠**useless**: effective, fruitful, productive, profitable, useful ≠**barren**: abundant, fecund, fertile, fruitful, productive, prolific

fruity *adjective* 1 = **rich**, full, mellow, resonant 2 *Informal, chiefly Brit.* = **risqué**, bawdy, blue, hot, indecent, indelicate, juicy, near the knuckle (*informal*), racy, ripe, salacious, sexy, smutty, spicy (*informal*), suggestive, titillating, vulgar

frumpy, frumpish *adjective* = **dowdy**, badly-dressed, dated, dingy, drab, dreary, mumsy, out of date

frustrate *verb* = **thwart**, baffle, balk, block, check, circumvent, confront, counter, defeat, disappoint, foil, forestall, inhibit, neutralize, nullify, render null and void, stymie

➤ **Antonyms**
advance, encourage, endorse, forward, further, promote, satisfy, stimulate

frustrated *adjective* = **disappointed**, carrying a chip on one's shoulder (*informal*), choked, discontented, discouraged, disheartened, embittered, foiled, irked, resentful, sick as a parrot (*informal*)

frustration *noun* 1 = **annoyance**, disappointment, dissatisfaction, grievance, irritation, resentment, vexation 2 = **obstruction**, blocking, circumvention, contravention, curbing, failure, foiling, nonfulfilment, nonsuccess, thwarting

fuddled *adjective* 1 = **confused**, muddled, muzzy 2 = **drunk**, bevvied (*dialect*), blitzed (*slang*), blotto (*slang*), bombed (*slang*), flying (*slang*), inebriated, intoxicated, legless (*informal*), lit up (*slang*), out of it (*slang*), paralytic (*informal*), pissed (*taboo slang*), rat-arsed (*taboo slang*), smashed (*slang*), sozzled (*informal*), steamboats (*Scot. slang*), steaming (*slang*), stupefied, tipsy, wasted (*slang*), woozy (*informal*), wrecked (*slang*), zonked (*slang*)

fuddy-duddy *noun Informal* = **conservative**, dinosaur, dodo (*informal*), fossil, museum piece, (old) fogey, square (*informal*), stick-in-the-mud (*informal*), stuffed shirt (*informal*)

fudge *verb* = **misrepresent**, avoid, cook (*slang*), dodge, equivocate, evade, fake, falsify, flannel (*Brit. informal*), hedge, stall

fuel *noun* 1 = **incitement**, ammunition, encouragement, fodder, food, material, means, nourishment, provocation ◆ *verb* 2 = **inflame**, charge, fan, feed, fire, incite, nourish, stoke up, sustain

fug *noun* = **stale air**, fetidity, fetor, frowst, frowstiness, fustiness, reek, staleness, stink

fuggy *adjective* = **stuffy**, airless, fetid, foul, frowsty, noisome, noxious, stale, suffocating, unventilated

fugitive *noun* 1 = **runaway**, deserter, escapee, refugee ◆ *adjective* 2 = **momentary**, brief, ephemeral, evanescent, fleeing, fleeting, flitting, flying, passing, short, short-lived, temporary, transient, transitory

fulfil *verb* 1 = **achieve**, accomplish, bring to completion, carry out, complete, conclude, discharge, effect, execute, finish, keep, perfect, perform, realise, satisfy 2 = **comply with**, answer, conform to, fill, meet, obey, observe
➤ **Antonyms**
disappoint, dissatisfy, fail in, fail to meet, fall short of, neglect

fulfilment *noun* = **achievement**, accomplishment, attainment, carrying out *or* through, completion, consummation, discharge, discharging, effecting, end, implementation, observance, perfection, realization

full *adjective* 1 = **filled**, brimful, brimming, bursting at the seams, complete, entire, gorged, intact, loaded, replete, sated, satiated, satisfied, saturated, stocked, sufficient 2 = **crammed**, chock-a-block, chock-full, crowded, in use, jammed, occupied, packed, taken 3 = **extensive**, abundant, adequate, all-inclusive, ample, broad, comprehensive, copious, detailed, exhaustive, generous, maximum, plenary, plenteous, plentiful, thorough, unabridged 4 = **plump**, buxom, curvaceous, rounded, voluptuous 5 = **rich**, clear, deep, distinct, loud, resonant, rounded 6 = **voluminous**, baggy, balloon-like, capacious, large, loose, puffy ◆ *noun* 7 **in full** = **completely**, in its entirety, in total, *in toto*, without exception 8 **to the full** = **thoroughly**, completely, entirely, fully, to the utmost, without reservation
➤ **Antonyms**
adjective ≠**filled**, **crammed**: blank, devoid, empty, vacant, void ≠**extensive**: abridged, incomplete, limited, partial ≠**rich**: faint, thin ≠**voluminous**: restricted, tight

full-blooded *adjective* = **vigorous**, ballsy (*taboo slang*), gutsy (*slang*), hearty, lusty, mettlesome, red-blooded, virile

full-blown *adjective* = **fully developed**, advanced, complete, developed, entire, full, full-scale, full-sized, fully fledged, fully formed, fully grown, progressed, total, whole
➤ **Antonyms**
dormant, latent, potential, undeveloped

full-bodied *adjective* = **rich**, fruity, full-flavoured, heady, heavy, mellow, redolent, strong, well-matured

fullness *noun* 1 = **plenty**, abundance, adequateness, ampleness, copiousness, fill, glut, profusion, repletion, satiety, saturation, sufficiency 2 = **completeness**, broadness, comprehensiveness, entirety, extensiveness, totality, vastness, wealth, wholeness 3 = **roundness**, curvaceousness, voluptuousness 4 = **richness**, clearness, loudness, resonance, strength

full-scale *adjective* = **major**, all-encompassing, all-out, comprehensive, exhaustive, extensive, full-dress, in-depth, proper, sweeping, thorough, thoroughgoing, wide-ranging

fully *adverb* 1 = **totally**, absolutely, altogether, completely, entirely, every inch, from first to last, heart and soul, in all respects, intimately, lock, stock and barrel, one hundred per cent, perfectly, positively,

thoroughly, to the hilt, utterly, wholly 2 = **adequately**, abundantly, amply, comprehensively, enough, plentifully, satisfactorily, sufficiently 3 = **at least**, quite, without (any) exaggeration, without a word of a lie (*informal*)

fulminate *verb* = **criticize**, berate, blast, castigate, censure, denounce, denunciate, fume, inveigh against, lambast(e), protest against, rage, rail against, tear into (*informal*), upbraid, vilify, vituperate

fulmination *noun* = **condemnation**, denunciation, diatribe, invective, reprobation, tirade

fulsome *adjective* = **extravagant**, adulatory, cloying, excessive, fawning, gross, icky (*informal*), immoderate, ingratiating, inordinate, insincere, nauseating, overdone, over the top, saccharine, sickening, smarmy (*Brit. informal*), sycophantic, unctuous

fumble *verb* 1 = **grope**, feel around, flounder, paw (*informal*), scrabble 2 = **bungle**, bodge (*informal*), botch, cock up (*Brit. slang*), fuck up (*offensive taboo slang*), make a hash of (*informal*), make a nonsense of, mess up, misfield, mishandle, mismanage, muff, spoil

fume *verb* = **rage**, blow a fuse (*slang, chiefly U.S.*), boil, chafe, champ at the bit (*informal*), crack up (*informal*), fly off the handle (*informal*), get hot under the collar (*informal*), get steamed up about (*slang*), go ballistic (*slang, chiefly U.S.*), go off the deep end (*informal*), go up the wall (*slang*), rant, rave, see red (*informal*), seethe, smoulder, storm, wig out (*slang*)

fumes *noun* = **smoke**, effluvium, exhalation, exhaust, gas, haze, miasma, pollution, reek, smog, stench, vapour

fumigate *verb* = **disinfect**, clean out *or* up, cleanse, purify, sanitize, sterilize

fuming *adjective* = **furious**, all steamed up (*slang*), angry, at boiling point (*informal*), choked, enraged, fit to be tied (*slang*), foaming at the mouth, in a rage, incandescent, incensed, on the warpath (*informal*), pissed (*taboo slang*), pissed off (*taboo slang*), raging, roused, seething, up in arms

fun *noun* 1 = **enjoyment**, amusement, beer and skittles (*informal*), cheer, distraction, diversion, entertainment, frolic, gaiety, good time, high jinks, jollity, joy, living it up, merriment, merrymaking, mirth, pleasure, recreation, romp, sport, treat 2 = **joking**, clowning, foolery, game, horseplay, jesting, jocularity, nonsense, play, playfulness, skylarking (*informal*), sport, teasing 3 **in** *or* **for fun** = **for a joke**, facetiously, for a laugh, in jest, jokingly, light-heartedly,

mischievously, playfully, roguishly, teasingly, tongue in cheek, with a gleam *or* twinkle in one's eye, with a straight face **4 make fun of** = **mock**, deride, hold up to ridicule, lampoon, laugh at, make a fool of, make a monkey of, make game of, make sport of, parody, poke fun at, rag, rib (*informal*), ridicule, satirize, scoff at, send up (*Brit. informal*), sneer at, take off, take the piss out of (*taboo slang*), taunt ♦ *adjective* **5** = **enjoyable**, amusing, convivial, diverting, entertaining, lively, witty
➤ **Antonyms**
noun ≠**enjoyment**: depression, desolation, despair, distress, gloom, grief, melancholy, misery, sadness, sorrow, unhappiness, woe

function *noun* **1** = **purpose**, activity, business, capacity, charge, concern, duty, employment, exercise, job, mission, occupation, office, operation, part, post, province, *raison d'être,* responsibility, role, situation, task **2** = **reception**, affair, do (*informal*), gathering, social occasion ♦ *verb* **3** = **work**, act, act the part of, behave, be in business, be in commission, be in operation *or* action, be in running order, do duty, go, officiate, operate, perform, run, serve, serve one's turn

functional *adjective* **1** = **practical**, hard-wearing, serviceable, useful, utilitarian, utility **2** = **working**, operative

functionary *noun* = **officer**, dignitary, employee, office bearer, office holder, official

fund *noun* **1** = **reserve**, capital, endowment, fall-back, foundation, kitty, pool, stock, store, supply **2** = **store**, hoard, mine, repository, reserve, reservoir, source, treasury, vein ♦ *verb* **3** = **finance**, capitalize, endow, float, pay for, promote, stake, subsidize, support

fundamental *adjective* **1** = **essential**, basic, cardinal, central, constitutional, crucial, elementary, first, important, indispensable, integral, intrinsic, key, necessary, organic, primary, prime, principal, radical, rudimentary, underlying, vital ♦ *noun* **2** = **principle**, axiom, basic, cornerstone, essential, first principle, law, rudiment, rule, *sine qua non*
➤ **Antonyms**
adjective ≠**essential**: advanced, back-up, extra, incidental, lesser, secondary, subsidiary, superfluous

fundamentally *adverb* = **essentially**, at bottom, at heart, basically, intrinsically, primarily, radically

funds *plural noun* = **money**, brass (*Northern English dialect*), bread (*slang*), capital, cash, dosh (*Brit. & Austral. slang*), dough (*slang*), finance, hard cash, necessary (*informal*), needful (*informal*), ready money, resources, savings, the ready

(*informal*), the wherewithal

funeral *noun* = **burial**, cremation, inhumation, interment, obsequies

funereal *adjective* = **gloomy**, dark, depressing, dismal, dreary, grave, lugubrious, mournful, sad, sepulchral, solemn, sombre, woeful

funk *verb* = **chicken out of** (*informal*), dodge, duck out of (*informal*), flinch from, recoil from, take fright, turn tail

funnel *verb* = **channel**, conduct, convey, direct, filter, move, pass, pour

funny *adjective* **1** = **humorous**, absurd, a card (*informal*), a caution (*informal*), amusing, a scream, comic, comical, diverting, droll, entertaining, facetious, farcical, hilarious, jocose, jocular, jolly, laughable, ludicrous, rich, ridiculous, riotous, risible, side-splitting, silly, witty **2** = **peculiar**, curious, dubious, mysterious, odd, perplexing, puzzling, queer, remarkable, rum (*Brit. slang*), strange, suspicious, unusual, weird
➤ **Antonyms**
≠**humorous**: grave, humourless, melancholy, serious, sober, solemn, stern, unfunny

furbish *verb Formal* = **renovate**, brighten, burnish, polish, restore, rub, shine, smarten up, spruce up

furious *adjective* **1** = **angry**, beside oneself, boiling, choked, cross, enraged, fit to be tied (*slang*), foaming at the mouth, frantic, frenzied, fuming, incandescent, incensed, infuriated, in high dudgeon, livid (*informal*), mad, maddened, on the warpath (*informal*), pissed (*taboo slang*), pissed off (*taboo slang*), raging, up in arms, wrathful **2** = **violent**, agitated, boisterous, fierce, impetuous, intense, savage, stormy, tempestuous, tumultuous, turbulent, ungovernable, unrestrained, vehement, wild
➤ **Antonyms**
≠**angry**: calm, dispassionate, impassive, imperturbable, mild, placated, pleased, serene, tranquil

furnish *verb* **1** = **decorate**, appoint, equip, fit, fit out, fit up, outfit, provide, provision, purvey, rig, stock, store, supply **2** = **supply**, afford, bestow, endow, give, grant, hand out, offer, present, provide, reveal

furniture *noun* = **household goods**, appliances, appointments, chattels, effects, equipment, fittings, furnishings, goods, movable property, movables, possessions, things (*informal*)

furore *noun* = **commotion**, brouhaha, disturbance, excitement, flap (*informal*), frenzy, fury, hullabaloo, outburst, outcry, stir, to-do, uproar

furrow *noun* **1** = **groove**, channel,

corrugation, crease, hollow, line, rut, seam, trench, wrinkle ♦ *verb* **2 = wrinkle**, corrugate, crease, draw together, knit, seam

further *adverb* **1 = in addition**, additionally, also, as well as, besides, furthermore, into the bargain, moreover, on top of, over and above, to boot, what's more, yet ♦ *adjective* **2 = additional**, extra, fresh, more, new, other, supplementary ♦ *verb* **3 = promote**, advance, aid, assist, champion, contribute to, encourage, expedite, facilitate, forward, foster, hasten, help, lend support to, pave the way for, plug (*informal*), push, speed, succour, work for
➤ **Antonyms**
verb ≠ **promote**: foil, frustrate, hinder, hobble, impede, obstruct, oppose, prevent, retard, stop, thwart

furtherance *noun* **= promotion**, advancement, advocacy, backing, boosting, carrying-out, championship, prosecution, pursuit

furthermore *adverb* **= besides**, additionally, as well, further, in addition, into the bargain, moreover, not to mention, to boot, too, what's more

furthest *adjective* **= most distant**, extreme, farthest, furthermost, outermost, outmost, remotest, ultimate, uttermost

furtive *adjective* **= sly**, behind someone's back, clandestine, cloaked, conspiratorial, covert, hidden, secret, secretive, skulking, slinking, sneaking, sneaky, stealthy, surreptitious, underhand, under-the-table
➤ **Antonyms**
above-board, candid, forthright, frank, open, public, straightforward, undisguised, unreserved

fury *noun* **1 = anger**, frenzy, impetuosity, ire, madness, passion, rage, red mist (*informal*), wrath **2 = violence**, ferocity, fierceness, force, intensity, power, savagery, severity, tempestuousness, turbulence, vehemence **3 = spitfire**, hellcat, shrew, termagant, virago, vixen
➤ **Antonyms**
≠ **anger**: calm, calmness, composure, equanimity ≠ **violence**: hush, peace, peacefulness, serenity, stillness, tranquillity

fuse *verb* **= join**, amalgamate, blend, coalesce, combine, commingle, dissolve, integrate, intermingle, intermix, meld, melt, merge, run together, solder, unite, weld
➤ **Antonyms**
diffuse, dispense, disseminate, dissipate, disunite, scatter, separate, spread, strew

fusillade *noun* **= barrage**, broadside, burst, fire, hail, outburst, salvo, volley

fusion *noun* **= merging**, alloy, amalgam, amalgamation, blend, blending, coalescence, commingling, commixture, integration, meld, merger, mixture, smelting, union, uniting, welding

fuss *noun* **1 = bother**, ado, agitation, bustle, commotion, confusion, excitement, fidget, flap (*informal*), flurry, fluster, flutter, hue and cry, hurry, palaver, stir, storm in a teacup (*Brit.*), to-do, upset, worry **2 = argument**, altercation, bother, complaint, difficulty, display, furore, hassle (*informal*), objection, row, squabble, trouble, unrest, upset ♦ *verb* **3 = worry**, bustle, chafe, fidget, flap (*informal*), fret, fume, get in a stew (*informal*), get worked up, labour over, make a meal of (*informal*), make a thing of (*informal*), niggle, take pains

fusspot *noun Brit. informal* **= nit-picker** (*informal*), fidget, old woman, perfectionist, worrier

fussy *adjective* **1 = particular**, choosy (*informal*), dainty, difficult, discriminating, exacting, faddish, faddy, fastidious, finicky, hard to please, nit-picking (*informal*), old-maidish, old womanish, overparticular, pernickety, picky (*informal*), squeamish **2 = overelaborate**, busy, cluttered, overdecorated, overembellished, overworked, rococo

fusty *adjective* **1 = stale**, airless, damp, frowsty, mildewed, mouldering, mouldy, musty, stuffy **2 = old-fashioned**, antediluvian, antiquated, archaic, old-fogeyish, outdated, out-of-date, out of the ark (*informal*), passé

futile *adjective* **1 = useless**, abortive, barren, bootless, empty, forlorn, fruitless, hollow, ineffectual, in vain, profitless, to no avail, unavailing, unproductive, unprofitable, unsuccessful, vain, valueless, worthless **2 = trivial**, idle, pointless, trifling, unimportant
➤ **Antonyms**
≠ **useless**: constructive, effective, fruitful, profitable, purposeful, successful, useful, valuable, worthwhile ≠ **trivial**: important, significant

futility *noun* **1 = uselessness**, bootlessness, emptiness, fruitlessness, hollowness, ineffectiveness **2 = triviality**, pointlessness, unimportance, vanity

future *noun* **1 = time to come**, hereafter **2 = prospect**, expectation, outlook ♦ *adjective* **3 = forthcoming**, approaching, coming, destined, eventual, expected, fated, impending, in the offing, later, prospective, subsequent, to be, to come, ultimate, unborn
➤ **Antonyms**
adjective ≠ **forthcoming**: bygone, erstwhile, ex-, former, late, past, preceding, previous, quondam

fuzz *noun* = **fluff**, down, fibre, floss, hair, nap, pile

fuzzy *adjective* **1** = **fluffy**, down-covered, downy, flossy, frizzy, woolly **2** = **indistinct**, bleary, blurred, distorted, faint, ill-defined, muffled, out of focus, shadowy, unclear, unfocused, vague

➤ **Antonyms**

≠**indistinct:** clear, defined, detailed, distinct, in focus, precise

G g

gabble *verb* **1** = **prattle**, babble, blab, blabber, cackle, chatter, gaggle, gibber, gush, jabber, rabbit (*Brit. informal*), rattle, run off at the mouth (*slang*), splutter, spout, sputter, waffle (*informal, chiefly Brit.*) ◆ *noun* **2** = **gibberish**, babble, blabber, cackling, chatter, drivel, jargon, pap, prattle, twaddle, waffle (*informal, chiefly Brit.*)

gad *verb, with* **about** *or* **around** = **gallivant**, ramble, range, roam, rove, run around, stravaig (*Scot. & Northern English dialect*), stray, traipse (*informal*), wander

gadabout *noun* = **pleasure-seeker**, gallivanter, rambler, rover, wanderer

gadget *noun* = **device**, appliance, contraption (*informal*), contrivance, gimmick, gizmo (*slang, chiefly U.S.*), instrument, invention, novelty, thing, tool, waldo

gaffe *noun* = **blunder**, bloomer (*informal*), boob (*Brit. slang*), boo-boo (*informal*), clanger (*informal*), faux pas, gaucherie, howler, indiscretion, lapse, mistake, slip, solecism

gaffer *noun* **1** *Informal* = **manager**, boss (*informal*), foreman, ganger, overseer, superintendent, supervisor **2** = **old man**, granddad, greybeard, old boy (*informal*), old fellow, old-timer (*U.S.*)

gag ¹ *verb* **1** = **choke**, gasp, pant, struggle for breath **2** = **retch**, barf (*slang*), disgorge, heave, puke (*slang*), spew, throw up (*informal*), vomit **3** = **suppress**, curb, muffle, muzzle, quiet, silence, stifle, still, stop up, throttle

gag ² *noun* = **joke**, crack (*slang*), funny (*informal*), hoax, jest, wisecrack (*informal*), witticism

gaiety *noun* **1** = **cheerfulness**, animation, blitheness, blithesomeness (*literary*), effervescence, elation, exhilaration, glee, good humour, high spirits, hilarity, *joie de vivre*, jollity, joviality, joyousness, light-heartedness, liveliness, merriment, mirth, sprightliness, vivacity **2** = **merrymaking**, celebration, conviviality, festivity, fun, jollification, revelry, revels **3** = **colour**, brightness, brilliance, colourfulness, gaudiness, glitter, show, showiness, sparkle
➤ **Antonyms**
≠**cheerfulness**: despondency, gloom,

melancholy, misery, sadness

gaily *adverb* **1** = **cheerfully**, blithely, gleefully, happily, joyfully, light-heartedly, merrily **2** = **colourfully**, brightly, brilliantly, flamboyantly, flashily, gaudily, showily

gain *verb* **1** = **acquire**, achieve, attain, bag, bring in, capture, clear, collect, earn, gather, get, glean, harvest, land, make, net, obtain, procure, realize, reap, score (*slang*), secure, win **2** = **improve**, advance, build up, increase, pick up, profit **3** = **reach**, arrive at, attain, come to, get to **4 gain on** = **get nearer**, approach, catch up with, close, narrow the gap, overtake **5 gain time** = **stall**, delay, procrastinate, temporize, use delaying tactics ◆ *noun* **6** = **profit**, accretion, achievement, acquisition, advantage, attainment, benefit, dividend, earnings, emolument, headway, income, lucre, proceeds, produce, return, winnings, yield **7** = **increase**, advance, advancement, growth, improvement, increment, progress, rise
➤ **Antonyms**
verb ≠**acquire**: forfeit, lose ≠**improve**: fail, worsen ◆ *noun* ≠**profit**: forfeiture, loss ≠**increase**: damage, injury

gainful *adjective* = **profitable**, advantageous, beneficial, expedient, fruitful, lucrative, moneymaking, paying, productive, remunerative, rewarding, useful, worthwhile

gains *plural noun* = **profits**, booty, earnings, gainings, pickings, prize, proceeds, revenue, takings, winnings

gainsay *verb* = **contradict**, contravene, controvert, deny, disaffirm, disagree with, dispute, rebut, retract
➤ **Antonyms**
agree with, back, confirm, support

gait *noun* = **walk**, bearing, carriage, pace, step, stride, tread

gala *noun* **1** = **festival**, beano (*Brit. slang*), carnival, celebration, festivity, fête, hooley *or* hoolie (*chiefly Irish & N.Z.*), jamboree, pageant, party, rave (*Brit. slang*), rave-up (*Brit. slang*) ◆ *adjective* **2** = **festive**, celebratory, convivial, festal, gay, jovial, joyful, merry

gale *noun* **1** = **storm**, blast, cyclone, hurricane, squall, tempest, tornado, typhoon **2** *Informal* = **outburst**, burst, eruption, explosion, fit, howl, outbreak, paroxysm, peal, shout, shriek, storm

gall [1] *noun* **1** *Informal* = **impudence**, brass (*informal*), brass neck (*Brit. informal*), brazenness, cheek (*informal*), chutzpah (*U.S. & Canad. informal*), effrontery, face (*informal*), impertinence, insolence, neck (*informal*), nerve (*informal*), sassiness (*U.S. informal*), sauciness **2** = **bitterness**, acrimony, animosity, animus, antipathy, bad blood, bile, enmity, hostility, malevolence, malice, malignity, rancour, sourness, spite, spleen, venom

gall [2] *verb* **1** = **annoy**, aggravate (*informal*), be on one's back (*slang*), bother, exasperate, fret, get in one's hair (*informal*), get on one's nerves (*informal*), harass, hassle (*informal*), irk, irritate, nag, nark (*Brit., Austral., & N.Z. slang*), nettle, peeve (*informal*), pester, piss one off (*taboo slang*), plague, provoke, rankle, rile (*informal*), rub up the wrong way, ruffle, vex **2** = **scrape**, abrade, bark, chafe, excoriate, fret, graze, irritate, rub raw, skin ♦ *noun* **3** = **irritation**, aggravation (*informal*), annoyance, bother, botheration (*informal*), exasperation, harassment, irritant, nuisance, pest, provocation, vexation **4** = **sore**, abrasion, chafe, excoriation, raw spot, scrape, sore spot, wound

gallant *adjective* **1** = **brave**, bold, courageous, daring, dashing, dauntless, doughty, fearless, game (*informal*), heroic, high-spirited, honourable, intrepid, lion-hearted, manful, manly, mettlesome, noble, plucky, valiant, valorous **2** = **courteous**, attentive, chivalrous, courtly, gentlemanly, gracious, magnanimous, noble, polite **3** = **elegant**, august, dignified, glorious, grand, imposing, lofty, magnificent, noble, splendid, stately ♦ *noun* **4** = **ladies' man**, beau, blade (*archaic*), buck (*informal*), dandy, fop, lady-killer (*informal*), man about town, man of fashion
➤ **Antonyms**
adjective ≠**brave**: cowardly, fearful, ignoble ≠**courteous**: churlish, discourteous, ill-mannered, impolite, rude

gallantry *noun* **1** = **courtesy**, attentiveness, chivalry, courteousness, courtliness, elegance, gentlemanliness, graciousness, nobility, politeness **2** = **bravery**, audacity, boldness, courage, courageousness, daring, dauntlessness, derring-do (*archaic*), fearlessness, heroism, intrepidity, manliness, mettle, nerve, pluck, prowess, spirit, valiance, valour
➤ **Antonyms**
≠**courtesy**: churlishness, discourtesy, rudeness, ungraciousness ≠**bravery**: cowardice, irresolution

galling *adjective* = **annoying**, aggravating

(*informal*), bitter, bothersome, exasperating, harassing, humiliating, irksome, irritating, nettlesome, plaguing, provoking, rankling, vexatious, vexing

gallivant *verb* = **wander**, gad about, ramble, roam, rove

gallop *verb* = **run**, barrel (along) (*informal, chiefly U.S. & Canad.*), bolt, career, dart, dash, fly, hasten, hie (*archaic*), hurry, race, rush, scud, shoot, speed, sprint, tear along, zoom

galore *adverb* = **in abundance**, à gogo (*informal*), all over the place, aplenty, everywhere, in great quantity, in numbers, in profusion, to spare

galvanize *verb* = **stimulate**, arouse, awaken, electrify, excite, fire, inspire, invigorate, jolt, kick-start, move, prod, provoke, put a bomb under (*informal*), quicken, shock, spur, startle, stir, thrill, vitalize, wake

gamble *verb* **1** = **bet**, back, game, have a flutter (*informal*), lay *or* make a bet, play, punt, put one's shirt on, stake, try one's luck, wager **2** = **risk**, back, chance, hazard, put one's faith *or* trust in, skate on thin ice, speculate, stake, stick one's neck out (*informal*), take a chance, take the plunge, venture ♦ *noun* **3** = **bet**, flutter (*informal*), punt, wager **4** = **risk**, chance, leap in the dark, lottery, speculation, uncertainty, venture
➤ **Antonyms**
noun ≠**risk**: banker, certainty, foregone conclusion, safe bet, sure thing

gambol *verb* **1** = **frolic**, caper, cavort, curvet, cut a caper, frisk, hop, jump, prance, rollick, skip ♦ *noun* **2** = **frolic**, antic, caper, gambado, hop, jump, prance, skip, spring

game *noun* **1** = **pastime**, amusement, distraction, diversion, entertainment, frolic, fun, jest, joke, lark, merriment, play, recreation, romp, sport **2** = **match**, competition, contest, event, head-to-head, meeting, round, tournament **3** = **undertaking**, adventure, business, enterprise, line, occupation, plan, proceeding, scheme **4** = **wild animals**, chase, prey, quarry **5** = **scheme**, design, device, plan, plot, ploy, stratagem, strategy, tactic, trick ♦ *adjective* **6** = **brave**, ballsy (*taboo slang*), bold, courageous, dauntless, dogged, fearless, feisty (*informal, chiefly U.S. & Canad.*), gallant, gritty, have-a-go (*informal*), heroic, intrepid, persevering, persistent, plucky, resolute, spirited, unflinching, valiant, valorous **7** = **willing**, desirous, disposed, eager, inclined, interested, keen, prepared, ready, up for it (*informal*)

➤ **Antonyms**
noun ≠**pastime:** business, chore, duty, job, labour, toil, work ◆ *adjective* ≠**brave:** cowardly, fearful, irresolute

gamut *noun* = **range,** area, catalogue, compass, field, scale, scope, series, sweep

gang *noun* = **group,** band, bevy, camp, circle, clique, club, company, coterie, crew (*informal*), crowd, herd, horde, lot, mob, pack, party, posse (*slang*), ring, set, shift, squad, team, troupe

gangling, gangly *adjective* = **tall,** angular, awkward, lanky, loose-jointed, rangy, rawboned, skinny, spindly

gangster *noun* = **racketeer,** bandit, brigand, crook (*informal*), desperado, gang member, heavy (*slang*), hood (*U.S. slang*), hoodlum (*chiefly U.S.*), mobster (*U.S. slang*), robber, ruffian, thug, tough, tsotsi (*S. African*)

gap *noun* **1** = **opening,** blank, breach, break, chink, cleft, crack, cranny, crevice, discontinuity, divide, hole, interstice, rent, rift, space, vacuity, void **2** = **interval,** breathing space, entr'acte, hiatus, interlude, intermission, interruption, lacuna, lull, pause, recess, respite **3** = **difference,** disagreement, disparity, divergence, inconsistency

gape *verb* **1** = **stare,** gawk, gawp (*Brit. slang*), goggle, wonder **2** = **open,** crack, split, yawn

gaping *adjective* = **wide,** broad, cavernous, great, open, vast, wide open, yawning

garb *noun* **1** = **clothes,** apparel, array, attire, clothing, costume, dress, garment, gear (*slang*), habiliment, habit, outfit, raiment (*archaic*), robes, threads (*slang*), uniform, vestments, wear **2** = **fashion,** cut, look, mode, style **3** = **appearance,** aspect, attire, covering, guise, outward form ◆ *verb* **4** = **clothe,** apparel, attire, cover, dress, rig out, robe

garbage *noun* **1** = **junk,** bits and pieces, debris, detritus, litter, odds and ends, rubbish, scraps **2** = **waste,** dreck (*slang, chiefly U.S.*), dross, filth, muck, offal, refuse, rubbish, scourings, slops, sweepings, swill, trash (*chiefly U.S.*), wack (*U.S. slang*) **3** = **nonsense,** balderdash, balls (*taboo slang*), bilge (*informal*), bosh (*informal*), bull (*slang*), bullshit (*taboo slang*), bunkum *or* buncombe (*chiefly U.S.*), claptrap (*informal*), cobblers (*Brit. taboo slang*), codswallop (*Brit. slang*), crap (*slang*), drivel, eyewash (*informal*), flapdoodle (*slang*), gibberish, guff (*slang*), havers (*Scot.*), hogwash, hokum (*slang, chiefly U.S. & Canad.*), horsefeathers (*U.S. slang*), hot air (*informal*), kak (*S. African slang*), moonshine, pap, piffle (*informal*),

poppycock (*informal*), rot, shit (*taboo slang*), stuff and nonsense, tommyrot, tosh (*informal*), trash, tripe (*informal*), twaddle

garble *verb* **1** = **jumble,** confuse, mix up **2** = **distort,** corrupt, doctor, falsify, misinterpret, misquote, misreport, misrepresent, misstate, mistranslate, mutilate, pervert, slant, tamper with, twist ➤ **Antonyms** clarify, decipher, make intelligible

garbled *adjective* = **jumbled,** confused, distorted, double-Dutch, incomprehensible, mixed up, unintelligible

gargantuan *adjective* = **huge,** big, Brobdingnagian, colossal, elephantine, enormous, giant, gigantic, ginormous (*informal*), humongous *or* humungous (*U.S. slang*), immense, mammoth, massive, monstrous, monumental, mountainous, prodigious, stellar (*informal*), titanic, towering, tremendous, vast ➤ **Antonyms** little, meagre, miniature, minute, paltry, petite, puny, pygmy *or* pigmy, small, tiny

garish *adjective* = **gaudy,** brash, brassy, brummagem, cheap, flash (*informal*), flashy, flaunting, glaring, glittering, loud, meretricious, naff (*Brit. slang*), raffish, showy, tacky (*informal*), tasteless, tawdry, vulgar ➤ **Antonyms** conservative, elegant, modest, plain, refined, sedate, sombre, unobtrusive

garland *noun* **1** = **wreath,** bays, chaplet, coronal, crown, festoon, honours, laurels ◆ *verb* **2** = **adorn,** crown, deck, festoon, wreathe

garments *plural noun* = **clothes,** apparel, array, articles of clothing, attire, clothing, costume, dress, duds (*informal*), garb, gear (*slang*), habiliment, habit, outfit, raiment (*archaic*), robes, schmutter (*slang*), threads (*slang*), togs, uniform, vestments, wear

garner *verb* **1** = **collect,** accumulate, amass, assemble, deposit, gather, hoard, husband, lay in *or* up, put by, reserve, save, stockpile, store, stow away, treasure ◆ *noun* **2** *Literary* = **storehouse,** depository, granary, store, vault

garnish *verb* **1** = **decorate,** adorn, beautify, bedeck, deck, embellish, enhance, festoon, grace, ornament, set off, trim ◆ *noun* **2** = **decoration,** adornment, embellishment, enhancement, festoon, garniture, ornament, ornamentation, trim, trimming ➤ **Antonyms** *verb* ≠**decorate:** denude, spoil, strip

garrison *noun* **1** = **troops,** armed force, command, detachment, unit **2** = **fort,** base, camp, encampment, fortification, fortress, post, station, stronghold ◆ *verb* **3** = **station,**

assign, mount, position, post, put on duty **4** = **occupy**, defend, guard, man, protect, supply with troops

garrulity noun **1** = **talkativeness**, babble, babbling, chatter, chattering, chattiness, effusiveness, gabbiness (*informal*), garrulousness, gift of the gab (*informal*), glibness, loquacity, mouthiness, prating, prattle, verbosity, volubility **2** = **long-windedness**, diffuseness, prolixity, prosiness, verbosity, windiness, wordiness

garrulous adjective **1** = **talkative**, babbling, chattering, chatty, effusive, gabby (*informal*), glib, gossiping, gushing, loquacious, mouthy, prating, prattling, verbose, voluble **2** = **long-winded**, diffuse, gassy (*slang*), prolix, prosy, verbose, windy, wordy
➤ **Antonyms**
≠**talkative**: reserved, reticent, taciturn, tight-lipped, uncommunicative
≠**long-winded**: concise, succinct, terse

gash verb **1** = **cut**, cleave, gouge, incise, lacerate, rend, slash, slit, split, tear, wound
♦ noun **2** = **cut**, cleft, gouge, incision, laceration, rent, slash, slit, split, tear, wound

gasp verb **1** = **gulp**, blow, catch one's breath, choke, fight for breath, pant, puff
♦ noun **2** = **gulp**, blow, ejaculation, exclamation, intake of breath, pant, puff, sharp intake of breath

gate noun = **barrier**, access, door, doorway, egress, entrance, exit, gateway, opening, passage, port (*Scot.*), portal

gather verb **1** = **assemble**, accumulate, amass, bring or get together, collect, congregate, convene, flock, foregather, garner, group, heap, hoard, marshal, mass, muster, pile up, round up, stack up, stockpile **2** = **intensify**, build, deepen, enlarge, expand, grow, heighten, increase, rise, swell, thicken, wax **3** = **learn**, assume, be led to believe, conclude, deduce, draw, hear, infer, make, surmise, understand **4** = **fold**, pleat, pucker, ruffle, shirr, tuck **5** = **pick**, crop, cull, garner, glean, harvest, pluck, reap, select **6** = **enfold**, clasp, draw, embrace, hold, hug
➤ **Antonyms**
≠**assemble**: diffuse, disperse, dissipate, scatter, separate

gathering noun **1** = **assembly**, assemblage, company, conclave, concourse, congregation, congress, convention, convocation, crowd, flock, get-together (*informal*), group, knot, meeting, muster, party, rally, throng, turnout **2** = **accumulation**, acquisition, aggregate, collecting, collection, concentration, gain, heap, hoard, mass, pile, procuring, roundup, stock, stockpile **3** *Informal* = **pimple**,

abscess, boil, carbuncle, pustule, sore, spot, tumour, ulcer

gauche adjective = **awkward**, clumsy, graceless, ignorant, ill-bred, ill-mannered, inelegant, inept, insensitive, lacking in social graces, maladroit, tactless, uncultured, unpolished, unsophisticated
➤ **Antonyms**
elegant, gracious, polished, polite, refined, sophisticated, tasteful, urbane, well-mannered

gaudy adjective = **garish**, brash, bright, brilliant, brummagem, flash (*informal*), flashy, florid, gay, gimcrack, glaring, jazzy (*informal*), loud, meretricious, naff (*Brit. slang*), ostentatious, raffish, showy, tacky (*informal*), tasteless, tawdry, vulgar
➤ **Antonyms**
colourless, conservative, dull, elegant, modest, quiet, refined, sedate, subtle, tasteful

gauge verb **1** = **judge**, adjudge, appraise, assess, estimate, evaluate, guess, rate, reckon, value **2** = **measure**, ascertain, calculate, check, compute, count, determine, weigh ♦ noun **3** = **indicator**, basis, criterion, example, exemplar, guide, guideline, measure, meter, model, par, pattern, rule, sample, standard, test, touchstone, yardstick **4** = **size**, bore, capacity, degree, depth, extent, height, magnitude, measure, scope, span, thickness, width

gaunt adjective **1** = **thin**, angular, attenuated, bony, cadaverous, emaciated, haggard, lank, lean, macilent (*rare*), meagre, pinched, rawboned, scraggy, scrawny, skeletal, skin and bone, skinny, spare, wasted **2** = **bleak**, bare, desolate, dismal, dreary, forbidding, forlorn, grim, harsh, stark
➤ **Antonyms**
≠**thin**: chubby, corpulent, fat, lush, obese, plump, stout, well-fed ≠**bleak**: inviting, lush, luxurious

gawk verb **1** = **stare**, gape, gawp (*slang*), gaze open-mouthed, goggle ♦ noun **2** = **oaf**, boor, churl, clod, clodhopper (*informal*), dolt, dunderhead, galoot (*slang*), ignoramus, lout, lubber, lummox (*informal*)

gawky adjective = **awkward**, clownish, clumsy, gauche, loutish, lumbering, lumpish, maladroit, oafish, uncouth, ungainly
➤ **Antonyms**
elegant, graceful, self-assured, well-coordinated

gay adjective **1** = **homosexual**, bent (*offensive slang*), dykey (*slang*), lesbian, moffie (*S. African slang*), pink (*informal*), poofy (*offensive slang*), queer (*informal*, *derogatory*) **2** = **cheerful**, animated, blithe, carefree, debonair, full of beans (*informal*), glad, gleeful, happy, hilarious, insouciant, jolly, jovial, joyful, joyous, light-hearted,

lively, merry, sparkling, sunny, vivacious **3** = **colourful**, bright, brilliant, flamboyant, flashy, fresh, garish, gaudy, rich, showy, vivid **4** = **merry**, convivial, festive, frivolous, frolicsome, fun-loving, gamesome, playful, pleasure-seeking, rakish, rollicking, sportive, waggish ♦ *noun* **5** = **homosexual**, bull dyke (*offensive slang*), dyke (*offensive slang*), faggot (*U.S. offens. slang*), fairy (*offensive slang*), invert, lesbian, poof (*offensive slang*), queer (*offensive slang*)
➤ **Antonyms**
adjective, noun ≠**homosexual:** heterosexual, straight ♦ *adjective* ≠**cheerful:** cheerless, down in the dumps (*informal*), grave, grim, melancholy, miserable, sad, sedate, serious, sober, solemn, sombre, unhappy ≠**colourful:** colourless, conservative, drab, dull, sombre

gaze *verb* **1** = **stare**, contemplate, eyeball (*slang*), gape, look, look fixedly, regard, view, watch, wonder ♦ *noun* **2** = **stare**, fixed look, look

gazette *noun* = **newspaper**, journal, news-sheet, organ, paper, periodical

gear *noun* **1** = **cog**, cogwheel, gearwheel, toothed wheel **2** = **mechanism**, cogs, gearing, machinery, works **3** = **clothing**, apparel, array, attire, clothes, costume, dress, garb, garments, habit, outfit, rigout (*informal*), schmutter (*slang*), threads (*slang*), togs, wear **4** = **belongings**, baggage, effects, kit, luggage, stuff, things **5** = **equipment**, accessories, accoutrements, apparatus, harness, instruments, outfit, paraphernalia, rigging, supplies, tackle, tools, trappings ♦ *verb* **6** = **equip**, adapt, adjust, fit, rig, suit, tailor

gelatinous *adjective* = **jelly-like**, gluey, glutinous, gummy, mucilaginous, sticky, viscid, viscous

gem *noun* **1** = **precious stone**, jewel, semiprecious stone, stone **2** = **prize**, flower, jewel, masterpiece, pearl, pick, treasure

genealogy *noun* = **ancestry**, blood line, derivation, descent, extraction, family tree, line, lineage, pedigree, progeniture, stemma, stirps, stock, strain

general *adjective* **1** = **common**, accepted, broad, extensive, popular, prevailing, prevalent, public, universal, widespread **2** = **universal**, across-the-board, all-inclusive, blanket, broad, catholic, collective, comprehensive, encyclopedic, generic, indiscriminate, miscellaneous, overall, overarching, panoramic, sweeping, total **3** = **ordinary**, accustomed, conventional, customary, everyday, habitual, normal, regular, typical, usual **4** = **imprecise**, approximate, ill-defined, inaccurate, indefinite, inexact, loose, undetailed,

unspecific, vague
➤ **Antonyms**
≠**common**, **universal:** distinctive, exceptional, extraordinary, individual, peculiar, special, unusual ≠**ordinary:** infrequent, rare ≠**Imprecise:** definite, exact, particular, precise, specific

generality *noun* **1** = **generalization**, abstract principle, loose statement, sweeping statement, vague notion **2** = **commonness**, acceptedness, extensiveness, popularity, prevalence, ubiquity, universality **3** = **universality**, breadth, catholicity, completeness, comprehensiveness, miscellaneity, sweepingness **4** = **impreciseness**, approximateness, indefiniteness, inexactness, lack of detail, looseness, vagueness

generally *adverb* **1** = **usually**, almost always, as a rule, by and large, conventionally, customarily, for the most part, habitually, in most cases, largely, mainly, normally, on average, on the whole, ordinarily, regularly, typically **2** = **commonly**, extensively, popularly, publicly, universally, widely **3** = **broadly**, approximately, chiefly, for the most part, in the main, largely, mainly, mostly, on the whole, predominantly, principally
➤ **Antonyms**
≠**usually:** especially, occasionally, rarely, unusually ≠**commonly:** individually, particularly

generate *verb* = **produce**, beget, breed, bring about, cause, create, engender, form, give rise to, initiate, make, originate, procreate, propagate, spawn, whip up
➤ **Antonyms**
annihilate, crush, destroy, end, extinguish, kill, terminate

generation *noun* **1** = **age group**, breed, crop **2** = **age**, day, days, epoch, era, period, time, times **3** = **production**, begetting, breeding, creation, engenderment, formation, genesis, origination, procreation, propagation, reproduction

generic *adjective* = **collective**, all-encompassing, blanket, common, comprehensive, general, inclusive, sweeping, universal, wide
➤ **Antonyms**
individual, particular, precise, specific

generosity *noun* **1** = **liberality**, beneficence, benevolence, bounteousness, bounty, charity, kindness, largesse *or* largess, munificence, open-handedness **2** = **unselfishness**, disinterestedness, goodness, high-mindedness, magnanimity, nobleness

generous *adjective* **1** = **liberal**, beneficent, benevolent, bounteous, bountiful, charitable, free, hospitable, kind, lavish, munificent,

open-handed, princely, prodigal,
ungrudging, unstinting **2 = unselfish**,
big-hearted, disinterested, good,
high-minded, lofty, magnanimous, noble **3**
= plentiful, abundant, ample, copious, full,
fulsome, lavish, liberal, overflowing, rich,
unstinting
➤ **Antonyms**
≠**liberal:** avaricious, close-fisted, greedy,
mean, miserly, parsimonious, selfish, stingy,
tight ≠**plentiful:** cheap, minimal, scanty,
small, tiny

genesis noun **= beginning**, birth,
commencement, creation, dawn,
engendering, formation, generation,
inception, origin, outset, propagation, root,
source, start
➤ **Antonyms**
completion, conclusion, end, finish,
termination

genial adjective **= cheerful**, affable,
agreeable, amiable, cheery, congenial,
convivial, cordial, easy-going, enlivening,
friendly, glad, good-natured, happy, hearty,
jolly, jovial, joyous, kind, kindly, merry,
pleasant, sunny, warm, warm-hearted
➤ **Antonyms**
cheerless, cool, discourteous, frigid, morose,
rude, sardonic, sullen, unfriendly,
ungracious, unpleasant

geniality noun **= cheerfulness**, affability,
agreeableness, amiability, cheeriness,
congenialness, conviviality, cordiality,
friendliness, gladness, good cheer, good
nature, happiness, heartiness, jollity, joviality,
joy, joyousness, kindliness, kindness, mirth,
pleasantness, sunniness, warm-heartedness,
warmth

genitals plural noun **= sex organs**,
genitalia, loins, private parts, pudenda,
reproductive organs

genius noun **1 = master**, adept, brain
(informal), brainbox, buff (informal),
expert, hotshot (informal), intellect
(informal), maestro, master-hand,
mastermind, maven (U.S.), virtuoso, whiz
(informal) **2 = brilliance**, ability, aptitude,
bent, capacity, creative power, endowment,
faculty, flair, gift, inclination, knack,
propensity, talent, turn
➤ **Antonyms**
≠**master:** dolt, dunce, fool, half-wit, idiot,
imbecile, nincompoop, simpleton

genre noun **= type**, brand, category,
character, class, fashion, genus, group, kind,
school, sort, species, stamp, style

genteel adjective **= refined**, aristocratic,
civil, courteous, courtly, cultivated, cultured,
elegant, fashionable, formal, gentlemanly,
ladylike, mannerly, polished, polite,
respectable, sophisticated, stylish, urbane,

well-bred, well-mannered
➤ **Antonyms**
discourteous, ill-bred, impolite, inelegant,
low-bred, natural, plebeian, rude,
unaffected, uncultured, unmannerly,
unpolished, unrefined

gentility noun **1 = nobility**, blue blood,
gentle birth, good family, high birth, rank **2**
= refinement, breeding, civility, courtesy,
courtliness, cultivation, culture, decorum,
elegance, etiquette, formality, good
breeding, good manners, mannerliness,
polish, politeness, propriety, respectability,
sophistication, urbanity **3 = aristocracy**,
elite, gentlefolk, gentry, nobility, nobles,
ruling class, upper class

gentle adjective **1 = mild**, amiable, benign,
bland, compassionate, dove-like, humane,
kind, kindly, lenient, meek, merciful, pacific,
peaceful, placid, quiet, soft, sweet-tempered,
tender **2 = moderate**, balmy, calm, clement,
easy, light, low, mild, muted, placid, quiet,
serene, slight, smooth, soft, soothing,
temperate, tranquil, untroubled **3 = gradual**,
easy, imperceptible, light, mild, moderate,
slight, slow **4 = tame**, biddable, broken,
docile, manageable, placid, tractable **5**
Archaic **= well-bred**, aristocratic, civil,
courteous, cultured, elegant, genteel,
gentlemanlike, gentlemanly, high-born,
ladylike, noble, polished, polite, refined,
upper-class, well-born
➤ **Antonyms**
≠**mild:** aggressive, cruel, fierce, hard, harsh,
heartless, impolite, rough, savage, sharp,
unkind ≠**tame:** fierce, savage,
unmanageable, wild ≠**moderate:** powerful,
strong, violent, wild ≠**gradual:** sudden

gentlemanly adjective **= polite**, civil,
civilized, courteous, cultivated, debonair,
gallant, genteel, gentlemanlike, honourable,
mannerly, noble, obliging, polished, refined,
reputable, suave, urbane, well-bred,
well-mannered

gentleness noun **= tenderness**,
compassion, kindness, mildness, softness,
sweetness

gentry noun **= nobility**, aristocracy, elite,
upper class, upper crust (informal)

genuine adjective **1 = authentic**, actual,
bona fide, honest, legitimate, natural, on the
level, original, pure, real, sound, sterling, the
real McCoy, true, unadulterated, unalloyed,
veritable **2 = sincere**, artless, candid, earnest,
frank, heartfelt, honest, unaffected,
unfeigned
➤ **Antonyms**
≠**authentic:** artificial, bogus, counterfeit,
fake, false, fraudulent, imitation, phoney,
pseudo (informal), sham, simulated,
spurious ≠**sincere:** affected, false, feigned,

hypocritical, insincere, phoney

germ *noun* **1** = **microbe**, bacterium, bug (*informal*), microorganism, virus **2** = **embryo**, bud, egg, nucleus, ovule, ovum, seed, spore, sprout **3** = **beginning**, bud, cause, embryo, origin, root, rudiment, seed, source, spark

germane *adjective* = **relevant**, akin, allied, apposite, appropriate, apropos, apt, cognate, connected, fitting, kindred, material, pertinent, proper, related, suitable, to the point *or* purpose
➤ **Antonyms**
extraneous, foreign, immaterial, inappropriate, irrelevant, unrelated

germinate *verb* = **sprout**, bud, develop, generate, grow, originate, pullulate, shoot, swell, vegetate

gestation *noun* = **development**, evolution, incubation, maturation, pregnancy, ripening

gesticulate *verb* = **signal**, gesture, indicate, make a sign, motion, sign, wave

gesture *noun* **1** = **signal**, action, gesticulation, indication, motion, sign ♦ *verb* **2** = **signal**, gesticulate, indicate, motion, sign, wave

get *verb* **1** = **obtain**, achieve, acquire, attain, bag, bring, come by, come into possession of, earn, fall heir to, fetch, gain, glean, inherit, land, make, net, pick up, procure, realize, reap, receive, score (*slang*), secure, succeed to, win **2** = **contract**, be afflicted with, become infected with, be smitten by, catch, come down with, fall victim to, take **3** = **become**, come to be, grow, turn, wax **4** = **arrange**, contrive, fix, manage, succeed, wangle (*informal*) **5** = **understand**, catch, comprehend, fathom, follow, get the picture, hear, notice, perceive, see, suss (out) (*slang*), take in, work out **6** = **arrive**, come, make it (*informal*), reach **7** = **persuade**, coax, convince, induce, influence, prevail upon, sway, talk into, wheedle, win over **8** *Informal* = **annoy**, bother, bug (*informal*), gall, get (someone's) goat (*slang*), irk, irritate, nark (*Brit., Austral., & N.Z. slang*), pique, rub (someone) up the wrong way, upset, vex **9** = **puzzle**, baffle, confound, mystify, nonplus, perplex, stump **10** = **capture**, arrest, collar (*informal*), grab, lay hold of, nab (*informal*), nail (*informal*), seize, take, trap **11** *Informal* = **impress**, affect, arouse, excite, have an effect on, impact on, move, stimulate, stir, touch, tug at (someone's) heartstrings (*often facetious*) **12** = **contact**, communicate with, get in touch with, reach

get across *verb* **1** = **cross**, ford, negotiate, pass over, traverse **2** = **communicate**, bring home to, convey, get (something) through

to, impart, make clear *or* understood, put over, transmit

get ahead *verb* **1** = **prosper**, advance, be successful, cut it (*informal*), do well, flourish, get on, make good, make one's mark, progress, succeed, thrive **2** = **overtake**, excel, leave behind, outdo, outmanoeuvre, surpass

get along *verb* **1** = **go away**, be off, depart, get on one's bike (*Brit. slang*), go, go to hell (*informal*), leave, make tracks, move off, sling one's hook (*Brit. slang*), slope off **2** = **cope**, develop, fare, get by (*informal*), make out (*informal*), manage, progress, shift **3** = **be friendly**, agree, be compatible, be on good terms, get on, harmonize, hit it off (*informal*)

get at *verb* **1** = **gain access to**, acquire, attain, come to grips with, get, get hold of, reach **2** = **imply**, hint, intend, lead up to, mean, suggest **3** = **criticize**, annoy, attack, be on one's back (*slang*), blame, carp, find fault with, hassle (*informal*), irritate, nag, nark (*Brit., Austral., & N.Z. slang*), pick on, put the boot into (*slang*), taunt **4** = **corrupt**, bribe, buy off, influence, suborn, tamper with

getaway *noun* = **escape**, break, break-out, decampment, flight

get away *verb* = **escape**, abscond, break free, break out, decamp, depart, disappear, flee, leave, make good one's escape, slope off

get back *verb* **1** = **regain**, recoup, recover, repossess, retrieve **2** = **return**, arrive home, come back *or* home, revert, revisit **3 get back at** = **retaliate**, be avenged, get even with, get one's own back, give tit for tat, hit back, settle the score with, take vengeance on

get by *verb* **1** = **pass**, circumvent, get ahead of, go around, go past, overtake, round **2** = **manage**, contrive, cope, exist, fare, get along, keep one's head above water, make both ends meet, subsist, survive

get down *verb* **1** = **descend**, alight, bring down, climb down, disembark, dismount, get off, lower, step down **2** = **dishearten**, bring down, depress, dispirit

get in *verb* = **enter**, alight, appear, arrive, collect, come, embark, include, infiltrate, insert, interpose, land, make inroads (into), mount, penetrate

get off *verb* **1** = **leave**, alight, depart, descend, disembark, dismount, escape, exit **2** = **remove**, detach, shed, take off

get on *verb* **1** = **board**, ascend, climb, embark, mount **2** = **be friendly**, agree, be compatible, concur, get along, harmonize, hit it off (*informal*) **3** = **progress**, advance, cope, cut it (*informal*), fare, get along, make out (*informal*), manage, prosper, succeed

get out *verb* = **leave**, alight, break out, clear out (*informal*), decamp, escape, evacuate, extricate oneself, free oneself, vacate, withdraw

get out of *verb* = **avoid**, body-swerve (*Scot.*), dodge, escape, evade, shirk

get over *verb* **1** = **cross**, ford, get across, pass, pass over, surmount, traverse **2** = **recover from**, come round, get better, mend, pull through, rally, revive, survive **3** = **overcome**, defeat, get the better of, master, shake off **4** = **communicate**, convey, get *or* put across, impart, make clear *or* understood

get round *verb* **1** = **bypass**, circumvent, edge, evade, outmanoeuvre, skirt **2** *Informal* = **win over**, cajole, coax, convert, persuade, prevail upon, talk round, wheedle

get together *verb* = **meet**, accumulate, assemble, collect, congregate, convene, converge, gather, join, muster, rally, unite

get up *verb* = **arise**, ascend, climb, increase, mount, rise, scale, stand

ghastly *adjective* = **horrible**, ashen, cadaverous, deathlike, deathly pale, dreadful, frightful, from hell (*informal*), godawful (*slang*), grim, grisly, gruesome, hideous, horrendous, horrid, like death warmed up (*informal*), livid, loathsome, pale, pallid, repellent, shocking, spectral, terrible, terrifying, wan
➤ **Antonyms**
appealing, attractive, beautiful, blooming, charming, healthy, lovely, pleasing

ghost *noun* **1** = **spirit**, apparition, eidolon, manes, phantasm, phantom, revenant, shade (*literary*), soul, spectre, spook (*informal*), wraith **2** = **trace**, glimmer, hint, possibility, semblance, shadow, suggestion

ghostly *adjective* = **supernatural**, eerie, ghostlike, illusory, insubstantial, phantasmal, phantom, spectral, spooky (*informal*), uncanny, unearthly, weird, wraithlike

ghoulish *adjective* = **macabre**, disgusting, grisly, gruesome, morbid, sick (*informal*), unwholesome

giant *noun* **1** = **ogre**, behemoth, colossus, Hercules, leviathan, monster, titan
♦ *adjective* **2** = **huge**, Brobdingnagian, colossal, elephantine, enormous, gargantuan, gigantic, ginormous (*informal*), humongous *or* humungous (*U.S. slang*), immense, jumbo (*informal*), large, mammoth, monstrous, prodigious, stellar (*informal*), titanic, vast
➤ **Antonyms**
adjective ≠**huge**: dwarf, Lilliputian, miniature, pygmy *or* pigmy, tiny

gibberish *noun* = **nonsense**, all Greek (*informal*), babble, balderdash, balls (*taboo*

slang), bilge (*informal*), blather, bosh (*informal*), bull (*slang*), bullshit (*taboo slang*), bunkum *or* buncombe (*chiefly U.S.*), cobblers (*Brit. taboo slang*), crap (*slang*), double talk, drivel, eyewash (*informal*), gabble, garbage (*informal*), gobbledegook (*informal*), guff (*slang*), hogwash, hokum (*slang, chiefly U.S. & Canad.*), horsefeathers (*U.S. slang*), hot air (*informal*), jabber, jargon, moonshine, mumbo jumbo, pap, piffle (*informal*), poppycock (*informal*), prattle, shit (*taboo slang*), tommyrot, tosh (*slang, chiefly Brit.*), tripe (*informal*), twaddle, yammer (*informal*)

gibe, jibe *noun* **1** = **taunt**, barb, crack (*slang*), cutting remark, derision, dig, jeer, mockery, ridicule, sarcasm, scoffing, sneer
♦ *verb* **2** = **taunt**, deride, flout, jeer, make fun of, mock, poke fun at, ridicule, scoff, scorn, sneer, take the piss out of (*slang*), twit

giddiness *noun* = **dizziness**, faintness, light-headedness, vertigo

giddy *adjective* **1** = **dizzy**, dizzying, faint, light-headed, reeling, unsteady, vertiginous **2** = **scatterbrained**, capricious, careless, changeable, changeful, ditzy *or* ditsy (*slang*), dizzy, erratic, fickle, flighty, frivolous, heedless, impulsive, inconstant, irresolute, irresponsible, reckless, silly, thoughtless, unbalanced, unstable, unsteady, vacillating, volatile, wild
➤ **Antonyms**
≠**scatterbrained**: calm, constant, determined, earnest, resolute, serious, steady

gift *noun* **1** = **donation**, benefaction, bequest, bonus, boon, bounty, contribution, grant, gratuity, hand-out, largesse *or* largess, legacy, offering, present **2** = **talent**, ability, aptitude, attribute, bent, capability, capacity, endowment, faculty, flair, genius, knack, power, turn

gifted *adjective* = **talented**, able, accomplished, adroit, brilliant, capable, clever, expert, ingenious, intelligent, masterly, skilled
➤ **Antonyms**
amateur, backward, dull, incapable, inept, retarded, slow, talentless, unskilled

gigantic *adjective* = **enormous**, Brobdingnagian, colossal, Cyclopean, elephantine, gargantuan, giant, herculean, huge, humongous *or* humungous (*U.S. slang*), immense, mammoth, monstrous, prodigious, stellar (*informal*), stupendous, titanic, tremendous, vast
➤ **Antonyms**
diminutive, insignificant, little, miniature, puny, small, tiny, weak

giggle *verb, noun* = **laugh**, cackle, chortle, chuckle, snigger, tee-hee, titter, twitter

gild verb = **embellish**, adorn, beautify, bedeck, brighten, coat, deck, dress up, embroider, enhance, enrich, garnish, grace, ornament

gimmick noun = **stunt**, contrivance, device, dodge, gadget, gambit, gizmo (*slang, chiefly U.S.*), ploy, scheme, stratagem, trick

gingerly adverb **1** = **cautiously**, carefully, charily, circumspectly, daintily, delicately, fastidiously, hesitantly, reluctantly, squeamishly, suspiciously, timidly, warily ◆ adjective **2** = **cautious**, careful, chary, circumspect, dainty, delicate, fastidious, hesitant, reluctant, squeamish, suspicious, timid, wary
➤ Antonyms
adverb ≠**cautiously**: boldly, carelessly, confidently, rashly

gird verb **1** = **girdle**, belt, bind **2** = **surround**, blockade, encircle, enclose, encompass, enfold, engird, environ, hem in, pen, ring **3** As in **gird up one's loins** = **prepare**, brace, fortify, make ready, ready, steel

girdle noun **1** = **belt**, band, cincture, cummerbund, fillet, sash, waistband ◆ verb **2** = **surround**, bind, bound, encircle, enclose, encompass, engird, environ, enwreath, gird, hem, ring

girl noun = **female child**, bird (*slang*), chick (*slang*), colleen (*Irish*), damsel (*archaic*), daughter, lass, lassie (*informal*), maid (*archaic*), maiden (*archaic*), miss, wench

girth noun = **circumference**, bulk, measure, size

gist noun = **point**, core, drift, essence, force, idea, import, marrow, meaning, nub, pith, quintessence, sense, significance, substance

give verb **1** = **present**, accord, administer, allow, award, bestow, commit, confer, consign, contribute, deliver, donate, entrust, furnish, grant, hand over *or* out, make over, permit, provide, purvey, supply, vouchsafe **2** = **announce**, be a source of, communicate, emit, impart, issue, notify, pronounce, publish, render, transmit, utter **3** = **produce**, cause, do, engender, lead, make, occasion, perform **4** = **surrender**, cede, devote, hand over, lend, relinquish, yield **5** = **concede**, allow, grant **6** = **break**, bend, collapse, fall, recede, retire, sink **7** = **demonstrate**, display, evidence, indicate, manifest, offer, proffer, provide, set forth, show
➤ Antonyms
≠**present**: accept, get, hold, keep, receive, take, withdraw

give away verb = **reveal**, betray, disclose, divulge, expose, grass (*Brit. slang*), grass up (*slang*), inform on, leak, let out, let slip, let the cat out of the bag (*informal*), put the finger on (*informal*), shop (*slang, chiefly Brit.*), uncover

give in verb = **admit defeat**, capitulate, cave in (*informal*), collapse, comply, concede, quit, submit, succumb, surrender, yield

given adjective = **inclined**, addicted, apt, disposed, liable, likely, prone

give off verb = **emit**, discharge, exhale, exude, produce, release, send out, throw out, vent

give out verb **1** = **emit**, discharge, exhale, exude, produce, release, send out, throw out, vent **2** = **make known**, announce, broadcast, communicate, disseminate, impart, notify, publish, shout from the rooftops (*informal*), transmit, utter

give up verb = **abandon**, call it a day *or* night, capitulate, cave in (*informal*), cease, cede, cut out, desist, despair, fall by the wayside, forswear, hand over, kick (*informal*), kiss (something) goodbye, leave off, quit, relinquish, renounce, resign, say goodbye to, step down (*informal*), stop, surrender, throw in the sponge, throw in the towel, waive

glacial adjective **1** = **icy**, arctic, biting, bitter, chill, chilly, cold, freezing, frigid, frosty, frozen, gelid, piercing, polar, raw, wintry **2** = **unfriendly**, antagonistic, cold, frigid, hostile, icy, inimical

glad adjective **1** = **happy**, blithesome (*literary*), cheerful, chuffed (*slang*), contented, delighted, gay, gleeful, gratified, jocund, jovial, joyful, overjoyed, pleased, willing **2** Archaic = **pleasing**, animated, cheerful, cheering, cheery, delightful, felicitous, gratifying, joyous, merry, pleasant
➤ Antonyms
≠**happy**: depressed, discontented, displeased, melancholy, miserable, sad, sorrowful, unhappy

gladden verb = **please**, cheer, delight, elate, enliven, exhilarate, gratify, hearten, rejoice

gladly adverb = **happily**, cheerfully, freely, gaily, gleefully, jovially, joyfully, joyously, lief (*rare*), merrily, readily, willingly, with (a) good grace, with pleasure
➤ Antonyms
dolefully, grudgingly, reluctantly, sadly, unenthusiastically, unwillingly

gladness noun = **happiness**, animation, blitheness, cheerfulness, delight, felicity, gaiety, glee, high spirits, hilarity, jollity, joy, joyousness, mirth, pleasure

glamorous adjective = **elegant**, alluring, attractive, beautiful, bewitching, captivating, charming, dazzling, enchanting, entrancing, exciting, fascinating, glittering, glitzy (*slang*), glossy, lovely, prestigious, smart
➤ Antonyms
colourless, dull, plain, unattractive,

unexciting, unglamorous

glamour *noun* = **charm**, allure, appeal, attraction, beauty, bewitchment, enchantment, fascination, magnetism, prestige, ravishment, witchery

glance *noun* 1 = **peek**, brief look, butcher's (*Brit. slang*), dekko (*slang*), gander (*informal*), glimpse, look, peep, quick look, shufti (*Brit. slang*), squint, view 2 = **gleam**, flash, glimmer, glint, reflection, sparkle, twinkle 3 = **allusion**, passing mention, reference ◆ *verb* 4 = **peek**, check, check out (*informal*), clock (*Brit. informal*), gaze, glimpse, look, peep, scan, take a dekko at (*Brit. slang*), view 5 = **gleam**, flash, glimmer, glint, glisten, glitter, reflect, shimmer, shine, twinkle 6 = **graze**, bounce, brush, rebound, ricochet, skim 7 *with* **over, through,** *etc.* = **scan**, browse, dip into, flip through, leaf through, riffle through, run over *or* through, skim through, thumb through
➤ **Antonyms**
noun ≠**peek:** examination, good look, inspection, perusal ◆ *verb* ≠**peek:** peruse, scrutinize, study

glare *verb* 1 = **scowl**, frown, give a dirty look, glower, look daggers, lour *or* lower, stare angrily 2 = **dazzle**, blaze, flame, flare ◆ *noun* 3 = **scowl**, angry stare, black look, dirty look, frown, glower, lour *or* lower 4 = **dazzle**, blaze, brilliance, flame, flare, glow

glaring *adjective* 1 = **conspicuous**, audacious, blatant, egregious, flagrant, gross, manifest, obvious, open, outrageous, outstanding, overt, patent, rank, unconcealed, visible 2 = **dazzling**, blazing, bright, flashy, florid, garish, glowing, loud
➤ **Antonyms**
≠**conspicuous:** concealed, hidden, inconspicuous, obscure ≠**dazzling:** soft, subdued, subtle

glassy *adjective* 1 = **transparent**, clear, glossy, icy, shiny, slick, slippery, smooth 2 = **expressionless**, blank, cold, dazed, dull, empty, fixed, glazed, lifeless, vacant

glaze *verb* 1 = **coat**, burnish, enamel, furbish, gloss, lacquer, polish, varnish ◆ *noun* 2 = **coat**, enamel, finish, gloss, lacquer, lustre, patina, polish, shine, varnish

gleam *noun* 1 = **glow**, beam, flash, glimmer, ray, sparkle 2 = **trace**, flicker, glimmer, hint, inkling, ray, suggestion 3 = **brightness**, brilliance, coruscation, flash, gloss, lustre, sheen, splendour ◆ *verb* 4 = **shine**, coruscate, flare, flash, glance, glimmer, glint, glisten, glitter, glow, scintillate, shimmer, sparkle

glee *noun* = **delight**, cheerfulness, elation, exhilaration, exuberance, exultation, fun,

gaiety, gladness, hilarity, jocularity, jollity, joviality, joy, joyfulness, joyousness, liveliness, merriment, mirth, sprightliness, triumph, verve
➤ **Antonyms**
depression, gloom, melancholy, misery, sadness

gleeful *adjective* = **delighted**, cheerful, chirpy (*informal*), cock-a-hoop, elated, exuberant, exultant, gay, gratified, happy, jocund, jovial, joyful, joyous, jubilant, merry, mirthful, overjoyed, over the moon (*informal*), pleased, rapt, triumphant

glib *adjective* = **smooth**, artful, easy, fast-talking, fluent, garrulous, insincere, plausible, quick, ready, slick, slippery, smooth-tongued, suave, talkative, voluble
➤ **Antonyms**
halting, hesitant, implausible, sincere, tongue-tied

glide *verb* = **slide**, coast, drift, float, flow, fly, roll, run, sail, skate, skim, slip, soar

glimmer *verb* 1 = **flicker**, blink, gleam, glisten, glitter, glow, shimmer, shine, sparkle, twinkle ◆ *noun* 2 = **trace**, flicker, gleam, grain, hint, inkling, ray, suggestion 3 = **gleam**, blink, flicker, glow, ray, shimmer, sparkle, twinkle

glimpse *noun* 1 = **look**, brief view, butcher's (*Brit. slang*), gander (*informal*), glance, peek, peep, quick look, shufti (*Brit. slang*), sight, sighting, squint ◆ *verb* 2 = **catch sight of**, clock (*Brit. informal*), descry, espy, sight, spot, spy, view

glint *verb* 1 = **gleam**, flash, glimmer, glitter, shine, sparkle, twinkle ◆ *noun* 2 = **gleam**, flash, glimmer, glitter, shine, sparkle, twinkle, twinkling

glisten *verb* = **gleam**, coruscate, flash, glance, glare, glimmer, glint, glitter, scintillate, shimmer, shine, sparkle, twinkle

glitch *noun* = **problem**, blip, bug (*informal*), difficulty, fault, flaw, fly in the ointment, gremlin, hitch, interruption, kink, malfunction, snag

glitter *verb* 1 = **shine**, coruscate, flare, flash, glare, gleam, glimmer, glint, glisten, scintillate, shimmer, sparkle, twinkle ◆ *noun* 2 = **shine**, beam, brightness, brilliance, flash, glare, gleam, lustre, radiance, scintillation, sheen, shimmer, sparkle 3 = **glamour**, display, gaudiness, gilt, pageantry, show, showiness, splendour, tinsel

gloat *verb* = **relish**, crow, drool, exult, glory, revel in, rub it in (*informal*), rub one's hands, rub someone's nose in it, triumph, vaunt

global *adjective* 1 = **worldwide**, international, pandemic, planetary, universal, world 2 = **comprehensive**,

all-encompassing, all-inclusive, all-out, encyclopedic, exhaustive, general, thorough, total, unbounded, unlimited
➤ **Antonyms**
≠**comprehensive:** limited, narrow, parochial, restricted, sectional

globe *noun* = **sphere**, ball, earth, orb, planet, round, world

globule *noun* = **droplet**, bead, bubble, drop, particle, pearl, pellet

gloom *noun* **1** = **depression**, blues, dejection, desolation, despair, despondency, downheartedness, low spirits, melancholy, misery, sadness, sorrow, the hump (*Brit. informal*), unhappiness, woe **2** = **darkness**, blackness, cloud, cloudiness, dark, dimness, dullness, dusk, duskiness, gloominess, murk, murkiness, obscurity, shade, shadow, twilight
➤ **Antonyms**
≠**depression:** brightness, cheerfulness, delight, happiness, high spirits, jollity, joy, mirth ≠**darkness:** daylight, light, radiance

gloomy *adjective* **1** = **miserable**, blue, chapfallen, cheerless, crestfallen, dejected, despondent, dismal, dispirited, down, downcast, downhearted, down in the dumps (*informal*), down in the mouth, glum, in low spirits, low, melancholy, moody, morose, pessimistic, sad, saturnine, sullen **2** = **depressing**, bad, black, cheerless, comfortless, disheartening, dismal, dispiriting, dreary, funereal, joyless, sad, saddening, sombre **3** = **dark**, black, crepuscular, dim, dismal, dreary, dull, dusky, grey, murky, obscure, overcast, shadowy, sombre, Stygian, tenebrous
➤ **Antonyms**
≠**miserable:** blithe, bright, cheerful, chirpy (*informal*), happy, high-spirited, jolly, jovial, light, merry, upbeat (*informal*) ≠**dark:** brilliant, light, radiant, sunny

glorify *verb* **1** = **enhance**, add lustre to, adorn, aggrandize, augment, dignify, elevate, ennoble, illuminate, immortalize, lift up, magnify, raise **2** = **praise**, celebrate, crack up (*informal*), cry up (*informal*), eulogize, extol, hymn, laud, lionize, magnify, panegyrize, sing *or* sound the praises of **3** = **worship**, adore, apotheosize, beatify, bless, canonize, deify, enshrine, exalt, honour, idolize, pay homage to, revere, sanctify, venerate
➤ **Antonyms**
≠**enhance:** debase, defile, degrade ≠**praise:** condemn, humiliate, mock ≠**worship:** desecrate, dishonour

glorious *adjective* **1** = **splendid**, beautiful, bright, brilliant, dazzling, divine, effulgent, gorgeous, radiant, resplendent, shining, splendiferous (*facetious*), superb **2**

= **delightful**, enjoyable, excellent, fine, gorgeous, great, heavenly (*informal*), marvellous, pleasurable, splendid, splendiferous (*facetious*), wonderful **3** = **famous**, celebrated, distinguished, elevated, eminent, excellent, famed, grand, honoured, illustrious, magnificent, majestic, noble, noted, renowned, sublime, triumphant
➤ **Antonyms**
≠**splendid, delightful:** awful, dreary, dull, gloomy, horrible, unimpressive, unpleasant ≠**famous:** minor, ordinary, trivial, unimportant, unknown

glory *noun* **1** = **honour**, celebrity, dignity, distinction, eminence, exaltation, fame, illustriousness, immortality, kudos, praise, prestige, renown **2** = **splendour**, éclat, grandeur, greatness, magnificence, majesty, nobility, pageantry, pomp, sublimity, triumph **3** = **worship**, adoration, benediction, blessing, gratitude, homage, laudation, praise, thanksgiving, veneration **4** = **beauty**, brilliance, effulgence, gorgeousness, lustre, radiance, resplendence
♦ *verb* **5** = **triumph**, boast, crow, drool, exult, gloat, pride oneself, relish, revel, take delight
➤ **Antonyms**
noun ≠**honour:** condemnation, disgrace, dishonour, disrepute, infamy, shame ≠**splendour:** triviality ≠**worship:** blasphemy ≠**beauty:** ugliness

gloss[1] *noun* **1** = **shine**, brightness, brilliance, burnish, gleam, lustre, patina, polish, sheen, varnish, veneer **2** = **façade**, appearance, front, mask, semblance, show, surface
♦ *verb* **3** = **glaze**, burnish, finish, furbish, lacquer, polish, shine, varnish, veneer **4 gloss over** = **conceal**, camouflage, cover up, disguise, hide, mask, smooth over, sweep under the carpet (*informal*), veil, whitewash (*informal*)

gloss[2] *noun* **1** = **comment**, annotation, commentary, elucidation, explanation, footnote, interpretation, note, scholium, translation ♦ *verb* **2** = **interpret**, annotate, comment, construe, elucidate, explain, translate

glossy *adjective* = **shiny**, bright, brilliant, burnished, glassy, glazed, lustrous, polished, sheeny, shining, silken, silky, sleek, smooth
➤ **Antonyms**
drab, dull, mat *or* matt, subfusc

glow *noun* **1** = **light**, burning, gleam, glimmer, incandescence, lambency, luminosity, phosphorescence **2** = **radiance**, brightness, brilliance, effulgence, splendour, vividness **3** = **blush**, bloom, flush, reddening, rosiness **4** = **passion**, ardour, earnestness, enthusiasm, excitement, fervour, gusto,

impetuosity, intensity, vehemence, warmth
♦ *verb* 5 = **shine**, brighten, burn, gleam,
glimmer, redden, smoulder 6 = **blush**, be
suffused, colour, fill, flush, radiate, thrill,
tingle
➤ Antonyms
noun ≠**radiance**: dullness, greyness ≠**blush**:
paleness, pallor, wanness ≠**passion**: chill,
coolness, half-heartedness, iciness,
indifference

glower *verb* 1 = **scowl**, frown, give a dirty
look, glare, look daggers, lour *or* lower
♦ *noun* 2 = **scowl**, angry stare, black look,
dirty look, frown, glare, lour *or* lower

glowing *adjective* 1 = **bright**, aglow,
beaming, flaming, florid, flushed, lambent,
luminous, radiant, red, rich, ruddy, suffused,
vibrant, vivid, warm 2 = **complimentary**,
adulatory, ecstatic, enthusiastic, eulogistic,
laudatory, panegyrical, rave (*informal*),
rhapsodic
➤ Antonyms
≠**bright**: colourless, cool, dull, grey, pale,
pallid, wan ≠**complimentary**: cruel,
dispassionate, scathing, unenthusiastic

glue *noun* 1 = **adhesive**, cement, gum,
mucilage, paste ♦ *verb* 2 = **stick**, affix,
agglutinate, cement, fix, gum, paste, seal

glum *adjective* = **gloomy**, chapfallen,
churlish, crabbed, crestfallen, crusty,
dejected, doleful, down, gruff, grumpy,
huffy, ill-humoured, low, moody, morose,
pessimistic, saturnine, sour, sulky, sullen,
surly
➤ Antonyms
cheerful, cheery, chirpy (*informal*), jolly,
joyful, merry, upbeat (*informal*)

glut *noun* 1 = **surfeit**, excess,
overabundance, oversupply, plethora,
saturation, superabundance, superfluity,
surplus ♦ *verb* 2 = **saturate**, choke, clog,
deluge, flood, inundate, overload,
oversupply 3 = **overfeed**, cram, fill, gorge,
satiate, stuff
➤ Antonyms
noun ≠**surfeit**: dearth, lack, paucity, scarcity,
shortage, want

glutinous *adjective* = **sticky**, adhesive,
cohesive, gluey, gooey, gummy,
mucilaginous, viscid, viscous

glutton *noun* = **gourmand**, gannet (*slang*),
gobbler, gorger, gormandizer, pig (*informal*)

gluttonous *adjective* = **greedy**,
gormandizing, insatiable, piggish, ravenous,
voracious

gluttony *noun* = **greed**, edacity,
gormandizing, gourmandism, greediness,
piggishness, rapacity, voraciousness, voracity

gnarled *adjective* = **twisted**, contorted,
knotted, knotty, knurled, leathery, rough,
rugged, weather-beaten, wrinkled

gnaw *verb* 1 = **bite**, chew, munch, nibble,
worry 2 = **distress**, fret, harry, haunt, nag,
plague, prey on one's mind, trouble, worry 3
= **erode**, consume, devour, eat away *or* into,
fret, wear away *or* down

go *verb* 1 = **move**, advance, fare (*archaic*),
journey, make for, pass, proceed, repair, set
off, travel 2 = **leave**, decamp, depart, make
tracks, move out, slope off, withdraw 3
= **lead**, connect, extend, fit, give access,
reach, run, span, spread, stretch 4
= **function**, move, operate, perform, run,
work 5 = **fare**, develop, eventuate, fall out,
happen, pan out (*informal*), proceed, result,
turn out, work out 6 = **die**, buy it (*U.S.
slang*), check out (*U.S. slang*), croak
(*slang*), expire, give up the ghost, go
belly-up (*slang*), kick it (*slang*), kick the
bucket (*slang*), pass away, peg it (*informal*),
peg out (*informal*), perish, pop one's clogs
(*informal*), snuff it (*informal*) 7 = **elapse**,
expire, flow, lapse, pass, slip away 8
= **contribute**, avail, concur, conduce, incline,
lead to, serve, tend, work towards 9
= **harmonize**, accord, agree, blend, chime,
complement, correspond, fit, match, suit
♦ *noun* 10 = **attempt**, bid, crack (*informal*),
effort, essay, shot (*informal*), stab
(*informal*), try, turn, whack (*informal*), whirl
(*informal*) 11 *Informal* = **energy**, activity,
animation, brio, drive, force, get-up-and-go
(*informal*), life, oomph (*informal*), pep,
spirit, verve, vigour, vitality, vivacity
➤ Antonyms
verb ≠**move**: arrive, halt, reach, remain,
stay, stop ≠**function**: break (down), fail,
malfunction, stop

go about *verb* 1 = **move around**, circulate,
pass around, wander 2 = **tackle**, approach,
begin, get the show on the road, set about,
take the bit between one's teeth, undertake
3 = **busy** *or* **occupy oneself with**, devote
oneself to

goad *verb* 1 = **provoke**, annoy, arouse, be
on one's back (*slang*), drive, egg on, exhort,
harass, hassle (*informal*), hound, impel,
incite, instigate, irritate, lash, nark (*Brit.,
Austral., & N.Z. slang*), prick, prod,
prompt, propel, spur, stimulate, sting, urge,
worry ♦ *noun* 2 = **provocation**, impetus,
incentive, incitement, irritation, motivation,
pressure, spur, stimulation, stimulus, urge

go-ahead *noun* 1 *Informal* = **permission**,
assent, authorization, consent, green light,
leave, O.K. *or* okay (*informal*) ♦ *adjective* 2
= **enterprising**, ambitious, go-getting
(*informal*), pioneering, progressive,
up-and-coming

go ahead *verb* = **advance**, begin, continue,
go forward, go on, proceed, progress

goal noun = aim, ambition, design, destination, end, Holy Grail (informal), intention, limit, mark, object, objective, purpose, target

go along verb 1 = accompany, carry on, escort, join, keep up, move, pass, travel 2 = agree, acquiesce, assent, concur, cooperate, follow

go away verb = leave, decamp, depart, exit, get on one's bike (Brit. slang), go to hell (informal), hook it (slang), make tracks, move out, pack one's bags (informal), recede, sling one's hook (Brit. slang), slope off, withdraw

go back verb = return, retrocede, revert

go back on verb = repudiate, change one's mind about, desert, forsake, renege on, retract

gobble verb = devour, bolt, cram, gorge, gulp, guzzle, pig out on (U.S. & Canad. slang), stuff, swallow, wolf

gobbledegook noun = nonsense, babble, cant, gabble, gibberish, hocus-pocus, jargon, mumbo jumbo, twaddle

go-between noun = intermediary, agent, broker, dealer, factor, liaison, mediator, medium, middleman

go by verb 1 = pass, elapse, exceed, flow on, move onward, proceed 2 = follow, adopt, be guided by, heed, judge from, observe, take as guide

godforsaken adjective = desolate, abandoned, backward, bleak, deserted, dismal, dreary, forlorn, gloomy, lonely, neglected, remote, wretched

godless adjective 1 = wicked, depraved, evil, impious, unprincipled, unrighteous 2 = profane, atheistic, irreligious, ungodly

godlike adjective = divine, celestial, deific, deiform, heavenly, superhuman, transcendent

godly adjective = devout, god-fearing, good, holy, pious, religious, righteous, saintly

go down verb 1 = fall, be beaten, collapse, decline, decrease, drop, founder, go under, lose, set, sink, submerge, submit, suffer defeat 2 = be recorded, be commemorated, be recalled, be remembered

godsend noun = blessing, boon, manna, stroke of luck, windfall

go far verb = be successful, advance, cut it (informal), do well, get ahead (informal), get on (informal), make a name for oneself, make one's mark, progress, succeed

go for verb 1 = favour, admire, be attracted to, be fond of, choose, hold with, like, prefer 2 = attack, assail, assault, launch oneself at, rush upon, set about or upon, spring upon 3 = seek, clutch at, fetch, obtain, reach, stretch for

go in for verb = enter, adopt, embrace, engage in, espouse, practise, pursue, take up, undertake

go into verb 1 = enter, begin, develop, participate in, undertake 2 = investigate, analyse, consider, delve into, discuss, examine, inquire into, look into, probe, pursue, research, review, scrutinize, study, work over

golden adjective 1 = yellow, blond or blonde, bright, brilliant, flaxen, resplendent, shining 2 = successful, best, blissful, delightful, flourishing, glorious, halcyon, happy, joyful, joyous, precious, prosperous, rich 3 = promising, advantageous, auspicious, excellent, favourable, opportune, propitious, rosy, valuable
➤ **Antonyms**
≠yellow: black, brunette, dark, dull ≠successful: poorest, sad, unfavourable, worst ≠promising: black, dark, sad, unfavourable, untimely, wretched

gone adjective 1 = used up, consumed, done, finished, spent 2 = past, elapsed, ended, finished, over 3 = missing, absent, astray, away, lacking, lost, vanished 4 = dead, deceased, defunct, departed, extinct, no more

good adjective 1 = excellent, acceptable, admirable, agreeable, awesome (slang), bad (slang), bitchin' (U.S. slang), capital, choice, commendable, crucial (slang), divine, dope (slang), fine, first-class, first-rate, great, hunky-dory (informal), pleasant, pleasing, positive, precious, satisfactory, splendid, super (informal), superior, tiptop, valuable, wicked (slang), world-class, worthy 2 = honourable, admirable, estimable, ethical, exemplary, honest, moral, praiseworthy, right, righteous, trustworthy, upright, virtuous, worthy 3 = favourable, adequate, advantageous, auspicious, beneficial, convenient, fit, fitting, healthy, helpful, opportune, profitable, propitious, salubrious, salutary, suitable, useful, wholesome 4 = kind, altruistic, approving, beneficent, benevolent, charitable, friendly, gracious, humane, kind-hearted, kindly, merciful, obliging, well-disposed 5 = expert, able, accomplished, adept, adroit, capable, clever, competent, dexterous, efficient, first-rate, proficient, reliable, satisfactory, serviceable, skilled, sound, suitable, talented, thorough, useful 6 = well-behaved, decorous, dutiful, mannerly, obedient, orderly, polite, proper, seemly, well-mannered 7 = valid, authentic, bona fide, dependable, genuine, honest, legitimate, proper, real, reliable, sound, true, trustworthy 8 = full, adequate, ample, complete, considerable, entire, extensive,

large, long, sizable or sizeable, solid, substantial, sufficient, whole **9 = enjoyable**, agreeable, cheerful, congenial, convivial, gratifying, happy, pleasant, pleasing, pleasurable, satisfying **10 = best**, fancy, finest, newest, nicest, precious, smartest, special, valuable **11** Of weather **= sunny**, balmy, bright, calm, clear, clement, cloudless, fair, halcyon, mild, sunshiny, tranquil **12 = eatable**, fit to eat, sound, uncorrupted, untainted, whole ◆ noun **13 = benefit**, advantage, avail, behalf, gain, interest, mileage (informal), profit, service, use, usefulness, welfare, wellbeing, worth **14 = virtue**, excellence, goodness, merit, morality, probity, rectitude, right, righteousness, uprightness, worth **15 for good = permanently**, finally, for ever, irrevocably, never to return, once and for all, sine die
➤ **Antonyms**
adjective ≠**excellent**: awful, bad, boring, disagreeable, dull, inadequate, rotten, tedious, unpleasant ≠**honourable**: bad, base, corrupt, dishonest, dishonourable, evil, immoral, improper, sinful ≠**favourable**: inappropriate, pathetic, unbecoming, unbefitting, unfavourable, unfitting, unsuitable, useless ≠**kind**: cruel, evil, mean (informal), selfish, unkind, vicious, wicked ≠**expert**: bad, incompetent, inefficient, unsatisfactory, unskilled ≠**well-behaved**: ill-mannered, mischievous, naughty, rude ≠**valid**: counterfeit, false, fraudulent, invalid, phoney ≠**full**: scant, short ≠**eatable**: bad, decayed, mouldy, off, rotten, unsound ◆ noun ≠**benefit**: detriment, disadvantage, failure, ill-fortune, loss ≠**virtue**: badness, baseness, corruption, cruelty, dishonesty, evil, immorality, meanness, wickedness

goodbye noun **= farewell**, adieu, leave-taking, parting

good-for-nothing noun **1 = layabout**, black sheep, idler, ne'er-do-well, numb-nut (U.S. slang), profligate, rapscallion, scapegrace, skiver (Brit. slang), slacker (informal), waster, wastrel ◆ adjective **2 = worthless**, feckless, idle, irresponsible, useless

good-humoured adjective **= cheerful**, affable, amiable, congenial, genial, good-tempered, happy, pleasant

good-looking adjective **= attractive**, comely, fair, handsome, personable, pretty, well-favoured

goodly adjective **1 = considerable**, ample, large, significant, sizable or sizeable, substantial, tidy (informal) **2 = attractive**, agreeable, comely, desirable, elegant, fine, good-looking, graceful, handsome, personable, pleasant, pleasing, well-favoured

good-natured adjective **= kindly**, agreeable, amiable, benevolent, friendly, good-hearted, helpful, kind, tolerant, warm-hearted, well-disposed, willing to please

goodness noun **1 = excellence**, merit, quality, superiority, value, worth **2 = virtue**, honesty, honour, integrity, merit, morality, probity, rectitude, righteousness, uprightness **3 = benefit**, advantage, nourishment, nutrition, salubriousness, wholesomeness **4 = kindness**, beneficence, benevolence, friendliness, generosity, goodwill, graciousness, humaneness, kind-heartedness, kindliness, mercy, obligingness
➤ **Antonyms**
≠**virtue**: badness, corruption, dishonesty, evil, immorality, wickedness, worthlessness ≠**benefit**: detriment, disadvantage

goods plural noun **1 = merchandise**, commodities, stock, stuff, wares **2 = property**, appurtenances, belongings, chattels, effects, furnishings, furniture, gear, movables, paraphernalia, possessions, things, trappings

goodwill noun **= friendliness**, amity, benevolence, favour, friendship, heartiness, kindliness, zeal

go off verb **1 = leave**, decamp, depart, go away, hook it (slang), move out, pack one's bags (informal), part, quit, slope off **2 = explode**, blow up, detonate, fire **3 = happen**, occur, take place **4** Informal **= rot**, go bad, go stale

go on verb **1 = continue**, endure, happen, last, occur, persist, proceed, stay **2 = chatter**, blether, carry on, prattle, rabbit (Brit. informal), ramble on, waffle (informal, chiefly Brit.), witter (on) (informal)

go out verb **1 = leave**, depart, exit **2 = be extinguished**, die out, expire, fade out

go over verb **1 = examine**, inspect, rehearse, reiterate, review, revise, study, work over **2 = scan**, peruse, read, skim

gore[1] noun **= blood**, bloodshed, butchery, carnage, slaughter

gore[2] verb **= pierce**, impale, spit, stab, transfix, wound

gorge noun **1 = ravine**, canyon, chasm, cleft, clough (dialect), defile, fissure, pass ◆ verb **2 = overeat**, bolt, cram, devour, feed, fill, glut, gobble, gormandize, gulp, guzzle, pig out (U.S. & Canad. slang), raven, sate, satiate, stuff, surfeit, swallow, wolf

gorgeous adjective **1 = beautiful**, brilliant, dazzling, drop-dead (slang), elegant, glittering, grand, luxuriant, magnificent, opulent, ravishing, resplendent, showy, splendid, splendiferous (facetious), stunning

(*informal*), sumptuous, superb **2** *Informal* = **pleasing**, attractive, bright, delightful, enjoyable, exquisite, fine, glorious, good, good-looking, lovely
➤ **Antonyms**
cheap, dismal, dreary, dull, gloomy, homely, plain, repulsive, shabby, shoddy, sombre, ugly, unattractive, unsightly

gory *adjective* = **bloodthirsty**, blood-soaked, bloodstained, bloody, ensanguined (*literary*), murderous, sanguinary

gospel *noun* **1** = **doctrine**, credo, creed, message, news, revelation, tidings **2** = **truth**, certainty, fact, the last word, verity

gossamer *adjective* = **delicate**, airy, diaphanous, fine, flimsy, gauzy, light, sheer, silky, thin, transparent

gossip *noun* **1** = **idle talk**, blether, bush telegraph, buzz, chinwag (*Brit. informal*), chitchat, clishmaclaver (*Scot.*), dirt (*U.S. slang*), gen (*Brit. informal*), hearsay, jaw (*slang*), latest (*informal*), newsmongering (*old-fashioned*), prattle, scandal, scuttlebutt (*U.S. slang*), small talk, tittle-tattle **2** = **busybody**, babbler, blatherskite, blether, chatterbox (*informal*), chatterer, flibbertigibbet, gossipmonger, newsmonger (*old-fashioned*), prattler, quidnunc, scandalmonger, tattler, telltale ◆ *verb* **3** = **chat**, blather, blether, chew the fat or rag (*slang*), dish the dirt (*informal*), gabble, jaw (*slang*), prate, prattle, schmooze (*slang*), shoot the breeze (*slang, chiefly U.S.*), tattle

go through *verb* **1** = **suffer**, bear, brave, endure, experience, tolerate, undergo, withstand **2** = **examine**, check, explore, forage, hunt, look, search, work over **3** = **use up**, consume, exhaust, squander

gouge *verb* **1** = **scoop**, chisel, claw, cut, dig (out), hollow (out) ◆ *noun* **2** = **gash**, cut, furrow, groove, hollow, scoop, scratch, trench

go under *verb* = **sink**, default, die, drown, fail, fold (*informal*), founder, go down, submerge, succumb

gourmet *noun* = **connoisseur**, bon vivant, epicure, foodie (*informal*), gastronome

govern *verb* **1** = **rule**, administer, be in power, call the shots, call the tune, command, conduct, control, direct, guide, handle, hold sway, lead, manage, order, oversee, pilot, reign, steer, superintend, supervise **2** = **determine**, decide, guide, influence, rule, sway, underlie **3** = **restrain**, bridle, check, contain, control, curb, direct, discipline, get the better of, hold in check, inhibit, keep a tight rein on, master, regulate, subdue, tame

government *noun* **1** = **executive**, administration, ministry, powers-that-be,

regime **2** = **rule**, administration, authority, dominion, execution, governance, law, polity, sovereignty, state, statecraft **3** = **guidance**, authority, command, control, direction, domination, management, regulation, restraint, superintendence, supervision, sway

governor *noun* = **leader**, administrator, boss (*informal*), chief, commander, comptroller, controller, director, executive, head, manager, overseer, ruler, superintendent, supervisor

go with *verb* = **match**, agree, blend, complement, concur, correspond, fit, harmonize, suit

go without *verb* = **be deprived of**, abstain, be denied, deny oneself, do without, go short, lack, want

gown *noun* = **dress**, costume, frock, garb, garment, habit, robe

grab *verb* = **snatch**, bag, capture, catch, catch or take hold of, clutch, grasp, grip, latch on to, nab (*informal*), nail (*informal*), pluck, seize, snap up

grace *noun* **1** = **elegance**, attractiveness, beauty, charm, comeliness, ease, finesse, gracefulness, loveliness, pleasantness, poise, polish, refinement, shapeliness, tastefulness **2** = **manners**, breeding, consideration, cultivation, decency, decorum, etiquette, mannerliness, propriety, tact **3** = **indulgence**, charity, clemency, compassion, forgiveness, leniency, lenity, mercy, pardon, quarter, reprieve **4** = **goodwill**, benefaction, beneficence, benevolence, favour, generosity, goodness, kindliness, kindness **5** = **prayer**, benediction, blessing, thanks, thanksgiving ◆ *verb* **6** = **honour**, adorn, beautify, bedeck, deck, decorate, dignify, distinguish, elevate, embellish, enhance, enrich, favour, garnish, glorify, ornament, set off
➤ **Antonyms**
noun ≠**elegance**: awkwardness, clumsiness, inelegance, stiffness, tastelessness, ugliness, ungainliness ≠**manners**: bad manners, tactlessness ≠**goodwill**: disfavour, ill will ◆ *verb* ≠**honour**: desecrate, dishonour, insult, ruin, spoil

graceful *adjective* = **elegant**, agile, beautiful, becoming, charming, comely, easy, fine, flowing, gracile (*rare*), natural, pleasing, smooth, symmetrical, tasteful
➤ **Antonyms**
awkward, clumsy, gawky, inelegant, plain, ponderous, stiff, ugly, ungainly, ungraceful

gracious *adjective* = **kind**, accommodating, affable, amiable, beneficent, benevolent, benign, benignant, charitable, chivalrous, civil, compassionate, considerate, cordial,

courteous, courtly, friendly, hospitable, indulgent, kindly, lenient, loving, merciful, mild, obliging, pleasing, polite, well-mannered
➤ **Antonyms**
brusque, cold, discourteous, gruff, haughty, impolite, mean, remote, rude, surly, unfriendly, ungracious, unpleasant

grade noun 1 = **level**, brand, category, class, condition, degree, echelon, group, mark, notch, order, place, position, quality, rank, rung, size, stage, station, step 2 **make the grade** Informal = **succeed**, come through with flying colours, come up to scratch (informal), measure up, measure up to expectations, pass muster, prove acceptable, win through ♦ verb 3 = **classify**, arrange, brand, class, evaluate, group, order, range, rank, rate, sequence, sort, value

gradient noun = **slope**, acclivity, bank, declivity, grade, hill, incline, rise

gradual adjective = **steady**, continuous, even, gentle, graduated, moderate, piecemeal, progressive, regular, slow, successive, unhurried
➤ **Antonyms**
abrupt, broken, instantaneous, overnight, sudden

gradually adverb = **steadily**, bit by bit, by degrees, drop by drop, evenly, gently, little by little, moderately, piece by piece, piecemeal, progressively, slowly, step by step, unhurriedly

graduate verb 1 = **mark off**, calibrate, grade, measure out, proportion, regulate 2 = **classify**, arrange, grade, group, order, range, rank, sequence, sort

graft noun 1 = **shoot**, bud, implant, scion, splice, sprout ♦ verb 2 = **transplant**, affix, implant, ingraft, insert, join, splice

grain noun 1 = **seed**, grist, kernel 2 = **cereals**, corn 3 = **bit**, atom, crumb, fragment, granule, iota, jot, mite, modicum, molecule, morsel, mote, ounce, particle, piece, scintilla (rare), scrap, scruple, spark, speck, suspicion, trace, whit 4 = **texture**, fibre, nap, pattern, surface, weave 5 As in **go against the grain** = **inclination**, character, disposition, humour, make-up, temper

grand adjective 1 = **impressive**, ambitious, august, dignified, elevated, eminent, exalted, fine, glorious, gorgeous, grandiose, great, haughty, illustrious, imposing, large, lofty, lordly, luxurious, magnificent, majestic, monumental, noble, opulent, ostentatious, palatial, pompous, pretentious, princely, regal, splendid, splendiferous (facetious), stately, striking, sublime, sumptuous, superb 2 = **excellent**, admirable, awesome (slang), divine, fine, first-class, first-rate, great

(informal), hunky-dory (informal), marvellous (informal), outstanding, smashing (informal), splendid, splendiferous (facetious), super (informal), superb, terrific (informal), very good, wonderful, world-class 3 = **chief**, big-time (informal), head, highest, lead, leading, main, major league (informal), pre-eminent, principal, supreme
➤ **Antonyms**
≠**impressive**: undignified, unimposing ≠**excellent**: awful, bad, chickenshit (U.S. slang), common, contemptible, crappy (slang), mean, pants (informal), petty, poor, poxy (slang), terrible, worthless ≠**chief**: inferior, insignificant, little, secondary, small, trivial, unimportant

grandeur noun = **splendour**, augustness, dignity, greatness, importance, loftiness, magnificence, majesty, nobility, pomp, state, stateliness, sublimity
➤ **Antonyms**
commonness, inferiority, insignificance, lowliness, pettiness, smallness, triviality, unimportance

grandiose adjective 1 = **imposing**, ambitious, grand, impressive, lofty, magnificent, majestic, monumental, stately 2 = **pretentious**, affected, ambitious, bombastic, extravagant, flamboyant, high-flown, ostentatious, pompous, showy
➤ **Antonyms**
≠**imposing**: humble, modest, small-scale ≠**pretentious**: down-to-earth, unpretentious

grant verb 1 = **give**, allocate, allot, assign, award, bestow, confer, donate, hand out, impart, present, vouchsafe 2 = **consent to**, accede to, accord, agree to, allow, permit 3 = **admit**, acknowledge, cede, concede 4 Law = **transfer**, assign, convey, transmit ♦ noun 5 = **award**, admission, allocation, allotment, allowance, benefaction, bequest, boon, bounty, concession, donation, endowment, gift, hand-out, present, stipend, subsidy

granule noun = **grain**, atom, crumb, fragment, iota, jot, molecule, particle, scrap, speck

graphic adjective 1 = **vivid**, clear, descriptive, detailed, explicit, expressive, forcible, illustrative, lively, lucid, picturesque, striking, telling, well-drawn 2 = **pictorial**, delineated, diagrammatic, drawn, illustrative, representational, seen, visible, visual
➤ **Antonyms**
≠**vivid**: generalized, imprecise, unspecific, vague, woolly ≠**pictorial**: impressionistic

grapple verb 1 = **deal with**, address oneself to, attack, battle, clash, combat, confront, contend, cope, do battle, encounter, engage, face, fight, get to grips with, struggle, tackle, take on, tussle, wrestle 2

= **grip**, catch, clasp, clutch, come to grips,
fasten, grab, grasp, hold, hug, lay or take
hold, make fast, seize, wrestle

grasp verb 1 = **grip**, catch, clasp, clinch,
clutch, grab, grapple, hold, lay or take hold
of, seize, snatch 2 = **understand**, catch on,
catch or get the drift of, comprehend,
follow, get, get the hang of (informal), get
the message, get the picture, realize, see,
take in ♦ noun 3 = **grip**, clasp, clutches,
embrace, hold, possession, tenure 4
= **understanding**, awareness,
comprehension, grip, ken, knowledge,
mastery, perception, realization 5 = **control**,
capacity, compass, extent, mastery, power,
range, reach, scope, sway, sweep

grasping adjective = **greedy**, acquisitive,
avaricious, close-fisted, covetous, mean,
miserly, niggardly, penny-pinching
(informal), rapacious, selfish, snoep (S.
African informal), stingy, tight-arsed (taboo
slang), tight as a duck's arse (taboo slang),
tight-assed (U.S. taboo slang), tightfisted,
usurious, venal
➤ **Antonyms**
altruistic, generous, unselfish

grate verb 1 = **shred**, mince, pulverize,
triturate 2 = **scrape**, creak, grind, rasp, rub,
scratch 3 = **annoy**, aggravate (informal),
chafe, exasperate, fret, gall, get one down,
get on one's nerves (informal), get on one's
wick (Brit. slang), get under someone's skin
(informal), get up someone's nose
(informal), irk, irritate, jar, nark (Brit.,
Austral., & N.Z. slang), nettle, peeve,
rankle, rub one up the wrong way, set one's
teeth on edge, vex

grateful adjective = **thankful**, appreciative,
beholden, indebted, obliged

gratification noun = **satisfaction**, delight,
enjoyment, fruition, fulfilment, glee,
indulgence, joy, kick or kicks (informal),
pleasure, recompense, relish, reward, thrill
➤ **Antonyms**
control, denial, disappointment, discipline,
dissatisfaction, frustration, pain, restraint,
sorrow

gratify verb = **please**, cater to, delight,
favour, fawn on, feed, fulfil, give pleasure,
gladden, humour, indulge, pander to,
recompense, requite, satisfy, thrill

grating¹ noun = **grille**, grate, grid, gridiron,
lattice, trellis

grating² adjective = **irritating**, annoying,
disagreeable, discordant, displeasing,
grinding, harsh, irksome, jarring, offensive,
rasping, raucous, scraping, squeaky, strident,
unpleasant, vexatious
➤ **Antonyms**
agreeable, calming, mellifluous, musical,

pleasing, soft, soothing

gratis adjective = **free**, buckshee (Brit.
slang), for nothing, freely, free of charge,
gratuitously, on the house, unpaid

gratitude noun = **thankfulness**,
appreciation, gratefulness, indebtedness,
obligation, recognition, sense of obligation,
thanks
➤ **Antonyms**
ingratitude, ungratefulness, unthankfulness

gratuitous adjective 1 = **unjustified**,
assumed, baseless, causeless, groundless,
irrelevant, needless, superfluous,
uncalled-for, unfounded, unmerited,
unnecessary, unprovoked, unwarranted,
wanton 2 = **voluntary**, buckshee (Brit.
slang), complimentary, free, gratis,
spontaneous, unasked-for, unpaid,
unrewarded
➤ **Antonyms**
≠**unjustified**: justifiable, provoked, relevant,
well-founded ≠**voluntary**: compulsory,
involuntary, paid

gratuity noun = **tip**, baksheesh,
benefaction, bonsela (S. African), bonus,
boon, bounty, donation, gift, largesse or
largess, perquisite, pourboire, present,
recompense, reward

grave¹ adjective 1 = **important**, acute,
critical, crucial, dangerous, exigent,
hazardous, life-and-death, momentous, of
great consequence, perilous, pressing,
serious, severe, significant, threatening,
urgent, vital, weighty 2 = **solemn**, dignified,
dour, dull, earnest, gloomy, grim-faced,
heavy, leaden, long-faced, muted, quiet,
sage (obsolete), sedate, serious, sober,
sombre, staid, subdued, thoughtful,
unsmiling
➤ **Antonyms**
≠**important**: frivolous, insignificant, mild,
trifling, unimportant ≠**solemn**: carefree,
exciting, flippant, happy, joyous, merry,
undignified

grave² noun = **tomb**, burying place, crypt,
last resting place, mausoleum, pit, sepulchre,
vault

graveyard noun = **cemetery**, boneyard
(informal), burial ground, charnel house,
churchyard, God's acre (literary), necropolis

gravitas noun = **seriousness**, gravity,
solemnity

gravitate verb 1 with to or towards = **be
drawn**, be attracted, be influenced, be
pulled, incline, lean, move, tend 2 = **fall**, be
precipitated, descend, drop, precipitate,
settle, sink

gravity noun 1 = **importance**, acuteness,
consequence, exigency, hazardousness,
moment, momentousness, perilousness,

pressingness, seriousness, severity, significance, urgency, weightiness **2** = **solemnity**, demureness, dignity, earnestness, gloom, gravitas, grimness, reserve, sedateness, seriousness, sobriety, thoughtfulness
➤ Antonyms
≠**importance**: inconsequentiality, insignificance, triviality, unimportance ≠**solemnity**: flippancy, frivolity, gaiety, happiness, joy, levity, merriment, thoughtlessness

graze¹ verb = **feed**, browse, crop, pasture

graze² verb **1** = **scratch**, abrade, bark, chafe, scrape, skin **2** = **touch**, brush, glance off, kiss, rub, scrape, shave, skim ◆ noun **3** = **scratch**, abrasion, scrape

greasy adjective **1** = **fatty**, oily, oleaginous, slick, slimy, slippery **2** = **sycophantic**, fawning, glib, grovelling, ingratiating, oily, slick, smarmy (Brit. informal), smooth, toadying, unctuous

great adjective **1** = **large**, big, bulky, colossal, elephantine, enormous, extensive, gigantic, ginormous (informal), huge, humongous or humungous (U.S. slang), immense, mammoth, prodigious, stellar (informal), stupendous, tremendous, vast, voluminous **2** = **long**, extended, lengthy, prolonged, protracted **3** = **major**, big-time (informal), capital, chief, grand, head, lead, leading, main, major league (informal), paramount, primary, principal, prominent, superior **4** = **extreme**, considerable, decided, excessive, extravagant, grievous, high, inordinate, prodigious, pronounced, serious (informal), strong **5** = **important**, consequential, critical, crucial, grave, heavy, momentous, serious, significant, weighty **6** = **famous**, celebrated, distinguished, eminent, exalted, excellent, famed, glorious, illustrious, notable, noteworthy, outstanding, prominent, remarkable, renowned, superb, superlative, talented, world-class **7** = **skilful**, able, adept, adroit, crack (slang), expert, good, masterly, proficient, skilled **8** Informal = **excellent**, admirable, awesome (slang), bitchin', boffo (slang), brill (informal), chillin' (U.S. slang), cracking (Brit. informal), crucial (slang), def (informal), dope (slang), fantastic (informal), fine, first-rate, good, hunky-dory (informal), jim-dandy (slang), marvellous (informal), mean (slang), mega (slang), sovereign, superb, terrific (informal), the dog's bollocks (taboo slang), topping (Brit. slang), tremendous (informal), wonderful **9** = **noble**, august, chivalrous, dignified, distinguished, exalted, fine, glorious, grand, heroic, high-minded, idealistic, impressive, lofty, magnanimous, princely, sublime **10**

= **enthusiastic**, active, devoted, keen, zealous **11** = **utter**, absolute, arrant, complete, consummate, downright, egregious, flagrant, out-and-out, perfect, positive, thoroughgoing, thundering (informal), total, unmitigated, unqualified
➤ Antonyms
≠**large**: diminutive, little, small ≠**important**: inconsequential, inconsiderable, insignificant, petty, trivial, unimportant ≠**skilful**: inexperienced, unskilled, untrained ≠**excellent**: average, inferior, poor, secondary, second-rate, undistinguished, unnotable ≠**noble**: base, ignoble, inhumane, mean, unkind

greatly adverb = **very much**, abundantly, by leaps and bounds, by much, considerably, enormously, exceedingly, extremely, highly, hugely, immensely, markedly, mightily, much, notably, powerfully, remarkably, seriously (informal), to the nth degree, tremendously, vastly

greatness noun **1** = **immensity**, bulk, enormity, hugeness, largeness, length, magnitude, mass, prodigiousness, size, vastness **2** = **intensity**, amplitude, force, high degree, potency, power, strength **3** = **importance**, gravity, heaviness, import, moment, momentousness, seriousness, significance, urgency, weight **4** = **fame**, celebrity, distinction, eminence, glory, grandeur, illustriousness, lustre, note, renown **5** = **grandeur**, chivalry, dignity, disinterestedness, generosity, heroism, high-mindedness, idealism, loftiness, majesty, nobility, nobleness, stateliness, sublimity

greed, greediness noun **1** = **gluttony**, edacity, esurience, gormandizing, hunger, insatiableness, ravenousness, voracity **2** = **avarice**, acquisitiveness, avidity, covetousness, craving, cupidity, desire, eagerness, graspingness, longing, rapacity, selfishness
➤ Antonyms
≠**avarice**: altruism, benevolence, generosity, largesse or largess, munificence, self-restraint, unselfishness

greedy adjective **1** = **gluttonous**, edacious, esurient, gormandizing, hoggish, hungry, insatiable, piggish, ravenous, voracious **2** = **grasping**, acquisitive, avaricious, avid, covetous, craving, desirous, eager, hungry, impatient, rapacious, selfish
➤ Antonyms
≠**grasping**: altruistic, benevolent, generous, munificent, self-restrained, unselfish

Greek adjective **1** = **Hellenic** ◆ noun **2** = **Hellene**

green adjective **1** = **leafy**, blooming, budding, flourishing, fresh, grassy, new,

undecayed, verdant, verdurous **2**
= ecological, conservationist, ecologically
sound, environment-friendly, non-polluting,
ozone-friendly **3 = new**, fresh, immature,
raw, recent, unripe **4 = nauseous**, ill, pale,
sick, under the weather, unhealthy, wan **5**
– inexperienced, callow, credulous, gullible,
ignorant, immature, inexpert, ingenuous,
innocent, naive, new, raw, unpolished,
unpractised, unskilful, unsophisticated,
untrained, unversed, wet behind the ears
(*informal*) **6 = jealous**, covetous, envious,
grudging, resentful ◆ *noun* **7 = lawn**,
common, grassplot, sward, turf

green light *noun* **= permission**, approval,
authorization, blessing, clearance,
confirmation, go-ahead (*informal*),
imprimatur, O.K. *or* okay (*informal*), sanction

greet *verb* **= welcome**, accost, address,
compliment, hail, meet, nod to, receive,
salute, tip one's hat to

greeting *noun* **1 = welcome**, address, hail,
reception, salutation, salute **2 greetings**
= best wishes, compliments, devoirs, good
wishes, regards, respects, salutations

gregarious *adjective* **= outgoing**, affable,
companionable, convivial, cordial, friendly,
sociable, social
➤ **Antonyms**
antisocial, reserved, solitary, standoffish,
unsociable, withdrawn

grey *adjective* **1 = pale**, ashen, bloodless,
colourless, like death warmed up (*informal*),
livid, pallid, wan **2 = dismal**, cheerless,
cloudy, dark, depressing, dim, drab, dreary,
dull, foggy, gloomy, misty, murky, overcast,
sunless **3 = characterless**, anonymous,
colourless, dull, indistinct, neutral, unclear,
unidentifiable **4 = old**, aged, ancient, elderly,
experienced, hoary, mature, venerable

gridlock *noun* **= standstill**, deadlock, full
stop, halt, impasse, stalemate

grief *noun* **1 = sadness**, affliction, agony,
anguish, bereavement, dejection, distress,
grievance, hardship, heartache, heartbreak,
misery, mournfulness, mourning, pain,
regret, remorse, sorrow, suffering, trial,
tribulation, trouble, woe **2 come to grief**
Informal **= fail**, come unstuck, fall flat on
one's face, meet with disaster, miscarry
➤ **Antonyms**
≠**sadness:** cheer, comfort, consolation,
delight, gladness, happiness, joy, rejoicing,
solace

grievance *noun* **= complaint**, affliction, axe
to grind, beef (*slang*), chip on one's
shoulder (*informal*), damage, distress, grief,
gripe (*informal*), hardship, injury, injustice,
protest, resentment, sorrow, trial, tribulation,
trouble, unhappiness, wrong

grieve *verb* **1 = mourn**, ache, bemoan,
bewail, complain, deplore, lament, regret,
rue, sorrow, suffer, wail, weep **2 = sadden**,
afflict, agonize, break the heart of, crush,
distress, hurt, injure, make one's heart bleed,
pain, wound
➤ **Antonyms**
≠**sadden:** cheer, comfort, console, ease,
gladden, please, rejoice, solace

grievous *adjective* **1 = severe**, afflicting,
calamitous, damaging, distressing, dreadful,
grave, harmful, heavy, hurtful, injurious,
lamentable, oppressive, painful, wounding **2**
= deplorable, appalling, atrocious, dreadful,
egregious, flagrant, glaring, heinous,
intolerable, lamentable, monstrous, offensive,
outrageous, shameful, shocking, unbearable
➤ **Antonyms**
≠**severe:** insignificant, mild, trivial,
unimportant ≠**deplorable:** delightful,
pleasant

grim *adjective* **= forbidding**, cruel, ferocious,
fierce, formidable, frightful, ghastly,
godawful (*slang*), grisly, gruesome, hard,
harsh, hideous, horrible, horrid, implacable,
merciless, morose, relentless, resolute,
ruthless, severe, shocking, sinister, stern,
sullen, surly, terrible, unrelenting, unyielding
➤ **Antonyms**
amiable, attractive, benign, cheerful, easy,
genial, gentle, happy, kind, pleasant, soft,
sympathetic

grimace *noun* **1 = scowl**, face, frown,
mouth, sneer, wry face ◆ *verb* **2 = scowl**,
frown, lour *or* lower, make a face *or* faces,
mouth, sneer

grime *noun* **= dirt**, filth, grot (*slang*), smut,
soot

grimy *adjective* **= dirty**, begrimed,
besmeared, besmirched, filthy, foul, grubby,
scuzzy (*slang*), smutty, soiled, sooty, unclean

grind *verb* **1 = crush**, abrade, comminute,
granulate, grate, kibble, mill, pound,
powder, pulverize, triturate **2 = smooth**, file,
polish, sand, sharpen, whet **3 = scrape**,
gnash, grate, grit **4 grind down = oppress**,
afflict, harass, hold down, hound, persecute,
plague, trouble, tyrannize (over) ◆ *noun* **5**
Informal **= hard work**, chore, drudgery,
labour, sweat (*informal*), task, toil

grip *noun* **1 = clasp**, handclasp (*U.S.*), hold,
purchase **2 = control**, clutches, domination,
influence, keeping, possession, power,
tenure **3 = understanding**, command,
comprehension, grasp, mastery, perception
4 come *or* **get to grips (with) = tackle**,
close with, confront, contend with, cope
with, deal with, encounter, face up to,
grapple with, grasp, handle, meet, take on,
take the bit between one's teeth, undertake
◆ *verb* **5 = grasp**, clasp, clutch, hold, latch

on to, seize, take hold of **6** = **engross**, absorb, catch up, compel, enthral, entrance, fascinate, hold, involve, mesmerize, rivet, spellbind

gripping *adjective* = **fascinating**, compelling, compulsive, engrossing, enthralling, entrancing, exciting, riveting, spellbinding, thrilling, unputdownable (*informal*)

grisly *adjective* = **gruesome**, abominable, appalling, awful, dreadful, frightful, ghastly, grim, hellacious (*U.S. slang*), hideous, horrible, horrid, macabre, shocking, sickening, terrible, terrifying
➤ **Antonyms**
agreeable, attractive, charming, innocuous, nice, pleasant

grit *noun* **1** = **gravel**, dust, pebbles, sand **2** = **courage**, backbone, balls (*taboo slang*), determination, doggedness, fortitude, gameness, guts (*informal*), hardihood, mettle, nerve, perseverance, pluck, resolution, spirit, tenacity, toughness ◆ *verb* **3** = **grind**, clench, gnash, grate

gritty *adjective* **1** = **courageous**, ballsy (*taboo slang*), brave, determined, dogged, feisty (*informal, chiefly U.S. & Canad.*), game, hardy, mettlesome, plucky, resolute, spirited, steadfast, tenacious, tough **2** = **rough**, abrasive, dusty, grainy, granular, gravelly, rasping, sandy

groan *noun* **1** = **moan**, cry, sigh, whine **2** *Informal* = **complaint**, beef (*slang*), gripe (*informal*), grouse, grumble, objection, protest ◆ *verb* **3** = **moan**, cry, sigh, whine **4** *Informal* = **complain**, beef (*slang*), bemoan, bitch (*slang*), gripe (*informal*), grouse, grumble, lament, object

groggy *adjective* = **dizzy**, befuddled, confused, dazed, faint, muzzy, punch-drunk, reeling, shaky, staggering, stunned, stupefied, unsteady, weak, wobbly, woozy (*informal*)

groom *noun* **1** = **stableman**, currier (*rare*), hostler *or* ostler (*archaic*), stableboy ◆ *verb* **2** = **rub down**, brush, clean, curry, tend **3** = **smarten up**, clean, dress, get up (*informal*), gussy up (*slang, chiefly U.S.*), preen, primp, spruce up, tidy, turn out **4** = **train**, coach, drill, educate, make ready, nurture, prepare, prime, ready

groove *noun* = **indentation**, channel, cut, cutting, flute, furrow, gutter, hollow, rebate, rut, score, trench, trough

grope *verb* = **feel**, cast about, finger, fish, flounder, forage, fumble, grabble, scrabble, search

gross *adjective* **1** = **blatant**, apparent, arrant, downright, egregious, flagrant, glaring, grievous, heinous, manifest, obvious,

outrageous, plain, rank, serious, shameful, sheer, shocking, unmitigated, unqualified, utter **2** = **vulgar**, coarse, crude, improper, impure, indecent, indelicate, lewd, low, obscene, offensive, ribald, rude, sensual, smutty, unseemly, X-rated (*informal*) **3** = **fat**, big, bulky, corpulent, dense, great, heavy, hulking, large, lumpish, massive, obese, overweight, thick **4** = **total**, aggregate, before deductions, before tax, entire, whole **5** = **coarse**, boorish, callous, crass, dull, ignorant, imperceptive, insensitive, tasteless, uncultured, undiscriminating, unfeeling, unrefined, unsophisticated ◆ *verb* **6** = **earn**, bring in, make, rake in (*informal*), take
➤ **Antonyms**
≠**blatant**: partial, qualified ≠**vulgar**: decent, delicate, proper, pure *adjective* ≠**fat**: delicate, little, petite, slim, small, svelte, thin ≠**total**: net ≠**coarse**: cultivated, elegant

grotesque *adjective* = **unnatural**, absurd, bizarre, deformed, distorted, extravagant, fanciful, fantastic, freakish, incongruous, ludicrous, malformed, misshapen, odd, outlandish, preposterous, ridiculous, strange, weird, whimsical
➤ **Antonyms**
average, classic, graceful, natural, normal, realistic

ground *noun* **1** = **earth**, clod, dirt, dry land, dust, field, land, loam, mould, sod, soil, terra firma, terrain, turf **2** = **stadium**, arena, field, park (*informal*), pitch **3** *often plural* = **land**, area, country, district, domain, estate, fields, gardens, habitat, holding, property, realm, terrain, territory, tract **4** *usually plural* = **dregs**, deposit, grouts, lees, sediment, settlings **5 grounds** = **reason**, account, argument, base, basis, call, cause, excuse, factor, foundation, inducement, justification, motive, occasion, premise, pretext, rationale ◆ *verb* **6** = **instruct**, acquaint with, coach, familiarize with, inform, initiate, prepare, teach, train, tutor **7** = **base**, establish, fix, found, set, settle

groundless *adjective* = **unjustified**, baseless, chimerical, empty, false, idle, illusory, imaginary, unauthorized, uncalled-for, unfounded, unprovoked, unsupported, unwarranted
➤ **Antonyms**
justified, logical, proven, real, reasonable, substantial, supported, true, well-founded

groundwork *noun* = **preliminaries**, base, basis, cornerstone, footing, foundation, fundamentals, preparation, spadework, underpinnings

group *noun* **1** = **set**, aggregation, assemblage, association, band, batch, bevy, bunch, camp, category, circle, class, clique, clump, cluster, collection, company, congregation, coterie, crowd, faction, formation, gang, gathering, organization, pack, party, posse (*slang*), troop ♦ *verb* **2** = **arrange**, assemble, associate, assort, bracket, class, classify, dispose, gather, marshal, order, organize, put together, range, sort **3** = **get together**, associate, band together, cluster, congregate, consort, fraternize, gather

grouse *verb* **1** = **complain**, beef (*slang*), bellyache (*slang*), bitch (*slang*), bleat, carp, find fault, gripe (*informal*), grouch (*informal*), grumble, kvetch (*U.S. slang*), moan, whine, whinge (*informal*) ♦ *noun* **2** = **complaint**, beef (*slang*), grievance, gripe (*informal*), grouch (*informal*), grumble, moan, objection, protest

grove *noun* = **wood**, coppice, copse, covert, plantation, spinney, thicket

grovel *verb* = **humble oneself**, abase oneself, bootlick (*informal*), bow and scrape, brown-nose (*taboo slang*), cower, crawl, creep, cringe, crouch, demean oneself, fawn, flatter, kiss ass (*taboo slang*), kowtow, lick someone's arse (*taboo slang*), lick someone's boots, pander to, sneak, toady
➤ **Antonyms**
be proud, domineer, face, hold one's head high, intimidate

grow *verb* **1** = **increase**, develop, enlarge, expand, extend, fill out, get bigger, get taller, heighten, multiply, spread, stretch, swell, thicken, widen **2** = **spring up**, develop, flourish, germinate, shoot, sprout, vegetate **3** = **cultivate**, breed, farm, nurture, produce, propagate, raise **4** = **improve**, advance, expand, flourish, progress, prosper, succeed, thrive **5** = **originate**, arise, issue, spring, stem **6** = **become**, come to be, develop (into), get, turn, wax
➤ **Antonyms**
≠**increase**: decline, decrease, die, diminish, dwindle, fail, lessen, shrink, subside, wane

grown-up *adjective* **1** = **mature**, adult, fully-grown, of age ♦ *noun* **2** = **adult**, man, woman

growth *noun* **1** = **increase**, aggrandizement, augmentation, development, enlargement, evolution, expansion, extension, growing, heightening, multiplication, proliferation, stretching, thickening, widening **2** = **progress**, advance, advancement, expansion, improvement, prosperity, rise, success **3** = **cultivation**, crop, development, germination, produce, production, shooting, sprouting, vegetation **4** *Medical* = **tumour**, excrescence, lump
➤ **Antonyms**
≠**increase**: decline, decrease, drop, dwindling, failure, fall, lessening, shrinkage,

slackening, subsiding

grub *noun* **1** *Slang* = **food**, eats (*slang*), feed, nosebag (*slang*), nosh (*slang*), rations, sustenance, tack (*informal*), victuals, vittles (*obsolete or dialect*) **2** = **larva**, caterpillar, maggot ♦ *verb* **3** = **search**, ferret, forage, hunt, rummage, scour, uncover, unearth **4** = **dig up**, burrow, probe, pull up, root (*informal*), rootle (*Brit.*), search for, uproot

grubby *adjective* = **dirty**, besmeared, filthy, frowzy, grimy, grungy (*slang chiefly U.S. & Canad.*), manky (*Scot. dialect*), mean, messy, mucky, scruffy, scuzzy (*slang*), seedy, shabby, slovenly, smutty, soiled, sordid, squalid, unkempt, untidy, unwashed

grudge *noun* **1** = **resentment**, animosity, animus, antipathy, aversion, bitterness, chip on one's shoulder (*informal*), dislike, enmity, grievance, hard feelings, hate, ill will, malevolence, malice, pique, rancour, spite, venom ♦ *verb* **2** = **resent**, begrudge, be reluctant, complain, covet, envy, hold back, mind, stint
➤ **Antonyms**
noun ≠**resentment**: appreciation, goodwill, liking, thankfulness ♦ *verb* ≠**resent**: be glad for, celebrate, welcome

gruelling *adjective* = **exhausting**, arduous, backbreaking, brutal, crushing, demanding, difficult, fatiguing, fierce, grinding, hard, harsh, laborious, punishing, severe, stiff, strenuous, taxing, tiring, trying
➤ **Antonyms**
cushy (*informal*), easy, enjoyable, light, pleasant, undemanding

gruesome *adjective* = **horrific**, abominable, awful, fearful, from hell (*informal*), ghastly, grim, grisly, hellacious (*U.S. slang*), hideous, horrendous, horrible, horrid, horrifying, loathsome, macabre, obscene, repugnant, repulsive, shocking, spine-chilling, terrible
➤ **Antonyms**
appealing, benign, cheerful, pleasant, sweet

gruff *adjective* **1** = **surly**, bad-tempered, bearish, blunt, brusque, churlish, crabbed, crusty, curt, discourteous, grouchy (*informal*), grumpy, ill-humoured, ill-natured, impolite, rough, rude, sour, sullen, uncivil, ungracious, unmannerly **2** = **hoarse**, croaking, guttural, harsh, husky, low, rasping, rough, throaty
➤ **Antonyms**
≠**surly**: courteous, good-tempered, gracious, kind, pleasant, polite ≠**hoarse**: mellifluous, smooth, sweet

grumble *verb* **1** = **complain**, beef (*slang*), bellyache (*slang*), bitch (*slang*), bleat, carp, find fault, gripe (*informal*), grouch (*informal*), grouse, kvetch (*U.S. slang*), moan, repine, whine, whinge (*informal*) **2** = **rumble**, growl, gurgle, murmur, mutter, roar ◆ *noun* **3** = **complaint**, beef (*slang*), grievance, gripe (*informal*), grouch (*informal*), grouse, moan, objection, protest **4** = **rumble**, growl, gurgle, murmur, muttering, roar

grumpy *adjective* = **irritable**, bad-tempered, cantankerous, crotchety (*informal*), peevish, sulky, sullen, surly, testy

guarantee *noun* **1** = **assurance**, bond, certainty, collateral, covenant, earnest, guaranty, pledge, promise, security, surety, undertaking, warranty, word, word of honour ◆ *verb* **2** = **ensure**, answer for, assure, certify, insure, maintain, make certain, pledge, promise, protect, secure, stand behind, swear, vouch for, warrant

guarantor *noun* = **underwriter**, backer, bailsman (*rare*), bondsman (*Law*), guarantee, sponsor, supporter, surety, voucher, warrantor

guard *verb* **1** = **watch over**, cover, defend, escort, keep, mind, oversee, patrol, police, preserve, protect, safeguard, save, screen, secure, shelter, shield, supervise, tend, watch ◆ *noun* **2** = **protector**, custodian, defender, lookout, picket, sentinel, sentry, warder, watch, watchman **3** = **escort**, convoy, patrol **4** = **protection**, buffer, bulwark, bumper, defence, pad, rampart, safeguard, screen, security, shield **5** = **watchfulness**, attention, care, caution, heed, vigilance, wariness **6 off guard** = **unprepared**, napping, unready, unwary, with one's defences down **7 on guard** = **prepared**, alert, cautious, circumspect, on the alert, on the lookout, on the qui vive, ready, vigilant, wary, watchful

guarded *adjective* = **cautious**, cagey (*informal*), careful, circumspect, discreet, leery (*slang*), noncommittal, prudent, reserved, restrained, reticent, suspicious, wary

guardian *noun* = **keeper**, attendant, champion, curator, custodian, defender, escort, guard, preserver, protector, trustee, warden, warder

guerrilla *noun* = **freedom fighter**, irregular, member of the underground *or* resistance, partisan, underground fighter

guess *verb* **1** = **estimate**, conjecture, fathom, hypothesize, penetrate, predict, solve, speculate, work out **2** = **suppose**, believe, conjecture, dare say, deem, divine, fancy, hazard, imagine, judge, reckon, surmise, suspect, think ◆ *noun* **3** = **supposition**, ballpark figure (*informal*), conjecture, feeling, hypothesis, judgment, notion, prediction, reckoning, shot in the dark, speculation, surmise, suspicion, theory
➤ **Antonyms**
verb ≠**estimate**, **suppose**: be certain, be sure, know, prove, show ◆ *noun*

≠**supposition**: certainty, fact

guesswork *noun* = **speculation**, conjecture, estimation, presumption, supposition, surmise, suspicion, theory

guest *noun* = **visitor**, boarder, caller, company, lodger, visitant

guidance *noun* = **advice**, auspices, conduct, control, counsel, counselling, direction, government, help, instruction, intelligence, leadership, management, teaching

guide *noun* **1** = **escort**, adviser, attendant, chaperon, cicerone, conductor, controller, counsellor, director, dragoman, guru, leader, mentor, monitor, pilot, steersman, teacher, torchbearer, usher **2** = **pointer**, beacon, clue, guiding light, key, landmark, lodestar, mark, marker, sign, signal, signpost **3** = **guidebook**, Baedeker, catalogue, directory, handbook, instructions, key, manual, vade mecum **4** = **model**, criterion, example, exemplar, ideal, imago (*Psychoanalysis*), inspiration, lodestar, master, par, paradigm, standard ◆ *verb* **5** = **lead**, accompany, attend, conduct, convoy, direct, escort, pilot, shepherd, show the way, steer, usher **6** = **steer**, command, control, direct, handle, manage, manoeuvre **7** = **supervise**, advise, counsel, educate, govern, influence, instruct, oversee, regulate, rule, superintend, sway, teach, train

guild *noun* = **society**, association, brotherhood, club, company, corporation, fellowship, fraternity, league, lodge, order, organization, union

guile *noun* = **cunning**, art, artfulness, artifice, cleverness, craft, craftiness, deceit, deception, duplicity, gamesmanship (*informal*), knavery, ruse, sharp practice, slyness, treachery, trickery, trickiness, wiliness
➤ **Antonyms**
candour, frankness, honesty, sincerity, truthfulness

guileful *adjective* = **cunning**, artful, clever, crafty, deceitful, duplicitous, foxy, sly, sneaky, treacherous, tricky, underhand, wily

guilt *noun* **1** = **culpability**, blame, blameworthiness, criminality, delinquency, guiltiness, iniquity, misconduct, responsibility, sinfulness, wickedness, wrong, wrongdoing **2** = **remorse**, bad conscience, contrition, disgrace, dishonour, guiltiness, guilty conscience, infamy, regret, self-condemnation, self-reproach, shame, stigma
➤ **Antonyms**
≠**culpability**: blamelessness, innocence, righteousness, sinlessness, virtue ≠**remorse**: honour, pride, self-respect

guiltless *adjective* = **innocent**, blameless,

clean (*slang*), clear, immaculate, impeccable, irreproachable, pure, sinless, spotless, squeaky-clean, unimpeachable, unsullied, untainted, untarnished

guilty *adjective* **1** = **culpable**, at fault, blameworthy, convicted, criminal, delinquent, erring, evil, felonious, iniquitous, offending, reprehensible, responsible, sinful, to blame, wicked, wrong **2** = **remorseful**, ashamed, conscience-stricken, contrite, hangdog, regretful, rueful, shamefaced, sheepish, sorry
➤ Antonyms
≠**culpable**: blameless, innocent, moral, righteous, virtuous ≠**remorseful**: proud

guise *noun* = **form**, appearance, aspect, demeanour, disguise, mode, pretence, semblance, shape

gulf *noun* **1** = **bay**, bight, sea inlet **2** = **chasm**, abyss, breach, cleft, gap, opening, rent, rift, separation, split, void, whirlpool

gullibility *noun* = **credulity**, innocence, naïveté, simplicity, trustingness

gullible *adjective* = **naive**, as green as grass, born yesterday, credulous, easily taken in, foolish, green, innocent, silly, simple, trusting, unsceptical, unsophisticated, unsuspecting, wet behind the ears (*informal*)
➤ Antonyms
cynical, sophisticated, suspicious, untrusting, worldly

gully *noun* = **channel**, ditch, gutter, watercourse

gulp *verb* **1** = **swallow**, bolt, devour, gobble, guzzle, knock back (*informal*), quaff, swig (*informal*), swill, toss off, wolf **2** = **gasp**, choke, stifle, swallow ♦ *noun* **3** = **swallow**, draught, mouthful, swig (*informal*)

gum *noun* **1** = **glue**, adhesive, cement, exudate, mucilage, paste, resin ♦ *verb* **2** = **stick**, affix, cement, clog, glue, paste, stiffen

gumption *noun* = **resourcefulness**, ability, acumen, astuteness, cleverness, common sense, discernment, enterprise, get-up-and-go (*informal*), horse sense, initiative, mother wit, nous (*Brit. slang*), sagacity, savvy (*slang*), shrewdness, spirit, wit(s)

gun *noun* = **firearm**, handgun, piece (*slang*), shooter (*slang*)

gunman *noun* = **terrorist**, assassin, bandit, bravo, desperado, gangster, gunslinger (*U.S. slang*), heavy (*slang*), hit man (*slang*), killer, mobster (*U.S. slang*), murderer, thug

gurgle *verb* **1** = **murmur**, babble, bubble, burble, crow, lap, plash, purl, ripple, splash ♦ *noun* **2** = **murmur**, babble, purl, ripple

guru *noun* = **teacher**, authority, guiding light, leader, maharishi, mahatma, master, mentor, sage, Svengali, swami, torchbearer, tutor

gush *verb* **1** = **flow**, burst, cascade, flood, issue, jet, pour, run, rush, spout, spurt, stream **2** = **enthuse**, babble, blather, chatter, effervesce, effuse, jabber, overstate, spout ♦ *noun* **3** = **stream**, burst, cascade, flood, flow, issue, jet, outburst, outflow, rush, spout, spurt, torrent **4** = **babble**, blather, chatter, effusion, exuberance

gust *noun* **1** = **blast**, blow, breeze, flurry, gale, puff, rush, squall **2** = **surge**, burst, eruption, explosion, fit, gale, outburst, paroxysm, passion, storm ♦ *verb* **3** = **blow**, blast, puff, squall

gusto *noun* = **relish**, appetite, appreciation, brio, delight, enjoyment, enthusiasm, exhilaration, fervour, liking, pleasure, savour, verve, zeal, zest, zing (*informal*)
➤ Antonyms
apathy, coolness, disinterest, distaste, inertia

gusty *adjective* = **windy**, blowy, blustering, blustery, breezy, inclement, squally, stormy, tempestuous

gut *noun* **1** *Informal* = **paunch**, belly, potbelly, spare tyre (*Brit. slang*) **2 guts: a** = **intestines**, belly, bowels, entrails, innards (*informal*), insides (*informal*), inwards, stomach, viscera **b** *Informal* = **courage**, audacity, backbone, boldness, bottle (*slang*), daring, forcefulness, grit, hardihood, mettle, nerve, pluck, spirit, spunk (*informal*), willpower ♦ *verb* **3** = **disembowel**, clean, draw, dress, eviscerate **4** = **ravage**, clean out, despoil, empty, pillage, plunder, ransack, rifle, sack, strip ♦ *adjective* **5** *As in* **gut reaction** = **instinctive**, basic, deep-seated, emotional, heartfelt, innate, intuitive, involuntary, natural, spontaneous, unthinking, visceral

gutless *adjective* = **faint-hearted**, abject, chicken (*slang*), chickenshit (*U.S. slang*), cowardly, craven, feeble, irresolute, lily-livered, spineless, submissive, timid, weak
➤ Antonyms
bold, brave, courageous, determined, resolute

gutsy *adjective* = **brave**, bold, courageous, determined, gritty, indomitable, plucky, resolute, spirited

gutter *noun* = **drain**, channel, conduit, ditch, duct, pipe, sluice, trench, trough, tube

guttersnipe *noun* = **street urchin**, gamin, mudlark (*slang*), ragamuffin, street Arab (*offensive*), waif

guttural *adjective* = **throaty**, deep, gravelly, gruff, hoarse, husky, low, rasping, rough, thick

guy *noun Informal* = **man**, bloke (*Brit. informal*), cat (*slang*), chap, fellow, lad, person, youth

guzzle *verb* = **devour**, bolt, carouse, cram, drink, gobble, gorge, gormandize, knock back (*informal*), pig out (*U.S. & Canad. slang*), quaff, stuff (oneself), swill, tope, wolf

Gypsy, Gipsy *noun* = **traveller**, Bohemian, nomad, rambler, roamer, Romany, rover, vagabond, vagrant, wanderer

gyrate *verb* = **rotate**, circle, pirouette, revolve, spin, spiral, twirl, whirl

gyration *noun* = **rotation**, convolution, pirouette, revolution, spin, spinning, spiral, whirl, whirling

H h

habiliments *plural noun* = **clothes**, apparel, array, attire, clothing, costume, dress, garb, garment, habit, raiment (*archaic or poetic*), robes, uniform, vestments

habit *noun* 1 = **mannerism**, bent, custom, disposition, manner, practice, proclivity, propensity, quirk, tendency, way 2 = **custom**, convention, mode, practice, routine, rule, second nature, tradition, usage, wont 3 = **addiction**, dependence, fixation, obsession, weakness 4 = **disposition**, constitution, frame of mind, make-up, nature 5 = **dress**, apparel, garb, garment, habiliment, riding dress

habitat *noun* = **home**, abode, element, environment, home ground, locality, natural home, surroundings, terrain, territory

habitation *noun* 1 = **occupation**, inhabitance, inhabitancy, occupancy, tenancy 2 *Formal* = **dwelling**, abode, domicile, dwelling house, home, house, living quarters, lodging, pad (*slang*), quarters, residence

habit-forming *adjective* = **addictive**, compulsive, moreish (*informal*)

habitual *adjective* 1 = **customary**, accustomed, common, familiar, fixed, natural, normal, ordinary, regular, routine, standard, traditional, usual, wonted 2 = **persistent**, chronic, confirmed, constant, established, frequent, hardened, ingrained, inveterate, recurrent
➤ **Antonyms**
≠**customary**: abnormal, exceptional, extraordinary, irregular, rare, strange, uncommon, unusual ≠**persistent**: infrequent, irregular, occasional

habituate *verb* = **accustom**, acclimatize, acquaint, break in, condition, discipline, familiarize, harden, inure, make used to, school, season, train

habituated *adjective* = **accustomed**, acclimatized, adapted, broken in, conditioned, disciplined, familiarized, hardened, inured, schooled, seasoned, trained, used (to)
➤ **Antonyms**
unaccustomed, unfamiliar, unused (to)

habitué *noun* = **frequent visitor**, constant customer, frequenter, regular (*informal*), regular patron

hack[1] *verb* 1 = **cut**, chop, gash, hew, kick,

lacerate, mangle, mutilate, notch, slash
♦ *noun* 2 = **cut**, chop, gash, notch, slash

hack[2] *noun* 1 = **scribbler**, literary hack 2 = **horse**, crock, hired horse, jade, nag
♦ *adjective* 3 = **unoriginal**, banal, mediocre, pedestrian, poor, stereotyped, tired, undistinguished, uninspired

hackles *plural noun* **make one's hackles rise** = **infuriate**, anger, annoy, cause resentment, get one's dander up (*slang*), make one see red (*informal*), rub one up the wrong way

hackneyed *adjective* = **unoriginal**, banal, clichéd, common, commonplace, overworked, pedestrian, played out (*informal*), run-of-the-mill, stale, stereotyped, stock, threadbare, timeworn, tired, trite, worn-out
➤ **Antonyms**
fresh, imaginative, new, novel, original, striking, unusual

Hades *noun* = **underworld**, hell, infernal regions, lower world, nether regions, realm of Pluto, (the) inferno

haft *noun* = **handle**, shaft

hag *noun* = **witch**, crone, fury, harridan, shrew, termagant, virago, vixen

haggard *adjective* = **gaunt**, careworn, drawn, emaciated, ghastly, hollow-eyed, pinched, shrunken, thin, wan, wasted, wrinkled
➤ **Antonyms**
bright-eyed, brisk, energetic, fresh, hale, robust, sleek, vigorous

haggle *verb* 1 = **bargain**, barter, beat down, drive a hard bargain 2 = **wrangle**, bicker, dispute, quarrel, squabble

hag-ridden *adjective* = **careworn**, angst-ridden, anxiety-ridden, ground down, harassed, tormented, with all the troubles of the world on one's shoulders, worn down, worried

hail[1] *noun* 1 = **shower**, barrage, bombardment, downpour, pelting, rain, storm, volley ♦ *verb* 2 = **shower**, barrage, batter, beat down upon, bombard, pelt, rain, rain down on, storm, volley

hail[2] *verb* 1 = **salute**, greet, welcome 2 = **acclaim**, acknowledge, applaud, cheer, exalt, glorify, honour 3 = **flag down**, accost, address, call, halloo, shout to, signal to, sing out, speak to, wave down 4 **hail from**

= **come from**, be a native of, be born in, originate in

➤ **Antonyms**

≠ **salute:** avoid, cut (*informal*), ignore, snub
≠ **acclaim:** boo, condemn, criticize, hiss, insult, jeer

hail-fellow-well-met *adjective*
= **overfriendly**, back-slapping, familiar, free-and-easy, genial, hearty, unceremonious

hair *noun* 1 = **locks**, head of hair, mane, mop, shock, tresses 2 **by a hair** = **by a narrow margin**, by a fraction of an inch, by a hair's-breadth, by a split second, by a whisker, by the skin of one's teeth 3 **get in one's hair** *Informal* = **annoy**, aggravate (*informal*), be on one's back (*slang*), exasperate, get on one's nerves (*informal*), get on one's wick (*Brit. slang*), get up one's nose (*informal*), harass, hassle (*informal*), irritate, nark (*Brit., Austral., & N.Z. slang*), pester, piss one off (*taboo slang*), plague 4 **let one's hair down** = **let oneself go**, chill out (*slang, chiefly U.S.*), let it all hang out (*informal*), let off steam (*informal*), mellow out (*informal*), relax, veg out (*slang, chiefly U.S.*) 5 **not turn a hair** = **remain calm**, keep one's cool (*slang*), keep one's hair on (*Brit. informal*), not bat an eyelid 6 **split hairs** = **quibble**, cavil, find fault, pettifog

hairdresser *noun* = **stylist**, barber, coiffeur *or* coiffeuse

hairless *adjective* = **bare**, bald, baldheaded, beardless, clean-shaven, depilated, shorn

hairpiece *noun* = **wig**, toupee

hair-raising *adjective* = **frightening**, alarming, bloodcurdling, breathtaking, creepy, exciting, horrifying, petrifying, scary, shocking, spine-chilling, startling, terrifying, thrilling

hair's-breadth *noun* = **fraction**, hair, jot, narrow margin, whisker

hairsplitting *adjective* = **fault-finding**, captious, carping, cavilling, fine, finicky, nice, niggling, nit-picking (*informal*), overrefined, quibbling, subtle

hairstyle *noun* = **haircut**, coiffure, cut, hairdo, style

hairy *adjective* 1 = **shaggy**, bearded, bewhiskered, bushy, fleecy, furry, hirsute, stubbly, unshaven, woolly 2 *Slang* = **dangerous**, difficult, hazardous, perilous, risky, scaring

halcyon *adjective* 1 = **peaceful**, calm, gentle, mild, placid, quiet, serene, still, tranquil, undisturbed, unruffled 2 *As in* **halcyon days** = **happy**, carefree, flourishing, golden, palmy, prosperous

hale *adjective* = **healthy**, able-bodied, blooming, fit, flourishing, hearty, in fine fettle, in the pink, right as rain (*Brit.*

informal), robust, sound, strong, vigorous, well

half *noun* 1 = **equal part**, bisection, division, fifty per cent, fraction, hemisphere, portion, section 2 **by half** = **excessively**, considerably, very much ♦ *adjective* 3 = **partial**, divided, fractional, halved, incomplete, limited, moderate ♦ *adverb* 4 = **partially**, after a fashion, all but, barely, inadequately, incompletely, in part, partly, pretty nearly, slightly

half-baked *adjective Informal* = **poorly planned**, ill-conceived, ill-judged, impractical, short-sighted, unformed, unthought out *or* through

half-hearted *adjective* = **unenthusiastic**, apathetic, cool, half-arsed (*Brit. slang*), half-assed (*U.S. & Canad. slang*), indifferent, lacklustre, listless, lukewarm, neutral, passive, perfunctory, spiritless, tame, uninterested

➤ **Antonyms**

ambitious, animated, avid, concerned, determined, eager, emotional, energetic, enthusiastic, excited, spirited, warm, wholehearted, zealous

halfway *adverb* 1 = **midway**, to *or* in the middle, to the midpoint 2 = **partially**, incompletely, moderately, nearly, partly, rather 3 **meet halfway** = **compromise**, accommodate, come to terms, concede, give and take, strike a balance, trade off ♦ *adjective* 4 = **midway**, central, equidistant, intermediate, mid, middle 5 = **partial**, imperfect, incomplete, moderate, part-way

halfwit *noun* = **fool**, airhead (*slang*), berk (*Brit. slang*), charlie (*Brit. informal*), dickhead (*slang*), dimwit (*informal*), divvy (*Brit. slang*), dolt, dumb-ass (*slang*), dunce, dunderhead, fathead (*informal*), idiot, imbecile (*informal*), jerk (*slang, chiefly U.S. & Canad.*), lamebrain (*informal*), mental defective, moron, nerd *or* nurd (*slang*), nitwit (*informal*), numbskull *or* numskull, numpty (*Scot. informal*), oaf, pillock (*Brit. slang*), prat (*slang*), prick (*slang*), schmuck (*U.S. slang*), simpleton, twit (*informal, chiefly Brit.*), wally (*slang*)

half-witted *adjective* = **foolish**, addle-brained, barmy (*slang*), batty (*slang*), crazy, doltish, doolally (*slang*), dull, dull-witted, dumb (*informal*), dumb-ass (*slang*), feeble-minded, goofy (*informal*), idiotic, moronic, obtuse, silly, simple, simple-minded, stupid

hall *noun* 1 = **entrance hall**, corridor, entry, foyer, hallway, lobby, passage, passageway, vestibule 2 = **meeting place**, assembly room, auditorium, chamber, concert hall

hallmark noun 1 = indication, badge, emblem, sure sign, telltale sign 2 Brit. = seal, authentication, device, endorsement, mark, sign, signet, stamp, symbol

hallowed adjective = sanctified, blessed, consecrated, dedicated, holy, honoured, revered, sacred, sacrosanct

hallucinate verb = imagine, daydream, envision, fantasize, freak out (informal), have hallucinations, trip (informal)

hallucination noun = illusion, apparition, delusion, dream, fantasy, figment of the imagination, mirage, phantasmagoria, vision

hallucinogenic adjective = psychedelic, hallucinatory, mind-blowing (informal), mind-expanding, psychoactive

halo noun = ring of light, aura, aureole or aureola, corona, nimbus, radiance

halt verb 1 = stop, belay (Nautical), break off, call it a day, cease, close down, come to an end, desist, draw up, pull up, rest, stand still, wait 2 = hold back, arrest, block, bring to an end, check, curb, cut short, end, impede, nip in the bud, obstruct, staunch, stem, stem the flow, terminate ◆ noun 3 = stop, arrest, break, close, end, impasse, interruption, pause, stand, standstill, stoppage, termination
➤ Antonyms
verb ≠stop: begin, commence, continue, go ahead, maintain, proceed, resume, start ≠hold back: aid, boost, encourage, forward ◆ noun ≠stop: beginning, commencement, continuation, resumption, start

halting adjective = faltering, awkward, hesitant, imperfect, laboured, stammering, stumbling, stuttering

halve verb 1 = bisect, cut in half, divide equally, reduce by fifty per cent, share equally, split in two ◆ noun 2 plural **by halves** = incompletely, imperfectly, scrappily, skimpily

ham-fisted adjective Informal = clumsy, all fingers and thumbs (informal), awkward, bungling, butterfingered (informal), cack-handed (informal), ham-handed (informal), inept, maladroit

hammer verb 1 = hit, bang, beat, drive, knock, strike, tap 2 often with **into** = impress upon, din into, drive home, drub into, drum into, instruct, repeat 3 often with **away (at)** = work, beaver away (Brit. informal), drudge, grind, keep on, peg away (chiefly Brit.), persevere, persist, plug away (informal), pound away, stick at 4 Informal = defeat, beat, blow out of the water (slang), clobber (slang), drub, lick (informal), master, run rings around (informal), tank (slang), thrash, trounce, wipe the floor with (informal), worst

hammer out verb = work out, accomplish, bring about, come to a conclusion, complete, finish, form a resolution, make a decision, negotiate, produce, settle, sort out, thrash out

hamper verb = hinder, bind, cramp, curb, encumber, entangle, fetter, frustrate, hamstring, handicap, hold up, impede, interfere with, obstruct, prevent, restrain, restrict, slow down, thwart
➤ Antonyms
aid, assist, boost, encourage, expedite, forward, further, help, promote, speed

hamstring verb = thwart, balk, foil, frustrate, prevent, ruin, stop

hand noun 1 = palm, fist, hook, mitt (slang), paw (informal) 2 = penmanship, calligraphy, handwriting, longhand, script 3 = influence, agency, direction, part, participation, share 4 = assistance, aid, help, support 5 = worker, artificer, artisan, craftsman, employee, hired man, labourer, operative, workman 6 = round of applause, clap, ovation 7 **at** or **on hand** = nearby, approaching, at one's fingertips, available, close, handy, imminent, just round the corner, near, on tap (informal), ready, within reach 8 **from hand to mouth** = in poverty, by necessity, improvidently, insecurely, on the breadline (informal), precariously, uncertainly 9 **hand in glove** = in league, allied, in cahoots (informal), in partnership 10 **hand over fist** = steadily, by leaps and bounds, easily, swiftly 11 **in hand: a = under control**, in order, receiving attention **b = in reserve**, available for use, put by, ready ◆ verb 12 = give, deliver, hand over, pass

handbook noun = guidebook, guide, instruction book, manual

handcuff verb = shackle, fetter, manacle

handcuffs plural noun = shackles, cuffs (informal), fetters, manacles

hand down or **on** verb = pass on or down, bequeath, give, grant, transfer, will

handful noun = few, small number, small quantity, smattering, sprinkling
➤ Antonyms
a lot, crowd, heaps, horde, large number, large quantity, loads (informal), masses (informal), mob, plenty, scores, stacks

handicap noun 1 = disability, defect, impairment 2 = disadvantage, barrier, block, drawback, encumbrance, hazard, hindrance, impediment, limitation, millstone, obstacle, restriction, shortcoming, stumbling block 3 = advantage, edge, head start, odds, penalty ◆ verb 4 = hinder, burden, encumber, hamper, hamstring, hobble, hold back, impede, limit, place at a disadvantage,

restrict, retard
➤ **Antonyms**
noun ≠**disadvantage**: advantage, asset, benefit, boost, edge ◆ verb ≠**hinder**: aid, assist, benefit, boost, forward, further, help, promote

handicraft noun = **craftsmanship**, art, artisanship, craft, handiwork, skill, workmanship

handiwork noun 1 = **handicraft**, craft, handwork 2 = **creation**, achievement, artefact, design, invention, product, production, result

handkerchief noun = **hanky** (informal), tissue

handle noun 1 = **grip**, haft, handgrip, hilt, stock 2 **fly off the handle** Informal = **lose one's temper**, blow one's top, explode, flip one's lid (slang), fly into a rage, go ballistic (slang, chiefly U.S.), have a tantrum, hit or go through the roof (informal), let fly (informal), lose it (informal), lose one's cool (slang), lose the plot (informal), wig out (slang) ◆ verb 3 = **hold**, feel, finger, fondle, grasp, maul, paw (informal), pick up, poke, touch 4 = **control**, direct, guide, manage, manipulate, manoeuvre, operate, steer, use, wield 5 = **discuss**, discourse, treat 6 = **deal with**, administer, conduct, cope with, manage, supervise, take care of, treat 7 = **deal in**, carry, market, sell, stock, trade, traffic in

handling noun = **management**, administration, approach, conduct, direction, manipulation, running, treatment

hand-out noun 1 = **charity**, alms, dole 2 = **leaflet**, bulletin, circular, free sample, literature (informal), mailshot, press release

hand out verb = **distribute**, deal out, disburse, dish out (informal), dispense, disseminate, give out

hand over verb = **give**, deliver, donate, fork out or up (slang), present, release, surrender, transfer, turn over, yield

hand-picked adjective = **selected**, choice, chosen, elect, elite, select
➤ **Antonyms**
haphazard, indiscriminate, random, run-of-the-mill, wholesale

hands plural noun 1 = **control**, authority, care, charge, command, custody, disposal, guardianship, keeping, possession, power, supervision 2 **hands down** = **easily**, effortlessly, with no contest, with no trouble

handsome adjective 1 = **good-looking**, admirable, attractive, becoming, comely, dishy (informal, chiefly Brit.), elegant, fine, gorgeous, graceful, personable 2 = **generous**, abundant, ample, bountiful, considerable, gracious, large, liberal,

magnanimous, plentiful, sizable or sizeable
➤ **Antonyms**
≠**good-looking**: inelegant, tasteless, ugly, unattractive, unprepossessing, unsightly ≠**generous**: base, cheap, meagre, mean, miserly, selfish, small, stingy, ungenerous

handsomely adverb = **generously**, abundantly, amply, bountifully, liberally, magnanimously, munificently, plentifully, richly

handwriting noun = **penmanship**, calligraphy, fist, hand, longhand, scrawl, script

handy adjective 1 = **convenient**, accessible, at hand, at one's fingertips, available, close, just round the corner, near, nearby, on hand, within reach 2 = **useful**, convenient, easy to use, helpful, manageable, neat, practical, serviceable, user-friendly 3 = **skilful**, adept, adroit, clever, deft, dexterous, expert, proficient, ready, skilled
➤ **Antonyms**
≠**convenient**: awkward, inaccessible, inconvenient, out of the way, unavailable ≠**useful**: awkward, inconvenient, unwieldy, useless ≠**skilful**: clumsy, ham-fisted, incompetent, inept, inexpert, maladroit, unaccomplished, unskilful, unskilled, useless

handyman noun = **odd-jobman**, DIY expert, jack-of-all-trades

hang verb 1 = **suspend**, be pendent, dangle, depend, droop, incline 2 = **execute**, lynch, send to the gallows, string up (informal) 3 = **hover**, be poised, drift, float, remain, swing 4 = **fasten**, attach, cover, deck, decorate, drape, fix, furnish 5 **hang fire** = **put off**, be slow, be suspended, delay, hang back, procrastinate, stall, vacillate ◆ noun 6 **get the hang of** = **grasp**, comprehend, get the knack or technique, understand

hang about or **around** verb 1 = **loiter**, dally, linger, roam, tarry, waste time 2 = **associate with**, frequent, hang out (informal), hang with (informal, chiefly U.S.), haunt, resort

hang back verb = **be reluctant**, be backward, demur, hesitate, hold back, recoil

hangdog adjective = **guilty**, abject, browbeaten, cowed, cringing, defeated, downcast, furtive, shamefaced, sneaking, wretched

hanger-on noun = **parasite**, dependant, follower, freeloader (slang), lackey, leech, minion, sponger (informal), sycophant

hang on verb 1 Informal = **wait**, hold on, hold the line, remain, stop 2 = **continue**, carry on, endure, go on, hold on, hold out, persevere, persist, remain, stay the course 3 = **grasp**, cling, clutch, grip, hold fast 4

= **depend on**, be conditional upon, be contingent on, be dependent on, be determined by, hinge, rest, turn on **5** *Also* **hang onto** *or* **hang upon** = listen attentively, be rapt, give ear

hang-out *noun* = haunt, den, home, joint (*slang*), resort

hangover *noun* = aftereffects, head (*informal*), morning after (*informal*)

hang over *verb* = loom, be imminent, impend, menace, threaten

hang-up *noun Informal* = preoccupation, block, difficulty, inhibition, obsession, problem, thing (*informal*)

hank *noun* = coil, length, loop, piece, roll, skein

hanker *verb, with* for *or* after = desire, ache, covet, crave, eat one's heart out over, hope, hunger, itch, long, lust, pine, set one's heart on, thirst, want, wish, yearn, yen (*informal*)

hankering *noun* = desire, ache, craving, hope, hunger, itch, longing, pining, thirst, urge, wish, yearning, yen (*informal*)

hanky-panky *noun Informal* = mischief, chicanery, deception, funny business (*informal*), jiggery-pokery (*informal, chiefly Brit.*), monkey business (*informal*), shenanigans (*informal*), subterfuge, trickery

haphazard *adjective* **1** = random, accidental, arbitrary, chance, fluky (*informal*) **2** = unsystematic, aimless, careless, casual, disorderly, disorganized, hit or miss (*informal*), indiscriminate, slapdash, slipshod, unmethodical
➤ **Antonyms**
≠**random**: arranged, deliberate, planned ≠**unsystematic**: careful, considered, methodical, orderly, organized, systematic, thoughtful

hapless *adjective* = unlucky, cursed, ill-fated, ill-starred, jinxed, luckless, miserable, unfortunate, unhappy, wretched

happen *verb* **1** = occur, appear, arise, come about, come off (*informal*), come to pass, crop up (*informal*), develop, ensue, eventuate, follow, materialize, present itself, result, see the light of day, take place, transpire (*informal*), **2** = chance, fall out, have the fortune to be, pan out (*informal*), supervene, turn out **3** = befall, become of, betide

happening *noun* = event, accident, adventure, affair, case, chance, episode, escapade, experience, incident, occasion, occurrence, phenomenon, proceeding, scene

happily *adverb* **1** = joyfully, blithely, cheerfully, gaily, gleefully, joyously, merrily **2** = luckily, auspiciously, favourably,

fortunately, opportunely, propitiously, providentially **3** = willingly, agreeably, contentedly, delightedly, enthusiastically, freely, gladly, heartily, with pleasure

happiness *noun* = joy, blessedness, bliss, cheer, cheerfulness, cheeriness, contentment, delight, ecstasy, elation, enjoyment, exuberance, felicity, gaiety, gladness, high spirits, jubilation, light-heartedness, merriment, pleasure, prosperity, satisfaction, wellbeing
➤ **Antonyms**
annoyance, bane, depression, despondency, distress, grief, low spirits, misery, misfortune, sadness, sorrow, unhappiness

happy *adjective* **1** = joyful, blessed, blissful, blithe, cheerful, cock-a-hoop, content, contented, delighted, ecstatic, elated, floating on air, glad, gratified, jolly, joyous, jubilant, merry, on cloud nine (*informal*), overjoyed, over the moon (*informal*), pleased, thrilled, walking on air (*informal*) **2** = fortunate, advantageous, appropriate, apt, auspicious, befitting, convenient, favourable, felicitous, lucky, opportune, promising, propitious, satisfactory, seasonable, successful, timely, well-timed
➤ **Antonyms**
≠**joyful**: depressed, despondent, discontented, displeased, down in the dumps (*informal*), forlorn, gloomy, joyless, low, melancholy, miserable, mournful, sad, sombre, sorrowful, sorry, unhappy ≠**fortunate**: inapt, unfortunate, unhappy, unlucky

happy-go-lucky *adjective* = carefree, blithe, casual, devil-may-care, easy-going, heedless, improvident, insouciant, irresponsible, light-hearted, nonchalant, unconcerned, untroubled
➤ **Antonyms**
careworn, cheerless, gloomy, melancholy, morose, sad, serious, unhappy

harangue *verb* **1** = rant, address, declaim, exhort, hold forth, lecture, spout (*informal*) ♦ *noun* **2** = speech, address, declamation, diatribe, exhortation, lecture, oration, screed, spiel (*informal*), tirade

harass *verb* = annoy, badger, bait, be on one's back (*slang*), bother, breathe down someone's neck, chivvy (*Brit.*), disturb, fatigue, harry, hassle (*informal*), hound, persecute, pester, plague, tease, torment, trouble, vex, weary, worry

harassed *adjective* = hassled (*informal*), careworn, distraught, harried, plagued, strained, tormented, troubled, under pressure, under stress, vexed, worried

harassment *noun* = hassle (*informal*), aggravation (*informal*), annoyance, badgering, bedevilment, bother, grief (*informal*), irritation, molestation, nuisance, persecution, pestering, torment, trouble, vexation

harbinger *noun Literary* = **herald**, forerunner, foretoken, indication, messenger, omen, portent, precursor, sign

harbour *noun* 1 = **port**, anchorage, destination, haven 2 = **sanctuary**, asylum, covert, haven, refuge, retreat, sanctum, security, shelter ♦ *verb* 3 = **maintain**, believe, brood over, cherish, cling to, entertain, foster, hold, imagine, nurse, nurture, retain 4 = **shelter**, conceal, hide, lodge, protect, provide refuge, relieve, secrete, shield

hard *adjective* 1 = **tough**, compact, dense, firm, impenetrable, inflexible, rigid, rocklike, solid, stiff, stony, strong, unyielding 2 = **strenuous**, arduous, backbreaking, burdensome, exacting, exhausting, fatiguing, formidable, laborious, rigorous, toilsome, tough, uphill, wearying 3 = **difficult**, baffling, complex, complicated, intricate, involved, knotty, perplexing, puzzling, tangled, thorny, unfathomable 4 = **harsh**, callous, cold, cruel, exacting, grim, hardhearted, implacable, obdurate, pitiless, ruthless, severe, stern, strict, stubborn, unfeeling, unjust, unkind, unrelenting, unsparing, unsympathetic 5 = **grim**, calamitous, dark, disagreeable, disastrous, distressing, grievous, intolerable, painful, unpleasant 6 = **forceful**, driving, fierce, heavy, powerful, strong, violent 7 *Of truth or facts* = **indisputable**, actual, bare, cold, definite, plain, undeniable, unvarnished, verified 8 *Of feelings or words* = **bitter**, acrimonious, angry, antagonistic, hostile, rancorous, resentful ♦ *adverb* 9 = **energetically**, fiercely, forcefully, forcibly, heavily, intensely, powerfully, severely, sharply, strongly, vigorously, violently, with all one's might, with might and main 10 = **intently**, assiduously, determinedly, diligently, doggedly, earnestly, industriously, persistently, steadily, strenuously, untiringly 11 = **with difficulty**, agonizingly, badly, distressingly, harshly, laboriously, painfully, roughly, severely ➤ **Antonyms** *adjective* ≠ **tough**: flexible, malleable, pliable, soft, weak ≠ **strenuous**: easy, easy-peasy (*slang*), lazy, light, soft ≠ **difficult**: clear, direct, easy, easy-peasy (*slang*), simple, straightforward, uncomplicated ≠ **harsh**: agreeable, amiable, careless, flexible, friendly, gentle, good, humane, kind, lenient, merciful, mild, permissive, pleasant ♦ *adverb* ≠ **energetically**: lazily, lightly, loosely, softly, weakly ≠ **intently**: easily, gently, softly

hard-and-fast *adjective* = **fixed**, binding, immutable, incontrovertible, inflexible, invariable, rigid, set, strict, stringent, unalterable

hard-bitten *or* **hard-boiled** *adjective Informal* = **tough**, case-hardened, cynical, down-to-earth, hard-headed, hard-nosed (*informal*), matter-of-fact, practical, realistic, shrewd, unsentimental ➤ **Antonyms** benign, compassionate, gentle, humane, idealistic, mild, romantic, sympathetic

hard-core *adjective* 1 = **explicit**, obscene, X-rated (*informal*) 2 = **dyed-in-the-wool**, dedicated, die-hard, extreme, intransigent, obstinate, rigid, staunch, steadfast

harden *verb* 1 = **solidify**, anneal, bake, cake, freeze, set, stiffen 2 = **accustom**, brutalize, case-harden, habituate, inure, season, train 3 = **reinforce**, brace, buttress, fortify, gird, indurate, nerve, steel, strengthen, toughen

hardened *adjective* 1 = **habitual**, chronic, fixed, incorrigible, inveterate, irredeemable, shameless 2 = **seasoned**, accustomed, habituated, inured, toughened ➤ **Antonyms** infrequent, irregular, occasional, rare, unaccustomed

hard-headed *adjective* = **shrewd**, astute, cool, hard-boiled (*informal*), level-headed, practical, pragmatic, realistic, sensible, tough, unsentimental ➤ **Antonyms** idealistic, impractical, sentimental, unrealistic

hardhearted *adjective* = **unsympathetic**, affectless, callous, cold, cruel, hard, hard as nails, heartless, indifferent, inhuman, insensitive, intolerant, merciless, pitiless, stony, uncaring, unfeeling, unkind ➤ **Antonyms** compassionate, forgiving, gentle, humane, kind, loving, merciful, sensitive, soft-hearted, sympathetic, understanding, warm, warm-hearted

hardihood *noun* = **courage**, backbone, boldness, bottle (*Brit. slang*), bravery, daring, determination, firmness, grit, guts (*informal*), intrepidity, mettle, nerve, pluck, resolution, spirit, spunk (*informal*), strength

hardiness *noun* = **resilience**, boldness, courage, fortitude, intrepidity, resolution, robustness, ruggedness, sturdiness, toughness, valour

hardline *adjective* = **tough**, inflexible, intransigent, uncompromising, unyielding

hardly *adverb* = **barely**, almost not, at a push, by no means, faintly, infrequently, just, not at all, not quite, no way, only, only just, scarcely, with difficulty

➤ **Antonyms**
abundantly, amply, by all means, certainly, completely, easily, fully, indubitably, more than, really, truly, undoubtedly, well over

hard-pressed *adjective* = **under pressure**, harried, hotly pursued, in difficulties, pushed (*informal*), under attack, up against it (*informal*), with one's back to the wall

hardship *noun* = **suffering**, adversity, affliction, burden, calamity, destitution, difficulty, grievance, labour, misery, misfortune, need, oppression, persecution, privation, toil, torment, trial, tribulation, trouble, want
➤ **Antonyms**
aid, blessing, boon, comfort, ease, good fortune, happiness, help, prosperity, relief

hard up *adjective* = **poor**, bankrupt, broke (*informal*), bust (*informal*), cleaned out (*slang*), dirt-poor (*informal*), down and out, flat broke (*informal*), impecunious, impoverished, in the red (*informal*), on one's uppers (*informal*), on the breadline, out of pocket, penniless, short, short of cash *or* funds, skint (*Brit. slang*), strapped for cash (*informal*), without two pennies to rub together (*informal*)
➤ **Antonyms**
affluent, comfortable (*informal*), fortunate, loaded (*slang*), rich, wealthy, well-heeled (*informal*), well-off

hard-wearing *adjective* = **durable**, resilient, rugged, stout, strong, tough, well-made

hard-working *adjective* = **industrious**, assiduous, busy, conscientious, diligent, energetic
➤ **Antonyms**
careless, good-for-nothing, lazy

hardy *adjective* = **strong**, firm, fit, hale, healthy, hearty, lusty, robust, rugged, sound, stalwart, stout, sturdy, tough, vigorous
➤ **Antonyms**
delicate, feeble, fragile, frail, sickly, soft, weak, weedy

harebrained *adjective* = **foolish**, asinine, empty-headed, flighty, half-baked (*informal*), inane, mindless, rash, reckless, unstable, unsteady, wild

hark *verb Old-fashioned* = **listen**, attend, give ear, give heed, hear, mark, notice, pay attention

hark back *verb* = **return**, look back, recall, recollect, regress, remember, revert, think back

harlot *noun Literary* = **prostitute**, call girl, fallen woman, hussy, loose woman, pro (*slang*), scrubber (*Brit. & Austral. slang*), slag (*Brit. slang*), slapper (*Brit. slang*), streetwalker, strumpet, tart (*informal*), tramp (*slang*), whore, working girl (*facetious slang*)

harm *verb* 1 = **injure**, abuse, blemish, damage, hurt, ill-treat, ill-use, impair, lay a finger on, maltreat, mar, molest, ruin, spoil, wound ♦ *noun* 2 = **injury**, abuse, damage, detriment, hurt, ill, impairment, loss, mischief, misfortune
➤ **Antonyms**
verb ≠**injure**: aid, alleviate, ameliorate, assist, benefit, better, cure, heal, help, improve, repair ♦ *noun* ≠**injury**: aid, assistance, benefit, blessing, boon, gain, good, help, improvement, reparation

harmful *adjective* = **injurious**, baleful, baneful, damaging, deleterious, destructive, detrimental, disadvantageous, evil, hurtful, noxious, pernicious
➤ **Antonyms**
beneficial, good, harmless, healthy, helpful, innocuous, safe, wholesome

harmless *adjective* = **innocuous**, gentle, innocent, innoxious, inoffensive, nontoxic, not dangerous, safe, unobjectionable
➤ **Antonyms**
dangerous, destructive, harmful, unhealthy, unsafe, unwholesome

harmonious *adjective* 1 = **compatible**, agreeable, congruous, consonant, coordinated, correspondent, matching 2 = **friendly**, agreeable, amicable, compatible, concordant, congenial, cordial, *en rapport*, fraternal, in accord, in harmony, in unison, of one mind, sympathetic 3 = **melodious**, concordant, dulcet, euphonic, euphonious, harmonic, harmonizing, mellifluous, musical, sweet-sounding, tuneful
➤ **Antonyms**
≠**compatible**: contrasting, discordant, incompatible, inconsistent, unlike ≠**friendly**: discordant, unfriendly ≠**melodious**: cacophonous, discordant, grating, harsh, unmelodious

harmonize *verb* = **go together**, accord, adapt, agree, arrange, attune, be in unison, be of one mind, blend, coordinate, correspond, match, reconcile, suit, tally, tone in with

harmony *noun* 1 = **agreement**, accord, amicability, amity, assent, compatibility, concord, conformity, consensus, cooperation, friendship, goodwill, like-mindedness, order, peace, rapport, sympathy, unanimity, understanding, unity 2 = **tunefulness**, euphony, melodiousness, melody, tune, unison 3 = **compatibility**, balance, concord, congruity, consistency, consonance, coordination, correspondence, fitness, parallelism, suitability, symmetry
➤ **Antonyms**
≠**agreement**: antagonism, conflict, contention, disagreement, dissension,

hostility, opposition ≠**tunefulness:**
cacophony ≠**compatibility:** conflict,
disagreement, incongruity, inconsistency,
unsuitability

harness *noun* **1** = **equipment,** gear, tack,
tackle, trappings **2 in harness** = **working,**
active, at work, busy, in action ♦ *verb* **3**
= **put in harness,** couple, hitch up, saddle,
yoke **4** = **exploit,** apply, channel, control,
employ, make productive, mobilize, render
useful, turn to account, utilize

harp *verb,* **with on** *or* **upon** = **go on,** dwell
on, labour, press, reiterate, renew, repeat,
rub it in

harridan *noun* = **shrew,** ballbreaker (*slang*),
battle-axe (*informal*), nag, scold, tartar,
termagant, virago, witch

harrowing *adjective* = **distressing,**
agonizing, alarming, chilling, disturbing,
excruciating, frightening, gut-wrenching,
heartbreaking, heart-rending, nerve-racking,
painful, racking, scaring, terrifying,
tormenting, traumatic

harry *verb* = **pester,** annoy, badger, bedevil,
be on one's back (*slang*), bother, breathe
down someone's neck, chivvy, get in one's
hair (*informal*), harass, hassle (*informal*),
persecute, plague, tease, torment, trouble,
vex, worry

harsh *adjective* **1** = **severe,** abusive, austere,
bitter, bleak, brutal, comfortless, cruel, dour,
Draconian, drastic, grim, hard, pitiless,
punitive, relentless, ruthless, sharp, Spartan,
stern, stringent, tough, unfeeling, unkind,
unpleasant, unrelenting **2** = **raucous,** coarse,
croaking, crude, discordant, dissonant,
grating, guttural, jarring, rasping, rough,
strident, unmelodious
➤ **Antonyms**
≠**severe:** agreeable, gentle, kind, loving,
merciful, mild, pleasant, sweet ≠**raucous:**
harmonious, mellifluous, smooth, soft,
soothing, sweet

harshly *adverb* = **severely,** brutally, cruelly,
grimly, roughly, sharply, sternly, strictly

harshness *noun* = **severity,** acerbity,
acrimony, asperity, bitterness, brutality,
coarseness, hardness, ill-temper, rigour,
roughness, sourness, sternness

harum-scarum *adjective* = **reckless,**
careless, hasty, impetuous, imprudent,
inconstant, irresponsible, precipitate, rash,
scatterbrained, scatty (*Brit. informal*), wild

harvest *noun* **1** = **gathering,** harvesting,
harvest-time, reaping **2** = **crop,** produce,
yield **3** = **product,** consequence, effect,
fruition, result, return ♦ *verb* **4** = **gather,**
mow, pick, pluck, reap

hash *noun* **make a hash of** *Informal* = **mess
up,** bodge (*informal*), botch, bungle, cock

up (*Brit. slang*), flub (*U.S. slang*), fuck up
(*offensive taboo slang*), jumble, make a
nonsense of (*informal*), make a pig's ear of
(*informal*), mishandle, mismanage, mix,
muddle

hassle *Informal* ♦ *noun* **1** = **trouble,** bother,
difficulty, grief (*informal*), inconvenience,
problem, struggle, trial, upset **2**
= **argument,** altercation, bickering,
disagreement, dispute, fight, quarrel, row,
squabble, tussle, wrangle ♦ *verb* **3** = **bother,**
annoy, badger, be on one's back (*slang*),
breath down someone's neck, bug
(*informal*), get in one's hair (*informal*), get
on one's nerves (*informal*), harass, harry,
hound, pester

haste *noun* **1** = **speed,** alacrity, briskness,
dispatch, expedition, fleetness, nimbleness,
promptitude, quickness, rapidity, rapidness,
swiftness, urgency, velocity **2** = **rush,** bustle,
hastiness, hurry, hustle, impetuosity,
precipitateness, rashness, recklessness
➤ **Antonyms**
≠**speed:** slowness, sluggishness ≠**rush:**
calmness, care, delay, deliberation,
leisureliness, sureness

hasten *verb* **1** = **rush,** barrel (along)
(*informal, chiefly U.S. & Canad.*), beetle,
bolt, burn rubber (*informal*), dash, fly, get
one's skates on (*informal*), haste, hurry (up),
make haste, race, run, scurry, scuttle, speed,
sprint, step on it (*informal*), tear (along) **2**
= **hurry (up),** accelerate, advance, dispatch,
expedite, goad, precipitate, press, push
forward, quicken, speed (up), step up
(*informal*), urge
➤ **Antonyms**
≠**rush:** crawl, creep, dawdle, move slowly
≠**hurry (up):** decelerate, delay, hinder,
impede, retard, slow, slow down

hastily *adverb* **1** = **quickly,** apace,
double-quick, fast, hotfoot, pdq (*slang*),
posthaste, promptly, pronto (*informal*),
rapidly, speedily, straightaway **2** = **hurriedly,**
heedlessly, impetuously, impulsively, on the
spur of the moment, precipitately, rashly,
recklessly, too quickly

hasty *adjective* **1** = **speedy,** brisk, eager,
expeditious, fast, fleet, hurried, prompt,
rapid, swift, urgent **2** = **brief,** cursory,
fleeting, passing, perfunctory, rushed, short,
superficial **3** = **rash,** foolhardy, headlong,
heedless, impetuous, impulsive, indiscreet,
precipitate, reckless, thoughtless, unduly
quick
➤ **Antonyms**
≠**speedy:** leisurely, slow ≠**brief:** long,
protracted ≠**rash:** careful, cautious,
detailed, thorough, thoughtful

hatch *verb* **1** = **incubate,** breed, bring forth,
brood **2** = **devise,** conceive, concoct,

contrive, cook up (*informal*), design, dream up (*informal*), manufacture, plan, plot, project, scheme, think up, trump up

hatchet *noun* = axe, cleaver, machete, tomahawk

hate *verb* **1** = detest, abhor, abominate, be hostile to, be repelled by, be sick of, despise, dislike, have an aversion to, loathe, recoil from **2** = be unwilling, be loath, be reluctant, be sorry, dislike, feel disinclined, have no stomach for, shrink from ♦ *noun* **3** = dislike, abhorrence, abomination, animosity, animus, antagonism, antipathy, aversion, detestation, enmity, hatred, hostility, loathing, odium
➤ Antonyms
verb ≠detest: be fond of, cherish, dote on, enjoy, esteem, fancy, like, love, relish, treasure, wish ♦ *noun* ≠dislike: affection, amity, devotion, fondness, goodwill, liking, love

hateful *adjective* = despicable, abhorrent, abominable, detestable, disgusting, foul, heinous, horrible, loathsome, obnoxious, obscene, odious, offensive, repellent, repugnant, repulsive, revolting, vile
➤ Antonyms
attractive, beautiful, charming, desirable, good, likable *or* likeable, lovable, pleasant, wonderful

hatred *noun* = dislike, abomination, animosity, animus, antagonism, antipathy, aversion, detestation, enmity, hate, ill will, odium, repugnance, revulsion
➤ Antonyms
affection, amity, attachment, devotion, fondness, friendliness, goodwill, liking, love

haughtiness *noun* = pride, airs, aloofness, arrogance, conceit, contempt, contemptuousness, disdain, hauteur, insolence, loftiness, pomposity, snobbishness, superciliousness

haughty *adjective* = proud, arrogant, assuming, conceited, contemptuous, disdainful, high, high and mighty (*informal*), hoity-toity (*informal*), imperious, lofty, on one's high horse (*informal*), overweening, scornful, snobbish, snooty (*informal*), stuck-up (*informal*), supercilious, uppish (*Brit. informal*)
➤ Antonyms
humble, meek, mild, modest, self-effacing, subservient, wimpish *or* wimpy (*informal*)

haul *verb* **1** = drag, draw, hale, heave, lug, pull, tow, trail, tug **2** = transport, carry, cart, convey, hump (*Brit. slang*), move ♦ *noun* **3** = drag, heave, pull, tug **4** = yield, booty, catch, find, gain, harvest, loot, spoils, takings

haunt *verb* **1** = visit, walk **2** = plague, beset,

come back, obsess, possess, prey on, recur, stay with, torment, trouble, weigh on **3** = frequent, hang around *or* about, resort, visit ♦ *noun* **4** = meeting place, den, gathering place, hangout (*informal*), rendezvous, resort, stamping ground

haunted *adjective* **1** = possessed, cursed, eerie, ghostly, jinxed, spooky (*informal*) **2** = preoccupied, obsessed, plagued, tormented, troubled, worried

haunting *adjective* = evocative, disturbing, eerie, indelible, nostalgic, persistent, poignant, recurrent, recurring, unforgettable

hauteur *noun* = haughtiness, affectedness, airs, arrogance, contempt, dignity, disdain, loftiness, pride, snobbishness, stateliness, superciliousness

have *verb* **1** = possess, hold, keep, obtain, occupy, own, retain **2** = receive, accept, acquire, gain, get, obtain, procure, secure, take **3** = experience, endure, enjoy, feel, meet with, suffer, sustain, undergo **4** *Slang* = cheat, deceive, dupe, fool, outwit, swindle, take in (*informal*), trick **5** = put up with (*informal*), allow, consider, entertain, permit, think about, tolerate **6** = give birth to, bear, beget, bring forth, bring into the world, deliver **7 have to** = be obliged, be bound, be compelled, be forced, have got to, must, ought, should **8 have had it** *Informal* = be exhausted, be defeated, be finished, be out, be past it (*informal*)

haven *noun* **1** = sanctuary, asylum, refuge, retreat, sanctum, shelter **2** = harbour, anchorage, port

have on *verb* **1** = wear, be clothed in, be dressed in **2** = have planned, be committed to, be engaged to, have on the agenda **3** *Informal* = tease, deceive, kid (*informal*), play a joke on, pull someone's leg, take the mickey, trick, wind up (*Brit. slang*)

havoc *noun* **1** *Informal* = disorder, chaos, confusion, disruption, mayhem, shambles **2 play havoc (with)** = wreck, bring into chaos, confuse, convulse, demolish, destroy, devastate, disorganize, disrupt

haw *verb* **hem and haw** *or* **hum and haw** = hesitate, falter, fumble, pause, stammer, stutter

hawk *verb* = peddle, sell, tout (*informal*)

hawker *noun* = pedlar, barrow boy (*Brit.*), huckster, vendor

hawk-eyed *adjective* = sharp-eyed, Argus-eyed, gimlet-eyed, having eyes in the back of one's head (*informal*), keen-sighted, lynx-eyed, observant, perceptive, vigilant

haywire *adjective* **As in go haywire** = chaotic, confused, disordered, disorganized, mixed up, on the blink (*slang*), on the fritz (*slang*), out of order, shambolic (*informal*), topsy-turvy

hazard *noun* 1 = **danger**, jeopardy, peril, pitfall, risk, threat ♦ *verb* 2 = **jeopardize**, endanger, expose, imperil, risk, threaten 3 As in hazard a guess = **conjecture**, advance, offer, presume, throw out, venture, volunteer

hazardous *adjective* = **dangerous**, dicey (*informal, chiefly Brit.*), difficult, fraught with danger, insecure, perilous, precarious, risky, unsafe
➤ **Antonyms**
reliable, safe, secure, sound, stable, sure

haze *noun* = **mist**, cloud, dimness, film, fog, obscurity, smog, smokiness, steam, vapour

hazy *adjective* 1 = **misty**, blurry, cloudy, dim, dull, faint, foggy, nebulous, obscure, overcast, smoky, veiled 2 = **vague**, fuzzy, ill-defined, indefinite, indistinct, loose, muddled, muzzy, nebulous, uncertain, unclear
➤ **Antonyms**
≠**misty**: bright, clear, light, sunny ≠**vague**: certain, clear, detailed, well-defined

head *noun* 1 = **skull**, bean (*U.S. & Canad. slang*), cranium, crown, loaf (*slang*), noddle (*informal, chiefly Brit.*), noggin, nut (*slang*), pate 2 = **mind**, ability, aptitude, brain, brains (*informal*), capacity, faculty, flair, intellect, intelligence, mentality, talent, thought, understanding 3 = **front**, cutting edge, first place, fore, forefront, van, vanguard 4 = **top**, apex, crest, crown, height, peak, pinnacle, pitch, summit, tip, vertex 5 = **leader**, boss (*informal*), captain, chief, chieftain, commander, director, headmaster *or* headmistress, head teacher, manager, master, principal, superintendent, supervisor 6 = **culmination**, climax, conclusion, crisis, end, turning point 7 = **source**, beginning, commencement, origin, rise, start 8 *Geography* = **headland**, cape, foreland, point, promontory 9 = **heading**, branch, category, class, department, division, section, subject, topic 10 go to one's head = **excite**, dizzy, intoxicate, make conceited, puff up 11 head over heels = **completely**, intensely, thoroughly, uncontrollably, utterly, wholeheartedly 12 put (our, their, *etc.*) heads together *Informal* = **consult**, confab (*informal*), confabulate, confer, deliberate, discuss, palaver, powwow, talk over ♦ *adjective* 13 = **chief**, arch, first, foremost, front, highest, leading, main, pre-eminent, premier, prime, principal, supreme, topmost ♦ *verb* 14 = **lead**, be *or* go first, cap, crown, lead the way, precede, top 15 = **be in charge of**, command, control, direct, govern, guide, lead, manage, rule, run, supervise 16 = **make for**, aim, go to, make a beeline for, point, set off for, set out, start

towards, steer, turn

headache *noun* 1 = **migraine**, head (*informal*), neuralgia 2 *Informal* = **problem**, bane, bother, inconvenience, nuisance, trouble, vexation, worry

headfirst *adverb* 1 = **headlong**, diving, head-on 2 = **recklessly**, carelessly, hastily, head over heels, precipitately, rashly

heading *noun* 1 = **title**, caption, headline, name, rubric 2 = **division**, category, class, section

headland *noun* = **promontory**, bill, bluff, cape, cliff, foreland, head, mull (*Scot.*), point

headlong *adverb, adjective* 1 = **headfirst**, headforemost, head-on ♦ *adverb* 2 = **hastily**, heedlessly, helter-skelter, hurriedly, pell-mell, precipitately, rashly, thoughtlessly, wildly ♦ *adjective* 3 = **hasty**, breakneck, dangerous, impetuous, impulsive, inconsiderate, precipitate, reckless, thoughtless

headmaster *or* **headmistress** *noun* = **principal**, head, head teacher, rector

head off *verb* 1 = **intercept**, block off, cut off, deflect, divert, interpose, intervene 2 = **prevent**, avert, fend off, forestall, parry, stop, ward off

headstrong *adjective* = **obstinate**, contrary, foolhardy, heedless, imprudent, impulsive, intractable, mulish, perverse, pig-headed, rash, reckless, self-willed, stiff-necked, stubborn, ungovernable, unruly, wilful
➤ **Antonyms**
cautious, impressionable, manageable, pliant, subservient, tractable

headway *noun* 1 = **advance**, improvement, progress, progression, way 2 make headway = **progress**, advance, come *or* get on, cover ground, develop, gain, gain ground, make inroads (into), make strides

heady *adjective* 1 = **exciting**, exhilarating, intoxicating, overwhelming, stimulating, thrilling 2 = **intoxicating**, inebriating, potent, spirituous, strong 3 = **rash**, hasty, impetuous, impulsive, inconsiderate, precipitate, reckless, thoughtless

heal *verb* 1 = **cure**, make well, mend, regenerate, remedy, restore, treat 2 = **patch up**, alleviate, ameliorate, conciliate, harmonize, reconcile, settle, soothe
➤ **Antonyms**
aggravate, exacerbate, harm, hurt, inflame, injure, make worse, reopen, wound

healing *adjective* 1 = **medicinal**, curative, remedial, restorative, restoring, therapeutic 2 = **soothing**, assuaging, comforting, gentle, mild, mitigative, palliative

health *noun* 1 = **condition**, constitution,

fettle, form, shape, state, tone **2**
= **wellbeing**, fitness, good condition,
haleness, healthiness, robustness, soundness,
strength, vigour, wellness
➤ Antonyms
≠**wellbeing**: debility, disease, frailty, illness,
sickness, weakness

healthful adjective = **healthy**, beneficial,
bracing, good for one, health-giving,
invigorating, nourishing, nutritious,
salubrious, salutary, wholesome

healthy adjective **1** = **well**, active, alive and
kicking, blooming, fighting fit, fit, fit as a
fiddle (informal), flourishing, hale, hale and
hearty, hardy, hearty, in fine feather, in fine
fettle, in fine form, in good condition, in
good shape (informal), in the pink,
physically fit, right as rain (Brit. informal),
robust, sound, strong, sturdy, vigorous **2**
= **wholesome**, beneficial, bracing, good for
one, healthful, health-giving, hygienic,
invigorating, nourishing, nutritious,
salubrious, salutary
➤ Antonyms
≠**well**: ailing, at death's door, debilitated,
delicate, diseased, feeble, fragile, frail, ill,
infirm, poorly (informal), sick, sickly, unfit,
unhealthy, unsound, unwell, weak, weedy
(informal) ≠**wholesome**: unhealthy,
unwholesome

heap noun **1** = **pile**, accumulation,
aggregation, collection, hoard, lot, mass,
mound, mountain, rick, stack, stockpile,
store **2** often plural, Informal = **a lot**,
abundance, great deal, lashings (Brit.
informal), load(s) (informal), lots
(informal), mass, mint, ocean(s), oodles
(informal), plenty, pot(s) (informal),
quantities, stack(s), tons ♦ verb **3** = **pile**,
accumulate, amass, augment, bank, collect,
gather, hoard, increase, mound, stack,
stockpile, store **4** = **confer**, assign, bestow,
burden, load, shower upon

hear verb **1** = **listen to**, attend, be all ears
(informal), catch, eavesdrop, give attention,
hark, hearken (archaic), heed, listen in,
overhear **2** = **learn**, ascertain, be informed,
be told of, discover, find out, gather, get
wind of (informal), hear tell (dialect), pick
up, understand **3** Law = **try**, examine,
investigate, judge

hearing noun **1** = **perception**, audition, ear
2 = **chance to speak**, audience, audition,
interview **3** = **earshot**, auditory range,
hearing distance, range, reach, sound **4**
= **inquiry**, industrial tribunal, investigation,
review, trial

hearsay noun = **rumour**, buzz, dirt (U.S.
slang), gossip, grapevine (informal), idle
talk, mere talk, report, talk, talk of the town,
tittle-tattle, word of mouth

heart noun **1** = **nature**, character,
disposition, emotion, feeling, inclination,
sentiment, soul, sympathy, temperament **2**
= **tenderness**, affection, benevolence,
compassion, concern, humanity, love, pity,
understanding **3** = **courage**, balls (taboo
slang), boldness, bravery, fortitude, guts
(informal), mettle, mind, nerve, pluck,
purpose, resolution, spirit, spunk (informal),
will **4** = **centre**, central part, core, crux,
essence, hub, kernel, marrow, middle,
nucleus, pith, quintessence, root **5 by heart**
= **by memory**, by rote, off pat,
parrot-fashion (informal), pat, word for
word **6 take heart** = **be encouraged**, be
comforted, be heartened, brighten up, buck
up (informal), cheer up, perk up, revive

heartache noun = **sorrow**, affliction,
agony, anguish, despair, distress, grief,
heartbreak, pain, remorse, suffering,
torment, torture

heartbreak noun = **grief**, anguish,
desolation, despair, misery, pain, sorrow,
suffering

heartbreaking adjective = **sad**, agonizing,
bitter, desolating, disappointing, distressing,
grievous, gut-wrenching, harrowing,
heart-rending, pitiful, poignant, tragic
➤ Antonyms
cheerful, cheery, comic, glorious, happy,
jolly, joyful, joyous, light-hearted

heartbroken adjective = **miserable**,
brokenhearted, choked, crestfallen, crushed,
dejected, desolate, despondent,
disappointed, disconsolate, disheartened,
dismal, dispirited, downcast, down in the
dumps (informal), grieved, heartsick
➤ Antonyms
cheerful, cock-a-hoop, elated, exuberant,
happy, in seventh heaven, joyful, joyous, on
cloud nine, over the moon (informal)

hearten verb = **encourage**, buck up
(informal), buoy up, cheer, comfort,
console, gee up, raise someone's spirits,
reassure, rouse, stimulate

heartfelt adjective = **sincere**, ardent,
cordial, deep, devout, earnest, fervent,
genuine, hearty, honest, profound,
unfeigned, warm, wholehearted
➤ Antonyms
false, feigned, flippant, fraudulent, frivolous,
half-hearted, hypocritical, insincere, phoney
or phony (informal), pretended, put on

heartily adverb **1** = **sincerely**, cordially,
deeply, feelingly, genuinely, profoundly,
unfeignedly, warmly **2** = **enthusiastically**,
eagerly, earnestly, resolutely, vigorously,
zealously **3** = **thoroughly**, absolutely,
completely, totally, very

heartless adjective = **cruel**, brutal, callous,

cold, cold-blooded, cold-hearted, hard,
hardhearted, harsh, inhuman, merciless,
pitiless, uncaring, unfeeling, unkind
➤ **Antonyms**
compassionate, generous, humane, kind,
merciful, sensitive, sympathetic,
warm-hearted

heart-rending *adjective* = **moving**,
affecting, distressing, gut-wrenching,
harrowing, heartbreaking, pathetic, piteous,
pitiful, poignant, sad, tragic

heart-to-heart *adjective* 1 = **intimate**,
candid, open, personal, sincere, unreserved
♦ *noun* 2 = **cosy chat**, tête-à-tête

heart-warming *adjective* = **moving**,
affecting, cheering, encouraging, heartening,
touching, warming

hearty *adjective* 1 = **friendly**, affable,
ardent, back-slapping, cordial, eager,
ebullient, effusive, enthusiastic, generous,
genial, jovial, unreserved, warm 2
= **wholehearted**, earnest, genuine, heartfelt,
honest, real, sincere, true, unfeigned 3
= **substantial**, ample, filling, nourishing,
sizable *or* sizeable, solid, square
➤ **Antonyms**
≠**friendly**: cold, cool, unfriendly
≠**wholehearted**: half-hearted, insincere, mild

heat *verb* 1 = **warm up**, become warm,
chafe, flush, glow, grow hot, make hot,
reheat ♦ *noun* 2 = **hotness**, fever, fieriness,
high temperature, hot spell, sultriness,
swelter, torridity, warmness, warmth 3
= **passion**, agitation, ardour, earnestness,
excitement, fervour, fever, fury, impetuosity,
intensity, vehemence, violence, warmth, zeal
➤ **Antonyms**
verb ≠**warm up**: chill, cool, cool off, freeze
♦ *noun* ≠**hotness**: cold, coldness, coolness
≠**passion**: calmness, coldness, composure,
coolness

heated *adjective* = **impassioned**, angry,
bitter, excited, fierce, fiery, frenzied, furious,
intense, passionate, raging, stormy,
tempestuous, vehement, violent
➤ **Antonyms**
calm, civilized, dispassionate, friendly,
half-hearted, mellow, mild, peaceful, quiet,
rational, reasoned, serene, subdued,
unemotional, unfazed (*informal*), unruffled

heathen *noun* Old-fashioned 1 = **pagan**,
idolater, idolatress, infidel, unbeliever
♦ *adjective* 2 = **pagan**, godless, heathenish,
idolatrous, infidel, irreligious

heave *verb* 1 = **lift**, drag (up), elevate, haul
(up), heft (*informal*), hoist, lever, pull (up),
raise, tug 2 = **throw**, cast, fling, hurl, pitch,
send, sling, toss 3 = **sigh**, breathe heavily,
groan, puff, sob, utter wearily 4 = **surge**,
billow, breathe, dilate, exhale, expand,

palpitate, pant, rise, swell, throb 5 = **vomit**,
barf (*U.S. slang*), be sick, chuck (up) (*slang,
chiefly U.S.*), chunder (*slang, chiefly
Austral.*), do a technicolour yawn (*slang*),
gag, retch, spew, throw up (*informal*),
upchuck (*U.S. slang*)

heaven *noun* 1 = **paradise**, abode of God,
bliss, Elysium *or* Elysian fields (*Greek myth*),
happy hunting ground (*Native American
legend*), hereafter, life everlasting, life to
come, next world, nirvana (*Buddhism,
Hinduism*), Valhalla (*Norse myth*), Zion
(*Christianity*) 2 = **happiness**, bliss,
dreamland, ecstasy, enchantment, felicity,
paradise, rapture, seventh heaven, sheer
bliss, transport, utopia 3 **the heavens** = **sky**,
empyrean (*poetic*), ether, firmament, welkin
(*archaic*)

heavenly *adjective* 1 *Informal* = **wonderful**,
alluring, beautiful, blissful, delightful, divine
(*informal*), entrancing, exquisite, glorious,
lovely, rapturous, ravishing, sublime 2
= **celestial**, angelic, beatific, blessed, blest,
cherubic, divine, extraterrestrial, godlike,
holy, immortal, paradisaical, seraphic,
superhuman, supernatural
➤ **Antonyms**
≠**wonderful**: abominable, abysmal,
appalling, awful, bad, depressing, dire,
disagreeable, dreadful, dreary, dull, frightful,
gloomy, grim, hellacious (*U.S. slang*),
horrible, horrid, lousy (*slang*), miserable,
rotten (*informal*), terrible, unpleasant, vile
≠**celestial**: earthly, human, secular, worldly

heavily *adverb* 1 = **densely**, closely,
compactly, fast, hard, thick, thickly 2
= **considerably**, a great deal, copiously,
excessively, frequently, to excess, very much
3 = **laboriously**, painfully, with difficulty 4
= **ponderously**, awkwardly, clumsily,
weightily

heaviness *noun* 1 = **weight**, gravity,
heftiness, ponderousness 2 = **onerousness**,
arduousness, burdensomeness, grievousness,
oppressiveness, severity, weightiness 3
= **sluggishness**, deadness, dullness, languor,
lassitude, numbness, torpor 4 = **sadness**,
dejection, depression, despondency, gloom,
gloominess, glumness, melancholy,
seriousness

heavy *adjective* 1 = **weighty**, bulky, hefty,
massive, ponderous, portly 2
= **considerable**, abundant, copious,
excessive, large, profuse 3 = **onerous**,
burdensome, difficult, grievous, hard, harsh,
intolerable, laborious, oppressive, severe,
tedious, vexatious, wearisome 4 = **sluggish**,
apathetic, drowsy, dull, inactive, indolent,
inert, listless, slow, stupid, torpid, wooden 5
= **sad**, crestfallen, dejected, depressed,
despondent, disconsolate, downcast,

gloomy, grieving, melancholy, sorrowful **6 = overcast**, cloudy, dull, gloomy, leaden, louring or lowering **7 = serious**, complex, deep, difficult, grave, profound, solemn, weighty
➤ **Antonyms**
≠**weighty**: agile, compact, handy, light, slight, small ≠**considerable**: light, moderate, slight, sparse ≠**onerous**: bearable, easy, gentle, light, mild, moderate, soft ≠**sluggish**: agile, alert, brisk, quick ≠**sad**: calm, cheerful, happy, joyful ≠**serious**: inconsequential, trivial, unimportant

heavy-handed adjective **1 = clumsy**, awkward, bungling, graceless, ham-fisted (informal), ham-handed (informal), inept, inexpert, like a bull in a china shop (informal), maladroit **2 = tactless**, bungling, inconsiderate, insensitive, thoughtless
➤ **Antonyms**
≠**clumsy**: adept, adroit, competent, ⸠ dexterous, effectual, efficient, gentle, graceful, skilful, smooth ≠**tactless**: considered, diplomatic, prudent, sensible, tactful, well-advised, well-thought-out, wise

heavy-hearted adjective **= sad**, crushed, depressed, despondent, discouraged, disheartened, dismal, downcast, downhearted, down in the dumps (informal), forlorn, heartsick, melancholy, miserable, morose, mournful, sick as a parrot (informal), sorrowful

heckle verb **= jeer**, bait, barrack (informal), boo, disrupt, interrupt, pester, shout down, taunt

hectic adjective **= frantic**, animated, boisterous, chaotic, excited, fevered, feverish, flurrying, flustering, frenetic, frenzied, furious, heated, riotous, rumbustious, tumultuous, turbulent, wild
➤ **Antonyms**
calm, peaceful, relaxing, tranquil

hector verb **= bully**, bluster, boast, browbeat, intimidate, menace, provoke, ride roughshod over, threaten, worry

hedge noun **1 = hedgerow 2 = barrier**, boundary, screen, windbreak **3 = insurance cover**, compensation, counterbalance, guard, protection ◆ verb **4 = dodge**, beg the question, be noncommittal, duck, equivocate, evade, flannel (Brit. informal), prevaricate, pussyfoot (informal), quibble, sidestep, temporize, waffle (informal, chiefly Brit.) **5 = insure**, cover, fortify, guard, protect, safeguard, shield

hedonism noun **= pursuit of pleasure**, dolce vita, gratification, luxuriousness, pleasure-seeking, self-indulgence, sensualism, sensuality

hedonist noun **1 = pleasure seeker**, bon vivant, sensualist, voluptuary **2 = sybarite**, epicure, epicurean

heed Formal ◆ noun **1 = care**, attention, caution, consideration, ear, heedfulness, mind, note, notice, regard, respect, thought, watchfulness ◆ verb **2 = pay attention to**, attend, bear in mind, be guided by, consider, follow, listen to, mark, mind, note, obey, observe, regard, take notice of, take to heart
➤ **Antonyms**
noun ≠**care**: carelessness, disregard, inattention, laxity, laxness, neglect, thoughtlessness ◆ verb ≠**pay attention to**: be inattentive to, discount, disobey, disregard, flout, ignore, neglect, overlook, reject, shun, turn a deaf ear to

heedless adjective **= careless**, foolhardy, imprudent, inattentive, incautious, neglectful, negligent, oblivious, precipitate, rash, reckless, thoughtless, unmindful, unobservant, unthinking
➤ **Antonyms**
attentive, aware, careful, cautious, concerned, heedful, mindful, observant, thoughtful, vigilant, wary, watchful

heel¹ noun **1** Slang **= swine**, blackguard, bounder (old-fashioned Brit. slang), cad (Brit. informal), rotter (slang, chiefly Brit.), scally (Northwest English dialect), scoundrel, scumbag (slang) **2 down at heel = shabby**, dowdy, impoverished, out at elbows, run-down, seedy, slipshod, slovenly, worn **3 take to one's heels = flee**, escape, hook it (slang), run away or off, show a clean pair of heels, skedaddle (informal), take flight, turn tail, vamoose (slang, chiefly U.S.)

heel² verb **= lean over**, cant, careen, incline, keel over, list, tilt

hefty adjective Informal **1 = big**, beefy (informal), brawny, burly, hulking, husky (informal), massive, muscular, robust, strapping, strong **2 = heavy**, ample, awkward, bulky, colossal, cumbersome, large, massive, ponderous, substantial, tremendous, unwieldy, weighty **3 = forceful**, heavy, powerful, thumping (slang), vigorous
➤ **Antonyms**
≠**big**: diminutive, inconsequential, ineffectual, infinitesimal, insignificant, little, minute, narrow, pocket-sized, scanty, short, slight, slim, small, thin, tiny ≠**heavy**: agile, light ≠**forceful**: feeble, frail, mild, soft, weak, weedy (informal), wimpish or wimpy (informal)

height noun **1 = altitude**, elevation, highness, loftiness, stature, tallness **2 = peak**, apex, apogee, crest, crown, elevation, hill, mountain, pinnacle, summit, top, vertex,

zenith **3 = culmination,** climax, extremity, limit, maximum, *ne plus ultra,* ultimate, utmost degree, uttermost
➤ **Antonyms**
≠**altitude:** depth, lowness, shortness, smallness ≠**peak:** abyss, base, bottom, canyon, chasm, depth, lowland, nadir, ravine, valley ≠**culmination:** low point, minimum, nadir

heighten *verb* **= intensify,** add to, aggravate, amplify, augment, enhance, improve, increase, magnify, sharpen, strengthen

heinous *adjective* **= shocking,** abhorrent, abominable, atrocious, awful, evil, execrable, flagrant, grave, hateful, hideous, infamous, iniquitous, monstrous, nefarious, odious, outrageous, revolting, unspeakable, vicious, villainous

heir *noun* **= successor,** beneficiary, heiress (*fem.*), inheritor, inheritress *or* inheritrix (*fem.*), next in line, scion

hell *noun* **1 = underworld,** abode of the damned, abyss, bottomless pit, fire and brimstone, Gehenna (*New Testament, Judaism*), Hades (*Greek myth*), hellfire, infernal regions, inferno, lower world, nether world, Tartarus (*Greek myth*) **2** *Informal* **= torment,** affliction, agony, anguish, martyrdom, misery, nightmare, ordeal, suffering, trial, wretchedness **3 hell for leather = speedily,** at a rate of knots, at the double, full-tilt, headlong, hotfoot, hurriedly, like a bat out of hell (*slang*), pell-mell, posthaste, quickly, swiftly

hellbent *adjective Informal* **= intent,** bent, determined, fixed, resolved, set, settled

hellish *adjective* **1 = devilish,** damnable, damned, demoniacal, diabolical, fiendish, infernal **2** *Informal* **= atrocious,** abominable, accursed, barbarous, cruel, detestable, execrable, inhuman, monstrous, nefarious, vicious, wicked
➤ **Antonyms**
≠**atrocious:** admirable, agreeable, delightful, fine, good, humane, innocuous, kind, merciful, pleasant, wonderful

hello *interjection* **= hi** (*Informal*), good afternoon, good evening, good morning, greetings, how do you do?, welcome

helm *noun* **1** *Nautical* **= tiller,** rudder, steering gear, wheel **2 at the helm = in charge,** at the wheel, directing, in command, in control, in the driving seat, in the saddle

help *verb* **1 = aid,** abet, assist, back, befriend, cooperate, encourage, give a leg up (*informal*), lend a hand, lend a helping hand, promote, relieve, save, second, serve, stand by, succour, support **2 = improve,**

alleviate, ameliorate, cure, ease, facilitate, heal, mitigate, relieve, remedy, restore **3 = refrain from,** abstain, avoid, control, eschew, forbear, hinder, keep from, prevent, resist, shun, withstand ♦ *noun* **4 = assistance,** advice, aid, avail, benefit, cooperation, guidance, helping hand, promotion, service, support, use, utility **5 = assistant,** employee, hand, helper, worker **6 = remedy,** cure, relief, restorative
➤ **Antonyms**
verb ≠**aid:** bar, block, discourage, fight, foil, frustrate, hinder, hobble, impede, obstruct, oppose ≠**improve:** aggravate, harm, hurt, injure, irritate, make worse ♦ *noun* ≠**assistance:** aggravation, bane, block, discouragement, hindrance, irritant, obstruction, opposition

helper *noun* **= assistant,** abettor, aide, aider, ally, attendant, auxiliary, collaborator, colleague, deputy, helpmate, henchman, mate, partner, protagonist, right-hand man, second, subsidiary, supporter

helpful *adjective* **1 = useful,** advantageous, beneficial, constructive, favourable, fortunate, practical, productive, profitable, serviceable, timely **2 = cooperative,** accommodating, beneficent, benevolent, caring, considerate, friendly, kind, neighbourly, supportive, sympathetic

helpfulness *noun* **1 = usefulness,** advantage, assistance, benefit **2 = kindness,** cooperation, friendliness, rallying round, support

helping *noun* **= portion,** dollop (*informal*), piece, plateful, ration, serving

helpless *adjective* **1 = vulnerable,** abandoned, defenceless, dependent, destitute, exposed, forlorn, stranded, unprotected, wide open **2 = powerless,** debilitated, disabled, feeble, impotent, incapable, incompetent, infirm, paralysed, unfit, weak
➤ **Antonyms**
≠**vulnerable:** invulnerable, safe, secure, well-protected ≠**powerless:** able, capable, competent, equipped, fit, hardy, healthy, hearty, mighty, powerful, robust, solid, strong, sturdy, thriving, tough

helplessness *noun* **1 = vulnerability,** defencelessness, exposed position, forlornness **2 = weakness,** disability, feebleness, impotence, infirmity, powerlessness

helpmate *noun* **= partner,** assistant, associate, companion, consort, helper, helpmeet, husband, significant other (*U.S. informal*), spouse, support, wife

helter-skelter *adjective* **1 = haphazard,** confused, disordered, higgledy-piggledy (*informal*), hit-or-miss, jumbled, muddled, random, topsy-turvy ◆ *adverb* **2** = **carelessly**, anyhow, hastily, headlong, hurriedly, pell-mell, rashly, recklessly, wildly

hem *noun* = **edge**, border, fringe, margin, trimming

he-man *noun Informal* = **muscle man**, Atlas, bit of beefcake, Hercules, hunk (*slang*), Tarzan (*informal*)

hem in *verb* = **surround**, beset, border, circumscribe, confine, edge, enclose, environ, hedge in, restrict, shut in, skirt

hence *conjunction* = **therefore**, ergo, for this reason, on that account, thus

henceforth *adverb* = **from now on**, from this day forward, hence, hereafter, in the future

henchman *noun* = **attendant**, aide, associate, bodyguard, follower, heavy (*slang*), minder (*slang*), right-hand man, sidekick (*slang*), subordinate, supporter

henpecked *adjective* = **dominated**, browbeaten, bullied, cringing, led by the nose, meek, subject, subjugated, tied to someone's apron strings, timid, treated like dirt
➤ Antonyms
aggressive, assertive, bossy (*informal*), dominating, domineering, forceful, macho, overbearing, self-assertive, spirited, wilful

herald *noun* **1** = **messenger**, bearer of tidings, crier **2** *Often literary* = **forerunner**, harbinger, indication, omen, precursor, sign, signal, token ◆ *verb* **3** = **announce**, advertise, broadcast, proclaim, publicize, publish, trumpet **4** = **indicate**, foretoken, harbinger, pave the way, portend, precede, presage, promise, show, usher in

herculean *adjective* **1** = **arduous**, demanding, difficult, exhausting, formidable, gruelling, hard, heavy, laborious, onerous, prodigious, strenuous, toilsome, tough **2** = **strong**, athletic, brawny, husky (*informal*), mighty, muscular, powerful, rugged, sinewy, stalwart, strapping, sturdy

herd *noun* **1** = **flock**, assemblage, collection, crowd, crush, drove, horde, mass, mob, multitude, press, swarm, throng **2** *Often disparaging* = **mob**, populace, rabble, riffraff, the hoi polloi, the masses, the plebs ◆ *verb* **3** = **congregate**, assemble, associate, collect, flock, gather, huddle, muster, rally **4** = **drive**, force, goad, guide, lead, shepherd, spur

herdsman *noun Chiefly Brit.* = **stockman**, cowherd, cowman, drover, grazier

hereafter *adverb* **1** = **in future**, after this, from now on, hence, henceforth, henceforward ◆ *noun* **2 the hereafter** = **afterlife**, future life, life after death, next world, the beyond

hereditary *adjective* **1** = **genetic**, family, inborn, inbred, inheritable, transmissible **2** *Law* = **inherited**, ancestral, bequeathed, handed down, patrimonial, traditional, transmitted, willed

heredity *noun* = **genetics**, congenital traits, constitution, genetic make-up, inheritance

heresy *noun* = **unorthodoxy**, apostasy, dissidence, error, heterodoxy, iconoclasm, impiety, revisionism, schism

heretic *noun* = **nonconformist**, apostate, dissenter, dissident, renegade, revisionist, schismatic, sectarian, separatist

heretical *adjective* = **unorthodox**, freethinking, heterodox, iconoclastic, idolatrous, impious, revisionist, schismatic

heritage *noun* = **inheritance**, bequest, birthright, endowment, estate, legacy, lot, patrimony, portion, share, tradition

hermaphrodite *noun* = **androgyne**, bisexual

hermaphroditic *adjective* = **androgynous**, AC/DC (*informal*), bisexual, gynandrous

hermetic, hermetical *adjective* = **airtight**, sealed, shut

hermit *noun* = **recluse**, anchoret, anchorite, eremite, loner (*informal*), monk, solitary, stylite

hero *noun* **1** = **leading man**, lead actor, male lead, principal male character, protagonist **2** = **idol**, celeb (*informal*), celebrity, champion, conqueror, great man, heart-throb (*Brit.*), man of the hour, megastar (*informal*), popular figure, star, superstar, victor

heroic *adjective* = **courageous**, bold, brave, daring, dauntless, doughty, fearless, gallant, intrepid, lion-hearted, stouthearted, undaunted, valiant, valorous
➤ Antonyms
base, chicken (*slang*), cowardly, craven, faint-hearted, ignoble, mean, timid

heroine *noun* **1** = **leading lady**, diva, female lead, lead actress, prima donna, principal female character, protagonist **2** = **idol**, celeb (*informal*), celebrity, goddess, megastar (*informal*), woman of the hour

heroism *noun* = **bravery**, boldness, courage, courageousness, daring, fearlessness, fortitude, gallantry, intrepidity, prowess, spirit, valour

hero worship *noun* = **idolization**, admiration, adoration, adulation, idealization, putting on a pedestal, veneration

hesitant *adjective* = **uncertain**, diffident, doubtful, half-hearted, halting, hanging back, hesitating, irresolute, lacking

confidence, reluctant, shy, timid, unsure, vacillating, wavering
➤ **Antonyms**
arrogant, avid, can-do (*informal*), clear, confident, definite, determined, dogmatic, eager, enthusiastic, firm, forceful, keen, positive, resolute, self-assured, spirited, sure, unhesitating, unwavering

hesitate *verb* **1** = **waver**, be uncertain, delay, dither (*chiefly Brit.*), doubt, haver (*Brit.*), hum and haw, pause, shillyshally (*informal*), swither (*Scot.*), vacillate, wait **2** = **be reluctant**, balk, be unwilling, boggle, demur, hang back, scruple, shrink from, think twice **3** = **falter**, fumble, hem and haw *or* hum and haw, stammer, stumble, stutter
➤ **Antonyms**
≠**waver**: be confident, be decisive, be firm, continue ≠**be reluctant**: be determined, resolve, welcome

hesitation *noun* **1** = **indecision**, delay, doubt, dubiety, hesitancy, irresolution, uncertainty, vacillation **2** = **reluctance**, demurral, misgiving(s), qualm(s), scruple(s), unwillingness **3** = **faltering**, fumbling, hemming and hawing, stammering, stumbling, stuttering

heterodox *adjective* = **unorthodox**, dissident, heretical, iconoclastic, revisionist, schismatic, unsound

heterogeneous *adjective* = **varied**, assorted, contrary, contrasted, different, disparate, dissimilar, divergent, diverse, diversified, incongruous, manifold, miscellaneous, mixed, motley, opposed, unlike, unrelated

hew *verb* **1** = **cut**, axe, chop, hack, lop, split **2** = **carve**, fashion, form, make, model, sculpt, sculpture, shape, smooth

heyday *noun* = **prime**, bloom, flowering, pink, prime of life, salad days

hiatus *noun* = **pause**, blank, breach, break, discontinuity, gap, interruption, interval, lacuna, lapse, opening, respite, space

hibernate *verb* = **lie dormant**, hole up, overwinter, remain torpid, sleep snug, vegetate, winter

hidden *adjective* = **concealed**, abstruse, clandestine, close, covered, covert, cryptic, dark, latent, masked, mysterious, mystic, mystical, obscure, occult, recondite, secret, shrouded, ulterior, under wraps, unrevealed, unseen, veiled

hide¹ *verb* **1** = **conceal**, cache, secrete, stash (*informal*) **2** = **go into hiding**, go to ground, go underground, hole up, lie low, take cover **3** = **suppress**, draw a veil over, hush up, keep dark, keep secret, keep under one's hat, withhold **4** = **disguise**, blot out, bury, camouflage, cloak, conceal, cover,

eclipse, mask, obscure, screen, shelter, shroud, veil
➤ **Antonyms**
admit, bare, confess, disclose, display, divulge, exhibit, expose, find, flaunt, reveal, show, uncover, unveil

hide² *noun* = **skin**, fell, pelt

hideaway *noun* = **hiding place**, haven, hide-out, nest, refuge, retreat, sanctuary, sequestered nook

hidebound *adjective* = **conventional**, narrow, narrow-minded, puritan, rigid, set, set in one's ways, strait-laced, ultraconservative
➤ **Antonyms**
broad-minded, flexible, liberal, open, receptive, tolerant, unconventional, unorthodox

hideous *adjective* = **ugly**, ghastly, grim, grisly, grotesque, gruesome, monstrous, repulsive, revolting, unsightly
➤ **Antonyms**
appealing, beautiful, captivating, charming, entrancing, lovely, pleasant, pleasing

hide-out *noun* = **hiding place**, den, hideaway, lair, secret place, shelter

hiding *noun* = **beating**, caning, drubbing, flogging, licking (*informal*), spanking, tanning (*slang*), thrashing, walloping (*informal*), whipping

hierarchy *noun* = **grading**, pecking order, ranking

hieroglyphic *adjective* = **indecipherable**, enigmatical, figurative, obscure, runic, symbolical

higgledy-piggledy *Informal* ♦ *adverb* **1** = **haphazardly**, all over the place, all over the shop (*informal*), anyhow, any old how, confusedly, helter-skelter, pell-mell, topsy-turvy ♦ *adjective* **2** = **haphazard**, helter-skelter, indiscriminate, jumbled, muddled, pell-mell, topsy-turvy

high *adjective* **1** = **tall**, elevated, lofty, soaring, steep, towering **2** = **extreme**, excessive, extraordinary, great, intensified, sharp, strong **3** = **expensive**, costly, dear, exorbitant, high-priced, steep (*informal*), stiff **4** = **high-pitched**, acute, penetrating, piercing, piping, sharp, shrill, soprano, strident, treble **5** = **gamey**, niffy (*Brit. slang*), pongy (*Brit. informal*), strong-flavoured, tainted, whiffy (*Brit. slang*) **6** = **important**, arch, big-time (*informal*), chief, consequential, distinguished, eminent, exalted, influential, leading, major league (*informal*), notable, powerful, prominent, ruling, significant, superior **7** = **cheerful**, boisterous, bouncy (*informal*), elated, excited, exhilarated, exuberant, joyful, light-hearted, merry **8** *Informal*

= **intoxicated**, delirious, euphoric, freaked out (*informal*), hyped up (*slang*), inebriated, on a trip (*informal*), spaced out (*slang*), stoned (*slang*), tripping (*informal*), turned on (*slang*), zonked (*slang*) **9** = **luxurious**, extravagant, grand, lavish, rich **10 high and dry** = **abandoned**, bereft, destitute, helpless, stranded **11 high and low** = **everywhere**, all over, exhaustively, far and wide, in every nook and cranny **12 high and mighty** *Informal* = **self-important**, arrogant, cavalier, conceited, disdainful, haughty, imperious, overbearing, snobbish, stuck-up (*informal*), superior ♦ *adverb* **13** = **aloft**, at great height, far up, way up ♦ *noun* **14** = **peak**, apex, crest, height, record level, summit, top **15** *Informal* = **intoxication**, delirium, ecstasy, euphoria, trip (*informal*)
➤ **Antonyms**
adjective ≠**tall**: dwarfed, low, short, stunted ≠**extreme**: average, low, mild, moderate, restrained, suppressed ≠**high-pitched**: alto, bass, deep, gruff, low, low-pitched ≠**important**: average, common, inconsequential, insignificant, low, lowly, low-ranking, menial, secondary, undistinguished, unimportant ≠**cheerful**: dejected, depressed, gloomy, low, melancholy, sad

highbrow *Often disparaging* ♦ *adjective* **1** = **intellectual**, bookish, brainy (*informal*), cultivated, cultured, deep, highbrowed, sophisticated ♦ *noun* **2** = **intellectual**, aesthete, Brahmin (*U.S.*), brain (*informal*), brainbox (*slang*), egghead (*informal*), mastermind, savant, scholar
➤ **Antonyms**
adjective ≠**intellectual**: ignorant, lowbrow, philistine, shallow, uncultivated, uninformed, unintellectual, unlearned, unsophisticated ♦ *noun* ≠**intellectual**: idiot, ignoramus, illiterate, imbecile (*informal*), lowbrow, moron, philistine

highfalutin *adjective* = **pompous**, big, bombastic, florid, grandiose, high-flown, high-sounding, lofty, magniloquent, pretentious

high-flown *adjective* = **extravagant**, arty-farty (*informal*), elaborate, exaggerated, florid, grandiose, high-falutin (*informal*), inflated, lofty, magniloquent, overblown, pretentious
➤ **Antonyms**
down-to-earth, moderate, modest, practical, pragmatic, realistic, reasonable, restrained, sensible, simple, straightforward, unpretentious

high-handed *adjective* = **dictatorial**, arbitrary, autocratic, bossy (*informal*), despotic, domineering, imperious,

oppressive, overbearing, peremptory, tyrannical, wilful

highlands *plural noun* = **uplands**, heights, hill country, hills, mesa, mountainous region, plateau, tableland

highlight *noun* **1** = **high point**, best part, climax, feature, focal point, focus, high spot, main feature, memorable part, peak ♦ *verb* **2** = **emphasize**, accent, accentuate, bring to the fore, feature, focus attention on, foreground, give prominence to, play up, set off, show up, spotlight, stress, underline
➤ **Antonyms**
noun ≠**high point**: disappointment, lowlight, low point ♦ *verb* ≠**emphasize**: de-emphasize, gloss over, neglect, overlook, play down

highly *adverb* **1** = **extremely**, decidedly, eminently, exceptionally, extraordinarily, greatly, immensely, seriously (*informal*), supremely, tremendously, vastly, very, very much **2** = **favourably**, appreciatively, approvingly, enthusiastically, warmly, well

highly strung *adjective* = **nervous**, easily upset, edgy, excitable, irascible, irritable, nervy (*Brit. informal*), neurotic, on pins and needles, on tenterhooks, restless, sensitive, stressed, taut, temperamental, tense, tetchy, twitchy (*informal*), wired (*slang*)
➤ **Antonyms**
calm, collected, easy-going, even-tempered, laid-back (*informal*), placid, relaxed, serene, unfazed (*informal*)

high-minded *adjective* = **principled**, elevated, ethical, fair, good, honourable, idealistic, magnanimous, moral, noble, pure, righteous, upright, virtuous, worthy
➤ **Antonyms**
dishonest, dishonourable, unethical, unfair

high-powered *adjective* = **dynamic**, aggressive, driving, effective, energetic, enterprising, fast-track, forceful, go-ahead, go-getting (*informal*), vigorous

high-pressure *Informal (of salesmanship)* *adjective* = **forceful**, aggressive, bludgeoning, coercive, compelling, high-powered, importunate, insistent, intensive, in-your-face (*slang*), persistent, persuasive, pushy (*informal*)

high-spirited *adjective* = **lively**, alive and kicking, animated, boisterous, bold, bouncy, daring, dashing, ebullient, effervescent, energetic, exuberant, frolicsome, full of beans (*informal*), full of life, fun-loving, gallant, mettlesome, sparky, spirited, spunky (*informal*), vibrant, vital, vivacious

hijack *verb* = **seize**, commandeer, expropriate, skyjack, take over

hike *noun* **1** = **walk**, journey on foot, march, ramble, tramp, trek ♦ *verb* **2** = **walk**, back-pack, hoof it (*slang*), leg it (*informal*), ramble, tramp **3 hike up = raise**, hitch up, jack up, lift, pull up

hiker *noun* = **walker**, backpacker, rambler

hilarious *adjective* = **funny**, amusing, comical, entertaining, humorous, jolly, merry, mirthful, rollicking, side-splitting, uproarious
➤ **Antonyms**
dull, gloomy, quiet, sad, sedate, serious

hilarity *noun* = **merriment**, amusement, cheerfulness, exhilaration, exuberance, gaiety, glee, high spirits, jollity, joviality, laughter, levity, mirth

hill *noun* **1** = **mount**, brae (*Scot.*), elevation, eminence, fell, height, hillock, hilltop, knoll, mound, prominence, tor **2** = **heap**, drift, hummock, mound, pile, rick, stack **3** = **slope**, brae (*Scot.*), climb, gradient, incline, rise

hillock *noun* = **mound**, barrow, hummock, knoll

hilly *adjective* = **mountainous**, rolling, steep, undulating

hilt *noun* **1** = **handle**, grip, haft, handgrip **2 to the hilt** = **fully**, completely, entirely, totally, wholly

hind *adjective* = **back**, after, hinder, posterior, rear

hinder *verb* = **obstruct**, arrest, block, check, debar, delay, deter, encumber, frustrate, hamper, hamstring, handicap, hobble, hold up *or* back, impede, interrupt, oppose, prevent, retard, slow down, stop, stymie, throw a spanner in the works, thwart, trammel
➤ **Antonyms**
accelerate, advance, aid, benefit, encourage, expedite, facilitate, further, help, hurry, promote, quicken, speed, support

hindmost *adjective* = **last**, concluding, final, furthest, furthest behind, most remote, rearmost, terminal, trailing, ultimate

hindrance *noun* = **obstacle**, bar, barrier, block, check, deterrent, difficulty, drag, drawback, encumbrance, handicap, hazard, hitch, impediment, interruption, limitation, obstruction, restraint, restriction, snag, stoppage, stumbling block, trammel
➤ **Antonyms**
advancement, advantage, aid, asset, assistance, benefit, boon, boost, encouragement, furtherance, help, support

hinge *verb* **hinge on = depend on**, be contingent on, be subject to, hang on, pivot on, rest on, revolve around, turn on

hint *noun* **1** = **indication**, allusion, clue, implication, inkling, innuendo, insinuation, intimation, mention, reminder, suggestion,

tip-off, word to the wise **2** = **advice**, help, pointer, suggestion, tip, wrinkle (*informal*) **3** = **trace**, breath, dash, *soupçon*, speck, suggestion, suspicion, taste, tinge, touch, undertone, whiff, whisper ◆ *verb* **4** = **suggest**, allude, cue, imply, indicate, insinuate, intimate, let it be known, mention, prompt, tip off, tip the wink (*informal*)

hip *adjective Slang* = **with it** (*informal*), aware, clued-up (*informal*), fashionable, in, informed, in on, knowledgeable, onto, trendy (*Brit. informal*), wise (*slang*)

hippy *noun* = **bohemian**, beatnik, dropout, flower child

hire *verb* **1** = **employ**, appoint, commission, engage, sign up, take on **2** = **rent**, charter, engage, lease, let ◆ *noun* **3** = **rental**, charge, cost, fee, price, rent

hirsute *adjective* = **hairy**, bearded, bewhiskered, bristly, shaggy, unshaven

hiss *noun* **1** = **sibilation**, buzz, hissing, sibilance **2** = **catcall**, boo, contempt, derision, jeer, raspberry ◆ *verb* **3** = **whistle**, rasp, shrill, sibilate, wheeze, whirr, whiz **4** = **jeer**, blow a raspberry, boo, catcall, condemn, damn, decry, deride, hoot, mock, revile, ridicule

historian *noun* = **chronicler**, annalist, biographer, historiographer, recorder

historic *adjective* = **significant**, celebrated, consequential, epoch-making, extraordinary, famous, ground-breaking, momentous, notable, outstanding, red-letter, remarkable
➤ **Antonyms**
ordinary, uncelebrated, unimportant, unknown

historical *adjective* = **factual**, actual, archival, attested, authentic, chronicled, documented, real, verifiable
➤ **Antonyms**
fabulous, fictional, legendary, mythical

history *noun* **1** = **chronicle**, account, annals, autobiography, biography, memoirs, narration, narrative, recapitulation, recital, record, relation, saga, story **2** = **the past**, ancient history, antiquity, bygone times, days of old, days of yore, olden days, the good old days, the old days, yesterday, yesteryear

histrionic *adjective* = **theatrical**, actorly, actressy, affected, artificial, bogus, camp (*informal*), dramatic, forced, insincere, melodramatic, sensational, unnatural

histrionics *plural noun* = **dramatics**, performance, scene, staginess, tantrums, temperament, theatricality

hit *verb* **1** = **strike**, bang, bash (*informal*), batter, beat, belt (*informal*), chin (*slang*), clip (*informal*), clobber (*slang*), clout (*informal*), cuff, deck (*slang*), flog, knock, lambast(e), lay one on (*slang*), lob, punch, slap, smack, smite (*archaic*), sock (*slang*), swat, thump, wallop (*informal*), whack **2** = **collide with**, bang into, bump, clash with, crash against, meet head-on, run into, smash into **3** = **affect**, damage, devastate, impact on, impinge on, influence, leave a mark on, make an impact *or* impression on, move, overwhelm, touch **4** = **reach**, accomplish, achieve, arrive at, attain, gain, secure, strike, touch **5 hit it off** *Informal* = **get on (well) with**, be on good terms, click (*slang*), get on like a house on fire (*informal*), take to, warm to ♦ *noun* **6** = **stroke**, belt (*informal*), blow, bump, clash, clout (*informal*), collision, cuff, impact, knock, rap, shot, slap, smack, swipe (*informal*), wallop (*informal*) **7** = **success**, sellout, sensation, smash (*informal*), smasheroo (*informal*), triumph, winner

hitch *noun* **1** = **problem**, catch, check, delay, difficulty, drawback, hassle (*informal*), hazard, hindrance, hold-up, impediment, mishap, obstacle, snag, trouble ♦ *verb* **2** *Informal* = **hitchhike**, thumb a lift **3** = **fasten**, attach, connect, couple, harness, join, make fast, tether, tie, unite, yoke **4 hitch up** = **pull up**, hoick, jerk, tug, yank

hither *adverb* = **here**, close, closer, near, nearer, nigh (*archaic*), over here, to this place

hitherto *adverb* Formal = **previously**, heretofore, so far, thus far, till now, until now, up to now

hit on *or* **upon** *verb* = **think up**, arrive at, chance upon, come upon, discover, guess, invent, light upon, realize, strike upon, stumble on

hit-or-miss *or* **hit-and-miss** *adjective* = **haphazard**, aimless, casual, cursory, disorganized, indiscriminate, perfunctory, random, undirected, uneven
➤ **Antonyms**
arranged, deliberate, organized, planned, systematic

hit out (at) *verb* = **attack**, assail, castigate, condemn, denounce, inveigh against, lash out, rail against, strike out at

hive *noun* **1** = **colony**, cluster, swarm **2** As in **hive of activity** = **centre**, heart, hub

hoard *noun* **1** = **store**, accumulation, cache, fall-back, fund, heap, mass, pile, reserve, stash, stockpile, supply, treasure-trove ♦ *verb* **2** = **save**, accumulate, amass, buy up, cache, collect, deposit, garner, gather, hive, lay up, put away, put by, stash away (*informal*), stockpile, store, treasure

hoarder *noun* = **saver**, collector, miser, niggard, tight-arse (*taboo slang*), tight-ass (*U.S. taboo slang*)

hoarse *adjective* = **rough**, croaky, discordant, grating, gravelly, growling, gruff, guttural, harsh, husky, rasping, raucous, throaty
➤ **Antonyms**
harmonious, mellifluous, mellow, melodious, smooth

hoarseness *noun* = **croakiness**, a frog in one's throat, gruffness, huskiness, rasping, sore throat, throatiness, wheeziness

hoary *adjective* **1** = **white-haired**, frosty, grey, grey-haired, grizzled, hoar, silvery, white **2** = **old**, aged, ancient, antiquated, antique, venerable

hoax *noun* **1** = **trick**, cheat, con (*informal*), deception, fast one (*informal*), fraud, imposture, joke, practical joke, prank, ruse, spoof (*informal*), swindle ♦ *verb* **2** = **deceive**, bamboozle (*informal*), befool, bluff, con (*slang*), delude, dupe, fool, hoodwink, hornswoggle (*slang*), kid (*informal*), swindle, take in (*informal*), take (someone) for a ride (*informal*), trick, wind up (*Brit. slang*)

hobble *verb* **1** = **limp**, dodder, falter, shamble, shuffle, stagger, stumble, totter **2** = **tie**, fasten, fetter, hamstring, restrict, shackle

hobby *noun* = **pastime**, diversion, favourite occupation, (leisure) activity, leisure pursuit, relaxation, sideline

hobgoblin *noun* = **imp**, bogey, goblin, hob, spectre, spirit, sprite

hobnob *verb* = **socialize**, associate, consort, fraternize, hang about, hang out (*informal*), keep company, mingle, mix

hocus-pocus *noun* Informal = **trickery**, artifice, cheat, chicanery, deceit, deception, delusion, hoax, humbug, imposture, swindle

hog *verb* Slang = **monopolize**, be a dog in the manger, corner, corner the market in, dominate, tie up

hogwash *noun* Informal = **nonsense**, balderdash, balls (*taboo slang*), bilge (*informal*), bosh (*informal*), bull (*slang*), bullshit (*taboo slang*), bunk (*informal*), bunkum *or* buncombe (*chiefly U.S.*), cobblers (*Brit. taboo slang*), crap (*slang*), drivel, eyewash (*informal*), garbage (*informal*), guff (*slang*), hot air (*informal*), moonshine, piffle (*informal*), poppycock (*informal*), rot, rubbish, shit (*taboo slang*), tommyrot, tosh (*slang, chiefly Brit.*), trash, tripe (*informal*), twaddle

hoi polloi *noun* = **the common people**, admass, *canaille*, commonalty, riffraff, the (common) herd, the great unwashed (*informal & derogatory*), the lower orders, the masses, the plebs, the populace, the proles (*derogatory slang, chiefly Brit.*), the proletariat, the rabble, the third estate, the underclass

hoist verb 1 = **raise**, elevate, erect, heave, lift, rear, upraise ♦ noun 2 = **lift**, crane, elevator, tackle, winch

hoity-toity adjective Informal = **haughty**, arrogant, conceited, disdainful, high and mighty (informal), lofty, overweening, proud, scornful, snobbish, snooty (informal), stuck-up (informal), supercilious, toffee-nosed (slang, chiefly Brit.), uppish (Brit. informal)

hold verb 1 = **grasp**, clasp, cleave, clinch, cling, clutch, cradle, embrace, enfold, grip 2 = **support**, bear, brace, carry, prop, shoulder, sustain, take 3 = **continue**, endure, last, persevere, persist, remain, resist, stay, wear 4 = **accommodate**, comprise, contain, have a capacity for, seat, take 5 = **restrain**, arrest, bind, check, confine, curb, detain, impound, imprison, pound, stay, stop, suspend 6 = **own**, have, keep, maintain, occupy, possess, retain 7 = **consider**, assume, believe, deem, entertain, esteem, judge, maintain, presume, reckon, regard, think, view 8 = **convene**, assemble, call, carry on, celebrate, conduct, have, officiate at, preside over, run 9 = **apply**, be in force, be the case, exist, hold good, operate, remain true, remain valid, stand up ♦ noun 10 = **grip**, clasp, clutch, grasp 11 = **foothold**, anchorage, footing, leverage, prop, purchase, stay, support, vantage 12 = **control**, ascendancy, authority, clout (informal), dominance, dominion, influence, mastery, pull (informal), sway
➤ **Antonyms**
verb ≠**support**: break, come undone, give way, loosen ≠**restrain**: free, let go, let loose, release ≠**own**: bestow, give, give away, give up, hand over, offer, turn over ≠**consider**: deny, disavow, disclaim, put down, refute, reject ≠**convene**: call off, cancel, postpone

hold back verb 1 = **restrain**, check, control, curb, inhibit, rein, repress, stem the flow, suppress 2 = **withhold**, desist, forbear, keep back, refuse

holder noun 1 = **case**, container, cover, housing, receptacle, sheath 2 = **owner**, bearer, custodian, incumbent, keeper, occupant, possessor, proprietor, purchaser

hold forth verb = **speak**, declaim, descant, discourse, go on, harangue, lecture, orate, preach, speechify, spiel (informal), spout (informal)

holding noun = **property**, assets, estate, investments, land interests, possessions, resources, securities, stocks and shares

hold off verb 1 = **fend off**, keep off, rebuff,

repel, repulse, stave off 2 = **put off**, avoid, defer, delay, keep from, postpone, refrain

hold out verb 1 = **offer**, extend, give, present, proffer 2 = **last**, carry on, continue, endure, hang on, persevere, persist, stand fast, stay the course, withstand

hold over verb = **postpone**, adjourn, defer, delay, put off, suspend, take a rain check on (U.S. & Canad. informal), waive

hold-up noun 1 = **robbery**, burglary, mugging (informal), stick-up (slang, chiefly U.S.), theft 2 = **delay**, bottleneck, difficulty, hitch, obstruction, setback, snag, stoppage, traffic jam, trouble, wait

hold up verb 1 = **delay**, detain, hinder, impede, retard, set back, slow down, stop 2 = **support**, bolster, brace, buttress, jack up, prop, shore up, sustain 3 = **rob**, mug (informal), stick up (slang, chiefly U.S.), waylay 4 = **exhibit**, display, flaunt, present, show

hold with verb = **approve of**, agree to or with, be in favour of, countenance, subscribe to, support, take kindly to
➤ **Antonyms**
be against, disagree with, disapprove of, hold out against, oppose

hole noun 1 = **cavity**, cave, cavern, chamber, depression, excavation, hollow, pit, pocket, scoop, shaft 2 = **opening**, aperture, breach, break, crack, fissure, gap, orifice, outlet, perforation, puncture, rent, split, tear, vent 3 = **burrow**, covert, den, earth, lair, nest, retreat, shelter 4 = **fault**, defect, discrepancy, error, fallacy, flaw, inconsistency, loophole 5 Informal = **hovel**, dive (slang), dump (informal), joint (slang), slum 6 Informal = **predicament**, dilemma, fix (informal), hot water (informal), jam (informal), mess, quandary, scrape (informal), spot (informal), tangle, tight spot 7 **pick holes in** = **criticize**, bad-mouth (slang, chiefly U.S. & Canad.), cavil, crab (informal), denigrate, disparage, disprove, find fault, knock (informal), pull to pieces, put down, rubbish (informal), run down, slag (off) (slang), slate (informal)

hole-and-corner adjective Informal = **furtive**, backstairs, clandestine, secret, secretive, sneaky (informal), stealthy, surreptitious, underhand, under the counter (informal)
➤ **Antonyms**
above-board, candid, frank, open, public

hole up verb = **hide**, go into hiding, go to earth, hibernate, shelter, take cover, take refuge

holiday noun 1 = **vacation**, away day, break, leave, recess, time off 2 = **festival**, anniversary, bank holiday, celebration, feast, festivity, fête, gala, name day, public holiday, red-letter day, saint's day

holier-than-thou *adjective* = **self-righteous**, goody-goody (*informal*), pietistic, pietistical, priggish, religiose, sanctimonious, self-satisfied, smug, squeaky-clean, unctuous

holiness *noun* = **sanctity**, blessedness, devoutness, divinity, godliness, piety, purity, religiousness, righteousness, sacredness, saintliness, spirituality, virtuousness

holler *Informal* ◆ *verb, noun* = **yell**, bawl, bellow, call, cheer, clamour, cry, hail, halloo, roar, shout, whoop

hollow *adjective* **1** = **empty**, not solid, unfilled, vacant, void **2** = **sunken**, cavernous, concave, deep-set, depressed, indented **3** = **toneless**, deep, dull, expressionless, flat, low, muffled, muted, reverberant, rumbling, sepulchral **4** = **worthless**, empty, fruitless, futile, meaningless, pointless, unavailing, useless, vain **5 beat (someone) hollow** *Brit. informal* = **defeat**, hammer (*informal*), outdo, overcome, rout, thrash, trounce, worst ◆ *noun* **6** = **cavity**, basin, bowl, cave, cavern, concavity, crater, cup, den, dent, depression, dimple, excavation, hole, indentation, pit, trough **7** = **valley**, bottom, dale, dell, dingle, glen ◆ *verb* **8** = **scoop**, channel, dig, excavate, furrow, gouge, groove, pit
➤ **Antonyms**
adjective ≠**empty**: full, occupied, solid ≠**sunken**: convex, rounded ≠**toneless**: expressive, vibrant ≠**worthless**: gratifying, meaningful, pleasing, satisfying, valuable, worthwhile ◆ *noun* ≠**cavity**: bump, mound, projection ≠**valley**: bluff, height, hill, knoll, mountain, rise

holocaust *noun* = **genocide**, annihilation, carnage, conflagration, destruction, devastation, fire, inferno, massacre, mass murder, pogrom

holy *adjective* **1** = **sacred**, blessed, consecrated, dedicated, hallowed, sacrosanct, sanctified, venerable, venerated **2** = **devout**, divine, faithful, god-fearing, godly, hallowed, pious, pure, religious, righteous, saintly, sublime, virtuous
➤ **Antonyms**
≠**sacred**: desecrated, unconsecrated, unhallowed, unholy, unsanctified ≠**devout**: blasphemous, corrupt, earthly, evil, human, immoral, impious, irreligious, sacrilegious, secular, sinful, unholy, wicked, worldly

homage *noun* = **respect**, admiration, adoration, adulation, awe, deference, devotion, duty, esteem, honour, reverence, worship
➤ **Antonyms**
condemnation, contempt, disdain, disregard,

disrespect, irreverence, scorn

home *noun* **1** = **dwelling**, abode, domicile, dwelling place, habitation, house, pad (*slang*), residence **2** = **birthplace**, family, fireside, hearth, homestead, home town, household **3** = **territory**, abode, element, environment, habitat, habitation, haunt, home ground, range, stamping ground **4 at home: a** = **in**, available, present **b** = **at ease**, comfortable, familiar, relaxed **c** = **having guests**, entertaining, giving a party, receiving **5 bring home to** = **make clear**, drive home, emphasize, impress upon, press home ◆ *adjective* **6** = **domestic**, central, familiar, family, household, inland, internal, local, national, native

homeland *noun* = **native land**, country of origin, fatherland, mother country, motherland

homeless *adjective* **1** = **destitute**, abandoned, displaced, dispossessed, down-and-out, exiled, forlorn, forsaken, outcast, unsettled ◆ *noun* **2 the homeless** = **vagrants**, dossers (*Brit. slang*), squatters

homely *adjective* = **comfortable**, comfy (*informal*), cosy, domestic, down-to-earth, everyday, familiar, friendly, homelike, homespun, homy, informal, modest, natural, ordinary, plain, simple, unaffected, unassuming, unfussy, unpretentious, welcoming
➤ **Antonyms**
affected, elaborate, elegant, grand, ostentatious, pretentious, refined, regal, sophisticated, splendid

homespun *adjective* = **unsophisticated**, artless, coarse, homely, home-made, inelegant, plain, rough, rude, rustic, unpolished

homicidal *adjective* = **murderous**, deadly, death-dealing, lethal, maniacal, mortal

homicide *noun* **1** = **murder**, bloodshed, killing, manslaughter, slaying **2** = **murderer**, killer, slayer

homily *noun* = **sermon**, address, discourse, lecture, preaching, preachment

homogeneity *noun* = **uniformity**, analogousness, comparability, consistency, correspondence, identicalness, oneness, sameness, similarity

homogeneous *adjective* = **uniform**, akin, alike, analogous, cognate, comparable, consistent, identical, kindred, similar, unvarying
➤ **Antonyms**
different, disparate, dissimilar, divergent, diverse, heterogeneous, manifold, mixed, unlike, unrelated, varied, various, varying

homologous *adjective* = **similar**, analogous, comparable, correspondent, corresponding, like, parallel, related

homosexual *adjective* = **gay**, bent (*slang*), camp (*informal*), dykey (*slang*), homoerotic, lesbian, moffie (*S. African slang*), pink (*informal*), queer (*informal, derogatory*), sapphic

hone *verb* = **sharpen**, edge, file, grind, point, polish, whet

honest *adjective* **1** = **trustworthy**, conscientious, decent, ethical, high-minded, honourable, law-abiding, reliable, reputable, scrupulous, trusty, truthful, upright, veracious, virtuous **2** = **open**, candid, direct, forthright, frank, ingenuous, outright, plain, round, sincere, straightforward, undisguised, unfeigned, upfront (*informal*) **3** = **fair**, equitable, fair and square, impartial, just
➤ **Antonyms**
≠**trustworthy**: bad, corrupt, crooked, deceitful, dishonest, guilty, immoral, treacherous, unethical, unfair, unfaithful, unlawful, unprincipled, unreliable, unrighteous, unscrupulous, untrustworthy, untruthful ≠**open**: disguised, false, insincere, secretive

honestly *adverb* **1** = **frankly**, candidly, in all sincerity, in plain English, plainly, straight (out), to one's face, truthfully **2** = **ethically**, by fair means, cleanly, honourably, in good faith, lawfully, legally, legitimately, on the level (*informal*), with clean hands

honesty *noun* **1** = **integrity**, faithfulness, fidelity, honour, incorruptibility, morality, probity, rectitude, reputability, scrupulousness, straightness, trustworthiness, truthfulness, uprightness, veracity, virtue **2** = **frankness**, bluntness, candour, equity, even-handedness, fairness, genuineness, openness, outspokenness, plainness, sincerity, straightforwardness

honorary *adjective* = **nominal**, complimentary, ex officio, in name *or* title only, titular, unofficial, unpaid

honour *noun* **1** = **integrity**, decency, fairness, goodness, honesty, morality, principles, probity, rectitude, righteousness, trustworthiness, uprightness **2** = **prestige**, credit, dignity, distinction, elevation, eminence, esteem, fame, glory, high standing, rank, renown, reputation, repute **3** = **tribute**, acclaim, accolade, adoration, Brownie points, commendation, deference, homage, kudos, praise, recognition, regard, respect, reverence, veneration **4** = **privilege**, compliment, credit, favour, pleasure, source of pride *or* satisfaction **5** *Old-fashioned* = **virginity**, chastity, innocence, modesty, purity, virtue ♦ *verb* **6** = **respect**, admire, adore, appreciate, esteem, exalt, glorify, hallow, prize, revere, reverence, value, venerate, worship **7** = **acclaim**, celebrate,

commemorate, commend, compliment, crack up (*informal*), decorate, dignify, exalt, glorify, laud, lionize, praise **8** = **pay**, accept, acknowledge, cash, clear, credit, pass, take **9** = **fulfil**, be as good as (*informal*), be faithful to, be true to, carry out, discharge, keep, live up to, observe
➤ **Antonyms**
noun ≠**integrity**: degradation, dishonesty, dishonour, insincerity, lowness, meanness, unscrupulousness ≠**prestige**: disgrace, dishonour, disrepute, disrespect, infamy, shame ≠**tribute**: condemnation, contempt, disfavour, insult, scorn, slight ♦ *verb* ≠**respect**, acclaim: condemn, defame, degrade, dishonour, insult, offend, scorn, slight ≠**pay**: refuse

honourable *adjective* **1** = **principled**, ethical, fair, high-minded, honest, just, moral, true, trustworthy, trusty, upright, upstanding, virtuous **2** = **respected**, creditable, estimable, proper, reputable, respectable, right, righteous, virtuous

honours *plural noun* = **titles**, awards, decorations, distinctions, laurels

hoodoo *noun Informal* = **jinx**, bad luck, curse, evil eye, evil star, hex (*U.S. & Canad. informal*), nemesis, voodoo

hoodwink *verb* = **deceive**, bamboozle (*informal*), befool, cheat, con (*informal*), delude, dupe, fool, hoax, kid (*informal*), lead up the garden path (*informal*), mislead, pull a fast one on (*informal*), rook (*slang*), sell a pup, swindle, take (someone) for a ride (*informal*), trick

hook *noun* **1** = **fastener**, catch, clasp, hasp, holder, link, lock, peg **2 by hook or by crook** = **by any means**, by fair means or foul, somehow, somehow or other, someway **3 hook, line, and sinker** *Informal* = **completely**, entirely, lock, stock and barrel, thoroughly, through and through, totally, utterly, wholly **4 off the hook** *Slang* = **let off**, acquitted, cleared, exonerated, in the clear, under no obligation, vindicated ♦ *verb* **5** = **fasten**, catch, clasp, fix, hasp, secure **6** = **catch**, enmesh, ensnare, entrap, snare, trap

hooked *adjective* **1** = **bent**, aquiline, curved, hook-shaped **2** *Slang* = **addicted**, devoted, enamoured, obsessed, taken, turned on (*slang*)

hooligan *noun* = **delinquent**, casual, hoodlum (*chiefly U.S.*), lager lout, ned (*Scot. slang*), rowdy, ruffian, tough, vandal, yob *or* yobbo (*Brit. slang*)

hooliganism *noun* = **delinquency**, disorder, loutishness, rowdiness, vandalism, violence, yobbishness

hoop *noun* = **ring**, band, circlet, girdle, loop,

round, wheel

hoot *noun* **1** = **toot 2** = **cry**, call **3** = **catcall**, boo, hiss, jeer, yell **4** *Informal* = **laugh**, card (*informal*), caution (*informal*), scream (*informal*) ♦ *verb* **5** = **toot 6** = **cry**, scream, shout, shriek, whoop, yell **7** = **jeer**, boo, catcall, condemn, decry, hiss, howl down, yell at

hop *verb* **1** = **jump**, bound, caper, dance, leap, skip, spring, trip, vault ♦ *noun* **2** = **jump**, bounce, bound, leap, skip, spring, step, vault

hope *verb* **1** = **desire**, anticipate, aspire, await, believe, contemplate, count on, cross one's fingers, expect, foresee, keep one's fingers crossed, long, look forward to, rely, set one's heart on, trust ♦ *noun* **2** = **belief**, ambition, anticipation, assumption, confidence, desire, dream, expectancy, expectation, faith, light at the end of the tunnel, longing
➤ **Antonyms**
noun ≠**belief**: despair, distrust, doubt, dread, hopelessness

hopeful *adjective* **1** = **optimistic**, anticipating, assured, buoyant, confident, expectant, looking forward to, sanguine **2** = **promising**, auspicious, bright, cheerful, encouraging, heartening, propitious, reassuring, rosy
➤ **Antonyms**
≠**optimistic**: cheerless, dejected, despairing, hopeless, pessimistic ≠**promising**: depressing, discouraging, disheartening, unpromising

hopefully *adverb* **1** = **optimistically**, confidently, expectantly, sanguinely **2** *Informal* = **it is hoped**, all being well, conceivably, expectedly, feasibly, probably

hopeless *adjective* **1** = **pessimistic**, abject, defeatist, dejected, demoralized, despairing, desperate, despondent, disconsolate, downhearted, forlorn, in despair, woebegone **2** = **impossible**, forlorn, futile, impracticable, not having a prayer, no-win, pointless, unachievable, unattainable, useless, vain **3** = **incurable**, helpless, irremediable, irreparable, irreversible, lost, past remedy, remediless **4** *Informal* = **no good**, inadequate, incompetent, ineffectual, inferior, pants (*informal*), pathetic, poor, useless (*informal*)
➤ **Antonyms**
≠**pessimistic**: assured, cheerful, confident, expectant, happy, heartened, hopeful, optimistic, uplifted ≠**incurable**: curable, remediable

hopelessly *adverb* **1** = **without hope**, beyond all hope, despairingly, in despair, irredeemably, irremediably **2** = **completely**, impossibly, totally, utterly

horde *noun* = **crowd**, band, crew, drove, gang, host, mob, multitude, pack, press, swarm, throng, troop

horizon *noun* **1** = **skyline**, field of vision, vista **2** *plural* = **scope**, ambit, compass, ken, perspective, prospect, purview, range, realm, sphere, stretch

horizontal *adjective* = **level**, flat, parallel

horny *adjective* = **aroused**, amorous, excited, lustful, randy (*informal, chiefly Brit.*), raunchy (*slang*), turned on (*slang*)

horrible *adjective* **1** = **dreadful**, awful, beastly (*informal*), cruel, disagreeable, ghastly (*informal*), horrid, mean, nasty, terrible, unkind, unpleasant **2** = **terrifying**, abhorrent, abominable, appalling, awful, dreadful, fearful, frightful, from hell (*informal*), ghastly, grim, grisly, gruesome, heinous, hideous, horrid, loathsome, obscene, repulsive, revolting, shameful, shocking, terrible
➤ **Antonyms**
agreeable, appealing, attractive, charming, cute, delightful, enchanting, fetching, lovely, pleasant, wonderful

horrid *adjective* **1** = **unpleasant**, awful, disagreeable, disgusting, dreadful, horrible, nasty, obscene, offensive, terrible, yucky *or* yukky (*slang*) **2** *Informal* = **unkind**, beastly (*informal*), cruel, mean, nasty

horrific *adjective* = **horrifying**, appalling, awful, dreadful, frightful, ghastly, grisly, horrendous, shocking, terrifying

horrify *verb* **1** = **terrify**, affright, alarm, frighten, gross out (*U.S. slang*), intimidate, make one's hair stand on end, petrify, put the wind up (*informal*), scare, terrorize **2** = **shock**, appal, disgust, dismay, outrage, sicken
➤ **Antonyms**
comfort, delight, enchant, encourage, gladden, hearten, please, reassure, soothe

horror *noun* **1** = **terror**, alarm, apprehension, awe, consternation, dismay, dread, fear, fright, panic **2** = **hatred**, abhorrence, abomination, antipathy, aversion, detestation, disgust, loathing, odium, repugnance, revulsion
➤ **Antonyms**
≠**hatred**: affinity, approval, attraction, delight, liking, love

horse *noun* = **nag**, colt, filly, gee-gee (*slang*), gelding, mare, mount, stallion, steed (*archaic or literary*)

horse around *or* **about** *verb Informal* = **play around**, clown, fool about *or* around, misbehave, play the fool, play the goat, roughhouse (*slang*)

horseman *noun* = **rider**, cavalier, cavalryman, dragoon, equestrian, horse-soldier, knight

horseplay *noun* = **rough-and-tumble**, buffoonery, clowning, fooling around, high jinks, pranks, romping, roughhousing (*slang*), skylarking (*informal*)

horse sense *noun* = **common sense**, gumption (*Brit. informal*), judgment, mother wit, nous (*Brit. slang*), practicality

hospitable *adjective* = **welcoming**, amicable, bountiful, cordial, friendly, generous, genial, gracious, kind, liberal, sociable
➤ **Antonyms**
inhospitable, parsimonious

hospitality *noun* = **welcome**, cheer, conviviality, cordiality, friendliness, heartiness, hospitableness, neighbourliness, sociability, warmth

host[1] *noun* **1** = **master of ceremonies**, entertainer, innkeeper, landlord *or* landlady, proprietor **2** = **presenter**, anchorman *or* anchorwoman, compere (*Brit.*) ◆ *verb* **3** = **present**, compere (*Brit.*), front (*informal*), introduce

host[2] *noun* = **multitude**, army, array, drove, horde, legion, myriad, swarm, throng

hostage *noun* = **prisoner**, captive, pawn, pledge, security, surety

hostile *adjective* **1** = **unfriendly**, antagonistic, anti (*informal*), bellicose, belligerent, contrary, ill-disposed, inimical, malevolent, opposed, opposite, rancorous, unkind, warlike **2** = **inhospitable**, adverse, alien, unpropitious, unsympathetic, unwelcoming
➤ **Antonyms**
≠**unfriendly:** affable, agreeable, amiable, approving, cordial, friendly, kind, peaceful, sympathetic, warm ≠**inhospitable:** congenial

hostilities *plural noun* = **warfare**, conflict, fighting, state of war, war
➤ **Antonyms**
alliance, ceasefire, peace, treaty, truce

hostility *noun* = **unfriendliness**, abhorrence, animosity, animus, antagonism, antipathy, aversion, bad blood, detestation, enmity, hatred, ill will, malevolence, malice, opposition, resentment
➤ **Antonyms**
agreement, amity, approval, congeniality, cordiality, friendliness, goodwill, sympathy

hot *adjective* **1** = **heated**, blistering, boiling, burning, fiery, flaming, piping hot, roasting, scalding, scorching, searing, steaming, sultry, sweltering, torrid, warm **2** = **spicy**, acrid, biting, peppery, piquant, pungent, sharp **3** = **passionate**, ablaze, animated, ardent, excited, fervent, fervid, fierce, fiery, flaming, impetuous, inflamed, intense,

irascible, lustful, raging, stormy, touchy, vehement, violent **4** = **new**, fresh, just out, latest, recent, up to the minute **5** = **popular**, approved, favoured, in demand, in vogue, sought-after **6** = **following closely**, close, in hot pursuit, near
➤ **Antonyms**
≠**heated:** chilly, cold, cool, freezing, frigid, frosty, icy, parky (*Brit. informal*) ≠**spicy:** mild ≠**passionate:** apathetic, calm, dispassionate, half-hearted, indifferent, mild, moderate ≠**new:** old, stale, trite ≠**popular:** out of favour, unpopular ≠**following closely:** cold

hot air *noun* = **empty talk**, blather, blether, bombast, bosh (*informal*), bunkum *or* buncombe (*chiefly U.S.*), claptrap (*informal*), gas (*informal*), guff (*slang*), rant, tall talk (*informal*), verbiage, wind

hotbed *noun* = **breeding ground**, den, forcing house, nest, nursery, seedbed

hot-blooded *adjective* = **passionate**, ardent, excitable, fervent, fiery, heated, impulsive, rash, spirited, temperamental, wild
➤ **Antonyms**
apathetic, calm, cold, cool, frigid, impassive, restrained, unenthusiastic

hotchpotch *noun* = **mixture**, conglomeration, farrago, hash, hodgepodge (*U.S.*), jumble, medley, *mélange*, mess, miscellany, mishmash, potpourri

hotfoot *adverb* = **speedily**, hastily, helter-skelter, hurriedly, pell-mell, posthaste, quickly

hot-headed *adjective* = **rash**, fiery, foolhardy, hasty, hot-tempered, impetuous, precipitate, quick-tempered, reckless, unruly, volatile

hothouse *noun* = **greenhouse**, conservatory, glasshouse

hotly *adverb* **1** = **passionately**, angrily, fiercely, heatedly, impetuously, indignantly, vehemently, with indignation **2** = **enthusiastically**, closely, eagerly, hotfoot, with enthusiasm

hound *verb* **1** = **pursue**, chase, drive, give chase, hunt, hunt down **2** = **harass**, badger, goad, harry, impel, persecute, pester, prod, provoke

house *noun* **1** = **home**, abode, building, domicile, dwelling, edifice, habitation, homestead, pad (*slang*), residence **2** = **household**, family, ménage **3** = **dynasty**, ancestry, clan, family tree, kindred, line, lineage, race, tribe **4** = **firm**, business, company, concern, establishment, organization, outfit (*informal*), partnership **5** = **assembly**, Commons, legislative body, parliament **6 on the house** = **free**, for nothing, gratis, without expense ♦ *verb* **7** = **accommodate**, billet, board, domicile, harbour, lodge, put up, quarter, take in **8** = **contain**, cover, keep, protect, sheathe, shelter, store

household *noun* **1** = **family**, home, house, ménage ♦ *adjective* **2** = **domestic**, family

householder *noun* = **occupant**, homeowner, resident, tenant

housekeeping *noun* = **household management**, home economy, homemaking (*U.S.*), housecraft, housewifery

housing *noun* **1** = **accommodation**, dwellings, homes, houses **2** = **case**, casing, container, cover, covering, enclosure, sheath

hovel *noun* = **hut**, cabin, den, hole, shack, shanty, shed

hover *verb* **1** = **float**, be suspended, drift, flutter, fly, hang, poise **2** = **linger**, hang about, wait nearby **3** = **waver**, alternate, dither (*chiefly Brit.*), falter, fluctuate, haver (*Brit.*), oscillate, pause, seesaw, swither (*Scot. dialect*), vacillate

however *adverb* = **nevertheless**, after all, anyhow, be that as it may, but, even though, nonetheless, notwithstanding, on the other hand, still, though, yet

howl *noun* **1** = **cry**, bawl, bay, bellow, clamour, groan, hoot, outcry, roar, scream, shriek, ululation, wail, yelp, yowl ♦ *verb* **2** = **cry**, bawl, bellow, cry out, lament, roar, scream, shout, shriek, ululate, wail, weep, yell, yelp

howler *noun Informal* = **mistake**, bloomer (*Brit. informal*), blunder, boob (*Brit. slang*), booboo (*informal*), bull (*slang*), clanger (*informal*), error, malapropism, schoolboy howler

hoyden *noun Old-fashioned* = **tomboy**

hoydenish *adjective Old-fashioned* = **unladylike**, boisterous, bold, ill-mannered, inelegant, uncouth, unfeminine, ungenteel, unruly

hub *noun* = **centre**, core, focal point, focus, heart, middle, nerve centre, pivot

hubbub *noun* = **noise**, babel, bedlam, brouhaha, clamour, confusion, din, disorder, disturbance, hue and cry, hullabaloo, hurly-burly, pandemonium, racket, riot, ruckus (*informal*), ruction (*informal*), rumpus, tumult, uproar

hubris *noun* = **pride**, arrogance, nemesis

huckster *noun* = **pedlar**, barker (*informal*), hawker, salesman, vendor

huddle *noun* **1** = **crowd**, confusion, disorder, heap, jumble, mass, mess, muddle **2** *Informal* = **conference**, confab (*informal*), discussion, meeting, powwow ♦ *verb* **3** = **crowd**, cluster, converge, flock, gather,

press, throng **4** = **curl up**, crouch, cuddle, hunch up, make oneself small, nestle, snuggle

hue *noun* = **colour**, dye, shade, tincture, tinge, tint, tone

hue and cry *noun* = **outcry**, brouhaha, clamour, furore, hullabaloo, much ado, ruction (*informal*), rumpus, uproar

huff *noun* **1** = **sulk**, anger, bad mood, miff (*informal*), passion, pet, pique, rage, temper **2 in a huff** = **offended**, angered, annoyed, hacked (off) (*U.S. slang*), hurt, in high dudgeon, irked, miffed (*informal*), nettled, peeved, piqued, pissed off (*taboo slang*), put out (*informal*), sulking (*informal*)

huffy *adjective* = **resentful**, angry, choked, cross, disgruntled, moody, moping, offended, peevish, pettish, petulant, querulous, snappy, sulky, sullen, surly
➤ **Antonyms**
amiable, cheerful, friendly, gay, good-humoured, happy, pleasant, sunny

hug *verb* **1** = **clasp**, cuddle, embrace, enfold, hold close, squeeze, take in one's arms **2** = **follow closely**, cling to, keep close, stay near ♦ *noun* **3** = **embrace**, bear hug, clasp, clinch (*slang*), squeeze

huge *adjective* = **enormous**, Brobdingnagian, bulky, colossal, elephantine, extensive, gargantuan, giant, gigantic, ginormous (*informal*), great, humongous *or* humungous (*U.S. slang*), immense, jumbo (*informal*), large, mammoth, massive, mega (*slang*), monumental, mountainous, prodigious, stellar (*informal*), stupendous, titanic, tremendous, vast
➤ **Antonyms**
insignificant, little, microscopic, minute, petty, puny, small, tiny

huggermugger *noun Archaic* = **confusion**, disarray, disorder, disorganization, guddle (*Scot.*), hodgepodge (*U.S.*), hotchpotch, huddle, jumble, mess, muddle, pig's breakfast (*informal*), shambles, state

hulk *noun* **1** = **wreck**, derelict, frame, hull, shell, shipwreck **2** *Disparaging* = **oaf**, lout, lubber, lump (*informal*)

hulking *adjective* = **ungainly**, awkward, bulky, clumsy, clunky (*informal*), cumbersome, gross, lubberly, lumbering, lumpish, massive, oafish, overgrown, ponderous, unwieldy

hull *noun* **1** = **frame**, body, casing, covering, framework, skeleton **2** = **husk**, peel, pod, rind, shell, shuck, skin ♦ *verb* **3** = **peel**, husk, shell, shuck, skin, trim

hullabaloo *noun* = **commotion**, babel, bedlam, brouhaha, clamour, confusion, din, disturbance, furore, hubbub, hue and cry, hurly-burly, noise, outcry, pandemonium, racket, ruckus (*informal*), ruction (*informal*), rumpus, to-do, tumult, turmoil, upheaval, uproar

hum *verb* **1** = **drone**, buzz, croon, mumble, murmur, purr, sing, throb, thrum, vibrate, whir **2** *Informal* = **be busy**, be active, bustle, buzz, move, pulsate, pulse, stir, vibrate

human *adjective* **1** = **mortal**, anthropoid, fleshly, manlike **2** = **kind**, approachable, compassionate, considerate, fallible, forgivable, humane, kindly, natural, understandable, understanding, vulnerable ♦ *noun* **3** = **human being**, body, child, creature, individual, man or woman, mortal, person, soul
➤ **Antonyms**
adjective ≠**mortal**: animal, nonhuman ≠**kind**: beastly, brutish, cruel, inhuman, unsympathetic ♦ *noun* ≠**human being**: animal, god, nonhuman

humane *adjective* = **kind**, benevolent, benign, charitable, clement, compassionate, forbearing, forgiving, gentle, good, good-natured, kind-hearted, kindly, lenient, merciful, mild, sympathetic, tender, understanding
➤ **Antonyms**
barbarous, brutal, cruel, inhuman, inhumane, ruthless, uncivilized, unkind, unmerciful, unsympathetic

humanitarian *adjective* **1** = **philanthropic**, altruistic, beneficent, benevolent, charitable, compassionate, humane, public-spirited ♦ *noun* **2** = **philanthropist**, altruist, benefactor, Good Samaritan

humanitarianism *noun* = **philanthropy**, beneficence, benevolence, charity, generosity, goodwill, humanism

humanities *plural noun* = **classical studies**, classics, liberal arts, literae humaniores

humanity *noun* **1** = **human race**, flesh, Homo sapiens, humankind, man, mankind, men, mortality, people **2** = **human nature**, humanness, mortality **3** = **kindness**, benevolence, benignity, brotherly love, charity, compassion, fellow feeling, kind-heartedness, mercy, philanthropy, sympathy, tenderness, tolerance, understanding

humanize *verb* = **civilize**, cultivate, educate, enlighten, improve, mellow, polish, reclaim, refine, soften, tame

humble *adjective* **1** = **modest**, meek, self-effacing, submissive, unassuming, unostentatious, unpretentious **2** = **lowly**, common, commonplace, insignificant, low, low-born, mean, modest, obscure, ordinary, plebeian, poor, simple, undistinguished, unimportant, unpretentious ♦ *verb* **3**

= **humiliate**, abase, abash, break, bring down, chagrin, chasten, crush, debase, degrade, demean, disgrace, lower, mortify, put down (*slang*), put (someone) in their place, reduce, shame, sink, subdue, take down a peg (*informal*)
➤ **Antonyms**
adjective ≠**modest**: arrogant, assuming, conceited, haughty, immodest, lordly, ostentatious, overbearing, pompous, presumptuous, pretentious, proud, snobbish, superior, vain ≠**lowly**: aristocratic, distinguished, elegant, famous, glorious, high, important, rich, significant, superior, wealthy ♦ *verb* ≠**humiliate**: elevate, exalt, magnify, raise

humbly *adverb* = **meekly**, cap in hand, deferentially, diffidently, modestly, obsequiously, on bended knee, respectfully, servilely, submissively, subserviently, unassumingly

humbug *noun* **1** = **nonsense**, baloney (*informal*), cant, claptrap (*informal*), eyewash (*informal*), hypocrisy, quackery, rubbish, trash **2** = **deception**, bluff, canard, cheat, deceit, dodge, feint, fraud, hoax, imposition, imposture, ruse, sham, swindle, trick, trickery, wile **3** = **fraud**, charlatan, cheat, con man (*informal*), faker, fraudster, impostor, phoney or phony (*informal*), quack, swindler, trickster

humdrum *adjective* = **dull**, banal, boring, commonplace, dreary, ho-hum (*informal*), mind-numbing, monotonous, mundane, ordinary, repetitious, routine, tedious, tiresome, uneventful, uninteresting, unvaried, wearisome
➤ **Antonyms**
dramatic, entertaining, exciting, extraordinary, interesting, lively, sexy (*informal*), stimulating

humid *adjective* = **damp**, clammy, dank, moist, muggy, steamy, sticky, sultry, watery, wet
➤ **Antonyms**
arid, dry, sunny, torrid

humidity *noun* = **damp**, clamminess, dampness, dankness, dew, humidness, moistness, moisture, mugginess, sogginess, wetness

humiliate *verb* = **embarrass**, abase, abash, bring low, chasten, crush, debase, degrade, discomfit, disgrace, humble, make (someone) eat humble pie, mortify, put down, put (someone) in their place, shame, subdue, take down a peg (*informal*), take the wind out of someone's sails
➤ **Antonyms**
elevate, honour, magnify, make proud

humiliating *adjective* = **embarrassing**, cringe-making (*Brit. informal*), cringeworthy

(*Brit. informal*), crushing, degrading, disgracing, humbling, ignominious, mortifying, shaming, toe-curling (*slang*)

humiliation *noun* = **embarrassment**, abasement, affront, chagrin, condescension, degradation, disgrace, dishonour, humbling, ignominy, indignity, loss of face, mortification, put-down, resignation, self-abasement, shame, submission, submissiveness

humility *noun* = **modesty**, diffidence, humbleness, lack of pride, lowliness, meekness, self-abasement, servility, submissiveness, unpretentiousness
➤ **Antonyms**
arrogance, conceit, disdain, haughtiness, pomposity, presumption, pretentiousness, pride, snobbishness, superciliousness, superiority, vanity

hummock *noun* = **hillock**, hump, knoll, mound

humorist *noun* = **comedian**, card (*informal*), comic, eccentric, funny man, jester, joker, wag, wit

humorous *adjective* = **funny**, amusing, comic, comical, droll, entertaining, facetious, farcical, hilarious, jocose, jocular, laughable, ludicrous, merry, playful, side-splitting, waggish, whimsical, witty
➤ **Antonyms**
earnest, grave, sad, serious, sober, solemn

humour *noun* **1** = **funniness**, amusement, comedy, drollery, facetiousness, fun, jocularity, ludicrousness **2** = **joking**, comedy, farce, gags (*informal*), jesting, jests, jokes, pleasantry, wisecracks (*informal*), wit, witticisms, wittiness **3** = **mood**, disposition, frame of mind, spirits, temper ◆ *verb* **4** = **indulge**, accommodate, cosset, favour, fawn on, feed, flatter, go along with, gratify, mollify, pamper, pander to, spoil
➤ **Antonyms**
noun ≠**funniness**: gravity, grief, melancholy, sadness, seriousness, sobriety, solemnity, sorrow ◆ *verb* ≠**indulge**: aggravate, excite, oppose, rouse, stand up to

humourless *adjective* = **serious**, dour, dry, heavy-going, intense, po-faced, solemn, straight, unamused, unamusing, unfunny, unsmiling

hump *noun* **1** = **lump**, bulge, bump, hunch, knob, mound, projection, protrusion, protuberance, swelling **2** *As in* **get the hump** *Brit. informal* = **sulks**, blues, doldrums, dumps (*informal*), grumps (*informal*), megrims (*rare*), mopes ◆ *verb* **3** *Slang* = **carry**, heave, hoist, lug, shoulder

hunch *noun* **1** = **feeling**, idea, impression, inkling, intuition, premonition, presentiment, suspicion ◆ *verb* **2** = **draw in**, arch, bend,

crouch, curve, huddle, hump, squat, stoop, tense

hunchback *noun* = **humpback**, Quasimodo

hunchbacked *adjective* = **humpbacked**, deformed, humped, malformed, misshapen, stooped

hunger *noun* **1** = **appetite**, emptiness, hungriness, ravenousness, voracity **2** = **starvation**, famine **3** = **desire**, ache, appetite, craving, greediness, itch, lust, thirst, yearning, yen (*informal*) ◆ *verb* **4** = **want**, ache, crave, desire, hanker, hope, itch, long, pine, starve, thirst, wish, yearn

hungry *adjective* **1** = **empty**, famished, famishing, hollow, peckish (*informal, chiefly Brit.*), ravenous, sharp-set, starved, starving, voracious **2** = **eager**, athirst, avid, covetous, craving, desirous, greedy, keen, yearning

hunk *noun* = **lump**, block, chunk, gobbet, mass, nugget, piece, slab, wedge, wodge (*Brit. informal*)

hunt *verb* **1** = **stalk**, chase, gun for, hound, pursue, track, trail **2** = **search**, ferret about, forage, go in quest of, look, look high and low, rummage through, scour, seek, try to find ◆ *noun* **3** = **search**, chase, hunting, investigation, pursuit, quest

hunter *noun* = **huntsman** *or* **huntress**, sportsman *or* sportswoman

hurdle *noun* **1** = **fence**, barricade, barrier, block, hedge, wall **2** = **obstacle**, barrier, block, complication, difficulty, handicap, hazard, hindrance, impediment, obstruction, snag, stumbling block

hurl *verb* = **throw**, cast, chuck (*informal*), fire, fling, heave, launch, let fly, pitch, project, propel, send, shy, sling, toss

hurly-burly *noun* = **commotion**, bedlam, brouhaha, chaos, confusion, disorder, furore, hubbub, pandemonium, tumult, turbulence, turmoil, upheaval, uproar
➤ **Antonyms**
composure, order, organization, tidiness

hurricane *noun* = **storm**, cyclone, gale, tempest, tornado, twister (*U.S. informal*), typhoon, windstorm

hurried *adjective* = **hasty**, breakneck, brief, cursory, hectic, perfunctory, precipitate, quick, quickie (*informal*), rushed, short, slapdash, speedy, superficial, swift

hurriedly *adverb* = **hastily**, hurry-scurry, in a rush, perfunctorily, quickly

hurry *verb* **1** = **rush**, barrel (along) (*informal, chiefly U.S. & Canad.*), burn rubber (*informal*), dash, fly, get a move on (*informal*), get one's skates on (*informal*), lose no time, make haste, scoot, scurry, step on it (*informal*) **2** = **speed (up)**, accelerate, expedite, goad, hasten, hustle, push on,

quicken, urge ♦ *noun* **3** = **haste**, bustle, celerity, commotion, dispatch, expedition, flurry, precipitation, promptitude, quickness, rush, speed, urgency
➤ **Antonyms**
verb ≠**rush**: crawl, creep, dawdle, drag one's feet, move slowly ≠**speed (up)**: delay, retard, slow, slow down ♦ *noun* ≠**haste**: calmness, slowness

hurt *verb* **1** = **harm**, bruise, damage, disable, impair, injure, lay a finger on, mar, spoil, wound **2** = **ache**, be sore, be tender, burn, smart, sting, throb **3** = **upset**, afflict, aggrieve, annoy, cut to the quick, distress, grieve, pain, sadden, sting, wound ♦ *noun* **4** = **distress**, discomfort, pain, pang, soreness, suffering ♦ *adjective* **5** = **injured**, bruised, cut, damaged, grazed, harmed, scarred, scraped, scratched, wounded **6** = **upset**, aggrieved, crushed, injured, miffed (*informal*), offended, pained, piqued, rueful, sad, wounded
➤ **Antonyms**
verb ≠**harm**: alleviate, cure, heal, relieve, repair, restore, soothe ♦ *noun* ≠**distress**: delight, happiness, joy, pleasure, pride, satisfaction ♦ *adjective* ≠**injured**: alleviated, assuaged, healed, relieved, repaired, restored, soothed ≠**upset**: calmed, consoled, placated

hurtful *adjective* = **unkind**, cruel, cutting, damaging, destructive, detrimental, disadvantageous, distressing, harmful, injurious, malicious, mean, mischievous, nasty, spiteful, upsetting, wounding

hurtle *verb* = **rush**, charge, crash, fly, plunge, race, shoot, speed, stampede, tear

husband *noun* **1** = **partner**, better half (*humorous*), bridegroom, man (*informal*), mate, old man (*informal*), significant other (*U.S. informal*), spouse ♦ *verb* **2** = **economize**, budget, conserve, hoard, manage thriftily, save, store, use sparingly
➤ **Antonyms**
verb ≠**economize**: be extravagant, fritter away, spend, splash out (*informal, chiefly Brit.*), squander

husbandry *noun* **1** = **farming**, agriculture, agronomy, cultivation, land management, tillage **2** = **thrift**, careful management, economy, frugality, good housekeeping

hush *verb* **1** = **quieten**, mute, muzzle, shush, silence, still, suppress ♦ *noun* **2** = **quiet**, calm, peace, peacefulness, silence, still (*poetic*), stillness, tranquillity

hush-hush *adjective* = **secret**, classified, confidential, restricted, top-secret, under wraps

hush up *verb* = **cover up**, conceal, draw a veil over, keep dark, keep secret, sit on

(*informal*), smother, squash, suppress, sweep under the carpet (*informal*)

husk *noun* = **rind**, bark, chaff, covering, hull, shuck

huskiness *noun* = **hoarseness**, dryness, harshness, raspingness, roughness

husky *adjective* **1** = **hoarse**, croaking, croaky, gruff, guttural, harsh, rasping, raucous, rough, throaty **2** *Informal* = **muscular**, beefy (*informal*), brawny, burly, hefty, powerful, rugged, stocky, strapping, thickset

hussy *noun* Old-fashioned = **slut**, baggage (*informal, old-fashioned*), floozy (*slang*), jade, scrubber (*Brit. & Austral. slang*), slapper (*Brit. slang*), strumpet, tart (*informal*), tramp (*slang*), trollop, wanton

hustle *verb* = **jostle**, bustle, crowd, elbow, force, haste, hasten, hurry, impel, jog, push, rush, shove, thrust

hut *noun* = **shed**, cabin, den, hovel, lean-to, refuge, shanty, shelter

hybrid *noun* = **crossbreed**, amalgam, composite, compound, cross, half-blood, half-breed, mixture, mongrel, mule

hygiene *noun* = **cleanliness**, hygienics, sanitary measures, sanitation

hygienic *adjective* = **clean**, aseptic, disinfected, germ-free, healthy, pure, salutary, sanitary, sterile
➤ **Antonyms**
dirty, filthy, germ-ridden, harmful, insanitary, polluted, unhealthy, unhygienic, unwholesome

hymn *noun* = **song of praise**, anthem, canticle, carol, chant, doxology, paean, psalm

hype *noun* Slang = **publicity**, ballyhoo (*informal*), brouhaha, build-up, plugging (*informal*), promotion, puffing, razzmatazz (*slang*)

hyperbole *noun* = **exaggeration**, amplification, enlargement, magnification, overstatement

hypercritical *adjective* = **fault-finding**, captious, carping, cavilling, censorious, finicky, fussy, hairsplitting, niggling, overcritical, overexacting, overscrupulous, pernickety (*informal*), strict

hypnotic *adjective* = **mesmerizing**, mesmeric, narcotic, sleep-inducing, somniferous, soothing, soporific, spellbinding

hypnotize *verb* **1** = **mesmerize**, put in a trance, put to sleep **2** = **fascinate**, absorb, entrance, magnetize, spellbind

hypochondria *noun* = **valetudinarianism**

hypochondriac *adjective, noun* = **valetudinarian**

hypocrisy *noun* = **insincerity**, cant, deceit,

deceitfulness, deception, dissembling, duplicity, falsity, imposture, phoneyness or phoniness (*informal*), pretence, sanctimoniousness, speciousness, two-facedness
➤ **Antonyms**
honesty, sincerity, truthfulness

hypocrite *noun* = **fraud**, charlatan, deceiver, dissembler, impostor, pharisee, phoney or phony (*informal*), pretender, whited sepulchre

hypocritical *adjective* = **insincere**, canting, deceitful, deceptive, dissembling, duplicitous, false, fraudulent, hollow, pharisaical, phoney or phony (*informal*), sanctimonious, specious, spurious, two-faced

hypodermic *noun* = **syringe**, needle

hypothesis *noun* = **assumption**, postulate, premise, premiss, proposition, supposition, theory, thesis

hypothetical *adjective* = **theoretical**, academic, assumed, conjectural, imaginary, putative, speculative, supposed
➤ **Antonyms**
actual, confirmed, established, known, proven, real, true

hysteria *noun* = **frenzy**, agitation, delirium, hysterics, madness, panic, unreason

hysterical *adjective* **1** = **frenzied**, berserk, beside oneself, convulsive, crazed, distracted, distraught, frantic, mad, overwrought, raving, uncontrollable **2** *Informal* = **hilarious**, comical, farcical, screaming, side-splitting, uproarious, wildly funny
➤ **Antonyms**
≠frenzied: calm, composed, poised, self-possessed, unfazed (*informal*)
≠hilarious: grave, melancholy, sad, serious

I i

ice *noun* **1 break the ice** = **begin**, initiate the proceedings, kick off (*informal*), lead the way, make a start, start *or* set the ball rolling (*informal*), take the plunge (*informal*) **2 on thin ice** = **unsafe**, at risk, in jeopardy, open to attack, out on a limb, sticking one's neck out (*informal*), vulnerable

ice-cold *adjective* = **freezing**, arctic, biting, bitter, chilled to the bone *or* marrow, frozen, glacial, icy, raw, refrigerated, shivering

icy *adjective* **1** = **cold**, arctic, biting, bitter, chill, chilling, chilly, freezing, frost-bound, frosty, frozen over, ice-cold, parky (*Brit. informal*), raw **2** = **slippery**, glacial, glassy, like a sheet of glass, rimy, slippy (*informal or dialect*) **3** = **unfriendly**, aloof, cold, distant, forbidding, frigid, frosty, glacial, hostile, indifferent, steely, stony, unwelcoming
➤ **Antonyms**
≠**cold**: blistering, boiling, hot, sizzling, warm ≠**unfriendly**: cordial, friendly, gracious, warm

idea *noun* **1** = **thought**, abstraction, concept, conception, conclusion, fancy, impression, judgment, perception, understanding **2** = **plan**, design, hypothesis, recommendation, scheme, solution, suggestion, theory **3** = **belief**, conviction, doctrine, interpretation, notion, opinion, teaching, view, viewpoint **4** = **impression**, approximation, ballpark figure, clue, estimate, guess, hint, inkling, intimation, notion, suspicion **5** = **intention**, aim, end, import, meaning, object, objective, plan, purpose, *raison d'être*, reason, sense, significance

ideal *noun* **1** = **model**, archetype, criterion, epitome, example, exemplar, last word, nonpareil, paradigm, paragon, pattern, perfection, prototype, standard, standard of perfection **2** *often plural* = **principle**, moral value, standard ♦ *adjective* **3** = **perfect**, archetypal, classic, complete, consummate, model, optimal, quintessential, supreme **4** = **imaginary**, fanciful, impractical, ivory-tower, unattainable, unreal, Utopian, visionary
➤ **Antonyms**
adjective ≠**perfect**: deficient, flawed, impaired, imperfect, unsuitable ≠**imaginary**: actual, factual, literal, mundane, ordinary, real

idealist *noun* = **romantic**, dreamer, Utopian, visionary

idealistic *adjective* = **perfectionist**, impracticable, optimistic, quixotic, romantic, starry-eyed, Utopian, visionary
➤ **Antonyms**
down-to-earth, practical, pragmatic, realistic, sensible

idealize *verb* = **romanticize**, apotheosize, ennoble, exalt, glorify, magnify, put on a pedestal, worship

ideally *adverb* = **in a perfect world**, all things being equal, if one had one's way, under the best of circumstances

identical *adjective* = **alike**, a dead ringer (*slang*), corresponding, duplicate, equal, equivalent, indistinguishable, interchangeable, like, like two peas in a pod, matching, selfsame, the dead spit (*informal*), the same, twin
➤ **Antonyms**
different, disparate, distinct, diverse, separate, unlike

identification *noun* **1** = **recognition**, cataloguing, classifying, establishment of identity, labelling, naming, pinpointing **2** = **sympathy**, association, connection, empathy, fellow feeling, involvement, rapport, relationship **3** = **identity card**, credentials, ID, letters of introduction, papers

identify *verb* **1** = **recognize**, catalogue, classify, diagnose, flag, label, make out, name, pick out, pinpoint, place, put one's finger on (*informal*), single out, spot, tag **2 identify with** = **relate to**, ally with, associate with, empathize with, feel for, put in the same category as, put oneself in the place *or* shoes of, respond to, see through another's eyes, think of in connection with

identity *noun* **1** = **existence**, distinctiveness, individuality, oneness, particularity, personality, self, selfhood, singularity, uniqueness **2** = **sameness**, accord, correspondence, empathy, rapport, unanimity, unity

idiocy *noun* = **foolishness**, abject stupidity, asininity, cretinism, fatuity, fatuousness, imbecility, inanity, insanity, lunacy, senselessness, tomfoolery
➤ **Antonyms**
acumen, sagacity, sanity, sense, soundness, wisdom

idiom *noun* **1** = **phrase**, expression, locution, set phrase, turn of phrase **2** = **language**, jargon, mode of expression, parlance, style, talk, usage, vernacular

idiomatic *adjective* = **vernacular**, dialectal, native

idiosyncrasy *noun* = **peculiarity**, affectation, characteristic, eccentricity, habit, mannerism, oddity, personal trait, quirk, singularity, trick

idiot *noun* = **fool**, airhead (*slang*), ass, berk (*Brit. slang*), blockhead, booby, charlie (*Brit. informal*), chump, coot, cretin, dickhead (*slang*), dickwit (*slang*), dimwit (*informal*), dipstick (*Brit. slang*), divvy (*Brit. slang*), dork (*slang*), dumb-ass (*slang*), dunderhead, dweeb (*U.S. slang*), fuckwit (*taboo slang*), geek (*slang*), gobshite (*Irish taboo slang*), gonzo (*slang*), halfwit, imbecile, jerk (*slang, chiefly U.S. & Canad.*), lamebrain (*informal*), mooncalf, moron, nerd *or* nurd (*slang*), nincompoop, nitwit (*informal*), numbskull *or* numskull, numpty (*Scot. informal*), oaf, pillock (*Brit. slang*), plank (*Brit. slang*), plonker (*slang*), prat (*slang*), prick (*derogatory slang*), schmuck (*U.S. slang*), simpleton, twit (*informal, chiefly Brit.*), wally (*slang*)

idiotic *adjective* = **foolish**, asinine, braindead (*informal*), crackpot (*informal*), crazy, daft (*informal*), dumb (*informal*), dumb-ass (*slang*), fatuous, foolhardy, halfwitted, harebrained, imbecile, imbecilic, inane, insane, loopy (*informal*), lunatic, moronic, senseless, stupid, unintelligent
➤ **Antonyms**
brilliant, commonsensical, intelligent, sensible, thoughtful, wise

idle *adjective* 1 = **inactive**, dead, empty, gathering dust, jobless, mothballed, out of action *or* operation, out of work, redundant, stationary, ticking over, unemployed, unoccupied, unused, vacant 2 = **lazy**, good-for-nothing, indolent, lackadaisical, shiftless, slothful, sluggish 3 = **useless**, abortive, bootless, fruitless, futile, groundless, ineffective, of no avail, otiose, pointless, unavailing, unproductive, unsuccessful, vain, worthless 4 = **trivial**, frivolous, insignificant, irrelevant, nugatory, superficial, unhelpful, unnecessary ◆ *verb* 5 *often with* **away** = **laze**, dally, dawdle, fool, fritter, hang out (*informal*), kill time, loaf, loiter, lounge, potter, waste, while 6 = **skive** (*Brit. slang*), bob off (*Brit. slang*), coast, drift, mark time, shirk, sit back and do nothing, slack, slow down, take it easy, vegetate, veg out (*slang*)
➤ **Antonyms**
adjective ≠**inactive**, lazy: active, busy, employed, energetic, functional, industrious, occupied, operative, working ≠**useless**: advantageous, effective, fruitful, profitable,

useful, worthwhile ≠**trivial**: important, meaningful

idleness *noun* 1 = **inactivity**, inaction, leisure, time on one's hands, unemployment 2 = **laziness**, hibernation, inertia, shiftlessness, sloth, sluggishness, torpor, vegetating 3 = **loafing**, dilly-dallying (*informal*), lazing, pottering, skiving (*Brit. slang*), time-wasting, trifling

idling *noun, adjective* = **loafing**, dawdling, drifting, pottering, resting, resting on one's oars, taking it easy, ticking over

idol *noun* 1 = **hero**, beloved, darling, fave (*informal*), favourite, pet, pin-up (*slang*), superstar 2 = **graven image**, deity, god, image, pagan symbol

idolater *noun* 1 = **heathen**, idol-worshipper, pagan 2 = **admirer**, adorer, devotee, idolizer, votary, worshipper

idolatrous *adjective* = **adoring**, adulatory, reverential, uncritical, worshipful

idolatry *noun* = **adoration**, adulation, apotheosis, deification, exaltation, glorification, hero worship, idolizing

idolize *verb* = **worship**, admire, adore, apotheosize, bow down before, deify, dote upon, exalt, glorify, hero-worship, look up to, love, revere, reverence, venerate, worship to excess

idyllic *adjective* = **idealized**, arcadian, charming, halcyon, heavenly, ideal, peaceful, picturesque, unspoiled

if *conjunction* 1 = **provided**, admitting, allowing, assuming, granting, in case, on condition that, on the assumption that, providing, supposing, though, whenever, wherever, whether ◆ *noun* 2 = **doubt**, condition, hesitation, stipulation, uncertainty

ignite *verb* 1 = **catch fire**, burn, burst into flames, fire, flare up, inflame, take fire 2 = **set fire to**, kindle, light, put a match to (*informal*), set alight, torch, touch off

ignominious *adjective* = **humiliating**, abject, despicable, discreditable, disgraceful, dishonourable, disreputable, indecorous, inglorious, mortifying, scandalous, shameful, sorry, undignified
➤ **Antonyms**
creditable, honourable, reputable, worthy

ignominy *noun* = **disgrace**, bad odour, contempt, discredit, dishonour, disrepute, humiliation, infamy, mortification, obloquy, odium, opprobrium, reproach, shame, stigma
➤ **Antonyms**
credit, honour, repute

ignorance *noun* 1 = **unawareness**, greenness, inexperience, innocence, nescience (*literary*), oblivion,

unconsciousness, unfamiliarity **2 = lack of education**, benightedness, blindness, illiteracy, mental darkness, unenlightenment, unintelligence
➤ **Antonyms**
≠**lack of education**: comprehension, enlightenment, insight, intelligence, knowledge, understanding, wisdom

ignorant *adjective* **1 = uninformed**, benighted, blind to, inexperienced, innocent, in the dark about, oblivious, out of the loop, unaware, unconscious, unenlightened, uninitiated, unknowing, unschooled, unwitting **2 = uneducated**, as green as grass, green, illiterate, naive, unaware, uncultivated, unknowledgeable, unlearned, unlettered, unread, untaught, untrained, untutored, wet behind the ears (*informal*) **3 = insensitive**, crass, crude, gross, half-baked (*informal*), rude, shallow, superficial, uncomprehending, unscholarly
➤ **Antonyms**
≠**uninformed**: aware, conscious, informed, in the loop ≠**uneducated**: astute, brilliant, cultured, educated, knowledgeable, learned, literate, sagacious, sophisticated, wise

ignore *verb* = **overlook**, be oblivious to, blank (*slang*), bury one's head in the sand, cold-shoulder, cut (*informal*), discount, disregard, give the cold shoulder to, neglect, pass over, pay no attention to, reject, send (someone) to Coventry, shut one's eyes to, take no notice of, turn a blind eye to, turn a deaf ear to, turn one's back on
➤ **Antonyms**
acknowledge, heed, note, pay attention to, recognize, regard

ill *adjective* **1 = unwell**, ailing, at death's door, dicky (*Brit. informal*), diseased, funny (*informal*), green about the gills, indisposed, infirm, laid up (*informal*), not up to snuff (*informal*), off-colour, on the sick list (*informal*), out of sorts (*informal*), poorly (*informal*), queasy, seedy (*informal*), sick, under the weather (*informal*), unhealthy, valetudinarian **2 = harmful**, bad, damaging, deleterious, detrimental, evil, foul, iniquitous, injurious, ruinous, unfortunate, unlucky, vile, wicked, wrong **3 = hostile**, acrimonious, adverse, antagonistic, cantankerous, cross, harsh, hateful, hurtful, inimical, malevolent, malicious, sullen, surly, unfriendly, unkind **4 = ominous**, bodeful, disturbing, foreboding, inauspicious, sinister, threatening, unfavourable, unhealthy, unlucky, unpromising, unpropitious, unwholesome
♦ *noun* **5 = harm**, affliction, hardship, hurt, injury, misery, misfortune, pain, trial, tribulation, trouble, unpleasantness, woe **6 = evil**, abuse, badness, cruelty, damage,

depravity, destruction, ill usage, malice, mischief, suffering, wickedness ♦ *adverb* **7 = badly**, hard, inauspiciously, poorly, unfavourably, unfortunately, unluckily **8 = hardly**, barely, by no means, insufficiently, scantily **9** As in **ill-gotten = illegally**, criminally, dishonestly, foully, fraudulently, illegitimately, illicitly, unlawfully, unscrupulously
➤ **Antonyms**
adjective ≠**unwell**: hale, healthy, strong, well ≠**harmful**: favourable, good ≠**hostile**: generous, kind ♦ *noun* ≠**evil**: good, kindness ♦ *adverb* ≠**hardly**: easily, well

ill-advised *adjective* = **misguided**, foolhardy, foolish, ill-considered, ill-judged, impolitic, imprudent, inappropriate, incautious, indiscreet, injudicious, overhasty, rash, reckless, short-sighted, thoughtless, unseemly, unwise, wrong-headed
➤ **Antonyms**
appropriate, cautious, discreet, judicious, politic, prudent, seemly, sensible, wise

ill-assorted *adjective* = **incompatible**, incongruous, inharmonious, mismatched, uncongenial, unsuited

ill at ease *adjective* = **uncomfortable**, antsy (*informal*), anxious, awkward, disquieted, disturbed, edgy, faltering, fidgety, hesitant, like a fish out of water, nervous, neurotic, on edge, on pins and needles (*informal*), on tenterhooks, out of place, restless, self-conscious, strange, tense, twitchy (*informal*), uneasy, unquiet, unrelaxed, unsettled, unsure, wired (*slang*)
➤ **Antonyms**
at ease, at home, comfortable, easy, quiet, relaxed, settled, sure

ill-bred *adjective* = **bad-mannered**, boorish, churlish, coarse, crass, discourteous, ill-mannered, impolite, indelicate, rude, uncivil, uncivilized, uncouth, ungallant, ungentlemanly, unladylike, unmannerly, unrefined, vulgar
➤ **Antonyms**
civil, courteous, delicate, mannerly, refined, urbane, well-bred

ill-defined *adjective* = **unclear**, blurred, dim, fuzzy, indistinct, nebulous, shadowy, vague, woolly
➤ **Antonyms**
apparent, bold, clear, conspicuous, cut-and-dried, distinct, evident, manifest, obvious, plain

ill-disposed *adjective* = **unfriendly**, against, antagonistic, anti (*informal*), antipathetic, averse, disobliging, down on (*informal*), hostile, inimical, opposed, uncooperative, unwelcoming
➤ **Antonyms**
amicable, cooperative, friendly, obliging,

welcoming, well-disposed

illegal *adjective* = **unlawful**, actionable (*Law*), banned, black-market, bootleg, criminal, felonious, forbidden, illicit, lawless, off limits, outlawed, prohibited, proscribed, unauthorized, unconstitutional, under-the-counter, under-the-table, unlicensed, unofficial, wrongful
➤ **Antonyms**
lawful, legal, licit, permissible

illegality *noun* = **crime**, criminality, felony, illegitimacy, illicitness, lawlessness, unlawfulness, wrong, wrongness

illegible *adjective* = **indecipherable**, crabbed, faint, hard to make out, hieroglyphic, obscure, scrawled, undecipherable, unreadable
➤ **Antonyms**
clear, decipherable, legible, plain, readable

illegitimate *adjective* **1** = **born out of wedlock**, baseborn (*archaic*), bastard, born on the wrong side of the blanket, fatherless, misbegotten (*literary*) **2** = **unlawful**, illegal, illicit, improper, unauthorized, unconstitutional, under-the-table, unsanctioned **3** = **invalid**, illogical, incorrect, spurious, unsound
➤ **Antonyms**
≠unlawful: authorized, constitutional, lawful, legal, legitimate, proper, sanctioned

ill-fated *adjective* = **doomed**, blighted, hapless, ill-omened, ill-starred, luckless, star-crossed, unfortunate, unhappy, unlucky

ill feeling *noun* = **hostility**, animosity, animus, antagonism, bad blood, bitterness, chip on one's shoulder, disgruntlement, dissatisfaction, dudgeon (*archaic*), enmity, frustration, hard feelings, ill will, indignation, offence, rancour, resentment
➤ **Antonyms**
amity, benevolence, favour, friendship, goodwill, satisfaction

ill-founded *adjective* = **groundless**, baseless, empty, idle, unjustified, unproven, unreliable, unsubstantiated, unsupported

ill-humoured *adjective* = **bad-tempered**, acrimonious, crabbed, crabby, cross, disagreeable, grumpy, huffy, impatient, irascible, irritable, like a bear with a sore head (*informal*), liverish, mardy (*dialect*), moody, morose, out of sorts, out of temper, petulant, ratty (*Brit. & N.Z. informal*), sharp, snappish, snappy, sulky, sullen, tart, testy, tetchy, thin-skinned, touchy, unpleasant, waspish
➤ **Antonyms**
affable, agreeable, amiable, charming, congenial, delightful, genial, good-humoured, good-natured, pleasant

illiberal *adjective* **1** = **intolerant**, bigoted,

hidebound, narrow-minded, prejudiced, reactionary, small-minded, uncharitable, ungenerous **2** = **mean**, close-fisted, miserly, niggardly, parsimonious, selfish, sordid, stingy, tight, tight-arsed (*taboo slang*), tight as a duck's arse (*taboo slang*), tight-assed (*U.S. taboo slang*), tightfisted, ungenerous
➤ **Antonyms**
≠intolerant: broad-minded, charitable, generous, liberal, open-minded, politically correct *or* PC, right-on (*informal*), tolerant

illicit *adjective* **1** = **illegal**, black-market, bootleg, contraband, criminal, felonious, illegitimate, off limits, prohibited, unauthorized, unlawful, unlicensed **2** = **forbidden**, clandestine, furtive, guilty, immoral, improper, wrong
➤ **Antonyms**
≠illegal: above-board, lawful, legal, legitimate, licit, permissible

illiteracy *noun* = **lack of education**, benightedness, ignorance, illiterateness

illiterate *adjective* = **uneducated**, benighted, ignorant, uncultured, unlettered, untaught, untutored
➤ **Antonyms**
cultured, educated, lettered, literate, taught, tutored

ill-judged *adjective* = **misguided**, foolish, ill-advised, ill-considered, injudicious, overhasty, rash, short-sighted, unwise, wrong-headed

ill-mannered *adjective* = **rude**, badly behaved, boorish, churlish, coarse, discourteous, ill-behaved, ill-bred, impolite, insolent, loutish, uncivil, uncouth, unmannerly
➤ **Antonyms**
civil, courteous, cultivated, mannerly, polished, polite, refined, well-mannered

ill-natured *adjective* = **unkind**, bad-tempered, catty (*informal*), churlish, crabbed, cross, cross-grained, disagreeable, disobliging, malevolent, malicious, mean, nasty, perverse, petulant, shrewish, spiteful, sulky, sullen, surly, unfriendly, unpleasant
➤ **Antonyms**
agreeable, amiable, cheerful, congenial, friendly, good-natured, kind, obliging, pleasant

illness *noun* = **sickness**, affliction, ailment, attack, complaint, disability, disease, disorder, ill health, indisposition, infirmity, lurgy (*informal*), malady, malaise, poor health

illogical *adjective* = **irrational**, absurd, fallacious, faulty, inconclusive, inconsistent, incorrect, invalid, meaningless, senseless, sophistical, specious, spurious, unreasonable, unscientific, unsound

> **Antonyms**
coherent, consistent, correct, logical,
rational, reasonable, scientific, sound,
valid

ill-starred *adjective* = **doomed**, hapless,
ill-fated, ill-omened, inauspicious,
star-crossed, unfortunate, unhappy, unlucky

ill temper *noun* = **irascibility**, annoyance,
bad temper, crossness, curtness, impatience,
irritability, petulance, sharpness, spitefulness,
tetchiness

ill-tempered *adjective* = **irascible**,
annoyed, bad-tempered, choleric, cross,
curt, grumpy, ill-humoured, impatient,
irritable, liverish, ratty (*Brit. & N.Z.*
informal), sharp, spiteful, testy, tetchy,
touchy
> **Antonyms**
benign, cheerful, good-natured,
mild-mannered, patient, pleasant,
sweet-tempered

ill-timed *adjective* = **inopportune**,
awkward, inappropriate, inconvenient, inept,
unseasonable, untimely, unwelcome
> **Antonyms**
appropriate, convenient, opportune,
seasonable, timely, well-timed

ill-treat *verb* = **abuse**, damage, dump on
(*slang, chiefly U.S.*), handle roughly, harass,
harm, harry, ill-use, injure, knock about *or*
around, maltreat, mishandle, misuse,
oppress, shit on (*taboo slang*), wrong

ill-treatment *noun* = **abuse**, damage,
harm, ill-use, injury, mistreatment, misuse,
rough handling

illuminate *verb* 1 = **light up**, brighten,
illumine (*literary*), irradiate, light 2 = **clarify**,
clear up, elucidate, enlighten, explain,
explicate, give insight into, instruct,
interpret, make clear, shed light on 3
= **decorate**, adorn, illustrate, ornament
> **Antonyms**
≠**light up:** black out, darken, dim, obscure,
overshadow ≠**clarify:** befog, cloud, dull,
obfuscate, overcast, shade, veil

illuminating *adjective* = **informative**,
enlightening, explanatory, helpful,
instructive, revealing
> **Antonyms**
confusing, obscuring, puzzling, unhelpful

illumination *noun* 1 = **light**, beam,
brightening, brightness, lighting, lighting
up, lights, radiance, ray 2 = **enlightenment**,
awareness, clarification, edification, insight,
inspiration, instruction, perception,
revelation, understanding

illusion *noun* 1 = **fantasy**, chimera,
daydream, figment of the imagination,
hallucination, ignis fatuus, mirage, mockery,
phantasm, semblance, will-o'-the-wisp 2

= **misconception**, deception, delusion, error,
fallacy, false impression, fancy,
misapprehension
> **Antonyms**
actuality, fact, reality, truth

illusory *or* **illusive** *adjective* = **unreal**,
apparent, Barmecide, beguiling, chimerical,
deceitful, deceptive, delusive, fallacious,
false, hallucinatory, misleading, mistaken,
seeming, sham, untrue
> **Antonyms**
authentic, down-to-earth, factual, genuine,
real, reliable, solid, true

illustrate *verb* 1 = **demonstrate**, bring
home, clarify, elucidate, emphasize,
exemplify, exhibit, explain, explicate,
instance, interpret, make clear, make plain,
point up, show 2 = **draw**, adorn, decorate,
depict, ornament, picture, sketch

illustrated *adjective* = **pictorial**, decorated,
embellished, graphic, illuminated, picture,
pictured, with illustrations

illustration *noun* 1 = **picture**, adornment,
decoration, figure, plate, sketch 2
= **example**, analogy, case, case in point,
clarification, demonstration, elucidation,
exemplification, explanation, instance,
interpretation, specimen

illustrious *adjective* = **famous**, brilliant,
celebrated, distinguished, eminent, exalted,
famed, glorious, great, noble, notable,
noted, prominent, remarkable, renowned,
resplendent, signal, splendid
> **Antonyms**
humble, ignoble, infamous, lowly, meek,
notorious, obscure, unassuming

ill will *noun* = **hostility**, acrimony, animosity,
animus, antagonism, antipathy, aversion,
bad blood, dislike, enmity, envy, grudge,
hard feelings, hatred, malevolence, malice,
no love lost, rancour, resentment, spite,
unfriendliness, venom
> **Antonyms**
amiability, amity, charity, congeniality,
cordiality, friendship, goodwill

image *noun* 1 = **concept**, conception, idea,
impression, mental picture, perception 2
= **figure**, conceit, trope 3 = **representation**,
appearance, effigy, figure, icon, idol,
likeness, picture, portrait, reflection, statue 4
= **replica**, chip off the old block (*informal*),
counterpart, (dead) ringer (*slang*),
Doppelgänger, double, facsimile, similitude,
spit (*informal, chiefly Brit.*), spitting image
(*informal*)

imaginable *adjective* = **possible**,
believable, comprehensible, conceivable,
credible, likely, plausible, supposable,
thinkable, under the sun, within the bounds
of possibility

> **Antonyms**
impossible, incomprehensible, inconceivable, incredible, unbelievable, unimaginable, unlikely, unthinkable

imaginary *adjective* = **fictional**, assumed, chimerical, dreamlike, fancied, fanciful, fictitious, hallucinatory, hypothetical, ideal, illusive, illusory, imagal (*Psychoanal.*), imagined, invented, legendary, made-up, mythological, nonexistent, phantasmal, shadowy, supposed, suppositious, supposititious, unreal, unsubstantial, visionary
> **Antonyms**
actual, factual, genuine, known, proven, real, substantial, tangible, true

imagination *noun* **1** = **unreality**, chimera, conception, idea, ideality, illusion, image, invention, notion, supposition **2** = **creativity**, enterprise, fancy, ingenuity, insight, inspiration, invention, inventiveness, originality, resourcefulness, vision, wit, wittiness

imaginative *adjective* = **creative**, clever, dreamy, enterprising, fanciful, fantastic, ingenious, inspired, inventive, original, poetical, visionary, vivid, whimsical
> **Antonyms**
literal, mundane, ordinary, uncreative, unimaginative, uninspired, unoriginal, unpoetical, unromantic

imagine *verb* **1** = **envisage**, conceive, conceptualize, conjure up, create, devise, dream up (*informal*), fantasize, form a mental picture of, frame, invent, picture, plan, project, scheme, see in the mind's eye, think of, think up, visualize **2** = **believe**, apprehend, assume, conjecture, deduce, deem, fancy, gather, guess (*informal, chiefly U.S. & Canad.*), infer, realize, suppose, surmise, suspect, take for granted, take it, think

imbecile *noun* **1** = **idiot**, berk (*Brit. slang*), bungler, charlie (*Brit. informal*), chump, coot, cretin, dickhead (*slang*), dickwit (*slang*), dipstick (*Brit. slang*), divvy (*Brit. slang*), dolt, dork (*slang*), dotard, dumb-ass (*slang*), dweeb (*U.S. slang*), fool, fuckwit (*taboo slang*), geek (*slang*), gobshite (*Irish taboo slang*), gonzo (*slang*), halfwit, jerk (*slang, chiefly U.S. & Canad.*), moron, nerd or nurd (*slang*), numbskull or numskull, numpty (*Scot. informal*), pillock (*Brit. slang*), plank (*Brit. slang*), plonker (*slang*), prat (*slang*), prick (*derogatory slang*), schmuck (*U.S. slang*), thickhead, tosser (*Brit. slang*), twit (*informal, chiefly Brit.*), wally (*slang*) ♦ *adjective* **2** = **stupid**, asinine, braindead (*informal*), dead from the neck up, dumb-ass (*slang*), fatuous, feeble-minded, foolish, idiotic, imbecilic, inane, ludicrous, moronic, simple,

simple-minded, thick, witless

imbecility *noun* = **stupidity**, asininity, childishness, cretinism, fatuity, foolishness, idiocy, inanity, incompetency
> **Antonyms**
comprehension, intelligence, perspicacity, reasonableness, sagacity, sense, soundness, wisdom

imbibe *verb Formal* **1** = **drink**, consume, knock back (*informal*), quaff, sink (*informal*), suck, swallow, swig (*informal*) **2** = **absorb**, acquire, assimilate, gain, gather, ingest, receive, take in

imbroglio *noun* = **complication**, complexity, embarrassment, entanglement, involvement, misunderstanding, quandary

imitate *verb* = **copy**, affect, ape, burlesque, caricature, counterfeit, do (*informal*), do an impression of, duplicate, echo, emulate, follow, follow in the footsteps of, follow suit, impersonate, mimic, mirror, mock, parody, personate, repeat, send up (*Brit. informal*), simulate, spoof (*informal*), take a leaf out of (someone's) book, take off (*informal*), travesty

imitation *noun* **1** = **replica**, carbon copy (*informal*), fake, forgery, impersonation, impression, mockery, parody, reflection, reproduction, sham, substitution, takeoff (*informal*), travesty **2** = **mimicry**, aping, copy, counterfeit, counterfeiting, duplication, echoing, likeness, resemblance, simulation ♦ *adjective* **3** = **artificial**, dummy, ersatz, man-made, mock, phoney *or* phony (*informal*), pseudo (*informal*), repro, reproduction, sham, simulated, synthetic
> **Antonyms**
adjective ≠**artificial**: authentic, genuine, original, real, true, valid

imitative *adjective* = **derivative**, copied, copycat (*informal*), copying, echoic, mimetic, mimicking, mock, onomatopoeic, parrot-like, plagiarized, pseudo (*informal*), put-on, second-hand, simulated, unoriginal

imitator *noun* = **impersonator**, aper, carbon copy (*informal*), copier, copycat (*informal*), echo, epigone (*rare*), follower, impressionist, mimic, parrot, shadow

immaculate *adjective* **1** = **clean**, impeccable, neat, neat as a new pin, spick-and-span, spotless, spruce, squeaky-clean, trim **2** = **pure**, above reproach, faultless, flawless, guiltless, impeccable, incorrupt, innocent, perfect, sinless, squeaky-clean, stainless, unblemished, uncontaminated, undefiled, unexceptionable, unpolluted, unsullied, untarnished, virtuous
> **Antonyms**
≠**clean**: dirty, filthy, unclean ≠**pure**:

contaminated, corrupt, impeachable,
impure, polluted, stained, tainted

immaterial *adjective* **1** = **irrelevant**, a
matter of indifference, extraneous,
impertinent, inapposite, inconsequential,
inconsiderable, inessential, insignificant, of
little account, of no consequence, of no
importance, trifling, trivial, unimportant,
unnecessary **2** = **spiritual**, airy, disembodied,
ethereal, ghostly, incorporeal, metaphysical,
unembodied, unsubstantial
➤ **Antonyms**
≠**irrelevant**: crucial, essential, germane,
important, material, relevant, significant,
substantial ≠**spiritual**: earthly, physical, real,
tangible

immature *adjective* **1** = **young**, adolescent,
crude, green, imperfect, premature, raw,
undeveloped, unfinished, unfledged,
unformed, unripe, unseasonable, untimely **2**
= **childish**, babyish, callow, inexperienced,
infantile, jejune, juvenile, puerile, wet behind
the ears (*informal*)
➤ **Antonyms**
adult, developed, fully-fledged, mature,
mellow, ripe

immaturity *noun* **1** = **unripeness**,
crudeness, crudity, greenness, imperfection,
rawness, unpreparedness **2** = **childishness**,
babyishness, callowness, inexperience,
juvenility, puerility

immeasurable *adjective* = **incalculable**,
bottomless, boundless, endless, illimitable,
immense, inestimable, inexhaustible, infinite,
limitless, measureless, unbounded,
unfathomable, unlimited, vast
➤ **Antonyms**
bounded, calculable, estimable, exhaustible,
fathomable, finite, limited, measurable

immediate *adjective* **1** = **instant**,
instantaneous **2** = **nearest**, adjacent, close,
contiguous, direct, near, next, primary,
proximate, recent **3** = **current**, actual,
existing, extant, on hand, present, pressing,
up to date, urgent
➤ **Antonyms**
≠**instant**: delayed, late, later, leisurely,
postponed, slow, tardy ≠**nearest**: distant,
far, remote

immediately *adverb* **1** = **at once**, before
you could say Jack Robinson (*informal*),
directly, forthwith, instantly, now, on the
nail, posthaste, promptly, pronto (*informal*),
right away, right now, straight away, this
instant, this very minute, *tout de suite,*
unhesitatingly, without delay, without
hesitation **2** = **closely**, at first hand, directly,
nearly

immemorial *adjective* = **age-old**, ancient,
archaic, fixed, long-standing, of yore, olden
(*archaic*), rooted, time-honoured, traditional

immense *adjective* = **huge**,
Brobdingnagian, colossal, elephantine,
enormous, extensive, giant, gigantic,
ginormous (*informal*), great, humongous or
humungous (*U.S. slang*), illimitable,
immeasurable, infinite, interminable, jumbo
(*informal*), large, mammoth, massive, mega
(*slang*), monstrous, monumental,
prodigious, stellar (*informal*), stupendous,
titanic, tremendous, vast
➤ **Antonyms**
infinitesimal, little, microscopic, minuscule,
minute, puny, small, tiny

immensity *noun* = **size**, bulk, enormity,
expanse, extent, greatness, hugeness,
infinity, magnitude, massiveness, scope,
sweep, vastness

immerse *verb* **1** = **plunge**, bathe, dip,
douse, duck, dunk, sink, submerge **2**
= **engross**, absorb, busy, engage, involve,
occupy, take up

immersion *noun* **1** = **dipping**, baptism,
bathe, dip, dousing, ducking, dunking,
plunging, submerging **2** = **involvement**,
absorption, concentration, preoccupation

immigrant *noun* = **settler**, incomer,
newcomer

imminent *adjective* = **near**, at hand,
brewing, close, coming, fast-approaching,
forthcoming, gathering, impending, in the
air, in the offing, in the pipeline, just round
the corner, looming, menacing, nigh
(*archaic*), on the cards, on the horizon, on
the way, threatening, upcoming
➤ **Antonyms**
delayed, distant, far-off, remote

immobile *adjective* = **stationary**, at a
standstill, at rest, fixed, frozen, immobilized,
immotile, immovable, like a statue,
motionless, rigid, riveted, rooted, stable,
static, stiff, still, stock-still, stolid, unmoving
➤ **Antonyms**
active, mobile, movable, on the move,
pliant, portable, vigorous

immobility *noun* = **stillness**, absence of
movement, firmness, fixity, immovability,
inertness, motionlessness, stability, steadiness

immobilize *verb* = **paralyse**, bring to a
standstill, cripple, disable, freeze, halt, lay up
(*informal*), put out of action, render
inoperative, stop, transfix

immoderate *adjective* = **excessive**,
egregious, enormous, exaggerated,
exorbitant, extravagant, extreme, inordinate,
intemperate, O.T.T. (*slang*), over the odds
(*informal*), over the top (*slang*), profligate,
steep (*informal*), uncalled-for,
unconscionable, uncontrolled, undue,
unjustified, unreasonable, unrestrained,
unwarranted, wanton

> Antonyms
controlled, judicious, mild, moderate,
reasonable, restrained, temperate

immodesty noun 1 = **lewdness**,
bawdiness, coarseness, impurity,
indecorousness, indelicacy, obscenity 2
= **shamelessness**, audacity, balls (taboo
slang), boldness, brass neck (Brit.
informal), forwardness, gall (informal), impudence,
temerity
> Antonyms
≠**lewdness**: decency, decorousness,
delicacy, modesty, restraint, sobriety

immoral adjective = **wicked**, abandoned,
bad, corrupt, debauched, degenerate,
depraved, dishonest, dissolute, evil, impure,
indecent, iniquitous, lewd, licentious,
nefarious, obscene, of easy virtue,
pornographic, profligate, reprobate, sinful,
sink, unchaste, unethical, unprincipled,
vicious, vile, wrong
> Antonyms
conscientious, good, honourable, inoffensive,
law-abiding, moral, pure, upright, virtuous

immorality noun = **wickedness**, badness,
corruption, debauchery, depravity,
dissoluteness, evil, iniquity, licentiousness,
profligacy, sin, turpitude, vice, wrong
> Antonyms
goodness, honesty, lawfulness, morality,
purity

immortal adjective 1 = **eternal**, abiding,
constant, death-defying, deathless, endless,
enduring, everlasting, imperishable,
incorruptible, indestructible, lasting,
perennial, perpetual, sempiternal (literary),
timeless, undying, unfading ◆ noun 2
= **great**, genius, hero, paragon 3 = **god**,
goddess, Olympian
> Antonyms
adjective ≠**eternal**: ephemeral, fading,
fleeting, mortal, passing, perishable,
temporary, transitory

immortality noun 1 = **eternity**,
deathlessness, endlessness, everlasting life,
incorruptibility, indestructibility, perpetuity,
timelessness 2 = **fame**, celebrity,
glorification, gloriousness, glory, greatness,
renown

immortalize verb = **commemorate**,
apotheosize, celebrate, enshrine, eternalize,
eternize, exalt, glorify, memorialize,
perpetuate, solemnize

immovable adjective 1 = **fixed**, fast, firm,
immutable, jammed, rooted, secure, set,
stable, stationary, stuck, unbudgeable 2
= **inflexible**, adamant, constant, impassive,
obdurate, resolute, steadfast, stony-hearted,
unchangeable, unimpressionable,
unshakable, unshaken, unwavering,
unyielding

> Antonyms
≠**inflexible**: changeable, flexible,
impressionable, movable, shakable,
wavering, yielding

immune adjective = **exempt**, clear, free,
insusceptible, invulnerable, let off (informal),
not affected, not liable, not subject, proof
(against), protected, resistant, safe,
unaffected
> Antonyms
exposed, liable, prone, susceptible,
unprotected, vulnerable

immunity noun 1 = **resistance**,
immunization, protection 2 = **exemption**,
amnesty, charter, exoneration, franchise,
freedom, indemnity, invulnerability, liberty,
licence, prerogative, privilege, release, right
> Antonyms
≠**resistance**: exposure, liability, openness,
proneness, susceptibility, vulnerability

immunize verb = **vaccinate**, inoculate,
protect, safeguard

imp noun 1 = **demon**, devil, sprite 2
= **rascal**, brat, gamin, minx, pickle (Brit.
informal), rogue, scamp, urchin

impact noun 1 = **effect**, brunt, burden,
consequences, full force, impression,
influence, meaning, power, repercussions,
significance, thrust, weight 2 = **collision**,
bang, blow, bump, concussion, contact,
crash, force, jolt, knock, shock, smash,
stroke, thump ◆ verb 3 = **hit**, clash, collide,
crash, crush, strike

impair verb = **worsen**, blunt, damage,
debilitate, decrease, deteriorate, diminish,
enervate, enfeeble, harm, hinder, injure,
lessen, mar, reduce, spoil, undermine,
vitiate, weaken
> Antonyms
ameliorate, amend, better, enhance,
facilitate, improve, strengthen

impaired adjective = **damaged**, defective,
faulty, flawed, imperfect, unsound

impart verb 1 = **communicate**, convey,
disclose, discover, divulge, make known,
pass on, relate, reveal, tell 2 = **give**, accord,
afford, bestow, confer, contribute, grant,
lend, offer, yield

impartial adjective = **neutral**, detached,
disinterested, equal, equitable, even-handed,
fair, just, nondiscriminating, nonpartisan,
objective, open-minded, unbiased,
unprejudiced, without fear or favour
> Antonyms
biased, bigoted, influenced, partial,
prejudiced, swayed, unfair, unjust

impartiality noun = **neutrality**,
detachment, disinterest, disinterestedness,
dispassion, equality, equity,
even-handedness, fairness, lack of bias,

nonpartisanship, objectivity,
open-mindedness
➤ **Antonyms**
bias, favouritism, partiality, partisanship,
subjectivity, unfairness

impassable *adjective* = **blocked**, closed,
impenetrable, obstructed, pathless, trackless,
unnavigable

impasse *noun* = **deadlock**, blind alley
(*informal*), dead end, stalemate, standoff,
standstill

impassioned *adjective* = **intense**, ablaze,
animated, ardent, blazing, excited, fervent,
fervid, fiery, flaming, furious, glowing,
heated, inflamed, inspired, passionate,
rousing, stirring, vehement, violent, vivid,
warm, worked up
➤ **Antonyms**
apathetic, cool, impassive, indifferent,
objective, reasoned

impatience *noun* 1 = **irritability**,
intolerance, irritableness, quick temper,
shortness, snappiness 2 = **haste**, hastiness,
heat, impetuosity, rashness, vehemence,
violence 3 = **restlessness**, agitation, anxiety,
avidity, disquietude, eagerness, edginess,
fretfulness, nervousness, restiveness,
uneasiness
➤ **Antonyms**
≠**irritability**: control, forbearance, patience,
restraint, tolerance ≠**restlessness**: calm,
composure, serenity

impatient *adjective* 1 = **irritable**,
demanding, hot-tempered, intolerant,
quick-tempered, snappy, testy 2 = **hasty**,
abrupt, brusque, curt, headlong, impetuous,
indignant, sudden, vehement, violent 3
= **restless**, agog, athirst, chafing, eager,
edgy, fretful, like a cat on hot bricks
(*informal*), straining at the leash
➤ **Antonyms**
≠**irritable**: easy-going, tolerant ≠**restless**:
calm, composed, cool, imperturbable,
patient, quiet, serene

impeach *verb* 1 = **charge**, accuse, arraign,
blame, censure, criminate (*rare*), denounce,
indict, tax 2 = **challenge**, call into question,
cast aspersions on, cast doubt on, disparage,
impugn, question

impeachment *noun* = **accusation**,
arraignment, indictment

impeccable *adjective* = **faultless**, above
suspicion, blameless, exact, exquisite,
flawless, immaculate, incorrupt, innocent,
irreproachable, perfect, precise, pure, sinless,
squeaky-clean, stainless, unblemished,
unerring, unimpeachable
➤ **Antonyms**
blameworthy, corrupt, defective, deficient,
faulty, flawed, shallow, sinful

impecunious *adjective* = **poor**, broke
(*informal*), cleaned out (*slang*), destitute,
dirt-poor (*informal*), down and out, flat
broke (*informal*), indigent, in queer street,
insolvent, penniless, poverty-stricken, short,
skint (*Brit. slang*), stony (*Brit. slang*),
strapped (*slang*), without two pennies to
rub together (*informal*)
➤ **Antonyms**
affluent, prosperous, rich, wealthy, well-off,
well-to-do

impede *verb* = **hinder**, bar, block, brake,
check, clog, cumber, curb, delay, disrupt,
encumber, hamper, hold up, obstruct,
restrain, retard, slow (down), stop, throw a
spanner in the works (*Brit. informal*), thwart
➤ **Antonyms**
advance, aid, assist, further, help, promote

impediment *noun* = **obstacle**, bar, barrier,
block, check, clog, curb, defect, difficulty,
encumbrance, fly in the ointment, hazard,
hindrance, millstone around one's neck,
obstruction, snag, stumbling block
➤ **Antonyms**
advantage, aid, assistance, benefit,
encouragement, relief, support

impedimenta *plural noun* = **baggage**,
accoutrements, belongings, effects,
equipment, gear, junk (*informal*), luggage,
odds and ends, paraphernalia, possessions,
stuff, things, trappings

impel *verb* = **force**, actuate, chivy, compel,
constrain, drive, goad, incite, induce,
influence, inspire, instigate, motivate, move,
oblige, power, prod, prompt, propel, push,
require, spur, stimulate, urge
➤ **Antonyms**
check, discourage, dissuade, rebuff, repulse,
restrain

impending *adjective* = **looming**,
approaching, brewing, coming,
forthcoming, gathering, hovering, imminent,
in the offing, in the pipeline, menacing,
near, nearing, on the horizon, threatening,
upcoming

impenetrable *adjective* 1 = **impassable**,
dense, hermetic, impermeable, impervious,
inviolable, solid, thick, unpierceable 2
= **incomprehensible**, arcane, baffling,
cabbalistic, dark, enigmatic, enigmatical,
hidden, indiscernible, inexplicable,
inscrutable, mysterious, obscure,
unfathomable, unintelligible
➤ **Antonyms**
≠**impassable**: accessible, enterable, passable,
penetrable, pierceable, vulnerable
≠**incomprehensible**: clear, explicable,
obvious, soluble, understandable

imperative *adjective* 1 = **urgent**,
compulsory, crucial, essential, exigent,
indispensable, insistent, obligatory, pressing,

vital **2** = **commanding**, authoritative,
autocratic, dictatorial, domineering,
high-handed, imperious, lordly, magisterial,
peremptory
➤ **Antonyms**
≠**urgent**: avoidable, discretional,
nonessential, optional, unimportant,
unnecessary

imperceptible *adjective* = **undetectable**,
faint, fine, gradual, impalpable,
inappreciable, inaudible, indiscernible,
indistinguishable, infinitesimal, insensible,
invisible, microscopic, minute, shadowy,
slight, small, subtle, teensy-weensy,
teeny-weeny, tiny, unnoticeable
➤ **Antonyms**
audible, detectable, discernible,
distinguishable, noticeable, perceptible,
visible

imperceptibly *adverb* = **invisibly**, by a
hair's-breadth, inappreciably, indiscernibly,
little by little, slowly, subtly, unnoticeably,
unobtrusively, unseen

imperfect *adjective* = **flawed**, broken,
damaged, defective, deficient, faulty,
immature, impaired, incomplete, inexact,
limited, partial, patchy, rudimentary,
sketchy, undeveloped, unfinished
➤ **Antonyms**
complete, developed, exact, finished,
flawless, perfect

imperfection *noun* = **fault**, blemish,
defect, deficiency, failing, fallibility, flaw,
foible, frailty, inadequacy, incompleteness,
infirmity, insufficiency, peccadillo, scar,
shortcoming, stain, taint, weakness, weak
point
➤ **Antonyms**
adequacy, completeness, consummation,
excellence, faultlessness, flawlessness,
perfection, sufficiency

imperial *adjective* **1** = **royal**, kingly,
majestic, princely, queenly, regal, sovereign
2 = **supreme**, august, exalted, grand, great,
high, imperious, lofty, magnificent, noble,
superior

imperil *verb* = **endanger**, expose, hazard,
jeopardize, risk
➤ **Antonyms**
care for, guard, protect, safeguard, secure

imperishable *adjective* = **indestructible**,
abiding, enduring, eternal, everlasting,
immortal, perennial, permanent, perpetual,
undying, unfading, unforgettable
➤ **Antonyms**
dying, fading, forgettable, mortal, perishable

impermeable *adjective* = **impenetrable**,
hermetic, impassable, impervious,
nonporous, proof, resistant

impersonal *adjective* = **detached**, aloof,

bureaucratic, businesslike, cold,
dispassionate, formal, inhuman, neutral,
remote
➤ **Antonyms**
friendly, intimate, outgoing, personal, warm

impersonate *verb* = **imitate**, act, ape,
caricature, do (*informal*), do an impression
of, enact, masquerade as, mimic, parody,
pass oneself off as, personate, pose as
(*informal*), take off (*informal*)

impersonation *noun* = **imitation**,
caricature, impression, mimicry, parody,
takeoff (*informal*)

impertinence *noun* = **rudeness**,
assurance, audacity, backchat (*informal*),
boldness, brass neck (*Brit. informal*),
brazenness, cheek (*informal*), chutzpah
(*U.S. & Canad. informal*), disrespect,
effrontery, face (*informal*), forwardness,
front, impudence, incivility, insolence, neck
(*informal*), nerve (*informal*), pertness,
presumption, sauce (*informal*)

impertinent *adjective* = **rude**, bold,
brazen, cheeky (*informal*), discourteous,
disrespectful, flip (*informal*), forward, fresh
(*informal*), impolite, impudent, insolent,
interfering, lippy (*U.S. & Canad. slang*),
pert, presumptuous, sassy (*U.S. informal*),
saucy (*informal*), uncivil, unmannerly
➤ **Antonyms**
mannerly, polite, respectful

imperturbable *adjective* = **calm**,
collected, complacent, composed, cool,
equanimous, nerveless, sedate,
self-possessed, serene, stoic, stoical, tranquil,
undisturbed, unexcitable, unfazed
(*informal*), unflappable (*informal*),
unmoved, unruffled
➤ **Antonyms**
agitated, excitable, frantic, jittery (*informal*),
nervous, panicky, ruffled, touchy, upset

impervious *adjective* **1** = **sealed**, hermetic,
impassable, impenetrable, impermeable,
imperviable, invulnerable, resistant **2**
= **unaffected**, closed, immune, invulnerable,
proof against, unmoved, unreceptive,
unswayable, untouched

impetuosity *noun* = **haste**, hastiness,
impulsiveness, precipitancy, precipitateness,
rashness, vehemence, violence

impetuous *adjective* = **rash**, ardent, eager,
fierce, furious, hasty, headlong, impassioned,
impulsive, passionate, precipitate,
spontaneous, spur-of-the-moment,
unbridled, unplanned, unpremeditated,
unreflecting, unrestrained, unthinking,
vehement, violent
➤ **Antonyms**
cautious, leisurely, mild, slow, wary

impetuously *adverb* = **rashly**,

helter-skelter, impulsively, in the heat of the moment, on the spur of the moment, passionately, recklessly, spontaneously, unthinkingly, vehemently, without thinking

impetus *noun* 1 = **incentive**, catalyst, goad, impulse, impulsion, motivation, push, spur, stimulus 2 = **force**, energy, momentum, power

impiety *noun* = **sacrilege**, godlessness, iniquity, irreligion, irreverence, profaneness, profanity, sinfulness, ungodliness, unholiness, unrighteousness, wickedness
➤ **Antonyms**
devoutness, godliness, holiness, piety, respect, reverence, righteousness

impinge *verb* 1 = **encroach**, infringe, invade, make inroads, obtrude, trespass, violate 2 = **affect**, bear upon, have a bearing on, impact, influence, relate to, touch, touch upon

impious *adjective* = **sacrilegious**, blasphemous, godless, iniquitous, irreligious, irreverent, profane, sinful, ungodly, unholy, unrighteous, wicked
➤ **Antonyms**
devout, godly, holy, pious, religious, reverent, righteous

impish *adjective* = **mischievous**, devilish, elfin, prankish, puckish, rascally, roguish, sportive, waggish

implacability *noun* = **pitilessness**, implacableness, inexorability, inflexibility, intractability, mercilessness, relentlessness, ruthlessness, unforgivingness, vengefulness

implacable *adjective* = **unyielding**, cruel, inexorable, inflexible, intractable, merciless, pitiless, rancorous, relentless, remorseless, ruthless, unappeasable, unbending, uncompromising, unforgiving, unrelenting
➤ **Antonyms**
appeasable, flexible, lenient, merciful, relenting, tolerant, yielding

implant *verb* 1 = **instil**, inculcate, infix, infuse, inseminate, sow 2 = **insert**, embed, fix, graft, ingraft, place, plant, root, sow

implement *verb* 1 = **carry out**, bring about, complete, effect, enforce, execute, fulfil, perform, put into action *or* effect, realize ◆ *noun* 2 = **tool**, agent, apparatus, appliance, device, gadget, instrument, utensil
➤ **Antonyms**
verb ≠**carry out**: delay, hamper, hinder, impede, weaken

implementation *noun* = **carrying out**, accomplishment, discharge, effecting, enforcement, execution, fulfilment, performance, performing, realization

implicate *verb* = **incriminate**, associate, compromise, concern, embroil, entangle,

imply, include, inculpate, involve, mire, stitch up (*slang*), tie up with
➤ **Antonyms**
acquit, disentangle, dissociate, eliminate, exclude, exculpate, rule out

implicated *adjective* = **involved**, incriminated, suspected, under suspicion

implication *noun* 1 = **suggestion**, conclusion, inference, innuendo, meaning, overtone, presumption, ramification, significance, signification 2 = **involvement**, association, connection, entanglement, incrimination

implicit *adjective* 1 = **implied**, contained, inferred, inherent, latent, tacit, taken for granted, undeclared, understood, unspoken 2 = **absolute**, constant, entire, firm, fixed, full, steadfast, total, unhesitating, unqualified, unreserved, unshakable, unshaken, wholehearted
➤ **Antonyms**
≠**implied**: declared, explicit, expressed, obvious, patent, spoken, stated

implicitly *adverb* = **absolutely**, completely, firmly, unconditionally, unhesitatingly, unreservedly, utterly, without reservation

implied *adjective* = **unspoken**, hinted at, implicit, indirect, inherent, insinuated, suggested, tacit, undeclared, unexpressed, unstated

implore *verb* = **beg**, beseech, conjure, crave, entreat, go on bended knee to, importune, plead with, pray, solicit, supplicate

imply *verb* 1 = **hint**, connote, give (someone) to understand, insinuate, intimate, signify, suggest 2 = **entail**, betoken, denote, evidence, import, include, indicate, involve, mean, point to, presuppose

impolite *adjective* = **bad-mannered**, boorish, churlish, discourteous, disrespectful, ill-bred, ill-mannered, indecorous, indelicate, insolent, loutish, rough, rude, uncivil, uncouth, ungallant, ungentlemanly, ungracious, unladylike, unmannerly, unrefined
➤ **Antonyms**
courteous, decorous, gallant, gracious, mannerly, polite, refined, respectful, well-bred

impoliteness *noun* = **bad manners**, boorishness, churlishness, discourtesy, disrespect, incivility, indelicacy, insolence, rudeness, unmannerliness
➤ **Antonyms**
civility, courtesy, delicacy, mannerliness, politeness, respect

impolitic *adjective* = **unwise**, ill-advised, ill-judged, imprudent, indiscreet, inexpedient, injudicious, maladroit,

misguided, undiplomatic, untimely
➤ **Antonyms**
diplomatic, discreet, expedient, judicious,
politic, prudent, timely, wise

import *verb* **1** = **bring in**, introduce, land
♦ *noun* **2** *Formal* = **importance**, bottom,
consequence, magnitude, moment,
significance, substance, weight **3**
= **meaning**, bearing, drift, gist, implication,
intention, message, purport, sense,
significance, thrust

importance *noun* **1** = **significance**,
concern, consequence, import, interest,
moment, momentousness, substance,
usefulness, value, weight, worth **2**
= **prestige**, bottom, distinction, eminence,
esteem, influence, mark, pre-eminence,
prominence, standing, status

important *adjective* **1** = **significant**,
far-reaching, grave, large, material,
meaningful, momentous, of substance,
primary, salient, seminal, serious, signal,
substantial, urgent, weighty **2** = **powerful**,
big-time (*informal*), eminent, foremost,
high-level, high-ranking, influential, leading,
major league (*informal*), notable,
noteworthy, of note, outstanding,
pre-eminent, prominent **3** *usually with* **to**
= **of concern**, basic, essential, of interest,
relevant, valuable, valued
➤ **Antonyms**
inconsequential, insignificant, minor,
needless, negligible, secondary, trivial,
undistinctive, unimportant, unnecessary

importunate *adjective Formal*
= **persistent**, burning, clamant, clamorous,
demanding, dogged, earnest, exigent,
insistent, pertinacious, pressing, solicitous,
troublesome, urgent

impose *verb* **1** = **establish**, decree, exact,
fix, institute, introduce, lay, levy, ordain,
place, promulgate, put, set **2** = **inflict**,
appoint, charge with, dictate, enforce,
enjoin, prescribe, saddle (someone) with **3**
impose on: a = **intrude on**, butt in on,
encroach on, foist on, force oneself on,
gate-crash (*informal*), horn in (*informal*),
inflict on, obtrude on, presume upon, take
liberties with, trespass on **b** = **take
advantage of**, abuse, exploit, play on, use
c = **deceive**, con (*informal*), dupe, hoodwink,
pull the wool over (somebody's) eyes, trick

imposing *adjective* = **impressive**, august,
commanding, dignified, effective, grand,
majestic, stately, striking
➤ **Antonyms**
insignificant, mean, modest, ordinary, petty,
poor, unimposing

imposition *noun* **1** = **application**, decree,
introduction, laying on, levying,
promulgation **2** = **intrusion**, cheek

(*informal*), encroachment, liberty,
presumption **3** = **constraint**, burden, charge,
duty, levy, tax

impossibility *noun* = **hopelessness**,
impracticability, inability, inconceivability

impossible *adjective* **1** = **inconceivable**,
beyond one, beyond the bounds of
possibility, hopeless, impracticable, not to be
thought of, out of the question,
unachievable, unattainable, unobtainable,
unthinkable **2** = **absurd**, inadmissible,
insoluble, intolerable, ludicrous, outrageous,
preposterous, unacceptable, unanswerable,
ungovernable, unreasonable, unsuitable,
unworkable
➤ **Antonyms**
≠**inconceivable**: conceivable, imaginable,
likely, plausible, possible, reasonable

impostor *noun* = **impersonator**, charlatan,
cheat, deceiver, fake, fraud, hypocrite, knave
(*archaic*), phoney *or* phony (*informal*),
pretender, quack, rogue, sham, trickster

impotence *noun* = **powerlessness**,
disability, enervation, feebleness, frailty,
helplessness, inability, inadequacy,
incapacity, incompetence, ineffectiveness,
inefficacy, inefficiency, infirmity, paralysis,
uselessness, weakness
➤ **Antonyms**
ability, adequacy, competence, effectiveness,
efficacy, efficiency, powerfulness, strength,
usefulness

impotent *adjective* = **powerless**, disabled,
emasculate, enervated, feeble, frail, helpless,
incapable, incapacitated, incompetent,
ineffective, infirm, nerveless, paralysed,
unable, unmanned, weak
➤ **Antonyms**
able, capable, competent, effective, potent,
powerful, strong

impoverish *verb* **1** = **bankrupt**, beggar,
break, pauperize, ruin **2** = **diminish**, deplete,
drain, exhaust, reduce, sap, use up, wear out

impoverished *adjective* **1** = **poor**,
bankrupt, destitute, distressed, impecunious,
indigent, in reduced *or* straitened
circumstances, necessitous, needy, on one's
uppers, penurious, poverty-stricken, ruined,
straitened **2** = **depleted**, barren, denuded,
drained, empty, exhausted, played out,
reduced, spent, sterile, worn out
➤ **Antonyms**
≠**poor**: affluent, rich, wealthy, well-off
≠**depleted**: fecund, fertile, productive

impracticability *noun* = **impracticality**,
futility, hopelessness, impossibility,
unsuitableness, unworkability, uselessness

impracticable *adjective* **1** = **unfeasible**,
impossible, out of the question,
unachievable, unattainable, unworkable **2**

= **unsuitable**, awkward, impractical, inapplicable, inconvenient, unserviceable, useless
➤ **Antonyms**
≠**unfeasible**: feasible, possible, practicable
≠**unsuitable**: practical, serviceable, suitable

impractical *adjective* 1 = **unworkable**, impossible, impracticable, inoperable, nonviable, unrealistic, unserviceable, visionary, wild 2 = **idealistic**, romantic, starry-eyed, unbusinesslike, unrealistic, visionary
➤ **Antonyms**
≠**unworkable**: possible, practical, serviceable, viable, workable ≠**idealistic**: down-to-earth, realistic, sensible

impracticality *noun* = **unworkability**, hopelessness, impossibility, inapplicability, romanticism

imprecise *adjective* = **indefinite**, ambiguous, blurred round the edges, careless, equivocal, estimated, fluctuating, hazy, ill-defined, inaccurate, indeterminate, inexact, inexplicit, loose, rough, sloppy (*informal*), vague, wide of the mark, woolly
➤ **Antonyms**
accurate, careful, definite, determinate, exact, explicit, precise

impregnable *adjective* = **invulnerable**, immovable, impenetrable, indestructible, invincible, secure, strong, unassailable, unbeatable, unconquerable, unshakable
➤ **Antonyms**
destructible, exposed, insecure, open, pregnable, shakable, vulnerable

impregnate *verb* 1 = **saturate**, fill, imbrue (*rare*), imbue, infuse, percolate, permeate, pervade, seep, soak, steep, suffuse 2 = **fertilize**, fecundate, fructify, get with child, inseminate, make pregnant

impress *verb* 1 = **excite**, affect, grab (*informal*), influence, inspire, make an impression, move, stir, strike, sway, touch 2 = **stress**, bring home to, emphasize, fix, inculcate, instil into 3 = **imprint**, emboss, engrave, indent, mark, print, stamp

impression *noun* 1 = **effect**, feeling, impact, influence, reaction, sway 2 = **idea**, belief, concept, conviction, fancy, feeling, funny feeling (*informal*), hunch, memory, notion, opinion, recollection, sense, suspicion 3 = **imitation**, impersonation, parody, send-up (*Brit. informal*), takeoff (*informal*) 4 = **mark**, brand, dent, hollow, impress, imprint, indentation, outline, stamp, stamping 5 = **edition**, imprinting, issue, printing 6 **make an impression** = **cause a stir**, arouse comment, be conspicuous, excite notice, find favour, make a hit (*informal*), make an impact, stand out

impressionable *adjective* = **suggestible**, feeling, gullible, ingenuous, open, receptive, responsive, sensitive, susceptible, vulnerable
➤ **Antonyms**
blasé, hardened, insensitive, jaded, unresponsive

impressive *adjective* = **grand**, affecting, awesome, dramatic, exciting, forcible, moving, powerful, stirring, striking, touching
➤ **Antonyms**
ordinary, unimposing, unimpressive, uninspiring, unmemorable, weak

imprint *noun* 1 = **mark**, impression, indentation, print, sign, stamp ◆ *verb* 2 = **fix**, engrave, establish, etch, impress, print, stamp

imprison *verb* = **jail**, confine, constrain, detain, immure, incarcerate, intern, lock up, put away, put under lock and key, send down (*informal*), send to prison
➤ **Antonyms**
discharge, emancipate, free, liberate, release

imprisoned *adjective* = **jailed**, behind bars, captive, confined, immured, incarcerated, in irons, in jail, inside (*slang*), interned, locked up, put away, under lock and key

imprisonment *noun* = **custody**, confinement, detention, durance (*archaic*), duress, incarceration, internment, porridge (*slang*)

improbability *noun* = **doubt**, doubtfulness, dubiety, uncertainty, unlikelihood

improbable *adjective* = **doubtful**, cock-and-bull (*informal*), dubious, fanciful, far-fetched, implausible, questionable, unbelievable, uncertain, unconvincing, unlikely, weak
➤ **Antonyms**
certain, convincing, doubtless, likely, plausible, probable, reasonable

impromptu *adjective* 1 = **unprepared**, ad-lib, extemporaneous, extempore, extemporized, improvised, offhand, off the cuff (*informal*), spontaneous, unpremeditated, unrehearsed, unscripted, unstudied ◆ *adverb* 2 = **spontaneously**, ad lib, off the cuff (*informal*), off the top of one's head (*informal*), on the spur of the moment, without preparation
➤ **Antonyms**
adjective ≠**unprepared**: considered, planned, premeditated, prepared, rehearsed

improper *adjective* 1 = **indecent**, impolite, indecorous, indelicate, off-colour, risqué, smutty, suggestive, unbecoming, unfitting, unseemly, untoward, vulgar 2 = **inappropriate**, ill-timed, inapplicable, inapposite, inapt, incongruous, infelicitous, inopportune, malapropos, out of place,

uncalled-for, unfit, unseasonable, unsuitable, unsuited, unwarranted **3 = incorrect,** abnormal, erroneous, false, inaccurate, irregular, wrong
➤ **Antonyms**
≠**indecent:** becoming, decent, decorous, delicate, fitting, proper, seemly
≠**inappropriate:** apposite, appropriate, apt, felicitous, opportune, seasoned, suitable
impropriety noun Formal **1 = indecency,** bad taste, immodesty, incongruity, indecorum, unsuitability, vulgarity **2 = lapse,** bloomer (Brit. informal), blunder, faux pas, gaffe, gaucherie, mistake, slip, solecism
➤ **Antonyms**
≠**indecency:** decency, decorum, delicacy, modesty, propriety, suitability
improve verb **1 = enhance,** ameliorate, amend, augment, better, correct, help, increase, mend, polish, rectify, touch up, upgrade **2 = progress,** advance, develop, gain strength, look up (informal), make strides, perk up, pick up, rally, reform, rise, take a turn for the better (informal), take on a new lease of life (informal) **3 = recuperate,** be on the mend, convalesce, gain ground, gain strength, grow better, make progress, mend, recover, turn the corner **4 = reform,** clean up one's act (informal), get it together (informal), get one's act together (informal), pull one's socks up (Brit. informal), shape up (informal), turn over a new leaf
➤ **Antonyms**
≠**enhance:** damage, harm, impair, injure, mar, worsen
improvement noun **1 = enhancement,** advancement, amelioration, amendment, augmentation, betterment, correction, face-lift, gain, increase, rectification **2 = progress,** advance, development, furtherance, rally, recovery, reformation, rise, upswing
improvident adjective **= imprudent,** careless, heedless, inconsiderate, negligent, prodigal, profligate, reckless, shiftless, short-sighted, spendthrift, thoughtless, thriftless, uneconomical, unthrifty, wasteful
➤ **Antonyms**
careful, considerate, economical, heedful, provident, prudent, thrifty
improvisation noun **1 = spontaneity,** ad-libbing, extemporizing, invention **2 = makeshift,** ad-lib, expedient, impromptu
improvise verb **1 = concoct,** contrive, devise, make do, throw together **2 = extemporize,** ad-lib, busk, coin, invent, play it by ear (informal), speak off the cuff (informal), vamp, wing it (informal)
improvised adjective **= unprepared,** ad-lib, extemporaneous, extempore,

extemporized, makeshift, off the cuff (informal), spontaneous, spur-of-the-moment, unrehearsed
imprudent adjective **= unwise,** careless, foolhardy, foolish, heedless, ill-advised, ill considered, ill-judged, impolitic, improvident, incautious, inconsiderate, indiscreet, injudicious, irresponsible, overhasty, rash, reckless, temerarious, unthinking
➤ **Antonyms**
careful, cautious, considerate, discreet, judicious, politic, provident, prudent, responsible, wise
impudence noun **= boldness,** assurance, audacity, backchat (informal), brass neck (Brit. informal), brazenness, bumptiousness, cheek (informal), chutzpah (U.S. & Canad. informal), effrontery, face (informal), front, impertinence, insolence, lip (slang), neck (informal), nerve (informal), pertness, presumption, rudeness, sassiness (U.S. informal), sauciness, shamelessness
impudent adjective **= bold,** audacious, bold-faced, brazen, bumptious, cheeky (informal), cocky (informal), forward, fresh (informal), immodest, impertinent, insolent, lippy (U.S. & Canad. slang), pert, presumptuous, rude, sassy (U.S. informal), saucy (informal), shameless
➤ **Antonyms**
courteous, modest, polite, respectful, retiring, self-effacing, timid, well-behaved
impulse noun **1 = urge,** caprice, drive, feeling, incitement, inclination, influence, instinct, motive, notion, passion, resolve, whim, wish **2 = force,** catalyst, impetus, momentum, movement, pressure, push, stimulus, surge, thrust
impulsive adjective **= instinctive,** devil-may-care, emotional, hasty, headlong, impetuous, intuitive, passionate, precipitate, quick, rash, spontaneous, unconsidered, unpredictable, unpremeditated
➤ **Antonyms**
calculating, cautious, considered, cool, deliberate, halting, planned, premeditated, rehearsed, restrained
impunity noun **= security,** dispensation, exemption, freedom, immunity, liberty, licence, nonliability, permission
impure adjective **1 = unrefined,** admixed, adulterated, alloyed, debased, mixed **2 = immoral,** carnal, coarse, corrupt, gross, immodest, indecent, indelicate, lascivious, lewd, licentious, lustful, obscene, prurient, ribald, salacious, smutty, unchaste, unclean, X-rated (informal) **3 = unclean,** contaminated, defiled, dirty, filthy, foul, infected, polluted, sullied, tainted, unwholesome, vitiated

➤ **Antonyms**

≠**immoral:** chaste, decent, delicate, modest, moral, pure, wholesome ≠**unclean:** clean, immaculate, spotless, squeaky-clean, undefiled, unsullied

impurity *noun* **1** *often plural* = **dirt**, bits, contaminant, dross, foreign body, foreign matter, grime, marks, pollutant, scum, spots, stains **2** = **contamination**, befoulment, defilement, dirtiness, filth, foulness, infection, pollution, taint, uncleanness **3** = **immorality**, carnality, coarseness, corruption, grossness, immodesty, indecency, lasciviousness, lewdness, licentiousness, obscenity, prurience, salaciousness, smuttiness, unchastity, vulgarity

imputation *noun* = **blame**, accusation, ascription, aspersion, attribution, censure, charge, insinuation, reproach, slander, slur

impute *verb* = **attribute**, accredit, ascribe, assign, credit, lay at the door of, refer, set down to

inability *noun* = **incapability**, disability, disqualification, impotence, inadequacy, incapacity, incompetence, ineptitude, powerlessness

➤ **Antonyms**

ability, adequacy, capability, capacity, competence, potential, power, talent

inaccessible *adjective* = **out of reach**, impassable, out of the way, remote, unapproachable, unattainable, un-get-at-able (*informal*), unreachable

➤ **Antonyms**

accessible, approachable, attainable, reachable

inaccuracy *noun* **1** = **imprecision**, erroneousness, incorrectness, inexactness, unfaithfulness, unreliability **2** = **error**, blunder, boob (*Brit. slang*), corrigendum, defect, erratum, fault, howler (*informal*), lapse, literal (*Printing*), miscalculation, mistake, slip, typo (*informal, Printing*)

inaccurate *adjective* = **incorrect**, careless, defective, discrepant, erroneous, faulty, imprecise, in error, inexact, mistaken, off base (*U.S. & Canad. informal*), off beam (*informal*), out, unfaithful, unreliable, unsound, way off beam (*informal*), wide of the mark, wild, wrong

➤ **Antonyms**

accurate, correct, exact, precise, reliable, sound

inaccurately *adverb* = **imprecisely**, carelessly, clumsily, inexactly, unfaithfully, unreliably

inaction *noun* = **inactivity**, dormancy, idleness, immobility, inertia, rest, torpidity, torpor

inactive *adjective* **1** = **unused**, abeyant,

dormant, idle, immobile, inert, inoperative, jobless, kicking one's heels, latent, mothballed, out of service, out of work, unemployed, unoccupied **2** = **slothful**, dull, indolent, lazy, lethargic, low-key (*informal*), passive, quiet, sedentary, slow, sluggish, somnolent, torpid

➤ **Antonyms**

≠**unused:** employed, mobile, occupied, operative, running, used, working ≠**slothful:** active, busy, diligent, energetic, industrious

inactivity *noun* **1** = **immobility**, dormancy, hibernation, inaction, passivity, unemployment **2** = **sloth**, dilatoriness, *dolce far niente,* dullness, heaviness, indolence, inertia, inertness, lassitude, laziness, lethargy, quiescence, sluggishness, stagnation, torpor, vegetation

➤ **Antonyms**

action, activeness, bustle, employment, exertion, mobility, movement

inadequacy *noun* **1** = **shortage**, dearth, inadequateness, incompleteness, insufficiency, meagreness, paucity, poverty, scantiness, skimpiness **2** = **incompetence**, defectiveness, deficiency, faultiness, inability, inaptness, incapacity, incompetency, ineffectiveness, inefficacy, unfitness, unsuitableness **3** = **shortcoming**, defect, failing, imperfection, lack, shortage, weakness

inadequate *adjective* **1** = **insufficient**, incommensurate, incomplete, insubstantial, meagre, niggardly, scant, scanty, short, sketchy, skimpy, sparse **2** = **incapable**, defective, deficient, faulty, found wanting, imperfect, inapt, incompetent, not up to scratch (*informal*), pathetic, unequal, unfitted, unqualified

➤ **Antonyms**

≠**insufficient:** adequate, ample, complete, perfect, satisfactory, substantial, sufficient ≠**incapable:** apt, capable, competent, equal, fit, qualified

inadequately *adverb* = **insufficiently**, imperfectly, meagrely, poorly, scantily, sketchily, skimpily, sparsely, thinly

inadmissible *adjective* = **unacceptable**, immaterial, improper, inappropriate, incompetent, irrelevant, unallowable, unqualified, unreasonable

inadvertently *adverb* **1** = **unintentionally**, accidentally, by accident, by mistake, involuntarily, mistakenly, unwittingly **2** = **carelessly**, heedlessly, in an unguarded moment, negligently, thoughtlessly, unguardedly, unthinkingly

➤ **Antonyms**

carefully, consciously, deliberately, heedfully, intentionally

inadvisable *adjective* = **unwise**, ill-advised,

impolitic, imprudent, inexpedient, injudicious

inane *adjective* = **senseless**, asinine, daft (*informal*), devoid of intelligence, empty, fatuous, frivolous, futile, goofy (*informal*), idiotic, imbecilic, mindless, puerile, silly, stupid, trifling, unintelligent, vacuous, vain, vapid, worthless
➤ Antonyms
meaningful, profound, sensible, serious, significant, weighty, worthwhile

inanimate *adjective* = **lifeless**, cold, dead, defunct, extinct, inactive, inert, insensate, insentient, quiescent, soulless, spiritless
➤ Antonyms
active, alive, alive and kicking, animate, full of beans (*informal*), lively, living, moving

inanity *noun* = **senselessness**, asininity, bêtise (*rare*), daftness (*informal*), emptiness, fatuity, folly, frivolity, imbecility, puerility, silliness, vacuity, vapidity, worthlessness

inapplicable *adjective* = **irrelevant**, inapposite, inappropriate, inapt, unsuitable, unsuited
➤ Antonyms
applicable, apposite, appropriate, apt, fitting, pertinent, relevant, suitable

inappropriate *adjective* = **unsuitable**, disproportionate, ill-fitted, ill-suited, ill-timed, improper, incongruous, malapropos, out of place, tasteless, unbecoming, unbefitting, unfit, unfitting, unseemly, untimely
➤ Antonyms
appropriate, becoming, congruous, fitting, proper, seemly, suitable, timely

inapt *adjective* **1** = **inappropriate**, ill-fitted, ill-suited, inapposite, infelicitous, unsuitable, unsuited **2** = **incompetent**, awkward, clumsy, dull, gauche, inept, inexpert, maladroit, slow, stupid
➤ Antonyms
≠inappropriate: apposite, appropriate, apt, felicitous, fitting, suitable, suited

inarticulate *adjective* **1** = **faltering**, halting, hesitant, tongue-tied **2** = **incoherent**, blurred, incomprehensible, indistinct, muffled, mumbled, poorly spoken, unclear, unintelligible
➤ Antonyms
≠incoherent: articulate, clear, coherent, comprehensible, intelligible, well-spoken

inattention *noun* = **neglect**, absent-mindedness, carelessness, daydreaming, disregard, forgetfulness, heedlessness, inadvertence, inattentiveness, indifference, preoccupation, thoughtlessness, woolgathering

inattentive *adjective* = **preoccupied**, absent-minded, careless, distracted, distrait, ditzy or ditsy (*slang*), dreamy, heedless, inadvertent, neglectful, negligent, regardless,

remiss, slapdash, slipshod, thoughtless, unheeding, unmindful, unobservant, vague
➤ Antonyms
attentive, aware, careful, considerate, heeding, mindful, observant, thoughtful

inaudible *adjective* = **indistinct**, low, mumbling, out of earshot, stifled, unheard
➤ Antonyms
audible, clear, discernible, distinct, perceptible

inaugural *adjective* = **first**, dedicatory, initial, introductory, maiden, opening

inaugurate *verb* **1** = **open**, commission, dedicate, ordain **2** = **invest**, induct, install, instate **3** = **launch**, begin, commence, get under way, initiate, institute, introduce, kick off (*informal*), originate, set in motion, set up, usher in

inauguration *noun* **1** = **investiture**, induction, installation **2** = **launch**, institution, launching, opening, setting up

inauspicious *adjective* = **unpromising**, bad, black, bodeful, discouraging, ill-omened, ominous, unfavourable, unfortunate, unlucky, unpropitious, untoward
➤ Antonyms
auspicious, encouraging, favourable, fortunate, good, lucky, promising, propitious

inborn *adjective* = **natural**, congenital, connate, hereditary, immanent, inbred, ingrained, inherent, inherited, innate, in one's blood, instinctive, intuitive, native

inbred *adjective* = **innate**, constitutional, deep-seated, immanent, ingrained, inherent, native, natural

incalculable *adjective* = **countless**, boundless, enormous, immense, incomputable, inestimable, infinite, innumerable, limitless, measureless, numberless, uncountable, untold, vast, without number

incantation *noun* = **chant**, abracadabra, charm, conjuration, formula, hex (*U.S. & Canad. informal*), invocation, spell

incapable *adjective* **1** = **incompetent**, feeble, inadequate, ineffective, inept, inexpert, insufficient, not equal to, not up to, unfit, unfitted, unqualified, weak **2** = **unable**, helpless, impotent, powerless, unfit **3 incapable of** = **not susceptible to**, impervious to, not admitting of, resistant to
➤ Antonyms
≠incompetent: adequate, capable, competent, efficient, expert, fit, qualified, sufficient

incapacitate *verb* = **disable**, cripple, disqualify, immobilize, lay up (*informal*), paralyse, prostrate, put out of action (*informal*), scupper (*Brit. slang*), unfit (*rare*)

incapacitated *adjective* = **indisposed**, disqualified, *hors de combat*, immobilized, laid up (*informal*), out of action (*informal*), unfit

incapacity *noun* = **inability**, disqualification, feebleness, impotence, inadequacy, incapability, incompetency, ineffectiveness, powerlessness, unfitness, weakness

incarcerate *verb* = **imprison**, commit, confine, coop up, detain, immure, impound, intern, jail *or* gaol, lock up, put under lock and key, restrain, restrict, send down (*Brit.*), throw in jail

incarceration *noun* = **imprisonment**, bondage, captivity, confinement, detention, internment, porridge (*slang*), restraint

incarnate *adjective* **1** = **made flesh**, in bodily form, in human form, in the flesh **2** = **personified**, embodied, typified

incarnation *noun* = **embodiment**, avatar, bodily form, epitome, exemplification, impersonation, manifestation, personification, type

incautious *adjective* = **careless**, hasty, heedless, ill-advised, ill-judged, improvident, imprudent, impulsive, inconsiderate, indiscreet, injudicious, negligent, precipitate, rash, reckless, thoughtless, unguarded, unthinking, unwary
➤ **Antonyms**
careful, cautious, considerate, discreet, guarded, heedful, judicious, prudent, thoughtful, wary

incautiously *adverb* = **rashly**, imprudently, impulsively, indiscreetly, precipitately, recklessly, thoughtlessly, unthinkingly

incendiary *adjective* **1** = **inflammatory**, dissentious, provocative, rabble-rousing, seditious, subversive ♦ *noun* **2** = **arsonist**, firebug (*informal*), fire raiser, pyromaniac

incense[1] *noun* = **perfume**, aroma, balm, bouquet, fragrance, redolence, scent

incense[2] *verb* = **anger**, enrage, exasperate, excite, gall, get one's hackles up, inflame, infuriate, irritate, madden, make one's blood boil (*informal*), make one see red (*informal*), make one's hackles rise, nark (*Brit., Austral., & N.Z. slang*), provoke, raise one's hackles, rile (*informal*), rub one up the wrong way

incensed *adjective* = **angry**, choked, cross, enraged, exasperated, fit to be tied (*slang*), fuming, furious, hot under the collar (*informal*), incandescent, indignant, infuriated, irate, ireful (*literary*), mad (*informal*), maddened, on the warpath (*informal*), pissed (*taboo slang*), pissed off (*taboo slang*), steamed up (*slang*), up in arms, wrathful

incentive *noun* = **encouragement**, bait, carrot (*informal*), carrot and stick, enticement, goad, impetus, impulse, inducement, lure, motivation, motive, spur, stimulant, stimulus
➤ **Antonyms**
deterrent, discouragement, disincentive, dissuasion, warning

inception *noun* = **beginning**, birth, commencement, dawn, inauguration, initiation, kickoff (*informal*), origin, outset, rise, start
➤ **Antonyms**
completion, conclusion, end, ending, finish, termination

incessant *adjective* = **endless**, ceaseless, constant, continual, continuous, eternal, everlasting, interminable, never-ending, nonstop, perpetual, persistent, relentless, unbroken, unceasing, unending, unrelenting, unremitting
➤ **Antonyms**
infrequent, intermittent, occasional, periodic, rare, sporadic

incessantly *adverb* = **endlessly**, all the time, ceaselessly, constantly, continually, eternally, everlastingly, interminably, nonstop, perpetually, persistently, without a break

incidence *noun* = **prevalence**, amount, degree, extent, frequency, occurrence, rate

incident *noun* **1** = **happening**, adventure, circumstance, episode, event, fact, matter, occasion, occurrence **2** = **disturbance**, brush, clash, commotion, confrontation, contretemps, mishap, scene, skirmish

incidental *adjective* **1** = **accompanying**, attendant, by-the-way, concomitant, contingent, contributory, related **2** = **secondary**, ancillary, minor, nonessential, occasional, subordinate, subsidiary **3** = **accidental**, casual, chance, fortuitous, odd, random
➤ **Antonyms**
≠secondary: crucial, essential, important, necessary, vital

incidentally *adverb* **1** = **parenthetically**, by the bye, by the way, in passing **2** = **accidentally**, by chance, casually, fortuitously

incidentals *plural noun* = **odds and ends**, contingencies, extras, minutiae

incinerate *verb* = **burn up**, carbonize, char, consume by fire, cremate, reduce to ashes

incipient *adjective* = **beginning**, commencing, developing, embryonic, inceptive, inchoate, nascent, originating, starting

incise *verb* = **cut into**, carve, chisel, engrave, etch, inscribe

incision noun = cut, gash, notch, opening, slash, slit

incisive adjective = penetrating, acute, keen, perspicacious, piercing, sharp, trenchant
➤ Antonyms
dense, dull, superficial, vague, woolly

incisiveness noun = perspicacity, keenness, penetration, sharpness, trenchancy

incite verb = provoke, agitate for or against, animate, drive, egg on, encourage, excite, foment, goad, impel, inflame, instigate, prod, prompt, put up to, rouse, set on, spur, stimulate, stir up, urge, whip up
➤ Antonyms
dampen, deter, discourage, dishearten, dissuade, restrain

incitement noun = provocation, agitation, clarion call, encouragement, goad, impetus, impulse, inducement, instigation, motivation, motive, prompting, spur, stimulus

incivility noun = rudeness, bad manners, boorishness, discourteousness, discourtesy, disrespect, ill-breeding, impoliteness, unmannerliness
➤ Antonyms
civility, courteousness, courtesy, good manners, mannerliness, politeness, respect

inclemency noun Formal 1 = storminess, bitterness, boisterousness, rawness, rigour, roughness, severity 2 = harshness, callousness, cruelty, mercilessness, severity, tyranny, unfeelingness

inclement adjective Formal 1 = stormy, bitter, boisterous, foul, harsh, intemperate, rigorous, rough, severe, tempestuous 2 = cruel, callous, draconian, harsh, intemperate, merciless, pitiless, rigorous, severe, tyrannical, unfeeling, unmerciful
➤ Antonyms
≠stormy: balmy, calm, clement, fine, mild, pleasant, temperate ≠cruel: compassionate, gentle, humane, kind, merciful, tender

inclination noun 1 = tendency, affection, aptitude, bent, bias, desire, disposition, fancy, fondness, leaning, liking, partiality, penchant, predilection, predisposition, prejudice, proclivity, proneness, propensity, stomach, taste, thirst, turn, turn of mind, wish 2 = slope, angle, bend, bending, deviation, gradient, incline, leaning, pitch, slant, tilt 3 = bow, bending, bowing, nod
➤ Antonyms
≠tendency: antipathy, aversion, disinclination, dislike, revulsion

incline verb 1 = slope, bend, bevel, cant, deviate, diverge, heel, lean, slant, tend, tilt, tip, veer 2 = predispose, be disposed or predisposed, bias, influence, persuade,

prejudice, sway, tend, turn 3 = bend, bow, lower, nod, nutate (rare), stoop ♦ noun 4 = slope, acclivity, ascent, declivity, descent, dip, grade, gradient, ramp, rise

inclined adjective = disposed, apt, given, liable, likely, minded, of a mind (informal), predisposed, prone, willing

inclose see ENCLOSE

include verb 1 = contain, comprehend, comprise, cover, embody, embrace, encompass, incorporate, involve, subsume, take in, take into account 2 = introduce, add, allow for, build in, count, enter, insert, number among
➤ Antonyms
eliminate, exclude, leave out, omit, rule out

including preposition = together with, as well as, containing, counting, inclusive of, plus, with

inclusion noun = addition, incorporation, insertion
➤ Antonyms
exception, exclusion, omission, rejection

inclusive adjective = comprehensive, across-the-board, all-embracing, all in, all together, blanket, catch-all (chiefly U.S.), full, general, global, in toto, overall, overarching, sweeping, umbrella, without exception
➤ Antonyms
confined, exclusive, limited, narrow, restricted, unique

incognito adjective = in disguise, disguised, under an assumed name, unknown, unrecognized

incoherence noun = unintelligibility, disconnectedness, disjointedness, inarticulateness

incoherent adjective = unintelligible, confused, disconnected, disjointed, disordered, inarticulate, inconsistent, jumbled, loose, muddled, rambling, stammering, stuttering, unconnected, uncoordinated, wandering, wild
➤ Antonyms
coherent, connected, intelligible, logical, rational

incombustible adjective = fireproof, flameproof, noncombustible, nonflammable, noninflammable

income noun = revenue, earnings, gains, interest, means, pay, proceeds, profits, receipts, salary, takings, wages

incoming adjective = arriving, approaching, entering, homeward, landing, new, returning, succeeding
➤ Antonyms
departing, exiting, leaving, outgoing

incomparable adjective = unequalled,

beyond compare, inimitable, matchless, paramount, peerless, superlative, supreme, transcendent, unmatched, unparalleled, unrivalled

incomparably *adverb* = **immeasurably**, beyond compare, by far, easily, eminently, far and away

incompatibility *noun* = **inconsistency**, antagonism, conflict, discrepancy, disparateness, incongruity, irreconcilability, uncongeniality

incompatible *adjective* = **inconsistent**, antagonistic, antipathetic, conflicting, contradictory, discordant, discrepant, disparate, ill-assorted, incongruous, inconsonant, irreconcilable, mismatched, uncongenial, unsuitable, unsuited
➤ **Antonyms**
alike, appropriate, compatible, congenial, consistent, harmonious, reconcilable, suitable, suited

incompetence *noun* = **ineptitude**, inability, inadequacy, incapability, incapacity, incompetency, ineffectiveness, ineptness, insufficiency, skill-lessness, unfitness, uselessness

incompetent *adjective* = **inept**, bungling, cowboy (*informal*), floundering, incapable, incapacitated, ineffectual, inexpert, insufficient, skill-less, unable, unfit, unfitted, unskilful, useless
➤ **Antonyms**
able, capable, competent, expert, fit, proficient, skilful

incomplete *adjective* = **unfinished**, broken, defective, deficient, fragmentary, imperfect, insufficient, lacking, partial, short, unaccomplished, undeveloped, undone, unexecuted, wanting
➤ **Antonyms**
accomplished, complete, developed, finished, perfect, unified, whole

incomprehensible *adjective* = **unintelligible**, above one's head, all Greek to one (*informal*), baffling, beyond comprehension, beyond one's grasp, enigmatic, impenetrable, inconceivable, inscrutable, mysterious, obscure, opaque, perplexing, puzzling, unfathomable, unimaginable, unthinkable
➤ **Antonyms**
apparent, clear, comprehensible, conceivable, evident, intelligible, manifest, obvious, understandable

inconceivable *adjective* = **unimaginable**, beyond belief, impossible, incomprehensible, incredible, mind-boggling (*informal*), not to be thought of, out of the question, staggering (*informal*), unbelievable, unheard-of, unknowable, unthinkable

➤ **Antonyms**
believable, comprehensible, conceivable, credible, imaginable, likely, plausible, possible, reasonable

inconclusive *adjective* = **indecisive**, ambiguous, indeterminate, open, uncertain, unconvincing, undecided, unsettled, up in the air (*informal*), vague

incongruity *noun* = **inappropriateness**, conflict, discrepancy, disparity, inaptness, incompatibility, inconsistency, inharmoniousness, unsuitability

incongruous *adjective* = **inappropriate**, absurd, conflicting, contradictory, contrary, disconsonant, discordant, extraneous, improper, inapt, incoherent, incompatible, inconsistent, out of keeping, out of place, unbecoming, unsuitable, unsuited
➤ **Antonyms**
appropriate, becoming, compatible, consistent, harmonious, suitable, suited

inconsiderable *adjective* = **insignificant**, exiguous, inconsequential, light, minor, negligible, petty, slight, small, small-time (*informal*), trifling, trivial, unimportant

inconsiderate *adjective* = **selfish**, careless, indelicate, insensitive, intolerant, rude, self-centred, tactless, thoughtless, uncharitable, ungracious, unkind, unthinking
➤ **Antonyms**
attentive, careful, considerate, gracious, kind, sensitive, tactful, thoughtful, tolerant

inconsistency *noun* **1** = **unreliability**, fickleness, instability, unpredictability, unsteadiness **2** = **incompatibility**, contrariety, disagreement, discrepancy, disparity, divergence, incongruity, inconsonance, paradox, variance

inconsistent *adjective* **1** = **changeable**, capricious, erratic, fickle, inconstant, irregular, uneven, unpredictable, unstable, unsteady, vagarious (*rare*), variable **2** = **incompatible**, at odds, at variance, conflicting, contradictory, contrary, discordant, discrepant, incoherent, in conflict, incongruous, inconstant, irreconcilable, out of step
➤ **Antonyms**
≠**changeable:** consistent, constant, predictable, reliable, stable, steady, unchanging ≠**incompatible:** coherent, compatible, homogeneous, orderly, reconcilable, uniform

inconsistently *adverb* = **unpredictably**, contradictorily, differently, eccentrically, erratically, inequably, randomly, unequally, unfairly, variably

inconsolable *adjective* = **heartbroken**, brokenhearted, desolate, despairing, heartsick, prostrate with grief, sick at heart

inconspicuous *adjective* = **unobtrusive**, camouflaged, hidden, insignificant, modest, muted, ordinary, plain, quiet, retiring, unassuming, unnoticeable, unostentatious
➤ **Antonyms**
bold, conspicuous, noticeable, obtrusive, obvious, salient, significant, visible

incontestable *adjective* = **certain**, beyond doubt, beyond question, incontrovertible, indisputable, indubitable, irrefutable, self-evident, sure, undeniable, unquestionable

incontinent *adjective* = **unrestrained**, unbridled, unchecked, uncontrollable, uncontrolled, ungovernable, ungoverned

incontrovertible *adjective* = **indisputable**, beyond dispute, certain, established, incontestable, indubitable, irrefutable, positive, sure, undeniable, unquestionable, unshakable

inconvenience *noun* 1 = **trouble**, annoyance, awkwardness, bother, difficulty, disadvantage, disruption, disturbance, downside, drawback, fuss, hassle (*informal*), hindrance, nuisance, uneasiness, upset, vexation 2 = **awkwardness**, cumbersomeness, unfitness, unhandiness, unsuitableness, untimeliness, unwieldiness ◆ *verb* 3 = **trouble**, bother, discommode, disrupt, disturb, give (someone) bother *or* trouble, hassle (*informal*), irk, make (someone) go out of his way, put out, put to trouble, upset

inconvenient *adjective* 1 = **troublesome**, annoying, awkward, bothersome, disadvantageous, disturbing, embarrassing, inopportune, tiresome, unseasonable, unsuitable, untimely, vexatious 2 = **difficult**, awkward, cumbersome, unhandy, unmanageable, unwieldy
➤ **Antonyms**
≠**troublesome**: convenient, handy, opportune, seasonable, suitable, timely

incorporate *verb* = **include**, absorb, amalgamate, assimilate, blend, coalesce, combine, consolidate, embody, fuse, integrate, meld, merge, mix, subsume, unite

incorrect *adjective* = **false**, erroneous, faulty, flawed, improper, inaccurate, inappropriate, inexact, mistaken, off base (*U.S. & Canad. informal*), off beam (*informal*), out, specious, unfitting, unsuitable, untrue, way off beam (*informal*), wide of the mark (*informal*), wrong
➤ **Antonyms**
accurate, correct, exact, faultless, fitting, flawless, right, suitable, true

incorrectness *noun* = **inaccuracy**, erroneousness, error, fallacy, faultiness, impreciseness, imprecision, impropriety, inexactness, speciousness, unsoundness, unsuitability, wrongness

incorrigible *adjective* = **incurable**, hardened, hopeless, intractable, inveterate, irredeemable, unreformed

incorruptibility *noun* = **integrity**, honesty, honour, justness, uprightness

incorruptible *adjective* 1 = **honest**, above suspicion, honourable, just, straight, trustworthy, unbribable, upright 2 = **imperishable**, everlasting, undecaying

increase *verb* 1 = **grow**, add to, advance, aggrandize, amplify, augment, boost, build up, develop, dilate, enhance, enlarge, escalate, expand, extend, heighten, inflate, intensify, magnify, mount, multiply, proliferate, prolong, raise, snowball, spread, step up (*informal*), strengthen, swell, wax ◆ *noun* 2 = **growth**, addition, augmentation, boost, development, enlargement, escalation, expansion, extension, gain, increment, intensification, rise, upsurge, upturn 3 **on the increase** = **growing**, developing, escalating, expanding, increasing, multiplying, on the rise, proliferating, spreading
➤ **Antonyms**
verb ≠**grow**: abate, abbreviate, abridge, condense, curtail, decline, decrease, deflate, diminish, dwindle, lessen, reduce, shorten, shrink

increasingly *adverb* = **progressively**, more and more, to an increasing extent

incredible *adjective* 1 = **implausible**, absurd, beyond belief, cock-and-bull (*informal*), far-fetched, impossible, improbable, inconceivable, not able to hold water, preposterous, unbelievable, unimaginable, unthinkable 2 *Informal* = **amazing**, ace (*informal*), astonishing, astounding, awe-inspiring, brilliant, def (*slang*), extraordinary, far-out (*slang*), great, marvellous, mega (*slang*), prodigious, rad (*informal*), sensational (*informal*), superhuman, wonderful

incredulity *noun* = **disbelief**, distrust, doubt, scepticism, unbelief

incredulous *adjective* = **disbelieving**, distrustful, doubtful, doubting, dubious, mistrustful, sceptical, suspicious, unbelieving, unconvinced
➤ **Antonyms**
believing, credulous, gullible, naive, trusting, unsuspecting, wet behind the ears (*informal*)

increment *noun* = **increase**, accretion, accrual, accruement, addition, advancement, augmentation, enlargement, gain, step up, supplement

incriminate *verb* = **implicate**, accuse, arraign, blacken the name of, blame, charge, impeach, inculpate, indict, involve, point the finger at (*informal*), stigmatize

incumbent *adjective Formal* = **obligatory**, binding, compulsory, mandatory, necessary

incur *verb* = **earn**, arouse, bring (upon oneself), contract, draw, expose oneself to, gain, induce, lay oneself open to, meet with, provoke

incurable *adjective* **1** = **fatal**, inoperable, irrecoverable, irremediable, remediless, terminal **2** = **incorrigible**, dyed-in-the-wool, hopeless, inveterate

indebted *adjective* = **grateful**, beholden, in debt, obligated, obliged, under an obligation

indecency *noun* = **obscenity**, bawdiness, coarseness, crudity, foulness, grossness, immodesty, impropriety, impurity, indecorum, indelicacy, lewdness, licentiousness, outrageousness, pornography, smut, smuttiness, unseemliness, vileness, vulgarity
➤ Antonyms
decency, decorum, delicacy, modesty, propriety, purity, seemliness

indecent *adjective* **1** = **lewd**, blue, coarse, crude, dirty, filthy, foul, gross, immodest, improper, impure, indelicate, licentious, pornographic, salacious, scatological, smutty, vile **2** = **unbecoming**, ill-bred, improper, in bad taste, indecorous, offensive, outrageous, tasteless, unseemly, vulgar
➤ Antonyms
decent, decorous, delicate, modest, proper, pure, respectable, seemly, tasteful

indecipherable *adjective* = **illegible**, crabbed, indistinguishable, unintelligible, unreadable

indecision *noun* = **hesitation**, ambivalence, dithering (*chiefly Brit.*), doubt, hesitancy, indecisiveness, irresolution, shilly-shallying (*informal*), uncertainty, vacillation, wavering

indecisive *adjective* **1** = **hesitating**, dithering (*chiefly Brit.*), doubtful, faltering, in two minds (*informal*), irresolute, pussyfooting (*informal*), tentative, uncertain, undecided, undetermined, vacillating, wavering **2** = **inconclusive**, indefinite, indeterminate, unclear, undecided
➤ Antonyms
≠hesitating: certain, decided, determined, positive, resolute, unhesitating
≠inconclusive: clear, conclusive, decisive, definite, determinate, final

indeed *adverb* = **really**, actually, certainly, doubtlessly, in point of fact, in truth, positively, strictly, to be sure, truly, undeniably, undoubtedly, verily (*archaic*), veritably

indefensible *adjective* = **unforgivable**, faulty, inexcusable, insupportable, unjustifiable, unpardonable, untenable,

unwarrantable, wrong
➤ Antonyms
defensible, excusable, forgivable, justifiable, legitimate, pardonable, supportable, tenable, warrantable

indefinable *adjective* = **inexpressible**, dim, hazy, impalpable, indescribable, indistinct, nameless, obscure, unrealized, vague

indefinite *adjective* = **unclear**, ambiguous, confused, doubtful, equivocal, evasive, general, ill-defined, imprecise, indeterminate, indistinct, inexact, loose, obscure, oracular, uncertain, undefined, undetermined, unfixed, unknown, unlimited, unsettled, vague
➤ Antonyms
certain, clear, definite, determinate, distinct, exact, fixed, settled, specific

indefinitely *adverb* = **endlessly**, ad infinitum, continually, for ever, *sine die*, till the cows come home (*informal*)

indelible *adjective* = **permanent**, enduring, indestructible, ineffaceable, ineradicable, inexpungible, inextirpable, ingrained, lasting
➤ Antonyms
eradicable, erasable, impermanent, removable, short-lived, temporary, washable

indelicacy *noun* = **vulgarity**, bad taste, coarseness, crudity, grossness, immodesty, impropriety, indecency, obscenity, offensiveness, rudeness, smuttiness, suggestiveness, tastelessness

indelicate *adjective* = **offensive**, blue, coarse, crude, embarrassing, gross, immodest, improper, indecent, indecorous, low, near the knuckle (*informal*), obscene, off-colour, risqué, rude, suggestive, tasteless, unbecoming, unseemly, untoward, vulgar, X-rated (*informal*)
➤ Antonyms
becoming, decent, decorous, delicate, modest, proper, refined, seemly

indemnify *verb* **1** = **insure**, endorse, guarantee, protect, secure, underwrite **2** = **compensate**, pay, reimburse, remunerate, repair, repay, requite, satisfy

indemnity *noun* **1** = **insurance**, guarantee, protection, security **2** = **compensation**, redress, reimbursement, remuneration, reparation, requital, restitution, satisfaction **3** *Law* = **exemption**, immunity, impunity, privilege

indent *verb* **1** = **order**, ask for, request, requisition **2** = **notch**, cut, dint, mark, nick, pink, scallop, score, serrate

independence *noun* = **freedom**, autarchy, autonomy, home rule, liberty, self-determination, self-government, self-reliance, self-rule, self-sufficiency, separation, sovereignty

> ➤ **Antonyms**
> bondage, dependence, subjection,
> subjugation, subordination, subservience

independent *adjective* **1** = **free**, absolute,
liberated, separate, unconnected,
unconstrained, uncontrolled, unrelated **2**
= **self-governing**, autarchic, autarchical,
autonomous, decontrolled, nonaligned,
self-determining, separated, sovereign **3**
= **self-sufficient**, bold, individualistic,
liberated, self-contained, self-reliant,
self-supporting, unaided, unconventional
> ➤ **Antonyms**
> ≠**free**: controlled, dependent, restrained,
> subject ≠**self-governing**: aligned,
> controlled, dependent, subject, submissive,
> subordinate, subservient, subsidiary

independently *adverb* = **separately**,
alone, autonomously, by oneself,
individually, on one's own, solo, unaided,
under one's own steam

indescribable *adjective* = **unutterable**,
beggaring description, beyond description,
beyond words, incommunicable, indefinable,
ineffable, inexpressible

indestructible *adjective* = **permanent**,
abiding, durable, enduring, everlasting,
immortal, imperishable, incorruptible,
indelible, indissoluble, lasting, nonperishable,
unbreakable, unfading
> ➤ **Antonyms**
> breakable, corruptible, destructible, fading,
> impermanent, mortal, perishable

indeterminate *adjective* = **uncertain**,
imprecise, inconclusive, indefinite, inexact,
undefined, undetermined, unfixed,
unspecified, unstipulated, vague
> ➤ **Antonyms**
> certain, clear, conclusive, definite,
> determinate, exact, fixed, precise, specified,
> stipulated

index *noun* = **indication**, clue, guide, mark,
sign, symptom, token

indicate *verb* **1** = **signify**, add up to
(*informal*), bespeak, be symptomatic of,
betoken, denote, evince, imply, manifest,
point to, reveal, show, signal, suggest **2**
= **point out**, designate, point to, specify **3**
= **show**, display, express, mark, read, record,
register

indication *noun* = **sign**, clue, evidence,
explanation, forewarning, hint, index,
inkling, intimation, manifestation, mark,
note, omen, portent, signal, suggestion,
symptom, warning

indicative *adjective* = **suggestive**,
exhibitive, indicatory, indicial, pointing to,
significant, symptomatic

indicator *noun* = **sign**, display, gauge,
guide, index, mark, marker, meter, pointer,

signal, signpost, symbol

indict *verb* = **charge**, accuse, arraign,
impeach, prosecute, serve with a summons,
summon, summons, tax

indictment *noun* = **charge**, accusation,
allegation, impeachment, prosecution,
summons

indifference *noun* **1** = **disregard**, absence
of feeling, aloofness, apathy, callousness,
carelessness, coldness, coolness, detachment,
heedlessness, inattention, lack of interest,
negligence, nonchalance, stoicalness,
unconcern **2** = **irrelevance**, insignificance,
triviality, unimportance **3** = **objectivity**,
disinterestedness, dispassion, equity,
impartiality, neutrality
> ➤ **Antonyms**
> ≠**disregard**: attention, care, commitment,
> concern, enthusiasm, heed, interest, regard

indifferent *adjective* **1** = **unconcerned**,
aloof, apathetic, callous, careless, cold, cool,
detached, distant, heedless, impervious,
inattentive, not giving a monkey's (*slang*),
regardless, uncaring, unimpressed,
uninterested, unmoved, unresponsive,
unsympathetic **2** = **mediocre**, average, fair,
middling, moderate, no great shakes
(*informal*), ordinary, passable, perfunctory,
so-so (*informal*), undistinguished, uninspired
3 = **unimportant**, immaterial, insignificant,
of no consequence **4** = **impartial**,
disinterested, dispassionate, equitable,
neutral, nonaligned, nonpartisan, objective,
unbiased, uninvolved, unprejudiced
> ➤ **Antonyms**
> ≠**unconcerned**: avid, compassionate,
> concerned, eager, enthusiastic, interested,
> keen, responsive, sensitive, susceptible,
> sympathetic ≠**mediocre**: excellent,
> exceptional, fine, first-class, notable,
> remarkable

indigent *adjective Formal* = **destitute**,
dirt-poor, down and out, down at heel
(*informal*), flat broke (*informal*),
impecunious, impoverished, in want,
necessitous, needy, on one's uppers
(*informal*), on the breadline, penniless,
penurious, poor, poverty-stricken, short,
straitened, without two pennies to rub
together (*informal*)
> ➤ **Antonyms**
> affluent, prosperous, rich, wealthy, well-off,
> well-to-do

indigestion *noun* = **heartburn**, dyspepsia,
dyspepsy, upset stomach

indignant *adjective* = **resentful**, angry,
annoyed, choked, disgruntled, exasperated,
fuming (*informal*), furious, hacked (off)
(*U.S. slang*), heated, hot under the collar
(*informal*), huffy (*informal*), in a huff,
incensed, in high dudgeon, irate, livid

(*informal*), mad (*informal*), miffed (*informal*), narked (*Brit., Austral., & N.Z. slang*), peeved (*informal*), pissed off (*taboo slang*), provoked, riled, scornful, seeing red (*informal*), sore (*informal*), up in arms (*informal*), wrathful

indignation *noun* = **resentment**, anger, exasperation, fury, ire (*literary*), pique, rage, righteous anger, scorn, umbrage, wrath

indignity *noun* = **humiliation**, abuse, affront, contumely, dishonour, disrespect, injury, insult, obloquy, opprobrium, outrage, reproach, slap in the face (*informal*), slight, snub

indirect *adjective* 1 = **incidental**, ancillary, collateral, contingent, secondary, subsidiary, unintended 2 = **circuitous**, backhanded, circumlocutory, crooked, devious, long-drawn-out, meandering, oblique, periphrastic, rambling, roundabout, tortuous, wandering, winding, zigzag
➤ **Antonyms**
≠ **circuitous**: direct, straight, straightforward, undeviating, uninterrupted

indirectly *adverb* = **second-hand**, by implication, circumlocutorily, in a roundabout way, obliquely, periphrastically

indiscernible *adjective* = **invisible**, hidden, impalpable, imperceptible, indistinct, indistinguishable, unapparent, undiscernible
➤ **Antonyms**
apparent, clear, discernible, distinct, distinguishable, perceptible, visible

indiscreet *adjective* = **tactless**, foolish, hasty, heedless, ill-advised, ill-considered, ill-judged, impolitic, imprudent, incautious, injudicious, naive, rash, reckless, undiplomatic, unthinking, unwise
➤ **Antonyms**
cautious, diplomatic, discreet, judicious, politic, prudent, tactful, wise

indiscretion *noun* = **mistake**, bloomer (*Brit. informal*), boob (*Brit. slang*), error, faux pas, folly, foolishness, gaffe, gaucherie, imprudence, lapse, rashness, recklessness, slip, slip of the tongue, tactlessness

indiscriminate *adjective* 1 = **random**, aimless, careless, desultory, general, hit or miss (*informal*), sweeping, uncritical, undiscriminating, unmethodical, unselective, unsystematic, wholesale 2 = **jumbled**, chaotic, confused, haphazard, higgledy-piggledy (*informal*), mingled, miscellaneous, mixed, mongrel, motley, promiscuous, undistinguishable
➤ **Antonyms**
≠ **random**: deliberate, discriminating, exclusive, methodical, selective, systematic

indispensable *adjective* = **essential**, crucial, imperative, key, necessary, needed,

needful, requisite, vital
➤ **Antonyms**
dispensable, disposable, nonessential, superfluous, unimportant, unnecessary

indisposed *adjective* 1 = **ill**, ailing, confined to bed, laid up (*informal*), on the sick list (*informal*), poorly (*informal*), sick, under the weather, unwell 2 = **unwilling**, averse, disinclined, loath, reluctant
➤ **Antonyms**
≠ **ill**: fine, fit, hardy, healthy, sound, well

indisposition *noun* 1 = **illness**, ailment, ill health, sickness 2 = **reluctance**, aversion, disinclination, dislike, distaste, hesitancy, unwillingness

indisputable *adjective* = **undeniable**, absolute, beyond doubt, certain, evident, incontestable, incontrovertible, indubitable, irrefutable, positive, sure, unassailable, unquestionable
➤ **Antonyms**
assailable, disputable, doubtful, indefinite, questionable, refutable, uncertain, vague

indissoluble *adjective* = **permanent**, abiding, binding, enduring, eternal, fixed, imperishable, incorruptible, indestructible, inseparable, lasting, solid, unbreakable

indistinct *adjective* = **unclear**, ambiguous, bleary, blurred, confused, dim, doubtful, faint, fuzzy, hazy, ill-defined, indefinite, indeterminate, indiscernible, indistinguishable, misty, muffled, obscure, out of focus, shadowy, undefined, unintelligible, vague, weak
➤ **Antonyms**
clear, defined, determinate, discernible, distinct, distinguishable, evident, intelligible

indistinguishable *adjective* 1 = **identical**, alike, cut from the same cloth, like as two peas in a pod (*informal*), (the) same, twin 2 = **imperceptible**, indiscernible, invisible, obscure

individual *adjective* 1 = **personal**, characteristic, discrete, distinct, distinctive, exclusive, identical, idiosyncratic, own, particular, peculiar, personalized, proper, respective, separate, several, single, singular, special, specific, unique ◆ *noun* 2 = **person**, being, body (*informal*), character, creature, mortal, party, personage, soul, type, unit
➤ **Antonyms**
adjective ≠ **personal**: collective, common, conventional, general, indistinct, ordinary, universal

individualism *noun* = **self-interest**, egocentricity, egoism, freethinking, independence, originality, self-direction, self-reliance

individualist *noun* = **maverick**, freethinker, independent, loner, lone wolf, nonconformist, original

individuality *noun* = **distinctiveness**, character, discreteness, distinction, originality, peculiarity, personality, separateness, singularity, uniqueness

individually *adverb* = **separately**, apart, independently, one at a time, one by one, personally, severally, singly

indoctrinate *verb* = **train**, brainwash, drill, ground, imbue, initiate, instruct, school, teach

indoctrination *noun* = **training**, brainwashing, drilling, grounding, inculcation, instruction, schooling

indolent *adjective* = **lazy**, fainéant, good-for-nothing, idle, inactive, inert, lackadaisical, languid, lethargic, listless, lumpish, slack, slothful, slow, sluggish, torpid, workshy
➤ **Antonyms**
active, assiduous, busy, conscientious, diligent, energetic, industrious, vigorous

indomitable *adjective* = **invincible**, bold, resolute, set, staunch, steadfast, unbeatable, unconquerable, unflinching, untameable, unyielding
➤ **Antonyms**
cowardly, faltering, feeble, shrinking, wavering, weak, yielding

indubitable *adjective* = **certain**, evident, incontestable, incontrovertible, indisputable, irrefutable, obvious, open-and-shut, sure, unarguable, undeniable, undoubted, unquestionable, veritable

induce *verb* **1** = **persuade**, actuate, convince, draw, encourage, get, impel, incite, influence, instigate, move, press, prevail upon, prompt, talk into **2** = **cause**, bring about, effect, engender, generate, give rise to, lead to, occasion, produce, set in motion, set off
➤ **Antonyms**
curb, deter, discourage, dissuade, hinder, prevent, restrain, stop, suppress

inducement *noun* = **incentive**, attraction, bait, carrot (*informal*), cause, clarion call, come-on (*informal*), consideration, encouragement, impulse, incitement, influence, lure, motive, reward, spur, stimulus, urge

indulge *verb* **1** = **gratify**, cater to, feed, give way to, pander to, regale, satiate, satisfy, treat oneself to, yield to **2** = **spoil**, baby, coddle, cosset, favour, fawn on, foster, give in to, go along with, humour, mollycoddle, pamper, pet

indulgence *noun* **1** = **luxury**, extravagance, favour, privilege, treat **2** = **gratification**, appeasement, fulfilment, satiation, satisfaction **3** = **intemperance**, excess,

fondness, immoderation, intemperateness, kindness, leniency, pampering, partiality, permissiveness, profligacy, profligateness, spoiling **4** = **tolerance**, courtesy, forbearance, goodwill, patience, understanding
➤ **Antonyms**
≠**intemperance**: moderation, strictness, temperance, temperateness

indulgent *adjective* = **lenient**, compliant, easy-going, favourable, fond, forbearing, gentle, gratifying, kind, kindly, liberal, mild, permissive, tender, tolerant, understanding
➤ **Antonyms**
austere, demanding, harsh, intolerant, rigorous, stern, strict, stringent, unmerciful

industrialist *noun* = **capitalist**, baron, big businessman, boss, captain of industry, financier, magnate, manufacturer, producer, tycoon

industrious *adjective* = **hard-working**, active, assiduous, busy, conscientious, diligent, energetic, laborious, persevering, persistent, productive, purposeful, sedulous, steady, tireless, zealous
➤ **Antonyms**
good-for-nothing, idle, indolent, lackadaisical, lazy, shiftless, slothful

industriously *adverb* = **diligently**, assiduously, conscientiously, doggedly, hard, like a Trojan, nose to the grindstone (*informal*), perseveringly, sedulously, steadily, without slacking

industry *noun* **1** = **business**, commerce, commercial enterprise, manufacturing, production, trade **2** = **effort**, activity, application, assiduity, determination, diligence, labour, perseverance, persistence, tirelessness, toil, vigour, zeal

inebriated *adjective* = **drunk**, babalas (*S. African*), befuddled, bevvied (*dialect*), blind drunk, blitzed (*slang*), blotto (*slang*), bombed (*slang*), Brahms and Liszt (*slang*), drunk as a skunk, flying (*slang*), fou *or* fu' (*Scot.*), half-cut (*informal*), half seas over (*informal*), high (*informal*), high as a kite (*informal*), inebriate, in one's cups, intoxicated, legless (*informal*), lit up (*slang*), merry (*Brit. informal*), out of it (*slang*), out to it (*Austral. & N.Z. slang*), paralytic (*informal*), pie-eyed (*slang*), pissed (*taboo slang*), plastered (*slang*), rat-arsed (*taboo slang*), smashed (*slang*), sozzled (*informal*), steamboats (*Scot. slang*), steaming (*slang*), stoned (*slang*), the worse for drink, three sheets in the wind (*informal*), tight (*informal*), tipsy, under the influence (*informal*), under the weather (*informal*), wasted (*slang*), wrecked (*slang*), zonked (*slang*)

ineffective *adjective* = **useless**, barren,

basket case, bootless, feeble, fruitless, futile, idle, impotent, inadequate, ineffectual, inefficacious, inefficient, pathetic, unavailing, unproductive, vain, weak, worthless
➤ **Antonyms**
effective, efficacious, efficient, fruitful, potent, productive, useful, worthwhile

ineffectual *adjective* = **weak**, abortive, basket case, bootless, emasculate, feeble, fruitless, futile, idle, impotent, inadequate, incompetent, ineffective, inefficacious, inefficient, inept, lame, pathetic, powerless, unavailing, useless, vain

inefficiency *noun* = **incompetence**, carelessness, disorganization, muddle, slackness, sloppiness

inefficient *adjective* = **incompetent**, cowboy (*informal*), disorganized, feeble, incapable, ineffectual, inefficacious, inept, inexpert, slipshod, sloppy, wasteful, weak
➤ **Antonyms**
able, capable, competent, effective, efficient, expert, organized, skilled

ineligible *adjective* = **unqualified**, disqualified, incompetent (*Law*), objectionable, ruled out, unacceptable, undesirable, unequipped, unfit, unfitted, unsuitable

inept *adjective* **1** = **incompetent**, awkward, bumbling, bungling, cack-handed (*informal*), clumsy, cowboy (*informal*), gauche, inexpert, maladroit, unhandy, unskilful, unworkmanlike **2** = **unsuitable**, absurd, improper, inappropriate, inapt, infelicitous, malapropos, meaningless, out of place, pointless, ridiculous, unfit
➤ **Antonyms**
≠**incompetent**: able, adroit, competent, dexterous, efficient, qualified, skilful, talented ≠**unsuitable**: appropriate, apt, effectual, germane, sensible, suitable

ineptitude *noun* **1** = **incompetence**, clumsiness, gaucheness, incapacity, inexpertness, unfitness, unhandiness **2** = **inappropriateness**, absurdity, pointlessness, uselessness

inequality *noun* = **disparity**, bias, difference, disproportion, diversity, imparity, irregularity, lack of balance, preferentiality, prejudice, unevenness

inequitable *adjective* = **unfair**, biased, discriminatory, one-sided, partial, partisan, preferential, prejudiced, unjust
➤ **Antonyms**
even-handed, fair, impartial, just, unbiased, unprejudiced

inert *adjective* = **inactive**, dead, dormant, dull, idle, immobile, inanimate, indolent, lazy, leaden, lifeless, motionless, passive, quiescent, slack, slothful, sluggish,

slumberous (*chiefly poetic*), static, still, torpid, unmoving, unreactive, unresponsive
➤ **Antonyms**
active, alive, alive and kicking, animated, energetic, full of beans (*informal*), living, mobile, moving, reactive, responsive, vital

inertia *noun* = **inactivity**, apathy, deadness, disinclination to move, drowsiness, dullness, idleness, immobility, indolence, languor, lassitude, laziness, lethargy, listlessness, passivity, sloth, sluggishness, stillness, stupor, torpor, unresponsiveness
➤ **Antonyms**
action, activity, animation, brio, energy, liveliness, vigour, vitality

inescapable *adjective* = **unavoidable**, certain, destined, fated, ineluctable, ineludible (*rare*), inevitable, inexorable, sure

inestimable *adjective* = **incalculable**, beyond price, immeasurable, invaluable, precious, priceless, prodigious

inevitable *adjective* = **unavoidable**, assured, certain, decreed, destined, fixed, ineluctable, inescapable, inexorable, necessary, ordained, settled, sure, unpreventable
➤ **Antonyms**
avoidable, escapable, evadable, preventable, uncertain

inevitably *adverb* = **unavoidably**, as a necessary consequence, as a result, automatically, certainly, necessarily, of necessity, perforce, surely, willy-nilly

inexcusable *adjective* = **unforgivable**, indefensible, inexpiable, outrageous, unjustifiable, unpardonable, unwarrantable
➤ **Antonyms**
defensible, excusable, forgivable, justifiable, pardonable

inexhaustible *adjective* **1** = **endless**, bottomless, boundless, illimitable, infinite, limitless, measureless, never-ending, unbounded **2** = **tireless**, indefatigable, undaunted, unfailing, unflagging, untiring, unwearied, unwearying
➤ **Antonyms**
≠**endless**: bounded, exhaustible, finite, limitable, limited, measurable ≠**tireless**: daunted, enervated, failing, flagging, tiring, wearied

inexorable *adjective* = **unrelenting**, adamant, cruel, hard, harsh, immovable, implacable, ineluctable, inescapable, inflexible, merciless, obdurate, pitiless, relentless, remorseless, severe, unappeasable, unbending, unyielding
➤ **Antonyms**
bending, flexible, lenient, movable, relenting, yielding

inexorably *adverb* = **relentlessly**,

implacably, inevitably, irresistibly, remorselessly, unrelentingly

inexpensive *adjective* = **cheap**, bargain, budget, economical, low-cost, low-priced, modest, reasonable
➤ **Antonyms**
costly, dear, exorbitant, expensive, high-priced, pricey, uneconomical

inexperience *noun* = **unfamiliarity**, callowness, greenness, ignorance, newness, rawness, unexpertness

inexperienced *adjective* = **immature**, amateur, callow, fresh, green, new, raw, unaccustomed, unacquainted, unfamiliar, unfledged, unpractised, unschooled, unseasoned, unskilled, untrained, untried, unused, unversed, wet behind the ears (*informal*)
➤ **Antonyms**
experienced, familiar, knowledgeable, practised, seasoned, skilled, trained, versed

inexpert *adjective* = **amateurish**, awkward, bungling, cack-handed (*informal*), clumsy, inept, maladroit, skill-less, unhandy, unpractised, unprofessional, unskilful, unskilled, unworkmanlike

inexplicable *adjective* = **unaccountable**, baffling, beyond comprehension, enigmatic, incomprehensible, inscrutable, insoluble, mysterious, mystifying, strange, unfathomable, unintelligible
➤ **Antonyms**
comprehensible, explainable, explicable, fathomable, intelligible, soluble, understandable

inexpressible *adjective* = **indescribable**, incommunicable, indefinable, ineffable, unspeakable, unutterable

inexpressive *adjective* = **impassive**, bland, blank, cold, dead, deadpan, emotionless, empty, expressionless, inanimate, inscrutable, lifeless, stony, vacant

inextricably *adverb* = **inseparably**, indissolubly, indistinguishably, intricately, irretrievably, totally

infallibility *noun* 1 = **perfection**, faultlessness, impeccability, irrefutability, omniscience, supremacy, unerringness 2 = **reliability**, dependability, safety, sureness, trustworthiness

infallible *adjective* 1 = **perfect**, faultless, impeccable, omniscient, unerring, unimpeachable 2 = **sure**, certain, dependable, foolproof, reliable, sure-fire (*informal*), trustworthy, unbeatable, unfailing
➤ **Antonyms**
≠**perfect**: errant, fallible, human, imperfect, mortal ≠**sure**: doubtful, dubious, uncertain, undependable, unreliable, unsure

infamous *adjective* = **notorious**, abominable, atrocious, base, detestable, disgraceful, dishonourable, disreputable, egregious, flagitious, hateful, heinous, ignominious, ill-famed, iniquitous, loathsome, monstrous, nefarious, odious, opprobrious, outrageous, scandalous, scurvy, shameful, shocking, vile, villainous, wicked
➤ **Antonyms**
esteemed, glorious, honourable, noble, reputable, virtuous

infancy *noun* 1 = **early childhood**, babyhood 2 = **beginnings**, cradle, dawn, early stages, emergence, inception, origins, outset, start
➤ **Antonyms**
≠**beginnings**: close, conclusion, death, end, expiration, finish, termination

infant *noun* 1 = **baby**, ankle-biter (*Austral. slang*), babe, babe in arms, bairn (*Scot.*), child, little one, neonate, newborn child, rug rat (*slang*), sprog (*slang*), suckling, toddler, tot, wean (*Scot.*) ♦ *adjective* 2 = **early**, baby, dawning, developing, emergent, growing, immature, initial, nascent, newborn, unfledged, young

infantile *adjective* = **childish**, babyish, immature, puerile, tender, weak, young
➤ **Antonyms**
adult, developed, mature

infatuate *verb* = **obsess**, befool, beguile, besot, bewitch, captivate, delude, enchant, enrapture, fascinate, make a fool of, mislead, stupefy, sweep one off one's feet, turn (someone's) head

infatuated *adjective* = **obsessed**, beguiled, besotted, bewitched, captivated, carried away, crazy about (*informal*), enamoured, enraptured, fascinated, head over heels in love with, inflamed, intoxicated, possessed, smitten (*informal*), spellbound, swept off one's feet, under the spell of

infatuation *noun* = **obsession**, crush (*informal*), fixation, folly, foolishness, madness, passion, thing (*informal*)

infect *verb* = **contaminate**, affect, blight, corrupt, defile, influence, poison, pollute, spread to *or* among, taint, touch, vitiate

infection *noun* = **contamination**, contagion, corruption, defilement, poison, pollution, septicity, virus

infectious *adjective* = **catching**, communicable, contagious, contaminating, corrupting, defiling, infective, pestilential, poisoning, polluting, spreading, transmittable, virulent, vitiating

infer *verb* = **deduce**, conclude, conjecture, derive, gather, presume, put two and two together, read between the lines, surmise, understand

inference *noun* = **deduction**, assumption, conclusion, conjecture, consequence, corollary, illation (*rare*), presumption, reading, surmise

inferior *adjective* **1** = **lower**, junior, lesser, menial, minor, secondary, subordinate, subsidiary, under, underneath **2** = **substandard**, bad, bush-league (*Austral. & N.Z. informal*), chickenshit (*U.S. slang*), crappy (*slang*), dime-a-dozen (*informal*), duff (*Brit. informal*), end-of-the-pier (*Brit. informal*), for the birds (*informal*), imperfect, indifferent, low-grade, low-rent (*informal, chiefly U.S.*), mean, mediocre, no great shakes (*informal*), not a patch on, not much cop (*Brit. slang*), of a sort *or* of sorts, pants (*informal*), piss-poor (*taboo slang*), poor, poorer, poxy (*slang*), second-class, second-rate, shoddy, strictly for the birds (*informal*), tinhorn (*U.S. slang*), two-bit (*U.S. & Canad. slang*), worse ♦ *noun* **3** = **underling**, junior, menial, subordinate
➤ **Antonyms**
adjective ≠**lower**: greater, higher, senior, superior, top ≠**substandard**: excellent, fine, first-class

inferiority *noun* **1** = **inadequacy**, badness, deficiency, imperfection, insignificance, meanness, mediocrity, shoddiness, unimportance, worthlessness **2** = **subservience**, abasement, inferior status *or* standing, lowliness, subordination
➤ **Antonyms**
≠**inadequacy**: eminence, excellence, superiority ≠**subservience**: advantage, ascendancy, dominance, superiority

infernal *adjective* **1** = **hellish**, chthonian, Hadean, lower, nether, Plutonian, Stygian, Tartarean (*literary*), underworld **2** = **devilish**, accursed, damnable, damned, demonic, diabolical, fiendish, hellish, malevolent, malicious, satanic
➤ **Antonyms**
≠**hellish**: celestial, heavenly ≠**devilish**: angelic, glorious, godlike, seraphic

infertile *adjective* = **barren**, infecund, nonproductive, sterile, unfruitful, unproductive
➤ **Antonyms**
fecund, fertile, fruitful, generative, productive

infertility *noun* = **sterility**, barrenness, infecundity, unfruitfulness, unproductiveness

infest *verb* = **overrun**, beset, flood, invade, penetrate, permeate, ravage, swarm, throng

infested *adjective* = **overrun**, alive, beset, crawling, lousy (*slang*), pervaded, plagued, ravaged, ridden, swarming, teeming

infiltrate *verb* = **penetrate**, creep in, filter through, insinuate oneself, make inroads (into), percolate, permeate, pervade, sneak

in (*informal*), work *or* worm one's way into

infinite *adjective* = **never-ending**, absolute, all-embracing, bottomless, boundless, enormous, eternal, everlasting, illimitable, immeasurable, immense, inestimable, inexhaustible, interminable, limitless, measureless, numberless, perpetual, stupendous, total, unbounded, uncounted, untold, vast, wide, without end, without number
➤ **Antonyms**
bounded, circumscribed, finite, limited, measurable, restricted

infinitesimal *adjective* = **microscopic**, atomic, inappreciable, insignificant, minuscule, minute, negligible, teensy-weensy, teeny, teeny-weeny, tiny, unnoticeable, wee
➤ **Antonyms**
enormous, great, huge, infinite, large, vast

infinity *noun* = **eternity**, boundlessness, endlessness, immensity, infinitude, perpetuity, vastness

infirm *adjective* **1** = **frail**, ailing, debilitated, decrepit, doddering, doddery, enfeebled, failing, feeble, lame, weak **2** = **irresolute**, faltering, indecisive, insecure, shaky, unsound, unstable, vacillating, wavering, weak, wobbly
➤ **Antonyms**
≠**frail**: healthy, hearty, robust, sound, strong, sturdy, vigorous

infirmity *noun* **1** = **frailty**, debility, decrepitude, deficiency, feebleness, ill health, imperfection, sickliness, vulnerability **2** = **ailment**, defect, disorder, failing, fault, malady, sickness, weakness
➤ **Antonyms**
≠**frailty**: health, soundness, stability, strength, vigour, wellness

inflame *verb* **1** = **enrage**, agitate, anger, arouse, embitter, exasperate, excite, fire, foment, heat, ignite, impassion, incense, infuriate, intoxicate, kindle, madden, make one's blood boil, provoke, rile, rouse, stimulate **2** = **aggravate**, exacerbate, exasperate, fan, increase, intensify, worsen
➤ **Antonyms**
allay, calm, cool, discourage, extinguish, pacify, quench, quiet, soothe, suppress

inflamed *adjective* = **sore**, angry, chafing, festering, fevered, heated, hot, infected, red, septic, swollen

inflammable *adjective* = **flammable**, combustible, incendiary

inflammation *noun* = **soreness**, burning, heat, painfulness, rash, redness, sore, tenderness

inflammatory *adjective* = **provocative**, anarchic, demagogic, explosive, fiery, incendiary, inflaming, instigative, insurgent, intemperate, like a red rag to a bull, rabble-rousing, rabid, riotous, seditious

inflate verb = **expand**, aerate, aggrandize, amplify, balloon, bloat, blow up, boost, dilate, distend, enlarge, escalate, exaggerate, increase, puff up or out, pump up, swell
➤ **Antonyms**
collapse, compress, contract, deflate, diminish, lessen, shrink

inflated adjective = **exaggerated**, bombastic, grandiloquent, ostentatious, overblown, swollen

inflation noun = **expansion**, aggrandizement, blowing up, distension, enhancement, enlargement, escalation, extension, increase, intensification, puffiness, rise, spread, swelling, tumefaction

inflection noun 1 = **intonation**, accentuation, modulation 2 Grammar = **conjugation**, declension 3 = **bend**, angle, arc, arch, bow, crook, curvature

inflexibility noun 1 = **obstinacy**, fixity, intransigence, obduracy, steeliness 2 = **rigidity**, hardness, immovability, inelasticity, stiffness, stringency

inflexible adjective 1 = **obstinate**, adamant, brassbound, dyed-in-the-wool, firm, fixed, hard and fast, immovable, immutable, implacable, inexorable, intractable, iron, obdurate, relentless, resolute, rigorous, set, set in one's ways, steadfast, steely, stiff-necked, strict, stringent, stubborn, unadaptable, unbending, unchangeable, uncompromising, unyielding 2 = **inelastic**, hard, hardened, nonflexible, rigid, stiff, taut
➤ **Antonyms**
≠**obstinate**: flexible, irresolute, movable, variable, yielding ≠**inelastic**: elastic, flexible, lissom(e), pliable, pliant, supple, yielding

inflict verb = **impose**, administer, apply, deliver, exact, levy, mete or deal out, visit, wreak

infliction noun 1 = **imposition**, administration, exaction, perpetration, wreaking 2 = **affliction**, penalty, punishment, trouble, visitation, worry

influence noun 1 = **effect**, hold, magnetism, power, rule, spell, sway, weight 2 = **control**, ascendancy, authority, direction, domination, mastery 3 = **power**, bottom, clout (informal), connections, good offices, importance, leverage, prestige, pull (informal), weight ♦ verb 4 = **affect**, act or work upon, control, direct, guide, impact on, manipulate, modify, sway 5 = **persuade**, arouse, dispose, incite, incline, induce, instigate, move, predispose, prompt, rouse 6 = **carry weight with**, bring pressure to bear upon, cut any ice with (informal), make

oneself felt, pull strings (informal)

influential adjective = **important**, authoritative, controlling, effective, efficacious, forcible, guiding, instrumental, leading, meaningful, momentous, moving, persuasive, potent, powerful, significant, telling, weighty
➤ **Antonyms**
impotent, ineffective, ineffectual, powerless, unimportant, uninfluential, unpersuasive, weak

influx noun = **arrival**, convergence, flow, incursion, inflow, inrush, inundation, invasion, rush

inform verb 1 = **tell**, acquaint, advise, apprise, clue in (informal), communicate, enlighten, give (someone) to understand, instruct, keep (someone) posted, leak to, let know, make conversant (with), notify, put (someone) in the picture (informal), send word to, teach, tip off 2 = **betray**, blab, blow the gaff (Brit. slang), blow the whistle on (informal), clype (Scot.), denounce, grass (Brit. slang), incriminate, inculpate, let the cat out of the bag, nark (Brit., Austral., & N.Z. slang), peach (slang), put the finger on (informal), rat (informal), shop (slang, chiefly Brit.), sing (slang, chiefly U.S.), snitch (slang), spill one's guts (slang), spill the beans (informal), squeal (slang), tell all, tell on (informal) 3 = **inspire**, animate, characterize, illuminate, imbue, permeate, suffuse, typify

informal adjective = **relaxed**, casual, colloquial, cosy, easy, familiar, natural, simple, unceremonious, unconstrained, unofficial
➤ **Antonyms**
ceremonious, constrained, conventional, formal, official, stiff

informality noun = **familiarity**, casualness, ease, lack of ceremony, naturalness, relaxation, simplicity

information noun = **facts**, advice, blurb, counsel, data, dope (informal), gen (Brit. informal), info (informal), inside story, instruction, intelligence, knowledge, latest (informal), lowdown (informal), material, message, news, notice, report, tidings, word

informative adjective = **instructive**, chatty, communicative, edifying, educational, enlightening, forthcoming, gossipy, illuminating, newsy, revealing

informed adjective = **knowledgeable**, abreast, acquainted, au courant, au fait, briefed, conversant, enlightened, erudite, expert, familiar, genned up (Brit. informal), in the know (informal), in the loop, in the picture, keeping one's finger on the pulse, learned, posted, primed, reliable, up, up to date, versed, well-read

informer *noun* = **betrayer**, accuser, grass (*Brit. slang*), Judas, nark (*Brit., Austral., & N.Z. slang*), sneak, squealer (*slang*), stool pigeon

infrequent *adjective* = **occasional**, few and far between, once in a blue moon, rare, sporadic, uncommon, unusual
➤ **Antonyms**
common, customary, frequent, habitual, often, regular, usual

infringe *verb* **1** = **break**, contravene, disobey, transgress, violate **2 infringe on** *or* **upon** = **intrude on**, encroach on, trespass on

infringement *noun* = **contravention**, breach, infraction, noncompliance, nonobservance, transgression, trespass, violation

infuriate *verb* = **enrage**, anger, be like a red rag to a bull, exasperate, gall, get one's back up, get one's goat (*slang*), incense, irritate, madden, make one's blood boil, make one see red (*informal*), make one's hackles rise, nark (*Brit., Austral., & N.Z. slang*), provoke, put one's back up, raise one's hackles, rile
➤ **Antonyms**
appease, calm, mollify, pacify, placate, propitiate, soothe

infuriating *adjective* = **annoying**, aggravating (*informal*), exasperating, galling, irritating, maddening, mortifying, pestilential, provoking, vexatious

ingenious *adjective* = **creative**, adroit, bright, brilliant, clever, crafty, dexterous, fertile, inventive, masterly, original, ready, resourceful, shrewd, skilful, subtle
➤ **Antonyms**
artless, clumsy, unimaginative, uninventive, unoriginal, unresourceful, unskilful

ingenuity *noun* = **originality**, adroitness, cleverness, faculty, flair, genius, gift, ingeniousness, inventiveness, knack, resourcefulness, sharpness, shrewdness, skill, turn
➤ **Antonyms**
clumsiness, dullness, incompetence, ineptitude, ineptness

ingenuous *adjective* = **naive**, artless, candid, childlike, frank, guileless, honest, innocent, open, plain, simple, sincere, trustful, trusting, unreserved, unsophisticated, unstudied
➤ **Antonyms**
artful, crafty, devious, insincere, reserved, sly, sophisticated, subtle, wily

ingenuousness *noun* = **naivety**, artlessness, candour, frankness, guilelessness, innocence, openness, trustingness, unsuspiciousness

➤ **Antonyms**
artfulness, craftiness, insincerity, slyness, sophistication, subterfuge, subtlety

inglorious *adjective* = **dishonourable**, discreditable, disgraceful, disreputable, failed, humiliating, ignoble, ignominious, infamous, obscure, shameful, unheroic, unknown, unsuccessful, unsung

ingratiate *verb* = **pander to**, be a yes man, blandish, brown-nose (*taboo slang*), crawl, curry favour, fawn, flatter, get in with, get on the right side of, grovel, insinuate oneself, keep (someone) sweet, kiss (someone's) ass (*U.S. & Canad. taboo slang*), lick someone's arse (*taboo slang*), lick (someone's) boots, play up to, rub (someone) up the right way (*informal*), seek the favour (of someone), suck up to (*informal*), toady, worm oneself into (someone's) favour

ingratiating *adjective* = **sycophantic**, bootlicking (*informal*), crawling, fawning, flattering, humble, obsequious, servile, timeserving, toadying, unctuous

ingratitude *noun* = **ungratefulness**, thanklessness, unappreciativeness
➤ **Antonyms**
appreciation, gratefulness, gratitude, thankfulness, thanks, thanksgiving

ingredient *noun* = **component**, constituent, element, part

inhabit *verb* = **live**, abide, dwell, lodge, make one's home, occupy, people, populate, possess, reside, take up residence in, tenant

inhabitant *noun* = **dweller**, aborigine, citizen, denizen, indigene, indweller, inmate, native, occupant, occupier, resident, tenant

inhabited *adjective* = **populated**, colonized, developed, held, occupied, peopled, settled, tenanted

inhale *verb* = **breathe in**, draw in, gasp, respire, suck in
➤ **Antonyms**
blow, breathe out, exhale, expire

inherent *adjective* = **innate**, basic, congenital, connate, essential, hereditary, immanent, inborn, inbred, inbuilt, ingrained, inherited, in one's blood, instinctive, intrinsic, native, natural
➤ **Antonyms**
alien, extraneous, extrinsic, imposed, superficial, supplementary

inherit *verb* = **be left**, accede to, be bequeathed, come into, fall heir to, succeed to

inheritance *noun* = **legacy**, bequest, birthright, heritage, patrimony

inhibit *verb* = **restrain**, arrest, bar, bridle, check, constrain, cramp (someone's) style (*informal*), curb, debar, discourage, forbid,

frustrate, hinder, hold back *or* in, impede, obstruct, prevent, prohibit, stem the flow, stop, throw a spanner in the works
➤ **Antonyms**
abet, allow, enable, encourage, further, let, permit, support

inhibited *adjective* = **shy**, constrained, frustrated, guarded, repressed, reserved, reticent, self-conscious, subdued, uptight (*informal*), withdrawn
➤ **Antonyms**
free, natural, outgoing, relaxed, spontaneous, uninhibited, unreserved

inhibition *noun* = **shyness**, bar, block, check, embargo, hang-up (*informal*), hindrance, interdict, mental blockage, obstacle, prohibition, reserve, restraint, restriction, reticence, self-consciousness

inhospitable *adjective* 1 = **unfriendly**, cool, uncongenial, ungenerous, unkind, unreceptive, unsociable, unwelcoming, xenophobic 2 = **bleak**, bare, barren, desolate, empty, forbidding, godforsaken, hostile, lonely, sterile, unfavourable, uninhabitable
➤ **Antonyms**
≠**unfriendly:** amicable, friendly, generous, genial, gracious, hospitable, sociable, welcoming

inhuman *adjective* = **cruel**, animal, barbaric, barbarous, bestial, brutal, cold-blooded, diabolical, fiendish, heartless, merciless, pitiless, remorseless, ruthless, savage, unfeeling, vicious
➤ **Antonyms**
charitable, compassionate, feeling, humane, merciful, sensitive, tender, warmhearted

inhumane *adjective* = **cruel**, brutal, heartless, pitiless, uncompassionate, unfeeling, unkind, unsympathetic

inhumanity *noun* = **cruelty**, atrocity, barbarism, brutality, brutishness, cold-bloodedness, cold-heartedness, hardheartedness, heartlessness, pitilessness, ruthlessness, unkindness, viciousness

inimical *adjective* = **hostile**, adverse, antagonistic, antipathetic, contrary, destructive, disaffected, harmful, hurtful, ill-disposed, injurious, noxious, opposed, oppugnant (*rare*), pernicious, repugnant, unfavourable, unfriendly, unwelcoming
➤ **Antonyms**
affable, amicable, congenial, favourable, friendly, good, helpful, kindly, sympathetic, welcoming

inimitable *adjective* = **unique**, consummate, incomparable, matchless, nonpareil, peerless, supreme, unequalled, unexampled, unmatched, unparalleled, unrivalled, unsurpassable

iniquitous *adjective* = **wicked**, abominable, accursed, atrocious, base, criminal, evil, heinous, immoral, infamous, nefarious, reprehensible, reprobate, sinful, unjust, unrighteous, vicious

iniquity *noun* = **wickedness**, abomination, baseness, crime, evil, evildoing, heinousness, infamy, injustice, misdeed, offence, sin, sinfulness, unrighteousness, wrong, wrongdoing
➤ **Antonyms**
fairness, goodness, honesty, integrity, justice, morality, righteousness, uprightness, virtue

initial *adjective* = **first**, beginning, commencing, early, inaugural, inceptive, inchoate, incipient, introductory, opening, primary
➤ **Antonyms**
closing, concluding, ending, final, last, terminal, ultimate

initially *adverb* = **at first**, at *or* in the beginning, at the outset, at the start, first, firstly, in the early stages, originally, primarily, to begin with

initiate *verb* 1 = **begin**, break the ice, commence, get under way, inaugurate, institute, kick off (*informal*), kick-start, launch, lay the foundations of, open, originate, pioneer, set going, set in motion, set the ball rolling, start 2 = **induct**, indoctrinate, instate, introduce, invest 3 = **instruct**, acquaint with, coach, familiarize with, teach, train ✦ *noun* 4 = **novice**, beginner, convert, entrant, learner, member, probationer, proselyte, tyro

initiation *noun* = **introduction**, admission, baptism of fire, commencement, debut, enrolment, entrance, inauguration, inception, induction, installation, instatement, investiture

initiative *noun* 1 = **first step**, advantage, beginning, commencement, first move, lead 2 = **resourcefulness**, ambition, drive, dynamism, enterprise, get-up-and-go (*informal*), inventiveness, leadership, originality, push (*informal*), resource

inject *verb* 1 = **vaccinate**, inoculate, jab (*informal*), shoot (*informal*) 2 = **introduce**, bring in, infuse, insert, instil, interject

injection *noun* 1 = **vaccination**, inoculation, jab (*informal*), shot (*informal*), vaccine 2 = **introduction**, dose, infusion, insertion, interjection

injudicious *adjective* = **unwise**, foolish, hasty, ill-advised, ill-judged, ill-timed, impolitic, imprudent, incautious, inconsiderate, indiscreet, inexpedient, rash, unthinking
➤ **Antonyms**
cautious, considerate, discreet, expedient,

judicious, prudent, well-timed, wise

injunction *noun* = **order**, admonition, command, dictate, exhortation, instruction, mandate, precept, ruling

injure *verb* = **hurt**, abuse, blemish, blight, break, damage, deface, disable, harm, impair, maltreat, mar, ruin, spoil, tarnish, undermine, vitiate, weaken, wound, wrong

injured *adjective* **1** = **hurt**, broken, damaged, disabled, lamed, undermined, weakened, wounded **2** = **wronged**, abused, blackened, blemished, defamed, ill-treated, maligned, maltreated, offended, tarnished, vilified **3** = **upset**, cut to the quick, disgruntled, displeased, hurt, long-suffering, put out, reproachful, stung, unhappy, wounded

injury *noun* = **harm**, abuse, damage, detriment, disservice, evil, grievance, hurt, ill, injustice, mischief, ruin, trauma (*Pathology*), wound, wrong

injustice *noun* = **unfairness**, bias, discrimination, favouritism, inequality, inequity, iniquity, one-sidedness, oppression, partiality, partisanship, prejudice, unjustness, unlawfulness, wrong
➤ **Antonyms**
equality, equity, fairness, impartiality, justice, lawfulness, rectitude, right

inkling *noun* = **suspicion**, clue, conception, faintest *or* foggiest idea, glimmering, hint, idea, indication, intimation, notion, suggestion, whisper

inland *adjective* = **interior**, domestic, internal, upcountry

inlet *noun* = **bay**, arm (of the sea), bight, cove, creek, entrance, firth *or* frith (*Scot.*), fjord, ingress, passage, sea loch (*Scot.*)

inmost *or* **innermost** *adjective* = **deepest**, basic, buried, central, deep, essential, intimate, personal, private, secret

innate *adjective* = **inborn**, congenital, connate, constitutional, essential, immanent, inbred, indigenous, ingrained, inherent, inherited, in one's blood, instinctive, intrinsic, intuitive, native, natural
➤ **Antonyms**
accidental, acquired, affected, assumed, cultivated, fostered, incidental, learned, nurtured, unnatural

inner *adjective* **1** = **inside**, central, essential, interior, internal, intestinal, inward, middle **2** = **mental**, emotional, psychological, spiritual **3** = **hidden**, esoteric, intimate, personal, private, repressed, secret, unrevealed
➤ **Antonyms**
≠**inside**: exterior, external, outer, outside, outward ≠**hidden**: exposed, obvious, overt, revealed, surface, unconcealed, unrepressed, visible

innkeeper *noun* = **publican**, host *or* hostess, hotelier, landlord *or* landlady, mine host

innocence *noun* **1** = **guiltlessness**, blamelessness, chastity, clean hands, incorruptibility, probity, purity, righteousness, sinlessness, stainlessness, uprightness, virginity, virtue **2** = **naïveté**, artlessness, credulousness, freshness, guilelessness, gullibility, inexperience, ingenuousness, simplicity, unsophistication, unworldliness **3** = **harmlessness**, innocuousness, innoxiousness, inoffensiveness **4** = **ignorance**, lack of knowledge, nescience (*literary*), unawareness, unfamiliarity
➤ **Antonyms**
≠**guiltlessness**: corruption, guilt, impurity, offensiveness, sinfulness, wrongness
≠**naïveté**: artfulness, cunning, disingenuousness, guile, wiliness, worldliness

innocent *adjective* **1** = **not guilty**, blameless, clear, faultless, guiltless, honest, in the clear, squeaky-clean, uninvolved, unoffending **2** = **pure**, chaste, immaculate, impeccable, incorrupt, pristine, righteous, sinless, spotless, stainless, unblemished, unsullied, upright, virgin, virginal **3** = **harmless**, innocuous, inoffensive, unmalicious, unobjectionable, well-intentioned, well-meant **4** = **naive**, artless, childlike, credulous, frank, guileless, gullible, ingenuous, open, simple, unsuspicious, unworldly, wet behind the ears (*informal*) **5** innocent of = **lacking**, clear of, empty of, free from, ignorant, nescient, unacquainted with, unaware, unfamiliar with, untouched by ♦ *noun* **6** = **child**, babe (in arms) (*informal*), greenhorn (*informal*), ingénue *or* (*masc.*) ingénu
➤ **Antonyms**
adjective ≠**not guilty**: blameworthy, culpable, guilty, responsible ≠**pure**: corrupt, dishonest, immoral, impure, sinful, wrong ≠**harmless**: evil, harmful, iniquitous, malicious, offensive, wicked ≠**naive**: artful, disingenuous, sophisticated, worldly

innovation *noun* = **modernization**, alteration, change, departure, introduction, modernism, newness, novelty, variation

innovative *adjective* = **novel**, inventive, new, transformational, variational

innuendo *noun* = **insinuation**, aspersion, hint, implication, imputation, intimation, overtone, suggestion, whisper

innumerable *adjective* = **countless**, beyond number, incalculable, infinite, many, multitudinous, myriad, numberless, numerous, unnumbered, untold
➤ **Antonyms**
calculable, computable, finite, limited,

measurable, numbered

inoffensive *adjective* = **harmless,** humble, innocent, innocuous, innoxious, mild, neutral, nonprovocative, peaceable, quiet, retiring, unobjectionable, unobtrusive, unoffending
➤ **Antonyms**
abrasive, harmful, irksome, irritating, malicious, objectionable, offensive, provocative

inoperative *adjective* = **out of action,** broken, broken-down, buggered (*slang, chiefly Brit.*), defective, *hors de combat*, ineffective, ineffectual, inefficacious, invalid, nonactive, null and void, on the fritz (*U.S. slang*), out of commission, out of order, out of service, unserviceable, unworkable, useless

inopportune *adjective* = **inconvenient,** ill-chosen, ill-timed, inappropriate, inauspicious, malapropos, mistimed, unfavourable, unfortunate, unpropitious, unseasonable, unsuitable, untimely
➤ **Antonyms**
appropriate, auspicious, convenient, favourable, fortunate, opportune, seasonable, suitable, timely, well-timed

inordinate *adjective* = **excessive,** disproportionate, exorbitant, extravagant, immoderate, intemperate, preposterous, unconscionable, undue, unreasonable, unrestrained, unwarranted
➤ **Antonyms**
inhibited, moderate, reasonable, restrained, rightful, sensible, temperate

inorganic *adjective* = **artificial,** chemical, man-made, mineral

inquest *noun* = **inquiry,** inquisition, investigation, probe

inquire, enquire *verb* **1** = **ask,** query, question, request information, seek information **2** = **investigate,** examine, explore, inspect, look into, make inquiries, probe, research, scrutinize, search

inquiring *adjective* = **inquisitive,** analytical, curious, doubtful, interested, investigative, nosy (*informal*), outward-looking, probing, questioning, searching, wondering

inquiry, enquiry *noun* **1** = **question,** query **2** = **investigation,** examination, exploration, inquest, interrogation, probe, research, scrutiny, search, study, survey

inquisition *noun* = **investigation,** cross-examination, examination, grilling (*informal*), inquest, inquiry, questioning, quizzing, third degree (*informal*)

inquisitive *adjective* = **curious,** inquiring, intrusive, nosy (*informal*), nosy-parkering (*informal*), peering, probing, prying, questioning, scrutinizing, snooping (*informal*), snoopy (*informal*)

➤ **Antonyms**
apathetic, incurious, indifferent, unconcerned, uninterested, unquestioning

inroad *noun* **make inroads upon** = **encroach upon,** consume, eat away, eat up *or* into, use up

insane *adjective* **1** = **mad,** barking (*slang*), barking mad (*slang*), cracked (*slang*), crackers (*Brit. slang*), crazed, crazy, cuckoo (*informal*), demented, deranged, doolally (*slang*), gaga (*informal*), having a screw loose (*informal*), loopy (*informal*), mental (*slang*), mentally disordered, mentally ill, *non compos mentis,* not right in the head, not the full shilling (*informal*), nuts (*slang*), off one's rocker (*slang*), off one's trolley (*slang*), of unsound mind, out of one's mind, round the bend (*informal*), round the twist (*informal*), screwy (*informal*) **2** = **stupid,** bizarre, daft (*informal*), dumb-ass (*slang*), fatuous, foolish, idiotic, impractical, inane, irrational, irresponsible, lunatic, preposterous, senseless
➤ **Antonyms**
logical, lucid, normal, practical, rational, reasonable, reasoned, sane, sensible, sound

insanitary *adjective* = **unhealthy,** contaminated, dirtied, dirty, disease-ridden, feculent, filthy, impure, infected, infested, insalubrious, noxious, polluted, unclean, unhygienic
➤ **Antonyms**
clean, healthy, hygienic, pure, salubrious, unpolluted

insanity *noun* **1** = **madness,** aberration, craziness, delirium, dementia, frenzy, mental derangement, mental disorder, mental illness **2** = **stupidity,** folly, irresponsibility, lunacy, preposterousness, senselessness
➤ **Antonyms**
logic, lucidity, normality, rationality, reason, sanity, sense, soundness, wisdom

insatiable *adjective* = **unquenchable,** edacious, gluttonous, greedy, insatiate, intemperate, quenchless, rapacious, ravenous, unappeasable, voracious
➤ **Antonyms**
appeasable, limited, quenchable, satiable, temperate

inscribe *verb* **1** = **carve,** cut, engrave, etch, impress, imprint **2** = **dedicate,** address **3** = **enrol,** engross, enlist, enter, record, register, write

inscription *noun* = **engraving,** dedication, label, legend, lettering, saying, words

inscrutable *adjective* **1** = **enigmatic,** blank, deadpan, impenetrable, poker-faced (*informal*), sphinxlike, unreadable **2** = **mysterious,** hidden, incomprehensible, inexplicable, undiscoverable, unexplainable,

unfathomable, unintelligible
➤ Antonyms
≠**enigmatic:** open, penetrable, readable,
revealing, transparent ≠**mysterious:** clear,
comprehensible, evident, explainable,
explicable, intelligible, lucid, manifest,
obvious, palpable, patent, plain,
understandable

insecure *adjective* **1** = **anxious**, afraid,
uncertain, unconfident, unsure **2** = **unsafe,**
dangerous, defenceless, exposed, hazardous,
ill-protected, open to attack, perilous,
unguarded, unprotected, unshielded,
vulnerable, wide-open **3** = **unstable,** built
upon sand, flimsy, frail, insubstantial, loose,
on thin ice, precarious, rickety, rocky, shaky,
unreliable, unsound, unsteady, weak, wobbly
➤ Antonyms
≠**anxious:** assured, certain, confident,
decisive, secure ≠**unsafe:** protected, safe,
secure ≠**unstable:** firm, reliable, secure,
sound, stable, steady, substantial, sure

insecurity *noun* **1** = **anxiety,** fear,
uncertainty, unsureness, worry **2**
= **vulnerability,** danger, defencelessness,
hazard, peril, risk, uncertainty, weakness **3**
= **unsteadiness,** dubiety, frailness, instability,
precariousness, shakiness, uncertainty,
unreliability, weakness
➤ Antonyms
≠**anxiety:** assurance, certainty, confidence,
security ≠**vulnerability:** dependability,
safety ≠**unsteadiness:** firmness, reliability,
security, stability, steadiness

insensibility *noun* **1** = **unconsciousness,**
inertness, numbness **2** = **insensitivity,**
apathy, callousness, dullness, indifference,
inertia, lethargy, torpor

insensible *adjective* **1** = **benumbed,**
anaesthetized, dull, inert, insensate,
numbed, torpid **2** = **unaware,** apathetic,
callous, cold, deaf, hard-hearted, impassive,
impervious, indifferent, oblivious, unaffected,
unconscious, unfeeling, unmindful,
unmoved, unresponsive, unsusceptible,
untouched **3** = **imperceptible,**
imperceivable, minuscule, negligible,
unnoticeable
➤ Antonyms
≠**unaware:** affected, aware, conscious,
feeling, mindful, responsive, sensible

insensitive *adjective* **1** = **unfeeling,**
callous, crass, hardened, imperceptive,
indifferent, obtuse, tactless, thick-skinned,
tough, uncaring, unconcerned,
unresponsive, unsusceptible **2 insensitive to**
= **unaffected by,** dead to, immune to,
impervious to, proof against, unmoved by
➤ Antonyms
≠**unfeeling:** caring, concerned, perceptive,
responsive, sensitive, susceptible,

sympathetic, tactful, tender

inseparable *adjective* **1** = **devoted,** bosom,
close, intimate **2** = **indivisible,** conjoined,
inalienable, indissoluble, inseverable

insert *verb* = **enter,** embed, implant, infix,
interject, interpolate, interpose, introduce,
place, pop in (*informal*), put, set, stick in,
tuck in, work in
➤ Antonyms
delete, extract, pull out, remove, take out,
withdraw

insertion *noun* = **inclusion,** addition,
implant, insert, inset, interpolation,
introduction, supplement

inside *adjective* **1** = **inner,** innermost,
interior, internal, intramural, inward **2**
= **confidential,** classified, esoteric, exclusive,
internal, limited, private, restricted, secret
♦ *adverb* **3** = **indoors,** under cover, within
♦ *noun* **4** = **interior,** contents, inner part **5
insides** *Informal* = **stomach,** belly, bowels,
entrails, gut, guts, innards (*informal*),
internal organs, viscera, vitals
➤ Antonyms
adjective ≠**inner:** exterior, external,
extramural, outer, outermost, outside,
outward

insidious *adjective* = **stealthy,** artful, crafty,
crooked, cunning, deceitful, deceptive,
designing, disingenuous, duplicitous,
guileful, intriguing, Machiavellian, slick, sly,
smooth, sneaking, subtle, surreptitious,
treacherous, tricky, wily
➤ Antonyms
artless, conspicuous, forthright, honest,
ingenuous, obvious, open, sincere,
straightforward, upright

insight *noun* = **understanding,** acumen,
awareness, comprehension, discernment,
intuition, intuitiveness, judgment,
observation, penetration, perception,
perspicacity, vision

insignia *noun* = **badge,** crest, decoration,
distinguishing mark, earmark, emblem,
ensign, symbol

insignificance *noun* = **unimportance,**
immateriality, inconsequence, irrelevance,
meaninglessness, negligibility, paltriness,
pettiness, triviality, worthlessness
➤ Antonyms
consequence, importance, matter,
meaningfulness, relevance, significance,
weight, worth

insignificant *adjective* = **unimportant,**
flimsy, immaterial, inconsequential,
inconsiderable, irrelevant, meagre,
meaningless, measly, minor, negligible,
nickel-and-dime (*U.S. slang*), nondescript,
nonessential, not worth mentioning,
nugatory, of no account, of no consequence,

of no moment, paltry, petty, scanty, small potatoes, trifling, trivial, unsubstantial, wanky (*taboo slang*)
➤ **Antonyms**
consequential, considerable, essential, important, meaningful, momentous, relevant, significant, substantial, vital, weighty
insincere *adjective* = **deceitful**, deceptive, devious, dishonest, disingenuous, dissembling, dissimulating, double-dealing, duplicitous, evasive, faithless, false, hollow, hypocritical, Janus-faced, lying, mendacious, perfidious, pretended, two-faced, unfaithful, untrue, untruthful, with tongue in cheek
➤ **Antonyms**
direct, earnest, faithful, genuine, honest, sincere, straightforward, true, truthful
insincerity *noun* = **deceitfulness**, deviousness, dishonesty, disingenuousness, dissimulation, duplicity, faithlessness, hypocrisy, lip service, mendacity, perfidy, pretence, untruthfulness
➤ **Antonyms**
directness, faithfulness, honesty, sincerity, truthfulness
insinuate *verb* 1 = **imply**, allude, hint, indicate, intimate, suggest 2 = **ingratiate**, curry favour, get in with, worm *or* work one's way in
insinuation *noun* = **implication**, allusion, aspersion, hint, innuendo, slur, suggestion
insipid *adjective* 1 = **bland**, anaemic, banal, characterless, colourless, drab, dry, dull, flat, ho-hum (*informal*), jejune, lifeless, limp, pointless, prosaic, prosy, spiritless, stale, stupid, tame, tedious, tiresome, trite, unimaginative, uninteresting, vapid, weak, wearisome, wishy-washy (*informal*) 2 = **tasteless**, bland, flavourless, savourless, unappetizing, watered down, watery, wishy-washy (*informal*)
➤ **Antonyms**
≠**bland**: colourful, engaging, exciting, interesting, lively, provocative, spirited, stimulating ≠**tasteless**: appetizing, fiery, palatable, piquant, pungent, savoury, tasty
insipidity, insipidness *noun* 1 = **dullness**, banality, colourlessness, flatness, lack of imagination, pointlessness, staleness, tameness, tediousness, triteness, uninterestingness, vapidity 2 = **tastelessness**, blandness, flavourlessness, lack of flavour
➤ **Antonyms**
≠**dullness**: animation, character, dynamism, gaiety, liveliness, spirit, vitality, vivacity
insist *verb* 1 = **demand**, be firm, brook no refusal, lay down the law, not take no for an answer, persist, press (someone), put one's foot down (*informal*), require, stand firm, stand one's ground, take *or* make a stand, urge 2 = **assert**, asseverate, aver, claim,

contend, hold, maintain, reiterate, repeat, swear, urge, vow
insistence *noun* = **persistence**, assertion, contention, demands, emphasis, importunity, insistency, pressing, reiteration, stress, urging
insistent *adjective* = **persistent**, demanding, dogged, emphatic, exigent, forceful, importunate, incessant, peremptory, persevering, pressing, unrelenting, urgent
insolence *noun* = **rudeness**, abuse, audacity, backchat (*informal*), boldness, cheek (*informal*), chutzpah (*U.S. & Canad. informal*), contemptuousness, contumely, disrespect, effrontery, front, gall (*informal*), impertinence, impudence, incivility, insubordination, offensiveness, pertness, sassiness (*U.S. informal*), sauce (*informal*), uncivility
➤ **Antonyms**
civility, courtesy, deference, esteem, mannerliness, politeness, respect, submission
insolent *adjective* = **rude**, abusive, bold, brazen-faced, contemptuous, fresh (*informal*), impertinent, impudent, insubordinate, insulting, pert, saucy, uncivil
➤ **Antonyms**
civil, courteous, deferential, mannerly, polite, respectful, submissive
insoluble *adjective* = **inexplicable**, baffling, impenetrable, indecipherable, mysterious, mystifying, obscure, unaccountable, unfathomable, unsolvable
➤ **Antonyms**
accountable, comprehensible, explicable, fathomable, penetrable, soluble, solvable
insolvency *noun* = **bankruptcy**, failure, liquidation, ruin
insolvent *adjective* = **bankrupt**, broke (*informal*), failed, gone bust (*informal*), gone to the wall, in queer street (*informal*), in receivership, in the hands of the receivers, on the rocks (*informal*), ruined
insomnia *noun* = **sleeplessness**, wakefulness
inspect *verb* = **examine**, audit, check, check out (*informal*), eye, eyeball (*slang*), give (something *or* someone) the once-over (*informal*), go over *or* through, investigate, look over, oversee, recce (*slang*), research, scan, scrutinize, search, superintend, supervise, survey, take a dekko at (*Brit. slang*), vet, work over
inspection *noun* = **examination**, check, checkup, investigation, look-over, once-over (*informal*), recce (*slang*), review, scan, scrutiny, search, superintendence, supervision, surveillance, survey
inspector *noun* = **examiner**, auditor, censor, checker, critic, investigator, overseer, scrutineer, scrutinizer,

superintendent, supervisor

inspiration *noun* 1 = **revelation**, arousal, awakening, creativity, elevation, encouragement, enthusiasm, exaltation, genius, illumination, insight, stimulation 2 = **influence**, muse, spur, stimulus
➤ **Antonyms**
depressant, deterrent, discouragement, disenchantment

inspire *verb* 1 = **stimulate**, animate, be responsible for, encourage, enliven, fire *or* touch the imagination of, galvanize, gee up, hearten, imbue, influence, infuse, inspirit, instil, rouse, spark off, spur 2 = **arouse**, enkindle, excite, give rise to, produce, quicken, rouse, stir
➤ **Antonyms**
≠**stimulate:** daunt, deflate, depress, discourage, disenchant, dishearten, dispirit

inspired *adjective* 1 = **brilliant**, dazzling, enthralling, exciting, impressive, memorable, of genius, outstanding, superlative, thrilling, wonderful 2 *Of a guess* = **instinctive**, instinctual, intuitive 3 = **uplifted**, aroused, elated, enthused, exalted, exhilarated, galvanized, possessed, stimulated, stirred up

inspiring *adjective* = **uplifting**, affecting, encouraging, exciting, exhilarating, heartening, moving, rousing, stimulating, stirring
➤ **Antonyms**
boring, depressing, discouraging, disheartening, dispiriting, dull, uninspiring

instability *noun* = **unpredictability**, capriciousness, changeableness, disequilibrium, fickleness, fitfulness, fluctuation, fluidity, frailty, imbalance, impermanence, inconstancy, insecurity, irresolution, mutability, oscillation, precariousness, restlessness, shakiness, transience, unsteadiness, vacillation, variability, volatility, wavering, weakness
➤ **Antonyms**
balance, constancy, equilibrium, permanence, predictability, resolution, security, stability, steadiness, strength

install *verb* 1 = **set up**, fix, lay, lodge, place, position, put in, station 2 = **induct**, establish, inaugurate, instate, institute, introduce, invest, set up 3 = **settle**, ensconce, position

installation *noun* 1 = **setting up**, establishment, fitting, instalment, placing, positioning 2 = **induction**, inauguration, instatement, investiture 3 = **equipment**, machinery, plant, system 4 *Military* = **establishment**, base, post, station

instalment *noun* = **portion**, chapter, division, episode, part, repayment, section

instance *noun* 1 = **example**, case, case in point, illustration, occasion, occurrence,

precedent, situation, time 2 = **insistence**, application, behest, demand, entreaty, importunity, impulse, incitement, instigation, pressure, prompting, request, solicitation, urging ◆ *verb* 3 = **quote**, adduce, cite, mention, name, specify

instant *noun* 1 = **second**, bat of an eye (*informal*), flash, jiffy (*informal*), moment, shake (*informal*), split second, tick (*Brit. informal*), trice, twinkling, twinkling of an eye (*informal*), two shakes of a lamb's tail (*informal*) 2 = **juncture**, moment, occasion, point, time ◆ *adjective* 3 = **immediate**, direct, instantaneous, on-the-spot, prompt, quick, quickie (*informal*), split-second, urgent 4 = **precooked**, convenience, fast, ready-mixed 5 = **urgent**, burning, exigent, imperative, importunate, pressing

instantaneous *adjective* = **immediate**, direct, instant, on-the-spot, prompt

instantaneously *adverb* = **immediately**, at once, forthwith, in a fraction of a second, instantly, in the bat of an eye (*informal*), in the same breath, in the twinkling of an eye (*informal*), like a bat out of hell (*slang*), like greased lightning (*informal*), on the instant, on the spot, posthaste, promptly, pronto (*informal*), quick as lightning, straight away, then and there

instantly *adverb* = **immediately**, at once, directly, forthwith, instantaneously, instanter (*Law*), now, on the spot, posthaste, pronto (*informal*), right away, right now, straight away, there and then, this minute, *tout de suite*, without delay

instead *adverb* 1 = **rather**, alternatively, in lieu, in preference, on second thoughts, preferably 2 **instead of** = **in place of**, as an alternative *or* equivalent to, in lieu of, rather than

instigate *verb* = **provoke**, actuate, bring about, encourage, foment, get going, impel, incite, influence, initiate, kick-start, kindle, move, persuade, prod, prompt, rouse, set off, set on, spur, start, stimulate, stir up, trigger, urge, whip up
➤ **Antonyms**
discourage, repress, restrain, stop, suppress

instigation *noun* = **prompting**, behest, bidding, encouragement, incentive, incitement, urging

instigator *noun* = **ringleader**, agitator, firebrand, fomenter, goad, incendiary, inciter, leader, mischief-maker, motivator, prime mover, spur, stirrer (*informal*), troublemaker

instil, instill *verb* = **introduce**, engender, engraft, imbue, implant, impress, inculcate, infix, infuse, insinuate, sow the seeds

instinct *noun* = **intuition**, aptitude, faculty,

feeling, gift, gut feeling (*informal*), gut reaction (*informal*), impulse, knack, natural inclination, predisposition, proclivity, sixth sense, talent, tendency, urge

instinctive *adjective* = **inborn**, automatic, inherent, innate, instinctual, intuitional, intuitive, involuntary, mechanical, native, natural, reflex, spontaneous, unlearned, unpremeditated, unthinking, visceral
➤ Antonyms
acquired, calculated, considered, learned, premeditated, thinking, voluntary, willed

instinctively *adverb* = **intuitively**, automatically, by instinct, in one's bones, involuntarily, naturally, without thinking

institute *noun* 1 = **society**, academy, association, college, conservatory, foundation, guild, institution, school, seat of learning, seminary 2 = **custom**, decree, doctrine, dogma, edict, law, maxim, precedent, precept, principle, regulation, rule, tenet ◆ *verb* 3 = **establish**, appoint, begin, bring into being, commence, constitute, enact, fix, found, induct, initiate, install, introduce, invest, launch, ordain, organize, originate, pioneer, put into operation, set in motion, settle, set up, start
➤ Antonyms
verb ≠**establish**: abandon, abolish, cancel, cease, discontinue, end, stop, suspend, terminate

institution *noun* 1 = **establishment**, academy, college, foundation, hospital, institute, school, seminary, society, university 2 = **custom**, convention, fixture, law, practice, ritual, rule, tradition 3 = **creation**, constitution, enactment, establishment, formation, foundation, initiation, introduction, investiture, investment, organization

institutional *adjective* 1 = **conventional**, accepted, bureaucratic, established, establishment (*informal*), formal, organized, orthodox, societal 2 = **routine**, cheerless, clinical, cold, drab, dreary, dull, forbidding, formal, impersonal, monotonous, regimented, uniform, unwelcoming

instruct *verb* 1 = **order**, bid, canon, charge, command, direct, enjoin, tell 2 = **teach**, coach, discipline, drill, educate, enlighten, ground, guide, inform, school, train, tutor 3 = **brief**, acquaint, advise, apprise, counsel, inform, notify, tell

instruction *noun* 1 = **order**, briefing, command, demand, direction, directive, injunction, mandate, ruling 2 = **teaching**, apprenticeship, coaching, discipline, drilling, education, enlightenment, grounding, guidance, information, lesson(s), preparation, schooling, training, tuition, tutelage

instructions *plural noun* = **orders**, advice, directions, guidance, information, key, recommendations, rules

instructive *adjective* = **informative**, cautionary, didactic, edifying, educational, enlightening, helpful, illuminating, instructional, revealing, useful

instructor *noun* = **teacher**, adviser, coach, demonstrator, exponent, guide, guru, handler, master *or* mistress, mentor, pedagogue, preceptor (*rare*), schoolmaster *or* schoolmistress, trainer, tutor

instrument *noun* 1 = **tool**, apparatus, appliance, contraption (*informal*), contrivance, device, gadget, implement, mechanism, utensil, waldo 2 *Informal* = **puppet**, cat's-paw, dupe, pawn, tool 3 = **means**, agency, agent, channel, factor, force, mechanism, medium, organ, vehicle

instrumental *adjective* = **active**, assisting, auxiliary, conducive, contributory, helpful, helping, influential, involved, of help *or* service, subsidiary, useful

insubordinate *adjective* = **disobedient**, contumacious, defiant, disorderly, fractious, insurgent, mutinous, rebellious, recalcitrant, refractory, riotous, seditious, turbulent, undisciplined, ungovernable, unruly
➤ Antonyms
compliant, deferential, disciplined, docile, obedient, orderly, submissive, subservient

insubordination *noun* = **disobedience**, defiance, indiscipline, insurrection, mutinousness, mutiny, rebellion, recalcitrance, revolt, riotousness, sedition, ungovernability
➤ Antonyms
acquiescence, compliance, deference, discipline, docility, obedience, submission, subordination

insubstantial *adjective* 1 = **flimsy**, feeble, frail, poor, slight, tenuous, thin, weak 2 = **imaginary**, chimerical, ephemeral, false, fanciful, idle, illusory, immaterial, incorporeal, unreal
➤ Antonyms
≠**flimsy**: firm, solid, strong, substantial, weighty

insufferable *adjective* = **unbearable**, detestable, dreadful, enough to test the patience of a saint, enough to try the patience of Job, impossible, insupportable, intolerable, more than flesh and blood can stand, outrageous, past bearing, too much, unendurable, unspeakable
➤ Antonyms
appealing, attractive, bearable, charming, disarming, pleasant

insufficient *adjective* = **inadequate**, deficient, incapable, incommensurate,

incompetent, lacking, scant, short, unfitted, unqualified
➤ **Antonyms**
adequate, ample, commensurate, competent, enough, plentiful, qualified, sufficient

insular *adjective* = **narrow-minded**, blinkered, circumscribed, closed, contracted, cut off, illiberal, inward-looking, isolated, limited, narrow, parish-pump, parochial, petty, prejudiced, provincial
➤ **Antonyms**
broad-minded, cosmopolitan, liberal, open-minded, tolerant, worldly

insulate *verb* = **isolate**, close off, cocoon, cushion, cut off, protect, sequester, shield, wrap up in cotton wool

insult *verb* **1** = **offend**, abuse, affront, call names, give offence to, injure, miscall (*dialect*), outrage, put down, revile, slag (off) (*slang*), slander, slight, snub ♦ *noun* **2** = **abuse**, affront, aspersion, contumely, indignity, insolence, offence, outrage, put-down, rudeness, slap in the face (*informal*), slight, snub
➤ **Antonyms**
verb ≠**offend**: flatter, please, praise ♦ *noun* ≠**abuse**: compliment, flattery, honour

insulting *adjective* = **offensive**, abusive, affronting, contemptuous, degrading, disparaging, insolent, rude, scurrilous, slighting
➤ **Antonyms**
complimentary, deferential, flattering, laudatory, respectful

insuperable *adjective* = **insurmountable**, impassable, invincible, unconquerable
➤ **Antonyms**
conquerable, possible, surmountable

insupportable *adjective* **1** = **intolerable**, insufferable, past bearing, unbearable, unendurable **2** = **unjustifiable**, indefensible, untenable

insurance *noun* = **protection**, assurance, cover, coverage, guarantee, indemnification, indemnity, provision, safeguard, security, something to fall back on (*informal*), warranty

insure *verb* = **protect**, assure, cover, guarantee, indemnify, underwrite, warrant

insurgent *adjective* **1** = **rebellious**, disobedient, insubordinate, insurrectionary, mutinous, revolting, revolutionary, riotous, seditious ♦ *noun* **2** = **rebel**, insurrectionist, mutineer, resister, revolter, revolutionary, revolutionist, rioter

insurmountable *adjective* = **insuperable**, hopeless, impassable, impossible, invincible, overwhelming, unconquerable

insurrection *noun* = **rebellion**, coup,

insurgency, mutiny, putsch, revolt, revolution, riot, rising, sedition, uprising

intact *adjective* = **undamaged**, all in one piece, complete, entire, perfect, scatheless, sound, together, unbroken, undefiled, unharmed, unhurt, unimpaired, uninjured, unscathed, untouched, unviolated, virgin, whole
➤ **Antonyms**
broken, damaged, harmed, impaired, injured

integral *adjective* **1** = **essential**, basic, component, constituent, elemental, fundamental, indispensable, intrinsic, necessary, requisite **2** = **whole**, complete, entire, full, intact, undivided
➤ **Antonyms**
≠**essential**: inessential, unimportant, unnecessary ≠**whole**: fractional

integrate *verb* = **join**, accommodate, amalgamate, assimilate, blend, coalesce, combine, fuse, harmonize, incorporate, intermix, knit, meld, merge, mesh, unite
➤ **Antonyms**
disperse, divide, segregate, separate

integration *noun* = **assimilation**, amalgamation, blending, combining, commingling, fusing, harmony, incorporation, mixing, unification

integrity *noun* **1** = **honesty**, candour, goodness, honour, incorruptibility, principle, probity, purity, rectitude, righteousness, uprightness, virtue **2** = **soundness**, coherence, cohesion, completeness, unity, wholeness
➤ **Antonyms**
≠**honesty**: corruption, deceit, dishonesty, disrepute, immorality

intellect *noun* **1** = **intelligence**, brains (*informal*), judgment, mind, reason, sense, understanding **2** *Informal* = **thinker**, brain (*informal*), egghead (*informal*), genius, intellectual, intelligence, mind

intellectual *adjective* **1** = **scholarly**, bookish, cerebral, highbrow, intelligent, mental, rational, studious, thoughtful ♦ *noun* **2** = **academic**, bluestocking (*usually disparaging*), egghead (*informal*), highbrow, thinker
➤ **Antonyms**
adjective ≠**scholarly**: ignorant, illiterate, material, physical, stupid, unintellectual, unlearned ♦ *noun* ≠**academic**: idiot, moron

intelligence *noun* **1** = **understanding**, acumen, alertness, aptitude, brain power, brains (*informal*), brightness, capacity, cleverness, comprehension, discernment, grey matter (*informal*), intellect, mind, nous (*Brit. slang*), penetration, perception, quickness, reason, sense, smarts (*slang, chiefly U.S.*) **2** = **information**, advice, data,

disclosure, facts, findings, gen (*Brit. informal*), knowledge, low-down (*informal*), news, notice, notification, report, rumour, tidings, tip-off, word
➤ **Antonyms**
≠**understanding:** dullness, ignorance, stupidity ≠**information:** concealment, misinformation

intelligent *adjective* = **clever**, acute, alert, apt, brainy (*informal*), bright, discerning, enlightened, instructed, knowing, penetrating, perspicacious, quick, quick-witted, rational, sharp, smart, thinking, well-informed
➤ **Antonyms**
dim-witted, dull, foolish, ignorant, obtuse, stupid, unintelligent

intelligentsia *noun* = **intellectuals**, eggheads (*informal*), highbrows, illuminati, literati, masterminds, the learned

intelligibility *noun* = **clarity**, clearness, comprehensibility, distinctness, explicitness, lucidity, plainness, precision, simplicity

intelligible *adjective* = **understandable**, clear, comprehensible, distinct, lucid, open, plain
➤ **Antonyms**
confused, garbled, incomprehensible, puzzling, unclear, unintelligible

intemperate *adjective* = **excessive**, extravagant, extreme, immoderate, incontinent, inordinate, intoxicated, O.T.T. (*slang*), over the top (*slang*), passionate, prodigal, profligate, self-indulgent, severe, tempestuous, unbridled, uncontrollable, ungovernable, unrestrained, violent, wild
➤ **Antonyms**
continent, disciplined, moderate, restrained, self-controlled, temperate

intend *verb* 1 = **plan**, aim, be resolved *or* determined, contemplate, determine, have in mind *or* view, mean, meditate, propose, purpose, scheme 2 *often with* **for** = **destine**, aim, consign, design, earmark, mark out, mean, set apart

intense *adjective* 1 = **extreme**, acute, agonizing, close, concentrated, deep, drastic, excessive, exquisite, fierce, forceful, great, harsh, intensive, powerful, profound, protracted, serious (*informal*), severe, strained, unqualified 2 = **passionate**, ardent, burning, consuming, eager, earnest, energetic, fanatical, fervent, fervid, fierce, flaming, forcible, heightened, impassioned, keen, speaking, vehement
➤ **Antonyms**
≠**extreme:** easy, gentle, mild, moderate, relaxed, slight ≠**passionate:** casual, cool, indifferent, subdued, weak

intensely *adverb* = **strongly**, deeply,

extremely, fiercely, passionately, profoundly, seriously (*informal*)

intensify *verb* = **increase**, add fuel to the flames (*informal*), add to, aggravate, augment, boost, concentrate, deepen, emphasize, enhance, escalate, exacerbate, fan the flames of, heighten, magnify, quicken, redouble, reinforce, set off, sharpen, step up (*informal*), strengthen, whet
➤ **Antonyms**
damp down, decrease, dilute, diminish, dull, lessen, minimize, weaken

intensity *noun* = **force**, ardour, concentration, depth, earnestness, emotion, energy, excess, extremity, fanaticism, fervency, fervour, fierceness, fire, intenseness, keenness, passion, potency, power, severity, strain, strength, tension, vehemence, vigour

intensive *adjective* = **concentrated**, all-out, comprehensive, demanding, exhaustive, in-depth, thorough, thoroughgoing

intent *noun* 1 = **intention**, aim, design, end, goal, meaning, object, objective, plan, purpose 2 **to all intents and purposes** = **virtually**, as good as, practically
♦ *adjective* 3 = **intense**, absorbed, alert, attentive, committed, concentrated, earnest, engrossed, fixed, industrious, occupied, piercing, preoccupied, rapt, steadfast, steady, watchful, wrapped up 4 = **resolved**, bent, determined, eager, hellbent (*informal*), resolute, set
➤ **Antonyms**
noun ≠**intention:** chance, fortune
♦ *adjective* ≠**intense:** casual, indifferent
≠**resolved:** irresolute, unsteady, wavering

intention *noun* = **purpose**, aim, design, end, end in view, goal, idea, intent, meaning, object, objective, point, scope, target, view

intentional *adjective* = **deliberate**, calculated, designed, done on purpose, intended, meant, planned, prearranged, preconcerted, premeditated, purposed, studied, wilful
➤ **Antonyms**
accidental, inadvertent, unintentional, unplanned

intentionally *adverb* = **deliberately**, by design, designedly, on purpose, wilfully

intently *adverb* = **attentively**, closely, fixedly, hard, keenly, searchingly, steadily, watchfully

inter *verb* = **bury**, entomb, inhume, inurn, lay to rest, sepulchre

intercede *verb* = **mediate**, advocate, arbitrate, interpose, intervene, plead, speak

intercept *verb* = **seize**, arrest, block, catch,

check, cut off, deflect, head off, interrupt, obstruct, stop, take

intercession noun = **pleading**, advocacy, entreaty, good offices, intervention, mediation, plea, prayer, solicitation, supplication

interchange verb 1 = **switch**, alternate, bandy, barter, exchange, reciprocate, swap, trade ♦ noun 2 = **junction**, alternation, crossfire, exchange, give and take, intersection, reciprocation

interchangeable adjective = **identical**, commutable, equivalent, exchangeable, reciprocal, synonymous, the same, transposable

intercourse noun 1 = **sexual intercourse**, carnal knowledge, coition, coitus, congress, copulation, intimacy, legover (slang), nookie (slang), rumpy-pumpy (slang), sex (informal), sexual act, sexual relations, the other (informal) 2 = **communication**, association, commerce, communion, connection, contact, converse, correspondence, dealings, intercommunication, trade, traffic, truck

interest noun 1 = **curiosity**, affection, attention, attentiveness, attraction, concern, notice, regard, suspicion, sympathy 2 = **importance**, concern, consequence, moment, note, relevance, significance, weight 3 = **hobby**, activity, diversion, leisure activity, pastime, preoccupation, pursuit, relaxation 4 often plural = **advantage**, benefit, boot (dialect), gain, good, profit 5 = **stake**, authority, claim, commitment, influence, investment, involvement, participation, portion, right, share 6 often plural = **business**, affair, care, concern, matter ♦ verb 7 = **arouse one's curiosity**, amuse, attract, catch one's eye, divert, engross, fascinate, hold the attention of, intrigue, move, touch 8 = **engage**, affect, concern, involve
➤ Antonyms
noun ≠**curiosity**: boredom, coolness, disinterest, dispassion, disregard, unconcern ≠**importance**: inconsequence, insignificance, irrelevance, worthlessness ♦ verb ≠**arouse one's curiosity**: bore, burden, irk, repel, tire, weary

interested adjective 1 = **curious**, affected, attentive, attracted, drawn, excited, fascinated, intent, into (informal), keen, moved, responsive, stimulated 2 = **involved**, biased, concerned, implicated, partial, partisan, predisposed, prejudiced
➤ Antonyms
≠**curious**: apathetic, bored, detached, inattentive, indifferent, unconcerned, uninterested, wearied

interesting adjective = **intriguing**,

absorbing, amusing, appealing, attractive, compelling, curious, engaging, engrossing, entertaining, gripping, pleasing, provocative, stimulating, stirring, suspicious, thought-provoking, unusual
➤ Antonyms
boring, dull, mind-numbing, tedious, tiresome, uninteresting

interface noun 1 = **connection**, border, boundary, frontier, link ♦ verb 2 = **connect**, combine, couple, join together, link

interfere verb 1 = **intrude**, butt in, get involved, intermeddle, intervene, meddle, poke one's nose in (informal), put one's two cents in (U.S. slang), stick one's oar in (informal), tamper 2 often with **with** = **conflict**, be a drag upon (informal), block, clash, collide, cramp, frustrate, get in the way of, hamper, handicap, hinder, impede, inhibit, obstruct, trammel

interference noun 1 = **intrusion**, intermeddling, intervention, meddlesomeness, meddling, prying 2 = **conflict**, clashing, collision, impedance, obstruction, opposition

interim adjective 1 = **temporary**, acting, caretaker, improvised, intervening, makeshift, pro tem, provisional, stopgap ♦ noun 2 = **interval**, entr'acte, interregnum, meantime, meanwhile, respite

interior noun 1 = **inside**, bosom, centre, contents, core, heart, innards (informal) 2 Geography = **heartland**, centre, upcountry ♦ adjective 3 = **inside**, inner, internal, inward 4 = **mental**, hidden, inner, intimate, personal, private, secret, spiritual 5 Politics = **domestic**, home
➤ Antonyms
adjective ≠**inside**: exterior, external, outer, outside, outward

interjection noun = **exclamation**, cry, ejaculation, interpolation, interposition

interloper noun = **trespasser**, gate-crasher (informal), intermeddler, intruder, meddler, uninvited guest, unwanted visitor

interlude noun = **interval**, break, breathing space, delay, entr'acte, episode, halt, hiatus, intermission, pause, respite, rest, spell, stop, stoppage, wait

intermediary noun = **mediator**, agent, broker, entrepreneur, go-between, middleman

intermediate adjective = **middle**, halfway, in-between (informal), intermediary, interposed, intervening, mean, mid, midway, transitional

interment noun = **burial**, burying, funeral, inhumation, sepulture

interminable adjective = **endless**, boundless, ceaseless, dragging, everlasting,

immeasurable, infinite, limitless, long, long-drawn-out, long-winded, never-ending, perpetual, protracted, unbounded, unlimited, wearisome
➤ **Antonyms**
bounded, finite, limited, measurable, restricted, temporary

intermingle verb = **mix**, amalgamate, blend, combine, commingle, commix, fuse, interlace, intermix, interweave, meld, merge

intermission noun = **interval**, break, breathing space, cessation, entr'acte, interlude, interruption, let-up (*informal*), lull, pause, recess, respite, rest, stop, stoppage, suspense, suspension

intermittent adjective = **periodic**, broken, discontinuous, fitful, irregular, occasional, punctuated, recurrent, recurring, spasmodic, sporadic, stop-go (*informal*)
➤ **Antonyms**
continuous, steady, unceasing

intern verb = **imprison**, confine, detain, hold, hold in custody

internal adjective **1** = **inner**, inside, interior **2** = **domestic**, civic, home, in-house, intramural **3** = **private**, intimate, subjective
➤ **Antonyms**
≠**inner:** exterior, external, outer, outermost, outside ≠**private:** exposed, revealed, unconcealed

international adjective = **universal**, cosmopolitan, ecumenical (*rare*), global, intercontinental, worldwide

Internet noun = **information superhighway**, cyberspace, the net (*informal*), the web (*informal*), World Wide Web

interpolate verb = **insert**, add, intercalate, introduce

interpolation noun = **insertion**, addition, aside, insert, intercalation, interjection, introduction

interpose verb **1** = **intervene**, come *or* place between, intercede, interfere, intermediate, intrude, mediate, step in **2** = **interrupt**, insert, interject, introduce, put forth, put one's oar in

interpret verb = **explain**, adapt, clarify, construe, decipher, decode, define, elucidate, explicate, expound, make sense of, paraphrase, read, render, solve, spell out, take, throw light on, translate, understand

interpretation noun = **explanation**, analysis, clarification, construction, diagnosis, elucidation, exegesis, explication, exposition, meaning, performance, portrayal, reading, rendering, rendition, sense, signification, translation, understanding, version

interpreter noun = **translator**, annotator,

commentator, exponent, scholiast

interrogate verb = **question**, ask, catechize, cross-examine, cross-question, enquire, examine, give (someone) the third degree (*informal*), grill (*informal*), inquire, investigate, pump, put the screws on (*informal*), quiz

interrogation noun = **questioning**, cross-examination, cross-questioning, examination, grilling (*informal*), inquiry, inquisition, probing, third degree (*informal*)

interrogative adjective = **questioning**, curious, inquiring, inquisitive, inquisitorial, quizzical

interrupt verb **1** = **intrude**, barge in (*informal*), break in, break (someone's) train of thought, butt in, disturb, heckle, hinder, interfere (with), obstruct, punctuate, separate, sever **2** = **suspend**, break, break off, check, cut, cut off, cut short, delay, disconnect, discontinue, disjoin, disunite, divide, hold up, lay aside, stay, stop

interrupted adjective = **disturbed**, broken, cut off, disconnected, discontinuous, incomplete, intermittent, uneven

interruption noun = **stoppage**, break, cessation, disconnection, discontinuance, disruption, dissolution, disturbance, disuniting, division, halt, hiatus, hindrance, hitch, impediment, intrusion, obstacle, obstruction, pause, separation, severance, stop, suspension

intersect verb = **cross**, bisect, crisscross, cut, cut across, divide, meet

intersection noun = **junction**, crossing, crossroads, interchange

interval noun = **break**, delay, distance, entr'acte, gap, hiatus, interim, interlude, intermission, meantime, meanwhile, opening, pause, period, playtime, respite, rest, season, space, spell, term, time, wait

intervene verb **1** = **step in** (*informal*), arbitrate, intercede, interfere, interpose oneself, intrude, involve oneself, mediate, put one's oar in, put one's two cents in (*U.S. slang*), take a hand (*informal*) **2** = **happen**, befall, come to pass, ensue, occur, succeed, supervene, take place

intervention noun = **mediation**, agency, intercession, interference, interposition, intrusion

interview noun **1** = **meeting**, audience, conference, consultation, dialogue, evaluation, oral (examination), press conference, talk ◆ verb **2** = **question**, examine, interrogate, sound out, talk to

interviewer noun = **questioner**, examiner, interlocutor, interrogator, investigator, reporter

interwoven *adjective* = **interconnected**, blended, connected, entwined, inmixed, interlaced, interlocked, intermingled, knit

intestinal *adjective* = **abdominal**, coeliac, duodenal, gut (*informal*), inner, stomachic, visceral

intestines *plural noun* = **guts**, bowels, entrails, innards (*informal*), insides (*informal*), internal organs, viscera, vitals

intimacy *noun* = **familiarity**, closeness, confidence, confidentiality, fraternization, understanding
➤ **Antonyms**
alienation, aloofness, coldness, detachment, distance, estrangement, remoteness, separation

intimate[1] *adjective* **1** = **close**, bosom, cherished, confidential, dear, friendly, near, nearest and dearest, thick (*informal*), warm **2** = **private**, confidential, personal, privy, secret **3** = **detailed**, deep, exhaustive, experienced, first-hand, immediate, in-depth, penetrating, personal, profound, thorough **4** = **snug**, comfy (*informal*), cosy, friendly, tête-à-tête, warm ♦ *noun* **5** = **friend**, bosom friend, buddy (*informal*), china (*Brit. slang*), chum (*informal*), close friend, cock (*Brit. informal*), comrade, confidant *or* confidante, (constant) companion, crony, familiar, gossip (*archaic*), homeboy (*slang, chiefly U.S.*), mate (*informal*), mucker (*Brit. slang*), pal
➤ **Antonyms**
adjective ≠**close**: distant, remote, superficial ≠**private**: known, open, public ♦ *noun* ≠**friend**: enemy, foe, stranger

intimate[2] *verb* **1** = **suggest**, allude, drop a hint, give (someone) to understand, hint, imply, indicate, insinuate, let it be known, tip (someone) the wink (*Brit. informal*), warn **2** = **announce**, communicate, declare, impart, make known, remind, state

intimately *adverb* **1** = **confidingly**, affectionately, closely, confidentially, familiarly, personally, tenderly, very well, warmly **2** = **in detail**, fully, inside out, thoroughly, through and through, to the core, very well

intimation *noun* **1** = **hint**, allusion, indication, inkling, insinuation, reminder, suggestion, warning **2** = **announcement**, communication, declaration, notice

intimidate *verb* = **frighten**, affright (*archaic*), alarm, appal, browbeat, bully, coerce, cow, daunt, dishearten, dismay, dispirit, lean on (*informal*), overawe, scare, scare off (*informal*), subdue, terrify, terrorize, threaten, twist someone's arm (*informal*)

intimidation *noun* = **bullying**, arm-twisting (*informal*), browbeating, coercion, fear, menaces, pressure, terror, terrorization, threat(s)

intolerable *adjective* = **unbearable**, beyond bearing, excruciating, impossible, insufferable, insupportable, more than flesh and blood can stand, not to be borne, painful, unendurable
➤ **Antonyms**
bearable, endurable, painless, possible, sufferable, supportable, tolerable

intolerance *noun* = **narrow-mindedness**, bigotry, chauvinism, discrimination, dogmatism, fanaticism, illiberality, impatience, jingoism, narrowness, prejudice, racialism, racism, xenophobia
➤ **Antonyms**
broad-mindedness, liberality, open-mindedness, patience, tolerance, understanding

intolerant *adjective* = **narrow-minded**, bigoted, chauvinistic, dictatorial, dogmatic, fanatical, illiberal, impatient, narrow, one-sided, prejudiced, racialist, racist, small-minded, uncharitable, xenophobic
➤ **Antonyms**
broad-minded, charitable, lenient, liberal, open-minded, patient, tolerant, understanding

intonation *noun* **1** = **tone**, accentuation, cadence, inflection, modulation **2** = **incantation**, chant

intone *verb* = **recite**, chant, croon, intonate, sing

intoxicate *verb* **1** = **go to one's head**, addle, befuddle, fuddle, inebriate, put (someone) under the table (*informal*), stupefy **2** = **exhilarate**, elate, excite, go to one's head, inflame, make one's head spin, stimulate

intoxicated *adjective* **1** = **drunk**, babalas (*S. African*), bevvied (*dialect*), blitzed (*slang*), blotto (*slang*), bombed (*slang*), Brahms and Liszt (*slang*), canned (*slang*), cut (*Brit. slang*), drunk as a skunk, drunken, flying (*slang*), fuddled, half seas over (*Brit. informal*), high (*informal*), inebriated, in one's cups (*informal*), legless (*informal*), lit up (*slang*), out of it (*slang*), out to it (*Austral. & N.Z. slang*), paralytic (*informal*), pissed (*taboo slang*), plastered (*slang*), rat-arsed (*taboo slang*), smashed (*slang*), sozzled (*informal*), steamboats (*Scot. slang*), steaming (*slang*), stewed (*slang*), stiff (*slang*), stoned (*slang*), the worse for drink, three sheets in the wind (*informal*), tight (*informal*), tipsy, under the influence, wasted (*slang*), wrecked (*slang*), zonked (*slang*) **2** = **euphoric**, dizzy, ecstatic, elated, enraptured, excited, exhilarated, high (*informal*), infatuated, sent (*slang*), stimulated

intoxicating *adjective* 1 = alcoholic, inebriant, intoxicant, spirituous, strong 2 = exciting, exhilarating, heady, sexy (*informal*), stimulating, thrilling

intoxication *noun* 1 = drunkenness, inebriation, inebriety, insobriety, tipsiness 2 = excitement, delirium, elation, euphoria, exaltation, exhilaration, infatuation

intransigent *adjective* = uncompromising, hardline, immovable, intractable, obdurate, obstinate, stiff-necked, stubborn, tenacious, tough, unbending, unbudgeable, unyielding
➤ Antonyms
acquiescent, compliant, compromising, flexible, open-minded

intrepid *adjective* = fearless, audacious, bold, brave, courageous, daring, dauntless, doughty, gallant, game (*informal*), have-a-go (*informal*), heroic, lion-hearted, nerveless, plucky, resolute, stalwart, stouthearted, unafraid, undaunted, unflinching, valiant, valorous
➤ Antonyms
afraid, cautious, cowardly, craven, daunted, faint-hearted, fearful, flinching, irresolute, timid

intricacy *noun* = complexity, complication, convolutions, elaborateness, entanglement, intricateness, involution, involvement, knottiness, obscurity

intricate *adjective* = complicated, baroque, Byzantine, complex, convoluted, daedal (*literary*), difficult, elaborate, fancy, involved, knotty, labyrinthine, obscure, perplexing, rococo, sophisticated, tangled, tortuous
➤ Antonyms
clear, easy, obvious, plain, simple, straightforward

intrigue *verb* 1 = interest, arouse the curiosity of, attract, charm, fascinate, pique, rivet, tickle one's fancy, titillate 2 = plot, connive, conspire, machinate, manoeuvre, scheme ♦ *noun* 3 = plot, cabal, chicanery, collusion, conspiracy, double-dealing, knavery, machination, manipulation, manoeuvre, ruse, scheme, sharp practice, stratagem, trickery, wile 4 = affair, amour, intimacy, liaison, romance

intriguing *adjective* = interesting, beguiling, compelling, diverting, exciting, fascinating, tantalizing, titillating

intrinsic *adjective* = inborn, basic, built-in, central, congenital, constitutional, elemental, essential, fundamental, genuine, inbred, inherent, native, natural, radical, real, true, underlying
➤ Antonyms
acquired, added, appended, artificial,

extraneous, extrinsic, incidental

introduce *verb* 1 = present, acquaint, do the honours, familiarize, make known, make the introduction 2 = bring up, advance, air, broach, moot, offer, propose, put forward, recommend, set forth, submit, suggest, ventilate 3 = bring in, begin, commence, establish, found, inaugurate, initiate, institute, launch, organize, pioneer, set up, start, usher in 4 = insert, add, inject, interpolate, interpose, put in, throw in (*informal*) 5 = lead into, announce, lead off, open, preface

introduction *noun* 1 = launch, baptism, debut, establishment, first acquaintance, inauguration, induction, initiation, institution, pioneering, presentation 2 = opening, commencement, exordium, foreword, intro (*informal*), lead-in, opening passage, opening remarks, overture, preamble, preface, preliminaries, prelude, proem, prolegomena, prolegomenon, prologue 3 = insertion, addition, interpolation
➤ Antonyms
≠launch: completion, elimination, termination ≠opening: conclusion, end, epilogue ≠insertion: extraction, removal, withdrawal

introductory *adjective* = preliminary, early, elementary, first, inaugural, initial, initiatory, opening, precursory, prefatory, preparatory, starting
➤ Antonyms
closing, concluding, final, last, terminating

introspective *adjective* = inward-looking, brooding, contemplative, inner-directed, introverted, meditative, pensive, subjective

introverted *adjective* = introspective, indrawn, inner-directed, inward-looking, self-centred, self-contained, withdrawn

intrude *verb* = interfere, butt in, encroach, infringe, interrupt, meddle, obtrude, push in, put one's two cents in (*U.S. slang*), thrust oneself in *or* forward, trespass, violate

intruder *noun* = trespasser, burglar, gate-crasher (*informal*), infiltrator, interloper, invader, prowler, raider, snooper (*informal*), squatter, thief

intrusion *noun* = invasion, encroachment, infringement, interference, interruption, trespass, violation

intrusive *adjective* = interfering, disturbing, forward, impertinent, importunate, invasive, meddlesome, nosy (*informal*), officious, presumptuous, pushy (*informal*), uncalled-for, unwanted

intuition *noun* = instinct, discernment, hunch, insight, perception, presentiment, sixth sense

intuitive *adjective* = **instinctive**, innate, instinctual, involuntary, spontaneous, unreflecting, untaught

inundate *verb* = **flood**, deluge, drown, engulf, glut, immerse, overflow, overrun, overwhelm, submerge, swamp

inundation *noun* = **flood**, deluge, overflow, tidal wave, torrent

invade *verb* **1** = **attack**, assail, assault, burst in, descend upon, encroach, infringe, make inroads, occupy, raid, violate **2** = **infest**, infect, overrun, overspread, penetrate, permeate, pervade, swarm over

invader *noun* = **attacker**, aggressor, alien, looter, plunderer, raider, trespasser

invalid [1] *noun* **1** = **patient**, convalescent, valetudinarian ◆ *adjective* **2** = **disabled**, ailing, bedridden, feeble, frail, ill, infirm, poorly (*informal*), sick, sickly, valetudinarian, weak

invalid [2] *adjective* = **null and void**, baseless, fallacious, false, ill-founded, illogical, inoperative, irrational, not binding, nugatory, null, unfounded, unscientific, unsound, untrue, void, worthless
➤ **Antonyms**
logical, operative, rational, solid, sound, true, valid, viable

invalidate *verb* = **nullify**, abrogate, annul, cancel, overrule, overthrow, quash, render null and void, rescind, undermine, undo, weaken
➤ **Antonyms**
authorize, empower, ratify, sanction, strengthen, validate

invaluable *adjective* = **precious**, beyond price, costly, inestimable, priceless, valuable, worth one's *or* its weight in gold
➤ **Antonyms**
cheap, rubbishy, valueless, worthless

invariable *adjective* = **regular**, changeless, consistent, constant, fixed, immutable, inflexible, rigid, set, unalterable, unchangeable, unchanging, unfailing, uniform, unvarying, unwavering
➤ **Antonyms**
alterable, changeable, changing, differing, flexible, inconsistent, irregular, uneven, variable, varying

invariably *adverb* = **consistently**, always, customarily, day in, day out, ever, every time, habitually, inevitably, on every occasion, perpetually, regularly, unfailingly, without exception

invasion *noun* **1** = **attack**, aggression, assault, campaign, foray, incursion, inroad, irruption, offensive, onslaught, raid **2** = **intrusion**, breach, encroachment, infiltration, infraction, infringement, overstepping, usurpation, violation

invective *noun* = **abuse**, berating, billingsgate, castigation, censure, contumely, denunciation, diatribe, obloquy, philippic(s), reproach, revilement, sarcasm, tirade, tongue-lashing, vilification, vituperation

invent *verb* **1** = **create**, coin, come up with (*informal*), conceive, contrive, design, devise, discover, dream up (*informal*), formulate, imagine, improvise, originate, think up **2** = **make up**, concoct, cook up (*informal*), fabricate, feign, forge, manufacture, trump up

invention *noun* **1** = **creation**, brainchild (*informal*), contraption, contrivance, design, development, device, discovery, gadget, instrument, waldo **2** = **creativity**, coinage, creativeness, genius, imagination, ingenuity, inspiration, inventiveness, originality, resourcefulness **3** = **fiction**, deceit, fabrication, fake, falsehood, fantasy, fib (*informal*), figment *or* product of (someone's) imagination, forgery, lie, prevarication, sham, story, tall story (*informal*), untruth, urban legend, urban myth, yarn

inventive *adjective* = **creative**, fertile, gifted, ground-breaking, imaginative, ingenious, innovative, inspired, original, resourceful
➤ **Antonyms**
imitative, pedestrian, trite, unimaginative, uninspired, uninventive

inventor *noun* = **creator**, architect, author, coiner, designer, father, framer, maker, originator

inventory *noun* = **list**, account, catalogue, file, record, register, roll, roster, schedule, stock book

inverse *adjective* = **opposite**, contrary, converse, inverted, reverse, reversed, transposed

inversion *noun* **1** = **reversal**, contraposition, contrariety, transposal, transposition **2** = **opposite**, antipode, antithesis, contrary

invert *verb* = **overturn**, capsize, introvert, intussuscept (*Pathology*), invaginate (*Pathology*), overset, reverse, transpose, turn inside out, turn turtle, turn upside down, upset, upturn

invest *verb* **1** = **spend**, advance, devote, lay out, put in, sink **2** = **empower**, authorize, charge, license, sanction, vest **3** = **install**, adopt, consecrate, enthrone, establish, inaugurate, induct, ordain **4** = **provide**, endow, endue, supply

investigate *verb* = **examine**, consider, explore, go into, inquire into, inspect, look into, make inquiries, probe, put to the test, recce (*slang*), research, scrutinize, search, sift, study, work over

investigation noun = **examination**, analysis, exploration, fact finding, hearing, inquest, inquiry, inspection, probe, recce (slang), research, review, scrutiny, search, study, survey

investigator noun = **examiner**, dick (slang, chiefly U.S.), gumshoe (U.S. slang), inquirer, (private) detective, private eye (informal), researcher, reviewer, sleuth

investiture noun = **installation**, admission, enthronement, inauguration, induction, instatement, investing, investment, ordination

investment noun 1 = **transaction**, asset, investing, speculation, venture 2 = **stake**, ante (informal), contribution

inveterate adjective = **long-standing**, chronic, confirmed, deep-dyed (usually derogatory), deep-rooted, deep-seated, dyed-in-the-wool, entrenched, established, habitual, hard-core, hardened, incorrigible, incurable, ineradicable, ingrained, obstinate

invidious adjective = **undesirable**, hateful, thankless, unpleasant
➤ Antonyms
desirable, pleasant, pleasing

invigilate verb = **watch over**, conduct, keep an eye on, oversee, preside over, run, superintend, supervise

invigorate verb = **refresh**, animate, brace, buck up (informal), energize, enliven, exhilarate, fortify, freshen (up), galvanize, harden, liven up, nerve, pep up, perk up, put new heart into, quicken, rejuvenate, revitalize, stimulate, strengthen

invincible adjective = **unbeatable**, impregnable, indestructible, indomitable, inseparable, insuperable, invulnerable, unassailable, unconquerable, unsurmountable, unyielding
➤ Antonyms
assailable, beatable, conquerable, defenceless, fallible, powerless, unprotected, vulnerable, weak, yielding

inviolable adjective = **sacrosanct**, hallowed, holy, inalienable, sacred, unalterable

inviolate adjective = **intact**, entire, pure, sacred, stainless, unbroken, undefiled, undisturbed, unhurt, unpolluted, unstained, unsullied, untouched, virgin, whole
➤ Antonyms
abused, broken, defiled, polluted, stained, sullied, touched, violated

invisible adjective 1 = **unseen**, imperceptible, indiscernible, out of sight, unperceivable 2 = **hidden**, concealed, disguised, inappreciable, inconspicuous, infinitesimal, microscopic
➤ Antonyms
≠unseen: discernible, distinct, obvious, perceptible, seen, visible

invitation noun 1 = **request**, asking, begging, bidding, call, invite (informal), solicitation, summons, supplication 2 = **inducement**, allurement, challenge, come-on (informal), coquetry, enticement, glad eye (informal), incitement, open door, overture, provocation, temptation

invite verb 1 = **request**, ask, beg, bid, call, request the pleasure of (someone's) company, solicit, summon 2 = **encourage**, allure, ask for (informal), attract, bring on, court, draw, entice, lead, leave the door open to, provoke, solicit, tempt, welcome

inviting adjective = **tempting**, alluring, appealing, attractive, beguiling, captivating, delightful, engaging, enticing, fascinating, intriguing, magnetic, mouthwatering, pleasing, seductive, warm, welcoming, winning
➤ Antonyms
disagreeable, offensive, off-putting (Brit. informal), repellent, unappealing, unattractive, undesirable, uninviting, unpleasant

invocation noun = **appeal**, beseeching, entreaty, petition, prayer, supplication

invoke verb 1 = **apply**, call in, have recourse to, implement, initiate, put into effect, resort to, use 2 = **call upon**, adjure, appeal to, beg, beseech, conjure, entreat, implore, petition, pray, solicit, supplicate

involuntary adjective = **unintentional**, automatic, blind, conditioned, instinctive, instinctual, reflex, spontaneous, unconscious, uncontrolled, unthinking
➤ Antonyms
calculated, deliberate, intentional, planned, purposed, volitional, voluntary, wilful

involve verb 1 = **include**, comprehend, comprise, contain, cover, embrace, incorporate, number among, take in 2 = **entail**, imply, mean, necessitate, presuppose, require 3 = **concern**, affect, associate, compromise, connect, draw in, implicate, incriminate, inculpate, mix up (informal), stitch up (slang), touch 4 = **complicate**, embroil, enmesh, entangle, link, mire, mix up, snarl up, tangle 5 = **preoccupy**, absorb, bind, commit, engage, engross, grip, hold, rivet, wrap up

involved adjective 1 = **complicated**, Byzantine, complex, confusing, convoluted, difficult, elaborate, intricate, knotty, labyrinthine, sophisticated, tangled, tortuous 2 = **concerned**, caught (up), implicated, in on (informal), mixed up in or with, occupied, participating, taking part, up to one's ears in

> ➤ Antonyms
≠ **complicated**: easy, easy-peasy (*slang*), elementary, simple, simplified, straightforward, uncomplicated, unsophisticated

involvement *noun* 1 = **connection**, association, commitment, concern, dedication, interest, participation, responsibility 2 = **complication**, complexity, difficulty, embarrassment, entanglement, imbroglio, intricacy, problem, ramification

invulnerable *adjective* = **safe**, impenetrable, indestructible, insusceptible, invincible, proof against, secure, unassailable
➤ Antonyms
assailable, defenceless, insecure, susceptible, unprotected, vulnerable, weak

inward *adjective* 1 = **incoming**, entering, inbound, inflowing, ingoing, inpouring, penetrating 2 = **internal**, inner, inside, interior 3 = **private**, confidential, hidden, inmost, innermost, personal, privy, secret
➤ Antonyms
≠ **internal**: exterior, external, outer, outermost, outside, outward ≠ **private**: open, public

inwardly *adverb* = **privately**, at heart, deep down, in one's head, in one's inmost heart, inside, secretly, to oneself, within

irate *adjective* = **angry**, annoyed, cross, enraged, furious, incensed, indignant, infuriated, livid

Irish *adjective* = **Hibernian**, green

irksome *adjective* = **irritating**, aggravating, annoying, boring, bothersome, burdensome, disagreeable, exasperating, tedious, tiresome, troublesome, trying, uninteresting, unwelcome, vexatious, vexing, wearisome
➤ Antonyms
agreeable, enjoyable, gratifying, interesting, pleasant, pleasing, welcome

iron *adjective* 1 = **ferrous**, chalybeate, ferric, irony 2 = **inflexible**, adamant, cruel, hard, heavy, immovable, implacable, indomitable, obdurate, rigid, robust, steel, steely, strong, tough, unbending, unyielding
➤ Antonyms
≠ **inflexible**: bending, easy, flexible, light, malleable, pliable, soft, weak, yielding

ironic, ironical *adjective* 1 = **sarcastic**, double-edged, mocking, mordacious, sardonic, satirical, scoffing, sneering, with tongue in cheek, wry 2 = **paradoxical**, incongruous

iron out *verb* = **settle**, clear up, eliminate, eradicate, erase, expedite, get rid of, harmonize, put right, reconcile, resolve, simplify, smooth over, sort out, straighten out, unravel

irons *plural noun* = **chains**, bonds, fetters, gyves (*archaic*), manacles, shackles

irony *noun* 1 = **sarcasm**, mockery, satire 2 = **paradox**, contrariness, incongruity

irrational *adjective* 1 = **illogical**, absurd, crackpot (*informal*), crazy, foolish, injudicious, loopy (*informal*), nonsensical, preposterous, silly, unreasonable, unreasoning, unsound, unthinking, unwise 2 = **senseless**, aberrant, brainless, crazy, demented, insane, mindless, muddle-headed, raving, unstable, wild
➤ Antonyms
≠ **illogical**: circumspect, judicious, logical, rational, reasonable, sensible, sound, wise

irrationality *noun* = **senselessness**, absurdity, brainlessness, illogicality, insanity, lack of judgment, lunacy, madness, preposterousness, unreasonableness, unsoundness

irreconcilable *adjective* 1 = **incompatible**, clashing, conflicting, diametrically opposed, incongruous, inconsistent, opposed 2 = **inflexible**, hardline, implacable, inexorable, intransigent, unappeasable, uncompromising

irrecoverable *adjective* = **lost**, gone for ever, irreclaimable, irredeemable, irremediable, irreparable, irretrievable, unregainable, unsalvageable, unsavable

irrefutable *adjective* = **undeniable**, apodeictic, apodictic, beyond question, certain, incontestable, incontrovertible, indisputable, indubitable, invincible, irrefragable, irresistible, sure, unanswerable, unassailable, unquestionable

irregular *adjective* 1 = **uneven**, asymmetrical, broken, bumpy, craggy, crooked, elliptic, elliptical, holey, jagged, lopsided, lumpy, pitted, ragged, rough, serrated, unequal, unsymmetrical 2 = **variable**, desultory, disconnected, eccentric, erratic, fitful, fluctuating, fragmentary, haphazard, inconstant, intermittent, nonuniform, occasional, out of order, patchy, random, shifting, spasmodic, sporadic, uncertain, uneven, unmethodical, unpunctual, unsteady, unsystematic, wavering 3 = **unconventional**, abnormal, anomalous, capricious, disorderly, eccentric, exceptional, extraordinary, immoderate, improper, inappropriate, inordinate, odd, peculiar, queer, quirky, rum (*Brit. slang*), unofficial, unorthodox, unsuitable, unusual ◆ *noun* 4 = **guerrilla**, partisan, volunteer
➤ Antonyms
adjective ≠ **uneven**: balanced, equal, even, regular, smooth, symmetrical ≠ **variable**: certain, invariable, methodical, punctual, reliable, steady, systematic
≠ **unconventional**: appropriate, conventional, normal, orthodox, proper,

regular, standard, usual

irregularity *noun* **1** = **unevenness**, asymmetry, bumpiness, crookedness, jaggedness, lack of symmetry, lopsidedness, lumpiness, patchiness, raggedness, roughness, spottiness **2** = **uncertainty**, confusion, desultoriness, disorderliness, disorganization, haphazardness, lack of method, randomness, unpunctuality, unsteadiness **3** = **abnormality**, aberration, anomaly, breach, deviation, eccentricity, freak, malfunction, malpractice, oddity, peculiarity, singularity, unconventionality, unorthodoxy

irregularly *adverb* = **erratically**, anyhow, by fits and starts, disconnectedly, eccentrically, fitfully, haphazardly, in snatches, intermittently, jerkily, now and again, occasionally, off and on, out of sequence, spasmodically, unevenly, unmethodically, unpunctually

irrelevance, irrelevancy *noun* = **inappropriateness**, inappositeness, inaptness, inconsequence, non sequitur
➤ **Antonyms**
appositeness, appropriateness, aptness, consequence, pertinence, point, relevance, suitability

irrelevant *adjective* = **unconnected**, beside the point, extraneous, immaterial, impertinent, inapplicable, inapposite, inappropriate, inapt, inconsequent, neither here nor there, unrelated
➤ **Antonyms**
applicable, apposite, appropriate, apt, connected, fitting, pertinent, related, relevant, suitable

irreparable *adjective* = **beyond repair**, incurable, irrecoverable, irremediable, irreplaceable, irretrievable, irreversible

irreplaceable *adjective* = **indispensable**, invaluable, priceless, unique, vital

irrepressible *adjective* = **ebullient**, boisterous, bubbling over, buoyant, effervescent, insuppressible, uncontainable, uncontrollable, unmanageable, unquenchable, unrestrainable, unstoppable

irreproachable *adjective* = **blameless**, beyond reproach, faultless, guiltless, impeccable, inculpable, innocent, irreprehensible, irreprovable, perfect, pure, squeaky-clean, unblemished, unimpeachable

irresistible *adjective* **1** = **overwhelming**, compelling, compulsive, imperative, overmastering, overpowering, potent, urgent **2** = **seductive**, alluring, beckoning, enchanting, fascinating, ravishing, tempting **3** = **inescapable**, ineluctable, inevitable, inexorable, unavoidable

irresolute *adjective* = **indecisive**, doubtful,

fickle, half-arsed (*Brit. slang*), half-assed (*U.S. & Canad. slang*), half-hearted, hesitant, hesitating, infirm, in two minds, tentative, undecided, undetermined, unsettled, unstable, unsteady, vacillating, wavering, weak
➤ **Antonyms**
decisive, determined, firm, fixed, resolute, resolved, settled, stable, stalwart, steadfast, steady, strong

irrespective of *preposition* = **despite**, apart from, discounting, in spite of, notwithstanding, regardless of, without reference to, without regard to

irresponsible *adjective* = **thoughtless**, careless, featherbrained, flighty, giddy, good-for-nothing, harebrained, harum-scarum, ill-considered, immature, reckless, scatterbrained, shiftless, undependable, unreliable, untrustworthy, wild
➤ **Antonyms**
careful, dependable, level-headed, mature, reliable, responsible, sensible, trustworthy

irreverence *noun* = **disrespect**, cheek (*informal*), cheekiness (*informal*), chutzpah (*U.S. & Canad. informal*), derision, flippancy, impertinence, impudence, lack of respect, mockery, sauce (*informal*)

irreverent *adjective* = **disrespectful**, cheeky (*informal*), contemptuous, derisive, flip (*informal*), flippant, fresh (*informal*), iconoclastic, impertinent, impious, impudent, mocking, sassy (*U.S. informal*), saucy, tongue-in-cheek
➤ **Antonyms**
awed, deferential, meek, pious, respectful, reverent, submissive

irreversible *adjective* = **irrevocable**, final, incurable, irreparable, unalterable

irrevocable *adjective* = **fixed**, changeless, fated, immutable, invariable, irremediable, irretrievable, irreversible, predestined, predetermined, settled, unalterable, unchangeable, unreversible

irrigate *verb* = **water**, flood, inundate, moisten, wet

irritability *noun* = **bad temper**, ill humour, impatience, irascibility, peevishness, petulance, prickliness, testiness, tetchiness, touchiness
➤ **Antonyms**
bonhomie, cheerfulness, complacence, good humour, patience

irritable *adjective* = **bad-tempered**, cantankerous, choleric, crabbed, crabby, cross, crotchety (*informal*), dyspeptic, edgy, exasperated, fiery, fretful, hasty, hot, ill-humoured, ill-tempered, irascible, narky (*Brit. slang*), out of humour, oversensitive,

peevish, petulant, prickly, ratty (*Brit. & N.Z. informal*), snappish, snappy, snarling, tense, testy, tetchy, touchy
➤ **Antonyms**
agreeable, calm, cheerful, complacent, composed, even-tempered, good-natured, imperturbable, patient, unexcitable

irritate *verb* **1 = annoy**, aggravate (*informal*), anger, bother, drive one up the wall (*slang*), enrage, exasperate, fret, gall, get in one's hair (*informal*), get one's back up, get one's dander up (*informal*), get one's goat (*slang*), get one's hackles up, get on one's nerves (*informal*), get on one's wick (*informal*), get under one's skin (*informal*), harass, incense, inflame, infuriate, nark (*Brit., Austral., & N.Z. slang*), needle (*informal*), nettle, offend, pester, piss one off (*taboo slang*), provoke, put one's back up, raise one's hackles, rankle with, rub up the wrong way (*informal*), ruffle, try one's patience, vex **2 = rub**, aggravate, chafe, fret, inflame, intensify, pain
➤ **Antonyms**
≠**annoy:** calm, comfort, gratify, mollify, placate, please, soothe

irritated *adjective* **= annoyed**, angry, bothered, cross, displeased, exasperated, flustered, hacked (off) (*U.S. slang*), harassed, impatient, irritable, nettled, out of humour, peeved (*informal*), piqued, pissed (*taboo slang*), pissed off (*taboo slang*), put out, ruffled, vexed

irritating *adjective* **= annoying**, aggravating (*informal*), displeasing, disquieting, disturbing, galling, infuriating, irksome, maddening, nagging, pestilential, provoking, thorny, troublesome, trying, upsetting, vexatious, worrisome
➤ **Antonyms**
agreeable, assuaging, calming, comforting, mollifying, pleasant, pleasing, quieting, soothing

irritation *noun* **1 = annoyance**, anger, crossness, displeasure, exasperation, ill humour, ill temper, impatience, indignation, irritability, resentment, shortness, snappiness, testiness, vexation, wrath **2 = nuisance**, aggravation (*informal*), annoyance, drag (*informal*), gall, goad, irritant, pain (*informal*), pain in the arse (*taboo informal*), pain in the neck (*informal*), pest, provocation, tease, thorn in one's flesh
➤ **Antonyms**
≠**annoyance:** calm, composure, ease, pleasure, quietude, satisfaction, serenity, tranquillity

island *noun* **= isle**, ait or eyot (*dialect*), atoll, cay or key, islet

isolate *verb* **= separate**, cut off, detach, disconnect, divorce, insulate, quarantine,

segregate, sequester, set apart

isolated *adjective* **1 = remote**, backwoods, hidden, incommunicado, in the middle of nowhere, lonely, off the beaten track, outlying, out-of-the-way, retired, secluded, unfrequented **2 = random**, abnormal, anomalous, exceptional, freak, out on a limb, single, solitary, special, unique, unrelated, untypical, unusual

isolation *noun* **= separation**, aloofness, detachment, disconnection, exile, insularity, insulation, ivory tower, loneliness, quarantine, remoteness, retirement, seclusion, segregation, self-sufficiency, solitude, withdrawal

issue *noun* **1 = topic**, affair, argument, bone of contention, can of worms (*informal*), concern, controversy, matter, matter of contention, point, point in question, problem, question, subject **2 = edition**, copy, impression, instalment, number, printing **3 = outcome**, conclusion, consequence, culmination, effect, end, end result, finale, pay-off (*informal*), result, termination, upshot **4 = children**, descendants, heirs, offspring, progeny, scions, seed (*chiefly biblical*) **5 = distribution**, circulation, delivery, dispersal, dissemination, granting, issuance, issuing, publication, sending out, supply, supplying **6 at issue = under discussion**, at variance, controversial, in disagreement, in dispute, to be decided, unsettled **7 take issue = disagree**, challenge, dispute, object, oppose, raise an objection, take exception ♦ *verb* **8 = give out**, announce, broadcast, circulate, deliver, distribute, emit, promulgate, publish, put in circulation, put out, release **9 = emerge**, arise, be a consequence of, come forth, emanate, flow, originate, proceed, rise, spring, stem
➤ **Antonyms**
noun ≠**outcome:** beginning, cause, inception, start ≠**children:** parent, sire ≠**distribution:** cancellation, recall ♦ *verb* ≠**give out:** revoke, withdraw ≠**emerge:** cause

isthmus *noun* **= strip**, spit

itch *noun* **1 = irritation**, itchiness, prickling, tingling **2 = desire**, craving, hankering, hunger, longing, lust, passion, restlessness, yearning, yen (*informal*) ♦ *verb* **3 = prickle**, crawl, irritate, tickle, tingle **4 = long**, ache, burn, crave, hanker, hunger, lust, pant, pine, yearn

itching *adjective* **= longing**, agog, aquiver, atremble, avid, burning, consumed with curiosity, eager, impatient, inquisitive, mad keen (*informal*), raring, spoiling for

itchy *adjective* **= impatient**, eager, edgy, fidgety, restive, restless, unsettled

item *noun* **1** = **detail**, article, aspect, component, consideration, entry, matter, particular, point, thing **2** = **report**, account, article, bulletin, dispatch, feature, note, notice, paragraph, piece

itemize *verb* = **list**, count, detail, document, enumerate, Instance, inventory, number, particularize, record, set out, specify

itinerant *adjective* = **wandering**, ambulatory, Gypsy, journeying, migratory, nomadic, peripatetic, roaming, roving, travelling, unsettled, vagabond, vagrant, wayfaring

➤ **Antonyms**
established, fixed, resident, rooted, settled, stable

itinerary *noun* **1** = **schedule**, circuit, journey, line, programme, route, timetable, tour **2** = **guidebook**, Baedeker, guide

J j

jab *verb, noun* = **poke**, dig, lunge, nudge, prod, punch, stab, tap, thrust

jabber *verb* = **chatter**, babble, blether, gabble, mumble, prate, rabbit (on) (*Brit. informal*), ramble, yap (*informal*)

jacket *noun* = **covering**, case, casing, coat, envelope, folder, sheath, skin, wrapper, wrapping

jackpot *noun* = **prize**, award, bonanza, kitty, pool, pot, pot of gold at the end of the rainbow, reward, winnings

jack up *verb* 1 = **lift**, elevate, heave, hoist, lift up, raise, rear 2 = **increase**, accelerate, augment, boost, escalate, inflate, put up, raise

jaded *adjective* 1 = **tired**, clapped out (*Austral. & N.Z. informal*), exhausted, fagged (out) (*informal*), fatigued, spent, tired-out, weary, zonked (*slang*) 2 = **bored**, cloyed, dulled, glutted, gorged, sated, satiated, surfeited, tired
➤ **Antonyms**
≠**tired**: bright-eyed and bushy-tailed (*informal*), fresh, refreshed ≠**bored**: eager, enthusiastic, keen

jagged *adjective* = **uneven**, barbed, broken, cleft, craggy, denticulate, indented, notched, pointed, ragged, ridged, rough, serrated, snaggy, spiked, toothed
➤ **Antonyms**
glassy, level, regular, rounded, smooth

jail, gaol *noun* 1 = **prison**, borstal, brig (*chiefly U.S.*), calaboose (*U.S. informal*), can (*slang*), clink (*slang*), cooler (*slang*), inside (*slang*), jailhouse (*Southern U.S.*), jug (*slang*), lockup, nick (*Brit. slang*), penitentiary (*U.S.*), poky *or* pokey (*U.S. & Canad. slang*), quod (*slang*), reformatory, slammer (*slang*), stir (*slang*) ◆ *verb* 2 = **imprison**, confine, detain, immure, impound, incarcerate, lock up, send down

jailer, gaoler *noun* = **guard**, captor, keeper, screw (*slang*), turnkey (*archaic*), warden, warder

jam *verb* 1 = **pack**, cram, force, press, ram, squeeze, stuff, wedge 2 = **crowd**, crush, throng 3 = **congest**, block, cease, clog, halt, obstruct, stall, stick ◆ *noun* 4 = **crush**, crowd, horde, mass, mob, multitude, pack, press, swarm, throng 5 = **predicament**, bind, deep water, dilemma, fix (*informal*), hole (*slang*), hot water, pickle (*informal*),

plight, quandary, scrape (*informal*), spot (*informal*), strait, tight spot, trouble

jamboree *noun* = **festival**, beano (*Brit. slang*), blast (*U.S. slang*), carnival, carousal, carouse, celebration, festivity, fête, frolic, hooley *or* hoolie (*chiefly Irish & N.Z.*), jubilee, merriment, party, rave (*Brit. slang*), rave-up (*Brit. slang*), revelry, spree

jangle *verb* 1 = **rattle**, chime, clank, clash, clatter, jingle, vibrate ◆ *noun* 2 = **clash**, cacophony, clang, clangour, din, dissonance, jar, racket, rattle, reverberation
➤ **Antonyms**
noun ≠**clash**: harmoniousness, mellifluousness, quiet, silence

janitor *noun* = **caretaker**, concierge, custodian, doorkeeper, porter

jar¹ *noun* = **pot**, amphora, carafe, container, crock, flagon, jug, pitcher, receptacle, urn, vase, vessel

jar² *verb* 1 = **irritate**, annoy, clash, discompose, gall, get on one's nerves (*informal*), grate, grind, irk, nark (*Brit., Austral., & N.Z. slang*), nettle, offend, piss one off (*taboo slang*) 2 = **clash**, bicker, contend, disagree, interfere, oppose, quarrel, wrangle 3 = **jolt**, agitate, bump, convulse, disturb, grate, rasp, rattle, rock, shake, vibrate ◆ *noun* 4 = **jolt**, bump, convulsion, shock, vibration

jargon *noun* 1 = **parlance**, argot, cant, dialect, idiom, lingo (*informal*), patois, patter, slang, tongue, usage 2 = **gobbledegook**, balderdash, bunkum *or* buncombe (*chiefly U.S.*), drivel, gabble, gibberish, Greek (*informal*), mumbo jumbo, nonsense, palaver, rigmarole, twaddle

jaundiced *adjective* 1 = **cynical**, preconceived, sceptical 2 = **bitter**, biased, bigoted, distorted, envious, hostile, jealous, partial, prejudiced, resentful, spiteful, suspicious
➤ **Antonyms**
≠**cynical**: credulous, ingenuous, naive, optimistic ≠**bitter**: open-minded, trusting, unbiased

jaunt *noun* = **outing**, airing, excursion, expedition, promenade, ramble, stroll, tour, trip

jaunty *adjective* = **sprightly**, airy, breezy, buoyant, carefree, dapper, gay, high-spirited, lively, perky, self-confident, showy, smart,

sparky, spruce, trim
➤ **Antonyms**
dignified, dull, lifeless, sedate, serious, staid
jaw *Slang* ♦ *noun* **1** = **chat**, chinwag (*Brit. informal*), conversation, gabfest (*informal, chiefly U.S. & Canad.*), gossip, natter, talk ♦ *verb* **2** = **talk**, babble, chat, chatter, chew the fat or rag (*slang*), gossip, lecture, run off at the mouth (*slang*), spout
jaws *plural noun* = **opening**, abyss, aperture, entrance, gates, ingress, maw, mouth, orifice
jazz up *verb* = **enliven**, animate, enhance, heighten, improve
jazzy *adjective* = **flashy**, animated, fancy, gaudy, lively, smart, snazzy (*informal*), spirited, vivacious, wild, zestful
jealous *adjective* **1** = **suspicious**, anxious, apprehensive, attentive, guarded, mistrustful, possessive, protective, solicitous, vigilant, wary, watchful, zealous **2** = **envious**, covetous, desirous, emulous, green, green-eyed, grudging, intolerant, invidious, resentful, rival
➤ **Antonyms**
≠**suspicious**: carefree, indifferent, trusting ≠**envious**: satisfied
jealousy *noun* = **envy**, covetousness, distrust, heart-burning, ill-will, mistrust, possessiveness, resentment, spite, suspicion
jeans *plural noun* = **denims**, Levis (*Trademark*)
jeer *verb* **1** = **mock**, banter, barrack, cock a snook at (*Brit.*), contemn (*formal*), deride, flout, gibe, heckle, hector, knock (*informal*), ridicule, scoff, sneer, taunt ♦ *noun* **2** = **mockery**, abuse, aspersion, boo, catcall, derision, gibe, hiss, hoot, obloquy, ridicule, scoff, sneer, taunt
➤ **Antonyms**
verb ≠**mock**: acclaim, applaud, cheer, clap, praise ♦ *noun* ≠**mockery**: adulation, applause, cheers, encouragement, praise
jell *verb* **1** = **take shape**, come together, crystallize, finalize, form, materialize **2** = **solidify**, congeal, harden, set, thicken
jeopardize *verb* = **endanger**, chance, expose, gamble, hazard, imperil, risk, stake, venture
jeopardy *noun* = **danger**, endangerment, exposure, hazard, insecurity, liability, peril, pitfall, precariousness, risk, venture, vulnerability
jeremiad *noun* = **complaint**, groan, keen, lament, lamentation, moan, plaint, wail
jerk *verb, noun* = **tug**, jolt, lurch, pull, throw, thrust, tweak, twitch, wrench, yank
jerky *adjective* = **bumpy**, bouncy, convulsive, fitful, jolting, jumpy, rough, shaky, spasmodic, tremulous, twitchy, uncontrolled

➤ **Antonyms**
flowing, frictionless, gliding, smooth
jerry-built *adjective* = **ramshackle**, cheap, defective, faulty, flimsy, rickety, shabby, slipshod, thrown together, unsubstantial
➤ **Antonyms**
sturdy, substantial, well-built, well-constructed
jest *noun* **1** = **joke**, banter, bon mot, crack (*slang*), fun, gag (*informal*), hoax, jape, josh (*slang, chiefly U.S. & Canad.*), play, pleasantry, prank, quip, sally, sport, wisecrack (*informal*), witticism ♦ *verb* **2** = **joke**, banter, chaff, deride, gibe, jeer, josh (*slang, chiefly U.S. & Canad.*), kid (*informal*), mock, quip, scoff, sneer, tease
jester *noun* **1** = **clown**, buffoon, fool, harlequin, madcap, mummer, pantaloon, prankster, zany **2** = **humorist**, comedian, comic, joculator or (*fem.*) joculatrix, joker, quipster, wag, wit
jet¹ *noun* **1** = **stream**, flow, fountain, gush, spout, spray, spring **2** = **nozzle**, atomizer, nose, rose, spout, sprayer, sprinkler ♦ *verb* **3** = **fly**, soar, zoom **4** = **stream**, flow, gush, issue, rush, shoot, spew, spout, squirt, surge
jet² *adjective* = **black**, coal-black, ebony, inky, pitch-black, raven, sable
jettison *verb* = **abandon**, discard, dump, eject, expel, heave, scrap, throw overboard, unload
jetty *noun* = **pier**, breakwater, dock, groyne, mole, quay, wharf
jewel *noun* **1** = **gemstone**, brilliant, ornament, precious stone, rock (*slang*), sparkler (*informal*), trinket **2** = **rarity**, charm, collector's item, find, gem, humdinger (*slang*), masterpiece, paragon, pearl, prize, treasure, wonder
jewellery *noun* = **jewels**, finery, gems, ornaments, precious stones, regalia, treasure, trinkets
Jezebel *noun* = **harlot**, harridan, hussy, jade, virago, wanton, witch
jib *verb* = **refuse**, balk, recoil, retreat, shrink, stop short
jibe *see* GIBE
jig *verb* = **skip**, bob, bounce, caper, jiggle, jounce, prance, shake, twitch, wiggle, wobble
jingle *noun* **1** = **song**, chorus, ditty, doggerel, limerick, melody, tune **2** = **rattle**, clang, clangour, clink, reverberation, ringing, tinkle ♦ *verb* **3** = **ring**, chime, clatter, clink, jangle, rattle, tinkle, tintinnabulate
jinx *noun* **1** = **curse**, black magic, evil eye, hex (*U.S. & Canad. informal*), hoodoo (*informal*), nemesis, plague, voodoo ♦ *verb* **2** = **curse**, bewitch, hex (*U.S. & Canad. informal*)

jitters *plural noun* = **nerves**, anxiety, butterflies (in one's stomach) (*informal*), cold feet (*informal*), fidgets, heebie-jeebies (*slang*), nervousness, tenseness, the shakes (*informal*), the willies (*informal*)

jittery *adjective* = **nervous**, agitated, antsy (*informal*), anxious, fidgety, hyper (*informal*), jumpy, neurotic, quivering, shaky, trembling, twitchy (*informal*), wired (*slang*)
➤ Antonyms
calm, composed, laid-back (*informal*), relaxed, together (*slang*), unfazed (*informal*), unflustered

job *noun* 1 = **occupation**, activity, bread and butter (*informal*), business, calling, capacity, career, craft, employment, function, livelihood, métier, office, position, post, profession, situation, trade, vocation 2 = **task**, affair, assignment, charge, chore, concern, contribution, duty, enterprise, errand, function, pursuit, responsibility, role, stint, undertaking, venture, work 3 = **consignment**, allotment, assignment, batch, commission, contract, lot, output, piece, portion, product, share

jobless *adjective* = **unemployed**, idle, inactive, out of work, unoccupied

jockey *verb* = **manoeuvre**, cajole, engineer, finagle (*informal*), ingratiate, insinuate, manage, manipulate, negotiate, trim, wheedle

jocular *adjective* = **humorous**, amusing, comical, droll, facetious, frolicsome, funny, jesting, jocose, jocund, joking, jolly, jovial, ludic (*literary*), playful, roguish, sportive, teasing, waggish, whimsical, witty
➤ Antonyms
earnest, humourless, serious, solemn

jog *verb* 1 = **run**, canter, dogtrot, lope, trot 2 = **nudge**, activate, arouse, prod, prompt, push, remind, shake, stimulate, stir, suggest 3 = **plod**, lumber, traipse (*informal*), tramp, trudge

joie de vivre *noun* = **enthusiasm**, ebullience, enjoyment, gaiety, gusto, joy, joyfulness, pleasure, relish, zest
➤ Antonyms
apathy, depression, distaste

join *verb* 1 = **enrol**, affiliate with, associate with, enlist, enter, sign up 2 = **meet**, adjoin, border, border on, butt, conjoin, extend, reach, touch, verge on 3 = **connect**, accompany, add, adhere, annex, append, attach, cement, combine, couple, fasten, knit, link, marry, splice, tie, unite, yoke
➤ Antonyms
≠enrol: leave, part, quit, resign ≠connect: detach, disconnect, disengage, disentangle, divide, separate, sever, unfasten

joint *adjective* 1 = **shared**, collective, combined, communal, concerted, consolidated, cooperative, joined, mutual, united ♦ *noun* 2 = **junction**, articulation, connection, hinge, intersection, juncture, knot, nexus, node, seam, union ♦ *verb* 3 = **join**, connect, couple, fasten, fit, unite 4 = **divide**, carve, cut up, dismember, dissect, segment, sever, sunder

jointly *adverb* = **collectively**, as one, in common, in conjunction, in league, in partnership, mutually, together, unitedly
➤ Antonyms
individually, separately, singly

joke *noun* 1 = **jest**, frolic, fun, gag (*informal*), jape, josh (*slang, chiefly U.S. & Canad.*), lark, play, prank, pun, quip, quirk, sally, sport, whimsy, wisecrack (*informal*), witticism, yarn 2 = **laughing stock**, buffoon, butt, clown, simpleton, target ♦ *verb* 3 = **jest**, banter, chaff, deride, frolic, gambol, josh (*slang, chiefly U.S. & Canad.*), kid (*informal*), mock, play the fool, quip, ridicule, taunt, tease, wind up (*Brit. slang*)

joker *noun* = **comedian**, buffoon, clown, comic, humorist, jester, kidder (*informal*), prankster, trickster, wag, wit

jolly *adjective* = **happy**, blithesome, carefree, cheerful, chirpy (*informal*), convivial, festive, frolicsome, funny, gay, genial, gladsome (*archaic*), hilarious, jocund, jovial, joyful, joyous, jubilant, ludic (*literary*), merry, mirthful, playful, sportive, sprightly, upbeat (*informal*)
➤ Antonyms
doleful, down in the dumps (*informal*), grave, lugubrious, miserable, morose, serious, solemn

jolt *noun* 1 = **surprise**, blow, bolt from the blue, bombshell, reversal, setback, shock, thunderbolt, whammy (*informal, chiefly U.S.*) 2 = **jerk**, bump, jar, jog, jump, lurch, quiver, shake, start ♦ *verb* 3 = **surprise**, astonish, discompose, disturb, perturb, stagger, startle, stun, upset 4 = **jerk**, jar, jog, jostle, knock, push, shake, shove

jostle *verb* = **push**, bump, butt, crowd, elbow, hustle, jog, joggle, jolt, press, scramble, shake, shove, squeeze, throng, thrust

jot *verb* 1 = **note down**, list, note, record, register, scribble, tally ♦ *noun* 2 = **bit**, ace, atom, detail, fraction, grain, iota, mite, morsel, particle, scintilla, scrap, smidgen or smidgin (*informal, chiefly U.S. & Canad.*), speck, tad (*informal, chiefly U.S.*), tittle, trifle, whit

journal *noun* 1 = **newspaper**, chronicle, daily, gazette, magazine, monthly, paper, periodical, record, register, review, tabloid, weekly, zine (*informal*) **2** = **diary**, chronicle, commonplace book, daybook, log, record

journalist *noun* = **reporter**, broadcaster, columnist, commentator, contributor, correspondent, hack, journo (*slang*), newsman *or* newswoman, newspaperman *or* newspaperwoman, pressman, scribe (*informal*), stringer

journey *noun* **1** = **trip**, excursion, expedition, jaunt, odyssey, outing, passage, peregrination, pilgrimage, progress, ramble, tour, travel, trek, voyage ◆ *verb* **2** = **travel**, fare, fly, go, peregrinate, proceed, ramble, range, roam, rove, tour, traverse, trek, voyage, wander, wend

jovial *adjective* = **cheerful**, airy, animated, blithe, buoyant, cheery, convivial, cordial, gay, glad, happy, hilarious, jocose, jocund, jolly, jubilant, merry, mirthful
➤ **Antonyms**
antisocial, doleful, grumpy, morose, solemn, unfriendly

joy *noun* **1** = **delight**, bliss, ecstasy, elation, exaltation, exultation, felicity, festivity, gaiety, gladness, glee, hilarity, pleasure, rapture, ravishment, satisfaction, transport **2** = **treasure**, charm, delight, gem, jewel, pride, prize, treat, wonder
➤ **Antonyms**
≠**delight**: despair, grief, misery, sorrow, tribulation, unhappiness ≠**treasure**: bane

joyful *adjective* = **delighted**, blithesome, cock-a-hoop, elated, enraptured, floating on air, glad, gladsome (*archaic*), gratified, happy, jocund, jolly, jovial, jubilant, light-hearted, merry, on cloud nine (*informal*), over the moon (*informal*), pleased, rapt, satisfied

joyless *adjective* = **unhappy**, cheerless, dejected, depressed, dismal, dispirited, downcast, down in the dumps (*informal*), dreary, gloomy, miserable, sad

joyous *adjective* = **joyful**, blithe, cheerful, festive, heartening, merry, rapturous

jubilant *adjective* = **overjoyed**, cock-a-hoop, elated, enraptured, euphoric, excited, exuberant, exultant, glad, joyous, over the moon (*informal*), rejoicing, rhapsodic, thrilled, triumphal, triumphant
➤ **Antonyms**
despondent, doleful, downcast, melancholy, sad, sorrowful

jubilation *noun* = **joy**, celebration, ecstasy, elation, excitement, exultation, festivity, jamboree, jubilee, triumph

jubilee *noun* = **celebration**, carnival, festival, festivity, fête, gala, holiday

judge *noun* **1** = **magistrate**, beak (*Brit. slang*), justice **2** = **referee**, adjudicator, arbiter, arbitrator, moderator, umpire **3**
= **critic**, appraiser, arbiter, assessor, authority, connoisseur, evaluator, expert ◆ *verb* **4** = **adjudicate**, adjudge, arbitrate, ascertain, conclude, decide, determine, discern, distinguish, mediate, referee, umpire **5** = **consider**, appraise, appreciate, assess, criticize, esteem, estimate, evaluate, examine, rate, review, value **6** = **try**, adjudge, condemn, decree, doom, find, pass sentence, pronounce sentence, rule, sentence, sit

judgment *noun* **1** = **opinion**, appraisal, assessment, belief, conviction, deduction, diagnosis, estimate, finding, valuation, view **2** = **verdict**, arbitration, award, conclusion, decision, decree, determination, finding, order, result, ruling, sentence **3** = **sense**, acumen, common sense, discernment, discrimination, intelligence, penetration, percipience, perspicacity, prudence, sagacity, shrewdness, smarts (*slang, chiefly U.S.*), taste, understanding, wisdom **4** = **punishment**, damnation, doom, fate, misfortune, retribution

judicial *adjective* **1** = **legal**, judiciary, juridical, official **2** = **discriminating**, distinguished, impartial, judgelike, magisterial, magistral

judicious *adjective* = **sensible**, acute, astute, careful, cautious, circumspect, considered, diplomatic, discerning, discreet, discriminating, enlightened, expedient, informed, politic, prudent, rational, reasonable, sagacious, sage, sane, sapient, shrewd, skilful, sober, sound, thoughtful, well-advised, well-judged, wise
➤ **Antonyms**
imprudent, indiscreet, injudicious, tactless, thoughtless

jug *noun* = **container**, carafe, crock, ewer, jar, pitcher, urn, vessel

juggle *verb* = **manipulate**, alter, change, disguise, doctor (*informal*), falsify, fix (*informal*), manoeuvre, misrepresent, modify, tamper with

juice *noun* = **liquid**, extract, fluid, liquor, nectar, sap, secretion, serum

juicy *adjective* **1** = **moist**, lush, sappy, succulent, watery **2** *Informal* = **interesting**, colourful, provocative, racy, risqué, sensational, spicy (*informal*), suggestive, vivid

jumble *noun* **1** = **muddle**, chaos, clutter, confusion, disarrangement, disarray, disorder, farrago, gallimaufry, hodgepodge, hotchpotch (*U.S.*), litter, medley, mélange, mess, miscellany, mishmash, mixture, pig's breakfast (*informal*) ◆ *verb* **2** = **mix**, confound, confuse, disarrange, dishevel, disorder, disorganize, entangle, mistake, muddle, ravel, shuffle, tangle

jumbo *adjective* = **giant**, elephantine, gigantic, ginormous (*informal*), huge, humongous *or* humungous (*U.S. slang*), immense, large, mega (*informal*), oversized
➤ **Antonyms**
baby, dwarf, micro, mini, pocket, tiny, wee

jump *verb* 1 = **leap**, bounce, bound, caper, clear, gambol, hop, hurdle, skip, spring, vault 2 = **recoil**, flinch, jerk, start, wince 3 = **increase**, advance, ascend, escalate, gain, hike, mount, rise, surge 4 = **miss**, avoid, digress, evade, omit, overshoot, skip, switch ♦ *noun* 5 = **leap**, bound, buck, caper, hop, skip, spring, vault 6 = **rise**, advance, augmentation, boost, increase, increment, upsurge, upturn 7 = **interruption**, breach, break, gap, hiatus, lacuna, space 8 = **jolt**, jar, jerk, lurch, shock, start, swerve, twitch, wrench 9 = **hurdle**, barricade, barrier, fence, impediment, obstacle, rail

jumped-up *adjective* = **conceited**, arrogant, cocky, immodest, insolent, overbearing, pompous, presumptuous, puffed up, self-opinionated, stuck-up, toffee-nosed, too big for one's boots *or* breeches

jumper *noun* = **sweater**, jersey, pullover, woolly

jumpy *adjective* = **nervous**, agitated, antsy (*informal*), anxious, apprehensive, fidgety, hyper (*informal*), jittery (*informal*), neurotic, on edge, restless, shaky, tense, timorous, twitchy (*informal*), wired (*slang*)
➤ **Antonyms**
calm, composed, laid-back (*informal*), together (*slang*), unfazed (*informal*), unflustered

junction *noun* = **connection**, alliance, combination, coupling, joint, juncture, linking, seam, union

juncture *noun* 1 = **moment**, conjuncture, contingency, crisis, crux, emergency, exigency, occasion, point, predicament, strait, time 2 = **junction**, bond, connection, convergence, edge, intersection, link, seam, weld

junior *adjective* = **minor**, inferior, lesser, lower, secondary, subordinate, younger
➤ **Antonyms**
elder, higher-ranking, older, senior, superior

junk *noun* = **rubbish**, clutter, debris, dreck (*slang, chiefly U.S.*), leavings, litter, oddments, odds and ends, refuse, rummage, scrap, trash, waste

jurisdiction *noun* 1 = **authority**, command, control, dominion, influence, power, prerogative, rule, say, sway 2 = **range**, area, bounds, circuit, compass, district, dominion, field, orbit, province, scope, sphere, zone

just *adverb* 1 = **recently**, hardly, lately, only now, scarcely 2 = **merely**, at a push, at most, but, by the skin of one's teeth, no more than, nothing but, only, simply, solely 3 = **exactly**, absolutely, completely, entirely, perfectly, precisely ♦ *adjective* 4 = **fair**, blameless, conscientious, decent, equitable, fair-minded, good, honest, honourable, impartial, lawful, pure, right, righteous, unbiased, upright, virtuous 5 = **correct**, accurate, exact, faithful, normal, precise, proper, regular, sound, true 6 = **fitting**, appropriate, apt, condign, deserved, due, justified, legitimate, merited, proper, reasonable, rightful, sensible, suitable, well-deserved
➤ **Antonyms**
adjective ≠**fair**: corrupt, devious, dishonest, inequitable, prejudiced, unfair, unjust, unlawful ≠**correct**: untrue ≠**fitting**: inappropriate, undeserved, unfit, unreasonable

just about *adverb* = **practically**, all but, almost, around, close to, nearly, not quite, virtually, well-nigh

justice *noun* 1 = **fairness**, equity, honesty, impartiality, integrity, justness, law, legality, legitimacy, reasonableness, rectitude, right 2 = **amends**, compensation, correction, penalty, recompense, redress, reparation 3 = **judge**, magistrate
➤ **Antonyms**
≠**fairness**: dishonesty, favouritism, inequity, injustice, partiality, unfairness, unlawfulness, unreasonableness, wrong

justifiable *adjective* = **reasonable**, acceptable, defensible, excusable, fit, lawful, legitimate, proper, right, sensible, sound, tenable, understandable, valid, vindicable, warrantable, well-founded
➤ **Antonyms**
arbitrary, capricious, indefensible, inexcusable, unreasonable, unwarranted

justification *noun* 1 = **explanation**, absolution, apology, approval, defence, exculpation, excuse, exoneration, extenuation, plea, rationalization, vindication 2 = **reason**, basis, defence, grounds, plea, warrant

justify *verb* = **explain**, absolve, acquit, approve, confirm, defend, establish, exculpate, excuse, exonerate, legalize, legitimize, maintain, substantiate, support, sustain, uphold, validate, vindicate, warrant

justly *adverb* = **properly**, accurately, correctly, equally, equitably, fairly, honestly, impartially, lawfully

jut *verb* = **stick out**, bulge, extend, impend, overhang, poke, project, protrude

juvenile *adjective* **1** = **young**, babyish, boyish, callow, childish, girlish, immature, inexperienced, infantile, jejune, puerile, undeveloped, unsophisticated, youthful ♦ *noun* **2** = **child**, adolescent, boy, girl, infant, minor, youth

➤ **Antonyms**
adjective ≠**young**: adult, grown-up, mature
♦ *noun* ≠**child**: adult, grown-up

juxtaposition *noun* = **proximity**, adjacency, closeness, contact, contiguity, nearness, propinquity, vicinity

K k

kaleidoscopic *adjective* **1** = **changeable**, fluctuating, fluid, many-coloured, mobile, motley, mutable, unstable, variegated **2** = **complicated**, complex, confused, convoluted, disordered, intricate, jumbled, varied

kamikaze *adjective* = **self-destructive**, foolhardy, suicidal

keel over *verb* = **collapse**, black out (*informal*), capsize, faint, founder, overturn, pass out, swoon (*literary*), topple over, upset

keen *adjective* **1** = **eager**, ardent, avid, bright-eyed and bushy-tailed (*informal*), devoted to, earnest, ebullient, enthusiastic, fervid, fierce, fond of, impassioned, intense, into (*informal*), zealous **2** = **astute**, brilliant, canny, clever, discerning, discriminating, perceptive, perspicacious, quick, sagacious, sapient, sensitive, shrewd, wise **3** = **sharp**, acid, acute, biting, caustic, cutting, edged, finely honed, incisive, penetrating, piercing, pointed, razor-like, sardonic, satirical, tart, trenchant, vitriolic
➤ **Antonyms**
≠**eager**: apathetic, half-hearted, indifferent, lukewarm, unenthusiastic, uninterested ≠**astute**: dull, obtuse, unperceptive ≠**sharp**: blunt, dull

keenness *noun* **1** = **eagerness**, ardour, avidity, avidness, diligence, earnestness, ebullience, enthusiasm, fervour, impatience, intensity, passion, zeal, zest **2** = **astuteness**, canniness, cleverness, discernment, insight, sagacity, sapience, sensitivity, shrewdness, wisdom **3** = **sharpness**, acerbity, harshness, incisiveness, mordancy, penetration, pungency, rigour, severity, sternness, trenchancy, unkindness, virulence

keep *verb* **1** = **retain**, conserve, control, hold, maintain, possess, preserve **2** = **look after**, care for, defend, guard, maintain, manage, mind, operate, protect, safeguard, shelter, shield, tend, watch over **3** = **store**, accumulate, amass, carry, deal in, deposit, furnish, garner, heap, hold, pile, place, stack, stock, trade in **4** = **support**, board, feed, foster, maintain, nourish, nurture, provide for, provision, subsidize, sustain, victual **5** = **detain**, arrest, block, check, constrain, control, curb, delay, deter, hamper, hamstring, hinder, hold, hold back, impede, inhibit, keep back, limit, obstruct, prevent, restrain, retard, shackle, stall, withhold **6** = **comply with**, adhere to, celebrate, commemorate, fulfil, hold, honour, obey, observe, perform, respect, ritualize, solemnize **7** = **associate with**, accompany, consort with, fraternize with ♦ *noun* **8** = **board**, food, livelihood, living, maintenance, means, nourishment, subsistence, support **9** = **tower**, castle, citadel, donjon, dungeon, fastness, stronghold
➤ **Antonyms**
verb ≠**retain**: abandon, discard, give up, lose ≠**detain**: free, liberate, release ≠**comply with**: disregard, ignore

keep at *verb* = **persist**, be steadfast, carry on, complete, continue, drudge, endure, finish, grind, labour, last, maintain, persevere, remain, slave, stay, stick, toil

keep back *verb* **1** = **restrain**, check, constrain, control, curb, delay, hold back, keep a tight rein on, limit, prohibit, restrict, retard, withhold **2** = **suppress**, censor, conceal, hide, keep dark, keep under one's hat, reserve, withhold

keeper *noun* = **guardian**, attendant, caretaker, curator, custodian, defender, governor, guard, jailer *or* gaoler, overseer, preserver, steward, superintendent, warden, warder

keeping *noun* **1** = **care**, aegis, auspices, charge, custody, guardianship, keep, maintenance, patronage, possession, protection, safekeeping, trust **2** *As in* **in keeping with** = **agreement**, accord, balance, compliance, conformity, congruity, consistency, correspondence, harmony, observance, proportion

keep on *verb* = **continue**, carry on, endure, last, persevere, persist, prolong, remain

keepsake *noun* = **souvenir**, emblem, favour, memento, relic, remembrance, reminder, symbol, token

keep up *verb* = **maintain**, balance, compete, contend, continue, emulate, keep pace, match, persevere, preserve, rival, sustain, vie

keg *noun* = **barrel**, cask, drum, firkin, hogshead, tun, vat

kernel *noun* = **essence**, core, germ, gist, grain, marrow, nub, pith, seed, substance

key *noun* **1** = **opener**, latchkey **2** = **answer**, clue, cue, explanation, guide, indicator,

interpretation, lead, means, pointer, sign, solution, translation ◆ *adjective* **3** = **essential**, basic, chief, crucial, decisive, fundamental, important, leading, main, major, pivotal, principal
➤ **Antonyms**
adjective ≠**essential**: minor, secondary, subsidiary, superficial

key in *verb* = **type**, enter, input, keyboard

keynote *noun* = **heart**, centre, core, essence, gist, kernel, marrow, pith, substance, theme

kick *verb* **1** = **boot**, punt, put the boot in(to) (*slang*) **2** *Informal* = **resist**, complain, gripe (*informal*), grumble, object, oppose, protest, rebel, spurn **3** *Informal* = **give up**, abandon, desist from, leave off, quit, stop ◆ *noun* **4** *Informal* = **thrill**, buzz (*slang*), enjoyment, excitement, fun, gratification, jollies (*slang*), pleasure, stimulation **5** *Informal* = **pungency**, force, intensity, pep, power, punch, snap (*informal*), sparkle, strength, tang, verve, vitality, zest

kickoff *noun Informal* = **start**, beginning, commencement, opening, outset

kick off *verb Informal* = **begin**, commence, get the show on the road, get under way, initiate, kick-start, open, start

kick out *verb Informal* = **dismiss**, discharge, eject, evict, expel, get rid of, give (someone) their marching orders, give the boot (*slang*), give the bum's rush (*slang*), give the push, kiss off (*slang, chiefly U.S. & Canad.*), oust, reject, remove, sack (*informal*), show one the door, throw out on one's ear (*informal*), toss out

kid¹ *noun Informal* = **child**, ankle-biter (*Austral. slang*), baby, bairn, boy, girl, infant, lad, lass, little one, rug rat (*U.S. & Canad. informal*), sprog (*slang*), stripling, teenager, tot, youngster, youth

kid² *verb* = **tease**, bamboozle, beguile, cozen, delude, fool, gull (*archaic*), hoax, hoodwink, jest, joke, mock, plague, pretend, rag (*Brit.*), ridicule, trick, wind up (*Brit. slang*)

kidnap *verb* = **abduct**, capture, hijack, hold to ransom, remove, seize, steal

kill *verb* **1** = **slay**, annihilate, assassinate, blow away (*slang, chiefly U.S.*), bump off (*slang*), butcher, destroy, dispatch, do away with, do in (*slang*), eradicate, execute, exterminate, extirpate, knock off (*slang*), liquidate, massacre, murder, neutralize, obliterate, slaughter, take out (*slang*), take (someone's) life, waste (*informal*), wipe from the face of the earth (*informal*) **2** *Informal* = **suppress**, cancel, cease, deaden, defeat, extinguish, halt, quash, quell, ruin, scotch, smother, stifle, still, stop, veto

killer *noun* = **assassin**, butcher, cut-throat,

destroyer, executioner, exterminator, gunman, hit man (*slang*), liquidator, murderer, slaughterer, slayer

killing *adjective* **1** *Informal* = **tiring**, debilitating, enervating, exhausting, fatiguing, punishing **2** *Informal* = **hilarious**, absurd, amusing, comical, ludicrous, uproarious **3** = **deadly**, death-dealing, deathly, fatal, lethal, mortal, murderous ◆ *noun* **4** = **slaughter**, bloodshed, carnage, execution, extermination, fatality, homicide, manslaughter, massacre, murder, necktie party (*informal*), slaying **5** *Informal* = **bonanza**, bomb (*slang*), cleanup (*informal*), coup, gain, profit, success, windfall

killjoy *noun* = **spoilsport**, dampener, damper, wet blanket (*informal*)

kin *noun* = **family**, connections, kindred, kinsfolk, kinsmen, kith, people, relations, relatives

kind¹ *adjective* = **considerate**, affectionate, amiable, amicable, beneficent, benevolent, benign, bounteous, charitable, clement, compassionate, congenial, cordial, courteous, friendly, generous, gentle, good, gracious, humane, indulgent, kind-hearted, kindly, lenient, loving, mild, neighbourly, obliging, philanthropic, propitious, sympathetic, tender-hearted, thoughtful, understanding
➤ **Antonyms**
cruel, hard-hearted, harsh, heartless, merciless, severe, unkind, unsympathetic, vicious

kind² *noun* **1** = **class**, brand, breed, family, genus, ilk, race, set, sort, species, stamp, variety **2** = **nature**, character, description, essence, habit, manner, mould, persuasion, sort, style, temperament, type

kind-hearted *adjective* = **sympathetic**, altruistic, amicable, compassionate, considerate, generous, good-natured, gracious, helpful, humane, kind, tender, tender-hearted
➤ **Antonyms**
cold, cold-hearted, cruel, hard-hearted, harsh, heartless, selfish, severe, unkind, unsympathetic

kindle *verb* **1** = **set fire to**, fire, ignite, inflame, light **2** = **arouse**, agitate, animate, awaken, bestir, enkindle, exasperate, excite, foment, incite, induce, inflame, inspire, provoke, rouse, sharpen, stimulate, stir, thrill
➤ **Antonyms**
douse, extinguish, quell, quench

kindliness *noun* = **kindness**, amiability, beneficence, benevolence, benignity, charity, compassion, friendliness, gentleness, humanity, kind-heartedness, sympathy

kindly *adjective* **1** = **benevolent**, affable, beneficial, benign, compassionate, cordial, favourable, genial, gentle, good-natured, hearty, helpful, kind, mild, pleasant, polite, sympathetic, warm ◆ *adverb* **2** = **benevolently**, agreeably, cordially, graciously, politely, tenderly, thoughtfully
➤ **Antonyms**
adjective ≠**benevolent**: cruel, harsh, malevolent, malicious, mean, severe, spiteful, unkindly, unsympathetic ◆ *adverb* ≠**benevolently**: cruelly, harshly, malevolently, maliciously, meanly, spitefully, unkindly, unsympathetically

kindness *noun* **1** = **goodwill**, affection, amiability, beneficence, benevolence, charity, clemency, compassion, decency, fellow-feeling, generosity, gentleness, goodness, grace, hospitality, humanity, indulgence, kindliness, magnanimity, patience, philanthropy, tenderness, tolerance, understanding **2** = **good deed**, aid, assistance, benefaction, bounty, favour, generosity, help, service
➤ **Antonyms**
≠**goodwill**: animosity, callousness, cold-heartedness, cruelty, hard-heartedness, heartlessness, ill will, inhumanity, malevolence, malice, misanthropy, viciousness

kindred *adjective* **1** = **similar**, affiliated, akin, allied, cognate, congenial, corresponding, kin, like, matching, related ◆ *noun* **2** = **relationship**, affinity, consanguinity **3** = **family**, connections, flesh, kin, kinsfolk, kinsmen, lineage, relations, relatives

king *noun* = **ruler**, crowned head, emperor, majesty, monarch, overlord, prince, sovereign

kingdom *noun* **1** = **country**, commonwealth, division, nation, province, realm, state, territory, tract **2** = **domain**, area, field, province, sphere, territory

kink *noun* **1** = **twist**, bend, coil, corkscrew, crimp, entanglement, frizz, knot, tangle, wrinkle **2** = **flaw**, complication, defect, difficulty, hitch, imperfection, knot, tangle **3** = **quirk**, crotchet, eccentricity, fetish, foible, idiosyncrasy, singularity, vagary, whim

kinky *adjective* **1** *Slang* = **perverted**, degenerated, depraved, deviant, licentious, pervy (*slang*), unnatural, warped **2** = **twisted**, coiled, crimped, curled, curly, frizzled, frizzy, tangled **3** *Slang* = **weird**, bizarre, eccentric, odd, oddball (*informal*), off-the-wall (*slang*), outlandish, outré, peculiar, queer, quirky, strange, unconventional, wacko (*slang*)

kinsfolk *plural noun* = **family**, connections, kin, kindred, kinsmen, relations, relatives

kinship *noun* **1** = **relation**, blood relationship, consanguinity, kin, ties of blood **2** = **similarity**, affinity, alliance, association, bearing, connection, correspondence, relationship

kinsman *noun* = **relative**, blood relative, fellow clansman, fellow tribesman, relation

kiosk *noun* = **booth**, bookstall, counter, newsstand, stall, stand

kiss *verb* **1** = **osculate**, buss (*archaic*), canoodle (*slang*), greet, neck (*informal*), peck (*informal*), salute, smooch (*informal*) **2** = **brush**, caress, glance, graze, scrape, touch ◆ *noun* **3** = **osculation**, buss (*archaic*), peck (*informal*), smacker (*slang*)

kit *noun* = **equipment**, accoutrements, apparatus, effects, gear, impedimenta, implements, instruments, outfit, paraphernalia, provisions, rig, supplies, tackle, tools, trappings, utensils

kitchen *noun* = **cookhouse**, galley, kitchenette

kit out *or* **up** *verb* = **equip**, accoutre, arm, deck out, fit out, fix up, furnish, outfit, provide with, supply

knack *noun* = **skill**, ability, adroitness, aptitude, bent, capacity, dexterity, expertise, expertness, facility, flair, forte, genius, gift, handiness, ingenuity, propensity, quickness, skilfulness, talent, trick
➤ **Antonyms**
awkwardness, clumsiness, disability, ineptitude

knave *noun Archaic* = **rogue**, blackguard, bounder (*old-fashioned Brit. slang*), cheat, cocksucker (*taboo slang*), rapscallion, rascal, reprobate, rotter (*slang, chiefly Brit.*), scally (*Northwest English dialect*), scallywag (*informal*), scamp, scapegrace, scoundrel, scumbag (*slang*), swindler, varlet (*archaic*), villain

knavery *noun Old-fashioned* = **dishonesty**, chicanery, corruption, deceit, deception, double-dealing, duplicity, fraud, imposture, rascality, roguery, trickery, villainy

knavish *adjective Old-fashioned* = **dishonest**, deceitful, deceptive, dishonourable, fraudulent, lying, rascally, roguish, scoundrelly, tricky, unprincipled, unscrupulous, villainous
➤ **Antonyms**
honest, honourable, noble, principled, trustworthy

knead *verb* = **squeeze**, blend, form, manipulate, massage, mould, press, rub, shape, stroke, work

kneel *verb* = **genuflect**, bow, bow down, curtsey, curtsy, get down on one's knees, kowtow, make obeisance, stoop

knell *noun* **1** = **ringing**, chime, peal, sound,

toll ♦ verb 2 = **ring**, announce, chime, herald, peal, resound, sound, toll

knickers plural noun = **underwear**, bloomers, briefs, drawers, panties, smalls

knick-knack noun = **trinket**, bagatelle, bauble, bibelot, bric-a-brac, gewgaw, gimcrack, kickshaw, plaything, trifle

knife noun 1 = **blade**, cutter, cutting tool ♦ verb 2 = **cut**, impale, lacerate, pierce, slash, stab, wound

knit verb 1 = **join**, affix, ally, bind, connect, contract, fasten, heal, interlace, intertwine, link, loop, mend, secure, tie, unite, weave 2 = **wrinkle**, crease, furrow, knot, pucker

knob noun = **lump**, boss, bulk, bump, bunch, hump, knot, knurl, nub, projection, protrusion, protuberance, snag, stud, swell, swelling, tumour

knock verb 1 = **hit**, belt (informal), buffet, chin (slang), clap, cuff, deck (slang), lay one on (slang), punch, rap, slap, smack, smite (archaic), strike, thump, thwack 2 Informal = **criticize**, abuse, asperse, belittle, carp, cavil, censure, condemn, denigrate, deprecate, disparage, find fault, have a go (at) (informal), lambast(e), run down, slag (off) (slang), slam (slang) ♦ noun 3 = **blow**, belt (informal), box, clip, clout (informal), cuff, hammering, rap, slap, smack, thump 4 Informal = **setback**, defeat, failure, rebuff, rejection, reversal 5 Informal = **criticism**, blame, censure, condemnation, heat (slang, chiefly U.S. & Canad.), slagging (off) (slang), stick (slang), stricture

knockabout adjective = **boisterous**, farcical, harum-scarum, rambunctious (informal), riotous, rollicking, rough-and-tumble, rumbustious, slapstick

knock about or **around** verb 1 = **wander**, ramble, range, roam, rove, traipse, travel 2 = **hit**, abuse, batter, beat up (informal), bruise, buffet, clobber (slang), damage, hurt, lambast(e), maltreat, manhandle, maul, mistreat, strike, work over (slang), wound

knock down verb = **demolish**, batter, clout (informal), deck (slang), destroy, fell, floor, level, pound, raze, smash, wallop (informal), wreck

knock off verb 1 Informal = **stop work**, clock off, clock out, complete, conclude, finish, terminate 2 Slang = **kill**, assassinate, blow away (slang, chiefly U.S.), bump off (slang), do away with, do in (slang), liquidate, murder, slay, take out (slang), waste (informal) 3 Slang = **steal**, blag (slang), cabbage (Brit. slang), filch, nick (slang, chiefly Brit.), pilfer, pinch, purloin, rob, thieve

knockout noun 1 = **killer blow**, coup de

grâce, kayo (slang), KO or K.O. (slang) 2 Informal = **success**, hit, sensation, smash, smasheroo (informal), smash hit, stunner (informal), triumph, winner
➤ **Antonyms**
≠**success**: clunker (informal), failure, flop (informal), turkey (informal)

knot noun 1 = **connection**, bond, bow, braid, joint, ligature, loop, rosette, tie 2 = **cluster**, aggregation, bunch, clump, collection, heap, mass, pile, tuft 3 = **group**, assemblage, band, circle, clique, company, crew (informal), crowd, gang, mob, pack, set, squad ♦ verb 4 = **tie**, bind, complicate, entangle, knit, loop, secure, tether, weave

know verb 1 = **understand**, apprehend, comprehend, experience, fathom, feel certain, ken (Scot.), learn, notice, perceive, realize, recognize, see, undergo 2 = **be acquainted with**, associate with, be familiar with, fraternize with, have dealings with, have knowledge of, recognize 3 = **distinguish**, differentiate, discern, identify, make out, perceive, recognize, see, tell
➤ **Antonyms**
≠**understand**: misunderstand ≠**be acquainted with**: be ignorant, be unfamiliar with

know-how noun Informal = **capability**, ability, adroitness, aptitude, craft, dexterity, experience, expertise, faculty, flair, ingenuity, knack, knowledge, proficiency, savoir-faire, skill, talent

knowing adjective 1 = **meaningful**, eloquent, expressive, significant 2 = **cunning**, acute, astute, perceptive, sagacious, shrewd 3 = **deliberate**, aware, conscious, intended, intentional 4 = **well-informed**, clever, clued-up (informal), competent, discerning, experienced, expert, intelligent, qualified, skilful
➤ **Antonyms**
≠**cunning**: ingenuous, naive, wet behind the ears (informal) ≠**deliberate**: accidental, unintentional ≠**well-informed**: ignorant, obtuse

knowingly adverb = **deliberately**, consciously, intentionally, on purpose, purposely, wilfully, wittingly

knowledge noun 1 = **learning**, education, enlightenment, erudition, instruction, intelligence, scholarship, schooling, science, tuition, wisdom 2 = **understanding**, ability, apprehension, cognition, comprehension, consciousness, discernment, grasp, judgment, recognition 3 = **acquaintance**, cognizance, familiarity, information, intimacy, notice
➤ **Antonyms**
≠**learning**: ignorance, illiteracy

≠**understanding:** misunderstanding, unawareness ≠**acquaintance:** unfamiliarity

knowledgeable *adjective* **1** = **well-informed**, acquainted, *au courant, au fait,* aware, clued-up (*informal*), cognizant, conscious, conversant, experienced, familiar, in the know (*informal*), in the loop, understanding **2** = **intelligent**, educated, erudite, learned, lettered, scholarly

known *adjective* = **famous**, acknowledged, admitted, avowed, celebrated, common, confessed, familiar, manifest, noted, obvious, patent, plain, popular, published, recognized, well-known

➤ **Antonyms**

closet (*informal*), concealed, hidden, secret, unfamiliar, unknown, unrecognized, unrevealed

knuckle under *verb* = **give way**, accede, acquiesce, capitulate, cave in (*informal*), give in, submit, succumb, surrender, yield

➤ **Antonyms**

be defiant, dig one's heels in (*informal*), hold out (against), kick up (a fuss *or* stink), rebel, resist

L l

label noun 1 = **tag**, docket (chiefly Brit.),
flag, marker, sticker, tally, ticket 2 = **epithet**,
characterization, classification, description
♦ verb 3 = **tag**, docket (chiefly Brit.), flag,
mark, stamp, sticker, tally 4 = **describe**,
brand, call, characterize, class, classify,
define, designate, identify, name

laborious adjective = **hard**, arduous,
backbreaking, burdensome, difficult,
exhausting, fatiguing, herculean, onerous,
strenuous, tiresome, tiring, toilsome, tough,
uphill, wearing, wearisome
➤ **Antonyms**
easy, easy-peasy (slang), effortless, light

labour noun 1 = **work**, industry, toil 2
= **workers**, employees, hands, labourers,
workforce, workmen 3 = **childbirth**,
contractions, delivery, labour pains, pains,
parturition, throes, travail 4 = **toil**,
donkey-work, drudgery, effort, exertion,
grind (informal), industry, pains,
painstaking, sweat (informal), travail 5
= **chore**, job, task, undertaking ♦ verb 6
= **work**, drudge, endeavour, grind
(informal), peg along or away (chiefly Brit.),
plod, plug along or away (informal), slave,
strive, struggle, sweat (informal), toil, travail
7 = **overemphasize**, dwell on, elaborate, go
on about, make a federal case of (U.S.
informal), make a production (out) of
(informal), overdo, strain 8 usually with
under = **be disadvantaged**, be a victim of,
be burdened by, suffer
➤ **Antonyms**
noun ≠toil: ease, idleness, leisure, relaxation,
repose, respite, rest ♦ verb ≠work: relax, rest

laboured adjective = **difficult**, awkward,
forced, heavy, stiff, strained

labourer noun = **worker**, blue-collar worker,
drudge, hand, labouring man, manual
worker, navvy (Brit. informal), unskilled
worker, working man, workman

labyrinth noun = **maze**, complexity,
complication, convolution, entanglement,
intricacy, jungle, perplexity, puzzle, riddle,
tangle

labyrinthine adjective = **complex**,
Byzantine, confused, convoluted, intricate,
involved, knotty, mazelike, perplexing,
puzzling, tangled, tortuous, winding

lace noun 1 = **netting**, filigree, openwork,
tatting 2 = **cord**, bootlace, shoelace, string,
thong, tie ♦ verb 3 = **fasten**, attach, bind,
close, do up, thread, tie 4 = **mix in**, add to,
fortify, spike 5 = **intertwine**, interweave,
twine

lacerate verb 1 = **tear**, claw, cut, gash, jag,
maim, mangle, rend, rip, slash, wound 2
= **hurt**, afflict, distress, harrow, rend,
torment, torture, wound

laceration noun = **cut**, gash, injury,
mutilation, rent, rip, slash, tear, wound

lachrymose adjective = **tearful**, crying,
mournful, sad, weeping, weepy (informal),
woeful

lack noun 1 = **shortage**, absence, dearth,
deficiency, deprivation, destitution,
insufficiency, need, privation, scantiness,
scarcity, shortcoming, shortness, want
♦ verb 2 = **need**, be deficient in, be short of,
be without, miss, require, want
➤ **Antonyms**
noun ≠shortage: abundance, adequacy,
excess, plentifulness, sufficiency, surplus
♦ verb ≠need: enjoy, have, own, possess

lackadaisical adjective 1 = **lethargic**,
apathetic, dull, enervated, half-hearted,
indifferent, languid, languorous, limp,
listless, spiritless 2 = **lazy**, abstracted,
dreamy, idle, indolent, inert
➤ **Antonyms**
ambitious, diligent, excited, inspired, spirited

lackey noun 1 = **hanger-on**, fawner,
flatterer, instrument, menial, minion,
parasite, pawn, sycophant, toady, tool, yes
man 2 = **manservant**, attendant, cohort
(chiefly U.S.), flunky, footman, valet, varlet
(archaic)

lacking adjective = **without**, defective,
deficient, flawed, impaired, inadequate,
minus (informal), missing, needing, sans
(archaic), wanting

lacklustre adjective = **flat**, boring, dim,
drab, dry, dull, leaden, lifeless, lustreless,
muted, prosaic, sombre, unimaginative,
uninspired, vapid

laconic adjective = **terse**, brief, clipped,
compact, concise, crisp, curt, monosyllabic,
pithy, sententious, short, succinct, to the
point
➤ **Antonyms**
long-winded, loquacious, rambling, verbose,
voluble, wordy

lacuna noun = **gap**, blank, break, hiatus,
omission, space, void

lacy *adjective* = **filigree**, delicate, fine, lace-like, meshy, net-like, open

lad *noun* = **boy**, chap (*informal*), fellow, guy (*informal*), juvenile, kid (*informal*), laddie (*Scot.*), schoolboy, stripling, youngster, youth

laden *adjective* = **loaded**, burdened, charged, encumbered, fraught, full, hampered, oppressed, taxed, weighed down, weighted

la-di-da *adjective Informal* = **affected**, arty-farty (*informal*), conceited, highfalutin (*informal*), mannered, mincing, overrefined, posh (*informal, chiefly Brit.*), precious, pretentious, snobbish, snooty (*informal*), stuck-up (*informal*), toffee-nosed (*slang, chiefly Brit.*)

lady *noun* 1 = **gentlewoman**, dame 2 = **woman**, female

lady-killer *noun* = **womanizer**, Casanova, Don Juan, heartbreaker, ladies' man, libertine, Lothario, philanderer, rake, roué, wolf (*informal*)

ladylike *adjective* = **refined**, courtly, cultured, decorous, elegant, genteel, modest, polite, proper, respectable, sophisticated, well-bred
➤ **Antonyms**
discourteous, ill-bred, ill-mannered, impolite, rude, uncultured, unladylike, unmannerly, unrefined

lag *verb* 1 = **hang back**, be behind, dawdle, delay, drag (behind), drag one's feet (*informal*), idle, linger, loiter, saunter, straggle, tarry, trail 2 = **flag**, decrease, diminish, ebb, fail, fall off, lose strength, slacken, wane

laggard *noun* = **straggler**, dawdler, idler, lingerer, loafer, loiterer, lounger, saunterer, skiver (*Brit. slang*), slowcoach (*Brit. informal*), slowpoke (*U.S. & Canad. informal*), sluggard, snail

laid-back *adjective* = **relaxed**, at ease, casual, easy-going, easy-oasy (*slang*), free and easy, together (*slang*), unflappable (*informal*), unhurried
➤ **Antonyms**
antsy (*informal*), edgy, jittery (*informal*), jumpy, keyed-up, nervous, on edge, tense, twitchy (*informal*), uptight (*informal*), wound-up (*informal*)

lair *noun* 1 = **nest**, burrow, den, earth, form, hole, resting place 2 *Informal* = **hide-out**, den, refuge, retreat, sanctuary

laissez faire *or* **laisser faire** *noun* = **nonintervention**, free enterprise, free trade, individualism, live and let live

lake *noun* = **pond**, lagoon, loch (*Scot.*), lough (*Irish*), mere, reservoir, tarn

lam *verb Slang* = **attack**, batter, beat, hit, knock, lambast(e), pelt, pound, strike, thrash

lambast(e) *verb* 1 = **beat**, bludgeon, cosh (*Brit.*), cudgel, drub, flog, strike, thrash, whip 2 = **reprimand**, bawl out (*informal*), berate, carpet (*informal*), castigate, censure, chew out (*U.S. & Canad. informal*), give a rocket (*Brit. & N.Z. informal*), rap over the knuckles, read the riot act, rebuke, scold, slap on the wrist, tear into (*informal*), tear (someone) off a strip (*Brit. informal*), upbraid

lambent *adjective* 1 = **flickering**, dancing, fluttering, twinkling 2 *Of wit or humour* = **brilliant**, light, sparkling

lame *adjective* 1 = **disabled**, crippled, defective, game, halt (*archaic*), handicapped, hobbling, limping 2 = **unconvincing**, feeble, flimsy, inadequate, insufficient, pathetic, poor, thin, unsatisfactory, weak

lament *verb* 1 = **bemoan**, bewail, complain, deplore, grieve, mourn, regret, sorrow, wail, weep ♦ *noun* 2 = **complaint**, keening, lamentation, moan, moaning, plaint, ululation, wail, wailing 3 = **dirge**, coronach (*Scot. & Irish*), elegy, requiem, threnody

lamentable *adjective* 1 = **regrettable**, deplorable, distressing, grievous, gut-wrenching, harrowing, mournful, sorrowful, tragic, unfortunate, woeful 2 = **disappointing**, low, meagre, mean, miserable, not much cop (*Brit. slang*), pitiful, poor, unsatisfactory, wretched

lamentation *noun* = **sorrow**, dirge, grief, grieving, keening, lament, moan, mourning, plaint, sobbing, ululation, wailing, weeping

laminate *verb* 1 = **cover**, coat, face, foliate, layer, stratify, veneer 2 = **split**, exfoliate, flake, separate

lampoon *noun* 1 = **satire**, burlesque, caricature, parody, send-up (*Brit. informal*), skit, takeoff (*informal*) ♦ *verb* 2 = **ridicule**, burlesque, caricature, make fun of, mock, parody, satirize, send up (*Brit. informal*), take off (*informal*)

land *noun* 1 = **ground**, dry land, earth, terra firma 2 = **soil**, dirt, ground, loam 3 = **countryside**, farming, farmland, rural districts 4 *Law* = **property**, acres, estate, grounds, real property, realty 5 = **country**, district, fatherland, motherland, nation, province, region, territory, tract ♦ *verb* 6 = **alight**, arrive, berth, come to rest, debark, disembark, dock, touch down 7 *Informal* = **obtain**, acquire, gain, get, score (*slang*), secure, win

landing *noun* 1 = **coming in**, arrival, disembarkation, disembarkment, touchdown 2 = **platform**, jetty, landing stage, quayside

landlord *noun* 1 = **owner**, freeholder,

lessor, proprietor **2 = innkeeper**, host, hotelier, hotel-keeper

landmark *noun* **1 = feature**, monument **2 = milestone**, crisis, turning point, watershed

landscape *noun* **= scenery**, countryside, outlook, panorama, prospect, scene, view, vista

landslide *noun* **= landslip**, avalanche, rockfall

land up *verb* **= end up**, arrive, lead, turn up, wind up

lane *noun* **= road**, alley, footpath, passageway, path, pathway, street, way

language *noun* **1 = speech**, communication, conversation, discourse, expression, interchange, parlance, talk, utterance, verbalization, vocalization **2 = tongue**, argot, cant, dialect, idiom, jargon, lingo (*informal*), lingua franca, patois, patter, speech, terminology, vernacular, vocabulary **3 = style**, diction, expression, phraseology, phrasing, wording

languid *adjective* **1 = feeble**, drooping, faint, languorous, limp, pining, sickly, weak, weary **2 = lazy**, indifferent, lackadaisical, languorous, listless, spiritless, unenthusiastic, uninterested **3 = lethargic**, dull, heavy, inactive, inert, sluggish, torpid
> Antonyms
active, alive and kicking, energetic, strong, tireless, vigorous

languish *verb* **1** *Literary* **= waste away**, be abandoned, be disregarded, be neglected, rot, suffer **2 = decline**, droop, fade, fail, faint, flag, sicken, waste, weaken, wilt, wither **3** *often with* **for = pine**, desire, eat one's heart out over, hanker, hunger, long, sigh, want, yearn
> Antonyms
≠**waste away, decline**: bloom, flourish, prosper, thrive

languishing *adjective* **1 = fading**, declining, deteriorating, drooping, droopy, failing, flagging, sickening, sinking, wasting away, weak, weakening, wilting, withering **2 = lovesick**, dreamy, longing, lovelorn, melancholic, nostalgic, pensive, pining, soulful, tender, wistful, woebegone, yearning

languor *noun Literary* **= relaxation**, dreaminess, drowsiness, indolence, laziness, lotus-eating, sleepiness, sloth

lank *adjective* **1 = limp**, dull, lifeless, long, lustreless, straggling **2 = thin**, emaciated, gaunt, lanky, lean, rawboned, scraggy, scrawny, skinny, slender, slim, spare

lanky *adjective* **= gangling**, angular, bony, gaunt, loose-jointed, rangy, rawboned, scraggy, scrawny, spare, tall, thin, weedy (*informal*)

> Antonyms
brawny, burly, chubby, fat, muscular, plump, portly, rotund, rounded, short, sinewy, stocky, stout

lap[1] *noun* **1 = circuit**, circle, course, distance, loop, orbit, round, tour ♦ *verb* **2 = wrap**, cover, enfold, envelop, fold, swaddle, swathe, turn, twist

lap[2] *verb* **1 = ripple**, gurgle, plash, purl, slap, splash, swish, wash **2 = drink**, lick, sip, sup

lapse *noun* **1 = mistake**, error, failing, fault, indiscretion, negligence, omission, oversight, slip **2 = interval**, break, breathing space, gap, intermission, interruption, lull, passage, pause **3 = drop**, backsliding, decline, descent, deterioration, fall, relapse ♦ *verb* **4 = drop**, decline, degenerate, deteriorate, fail, fall, sink, slide, slip **5 = end**, become obsolete, become void, expire, run out, stop, terminate

lapsed *adjective* **1 = expired**, discontinued, ended, finished, invalid, out of date, run out, unrenewed **2 = backsliding**, lacking faith, nonpractising

larceny *noun Law* **= theft**, burglary, misappropriation, pilfering, purloining, robbery, stealing

large *adjective* **1 = big**, bulky, colossal, considerable, elephantine, enormous, giant, gigantic, ginormous (*informal*), goodly, great, huge, humongous *or* humungous (*U.S. slang*), immense, jumbo (*informal*), king-size, man-size, massive, mega (*slang*), monumental, sizable *or* sizeable, substantial, tidy (*informal*), vast **2 = comprehensive**, abundant, ample, broad, capacious, copious, extensive, full, generous, grand, grandiose, liberal, plentiful, roomy, spacious, sweeping, wide **3 at large: a = in general**, as a whole, chiefly, generally, in the main, mainly **b = free**, at liberty, on the loose, on the run, roaming, unconfined **c = at length**, considerably, exhaustively, greatly, in full detail
> Antonyms
≠**big**: inconsiderable, infinitesimal, little, minute, petty, short, slender, slight, slim, small, tiny, trivial ≠**comprehensive**: brief, narrow, scanty, scarce, sparse, thin

largely *adverb* **= mainly**, as a rule, by and large, chiefly, considerably, extensively, generally, mostly, predominantly, primarily, principally, to a great extent, widely

large-scale *adjective* **= wide-ranging**, broad, extensive, far-reaching, global, sweeping, vast, wholesale, wide

largesse, largess *noun* **= generosity**, alms-giving, benefaction, bounty, charity, liberality, munificence, open-handedness, philanthropy

lark *Informal* ♦ *noun* **1 = prank**, antic, caper,

escapade, fling, frolic, fun, gambol, game, jape, mischief, revel, rollick, romp, skylark, spree ♦ *verb* **2 lark about** = **play**, caper, cavort, cut capers, frolic, gambol, have fun, make mischief, rollick, romp, sport

lascivious *adjective* **1** = **lustful**, horny (*slang*), lecherous, lewd, libidinous, licentious, prurient, randy (*informal, chiefly Brit.*), salacious, sensual, unchaste, voluptuous, wanton **2** = **bawdy**, blue, coarse, crude, dirty, indecent, obscene, offensive, pornographic, ribald, scurrilous, smutty, suggestive, vulgar, X-rated (*informal*)

lash[1] *noun* **1** = **blow**, hit, stripe, stroke, swipe (*informal*) ♦ *verb* **2** = **whip**, beat, birch, chastise, flagellate, flog, horsewhip, lam (*slang*), lambast(e), scourge, thrash **3** = **pound**, beat, buffet, dash, drum, hammer, hit, knock, lambast(e), larrup (*dialect*), punch, smack, strike **4** = **censure**, attack, belabour, berate, blast, castigate, criticize, flay, lambast(e), lampoon, put down, ridicule, satirize, scold, slate (*informal, chiefly Brit.*), tear into (*informal*), upbraid

lash[2] *verb* = **fasten**, bind, join, make fast, rope, secure, strap, tie

lass *noun* = **girl**, bird (*slang*), chick (*slang*), colleen (*Irish*), damsel, lassie (*informal*), maid, maiden, miss, schoolgirl, wench (*facetious*), young woman

lassitude *noun* = **weariness**, apathy, drowsiness, dullness, enervation, ennui, exhaustion, fatigue, heaviness, inertia, languor, lethargy, listlessness, sluggishness, tiredness, torpor

last[1] *adjective* **1** = **hindmost**, aftermost, at the end, rearmost **2** = **most recent**, latest **3** = **final**, closing, concluding, extreme, furthest, remotest, terminal, ultimate, utmost ♦ *adverb* **4** = **in** *or* **at the end**, after, behind, bringing up the rear, in the rear ♦ *noun* **5** = **end**, close, completion, conclusion, ending, finale, finish, termination **6 at last** = **finally**, at length, at the end of the day, eventually, in conclusion, in the end, in the fullness of time, ultimately
➤ **Antonyms**
adjective ≠**hindmost**: first, foremost, leading ≠**final**: earliest, first, initial, introductory, opening

last[2] *verb* = **continue**, abide, carry on, endure, hold on, hold out, keep, keep on, persist, remain, stand up, survive, wear
➤ **Antonyms**
cease, depart, die, end, expire, fade, fail, stop, terminate

last-ditch *adjective* = **final**, all-out (*informal*), desperate, frantic, heroic, straining, struggling

lasting *adjective* = **continuing**, abiding, deep-rooted, durable, enduring, eternal, indelible, lifelong, long-standing, long-term, perennial, permanent, perpetual, unceasing, undying, unending
➤ **Antonyms**
ephemeral, fleeting, momentary, passing, short-lived, transient, transitory

lastly *adverb* = **finally**, after all, all in all, at last, in conclusion, in the end, to conclude, to sum up, ultimately

last-minute *adjective* = **late**, deathbed, eleventh hour, last-ditch, last-gasp

latch *noun* **1** = **fastening**, bar, bolt, catch, clamp, hasp, hook, lock, sneck (*dialect*) ♦ *verb* **2** = **fasten**, bar, bolt, lock, make fast, secure, sneck (*dialect*)

late *adjective* **1** = **overdue**, behind, behindhand, belated, delayed, last-minute, slow, tardy, unpunctual **2** = **dead**, deceased, defunct, departed, ex-, former, old, past, preceding, previous **3** = **recent**, advanced, fresh, modern, new ♦ *adverb* **4** = **belatedly**, at the last minute, behindhand, behind time, dilatorily, slowly, tardily, unpunctually
➤ **Antonyms**
adjective ≠**overdue**: beforehand, early, prompt, punctual, seasoned, timely ≠**dead**: alive, existing ≠**recent**: old ♦ *adverb* ≠**belatedly**: beforehand, early, in advance

lately *adverb* = **recently**, in recent times, just now, latterly, not long ago, of late

lateness *noun* = **delay**, advanced hour, belatedness, late date, tardiness, unpunctuality

latent *adjective* = **hidden**, concealed, dormant, inherent, invisible, lurking, potential, quiescent, secret, undeveloped, unexpressed, unrealized, unseen, veiled
➤ **Antonyms**
apparent, conspicuous, developed, evident, expressed, manifest, obvious, realized

later *adverb* = **afterwards**, after, by and by, in a while, in time, later on, next, subsequently, thereafter

lateral *adjective* = **sideways**, edgeways, flanking, side, sideward

latest *adjective* = **up-to-date**, current, fashionable, happening (*informal*), in, modern, most recent, newest, now, up-to-the-minute, with it (*informal*)

lather *noun* **1** = **froth**, bubbles, foam, soap, soapsuds, suds **2** *Informal* = **fluster**, dither (*chiefly Brit.*), fever, flap (*informal*), fuss, state (*informal*), stew (*informal*), sweat, tizzy (*informal*) ♦ *verb* **3** = **froth**, foam, soap **4** *Informal* = **beat**, cane, drub, flog, lambast(e), strike, thrash, whip

latitude *noun* = **scope**, a free hand, elbowroom, freedom, indulgence, laxity, leeway, liberty, licence, play, room, space, unrestrictedness

latter *adjective* = **second**, closing, concluding, last, last-mentioned, later, latest, modern, recent
➤ **Antonyms**
antecedent, earlier, foregoing, former, preceding, previous, prior

latterly *adverb* = **recently**, hitherto, lately, of late

lattice *noun* = **grid**, fretwork, grating, grille, latticework, mesh, network, openwork, tracery, trellis, web

laud *verb Literary* = **praise**, acclaim, approve, celebrate, crack up (*informal*), extol, glorify, honour, sing *or* sound the praises of

laudable *adjective* = **praiseworthy**, admirable, commendable, creditable, estimable, excellent, meritorious, of note, worthy
➤ **Antonyms**
base, blameworthy, contemptible, ignoble, lowly, unworthy

laudatory *adjective* = **eulogistic**, acclamatory, adulatory, approbatory, approving, commendatory, complimentary, panegyrical

laugh *verb* 1 = **chuckle**, be convulsed (*informal*), be in stitches, be rolling in the aisles (*informal*), bust a gut (*informal*), chortle, crack up (*informal*), crease up (*informal*), giggle, guffaw, roar with laughter, snigger, split one's sides, titter 2 **laugh at** = **make fun of**, belittle, deride, jeer, lampoon, make a mock of, mock, ridicule, scoff at, take the mickey (out of) (*informal*), taunt ♦ *noun* 3 = **chuckle**, belly laugh (*informal*), chortle, giggle, guffaw, roar *or* shriek of laughter, snigger, titter 4 *Informal* = **clown**, card (*informal*), caution (*informal*), comedian, comic, entertainer, hoot (*informal*), humorist, scream (*informal*), wag, wit 5 *Informal* = **joke**, hoot (*informal*), lark, scream (*informal*)

laughable *adjective* = **ridiculous**, absurd, derisive, derisory, ludicrous, nonsensical, preposterous, risible, worthy of scorn

laughing stock *noun* = **figure of fun**, Aunt Sally (*Brit.*), butt, everybody's fool, fair game, target, victim

laugh off *verb* = **disregard**, brush aside, dismiss, ignore, minimize, pooh-pooh, shrug off

laughter *noun* 1 = **chuckling**, cachinnation, chortling, giggling, guffawing, laughing, tittering 2 = **amusement**, glee, hilarity, merriment, mirth

launch *verb* 1 = **propel**, cast, discharge, dispatch, fire, project, send off, set afloat, set in motion, throw 2 = **begin**, commence, embark upon, inaugurate, initiate, instigate, introduce, open, start

launder *verb* 1 = **wash**, clean 2 = **process**, cook (*slang*), doctor, manipulate

laurels *plural noun* = **glory**, acclaim, awards, Brownie points, commendation, credit, distinction, fame, honour, kudos, praise, prestige, recognition, renown, reward

lavatory *noun* = **toilet**, bathroom, bog (*slang*), can (*U.S. & Canad. slang*), cloakroom (*Brit.*), crapper (*taboo slang*), Gents *or* Ladies, john (*slang, chiefly U.S. & Canad.*), khazi (*slang*), latrine, little boy's room *or* little girl's room (*informal*), loo (*Brit. informal*), pissoir, powder room, privy, (public) convenience, washroom, water closet, W.C.

lavish *adjective* 1 = **plentiful**, abundant, copious, exuberant, lush, luxuriant, opulent, profuse, prolific, sumptuous 2 = **generous**, bountiful, effusive, free, liberal, munificent, open-handed, unstinting 3 = **extravagant**, exaggerated, excessive, immoderate, improvident, intemperate, prodigal, thriftless, unreasonable, unrestrained, wasteful, wild ♦ *verb* 4 = **spend**, deluge, dissipate, expend, heap, pour, shower, squander, waste
➤ **Antonyms**
adjective ≠**plentiful**: frugal, meagre, miserly, scanty, stingy ≠**generous**: cheap, miserly, parsimonious, stingy, tight-fisted ≠**extravagant**: sparing, thrifty ♦ *verb* ≠**spend**: begrudge, economize, stint, withhold

law *noun* 1 = **constitution**, charter, code, jurisprudence 2 = **rule**, act, canon, code, command, commandment, covenant, decree, demand, edict, enactment, order, ordinance, regulation, statute 3 = **principle**, axiom, canon, criterion, formula, precept, standard 4 **lay down the law** = **dictate**, dogmatize, emphasize, pontificate

law-abiding *adjective* = **obedient**, compliant, dutiful, good, honest, honourable, lawful, orderly, peaceable, peaceful

law-breaker *noun* = **criminal**, convict, crook (*informal*), culprit, delinquent, felon (*formerly criminal law*), miscreant, offender, sinner, transgressor, trespasser, villain, violater, wrongdoer

lawful *adjective* = **legal**, allowable, authorized, constitutional, just, legalized, legitimate, licit, permissible, proper, rightful, valid, warranted
➤ **Antonyms**
banned, forbidden, illegal, illegitimate, illicit, prohibited, unauthorized, unlawful

lawless *adjective* = **disorderly**, anarchic,

chaotic, insubordinate, insurgent, mutinous, rebellious, reckless, riotous, seditious, ungoverned, unrestrained, unruly, wild
➤ **Antonyms**
civilized, compliant, disciplined, law-abiding, obedient, orderly, restrained, well-governed

lawlessness *noun* = **anarchy**, chaos, disorder, mob rule

lawsuit *noun* = **case**, action, argument, cause, contest, dispute, industrial tribunal, litigation, proceedings, prosecution, suit, trial

lawyer *noun* = **legal adviser**, advocate, attorney, barrister, counsel, counsellor, solicitor

lax *adjective* = **slack**, careless, casual, easy-going, easy-oasy (*slang*), lenient, neglectful, negligent, overindulgent, remiss, slapdash, slipshod
➤ **Antonyms**
conscientious, disciplined, firm, heedful, rigid, scrupulous, severe, stern, strict, stringent

laxative *noun* = **purgative**, aperient, cathartic, physic (*rare*), purge, salts

lay[1] *verb* 1 = **place**, deposit, establish, leave, plant, put, set, set down, settle, spread 2 = **attribute**, allocate, allot, ascribe, assign, charge, impute 3 = **put forward**, advance, bring forward, lodge, offer, present, submit 4 = **devise**, concoct, contrive, design, hatch, plan, plot, prepare, work out 5 = **arrange**, dispose, locate, organize, position, set out 6 = **produce**, bear, deposit 7 = **bet**, gamble, give odds, hazard, risk, stake, wager 8 **lay bare** = **reveal**, disclose, divulge, explain, expose, show, unveil 9 **lay hold of** = **grasp**, get, get hold of, grab, grip, seize, snatch

lay[2] *adjective* 1 = **nonclerical**, laic, laical, secular 2 = **nonspecialist**, amateur, inexpert, nonprofessional

lay[3] *noun* = **poem**, ballad, lyric, ode, song

layabout *noun* = **idler**, couch potato (*slang*), good-for-nothing, laggard, loafer, lounger, ne'er-do-well, shirker, skiver (*Brit. slang*), vagrant, wastrel

lay aside *verb* = **abandon**, cast aside, dismiss, postpone, put aside, put off, reject, shelve

lay down *verb* 1 = **sacrifice**, give up, relinquish, surrender, yield 2 = **stipulate**, affirm, assume, establish, formulate, ordain, postulate, prescribe

layer *noun* 1 = **tier**, ply, row, seam, stratum, thickness 2 = **covering**, blanket, coat, coating, cover, film, mantle, sheet

lay in *verb* = **store (up)**, accumulate, amass, build up, collect, hoard, stockpile, stock up

lay into *verb Informal* = **attack**, assail, belabour, go for the jugular, hit out at,

lambast(e), let fly at, pitch into (*informal*), set about

layman *noun* = **nonprofessional**, amateur, lay person, outsider

lay-off *noun* = **unemployment**, discharge, dismissal

lay off *verb* 1 = **dismiss**, discharge, drop, give the boot to (*slang*), let go, make redundant, oust, pay off 2 *Informal* = **stop**, belay (*Nautical*), cease, desist, get off someone's back (*informal*), give it a rest (*informal*), give over (*informal*), give up, leave alone, leave off, let up, quit

lay on *verb* 1 = **provide**, cater (for), furnish, give, purvey, supply 2 **lay it on thick** *Slang* = **exaggerate**, butter up, flatter, overdo it, overpraise, soft-soap (*informal*)

layout *noun* = **arrangement**, design, draft, format, formation, geography, outline, plan

lay out *verb* 1 = **arrange**, design, display, exhibit, plan, spread out 2 *Informal* = **spend**, disburse, expend, fork out (*slang*), invest, pay, shell out (*informal*) 3 *Informal* = **knock out**, kayo (*slang*), knock for six (*informal*), knock unconscious, KO *or* K.O. (*slang*)

lay up *verb* 1 *Informal* = **confine (to bed)**, hospitalize, incapacitate 2 = **store up**, accumulate, amass, garner, hoard, keep, preserve, put away, save, treasure

laze *verb* 1 = **idle**, hang around, loaf, loll, lounge, stand around 2 *often with* **away** = **kill time**, fool away, fritter away, pass time, veg out (*slang, chiefly U.S.*), waste time, while away the hours

laziness *noun* = **idleness**, inactivity, indolence, lackadaisicalness, slackness, sloth, slothfulness, slowness, sluggishness, tardiness

lazy *adjective* 1 = **idle**, good-for-nothing, inactive, indolent, inert, remiss, shiftless, slack, slothful, slow, workshy 2 = **lethargic**, drowsy, languid, languorous, sleepy, slow-moving, sluggish, somnolent, torpid
➤ **Antonyms**
active, assiduous, diligent, energetic, industrious, quick, stimulated

lazybones *noun Informal* = **idler**, couch potato (*slang*), loafer, lounger, shirker, skiver (*Brit. slang*), sleepyhead, slugabed, sluggard

leach *verb* = **extract**, drain, filter, filtrate, percolate, seep, strain

lead *verb* 1 = **guide**, conduct, escort, pilot, precede, show the way, steer, usher 2 = **cause**, dispose, draw, incline, induce, influence, persuade, prevail, prompt 3 = **command**, direct, govern, head, manage, preside over, supervise 4 = **be ahead (of)**, blaze a trail, come first, exceed, excel, outdo, outstrip, surpass, transcend 5 = **live**, experience, have, pass, spend, undergo **6** = **result in**, bring on, cause, conduce, contribute, produce, serve, tend ♦ *noun* **7** = **first place**, cutting edge, precedence, primacy, priority, supremacy, van, vanguard **8** = **example**, direction, guidance, leadership, model **9** = **advantage**, advance, edge, margin, start **10** = **clue**, guide, hint, indication, suggestion, tip, trace **11** = **leading role**, principal, protagonist, star part, title role ♦ *adjective* **12** = **main**, chief, first, foremost, head, leading, most important, premier, primary, prime, principal

leaden *adjective* **1** = **heavy**, cumbersome, inert, onerous **2** = **grey**, greyish, lacklustre, louring *or* lowering, lustreless, overcast, sombre **3** = **lifeless**, dismal, dreary, dull, gloomy, languid, listless, spiritless

leader *noun* = **principal**, boss (*informal*), captain, chief, chieftain, commander, conductor, director, guide, head, number one, ringleader, ruler, superior
➤ **Antonyms**
adherent, disciple, follower, hanger-on, henchman, sidekick (*slang*), supporter

leadership *noun* **1** = **guidance**, administration, direction, directorship, domination, management, running, superintendency **2** = **authority**, command, control, influence, initiative, pre-eminence, supremacy, sway

leading *adjective* = **principal**, chief, dominant, first, foremost, governing, greatest, highest, main, number one, outstanding, pre-eminent, primary, ruling, superior
➤ **Antonyms**
following, hindmost, incidental, inferior, lesser, minor, secondary, subordinate

lead off *verb* = **begin**, commence, get going, get under way, inaugurate, initiate, kick off (*informal*), open, set out, start, start the ball rolling (*informal*)

lead on *verb* = **entice**, beguile, deceive, draw on, inveigle, lure, seduce, string along (*informal*), tempt

lead up to *verb* = **introduce**, approach, intimate, make advances, make overtures, pave the way, prepare for, prepare the way, work round to

leaf *noun* **1** = **frond**, blade, bract, flag, foliole, needle, pad **2** = **page**, folio, sheet **3 turn over a new leaf** = **reform**, amend, begin anew, change, change one's ways, improve ♦ *verb* **4 leaf through** = **skim**, browse, flip, glance, riffle, thumb (through) **5** = **put out leaves**, bud, green, turn green

leaflet *noun* = **booklet**, advert (*Brit. informal*), bill, brochure, circular, handbill, mailshot, pamphlet

leafy *adjective* = **green**, in foliage, leaved, shaded, shady, verdant, wooded

league *noun* **1** = **association**, alliance, band, coalition, combination, combine, compact, confederacy, confederation, consortium, federation, fellowship, fraternity, group, guild, order, partnership, union **2** *Informal* = **class**, ability group, category, level **3 in league (with)** = **collaborating**, allied, hand in glove, in cahoots (*informal*), leagued ♦ *verb* **4** = **unite**, ally, amalgamate, associate, band, collaborate, combine, confederate, join forces

leak *noun* **1** = **hole**, aperture, chink, crack, crevice, fissure, opening, puncture **2** = **leakage**, drip, leaking, oozing, percolation, seepage **3** = **disclosure**, divulgence ♦ *verb* **4** = **escape**, discharge, drip, exude, ooze, pass, percolate, seep, spill, trickle **5** = **disclose**, blow wide open (*slang*), divulge, give away, let slip, let the cat out of the bag, make known, make public, pass on, reveal, spill the beans (*informal*), tell

leaky *adjective* = **leaking**, cracked, holey, not watertight, perforated, porous, punctured, split, waterlogged

lean[1] *verb* **1** = **rest**, be supported, prop, recline, repose **2** = **bend**, heel, incline, slant, slope, tilt, tip **3** = **tend**, be disposed to, be prone to, favour, gravitate towards, have a propensity, prefer **4 lean on** = **depend on**, confide in, count on, have faith in, rely on, trust

lean[2] *adjective* **1** = **trim**, angular, bony, emaciated, gaunt, lank, rangy, scraggy, scrawny, skinny, slender, slim, spare, thin, unfatty, wiry **2** = **poor**, bare, barren, inadequate, infertile, meagre, pathetic, pitiful, scanty, sparse, unfruitful, unproductive
➤ **Antonyms**
≠**trim**: ample, brawny, burly, fat, full, obese, plump, portly ≠**poor**: abundant, fertile, plentiful, profuse, rich

leaning *noun* = **tendency**, aptitude, bent, bias, disposition, inclination, liking, partiality, penchant, predilection, proclivity, proneness, propensity, taste

leap *verb* **1** = **jump**, bounce, bound, caper, cavort, frisk, gambol, hop, skip, spring **2** = **jump over**, clear, vault ♦ *noun* **3** = **jump**, bound, caper, frisk, hop, skip, spring, vault **4** = **rise**, change, escalation, increase, surge, upsurge, upswing

learn *verb* **1** = **master**, acquire, attain, become able, grasp, imbibe, pick up **2** = **memorize**, commit to memory, con (*archaic*), get off pat, get (something) word-perfect, learn by heart **3** = **discover**, ascertain, detect, determine, discern, find out, gain, gather, hear, suss (out) (*slang*), understand

learned *adjective* = **scholarly**, academic, cultured, erudite, experienced, expert, highbrow, intellectual, lettered, literate, skilled, versed, well-informed, well-read
➤ **Antonyms**
ignorant, illiterate, uneducated, unlearned

learner *noun* 1 = **beginner**, apprentice, neophyte, novice, tyro 2 = **student**, disciple, pupil, scholar, trainee
➤ **Antonyms**
≠**beginner:** adept, expert, master, virtuoso, wizard ≠**student:** coach, guru, instructor, mentor, teacher, tutor

learning *noun* = **knowledge**, acquirements, attainments, culture, education, erudition, information, letters, literature, lore, research, scholarship, schooling, study, tuition, wisdom

lease *verb* = **hire**, charter, let, loan, rent

leash *noun* 1 = **lead**, rein, tether ♦ *verb* 2 = **tether**, fasten, secure, tie up

least *adjective* = **smallest**, feeblest, fewest, last, lowest, meanest, minimum, minutest, poorest, slightest, tiniest

leathery *adjective* = **tough**, durable, hard, hardened, leatherlike, rough, rugged, wrinkled

leave[1] *verb* 1 = **depart**, abandon, abscond, decamp, desert, disappear, do a bunk (*Brit. slang*), exit, flit (*informal*), forsake, go, go away, hook it (*slang*), make tracks, move, pack one's bags (*informal*), pull out, quit, relinquish, retire, set out, sling one's hook (*Brit. slang*), slope off, take off (*informal*), withdraw 2 = **forget**, lay down, leave behind, mislay 3 = **give up**, abandon, cease, desert, desist, drop, evacuate, forbear, refrain, relinquish, renounce, stop, surrender 4 = **cause**, deposit, generate, produce, result in 5 = **entrust**, allot, assign, cede, commit, consign, give over, refer 6 = **bequeath**, hand down, transmit, will
➤ **Antonyms**
≠**depart:** appear, arrive, come, emerge, stay ≠**give up:** assume, continue, hold, persist, remove, retain

leave[2] *noun* 1 = **permission**, allowance, authorization, concession, consent, dispensation, freedom, liberty, sanction 2 = **holiday**, furlough, leave of absence, sabbatical, time off, vacation 3 *As in* **take one's leave of** = **departure**, adieu, farewell, goodbye, leave-taking, parting, retirement, withdrawal
➤ **Antonyms**
≠**permission:** denial, prohibition, refusal, rejection ≠**holiday:** duty ≠**departure:** arrival, stay

leaven *noun* 1 = **yeast**, barm, ferment,

leavening 2 = **catalyst**, influence, inspiration ♦ *verb* 3 = **ferment**, lighten, raise, work 4 = **stimulate**, elevate, imbue, inspire, permeate, pervade, quicken, suffuse

leave off *verb* = **stop**, abstain, belay (*Nautical*), break off, cease, desist, discontinue, end, give over (*informal*), give up, halt, kick (*informal*), knock off (*informal*), refrain

leave out *verb* = **omit**, bar, cast aside, count out, disregard, except, exclude, ignore, neglect, overlook, reject

leave-taking *noun* = **departure**, farewell, going, goodbye, leaving, parting, sendoff (*informal*), valediction

leavings *plural noun* = **leftovers**, bits, dregs, fragments, pieces, refuse, remains, remnants, residue, scraps, spoil, sweepings, waste

lecher *noun* = **womanizer**, adulterer, Casanova, debauchee, dirty old man (*slang*), Don Juan, fornicator, goat (*informal*), lech *or* letch (*informal*), libertine, profligate, rake, roué, satyr, seducer, sensualist, wanton, wolf (*informal*)

lecherous *adjective* = **lustful**, carnal, lascivious, lewd, libidinous, licentious, prurient, randy (*informal, chiefly Brit.*), raunchy (*slang*), salacious, unchaste, wanton
➤ **Antonyms**
prim, proper, prudish, puritanical, strait-laced, virginal, virtuous

lechery *noun* = **lustfulness**, carnality, debauchery, lasciviousness, lecherousness, leching (*informal*), lewdness, libertinism, libidinousness, licentiousness, lubricity, lust, profligacy, prurience, rakishness, randiness (*informal, chiefly Brit.*), salaciousness, sensuality, wantonness, womanizing

lecture *noun* 1 = **talk**, address, discourse, disquisition, harangue, instruction, lesson, speech 2 = **telling off** (*informal*), castigation, censure, chiding, dressing-down (*informal*), going-over (*informal*), heat (*slang, chiefly U.S. & Canad.*), rebuke, reprimand, reproof, scolding, talking-to (*informal*) ♦ *verb* 3 = **talk**, address, discourse, expound, give a talk, harangue, hold forth, speak, spout, teach 4 = **tell off** (*informal*), admonish, bawl out (*informal*), berate, carpet (*informal*), castigate, censure, chew out (*U.S. & Canad. informal*), chide, give a rocket (*Brit. & N.Z. informal*), rate, read the riot act, reprimand, reprove, scold, tear into (*informal*), tear (someone) off a strip (*Brit. informal*)

ledge *noun* = **shelf**, mantle, projection, ridge, sill, step

lee *noun* = **shelter**, cover, protection, refuge, screen, shade, shadow, shield

leech *noun* = **parasite**, bloodsucker (*informal*), freeloader (*slang*), hanger-on, sponger (*informal*), sycophant

leer *noun, verb* = **grin**, drool, eye, gloat, goggle, ogle, smirk, squint, stare, wink

leery *adjective Slang* = **wary**, careful, cautious, chary, distrustful, doubting, dubious, on one's guard, sceptical, shy, suspicious, uncertain, unsure

lees *plural noun* = **sediment**, deposit, dregs, grounds, precipitate, refuse, settlings

leeway *noun* = **room**, elbowroom, latitude, margin, play, scope, space

left *adjective* **1** = **left-hand**, larboard (*Nautical*), port, sinistral **2** *Of politics* = **socialist**, leftist, left-wing, liberal, progressive, radical

left-handed *adjective* **1** *Archaic* = **awkward**, cack-handed (*informal*), careless, clumsy, fumbling, gauche, maladroit **2** = **ambiguous**, backhanded, double-edged, enigmatic, equivocal, indirect, ironic, sardonic

leftover *noun* **1** = **remnant**, leaving, oddment, remains, scrap ♦ *adjective* **2** = **surplus**, excess, extra, remaining, uneaten, unused, unwanted

left-wing *adjective* = **socialist**, communist, Marxist, radical, red (*informal*)

leg *noun* **1** = **limb**, lower limb, member, pin (*informal*), stump (*informal*) **2** = **support**, brace, prop, upright **3** = **stage**, lap, part, portion, section, segment, stretch **4 not have a leg to stand on** *Informal* = **have no basis**, be defenceless, be full of holes, be illogical, be invalid, be undermined, be vulnerable, lack support **5 on one's (its) last legs** = **worn out**, about to break down, about to collapse, at death's door, dying, exhausted, failing, giving up the ghost **6 pull someone's leg** *Informal* = **tease**, chaff, deceive, fool, have (someone) on, joke, kid (*informal*), make fun of, poke fun at, rag, rib (*informal*), trick, twit, wind up (*Brit. slang*) **7 shake a leg** *Informal* = **hurry**, get a move on (*informal*), get cracking (*informal*), hasten, look lively (*informal*), rush, stir one's stumps **8 stretch one's legs** = **take a walk**, exercise, go for a walk, move about, promenade, stroll, take the air ♦ *verb* **9 leg it** *Informal* = **run**, go on foot, hotfoot, hurry, skedaddle (*informal*), walk

legacy *noun* **1** = **bequest**, devise (*Law*), estate, gift, heirloom, inheritance **2** = **heritage**, birthright, endowment, inheritance, patrimony, throwback, tradition

legal *adjective* **1** = **lawful**, allowable, allowed, authorized, constitutional, legalized, legitimate, licit, permissible, proper, rightful, sanctioned, valid **2** = **judicial**, forensic,

judiciary, juridical

legality *noun* = **lawfulness**, accordance with the law, admissibleness, legitimacy, permissibility, rightfulness, validity

legalize *verb* = **permit**, allow, approve, authorize, decriminalize, legitimate, legitimize, license, sanction, validate

legal tender *noun* = **currency**, medium, money, payment, specie

legate *noun* = **messenger**, ambassador, delegate, depute (*Scot.*), deputy, emissary, envoy

legatee *noun* = **beneficiary**, heir, inheritor, recipient

legation *noun* = **delegation**, consulate, diplomatic mission, embassy, envoys, ministry, representation

legend *noun* **1** = **myth**, fable, fiction, folk tale, narrative, saga, story, tale, urban legend, urban myth **2** = **celebrity**, big name, celeb (*informal*), luminary, marvel, megastar (*informal*), phenomenon, prodigy, spectacle, wonder **3** = **inscription**, caption, device, motto **4** = **key**, cipher, code, table of symbols

legendary *adjective* **1** = **famous**, celebrated, famed, illustrious, immortal, renowned, well-known **2** = **mythical**, apocryphal, fabled, fabulous, fanciful, fictitious, romantic, traditional
➤ **Antonyms**
≠**famous**: unknown ≠**mythical**: factual, genuine, historical

legerdemain *noun* **1** = **sleight of hand**, prestidigitation **2** = **deception**, artfulness, artifice, chicanery, contrivance, craftiness, cunning, feint, hocus-pocus, manipulation, manoeuvring, subterfuge, trickery

legibility *noun* = **readability**, clarity, decipherability, ease of reading, legibleness, neatness, plainness, readableness

legible *adjective* = **readable**, bold, clear, decipherable, distinct, easily read, easy to read, neat, plain

legion *noun* **1** = **army**, brigade, company, division, force, troop **2** = **multitude**, drove, horde, host, mass, myriad, number, throng

legislate *verb* = **make laws**, codify, constitute, enact, establish, ordain, pass laws, prescribe, put in force

legislation *noun* **1** = **lawmaking**, codification, enactment, prescription, regulation **2** = **law**, act, bill, charter, measure, regulation, ruling, statute

legislative *adjective* = **law-making**, congressional, judicial, law-giving, parliamentary

legislator *noun* = **lawmaker**, lawgiver, parliamentarian

legislature noun = **parliament**, assembly, chamber, congress, diet, house, law-making body, senate

legitimate adjective **1** = **lawful**, acknowledged, authentic, authorized, genuine, kosher (informal), legal, legit (slang), licit, proper, real, rightful, sanctioned, statutory, true **2** = **reasonable**, admissible, correct, just, justifiable, logical, sensible, valid, warranted, well-founded ♦ verb **3** = **legitimize**, authorize, give the green light for, legalize, legitimatize, permit, pronounce lawful, sanction
➤ **Antonyms**
adjective ≠**lawful**: false, fraudulent, illegal, illegitimate, unlawful ≠**reasonable**: unfair, unfounded, unjustified, unreasonable, unsound

legitimize, legitimise verb = **legalize**, authorize, give the green light for, legitimate, permit, pronounce lawful, sanction

leisure noun **1** = **spare time**, breathing space, ease, freedom, free time, holiday, liberty, opportunity, pause, quiet, recreation, relaxation, respite, rest, retirement, spare moments, time off, vacation **2 at leisure: a** = **free**, available, not booked up, on holiday, unengaged, unoccupied **b at one's leisure** = **in one's own (good) time**, at an unhurried pace, at one's convenience, deliberately, unhurriedly, when it suits one, when one gets round to it (informal), without hurry
➤ **Antonyms**
≠**spare time**: business, duty, employment, labour, obligation, occupation, work

leisurely adjective **1** = **unhurried**, comfortable, easy, gentle, laid-back (informal), lazy, relaxed, restful, slow ♦ adverb **2** = **unhurriedly**, at one's convenience, at one's leisure, comfortably, deliberately, easily, indolently, lazily, lingeringly, slowly, without haste
➤ **Antonyms**
adjective ≠**unhurried**: brisk, fast, hasty, hectic, hurried, quick, rapid, rushed ♦ adverb ≠**unhurriedly**: briskly, hastily, hurriedly, quickly, rapidly

leitmotif or **leitmotiv** noun, with **recurrent** or **recurring** = **theme**, air, convention, device, idea, melody, motif, phrase, strain

lend verb **1** = **loan**, accommodate one with, advance **2** = **give**, add, afford, bestow, confer, contribute, furnish, grant, hand out, impart, present, provide, supply **3 lend an ear** = **listen**, give ear, hearken (archaic), heed, take notice **4 lend a hand** = **help**, aid, assist, give a (helping) hand, help out **5 lend itself to** = **be appropriate**, be adaptable, be

serviceable, fit, present opportunities of, suit

length noun **1** Of linear extent = **distance**, extent, longitude, measure, reach, span **2** Of time = **duration**, period, space, span, stretch, term **3** = **piece**, measure, portion, section, segment **4** = **lengthiness**, elongation, extensiveness, protractedness **5 at length: a** = **at last**, at long last, eventually, finally, in the end **b** = **in detail**, completely, fully, in depth, thoroughly, to the full **c** = **for a long time**, for ages, for hours, interminably

lengthen verb = **extend**, continue, draw out, elongate, expand, increase, make longer, prolong, protract, spin out, stretch
➤ **Antonyms**
abbreviate, abridge, curtail, cut, cut down, diminish, shorten, trim

lengthy adjective = **long**, diffuse, drawn-out, extended, interminable, lengthened, long-drawn-out, long-winded, overlong, prolix, prolonged, protracted, tedious, verbose, very long
➤ **Antonyms**
brief, concise, condensed, limited, short, succinct, terse, to the point

leniency noun = **mercy**, clemency, compassion, forbearance, gentleness, indulgence, lenity, mildness, moderation, pity, quarter, tenderness, tolerance

lenient adjective = **merciful**, clement, compassionate, forbearing, forgiving, gentle, indulgent, kind, mild, sparing, tender, tolerant
➤ **Antonyms**
harsh, merciless, rigid, rigorous, severe, stern, strict, stringent

leper noun = **outcast**, pariah, untouchable

lesbian noun **1** = **dyke** (slang), butch (slang), sapphist ♦ adjective **2** = **homosexual**, butch (slang), dykey (slang), gay, sapphic

lesion noun = **injury**, abrasion, bruise, contusion, hurt, trauma (Pathology), wound

less adjective **1** = **smaller**, shorter, slighter ♦ adverb **2** = **to a smaller extent**, barely, little, meagrely ♦ preposition **3** = **minus**, excepting, lacking, subtracting, without

lessen verb = **reduce**, abate, abridge, contract, curtail, decrease, de-escalate, die down, diminish, downsize, dwindle, ease, grow less, impair, lighten, lower, minimize, moderate, narrow, relax, shrink, slacken, slow down, weaken, wind down
➤ **Antonyms**
add to, augment, boost, enhance, enlarge, expand, increase, magnify, multiply, raise

lessening noun = **reduction**, abatement, contraction, curtailment, decline, decrease, diminution, dwindling, ebbing, let-up (*informal*), minimization, moderation, petering out, shrinkage, slackening, slowing down, waning, weakening

lesser *adjective* = **lower**, inferior, less important, minor, secondary, slighter, subordinate, under-
➤ Antonyms
greater, higher, major, primary, superior

lesson *noun* **1** = **class**, coaching, instruction, period, schooling, teaching, tutoring **2** = **exercise**, assignment, drill, homework, lecture, practice, reading, recitation, task **3** = **example**, deterrent, exemplar, message, model, moral, precept **4** = **punishment**, admonition, censure, chiding, rebuke, reprimand, reproof, scolding, warning

let[1] *verb* **1** = **allow**, authorize, entitle, give leave, give permission, give the go-ahead, give the green light, give the O.K. *or* okay (*informal*), grant, permit, sanction, suffer (*archaic*), tolerate, warrant **2** = **lease**, hire, rent **3** = **enable**, allow, cause, grant, make, permit

let[2] *noun* = **hindrance**, constraint, impediment, interference, obstacle, obstruction, prohibition, restriction

letdown *noun* = **disappointment**, anticlimax, bitter pill, blow, comedown (*informal*), frustration, setback, washout (*informal*), whammy (*informal, chiefly U.S.*)

let down *verb* = **disappoint**, disenchant, disillusion, dissatisfy, fail, fall short, leave in the lurch, leave stranded

lethal *adjective* = **deadly**, baneful, dangerous, deathly, destructive, devastating, fatal, mortal, murderous, noxious, pernicious, poisonous, virulent
➤ Antonyms
harmless, healthy, innocuous, safe, wholesome

lethargic *adjective* = **sluggish**, apathetic, comatose, debilitated, drowsy, dull, enervated, heavy, inactive, indifferent, inert, languid, lazy, listless, sleepy, slothful, slow, torpid
➤ Antonyms
active, alert, animated, energetic, responsive, spirited, stimulated, vigorous

lethargy *noun* = **sluggishness**, apathy, drowsiness, dullness, inaction, indifference, inertia, languor, lassitude, listlessness, sleepiness, sloth, slowness, stupor, torpidity, torpor
➤ Antonyms
animation, brio, energy, life, liveliness, spirit, verve, vigour, vim, vitality, vivacity, zeal, zest

let in *verb* = **admit**, allow to enter, give access to, greet, include, incorporate, receive, take in, welcome

let off *verb* **1** = **excuse**, absolve, discharge, dispense, exempt, exonerate, forgive, pardon, release, spare **2** = **fire**, detonate, discharge, explode **3** = **emit**, exude, give off, leak, release

let on *verb Informal* **1** = **reveal**, admit, disclose, divulge, give away, let the cat out of the bag (*informal*), make known, say **2** = **pretend**, act, counterfeit, dissemble, dissimulate, feign, make believe, make out, profess, simulate

let out *verb* **1** = **emit**, give vent to, produce **2** = **release**, discharge, free, let go, liberate **3** = **reveal**, betray, blow wide open (*slang*), disclose, leak, let fall, let slip, make known

letter *noun* **1** = **message**, acknowledgment, answer, billet (*archaic*), communication, dispatch, epistle, line, missive, note, reply **2** = **character**, sign, symbol **3 to the letter** = **precisely**, accurately, exactly, literally, strictly, word for word

lettered *adjective* = **educated**, accomplished, cultivated, cultured, erudite, informed, knowledgeable, learned, literate, scholarly, versed, well-educated, well-read

letters *plural noun* = **learning**, belles-lettres, culture, erudition, humanities, literature, scholarship

let-up *noun Informal* = **lessening**, abatement, break, breathing space, cessation, interval, lull, pause, recess, remission, respite, slackening

let up *verb* = **stop**, abate, decrease, diminish, ease (up), moderate, relax, slacken, subside

levee *noun* = **reception**, ceremony, entertainment, gathering, party

level *adjective* **1** = **horizontal**, as flat as a pancake, flat, plane **2** = **even**, consistent, plain, smooth, uniform **3** = **equal**, aligned, balanced, commensurate, comparable, equivalent, even, flush, in line, neck and neck, on a line, on a par, proportionate ♦ *verb* **4** = **flatten**, even off *or* out, make flat, plane, smooth **5** = **equalize**, balance, even up **6** = **direct**, aim, beam, focus, point, train **7** = **destroy**, bulldoze, demolish, devastate, flatten, knock down, lay low, pull down, raze, tear down, wreck ♦ *noun* **8** = **position**, achievement, degree, grade, rank, stage, standard, standing, status **9** = **height**, altitude, elevation, vertical position **10** = **flat surface**, horizontal, plain, plane **11 on the level** *Informal* = **honest**, above board, fair, genuine, open, sincere, square, straight, straightforward, up front (*slang*)
➤ Antonyms
adjective ≠**horizontal:** slanted, tilted, vertical ≠**even:** bumpy, uneven ≠**equal:** above, below ♦ *verb* ≠**destroy:** build, erect, raise, roughen

level-headed *adjective* = **calm**, balanced,

collected, composed, cool, dependable,
even-tempered, reasonable, sane,
self-possessed, sensible, steady, together
(*slang*), unflappable (*informal*)

lever *noun* 1 = **handle**, bar, crowbar, jemmy
♦ *verb* 2 = **prise**, force, jemmy, move, pry
(*U.S.*), raise

leverage *noun* = **influence**, authority, clout
(*informal*), pull (*informal*), purchasing
power, rank, weight

leviathan *noun* = **monster**, behemoth,
colossus, hulk, mammoth, Titan, whale

levity *noun* = **light-heartedness**, buoyancy,
facetiousness, flightiness, flippancy, frivolity,
giddiness, light-mindedness, silliness,
skittishness, triviality
➤ **Antonyms**
earnestness, gravity, seriousness, solemnity

levy *verb* 1 = **impose**, charge, collect,
demand, exact, gather, tax 2 = **conscript**,
call, call up, mobilize, muster, press, raise,
summon ♦ *noun* 3 = **imposition**,
assessment, collection, exaction, gathering 4
= **tax**, assessment, duty, excise, fee,
imposition, impost, tariff, toll

lewd *adjective* = **indecent**, bawdy, blue,
dirty, impure, lascivious, libidinous,
licentious, loose, lustful, obscene,
pornographic, salacious, smutty, unchaste,
vile, vulgar, wanton, wicked, X-rated
(*informal*)

lewdness *noun* = **indecency**, bawdiness,
carnality, crudity, debauchery, depravity,
impurity, lasciviousness, lechery,
licentiousness, lubricity, obscenity,
pornography, salaciousness, smut,
smuttiness, unchastity, vulgarity, wantonness

lexicon *noun* = **vocabulary**, dictionary,
glossary, wordbook, word list

liabilities *plural noun* = **debts**, accounts
payable, expenditure, obligations

liability *noun* 1 = **disadvantage**, albatross,
burden, drag, drawback, encumbrance,
handicap, hindrance, impediment,
inconvenience, millstone, minus (*informal*),
nuisance 2 = **responsibility**, accountability,
answerability, culpability, duty, obligation,
onus 3 = **debt**, arrear, debit, obligation

liable *adjective* 1 = **likely**, apt, disposed,
inclined, prone, tending 2 = **vulnerable**,
exposed, open, subject, susceptible 3
= **responsible**, accountable, answerable,
bound, chargeable, obligated

liaise *verb* = **communicate**, keep contact,
link, mediate

liaison *noun* 1 = **communication**,
connection, contact, go-between, hook-up,
interchange, intermediary 2 = **affair**, amour,
entanglement, fling, illicit romance, intrigue,

love affair, romance

liar *noun* = **falsifier**, fabricator, fibber,
perjurer, prevaricator, storyteller (*informal*)

libel *noun* 1 = **defamation**, aspersion,
calumny, denigration, obloquy, slander,
smear, vituperation ♦ *verb* 2 = **defame**,
blacken, calumniate, derogate, drag
(someone's) name through the mud,
malign, revile, slander, slur, smear, traduce,
vilify

libellous *adjective* = **defamatory**,
derogatory, false, injurious, malicious,
maligning, scurrilous, slanderous, traducing,
untrue, vilifying, vituperative

liberal *adjective* 1 = **progressive**, advanced,
humanistic, latitudinarian, libertarian,
politically correct *or* PC, radical, reformist,
right-on (*informal*) 2 = **generous**,
beneficent, bounteous, bountiful, charitable,
free-handed, kind, open-handed,
open-hearted, prodigal, unstinting 3
= **tolerant**, advanced, broad-minded,
catholic, enlightened, high-minded,
humanitarian, indulgent, magnanimous,
permissive, politically correct *or* PC, right-on
(*informal*), unbiased, unbigoted,
unprejudiced 4 = **abundant**, ample,
bountiful, copious, handsome, lavish,
munificent, plentiful, profuse, rich 5
= **flexible**, broad, free, general, inexact,
lenient, loose, not close, not literal, not strict
➤ **Antonyms**
≠**progressive**: conservative, reactionary,
right-wing ≠**generous**: cheap, stingy
≠**tolerant**: biased, bigoted, intolerant,
prejudiced ≠**abundant**: inadequate, limited,
skimpy, small ≠**flexible**: fixed, inflexible,
literal, strict

liberalism *noun* = **progressivism**,
freethinking, humanitarianism,
latitudinarianism, libertarianism, radicalism

liberality *noun* 1 = **generosity**,
beneficence, benevolence, bounty, charity,
free-handedness, kindness, largesse *or*
largess, munificence, open-handedness,
philanthropy 2 = **broad-mindedness**,
breadth, candour, catholicity, impartiality,
latitude, liberalism, libertarianism,
magnanimity, permissiveness, progressivism,
toleration

liberalize *verb* = **relax**, ameliorate, broaden,
ease, expand, extend, loosen, mitigate,
moderate, modify, slacken, soften, stretch

liberate *verb* = **free**, deliver, discharge,
emancipate, let loose, let out, redeem,
release, rescue, set free
➤ **Antonyms**
confine, detain, immure, imprison,
incarcerate, intern, jail, lock up, put away

liberation *noun* = **freeing**, deliverance,

emancipation, enfranchisement, freedom, liberating, liberty, manumission, redemption, release, unfettering, unshackling

liberator *noun* = **deliverer**, emancipator, freer, manumitter, redeemer, rescuer, saviour

libertine *noun* 1 = **reprobate**, debauchee, lech *or* letch (*informal*), lecher, loose liver, profligate, rake, roué, seducer, sensualist, swinger (*slang*), voluptuary, womanizer ♦ *adjective* 2 = **promiscuous**, abandoned, corrupt, debauched, decadent, degenerate, depraved, dissolute, immoral, licentious, profligate, rakish, reprobate, voluptuous, wanton

liberty *noun* 1 = **freedom**, autonomy, emancipation, immunity, independence, liberation, release, self-determination, sovereignty 2 = **permission**, authorization, blank cheque, carte blanche, dispensation, exemption, franchise, freedom, leave, licence, prerogative, privilege, right, sanction 3 = **impertinence**, disrespect, familiarity, forwardness, impropriety, impudence, insolence, overfamiliarity, presumption, presumptuousness 4 **at liberty** = **free**, not confined, on the loose, unlimited, unoccupied, unrestricted
➤ **Antonyms**
≠**freedom**: captivity, constraint, enslavement, imprisonment, restraint, slavery, tyranny ≠**permission**: compulsion, duress, restriction

libidinous *adjective* = **lustful**, carnal, debauched, impure, incontinent, lascivious, lecherous, loose, prurient, randy (*informal, chiefly Brit.*), ruttish, salacious, sensual, unchaste, wanton, wicked

libretto *noun* = **words**, book, lines, lyrics, script

licence *noun* 1 = **certificate**, charter, permit, warrant 2 = **permission**, a free hand, authority, authorization, blank cheque, carte blanche, dispensation, entitlement, exemption, immunity, leave, liberty, privilege, right 3 = **freedom**, independence, latitude, leeway, liberty 4 = **laxity**, abandon, anarchy, disorder, excess, immoderation, impropriety, indulgence, irresponsibility, lawlessness, profligacy, unruliness
➤ **Antonyms**
≠**permission**: denial, prohibition, restriction ≠**freedom**: constraint, restraint ≠**laxity**: moderation, strictness

license *verb* = **permit**, accredit, allow, authorize, certify, commission, empower, enable, entitle, give a blank cheque to, sanction, warrant
➤ **Antonyms**
ban, debar, disallow, forbid, outlaw, prohibit, proscribe, rule out, veto

licentious *adjective* = **promiscuous**, abandoned, debauched, dissolute, immoral, impure, lascivious, lewd, libertine, libidinous, lustful, profligate, sensual, uncontrollable, uncontrolled, unruly, wanton
➤ **Antonyms**
chaste, law-abiding, lawful, moral, principled, proper, scrupulous, virtuous

licentiousness *noun* = **promiscuity**, abandon, debauchery, dissipation, dissoluteness, lechery, lewdness, libertinism, libidinousness, lust, lustfulness, profligacy, prurience, salaciousness, salacity, wantonness

lick *verb* 1 = **taste**, brush, lap, tongue, touch, wash 2 *Of flames* = **flicker**, dart, flick, ignite, kindle, play over, ripple, touch 3 *Informal* = **beat**, best, blow out of the water (*slang*), clobber (*slang*), defeat, master, outdo, outstrip, overcome, rout, run rings around (*informal*), stuff (*slang*), surpass, tank (*slang*), top, trounce, vanquish, wipe the floor with (*informal*) 4 *Informal* = **thrash**, beat, clobber (*slang*), flog, slap, spank, strike, wallop (*informal*) ♦ *noun* 5 = **dab**, bit, brush, little, sample, speck, stroke, taste, touch 6 *Informal* = **pace**, clip (*informal*), rate, speed

lie[1] *verb* 1 = **fib**, dissimulate, equivocate, fabricate, falsify, forswear oneself, invent, misrepresent, perjure, prevaricate, tell a lie, tell untruths ♦ *noun* 2 = **falsehood**, deceit, fabrication, falsification, falsity, fib, fiction, invention, mendacity, pork pie (*Brit. slang*), porky (*Brit. slang*), prevarication, untruth, white lie

lie[2] *verb* 1 = **recline**, be prone, be prostrate, be recumbent, be supine, couch, loll, lounge, repose, rest, sprawl, stretch out 2 = **be situated**, be, be buried, be found, be interred, be located, belong, be placed, exist, extend, remain 3 *usually with* **in** = **exist**, be present, consist, dwell, inhere, pertain

liege *noun* = **feudal lord**, chieftain, master, overlord, sovereign, superior

lieu *noun* **in lieu of** = **instead of**, in place of

life *noun* 1 = **being**, animation, breath, entity, sentience, viability, vitality 2 = **existence**, being, continuance, course, duration, lifetime, span, time 3 = **person**, human, human being, individual, mortal, soul 4 = **behaviour**, conduct, life style, way of life 5 = **biography**, autobiography, career, confessions, history, life story, memoirs, story 6 = **the human condition**, the times, the world, this mortal coil 7 = **liveliness**, activity, animation, brio, energy, get-up-and-go (*informal*), go (*informal*), high spirits, pep, sparkle, spirit, verve, vigour, vitality, vivacity, zest 8 = **spirit**, animating spirit, *élan vital*, essence, heart, lifeblood, soul, vital spark 9

= **living things**, creatures, living beings, organisms, wildlife

lifeblood *noun* = **animating force**, driving force, essence, guts (*informal*), heart, inspiration, life, stimulus, vital spark

lifeless *adjective* **1** = **dead**, cold, deceased, defunct, extinct, inanimate, inert **2** = **dull**, cold, colourless, flat, heavy, hollow, lacklustre, lethargic, listless, passive, slow, sluggish, spiritless, static, stiff, torpid, wooden **3** = **unconscious**, comatose, dead to the world (*informal*), in a faint, inert, insensate, insensible, out cold, out for the count
➤ **Antonyms**
≠**dead**: alive, alive and kicking, animate, live, living, vital ≠**dull**: active, animated, lively, spirited

lifelike *adjective* = **realistic**, authentic, exact, faithful, graphic, natural, photographic, real, true-to-life, undistorted, vivid

lifelong *adjective* = **long-lasting**, constant, deep-rooted, enduring, for all one's life, for life, lasting, lifetime, long-standing, perennial, permanent, persistent

lifetime *noun* = **existence**, all one's born days, career, course, day(s), life span, one's natural life, period, span, time

lift *verb* **1** = **raise**, bear aloft, buoy up, draw up, elevate, heft (*informal*), hoist, pick up, raise high, rear, upheave, uplift, upraise **2** = **exalt**, advance, ameliorate, boost, dignify, elevate, enhance, improve, promote, raise, upgrade **3** = **revoke**, annul, cancel, countermand, end, relax, remove, rescind, stop, terminate **4** = **disappear**, be dispelled, disperse, dissipate, vanish **5** *Informal* = **steal**, appropriate, blag (*slang*), copy, crib (*informal*), nick (*slang, chiefly Brit.*), pilfer, pinch (*informal*), pirate, plagiarize, purloin, take, thieve ♦ *noun* **6** = **elevator** (*chiefly U.S.*) **7** = **ride**, car ride, drive, run, transport **8** = **boost**, encouragement, fillip, gee-up, pick-me-up, reassurance, shot in the arm (*informal*), uplift
➤ **Antonyms**
verb ≠**raise**: dash, descend, drop, fall, hang, lower ≠**exalt**: depress ≠**revoke**: establish, impose ♦ *noun* ≠**boost**: blow, letdown

ligature *noun* = **link**, band, bandage, binding, bond, connection, ligament, tie

light[1] *noun* **1** = **brightness**, blaze, brilliance, flash, glare, gleam, glint, glow, illumination, incandescence, luminescence, luminosity, lustre, phosphorescence, radiance, ray, scintillation, shine, sparkle **2** = **lamp**, beacon, bulb, candle, flare, lantern, lighthouse, star, taper, torch **3** = **daybreak**, broad day, cockcrow, dawn, daylight, daytime, morn (*poetic*), morning, sun, sunrise **4** = **aspect**,

angle, approach, attitude, context, interpretation, point of view, slant, vantage point, viewpoint **5** = **understanding**, awareness, comprehension, elucidation, explanation, insight, knowledge **6** = **shining example**, example, exemplar, guiding light, model, paragon **7** = **match**, flame, lighter **8 in (the) light of** = **considering**, bearing in mind, because of, in view of, taking into account, with knowledge of ♦ *adjective* **9** = **bright**, aglow, brilliant, glowing, illuminated, luminous, lustrous, shining, sunny, well-lighted, well-lit **10** = **pale**, bleached, blond, faded, fair, light-hued, light-toned, pastel ♦ *verb* **11** = **ignite**, fire, inflame, kindle, set a match to, torch **12** = **illuminate**, brighten, floodlight, flood with light, illumine, lighten, light up
➤ **Antonyms**
noun ≠**brightness**: cloud, dark, darkness, dusk, obscurity, shade, shadow
≠**understanding**: mystery ♦ *adjective* ≠**bright**: dark, dim, dusky, gloomy ≠**pale**: dark, deep ♦ *verb* ≠**ignite**: douse, extinguish, put out, quench ≠**illuminate**: cloud, darken, dull

light[2] *adjective* **1** = **insubstantial**, airy, buoyant, delicate, easy, flimsy, imponderous, lightsome, lightweight, portable, slight, underweight **2** = **weak**, faint, gentle, indistinct, mild, moderate, slight, soft **3** = **insignificant**, inconsequential, inconsiderable, minute, scanty, slight, small, thin, tiny, trifling, trivial, unsubstantial, wee **4** = **undemanding**, cushy (*informal*), easy, effortless, manageable, moderate, simple, unexacting, untaxing **5** = **light-hearted**, amusing, diverting, entertaining, frivolous, funny, gay, humorous, pleasing, superficial, trifling, trivial, witty **6** = **nimble**, agile, airy, graceful, light-footed, lithe, sprightly, sylphlike **7** = **digestible**, frugal, modest, not heavy, not rich, small **8** = **carefree**, airy, animated, blithe, cheerful, cheery, frivolous, gay, lively, merry, sunny **9** = **dizzy**, giddy, light-headed, reeling, unsteady ♦ *verb* **10** = **settle**, alight, land, perch **11 light on** *or* **upon** = **come across**, chance upon, discover, encounter, find, happen upon, hit upon, stumble on
➤ **Antonyms**
adjective ≠**insubstantial**: heavy ≠**weak**: forceful, strong ≠**insignificant**: deep, profound, serious, weighty ≠**undemanding**: burdensome, strenuous ≠**light-hearted**: serious, sombre ≠**nimble**: clumsy ≠**digestible**: rich, substantial

lighten[1] *verb* = **brighten**, become light, flash, gleam, illuminate, irradiate, light up, make bright, shine

lighten[2] *verb* **1** = **make lighter**, ease, reduce

in weight, unload **2** = **ease**, allay, alleviate, ameliorate, assuage, facilitate, lessen, mitigate, reduce, relieve **3** = **cheer**, brighten, buoy up, encourage, gladden, hearten, inspire, lift, perk up, revive
➤ **Antonyms**
≠**make lighter:** burden, encumber, handicap ≠**ease:** aggravate, heighten, increase, intensify, make worse, worsen ≠**cheer:** depress, oppress, sadden, weigh down

light-fingered *adjective* = **thieving**, dishonest, pilfering, pinching (*informal*), stealing

light-footed *adjective* = **nimble**, agile, graceful, lithe, sprightly, spry, swift

light-headed *adjective* = **faint**, delirious, dizzy, giddy, hazy, vertiginous, woozy (*informal*)

light-hearted *adjective* = **carefree**, blithe, bright, cheerful, chirpy (*informal*), effervescent, frolicsome, gay, genial, glad, happy-go-lucky, insouciant, jocund, jolly, jovial, joyful, joyous, merry, playful, sunny, untroubled, upbeat (*informal*)
➤ **Antonyms**
cheerless, dejected, depressed, despondent, gloomy, heavy-hearted, low, melancholy, morose, sad

lightly *adverb* **1** = **moderately**, sparingly, sparsely, thinly **2** = **gently**, airily, delicately, faintly, gingerly, slightly, softly, timidly **3** = **easily**, effortlessly, readily, simply **4** = **carelessly**, breezily, flippantly, frivolously, heedlessly, indifferently, slightingly, thoughtlessly
➤ **Antonyms**
≠**moderately:** abundantly, heavily, thickly ≠**gently:** firmly, forcefully, heavily ≠**easily:** arduously, awkwardly, slowly, with difficulty ≠**carelessly:** carefully, earnestly, ponderously, seriously

lightweight *adjective* = **unimportant**, inconsequential, insignificant, nickel-and-dime (*U.S. slang*), of no account, paltry, petty, slight, trifling, trivial, worthless
➤ **Antonyms**
important, momentous, serious, significant, substantial, weighty

likable, likeable *adjective* = **attractive**, agreeable, amiable, appealing, charming, engaging, friendly, genial, nice, pleasant, pleasing, sympathetic, winning, winsome

like[1] *adjective* **1** = **similar**, akin, alike, allied, analogous, approximating, cognate, corresponding, equivalent, identical, parallel, relating, resembling, same ♦ *noun* **2** = **equal**, counterpart, fellow, match, parallel, twin

➤ **Antonyms**
adjective ≠**similar:** contrasted, different, dissimilar, divergent, diverse, opposite, unlike ♦ *noun* ≠**equal:** opposite

like[2] *verb* **1** – **enjoy**, adore (*Informal*), be fond of, be keen on, be partial to, delight in, dig (*slang*), go for, love, relish, revel in **2** = **admire**, appreciate, approve, cherish, esteem, hold dear, prize, take a shine to (*informal*), take to **3** = **wish**, care to, choose, choose to, desire, fancy, feel inclined, prefer, select, want ♦ *noun* **4** *usually plural* = **preference**, cup of tea (*informal*), favourite, liking, partiality, predilection
➤ **Antonyms**
verb ≠**enjoy**, **admire:** abominate, despise, detest, dislike, hate, loathe

likelihood *noun* = **probability**, chance, good chance, liability, likeliness, possibility, prospect, strong possibility

likely *adjective* **1** = **inclined**, apt, disposed, liable, prone, tending **2** = **probable**, anticipated, expected, odds-on, on the cards, to be expected **3** = **plausible**, believable, credible, feasible, possible, reasonable **4** = **appropriate**, acceptable, agreeable, befitting, fit, pleasing, proper, qualified, suitable **5** = **promising**, fair, favourite, hopeful, up-and-coming ♦ *adverb* **6** = **probably**, doubtlessly, in all probability, like as not (*informal*), like enough (*informal*), no doubt, presumably

like-minded *adjective* = **agreeing**, compatible, *en rapport*, harmonious, in accord, in harmony, of one mind, of the same mind, unanimous

liken *verb* = **compare**, equate, juxtapose, match, mention in the same breath, parallel, relate, set beside

likeness *noun* **1** = **resemblance**, affinity, correspondence, similarity, similitude **2** = **portrait**, copy, counterpart, depiction, effigy, facsimile, image, model, photograph, picture, replica, representation, reproduction, study **3** = **appearance**, form, guise, semblance

likewise *adverb* **1** = **also**, besides, further, furthermore, in addition, moreover, too **2** = **similarly**, in like manner, in the same way

liking *noun* = **fondness**, affection, affinity, appreciation, attraction, bent, bias, desire, inclination, love, partiality, penchant, predilection, preference, proneness, propensity, soft spot, stomach, taste, tendency, thirst, weakness
➤ **Antonyms**
abhorrence, aversion, dislike, hatred, loathing, repugnance

Lilliputian *noun* **1** = **midget**, dwarf, homunculus, hop-o'-my-thumb, manikin, pygmy or pigmy ♦ adjective 2 = **tiny**, baby, diminutive, dwarf, little, mini, miniature, minuscule, petite, pocket-sized, pygmy or pigmy, small, wee

lilt noun = **rhythm**, beat, cadence, sway, swing

lily-livered adjective Old-fashioned = **cowardly**, abject, chicken (slang), chicken-hearted, craven, faint-hearted, fearful, gutless (informal), pusillanimous, scared, spineless, timid, timorous, yellow (informal), yellow-bellied (slang)

limb noun 1 = **part**, appendage, arm, extension, extremity, leg, member, wing 2 = **branch**, bough, offshoot, projection, spur

limber adjective 1 = **pliant**, elastic, flexible, plastic, pliable, supple 2 = **agile**, graceful, lissom(e), lithe, loose-jointed, loose-limbed, supple ♦ verb 3 **limber up** = **loosen up**, exercise, get ready, prepare, warm up

limelight noun = **publicity**, attention, celebrity, fame, glare of publicity, prominence, public eye, public notice, recognition, stardom, the spotlight

limit noun 1 = **end**, bound, breaking point, cutoff point, deadline, end point, furthest bound, greatest extent, termination, the bitter end, ultimate, utmost 2 = **boundary**, border, confines, edge, end, extent, frontier, pale, perimeter, periphery, precinct 3 = **maximum**, ceiling, check, curb, limitation, obstruction, restraint, restriction 4 **the limit** Informal = **the last straw**, enough, it (informal), the end ♦ verb 5 = **restrict**, bound, check, circumscribe, confine, curb, delimit, demarcate, fix, hem in, hinder, ration, restrain, specify, straiten

limitation noun = **restriction**, block, check, condition, constraint, control, curb, disadvantage, drawback, impediment, obstruction, qualification, reservation, restraint, snag

limited adjective 1 = **restricted**, bounded, checked, circumscribed, confined, constrained, controlled, curbed, defined, finite, fixed, hampered, hemmed in 2 = **narrow**, cramped, diminished, inadequate, insufficient, minimal, reduced, restricted, scant, short, unsatisfactory
➤ **Antonyms**
≠**restricted**: boundless, limitless, unlimited, unrestricted

limitless adjective = **infinite**, boundless, countless, endless, illimitable, immeasurable, immense, inexhaustible, measureless, never-ending, numberless, unbounded, uncalculable, undefined, unending, unlimited, untold, vast

limp[1] verb 1 = **hobble**, falter, halt (archaic), hirple (Scot.), hop, shamble, shuffle ♦ noun

2 = **lameness**, hirple (Scot.), hobble

limp[2] adjective 1 = **floppy**, drooping, flabby, flaccid, flexible, lax, limber, loose, pliable, relaxed, slack, soft 2 = **weak**, debilitated, enervated, exhausted, lethargic, spent, tired, worn out
➤ **Antonyms**
≠**floppy**: firm, hard, rigid, solid, stiff, taut, tense, unyielding ≠**weak**: hardy, powerful, robust, strong, sturdy, tough

limpid adjective 1 = **clear**, bright, crystal-clear, crystalline, pure, translucent, transparent 2 = **understandable**, clear, comprehensible, intelligible, lucid, perspicuous, unambiguous

line[1] noun 1 = **stroke**, band, bar, channel, dash, groove, mark, rule, score, scratch, streak, stripe, underline 2 = **wrinkle**, crease, crow's foot, furrow, mark 3 = **boundary**, border, borderline, demarcation, edge, frontier, limit, mark 4 = **outline**, configuration, contour, features, figure, profile, silhouette 5 = **string**, cable, cord, filament, rope, strand, thread, wire, wisp 6 = **trajectory**, axis, course, direction, path, route, track 7 = **approach**, avenue, belief, course, course of action, ideology, method, policy, position, practice, procedure, scheme, system 8 = **occupation**, activity, area, bag (slang), business, calling, department, employment, field, forte, interest, job, profession, province, pursuit, specialization, trade, vocation 9 = **row**, column, crocodile (Brit.), file, procession, queue, rank, sequence, series 10 Military = **formation**, disposition, firing line, front, front line, position, trenches 11 **draw the line** = **object**, lay down the law, prohibit, put one's foot down, restrict, set a limit 12 **in line: a** = **in alignment**, in a row, plumb, straight, true **b** = **in accord**, in agreement, in conformity, in harmony, in step 13 **in line for** = **due for**, a candidate for, being considered for, in the running for, next in succession to, on the short list for ♦ verb 14 = **mark**, crease, cut, draw, furrow, rule, score, trace, underline 15 = **border**, bound, edge, fringe, rim, skirt, verge

line[2] verb = **fill**, ceil, cover, face, interline

lineage noun = **descent**, ancestry, birth, descendants, extraction, family, forebears, forefathers, genealogy, house, line, offspring, pedigree, progeny

lineaments plural noun = **features**, configuration, countenance, face, line, outline, physiognomy, visage

lined adjective 1 = **ruled**, feint 2 = **wrinkled**, furrowed, wizened, worn

lines plural noun = **words**, part, script

line-up noun = **arrangement**, array, row,

selection, team

line up *verb* **1** = **queue up**, fall in, form ranks **2** = **produce**, assemble, come up with, lay on, obtain, organize, prepare, procure, secure

linger *verb* **1** = **stay**, hang around, hang in the air, loiter, remain, stop, tarry, wait **2** = **continue**, abide, endure, persist, remain, stay **3** = **hang on**, cling to life, die slowly, last, survive **4** = **delay**, dally, dawdle, drag one's feet *or* heels, idle, lag, procrastinate, take one's time

lingering *adjective* = **slow**, dragging, long-drawn-out, protracted, remaining

lingo *noun Informal* = **language**, argot, cant, dialect, idiom, jargon, patois, patter, speech, talk, tongue

liniment *noun* = **ointment**, balm, balsam, cream, embrocation, emollient, lotion, salve, unguent

link *noun* **1** = **component**, constituent, division, element, member, part, piece **2** = **connection**, affiliation, affinity, association, attachment, bond, joint, knot, liaison, relationship, tie, tie-up ♦ *verb* **3** = **connect**, attach, bind, couple, fasten, join, tie, unite, yoke **4** = **associate**, bracket, connect, identify, relate
➤ **Antonyms**
verb ≠ **connect**: detach, disconnect, divide, separate, sever, split, sunder

lion *noun* **1** = **hero**, brave person, champion, conqueror, fighter, warrior **2** = **celebrity**, big name, celeb (*informal*), idol, luminary, megastar (*informal*), notable, prodigy, star, superstar, V.I.P., wonder

lion-hearted *adjective* = **brave**, bold, courageous, daring, dauntless, heroic, intrepid, resolute, stalwart, valiant, valorous
➤ **Antonyms**
abject, chicken-hearted, chickenshit (*U.S. slang*), cowardly, craven, faint-hearted, gutless (*informal*), lily-livered, pusillanimous, spineless, timorous, wimpish *or* wimpy (*informal*), wussy (*slang*), yellow (*informal*)

lionize *verb* = **idolize**, acclaim, celebrate, crack up (*informal*), eulogize, exalt, fête, glorify, hero-worship, honour, make much of, sing *or* sound the praises of

lip *noun* **1** = **edge**, brim, brink, flange, margin, rim **2** *Slang* = **impudence**, backchat (*informal*), cheek (*informal*), effrontery, impertinence, insolence, rudeness, sauce (*informal*) **3** **smack** *or* **lick one's lips** = **relish**, anticipate, delight in, drool over, enjoy, gloat over, savour, slaver over

liquefaction *noun* = **melting**, dissolving, thawing

liquefy *verb* = **melt**, dissolve, run, thaw

liquid *noun* **1** = **fluid**, juice, liquor, solution ♦ *adjective* **2** = **fluid**, aqueous, flowing, liquefied, melted, molten, running, runny, thawed, wet **3** = **clear**, bright, brilliant, limpid, shining, translucent, transparent **4** = **smooth**, dulcet, flowing, fluent, mellifluent, mellifluous, melting, soft, sweet **5** *Of assets* = **convertible**, negotiable

liquidate *verb* **1** = **pay**, clear, discharge, honour, pay off, settle, square **2** = **dissolve**, abolish, annul, cancel, terminate **3** = **convert to cash**, cash, realize, sell off, sell up **4** = **kill**, annihilate, blow away (*slang, chiefly U.S.*), bump off (*slang*), destroy, dispatch, do away with, do in (*slang*), eliminate, exterminate, finish off, get rid of, murder, wipe out (*informal*)

liquor *noun* **1** = **alcohol**, booze (*informal*), drink, Dutch courage (*informal*), grog, hard stuff (*informal*), hooch *or* hootch (*informal, chiefly U.S. & Canad.*), intoxicant, spirits, strong drink **2** = **juice**, broth, extract, gravy, infusion, liquid, stock

lissom(e) *adjective* = **supple**, agile, flexible, graceful, light, limber, lithe, loose-jointed, loose-limbed, nimble, pliable, pliant, willowy

list¹ *noun* **1** = **inventory**, catalogue, directory, file, index, invoice, leet (*Scot.*), listing, record, register, roll, schedule, series, syllabus, tally ♦ *verb* **2** = **itemize**, catalogue, enrol, enter, enumerate, file, index, note, record, register, schedule, set down, tabulate, write down

list² *verb* **1** = **lean**, cant, careen, heel, heel over, incline, tilt, tip ♦ *noun* **2** = **tilt**, cant, leaning, slant

listen *verb* **1** = **hear**, attend, be all ears, be attentive, give ear, hang on (someone's) words, hark, hearken (*archaic*), keep one's ears open, lend an ear, prick up one's ears **2** = **pay attention**, concentrate, do as one is told, give heed to, heed, mind, obey, observe, take notice

listless *adjective* = **languid**, apathetic, enervated, impassive, inattentive, indifferent, indolent, inert, languishing, lethargic, lifeless, limp, sluggish, spiritless
➤ **Antonyms**
active, alert, alive and kicking, attentive, energetic, full of beans (*informal*), lively, sparky, spirited, wide-awake

litany *noun* **1** = **prayer**, invocation, petition, supplication **2** = **recital**, account, catalogue, enumeration, list, recitation

literacy *noun* = **education**, articulacy, articulateness, knowledge, learning, scholarship

literal *adjective* **1** = **exact**, accurate, close, faithful, strict, verbatim, word for word **2** = **unimaginative**, boring, colourless, down-to-earth, dull, factual, matter-of-fact, prosaic, prosy, uninspired **3 = actual**, bona fide, genuine, gospel, plain, real, simple, true, unexaggerated, unvarnished

literally *adverb* **= exactly**, actually, faithfully, plainly, precisely, really, simply, strictly, to the letter, truly, verbatim, word for word

literary *adjective* **= well-read**, bookish, erudite, formal, learned, lettered, literate, scholarly

literate *adjective* **= educated**, cultivated, cultured, erudite, informed, knowledgeable, learned, lettered, scholarly, well-informed, well-read

literature *noun* **1 = writings**, letters, lore, written works **2 = information**, brochure, leaflet, mailshot, pamphlet

lithe *adjective* **= supple**, flexible, limber, lissom(e), loose-jointed, loose-limbed, pliable, pliant

litigant *noun* **= claimant**, contestant, disputant, litigator, party, plaintiff

litigate *verb* **= sue**, contest at law, file a suit, go to court, go to law, institute legal proceedings, press charges, prosecute

litigation *noun* **= lawsuit**, action, case, contending, disputing, process, prosecution

litigious *adjective* **= contentious**, argumentative, belligerent, disputatious, quarrelsome

litter *noun* **1 = rubbish**, debris, detritus, fragments, garbage (*chiefly U.S.*), muck, refuse, shreds, trash **2 = jumble**, clutter, confusion, disarray, disorder, mess, scatter, untidiness **3 = brood**, family, offspring, progeny, young **4 = bedding**, couch, floor cover, mulch, straw-bed **5 = stretcher**, palanquin ◆ *verb* **6 = clutter**, derange, disarrange, disorder, mess up **7 = scatter**, strew

little *adjective* **1 = small**, diminutive, dwarf, elfin, infinitesimal, Lilliputian, mini, miniature, minute, petite, pygmy *or* pigmy, short, slender, tiny, wee **2 = young**, babyish, immature, infant, junior, undeveloped **3 = mean**, base, cheap, illiberal, narrow-minded, petty, small-minded **4 = unimportant**, inconsiderable, insignificant, minor, negligible, paltry, trifling, trivial **5 = not much**, hardly any, insufficient, meagre, measly, scant, skimpy, small, sparse **6 = short**, brief, fleeting, hasty, passing, short-lived ◆ *adverb* **7 = hardly**, barely, not much, not quite, only just **8 = rarely**, hardly ever, not often, scarcely, seldom **9 little by little = gradually**, bit by bit, by degrees, imperceptibly, piecemeal, progressively, slowly, step by step ◆ *noun* **10 = bit**, dab, dash, fragment, hint, modicum, particle, pinch, small amount, snippet, speck, spot,

tad (*informal, chiefly U.S.*), taste, touch, trace, trifle

➤ **Antonyms**
adjective ≠**small**: big, colossal, considerable, enormous, giant, ginormous (*informal*), great, huge, immense, large, mega (*slang*) ≠**unimportant**: grave, important, major, momentous, serious, significant ≠**not much**: abundant, ample, much, plentiful ≠**short**: long ◆ *adverb* ≠**hardly**: certainly, much, surely ≠**rarely**: always, much ◆ *noun* ≠**bit**: lot, many, much

liturgy *noun* **= ceremony**, celebration, form of worship, formula, rite, ritual, sacrament, service, services, worship

livable *adjective* **1 = tolerable**, acceptable, bearable, endurable, passable, sufferable **2** *with* **with = congenial**, companionable, compatible, easy, easy to live with, harmonious, sociable

live[1] *verb* **1 = exist**, be, be alive, breathe, draw breath, have life **2 = persist**, be permanent, be remembered, last, prevail, remain alive **3 = dwell**, abide, hang out (*informal*), inhabit, lodge, occupy, reside, settle, stay (*chiefly Scot.*) **4 = survive**, abide, continue, earn a living, endure, fare, feed, get along, lead, make ends meet, pass, remain, subsist, support oneself **5 = thrive**, be happy, enjoy life, flourish, luxuriate, make the most of life, prosper

live[2] *adjective* **1 = living**, alive, animate, breathing, existent, quick (*archaic*), vital **2 = topical**, active, burning, controversial, current, hot, pertinent, pressing, prevalent, vital **3 = burning**, active, alight, blazing, connected, glowing, hot, ignited, smouldering, switched on

livelihood *noun* **= occupation**, bread and butter (*informal*), employment, job, living, maintenance, means, (means of) support, (source of) income, subsistence, sustenance, work

liveliness *noun* **= energy**, activity, animation, boisterousness, brio, briskness, dynamism, gaiety, spirit, sprightliness, vitality, vivacity

livelong *adjective Chiefly poetic* **= everlasting**, complete, entire, full, long-drawn-out, whole

lively *adjective* **1 = vigorous**, active, agile, alert, alive and kicking, bright-eyed and bushy-tailed, brisk, chirpy (*informal*), energetic, full of beans (*informal*), full of pep (*informal*), keen, nimble, perky, quick, sprightly, spry **2 = animated**, blithe, cheerful, chirpy (*informal*), frisky, gay, merry, sparkling, sparky, spirited, upbeat (*informal*), vivacious **3 = busy**, astir, bustling, buzzing, crowded, eventful,

moving, stirring **4 = vivid**, bright, colourful, exciting, forceful, invigorating, racy, refreshing, stimulating
➤ **Antonyms**
≠**vigorous**: debilitated, disabled, inactive, slow, sluggish, torpid ≠**animated**: apathetic, dull, lifeless, listless ≠**busy**: dull, slow ≠**vivid**: dull

liven up verb **= stir**, animate, brighten, buck up (informal), enliven, pep up, perk up, put life into, rouse, vitalize

liverish adjective **1** Informal **= sick**, bilious, queasy **2 = irritable**, crotchety (informal), crusty, disagreeable, grumpy, ill-humoured, irascible, like a bear with a sore head, peevish, ratty (Brit. & N.Z. informal), snappy, splenetic, tetchy

livery noun **= costume**, attire, clothing, dress, garb, raiment (archaic or poetic), regalia, suit, uniform, vestments

live wire noun Informal **= dynamo**, ball of fire (informal), go-getter (informal), hustler (U.S. & Canad. slang)

livid adjective **1** Informal **= angry**, beside oneself, cross, enraged, exasperated, fuming, furious, hot under the collar (informal), incandescent, incensed, indignant, infuriated, mad (informal), outraged, pissed (taboo slang), pissed off (taboo slang) **2 = discoloured**, angry, black-and-blue, bruised, contused, purple
➤ **Antonyms**
≠**angry**: assuaged, blissful, content, delighted, enchanted, forgiving, happy, mollified, overjoyed, pleased

living adjective **1 = alive**, active, alive and kicking, animated, breathing, existing, lively, quick (archaic), strong, vigorous, vital **2 = current**, active, contemporary, continuing, developing, extant, in use, ongoing, operative, persisting ♦ noun **3 = existence**, animation, being, existing, life, subsistence **4 = lifestyle**, mode of living, way of life **5 = livelihood**, bread and butter (informal), job, maintenance, (means of) support, occupation, (source of) income, subsistence, sustenance, work **6** Church of England **= benefice**, incumbency, stipend
➤ **Antonyms**
adjective ≠**alive**: dead, deceased, defunct, departed, expired, late, lifeless, perished ≠**current**: obsolescent, obsolete, out-of-date, vanishing

load noun **1 = cargo**, bale, consignment, freight, lading, shipment **2 = burden**, affliction, albatross, encumbrance, millstone, onus, oppression, pressure, trouble, weight, worry ♦ verb **3 = fill**, cram, freight, heap, pack, pile, stack, stuff **4 = burden**, encumber, hamper, oppress, saddle with, trouble, weigh down, worry **5** Of firearms **= make ready**, charge, prepare to fire, prime

loaded adjective **1 = laden**, burdened, charged, freighted, full, weighted **2 = charged**, at the ready, primed, ready to shoot or fire **3 = tricky**, artful, insidious, manipulative, prejudicial **4 = biased**, distorted, weighted **5** Slang **= rich**, affluent, flush (informal), moneyed, rolling (slang), wealthy, well-heeled (informal), well off, well-to-do

loaf[1] noun **1 = lump**, block, cake, cube, slab **2** Slang **= head**, block (informal), chump (Brit. slang), gumption (Brit. informal), noddle (informal, chiefly Brit.), nous (Brit. slang), sense

loaf[2] verb **= idle**, laze, lie around, loiter, lounge around, take it easy

loafer noun **= idler**, bum (informal), couch potato (slang), drone (Brit.), layabout, lazybones (informal), lounger, ne'er-do-well, shirker, skiver (Brit. slang), time-waster

loan noun **1 = advance**, accommodation, allowance, credit, mortgage ♦ verb **2 = lend**, accommodate, advance, allow, credit, let out

loath, loth adjective **= unwilling**, against, averse, backward, disinclined, indisposed, opposed, reluctant, resisting
➤ **Antonyms**
anxious, avid, desirous, eager, enthusiastic, keen, willing

loathe verb **= hate**, abhor, abominate, despise, detest, dislike

loathing noun **= hatred**, abhorrence, abomination, antipathy, aversion, detestation, disgust, horror, odium, repugnance, repulsion, revulsion

loathsome adjective **= hateful**, abhorrent, abominable, detestable, disgusting, horrible, nasty, nauseating, obnoxious, odious, offensive, repugnant, repulsive, revolting, vile, yucky or yukky (slang)
➤ **Antonyms**
adorable, amiable, attractive, charming, delightful, enchanting, engaging, fetching, likable or likeable, lovable, lovely

lob verb Informal **= throw**, fling, launch, lift, loft, pitch, shy (informal), toss

lobby noun **1 = corridor**, entrance hall, foyer, hall, hallway, passage, passageway, porch, vestibule **2 = pressure group** ♦ verb **3 = campaign**, influence, persuade, press, pressure, promote, pull strings (Brit. informal), push, urge

local adjective **1 = regional**, community, district, neighbourhood, parish, provincial **2 = restricted**, confined, limited, narrow, parochial, provincial, small-town (chiefly U.S.) ♦ noun **3 = resident**, character (informal), inhabitant, local yokel (*disparaging*), native

locale *noun* = site, locality, location, locus, place, position, scene, setting, spot, venue

locality *noun* 1 = **neighbourhood**, area, district, neck of the woods (*informal*), region, vicinity 2 = site, locale, location, place, position, scene, setting, spot

localize *verb* = **restrict**, circumscribe, concentrate, confine, contain, delimit, delimitate, limit, restrain

locate *verb* 1 = **find**, come across, detect, discover, lay one's hands on, pin down, pinpoint, track down, unearth 2 = **place**, establish, fix, put, seat, set, settle, situate

location *noun* = site, bearings, locale, locus, place, point, position, situation, spot, venue, whereabouts

lock[1] *noun* 1 = **fastening**, bolt, clasp, padlock ♦ *verb* 2 = **fasten**, bolt, close, latch, seal, secure, shut 3 = **unite**, clench, engage, entangle, entwine, join, link, mesh 4 = **embrace**, clasp, clutch, encircle, enclose, grapple, grasp, hug, press

lock[2] *noun* = **strand**, curl, ringlet, tress, tuft

lock out *verb* = **shut out**, ban, bar, debar, exclude, keep out, refuse admittance to

lockup *noun* = **prison**, can (*slang*), cell, cooler (*slang*), jail *or* gaol, jug (*slang*), police cell

lock up *verb* = **imprison**, cage, confine, detain, incarcerate, jail, put behind bars, shut up

locomotion *noun* = **movement**, motion, moving, progress, progression, travel, travelling

locution *noun* 1 = **manner of speech**, accent, articulation, diction, inflection, intonation, phrasing, style 2 = **expression**, collocation, idiom, phrase, term, turn of speech, wording

lodestar *noun* = **guide**, beacon, model, pattern, standard

lodestone *noun* = **focus**, focal point, magnet

lodge *noun* 1 = **cabin**, chalet, cottage, gatehouse, house, hunting lodge, hut, shelter 2 = **society**, association, branch, chapter, club, group 3 = **den**, haunt, lair ♦ *verb* 4 = **stay**, board, room, sojourn, stop 5 = **accommodate**, billet, entertain, harbour, put up, quarter, shelter 6 = **stick**, become fixed, catch, come to rest, imbed, implant 7 = **register**, deposit, file, lay, place, put, put on record, set, submit

lodger *noun* = **tenant**, boarder, guest, paying guest, P.G., resident

lodging *noun, often plural* = **accommodation**, abode, apartments, boarding, digs (*Brit. informal*), dwelling, habitation, quarters, residence, rooms, shelter

lofty *adjective* 1 = **high**, elevated, raised, sky-high, soaring, tall, towering 2 = **noble**, dignified, distinguished, elevated, exalted, grand, illustrious, imposing, majestic, renowned, stately, sublime, superior 3 = **haughty**, arrogant, condescending, disdainful, high and mighty (*informal*), lordly, patronizing, proud, snooty (*informal*), supercilious, toffee-nosed (*slang, chiefly Brit.*)
➤ **Antonyms**
≠**high**: dwarfed, low, short, stunted ≠**noble**: debased, degraded, humble, low, lowly, mean ≠**haughty**: friendly, modest, unassuming, warm

log *noun* 1 = **stump**, block, bole, chunk, piece of timber, trunk 2 = **record**, account, chart, daybook, journal, logbook, tally ♦ *verb* 3 = **chop**, cut, fell, hew 4 = **record**, book, chart, make a note of, note, register, report, set down

loggerheads *plural noun* **at loggerheads** = **quarrelling**, at daggers drawn, at each other's throats, at odds, feuding, in dispute, opposed

logic *noun* 1 = **science of reasoning**, argumentation, deduction, dialectics 2 = **reason**, good reason, good sense, sense, sound judgment 3 = **connection**, chain of thought, coherence, link, rationale, relationship

logical *adjective* 1 = **rational**, clear, cogent, coherent, consistent, deducible, reasonable, sound, valid, well-organized 2 = **reasonable**, judicious, most likely, necessary, obvious, plausible, sensible, wise
➤ **Antonyms**
≠**rational**: illogical, instinctive, irrational, unorganized, unreasonable ≠**reasonable**: illogical, implausible, unlikely, unreasonable

logistics *noun* = **organization**, coordination, engineering, management, masterminding, orchestration, plans, strategy

loiter *verb* = **linger**, dally, dawdle, delay, dilly-dally (*informal*), hang about *or* around, idle, lag, loaf, loll, skulk

loll *verb* 1 = **lounge**, flop, loaf, recline, relax, slouch, slump, sprawl 2 = **droop**, dangle, drop, flap, flop, hang, hang loosely, sag

lone *adjective* 1 = **solitary**, by oneself, one, only, separate, separated, single, sole, unaccompanied 2 = **isolated**, deserted, lonesome

loneliness *noun* = **solitude**, aloneness, desertedness, desolation, forlornness, isolation, lonesomeness, seclusion, solitariness

lonely *adjective* 1 = **abandoned**, destitute, estranged, forlorn, forsaken, friendless,

lonesome, outcast **2 = solitary**, alone, apart, by oneself, companionless, isolated, lone, single, withdrawn **3 = desolate**, deserted, godforsaken, isolated, off the beaten track (*informal*), out-of-the-way, remote, secluded, solitary, unfrequented, uninhabited
➤ Antonyms
≠**abandoned**: befriended, popular
≠**solitary**: accompanied, together
≠**desolate**: bustling, crowded, frequented, populous, teeming

loner *noun Informal* = **individualist**, lone wolf, maverick, outsider, recluse

lonesome *adjective Chiefly U.S. & Canad.* = **lonely**, companionless, desolate, dreary, forlorn, friendless, gloomy

long[1] *adjective* **1 = elongated**, expanded, extended, extensive, far-reaching, lengthy, spread out, stretched **2 = prolonged**, dragging, interminable, late, lengthy, lingering, long-drawn-out, protracted, slow, sustained, tardy **3 by a long shot: a = by far**, easily, far and away, indubitably, undoubtedly, without doubt **b = by any means**, in any circumstances, on any account
➤ Antonyms
≠**elongated**: compressed, contracted, little, short, small ≠**prolonged**: abbreviated, abridged, brief, momentary, quick, short, short-lived

long[2] *verb* = **desire**, ache, covet, crave, dream of, eat one's heart out over, hanker, hunger, itch, lust, pine, set one's heart on, want, wish, yearn

longing *noun* **1 = desire**, ache, ambition, aspiration, coveting, craving, hankering, hope, hungering, itch, thirst, urge, wish, yearning, yen (*informal*) ♦ *adjective* **2 = yearning**, ardent, avid, craving, desirous, eager, hungry, languishing, pining, wishful, wistful
➤ Antonyms
noun ≠**desire**: abhorrence, antipathy, apathy, disgust, disregard, indifference, loathing, revulsion, unconcern ♦ *adjective* ≠**yearning**: apathetic, cold, disgusted, hateful, indifferent, loathing, unconcerned, uninterested

long-lived *adjective* = **long-lasting**, enduring

long shot *noun* = **outsider**, dark horse

long-standing *adjective* = **established**, abiding, enduring, fixed, long-established, long-lasting, long-lived, time-honoured

long-suffering *adjective* = **uncomplaining**, easy-going, forbearing, forgiving, patient, resigned, stoical, tolerant

long-winded *adjective* = **rambling**, garrulous, lengthy, long-drawn-out,

overlong, prolix, prolonged, repetitious, tedious, tiresome, verbose, wordy
➤ Antonyms
brief, concise, crisp, curt, laconic, pithy, sententious, short, succinct, terse, to the point

look *verb* **1 = see**, behold (*archaic*), check, check out (*informal*), clock (*Brit. slang*), examine, eye, gaze, get a load of (*informal*), glance, inspect, observe, peep, regard, scan, scrutinize, study, survey, take a dekko at (*Brit. slang*), take a gander at (*informal*), view, watch **2 = stare**, gape, gawk, gawp (*Brit. slang*), goggle, ogle **3 = consider**, contemplate **4 = seem**, appear, display, exhibit, look like, seem to be, show, strike one as **5 = face**, front, front on, give onto, overlook **6 = search**, forage, hunt, seek **7 = hope**, anticipate, await, expect, reckon on **8 look like = resemble**, be the image of, favour, make one think of, put one in mind of, remind one of, take after ♦ *noun* **9 = glimpse**, examination, eyeful (*informal*), gander (*informal*), gaze, glance, inspection, observation, once-over (*informal*), peek, recce (*slang*), review, shufti (*Brit. slang*), sight, survey, view **10 = appearance**, air, aspect, bearing, cast, complexion, countenance, demeanour, effect, expression, face, fashion, guise, manner, mien (*literary*), semblance

look after *verb* = **take care of**, attend to, care for, guard, keep an eye on, mind, nurse, protect, sit with, supervise, take charge of, tend, watch

lookalike *noun* = **double**, clone, dead ringer (*slang*), living image, replica, spitting image (*informal*), twin

look down on *or* **upon** *verb* = **disdain**, contemn, despise, hold in contempt, look down one's nose at (*informal*), scorn, sneer, spurn, treat with contempt, turn one's nose up (at) (*informal*)

look forward to *verb* = **anticipate**, await, count on, count the days until, expect, hope for, long for, look for, set one's heart on, wait for

lookout *noun* **1 = watch**, guard, qui vive, readiness, vigil **2 = watchman**, guard, sentinel, sentry **3 = watchtower**, beacon, citadel, observation post, observatory, post, tower **4** *Informal* = **concern**, business, funeral (*informal*), pigeon (*Brit. informal*), worry **5** *Chiefly Brit.* = **prospect**, chances, future, likelihood, outlook, view

look out *verb* = **be careful**, be alert, be on guard, be vigilant, beware, keep an eye out, keep one's eyes open, keep one's eyes peeled, keep one's eyes skinned, pay attention, watch out

look over *verb* = **examine**, cast an eye over, check, check out (*informal*), inspect, look through, peruse, scan, take a dekko at (*Brit. slang*), view

look up *verb* **1** = **research**, find, hunt for, search for, seek out, track down **2** = **improve**, come along, get better, perk up, pick up, progress, shape up (*informal*), show improvement **3** = **visit**, call on, drop in on (*informal*), go to see, look in on, pay a visit to **4 look up to** = **respect**, admire, defer to, esteem, have a high opinion of, honour, regard highly, revere

loom *verb* = **appear**, become visible, be imminent, bulk, emerge, hover, impend, menace, take shape, threaten

loop *noun* **1** = **curve**, bend, circle, coil, convolution, curl, eyelet, hoop, kink, loophole, noose, ring, spiral, twirl, twist, whorl ◆ *verb* **2** = **twist**, bend, circle, coil, curl, curve round, encircle, fold, join, knot, roll, spiral, turn, wind round

loophole *noun* = **let-out**, avoidance, escape, evasion, excuse, means of escape, plea, pretence, pretext, subterfuge

loose *adjective* **1** = **slack**, baggy, easy, hanging, loosened, not fitting, not tight, relaxed, slackened, sloppy **2** = **free**, floating, insecure, movable, released, unattached, unbound, unconfined, unfastened, unfettered, unrestricted, unsecured, untied, wobbly **3** = **vague**, ill-defined, imprecise, inaccurate, indefinite, indistinct, inexact, rambling, random **4** *Old-fashioned* = **promiscuous**, abandoned, debauched, disreputable, dissipated, dissolute, fast, immoral, lewd, libertine, licentious, profligate, unchaste, wanton **5** = **careless**, heedless, imprudent, lax, negligent, rash, thoughtless, unmindful ◆ *verb* **6** = **free**, detach, disconnect, disengage, ease, let go, liberate, loosen, release, set free, slacken, unbind, unbridle, undo, unfasten, unleash, unloose, untie

➤ Antonyms

adjective ≠**slack**: tight ≠**free**: bound, curbed, fastened, fettered, restrained, secured, tethered, tied ≠**vague**: accurate, clear, concise, exact, precise ≠**promiscuous**: chaste, disciplined, moral, virtuous ◆ *verb* ≠**free**: bind, cage, capture, fasten, fetter, imprison, tether

loose-jointed *adjective* = **supple**, agile, elastic, flexible, limber, lissom(e), lithe, pliable, pliant

loosen *verb* **1** = **free**, deliver, let go, liberate, release, set free **2** = **untie**, detach, let out, separate, slacken, unbind, undo, unloose, work free, work loose **3 loosen up** = **relax**, ease up *or* off, go easy (*informal*), lessen, let up, lighten up (*slang*), mitigate, moderate, soften, weaken

loot *noun* **1** = **plunder**, booty, goods, haul, prize, spoils, swag (*slang*) ◆ *verb* **2** = **plunder**, despoil, pillage, raid, ransack, ravage, rifle, rob, sack

lop *verb* = **cut**, chop, crop, detach, dock, hack, prune, sever, shorten, trim

lope *verb* = **stride**, bound, lollop, spring

lopsided *adjective* = **crooked**, askew, asymmetrical, awry, cockeyed, disproportionate, off balance, one-sided, out of shape, out of true, skewwhiff (*Brit. informal*), squint, tilting, unbalanced, unequal, uneven, warped

loquacious *adjective* = **talkative**, babbling, blathering, chattering, chatty, gabby (*informal*), garrulous, voluble, wordy

loquacity *noun* = **talkativeness**, babbling, chattering, chattiness, effusiveness, garrulity, volubility

lord *noun* **1** = **master**, commander, governor, king, leader, liege, monarch, overlord, potentate, prince, ruler, sovereign, superior **2** = **nobleman**, earl, noble, peer, viscount **3 Our Lord** *or* **the Lord** = **Jesus Christ**, Christ, God, Jehovah, the Almighty, the Galilean, the Good Shepherd, the Nazarene ◆ *verb* **4 lord it over** = **order around**, be overbearing, boss around (*informal*), domineer, pull rank, put on airs, swagger

lordly *adjective* **1** = **proud**, arrogant, condescending, dictatorial, disdainful, domineering, haughty, high and mighty (*informal*), high-handed, imperious, lofty, overbearing, patronizing, stuck-up (*informal*), supercilious, tyrannical **2** = **noble**, aristocratic, gracious, grand, imperial, lofty, majestic, princely, regal, stately

lore *noun* = **traditions**, beliefs, doctrine, experience, folk-wisdom, mythos, sayings, teaching, traditional wisdom, wisdom

lose *verb* **1** = **mislay**, be deprived of, displace, drop, fail to keep, forget, misplace, miss, suffer loss **2** = **forfeit**, fail, fall short, lose out on (*informal*), miss, pass up (*informal*), yield **3** = **be defeated**, be the loser, come a cropper (*informal*), come to grief, get the worst of, lose out, suffer defeat, take a licking (*informal*) **4** = **waste**, consume, dissipate, drain, exhaust, expend, lavish, misspend, squander, use up **5** = **stray from**, wander from **6** = **outdistance**, lap, leave behind, outrun, outstrip, overtake, pass **7** = **escape**, dodge, duck, elude, evade, give someone the slip, shake off, slip away, throw off

loser *noun* = **failure**, also-ran, dud (*informal*), flop (*informal*), no-hoper

(*Austral. slang*), underdog, washout (*informal*)

loss *noun* **1** = **losing**, defeat, deprivation, disappearance, drain, failure, forfeiture, misfortune, mislaying, squandering, waste **2** = **damage**, cost, destruction, detriment, disadvantage, harm, hurt, impairment, injury, ruin **3** *sometimes plural* = **deficit**, debit, debt, deficiency, depletion, shrinkage **4 at a loss** = **confused**, at one's wits' end, baffled, bewildered, helpless, nonplussed, perplexed, puzzled, stuck (*informal*), stumped
➤ **Antonyms**
≠**losing**: acquisition, finding, gain, preservation, reimbursement, saving, winning   ≠**damage**: advantage, recovery, restoration   ≠**deficit**: gain

lost *adjective* **1** = **missing**, disappeared, forfeited, mislaid, misplaced, missed, strayed, vanished, wayward **2** = **off-course**, adrift, astray, at sea, disoriented, off-track **3** = **bewildered**, baffled, clueless (*slang*), confused, helpless, ignorant, mystified, perplexed, puzzled **4** = **wasted**, consumed, dissipated, frittered away, misapplied, misdirected, misspent, misused, squandered **5** = **engrossed**, absent, absorbed, abstracted, distracted, dreamy, entranced, preoccupied, rapt, spellbound, taken up **6** = **fallen**, abandoned, corrupt, damned, depraved, dissolute, irreclaimable, licentious, profligate, unchaste, wanton

lot *noun* **1** = **collection**, assortment, batch, bunch (*informal*), consignment, crowd, group, quantity, set **2** = **destiny**, accident, chance, doom, fate, fortune **3 a lot** *or* **lots** = **plenty**, abundance, a great deal, heap(s), large amount, load(s) (*informal*), masses (*informal*), numbers, ocean(s), piles (*informal*), quantities, scores, stack(s) **4 throw in one's lot with** = **join with**, ally *or* align oneself with, join forces with, join fortunes with, support

loth *see* LOATH

lotion *noun* = **cream**, balm, embrocation, liniment, salve, solution

lottery *noun* **1** = **raffle**, draw, sweepstake **2** = **gamble**, chance, hazard, risk, toss-up (*informal*), venture

loud *adjective* **1** = **noisy**, blaring, booming, clamorous, deafening, ear-piercing, ear-splitting, forte (*Music*), piercing, resounding, rowdy, sonorous, stentorian, strident, thundering, tumultuous, vociferous **2** = **garish**, brash, flamboyant, flashy, gaudy, glaring, lurid, ostentatious, showy, tasteless, tawdry, vulgar **3** = **loud-mouthed** (*informal*), brash, brazen, coarse, crass, crude, offensive, raucous, vulgar
➤ **Antonyms**
≠**noisy**: gentle, inaudible, low, low-pitched,

quiet, silent, soft, soundless, subdued   ≠**garish**: conservative, dull, sober, sombre   ≠**loud-mouthed**: quiet, reserved, retiring, shy, unassuming

loudly *adverb* = **noisily**, at full volume, at the top of one's voice, deafeningly, fortissimo (*Music*), lustily, shrilly, uproariously, vehemently, vigorously, vociferously

loudmouth *noun* = **bigmouth** (*slang*), blowhard (*informal*), braggart, bullshit artist (*taboo slang*), bullshitter (*taboo slang*), windbag (*slang*)

lounge *verb* **1** = **relax**, laze, lie about, loaf, loiter, loll, make oneself at home, recline, sprawl, take it easy **2** = **pass time**, dawdle, hang out (*informal*), idle, kill time, potter, veg out (*slang, chiefly U.S.*), waste time

lour *see* LOWER[2]

louring *see* LOWERING

lousy *adjective* **1** *Slang* = **mean**, base, contemptible, despicable, dirty, hateful, low, rotten (*informal*), vicious, vile **2** *Slang* = **inferior**, awful, bad, miserable, no good, poor, poxy (*slang*), rotten (*informal*), second-rate, terrible **3** = **lice-infested**, lice-infected, lice-ridden

lout *noun* = **oaf**, bear, boor, bumpkin, churl, clod, dolt, ned (*Scot. slang*), yahoo, yob *or* yobbo (*Brit. slang*)

loutish *adjective* = **oafish**, boorish, coarse, gross, ill-bred, ill-mannered, rough, uncouth, unmannerly

lovable, loveable *adjective* = **endearing**, adorable, amiable, attractive, captivating, charming, cuddly, cute, delightful, enchanting, engaging, fetching (*informal*), likable *or* likeable, lovely, pleasing, sweet, winning, winsome
➤ **Antonyms**
abhorrent, abominable, detestable, hateful, loathsome, obnoxious, odious, offensive, revolting

love *verb* **1** = **adore**, be attached to, be in love with, cherish, dote on, have affection for, hold dear, idolize, prize, think the world of, treasure, worship **2** = **enjoy**, appreciate, delight in, desire, fancy, have a weakness for, like, relish, savour, take pleasure in
♦ *noun* **3** = **passion**, adoration, adulation, affection, ardour, attachment, devotion, fondness, friendship, infatuation, liking, rapture, regard, tenderness, warmth **4** = **liking**, delight, devotion, enjoyment, fondness, inclination, partiality, relish, soft spot, taste, weakness **5** = **beloved**, angel, darling, dear, dearest, dear one, loved one, lover, sweet, sweetheart, truelove **6 for love or money** = **by any means**, ever, under any

conditions **7 fall in love (with) = lose one's heart (to)**, bestow one's affections on, be taken with, fall for, take a shine to (*informal*) **8 in love = enamoured**, besotted, charmed, enraptured, infatuated, smitten
➤ **Antonyms**
verb ≠ **adore, enjoy:** abhor, abominate, detest, dislike, hate, scorn ♦ *noun* ≠ **passion, liking:** abhorrence, abomination, animosity, antagonism, antipathy, aversion, bad blood, bitterness, detestation, disgust, dislike, hate, hatred, hostility, ill will, incompatibility, loathing, malice, repugnance, resentment, scorn ≠ **beloved:** enemy, foe

love affair *noun* **= romance**, affair, *affaire de coeur*, amour, intrigue, liaison, relationship

loveless *adjective* **= unloving**, cold, cold-hearted, frigid, hard, heartless, icy, insensitive, unfeeling, unresponsive

lovelorn *adjective* **= lovesick**, languishing, pining, slighted, spurned, unrequited, yearning

lovely *adjective* **1 = beautiful**, admirable, adorable, amiable, attractive, captivating, charming, comely, enchanting, exquisite, graceful, handsome, pretty, sweet, winning **2 = enjoyable**, agreeable, delightful, engaging, gratifying, nice, pleasant, pleasing
➤ **Antonyms**
≠ **beautiful:** hideous, ugly, unattractive ≠ **enjoyable:** abhorrent, detestable, hateful, loathsome, odious, repellent, repugnant, revolting

lovemaking *noun* **= sexual intercourse**, act of love, carnal knowledge, coitus, copulation, intercourse, intimacy, sexual relations, sexual union *or* congress

lover *noun* **= sweetheart**, admirer, beau, beloved, boyfriend *or* girlfriend, fancy man *or* fancy woman (*slang*), fiancé *or* fiancée, flame (*informal*), mistress, paramour, suitor, swain (*archaic*), toy boy

lovesick *adjective* **= lovelorn**, desiring, languishing, longing, pining, yearning

loving *adjective* **= affectionate**, amorous, ardent, dear, demonstrative, devoted, doting, fond, friendly, kind, solicitous, tender, warm, warm-hearted
➤ **Antonyms**
aloof, cold, contemptuous, cruel, detached, distasteful, hateful, hostile, indifferent, mean, scornful, unconcerned, unloving

low[1] *adjective* **1 = small**, little, short, squat, stunted **2 = low-lying**, deep, depressed, ground-level, shallow, subsided, sunken **3 = inexpensive**, cheap, economical, moderate, modest, reasonable **4 = meagre**, depleted, insignificant, little, measly, paltry, reduced, scant, small, sparse, trifling **5**

= inferior, deficient, inadequate, low-grade, mediocre, pathetic, poor, puny, second-rate, shoddy, substandard, worthless **6 = coarse**, common, crude, disgraceful, dishonourable, disreputable, gross, ill-bred, obscene, rough, rude, unbecoming, undignified, unrefined, vulgar **7 = contemptible**, abject, base, cowardly, dastardly, degraded, depraved, despicable, ignoble, mean, menial, nasty, scurvy, servile, sordid, unworthy, vile, vulgar **8 = lowly**, humble, lowborn, meek, plain, plebeian, poor, simple, unpretentious **9 = dejected**, blue, depressed, despondent, disheartened, dismal, down, downcast, down in the dumps (*informal*), fed up, forlorn, gloomy, glum, miserable, morose, sad, unhappy **10 = ill**, debilitated, dying, exhausted, feeble, frail, prostrate, reduced, sinking, stricken, weak **11 = quiet**, gentle, hushed, muffled, muted, soft, subdued, whispered ♦ *adverb* **12 lie low = hide**, conceal oneself, go underground, hide away, hide out, hole up, keep a low profile, keep out of sight, lurk, skulk, take cover
➤ **Antonyms**
adjective ≠ **small:** tall, towering ≠ **low-lying:** elevated ≠ **meagre:** important, significant ≠ **contemptible:** brave, eminent, exalted, fine, grand, high-ranking, honourable, laudable, lofty, praiseworthy, superior, worthy ≠ **dejected:** cheerful, elated, happy, high ≠ **ill:** alert, energetic, enthusiastic, strong ≠ **quiet:** loud, noisy

low[2] *noun* **1 = mooing**, bellow, bellowing, lowing, moo ♦ *verb* **2 = moo**, bellow

lowdown *noun Informal* **= information**, dope (*informal*), gen (*Brit. informal*), info (*informal*), inside story, intelligence

low-down *adjective* **= mean**, base, cheap (*informal*), contemptible, despicable, low, nasty, reprehensible, scurvy, ugly, underhand

lower[1] *adjective* **1 = under**, inferior, junior, lesser, low-level, minor, secondary, second-class, smaller, subordinate **2 = reduced**, curtailed, decreased, diminished, lessened, pared down ♦ *verb* **3 = drop**, depress, fall, let down, make lower, sink, submerge, take down **4 = demean**, abase, belittle, condescend, debase, degrade, deign, devalue, disgrace, downgrade, humble, humiliate, stoop **5 = lessen**, abate, curtail, cut, decrease, diminish, minimize, moderate, prune, reduce, slash **6 = quieten**, soften, tone down
➤ **Antonyms**
adjective ≠ **reduced:** enlarged, higher, increased ♦ *verb* ≠ **drop:** elevate, hoist, lift, raise ≠ **lessen:** amplify, augment, boost, enlarge, extend, increase, inflate, magnify, raise

lower[2], **lour** *verb* **= darken**, blacken, cloud

up *or* over, loom, menace, threaten

lowering, louring *adjective* = **darkening**, black, clouded, cloudy, dark, forbidding, gloomy, grey, heavy, menacing, ominous, overcast, threatening

low-key *adjective* = **subdued**, keeping a low profile, low-pitched, muffled, muted, played down, quiet, restrained, toned down, understated

lowly *adjective* 1 = **lowborn**, ignoble, inferior, mean, plebeian, proletarian, subordinate 2 = **humble**, meek, mild, modest, unassuming 3 = **unpretentious**, average, common, homespun, modest, ordinary, plain, poor, simple

low-minded *adjective* = **vulgar**, coarse, crude, dirty, disgusting, filthy, foul, gross, indecent, obscene, rude, smutty, uncouth

low-spirited *adjective* = **depressed**, apathetic, blue, dejected, despondent, dismal, down, down-hearted, down in the dumps (*informal*), down in the mouth, fed up, gloomy, heavy-hearted, low, miserable, moody, sad, unhappy

low-tech *adjective* = **unsophisticated**, basic, simple
➤ **Antonyms**
high-tech *or* hi-tech, scientific, technical, technological

loyal *adjective* = **faithful**, constant, dependable, devoted, dutiful, immovable, patriotic, staunch, steadfast, tried and true, true, true-blue, true-hearted, trustworthy, trusty, unswerving, unwavering
➤ **Antonyms**
disloyal, false, perfidious, traitorous, treacherous, unfaithful, untrustworthy

loyalty *noun* = **faithfulness**, allegiance, constancy, dependability, devotion, fealty, fidelity, patriotism, reliability, staunchness, steadfastness, true-heartedness, trueness, trustiness, trustworthiness

lozenge *noun* = **tablet**, cough drop, jujube, pastille

lubberly *adjective* = **oafish**, awkward, clodhopping (*informal*), clownish, clumsy, loutish, lumbering, lumpen (*informal*), lumpish, uncouth, ungainly

lubricate *verb* = **oil**, grease, make slippery, make smooth, smear

lucid *adjective* 1 = **clear**, clear-cut, comprehensible, crystal clear, distinct, evident, explicit, intelligible, obvious, plain, transparent 2 = **translucent**, clear, crystalline, diaphanous, glassy, limpid, pellucid, pure, transparent 3 = **bright**, beaming, brilliant, effulgent, gleaming, luminous, radiant, resplendent, shining 4 = **clear-headed**, all there, *compos mentis,* in one's right mind, rational, reasonable, sane,

sensible, sober, sound
➤ **Antonyms**
≠**clear**: ambiguous, clear as mud (*informal*), confused, equivocal, incomprehensible, indistinct, muddled, unclear, unintelligible, vague ≠**translucent**: unclear ≠**bright**: dull ≠**clear-headed**: confused, irrational, muddled, unclear, unperceptive, vague

luck *noun* 1 = **fortune**, accident, chance, destiny, fate, fortuity 2 = **good fortune**, advantage, blessing, break (*informal*), fluke, godsend, good luck, prosperity, serendipity, stroke, success, windfall

luckily *adverb* 1 = **fortunately**, favourably, happily, opportunely, propitiously, providentially 2 = **by chance**, as it chanced, as luck would have it, fortuitously

luckless *adjective* = **unlucky**, calamitous, cursed, disastrous, doomed, hapless, hopeless, ill-fated, ill-starred, jinxed, star-crossed, unfortunate, unhappy, unpropitious, unsuccessful

lucky *adjective* 1 = **fortunate**, advantageous, blessed, charmed, favoured, jammy (*Brit. slang*), on a roll (*informal*), prosperous, serendipitous, successful 2 = **fortuitous**, adventitious, auspicious, opportune, propitious, providential, timely
➤ **Antonyms**
≠**fortunate**: bad, detrimental, ominous, unfavourable, unfortunate, unhappy, unlucky, unpromising ≠**fortuitous**: unlucky, untimely

lucrative *adjective* = **profitable**, advantageous, fat, fruitful, gainful, high-income, money-making, paying, productive, remunerative, well-paid

lucre *noun Usually facetious* = **money**, gain, mammon, pelf, profit, riches, spoils, wealth

ludicrous *adjective* = **ridiculous**, absurd, comic, comical, crazy, droll, farcical, funny, incongruous, laughable, nonsensical, odd, outlandish, preposterous, silly
➤ **Antonyms**
grave, logical, sad, sensible, serious, solemn

lug *verb* = **carry**, drag, haul, heave, hump (*Brit. slang*), pull, tow, yank

luggage *noun* = **baggage**, bags, cases, gear, impedimenta, paraphernalia, suitcases, things, trunks

lugubrious *adjective* = **gloomy**, dismal, doleful, dreary, funereal, melancholy, morose, mournful, sad, serious, sombre, sorrowful, woebegone, woeful

lukewarm *adjective* 1 = **tepid**, blood-warm, warm 2 = **half-hearted**, apathetic, cold, cool, indifferent, phlegmatic, unconcerned, unenthusiastic, uninterested, unresponsive

lull *verb* 1 = **calm**, allay, compose, hush,

pacify, quell, quiet, soothe, still, subdue, tranquillize ♦ *noun* **2** = **respite**, calm, calmness, hush, let-up (*informal*), pause, quiet, silence, stillness, tranquillity

lullaby *noun* = **cradlesong**, berceuse

lumber[1] *noun* **1** *Brit.* = **junk**, castoffs, clutter, jumble, refuse, rubbish, trash ♦ *verb* **2** *Brit. informal* = **burden**, encumber, impose upon, land, load, saddle

lumber[2] *verb* = **plod**, clump, shamble, shuffle, stump, trudge, trundle, waddle

lumbering *adjective* = **awkward**, blundering, bumbling, clumsy, elephantine, heavy, heavy-footed, hulking, lubberly, overgrown, ponderous, ungainly, unwieldy

luminary *noun* = **celebrity**, big name, celeb (*informal*), dignitary, leading light, megastar (*informal*), notable, personage, star, V.I.P., worthy

luminescent *adjective* = **glowing**, Day-Glo, fluorescent, luminous, phosphorescent, radiant, shining

luminous *adjective* = **bright**, brilliant, glowing, illuminated, lighted, lit, luminescent, lustrous, radiant, resplendent, shining, vivid

lump[1] *noun* **1** = **piece**, ball, bunch, cake, chunk, clod, cluster, dab, gob, group, hunk, mass, nugget, spot, wedge **2** = **swelling**, bulge, bump, growth, hump, protrusion, protuberance, tumescence, tumour ♦ *verb* **3** = **group**, aggregate, bunch, coalesce, collect, combine, conglomerate, consolidate, mass, pool, unite

lump[2] *verb* = **put up with**, bear, endure, stand, suffer, take, tolerate

lumpish *adjective* = **clumsy**, awkward, bungling, elephantine, gawky, heavy, lethargic, lumbering, oafish, ungainly

lumpy *adjective* = **bumpy**, knobbly, uneven

lunacy *noun* **1** = **foolishness**, aberration, absurdity, craziness, folly, foolhardiness, idiocy, imbecility, madness, senselessness, stupidity, tomfoolery **2** = **insanity**, dementia, derangement, idiocy, madness, mania, psychosis

➤ **Antonyms**

≠**foolishness**: prudence, reason, sense ≠**insanity**: reason, sanity

lunatic *adjective* **1** = **irrational**, barking (*slang*), barking mad (*slang*), barmy (*slang*), bonkers (*slang, chiefly Brit.*), crackbrained, crackpot (*informal*), crazy, daft, demented, deranged, insane, loopy (*informal*), mad, maniacal, not the full shilling (*informal*), nuts (*slang*), off one's trolley (*slang*), out to lunch (*informal*), psychotic, unhinged, up the pole (*informal*), wacko *or* whacko (*informal*) ♦ *noun* **2**

= **madman**, headbanger (*informal*), headcase (*informal*), loony (*slang*), maniac, nut (*slang*), nutcase (*slang*), nutter (*Brit. slang*), psychopath

lunge *noun* **1** = **thrust**, charge, cut, jab, pass, pounce, spring, stab, swing, swipe (*informal*) ♦ *verb* **2** = **pounce**, bound, charge, cut, dash, dive, fall upon, hit at, jab, leap, plunge, poke, stab, strike at, thrust

lurch *verb* **1** = **tilt**, heave, heel, lean, list, pitch, rock, roll **2** = **stagger**, reel, stumble, sway, totter, weave

lure *verb* **1** = **tempt**, allure, attract, beckon, decoy, draw, ensnare, entice, inveigle, invite, lead on, seduce ♦ *noun* **2** = **temptation**, allurement, attraction, bait, carrot (*informal*), come-on (*informal*), decoy, enticement, incentive, inducement, magnet

lurid *adjective* **1** = **sensational**, graphic, melodramatic, shock-horror (*facetious*), shocking, startling, vivid **2** = **glaring**, fiery, flaming, intense, overbright **3** = **gruesome**, disgusting, ghastly, gory, grim, grisly, macabre, revolting, savage, violent

➤ **Antonyms**

≠**sensational**: breezy, factual, jaunty, light-hearted, mild ≠**glaring**: pale, pastel, watery

lurk *verb* = **hide**, conceal oneself, crouch, lie in wait, prowl, skulk, slink, sneak

luscious *adjective* = **delicious**, appetizing, delectable, juicy, mouth-watering, palatable, rich, savoury, scrumptious (*informal*), succulent, sweet, toothsome, yummy (*slang*)

lush *adjective* **1** = **abundant**, dense, flourishing, green, lavish, overgrown, prolific, rank, teeming, verdant **2** = **luxurious**, elaborate, extravagant, grand, lavish, opulent, ornate, palatial, plush (*informal*), ritzy (*slang*), sumptuous

lust *noun* **1** = **lechery**, carnality, lasciviousness, lewdness, libido, licentiousness, randiness (*informal, chiefly Brit.*), salaciousness, sensuality, the hots (*slang*), wantonness **2** = **desire**, appetite, avidity, covetousness, craving, greed, longing, passion, thirst ♦ *verb* **3** = **desire**, be consumed with desire for, covet, crave, hunger for *or* after, need, want, yearn

lustful *adjective* = **lascivious**, carnal, horny (*slang*), hot-blooded, lecherous, lewd, libidinous, licentious, passionate, randy (*informal, chiefly Brit.*), unchaste, wanton

lustily *adverb* = **vigorously**, forcefully, hard, powerfully, strongly, with all one's might

lustre *noun* **1** = **sparkle**, burnish, gleam, glint, glitter, gloss, glow, sheen, shimmer, shine **2** = **glory**, distinction, fame, honour, illustriousness, prestige, renown

lustrous *adjective* = **shining**, bright,

burnished, dazzling, gleaming, glistening, glossy, glowing, luminous, radiant, shimmering, shiny, sparkling

lusty *adjective* = **vigorous**, brawny, energetic, hale, healthy, hearty, powerful, red-blooded (*informal*), robust, rugged, stalwart, stout, strapping, strong, sturdy, virile

luxuriant *adjective* **1** = **abundant**, ample, copious, excessive, lavish, plenteous, plentiful, prodigal, profuse **2** = **lush**, dense, fecund, fertile, flourishing, fruitful, overflowing, productive, prolific, rank, rich, riotous, teeming **3** = **elaborate**, baroque, decorated, extravagant, fancy, flamboyant, ornate, rococo, sumptuous
➤ **Antonyms**
≠**abundant, lush:** meagre, scanty, sparse, thin ≠**elaborate:** plain, simple, unadorned

luxuriate *verb* **1** = **enjoy**, bask, delight, indulge, relish, revel, wallow **2** = **flourish**, grow, prosper, thrive

luxurious *adjective* **1** = **sumptuous**, comfortable, costly, de luxe, expensive, lavish, magnificent, opulent, plush (*informal*), rich, ritzy (*slang*), splendid, well-appointed **2** = **pleasure-loving**, epicurean, pampered, self-indulgent, sensual, sybaritic, voluptuous
➤ **Antonyms**
ascetic, austere, deprived, economical, plain, poor, sparing, Spartan, thrifty

luxury *noun* **1** = **opulence**, affluence, hedonism, richness, splendour,

sumptuousness, voluptuousness **2** = **pleasure**, bliss, comfort, delight, enjoyment, gratification, indulgence, satisfaction, wellbeing **3** = **extravagance**, extra, frill, indulgence, nonessential, treat
➤ **Antonyms**
≠**opulence:** austerity, deprivation, destitution, poverty, privation, want ≠**pleasure:** burden, difficulty, discomfort, hardship, infliction, misery ≠**extravagance:** necessity, need

lying *noun* **1** = **dishonesty**, deceit, dissimulation, double-dealing, duplicity, fabrication, fibbing, mendacity, perjury, prevarication, untruthfulness ♦ *adjective* **2** = **deceitful**, dishonest, dissembling, double-dealing, false, mendacious, perfidious, treacherous, two-faced, untruthful
➤ **Antonyms**
adjective ≠**deceitful:** candid, forthright, frank, honest, reliable, sincere, straight, straightforward, truthful, veracious

lynchpin, linchpin *noun* = **driving force**, chief, co-ordinator, cornerstone, director, principal

lyric *adjective* **1** *Of poetry* = **songlike**, expressive, lyrical, melodic, musical **2** *Of a voice* = **melodic**, clear, dulcet, flowing, graceful, light ♦ *noun* **3** *plural* = **words**, book, libretto, text, words of a song

lyrical *adjective* = **enthusiastic**, carried away, ecstatic, effusive, emotional, expressive, impassioned, inspired, poetic, rapturous, rhapsodic

M m

macabre *adjective* = **gruesome**, cadaverous, deathlike, deathly, dreadful, eerie, frightening, frightful, ghastly, ghostly, ghoulish, grim, grisly, hideous, horrid, morbid, unearthly, weird
➤ **Antonyms**
appealing, beautiful, charming, delightful, lovely, pleasant

machiavellian *adjective* = **scheming**, astute, crafty, cunning, cynical, double-dealing, opportunist, sly, underhand, unscrupulous

machination *noun* = **plot**, artifice, cabal, conspiracy, design, device, dodge, intrigue, manoeuvre, ploy, ruse, scheme, stratagem, trick

machine *noun* 1 = **appliance**, apparatus, contraption, contrivance, device, engine, instrument, mechanism, tool 2 = **system**, agency, machinery, organization, party, setup (*informal*), structure

machinery *noun* 1 = **equipment**, apparatus, gear, instruments, mechanism, tackle, tools, works 2 = **procedure**, agency, channels, machine, organization, structure, system

macho *adjective* = **manly**, chauvinist, masculine, virile

mad *adjective* 1 = **insane**, aberrant, as daft as a brush (*informal, chiefly Brit.*), bananas (*slang*), barking (*slang*), barking mad (*slang*), barmy (*slang*), batty (*slang*), bonkers (*slang, chiefly Brit.*), crackers (*Brit. slang*), crackpot (*informal*), crazed, crazy (*informal*), cuckoo (*informal*), delirious, demented, deranged, distracted, doolally (*slang*), flaky (*U.S. slang*), frantic, frenzied, gonzo (*slang*), loony (*slang*), loopy (*informal*), lost one's marbles (*informal*), lunatic, mental (*slang*), *non compos mentis*, not right in the head, not the full shilling (*informal*), nuts (*slang*), nutty (*slang*), off one's chump (*slang*), off one's head (*slang*), off one's nut (*slang*), off one's rocker (*slang*), off one's trolley (*slang*), of unsound mind, out of one's mind, out to lunch (*informal*), psychotic, rabid, raving, round the bend (*Brit. slang*), round the twist (*Brit. slang*), screwy (*informal*), unbalanced, unhinged, unstable, up the pole (*informal*), wacko *or* whacko (*informal*) 2 = **foolish**, absurd, as daft as a brush (*informal, chiefly Brit.*), asinine, daft

(*informal*), foolhardy, imprudent, inane, irrational, ludicrous, nonsensical, preposterous, senseless, unreasonable, unsafe, unsound, wild 3 *Informal* = **angry**, ape (*slang*), apeshit (*slang*), berserk, choked, cross, enraged, exasperated, fit to be tied (*slang*), fuming, furious, in a wax (*informal, chiefly Brit.*), incandescent, incensed, infuriated, irate, irritated, livid (*informal*), pissed (*taboo slang*), pissed off (*taboo slang*), raging, resentful, seeing red (*informal*), wild, wrathful 4 = **enthusiastic**, ardent, avid, crazy (*informal*), daft (*informal*), devoted, dotty (*slang, chiefly Brit.*), enamoured, fanatical, fond, hooked, impassioned, infatuated, in love with, keen, nuts (*slang*), wild, zealous 5 = **frenzied**, abandoned, agitated, boisterous, ebullient, energetic, excited, frenetic, full-on (*informal*), gay, riotous, uncontrolled, unrestrained, wild 6 **like mad** *Informal* = **energetically**, enthusiastically, excitedly, furiously, hell for leather, like greased lightning (*informal*), like lightning, like nobody's business (*informal*), like the clappers (*Brit. informal*), madly, quickly, rapidly, speedily, unrestrainedly, violently, wildly, with might and main
➤ **Antonyms**
≠**insane**: rational, sane ≠**foolish**: sensible, sound ≠**angry**: appeased, calm, composed, cool, mollified ≠**enthusiastic**: nonchalant, uncaring

madcap *adjective* = **reckless**, crazy, foolhardy, hare-brained, imprudent, impulsive, rash, thoughtless

madden *verb* = **infuriate**, aggravate (*informal*), annoy, craze, dement, derange, drive one crazy, drive one off one's head (*slang*), drive one out of one's mind, drive one round the bend (*Brit. slang*), drive one round the twist (*Brit. slang*), drive one to distraction (*informal*), enrage, exasperate, gall, get one's back up, get one's dander up (*informal*), get one's goat (*slang*), get one's hackles up, incense, inflame, irritate, make one's blood boil, make one see red (*informal*), make one's hackles rise, nark (*Brit., Austral., & N.Z. slang*), piss one off (*taboo slang*), provoke, put one's back up, raise one's hackles, unhinge, upset, vex
➤ **Antonyms**
appease, calm, mollify, pacify, soothe

made-up *adjective* = **false**, fabricated, fictional, imaginary, invented, make-believe, mythical, specious, trumped-up, unreal, untrue

madly *adverb* **1** = **insanely**, crazily, deliriously, dementedly, distractedly, frantically, frenziedly, hysterically, rabidly **2** = **foolishly**, absurdly, irrationally, ludicrously, nonsensically, senselessly, unreasonably, wildly **3** = **energetically**, excitedly, furiously, hastily, hell for leather, hotfoot, hurriedly, like greased lightning (*informal*), like lightning, like mad (*informal*), like nobody's business (*informal*), like the clappers (*Brit. informal*), quickly, rapidly, recklessly, speedily, violently, wildly **4** *Informal* = **passionately**, desperately, devotedly, exceedingly, excessively, extremely, intensely, to distraction

madman *or* **madwoman** *noun* = **lunatic**, headbanger (*informal*), headcase (*informal*), loony (*slang*), maniac, mental case (*slang*), nut (*slang*), nutcase (*slang*), nutter (*Brit. slang*), psycho (*slang*), psychopath, psychotic

madness *noun* **1** = **insanity**, aberration, craziness, delusion, dementia, derangement, distraction, lunacy, mania, mental illness, psychopathy, psychosis **2** = **foolishness**, absurdity, daftness (*informal*), folly, foolhardiness, idiocy, nonsense, preposterousness, wildness **3** *Informal* = **anger**, exasperation, frenzy, fury, ire, rage, raving, wildness, wrath **4** = **passion**, ardour, craze, enthusiasm, fanaticism, fondness, infatuation, keenness, rage, zeal **5** = **frenzy**, abandon, agitation, excitement, furore, intoxication, riot, unrestraint, uproar

maelstrom *noun* **1** = **whirlpool**, vortex **2** = **turmoil**, chaos, confusion, disorder, tumult, upheaval

maestro *noun* = **master**, expert, genius, virtuoso

magazine *noun* **1** = **journal**, pamphlet, paper, periodical **2** = **storehouse**, ammunition dump, arsenal, depot, powder room (*obsolete*), store, warehouse

magic *noun* **1** = **sorcery**, black art, enchantment, necromancy, occultism, sortilege, spell, theurgy, witchcraft, wizardry **2** = **conjuring**, hocus-pocus, illusion, jiggery-pokery (*informal, chiefly Brit.*), jugglery, legerdemain, prestidigitation, sleight of hand, trickery **3** = **charm**, allurement, enchantment, fascination, glamour, magnetism, power ◆ *adjective* **4** *Also* **magical** = **miraculous**, bewitching, charismatic, charming, enchanting, entrancing, fascinating, magnetic, marvellous, sorcerous, spellbinding

magician *noun* **1** = **sorcerer**, archimage (*rare*), conjuror *or* conjurer, enchanter *or* enchantress, illusionist, necromancer, thaumaturge (*rare*), theurgist, warlock, witch, wizard **2** = **miracle-worker**, genius, marvel, spellbinder, virtuoso, wizard, wonder-worker

magisterial *adjective* = **authoritative**, commanding, imperious, lordly, masterful
➤ **Antonyms**
deferential, diffident, humble, servile, shy, submissive, subservient, wimpish *or* wimpy (*informal*)

magistrate *noun* = **judge**, bailie (*Scot.*), J.P., justice, justice of the peace, provost (*Scot.*)

magnanimity *noun* = **generosity**, beneficence, benevolence, big-heartedness, bountifulness, charitableness, high-mindedness, largesse *or* largess, munificence, nobility, open-handedness, selflessness, unselfishness

magnanimous *adjective* = **generous**, beneficent, big, big-hearted, bountiful, charitable, free, great-hearted, handsome, high-minded, kind, kindly, munificent, noble, open-handed, selfless, ungrudging, unselfish, unstinting
➤ **Antonyms**
miserly, petty, resentful, selfish, small, unforgiving, vindictive

magnate *noun* **1** = **tycoon**, baron, big cheese (*slang, old-fashioned*), big hitter (*informal*), big noise (*informal*), big shot (*informal*), big wheel (*slang*), bigwig (*informal*), captain of industry, chief, fat cat (*slang, chiefly U.S.*), heavy hitter (*informal*), leader, Mister Big (*slang, chiefly U.S.*), mogul, nabob (*informal*), notable, plutocrat, V.I.P. **2** = **aristocrat**, aristo (*informal*), baron, bashaw, grandee, magnifico, nob (*slang, chiefly Brit.*), noble, notable, personage, prince

magnetic *adjective* = **attractive**, alluring, captivating, charismatic, charming, enchanting, entrancing, fascinating, hypnotic, irresistible, mesmerizing, seductive
➤ **Antonyms**
disagreeable, offensive, repellent, repulsive, unappealing, unattractive, unlikable *or* unlikeable, unpleasant

magnetism *noun* = **charm**, allure, appeal, attraction, attractiveness, captivatingness, charisma, draw, drawing power, enchantment, fascination, hypnotism, magic, mesmerism, power, pull, seductiveness, spell

magnification *noun* = **increase**, aggrandizement, amplification, augmentation, blow-up (*informal*), boost, build-up, deepening, dilation, enhancement, enlargement, exaggeration, expansion, heightening, inflation, intensification

magnificence *noun* = **splendour**, brilliance, éclat, glory, gorgeousness, grandeur, luxuriousness, luxury, majesty, nobility, opulence, pomp, resplendence, stateliness, sublimity, sumptuousness

magnificent *adjective* **1** = **splendid**, august, elegant, elevated, exalted, glorious, gorgeous, grand, grandiose, imposing, impressive, lavish, luxurious, majestic, noble, opulent, princely, regal, resplendent, rich, splendiferous (*facetious*), stately, striking, sublime, sumptuous, transcendent **2** = **excellent**, brilliant, divine (*informal*), fine, outstanding, splendid, superb, superior
➤ **Antonyms**
bad, humble, ignoble, lowly, mean, modest, ordinary, petty, poor, trivial, undistinguished, unimposing

magnify *verb* **1** = **enlarge**, aggrandize, amplify, augment, blow up (*informal*), boost, build up, deepen, dilate, expand, heighten, increase, intensify **2** = **overstate**, aggravate, blow up, blow up out of all proportion, dramatize, enhance, exaggerate, inflate, make a federal case of (*U.S. informal*), make a mountain out of a molehill, make a production (out) of (*informal*), overdo, overemphasize, overestimate, overplay, overrate
➤ **Antonyms**
≠**enlarge**: decrease, diminish, lessen, lower, minimize, reduce, shrink ≠**overstate**: belittle, deflate, denigrate, deprecate, disparage, understate

magniloquent *adjective* = **pompous**, arty-farty (*informal*), bombastic, declamatory, elevated, exalted, grandiloquent, high-flown, high-sounding, lofty, orotund, overblown, pretentious, rhetorical, sonorous, stilted, turgid

magnitude *noun* **1** = **importance**, consequence, eminence, grandeur, greatness, mark, moment, note, significance, weight **2** = **size**, amount, amplitude, bigness, bulk, capacity, dimensions, enormity, expanse, extent, hugeness, immensity, intensity, largeness, mass, measure, proportions, quantity, space, strength, vastness, volume
➤ **Antonyms**
≠**importance**: insignificance, triviality, unimportance ≠**size**: meanness, smallness

maid *noun* **1** = **servant**, abigail (*archaic*), handmaiden (*archaic*), housemaid, maidservant, serving-maid **2** *Literary* = **girl**, damsel, lass, lassie (*informal*), maiden, miss, nymph (*poetic*), wench

maiden *noun* **1** *Literary* = **girl**, damsel, lass, lassie (*informal*), maid, miss, nymph

(*poetic*), virgin, wench ♦ *adjective* **2** = **unmarried**, chaste, intact, pure, undefiled, unwed, virgin, virginal **3** = **first**, inaugural, initial, initiatory, introductory

maidenly *adjective* = **modest**, chaste, decent, decorous, demure, gentle, girlish, pure, reserved, undefiled, unsullied, vestal, virginal, virtuous
➤ **Antonyms**
brazen, corrupt, defiled, depraved, dirty, immodest, immoral, impure, indecent, loose, promiscuous, shameless, sinful, unchaste, wanton, wicked

mail *noun* **1** = **letters**, correspondence, packages, parcels, post **2** = **postal service**, post, postal system ♦ *verb* **3** = **post**, dispatch, forward, send, send by mail *or* post

maim *verb* = **cripple**, disable, hamstring, hurt, impair, incapacitate, injure, lame, mangle, mar, mutilate, put out of action, wound

main *adjective* **1** = **chief**, capital, cardinal, central, critical, crucial, essential, foremost, head, leading, major, necessary, outstanding, paramount, particular, predominant, pre-eminent, premier, primary, prime, principal, special, supreme, vital ♦ *noun* **2** = **conduit**, cable, channel, duct, line, pipe **3** = **force**, effort, might, potency, power, puissance, strength **4 in the main** = **on the whole**, for the most part, generally, in general, mainly, mostly
➤ **Antonyms**
adjective ≠**chief**: auxiliary, dependent, insignificant, least, lesser, minor, secondary, subordinate, trivial, unimportant

mainly *adverb* = **chiefly**, above all, first and foremost, for the most part, generally, in general, in the main, largely, mostly, most of all, on the whole, overall, predominantly, primarily, principally, substantially, to the greatest extent, usually

mainstay *noun* = **pillar**, anchor, backbone, bulwark, buttress, chief support, lynchpin, prop

mainstream *adjective* = **conventional**, accepted, central, current, established, general, orthodox, prevailing, received
➤ **Antonyms**
fringe, marginal, peripheral, unconventional, unorthodox

maintain *verb* **1** = **continue**, carry on, conserve, keep, keep up, nurture, perpetuate, preserve, prolong, retain, sustain, uphold **2** = **look after**, care for, finance, provide for, supply, support, take care of **3** = **assert**, affirm, allege, asseverate, aver, avow, claim, contend, declare, hold, insist, profess, state **4** = **support**, advocate, argue for, back, champion, defend, fight for,

justify, plead for, stand by, take up the
cudgels for, uphold, vindicate
> **Antonyms**
≠**continue**: abolish, break off, conclude,
discontinue, drop, end, finish, give up,
relinquish, suspend, terminate ≠**assert**:
disavow ≠**support**: abandon, desert

maintenance *noun* 1 = **continuation**,
carrying-on, continuance, perpetuation,
prolongation, retainment, support,
sustainment, sustention 2 = **upkeep**, care,
conservation, keeping, nurture, preservation,
provision, repairs, supply 3 = **allowance**,
aliment, alimony, food, keep, livelihood,
living, subsistence, support, sustenance,
upkeep

majestic *adjective* = **grand**, august,
awesome, dignified, elevated, exalted,
grandiose, imperial, imposing, impressive,
kingly, lofty, magnificent, monumental,
noble, pompous, princely, regal, royal,
splendid, splendiferous (*facetious*), stately,
sublime, superb
> **Antonyms**
humble, ignoble, lowly, mean, modest,
ordinary, unassuming, undistinguished,
unimposing

majesty *noun* = **grandeur**, augustness,
awesomeness, dignity, exaltedness, glory,
imposingness, impressiveness, kingliness,
loftiness, magnificence, nobility, pomp,
queenliness, royalty, splendour, state,
stateliness, sublimity
> **Antonyms**
meanness, triviality

major *adjective* 1 = **main**, better, bigger,
chief, elder, greater, head, higher, larger,
lead, leading, most, senior, superior,
supreme, uppermost 2 = **important**, critical,
crucial, grave, great, mega (*slang*), notable,
outstanding, pre-eminent, radical, serious,
significant, vital, weighty
> **Antonyms**
≠**main**: auxiliary, lesser, minor, secondary,
smaller, subordinate ≠**important**:
inconsequential, insignificant, trivial,
unimportant

majority *noun* 1 = **most**, best part, bulk,
greater number, mass, more, plurality,
preponderance, superiority 2 = **adulthood**,
manhood *or* womanhood, maturity, seniority

make *verb* 1 = **create**, assemble, build,
compose, constitute, construct, fabricate,
fashion, forge, form, frame, manufacture,
mould, originate, produce, put together,
shape, synthesize 2 = **force**, cause, coerce,
compel, constrain, dragoon, drive, impel,
induce, oblige, press, pressurize, prevail
upon, railroad (*informal*), require 3
= **produce**, accomplish, beget, bring about,
cause, create, effect, engender, generate,

give rise to, lead to, occasion 4 = **perform**,
act, carry out, do, effect, engage in, execute,
practise, prosecute 5 = **appoint**, assign,
create, designate, elect, install, invest,
nominate, ordain 6 = **amount to**, add up to,
compose, constitute, embody, form,
represent 7 = **earn**, acquire, clear, gain, get,
net, obtain, realize, secure, take in, win 8
= **calculate**, estimate, gauge, judge, reckon,
suppose, think 9 = **get to**, arrive at, arrive in
time for, attain, catch, meet, reach 10
= **enact**, draw up, establish, fix, form, frame,
pass 11 **make as if** *or* **though** = **pretend**,
act as if *or* though, affect, feign, feint, give
the impression that, make a show of 12
make it *Informal* = **succeed**, arrive
(*informal*), be successful, come through,
crack it (*informal*), cut it (*informal*), get on,
get somewhere, prosper, pull through,
survive ♦ *noun* 13 = **brand**, build, character,
composition, constitution, construction, cut,
designation, form, kind, make-up, mark,
model, shape, sort, structure, style, type,
variety 14 = **nature**, cast of mind, character,
disposition, frame of mind, humour, kidney,
make-up, stamp, temper, temperament

make away *verb* 1 = **depart**, abscond,
beat a hasty retreat, clear out (*informal*), cut
and run (*informal*), decamp, do a runner
(*slang*), flee, fly, fly the coop (*U.S. &
Canad. informal*), hook it (*slang*), make off,
run away *or* off, run for it (*informal*), scoot,
skedaddle (*informal*), slope off, take a
powder (*U.S. & Canad. slang*), take it on
the lam (*U.S. & Canad. slang*), take to
one's heels 2 **with** = **steal**, abduct,
cabbage (*Brit. slang*), carry off, cart off
(*slang*), filch, kidnap, knock off (*slang*),
make off with, nab (*informal*), nick (*slang,
chiefly Brit.*), pilfer, pinch (*informal*),
purloin, swipe (*slang*) 3 **with** = **kill**,
blow away (*slang, chiefly U.S.*), bump off
(*slang*), destroy, dispose of, do away with,
do in (*slang*), eliminate, get rid of, murder,
rub out (*U.S. slang*)

make-believe *noun* 1 = **fantasy**, charade,
dream, imagination, play-acting, pretence,
unreality ♦ *adjective* 2 = **imaginary**, dream,
fantasized, fantasy, imagined, made-up,
mock, pretend, pretended, sham, unreal
> **Antonyms**
noun ≠**fantasy**: actuality, fact, reality,
truthfulness ♦ *adjective* ≠**imaginary**:
authentic, genuine, real, unfeigned

make believe *verb* = **pretend**, act as if *or*
though, dream, enact, fantasize, imagine,
play, play-act

make do *verb* = **manage**, cope, get along
or by, improvise, muddle through, scrape
along *or* by

make for *verb* 1 = **head for**, aim for, be

bound for, head towards, proceed towards, steer (a course) for **2** = **attack**, assail, assault, fall on, fly at, go for, have a go at (*informal*), lunge at, set upon **3** = **contribute to**, be conducive to, conduce to, facilitate, favour, promote

make off *verb* **1** = **flee**, abscond, beat a hasty retreat, bolt, clear out (*informal*), cut and run (*informal*), decamp, do a runner (*slang*), fly, fly the coop (*U.S. & Canad. informal*), hook it (*slang*), make away, run away *or* off, run for it (*informal*), skedaddle (*informal*), slope off, take a powder (*U.S. & Canad. slang*), take it on the lam (*U.S. & Canad. slang*), take to one's heels **2 make off with** = **steal**, abduct, cabbage (*Brit. slang*), carry off, cart off (*slang*), filch, kidnap, knock off (*slang*), make away with, nab (*informal*), nick (*slang, chiefly Brit.*), pilfer, pinch (*informal*), purloin, run away *or* off with, swipe (*slang*)

make out *verb* **1** = **see**, descry, detect, discern, discover, distinguish, espy, perceive, recognize **2** = **understand**, comprehend, decipher, fathom, follow, grasp, perceive, realize, see, suss (out) (*slang*), work out **3** = **write out**, complete, draw up, fill in *or* out, inscribe **4** = **prove**, demonstrate, describe, represent, show **5** = **pretend**, assert, claim, let on, make as if *or* though **6** = **fare**, get on, manage, prosper, succeed, thrive

maker *noun* = **manufacturer**, author, builder, constructor, director, fabricator, framer, producer

Maker *noun* = **God**, Creator

makeshift *adjective* **1** = **temporary**, expedient, jury (*chiefly Nautical*), make-do, provisional, rough and ready, stopgap, substitute ♦ *noun* **2** = **stopgap**, expedient, shift, substitute

make-up *noun* **1** = **cosmetics**, face (*informal*), greasepaint (*Theatre*), maquillage, paint (*informal*), powder, war paint (*informal, humorous*) **2** = **structure**, arrangement, assembly, composition, configuration, constitution, construction, form, format, formation, organization **3** = **nature**, build, cast of mind, character, constitution, disposition, figure, frame of mind, make, stamp, temper, temperament

make up *verb* **1** = **form**, compose, comprise, constitute **2** = **invent**, coin, compose, concoct, construct, cook up (*informal*), create, devise, dream up, fabricate, formulate, frame, hatch, manufacture, originate, trump up, write **3** = **complete**, fill, meet, supply **4** = **settle**, bury the hatchet, call it quits, come to terms, compose, forgive and forget, make peace, mend, reconcile, shake hands **5 make**

up for = **compensate for**, atone for, balance, make amends for, offset, recompense, redeem, redress, requite **6 make up one's mind** = **decide**, choose, come to a decision, determine, make a decision, reach a decision, resolve, settle **7 make up to** *Informal* = **court**, chat up (*informal*), curry favour with, flirt with, make overtures to, woo

making *noun* **1** = **creation**, assembly, building, composition, construction, fabrication, forging, manufacture, production **2 in the making** = **budding**, coming, emergent, growing, nascent, potential

makings *plural noun* = **beginnings**, capability, capacity, ingredients, materials, potential, potentiality, qualities

maladjusted *adjective* = **disturbed**, alienated, estranged, hung-up (*slang*), neurotic, unstable

maladministration *noun* = **mismanagement**, blundering, bungling, corruption, dishonesty, incompetence, inefficiency, malfeasance (*Law*), malpractice, misgovernment, misrule

maladroit *adjective* = **clumsy**, awkward, cack-handed (*informal*), ham-fisted *or* ham-handed (*informal*), inept, inexpert, unskilful

malady *noun* = **disease**, affliction, ailment, complaint, disorder, ill, illness, indisposition, infirmity, lurgy (*informal*), sickness

malaise *noun* = **unease**, angst, anxiety, depression, discomfort, disquiet, doldrums, enervation, illness, lassitude, melancholy, sickness, weakness

malcontent *noun* **1** = **troublemaker**, agitator, complainer, fault-finder, grouch (*informal*), grouser, grumbler, mischief-maker, rebel, stirrer (*informal*) ♦ *adjective* **2** = **discontented**, disaffected, disgruntled, disgusted, dissatisfied, dissentious, factious, ill-disposed, rebellious, resentful, restive, unhappy, unsatisfied

male *adjective* = **masculine**, manful, manlike, manly, virile
➤ **Antonyms**
camp (*informal*), effeminate, female, feminine, girlie, unmanly, wimpish *or* wimpy (*informal*), womanish, womanly, wussy (*slang*)

malefactor *noun* = **wrongdoer**, convict, criminal, crook (*informal*), culprit, delinquent, evildoer, felon, lawbreaker, miscreant, offender, outlaw, transgressor, villain

malevolence *noun* = **malice**, hate, hatred, ill will, maliciousness, malignity, nastiness, rancour, spite, spitefulness, vengefulness, vindictiveness

malevolent *adjective* = **spiteful**, baleful, evil-minded, hateful (*archaic*), hostile, ill-natured, maleficent, malicious, malign, malignant, pernicious, rancorous, vengeful, vicious, vindictive
➤ **Antonyms**
amiable, benevolent, benign, friendly, gracious, kind, warm-hearted

malformation *noun* = **deformity**, crookedness, distortion, misshape, misshapenness

malformed *adjective* = **misshapen**, abnormal, contorted, crooked, deformed, distorted, irregular, twisted

malfunction *verb* 1 = **break down**, develop a fault, fail, go wrong ◆ *noun* 2 = **fault**, breakdown, defect, failure, flaw, glitch, impairment

malice *noun* = **spite**, animosity, animus, bad blood, bitterness, enmity, evil intent, hate, hatred, ill will, malevolence, maliciousness, malignity, rancour, spitefulness, spleen, vengefulness, venom, vindictiveness

malicious *adjective* = **spiteful**, baleful, bitchy (*informal*), bitter, catty (*informal*), evil-minded, hateful, ill-disposed, ill-natured, injurious, malevolent, malignant, mischievous, pernicious, rancorous, resentful, shrewish, vengeful, vicious
➤ **Antonyms**
amiable, benevolent, friendly, kind, warm-hearted

malign *verb* 1 = **disparage**, abuse, asperse, bad-mouth (*slang, chiefly U.S. & Canad.*), blacken (someone's name), calumniate, defame, denigrate, derogate, do a hatchet job on (*informal*), harm, injure, knock (*informal*), libel, revile, rubbish (*informal*), run down, slag (off) (*slang*), slander, smear, speak ill of, traduce, vilify ◆ *adjective* 2 = **evil**, bad, baleful, baneful, deleterious, destructive, harmful, hostile, hurtful, injurious, maleficent, malevolent, malignant, pernicious, vicious, wicked
➤ **Antonyms**
verb ≠**disparage:** commend, compliment, extol, praise ◆ *adjective* ≠**evil:** agreeable, amiable, beneficial, benevolent, benign, friendly, good, harmless, innocuous, kind, virtuous, warm-hearted, wholesome

malignant *adjective* 1 = **hostile**, baleful, bitter, destructive, harmful, hurtful, inimical, injurious, maleficent, malevolent, malicious, malign, of evil intent, pernicious, spiteful, vicious 2 *Medical* = **uncontrollable**, cancerous, dangerous, deadly, evil, fatal, irremediable, metastatic, virulent
➤ **Antonyms**
≠**hostile:** amicable, benevolent, benign,

friendly, kind, warm-hearted

malleable *adjective* 1 = **workable**, ductile, plastic, soft, tensile 2 = **manageable**, adaptable, biddable, compliant, impressionable, pliable, tractable

malodorous *adjective* = **smelly**, fetid, mephitic, nauseating, noisome, offensive, putrid, reeking, stinking

malpractice *noun* = **misconduct**, abuse, dereliction, misbehaviour, mismanagement, negligence

maltreat *verb* = **abuse**, bully, damage, handle roughly, harm, hurt, ill-treat, injure, mistreat

mammoth *adjective* = **colossal**, Brobdingnagian, elephantine, enormous, gargantuan, giant, gigantic, ginormous (*informal*), huge, humongous *or* humungous (*U.S. slang*), immense, jumbo (*informal*), massive, mega (*slang*), mighty, monumental, mountainous, prodigious, stellar (*informal*), stupendous, titanic, vast
➤ **Antonyms**
diminutive, insignificant, little, miniature, minute, puny, small, tiny, trivial

man *noun* 1 = **male**, bloke (*Brit. informal*), chap (*informal*), gentleman, guy (*informal*) 2 = **human**, adult, being, body, human being, individual, one, person, personage, somebody, soul 3 = **mankind**, Homo sapiens, humanity, humankind, human race, mortals, people 4 = **manservant**, attendant, follower, retainer, servant, valet 5 = **employee**, hand, hireling, liegeman, soldier, subject, subordinate, vassal, worker, workman 6 = **boyfriend**, beau, husband, lover, partner, significant other (*U.S. informal*), spouse 7 **to a man** = **without exception**, bar none, every one, one and all, unanimously ◆ *verb* 8 = **staff**, crew, fill, furnish with men, garrison, occupy, people

manacle *noun* 1 = **handcuff**, bond, chain, fetter, gyve (*archaic*), iron, shackle, tie ◆ *verb* 2 = **handcuff**, bind, chain, check, clap *or* put in irons, confine, constrain, curb, fetter, hamper, inhibit, put in chains, restrain, shackle, tie one's hands

manage *verb* 1 = **succeed**, accomplish, arrange, bring about *or* off, contrive, cope with, crack it (*informal*), cut it (*informal*), deal with, effect, engineer 2 = **administer**, be in charge (of), call the shots, call the tune, command, concert, conduct, direct, govern, handle, manipulate, oversee, preside over, rule, run, superintend, supervise 3 = **handle**, control, dominate, govern, guide, influence, manipulate, operate, pilot, ply, steer, train, use, wield 4 = **cope**, carry on, fare, get along, get by (*informal*), get on, get through, make do, make out, muddle

through, shift, survive
➤ **Antonyms**
≠**succeed:** bodge (*informal*), botch, fail, make a mess of, make a nonsense of, mismanage, muff, spoil

manageable *adjective* 1 = **easy**, convenient, handy, user-friendly, wieldy 2 = **docile**, amenable, compliant, controllable, governable, submissive, tamable, tractable
➤ **Antonyms**
≠**easy:** demanding, difficult, hard ≠**docile:** disobedient, headstrong, obstinate, refractory, stubborn, ungovernable, unruly, unyielding, wild

management *noun* 1 = **directors**, administration, board, bosses (*informal*), directorate, employers, executive(s) 2 = **administration**, care, charge, command, conduct, control, direction, governance, government, guidance, handling, manipulation, operation, rule, running, superintendence, supervision

manager *noun* = **supervisor**, administrator, boss (*informal*), comptroller, conductor, controller, director, executive, gaffer (*informal, chiefly Brit.*), governor, head, organizer, overseer, proprietor, superintendent

mandate *noun* = **command**, authority, authorization, bidding, canon, charge, commission, decree, directive, edict, fiat, injunction, instruction, order, precept, sanction, warrant

mandatory *adjective* = **compulsory**, binding, obligatory, required, requisite
➤ **Antonyms**
discretionary, nonbinding, noncompulsory, nonobligatory, optional, unnecessary, voluntary

manful *adjective* = **brave**, bold, courageous, daring, determined, gallant, hardy, heroic, indomitable, intrepid, manly, noble, powerful, resolute, stalwart, stout, stout-hearted, strong, valiant, vigorous

manfully *adverb* = **bravely**, boldly, courageously, desperately, determinedly, gallantly, hard, heroically, intrepidly, like a Trojan, like one possessed, like the devil, nobly, powerfully, resolutely, stalwartly, stoutly, strongly, to the best of one's ability, valiantly, vigorously, with might and main

mangle *verb* = **crush**, butcher, cripple, cut, deform, destroy, disfigure, distort, hack, lacerate, maim, mar, maul, mutilate, rend, ruin, spoil, tear, total (*slang*), trash (*slang*), wreck

mangy *adjective* = **scruffy**, dirty, grungy (*slang, chiefly U.S.*), mean, moth-eaten, scabby (*informal*), scuzzy (*slang, chiefly U.S.*), seedy, shabby, shoddy, squalid

➤ **Antonyms**
attractive, choice, clean, de luxe, fine, splendid, spotless, superb, tidy, well-dressed, well-kept

manhandle *verb* 1 = **rough up**, handle roughly, knock about or around, maul, paw (*informal*), pull, push 2 = **haul**, carry, heave, hump (*Brit. slang*), lift, manoeuvre, pull, push, shove, tug

manhood *noun* = **manliness**, bravery, courage, determination, firmness, fortitude, hardihood, manfulness, masculinity, maturity, mettle, resolution, spirit, strength, valour, virility

mania *noun* 1 = **obsession**, cacoethes, craving, craze, desire, enthusiasm, fad (*informal*), fetish, fixation, partiality, passion, preoccupation, rage, thing (*informal*) 2 = **madness**, aberration, craziness, delirium, dementia, derangement, disorder, frenzy, insanity, lunacy

maniac *noun* 1 = **madman** or **madwoman**, headbanger (*informal*), headcase (*informal*), loony (*slang*), lunatic, nutcase (*slang*), nutter (*Brit. slang*), psycho (*slang*), psychopath 2 = **fanatic**, energumen, enthusiast, fan, fiend (*informal*), freak (*informal*)

manifest *adjective* 1 = **obvious**, apparent, blatant, bold, clear, conspicuous, distinct, evident, glaring, noticeable, open, palpable, patent, plain, salient, unmistakable, visible
♦ *verb* 2 = **display**, declare, demonstrate, establish, evince, exhibit, expose, express, make plain, prove, reveal, set forth, show
➤ **Antonyms**
adjective ≠**obvious:** concealed, disguised, hidden, inconspicuous, indistinct, masked, suppressed, unapparent, vague, veiled
♦ *verb* ≠**display:** conceal, cover, cover up, deny, hide, mask, obscure, refute

manifestation *noun* = **display**, appearance, demonstration, disclosure, exhibition, exposure, expression, indication, instance, mark, materialization, revelation, show, sign, symptom, token

manifold *adjective Formal* = **numerous**, abundant, assorted, copious, diverse, diversified, many, multifarious, multifold, multiple, multiplied, multitudinous, varied, various

manipulate *verb* 1 = **work**, employ, handle, operate, ply, use, wield 2 = **influence**, conduct, control, direct, do a number on (*chiefly U.S.*), engineer, guide, manoeuvre, negotiate, steer, twist around one's little finger

mankind *noun* = **people**, Homo sapiens, humanity, humankind, human race, man

manliness *noun* = **virility**, boldness,

manly

51

marauder

bravery, courage, fearlessness, firmness, hardihood, heroism, independence, intrepidity, machismo, manfulness, manhood, masculinity, mettle, resolution, stouthearted, valour, vigour

manly *adjective* = **virile**, bold, brave, butch (*slang*), courageous, daring, dauntless, fearless, gallant, hardy, heroic, macho, male, manful, masculine, muscular, noble, powerful, red-blooded (*informal*), resolute, robust, stout-hearted, strapping, strong, valiant, valorous, vigorous, well-built
➤ **Antonyms**
camp (*informal*), cowardly, craven, delicate, effeminate, faint-hearted, feeble, feminine, frail, girlie, ignoble, irresolute, sickly, soft, timid, unmanly, weak, wimpish *or* wimpy (*informal*), womanish, wussy (*slang*)

man-made *adjective* = **artificial**, ersatz, manufactured, mock, plastic (*slang*), synthetic

manner *noun* 1 = **behaviour**, air, appearance, aspect, bearing, comportment, conduct, demeanour, deportment, look, mien (*literary*), presence, tone 2 = **style**, approach, custom, fashion, form, genre, habit, line, means, method, mode, practice, procedure, process, routine, tack, tenor, usage, way, wont 3 = **type**, brand, breed, category, form, kind, nature, sort, variety

mannered *adjective* = **affected**, artificial, arty-farty (*informal*), posed, pretentious, pseudo (*informal*), put-on, stilted
➤ **Antonyms**
genuine, honest, natural, real, sincere, unaffected, unpretentious

mannerism *noun* = **habit**, characteristic, foible, idiosyncrasy, peculiarity, quirk, trait, trick

mannerly *adjective* = **polite**, civil, civilized, courteous, decorous, genteel, gentlemanly, gracious, ladylike, polished, refined, respectful, well-behaved, well-bred, well-mannered
➤ **Antonyms**
boorish, discourteous, disrespectful, ill-mannered, impertinent, impolite, impudent, insolent, rude, unmannerly

manners *plural noun* 1 = **behaviour**, bearing, breeding, carriage, comportment, conduct, demeanour, deportment 2 = **politeness**, ceremony, courtesy, decorum, etiquette, formalities, good form, polish, politesse, proprieties, protocol, p's and q's, refinement, social graces, the done thing

manoeuvre *verb* 1 = **manipulate**, contrive, devise, engineer, intrigue, machinate, manage, plan, plot, pull strings, scheme, wangle (*informal*) 2 = **move**, deploy, exercise 3 = **steer**, direct, drive, guide,

handle, navigate, negotiate, pilot ♦ *noun* 4 = **movement**, deployment, evolution, exercise, operation 5 = **stratagem**, action, artifice, dodge, intrigue, machination, move, movement, plan, plot, ploy, ruse, scheme, subterfuge, tactic, trick

mansion *noun* = **residence**, abode, dwelling, habitation, hall, manor, seat, villa

mantle *noun* 1 = **cloak**, cape, hood, shawl, wrap 2 = **covering**, blanket, canopy, cloud, cover, curtain, envelope, pall, screen, shroud, veil ♦ *verb* 3 = **cover**, blanket, cloak, cloud, disguise, envelop, hide, mask, overspread, screen, shroud, veil, wrap

manual *adjective* 1 = **hand-operated**, done by hand, human, physical ♦ *noun* 2 = **handbook**, bible, guide, guidebook, instructions, workbook

manufacture *verb* 1 = **make**, assemble, build, compose, construct, create, fabricate, forge, form, mass-produce, mould, process, produce, put together, shape, turn out 2 = **concoct**, cook up (*informal*), devise, fabricate, hatch, invent, make up, think up, trump up ♦ *noun* 3 = **making**, assembly, construction, creation, fabrication, mass-production, produce, production

manufacturer *noun* = **maker**, builder, constructor, creator, fabricator, factory-owner, industrialist, producer

manure *noun* = **compost**, droppings, dung, excrement, fertilizer, muck, ordure

many *adjective* 1 = **numerous**, abundant, copious, countless, divers (*archaic*), frequent, innumerable, manifold, multifarious, multifold, multitudinous, myriad, profuse, sundry, umpteen (*informal*), varied, various ♦ *noun* 2 = **a lot**, a horde, a mass, a multitude, a thousand and one, heaps (*informal*), large numbers, lots (*informal*), piles (*informal*), plenty, scores, tons (*informal*), umpteen (*informal*) 3 **the many** = **the masses**, the crowd, (the) hoi polloi, the majority, the multitude, the people, the rank and file

mar *verb* = **spoil**, blemish, blight, blot, damage, deface, detract from, disfigure, harm, hurt, impair, injure, maim, mangle, mutilate, put a damper on, ruin, scar, stain, sully, taint, tarnish, vitiate
➤ **Antonyms**
adorn, ameliorate, better, embellish, improve, ornament

maraud *verb* = **raid**, despoil, forage, foray, harry, loot, pillage, plunder, ransack, ravage, reive (*dialect*), sack

marauder *noun* = **raider**, bandit, brigand, buccaneer, cateran (*Scot.*), corsair, freebooter, mosstrooper, outlaw, pillager, pirate, plunderer, ravager, reiver (*dialect*), robber, sea wolf

march *verb* 1 = **walk**, file, footslog, pace, parade, stalk, stride, strut, tramp, tread ♦ *noun* 2 = **stride**, gait, pace, step 3 = **walk**, hike, routemarch, tramp, trek 4 = **progress**, advance, development, evolution, progression 5 = **demonstration**, demo (*informal*), parade, procession 6 **on the march** = **advancing**, afoot, astir, en route, marching, on one's way, on the way, proceeding, progressing, under way

marches *plural noun* = **borders**, borderland, boundaries, confines, frontiers, limits, marchlands

margin *noun* 1 = **edge**, border, bound, boundary, brim, brink, confine, limit, perimeter, periphery, rim, side, verge 2 = **room**, allowance, compass, elbowroom, extra, latitude, leeway, play, scope, space, surplus

marginal *adjective* 1 = **borderline**, bordering, on the edge, peripheral 2 = **insignificant**, low, minimal, minor, negligible, slight, small

marijuana *noun* = **cannabis**, bhang, blow (*slang*), charas, chronic (*U.S. slang*), dope (*slang*), gage (*U.S. old-fashioned slang*), ganja, grass (*slang*), hash (*slang*), hashish, hemp, kif, leaf (*slang*), mary jane (*U.S. slang*), pot (*slang*), sinsemilla, smoke (*informal*), stuff (*slang*), tea (*U.S. slang*), wacky baccy (*slang*), weed (*slang*)

marine *adjective* = **nautical**, maritime, naval, ocean-going, oceanic, pelagic, saltwater, sea, seafaring, seagoing, thalassic

mariner *noun* = **sailor**, bluejacket, gob (*U.S. slang*), hand, Jack Tar, matelot (*slang, chiefly Brit.*), navigator, salt, sea dog, seafarer, seafaring man, seaman, tar

marital *adjective* = **matrimonial**, conjugal, connubial, married, nuptial, spousal, wedded

maritime *adjective* 1 = **nautical**, marine, naval, oceanic, sea, seafaring 2 = **coastal**, littoral, seaside

mark *noun* 1 = **spot**, blemish, blot, blotch, bruise, dent, impression, line, nick, pock, scar, scratch, smirch, smudge, splotch, stain, streak 2 = **sign**, badge, blaze, brand, characteristic, device, earmark, emblem, evidence, feature, flag, hallmark, impression, incision, index, indication, label, note, print, proof, seal, signet, stamp, symbol, symptom, token 3 = **criterion**, level, measure, norm, par, standard, yardstick 4 = **target**, aim, end, goal, object, objective, purpose 5 = **influence**, consequence, dignity, distinction, eminence, fame, importance, notability, note, notice, prestige, quality, regard, standing 6 = **track**, footmark, footprint, sign, trace, trail, vestige 7 **make** **one's mark** = **succeed**, achieve recognition, be a success, find a place in the sun, get on in the world, make a success of oneself, make good, make it (*informal*), make something of oneself, prosper ♦ *verb* 8 = **scar**, blemish, blot, blotch, brand, bruise, dent, impress, imprint, nick, scratch, smirch, smudge, splotch, stain, streak 9 = **characterize**, brand, flag, identify, label, stamp 10 = **distinguish**, betoken, denote, evince, exemplify, illustrate, show 11 = **observe**, attend, hearken (*archaic*), mind, note, notice, pay attention, pay heed, regard, remark, watch 12 = **grade**, appraise, assess, correct, evaluate

marked *adjective* = **noticeable**, apparent, blatant, clear, considerable, conspicuous, decided, distinct, dramatic, evident, manifest, notable, noted, obvious, outstanding, patent, prominent, pronounced, remarkable, salient, signal, striking

➤ **Antonyms**
concealed, doubtful, dubious, hidden, imperceptible, inconspicuous, indistinct, insignificant, obscure, unclear, unnoticeable, vague

markedly *adverb* = **noticeably**, clearly, considerably, conspicuously, decidedly, distinctly, evidently, greatly, manifestly, notably, obviously, outstandingly, patently, remarkably, seriously (*informal*), signally, strikingly, to a great extent

market *noun* 1 = **fair**, bazaar, mart ♦ *verb* 2 = **sell**, offer for sale, retail, vend

marketable *adjective* = **sought after**, in demand, merchantable, saleable, vendible, wanted

marksman, markswoman *noun* = **sharpshooter**, crack shot (*informal*), deadeye (*informal, chiefly U.S.*), dead shot (*informal*), good shot

maroon *verb* = **abandon**, cast ashore, cast away, desert, leave, leave high and dry (*informal*), strand

marriage *noun* 1 = **wedding**, espousal, match, matrimony, nuptial rites, nuptials, wedding ceremony, wedlock 2 = **union**, alliance, amalgamation, association, confederation, coupling, link, merger

married *adjective* 1 = **wedded**, hitched (*slang*), joined, one, spliced (*informal*), united, wed 2 = **marital**, conjugal, connubial, husbandly, matrimonial, nuptial, spousal, wifely

marrow *noun* = **core**, cream, essence, gist, heart, kernel, pith, quick, quintessence, soul, spirit, substance

marry *verb* 1 = **wed**, become man and wife, espouse, get hitched (*slang*), get spliced (*informal*), plight one's troth (*old-fashioned*), take the plunge (*informal*), take to wife, tie the knot (*informal*), walk down the aisle (*informal*), wive (*archaic*) **2** = **unite**, ally, bond, join, knit, link, match, merge, splice, tie, unify, yoke

marsh *noun* = **swamp**, bog, fen, morass, moss (*Scot. & Northern English dialect*), quagmire, slough

marshal *verb* **1** = **arrange**, align, array, assemble, collect, deploy, dispose, draw up, gather, group, line up, muster, order, organize, rank, sequence **2** = **conduct**, escort, guide, lead, shepherd, usher

marshy *adjective* = **swampy**, boggy, fenny, miry, paludal, quaggy, spongy, waterlogged, wet

martial *adjective* = **military**, bellicose, belligerent, brave, heroic, soldierly, warlike

martinet *noun* = **disciplinarian**, drillmaster, stickler

martyrdom *noun* = **persecution**, agony, anguish, ordeal, suffering, torment, torture
➤ **Antonyms**
bliss, ecstasy, happiness, joy

marvel *verb* **1** = **wonder**, be amazed, be awed, be filled with surprise, gape, gaze, goggle ♦ *noun* **2** = **wonder**, genius, miracle, phenomenon, portent, prodigy, whizz (*informal*)

marvellous *adjective* **1** = **excellent**, awesome (*slang*), bad (*slang*), bodacious (*slang, chiefly U.S.*), boffo (*slang*), brill (*informal*), chillin' (*U.S. slang*), colossal, cracking (*Brit. informal*), crucial (*slang*), def (*slang*), divine (*informal*), fabulous (*informal*), fantastic (*informal*), glorious, great (*informal*), jim-dandy (*slang*), magnificent, mean (*slang*), mega (*slang*), sensational (*informal*), smashing (*informal*), sovereign, splendid, stupendous, super (*informal*), superb, terrific (*informal*), topping (*Brit. slang*), wicked (*informal*), wonderful **2** = **amazing**, astonishing, astounding, breathtaking, brilliant, extraordinary, jaw-dropping, miraculous, phenomenal, prodigious, remarkable, sensational (*informal*), singular, spectacular, stupendous, wondrous (*archaic or literary*)
➤ **Antonyms**
≠**excellent**: awful, bad, terrible ≠**amazing**: believable, commonplace, credible, everyday, ordinary

masculine *adjective* **1** = **male**, manful, manlike, manly, mannish, virile **2** = **strong**, bold, brave, butch (*slang*), gallant, hardy, macho, muscular, powerful, red-blooded (*informal*), resolute, robust, stout-hearted, strapping, vigorous, well-built

mask *noun* **1** = **visor**, domino, false face,

vizard (*archaic*) **2** = **disguise**, blind, camouflage, cloak, concealment, cover, cover-up, façade, front, guise, screen, semblance, show, veil, veneer ♦ *verb* **3** = **disguise**, camouflage, cloak, conceal, cover, hide, obscure, screen, veil

masquerade *verb* **1** = **pose**, disguise, dissemble, dissimulate, impersonate, pass oneself off, pretend (to be) ♦ *noun* **2** = **pretence**, cloak, cover-up, deception, disguise, mask, pose, screen, subterfuge **3** = **masked ball**, fancy dress party, revel

mass *noun* **1** = **piece**, block, chunk, concretion, hunk, lump **2** = **collection**, aggregate, body, entirety, sum, sum total, totality, whole **3** = **lot**, accumulation, aggregation, assemblage, batch, bunch, collection, combination, conglomeration, heap, load, pile, quantity, rick, stack **4** = **crowd**, assemblage, band, body, bunch (*informal*), group, horde, host, lot, mob, number, throng, troop **5** = **majority**, body, bulk, greater part, lion's share, preponderance **6** = **size**, bulk, dimension, greatness, magnitude **7** **the masses** = **the multitude**, the commonalty, the common people, the crowd, (the) hoi polloi ♦ *adjective* **8** = **large-scale**, extensive, general, indiscriminate, pandemic, popular, wholesale, widespread ♦ *verb* **9** = **gather**, accumulate, amass, assemble, collect, congregate, foregather, mob, muster, rally, swarm, throng

massacre *noun* **1** = **slaughter**, annihilation, blood bath, butchery, carnage, extermination, holocaust, killing, mass slaughter, murder ♦ *verb* **2** = **slaughter**, annihilate, blow away (*slang, chiefly U.S.*), butcher, cut to pieces, exterminate, kill, mow down, murder, slay, take out (*slang*), wipe out

massage *noun* **1** = **rub-down**, acupressure, kneading, manipulation, reflexology, rubbing, shiatsu ♦ *verb* **2** = **rub down**, knead, manipulate, rub

massive *adjective* = **huge**, big, bulky, colossal, elephantine, enormous, extensive, gargantuan, gigantic, ginormous (*informal*), great, heavy, hefty, hulking, humongous *or* humungous (*U.S. slang*), immense, imposing, impressive, mammoth, mega (*slang*), monster, monumental, ponderous, solid, stellar (*informal*), substantial, titanic, vast, weighty, whacking (*informal*), whopping (*informal*)
➤ **Antonyms**
frail, light, little, minute, petty, slight, small, thin, tiny, trivial

master *noun* **1** = **head**, boss (*informal*), captain, chief, commander, controller, director, employer, governor, lord, manager,

overlord, overseer, owner, principal, ruler, skipper (*informal*), superintendent **2 = expert**, ace (*informal*), adept, dab hand (*Brit. informal*), doyen, genius, grandmaster, maestro, maven (*U.S.*), past master, pro (*informal*), virtuoso, wizard **3 = teacher**, guide, guru, instructor, pedagogue, preceptor, schoolmaster, spiritual leader, swami, torchbearer, tutor ♦ *adjective* **4 = main**, chief, controlling, foremost, grand, great, leading, predominant, prime, principal **5 = expert**, adept, crack (*informal*), masterly, proficient, skilful, skilled ♦ *verb* **6 = learn**, acquire, become proficient in, get the hang of (*informal*), grasp **7 = overcome**, bridle, check, conquer, curb, defeat, lick (*informal*), overpower, quash, quell, subdue, subjugate, suppress, tame, triumph over, vanquish **8 = control**, command, direct, dominate, govern, manage, regulate, rule
➤ Antonyms
noun ≠**head**: crew, servant, slave, subject ≠**expert**: amateur, novice ≠**teacher**: student ♦ *adjective* ≠**main**: lesser, minor ≠**expert**: amateurish, clumsy, incompetent, inept, novice, unaccomplished, unskilled, untalented ♦ *verb* ≠**overcome**: cave in (*informal*), give in, surrender, yield

masterful *adjective* **1 = skilful**, adept, adroit, clever, consummate, crack (*informal*), deft, dexterous, excellent, expert, exquisite, fine, finished, first-rate, masterly, skilled, superior, superlative, supreme, world-class **2 = domineering**, arrogant, authoritative, bossy (*informal*), despotic, dictatorial, high-handed, imperious, magisterial, overbearing, overweening, peremptory, self-willed, tyrannical
➤ Antonyms
≠**skilful**: amateurish, clumsy, incompetent, inept, unaccomplished, unskilled, untalented ≠**domineering**: irresolute, meek, spineless, weak, wimpish *or* wimpy (*informal*), wussy (*slang*)

masterly *adjective* **= skilful**, adept, adroit, clever, consummate, crack (*informal*), dexterous, excellent, expert, exquisite, fine, finished, first-rate, masterful, skilled, superior, superlative, supreme, world-class

mastermind *verb* **1 = plan**, be the brains behind (*informal*), conceive, devise, direct, manage, organize ♦ *noun* **2 = organizer**, architect, authority, brain(s) (*informal*), brainbox, director, engineer, genius, intellect, manager, planner, virtuoso

masterpiece *noun* **= classic**, chef-d'oeuvre, jewel, magnum opus, master work, *pièce de résistance, tour de force*

mastery *noun* **1 = expertise**, ability, acquirement, attainment, cleverness, deftness, dexterity, finesse, know-how,

(*informal*), proficiency, prowess, skill, virtuosity **2 = control**, ascendancy, authority, command, conquest, domination, dominion, pre-eminence, rule, superiority, supremacy, sway, triumph, upper hand, victory, whip hand **3 = understanding**, command, comprehension, familiarity, grasp, grip, knowledge

match *noun* **1 = game**, bout, competition, contest, head-to-head, test, trial **2 = equal**, competitor, counterpart, equivalent, peer, rival **3 = companion**, complement, counterpart, equal, equivalent, fellow, mate, tally **4 = replica**, copy, dead ringer (*slang*), double, duplicate, equal, lookalike, ringer (*slang*), spit (*informal, chiefly Brit.*), spit and image (*informal*), spitting image (*informal*), twin **5 = marriage**, affiliation, alliance, combination, couple, duet, item (*informal*), pair, pairing, partnership, union ♦ *verb* **6 = correspond**, accompany, accord, adapt, agree, blend, coordinate, fit, go with, harmonize, suit, tally, tone with **7 = pair**, ally, combine, couple, join, link, marry, mate, unite, yoke **8 = rival**, compare, compete, contend, emulate, equal, measure up to, oppose, pit against, vie

matching *adjective* **= identical**, analogous, comparable, coordinating, corresponding, double, duplicate, equal, equivalent, like, paired, parallel, same, toning, twin
➤ Antonyms
different, disparate, dissimilar, distinct, divergent, diverse, nonparallel, other, unequal, unlike

matchless *adjective* **= unequalled**, consummate, exquisite, incomparable, inimitable, peerless, perfect, superlative, supreme, unique, unmatched, unparalleled, unrivalled, unsurpassed
➤ Antonyms
average, common, commonplace, comparable, equalled, everyday, excelled, inferior, lesser, mediocre, no great shakes (*informal*), ordinary, second-class, surpassed

mate *noun* **1** *Informal* **= friend**, buddy (*informal*), china (*Brit. slang*), chum (*informal*), cock (*Brit. informal*), comrade, crony, homeboy (*slang, chiefly U.S.*), pal (*informal*) **2 = colleague**, associate, companion, compeer, co-worker, fellow-worker **3 = partner**, better half (*humorous*), husband *or* wife, significant other (*U.S. informal*), spouse **4 = assistant**, helper, subordinate **5 = double**, companion, fellow, match, twin ♦ *verb* **6 = pair**, breed, copulate, couple **7 = marry**, match, wed **8 = join**, couple, match, pair, yoke

material *noun* **1 = substance**, body, constituents, element, matter, stuff **2 = cloth**, fabric, stuff **3 = information**, data, evidence, facts, notes, work ◆ *adjective* **4** = **physical**, bodily, concrete, corporeal, fleshly, nonspiritual, palpable, substantial, tangible, worldly **5** = **relevant**, applicable, apposite, apropos, germane, pertinent **6** = **important**, consequential, essential, grave, indispensable, key, meaningful, momentous, serious, significant, vital, weighty

materialize *verb* = **occur**, appear, come about, come into being, come to pass, happen, take place, take shape, turn up

materially *adverb* = **significantly**, considerably, essentially, gravely, greatly, much, seriously, substantially
➤ **Antonyms**
barely, hardly, insignificantly, little, scarcely, superficially, unsubstantially

maternal *adjective* = **motherly**

maternity *noun* = **motherhood**, motherliness

matey *adjective Brit. informal* = **friendly**, amiable, chummy (*informal*), companionable, comradely, free-and-easy, hail-fellow-well-met, intimate, pally (*informal*), palsy-walsy (*informal*), sociable, thick (*informal*)

matrimonial *adjective* = **marital**, conjugal, connubial, hymeneal, married, nuptial, spousal, wedded, wedding

matrimony *noun* = **marriage**, marital rites, nuptials, wedding ceremony, wedlock

matted *adjective* = **tangled**, knotted, tousled, uncombed

matter *noun* **1** = **substance**, body, material, stuff **2** = **situation**, affair, business, concern, episode, event, incident, issue, occurrence, proceeding, question, subject, thing, topic, transaction **3** = **amount**, quantity, sum **4** = **content**, argument, purport, sense, subject, substance, text, thesis **5** *Medical* = **pus**, discharge, purulence, secretion **6** = **importance**, consequence, import, moment, note, significance, weight **7** *As in* **what's the matter?** = **problem**, complication, difficulty, distress, trouble, upset, worry ◆ *verb* **8** = **be important**, be of consequence, carry weight, count, have influence, make a difference, mean something, signify

matter-of-fact *adjective* = **unsentimental**, deadpan, down-to-earth, dry, dull, emotionless, flat, lifeless, mundane, plain, prosaic, sober, unembellished, unimaginative, unvarnished

mature *adjective* **1** = **grown-up**, adult, complete, fit, full-blown, full-grown, fully fledged, grown, matured, mellow, of age, perfect, prepared, ready, ripe, ripened, seasoned ◆ *verb* **2** = **develop**, age, become adult, bloom, blossom, come of age, grow

up, maturate, mellow, perfect, reach adulthood, ripen, season
➤ **Antonyms**
adjective ≠**grown-up**: adolescent, childish, green, immature, incomplete, juvenile, puerile, undeveloped, unfinished, unperfected, unripe, young, youthful

maturity *noun* = **adulthood**, completion, experience, full bloom, full growth, fullness, majority, manhood *or* womanhood, maturation, matureness, perfection, ripeness, wisdom
➤ **Antonyms**
childishness, immaturity, imperfection, incompletion, juvenility, puerility, youthfulness

maudlin *adjective* = **sentimental**, icky (*informal*), lachrymose, mawkish, mushy (*informal*), overemotional, slushy (*informal*), soppy (*Brit. informal*), tearful, weepy (*informal*)

maul *verb* **1** = **tear**, claw, lacerate, mangle **2** = **ill-treat**, abuse, batter, beat, beat up (*informal*), handle roughly, knock about *or* around, manhandle, molest, pummel, rough up, thrash, work over (*slang*)

maunder *verb* **1** = **idle**, dawdle, dilly-dally (*informal*), drift, loaf, meander, mooch (*slang*), potter, ramble, straggle, stray, traipse (*Informal*) **2** = **chatter**, babble, blather, blether, gabble, prattle, rabbit (on) (*Brit. informal*), ramble, rattle on, waffle (*informal, chiefly Brit.*), witter (*informal*)

maverick *noun* **1** = **rebel**, dissenter, dissentient, eccentric, heretic, iconoclast, individualist, nonconformist, protester, radical ◆ *adjective* **2** = **rebel**, dissenting, eccentric, heretical, iconoclastic, individualistic, nonconformist, radical
➤ **Antonyms**
noun ≠**rebel**: Babbitt (*U.S.*), conventionalist, stick-in-the-mud (*informal*), traditionalist, yes man

mawkish *adjective* = **sentimental**, emotional, feeble, gushy (*informal*), icky (*informal*), maudlin, mushy (*informal*), schmaltzy (*slang*), slushy (*informal*), soppy (*Brit. informal*), three-hankie (*informal*)

maxim *noun* = **saying**, adage, aphorism, apophthegm, axiom, byword, dictum, gnome, motto, proverb, rule, saw

maximum *noun* **1** = **top**, apogee, ceiling, crest, extremity, height, most, peak, pinnacle, summit, upper limit, utmost, uttermost, zenith ◆ *adjective* **2** = **greatest**, highest, maximal, most, paramount, supreme, topmost, utmost
➤ **Antonyms**
noun ≠**top**: bottom, minimum ◆ *adjective* ≠**greatest**: least, lowest, minimal

maybe *adverb* = **perhaps**, it could be, mayhap (*archaic*), peradventure (*archaic*), perchance (*archaic*), possibly

mayhem *noun* = **chaos**, commotion, confusion, destruction, disorder, fracas, havoc, trouble, violence

maze *noun* 1 = **labyrinth**, convolutions, intricacy, meander 2 = **web**, bewilderment, confusion, imbroglio, mesh, perplexity, puzzle, snarl, tangle, uncertainty

meadow *noun* = **field**, grassland, lea (*poetic*), ley, pasture

meagre *adjective* 1 = **insubstantial**, deficient, exiguous, inadequate, little, measly, paltry, pathetic, poor, puny, scant, scanty, scrimpy, short, skimpy, slender, slight, small, spare, sparse 2 = **thin**, bony, emaciated, gaunt, hungry, lank, lean, scraggy, scrawny, skinny, starved, underfed

mean[1] *verb* 1 = **intend**, aim, aspire, contemplate, design, desire, have in mind, plan, propose, purpose, set out, want, wish 2 = **signify**, betoken, connote, convey, denote, drive at, express, hint at, imply, indicate, purport, represent, say, spell, stand for, suggest, symbolize 3 = **destine**, design, fate, fit, make, match, predestine, preordain, suit 4 = **result in**, bring about, cause, engender, entail, give rise to, involve, lead to, necessitate, produce 5 = **foretell**, adumbrate, augur, betoken, foreshadow, herald, portend, presage, promise

mean[2] *adjective* 1 = **miserly**, beggarly, close (*informal*), mercenary, mingy (*Brit. informal*), near (*informal*), niggardly, parsimonious, penny-pinching, penurious, selfish, skimpy, snoep (*S. African informal*), stingy, tight, tight-arsed (*taboo slang*), tight as a duck's arse (*taboo slang*), tight-assed (*U.S. taboo slang*), tight-fisted, ungenerous 2 = **dishonourable**, abject, base, callous, contemptible, degenerate, degraded, despicable, disgraceful, hard-hearted, ignoble, low-minded, narrow-minded, petty, scurvy, shabby, shameful, sordid, vile, wretched 3 = **malicious**, bad-tempered, cantankerous, churlish, disagreeable, hostile, ill-tempered, nasty, rude, sour, unfriendly, unpleasant 4 = **shabby**, beggarly, contemptible, down-at-heel, grungy (*slang, chiefly U.S.*), insignificant, low-rent (*informal, chiefly U.S.*), miserable, paltry, poor, run-down, scruffy, scuzzy (*slang, chiefly U.S.*), seedy, sordid, squalid, tawdry, wretched 5 = **lowly**, base, baseborn (*archaic*), common, humble, ignoble, inferior, low, lowborn, menial, modest, obscure, ordinary, plebeian, proletarian, servile, undistinguished, vulgar

➤ **Antonyms**

≠**miserly**: altruistic, big, bountiful, generous,

munificent, prodigal, unselfish ≠**dishonourable**: good, honourable, praiseworthy ≠**malicious**: compassionate, gentle, humane, kind, sympathetic, warm-hearted ≠**shabby**: attractive, choice, de luxe, excellent, first-rate, pleasing, superb, superior ≠**lowly**: consequential, high, important, noble, princely, significant

mean[3] *noun* 1 = **average**, balance, compromise, happy medium, median, middle, middle course or way, midpoint, norm ♦ *adjective* 2 = **average**, intermediate, medial, median, medium, middle, middling, normal, standard

meander *verb* 1 = **wind**, snake, turn, zigzag 2 = **wander**, ramble, stravaig (*Scot. & Northern English dialect*), stray, stroll ♦ *noun* 3 = **curve**, bend, coil, loop, turn, twist, zigzag

meandering *adjective* = **winding**, anfractuous, circuitous, convoluted, indirect, roundabout, serpentine, snaking, tortuous, wandering

➤ **Antonyms**

direct, straight, straightforward, undeviating

meaning *noun* 1 = **sense**, connotation, denotation, drift, explanation, gist, implication, import, interpretation, message, purport, significance, signification, substance, upshot, value 2 = **purpose**, aim, design, end, goal, idea, intention, object, plan, point, trend 3 = **force**, effect, efficacy, point, thrust, use, usefulness, validity, value, worth ♦ *adjective* 4 = **expressive**, eloquent, meaningful, pointed, pregnant, speaking, suggestive

meaningful *adjective* 1 = **significant**, important, material, purposeful, relevant, serious, useful, valid, worthwhile 2 = **expressive**, eloquent, meaning, pointed, pregnant, speaking, suggestive

➤ **Antonyms**

≠**significant**: inconsequential, insignificant, meaningless, senseless, superficial, trivial, unimportant, useless, worthless

meaningless *adjective* = **pointless**, aimless, empty, futile, hollow, inane, inconsequential, insignificant, insubstantial, nonsensical, nugatory, purposeless, senseless, trifling, trivial, useless, vain, valueless, wanky (*taboo slang*), worthless

➤ **Antonyms**

consequential, deep, evident, important, meaningful, obvious, purposeful, sensible, significant, useful, valuable, worthwhile

meanness *noun* 1 = **miserliness**, minginess (*Brit. informal*), niggardliness, parsimony, penuriousness, selfishness, stinginess, tight-fistedness 2 = **pettiness**, abjectness, baseness, degeneracy, degradation, despicableness, disgracefulness, dishonourableness, ignobility, low-mindedness, narrow-mindedness, scurviness, shabbiness, shamefulness, sordidness, vileness, wretchedness **3 = malice**, bad temper, cantankerousness, churlishness, disagreeableness, hostility, ill temper, maliciousness, nastiness, rudeness, sourness, unfriendliness, unpleasantness **4 = shabbiness**, beggarliness, contemptibleness, insignificance, paltriness, pettiness, poorness, scruffiness, seediness, sordidness, squalor, tawdriness, wretchedness **5 = lowliness**, baseness, humbleness, obscurity, servility

means *noun* **1 = method**, agency, avenue, channel, course, expedient, instrument, measure, medium, mode, process, way ◆ *plural noun* **2 = money**, affluence, capital, estate, fortune, funds, income, property, resources, riches, substance, wealth, wherewithal **3 by all means = certainly**, absolutely, definitely, doubtlessly, of course, positively, surely **4 by means of = by way of**, by dint of, through, using, utilizing, via, with the aid of **5 by no means = in no way**, absolutely not, definitely not, not at all, not in the least, not in the slightest, not the least bit, no way, on no account

meantime, meanwhile *adverb* **= at the same time**, concurrently, for now, for the duration, for the moment, for then, in the interim, in the interval, in the intervening time, in the meantime, in the meanwhile, simultaneously

measly *adjective* **= meagre**, miserable, paltry, pathetic, pitiful, poor, puny, scanty, skimpy

measurable *adjective* **= quantifiable**, assessable, computable, determinable, gaugeable, material, mensurable, perceptible, quantitative, significant

measure *noun* **1 = quantity**, allotment, allowance, amount, amplitude, capacity, degree, extent, magnitude, portion, proportion, quota, range, ration, reach, scope, share, size **2 = gauge**, metre, rule, scale, yardstick **3 = standard**, criterion, example, model, norm, par, test, touchstone, yardstick **4 = action**, act, course, deed, expedient, manoeuvre, means, procedure, proceeding, step **5 = law**, act, bill, enactment, resolution, statute **6 = rhythm**, beat, cadence, foot, metre, verse **7** *As in* **beyond measure = limit**, bounds, control, limitation, moderation, restraint **8 for good measure = in addition**, as a bonus, besides, into the bargain, to boot ◆ *verb* **9 = quantify**, appraise, assess, calculate, calibrate, compute, determine, estimate, evaluate, gauge, judge, mark out, rate, size, sound, survey, value, weigh

measured *adjective* **1 = steady**, dignified, even, leisurely, regular, sedate, slow, solemn, stately, unhurried **2 = considered**, calculated, deliberate, reasoned, sober, studied, well-thought-out

measureless *adjective* **= infinite**, beyond measure, boundless, endless, immeasurable, immense, incalculable, inestimable, limitless, unbounded, vast

measurement *noun* **1 = calculation**, appraisal, assessment, calibration, computation, estimation, evaluation, judgment, mensuration, metage, survey, valuation **2 = size**, amount, amplitude, area, capacity, depth, dimension, extent, height, length, magnitude, volume, weight, width

measure out *verb* **= dispense**, allot, apportion, assign, deal out, distribute, divide, divvy up (*informal*), dole out, issue, mete out, parcel out, pour out, share out

measure up to *verb* **= fulfil the expectations**, be adequate, be capable, be equal to, be fit, be suitable, be suited, come up to scratch (*informal*), come up to standard, compare, cut the mustard (*U.S. slang*), equal, fit *or* fit the bill, make the grade (*informal*), match, meet, rival

meat *noun* **1 = food**, aliment, cheer, chow (*informal*), comestibles, eats (*slang*), fare, flesh, grub (*slang*), nosh (*slang*), nourishment, nutriment, provender, provisions, rations, subsistence, sustenance, viands, victuals **2 = gist**, core, essence, heart, kernel, marrow, nub, nucleus, pith, point, substance

meaty *adjective* **1 = brawny**, beefy (*informal*), burly, fleshy, heavily built, heavy, husky (*informal*), muscular, solid, strapping, sturdy **2 = interesting**, meaningful, pithy, profound, rich, significant, substantial **3 = substantial**, hearty, nourishing, rich

mechanical *adjective* **1 = automatic**, automated, machine-driven **2 = unthinking**, automatic, cold, cursory, dead, emotionless, habitual, impersonal, instinctive, involuntary, lacklustre, lifeless, machine-like, matter-of-fact, perfunctory, routine, spiritless, unconscious, unfeeling ➤ **Antonyms** ≠**automatic:** manual ≠**unthinking:** conscious, genuine, sincere, thinking, voluntary, warm, wholehearted

mechanism *noun* **1 = workings**, action, components, gears, innards (*informal*), machinery, motor, works **2 = machine**, apparatus, appliance, contrivance, device, instrument, structure, system, tool **3 = process**, agency, execution, functioning, means, medium, method, methodology, operation, performance, procedure, system, technique, way, workings

meddle *verb* = **interfere**, butt in, intermeddle, interpose, intervene, intrude, pry, put one's oar in, put one's two cents in (*U.S. slang*), stick one's nose in (*informal*), tamper

meddlesome *adjective* = **interfering**, intrusive, meddling, mischievous, officious, prying

mediate *verb* = **intervene**, act as middleman, arbitrate, bring to an agreement, bring to terms, conciliate, intercede, interpose, make peace between, moderate, reconcile, referee, resolve, restore harmony, settle, step in (*informal*), umpire

mediation *noun* = **arbitration**, conciliation, intercession, intervention, reconciliation

mediator *noun* = **negotiator**, advocate, arbiter, arbitrator, go-between, honest broker, interceder, intermediary, judge, middleman, moderator, peacemaker, referee, umpire

medicinal *adjective* = **therapeutic**, analeptic, curative, healing, medical, remedial, restorative, roborant, sanative

medicine *noun* = **remedy**, cure, drug, medicament, medication, nostrum, physic

medieval *adjective* **1** = **Gothic 2** *Informal* = **old-fashioned**, antediluvian, antiquated, antique, archaic, primitive, unenlightened

mediocre *adjective* = **second-rate**, average, banal, bog-standard (*Brit. & Irish slang*), commonplace, fair to middling (*informal*), indifferent, inferior, insignificant, mean, medium, middling, no great shakes (*informal*), ordinary, passable, pedestrian, run-of-the-mill, so-so (*informal*), tolerable, undistinguished, uninspired, vanilla (*slang*)
➤ **Antonyms**
distinctive, distinguished, excellent, extraordinary, fine, incomparable, superb, superior, unexcelled, unique, unrivalled, unsurpassed

mediocrity *noun* = **insignificance**, commonplaceness, indifference, inferiority, meanness, ordinariness, poorness, unimportance

meditate *verb* **1** = **reflect**, be in a brown study, cogitate, consider, contemplate, deliberate, muse, ponder, ruminate, study, think **2** = **plan**, consider, contemplate, design, devise, have in mind, intend, mull over, purpose, scheme, think over

meditation *noun* = **reflection**, brown study, cerebration, cogitation, concentration, contemplation, musing, pondering, reverie, ruminating, rumination, study, thought

medium *adjective* **1** = **average**, fair, intermediate, mean, medial, median,

mediocre, middle, middling, midway
♦ *noun* **2** = **middle**, average, centre, compromise, mean, middle course, middle ground, middle path, middle way, midpoint **3** = **means**, agency, avenue, channel, form, instrument, instrumentality, mode, organ, vehicle, way **4** = **spiritualist**, channeller, spiritist **5** = **environment**, atmosphere, conditions, element, habitat, influences, milieu, setting, surroundings
➤ **Antonyms**
adjective ≠**average**: curious, distinctive, extraordinary, extreme, uncommon, unique, unusual, utmost

medley *noun* = **mixture**, assortment, confusion, farrago, gallimaufry, hodgepodge, hotchpotch, jumble, *mélange*, miscellany, mishmash, mixed bag (*informal*), olio, omnium-gatherum, pastiche, patchwork, potpourri, salmagundi

meek *adjective* = **submissive**, acquiescent, compliant, deferential, docile, forbearing, gentle, humble, long-suffering, mild, modest, patient, peaceful, soft, timid, unassuming, unpretentious, yielding
➤ **Antonyms**
arrogant, bold, bossy, domineering, feisty (*informal, chiefly U.S. & Canad.*), forward, immodest, overbearing, presumptuous, pretentious, proud, self-assertive, spirited, wilful

meekness *noun* = **submissiveness**, acquiescence, compliance, deference, docility, forbearance, gentleness, humbleness, humility, long-suffering, lowliness, mildness, modesty, patience, peacefulness, resignation, softness, submission, timidity

meet *verb* **1** = **encounter**, bump into, chance on, come across, confront, contact, find, happen on, run across, run into **2** = **converge**, abut, adjoin, come together, connect, cross, intersect, join, link up, touch, unite **3** = **gather**, assemble, collect, come together, congregate, convene, foregather, muster, rally **4** = **fulfil**, answer, carry out, come up to, comply with, cope with, discharge, equal, gratify, handle, match, measure up to, perform, satisfy **5** = **experience**, bear, encounter, endure, face, go through, suffer, undergo
➤ **Antonyms**
≠**encounter**: avoid, elude, escape, miss ≠**converge**: diverge ≠**gather**: adjourn, disperse, scatter ≠**fulfil**: fail, fall short, renege

meeting *noun* **1** = **encounter**, assignation, confrontation, engagement, introduction, rendezvous, tryst **2** = **conference**, assembly, audience, company, conclave, congregation, congress, convention, convocation, gathering, get-together (*informal*), meet, powwow, rally, reunion, session **3** = **convergence**, concourse, confluence, conjunction, crossing, intersection, junction, union

melancholy *noun* **1** = **sadness**, blues, dejection, depression, despondency, gloom, gloominess, low spirits, misery, pensiveness, sorrow, the hump (*Brit. informal*), unhappiness, woe ♦ *adjective* **2** = **sad**, blue, dejected, depressed, despondent, disconsolate, dismal, dispirited, doleful, down, downcast, downhearted, down in the dumps (*informal*), down in the mouth, gloomy, glum, heavy-hearted, joyless, low, low-spirited, lugubrious, melancholic, miserable, moody, mournful, pensive, sombre, sorrowful, unhappy, woebegone, woeful
➤ **Antonyms**
noun ≠ **sadness**: delight, gladness, happiness, joy, pleasure ♦ *adjective* ≠ **sad**: blithe, bright, cheerful, gay, glad, happy, jolly, joyful, joyous, light-hearted, lively, merry, sunny

melee, mêlée *noun* = **fight**, brawl, fracas, free-for-all (*informal*), rumpus, scrimmage, scuffle, set-to (*informal*), skirmish, tussle

mellifluous *adjective* = **sweet**, dulcet, euphonious, honeyed, silvery, smooth, soft, soothing, sweet-sounding

mellow *adjective* **1** = **tuneful**, dulcet, euphonic, full, mellifluous, melodious, rich, rounded, smooth, sweet, well-tuned **2** = **relaxed**, cheerful, cordial, elevated, expansive, genial, half-tipsy, happy, jolly, jovial, merry (*Brit. informal*) **3** = **ripe**, delicate, full-flavoured, juicy, mature, perfect, rich, soft, sweet, well-matured ♦ *verb* **4** = **mature**, develop, improve, perfect, ripen, season, soften, sweeten
➤ **Antonyms**
adjective ≠ **ripe**: green, immature, raw, sour, unripe

melodious *adjective* = **musical**, concordant, dulcet, euphonic, euphonious, harmonious, melodic, silvery, sweet-sounding, sweet-toned, tuneful
➤ **Antonyms**
cacophonous, discordant, grating, harsh, unharmonious, unmelodic, unmelodious, unmusical, untuneful

melodramatic *adjective* = **theatrical**, actorly, actressy, blood-and-thunder, extravagant, hammy (*informal*), histrionic, overdramatic, overemotional, sensational, stagy

melody *noun* **1** = **tune**, air, descant, music, refrain, song, strain, theme **2** = **tunefulness**, euphony, harmony, melodiousness, music, musicality

melt *verb* **1** = **dissolve**, deliquesce, diffuse, flux, fuse, liquefy, soften, thaw **2** *often with* **away** = **disappear**, disperse, dissolve, evanesce, evaporate, fade, vanish **3** = **soften**, disarm, mollify, relax, touch

member *noun* **1** = **representative**, associate, fellow **2** = **limb**, appendage, arm, component, constituent, element, extremity, leg, organ, part, portion

membership *noun* **1** = **members**, associates, body, fellows **2** = **participation**, belonging, enrolment, fellowship

memento *noun* = **souvenir**, keepsake, memorial, relic, remembrance, reminder, token, trophy

memoir *noun* = **account**, biography, essay, journal, life, monograph, narrative, record, register

memoirs *plural noun* = **autobiography**, diary, experiences, journals, life, life story, memories, recollections, reminiscences

memorable *adjective* = **noteworthy**, catchy, celebrated, distinguished, extraordinary, famous, historic, illustrious, important, impressive, momentous, notable, remarkable, signal, significant, striking, unforgettable
➤ **Antonyms**
commonplace, forgettable, insignificant, ordinary, trivial, undistinguished, unimportant, unimpressive, unmemorable

memorandum *noun* = **note**, communication, jotting, memo, message, minute, reminder

memorial *noun* **1** = **monument**, cairn, memento, plaque, record, remembrance, souvenir ♦ *adjective* **2** = **commemorative**, monumental

memorize *verb* = **remember**, commit to memory, con (*archaic*), get by heart, learn, learn by heart, learn by rote

memory *noun* **1** = **recall**, recollection, remembrance, reminiscence, retention **2** = **commemoration**, honour, remembrance **3** = **reputation**, celebrity, fame, glory, name, renown, repute

menace *verb* **1** = **threaten**, alarm, bode ill, browbeat, bully, frighten, impend, intimidate, loom, lour *or* lower, terrorize, utter threats to ♦ *noun* **2** = **threat**, commination, intimidation, scare, warning **3** = **danger**, hazard, jeopardy, peril **4** *Informal* = **nuisance**, annoyance, pest, plague, troublemaker

menacing *adjective* = **threatening**, alarming, baleful, bodeful, dangerous, forbidding, frightening, intimidating, intimidatory, looming, louring *or* lowering, minacious, minatory, ominous

> ➤ **Antonyms**
auspicious, encouraging, favourable,
promising

mend *verb* **1** = **repair**, cure, darn, fix, heal,
patch, rectify, refit, reform, remedy, renew,
renovate, restore, retouch **2** = **heal**,
convalesce, get better, recover, recuperate **3**
= **improve**, ameliorate, amend, better,
correct, emend, rectify, reform, revise
♦ *noun* **4** = **repair**, darn, patch, stitch **5 on
the mend** = **convalescent**, convalescing,
getting better, improving, recovering,
recuperating

mendacious *adjective* = **lying**, deceitful,
deceptive, dishonest, duplicitous, fallacious,
false, fraudulent, insincere, perfidious,
perjured, untrue, untruthful
> ➤ **Antonyms**
genuine, honest, true, truthful

menial *adjective* **1** = **unskilled**, boring, dull,
humdrum, low-status, routine **2** = **humble**,
abject, base, degrading, demeaning,
fawning, grovelling, ignoble, ignominious,
low, lowly, mean, obsequious, servile,
slavish, sorry, subservient, sycophantic, vile
♦ *noun* **3** = **servant**, attendant, dogsbody
(*informal*), domestic, drudge, flunky,
labourer, lackey, serf, skivvy (*chiefly Brit.*),
slave, underling, varlet (*archaic*), vassal
> ➤ **Antonyms**
adjective ≠**humble**: aristocratic, autocratic,
bossy, dignified, domineering, elevated,
haughty, high, noble, overbearing, proud
♦ *noun* ≠**servant**: boss, chief, commander,
lord, master, superior

menstruation *noun* = **period**, catamenia
(*Physiology*), courses (*Physiology*), the curse
(*informal*), flow (*informal*), menses,
menstrual cycle, monthly (*informal*)

mental *adjective* **1** = **intellectual**, cerebral **2**
Informal = **insane**, as daft as a brush
(*informal, chiefly Brit.*), deranged, disturbed,
lunatic, mad, mentally ill, not right in the
head, psychiatric, psychotic, round the bend
(*Brit. slang*), unbalanced, unstable

mentality *noun* = **attitude**, cast of mind,
character, disposition, frame of mind,
make-up, outlook, personality, psychology,
turn of mind, way of thinking

mentally *adverb* = **in the mind**, in one's
head, intellectually, inwardly,
psychologically, rationally, subjectively

mention *verb* **1** = **refer to**, acknowledge,
adduce, allude to, bring up, broach, call
attention to, cite, communicate, declare,
disclose, divulge, hint at, impart, intimate,
make known, name, point out, recount,
report, reveal, speak about *or* of, state, tell,
touch upon **2 not to mention** = **to say
nothing of**, as well as, besides, not counting

♦ *noun* **3** = **reference**, allusion,
announcement, indication, notification,
observation, remark **4** = **acknowledgment**,
citation, recognition, tribute

mentor *noun* = **guide**, adviser, coach,
counsellor, guru, instructor, teacher, tutor

menu *noun* = **bill of fare**, carte du jour,
tariff (*chiefly Brit.*)

mercantile *adjective* = **commercial**,
marketable, trade, trading

mercenary *noun* **1** = **hireling**, condottiere
(*History*), free companion (*History*),
freelance (*History*), soldier of fortune
♦ *adjective* **2** = **greedy**, acquisitive,
avaricious, bribable, covetous, grasping,
money-grubbing (*informal*), sordid, venal **3**
= **hired**, bought, paid, venal
> ➤ **Antonyms**
adjective ≠**greedy**: altruistic, benevolent,
generous, idealistic, liberal, munificent,
philanthropic, unselfish

merchandise *noun* **1** = **goods**,
commodities, produce, products, staples,
stock, stock in trade, truck, vendibles, wares
♦ *verb* **2** = **trade**, buy and sell, deal in,
distribute, do business in, market, retail, sell,
traffic in, vend

merchant *noun* = **tradesman**, broker,
dealer, purveyor, retailer, salesman, seller,
shopkeeper, supplier, trader, trafficker,
vendor, wholesaler

merciful *adjective* = **compassionate**,
beneficent, benignant, clement, forbearing,
forgiving, generous, gracious, humane, kind,
lenient, liberal, mild, pitying, soft, sparing,
sympathetic, tender-hearted
> ➤ **Antonyms**
cruel, hard-hearted, inhumane, merciless,
pitiless, uncompassionate, unfeeling

merciless *adjective* = **cruel**, barbarous,
callous, fell (*archaic*), hard, hard-hearted,
harsh, heartless, implacable, inexorable,
inhumane, pitiless, relentless, ruthless,
severe, unappeasable, unfeeling, unforgiving,
unmerciful, unpitying, unsparing,
unsympathetic

mercurial *adjective* = **lively**, active,
capricious, changeable, erratic, fickle, flighty,
gay, impulsive, inconstant, irrepressible,
light-hearted, mobile, quicksilver, spirited,
sprightly, temperamental, unpredictable,
unstable, variable, volatile
> ➤ **Antonyms**
consistent, constant, dependable, predictable,
reliable, stable, steady, unchanging

mercy *noun* **1** = **compassion**, benevolence,
charity, clemency, favour, forbearance,
forgiveness, grace, kindness, leniency, pity,
quarter **2** = **blessing**, benison (*archaic*),
boon, godsend, piece of luck, relief **3 at the**

mercy of = in the power of, defenceless against, exposed to, in the clutches of, naked before, open to, prey to, subject to, threatened by, unprotected against, vulnerable to
> **Antonyms**
≠compassion: brutality, cruelty, harshness, inhumanity, pitilessness, severity

mere *adjective* = **simple**, absolute, bare, common, complete, entire, nothing more than, plain, pure, pure and simple, sheer, stark, unadulterated, unmitigated, unmixed, utter

meretricious *adjective* = **trashy**, flashy, garish, gaudy, gimcrack, showy, tawdry, tinsel

merge *verb* = **combine**, amalgamate, become lost in, be swallowed up by, blend, coalesce, consolidate, converge, fuse, incorporate, intermix, join, meet, meld, melt into, mingle, mix, tone with, unite
> **Antonyms**
detach, diverge, divide, part, separate, sever

merger *noun* = **union**, amalgamation, coalition, combination, consolidation, fusion, incorporation

merit *noun* 1 = **worth**, advantage, asset, excellence, good, goodness, integrity, quality, strong point, talent, value, virtue, worthiness 2 = **claim**, credit, desert, due, right ♦ *verb* 3 = **deserve**, be entitled to, be worthy of, earn, have a claim to, have a right to, have coming to one, incur, rate, warrant

meritorious *adjective* = **praiseworthy**, admirable, commendable, creditable, deserving, excellent, exemplary, good, honourable, laudable, right, righteous, virtuous, worthy
> **Antonyms**
discreditable, dishonourable, ignoble, undeserving, unexceptional, unpraiseworthy

merriment *noun* = **fun**, amusement, conviviality, festivity, frolic, gaiety, glee, hilarity, jocularity, jollity, joviality, laughter, levity, liveliness, merrymaking, mirth, revelry, sport

merry *adjective* 1 = **cheerful**, blithe, blithesome, carefree, chirpy (*informal*), convivial, festive, frolicsome, fun-loving, gay, genial, glad, gleeful, happy, jocund, jolly, joyful, joyous, light-hearted, mirthful, rollicking, sportive, upbeat (*informal*), vivacious 2 *Brit. informal* = **tipsy**, elevated (*informal*), happy, mellow, squiffy (*Brit. informal*), tiddly (*slang, chiefly Brit.*) 3 = **comical**, amusing, comic, facetious, funny, hilarious, humorous, jocular, mirthful 4 **make merry = have fun**, carouse, celebrate, enjoy oneself, feast, frolic, have a good time,

make whoopee (*informal*), revel
> **Antonyms**
≠cheerful: dejected, dismal, down in the dumps (*informal*), gloomy, miserable, sad, unhappy

mesh *noun* 1 = **net**, netting, network, plexus, reticulation, tracery, web 2 = **trap**, entanglement, snare, tangle, toils, web ♦ *verb* 3 = **entangle**, catch, enmesh, ensnare, net, snare, tangle, trap 4 = **engage**, combine, come together, connect, coordinate, dovetail, fit together, harmonize, interlock, knit

mesmerize *verb* = **entrance**, absorb, captivate, enthral, fascinate, grip, hold spellbound, hypnotize, magnetize, spellbind

mess *noun* 1 = **disorder**, balls-up (*taboo slang*), bodge (*informal*), botch, chaos, clutter, cock-up (*Brit. slang*), confusion, dirtiness, disarray, disorganization, fuck-up (*offensive taboo slang*), grot (*slang*), hash, hodgepodge (*U.S.*), hotchpotch, jumble, litter, mishmash, pig's breakfast (*informal*), shambles, state, turmoil, untidiness 2 = **difficulty**, deep water, dilemma, fine kettle of fish (*informal*), fix (*informal*), hole (*informal*), hot water (*informal*), imbroglio, jam (*informal*), mix-up, muddle, perplexity, pickle (*informal*), plight, predicament, spot (*informal*), stew (*informal*), tight spot ♦ *verb* 3 *often with* **up = dirty**, befoul, besmirch, botch, bungle, clutter, cock up (*Brit. slang*), disarrange, dishevel, foul, fuck up (*offensive taboo slang*), litter, make a hash of (*informal*), make a nonsense of, make a pig's ear of (*informal*), muck up (*Brit. slang*), muddle, pollute, scramble 4 *often with* **with = interfere**, fiddle (*informal*), meddle, play, tamper, tinker

mess about or **around** *verb* 1 = **potter**, amuse oneself, dabble, fool (about *or* around), footle (*informal*), muck about (*informal*), piss about *or* around (*taboo slang*), play about *or* around, trifle 2 = **meddle**, fiddle (*informal*), fool (about *or* around), interfere, piss about *or* around (*taboo slang*), play, tamper, tinker, toy

message *noun* 1 = **communication**, bulletin, communiqué, dispatch, intimation, letter, memorandum, missive, note, notice, tidings, word 2 = **point**, idea, import, meaning, moral, purport, theme 3 *Scot.* = **errand**, commission, job, mission, task 4 **get the message = understand**, catch on (*informal*), comprehend, get it, get the point, see, take the hint, twig (*Brit. informal*)

messenger *noun* = **courier**, agent, bearer, carrier, delivery boy, emissary, envoy, errand-boy, go-between, harbinger, herald, runner

messy *adjective* = **untidy**, chaotic, cluttered,

confused, dirty, dishevelled, disordered, disorganized, grubby, littered, muddled, scuzzy (*slang, chiefly U.S.*), shambolic, sloppy (*informal*), slovenly, unkempt
➤ **Antonyms**
clean, meticulous, neat, ordered, orderly, shipshape, smart, squeaky-clean, tidy

metamorphosis *noun* = **transformation**, alteration, change, conversion, mutation, transmutation

metaphor *noun* = **figure of speech**, allegory, analogy, emblem, image, symbol, trope

metaphorical *adjective* = **figurative**, allegorical, emblematic, emblematical, symbolic, tropical (*rhetoric*)

metaphysical *adjective* **1** = **philosophical**, basic, esoteric, essential, eternal, fundamental, general, ideal, intellectual, profound, speculative, spiritual, subjective, universal **2** = **abstract**, abstruse, deep, high-flown, oversubtle, recondite, theoretical, transcendental **3** = **supernatural**, immaterial, impalpable, incorporeal, intangible, spiritual, unreal, unsubstantial

mete *verb* = **distribute**, administer, allot, apportion, assign, deal, dispense, divide, dole, measure, parcel, portion, ration, share

meteoric *adjective* = **spectacular**, brief, brilliant, dazzling, ephemeral, fast, flashing, fleeting, momentary, overnight, rapid, speedy, sudden, swift, transient
➤ **Antonyms**
gradual, lengthy, long, prolonged, slow, steady, unhurried

method *noun* **1** = **manner**, approach, arrangement, course, fashion, form, mode, modus operandi, plan, practice, procedure, process, programme, routine, rule, scheme, style, system, technique, way **2** = **orderliness**, design, form, order, organization, pattern, planning, purpose, regularity, structure, system

methodical *adjective* = **orderly**, businesslike, deliberate, disciplined, efficient, meticulous, neat, ordered, organized, painstaking, planned, precise, regular, structured, systematic, tidy, well-regulated
➤ **Antonyms**
casual, chaotic, confused, disordered, disorderly, haphazard, irregular, random, unmethodical

meticulous *adjective* = **thorough**, detailed, exact, fastidious, fussy, microscopic, painstaking, particular, perfectionist, precise, punctilious, scrupulous, strict
➤ **Antonyms**
careless, haphazard, imprecise, inexact, loose, negligent, slapdash, sloppy

métier *noun* **1** = **profession**, calling, craft,

line, occupation, pursuit, trade, vocation **2** = **strong point**, forte, long suit (*informal*), speciality, specialty, strong suit

metropolis *noun* = **city**, capital

mettle *noun* **1** = **courage**, ardour, balls (*taboo slang*), boldness, bottle (*Brit. slang*), bravery, daring, fire, fortitude, gallantry, gameness, grit, guts (*informal*), hardihood, heart, indomitability, life, nerve, pluck, resolution, resolve, spirit, spunk (*informal*), valour, vigour **2** = **character**, calibre, disposition, kidney, make-up, nature, quality, stamp, temper, temperament

microbe *noun* = **microorganism**, bacillus, bacterium, bug (*informal*), germ, virus

microscopic *adjective* = **tiny**, imperceptible, infinitesimal, invisible, minuscule, minute, negligible, teensy-weensy, teeny-weeny
➤ **Antonyms**
enormous, gigantic, ginormous (*informal*), great, huge, immense, large, vast

midday *noun* = **noon**, noonday, noontide, noontime, twelve noon, twelve o'clock

middle *noun* **1** = **centre**, focus, halfway point, heart, inside, mean, midpoint, midsection, midst, thick **2** = **waist**, midriff, midsection ◆ *adjective* **3** = **central**, halfway, inner, inside, intermediate, intervening, mean, medial, median, medium, mid

middle-class *adjective* = **bourgeois**, conventional, petit-bourgeois, suburban, traditional

middleman *noun* = **intermediary**, broker, distributor, entrepreneur, go-between

middling *adjective* **1** = **mediocre**, indifferent, run-of-the-mill, so-so (*informal*), tolerable, unexceptional, unremarkable **2** = **moderate**, adequate, all right, average, bog-standard (*Brit. & Irish slang*), fair, medium, modest, O.K. *or* okay (*informal*), ordinary, passable, serviceable

midget *noun* **1** = **dwarf**, gnome, homuncule, homunculus, manikin, munchkin (*informal, chiefly U.S.*), pygmy *or* pigmy, shrimp (*informal*), Tom Thumb ◆ *adjective* **2** = **tiny**, baby, dwarf, Lilliputian, little, miniature, pocket, pygmy *or* pigmy, small, teensy-weensy, teeny-weeny

midnight *noun* = **twelve o'clock**, dead of night, middle of the night, the witching hour, twelve o'clock at night

midst *noun* **1** = **middle**, bosom, centre, core, depths, heart, hub, interior, thick **2 in the midst of** = **among**, amidst, during, enveloped by, in the middle of, in the thick of, surrounded by

midway *adjective, adverb* = **halfway**, betwixt and between, in the middle

might *noun* 1 = **power**, ability, capability, capacity, clout (*informal*), efficacy, efficiency, energy, force, potency, prowess, puissance, strength, sway, valour, vigour 2 **with might and main** = **forcefully**, as hard as one can, as hard as possible, full blast, full force, lustily, manfully, mightily, vigorously, with all one's might *or* strength

mightily *adverb* 1 = **very**, decidedly, exceedingly, extremely, greatly, highly, hugely, intensely, much, seriously (*informal*), very much 2 = **powerfully**, energetically, forcefully, lustily, manfully, strongly, vigorously, with all one's might and main, with all one's strength

mighty *adjective* 1 = **powerful**, doughty, forceful, hardy, indomitable, lusty, manful, potent, puissant, robust, stalwart, stout, strapping, strong, sturdy, vigorous 2 = **great**, bulky, colossal, elephantine, enormous, gigantic, ginormous (*informal*), grand, huge, humongous *or* humungous (*U.S. slang*), immense, large, massive, mega (*slang*), monumental, prodigious, stellar (*informal*), stupendous, titanic, towering, tremendous, vast
➤ **Antonyms**
≠**powerful:** feeble, impotent, weak, weedy (*informal*), wimpish *or* wimpy (*informal*), wussy (*slang*) ≠**great:** small, tiny, unimposing, unimpressive

migrant *noun* 1 = **wanderer**, drifter, emigrant, gypsy, immigrant, itinerant, nomad, rover, tinker, transient, traveller, vagrant ♦ *adjective* 2 = **travelling**, drifting, gypsy, immigrant, itinerant, migratory, nomadic, roving, shifting, transient, vagrant, wandering

migrate *verb* = **move**, drift, emigrate, journey, roam, rove, shift, travel, trek, voyage, wander

migration *noun* = **wandering**, emigration, journey, movement, roving, shift, travel, trek, voyage

migratory *adjective* = **nomadic**, gypsy, itinerant, migrant, peripatetic, roving, shifting, transient, travelling, unsettled, vagrant, wandering

mild *adjective* 1 = **bland**, smooth 2 = **gentle**, amiable, calm, compassionate, docile, easy, easy-going, easy-oasy (*slang*), equable, forbearing, forgiving, indulgent, kind, meek, mellow, merciful, moderate, pacific, peaceable, placid, pleasant, serene, soft, tender 3 = **temperate**, balmy, calm, clement, moderate, tranquil, warm
➤ **Antonyms**
≠**gentle:** harsh, powerful, severe, sharp, strong, unkind, unpleasant, violent
≠**temperate:** bitter, cold, fierce, harsh, rough, stormy, violent, wild

mildness *noun* = **gentleness**, blandness, calmness, clemency, docility, forbearance, indulgence, kindness, leniency, lenity, meekness, mellowness, moderation, placidity, smoothness, softness, temperateness, tenderness, tranquillity, warmth

milieu *noun* = **surroundings**, background, element, environment, locale, location, *mise en scène*, scene, setting, sphere

militant *adjective* 1 = **aggressive**, active, assertive, combative, vigorous 2 = **warring**, belligerent, combating, contending, embattled, fighting, in arms ♦ *noun* 3 = **activist**, partisan 4 = **warrior**, belligerent, combatant, fighter, gladiator
➤ **Antonyms**
adjective ≠**aggressive, warring:** pacific, pacifist, peaceful

military *adjective* 1 = **warlike**, armed, martial, soldierlike, soldierly ♦ *noun* 2 = **armed forces**, army, forces, services

militate *verb* 1 **militate against** = **counteract**, be detrimental to, conflict with, contend with, count against, counter, oppose, resist, tell against, weigh against 2 **militate for** = **promote**, advance, aid, further, help

militia *noun* = **reserve(s)**, fencibles (*History*), National Guard (*U.S.*), Territorial Army (*Brit.*), trainband (*History*), yeomanry (*History*)

milk *verb* 1 = **siphon**, drain, draw off, express, extract, let out, press, tap 2 = **exploit**, bleed, drain, extract, impose on, pump, take advantage of, use, wring

milk-and-water *adjective* = **weak**, feeble, innocuous, insipid, jejune, nerdy *or* nurdy (*slang*), vapid, weedy (*informal*), wimpish *or* wimpy (*informal*), wishy-washy (*informal*), wussy (*slang*)
➤ **Antonyms**
effective, energetic, forceful, healthy, strong

milksop *noun* = **weakling**, chinless wonder (*Brit. informal*), coward, dastard (*archaic*), jessie (*Scot. slang*), namby-pamby, sissy, wimp (*informal*), wuss (*slang*)

mill *noun* 1 = **factory**, foundry, plant, shop, works 2 = **grinder**, crusher 3 **run of the mill** = **commonplace**, average, bog-standard (*Brit. & Irish slang*), everyday, fair, middling, ordinary, routine, unexceptional, unremarkable ♦ *verb* 4 = **grind**, comminute, crush, granulate, grate, pound, powder, press, pulverize 5 = **swarm**, crowd, seethe, throng

millstone *noun* 1 = **grindstone**, quernstone 2 = **burden**, affliction, albatross, dead weight, drag, encumbrance, load, weight

mime *noun* 1 = **dumb show**, gesture,

mummery, pantomime ♦ *verb* **2** = **act out**, gesture, pantomime, represent, simulate

mimic *verb* **1** = **imitate**, ape, caricature, do (*informal*), impersonate, parody, take off (*informal*) **2** = **resemble**, echo, look like, mirror, simulate, take on the appearance of ♦ *noun* **3** = **imitator**, caricaturist, copycat (*informal*), impersonator, impressionist, parodist, parrot

mimicry *noun* = **imitation**, burlesque, caricature, impersonation, mimicking, mockery, parody, take-off (*informal*)

mince *verb* **1** = **cut**, chop, crumble, grind, hash **2** = **posture**, attitudinize, give oneself airs, ponce (*slang*), pose **3** *As in* **mince one's words** = **tone down**, diminish, euphemize, extenuate, hold back, moderate, palliate, soften, spare, weaken

mincing *adjective* = **affected**, arty-farty (*informal*), camp (*informal*), dainty, effeminate, foppish, lah-di-dah (*informal*), nice, niminy-piminy, poncy (*slang*), precious, pretentious, sissy

mind *noun* **1** = **brain**, head, imagination, psyche **2** = **intelligence**, brain(s) (*informal*), grey matter (*informal*), intellect, mentality, ratiocination, reason, sense, spirit, understanding, wits **3** = **memory**, recollection, remembrance **4** = **thinker**, brain (*informal*), brainbox, genius, intellect, intellectual **5** = **attitude**, belief, feeling, judgment, opinion, outlook, point of view, sentiment, thoughts, view, way of thinking **6** = **intention**, bent, desire, disposition, fancy, inclination, leaning, notion, purpose, tendency, urge, will, wish **7** = **attention**, concentration, thinking, thoughts **8** = **sanity**, judgment, marbles (*informal*), mental balance, rationality, reason, senses, wits **9 bear** *or* **keep in mind** = **remember**, be cognizant of, be mindful of, take note of **10 in** *or* **of two minds** = **undecided**, dithering (*chiefly Brit.*), hesitant, shillyshallying (*informal*), swithering (*Scot.*), uncertain, unsure, vacillating, wavering **11 make up one's mind** = **decide**, choose, come to a decision, determine, reach a decision, resolve ♦ *verb* **12** = **take offence**, be affronted, be bothered, care, disapprove, dislike, look askance at, object, resent **13** = **pay attention**, adhere to, attend, comply with, follow, heed, listen to, mark, note, notice, obey, observe, pay heed to, regard, respect, take heed, watch **14** = **be sure**, ensure, make certain **15** = **guard**, attend to, have charge of, keep an eye on, look after, take care of, tend, watch **16** = **be careful**, be cautious, be on (one's) guard, be wary, take care, watch **17 never mind** = **forget (it)**, disregard, do not concern yourself, don't bother, don't give (it) a second thought, it

does not matter, it's none of your business, it's nothing to do with you, pay no attention

mindful *adjective* = **aware**, alert, alive to, attentive, careful, chary, cognizant, conscious, heedful, regardful, respectful, sensible, thoughtful, wary, watchful
➤ **Antonyms**
heedless, inattentive, incautious, mindless, oblivious, thoughtless, unaware

mindless *adjective* **1** = **unthinking**, asinine, braindead (*informal*), brutish, careless, dead from the neck up (*informal*), dumb-ass (*slang*), foolish, forgetful, gratuitous, heedless, idiotic, imbecilic, inane, inattentive, moronic, neglectful, negligent, oblivious, obtuse, stupid, thoughtless, unintelligent, unmindful, witless **2** = **mechanical**, automatic, brainless
➤ **Antonyms**
≠**unthinking:** attentive, aware, intelligent, mindful, sane, thinking

mind out *verb* = **be careful**, be on one's guard, beware, keep one's eyes open, look out, pay attention, take care, watch

mine *noun* **1** = **pit**, coalfield, colliery, deposit, excavation, lode, shaft, vein **2** = **source**, abundance, fund, hoard, reserve, stock, store, supply, treasury, wealth ♦ *verb* **3** = **dig up**, delve, dig for, excavate, extract, hew, quarry, unearth **4** = **tunnel**, sap, subvert, undermine, weaken **5** = **lay mines in** *or* **under**, sow with mines

miner *noun* = **coalminer**, collier (*Brit.*), pitman (*Brit.*)

mingle *verb* **1** = **mix**, admix, alloy, blend, coalesce, combine, commingle, compound, intermingle, intermix, interweave, join, marry, meld, merge, unite **2** = **associate**, circulate, consort, fraternize, hang about *or* around, hang out (*informal*), hobnob, rub shoulders (*informal*), socialize
➤ **Antonyms**
≠**mix:** detach, dissolve, divide, part, separate ≠**associate:** avoid, dissociate, estrange

miniature *adjective* = **small**, baby, diminutive, dwarf, Lilliputian, little, midget, mini, minuscule, minute, pocket, pygmy *or* pigmy, reduced, scaled-down, teensy-weensy, teeny-weeny, tiny, toy, wee
➤ **Antonyms**
big, enlarged, enormous, giant, gigantic, ginormous (*informal*), great, huge, immense, large, mega (*slang*), oversize

minimal *adjective* = **minimum**, least, least possible, littlest, nominal, slightest, smallest, token

minimize *verb* **1** = **reduce**, abbreviate, attenuate, curtail, decrease, diminish, downsize, miniaturize, prune, shrink **2** = **play down**, belittle, decry, deprecate, depreciate,

discount, disparage, make light *or* little of, underestimate, underrate
> **Antonyms**
≠**reduce:** augment, enlarge, expand, extend, heighten, increase, magnify ≠**play down:** boast about, elevate, enhance, exalt, praise, vaunt

minimum *noun* **1** = **least**, bottom, depth, lowest, nadir, slightest ♦ *adjective* **2** = **least**, least possible, littlest, lowest, minimal, slightest, smallest
> **Antonyms**
adjective ≠**least:** greatest, highest, largest, maximum, most

minion *noun* = **follower**, bootlicker (*informal*), cohort (*chiefly U.S.*), creature, darling, dependant, favourite, flatterer, flunky, hanger-on, henchman, hireling, lackey, lickspittle, parasite, pet, sycophant, toady, underling, yes man

minister *noun* **1** = **clergyman**, chaplain, churchman, cleric, divine, ecclesiastic, padre (*informal*), parson, pastor, preacher, priest, rector, vicar **2** = **official**, administrator, ambassador, cabinet member, delegate, diplomat, envoy, executive, office-holder, plenipotentiary ♦ *verb* **3** = **attend**, accommodate, administer, answer, be solicitous of, cater to, pander to, serve, take care of, tend

ministrations *plural noun* = **help**, aid, assistance, favour, patronage, relief, service, succour, support

ministry *noun* **1** = **the priesthood**, holy orders, the church, the pulpit **2** = **department**, administration, bureau, cabinet, council, government, office, quango

minor *adjective* = **small**, inconsequential, inconsiderable, inferior, insignificant, junior, lesser, light, negligible, nickel-and-dime (*U.S. slang*), paltry, petty, secondary, slight, smaller, subordinate, trifling, trivial, unimportant, younger
> **Antonyms**
appreciable, consequential, considerable, essential, grand, great, heavy, important, major, profound, serious, significant, substantial, superior, vital, weighty

minstrel *noun* = **musician**, bard, harper, jongleur, singer, songstress, troubadour

mint *noun* **1** = **fortune**, bomb (*Brit. slang*), bundle (*slang*), heap (*informal*), King's ransom, million, packet (*slang*), pile (*informal*) ♦ *adjective* **2** = **perfect**, brand-new, excellent, first-class, fresh, unblemished, undamaged, untarnished ♦ *verb* **3** = **make**, cast, coin, produce, punch, stamp, strike **4** = **invent**, coin, construct, devise, fabricate, fashion, forge, make up, produce, think up

minuscule *adjective* = **tiny**, diminutive, infinitesimal, little, microscopic, miniature, minute

minute[1] *noun* **1** = **sixty seconds**, sixtieth of an hour **2** = **moment**, flash, instant, jiffy (*informal*), second, shake (*informal*), tick (*Brit. informal*), trice **3** any minute = **very soon**, any moment, any second, any time, at any time, before long **4** up to the minute = **latest**, all the rage, in, modish, (most) fashionable, newest, now (*informal*), smart, stylish, trendiest, trendy (*Brit. informal*), up to date, vogue, with it (*informal*)

minute[2] *adjective* **1** = **small**, diminutive, fine, infinitesimal, Lilliputian, little, microscopic, miniature, minuscule, slender, teensy-weensy, teeny-weeny, tiny **2** = **negligible**, inconsiderable, paltry, petty, picayune (*U.S.*), piddling (*informal*), puny, slight, trifling, trivial, unimportant **3** = **precise**, close, critical, detailed, exact, exhaustive, meticulous, painstaking, punctilious
> **Antonyms**
≠**small:** enormous, generous, gigantic, ginormous (*informal*), grand, great, huge, immense, mega (*slang*), monstrous ≠**negligible:** important, major, significant, vital ≠**precise:** careless, haphazard, imprecise, inexact, loose, quick, rough, superficial

minutely *adverb* = **precisely**, closely, critically, exactly, exhaustively, in detail, meticulously, painstakingly, with a fine-tooth comb

minutes *plural noun* = **record**, memorandum, notes, proceedings, transactions, transcript

minutiae *plural noun* = **details**, finer points, ins and outs, niceties, particulars, subtleties, trifles, trivia

minx *noun* = **flirt**, baggage (*informal, old-fashioned*), coquette, hoyden, hussy, jade, tomboy, wanton

miracle *noun* = **wonder**, marvel, phenomenon, prodigy, thaumaturgy

miraculous *adjective* = **wonderful**, amazing, astonishing, astounding, extraordinary, incredible, inexplicable, magical, marvellous, phenomenal, preternatural, prodigious, superhuman, supernatural, thaumaturgic, unaccountable, unbelievable, wondrous (*archaic or literary*)
> **Antonyms**
awful, bad, banal, common, commonplace, everyday, normal, ordinary, run-of-the-mill, terrible, unexceptional, unremarkable, usual

mirage *noun* = **illusion**, hallucination, optical illusion, phantasm

mire *noun* **1** = **swamp**, bog, marsh, morass,

quagmire **2** = **mud**, dirt, gloop (*informal*), grot (*slang*), muck, ooze, slime, slob (*Irish*) **3 in the mire** = **in trouble**, encumbered, entangled, in difficulties ◆ *verb* **4** = **bog down**, flounder, sink, stick in the mud **5** = **begrime**, besmirch, bespatter, cake, dirty, muddy, soil **6** = **entangle**, catch up, enmesh, involve

mirror *noun* **1** = **looking-glass**, glass, reflector, speculum **2** = **reflection**, copy, double, image, likeness, replica, representation, twin ◆ *verb* **3** = **reflect**, copy, depict, echo, emulate, follow, represent, show

mirth *noun* = **merriment**, amusement, cheerfulness, festivity, frolic, fun, gaiety, gladness, glee, hilarity, jocularity, jollity, joviality, joyousness, laughter, levity, merrymaking, pleasure, rejoicing, revelry, sport

mirthful *adjective* = **merry**, amused, amusing, blithe, cheerful, cheery, festive, frolicsome, funny, gay, glad, gladsome (*archaic*), happy, hilarious, jocund, jolly, jovial, laughable, light-hearted, ludic (*literary*), playful, sportive, uproarious, vivacious
➤ **Antonyms**
dejected, depressed, despondent, dismal, down in the dumps (*informal*), gloomy, grave, lugubrious, melancholy, miserable, morose, sad, saturnine, serious, solemn, sombre, sorrowful, unhappy

misadventure *noun* = **misfortune**, accident, bad break (*informal*), bad luck, bummer (*slang*), calamity, catastrophe, debacle, disaster, failure, ill fortune, ill luck, mischance, mishap, reverse, setback

misanthrope *noun* = **cynic**, egoist, egotist, mankind-hater, misanthropist

misanthropic *adjective* = **antisocial**, cynical, malevolent, unfriendly

misapprehend *verb* = **misunderstand**, get hold of the wrong end of the stick, get one's lines crossed, get the wrong idea *or* impression, misconceive, misconstrue, misinterpret, misread, mistake

misapprehension *noun* = **misunderstanding**, delusion, error, fallacy, false belief, false impression, misconception, misconstruction, misinterpretation, misreading, mistake, wrong idea *or* impression

misappropriate *verb* = **steal**, cabbage (*Brit. slang*), defalcate (*Law*), embezzle, misapply, misspend, misuse, peculate, pocket, swindle

misbegotten *adjective* **1** = **ill-conceived**, abortive, hare-brained, ill-advised, poorly thought-out **2** *Literary* = **illegitimate**, bastard, born out of wedlock, natural, spurious (*rare*)

misbehave *verb* = **be naughty**, act up (*informal*), be bad, be insubordinate, carry on (*informal*), get up to mischief (*informal*), muck about (*Brit. slang*)
➤ **Antonyms**
act correctly, be good, behave, conduct oneself properly, mind one's manners, mind one's p's and q's, toe the line

misbehaviour *noun* = **misconduct**, acting up (*informal*), bad behaviour, impropriety, incivility, indiscipline, insubordination, mischief, misdeeds, misdemeanour, monkey business (*informal*), naughtiness, rudeness, shenanigans (*informal*)

miscalculate *verb* = **misjudge**, blunder, calculate wrongly, err, get (it) wrong, go wrong, make a mistake, overestimate, overrate, slip up, underestimate, underrate

miscarriage *noun* **1** = **spontaneous abortion**, miss (*informal*) **2** = **failure**, botch (*informal*), breakdown, error, misadventure, mischance, misfire, mishap, mismanagement, nonsuccess, perversion, thwarting, undoing

miscarry *verb* **1** = **abort 2** = **fail**, come to grief, come to nothing, fall through, gang agley (*Scot.*), go amiss, go astray, go awry, go pear-shaped (*informal*), go wrong, misfire

miscellaneous *adjective* = **mixed**, assorted, confused, diverse, diversified, farraginous, heterogeneous, indiscriminate, jumbled, manifold, many, mingled, motley, multifarious, multiform, promiscuous, sundry, varied, various

miscellany *noun* = **assortment**, anthology, collection, diversity, farrago, gallimaufry, hotchpotch, jumble, medley, *mélange,* mixed bag, mixture, omnium-gatherum, potpourri, salmagundi, variety

mischance *noun* = **misfortune**, accident, bad break (*informal*), bad luck, bummer (*slang*), calamity, contretemps, disaster, ill chance, ill fortune, ill luck, infelicity, misadventure, mishap

mischief *noun* **1** = **misbehaviour**, devilment, impishness, monkey business (*informal*), naughtiness, pranks, roguery, roguishness, shenanigans (*informal*), trouble, waywardness **2** = **harm**, damage, detriment, disadvantage, disruption, evil, hurt, injury, misfortune, trouble

mischievous *adjective* **1** = **naughty**, arch, bad, badly behaved, exasperating, frolicsome, impish, ludic (*literary*), playful, puckish, rascally, roguish, sportive, teasing, troublesome, vexatious, wayward **2** = **malicious**, bad, damaging, deleterious, destructive, detrimental, evil, harmful, hurtful, injurious, malignant, pernicious, sinful, spiteful, troublesome, vicious, wicked

misconception *noun* = **delusion**, error, fallacy, misapprehension, misconstruction, mistaken belief, misunderstanding, wrong end of the stick, wrong idea

misconduct *noun* = **immorality**, delinquency, dereliction, impropriety, malfeasance (*Law*), malpractice, misbehaviour, misdemeanour, mismanagement, naughtiness, rudeness, transgression, unethical behaviour, wrongdoing

misconstrue *verb* = **misinterpret**, get a false impression, get one's lines crossed, make a wrong interpretation, misapprehend, misconceive, misjudge, misread, mistake, mistranslate, misunderstand, take the wrong way (*informal*)

miscreant *noun* = **wrongdoer**, blackguard, caitiff (*archaic*), criminal, evildoer, knave (*archaic*), malefactor, rascal, reprobate, rogue, scally (*Northwest English dialect*), scoundrel, sinner, skelm (*S. African*), vagabond, villain

misdeed *noun* = **offence**, crime, fault, misconduct, misdemeanour, sin, transgression, trespass, villainy, wrong

misdemeanour *noun* = **offence**, fault, infringement, misbehaviour, misconduct, misdeed, peccadillo, transgression, trespass

miser *noun* = **hoarder**, cheapskate (*informal*), churl (*archaic*), curmudgeon, hunks (*rare*), niggard, penny-pincher (*informal*), screw (*slang*), Scrooge, skinflint, tight-arse (*taboo slang*), tight-ass (*U.S. taboo slang*), tightwad (*U.S. & Canad. slang*)

miserable *adjective* 1 = **unhappy**, afflicted, broken-hearted, crestfallen, dejected, depressed, desolate, despondent, disconsolate, dismal, distressed, doleful, down, downcast, down in the dumps (*informal*), down in the mouth (*informal*), forlorn, gloomy, heartbroken, low, melancholy, mournful, sorrowful, woebegone, wretched 2 = **despicable**, abject, bad, contemptible, deplorable, detestable, disgraceful, lamentable, low, mean, pathetic, piteous, pitiable, scurvy, shabby, shameful, sordid, sorry, squalid, vile, worthless, wretched
➤ Antonyms
≠unhappy: cheerful, happy ≠despicable: admirable, good, respectable

miserly *adjective* = **mean**, avaricious, beggarly, close, close-fisted, covetous, grasping, illiberal, mingy (*Brit. informal*), near, niggardly, parsimonious, penny-pinching (*informal*), penurious, snoep

(*S. African informal*), sordid, stingy, tight-arsed (*taboo slang*), tight as a duck's arse (*taboo slang*), tight-assed (*U.S. taboo slang*), tightfisted, ungenerous
➤ Antonyms
charitable, extravagant, generous, prodigal, unselfish

misery *noun* 1 = **unhappiness**, agony, anguish, depression, desolation, despair, discomfort, distress, gloom, grief, hardship, melancholy, sadness, sorrow, suffering, torment, torture, woe, wretchedness 2 = **misfortune**, affliction, bitter pill (*informal*), burden, calamity, catastrophe, curse, disaster, hardship, load, ordeal, sorrow, trial, tribulation, trouble, woe 3 = **poverty**, destitution, indigence, need, penury, privation, sordidness, squalor, want, wretchedness 4 *Brit. informal* = **moaner**, grouch (*informal*), killjoy, pessimist, prophet of doom, sourpuss (*informal*), spoilsport, wet blanket (*informal*), wowser (*Austral. & N.Z. slang*)
➤ Antonyms
≠unhappiness: comfort, contentment, ease, enjoyment, happiness, joy, pleasure
≠poverty: luxury

misfire *verb* = **fail**, fail to go off, fall through, go pear-shaped (*informal*), go phut (*informal*), go wrong, miscarry

misfit *noun* = **nonconformist**, eccentric, fish out of water (*informal*), oddball (*informal*), square peg (in a round hole) (*informal*)

misfortune *noun* 1 = **bad luck**, adversity, evil fortune, hard luck, ill luck, infelicity 2 = **mishap**, accident, affliction, blow, bummer (*slang*), calamity, disaster, evil chance, failure, hardship, harm, loss, misadventure, mischance, misery, reverse, setback, stroke of bad luck, tragedy, trial, tribulation, trouble, whammy (*informal, chiefly U.S.*)
➤ Antonyms
fortune, good luck, relief

misgiving *noun* = **unease**, anxiety, apprehension, distrust, doubt, dubiety, hesitation, qualm, reservation, scruple, suspicion, trepidation, uncertainty, worry

misguided *adjective* = **unwise**, deluded, erroneous, foolish, ill-advised, imprudent, injudicious, labouring under a delusion *or* misapprehension, misled, misplaced, mistaken, uncalled-for, unreasonable, unwarranted

mishandle *verb* = **mismanage**, bodge (*informal*), botch, bungle, flub (*U.S. slang*), make a hash of (*informal*), make a mess of, make a nonsense of, mess up (*informal*), muff, screw (up) (*informal*)

mishap *noun* = **accident**, adversity, bad

luck, calamity, contretemps, disaster, evil chance, evil fortune, hard luck, ill fortune, ill luck, infelicity, misadventure, mischance, misfortune

misinform verb = **mislead**, deceive, give (someone) a bum steer (informal, chiefly U.S.), give (someone) duff gen (Brit. informal), misdirect, misguide

misinterpret verb = **misunderstand**, distort, falsify, get wrong, misapprehend, misconceive, misconstrue, misjudge, misread, misrepresent, mistake, pervert

misjudge verb = **miscalculate**, be wrong about, get the wrong idea about, overestimate, overrate, underestimate, underrate

mislay verb = **lose**, be unable to find, be unable to put or lay one's hand on, forget the whereabouts of, lose track of, misplace, miss

mislead verb = **deceive**, beguile, bluff, delude, fool, give (someone) a bum steer (informal, chiefly U.S.), hoodwink, lead astray, misdirect, misguide, misinform, pull the wool over (someone's) eyes (informal), take for a ride (informal), take in (informal)

misleading adjective = **confusing**, ambiguous, casuistical, deceitful, deceptive, delusive, delusory, disingenuous, evasive, false, sophistical, specious, spurious, tricky (informal), unstraightforward
➤ **Antonyms**
candid, clear, correct, direct, explicit, frank, genuine, honest, obvious, open, plain, simple, sincere, straightforward, true, truthful

mismanage verb = **mishandle**, be incompetent, be inefficient, bodge (informal), botch, bungle, make a hash of (informal), make a mess of, make a nonsense of, maladminister, mess up, misconduct, misdirect, misgovern

misplace verb 1 = **lose**, be unable to find, be unable to put or lay one's hand on, forget the whereabouts of, lose track of, misfile, mislay, miss, put in the wrong place 2 = **place wrongly**, place unwisely

misprint noun = **mistake**, corrigendum, erratum, literal, printing error, typo (informal), typographical error

misquote verb = **misrepresent**, distort, falsify, garble, mangle, misreport, misstate, muddle, pervert, quote or take out of context, twist

misrepresent verb = **distort**, belie, disguise, falsify, garble, misinterpret, misstate, pervert, twist

misrule noun 1 = **mismanagement**, bad government, maladministration, misgovernment 2 = **disorder**, anarchy, chaos, confusion, lawlessness, tumult, turmoil

miss[1] verb 1 = **omit**, be late for, blunder, err, fail, fail to grasp, fail to notice, forego, lack, leave out, let go, let slip, lose, miscarry, mistake, overlook, pass over, pass up, skip, slip, trip 2 = **long for**, feel the loss of, hunger for, need, pine for, want, wish, yearn for 3 = **avoid**, escape, evade ♦ noun 4 = **mistake**, blunder, error, failure, fault, loss, omission, oversight, want

miss[2] noun = **girl**, damsel, lass, lassie (informal), maid, maiden, schoolgirl, spinster, young lady

misshapen adjective = **deformed**, contorted, crippled, crooked, distorted, grotesque, ill-made, ill-proportioned, malformed, twisted, ugly, ungainly, unshapely, unsightly, warped, wry

missile noun = **rocket**, projectile, weapon

missing adjective = **absent**, astray, gone, lacking, left behind, left out, lost, mislaid, misplaced, not present, nowhere to be found, unaccounted-for, wanting
➤ **Antonyms**
accounted for, at hand, available, here, in attendance, on hand, present, there, to hand

mission noun 1 = **task**, aim, assignment, business, calling, charge, commission, duty, errand, goal, job, office, operation, purpose, pursuit, quest, trust, undertaking, vocation, work 2 = **delegation**, commission, deputation, embassy, legation, ministry, task force

missionary noun = **evangelist**, apostle, converter, preacher, propagandist, proselytizer

missive noun = **letter**, communication, dispatch, epistle, memorandum, message, note, report

misspent adjective = **wasted**, dissipated, idle, imprudent, misapplied, prodigal, profitless, squandered, thrown away
➤ **Antonyms**
active, fruitful, industrious, meaningful, profitable, unwasted, useful, worthwhile

mist noun 1 = **fog**, cloud, condensation, dew, drizzle, film, haar (Eastern Brit.), haze, smog, smur or smir (Scot.), spray, steam, vapour ♦ verb 2 = **steam** (up), becloud, befog, blear, blur, cloud, film, fog, obscure

mistake noun 1 = **error**, bloomer (Brit. informal), blunder, boob (Brit. slang), boo-boo (informal), clanger (informal), erratum, error of judgment, false move, fault, faux pas, gaffe, goof (informal), howler (informal), inaccuracy, miscalculation, misconception, misstep, misunderstanding, oversight, slip, slip-up (informal), solecism ♦ verb 2 = **misunderstand**, get wrong, misapprehend, misconceive, misconstrue, misinterpret, misjudge, misread **3 = confuse with**, accept as, confound, misinterpret as, mix up with, take for **4 = miscalculate**, be wide of *or* be off the mark, be wrong, blunder, boob (*Brit. slang*), drop a clanger (*informal*), err, goof (*informal*), misjudge, put one's foot in it (*informal*), slip up (*informal*)

mistaken *adjective* **= wrong**, barking up the wrong tree (*informal*), erroneous, fallacious, false, faulty, getting the wrong end of the stick (*informal*), inaccurate, inappropriate, incorrect, in the wrong, labouring under a misapprehension, misguided, misinformed, misled, off base (*U.S. & Canad. informal*), off beam (*informal*), off target, off the mark, unfounded, unsound, way off beam (*informal*), wide of the mark
➤ **Antonyms**
accurate, correct, logical, right, sound, true

mistakenly *adverb* **= incorrectly**, by mistake, erroneously, fallaciously, falsely, inaccurately, inappropriately, in error, misguidedly, wrongly

mistimed *adjective* **= inopportune**, badly timed, ill-timed, inconvenient, unseasonable, unsynchronized, untimely

mistreat *verb* = **abuse**, brutalize, handle roughly, harm, ill-treat, ill-use, injure, knock about *or* around, maltreat, manhandle, maul, misuse, molest, rough up, wrong

mistress *noun* **= lover**, concubine, doxy (*archaic*), fancy bit (*slang*), fancy woman (*slang*), floozy (*slang*), girlfriend, inamorata, kept woman, ladylove (*rare*), paramour

mistrust *verb* **1 = doubt**, apprehend, beware, be wary of, distrust, fear, have doubts about, suspect ◆ *noun* **2** = **suspicion**, apprehension, distrust, doubt, dubiety, fear, misgiving, scepticism, uncertainty, wariness

mistrustful *adjective* **= suspicious**, apprehensive, cautious, chary, cynical, distrustful, doubtful, dubious, fearful, hesitant, leery (*slang*), nervous, sceptical, uncertain, wary
➤ **Antonyms**
certain, definite, positive, sure, unafraid

misty *adjective* **= foggy**, bleary, blurred, cloudy, dark, dim, fuzzy, hazy, indistinct, murky, nebulous, obscure, opaque, overcast, unclear, vague
➤ **Antonyms**
bright, clear, distinct, lucid, obvious, plain, sunny, well-defined

misunderstand *verb* **= misinterpret**, be at cross-purposes, get (it) wrong, get one's lines crossed, get one's wires crossed, get the wrong end of the stick, get the wrong

idea (about), misapprehend, misconceive, misconstrue, mishear, misjudge, misread, miss the point (of), mistake

misunderstanding *noun* **1 = mistake**, error, false impression, misapprehension, misconception, misconstruction, misinterpretation, misjudgment, misreading, mix-up, wrong idea **2 = disagreement**, argument, breach, conflict, difference, difficulty, discord, dissension, falling-out (*informal*), quarrel, rift, rupture, squabble, variance

misunderstood *adjective* **= misjudged**, misconstrued, misheard, misinterpreted, misread, unappreciated, unrecognized

misuse *noun* **1 = waste**, abuse, barbarism, catachresis, corruption, desecration, dissipation, malapropism, misapplication, misemployment, misusage, perversion, profanation, solecism, squandering **2** = **mistreatment**, abuse, cruel treatment, exploitation, harm, ill-treatment, ill-usage, inhumane treatment, injury, maltreatment, manhandling, rough handling ◆ *verb* **3** = **waste**, abuse, corrupt, desecrate, dissipate, misapply, misemploy, pervert, profane, prostitute, squander **4 = mistreat**, abuse, brutalize, exploit, handle roughly, harm, ill-treat, ill-use, injure, maltreat, manhandle, maul, molest, wrong
➤ **Antonyms**
verb ≠**waste**: appreciate, prize, treasure, use ≠**mistreat**: cherish, honour, respect

mitigate *verb* **= ease**, abate, allay, appease, assuage, blunt, calm, check, diminish, dull, extenuate, lessen, lighten, moderate, modify, mollify, pacify, palliate, placate, quiet, reduce the force of, remit, soften, soothe, subdue, take the edge off, temper, tone down, tranquillize, weaken
➤ **Antonyms**
aggravate, augment, enhance, heighten, increase, intensify, strengthen

mitigation *noun* **= relief**, abatement, allaying, alleviation, assuagement, diminution, easement, extenuation, moderation, mollification, palliation, remission

mix *verb* **1 = combine**, alloy, amalgamate, associate, blend, coalesce, commingle, commix, compound, cross, fuse, incorporate, intermingle, interweave, join, jumble, meld, merge, mingle, put together, unite **2 = socialize**, associate, come together, consort, fraternize, hang out (*informal*), hobnob, join, mingle ◆ *noun* **3** = **mixture**, alloy, amalgam, assortment, blend, combination, compound, fusion, medley, meld, mixed bag (*informal*)

mixed *adjective* **1 = combined**, alloyed, amalgamated, blended, composite,

compound, fused, incorporated, joint, mingled, united **2 = varied**, assorted, cosmopolitan, diverse, diversified, heterogeneous, manifold, miscellaneous, motley **3 = crossbred**, hybrid, interbred, interdenominational, mongrel **4 = uncertain**, ambivalent, equivocal, indecisive
➤ **Antonyms**
≠**combined**: isolated, pure, straight, unmixed ≠**varied**: homogeneous, unmixed ≠**crossbred**: pure

mixed-up *adjective* = **confused**, at sea, bewildered, distraught, disturbed, maladjusted, muddled, perplexed, puzzled, upset

mixture *noun* = **blend**, admixture, alloy, amalgam, amalgamation, association, assortment, brew, combine, composite, compound, concoction, conglomeration, cross, fusion, hotchpotch, jumble, medley, *mélange*, meld, miscellany, mix, mixed bag (*informal*), potpourri, salmagundi, union, variety

mix-up *noun* = **confusion**, disorder, fankle (*Scot.*), jumble, mess, mistake, misunderstanding, muddle, snarl-up (*informal, chiefly Brit.*), tangle

mix up *verb* **1 = combine**, blend, commix, mix **2 = confuse**, confound, muddle **3 = bewilder**, confuse, disturb, fluster, muddle, perplex, puzzle, throw into confusion, unnerve, upset **4 = entangle**, embroil, implicate, involve, rope in

moan *noun* **1 = groan**, lament, lamentation, sigh, sob, sough, wail, whine **2** *Informal* = **grumble**, beef (*slang*), bitch (*slang*), complaint, gripe (*informal*), grouch (*informal*), grouse, kvetch (*U.S. slang*), protest, whine ◆ *verb* **3 = groan**, bemoan, bewail, deplore, grieve, keen, lament, mourn, sigh, sob, sough, whine **4** *Informal* = **grumble**, beef (*slang*), bitch (*slang*), bleat, carp, complain, gripe (*informal*), groan, grouch (*informal*), grouse, moan and groan, whine, whinge (*informal*)

mob *noun* **1 = crowd**, assemblage, body, collection, drove, flock, gang, gathering, herd, horde, host, mass, multitude, pack, press, swarm, throng **2 = masses**, *canaille*, commonalty, great unwashed (*informal & derogatory*), hoi polloi, rabble, riffraff, scum **3** *Slang* = **gang**, class, company, crew (*informal*), group, lot, set, troop ◆ *verb* **4 = surround**, crowd around, jostle, overrun, set upon, swarm around

mobile *adjective* **1 = movable**, ambulatory, itinerant, locomotive, migrant, motile, moving, peripatetic, portable, travelling, wandering **2 = changeable**, animated, ever-changing, expressive

mobilize *verb* = **prepare**, activate, animate, call to arms, call up, get *or* make ready, marshal, muster, organize, put in motion, rally, ready

mock *verb* **1 = laugh at**, chaff, deride, flout, insult, jeer, laugh to scorn, make a monkey out of, make fun of, poke fun at, ridicule, scoff, scorn, show contempt for, sneer, take the mickey (out of) (*informal*), take the piss (out of) (*taboo slang*), taunt, tease, wind up (*Brit. slang*) **2 = mimic**, ape, burlesque, caricature, counterfeit, do (*informal*), imitate, lampoon, parody, satirize, send up (*Brit. informal*), take off (*informal*), travesty **3 = foil**, defeat, defy, disappoint, frustrate, thwart ◆ *adjective* **4 = imitation**, artificial, bogus, counterfeit, dummy, ersatz, fake, faked, false, feigned, forged, fraudulent, phoney *or* phony (*informal*), pretended, pseudo (*informal*), sham, spurious
➤ **Antonyms**
verb ≠**laugh at**: encourage, praise, respect, revere ◆ *adjective* ≠**imitation**: authentic, genuine, natural, real, sincere, true, unfeigned

mockery *noun* **1 = derision**, contempt, contumely, disdain, disrespect, gibes, insults, jeering, ridicule, scoffing, scorn **2 = parody**, burlesque, caricature, deception, farce, imitation, lampoon, mimicry, pretence, send-up (*Brit. informal*), sham, spoof (*informal*), take-off (*informal*), travesty **3 = farce**, apology (*informal*), disappointment, joke, laughing stock, letdown

mocking *adjective* = **scornful**, contemptuous, contumelious, derisive, derisory, disdainful, disrespectful, insulting, irreverent, sarcastic, sardonic, satiric, satirical, scoffing, taunting

mode *noun* **1 = method**, form, manner, procedure, process, style, system, technique, way **2 = fashion**, craze, look, rage, style, trend, vogue

model *noun* **1 = representation**, copy, dummy, facsimile, image, imitation, miniature, mock-up, replica **2 = pattern**, archetype, design, epitome, example, exemplar, gauge, ideal, lodestar, mould, norm, original, par, paradigm, paragon, prototype, standard, type **3 = sitter**, poser, subject **4 = mannequin 5 = version**, configuration, design, form, kind, mark, mode, stamp, style, type, variety ◆ *adjective* **6 = ideal**, archetypal, exemplary, illustrative, paradigmatic, perfect, standard, typical **7 = imitation**, copy, dummy, facsimile, miniature ◆ *verb* **8 = shape**, carve, cast, design, fashion, form, mould, sculpt, stamp **9 = base**, pattern, plan **10 = show off**, display, sport (*informal*), wear

➤ **Antonyms**
adjective ≠**ideal**: deficient, flawed, impaired, imperfect

moderate *adjective* **1** = **mild**, calm, controlled, cool, deliberate, equable, gentle, judicious, limited, middle-of-the-road, modest, peaceable, reasonable, restrained, sober, steady, temperate **2** = **average**, fair, fairish, fair to middling (*informal*), indifferent, mediocre, medium, middling, ordinary, passable, so-so (*informal*), unexceptional ✦ *verb* **3** = **lessen**, abate, allay, appease, assuage, calm, clear the air, control, curb, decrease, diminish, ease, mitigate, modulate, pacify, play down, quiet, regulate, relax, repress, restrain, soften, soft-pedal (*informal*), subdue, tame, temper, tone down **4** = **arbitrate**, chair, judge, mediate, preside, referee, take the chair
➤ **Antonyms**
adjective ≠**mild**: extreme, intemperate, ruffled, unreasonable, wild ≠**average**: excessive, extreme, immoderate, inordinate, unusual ✦ *verb* ≠**lessen**: heighten, increase, intensify

moderately *adverb* = **reasonably**, fairly, gently, in moderation, passably, quite, rather, slightly, somewhat, to a degree, tolerably, to some extent, within limits, within reason

moderation *noun* **1** = **restraint**, calmness, composure, coolness, equanimity, fairness, judiciousness, justice, justness, mildness, moderateness, reasonableness, sedateness, temperance **2 in moderation** = **moderately**, within limits, within reason

modern *adjective* = **current**, contemporary, fresh, late, latest, neoteric (*rare*), new, newfangled, novel, present, present-day, recent, twentieth-century, up-to-date, up-to-the-minute, with it (*informal*)
➤ **Antonyms**
ancient, antiquated, archaic, former, obsolete, old, old-fashioned, old hat, outmoded, passé, past, square (*informal*), uncool (*slang*)

modernity *noun* = **novelty**, currency, freshness, innovation, newness

modernize *verb* = **update**, bring into the twentieth century, bring up to date, face-lift, make over, rebrand, rejuvenate, remake, remodel, renew, renovate, revamp

modest *adjective* **1** = **unpretentious**, bashful, blushing, coy, demure, diffident, discreet, humble, meek, quiet, reserved, reticent, retiring, self-conscious, self-effacing, shy, simple, unassuming **2** = **moderate**, fair, limited, middling, ordinary, small, unexceptional

modesty *noun* = **reserve**, bashfulness, coyness, decency, demureness, diffidence, discreetness, humbleness, humility, lack of pretension, meekness, propriety, quietness, reticence, self-effacement, shyness, simplicity, timidity, unobtrusiveness, unpretentiousness
➤ **Antonyms**
arrogance, assurance, boastfulness, boldness, conceit, confidence, egotism, forwardness, haughtiness, immodesty, indecency, ostentation, presumption, pretentiousness, pride, showiness, vanity

modicum *noun* = **little**, atom, bit, crumb, dash, drop, fragment, grain, inch, iota, mite, ounce, particle, pinch, scrap, shred, small amount, speck, tad (*informal, chiefly U.S.*), tinge, touch

modification *noun* = **change**, adjustment, alteration, modulation, mutation, qualification, refinement, reformation, restriction, revision, variation

modify *verb* **1** = **change**, adapt, adjust, alter, convert, recast, redo, refashion, reform, remodel, reorganize, reshape, revise, rework, transform, tweak (*informal*), vary **2** = **tone down**, abate, ease, lessen, limit, lower, moderate, qualify, reduce, relax, restrain, restrict, soften, temper

modish *adjective* = **fashionable**, contemporary, current, in, smart, stylish, trendy (*Brit. informal*), up-to-the-minute, voguish

modulate *verb* = **adjust**, attune, balance, regulate, tune, vary

mogul *noun* = **tycoon**, baron, bashaw, big cheese (*slang, old-fashioned*), big gun (*informal*), big hitter (*informal*), big noise (*informal*), big shot (*informal*), big wheel (*slang*), heavy hitter (*informal*), lord, magnate, nabob (*informal*), nob (*slang, chiefly Brit.*), notable, personage, potentate, V.I.P.

moist *adjective* = **damp**, clammy, dampish, dank, dewy, dripping, drizzly, humid, not dry, rainy, soggy, wet, wettish

moisten *verb* = **dampen**, bedew, damp, humidify, lick, moisturize, soak, water, wet

moisture *noun* = **damp**, dampness, dankness, dew, humidity, liquid, perspiration, sweat, water, wateriness, wetness

molecule *noun* = **particle**, atom, iota, jot, mite, mote, speck

molest *verb* **1** = **abuse**, accost, assail, attack, harm, hurt, ill-treat, injure, interfere with, maltreat, manhandle **2** = **annoy**, abuse, afflict, badger, beset, bother, bug (*informal*), disturb, harass, harry, hector, irritate, persecute, pester, plague, tease, torment, upset, vex, worry

mollify *verb* = pacify, appease, calm, conciliate, placate, quiet, soothe, sweeten

mollycoddle *verb* = pamper, baby, cosset, indulge, spoil

moment *noun* 1 = instant, bat of an eye (*informal*), flash, jiffy (*informal*), minute, no time, second, shake (*informal*), split second, tick (*Brit. informal*), trice, twinkling, two shakes (*informal*), two shakes of a lamb's tail (*informal*) 2 = time, hour, instant, juncture, point, point in time, stage 3 = importance, concern, consequence, gravity, import, seriousness, significance, substance, value, weight, weightiness, worth

momentarily *adverb* = briefly, for a little while, for a minute, for a moment, for an instant, for a second, for a short time, for a short while, for the nonce, temporarily

momentary *adjective* = short-lived, brief, ephemeral, evanescent, fleeting, flying, fugitive, hasty, passing, quick, short, temporary, transitory
➤ **Antonyms**
lasting, lengthy, long-lived, permanent

momentous *adjective* = significant, consequential, critical, crucial, decisive, earth-shaking (*informal*), fateful, grave, historic, important, of moment, pivotal, serious, vital, weighty
➤ **Antonyms**
inconsequential, insignificant, trifling, trivial, unimportant

momentum *noun* = impetus, drive, energy, force, power, propulsion, push, strength, thrust

monarch *noun* = ruler, crowned head, emperor *or* empress, king, potentate, prince *or* princess, queen, sovereign

monarchy *noun* 1 = sovereignty, absolutism, autocracy, despotism, kingship, monocracy, royalism 2 = kingdom, empire, principality, realm

monastery *noun* = abbey, cloister, convent, friary, house, nunnery, priory, religious community

monastic *adjective* = monkish, ascetic, austere, celibate, cloistered, cloistral, contemplative, conventual, hermit-like, recluse, reclusive, secluded, sequestered, withdrawn

monetary *adjective* = financial, budgetary, capital, cash, fiscal, pecuniary

money *noun* 1 = cash, ackers (*slang*), banknotes, brass (*Northern English dialect*), bread (*slang*), capital, coin, currency, dibs (*slang*), dosh (*Brit. & Austral. slang*), dough (*slang*), filthy lucre (*facetious*), funds, gelt (*slang, chiefly U.S.*), green (*slang*), hard cash, legal tender, lolly (*Brit. slang*), loot (*informal*), mazuma (*slang,*

chiefly *U.S.*), megabucks (*U.S. & Canad. slang*), moolah (*slang*), necessary (*informal*), needful (*informal*), pelf (*contemptuous*), readies (*informal*), rhino (*Brit. slang*), riches, shekels (*informal*), silver, specie, spondulicks (*slang*), the ready (*informal*), the wherewithal, tin (*slang*), wealth 2 **in the money** = rich, affluent, flush (*informal*), in clover (*informal*), loaded (*slang*), on Easy Street (*informal*), prosperous, rolling (*slang*), wealthy, well-heeled (*informal*), well-off, well-to-do

moneymaking *adjective* = profitable, gainful, going, lucrative, paying, remunerative, successful, thriving

mongrel *noun* 1 = hybrid, bigener (*Biology*), cross, crossbreed, half-breed, mixed breed ◆ *adjective* 2 = hybrid, bastard, crossbred, half-breed, of mixed breed

monitor *noun* 1 = watchdog, guide, invigilator, overseer, prefect (*Brit.*), supervisor ◆ *verb* 2 = check, follow, keep an eye on, keep tabs on, keep track of, observe, oversee, record, scan, supervise, survey, watch

monk *noun* = friar (*loosely*), brother, monastic, religious

monkey *noun* 1 = simian, jackanapes (*archaic*), primate 2 = rascal, devil, imp, mischief maker, pickle (*Brit. informal*), rogue, scamp 3 **make a monkey of** = make a fool of, make fun of, make (someone) a laughing stock, make (someone) look foolish, make (someone) look ridiculous, make (someone) look silly, play a trick on, ridicule ◆ *verb* 4 **with around** *or* **about with** = fool, fiddle (*informal*), interfere, meddle, mess, play, tamper, tinker, trifle

monkey business *noun* 1 = mischief, carry-on (*informal, chiefly Brit.*), clowning, horseplay, monkey tricks, pranks, shenanigans (*informal*), skylarking (*informal*), tomfoolery 2 = dishonesty, chicanery, funny business, hanky-panky (*informal*), skulduggery (*informal*), trickery

monolithic *adjective* = huge, colossal, giant, gigantic, immovable, impenetrable, imposing, intractable, massive, monumental, solid, substantial, undifferentiated, undivided, unitary

monologue *noun* = speech, harangue, lecture, sermon, soliloquy

monopolize *verb* = control, corner, corner the market in, dominate, engross, exercise *or* have a monopoly of, hog (*slang*), keep to oneself, take over, take up

monotonous *adjective* = tedious, all the same, boring, colourless, droning, dull, flat, ho-hum (*informal*), humdrum,

mind-numbing, plodding, repetitious, repetitive, samey (*informal*), soporific, tiresome, toneless, unchanging, uniform, uninflected, unvaried, wearisome
➤ **Antonyms**
animated, enjoyable, entertaining, enthralling, exciting, exhilarating, interesting, lively, sexy (*informal*), stimulating

monotony *noun* = **tedium**, boredom, colourlessness, dullness, flatness, humdrumness, monotonousness, repetitiousness, repetitiveness, routine, sameness, tediousness, tiresomeness, uniformity, wearisomeness

monster *noun* **1** = **giant**, behemoth, Brobdingnagian, colossus, leviathan, mammoth, titan **2** = **brute**, barbarian, beast, bogeyman, demon, devil, fiend, ghoul, ogre, savage, villain **3** = **freak**, abortion, lusus naturae, miscreation, monstrosity, mutant, teratism ♦ *adjective* **4** = **huge**, Brobdingnagian, colossal, elephantine, enormous, gargantuan, giant, gigantic, ginormous (*informal*), humongous *or* humungous (*U.S. slang*), immense, jumbo (*informal*), mammoth, massive, mega (*slang*), monstrous, stellar (*informal*), stupendous, titanic, tremendous

monstrosity *noun* **1** = **eyesore**, abortion, freak, horror, lusus naturae, miscreation, monster, mutant, ogre, teratism **2** = **hideousness**, abnormality, atrocity, dreadfulness, evil, frightfulness, heinousness, hellishness, horror, loathsomeness, obscenity

monstrous *adjective* **1** = **unnatural**, abnormal, dreadful, enormous, fiendish, freakish, frightful, grotesque, gruesome, hellish, hideous, horrendous, horrible, miscreated, obscene, teratoid, terrible **2** = **outrageous**, atrocious, cruel, devilish, diabolical, disgraceful, egregious, evil, fiendish, foul, heinous, horrifying, infamous, inhuman, intolerable, loathsome, odious, satanic, scandalous, shocking, vicious, villainous **3** = **huge**, colossal, elephantine, enormous, gargantuan, giant, gigantic, ginormous (*informal*), great, humongous *or* humungous (*U.S. slang*), immense, mammoth, massive, mega (*slang*), prodigious, stellar (*informal*), stupendous, titanic, towering, tremendous, vast
➤ **Antonyms**
≠**unnatural**: appealing, attractive, beautiful, delightful, lovely, natural, normal, ordinary, pleasant ≠**outrageous**: admirable, decent, fine, good, honourable, humane, kind, merciful, mild ≠**huge**: diminutive, insignificant, little, meagre, miniature, minute, puny, slight, small, tiny

month *noun* = **four weeks**, moon, thirty days

monument *noun* **1** = **memorial**, cairn, cenotaph, commemoration, gravestone, headstone, marker, mausoleum, obelisk, pillar, shrine, statue, tombstone **2** = **testament**, memento, record, remembrance, reminder, token, witness

monumental *adjective* **1** = **important**, awe-inspiring, awesome, classic, enduring, enormous, epoch-making, historic, immortal, lasting, majestic, memorable, outstanding, prodigious, significant, stupendous, unforgettable **2** = **commemorative**, cyclopean, funerary, memorial, monolithic, statuary **3** *Informal* = **immense**, catastrophic, colossal, egregious, gigantic, great, horrible, indefensible, massive, staggering, terrible, tremendous, unforgivable, whopping (*informal*)
➤ **Antonyms**
≠**important**: ephemeral, inconsequential, insignificant, modest, negligible, ordinary, trivial, undistinguished, unimportant, unimpressive, unremarkable ≠**immense**: average, insignificant, mild, petty, slight, small, tiny, trivial

mood *noun* **1** = **state of mind**, disposition, frame of mind, humour, spirit, temper, tenor, vein **2** = **depression**, bad temper, bate (*Brit. slang*), blues, doldrums, dumps (*informal*), fit of pique, grumps (*informal*), low spirits, melancholy, sulk, the hump (*Brit. informal*), the sulks, wax (*informal, chiefly Brit.*) **3** **in the mood** = **inclined**, disposed (towards), eager, favourable, interested, in the (right) frame of mind, keen, minded, willing

moody *adjective* **1** = **sulky**, angry, cantankerous, crabbed, crabby, cross, crotchety (*informal*), crusty, curt, huffish, huffy, ill-humoured, ill-tempered, in a huff, irascible, irritable, offended, petulant, piqued, pissed (*taboo slang*), pissed off (*taboo slang*), short-tempered, splenetic, temperamental, testy, tetchy, touchy, waspish, wounded **2** = **gloomy**, broody, crestfallen, dismal, doleful, dour, downcast, down in the dumps (*informal*), down in the mouth (*informal*), frowning, glum, in the doldrums, introspective, lugubrious, melancholy, miserable, mopish, mopy, morose, out of sorts (*informal*), pensive, sad, saturnine, sullen **3** = **changeable**, capricious, erratic, faddish, fickle, fitful, flighty, impulsive, inconstant, mercurial, temperamental, unpredictable, unstable, unsteady, volatile
➤ **Antonyms**
≠**sulky, gloomy**: amiable, cheerful, gay, happy, optimistic ≠**changeable**: constant, stable, steady

moon *noun* **1** = **satellite 2 once in a blue**

moon = **rarely**, almost never, hardly ever, very seldom ♦ *verb* 3 = **idle**, daydream, languish, mooch (*slang*), mope, waste time

moor¹ *noun* = **moorland**, fell (*Brit.*), heath, muir (*Scot.*)

moor² *verb* = **tie up**, anchor, berth, dock, fasten, fix, lash, make fast, secure

moot *adjective* 1 = **debatable**, arguable, at issue, contestable, controversial, disputable, doubtful, open, open to debate, undecided, unresolved, unsettled ♦ *verb* 2 = **bring up**, broach, introduce, propose, put forward, suggest, ventilate

mop *noun* 1 = **squeegee**, sponge, swab 2 = **mane**, shock, tangle, thatch ♦ *verb* 3 = **clean**, soak up, sponge, swab, wash, wipe

mope *verb* = **brood**, fret, languish, moon, pine, pout, sulk

mop up *verb* 1 = **clean up**, mop, soak up, sponge, swab, wash, wipe 2 *Military* = **finish off**, account for, clean out, clear, eliminate, neutralize, pacify, round up, secure

moral *adjective* 1 = **ethical** 2 = **good**, blameless, chaste, decent, ethical, high-minded, honest, honourable, incorruptible, innocent, just, meritorious, noble, principled, proper, pure, right, righteous, upright, upstanding, virtuous ♦ *noun* 3 = **lesson**, meaning, message, point, significance
➤ **Antonyms**
adjective ≠**good**: amoral, dishonest, dishonourable, immoral, improper, sinful, unethical, unfair, unjust, wrong

morale *noun* = **confidence**, esprit de corps, heart, mettle, self-esteem, spirit, temper

morality *noun* 1 = **integrity**, chastity, decency, ethicality, ethicalness, goodness, honesty, justice, principle, rectitude, righteousness, rightness, uprightness, virtue 2 = **standards**, conduct, ethics, habits, ideals, manners, moral code, morals, mores, philosophy, principles

morals *plural noun* = **morality**, behaviour, conduct, ethics, habits, integrity, manners, mores, principles, scruples, standards

morass *noun* 1 = **marsh**, bog, fen, quagmire, slough, swamp 2 = **mess**, confusion, mix-up, muddle, tangle

moratorium *noun* = **postponement**, freeze, halt, respite, standstill, stay, suspension

morbid *adjective* 1 = **unwholesome**, brooding, funereal, ghoulish, gloomy, grim, melancholy, pessimistic, sick, sombre, unhealthy 2 = **gruesome**, dreadful, ghastly, grisly, hideous, horrid, macabre 3 = **diseased**, ailing, deadly, infected, malignant, pathological, sick, sickly,

unhealthy, unsound
➤ **Antonyms**
≠**unwholesome**: bright, cheerful, happy, healthy, wholesome ≠**diseased**: healthy, salubrious

mordant *adjective* = **sarcastic**, biting, caustic, cutting, incisive, pungent, scathing, stinging, trenchant

more *adjective* 1 = **extra**, added, additional, fresh, further, new, new-found, other, spare, supplementary ♦ *adverb* 2 = **to a greater extent**, better, further, longer

moreover *adverb* = **furthermore**, additionally, also, as well, besides, further, in addition, into the bargain, likewise, to boot, too, what is more, withal (*literary*)

morgue *noun* = **mortuary**

moribund *adjective* 1 = **dying**, at death's door, breathing one's last, doomed, fading fast, failing, (having) one foot in the grave, *in extremis*, near death, near the end, on one's deathbed, on one's last legs 2 = **declining**, at a standstill, forceless, obsolescent, on its last legs, on the way out, stagnant, stagnating, standing still, waning, weak

morning *noun* = **dawn**, a.m., break of day, daybreak, forenoon, morn (*poetic*), morrow (*archaic*), sunrise

moron *noun* = **fool**, airhead (*slang*), ass, berk (*Brit. slang*), blockhead, bonehead (*slang*), charlie (*Brit. informal*), chump, coot, cretin, dickhead (*slang*), dickwit (*slang*), dimwit (*informal*), dipstick (*Brit. slang*), divvy (*Brit. slang*), dolt, dope (*informal*), dork (*slang*), dumb-ass (*slang*), dummy (*slang*), dunce, dunderhead, dweeb (*U.S. slang*), fathead (*informal*), fuckwit (*taboo slang*), geek (*slang*), gobshite (*Irish taboo slang*), gonzo (*slang*), halfwit, idiot, imbecile, jerk (*slang, chiefly U.S. & Canad.*), lamebrain (*informal*), mental defective, muttonhead (*slang*), nerd or nurd (*slang*), nitwit (*informal*), numbskull or numskull, numpty (*Scot. informal*), oaf, pillock (*Brit. slang*), plank (*Brit. slang*), plonker (*slang*), prat (*slang*), prick (*derogatory slang*), schmuck (*U.S. slang*), simpleton, thickhead, tosser (*Brit. slang*), twit (*informal, chiefly Brit.*), wally (*slang*), weenie (*U.S. informal*)

moronic *adjective* = **idiotic**, cretinous, dumb-ass (*slang*), foolish, halfwitted, imbecilic, mindless, stupid, unintelligent

morose *adjective* = **sullen**, blue, churlish, crabbed, crabby, cross, crusty, depressed, dour, down, down in the dumps (*informal*), gloomy, glum, grouchy (*informal*), gruff, ill-humoured, ill-natured, ill-tempered, in a bad mood, low, melancholy, miserable, moody, mournful, perverse, pessimistic,

saturnine, sour, sulky, surly, taciturn
➤ **Antonyms**
amiable, blithe, cheerful, chirpy (*informal*),
friendly, gay, genial, good-humoured,
good-natured, happy, pleasant, sweet

morsel *noun* = piece, bit, bite, crumb,
fraction, fragment, grain, mouthful, nibble,
part, scrap, segment, slice, snack, soupçon,
tad (*informal, chiefly U.S.*), taste, titbit

mortal *adjective* 1 = human, corporeal,
earthly, ephemeral, impermanent, passing,
sublunary, temporal, transient, worldly 2
= fatal, deadly, death-dealing, destructive,
killing, lethal, murderous, terminal 3
= unrelenting, bitter, deadly, implacable,
irreconcilable, out-and-out, remorseless,
sworn, to the death 4 = great, agonizing,
awful, dire, enormous, extreme, grave,
intense, serious, severe, terrible ♦ *noun* 5
= human being, being, body, earthling,
human, individual, man, person, woman

mortality *noun* 1 = humanity,
ephemerality, impermanence, temporality,
transience 2 = killing, bloodshed, carnage,
death, destruction, fatality, loss of life

mortification *noun* 1 = humiliation,
abasement, annoyance, chagrin,
discomfiture, dissatisfaction, embarrassment,
loss of face, shame, vexation 2 = discipline,
abasement, chastening, control, denial,
subjugation 3 *Medical* = gangrene,
corruption, festering, necrosis, putrescence

mortified *adjective* 1 = humiliated,
abashed, affronted, annoyed, ashamed,
chagrined, chastened, confounded, crushed,
deflated, discomfited, displeased,
embarrassed, given a showing-up
(*informal*), humbled, made to eat humble
pie (*informal*), pissed (*taboo slang*), pissed
off (*taboo slang*), put down, put out
(*informal*), put to shame, rendered
speechless, shamed, vexed 2 = disciplined,
abased, chastened, conquered, controlled,
crushed, subdued 3 *Of flesh* = gangrenous,
decayed, necrotic, rotted

mortify *verb* 1 = humiliate, abase, abash,
affront, annoy, chagrin, chasten, confound,
crush, deflate, disappoint, discomfit,
displease, embarrass, humble, make
(someone) eat humble pie (*informal*), put
down, put to shame, shame, take (someone)
down a peg (*informal*), vex 2 = discipline,
abase, chasten, control, deny, subdue 3 *Of
flesh* = putrefy, become gangrenous,
corrupt, deaden, die, fester, gangrene,
necrose

mortuary *noun* = morgue, funeral home
(*U.S.*), funeral parlour

mostly *adverb* = generally, above all,
almost entirely, as a rule, chiefly,

customarily, for the most part, largely,
mainly, most often, on the whole,
particularly, predominantly, primarily,
principally, usually

moth-eaten *adjective* = decayed,
antiquated, decrepit, dilapidated, grungy
(*slang, chiefly U.S.*), obsolete, outdated,
outworn, ragged, scuzzy (*slang, chiefly
U.S.*), seedy, shabby, stale, tattered,
threadbare, worn-out

mother *noun* 1 = parent, dam, ma
(*informal*), mater, mom (*U.S. informal*),
mum (*Brit. informal*), mummy (*Brit.
informal*), old lady (*informal*), old woman
(*informal*) ♦ *adjective* 2 = native, connate,
inborn, innate, natural ♦ *verb* 3 = give birth
to, bear, bring forth, drop, produce 4
= nurture, care for, cherish, nurse, protect,
raise, rear, tend 5 = pamper, baby, fuss
over, indulge, spoil

motherly *adjective* = maternal,
affectionate, caring, comforting, fond,
gentle, kind, loving, protective, sheltering,
tender, warm

mother wit *noun* = common sense,
brains, gumption (*Brit. informal*), horse
sense, judgment, native intelligence, nous
(*Brit. slang*), savvy (*slang*), smarts (*slang,
chiefly U.S.*)

motif *noun* 1 = theme, concept, idea,
leitmotif, subject 2 = design, decoration,
ornament, shape

motion *noun* 1 = movement, action,
change, flow, kinesics, locomotion, mobility,
motility, move, passage, passing, progress,
travel 2 = gesture, gesticulation, sign, signal,
wave 3 = proposal, proposition,
recommendation, submission, suggestion 4
in motion = moving, afoot, functioning,
going, in progress, on the go (*informal*), on
the move (*informal*), operational, travelling,
under way, working ♦ *verb* 5 = gesture,
beckon, direct, gesticulate, nod, signal, wave

motionless *adjective* = still, at a standstill,
at rest, calm, fixed, frozen, halted, immobile,
inanimate, inert, lifeless, paralysed, standing,
static, stationary, stock-still, transfixed,
unmoved, unmoving
➤ **Antonyms**
active, agitated, animated, frantic, lively,
mobile, moving, restless, travelling

motivate *verb* = inspire, actuate, arouse,
bring, cause, draw, drive, get going, give
incentive to, impel, induce, inspirit, instigate,
lead, move, persuade, prod, prompt,
provoke, set off, set on, stimulate, stir, trigger

motivation *noun* 1 = inspiration,
ambition, desire, drive, hunger, interest,
wish 2 = incentive, carrot and stick, impulse,
incitement, inducement, inspiration,

instigation, motive, persuasion, reason, spur, stimulus

motive *noun* 1 = **reason**, cause, design, ground(s), incentive, incitement, inducement, influence, inspiration, intention, mainspring, motivation, object, occasion, purpose, rationale, spur, stimulus, the why and wherefore, thinking ◆ *adjective* 2 = **moving**, activating, driving, impelling, motivating, operative, prompting

motley *adjective* 1 = **miscellaneous**, assorted, disparate, dissimilar, diversified, heterogeneous, mingled, mixed, unlike, varied 2 = **multicoloured**, chequered, particoloured, polychromatic, polychrome, polychromous, rainbow, variegated
➤ **Antonyms**
≠**miscellaneous**: homogeneous, similar, uniform ≠**multicoloured**: monochromatic, plain, self-coloured, solid

mottled *adjective* = **blotchy**, brindled, chequered, dappled, flecked, freckled, marbled, piebald, pied, speckled, spotted, stippled, streaked, tabby, variegated

motto *noun* = **saying**, adage, byword, cry, dictum, formula, gnome, maxim, precept, proverb, rule, saw, slogan, tag-line, watchword

mould[1] *noun* 1 = **cast**, die, form, matrix, pattern, shape, stamp 2 = **design**, brand, build, configuration, construction, cut, fashion, form, format, frame, kind, line, make, pattern, shape, stamp, structure, style 3 = **nature**, calibre, character, ilk, kidney, kind, quality, sort, stamp, type ◆ *verb* 4 = **shape**, carve, cast, construct, create, fashion, forge, form, make, model, sculpt, stamp, work 5 = **influence**, affect, control, direct, form, make, shape

mould[2] *noun* = **fungus**, blight, mildew, mouldiness, mustiness

mouldy *adjective* = **stale**, bad, blighted, decaying, fusty, mildewed, musty, rotten, rotting, spoiled

mound *noun* 1 = **heap**, bing (*Scot.*), drift, pile, rick, stack 2 = **hill**, bank, dune, embankment, hillock, knoll, rise 3 = **earthwork**, bulwark, motte (*History*), rampart 4 *Archaeology* = **barrow**, tumulus

mount *verb* 1 = **ascend**, clamber up, climb, escalade, go up, make one's way up, scale 2 = **get (up) on**, bestride, climb onto, climb up on, get astride, jump on 3 = **increase**, accumulate, build, escalate, grow, intensify, multiply, pile up, swell 4 = **display**, frame, set, set off 5 = **fit**, emplace, install, place, position, put in place, set up 6 = **stage**, exhibit, get up (*informal*), prepare, produce, put on 7 *Military* = **launch**, deliver, prepare, ready, set in motion, stage ◆ *noun* 8

= **backing**, base, fixture, foil, frame, mounting, setting, stand, support 9 = **horse**, steed (*literary*)
➤ **Antonyms**
verb ≠**ascend**: descend, drop, go down, make one's way down ≠**get (up) on**: climb down from, climb off, dismount, get down from, get off, jump off ≠**increase**: contract, decline, decrease, diminish, dwindle, fall, lessen, lower, reduce, shrink, wane

mountain *noun* 1 = **peak**, alp, ben (*Scot.*), berg (*S. Afr.*), elevation, eminence, fell (*Brit.*), height, mount, Munro 2 = **heap**, abundance, mass, mound, pile, stack, ton

mountainous *adjective* 1 = **high**, alpine, highland, rocky, soaring, steep, towering, upland 2 = **huge**, daunting, enormous, gigantic, great, hulking, immense, mammoth, mighty, monumental, ponderous, prodigious
➤ **Antonyms**
≠**huge**: diminutive, insignificant, little, minute, petty, puny, small, tiny, trivial, weak

mourn *verb* = **grieve**, bemoan, bewail, deplore, keen, lament, miss, rue, sorrow, wail, wear black, weep

mournful *adjective* 1 = **sad**, afflicting, calamitous, deplorable, distressing, grievous, harrowing, lamentable, melancholy, painful, piteous, plaintive, sorrowful, tragic, unhappy, woeful 2 = **dismal**, brokenhearted, cheerless, desolate, disconsolate, downcast, down in the dumps (*informal*), funereal, gloomy, grief-stricken, grieving, heartbroken, heavy, heavy-hearted, joyless, lugubrious, melancholy, miserable, rueful, sad, sombre, unhappy, woeful
➤ **Antonyms**
≠**sad**: agreeable, cheerful, fortunate, happy, lucky, pleasant, satisfying ≠**dismal**: bright, cheerful, chirpy (*informal*), genial, happy, jolly, joyful, light-hearted, sunny, upbeat (*informal*)

mourning *noun* 1 = **grieving**, bereavement, grief, keening, lamentation, weeping, woe 2 = **black**, sackcloth and ashes, weeds, widow's weeds

mouth *noun* 1 = **lips**, chops (*slang*), gob (*slang, especially Brit.*), jaws, maw, trap (*slang*), yap (*slang*) 2 *Informal* = **boasting**, braggadocio, bragging, empty talk, gas (*informal*), hot air (*slang*), idle talk 3 *Informal* = **insolence**, backchat (*informal*), cheek (*informal*), impudence, lip (*slang*), rudeness, sauce (*informal*) 4 = **opening**, aperture, cavity, crevice, door, entrance, gateway, inlet, lips, orifice, rim 5 **down in** or **at the mouth** = **depressed**, blue, crestfallen, dejected, disheartened, dispirited, down, downcast, down in the dumps (*informal*), in low spirits, melancholy, miserable, sad, sick as a parrot (*informal*), unhappy

mouthful *noun* = **taste**, bit, bite, drop, forkful, little, morsel, sample, sip, spoonful, sup, swallow

mouthpiece *noun* **1** = **spokesperson**, agent, delegate, representative, spokesman *or* spokeswoman **2** = **publication**, journal, organ, periodical

movable *adjective* = **portable**, detachable, mobile, not fixed, portative, transferable, transportable

move *verb* **1** = **go**, advance, budge, change position, drift, march, proceed, progress, shift, stir, walk **2** = **change**, carry, shift, switch, transfer, transport, transpose **3** = **relocate**, change residence, flit (*Scot. & Northern English dialect*), go away, leave, migrate, move house, pack one's bags (*informal*), quit, remove **4** = **drive**, activate, impel, motivate, operate, prod, propel, push, set going, shift, shove, start, turn **5** = **prompt**, actuate, cause, give rise to, impel, incite, induce, influence, inspire, instigate, lead, motivate, persuade, rouse, stimulate, urge **6** = **touch**, affect, agitate, excite, impress, make an impression on, tug at (someone's) heartstrings (*often facetious*) **7** = **propose**, advocate, put forward, recommend, suggest, urge ◆ *noun* **8** = **action**, act, deed, manoeuvre, measure, motion, movement, ploy, shift, step, stratagem, stroke, turn **9** = **transfer**, change of address, flit (*Scot. & Northern English dialect*), flitting (*Scot. & Northern English dialect*), migration, relocation, removal, shift **10 get a move on** = **speed up**, get cracking (*informal*), get going, hurry (up), make haste, shake a leg (*informal*), step on it (*informal*), stir oneself **11 on the move** *Informal* **a** = **in transit**, journeying, moving, on the road (*informal*), on the run, on the wing, travelling, under way, voyaging **b** = **active**, advancing, astir, going forward, moving, progressing, stirring, succeeding
➤ **Antonyms**
verb ≠**prompt**: deter, discourage, dissuade, prevent, stop

movement *noun* **1** = **motion**, act, action, activity, advance, agitation, change, development, displacement, exercise, flow, gesture, manoeuvre, move, moving, operation, progress, progression, shift, steps, stir, stirring, transfer **2** = **group**, camp, campaign, crusade, drive, faction, front, grouping, organization, party **3** = **trend**, current, drift, flow, swing, tendency **4** *Music* = **section**, division, part, passage **5** = **workings**, action, innards (*informal*), machinery, mechanism, works **6** = **rhythm**, beat, cadence, measure (*Prosody*), metre, pace, swing, tempo

movie *noun* = **film**, feature, flick (*slang*), picture

moving *adjective* **1** = **emotional**, affecting, arousing, emotive, exciting, impelling, impressive, inspiring, pathetic, persuasive, poignant, stirring, touching **2** = **mobile**, motile, movable, portable, running, unfixed
➤ **Antonyms**
≠**emotional**: unemotional, unexciting, unimpressive, uninspiring ≠**mobile**: fixed, immobile, immovable, stationary, still, unmoving

mow *verb* = **cut**, crop, scythe, shear, trim

mow down *verb* = **massacre**, blow away (*slang, chiefly U.S.*), butcher, cut down, cut to pieces, shoot down, slaughter

much *adjective* **1** = **great**, abundant, a lot of, ample, considerable, copious, plenteous, plenty of, sizable *or* sizeable, substantial ◆ *noun* **2** = **a lot**, a good deal, a great deal, an appreciable amount, heaps (*informal*), loads (*informal*), lots (*informal*), plenty ◆ *adverb* **3** = **greatly**, a great deal, a lot, considerably, decidedly, exceedingly, frequently, indeed, often, regularly
➤ **Antonyms**
adjective ≠**great**: inadequate, insufficient, little, scant ◆ *noun* ≠**a lot**: hardly anything, little, next to nothing, not a lot, not much, practically nothing, very little ◆ *adverb* ≠**greatly**: barely, hardly, infrequently, irregularly, not a lot, not much, occasionally, only just, rarely, scarcely, seldom, slightly

muck *noun* **1** = **dirt**, crap (*slang*), crud (*slang*), filth, grot (*slang*), gunge (*informal*), gunk (*informal*), kak (*S. African informal*), mire, mud, ooze, scum, sewage, shit (*taboo slang*), slime, slob (*Irish*), sludge **2** = **manure**, crap (*taboo slang*), dung, ordure, shit (*taboo slang*) **3 make a muck of** *Slang* = **spoil**, blow (*slang*), botch, bungle, cock up (*Brit. slang*), flub (*U.S. slang*), fuck up (*offensive taboo slang*), make a mess of, make a nonsense of, make a pig's ear of (*informal*), mar, mess up, muff, ruin, screw up (*informal*)

muck up *verb* = **ruin**, blow (*slang*), bodge (*informal*), botch, bungle, cock up (*Brit. slang*), flub (*U.S. slang*), fuck up (*offensive taboo slang*), make a mess of, make a muck of (*slang*), make a nonsense of, make a pig's ear of (*informal*), mar, mess up, muff, screw up (*informal*), spoil

mucky *adjective* = **dirty**, begrimed, filthy, grimy, messy, muddy

mud *noun* = **dirt**, clay, gloop (*informal*), mire, ooze, silt, slime, slob (*Irish*), sludge

muddle *noun* **1** = **confusion**, chaos, clutter, daze, disarray, disorder, disorganization, fankle (*Scot.*), hodgepodge (*U.S.*), hotchpotch, jumble, mess, mix-up, perplexity, pig's breakfast (*informal*), plight, predicament, ravel, tangle ♦ *verb* 2 = **jumble**, confuse, disarrange, disorder, disorganize, make a mess of, mess, mix up, ravel, scramble, spoil, tangle 3 = **confuse**, befuddle, bewilder, confound, daze, disorient, perplex, stupefy

muddled *adjective* 1 = **jumbled**, chaotic, confused, disarrayed, disordered, disorganized, higgledy-piggledy (*informal*), messy, mixed-up, scrambled, tangled 2 = **bewildered**, at sea, befuddled, confused, dazed, disoriented, perplexed, stupefied, vague 3 = **incoherent**, confused, loose, muddleheaded, unclear, woolly
➤ **Antonyms**
≠**jumbled**: cut-and-dried (*informal*), orderly, organized ≠**incoherent**: clear, exact, precise

muddy *adjective* 1 = **dirty**, bespattered, clarty (*Scot., & Northern English dialect*), grimy, mucky, mud-caked, soiled 2 = **boggy**, marshy, miry, quaggy, swampy 3 = **dull**, blurred, dingy, flat, lustreless, smoky, unclear, washed-out 4 = **cloudy**, dirty, foul, impure, opaque, turbid 5 = **confused**, fuzzy, hazy, indistinct, muddled, unclear, vague, woolly ♦ *verb* 6 = **smear**, begrime, bespatter, cloud, dirty, smirch, soil

muffle *verb* 1 = **deaden**, dull, gag, hush, muzzle, quieten, silence, soften, stifle, suppress 2 = **wrap up**, cloak, conceal, cover, disguise, envelop, hood, mask, shroud, swaddle, swathe

muffled *adjective* = **indistinct**, dim, dull, faint, muted, stifled, strangled, subdued, suppressed

mug[1] *noun* = **cup**, beaker, flagon, jug, pot, stein, tankard, toby jug

mug[2] *noun* 1 = **face**, countenance, features, visage 2 = **fool**, chump (*informal*), easy *or* soft touch (*slang*), simpleton, sucker (*slang*)

mug[3] *verb* = **attack**, assault, beat up, rob, set about *or* upon

muggy *adjective* = **humid**, clammy, close, damp, moist, oppressive, sticky, stuffy, sultry

mug up *verb* = **study**, bone up on (*informal*), burn the midnight oil (*informal*), cram (*informal*), get up (*informal*), swot (*Brit. informal*)

mull *verb* = **ponder**, consider, contemplate, deliberate, examine, meditate, muse on, reflect on, review, ruminate, study, think about, think over, turn over in one's mind, weigh

multifarious *adjective* = **diverse**, different, diversified, legion, manifold, many, miscellaneous, multiform, multiple, multitudinous, numerous, sundry, varied, variegated

multiple *adjective* = **many**, collective, manifold, multitudinous, numerous, several, sundry, various

multiply *verb* 1 = **increase**, accumulate, augment, build up, expand, extend, proliferate, spread 2 = **reproduce**, breed, propagate
➤ **Antonyms**
≠**increase**: abate, decline, decrease, diminish, lessen, reduce

multitude *noun* 1 = **mass**, army, assemblage, assembly, collection, concourse, congregation, crowd, great number, horde, host, legion, lot, lots (*informal*), mob, myriad, sea, swarm, throng 2 = **public**, commonalty, common people, herd, hoi polloi, mob, populace, proletariat, rabble

munch *verb* = **chew**, champ, chomp, crunch, masticate, scrunch

mundane *adjective* 1 = **ordinary**, banal, commonplace, day-to-day, everyday, humdrum, prosaic, routine, vanilla (*slang*), workaday 2 = **earthly**, fleshly, human, material, mortal, secular, sublunary, temporal, terrestrial, worldly
➤ **Antonyms**
≠**ordinary**: dramatic, exciting, extraordinary, ground-breaking, imaginative, interesting, left-field (*informal*), novel, original, special, uncommon, unusual ≠**earthly**: ethereal, heavenly, spiritual, unworldly

municipal *adjective* = **civic**, borough, city, community, public, town, urban

municipality *noun* = **town**, borough, burgh (*Scot.*), city, district, township, urban community

munificence *noun* = **generosity**, beneficence, benevolence, big-heartedness, bounteousness, bounty, generousness, largesse *or* largess, liberality, magnanimousness, open-handedness, philanthropy

munificent *adjective* = **generous**, beneficent, benevolent, big-hearted, bounteous, bountiful, free-handed, lavish, liberal, magnanimous, open-handed, philanthropic, princely, rich, unstinting
➤ **Antonyms**
cheap, mean, miserly, parsimonious, small, stingy

murder *noun* 1 = **killing**, assassination, bloodshed, butchery, carnage, homicide, manslaughter, massacre, slaying 2 *Informal* = **agony**, an ordeal, a trial, danger, difficulty, hell (*informal*), misery, trouble ♦ *verb* 3 = **kill**, assassinate, blow away (*slang, chiefly U.S.*), bump off (*slang*), butcher, destroy, dispatch, do in (*informal*), do to death, eliminate (*slang*), hit (*slang*), massacre, rub out (*U.S. slang*), slaughter, slay, take out (*slang*), take the life of, waste (*informal*) **4** = **ruin**, abuse, butcher, destroy, mangle, mar, misuse, spoil **5** *Informal* = **beat decisively**, blow out of the water (*slang*), cream (*slang, chiefly U.S.*), defeat utterly, drub, hammer (*informal*), lick (*informal*), make mincemeat of (*informal*), slaughter, stuff (*slang*), tank (*slang*), thrash, wipe the floor with (*informal*)

murderer *noun* = **killer**, assassin, butcher, cut-throat, hit man (*slang*), homicide, slaughterer, slayer

murderous *adjective* **1** = **deadly**, barbarous, bloodthirsty, bloody, brutal, cruel, cut-throat, death-dealing, destructive, devastating, fatal, fell (*archaic*), ferocious, internecine, lethal, sanguinary, savage, slaughterous, withering **2** *Informal* = **unpleasant**, arduous, dangerous, difficult, exhausting, harrowing, hellish (*informal*), killing (*informal*), sapping, strenuous

murky *adjective* = **dark**, cheerless, cloudy, dim, dismal, dreary, dull, dusky, foggy, gloomy, grey, impenetrable, misty, nebulous, obscure, overcast
➤ **Antonyms**
bright, cheerful, clear, distinct, sunny

murmur *verb* **1** = **mumble**, babble, buzz, drone, hum, mutter, purr, rumble, speak in an undertone, whisper **2** = **grumble**, beef (*slang*), carp, cavil, complain, gripe (*informal*), grouse, moan (*informal*) ♦ *noun* **3** = **drone**, babble, buzzing, humming, mumble, muttering, purr, rumble, susurrus (*literary*), undertone, whisper, whispering **4** = **complaint**, beef (*slang*), gripe (*informal*), grouse, grumble, moan (*informal*), word

muscle *noun* **1** = **tendon**, muscle tissue, sinew, thew **2** = **strength**, brawn, clout (*informal*), force, forcefulness, might, potency, power, stamina, sturdiness, weight ♦ *verb* **3 muscle in** *Informal* = **impose oneself**, butt in, elbow one's way in, force one's way in

muscular *adjective* = **strong**, athletic, beefy (*informal*), brawny, husky (*informal*), lusty, powerful, powerfully built, robust, sinewy, stalwart, strapping, sturdy, thickset, vigorous, well-knit

muse *verb* = **ponder**, be in a brown study, be lost in thought, brood, cogitate, consider, contemplate, deliberate, dream, meditate, mull over, reflect, ruminate, speculate, think, think over, weigh

mushroom *verb* = **expand**, boom, burgeon, flourish, grow rapidly, increase, luxuriate, proliferate, shoot up, spread, spring up, sprout

mushy *adjective* **1** = **soft**, pulpy, semi-solid, slushy, squashy, squelchy, squidgy

(*informal*) **2** *Informal* = **sentimental**, icky (*informal*), maudlin, mawkish, saccharine, schmaltzy (*slang*), sloppy (*informal*), slushy (*informal*)

musical *adjective* = **melodious**, dulcet, euphonic, euphonious, harmonious, lilting, lyrical, melodic, sweet-sounding, tuneful
➤ **Antonyms**
discordant, grating, harsh, unmelodious, unmusical

musing *noun* = **thinking**, absent-mindedness, abstraction, brown study, cerebration, cogitation, contemplation, day-dreaming, dreaming, introspection, meditation, reflection, reverie, rumination, woolgathering

must *noun* = **necessity**, duty, essential, fundamental, imperative, necessary thing, obligation, prerequisite, requirement, requisite, *sine qua non*

muster *verb* **1** = **assemble**, call together, call up, collect, come together, congregate, convene, convoke, enrol, gather, group, marshal, meet, mobilize, rally, round up, summon ♦ *noun* **2** = **assembly**, assemblage, collection, concourse, congregation, convention, convocation, gathering, meeting, mobilization, rally, roundup **3 pass muster** = **be acceptable**, be or come up to scratch, fill the bill (*informal*), make the grade, measure up, qualify

musty *adjective* **1** = **stale**, airless, dank, decayed, frowsty, fusty, mildewed, mildewy, mouldy, old, smelly, stuffy **2** = **old-fashioned**, ancient, antediluvian, antiquated, banal, clichéd, dull, hackneyed, hoary, moth-eaten, obsolete, stale, threadbare, trite, worn-out
➤ **Antonyms**
≠**old-fashioned**: current, exciting, fashionable, fresh, imaginative, interesting, lively, modern, modish, new, novel, original, unusual, up-to-date, with it (*informal*)

mutability *noun* = **change**, alteration, evolution, metamorphosis, transition, variation, vicissitude

mutable *adjective* = **changeable**, adaptable, alterable, changing, fickle, flexible, inconsistent, inconstant, irresolute, uncertain, undependable, unreliable, unsettled, unstable, unsteady, vacillating, variable, volatile, wavering

mutation *noun* **1** = **change**, alteration, deviation, evolution, metamorphosis, modification, transfiguration, transformation, variation **2** = **mutant**, anomaly, deviant

mute *adjective* **1** = **silent**, aphasiac, aphasic, aphonic, dumb, mum, speechless, unexpressed, unspeaking, unspoken, voiceless, wordless ♦ *verb* **2** = **muffle**, dampen, deaden, lower, moderate, soften, soft-pedal, subdue, tone down, turn down

mutilate *verb* **1** = **maim**, amputate, butcher, cripple, cut to pieces, cut up, damage, disable, disfigure, dismember, hack, injure, lacerate, lame, mangle **2** = **distort**, adulterate, bowdlerize, butcher, censor, cut, damage, expurgate, hack, mar, spoil

mutinous *adjective* = **rebellious**, bolshie (*Brit. informal*), contumacious, disobedient, insubordinate, insurgent, refractory, revolutionary, riotous, seditious, subversive, turbulent, ungovernable, unmanageable, unruly

mutiny *noun* **1** = **rebellion**, defiance, disobedience, insubordination, insurrection, refusal to obey orders, resistance, revolt, revolution, riot, rising, strike, uprising ♦ *verb* **2** = **rebel**, be insubordinate, defy authority, disobey, refuse to obey orders, resist, revolt, rise up, strike

mutter *verb* = **grumble**, complain, grouch (*informal*), grouse, mumble, murmur, rumble

mutual *adjective* = **shared**, common, communal, correlative, interactive, interchangeable, interchanged, joint, reciprocal, reciprocated, requited, returned

muzzle *noun* **1** = **jaws**, mouth, nose, snout **2** = **gag**, guard ♦ *verb* **3** = **suppress**, censor, choke, curb, gag, restrain, silence, stifle

myopic *adjective* = **short-sighted**, near-sighted

myriad *adjective* **1** = **innumerable**, a thousand and one, countless, immeasurable, incalculable, multitudinous, untold ♦ *noun* **2** = **multitude**, a million, army, a thousand, flood, horde, host, millions, mountain, scores, sea, swarm, thousands

mysterious *adjective* **1** = **strange**, abstruse, arcane, baffling, concealed, cryptic, curious, Delphic, enigmatic, hidden, impenetrable, incomprehensible, inexplicable, inscrutable, insoluble, mystical, mystifying, obscure, perplexing, puzzling, recondite, secret, sphinxlike, uncanny, unfathomable, unknown, veiled, weird **2** = **secretive**, cloak-and-dagger, covert, furtive ➤ **Antonyms**
apparent, clear, manifest, open, plain

mystery *noun* = **puzzle**, cloak and dagger, closed book, conundrum, enigma, problem, question, riddle, secrecy, secret, teaser

mystic, mystical *adjective*
= **supernatural**, abstruse, arcane, cabalistic, cryptic, enigmatical, esoteric, hidden, inscrutable, metaphysical, mysterious, nonrational, occult, otherworldly, paranormal, preternatural, transcendental

mystify *verb* = **puzzle**, baffle, bamboozle (*informal*), be all Greek to (*informal*), beat (*slang*), befog, bewilder, confound, confuse, elude, escape, flummox, nonplus, perplex, stump

mystique *noun* = **fascination**, awe, charisma, charm, glamour, magic, spell

myth *noun* **1** = **legend**, allegory, fable, fairy story, fiction, folk tale, parable, saga, story, tradition, urban legend, urban myth **2** = **illusion**, delusion, fancy, fantasy, figment, imagination, superstition, tall story

mythical *adjective* **1** = **legendary**, allegorical, chimerical, fabled, fabulous, fairy-tale, mythological, storied **2** = **imaginary**, fabricated, fanciful, fantasy, fictitious, invented, made-up, make-believe, nonexistent, pretended, unreal, untrue

mythological *adjective* = **legendary**, fabulous, mythic, mythical, traditional

mythology *noun* = **legend**, folklore, folk tales, lore, mythos, myths, stories, tradition

N n

nab *verb* = **catch**, apprehend, arrest, capture, catch in the act, collar (*informal*), feel one's collar (*slang*), grab, lift (*slang*), nail (*informal*), nick (*slang, chiefly Brit.*), seize, snatch

nadir *noun* = **bottom**, depths, lowest point, minimum, rock bottom, zero
➤ **Antonyms**
acme, apex, climax, crest, height, high point, peak, pinnacle, summit, top, vertex, zenith

naevus *noun* = **birthmark**, mole

naff *adjective Brit. slang* = **bad**, duff (*Brit. informal*), inferior, low-grade, pants (*slang*), poor, rubbishy, second-rate, shabby, shoddy, substandard, trashy, worthless
➤ **Antonyms**
excellent, exceptional, fine, first-class, first-rate, high-quality, superior

nag[1] *verb* 1 = **scold**, annoy, badger, bend someone's ear (*informal*), be on one's back (*slang*), berate, breathe down someone's neck, chivvy, goad, harass, harry, hassle (*informal*), henpeck, irritate, nark (*Brit., Austral., & N.Z. slang*), pester, plague, provoke, torment, upbraid, vex, worry
♦ *noun* 2 = **scold**, harpy, shrew, tartar, termagant, virago

nag[2] *noun* = **horse**, hack, jade, plug (*U.S.*)

nagging *adjective* = **irritating**, continuous, critical, distressing, on someone's back (*informal*), painful, persistent, scolding, shrewish, worrying

nail *verb* = **fasten**, attach, beat, fix, hammer, join, pin, secure, tack

naive *adjective* 1 = **gullible**, as green as grass, callow, credulous, green, unsuspicious, wet behind the ears (*informal*) 2 = **innocent**, artless, candid, childlike, confiding, frank, guileless, ingenuous, jejune, natural, open, simple, trusting, unaffected, unpretentious, unsophisticated, unworldly
➤ **Antonyms**
≠**innocent:** artful, disingenuous, experienced, sly, sophisticated, urbane, worldly, worldly-wise

naivety, naïveté *noun* 1 = **gullibility**, callowness, credulity 2 = **innocence**, artlessness, candour, frankness, guilelessness, inexperience, ingenuousness, naturalness, openness, simplicity

naked *adjective* 1 = **nude**, bare, buck naked (*slang*), denuded, disrobed, divested, exposed, in one's birthday suit (*informal*), in the altogether (*informal*), in the bare scud (*slang*), in the buff (*informal*), in the raw (*informal*), naked as the day one was born (*informal*), scuddy (*slang*), starkers (*informal*), stripped, unclothed, uncovered, undraped, undressed, without a stitch on (*informal*) 2 = **undisguised**, blatant, evident, manifest, open, overt, patent, plain, simple, stark, unadorned, unconcealed, unexaggerated, unmistakable, unqualified, unvarnished
➤ **Antonyms**
≠**nude:** clothed, concealed, covered, dressed, wrapped up ≠**undisguised:** concealed, disguised

nakedness *noun* 1 = **nudity**, baldness, bareness, undress 2 = **openness**, plainness, simplicity, starkness

namby-pamby *adjective* = **feeble**, anaemic, boneless, colourless, insipid, mawkish, niminy-piminy, prim, prissy (*informal*), sentimental, spineless, vapid, weak, weedy (*informal*), wimpish *or* wimpy (*informal*), wishy-washy (*informal*), wussy (*slang*)

name *noun* 1 = **title**, appellation, cognomen, denomination, designation, epithet, handle (*slang*), moniker *or* monicker (*slang*), nickname, sobriquet, term 2 = **fame**, distinction, eminence, esteem, honour, note, praise, renown, repute 3 = **reputation**, character, credit ♦ *verb* 4 = **call**, baptize, christen, denominate, dub, entitle, label, style, term 5 = **nominate**, appoint, choose, cite, classify, commission, designate, flag, identify, mention, select, specify

named *adjective* 1 = **called**, baptized, christened, denominated, dubbed, entitled, known as, labelled, styled, termed 2 = **nominated**, appointed, chosen, cited, classified, commissioned, designated, identified, mentioned, picked, selected, singled out, specified

nameless *adjective* 1 = **anonymous**, innominate, undesignated, unnamed, untitled 2 = **unknown**, incognito, obscure, undistinguished, unheard-of, unsung 3 = **horrible**, abominable, indescribable, ineffable, inexpressible, unmentionable, unspeakable, unutterable

namely *adverb* = **specifically**, i.e., that is to say, to wit, viz.

nap[1] *noun* **1** = **sleep**, catnap, forty winks (*informal*), kip (*Brit. slang*), rest, shuteye (*slang*), siesta, zizz (*Brit. informal*) ◆ *verb* **2** = **sleep**, catnap, doze, drop off (*informal*), drowse, kip (*Brit. slang*), nod, nod off (*informal*), rest, snooze (*informal*), zizz (*Brit. informal*)

nap[2] *noun* = **weave**, down, fibre, grain, pile, shag

napkin *noun* = **serviette**, cloth

narcissism *noun* = **egotism**, self-admiration, self-love, vanity

narcotic *noun* **1** = **drug**, anaesthetic, analgesic, anodyne, opiate, painkiller, sedative, tranquillizer ◆ *adjective* **2** = **sedative**, analgesic, calming, dulling, hypnotic, Lethean, numbing, painkilling, somnolent, soporific, stupefacient, stupefactive, stupefying

nark *verb* = **annoy**, aggravate (*informal*), bother, bug, exasperate, gall, get on one's nerves (*informal*), irk, irritate, miff (*informal*), nettle, peeve, pique, piss one off (*taboo slang*), provoke, rile

narrate *verb* = **tell**, chronicle, describe, detail, recite, recount, rehearse, relate, repeat, report, set forth, unfold

narration *noun* = **telling**, description, explanation, reading, recital, rehearsal, relation, storytelling, voice-over (*in film*)

narrative *noun* = **story**, account, chronicle, detail, history, report, statement, tale

narrator *noun* = **storyteller**, annalist, author, bard, chronicler, commentator, raconteur, reciter, relater, reporter, writer

narrow *adjective* **1** = **thin**, attenuated, fine, slender, slim, spare, tapering **2** = **limited**, circumscribed, close, confined, constricted, contracted, cramped, incapacious, meagre, near, pinched, restricted, scanty, straitened, tight **3** = **exclusive**, select **4** = **insular**, biased, bigoted, dogmatic, illiberal, intolerant, narrow-minded, partial, prejudiced, puritan, reactionary, small-minded ◆ *verb* **5** = **tighten**, circumscribe, constrict, diminish, limit, reduce, simplify, straiten
➤ **Antonyms**
adjective ≠**thin**: broad, wide ≠**limited**: ample, big, broad, generous, open, spacious, wide ≠**insular**: broad-minded, generous, liberal, receptive, tolerant

narrowly *adverb* = **just**, barely, by a whisker *or* hair's-breadth, by the skin of one's teeth, only just, scarcely

narrow-minded *adjective* = **intolerant**, biased, bigoted, conservative, hidebound, illiberal, insular, opinionated, parochial, petty, prejudiced, provincial, reactionary, short-sighted, small-minded, strait-laced
➤ **Antonyms**
broad-minded, catholic, cosmopolitan, freethinking, indulgent, open-minded, permissive, tolerant, unprejudiced

narrows *plural noun* = **channel**, gulf, passage, sound, straits

nastiness *noun* = **unpleasantness**, disagreeableness, malice, meanness, offensiveness, spitefulness

nasty *adjective* **1** = **objectionable**, dirty, disagreeable, disgusting, filthy, foul, grotty (*slang*), horrible, loathsome, malodorous, mephitic, nauseating, noisome, obnoxious, odious, offensive, polluted, repellent, repugnant, sickening, unappetizing, unpleasant, vile, yucky *or* yukky (*slang*) **2** = **painful**, bad, critical, dangerous, serious, severe **3** = **spiteful**, abusive, annoying, bad-tempered, despicable, disagreeable, distasteful, malicious, mean, unpleasant, vicious, vile
➤ **Antonyms**
≠**objectionable**: admirable, agreeable, enjoyable, nice, pleasant, sweet ≠**spiteful**: decent, kind, nice, pleasant, sweet

nation *noun* = **country**, commonwealth, community, people, population, race, realm, society, state, tribe

national *adjective* **1** = **nationwide**, civil, countrywide, governmental, public, state, widespread **2** = **domestic**, internal, social ◆ *noun* **3** = **citizen**, inhabitant, native, resident, subject

nationalism *noun* = **patriotism**, allegiance, chauvinism, fealty, jingoism, loyalty, nationality

nationality *noun* = **race**, birth, ethnic group, nation

nationwide *adjective* = **national**, countrywide, general, overall, widespread

native *adjective* **1** = **local**, domestic, home, home-grown, home-made, indigenous, mother, vernacular **2** = **original**, genuine, real **3** = **inborn**, built-in, congenital, endemic, hereditary, immanent, inbred, ingrained, inherent, inherited, innate, instinctive, intrinsic, inveterate, natal, natural **4** = **indigenous**, aboriginal, autochthonous ◆ *noun* **5** = **inhabitant**, aborigine, autochthon, citizen, countryman, dweller, national, resident

nativity *noun* **1** = **birth**, delivery, parturition **2** = **crèche**, manger scene
➤ **Antonyms**
≠**birth**: death, demise, dying, expiration

natter *verb* **1** = **gossip**, blather, blether, chatter, chew the fat *or* rag (*slang*), gabble, jabber, jaw (*slang*), palaver, prate, prattle, rabbit (on) (*Brit. informal*), run off at the mouth (*slang*), shoot the breeze (*informal*), talk, talk idly, witter (*informal*) ♦ noun 2 = **gossip**, blather, blether, chat, chinwag (*Brit. informal*), chitchat, confabulation, conversation, gab (*informal*), gabble, gabfest (*informal, chiefly U.S. & Canad.*), jabber, jaw (*slang*), palaver, prattle, talk

natty *adjective* = **smart**, chic, crucial (*slang*), dapper, elegant, fashionable, neat, snazzy (*informal*), spruce, stylish, trendy (*Brit. informal*), trim, well-dressed, well-turned-out

natural *adjective* 1 = **normal**, common, everyday, legitimate, logical, ordinary, regular, typical, usual 2 = **unaffected**, artless, candid, frank, genuine, ingenuous, open, real, simple, spontaneous, unpretentious, unsophisticated, unstudied 3 = **innate**, characteristic, congenital, essential, immanent, inborn, indigenous, inherent, in one's blood, instinctive, intuitive, natal, native 4 = **pure**, organic, plain, unbleached, unmixed, unpolished, unrefined, whole
➤ **Antonyms**
≠**normal**: abnormal, irregular, out of the ordinary, strange, untypical ≠**unaffected**: affected, artificial, assumed, counterfeit, feigned, phoney *or* phony (*informal*), unnatural ≠**pure**: manufactured, processed, synthetic, unnatural

naturalism *noun* = **realism**, factualism, verisimilitude

naturalist *noun* 1 = **biologist**, botanist, ecologist, zoologist 2 = **realist**, factualist

naturalistic *adjective* = **realistic**, lifelike, true-to-life

naturalize *verb* = **adopt**, acclimate, acclimatize, acculturate, accustom, adapt, domesticate, enfranchise, familiarize, grant citizenship, habituate

naturally *adverb* 1 = **of course**, absolutely, as a matter of course, certainly 2 = **genuinely**, as anticipated, customarily, informally, normally, simply, spontaneously, typically, unaffectedly, unpretentiously

nature *noun* 1 = **creation**, cosmos, earth, environment, universe, world 2 = **make-up**, attributes, character, complexion, constitution, essence, features, quality, traits 3 = **kind**, category, description, sort, species, style, type, variety 4 = **temperament**, disposition, humour, mood, outlook, temper 5 = **country**, countryside, landscape, natural history, scenery

naturist *noun* = **nudist**

naughty *adjective* 1 = **disobedient**, annoying, bad, exasperating, fractious, impish, misbehaved, mischievous, perverse, playful, refractory, roguish, sinful, teasing,

wayward, wicked, worthless 2 = **obscene**, bawdy, blue, improper, lewd, off-colour, ribald, risqué, smutty, vulgar, X-rated (*informal*)
➤ **Antonyms**
≠**disobedient**: good, obedient, polite, proper, seemly, well-behaved, well-mannered ≠**obscene**: polite, proper

nausea *noun* 1 = **sickness**, biliousness, qualm(s), queasiness, retching, squeamishness, vomiting 2 = **disgust**, abhorrence, aversion, loathing, odium, repugnance, revulsion

nauseate *verb* = **sicken**, disgust, gross out (*U.S. slang*), horrify, offend, repel, repulse, revolt, turn one's stomach

nauseous *adjective* = **sickening**, abhorrent, disgusting, distasteful, nauseating, offensive, repugnant, repulsive, revolting

nautical *adjective* = **maritime**, marine, naval, oceanic, seafaring, seagoing, yachting

naval *adjective* = **nautical**, marine, maritime, oceanic

navel *noun* = **umbilicus**, bellybutton (*informal*), omphalos (*literary*)

navigable *adjective* 1 = **passable**, clear, negotiable, traversable, unobstructed 2 = **sailable**, controllable, dirigible, steerable

navigate *verb* = **sail**, con (*Nautical*), cross, cruise, direct, drive, guide, handle, journey, manoeuvre, pilot, plan, plot, skipper, steer, voyage

navigation *noun* = **sailing**, cruising, helmsmanship, pilotage, seamanship, steering, voyaging

navigator *noun* = **pilot**, mariner, seaman

navvy *noun* = **labourer**, ganger, worker, workman

navy *noun* = **fleet**, argosy (*archaic*), armada, flotilla, warships

near *adjective* 1 = **close**, adjacent, adjoining, a hop, skip and a jump away (*informal*), alongside, at close quarters, beside, bordering, close by, contiguous, just round the corner, nearby, neighbouring, proximate, touching, within sniffing distance (*informal*) 2 = **forthcoming**, approaching, imminent, impending, in the offing, looming, near-at-hand, next, nigh, on the cards (*informal*), upcoming 3 = **intimate**, akin, allied, attached, connected, dear, familiar, related
➤ **Antonyms**
≠**close**: distant, far, faraway, far-flung, far-off, far-removed, outlying, out-of-the-way, remote, removed ≠**forthcoming**: distant, faraway, far-off, remote ≠**intimate**: distant, remote

nearby *adjective* 1 = **neighbouring**,

adjacent, adjoining, convenient, handy
♦ *adverb* **2 = close at hand**, at close
quarters, just round the corner, not far away,
proximate, within reach, within sniffing
distance (*informal*)

nearly *adverb* **= almost**, about, all but,
approaching, approximately, as good as,
closely, just about, not quite, practically,
roughly, virtually, well-nigh

nearness *noun* **1 = closeness**, accessibility,
availability, contiguity, handiness,
juxtaposition, propinquity, proximity, vicinity
2 = immediacy, imminence **3 = intimacy**,
dearness, familiarity

near-sighted *adjective* **= short-sighted**,
myopic

near thing *noun* **= narrow escape**, close
shave (*informal*), near miss

neat *adjective* **1 = tidy**, accurate, dainty,
fastidious, methodical, nice, orderly,
shipshape, smart, spick-and-span, spruce,
straight, systematic, trim, uncluttered **2**
= elegant, adept, adroit, agile, apt, clever,
deft, dexterous, efficient, effortless, expert,
graceful, handy, nimble, practised, precise,
skilful, stylish, well-judged **3** *Of alcoholic*
drinks **= undiluted**, pure, straight, unmixed
➤ **Antonyms**
≠**tidy**: clumsy, cluttered, disarrayed,
disorderly, disorganized, messy, slobby
(*informal*), sloppy (*informal*), untidy
≠**elegant**: awful, bad, clumsy, incompetent,
inefficient, inelegant, terrible

neatly *adverb* **1 = tidily**, accurately, daintily,
fastidiously, methodically, nicely, smartly,
sprucely, systematically **2 = elegantly**,
adeptly, adroitly, agilely, aptly, cleverly,
deftly, dexterously, efficiently, effortlessly,
expertly, gracefully, handily, nimbly,
precisely, skilfully, stylishly

neatness *noun* **1 = tidiness**, accuracy,
daintiness, fastidiousness, methodicalness,
niceness, nicety, orderliness, smartness,
spruceness, straightness, trimness **2**
= elegance, adeptness, adroitness, agility,
aptness, cleverness, deftness, dexterity,
efficiency, effortlessness, expertness, grace,
gracefulness, handiness, nimbleness,
preciseness, precision, skilfulness, skill, style,
stylishness

nebulous *adjective* **= vague**, ambiguous,
amorphous, cloudy, confused, dim, hazy,
imprecise, indefinite, indeterminate,
indistinct, misty, murky, obscure, shadowy,
shapeless, uncertain, unclear, unformed

necessarily *adverb* **= certainly**,
accordingly, automatically, axiomatically, by
definition, compulsorily, consequently,
incontrovertibly, ineluctably, inevitably,
inexorably, irresistibly, naturally, *nolens*

volens, of course, of necessity, perforce,
undoubtedly, willy-nilly

necessary *adjective* **1 = needed**,
compulsory, *de rigueur*, essential,
imperative, indispensable, mandatory,
needful, obligatory, required, requisite, vital
2 = certain, fated, inescapable, inevitable,
inexorable, unavoidable
➤ **Antonyms**
≠**needed**: dispensable, expendable,
inessential, nonessential, superfluous,
unnecessary ≠**certain**: unnecessary

necessitate *verb* **= compel**, call for, coerce,
constrain, demand, entail, force, impel,
make necessary, oblige, require

necessities *plural noun* **= essentials**,
exigencies, fundamentals, indispensables,
needs, requirements

necessity *noun* **1 = inevitability**,
compulsion, destiny, fate, inexorableness,
obligation **2 = essential**, desideratum,
fundamental, necessary, need, prerequisite,
requirement, requisite, *sine qua non*, want **3**
= needfulness, demand, exigency,
indispensability, need, requirement **4**
= poverty, destitution, extremity, indigence,
need, penury, privation

necromancy *noun* **= magic**, black art,
black magic, demonology, divination,
enchantment, sorcery, thaumaturgy (*rare*),
voodoo, witchcraft, witchery, wizardry

necropolis *noun* **= cemetery**, burial
ground, churchyard, God's acre, graveyard

need *verb* **1 = require**, call for, demand,
entail, have occasion to *or* for, lack, miss,
necessitate, want ♦ *noun* **2 = lack**,
inadequacy, insufficiency, paucity, shortage
3 = requirement, demand, desideratum,
essential, necessity, requisite **4 = emergency**,
exigency, necessity, obligation, urgency,
want **5 = poverty**, deprivation, destitution,
distress, extremity, impecuniousness,
indigence, neediness, penury, privation

needed *adjective* **= necessary**, called for,
desired, lacked, required, wanted

needful *adjective* **= necessary**, essential,
indispensable, needed, required, requisite,
stipulated, vital

needle *verb* **= irritate**, aggravate (*informal*),
annoy, bait, be on one's back (*slang*), gall,
get in one's hair (*informal*), get on one's
nerves (*informal*), get under one's skin
(*informal*), goad, harass, hassle (*informal*),
irk, nag, nark (*Brit., Austral., & N.Z. slang*),
nettle, pester, piss one off (*taboo slang*),
prick, prod, provoke, rile, ruffle, spur, sting,
taunt

needless *adjective* **= unnecessary**,
causeless, dispensable, excessive,
expendable, gratuitous, groundless,

nonessential, pointless, redundant, superfluous, uncalled-for, undesired, unwanted, useless
➤ **Antonyms**
beneficial, essential, obligatory, required, useful

needlework *noun* = **embroidery**, fancywork, needlecraft, sewing, stitching, tailoring

needy *adjective* = **poor**, deprived, destitute, dirt-poor, disadvantaged, down at heel (*informal*), impecunious, impoverished, indigent, on the breadline (*informal*), penniless, poverty-stricken, underprivileged
➤ **Antonyms**
affluent, comfortable, moneyed, prosperous, rich, wealthy, well-off, well-to-do

ne'er-do-well *noun* = **layabout**, black sheep, good-for-nothing, idler, loafer, loser, skiver (*Brit. slang*), wastrel

nefarious *adjective* = **wicked**, abominable, atrocious, base, criminal, depraved, detestable, dreadful, evil, execrable, foul, heinous, horrible, infamous, infernal, iniquitous, monstrous, odious, opprobrious, shameful, sinful, vicious, vile, villainous
➤ **Antonyms**
admirable, good, honest, honourable, just, noble, praiseworthy, upright, virtuous

negate *verb* **1** = **invalidate**, abrogate, annul, cancel, countermand, neutralize, nullify, obviate, repeal, rescind, retract, reverse, revoke, void, wipe out **2** = **deny**, contradict, disallow, disprove, gainsay (*archaic or literary*), oppose, rebut, refute
➤ **Antonyms**
≠**deny**: affirm, assert, attest, avouch, avow, certify, confirm, declare, maintain, pronounce, ratify, state, swear, testify

negation *noun* **1** = **cancellation**, neutralization, nullification **2** = **denial**, antithesis, antonym, contradiction, contrary, converse, counterpart, disavowal, disclaimer, inverse, opposite, rejection, renunciation, reverse

negative *adjective* **1** = **contradictory**, contrary, denying, dissenting, opposing, recusant, refusing, rejecting, resisting **2** = **pessimistic**, antagonistic, colourless, contrary, cynical, gloomy, jaundiced, neutral, uncooperative, unenthusiastic, uninterested, unwilling, weak **3** = **neutralizing**, annulling, counteractive, invalidating, nullifying ◆ *noun* **4** = **contradiction**, denial, refusal
➤ **Antonyms**
adjective ≠**contradictory**: affirmative, approving, assenting, concurring, positive ≠**pessimistic**: cheerful, enthusiastic, optimistic, positive

negativeness, negativity *noun* **1**

= **contradictoriness**, contradiction, contrariness, denial, dissent, opposition, recusancy, refusal, rejection, resistance **2** = **pessimism**, antagonism, colourlessness, contrariness, cynicism, gloom, neutrality, uncooperativeness, uninterestedness, unwillingness, weakness

neglect *verb* **1** = **forget**, be remiss, evade, let slide, omit, pass over, procrastinate, shirk, skimp **2** = **disregard**, contemn, discount, disdain, ignore, leave alone, overlook, pass by, rebuff, scorn, slight, spurn, turn one's back on ◆ *noun* **3** = **negligence**, carelessness, default, dereliction, failure, forgetfulness, laxity, laxness, neglectfulness, oversight, remissness, slackness, slovenliness **4** = **disregard**, disdain, disrespect, heedlessness, inattention, indifference, slight, unconcern
➤ **Antonyms**
verb ≠**disregard**: appreciate, attend to, notice, observe, regard, remember, value ◆ *noun* ≠**negligence**, disregard: attention, care, consideration, notice, regard, respect

neglected *adjective* **1** = **abandoned**, derelict, overgrown **2** = **disregarded**, unappreciated, underestimated, undervalued

neglectful *adjective* = **careless**, disregardful, heedless, inattentive, indifferent, lax, negligent, remiss, thoughtless, uncaring, unmindful

negligence *noun* = **carelessness**, default, dereliction, disregard, failure, forgetfulness, heedlessness, inadvertence, inattention, inattentiveness, indifference, laxity, laxness, neglect, omission, oversight, remissness, shortcoming, slackness, thoughtlessness

negligent *adjective* = **careless**, cursory, disregardful, forgetful, heedless, inadvertent, inattentive, indifferent, neglectful, nonchalant, offhand, regardless, remiss, slack, slapdash, slipshod, thoughtless, unmindful, unthinking
➤ **Antonyms**
attentive, careful, considerate, mindful, painstaking, rigorous, thorough, thoughtful

negligible *adjective* = **insignificant**, imperceptible, inconsequential, minor, minute, nickel-and-dime (*U.S. slang*), petty, small, trifling, trivial, unimportant
➤ **Antonyms**
important, noteworthy, significant, vital

negotiable *adjective* = **debatable**, discussable *or* discussible, transactional, transferable, variable

negotiate *verb* **1** = **deal**, adjudicate, arbitrate, arrange, bargain, conciliate, confer, consult, contract, cut a deal, debate, discuss, handle, manage, mediate, parley, settle, transact, work out **2** = **get round**, clear, cross, get over, get past, pass, pass through, surmount

negotiation *noun* = **bargaining**, arbitration, debate, diplomacy, discussion, mediation, transaction, wheeling and dealing (*informal*)

negotiator *noun* = **mediator**, ambassador, delegate, diplomat, honest broker, intermediary, moderator

neighbourhood *noun* = **district**, community, confines, environs, locale, locality, precincts, proximity, purlieus, quarter, region, surroundings, vicinity

neighbouring *adjective* = **nearby**, abutting, adjacent, adjoining, bordering, connecting, contiguous, near, nearest, next, surrounding
➤ **Antonyms**
distant, far, far-off, remote

neighbourly *adjective* = **helpful**, considerate, friendly, harmonious, hospitable, kind, obliging, sociable

nemesis *noun* = **retribution**, destiny, destruction, fate, vengeance

nepotism *noun* = **favouritism**, bias, partiality, patronage, preferential treatment

nerd, nurd *noun Slang* = **bore**, anorak (*informal*), dork (*slang*), geek (*informal*), obsessive, trainspotter (*informal*), wonk (*informal*)

nerve *noun* **1** = **bravery**, balls (*taboo slang*), ballsiness (*taboo slang*), bottle (*Brit. slang*), coolness, courage, daring, determination, endurance, energy, face (*informal*), fearlessness, firmness, force, fortitude, gameness, grit, guts (*informal*), hardihood, intrepidity, mettle, might, pluck, resolution, spirit, spunk (*informal*), steadfastness, vigour, will **2** *Informal* = **impudence**, audacity, boldness, brass (*informal*), brass neck (*Brit. informal*), brazenness, cheek (*informal*), chutzpah (*U.S. & Canad. informal*), effrontery, front, gall, impertinence, insolence, neck (*informal*), sassiness (*U.S. slang*), sauce (*informal*), temerity ◆ *verb* **3 nerve oneself** = **brace oneself**, embolden oneself, encourage oneself, fortify oneself, gee oneself up, hearten oneself, invigorate oneself, steel oneself, strengthen oneself

nerveless *adjective* **1** = **calm**, composed, controlled, cool, impassive, imperturbable, self-possessed, unemotional **2** = **fearless**, brave, courageous, daring, gutsy (*slang*), plucky, unafraid

nerve-racking *adjective* = **tense**, annoying, difficult, distressing, frightening, gut-wrenching, harassing, harrowing, maddening, stressful, trying, worrying

nerves *plural noun* = **tension**, anxiety,

butterflies (in one's stomach) (*informal*), cold feet (*informal*), fretfulness, heebie-jeebies (*slang*), imbalance, nervousness, strain, stress, worry

nervous *adjective* = **apprehensive**, agitated, antsy (*informal*), anxious, edgy, excitable, fearful, fidgety, flustered, hesitant, highly strung, hyper (*informal*), hysterical, jittery (*informal*), jumpy, nervy (*Brit. informal*), neurotic, on edge, ruffled, shaky, tense, timid, timorous, twitchy (*informal*), uneasy, uptight (*informal*), weak, wired (*slang*), worried
➤ **Antonyms**
bold, calm, confident, constant, cool, equable, even, laid-back (*informal*), peaceful, relaxed, steady, together (*slang*), unfazed (*informal*)

nervous breakdown *noun* = **collapse**, breakdown, crack-up (*informal*), nervous disorder, neurasthenia (*obsolete*)

nervousness *noun* = **anxiety**, agitation, antsiness (*informal*), disquiet, excitability, fluster, perturbation, tension, timidity, touchiness, tremulousness, worry

nervy *adjective* = **anxious**, agitated, fidgety, jittery (*informal*), jumpy, nervous, on edge, tense, twitchy (*informal*)

nest *noun* = **refuge**, den, haunt, hideaway, resort, retreat, snuggery

nest egg *noun* = **reserve**, cache, deposit, fall-back, fund(s), savings, store

nestle *verb* = **snuggle**, cuddle, curl up, huddle, nuzzle

nestling *noun* = **chick**, fledgling

net¹ *noun* **1** = **mesh**, lacework, lattice, netting, network, openwork, reticulum, tracery, web ◆ *verb* **2** = **catch**, bag, capture, enmesh, ensnare, entangle, nab (*informal*), trap

net², **nett** *adjective* **1** = **take-home**, after taxes, clear, final **2** = **conclusive**, closing, final ◆ *verb* **3** = **earn**, accumulate, bring in, clear, gain, make, realize, reap

nether *adjective* = **lower**, basal, below, beneath, bottom, inferior, Stygian, under, underground

nether world *noun* = **hell**, Avernus, Hades, infernal regions, nether regions, underworld

nettle *verb* = **irritate**, aggravate (*informal*), annoy, chafe, exasperate, fret, gall, get on one's nerves (*informal*), goad, harass, hassle (*informal*), incense, nark (*Brit., Austral., & N.Z. slang*), pique, piss one off (*taboo slang*), provoke, ruffle, sting, tease, vex

nettled *adjective* = **irritated**, aggrieved, angry, annoyed, chafed, choked, cross, exasperated, galled, goaded, hacked (off) (*U.S. slang*), harassed, huffy, incensed, irritable, peeved, peevish, piqued, pissed (*taboo slang*), pissed off (*taboo slang*), provoked, put out, ratty (*Brit. & N.Z. informal*), riled, ruffled, stung, teased, tetchy, touchy, vexed

network *noun* = **system**, arrangement, channels, circuitry, complex, convolution, grid, grill, interconnections, labyrinth, lattice, maze, mesh, net, nexus, organization, plexus, structure, tracks, web

neurosis *noun* = **obsession**, abnormality, affliction, derangement, deviation, instability, maladjustment, mental disturbance, mental illness, phobia, psychological *or* emotional disorder

neurotic *adjective* = **unstable**, abnormal, antsy (*informal*), anxious, compulsive, deviant, disordered, distraught, disturbed, hyper (*informal*), maladjusted, manic, nervous, obsessive, overwrought, twitchy (*informal*), unhealthy
➤ Antonyms
calm, laid-back (*informal*), level-headed, normal, rational, sane, stable, together (*slang*), well-adjusted, well-balanced

neuter *verb* = **castrate**, doctor (*informal*), dress, emasculate, fix (*informal*), geld, spay

neutral *adjective* 1 = **unbiased**, disinterested, dispassionate, even-handed, impartial, indifferent, nonaligned, nonbelligerent, noncombatant, noncommittal, nonpartisan, sitting on the fence, unaligned, uncommitted, undecided, uninvolved, unprejudiced 2 = **indeterminate**, achromatic, colourless, dull, expressionless, indistinct, indistinguishable, intermediate, toneless, undefined
➤ Antonyms
≠unbiased: active, belligerent, biased, decided, interested, interfering, partial, participating, positive, prejudiced

neutrality *noun* = **impartiality**, detachment, disinterestedness, nonalignment, noninterference, noninterventionism, noninvolvement, nonpartisanship

neutralize *verb* = **counteract**, cancel, compensate for, counterbalance, frustrate, invalidate, negate, nullify, offset, undo

never *adverb* = **at no time**, not at all, not for love nor money (*informal*), not on your life (*informal*), not on your nelly (*Brit. slang*), no way, on no account, under no circumstances
➤ Antonyms
always, aye (*Scot.*), constantly, continually, every time, forever, perpetually, without exception

never-ending *adjective* = **eternal**,

boundless, ceaseless, constant, continual, continuous, everlasting, incessant, interminable, nonstop, perpetual, persistent, relentless, unbroken, unceasing, unchanging, uninterrupted, unremitting

never-never *noun Informal* = **hire-purchase** (*Brit.*), H.P. (*Brit.*)

nevertheless *adverb* = **nonetheless**, but, even so, (even) though, however, notwithstanding, regardless, still, yet

new *adjective* 1 = **modern**, advanced, all-singing, all-dancing, contemporary, current, different, fresh, ground-breaking, happening (*informal*), latest, modernistic, modish, newfangled, novel, original, recent, state-of-the-art, topical, ultramodern, unfamiliar, unknown, unused, unusual, up-to-date, virgin 2 = **extra**, added, more, new-found, supplementary 3 = **changed**, altered, improved, modernized, rebranded, redesigned, renewed, restored
➤ Antonyms
≠modern: aged, ancient, antiquated, antique, hackneyed, old, old-fashioned, outmoded, passé, stale, trite

newcomer *noun* = **novice**, alien, arrival, beginner, foreigner, immigrant, incomer, Johnny-come-lately (*informal*), outsider, parvenu, settler, stranger

newfangled *adjective* = **new**, all-singing, all-dancing, contemporary, fashionable, gimmicky, modern, new-fashioned, novel, recent, state-of-the-art
➤ Antonyms
antiquated, dated, obsolete, old-fashioned, outmoded, out-of-date, passé

newly *adverb* = **recently**, anew, freshly, just, lately, latterly

newness *noun* = **novelty**, freshness, innovation, oddity, originality, strangeness, unfamiliarity, uniqueness

news *noun* = **information**, account, advice, bulletin, buzz, communiqué, dirt (*U.S. slang*), disclosure, dispatch, exposé, gen (*Brit. informal*), gossip, hearsay, intelligence, latest (*informal*), leak, news flash, release, report, revelation, rumour, scandal, scuttlebutt (*U.S. slang*), statement, story, tidings, word

newsworthy *adjective* = **interesting**, arresting, important, notable, noteworthy, remarkable, significant, stimulating

next *adjective* 1 = **following**, consequent, ensuing, later, subsequent, succeeding 2 = **nearest**, adjacent, adjoining, closest, neighbouring ◆ *adverb* 3 = **afterwards**, closely, following, later, subsequently, thereafter

next world *noun* = **afterlife**, afterworld, heaven, hereafter, nirvana, paradise

nibble *verb* 1 = **bite**, eat, gnaw, munch, nip, peck, pick at ♦ *noun* 2 = **snack**, bite, crumb, morsel, peck, *soupçon*, taste, titbit

nice *adjective* 1 = **pleasant**, agreeable, attractive, charming, delightful, good, pleasurable 2 = **kind**, amiable, commendable, courteous, friendly, likable *or* likeable, polite, prepossessing, refined, well-mannered 3 = **neat**, dainty, fine, tidy, trim 4 = **subtle**, accurate, careful, critical, delicate, discriminating, exact, exacting, fastidious, fine, meticulous, precise, rigorous, scrupulous, strict
➤ **Antonyms**
≠**pleasant**: awful, disagreeable, dreadful, miserable, unpleasant ≠**kind**: disagreeable, mean, unfriendly, unkind, unpleasant, vulgar ≠**neat**: coarse, crude, rough, shabby, sloppy (*informal*) ≠**subtle**: careless, rough, sloppy (*informal*), vague

nicely *adverb* 1 = **pleasantly**, acceptably, agreeably, attractively, charmingly, delightfully, pleasingly, pleasurably, well 2 = **kindly**, amiably, commendably, courteously, likably, politely, prepossessingly 3 = **neatly**, daintily, finely, tidily, trimly 4 = **subtly**, accurately, carefully, critically, delicately, exactingly, exact, fastidiously, finely, meticulously, precisely, rigorously, scrupulously, strictly
➤ **Antonyms**
≠**pleasantly**: unattractively, unpleasantly ≠**neatly**: sloppily (*informal*) ≠**subtly**: carelessly, sloppily (*informal*)

niceness *noun* 1 = **kindness**, agreeableness, amiability, attractiveness, charm, courtesy, delightfulness, friendliness, good manners, goodness, likableness *or* likeableness, pleasantness, pleasurableness, politeness, refinement 2 = **neatness**, daintiness, fineness, tidiness, trimness 3 = **precision**, accuracy, care, carefulness, criticalness, delicacy, discrimination, exactingness, exactitude, exactness, fastidiousness, fineness, meticulosity, meticulousness, preciseness, rigorousness, rigour, scrupulosity, scrupulousness, strictness, subtleness, subtlety

nicety *noun* 1 = **subtlety**, daintiness, delicacy, discrimination, distinction, nuance, refinement 2 = **precision**, accuracy, exactness, fastidiousness, finesse, meticulousness, minuteness

niche *noun* 1 = **alcove**, corner, hollow, nook, opening, recess 2 = **position**, calling, pigeonhole (*informal*), place, slot (*informal*), vocation

nick *verb* 1 = **cut**, chip, damage, dent, mark, notch, scar, score, scratch, snick 2 *Slang* = **steal**, finger (*slang*), knock off (*slang*), pilfer, pinch (*informal*), snitch (*slang*),

swipe (*slang*) ♦ *noun* 3 = **cut**, chip, dent, mark, notch, scar, score, scratch, snick

nickname *noun* = **pet name**, diminutive, epithet, familiar name, handle (*slang*), label, moniker *or* monicker (*slang*), sobriquet

nifty *adjective Informal* = **neat**, agile, apt, attractive, chic, clever, deft, enjoyable, excellent, pleasing, quick, sharp, smart, spruce, stylish

niggard *noun* = **miser**, cheapskate (*informal*), cheeseparer, churl (*archaic*), meanie *or* meany (*informal, chiefly Brit.*), penny-pincher (*informal*), screw (*slang*), Scrooge, skinflint, tight-arse (*taboo slang*), tight-ass (*U.S. taboo slang*)

niggardliness *noun* = **miserliness**, avarice, avariciousness, closeness, covetousness, frugality, grudgingness, meanness, mercenariness, nearness (*informal*), parsimony, penuriousness, sordidness, sparingness, stinginess, thrift, tightfistedness, ungenerousness

niggardly *adjective* 1 = **stingy**, avaricious, close, covetous, frugal, grudging, mean, mercenary, miserly, near (*informal*), parsimonious, penurious, Scrooge-like, snoep (*S. African informal*), sordid, sparing, stinging, tight-arse (*taboo slang*), tight-arsed (*taboo slang*), tight as a duck's arse (*taboo slang*), tight-ass (*U.S. taboo slang*), tight-assed (*U.S. taboo slang*), tightfisted, ungenerous 2 = **paltry**, beggarly, inadequate, insufficient, meagre, mean, measly, miserable, pathetic, scant, scanty, skimpy, small, wretched
➤ **Antonyms**
≠**stingy**: bountiful, generous, lavish, liberal, munificent, prodigal ≠**paltry**: abundant, ample, bountiful, copious, generous, handsome, liberal, plentiful, profuse

niggle *verb* 1 = **worry**, annoy, irritate, rankle 2 = **criticize**, carp, cavil, find fault, fuss

niggling *adjective* 1 = **persistent**, gnawing, irritating, troubling, worrying 2 = **petty**, cavilling, finicky, fussy, insignificant, minor, nit-picking (*informal*), pettifogging, picky (*informal*), piddling (*informal*), quibbling, trifling, unimportant

night *noun* = **darkness**, dark, dead of night, hours of darkness, night-time, night watches

night and day *adverb* = **constantly**, all the time, ceaselessly, continually, continuously, day in, day out, endlessly, incessantly, interminably, unremittingly

nightfall *noun* = **evening**, crepuscule, dusk, eve (*archaic*), eventide, gloaming (*Scot. or poetic*), sundown, sunset, twilight, vespers
➤ **Antonyms**
aurora (*poetic*), cockcrow, dawn, dawning, daybreak, daylight, morning, sunrise

nightly *adjective* **1** = **nocturnal**, night-time
♦ *adverb* **2** = **every night**, each night, night after night, nights (*informal*)

nightmare *noun* **1** = **bad dream**, hallucination, incubus, night terror, succubus **2** = **ordeal**, hell on earth, horror, torment, trial, tribulation

nihilism *noun* = **nonbelief**, abnegation, agnosticism, atheism, denial, disbelief, rejection, renunciation, repudiation, scepticism

nil *noun* = **nothing**, duck, love, naught, *nihil*, none, zero, zilch (*slang*)

nimble *adjective* = **agile**, active, alert, bright (*informal*), brisk, deft, dexterous, lively, nippy (*Brit. informal*), pdq (*slang*), proficient, prompt, quick, quick-witted, ready, smart, sprightly, spry, swift
➤ **Antonyms**
awkward, clumsy, dull, heavy, inactive, indolent, lethargic, slow

nimbleness *noun* = **agility**, adroitness, alacrity, alertness, dexterity, finesse, grace, lightness, nippiness (*Brit. informal*), skill, smartness, sprightliness, spryness

nimbly *adverb* = **quickly**, actively, acutely, agilely, alertly, briskly, deftly, dexterously, easily, fast, fleetly, hotfoot, pdq (*slang*), posthaste, proficiently, promptly, pronto (*informal*), quick-wittedly, readily, sharply, smartly, speedily, spryly, swiftly

nimbus *noun* **1** = **cloud 2** = **halo**, ambience, atmosphere, aura, aureole, corona, glow, irradiation

nincompoop *noun* = **idiot**, berk (*Brit. slang*), blockhead, charlie (*Brit. informal*), chump, coot, dickhead (*slang*), dimwit (*informal*), dipstick (*Brit. slang*), divvy (*slang*), dolt, dork (*slang*), dumb-ass (*slang*), dunce, dweeb (*U.S. slang*), fathead (*informal*), fool, fuckwit (*taboo slang*), geek (*slang*), gobshite (*Irish taboo slang*), gonzo (*slang*), jerk (*slang, chiefly U.S. & Canad.*), lamebrain (*informal*), nerd *or* nurd (*slang*), ninny, nitwit (*informal*), noodle, numbskull *or* numskull, numpty (*Scot. informal*), oaf, pillock (*Brit. slang*), plank (*Brit. slang*), plonker (*slang*), prat (*slang*), prick (*slang*), schmuck (*U.S. slang*), simpleton, twit (*informal, chiefly Brit.*), wally (*slang*)

nip¹ *verb* **1** = **pinch**, bite, catch, clip, compress, grip, nibble, snag, snap, snip, squeeze, tweak, twitch **2** = **thwart**, check, frustrate

nip² *noun* = **dram**, draught, drop, finger, mouthful, peg (*Brit.*), portion, shot (*informal*), sip, snifter (*informal*), soupçon, sup, swallow, taste

nipper *noun Informal* = **child**, ankle-biter (*Austral. slang*), baby, boy, girl, infant, kid

(*informal*), little one, rug rat (*slang*), sprog (*slang*), tot

nipple *noun* = **teat**, boob (*slang*), breast, dug, mamilla, pap, papilla, tit, udder

nippy *adjective* **1** = **chilly**, biting, nipping, sharp, stinging **2** *Informal* = **quick**, active, agile, fast, nimble, pdq (*slang*), spry

nirvana *noun* = **paradise**, bliss, joy, peace, serenity, tranquillity

nit-picking *adjective* = **fussy**, captious, carping, cavilling, finicky, hairsplitting, pedantic, pettifogging, quibbling

nitty-gritty *noun* = **basics**, bottom line, brass tacks (*informal*), core, crux, essence, essentials, facts, fundamentals, gist, heart of the matter, ins and outs, nuts and bolts, reality, substance

nitwit *noun Informal* = **fool**, dickhead (*slang*), dickwit (*slang*), dimwit (*informal*), dipstick (*Brit. slang*), divvy (*slang*), dork (*slang*), dummy (*slang*), fuckwit (*taboo slang*), geek (*slang*), gobshite (*Irish taboo slang*), halfwit, lamebrain (*informal*), nincompoop, ninny, numpty (*Scot. informal*), oaf, plank (*Brit. slang*), simpleton

no *interjection* **1** = **never**, nay, not at all, no way ♦ *noun* **2** = **refusal**, denial, negation, rejection, veto **3** = **objector**, dissenter, dissident, protester
➤ **Antonyms**
interjection ≠ **never**: certainly, of course, yes ♦ *noun* ≠ **refusal**: acceptance, assent, consent

nob *noun Slang* = **aristocrat**, aristo (*informal*), big hitter (*informal*), big shot (*informal*), bigwig (*informal*), celeb (*informal*), fat cat (*slang, chiefly U.S.*), heavy hitter (*informal*), nabob (*informal*), toff (*Brit. slang*), V.I.P.

nobble *verb* **1** *Brit. slang* = **bribe**, get at, influence, intimidate, outwit, win over **2** *Brit. slang* = **disable**, handicap, incapacitate, weaken **3** *Brit. slang* = **steal**, filch, knock off (*slang*), nick (*slang, chiefly Brit.*), pilfer, pinch (*informal*), purloin, snitch (*slang*), swipe (*slang*)

nobility *noun* **1** = **dignity**, eminence, excellence, grandeur, greatness, illustriousness, loftiness, magnificence, majesty, nobleness, stateliness, sublimity, superiority, worthiness **2** = **integrity**, honour, incorruptibility, uprightness, virtue **3** = **aristocracy**, elite, high society, lords, nobles, patricians, peerage, ruling class, upper class

noble *adjective* **1** = **worthy**, generous, honourable, magnanimous, upright, virtuous **2** = **aristocratic**, blue-blooded, gentle (*archaic*), highborn, lordly, patrician, titled **3** = **impressive**, august, dignified,

distinguished, elevated, eminent, excellent, grand, great, imposing, lofty, splendid, stately, superb ♦ *noun* **4** = **lord**, aristo (*informal*), aristocrat, childe (*archaic*), nobleman, peer
➤ **Antonyms**
adjective ≠**worthy**: contemptible, despicable, dishonest, selfish ≠**aristocratic**: base, humble, ignoble, lowborn, lowly, peasant, plebeian, vulgar ≠**impressive**: base, humble, ignoble, insignificant, lowly, mean, modest, plain ♦ *noun* ≠**lord**: commoner, peasant, serf

nobody *pronoun* **1** = **no-one** ♦ *noun* **2** = **nonentity**, cipher, lightweight (*informal*), menial, nothing (*informal*)
➤ **Antonyms**
noun ≠**nonentity**: big name, big noise (*informal*), big shot (*slang*), celeb (*informal*), celebrity, megastar (*informal*), personage, star, superstar, V.I.P.

nocturnal *adjective* = **nightly**, night, night-time, of the night

nod *verb* **1** = **acknowledge**, bob, bow, dip, duck, gesture, indicate, salute, signal **2** = **agree**, assent, concur, show agreement **3** = **sleep**, be sleepy, doze, droop, drowse, kip (*Brit. slang*), nap, slump, zizz (*Brit. informal*) ♦ *noun* **4** = **gesture**, acknowledgment, beck, greeting, indication, salute, sign, signal

noggin *noun* **1** *Informal* = **head**, bean (*U.S. & Canad. slang*), block (*informal*), bonce (*Brit. slang*), conk (*slang*), dome (*slang*), napper (*slang*), noddle (*informal, chiefly Brit.*), nut (*slang*) **2** = **quarter-pint**, gill **3** = **cup**, dram, mug, nip, tot

no go *adjective* = **impossible**, futile, hopeless, not on (*informal*), vain

noise *noun* **1** = **sound**, babble, blare, clamour, clatter, commotion, cry, din, fracas, hubbub, outcry, pandemonium, racket, row, rumpus, talk, tumult, uproar ♦ *verb* **2** = **report**, advertise, bruit, circulate, gossip, publicize, repeat, rumour

noiseless *adjective* = **silent**, hushed, inaudible, mute, muted, quiet, soundless, still

noisome *adjective* **1** = **offensive**, disgusting, fetid, foul, malodorous, noxious, putrid, smelly, stinking **2** = **poisonous**, bad, harmful, pernicious, pestilential, unhealthy, unwholesome

noisy *adjective* = **loud**, boisterous, cacophonous, chattering, clamorous, deafening, ear-splitting, obstreperous, piercing, riotous, strident, tumultuous, turbulent, uproarious, vociferous
➤ **Antonyms**
hushed, quiet, silent, still, subdued, tranquil, tuneful

nomad *noun* = **wanderer**, drifter, itinerant, migrant, rambler, rover, vagabond

nomadic *adjective* = **wandering**, itinerant, migrant, migratory, pastoral, peripatetic, roaming, roving, travelling, vagrant

nom de plume *noun* = **pseudonym**, alias, assumed name, nom de guerre, pen name

nomenclature *noun* = **terminology**, classification, codification, locution, phraseology, taxonomy, vocabulary

nominal *adjective* **1** = **so-called**, formal, ostensible, pretended, professed, puppet, purported, self-styled, *soi-disant,* supposed, theoretical, titular **2** = **small**, inconsiderable, insignificant, minimal, symbolic, token, trifling, trivial

nominate *verb* = **name**, appoint, assign, choose, commission, designate, elect, elevate, empower, present, propose, recommend, select, submit, suggest, term

nomination *noun* = **choice**, appointment, designation, election, proposal, recommendation, selection, suggestion

nominee *noun* = **candidate**, aspirant, contestant, entrant, favourite, protégé, runner

nonaligned *adjective* = **neutral**, impartial, uncommitted, undecided

nonchalance *noun* = **indifference**, calm, composure, cool (*slang*), equanimity, imperturbability, sang-froid, self-possession, unconcern

nonchalant *adjective* = **casual**, airy, apathetic, blasé, calm, careless, collected, cool, detached, dispassionate, indifferent, insouciant, laid-back (*informal*), offhand, unconcerned, unemotional, unfazed (*informal*), unperturbed
➤ **Antonyms**
anxious, caring, concerned, involved, worried

noncombatant *noun* = **civilian**, neutral, nonbelligerent

noncommittal *adjective* = **evasive**, ambiguous, careful, cautious, circumspect, discreet, equivocal, guarded, indefinite, neutral, politic, reserved, tactful, temporizing, tentative, unrevealing, vague, wary

non compos mentis *adjective* = **insane**, crazy, deranged, mentally ill, of unsound mind, unbalanced, unhinged
➤ **Antonyms**
all there (*informal*), compos mentis, in one's right mind, lucid, mentally sound, rational, sane

nonconformist *noun* = **maverick**, dissenter, dissentient, eccentric, heretic, iconoclast, individualist, protester, radical, rebel

➤ **Antonyms**
Babbitt (*U.S.*), conventionalist,
stick-in-the-mud (*informal*), traditionalist,
yes man

nonconformity *noun* = **dissent**,
eccentricity, heresy, heterodoxy

nondescript *adjective* = **ordinary**,
bog-standard (*Brit. & Irish slang*),
characterless, common or garden (*informal*),
commonplace, dull, featureless,
indeterminate, mousy, nothing to write
home about, run-of-the-mill, unclassifiable,
unclassified, undistinguished, unexceptional,
uninspiring, uninteresting, unmemorable,
unremarkable, vague, vanilla (*informal*)
➤ **Antonyms**
distinctive, extraordinary, memorable,
remarkable, unique, unusual

none *pronoun* = **not any**, bugger all (*slang*),
diddly (*U.S. slang*), f.a. (*Brit. slang*), fuck all
(*Brit. taboo slang*), nil, nobody, no-one, no
part, not a bit, nothing, not one, sweet F.A.
(*Brit. slang*), sweet Fanny Adams (*Brit.
slang*), zero, zilch (*slang, chiefly U.S. &
Canad.*)

nonentity *noun* = **nobody**, cipher,
lightweight (*informal*), mediocrity, small fry,
unimportant person

nonessential *adjective* = **unnecessary**,
dispensable, excessive, expendable,
extraneous, inessential, peripheral,
superfluous, unimportant
➤ **Antonyms**
appropriate, essential, important,
indispensable, significant, vital

nonetheless *adverb* = **nevertheless**,
despite that, even so, however, in spite of
that, yet

nonevent *noun* = **flop** (*informal*), clunker
(*informal*), disappointment, dud (*informal*),
failure, fiasco, washout

nonexistent *adjective* = **imaginary**,
chimerical, fancied, fictional, hallucinatory,
hypothetical, illusory, imagined,
insubstantial, legendary, missing, mythical,
unreal
➤ **Antonyms**
actual, existent, existing, genuine, real, true,
veritable

nonplus *verb* = **take aback**, astonish,
astound, baffle, be all Greek to (*informal*),
bewilder, confound, confuse, discomfit,
disconcert, discountenance, dismay,
dumbfound, embarrass, faze, flummox,
mystify, perplex, puzzle, stump, stun

nonsense *noun* = **rubbish**, absurdity,
balderdash, balls (*taboo slang*), bilge
(*informal*), blather, bollocks (*Brit. taboo
slang*), bombast, bosh (*informal*), bull
(*slang*), bullshit (*taboo slang*), bunk

(*informal*), bunkum or buncombe (*chiefly
U.S.*), claptrap (*informal*), cobblers (*Brit.
taboo slang*), crap (*slang*), double Dutch
(*Brit. informal*), drivel, eyewash (*informal*),
fatuity, folly, foolishness, garbage (*informal*),
gibberish, guff (*slang*), hogwash, hokum
(*slang, chiefly U.S. & Canad.*), horsefeathers
(*U.S. slang*), hot air (*informal*), idiocy,
inanity, jest, ludicrousness, moonshine, pants
(*slang*), pap, piffle (*informal*), poppycock
(*informal*), rhubarb, ridiculousness, rot,
senselessness, shit (*taboo slang*), silliness,
stuff, stupidity, tommyrot, tosh (*slang,
chiefly Brit.*), trash, tripe (*informal*),
twaddle, waffle (*informal, chiefly Brit.*)
➤ **Antonyms**
fact, reality, reason, sense, seriousness, truth,
wisdom

nonsensical *adjective* = **senseless**, absurd,
asinine, crazy, foolish, inane,
incomprehensible, irrational, ludicrous,
meaningless, ridiculous, silly

nonstarter *noun* = **dead loss**, dud
(*informal*), lemon (*informal*), loser,
no-hoper (*informal*), turkey (*informal*),
washout (*informal*)

nonstop *adjective* **1** = **continuous**,
ceaseless, constant, direct, endless, incessant,
interminable, relentless, steady, unbroken,
unending, unfaltering, uninterrupted,
unremitting ♦ *adverb* **2** = **continuously**,
ceaselessly, constantly, directly, endlessly,
incessantly, interminably, perpetually,
relentlessly, steadily, unbrokenly, unendingly,
unfalteringly, uninterruptedly, unremittingly,
without stopping
➤ **Antonyms**
adjective ≠ **continuous**: broken,
discontinuous, fitful, intermittent, irregular,
occasional, periodic, punctuated, recurrent,
spasmodic, sporadic, stop-go (*informal*)

nook *noun* = **niche**, alcove, cavity, corner,
cranny, crevice, cubbyhole, hide-out,
inglenook (*Brit.*), opening, recess, retreat

noon *noun* = **midday**, high noon, noonday,
noontide, noontime, twelve noon

norm *noun* = **standard**, average,
benchmark, criterion, mean, measure,
model, par, pattern, rule, type, yardstick

normal *adjective* **1** = **usual**, accustomed,
acknowledged, average, bog-standard (*Brit.
& Irish slang*), common, conventional,
habitual, natural, ordinary, popular, regular,
routine, run-of-the-mill, standard, typical **2**
= **sane**, rational, reasonable, well-adjusted
➤ **Antonyms**
≠ **usual**: abnormal, exceptional, irregular,
peculiar, rare, remarkable, singular,
uncommon, unnatural, unusual

normality *noun* **1** = **regularity**,

accustomedness, averageness, commonness, commonplaceness, conventionality, habitualness, naturalness, ordinariness, popularity, routineness, typicality, usualness **2 = sanity**, adjustment, balance, rationality, reason

normally *adverb* **= usually**, as a rule, commonly, generally, habitually, ordinarily, regularly, typically

north *adjective* **1 = northern**, Arctic, boreal, northerly, polar ♦ *adverb* **2 = northward(s)**, northerly

nose *noun* **1 = snout**, beak, bill, conk (*slang*), hooter (*slang*), neb (*archaic or dialect*), proboscis, schnozzle (*slang, chiefly U.S.*), snitch (*slang*) ♦ *verb* **2 = ease forward**, nudge, nuzzle, push, shove **3 = pry**, meddle, snoop (*informal*)

nose-dive *verb* **= drop**, dive, plummet, plunge

nosegay *noun* **= posy**, bouquet

nose out *verb* **= detect**, scent, search (for), smell, sniff

nosey, nosy *adjective* **= inquisitive**, curious, eavesdropping, interfering, intrusive, meddlesome, prying, snooping (*informal*)

nosh *Slang* ♦ *noun* **1 = food**, aliment, chow (*informal*), comestibles, eats (*slang*), fare, feed, grub (*slang*), meal, nosebag (*slang*), repast, scoff (*slang*), sustenance, tack (*informal*), viands, victuals, vittles (*obsolete or dialect*) ♦ *verb* **2 = eat**, consume, scoff (*slang*)

nostalgia *noun* **= reminiscence**, homesickness, longing, pining, regret, regretfulness, remembrance, wistfulness, yearning

nostalgic *adjective* **= sentimental**, emotional, homesick, longing, maudlin, regretful, wistful

nostrum *noun* **= medicine**, cure, cure-all, drug, elixir, panacea, patent medicine, potion, quack medicine, remedy, sovereign cure, specific, treatment

notability *noun* **1 = fame**, celebrity, distinction, eminence, esteem, renown **2 = celebrity**, big name, celeb (*informal*), dignitary, megastar (*informal*), notable, personage, V.I.P., worthy

notable *adjective* **1 = remarkable**, celebrated, conspicuous, distinguished, eminent, evident, extraordinary, famous, manifest, marked, memorable, noteworthy, noticeable, notorious, outstanding, pre-eminent, pronounced, rare, renowned, salient, striking, uncommon, unusual, well-known ♦ *noun* **2 = celebrity**, big name, celeb (*informal*), dignitary, luminary, megastar (*informal*), notability, personage,

V.I.P., worthy
> **Antonyms**
adjective ≠**remarkable**: anonymous, concealed, hidden, imperceptible, obscure, unknown, vague

notably *adverb* **= particularly**, conspicuously, distinctly, especially, markedly, noticeably, outstandingly, remarkably, seriously (*informal*), signally, strikingly, uncommonly

notation *noun* **= signs**, characters, code, script, symbols, system

notch *noun* **1 = cut**, cleft, incision, indentation, mark, nick, score **2** *Informal* **= level**, cut (*informal*), degree, grade, step ♦ *verb* **3 = cut**, indent, mark, nick, score, scratch

notch up *verb* **= register**, achieve, gain, make, score

note *noun* **1 = message**, annotation, comment, communication, epistle, gloss, jotting, letter, memo, memorandum, minute, record, remark, reminder **2 = symbol**, indication, mark, sign, token **3** *As in* **of note = fame**, celebrity, character, consequence, distinction, eminence, prestige, renown, reputation **4** *As in* **take note of = notice**, heed, observation, regard ♦ *verb* **5 = see**, notice, observe, perceive **6 = mark**, denote, designate, indicate, record, register **7 = mention**, remark

notebook *noun* **= jotter**, commonplace book, diary, exercise book, Filofax (*Trademark*), journal, memorandum book, notepad, record book

noted *adjective* **= famous**, acclaimed, celebrated, conspicuous, distinguished, eminent, illustrious, notable, notorious, prominent, recognized, renowned, well-known
> **Antonyms**
infamous, obscure, undistinguished, unknown

notes *plural noun* **= jottings**, impressions, outline, record, report, sketch

noteworthy *adjective* **= remarkable**, exceptional, extraordinary, important, notable, outstanding, significant, unusual
> **Antonyms**
commonplace, insignificant, normal, ordinary, pedestrian, run-of-the-mill, unexceptional, unremarkable

nothing *noun* **= nought**, bagatelle, cipher, emptiness, naught, nil, nobody, nonentity, nonexistence, nothingness, nullity, trifle, void, zero

nothingness *noun* **1 = oblivion**, nihility, nonbeing, nonexistence, nullity **2 = insignificance**, unimportance, worthlessness

notice *noun* **1 = interest**, cognizance,

consideration, heed, note, observation, regard **2 = attention**, civility, respect **3 = announcement**, advice, communication, instruction, intelligence, intimation, news, notification, order, warning **4 = review**, advertisement, comment, criticism, poster, sign ♦ *verb* **5 = observe**, behold (*archaic or literary*), detect, discern, distinguish, eyeball (*slang*), heed, mark, mind, note, perceive, remark, see, spot
➤ Antonyms
noun ≠**interest**: disregard, ignorance, neglect, omission, oversight ♦ *verb*
≠**observe**: disregard, ignore, neglect, overlook

noticeable *adjective* **= obvious**, appreciable, blatant, bold, clear, conspicuous, distinct, evident, manifest, observable, perceptible, plain, salient, striking, unmistakable

notification *noun* **= announcement**, advice, alert, declaration, information, intelligence, message, notice, notifying, publication, statement, telling, warning

notify *verb* **= inform**, acquaint, advise, alert, announce, apprise, declare, make known, publish, tell, warn

notion *noun* **1 = idea**, apprehension, belief, concept, conception, impression, inkling, judgment, knowledge, opinion, sentiment, understanding, view **2 = whim**, caprice, desire, fancy, impulse, inclination, wish

notional *adjective* **= speculative**, abstract, conceptual, fanciful, hypothetical, ideal, imaginary, theoretical, unreal, visionary
➤ Antonyms
actual, factual, genuine, real

notoriety *noun* **= scandal**, dishonour, disrepute, infamy, obloquy, opprobrium

notorious *adjective* **= infamous**, dishonourable, disreputable, opprobrious, scandalous

notoriously *adverb* **= infamously**, dishonourably, disreputably, opprobriously, scandalously

notwithstanding *preposition* **1 = despite**, in spite of ♦ *adverb* **2 = nevertheless**, although, (even) though, however, nonetheless, though, yet

nought *noun* **= zero**, naught, nil, nothing, nothingness

nourish *verb* **1 = feed**, attend, furnish, nurse, nurture, supply, sustain, tend **2 = encourage**, comfort, cultivate, foster, maintain, promote, support

nourishing *adjective* **= nutritious**, alimentative, beneficial, healthful, health-giving, nutritive, wholesome

nourishment *noun* **= food**, aliment, diet,

nutriment, nutrition, sustenance, tack (*informal*), viands, victuals, vittles (*obsolete or dialect*)

nouveau riche *noun* **= new-rich**, arriviste, parvenu, upstart

novel[1] *noun* **= story**, fiction, narrative, romance, tale

novel[2] *adjective* **= new**, different, fresh, ground-breaking, innovative, left-field (*informal*), original, rare, singular, strange, uncommon, unfamiliar, unusual
➤ Antonyms
ancient, common, customary, familiar, habitual, old-fashioned, ordinary, run-of-the-mill, traditional, usual

novelty *noun* **1 = newness**, freshness, innovation, oddity, originality, strangeness, surprise, unfamiliarity, uniqueness **2 = gimmick**, curiosity, gadget **3 = knick-knack**, bagatelle, bauble, gewgaw, gimcrack, memento, souvenir, trifle, trinket

novice *noun* **= beginner**, amateur, apprentice, convert, learner, neophyte, newcomer, novitiate, probationer, proselyte, pupil, trainee, tyro
➤ Antonyms
ace, doyen, expert, grandmaster, guru, master, maven, old hand, professional, teacher

novitiate *noun* **= apprenticeship**, probation, training

now *adverb* **1 = nowadays**, any more, at the moment, these days **2 = immediately**, at once, instanter (*Law*), instantly, presently (*Scot. & U.S.*), promptly, straightaway **3 now and again** *or* **then = occasionally**, at times, from time to time, infrequently, intermittently, on and off, once in a while, on occasion, sometimes, sporadically

nowadays *adverb* **= now**, any more, at the moment, in this day and age, these days, today

noxious *adjective* **= harmful**, baneful (*archaic*), corrupting, deadly, deleterious, destructive, detrimental, foul, hurtful, injurious, insalubrious, noisome, pernicious, pestilential, poisonous, unhealthy, unwholesome
➤ Antonyms
innocuous, innoxious, inoffensive, nontoxic, not dangerous, safe, unobjectionable

nuance *noun* **= subtlety**, degree, distinction, gradation, nicety, refinement, shade, tinge

nubile *adjective* **= marriageable**, ripe (*informal*)

nucleus *noun* **= centre**, basis, core, focus, heart, kernel, nub, pivot

nude *adjective* **= naked**, *au naturel*, bare,

buck naked (*slang*), disrobed, exposed, in one's birthday suit (*informal*), in the altogether (*informal*), in the bare scud (*slang*), in the buff (*informal*), in the raw (*informal*), naked as the day one was born (*informal*), scuddy (*slang*), starkers (*informal*), stark-naked, stripped, unclad, unclothed, uncovered, undraped, undressed, without a stitch on (*informal*)
➤ **Antonyms**
attired, clothed, covered, dressed

nudge *verb, noun* = **push**, bump, dig, elbow, jog, poke, prod, shove, touch

nudity *noun* = **nakedness**, bareness, deshabille, nudism, undress

nugget *noun* = **lump**, chunk, clump, hunk, mass, piece

nuisance *noun* = **problem**, annoyance, bore, bother, drag (*informal*), gall, hassle (*informal*), inconvenience, infliction, irritation, offence, pain in the arse (*taboo informal*), pain in the backside, pain in the butt (*informal*), pain in the neck, pest, plague, trouble, vexation
➤ **Antonyms**
benefit, blessing, delight, happiness, joy, pleasure, satisfaction

null *adjective* **null and void** = **invalid**, characterless, ineffectual, inoperative, nonexistent, powerless, useless, vain, valueless, void, worthless

nullify *verb* = **cancel**, abolish, abrogate, annul, bring to naught, counteract, countervail, invalidate, negate, neutralize, obviate, quash, rebut, render null and void, repeal, rescind, revoke, veto, void
➤ **Antonyms**
authorize, confirm, endorse, ratify, validate

nullity *noun* = **nonexistence**, characterlessness, ineffectualness, invalidity, powerlessness, uselessness, valuelessness, voidness, worthlessness

numb *adjective* **1** = **unfeeling**, benumbed, dead, deadened, frozen, immobilized, insensible, insensitive, paralysed, stupefied, torpid ◆ *verb* **2** = **deaden**, benumb, dull, freeze, immobilize, paralyse, stun, stupefy
➤ **Antonyms**
adjective ≠**unfeeling**: feeling, responsive, sensitive, sentient

number *noun* **1** = **numeral**, character, count, digit, figure, integer, sum, total, unit **2** = **quantity**, aggregate, amount, collection, company, crowd, horde, many, multitude, throng **3** = **issue**, copy, edition, imprint, printing ◆ *verb* **4** = **calculate**, account, add, compute, count, enumerate, include, reckon, tell, total
➤ **Antonyms**
noun ≠**quantity**: insufficiency, lack,

scantiness, scarcity, shortage, want ◆ *verb* ≠**calculate**: conjecture, guess, theorize

numbered *adjective* **1** = **included**, categorized, contained, counted, designated, fixed, specified, totalled **2** = **limited**, limited in number

numberless *adjective* = **infinite**, countless, endless, innumerable, multitudinous, myriad, unnumbered, untold

numbness *noun* = **deadness**, dullness, insensibility, insensitivity, paralysis, stupefaction, torpor, unfeelingness

numbskull, numskull *noun* = **fool**, blockhead, clot (*Brit. informal*), dolt, dummy (*slang*), dunce, oaf, twit (*informal*)

numeral *noun* = **number**, character, cipher, digit, figure, integer, symbol

numerous *adjective* = **many**, abundant, copious, plentiful, profuse, several, thick on the ground
➤ **Antonyms**
few, not many, scarcely any

nuncio *noun* = **ambassador**, envoy, legate, messenger

nunnery *noun* = **convent**, abbey, cloister, house, monastery

nuptial *adjective* = **marital**, bridal, conjugal, connubial, hymeneal (*poetic*), matrimonial, wedded, wedding

nuptials *plural noun* = **wedding**, espousal (*archaic*), marriage, matrimony

nurse *verb* **1** = **look after**, care for, minister to, tend, treat **2** = **breast-feed**, feed, nourish, nurture, suckle, wet-nurse **3** = **foster**, cherish, cultivate, encourage, harbour, keep alive, preserve, promote, succour, support

nursery *noun* = **crèche**, kindergarten, playgroup

nurture *noun* **1** = **development**, discipline, education, instruction, rearing, training, upbringing ◆ *verb* **2** = **develop**, bring up, cultivate, discipline, educate, instruct, rear, school, train **3** = **nourish**, feed, nurse, support, sustain, tend
➤ **Antonyms**
verb ≠**develop**, **nourish**: deprive, disregard, ignore, neglect, overlook

nut *noun* **1** = **kernel**, pip, seed, stone **2** *Slang* = **madman**, crackpot (*informal*), crank (*informal*), eccentric, headbanger (*informal*), headcase (*informal*), loony (*slang*), lunatic, maniac, nutcase (*slang*), nutter (*Brit. slang*), oddball (*informal*), psycho (*slang*), wacko (*slang*) **3** *Slang* = **head**, brain, mind, reason, senses

nutrition *noun* = **food**, nourishment, nutriment, sustenance

nutritious *adjective* = **nourishing**,

alimental, alimentative, beneficial, healthful, health-giving, invigorating, nutritive, strengthening, wholesome

nuts *adjective Slang* = **insane**, as daft as a brush (*informal, chiefly Brit.*), bananas (*slang*), barking (*slang*), barking mad (*slang*), batty (*slang*), crazy (*informal*), demented, deranged, doolally (*slang*), eccentric, gonzo (*slang*), irrational, loony (*slang*), loopy (*informal*), mad, not the full

shilling (*informal*), nutty (*slang*), off one's trolley (*slang*), out to lunch (*informal*), psycho (*slang*), psychopathic, up the pole (*informal*), wacko *or* whacko (*informal*)

nuzzle *verb* = **snuggle**, burrow, cuddle, fondle, nestle, pet

nymph *noun* = **sylph**, damsel, dryad, girl, hamadryad, lass, maid, maiden, naiad, Oceanid (*Greek myth*), oread

O o

oaf *noun* = **dolt**, blockhead, bonehead (*slang*), brute, clod, dullard, dumb-ass (*slang*), dunce, fathead (*informal*), fool, galoot (*slang, chiefly U.S.*), gawk, geek (*slang*), gobshite (*Irish taboo slang*), goon, halfwit, idiot, jerk (*slang, chiefly U.S. & Canad.*), lout, lummox (*informal*), moron, nerd *or* nurd (*slang*), numbskull *or* numskull, numpty (*Scot. informal*), schmuck (*U.S. slang*), wally (*slang*)
➤ **Antonyms**
brain (*informal*), egghead (*informal*), genius, intellect, smart aleck (*informal*), wiseacre

oafish *adjective* = **stupid**, boneheaded (*slang*), bovine, brutish, dense, dim, dim-witted (*informal*), doltish, dozy (*Brit. informal*), dull, dumb (*informal*), dumb-ass (*slang*), loutish, lubberly, lumbering, moronic, obtuse, slow on the uptake (*informal*), thick
➤ **Antonyms**
acute, brainy (*informal*), bright, clever, intelligent, quick-witted, sharp, smart

oasis *noun* = **haven**, island, refuge, resting place, retreat, sanctuary, sanctum

oath *noun* **1** = **promise**, affirmation, avowal, bond, pledge, sworn statement, vow, word **2** = **swearword**, blasphemy, curse, cuss (*informal*), expletive, imprecation, malediction, profanity, strong language

obdurate *adjective* = **stubborn**, adamant, dogged, firm, fixed, hard, hard-hearted, immovable, implacable, inexorable, inflexible, mulish, obstinate, perverse, pig-headed, relentless, stiff-necked, unbending, unfeeling, unimpressible, unrelenting, unshakable, unyielding
➤ **Antonyms**
amenable, biddable, compliant, flexible, malleable, pliant, soft-hearted, submissive, tender, tractable, yielding

obedience *noun* = **submissiveness**, accordance, acquiescence, agreement, assent, compliance, deference, docility, dutifulness, duty, observance, respect, reverence, submission, subservience, tractability
➤ **Antonyms**
defiance, disobedience, insubordination, obstinacy, recalcitrance, stubbornness, wilfulness

obedient *adjective* = **submissive**, acquiescent, amenable, biddable, compliant, deferential, docile, duteous, dutiful, law-abiding, observant, regardful, respectful, subservient, tractable, under control, well-trained, yielding
➤ **Antonyms**
arrogant, contrary, disobedient, disrespectful, intractable, obdurate, obstinate, rebellious, stubborn, undutiful, ungovernable, unmanageable, unruly, wayward

obeisance *noun Formal* **1** = **respect**, deference, homage, reverence **2** = **bow**, bending of the knee, curtsy *or* curtsey, genuflection, salaam

obelisk *noun* = **column**, monolith, monument, needle, pillar, shaft

obese *adjective* = **fat**, corpulent, fleshy, gross, heavy, outsize, overweight, paunchy, plump, podgy, portly, roly-poly, rotund, stout, tubby, well-upholstered (*informal*)
➤ **Antonyms**
emaciated, gaunt, lean, scraggy, skeletal, skinny, slender, thin

obesity *noun* = **fatness**, beef (*informal*), bulk, corpulence, fleshiness, grossness, overweight, portliness, stoutness, tubbiness, weight problem
➤ **Antonyms**
emaciation, gauntness, leanness, skinniness, slenderness, thinness

obey *verb* **1** = **do what one is told**, bow to, cave in (*informal*), come to heel, get into line, give in, give way, knuckle under (*informal*), submit, succumb, surrender (to), take orders from, toe the line, yield **2** = **carry out**, abide by, act upon, adhere to, be ruled by, comply, conform, discharge, do what is expected, execute, follow, fulfil, heed, keep, mind, observe, perform, respond, serve
➤ **Antonyms**
≠**do what one is told**: disobey, rebel
≠**carry out**: contravene, defy, disobey, disregard, ignore, transgress, violate

obfuscate *verb Formal* = **confuse**, befog, cloud, darken, muddy the waters, obscure, perplex

object[1] *noun* **1** = **thing**, article, body, entity, fact, item, phenomenon, reality **2** = **target**, butt, focus, recipient, victim **3** = **purpose**, aim, design, end, end purpose, goal, idea, intent, intention, motive, objective, point, reason

object[2] *verb* = **protest**, argue against, demur, draw the line (at something), expostulate, oppose, raise objections, take exception
➤ Antonyms
accept, acquiesce, agree, approve, assent, comply, concur, consent, like, take on board, welcome

objection *noun* = **protest**, cavil, censure, counter-argument, demur, doubt, exception, opposition, remonstrance, scruple
➤ Antonyms
acceptance, affirmation, agreement, approbation, assent, endorsement, support

objectionable *adjective* = **unpleasant**, abhorrent, deplorable, disagreeable, displeasing, distasteful, exceptionable, insufferable, intolerable, noxious, obnoxious, offensive, regrettable, repugnant, unacceptable, undesirable, unseemly, unsociable
➤ Antonyms
acceptable, agreeable, desirable, likable *or* likeable, pleasant, pleasing, welcome

objective *noun* 1 = **purpose**, aim, ambition, aspiration, design, end, end in view, goal, Holy Grail (*informal*), intention, mark, object, target ♦ *adjective* 2 = **unbiased**, detached, disinterested, dispassionate, equitable, even-handed, fair, impartial, impersonal, judicial, just, open-minded, unemotional, uninvolved, unprejudiced
➤ Antonyms
adjective ≠**unbiased:** biased, personal, prejudiced, subjective, unfair, unjust

objectively *adverb* = **impartially**, disinterestedly, dispassionately, even-handedly, with an open mind, with objectivity *or* impartiality

objectivity *noun* = **impartiality**, detachment, disinterest, disinterestedness, dispassion, equitableness, impersonality
➤ Antonyms
bent, bias, partiality, predisposition, prejudice, subjectivity

obligation *noun* = **duty**, accountability, accountableness, burden, charge, compulsion, culpability, liability, must, onus, pigeon (*informal*), requirement, responsibility, trust

obligatory *adjective* = **compulsory**, binding, coercive, de rigueur, enforced, essential, imperative, mandatory, necessary, required, requisite, unavoidable
➤ Antonyms
discretionary, elective, noncompulsory, optional, voluntary

oblige *verb* 1 = **compel**, bind, coerce, constrain, dragoon, force, impel, make, necessitate, obligate, railroad (*informal*), require 2 = **do (someone) a favour** *or* a **kindness**, accommodate, benefit, favour, gratify, indulge, please, put oneself out for, serve
➤ Antonyms
≠**do (someone) a favour** *or* a **kindness:** bother, discommode, disoblige, disrupt, inconvenience, put out, trouble

obliged *adjective* 1 = **grateful**, appreciative, beholden, gratified, indebted, in (someone's) debt, thankful 2 = **bound**, compelled, forced, required, under an obligation, under compulsion

obliging *adjective* = **cooperative**, accommodating, agreeable, amiable, civil, complaisant, considerate, courteous, eager to please, friendly, good-natured, helpful, kind, polite, willing
➤ Antonyms
discourteous, disobliging, inconsiderate, rude, sullen, surly, unaccommodating, uncooperative, unhelpful, unobliging

oblique *adjective* 1 = **slanting**, angled, aslant, at an angle, atilt, inclined, slanted, sloped, sloping, tilted 2 = **indirect**, backhanded, circuitous, circumlocutory, evasive, implied, roundabout, sidelong
➤ Antonyms
≠**indirect:** blunt, candid, direct, downright, forthright, frank, open, straightforward

obliquely *adverb* 1 = **at an angle**, aslant, aslope, diagonally, slantwise 2 = **indirectly**, circuitously, evasively, in a roundabout manner *or* way, not in so many words

obliterate *verb* = **destroy**, annihilate, blot out, cancel, delete, efface, eradicate, erase, expunge, extirpate, root out, wipe from *or* off the face of the earth, wipe out
➤ Antonyms
build, construct, create, establish, form, formulate, generate, make

obliteration *noun* = **annihilation**, blotting out, deletion, effacement, elimination, eradication, erasure, extirpation, rooting out, wiping out
➤ Antonyms
building, construction, creation, establishment, formation, generation, making

oblivion *noun* 1 = **neglect**, abeyance, disregard, forgetfulness, (waters of) Lethe 2 = **unconsciousness**, insensibility, obliviousness, unawareness
➤ Antonyms
≠**unconsciousness:** awareness, consciousness, perception, realization, recognition, sensibility

oblivious *adjective* = **unaware**, blind, careless, deaf, disregardful, forgetful, heedless, ignorant, inattentive, insensible,

neglectful, negligent, regardless, unconcerned, unconscious, unmindful, unobservant
➤ **Antonyms**
alert, attentive, aware, conscious, heedful, mindful, observant, watchful

obloquy *noun Formal* **1** = **abuse**, aspersion, attack, blame, censure, criticism, invective, reproach, slander, vilification **2** = **disgrace**, discredit, dishonour, humiliation, ignominy, infamy, shame, stigma

obnoxious *adjective* = **offensive**, abhorrent, abominable, detestable, disagreeable, disgusting, foul, hateful, horrid, insufferable, loathsome, nasty, nauseating, objectionable, obscene, odious, repellent, reprehensible, repugnant, repulsive, revolting, sickening, unpleasant
➤ **Antonyms**
agreeable, amiable, charming, congenial, delightful, likable *or* likeable, pleasant, pleasing

obscene *adjective* **1** = **indecent**, bawdy, blue, coarse, dirty, filthy, foul, gross, immodest, immoral, improper, impure, lewd, licentious, loose, offensive, pornographic, prurient, ribald, salacious, shameless, smutty, suggestive, unchaste, unwholesome, X-rated (*informal*) **2** = **disgusting**, atrocious, evil, heinous, loathsome, outrageous, shocking, sickening, vile, wicked
➤ **Antonyms**
≠**indecent**: chaste, decent, decorous, inoffensive, modest, proper, pure, refined, respectable, seemly

obscenity *noun* **1** = **indecency**, bawdiness, blueness, coarseness, dirtiness, filthiness, foulness, grossness, immodesty, impropriety, impurity, indelicacy, lewdness, licentiousness, pornography, prurience, salacity, smut, smuttiness, suggestiveness, vileness **2** = **swearword**, four-letter word, profanity, vulgarism **3** = **atrocity**, abomination, affront, blight, evil, offence, outrage, vileness, wrong
➤ **Antonyms**
≠**indecency**: chastity, decency, decorum, delicacy, innocence, modesty, propriety, purity

obscure *adjective* **1** = **little-known**, humble, inconspicuous, lowly, minor, nameless, out-of-the-way, remote, undistinguished, unheard-of, unimportant, unknown **2** = **vague**, abstruse, ambiguous, arcane, concealed, confusing, cryptic, deep, Delphic, doubtful, enigmatic, esoteric, hazy, hidden, incomprehensible, indefinite, intricate, involved, mysterious, occult, opaque, recondite, unclear **3** = **dark**, blurred, clouded, cloudy, dim, faint, gloomy,

indistinct, murky, shadowy, shady, sombre
♦ *verb* **4** = **conceal**, cover, disguise, hide, obfuscate, screen, throw a veil over, veil **5** = **cover**, bedim, block, block out, blur, cloak, cloud, darken, dim, dull, eclipse, mask, overshadow, shade, shroud
➤ **Antonyms**
adjective ≠**little-known**: celebrated, distinguished, eminent, familiar, famous, illustrious, important, major, prominent, renowned, significant, well-known, widely-known ≠**vague**: apparent, clear, definite, distinct, evident, explicit, intelligible, lucid, manifest, obvious, plain, prominent, straightforward, transparent, unmistakable ≠**dark**: bright, clear, sharp, transparent, well-defined ♦ *verb* ≠**conceal**: clarify, disclose, explain, explicate, expose, interpret, reveal, show ≠**cover**: expose, reveal, uncover, unmask, unveil

obscurity *noun* **1** = **insignificance**, inconspicuousness, lowliness, namelessness, nonrecognition, unimportance **2** = **vagueness**, abstruseness, ambiguity, complexity, impenetrableness, incomprehensibility, intricacy, reconditeness **3** = **darkness**, dimness, dusk, duskiness, gloom, haze, haziness, indistinctness, murkiness, shadows
➤ **Antonyms**
≠**vagueness**: clarity, clearness, comprehensibility, explicitness, lucidity, obviousness

obsequies *plural noun Formal* = **funeral rites**, burial, burial service, funeral, last offices

obsequious *adjective* = **sycophantic**, cringing, deferential, fawning, flattering, grovelling, ingratiating, servile, submissive, unctuous

observable *adjective* = **noticeable**, apparent, appreciable, blatant, clear, detectable, discernible, evident, obvious, open, patent, perceivable, perceptible, recognizable, visible

observance *noun* **1** = **carrying out**, adherence to, attention, celebration, compliance, discharge, fulfilment, heeding, honouring, notice, observation, performance **2** = **ritual**, ceremonial, ceremony, custom, fashion, form, formality, practice, rite, service, tradition
➤ **Antonyms**
≠**carrying out**: disdain, disregard, evasion, heedlessness, inattention, neglect, nonobservance, omission, oversight

observant *adjective* = **attentive**, alert, eagle-eyed, heedful, mindful, obedient, perceptive, quick, sharp-eyed, submissive, vigilant, watchful, wide-awake
➤ **Antonyms**
distracted, dreamy, heedless, inattentive,

indifferent, negligent, preoccupied, unobservant, vague

observation *noun* **1** = **study**, attention, consideration, examination, experience, information, inspection, knowledge, monitoring, notice, review, scrutiny, surveillance, watching **2** = **comment**, annotation, finding, note, opinion, pronouncement, reflection, remark, thought, utterance

observe *verb* **1** = **see**, detect, discern, discover, espy, note, notice, perceive, spot, witness **2** = **watch**, behold (*archaic or literary*), check, check out (*informal*), contemplate, eye, eyeball (*slang*), get a load of (*informal*), keep an eye on (*informal*), keep tabs on (*informal*), keep track of, keep under observation, look at, monitor, pay attention to, regard, scrutinize, study, survey, take a dekko at (*Brit. slang*), view **3** = **remark**, comment, declare, mention, note, opine, say, state **4** = **carry out**, abide by, adhere to, comply, conform to, follow, fulfil, heed, honour, keep, mind, obey, perform, respect **5** = **celebrate**, commemorate, keep
> **Antonyms**
≠**carry out**: disregard, ignore, miss, neglect, omit, overlook, violate

observer *noun* = **spectator**, beholder, bystander, commentator, eyewitness, fly on the wall, looker-on, onlooker, viewer, watcher, witness

obsessed *adjective* = **preoccupied**, beset, dominated, gripped, haunted, having a one-track mind, hung up on (*slang*), infatuated, in the grip of, troubled
> **Antonyms**
aloof, apathetic, detached, disinterested, impassive, indifferent, uncaring, unconcerned

obsession *noun* = **preoccupation**, addiction, bee in one's bonnet (*informal*), complex, enthusiasm, fetish, fixation, hang-up (*informal*), infatuation, mania, phobia, ruling passion, thing (*informal*)

obsessive *adjective* = **compulsive**, besetting, consuming, fixed, gripping, haunting, tormenting

obsolescent *adjective* = **becoming obsolete**, ageing, declining, dying out, not with it (*informal*), on the decline, on the wane, on the way out, past its prime, waning

obsolete *adjective* = **out of date**, anachronistic, ancient, antediluvian, antiquated, antique, archaic, bygone, dated, discarded, disused, extinct, old, old-fashioned, old hat, out, outmoded, out of fashion, out of the ark (*informal*), outworn, passé, past it
> **Antonyms**
à la mode, contemporary, current,

fashionable, in, in vogue, modern, new, present day, trendy (*Brit. informal*), up-to-date

obstacle *noun* = **difficulty**, bar, barrier, block, check, hindrance, hitch, hurdle, impediment, interference, interruption, obstruction, snag, stumbling block
> **Antonyms**
advantage, aid, asset, assistance, benefit, help, support

obstinacy *noun* = **stubbornness**, doggedness, firmness, inflexibility, intransigence, mulishness, obduracy, perseverance, persistence, pertinacity, pig-headedness, resoluteness, tenacity, wilfulness
> **Antonyms**
compliance, cooperativeness, docility, flexibility, meekness, submissiveness, tractability

obstinate *adjective* = **stubborn**, cussed, determined, dogged, firm, headstrong, immovable, inflexible, intractable, intransigent, mulish, persistent, pertinacious, perverse, pig-headed, recalcitrant, refractory, self-willed, steadfast, stiff-necked, strong-minded, tenacious, unyielding, wilful
> **Antonyms**
amenable, biddable, complaisant, compliant, docile, flexible, irresolute, manageable, obedient, submissive, tractable, undecided, wavering

obstreperous *adjective* = **unruly**, boisterous, disorderly, loud, noisy, out of control, out of hand, raucous, restive, riotous, rough, rowdy, tumultuous, turbulent, uncontrolled, undisciplined, unmanageable, uproarious, vociferous, wild
> **Antonyms**
calm, controlled, disciplined, docile, gentle, orderly, peaceful, placid, quiet

obstruct *verb* = **block**, arrest, bar, barricade, bring to a standstill, bung, check, choke, clog, cut off, frustrate, get in the way of, hamper, hamstring, hide, hinder, hold up, impede, inhibit, interfere with, interrupt, obscure, prevent, restrict, retard, shield, shut off, slow down, stop, thwart
> **Antonyms**
abet, advance, aid, assist, encourage, favour, further, gee up, help, promote, support

obstruction *noun* = **obstacle**, bar, barricade, barrier, block, blockage, check, difficulty, hazard, hindrance, impediment, occlusion, snag, stop, stoppage
> **Antonyms**
aid, assistance, cooperation, encouragement, favour, furtherance, geeing-up, help, support

obstructive *adjective* = **unhelpful**, awkward, blocking, delaying, difficult, hindering, inhibiting, preventative,

restrictive, stalling, uncooperative
➤ Antonyms
cooperative, encouraging, favourable,
helpful, obliging, supportive

obtain verb 1 = get, achieve, acquire, attain,
come by, earn, gain, get hold of, get one's
hands on, land, procure, score (slang),
secure 2 Formal = exist, be in force, be
prevalent, be the case, hold, prevail, stand
➤ Antonyms
≠get: forfeit, forgo, give up, hand over, lose,
relinquish, renounce, surrender

obtainable adjective = available,
achievable, at hand, attainable, on tap
(informal), procurable, ready, to be had

obtrusive adjective = noticeable, blatant,
obvious, prominent, protruding,
protuberant, sticking out
➤ Antonyms
concealed, covert, hidden, inconspicuous,
low-key, muted, unnoticeable, unobtrusive

obtuse adjective 1 = stupid, dense, dopey
(informal), dull, dull-witted, dumb
(informal), dumb-ass (informal), heavy,
imperceptive, insensitive, retarded, slow,
slow on the uptake (informal), stolid, thick,
uncomprehending, unintelligent 2 = blunt,
rounded
➤ Antonyms
≠stupid: astute, bright, clever, keen, quick,
sensitive, sharp, shrewd, smart

obviate verb Formal = preclude, avert,
prevent, remove

obvious adjective = evident, apparent,
blatant, bold, clear, conspicuous, distinct,
indisputable, manifest, much in evidence,
noticeable, open, overt, palpable, patent,
perceptible, plain, plain as the nose on your
face (informal), pronounced, recognizable,
salient, self-evident, self-explanatory, staring
one in the face (informal), sticking out a
mile (informal), straightforward, transparent,
unconcealed, undeniable, undisguised,
unmistakable, visible
➤ Antonyms
ambiguous, clear as mud (informal),
concealed, dark, hidden, imperceptible,
inconspicuous, indistinct, invisible, obscure,
unapparent, unclear, vague

obviously adverb = clearly, certainly,
distinctly, manifestly, needless to say, of
course, palpably, patently, plainly,
undeniably, unmistakably, unquestionably,
without doubt

occasion noun 1 = time, chance,
convenience, incident, moment, occurrence,
opening, opportunity, window 2 = reason,
call, cause, excuse, ground(s), justification,
motive, prompting, provocation 3 = event,
affair, celebration, experience, happening,
occurrence ◆ verb 4 Formal = cause, bring
about, create, effect, elicit, engender, evoke,
generate, give rise to, induce, inspire, lead
to, move, produce, prompt, provoke

occasional adjective = infrequent, casual,
desultory, incidental, intermittent, irregular,
odd, rare, sporadic, uncommon
➤ Antonyms
constant, continual, customary, frequent,
habitual, incessant, regular, routine, usual

occasionally adverb = sometimes, at
intervals, at times, (every) now and then,
every so often, from time to time, irregularly,
now and again, off and on, on and off, once
in a while, on occasion, periodically
➤ Antonyms
constantly, continually, continuously,
frequently, habitually, often, regularly,
routinely

occult adjective = supernatural, abstruse,
arcane, cabbalistic, esoteric, magical,
mysterious, mystic, mystical, preternatural,
recondite, unknown

occultism noun = black magic, diabolism,
magic, sorcery, supernaturalism, the black
arts, witchcraft

occupancy noun = tenancy, possession,
residence, tenure, use

occupant noun = inhabitant, addressee,
incumbent, indweller, inmate, lessee,
occupier, resident, tenant, user

occupation noun 1 = profession, activity,
business, calling, craft, employment, job, line
(of work), post, pursuit, trade, vocation, walk
of life, work 2 = possession, control,
holding, occupancy, residence, tenancy,
tenure, use 3 = invasion, conquest, foreign
rule, seizure, subjugation

occupied adjective 1 = busy, employed,
engaged, tied up (informal), working 2 = in
use, engaged, full, taken, unavailable 3
= inhabited, full, lived-in, peopled, settled,
tenanted
➤ Antonyms
≠inhabited: deserted, empty, tenantless,
uninhabited, unoccupied, untenanted, vacant

occupy verb 1 = live in, be established in,
be in residence in, dwell in, inhabit, own,
possess, reside in, stay in (Scot.), tenant 2
often passive = take up, absorb, amuse,
busy, divert, employ, engage, engross,
entertain, hold the attention of, immerse,
interest, involve, keep busy or occupied,
monopolize, preoccupy, tie up 3 = fill,
cover, hold, permeate, pervade, take up,
use, utilize 4 = invade, capture, hold,
overrun, seize, take over, take possession of
➤ Antonyms
≠live in: abandon, depart, desert, evacuate,
quit, vacate ≠invade: retreat, withdraw

occur _verb_ **1** = **happen**, arise, befall, betide, chance, come about, come off (_informal_), come to pass (_archaic_), crop up (_informal_), materialize, result, take place, turn up (_informal_) **2** = **exist**, appear, be found, be present, develop, manifest itself, obtain, show itself **3 occur to** = **come to mind**, come to one, cross one's mind, dawn on, enter one's head, spring to mind, strike one, suggest itself

occurrence _noun_ **1** = **incident**, adventure, affair, circumstance, episode, event, happening, instance, proceeding, transaction **2** = **existence**, appearance, development, manifestation, materialization

odd _adjective_ **1** = **unusual**, abnormal, atypical, bizarre, curious, deviant, different, eccentric, exceptional, extraordinary, fantastic, freak, freakish, funny, irregular, kinky (_informal_), left-field (_informal_), oddball (_informal_), off-the-wall (_slang_), outlandish, out of the ordinary, peculiar, quaint, queer, rare, remarkable, singular, strange, uncommon, unconventional, weird **2** = **occasional**, casual, incidental, irregular, miscellaneous, periodic, random, sundry, varied, various **3** = **spare**, leftover, remaining, single, solitary, surplus, unmatched, unpaired
➤ **Antonyms**
≠**unusual**: common, customary, familiar, natural, normal, ordinary, regular, typical, unexceptional, unremarkable, usual ≠**occasional**: habitual, permanent, regular, steady ≠**spare**: even, matched, paired

oddity _noun_ **1** = **irregularity**, abnormality, anomaly, eccentricity, freak, idiosyncrasy, kink, peculiarity, phenomenon, quirk, rarity **2** = **misfit**, card (_informal_), crank (_informal_), maverick, nut (_slang_), oddball (_informal_), wacko (_slang_), weirdo _or_ weirdie (_informal_) **3** = **strangeness**, abnormality, bizarreness, eccentricity, extraordinariness, freakishness, incongruity, oddness, outlandishness, peculiarity, queerness, singularity, unconventionality, unnaturalness

odd man out _noun_ = **misfit**, exception, freak, maverick, nonconformist, outsider, square peg in a round hole (_informal_)

oddment _noun_ = **leftover**, bit, fag end, fragment, off cut, remnant, scrap, snippet

odds _plural noun_ **1** = **probability**, balance, chances, likelihood **2** _Brit._ = **difference**, disparity, dissimilarity **3** = **advantage**, edge, lead, superiority **4 at odds** = **in conflict**, at daggers drawn, at loggerheads, at sixes and sevens, at variance, in disagreement, in opposition to, on bad terms, out of line

odds and ends _plural noun_ = **scraps**, bits, bits and pieces, debris, leavings, litter, oddments, remnants, rubbish, sundry _or_ miscellaneous items

odious _adjective_ = **offensive**, abhorrent, abominable, detestable, disgusting, execrable, foul, hateful, horrible, horrid, loathsome, obnoxious, obscene, repellent, repugnant, repulsive, revolting, unpleasant, vile, yucky _or_ yukky (_slang_)
➤ **Antonyms**
agreeable, charming, congenial, delightful, enchanting, enjoyable, pleasant, pleasing, winsome

odium _noun_ _Formal_ = **hatred**, abhorrence, antipathy, censure, condemnation, detestation, disapprobation, disapproval, disfavour, dislike, obloquy, opprobrium

odour _noun_ = **smell**, aroma, bouquet, essence, fragrance, perfume, redolence, scent, stench, stink

odyssey _noun_ = **journey**, crusade, peregrination, pilgrimage, quest, trek, voyage

off _adverb_ **1** = **away**, apart, aside, elsewhere, out ♦ _adjective_ **2** = **cancelled**, absent, finished, gone, inoperative, postponed, unavailable **3** = **substandard**, bad, below par, disappointing, low-quality, poor, unsatisfactory **4** = **bad**, decomposed, high, mouldy, rancid, rotten, sour, turned

off and on _adverb_ = **occasionally**, (every) now and again, every once in a while, from time to time, intermittently, now and then, on and off, sometimes, sporadically

offbeat _adjective_ = **unusual**, bizarre, eccentric, far-out (_slang_), idiosyncratic, kinky (_informal_), left-field (_informal_), novel, oddball (_informal_), off-the-wall (_slang_), outré, strange, uncommon, unconventional, unorthodox, wacko (_slang_), way-out (_informal_), weird
➤ **Antonyms**
common, conventional, normal, ordinary, orthodox, run-of-the-mill, stereotyped, traditional, unoriginal, usual

off colour _adjective_ = **ill**, green about the gills, not up to par, off form, out of sorts, peaky, peely-wally (_Scot._), poorly (_informal_), queasy, run down, sick, under par, under the weather (_informal_), unwell, washed out

offence _noun_ **1** = **crime**, breach of conduct, delinquency, fault, lapse, misdeed, misdemeanour, peccadillo, sin, transgression, trespass, wrong, wrongdoing **2** = **annoyance**, anger, displeasure, hard feelings, huff, indignation, pique, resentment, umbrage, wounded feelings, wrath **3** = **insult**, affront, displeasure, harm, hurt, indignity, injury, injustice, outrage, put-down (_slang_), slight, snub **4 take offence** = **be offended**, be disgruntled, go into a huff, resent, take the huff, take umbrage

offend verb 1 = **insult**, affront, annoy, cut to the quick, disgruntle, displease, give offence, hurt (someone's) feelings, miff (informal), outrage, pique, piss one off (taboo slang), put (someone's) back up, put (someone's) nose out of joint, slight, snub, tread on (someone's) toes (informal), upset, wound 2 = **disgust**, be disagreeable to, gross out (U.S. slang), make (someone) sick, nauseate, repel, repulse, sicken, turn (someone) off (informal)
➤ **Antonyms**
≠**insult**: appease, assuage, conciliate, delight, mollify, placate, please, soothe

offended adjective = **resentful**, affronted, disgruntled, displeased, huffy, in a huff, miffed (informal), outraged, piqued, put out (informal), smarting, stung, upset

offender noun = **criminal**, crook, culprit, delinquent, lawbreaker, miscreant, sinner, transgressor, villain, wrongdoer

offensive adjective 1 = **disgusting**, abominable, detestable, disagreeable, grisly, loathsome, nasty, nauseating, noisome, obnoxious, odious, repellent, revolting, sickening, unpalatable, unpleasant, unsavoury, vile, yucky or yukky (slang) 2 = **insulting**, abusive, annoying, discourteous, displeasing, disrespectful, impertinent, insolent, irritating, objectionable, rude, uncivil, unmannerly 3 = **attacking**, aggressive, invading ♦ noun 4 = **attack**, campaign, drive, onslaught, push (informal) 5 As in on the offensive = **aggression**, attack
➤ **Antonyms**
adjective ≠**disgusting**: agreeable, attractive, captivating, charming, delightful, pleasant ≠**insulting**: civil, conciliatory, courteous, deferential, polite, respectful ≠**attacking**: defensive ♦ noun ≠**aggression**: defensive

offer verb 1 = **proffer**, bid, extend, give, hold out, put on the market, put up for sale, tender 2 = **provide**, afford, furnish, make available, place at (someone's) disposal, present, purvey, show 3 = **volunteer**, be at (someone's) service, come forward, offer one's services 4 = **propose**, advance, extend, move, put forth, put forward, submit, suggest ♦ noun 5 = **proposal**, attempt, bid, endeavour, essay, overture, proposition, submission, suggestion, tender
➤ **Antonyms**
verb ≠**proffer**: refuse, retract, revoke, take back, withdraw, withhold

offering noun 1 = **contribution**, donation, gift, hand-out, present, subscription, widow's mite 2 = **sacrifice**, oblation (in religious contexts)

offhand adjective 1 = **casual**, abrupt, aloof, brusque, careless, cavalier, couldn't-care-less, curt, glib, informal, offhanded, perfunctory, take-it-or-leave-it (informal), unceremonious, unconcerned, uninterested ♦ adverb 2 = **impromptu**, ad lib, extempore, just like that (informal), off the cuff (informal), off the top of one's head (informal), without preparation
➤ **Antonyms**
adjective ≠**casual**: attentive, careful, grave, intent, planned, premeditated, prepared, responsible, serious, thoughtful

office noun 1 = **post**, business, capacity, duty, employment, function, occupation, place, responsibility, role, service, situation, station, work 2 good offices = **help**, aid, backing, intercession, intervention, mediation, support

officer noun = **official**, agent, appointee, bureaucrat, dignitary, executive, functionary, office-holder, public servant, representative

official adjective 1 = **authorized**, accredited, authentic, authoritative, bona fide, certified, endorsed, formal, legitimate, licensed, proper, sanctioned, signed and sealed ♦ noun 2 = **officer**, agent, bureaucrat, executive, functionary, office bearer, representative
➤ **Antonyms**
adjective ≠**authorized**: casual, doubtful, dubious, informal, unauthorized, unofficial, unreliable

officiate verb = **preside**, chair, conduct, manage, oversee, serve, superintend

officious adjective = **interfering**, dictatorial, forward, impertinent, intrusive, meddlesome, meddling, obtrusive, overzealous, pushy (informal), self-important
➤ **Antonyms**
aloof, detached, indifferent, reserved, reticent, retiring, shy, taciturn, unforthcoming, withdrawn

offing noun in the offing = **imminent**, close at hand, coming up, hovering, in prospect, in the immediate future, in the wings, on the horizon, on the way, upcoming

off key adjective = **out of tune**, discordant, dissonant, inharmonious, jarring

off-load verb = **get rid of**, discharge, dump, jettison, shift, take off, transfer, unburden, unload

off-putting adjective Informal = **discouraging**, daunting, discomfiting, disconcerting, dismaying, dispiriting, disturbing, formidable, frustrating, intimidating, unnerving, unsettling, upsetting

offset verb = **cancel out**, balance out, compensate for, counteract, counterbalance, make up for, neutralize

offshoot noun 1 = **outgrowth**, branch, limb, sprout 2 = **by-product**, adjunct, appendage, development, spin-off

offspring *noun* **1** = **child**, descendant, heir, scion, successor **2** = **children**, brood, descendants, family, heirs, issue, kids (*informal*), progeny, seed (*chiefly biblical*), spawn, successors, young
➤ **Antonyms**
ancestor, begetter, forebear, forefather, forerunner, parent, predecessor, procreator, progenitor

often *adverb* = **frequently**, again and again, generally, many a time, much, oft (*archaic or poetic*), oftentimes (*archaic*), ofttimes (*archaic*), over and over again, repeatedly, time after time, time and again
➤ **Antonyms**
hardly ever, infrequently, irregularly, never, now and then, occasionally, rarely, scarcely, seldom

ogle *verb* = **leer**, eye up (*informal*), give the glad eye (*informal*), give the once-over (*informal*), make sheep's eyes at (*informal*)

ogre *noun* = **monster**, bogey, bogeyman, bugbear, demon, devil, giant, spectre

oil *verb* = **lubricate**, grease

oily *adjective* **1** = **greasy**, fatty, oleaginous **2** = **obsequious**, flattering, plausible, servile, smarmy (*Brit. informal*), smooth, unctuous

ointment *noun* = **lotion**, balm, cream, embrocation, emollient, liniment, salve, unguent

O.K., okay *Informal* ♦ *interjection* **1** = **all right**, agreed, right, roger, very good, very well, yes ♦ *adjective* **2** = **fine**, acceptable, accurate, adequate, all right, approved, convenient, correct, fair, good, in order, middling, not bad (*informal*), passable, permitted, satisfactory, so-so (*informal*), tolerable, up to scratch (*informal*) ♦ *verb* **3** = **approve**, agree to, authorize, consent to, endorse, entitle, give one's consent to, give the go-ahead, give the green light, give the thumbs up (*informal*), pass, rubber-stamp (*informal*), sanction, say yes to ♦ *noun* **4** = **approval**, agreement, approbation, assent, authorization, consent, endorsement, go-ahead (*informal*), green light, permission, sanction, say-so (*informal*), seal of approval
➤ **Antonyms**
adjective ≠**fine:** displeasing, inaccurate, inadequate, incorrect, not up to scratch (*informal*), poor, unacceptable, unsatisfactory, unsuitable

old *adjective* **1** = **aged**, advanced in years, ancient, decrepit, elderly, getting on, grey, grey-haired, hoary, mature, over the hill (*informal*), past it, past one's prime, senile, venerable **2** = **worn-out**, crumbling, done **3** = **early**, aboriginal, antique, archaic, bygone,

of old, olden (*archaic*), original, primeval, primitive, primordial **4** = **out of date**, antediluvian, antiquated, antique, dated, hackneyed, obsolete, old-fashioned, outdated, outmoded, out of the ark (*informal*), passé, stale, superannuated, timeworn, unfashionable **5** = **former**, earlier, erstwhile, ex-, one-time, previous, quondam **6** = **long-established**, age-old, experienced, familiar, of long standing, practised, skilled, time-honoured, traditional, veteran, vintage
➤ **Antonyms**
≠**aged:** immature, juvenile, young, youthful ≠**out of date:** current, fashionable, modern, modish, new, novel, recent, up-to-date

old age *noun* = **declining years**, advancing years, age, autumn *or* evening of one's life, dotage, senility, Third Age
➤ **Antonyms**
adolescence, childhood, early life, immaturity, young days, youth

old-fashioned *adjective* = **out of date**, ancient, antiquated, archaic, behind the times, dated, dead, démodé, not with it (*informal*), obsolescent, obsolete, old hat, old-time, outdated, outmoded, out of style, out of the ark (*informal*), passé, past, square (*informal*), unfashionable
➤ **Antonyms**
chic, contemporary, current, fashionable, happening (*informal*), modern, modish, trendy (*Brit. informal*), up-to-date, voguish, with it (*informal*)

old hand *noun* = **expert**, past master, veteran

old-time *adjective* = **old-fashioned**, ancient, antique, bygone, former, past, vintage

old-world *adjective* = **traditional**, archaic, ceremonious, chivalrous, courtly, gallant, old-fashioned, picturesque, quaint

oleaginous *adjective* = **oily**, fat, fatty, greasy, sebaceous

Olympian *adjective* = **majestic**, elevated, exalted, glorious, godlike, lofty, sublime

omen *noun* = **sign**, augury, foreboding, foretoken, indication, portent, premonition, presage, prognostication, warning

ominous *adjective* = **threatening**, baleful, dark, fateful, forbidding, foreboding, inauspicious, menacing, portentous, premonitory, sinister, unpromising, unpropitious
➤ **Antonyms**
auspicious, encouraging, favourable, promising, propitious

omission *noun* = **exclusion**, default, failure, forgetfulness, lack, leaving out, neglect, noninclusion, oversight

➤ **Antonyms**
addition, inclusion, incorporation, insertion

omit *verb* = **leave out**, disregard, drop, eliminate, exclude, fail, forget, give (something) a miss (*informal*), leave (something) undone, miss (out), neglect, overlook, pass over, skip
➤ **Antonyms**
add, enter, include, incorporate, insert, put in

omnipotence *noun* = **supremacy**, divine right, invincibility, mastery, sovereignty, supreme power
➤ **Antonyms**
frailty, impotence, inability, inferiority, powerlessness, vulnerability, weakness

omnipotent *adjective* = **almighty**, all-powerful, supreme
➤ **Antonyms**
feeble, frail, impotent, incapable, inferior, powerless, vulnerable, weak

omniscient *adjective* = **all-knowing**, all-wise

on and off *adverb* = **occasionally**, by fits and starts, discontinuously, (every) now and again, fitfully, from time to time, intermittently, now and then, off and on, sometimes, spasmodically

once *adverb* 1 = **at one time**, formerly, in the old days, in the past, in times gone by, in times past, long ago, once upon a time, previously 2 **once and for all** = **for the last time**, conclusively, decisively, finally, for all time, for good, permanently, positively, with finality 3 **once in a while** = **occasionally**, at intervals, at times, every now and then, from time to time, now and again, on occasion, sometimes ♦ *noun* 4 **at once**: a = **immediately**, directly, forthwith, instantly, now, right away, straight away, straightway (*archaic*), this (very) minute, without delay, without hesitation b = **simultaneously**, at *or* in one go (*informal*), at the same time, together

oncoming *adjective* = **approaching**, advancing, forthcoming, looming, onrushing

one-horse *adjective Informal* = **small**, backwoods, inferior, minor, obscure, quiet, sleepy, slow, small-time (*informal*), tinpot (*Brit. informal*), unimportant

onerous *adjective* = **difficult**, backbreaking, burdensome, crushing, demanding, exacting, exhausting, formidable, hard, heavy, laborious, oppressive, responsible, taxing, weighty
➤ **Antonyms**
cushy (*informal*), easy, effortless, facile, light, painless, simple, trifling, undemanding, unexacting, untaxing

one-sided *adjective* = **biased**, coloured, discriminatory, inequitable, lopsided, partial, partisan, prejudiced, unequal, unfair, unjust

➤ **Antonyms**
equal, equitable, fair, impartial, just, unbiased, uncoloured, unprejudiced

one-time *adjective* = **former**, erstwhile, ex-, late, previous, quondam, sometime

one-track *adjective Informal* = **obsessed**, fanatical, fixated, single-track

ongoing *adjective* = **in progress**, continuous, developing, evolving, progressing, unfinished, unfolding

onlooker *noun* = **observer**, bystander, eyewitness, looker-on, spectator, viewer, watcher, witness

only *adjective* 1 = **sole**, exclusive, individual, lone, one and only, single, solitary, unique ♦ *adverb* 2 = **merely**, at most, barely, exclusively, just, purely, simply

onomatopoeic *adjective* = **imitative**, echoic, onomatopoetic

onrush *noun* = **surge**, charge, flood, flow, onset, onslaught, push, rush, stampede, stream

onset *noun* = **beginning**, inception, kick-off (*informal*), outbreak, start
➤ **Antonyms**
conclusion, culmination, end, ending, finish, outcome, termination, wind-up

onslaught *noun* = **attack**, assault, blitz, charge, offensive, onrush, onset
➤ **Antonyms**
defensive, escape, flight, retreat, rout, stampede, withdrawal

onus *noun* = **burden**, liability, load, obligation, responsibility, task
➤ **Antonyms**
exemption, exoneration, liberation, pardon, release, relief, remission

onward, onwards *adverb* = **ahead**, beyond, forth, forward, in front, on

ooze[1] *verb* = **seep**, bleed, discharge, drain, dribble, drip, drop, emit, escape, exude, filter, leak, sweat, weep

ooze[2] *noun* = **mud**, alluvium, mire, muck, silt, slime, sludge

opacity *noun* = **opaqueness**, cloudiness, dullness, impermeability, murkiness, obscurity

opalescent *adjective* = **iridescent**, lustrous, nacreous, opaline, pearly

opaque *adjective* 1 = **cloudy**, clouded, dim, dull, filmy, hazy, impenetrable, murky 2 = **incomprehensible**, abstruse, baffling, cryptic, difficult, enigmatic, obscure, unclear, unfathomable, unintelligible
➤ **Antonyms**
≠**cloudy**: bright, clear, crystal clear, limpid, lucid, pellucid, transparent
≠**incomprehensible**: clear, crystal clear, lucid

open *adjective* 1 = **unclosed**, agape, ajar,

gaping, revealed, unbarred, uncovered, unfastened, unlocked, unobstructed, unsealed, yawning **2 = extended**, expanded, spread out, unfolded, unfurled **3 = unenclosed**, clear, exposed, extensive, free, rolling, spacious, sweeping, uncrowded, wide, wide-open **4 = accessible**, available, free, free to all, general, public, unengaged, unoccupied, unrestricted, up for grabs (*informal*), vacant **5 = unresolved**, arguable, debatable, moot, undecided, unsettled, up in the air, yet to be decided **6 = objective**, disinterested, free, impartial, receptive, unbiased, uncommitted, unprejudiced **7 = frank**, above board, artless, candid, fair, guileless, honest, ingenuous, innocent, natural, sincere, transparent, unreserved **8 = generous**, bounteous, bountiful, liberal, munificent, prodigal **9 = obvious**, apparent, barefaced, blatant, bold, clear, conspicuous, downright, evident, flagrant, frank, manifest, noticeable, overt, plain, unconcealed, undisguised, visible **10 = unprotected**, exposed, undefended, unfortified **11** *with* **to = susceptible**, an easy target for, at the mercy of, defenceless against, disposed, exposed, liable, vulnerable **12 = gappy**, filigree, lacy, loose, porous, spongy ♦ *verb* **13 = unfasten**, clear, throw wide, unbar, unblock, unclose, uncork, uncover, undo, unlock, unseal, untie, unwrap **14 = unfold**, expand, spread (out), unfurl, unroll **15 = split**, come apart, crack, rupture, separate **16 = start**, begin, commence, get *or* start the ball rolling, inaugurate, initiate, kick off (*informal*), launch, set in motion
➤ **Antonyms**
adjective ≠**unclosed:** closed, fastened, locked, sealed, shut ≠**unenclosed:** bounded, confined, covered, crowded, enclosed, limited, obstructed, restricted ≠**accessible:** inaccessible, private, protected, restricted ≠**objective:** biased, partial, prejudiced ≠**frank:** artful, cunning, introverted, reserved, secretive, sly, withdrawn ≠**obvious:** covert, disguised, hidden, secret, veiled ≠**unprotected:** defended, protected ♦ *verb* ≠**unfasten:** block, close, fasten, lock, obstruct, seal, shut ≠**unfold:** fold ≠**start:** close, conclude, end, finish, terminate

open-air *adjective* **= outdoor**, alfresco

open-and-shut *adjective* **= straightforward**, foregone, obvious, simple

open-handed *adjective* **= generous**, bountiful, free, lavish, liberal, munificent, prodigal, unstinting
➤ **Antonyms**
avaricious, close-fisted, grasping, grudging, mean, miserly, parsimonious, penny-pinching (*informal*), penurious,

stingy, tight-fisted

opening *noun* **1 = beginning**, birth, commencement, dawn, inauguration, inception, initiation, kickoff (*informal*), launch, launching, onset, opening move, outset, overture, start **2 = opportunity**, break (*informal*), chance, look-in (*informal*), occasion, place, vacancy, window **3 = hole**, aperture, breach, break, chink, cleft, crack, fissure, gap, orifice, perforation, rent, rupture, slot, space, split, vent ♦ *adjective* **4 = first**, beginning, commencing, early, inaugural, initial, introductory, maiden, primary
➤ **Antonyms**
noun ≠**beginning:** cessation, close, completion, conclusion, culmination, ending, finale, finish, termination, winding up (*informal*) ≠**hole:** blockage, closing, closure, obstruction, occlusion, plug, seal, stoppage

openly *adverb* **1 = candidly**, face to face, forthrightly, frankly, overtly, plainly, straight from the shoulder (*informal*), unhesitatingly, unreservedly **2 = blatantly**, brazenly, flagrantly, in full view, in public, publicly, shamelessly, unabashedly, unashamedly
➤ **Antonyms**
covertly, furtively, in camera, privately, quietly, secretly, slyly, surreptitiously

open-minded *adjective* **= unprejudiced**, broad, broad-minded, catholic, dispassionate, enlightened, free, impartial, liberal, reasonable, receptive, tolerant, unbiased, undogmatic
➤ **Antonyms**
biased, bigoted, dogmatic, intolerant, narrow-minded, opinionated, pig-headed, prejudiced, uncompromising

openness *noun* **= frankness**, candour *or* (*U.S.*) candor, honesty, sincerity *or* sincereness

operate *verb* **1 = work**, act, be in action, be in business, function, go, perform, run **2 = handle**, be in charge of, manage, manoeuvre, use, work **3 = perform surgery**
➤ **Antonyms**
≠**work:** break down, conk out (*informal*), cut out (*informal*), fail, falter, halt, seize up, stall, stop

operation *noun* **1 = procedure**, affair, course, exercise, motion, movement, performance, process, use, working **2 = effect**, activity, agency, force, influence **3 = undertaking**, affair, business, deal, enterprise, proceeding, transaction **4 = surgery 5 = manoeuvre**, assault, campaign, exercise **6 in operation = in action**, effective, functioning, going, in business, in force, operative

operational *adjective* **= working**,

functional, going, in working order,
operative, prepared, ready, up and running,
usable, viable, workable
> **Antonyms**
broken, ineffective, inoperative, kaput
(*informal*), nonfunctional, on the blink
(*slang*), on the fritz (*slang*), out of order

operative *adjective* 1 = **in force**, active,
current, effective, efficient, functional,
functioning, in business, in operation,
operational, serviceable, workable 2
= **relevant**, crucial, important, indicative,
influential, key, significant ♦ *noun* 3
= **worker**, artisan, employee, hand, labourer,
machinist, mechanic
> **Antonyms**
adjective ≠**in force**: ineffective, inefficient,
inoperative, nonfunctional, powerless,
unusable, unworkable

operator *noun* 1 = **worker**, conductor,
driver, handler, mechanic, operative,
practitioner, technician 2 = **manager**,
administrator, contractor, dealer, director 3
Informal = **manipulator**, Machiavellian,
mover, shyster (*slang, chiefly U.S.*),
wheeler-dealer (*informal*), worker

opiate *noun* = **narcotic**, downer (*slang*),
drug, sedative, tranquillizer

opine *verb Formal* = **give as one's opinion**,
believe, conjecture, declare, say, suggest,
suppose, venture, volunteer

opinion *noun* 1 = **belief**, assessment,
conception, conjecture, estimation, feeling,
idea, impression, judgment, mind, notion,
persuasion, point of view, sentiment, theory,
view 2 **matter of opinion** = **debatable
point**, matter of judgment, moot point,
open question

opinionated *adjective* = **dogmatic**,
adamant, biased, bigoted, bull-headed,
cocksure, dictatorial, doctrinaire, inflexible,
obdurate, obstinate, overbearing,
pig-headed, prejudiced, self-assertive,
single-minded, stubborn, uncompromising
> **Antonyms**
broad-minded, compliant, compromising,
dispassionate, flexible, open-minded,
receptive, tolerant, unbiased, unbigoted,
unprejudiced

opponent *noun* = **adversary**, antagonist,
challenger, competitor, contestant,
disputant, enemy, foe, opposer, rival, the
opposition
> **Antonyms**
accomplice, ally, associate, colleague, friend,
helper, mate, supporter

opportune *adjective Formal* = **timely**,
advantageous, appropriate, apt, auspicious,
convenient, falling into one's lap, favourable,
felicitous, fit, fitting, fortunate, happy, lucky,

proper, propitious, seasonable, suitable,
well-timed
> **Antonyms**
inappropriate, inconvenient, inopportune,
unfavourable, unfortunate, unsuitable,
untimely

opportunism *noun* = **expediency**,
exploitation, Machiavellianism, pragmatism,
realism, unscrupulousness

opportunity *noun* = **chance**, break
(*informal*), convenience, moment, occasion,
opening, scope, time, window

oppose *verb* = **fight**, bar, block, check,
combat, confront, contradict, counter,
counterattack, defy, face, fly in the face of,
hinder, obstruct, prevent, resist, set one's
face against, speak against, stand up to, take
a stand against, take issue with, take on,
thwart, withstand
> **Antonyms**
advance, advocate, aid, back, defend,
espouse, help, promote, support

opposed *adjective* = **against**, antagonistic,
anti (*informal*), antipathetic, antithetical, at
daggers drawn, averse, clashing, conflicting,
contra (*informal*), contrary, dissentient,
hostile, incompatible, inimical, in opposition,
opposing, opposite

opposing *adjective* = **conflicting**,
antagonistic, antipathetic, clashing,
combatant, contrary, enemy, hostile,
incompatible, irreconcilable, opposed,
opposite, rival, warring

opposite *adjective* 1 = **facing**,
corresponding, fronting 2 = **different**,
adverse, antagonistic, antithetical,
conflicting, contradictory, contrary,
contrasted, diametrically opposed, differing,
diverse, hostile, inconsistent, inimical,
irreconcilable, opposed, reverse, unlike
♦ *noun* 3 = **reverse**, antithesis,
contradiction, contrary, converse, inverse,
the other extreme
> **Antonyms**
adjective ≠**different**: alike, consistent,
corresponding, identical, like, matching,
same, similar, uniform

opposition *noun* 1 = **hostility**, antagonism,
competition, counteraction, disapproval,
obstruction, obstructiveness, prevention,
resistance, unfriendliness 2 = **opponent**,
antagonist, competition, foe, other side, rival
> **Antonyms**
≠**hostility**: agreement, approval, assent,
collaboration, concurrence, cooperation,
friendliness, responsiveness

oppress *verb* 1 = **subjugate**, abuse, crush,
maltreat, overpower, overwhelm, persecute,
subdue, suppress, wrong 2 = **depress**, afflict,
burden, dispirit, harass, lie *or* weigh heavy

upon, sadden, take the heart out of,
torment, vex
➤ Antonyms
≠**subjugate:** deliver, emancipate, free,
liberate, loose, release, set free ≠**depress:**
unburden

oppressed *adjective* = downtrodden,
abused, browbeaten, burdened,
disadvantaged, enslaved, harassed,
maltreated, misused, slave, subject,
tyrannized, underprivileged
➤ Antonyms
advantaged, exalted, favoured, honoured,
liberated, privileged

oppression *noun* = subjugation, abuse,
brutality, cruelty, hardship, harshness, injury,
injustice, iron hand, maltreatment,
persecution, subjection, suffering, tyranny
➤ Antonyms
benevolence, clemency, compassion,
goodness, humaneness, justice, kindness,
mercy, sympathy, tenderness

oppressive *adjective* 1 = tyrannical, brutal,
cruel, despotic, harsh, heavy, inhuman,
overbearing, repressive, severe, unjust 2
= stifling, airless, close, heavy, muggy,
overpowering, stuffy, suffocating, sultry,
torrid
➤ Antonyms
≠**tyrannical:** gentle, humane, just, lenient,
merciful, soft

oppressor *noun* = persecutor, autocrat,
bully, despot, scourge, slave-driver,
taskmaster, tormentor, tyrant

opprobrious *adjective* 1 = contemptuous,
abusive, damaging, defamatory, insulting,
vitriolic 2 = shameful, abominable,
contemptible, despicable, dishonourable,
disreputable, ignominious, reprehensible

opprobrium *noun Formal* = disgrace,
calumny, censure, discredit, disfavour,
dishonour, disrepute, ignominy, ill repute,
infamy, shame, stigma

oppugn *verb Formal* = dispute, argue,
attack, call into question, cast doubt on,
oppose

opt *verb, often with* **for** = choose, decide
(on), elect, go for, plump for, prefer
➤ Antonyms
decide against, dismiss, eliminate, exclude,
preclude, reject, rule out, turn down

optimistic *adjective* 1 = idealistic, Utopian
2 = hopeful, bright, buoyant, can-do
(*informal*), cheerful, confident, encouraged,
expectant, looking on the bright side,
positive, rosy, sanguine
➤ Antonyms
≠**hopeful:** bleak, cynical, despairing,
despondent, downhearted, fatalistic,
gloomy, glum, hopeless, pessimistic, resigned

optimum *adjective* = ideal, best, choicest,
highest, most favourable *or* advantageous,
optimal, peak, perfect, superlative
➤ Antonyms
inferior, least, lowest, minimal, poorest, worst

option *noun* = choice, alternative, election,
preference, selection

optional *adjective* = voluntary,
discretionary, elective, extra, noncompulsory,
open, possible, up to the individual
➤ Antonyms
compulsory, *de rigueur*, mandatory,
obligatory, required

opulence *noun* 1 = wealth, affluence, big
bucks (*informal, chiefly U.S.*), big money,
fortune, lavishness, luxuriance, luxury,
megabucks (*U.S. & Canad. slang*), plenty,
prosperity, riches, richness, sumptuousness,
tidy sum (*informal*) 2 = abundance,
copiousness, cornucopia, fullness, profusion,
richness, superabundance
➤ Antonyms
≠**wealth:** impecuniousness, indigence, lack,
penury, poverty, privation, want
≠**abundance:** dearth, lack, paucity,
scantiness, scarcity, want

opulent *adjective* 1 = rich, affluent, lavish,
luxurious, moneyed, prosperous, sumptuous,
wealthy, well-heeled (*informal*), well-off,
well-to-do 2 = abundant, copious, lavish,
luxuriant, plentiful, profuse, prolific
➤ Antonyms
≠**rich:** broke (*informal*), destitute, down and
out, indigent, moneyless, needy, on the
rocks, penurious, poor, poverty-stricken

opus *noun* = work, brainchild, composition,
creation, *oeuvre*, piece, production

oracle *noun* 1 = prophet, seer, sibyl,
soothsayer 2 = prophecy, answer, augury,
divination, prediction, prognostication,
revelation, vision 3 = authority, adviser,
guru, high priest, horse's mouth,
mastermind, mentor, pundit, source, wizard

oracular *adjective* 1 = prophetic,
portentous, prescient, sibylline 2 = wise,
authoritative, sage 3 = mysterious,
ambiguous, arcane, cryptic, Delphic,
equivocal, obscure, two-edged

oral *adjective* = spoken, verbal, viva voce,
vocal

oration *noun* = speech, address,
declamation, discourse, harangue, homily,
lecture, spiel (*informal*)

orator *noun* = public speaker, declaimer,
lecturer, rhetorician, speaker

oratorical *adjective* = rhetorical,
bombastic, declamatory, eloquent,
grandiloquent, high-flown, magniloquent,
silver-tongued, sonorous

oratory *noun* = eloquence, declamation,

elocution, grandiloquence, public speaking, rhetoric, speechifying, speech-making

orb *noun* = **sphere**, ball, circle, globe, ring, round

orbit *noun* **1** = **path**, circle, course, cycle, ellipse, revolution, rotation, track, trajectory **2** = **sphere of influence**, ambit, compass, course, domain, influence, range, reach, scope, sphere, sweep ♦ *verb* **3** = **circle**, circumnavigate, encircle, revolve around

orchestrate *verb* **1** = **score**, arrange **2** = **organize**, arrange, concert, coordinate, integrate, present, put together, set up, stage-manage

ordain *verb* **1** = **appoint**, anoint, consecrate, invest, nominate **2** *Formal* = **order**, decree, demand, dictate, establish, fix, lay down, legislate, prescribe, pronounce, rule, set, will

ordeal *noun* = **hardship**, affliction, agony, anguish, baptism of fire, nightmare, suffering, test, torture, trial, tribulation(s), trouble(s)
➤ **Antonyms**
bliss, delight, elation, enjoyment, gladness, happiness, joy, pleasure

order *noun* **1** = **instruction**, behest, command, decree, dictate, direction, directive, injunction, law, mandate, ordinance, precept, regulation, rule, say-so (*informal*), stipulation **2** = **tidiness**, arrangement, harmony, method, neatness, orderliness, organization, pattern, plan, regularity, symmetry, system **3** = **sequence**, arrangement, array, categorization, classification, codification, grouping, layout, line-up, ordering, placement, progression, series, setup (*informal*), structure, succession **4** = **peace**, calm, control, discipline, law, law and order, quiet, tranquillity **5** = **request**, application, booking, commission, requisition, reservation **6** = **class**, caste, degree, grade, hierarchy, pecking order (*informal*), position, rank, status **7** = **kind**, breed, cast, class, family, genre, genus, ilk, sort, species, subclass, taxonomic group, tribe, type **8** = **society**, association, brotherhood, community, company, fraternity, guild, league, lodge, organization, sect, sisterhood, sodality, union **9 in order: a** = **tidy**, arranged, in sequence, neat, orderly, shipshape **b** = **appropriate**, acceptable, called for, correct, fitting, O.K. or okay (*informal*), right, suitable **10 out of order: a** = **not working**, broken, broken-down, bust (*informal*), gone haywire (*informal*), in disrepair, inoperative, kaput (*informal*), nonfunctional, on the blink (*slang*), on the fritz (*U.S. slang*), out of commission, U.S. (*informal*), wonky (*Brit. slang*) **b** = **improper**, indecorous, not cricket (*informal*), not done, not on

(*informal*), out of place, out of turn, uncalled-for, wrong ♦ *verb* **11** = **command**, adjure, bid, charge, decree, demand, direct, enjoin, instruct, ordain, prescribe, require **12** = **request**, apply for, book, call for, contract for, demand, engage, prescribe, reserve, send away for **13** = **arrange**, adjust, align, catalogue, class, classify, conduct, control, group, lay out, marshal, neaten, organize, put to rights, regulate, sequence, set in order, sort out, systematize, tabulate, tidy
➤ **Antonyms**
noun ≠**tidiness:** chaos, clutter, confusion, disarray, disorder, jumble, mess, muddle, pandemonium, shambles ♦ *verb* ≠**arrange:** clutter, confuse, disarrange, disorder, disturb, jumble up, mess up, mix up, muddle, scramble

orderly *adjective* **1** = **well-organized**, businesslike, in apple-pie order (*informal*), in order, methodical, neat, regular, scientific, shipshape, systematic, systematized, tidy, trim, well-regulated **2** = **well-behaved**, controlled, decorous, disciplined, law-abiding, nonviolent, peaceable, quiet, restrained
➤ **Antonyms**
≠**well-organized:** chaotic, disorderly, disorganized, higgledy-piggledy (*informal*), messy, sloppy, unsystematic
≠**well-behaved:** disorderly, riotous, uncontrolled, undisciplined

ordinance *noun* = **rule**, command, decree, dictum, edict, law, order, precept, regulation, ruling, statute

ordinarily *adverb* = **usually**, as a rule, commonly, customarily, generally, habitually, in general, in the usual way, normally
➤ **Antonyms**
hardly ever, infrequently, occasionally, rarely, scarcely, seldom, uncommonly

ordinary *adjective* **1** = **usual**, accustomed, common, conventional, customary, established, everyday, familiar, habitual, normal, regular, routine, standard, stock, typical **2** = **commonplace**, banal, common or garden (*informal*), humble, humdrum, modest, mundane, pedestrian, plain, prosaic, run-of-the-mill, unremarkable, workaday **3** = **average**, fair, indifferent, inferior, mean, mediocre, no great shakes (*informal*), second-rate, undistinguished, unexceptional, uninspired, unremarkable **4 out of the ordinary** = **unusual**, atypical, exceptional, exciting, extraordinary, noteworthy, outstanding, rare, remarkable, significant, special, striking, uncommon
➤ **Antonyms**
≠**commonplace, average:** distinguished, exceptional, extraordinary, important,

impressive, inspired, notable, novel, outstanding, rare, significant, superior, uncommon, unconventional, unique, unusual

ordnance noun = **weapons**, arms, artillery, big guns, guns, materiel, munitions

organ noun 1 = **part**, element, member, process, structure, unit 2 = **medium**, agency, channel, forum, journal, means, mouthpiece, newspaper, paper, periodical, publication, vehicle, voice

organic adjective 1 = **natural**, animate, biological, live, living 2 = **systematic**, integrated, methodical, ordered, organized, structured

organism noun = **creature**, animal, being, body, entity, living thing, structure

organization noun 1 = **group**, association, body, company, concern, confederation, consortium, corporation, federation, institution, league, outfit (informal), syndicate 2 = **management**, construction, coordination, direction, formation, forming, formulation, methodology, organizing, planning, regulation, running, structuring 3 = **structure**, arrangement, chemistry, composition, configuration, conformation, constitution, design, format, framework, grouping, make-up, pattern, plan, system, unity, whole

organize verb 1 = **plan**, arrange, be responsible for, constitute, construct, coordinate, establish, form, frame, get going, get together, marshal, put together, run, see to (informal), set up, shape, take care of 2 = **put in order**, arrange, catalogue, classify, codify, group, systematize
➤ **Antonyms**
≠**plan**: confuse, derange, disrupt, upset ≠**put in order**: disorganize, jumble, mix up, muddle, scramble

orgasm noun = **climax**, coming (taboo slang), pleasure

orgy noun 1 = **revel**, bacchanalia, carousal, debauch, revelry, Saturnalia 2 = **spree**, binge (informal), bout, excess, indulgence, overindulgence, splurge, surfeit

orient verb = **adjust**, acclimatize, adapt, align, familiarize, get one's bearings, orientate

orientation noun 1 = **position**, bearings, coordination, direction, location, sense of direction 2 = **adjustment**, acclimatization, adaptation, assimilation, breaking in, familiarization, introduction, settling in

orifice noun = **opening**, aperture, cleft, hole, mouth, perforation, pore, rent, vent

origin noun 1 = **root**, base, basis, cause, derivation, font (poetic), fount, fountain, fountainhead, provenance, roots, source, spring, wellspring 2 = **beginning**, birth,

commencement, creation, dawning, early stages, emergence, foundation, genesis, inauguration, inception, launch, origination, outset, start 3 = **ancestry**, beginnings, birth, descent, extraction, family, heritage, lineage, parentage, pedigree, stirps, stock
➤ **Antonyms**
≠**beginning**: conclusion, culmination, death, end, expiry, finale, finish, outcome, termination

original adjective 1 = **first**, aboriginal, earliest, early, infant, initial, introductory, opening, primary, primitive, primordial, rudimentary, starting 2 = **new**, fresh, ground-breaking, innovative, innovatory, novel, seminal, unconventional, unprecedented, untried, unusual 3 = **creative**, fertile, imaginative, ingenious, inventive, resourceful 4 = **authentic**, archetypal, first, first-hand, genuine, master, primary, prototypical ♦ noun 5 = **prototype**, archetype, master, model, paradigm, pattern, precedent, standard, type
➤ **Antonyms**
adjective ≠**first**: final, last, latest ≠**new**: antiquated, banal, commonplace, conventional, familiar, normal, old, old-fashioned, ordinary, stale, standard, stock, traditional, typical, unimaginative, unoriginal, usual ≠**authentic**: borrowed, copied, secondary, unoriginal ♦ noun ≠**prototype**: copy, imitation, replica, reproduction

originality noun = **novelty**, creativeness, creative spirit, creativity, freshness, imagination, imaginativeness, individuality, ingenuity, innovation, innovativeness, inventiveness, new ideas, newness, unconventionality, unorthodoxy
➤ **Antonyms**
conformity, conventionality, imitativeness, normality, orthodoxy, regularity, staleness, traditionalism

originally adverb = **initially**, at first, at the outset, at the start, by origin, first, in the beginning, in the first place, to begin with

originate verb 1 = **begin**, arise, be born, come, derive, emanate, emerge, flow, issue, proceed, result, rise, spring, start, stem 2 = **introduce**, bring about, conceive, create, develop, discover, evolve, form, formulate, generate, give birth to, inaugurate, initiate, institute, invent, launch, pioneer, produce, set in motion, set up
➤ **Antonyms**
cease, conclude, end, finish, terminate, wind up

originator noun = **creator**, architect, author, father or mother, founder, generator, innovator, inventor, maker, pioneer, prime mover

ornament *noun* 1 = **decoration**, accessory, adornment, bauble, embellishment, festoon, frill, garnish, knick-knack, trimming, trinket 2 = **leading light**, flower, honour, jewel, pride, treasure ◆ *verb* 3 = **decorate**, adorn, beautify, brighten, deck, dress up, embellish, festoon, garnish, grace, prettify, trim

ornamental *adjective* = **decorative**, attractive, beautifying, embellishing, for show, showy

ornamentation *noun* = **decoration**, adornment, elaboration, embellishment, embroidery, frills, ornateness

ornate *adjective* = **elaborate**, baroque, beautiful, bedecked, busy, decorated, elegant, fancy, florid, fussy, ornamented, overelaborate, rococo
➤ **Antonyms**
austere, bare, basic, ordinary, plain, severe, simple, spartan, stark, subdued, unadorned, unfussy

orthodox *adjective* = **established**, accepted, approved, conformist, conventional, customary, kosher (*informal*), official, received, traditional, well-established
➤ **Antonyms**
eccentric, heretical, left-field (*informal*), liberal, nonconformist, novel, off-the-wall (*slang*), original, radical, unconventional, unorthodox, unusual

orthodoxy *noun* = **conformity**, authoritativeness, authority, conformism, conventionality, inflexibility, received wisdom, traditionalism
➤ **Antonyms**
flexibility, heresy, heterodoxy, impiety, nonconformism, nonconformity, unconventionality

oscillate *verb* = **fluctuate**, seesaw, sway, swing, vacillate, vary, vibrate, waver
➤ **Antonyms**
commit oneself, decide, determine, purpose, resolve, settle

oscillation *noun* = **swing**, fluctuation, instability, seesawing, vacillation, variation, wavering

ossify *verb* = **harden**, fossilize, freeze, petrify, solidify, stiffen

ostensible *adjective* = **apparent**, alleged, avowed, exhibited, manifest, outward, pretended, professed, purported, seeming, so-called, superficial, supposed

ostensibly *adverb* = **apparently**, on the face of it, on the surface, professedly, seemingly, supposedly, to all intents and purposes

ostentation *noun* = **display**, affectation, boasting, exhibitionism, flamboyance, flashiness, flaunting, flourish, pageantry, parade, pomp, pretension, pretentiousness,
show, showiness, showing off (*informal*), swank (*informal*), vaunting
➤ **Antonyms**
humility, inconspicuousness, modesty, plainness, reserve, simplicity, unpretentiousness

ostentatious *adjective* = **pretentious**, boastful, brash, conspicuous, extravagant, flamboyant, flash (*informal*), flashy, gaudy, loud, obtrusive, pompous, showy, swanky (*informal*), vain, vulgar
➤ **Antonyms**
conservative, inconspicuous, low-key, modest, plain, reserved, simple, sombre

ostracism *noun* = **exclusion**, avoidance, banishment, boycott, cold-shouldering, exile, expulsion, isolation, rejection
➤ **Antonyms**
acceptance, admission, approval, inclusion, invitation, reception, welcome

ostracize *verb* = **exclude**, avoid, banish, blackball, blacklist, boycott, cast out, cold-shoulder, excommunicate, exile, expatriate, expel, give (someone) the cold shoulder, reject, send to Coventry, shun, snub
➤ **Antonyms**
accept, admit, approve, embrace, greet, include, invite, receive, welcome

other *adjective* 1 = **additional**, added, alternative, auxiliary, extra, further, more, spare, supplementary 2 = **different**, contrasting, dissimilar, distinct, diverse, remaining, separate, unrelated, variant

otherwise *conjunction* 1 = **or else**, if not, or then ◆ *adverb* 2 = **differently**, any other way, contrarily

ounce *noun* = **shred**, atom, crumb, drop, grain, iota, particle, scrap, speck, trace, whit

oust *verb* = **expel**, depose, dislodge, displace, dispossess, eject, throw out, topple, turn out, unseat

out *adjective* 1 = **away**, abroad, absent, elsewhere, gone, not at home, outside 2 = **extinguished**, at an end, cold, dead, doused, ended, exhausted, expired, finished, used up 3 = **old-fashioned**, antiquated, behind the times, dated, dead, *démodé*, old hat, passé, square (*informal*), unfashionable 4 = **not allowed**, impossible, not on (*informal*), ruled out, unacceptable
➤ **Antonyms**
≠**old-fashioned**: à la mode, fashionable, in, in fashion, latest, modern, trendy (*Brit. informal*), up-to-date, with it (*informal*)

out-and-out *adjective* = **absolute**, arrant, complete, consummate, deep-dyed (*usually derogatory*), downright, outright, perfect, thorough, total, unmitigated, unqualified, utter

outbreak *noun* = **eruption**, burst, epidemic, explosion, flare-up, flash, outburst, rash, spasm, upsurge

outburst *noun* = **outpouring**, attack, discharge, eruption, explosion, fit of temper, flare-up, outbreak, paroxysm, spasm, storm, surge

outcast *noun* = **pariah**, castaway, exile, leper, *persona non grata*, refugee, untouchable, vagabond, wretch

outclass *verb* = **surpass**, be a cut above (*informal*), beat, eclipse, exceed, excel, leave *or* put in the shade, leave standing (*informal*), outdistance, outdo, outrank, outshine, outstrip, overshadow, run rings around (*informal*)

outcome *noun* = **result**, aftereffect, aftermath, conclusion, consequence, end, end result, issue, payoff (*informal*), sequel, upshot

outcry *noun* = **protest**, clamour, commotion, complaint, exclamation, hue and cry, hullaballoo, outburst, uproar

outdated *adjective* = **old-fashioned**, antiquated, antique, archaic, behind the times, *démodé*, obsolete, outmoded, out of date, out of style, out of the ark (*informal*), passé, unfashionable
➤ **Antonyms**
à la mode, all the rage, contemporary, current, fashionable, in vogue, modern, modish, stylish, trendy (*Brit. informal*), up-to-date, with it (*informal*)

outdistance *verb* = **leave behind**, leave standing (*informal*), lose, outrun, outstrip, shake off

outdo *verb* = **surpass**, beat, be one up on, best, eclipse, exceed, excel, get the better of, go one better than (*informal*), outclass, outdistance, outmanoeuvre, outshine, outsmart (*informal*), overcome, run rings around (*informal*), top, transcend

outdoor *adjective* = **open-air**, alfresco, out-of-door(s), outside
➤ **Antonyms**
indoor, inside, interior, within

outer *adjective* = **external**, exposed, exterior, outlying, outside, outward, peripheral, superficial, surface
➤ **Antonyms**
central, closer, inner, inside, interior, internal, inward, nearer

outface *verb* = **outstare**, confront, defy, look straight in the eye, square up to, stare down, stare out

outfit *noun* **1** = **costume**, clothes, ensemble, garb, gear (*informal*), get-up (*informal*), kit, rigout (*informal*), suit, threads (*slang*) **2** *Informal* = **group**, company, corps, coterie, crew, organization, set, setup (*informal*), squad, team, unit

outfitter *noun* *Old-fashioned* = **clothier**, costumier, couturier, dressmaker, tailor

outflow *noun* = **discharge**, ebb, effluence, effusion, emanation, gush, issue, jet, outpouring, rush, spout

outgoing *adjective* **1** = **leaving**, departing, ex-, former, last, past, retiring, withdrawing **2** = **sociable**, approachable, communicative, cordial, demonstrative, easy, expansive, extrovert, friendly, genial, gregarious, informal, open, unreserved, warm
➤ **Antonyms**
≠**leaving**: arriving, entering, incoming
≠**sociable**: austere, cold, indifferent, reserved, retiring, withdrawn

outgoings *plural noun* = **expenses**, costs, expenditure, outlay, overheads

outgrowth *noun* **1** = **product**, by-product, consequence, development, result, spin-off **2** = **offshoot**, bulge, excrescence, outcrop, process, shoot, sprout

outing *noun* = **trip**, excursion, expedition, jaunt, pleasure trip, spin (*informal*)

outlandish *adjective* = **strange**, alien, bizarre, eccentric, exotic, fantastic, far-out (*slang*), foreign, freakish, grotesque, outré, preposterous, queer, unheard-of, weird
➤ **Antonyms**
banal, commonplace, everyday, familiar, humdrum, mundane, normal, ordinary, usual, well-known

outlast *verb* = **outlive**, outstay, outwear, survive

outlaw *noun* **1** *History* = **bandit**, brigand, desperado, footpad (*archaic*), fugitive, highwayman, marauder, outcast, pariah, robber ◆ *verb* **2** = **forbid**, ban, banish, bar, disallow, embargo, exclude, interdict, make illegal, prohibit, proscribe **3** = **put a price on (someone's) head**
➤ **Antonyms**
verb ≠**forbid**: allow, approve, authorize, consent, endorse, legalise, permit, sanction, support

outlay *noun* = **expenditure**, cost, disbursement, expenses, investment, outgoings, spending

outlet *noun* **1** = **release**, means of expression, safety valve, vent **2** = **shop**, market, store **3** = **opening**, avenue, channel, duct, egress, exit, orifice, release, way out

outline *noun* **1** = **summary**, bare facts, main features, recapitulation, résumé, rough idea, rundown, synopsis, thumbnail sketch **2** = **shape**, configuration, contour, delineation, figure, form, profile, silhouette ◆ *verb* **3** = **summarize**, adumbrate, delineate, draft, plan, rough out, sketch (in), trace

outlive *verb* = **survive**, outlast

outlook *noun* **1** = **attitude**, angle, frame of mind, perspective, point of view, slant, standpoint, viewpoint, views **2** = **prospect**, expectations, forecast, future **3** = **view**, aspect, panorama, prospect, scene, vista

outlying *adjective* = **remote**, backwoods, distant, far-flung, in the middle of nowhere, outer, out-of-the-way, peripheral, provincial

outmanoeuvre *verb* = **outwit**, get the better of, outdo, outflank, outsmart (*informal*), run rings round (*informal*), steal a march on (*informal*)

outmoded *adjective* = **old-fashioned**, anachronistic, antediluvian, antiquated, antique, archaic, behind the times, dated, *démodé*, obsolescent, obsolete, old-time, out-of-date, out of style, outworn, passé, square (*informal*), unfashionable
➤ **Antonyms**
all the rage, fashionable, fresh, in vogue, latest, modern, modish, new, recent

out-of-date *adjective* = **old-fashioned**, antiquated, archaic, dated, discarded, elapsed, expired, invalid, lapsed, obsolete, outmoded, out of the ark (*informal*), outworn, passé, stale, unfashionable
➤ **Antonyms**
contemporary, current, fashionable, in, new, now (*informal*), trendy (*Brit. informal*), up to date, valid

out-of-the-way *adjective* = **remote**, distant, far-flung, inaccessible, isolated, lonely, obscure, off the beaten track, outlying, secluded, unfrequented
➤ **Antonyms**
accessible, close, convenient, frequented, handy, near, nearby, proximate, reachable, within sniffing distance (*informal*)

out-of-work *adjective* = **unemployed**, idle, jobless, laid off, on the dole (*Brit.*), out of a job, redundant

outpouring *noun* = **stream**, cascade, deluge, effluence, effusion, emanation, flow, flux, issue, outflow, spate, spurt, torrent

output *noun* = **production**, achievement, manufacture, product, productivity, yield

outrage *noun* **1** = **indignation**, anger, fury, hurt, resentment, shock, wrath **2** = **atrocity**, barbarism, enormity, evil, inhumanity **3** = **violation**, abuse, affront, desecration, indignity, injury, insult, offence, profanation, sacrilege, shock, violence ◆ *verb* **4** = **offend**, affront, incense, infuriate, madden, scandalize, shock

outrageous *adjective* **1** = **unreasonable**, excessive, exorbitant, extravagant, immoderate, O.T.T. (*slang*), over the top (*slang*), preposterous, scandalous, shocking, steep (*informal*) **2** = **atrocious**, abominable,

barbaric, disgraceful, egregious, flagrant, heinous, horrible, infamous, inhuman, iniquitous, nefarious, offensive, scandalous, shocking, unspeakable, villainous, violent, wicked
➤ **Antonyms**
≠**unreasonable**: equitable, fair, moderate, reasonable ≠**atrocious**: just, mild, minor, tolerable, trivial

outré *adjective* = **eccentric**, bizarre, fantastic, freakish, odd, off-the-wall (*slang*), outlandish, unconventional, weird

outrider *noun* = **escort**, advance guard, attendant, bodyguard

outright *adjective* **1** = **absolute**, arrant, complete, consummate, downright, out-and-out, perfect, pure, thorough, thoroughgoing, total, unconditional, undeniable, unmitigated, unqualified, utter, wholesale **2** = **direct**, definite, flat, straightforward, unequivocal, unqualified ◆ *adverb* **3** = **absolutely**, completely, straightforwardly, thoroughly, to the full, without hesitation, without restraint **4** = **instantly**, at once, immediately, instantaneously, on the spot, straight away, there and then, without more ado **5** = **openly**, explicitly, overtly

outrun *verb* **1** = **outdistance**, beat, escape, get away from, lose, outpace, outstrip, shake off **2** = **surpass**, exceed, leave behind, outdo

outset *noun* = **beginning**, commencement, early days, inauguration, inception, kickoff (*informal*), onset, opening, start, starting point
➤ **Antonyms**
closing, completion, conclusion, consummation, end, finale, finish, termination

outshine *verb* = **outdo**, be head and shoulders above, be superior to, eclipse, leave *or* put in the shade, outclass, outstrip, overshadow, surpass, top, transcend, upstage

outside *adjective* **1** = **external**, exterior, extraneous, extreme, out, outdoor, outer, outermost, outward, surface **2** *As in an* **outside chance** = **remote**, distant, faint, marginal, negligible, slight, slim, small, unlikely ◆ *noun* **3** = **exterior**, façade, face, front, skin, surface, topside
➤ **Antonyms**
adjective ≠**external**: in, indoor, inner, innermost, inside, interior, internal, inward

outsider *noun* = **interloper**, alien, foreigner, incomer, intruder, newcomer, nonmember, odd one out, outlander, stranger

outsize *adjective* = **extra-large**, enormous, gargantuan, giant, gigantic, huge, humongous *or* humungous (*U.S. slang*), immense, jumbo (*informal*), large,

mammoth, monster, oversized
➤ **Antonyms**
baby, dwarf, micro, mini, pocket, tiny, undersized

outskirts *plural noun* = **edge**, borders, boundary, environs, periphery, purlieus, suburbia, suburbs, vicinity

outsmart *verb Informal* = **outwit**, get the better of, outfox, outmanoeuvre, pull a fast one on (*informal*), put one over on (*informal*), run rings round (*informal*), trick

outspoken *adjective* = **forthright**, abrupt, blunt, candid, direct, downright, explicit, frank, free, free-spoken, open, plain-spoken, round, unceremonious, unequivocal, unreserved
➤ **Antonyms**
diplomatic, gracious, judicious, reserved, reticent, tactful

outspread *adjective* = **outstretched**, expanded, extended, fanlike, fanned out, flared, open, opened up, unfolded, unfurled, wide-open

outstanding *adjective* 1 = **excellent**, celebrated, distinguished, eminent, exceptional, great, important, impressive, pre-eminent, special, superior, superlative, well-known 2 = **unpaid**, due, owing, payable, pending, remaining, uncollected, unresolved, unsettled 3 = **conspicuous**, arresting, eye-catching, marked, memorable, notable, noteworthy, prominent, salient, signal, striking
➤ **Antonyms**
≠**excellent**: dull, inferior, insignificant, mediocre, no great shakes (*informal*), ordinary, pedestrian, run-of-the-mill, unexceptional, unimpressive

outstrip *verb* 1 = **surpass**, better, eclipse, exceed, excel, outdo, overtake, transcend 2 = **outdistance**, outpace, outrun, shake off

outward *adjective* = **apparent**, evident, exterior, external, noticeable, observable, obvious, ostensible, outer, outside, perceptible, superficial, surface, visible
➤ **Antonyms**
inner, inside, interior, internal, invisible, inward, obscure, unnoticeable

outwardly *adverb* = **apparently**, as far as one can see, externally, officially, on the face of it, on the surface, ostensibly, professedly, seemingly, superficially, to all appearances, to all intents and purposes, to the eye

outweigh *verb* = **override**, cancel (out), compensate for, eclipse, make up for, outbalance, overcome, predominate, preponderate, prevail over, take precedence over, tip the scales

outwit *verb* = **outsmart** (*informal*), cheat, deceive, dupe, get the better of, make a fool

or monkey of, outfox, outmanoeuvre, outthink, put one over on (*informal*), run rings round (*informal*), swindle, take in (*informal*)

outworn *adjective* = **outdated**, antiquated, behind the times, discredited, disused, hackneyed, obsolete, outmoded, out-of-date, threadbare, worn-out
➤ **Antonyms**
fresh, modish, new, recent, up to date

oval *adjective* = **elliptical**, egg-shaped, ovate, oviform, ovoid

ovation *noun* = **applause**, acclaim, acclamation, big hand, cheering, cheers, clapping, plaudits, tribute
➤ **Antonyms**
abuse, booing, catcalls, derision, heckling, jeers, jibes, mockery, ridicule

over *preposition* 1 = **on top of**, above, on, superior to, upon 2 = **more than**, above, exceeding, in excess of 3 **over and above** = **In addition to**, added to, as well as, besides, let alone, not to mention, on top of, plus ♦ *adverb* 4 = **above**, aloft, on high, overhead 5 = **extra**, beyond, in addition, in excess, left over 6 **over and over (again)** = **repeatedly**, ad nauseam, again and again, frequently, often, time and again ♦ *adjective* 7 = **finished**, accomplished, at an end, by, bygone, closed, completed, concluded, done (with), ended, gone, past, settled, up (*informal*) 8 = **extra**, remaining, superfluous, surplus, unused

overabundance *noun* = **excess**, glut, plethora, profusion, superabundance, superfluity, surfeit, surplus

overact *verb* = **exaggerate**, ham or ham up (*informal*), overdo, overplay

overall *adjective* 1 = **total**, all-embracing, blanket, complete, comprehensive, general, global, inclusive, long-range, long-term, overarching ♦ *adverb* 2 = **in general**, generally speaking, in (the) large, in the long term, on the whole

overawe *verb* = **intimidate**, abash, alarm, browbeat, cow, daunt, frighten, scare, terrify
➤ **Antonyms**
bolster, buoy up, cheer up, comfort, console, hearten, reassure

overbalance *verb* = **topple over**, capsize, keel over, lose one's balance, lose one's footing, overturn, slip, take a tumble, tip over, tumble, turn turtle, upset

overbearing *adjective* = **dictatorial**, arrogant, autocratic, bossy (*informal*), cavalier, dogmatic, domineering, haughty, high-handed, imperious, lordly, officious, peremptory, supercilious, superior, tyrannical
➤ **Antonyms**
deferential, humble, modest, self-effacing,

submissive, unassertive, unassuming

overblown *adjective* = **excessive**, disproportionate, immoderate, inflated, overdone, over the top, undue

overcast *adjective* = **cloudy**, clouded, clouded over, dismal, dreary, dull, grey, hazy, leaden, louring *or* lowering, murky, threatening
➤ **Antonyms**
bright, brilliant, clear, cloudless, fine, sunny, unclouded

overcharge *verb* = **cheat**, diddle (*informal*), do (*slang*), fleece, rip off (*slang*), rook (*slang*), short-change, skin (*slang*), sting (*informal*), surcharge

overcome *verb* 1 = **conquer**, beat, crush, defeat, get the better of, lick (*informal*), master, overpower, overthrow, overwhelm, prevail, rise above, subdue, subjugate, surmount, triumph over, undo, vanquish
♦ *adjective* 2 = **affected**, at a loss for words, bowled over (*informal*), overwhelmed, speechless, swept off one's feet

overconfident *adjective* = **cocksure**, brash, foolhardy, overweening, presumptuous, riding for a fall (*informal*), uppish (*Brit. informal*)
➤ **Antonyms**
cautious, diffident, doubtful, hesitant, insecure, timid, timorous, uncertain, unsure

overcrowded *adjective* = **packed (out)**, bursting at the seams, choked, congested, crammed full, jam-packed, overloaded, overpopulated, swarming
➤ **Antonyms**
abandoned, deserted, desolate, empty, forsaken, unoccupied, vacant

overdo *verb* 1 = **exaggerate**, be intemperate, belabour, carry too far, do to death (*informal*), gild the lily, go overboard (*informal*), go to extremes, not know when to stop, overindulge, overplay, overreach, overstate, overuse 2 **overdo it** = **overwork**, bite off more than one can chew, burn the candle at both ends (*informal*), drive oneself, go too far, overload oneself, overtax one's strength, overtire oneself, strain *or* overstrain oneself, wear oneself out
➤ **Antonyms**
≠**exaggerate**: belittle, disparage, minimize, play down, underplay, underrate, understate, underuse, undervalue

overdone *adjective* 1 = **excessive**, beyond all bounds, exaggerated, fulsome, immoderate, inordinate, overelaborate, preposterous, too much, undue, unnecessary 2 = **overcooked**, burnt, burnt to a cinder, charred, dried up, spoiled
➤ **Antonyms**
≠**excessive**: belittled, minimized,

moderated, played down, underdone, underplayed, understated

overdue *adjective* = **late**, behindhand, behind schedule, behind time, belated, not before time (*informal*), owing, tardy, unpunctual
➤ **Antonyms**
ahead of time, beforehand, early, in advance, in good time, punctual

overeat *verb* = **overindulge**, binge (*informal*), eat like a horse (*informal*), gorge, gormandize, guzzle, make a pig of oneself (*informal*), pig out (*slang*), stuff, stuff oneself

overemphasize *verb* = **overstress**, belabour, blow up out of all proportion, lay too much stress on, make a big thing of (*informal*), make a mountain out of a molehill (*informal*), make something out of nothing, make too much of, overdramatize
➤ **Antonyms**
belittle, downplay, make light of, minimize, play down, underplay, underrate, understate

overexert *verb* = **do too much**, burn the candle at both ends (*informal*), drive oneself, knock oneself out, overstrain oneself, overtax oneself, overtire oneself, overwork, push oneself too hard, strain oneself, wear oneself out, work oneself to death

overflow *verb* 1 = **spill**, brim over, bubble over, discharge, fall over, pour out, pour over, run over, run with, spray, surge, well over ♦ *noun* 2 = **surplus**, flood, flooding, inundation, overabundance, spill, spilling over

overhang *verb* = **project**, beetle, bulge, extend, impend, jut, loom, protrude, stick out

overhaul *verb* 1 = **check**, do up (*informal*), examine, inspect, recondition, re-examine, repair, restore, service, survey 2 = **overtake**, catch up with, draw level with, get ahead of, pass ♦ *noun* 3 = **checkup**, check, examination, going-over (*informal*), inspection, reconditioning, service

overhead *adverb* 1 = **above**, aloft, atop, in the sky, on high, skyward, up above, upward ♦ *adjective* 2 = **aerial**, overhanging, upper
➤ **Antonyms**
adverb ≠**above**: below, beneath, downward, underfoot, underneath

overheads *plural noun* = **running costs**, operating costs

overheated *adjective* = **agitated**, fiery, flaming, impassioned, inflamed, overexcited, roused
➤ **Antonyms**
calm, collected, composed, cool, dispassionate, unemotional, unexcited, unfazed (*informal*), unruffled

overindulge *verb* = **be immoderate** *or*

intemperate, drink *or* eat too much, have a binge (*informal*), live it up (*informal*), make a pig of oneself (*informal*), overdo it, pig out (*slang*)

overindulgence *noun* = **immoderation**, excess, intemperance, overeating, surfeit

overjoyed *adjective* = **delighted**, cock-a-hoop, deliriously happy, elated, euphoric, floating on air, happy as a lark, in raptures, joyful, jubilant, on cloud nine (*informal*), over the moon (*informal*), rapt, rapturous, thrilled, tickled pink (*informal*), transported
➤ **Antonyms**
crestfallen, dejected, disappointed, downcast, down in the dumps (*informal*), heartbroken, miserable, sad, unhappy, woebegone

overlay *verb* 1 = **cover**, adorn, blanket, inlay, laminate, ornament, veneer ♦ *noun* 2 = **covering**, adornment, decoration, ornamentation, veneer

overload *verb* = **overburden**, burden, encumber, oppress, overcharge, overtax, saddle (with), strain, weigh down

overlook *verb* 1 = **miss**, disregard, fail to notice, forget, neglect, omit, pass, slip up on 2 = **ignore**, blink at, condone, disregard, excuse, forgive, let bygones be bygones, let one off with, let pass, let ride, make allowances for, pardon, turn a blind eye to, wink at 3 = **have a view of**, afford a view of, command a view of, front on to, look over *or* out on
➤ **Antonyms**
≠miss: discern, heed, mark, note, notice, observe, perceive, regard, spot

overly *adverb* = **excessively**, exceedingly, immoderately, inordinately, over, too, unduly, very much

overpower *verb* = **overwhelm**, beat, clobber (*slang*), conquer, crush, defeat, get the upper hand over, knock out, lick (*informal*), master, overcome, overthrow, quell, subdue, subjugate, vanquish

overpowering *adjective* = **overwhelming**, compelling, compulsive, extreme, forceful, invincible, irrefutable, irresistible, powerful, strong, uncontrollable

overrate *verb* = **overestimate**, assess too highly, exaggerate, make too much of, oversell, overvalue, rate too highly, think or expect too much of, think too highly of

overreach *verb* **overreach oneself** = **try to be too clever**, be hoist with one's own petard, bite off more than one can chew, defeat one's own ends, go too far, have one's schemes backfire *or* boomerang *or* rebound on one

override *verb* = **overrule**, annul, cancel, countermand, discount, disregard, ignore, nullify, outweigh, quash, reverse, set aside, supersede, take no account of

overriding *adjective* = **predominant**, cardinal, compelling, dominant, major, number one, paramount, pivotal, prevailing, primary, prime, supreme, ultimate
➤ **Antonyms**
immaterial, inconsequential, insignificant, irrelevant, minor, negligible, paltry, petty, trifling, trivial, unimportant

overrule *verb* = **reverse**, alter, annul, cancel, countermand, disallow, invalidate, make null and void, outvote, override, overturn, recall, repeal, rescind, revoke, rule against, set aside, veto
➤ **Antonyms**
allow, approve, consent to, endorse, pass, permit, sanction

overrun *verb* 1 = **overwhelm**, invade, massacre, occupy, put to flight, rout, swamp 2 = **spread over**, choke, infest, inundate, overflow, overgrow, permeate, ravage, spread like wildfire, swarm over 3 = **exceed**, go beyond, overshoot, run over *or* on

overseer *noun* = **supervisor**, boss (*informal*), chief, foreman, gaffer (*informal, chiefly Brit.*), manager, master, superintendent, superior

overshadow *verb* 1 = **outshine**, dominate, dwarf, eclipse, excel, leave *or* put in the shade, outweigh, surpass, take precedence over, throw into the shade, tower above 2 = **spoil**, blight, cast a gloom upon, mar, put a damper on, ruin, take the pleasure *or* enjoyment out of, temper

oversight *noun* = **mistake**, blunder, carelessness, delinquency, error, fault, inattention, lapse, laxity, neglect, omission, slip

overt *adjective* = **open**, apparent, blatant, bold, manifest, observable, obvious, patent, plain, public, unconcealed, undisguised, visible
➤ **Antonyms**
concealed, covert, disguised, hidden, hush-hush (*informal*), invisible, secret, surreptitious, underhand

overtake *verb* 1 = **pass**, catch up with, draw level with, get past, leave behind, outdistance, outdo, outstrip, overhaul 2 = **befall**, catch unprepared, come upon, engulf, happen, hit, overwhelm, strike, take by surprise

overthrow *verb* 1 = **defeat**, abolish, beat, bring down, conquer, crush, depose, dethrone, do away with, master, oust, overcome, overpower, overwhelm, subdue, subjugate, topple, unseat, vanquish ♦ *noun* 2 = **downfall**, defeat, deposition,

destruction, dethronement, discomfiture, displacement, end, fall, ousting, rout, ruin, subversion, undoing, unseating
➤ **Antonyms**
verb ≠**defeat**: defend, guard, keep, maintain, preserve, protect, restore, support, uphold ♦ *noun* ≠**downfall**: defence, preservation, protection

overtone *noun, often plural* = **hint**, association, connotation, flavour, implication, innuendo, intimation, nuance, sense, suggestion, undercurrent

overture *noun* **1** *Music* = **introduction**, opening, prelude **2 overtures** = **approach**, advance, invitation, offer, opening move, proposal, proposition
➤ **Antonyms**
≠**introduction**: coda, finale ≠**approach**: rejection, withdrawal

overturn *verb* **1** = **tip over**, capsize, keel over, knock over *or* down, overbalance, reverse, spill, topple, tumble, upend, upset, upturn **2** = **overthrow**, abolish, annul, bring down, countermand, depose, destroy, invalidate, obviate, repeal, rescind, reverse, set aside, unseat

overweening *adjective* = **excessive**, blown up out of all proportion, extravagant, immoderate

overweight *adjective* = **fat**, bulky, buxom, chubby, chunky, corpulent, fleshy, gross, heavy, hefty, huge, massive, obese, outsize, plump, podgy, portly, stout, tubby (*informal*)
➤ **Antonyms**
emaciated, gaunt, lean, pinched, scraggy, scrawny, skinny, thin, underweight

overwhelm *verb* **1** = **overcome**, bowl over (*informal*), devastate, knock (someone) for six (*informal*), overpower, prostrate, render speechless, stagger, sweep (someone) off his *or* her feet, take (someone's) breath away **2** = **destroy**, crush, cut to pieces, massacre, overpower, overrun, rout

overwhelming *adjective* = **overpowering**, breathtaking, crushing, devastating, invincible, irresistible, shattering, stunning, towering, uncontrollable
➤ **Antonyms**
commonplace, incidental, insignificant,

negligible, paltry, resistible, trivial, unimportant

overwork *verb* **1** = **strain oneself**, burn the candle at both ends, burn the midnight oil, overstrain oneself, sweat (*informal*), work one's fingers to the bone **2** = **overuse**, drive into the ground, exhaust, exploit, fatigue, oppress, overtax, wear out, weary

overwrought *adjective* = **agitated**, beside oneself, distracted, excited, frantic, in a state, in a tizzy (*informal*), keyed up, on edge, overexcited, overworked, stirred, strung out (*informal*), tense, uptight (*informal*), wired (*slang*), worked up (*informal*), wound up (*informal*)
➤ **Antonyms**
calm, collected, controlled, cool, dispassionate, emotionless, impassive, self-contained, unfazed (*informal*), unmoved

owe *verb* = **be in debt**, be beholden to, be in arrears, be obligated *or* indebted, be under an obligation to

owing *adjective* = **unpaid**, due, outstanding, overdue, owed, payable, unsettled

owing to *preposition* = **because of**, as a result of, on account of

own *adjective* **1** = **personal**, individual, particular, private ♦ *pronoun* **2 hold one's own** = **keep going**, compete, keep one's end up, keep one's head above water, maintain one's position **3 on one's own** = **alone**, by oneself, independently, off one's own bat, on one's tod (*Brit. slang*), singly, unaided, unassisted, under one's own steam ♦ *verb* **4** = **possess**, be in possession of, be responsible for, enjoy, have, hold, keep, retain **5** = **acknowledge**, admit, allow, allow to be valid, avow, concede, confess, disclose, go along with, grant, recognize **6 own up** = **confess**, admit, come clean, tell the truth

owner *noun* = **possessor**, holder, landlord *or* landlady, lord, master *or* mistress, proprietor, proprietress, proprietrix

ownership *noun* = **possession**, dominion, proprietary rights, proprietorship, right of possession, title

P p

pace *noun* **1** = **step**, gait, measure, stride, tread, walk **2** = **speed**, clip (*informal*), lick (*informal*), momentum, motion, movement, progress, rate, tempo, time, velocity ♦ *verb* **3** = **stride**, march, patrol, pound, walk back and forth, walk up and down **4 pace out** = **measure**, count, determine, mark out, step

pacific *adjective Formal* **1** = **peacemaking**, appeasing, conciliatory, diplomatic, irenic, pacificatory, placatory, propitiatory **2** = **nonaggressive**, dovelike, dovish, friendly, gentle, mild, nonbelligerent, nonviolent, pacifist, peaceable, peace-loving **3** = **peaceful**, at peace, calm, halcyon, placid, quiet, serene, smooth, still, tranquil, unruffled
➤ **Antonyms**
≠**nonaggressive**: aggressive, antagonistic, belligerent, hostile, nonconciliatory, pugnacious, unforgiving, unfriendly, violent, warlike

pacifist *noun* = **peace lover**, conchie (*informal*), conscientious objector, dove, passive resister, peacemonger, peacenik (*informal*), satyagrahi

pacify *verb* = **calm**, allay, appease, assuage, mollify, placate, propitiate, soothe

pack *verb* **1** = **package**, batch, bundle, burden, load, store, stow **2** = **cram**, charge, compact, compress, crowd, fill, jam, mob, press, ram, stuff, tamp, throng, wedge **3 pack off** = **send away**, bundle out, dismiss, hustle out, send packing (*informal*), send someone about his business **4 send (someone) packing** = **send away**, discharge, dismiss, give (someone) the brushoff (*slang*), send (someone) about his or her business ♦ *noun* **5** = **bundle**, back pack, bale, burden, fardel (*archaic*), kit, kitbag, knapsack, load, parcel, rucksack, truss **6** = **packet**, package **7** = **group**, assemblage, band, bunch, collection, company, crew, crowd, deck, drove, flock, gang, herd, lot, mob, set, troop

package *noun* **1** = **parcel**, box, carton, container, packet **2** = **unit**, amalgamation, combination, entity, whole ♦ *verb* **3** = **pack**, batch, box, parcel (up), wrap, wrap up

packed *adjective* = **full**, brimful, bursting at the seams, chock-a-block, chock-full, congested, cram-full, crammed, crowded, filled, hoatching (*Scot.*), jammed, jam-packed, loaded *or* full to the gunwales,

overflowing, overloaded, packed like sardines, seething, swarming
➤ **Antonyms**
deserted, empty, uncongested, uncrowded

packet *noun* **1** = **package**, bag, carton, container, parcel, poke (*dialect*), wrapper, wrapping **2** *Slang* = **fortune**, a bob or two (*Brit. informal*), an arm and a leg (*informal*), big bucks (*informal, chiefly U.S.*), big money, bomb (*Brit. slang*), bundle (*slang*), king's ransom (*informal*), lot(s), megabucks (*U.S. & Canad. slang*), mint, pile (*informal*), pot(s) (*informal*), pretty penny (*informal*), small fortune, tidy sum (*informal*), wad (*U.S. & Canad. slang*)

pack in *verb* **1** *Brit. informal* = **stop**, cease, chuck (*informal*), desist, give up *or* over, jack in, kick (*informal*), leave off **2** = **attract**, cram, draw, fill to capacity, squeeze in

pack up *verb* **1** = **put away**, store, tidy up **2** *Informal* = **stop**, call it a day (*informal*), call it a night (*informal*), finish, give up, pack in (*Brit. informal*) **3** = **break down**, conk out (*informal*), fail, give out, stall, stop

pact *noun* = **agreement**, alliance, arrangement, bargain, bond, compact, concord, concordat, contract, convention, covenant, deal, league, protocol, treaty, understanding

pad[1] *noun* **1** = **cushion**, buffer, protection, stiffening, stuffing, wad **2** = **notepad**, block, jotter, tablet, writing pad **3** = **paw**, foot, sole **4** *Slang* = **home**, apartment, flat, hang-out (*informal*), place, quarters, room ♦ *verb* **5** = **pack**, cushion, fill, line, protect, shape, stuff **6 pad out** = **lengthen**, amplify, augment, eke, elaborate, fill out, flesh out, inflate, protract, spin out, stretch

pad[2] *verb* = **sneak**, creep, go barefoot, steal

padding *noun* **1** = **filling**, packing, stuffing, wadding **2** = **waffle** (*informal, chiefly Brit.*), hot air (*informal*), prolixity, verbiage, verbosity, wordiness

paddle[1] *noun* **1** = **oar**, scull, sweep ♦ *verb* **2** = **row**, oar, propel, pull, scull

paddle[2] *verb* **1** = **wade**, plash, slop, splash (about) **2** = **dabble**, stir

pagan *adjective* **1** = **heathen**, Gentile, heathenish, idolatrous, infidel, irreligious, polytheistic ♦ *noun* **2** = **heathen**, Gentile, idolater, infidel, polytheist, unbeliever

page[1] *noun* **1** = **folio**, leaf, sheet, side **2**

Literary = **period**, chapter, episode, epoch, era, event, incident, phase, point, stage, time ♦ *verb* **3** = **paginate**, foliate, number

page² *noun* **1** = **attendant**, bellboy (*U.S.*), footboy, pageboy, servant, squire ♦ *verb* **2** = **call**, announce, call out, preconize, seek, send for, summon

pageant *noun* = **show**, display, extravaganza, parade, procession, ritual, spectacle, tableau

pageantry *noun* = **spectacle**, display, drama, extravagance, glamour, glitter, grandeur, magnificence, parade, pomp, show, showiness, splash (*informal*), splendour, state, theatricality

pain *noun* **1** = **hurt**, ache, cramp, discomfort, irritation, pang, smarting, soreness, spasm, suffering, tenderness, throb, throe (*rare*), trouble, twinge **2** = **suffering**, affliction, agony, anguish, bitterness, distress, grief, hardship, heartache, misery, torment, torture, tribulation, woe, wretchedness **3** *Informal* = **nuisance**, aggravation, annoyance, bore, bother, drag (*informal*), gall, headache (*informal*), irritation, pain in the arse (*taboo informal*), pain in the neck (*informal*), pest, vexation ♦ *verb* **4** = **hurt**, ail, chafe, discomfort, harm, inflame, injure, smart, sting, throb **5** = **distress**, afflict, aggrieve, agonize, cut to the quick, disquiet, grieve, hurt, sadden, torment, torture, vex, worry, wound **6** *Informal* = **irritate**, annoy, exasperate, gall, harass, nark (*Brit., Austral., & N.Z. slang*), rile, vex

pained *adjective* = **distressed**, aggrieved, anguished, hurt, injured, miffed (*informal*), offended, reproachful, stung, unhappy, upset, worried, wounded

painful *adjective* **1** = **distressing**, afflictive, disagreeable, distasteful, grievous, saddening, unpleasant **2** = **sore**, aching, agonizing, excruciating, harrowing, hurting, inflamed, raw, smarting, tender, throbbing **3** = **difficult**, arduous, hard, laborious, severe, tedious, troublesome, trying, vexatious **4** *Informal* = **terrible**, abysmal, awful, dire, dreadful, excruciating, extremely bad, godawful, gut-wrenching
➤ **Antonyms**
≠**distressing**: agreeable, enjoyable, pleasant, satisfying ≠**sore**: comforting, painless, relieving, soothing ≠**difficult**: a piece of cake (*informal*), easy, effortless, interesting, short, simple, straightforward, undemanding

painfully *adverb* = **distressingly**, alarmingly, clearly, deplorably, dreadfully, excessively, markedly, sadly, unfortunately, woefully

painkiller *noun* = **analgesic**, anaesthetic, anodyne, drug, palliative, remedy, sedative

painless *adjective* = **simple**, easy, effortless, fast, no trouble, pain-free, quick, trouble-free

pains *plural noun* **1** = **trouble**, assiduousness, bother, care, diligence, effort, industry, labour, special attention **2** = **contractions**, birth-pangs, childbirth, labour

painstaking *adjective* = **thorough**, assiduous, careful, conscientious, diligent, earnest, exacting, hard-working, industrious, meticulous, persevering, punctilious, scrupulous, sedulous, strenuous, thoroughgoing
➤ **Antonyms**
careless, half-hearted, haphazard, heedless, lazy, negligent, slapdash, slipshod, thoughtless

paint *noun* **1** = **colouring**, colour, dye, emulsion, pigment, stain, tint **2** *Informal* = **make-up**, cosmetics, face (*informal*), greasepaint, *maquillage*, war paint (*informal*) ♦ *verb* **3** = **depict**, catch a likeness, delineate, draw, figure, picture, portray, represent, sketch **4** = **coat**, apply, colour, cover, daub, decorate, slap on (*informal*) **5** = **describe**, bring to life, capture, conjure up a vision, depict, evoke, make one see, portray, put graphically, recount, tell vividly **6 paint the town red** *Informal* = **celebrate**, carouse, go on a binge (*informal*), go on a spree, go on the town, live it up (*informal*), make merry, make whoopee (*informal*), revel

pair *noun* **1** = **couple**, brace, combination, doublet, duo, match, matched set, span, twins, two of a kind, twosome, yoke ♦ *verb* **2** = **couple**, bracket, join, marry, match (up), mate, pair off, put together, team, twin, wed, yoke

pal *noun* *Informal* = **friend**, buddy (*informal*), chum (*informal*), companion, comrade, crony, mate (*informal*)

palatable *adjective* **1** = **delicious**, appetizing, delectable, luscious, mouthwatering, savoury, tasty, toothsome **2** = **acceptable**, agreeable, attractive, enjoyable, fair, pleasant, satisfactory
➤ **Antonyms**
≠**delicious**: bland, flat, insipid, stale, tasteless, unappetizing, unpalatable

palate *noun* **1** = **taste**, appetite, heart, stomach **2** = **enjoyment**, appreciation, gusto, liking, relish, zest

palatial *adjective* = **magnificent**, de luxe, gorgeous, grand, grandiose, illustrious, imposing, luxurious, majestic, opulent, plush (*informal*), regal, spacious, splendid, splendiferous (*facetious*), stately, sumptuous

palaver *noun* = **fuss**, business (*informal*), carry-on (*informal, chiefly Brit.*), pantomime (*informal, chiefly Brit.*), performance (*informal*), rigmarole, song and dance (*Brit. informal*), to-do

pale *adjective* **1** = **white**, anaemic, ashen, ashy, bleached, bloodless, colourless, faded, light, like death warmed up (*informal*), pallid, pasty, sallow, wan, washed-out, whitish **2** = **poor**, feeble, inadequate, pathetic, thin, weak ♦ *verb* **3** = **become pale**, blanch, go white, lose colour, whiten **4** = **fade**, decrease, dim, diminish, dull, grow dull, lessen, lose lustre
➤ **Antonyms**
adjective ≠ **white**: blooming, florid, flushed, glowing, rosy-cheeked, rubicund, ruddy, sanguine

pall[1] *noun* **1** = **cloud**, mantle, shadow, shroud, veil **2** = **gloom**, check, damp, damper

pall[2] *verb* = **become boring**, become dull, become tedious, cloy, glut, jade, satiate, sicken, surfeit, tire, weary

pallid *adjective* = **pale**, anaemic, ashen, colourless, pasty, wan

pallor *noun* = **paleness**, lack of colour, pallidness, wanness, whiteness

palm[1] *noun* **1** = **hand**, hook, meathook (*slang*), mitt (*slang*), paw (*informal*) **2 grease someone's palm** *Slang* = **bribe**, buy, corrupt, fix (*informal*), give a backhander (*slang*), induce, influence, pay off (*informal*), square, suborn **3 in the palm of one's hand** = **in one's power**, at one's mercy, in one's clutches, in one's control

palm[2] *noun* = **victory**, bays, crown, fame, glory, honour, laurels, merit, prize, success, triumph, trophy

palm off *verb* **1** = **fob off**, foist off, pass off **2 palm off on** = **foist on**, force upon, impose upon, thrust upon, unload upon

palmy *adjective* = **prosperous**, flourishing, fortunate, glorious, golden, halcyon, happy, joyous, luxurious, thriving, triumphant

palpable *adjective* **1** = **obvious**, apparent, blatant, clear, conspicuous, evident, manifest, open, patent, plain, salient, unmistakable, visible **2** = **tangible**, concrete, material, real, solid, substantial, touchable

palpitate *verb* = **beat**, flutter, pitapat, pitter-patter, pound, pulsate, pulse, quiver, shiver, throb, tremble, vibrate

palsied *adjective* = **paralysed**, arthritic, atonic (*Pathology*), crippled, debilitated, disabled, helpless, paralytic, rheumatic, sclerotic, shaking, shaky, spastic, trembling

paltry *adjective* = **insignificant**, base, beggarly, chickenshit (*U.S. slang*), contemptible, crappy (*slang*), derisory, despicable, inconsiderable, low, meagre,

mean, measly, Mickey Mouse (*slang*), minor, miserable, nickel-and-dime (*U.S. slang*), petty, picayune (*U.S.*), piddling (*informal*), pitiful, poor, poxy (*slang*), puny, slight, small, sorry, toytown (*slang*), trifling, trivial, twopenny-halfpenny (*Brit. informal*), unimportant, worthless, wretched
➤ **Antonyms**
consequential, considerable, essential, grand, important, major, mega (*slang*), significant, valuable

pamper *verb* = **spoil**, baby, cater to one's every whim, coddle, cosset, fondle, gratify, humour, indulge, mollycoddle, pander to, pet, wait on (someone) hand and foot

pamphlet *noun* = **booklet**, brochure, circular, folder, leaflet, tract

pan[1] *noun* **1** = **pot**, container, saucepan, vessel ♦ *verb* **2** = **sift out**, look for, search for, separate, wash **3** *Informal* = **criticize**, blast, censure, flay, hammer (*Brit. informal*), knock (*informal*), lambast(e), put down, roast (*informal*), rubbish (*informal*), slag (off) (*slang*), slam (*slang*), slate (*informal*), tear into (*informal*), throw brickbats at (*informal*)

pan[2] *verb* = **move**, follow, scan, sweep, swing, track, traverse

panacea *noun* = **cure-all**, catholicon, elixir, nostrum, sovereign remedy, universal cure

panache *noun* = **style**, a flourish, brio, dash, élan, flair, flamboyance, spirit, swagger, verve

pandemonium *noun* = **uproar**, babel, bedlam, chaos, clamour, commotion, confusion, din, hubbub, hue and cry, hullabaloo, racket, ruckus (*informal*), ruction (*informal*), rumpus, tumult, turmoil
➤ **Antonyms**
calm, hush, order, peace, peacefulness, quietude, repose, stillness, tranquillity

pander *verb* **pander to** = **indulge**, cater to, gratify, play up to (*informal*), please, satisfy

pang *noun* = **twinge**, ache, agony, anguish, discomfort, distress, gripe, pain, prick, spasm, stab, sting, stitch, throe (*rare*), wrench

panic *noun* **1** = **fear**, agitation, alarm, consternation, dismay, fright, horror, hysteria, scare, terror ♦ *verb* **2** = **go to pieces**, become hysterical, be terror-stricken, have kittens (*informal*), lose one's bottle (*Brit. slang*), lose one's nerve, overreact **3** = **alarm**, put the wind up (someone) (*informal*), scare, startle, terrify, unnerve

panicky *adjective* = **frightened**, afraid, agitated, antsy (*informal*), distressed, fearful, frantic, frenzied, hysterical, in a flap (*informal*), in a tizzy (*informal*), jittery (*informal*), nervous, windy (*slang*), worked up, worried

➤ **Antonyms**

calm, collected, composed, confident, cool, imperturbable, self-controlled, together (*slang*), unexcitable, unfazed (*informal*), unflappable, unruffled

panic-stricken *adjective* = **frightened**, aghast, agitated, alarmed, appalled, fearful, frenzied, frightened out of one's wits, frightened to death, horrified, horror-stricken, hysterical, in a cold sweat (*informal*), panicky, petrified, scared, scared shitless (*taboo slang*), scared stiff, shit-scared (*taboo slang*), startled, terrified, terror-stricken, unnerved

panoply *noun* = **array**, attire, dress, garb, get-up (*informal*), insignia, raiment (*archaic or poetic*), regalia, show, trappings, turnout

panorama *noun* 1 = **view**, bird's-eye view, prospect, scenery, scenic view, vista 2 = **survey**, overall picture, overview, perspective

panoramic *adjective* = **wide**, all-embracing, bird's-eye, comprehensive, extensive, far-reaching, general, inclusive, overall, scenic, sweeping

pant *verb* 1 = **puff**, blow, breathe, gasp, heave, huff, palpitate, throb, wheeze 2 *with* **for** = **long**, ache, covet, crave, desire, eat one's heart out over, hanker after, hunger, pine, set one's heart on, sigh, suspire (*archaic or poetic*), thirst, want, yearn ♦ *noun* 3 = **puff**, gasp, huff, wheeze

panting *adjective* 1 = **out of breath**, breathless, gasping, out of puff, out of whack (*informal*), puffed, puffed out, puffing, short of breath, winded 2 = **eager**, agog, all agog, anxious, champing at the bit (*informal*), impatient, raring to go

pants *plural noun* 1 *Brit.* = **underpants**, boxer shorts, briefs, broekies (*S. African*), drawers, knickers, panties, Y-fronts (*Trademark*) 2 *U.S.* = **trousers**, slacks

pap *noun* 1 = **mush**, baby food, mash, pulp 2 = **rubbish**, drivel, trash, trivia

paper *noun* 1 = **newspaper**, blat, daily, gazette, journal, news, organ, rag (*informal*) 2 = **essay**, analysis, article, assignment, composition, critique, dissertation, examination, monograph, report, script, study, thesis, treatise 3 **on paper** = **in theory**, ideally, in the abstract, theoretically 4 **papers: a** = **documents**, certificates, deeds, instruments, records **b** = **letters**, archive, diaries, documents, dossier, file, records ♦ *adjective* 5 = **disposable**, cardboard, flimsy, insubstantial, paper-thin, papery, thin ♦ *verb* 6 = **wallpaper**, cover with paper, hang, line, paste up

papery *adjective* = **thin**, flimsy, fragile, frail, insubstantial, light, lightweight, paperlike, paper-thin, wafer-thin

par *noun* 1 = **average**, level, mean, median, norm, standard, usual 2 = **equivalence**, balance, equal footing, equality, equilibrium, parity 3 **above par** = **excellent**, first-rate (*informal*), outstanding, superior 4 **below par: a** = **inferior**, below average, bush-league (*Austral. & N.Z. informal*), dime-a-dozen (*informal*), lacking, not up to scratch (*informal*), poor, second-rate, substandard, tinhorn (*U.S. slang*), two-bit (*U.S. & Canad. slang*), wanting **b** = **under the weather** (*informal*), not oneself, off colour (*chiefly Brit.*), off form, poorly (*informal*), sick, unfit, unhealthy 5 **on a par with** = **equal to**, much the same as, the same as, well-matched with 6 **par for the course** = **usual**, average, expected, ordinary, predictable, standard, typical 7 **up to par** = **satisfactory**, acceptable, adequate, good enough, passable, up to scratch (*informal*), up to the mark

parable *noun* = **lesson**, allegory, exemplum, fable, moral tale, story

parade *noun* 1 = **procession**, array, cavalcade, ceremony, column, march, pageant, review, spectacle, train 2 = **show**, array, display, exhibition, flaunting, ostentation, pomp, spectacle, vaunting ♦ *verb* 3 = **flaunt**, air, brandish, display, exhibit, make a show of, show, show off (*informal*), strut, swagger, vaunt 4 = **march**, defile, process

paradigm *noun* = **model**, example, ideal, pattern

paradise *noun* 1 = **heaven**, City of God, divine abode, Elysian fields, garden of delights, Happy Valley (*Islam*), heavenly kingdom, Olympus (*poetic*), Promised Land, Zion (*Christianity*) 2 = **Garden of Eden**, Eden 3 = **bliss**, delight, felicity, heaven, seventh heaven, utopia

paradox *noun* = **contradiction**, absurdity, ambiguity, anomaly, enigma, inconsistency, mystery, oddity, puzzle

paradoxical *adjective* = **contradictory**, absurd, ambiguous, baffling, confounding, enigmatic, equivocal, illogical, impossible, improbable, inconsistent, oracular, puzzling, riddling

paragon *noun* = **model**, apotheosis, archetype, best thing since sliced bread (*informal*), criterion, cynosure, epitome, exemplar, greatest thing since sliced bread (*informal*), ideal, jewel, masterpiece, nonesuch (*archaic*), nonpareil, norm, paradigm, pattern, prototype, quintessence, standard

paragraph *noun* = **section**, clause, item, notice, part, passage, portion, subdivision

parallel *adjective* **1** = **equidistant**, aligned, alongside, coextensive, side by side **2** = **matching**, akin, analogous, complementary, correspondent, corresponding, like, resembling, similar, uniform ♦ *noun* **3** = **equivalent**, analogue, complement, corollary, counterpart, duplicate, equal, likeness, match, twin **4** = **similarity**, analogy, comparison, correlation, correspondence, likeness, parallelism, resemblance ♦ *verb* **5** = **correspond**, agree, be alike, chime with, compare, complement, conform, correlate, equal, keep pace (with), match
➤ **Antonyms**
adjective ≠**matching**: different, dissimilar, divergent, non-parallel, unlike ♦ *noun* ≠**equivalent**: opposite, reverse ≠**similarity**: difference, dissimilarity, divergence ♦ *verb* ≠**correspond**: be unlike, differ, diverge

paralyse *verb* **1** = **disable**, cripple, debilitate, incapacitate, lame **2** = **immobilize**, anaesthetize, arrest, benumb, freeze, halt, numb, petrify, stop dead, stun, stupefy, transfix

paralysis *noun* **1** = **immobility**, palsy, paresis (*Pathology*) **2** = **standstill**, arrest, breakdown, halt, inactivity, shutdown, stagnation, stoppage

paralytic *adjective* **1** = **paralysed**, crippled, disabled, immobile, immobilized, incapacitated, lame, numb, palsied **2** *Brit. informal* = **drunk**, bevvied (*dialect*), blitzed (*slang*), blotto (*slang*), bombed (*slang*), Brahms and Liszt (*slang*), canned (*slang*), flying (*slang*), inebriated, intoxicated, legless (*informal*), lit up (*slang*), out of it (*slang*), out to it (*Austral. & N.Z. slang*), pie-eyed (*slang*), pissed (*taboo slang*), plastered (*slang*), rat-arsed (*taboo slang*), sloshed (*slang*), smashed (*slang*), steamboats (*Scot. slang*), steaming (*slang*), stewed (*slang*), stoned (*slang*), tired and emotional (*euphemistic*), wasted (*slang*), wrecked (*slang*), zonked (*slang*)

parameter *noun Informal* = **limit**, constant, criterion, framework, guideline, limitation, restriction, specification

paramount *adjective* = **principal**, capital, cardinal, chief, dominant, eminent, first, foremost, main, outstanding, predominant, pre-eminent, primary, prime, superior, supreme
➤ **Antonyms**
inferior, insignificant, least, minor, negligible, secondary, slight, subordinate, trifling, unimportant

paranoid *adjective* **1** = **mentally ill**, deluded, disturbed, manic, neurotic, obsessive, paranoiac, psychotic, unstable **2** *Informal* = **suspicious**, antsy (*informal*), apprehensive, fearful, nervous, worried

paraphernalia *noun* = **equipment**, accoutrements, apparatus, appurtenances, baggage, belongings, clobber (*Brit. slang*), effects, equipage, gear, impedimenta, material, stuff, tackle, things, trappings

paraphrase *noun* **1** = **rewording**, interpretation, rehash, rendering, rendition, rephrasing, restatement, translation, version ♦ *verb* **2** = **reword**, express in other words or one's own words, interpret, rehash, render, rephrase, restate

parasite *noun* = **sponger** (*informal*), bloodsucker (*informal*), cadger, drone (*Brit.*), hanger-on, leech, scrounger (*informal*), sponge (*informal*)

parasitic, parasitical *adjective* = **scrounging** (*informal*), bloodsucking (*informal*), cadging, leechlike, sponging (*informal*)

parcel *noun* **1** = **package**, bundle, carton, pack, packet **2** = **group**, band, batch, bunch, collection, company, crew, crowd, gang, lot, pack **3** = **plot**, piece of land, property, tract ♦ *verb* **4** *often with* **up** = **wrap**, do up, pack, package, tie up **5** **parcel out** = **distribute**, allocate, allot, apportion, carve up, deal out, dispense, divide, dole out, mete out, portion, share out, split up

parch *verb* = **dry up**, blister, burn, dehydrate, desiccate, evaporate, make thirsty, scorch, sear, shrivel, wither

parched *adjective* = **dried out** or **up**, arid, dehydrated, drouthy (*Scot.*), dry, scorched, shrivelled, thirsty, torrid, waterless, withered

parching *adjective* = **drying**, baking, blistering, burning, dry, hot, roasting (*informal*), scorching, searing, sweltering, withering

pardon *verb* **1** = **forgive**, absolve, acquit, amnesty, condone, exculpate, excuse, exonerate, free, let off (*informal*), liberate, overlook, release, remit, reprieve ♦ *noun* **2** = **forgiveness**, absolution, acquittal, allowance, amnesty, condonation, discharge, excuse, exoneration, grace, indulgence, mercy, release, remission, reprieve
➤ **Antonyms**
verb ≠**forgive**: admonish, blame, castigate, censure, chasten, chastise, condemn, discipline, fine, penalize, punish, rebuke ♦ *noun* ≠**forgiveness**: condemnation, guilt, penalty, punishment, redress, retaliation, retribution, revenge, vengeance

pardonable *adjective* = **forgivable**, allowable, condonable, excusable, minor, not serious, permissible, understandable, venial

pare *verb* **1** = **peel**, clip, cut, shave, skin, trim

2 = **cut back**, crop, cut, decrease, dock, reduce

parent *noun* **1** = **father** *or* **mother**, begetter, procreator, progenitor, sire **2** = **source**, architect, author, cause, creator, forerunner, origin, originator, prototype, root, wellspring

parentage *noun* = **family**, ancestry, birth, derivation, descent, extraction, line, lineage, origin, paternity, pedigree, race, stirps, stock

pariah *noun* = **outcast**, exile, leper, outlaw, undesirable, unperson, untouchable

parish *noun* = **community**, church, churchgoers, congregation, flock, fold, parishioners

parity *noun* **1** = **equality**, consistency, equal terms, equivalence, par, parallelism, quits (*informal*), uniformity, unity **2** = **correspondence**, affinity, agreement, analogy, conformity, congruity, likeness, resemblance, sameness, similarity, similitude

park *noun* **1** = **parkland**, estate, garden, grounds, pleasure garden, recreation ground, woodland ♦ *verb* **2** = **leave**, manoeuvre, position, station

parlance *noun* = **language**, idiom, jargon, phraseology, speech, talk, tongue

parley *Old-fashioned* ♦ *noun* **1** = **discussion**, colloquy, confab (*informal*), conference, congress, council, dialogue, meeting, palaver, powwow, seminar, talk(s) ♦ *verb* **2** = **discuss**, confabulate, confer, deliberate, negotiate, palaver, powwow, speak, talk

parliament *noun* **1** = **assembly**, congress, convention, convocation, council, diet, legislature, senate, talking shop (*informal*) **2 Parliament** = **Houses of Parliament**, Mother of Parliaments, the House, the House of Commons and the House of Lords, Westminster

parliamentary *adjective* = **governmental**, congressional, deliberative, law-giving, law-making, legislative

parlour *noun Old-fashioned* = **sitting room**, best room, drawing room, front room, living room, lounge, reception room

parlous *adjective Archaic or humorous* = **dangerous**, chancy (*informal*), desperate, difficult, dire, hairy (*slang*), hazardous, perilous, risky

parochial *adjective* = **provincial**, insular, inward-looking, limited, narrow, narrow-minded, parish-pump, petty, restricted, small-minded
➤ **Antonyms**
all-embracing, broad, broad-minded, cosmopolitan, international, liberal, national, universal, world-wide

parodist *noun* = **mimic**, burlesquer, caricaturist, humorist, impressionist, ironist, lampooner, mocker, pasquinader, satirist

parody *noun* **1** = **takeoff** (*informal*), burlesque, caricature, imitation, lampoon, satire, send-up (*Brit. informal*), skit, spoof (*informal*) **2** = **travesty**, apology, caricature, farce, mockery ♦ *verb* **3** = **take off** (*informal*), burlesque, caricature, do a takeoff of (*informal*), lampoon, mimic, poke fun at, satirize, send up (*Brit. informal*), spoof (*informal*), take the piss out of (*taboo slang*), travesty

paroxysm *noun* = **outburst**, attack, convulsion, eruption, fit, flare-up (*informal*), seizure, spasm

parrot *noun* **1** = **mimic**, copycat (*informal*), imitator, (little) echo **2 parrot-fashion** *Informal* = **by rote**, mechanically, mindlessly ♦ *verb* **3** = **repeat**, copy, echo, imitate, mimic, reiterate

parry *verb* **1** = **ward off**, block, deflect, fend off, hold at bay, rebuff, repel, repulse, stave off **2** = **evade**, avoid, circumvent, dodge, duck (*informal*), fence, fight shy of, shun, sidestep

parsimonious *adjective* = **mean**, cheeseparing, close, close-fisted, frugal, grasping, mingy (*Brit. informal*), miserable, miserly, near (*informal*), niggardly, penny-pinching (*informal*), penurious, saving, scrimpy, skinflinty, snoep (*S. African informal*), sparing, stingy, stinting, tight-arse (*taboo slang*), tight-arsed (*taboo slang*), tight as a duck's arse (*taboo slang*), tight-ass (*U.S. taboo slang*), tight-assed (*U.S. taboo slang*), tightfisted
➤ **Antonyms**
extravagant, generous, lavish, munificent, open-handed, spendthrift, wasteful

parsimony *noun Formal* = **meanness**, frugality, minginess (*Brit. informal*), miserliness, nearness (*informal*), niggardliness, penny-pinching (*informal*), stinginess, tightness

parson *noun* = **clergyman**, churchman, cleric, divine, ecclesiastic, incumbent, man of God, man of the cloth, minister, pastor, preacher, priest, rector, reverend (*informal*), vicar

part *noun* **1** = **piece**, bit, fraction, fragment, lot, particle, portion, scrap, section, sector, segment, share, slice **2** = **component**, branch, constituent, department, division, element, ingredient, limb, member, module, organ, piece, unit **3** *Theatre* = **role**, character, lines **4** = **duty**, bit, business, capacity, charge, function, involvement, office, place, responsibility, role, say, share, task, work **5** = **side**, behalf, cause, concern,

faction, interest, party **6** *often plural*
= **region**, airt (*Scot.*), area, district, neck of
the woods (*informal*), neighbourhood,
quarter, territory, vicinity **7 for the most
part** = **mainly**, chiefly, generally, in the
main, largely, mostly, on the whole,
principally **8 in good part**
= **good-naturedly**, cheerfully, cordially, well,
without offence **9 in part** = **partly**, a little, in
some measure, partially, slightly, somewhat,
to a certain extent, to some degree **10 on
the part of** = **on behalf of**, for the sake of,
in support of, in the name of **11 take part in**
= **participate in**, associate oneself with, be
instrumental in, be involved in, have a hand
in, join in, partake in, play a part in, put
one's twopence-worth in, take a hand in
♦ *verb* **12** = **divide**, break, cleave, come
apart, detach, disconnect, disjoin, dismantle,
disunite, rend, separate, sever, split, tear **13**
= **leave**, break up, depart, go, go away, go
(their) separate ways, part company, quit,
say goodbye, separate, split up, take one's
leave, withdraw **14 part with** = **give up**,
abandon, discard, forgo, let go of,
relinquish, renounce, sacrifice, surrender,
yield
➤ **Antonyms**
noun ≠**piece**: bulk, entirety, mass, totality,
whole ♦ *verb* ≠**divide**: adhere, close,
combine, hold, join, stick, unite ≠**leave**:
appear, arrive, come, gather, remain, show
up (*informal*), stay, turn up

partake *verb* **1 partake of** = **consume**, eat,
receive, share, take **2 partake in**
= **participate in**, engage in, enter into, share
in, take part in

partial *adjective* **1** = **incomplete**,
fragmentary, imperfect, limited,
uncompleted, unfinished **2** = **biased**,
discriminatory, influenced, interested,
one-sided, partisan, predisposed, prejudiced,
tendentious, unfair, unjust **3 be partial to**
= **have a liking for**, be fond of, be keen on,
be taken with, care for, have a soft spot for,
have a weakness for
➤ **Antonyms**
≠**incomplete**: complete, entire, finished, full,
total, whole ≠**biased**: impartial, objective,
unbiased, unprejudiced

partiality *noun* **1** = **bias**, favouritism,
partisanship, predisposition, preference,
prejudice **2** = **liking**, affinity, fondness,
inclination, love, penchant, predilection,
predisposition, preference, proclivity, taste,
weakness
➤ **Antonyms**
≠**bias**: disinterest, equity, fairness,
impartiality, objectivity ≠**liking**: abhorrence,
antipathy, aversion, disgust, disinclination,
dislike, distaste, loathing, revulsion

partially *adverb* = **partly**, fractionally,
halfway, incompletely, in part, moderately,
not wholly, piecemeal, somewhat, to a
certain extent *or* degree

participant *noun* = **participator**, associate,
contributor, member, partaker, party, player,
shareholder, stakeholder

participate *verb* = **take part**, be a
participant, be a party to, be involved in,
engage in, enter into, get in on the act, have
a hand in, join in, partake, perform, share
➤ **Antonyms**
abstain, boycott, forgo, forsake, forswear,
opt out, pass up, refrain from, take no part of

participation *noun* = **taking part**,
assistance, contribution, involvement, joining
in, partaking, partnership, sharing in

particle *noun* = **bit**, atom, crumb, grain,
iota, jot, mite, molecule, mote, piece, scrap,
shred, speck, tittle, whit

particular *adjective* **1** = **specific**, distinct,
exact, express, peculiar, precise, special **2**
= **special**, especial, exceptional, marked,
notable, noteworthy, remarkable, singular,
uncommon, unusual **3** = **detailed**,
blow-by-blow, circumstantial, itemized,
minute, painstaking, precise, selective,
thorough **4** = **fussy**, choosy (*informal*),
critical, dainty, demanding, discriminating,
exacting, fastidious, finicky, meticulous, nice
(*rare*), overnice, pernickety (*informal*), picky
(*informal*) ♦ *noun* **5** *usually plural* = **detail**,
circumstance, fact, feature, item,
specification **6 in particular** = **especially**,
distinctly, exactly, expressly, particularly,
specifically
➤ **Antonyms**
adjective ≠**specific**: general, imprecise,
indefinite, indistinct, inexact, unspecified,
vague ≠**fussy**: casual, easy, easy to please,
indiscriminate, negligent, slack, sloppy,
uncritical

particularly *adverb* **1** = **especially**,
decidedly, exceptionally, markedly, notably,
outstandingly, peculiarly, singularly,
surprisingly, uncommonly, unusually **2**
= **specifically**, distinctly, especially, explicitly,
expressly, in particular

parting *noun* **1** = **going**, adieu, departure,
farewell, goodbye, leave-taking, valediction **2**
= **division**, breaking, detachment,
divergence, partition, rift, rupture,
separation, split ♦ *adjective* **3** = **farewell**,
departing, final, last, valedictory

partisan *noun* **1** = **supporter**, adherent,
backer, champion, devotee, disciple,
follower, stalwart, upholder, votary **2**
= **underground fighter**, guerrilla, irregular,
resistance fighter ♦ *adjective* **3**
= **prejudiced**, biased, factional, interested,

one-sided, partial, sectarian, tendentious **4**
= underground, guerrilla, irregular,
resistance
➤ **Antonyms**
noun ≠**supporter:** adversary, contender,
critic, detractor, foe, knocker (*informal*),
leader, opponent, rival ♦ *adjective*
≠**prejudiced:** bipartisan, broad-minded,
disinterested, impartial, non-partisan,
unbiased, unprejudiced

partition *noun* **1 = screen**, barrier, divider,
room divider, wall **2 = division**, dividing,
segregation, separation, severance, splitting
3 = allotment, apportionment, distribution,
portion, rationing out, share ♦ *verb* **4**
= separate, divide, fence off, screen, wall off
5 = divide, apportion, cut up, parcel out,
portion, section, segment, separate, share,
split up, subdivide

partly *adverb* **= partially**, halfway,
incompletely, in part, in some measure, not
fully, relatively, slightly, somewhat, to a
certain degree *or* extent, up to a certain
point
➤ **Antonyms**
completely, entirely, fully, in full, totally,
wholly

partner *noun* **1 = spouse**, bedfellow, better
half (*Brit. informal*), consort, helpmate, her
indoors (*Brit. slang*), husband *or* wife, mate,
significant other (*U.S. informal*) **2**
= companion, accomplice, ally, associate,
bedfellow, collaborator, colleague, comrade,
confederate, copartner, helper, mate,
participant, team-mate

partnership *noun* **1 = company**, alliance,
association, combine, conglomerate,
cooperative, corporation, firm, house,
society, union **2 = cooperation**,
companionship, connection, copartnership,
fellowship, interest, participation, sharing

parts *plural noun* **1** *Literary* **= talents**,
abilities, accomplishments, attributes, calibre,
capabilities, endowments, faculties, genius,
gifts, intellect, intelligence **2 = components**,
bits and pieces, spare parts, spares

party *noun* **1 = get-together** (*informal*),
at-home, bash (*informal*), beano (*Brit.
slang*), celebration, do (*informal*), festivity,
function, gathering, hooley *or* hoolie (*chiefly
Irish & N.Z.*), knees-up (*Brit. informal*), rave
(*Brit. slang*), rave-up (*Brit. slang*),
reception, shindig (*informal*), social, social
gathering, soirée **2 = group**, band, body,
bunch (*informal*), company, crew,
detachment (*Military*), gang, gathering,
squad, team, unit **3 = faction**, alliance,
association, cabal, camp, clique, coalition,
combination, confederacy, coterie, grouping,
league, schism, set, side **4** *Law* **= litigant**,
contractor (*Law*), defendant, participant,

plaintiff **5** *Informal* **= person**, individual,
somebody, someone

pass *verb* **1 = go by** *or* **past**, depart, elapse,
flow, go, lapse, leave, move, move onwards,
proceed, roll, run **2 = qualify**, answer, come
up to scratch (*informal*), do, get through,
graduate, pass muster, succeed, suffice, suit
3 = spend, beguile, devote, employ,
experience, fill, occupy, suffer, undergo,
while away **4 = give**, convey, deliver,
exchange, hand, kick, let have, reach, send,
throw, transfer, transmit **5 = approve**,
accept, adopt, authorize, decree, enact,
establish, legislate, ordain, ratify, sanction,
validate **6 = pronounce**, declare, deliver,
express, utter **7 = exceed**, beat, excel, go
beyond, outdistance, outdo, outstrip,
overtake, surmount, surpass, transcend **8**
= ignore, disregard, miss, neglect, not heed,
omit, overlook, skip (*informal*) **9 = excrete**,
crap (*taboo slang*), defecate, discharge,
eliminate, empty, evacuate, expel, shit
(*taboo slang*), void **10 = end**, blow over,
cease, die, disappear, dissolve, dwindle, ebb,
evaporate, expire, fade, go, melt away,
terminate, vanish, wane **11** *with* **for** *or* **as**
= be mistaken for, be accepted as, be
regarded as, be taken for, impersonate, serve
as **12** *Old-fashioned* **= happen**, befall, come
up, develop, fall out, occur, take place
♦ *noun* **13 = gap**, canyon, col, defile, gorge,
ravine, route **14 = licence**, authorization,
identification, identity card, passport,
permission, permit, safe-conduct, ticket,
warrant **15 = thrust**, feint, jab, lunge, push,
swing **16** *Informal As in* **make a pass at**
= advances, approach, overture, play
(*informal*), proposition, suggestion **17** *As in*
a pretty pass = predicament, condition,
juncture, pinch, plight, situation, stage,
state, state of affairs, straits
➤ **Antonyms**
verb ≠**go by** *or* **past:** bring *or* come to a
standstill, cease, halt, pause, stop ≠**qualify:**
be inadequate, be inferior to, be
unsuccessful, come a cropper (*informal*),
fail, lose, suffer defeat ≠**approve:** ban,
disallow, invalidate, overrule, prohibit,
refuse, reject, veto ≠**ignore:** acknowledge,
heed, note, notice, observe, pay attention to

passable *adjective* **1 = adequate**,
acceptable, admissible, allowable, all right,
average, fair, fair enough, mediocre,
middling, moderate, not too bad, ordinary,
presentable, so-so (*informal*), tolerable,
unexceptional **2 = clear**, crossable,
navigable, open, traversable, unobstructed
➤ **Antonyms**
≠**adequate:** A1 *or* A-one (*informal*),
exceptional, extraordinary, first-class,
inadequate, inadmissible, marvellous,
outstanding, superb, tops (*slang*),

unacceptable, unsatisfactory ≠ **clear:** blocked, closed, impassable, obstructed, sealed off, unnavigable

passage noun 1 = **way,** alley, avenue, channel, course, lane, opening, path, road, route, thoroughfare 2 = **corridor,** aisle, doorway, entrance, entrance hall, exit, hall, hallway, lobby, passageway, vestibule 3 = **extract,** clause, excerpt, paragraph, piece, quotation, reading, section, sentence, text, verse 4 = **journey,** crossing, tour, trek, trip, voyage 5 = **movement,** advance, change, conversion, flow, motion, passing, progress, progression, transit, transition 6 = **safe-conduct,** allowance, authorization, freedom, permission, right, visa, warrant 7 = **establishment,** acceptance, enactment, legalization, legislation, passing, ratification

passageway noun = **corridor,** aisle, alley, hall, hallway, lane, passage

pass away verb Euphemistic = **die,** buy it (U.S. slang), buy the farm (U.S. slang), check out (U.S. slang), croak (slang), decease, depart (this life), expire, go belly-up (slang), kick it (slang), kick the bucket (slang), pass on, pass over, peg it (informal), peg out (informal), pop one's clogs (informal), shuffle off this mortal coil, snuff it (informal)

pass by verb 1 = **go past,** leave, move past, pass 2 = **disregard,** miss, neglect, not choose, overlook, pass over

passé adjective = **out-of-date,** dated, obsolete, old-fashioned, old hat, outdated, outmoded, unfashionable

passenger noun = **traveller,** fare, hitchhiker, pillion rider, rider

passer-by noun = **bystander,** onlooker, witness

passing adjective 1 = **momentary,** brief, ephemeral, fleeting, short, short-lived, temporary, transient, transitory 2 = **superficial,** casual, cursory, glancing, hasty, quick, shallow, short, slight ◆ noun 3 = **end,** death, decease, demise, finish, loss, termination 4 **in passing** = **incidentally,** accidentally, by the bye, by the way, en passant, on the way

passion noun 1 = **love,** adoration, affection, ardour, attachment, concupiscence, desire, fondness, infatuation, itch, keenness, lust, the hots (slang) 2 = **emotion,** animation, ardour, eagerness, excitement, feeling, fervour, fire, heat, intensity, joy, rapture, spirit, transport, warmth, zeal, zest 3 = **rage,** anger, fit, flare-up (informal), frenzy, fury, indignation, ire, outburst, paroxysm, resentment, storm, vehemence, wrath 4 = **mania,** bug (informal), craving, craze, enthusiasm, fancy, fascination, idol,

infatuation, obsession
➤ **Antonyms**
≠ **emotion:** apathy, calmness, coldness, coolness, frigidity, hate, indifference, unconcern

passionate adjective 1 = **loving,** amorous, ardent, aroused, desirous, erotic, hot, lustful, sensual, sexy (informal), steamy (informal), wanton 2 = **emotional,** ablaze, animated, ardent, eager, enthusiastic, excited, fervent, fervid, fierce, flaming, frenzied, heartfelt, impassioned, impetuous, impulsive, intense, strong, vehement, warm, wild, zealous 3 = **quick-tempered,** choleric, excitable, fiery, hot-headed, hot-tempered, irascible, irritable, peppery, stormy, tempestuous, violent
➤ **Antonyms**
≠ **loving:** cold, frigid, passionless, unloving, unresponsive ≠ **emotional:** apathetic, calm, cold, half-hearted, indifferent, languorous, nonchalant, unemotional, unenthusiastic ≠ **quick-tempered:** agreeable, calm, easy-going, even-tempered, nonviolent, placid, unexcitable

passive adjective = **submissive,** acquiescent, compliant, docile, enduring, inactive, inert, lifeless, long-suffering, nonviolent, patient, quiescent, receptive, resigned, unassertive, uninvolved, unresisting
➤ **Antonyms**
active, alive, assertive, bossy (informal), defiant, domineering, energetic, feisty (informal, chiefly U.S. & Canad.), impatient, involved, lively, rebellious, spirited, violent, zippy (informal)

pass off verb 1 = **fake,** counterfeit, feign, make a pretence of, palm off 2 = **come to an end,** die away, disappear, fade out, vanish 3 = **take place,** be completed, go off, happen, occur, turn out

pass out verb 1 Informal = **faint,** become unconscious, black out (informal), drop, flake out (informal), keel over (informal), lose consciousness, swoon (literary) 2 = **hand out,** deal out, distribute, dole out

pass over verb = **disregard,** discount, forget, ignore, not dwell on, omit, overlook, pass by, take no notice of

pass up verb Informal = **miss,** abstain, decline, forgo, give (something) a miss (informal), ignore, let slip, let (something) go by, neglect, refuse, reject

password noun = **signal,** countersign, key word, open sesame, watchword

past adjective 1 = **former,** ancient, bygone, early, erstwhile, foregoing, late, long-ago, olden, preceding, previous, prior, quondam, recent 2 = **over,** accomplished, completed, done, elapsed, ended, extinct, finished,

forgotten, gone, over and done with, spent
♦ *noun* 3 = **background**, experience,
history, life, past life 4 **the past = former
times**, antiquity, days gone by, days of yore,
good old days, history, long ago, olden
days, old times, times past, yesteryear
(*literary*) ♦ *preposition* 5 = **after**, beyond,
farther than, later than, outside, over,
subsequent to 6 = **beyond**, across, by, on,
over
➤ **Antonyms**
adjective ≠**former:** arrived, begun, coming,
future, now, present ♦ *noun* ≠**former
times:** future, now, present, time to come,
today, tomorrow

paste *noun* 1 = **adhesive**, cement, glue,
gum, mucilage ♦ *verb* 2 = **stick**, cement,
fasten, fix, glue, gum

pastel *adjective* = **pale**, delicate, light,
muted, soft, soft-hued
➤ **Antonyms**
bright, deep, rich, strong, vibrant, vivid

pastiche *noun* = **medley**, blend, farrago,
gallimaufry, hotchpotch, *mélange,*
miscellany, mixture, motley

pastille *noun* = **lozenge**, cough drop,
jujube, tablet, troche (*Medical*)

pastime *noun* = **activity**, amusement,
distraction, diversion, entertainment, game,
hobby, leisure, play, recreation, relaxation,
sport

past master *noun* = **expert**, ace
(*informal*), artist, dab hand (*Brit. informal*),
old hand, virtuoso, wizard

pastor *noun* = **clergyman**, churchman,
divine, ecclesiastic, minister, parson, priest,
rector, vicar

pastoral *adjective* 1 = **rustic**, agrestic,
Arcadian, bucolic, country, georgic
(*literary*), idyllic, rural, simple 2
= **ecclesiastical**, clerical, ministerial, priestly

pasture *noun* = **grassland**, grass, grazing,
grazing land, lea (*poetic*), meadow,
pasturage, shieling (*Scot.*)

pasty *adjective* = **pale**, anaemic, pallid,
sickly, wan

pat *verb* 1 = **stroke**, caress, dab, fondle, pet,
slap, tap, touch ♦ *noun* 2 = **stroke**, clap,
dab, light blow, slap, tap 3 = **lump**, cake,
dab, portion, small piece

patch *noun* 1 = **reinforcement**, piece of
material 2 = **spot**, bit, scrap, shred, small
piece, stretch 3 = **plot**, area, ground, land,
tract ♦ *verb* 4 = **mend**, cover, fix, reinforce,
repair, sew up 5 **patch up = settle**, bury the
hatchet, conciliate, make friends, placate,
restore, settle differences, smooth

patchwork *noun* = **mixture**, confusion,
hash, hotchpotch, jumble, medley,

mishmash, pastiche

patchy *adjective* = **uneven**, bitty, erratic,
fitful, inconstant, irregular, random, sketchy,
spotty, variable, varying
➤ **Antonyms**
constant, even, regular, unbroken, unvarying

patent *noun* 1 = **copyright**, invention,
licence ♦ *adjective* 2 = **obvious**, apparent,
blatant, clear, conspicuous, downright,
evident, flagrant, glaring, indisputable,
manifest, open, palpable, transparent,
unconcealed, unequivocal, unmistakable

paternal *adjective* 1 = **fatherly**, benevolent,
concerned, fatherlike, protective, solicitous,
vigilant 2 = **patrilineal**, patrimonial

paternity *noun* 1 = **fatherhood**, fathership
2 = **parentage**, descent, extraction, family,
lineage 3 = **origin**, authorship, derivation,
source

path *noun* 1 = **way**, footpath, footway,
pathway, road, towpath, track, trail, walkway
(*chiefly U.S.*) 2 = **walk**, avenue 3 = **course**,
avenue, direction, passage, procedure, road,
route, track, way

pathetic *adjective* 1 = **sad**, affecting,
distressing, gut-wrenching, harrowing,
heartbreaking, heart-rending, melting,
moving, pitiable, plaintive, poignant, tender,
touching 2 = **inadequate**, deplorable, feeble,
lamentable, meagre, measly, miserable, not
much cop (*Brit. slang*), paltry, petty, pitiful,
poor, puny, sorry, wet (*Brit. informal*),
woeful 3 *Slang* = **worthless**, chickenshit
(*U.S. slang*), crappy (*slang*), crummy
(*slang*), pants (*informal*), poxy (*slang*),
rubbishy, trashy, uninteresting, useless,
wanky (*taboo slang*)
➤ **Antonyms**
≠**sad:** amusing, comical, droll, entertaining,
funny, laughable, ludicrous, ridiculous

pathfinder *noun* = **pioneer**, discoverer,
explorer, guide, scout, trailblazer

pathos *noun* = **sadness**, pitiableness,
pitifulness, plaintiveness, poignancy

patience *noun* 1 = **forbearance**, calmness,
composure, cool (*slang*), equanimity, even
temper, imperturbability, restraint, serenity,
sufferance, tolerance, toleration 2
= **endurance**, constancy, fortitude,
long-suffering, perseverance, persistence,
resignation, stoicism, submission
➤ **Antonyms**
≠**forbearance:** agitation, exasperation,
excitement, impatience, irritation,
nervousness, passion, restlessness

patient *adjective* 1 = **long-suffering**, calm,
composed, enduring, persevering, persistent,
philosophical, quiet, resigned, self-possessed,
serene, stoical, submissive, uncomplaining,
untiring 2 = **forbearing**, accommodating,

even-tempered, forgiving, indulgent, lenient, mild, tolerant, understanding ♦ *noun* **3** = **sick person**, case, invalid, sufferer

patriot *noun* = **nationalist**, chauvinist, flag-waver (*informal*), jingo, lover of one's country, loyalist

patriotic *adjective* = **nationalistic**, chauvinistic, flag-waving (*informal*), jingoistic, loyal

patriotism *noun* = **nationalism**, flag-waving (*Informal*), jingoism, love of one's country, loyalty

patrol *noun* **1** = **policing**, guarding, protecting, rounds, safeguarding, vigilance, watching **2** = **guard**, garrison, patrolman, sentinel, watch, watchman ♦ *verb* **3** = **police**, cruise, guard, inspect, keep guard, keep watch, make the rounds, pound, range, safeguard, walk the beat

patron *noun* **1** = **supporter**, advocate, angel (*informal*), backer, benefactor, champion, defender, friend, guardian, helper, philanthropist, protagonist, protector, sponsor **2** = **customer**, buyer, client, frequenter, habitué, shopper

patronage *noun* **1** = **support**, aid, assistance, backing, benefaction, championship, encouragement, espousal, help, promotion, sponsorship **2** = **custom**, business, clientele, commerce, trade, trading, traffic **3** = **condescension**, deigning, disdain, patronizing, stooping

patronize *verb* **1** = **talk down to**, be lofty with, look down on, treat as inferior, treat condescendingly, treat like a child **2** = **be a customer** *or* **client of**, buy from, deal with, do business with, frequent, shop at, trade with **3** = **support**, assist, back, befriend, foster, fund, help, maintain, promote, sponsor, subscribe to

patronizing *adjective* = **condescending**, contemptuous, disdainful, gracious, haughty, lofty, snobbish, stooping, supercilious, superior, toffee-nosed (*slang, chiefly Brit.*)
➤ **Antonyms**
deferential, humble, obsequious, respectful, servile

patter[1] *verb* **1** = **tap**, beat, pat, pelt, pitapat, pitter-patter, rat-a-tat, spatter **2** = **walk lightly**, scurry, scuttle, skip, tiptoe, trip ♦ *noun* **3** = **tapping**, pattering, pitapat, pitter-patter

patter[2] *noun* **1** = **spiel** (*informal*), line, monologue, pitch **2** = **chatter**, gabble, jabber, nattering, prattle, yak (*slang*) **3** = **jargon**, argot, cant, lingo (*informal*), patois, slang, vernacular ♦ *verb* **4** = **chatter**, babble, blab, hold forth, jabber, prate, rattle off, rattle on, spiel (*informal*), spout (*informal*), tattle

pattern *noun* **1** = **design**, arrangement, decoration, decorative design, device, figure, motif, ornament **2** = **order**, arrangement, method, orderliness, plan, sequence, system **3** = **plan**, design, diagram, guide, instructions, original, stencil, template **4** = **model**, archetype, criterion, cynosure, example, exemplar, guide, norm, original, par, paradigm, paragon, prototype, standard **5** = **sample**, example, specimen **6** = **type**, kind, shape, sort, style, variety ♦ *verb* **7** = **model**, copy, emulate, follow, form, imitate, mould, order, shape, style **8** = **decorate**, design, trim

paucity *noun Formal* = **scarcity**, dearth, deficiency, fewness, insufficiency, lack, meagreness, paltriness, poverty, rarity, scantiness, shortage, slenderness, slightness, smallness, sparseness, sparsity

paunch *noun* = **belly**, abdomen, beer-belly (*informal*), corporation (*informal*), middle-age spread (*informal*), pot, potbelly, spare tyre (*Brit. slang*), spread (*informal*)

pauper *noun* = **down-and-out**, bankrupt, beggar, have-not, indigent, insolvent, mendicant, poor person

pause *verb* **1** = **stop briefly**, break, cease, delay, deliberate, desist, discontinue, halt, have a breather (*informal*), hesitate, interrupt, rest, take a break, wait, waver ♦ *noun* **2** = **stop**, break, breather (*informal*), breathing space, caesura, cessation, delay, discontinuance, entr'acte, gap, halt, hesitation, interlude, intermission, interruption, interval, let-up (*informal*), lull, respite, rest, stay, stoppage, wait
➤ **Antonyms**
verb ≠**stop briefly**: advance, continue, proceed, progress ♦ *noun* ≠**stop**: advancement, continuance, progression

pave *verb* = **cover**, asphalt, concrete, flag, floor, macadamize, surface, tar, tile

paw *verb Informal* = **manhandle**, grab, handle roughly, maul, molest

pawn[1] *verb* **1** = **hock** (*informal, chiefly U.S.*), deposit, gage (*archaic*), hazard, mortgage, pledge, pop (*informal*), stake, wager ♦ *noun* **2** = **security**, assurance, bond, collateral, gage, guarantee, guaranty, pledge

pawn[2] *noun* = **tool**, cat's-paw, creature, dupe, instrument, plaything, puppet, stooge (*slang*), toy

pay *verb* **1** = **reimburse**, clear, compensate, cough up (*informal*), discharge, foot, give, honour, liquidate, meet, offer, recompense, remit, remunerate, render, requite, reward, settle, square up **2** *often with* **for** = **suffer**, answer for, atone, be punished, compensate, get one's deserts, make amends, suffer the consequences **3** = **give**, bestow, extend, grant, hand out, present, proffer, render **4** = **benefit**, be advantageous, be worthwhile, repay, serve **5** = **be profitable**, be remunerative, make a return, make money, provide a living **6** = **yield**, bring in, produce, profit, return **7** = **pay back**, avenge oneself for, get even with (*informal*), get revenge on, punish, reciprocate, repay, requite, settle a score ◆ *noun* **8** = **wages**, allowance, compensation, earnings, emoluments, fee, hand-out, hire, income, meed (*archaic*), payment, recompense, reimbursement, remuneration, reward, salary, stipend, takings

payable *adjective* = **due**, mature, obligatory, outstanding, owed, owing, receivable, to be paid

pay back *verb* **1** = **repay**, refund, reimburse, return, settle up, square **2** = **get even with** (*informal*), get one's own back, hit back, reciprocate, recompense, retaliate, settle a score with

payment *noun* **1** = **paying**, defrayal, discharge, outlay, remittance, settlement **2** = **remittance**, advance, deposit, instalment, portion, premium **3** = **wage**, fee, hire, remuneration, reward

pay off *verb* **1** = **settle**, clear, discharge, liquidate, pay in full, square **2** = **succeed**, be effective, be profitable, be successful, work **3** = **dismiss**, discharge, fire, lay off, let go, sack (*informal*) **4** *Informal* = **bribe**, buy off, corrupt, get at, grease the palm of (*slang*), oil (*informal*), suborn **5** = **get even with** (*informal*), pay back, retaliate, settle a score

pay out *verb* = **spend**, cough up (*informal*), disburse, expend, fork out *or* over *or* up (*slang*), lay out (*informal*), shell out (*informal*)

peace *noun* **1** = **stillness**, calm, calmness, hush, peacefulness, quiet, quietude, repose, rest, silence, tranquillity **2** = **serenity**, calm, composure, contentment, placidity, relaxation, repose **3** = **harmony**, accord, agreement, amity, concord **4** = **truce**, armistice, cessation of hostilities, conciliation, pacification, treaty

peaceable *adjective* **1** = **peace-loving**, amiable, amicable, conciliatory, dovish, friendly, gentle, inoffensive, mild, nonbelligerent, pacific, peaceful, placid, unwarlike **2** = **calm**, balmy, peaceful, quiet, restful, serene, still, tranquil, undisturbed

peaceful *adjective* **1** = **at peace**, amicable, free from strife, friendly, harmonious, nonviolent, on friendly *or* good terms, without hostility **2** = **calm**, gentle, placid, quiet, restful, serene, still, tranquil, undisturbed, unruffled, untroubled **3** = **peace-loving**, conciliatory, irenic, pacific,

peaceable, placatory, unwarlike
➤ **Antonyms**
≠**at peace**: antagonistic, bitter, hostile, unfriendly, violent, warring, wartime ≠**calm**: agitated, disquieted, disturbed, loud, nervous, noisy, raucous, restless, upset ≠**peace-loving**: belligerent, warlike

peacemaker *noun* = **mediator**, appeaser, arbitrator, conciliator, pacifier, peacemonger

peak *noun* **1** = **point**, aiguille, apex, brow, crest, pinnacle, summit, tip, top **2** = **high point**, acme, apogee, climax, crown, culmination, maximum point, *ne plus ultra*, zenith ◆ *verb* **3** = **culminate**, be at its height, climax, come to a head, reach its highest point, reach the zenith

peal *noun* **1** = **ring**, blast, carillon, chime, clamour, clang, clap, crash, resounding, reverberation, ringing, roar, rumble, sound, tintinnabulation ◆ *verb* **2** = **ring**, chime, crack, crash, resonate, resound, reverberate, roar, roll, rumble, sound, tintinnabulate, toll

peasant *noun* **1** = **rustic**, churl (*archaic*), countryman, hind (*obsolete*), son of the soil, swain (*archaic*) **2** *Informal* = **boor**, churl, country bumpkin, hayseed (*U.S. & Canad. informal*), hick (*informal, chiefly U.S. & Canad.*), lout, provincial, yokel

peccadillo *noun* = **misdeed**, error, indiscretion, infraction, lapse, misdemeanour, petty sin, slip, trifling fault

peck *verb, noun* = **pick**, bite, dig, hit, jab, kiss, nibble, poke, prick, strike, tap

peculiar *adjective* **1** = **odd**, abnormal, bizarre, curious, eccentric, exceptional, extraordinary, far-out (*slang*), freakish, funny, offbeat, off-the-wall (*slang*), outlandish, out-of-the-way, outré, quaint, queer, singular, strange, uncommon, unconventional, unusual, wacko (*slang*), weird **2** = **specific**, appropriate, characteristic, distinct, distinctive, distinguishing, endemic, idiosyncratic, individual, local, particular, personal, private, restricted, special, unique
➤ **Antonyms**
≠**odd**: commonplace, conventional, expected, familiar, ordinary, usual ≠**specific**: common, general, indistinctive, unspecific

peculiarity *noun* **1** = **eccentricity**, abnormality, bizarreness, foible, freakishness, idiosyncrasy, mannerism, oddity, odd trait, queerness, quirk **2** = **characteristic**, attribute, distinctiveness, feature, mark, particularity, property, quality, singularity, speciality, trait

pedagogue *noun* = **teacher**, dogmatist, dominie (*Scot.*), educator, instructor, master *or* mistress, pedant, schoolmaster *or* schoolmistress

pedant noun = hairsplitter, casuist, doctrinaire, dogmatist, literalist, nit-picker (informal), pedagogue, pettifogger, precisian, quibbler, scholastic, sophist

pedantic adjective = hairsplitting, abstruse, academic, bookish, didactic, donnish, erudite, formal, fussy, nit-picking (informal), overnice, particular, pedagogic, picky (informal), pompous, precise, priggish, punctilious, scholastic, schoolmasterly, sententious, stilted

pedantry noun = hairsplitting, bookishness, finicality, overnicety, pedagogism, pettifoggery, pomposity, punctiliousness, quibbling, sophistry, stuffiness

peddle verb = sell, flog (slang), hawk, huckster, market, push (informal), sell door to door, trade, vend

pedestal noun 1 = support, base, dado (Architecture), foot, foundation, mounting, pier, plinth, socle, stand 2 **put on a pedestal** = worship, apotheosize, deify, dignify, ennoble, exalt, glorify, idealize

pedestrian noun 1 = walker, footslogger, foot-traveller ◆ adjective 2 = dull, banal, boring, commonplace, flat, ho-hum (informal), humdrum, mediocre, mundane, no great shakes (informal), ordinary, plodding, prosaic, run-of-the-mill, unimaginative, uninspired, uninteresting
➤ Antonyms
noun ≠walker: driver, motorist ◆ adjective ≠dull: exciting, fascinating, imaginative, important, interesting, noteworthy, outstanding, remarkable, significant

pedigree noun 1 = lineage, ancestry, blood, breed, derivation, descent, extraction, family, family tree, genealogy, heritage, line, race, stemma, stirps, stock ◆ adjective 2 = purebred, full-blooded, thoroughbred

pedlar noun = seller, door-to-door salesman, hawker, huckster, vendor

peek verb 1 = glance, eyeball (slang), keek (Scot.), look, peep, peer, snatch a glimpse, sneak a look, spy, take a look, take or have a gander (informal) ◆ noun 2 = glance, blink, butcher's (Brit. slang), gander (informal), glim (Scot.), glimpse, keek (Scot.), look, look-see (slang), peep, shufti (Brit. slang)

peel verb 1 = skin, decorticate, desquamate, flake off, pare, scale, strip off ◆ noun 2 = skin, epicarp, exocarp, peeling, rind

peep¹ verb 1 = peek, eyeball (slang), keek (Scot.), look, look from hiding, look surreptitiously, peer, sneak a look, spy, steal a look 2 = appear briefly, emerge, peer out, show partially ◆ noun 3 = look, butcher's (Brit. slang), gander (informal), glim

(Scot.), glimpse, keek (Scot.), look-see (slang), peek, shufti (Brit. slang)

peep² verb, noun = tweet, cheep, chirp, chirrup, pipe, squeak, twitter

peephole noun = spyhole, aperture, chink, crack, crevice, fissure, hole, keyhole, opening, pinhole, slit

peer¹ noun 1 = noble, aristo (informal), aristocrat, baron, count, duke, earl, lord, marquess, marquis, nobleman, viscount 2 = equal, coequal, compeer, fellow, like, match

peer² verb 1 = squint, gaze, inspect, peep, scan, scrutinize, snoop, spy, squinny 2 = appear, become visible, emerge, peep out

peerage noun = aristocracy, lords and ladies, nobility, peers, titled classes

peerless adjective = unequalled, beyond compare, excellent, incomparable, matchless, nonpareil, outstanding, second to none, superlative, unique, unmatched, unparalleled, unrivalled, unsurpassed
➤ Antonyms
commonplace, inferior, mediocre, no great shakes (informal), ordinary, poor, second-rate

peeved adjective = irritated, annoyed, exasperated, galled, hacked (off) (U.S. slang), irked, nettled, piqued, pissed (taboo slang), pissed off (taboo slang), put out, riled, sore, upset, vexed

peevish adjective = irritable, acrimonious, cantankerous, captious, childish, churlish, crabbed, cross, crotchety (informal), crusty, fractious, fretful, grumpy, huffy, ill-natured, ill-tempered, liverish, pettish, petulant, querulous, ratty (Brit. & N.Z. informal), short-tempered, shrewish, snappy, splenetic, sulky, sullen, surly, testy, tetchy, touchy, waspish, whingeing (informal)
➤ Antonyms
affable, agreeable, cheerful, cheery, easy-going, even-tempered, genial, good-natured, happy, merry, pleasant, sweet

peg verb 1 = fasten, attach, fix, join, make fast, secure 2 **with along or away** = work at, apply oneself to, beaver away (Brit. informal), keep at it, keep going, keep on, persist, plod along, plug away at (informal), stick to it, work away 3 **Of prices, etc.** = fix, control, freeze, limit, set

pejorative adjective = derogatory, deprecatory, depreciatory, disparaging, negative, uncomplimentary, unpleasant

pelt¹ verb 1 = throw, assail, batter, beat, belabour, bombard, cast, hurl, pepper, pummel, shower, sling, strike, thrash, wallop (informal) 2 = rush, barrel (along) (informal, chiefly U.S. & Canad.), belt (slang), burn rubber (informal), career, charge, dash, hurry, run fast, shoot, speed, stampede, tear, whizz (*informal*) **3 = pour**, bucket down (*informal*), rain cats and dogs (*informal*), rain hard, teem

pelt² *noun* = **coat**, fell, hide, skin

pen¹ *verb* = **write**, commit to paper, compose, draft, draw up, jot down

pen² *noun* **1** = **enclosure**, cage, coop, corral (*chiefly U.S. & Canad.*), fold, hutch, pound, sty ♦ *verb* **2** = **enclose**, cage, confine, coop up, fence in, hedge, hem in, hurdle, impound, mew (up), pound, shut up *or* in

penal *adjective* = **disciplinary**, corrective, penalizing, punitive, retributive

penalize *verb* = **punish**, award a penalty against (*Sport*), correct, discipline, handicap, impose a penalty on, inflict a handicap on, put at a disadvantage

penalty *noun* = **punishment**, disadvantage, fine, forfeit, forfeiture, handicap, mulct, price, retribution

penance *noun* **1** = **atonement**, mortification, penalty, punishment, reparation, sackcloth and ashes **2 do penance** = **atone**, accept punishment, make amends, make reparation, mortify oneself, show contrition, suffer

penchant *noun* = **liking**, affinity, bent, bias, disposition, fondness, inclination, leaning, partiality, predilection, predisposition, proclivity, proneness, propensity, taste, tendency, turn

pending *adjective* = **undecided**, awaiting, forthcoming, hanging fire, imminent, impending, in the balance, in the offing, undetermined, unsettled, up in the air

penetrate *verb* **1** = **pierce**, bore, enter, go through, impale, perforate, prick, probe, stab **2** = **permeate**, diffuse, enter, get in, infiltrate, make inroads (into), pervade, seep, suffuse **3** = **grasp**, comprehend, decipher, discern, fathom, figure out (*informal*), get to the bottom of, suss (out) (*slang*), understand, unravel, work out **4** = **be understood**, affect, become clear, come across, get through to, impress, touch

penetrating *adjective* **1** = **sharp**, biting, carrying, harsh, intrusive, pervasive, piercing, pungent, shrill, stinging, strong **2** = **perceptive**, acute, astute, critical, discerning, discriminating, incisive, intelligent, keen, perspicacious, profound, quick, sagacious, searching, sharp, sharp-witted, shrewd
➤ **Antonyms**
≠**sharp**: blunt, dull, mild, sweet
≠**perceptive**: apathetic, dull, indifferent, obtuse, shallow, stupid, uncomprehending, unperceptive

penetration *noun* **1** = **piercing**, entrance,

entry, incision, inroad, invasion, perforation, puncturing **2** = **perception**, acuteness, astuteness, discernment, insight, keenness, perspicacity, sharpness, shrewdness, wit

penis *noun* = **phallus**, chopper (*Brit. slang*), cock (*taboo slang*), dick (*taboo slang*), dong (*slang*), John Thomas (*taboo slang*), joystick (*slang*), knob (*Brit. taboo slang*), member, organ, pecker (*U.S. & Canad. taboo slang*), pizzle (*archaic & dialect*), plonker (*slang*), prick (*taboo slang*), schlong (*U.S. slang*), tadger (*Brit. slang*), tool (*taboo slang*), wang (*U.S. slang*), weenie (*U.S. slang*), whang (*U.S. slang*), willie *or* willy (*Brit. informal*), winkle (*Brit. slang*)

penitence *noun* = **repentance**, compunction, contrition, regret, remorse, ruefulness, self-reproach, shame, sorrow

penitent *adjective* = **repentant**, abject, apologetic, atoning, conscience-stricken, contrite, regretful, remorseful, rueful, sorrowful, sorry
➤ **Antonyms**
callous, impenitent, remorseless, unrepentant

penmanship *noun Formal* = **handwriting**, calligraphy, chirography, fist (*informal*), hand, longhand, script, writing

pen name *noun* = **pseudonym**, allonym, nom de plume

pennant *noun* = **flag**, banderole, banner, burgee (*Nautical*), ensign, jack, pennon, streamer

penniless *adjective* = **poor**, bankrupt, broke (*informal*), cleaned out (*slang*), destitute, dirt-poor (*informal*), down and out, down at heel, flat broke (*informal*), impecunious, impoverished, indigent, in queer street, moneyless, necessitous, needy, on one's uppers, on the breadline, penurious, poverty-stricken, ruined, short, skint (*Brit. slang*), stony-broke (*Brit. slang*), strapped (*slang*), without a penny to one's name, without two pennies to rub together (*informal*)
➤ **Antonyms**
affluent, filthy rich, loaded (*slang*), rich, rolling (*slang*), wealthy, well-heeled (*informal*)

penny-pinching *adjective* = **miserly**, cheeseparing, close, frugal, mean, mingy (*Brit. informal*), near (*informal*), niggardly, scrimping, Scrooge-like, snoep (*S. African informal*), stingy, tight-arse (*taboo slang*), tight-arsed (*taboo slang*), tight as a duck's arse (*taboo slang*), tight-ass (*U.S. taboo slang*), tight-assed (*U.S. taboo slang*), tightfisted
➤ **Antonyms**
generous, kind, liberal, munificent,

open-handed, prodigal, unstinting

pennyworth noun = bit, crumb, jot, little, mite, modicum, particle, scrap, small amount, tittle

pension noun = allowance, annuity, benefit, superannuation

pensioner noun = senior citizen, O.A.P., retired person

pensive adjective = thoughtful, blue (informal), cogitative, contemplative, dreamy, grave, in a brown study (informal), meditative, melancholy, mournful, musing, preoccupied, reflective, ruminative, sad, serious, sober, solemn, sorrowful, wistful
➤ Antonyms
active, carefree, cheerful, frivolous, gay, happy, joyous, light-hearted

pent-up adjective = suppressed, bottled up, bridled, checked, constrained, curbed, held back, inhibited, repressed, smothered, stifled

penurious adjective Formal 1 = mean, cheeseparing, close, close-fisted, frugal, grudging, miserly, near (informal), niggardly, parsimonious, skimping, stingy, tight-arse (taboo slang), tight-arsed (taboo slang), tight as a duck's arse (taboo slang), tight-ass (U.S. taboo slang), tight-assed (U.S. taboo slang), tightfisted, ungenerous 2 = poor, destitute, down and out, down at heel, impecunious, impoverished, indigent, needy, on the breadline, penniless, poverty-stricken 3 = meagre, beggarly, deficient, inadequate, miserable, miserly, paltry, pathetic, poor, scanty

penury noun 1 = poverty, beggary, destitution, indigence, need, pauperism, privation, straitened circumstances, want 2 = scarcity, dearth, deficiency, lack, paucity, scantiness, shortage, sparseness

people plural noun 1 = persons, human beings, humanity, humans, mankind, men and women, mortals 2 = nation, citizens, community, folk, inhabitants, population, public 3 = family, clan, race, tribe 4 the people = the public, the commonalty, the crowd, the general public, the grass roots, the herd, (the) hoi polloi, the masses, the mob, the multitude, the plebs, the populace, the proles (derogatory slang, chiefly Brit.), the proletariat, the rabble, the rank and file ♦ verb 5 = inhabit, colonize, occupy, populate, settle

pepper noun 1 = seasoning, flavour, spice ♦ verb 2 = sprinkle, bespatter, dot, fleck, spatter, speck, stipple, stud 3 = pelt, bombard, riddle, scatter, shower

peppery adjective 1 = hot, fiery, highly seasoned, piquant, pungent, spicy 2 = irritable, choleric, hot-tempered, irascible, quick-tempered, snappish, testy, touchy,

vitriolic, waspish 3 = sharp, astringent, biting, caustic, incisive, sarcastic, stinging, trenchant, vitriolic
➤ Antonyms
≠hot: bland, insipid, mild, tasteless, vapid

perceive verb 1 = see, be aware of, behold, descry, discern, discover, distinguish, espy, make out, note, notice, observe, recognize, remark, spot 2 = understand, appreciate, apprehend, comprehend, conclude, deduce, feel, gather, get (informal), get the message, get the picture, grasp, know, learn, realize, see, sense, suss (out) (slang)

perceptible adjective = visible, apparent, appreciable, blatant, clear, conspicuous, detectable, discernible, distinct, evident, noticeable, observable, obvious, palpable, perceivable, recognizable, tangible
➤ Antonyms
concealed, hidden, imperceptible, inconspicuous, indiscernible, invisible, unapparent, undetectable, unnoticeable

perception noun = understanding, apprehension, awareness, conception, consciousness, discernment, feeling, grasp, idea, impression, insight, notion, observation, recognition, sensation, sense, taste

perceptive adjective = observant, acute, alert, astute, aware, discerning, insightful, intuitive, penetrating, percipient, perspicacious, quick, responsive, sensitive, sharp
➤ Antonyms
dull, indifferent, insensitive, obtuse, slow-witted, stupid, thick

perch noun 1 = resting place, branch, pole, post, roost ♦ verb 2 = sit, alight, balance, land, rest, roost, settle

perchance adverb Archaic or poetic = perhaps, by chance, for all one knows, haply (archaic), maybe, mayhap (archaic), peradventure (archaic), possibly, probably

percipient adjective Formal = perceptive, alert, alive, astute, aware, bright (informal), discerning, discriminating, intelligent, observant, penetrating, perspicacious, quick-witted, sharp, wide-awake

percolate verb = filter, drain, drip, exude, filtrate, leach, ooze, penetrate, perk (of coffee, informal), permeate, pervade, seep, strain, transfuse

percussion noun = impact, blow, brunt, bump, clash, collision, concussion, crash, jolt, knock, shock, smash, thump

peremptory adjective 1 = imperative, absolute, binding, categorical, commanding, compelling, decisive, final, incontrovertible, irrefutable, obligatory, undeniable 2 = imperious, arbitrary, assertive, authoritative, autocratic, bossy (*informal*), dictatorial, dogmatic, domineering, high-handed, intolerant, overbearing

perennial *adjective* **1** = **lasting**, abiding, chronic, constant, continual, continuing, enduring, incessant, inveterate, lifelong, persistent, recurrent, unchanging **2** = **eternal**, ceaseless, deathless, everlasting, immortal, imperishable, never-ending, permanent, perpetual, unceasing, undying, unfailing, uninterrupted

perfect *adjective* **1** = **complete**, absolute, completed, consummate, entire, finished, full, out-and-out, sheer, unadulterated, unalloyed, unmitigated, utter, whole **2** = **faultless**, blameless, clean, flawless, immaculate, impeccable, pure, spotless, unblemished, unmarred, untarnished **3** = **excellent**, ideal, splendid, sublime, superb, superlative, supreme **4** = **exact**, accurate, close, correct, faithful, on the money (*U.S.*), precise, right, spot-on (*Brit. informal*), strict, true, unerring **5** = **expert**, accomplished, adept, experienced, finished, masterly, polished, practised, skilful, skilled ♦ *verb* **6** = **improve**, ameliorate, cultivate, develop, elaborate, hone, polish, refine **7** = **accomplish**, achieve, carry out, complete, consummate, effect, finish, fulfil, perform, realize
➤ **Antonyms**
adjective ≠ **complete**: incomplete, partial, unfinished ≠ **faultless**: damaged, defective, deficient, faulty, flawed, impaired, imperfect, impure, ruined, spoiled ≠ **excellent**: bad, inferior, poor, unskilled, worthless ♦ *verb* ≠ **improve**: mar

perfection *noun* **1** = **accomplishment**, achievement, achieving, completion, consummation, evolution, fulfilment, realization **2** = **completeness**, maturity **3** = **purity**, integrity, perfectness, wholeness **4** = **excellence**, exquisiteness, sublimity, superiority **5** = **exactness**, faultlessness, precision **6** = **ideal**, acme, crown, paragon

perfectionist *noun* = **stickler**, formalist, precisian, precisionist, purist

perfectly *adverb* **1** = **completely**, absolutely, altogether, consummately, entirely, every inch, fully, quite, thoroughly, totally, utterly, wholly **2** = **flawlessly**, admirably, exquisitely, faultlessly, ideally, impeccably, like a dream, superbly, superlatively, supremely, to perfection, wonderfully
➤ **Antonyms**
≠ **completely**: inaccurately, incompletely, mistakenly, partially ≠ **flawlessly**: badly, defectively, faultily, imperfectly, poorly

perfidious *adjective Literary* = **treacherous**, corrupt, deceitful, dishonest, disloyal,

double-dealing, double-faced, faithless, false, recreant (*archaic*), traitorous, treasonous, two-faced, unfaithful, untrustworthy

perfidy *noun Literary* = **treachery**, betrayal, deceit, disloyalty, double-dealing, duplicity, faithlessness, falsity, infidelity, perfidiousness, treason

perforate *verb* = **pierce**, bore, drill, hole, honeycomb, penetrate, punch, puncture

perform *verb* **1** = **carry out**, accomplish, achieve, act, bring about, complete, comply with, discharge, do, effect, execute, fulfil, function, observe, pull off, satisfy, transact, work **2** = **present**, act, appear as, depict, enact, play, produce, put on, render, represent, stage

performance *noun* **1** = **carrying out**, accomplishment, achievement, act, completion, conduct, consummation, discharge, execution, exploit, feat, fulfilment, work **2** = **presentation**, acting, appearance, exhibition, gig (*informal*), interpretation, play, portrayal, production, representation, show **3** = **functioning**, action, conduct, efficiency, operation, practice, running, working **4** *Informal* = **carry-on** (*informal, chiefly Brit.*), act, behaviour, bother, business, fuss, pantomime (*informal, chiefly Brit.*), pother, rigmarole, to-do

performer *noun* = **artiste**, actor *or* actress, play-actor, player, Thespian, trouper

perfume *noun* = **fragrance**, aroma, attar, balminess, bouquet, cologne, essence, incense, niff (*Brit. slang*), odour, redolence, scent, smell, sweetness

perfunctory *adjective* = **offhand**, automatic, careless, cursory, heedless, inattentive, indifferent, mechanical, negligent, routine, sketchy, slipshod, slovenly, stereotyped, superficial, unconcerned, unthinking, wooden
➤ **Antonyms**
ardent, assiduous, attentive, careful, diligent, keen, spirited, thorough, thoughtful, zealous

perhaps *adverb* = **maybe**, as the case may be, conceivably, feasibly, for all one knows, it may be, perchance (*archaic*), possibly

peril *noun* = **danger**, exposure, hazard, insecurity, jeopardy, menace, pitfall, risk, uncertainty, vulnerability
➤ **Antonyms**
certainty, impregnability, invulnerability, safety, security, surety

perilous *adjective* = **dangerous**, chancy (*informal*), exposed, fraught with danger, hairy (*slang*), hazardous, parlous (*archaic*), precarious, risky, threatening, unsafe, unsure, vulnerable

perimeter *noun* = **boundary**, ambit, border, borderline, bounds, circumference,

confines, edge, limit, margin, periphery
➤ **Antonyms**
central part, centre, core, heart, hub,
middle, nucleus

period *noun* **1** = **time**, interval, season,
space, span, spell, stretch, term, while **2**
= **age**, aeon, course, cycle, date, days,
epoch, era, generation, season, stage, term,
time, years

periodic *adjective* = **recurrent**, at fixed
intervals, cyclic, cyclical, every once in a
while, every so often, infrequent,
intermittent, occasional, periodical, regular,
repeated, seasonal, spasmodic, sporadic

periodical *noun* = **publication**, journal,
magazine, monthly, organ, paper, quarterly,
review, serial, weekly, zine (*informal*)

peripheral *adjective* **1** = **incidental**,
inessential, irrelevant, marginal, minor,
secondary, unimportant **2** = **outermost**,
exterior, external, outer, outside

perish *verb* **1** = **die**, be killed, be lost,
decease, expire, lose one's life, pass away **2**
= **be destroyed**, collapse, decline, disappear,
fall, go under, vanish **3** = **rot**, break down,
decay, decompose, disintegrate, moulder,
waste, wither

perishable *adjective* = **short-lived**,
decaying, decomposable, destructible, easily
spoilt, liable to rot, unstable
➤ **Antonyms**
durable, lasting, long-life, long-lived,
non-perishable

perjure *verb* **perjure oneself** *Criminal law*
= **commit perjury**, bear false witness,
forswear, give false testimony, lie under
oath, swear falsely

perjured *adjective* = **lying**, deceitful, false,
forsworn, mendacious, perfidious, traitorous,
treacherous, untrue, untruthful

perjury *noun* = **lying under oath**, bearing
false witness, false oath, false statement, false
swearing, forswearing, giving false
testimony, oath breaking, violation of an
oath, wilful falsehood

perk *noun Brit. informal* = **bonus**, benefit,
extra, fringe benefit, perquisite, plus

perk up *verb* = **cheer up**, brighten, buck up
(*informal*), liven up, look up, pep up, rally,
recover, recuperate, revive, take heart

permanence *noun* = **continuity**,
constancy, continuance, dependability,
durability, duration, endurance, finality,
fixedness, fixity, immortality, indestructibility,
lastingness, perdurability (*rare*),
permanency, perpetuity, stability, survival

permanent *adjective* = **lasting**, abiding,
constant, durable, enduring, eternal,
everlasting, fixed, immovable, immutable,

imperishable, indestructible, invariable,
long-lasting, perennial, perpetual, persistent,
stable, steadfast, unchanging, unfading
➤ **Antonyms**
brief, changing, ephemeral, finite, fleeting,
impermanent, inconstant, momentary,
mortal, passing, short-lived, temporary,
transitory, variable

permeate *verb* = **pervade**, charge, diffuse
throughout, fill, filter through, imbue,
impregnate, infiltrate, pass through,
penetrate, percolate, saturate, seep through,
soak through, spread through

permissible *adjective* = **permitted**,
acceptable, admissible, allowable, all right,
authorized, kosher (*informal*), lawful, legal,
legit (*slang*), legitimate, licit, O.K. *or* okay
(*informal*), proper, sanctioned
➤ **Antonyms**
banned, forbidden, illegal, illicit, prohibited,
unauthorized, unlawful

permission *noun* = **authorization**,
allowance, approval, assent, blank cheque,
carte blanche, consent, dispensation,
freedom, go-ahead (*informal*), green light,
leave, liberty, licence, permit, sanction,
sufferance, tolerance

permissive *adjective* = **tolerant**,
acquiescent, easy-going, easy-oasy (*slang*),
forbearing, free, indulgent, latitudinarian,
lax, lenient, liberal, open-minded
➤ **Antonyms**
authoritarian, denying, domineering,
forbidding, grudging, rigid, strict

permit *verb* **1** = **allow**, admit, agree,
authorize, consent, empower, enable,
endorse, endure, entitle, give leave *or*
permission, give the green light to, grant,
let, license, own, sanction, suffer, tolerate,
warrant ◆ *noun* **2** = **licence**, authorization,
liberty, pass, passport, permission, sanction,
warrant

permutation *noun* = **transformation**,
alteration, change, shift, transmutation,
transposition

pernicious *adjective Formal* = **wicked**, bad,
baleful, baneful (*archaic*), damaging,
dangerous, deadly, deleterious, destructive,
detrimental, evil, fatal, harmful, hurtful,
injurious, maleficent, malevolent, malicious,
malign, malignant, noisome, noxious,
offensive, pestilent, poisonous, ruinous,
venomous

pernickety *adjective Informal* **1** = **fussy**,
careful, carping, difficult to please, exacting,
fastidious, finicky, hairsplitting, nice,
nit-picking (*informal*), overprecise,
painstaking, particular, picky (*informal*),
punctilious **2** = **tricky**, detailed, exacting,
fiddly, fine

> ➤ **Antonyms**
≠**fussy**: careless, easy to please, haphazard, heedless, inattentive, lax, slack, slapdash, slipshod, sloppy, uncritical ≠**tricky**: easy, simple

peroration *noun Formal* = **summing-up**, closing remarks, conclusion, recapitulation, recapping (*informal*), reiteration

perpendicular *adjective* = **upright**, at right angles to, on end, plumb, straight, vertical

perpetrate *verb* = **commit**, be responsible for, bring about, carry out, do, effect, enact, execute, inflict, perform, wreak

perpetual *adjective* **1** = **everlasting**, abiding, endless, enduring, eternal, immortal, infinite, lasting, never-ending, perennial, permanent, sempiternal (*literary*), unchanging, undying, unending **2** = **continual**, ceaseless, constant, continuous, endless, incessant, interminable, never-ending, perennial, persistent, recurrent, repeated, unceasing, unfailing, uninterrupted, unremitting
> ➤ **Antonyms**
brief, ephemeral, fleeting, impermanent, momentary, passing, short-lived, temporary, transitory

perpetuate *verb* = **maintain**, continue, eternalize, immortalize, keep alive, keep going, keep up, preserve, sustain
> ➤ **Antonyms**
abolish, destroy, end, forget, ignore, put an end to, stamp out, suppress

perplex *verb* **1** = **puzzle**, baffle, befuddle, bemuse, beset, bewilder, confound, confuse, dumbfound, faze, flummox, mix up, muddle, mystify, nonplus, stump **2** = **complicate**, encumber, entangle, involve, jumble, mix up, snarl up, tangle, thicken

perplexing *adjective* = **puzzling**, baffling, bewildering, complex, complicated, confusing, difficult, enigmatic, hard, inexplicable, intricate, involved, knotty, labyrinthine, mysterious, mystifying, paradoxical, strange, taxing, thorny, unaccountable, weird

perplexity *noun* **1** = **puzzlement**, bafflement, bewilderment, confusion, incomprehension, mystification, stupefaction **2** = **puzzle**, can of worms (*informal*), difficulty, dilemma, enigma, fix (*informal*), how-do-you-do (*informal*), knotty problem, mystery, paradox, snarl **3** = **complexity**, difficulty, inextricability, intricacy, involvement, obscurity

perquisite *noun Formal* = **bonus**, benefit, dividend, extra, fringe benefit, icing on the cake, perk (*Brit. informal*), plus

persecute *verb* **1** = **victimize**, afflict, be on

one's back (*slang*), distress, dragoon, hound, hunt, ill-treat, injure, maltreat, martyr, molest, oppress, pick on, pursue, torment, torture **2** = **harass**, annoy, badger, bait, bother, hassle (*informal*), pester, tease, vex, worry
> ➤ **Antonyms**
accommodate, coddle, comfort, console, cosset, humour, indulge, leave alone, let alone, mollycoddle, pamper, pet, spoil

perseverance *noun* = **persistence**, constancy, dedication, determination, diligence, doggedness, endurance, indefatigability, pertinacity, purposefulness, resolution, sedulity, stamina, steadfastness, tenacity

persevere *verb* = **keep going**, be determined *or* resolved, carry on, continue, endure, go on, hang on, hold fast, hold on (*informal*), keep on *or* at, keep one's hand in, maintain, persist, plug away (*informal*), pursue, remain, stand firm, stay the course, stick at *or* to
> ➤ **Antonyms**
be irresolute, dither (*chiefly Brit.*), end, falter, give in, give up, hesitate, quit, shillyshally (*informal*), swither (*Scot.*), throw in the towel, vacillate, waver

persist *verb* **1** = **continue**, abide, carry on, endure, keep up, last, linger, remain **2** = **persevere**, be resolute, continue, hold on (*informal*), insist, stand firm, stay the course

persistence *noun* = **determination**, constancy, diligence, doggedness, endurance, grit, indefatigability, perseverance, pertinacity, pluck, resolution, stamina, steadfastness, tenacity, tirelessness

persistent *adjective* **1** = **continuous**, constant, continual, endless, incessant, interminable, lasting, never-ending, perpetual, relentless, repeated, unrelenting, unremitting **2** = **determined**, assiduous, dogged, enduring, fixed, immovable, indefatigable, obdurate, obstinate, persevering, pertinacious, resolute, steadfast, steady, stiff-necked, stubborn, tenacious, tireless, unflagging
> ➤ **Antonyms**
≠**continuous**: inconstant, intermittent, irregular, occasional, off-and-on, periodic ≠**determined**: changeable, flexible, irresolute, tractable, yielding

person *noun* **1** = **individual**, being, body, human, human being, living soul, soul **2 in person** = **personally**, bodily, in the flesh, oneself

persona *noun* = **personality**, assumed role, character, façade, face, front, mask, part, public face, role

personable *adjective* = **pleasant**, affable,

agreeable, amiable, attractive, charming, good-looking, handsome, likable or likeable, nice, pleasing, presentable, winning
➤ **Antonyms**
disagreeable, sullen, surly, ugly, unattractive, unpleasant, unsightly

personage noun = **personality**, big name, big noise (informal), big shot (informal), celeb (informal), celebrity, dignitary, luminary, megastar (informal), notable, public figure, somebody, V.I.P., well-known person, worthy

personal adjective **1** = **private**, exclusive, individual, intimate, own, particular, peculiar, privy, special **2** = **physical**, bodily, corporal, corporeal, exterior, material **3** = **offensive**, derogatory, disparaging, insulting, nasty, pejorative, slighting

personality noun **1** = **nature**, character, disposition, identity, individuality, make-up, psyche, temper, temperament, traits **2** = **character**, attraction, attractiveness, charisma, charm, dynamism, likableness or likeableness, magnetism, pleasantness **3** = **celebrity**, big name, celeb (informal), famous name, household name, megastar (informal), notable, personage, star, well-known face, well-known person

personally adverb **1** = **by oneself**, alone, independently, in person, in the flesh, on one's own, solely **2** = **in one's opinion**, for oneself, for one's part, from one's own viewpoint, in one's books, in one's own view **3** = **individually**, individualistically, privately, specially, subjectively

personate verb Criminal law = **impersonate**, act, depict, do (informal), enact, feign, imitate, play-act, portray, represent

personification noun = **embodiment**, epitome, image, incarnation, likeness, portrayal, recreation, representation, semblance

personify verb = **embody**, body forth, epitomize, exemplify, express, image (rare), incarnate, mirror, represent, symbolize, typify

personnel noun = **employees**, helpers, human resources, liveware, members, men and women, people, staff, workers, workforce

perspective noun **1** = **outlook**, angle, attitude, broad view, context, frame of reference, overview, way of looking **2** = **objectivity**, proportion, relation, relative importance, relativity **3** = **view**, outlook, panorama, prospect, scene, vista

perspicacious adjective Formal = **perceptive**, acute, alert, astute, aware, clear-sighted, clever, discerning, keen, observant, penetrating, percipient, sagacious, sharp, sharp-witted, shrewd

perspicacity noun Formal = **insight**, acumen, acuteness, discernment, discrimination, keenness, penetration, perceptiveness, percipience, perspicaciousness, perspicuity, sagaciousness, sagacity, sharpness, shrewdness, smarts (slang, chiefly U.S.), suss (slang), wit

perspiration noun = **sweat**, exudation, moisture, wetness

perspire verb = **sweat**, be damp, be wet, drip, exude, glow, pour with sweat, secrete, swelter

persuade verb **1** = **talk into**, actuate, advise, allure, bring round (informal), coax, counsel, entice, impel, incite, induce, influence, inveigle, prevail upon, prompt, sway, twist (someone's) arm, urge, win over **2** = **convince**, cause to believe, convert, satisfy
➤ **Antonyms**
≠**talk into**: deter, discourage, dissuade, forbid, prohibit

persuasion noun **1** = **urging**, blandishment, cajolery, conversion, enticement, exhortation, inducement, influencing, inveiglement, wheedling **2** = **persuasiveness**, cogency, force, potency, power, pull (informal) **3** = **creed**, belief, certitude, conviction, credo, faith, firm belief, fixed opinion, opinion, tenet, views **4** = **faction**, camp, cult, denomination, party, school, school of thought, sect, side

persuasive adjective = **convincing**, cogent, compelling, credible, effective, eloquent, forceful, impelling, impressive, inducing, influential, logical, moving, plausible, sound, telling, touching, valid, weighty, winning
➤ **Antonyms**
feeble, flimsy, illogical, implausible, incredible, ineffective, invalid, unconvincing, unimpressive, weak

pert adjective = **impudent**, bold, cheeky, forward, impertinent, insolent, sassy (U.S. informal), saucy

pertain verb = **relate**, appertain, apply, be appropriate, bear on, befit, belong, be part of, be relevant, concern, refer, regard

pertinacious adjective = **determined**, bull-headed, dogged, headstrong, inflexible, intractable, mulish, obdurate, obstinate, persevering, persistent, perverse, pig-headed, relentless, resolute, self-willed, stiff-necked, strong-willed, stubborn, tenacious, unyielding, wilful

pertinent adjective = **relevant**, admissible, ad rem, applicable, apposite, appropriate, apropos, apt, fit, fitting, germane, material, pat, proper, suitable, to the point, to the purpose
➤ **Antonyms**
immaterial, inappropriate, incongruous,

irrelevant, unfitting, unrelated, unsuitable

pertness noun = **impudence**, audacity, brashness, brass (informal), bumptiousness, cheek (informal), cheekiness, chutzpah (U.S. & Canad. informal), cockiness, effrontery, forwardness, front, impertinence, insolence, presumption, rudeness, sauciness

perturb verb 1 = **disturb**, agitate, alarm, bother, discompose, disconcert, discountenance, disquiet, faze, fluster, ruffle, trouble, unnerve, unsettle, upset, vex, worry 2 = **disorder**, confuse, disarrange, muddle, unsettle

perturbed adjective = **disturbed**, agitated, alarmed, antsy (informal), anxious, disconcerted, disquieted, fearful, flurried, flustered, ill at ease, nervous, restless, shaken, troubled, uncomfortable, uneasy, upset, worried
➤ **Antonyms**
assured, at ease, comfortable, composed, cool, impassive, relaxed, unperturbed, unruffled

perusal noun = **read**, browse, check, examination, inspection, look through, scrutiny, study

peruse verb = **read**, browse, check, examine, eyeball (slang), inspect, look through, run one's eye over, scan, scrutinize, study, work over

pervade verb = **spread through**, affect, charge, diffuse, extend, fill, imbue, infuse, overspread, penetrate, percolate, permeate, suffuse

pervasive adjective = **widespread**, common, extensive, general, inescapable, omnipresent, permeating, pervading, prevalent, rife, ubiquitous, universal

perverse adjective 1 = **abnormal**, depraved, deviant, improper, incorrect, unhealthy 2 = **stubborn**, contradictory, contrary, cussed (informal), delinquent, disobedient, dogged, headstrong, intractable, intransigent, miscreant, mulish, obdurate, obstinate, pig-headed, rebellious, refractory, stiff-necked, troublesome, unmanageable, unreasonable, unyielding, wayward, wilful 3 = **ill-natured**, cantankerous, churlish, crabbed, cross, fractious, ill-tempered, peevish, petulant, shrewish, spiteful, stroppy (Brit. slang), surly
➤ **Antonyms**
≠**stubborn**: accommodating, agreeable, complaisant, cooperative, flexible, malleable, obedient, obliging ≠**ill-natured**: agreeable, amiable, good-natured

perversion noun 1 = **deviation**, aberration, abnormality, debauchery, depravity, immorality, kink (Brit. informal), kinkiness

(slang), unnaturalness, vice, vitiation, wickedness 2 = **distortion**, corruption, falsification, misinterpretation, misrepresentation, misuse, twisting

perversity noun = **contrariness**, contradictiveness, contradictoriness, contumacy, frowardness (archaic), intransigence, obduracy, refractoriness, waywardness, wrong-headedness

pervert verb 1 = **distort**, abuse, falsify, garble, misconstrue, misinterpret, misrepresent, misuse, twist, warp 2 = **corrupt**, debase, debauch, degrade, deprave, desecrate, initiate, lead astray, subvert ♦ noun 3 = **deviant**, debauchee, degenerate, sicko (informal), sleazeball (slang), weirdo or weirdie (informal)

perverted adjective = **unnatural**, aberrant, abnormal, corrupt, debased, debauched, depraved, deviant, distorted, evil, immoral, impaired, kinky (slang), misguided, pervy (slang), sick, sicko (slang), twisted, unhealthy, vicious, vitiated, warped, wicked

pessimism noun = **gloominess**, cynicism, dejection, depression, despair, despondency, distrust, gloom, gloomy outlook, glumness, hopelessness, melancholy, the hump (Brit. informal)

pessimist noun = **wet blanket** (informal), cynic, defeatist, doomster, gloom merchant (informal), killjoy, melancholic, misanthrope, prophet of doom, worrier

pessimistic adjective = **gloomy**, bleak, cynical, dark, dejected, depressed, despairing, despondent, distrustful, downhearted, fatalistic, foreboding, glum, hopeless, melancholy, misanthropic, morose, resigned, sad
➤ **Antonyms**
assured, bright, buoyant, cheerful, cheery, encouraged, exhilarated, hopeful, in good heart, optimistic, sanguine

pest noun 1 = **nuisance**, annoyance, bane, bore, bother, drag (informal), gall, irritation, pain (informal), pain in the arse (taboo informal), pain in the neck (informal), thorn in one's flesh, trial, vexation 2 = **infection**, bane, blight, bug, curse, epidemic, pestilence, plague, scourge

pester verb = **annoy**, aggravate (informal), badger, bedevil, bend someone's ear (informal), be on one's back (slang), bother, bug (informal), chivvy, disturb, drive one up the wall (slang), fret, get at, get in one's hair (informal), get on one's nerves (informal), harass, harry, hassle (informal), irk, nag, pick on, plague, ride (informal), torment, worry

pestilence noun 1 = **plague**, Black Death, epidemic, pandemic, visitation 2 = **affliction**, bane, blight, cancer, canker, curse, scourge

pestilent *adjective* 1 = **annoying**, bothersome, galling, irksome, irritating, plaguy (*informal*), tiresome, vexing 2 = **harmful**, corrupting, deleterious, destructive, detrimental, evil, injurious, pernicious, ruinous, vicious 3 = **contaminated**, catching, contagious, diseased, disease-ridden, infected, infectious, plague-ridden, tainted

pestilential *adjective* 1 = **deadly**, dangerous, deleterious, destructive, detrimental, evil, foul, harmful, hazardous, injurious, pernicious, ruinous 2 = **contaminated**, catching, contagious, disease-ridden, infectious, malignant, noxious, pestiferous, poisonous, venomous

pet[1] *noun* 1 = **favourite**, apple of one's eye, blue-eyed boy (*informal*), darling, fave (*informal*), idol, jewel, treasure ◆ *adjective* 2 = **tame**, domesticated, house, house-broken, house-trained (*Brit.*), trained 3 = **favourite**, cherished, dearest, dear to one's heart, fave (*informal*), favoured, particular, preferred, special ◆ *verb* 4 = **pamper**, baby, coddle, cosset, mollycoddle, spoil 5 = **fondle**, caress, pat, stroke 6 *Informal* = **cuddle**, canoodle (*slang*), kiss, neck (*informal*), smooch (*informal*), snog (*Brit. slang*)

pet[2] *noun* = **sulk**, bad mood, bate (*Brit. slang*), huff, ill temper, miff (*informal*), paddy (*Brit. informal*), paddywhack (*Brit. informal*), pique, pout, sulks, tantrum, temper

peter out *verb* = **die out**, come to nothing, dwindle, ebb, evaporate, fade, fail, give out, run dry, run out, stop, taper off, wane

petite *adjective* = **small**, dainty, delicate, dinky (*Brit. informal*), elfin, little, slight

petition *noun* 1 = **appeal**, address, application, entreaty, invocation, memorial, plea, prayer, request, round robin, solicitation, suit, supplication ◆ *verb* 2 = **appeal**, adjure, ask, beg, beseech, call upon, crave, entreat, plead, pray, press, solicit, sue, supplicate, urge

petrified *adjective* 1 = **terrified**, aghast, appalled, dazed, dumbfounded, frozen, horrified, numb, scared shitless (*taboo slang*), scared stiff, shit-scared (*taboo slang*), shocked, speechless, stunned, stupefied, terror-stricken 2 = **fossilized**, ossified, rocklike

petrify *verb* 1 = **terrify**, amaze, appal, astonish, astound, confound, dumbfound, horrify, immobilize, paralyse, stun, stupefy, transfix 2 = **fossilize**, calcify, harden, set, solidify, turn to stone

petty *adjective* 1 = **trivial**, contemptible, inconsiderable, inessential, inferior,

insignificant, little, measly (*informal*), negligible, nickel-and-dime (*U.S. slang*), paltry, piddling (*informal*), slight, small, trifling, unimportant 2 = **small-minded**, cheap, grudging, mean, mean-minded, shabby, spiteful, stingy, ungenerous 3 = **minor**, inferior, junior, lesser, lower, secondary, subordinate
➤ **Antonyms**
≠**trivial**: consequential, considerable, essential, important, major, momentous, significant ≠**small-minded**: broad-minded, generous, liberal, magnanimous, open-minded, tolerant

petulance *noun* = **sulkiness**, bad temper, crabbiness, ill humour, irritability, peevishness, pettishness, pique, pouts, querulousness, spleen, sullenness, waspishness

petulant *adjective* = **sulky**, bad-tempered, captious, cavilling, crabbed, cross, crusty, fault-finding, fretful, huffy, ill-humoured, impatient, irritable, moody, peevish, perverse, pouting, querulous, ratty (*Brit. & N.Z. informal*), snappish, sour, sullen, ungracious, waspish
➤ **Antonyms**
affable, cheerful, congenial, easy-going, even-tempered, good-humoured, good-natured, happy, patient, smiling

phantom *noun* 1 = **spectre**, apparition, eidolon, ghost, phantasm, revenant, shade (*literary*), spirit, spook (*informal*), wraith 2 = **illusion**, chimera, figment, figment of the imagination, hallucination, vision

pharisee *noun* = **hypocrite**, canter, dissembler, dissimulator, fraud, humbug, phoney *or* phony (*informal*), pietist, whited sepulchre

phase *noun* = **stage**, aspect, chapter, condition, development, juncture, period, point, position, state, step, time

phase out *verb* = **wind down**, axe (*informal*), close, deactivate, dispose of gradually, ease off, eliminate, pull, pull out, remove, replace, run down, taper off, terminate, wind up, withdraw
➤ **Antonyms**
activate, begin, create, establish, form, initiate, open, set up, start

phenomenal *adjective* = **extraordinary**, exceptional, fantastic, marvellous, miraculous, notable, outstanding, prodigious, remarkable, sensational, singular, stellar (*informal*), uncommon, unique, unparalleled, unusual, wondrous (*archaic or literary*)
➤ **Antonyms**
average, common, mediocre, no great shakes (*informal*), ordinary, poor, run-of-the-mill, second-rate, unexceptional,

unremarkable, usual

phenomenon *noun* **1** = **occurrence**, circumstance, episode, event, fact, happening, incident **2** = **wonder**, exception, marvel, miracle, nonpareil, prodigy, rarity, sensation, sight, spectacle

philander *verb* = **womanize** (*informal*), coquet, court, dally, flirt, fool around (*informal*), toy, trifle

philanderer *noun* = **womanizer** (*informal*), Casanova, dallier, Don Juan, flirt, gallant, gay dog, ladies' man, lady-killer (*informal*), Lothario, playboy, stud (*slang*), trifler, wolf (*informal*)

philanthropic *adjective* = **humanitarian**, almsgiving, altruistic, beneficent, benevolent, benignant, charitable, eleemosynary, generous, gracious, humane, kind, kind-hearted, munificent, public-spirited
➤ **Antonyms**
egoistic, mean, miserly, niggardly, penurious, selfish, self-seeking, stingy

philanthropist *noun* = **humanitarian**, almsgiver, altruist, benefactor, contributor, donor, giver, patron

philanthropy *noun* = **humanitarianism**, almsgiving, altruism, beneficence, benevolence, benignity, bounty, brotherly love, charitableness, charity, generosity, generousness, kind-heartedness, largesse *or* largess, liberality, munificence, open-handedness, patronage, public-spiritedness

philistine *noun* **1** = **boor**, barbarian, bourgeois, Goth, ignoramus, lout, lowbrow, vulgarian, yahoo ◆ *adjective* **2** = **uncultured**, anti-intellectual, boorish, bourgeois, crass, ignorant, inartistic, lowbrow, tasteless, uncultivated, uneducated, unrefined

philosopher *noun* = **thinker**, dialectician, logician, mahatma, metaphysician, sage, seeker after truth, theorist, wise man

philosophical, philosophic *adjective* **1** = **rational**, abstract, erudite, learned, logical, sagacious, theoretical, thoughtful, wise **2** = **stoical**, calm, collected, composed, cool, impassive, imperturbable, patient, resigned, sedate, serene, tranquil, unruffled
➤ **Antonyms**
≠**rational:** factual, illogical, irrational, practical, pragmatic, scientific ≠**stoical:** emotional, hot-headed, impulsive, restless, upset

philosophy *noun* **1** = **thought**, aesthetics, knowledge, logic, metaphysics, rationalism, reason, reasoning, thinking, wisdom **2** = **outlook**, attitude to life, basic idea, beliefs, convictions, doctrine, ideology, principles, tenets, thinking, values, viewpoint,

Weltanschauung, world view **3** = **stoicism**, calmness, composure, coolness, dispassion, equanimity, resignation, restraint, self-possession, serenity

phlegmatic *adjective* = **unemotional**, apathetic, bovine, cold, dull, frigid, heavy, impassive, indifferent, lethargic, listless, lymphatic, matter-of-fact, placid, sluggish, stoical, stolid, undemonstrative, unfeeling
➤ **Antonyms**
active, alert, animated, emotional, energetic, excited, hyper (*informal*), lively, passionate

phobia *noun* = **terror**, aversion, detestation, dislike, distaste, dread, fear, hatred, horror, irrational fear, loathing, obsession, overwhelming anxiety, repulsion, revulsion, thing (*informal*)
➤ **Antonyms**
bent, fancy, fondness, inclination, liking, love, partiality, passion, penchant, soft spot

phone *noun* **1** = **telephone**, blower (*informal*) **2** = **call**, bell (*Brit. slang*), buzz (*informal*), ring (*informal, chiefly Brit.*), tinkle (*Brit. informal*) ◆ *verb* **3** = **call**, buzz (*informal*), get on the blower (*informal*), give someone a bell (*Brit. slang*), give someone a buzz (*informal*), give someone a call, give someone a ring (*informal, chiefly Brit.*), give someone a tinkle (*Brit. informal*), make a call, ring (up) (*informal, chiefly Brit.*), telephone

phoney *Informal* ◆ *adjective* **1** = **fake**, affected, assumed, bogus, counterfeit, ersatz, false, feigned, forged, imitation, pseudo (*informal*), put-on, sham, spurious, trick ◆ *noun* **2** = **fake**, counterfeit, faker, forgery, fraud, humbug, impostor, pretender, pseud (*informal*), sham
➤ **Antonyms**
adjective ≠**fake:** authentic, bona fide, genuine, original, real, sincere, unaffected, unassumed, unfeigned

photograph *noun* **1** = **picture**, image, likeness, photo (*informal*), print, shot, slide, snap (*informal*), snapshot, transparency ◆ *verb* **2** = **take a picture of**, capture on film, film, get a shot of, record, shoot, snap (*informal*), take, take (someone's) picture

photographic *adjective* **1** = **lifelike**, graphic, natural, pictorial, realistic, visual, vivid **2** *Of a person's memory* = **accurate**, detailed, exact, faithful, minute, precise, retentive

phrase *noun* **1** = **expression**, group of words, idiom, locution, motto, remark, saying, tag, utterance, way of speaking ◆ *verb* **2** = **express**, couch, formulate, frame, present, put, put into words, say, term, utter, voice, word

phraseology *noun* = **wording**, choice of

words, diction, expression, idiom, language, parlance, phrase, phrasing, speech, style, syntax

physical *adjective* 1 = **bodily**, carnal, corporal, corporeal, earthly, fleshly, incarnate, mortal, somatic, unspiritual 2 = **material**, natural, palpable, real, sensible, solid, substantial, tangible, visible

physician *noun* = **doctor**, doc (*informal*), doctor of medicine, general practitioner, G.P., healer, M.D., medic (*informal*), medical practitioner, medico (*informal*), sawbones (*slang*), specialist

physique *noun* = **build**, body, constitution, figure, form, frame, make-up, shape, structure

pick *verb* 1 = **select**, cherry-pick, choose, decide upon, elect, fix upon, hand-pick, mark out, opt for, settle upon, sift out, single out, sort out 2 = **gather**, collect, cull, cut, harvest, pluck, pull 3 = **nibble**, have no appetite, peck at, play *or* toy with, push the food round the plate 4 = **provoke**, foment, incite, instigate, start 5 = **open**, break into, break open, crack, force, jemmy, prise open 6 **pick one's way** = **tread carefully**, be tentative, find *or* make one's way, move cautiously, work through ♦ *noun* 7 = **choice**, choosing, decision, option, preference, selection 8 = **the best**, choicest, *crème de la crème*, elect, elite, flower, pride, prize, the cream, the tops (*slang*)
> **Antonyms**
verb ≠ **select**: cast aside, decline, discard, dismiss, reject, spurn, turn down

picket *noun* 1 = **protester**, demonstrator, flying picket, picketer 2 = **lookout**, guard, patrol, scout, sentinel, sentry, spotter, vedette (*Military*), watch 3 = **stake**, pale, paling, palisade, peg, post, stanchion, upright ♦ *verb* 4 = **blockade**, boycott, demonstrate 5 = **fence**, corral (*U.S.*), enclose, hedge in, palisade, pen in, rail in, shut in, wall in

pickle *noun* 1 *Informal* = **predicament**, bind (*informal*), difficulty, dilemma, fix (*informal*), hot water (*informal*), jam (*informal*), quandary, scrape (*informal*), spot (*informal*), tight spot ♦ *verb* 2 = **preserve**, cure, keep, marinade, steep

pick-me-up *noun Informal* = **tonic**, bracer (*informal*), drink, pick-up (*slang*), refreshment, restorative, roborant, shot in the arm (*informal*), stimulant

pick on *verb* = **torment**, badger, bait, blame, bully, goad, hector, tease

pick out *verb* 1 = **select**, choose, cull, hand-pick, separate the sheep from the goats, single out, sort out 2 = **identify**, discriminate, distinguish, make distinct,

make out, notice, perceive, recognize, tell apart

pick up *verb* 1 = **lift**, gather, grasp, hoist, raise, take up, uplift 2 = **obtain**, buy, come across, find, garner, happen upon, purchase, score (*slang*) 3 = **recover**, be on the mend, gain, gain ground, get better, improve, make a comeback (*informal*), mend, perk up, rally, take a turn for the better, turn the corner 4 = **learn**, acquire, get the hang of (*informal*), master 5 = **collect**, call for, get, give someone a lift, go to get, uplift (*Scot.*) 6 *Informal* = **arrest**, apprehend, bust (*informal*), collar (*informal*), do (*slang*), feel one's collar (*slang*), lift (*slang*), nab (*informal*), nail (*informal*), nick (*slang, chiefly Brit.*), pinch (*informal*), pull in (*Brit. slang*), run in (*slang*), take into custody

pick-up *noun* 1 = **acceleration**, response, revving (*informal*), speed-up 2 = **improvement**, change for the better, gain, rally, recovery, revival, rise, strengthening, upswing, upturn

picnic *noun* 1 = **excursion**, *fête champêtre*, outdoor meal, outing 2 *Informal* = **walkover** (*informal*), breeze (*U.S. & Canad. informal*), cakewalk (*informal*), child's play (*informal*), cinch (*slang*), duck soup (*U.S. slang*), piece of cake (*Brit. informal*), pushover (*slang*), snap (*informal*)

pictorial *adjective* = **graphic**, expressive, illustrated, picturesque, representational, scenic, striking, vivid

picture *noun* 1 = **representation**, delineation, drawing, effigy, engraving, illustration, image, likeness, painting, photograph, portrait, portrayal, print, similitude, sketch 2 = **description**, account, depiction, image, impression, re-creation, report 3 = **double**, carbon copy, copy, dead ringer (*slang*), duplicate, image, likeness, living image, lookalike, replica, ringer (*slang*), spit (*informal, chiefly Brit.*), spit and image (*informal*), spitting image (*informal*), twin 4 = **personification**, archetype, embodiment, epitome, essence, living example, perfect example 5 = **film**, flick (*slang*), motion picture, movie (*U.S. informal*) ♦ *verb* 6 = **imagine**, conceive of, envision, see, see in the mind's eye, visualize 7 = **represent**, delineate, depict, describe, draw, illustrate, paint, photograph, portray, render, show, sketch

picturesque *adjective* 1 = **interesting**, attractive, beautiful, charming, pretty, quaint, scenic, striking 2 = **vivid**, colourful, graphic
> **Antonyms**
≠ **interesting**: commonplace, everyday, inartistic, unattractive, uninteresting ≠ **vivid**: drab, dull

piddling *adjective Informal* = **trivial**, chickenshit (*U.S. slang*), crappy (*slang*), derisory, fiddling, insignificant, little, measly (*informal*), Mickey Mouse (*slang*), nickel-and-dime (*U.S. slang*), paltry, pants (*informal*), petty, piffling, poxy (*slang*), puny, toytown (*slang*), trifling, unimportant, useless, wanky (*taboo slang*), worthless
➤ **Antonyms**
considerable, important, major, significant, sizable *or* sizeable, substantial, tidy (*informal*), useful, valuable

piebald *adjective* = **pied**, black and white, brindled, dappled, flecked, mottled, speckled, spotted

piece *noun* **1** = **bit**, allotment, chunk, division, fraction, fragment, length, morsel, mouthful, part, portion, quantity, scrap, section, segment, share, shred, slice **2** = **instance**, case, example, occurrence, sample, specimen, stroke **3** = **work**, article, bit (*informal*), composition, creation, item, production, study, work of art **4 go to pieces** = **break down**, crack up (*informal*), crumple, disintegrate, fall apart, lose control, lose one's head **5 in pieces** = **smashed**, broken, bust (*informal*), damaged, disintegrated, in bits, in smithereens, ruined, shattered **6 of a piece** = **alike**, analogous, consistent, identical, of the same kind, similar, the same, uniform ♦ *verb* **7 piece together** = **assemble**, compose, fix, join, mend, patch, repair, restore, unite

pièce de résistance *noun*
= **masterpiece**, *chef-d'oeuvre*, jewel, masterwork, showpiece

piecemeal *adverb* **1** = **bit by bit**, at intervals, by degrees, by fits and starts, fitfully, gradually, intermittently, little by little, partially, slowly ♦ *adjective* **2** = **unsystematic**, fragmentary, intermittent, interrupted, partial, patchy, spotty

pied *adjective* = **variegated**, dappled, flecked, irregular, motley, mottled, multicoloured, parti-coloured, piebald, spotted, streaked, varicoloured

pier *noun* **1** = **jetty**, landing place, promenade, quay, wharf **2** = **pillar**, buttress, column, pile, piling, post, support, upright

pierce *verb* **1** = **penetrate**, bore, drill, enter, impale, lance, perforate, prick, probe, puncture, run through, spike, stab, stick into, transfix **2** = **hurt**, affect, cut, cut to the quick, excite, move, pain, rouse, sting, stir, strike, thrill, touch, wound

piercing *adjective* **1** *Usually of sound* = **penetrating**, ear-splitting, high-pitched, loud, sharp, shattering, shrill **2** = **perceptive**, alert, aware, bright (*informal*), keen, penetrating, perspicacious, probing, quick-witted, searching, sharp, shrewd **3** *Usually of weather* = **cold**, arctic, biting, bitter, freezing, frosty, keen, nipping, nippy, numbing, raw, wintry **4** = **sharp**, acute, agonizing, excruciating, exquisite, fierce, intense, painful, powerful, racking, severe, shooting, stabbing
➤ **Antonyms**
≠**penetrating**: inaudible, low, low-pitched, mellifluous, quiet, soundless ≠**perceptive**: obtuse, slow, slow-witted, thick, unperceptive

piety *noun* = **holiness**, devotion, devoutness, dutifulness, duty, faith, godliness, grace, piousness, religion, reverence, sanctity, veneration

pig *noun* **1** = **hog**, boar, grunter, piggy, piglet, porker, shoat, sow, swine **2** *Informal* = **slob** (*slang*), animal, beast, boor, brute, glutton, greedy guts (*slang*), guzzler, hog (*informal*), sloven, swine

pigeon¹ *noun* **1** = **dove**, bird, culver (*archaic*), cushat, squab **2** *Slang* = **victim**, dupe, fall guy (*informal*), gull (*archaic*), mug (*Brit. slang*), sitting duck, sitting target, sucker (*slang*)

pigeon² *noun Brit. informal*
= **responsibility**, baby (*slang*), business, concern, lookout (*informal*), worry

pigeonhole *noun* **1** = **compartment**, cubbyhole, cubicle, locker, niche, place, section **2** *Informal* = **classification**, category, class, slot (*informal*) ♦ *verb* **3** = **classify**, catalogue, categorize, characterize, codify, compartmentalize, ghettoize, label, slot (*informal*), sort **4** = **put off**, defer, file, postpone, shelve

pig-headed *adjective* = **stubborn**, bull-headed, contrary, cross-grained, dense, froward (*archaic*), inflexible, mulish, obstinate, perverse, self-willed, stiff-necked, stupid, unyielding, wilful, wrong-headed
➤ **Antonyms**
agreeable, amiable, complaisant, cooperative, flexible, obliging, open-minded, tractable

pigment *noun* = **colour**, colorant, colouring, colouring matter, dye, dyestuff, paint, stain, tincture, tint

pile¹ *noun* **1** = **heap**, accumulation, assemblage, assortment, collection, hoard, mass, mound, mountain, rick, stack, stockpile **2** *often plural Informal* = **a lot**, great deal, ocean, oodles (*informal*), quantity, stacks **3** = **building**, edifice, erection, structure **4** *Informal* = **fortune**, big bucks (*informal, chiefly U.S.*), big money, bomb (*Brit. slang*), megabucks (*U.S. & Canad. slang*), mint, money, packet (*slang*), pot, pretty penny (*informal*), tidy sum (*informal*), wad (*U.S. & Canad. slang*), wealth ♦ *verb* **5** = **collect,** accumulate, amass, assemble, gather, heap, hoard, load up, mass, stack, store **6** = **crowd,** charge, crush, flock, flood, jam, pack, rush, stream

pile² *noun* = **foundation,** beam, column, pier, piling, pillar, post, support, upright

pile³ *noun* = **nap,** down, fibre, filament, fur, hair, plush, shag, surface

piles *plural noun* = **haemorrhoids**

pile-up *noun Informal* = **collision,** accident, crash, multiple collision, smash, smash-up (*informal*)

pilfer *verb* = **steal,** appropriate, blag (*slang*), cabbage (*Brit. slang*), embezzle, filch, knock off (*slang*), lift (*informal*), nick (*slang, chiefly Brit.*), pinch (*informal*), purloin, rifle, rob, snaffle (*Brit. informal*), snitch (*slang*), swipe (*slang*), take, thieve, walk off with

pilgrim *noun* = **traveller,** crusader, hajji, palmer, wanderer, wayfarer

pilgrimage *noun* = **journey,** crusade, excursion, expedition, hajj, mission, tour, trip

pill *noun* **1** = **tablet,** bolus, capsule, pellet, pilule **2 the pill** = **oral contraceptive 3** *Slang* = **trial,** bore, drag (*informal*), nuisance, pain (*informal*), pain in the neck (*informal*), pest

pillage *verb* **1** = **plunder,** depredate (*rare*), despoil, freeboot, loot, maraud, raid, ransack, ravage, reive (*dialect*), rifle, rob, sack, spoil (*archaic*), spoliate, strip ♦ *noun* **2** = **plunder,** depredation, devastation, marauding, rapine, robbery, sack, spoliation **3** = **booty,** loot, plunder, spoils

pillar *noun* **1** = **support,** column, obelisk, pier, pilaster, piling, post, prop, shaft, stanchion, upright **2** = **supporter,** leader, leading light (*informal*), mainstay, rock, torchbearer, tower of strength, upholder, worthy

pillory *verb* = **ridicule,** brand, cast a slur on, denounce, expose to ridicule, heap or pour scorn on, hold up to shame, lash, show up, stigmatize

pilot *noun* **1** = **airman,** aviator, captain, flyer **2** = **helmsman,** conductor, coxswain, director, guide, leader, navigator, steersman ♦ *adjective* **3** = **trial,** experimental, model, test ♦ *verb* **4** = **fly,** conduct, control, direct, drive, guide, handle, lead, manage, navigate, operate, shepherd, steer

pimple *noun* = **spot,** boil, papule (*Pathology*), plook (*Scot.*), pustule, swelling, zit (*slang*)

pin *verb* **1** = **fasten,** affix, attach, fix, join, secure **2** = **hold fast,** fix, hold down, immobilize, pinion, press, restrain

pinch *verb* **1** = **squeeze,** compress, grasp, nip, press, tweak **2** = **hurt,** chafe, confine,

cramp, crush, pain **3** *Informal* = **steal,** blag (*slang*), cabbage (*Brit. slang*), filch, knock off (*slang*), lift (*informal*), nick (*slang, chiefly Brit.*), pilfer, purloin, rob, snaffle (*Brit. informal*), snatch, snitch (*slang*), swipe (*slang*) **4** *Informal* = **arrest,** apprehend, bust (*informal*), collar (*informal*), do (*slang*), feel one's collar (*slang*), lift (*slang*), nab (*informal*), nail (*informal*), nick (*slang, chiefly Brit.*), pick up (*slang*), pull in (*Brit. slang*), run in (*slang*), take into custody **5** = **scrimp,** afflict, be stingy, distress, economize, oppress, pinch pennies, press, skimp, spare, stint, tighten one's belt ♦ *noun* **6** = **squeeze,** nip, tweak **7** = **dash,** bit, jot, mite, small quantity, soupçon, speck, taste **8** = **hardship,** crisis, difficulty, emergency, exigency, necessity, oppression, pass, plight, predicament, pressure, strait, stress
➤ **Antonyms**
verb ≠**arrest:** free, let go, let out, release, set free ≠**scrimp:** be extravagant, blow (*slang*), fritter away, spend like water, squander, waste

pinched *adjective* = **thin,** careworn, drawn, gaunt, haggard, peaky, starved, worn
➤ **Antonyms**
blooming, chubby, fat, glowing, hale and hearty, healthy, plump, radiant, ruddy, well-fed

pin down *verb* **1** = **force,** compel, constrain, make, press, pressurize **2** = **determine,** designate, home in on, identify, locate, name, pinpoint, specify **3** = **fix,** bind, confine, constrain, hold, hold down, immobilize, nail down, tie down

pine *verb* **1** *often with* **for** = **long,** ache, carry a torch for, covet, crave, desire, eat one's heart out over, hanker, hunger for, lust after, sigh, suspire (*archaic or poetic*), thirst for, wish for, yearn for **2** = **waste,** decay, decline, droop, dwindle, fade, flag, languish, peak, sicken, sink, weaken, wilt, wither

pinion *verb* = **immobilize,** bind, chain, confine, fasten, fetter, manacle, pin down, shackle, tie

pink¹ *noun* **1** = **best,** acme, height, peak, perfection, summit ♦ *adjective* **2** = **rosy,** flesh, flushed, reddish, rose, roseate, salmon

pink² *verb* = **cut,** incise, notch, perforate, prick, punch, scallop, score

pinnacle *noun* **1** = **peak,** acme, apex, apogee, crest, crown, eminence, height, meridian, summit, top, vertex, zenith **2** = **spire,** belfry, cone, needle, obelisk, pyramid, steeple

pinpoint *verb* = **identify,** define, distinguish, get a fix on, home in on, locate, spot

pint *noun Brit. informal* = **beer,** ale, jar (*Brit.*

informal), jug (*Brit. informal*)

pint-size *adjective Informal* = **small**, diminutive, little, midget, miniature, pocket, pygmy *or* pigmy, teensy-weensy, teeny-weeny, tiny, wee

pioneer *noun* 1 = **settler**, colonist, colonizer, explorer, frontiersman 2 = **founder**, developer, founding father, innovator, leader, trailblazer ◆ *verb* 3 = **develop**, create, discover, establish, initiate, instigate, institute, invent, launch, lay the groundwork, map out, open up, originate, prepare, show the way, start, take the lead

pious *adjective* 1 = **religious**, dedicated, devoted, devout, God-fearing, godly, holy, reverent, righteous, saintly, spiritual 2 = **self-righteous**, goody-goody, holier-than-thou, hypocritical, pietistic, sanctimonious
➤ **Antonyms**
≠**religious**: impious, irreligious, irreverent, ungodly, unholy ≠**self-righteous**: humble, meek, sincere

pipe *noun* 1 = **tube**, conduit, conveyor, duct, hose, line, main, passage, pipeline 2 = **clay**, briar, meerschaum 3 = **whistle**, fife, horn, tooter, wind instrument ◆ *verb* 4 = **whistle**, cheep, peep, play, sing, sound, tootle, trill, tweet, twitter, warble 5 = **convey**, bring in, channel, conduct, siphon, supply, transmit

pipe down *verb Informal* = **be quiet**, belt up (*slang*), button it (*slang*), button one's lip (*slang*), hold one's tongue, hush, put a sock in it (*Brit. slang*), quieten down, shush, shut one's mouth, shut up (*informal*)

pipe dream *noun* = **daydream**, castle in the air, chimera, delusion, dream, fantasy, notion, reverie, vagary

pipeline *noun* 1 = **tube**, conduit, conveyor, duct, line, passage, pipe 2 **in the pipeline** = **on the way**, brewing, coming, getting ready, in preparation, in process, in production, under way

piquancy *noun* 1 = **spiciness**, bite (*informal*), edge, flavour, kick (*informal*), pungency, relish, sharpness, spice, tang, zest 2 = **interest**, colour, excitement, pep, pizzazz *or* pizazz (*informal*), raciness, spirit, vigour, vitality, zing (*informal*), zip (*informal*)

piquant *adjective* 1 = **spicy**, acerb, biting, highly-seasoned, peppery, pungent, savoury, sharp, stinging, tangy, tart, with a kick (*informal*), zesty 2 = **interesting**, lively, provocative, racy, salty, scintillating, sparkling, spirited, stimulating
➤ **Antonyms**
≠**spicy**: bland, insipid, mild ≠**interesting**: banal, bland, boring, dull, insipid, tame,

uninteresting, vapid

pique *noun* 1 = **resentment**, annoyance, displeasure, huff, hurt feelings, irritation, miff (*informal*), offence, umbrage, vexation, wounded pride ◆ *verb* 2 = **displease**, affront, annoy, gall, get (*informal*), incense, irk, irritate, miff (*informal*), mortify, nark (*Brit., Austral., & N.Z. slang*), nettle, offend, peeve (*informal*), provoke, put out, put someone's nose out of joint (*informal*), rile, sting, vex, wound 3 = **arouse**, excite, galvanize, goad, kindle, provoke, rouse, spur, stimulate, stir, whet

piracy *noun* = **robbery**, buccaneering, freebooting, hijacking, infringement, rapine, stealing, theft

pirate *noun* 1 = **buccaneer**, corsair, filibuster, freebooter, marauder, raider, rover, sea robber, sea rover, sea wolf 2 = **plagiarist**, cribber (*informal*), infringer, plagiarizer ◆ *verb* 3 = **copy**, appropriate, borrow, crib (*informal*), lift (*informal*), plagiarize, poach, reproduce, steal

pit *noun* 1 = **hole**, abyss, cavity, chasm, coal mine, crater, dent, depression, dimple, excavation, gulf, hollow, indentation, mine, pockmark, pothole, trench ◆ *verb* 2 *often with* **against** = **set against**, match, oppose, put in opposition 3 = **scar**, dent, dint, gouge, hole, indent, mark, nick, notch, pockmark

pitch *verb* 1 = **throw**, bung (*Brit. slang*), cast, chuck (*informal*), fling, heave, hurl, launch, lob (*informal*), sling, toss 2 = **set up**, erect, fix, locate, place, plant, put up, raise, settle, station 3 = **fall**, dive, drop, stagger, topple, tumble 4 = **toss**, flounder, lurch, make heavy weather, plunge, roll, wallow, welter ◆ *noun* 5 = **sports field**, field of play, ground, park (*U.S. & Canad.*) 6 = **level**, degree, height, highest point, point, summit 7 = **slope**, angle, cant, dip, gradient, incline, steepness, tilt 8 = **tone**, harmonic, modulation, sound, timbre 9 = **sales talk**, line, patter, spiel (*informal*)

pitch-black *adjective* = **jet-black**, dark, ebony, inky, jet, pitch-dark, raven, sable, unlit

pitch in *verb* 1 = **help**, chip in (*informal*), contribute, cooperate, do one's bit, join in, lend a hand, lend a helping hand, participate 2 = **begin**, fall to, get busy, get cracking (*informal*), plunge into, set about, set to, tackle

pitch into *verb Informal* = **attack**, assail, assault, get stuck into (*informal*), tear into (*informal*)

piteous *adjective* = **pathetic**, affecting, deplorable, dismal, distressing, doleful, grievous, gut-wrenching, harrowing, heartbreaking, heart-rending, lamentable, miserable, mournful, moving, pitiable, pitiful, plaintive, poignant, sad, sorrowful, woeful, wretched

pitfall noun 1 = **danger**, banana skin (informal), catch, difficulty, drawback, hazard, peril, snag, trap 2 = **trap**, deadfall, downfall, pit, snare

pith noun 1 = **essence**, core, crux, gist, heart, heart of the matter, kernel, marrow, meat, nub, point, quintessence, salient point, the long and the short of it 2 = **importance**, consequence, depth, force, import, matter, moment, power, significance, strength, substance, value, weight

pithy adjective = **succinct**, brief, cogent, compact, concise, epigrammatic, expressive, finely honed, forceful, laconic, meaningful, pointed, short, terse, to the point, trenchant
➤ **Antonyms**
diffuse, garrulous, long, long-winded, loquacious, prolix, verbose, wordy

pitiful adjective 1 = **pathetic**, deplorable, distressing, grievous, gut-wrenching, harrowing, heartbreaking, heart-rending, lamentable, miserable, piteous, pitiable, sad, woeful, wretched 2 = **contemptible**, abject, base, beggarly, despicable, dismal, inadequate, insignificant, low, mean, measly, miserable, paltry, scurvy, shabby, sorry, vile, worthless
➤ **Antonyms**
≠**pathetic**: amusing, cheerful, cheering, comical, funny, happy, heartening, laughable, merry ≠**contemptible**: adequate, admirable, honourable, laudable, praiseworthy, significant, valuable

pitiless adjective = **merciless**, brutal, callous, cold-blooded, cold-hearted, cruel, hardhearted, harsh, heartless, implacable, inexorable, inhuman, relentless, ruthless, uncaring, unfeeling, unmerciful, unsympathetic
➤ **Antonyms**
caring, compassionate, kind, merciful, relenting, responsive, soft-hearted, sparing

pittance noun = **peanuts** (slang), allowance, chicken feed (slang), drop, mite, modicum, portion, ration, slave wages, trifle

pity noun 1 = **compassion**, charity, clemency, commiseration, condolence, fellow feeling, forbearance, kindness, mercy, quarter, sympathy, tenderness, understanding 2 = **shame**, bummer (slang), crime (informal), crying shame, misfortune, regret, sad thing, sin 3 **take pity on** = **have mercy on**, feel compassion for, forgive, melt, pardon, put out of one's misery, relent, reprieve, show mercy, spare ◆ verb 4 = **feel sorry for**, bleed for, commiserate with, condole with, feel for, grieve for, have

compassion for, sympathize with, weep for
➤ **Antonyms**
noun ≠**compassion**: anger, apathy, brutality, cruelty, disdain, fury, hard-heartedness, indifference, inhumanity, mercilessness, pitilessness, ruthlessness, scorn, severity, unconcern, wrath

pivot noun 1 = **axis**, axle, fulcrum, spindle, swivel 2 = **hub**, centre, focal point, heart, hinge, kingpin ◆ verb 3 = **turn**, revolve, rotate, spin, swivel, twirl 4 = **rely**, be contingent, depend, hang, hinge, revolve round, turn

pivotal adjective = **crucial**, central, critical, decisive, vital

pixie noun = **elf**, brownie, fairy, peri, sprite

placard noun = **notice**, advertisement, affiche, bill, poster, public notice, sticker

placate verb = **calm**, appease, assuage, conciliate, humour, mollify, pacify, propitiate, satisfy, soothe, win over

place noun 1 = **spot**, area, location, locus, point, position, site, situation, station, venue, whereabouts 2 = **region**, city, district, hamlet, locale, locality, neighbourhood, quarter, town, vicinity, village 3 = **position**, grade, rank, station, status 4 = **space**, accommodation, room, stead 5 = **home**, abode, apartment, domicile, dwelling, flat, house, manor, mansion, pad (slang), property, residence, seat 6 = **duty**, affair, charge, concern, function, prerogative, responsibility, right, role 7 = **job**, appointment, berth (informal), billet (informal), employment, position, post 8 **in place of** = **instead of**, as an alternative to, as a substitute for, in exchange for, in lieu of, taking the place of 9 **put (someone) in his place** = **humble**, bring down, cut down to size, humiliate, make (someone) eat humble pie, make (someone) swallow his pride, mortify, take down a peg (informal) 10 **take place** = **happen**, befall, betide, come about, come to pass (archaic), go on, occur, transpire (informal) ◆ verb 11 = **put**, bung (Brit. slang), deposit, dispose, establish, fix, install, lay, locate, plant, position, rest, set, settle, situate, stand, station, stick (informal) 12 = **classify**, arrange, class, grade, group, order, rank, sort 13 = **identify**, associate, know, put one's finger on, recognize, remember, set in context 14 = **assign**, allocate, appoint, charge, commission, entrust, give

placid adjective = **calm**, collected, composed, cool, equable, even, even-tempered, gentle, halcyon, imperturbable, mild, peaceful, quiet, self-possessed, serene, still, tranquil, undisturbed, unexcitable, unfazed (informal), unmoved, unruffled, untroubled

> **Antonyms**
agitated, disturbed, emotional, excitable,
impulsive, passionate, rough,
temperamental, tempestuous

plagiarism *noun* = **copying**, borrowing,
cribbing (*informal*), infringement, piracy,
theft

plagiarize *verb* = **copy**, appropriate,
borrow, crib (*informal*), infringe, lift
(*informal*), pirate, steal, thieve

plague *noun* **1** = **disease**, contagion,
epidemic, infection, lurgy (*informal*),
pandemic, pestilence **2** = **affliction**, bane,
blight, calamity, cancer, curse, evil, scourge,
torment, trial **3** *Informal* = **nuisance**,
aggravation (*informal*), annoyance, bother,
hassle (*informal*), irritant, pain (*informal*),
pest, problem, thorn in one's flesh, vexation
♦ *verb* **4** = **pester**, afflict, annoy, badger,
bedevil, be on one's back (*slang*), bother,
disturb, fret, get in one's hair (*informal*), get
on one's nerves (*informal*), harass, harry,
hassle (*informal*), haunt, molest, pain,
persecute, tease, torment, torture, trouble,
vex

plain *adjective* **1** = **clear**, apparent, bold,
comprehensible, distinct, evident, legible,
lucid, manifest, obvious, overt, patent,
transparent, unambiguous, understandable,
unmistakable, visible **2** = **straightforward**,
artless, blunt, candid, direct, downright,
forthright, frank, guileless, honest,
ingenuous, open, outspoken, round, sincere,
upfront (*informal*) **3** = **unadorned**, austere,
bare, basic, discreet, modest, muted, pure,
restrained, severe, simple, Spartan, stark,
unembellished, unfussy, unornamented,
unpatterned, unvarnished **4** = **ugly**,
ill-favoured, no oil painting (*informal*), not
beautiful, not striking, ordinary, unalluring,
unattractive, unlovely, unprepossessing **5**
= **ordinary**, common, commonplace,
everyday, frugal, homely, lowly, modest,
simple, unaffected, unpretentious, workaday
6 = **flat**, even, level, plane, smooth ♦ *noun* **7**
= **flatland**, grassland, llano, lowland, mesa,
open country, pampas, plateau, prairie,
steppe, tableland, veld
> **Antonyms**
adjective ≠**clear**: ambiguous, complex,
concealed, deceptive, difficult, disguised,
hidden, illegible, incomprehensible,
inconspicuous, indiscernible, indistinct,
obscure, vague, veiled ≠**straightforward**:
circuitous, indirect, meandering, rambling,
roundabout ≠**unadorned**: adorned,
decorated, fancy, ornate ≠**ugly**: attractive,
beautiful, comely, good-looking, gorgeous,
handsome ≠**ordinary**: affected,
distinguished, egotistic, ostentatious,
pretentious, sophisticated, worldly ≠**flat**:

bumpy, not level, uneven

plain-spoken *adjective* = **blunt**, candid,
direct, downright, explicit, forthright, frank,
open, outright, outspoken, straightforward,
unequivocal, upfront (*informal*)
> **Antonyms**
diplomatic, discreet, evasive, guarded,
indirect, reticent, subtle, tactful, thoughtful

plaintive *adjective* = **sorrowful**,
disconsolate, doleful, grief-stricken, grievous,
heart-rending, melancholy, mournful,
pathetic, piteous, pitiful, rueful, sad, wistful,
woebegone, woeful

plan *noun* **1** = **scheme**, contrivance, design,
device, idea, method, plot, procedure,
programme, project, proposal, proposition,
scenario, strategy, suggestion, system **2**
= **diagram**, blueprint, chart, delineation,
drawing, illustration, layout, map,
representation, scale drawing, sketch ♦ *verb*
3 = **devise**, arrange, concoct, contrive,
design, draft, formulate, frame, invent,
organize, outline, plot, prepare, represent,
scheme, think out **4** = **intend**, aim,
contemplate, envisage, foresee, mean,
propose, purpose

plane *noun* **1** = **aeroplane**, aircraft, jet **2**
= **flat surface**, level surface **3** = **level**,
condition, degree, footing, position, stratum
♦ *adjective* **4** = **level**, even, flat, flush,
horizontal, plain, regular, smooth, uniform
♦ *verb* **5** = **skim**, glide, sail, skate, volplane

plant *noun* **1** = **vegetable**, bush, flower,
herb, shrub, weed **2** = **factory**, foundry, mill,
shop, works, yard **3** = **machinery**, apparatus,
equipment, gear ♦ *verb* **4** = **sow**, implant,
put in the ground, scatter, seed, set out,
transplant **5** = **place**, establish, fix, found,
imbed, insert, institute, lodge, put, root, set,
settle, sow the seeds

plaque *noun* = **plate**, badge, brooch,
cartouch(e), medal, medallion, panel, slab,
tablet

plaster *noun* **1** = **mortar**, gesso, gypsum,
plaster of Paris, stucco **2** = **bandage**,
adhesive plaster, dressing, Elastoplast
(*Trademark*), sticking plaster ♦ *verb* **3**
= **cover**, bedaub, besmear, coat, daub,
overlay, smear, spread

plastic *adjective* **1** = **manageable**,
compliant, docile, easily influenced,
impressionable, malleable, pliable, receptive,
responsive, tractable **2** = **pliant**, ductile,
fictile, flexible, mouldable, pliable, soft,
supple, tensile **3** *Slang* = **false**, artificial,
meretricious, mock, phoney or phony
(*informal*), pseudo (*informal*), sham,
specious, spurious, superficial, synthetic
> **Antonyms**
≠**manageable**: intractable, rebellious,

plate 545 **plaything**

recalcitrant, refractory, unmanageable, unreceptive ≠**pliant**: brittle, hard, inflexible, rigid, stiff, unbending, unyielding ≠**false**: authentic, genuine, natural, real, sincere, true

plate noun **1** = **platter**, dish, trencher (archaic) **2** = **helping**, course, dish, portion, serving **3** = **layer**, panel, sheet, slab **4** = **illustration**, lithograph, print ♦ verb **5** = **coat**, anodize, cover, electroplate, face, gild, laminate, nickel, overlay, platinize, silver

plateau noun **1** = **upland**, highland, mesa, table, tableland **2** = **levelling off**, level, stability, stage

platform noun **1** = **stage**, dais, podium, rostrum, stand **2** = **policy**, manifesto, objective(s), party line, principle, programme, tenet(s)

platitude noun = **cliché**, banality, bromide, commonplace, hackneyed saying, inanity, stereotype, trite remark, truism

platitudinous adjective = **clichéd**, banal, commonplace, corny (slang), hack, hackneyed, overworked, set, stale, stereotyped, stock, tired, trite, truistic, vapid, well-worn

platoon noun = **squad**, company, group, outfit (informal), patrol, squadron, team

platter noun = **plate**, charger, dish, salver, tray, trencher (archaic)

plaudits plural noun = **approval**, acclaim, acclamation, applause, approbation, clapping, commendation, congratulation, hand, kudos, ovation, praise, round of applause

plausible adjective **1** = **believable**, colourable, conceivable, credible, likely, persuasive, possible, probable, reasonable, tenable, verisimilar **2** = **glib**, fair-spoken, smooth, smooth-talking, smooth-tongued, specious

➤ **Antonyms**
≠**believable**: genuine, illogical, implausible, impossible, improbable, inconceivable, incredible, real, unbelievable, unlikely

play verb **1** = **amuse oneself**, caper, engage in games, entertain oneself, fool, frisk, frolic, gambol, have fun, revel, romp, sport, trifle **2** = **compete**, be in a team, challenge, contend against, participate, rival, take on, take part, vie with **3** = **act**, act the part of, execute, impersonate, perform, personate, portray, represent, take the part of **4** = **gamble**, bet, chance, hazard, punt (chiefly Brit.), risk, speculate, take, wager **5 play ball** Informal = **cooperate**, collaborate, go along, play along, reciprocate, respond, show willing **6 play by ear** = **improvise**, ad lib, extemporize, rise to the occasion, take it as it comes **7 play for time** = **stall**, delay, drag one's feet (informal), filibuster, hang fire,

procrastinate, temporize **8 play the fool** = **mess about**, act the goat (informal), clown, clown around, horse around (informal), lark (about) (informal), monkey around, skylark (informal) **9 play the game** Informal = **play fair**, conform, follow the rules, go along with, keep in step, play by the rules, toe the line ♦ noun **10** = **drama**, comedy, dramatic piece, entertainment, farce, masque, pantomime, performance, piece, radio play, show, soap opera, stage show, television drama, tragedy **11** = **amusement**, caper, diversion, entertainment, frolic, fun, gambol, game, jest, pastime, prank, recreation, romp, sport **12** = **gambling**, gaming **13** = **action**, activity, employment, function, operation, transaction, working **14** = **fun**, foolery, humour, jest, joking, lark (informal), prank, sport, teasing **15** = **space**, elbowroom, give (informal), latitude, leeway, margin, motion, movement, range, room, scope, sweep, swing

play around verb = **philander**, dally, fool around, mess around, take lightly, trifle, womanize

playboy noun = **womanizer**, ladies' man, lady-killer (informal), lover boy (slang), man about town, philanderer, pleasure seeker, rake, roué, socialite

play down verb = **minimize**, gloss over, make light of, make little of, set no store by, soft-pedal (informal), underplay, underrate

player noun **1** = **sportsman** or **sportswoman**, competitor, contestant, participant, team member **2** = **musician**, artist, instrumentalist, music maker, performer, virtuoso **3** = **performer**, actor or actress, entertainer, Thespian, trouper

playful adjective **1** = **joking**, arch, coy, flirtatious, good-natured, humorous, jesting, jokey, roguish, teasing, tongue-in-cheek, waggish **2** = **lively**, cheerful, coltish, frisky, frolicsome, gay, impish, joyous, kittenish, larkish (informal), ludic (literary), merry, mischievous, puckish, rollicking, spirited, sportive, sprightly, vivacious

➤ **Antonyms**
despondent, gloomy, grave, morose, sedate, serious

playmate noun = **friend**, chum (informal), companion, comrade, neighbour, pal (informal), playfellow

play on or **upon** verb = **take advantage of**, abuse, capitalize on, exploit, impose on, milk, profit by, trade on, turn to account, utilize

plaything noun = **toy**, amusement, bauble, game, gewgaw, gimcrack, pastime, trifle, trinket

play up *verb* **1** = **emphasize**, accentuate, bring to the fore, call attention to, highlight, magnify, point up, stress, turn the spotlight on, underline **2** *Brit. informal* = **be awkward**, be bolshie (*Brit. informal*), be cussed (*informal*), be disobedient, be stroppy (*Brit. slang*), give trouble, misbehave **3** *Brit. informal* = **hurt**, be painful, be sore, bother, give one gyp (*Brit. & N.Z. slang*), give one trouble, pain, trouble **4** *Brit. informal* = **malfunction**, be on the blink (*slang*), be wonky (*Brit. slang*), not work properly **5 play up to** *Informal* = **butter up**, bootlick (*informal*), brown-nose (*taboo slang*), crawl to, curry favour, fawn, flatter, get in with, ingratiate oneself, keep (someone) sweet, kiss (someone's) ass (*U.S. & Canad. taboo slang*), pander to, suck up to (*informal*), toady

play with *verb* **1** = **string along**, amuse oneself with, flirt with, toy with, trifle with **2** = **fiddle with** (*informal*), fidget with, fool around, interfere with, jiggle, mess about, waggle, wiggle

playwright *noun* = **dramatist**, dramaturge, dramaturgist

plea *noun* **1** = **appeal**, begging, entreaty, intercession, overture, petition, prayer, request, suit, supplication **2** *Law* = **suit**, action, allegation, cause **3** = **excuse**, apology, claim, defence, explanation, extenuation, justification, pretext, vindication

plead *verb* **1** = **appeal**, ask, beg, beseech, crave, entreat, implore, importune, petition, request, solicit, supplicate **2** = **allege**, adduce, argue, assert, maintain, put forward, use as an excuse

pleasant *adjective* **1** = **pleasing**, acceptable, agreeable, amusing, delectable, delightful, enjoyable, fine, gratifying, lovely, nice, pleasurable, refreshing, satisfying, welcome **2** = **friendly**, affable, agreeable, amiable, charming, cheerful, cheery, congenial, engaging, genial, good-humoured, likable *or* likeable, nice
➤ **Antonyms**
≠**pleasing**: awful, disagreeable, distasteful, horrible, horrid, miserable, offensive, repulsive, unpleasant ≠**friendly**: cold, disagreeable, horrible, horrid, impolite, offensive, rude, unfriendly, unlikable *or* unlikeable

pleasantry *noun* = **joke**, badinage, banter, bon mot, good-natured remark, jest, josh (*slang, chiefly U.S. & Canad.*), quip, sally, witticism

please *verb* **1** = **delight**, amuse, charm, cheer, content, entertain, give pleasure to, gladden, gratify, humour, indulge, rejoice, satisfy, suit, tickle, tickle pink (*informal*) **2**

= **want**, be inclined, choose, desire, like, opt, prefer, see fit, will, wish
➤ **Antonyms**
≠**delight**: anger, annoy, depress, disgust, displease, dissatisfy, grieve, incense, offend, provoke, sadden, vex

pleased *adjective* = **happy**, chuffed (*Brit. slang*), contented, delighted, euphoric, glad, gratified, in high spirits, over the moon (*informal*), pleased as punch (*informal*), rapt, satisfied, thrilled, tickled, tickled pink (*informal*)

pleasing *adjective* = **enjoyable**, agreeable, amiable, amusing, attractive, charming, delightful, engaging, entertaining, gratifying, likable *or* likeable, pleasurable, polite, satisfying, winning
➤ **Antonyms**
boring, disagreeable, dull, monotonous, rude, unattractive, unlikable *or* unlikeable, unpleasant

pleasurable *adjective* = **enjoyable**, agreeable, delightful, fun, good, lovely, nice, pleasant

pleasure *noun* **1** = **happiness**, amusement, beer and skittles (*informal*), bliss, comfort, contentment, delectation, delight, diversion, ease, enjoyment, gladness, gratification, jollies (*slang*), joy, recreation, satisfaction, solace **2** = **wish**, choice, command, desire, inclination, mind, option, preference, purpose, will
➤ **Antonyms**
≠**happiness**: abstinence, anger, displeasure, duty, labour, misery, necessity, obligation, pain, sadness, sorrow, suffering, unhappiness

plebeian *adjective* **1** = **common**, base, coarse, ignoble, low, lowborn, lower-class, mean, non-U (*Brit. informal*), proletarian, uncultivated, unrefined, vulgar, working-class ♦ *noun* **2** = **commoner**, common man, man in the street, peasant, pleb, prole (*derogatory slang, chiefly Brit.*), proletarian
➤ **Antonyms**
adjective ≠**common**: aristocratic, cultivated, highborn, high-class, patrician, polished, refined, upper-class, well-bred

pledge *noun* **1** = **promise**, assurance, covenant, oath, undertaking, vow, warrant, word, word of honour **2** = **guarantee**, bail, bond, collateral, deposit, earnest, gage, pawn, security, surety **3** = **toast**, health ♦ *verb* **4** = **promise**, contract, engage, give one's oath, give one's word, give one's word of honour, swear, undertake, vouch, vow **5** = **bind**, engage, gage (*archaic*), guarantee, mortgage, plight **6** = **drink to**, drink the health of, toast

plenteous *adjective* **1** = **plentiful**, abundant, ample, bounteous (*literary*), bountiful, copious, generous, inexhaustible, infinite, lavish, liberal, overflowing, profuse, thick on the ground **2 = productive,** bumper, fertile, fruitful, luxuriant, plentiful, prolific

plentiful *adjective* **1 = abundant,** ample, bounteous (*literary*), bountiful, complete, copious, generous, inexhaustible, infinite, lavish, liberal, overflowing, plenteous, profuse, thick on the ground **2 = productive,** bumper, fertile, fruitful, luxuriant, plenteous, prolific
➤ Antonyms
≠**abundant:** deficient, inadequate, insufficient, scant, scarce, skimpy, small, sparing, sparse, thin on the ground

plenty *noun* **1 = lots** (*informal*), abundance, enough, fund, good deal, great deal, heap(s) (*informal*), mass, masses, mine, mountain(s), oodles (*informal*), pile(s) (*informal*), plethora, quantities, quantity, stack(s), store, sufficiency, volume **2 = abundance,** affluence, copiousness, fertility, fruitfulness, luxury, opulence, plenitude, plenteousness, plentifulness, profusion, prosperity, wealth

plethora *noun* **= excess,** glut, overabundance, profusion, superabundance, superfluity, surfeit, surplus
➤ Antonyms
dearth, deficiency, lack, scarcity, shortage, want

pliable *adjective* **1 = flexible,** bendable, bendy, ductile, limber, lithe, malleable, plastic, pliant, supple, tensile **2 = compliant,** adaptable, docile, easily led, impressionable, influenceable, like putty in one's hands, manageable, persuadable, pliant, receptive, responsive, susceptible, tractable, yielding
➤ Antonyms
≠**flexible:** rigid, stiff ≠**compliant:** headstrong, inflexible, intractable, obdurate, obstinate, stubborn, unadaptable, unbending, unyielding, wilful

pliant *adjective* **1 = flexible,** bendable, bendy, ductile, lithe, plastic, pliable, supple, tensile **2 = impressionable,** adaptable, biddable, compliant, easily led, influenceable, manageable, persuadable, pliable, susceptible, tractable, yielding

plight *noun* **= difficulty,** case, circumstances, condition, dilemma, extremity, hole (*slang*), hot water (*informal*), jam (*informal*), perplexity, pickle (*informal*), predicament, scrape (*informal*), situation, spot (*informal*), state, straits, tight spot, trouble

plod *verb* **1 = trudge,** clump, drag, lumber, slog, stomp (*informal*), tramp, tread **2 = slog,** drudge, grind (*informal*), grub, labour, peg away, persevere, plough through, plug away (*informal*), soldier on, toil

plot[1] *noun* **1 = plan,** cabal, conspiracy, covin (*Law*), intrigue, machination, scheme, stratagem **2 = story,** action, narrative, outline, scenario, story line, subject, theme, thread ♦ *verb* **3 = plan,** cabal, collude, conspire, contrive, hatch, intrigue, machinate, manoeuvre, scheme **4 = devise,** brew, conceive, concoct, contrive, cook up (*informal*), design, frame, hatch, imagine, lay, project **5 = chart,** calculate, compute, draft, draw, locate, map, mark, outline

plot[2] *noun* **= patch,** allotment, area, ground, lot, parcel, tract

plough *verb* **1 = turn over,** break ground, cultivate, dig, furrow, ridge, till **2** *usually with* **through = forge,** cut, drive, flounder, plod, plunge, press, push, stagger, surge, wade **3 plough into = plunge into,** bulldoze into, career into, crash into, hurtle into, shove into, smash into

ploy *noun* **= tactic,** device, dodge, manoeuvre, move, ruse, scheme, stratagem, trick, wile

pluck *verb* **1 = pull out** *or* **off,** collect, draw, gather, harvest, pick **2 = tug,** catch, clutch, jerk, pull at, snatch, tweak, yank **3 = strum,** finger, pick, plunk, thrum, twang ♦ *noun* **4 = courage,** backbone, balls (*taboo slang*), ballsiness (*taboo slang*), boldness, bottle (*Brit. slang*), bravery, determination, grit, guts (*informal*), hardihood, heart, intrepidity, mettle, nerve, resolution, spirit, spunk (*informal*)

plucky *adjective* **= courageous,** ballsy (*taboo slang*), bold, brave, daring, doughty, feisty (*informal, chiefly U.S. & Canad.*), game, gritty, gutsy (*slang*), hardy, have-a-go (*informal*), heroic, intrepid, mettlesome, spirited, spunky (*informal*), undaunted, unflinching, valiant
➤ Antonyms
afraid, chicken (*slang*), cowardly, dastardly, dispirited, scared, spineless, spiritless, timid, yellow (*informal*)

plug *noun* **1 = stopper,** bung, cork, spigot, stopple **2** *Informal* **= mention,** advert (*Brit. informal*), advertisement, good word, hype, publicity, puff, push **3 = wad,** cake, chew, pigtail, quid, twist ♦ *verb* **4 = seal,** block, bung, choke, close, cork, cover, fill, pack, stop, stopper, stopple, stop up, stuff **5** *Informal* **= mention,** advertise, build up, hype, promote, publicize, puff, push, write up **6** *Slang* **= shoot,** blow away (*slang, chiefly U.S.*), gun down, pick off, pop, pot, put a bullet in **7 plug away** *Informal* **= slog,** drudge, grind (*informal*), labour, peg away, plod, toil

plum *noun* **1 = prize,** bonus, cream, find, pick, treasure ♦ *adjective* **2 = choice,** best, first-class, prize

plumb verb 1 = **delve**, explore, fathom, gauge, go into, measure, penetrate, probe, search, sound, unravel ◆ noun 2 = **weight**, lead, plumb bob, plummet ◆ adverb 3 = **vertically**, perpendicularly, up and down 4 = **exactly**, bang, precisely, slap, spot-on (Brit. informal)

plume noun 1 = **feather**, aigrette, crest, pinion, quill ◆ verb 2 with on or upon = **pride oneself**, congratulate oneself, pat oneself on the back, pique oneself, preen oneself

plummet verb = **plunge**, crash, descend, dive, drop down, fall, nose-dive, stoop, swoop, tumble

plump adjective = **chubby**, beefy (informal), burly, buxom, corpulent, dumpy, fat, fleshy, full, obese, podgy, portly, roly-poly, rotund, round, stout, tubby, well-covered, well-upholstered (informal)
➤ **Antonyms**
anorexic, bony, emaciated, lanky, lean, scrawny, skinny, slender, slim, sylphlike, thin

plunder verb 1 = **loot**, despoil, devastate, pillage, raid, ransack, ravage, rifle, rob, sack, spoil, steal, strip ◆ noun 2 = **loot**, booty, ill-gotten gains, pillage, prey, prize, rapine, spoils, swag (slang)

plunge verb 1 = **throw**, cast, pitch 2 = **hurtle**, career, charge, dash, jump, lurch, rush, swoop, tear 3 = **descend**, dip, dive, douse, drop, fall, go down, immerse, nose-dive, plummet, sink, submerge, tumble ◆ noun 4 = **dive**, descent, drop, fall, immersion, jump, submersion, swoop

plus preposition 1 = **and**, added to, coupled with, with, with the addition of ◆ adjective 2 = **additional**, added, add-on, extra, positive, supplementary ◆ noun 3 Informal = **advantage**, asset, benefit, bonus, extra, gain, good point, icing on the cake, perk (Brit. informal), surplus

plush adjective = **luxurious**, costly, de luxe, lavish, luxury, opulent, palatial, rich, ritzy (slang), sumptuous
➤ **Antonyms**
cheap, cheap and nasty, inexpensive, ordinary, plain, spartan

plutocrat noun = **rich man**, capitalist, Croesus, Dives, fat cat (slang, chiefly U.S.), magnate, millionaire, moneybags (slang), tycoon

ply verb 1 = **work at**, carry on, exercise, follow, practise, pursue 2 = **use**, employ, handle, manipulate, swing, utilize, wield 3 = **bombard**, assail, beset, besiege, harass, importune, press, urge

poach verb 1 = **steal**, hunt or fish illegally, plunder, rob, steal game 2 = **encroach**, appropriate, infringe, intrude, trespass

pocket noun 1 = **pouch**, bag, compartment, hollow, receptacle, sack ◆ verb 2 = **steal**, appropriate, cabbage (Brit. slang), filch, help oneself to, lift (informal), pilfer, purloin, snaffle (Brit. informal), take 3 = **bear**, accept, brook, endure, put up with (informal), stomach, swallow, take, tolerate ◆ adjective 4 = **small**, abridged, compact, concise, little, miniature, pint-size(d) (informal), portable, potted (informal)

pod noun, verb = **shell**, hull, husk, shuck

podgy adjective = **tubby**, chubby, chunky, dumpy, fat, fleshy, fubsy (archaic or dialect), plump, roly-poly, rotund, short and fat, squat, stout, stubby, stumpy

podium noun = **platform**, dais, rostrum, stage

poem noun = **verse**, lyric, ode, rhyme, song, sonnet

poet noun = **bard**, lyricist, maker (archaic), rhymer, versifier

poetic adjective = **lyrical**, elegiac, lyric, metrical, rhythmic, rhythmical, songlike

poetry noun = **verse**, metrical composition, poems, poesy (archaic), rhyme, rhyming

poignancy noun 1 = **sadness**, emotion, emotionalism, evocativeness, feeling, pathos, piteousness, plaintiveness, sentiment, tenderness 2 = **sharpness**, bitterness, intensity, keenness 3 = **pungency**, piquancy, sharpness

poignant adjective 1 = **moving**, affecting, agonizing, bitter, distressing, gut-wrenching, harrowing, heartbreaking, heart-rending, intense, painful, pathetic, sad, touching, upsetting 2 = **cutting**, acute, biting, caustic, keen, penetrating, piercing, pointed, sarcastic, severe, sharp 3 = **pungent**, acrid, piquant, sharp, stinging, tangy

point noun 1 = **essence**, burden, core, crux, drift, gist, heart, import, main idea, marrow, matter, meaning, nub, pith, proposition, question, subject, text, theme, thrust 2 = **aim**, design, end, goal, intent, intention, motive, object, objective, purpose, reason, use, usefulness, utility 3 = **item**, aspect, detail, facet, feature, instance, nicety, particular 4 = **characteristic**, aspect, attribute, peculiarity, property, quality, respect, side, trait 5 = **place**, location, position, site, spot, stage, station 6 = **full stop**, dot, mark, period, speck, stop 7 = **end**, apex, nib, prong, sharp end, spike, spur, summit, tine, tip, top 8 = **headland**, bill, cape, foreland, head, ness (archaic), promontory 9 = **stage**, circumstance, condition, degree, extent, position 10 = **moment**, instant, juncture, time, very minute 11 = **unit**, score, tally 12 **beside the point = irrelevant**, immaterial, incidental, inconsequential, not to the purpose, off the subject, out of the way, pointless, unimportant, without connection **13 to the point** = **relevant**, applicable, apposite, appropriate, apropos, apt, brief, fitting, germane, pertinent, pithy, pointed, short, suitable, terse ◆ *verb* **14** = **indicate**, bespeak, call attention to, denote, designate, direct, show, signify **15** = **aim**, bring to bear, direct, level, train

point-blank *adjective* **1** = **direct**, abrupt, blunt, categorical, downright, explicit, express, plain, straight-from-the-shoulder, unreserved ◆ *adverb* **2** = **directly**, bluntly, brusquely, candidly, explicitly, forthrightly, frankly, openly, overtly, plainly, straight, straightforwardly

pointed *adjective* **1** = **sharp**, acicular, acuminate, acute, barbed, cuspidate, edged **2** = **cutting**, accurate, acute, biting, incisive, keen, penetrating, pertinent, sharp, telling, trenchant

pointer *noun* **1** = **hint**, advice, caution, information, recommendation, suggestion, tip, warning **2** = **indicator**, guide, hand, needle

pointless *adjective* = **senseless**, absurd, aimless, dumb-ass (*slang*), fruitless, futile, inane, ineffectual, irrelevant, meaningless, nonsensical, silly, stupid, unavailing, unproductive, unprofitable, useless, vague, vain, without rhyme or reason, worthless
➤ **Antonyms**
appropriate, beneficial, desirable, fitting, fruitful, logical, meaningful, productive, profitable, proper, sensible, to the point, useful, worthwhile

point of view *noun* **1** = **perspective**, angle, orientation, outlook, position, standpoint **2** = **opinion**, approach, attitude, belief, judgment, slant, view, viewpoint, way of looking at it

point out *verb* = **mention**, allude to, bring up, call attention to, identify, indicate, remind, reveal, show, specify

poise *noun* **1** = **composure**, aplomb, assurance, calmness, cool (*slang*), coolness, dignity, elegance equanimity, equilibrium, grace, presence, presence of mind, sang-froid, savoir-faire, self-possession, serenity ◆ *verb* **2** = **position**, balance, float, hang, hang in midair, hang suspended, hold, hover, support, suspend

poised *adjective* **1** = **ready**, all set, in the wings, on the brink, prepared, standing by, waiting **2** = **composed**, calm, collected, debonair, dignified, graceful, nonchalant, self-confident, self-possessed, serene, suave, together (*informal*), unfazed (*informal*), unruffled, urbane

➤ **Antonyms**
≠**composed**: agitated, annoyed, discomposed, disturbed, excited, irritated, ruffled, worked up

poison *noun* **1** = **toxin**, bane, venom **2** = **contamination**, bane, blight, cancer, canker, contagion, corruption, malignancy, miasma, virus ◆ *verb* **3** = **murder**, give (someone) poison, kill **4** = **contaminate**, adulterate, envenom, infect, pollute **5** = **corrupt**, defile, deprave, pervert, subvert, taint, undermine, vitiate, warp ◆ *adjective* **6** = **poisonous**, deadly, lethal, toxic, venomous

poisonous *adjective* **1** = **toxic**, baneful (*archaic*), deadly, fatal, lethal, mephitic, mortal, noxious, venomous, virulent **2** = **evil**, baleful, baneful (*archaic*), corrupting, malicious, noxious, pernicious, pestiferous, pestilential, vicious

poke *verb* **1** = **jab**, butt, dig, elbow, hit, nudge, prod, punch, push, shove, stab, stick, thrust **2** = **interfere**, butt in, intrude, meddle, nose, peek, poke one's nose into (*informal*), pry, put one's two cents in (*U.S. slang*), snoop (*informal*), tamper **3 poke fun at** = **make fun of**, chaff, jeer, make a mock of, mock, rib (*informal*), ridicule, send up (*Brit. informal*), take the mickey (*informal*), take the piss (out of) (*taboo slang*), tease ◆ *noun* **4** = **jab**, butt, dig, hit, nudge, prod, punch, thrust

poky *adjective* = **small**, confined, cramped, incommodious, narrow, tiny
➤ **Antonyms**
capacious, commodious, large, open, roomy, spacious, wide

polar *adjective* **1** = **freezing**, Antarctic, Arctic, cold, extreme, frozen, furthest, glacial, icy, terminal **2** = **opposite**, antagonistic, antipodal, antithetical, contradictory, contrary, diametric, opposed

polarity *noun* = **opposition**, ambivalence, contradiction, contrariety, dichotomy, duality, paradox

pole[1] *noun* = **rod**, bar, mast, post, shaft, spar, staff, standard, stick

pole[2] *noun* **1** = **extremity**, antipode, limit, terminus **2 poles apart** = **at opposite extremes**, at opposite ends of the earth, incompatible, irreconcilable, miles apart, widely separated, worlds apart

polemic *noun* **1** = **argument**, controversy, debate, dispute ◆ *adjective* **2** = **controversial**, argumentative, contentious, disputatious, polemical

polemics *noun* = **dispute**, argument, argumentation, contention, controversy, debate, disputation

police *noun* **1** = **the law** (*informal*), boys in blue (*informal*), constabulary, fuzz (*slang*), law enforcement agency, police force, the Old Bill (*slang*) ♦ *verb* 2 = **control**, guard, keep in order, keep the peace, patrol, protect, regulate, watch 3 = **monitor**, check, observe, oversee, supervise

policeman *noun* = **cop** (*slang*), bizzy (*informal*), bobby (*informal*), bogey (*slang*), constable, copper (*slang*), flatfoot (*slang*), fuzz (*slang*), gendarme (*slang*), officer, peeler (*obsolete Brit. slang*), pig (*slang*), rozzer (*slang*), woodentop (*slang*)

policy *noun* 1 = **procedure**, action, approach, code, course, custom, guideline, line, plan, practice, programme, protocol, rule, scheme, stratagem, theory 2 *Archaic* = **wisdom**, discretion, good sense, prudence, sagacity, shrewdness

polish *verb* 1 = **shine**, brighten, buff, burnish, clean, furbish, rub, smooth, wax 2 = **perfect**, brush up, correct, cultivate, emend, enhance, finish, improve, refine, touch up ♦ *noun* 3 = **varnish**, wax 4 = **sheen**, brightness, brilliance, finish, glaze, gloss, lustre, smoothness, sparkle, veneer 5 = **style**, breeding, class (*informal*), elegance, finesse, finish, grace, politesse, refinement, suavity, urbanity

polished *adjective* 1 = **accomplished**, adept, expert, faultless, fine, flawless, impeccable, masterly, outstanding, professional, skilful, superlative 2 = **shining**, bright, burnished, furbished, glassy, gleaming, glossy, slippery, smooth 3 = **elegant**, civilized, courtly, cultivated, finished, genteel, polite, refined, sophisticated, urbane, well-bred
➤ **Antonyms**
≠**accomplished**: amateurish, inept, inexpert, unaccomplished, unskilled ≠**shining**: dark, dull, matt, rough ≠**elegant**: inelegant, uncivilized, uncultivated, unrefined, unsophisticated

polish off *verb Informal* 1 = **finish**, consume, down, eat up, put away, shift (*informal*), swill, wolf 2 = **kill**, blow away (*slang, chiefly U.S.*), bump off (*informal*), dispose of, do away with, do in (*slang*), eliminate, get rid of, liquidate, murder, take out (*slang*)

polite *adjective* 1 = **mannerly**, affable, civil, complaisant, courteous, deferential, gracious, obliging, respectful, well-behaved, well-mannered 2 = **refined**, civilized, courtly, cultured, elegant, genteel, polished, sophisticated, urbane, well-bred
➤ **Antonyms**
≠**mannerly**: crude, discourteous, ill-mannered, impertinent, impolite, impudent, insulting, rude ≠**refined**: uncultured, unrefined

politeness *noun* = **courtesy**, civility,

courteousness, decency, etiquette, mannerliness

politic *adjective* 1 = **wise**, advisable, diplomatic, discreet, expedient, in one's best interests, judicious, prudent, sagacious, sensible, tactful 2 = **shrewd**, artful, astute, canny, crafty, cunning, designing, ingenious, intriguing, Machiavellian, scheming, sly, subtle, unscrupulous

political *adjective* 1 = **governmental**, parliamentary, policy-making 2 = **factional**, partisan, party

politician *noun* = **statesman**, legislator, Member of Parliament, M.P., office bearer, politico (*informal, chiefly U.S.*), public servant

politics *noun* 1 = **statesmanship**, affairs of state, civics, government, government policy, political science, polity, statecraft 2 = **power struggle**, Machiavellianism, machination, Realpolitik

poll *noun* 1 = **canvass**, ballot, census, count, Gallup Poll, (public) opinion poll, sampling, survey 2 = **vote**, figures, returns, tally, voting ♦ *verb* 3 = **tally**, register 4 = **question**, ballot, canvass, fly a kite, interview, sample, survey

pollute *verb* 1 = **contaminate**, adulterate, befoul, dirty, foul, infect, make filthy, mar, poison, smirch, soil, spoil, stain, taint 2 = **defile**, besmirch, corrupt, debase, debauch, deprave, desecrate, dishonour, profane, sully, violate
➤ **Antonyms**
≠**contaminate**: clean, cleanse, decontaminate, disinfect, purge, sanitize, sterilize ≠**defile**: esteem, honour

pollution *noun* = **contamination**, adulteration, corruption, defilement, dirtying, foulness, impurity, taint, uncleanness

poltroon *noun Obsolete* = **coward**, chicken (*slang*), craven, yellow-belly (*slang*)

polychromatic *adjective* = **multicoloured**, many-coloured, many-hued, of all the colours of the rainbow, polychrome, rainbow, varicoloured, variegated

pomp *noun* 1 = **ceremony**, éclat, flourish, grandeur, magnificence, pageant, pageantry, parade, solemnity, splendour, state 2 = **show**, display, grandiosity, ostentation, pomposity, vainglory

pomposity *noun* 1 = **self-importance**, affectation, airs, arrogance, flaunting, grandiosity, haughtiness, pompousness, portentousness, presumption, pretension, pretentiousness, vainglory, vanity 2 = **grandiloquence**, bombast, hot air (*informal*), loftiness, magniloquence, rant, turgidity

pompous *adjective* 1 = **self-important**,

affected, arrogant, bloated, grandiose, imperious, magisterial, ostentatious, overbearing, pontifical, portentous, pretentious, puffed up, showy, supercilious, vainglorious **2 = grandiloquent**, arty-farty (*informal*), boastful, bombastic, high-flown, inflated, magniloquent, overblown, turgid
➤ **Antonyms**
≠**self-important**: humble, modest, natural, self-effacing, simple, unaffected, unpretentious ≠**grandiloquent**: direct, plain-spoken, simple, succinct

ponce *Offensive slang, chiefly Brit. noun* **1** = **fop**, beau, coxcomb (*archaic*), dandy, popinjay, swell **2 = pimp**, bawd (*archaic*), pander, procurer

pond *noun* = **pool**, dew pond, duck pond, fish pond, lochan (*Scot.*), millpond, small lake, tarn

ponder *verb* = **think**, brood, cerebrate, cogitate, consider, contemplate, deliberate, examine, excogitate, give thought to, meditate, mull over, muse, puzzle over, rack one's brains, reflect, ruminate, study, weigh

ponderous *adjective* **1 = dull**, dreary, heavy, laboured, lifeless, long-winded, pedantic, pedestrian, plodding, prolix, stilted, stodgy, tedious, tiresome, verbose **2 = unwieldy**, bulky, clunky (*informal*), cumbersome, cumbrous, heavy, hefty, huge, massive, weighty **3 = clumsy**, awkward, elephantine, graceless, heavy-footed, laborious, lumbering
➤ **Antonyms**
≠**unwieldy**: handy, light, little, small, tiny, weightless ≠**clumsy**: graceful, light, light-footed

pontifical *adjective* **1 = papal**, apostolic, ecclesiastical **2 = pompous**, dogmatic, imperious, magisterial, overbearing, portentous, pretentious, self-important

pontificate *verb* = **expound**, declaim, dogmatize, hold forth, lay down the law, pontify, preach, pronounce, sound off

pooh-pooh *verb* = **scorn**, belittle, brush aside, deride, disdain, dismiss, disregard, make little of, play down, scoff, slight, sneer, sniff at, spurn, turn up one's nose at (*informal*)
➤ **Antonyms**
exalt, extol, glorify, praise

pool¹ *noun* **1 = pond**, lake, mere, puddle, splash, tarn **2 = swimming pool**, swimming bath

pool² *noun* **1** = **syndicate**, collective, combine, consortium, group, team, trust **2 = kitty**, bank, funds, jackpot, pot, stakes ◆ *verb* **3 = combine**, amalgamate, join forces, league, merge, put together, share

poor *adjective* **1 = impoverished**, badly off,

broke (*informal*), destitute, dirt-poor (*informal*), down and out, down at heel, flat broke (*informal*), hard up (*informal*), impecunious, indigent, in need, in queer street, in want, necessitous, needy, on one's beam-ends, on one's uppers, on the breadline, on the rocks, penniless, penurious, poverty-stricken, short, skint (*Brit. slang*), stony-broke (*Brit. slang*), without two pennies to rub together (*informal*) **2 = meagre**, deficient, exiguous, inadequate, incomplete, insufficient, lacking, measly, miserable, niggardly, pathetic, pitiable, reduced, scant, scanty, skimpy, slight, sparse, straitened **3 = inferior**, below par, chickenshit (*U.S. slang*), crappy (*slang*), faulty, feeble, for the birds (*informal*), low-grade, low-rent (*informal chiefly U.S.*), mediocre, no great shakes (*informal*), not much cop (*Brit. slang*), pants (*informal*), piss-poor (*taboo slang*), poxy (*slang*), rotten (*informal*), rubbishy, second-rate, shabby, shoddy, sorry, strictly for the birds (*informal*), substandard, unsatisfactory, valueless, weak, worthless **4 = unfortunate**, hapless, ill-fated, luckless, miserable, pathetic, pitiable, unhappy, unlucky, wretched
➤ **Antonyms**
≠**impoverished**: affluent, comfortable (*informal*), prosperous, rich, wealthy, well-heeled (*informal*), well-off ≠**meagre**: abundant, adequate, ample, complete, dense, plentiful, satisfactory, sufficient, thick ≠**inferior**: excellent, exceptional, first-class, first-rate, satisfactory, superior, valuable ≠**unfortunate**: fortunate, happy, lucky, successful

poorly *adverb* **1 = badly**, crudely, inadequately, incompetently, inexpertly, inferiorly, insufficiently, meanly, shabbily, unsatisfactorily, unsuccessfully ◆ *adjective* **2** *Informal* = **ill**, ailing, below par, indisposed, off colour, out of sorts, rotten (*informal*), seedy (*informal*), sick, under the weather (*informal*), unwell
➤ **Antonyms**
adverb ≠**badly**: acceptably, adequately, competently, expertly, satisfactorily, sufficiently, well ◆ *adjective* ≠**ill**: fit, hale and hearty, healthy, in good health, in the pink, well

pop *verb* **1 = burst**, bang, crack, explode, go off, report, snap **2 = put**, insert, push, shove, slip, stick, thrust, tuck **3** *often with* **in, out,** *etc. Informal* = **call**, appear, come *or* go suddenly, drop in (*informal*), leave quickly, nip in *or* out (*Brit. informal*), visit **4** *Especially of eyes* = **protrude**, bulge, stick out ◆ *noun* **5 = bang**, burst, crack, explosion, noise, report **6** *Informal* = **soft drink**, fizzy drink, ginger (*Scot.*), lemonade, mineral water, soda water

pope *noun* = **Holy Father,** Bishop of Rome, pontiff, Vicar of Christ

popinjay *noun* = **fop,** buck (*archaic*), coxcomb (*archaic*), dandy, peacock, swell (*informal*)

poppycock *noun Informal* = **nonsense,** babble, balderdash, balls (*taboo slang*), baloney (*informal*), bilge (*informal*), bollocks (*Brit. taboo slang*), bosh (*informal*), bull (*slang*), bullshit (*taboo slang*), bunk (*informal*), bunkum *or* buncombe (*chiefly U.S.*), cobblers (*Brit. taboo slang*), crap (*slang*), drivel, eyewash (*informal*), garbage (*informal*), hogwash, hokum (*slang, chiefly U.S. & Canad.*), hooey (*slang*), horsefeathers (*U.S. slang*), hot air (*informal*), moonshine, pants (*informal*), pap, piffle (*informal*), rot, rubbish, shit (*taboo slang*), tommyrot, tosh (*slang, chiefly Brit.*), trash, tripe (*informal*), twaddle

populace *noun* = **people,** commonalty, crowd, general public, hoi polloi, inhabitants, Joe (and Eileen) Public (*slang*), Joe Six-Pack (*U.S. slang*), masses, mob, multitude, rabble, throng

popular *adjective* 1 = **well-liked,** accepted, approved, celebrated, famous, fashionable, fave (*informal*), favoured, favourite, in, in demand, in favour, liked, sought-after 2 = **common,** conventional, current, general, prevailing, prevalent, public, standard, stock, ubiquitous, universal, widespread
➤ **Antonyms**
≠**well-liked:** despised, detested, disliked, hated, loathed, unaccepted, unpopular ≠**common:** infrequent, rare, uncommon, unusual

popularity *noun* = **favour,** acceptance, acclaim, adoration, approval, celebrity, currency, esteem, fame, idolization, lionization, recognition, regard, renown, reputation, repute, vogue

popularize *verb* = **make popular,** disseminate, familiarize, give currency to, give mass appeal, make available to all, simplify, spread, universalize

popularly *adverb* = **generally,** commonly, conventionally, customarily, ordinarily, regularly, traditionally, universally, usually, widely

populate *verb* = **inhabit,** colonize, live in, occupy, people, settle

population *noun* = **inhabitants,** citizenry, community, denizens, folk, natives, people, populace, residents, society

populous *adjective* = **populated,** crowded, heavily populated, overpopulated, packed, swarming, teeming, thronged

pore[1] *verb* **pore over** = **study,** brood, contemplate, dwell on, examine, go over, peruse, ponder, read, scrutinize, work over

pore[2] *noun* = **opening,** hole, orifice, outlet, stoma

pornographic *adjective* = **obscene,** blue, dirty, filthy, indecent, lewd, offensive, prurient, salacious, smutty, X-rated (*informal*)

pornography *noun* = **obscenity,** dirt, erotica, filth, indecency, porn (*informal*), porno (*informal*), smut

porous *adjective* = **permeable,** absorbent, absorptive, penetrable, pervious, spongy
➤ **Antonyms**
impenetrable, impermeable, impervious, nonporous

port *noun* = **harbour,** anchorage, haven, roads, roadstead, seaport

portable *adjective* = **light,** compact, convenient, easily carried, handy, lightweight, manageable, movable, portative

portal *noun Literary* = **doorway,** door, entrance, entrance way, entry, gateway, way in

portend *verb* = **foretell,** adumbrate, augur, bespeak, betoken, bode, foreshadow, foretoken, forewarn, harbinger, herald, indicate, omen, point to, predict, presage, prognosticate, promise, threaten, vaticinate (*rare*), warn of

portent *noun* = **omen,** augury, foreboding, foreshadowing, forewarning, harbinger, indication, premonition, presage, presentiment, prognostic, prognostication, sign, threat, warning

portentous *adjective* 1 = **significant,** alarming, bodeful, crucial, fateful, forbidding, important, menacing, minatory, momentous, ominous, sinister, threatening 2 = **pompous,** bloated, elephantine, heavy, ponderous, pontifical, self-important, solemn

porter[1] *noun* = **baggage attendant,** bearer, carrier

porter[2] *noun Chiefly Brit.* = **doorman,** caretaker, concierge, gatekeeper, janitor

portion *noun* 1 = **part,** bit, fraction, fragment, morsel, piece, scrap, section, segment 2 = **share,** allocation, allotment, allowance, division, lot, measure, parcel, quantity, quota, ration 3 = **helping,** piece, serving 4 *Literary* = **destiny,** cup, fate, fortune, lot, luck ◆ *verb* 5 = **divide,** allocate, allot, apportion, assign, deal, distribute, divvy up (*informal*), dole out, parcel out, partition, share out

portly *adjective* = **stout,** burly, corpulent, fat, fleshy, heavy, large, plump

portrait *noun* 1 = **picture,** image, likeness, painting, photograph, portraiture, representation, sketch **2 = description,** account, characterization, depiction, portrayal, profile, thumbnail sketch, vignette

portray verb **1 = represent,** delineate, depict, draw, figure, illustrate, limn, paint, picture, render, sketch **2 - describe,** characterize, depict, paint a mental picture of, put in words **3 = play,** act the part of, represent

portrayal noun **= representation,** characterization, delineation, depiction, description, impersonation, interpretation, performance, picture, rendering, take (informal, chiefly U.S.)

pose verb **1 = position,** arrange, model, sit, sit for **2 = put on airs,** affect, attitudinize, posture, show off (informal), strike an attitude **3** often with **as = impersonate,** feign, masquerade as, pass oneself off as, pretend to be, profess to be, sham **4 = present,** advance, ask, posit, propound, put, put forward, set, state, submit ♦ noun **5 = posture,** attitude, bearing, mien (literary), position, stance **6 = act,** affectation, air, attitudinizing, façade, front, mannerism, masquerade, posturing, pretence, role

poser noun **= puzzle,** brain-teaser (informal), conundrum, enigma, knotty point, problem, question, riddle, teaser, tough one, vexed question

poseur noun **= show-off** (informal), exhibitionist, impostor, poser, posturer

posh adjective Informal, chiefly Brit. **= upper-class,** classy (slang), elegant, exclusive, fashionable, grand, high-class, high-toned, la-di-da (informal), luxurious, luxury, ritzy (slang), smart, stylish, swanky (informal), swish (informal, chiefly Brit.), top-drawer, up-market

posit verb **= put forward,** advance, assume, postulate, presume, propound, state

position noun **1 = place,** area, bearings, locale, locality, location, point, post, reference, site, situation, spot, station, whereabouts **2 = posture,** arrangement, attitude, disposition, pose, stance **3 = attitude,** angle, belief, opinion, outlook, point of view, slant, stance, stand, standpoint, view, viewpoint **4 = status,** caste, class, consequence, eminence, importance, place, prestige, rank, reputation, standing, station, stature **5 = job,** berth (informal), billet (informal), capacity, duty, employment, function, occupation, office, place, post, role, situation **6 = situation,** circumstances, condition, lie of the land, pass, plight, predicament, state, strait(s) ♦ verb **7 = place,** arrange, array, dispose, fix, lay out, locate, put, sequence, set, settle, stand, stick (informal)

positive adjective **1 = certain,** assured, confident, convinced, sure **2 = definite,** absolute, actual, affirmative, categorical, certain, clear, clear-cut, conclusive, concrete, decisive, direct, explicit, express, firm, incontrovertible, indisputable, real, unequivocal, unmistakable **3 = helpful,** beneficial, constructive, effective, efficacious, forward-looking, practical, productive, progressive, useful **4** Informal **= absolute,** complete, consummate, downright, out-and-out, perfect, rank, thorough, thoroughgoing, unmitigated, utter
➤ Antonyms
≠ **certain:** not confident, unassured, uncertain, unconvinced, unsure ≠ **definite:** contestable, disputable, doubtful, inconclusive, indecisive, indefinite, uncertain ≠ **helpful:** conservative, detrimental, harmful, impractical, reactionary, unhelpful, useless

positively adverb **= definitely,** absolutely, assuredly, categorically, certainly, emphatically, firmly, surely, undeniably, unequivocally, unmistakably, unquestionably, with certainty, without qualification

possess verb **1 = have,** be blessed with, be born with, be endowed with, enjoy, have to one's name, hold, own **2 = seize,** acquire, control, dominate, hold, occupy, take over, take possession of **3 = control,** bewitch, consume, dominate, enchant, fixate, influence, mesmerize, obsess, put under a spell

possessed adjective **= crazed,** bedevilled, berserk, bewitched, consumed, cursed, demented, enchanted, frenetic, frenzied, hag-ridden, haunted, maddened, obsessed, raving, under a spell

possession noun **1 = ownership,** control, custody, hold, occupancy, occupation, proprietorship, tenure, title **2 possessions = property,** assets, belongings, chattels, effects, estate, goods and chattels, things, wealth **3 = province,** colony, dominion, protectorate, territory

possessive adjective **= jealous,** acquisitive, controlling, covetous, dominating, domineering, grasping, overprotective, selfish

possibility noun **1 = feasibility,** likelihood, plausibility, potentiality, practicability, workableness **2 = likelihood,** chance, hazard, hope, liability, odds, probability, prospect, risk **3** often plural **= potential,** capabilities, potentiality, promise, prospects, talent

possible adjective **1 = conceivable,** credible, hypothetical, imaginable, likely, potential **2 = likely,** hopeful, potential, probable, promising **3 = feasible,** attainable, doable, on (informal), practicable, realizable, viable, within reach, workable

> ➤ **Antonyms**
> ≠**conceivable:** impossible, inconceivable, incredible, unimaginable, unlikely, unthinkable ≠**likely:** impossible, improbable ≠**feasible:** impossible, impracticable, unfeasible, unobtainable, unreasonable

possibly adverb 1 = **perhaps**, God willing, haply (archaic), maybe, mayhap (archaic), peradventure (archaic), perchance (archaic) 2 = **at all**, by any chance, by any means, in any way

post[1] noun 1 = **mail**, collection, delivery, postal service ♦ verb 2 = **send**, dispatch, mail, transmit 3 **keep someone posted** = **notify**, advise, brief, fill in on (informal), inform, report to

post[2] noun 1 = **support**, column, newel, pale, palisade, picket, pillar, pole, shaft, stake, standard, stock, upright ♦ verb 2 = **put up**, advertise, affix, announce, display, make known, pin up, proclaim, promulgate, publicize, publish, stick up

post[3] noun 1 = **job**, appointment, assignment, berth (informal), billet (informal), employment, office, place, position, situation 2 = **station**, beat, place, position ♦ verb 3 = **station**, assign, establish, locate, place, position, put, situate

poster noun = **notice**, advertisement, announcement, bill, placard, public notice, sticker

posterior adjective 1 = **behind**, after, back, hind, hinder, rear 2 = **later**, ensuing, following, latter, subsequent

posterity noun 1 = **future**, future generations, succeeding generations 2 = **descendants**, children, family, heirs, issue, offspring, progeny, scions, seed (chiefly biblical)

posthaste adverb = **speedily**, at once, before one can say Jack Robinson, directly, double-quick, hastily, hotfoot, pdq (slang), promptly, pronto (informal), quickly, straightaway, swiftly

postmortem noun = **examination**, analysis, autopsy, dissection, necropsy

postpone verb = **put off**, adjourn, defer, delay, hold over, put back, put on ice (informal), put on the back burner (informal), shelve, suspend, table, take a rain check on (U.S. & Canad. informal)
> ➤ **Antonyms**
> advance, bring forward, carry out, go ahead with

postponement noun = **delay**, adjournment, deferment, deferral, moratorium, respite, stay, suspension

postscript noun = **P.S.**, addition, afterthought, afterword, appendix, supplement

postulate verb Formal = **presuppose**, advance, assume, hypothesize, posit, predicate, propose, put forward, suppose, take for granted, theorize

posture noun 1 = **bearing**, attitude, carriage, disposition, mien (literary), pose, position, set, stance 2 = **attitude**, disposition, feeling, frame of mind, inclination, mood, outlook, point of view, stance, standpoint ♦ verb 3 = **show off** (informal), affect, attitudinize, do for effect, make a show, pose, put on airs, try to attract attention

posy noun = **bouquet**, boutonniere, buttonhole, corsage, nosegay, spray

pot noun 1 = **container**, bowl, pan, vessel 2 = **pool**, bank, jackpot, kitty, stakes 3 Informal = **trophy**, cup 4 **go to pot** = **decline**, deteriorate, go downhill (informal), go to rack and ruin, go to the dogs (informal), run to seed, slump, worsen ♦ verb 5 = **shoot**, hit, plug (informal), strike

potbelly noun = **paunch**, beer belly (informal), gut, middle-age spread (informal), pot, spare tyre (Brit. slang), spread (informal)

potency noun = **power**, authority, capacity, control, effectiveness, efficacy, energy, force, influence, might, muscle, potential, puissance, strength, sway, vigour

potent adjective 1 = **powerful**, authoritative, commanding, dominant, dynamic, influential 2 = **persuasive**, cogent, compelling, convincing, effective, forceful, impressive, telling 3 = **strong**, efficacious, forceful, mighty, powerful, puissant, vigorous
> ➤ **Antonyms**
> ≠**persuasive:** ineffective, unconvincing ≠**strong:** impotent, weak

potentate noun = **ruler**, emperor, king, mogul, monarch, overlord, prince, sovereign

potential adjective 1 = **possible**, budding, dormant, embryonic, future, hidden, inherent, latent, likely, promising, undeveloped, unrealized ♦ noun 2 = **ability**, aptitude, capability, capacity, possibility, potentiality, power, the makings, what it takes (informal), wherewithal

potentiality noun = **capacity**, ability, aptitude, capability, likelihood, potential, promise, prospect, the makings

pother noun Literary = **fuss**, bother, carry-on (informal, chiefly Brit.), commotion, disturbance, flap (informal), hoo-ha, stew (informal), tizzy (informal), to-do

potion noun = **concoction**, brew, cup, dose, draught, elixir, mixture, philtre, tonic

potpourri noun = **mixture**, collection, combination, hotchpotch, medley, mélange, miscellany, mixed bag (*informal*), pastiche, patchwork

potter *verb* = **mess about**, dabble, fiddle (*informal*), footle (*informal*), fribble, fritter, poke along, tinker

pottery *noun* = **ceramics**, earthenware, stoneware, terracotta

potty *adjective Brit. informal* **1** = **crazy**, barmy (*slang*), crackers (*Brit. slang*), crackpot (*informal*), daft (*informal*), dippy (*slang*), doolally (*slang*), dotty (*slang, chiefly Brit.*), eccentric, loopy (*informal*), oddball (*informal*), off one's chump (*slang*), off one's trolley (*slang*), off the rails, off-the-wall (*slang*), touched, up the pole (*informal*), wacko *or* whacko (*informal*) **2** = **trivial**, footling (*informal*), insignificant, petty, piddling (*informal*), trifling

pouch *noun* = **bag**, container, pocket, poke (*dialect*), purse, sack

pounce *verb* **1** = **spring**, ambush, attack, bound onto, dash at, drop, fall upon, jump, leap at, snatch, strike, swoop, take by surprise, take unawares ◆ *noun* **2** = **spring**, assault, attack, bound, jump, leap, swoop

pound[1] *verb* **1** = **beat**, batter, beat the living daylights out of, belabour, clobber (*slang*), hammer, pelt, pummel, strike, thrash, thump **2** = **crush**, bray (*dialect*), bruise, comminute, powder, pulverize, triturate **3** with out = **thump**, bang, beat, hammer **4** = **pulsate**, beat, palpitate, pitapat, pulse, throb **5** = **stomp** (*informal*), clomp, march, thunder, tramp

pound[2] *noun* = **enclosure**, compound, corral (*chiefly U.S. & Canad.*), pen, yard

pour *verb* **1** = **flow**, course, emit, gush, run, rush, spew, spout, stream **2** = **let flow**, decant, spill, splash **3** = **rain**, bucket down (*informal*), come down in torrents, pelt (down), rain cats and dogs (*informal*), rain hard *or* heavily, sheet, teem **4** = **stream**, crowd, swarm, teem, throng

pout *verb* **1** = **sulk**, glower, look petulant, look sullen, lour *or* lower, make a *moue*, mope, pull a long face, purse one's lips, turn down the corners of one's mouth ◆ *noun* **2** = **sullen look**, glower, long face, *moue*

poverty *noun* **1** = **pennilessness**, beggary, destitution, distress, hand-to-mouth existence, hardship, indigence, insolvency, necessitousness, necessity, need, pauperism, penury, privation, want **2** = **scarcity**, dearth, deficiency, insufficiency, lack, paucity, shortage
➤ **Antonyms**
≠**pennilessness:** affluence, comfort, luxury, opulence, richness, wealth ≠**scarcity:** abundance, plethora, sufficiency

poverty-stricken *adjective* = **penniless**, bankrupt, beggared, broke (*informal*), destitute, dirt-poor (*informal*), distressed, down and out, down at heel, flat broke (*informal*), impecunious, impoverished, indigent, in queer street, needy, on one's beam-ends, on one's uppers, on the breadline, penurious, poor, short, skint (*Brit. slang*), stony-broke (*Brit. slang*), without two pennies to rub together (*informal*)

powder *noun* **1** = **dust**, fine grains, loose particles, pounce, talc ◆ *verb* **2** = **dust**, cover, dredge, scatter, sprinkle, strew

powdery *adjective* = **fine**, chalky, crumbling, crumbly, dry, dusty, friable, grainy, granular, loose, pulverized, sandy

power *noun* **1** = **ability**, capability, capacity, competence, competency, faculty, potential **2** = **control**, ascendancy, authority, bottom, command, dominance, domination, dominion, influence, mastery, rule, sovereignty, supremacy, sway **3** = **authority**, authorization, licence, prerogative, privilege, right, warrant **4** = **strength**, brawn, energy, force, forcefulness, intensity, might, muscle, potency, vigour, weight
➤ **Antonyms**
≠**ability:** inability, incapability, incapacity, incompetence ≠**strength:** enervation, feebleness, impotence, listlessness, weakness

powerful *adjective* **1** = **controlling**, authoritative, commanding, dominant, influential, prevailing, puissant, sovereign, supreme **2** = **strong**, energetic, mighty, potent, robust, stalwart, strapping, sturdy, vigorous **3** = **persuasive**, cogent, compelling, convincing, effective, effectual, forceful, forcible, impressive, storming, striking, telling, weighty

powerfully *adverb* = **strongly**, forcefully, forcibly, hard, mightily, vigorously, with might and main

powerless *adjective* **1** = **defenceless**, dependent, disenfranchised, disfranchised, ineffective, over a barrel (*informal*), subject, tied, unarmed, vulnerable **2** = **weak**, debilitated, disabled, etiolated, feeble, frail, helpless, impotent, incapable, incapacitated, ineffectual, infirm, paralysed, prostrate
➤ **Antonyms**
≠**weak:** able-bodied, fit, healthy, lusty, powerful, robust, strong, sturdy

powwow *noun* **1** = **meeting**, confab (*informal*), confabulation, conference, congress, consultation, council, discussion, get-together (*informal*), talk ◆ *verb* **2** = **meet**, confer, discuss, get together, talk

practicability *noun* = **feasibility**, advantage, operability, possibility, practicality, use, usefulness, value, viability, workability

practicable *adjective* = feasible, achievable, attainable, doable, performable, possible, viable, within the realm of possibility, workable
➤ Antonyms
beyond the bounds of possibility, impossible, out of the question, unachievable, unattainable, unfeasible, unworkable

practical *adjective* 1 = functional, applied, efficient, empirical, experimental, factual, pragmatic, realistic, utilitarian 2 = sensible, businesslike, down-to-earth, everyday, hard-headed, matter-of-fact, mundane, ordinary, realistic, workaday 3 = feasible, doable, practicable, serviceable, sound, useful, workable 4 = skilled, accomplished, efficient, experienced, proficient, qualified, seasoned, trained, veteran, working
➤ Antonyms
≠functional: impracticable, impractical, inefficient, speculative, theoretical, unpractical, unrealistic ≠sensible: impractical, unpractical, unrealistic ≠feasible: impossible, impractical, unpractical, unsound, unworkable, useless ≠skilled: inefficient, inexperienced, unaccomplished, unqualified, unskilled, untrained

practically *adverb* 1 = almost, all but, basically, close to, essentially, fundamentally, in effect, just about, nearly, to all intents and purposes, very nearly, virtually, well-nigh 2 = sensibly, clearly, matter-of-factly, rationally, realistically, reasonably, unsentimentally, with common sense

practice *noun* 1 = custom, habit, method, mode, praxis, routine, rule, system, tradition, usage, use, usual procedure, way, wont 2 = rehearsal, discipline, drill, exercise, preparation, repetition, study, training, work-out 3 = profession, business, career, vocation, work 4 = use, action, application, effect, exercise, experience, operation

practise *verb* 1 = rehearse, discipline, drill, exercise, go over, go through, keep one's hand in, polish, prepare, repeat, study, train, warm up, work out 2 = do, apply, carry out, follow, live up to, observe, perform, put into practice 3 = work at, carry on, engage in, ply, pursue, specialize in, undertake

practised *adjective* = skilled, able, accomplished, experienced, expert, proficient, qualified, seasoned, trained, versed
➤ Antonyms
amateurish, bungling, incompetent, inexperienced, inexpert, unqualified, unskilled, untrained

pragmatic *adjective* = practical, businesslike, down-to-earth, efficient, hard-headed, matter-of-fact, realistic, sensible, utilitarian

➤ Antonyms
airy-fairy, idealistic, impractical, inefficient, starry-eyed, stupid, theoretical, unprofessional, unrealistic

praise *verb* 1 = approve, acclaim, admire, applaud, cheer, compliment, congratulate, crack up (*informal*), cry up, eulogize, extol, honour, laud, pat on the back, pay tribute to, sing the praises of, take one's hat off to 2 = give thanks to, adore, bless, exalt, glorify, magnify (*archaic*), pay homage to, worship ♦ *noun* 3 = approval, acclaim, acclamation, accolade, applause, approbation, cheering, commendation, compliment, congratulation, encomium, eulogy, good word, kudos, laudation, ovation, panegyric, plaudit, tribute 4 = thanks, adoration, devotion, glory, homage, worship

praiseworthy *adjective* = creditable, admirable, commendable, estimable, excellent, exemplary, fine, honourable, laudable, meritorious, worthy
➤ Antonyms
condemnable, deplorable, despicable, discreditable, disgraceful, dishonourable, ignoble, reprehensible

prance *verb* 1 = dance, bound, caper, cavort, cut a rug (*informal*), frisk, gambol, jump, leap, romp, skip, spring, trip 2 = strut, parade, show off (*informal*), stalk, swagger, swank (*informal*)

prank *noun* = trick, antic, caper, escapade, frolic, jape, lark (*informal*), practical joke, skylarking (*informal*)

prate *verb* = chatter, babble, blather, blether, go on, jaw (*slang*), rabbit (on) (*Brit. informal*), waffle (*informal, chiefly Brit.*), witter on (*informal*), yak (*slang*)

prattle *verb* = chatter, babble, blather, blether, drivel, gabble, jabber, rabbit (on) (*Brit. informal*), rattle on, run on, waffle (*informal, chiefly Brit.*), witter (*informal*)

pray *verb* 1 = say one's prayers, offer a prayer, recite the rosary 2 = beg, adjure, ask, beseech, call upon, crave, cry for, entreat, implore, importune, invoke, petition, plead, request, solicit, sue, supplicate, urge

prayer *noun* 1 = orison, communion, devotion, invocation, litany, supplication 2 = plea, appeal, entreaty, petition, request, suit, supplication

preach *verb* 1 = deliver a sermon, address, evangelize, exhort, orate 2 = lecture, admonish, advocate, exhort, harangue, moralize, sermonize, urge

preacher *noun* = clergyman, evangelist, minister, missionary, parson, revivalist

preamble *noun* = introduction, exordium, foreword, opening move, opening statement *or* remarks, overture, preface, prelude, proem, prolegomenon

precarious *adjective* = **dangerous**, built on sand, chancy (*informal*), dicey (*informal*, chiefly *Brit.*), dodgy (*Brit., Austral., & N.Z. informal*), doubtful, dubious, hairy (*slang*), hazardous, insecure, perilous, risky, shaky, slippery, touch and go, tricky, uncertain, unreliable, unsafe, unsettled, unstable, unsteady, unsure
➤ **Antonyms**
certain, dependable, reliable, safe, secure, stable, steady

precaution *noun* 1 = **safeguard**, belt and braces (*informal*), insurance, preventative measure, protection, provision, safety measure 2 = **forethought**, anticipation, care, caution, circumspection, foresight, providence, prudence, wariness

precede *verb* = **go before**, antecede, antedate, come first, forerun, go ahead of, head, herald, introduce, lead, pave the way, preface, take precedence, usher

precedence *noun* = **priority**, antecedence, lead, pre-eminence, preference, primacy, rank, seniority, superiority, supremacy

precedent *noun* = **instance**, antecedent, authority, criterion, example, exemplar, model, paradigm, pattern, previous example, prototype, standard

preceding *adjective* = **previous**, above, aforementioned, aforesaid, anterior, earlier, foregoing, former, past, prior

precept *noun* 1 = **rule**, behest, canon, command, commandment, decree, dictum, direction, instruction, law, mandate, order, ordinance, principle, regulation, statute 2 = **maxim**, axiom, byword, dictum, guideline, motto, principle, rule, saying

precinct *noun* 1 = **enclosure**, bound, boundary, confine, limit 2 = **area**, district, quarter, section, sector, zone

precincts *plural noun* = **district**, borders, bounds, confines, environs, limits, milieu, neighbourhood, purlieus, region, surrounding area

precious *adjective* 1 = **valuable**, choice, costly, dear, expensive, exquisite, fine, high-priced, inestimable, invaluable, priceless, prized, rare, recherché 2 = **loved**, adored, beloved, cherished, darling, dear, dearest, fave (*informal*), favourite, idolized, prized, treasured, valued, worth one's *or* its weight in gold 3 = **affected**, alembicated, artificial, chichi, fastidious, overnice, overrefined, twee (*Brit. informal*)

precipice *noun* = **cliff**, bluff, brink, cliff face, crag, height, rock face, sheer drop, steep

precipitate *verb* 1 = **quicken**, accelerate, advance, bring on, dispatch, expedite, further, hasten, hurry, press, push forward,

speed up, trigger 2 = **throw**, cast, discharge, fling, hurl, launch, let fly, send forth ◆ *adjective* 3 = **hasty**, frantic, harum-scarum, heedless, hurried, ill-advised, impetuous, impulsive, indiscreet, madcap, precipitous, rash, reckless 4 = **swift**, breakneck, headlong, plunging, rapid, rushing, violent 5 = **sudden**, abrupt, brief, quick, unexpected, without warning

precipitous *adjective* 1 = **sheer**, abrupt, dizzy, falling sharply, high, perpendicular, steep 2 = **hasty**, abrupt, careless, harum-scarum, heedless, hurried, ill-advised, precipitate, rash, reckless, sudden

précis *noun* 1 = **summary**, abridgment, abstract, aperçu, compendium, condensation, digest, outline, résumé, rundown, sketch, synopsis ◆ *verb* 2 = **summarize**, abridge, abstract, compress, condense, outline, shorten, sum up

precise *adjective* 1 = **exact**, absolute, accurate, actual, clear-cut, correct, definite, explicit, express, fixed, literal, particular, specific, strict, unequivocal 2 = **strict**, careful, ceremonious, exact, fastidious, finicky, formal, inflexible, meticulous, nice, particular, prim, punctilious, puritanical, rigid, scrupulous, stiff
➤ **Antonyms**
≠**exact:** ambiguous, equivocal, incorrect, indefinite, indistinct, inexact, loose, vague ≠**strict:** careless, flexible, haphazard, inexact, informal, relaxed, unceremonious

precisely *adverb* = **exactly**, absolutely, accurately, bang, correctly, just, just so, literally, neither more nor less, on the button (*informal*), plumb (*informal*), slap (*informal*), smack (*informal*), square, squarely, strictly, to the letter

precision *noun* = **exactness**, accuracy, care, correctness, definiteness, dotting the i's and crossing the t's, exactitude, fidelity, meticulousness, nicety, particularity, preciseness, rigour

preclude *verb* = **prevent**, check, debar, exclude, forestall, hinder, inhibit, make impossible, make impracticable, obviate, prohibit, put a stop to, restrain, rule out, stop

precocious *adjective* = **advanced**, ahead, bright, developed, forward, quick, smart
➤ **Antonyms**
backward, dense, dull, retarded, slow, underdeveloped

preconceived *adjective* = **presumed**, forejudged, prejudged, presupposed

preconception *noun* = **preconceived idea** *or* **notion**, bias, notion, predisposition, prejudice, prepossession, presumption, presupposition

precondition *noun* = **necessity**, essential,

must, prerequisite, requirement, *sine qua non*

precursor *noun* 1 = **herald**, forerunner, harbinger, messenger, usher, vanguard 2 = **forerunner**, antecedent, forebear, originator, pioneer, predecessor

predatory *adjective* 1 = **hunting**, carnivorous, predacious, rapacious, raptorial, ravening 2 = **rapacious**, despoiling, greedy, marauding, pillaging, plundering, ravaging, thieving, voracious

predecessor *noun* 1 = **previous job holder**, antecedent, forerunner, former job holder, precursor, prior job holder 2 = **ancestor**, antecedent, forebear, forefather

predestination *noun* = **fate**, destiny, doom, election (*Theology*), foreordainment, foreordination, lot, necessity, predetermination

predestined *adjective* = **fated**, doomed, foreordained, meant, predestinated, predetermined, pre-elected, preordained

predetermined *adjective* = **prearranged**, agreed, arranged in advance, cut and dried (*informal*), decided beforehand, fixed, preplanned, set, settled, set up

predicament *noun* = **fix** (*informal*), corner, dilemma, emergency, hole (*slang*), hot water (*informal*), how-do-you-do (*informal*), jam (*informal*), mess, pickle (*informal*), pinch, plight, quandary, scrape (*informal*), situation, spot (*informal*), state, tight spot

predicate *verb* 1 *with* **on** *or* **upon** = **base**, build, establish, found, ground, postulate, rest 2 = **declare**, affirm, assert, aver, avouch, avow, contend, maintain, proclaim, state

predict *verb* = **foretell**, augur, call, divine, forebode, forecast, foresee, portend, presage, prognosticate, prophesy, soothsay, vaticinate (*rare*)

predictable *adjective* = **likely**, anticipated, calculable, certain, expected, foreseeable, foreseen, on the cards, reliable, sure, sure-fire (*informal*)
➤ **Antonyms**
out of the blue, surprising, unexpected, unforeseen, unlikely, unpredictable

prediction *noun* = **prophecy**, augury, divination, forecast, prognosis, prognostication, soothsaying, sortilege

predilection *noun* = **liking**, bag (*slang*), bias, cup of tea (*informal*), fancy, fondness, inclination, leaning, love, partiality, penchant, predisposition, preference, proclivity, proneness, propensity, taste, tendency, weakness

predispose *verb* = **incline**, affect, bias, dispose, induce, influence, lead, make (one)

of a mind to, prejudice, prepare, prime, prompt, sway

predisposed *adjective* = **inclined**, agreeable, amenable, given, liable, minded, prone, ready, subject, susceptible, willing

predisposition *noun* = **inclination**, bent, bias, disposition, likelihood, penchant, potentiality, predilection, proclivity, proneness, propensity, susceptibility, tendency, willingness

predominance *noun* = **prevalence**, ascendancy, control, dominance, dominion, edge, greater number, hold, leadership, mastery, paramountcy, preponderance, supremacy, sway, upper hand, weight

predominant *adjective* = **main**, ascendant, capital, chief, controlling, dominant, important, leading, notable, paramount, preponderant, prevailing, prevalent, primary, prime, principal, prominent, ruling, sovereign, superior, supreme, top-priority
➤ **Antonyms**
inferior, minor, secondary, subordinate, unimportant, uninfluential

predominantly *adverb* = **mainly**, chiefly, for the most part, generally, largely, mostly, primarily, principally

predominate *verb* = **prevail**, be most noticeable, carry weight, get the upper hand, hold sway, outweigh, overrule, overshadow, preponderate, reign, rule, tell

pre-eminence *noun* = **superiority**, distinction, excellence, paramountcy, predominance, prestige, prominence, renown, supremacy, transcendence

pre-eminent *adjective* = **outstanding**, chief, consummate, distinguished, excellent, foremost, incomparable, matchless, paramount, peerless, predominant, renowned, superior, supreme, transcendent, unequalled, unrivalled, unsurpassed

pre-empt *verb* = **anticipate**, acquire, appropriate, arrogate, assume, seize, take over, usurp

preen *verb* 1 *Of birds* = **clean**, plume 2 = **smarten**, array, deck out, doll up (*slang*), dress up, prettify, primp, prink, spruce up, titivate, trig (*archaic or dialect*), trim 3 **preen oneself (on)** = **pride oneself**, congratulate oneself, pique oneself, plume oneself

preface *noun* 1 = **introduction**, exordium, foreword, preamble, preliminary, prelude, proem, prolegomenon, prologue ◆ *verb* 2 = **introduce**, begin, launch, lead up to, open, precede, prefix

prefatory *adjective* = **introductory**, antecedent, opening, precursory, preliminary, preparatory

prefer *verb* **1** = **like better**, adopt, be partial to, choose, desire, elect, fancy, favour, go for, incline towards, opt for, pick, plump for, select, single out, wish, would rather, would sooner **2** *Law* = **put forward**, file, lodge, place, present, press **3** = **promote**, advance, aggrandize, elevate, move up, raise, upgrade

preferable *adjective* = **better**, best, choice, chosen, favoured, more desirable, more eligible, superior, worthier
➤ **Antonyms**
average, fair, ineligible, inferior, mediocre, poor, second-rate, undesirable

preferably *adverb* = **rather**, as a matter of choice, by choice, first, in or for preference, much rather, much sooner, sooner, willingly

preference *noun* **1** = **first choice**, bag (*slang*), choice, cup of tea (*informal*), desire, election, fave (*informal*), favourite, option, partiality, pick, predilection, selection, top of the list **2** = **priority**, advantage, favoured treatment, favouritism, first place, precedence, pride of place

preferential *adjective* = **privileged**, advantageous, better, favoured, partial, partisan, special, superior

preferment *noun* = **promotion**, advancement, dignity, elevation, exaltation, rise, upgrading

prefigure *verb* **1** = **foreshadow**, foretoken, indicate, intimate, portend, presage, suggest **2** = **imagine**, consider, fancy, picture, presuppose

pregnancy *noun* = **gestation**

pregnant *adjective* **1** = **expectant**, big *or* heavy with child, enceinte, expecting (*informal*), gravid, in the club (*Brit. slang*), in the family way (*informal*), in the pudding club (*slang*), preggers (*Brit. informal*), with child **2** = **meaningful**, charged, eloquent, expressive, loaded, pointed, significant, suggestive, telling, weighty

prehistoric *adjective* = **earliest**, early, primeval, primitive, primordial

prejudge *verb* = **jump to conclusions**, anticipate, forejudge, make a hasty assessment, presume, presuppose

prejudice *noun* **1** = **bias**, jaundiced eye, partiality, preconceived notion, preconception, prejudgment, warp **2** = **discrimination**, bigotry, chauvinism, injustice, intolerance, narrow-mindedness, racism, sexism, unfairness **3** = **harm**, damage, detriment, disadvantage, hurt, impairment, loss, mischief ◆ *verb* **4** = **bias**, colour, distort, influence, jaundice, poison, predispose, prepossess, slant, sway, warp **5** = **harm**, damage, hinder, hurt, impair, injure, mar, spoil, undermine

prejudiced *adjective* = **biased**, bigoted, conditioned, discriminatory, influenced, intolerant, jaundiced, narrow-minded, one-sided, opinionated, partial, partisan, prepossessed, unfair
➤ **Antonyms**
fair, impartial, just, neutral, not bigoted, not prejudiced, open-minded, unbiased

prejudicial *adjective* = **harmful**, counterproductive, damaging, deleterious, detrimental, disadvantageous, hurtful, inimical, injurious, undermining, unfavourable

preliminary *adjective* **1** = **first**, exploratory, initial, initiatory, introductory, opening, pilot, precursory, prefatory, preparatory, prior, qualifying, test, trial ◆ *noun* **2** = **introduction**, beginning, first round, foundation, groundwork, initiation, opening, overture, preamble, preface, prelims, prelude, preparation, start

prelude *noun* = **introduction**, beginning, commencement, curtain-raiser, exordium, foreword, intro (*informal*), overture, preamble, preface, preliminary, preparation, proem, prolegomenon, prologue, start

premature *adjective* **1** = **early**, forward, unseasonable, untimely **2** = **hasty**, ill-considered, ill-timed, impulsive, inopportune, jumping the gun, overhasty, precipitate, previous (*informal*), rash, too soon, untimely **3** = **immature**, abortive, embryonic, incomplete, predeveloped, undeveloped, unfledged

prematurely *adverb* **1** = **too early**, before one's time, too soon, untimely **2** = **overhastily**, at half-cock, half-cocked, precipitately, rashly, too hastily, too soon

premeditated *adjective* = **planned**, aforethought, calculated, conscious, considered, contrived, deliberate, intended, intentional, prepense, studied, wilful
➤ **Antonyms**
accidental, inadvertent, unintentional, unplanned, unpremeditated, unwitting

premeditation *noun* = **planning**, deliberation, design, determination, forethought, intention, malice aforethought, plotting, prearrangement, predetermination, purpose

premier *noun* **1** = **head of government**, chancellor, chief minister, P.M., prime minister ◆ *adjective* **2** = **chief**, arch, first, foremost, head, highest, leading, main, primary, prime, principal, top **3** = **first**, earliest, inaugural, initial, original

premiere *noun* = **first night**, debut, first performance, first showing, opening

premise *noun* = **assumption**, argument, assertion, ground, hypothesis, postulate, postulation, presupposition, proposition, supposition, thesis

premises *plural noun* = **building**, establishment, place, property, site

premium *noun* **1** = **bonus**, boon, bounty, fee, percentage (*informal*), perk (*Brit. informal*), perquisite, prize, recompense, remuneration, reward **2** = **regard**, appreciation, stock, store, value **3 at a premium** = **in great demand**, beyond one's means, costly, expensive, hard to come by, in short supply, like gold dust, not to be had for love or money, rare, scarce, valuable

premonition *noun* = **feeling**, apprehension, feeling in one's bones, foreboding, forewarning, funny feeling (*informal*), hunch, idea, intuition, misgiving, omen, portent, presage, presentiment, sign, suspicion, warning

preoccupation *noun* **1** = **obsession**, bee in one's bonnet, concern, fixation, hang-up (*informal*), hobbyhorse, *idée fixe*, pet subject **2** = **absorption**, absence of mind, absent-mindedness, abstraction, brown study, daydreaming, engrossment, immersion, inattentiveness, musing, oblivion, pensiveness, prepossession, reverie, woolgathering

preoccupied *adjective* = **absorbed**, absent-minded, abstracted, caught up in, distracted, distrait, engrossed, faraway, heedless, immersed, in a brown study, intent, lost in, lost in thought, oblivious, rapt, taken up, unaware, wrapped up

preordained *adjective* = **predetermined**, destined, doomed, fated, mapped out in advance, predestined

preparation *noun* **1** = **groundwork**, development, getting ready, preparing, putting in order **2** = **readiness**, alertness, anticipation, expectation, foresight, precaution, preparedness, provision, safeguard **3** *often plural* = **arrangement**, measure, plan, provision **4** = **mixture**, composition, compound, concoction, medicine, tincture **5** *Old-fashioned* = **homework**, prep (*informal*), revision, schoolwork, study, swotting (*Brit. informal*)

preparatory *adjective* **1** = **introductory**, basic, elementary, opening, prefatory, preliminary, preparative, primary **2 preparatory to** = **before**, in advance of, in anticipation of, in preparation for, prior to

prepare *verb* **1** = **make** *or* **get ready**, adapt, adjust, anticipate, arrange, coach, dispose, form, groom, make provision, plan, practise, prime, put in order, train, warm up **2** = **put together**, assemble, concoct, construct, contrive, draw up, fashion, fix up, get up (*informal*), make, produce, turn out **3** = **equip**, accoutre, fit, fit out, furnish, outfit, provide, supply

prepared *adjective* **1** = **ready**, all set, all systems go (*informal*), arranged, fit, in order, in readiness, planned, primed, set **2** = **willing**, able, disposed, inclined, minded, of a mind, predisposed

preponderance *noun* = **predominance**, ascendancy, bulk, dominance, domination, dominion, extensiveness, greater numbers, greater part, lion's share, mass, power, prevalence, superiority, supremacy, sway, weight

preponderant *adjective* = **prevalent**, ascendant, dominant, extensive, foremost, greater, important, larger, paramount, predominant, prevailing, significant

preponderate *verb* = **predominate**, dominate, hold sway, outnumber, prevail, reign supreme, rule

prepossessing *adjective* = **attractive**, alluring, amiable, appealing, beautiful, bewitching, captivating, charming, engaging, fair, fascinating, fetching, glamorous, good-looking, handsome, inviting, likable *or* likeable, lovable, magnetic, pleasing, striking, taking, winning ➤ **Antonyms** disagreeable, displeasing, objectionable, offensive, repulsive, ugly, unattractive, uninviting, unlikable *or* unlikeable

prepossession *noun* **1** = **partiality**, bias, inclination, liking, predilection, predisposition, prejudice **2** = **preoccupation**, absorption, engrossment

preposterous *adjective* = **ridiculous**, absurd, asinine, bizarre, crazy, excessive, exorbitant, extravagant, extreme, foolish, impossible, incredible, insane, irrational, laughable, ludicrous, monstrous, nonsensical, out of the question, outrageous, risible, senseless, shocking, unreasonable, unthinkable

prerequisite *noun* **1** = **requirement**, condition, essential, imperative, must, necessity, precondition, qualification, requisite, *sine qua non* ♦ *adjective* **2** = **required**, called for, essential, imperative, indispensable, mandatory, necessary, needful, obligatory, of the essence, requisite, vital

prerogative *noun* = **right**, advantage, authority, birthright, choice, claim, due, exemption, immunity, liberty, perquisite, privilege, sanction, title

presage *verb* **1** = **portend**, augur, betoken, bode, foreshadow, foretoken, signify ♦ *noun* **2** = **omen**, augury, auspice, forecast, forewarning, harbinger, intimation, portent, prediction, prognostication, prophecy, sign, warning **3** = **misgiving**, apprehension, feeling, foreboding, forewarning, intuition, premonition, presentiment

prescience *noun Formal* = **foresight**, clairvoyance, foreknowledge, precognition, second sight

prescient *adjective* = **foresighted**, clairvoyant, discerning, divinatory, divining, far-sighted, perceptive, prophetic, psychic

prescribe *verb* = **order**, appoint, assign, command, decree, define, dictate, direct, enjoin, establish, fix, impose, lay down, ordain, recommend, require, rule, set, specify, stipulate

prescript *noun* = **rule**, canon, command, dictate, dictum, direction, directive, edict, instruction, law, mandate, order, ordinance, precept, regulation, requirement

prescription *noun* **1** = **instruction**, direction, formula, recipe **2** = **medicine**, drug, mixture, preparation, remedy

prescriptive *adjective* = **dictatorial**, authoritarian, didactic, dogmatic, legislating, preceptive, rigid

presence *noun* **1** = **being**, attendance, companionship, company, existence, habitation, inhabitance, occupancy, residence **2** = **personality**, air, appearance, aspect, aura, bearing, carriage, comportment, demeanour, ease, mien (*literary*), poise, self-assurance **3** = **proximity**, closeness, immediate circle, nearness, neighbourhood, propinquity, vicinity **4** = **spirit**, apparition, eidolon, ghost, manifestation, revenant, shade (*literary*), spectre, supernatural being, wraith

presence of mind *noun* = **level-headedness**, alertness, aplomb, calmness, composure, cool (*slang*), coolness, imperturbability, phlegm, quickness, sang-froid, self-assurance, self-command, self-possession, wits

present[1] *adjective* **1** = **here**, accounted for, at hand, available, in attendance, near, nearby, ready, there, to hand **2** = **current**, contemporary, existent, existing, extant, immediate, instant, present-day ♦ *noun* **3** **the present** = **now**, here and now, the present moment, the time being, this day and age, today **4 at present** = **just now**, at the moment, now, nowadays, right now **5 for the present** = **for now**, for a while, for the moment, for the nonce, for the time being, in the meantime, not for long, provisionally, temporarily

present[2] *noun* **1** = **gift**, benefaction, bonsela (*S. African*), boon, bounty, donation, endowment, favour, grant, gratuity, hand-out, largesse *or* largess, offering, prezzie (*informal*) ♦ *verb* **2** = **introduce**, acquaint with, make known **3** = **put on**, demonstrate, display, exhibit,

give, mount, put before the public, show, stage **4** = **give**, award, bestow, confer, donate, entrust, furnish, grant, hand out, hand over, offer, proffer, put at (someone's) disposal **5** = **put forward**, adduce, advance, declare, expound, extend, hold out, introduce, offer, pose, produce, proffer, raise, recount, relate, state, submit, suggest, tender

presentable *adjective* = **decent**, acceptable, becoming, fit to be seen, good enough, not bad (*informal*), O.K. *or* okay (*informal*), passable, proper, respectable, satisfactory, suitable, tolerable
➤ **Antonyms**
below par, not good enough, not up to scratch, poor, rubbishy, unacceptable, unpresentable, unsatisfactory

presentation *noun* **1** = **giving**, award, bestowal, conferral, donation, investiture, offering **2** = **performance**, demonstration, display, exhibition, production, representation, show **3** = **portrayal**, appearance, arrangement, delivery, exposition, production, rendition, staging, submission

present-day *adjective* = **current**, contemporary, latter-day, modern, newfangled, present, recent, up-to-date

presentiment *noun* = **premonition**, anticipation, apprehension, expectation, fear, feeling, foreboding, forecast, forethought, hunch, intuition, misgiving, presage

presently *adverb* = **soon**, anon (*archaic*), before long, by and by, erelong (*archaic or poetic*), in a minute, in a moment, in a short while, pretty soon (*informal*), shortly

preservation *noun* = **protection**, conservation, defence, keeping, maintenance, perpetuation, safeguarding, safekeeping, safety, salvation, security, storage, support, upholding

preserve *verb* **1** = **protect**, care for, conserve, defend, guard, keep, safeguard, save, secure, shelter, shield **2** = **maintain**, continue, keep, keep up, perpetuate, retain, sustain, uphold **3** = **keep**, conserve, put up, save, store ♦ *noun* **4** = **area**, domain, field, realm, specialism, sphere **5** *often plural* = **jam**, confection, confiture, conserve, jelly, marmalade, sweetmeat **6** = **reserve**, game reserve, reservation, sanctuary
➤ **Antonyms**
verb ≠**protect**: assail, assault, attack, leave unprotected ≠**maintain**: abandon, discontinue, drop, end, give up ≠**keep**: blow (*slang*), consume, fritter away, spend, squander, waste

preside *verb* = **run**, administer, be at the head of, be in authority, chair, conduct, control, direct, govern, head, lead, manage, officiate, supervise

press *verb* 1 = **compress**, bear down on, condense, crush, depress, force down, jam, mash, push, reduce, squeeze, stuff 2 = **hug**, clasp, crush, embrace, encircle, enfold, fold in one's arms, hold close, squeeze 3 = **smooth**, calender, finish, flatten, iron, mangle, put the creases in, steam 4 = **urge**, beg, entreat, exhort, implore, importune, petition, plead, pressurize, sue, supplicate 5 = **force**, compel, constrain, demand, enforce, enjoin, insist on 6 = **crowd**, cluster, flock, gather, hasten, herd, hurry, mill, push, rush, seethe, surge, swarm, throng 7 **be pressed** = **be hard put**, be hurried, be pushed, be rushed (*informal*), be short of ♦ *noun* 8 **the press: a** = **newspapers**, Fleet Street, fourth estate, journalism, news media, the papers **b** = **journalists**, columnists, correspondents, gentlemen of the press, journos (*slang*), newsmen, photographers, pressmen, reporters 9 = **crowd**, bunch, crush, flock, herd, horde, host, mob, multitude, pack, push (*informal*), swarm, throng

pressing *adjective* = **urgent**, burning, constraining, crucial, exigent, high-priority, imperative, important, importunate, now or never, serious, vital
➤ **Antonyms**
regular, routine, unimportant, unnecessary

pressure *noun* 1 = **force**, compressing, compression, crushing, heaviness, squeezing, weight 2 = **power**, coercion, compulsion, constraint, force, influence, obligation, sway 3 = **stress**, adversity, affliction, burden, demands, difficulty, distress, exigency, hassle (*informal*), heat, hurry, load, press, strain, urgency

pressurize *verb* 1 = **compress**, condense, constrict, press, squash, squeeze 2 = **force**, breathe down someone's neck, browbeat, coerce, compel, dragoon, drive, intimidate, press-gang, put the screws on (*slang*), turn on the heat (*informal*), twist one's arm (*informal*)

prestige *noun* = **status**, authority, bottom, Brownie points, cachet, celebrity, credit, distinction, eminence, esteem, fame, honour, importance, influence, kudos, regard, renown, reputation, standing, stature, weight

prestigious *adjective* = **celebrated**, eminent, esteemed, exalted, great, illustrious, important, imposing, impressive, influential, notable, prominent, renowned, reputable, respected
➤ **Antonyms**
humble, lowly, minor, obscure, unimportant, unimpressive, unknown

presumably *adverb* = **it would seem**, apparently, doubtless, doubtlessly, in all likelihood, in all probability, likely, most likely, on the face of it, probably, seemingly

presume *verb* 1 = **believe**, assume, conjecture, guess (*informal, chiefly U.S. & Canad.*), infer, posit, postulate, presuppose, suppose, surmise, take for granted, take it, think 2 = **dare**, go so far, have the audacity, make bold, make so bold, take the liberty, undertake, venture 3 = **depend**, bank on, count on, rely, trust

presumption *noun* 1 = **cheek** (*informal*), assurance, audacity, boldness, brass (*informal*), brass neck (*Brit. informal*), chutzpah (*U.S. & Canad. informal*), effrontery, forwardness, front, gall (*informal*), impudence, insolence, neck (*informal*), nerve (*informal*), presumptuousness, sassiness (*U.S. informal*), temerity 2 = **probability**, basis, chance, grounds, likelihood, plausibility, reason 3 = **assumption**, anticipation, belief, conjecture, guess, hypothesis, opinion, premiss, presupposition, supposition, surmise

presumptive *adjective* = **assumed**, believed, expected, hypothetical, inferred, supposed, understood

presumptuous *adjective* = **pushy** (*informal*), arrogant, audacious, bigheaded (*informal*), bold, conceited, foolhardy, forward, insolent, overconfident, overfamiliar, overweening, presuming, rash, too big for one's boots, uppish (*Brit. informal*)
➤ **Antonyms**
bashful, humble, modest, retiring, shy, timid, unassuming

presuppose *verb* = **presume**, accept, assume, consider, imply, posit, postulate, suppose, take as read, take for granted, take it

presupposition *noun* = **assumption**, belief, hypothesis, preconceived idea, preconception, premise, presumption, supposition, theory

pretence *noun* 1 = **deception**, acting, charade, deceit, fabrication, fakery, faking, falsehood, feigning, invention, make-believe, sham, simulation, subterfuge, trickery 2 = **show**, affectation, appearance, artifice, display, façade, hokum (*slang, chiefly U.S. & Canad.*), posing, posturing, pretentiousness, veneer 3 = **pretext**, claim, cloak, colour, cover, excuse, façade, garb, guise, mask, masquerade, ruse, semblance, show, veil, wile
➤ **Antonyms**
≠**deception**: candour, frankness, honesty, ingenuousness, openness ≠**show**: actuality, fact, reality

pretend verb 1 = **feign**, affect, allege, assume, counterfeit, dissemble, dissimulate, fake, falsify, impersonate, make out, pass oneself off as, profess, put on, sham, simulate 2 = **make believe**, act, imagine, make up, play, play the part of, suppose 3 = **lay claim**, allege, aspire, claim, profess, purport

pretended adjective = **feigned**, alleged, avowed, bogus, counterfeit, fake, false, fictitious, imaginary, ostensible, phoney or phony (informal), pretend (informal), professed, pseudo (informal), purported, sham, so-called, spurious

pretender noun = **claimant**, aspirant, claimer

pretension noun 1 = **claim**, aspiration, assertion, assumption, demand, pretence, profession 2 = **affectation**, airs, conceit, hypocrisy, ostentation, pomposity, pretentiousness, self-importance, show, showiness, snobbery, snobbishness, vainglory, vanity

pretentious adjective = **affected**, arty-farty (informal), assuming, bombastic, conceited, exaggerated, extravagant, flaunting, grandiloquent, grandiose, highfalutin (informal), high-flown, high-sounding, hollow, inflated, magniloquent, mannered, ostentatious, overambitious, pompous, puffed up, showy, snobbish, specious, vainglorious
➤ **Antonyms**
modest, natural, plain, simple, unaffected, unassuming, unpretentious

pretext noun = **guise**, affectation, alleged reason, appearance, cloak, cover, device, excuse, mask, ploy, pretence, red herring, ruse, semblance, show, simulation, veil

prettify verb = **adorn**, deck out, decorate, doll up (slang), do up, embellish, garnish, gild, ornament, tart up (Brit. slang), titivate, trick out, trim

pretty adjective 1 = **attractive**, appealing, beautiful, bonny, charming, comely, cute, fair, good-looking, graceful, lovely, personable 2 = **pleasant**, bijou, dainty, delicate, elegant, fine, neat, nice, pleasing, tasteful, trim ♦ adverb 3 Informal = **fairly**, kind of (informal), moderately, quite, rather, reasonably, somewhat
➤ **Antonyms**
adjective ≠ **attractive**: plain, ugly, unattractive, unshapely, unsightly

prevail verb 1 = **win**, be victorious, carry the day, gain mastery, overcome, overrule, prove superior, succeed, triumph 2 = **be widespread**, abound, be current, be prevalent, exist generally, obtain, predominate, preponderate 3 **prevail on** or

upon = **persuade**, bring round, convince, dispose, incline, induce, influence, prompt, sway, talk into, win over

prevailing adjective 1 = **widespread**, common, current, customary, established, fashionable, general, in style, in vogue, ordinary, popular, prevalent, set, usual 2 = **predominating**, dominant, influential, main, operative, preponderating, principal, ruling

prevalence noun = **commonness**, acceptance, common occurrence, currency, frequency, pervasiveness, popularity, profusion, regularity, ubiquity, universality

prevalent adjective = **common**, accepted, commonplace, current, customary, established, everyday, extensive, frequent, general, habitual, popular, rampant, rife, ubiquitous, universal, usual, widespread
➤ **Antonyms**
confined, infrequent, limited, localized, rare, restricted, uncommon, unusual

prevaricate verb = **evade**, beat about the bush, beg the question, cavil, deceive, dodge, equivocate, flannel (Brit. informal), give a false colour to, hedge, lie, palter, quibble, shift, shuffle, stretch the truth, tergiversate
➤ **Antonyms**
be blunt, be direct, be frank, be straightforward, come straight to the point, not beat about the bush

prevarication noun = **evasion**, cavilling, deceit, deception, equivocation, falsehood, falsification, lie, misrepresentation, pretence, quibbling, tergiversation, untruth

prevent verb = **stop**, anticipate, avert, avoid, balk, bar, block, check, counteract, defend against, foil, forestall, frustrate, hamper, head off, hinder, impede, inhibit, intercept, nip in the bud, obstruct, obviate, preclude, restrain, stave off, thwart, ward off
➤ **Antonyms**
allow, encourage, help, incite, permit, support, urge

prevention noun = **elimination**, anticipation, avoidance, deterrence, forestalling, obviation, precaution, preclusion, prophylaxis, safeguard, thwarting

preventive, preventative adjective 1 = **hindering**, hampering, impeding, obstructive 2 = **protective**, counteractive, deterrent, inhibitory, precautionary, prophylactic, shielding ♦ noun 3 = **hindrance**, block, impediment, obstacle, obstruction 4 = **protection**, deterrent, neutralizer, prevention, prophylactic, protective, remedy, safeguard, shield

preview noun 1 = **sample**, advance showing, foretaste, sneak preview, taster, trailer ♦ *verb* **2** = **sample**, foretaste, taste

previous *adjective* **1** = **earlier**, antecedent, anterior, erstwhile, ex-, foregoing, former, one-time, past, preceding, prior, quondam, sometime **2** *Informal* = **premature**, ahead of oneself, precipitate, too early, too soon, untimely
➤ Antonyms
≠**earlier**: consequent, following, later, subsequent, succeeding

previously *adverb* = **before**, at one time, a while ago, beforehand, earlier, formerly, heretofore, hitherto, in advance, in anticipation, in days *or* years gone by, in the past, once, then, until now

prey *noun* **1** = **quarry**, game, kill **2** = **victim**, dupe, fall guy (*informal*), mark, mug (*Brit. slang*), target ♦ *verb* **3** = **hunt**, devour, eat, feed upon, live off, seize **4** = **worry**, burden, distress, hang over, haunt, oppress, trouble, weigh down, weigh heavily **5** = **victimize**, blackmail, bully, exploit, intimidate, take advantage of, terrorize

price *noun* **1** = **cost**, amount, asking price, assessment, bill, charge, damage (*informal*), estimate, expenditure, expense, face value, fee, figure, outlay, payment, rate, valuation, value, worth **2** = **consequences**, cost, penalty, sacrifice, toll **3 at any price** = **whatever the cost**, anyhow, cost what it may, expense no object, no matter what the cost, regardless ♦ *verb* **4** = **evaluate**, assess, cost, estimate, put a price on, rate, value

priceless *adjective* **1** = **valuable**, beyond price, cherished, costly, dear, expensive, incalculable, inestimable, invaluable, irreplaceable, precious, prized, rare, rich, treasured, worth a king's ransom, worth one's *or* its weight in gold **2** *Informal* = **hilarious**, absurd, amusing, comic, droll, funny, killing (*informal*), rib-tickling, ridiculous, riotous, side-splitting
➤ Antonyms
≠**valuable**: cheap, cheapo (*informal*), common, inexpensive, worthless

pricey, pricy *adjective* = **expensive**, costly, dear, high-priced, steep (*informal*)

prick *verb* **1** = **pierce**, bore, impale, jab, lance, perforate, pink, punch, puncture, stab **2** = **sting**, bite, itch, prickle, smart, tingle **3** = **distress**, cut, grieve, move, pain, stab, touch, trouble, wound **4** *usually with* **up** = **raise**, point, rise, stand erect ♦ *noun* **5** = **puncture**, cut, gash, hole, perforation, pinhole, wound **6** = **pang**, gnawing, prickle, smart, spasm, sting, twinge

prickle *noun* **1** = **spike**, barb, needle, point, spine, spur, thorn **2** = **tingling**, chill, goose bumps, goose flesh, pins and needles (*informal*), smart, tickle, tingle ♦ *verb* **3**

= **tingle**, itch, smart, sting, twitch **4** = **prick**, jab, nick, stick

prickly *adjective* **1** = **spiny**, barbed, brambly, briery, bristly, thorny **2** = **itchy**, crawling, pricking, prickling, scratchy, sharp, smarting, stinging, tingling **3** = **irritable**, bad-tempered, cantankerous, edgy, fractious, grumpy, liverish, peevish, pettish, petulant, ratty (*Brit. & N.Z. informal*), shirty (*slang, chiefly Brit.*), snappish, stroppy (*Brit. slang*), tetchy, touchy, waspish

pride *noun* **1** = **satisfaction**, delight, gratification, joy, pleasure **2** = **self-respect**, amour-propre, dignity, honour, self-esteem, self-worth **3** = **conceit**, arrogance, bigheadedness (*informal*), egotism, haughtiness, hauteur, hubris, loftiness, morgue, presumption, pretension, pretentiousness, self-importance, self-love, smugness, snobbery, superciliousness, vainglory, vanity **4** = **gem**, boast, jewel, pride and joy, prize, treasure **5** = **elite**, best, choice, cream, flower, glory, pick ♦ *verb* **6 pride oneself on** = **be proud of**, boast of, brag about, congratulate oneself on, crow about, exult in, flatter oneself, glory in, revel in, take pride in
➤ Antonyms
noun ≠**conceit**: humility, meekness, modesty

priest *noun* = **clergyman**, churchman, cleric, curate, divine, ecclesiastic, father, father confessor, holy man, man of God, man of the cloth, minister, padre (*informal*), pastor, vicar

priestly *adjective* = **ecclesiastic**, canonical, clerical, pastoral, priestlike, sacerdotal

prig *noun* = **goody-goody** (*informal*), Holy Joe (*informal*), Holy Willie (*informal*), Mrs Grundy, old maid (*informal*), pedant, prude, puritan, stuffed shirt (*informal*)

priggish *adjective* = **self-righteous**, goody-goody (*informal*), holier-than-thou, narrow-minded, pedantic, prim, prudish, puritanical, self-satisfied, smug, starchy (*informal*), stiff, stuffy

prim *adjective* = **prudish**, demure, fastidious, formal, fussy, niminy-piminy, old-maidish (*informal*), particular, precise, priggish, prissy (*informal*), proper, puritanical, schoolmarmish (*Brit. informal*), starchy (*informal*), stiff, strait-laced
➤ Antonyms
carefree, casual, easy-going, informal, laid-back, relaxed

primacy *noun* = **supremacy**, ascendancy, command, dominance, dominion, leadership, pre-eminence, superiority

prima donna *noun* = **diva**, leading lady, star

primal *adjective* **1** = **first**, earliest, initial, original, primary, prime, primitive, primordial **2 = chief**, central, first, greatest, highest, main, major, most important, paramount, prime, principal

primarily *adverb* **1 = chiefly**, above all, basically, especially, for the most part, fundamentally, generally, largely, mainly, mostly, on the whole, principally **2 = at first**, at *or* from the start, first and foremost, initially, in the beginning, in the first place, originally

primary *adjective* **1 = chief**, best, capital, cardinal, dominant, first, greatest, highest, leading, main, paramount, prime, principal, top **2 = elementary**, introductory, rudimentary, simple **3 = basic**, beginning, bog-standard (*informal*), elemental, essential, fundamental, radical, ultimate, underlying
➤ **Antonyms**
≠**chief**: inferior, lesser, lowest, subordinate, supplementary, unimportant ≠**elementary**: ensuing, following, later, secondary, subsequent, succeeding

prime *adjective* **1 = main**, chief, leading, predominant, pre-eminent, primary, principal, ruling, senior **2 = best**, capital, choice, excellent, first-class, first-rate, grade A, highest, quality, select, selected, superior, top ◆ *noun* **3 = peak**, best days, bloom, flower, full flowering, height, heyday, maturity, perfection, zenith ◆ *verb* **4 = inform**, brief, clue in (*informal*), clue up (*informal*), fill in (*informal*), gen up (*Brit. informal*), give someone the lowdown (*informal*), notify, tell **5 = prepare**, break in, coach, fit, get ready, groom, make ready, train

primeval, primaeval *adjective* **= earliest**, ancient, early, first, old, original, prehistoric, primal, primitive, primordial, pristine

primitive *adjective* **1 = early**, earliest, elementary, first, original, primary, primeval, primordial, pristine **2 = crude**, rough, rude, rudimentary, simple, unrefined
➤ **Antonyms**
≠**early**: advanced, later, modern ≠**crude**: comfortable, elaborate, refined

primordial *adjective* **= primeval**, earliest, first, prehistoric, primal, primitive, pristine

primp *verb* **= preen**, deck out, doll up (*slang*), dress up

prince *noun* **= ruler**, lord, monarch, potentate, sovereign

princely *adjective* **1 = regal**, august, dignified, grand, high-born, imperial, imposing, lofty, magnificent, majestic, noble, royal, sovereign, stately **2 = generous**, bounteous, bountiful, gracious, lavish, liberal, magnanimous, munificent,

open-handed, rich

principal *adjective* **1 = main**, arch, capital, cardinal, chief, controlling, dominant, essential, first, foremost, highest, key, leading, most important, paramount, pre-eminent, primary, prime, strongest ◆ *noun* **2 = headmaster** *or* **headmistress**, dean, director, head (*informal*), head teacher, master *or* mistress, rector **3 = head**, boss (*informal*), chief, director, leader, master, ruler, superintendent **4 = star**, first violin, lead, leader **5 = capital**, assets, capital funds, money
➤ **Antonyms**
adjective ≠**main**: auxiliary, inferior, minor, subordinate, subsidiary, supplementary

principally *adverb* **= mainly**, above all, chiefly, especially, first and foremost, for the most part, in the main, largely, mostly, particularly, predominantly, primarily

principle *noun* **1 = rule**, assumption, axiom, canon, criterion, dictum, doctrine, dogma, ethic, formula, fundamental, golden rule, law, maxim, moral law, precept, proposition, standard, truth, verity **2 = morals**, conscience, integrity, probity, rectitude, scruples, sense of duty, sense of honour, uprightness **3 in principle = in theory**, ideally, in essence, theoretically

principled *adjective* **= moral**, conscientious, correct, decent, ethical, high-minded, honourable, just, righteous, right-minded, scrupulous, upright, virtuous

prink *verb* **1 = dress up**, deck, dress to kill (*informal*), dress (up) to the nines (*informal*) **2 = preen**, adorn, doll up (*slang*), groom, primp, titivate

print *verb* **1 = publish**, engrave, go to press, impress, imprint, issue, mark, put to bed (*informal*), run off, stamp ◆ *noun* **2 = publication**, book, magazine, newspaper, newsprint, periodical, printed matter, typescript, zine (*informal*) **3 in print: a = published**, in black and white, on paper, on the streets, out, printed **b = available**, current, in the shops, obtainable, on the market, on the shelves **4 out of print = unavailable**, no longer published, o.p., unobtainable **5 = reproduction**, copy, engraving, photo (*informal*), photograph, picture **6 = typeface**, characters, face, font (*chiefly U.S.*), fount, lettering, letters, type

prior *adjective* **1 = earlier**, foregoing, former, preceding, pre-existent, pre-existing, previous **2 prior to = before**, earlier than, preceding, previous to

priority *noun* **= precedence**, first concern, greater importance, pre-eminence, preference, prerogative, rank, right of way, seniority, superiority, supremacy, the lead

priory noun = **monastery**, abbey, cloister, convent, nunnery, religious house

prison noun = **jail**, calaboose (*U.S. informal*), can (*slang*), choky (*slang*), clink (*slang*), confinement, cooler (*slang*), dungeon, glasshouse (*Military informal*), jug (*slang*), lockup, nick (*Brit. slang*), penal institution, penitentiary (*U.S.*), poky or pokey (*U.S. & Canad. slang*), pound, quod (*slang*), slammer (*slang*), stir (*slang*)

prisoner noun 1 = **convict**, con (*slang*), jailbird, lag (*slang*) 2 = **captive**, detainee, hostage, internee

prissy adjective = **prim**, old-maidish (*informal*), prim and proper, prudish, strait-laced

pristine adjective 1 = **new**, immaculate, pure, uncorrupted, undefiled, unspoiled, unsullied, untouched, virginal 2 = **original**, earliest, first, former, initial, primal, primary, primeval, primitive, primordial

privacy noun 1 = **seclusion**, isolation, privateness, retirement, retreat, separateness, sequestration, solitude 2 = **secrecy**, clandestineness, concealment, confidentiality

private adjective 1 = **exclusive**, individual, intimate, own, particular, personal, reserved, special 2 = **secret**, clandestine, closet, confidential, covert, hush-hush (*informal*), in camera, inside, off the record, privy (*archaic*), unofficial 3 = **nonpublic**, independent 4 = **secluded**, concealed, isolated, not overlooked, retired, secret, separate, sequestered 5 = **solitary**, withdrawn 6 **in private** = **in secret**, behind closed doors, confidentially, in camera, personally, privately ◆ noun 7 = **enlisted man** (*U.S.*), private soldier, squaddie or squaddy (*Brit. slang*), tommy (*Brit. informal*), Tommy Atkins (*Brit. informal*)
➤ **Antonyms**
adjective ≠**exclusive**: common, general, open, public, unlimited, unrestricted ≠**secret**: disclosed, known, official, open, public, revealed ≠**secluded**: bustling, busy, frequented, unsecluded ≠**solitary**: outgoing, sociable

privation noun Formal = **want**, destitution, distress, hardship, indigence, lack, loss, misery, necessity, need, neediness, penury, poverty, suffering

privilege noun = **right**, advantage, benefit, birthright, claim, concession, due, entitlement, franchise, freedom, immunity, liberty, prerogative, sanction

privileged adjective 1 = **special**, advantaged, elite, entitled, favoured, honoured, indulged, powerful, ruling 2 = **allowed**, empowered, exempt, free, granted, licensed, sanctioned, vested

privy adjective 1 Archaic = **secret**, confidential, hidden, hush-hush (*informal*), off the record, personal, private 2 **privy to** = **informed of**, apprised of, aware of, cognizant of, in on, in the know about (*informal*), in the loop, wise to (*slang*) ◆ noun 3 Obsolete = **lavatory**, latrine, outside toilet

prize[1] noun 1 = **reward**, accolade, award, honour, premium, trophy 2 = **winnings**, haul, jackpot, purse, stakes, windfall 3 = **goal**, aim, ambition, conquest, desire, gain, Holy Grail (*informal*), hope ◆ adjective 4 = **champion**, award-winning, best, first-rate, outstanding, top, top-notch (*informal*), winning

prize[2] verb = **value**, appreciate, cherish, esteem, hold dear, regard highly, set store by, treasure

prizefighter noun = **boxer**, fighter, pugilist

probability noun = **likelihood**, chance(s), expectation, liability, likeliness, odds, presumption, prospect

probable adjective = **likely**, apparent, credible, feasible, most likely, odds-on, on the cards, ostensible, plausible, possible, presumable, presumed, reasonable, seeming, verisimilar
➤ **Antonyms**
doubtful, improbable, not likely, unlikely

probably adverb = **likely**, as likely as not, doubtless, in all likelihood, in all probability, maybe, most likely, perchance (*archaic*), perhaps, possibly, presumably

probation noun = **trial period**, apprenticeship, examination, initiation, novitiate, test, trial

probe verb 1 = **examine**, explore, go into, investigate, look into, query, research, scrutinize, search, sift, sound, test, verify, work over 2 = **explore**, feel around, poke, prod ◆ noun 3 = **examination**, detection, exploration, inquest, inquiry, investigation, research, scrutiny, study

probity noun Formal = **integrity**, goodness, honesty, honour, morality, rectitude, righteousness, sincerity, trustworthiness, truthfulness, uprightness, virtue, worth

problem noun 1 = **difficulty**, can of worms (*informal*), complication, dilemma, disagreement, dispute, disputed point, doubt, Gordian knot, hard nut to crack (*informal*), how-do-you-do (*informal*), point at issue, predicament, quandary, trouble 2 = **puzzle**, brain-teaser (*informal*), conundrum, enigma, poser, question, riddle, teaser ◆ adjective 3 = **difficult**, delinquent, intractable, uncontrollable, unmanageable, unruly

problematic adjective = **tricky**, chancy

(*informal*), debatable, doubtful, dubious, enigmatic, moot, open to doubt, problematical, puzzling, questionable, uncertain, unsettled
➤ **Antonyms**
beyond question, certain, clear, definite, indisputable, settled, undebatable, unquestionable

procedure *noun* = **method**, action, conduct, course, custom, form, formula, modus operandi, operation, performance, plan of action, policy, practice, process, routine, scheme, step, strategy, system, transaction

proceed *verb* 1 = **go on**, advance, carry on, continue, get going, get on with, get under way with, go ahead, make a start, move on, press on, progress, set in motion 2 = **arise**, come, derive, emanate, ensue, flow, follow, issue, originate, result, spring, stem
➤ **Antonyms**
≠**go on**: break off, cease, discontinue, end, get behind, halt, leave off, pack in (*Brit. informal*), retreat, stop

proceeding *noun* 1 = **action**, act, course of action, deed, measure, move, occurrence, procedure, process, step, undertaking, venture 2 **proceedings** = **business**, account, affairs, annals, archives, dealings, doings, matters, minutes, records, report, transactions

proceeds *plural noun* = **income**, earnings, gain, produce, products, profit, receipts, returns, revenue, takings, yield

process *noun* 1 = **procedure**, action, course, course of action, manner, means, measure, method, mode, operation, performance, practice, proceeding, system, transaction 2 = **development**, advance, course, evolution, formation, growth, movement, progress, progression, stage, step, unfolding ♦ *verb* 3 = **handle**, deal with, dispose of, fulfil, take care of 4 = **prepare**, alter, convert, refine, transform, treat

procession *noun* 1 = **parade**, cavalcade, column, cortege, file, march, motorcade, train 2 = **sequence**, course, cycle, run, series, string, succession, train

proclaim *verb* = **declare**, advertise, affirm, announce, blaze (abroad), blazon (abroad), circulate, enunciate, give out, herald, indicate, make known, profess, promulgate, publish, shout from the housetops (*informal*), show, trumpet
➤ **Antonyms**
conceal, hush up, keep back, keep secret, suppress, withhold

proclamation *noun* = **declaration**, announcement, decree, edict, manifesto, notice, notification, promulgation,

pronouncement, pronunciamento, publication

proclivity *noun Formal* = **tendency**, bent, bias, disposition, inclination, leaning, liableness, penchant, predilection, predisposition, proneness, propensity, weakness

procrastinate *verb* = **delay**, adjourn, be dilatory, dally, defer, drag one's feet (*informal*), gain time, play a waiting game, play for time, postpone, prolong, protract, put off, retard, stall, temporize
➤ **Antonyms**
advance, expedite, get on with, hasten, hurry (up), proceed, speed up

procrastination *noun* = **delay**, dilatoriness, hesitation, slackness, slowness, temporization *or* temporisation

procreate *verb Formal* = **reproduce**, beget, breed, bring into being, engender, father, mother, produce

procure *verb* = **obtain**, acquire, appropriate, buy, come by, earn, effect, find, gain, get, get hold of, land, lay hands on, manage to get, pick up, purchase, score (*slang*), secure, win

procurer *or* **procuress** *noun* = **pimp**, bawd (*archaic*), madam, pander, panderer, white-slaver, whoremaster (*archaic*)

prod *verb* 1 = **poke**, dig, drive, elbow, jab, nudge, prick, propel, push, shove 2 = **prompt**, egg on, goad, impel, incite, motivate, move, put a bomb under (*informal*), rouse, spur, stimulate, stir up, urge ♦ *noun* 3 = **poke**, boost, dig, elbow, jab, nudge, push, shove 4 = **prompt**, boost, cue, reminder, signal, stimulus 5 = **goad**, poker, spur, stick

prodigal *adjective* 1 = **extravagant**, excessive, immoderate, improvident, intemperate, profligate, reckless, spendthrift, squandering, wanton, wasteful 2 *often with* **of** = **lavish**, bounteous, bountiful, profuse ♦ *noun* 3 = **spendthrift**, big spender, profligate, squanderer, wastrel
➤ **Antonyms**
adjective ≠**extravagant**: economical, frugal, miserly, parsimonious, sparing, stingy, thrifty, tight ≠**lavish**: deficient, lacking, meagre, scanty, scarce, short, sparse

prodigality *noun* 1 = **wastefulness**, abandon, dissipation, excess, extravagance, immoderation, intemperance, profligacy, recklessness, squandering, wantonness, waste 2 = **lavishness**, bounteousness, profusion

prodigious *adjective* 1 = **huge**, colossal, enormous, giant, gigantic, immeasurable, immense, inordinate, mammoth, massive, monstrous, monumental, stellar (*informal*),

stupendous, tremendous, vast **2 = wonderful**, abnormal, amazing, astounding, dramatic, exceptional, extraordinary, fabulous, fantastic (*informal*), flabbergasting (*informal*), impressive, marvellous, miraculous, phenomenal, remarkable, staggering, startling, striking, stupendous, unusual
➤ **Antonyms**
≠**huge**: negligible, small, tiny ≠**wonderful**: normal, ordinary, unexceptional, unimpressive, unremarkable, usual

prodigy *noun* **1 = genius**, brainbox, child genius, mastermind, talent, whizz (*informal*), whizz kid (*informal*), wizard, wonder child, wunderkind **2 = wonder**, marvel, miracle, one in a million, phenomenon, rare bird (*informal*), sensation

produce *verb* **1 = cause**, bring about, effect, generate, give rise to, make for, occasion, provoke, set off **2 = show**, advance, bring forward, bring to light, demonstrate, exhibit, offer, present, put forward, set forth **3 = yield**, afford, engender, furnish, give, render, supply **4 = make**, compose, construct, create, develop, fabricate, invent, manufacture, originate, put together, turn out **5 = bring forth**, bear, beget, breed, deliver **6 = present**, direct, do, exhibit, mount, put before the public, put on, show, stage ◆ *noun* **7 = fruit and vegetables**, crop, greengrocery, harvest, product, yield

producer *noun* **1 = director**, impresario, *régisseur* **2 = maker**, farmer, grower, manufacturer

product *noun* **1 = goods**, artefact, commodity, concoction, creation, invention, merchandise, produce, production, work **2 = result**, consequence, effect, end result, fruit, issue, legacy, offshoot, outcome, returns, spin-off, upshot, yield

production *noun* **1 = producing**, assembly, construction, creation, fabrication, formation, making, manufacture, manufacturing, origination, preparation **2 = presentation**, direction, management, staging

productive *adjective* **1 = fertile**, creative, dynamic, energetic, fecund, fruitful, generative, inventive, plentiful, producing, prolific, rich, teeming, vigorous **2 = useful**, advantageous, beneficial, constructive, effective, fruitful, gainful, gratifying, profitable, rewarding, valuable, worthwhile
➤ **Antonyms**
≠**fertile**: barren, poor, sterile, unfertile, unfruitful, unproductive ≠**useful**: unproductive, unprofitable, useless

productivity *noun* **= output**, abundance, mass production, production, productive capacity, productiveness, work rate, yield

profane *adjective* **1 = sacrilegious**, disrespectful, godless, heathen, idolatrous, impious, impure, irreligious, irreverent, pagan, sinful, ungodly, wicked **2 = secular**, lay, temporal, worldly **3 = crude**, abusive, blasphemous, coarse, filthy, foul, obscene, vulgar ◆ *verb* **4 = desecrate**, abuse, commit sacrilege, contaminate, debase, defile, misuse, pervert, pollute, prostitute, violate, vitiate
➤ **Antonyms**
adjective ≠**sacrilegious**: clean, holy, proper, religious, respectful, reverent, sacred, spiritual

profanity *noun* **1 = sacrilege**, blasphemy, impiety, profaneness **2 = swearing**, abuse, curse, cursing, execration, foul language, four-letter word, imprecation, irreverence, malediction, obscenity, swearword

profess *verb* **1 = claim**, act as if, allege, call oneself, dissemble, fake, feign, let on, make out, pretend, purport, sham **2 = state**, acknowledge, admit, affirm, announce, assert, asseverate, aver, avow, certify, confess, confirm, declare, maintain, own, proclaim, vouch

professed *adjective* **1 = supposed**, alleged, apparent, ostensible, pretended, purported, self-styled, so-called, *soi-disant*, would-be **2 = declared**, avowed, certified, confessed, confirmed, proclaimed, self-acknowledged, self-confessed

profession *noun* **1 = occupation**, business, calling, career, employment, line, line of work, métier, office, position, sphere, vocation, walk of life **2 = declaration**, acknowledgment, affirmation, assertion, attestation, avowal, claim, confession, statement, testimony, vow

professional *adjective* **1 = expert**, ace (*informal*), adept, competent, crack (*slang*), efficient, experienced, finished, masterly, polished, practised, proficient, qualified, skilled, slick, trained ◆ *noun* **2 = expert**, adept, authority, buff (*informal*), dab hand (*Brit. informal*), guru, hotshot (*informal*), maestro, master, maven (*U.S.*), past master, pro (*informal*), specialist, virtuoso, whizz (*informal*), wizard
➤ **Antonyms**
adjective ≠**expert**: amateurish, incapable, incompetent, inefficient, inept, inexperienced, unpolished, unqualified, unskilled, untrained

professor *noun* **= don** (*Brit.*), fellow (*Brit.*), head of faculty, prof (*informal*)

proffer *verb Formal* **= offer**, extend, hand, hold out, present, propose, propound, submit, suggest, tender, volunteer

proficiency *noun* **= skill**, ability, accomplishment, aptitude, competence, craft, dexterity, expertise, expertness, facility, knack, know-how (*informal*), mastery, skilfulness, talent

proficient *adjective* = **skilled**, able, accomplished, adept, apt, capable, clever, competent, conversant, efficient, experienced, expert, gifted, masterly, qualified, skilful, talented, trained, versed
➤ **Antonyms**
bad, incapable, incompetent, inept, unaccomplished, unskilled

profile *noun* 1 = **outline**, contour, drawing, figure, form, portrait, shape, side view, silhouette, sketch 2 = **biography**, characterization, character sketch, sketch, thumbnail sketch, vignette

profit *noun* 1 *often plural* = **earnings**, boot (*dialect*), bottom line, emoluments, gain, percentage (*informal*), proceeds, receipts, return, revenue, surplus, takings, winnings, yield 2 = **benefit**, advancement, advantage, avail, gain, good, interest, mileage (*informal*), use, value ♦ *verb* 3 = **benefit**, aid, avail, be of advantage to, better, contribute, gain, help, improve, promote, serve, stand in good stead 4 = **capitalize on**, cash in on (*informal*), exploit, make capital of, make good use of, make the most of, put to good use, reap the benefit of, take advantage of, turn to advantage *or* account, use, utilize 5 = **make money**, clean up (*informal*), clear, earn, gain, make a good thing of (*informal*), make a killing (*informal*), rake in (*informal*)

profitable *adjective* 1 = **money-making**, commercial, cost-effective, fruitful, gainful, lucrative, paying, remunerative, rewarding, worthwhile 2 = **beneficial**, advantageous, economic, expedient, fruitful, productive, rewarding, serviceable, useful, valuable, worthwhile
➤ **Antonyms**
disadvantageous, fruitless, unremunerative, unrewarding, useless, vain, worthless

profiteer *noun* 1 = **racketeer**, exploiter ♦ *verb* 2 = **exploit**, fleece, make a quick buck (*slang*), make someone pay through the nose, overcharge, racketeer, skin (*slang*), sting (*informal*)

profligacy *noun* 1 = **extravagance**, excess, improvidence, lavishness, prodigality, recklessness, squandering, waste, wastefulness 2 = **immorality**, abandon, corruption, debauchery, degeneracy, depravity, dissipation, dissoluteness, laxity, libertinism, licentiousness, promiscuity, wantonness

profligate *adjective* 1 = **extravagant**, immoderate, improvident, prodigal, reckless, spendthrift, squandering, wasteful 2 = **depraved**, abandoned, corrupt,

debauched, degenerate, dissipated, dissolute, immoral, iniquitous, libertine, licentious, loose, promiscuous, shameless, sink, unprincipled, vicious, vitiated, wanton, wicked, wild ♦ *noun* 3 = **spendthrift**, prodigal, squanderer, waster, wastrel 4 = **degenerate**, debauchee, dissipater, libertine, rake, reprobate, roué, swinger (*slang*)
➤ **Antonyms**
adjective ≠**depraved**: chaste, decent, moral, principled, pure, upright, virginal, virtuous

profound *adjective* 1 = **wise**, abstruse, deep, discerning, erudite, learned, penetrating, philosophical, recondite, sagacious, sage, serious, skilled, subtle, thoughtful, weighty 2 = **sincere**, abject, acute, deeply felt, extreme, great, heartfelt, heartrending, hearty, intense, keen 3 = **complete**, absolute, consummate, exhaustive, extensive, extreme, far-reaching, intense, out-and-out, pronounced, serious (*informal*), thoroughgoing, total, unqualified, utter 4 = **deep**, abysmal, bottomless, cavernous, fathomless, yawning
➤ **Antonyms**
≠**wise**: imprudent, stupid, thoughtless, uneducated, uninformed, unknowledgeable, unwise ≠**sincere**: insincere, shallow ≠**complete**: slight, superficial

profoundly *adverb* = **greatly**, abjectly, acutely, deeply, extremely, from the bottom of one's heart, heartily, intensely, keenly, seriously, sincerely, thoroughly, to the core, to the nth degree, very

profundity *noun* = **insight**, acuity, erudition, intelligence, learning, penetration, perceptiveness, perspicacity, perspicuity, sagacity, wisdom

profuse *adjective* 1 = **plentiful**, abundant, ample, bountiful, copious, luxuriant, overflowing, prolific, teeming 2 = **extravagant**, excessive, exuberant, fulsome, generous, immoderate, lavish, liberal, open-handed, prodigal, unstinting
➤ **Antonyms**
≠**plentiful**: deficient, inadequate, meagre, scanty, scarce, skimpy, sparse ≠**extravagant**: frugal, illiberal, moderate, provident, thrifty

profusion *noun* = **abundance**, bounty, copiousness, cornucopia, excess, extravagance, exuberance, glut, lavishness, luxuriance, multitude, oversupply, plenitude, plethora, prodigality, quantity, riot, superabundance, superfluity, surplus, wealth

progenitor *noun* 1 = **ancestor**, forebear, forefather, parent, primogenitor 2 = **originator**, instigator, source

progeny *noun* = **children**, breed, descendants, family, issue, lineage, offspring, posterity, race, scions, seed (*chiefly biblical*), stock, young

prognosis *noun* = **forecast**, diagnosis, prediction, prognostication, projection

prognosticate *verb* **1** = **foretell**, divine, forecast, predict, presage, prophesy **2** = **indicate**, betoken, forebode, foreshadow, point to, portend, presage

prognostication *noun* = **prediction**, forecast, prognosis, projection, prophecy, speculation

programme *noun* **1** = **schedule**, agenda, curriculum, line-up, list, listing, list of players, order of events, order of the day, plan, syllabus, timetable **2** = **show**, broadcast, performance, presentation, production ♦ *verb* **3** = **schedule**, arrange, line up, list, map out, plan, prearrange, work out

progress *noun* **1** = **development**, advance, advancement, amelioration, betterment, breakthrough, gain, gaining ground, growth, headway, improvement, increase, progression, promotion, step forward **2** = **movement**, advance, course, onward course, passage, progression, way **3 in progress** = **going on**, being done, happening, occurring, proceeding, taking place, under way ♦ *verb* **4** = **develop**, advance, ameliorate, better, blossom, gain, grow, improve, increase, mature **5** = **move on**, advance, come on, continue, cover ground, forge ahead, gain ground, gather way, get on, go forward, make headway, make inroads (into), make one's way, make strides, proceed, travel
➤ **Antonyms**
noun ≠**development**: decline, failure, recession, regression, relapse, retrogression ≠**movement**: regression, retrogression ♦ *verb* ≠**develop**: decrease, get behind, lose, lose ground, regress, retrogress ≠**move on**: get behind, recede, regress, retrogress

progression *noun* **1** = **progress**, advance, advancement, furtherance, gain, headway, movement forward **2** = **sequence**, chain, course, cycle, order, series, string, succession

progressive *adjective* **1** = **enlightened**, advanced, avant-garde, dynamic, enterprising, forward-looking, go-ahead, liberal, modern, radical, reformist, revolutionary, up-and-coming **2** = **growing**, accelerating, advancing, continuing, continuous, developing, escalating, increasing, intensifying, ongoing

prohibit *verb* **1** = **forbid**, ban, debar, disallow, interdict, outlaw, proscribe, veto **2** = **prevent**, constrain, hamper, hinder, impede, make impossible, obstruct, preclude, restrict, rule out, stop

➤ **Antonyms**
≠**forbid**: allow, authorize, command, consent to, endure, further, give leave, let, license, order, permit, suffer, tolerate ≠**prevent**: allow, let, permit

prohibited *adjective* = **forbidden**, banned, barred, not allowed, off limits, proscribed, taboo, *verboten*, vetoed

prohibition *noun* **1** = **prevention**, constraint, disqualification, exclusion, forbiddance, interdiction, negation, obstruction, restriction **2** = **ban**, bar, boycott, disallowance, embargo, injunction, interdict, proscription, veto

prohibitive *adjective* **1** = **exorbitant**, beyond one's means, excessive, extortionate, high-priced, preposterous, sky-high, steep (*informal*) **2** = **prohibiting**, forbidding, proscriptive, repressive, restraining, restrictive, suppressive

project *noun* **1** = **scheme**, activity, assignment, design, enterprise, job, occupation, plan, programme, proposal, task, undertaking, venture, work ♦ *verb* **2** = **forecast**, calculate, call, estimate, extrapolate, gauge, predetermine, predict, reckon **3** = **stick out**, beetle, bulge, extend, jut, overhang, protrude, stand out

projectile *noun* = **missile**, bullet, rocket, shell

projection *noun* **1** = **protrusion**, bulge, eaves, jut, ledge, overhang, protuberance, ridge, shelf, sill **2** = **forecast**, calculation, computation, estimate, estimation, extrapolation, prediction, reckoning

proletarian *adjective* **1** = **working-class**, cloth-cap (*informal*), common, plebeian ♦ *noun* **2** = **worker**, commoner, Joe Bloggs (*Brit. informal*), man of the people, pleb, plebeian, prole (*derogatory slang, chiefly Brit.*)

proletariat *noun* = **working class**, commonalty, commoners, hoi polloi, labouring classes, lower classes, lower orders, plebs, proles (*derogatory slang, chiefly Brit.*), the common people, the great unwashed (*informal & derogatory*), the herd, the masses, the rabble, wage-earners
➤ **Antonyms**
aristo (*informal*), aristocracy, gentry, nobility, peerage, ruling class, upper class, upper crust (*informal*)

proliferate *verb* = **increase**, breed, burgeon, escalate, expand, grow rapidly, multiply, mushroom, run riot, snowball

proliferation *noun* = **multiplication**, build-up, concentration, escalation, expansion, extension, increase, intensification, spread, step-up (*informal*)

prolific *adjective* = **productive**, abundant,

bountiful, copious, fecund, fertile, fruitful, generative, luxuriant, profuse, rank, rich, teeming
➤ **Antonyms**
barren, fruitless, infertile, sterile, unfruitful, unproductive, unprolific

prolix *adjective* = **long-winded**, boring, lengthy, long, long-drawn-out, prolonged, protracted, rambling, tedious, verbose, wordy

prologue *noun* = **introduction**, exordium, foreword, preamble, preface, preliminary, prelude, proem

prolong *verb* = **lengthen**, carry on, continue, delay, drag out, draw out, extend, make longer, perpetuate, protract, spin out, stretch
➤ **Antonyms**
abbreviate, abridge, curtail, cut, cut down, shorten

promenade *noun* 1 = **walkway**, boulevard, esplanade, parade, prom, public walk 2 = **stroll**, airing, constitutional, saunter, turn, walk ◆ *verb* 3 = **stroll**, perambulate, saunter, stretch one's legs, take a walk, walk

prominence *noun* 1 = **conspicuousness**, markedness, outstandingness, precedence, salience, specialness, top billing, weight 2 = **fame**, celebrity, distinction, eminence, greatness, importance, name, notability, pre-eminence, prestige, rank, reputation, standing 3 = **protrusion**, bulge, jutting, projection, protuberance, swelling

prominent *adjective* 1 = **noticeable**, blatant, conspicuous, easily seen, eye-catching, in the foreground, obtrusive, obvious, outstanding, pronounced, remarkable, salient, striking, to the fore, unmistakable 2 = **famous**, big-time (*informal*), celebrated, chief, distinguished, eminent, foremost, important, leading, main, major league (*informal*), notable, noted, outstanding, popular, pre-eminent, renowned, respected, top, well-known, well-thought-of 3 = **jutting**, bulging, hanging over, projecting, protruding, protrusive, protuberant, standing out
➤ **Antonyms**
≠**noticeable**: inconspicuous, indistinct, insignificant, unnoticeable ≠**famous**: insignificant, minor, secondary, undistinguished, unimportant, unknown, unnotable ≠**jutting**: concave, indented, receding

promiscuity *noun* = **licentiousness**, debauchery, immorality, looseness, permissiveness, promiscuousness, wantonness

promiscuous *adjective* 1 = **licentious**, abandoned, debauched, dissipated, dissolute, fast, immoral, lax, libertine, loose, of easy virtue, profligate, unbridled,

unchaste, wanton, wild 2 *Formal* = **mixed**, chaotic, confused, disordered, diverse, heterogeneous, ill-assorted, indiscriminate, intermingled, intermixed, jumbled, mingled, miscellaneous, motley
➤ **Antonyms**
≠**licentious**: chaste, decent, innocent, modest, moral, pure, undefiled, unsullied, vestal, virginal, virtuous ≠**mixed**: homogeneous, identical, neat, ordered, orderly, organized, shipshape, uniform, unmixed

promise *verb* 1 = **guarantee**, assure, contract, cross one's heart, engage, give an undertaking, give one's word, pledge, plight, stipulate, swear, take an oath, undertake, vouch, vow, warrant 2 = **seem likely**, augur, bespeak, betoken, bid fair, denote, give hope of, hint at, hold a probability, hold out hopes of, indicate, lead one to expect, look like, show signs of, suggest ◆ *noun* 3 = **guarantee**, assurance, bond, commitment, compact, covenant, engagement, oath, pledge, undertaking, vow, word, word of honour 4 = **potential**, ability, aptitude, capability, capacity, flair, talent

promising *adjective* 1 = **encouraging**, auspicious, bright, favourable, full of promise, hopeful, likely, propitious, reassuring, rosy 2 = **talented**, able, gifted, likely, rising, up-and-coming
➤ **Antonyms**
≠**encouraging**: discouraging, unauspicious, unfavourable, unpromising

promontory *noun* = **point**, cape, foreland, head, headland, ness (*archaic*), spur

promote *verb* 1 = **help**, advance, aid, assist, back, boost, contribute to, develop, encourage, forward, foster, further, gee up, nurture, stimulate, support 2 = **raise**, aggrandize, dignify, elevate, exalt, honour, kick upstairs (*informal*), prefer, upgrade 3 = **advertise**, beat the drum for (*informal*), hype, plug (*informal*), publicize, puff, push, sell 4 = **work for**, advocate, call attention to, champion, endorse, espouse, popularize, prescribe, push for, recommend, speak for, sponsor, support, urge
➤ **Antonyms**
≠**help**: discourage, hinder, hold back, impede, obstruct, oppose, prevent ≠**raise**: demote, downgrade, lower *or* reduce in rank

promoter *noun* 1 = **organizer**, arranger, entrepreneur, impresario 2 = **supporter**, advocate, campaigner, champion, proponent, upholder

promotion *noun* 1 = **rise**, advancement, aggrandizement, elevation, ennoblement, exaltation, honour, move up, preferment, upgrading 2 = **publicity**, advertising, advertising campaign, ballyhoo (*informal*), hard sell, hype, media hype, plugging (*informal*), propaganda, puffery (*informal*), pushing **3** = **encouragement**, advancement, advocacy, backing, boosting, cultivation, development, espousal, furtherance, progress, support

prompt *verb* **1** = **cause**, call forth, elicit, evoke, give rise to, occasion, provoke **2** = **motivate**, cause, impel, incite, induce, inspire, instigate, move, provoke, spur, stimulate, urge **3** = **remind**, assist, cue, help out, jog the memory, prod, refresh the memory ◆ *adjective* **4** = **immediate**, early, instant, instantaneous, on time, pdq (*slang*), punctual, quick, rapid, speedy, swift, timely, unhesitating **5** = **quick**, alert, brisk, eager, efficient, expeditious, ready, responsive, smart, willing ◆ *adverb* **6** *Informal* = **exactly**, on the dot, promptly, punctually, sharp ◆ *noun* **7** = **reminder**, cue, help, hint, jog, jolt, prod, spur
➤ **Antonyms**
verb ≠**motivate**: deter, discourage, prevent, restrain, talk out of ◆ *adjective* ≠**immediate**: hesitating, late, slow ≠**quick**: inefficient, remiss, slack, tardy, unresponsive

promptly *adverb* = **immediately**, at once, by return, directly, hotfoot, instantly, on the dot, on time, pdq (*slang*), posthaste, pronto (*informal*), punctually, quickly, speedily, swiftly, unhesitatingly

promptness *noun* = **swiftness**, alacrity, alertness, briskness, dispatch, eagerness, haste, promptitude, punctuality, quickness, readiness, speed, willingness

promulgate *verb* = **make known**, advertise, announce, broadcast, circulate, communicate, declare, decree, disseminate, issue, make public, notify, proclaim, promote, publish, spread

prone *adjective* **1** = **liable**, apt, bent, disposed, given, inclined, likely, predisposed, subject, susceptible, tending **2** = **face down**, flat, horizontal, lying down, procumbent, prostrate, recumbent
➤ **Antonyms**
≠**liable**: averse, disinclined, indisposed, not likely, unlikely ≠**face down**: erect, face up, perpendicular, supine, upright, vertical

prong *noun* = **point**, projection, spike, tine, tip

pronounce *verb* **1** = **say**, accent, articulate, enunciate, sound, speak, stress, utter, vocalize, voice **2** = **declare**, affirm, announce, assert, decree, deliver, judge, proclaim

pronounced *adjective* = **noticeable**, broad, clear, conspicuous, decided, definite, distinct, evident, marked, obvious, salient, striking, strong, unmistakable

➤ **Antonyms**
concealed, hidden, imperceptible, inconspicuous, unapparent, unnoticeable, vague

pronouncement *noun* = **announcement**, declaration, decree, dictum, edict, judgment, manifesto, notification, proclamation, promulgation, pronunciamento, statement

pronunciation *noun* = **intonation**, accent, accentuation, articulation, diction, elocution, enunciation, inflection, speech, stress

proof *noun* **1** = **evidence**, attestation, authentication, certification, confirmation, corroboration, demonstration, substantiation, testimony, verification **2** *As in* **put to the proof** = **test**, assay, examination, experiment, ordeal, scrutiny, trial **3** *Printing* = **trial print**, galley, galley proof, page proof, pull, slip, trial impression ◆ *adjective* **4** = **impervious**, impenetrable, repellent, resistant, strong, tight, treated **5** **be proof against** = **withstand**, hold out against, resist, stand firm against, stand up to

prop *verb* **1** = **support**, bolster, brace, buttress, hold up, maintain, shore, stay, sustain, truss, uphold **2** = **rest**, lean, set, stand ◆ *noun* **3** = **support**, brace, buttress, mainstay, stanchion, stay, truss

propaganda *noun* = **information**, advertising, agitprop, ballyhoo (*informal*), brainwashing, disinformation, hype, newspeak, promotion, publicity

propagate *verb* **1** = **spread**, broadcast, circulate, diffuse, disseminate, make known, proclaim, promote, promulgate, publicize, publish, transmit **2** = **reproduce**, beget, breed, engender, generate, increase, multiply, procreate, produce, proliferate
➤ **Antonyms**
≠**spread**: cover up, hide, hush up, keep under wraps, stifle, suppress, withhold

propagation *noun* **1** = **spreading**, circulation, communication, diffusion, dissemination, distribution, promotion, promulgation, spread, transmission **2** = **reproduction**, breeding, generation, increase, multiplication, procreation, proliferation

propel *verb* = **drive**, force, impel, launch, push, send, set in motion, shoot, shove, start, thrust
➤ **Antonyms**
check, delay, hold back, pull, slow, stop

propensity *noun* = **tendency**, aptness, bent, bias, disposition, inclination, leaning, liability, penchant, predisposition, proclivity, proneness, susceptibility, weakness

proper *adjective* **1** = **suitable**, appropriate, apt, becoming, befitting, fit, fitting, legitimate, meet (*archaic*), right, suited **2**

= **correct**, accepted, accurate, conventional, established, exact, formal, kosher (*informal*), orthodox, precise, right **3** = **polite**, *comme il faut*, decent, decorous, *de rigueur*, genteel, gentlemanly, ladylike, mannerly, punctilious, refined, respectable, seemly

➤ Antonyms

≠**suitable**: improper, inappropriate, unbecoming, unsuitable ≠**correct**: unconventional, unorthodox, wrong ≠**polite**: coarse, common, crude, discourteous, impolite, indecent, rude, ungentlemanly, unladylike, unrefined, unseemly

properly *adverb* **1** = **suitably**, appropriately, aptly, fittingly, rightly **2** = **correctly**, accurately **3** = **politely**, decently, decorously, respectably

➤ Antonyms

≠**suitably**: improperly, inappropriately, inaptly, unfittingly, unsuitably, wrongly ≠**correctly**: improperly, inaccurately, incorrectly, wrongly ≠**politely**: badly, impolitely, improperly, indecently, indecorously

property *noun* **1** = **possessions**, assets, belongings, building(s), capital, chattels, effects, estate, goods, holdings, house(s), means, resources, riches, wealth **2** = **land**, acres, estate, freehold, holding, real estate, real property, realty, title **3** = **quality**, ability, attribute, characteristic, feature, hallmark, idiosyncrasy, mark, peculiarity, trait, virtue

prophecy *noun* = **prediction**, augury, divination, forecast, foretelling, prognosis, prognostication, revelation, second sight, soothsaying, sortilege, vaticination (*rare*)

prophesy *verb* = **predict**, augur, call, divine, forecast, foresee, foretell, forewarn, presage, prognosticate, soothsay, vaticinate (*rare*)

prophet *noun* = **soothsayer**, augur, Cassandra, clairvoyant, diviner, forecaster, oracle, prognosticator, prophesier, seer, sibyl

prophetic *adjective* = **predictive**, augural, divinatory, foreshadowing, mantic, oracular, presaging, prescient, prognostic, sibylline

propinquity *noun Formal* **1** = **nearness**, adjacency, closeness, contiguity, neighbourhood, proximity, vicinity **2** = **relationship**, affiliation, affinity, blood, connection, consanguinity, kindred, kinship, relation, tie, ties of blood

propitiate *verb* = **appease**, conciliate, make peace, mollify, pacify, placate, reconcile, satisfy

propitiation *noun* = **appeasement**, conciliation, mollification, peacemaking, placation, reconciliation

propitious *adjective* **1** = **favourable**, advantageous, auspicious, bright, encouraging, fortunate, full of promise, happy, lucky, opportune, promising, prosperous, rosy, timely **2** = **well-disposed**, benevolent, benign, favourably inclined, friendly, gracious, kind

proponent *noun* = **supporter**, advocate, champion, defender, enthusiast, exponent, partisan, spokesman *or* spokeswoman, upholder

proportion *noun* **1** = **relative amount**, distribution, ratio, relationship **2** = **balance**, agreement, congruity, correspondence, harmony, symmetry **3** = **part**, amount, cut (*informal*), division, fraction, measure, percentage, quota, segment, share **4** **proportions** = **dimensions**, amplitude, breadth, bulk, capacity, expanse, extent, magnitude, measurements, range, scope, size, volume

proportional, proportionate *adjective* = **balanced**, commensurate, comparable, compatible, consistent, correspondent, corresponding, equitable, equivalent, even, in proportion, just

➤ Antonyms

different, discordant, disproportionate, dissimilar, incommensurable, incompatible, inconsistent, unequal

proposal *noun* = **suggestion**, bid, design, motion, offer, overture, plan, presentation, proffer, programme, project, proposition, recommendation, scheme, tender, terms

propose *verb* **1** = **put forward**, advance, come up with, present, proffer, propound, submit, suggest, tender **2** = **nominate**, introduce, invite, name, present, put up, recommend **3** = **intend**, aim, design, have every intention, have in mind, mean, plan, purpose, scheme **4** = **offer marriage**, ask for someone's hand (in marriage), pay suit, pop the question (*informal*)

proposition *noun* **1** = **proposal**, motion, plan, programme, project, recommendation, scheme, suggestion ♦ *verb* **2** = **make a pass at**, accost, make an improper suggestion, make an indecent proposal, solicit

propound *verb* = **put forward**, advance, advocate, contend, lay down, postulate, present, propose, set forth, submit, suggest

proprietor, proprietress *noun* = **owner**, deed holder, freeholder, landlord *or* landlady, landowner, possessor, titleholder

propriety *noun* **1** = **correctness**, appropriateness, aptness, becomingness, fitness, rightness, seemliness, suitableness **2** = **decorum**, breeding, courtesy, decency, delicacy, etiquette, good form, good manners, manners, modesty, politeness, protocol, punctilio, rectitude, refinement,

respectability, seemliness **3 the proprieties = etiquette**, accepted conduct, amenities, civilities, niceties, rules of conduct, social code, social conventions, social graces, the done thing
➤ Antonyms
≠**decorum**: bad form, bad manners, immodesty, impoliteness, indecency, indecorum, indelicacy, vulgarity

propulsion *noun* = **drive**, impetus, impulse, impulsion, momentum, motive power, power, pressure, propelling force, push, thrust

prosaic *adjective* = **dull**, banal, boring, commonplace, dry, everyday, flat, hackneyed, humdrum, matter-of-fact, mundane, ordinary, pedestrian, routine, stale, tame, trite, unimaginative, uninspiring, vapid, workaday
➤ Antonyms
entertaining, exciting, extraordinary, fascinating, imaginative, interesting, poetical, unusual

proscribe *verb* **1** = **prohibit**, ban, boycott, censure, condemn, damn, denounce, doom, embargo, forbid, interdict, reject **2** = **outlaw**, attaint (*archaic*), banish, blackball, deport, exclude, excommunicate, exile, expatriate, expel, ostracize
➤ Antonyms
≠**prohibit**: allow, authorize, endorse, give leave, give permission, license, permit, sanction, warrant

proscription *noun* **1** = **prohibition**, ban, boycott, censure, condemnation, damning, denunciation, dooming, embargo, interdict, rejection **2** = **banishment**, deportation, ejection, eviction, exclusion, excommunication, exile, expatriation, expulsion, ostracism

prosecute *verb* **1** *Law* = **put on trial**, arraign, bring action against, bring suit against, bring to trial, do (*slang*), indict, litigate, prefer charges, put in the dock, seek redress, sue, summon, take to court, try **2** = **conduct**, carry on, direct, discharge, engage in, manage, perform, practise, work at **3** = **continue**, carry through, follow through, persevere, persist, pursue, see through

proselyte *noun* = **convert**, initiate, neophyte, new believer, novice, tyro

proselytize *verb* = **convert**, bring to God, evangelize, make converts, spread the gospel

prospect *noun* **1** = **expectation**, anticipation, calculation, contemplation, future, hope, odds, opening, outlook, plan, presumption, probability, promise, proposal, thought **2** *sometimes plural* = **likelihood**, chance, possibility **3** = **view**, landscape, outlook, panorama, perspective, scene, sight, spectacle, vision, vista ♦ *verb* **4** = **look for**, explore, go after, search for, seek, survey

prospective *adjective* = **future**, about to be, anticipated, approaching, awaited, coming, destined, eventual, expected, forthcoming, hoped-for, imminent, intended, likely, looked-for, on the cards, possible, potential, soon-to-be, -to-be, to come, upcoming

prospectus *noun* = **catalogue**, announcement, conspectus, list, outline, plan, programme, scheme, syllabus, synopsis

prosper *verb* = **succeed**, advance, be fortunate, bloom, do well, fare well, flourish, flower, get on, grow rich, make good, make it (*informal*), progress, thrive

prosperity *noun* = **success**, affluence, boom, ease, fortune, good fortune, good times, life of luxury, life of Riley (*informal*), luxury, plenty, prosperousness, riches, the good life, wealth, well-being
➤ Antonyms
adversity, depression, destitution, failure, indigence, misfortune, poverty, shortage, want

prosperous *adjective* **1** = **wealthy**, affluent, in clover (*informal*), in the money (*informal*), moneyed, opulent, rich, well-heeled (*informal*), well-off, well-to-do **2** = **successful**, blooming, booming, doing well, flourishing, fortunate, lucky, on a roll, on the up and up (*Brit.*), palmy, prospering, thriving
➤ Antonyms
≠**wealthy**: impoverished, poor ≠**successful**: defeated, failing, inauspicious, unfavourable, unfortunate, unlucky, unpromising, unsuccessful, untimely

prostitute *noun* **1** = **whore**, bawd (*archaic*), brass (*slang*), call girl, camp follower, cocotte, courtesan, fallen woman, *fille de joie*, harlot, hooker (*U.S. slang*), hustler (*U.S. & Canad. slang*), loose woman, moll (*slang*), pro (*slang*), scrubber (*Brit. & Austral. slang*), streetwalker, strumpet, tart (*informal*), trollop, white slave, working girl (*facetious slang*) ♦ *verb* **2** = **cheapen**, debase, degrade, demean, devalue, misapply, pervert, profane

prostitution *noun* = **harlotry**, harlot's trade, Mrs. Warren's profession, streetwalking, the game (*slang*), the oldest profession, vice, whoredom

prostrate *adjective* **1** = **prone**, abject, bowed low, flat, horizontal, kowtowing, procumbent **2** = **exhausted**, at a low ebb, dejected, depressed, desolate, drained, fagged out (*informal*), fallen, inconsolable, overcome, spent, worn out ♦ *verb* **3**

= **exhaust**, drain, fag out (*informal*), fatigue, sap, tire, wear out, weary **4 prostrate oneself** = **bow down to**, abase oneself, bend the knee to, bow before, cast oneself before, cringe, fall at (someone's) feet, fall on one's knees before, grovel, kneel, kowtow, submit

prosy *adjective* = **dull**, boring, flat, humdrum, long, long-drawn-out, long-winded, monotonous, overlong, pedestrian, prosaic, tedious, tiresome, unimaginative, uninteresting, wordy

protagonist *noun* **1** = **supporter**, advocate, champion, exponent, leader, mainstay, moving spirit, prime mover, standard-bearer, torchbearer **2** = **leading character**, central character, hero *or* heroine, lead, principal

protean *adjective* = **changeable**, ever-changing, many-sided, mercurial, multiform, mutable, polymorphous, temperamental, variable, versatile, volatile

protect *verb* = **keep safe**, care for, chaperon, cover, cover up for, defend, foster, give sanctuary, guard, harbour, keep, look after, mount *or* stand guard over, preserve, safeguard, save, screen, secure, shelter, shield, stick up for (*informal*), support, take under one's wing, watch over
➤ **Antonyms**
assail, assault, attack, betray, endanger, expose, expose to danger, threaten

protection *noun* **1** = **safety**, aegis, care, charge, custody, defence, guardianship, guarding, preservation, protecting, safeguard, safekeeping, security **2** = **safeguard**, armour, barrier, buffer, bulwark, cover, guard, refuge, screen, shelter, shield

protective *adjective* = **protecting**, careful, covering, defensive, fatherly, insulating, jealous, maternal, motherly, paternal, possessive, safeguarding, sheltering, shielding, vigilant, warm, watchful

protector *noun* = **defender**, advocate, benefactor, bodyguard, champion, counsel, guard, guardian, guardian angel, knight in shining armour, patron, safeguard, tower of strength

protégé, protégée *noun* = **charge**, dependant, discovery, pupil, student, ward

protest *noun* **1** = **objection**, complaint, declaration, demur, demurral, disapproval, dissent, formal complaint, outcry, protestation, remonstrance ◆ *verb* **2** = **object**, complain, cry out, demonstrate, demur, disagree, disapprove, expostulate, express disapproval, kick (against) (*informal*), oppose, remonstrate, say no to, take exception, take up the cudgels **3**

= **assert**, affirm, argue, asseverate, attest, avow, contend, declare, insist, maintain, profess, testify, vow

protestation *noun Formal* = **declaration**, affirmation, asseveration, avowal, oath, pledge, profession, vow

protester *noun* = **demonstrator**, agitator, dissenter, dissident, protest marcher, rebel

protocol *noun* **1** = **code of behaviour**, conventions, courtesies, customs, decorum, etiquette, formalities, good form, manners, politesse, propriety, p's and q's, rules of conduct **2** = **agreement**, compact, concordat, contract, covenant, pact, treaty

prototype *noun* = **original**, archetype, example, first, mock-up, model, norm, paradigm, pattern, precedent, standard, type

protract *verb* = **extend**, continue, drag on *or* out, draw out, keep going, lengthen, prolong, spin out, stretch out
➤ **Antonyms**
abbreviate, abridge, compress, curtail, reduce, shorten, summarize

protracted *adjective* = **extended**, dragged out, drawn-out, interminable, lengthy, long, long-drawn-out, never-ending, overlong, prolonged, spun out, time-consuming

protrude *verb* = **stick out**, bulge, come through, extend, jut, obtrude, point, pop (*of eyes*), project, shoot out, stand out, start (from), stick out like a sore thumb

protrusion *noun* = **projection**, bulge, bump, hump, jut, lump, outgrowth, protuberance, swelling

protuberance *noun* = **bulge**, bump, excrescence, hump, knob, lump, outgrowth, process, projection, prominence, protrusion, swelling, tumour

protuberant *adjective* = **bulging**, beetling, bulbous, gibbous, hanging over, jutting, popping (*of eyes*), prominent, protruding, protrusive, proud (*dialect*), swelling, swollen
➤ **Antonyms**
concave, flat, indented, receding, sunken

proud *adjective* **1** = **satisfied**, appreciative, content, contented, glad, gratified, honoured, pleased, self-respecting, well-pleased **2** = **conceited**, arrogant, boastful, disdainful, egotistical, haughty, high and mighty (*informal*), imperious, lordly, narcissistic, overbearing, presumptuous, self-important, self-satisfied, snobbish, snooty (*informal*), stuck-up (*informal*), supercilious, toffee-nosed (*slang, chiefly Brit.*), too big for one's boots *or* breeches, vain **3** = **glorious**, exalted, gratifying, illustrious, memorable, pleasing, red-letter, rewarding, satisfying **4** = **distinguished**, august, eminent, grand, great, illustrious, imposing, magnificent,

majestic, noble, splendid, stately
➤ **Antonyms**
≠**satisfied**: discontented, displeased,
dissatisfied ≠**conceited**: abject, ashamed,
deferential, humble, meek, modest,
submissive, unobtrusive ≠**distinguished**:
base, humble, ignoble, ignominious, lowly,
unassuming, undignified

provable *adjective* = **verifiable**, attestable,
demonstrable, evincible, testable

prove *verb* **1** = **verify**, ascertain, attest,
authenticate, bear out, confirm, corroborate,
demonstrate, determine, establish, evidence,
evince, justify, show, show clearly,
substantiate **2** = **test**, analyse, assay, check,
examine, experiment, put to the test, put to
trial, try **3** = **turn out**, be found to be, come
out, end up, result
➤ **Antonyms**
≠**verify**: discredit, disprove, give the lie to,
refute, rule out

proven *adjective* = **established**, attested,
confirmed, definite, proved, reliable, tested,
verified

provenance *noun* = **origin**, birthplace,
derivation, source

provender *noun* = **fodder**, feed, forage

proverb *noun* = **saying**, adage, aphorism,
apophthegm, byword, dictum, gnome,
maxim, saw

proverbial *adjective* = **conventional**,
accepted, acknowledged, archetypal,
axiomatic, current, customary, famed,
famous, legendary, notorious, self-evident,
time-honoured, traditional, typical,
unquestioned, well-known

provide *verb* **1** = **supply**, accommodate,
cater, contribute, equip, furnish, outfit,
provision, purvey, stock up **2** = **give**, add,
afford, bring, impart, lend, present, produce,
render, serve, yield **3 provide for** or **against**
= **take precautions**, anticipate, arrange for,
forearm, get ready, make arrangements,
make plans, plan ahead, plan for, prepare
for, take measures **4 provide for** = **support**,
care for, keep, look after, maintain, sustain,
take care of
➤ **Antonyms**
≠**supply**: deprive, keep back, refuse,
withhold ≠**take precautions**: disregard, fail
to notice, miss, neglect, overlook ≠**support**:
neglect

providence *noun* **1** = **fate**, destiny, divine
intervention, fortune, God's will,
predestination **2** = **foresight**, care, caution,
discretion, far-sightedness, forethought,
perspicacity, presence of mind, prudence

provident *adjective* **1** = **thrifty**, economical,
frugal, prudent **2** = **foresighted**, canny,
careful, cautious, discreet, equipped,

far-seeing, far-sighted, forearmed, sagacious,
shrewd, vigilant, well-prepared, wise
➤ **Antonyms**
≠**thrifty**: improvident, imprudent, prodigal,
profligate, spendthrift, uneconomical,
wasteful ≠**foresighted**: careless, heedless,
improvident, negligent, reckless,
short-sighted, thoughtless

providential *adjective* = **lucky**, fortuitous,
fortunate, happy, heaven-sent, opportune,
timely, welcome

provider *noun* **1** = **supplier**, benefactor,
donor, giver, source **2** = **breadwinner**,
earner, mainstay, supporter, wage earner

providing, provided *conjunction* = **on
condition that**, as long as, contingent upon,
given, if and only if, in case, in the event, on
the assumption, subject to, upon these
terms, with the proviso, with the
understanding

province *noun* **1** = **region**, colony, county,
department, dependency, district, division,
domain, patch, section, territory, tract, turf
(*U.S. slang*), zone **2** = **area**, business,
capacity, charge, concern, duty,
employment, field, function, line, orbit, part,
pigeon (*Brit. informal*), post, responsibility,
role, sphere, turf (*U.S. slang*)

provincial *adjective* **1** = **rural**, country, hick
(*informal, chiefly U.S. & Canad.*),
home-grown, homespun, local, rustic **2**
= **parochial**, insular, inward-looking, limited,
narrow, narrow-minded, parish-pump,
small-minded, small-town (*chiefly U.S.*),
uninformed, unsophisticated, upcountry
♦ *noun* **3** = **yokel**, country cousin, hayseed
(*U.S. & Canad. informal*), hick (*informal,
chiefly U.S. & Canad.*), rustic
➤ **Antonyms**
adjective ≠**rural**: urban ≠**parochial**:
cosmopolitan, fashionable, polished, refined,
sophisticated, urbane

provision *noun* **1** = **supplying**,
accoutrement, catering, equipping, fitting
out, furnishing, providing, victualling **2**
= **condition**, agreement, clause, demand,
proviso, requirement, rider, specification,
stipulation, term **3** *As in* **make provision for**
= **arrangement**, plan, prearrangement,
precaution, preparation

provisional *adjective* **1** = **temporary**,
interim, pro tem, stopgap, transitional **2**
= **conditional**, contingent, limited,
provisory, qualified, tentative
➤ **Antonyms**
≠**temporary**: permanent ≠**conditional**:
definite, fixed

provisions *plural noun* = **food**,
comestibles, eatables, eats (*slang*), edibles,
fare, feed, foodstuff, groceries, grub (*slang*),

nosebag (*slang*), provender, rations, stores, supplies, sustenance, tack (*informal*), viands, victuals, vittles (*obsolete or dialect*)

proviso *noun* = **condition**, clause, limitation, provision, qualification, requirement, reservation, restriction, rider, stipulation, strings

provocation *noun* **1** = **cause**, *casus belli*, grounds, incitement, inducement, instigation, justification, motivation, reason, stimulus **2** = **offence**, affront, annoyance, challenge, dare, grievance, indignity, injury, insult, red rag, taunt, vexation

provocative *adjective* **1** = **offensive**, aggravating (*informal*), annoying, challenging, disturbing, galling, goading, incensing, insulting, outrageous, provoking, stimulating **2** = **suggestive**, alluring, arousing, erotic, exciting, inviting, seductive, sexy (*informal*), stimulating, tantalizing, tempting

provoke *verb* **1** = **anger**, affront, aggravate (*informal*), annoy, chafe, enrage, exasperate, gall, get in one's hair (*informal*), get one's back up, get on one's nerves (*informal*), hassle (*informal*), incense, infuriate, insult, irk, irritate, madden, make one's blood boil, nark (*Brit., Austral., & N.Z. slang*), offend, pique, piss one off (*taboo slang*), put one's back up, put out, rile, rub (someone) up the wrong way (*Informal*), take a rise out of, try one's patience, vex **2** = **rouse**, bring about, bring on *or* down, call forth, cause, draw forth, elicit, evoke, excite, fire, foment, generate, give rise to, incite, induce, inflame, inspire, instigate, kindle, lead to, motivate, move, occasion, precipitate, produce, promote, prompt, stimulate, stir
> **Antonyms**
≠**anger:** appease, calm, conciliate, mollify, pacify, placate, propitiate, quiet, soothe, sweeten ≠**rouse:** abate, allay, assuage, blunt, curb, ease, lessen, lull, mitigate, moderate, modify, relieve, temper

provoking *adjective* = **annoying**, aggravating (*informal*), exasperating, galling, irking, irksome, irritating, maddening, obstructive, offensive, tiresome, vexatious, vexing

prow *noun* = **bow(s)**, fore, forepart, front, head, nose, sharp end (*jocular*), stem

prowess *noun* **1** = **skill**, ability, accomplishment, adeptness, adroitness, aptitude, attainment, command, dexterity, excellence, expertise, expertness, facility, genius, mastery, talent **2** = **bravery**, boldness, courage, daring, dauntlessness, doughtiness, fearlessness, gallantry, hardihood, heroism, intrepidity, mettle, valiance, valour

> **Antonyms**
≠**skill:** clumsiness, inability, incapability, incompetence, ineptitude, ineptness, inexpertise ≠**bravery:** cowardice, faint-heartedness, fear, gutlessness, timidity

prowl *verb* = **move stealthily**, cruise, hunt, lurk, nose around, patrol, range, roam, rove, scavenge, skulk, slink, sneak, stalk, steal

proximity *noun* = **nearness**, adjacency, closeness, contiguity, juxtaposition, neighbourhood, propinquity, vicinity

proxy *noun* = **representative**, agent, attorney, delegate, deputy, factor, substitute, surrogate

prude *noun* = **prig**, old maid (*informal*), puritan, schoolmarm (*Brit. informal*)

prudence *noun* **1** = **common sense**, canniness, care, caution, circumspection, discretion, good sense, heedfulness, judgment, judiciousness, sagacity, vigilance, wariness, wisdom **2** = **thrift**, careful budgeting, economizing, economy, far-sightedness, foresight, forethought, frugality, good management, husbandry, planning, precaution, preparedness, providence, saving

prudent *adjective* **1** = **sensible**, canny, careful, cautious, circumspect, discerning, discreet, judicious, politic, sagacious, sage, shrewd, vigilant, wary, wise **2** = **thrifty**, canny, careful, economical, far-sighted, frugal, provident, sparing
> **Antonyms**
≠**sensible:** careless, heedless, impolitic, imprudent, inconsiderate, indiscreet, injudicious, irrational, rash, thoughtless, unwise ≠**thrifty:** careless, extravagant, improvident, imprudent, wasteful

prudery *noun* = **primness**, overmodesty, priggishness, prudishness, puritanicalness, squeamishness, starchiness (*informal*), strictness, stuffiness

prudish *adjective* = **prim**, demure, formal, narrow-minded, old-maidish (*informal*), overmodest, overnice, priggish, prissy (*informal*), proper, puritanical, schoolmarmish (*Brit. informal*), squeamish, starchy (*informal*), strait-laced, stuffy, Victorian
> **Antonyms**
broad-minded, liberal, open-minded, permissive

prune *verb* = **cut**, clip, cut back, dock, lop, pare down, reduce, shape, shorten, snip, trim

prurient *adjective* **1** = **lecherous**, lascivious, libidinous, lustful, salacious **2** = **indecent**, dirty, erotic, lewd, obscene, pornographic, salacious, smutty

pry *verb* = **be inquisitive**, be a busybody, be nosy (*informal*), interfere, intrude, meddle, nose into, peep, peer, poke, poke one's nose in or into (*informal*), snoop (*informal*)

prying *adjective* = **inquisitive**, curious, eavesdropping, impertinent, interfering, intrusive, meddlesome, meddling, nosy (*informal*), snooping (*informal*), snoopy (*informal*), spying

psalm *noun* = **hymn**, carol, chant, paean, song of praise

pseud *noun Informal* = **poser** (*informal*), fraud, humbug, phoney or phony (*informal*), trendy (*Brit. informal*)

pseudo- *adjective* = **false**, artificial, bogus, counterfeit, ersatz, fake, imitation, mock, not genuine, phoney or phony (*informal*), pretended, quasi-, sham, spurious
➤ **Antonyms**
actual, authentic, bona fide, genuine, heartfelt, honest, real, sincere, true, unfeigned

pseudonym *noun* = **false name**, alias, assumed name, incognito, nom de guerre, nom de plume, pen name, professional name, stage name

psyche *noun* = **soul**, anima, essential nature, individuality, inner man, innermost self, mind, personality, self, spirit, subconscious, true being

psychedelic *adjective* **1** = **hallucinogenic**, consciousness-expanding, hallucinatory, mind-bending (*informal*), mind-blowing (*informal*), mind-expanding, psychoactive **2** *Informal* = **multicoloured**, crazy, freaky (*slang*), kaleidoscopic, wild

psychiatrist *noun* = **psychotherapist**, analyst, headshrinker (*slang*), psychoanalyser, psychoanalyst, psychologist, shrink (*slang*), therapist

psychic *adjective* **1** = **supernatural**, clairvoyant, extrasensory, mystic, occult, preternatural, telekinetic, telepathic **2** = **mental**, psychogenic, psychological, spiritual

psychological *adjective* **1** = **mental**, cerebral, cognitive, intellectual **2** = **imaginary**, all in the mind, emotional, irrational, psychosomatic, subconscious, subjective, unconscious, unreal

psychology *noun* **1** = **behaviourism**, science of mind, study of personality **2** *Informal* = **way of thinking**, attitude, mental make-up, mental processes, thought processes, what makes one tick

psychopath *noun* = **madman**, headbanger (*informal*), headcase (*informal*), insane person, lunatic, maniac, mental case (*slang*), nutcase (*slang*), nutter (*Brit. slang*), psychotic, sociopath

psychotic *adjective* = **mad**, certifiable,

demented, deranged, insane, lunatic, mental (*slang*), *non compos mentis,* not right in the head, off one's chump, off one's head (*slang*), off one's rocker (*slang*), off one's trolley (*slang*), psychopathic, round the bend (*Brit. slang*), unbalanced

pub or **public house** *noun* = **tavern**, alehouse (*archaic*), bar, boozer (*Brit., Austral., & N.Z. informal*), hostelry (*archaic or facetious*), inn, local (*Brit. informal*), roadhouse, taproom, watering hole (*facetious slang*)

puberty *noun* = **adolescence**, awkward age, juvenescence, pubescence, teenage, teens, young adulthood

public *adjective* **1** = **general**, civic, civil, common, national, popular, social, state, universal, widespread **2** = **open**, accessible, communal, community, free to all, not private, open to the public, unrestricted **3** = **well-known**, important, prominent, respected **4** = **known**, acknowledged, exposed, in circulation, notorious, obvious, open, overt, patent, plain, published, recognized ◆ *noun* **5** = **people**, citizens, commonalty, community, country, electorate, everyone, hoi polloi, Joe (and Eileen) Public (*slang*), Joe Six-Pack (*U.S. slang*), masses, multitude, nation, populace, population, society, voters **6** = **clientele**, audience, buyers, followers, following, patrons, supporters, trade
➤ **Antonyms**
adjective ≠**open**: barred, closed, exclusive, inaccessible, personal, private, restricted, unavailable ≠**known**: hidden, secluded, secret, unknown, unrevealed

publication *noun* **1** = **pamphlet**, book, booklet, brochure, handbill, hardback, issue, leaflet, magazine, newspaper, paperback, periodical, title, zine (*informal*) **2** = **announcement**, advertisement, airing, appearance, broadcasting, declaration, disclosure, dissemination, notification, proclamation, promulgation, publishing, reporting

publicity *noun* = **advertising**, attention, ballyhoo (*informal*), boost, build-up, hype, plug (*informal*), press, promotion, public notice

publicize *verb* = **advertise**, bring to public notice, broadcast, give publicity to, hype, make known, play up, plug (*informal*), promote, push, spotlight, write up
➤ **Antonyms**
conceal, contain, cover up, keep dark, keep secret, smother, stifle, suppress, withhold

public-spirited *adjective* = **altruistic**, charitable, community-minded, generous, humanitarian, philanthropic, unselfish

publish *verb* **1** = **put out**, bring out, issue, print, produce **2** = **announce**, advertise, blow wide open (*slang*), broadcast, circulate, communicate, declare, disclose, distribute, divulge, impart, leak, proclaim, promulgate, publicize, reveal, spread

pucker *verb* **1** = **wrinkle**, contract, crease, draw together, gather, knit, purse, screw up, tighten ◆ *noun* **2** = **wrinkle**, crease, fold

pudding *noun* = **dessert**, afters (*Brit. informal*), last course, pud (*informal*), second course, sweet

puerile *adjective* = **childish**, babyish, foolish, immature, inane, infantile, irresponsible, jejune, juvenile, naive, petty, ridiculous, silly, trivial, weak
➤ **Antonyms**
adult, grown-up, mature, responsible, sensible

puff *noun* **1** = **blast**, breath, draught, emanation, flurry, gust, whiff **2** = **smoke**, drag (*slang*), pull ◆ *verb* **3** = **blow**, breathe, exhale, gasp, gulp, pant, wheeze **4** = **smoke**, drag (*slang*), draw, inhale, pull at *or* on, suck **5** *usually with* **up** = **swell**, bloat, dilate, distend, expand, inflate **6** = **promote**, crack up (*informal*), hype, overpraise, plug (*informal*), praise, publicize, push

puffy *adjective* = **swollen**, bloated, distended, enlarged, inflamed, inflated, puffed up

pugilism *noun* = **boxing**, fighting, prizefighting, the noble art *or* science, the ring

pugilist *noun* = **boxer**, bruiser (*informal*), fighter, prizefighter

pugnacious *adjective* = **aggressive**, antagonistic, argumentative, bellicose, belligerent, combative, contentious, hot-tempered, irascible, irritable, quarrelsome
➤ **Antonyms**
calm, conciliatory, gentle, peaceable, peaceful, peace-loving, placatory, placid, quiet

puke *verb Slang* = **vomit**, barf (*U.S. slang*), be nauseated, be sick, chuck (up) (*slang, chiefly U.S.*), chunder (*slang, chiefly Austral.*), disgorge, heave, regurgitate, retch, spew, throw up (*informal*), upchuck (*U.S. slang*)

pukka *adjective Anglo-Indian* = **genuine**, authentic, bona fide, official, on the level (*informal*), proper, real, the real McCoy

pull *verb* **1** = **draw**, drag, haul, jerk, tow, trail, tug, yank **2** = **strain**, dislocate, rend, rip, sprain, stretch, tear, wrench **3** = **extract**, draw out, gather, pick, pluck, remove, take out, uproot, weed **4** *Informal* = **attract**, draw, entice, lure, magnetize **5 pull apart** *or*

to pieces = **criticize**, attack, blast, find fault, lambast(e), lay into (*informal*), pan (*informal*), pick holes in, put down, run down, slam (*slang*), slate (*informal*), tear into (*informal*) **6 pull oneself together** *Informal* = **get a grip on oneself**, buck up (*informal*), get over it, regain composure, snap out of it (*informal*) ◆ *noun* **7** = **tug**, jerk, twitch, yank **8** = **puff**, drag (*slang*), inhalation **9** *Informal* = **influence**, advantage, bottom, clout (*informal*), leverage, muscle, power, weight **10** = **attraction**, drawing power, effort, exertion, force, forcefulness, influence, lure, magnetism
➤ **Antonyms**
verb ≠**draw**: drive, nudge, push, ram, shove, thrust ≠**extract**: implant, insert, plant ≠**attract**: deter, discourage, put one off, repel ◆ *noun* ≠**tug**: nudge, push, shove, thrust

pull down *verb* = **demolish**, bulldoze, destroy, raze, remove
➤ **Antonyms**
build, construct, erect, put up, raise, set up

pull in *verb* **1** = **draw in**, arrive, come in, draw up, reach, stop **2** = **attract**, bring in, draw **3** *Brit. slang* = **arrest**, bust (*informal*), collar (*informal*), feel one's collar (*slang*), lift (*slang*), nab (*informal*), nail (*informal*), pinch (*informal*), run in (*slang*), take into custody **4** = **earn**, clear, gain, gross, make, net, pocket, take home

pull off *verb Informal* = **succeed**, accomplish, bring off, carry out, crack it (*informal*), cut it (*informal*), do the trick, manage, score a success, secure one's object

pull out *verb* = **withdraw**, abandon, back off, depart, evacuate, leave, quit, rat on, retreat, stop participating

pull through *verb* = **survive**, come through, get better, get over, pull round, rally, recover, turn the corner, weather

pull up *verb* **1** = **stop**, brake, come to a halt, halt, reach a standstill **2** = **uproot**, dig out, lift, raise **3** = **reprimand**, admonish, bawl out (*informal*), carpet (*informal*), castigate, chew out (*U.S. & Canad. informal*), dress down (*informal*), rap over the knuckles, read the riot act, rebuke, reprove, slap on the wrist, take to task, tear into (*informal*), tear (someone) off a strip (*Brit. informal*), tell off (*informal*), tick off (*informal*)

pulp *noun* **1** = **paste**, mash, mush, pap, semiliquid, semisolid, triturate **2** = **flesh**, marrow, soft part ◆ *verb* **3** = **crush**, mash, pulverize, squash ◆ *adjective* **4** = **cheap**, lurid, mushy (*informal*), rubbishy, sensational, trashy

pulpy *adjective* = **soft**, fleshy, mushy, pappy,

squashy, succulent

pulsate verb = **throb**, beat, palpitate, pound, pulse, quiver, thump

pulse noun 1 = **beat**, beating, oscillation, pulsation, rhythm, throb, throbbing, vibration ♦ verb 2 = **beat**, pulsate, throb, tick, vibrate

pulverize verb 1 = **crush**, granulate, grind, mill, pestle, pound 2 = **defeat**, annihilate, blow out of the water (slang), crush, demolish, destroy, flatten, lick (informal), smash, stuff (slang), tank (slang), vanquish, wipe the floor with (informal), wreck

pummel verb = **beat**, batter, hammer, pound, punch, strike, thump

pump verb 1 often with **out** = **drive out**, bail out, drain, draw off, empty, force out, siphon 2 with **up** = **inflate**, blow up, dilate 3 often with **into** = **drive**, force, inject, pour, push, send, supply 4 = **interrogate**, cross-examine, give (someone) the third degree, grill (informal), probe, question closely, quiz, worm out of

pun noun = **play on words**, double entendre, quip, witticism

punch[1] verb 1 = **hit**, bash (informal), belt (informal), biff (slang), bop (informal), box, clout (informal), pummel, slam, slug, smash, sock (slang), strike, swipe (informal), wallop (informal) ♦ noun 2 = **blow**, bash (informal), biff (slang), bop (informal), clout (informal), hit, jab, knock, sock (slang), swipe (informal), thump, wallop (informal) 3 Informal = **effectiveness**, bite, drive, force, forcefulness, impact, point, verve, vigour

punch[2] verb = **pierce**, bore, cut, drill, perforate, prick, puncture, stamp

punch-drunk adjective = **dazed**, confused, groggy (informal), in a daze, punchy (informal), reeling, staggering, stupefied, unsteady, woozy (informal)

punch-up noun Brit. informal = **fight**, argument, brawl, dust-up (informal), free-for-all (informal), row, scrap (informal), set-to (informal), stand-up fight (informal)

punchy adjective Informal = **effective**, dynamic, forceful, in-your-face (slang), storming (informal)

punctilious adjective Formal = **particular**, careful, ceremonious, conscientious, exact, finicky, formal, fussy, meticulous, nice, precise, proper, scrupulous, strict

punctual adjective = **on time**, early, exact, in good time, on the dot, precise, prompt, seasonable, strict, timely
  ➤ **Antonyms**
  behind, behindhand, belated, delayed, late, overdue, tardy, unpunctual

punctuality noun = **promptness**, promptitude, readiness, regularity

punctuate verb 1 = **interrupt**, break, interject, intersperse, pepper, sprinkle 2 = **emphasize**, accentuate, lay stress on, mark, point up, stress, underline

puncture noun 1 = **hole**, break, cut, damage, leak, nick, opening, perforation, rupture, slit 2 = **flat tyre**, flat ♦ verb 3 = **pierce**, bore, cut, impale, nick, penetrate, perforate, prick, rupture

pundit noun = **expert**, buff (informal), guru, (self-appointed) expert or authority

pungent adjective 1 = **strong**, acerb, acid, acrid, aromatic, bitter, highly flavoured, hot, peppery, piquant, seasoned, sharp, sour, spicy, stinging, tangy, tart 2 = **cutting**, acrimonious, barbed, biting, caustic, incisive, keen, pointed, sarcastic, scathing, sharp, stinging, telling, trenchant
  ➤ **Antonyms**
  ≠strong: bland, dull, mild, moderate, tasteless, unsavoury, unstimulating, weak
  ≠cutting: dull, inane

punish verb 1 = **discipline**, castigate, chasten, chastise, correct, penalize, rap someone's knuckles, sentence, slap someone's wrist, throw the book at 2 = **mistreat**, abuse, batter, give (someone) a going-over (informal), harm, hurt, injure, knock about, manhandle, misuse, oppress, rough up

punishable adjective = **culpable**, blameworthy, chargeable, convictable, criminal, indictable

punishing adjective = **hard**, arduous, backbreaking, burdensome, demanding, exhausting, grinding, gruelling, strenuous, taxing, tiring, uphill, wearing
  ➤ **Antonyms**
  cushy (informal), easy, effortless, light, simple, undemanding, unexacting, untaxing

punishment noun 1 = **penalty**, chastening, chastisement, comeuppance (slang), correction, discipline, just deserts, penance, punitive measures, retribution, sanction, what for (informal) 2 Informal = **rough treatment**, abuse, beating, hard work, maltreatment, manhandling, pain, slave labour, torture, victimization

punitive adjective = **retaliatory**, in reprisal, in retaliation, retaliative, revengeful, vindictive

punt verb 1 = **bet**, back, gamble, lay, stake, wager ♦ noun 2 = **bet**, gamble, stake, wager

punter noun 1 = **gambler**, backer, better, punt (chiefly Brit.) 2 Informal = **person**, bloke (Brit. informal), fellow, guy (informal), man in the street 3 Informal = **customer**, client

puny adjective = **feeble**, diminutive,

dwarfish, frail, little, pint-sized (*informal*), pygmy or pigmy, sickly, stunted, tiny, undersized, undeveloped, weak, weakly
➤ Antonyms
brawny, burly, healthy, hefty (*informal*), husky (*informal*), powerful, robust, strong, sturdy, well-built, well-developed

pupil *noun* = **learner**, beginner, disciple, novice, scholar, schoolboy or schoolgirl, student, trainee, tyro
➤ Antonyms
coach, guru, instructor, master or mistress, schoolmaster or schoolmistress, schoolteacher, teacher, trainer, tutor

puppet *noun* 1 = **marionette**, doll 2 = **pawn**, cat's-paw, creature, dupe, figurehead, gull (*archaic*), instrument, mouthpiece, stooge, tool

purchase *verb* 1 = **buy**, acquire, come by, gain, get, get hold of, invest in, make a purchase, obtain, pay for, pick up, procure, score (*slang*), secure 2 = **achieve**, attain, earn, gain, realize, win ♦ *noun* 3 = **buy**, acquisition, asset, gain, investment, possession, property 4 = **grip**, advantage, edge, foothold, footing, grasp, hold, influence, lever, leverage, support, toehold
➤ Antonyms
verb ≠**buy**: hawk, market, merchandise, peddle, retail, sell, trade in, vend

purchaser *noun* = **buyer**, consumer, customer
➤ Antonyms
dealer, merchant, retailer, salesman or saleswoman, salesperson, seller, shopkeeper, tradesman, vendor

pure *adjective* 1 = **unmixed**, authentic, clear, flawless, genuine, natural, neat, perfect, real, simple, straight, true, unalloyed 2 = **clean**, disinfected, germ-free, immaculate, pasteurized, sanitary, spotless, squeaky-clean, sterile, sterilized, unadulterated, unblemished, uncontaminated, unpolluted, untainted, wholesome 3 = **innocent**, blameless, chaste, guileless, honest, immaculate, impeccable, maidenly, modest, squeaky-clean, true, uncorrupted, undefiled, unspotted, unstained, unsullied, upright, virgin, virginal, virtuous 4 = **complete**, absolute, mere, outright, sheer, thorough, unmitigated, unqualified, utter 5 = **theoretical**, abstract, academic, philosophical, speculative
➤ Antonyms
≠**unmixed**: adulterated, alloyed, flawed, imperfect, mixed ≠**clean**: contaminated, dirty, filthy, impure, infected, polluted, tainted ≠**innocent**: contaminated, corrupt, defiled, guilty, immodest, immoral, impure, indecent, obscene, sinful, unchaste, unclean, untrue ≠**complete**: qualified ≠**theoretical**:

applied, practical

purebred *adjective* = **thoroughbred**, blood, full-blooded, pedigree

purely *adverb* = **absolutely**, completely, entirely, exclusively, just, merely, only, plainly, simply, solely, totally, wholly

purgative *noun* 1 = **purge**, aperient (*Medical*), cathartic, laxative ♦ *adjective* 2 = **purging**, aperient (*Medical*), cleansing, laxative

purgatory *noun* = **torment**, agony, hell (*informal*), hell on earth, misery, murder (*informal*), torture

purge *verb* 1 = **get rid of**, axe (*informal*), dismiss, do away with, eject, eradicate, expel, exterminate, kill, liquidate, remove, rid of, rout out, wipe from the face of the earth, wipe out 2 = **cleanse**, clean out, clear, expiate, purify, wash 3 = **absolve**, exonerate, forgive, pardon ♦ *noun* 4 = **removal**, cleanup, ejection, elimination, eradication, expulsion, liquidation, witch hunt 5 = **purgative** (*Medical*), aperient (*Medical*), cathartic, dose of salts, laxative

purify *verb* 1 = **clean**, clarify, cleanse, decontaminate, disinfect, filter, fumigate, refine, sanitize, wash 2 = **absolve**, cleanse, exculpate, exonerate, redeem, sanctify
➤ Antonyms
≠**clean**: adulterate, befoul, contaminate, corrupt, defile, foul, infect, pollute, soil, taint ≠**absolve**: stain, sully, taint, vitiate

purist *noun* = **stickler**, classicist, formalist, pedant, precisian

puritan *noun* 1 = **moralist**, fanatic, prude, rigorist, zealot ♦ *adjective* 2 = **strict**, ascetic, austere, hidebound, intolerant, moralistic, narrow, narrow-minded, prudish, puritanical, severe, strait-laced

puritanical *adjective* = **strict**, ascetic, austere, bigoted, disapproving, fanatical, forbidding, narrow, narrow-minded, prim, proper, prudish, puritan, rigid, severe, stiff, strait-laced, stuffy
➤ Antonyms
broad-minded, hedonistic, indulgent, latitudinarian, liberal, permissive, tolerant

purity *noun* 1 = **cleanness**, brilliance, clarity, cleanliness, clearness, faultlessness, fineness, genuineness, immaculateness, pureness, untaintedness, wholesomeness 2 = **innocence**, blamelessness, chasteness, chastity, decency, honesty, integrity, piety, rectitude, sincerity, virginity, virtue, virtuousness
➤ Antonyms
≠**cleanness**: cloudiness, contamination, impurity ≠**innocence**: immodesty, immorality, impurity, unchasteness, vice, wickedness

purlieu noun Literary 1 usually plural = **outskirts**, borders, confines, environs, fringes, limits, neighbourhood, periphery, precincts, suburbs, vicinity 2 often plural = **stamping ground**, hang-out (informal), haunt, patch, resort, territory

purloin verb Formal = **steal**, appropriate, filch, nick (slang, chiefly Brit.), pilfer, pinch (informal), swipe (slang), thieve

purport verb 1 = **claim**, allege, assert, declare, maintain, pose as, pretend, proclaim, profess 2 = **signify**, betoken, convey, denote, express, imply, import, indicate, intend, mean, point to, suggest ♦ noun 3 = **significance**, bearing, drift, gist, idea, implication, import, meaning, sense

purpose noun 1 = **reason**, aim, design, function, idea, intention, object, point, principle, the why and wherefore 2 = **aim**, ambition, aspiration, design, desire, end, goal, Holy Grail (informal), hope, intention, object, objective, plan, project, scheme, target, view, wish 3 = **determination**, constancy, firmness, persistence, resolution, resolve, single-mindedness, steadfastness, tenacity, will 4 = **use**, advantage, avail, benefit, effect, gain, good, outcome, profit, result, return 5 **on purpose** = **deliberately**, by design, designedly, intentionally, knowingly, purposely, wilfully, wittingly ♦ verb 6 = **intend**, aim, aspire, contemplate, decide, design, determine, have a mind to, make up one's mind, mean, plan, propose, resolve, set one's sights on, work towards

purposeful adjective = **determined**, decided, deliberate, firm, fixed, immovable, resolute, resolved, settled, single-minded, steadfast, unfaltering
➤ Antonyms
aimless, faltering, irresolute, purposeless, undecided, undetermined, vacillating, wavering

purposeless adjective = **pointless**, aimless, empty, motiveless, needless, senseless, uncalled-for, unnecessary, useless, wanton

purposely adverb = **deliberately**, by design, calculatedly, consciously, designedly, expressly, intentionally, knowingly, on purpose, wilfully, with intent
➤ Antonyms
accidentally, by accident, by chance, by mistake, inadvertently, unconsciously, unintentionally, unknowingly, unwittingly

purse noun 1 = **pouch**, money-bag, wallet 2 = **money**, coffers, exchequer, funds, means, resources, treasury, wealth, wherewithal 3 = **prize**, award, gift, reward ♦ verb 4 = **pucker**, close, contract, knit, pout, press together, tighten, wrinkle

pursuance noun Formal = **carrying out**, bringing about, discharge, doing, effecting, execution, following, performance, pursuing

pursue verb 1 = **follow**, accompany, attend, chase, dog, give chase to, go after, harass, harry, haunt, hound, hunt, hunt down, plague, run after, shadow, stalk, tail (informal), track 2 = **try for**, aim for, aspire to, desire, have as one's goal, purpose, seek, strive for, work towards 3 = **engage in**, apply oneself, carry on, conduct, perform, ply, practise, wage, work at 4 = **court**, chase after, pay attention to, pay court to, set one's cap at, woo 5 = **continue**, adhere to, carry on, cultivate, hold to, keep on, maintain, persevere in, persist in, proceed, see through
➤ Antonyms
≠follow: avoid, flee, give (someone or something) a wide berth, keep away from, run away from, shun, steer clear of ≠try for: eschew, fight shy of

pursuit noun 1 = **pursuing**, chase, hunt, hunting, inquiry, quest, search, seeking, tracking, trail, trailing 2 = **occupation**, activity, hobby, interest, line, pastime, pleasure, vocation

purvey verb 1 = **supply**, cater, deal in, furnish, provide, sell, trade in 2 = **communicate**, make available, pass on, publish, retail, spread, transmit

purview noun 1 = **scope**, compass, confine(s), extent, field, limit, province, range, reach, sphere 2 = **understanding**, comprehension, overview, perspective, range of view

push verb 1 = **shove**, depress, drive, poke, press, propel, ram, thrust 2 = **make or force one's way**, elbow, jostle, move, shoulder, shove, squeeze, thrust 3 = **promote**, advertise, boost, hype, make known, plug (informal), publicize 4 = **urge**, egg on, encourage, expedite, gee up, hurry, impel, incite, persuade, press, prod, speed (up), spur 5 = **drive**, browbeat, coerce, constrain, encourage, exert influence on, influence ♦ noun 6 = **shove**, butt, jolt, nudge, poke, prod, thrust 7 Informal = **drive**, ambition, determination, dynamism, energy, enterprise, get-up-and-go (informal), go (informal), gumption (informal), initiative, pep, vigour, vitality 8 Informal = **effort**, advance, assault, attack, campaign, charge, offensive, onset, thrust 9 **the push** Informal, chiefly Brit. = **dismissal**, discharge, marching orders (informal), one's books (informal), one's cards (informal), the boot (slang), the (old) heave-ho (informal), the order of the boot (slang), the sack (informal)
➤ Antonyms
verb ≠shove: drag, draw, haul, jerk, pull, tow, trail, tug, yank ≠urge: deter,

discourage, dissuade, put off ♦ *noun*
≠**shove:** jerk, pull, tug, yank

pushed *adjective Informal, often with* **for**
= **short of,** hurried, in difficulty, pressed,
rushed, tight, under pressure, up against it
(*informal*)

pushing *adjective* = **ambitious,** determined,
driving, dynamic, enterprising, go-ahead, on
the go, purposeful, resourceful

push off *verb Informal* = **go away,** beat it
(*slang*), depart, get lost (*informal*), hit the
road (*slang*), leave, make oneself scarce
(*informal*), make tracks, pack one's bags
(*informal*), shove off (*informal*), slope off,
take off (*informal*)

pushover *noun Informal* **1** = **piece of cake**
(*Brit. informal*), breeze (*U.S. & Canad.
informal*), cakewalk (*informal*), child's play
(*informal*), cinch (*slang*), doddle (*Brit.
slang*), picnic (*informal*), plain sailing,
walkover (*informal*) **2** = **sucker** (*slang*),
chump (*informal*), easy game (*informal*),
easy *or* soft mark (*informal*), mug (*Brit.
slang*), soft touch (*slang*), stooge (*slang*),
walkover (*informal*)
➤ **Antonyms**
≠**piece of cake:** challenge, hassle (*informal*),
ordeal, test, trial, undertaking

pushy *adjective* = **forceful,** aggressive,
ambitious, assertive, bold, brash, bumptious,
loud, obnoxious, obtrusive, offensive,
officious, presumptuous, pushing,
self-assertive
➤ **Antonyms**
diffident, inoffensive, meek, mousy, quiet,
reserved, retiring, self-effacing, shy, timid,
unassertive, unassuming, unobtrusive

pusillanimous *adjective Formal*
= **cowardly,** abject, chicken-hearted, craven,
faint-hearted, fearful, feeble, gutless
(*informal*), lily-livered, recreant (*archaic*),
spineless, timid, timorous, weak, yellow
(*informal*)
➤ **Antonyms**
bold, brave, courageous, daring, dauntless,
fearless, gallant, heroic, intrepid, plucky,
valiant, valorous

pussyfoot *verb* **1** = **creep,** prowl, slink,
steal, tiptoe, tread warily **2** = **hedge,** beat
about the bush, be noncommittal,
equivocate, flannel (*Brit. informal*), hum and
haw, prevaricate, sit on the fence

pustule *noun* = **boil,** gathering, pimple, zit
(*slang*)

put *verb* **1** = **place,** bring, deposit, establish,
fix, lay, position, rest, set, settle, situate **2**
= **impose,** commit, condemn, consign,
doom, enjoin, inflict, levy, subject **3** = **make,**
assign, constrain, employ, force, induce,
oblige, require, set, subject to **4** = **express,**

phrase, set, state, utter, word **5** = **present,**
advance, bring forward, forward, offer, posit,
propose, set before, submit, tender **6**
= **throw,** cast, fling, heave, hurl, lob, pitch,
toss

put across *or* **over** *verb* = **communicate,**
convey, explain, get across, get through,
make clear, make oneself understood, spell
out

put aside *or* **by** *verb* **1** = **save,** cache,
deposit, keep in reserve, lay by, squirrel
away, stockpile, store, stow away **2**
= **disregard,** bury, discount, forget, ignore

putative *adjective Formal* = **supposed,**
alleged, assumed, commonly believed,
imputed, presumed, presumptive, reported,
reputed

put away *verb* **1** = **save,** deposit, keep, lay
in, put by, set aside, store away **2** *Informal*
= **commit,** certify, confine, institutionalize,
lock up **3** *Informal* = **consume,** devour, eat
up, gobble, gulp down, wolf down **4** = **put
back,** replace, return to (its) place, tidy
away

put-down *noun Informal* = **humiliation,**
barb, dig, gibe, kick in the teeth (*slang*),
knock (*informal*), one in the eye (*informal*),
rebuff, slight, sneer, snub

put down *verb* **1** = **record,** enter, inscribe,
log, set down, take down, transcribe, write
down **2** = **repress,** crush, quash, quell,
silence, stamp out, suppress **3** *usually with*
to = **attribute,** ascribe, impute, set down **4**
= **put to sleep,** destroy, do away with, put
away, put out of its misery **5** *Slang*
= **humiliate,** condemn, crush, deflate,
dismiss, disparage, mortify, reject, shame,
slight, snub

put forward *verb* = **recommend,** advance,
introduce, move, nominate, prescribe,
present, press, proffer, propose, submit,
suggest, tender

put off *verb* **1** = **postpone,** defer, delay,
hold over, put back, put on ice, put on the
back burner (*informal*), reschedule, take a
rain check on (*U.S. & Canad. informal*) **2**
= **disconcert,** abash, confuse, discomfit,
dismay, distress, faze, nonplus, perturb,
rattle (*informal*), take the wind out of
someone's sails, throw (*informal*), unsettle **3**
= **discourage,** dishearten, dissuade
➤ **Antonyms**
≠**discourage:** egg on, encourage, gee up,
incite, persuade, prompt, push, spur, urge

put on *verb* **1** = **don,** change into, dress, get
dressed in, slip into **2** = **fake,** affect, assume,
feign, make believe, play-act, pretend, sham,
simulate **3** = **present,** do, mount, produce,
show, stage **4** = **add,** gain, increase by **5**
= **bet,** back, lay, place, wager

> **Antonyms**

≠**don:** cast off, doff, remove, shed, slip off, slip out of, take off, throw off, undress

put out *verb* **1** = **annoy**, anger, confound, disturb, exasperate, harass, irk, irritate, nettle, perturb, provoke, vex **2** = **disconcert**, discompose, discountenance, disturb, embarrass, put on the spot, take the wind out of someone's sails **3** = **extinguish**, blow out, douse, quench, smother, snuff out, stamp out **4** = **inconvenience**, bother, discomfit, discommode, disturb, impose upon, incommode, trouble, upset **5** = **issue**, bring out, broadcast, circulate, make known, make public, publish, release

putrefy *verb Formal* = **rot**, break down, corrupt, decay, decompose, deteriorate, go bad, spoil

putrescent *adjective Formal* = **rotting**, decaying, decomposing, going bad, stinking

putrid *adjective* = **rotten**, bad, contaminated, corrupt, decayed, decomposed, fetid, foul, off, putrefied, rancid, rank, reeking, rotting, spoiled, stinking, tainted

> **Antonyms**

clean, fresh, pure, sweet, uncontaminated, untainted, wholesome

put through *verb* = **carry out**, accomplish, achieve, bring off, conclude, do, effect, execute, manage, pull off

put up *verb* **1** = **build**, construct, erect, fabricate, raise **2** = **accommodate**, board, entertain, give one lodging, house, lodge, take in **3** = **submit**, float, nominate, offer, present, propose, put forward, recommend **4** = **provide**, advance, give, invest, pay, pledge, supply **5 put up to** = **encourage**, egg on, goad, incite, instigate, prompt, put the idea into one's head, urge **6 put up with** *Informal* = **stand**, abide, bear, brook, endure, lump (*informal*), stand for, stomach, suffer, swallow, take, tolerate

> **Antonyms**

≠**build:** demolish, destroy, flatten, knock down, level, pull down, raze, tear down

≠**stand:** not stand for, object to, oppose,

protest against, reject, take exception to

put upon *verb* = **take advantage of**, abuse, exploit, impose upon, take for granted

puzzle *verb* **1** = **perplex**, baffle, beat (*slang*), bewilder, confound, confuse, flummox, mystify, nonplus, stump **2** *usually with* **out** = **solve**, clear up, crack, crack the code, decipher, figure out, find the key, get it, get the answer, resolve, see, sort out, suss (out) (*slang*), think through, unravel, work out **3** *usually with* **over** = **think about**, ask oneself, brood, cudgel *or* rack one's brains, mull over, muse, ponder, study, think hard, wonder ♦ *noun* **4** = **problem**, brain-teaser (*informal*), conundrum, enigma, mystery, paradox, poser, question, riddle, teaser

puzzled *adjective* = **perplexed**, at a loss, at sea, baffled, beaten, bewildered, clueless, confused, doubtful, flummoxed, in a fog, lost, mixed up, mystified, nonplussed, stuck, stumped, without a clue

puzzlement *noun* = **perplexity**, bafflement, bewilderment, confusion, disorientation, doubt, doubtfulness, mystification, questioning, surprise, uncertainty, wonder

puzzling *adjective* = **perplexing**, abstruse, ambiguous, baffling, bewildering, beyond one, enigmatic, full of surprises, hard, incomprehensible, inexplicable, involved, knotty, labyrinthine, misleading, mystifying, oracular, unaccountable, unclear, unfathomable

> **Antonyms**

clear, comprehensible, easy, evident, intelligible, lucid, manifest, obvious, patent, plain, simple, unambiguous, unequivocal, unmistakable

pygmy, pigmy *noun* **1** = **midget**, dwarf, Lilliputian, manikin **2** = **nonentity**, cipher, lightweight (*informal*), nobody, pipsqueak (*informal*), small fry ♦ *adjective* **3** = **small**, diminutive, dwarf, Lilliputian, midget, miniature, minuscule, tiny, undersized, wee

pyromaniac *noun* = **arsonist**, firebug (*informal*), fire raiser, incendiary

Q q

quack *noun* **1** = **charlatan**, fake, fraud, humbug, impostor, mountebank, phoney *or* phony (*informal*), pretender, quacksalver (*archaic*) ◆ *adjective* **2** = **fake**, counterfeit, fraudulent, phoney *or* phony (*informal*), pretended, sham

quaff *verb* = **drink**, down, gulp, imbibe, swallow, swig (*informal*)

quagmire *noun* **1** = **bog**, fen, marsh, mire, morass, quicksand, slough, swamp **2** = **entanglement**, difficulty, dilemma, fix (*informal*), imbroglio, impasse, jam (*informal*), muddle, pass, pickle (*informal*), pinch, plight, predicament, quandary, scrape (*informal*)

quail *verb* = **shrink**, blanch, blench, cower, cringe, droop, faint, falter, flinch, have cold feet (*informal*), quake, recoil, shake, shudder, tremble

quaint *adjective* **1** = **unusual**, bizarre, curious, droll, eccentric, fanciful, fantastic, odd, old-fashioned, original, peculiar, queer, rum (*Brit. slang*), singular, strange, whimsical **2** = **old-fashioned**, antiquated, antique, artful, charming, gothic, ingenious, old-world, picturesque
➤ **Antonyms**
≠**unusual**: normal, ordinary
≠**old-fashioned**: fashionable, modern, new, up-to-date

quake *verb* = **shake**, convulse, move, pulsate, quail, quiver, rock, shiver, shudder, throb, totter, tremble, vibrate, waver, wobble

qualification *noun* **1** = **attribute**, ability, accomplishment, aptitude, capability, capacity, eligibility, endowment(s), fitness, quality, skill, suitability, suitableness **2** = **condition**, allowance, caveat, criterion, exception, exemption, limitation, modification, objection, prerequisite, proviso, requirement, reservation, restriction, rider, stipulation

qualified *adjective* **1** = **capable**, able, accomplished, adept, certificated, competent, efficient, eligible, equipped, experienced, expert, fit, knowledgeable, licensed, practised, proficient, skilful, talented, trained **2** = **restricted**, bounded, circumscribed, conditional, confined, contingent, equivocal, guarded, limited, modified, provisional, reserved
➤ **Antonyms**
≠**capable**: amateur, apprentice, self-styled, self-taught, trainee, uncertificated, unqualified, untrained ≠**restricted**: categorical, outright, unconditional, unequivocal, whole-hearted

qualify *verb* **1** = **certify**, capacitate, commission, condition, empower, endow, equip, fit, ground, permit, prepare, ready, sanction, train **2** = **moderate**, abate, adapt, assuage, circumscribe, diminish, ease, lessen, limit, mitigate, modify, modulate, reduce, regulate, restrain, restrict, soften, temper, vary **3** = **be described**, be characterized, be designated, be distinguished, be named
➤ **Antonyms**
≠**certify**: ban, debar, disqualify, forbid, preclude, prevent

quality *noun* **1** = **excellence**, calibre, distinction, grade, merit, position, pre-eminence, rank, standing, status, superiority, value **2** = **characteristic**, aspect, attribute, condition, feature, mark, peculiarity, property, trait **3** = **nature**, character, constitution, description, essence, kind, make, sort, worth **4** *Obsolete* = **nobility**, aristocracy, gentry, ruling class, upper class

qualm *noun* **1** = **misgiving**, anxiety, apprehension, compunction, disquiet, doubt, hesitation, regret, reluctance, remorse, scruple, twinge *or* pang of conscience, uncertainty, uneasiness **2** = **nausea**, agony, attack, pang, queasiness, sickness, spasm, throe (*rare*), twinge

quandary *noun* = **difficulty**, bewilderment, cleft stick, delicate situation, dilemma, doubt, embarrassment, impasse, perplexity, plight, predicament, puzzle, strait, uncertainty

quantity *noun* **1** = **amount**, aggregate, allotment, lot, number, part, portion, quota, sum, total **2** = **size**, bulk, capacity, expanse, extent, greatness, length, magnitude, mass, measure, volume

quarrel *noun* **1** = **disagreement**, affray, altercation, argument, *bagarre*, brawl, breach, broil, commotion, contention, controversy, difference (of opinion), discord, disputation, dispute, dissension, dissidence, disturbance, feud, fight, fracas, fray, misunderstanding, row, scrap (*informal*), shindig (*informal*), shindy (*informal*), skirmish, spat, squabble, strife, tiff, tumult, vendetta, wrangle ◆ *verb* **2** = **disagree**,

altercate, argue, bicker, brawl, clash, differ, dispute, fall out (*informal*), fight, fight like cat and dog, go at it hammer and tongs, row, spar, squabble, wrangle **3 = object to**, carp, cavil, complain, decry, disapprove, find fault, take exception to
➤ **Antonyms**
noun ≠**disagreement:** accord, agreement, concord ♦ *verb* ≠**disagree:** agree, get on *or* along (with)

quarrelsome *adjective* = **argumentative**, belligerent, cantankerous, cat-and-dog (*informal*), choleric, combative, contentious, cross, disputatious, fractious, ill-tempered, irascible, irritable, litigious, peevish, petulant, pugnacious, querulous
➤ **Antonyms**
easy-going, equable, even-tempered, placid

quarry *noun* = **prey**, aim, game, goal, objective, prize, victim

quarter *noun* **1 = district**, area, direction, locality, location, neighbourhood, part, place, point, position, province, region, side, spot, station, territory, zone **2 = mercy**, clemency, compassion, favour, forgiveness, leniency, pity ♦ *verb* **3 = accommodate**, billet, board, house, install, lodge, place, post, put up, station

quarters *plural noun* = **lodgings**, abode, accommodation, barracks, billet, cantonment (*Military*), chambers, digs (*Brit. informal*), domicile, dwelling, habitation, lodging, post, residence, rooms, shelter, station

quash *verb* **1 = annul**, cancel, declare null and void, invalidate, nullify, overrule, overthrow, rescind, reverse, revoke, set aside, void **2 = suppress**, beat, crush, destroy, extinguish, extirpate, overthrow, put down, quell, quench, repress, squash, subdue

quasi- *adverb* **1 = almost**, apparently, partly, seemingly, supposedly ♦ *adjective* **2 = pseudo-**, apparent, fake, mock, near, nominal, pretended, seeming, semi-, sham, so-called, synthetic, virtual, would-be

quaver *verb* **1 = tremble**, flicker, flutter, oscillate, pulsate, quake, quiver, shake, shudder, thrill, trill, twitter, vibrate, waver ♦ *noun* **2 = trembling**, break, quiver, shake, sob, throb, tremble, tremor, trill, vibration, warble

queasy *adjective* **1 = sick**, bilious, green around the gills (*informal*), ill, nauseated, off colour, squeamish, upset **2 = uneasy**, anxious, fidgety, ill at ease, restless, troubled, uncertain, worried

queen *noun* **1 = sovereign**, consort, monarch, ruler **2 = ideal**, diva, doyenne, idol, mistress, model, perfection, prima donna, star

queenly *adjective* = **majestic**, grand, imperial, noble, regal, royal, stately

queer *adjective* **1 = strange**, abnormal, anomalous, atypical, curious, disquieting, droll, eerie, erratic, extraordinary, funny, left-field (*informal*), odd, outlandish, outré, peculiar, remarkable, rum (*Brit. slang*), singular, uncanny, uncommon, unconventional, unnatural, unorthodox, unusual, weird **2 = dubious**, doubtful, fishy (*informal*), irregular, mysterious, puzzling, questionable, shady (*informal*), suspicious **3 = faint**, dizzy, giddy, light-headed, queasy, reeling, uneasy **4 = eccentric**, crazy, demented, idiosyncratic, irrational, mad, odd, touched, unbalanced, unhinged ♦ *verb* **5** *As in* **queer someone's pitch** = **spoil**, bodge (*informal*), botch, endanger, harm, impair, imperil, injure, jeopardize, mar, ruin, thwart, wreck
➤ **Antonyms**
adjective ≠**strange:** believable, common, conventional, customary, natural, normal, ordinary, orthodox, rational, regular, straight, unexceptional, unoriginal ♦ *verb* ≠**spoil:** aid, boost, enhance, help

quell *verb* **1 = suppress**, conquer, crush, defeat, extinguish, overcome, overpower, put down, quash, squelch, stamp out, stifle, subdue, vanquish **2 = assuage**, allay, alleviate, appease, calm, compose, deaden, dull, mitigate, moderate, mollify, pacify, quiet, silence, soothe

quench *verb* **1 = satisfy**, allay, appease, cool, sate, satiate, slake **2 = put out**, check, crush, destroy, douse, end, extinguish, smother, snuff out, squelch, stifle, suppress

querulous *adjective* = **complaining**, cantankerous, captious, carping, censorious, critical, cross, discontented, dissatisfied, fault-finding, fretful, grouchy (*informal*), grumbling, hard to please, irascible, irritable, murmuring, peevish, petulant, plaintive, ratty (*Brit. & N.Z. informal*), sour, testy, tetchy, touchy, waspish, whining
➤ **Antonyms**
contented, easy to please, equable, placid, uncomplaining, uncritical, undemanding

query *noun* **1 = question**, demand, doubt, hesitation, inquiry, objection, problem, reservation, scepticism, suspicion ♦ *verb* **2 = doubt**, challenge, disbelieve, dispute, distrust, mistrust, suspect **3 = ask**, inquire *or* enquire, question

quest *noun* = **search**, adventure, crusade, enterprise, expedition, exploration, hunt, journey, mission, pilgrimage, pursuit, voyage

question *noun* **1 = issue**, bone of contention, motion, point, point at issue, proposal, proposition, subject, theme, topic **2 = difficulty**, argument, can of worms

(*informal*), confusion, contention, controversy, debate, dispute, doubt, dubiety, misgiving, problem, query, uncertainty **3** = **inquiry**, examination, interrogation, investigation **4 in question** = **under discussion**, at issue, in doubt, open to debate **5 out of the question** = **impossible**, inconceivable, not to be thought of, unthinkable ♦ *verb* **6** = **ask**, catechize, cross-examine, examine, grill (*informal*), inquire, interrogate, interview, investigate, probe, pump (*informal*), quiz, sound out **7** = **dispute**, call into question, cast doubt upon, challenge, controvert, disbelieve, distrust, doubt, impugn, mistrust, oppose, query, suspect
➤ **Antonyms**
noun ≠**inquiry**: answer, reply ♦ *verb* ≠**ask**: answer, reply ≠**dispute**: accept, believe, buy (*slang*), swallow (*informal*), take on board, take on trust

questionable *adjective* = **dubious**, arguable, controversial, controvertible, debatable, disputable, dodgy (*Brit., Austral., & N.Z. informal*), doubtful, dubitable, equivocal, fishy (*informal*), iffy (*informal*), moot, paradoxical, problematical, shady (*informal*), suspect, suspicious, uncertain, unproven, unreliable
➤ **Antonyms**
authoritative, certain, incontrovertible, indisputable, straightforward, unequivocal

queue *noun* = **line**, chain, concatenation, file, order, progression, sequence, series, string, succession, train

quibble *verb* **1** = **split hairs**, carp, cavil, equivocate, evade, pretend, prevaricate, shift ♦ *noun* **2** = **objection**, artifice, cavil, complaint, criticism, duplicity, equivocation, evasion, nicety, niggle, pretence, prevarication, protest, quiddity, quirk, shift, sophism, subterfuge, subtlety

quick *adjective* **1** = **fast**, active, brisk, express, fleet, hasty, headlong, pdq (*slang*), rapid, speedy, swift **2** = **brief**, cursory, hasty, hurried, perfunctory **3** = **sudden**, expeditious, prompt **4** = **intelligent**, acute, alert, all there (*informal*), astute, bright (*informal*), clever, discerning, nimble-witted, perceptive, quick on the uptake (*informal*), quick-witted, receptive, sharp, shrewd, smart **5** = **deft**, able, adept, adroit, apt, dexterous, skilful **6** = **excitable**, abrupt, curt, hasty, impatient, irascible, irritable, passionate, petulant, testy, touchy **7** = **nimble**, agile, alert, animated, energetic, flying, keen, lively, spirited, sprightly, spry, vivacious, winged **8** *Archaic* = **alive**, animate, existing, live, living, viable
➤ **Antonyms**
≠**fast**: slow, sluggish ≠**brief**: gradual, long

≠**intelligent**, deft: inexpert, maladroit, stupid, unintelligent, unskilful ≠**excitable**: calm, deliberate, patient, restrained ≠**nimble**: dull, heavy, inactive, lazy, lethargic, sluggish, unresponsive

quicken *verb* **1** = **speed**, accelerate, dispatch, expedite, hasten, hurry, impel, precipitate **2** = **invigorate**, activate, animate, arouse, energize, excite, galvanize, incite, inspire, kindle, refresh, reinvigorate, resuscitate, revitalize, revive, rouse, stimulate, strengthen, vitalize, vivify

quickly *adverb* = **swiftly**, abruptly, apace, at a rate of knots (*informal*), at or on the double, at speed, briskly, expeditiously, fast, hastily, hell for leather (*informal*), hotfoot, hurriedly, immediately, instantly, like greased lightning (*informal*), like lightning, like nobody's business (*informal*), like the clappers (*Brit. informal*), pdq (*slang*), posthaste, promptly, pronto (*informal*), quick, rapidly, soon, speedily, with all speed
➤ **Antonyms**
carefully, eventually, slowly, sluggishly, unhurriedly

quick-tempered *adjective* = **hot-tempered**, cantankerous, choleric, excitable, fiery, impatient, impulsive, irascible, irritable, petulant, quarrelsome, ratty (*Brit. & N.Z. informal*), shrewish, splenetic, testy, tetchy, waspish
➤ **Antonyms**
cool, dispassionate, phlegmatic, placid, slow to anger, tolerant

quick-witted *adjective* = **clever**, alert, astute, bright (*informal*), keen, perceptive, sharp, shrewd, smart
➤ **Antonyms**
dull, obtuse, slow, slow-witted, stupid, thick (*informal*), unperceptive

quid pro quo *noun* = **exchange**, compensation, equivalent, interchange, reprisal, retaliation, substitution, tit for tat

quiescent *adjective* = **quiet**, calm, dormant, in abeyance, inactive, latent, motionless, peaceful, placid, resting, serene, silent, smooth, still, tranquil, unagitated, undisturbed, unmoving, unruffled

quiet *adjective* **1** = **silent**, dumb, hushed, inaudible, low, low-pitched, noiseless, peaceful, soft, soundless **2** = **calm**, contented, gentle, mild, motionless, pacific, peaceful, placid, restful, serene, smooth, tranquil, untroubled **3** = **undisturbed**, isolated, private, retired, secluded, secret, sequestered, unfrequented **4** = **subdued**, conservative, modest, plain, restrained, simple, sober, unassuming, unobtrusive, unpretentious **5** = **reserved**, collected, docile, even-tempered, gentle, imperturbable, meek, mild, phlegmatic,

retiring, sedate, shy, unexcitable ◆ *noun* **6**
= **peace**, calmness, ease, quietness, repose,
rest, serenity, silence, stillness, tranquillity
➤ **Antonyms**
adjective ≠**silent**: deafening, ear-splitting,
high-decibel, high-volume, loud, noisy,
stentorian ≠**calm**: agitated, alert, excitable,
exciting, frenetic, troubled, turbulent, violent
≠**undisturbed**: bustling, busy, crowded,
exciting, fashionable, lively, popular, vibrant
≠**subdued**: blatant, brash, bright,
conspicuous, glaring, loud, obtrusive,
ostentatious, pretentious, showy ≠**reserved**:
excitable, excited, high-spirited, impatient,
loquacious, passionate, restless, talkative,
verbose, violent ◆ *noun* ≠**peace**: activity,
bustle, commotion, din, disturbance, noise,
racket

quieten *verb* **1** = **silence**, compose, hush,
muffle, mute, quell, quiet, shush (*informal*),
stifle, still, stop, subdue **2** = **soothe**, allay,
alleviate, appease, assuage, blunt, calm,
deaden, dull, lull, mitigate, mollify, palliate,
tranquillize
➤ **Antonyms**
≠**soothe**: aggravate, exacerbate, intensify,
provoke, upset, worsen

quietly *adverb* **1** = **silently**, confidentially,
dumbly, in a low voice *or* whisper, in an
undertone, inaudibly, in hushed tones, in
silence, mutely, noiselessly, privately,
secretly, softly, without talking **2** = **calmly**,
contentedly, dispassionately, meekly, mildly,
patiently, placidly, serenely,
undemonstratively **3** = **unobtrusively**, coyly,
demurely, diffidently, humbly, modestly,
unassumingly, unostentatiously,
unpretentiously

quietness *noun* = **peace**, calm, calmness,
hush, placidity, quiescence, quiet, quietude,
repose, rest, serenity, silence, still, stillness,
tranquillity

quilt *noun* = **bedspread**, comforter (*U.S.*),
continental quilt, counterpane, coverlet,
doona (*Austral.*), downie (*informal*), duvet,
eiderdown

quintessence *noun* = **essence**, core,
distillation, extract, gist, heart, kernel,
lifeblood, marrow, pith, soul, spirit

quintessential *adjective* = **ultimate**,
archetypal, definitive, prototypical, typical

quip *noun* = **joke**, badinage, bon mot,
counterattack, gibe, jest, pleasantry,
repartee, retort, riposte, sally, wisecrack
(*informal*), witticism

quirk *noun* = **peculiarity**, aberration, bee in
one's bonnet, caprice, characteristic,

eccentricity, fancy, fetish, foible, habit, *idée
fixe*, idiosyncrasy, kink, mannerism, oddity,
singularity, trait, vagary, whim

quirky *adjective* = **odd**, capricious, curious,
eccentric, fanciful, idiosyncratic, offbeat,
peculiar, rum (*Brit. slang*), singular,
unpredictable, unusual, whimsical

quisling *noun* = **traitor**, betrayer,
collaborator, fifth columnist, Judas,
renegade, turncoat

quit *verb* **1** = **stop**, abandon, belay
(*Nautical*), cease, conclude, discontinue,
drop, end, give up, halt, suspend, throw in
the towel **2** = **resign**, abdicate, go, leave,
pull out, relinquish, renounce, retire, step
down (*informal*), surrender **3** = **depart**,
abandon, decamp, desert, exit, forsake, go,
leave, pack one's bags (*informal*), pull out,
take off (*informal*), withdraw
➤ **Antonyms**
≠**stop**: complete, continue, finish, go on
with, see through

quite *adverb* **1** = **somewhat**, fairly,
moderately, rather, reasonably, relatively, to
a certain extent, to some degree **2**
= **absolutely**, completely, considerably,
entirely, fully, in all respects, largely,
perfectly, precisely, totally, wholly, without
reservation **3** = **truly**, in fact, in reality, in
truth, really

quiver *verb* **1** = **shake**, agitate, convulse,
oscillate, palpitate, pulsate, quake, quaver,
shiver, shudder, tremble, vibrate ◆ *noun* **2**
= **shake**, convulsion, oscillation, palpitation,
pulsation, shiver, shudder, spasm, throb, tic,
tremble, tremor, vibration

quixotic *adjective* = **unrealistic**, dreamy,
fanciful, idealistic, impractical, romantic

quiz *noun* **1** = **examination**, investigation,
questioning, test ◆ *verb* **2** = **question**, ask,
catechize, examine, grill (*informal*),
interrogate, investigate, pump (*informal*)

quizzical *adjective* = **mocking**, arch,
questioning, sardonic, teasing

quota *noun* = **share**, allocation, allowance,
assignment, cut (*informal*), part, portion,
proportion, ration, slice, whack (*informal*)

quotation *noun* **1** = **passage**, citation,
cutting, excerpt, extract, quote (*informal*),
reference, selection **2** *Commerce* = **estimate**,
bid price, charge, cost, figure, price, quote
(*informal*), rate, tender

quote *verb* = **repeat**, adduce, attest, cite,
detail, extract, instance, name, paraphrase,
proclaim, recall, recite, recollect, refer to,
retell

R r

rabble noun 1 = **mob**, canaille, crowd, herd, horde, swarm, throng 2 *Derogatory* = **commoners**, canaille, common people, crowd, hoi polloi, lower classes, lumpenproletariat, masses, peasantry, populace, proletariat, riffraff, scum, the great unwashed (*informal & derogatory*), trash (*chiefly U.S. & Canad.*)
➤ Antonyms
≠**commoners**: aristocracy, bourgeoisie, elite, gentry, high society, nobility, upper classes

rabble-rouser noun = **agitator**, demagogue, firebrand, incendiary, stirrer (*informal*), troublemaker

Rabelaisian adjective = **bawdy**, broad, coarse, earthy, gross, lusty, raunchy (*slang*), satirical, uninhibited, unrestrained

rabid adjective 1 = **fanatical**, bigoted, extreme, fervent, intemperate, intolerant, irrational, narrow-minded, zealous 2 = **mad**, hydrophobic
➤ Antonyms
≠**fanatical**: half-hearted, moderate, wishy-washy (*informal*)

race[1] noun 1 = **contest**, chase, competition, contention, dash, pursuit, rivalry ♦ verb 2 = **compete**, contest, run 3 = **run**, career, dart, dash, fly, gallop, go like a bomb (*Brit. & N.Z. informal*), hare (*Brit. informal*), hasten, hurry, run like mad (*informal*), speed, tear, zoom

race[2] noun = **people**, blood, breed, clan, ethnic group, family, folk, house, issue, kin, kindred, line, lineage, nation, offspring, progeny, seed (*chiefly biblical*), stock, tribe, type

racial adjective = **ethnic**, ethnological, folk, genealogical, genetic, national, tribal

rack noun 1 = **frame**, framework, stand, structure ♦ verb 2 = **torture**, afflict, agonize, crucify, distress, harrow, oppress, pain, torment

racket noun 1 = **noise**, babel, ballyhoo (*informal*), clamour, commotion, din, disturbance, fuss, hubbub, hullabaloo, outcry, pandemonium, row, rumpus, shouting, tumult, uproar 2 = **fraud**, criminal activity, illegal enterprise, scheme 3 *Slang* = **business**, game (*informal*), line, occupation

racy adjective 1 = **risqué**, bawdy, blue, broad, immodest, indecent, indelicate, naughty, near the knuckle (*informal*), off colour, smutty, spicy (*informal*), suggestive 2 = **lively**, animated, dramatic, energetic, entertaining, exciting, exhilarating, heady, sparkling, spirited, stimulating, vigorous

raddled adjective = **run-down**, broken-down, coarsened, dilapidated, dishevelled, haggard, tattered, the worse for wear, unkempt

radiance noun 1 = **happiness**, delight, gaiety, joy, pleasure, rapture, warmth 2 = **brightness**, brilliance, effulgence, glare, gleam, glitter, glow, incandescence, light, luminosity, lustre, resplendence, shine

radiant adjective 1 = **happy**, beaming, beatific, blissful, delighted, ecstatic, gay, glowing, joyful, joyous, on cloud nine (*informal*), rapturous, sent 2 = **bright**, beaming, brilliant, effulgent, gleaming, glittering, glorious, glowing, incandescent, luminous, lustrous, resplendent, shining, sparkling, sunny
➤ Antonyms
≠**happy**: disconsolate, down in the dumps (*informal*), gloomy, joyless, low, miserable, sad, sombre, sorrowful ≠**bright**: black, dark, dull, gloomy, sombre

radiate verb 1 = **spread out**, branch out, diverge, issue 2 = **emit**, diffuse, disseminate, emanate, give off or out, gleam, glitter, pour, scatter, send out, shed, shine, spread

radiation noun = **emission**, emanation, rays

radical adjective 1 = **revolutionary**, extremist, fanatical 2 = **fundamental**, basic, constitutional, deep-seated, essential, innate, native, natural, organic, profound, thoroughgoing 3 = **extreme**, complete, drastic, entire, excessive, severe, sweeping, thorough, violent ♦ noun 4 = **extremist**, fanatic, militant, revolutionary
➤ Antonyms
adjective ≠**fundamental**: insignificant, minor, superficial, token, trivial ♦ noun ≠**extremist**: conservative, moderate, reactionary

raffish adjective = **dashing**, bohemian, careless, casual, devil-may-care, disreputable, jaunty, rakish, sporty, unconventional

raffle noun = **draw**, lottery, sweep, sweepstake

ragamuffin noun = **urchin**, gamin, guttersnipe, scarecrow (*informal*), street arab (*Offensive*)

ragbag *noun* = **mixture**, confusion, hotchpotch, jumble, medley, miscellany, mixed bag (*informal*), potpourri

rage *noun* 1 = **fury**, agitation, anger, frenzy, ire, madness, mania, obsession, passion, rampage, raving, vehemence, violence, wrath 2 = **craze**, enthusiasm, fad (*informal*), fashion, latest thing, vogue ♦ *verb* 3 = **be furious**, be beside oneself, be incandescent, blow one's top, blow up (*informal*), crack up (*informal*), fly off the handle (*informal*), foam at the mouth, fret, fume, go ballistic (*slang, chiefly U.S.*), go off the deep end (*informal*), go up the wall (*slang*), lose it (*informal*), lose one's rag (*slang*), lose one's temper, lose the plot (*informal*), rant and rave, rave, see red (*informal*), seethe, storm, throw a fit (*informal*) 4 = **be at its height**, be uncontrollable, rampage, storm, surge
➤ **Antonyms**
noun ≠**fury**: acceptance, calmness, equanimity, gladness, good humour, joy, pleasure, resignation ♦ *verb* ≠**be furious**: accept, keep one's cool, remain unruffled, resign oneself to, stay calm

ragged *adjective* 1 = **shabby**, contemptible, down at heel, frayed, in holes, in rags, in tatters, mean, poor, scraggy, shaggy, tattered, tatty, threadbare, torn, unkempt, worn-out 2 = **rough**, crude, jagged, notched, rugged, serrated, uneven, unfinished
➤ **Antonyms**
≠**shabby**: fashionable, smart, well-dressed

raging *adjective* = **furious**, beside oneself, doing one's nut (*Brit. slang*), enraged, foaming at the mouth, frenzied, fuming, incandescent, incensed, infuriated, mad, raving, seething

rags *plural noun* = **old clothes**, castoffs, tattered clothing, tatters
➤ **Antonyms**
finery, gladrags, Sunday best

raid *noun* 1 = **attack**, break-in, foray, hit-and-run attack, incursion, inroad, invasion, onset, sally, sortie, surprise attack ♦ *verb* 2 = **attack**, assault, break into, foray, invade, pillage, plunder, rifle, sack, sally forth, swoop down upon

raider *noun* = **attacker**, invader, marauder, plunderer, robber, thief

rail *verb* = **complain**, attack, blast, castigate, censure, criticize, fulminate, revile, vociferate

railing *noun* = **fence**, balustrade, barrier, paling, rails

raillery *noun* = **teasing**, badinage, banter, chaff, joke, joking, kidding (*informal*), repartee, sport

rain *noun* 1 = **rainfall**, cloudburst, deluge,

downpour, drizzle, fall, precipitation, raindrops, showers 2 = **shower**, deluge, flood, hail, spate, stream, torrent, volley ♦ *verb* 3 = **pour**, bucket down (*informal*), come down in buckets (*informal*), drizzle, fall, pelt (down), rain cats and dogs (*informal*), shower, teem 4 = **fall**, deposit, drop, shower, sprinkle

rainy *adjective* = **wet**, damp, drizzly, showery
➤ **Antonyms**
arid, dry, fine, sunny

raise *verb* 1 = **lift**, elevate, exalt, heave, hoist, move up, rear, set upright, uplift 2 = **increase**, advance, amplify, augment, boost, enhance, enlarge, escalate, exaggerate, heighten, hike (up) (*informal*), inflate, intensify, jack up, magnify, put up, reinforce, strengthen 3 = **collect**, assemble, form, gather, get, levy, mass, mobilize, muster, obtain, rally, recruit 4 = **cause**, bring about, create, engender, give rise to, occasion, originate, produce, provoke, start 5 = **stir up**, activate, arouse, awaken, cause, evoke, excite, foment, foster, incite, instigate, kindle, motivate, provoke, rouse, set on foot, summon up, whip up 6 = **bring up**, develop, nurture, rear 7 = **grow**, breed, cultivate, produce, propagate, rear 8 = **put forward**, advance, bring up, broach, introduce, moot, suggest 9 = **build**, construct, erect, put up 10 = **end**, abandon, give up, lift, relieve, remove, terminate 11 = **promote**, advance, aggrandize, elevate, exalt, prefer, upgrade
➤ **Antonyms**
≠**increase**: cut, decrease, diminish, drop, lessen, lower, reduce, sink ≠**stir up**: calm, depress, lessen, lower, quash, quell, reduce, sink, soothe, suppress ≠**build**: demolish, destroy, level, ruin, wreck ≠**end**: begin, establish, start ≠**promote**: demote, downgrade, reduce

rake[1] *verb* 1 = **gather**, collect, remove, scrape up 2 = **scrape**, break up, harrow, hoe, scour, scratch 3 *with* **together** *or* **up** = **collect**, assemble, dig up, dredge up, gather, scrape together 4 = **search**, comb, examine, forage, hunt, ransack, scan, scour, scrutinize 5 = **sweep**, pepper 6 = **graze**, scrape, scratch

rake[2] *noun* = **libertine**, debauchee, lech *or* letch (*informal*), lecher, playboy, profligate, roué, swinger (*slang*)
➤ **Antonyms**
ascetic, celibate, puritan

rakish[1] *adjective* = **dashing**, breezy, dapper, debonair, devil-may-care, flashy, jaunty, natty (*informal*), raffish, smart, snazzy (*informal*), sporty

rakish[2] *adjective* = **immoral**, abandoned,

debauched, depraved, dissipated, dissolute, lecherous, licentious, loose, sinful, wanton

rally¹ *noun* **1** = **gathering**, assembly, conference, congregation, congress, convention, convocation, mass meeting, meeting, muster **2** = **recovery**, comeback (*informal*), improvement, recuperation, renewal, resurgence, revival, turn for the better ◆ *verb* **3** = **reassemble**, bring *or* come to order, re-form, regroup, reorganize, unite **4** = **gather**, assemble, bond together, bring *or* come together, collect, convene, get together, marshal, mobilize, muster, organize, round up, summon, unite **5** = **recover**, be on the mend, come round, get better, improve, perk up, pick up, pull through, recuperate, regain one's strength, revive, take a turn for the better, turn the corner
➤ **Antonyms**
noun ≠**recovery**: collapse, deterioration, relapse, turn for the worse ◆ *verb* ≠**gather**: disband, disperse, separate, split up ≠**recover**: deteriorate, fail, get worse, relapse, take a turn for the worse, worsen

rally² *verb* = **tease**, chaff, make fun of, mock, poke fun at, ridicule, send up (*Brit. informal*), take the mickey out of (*informal*), taunt

ram *verb* **1** = **hit**, butt, collide with, crash, dash, drive, force, impact, run into, slam, smash, strike **2** = **cram**, crowd, force, hammer, jam, pack, pound, stuff, thrust

ramble *verb* **1** = **walk**, amble, drift, perambulate, range, roam, rove, saunter, straggle, stray, stroll, traipse (*informal*), wander **2** = **babble**, chatter, digress, rabbit (on) (*Brit. informal*), rattle on, run off at the mouth (*slang*), waffle (*informal, chiefly Brit.*), wander, witter on (*informal*) **3** = **meander**, snake, twist and turn, wind, zigzag ◆ *noun* **4** = **walk**, excursion, hike, perambulation, roaming, roving, saunter, stroll, tour, traipse (*informal*), trip

rambler *noun* = **walker**, drifter, hiker, roamer, rover, stroller, wanderer, wayfarer

rambling *adjective* **1** = **sprawling**, irregular, spreading, straggling, trailing **2** = **long-winded**, circuitous, desultory, diffuse, digressive, disconnected, discursive, disjointed, incoherent, irregular, periphrastic, prolix, wordy
➤ **Antonyms**
≠**long-winded**: coherent, concise, direct, to the point

ramification *noun* **ramifications** = **consequences**, complications, developments, results, sequel, upshot

ramify *verb* **1** = **become complicated**, multiply, thicken **2** = **divide**, branch, fork,

separate, split up

ramp *noun* = **slope**, grade, gradient, incline, inclined plane, rise

rampage *verb* **1** = **go berserk**, go ballistic (*slang, chiefly U.S.*), rage, run amok, run riot, run wild, storm, tear ◆ *noun* **2 on the rampage** = **berserk**, amok, destructive, out of control, raging, rampant, riotous, violent, wild

rampant *adjective* **1** = **widespread**, epidemic, exuberant, luxuriant, prevalent, profuse, rank, rife, spreading like wildfire, unchecked, uncontrolled, unrestrained **2** *Heraldry* = **upright**, erect, rearing, standing

rampart *noun* = **defence**, barricade, bastion, bulwark, earthwork, embankment, fence, fort, fortification, guard, parapet, security, stronghold, wall

ramshackle *adjective* = **rickety**, broken-down, crumbling, decrepit, derelict, dilapidated, flimsy, jerry-built, shaky, tottering, tumbledown, unsafe, unsteady
➤ **Antonyms**
solid, stable, steady, well-built

rancid *adjective* = **rotten**, bad, fetid, foul, frowsty, fusty, musty, off, putrid, rank, sour, stale, strong-smelling, tainted
➤ **Antonyms**
fresh, pure, undecayed

rancorous *adjective* = **bitter**, acrimonious, malicious, malignant, resentful, spiteful, venomous, vindictive

rancour *noun* = **hatred**, animosity, animus, antipathy, bad blood, bitterness, chip on one's shoulder (*informal*), enmity, grudge, hate, hostility, ill feeling, ill will, malice, resentfulness, resentment, spite, spleen, venom

random *adjective* **1** = **chance**, accidental, adventitious, aimless, arbitrary, casual, desultory, fortuitous, haphazard, hit or miss, incidental, indiscriminate, purposeless, spot, stray, unplanned, unpremeditated ◆ *noun* **2 at random** = **haphazardly**, accidentally, adventitiously, aimlessly, arbitrarily, by chance, casually, indiscriminately, irregularly, purposelessly, randomly, unsystematically, willy-nilly
➤ **Antonyms**
adjective ≠**chance**: definite, deliberate, intended, planned, premeditated, specific

randy *adjective* *Informal* = **lustful**, amorous, aroused, concupiscent, horny (*slang*), hot, lascivious, lecherous, raunchy (*slang*), sexually excited, sexy (*informal*), turned-on (*slang*)

range *noun* **1** = **limits**, ambit, amplitude, area, bounds, compass, confines, distance, domain, extent, field, latitude, orbit, pale, parameters (*informal*), province, purview, radius, reach, scope, span, sphere, sweep **2** = **series**, assortment, class, collection, gamut, kind, lot, order, selection, sort, variety ♦ *verb* **3** = **vary**, extend, fluctuate, go, reach, run, stretch **4** = **roam**, cruise, explore, ramble, rove, stroll, sweep, traverse, wander **5** = **arrange**, align, array, dispose, draw up, line up, order, sequence **6** = **group**, arrange, bracket, catalogue, categorize, class, classify, file, grade, pigeonhole, rank

rangy *adjective* = **long-limbed**, gangling, lanky, leggy, long-legged

rank [1] *noun* **1** = **status**, caste, class, classification, degree, division, echelon, grade, level, nobility, order, position, quality, sort, standing, station, stratum, type **2** = **row**, column, file, formation, group, line, range, series, tier ♦ *verb* **3** = **arrange**, align, array, class, classify, dispose, grade, line up, marshal, order, position, range, sequence, sort

rank [2] *adjective* **1** = **absolute**, arrant, blatant, complete, downright, egregious, flagrant, gross, rampant, sheer, thorough, total, undisguised, unmitigated, utter **2** = **foul**, bad, disagreeable, disgusting, fetid, fusty, musty, noisome, noxious, off, offensive, pungent, putrid, rancid, revolting, stale, stinking, strong-smelling, yucky *or* yukky (*slang*) **3** = **abundant**, dense, exuberant, flourishing, lush, luxuriant, productive, profuse, strong-growing, vigorous

rank and file *noun* = **general public**, body, Joe (and Eileen) Public (*slang*), Joe Six-Pack (*U.S. slang*), majority, mass, masses

rankle *verb* = **annoy**, anger, embitter, fester, gall, get one's goat (*slang*), get on one's nerves (*informal*), irk, irritate, rile

ransack *verb* **1** = **search**, comb, explore, forage, go through, rake, rummage, scour, turn inside out **2** = **plunder**, despoil, gut, loot, pillage, raid, ravage, rifle, sack, strip

ransom *noun* **1** = **payment**, money, payoff, price ♦ *verb* **2** = **buy the freedom of**, buy (someone) out (*informal*), deliver, liberate, obtain *or* pay for the release of, redeem, release, rescue, set free

rant *verb* **1** = **shout**, bellow, bluster, cry, declaim, rave, roar, spout (*informal*), yell ♦ *noun* **2** = **tirade**, bluster, bombast, diatribe, harangue, rhetoric, vociferation

rap *verb* **1** = **hit**, crack, knock, strike, tap **2** = **bark**, speak abruptly, spit **3** *Slang, chiefly U.S.* = **talk**, chat, confabulate, converse, discourse **4** = **reprimand**, blast, castigate, censure, criticize, knock (*informal*), lambast(e), pan (*informal*), read the riot act, scold, tick off (*informal*) ♦ *noun* **5** = **blow**, clout (*informal*), crack, knock, tap **6** *Slang*

= **rebuke**, blame, censure, chiding, punishment, responsibility, sentence

rapacious *adjective* = **greedy**, avaricious, grasping, insatiable, marauding, plundering, predatory, preying, ravenous, voracious

rapacity *noun* = **greed**, avarice, avidity, greediness, insatiableness, rapaciousness, voraciousness, voracity

rape *verb* **1** = **sexually assault**, abuse, force, outrage, ravish, violate ♦ *noun* **2** = **sexual assault**, outrage, ravishment, violation **3** = **desecration**, abuse, defilement, maltreatment, perversion, violation

rapid *adjective* = **quick**, brisk, express, fast, fleet, flying, hasty, hurried, pdq (*slang*), precipitate, prompt, quickie (*informal*), speedy, swift
➤ **Antonyms**
deliberate, gradual, leisurely, slow, tardy, unhurried

rapidity *noun* = **speed**, alacrity, briskness, celerity, fleetness, haste, hurry, precipitateness, promptitude, promptness, quickness, rush, speediness, swiftness, velocity

rapidly *adverb* = **quickly**, apace, at speed, briskly, fast, hastily, hotfoot, hurriedly, in a hurry, in a rush, in haste, like a shot, like lightning, pdq (*slang*), posthaste, precipitately, promptly, pronto (*informal*), speedily, swiftly

rapine *noun* = **pillage**, despoilment, looting, marauding, plundering, ransacking, robbery, sack

rapport *noun* = **bond**, affinity, empathy, harmony, interrelationship, link, relationship, sympathy, tie, understanding

rapprochement *noun* = **reconciliation**, detente, reconcilement, restoration of harmony, reunion
➤ **Antonyms**
antagonism, dissension, exacerbation, falling-out, quarrel, resumption of hostilities, schism

rapscallion *noun Old-fashioned* = **rogue**, blackguard, cad, disgrace, good-for-nothing, knave (*archaic*), ne'er-do-well, rascal, scallywag (*informal*), scamp, scoundrel

rapt *adjective* **1** = **spellbound**, absorbed, carried away, engrossed, enthralled, entranced, fascinated, gripped, held, intent, preoccupied **2** = **blissful**, bewitched, captivated, charmed, delighted, ecstatic, enchanted, enraptured, rapturous, transported
➤ **Antonyms**
≠**spellbound**: bored, detached, left cold, unaffected, uninterested, uninvolved, unmoved

rapture *noun* = **ecstasy**, beatitude, bliss,

cloud nine (*informal*), delight, enthusiasm, euphoria, exaltation, felicity, happiness, joy, rhapsody, seventh heaven, spell, transport

rapturous *adjective* = **ecstatic**, blissful, delighted, enthusiastic, euphoric, happy, in seventh heaven, joyful, joyous, on cloud nine (*informal*), overjoyed, over the moon (*informal*), rapt, transported

rare[1] *adjective* **1** = **uncommon**, exceptional, few, infrequent, out of the ordinary, recherché, scarce, singular, sparse, sporadic, strange, unusual **2** = **superb**, admirable, choice, excellent, exquisite, extreme, fine, great, incomparable, peerless, superlative
➤ Antonyms
≠**uncommon**: abundant, bountiful, common, frequent, habitual, manifold, many, plentiful, profuse, regular

rare[2] *adjective* = **underdone**, bloody, half-cooked, half-raw, undercooked

rarefied *adjective* **1** = **exalted**, elevated, high, lofty, noble, spiritual, sublime **2** = **exclusive**, esoteric, private, select

rarely *adverb* **1** = **seldom**, almost never, hardly, hardly ever, infrequently, little, once in a blue moon, once in a while, only now and then, on rare occasions, scarcely ever **2** = **exceptionally**, extraordinarily, notably, remarkably, singularly, uncommonly, unusually
➤ Antonyms
≠**seldom**: commonly, frequently, often, regularly, usually

raring *adjective* As in **raring to** = **eager**, avid, champing at the bit (*informal*), desperate, enthusiastic, impatient, keen, keen as mustard, longing, ready, willing, yearning

rarity *noun* **1** = **curio**, collector's item, curiosity, find, gem, one-off, pearl, treasure **2** = **uncommonness**, infrequency, scarcity, shortage, singularity, sparseness, strangeness, unusualness **3** = **excellence**, choiceness, exquisiteness, fineness, incomparability, peerlessness, quality, superbness

rascal *noun* = **rogue**, blackguard, devil, disgrace, good-for-nothing, imp, knave (*archaic*), miscreant, ne'er-do-well, rapscallion, reprobate, scallywag (*informal*), scamp, scoundrel, varmint (*informal*), villain

rash[1] *adjective* = **reckless**, brash, careless, foolhardy, harebrained, hasty, headlong, heedless, helter-skelter, hot-headed, ill-advised, ill-considered, impetuous, imprudent, impulsive, incautious, injudicious, precipitate, premature, thoughtless, unthinking, unwary
➤ Antonyms
canny, careful, cautious, considered,

premeditated, prudent, well-thought-out

rash[2] *noun* **1** = **outbreak**, eruption **2** = **spate**, epidemic, flood, outbreak, plague, series, succession, wave

rashness *noun* = **recklessness**, carelessness, foolhardiness, hastiness, heedlessness, indiscretion, temerity, thoughtlessness

rasp *noun* **1** = **grating**, grinding, scrape, scratch ◆ *verb* **2** = **scrape**, file, grind, rub, scour **3** = **irritate**, grate (upon), irk, jar (upon), rub (someone) up the wrong way, set one's teeth on edge, wear upon

rasping *or* **raspy** *adjective* = **harsh**, grating, gravelly, gruff, hoarse, husky, rough

rat *Informal* ◆ *noun* **1** *Informal* = **traitor**, betrayer, double-crosser, grass (*Brit. informal*), informer, nark (*slang*), two-timer (*informal*) **2** = **rogue**, bad lot, bastard (*offensive*), bounder (*old-fashioned Brit. slang*), cad (*old-fashioned Brit. informal*), heel (*slang*), rotter (*slang, chiefly Brit.*), scoundrel ◆ *verb* **3 rat on** = **betray**, do the dirty on (*Brit. informal*), sell down the river (*informal*)

rate[1] *noun* **1** = **degree**, percentage, proportion, ratio, relation, scale, standard **2** = **speed**, gait, measure, pace, tempo, time, velocity **3** = **charge**, cost, dues, duty, fee, figure, hire, price, tariff, tax, toll **4** = **grade**, class, classification, degree, position, quality, rank, rating, status, value, worth **5 at any rate** = **in any case**, anyhow, anyway, at all events, nevertheless ◆ *verb* **6** = **evaluate**, adjudge, appraise, assess, class, classify, consider, count, esteem, estimate, grade, measure, rank, reckon, regard, value, weigh **7** = **deserve**, be entitled to, be worthy of, merit **8** *Slang* = **think highly of**, admire, esteem, respect, value

rate[2] *verb* = **scold**, bawl out (*informal*), berate, castigate, censure, criticize severely, haul over the coals (*informal*), read the riot act, rebuke, reprimand, reprove, take to task, tear into (*informal*), tear (someone) off a strip (*informal*)

rather *adverb* **1** = **to some extent**, a bit, a little, fairly, kind of (*informal*), moderately, pretty (*informal*), quite, relatively, slightly, somewhat, sort of (*informal*), to some degree **2** = **preferably**, instead, more readily, more willingly, sooner

ratify *verb* = **approve**, affirm, authenticate, authorize, bear out, bind, certify, confirm, consent to, corroborate, endorse, establish, sanction, sign, uphold, validate
➤ Antonyms
abrogate, annul, cancel, reject, repeal, repudiate, revoke

rating *noun* = **position**, class, classification, degree, designation, estimate, evaluation, grade, order, placing, rank, rate, standing, status

ratio *noun* = **proportion**, correlation, correspondence, equation, fraction, percentage, rate, relation, relationship

ration *noun* 1 = **allowance**, allotment, dole, helping, measure, part, portion, provision, quota, share 2 **rations** = **provisions**, commons (*Brit.*), food, provender, stores, supplies ♦ *verb* 3 = **limit**, budget, conserve, control, restrict, save 4 = **distribute**, allocate, allot, apportion, deal, dole, give out, issue, measure out

rational *adjective* 1 = **sensible**, enlightened, intelligent, judicious, logical, lucid, realistic, reasonable, sagacious, sane, sound, wise 2 = **reasoning**, cerebral, cognitive, thinking 3 = **sane**, all there (*informal*), balanced, *compos mentis,* in one's right mind, lucid, normal, of sound mind
➤ Antonyms
insane, irrational, unreasonable, unsound

rationale *noun* = **reason**, grounds, logic, motivation, philosophy, principle, *raison d'être,* theory

rationalize *verb* 1 = **justify**, account for, excuse, explain away, extenuate, make allowance for, make excuses for, vindicate 2 = **reason out**, apply logic to, elucidate, resolve, think through 3 = **streamline**, make cuts, make more efficient, trim

rattle *verb* 1 = **clatter**, bang, jangle 2 = **shake**, bounce, jar, jiggle, jolt, jounce, vibrate 3 *Informal* = **fluster**, discomfit, discompose, disconcert, discountenance, disturb, faze, frighten, perturb, scare, shake, upset 4 *with* **off** *or* **out** = **recite**, list, reel off, run through 5 *with* **on** *or* **away** = **prattle**, blether, chatter, gabble, gibber, jabber, rabbit (on) (*Brit. informal*), run on, witter (*informal*), yak (away) (*slang*)

ratty *adjective* = **irritable**, angry, annoyed, crabbed, cross, impatient, pissed (*taboo slang*), pissed off (*taboo slang*), short-tempered, snappy, testy, tetchy, touchy

raucous *adjective* = **harsh**, grating, hoarse, husky, loud, noisy, rasping, rough, strident
➤ Antonyms
dulcet, mellifluous, quiet, smooth, sweet

raunchy *adjective Slang* = **sexy**, bawdy, coarse, earthy, lecherous, lewd, lustful, lusty, ribald, salacious, sexual, smutty, steamy (*informal*), suggestive

ravage *verb* 1 = **destroy**, demolish, desolate, despoil, devastate, gut, lay waste, leave in ruins, loot, pillage, plunder, ransack, raze, ruin, sack, spoil, wreak havoc on, wreck ♦ *noun* 2 **ravages** = **damage**, demolition, depredation, desolation, destruction, devastation, havoc, pillage, plunder, rapine,

ruin, ruination, spoliation, waste

rave *verb* 1 = **rant**, babble, be delirious, go mad (*informal*), rage, roar, storm, talk wildly, thunder 2 *Informal* = **enthuse**, be mad about (*informal*), be wild about (*informal*), cry up, gush, praise ♦ *noun* 3 *Informal* = **praise**, acclaim, applause, encomium

ravenous *adjective* 1 = **starving**, famished, starved, very hungry 2 = **voracious**, devouring, predatory, rapacious, ravening
➤ Antonyms
≠**starving:** full, glutted, sated, satiated

ravine *noun* = **canyon**, defile, gap (*U.S.*), gorge, gulch (*U.S.*), gully, pass

raving *adjective* = **mad**, berserk, crazed, crazy, delirious, frantic, frenzied, furious, hysterical, insane, irrational, out of one's mind, rabid, raging, wild

ravish *verb* 1 = **enchant**, captivate, charm, delight, enrapture, entrance, fascinate, overjoy, spellbind, transport 2 *Literary* = **rape**, abuse, force, outrage, sexually assault, violate

ravishing *adjective* = **enchanting**, beautiful, bewitching, charming, dazzling, delightful, drop-dead (*slang*), entrancing, gorgeous, lovely, radiant, stunning (*informal*)

raw *adjective* 1 = **uncooked**, bloody (*of meat*), fresh, natural, unprepared 2 = **unrefined**, basic, coarse, crude, natural, organic, rough, unfinished, unprocessed, unripe, untreated 3 = **sore**, chafed, grazed, open, scratched, sensitive, skinned, tender 4 = **inexperienced**, callow, green, ignorant, immature, new, undisciplined, unpractised, unseasoned, unskilled, untrained, untried 5 = **chilly**, biting, bitter, bleak, chill, cold, damp, freezing, harsh, parky (*Brit. informal*), piercing, unpleasant, wet 6 = **frank**, bare, blunt, brutal, candid, naked, plain, realistic, unembellished, unvarnished
➤ Antonyms
≠**uncooked:** baked, cooked, done ≠**unrefined:** finished, prepared, refined ≠**inexperienced:** experienced, practised, professional, skilled, trained ≠**frank:** embellished, gilded

ray *noun* 1 = **beam**, bar, flash, gleam, shaft 2 = **trace**, flicker, glimmer, hint, indication, scintilla, spark

raze *verb* = **destroy**, bulldoze, demolish, flatten, knock down, level, pull down, remove, ruin, tear down, throw down

razzle-dazzle *or* **razzmatazz** *noun Slang* = **fuss**, carry-on (*informal, chiefly Brit.*), commotion, hullabaloo, performance (*informal*), rigmarole, song and dance (*informal*), to-do

re *preposition* = **concerning**, about, apropos,

in respect of, on the subject of, regarding, respecting, with reference to, with regard to

reach verb 1 = **arrive at**, attain, get as far as, get to, land at, make 2 = **touch**, contact, extend to, get (a) hold of, go as far as, grasp, stretch to 3 = **contact**, communicate with, establish contact with, find, get, get hold of, get in touch with, get through to, make contact with 4 = **come to**, amount to, arrive at, attain, climb to, drop to, fall to, move to, rise to, sink to 5 *Informal* = **pass**, hand, hold out, stretch ♦ noun 6 = **range**, ambit, capacity, command, compass, distance, extension, extent, grasp, influence, power, scope, spread, stretch, sweep

react verb 1 = **act**, behave, conduct oneself, function, operate, proceed, work 2 = **respond**, acknowledge, answer, reply, rise to the bait, take the bait

reaction noun 1 = **response**, acknowledgment, answer, feedback, reply 2 = **counteraction**, backlash, compensation, counterbalance, counterpoise, recoil 3 = **conservatism**, counter-revolution, the right

reactionary adjective 1 = **conservative**, blimpish, counter-revolutionary, right-wing ♦ noun 2 = **conservative**, Colonel Blimp, counter-revolutionary, die-hard, rightist, right-winger
➤ **Antonyms**
adjective, noun ≠**conservative**: leftist, progressive, radical, reformist, revolutionary, socialist

read verb 1 = **look at**, glance at, peruse, pore over, refer to, run one's eye over, scan, study 2 = **recite**, announce, declaim, deliver, speak, utter 3 = **understand**, comprehend, construe, decipher, discover, interpret, perceive the meaning of, see 4 = **register**, display, indicate, record, show

readable adjective 1 = **enjoyable**, easy to read, entertaining, enthralling, gripping, interesting 2 = **legible**, clear, comprehensible, decipherable, intelligible, plain, understandable
➤ **Antonyms**
≠**enjoyable**: as dry as dust, badly-written, boring, dull, heavy, heavy going, pretentious, turgid, unreadable ≠**legible**: illegible, incomprehensible, indecipherable, unintelligible, unreadable

readily adverb 1 = **willingly**, cheerfully, eagerly, freely, gladly, quickly, voluntarily, with good grace, with pleasure 2 = **promptly**, at once, easily, effortlessly, in no time, quickly, right away, smoothly, speedily, straight away, unhesitatingly, without delay, without demur, without difficulty, without hesitation
➤ **Antonyms**
≠**willingly**: reluctantly, unwillingly

≠**promptly**: hesitatingly, slowly, with difficulty

readiness noun 1 = **preparedness**, fitness, maturity, preparation, ripeness 2 = **willingness**, aptness, eagerness, inclination, keenness 3 = **promptness**, adroitness, dexterity, ease, facility, quickness, rapidity, skill

reading noun 1 = **learning**, book-learning, education, erudition, knowledge, scholarship 2 = **perusal**, examination, inspection, review, scrutiny, study 3 = **recital**, homily, lecture, lesson, performance, rendering, rendition, sermon 4 = **interpretation**, conception, construction, grasp, impression, take (*informal, chiefly U.S.*), treatment, understanding, version

ready adjective 1 = **prepared**, all set, arranged, completed, fit, in readiness, organized, primed, ripe, set 2 = **willing**, agreeable, apt, disposed, eager, game (*informal*), glad, happy, have-a-go (*informal*), inclined, keen, minded, predisposed, prone 3 = **prompt**, acute, adroit, alert, apt, astute, bright, clever, deft, dexterous, expert, handy, intelligent, keen, perceptive, quick, quick-witted, rapid, resourceful, sharp, skilful, smart 4 = **available**, accessible, at or on hand, at one's fingertips, at the ready, close to hand, convenient, handy, near, on call, on tap (*informal*), present 5 **ready to** = **on the point of**, about to, close to, in danger of, liable to, likely to, on the brink of, on the verge of ♦ noun 6 **at the ready** = **poised**, all systems go, in readiness, prepared, ready for action, waiting ♦ verb 7 = **prepare**, arrange, equip, fit out, get ready, make ready, order, organize, set
➤ **Antonyms**
adjective ≠**prepared**: immature, unequipped, unfit, unprepared ≠**willing**: disinclined, hesitant, loath, reluctant, unprepared, unwilling ≠**prompt**: slow ≠**available**: distant, inaccessible, late, unavailable

real adjective = **genuine**, absolute, actual, authentic, bona fide, certain, essential, existent, factual, heartfelt, honest, legitimate, positive, right, rightful, sincere, true, unaffected, unfeigned, valid, veritable
➤ **Antonyms**
affected, counterfeit, fake, faked, false, feigned, imaginary, imitation, insincere

realistic adjective 1 = **practical**, businesslike, common-sense, down-to-earth, hard-headed, level-headed, matter-of-fact, pragmatic, rational, real, sensible, sober, unromantic, unsentimental 2 = **lifelike**, authentic, faithful, genuine, graphic, natural, naturalistic, representational, true, true to

life, truthful, vérité
➤ **Antonyms**
≠**practical:** fanciful, idealistic, impractical, unrealistic

reality *noun* **1 = truth,** actuality, authenticity, certainty, fact, genuineness, materiality, realism, validity, verisimilitude, verity **2 in reality = in fact,** actually, as a matter of fact, in actuality, in point of fact, in truth, really

realization *noun* **1 = awareness,** appreciation, apprehension, cognizance, comprehension, conception, consciousness, grasp, imagination, perception, recognition, understanding **2 = achievement,** accomplishment, carrying-out, completion, consummation, effectuation, fulfilment

realize *verb* **1 = become aware of,** appreciate, apprehend, be cognizant of, become conscious of, catch on (*informal*), comprehend, conceive, get the message, grasp, imagine, recognize, take in, twig (*Brit. informal*), understand **2 = achieve,** accomplish, actualize, bring about, bring off, bring to fruition, carry out *or* through, complete, consummate, do, effect, effectuate, fulfil, make happen, perform **3 = sell for,** bring *or* take in, clear, earn, gain, get, go for, make, net, produce

really *adverb* **= truly,** absolutely, actually, assuredly, categorically, certainly, genuinely, in actuality, indeed, in fact, in reality, positively, surely, undoubtedly, verily, without a doubt

realm *noun* **1 = kingdom,** country, domain, dominion, empire, land, monarchy, principality, province, state **2 = field,** area, branch, department, orbit, patch, province, region, sphere, territory, turf (*U.S. slang*), world, zone

reap *verb* **1 = collect,** bring in, cut, garner, gather, harvest **2 = get,** acquire, derive, gain, obtain, win

rear[1] *noun* **1 = back,** back end, end, rearguard, stern, tail, tail end ♦ *adjective* **2 = back,** aft, following, hind, hindmost, last, trailing
➤ **Antonyms**
noun ≠**back:** bow, forward end, front, nose, stem, vanguard ♦ *adjective* ≠**back:** foremost, forward, front, leading

rear[2] *verb* **1 = bring up,** breed, care for, cultivate, educate, foster, grow, nurse, nurture, raise, train **2 = raise,** elevate, hoist, hold up, lift, set upright **3 = rise,** loom, soar, tower

reason *noun* **1 = cause,** aim, basis, design, end, goal, grounds, impetus, incentive, inducement, intention, motive, object, occasion, purpose **2 = sense,** apprehension,

brains, comprehension, intellect, judgment, logic, mentality, mind, rationality, reasoning, sanity, sound mind, soundness, understanding **3 = justification,** argument, case, defence, excuse, explanation, ground, rationale, vindication **4 in** *or* **within reason = in moderation,** proper, reasonable, sensible, warrantable, within bounds, within limits ♦ *verb* **5 = deduce,** conclude, draw conclusions, infer, make out, resolve, solve, think, work out **6 reason with = persuade,** argue with, bring round (*informal*), debate with, dispute with, move, prevail upon, talk into *or* out of, urge, win over
➤ **Antonyms**
noun ≠**sense:** emotion, feeling, instinct, sentiment

reasonable *adjective* **1 = sensible,** advisable, arguable, believable, credible, intelligent, judicious, justifiable, logical, plausible, practical, rational, reasoned, sane, sober, sound, tenable, well-advised, well-thought-out, wise **2 = fair,** acceptable, equitable, fit, just, moderate, proper, right, within reason **3 = average,** fair, moderate, modest, O.K. *or* okay (*informal*), tolerable
➤ **Antonyms**
≠**sensible:** impossible, irrational, unintelligent, unreasonable, unsound ≠**fair:** unfair, unreasonable

reasoned *adjective* **= sensible,** clear, judicious, logical, systematic, well-expressed, well-presented, well-thought-out

reasoning *noun* **1 = thinking,** analysis, cogitation, deduction, logic, reason, thought **2 = case,** argument, exposition, hypothesis, interpretation, proof, train of thought

reassure *verb* **= encourage,** bolster, buoy up, cheer up, comfort, gee up, hearten, inspirit, put *or* set one's mind at rest, relieve (someone) of anxiety, restore confidence to

rebate *noun* **= refund,** allowance, bonus, deduction, discount, reduction

rebel *verb* **1 = revolt,** mutiny, resist, rise up, take to the streets, take up arms **2 = defy,** come out against, dig one's heels in (*informal*), disobey, dissent, refuse to obey ♦ *noun* **3 = revolutionary,** insurgent, insurrectionary, mutineer, resistance fighter, revolutionist, secessionist **4 = nonconformist,** apostate, dissenter, heretic, schismatic ♦ *adjective* **5 = rebellious,** insurgent, insurrectionary, mutinous, revolutionary

rebellion *noun* **1 = resistance,** insurgence, insurrection, mutiny, revolt, revolution, rising, uprising **2 = nonconformity,** apostasy, defiance, disobedience, dissent, heresy, schism

rebellious *adjective* **1 = revolutionary,**

disaffected, disloyal, disobedient, disorderly, insubordinate, insurgent, insurrectionary, mutinous, rebel, recalcitrant, seditious, turbulent, ungovernable, unruly **2 = defiant**, difficult, incorrigible, intractable, obstinate, recalcitrant, refractory, resistant, unmanageable
➤ **Antonyms**
≠**revolutionary**: dutiful, loyal, obedient, patriotic, subordinate ≠**defiant**: dutiful, obedient, subservient

rebirth *noun* **= revival**, new beginning, regeneration, renaissance, renewal, restoration, resurgence, resurrection, revitalization

rebound *verb* **1 = bounce**, recoil, resound, return, ricochet, spring back **2 = misfire**, backfire, boomerang, recoil ♦ *noun* **3 = bounce**, comeback, kickback, repercussion, return, ricochet

rebuff *verb* **1 = reject**, brush off (*slang*), cold-shoulder, cut, decline, discourage, knock back (*slang*), put off, refuse, repulse, resist, slight, snub, spurn, turn down ♦ *noun* **2 = rejection**, brush-off (*slang*), cold shoulder, discouragement, kick in the teeth (*slang*), knock-back (*slang*), opposition, refusal, repulse, slap in the face (*informal*), slight, snub, thumbs down
➤ **Antonyms**
verb ≠**reject**: encourage, lead on (*informal*), submit to, welcome ♦ *noun* ≠**rejection**: come-on (*informal*), encouragement, thumbs up, welcome

rebuke *verb* **1 = scold**, admonish, bawl out (*informal*), berate, blame, castigate, censure, chide, dress down (*informal*), give a rocket (*Brit. & N.Z. informal*), haul (someone) over the coals (*informal*), lecture, read the riot act, reprehend, reprimand, reproach, reprove, take to task, tear into (*informal*), tear (someone) off a strip (*informal*), tell off (*informal*), tick off (*informal*), upbraid ♦ *noun* **2 = scolding**, admonition, blame, castigation, censure, dressing down (*informal*), lecture, reprimand, reproach, reproof, reproval, row, telling-off (*informal*), ticking-off (*informal*)
➤ **Antonyms**
verb ≠**scold**: applaud, approve, commend, compliment, congratulate, laud, praise ♦ *noun* ≠**scolding**: commendation, compliment, laudation, praise

rebut *verb* **= disprove**, confute, defeat, invalidate, negate, overturn, prove wrong, quash, refute

rebuttal *noun* **= disproof**, confutation, defeat, invalidation, negation, refutation

recalcitrant *adjective* **= disobedient**, contrary, defiant, insubordinate, intractable, obstinate, refractory, stubborn,

uncontrollable, ungovernable, unmanageable, unruly, unwilling, wayward, wilful
➤ **Antonyms**
amenable, compliant, docile, obedient, submissive

recall *verb* **1 = recollect**, bring or call to mind, call or summon up, evoke, look or think back to, mind (*dialect*), remember, reminisce about **2 = annul**, abjure, call back, call in, cancel, countermand, nullify, repeal, rescind, retract, revoke, take back, withdraw ♦ *noun* **3 = recollection**, memory, remembrance **4 = annulment**, cancellation, nullification, recision, repeal, rescindment, rescission, retraction, revocation, withdrawal

recant *verb* **= withdraw**, abjure, apostatize, deny, disavow, disclaim, disown, forswear, recall, renege, renounce, repudiate, retract, revoke, take back, unsay
➤ **Antonyms**
insist, maintain, profess, reaffirm, reiterate, repeat, restate, uphold

recapitulate *verb* **= restate**, go over again, outline, recap (*informal*), recount, reiterate, repeat, review, run over, run through again, summarize, sum up

recede *verb* **1 = fall back**, abate, back off, draw back, ebb, go back, regress, retire, retreat, retrogress, return, subside, withdraw **2 = lessen**, decline, diminish, dwindle, fade, shrink, sink, wane

receipt *noun* **1 = sales slip**, acknowledgment, counterfoil, proof of purchase, stub, voucher **2 = receiving**, acceptance, delivery, reception, recipience **3 receipts = takings**, gains, gate, income, proceeds, profits, return

receive *verb* **1 = get**, accept, accept delivery of, acquire, be given, be in receipt of, collect, derive, obtain, pick up, take **2 = experience**, bear, be subjected to, encounter, go through, meet with, suffer, sustain, undergo **3 = greet**, accommodate, admit, be at home to, entertain, meet, take in, welcome **4 = be informed of**, apprehend, be told, gather, hear, perceive

recent *adjective* **= new**, contemporary, current, fresh, happening (*informal*), late, latter, latter-day, modern, novel, present-day, up-to-date, young
➤ **Antonyms**
ancient, antique, earlier, early, former, historical, old

recently *adverb* **= newly**, currently, freshly, lately, latterly, not long ago, of late

receptacle *noun* **= container**, holder, repository

reception *noun* **1 = party**, do (*informal*), entertainment, function, levee, soirée **2**

= **response**, acknowledgment, greeting, reaction, recognition, treatment, welcome **3** = **receiving**, acceptance, admission, receipt

receptive *adjective* = **open**, accessible, amenable, approachable, favourable, friendly, hospitable, interested, open-minded, open to suggestions, susceptible, sympathetic, welcoming
➤ **Antonyms**
biased, narrow-minded, prejudiced, unreceptive, unresponsive

recess *noun* **1** = **alcove**, bay, cavity, corner, depression, hollow, indentation, niche, nook **2** = **break**, cessation of business, closure, holiday, intermission, interval, respite, rest, vacation **3 recesses** = **depths**, heart, innermost parts, secret places

recession *noun* = **depression**, decline, downturn, drop, slump
➤ **Antonyms**
boom, upturn

recherché *adjective* = **refined**, choice, esoteric, exotic, rare

recipe *noun* **1** = **directions**, ingredients, instructions **2** = **method**, formula, modus operandi, prescription, procedure, process, programme, technique

reciprocal *adjective* = **mutual**, alternate, complementary, correlative, corresponding, equivalent, exchanged, give-and-take, interchangeable, interdependent
➤ **Antonyms**
one-way, unilateral, unreciprocated

reciprocate *verb* = **return**, exchange, feel in return, interchange, reply, requite, respond, return the compliment, swap, trade

recital *noun* **1** = **performance**, rehearsal, rendering **2** = **recitation**, account, description, detailing, enumeration, narration, narrative, reading, relation, repetition, statement, story, tale, telling

recitation *noun* = **recital**, lecture, narration, passage, performance, piece, reading, rendering, telling

recite *verb* = **repeat**, declaim, deliver, describe, detail, enumerate, itemize, narrate, perform, recapitulate, recount, rehearse, relate, speak, tell

reckless *adjective* = **careless**, daredevil, devil-may-care, foolhardy, hasty, headlong, heedless, ill-advised, imprudent, inattentive, incautious, indiscreet, irresponsible, madcap, mindless, negligent, precipitate, rash, regardless, thoughtless, wild
➤ **Antonyms**
careful, cautious, heedful, mindful, observant, responsible, thoughtful, wary

reckon *verb* **1** *Informal* = **think**, assume, believe, be of the opinion, conjecture, expect, fancy, guess (*informal, chiefly U.S.*

& *Canad.*), imagine, suppose, surmise **2** = **consider**, account, appraise, count, deem, esteem, estimate, evaluate, gauge, hold, judge, look upon, rate, regard, think of **3** = **count**, add up, calculate, compute, enumerate, figure, number, tally, total **4 reckon on** *or* **upon** = **rely on**, bank on, calculate, count on, depend on, hope for, take for granted, trust in **5 reckon with: a** = **deal**, cope, face, handle, settle accounts, treat **b** = **take into account**, anticipate, bargain for, bear in mind, be prepared for, expect, foresee, plan for, take cognizance of

reckoning *noun* **1** = **count**, adding, addition, calculation, computation, counting, estimate **2** = **retribution**, doom, judgment, last judgment **3** = **bill**, account, charge, due, score, settlement

reclaim *verb* = **regain**, get *or* take back, recapture, recover, redeem, reform, regenerate, reinstate, rescue, restore, retrieve, salvage

recline *verb* = **lean**, be recumbent, lay (something) down, lie (down), loll, lounge, repose, rest, sprawl, stretch out
➤ **Antonyms**
get up, rise, sit up, stand, stand up, stand upright

recluse *noun* = **hermit**, anchoress, anchorite, monk, solitary

reclusive *adjective* = **solitary**, cloistered, hermit-like, isolated, monastic, recluse, retiring, secluded, sequestered, withdrawn
➤ **Antonyms**
gregarious, sociable

recognition *noun* **1** = **identification**, detection, discovery, recall, recollection, remembrance **2** = **acceptance**, admission, allowance, avowal, awareness, concession, confession, perception, realization, understanding **3** = **approval**, acknowledgment, appreciation, gratitude, greeting, honour, salute **4** *As in* **in recognition of** = **appreciation**, cognizance, notice, respect

recognize *verb* **1** = **identify**, know, know again, make out, notice, place, put one's finger on, recall, recollect, remember, spot **2** = **acknowledge**, accept, admit, allow, avow, be aware of, concede, confess, grant, own, perceive, realize, see, take on board, understand **3** = **approve**, acknowledge, appreciate, greet, honour, salute **4** = **appreciate**, notice, respect
➤ **Antonyms**
≠**acknowledge:** be unaware of, forget, ignore, overlook

recoil *verb* **1** = **jerk back**, kick, react, rebound, spring back **2** = **draw back**, balk at, falter, flinch, quail, shrink, shy away **3**

= backfire, boomerang, go pear-shaped (*informal*), go wrong, misfire, rebound ♦ *noun* **4** = **reaction**, backlash, kick, rebound, repercussion

recollect *verb* = **remember**, call to mind, place, recall, reminisce, summon up

recollection *noun* = **memory**, impression, mental Image, recall, remembrance, reminiscence

recommend *verb* **1** = **advise**, advance, advocate, counsel, prescribe, propose, put forward, suggest, urge **2** = **commend**, approve, endorse, praise, put in a good word for, speak well of, vouch for **3** = **make attractive**, make acceptable, make appealing, make interesting
➤ **Antonyms**
≠**advise, commend**: argue against, disapprove of, reject, veto

recommendation *noun* **1** = **advice**, counsel, proposal, suggestion, urging **2** = **commendation**, advocacy, approbation, approval, endorsement, favourable mention, good word, plug (*informal*), praise, reference, sanction, testimonial

recompense *verb* **1** = **reward**, pay, remunerate **2** = **compensate**, indemnify, make amends for, make good, make restitution for, make up for, pay for, redress, reimburse, repay, requite, satisfy ♦ *noun* **3** = **compensation**, amends, damages, emolument, indemnity, pay, payment, remuneration, reparation, repayment, requital, restitution, satisfaction **4** = **reward**, meed (*archaic*), pay, payment, return, wages

reconcile *verb* **1** = **resolve**, adjust, compose, harmonize, patch up, put to rights, rectify, settle, square **2** = **make peace between**, appease, conciliate, pacify, placate, propitiate, re-establish friendly relations between, restore harmony between, reunite **3** = **accept**, get used, make the best of, put up with (*informal*), resign oneself, submit, yield

reconciliation *noun* **1** = **pacification**, appeasement, conciliation, détente, propitiation, *rapprochement*, reconcilement, reunion, understanding **2** = **accommodation**, adjustment, compromise, settlement
➤ **Antonyms**
≠**pacification**: alienation, antagonism, break-up, estrangement, falling-out, separation

recondite *adjective* = **obscure**, abstruse, arcane, cabbalistic, concealed, dark, deep, difficult, esoteric, hidden, involved, mysterious, mystical, occult, profound, secret
➤ **Antonyms**
exoteric, simple, straightforward

recondition *verb* = **restore**, do up (*informal*), fix up (*informal, chiefly U.S. & Canad.*), overhaul, remodel, renew, renovate, repair, revamp

reconnaissance *noun* = **Inspection**, exploration, investigation, observation, patrol, recce (*slang*), reconnoitring, scan, scouting, scrutiny, survey

reconnoitre *verb* = **inspect**, case (*slang*), explore, get the lie of the land, investigate, make a reconnaissance (of), observe, patrol, recce (*slang*), scan, scout, scrutinize, see how the land lies, spy out, survey

reconsider *verb* = **rethink**, change one's mind, have second thoughts, reassess, re-evaluate, re-examine, review, revise, take another look at, think again, think better of, think over, think twice

reconstruct *verb* **1** = **rebuild**, reassemble, recreate, re-establish, reform, regenerate, remake, remodel, renovate, reorganize, restore **2** = **deduce**, build up, build up a picture of, piece together

record *noun* **1** = **document**, account, annals, archives, chronicle, diary, entry, file, journal, log, memoir, memorandum, memorial, minute, register, report **2** = **evidence**, documentation, memorial, remembrance, testimony, trace, witness **3** = **disc**, album, black disc, EP, forty-five, gramophone record, LP, recording, release, seventy-eight, single, vinyl **4** = **background**, career, curriculum vitae, history, performance, track record (*informal*) **5 off the record** = **not for publication**, confidential, confidentially, in confidence, in private, private, sub rosa, under the rose, unofficial, unofficially ♦ *verb* **6** = **set down**, chalk up (*informal*), chronicle, document, enrol, enter, inscribe, log, minute, note, preserve, put down, put on file, put on record, register, report, take down, transcribe, write down **7** = **make a recording of**, tape, tape-record, video, video-tape **8** = **register**, contain, give evidence of, indicate, read, say, show

recorder *noun* = **chronicler**, annalist, archivist, clerk, diarist, historian, registrar, scorekeeper, scorer, scribe

recording *noun* = **record**, cut (*informal*), disc, gramophone record, tape, video

recount *verb* = **tell**, delineate, depict, describe, detail, enumerate, give an account of, narrate, portray, recite, rehearse, relate, repeat, report, tell the story of

recoup *verb* **1** = **regain**, make good, recover, redeem, retrieve, win back **2** = **compensate**, make redress for, make up for, refund, reimburse, remunerate, repay, requite, satisfy

recourse *noun* = **option**, alternative, appeal, choice, expedient, refuge, remedy, resort, resource, way out

recover *verb* **1** = **get better**, be on the mend, bounce back, come round, convalesce, feel oneself again, get back on one's feet, get well, heal, improve, mend, pick up, pull through, rally, recuperate, regain one's health *or* strength, revive, take a turn for the better, turn the corner **2** = **regain**, find again, get back, make good, recapture, reclaim, recoup, redeem, repair, repossess, restore, retake, retrieve, take back, win back
➤ **Antonyms**
≠**get better**: deteriorate, go downhill, relapse, take a turn for the worse, weaken, worsen ≠**regain**: abandon, forfeit, lose

recovery *noun* **1** = **improvement**, convalescence, healing, mending, rally, recuperation, return to health, revival, turn for the better **2** = **revival**, amelioration, betterment, improvement, rally, rehabilitation, restoration, upturn **3** = **retrieval**, recapture, reclamation, redemption, repair, repossession, restoration

recreation *noun* = **pastime**, amusement, beer and skittles (*informal*), distraction, diversion, enjoyment, entertainment, exercise, fun, hobby, leisure activity, play, pleasure, refreshment, relaxation, relief, sport

recrimination *noun* = **bickering**, counterattack, countercharge, mutual accusation, name-calling, quarrel, retaliation, retort, squabbling

recruit *verb* **1** = **enlist**, draft, enrol, levy, mobilize, muster, raise, strengthen **2** = **win (over)**, engage, enrol, gather, obtain, procure, proselytize, round up, take on ♦ *noun* **3** = **beginner**, apprentice, convert, greenhorn (*informal*), helper, initiate, learner, neophyte, novice, proselyte, rookie (*informal*), trainee, tyro
➤ **Antonyms**
verb ≠**enlist**: dismiss, fire, lay off, make redundant, sack (*informal*)

rectify *verb* **1** = **correct**, adjust, amend, emend, fix, improve, make good, mend, put right, redress, reform, remedy, repair, right, set the record straight, square **2** *Chemistry* = **separate**, distil, purify, refine

rectitude *noun* = **morality**, correctness, decency, equity, goodness, honesty, honour, incorruptibility, integrity, justice, principle, probity, righteousness, scrupulousness, uprightness, virtue
➤ **Antonyms**
baseness, corruption, dishonesty, dishonour, immorality, scandalousness

recumbent *adjective* = **lying down**, flat, flat on one's back, horizontal, leaning, lying, prone, prostrate, reclining, resting, stretched out, supine

recuperate *verb* = **recover**, be on the mend, convalesce, get back on one's feet, get better, improve, mend, pick up, regain one's health, turn the corner

recur *verb* **1** = **happen again**, come again, come and go, come back, persist, reappear, repeat, return, revert **2** = **return to mind**, be remembered, come back

recurrent *adjective* = **periodic**, continued, cyclical, frequent, habitual, recurring, regular, repeated, repetitive
➤ **Antonyms**
isolated, one-off

recycle *verb* = **reprocess**, reclaim, reuse, salvage, save

red *adjective* **1** = **crimson**, cardinal, carmine, cherry, claret, coral, maroon, pink, rose, ruby, scarlet, vermilion, wine **2** *Of hair* = **chestnut**, bay, carroty, flame-coloured, flaming, foxy, reddish, sandy, titian **3** = **flushed**, blushing, embarrassed, florid, rubicund, shamefaced, suffused **4** = **bloodshot**, inflamed, red-rimmed ♦ *noun* **5** = **redness**, colour **6 in the red** *Informal* = **in debt**, bankrupt, in arrears, in debit, in deficit, insolvent, on the rocks, overdrawn, owing money, showing a loss **7 see red** *Informal* = **lose one's temper**, be beside oneself with rage (*informal*), become enraged, be *or* get pissed (off) (*taboo slang*), be *or* get very angry, blow a fuse (*slang, chiefly U.S.*), blow one's top, crack up (*informal*), fly off the handle (*informal*), go ballistic (*slang, chiefly U.S.*), go mad (*informal*), go off one's head (*slang*), go off the deep end (*informal*), go up the wall (*slang*), lose it (*informal*), lose one's rag (*slang*), lose the plot (*informal*)

red-blooded *adjective Informal* = **vigorous**, hearty, lusty, manly, robust, strong, virile, vital

redden *verb* = **flush**, blush, colour (up), crimson, go red

redeem *verb* **1** = **make up for**, atone for, compensate for, defray, make amends for, make good, offset, outweigh, redress, save **2** = **reinstate**, absolve, rehabilitate, restore to favour **3** = **save**, buy the freedom of, deliver, emancipate, extricate, free, liberate, pay the ransom of, ransom, rescue, set free **4** = **buy back**, reclaim, recover, recover possession of, regain, repossess, repurchase, retrieve, win back **5** = **trade in**, cash (in), change, exchange **6** = **fulfil**, abide by, adhere to, be faithful to, carry out, discharge, hold to, keep, make good, meet, perform

redemption *noun* **1** = **compensation**,

amends, atonement, expiation, reparation **2** = **salvation**, deliverance, emancipation, liberation, ransom, release, rescue **3** = **repurchase**, reclamation, recovery, repossession, retrieval **4** = **trade-in**, quid pro quo **5** = **fulfilment**, discharge, exchange, performance

red-handed *adjective* = **in the act**, bang to rights (*slang*), (in) flagrante delicto, with one's fingers *or* hand in the till (*informal*), with one's pants down (*U.S. slang*)

redolent *adjective* **1** = **reminiscent**, evocative, remindful, suggestive **2** = **scented**, aromatic, fragrant, odorous, perfumed, sweet-smelling

redoubtable *adjective* = **formidable**, dreadful, fearful, fearsome, mighty, powerful, strong, terrible

redound *verb* **1 redound on** *or* **upon** = **rebound**, come back, ensue, recoil, reflect, result **2 redound to** = **contribute to**, conduce, effect, lead to, tend towards

redress *verb* **1** = **make amends for**, compensate for, make reparation for, make restitution for, make up for, pay for, put right, recompense for **2** = **put right**, adjust, amend, balance, correct, even up, mend, rectify, regulate, relieve, remedy, repair, restore the balance, square ♦ *noun* **3** = **amends**, atonement, compensation, payment, quittance, recompense, reparation, requital, restitution **4** = **rectification**, correction, cure, ease, help, remedy

reduce *verb* **1** = **lessen**, abate, abridge, contract, curtail, cut, cut down, decrease, depress, dilute, diminish, downsize, impair, lower, moderate, shorten, slow down, tone down, truncate, turn down, weaken, wind down **2** = **degrade**, break, bring low, demote, downgrade, humble, humiliate, lower in rank, lower the status of, take down a peg (*informal*) **3** = **drive**, bring, bring to the point of, force **4** = **slim**, be *or* go on a diet, diet, lose weight, shed weight, slenderize (*chiefly U.S.*), trim **5** = **impoverish**, bankrupt, break, pauperize, ruin
➤ **Antonyms**
≠**lessen**: augment, enhance, enlarge, extend, heighten, increase ≠**degrade**: elevate, enhance, exalt, promote

redundancy *noun* = **unemployment**, joblessness, layoff, the axe (*informal*), the sack (*informal*)

redundant *adjective* = **superfluous**, de trop, excessive, extra, inessential, supernumerary, surplus, unnecessary, unwanted
➤ **Antonyms**
essential, necessary, needed, vital

reek *verb* **1** = **stink**, hum (*slang*), pong (*Brit. informal*), smell, smell to high heaven **2** **reek of** = **be redolent of**, be characterized by, be permeated by ♦ *noun* **3** = **stink**, fetor, malodour, niff (*Brit. slang*), odour, pong (*Brit. informal*), smell, stench **4** *Dialect* = **smoke**, exhalation, fumes, steam, vapour

reel *verb* **1** = **stagger**, falter, lurch, pitch, rock, roll, stumble, sway, totter, waver, wobble **2** = **whirl**, go round and round, revolve, spin, swim, swirl, twirl

refer *verb* **1** = **allude**, bring up, cite, hint, make mention of, make reference, mention, speak of, touch on **2** = **relate**, apply, be directed to, belong, be relevant to, concern, pertain **3** = **consult**, apply, go, have recourse to, look up, seek information from, turn to **4** = **direct**, guide, point, recommend, send **5** = **pass on**, commit, consign, deliver, hand over, submit, transfer, turn over

referee *noun* **1** = **umpire**, adjudicator, arbiter, arbitrator, judge, ref (*informal*) ♦ *verb* **2** = **umpire**, adjudicate, arbitrate, judge, mediate

reference *noun* **1** = **citation**, allusion, mention, note, quotation, remark **2** = **testimonial**, certification, character, credentials, endorsement, good word, recommendation **3** *As in* **with reference to** = **relevance**, applicability, bearing, concern, connection, consideration, regard, relation, respect

referendum *noun* = **public vote**, plebiscite, popular vote

refine *verb* **1** = **purify**, clarify, cleanse, distil, filter, process, rarefy **2** = **improve**, civilize, cultivate, hone, perfect, polish, temper

refined *adjective* **1** = **cultured**, civil, civilized, courtly, cultivated, elegant, genteel, gentlemanly, gracious, ladylike, polished, polite, sophisticated, urbane, well-bred, well-mannered **2** = **purified**, clarified, clean, distilled, filtered, processed, pure **3** = **discerning**, delicate, discriminating, exact, fastidious, fine, nice, precise, punctilious, sensitive, sublime, subtle
➤ **Antonyms**
≠**cultured**: boorish, coarse, common, ill-bred, inelegant, uncultured, ungentlemanly, unladylike, unmannerly, unrefined ≠**purified**: coarse, impure, unrefined

refinement *noun* **1** = **sophistication**, breeding, civility, civilization, courtesy, cultivation, culture, delicacy, discrimination, elegance, fastidiousness, finesse, finish, gentility, good breeding, good manners, grace, graciousness, polish, politeness, style, taste, urbanity **2** = **subtlety**, fine point, fine tuning, nicety, nuance **3** = **purification**, clarification, cleansing, distillation, filtering, processing

reflect *verb* **1** = **throw back**, echo, give back, imitate, mirror, reproduce, return **2** = **show**, bear out, bespeak, communicate, demonstrate, display, evince, exhibit, express, indicate, manifest, reveal **3** = **consider**, cogitate, contemplate, deliberate, meditate, mull over, muse, ponder, ruminate, think, wonder

reflection *noun* **1** = **image**, counterpart, echo, mirror image **2** = **consideration**, cerebration, cogitation, contemplation, deliberation, idea, meditation, musing, observation, opinion, perusal, pondering, rumination, study, thinking, thought, view **3** = **criticism**, aspersion, censure, imputation, reproach, slur

reflective *adjective* = **thoughtful**, cogitating, contemplative, deliberative, meditative, pensive, pondering, ruminative

reform *noun* **1** = **improvement**, amelioration, amendment, betterment, correction, rectification, rehabilitation, renovation ♦ *verb* **2** = **improve**, ameliorate, amend, better, correct, emend, mend, reconstruct, rectify, rehabilitate, remodel, reorganize, repair, restore, revolutionize **3** = **mend one's ways**, clean up one's act (*informal*), get back on the straight and narrow (*informal*), get it together (*informal*), get one's act together (*informal*), go straight (*informal*), pull one's socks up (*Brit. informal*), shape up (*informal*), turn over a new leaf

refractory *adjective* = **unmanageable**, difficult, disobedient, headstrong, intractable, mulish, obstinate, perverse, recalcitrant, stiff-necked, stubborn, uncontrollable, uncooperative, unruly, wilful

refrain[1] *verb* = **stop**, abstain, avoid, cease, desist, do without, eschew, forbear, give up, kick (*informal*), leave off, renounce

refrain[2] *noun* = **chorus**, burden, melody, song, tune

refresh *verb* **1** = **revive**, brace, breathe new life into, cheer, cool, enliven, freshen, inspirit, invigorate, kick-start (*informal*), reanimate, rejuvenate, revitalize, revivify, stimulate **2** = **stimulate**, brush up (*informal*), jog, prod, prompt, renew

refreshing *adjective* **1** = **stimulating**, bracing, cooling, fresh, inspiriting, invigorating, revivifying, thirst-quenching **2** = **new**, different, novel, original
➤ **Antonyms**
≠ **stimulating**: enervating, exhausting, soporific, tiring, wearisome

refreshment *noun* **1** = **revival**, enlivenment, freshening, reanimation,

renewal, renovation, repair, restoration, stimulation **2 refreshments** = **food and drink**, drinks, snacks, titbits

refrigerate *verb* = **cool**, chill, freeze, keep cold

refuge *noun* = **shelter**, asylum, bolt hole, harbour, haven, hide-out, protection, resort, retreat, sanctuary, security

refugee *noun* = **exile**, displaced person, émigré, escapee, fugitive, runaway

refulgent *adjective Literary* = **shining**, bright, brilliant, gleaming, lustrous, radiant, resplendent

refund *verb* **1** = **repay**, give back, make good, pay back, reimburse, restore, return ♦ *noun* **2** = **repayment**, reimbursement, return

refurbish *verb* = **renovate**, clean up, do up (*informal*), fix up (*informal, chiefly U.S. & Canad.*), mend, overhaul, re-equip, refit, remodel, repair, restore, revamp, set to rights, spruce up

refusal *noun* **1** = **rejection**, defiance, denial, kick in the teeth (*slang*), knock-back (*slang*), negation, no, rebuff, repudiation, thumbs down **2** = **option**, choice, consideration, opportunity

refuse[1] *verb* = **reject**, abstain, decline, deny, repel, repudiate, say no, spurn, turn down, withhold
➤ **Antonyms**
accept, agree, allow, approve, consent, give, permit

refuse[2] *noun* = **rubbish**, dreck (*slang, chiefly U.S.*), dregs, dross, garbage, junk (*informal*), leavings, lees, litter, scum, sediment, sweepings, trash, waste

refute *verb* = **disprove**, blow out of the water (*slang*), confute, counter, discredit, give the lie to, negate, overthrow, prove false, rebut, silence
➤ **Antonyms**
confirm, prove, substantiate

regain *verb* **1** = **recover**, get back, recapture, recoup, redeem, repossess, retake, retrieve, take back, win back **2** = **get back to**, reach again, reattain, return to

regal *adjective* = **royal**, fit for a king *or* queen, kingly *or* queenly, magnificent, majestic, noble, princely, proud, sovereign

regale *verb* **1** = **entertain**, amuse, delight, divert, gratify **2** = **serve**, feast, ply, refresh

regalia *plural noun* = **trappings**, accoutrements, apparatus, decorations, emblems, finery, garb, gear, paraphernalia, rigout (*informal*)

regard *verb* **1** = **consider**, account, adjudge, believe, deem, esteem, estimate, hold, imagine, judge, look upon, rate, see, suppose, think, treat, value, view **2 = look at**, behold, check, check out (*informal*), clock (*Brit. slang*), eye, eyeball (*U.S. slang*), gaze at, get a load of (*informal*), mark, notice, observe, remark, scrutinize, take a dekko at (*Brit. slang*), view, watch **3 = heed**, attend, listen to, mind, note, pay attention to, respect, take into consideration, take notice of **4 as regards = concerning**, pertaining to, regarding, relating to ♦ *noun* **5 = respect**, affection, attachment, care, concern, consideration, deference, esteem, honour, love, store, thought **6 = heed**, attention, interest, mind, notice **7 = look**, gaze, glance, scrutiny, stare **8 = relation**, bearing, concern, connection, reference, relevance

regardful *adjective* = **mindful**, attentive, aware, careful, considerate, dutiful, heedful, observant, respectful, thoughtful, watchful

regarding *preposition* = **concerning**, about, apropos, as regards, as to, in *or* with regard to, in re, in respect of, in the matter of, on the subject of, re, respecting, with reference to

regardless *adjective* **1 = heedless**, disregarding, inattentive, inconsiderate, indifferent, neglectful, negligent, rash, reckless, remiss, unconcerned, unmindful ♦ *adverb* **2 = in spite of everything**, anyway, come what may, despite everything, for all that, in any case, nevertheless, no matter what, nonetheless, rain or shine
➤ **Antonyms**
adjective ≠**heedless**: heedful, mindful, regardful

regards *plural noun* = **good wishes**, best wishes, compliments, greetings, respects, salutations

regenerate *verb* = **renew**, breathe new life into, change, give a shot in the arm, inspirit, invigorate, kick-start (*informal*), reawaken, reinvigorate, rejuvenate, renovate, restore, revive, revivify, uplift
➤ **Antonyms**
become moribund, decline, degenerate, stagnate, stultify

regime *noun* = **government**, administration, establishment, leadership, management, reign, rule, system

regimented *adjective* = **controlled**, disciplined, ordered, organized, regulated, systematized

region *noun* **1 = area**, country, district, division, expanse, land, locality, part, patch, place, province, quarter, section, sector, territory, tract, zone **2 = sphere**, domain, field, province, realm, world **3** *As in* **in the region of = vicinity**, area, neighbourhood, range, scope, sphere

regional *adjective* = **local**, district, parochial, provincial, zonal

register *noun* **1 = list**, annals, archives, catalogue, chronicle, diary, file, ledger, log, memorandum, record, roll, roster, schedule ♦ *verb* **2 = record**, catalogue, check in, chronicle, enlist, enrol, enter, inscribe, list, note, set down, sign on *or* up, take down **3 = show**, be shown, bespeak, betray, display, exhibit, express, indicate, manifest, mark, read, reflect, reveal, say **4** *Informal* = **have an effect**, come home, dawn on, get through, impress, make an impression, sink in, tell

regress *verb* = **revert**, backslide, degenerate, deteriorate, ebb, fall away *or* off, fall back, go back, lapse, recede, relapse, retreat, retrogress, return, wane
➤ **Antonyms**
advance, improve, progress, wax

regret *verb* **1 = feel sorry about**, bemoan, be upset, bewail, cry over spilt milk, deplore, feel remorse about, grieve, lament, miss, mourn, repent, rue, weep over ♦ *noun* **2 = sorrow**, bitterness, compunction, contrition, disappointment, grief, lamentation, pang of conscience, penitence, remorse, repentance, ruefulness, self-reproach
➤ **Antonyms**
verb ≠**feel sorry about**: be happy, be satisfied, feel satisfaction, have not looked back, rejoice ♦ *noun* ≠**sorrow**: callousness, contentment, impenitence, lack of compassion, pleasure, satisfaction

regretful *adjective* = **sorry**, apologetic, ashamed, contrite, disappointed, mournful, penitent, remorseful, repentant, rueful, sad, sorrowful

regrettable *adjective* = **unfortunate**, deplorable, disappointing, distressing, ill-advised, lamentable, pitiable, sad, shameful, unhappy

regular *adjective* **1 = normal**, common, commonplace, customary, daily, everyday, habitual, ordinary, routine, typical, unvarying, usual **2 = even**, balanced, flat, level, smooth, straight, symmetrical, uniform **3 = systematic**, consistent, constant, established, even, fixed, ordered, periodic, rhythmic, set, stated, steady, uniform **4 = methodical**, dependable, efficient, formal, orderly, standardized, steady, systematic **5 = official**, approved, bona fide, correct, established, formal, orthodox, proper, sanctioned, standard, traditional
➤ **Antonyms**
≠**normal**: abnormal, exceptional, infrequent, irregular, occasional, rare, uncommon, unconventional, unusual ≠**even**: erratic,

irregular, uneven ≠**systematic**: erratic, inconsistent, inconstant, irregular, varied ≠**methodical**: disorderly, unmethodical

regulate *verb* 1 = **control**, administer, arrange, conduct, direct, govern, guide, handle, manage, monitor, order, organize, oversee, rule, run, settle, superintend, supervise, systematize 2 = **adjust**, balance, fit, moderate, modulate, tune

regulation *noun* 1 = **rule**, canon, commandment, decree, dictate, direction, edict, law, order, ordinance, precept, procedure, requirement, standing order, statute 2 = **control**, administration, arrangement, direction, governance, government, management, supervision 3 = **adjustment**, modulation, tuning ♦ *adjective* 4 = **conventional**, customary, mandatory, normal, official, prescribed, required, standard, usual

regurgitate *verb* = **vomit**, barf (*U.S. slang*), chuck (up) (*slang, chiefly U.S.*), chunder (*slang, chiefly Austral.*), disgorge, puke (*slang*), sick up (*informal*), spew (out *or* up), throw up (*informal*)

rehabilitate *verb* 1 = **reintegrate**, adjust 2 = **restore**, re-establish, reinstate 3 = **redeem**, clear, reform, restore, save

rehash *verb* 1 = **rework**, alter, change, make over, rearrange, refashion, rejig (*informal*), reshuffle, reuse, rewrite ♦ *noun* 2 = **reworking**, new version, rearrangement, rewrite

rehearsal *noun* 1 = **practice**, drill, going-over (*informal*), practice session, preparation, reading, rehearsing, run-through 2 = **recital**, account, catalogue, description, enumeration, list, narration, recounting, relation, telling

rehearse *verb* 1 = **practise**, act, drill, go over, prepare, ready, recite, repeat, run through, study, train, try out 2 = **recite**, delineate, depict, describe, detail, enumerate, go over, list, narrate, recount, relate, review, run through, tell

reign *noun* 1 = **rule**, ascendancy, command, control, dominion, empire, hegemony, influence, monarchy, power, sovereignty, supremacy, sway ♦ *verb* 2 = **rule**, administer, be in power, command, govern, hold sway, influence, occupy *or* sit on the throne, wear the crown, wield the sceptre 3 = **be supreme**, be rampant, be rife, hold sway, obtain, predominate, prevail

reimburse *verb* = **pay back**, compensate, indemnify, recompense, refund, remunerate, repay, restore, return, square up

rein *noun* 1 = **control**, brake, bridle, check, curb, harness, hold, restraint, restriction 2 **give (a) free rein (to)** = **give a free hand**,

free, give a blank cheque (to), give carte blanche, give (someone) his *or* her head, give way to, indulge, let go, remove restraints ♦ *verb* 3 = **control**, bridle, check, curb, halt, hold, hold back, limit, restrain, restrict, slow down

reincarnation *noun* = **rebirth**, metempsychosis, transmigration of souls

reinforce *verb* = **support**, augment, bolster, buttress, emphasize, fortify, harden, increase, prop, shore up, stiffen, strengthen, stress, supplement, toughen, underline
➤ **Antonyms**
contradict, undermine, weaken

reinforcement *noun* 1 = **strengthening**, addition, amplification, augmentation, enlargement, fortification, increase, supplement 2 = **support**, brace, buttress, prop, shore, stay 3 **reinforcements** = **reserves**, additional *or* fresh troops, auxiliaries, support

reinstate *verb* = **restore**, bring back, recall, re-establish, rehabilitate, replace, return

reiterate *verb Formal* = **repeat**, do again, iterate, recapitulate, restate, retell, say again

reject *verb* 1 = **deny**, decline, disallow, exclude, renounce, repudiate, veto 2 = **rebuff**, jilt, refuse, repulse, say no to, spurn, turn down 3 = **discard**, bin, cast aside, eliminate, jettison, scrap, throw away *or* out ♦ *noun* 4 = **castoff**, clunker (*informal*), discard, failure, flotsam, second
➤ **Antonyms**
verb ≠**deny**: accept, agree, allow, approve, permit ≠**rebuff**: accept ≠**discard**: accept, receive, select ♦ *noun* ≠**castoff**: prize, treasure

rejection *noun* 1 = **denial**, dismissal, exclusion, renunciation, repudiation, thumbs down, veto 2 = **rebuff**, brushoff (*slang*), bum's rush (*slang*), kick in the teeth (*slang*), knock-back (*slang*), refusal
➤ **Antonyms**
≠**denial**: acceptance, affirmation, approval ≠**rebuff**: acceptance, selection

rejig *verb Informal* = **rearrange**, alter, juggle, manipulate, massage, reorganize, reshuffle, tweak

rejoice *verb* = **be glad**, be happy, be overjoyed, celebrate, delight, exult, glory, joy, jump for joy, make merry, revel, triumph
➤ **Antonyms**
be sad, be unhappy, be upset, grieve, lament, mourn

rejoicing *noun* = **happiness**, celebration, cheer, delight, elation, exultation, festivity, gaiety, gladness, joy, jubilation, merrymaking, revelry, triumph

rejoin *verb* = **reply**, answer, come back with, respond, retort, return, riposte

rejoinder noun = reply, answer, comeback (informal), counter, counterattack, response, retort, riposte

rejuvenate verb = revitalize, breathe new life into, give new life to, make young again, reanimate, refresh, regenerate, reinvigorate, renew, restore, restore vitality to, revivify

relapse verb 1 = lapse, backslide, degenerate, fail, fall back, regress, retrogress, revert, slip back, weaken 2 = worsen, deteriorate, fade, fail, sicken, sink, weaken ♦ noun 3 = lapse, backsliding, fall from grace, recidivism, regression, retrogression, reversion 4 = worsening, deterioration, recurrence, setback, turn for the worse, weakening
➤ Antonyms
verb ≠worsen: get better, improve, rally, recover ♦ noun ≠worsening: improvement, rally, recovery, turn for the better

relate verb 1 = connect, ally, associate, correlate, couple, join, link 2 = concern, appertain, apply, bear upon, be relevant to, have reference to, have to do with, pertain, refer 3 = tell, chronicle, describe, detail, give an account of, impart, narrate, present, recite, recount, rehearse, report, set forth
➤ Antonyms
≠connect: detach, disconnect, dissociate, divorce ≠concern: be irrelevant to, be unconnected, have nothing to do with

related adjective 1 = akin, agnate, cognate, consanguineous, kin, kindred 2 = associated, accompanying, affiliated, akin, allied, cognate, concomitant, connected, correlated, interconnected, joint, linked
➤ Antonyms
≠akin: unrelated ≠associated: separate, unconnected, unrelated

relation noun 1 = connection, application, bearing, bond, comparison, correlation, interdependence, link, pertinence, reference, regard, similarity, tie-in 2 = relative, kin, kinsman or kinswoman 3 = kinship, affiliation, affinity, consanguinity, kindred, propinquity, relationship 4 = account, description, narration, narrative, recital, recountal, report, story, tale

relations plural noun 1 = dealings, affairs, associations, connections, contact, interaction, intercourse, rapport, relationship, terms 2 = family, clan, kin, kindred, kinsfolk, kinsmen, relatives, tribe

relationship noun 1 = association, affinity, bond, communications, conjunction, connection, kinship, rapport 2 = affair, liaison 3 = connection, correlation, link, parallel, proportion, ratio, similarity, tie-up

relative adjective 1 = dependent, allied, associated, comparative, connected, contingent, corresponding, proportionate, reciprocal, related, respective 2 = relevant, applicable, apposite, appropriate, appurtenant, apropos, germane, pertinent 3 relative to = in proportion to, corresponding to, proportional to ♦ noun 4 = relation, connection, kinsman or kinswoman, member of one's or the family

relatively adverb = comparatively, in or by comparison, rather, somewhat, to some extent

relax verb 1 = be or feel at ease, calm, chill out (slang, chiefly U.S.), hang loose (slang), laze, let oneself go (informal), let one's hair down (informal), lighten up (slang), loosen up, make oneself at home, mellow out (informal), put one's feet up, rest, take it easy, take one's ease, unbend, unwind 2 = lessen, abate, diminish, ease, ebb, let up, loosen, lower, mitigate, moderate, reduce, relieve, slacken, weaken
➤ Antonyms
≠be or feel at ease: be alarmed, be alert ≠lessen: heighten, increase, intensify, tense, tighten, work

relaxation noun 1 = leisure, amusement, enjoyment, entertainment, fun, pleasure, recreation, refreshment, rest 2 = lessening, abatement, diminution, easing, let-up (informal), moderation, reduction, slackening, weakening

relaxed adjective = easy-going, casual, comfortable, downbeat (informal), easy, free and easy, informal, insouciant, laid-back (informal), leisurely, mellow, mild, nonchalant, unhurried, untaxing

relay noun 1 = shift, relief, turn 2 = message, communication, dispatch, transmission ♦ verb 3 = pass on, broadcast, carry, communicate, hand on, send, spread, transmit

release verb 1 = set free, deliver, discharge, disengage, drop, emancipate, extricate, free, let go, let out, liberate, loose, manumit, turn loose, unbridle, unchain, undo, unfasten, unfetter, unloose, unshackle, untie 2 = acquit, absolve, dispense, excuse, exempt, exonerate, let go, let off 3 = issue, break, circulate, disseminate, distribute, launch, make known, make public, present, publish, put out, unveil ♦ noun 4 = liberation, deliverance, delivery, discharge, emancipation, freedom, liberty, manumission, relief 5 = acquittal, absolution, acquittance, dispensation, exemption, exoneration, let-off (informal) 6 = issue, announcement, offering, proclamation, publication
➤ Antonyms
verb ≠set free: detain, engage, fasten, hold, imprison, incarcerate, keep ≠issue:

suppress, withhold ♦ *noun* ≠**liberation:** detention, imprisonment, incarceration, internment

relegate *verb* = **demote**, downgrade

relent *verb* **1** = **be merciful**, acquiesce, capitulate, change one's mind, come round, forbear, give in, give quarter, give way, have pity, melt, show mercy, soften, unbend, yield **2** = **ease**, die down, drop, fall, let up, relax, slacken, slow, weaken
➤ **Antonyms**
≠**be merciful:** be unyielding, give no quarter, remain firm, show no mercy ≠**ease:** increase, intensify, strengthen

relentless *adjective* **1** = **unremitting**, incessant, nonstop, persistent, punishing, sustained, unabated, unbroken, unfaltering, unflagging, unrelenting, unrelieved, unstoppable **2** = **merciless**, cruel, fierce, grim, hard, harsh, implacable, inexorable, inflexible, pitiless, remorseless, ruthless, uncompromising, undeviating, unforgiving, unrelenting, unstoppable, unyielding
➤ **Antonyms**
≠**merciless:** compassionate, forgiving, merciful, submissive, yielding

relevant *adjective* = **significant**, applicable, apposite, appropriate, appurtenant, apt, fitting, germane, material, pertinent, proper, related, relative, suited, to the point, to the purpose
➤ **Antonyms**
beside the point, extraneous, extrinsic, immaterial, inapplicable, inappropriate, irrelevant, unconnected, unrelated

reliable *adjective* = **dependable**, certain, faithful, honest, predictable, regular, reputable, responsible, safe, sound, stable, staunch, sure, tried and true, true, trustworthy, trusty, unfailing, upright
➤ **Antonyms**
irresponsible, undependable, unreliable, untrustworthy

reliance *noun* = **trust**, assurance, belief, confidence, credence, credit, dependence, faith

relic *noun* = **remnant**, fragment, keepsake, memento, remembrance, scrap, souvenir, survival, token, trace, vestige

relief *noun* **1** = **ease**, abatement, alleviation, assuagement, comfort, cure, deliverance, easement, mitigation, palliation, release, remedy, solace **2** = **rest**, break, breather (*informal*), diversion, let-up (*informal*), refreshment, relaxation, remission, respite **3** = **aid**, assistance, help, succour, support, sustenance

relieve *verb* **1** = **ease**, abate, allay, alleviate, assuage, calm, comfort, console, cure, diminish, dull, mitigate, mollify, palliate,

relax, soften, solace, soothe **2** = **help**, aid, assist, bring aid to, succour, support, sustain **3** = **free**, deliver, discharge, disencumber, exempt, release, unburden **4** = **take over from**, give (someone) a break *or* rest, stand in for, substitute for, take the place of **5** = **interrupt**, break, brighten, let up on (*informal*), lighten, slacken, vary
➤ **Antonyms**
≠**ease:** aggravate, exacerbate, heighten, intensify, worsen

religious *adjective* **1** = **devout**, churchgoing, devotional, divine, doctrinal, faithful, god-fearing, godly, holy, pious, pure, reverent, righteous, sacred, scriptural, sectarian, spiritual, theological **2** = **conscientious**, exact, faithful, fastidious, meticulous, punctilious, rigid, rigorous, scrupulous, unerring, unswerving
➤ **Antonyms**
≠**devout:** godless, infidel, irreligious, rational, secular, unbelieving

relinquish *verb* Formal = **give up**, abandon, abdicate, cast off, cede, desert, drop, forgo, forsake, hand over, leave, let go, quit, release, renounce, repudiate, resign, retire from, say goodbye to, surrender, vacate, waive, withdraw from, yield

relish *verb* **1** = **enjoy**, appreciate, delight in, fancy, lick one's lips, like, look forward to, luxuriate in, prefer, revel in, savour, taste ♦ *noun* **2** = **enjoyment**, appetite, appreciation, fancy, fondness, gusto, liking, love, partiality, penchant, predilection, stomach, taste, zest, zing (*informal*) **3** = **condiment**, appetizer, sauce, seasoning **4** = **flavour**, piquancy, savour, smack, spice, tang, taste, trace
➤ **Antonyms**
verb ≠**enjoy:** be unenthusiastic about, dislike, loathe ♦ *noun* ≠**enjoyment:** dislike, distaste, loathing

reluctance *noun* = **unwillingness**, aversion, backwardness, disinclination, dislike, disrelish, distaste, hesitancy, loathing, repugnance

reluctant *adjective* = **unwilling**, averse, backward, disinclined, grudging, hesitant, loath, recalcitrant, slow, unenthusiastic
➤ **Antonyms**
eager, enthusiastic, inclined, keen, willing

rely *verb* = **depend**, bank, be confident of, be sure of, bet, count, have confidence in, lean, reckon, swear by, trust

remain *verb* **1** = **continue**, abide, bide, dwell, endure, go on, last, persist, prevail, stand, stay, survive **2** = **stay behind**, be left, delay, hang in the air, linger, stay put (*informal*), tarry, wait

➤ **Antonyms**
≠ **stay behind:** depart, go, leave

remainder *noun* = **rest**, balance, butt, dregs, excess, leavings, oddment, relic, remains, remnant, residue, residuum, stub, surplus, tail end, trace, vestige(s)

remaining *adjective* = **left-over**, abiding, extant, lasting, lingering, outstanding, persisting, residual, surviving, unfinished

remains *plural noun* **1** = **remnants**, balance, crumbs, debris, detritus, dregs, fragments, leavings, leftovers, oddments, odds and ends, pieces, relics, remainder, residue, rest, scraps, traces, vestiges **2** = **corpse**, body, cadaver, carcass

remark *verb* **1** = **comment**, declare, mention, observe, pass comment, reflect, say, state **2** = **notice**, espy, make out, mark, note, observe, perceive, regard, see, take note *or* notice of ♦ *noun* **3** = **comment**, assertion, declaration, observation, opinion, reflection, statement, thought, utterance, word

remarkable *adjective* = **extraordinary**, conspicuous, distinguished, famous, impressive, miraculous, notable, noteworthy, odd, outstanding, phenomenal, pre-eminent, prominent, rare, signal, singular, strange, striking, surprising, uncommon, unusual, wonderful
➤ **Antonyms**
banal, common, commonplace, everyday, insignificant, mundane, ordinary, unexceptional, unimpressive, unsurprising, usual

remedy *noun* **1** = **cure**, antidote, counteractive, medicament, medicine, nostrum, panacea, relief, restorative, therapy, treatment **2** = **solution**, antidote, corrective, countermeasure, panacea, redress, relief ♦ *verb* **3** = **put right**, ameliorate, correct, fix, rectify, redress, reform, relieve, repair, set to rights, solve **4** = **cure**, alleviate, assuage, control, ease, heal, help, mitigate, palliate, relieve, restore, soothe, treat

remember *verb* **1** = **recall**, call to mind, call up, commemorate, look back (on), put one's finger on, recognize, recollect, reminisce, retain, summon up, think back **2** = **bear in mind**, keep in mind
➤ **Antonyms**
disregard, forget, ignore, neglect, overlook

remembrance *noun* **1** = **memory**, mind, recall, recognition, recollection, regard, reminiscence, retrospect, thought **2** = **souvenir**, commemoration, keepsake, memento, memorial, monument, relic, reminder, testimonial, token

remind *verb* = **call to mind**, awaken memories of, bring back to, bring to mind, call up, jog one's memory, make (someone)

remember, prompt, put in mind, refresh one's memory

reminisce *verb* = **recall**, go over in the memory, hark back, live in the past, look back, recollect, remember, review, think back

reminiscence *noun* = **recollection**, anecdote, memoir, memory, recall, reflection, remembrance

reminiscent *adjective* = **suggestive**, evocative, redolent, remindful, similar

remiss *adjective Formal* = **careless**, derelict, dilatory, forgetful, heedless, inattentive, indifferent, lackadaisical, lax, neglectful, negligent, regardless, slack, slapdash, slipshod, sloppy (*informal*), slothful, slow, tardy, thoughtless, unmindful
➤ **Antonyms**
attentive, careful, diligent, painstaking, scrupulous

remission *noun* **1** = **reduction**, decrease, diminution, lessening, suspension **2** = **pardon**, absolution, acquittal, amnesty, discharge, excuse, exemption, exoneration, forgiveness, indulgence, release, reprieve **3** = **lessening**, abatement, abeyance, alleviation, amelioration, ebb, let-up (*informal*), lull, moderation, relaxation, respite

remit *verb* **1** = **send**, dispatch, forward, mail, post, transmit **2** = **cancel**, desist, halt, repeal, rescind, stop **3** = **lessen**, abate, alleviate, decrease, diminish, dwindle, ease up, fall away, mitigate, moderate, reduce, relax, sink, slacken, soften, wane, weaken **4** = **postpone**, defer, delay, put off, put on the back burner (*informal*), shelve, suspend, take a rain check on (*U.S. & Canad. informal*) ♦ *noun* **5** = **instructions**, authorization, brief, guidelines, orders, terms of reference

remittance *noun* = **payment**, allowance, consideration, fee

remnant *noun* = **remainder**, bit, butt, end, fragment, hangover, leftovers, oddment, piece, remains, residue, residuum, rest, rump, scrap, shred, stub, tail end, trace, vestige

remonstrance *noun Formal* = **protest**, complaint, expostulation, grievance, objection, protestation, reprimand, reproof

remonstrate *verb Formal* = **protest**, argue, challenge, complain, dispute, dissent, expostulate, object, take exception, take issue

remorse *noun* = **regret**, anguish, bad *or* guilty conscience, compassion, compunction, contrition, grief, guilt, pangs of conscience, penitence, pity, repentance, ruefulness, self-reproach, shame, sorrow

remorseful *adjective* = **regretful**, apologetic, ashamed, conscience-stricken, contrite, guilt-ridden, guilty, penitent, repentant, rueful, sad, self-reproachful, sorrowful, sorry

remorseless *adjective* 1 = **pitiless**, callous, cruel, hard, hardhearted, harsh, implacable, inhumane, merciless, ruthless, savage, uncompassionate, unforgiving, unmerciful 2 = **relentless**, inexorable, unrelenting, unremitting, unstoppable

remote *adjective* 1 = **distant**, backwoods, far, faraway, far-off, godforsaken, inaccessible, in the middle of nowhere, isolated, lonely, off the beaten track, outlying, out-of-the-way, secluded 2 = **irrelevant**, extraneous, extrinsic, immaterial, outside, removed, unconnected, unrelated 3 = **aloof**, abstracted, cold, detached, distant, faraway, indifferent, removed, reserved, standoffish, unapproachable, uncommunicative, uninterested, uninvolved, withdrawn 4 = **slight**, doubtful, dubious, faint, implausible, inconsiderable, meagre, negligible, outside, poor, slender, slim, small, unlikely
➤ Antonyms
≠**distant**: adjacent, central, close, just round the corner, near, nearby, neighbouring ≠**irrelevant**: intrinsic, related, relevant ≠**aloof**: alert, attentive, aware, gregarious, interested, involved, outgoing, sociable ≠**slight**: considerable, good, likely, strong

removal *noun* 1 = **taking away** *or* **off** *or* **out**, abstraction, dislodgment, displacement, dispossession, ejection, elimination, eradication, erasure, expunction, extraction, purging, stripping, subtraction, uprooting, withdrawal 2 = **dismissal**, expulsion 3 = **move**, departure, flitting (*Scot. & Northern English dialect*), relocation, transfer

remove *verb* 1 = **take away** *or* **off** *or* **out**, abolish, abstract, amputate, carry off *or* away, cart off (*slang*), delete, detach, dislodge, displace, do away with, efface, eject, eliminate, erase, excise, expunge, extract, get rid of, move, pull, purge, shed, strike out, transfer, wipe from the face of the earth, wipe out, withdraw 2 = **dismiss**, depose, dethrone, discharge, expel, oust, relegate, show one the door, throw out, throw out on one's ear (*informal*), unseat 3 = **move**, depart, flit (*Scot. & Northern English dialect*), move away, quit, relocate, shift, transfer, transport, vacate
➤ Antonyms
≠**take away** *or* **off** *or* **out**: don, insert, join, link, place, put, put back, put in, put on, replace, set ≠**dismiss**: appoint, install

remunerate *verb Formal* = **pay**, compensate, indemnify, recompense, redress, reimburse, repay, requite, reward

remuneration *noun* = **payment**, compensation, earnings, fee, income, indemnity, pay, profit, recompense, reimbursement, reparation, repayment, return, reward, salary, stipend, wages

remunerative *adjective* = **profitable**, economic, gainful, lucrative, moneymaking, paying, recompensing, rewarding, rich, worthwhile

renaissance, renascence *noun* = **rebirth**, awakening, new birth, new dawn, reappearance, reawakening, re-emergence, regeneration, renewal, restoration, resurgence, resurrection, revival

renascent *adjective Literary* = **resurgent**, reanimated, reawakening, reborn, re-emerging, renewed, resurrected, reviving

rend *verb Literary* = **tear**, break, burst, cleave, crack, dissever, divide, fracture, lacerate, pierce, pull, rip, rupture, separate, sever, shatter, smash, splinter, split, sunder (*literary*), tear to pieces, wrench

render *verb* 1 = **make**, cause to become, leave 2 = **provide**, contribute, deliver, furnish, give, hand out, make available, pay, present, show, submit, supply, tender, turn over, yield 3 = **translate**, construe, explain, interpret, put, reproduce, restate, transcribe 4 = **represent**, act, depict, do, give, interpret, perform, play, portray, present 5 = **give up**, cede, deliver, give, hand over, relinquish, surrender, turn over, yield

rendezvous *noun* 1 = **appointment**, assignation, date, engagement, meeting, tryst (*archaic*) 2 = **meeting place**, gathering point, place of assignation, trysting-place (*archaic*), venue ◆ *verb* 3 = **meet**, assemble, be reunited, collect, come together, converge, gather, get together, join up, muster, rally

rendition *noun Formal* 1 = **performance**, arrangement, delivery, depiction, execution, interpretation, portrayal, presentation, reading, rendering, take (*informal, chiefly U.S.*), version 2 = **translation**, explanation, interpretation, reading, transcription, version

renegade *noun* 1 = **deserter**, apostate, backslider, betrayer, defector, dissident, mutineer, outlaw, rebel, recreant (*archaic*), runaway, traitor, turncoat ◆ *adjective* 2 = **traitorous**, apostate, backsliding, disloyal, dissident, mutinous, outlaw, rebel, rebellious, recreant (*archaic*), runaway, unfaithful

renege *verb* = **break one's word**, back out, break a promise, default, go back, repudiate, welsh (*slang*)

renew *verb* 1 = **recommence**, begin again, breathe new life into, bring up to date, continue, extend, prolong, reaffirm, recreate, re-establish, regenerate, rejuvenate, reopen,

repeat, restate, resume, revitalize **2**
= **restore**, fix up (*informal, chiefly U.S. &
Canad.*), mend, modernize, overhaul, refit,
refurbish, renovate, repair, transform **3**
= **replace**, refresh, replenish, restock

renounce *verb* = **give up**, abandon,
abdicate, abjure, abnegate, abstain from,
cast off, decline, deny, discard, disclaim,
disown, eschew, forgo, forsake, forswear,
leave off, quit, recant, reject, relinquish,
renege, repudiate, resign, retract, spurn,
swear off, throw off, waive, wash one's
hands of
➤ **Antonyms**
assert, avow, claim, maintain, reassert

renovate *verb* = **restore**, do up (*informal*),
fix up (*informal, chiefly U.S. & Canad.*),
modernize, overhaul, recondition, recreate,
refit, reform, refurbish, rehabilitate, remodel,
renew, repair, revamp

renown *noun* = **fame**, acclaim, celebrity,
distinction, eminence, glory, honour,
illustriousness, mark, note, reputation,
repute, stardom

renowned *adjective* = **famous**, acclaimed,
celebrated, distinguished, eminent,
esteemed, famed, illustrious, notable, noted,
well-known
➤ **Antonyms**
forgotten, little-known, neglected, obscure,
unknown

rent[1] *verb* **1** = **hire**, charter, lease, let ♦ *noun*
2 = **hire**, fee, lease, payment, rental, tariff

rent[2] *noun* = **tear**, breach, break, chink,
crack, flaw, gash, hole, opening, perforation,
rip, slash, slit, split

renunciation *noun* = **giving up**,
abandonment, abdication, abjuration,
abnegation, denial, disavowal, disclaimer,
eschewal, forswearing, rejection,
relinquishment, repudiation, spurning,
surrender, waiver

reorganize *verb* = **rearrange**, make a clean
sweep, rationalize, reshuffle, restructure,
shake up, spring-clean

repair[1] *verb* **1** = **mend**, fix, heal, make good,
patch, patch up, put back together, recover,
renew, renovate, restore, restore to working
order **2** = **put right**, compensate for, make
up for, rectify, redress, retrieve, square
♦ *noun* **3** = **mend**, adjustment, darn,
overhaul, patch, restoration **4** = **condition**,
fettle, form, nick (*informal*), shape
(*informal*), state
➤ **Antonyms**
verb ≠**mend**: damage, destroy, harm, ruin,
wreck

repair[2] *verb* = **go**, betake oneself, head for,
leave for, move, remove, retire, set off for,
withdraw

reparable *adjective* = **curable**, recoverable,
rectifiable, remediable, restorable,
retrievable, salvageable

reparation *noun* = **compensation**, amends,
atonement, damages, indemnity,
recompense, redress, repair, requital,
restitution, satisfaction

repartee *noun* = **wit**, badinage, banter, bon
mot, pleasantry, raillery, riposte, sally,
witticism, wittiness, wordplay

repast *noun* = **meal**, collation, food,
nourishment, spread (*informal*), victuals

repay *verb* **1** = **pay back**, compensate, make
restitution, recompense, refund, reimburse,
remunerate, requite, restore, return, reward,
settle up with, square **2** = **reciprocate**,
avenge, even or settle the score with, get
back at, get even with (*informal*), get one's
own back on (*informal*), hit back, make
reprisal, pay (someone) back in his or her
own coin, retaliate, return the compliment,
revenge

repeal *verb* **1** = **abolish**, abrogate, annul,
cancel, countermand, declare null and void,
invalidate, nullify, obviate, recall, rescind,
reverse, revoke, set aside, withdraw ♦ *noun*
2 = **abolition**, abrogation, annulment,
cancellation, invalidation, nullification,
rescinding, rescindment, revocation,
withdrawal
➤ **Antonyms**
verb ≠**abolish**: confirm, enact, introduce,
pass, ratify, reaffirm, validate ♦ *noun*
≠**abolition**: confirmation, enactment,
introduction, passing, ratification,
reaffirmation, validation

repeat *verb* **1** = **reiterate**, duplicate, echo,
quote, recapitulate, recite, redo, rehearse,
relate, renew, replay, reproduce, rerun,
reshow, restate, retell ♦ *noun* **2**
= **repetition**, duplicate, echo, recapitulation,
reiteration, replay, reproduction, rerun,
reshowing

repeatedly *adverb* = **over and over**, again
and again, frequently, many times, often,
time after time, time and (time) again

repel *verb* **1** = **disgust**, give one the creeps
(*informal*), gross out (*U.S. slang*), make one
shudder, make one sick, nauseate, offend,
put one off, revolt, sicken, turn one off
(*informal*), turn one's stomach **2** = **drive
off**, beat off, check, fight, hold off, keep at
arm's length, oppose, parry, put to flight,
rebuff, refuse, reject, repulse, resist, ward off
➤ **Antonyms**
≠**disgust**: attract, delight, draw, entrance,
fascinate, invite, please ≠**drive off**: submit

repellent *adjective* **1** = **disgusting**,
abhorrent, abominable, discouraging,
distasteful, hateful, horrid, loathsome,

nauseating, noxious, obnoxious, obscene, odious, offensive, off-putting (*Brit. informal*), repugnant, repulsive, revolting, sickening, yucky *or* yukky (*slang*) **2 = proof**, impermeable, repelling, resistant

repent *verb* = **regret**, atone, be ashamed, be contrite, be sorry, deplore, feel remorse, lament, relent, reproach oneself, rue, see the error of one's ways, show penitence, sorrow

repentance *noun* = **regret**, compunction, contrition, grief, guilt, penitence, remorse, sackcloth and ashes, self-reproach, sorriness, sorrow

repentant *adjective* = **regretful**, apologetic, ashamed, contrite, penitent, remorseful, rueful, self-reproachful, sorry

repercussion *noun* **1 repercussions** = **consequences**, backlash, result, sequel, side effects **2 = reverberation**, echo, rebound, recoil

repertoire *noun* = **range**, collection, list, repertory, repository, stock, store, supply

repertory *noun* = **repertoire**, collection, list, range, repository, stock, store, supply

repetition *noun* = **repeating**, duplication, echo, reappearance, recapitulation, recital, recurrence, rehearsal, reiteration, relation, renewal, replication, restatement, tautology

repetitious *adjective* = **long-winded**, pleonastic, prolix, redundant, tautological, tedious, verbose, wordy

repetitive *adjective* = **monotonous**, boring, dull, mechanical, recurrent, samey (*informal*), tedious, unchanging, unvaried

rephrase *verb* = **reword**, paraphrase, put differently, recast, say in other words

repine *verb Literary* = **complain**, brood, eat one's heart out, fret, grieve, grumble, lament, languish, moan, mope, sulk

replace *verb* **1 = take the place of**, fill (someone's) shoes *or* boots, follow, oust, stand in lieu of, step into (someone's) shoes *or* boots, substitute, succeed, supersede, supplant, supply, take over from **2 = put back**, re-establish, reinstate, restore

replacement *noun* = **successor**, double, fill-in, proxy, stand-in, substitute, surrogate, understudy

replenish *verb* = **refill**, fill, furnish, make up, provide, reload, renew, replace, restock, restore, stock, supply, top up
➤ **Antonyms**
consume, drain, empty, exhaust, use up

replete *adjective* **1 = sated**, full, full up, gorged, satiated **2 = filled**, abounding, brimful, brimming, charged, chock-full, crammed, full to bursting, glutted, jammed, jam-packed, stuffed, teeming, well-provided, well-stocked

➤ **Antonyms**
≠**sated**: empty, esurient, famished, hungry, starving ≠**filled**: bare, barren, empty, lacking, wanting

repletion *noun* **1 = fullness**, overfullness, satiation, satiety **2 = surfeit**, completeness, glut, plethora, superfluity

replica *noun* = **duplicate**, carbon copy (*informal*), copy, facsimile, imitation, model, reproduction
➤ **Antonyms**
master, original, prototype

replicate *verb* = **copy**, ape, duplicate, follow, mimic, recreate, reduplicate, repeat, reproduce

reply *verb* **1 = answer**, acknowledge, come back, counter, echo, react, reciprocate, rejoin, respond, retaliate, retort, return, riposte, write back ♦ *noun* **2 = answer**, acknowledgment, comeback (*informal*), counter, counterattack, echo, reaction, reciprocation, rejoinder, response, retaliation, retort, return, riposte

report *verb* **1 = communicate**, air, announce, bring word, broadcast, circulate, cover, declare, describe, detail, document, give an account of, inform of, mention, narrate, note, notify, pass on, proclaim, publish, recite, record, recount, relate, relay, state, tell, write up **2 = present oneself**, appear, arrive, be present, clock in *or* on, come, show up (*informal*), turn up ♦ *noun* **3 = account**, announcement, communication, declaration, description, detail, information, narrative, news, note, recital, record, relation, statement, summary, tale, tidings, version, word **4 = article**, communiqué, dispatch, message, paper, piece, story, write-up **5 = rumour**, buzz, gossip, hearsay, talk **6 = bang**, blast, boom, crack, crash, detonation, discharge, explosion, noise, reverberation, sound **7 = repute**, character, eminence, esteem, fame, regard, reputation

reporter *noun* = **journalist**, announcer, correspondent, hack (*derogatory*), journo (*slang*), newscaster, newshound (*informal*), newspaperman *or* newspaperwoman, pressman, writer

repose *noun* **1 = peace**, ease, inactivity, quiet, quietness, quietude, relaxation, respite, rest, restfulness, stillness, tranquillity **2 = composure**, aplomb, calmness, dignity, equanimity, peace of mind, poise, self-possession, serenity, tranquillity **3 = sleep**, slumber ♦ *verb* **4 = rest**, drowse, lay down, lie, lie down, lie upon, recline, relax, rest upon, sleep, slumber, take it easy

repository *noun* = **store**, archive, depository, depot, magazine, receptacle, storehouse, treasury, vault, warehouse

reprehensible *adjective* = **blameworthy**, bad, censurable, condemnable, culpable, discreditable, disgraceful, ignoble, objectionable, opprobrious, remiss, shameful, unworthy
➤ **Antonyms**
acceptable, admirable, forgivable, laudable, pardonable, praiseworthy, unobjectionable

represent *verb* **1** = **stand for**, act for, be, betoken, correspond to, equal, equate with, express, mean, serve as, speak for, substitute for, symbolize **2** = **exemplify**, embody, epitomize, personify, symbolize, typify **3** = **depict**, delineate, denote, describe, designate, express, illustrate, outline, picture, portray, render, reproduce, show, sketch

representation *noun* **1** = **portrayal**, account, delineation, depiction, description **2** = **picture**, illustration, image, likeness, model, portrait, sketch **3** *often plural* = **statement**, account, argument, explanation, exposition

representative *noun* **1** = **delegate**, agent, commissioner, councillor, depute (*Scot.*), deputy, member, member of parliament, M.P., proxy, spokesman *or* spokeswoman **2** = **salesman**, agent, commercial traveller, rep, traveller **3** = **typical example**, archetype, embodiment, epitome, exemplar, personification, type ♦ *adjective* **4** = **typical**, archetypal, characteristic, emblematic, exemplary, illustrative, symbolic **5** = **chosen**, delegated, elected, elective
➤ **Antonyms**
adjective ≠**typical**: atypical, extraordinary, uncharacteristic

repress *verb* **1** = **control**, bottle up, check, curb, hold back, hold in, inhibit, keep in check, master, muffle, overcome, overpower, restrain, silence, smother, stifle, suppress, swallow **2** = **subdue**, crush, quash, quell, subjugate
➤ **Antonyms**
≠**control**: encourage, express, give free rein to, let out, release ≠**subdue**: free, liberate

repression *noun* = **subjugation**, authoritarianism, constraint, control, despotism, domination, inhibition, restraint, suppression, tyranny

repressive *adjective* = **oppressive**, absolute, authoritarian, despotic, dictatorial, harsh, severe, tough, tyrannical
➤ **Antonyms**
democratic, liberal, libertarian

reprieve *verb* **1** = **grant a stay of execution to**, let off the hook (*slang*), pardon, postpone *or* remit the punishment of **2** = **relieve**, abate, allay, alleviate, mitigate, palliate, respite ♦ *noun* **3** = **stay of**

execution, abeyance, amnesty, deferment, pardon, postponement, remission, suspension **4** = **relief**, abatement, alleviation, let-up (*informal*), mitigation, palliation, respite

reprimand *verb* **1** = **blame**, admonish, bawl out (*informal*), carpet (*informal*), castigate, censure, chide, dress down (*informal*), give a rocket (*Brit. & N.Z. informal*), give (someone) a row (*informal*), haul over the coals (*informal*), lecture, rap over the knuckles, read the riot act, rebuke, reprehend, reproach, reprove, scold, slap on the wrist (*informal*), take to task, tear into (*informal*), tear (someone) off a strip (*Brit. informal*), tell off (*informal*), tick off (*informal*), upbraid ♦ *noun* **2** = **blame**, admonition, castigation, censure, dressing-down (*informal*), lecture, rebuke, reprehension, reproach, reproof, row, talking-to (*informal*), telling-off (*informal*), ticking-off (*informal*)
➤ **Antonyms**
verb ≠**blame**: applaud, commend, compliment, congratulate, praise ♦ *noun* ≠**blame**: commendation, compliment, congratulations, praise

reprisal *noun* = **retaliation**, an eye for an eye, counterstroke, requital, retribution, revenge, vengeance

reproach *noun* **1** = **blame**, censure, condemnation, contempt, disapproval, discredit, disgrace, dishonour, disrepute, ignominy, indignity, opprobrium, rebuke, scorn, shame ♦ *verb* **2** = **blame**, bawl out (*informal*), blast, carpet (*informal*), censure, chide, condemn, criticize, disparage, find fault with, give a rocket (*Brit. & N.Z. informal*), have a go at (*informal*), lambast(e), read the riot act, rebuke, reprehend, reprimand, reprove, scold, take to task, tear into (*informal*), tear (someone) off a strip (*Brit. informal*), upbraid

reproachful *adjective* = **critical**, castigatory, censorious, condemnatory, contemptuous, disappointed, disapproving, fault-finding, reproving, scolding, upbraiding

reprobate *noun* **1** = **scoundrel**, asshole (*U.S. & Canad. taboo slang*), bad egg (*old-fashioned informal*), bastard (*offensive*), blackguard, bugger (*taboo slang*), degenerate, evildoer, miscreant, ne'er-do-well, profligate, rake, rascal, scumbag (*slang*), sinner, son-of-a-bitch (*slang, chiefly U.S. & Canad.*), villain, wretch, wrongdoer ♦ *adjective* **2** = **unprincipled**, abandoned, bad, base, corrupt, damned, degenerate, depraved, dissolute, hardened, immoral, incorrigible, profligate, shameless, sinful, vile, wicked

reproduce *verb* **1** = **copy**, duplicate, echo,

emulate, imitate, match, mirror, parallel, print, recreate, repeat, replicate, represent, transcribe **2** *Biology* = **breed**, generate, multiply, procreate, produce young, proliferate, propagate, spawn

reproduction *noun* **1** *Biology* = **breeding**, generation, increase, multiplication, procreation, proliferation, propagation **2** = **copy**, duplicate, facsimile, imitation, picture, print, replica
➤ **Antonyms**
≠**copy**: master, original, prototype

reproof *noun* = **rebuke**, admonition, blame, castigation, censure, chiding, condemnation, criticism, dressing-down (*informal*), reprimand, reproach, reproval, scolding, ticking-off (*informal*), tongue-lashing
➤ **Antonyms**
commendation, compliment, encouragement, praise

reprove *verb* = **rebuke**, admonish, bawl out (*informal*), berate, blame, carpet (*informal*), censure, chide, condemn, give a rocket (*Brit. & N.Z. informal*), reprehend, reprimand, scold, take to task, tear into (*informal*), tear (someone) off a strip (*Brit. informal*), tell off (*informal*), tick off (*informal*), upbraid
➤ **Antonyms**
applaud, commend, compliment, encourage, praise

repudiate *verb* = **reject**, abandon, abjure, cast off, cut off, deny, desert, disavow, discard, disclaim, disown, forsake, renounce, rescind, retract, reverse, revoke, turn one's back on, wash one's hands of
➤ **Antonyms**
accept, acknowledge, admit, assert, avow, defend, own, proclaim, ratify

repugnance *noun* = **distaste**, abhorrence, antipathy, aversion, disgust, dislike, disrelish, hatred, loathing, odium, reluctance, repulsion, revulsion

repugnant *adjective* = **distasteful**, abhorrent, abominable, disgusting, foul, hateful, horrid, loathsome, nauseating, objectionable, obnoxious, odious, offensive, repellent, revolting, sickening, vile, yucky *or* yukky (*slang*)
➤ **Antonyms**
agreeable, attractive, pleasant, unobjectionable

repulse *verb* **1** = **disgust**, fill with loathing, gross out (*U.S. Slang*), nauseate, offend, put off, repel, revolt, sicken, turn one's stomach **2** = **drive back**, beat off, check, defeat, fight off, rebuff, repel, throw back, ward off **3** = **reject**, disdain, disregard, give the cold shoulder to, rebuff, refuse, snub, spurn, turn down ◆ *noun* **4** = **defeat**, check, disappointment, failure, reverse **5**

= **rejection**, cold shoulder, kick in the teeth (*slang*), knock-back (*slang*), rebuff, refusal, snub

repulsion *noun* = **disgust**, abhorrence, aversion, detestation, disrelish, distaste, hatred, loathing, odium, repugnance, revulsion

repulsive *adjective* = **disgusting**, abhorrent, abominable, disagreeable, distasteful, foul, hateful, hideous, horrid, loathsome, nauseating, objectionable, obnoxious, odious, offensive, repellent, revolting, sickening, ugly, unpleasant, vile
➤ **Antonyms**
appealing, attractive, delightful, enticing, lovely, pleasant

reputable *adjective* = **respectable**, creditable, estimable, excellent, good, honourable, honoured, legitimate, of good repute, reliable, trustworthy, upright, well-thought-of, worthy
➤ **Antonyms**
cowboy (*informal*), disreputable, fly-by-night, shady (*informal*), unreliable, untrustworthy

reputation *noun* **1** = **name**, character, esteem, estimation, opinion, renown, repute, standing, stature **2** = **fame**, credit, distinction, eminence, honour

repute *noun* = **reputation**, celebrity, distinction, eminence, esteem, estimation, fame, name, renown, standing, stature

reputed *adjective* = **supposed**, accounted, alleged, believed, considered, deemed, estimated, held, ostensible, putative, reckoned, regarded, rumoured, said, seeming, thought

reputedly *adverb* = **supposedly**, allegedly, apparently, ostensibly, seemingly

request *verb* **1** = **ask (for)**, appeal for, apply for, beg, beseech, call for, demand, desire, entreat, invite, petition, pray, put in for, requisition, seek, solicit ◆ *noun* **2** = **asking**, appeal, application, begging, call, demand, desire, entreaty, petition, prayer, requisition, suit
➤ **Antonyms**
verb ≠**ask (for)**: command, order ◆ *noun* ≠**asking**: command, order

require *verb* **1** = **need**, crave, depend upon, desire, have need of, lack, miss, stand in need of, want, wish **2** = **demand**, call for, entail, involve, necessitate, take **3** = **order**, ask, bid, call upon, command, compel, constrain, demand, direct, enjoin, exact, insist upon, instruct, oblige

required *adjective* = **needed**, called for, compulsory, demanded, *de rigueur*, essential, mandatory, necessary, obligatory, prescribed, recommended, requisite, set, unavoidable, vital

➤ **Antonyms**

elective, noncompulsory, not necessary, not vital, optional, unimportant, voluntary

requirement *noun* = **necessity**, demand, essential, lack, must, need, precondition, prerequisite, qualification, requisite, *sine qua non*, specification, stipulation, want

requisite *adjective* **1** = **necessary**, called for, essential, indispensable, mandatory, needed, needful, obligatory, prerequisite, required, vital ◆ *noun* **2** = **necessity**, condition, essential, must, need, precondition, prerequisite, requirement, *sine qua non*

requisition *verb* **1** = **demand**, apply for, call for, put in for, request **2** = **take over**, appropriate, commandeer, occupy, seize, take possession of ◆ *noun* **3** = **demand**, application, call, request, summons **4** = **takeover**, appropriation, commandeering, occupation, seizure

requital *noun* = **return**, amends, compensation, payment, recompense, redress, reimbursement, remuneration, repayment, restitution, reward

requite *verb* = **return**, compensate, get even, give in return, give tit for tat, make amends, make good, make restitution, pay, pay (someone) back in his *or* her own coin, reciprocate, recompense, redress, reimburse, remunerate, repay, respond, retaliate, return like for like, reward, satisfy

rescind *verb* = **annul**, abrogate, cancel, countermand, declare null and void, invalidate, obviate, overturn, quash, recall, repeal, retract, reverse, revoke, set aside, void

➤ **Antonyms**

confirm, enact, implement, reaffirm, support, uphold, validate

rescue *verb* **1** = **save**, deliver, extricate, free, get out, liberate, recover, redeem, release, salvage, save the life of, set free ◆ *noun* **2** = **liberation**, deliverance, extrication, recovery, redemption, release, relief, salvage, salvation, saving

➤ **Antonyms**

verb ≠ **save**: abandon, desert, leave, leave behind, lose, strand

research *noun* **1** = **investigation**, analysis, examination, experimentation, exploration, fact-finding, groundwork, inquiry, probe, scrutiny, study ◆ *verb* **2** = **investigate**, analyse, do tests, examine, experiment, explore, look into, make inquiries, probe, scrutinize, study, work over

resemblance *noun* = **similarity**, affinity, analogy, closeness, comparability, comparison, conformity, correspondence,

counterpart, facsimile, image, kinship, likeness, parallel, parity, sameness, semblance, similitude

➤ **Antonyms**

difference, disparity, dissimilarity, heterogeneity, unlikeness, variation

resemble *verb* = **be like**, bear a resemblance to, be similar to, duplicate, echo, favour (*informal*), look like, mirror, parallel, put one in mind of, remind one of, take after

resent *verb* = **be bitter about**, be angry about, bear a grudge about, begrudge, be in a huff about, be offended by, be pissed (off) about (*taboo slang*), dislike, grudge, harbour a grudge against, have hard feelings about, object to, take amiss, take as an insult, take exception to, take offence at, take umbrage at

➤ **Antonyms**

accept, approve, be content with, be pleased by, feel flattered by, like, welcome

resentful *adjective* = **bitter**, aggrieved, angry, embittered, grudging, huffish, huffy, hurt, in a huff, indignant, in high dudgeon, jealous, miffed (*informal*), offended, peeved (*informal*), piqued, pissed (*taboo slang*), pissed off (*taboo slang*), put out, unforgiving, wounded

➤ **Antonyms**

content, flattered, gratified, pleased, satisfied

resentment *noun* = **bitterness**, anger, animosity, bad blood, chip on one's shoulder (*informal*), displeasure, grudge, huff, hurt, ill feeling, ill will, indignation, pique, rage, rancour, umbrage

reservation *noun* **1** = **doubt**, demur, hesitancy, scepticism, scruple **2** = **condition**, proviso, qualification, rider, stipulation **3** = **reserve**, homeland, preserve, sanctuary, territory, tract

reserve *verb* **1** = **keep**, conserve, hang on to, hoard, hold, husband, keep back, lay up, preserve, put by, retain, save, set aside, stockpile, store, withhold **2** = **book**, bespeak, engage, prearrange, pre-engage, retain, secure **3** = **delay**, defer, keep back, postpone, put off, withhold ◆ *noun* **4** = **store**, backlog, cache, capital, fall-back, fund, hoard, reservoir, savings, stock, stockpile, supply **5** = **reservation**, park, preserve, sanctuary, tract **6** = **shyness**, aloofness, constraint, coolness, formality, modesty, reluctance, reservation, restraint, reticence, secretiveness, silence, taciturnity ◆ *adjective* **7** = **substitute**, alternate, auxiliary, extra, fall-back, secondary, spare

reserved *adjective* **1** = **uncommunicative**, aloof, cautious, close-mouthed, cold, cool, demure, formal, modest, prim, restrained, reticent, retiring, secretive, shy, silent,

standoffish, taciturn, unapproachable, undemonstrative, unforthcoming, unresponsive, unsociable **2 = set aside**, booked, engaged, held, kept, restricted, retained, spoken for, taken
➤ **Antonyms**
≠**uncommunicative:** ardent, demonstrative, forward, open, sociable, uninhibited, unreserved, warm

reservoir *noun* **1 = lake**, basin, pond, tank **2 = store**, accumulation, fund, pool, reserves, source, stock, stockpile, supply

reshuffle *noun* **1 = reorganization**, change, interchange, realignment, rearrangement, redistribution, regrouping, restructuring, revision, shake-up (*informal*) ◆ *verb* **2 = reorganize**, change around, change the line-up of, interchange, realign, rearrange, redistribute, regroup, restructure, revise, shake up (*informal*)

reside *verb* **1** *Formal* **= live**, abide, dwell, hang out (*informal*), have one's home, inhabit, lodge, remain, settle, sojourn, stay **2 = be present**, abide, be vested, consist, dwell, exist, lie
➤ **Antonyms**
≠**live:** holiday in, visit

residence *noun* **1 = home**, abode, domicile, dwelling, flat, habitation, house, household, lodging, pad (*slang*), place, quarters **2 = mansion**, hall, manor, palace, seat, villa **3 = stay**, occupancy, occupation, sojourn, tenancy

resident *noun* **1 = inhabitant**, citizen, denizen, local, lodger, occupant, tenant ◆ *adjective* **2 = inhabiting**, dwelling, living, local, neighbourhood, settled
➤ **Antonyms**
noun ≠**inhabitant:** nonresident, visitor ◆ *adjective* ≠**inhabiting:** nonresident, visiting

residual *adjective* **= remaining**, leftover, net, nett, unconsumed, unused, vestigial

residue *noun* **= remainder**, balance, dregs, excess, extra, leftovers, remains, remnant, residuum, rest, surplus

resign *verb* **1 = quit**, abdicate, give in one's notice, leave, step down (*informal*), vacate **2 = give up**, abandon, cede, forgo, forsake, hand over, relinquish, renounce, surrender, turn over, yield **3 resign oneself = accept**, acquiesce, bow, give in, give up, reconcile, submit, succumb, yield

resignation *noun* **1 = leaving**, abandonment, abdication, departure, notice, relinquishment, renunciation, retirement, surrender **2 = acceptance**, acquiescence, compliance, endurance, forbearing, fortitude, nonresistance, passivity, patience, submission, sufferance

➤ **Antonyms**
≠**acceptance:** defiance, dissent, kicking up a fuss, protest, resistance

resigned *adjective* **= stoical**, acquiescent, compliant, long-suffering, patient, subdued, submissive, unprotesting, unresisting

resilient *adjective* **1 = tough**, bouncy, buoyant, feisty (*informal, chiefly U.S. & Canad.*), hardy, irrepressible, quick to recover, strong **2 = flexible**, bouncy, elastic, plastic, pliable, rubbery, springy, supple
➤ **Antonyms**
≠**tough:** delicate, effete, sensitive, sickly, weak ≠**flexible:** flaccid, inflexible, limp, rigid, stiff

resist *verb* **1 = oppose**, battle, check, combat, confront, contend with, counteract, countervail, defy, dispute, fight, hinder, hold out against, put up a fight (against), refuse, stand up to, struggle against, thwart, weather **2 = refrain from**, abstain from, avoid, forbear, forgo, keep from, leave alone, prevent oneself from, refuse, turn down **3 = withstand**, be proof against, repel
➤ **Antonyms**
≠**oppose:** accept, acquiesce, cave in (*informal*), give in, submit, succumb, surrender, welcome, yield ≠**refrain from:** enjoy, give in to, indulge in, surrender to

resistance *noun* **= fighting**, battle, combat, contention, counteraction, defiance, fight, hindrance, impediment, intransigence, obstruction, opposition, refusal, struggle

Resistance *noun* **= freedom fighters**, guerrillas, maquis, partisans, underground

resistant *adjective* **1 = impervious**, hard, insusceptible, proof against, strong, tough, unaffected by, unyielding **2 = opposed**, antagonistic, defiant, dissident, hostile, intractable, intransigent, recalcitrant, unwilling

resolute *adjective* **= determined**, bold, constant, dogged, firm, fixed, immovable, inflexible, obstinate, persevering, purposeful, relentless, set, stalwart, staunch, steadfast, strong-willed, stubborn, tenacious, unbending, undaunted, unflinching, unshakable, unshaken, unwavering
➤ **Antonyms**
doubtful, irresolute, undecided, undetermined, unresolved, unsteady, weak

resolution *noun* **1 = determination**, boldness, constancy, courage, dedication, doggedness, earnestness, energy, firmness, fortitude, obstinacy, perseverance, purpose, relentlessness, resoluteness, resolve, sincerity, staunchness, staying power, steadfastness, stubbornness, tenacity, willpower **2 = decision**, aim, declaration, determination, intent, intention, judgment, motion, purpose, resolve, verdict **3 = solution**, answer, outcome, settlement, solving, sorting out, upshot, working out

resolve *verb* **1** = **decide**, agree, conclude, design, determine, fix, intend, make up one's mind, purpose, settle, undertake **2** = **break down**, analyse, clear, disintegrate, dissolve, liquefy, melt, reduce, separate, solve, split up **3** = **work out**, answer, clear up, crack, elucidate, fathom, find the solution to, suss (out) (*slang*) **4** = **dispel**, banish, clear up, explain, remove ♦ *noun* **5** = **determination**, boldness, courage, earnestness, firmness, resoluteness, resolution, steadfastness, willpower **6** = **decision**, conclusion, design, intention, objective, project, purpose, resolution, undertaking
➤ **Antonyms**
noun ≠**determination**: cowardice, half-heartedness, indecision, vacillation, wavering

resonant *adjective* = **echoing**, booming, full, resounding, reverberant, reverberating, rich, ringing, sonorous, vibrant

resort *verb* **1 resort to** = **have recourse to**, avail oneself of, bring into play, employ, exercise, fall back on, look to, make use of, turn to, use, utilize **2** = **go**, frequent, haunt, head for, visit ♦ *noun* **3** = **holiday centre**, haunt, refuge, retreat, spot, tourist centre, watering place (*Brit.*) **4** = **recourse**, reference **5** *As in* **last resort** = **course**, alternative, chance, expedient, hope, possibility

resound *verb* = **echo**, fill the air, re-echo, resonate, reverberate, ring

resounding *adjective* = **echoing**, booming, full, powerful, resonant, reverberating, rich, ringing, sonorous, sounding, vibrant

resource *noun* **1** = **supply**, hoard, reserve, source, stockpile **2** = **ingenuity**, ability, capability, cleverness, initiative, inventiveness, quick-wittedness, resourcefulness, talent **3** = **means**, course, device, expedient, resort

resourceful *adjective* = **ingenious**, able, bright, capable, clever, creative, imaginative, inventive, quick-witted, sharp, talented
➤ **Antonyms**
gormless (*Brit. informal*), unimaginative, uninventive

resources *plural noun* = **funds**, assets, capital, holdings, materials, means, money, property, reserves, riches, supplies, wealth, wherewithal

respect *noun* **1** = **regard**, admiration, appreciation, approbation, consideration, deference, esteem, estimation, honour, recognition, reverence, veneration **2** = **particular**, aspect, characteristic, detail,

facet, feature, matter, point, sense, way **3** *As in* **in respect of** *or* **with respect to** = **relation**, bearing, connection, reference, regard **4 respects** = **greetings**, compliments, good wishes, regards, salutations ♦ *verb* **5** = **think highly of**, admire, adore, appreciate, defer to, esteem, have a good *or* high opinion of, honour, look up to, recognize, regard, revere, reverence, set store by, value, venerate **6** = **abide by**, adhere to, attend, comply with, follow, heed, honour, notice, obey, observe, pay attention to, regard, show consideration for
➤ **Antonyms**
noun ≠**regard**: contempt, disdain, disregard, disrespect, irreverence, scorn ♦ *verb* ≠**abide by**: abuse, disregard, disrespect, ignore, neglect, scorn

respectable *adjective* **1** = **honourable**, admirable, decent, decorous, dignified, estimable, good, honest, proper, reputable, respected, upright, venerable, worthy **2** = **reasonable**, ample, appreciable, considerable, decent, fair, fairly good, goodly, presentable, sizable *or* sizeable, substantial, tidy (*informal*), tolerable
➤ **Antonyms**
≠**honourable**: dishonourable, disreputable, ignoble, impolite, improper, indecent, unrefined, unworthy ≠**reasonable**: paltry, poor, small

respectful *adjective* = **polite**, civil, courteous, courtly, deferential, dutiful, gracious, humble, mannerly, obedient, reverent, reverential, self-effacing, well-mannered

respective *adjective* = **specific**, corresponding, individual, own, particular, personal, relevant, separate, several, various

respite *noun* **1** = **pause**, break, breather (*informal*), breathing space, cessation, halt, hiatus, intermission, interruption, interval, let-up (*informal*), lull, recess, relaxation, relief, rest **2** = **delay**, adjournment, moratorium, postponement, reprieve, stay, suspension

resplendent *adjective* = **brilliant**, beaming, bright, dazzling, effulgent, gleaming, glittering, glorious, luminous, lustrous, radiant, shining, splendid

respond *verb* = **answer**, acknowledge, act in response, come back, counter, react, reciprocate, rejoin, reply, retort, return
➤ **Antonyms**
ignore, remain silent, turn a blind eye

response *noun* = **answer**, acknowledgment, comeback (*informal*), counterattack, counterblast, feedback, reaction, rejoinder, reply, retort, return, riposte

responsibility *noun* 1 = authority, importance, power 2 = accountability, amenability, answerability, liability 3 = fault, blame, burden, culpability, guilt, liability 4 = level-headedness, conscientiousness, dependability, maturity, rationality, reliability, sensibleness, soberness, stability, trustworthiness 5 = duty, care, charge, liability, obligation, onus, pigeon (*informal*), trust

responsible *adjective* 1 = in charge, at the helm, carrying the can (*informal*), in authority, in control 2 = to blame, at fault, culpable, guilty 3 = accountable, amenable, answerable, bound, chargeable, duty-bound, liable, subject, under obligation 4 = sensible, adult, conscientious, dependable, level-headed, mature, rational, reliable, sober, sound, stable, trustworthy 5 = authoritative, decision-making, executive, high, important
➤ Antonyms
≠accountable: unaccountable ≠sensible: irresponsible, unconscientious, undependable, unreliable, untrustworthy

responsive *adjective* = sensitive, alive, awake, aware, forthcoming, impressionable, open, perceptive, quick to react, reactive, receptive, sharp, susceptible, sympathetic
➤ Antonyms
apathetic, impassive, insensitive, silent, unresponsive, unsympathetic

rest[1] *noun* 1 = relaxation, doze, forty winks (*informal*), idleness, kip (*Brit. slang*), leisure, lie-down, nap, repose, siesta, sleep, slumber, snooze (*informal*) 2 = inactivity, motionlessness, standstill 3 = refreshment, relief 4 = calm, somnolence, stillness, tranquillity 5 = pause, break, breather (*informal*), breathing space, cessation, halt, holiday, interlude, intermission, interval, lull, respite, stop, time off, vacation 6 = support, base, holder, prop, shelf, stand, trestle 7 at rest: a = motionless, at a standstill, still, stopped, unmoving b = calm, peaceful, tranquil c = dead, at peace d = asleep, resting, sleeping ◆ *verb* 8 = relax, be at ease, be calm, doze, drowse, have a snooze (*informal*), have forty winks (*informal*), idle, kip (*Brit. slang*), laze, lie down, lie still, nap, put one's feet up, refresh oneself, sit down, sleep, slumber, snooze (*informal*), take a nap, take it easy, take one's ease 9 = place, be supported, lay, lean, lie, prop, recline, repose, sit, stand, stretch out 10 = depend, base, be based, be founded, found, hang, hinge, lie, rely, reside, turn 11 = stop, break off, cease, come to a standstill, desist, discontinue, halt, have a break, knock off (*informal*), stay, take a breather (*informal*)
➤ Antonyms
noun ≠relaxation, pause: activity, bustle,

work ◆ *verb* ≠relax, stop: keep going, slog away (*informal*), work

rest[2] *noun* 1 = remainder, balance, excess, leftovers, others, remains, remnants, residue, residuum, rump, surplus ◆ *verb* 2 = continue being, be left, go on being, keep, remain, stay

restaurant *noun* = café, bistro, cafeteria, diner (*chiefly U.S. & Canad.*), eatery *or* eaterie, tearoom, trattoria

restful *adjective* = relaxing, calm, calming, comfortable, peaceful, placid, quiet, relaxed, serene, sleepy, soothing, tranquil, tranquillizing, undisturbed, unhurried
➤ Antonyms
agitated, busy, disturbing, restless, uncomfortable, unrelaxed

restitution *noun* 1 *Law* = compensation, amends, indemnification, indemnity, recompense, redress, refund, reimbursement, remuneration, reparation, repayment, requital, satisfaction 2 = return, restoration

restive *adjective* = restless, agitated, antsy (*informal*), edgy, fidgety, fractious, fretful, ill at ease, impatient, jittery (*informal*), jumpy, nervous, on edge, uneasy, unquiet, unruly
➤ Antonyms
at ease, calm, content, peaceful, relaxed, satisfied, serene, tranquil

restless *adjective* 1 = moving, active, bustling, changeable, footloose, having itchy feet, hurried, inconstant, irresolute, nomadic, roving, transient, turbulent, unsettled, unstable, unsteady, wandering 2 = unsettled, agitated, antsy (*informal*), anxious, disturbed, edgy, fidgeting, fidgety, fitful, fretful, ill at ease, jumpy, nervous, on edge, restive, sleepless, tossing and turning, troubled, uneasy, unquiet, unruly, worried
➤ Antonyms
≠moving: settled, stable, steady ≠unsettled: comfortable, composed, easy, quiet, relaxed, restful, undisturbed

restlessness *noun* 1 = movement, activity, bustle, hurry, hurry-scurry, inconstancy, instability, transience, turbulence, turmoil, unrest, unsettledness 2 = restiveness, agitation, ants in one's pants (*slang*), anxiety, disquiet, disturbance, edginess, fitfulness, fretfulness, heebie-jeebies (*slang*), inquietude, insomnia, jitters (*informal*), jumpiness, nervousness, uneasiness, worriedness

restoration *noun* 1 = repair, reconstruction, recovery, refreshment, refurbishing, rehabilitation, rejuvenation, renewal, renovation, revitalization, revival 2 = reinstatement, re-establishment, reinstallation, replacement, restitution, return

> **Antonyms**
≠**repair:** demolition, scrapping, wrecking
≠**reinstatement:** abolition, overthrow

restore *verb* **1** = **repair**, fix, mend, rebuild, recondition, reconstruct, recover, refurbish, rehabilitate, renew, renovate, retouch, set to rights, touch up **2** = **revive**, bring back to health, build up, reanimate, refresh, rejuvenate, revitalize, revivify, strengthen **3** = **return**, bring back, give back, hand back, recover, re-establish, reinstate, replace, send back **4** = **reinstate**, reconstitute, re-enforce, re-establish, reimpose, reintroduce
> **Antonyms**
≠**repair:** demolish, scrap, wreck ≠**revive:** make worse, sicken, weaken ≠**reinstate:** abolish, abrogate, repeal, rescind

restrain *verb* **1** = **hold back**, check, confine, constrain, contain, control, curb, curtail, hamper, have on a tight leash, hinder, hold, inhibit, keep, keep under control, limit, prevent, rein, repress, restrict, straiten, subdue, suppress **2** = **imprison**, arrest, bind, chain, confine, detain, fetter, hold, jail, lock up, manacle, pinion, tie up
> **Antonyms**
≠**hold back:** assist, encourage, gee up, help, incite, urge on ≠**imprison:** free, liberate, release

restrained *adjective* **1** = **controlled**, calm, mild, moderate, muted, reasonable, reticent, self-controlled, soft, steady, temperate, undemonstrative **2** = **unobtrusive**, discreet, quiet, subdued, tasteful
> **Antonyms**
≠**controlled:** fiery, hot-headed, intemperate, unrestrained, wild ≠**unobtrusive:** garish, loud, over-the-top, self-indulgent, tasteless

restraint *noun* **1** = **limitation**, ban, boycott, bridle, check, curb, disqualification, embargo, interdict, limit, rein, taboo **2** = **bonds**, chains, manacles, pinions, straitjacket **3** = **self-control**, coercion, command, compulsion, constraint, control, curtailment, hindrance, hold, inhibition, limitation, moderation, prevention, pulling one's punches, restriction, self-discipline, self-possession, self-restraint, suppression **4** = **confinement**, arrest, bondage, captivity, detention, fetters, imprisonment
> **Antonyms**
≠**limitation:** freedom, liberty ≠**self-control:** excess, immoderation, intemperance, licence, self-indulgence

restrict *verb* = **limit**, bound, circumscribe, clip someone's wings, confine, contain, cramp, demarcate, hamper, handicap, hem in, impede, inhibit, keep within bounds *or* limits, regulate, restrain, straiten
> **Antonyms**
allow, broaden, encourage, foster, free,

permit, promote, widen

restriction *noun* = **limitation**, check, condition, confinement, constraint, containment, control, curb, demarcation, handicap, inhibition, regulation, restraint, rule, stipulation

result *noun* **1** = **consequence**, conclusion, decision, development, effect, end, end result, event, fruit, issue, outcome, product, reaction, sequel, termination, upshot ♦ *verb* **2** = **arise**, appear, derive, develop, emanate, ensue, eventuate, flow, follow, happen, issue, spring, stem, turn out **3** **result in** = **end in**, culminate in, finish with, pan out (*informal*), terminate in, wind up
> **Antonyms**
noun ≠**consequence:** beginning, cause, germ, origin, outset, root, source

resume *verb* **1** = **begin again**, carry on, continue, go on, proceed, recommence, reinstitute, reopen, restart, take up *or* pick up where one left off **2** = **occupy again**, assume again, reoccupy, take back, take up again
> **Antonyms**
≠**begin again:** cease, discontinue, stop

résumé *noun* = **summary**, abstract, digest, epitome, précis, recapitulation, review, rundown, synopsis

resumption *noun* = **continuation**, carrying on, re-establishment, renewal, reopening, restart, resurgence

resurgence *noun* = **revival**, rebirth, re-emergence, renaissance, renascence, resumption, resurrection, return

resurrect *verb* **1** = **restore to life**, raise from the dead **2** = **revive**, breathe new life into, bring back, reintroduce, renew

resurrection *noun* **1** = **raising** *or* **rising from the dead**, return from the dead **2** = **revival**, comeback (*informal*), reappearance, rebirth, renaissance, renascence, renewal, restoration, resurgence, resuscitation, return
> **Antonyms**
≠**raising** *or* **rising from the dead:** burial, demise ≠**revival:** killing off

resuscitate *verb* = **revive**, bring round, bring to life, give artificial respiration to, give the kiss of life, rescue, resurrect, revitalize, revivify, save

retain *verb* **1** = **keep**, contain, detain, grasp, grip, hang *or* hold onto, hold, hold back, hold fast, keep possession of, maintain, preserve, reserve, restrain, save **2** = **hire**, commission, employ, engage, pay, reserve **3** = **remember**, memorize, recall, recollect
> **Antonyms**
≠**keep:** let go, lose, release, use up
≠**remember:** forget

retainer *noun* **1** = **fee**, advance, deposit **2** = **servant**, attendant, dependant, domestic, flunky, footman, henchman, lackey, supporter, valet, vassal

retaliate *verb* = **pay (someone) back**, even the score, exact retribution, get back at, get even with (*informal*), get one's own back (*informal*), give as good as one gets (*informal*), give (someone) a taste of his *or* her own medicine, give tit for tat, hit back, reciprocate, return like for like, strike back, take an eye for an eye, take revenge, wreak vengeance
➤ **Antonyms**
accept, submit, turn the other cheek

retaliation *noun* = **revenge**, an eye for an eye, a taste of one's own medicine, counterblow, counterstroke, reciprocation, repayment, reprisal, requital, retribution, tit for tat, vengeance

retard *verb* = **slow down**, arrest, brake, check, decelerate, delay, encumber, handicap, hinder, hold back *or* up, impede, obstruct, set back
➤ **Antonyms**
accelerate, advance, expedite, hasten, speed, speed up, stimulate

retch *verb* = **gag**, barf (*U.S. slang*), be sick, chuck (up) (*slang, chiefly U.S.*), chunder (*slang, chiefly Austral.*), heave, puke (*slang*), regurgitate, spew, throw up (*informal*), vomit

reticence *noun* = **silence**, quietness, reserve, restraint, secretiveness, taciturnity, uncommunicativeness

reticent *adjective* = **uncommunicative**, close-lipped, mum, quiet, reserved, restrained, secretive, silent, taciturn, tight-lipped, unforthcoming, unspeaking
➤ **Antonyms**
candid, communicative, expansive, frank, open, talkative, voluble

retinue *noun* = **attendants**, aides, cortege, entourage, escort, followers, following, servants, suite, train

retire *verb* **1** = **stop working**, be pensioned off, (be) put out to grass (*informal*), give up work **2** = **withdraw**, absent oneself, betake oneself, depart, exit, go away, leave, remove **3** = **go to bed**, go to one's room, go to sleep, hit the hay (*slang*), hit the sack (*slang*), kip down (*Brit. slang*), turn in (*informal*) **4** = **fall back**, back off, decamp, give ground, give way, pull back, pull out, recede, retreat, withdraw

retirement *noun* = **withdrawal**, loneliness, obscurity, privacy, retreat, seclusion, solitude

retiring *adjective* = **shy**, bashful, coy, demure, diffident, humble, meek, modest, quiet, reclusive, reserved, reticent, self-effacing, shrinking, timid, timorous, unassertive, unassuming
➤ **Antonyms**
audacious, bold, brassy, forward, gregarious, outgoing, sociable

retort *verb* **1** = **reply**, answer, answer back, come back with, counter, rejoin, respond, retaliate, return, riposte ◆ *noun* **2** = **reply**, answer, comeback (*informal*), rejoinder, response, riposte

retouch *verb* = **touch up**, brush up, correct, finish, improve, recondition, renovate, restore

retract *verb* **1** = **withdraw**, abjure, cancel, deny, disavow, disclaim, disown, eat one's words, recall, recant, renege, renounce, repeal, repudiate, rescind, reverse, revoke, take back, unsay **2** = **go back on**, back out of, renege on **3** = **draw in**, pull back, pull in, reel in, sheathe

retreat *verb* **1** = **withdraw**, back away, back off, depart, draw back, fall back, give ground, go back, leave, pull back, recede, recoil, retire, shrink, turn tail ◆ *noun* **2** = **withdrawal**, departure, evacuation, flight, retirement **3** = **refuge**, asylum, den, haunt, haven, hideaway, privacy, resort, retirement, sanctuary, seclusion, shelter
➤ **Antonyms**
verb ≠**withdraw:** advance, engage, move forward ◆ *noun* ≠**withdrawal:** advance, charge, entrance

retrench *verb* = **cut back**, curtail, cut, decrease, diminish, economize, husband, lessen, limit, make economies, reduce, save, tighten one's belt, trim

retrenchment *noun* = **cutback**, contraction, cost-cutting, curtailment, cut, economy, reduction, tightening one's belt
➤ **Antonyms**
expansion, investment

retribution *noun* = **punishment**, an eye for an eye, compensation, justice, Nemesis, reckoning, recompense, redress, repayment, reprisal, requital, retaliation, revenge, reward, satisfaction, vengeance

retrieve *verb* = **get back**, fetch back, recall, recapture, recoup, recover, redeem, regain, repair, repossess, rescue, restore, salvage, save, win back

retro *adjective* = **old-time**, antique, bygone, former, nostalgia, of yesteryear, old, old-fashioned, old-world, past, period

retrograde *adjective* **1** = **deteriorating**, backward, declining, degenerative, downward, inverse, negative, regressive, relapsing, retreating, retrogressive, reverse, waning, worsening ◆ *verb* **2** = **deteriorate**, backslide, decline, degenerate, go downhill (*informal*), regress, relapse, retreat, retrogress, revert, wane, worsen

retrogress verb = **deteriorate**, backslide, decline, go back, go downhill (informal), regress, relapse, retrocede, retrograde, return, revert, worsen

retrospect noun = **hindsight**, afterthought, recollection, re-examination, remembrance, reminiscence, review, survey
➤ Antonyms
anticipation, foresight

return verb 1 = **come back**, come round again, go back, reappear, rebound, recoil, recur, repair, retreat, revert, turn back 2 = **put back**, carry back, convey, give back, re-establish, reinstate, remit, render, replace, restore, send, send back, take back, transmit 3 = **give back**, pay back, reciprocate, recompense, refund, reimburse, repay, requite 4 = **earn**, bring in, make, net, repay, yield 5 = **reply**, answer, come back (with), communicate, rejoin, respond, retort 6 = **elect**, choose, pick, vote in 7 As in return a verdict = **announce**, arrive at, bring in, come to, deliver, render, report, submit ♦ noun 8 = **retreat**, rebound, recoil, reversion 9 = **restoration**, re-establishment, reinstatement, replacement 10 = **reappearance**, recurrence 11 = **profit**, advantage, benefit, gain, income, interest, proceeds, revenue, takings, yield 12 = **statement**, account, form, list, report, summary 13 = **reply**, answer, comeback (informal), rejoinder, response, retort, riposte
➤ Antonyms
verb ≠come back: depart, disappear, go away, leave ≠put back, give back: hold, keep, leave, remove, retain ≠earn: lose ♦ noun ≠restoration: removal ≠reappearance: departure, leaving

revamp verb = **renovate**, do up (informal), fix up (informal, chiefly U.S. & Canad.), give a face-lift to, overhaul, patch up, recondition, refit, refurbish, rehabilitate, repair, restore

reveal verb 1 = **make known**, announce, betray, blow wide open (slang), broadcast, communicate, disclose, divulge, get off one's chest (informal), give away, give out, impart, leak, let on, let out, let slip, make public, proclaim, publish, tell 2 = **show**, bare, bring to light, display, exhibit, expose to view, lay bare, manifest, open, uncover, unearth, unmask, unveil
➤ Antonyms
≠make known: conceal, cover up, hide, keep quiet about, sweep under the carpet (informal) ≠show: conceal, cover up, hide

revel verb 1 revel in = **enjoy**, bask in, delight in, gloat about, indulge in, lap up, luxuriate in, rejoice over, relish, savour, take pleasure

in, thrive on, wallow in 2 = **celebrate**, carouse, go on a spree, live it up (informal), make merry, paint the town red (informal), push the boat out (Brit. informal), rave (Brit. slang), roister, whoop it up (informal) ♦ noun 3 often plural = **merrymaking**, bacchanal, beano (Brit. slang), carousal, carouse, celebration, debauch, festivity, gala, jollification, party, rave (Brit. slang), rave-up (Brit. slang), saturnalia, spree
➤ Antonyms
verb ≠enjoy: abhor, be uninterested in, dislike, hate, have no taste for

revelation noun = **disclosure**, announcement, betrayal, broadcasting, communication, discovery, display, exhibition, exposé, exposition, exposure, giveaway, leak, manifestation, news, proclamation, publication, telling, uncovering, unearthing, unveiling

reveller noun = **merrymaker**, carouser, celebrator, partygoer, pleasure-seeker, roisterer

revelry noun = **merrymaking**, beano (Brit. slang), carousal, carouse, celebration, debauch, debauchery, festivity, fun, jollification, jollity, party, rave (Brit. slang), rave-up (Brit. slang), roistering, saturnalia, spree

revenge noun 1 = **retaliation**, an eye for an eye, reprisal, requital, retribution, satisfaction, vengeance ♦ verb 2 = **avenge**, even the score for, get even, get one's own back for (informal), hit back, pay (someone) back, repay, requite, retaliate, take an eye for an eye for, take revenge for, vindicate

revengeful adjective = **vengeful**, bitter, merciless, pitiless, resentful, unforgiving, unmerciful

revenue noun = **income**, gain, interest, proceeds, profits, receipts, returns, rewards, takings, yield
➤ Antonyms
expenditure, expenses, outgoings

reverberate verb = **echo**, rebound, recoil, re-echo, resound, ring, vibrate

reverberation noun = **echo**, rebound, recoil, re-echoing, reflection, resonance, resounding, ringing, vibration

revere verb = **be in awe of**, adore, defer to, exalt, have a high opinion of, honour, look up to, put on a pedestal, respect, reverence, think highly of, venerate, worship
➤ Antonyms
deride, despise, hold in contempt, scorn, sneer at

reverence noun = **respect**, admiration, adoration, awe, deference, devotion, high esteem, homage, honour, veneration, worship

➤ **Antonyms**
contempt, contumely, derision, disdain, scorn

reverent *adjective* = **respectful**, adoring, awed, deferential, devout, humble, loving, meek, pious, reverential
➤ **Antonyms**
cheeky, disrespectful, flippant, impious, irreverent, mocking, sacrilegious

reverie *noun* = **daydream**, absent-mindedness, abstraction, brown study, castles in the air *or* Spain, daydreaming, inattention, musing, preoccupation, trance, woolgathering

reverse *verb* 1 = **turn round**, invert, transpose, turn back, turn over, turn upside down, upend 2 = **go backwards**, back, backtrack, back up, move backwards, retreat 3 *Law* = **change**, alter, annul, cancel, countermand, declare null and void, invalidate, negate, obviate, overrule, overset, overthrow, overturn, quash, repeal, rescind, retract, revoke, set aside, undo, upset ◆ *noun* 4 = **opposite**, antithesis, contradiction, contrary, converse, inverse 5 = **back**, flip side, other side, rear, underside, verso, wrong side 6 = **misfortune**, adversity, affliction, blow, check, defeat, disappointment, failure, hardship, misadventure, mishap, repulse, reversal, setback, trial, vicissitude ◆ *adjective* 7 = **opposite**, back to front, backward, contrary, converse, inverse, inverted
➤ **Antonyms**
verb ≠ **go backwards:** advance, go forward, move forward ≠ **change:** carry out, enforce, implement, validate ◆ *noun* ≠ **back:** forward side, front, obverse, recto, right side

revert *verb* = **return**, backslide, come back, go back, hark back, lapse, recur, regress, relapse, resume, take up where one left off

review *noun* 1 = **critique**, commentary, critical assessment, criticism, evaluation, judgment, notice, study 2 = **magazine**, journal, periodical, zine (*informal*) 3 = **survey**, analysis, examination, perusal, report, scrutiny, study 4 = **inspection**, display, march past, parade, procession 5 = **re-examination**, another look, fresh look, reassessment, recapitulation, reconsideration, re-evaluation, rethink, retrospect, revision, second look ◆ *verb* 6 = **assess**, criticize, discuss, evaluate, give one's opinion of, judge, read through, study, weigh, write a critique of 7 = **reconsider**, go over again, look at again, reassess, recapitulate, re-evaluate, re-examine, rethink, revise, run over, take another look at, think over 8 = **look back on**, call to mind, recall, recollect, reflect on, remember, summon up 9 = **inspect**, examine, scrutinize

reviewer *noun* = **critic**, arbiter,

commentator, connoisseur, essayist, judge

revile *verb* = **malign**, abuse, asperse, bad-mouth (*slang, chiefly U.S. & Canad.*), calumniate, defame, denigrate, knock (*informal*), libel, reproach, rubbish (*informal*), run down, scorn, slag (off) (*slang*), slander, smear, traduce, vilify

revise *verb* 1 = **change**, alter, amend, correct, edit, emend, modify, reconsider, redo, re-examine, revamp, review, rework, rewrite, update 2 = **study**, cram (*informal*), go over, memorize, reread, run through, swot up (*Brit. informal*)

revision *noun* 1 = **change**, alteration, amendment, correction, editing, emendation, modification, re-examination, review, rewriting, updating 2 = **studying**, cramming (*informal*), homework, memorizing, rereading, swotting (*Brit. informal*)

revitalize *verb* = **reanimate**, breathe new life into, bring back to life, refresh, rejuvenate, renew, restore, resurrect, revivify

revival *noun* = **renewal**, awakening, quickening, reanimation, reawakening, rebirth, refreshment, renaissance, restoration, resurgence, resurrection, resuscitation, revitalization, revivification
➤ **Antonyms**
disappearance, extinction, falling off, suppression

revive *verb* = **revitalize**, animate, awaken, breathe new life into, bring back to life, bring round, come round, comfort, invigorate, kick-start (*informal*), quicken, rally, reanimate, recover, refresh, rekindle, renew, renovate, restore, resuscitate, rouse
➤ **Antonyms**
die out, disappear, enervate, exhaust, tire out, weary

revivify *verb* = **revive**, breathe new life into, give new life to, inspirit, invigorate, kick-start (*informal*), reanimate, refresh, renew, restore, resuscitate

revoke *verb* = **cancel**, abolish, abrogate, annul, call back, countermand, declare null and void, disclaim, invalidate, negate, nullify, obviate, quash, recall, recant, renege, renounce, repeal, repudiate, rescind, retract, reverse, set aside, take back, withdraw
➤ **Antonyms**
confirm, endorse, implement, maintain, put into effect, uphold

revolt *noun* 1 = **uprising**, defection, insurgency, insurrection, mutiny, putsch, rebellion, revolution, rising, sedition ◆ *verb* 2 = **rebel**, defect, mutiny, resist, rise, take to the streets, take up arms (*against*) 3 = **disgust**, give one the creeps (*informal*), gross out (*U.S. slang*), make one's flesh creep, nauseate, offend, repel, repulse, shock, sicken, turn off (*informal*), turn one's stomach

revolting *adjective* = **disgusting**, abhorrent, abominable, appalling, distasteful, foul, horrible, horrid, loathsome, nasty, nauseating, nauseous, noisome, obnoxious, obscene, offensive, repellent, repugnant, repulsive, shocking, sickening, yucky *or* yukky (*slang*)
➤ **Antonyms**
agreeable, attractive, delightful, fragrant, palatable, pleasant

revolution *noun* 1 = **revolt**, coup, coup d'état, insurgency, mutiny, putsch, rebellion, rising, uprising 2 = **transformation**, drastic *or* radical change, innovation, metamorphosis, reformation, sea change, shift, upheaval 3 = **rotation**, circle, circuit, cycle, gyration, lap, orbit, round, spin, turn, wheel, whirl

revolutionary *adjective* 1 = **rebel**, extremist, insurgent, insurrectionary, mutinous, radical, seditious, subversive 2 = **innovative**, avant-garde, different, drastic, experimental, fundamental, ground-breaking, new, novel, progressive, radical, thoroughgoing ♦ *noun* 3 = **rebel**, insurgent, insurrectionary, insurrectionist, mutineer, revolutionist
➤ **Antonyms**
adjective, noun ≠**rebel**:
counter-revolutionary, loyalist, reactionary ♦ *adjective* ≠**innovative**: conservative, conventional, mainstream, minor, traditional, trivial

revolutionize *verb* = **transform**, break with the past, metamorphose, modernize, reform, revamp

revolve *verb* 1 = **go round**, circle, gyrate, orbit, rotate, spin, turn, twist, wheel, whirl 2 = **consider**, deliberate, meditate, mull over, ponder, reflect, ruminate, study, think about, think over, turn over (in one's mind)

revulsion *noun* = **disgust**, abhorrence, abomination, aversion, detestation, distaste, loathing, odium, recoil, repugnance, repulsion
➤ **Antonyms**
attraction, desire, fascination, liking, pleasure

reward *noun* 1 = **payment**, benefit, bonus, bounty, compensation, gain, honour, merit, premium, prize, profit, recompense, remuneration, repayment, requital, return, wages 2 = **punishment**, comeuppance (*slang*), desert, just deserts, requital, retribution ♦ *verb* 3 = **compensate**, honour, make it worth one's while, pay, recompense, remunerate, repay, requite
➤ **Antonyms**
noun ≠**payment**: fine, penalty, punishment ♦ *verb* ≠**compensate**: fine, penalize, punish

rewarding *adjective* = **satisfying**, advantageous, beneficial, economic, edifying, enriching, fruitful, fulfilling, gainful, gratifying, pleasing, productive, profitable, remunerative, valuable, worthwhile
➤ **Antonyms**
barren, boring, fruitless, unproductive, unprofitable, unrewarding, vain

reword *verb* = **put in other words**, express differently, paraphrase, put another way, recast, rephrase

rewrite *verb* = **revise**, correct, edit, emend, recast, redraft, touch up

rhapsodize *verb* = **enthuse**, go into ecstasies, gush, rave (*informal*), wax lyrical

rhetoric *noun* 1 = **oratory**, eloquence 2 = **hyperbole**, bombast, grandiloquence, hot air (*informal*), magniloquence, pomposity, rant, verbosity, wordiness

rhetorical *adjective* 1 = **oratorical**, linguistic, stylistic, verbal 2 = **high-flown**, arty-farty (*informal*), bombastic, declamatory, flamboyant, flashy, florid, flowery, grandiloquent, high-sounding, hyperbolic, magniloquent, oratorical, pompous, pretentious, showy, verbose, windy

rhyme *noun* 1 = **poetry**, ode, poem, song, verse 2 **rhyme or reason** = **sense**, logic, meaning, method, plan ♦ *verb* 3 = **sound like**, chime, harmonize

rhythm *noun* = **beat**, accent, cadence, flow, lilt, measure (*Prosody*), metre, movement, pattern, periodicity, pulse, swing, tempo, time

rhythmic, rhythmical *adjective* = **cadenced**, flowing, harmonious, lilting, melodious, metrical, musical, periodic, pulsating, throbbing

ribald *adjective* = **coarse**, bawdy, blue, broad, earthy, filthy, gross, indecent, licentious, naughty, near the knuckle (*informal*), obscene, off colour, Rabelaisian, racy, raunchy (*slang*), risqué, rude, scurrilous, smutty, vulgar, X-rated (*informal*)
➤ **Antonyms**
chaste, decent, decorous, genteel, inoffensive, polite, proper, refined, tasteful

ribaldry *noun* = **coarseness**, bawdiness, earthiness, filth, grossness, indecency, licentiousness, naughtiness, obscenity, raciness, rudeness, scurrility, smut, smuttiness, vulgarity

rich *adjective* 1 = **wealthy**, affluent, filthy rich, flush (*informal*), loaded (*slang*), made of money (*informal*), moneyed, opulent, propertied, prosperous, rolling (*slang*), stinking rich (*informal*), well-heeled (*informal*), well-off, well-to-do 2 = **well-stocked**, abounding, full, productive,

well-endowed, well-provided, well-supplied **3 = fruitful**, abounding, abundant, ample, copious, exuberant, fecund, fertile, full, lush, luxurious, plenteous, plentiful, productive, prolific **4 = full-bodied**, creamy, delicious, fatty, flavoursome, heavy, highly-flavoured, juicy, luscious, savoury, spicy, succulent, sweet, tasty **5 = vivid**, bright, deep, gay, intense, strong, vibrant, warm **6 = resonant**, deep, dulcet, full, mellifluous, mellow **7 = funny**, amusing, comical, hilarious, humorous, laughable, ludicrous, ridiculous, risible, side-splitting
➤ **Antonyms**
≠**wealthy**: destitute, impoverished, needy, penniless, poor ≠**well-stocked**: lacking, poor, scarce, wanting ≠**fruitful**: barren, poor, unfertile, unfruitful, unproductive ≠**full-bodied**: bland, dull ≠**vivid**: dull, insipid, weak ≠**resonant**: high-pitched

riches plural noun **= wealth**, abundance, affluence, assets, fortune, gold, money, opulence, plenty, property, resources, richness, substance, treasure
➤ **Antonyms**
dearth, indigence, lack, need, paucity, poverty, scantiness, scarcity, want

richly adverb **1 = elaborately**, elegantly, expensively, exquisitely, gorgeously, lavishly, luxuriously, opulently, palatially, splendidly, sumptuously **2 = fully**, amply, appropriately, in full measure, properly, suitably, thoroughly, well

rickety adjective **= shaky**, broken, broken-down, decrepit, derelict, dilapidated, feeble, flimsy, frail, imperfect, infirm, insecure, jerry-built, precarious, ramshackle, tottering, unsound, unsteady, weak, wobbly

rid verb **1 = free**, clear, deliver, disabuse, disburden, disencumber, lighten, make free, purge, relieve, unburden **2 get rid of = dispose of**, dispense with, do away with, dump, eject, eliminate, expel, jettison, remove, shake off, throw away or out, unload, weed out, wipe from the face of the earth

riddle¹ noun **= puzzle**, brain-teaser (informal), conundrum, enigma, mystery, poser, problem, teaser

riddle² verb **1 = pierce**, honeycomb, pepper, perforate, puncture **2 = sieve**, filter, screen, sift, strain, winnow ◆ noun **3 = sieve**, filter, screen, strainer

riddled adjective **= filled**, corrupted, damaged, impaired, infested, marred, permeated, pervaded, spoilt

ride verb **1 = control**, handle, manage, sit on **2 = travel**, be borne, be carried, be supported, float, go, journey, move, progress, sit **3 = dominate**, enslave, grip,

haunt, oppress, tyrannize over ◆ noun **4 = journey**, drive, jaunt, lift, outing, spin (informal), trip, whirl (informal)

ridicule noun **1 = mockery**, banter, chaff, derision, gibe, irony, jeer, laughter, raillery, sarcasm, satire, scorn, sneer, taunting ◆ verb **2 = laugh at**, banter, caricature, chaff, deride, humiliate, jeer, lampoon, laugh to scorn, make a fool of, make a monkey out of, make fun of, make one a laughing stock, mock, parody, poke fun at, pooh-pooh, satirize, scoff, send up (Brit. informal), sneer, take the mickey out of (informal), take the piss (out of) (taboo slang), taunt

ridiculous adjective **= laughable**, absurd, comical, contemptible, derisory, farcical, foolish, funny, hilarious, inane, incredible, ludicrous, nonsensical, outrageous, preposterous, risible, silly, stupid, unbelievable
➤ **Antonyms**
bright, clever, intelligent, logical, prudent, rational, reasonable, sagacious, sane, sensible, serious, smart, solemn, well-thought-out, wise

rife adjective **= widespread**, abundant, common, current, epidemic, frequent, general, plentiful, prevailing, prevalent, raging, rampant, teeming, ubiquitous, universal

riffraff noun **= rabble**, canaille, dregs of society, hoi polloi, ragtag and bobtail, scum, undesirables

rifle verb **= ransack**, burgle, despoil, go through, gut, loot, pillage, plunder, rob, rummage, sack, strip

rift noun **1 = breach**, alienation, difference, disagreement, division, estrangement, falling out (informal), quarrel, schism, separation, split **2 = split**, breach, break, chink, cleavage, cleft, crack, cranny, crevice, fault, fissure, flaw, fracture, gap, opening, space

rig verb **1 = fix**, arrange, doctor, engineer, fake, falsify, fiddle with (informal), gerrymander, juggle, manipulate, tamper with, trump up **2** Nautical **= equip**, accoutre, fit out, furnish, kit out, outfit, provision, supply, turn out ◆ noun **3 = apparatus**, accoutrements, equipage, equipment, fitments, fittings, fixtures, gear, machinery, outfit, tackle

right adjective **1 = just**, equitable, ethical, fair, good, honest, honourable, lawful, moral, proper, righteous, true, upright, virtuous **2 = correct**, accurate, exact, factual, genuine, precise, satisfactory, sound, spot-on (Brit. informal), true, unerring, valid, veracious **3 = proper**, appropriate, becoming, comme il faut, desirable, done, fit, fitting, seemly, suitable **4 = favourable**,

advantageous, convenient, deserved, due, ideal, opportune, propitious, rightful **5 = healthy**, all there (*informal*), balanced, *compos mentis*, fine, fit, in good health, in the pink, lucid, normal, rational, reasonable, sane, sound, unimpaired, up to par, well **6 = conservative**, reactionary, Tory ♦ *adverb* **7 = correctly**, accurately, aright, exactly, factually, genuinely, precisely, truly **8 = suitably**, appropriately, aptly, befittingly, fittingly, properly, satisfactorily **9 = straight**, directly, immediately, instantly, promptly, quickly, straightaway, without delay **10 = exactly**, bang, precisely, slap-bang (*informal*), squarely **11 = properly**, ethically, fairly, fittingly, honestly, honourably, justly, morally, righteously, virtuously **12 = favourably**, advantageously, beneficially, for the better, fortunately, to advantage, well ♦ *noun* **13 = prerogative**, authority, business, claim, due, freedom, interest, liberty, licence, permission, power, privilege, title **14 = justice**, equity, fairness, good, goodness, honour, integrity, lawfulness, legality, morality, propriety, reason, rectitude, righteousness, truth, uprightness, virtue **15 by rights = in fairness**, equitably, justly, properly **16 to rights = in order**, arranged, straight, tidy ♦ *verb* **17 = rectify**, compensate for, correct, fix, put right, redress, repair, settle, sort out, straighten, vindicate
➤ **Antonyms**
adjective ≠**just**: bad, dishonest, immoral, improper, indecent, unethical, unfair, unjust, wrong ≠**correct**: counterfeit, erroneous, fake, false, fraudulent, illegal, illicit, inaccurate, incorrect, inexact, invalid, mistaken, questionable, uncertain, unlawful, untruthful, wrong ≠**proper**: inappropriate, undesirable, unfitting, unseemly, unsuitable, wrong ≠**favourable**: disadvantageous, inconvenient, unfavourable ≠**healthy**: abnormal, unsound ≠**conservative**: left, leftist, left-wing, liberal, radical, socialist ♦ *adverb* ≠**correctly**: inaccurately, incorrectly ≠**suitably**: improperly, incompletely ≠**straight**: indirectly, slowly ≠**favourably**: badly, poorly, unfavourably ♦ *noun* ≠**justice**: badness, dishonour, evil, immorality, impropriety ♦ *verb* ≠**rectify**: make crooked, topple

right away *adverb* **= immediately**, at once, directly, forthwith, instantly, now, posthaste, promptly, pronto (*informal*), right off, straightaway, straight off (*informal*), this instant, without delay, without hesitation

righteous *adjective* **= virtuous**, blameless, equitable, ethical, fair, good, honest, honourable, just, law-abiding, moral, pure, squeaky-clean, upright

➤ **Antonyms**
bad, corrupt, dishonest, dishonourable, evil, false, guilty, immoral, improper, indecent, insincere, sinful, unethical, unfair, unjust, unprincipled, unrighteous, unscrupulous, unseemly, wicked

righteousness *noun* **= virtue**, blamelessness, equity, ethicalness, faithfulness, goodness, honesty, honour, integrity, justice, morality, probity, purity, rectitude, uprightness

rightful *adjective* **= lawful**, authorized, bona fide, due, just, legal, legitimate, proper, real, suitable, true, valid

rigid *adjective* **1 = strict**, adamant, exact, fixed, harsh, inflexible, intransigent, invariable, rigorous, set, severe, stern, stringent, unalterable, unbending, uncompromising, undeviating, unrelenting, unyielding **2 = stiff**, inelastic, inflexible, unyielding
➤ **Antonyms**
≠**strict**: flexible, indulgent, lax, lenient, merciful, soft, tolerant ≠**stiff**: bending, elastic, flexible, limber, lissom(e), mobile, pliable, pliant, soft, supple, yielding

rigmarole *noun* **1 = procedure**, bother, carry-on (*informal, chiefly Brit.*), fuss, hassle (*informal*), nonsense, palaver, pantomime (*informal*), performance (*informal*), red tape, to-do **2 = twaddle**, balderdash, gibberish, jargon, trash

rigorous *adjective* **1 = strict**, challenging, demanding, exacting, firm, hard, harsh, inflexible, rigid, severe, stern, stringent, tough **2 = thorough**, accurate, conscientious, exact, meticulous, nice, painstaking, precise, punctilious, scrupulous
➤ **Antonyms**
≠**strict**: easy, flexible, friendly, genial, gentle, humane, indulgent, kind, lax, lenient, loose, mild, permissive, relaxed, soft, sympathetic, tolerant, weak ≠**thorough**: careless, half-hearted, haphazard, imperfect, inaccurate, incorrect, inexact, loose, negligent, slapdash, sloppy, slovenly, unscrupulous

rigour *noun* **1 = hardship**, ordeal, privation, suffering, trial **2 = strictness**, asperity, firmness, hardness, harshness, inflexibility, rigidity, sternness, stringency **3 = thoroughness**, accuracy, conscientiousness, exactitude, exactness, meticulousness, preciseness, precision, punctiliousness

rigout *noun Informal* **= outfit**, apparel, clobber (*Brit. slang*), clothing, costume, dress, garb, gear (*informal*), get-up (*informal*), habit, togs

rig out *verb* **1 = dress**, array, attire, clothe,

costume, kit out **2 = equip**, accoutre, fit, furnish, kit out, outfit, set up

rig up *verb* **= set up**, arrange, assemble, build, cobble together, construct, erect, fix up, improvise, put together, put up, throw together

rile *verb* **= anger**, aggravate (*informal*), annoy, bug (*informal*), gall, get *or* put one's back up, get one's goat (*slang*), get on one's nerves (*informal*), get under one's skin (*informal*), irk, irritate, nark (*Brit., Austral., & N.Z. slang*), nettle, peeve (*informal*), pique, provoke, rub one up the wrong way, try one's patience, upset, vex

rim *noun* **= edge**, border, brim, brink, circumference, flange, lip, margin, verge

rind *noun* **= skin**, crust, husk, integument, outer layer, peel

ring¹ *verb* **1 = chime**, clang, peal, resonate, resound, reverberate, sound, toll **2 = phone**, buzz (*informal, chiefly Brit.*), call, telephone ♦ *noun* **3 = chime**, knell, peal **4 = call**, buzz (*informal, chiefly Brit.*), phone call

ring² *noun* **1 = circle**, band, circuit, halo, hoop, loop, round **2 = arena**, circus, enclosure, rink **3 = gang**, association, band, cabal, cartel, cell, circle, clique, combine, coterie, crew (*informal*), group, junta, knot, mob, organization, syndicate ♦ *verb* **4 = encircle**, circumscribe, enclose, encompass, gird, girdle, hem in, seal off, surround

rinse *verb* **1 = wash**, bathe, clean, cleanse, dip, splash, wash out, wet ♦ *noun* **2 = wash**, bath, dip, splash, wetting

riot *noun* **1 = disturbance**, anarchy, commotion, confusion, disorder, fray, lawlessness, mob violence, quarrel, row, street fighting, strife, tumult, turbulence, turmoil, upheaval, uproar **2 = merrymaking**, blast (*U.S. slang*), boisterousness, carousal, excess, festivity, frolic, high jinks, jollification, revelry, romp **3 = display**, extravaganza, flourish, profusion, show, splash **4 run riot: a = rampage**, be out of control, break *or* cut loose, go wild, let oneself go, raise hell, throw off all restraint **b = grow profusely**, grow like weeds, luxuriate, spread like wildfire ♦ *verb* **5 = rampage**, fight in the streets, go on the rampage, raise an uproar, run riot, take to the streets

riotous *adjective* **1 = unrestrained**, boisterous, loud, luxurious, noisy, orgiastic, roisterous, rollicking, saturnalian, side-splitting, uproarious, wanton, wild **2 = unruly**, anarchic, disorderly, lawless, mutinous, rampageous, rebellious, refractory, rowdy, tumultuous, ungovernable, uproarious, violent

➤ **Antonyms**

calm, civilized, disciplined, gentle, lawful,

mild, obedient, orderly, peaceful, quiet, restrained, well-behaved

rip *verb* **1 = tear**, be rent, burst, claw, cut, gash, hack, lacerate, rend, score, slash, slit, split ♦ *noun* **2 = tear**, cleavage, cut, gash, hole, laceration, rent, slash, slit, split

ripe *adjective* **1 = mature**, fully developed, fully grown, mellow, ready, ripened, seasoned **2 = suitable**, auspicious, favourable, ideal, opportune, right, timely **3 ripe for = ready for**, eager for, in readiness for, prepared for

➤ **Antonyms**

≠**mature:** green, immature, undeveloped, unripe   ≠**suitable:** disadvantageous, inappropriate, inconvenient, inopportune, unfavourable, unfitting, unseemly, unsuitable, untimely

ripen *verb* **= mature**, burgeon, come of age, come to fruition, develop, get ready, grow ripe, make ripe, prepare, season

rip-off *noun Slang* **= cheat**, con (*informal*), con trick (*informal*), daylight robbery (*informal*), exploitation, fraud, robbery, scam (*slang*), sting (*informal*), swindle, theft

rip off *verb Slang* **1 = cheat**, con (*informal*), defraud, diddle (*informal*), dupe, fleece, rob, skin (*slang*), steal from, swindle, trick **2 = steal**, filch, knock off (*slang*), lift (*informal*), pilfer, pinch (*informal*), swipe (*slang*), thieve

riposte *noun* **1 = retort**, answer, comeback (*informal*), counterattack, rejoinder, repartee, reply, response, return, sally ♦ *verb* **2 = retort**, answer, come back, rejoin, reply, respond, return

ripple *noun* **1 = wave**, undulation **2 = flutter**, frisson, thrill, tingle, tremor

rise *verb* **1 = get up**, arise, get out of bed, get to one's feet, rise and shine, stand up, surface **2 = go up**, ascend, climb, levitate, move up **3 = advance**, be promoted, get on, get somewhere, go places (*informal*), progress, prosper, work one's way up **4 = get steeper**, ascend, climb, go uphill, mount, slope upwards **5 = increase**, enlarge, go up, grow, intensify, lift, mount, soar, swell, wax **6 = rebel**, mutiny, resist, revolt, take up arms **7 = originate**, appear, crop up, emanate, emerge, flow, happen, issue, occur, spring, turn up ♦ *noun* **8 = upward slope**, acclivity, ascent, elevation, hillock, incline, rising ground **9 = pay increase**, increment, raise (*U.S.*) **10 = increase**, advance, ascent, climb, improvement, upsurge, upswing, upturn, upward turn **11 = advancement**, aggrandizement, climb, progress, promotion **12 give rise to = cause**, bring about, bring on, effect, produce, provoke, result in

> ➤ **Antonyms**
> *verb* ≠**go up, get steeper:** descend, drop, fall, plunge, sink ≠**increase:** abate, abbreviate, abridge, condense, curtail, decline, decrease, descend, diminish, drop, dwindle, fall, lessen, plunge, reduce, shrink, sink, wane ♦ *noun* ≠**increase:** blip, decline, decrease, downswing, downturn, drop, fall

risible *adjective Formal* = **ridiculous,** absurd, amusing, comical, droll, farcical, funny, hilarious, humorous, laughable, ludicrous, rib-tickling (*informal*), side-splitting

risk *noun* 1 = **danger,** chance, gamble, hazard, jeopardy, peril, pitfall, possibility, speculation, uncertainty, venture ♦ *verb* 2 = **dare,** chance, endanger, expose to danger, gamble, hazard, imperil, jeopardize, put in jeopardy, take a chance on, take the plunge, venture

risky *adjective* = **dangerous,** chancy (*informal*), dicey (*informal, chiefly Brit.*), dodgy (*Brit., Austral., & N.Z. informal*), fraught with danger, hazardous, perilous, precarious, touch-and-go, tricky, uncertain, unsafe
> ➤ **Antonyms**
> certain, reliable, safe, secure, stable, sure

risqué *adjective* = **suggestive,** bawdy, blue, daring, immodest, improper, indelicate, naughty, near the knuckle (*informal*), off colour, Rabelaisian, racy, ribald

rite *noun* = **ceremony,** act, ceremonial, custom, formality, liturgy, mystery, observance, practice, procedure, ritual, sacrament, service

ritual *noun* 1 = **ceremony,** ceremonial, liturgy, mystery, observance, rite, sacrament, service 2 = **custom,** convention, form, formality, habit, practice, procedure, protocol, red tape, routine, stereotype, tradition, usage ♦ *adjective* 3 = **ceremonial,** ceremonious, conventional, customary, formal, habitual, prescribed, routine, stereotyped

ritzy *adjective Slang* = **luxurious,** de luxe, elegant, glamorous, glittering, grand, high-class, luxury, opulent, plush (*informal*), posh (*informal, chiefly Brit.*), stylish, sumptuous, swanky (*informal*)

rival *noun* 1 = **opponent,** adversary, antagonist, challenger, competitor, contender, contestant 2 = **equal,** compeer, equivalent, fellow, match, peer ♦ *adjective* 3 = **competing,** competitive, conflicting, opposed, opposing ♦ *verb* 4 = **compete,** be a match for, bear comparison with, come up to, compare with, contend, emulate, equal, match, measure up to, oppose, seek to displace, vie with

> ➤ **Antonyms**
> *noun* ≠**opponent:** ally, friend, helper, supporter ♦ *verb* ≠**compete:** aid, back, help, support

rivalry *noun* = **competition,** competitiveness, conflict, contention, contest, duel, opposition, struggle, vying

river *noun* 1 = **stream,** beck, brook, burn (*Scot.*), creek, rivulet, tributary, waterway 2 = **flow,** flood, rush, spate, torrent

riveting *adjective* = **enthralling,** absorbing, arresting, captivating, engrossing, fascinating, gripping, hypnotic, spellbinding

road *noun* 1 = **way,** avenue, course, direction, highway, lane, motorway, path, pathway, roadway, route, street, thoroughfare, track 2 *Nautical* = **roadstead,** anchorage

roam *verb* = **wander,** drift, meander, prowl, ramble, range, rove, stray, stroll, travel, walk

roar *verb* 1 = **cry,** bawl, bay, bell, bellow, clamour, crash, howl, rumble, shout, thunder, yell 2 = **guffaw,** bust a gut (*informal*), crack up (*informal*), hoot, laugh heartily, split one's sides (*informal*) ♦ *noun* 3 = **cry,** bellow, clamour, crash, howl, outcry, rumble, shout, thunder, yell 4 = **guffaw,** belly laugh (*informal*), hoot

rob *verb* = **steal from,** burgle, cheat, con (*informal*), defraud, deprive, despoil, dispossess, do out of (*informal*), hold up, loot, mug (*informal*), pillage, plunder, raid, ransack, rifle, rip off (*slang*), sack, skin (*slang*), stiff (*slang*), swindle

robber *noun* = **thief,** bandit, brigand, burglar, cheat, con man (*informal*), fraud, fraudster, highwayman, looter, mugger (*informal*), pirate, plunderer, raider, stealer, swindler

robbery *noun* = **theft,** burglary, embezzlement, filching, hold-up, larceny, mugging (*informal*), pillage, plunder, raid, rip-off (*slang*), stealing, steaming (*informal*), stick-up (*slang, chiefly U.S.*), swindle, thievery

robe *noun* 1 = **gown,** costume, habit, vestment 2 = **dressing gown,** bathrobe, housecoat, negligee, peignoir, wrapper ♦ *verb* 3 = **clothe,** apparel (*archaic*), attire, drape, dress, garb

robot *noun* = **machine,** android, automaton, mechanical man

robust *adjective* = **strong,** able-bodied, athletic, brawny, fighting fit, fit, fit as a fiddle (*informal*), hale, hardy, healthy, husky (*informal*), in good health, lusty, muscular, powerful, rugged, sound, staunch, stout, strapping, sturdy, tough, vigorous, well
> ➤ **Antonyms**
> delicate, feeble, frail, hothouse (*informal, often disparaging*), infirm, sickly, slender,

unfit, unhealthy, unsound, weak, weedy (*informal*), wimpish *or* wimpy (*informal*), wussy (*slang*)

rock¹ *noun* 1 = **stone**, boulder 2 = **tower of strength**, anchor, bulwark, cornerstone, foundation, mainstay, protection, support

rock² *verb* 1 = **sway**, lurch, pitch, reel, roll, swing, toss, wobble 2 = **shock**, astonish, astound, daze, dumbfound, shake, stagger, stun, surprise

rocky¹ *adjective* = **rough**, boulder-strewn, craggy, pebbly, rugged, stony

rocky² *adjective* = **unstable**, doubtful, rickety, shaky, uncertain, undependable, unreliable, unsteady, weak, wobbly

rod *noun* = **stick**, bar, baton, birch, cane, crook, mace, pole, sceptre, shaft, staff, switch, wand

rogue *noun* = **scoundrel**, blackguard, charlatan, cheat, con man (*informal*), crook (*informal*), deceiver, fraud, fraudster, knave (*archaic*), ne'er-do-well, rapscallion, rascal, scally (*Northwest English dialect*), scamp, scumbag (*slang*), skelm (*S. African*), swindler, villain

roguish *adjective* 1 = **unprincipled**, criminal, crooked, deceitful, deceiving, dishonest, fraudulent, knavish, rascally, shady (*informal*), swindling, unscrupulous, villainous 2 = **mischievous**, arch, cheeky, coquettish, frolicsome, impish, playful, waggish

roister *verb Old-fashioned* = **make merry**, carouse, celebrate, frolic, go on a spree, live it up (*informal*), paint the town red (*informal*), push the boat out (*Brit. informal*), rave (*Brit. slang*), revel, rollick, romp, whoop it up (*informal*)

role *noun* 1 = **job**, capacity, duty, function, part, position, post, task 2 = **part**, character, impersonation, portrayal, representation

roll *verb* 1 = **turn**, go round, gyrate, pivot, reel, revolve, rotate, spin, swivel, trundle, twirl, wheel, whirl 2 = **wind**, bind, coil, curl, enfold, entwine, envelop, furl, swathe, twist, wrap 3 = **flow**, run, undulate 4 = **level**, even, flatten, press, smooth, spread 5 = **toss**, billow, lurch, reel, rock, sway, swing, tumble, wallow, welter 6 = **rumble**, boom, drum, echo, grumble, resound, reverberate, roar, thunder 7 = **sway**, lumber, lurch, reel, stagger, swagger, waddle 8 = **pass**, elapse, go past ♦ *noun* 9 = **turn**, cycle, gyration, reel, revolution, rotation, run, spin, twirl, undulation, wheel, whirl 10 = **spool**, ball, bobbin, cylinder, reel, scroll 11 = **register**, annals, catalogue, census, chronicle, directory, index, inventory, list, record, roster, schedule, scroll, table 12 = **tossing**, billowing, lurching, pitching, rocking, rolling,

swell, undulation, wallowing, waves 13 = **rumble**, boom, drumming, growl, grumble, resonance, reverberation, roar, thunder

rollicking *adjective* = **boisterous**, carefree, cavorting, devil-may-care, exuberant, frisky, frolicsome, full of beans (*informal*), hearty, jaunty, jovial, joyous, lively, merry, playful, rip-roaring (*informal*), romping, spirited, sprightly, swashbuckling
➤ **Antonyms**
cheerless, despondent, dull, gloomy, lifeless, melancholy, morose, sad, sedate, serious, unhappy

roly-poly *adjective* = **plump**, buxom, chubby, fat, overweight, podgy, pudgy, rotund, rounded, tubby

romance *noun* 1 = **love affair**, affair, *affaire (du coeur)*, affair of the heart, amour, attachment, intrigue, liaison, passion, relationship 2 = **excitement**, adventure, charm, colour, exoticness, fascination, glamour, mystery, nostalgia, sentiment 3 = **story**, fairy tale, fantasy, fiction, idyll, legend, love story, melodrama, novel, tale, tear-jerker (*informal*) 4 = **tall story** (*informal*), absurdity, exaggeration, fabrication, fairy tale, falsehood, fiction, flight of fancy, invention, lie, trumped-up story, urban legend, urban myth ♦ *verb* 5 = **exaggerate**, be economical with the truth, fantasize, let one's imagination run away with one, lie, make up stories, stretch the truth, tell stories

romantic *adjective* 1 = **loving**, amorous, fond, icky (*informal*), lovey-dovey, mushy (*informal*), passionate, sentimental, sloppy (*informal*), soppy (*Brit. informal*), tender 2 = **idealistic**, dreamy, high-flown, impractical, quixotic, starry-eyed, unrealistic, utopian, visionary, whimsical 3 = **exciting**, charming, colourful, exotic, fascinating, glamorous, mysterious, nostalgic, picturesque ♦ *noun* 4 = **idealist**, Don Quixote, dreamer, romancer, sentimentalist, utopian, visionary
➤ **Antonyms**
adjective ≠ **loving**: cold-hearted, insensitive, unaffectionate, unimpassioned, unloving, unromantic, unsentimental ≠ **idealistic**: practical, realistic ≠ **exciting**: uninspiring

romp *verb* 1 = **frolic**, caper, cavort, frisk, gambol, have fun, make merry, revel, roister, skip, sport 2 **romp home** *or* **in** = **win easily**, run away with it, walk it (*informal*), win by a mile (*informal*), win hands down ♦ *noun* 3 = **frolic**, caper, lark (*informal*)

rook *verb Old-fashioned slang* = **cheat**, bilk, defraud, diddle (*informal*), do (*slang*), fleece, overcharge, rip off (*slang*), skin (*slang*), sting (*informal*), swindle

room *noun* 1 = **chamber**, apartment, office

2 = space, allowance, area, capacity, compass, elbowroom, expanse, extent, latitude, leeway, margin, range, scope, territory, volume **3 = opportunity**, chance, occasion, scope

roomy *adjective* = **spacious**, ample, broad, capacious, commodious, extensive, generous, large, sizable *or* sizeable, wide
➤ Antonyms
bounded, confined, cramped, narrow, small, tiny

root¹ *noun* **1 = stem**, radicle, radix, rhizome, tuber **2 = source**, base, beginnings, bottom, cause, core, crux, derivation, foundation, fountainhead, fundamental, germ, heart, mainspring, nub, nucleus, origin, seat, seed, starting point **3 roots = sense of belonging**, birthplace, cradle, family, heritage, home, origins **4 root and branch = completely**, entirely, finally, radically, thoroughly, totally, utterly, wholly, without exception ◆ *verb* **5 = become established**, anchor, become settled, embed, entrench, establish, fasten, fix, ground, implant, moor, set, stick, take root

root² *verb* = **dig**, burrow, delve, ferret, forage, hunt, nose, poke, pry, rootle, rummage

rooted *adjective* = **deep-seated**, confirmed, deep, deeply felt, entrenched, established, firm, fixed, ingrained, radical, rigid

rootless *adjective* = **footloose**, homeless, itinerant, roving, transient, vagabond

root out *verb* = **get rid of**, abolish, cut out, destroy, dig up by the roots, do away with, efface, eliminate, eradicate, erase, exterminate, extirpate, remove, tear out by the roots, uproot, weed out, wipe from the face of the earth

rope *noun* **1 = cord**, cable, hawser, line, strand **2 the rope = hanging**, capital punishment, halter, lynching, noose **3 know the ropes = be experienced**, be an old hand, be knowledgeable, know all the ins and outs, know one's way around, know the score (*informal*), know what's what ◆ *verb* **4 = tie**, bind, fasten, hitch, lash, lasso, moor, tether

rope in *verb Brit.* = **persuade**, drag in, engage, enlist, inveigle, involve, talk into

ropey, ropy *adjective Informal* **1 = inferior**, deficient, inadequate, indifferent, mediocre, no great shakes (*informal*), of poor quality, poor, sketchy, substandard **2 = unwell**, below par, off colour, poorly (*informal*), rough (*informal*), sickish, under the weather (*informal*)

roseate *adjective* = **pink**, pinkish, red, rose-coloured, rosy

roster *noun* = **rota**, agenda, catalogue,

inventory, list, listing, register, roll, schedule, scroll, table

rostrum *noun* = **stage**, dais, platform, podium, stand

rosy *adjective* **1 = pink**, red, roseate, rose-coloured **2 = glowing**, blooming, blushing, flushed, fresh, healthy-looking, radiant, reddish, roseate, rubicund, ruddy **3 = promising**, auspicious, bright, cheerful, encouraging, favourable, hopeful, optimistic, reassuring, roseate, rose-coloured, sunny
➤ Antonyms
≠**glowing**: ashen, colourless, grey, pale, pallid, sickly, wan, white ≠**promising**: cheerless, depressing, discouraging, dismal, down in the dumps (*informal*), dull, gloomy, hopeless, miserable, pessimistic, unhappy, unpromising

rot *verb* **1 = decay**, break down, corrode, corrupt, crumble, decompose, degenerate, deteriorate, disintegrate, fester, go bad, moulder, perish, putrefy, spoil, taint **2 = deteriorate**, decline, degenerate, languish, waste away, wither away ◆ *noun* **3 = decay**, blight, canker, corrosion, corruption, decomposition, deterioration, disintegration, mould, putrefaction, putrescence **4 Informal = nonsense**, balderdash, balls (*taboo slang*), bilge (*informal*), bosh (*informal*), bullshit (*taboo slang*), bunk (*informal*), claptrap (*informal*), cobblers (*Brit. taboo slang*), codswallop (*Brit. slang*), crap (*slang*), drivel, garbage (*chiefly U.S.*), guff (*slang*), hogwash, hot air (*informal*), moonshine, pants (*slang*), piffle (*informal*), poppycock (*informal*), rubbish, shit (*taboo slang*), stuff and nonsense, tommyrot, tosh (*slang, chiefly Brit.*), trash, tripe (*informal*), twaddle

rotary *adjective* = **revolving**, gyratory, rotating, rotational, rotatory, spinning, turning

rotate *verb* **1 = revolve**, go round, gyrate, pirouette, pivot, reel, spin, swivel, turn, wheel **2 = follow in sequence**, alternate, interchange, switch, take turns

rotation *noun* **1 = revolution**, gyration, orbit, pirouette, reel, spin, spinning, turn, turning, wheel **2 = sequence**, alternation, cycle, interchanging, succession, switching

rotten *adjective* **1 = decaying**, bad, corroded, corrupt, crumbling, decayed, decomposed, decomposing, disintegrating, festering, fetid, foul, mouldering, mouldy, perished, putrescent, putrid, rank, sour, stinking, tainted, unsound **2 Informal = bad**, deplorable, disappointing, regrettable, unfortunate, unlucky **3 Informal = despicable**, base, contemptible, dirty, disagreeable, filthy, mean, nasty, unpleasant, vile, wicked **4 Informal = inferior**, crummy (*slang*), duff (*Brit. informal*), ill-considered,

ill-thought-out, inadequate, lousy (*slang*), poor, poxy (*slang*), ropey or ropy (*Brit. informal*), sorry, substandard, unacceptable, unsatisfactory **5 = corrupt**, bent (*slang*), crooked (*informal*), deceitful, dishonest, dishonourable, disloyal, faithless, immoral, perfidious **6** *Informal* **= unwell**, bad, below par, ill, off colour, poorly (*informal*), ropey or ropy (*Brit. informal*), rough (*informal*), sick, under the weather (*informal*)
➤ Antonyms
≠**decaying**: fresh, good, pure, sweet, wholesome ≠**corrupt**: decent, honest, honourable, moral, scrupulous, trustworthy

rotter *noun* Old-fashioned **= scoundrel**, bad lot, blackguard, blighter (*Brit. informal*), bounder (*old-fashioned Brit. slang*), cad (*Brit. informal*), cur, louse (*slang*), rat (*informal*), scumbag (*slang*), stinker (*slang*), swine

rotund *adjective* **1 = round**, bulbous, globular, orbicular, rounded, spherical **2 = plump**, chubby, corpulent, fat, fleshy, heavy, obese, podgy, portly, roly-poly, rounded, stout, tubby **3 = pompous**, full, grandiloquent, magniloquent
➤ Antonyms
≠**plump**: angular, gaunt, lank, lanky, lean, scrawny, skinny, slender, slight, slim, thin

roué *noun* **= libertine**, debauchee, dirty old man (*slang*), lech or letch (*informal*), lecher, profligate, rake, sensualist, swinger (*slang*), wanton

rough *adjective* **1 = uneven**, broken, bumpy, craggy, irregular, jagged, rocky, rugged, stony **2 = ungracious**, bluff, blunt, brusque, churlish, coarse, curt, discourteous, ill-bred, ill-mannered, impolite, inconsiderate, indelicate, loutish, rude, unceremonious, uncivil, uncouth, uncultured, unmannerly, unpolished, unrefined **3 = unpleasant**, arduous, difficult, hard, tough, uncomfortable **4 = approximate**, estimated, foggy, general, hazy, imprecise, inexact, sketchy, vague **5 = stormy**, agitated, boisterous, choppy, inclement, squally, tempestuous, turbulent, wild **6 = basic**, crude, cursory, hasty, imperfect, incomplete, quick, raw, rough-and-ready, rough-hewn, rudimentary, shapeless, sketchy, unfinished, unpolished, unrefined **7 = rough-hewn**, crude, raw, uncut, undressed, unhewn, unpolished, unprocessed, unwrought **8 = grating**, cacophonous, discordant, gruff, harsh, husky, inharmonious, jarring, rasping, raucous, unmusical **9 = harsh**, boisterous, cruel, curt, drastic, extreme, hard, nasty, rowdy, severe, sharp, tough, unfeeling, unjust, unpleasant, violent **10** *Informal* **= unwell**, below par, ill, not a hundred per

cent (*informal*), off colour, poorly (*informal*), ropey or ropy (*Brit. informal*), rotten (*informal*), sick, under the weather (*informal*), upset **11 = coarse**, bristly, fuzzy, hairy, shaggy ◆ *verb* **12 rough out = outline**, block out, delineate, draft, plan, sketch, suggest **13 rough up** *Informal* **= beat up**, bash up (*informal*), batter, do over (*Brit., Austral., & N.Z. slang*), knock about or around, maltreat, manhandle, mistreat, thrash, work over (*slang*) ◆ *noun* **14 = outline**, draft, mock-up, preliminary sketch, suggestion **15** *Informal* **= thug**, bruiser, bully boy, casual, lager lout, ned (*slang*), roughneck (*slang*), rowdy, ruffian, tough
➤ Antonyms
adjective ≠**uneven**: even, level, regular, smooth, unbroken ≠**ungracious**: civil, considerate, courteous, courtly, delicate, elegant, graceful, gracious, pleasant, polite, refined, smooth, sophisticated, urbane, well-bred, well-mannered ≠**unpleasant**: comfortable, cushy (*informal*), easy, pleasant, soft ≠**approximate**: exact, perfected, specific ≠**stormy**: calm, gentle, quiet, smooth, tranquil ≠**basic**: complete, detailed, finished, perfected, polished, refined, specific ≠**rough-hewn**: smooth ≠**grating**: harmonious, smooth ≠**harsh**: gentle, just, kind, mild, pleasant, quiet, soft ≠**coarse**: smooth, soft

rough-and-ready *adjective* **= makeshift**, adequate, cobbled together, crude, improvised, provisional, sketchy, stopgap, thrown together, unpolished, unrefined

rough-and-tumble *noun* **= fight**, affray (*Law*), brawl, donnybrook, dust-up (*informal*), fracas, melee or mêlée, punch-up (*Brit. informal*), roughhouse (*slang*), scrap (*informal*), scrimmage, scuffle, shindig (*informal*), shindy (*informal*), struggle

roughhouse *noun* Slang **= rough behaviour**, boisterousness, brawl, brawling, disorderliness, disturbance, horseplay, row, rowdiness, rowdyism

roughneck *noun* Slang **= thug**, bruiser (*informal*), bully boy, heavy (*slang*), rough (*informal*), rowdy, ruffian, tough

round *adjective* **1 = spherical**, ball-shaped, bowed, bulbous, circular, curved, curvilinear, cylindrical, discoid, disc-shaped, globular, orbicular, ring-shaped, rotund, rounded **2 = plump**, ample, fleshy, full, full-fleshed, roly-poly, rotund, rounded **3 = complete**, entire, full, solid, unbroken, undivided, whole ◆ *verb* **4 = go round**, bypass, circle, circumnavigate, encircle, flank, skirt, turn ◆ *noun* **5 = sphere**, ball, band, circle, disc, globe, orb, ring **6 = series**, bout, cycle, sequence, session, succession **7 = stage**,

division, lap, level, period, session, turn **8**
= **course**, ambit, beat, circuit, compass,
routine, schedule, series, tour, turn **9**
= **bullet**, cartridge, discharge, shell, shot

roundabout *adjective* = **indirect**,
circuitous, circumlocutory, devious,
discursive, evasive, meandering, oblique,
periphrastic, tortuous
➤ **Antonyms**
direct, straight, straightforward

round off *verb* = **complete**, bring to a
close, cap, close, conclude, crown, finish off,
put the finishing touch to, settle
➤ **Antonyms**
begin, commence, initiate, open, start

round on *verb* = **attack**, abuse, bite
(someone's) head off (*informal*), have a go
at (*Brit. slang*), lose one's temper with,
retaliate, snap at, turn on, wade into

roundup *noun* **1** *Informal* = **summary**,
survey **2** = **gathering**, assembly, collection,
herding, marshalling, muster, rally

round up *verb* = **gather**, assemble, bring
together, collect, drive, group, herd,
marshal, muster, rally

rouse *verb* **1** = **wake up**, arouse, awaken,
call, get up, rise, wake **2** = **excite**, agitate,
anger, animate, arouse, bestir, disturb,
exhilarate, galvanize, get going, incite,
inflame, instigate, move, prod, provoke,
startle, stimulate, stir, whip up

rousing *adjective* = **lively**, brisk, electrifying,
exciting, exhilarating, inspiring, moving,
spirited, stimulating, stirring, vigorous
➤ **Antonyms**
boring, dreary, dull, lifeless, sluggish,
spiritless, unenergetic, wearisome,
wishy-washy (*informal*)

rout *noun* **1** = **defeat**, beating, debacle,
disorderly retreat, drubbing, headlong flight,
hiding (*informal*), licking (*informal*),
overthrow, overwhelming defeat, pasting
(*slang*), ruin, shambles, thrashing ♦ *verb* **2**
= **defeat**, beat, chase, clobber (*slang*),
conquer, crush, destroy, dispel, drive off,
drub, lick (*informal*), overpower, overthrow,
put to flight, tank (*slang*), thrash, throw
back in confusion, wipe the floor with
(*informal*), worst

route *noun* **1** = **way**, avenue, beat, circuit,
course, direction, itinerary, journey, passage,
path, road, round, run ♦ *verb* **2** = **send**,
convey, direct, dispatch, forward, steer

routine *noun* **1** = **procedure**, custom,
formula, grind (*informal*), method, order,
pattern, practice, programme, usage, way,
wont ♦ *adjective* **2** = **usual**, conventional,
customary, everyday, familiar, habitual,
normal, ordinary, standard, typical, wonted,
workaday **3** = **boring**, clichéd, dull,

hackneyed, humdrum, mind-numbing,
predictable, run-of-the-mill, tedious,
tiresome, unimaginative, uninspired,
unoriginal
➤ **Antonyms**
adjective ≠**usual**: abnormal, different,
exceptional, irregular, special, unusual

rove *verb* = **wander**, cruise, drift, meander,
ramble, range, roam, stray, stroll, traipse
(*informal*)

rover *noun* = **wanderer**, drifter, gypsy,
itinerant, nomad, rambler, ranger, rolling
stone, transient, traveller, vagrant

row[1] *noun* **1** = **line**, bank, column, file,
queue, range, rank, sequence, series, string,
tier **2 in a row** = **consecutively**, one after
the other, successively

row[2] *noun Informal* **1** = **quarrel**, altercation,
brawl, controversy, dispute, falling-out
(*informal*), fracas, fuss, ruckus (*informal*),
ruction (*informal*), scrap (*informal*), shindig
(*informal*), shindy (*informal*), shouting
match (*informal*), slanging match (*Brit.*),
squabble, tiff, trouble **2** = **disturbance**,
commotion, noise, racket, rumpus, tumult,
uproar **3** = **telling-off** (*informal*),
castigation, dressing-down (*informal*),
lecture, reprimand, reproof, rollicking (*Brit.
informal*), talking-to (*informal*), ticking-off
(*informal*), tongue-lashing ♦ *verb* **4**
= **quarrel**, argue, brawl, dispute, fight, go at
it hammer and tongs, scrap (*informal*), spar,
squabble, wrangle

rowdy *adjective* **1** = **disorderly**, boisterous,
loud, loutish, noisy, obstreperous, rough,
unruly, uproarious, wild ♦ *noun* **2**
= **hooligan**, brawler, casual, lager lout, lout,
ned (*Scot. slang*), rough (*informal*), ruffian,
tearaway (*Brit.*), tough, troublemaker,
yahoo, yob *or* yobbo (*Brit. slang*)
➤ **Antonyms**
adjective ≠**disorderly**: decorous, gentle,
law-abiding, mannerly, orderly, peaceful,
refined

royal *adjective* **1** = **regal**, imperial, kinglike,
kingly, monarchical, princely, queenly,
sovereign **2** = **splendid**, august, grand,
impressive, magnificent, majestic, stately,
superb, superior

rub *verb* **1** = **stroke**, caress, knead, massage,
smooth **2** = **polish**, clean, scour, shine, wipe
3 = **spread**, apply, put, smear **4** = **chafe**,
abrade, fray, grate, scrape **5 rub up the
wrong way** = **annoy**, aggravate (*informal*),
anger, bug (*informal*), get one's goat
(*slang*), get on one's nerves (*informal*), get
under one's skin (*informal*), irk, irritate, nark
(*Brit., Austral., & N.Z. slang*), peeve
(*informal*), piss one off (*taboo slang*), vex
♦ *noun* **6** = **massage**, caress, kneading **7**
= **polish**, shine, stroke, wipe **8** *As in* **the rub**

= **difficulty**, catch, drawback, hazard, hindrance, hitch, impediment, obstacle, problem, snag, trouble

rubbish *noun* **1** = **waste**, crap (*slang*), debris, dregs, dross, flotsam and jetsam, garbage (*chiefly U.S.*), grot (*slang*), junk (*informal*), litter, lumber, offal, refuse, scrap, trash **2** = **nonsense**, balderdash, balls (*taboo slang*), bollocks (*Brit. taboo slang*), bosh (*informal*), bullshit (*taboo slang*), bunkum *or* buncombe (*chiefly U.S.*), claptrap (*informal*), cobblers (*Brit. taboo slang*), codswallop (*Brit. slang*), crap (*slang*), drivel, garbage (*chiefly U.S.*), gibberish, guff (*slang*), hogwash, hot air (*informal*), moonshine, pants (*slang*), piffle (*informal*), poppycock (*informal*), rot, shit (*taboo slang*), stuff and nonsense, tommyrot, tosh (*slang, chiefly Brit.*), trash, tripe (*informal*), twaddle

rubbishy *adjective* = **trashy**, cheap, shoddy, tatty, tawdry, throwaway, twopenny-halfpenny, valueless, worthless

rubicund *adjective* Old-fashioned = **reddish**, blushing, florid, flushed, pink, roseate, rosy, ruddy

rub out *verb* **1** = **erase**, cancel, delete, efface, excise, expunge, obliterate, remove, wipe out **2** *U.S. slang* = **murder**, assassinate, blow away (*slang, chiefly U.S.*), bump off (*slang*), dispatch, do in (*informal*), eliminate (*slang*), kill, knock off (*slang*), slaughter, slay, take out (*slang*), waste (*informal*)

ructions *plural noun Informal* = **row**, altercation, brawl, commotion, dispute, disturbance, fracas, fuss, hue and cry, quarrel, racket, rumpus, scrap (*informal*), scrimmage, shindig (*informal*), shindy (*informal*), storm, to-do, trouble, uproar

ruddy *adjective* **1** = **rosy**, blooming, blushing, florid, flushed, fresh, glowing, healthy, radiant, red, reddish, rosy-cheeked, rubicund, sanguine **2** = **red**, crimson, pink, reddish, roseate, ruby, scarlet
➤ **Antonyms**
≠**rosy**: anaemic, ashen, colourless, grey, pale, pallid, sickly, wan, white

rude *adjective* **1** = **impolite**, abrupt, abusive, blunt, brusque, cheeky, churlish, curt, discourteous, disrespectful, ill-mannered, impertinent, impudent, inconsiderate, insolent, insulting, offhand, peremptory, short, uncivil, unmannerly **2** = **vulgar**, barbarous, boorish, brutish, coarse, crude, graceless, gross, ignorant, loutish, low, oafish, rough, scurrilous, uncivilized, uncouth, uncultured, uneducated, ungracious, unpolished, unrefined **3** = **unpleasant**, abrupt, harsh, sharp, startling, sudden, violent **4** = **roughly-made**, artless, crude, inartistic, inelegant, makeshift,

primitive, raw, rough, rough-hewn, simple
➤ **Antonyms**
≠**impolite**: civil, considerate, cordial, courteous, courtly, decent, gentlemanly, gracious, ladylike, mannerly, polite, respectful, sociable, urbane, well-bred ≠**vulgar**: civilized, cultured, educated, elegant, learned, polished, refined, sophisticated, urbane ≠**roughly-made**: artful, even, finished, shapely, smooth, well-made

rudimentary *adjective* = **basic**, early, elementary, fundamental, immature, initial, introductory, primary, primitive, undeveloped
➤ **Antonyms**
advanced, complete, developed, higher, later, mature, refined, secondary, sophisticated, supplementary

rudiments *plural noun* = **basics**, beginnings, elements, essentials, first principles, foundation, fundamentals, nuts and bolts

rue *verb Literary* = **regret**, bemoan, be sorry for, bewail, deplore, grieve, kick oneself for, lament, mourn, repent, reproach oneself for

rueful *adjective* = **regretful**, conscience-stricken, contrite, dismal, melancholy, mournful, penitent, remorseful, repentant, sad, self-reproachful, sorrowful, sorry, woebegone, woeful
➤ **Antonyms**
cheerful, delighted, glad, happy, joyful, pleased, unrepentant

ruffian *noun* = **thug**, bruiser (*informal*), brute, bully, bully boy, casual, heavy (*slang*), hoodlum, hooligan, lager lout, ned (*Scot. slang*), rascal, rogue, rough (*informal*), roughneck (*slang*), rowdy, scoundrel, tough, tsotsi (*S. African*), villain, wretch, yardie

ruffle *verb* **1** = **disarrange**, derange, discompose, dishevel, disorder, mess up, rumple, tousle, wrinkle **2** = **annoy**, agitate, confuse, disconcert, disquiet, disturb, faze, fluster, harass, hassle (*informal*), irritate, nettle, peeve (*informal*), perturb, put out, rattle (*informal*), shake up (*informal*), stir, trouble, unnerve, unsettle, upset, vex, worry
➤ **Antonyms**
≠**annoy**: appease, calm, comfort, compose, console, ease, mollify, solace, soothe

rugged *adjective* **1** = **rocky**, broken, bumpy, craggy, difficult, irregular, jagged, ragged, rough, stark, uneven **2** = **strong-featured**, furrowed, leathery, lined, rough-hewn, weather-beaten, weathered, worn, wrinkled **3** = **stern**, austere, crabbed, dour, gruff, hard, harsh, rough, rude, severe, sour, surly **4** = **tough**, beefy (*informal*), brawny, burly, hale, hardy, husky (*informal*), muscular,

robust, strong, sturdy, vigorous, well-built
➤ **Antonyms**
≠**rocky**: even, gentle, level, regular, smooth, unbroken ≠**strong-featured**: delicate, pretty, refined, smooth, unmarked, youthful ≠**tough**: delicate, feeble, fragile, frail, infirm, sickly, skinny, soft, weak

ruin *verb* **1** = **destroy**, break, bring down, bring to nothing, bring to ruin, crush, defeat, demolish, devastate, lay in ruins, lay waste, overthrow, overturn, overwhelm, raze, shatter, smash, total (*slang*), trash (*slang*), wreak havoc upon, wreck **2** = **bankrupt**, impoverish, pauperize **3** = **spoil**, blow (*slang*), botch, damage, disfigure, injure, make a mess of, mangle, mar, mess up, screw up (*informal*), undo ◆ *noun* **4** = **destruction**, breakdown, collapse, crackup (*informal*), crash, damage, defeat, devastation, downfall, failure, fall, the end, undoing, wreck **5** = **disrepair**, decay, disintegration, ruination, wreckage **6** = **bankruptcy**, destitution, insolvency
➤ **Antonyms**
verb ≠**destroy**: build, construct, create, keep, preserve, save ≠**spoil**: enhance, enrich, improve, mend, repair, restore, strengthen, support ◆ *noun* ≠**destruction**: creation, preservation, success, triumph, victory

ruinous *adjective* **1** = **destructive**, baleful, calamitous, catastrophic, deadly, deleterious, devastating, dire, disastrous, fatal, injurious, pernicious, shattering **2** = **extravagant**, crippling, immoderate, wasteful

rule *noun* **1** = **regulation**, axiom, canon, criterion, decree, dictum, direction, guide, guideline, law, maxim, order, ordinance, precept, principle, ruling, standard, tenet **2** = **procedure**, course, formula, method, policy, way **3** = **custom**, condition, convention, form, habit, order *or* way of things, practice, procedure, routine, tradition, wont **4** = **government**, administration, ascendancy, authority, command, control, direction, domination, dominion, empire, influence, jurisdiction, leadership, mastery, power, regime, reign, supremacy, sway **5 as a rule** = **usually**, customarily, for the most part, generally, mainly, normally, on the whole, ordinarily ◆ *verb* **6** = **govern**, administer, be in authority, be in power, command, control, direct, guide, hold sway, lead, manage, preside over, regulate, reign **7** = **be pre-eminent**, be superior, dominate **8** = **be prevalent**, be customary, hold sway, obtain, predominate, preponderate, prevail **9** = **decree**, adjudge, adjudicate, decide, determine, establish, find, judge, lay down, pronounce, resolve, settle

rule out *verb* = **exclude**, ban, debar, dismiss, disqualify, eliminate, forbid, leave out, obviate, preclude, prevent, prohibit, proscribe, reject
➤ **Antonyms**
allow, approve, authorize, let, license, order, permit, sanction

ruler *noun* **1** = **governor**, commander, controller, crowned head, emperor *or* empress, head of state, king *or* queen, leader, lord, monarch, potentate, prince *or* princess, sovereign **2** = **measure**, rule, straight edge, yardstick

ruling *adjective* **1** = **governing**, commanding, controlling, dominant, leading, reigning, upper **2** = **predominant**, chief, current, dominant, main, pre-eminent, preponderant, prevailing, prevalent, principal, supreme ◆ *noun* **3** = **decision**, adjudication, decree, finding, judgment, pronouncement, resolution, verdict
➤ **Antonyms**
adjective ≠**predominant**: auxiliary, inferior, least, minor, secondary, subordinate, subsidiary, unimportant

rum *adjective Brit. slang* = **strange**, curious, dodgy (*Brit., Austral., & N.Z. informal*), funny, odd, peculiar, queer, singular, suspect, suspicious, unusual, weird

rumbustious *adjective* = **unruly**, boisterous, disorderly, loud, noisy, obstreperous, rough, rowdy, unmanageable, uproarious, wild

ruminate *verb* = **ponder**, brood, chew over, cogitate, consider, contemplate, deliberate, meditate, mull over, muse, rack one's brains, reflect, revolve, think, turn over in one's mind, weigh

rummage *verb* = **search**, delve, examine, explore, forage, hunt, ransack, root

rumour *noun* **1** = **story**, bush telegraph, buzz, dirt (*U.S. slang*), gossip, hearsay, news, report, talk, tidings, whisper, word ◆ *verb* **2 be rumoured** = **be said**, be circulated, be passed around, be put about, be reported, be told, be whispered

rump *noun* = **buttocks**, arse (*taboo slang*), ass (*U.S. & Canad. taboo slang*), backside (*informal*), bottom, bum (*Brit. slang*), buns (*U.S. slang*), butt (*U.S. & Canad. informal*), derrière (*euphemistic*), haunch, hindquarters, posterior, rear, rear end, seat, tail (*informal*)

rumple *verb* = **ruffle**, crease, crinkle, crumple, crush, derange, dishevel, disorder, mess up, pucker, screw up, scrunch, tousle, wrinkle

rumpus *noun* = **commotion**, brouhaha, confusion, disruption, disturbance, furore, fuss, hue and cry, noise, row, shindig (*informal*), shindy (*informal*), tumult, uproar

run *verb* **1** = **race**, barrel (along) (*informal, chiefly U.S. & Canad.*), bolt, career, dart, dash, gallop, hare (*Brit. informal*), hasten, hurry, jog, leg it (*informal*), lope, rush, scamper, scramble, scurry, speed, sprint, stampede **2** = **flee**, abscond, beat a retreat, beat it (*slang*), bolt, clear out, cut and run (*informal*), decamp, depart, do a runner (*slang*), escape, fly the coop (*U.S. & Canad. informal*), leg it (*informal*), make a run for it, make off, scarper (*Brit. slang*), skedaddle (*informal*), slope off, take flight, take off (*informal*), take to one's heels **3** = **give a lift to**, bear, carry, convey, drive, manoeuvre, operate, propel, transport **4** = **operate**, go **5** = **move**, course, glide, go, pass, roll, skim, slide **6** = **work**, function, go, operate, perform **7** = **manage**, administer, be in charge of, boss (*informal*), carry on, conduct, control, coordinate, direct, handle, head, lead, look after, mastermind, operate, oversee, own, regulate, superintend, supervise, take care of **8** = **continue**, extend, go, last, lie, proceed, range, reach, stretch **9** = **flow**, cascade, discharge, go, gush, issue, leak, move, pour, proceed, spill, spout, stream **10** = **melt**, dissolve, fuse, go soft, liquefy, turn to liquid **11** = **spread**, be diffused, bleed, lose colour, mix **12** = **unravel**, come apart, come undone, ladder, tear **13** = **circulate**, be current, climb, creep, go round, spread, trail **14** = **publish**, display, feature, print **15** *chiefly U.S. & Canad.* = **compete**, be a candidate, challenge, contend, put oneself up for, stand, take part **16** = **smuggle**, bootleg, deal in, ship, sneak, traffic in ♦ *noun* **17** = **race**, dash, gallop, jog, rush, sprint, spurt **18** = **ride**, drive, excursion, jaunt, journey, joy ride (*informal*), lift, outing, round, spin (*informal*), trip **19** = **sequence**, chain, course, cycle, passage, period, round, season, series, spell, streak, stretch, string **20** = **type**, category, class, kind, order, sort, variety **21** = **demand**, pressure, rush **22** = **tear**, ladder, rip, snag **23** = **enclosure**, coop, pen **24 in the long run** = **in the end**, at the end of the day, eventually, in the fullness of time, in time, ultimately, when all is said and done **25 on the run: a** = **escaping**, at liberty, fugitive, in flight, on the lam (*U.S. slang*), on the loose **b** = **in retreat**, defeated, falling back, fleeing, in flight, retreating, running away
➤ **Antonyms**
verb ≠**race:** crawl, creep, dawdle, walk ≠**flee:** remain, stay ≠**continue:** cease, stop

run across *verb* = **meet**, bump into, chance upon, come across, come upon, encounter, meet with, run into

runaway *noun* **1** = **fugitive**, absconder, deserter, escapee, escaper, refugee, truant ♦ *adjective* **2** = **escaped**, fleeing, fugitive, loose, out of control, uncontrolled, wild **3** = **easily won**, easy, effortless

run away *verb* **1** = **flee**, abscond, beat it (*slang*), bolt, clear out, decamp, do a bunk (*Brit. slang*), do a runner (*slang*), escape, fly the coop (*U.S. & Canad. informal*), make a run for it, run off, scarper (*Brit. slang*), scram (*informal*), skedaddle (*informal*), take flight, take it on the lam (*U.S. & Canad. slang*), take off, take to one's heels, turn tail **2 run away with: a** = **abscond**, abduct, elope **b** = **win easily**, romp home, walk it (*informal*), win by a mile (*informal*), win hands down

rundown *noun* = **summary**, briefing, outline, précis, recap (*informal*), résumé, review, run-through, sketch, synopsis

run-down *adjective* **1** = **exhausted**, below par, debilitated, drained, enervated, fatigued, out of condition, peaky, tired, under the weather (*informal*), unhealthy, weak, weary, worn-out **2** = **dilapidated**, broken-down, decrepit, dingy, ramshackle, seedy, shabby, tumbledown, worn-out
➤ **Antonyms**
≠**exhausted:** fighting fit, fine, fit, fit as a fiddle, full of beans (*informal*), healthy, well

run down *verb* **1** = **criticize**, bad-mouth (*slang, chiefly U.S. & Canad.*), belittle, decry, defame, denigrate, disparage, knock (*informal*), put down, revile, rubbish (*informal*), slag (off) (*slang*), speak ill of, vilify **2** = **reduce**, curtail, cut, cut back, decrease, downsize, drop, pare down, trim **3** = **knock down**, hit, knock over, run into, run over, strike **4** = **weaken**, debilitate, exhaust, sap the strength of, tire, undermine the health of

run-in *noun Informal* = **fight**, altercation, argument, brush, confrontation, contretemps, dispute, face-off (*slang*), quarrel, row, set-to (*informal*), skirmish, tussle

run in *verb* **1** = **break in gently**, run gently **2** *Informal* = **arrest**, apprehend, bust (*informal*), collar (*informal*), jail, lift (*slang*), nab (*informal*), nail (*informal*), pick up, pinch (*informal*), pull in (*Brit. slang*), take into custody, take to jail, throw in jail

run into *verb* **1** = **meet**, be beset by, be confronted by, bump into, chance upon, come across or upon, encounter, meet with, run across **2** = **collide with**, bump into, crash into, dash against, hit, ram, strike

runner *noun* **1** = **athlete**, jogger, sprinter **2** = **messenger**, courier, dispatch bearer, errand boy **3** *Botany* = **stem**, offshoot,

shoot, sprig, sprout, tendril

running *adjective* 1 = **continuous**, constant, incessant, in succession, on the trot (*informal*), perpetual, together, unbroken, unceasing, uninterrupted 2 = **flowing**, moving, streaming ♦ *noun* 3 = **management**, administration, charge, conduct, control, coordination, direction, leadership, organization, regulation, superintendency, supervision 4 = **working**, functioning, maintenance, operation, performance

runny *adjective* = **flowing**, diluted, fluid, liquefied, liquid, melted, streaming, watery

run off *verb* 1 = **flee**, bolt, clear out, decamp, do a runner (*slang*), escape, fly the coop (*U.S. & Canad. informal*), make off, run away, scarper (*Brit. slang*), skedaddle (*informal*), take flight, take it on the lam (*U.S. & Canad. slang*), take to one's heels, turn tail 2 = **produce**, churn out (*informal*), duplicate, print 3 = **drain**, bleed, flow away, siphon, tap 4 **run off with: a** = **run away with**, abscond with, elope with **b** = **steal**, lift (*informal*), make off with, pinch (*informal*), purloin, run away with, swipe (*slang*)

run-of-the-mill *adjective* = **ordinary**, average, banal, bog-standard (*Brit. & Irish slang*), common, commonplace, dime-a-dozen (*informal*), fair, mediocre, middling, modest, no great shakes (*informal*), passable, tolerable, undistinguished, unexceptional, unexciting, unimpressive, vanilla (*informal*)
➤ **Antonyms**
excellent, exceptional, extraordinary, marvellous, out of the ordinary, splendid, unusual

run out *verb* 1 = **be used up**, be exhausted, cease, dry up, fail, finish, give out, peter out 2 = **expire**, close, end, terminate 3 **run out of** = **exhaust one's supply of**, be cleaned out, be out of, have no more of, have none left, have no remaining 4 **run out on** *Informal* = **desert**, abandon, forsake, leave high and dry, leave holding the baby, leave in the lurch, rat on (*informal*), run away from, strand

run over *verb* 1 = **knock down**, hit, knock over, run down, strike 2 = **overflow**, brim over, spill, spill over 3 = **review**, check, examine, go over, go through, rehearse, run through, survey

run through *verb* 1 = **rehearse**, go over, practise, read, run over 2 = **pierce**, impale, spit, stab, stick, transfix

run-up *noun* = **build-up**, approach, preliminaries

rupture *noun* 1 = **break**, breach, burst, cleavage, cleft, crack, fissure, fracture, rent, split, tear 2 = **breach**, altercation, break, bust-up (*informal*), contention, disagreement, disruption, estrangement, falling-out (*informal*), feud, hostility, quarrel, rift, schism, split 3 *Medical* = **hernia** ♦ *verb* 4 = **break**, burst, cleave, crack, fracture, puncture, rend, separate, sever, split, tear 5 = **cause a breach**, break off, come between, disrupt, divide, split

rural *adjective* = **rustic**, agrarian, agricultural, Arcadian, bucolic, countrified, country, hick (*informal, chiefly U.S. & Canad.*), pastoral, sylvan, upcountry
➤ **Antonyms**
city, cosmopolitan, town, urban

ruse *noun* = **trick**, artifice, blind, deception, device, dodge, hoax, manoeuvre, ploy, sham, stratagem, subterfuge, wile

rush *verb* 1 = **hurry**, barrel (along) (*informal, chiefly U.S. & Canad.*), bolt, burn rubber (*informal*), career, dart, dash, fly, hasten, lose no time, make haste, race, run, scramble, scurry, shoot, speed, sprint, stampede, tear 2 = **push**, accelerate, dispatch, expedite, hurry, hustle, press, quicken, speed up 3 = **attack**, capture, charge, overcome, storm, take by storm ♦ *noun* 4 = **hurry**, charge, dash, dispatch, expedition, haste, race, scramble, speed, stampede, surge, swiftness, urgency 5 = **attack**, assault, charge, onslaught, push, storm, surge ♦ *adjective* 6 = **hasty**, brisk, cursory, emergency, expeditious, fast, hurried, prompt, quick, rapid, swift, urgent
➤ **Antonyms**
verb ≠**hurry**: dally, dawdle, delay, procrastinate, slow down, tarry, wait ♦ *adjective* ≠**hasty**: careful, detailed, leisurely, not urgent, slow, thorough, unhurried

rust *noun* 1 = **corrosion**, oxidation 2 = **mildew**, blight, mould, must, rot ♦ *verb* 3 = **corrode**, oxidize 4 = **deteriorate**, atrophy, decay, decline, go stale, stagnate, tarnish

rustic *adjective* 1 = **simple**, artless, homely, homespun, plain, unaffected, unpolished, unrefined, unsophisticated 2 = **rural**, Arcadian, bucolic, countrified, country, pastoral, sylvan 3 = **uncouth**, awkward, boorish, churlish, cloddish, clodhopping (*informal*), clownish, coarse, crude, graceless, hick (*informal, chiefly U.S. & Canad.*), loutish, lumpish, rough, uncultured, unmannerly ♦ *noun* 4 = **yokel**, boor, bumpkin, clod, clodhopper (*informal*), hayseed (*U.S. & Canad. informal*), hick (*informal, chiefly U.S. & Canad.*), hillbilly, peasant, son of the soil
➤ **Antonyms**
adjective ≠**simple**: elegant, grand, polished, refined, sophisticated ≠**rural**: cosmopolitan,

urban ≠**uncouth:** courtly, polished, refined, sophisticated, urbane ♦ *noun* ≠**yokel:** city slicker, cosmopolitan, courtier, sophisticate, townie, townsman

rustle *verb* 1 = **crackle**, crinkle, swish, whish, whisper, whoosh ♦ *noun* 2 = **crackle**, crinkling, rustling, whisper

rusty *adjective* 1 = **corroded**, oxidized, rust-covered, rusted 2 = **reddish-brown**, chestnut, coppery, reddish, russet, rust-coloured 3 = **out of practice**, not what it was, sluggish, stale, unpractised, weak

rut *noun* 1 = **groove**, furrow, gouge, indentation, pothole, score, track, trough,

wheel mark 2 = **habit**, dead end, groove, humdrum existence, pattern, routine, system

ruthless *adjective* = **merciless**, brutal, callous, cruel, hard, hard-hearted, harsh, heartless, inexorable, inhuman, pitiless, relentless, remorseless, severe, stern, unfeeling, unmerciful, unpitying, unrelenting, without pity
➤ **Antonyms**
compassionate, forgiving, gentle, humane, kind, lenient, merciful, pitying, sparing

rutted *adjective* = **grooved**, cut, furrowed, gouged, holed, indented, marked, scored

S s

sable *adjective* = **black**, dark, dusty, ebony, jet, raven, sombre

sabotage *noun* 1 = **damage**, destruction, disruption, subversion, treachery, treason, wrecking ♦ *verb* 2 = **damage**, cripple, destroy, disable, disrupt, incapacitate, subvert, throw a spanner in the works (*Brit. informal*), undermine, vandalize, wreck

sac *noun* = **pouch**, bag, bladder, cyst, pocket, pod, vesicle

saccharine *adjective* = **oversweet**, cloying, honeyed, icky (*informal*), maudlin, mawkish, nauseating, sentimental, sickly, soppy (*Brit. informal*), sugary, syrupy (*informal*), treacly

sack¹ *noun* 1 **the sack** = **dismissal**, discharge, termination of employment, the axe (*informal*), the boot (*slang*), the chop (*Brit. slang*), the (old) heave-ho (*informal*), the order of the boot (*slang*), the push (*slang*) 2 **hit the sack** *Slang* = **go to bed**, bed down, hit the hay (*slang*), retire, turn in (*informal*) ♦ *verb* 3 *Informal* = **dismiss**, axe (*informal*), discharge, fire (*informal*), give (someone) his books (*informal*), give (someone) his cards, give (someone) the elbow, give (someone) the push (*informal*), kick out (*informal*)

sack² *noun* 1 = **plundering**, despoliation, destruction, devastation, looting, pillage, plunder, ravage, ruin, waste ♦ *verb* 2 = **plunder**, demolish, despoil, destroy, devastate, lay waste, loot, maraud, pillage, raid, ravage, rifle, rob, ruin, spoil, strip

sackcloth and ashes *noun* = **penitence**, compunction, contrition, grief, mortification, mourning, penance, remorse, repentance

sacred *adjective* 1 = **holy**, blessed, consecrated, divine, hallowed, revered, sanctified, venerable 2 = **religious**, ecclesiastical, holy, solemn 3 = **inviolable**, inviolate, invulnerable, protected, sacrosanct, secure
➤ **Antonyms**
≠**holy, religious**: lay, nonspiritual, profane, secular, temporal, unconsecrated, worldly

sacrifice *noun* 1 = **surrender**, destruction, loss, renunciation 2 = **offering**, immolation, oblation ♦ *verb* 3 = **give up**, forego, forfeit, let go, lose, say goodbye to, surrender 4 = **offer**, immolate, offer up

sacrificial *adjective* = **propitiatory**, atoning, expiatory

sacrilege *noun* = **desecration**, blasphemy, heresy, impiety, irreverence, mockery, profanation, profaneness, profanity, violation
➤ **Antonyms**
piety, respect, reverence

sacrilegious *adjective* = **profane**, blasphemous, desecrating, godless, impious, irreligious, irreverent, ungodly, unholy

sacrosanct *adjective* = **inviolable**, hallowed, inviolate, sacred, sanctified, set apart, untouchable

sad *adjective* 1 = **unhappy**, blue, cheerless, dejected, depressed, disconsolate, dismal, doleful, down, downcast, down in the dumps (*informal*), down in the mouth (*informal*), gloomy, glum, grief-stricken, grieved, heavy-hearted, low, low-spirited, lugubrious, melancholy, mournful, pensive, sick at heart, sombre, wistful, woebegone 2 = **tragic**, calamitous, dark, depressing, disastrous, dismal, grievous, harrowing, heart-rending, moving, pathetic, pitiable, pitiful, poignant, sorry, tearful, upsetting 3 = **deplorable**, bad, dismal, lamentable, miserable, shabby, sorry, to be deplored, wretched 4 = **regrettable**, distressing, unfortunate, unhappy, unsatisfactory
➤ **Antonyms**
≠**unhappy**: blithe, cheerful, cheery, chirpy (*informal*), glad, happy, in good spirits, jolly, joyful, joyous, light-hearted, merry, pleased ≠**deplorable**: good ≠**regrettable**: fortunate

sadden *verb* = **upset**, aggrieve, bring tears to one's eyes, cast a gloom upon, cast down, dash, deject, depress, desolate, dispirit, distress, grieve, make one's heart bleed, make sad

saddle *verb* = **burden**, charge, encumber, load, lumber (*Brit. informal*), task, tax

sadistic *adjective* = **cruel**, barbarous, beastly, brutal, fiendish, inhuman, perverse, perverted, ruthless, savage, vicious

sadness *noun* = **unhappiness**, bleakness, cheerlessness, dejection, depression, despondency, dolefulness, gloominess, grief, heavy heart, melancholy, misery, mournfulness, poignancy, sorrow, sorrowfulness, the blues, the dumps (*informal*), tragedy, wretchedness

safe *adjective* 1 = **secure**, free from harm, impregnable, in safe hands, in safety, out of danger, out of harm's way, out of the

woods, protected, safe and sound **2 = unharmed**, all right, intact, O.K. or okay (informal), undamaged, unhurt, unscathed **3 = cautious**, circumspect, conservative, dependable, discreet, on the safe side, prudent, realistic, reliable, sure, tried and true, trustworthy, unadventurous **4 = risk-free**, certain, impregnable, riskless, secure, sound **5 = harmless**, innocuous, nonpoisonous, nontoxic, pure, tame, unpolluted, wholesome ♦ noun **6 = strongbox**, coffer, deposit box, repository, safe-deposit box, vault
➤ Antonyms
adjective ≠**secure**: at risk, damaged, endangered, imperilled, insecure, jeopardized, put at risk, put in danger, threatened ≠**cautious**: imprudent, incautious, reckless, risky, unsafe ≠**harmless**: baneful, dangerous, harmful, hazardous, hurtful, injurious, noxious, pernicious, unsafe

safe-conduct noun = **permit**, authorization, licence, pass, passport, safeguard, warrant

safeguard verb **1 = protect**, defend, guard, look after, preserve, screen, shield, watch over ♦ noun **2 = protection**, aegis, armour, bulwark, convoy, defence, escort, guard, security, shield, surety

safekeeping noun = **protection**, care, charge, custody, guardianship, keeping, supervision, surveillance

safely adverb = **in safety**, in one piece, safe and sound, securely, with impunity, without risk, with safety

safety noun **1 = security**, assurance, immunity, impregnability, protection **2 = shelter**, cover, refuge, sanctuary

sag verb **1 = sink**, bag, bulge, cave in, dip, droop, drop, fall, fall unevenly, give way, hang loosely, settle, slump, swag **2 = tire**, decline, droop, fall, flag, slide, slip, slump, wane, weaken, wilt ♦ noun **3 = drop**, decline, depression, dip, downturn, fall, lapse, slip, slump

saga noun = **tale**, adventure, chronicle, epic, narrative, story, yarn

sagacious adjective Formal = **wise**, astute, canny, clear-sighted, discerning, far-sighted, insightful, intelligent, judicious, knowing, perceptive, perspicacious, sage, sharp, sharp-witted, shrewd, smart

sagacity noun = **wisdom**, acuteness, astuteness, canniness, discernment, insight, judiciousness, perspicacity, sapience, sense, sharpness, shrewdness, understanding

sage noun **1 = wise man**, authority, elder, expert, guru, mahatma, man of learning, master, philosopher, pundit, savant,

Solomon ♦ adjective **2 = wise**, acute, canny, discerning, intelligent, judicious, learned, perspicacious, politic, prudent, sagacious, sapient, sensible

sail verb **1 = go by water**, cruise, ride the waves, voyage **2 = embark**, cast or weigh anchor, get under way, put to sea, set sail **3 = pilot**, captain, navigate, skipper, steer **4 = glide**, drift, float, fly, scud, shoot, skim, skirr, soar, sweep, wing **5 sail into** Informal = **attack**, assault, fall upon, get going, get to work on, lambast(e), set about, tear into (informal)

sailor noun = **mariner**, Jack Tar, lascar, marine, matelot (slang, chiefly Brit.), navigator, salt, sea dog, seafarer, seafaring man, seaman, tar (informal)

saintly adjective = **virtuous**, angelic, beatific, blameless, blessed, devout, god-fearing, godly, holy, pious, religious, righteous, sainted, saintlike, sinless, worthy

sake noun **1** As in **for someone's** or **one's own sake = benefit**, account, advantage, behalf, consideration, gain, good, interest, profit, regard, respect, welfare, wellbeing **2** As in **for the sake of = purpose**, aim, cause, end, motive, objective, principle, reason

salacious adjective = **lascivious**, bawdy, blue, carnal, erotic, indecent, lecherous, lewd, libidinous, lustful, obscene, pornographic, prurient, ribald, ruttish, smutty, steamy (informal), wanton, X-rated (informal)

salary noun = **pay**, earnings, emolument, income, remuneration, stipend, wage, wages

sale noun **1 = selling**, auction, deal, disposal, marketing, transaction, vending **2 for sale = available**, in stock, obtainable, on offer, on sale, on the market

salient adjective = **prominent**, arresting, conspicuous, important, marked, noticeable, outstanding, projecting, pronounced, remarkable, signal, striking

sallow adjective = **wan**, anaemic, bilious, jaundiced-looking, pale, pallid, pasty, peely-wally (Scot.), sickly, unhealthy, yellowish
➤ Antonyms
glowing, healthy-looking, radiant, rosy, ruddy

sally noun **1 = witticism**, bon mot, crack (informal), jest, joke, quip, retort, riposte, smart remark, wisecrack (informal) **2 = attack**, campaign, foray, incursion, offensive, raid, sortie, thrust **3 = excursion**, frolic, jaunt, trip ♦ verb **4 = go forth**, erupt, issue, rush, set out, surge

salt noun **1 = seasoning**, flavour, relish, savour, taste **2 = wit**, bite, dry humour, liveliness, piquancy, punch, pungency, sarcasm, sharpness **3 = sailor**, mariner, sea dog, seaman, tar (*informal*) **4 with a grain or pinch of salt = sceptically**, cynically, disbelievingly, doubtfully, suspiciously, with reservations ♦ *adjective* **5 = salty**, brackish, briny, saline, salted

salt away *verb* **= save**, accumulate, amass, bank, cache, hide, hoard up, lay by, lay in, lay up, put by, save for a rainy day, stash away (*informal*), stockpile

salty *adjective* **1 = salt**, brackish, brak (*S. African*), briny, over-salted, saline, salted **2 = witty**, colourful, humorous, lively, piquant, pungent, racy, sharp, snappy (*informal*), spicy, tangy, tart, zestful

salubrious *adjective* **= health-giving**, beneficial, good for one, healthful, healthy, invigorating, salutary, wholesome

salutary *adjective* **1 = beneficial**, advantageous, good, good for one, helpful, practical, profitable, timely, useful, valuable **2 = healthy**, healthful, salubrious

salutation *noun Formal* **= greeting**, address, salute, welcome

salute *verb* **1 = greet**, accost, acknowledge, address, doff one's cap to, hail, kiss, pay one's respects to, welcome **2 = honour**, acknowledge, pay tribute *or* homage to, recognize ♦ *noun* **3 = greeting**, address, recognition, salutation

salvage *verb* **= save**, glean, recover, redeem, rescue, restore, retrieve

salvation *noun* **= saving**, deliverance, escape, lifeline, preservation, redemption, rescue, restoration
➤ **Antonyms**
condemnation, damnation, doom, downfall, hell, loss, perdition, ruin

salve *noun* **= ointment**, balm, cream, dressing, emollient, liniment, lotion, lubricant, medication, unguent

same *adjective* **1 = aforementioned**, aforesaid, selfsame, very **2 = identical**, alike, corresponding, duplicate, equal, equivalent, indistinguishable, interchangeable, synonymous, twin **3 = unchanged**, changeless, consistent, constant, invariable, unaltered, unfailing, uniform, unvarying **4 all the same = nevertheless**, after all, anyhow, be that as it may, in any event, just the same, nonetheless, still **5 be all the same = be unimportant**, be immaterial, be of no consequence, not be worth mentioning
➤ **Antonyms**
≠**identical**: different, dissimilar, diverse, miscellaneous, other ≠**unchanged**: altered, inconsistent, variable

sameness *noun* **1 = similarity**, identicalness, identity, indistinguishability, likeness, oneness, resemblance, standardization, uniformity **2 = lack of**

variety, consistency, monotony, predictability, repetition, tedium

sample *noun* **1 = specimen**, cross section, example, exemplification, illustration, indication, instance, model, pattern, representative, sign ♦ *verb* **2 = test**, experience, inspect, partake of, taste, try ♦ *adjective* **3 = test**, illustrative, pilot, representative, specimen, trial

sanctify *verb* **= consecrate**, absolve, anoint, bless, cleanse, hallow, purify, set apart

sanctimonious *adjective*
= holier-than-thou, canting, false, goody-goody (*informal*), hypocritical, pi (*Brit. slang*), pietistic, pious, priggish, self-righteous, self-satisfied, smug, too good to be true, unctuous

sanction *noun* **1 = permission**, allowance, approbation, approval, authority, authorization, backing, confirmation, countenance, endorsement, O.K. *or* okay (*informal*), ratification, stamp *or* seal of approval, support **2** *often plural* **= ban**, boycott, coercive measures, embargo, penalty ♦ *verb* **3 = permit**, allow, approve, authorize, back, countenance, endorse, entitle, lend one's name to, support, vouch for **4 = confirm**, ratify, warrant
➤ **Antonyms**
noun ≠**permission**: ban, disapproval, embargo, prohibition, proscription, refusal, veto ≠**ban**: approbation, approval, authority, authorization, dispensation, licence, permission ♦ *verb* ≠**permit**: ban, boycott, disallow, forbid, refuse, reject, veto

sanctity *noun* **1 = sacredness**, inviolability, solemnity **2 = holiness**, devotion, godliness, goodness, grace, piety, purity, religiousness, righteousness, sanctitude, spirituality

sanctuary *noun* **1 = shrine**, altar, church, Holy of Holies, sanctum, temple **2 = protection**, asylum, haven, refuge, retreat, shelter **3 = reserve**, conservation area, national park, nature reserve

sanctum *noun* **1 = sanctuary**, Holy of Holies, shrine **2 = refuge**, den, private room, retreat, study

sane *adjective* **1 = rational**, all there (*informal*), compos mentis, in one's right mind, in possession of all one's faculties, lucid, mentally sound, normal, of sound mind **2 = sensible**, balanced, judicious, level-headed, moderate, reasonable, sober, sound
➤ **Antonyms**
≠**rational**: bonkers (*slang, chiefly Brit.*), crackpot (*informal*), crazy, daft (*informal*), insane, loony (*slang*), mad, mentally ill, *non compos mentis*, nuts (*slang*), off one's head (*slang*), off one's trolley (*slang*), out to

lunch (*informal*), round the bend *or* twist (*slang*) ≠**sensible:** dumb-ass (*slang*), foolish, stupid, unreasonable, unsound, up the pole (*informal*), wacko *or* whacko (*informal*)

sang-froid *noun* = **composure**, aplomb, calmness, cool (*slang*), cool-headedness, coolness, equanimity, imperturbability, indifference, nonchalance, phlegm, poise, self-possession

sanguinary *adjective Formal* **1** = **savage**, bloodthirsty, cruel, grim **2** = **bloody**, bloodied, gory

sanguine *adjective* **1** = **cheerful**, animated, assured, buoyant, confident, hopeful, in good heart, lively, optimistic, spirited **2** = **ruddy**, florid, red, rubicund
➤ **Antonyms**
≠**cheerful:** despondent, dispirited, down, gloomy, heavy-hearted, melancholy, pessimistic ≠**ruddy:** anaemic, ashen, pale, pallid, peely-wally (*Scot.*)

sanitary *adjective* = **hygienic**, clean, germ-free, healthy, salubrious, unpolluted, wholesome

sanity *noun* **1** = **mental health**, normality, rationality, reason, right mind (*informal*), saneness, stability **2** = **good sense**, common sense, judiciousness, level-headedness, rationality, sense, soundness of judgment
➤ **Antonyms**
≠**mental health:** craziness, dementia, insanity, lunacy, madness, mental derangement, mental illness ≠**good sense:** folly, senselessness, stupidity

sap[1] *noun* **1** = **vital fluid**, animating force, essence, lifeblood **2** *Slang* = **fool**, charlie (*Brit. informal*), chump (*informal*), dumb-ass (*slang*), dweeb (*U.S. slang*), idiot, jerk (*slang, chiefly U.S. & Canad.*), muggins (*Brit. slang*), nerd *or* nurd (*slang*), nincompoop, ninny, nitwit (*informal*), numpty (*Scot. informal*), numskull *or* numbskull, oaf, plonker (*slang*), prat (*slang*), simpleton, twit (*informal*), wally (*slang*)

sap[2] *verb* = **weaken**, bleed, deplete, devitalize, drain, enervate, erode, exhaust, rob, undermine, wear down

sapience *noun, often used ironically* = **wisdom**, discernment, insight, nous (*Brit. slang*), perspicacity, sagacity, sense, shrewdness, understanding

sapient *adjective, often used ironically* = **wise**, canny, discerning, discriminating, intelligent, judicious, knowing, perspicacious, sagacious, sage, shrewd

sarcasm *noun* = **irony**, bitterness, contempt, cynicism, derision, mockery, mordancy, ridicule, satire, scorn, sneering,

venom, vitriol

sarcastic *adjective* = **ironical**, acerb, acerbic, acid, acrimonious, bitchy (*informal*), biting, caustic, contemptuous, cutting, cynical, derisive, disparaging, mocking, mordacious, mordant, sardonic, sarky (*Brit. informal*), satirical, sharp, sneering, taunting, vitriolic

sardonic *adjective* = **mocking**, bitter, cynical, derisive, dry, ironical, jeering, malicious, mordacious, mordant, sarcastic, sneering, wry

Satan *noun* = **The Devil**, Beelzebub, Lord of the Flies, Lucifer, Mephistopheles, Old Nick (*informal*), Prince of Darkness, The Evil One

satanic *adjective* = **evil**, accursed, black, demoniac, demoniacal, demonic, devilish, diabolic, fiendish, hellish, infernal, inhuman, iniquitous, malevolent, malignant, wicked
➤ **Antonyms**
benevolent, benign, divine, godly, holy

sate *verb* = **satisfy**, indulge to the full, satiate, slake

satellite *noun* **1** = **sputnik**, communications satellite **2** = **moon**

satiate *verb* **1** = **glut**, cloy, gorge, jade, nauseate, overfill, stuff, surfeit **2** = **satisfy**, sate, slake

satiety *noun Formal* **1** = **surfeit**, overindulgence, saturation **2** = **fullness**, gratification, repletion, satiation, satisfaction

satire *noun* = **mockery**, burlesque, caricature, irony, lampoon, parody, ridicule, sarcasm, send-up (*Brit. informal*), skit, spoof (*informal*), takeoff (*informal*), travesty, wit

satirical, satiric *adjective* = **mocking**, biting, bitter, burlesque, caustic, censorious, cutting, cynical, incisive, ironical, mordacious, mordant, pungent, Rabelaisian, sarcastic, sardonic, taunting, vitriolic

satirize *verb* = **ridicule**, abuse, burlesque, censure, criticize, deride, hold up to ridicule, lampoon, lash, parody, pillory, send up (*Brit. informal*), take off (*informal*), travesty

satisfaction *noun* **1** = **contentment**, comfort, complacency, content, contentedness, ease, enjoyment, gratification, happiness, peace of mind, pleasure, pride, repletion, satiety, well-being **2** = **fulfilment**, achievement, assuaging, gratification, resolution, settlement **3** = **compensation**, amends, atonement, damages, indemnification, justice, recompense, redress, reimbursement, remuneration, reparation, requital, restitution, settlement, vindication
➤ **Antonyms**
≠**contentment:** annoyance, discontent, displeasure, dissatisfaction, frustration, grief, misgivings, pain, shame, unhappiness

≠**compensation**: injury

satisfactory *adjective* = **adequate**, acceptable, all right, average, competent, fair, good enough, passable, sufficient, suitable, up to scratch, up to standard, up to the mark
➤ Antonyms
bad, below par, inadequate, insufficient, leaving a lot to be desired, mediocre, no great shakes (*informal*), not up to scratch (*informal*), poor, sub-standard, unacceptable, unsatisfactory, unsuitable

satisfied *adjective* = **contented**, at ease, complacent, content, convinced, easy in one's mind, happy, like the cat that swallowed the canary (*informal*), pacified, positive, smug, sure

satisfy *verb* **1** = **content**, appease, assuage, feed, fill, gratify, indulge, mollify, pacify, pander to, please, quench, sate, satiate, slake, surfeit **2** = **be sufficient**, answer, be adequate, be enough, come up to expectations, do, fill the bill (*informal*), fulfil, meet, qualify, serve, serve the purpose, suffice **3** = **convince**, assure, dispel (someone's) doubts, persuade, put (someone's) mind at rest, quiet, reassure **4** = **fulfil**, answer, comply with, discharge, meet
➤ Antonyms
≠**content**: annoy, displease, dissatisfy, exasperate, frustrate, give cause for complaint ≠**be sufficient**: fail to meet ≠**convince**: dissuade, fail to persuade

satisfying *adjective* = **satisfactory**, cheering, convincing, filling, gratifying, pleasing, pleasurable

saturate *verb* = **soak**, douse, drench, imbue, impregnate, seep, souse, steep, suffuse, waterlog, wet through

saturated *adjective* = **soaked**, drenched, dripping, droukit *or* drookit (*Scot.*), soaked to the skin, soaking (wet), sodden, sopping (wet), waterlogged, wet through, wringing wet

saturnine *adjective* = **gloomy**, dour, dull, glum, grave, heavy, morose, phlegmatic, sedate, sluggish, sombre, taciturn, uncommunicative

sauce *noun Informal* = **impudence**, audacity, backchat (*informal*), cheek (*informal*), cheekiness, disrespectfulness, front, impertinence, insolence, lip (*slang*), nerve (*informal*), rudeness

sauciness *noun* = **impudence**, backchat (*informal*), brazenness, cheek (*informal*), flippancy, impertinence, insolence, lip (*slang*), pertness, rudeness, sauce (*informal*)

saucy *adjective* **1** = **impudent**, cheeky (*informal*), disrespectful, flip (*informal*),
flippant, forward, fresh (*informal*), impertinent, insolent, lippy (*U.S. & Canad. slang*), pert, presumptuous, rude, sassy (*U.S. informal*), smart-alecky (*informal*) **2** = **jaunty**, dashing, gay, natty (*informal*), perky, rakish, sporty

saunter *verb* **1** = **stroll**, amble, dally, meander, mosey (*informal*), ramble, roam, rove, take a stroll, wander ◆ *noun* **2** = **stroll**, airing, amble, constitutional, perambulation, promenade, ramble, turn, walk

savage *adjective* **1** = **wild**, feral, undomesticated, untamed **2** = **cruel**, barbarous, beastly, bestial, bloodthirsty, bloody, brutal, brutish, devilish, ferocious, fierce, harsh, inhuman, merciless, murderous, pitiless, ruthless, sadistic, vicious **3** = **primitive**, in a state of nature, nonliterate, rude, unspoilt **4** = **uncultivated**, rough, rugged, uncivilized ◆ *noun* **5** = **primitive**, autochthon, barbarian, heathen, indigene, native **6** = **lout**, barbarian, bear, boor, roughneck (*slang*), yahoo, yob (*Brit. slang*), yobbo (*Brit. slang*) **7** = **brute**, beast, fiend, monster ◆ *verb* **8** = **attack**, lacerate, mangle, maul **9** = **criticise**, attack, tear into (*informal*)
➤ Antonyms
adjective ≠**wild**: domesticated, tame ≠**cruel**: gentle, humane, kind, merciful, mild, restrained ≠**uncultivated**: civilized, cultivated, refined ◆ *verb* ≠**criticise**: acclaim, celebrate, praise, rave about (*informal*)

savagery *noun* = **cruelty**, barbarity, bestiality, bloodthirstiness, brutality, ferocity, fierceness, inhumanity, ruthlessness, sadism, viciousness

savant *noun* = **sage**, authority, intellectual, mahatma, master, mastermind, philosopher, scholar

save *verb* **1** = **rescue**, bail (someone) out, come to (someone's) rescue, deliver, free, liberate, recover, redeem, salvage, save (someone's) bacon (*British informal*), set free **2** = **protect**, conserve, guard, keep safe, look after, preserve, safeguard, screen, shield, take care of **3** = **keep**, be frugal, be thrifty, collect, economize, gather, hide away, hoard, hold, husband, lay by, put aside for a rainy day, put by, reserve, retrench, salt away, set aside, store, treasure up **4** = **prevent**, hinder, obviate, rule out, spare
➤ Antonyms
≠**rescue, protect**: abandon, endanger, expose, imperil, risk, threaten ≠**keep**: be extravagant (with), blow (*slang*), consume, discard, fritter away, spend, splurge, squander, use, use up, waste

saving *noun* **1** = **economy**, bargain, discount, reduction ◆ *adjective* **2** As in

saving grace = redeeming, compensatory, extenuating, qualifying

savings *plural noun* = **nest egg**, fall-back, fund, provision for a rainy day, reserves, resources, store

saviour *noun* = **rescuer**, defender, deliverer, friend in need, Good Samaritan, guardian, knight in shining armour, liberator, preserver, protector, redeemer, salvation

Saviour *noun* = **Christ**, Jesus, Messiah, Redeemer

savoir-faire *noun* = **social know-how** (*informal*), accomplishment, diplomacy, discretion, finesse, poise, social graces, tact, urbanity

savour *verb* 1 = **enjoy**, appreciate, delight in, drool, enjoy to the full, gloat over, like, luxuriate in, partake, relish, revel in 2 **savour of** = **suggest**, bear the hallmarks of, be indicative of, be suggestive of, partake of, show signs of, smack of, verge on ◆ *noun* 3 = **flavour**, piquancy, relish, smack, smell, tang, taste, zest, zing (*informal*) 4 = **trace**, distinctive quality

savoury *adjective* 1 = **spicy**, agreeable, appetizing, dainty, delectable, delicious, full-flavoured, good, luscious, mouthwatering, palatable, piquant, rich, scrumptious (*informal*), tangy, tasty, toothsome 2 = **wholesome**, decent, honest, reputable, respectable
➤ **Antonyms**
≠**spicy**: insipid, tasteless, unappetizing, unpalatable, unpleasant ≠**wholesome**: disreputable, distasteful, nasty, unpleasant, unsavoury

savvy *Slang* ◆ *verb* 1 = **understand**, apprehend, catch on, comprehend, get the gist, grasp, perceive, take in ◆ *noun* 2 = **understanding**, apprehension, comprehension, grasp, ken, perception

saw *noun* *Old-fashioned* = **saying**, adage, aphorism, apophthegm, axiom, dictum, maxim, proverb

say *verb* 1 = **speak**, add, affirm, announce, assert, asseverate, come out with (*informal*), declare, express, give voice *or* utterance to, maintain, mention, pronounce, put into words, remark, state, utter, voice 2 = **tell**, answer, disclose, divulge, give as one's opinion, make known, reply, respond, reveal 3 = **recite**, deliver, do, orate, perform, read, rehearse, render, repeat 4 = **report**, allege, bruit, claim, noise abroad, put about, rumour, suggest 5 = **suppose**, assume, conjecture, dare say, estimate, guess, hazard a guess, imagine, judge, presume, surmise 6 = **express**, communicate, convey, give the impression that, imply 7 **go without saying** = **be obvious**, be accepted, be a matter of course, be self-evident, be taken as read, be taken for granted, be understood 8 **to say the least** = **at the very least**, to put it mildly, without any exaggeration ◆ *noun* 9 = **chance to speak**, crack (*informal*), opportunity to speak, turn to speak, voice, vote 10 = **influence**, authority, clout (*informal*), power, sway, weight

saying *noun* = **proverb**, adage, aphorism, apophthegm, axiom, byword, dictum, maxim, saw, slogan

scale¹ *noun* = **flake**, lamina, layer, plate

scale² *noun* 1 = **graduation**, calibration, degrees, gamut, gradation, graduated system, hierarchy, ladder, progression, ranking, register, seniority system, sequence, series, spectrum, spread, steps 2 = **ratio**, proportion 3 = **degree**, extent, range, reach, scope, way ◆ *verb* 4 = **climb**, ascend, clamber, escalade, mount, surmount 5 = **adjust**, proportion, prorate (*chiefly U.S.*), regulate

scam *noun* *Slang* = **swindle**, diddle, fiddle, racket, stratagem

scamp *noun* = **rascal**, devil, imp, mischief-maker, monkey, rogue, scallywag (*informal*), scapegrace, toerag (*slang*), tyke (*informal*)

scamper *verb* = **run**, beetle, dart, dash, fly, hasten, hurry, romp, scoot, scurry, scuttle, sprint

scan *verb* 1 = **glance over**, check, check out (*informal*), clock (*Brit. slang*), examine, eye, eyeball (*slang*), get a load of (*informal*), look one up and down, look through, run one's eye over, run over, size up (*informal*), skim, take a dekko at (*Brit. slang*) 2 = **scrutinize**, con (*archaic*), investigate, recce (*slang*), scour, search, survey, sweep, take stock of

scandal *noun* 1 = **crime**, disgrace, embarrassment, offence, sin, skeleton in the cupboard, wrongdoing 2 = **shame**, calumny, defamation, detraction, discredit, disgrace, dishonour, ignominy, infamy, obloquy, offence, opprobrium, reproach, stigma 3 = **gossip**, abuse, aspersion, backbiting, dirt, dirty linen (*informal*), rumours, slander, talk, tattle

scandalize *verb* = **shock**, affront, appal, disgust, horrify, offend, outrage, raise eyebrows

scandalmonger *noun* = **gossip**, muckraker, tattler

scandalous *adjective* 1 = **shocking**, atrocious, disgraceful, disreputable, highly improper, infamous, monstrous, odious, opprobrious, outrageous, shameful, unseemly 2 = **slanderous**, defamatory, gossiping, libellous, scurrilous, untrue

> ➤ **Antonyms**
> ≠**shocking**: decent, proper, reputable, respectable, seemly, upright ≠**slanderous**: laudatory, unimpeachable

scant adjective = **meagre**, bare, barely sufficient, deficient, inadequate, insufficient, limited, little, minimal, sparse
> ➤ **Antonyms**
> abundant, adequate, ample, full, generous, plentiful, satisfactory, sufficient

scanty adjective = **meagre**, bare, deficient, inadequate, insufficient, pathetic, poor, restricted, scant, short, skimpy, slender, sparing, sparse, thin

scapegoat noun = **whipping boy**, fall guy (informal)

scar noun **1** = **mark**, blemish, cicatrix, injury, trauma (Pathology), wound ♦ verb **2** = **mark**, brand, damage, disfigure, traumatize

scarce adjective = **rare**, at a premium, deficient, few, few and far between, infrequent, in short supply, insufficient, thin on the ground, uncommon, unusual, wanting
> ➤ **Antonyms**
> abundant, ample, common, commonplace, frequent, numerous, plenteous, plentiful, sufficient

scarcely adverb **1** = **hardly**, barely, only just, scarce (archaic) **2** often used ironically = **definitely not**, by no means, hardly, not at all, on no account, under no circumstances

scarcity noun = **shortage**, dearth, deficiency, infrequency, insufficiency, lack, paucity, poverty, rareness, undersupply, want
> ➤ **Antonyms**
> abundance, excess, glut, superfluity, surfeit, surplus

scare verb **1** = **frighten**, alarm, daunt, dismay, give (someone) a fright, give (someone) a turn (informal), intimidate, panic, put the wind up (someone) (informal), shock, startle, terrify, terrorize ♦ noun **2** = **fright**, alarm, alert, panic, shock, start, terror

scared adjective = **frightened**, fearful, panicky, panic-stricken, petrified, shaken, startled, terrified

scaremonger noun = **alarmist**, doom merchant (informal), prophet of doom

scarper verb Brit slang = **run away**, abscond, beat a hasty retreat, beat it (slang), clear off (informal), decamp, depart, disappear, do a bunk (Brit. slang), flee, go, hook it (slang), make off, make oneself scarce (informal), run for it, scram (informal), skedaddle (informal), slope off, take flight, take oneself off, take to one's heels, vamoose (slang, chiefly U.S.)

scary adjective Informal = **frightening**, alarming, bloodcurdling, chilling, creepy (informal), hair-raising, hairy (slang), horrendous, horrifying, intimidating, shocking, spine-chilling, spooky (informal), terrifying, unnerving

scathing adjective = **critical**, belittling, biting, caustic, cutting, harsh, mordacious, mordant, sarcastic, savage, scornful, searing, trenchant, vitriolic, withering

scatter verb **1** = **throw about**, broadcast, diffuse, disseminate, fling, litter, shower, sow, spread, sprinkle, strew **2** = **disperse**, disband, dispel, dissipate, disunite, put to flight, separate
> ➤ **Antonyms**
> ≠**throw about**: cluster, collect ≠**disperse**: assemble, congregate, converge, rally, unite

scatterbrain noun = **featherbrain**, bird-brain (informal), butterfly, flibbertigibbet, madcap

scatterbrained adjective = **empty-headed**, bird-brained (informal), careless, featherbrained, forgetful, frivolous, giddy, madcap, scatty (Brit. informal), silly, slaphappy (informal), thoughtless

scattering noun = **sprinkling**, few, handful, scatter, smatter, smattering

scenario noun = **story line**, master plan, outline, résumé, rundown, scheme, sequence of events, sketch, summary, synopsis

scene noun **1** = **site**, area, locality, place, position, setting, situation, spot, stage, whereabouts **2** = **setting**, backdrop, background, location, mise en scène, set **3** = **show**, display, drama, exhibition, pageant, picture, representation, sight, spectacle, tableau **4** = **act**, division, episode, part **5** = **view**, landscape, panorama, prospect, vista **6** = **fuss**, carry-on (informal, chiefly Brit.), commotion, confrontation, display of emotion, drama, exhibition, hue and cry, performance, row, tantrum, to-do, upset **7** Informal = **world**, arena, business, environment, field of interest, milieu

scenery noun **1** = **landscape**, surroundings, terrain, view, vista **2** Theatre = **set**, backdrop, décor, flats, setting, stage set

scenic adjective = **picturesque**, beautiful, breathtaking, grand, impressive, panoramic, spectacular, striking

scent noun **1** = **fragrance**, aroma, bouquet, niff (Brit. slang), odour, perfume, redolence, smell **2** = **trail**, spoor, track ♦ verb **3** = **detect**, be on the track or trail of, discern, get wind of (informal), nose out, recognize, sense, smell, sniff, sniff out

scented adjective = **fragrant**, ambrosial, aromatic, odoriferous, perfumed, redolent, sweet-smelling

sceptic *noun* = **doubter**, agnostic, cynic, disbeliever, doubting Thomas, scoffer, unbeliever

sceptical *adjective* = **doubtful**, cynical, disbelieving, doubting, dubious, hesitating, incredulous, mistrustful, questioning, quizzical, scoffing, unbelieving, unconvinced
➤ **Antonyms**
believing, certain, convinced, credulous, dogmatic, free from doubt, of fixed mind, sure, trusting, undoubting, unquestioning

scepticism *noun* = **doubt**, agnosticism, cynicism, disbelief, incredulity, suspicion, unbelief

schedule *noun* 1 = **plan**, agenda, calendar, catalogue, inventory, itinerary, list, list of appointments, programme, timetable ♦ *verb* 2 = **plan**, appoint, arrange, book, organize, programme, slot (*informal*), time

schematic *adjective* = **diagrammatic**, diagrammatical, graphic, illustrative, representational

schematize *verb* = **systematize**, arrange, catalogue, categorize, classify, file, grade, methodize, order, pigeonhole, put into order, regulate, sort, standardize, systemize, tabulate

scheme *noun* 1 = **plan**, contrivance, course of action, design, device, programme, project, proposal, strategy, system, tactics, theory 2 = **plot**, conspiracy, dodge, game (*informal*), intrigue, machinations, manoeuvre, ploy, ruse, shift, stratagem, subterfuge 3 = **diagram**, arrangement, blueprint, chart, codification, draft, layout, outline, pattern, schedule, schema, system ♦ *verb* 4 = **plan**, contrive, design, devise, frame, imagine, lay plans, project, work out 5 = **plot**, collude, conspire, intrigue, machinate, manoeuvre, wheel and deal (*informal*)

scheming *adjective* = **calculating**, artful, conniving, cunning, deceitful, designing, duplicitous, foxy, Machiavellian, slippery, sly, tricky, underhand, wily
➤ **Antonyms**
above-board, artless, guileless, honest, ingenuous, naive, straightforward, trustworthy, undesigning

schism *noun* = **division**, breach, break, discord, disunion, rift, rupture, separation, splintering, split

schmaltzy *adjective* = **sentimental**, corny (*slang*), icky (*informal*), maudlin, mawkish, mushy (*informal*), overemotional, sloppy (*informal*), slushy (*informal*), soppy (*informal*), tear-jerking

scholar *noun* 1 = **intellectual**, academic, bluestocking (*usually disparaging*),

bookworm, egghead (*informal*), man of letters, savant 2 = **student**, disciple, learner, pupil, schoolboy *or* schoolgirl

scholarly *adjective* = **learned**, academic, bookish, erudite, intellectual, lettered, scholastic, studious, well-read
➤ **Antonyms**
lowbrow, middlebrow, philistine, unacademic, uneducated, unintellectual, unlettered

scholarship *noun* 1 = **learning**, accomplishments, attainments, book-learning, education, erudition, knowledge, lore 2 = **bursary**, fellowship

scholastic *adjective* = **learned**, academic, bookish, lettered, literary, scholarly

school *noun* 1 = **academy**, alma mater, college, department, discipline, faculty, institute, institution, seminary 2 = **group**, adherents, circle, class, clique, denomination, devotees, disciples, faction, followers, following, schism, sect, set ♦ *verb* 3 = **train**, coach, discipline, drill, educate, indoctrinate, instruct, prepare, prime, tutor, verse

schooling *noun* 1 = **teaching**, book-learning, education, formal education, tuition 2 = **training**, coaching, drill, grounding, guidance, instruction, preparation

schoolteacher *noun* = **schoolmaster** *or* **schoolmistress**, instructor, pedagogue, schoolmarm (*informal*)

science *noun* 1 = **discipline**, body of knowledge, branch of knowledge 2 = **skill**, art, technique

scientific *adjective* = **systematic**, accurate, controlled, exact, mathematical, precise

scientist *noun* = **inventor**, boffin (*informal*), technophile

scintillate *verb* = **sparkle**, blaze, coruscate, flash, give off sparks, gleam, glint, glisten, glitter, twinkle

scintillating *adjective* = **brilliant**, animated, bright, dazzling, ebullient, exciting, glittering, lively, sparkling, stimulating, witty

scion *noun* 1 = **descendant**, child, heir, offspring, successor 2 = **offshoot**, branch, graft, shoot, slip, sprout, twig

scoff [1] *verb* = **scorn**, belittle, deride, despise, flout, gibe, jeer, knock (*informal*), laugh at, make light of, mock, poke fun at, pooh-pooh, revile, ridicule, slag (off) (*slang*), sneer, take the piss (out of) (*taboo slang*)

scoff [2] *verb* = **gobble (up)**, bolt, cram, devour, gollop, gorge oneself on, gulp down, guzzle, put away, stuff oneself with, wolf

scold *verb* 1 = **reprimand**, bawl out (*informal*), berate, blame, castigate, censure,

chide, find fault with, give (someone) a dressing-down, give (someone) a row, give (someone) a talking-to (*informal*), go on at, haul (someone) over the coals (*informal*), lecture, nag, rebuke, reproach, reprove, slate (*informal, chiefly Brit.*), take (someone) to task, tear into (*informal*), tear (someone) off a strip (*Brit. informal*), tell off (*informal*), tick off (*informal*), upbraid ♦ *noun* **2** = **nag**, shrew, termagant (*rare*)
➤ **Antonyms**
verb ≠ **reprimand**: acclaim, applaud, approve, commend, compliment, extol, laud, praise

scolding *noun* = **rebuke**, dressing-down (*informal*), (good) talking-to (*informal*), lecture, piece of one's mind, row, telling-off (*informal*), ticking-off (*informal*), tongue-lashing

scoop *noun* **1** = **ladle**, dipper, spoon **2** = **exclusive**, coup, exposé, inside story, revelation, sensation ♦ *verb* **3** *often with* **up** = **lift**, clear away, gather up, pick up, remove, sweep up *or* away, take up **4 scoop out** = **hollow**, bail, dig, dip, empty, excavate, gouge, ladle, scrape, shovel

scoot *verb* = **dash**, bolt, dart, run, scamper, scurry, scuttle, skedaddle (*informal*), skitter

scope *noun* **1** = **opportunity**, elbowroom, freedom, latitude, liberty, room, space **2** = **range**, ambit, area, capacity, orbit, outlook, purview, reach, span, sphere **3** = **extent**, compass, confines, range

scorch *verb* = **burn**, blacken, blister, char, parch, roast, sear, shrivel, singe, wither

scorching *adjective* = **burning**, baking, boiling, broiling, fiery, flaming, red-hot, roasting, searing, sizzling, sweltering, torrid, tropical, unbearably hot

score *noun* **1** = **points**, grade, mark, outcome, record, result, total **2 the score** *Informal* = **the situation**, the equation, the facts, the lie of the land, the reality, the setup (*informal*), the truth **3** = **amount due**, account, bill, charge, debt, obligation, reckoning, tab (*U.S. informal*), tally, total **4** = **grounds**, account, basis, cause, ground, reason **5** = **grievance**, a bone to pick, grudge, injury, injustice, wrong **6 scores** = **lots**, a flock, a great number, an army, a throng, crowds, droves, hosts, hundreds, legions, masses, millions, multitudes, myriads, swarms, very many ♦ *verb* **7** = **gain**, achieve, amass, chalk up (*informal*), make, notch up (*informal*), win **8** = **keep count**, count, keep a tally of, record, register, tally **9** = **cut**, deface, gouge, graze, indent, mar, mark, nick, notch, scrape, scratch, slash **10** *with* **out** *or* **through** = **cross out**, cancel, delete, obliterate, put a line through, strike out **11** *Music* = **arrange**,

adapt, orchestrate, set **12** = **go down well with (someone)**, gain an advantage, impress, make a hit (*informal*), make an impact *or* impression, make a point, put oneself across, triumph

score off *verb* = **get the better of**, be one up on (*informal*), make a fool of

scorn *noun* **1** = **contempt**, contemptuousness, derision, despite, disdain, disparagement, mockery, sarcasm, scornfulness, slight, sneer ♦ *verb* **2** = **despise**, be above, consider beneath one, contemn, deride, disdain, flout, hold in contempt, look down on, make fun of, reject, scoff at, slight, sneer at, spurn, turn up one's nose at (*informal*)
➤ **Antonyms**
noun ≠ **contempt**: acceptance, admiration, affection, esteem, high regard, respect, tolerance, toleration, veneration, worship ♦ *verb* ≠ **despise**: accept, admire, esteem, look favourably on, respect, revere, tolerate, venerate, worship

scornful *adjective* = **contemptuous**, defiant, derisive, disdainful, haughty, insolent, insulting, jeering, mocking, sarcastic, sardonic, scathing, scoffing, slighting, sneering, supercilious, withering

scornfully *adverb* = **contemptuously**, disdainfully, dismissively, scathingly, slightingly, with a sneer, with contempt, with disdain, witheringly

scot-free *adjective* = **unharmed**, safe, undamaged, unhurt, uninjured, unpunished, unscathed, without a scratch

Scots *adjective* = **Scottish**, Caledonian

scoundrel *noun* Old-fashioned = **rogue**, bad egg (*old-fashioned informal*), bastard (*offensive*), blackguard, bugger (*taboo slang*), good-for-nothing, heel (*slang*), knave (*archaic*), miscreant, ne'er-do-well, rascal, reprobate, rotter (*slang, chiefly Brit.*), scally (*Northwest English dialect*), scamp, scumbag (*slang*), skelm (*S. African*), son-of-a-bitch (*slang, chiefly U.S. & Canad.*), swine, villain, wretch

scour[1] *verb* **1** = **rub**, abrade, buff, burnish, clean, cleanse, polish, scrub **2** = **wash**, cleanse, flush, purge

scour[2] *verb* = **search**, beat, comb, forage, go over with a fine-tooth comb, hunt, look high and low, rake, ransack

scourge *noun* **1** = **affliction**, bane, curse, infliction, misfortune, pest, plague, punishment, terror, torment **2** = **whip**, cat, cat-o'-nine-tails, lash, strap, switch, thong ♦ *verb* **3** = **afflict**, curse, harass, plague, terrorize, torment **4** = **whip**, beat, belt (*informal*), cane, castigate, chastise, discipline, flog, horsewhip, lash, leather,

punish, take a strap to, tan (someone's) hide (*slang*), thrash, trounce, wallop (*informal*)
➤ **Antonyms**
noun ≠**affliction**: benefit, blessing, boon, favour, gift, godsend

scout *noun* 1 = **vanguard**, advance guard, escort, lookout, outrider, precursor, reconnoitrer 2 = **recruiter**, talent scout ♦ *verb* 3 = **reconnoitre**, case (*slang*), check out, investigate, make a reconnaissance, observe, probe, recce (*slang*), see how the land lies, spy, spy out, survey, watch 4 **scout about** *or* **around** = **search for**, cast around for, ferret out, hunt for, look for, rustle up, search out, seek, track down

scowl *verb* 1 = **glower**, frown, grimace, look daggers at, lour *or* lower ♦ *noun* 2 = **glower**, black look, dirty look, frown, grimace

scrabble *verb* = **scrape**, clamber, claw, dig, grope, paw, scramble, scratch

scraggy *adjective* = **scrawny**, angular, bony, emaciated, gangling, gaunt, lanky, lean, rawboned, skinny, undernourished

scram *verb Informal* = **go away**, abscond, beat it (*slang*), bugger off (*taboo slang*), clear off (*informal*), depart, disappear, get lost (*informal*), go to hell (*informal*), leave, make oneself scarce (*informal*), make tracks, quit, scarper (*Brit. slang*), scoot, skedaddle (*informal*), sling one's hook (*Brit. slang*), take oneself off, vamoose (*slang, chiefly U.S.*)

scramble *verb* 1 = **struggle**, clamber, climb, crawl, move with difficulty, push, scrabble, swarm 2 = **strive**, contend, hasten, jockey for position, jostle, make haste, push, run, rush, vie ♦ *noun* 3 = **climb**, trek 4 = **struggle**, commotion, competition, confusion, free-for-all (*informal*), hassle (*informal*), hustle, melee *or* mêlée, muddle, race, rush, tussle

scrap¹ *noun* 1 = **piece**, atom, bit, bite, crumb, fragment, grain, iota, mite, modicum, morsel, mouthful, part, particle, portion, remnant, sliver, snatch, snippet, trace 2 = **waste**, junk, off cuts 3 **scraps** = **leftovers**, bits, leavings, remains, scrapings ♦ *verb* 4 = **get rid of**, abandon, break up, chuck (*informal*), discard, dispense with, ditch (*slang*), drop, jettison, junk (*informal*), shed, throw away *or* out, toss out, trash (*slang*), write off
➤ **Antonyms**
verb ≠**get rid of**: bring back, recall, re-establish, reinstall, reinstate, restore, return

scrap² *Informal* ♦ *noun* 1 = **fight**, argument, battle, brawl, disagreement, dispute, quarrel, row, scrimmage, scuffle, set-to (*informal*), shindig (*informal*), shindy (*informal*), squabble, tiff, wrangle ♦ *verb* 2 = **fight**,

argue, barney (*informal*), bicker, come to blows, fall out (*informal*), have a shouting match (*informal*), have words, row, spar, squabble, wrangle

scrape *verb* 1 = **rub**, abrade, bark, graze, scratch, scuff, skin 2 = **scour**, clean, erase, file, remove, rub 3 = **grate**, grind, rasp, scratch, screech, set one's teeth on edge, squeak 4 = **scrimp**, live from hand to mouth, pinch, save, skimp, stint, tighten one's belt 5 **scrape through** = **get by** (*informal*), cut it fine (*informal*), have a close shave (*informal*), just make it, struggle ♦ *noun* 6 *Informal* = **predicament**, awkward situation, difficulty, dilemma, distress, fix (*informal*), mess, plight, spot (*informal*), tight spot, trouble

scrape together *verb* = **collect**, amass, dredge up, get hold of, glean, hoard, muster, rake up *or* together, save

scrapheap *noun* **on the scrapheap** = **discarded**, ditched (*slang*), jettisoned, put out to grass (*informal*), redundant, written off

scrappy *adjective* = **incomplete**, bitty, disjointed, fragmentary, perfunctory, piecemeal, sketchy, thrown together

scratch *verb* 1 = **mark**, claw, cut, damage, etch, grate, graze, incise, lacerate, make a mark on, rub, score, scrape 2 = **erase**, annul, cancel, cross out, delete, eliminate, strike off 3 = **withdraw**, pull out, stand down ♦ *noun* 4 = **mark**, blemish, claw mark, gash, graze, laceration, scrape 5 **up to scratch** *Informal* = **adequate**, acceptable, capable, competent, satisfactory, sufficient, up to standard ♦ *adjective* 6 = **improvised**, haphazard, hastily prepared, impromptu, rough, rough-and-ready

scrawl *verb, noun* = **scribble**, doodle, scratch, squiggle

scrawny *adjective* = **thin**, angular, bony, gaunt, lanky, lean, scraggy, skeletal, skin-and-bones (*informal*), skinny, undernourished

scream *verb* 1 = **cry**, bawl, holler (*informal*), screech, shriek, shrill, sing out, squeal, yell 2 = **be conspicuous**, clash, jar, shriek ♦ *noun* 3 = **cry**, howl, outcry, screech, shriek, wail, yell, yelp 4 *Informal* = **laugh**, card (*informal*), caution (*informal*), character (*informal*), comedian, comic, entertainer, hoot (*informal*), joker, riot (*slang*), sensation, wag, wit

screech *noun, verb* = **cry**, scream, shriek, squawk, squeal, yelp

screed *noun* = **passage**, speech

screen *noun* 1 = **cover**, awning, canopy, cloak, concealment, guard, hedge, mantle, partition, room divider, shade, shelter,

shield, shroud 2 = **mesh**, net ♦ *verb* 3
= **cover**, cloak, conceal, hide, mask, shade,
shroud, shut out, veil 4 = **protect**, defend,
guard, safeguard, shelter, shield 5 = **vet**, cull,
evaluate, examine, filter, gauge, grade,
process, scan, sieve, sift, sort 6 = **broadcast**,
present, put on, show

screw *verb* 1 = **turn**, tighten, twist, work in
2 *Informal* = **coerce**, bring pressure to bear
on, constrain, force, hold a knife to
(someone's) throat, oppress, pressurize, put
the screws on (*informal*), squeeze 3
Informal = **contort**, contract, crumple,
distort, pucker, wrinkle 4 *Informal, often
with* **out of** = **extract**, extract, wrest, wring

screw up *verb* 1 *Informal* = **bungle**, bodge
(*informal*), botch, make a hash of
(*informal*), make a mess of (*slang*), make a
nonsense of, mess up, mishandle,
mismanage, spoil 2 = **contort**, contract,
crumple, distort, knit, knot, pucker, wrinkle

screwy *adjective Informal* = **crazy**, batty
(*slang*), cracked (*slang*), crackers (*Brit.
slang*), crackpot (*informal*), dotty (*slang,
chiefly Brit.*), eccentric, loopy (*informal*),
nutty (*slang*), odd, oddball (*informal*),
off-the-wall (*slang*), out to lunch (*informal*),
queer (*informal*), round the bend (*Brit.
slang*), up the pole (*informal*), wacko *or*
whacko (*informal*), weird

scribble *verb* = **scrawl**, dash off, doodle, jot,
pen, scratch, write

scribe *noun* = **copyist**, amanuensis, clerk,
notary (*archaic*), secretary, writer

scrimmage *noun* = **fight**, brawl,
disturbance, fray, free-for-all (*informal*),
melee *or* mêlée, riot, row, scrap (*informal*),
scuffle, set-to (*informal*), shindig (*informal*),
shindy (*informal*), skirmish, struggle

scrimp *verb* = **economize**, be frugal, curtail,
limit, pinch, pinch pennies, reduce, save,
scrape, shorten, skimp, stint, straiten, tighten
one's belt

script *noun* 1 = **text**, book, copy, dialogue,
libretto, lines, manuscript, words 2
= **handwriting**, calligraphy, hand, letters,
longhand, penmanship, writing

Scripture *noun* = **The Bible**, Holy Bible,
Holy Scripture, Holy Writ, The Book of
Books, The Good Book, The Gospels, The
Scriptures, The Word, The Word of God

scroll *noun* = **roll**, parchment

Scrooge *noun* = **miser**, cheapskate
(*informal*), meanie *or* meany (*informal,
chiefly Brit.*), niggard, penny-pincher
(*informal*), skinflint, tightwad (*U.S. &
Canad. slang*)

scrounge *verb Informal* = **cadge**, beg, blag
(*slang*), bum (*informal*), forage for, freeload
(*slang*), hunt around (for), mooch (*slang*),
sponge (*informal*), touch (someone) for
(*slang*)

scrounger *adjective* = **cadger**, bum
(*informal*), freeloader (*slang*), parasite,
sponger (*informal*)

scrub *verb* 1 = **scour**, clean, cleanse, rub 2
Informal = **cancel**, abandon, abolish, call off,
delete, discontinue, do away with, drop,
forget about, give up

scrubby *adjective* = **stunted**, meagre,
scrawny, spindly, underdeveloped, undersized

scruff[1] *noun* = **nape**, scrag (*informal*)

scruff[2] *noun Informal* = **ragamuffin**, ragbag
(*informal*), scarecrow, sloven, tatterdemalion
(*rare*), tramp

scruffy *adjective* = **tatty**, disreputable,
grungy, ill-groomed, mangy, messy, ragged,
run-down, scrubby (*Brit. informal*), seedy,
shabby, sloppy (*informal*), slovenly, squalid,
tattered, ungroomed, unkempt, untidy
➤ **Antonyms**
chic, dapper, natty, neat, soigné *or* soignée,
spruce, tidy, well-dressed, well-groomed,
well-turned-out

scrumptious *adjective Informal*
= **delicious**, appetizing, delectable, exquisite,
inviting, luscious, magnificent, moreish
(*informal*), mouthwatering, succulent,
yummy (*slang*)

scrunch *verb* = **crumple**, crush, ruck up,
squash

scruple *noun* 1 = **misgiving**, caution,
compunction, difficulty, doubt, hesitation,
perplexity, qualm, reluctance, second
thoughts, squeamishness, twinge of
conscience, uneasiness ♦ *verb* 2 = **have
misgivings about**, balk at, be loath, be
reluctant, demur, doubt, falter, have qualms
about, hesitate, stick at, think twice about,
vacillate, waver

scrupulous *adjective* 1 = **moral**,
conscientious, honourable, principled,
upright 2 = **careful**, exact, fastidious,
meticulous, minute, nice, painstaking,
precise, punctilious, rigorous, strict
➤ **Antonyms**
≠**moral**: amoral, dishonest, uncaring,
unconscientious, unprincipled, unscrupulous,
without scruples ≠**careful**: careless, inexact,
reckless, slapdash, superficial

scrutinize *verb* = **examine**, analyse, dissect,
explore, go over with a fine-tooth comb,
inquire into, inspect, investigate, peruse,
pore over, probe, research, scan, search, sift,
study, work over

scrutiny *noun* = **examination**, analysis,
close study, exploration, inquiry, inspection,
investigation, once-over (*informal*), perusal,
search, sifting, study

scud *verb* = **fly**, blow, race, sail, shoot, skim, speed

scuffle *verb* 1 = **fight**, clash, come to blows, contend, exchange blows, grapple, jostle, struggle, tussle ♦ *noun* 2 = **fight**, barney (*informal*), brawl, commotion, disturbance, fray, ruck (*slang*), ruckus (*informal*), rumpus, scrap (*informal*), scrimmage, set-to (*informal*), shindig (*informal*), shindy (*informal*), skirmish, tussle

sculpture *verb* = **sculpt**, carve, chisel, cut, fashion, form, hew, model, mould, shape

scum *noun* 1 = **impurities**, algae, crust, dross, film, froth, offscourings 2 = **rabble**, canaille, dregs of society, dross, lowest of the low, ragtag and bobtail, riffraff, rubbish, trash (*chiefly U.S. & Canad.*)

scupper *verb Brit. slang* = **destroy**, defeat, demolish, overthrow, overwhelm, put paid to, ruin, torpedo, undo, wreck

scurrility *noun* = **slanderousness**, abusiveness, invective, obloquy, offensiveness, scurrilousness, vituperation

scurrilous *adjective* = **slanderous**, abusive, coarse, defamatory, foul, gross, indecent, infamous, insulting, low, obscene, offensive, scandalous, vituperative, vulgar
➤ **Antonyms**
decent, polite, proper, refined, respectful

scurry *verb* 1 = **hurry**, beetle, dart, dash, fly, race, scamper, scoot, scud, scuttle, sprint, whisk ♦ *noun* 2 = **flurry**, bustle, scampering, whirl
➤ **Antonyms**
verb ≠**hurry**: amble, mooch (*slang*), mosey (*informal*), saunter, stroll, toddle, wander

scurvy *adjective Old-fashioned* = **contemptible**, bad, base, despicable, dishonourable, ignoble, low, low-down (*informal*), mean, rotten, shabby, vile

scuttle *verb* = **run**, bustle, hare (*Brit. informal*), hasten, hurry, rush, scamper, scoot, scramble, scud, scurry

sea *noun* 1 = **ocean**, main, the briny (*informal*), the deep, the drink (*informal*), the waves 2 = **expanse**, abundance, mass, multitude, plethora, profusion, sheet, vast number 3 **at sea** = **bewildered**, adrift, astray, at a loss, baffled, confused, disoriented, lost, mystified, puzzled, upset

seafaring *adjective* = **nautical**, marine, maritime, naval, oceanic

seal *noun* 1 = **authentication**, assurance, attestation, confirmation, imprimatur, insignia, notification, ratification, stamp ♦ *verb* 2 = **close**, bung, cork, enclose, fasten, make airtight, plug, secure, shut, stop, stopper, stop up, waterproof 3 = **authenticate**, assure, attest, confirm, establish, ratify, stamp, validate 4 = **settle**,

clinch, conclude, consummate, finalize, shake hands on (*informal*) 5 **seal off** = **isolate**, board up, fence off, put out of bounds, quarantine, segregate

seam *noun* 1 = **joint**, closure, suture (*Surgery*) 2 = **layer**, lode, stratum, vein 3 = **ridge**, furrow, line, scar, wrinkle

seamy *adjective* = **sordid**, corrupt, dark, degraded, disreputable, low, nasty, squalid, unpleasant, unwholesome

sear *verb* 1 = **scorch**, brand, burn, cauterize, desiccate, dry up *or* out, sizzle 2 = **wither**, blight, shrivel, wilt

search *verb* 1 = **look**, cast around, check, comb, examine, explore, forage, hunt, inquire, inspect, investigate, look high and low, probe, ransack, scour, scrutinize, seek, sift, turn inside out, turn upside down ♦ *noun* 2 = **look**, examination, exploration, going-over (*informal*), hunt, inquiry, inspection, investigation, pursuit, quest, scrutiny

searching *adjective* = **keen**, close, intent, minute, penetrating, piercing, probing, quizzical, severe, sharp, thorough
➤ **Antonyms**
cursory, perfunctory, peripheral, sketchy, superficial

season *noun* 1 = **period**, division, interval, spell, term, time, time of year ♦ *verb* 2 = **flavour**, colour, enliven, lace, pep up, salt, salt and pepper, spice 3 = **make experienced**, acclimatize, accustom, habituate, harden, mature, prepare, toughen, train

seasonable *adjective* = **appropriate**, convenient, fit, opportune, providential, suitable, timely, welcome, well-timed

seasoned *adjective* = **experienced**, hardened, long-serving, mature, old, practised, time-served, veteran, weathered, well-versed
➤ **Antonyms**
callow, green, inexperienced, new, novice, unpractised, unseasoned, unskilled

seasoning *noun* = **flavouring**, condiment, dressing, relish, salt and pepper, sauce, spice

seat *noun* 1 = **chair**, bench, pew, settle, stall, stool, throne 2 = **base**, bed, bottom, cause, footing, foundation, ground, groundwork 3 = **centre**, axis, capital, headquarters, heart, hub, location, place, site, situation, source, station 4 = **mansion**, abode, ancestral hall, house, residence 5 = **membership**, chair, constituency, incumbency, place ♦ *verb* 6 = **sit**, deposit, fix, install, locate, place, set, settle 7 = **hold**, accommodate, cater for, contain, have room *or* capacity for, sit, take

seating *noun* = **accommodation**, chairs, places, room, seats

secede verb = **withdraw**, break with, leave, pull out, quit, resign, retire, separate, split from

secession noun = **withdrawal**, apostasy, break, defection, disaffiliation, seceding, split

secluded adjective = **private**, cloistered, cut off, isolated, lonely, off the beaten track, out-of-the-way, reclusive, remote, retired, sequestered, sheltered, solitary, tucked away, unfrequented
➤ **Antonyms**
accessible, busy, frequented, open, public

seclusion noun = **privacy**, concealment, hiding, isolation, retirement, retreat, shelter, solitude

second[1] adjective 1 = **next**, following, subsequent, succeeding 2 = **additional**, alternative, extra, further, other, repeated 3 = **inferior**, lesser, lower, secondary, subordinate, supporting ◆ noun 4 = **supporter**, assistant, backer, helper ◆ verb 5 = **support**, advance, aid, approve, assist, back, commend, encourage, endorse, forward, further, give moral support to, go along with, help, promote

second[2] noun = **moment**, bat of an eye (informal), flash, instant, jiffy (informal), minute, sec (informal), split second, tick (Brit. informal), trice

secondary adjective 1 = **subordinate**, inferior, lesser, lower, minor, second-rate, unimportant 2 = **resultant**, consequential, contingent, derivative, derived, indirect, resulting, second-hand 3 = **backup**, alternate, auxiliary, extra, fall-back, relief, reserve, second, subsidiary, supporting
➤ **Antonyms**
≠subordinate: cardinal, chief, head, larger, main, major, more important, prime, principal, superior ≠resultant: original, preceding ≠backup: only, primary

second childhood noun = **senility**, Alzheimer's disease, dotage

second-class adjective = **inferior**, déclassé, indifferent, mediocre, no great shakes (informal), outclassed, second-best, second-rate, undistinguished, uninspiring

second-hand adjective 1 = **used**, handed down, hand-me-down (informal), nearly new, reach-me-down (informal) ◆ adverb 2 = **indirectly**, at second-hand

second in command noun = **deputy**, depute (Scot.), number two, right-hand man, successor designate

secondly adverb = **next**, in the second place, second

second-rate adjective = **inferior**, bush-league (Austral. & N.Z. informal), cheap, cheap and nasty (informal), commonplace, dime-a-dozen (informal),

low-grade, low-quality, mediocre, no great shakes (informal), not much cop (Brit. slang), pants (slang), poor, rubbishy, shoddy, substandard, tacky (informal), tawdry, two-bit (U.S. & Canad. slang)
➤ **Antonyms**
a cut above (informal), choice, de luxe, excellent, fine, first-class, first-rate, good quality, high-class, quality, superior

secrecy noun 1 = **mystery**, cloak and dagger, concealment, confidentiality, privacy, retirement, seclusion, silence, solitude, surreptitiousness 2 = **secretiveness**, clandestineness, covertness, furtiveness, stealth

secret adjective 1 = **concealed**, behind someone's back, camouflaged, cloak-and-dagger, close, closet (informal), confidential, conspiratorial, covered, covert, disguised, furtive, hidden, hole-and-corner (informal), hush-hush (informal), reticent, shrouded, undercover, underground, under wraps, undisclosed, unknown, unpublished, unrevealed, unseen 2 = **stealthy**, close, deep, discreet, reticent, secretive, sly, underhand 3 = **mysterious**, abstruse, arcane, cabbalistic, clandestine, classified, cryptic, esoteric, occult, recondite ◆ noun 4 = **mystery**, code, confidence, enigma, key, skeleton in the cupboard 5 **in secret** = **secretly**, behind closed doors, by stealth, in camera, incognito, slyly, surreptitiously
➤ **Antonyms**
adjective ≠concealed, stealthy: apparent, candid, disclosed, frank, manifest, obvious, open, overt, public, unconcealed, visible ≠mysterious: straightforward, well-known

secret agent noun = **spy**, nark (Brit., Austral., & N.Z. slang), undercover agent

secrete[1] verb = **give off**, emanate, emit, extrude, exude

secrete[2] verb = **hide**, bury, cache, conceal, cover, disguise, harbour, screen, secure, stash (informal), stash away (informal), stow, veil
➤ **Antonyms**
bare, display, exhibit, expose to view, leave in the open, reveal, show, uncover, unmask, unveil

secretion noun = **discharge**, emission, excretion, exudation

secretive adjective = **reticent**, cagey (informal), close, cryptic, deep, enigmatic, playing one's cards close to one's chest, reserved, tight-lipped, uncommunicative, unforthcoming, withdrawn
➤ **Antonyms**
candid, communicative, expansive, forthcoming, frank, open, unreserved

secretly adverb = **in secret**, behind closed

doors, behind (someone's) back, clandestinely, confidentially, covertly, furtively, in camera, in confidence, on the fly (*slang, chiefly Brit.*), on the q.t. (*informal*), on the sly, privately, quietly, stealthily, surreptitiously, unobserved

sect *noun* = **group**, camp, denomination, division, faction, party, schism, school, school of thought, splinter group, wing

sectarian *adjective* **1** = **narrow-minded**, bigoted, clannish, cliquish, doctrinaire, dogmatic, exclusive, factional, fanatic, fanatical, hidebound, insular, limited, parochial, partisan, rigid ♦ *noun* **2** = **bigot**, adherent, disciple, dogmatist, extremist, fanatic, partisan, zealot
➤ **Antonyms**
adjective ≠**narrow-minded**: broad-minded, catholic, free-thinking, liberal, non-sectarian, open-minded, tolerant, unbigoted, unprejudiced

section *noun* **1** = **part**, component, cross section, division, fraction, fragment, instalment, passage, piece, portion, sample, segment, slice, subdivision **2** = **district**, area, department, region, sector, zone

sectional *adjective* = **regional**, divided, exclusive, factional, local, localized, partial, separate, separatist

sector *noun* = **part**, area, category, district, division, quarter, region, stratum, subdivision, zone

secular *adjective* = **worldly**, civil, earthly, laic, laical, lay, nonspiritual, profane, state, temporal
➤ **Antonyms**
divine, holy, religious, sacred, spiritual, theological

secure *adjective* **1** = **safe**, immune, impregnable, in safe hands, out of harm's way, protected, sheltered, shielded, unassailable, undamaged, unharmed **2** = **sure**, assured, certain, confident, easy, reassured **3** = **fixed**, dependable, fast, fastened, firm, fortified, immovable, stable, steady, tight **4** = **reliable**, definite, in the bag (*informal*), solid, tried and true ♦ *verb* **5** = **obtain**, acquire, come by, gain, get, get hold of, land (*informal*), make sure of, pick up, procure, score (*slang*), win possession of **6** = **fasten**, attach, batten down, bolt, chain, fix, lash, lock, lock up, make fast, moor, padlock, tie up **7** = **guarantee**, assure, ensure, insure
➤ **Antonyms**
adjective ≠**safe**: endangered, unprotected, unsafe ≠**sure**: ill-at-ease, insecure, unassured, uncertain, uneasy, unsure ≠**fixed**: insecure, loose, not fastened, precarious, unfixed, unsafe, unsound ♦ *verb* ≠**obtain**: give up, let (something) slip

through (one's) fingers, lose ≠**fasten**: loose, unloose, untie ≠**guarantee**: endanger, imperil, leave unguaranteed

security *noun* **1** = **precautions**, defence, guards, protection, safeguards, safety measures, surveillance **2** = **safety**, asylum, care, cover, custody, immunity, preservation, protection, refuge, retreat, safekeeping, sanctuary **3** = **assurance**, certainty, confidence, conviction, ease of mind, freedom from doubt, positiveness, reliance, sureness **4** = **pledge**, collateral, gage, guarantee, hostage, insurance, pawn, surety
➤ **Antonyms**
≠**safety**: exposure, jeopardy, vulnerability ≠**assurance**: insecurity, uncertainty

sedate *adjective* **1** = **calm**, collected, composed, cool, decorous, dignified, imperturbable, placid, proper, quiet, seemly, serene, staid, tranquil, unflappable (*informal*), unruffled **2** = **unhurried**, deliberate, slow-moving
➤ **Antonyms**
≠**calm**: agitated, antsy (*informal*), excitable, excited, flighty, impassioned, jumpy, nervous, undignified, unsteady, wild

sedative *adjective* **1** = **calming**, allaying, anodyne, calmative, lenitive, relaxing, sleep-inducing, soothing, soporific, tranquillizing ♦ *noun* **2** = **tranquillizer**, anodyne, calmative, downer *or* down (*slang*), narcotic, opiate, sleeping pill

sedentary *adjective* = **inactive**, desk, desk-bound, motionless, seated, sitting, torpid
➤ **Antonyms**
active, mobile, motile, moving, on the go (*informal*)

sediment *noun* = **dregs**, deposit, grounds, lees, precipitate, residue, settlings

sedition *noun* = **rabble-rousing**, agitation, disloyalty, incitement to riot, subversion, treason

seditious *adjective* = **revolutionary**, disloyal, dissident, insubordinate, mutinous, rebellious, refractory, subversive, treasonable

seduce *verb* **1** = **corrupt**, betray, debauch, deflower, deprave, dishonour, ruin (*archaic*) **2** = **tempt**, allure, attract, beguile, deceive, decoy, ensnare, entice, inveigle, lead astray, lure, mislead

seduction *noun* **1** = **corruption**, defloration, ruin (*archaic*) **2** = **temptation**, allure, enticement, lure, snare

seductive *adjective* = **alluring**, attractive, beguiling, bewitching, captivating, come-hither (*informal*), come-to-bed (*informal*), enticing, flirtatious, inviting, irresistible, provocative, ravishing, sexy (*informal*), siren, specious, tempting

seductress *noun* = temptress, Circe, enchantress, *femme fatale,* Lorelei, siren, vamp *(informal)*

sedulous *adjective* = diligent, assiduous, conscientious, industrious, laborious, painstaking

see [1] *verb* **1** = perceive, behold, catch a glimpse of, catch sight of, check, check out *(informal)*, clock *(Brit. slang)*, descry, discern, distinguish, espy, eye, eyeball *(slang)*, get a load of *(slang)*, glimpse, identify, lay *or* clap eyes on *(informal)*, look, make out, mark, note, notice, observe, recognize, regard, sight, spot, take a dekko at *(Brit. slang)*, view, witness **2** = understand, appreciate, catch on *(informal)*, comprehend, fathom, feel, follow, get, get the drift of, get the hang of *(informal)*, grasp, know, make out, realize, take in **3** = foresee, anticipate, divine, envisage, foretell, imagine, picture, visualize **4** = find out, ascertain, determine, discover, investigate, learn, make inquiries, refer to **5** = make sure, ensure, guarantee, make certain, mind, see to it, take care **6** = consider, decide, deliberate, give some thought to, judge, make up one's mind, mull over, reflect, think over **7** = visit, confer with, consult, encounter, interview, meet, receive, run into, speak to **8** = go out with, consort *or* associate with, court, date *(informal, chiefly U.S.)*, go steady with *(informal)*, keep company with, walk out with *(obsolete)* **9** = accompany, attend, escort, lead, show, usher, walk

see [2] *noun* = diocese, bishopric

see about *verb* **1** = take care of, attend to, consider, deal with, give some thought to, look after, see to **2** = investigate, look into, make inquiries, research

seed *noun* **1** = grain, egg, egg cell, embryo, germ, kernel, ovule, ovum, pip, spore **2** = origin, beginning, germ, inkling, nucleus, source, start, suspicion **3** *chiefly Biblical* = offspring, children, descendants, heirs, issue, progeny, race, scions, spawn, successors **4 go** *or* **run to seed** = decline, decay, degenerate, deteriorate, go downhill *(informal)*, go to pieces, go to pot, go to rack and ruin, go to waste, let oneself go

seedy *adjective* **1** = shabby, crummy *(slang)*, decaying, dilapidated, down at heel, faded, grotty *(slang)*, grubby, mangy, manky *(Scot. dialect)*, old, run-down, scruffy, sleazy, slovenly, squalid, tatty, unkempt, worn **2** *Informal* = unwell, ailing, ill, off colour, out of sorts, peely-wally *(Scot.)*, poorly *(informal)*, sickly, under the weather *(informal)*

➤ **Antonyms**

≠**shabby:** classy, elegant, fashionable,

high-toned, posh *(informal, chiefly Brit.)*, ritzy *(slang)*, smart, swanky *(informal)*, swish *(informal, chiefly Brit.)*, top-drawer, up-market

seeing *conjunction* = since, as, inasmuch as, in view of the fact that

seek *verb* **1** = look for, be after, follow, go gunning for, go in pursuit of, go in quest of, go in search of, hunt, inquire, pursue, search for **2** = try, aim, aspire to, attempt, endeavour, essay, have a go *(informal)*, strive

seem *verb* = appear, assume, give the impression, have the *or* every appearance of, look, look as if, look like, look to be, pretend, sound like, strike one as being

seeming *adjective* = apparent, appearing, illusory, ostensible, outward, quasi-, specious, surface

seemingly *adverb* = apparently, as far as anyone could tell, on the face of it, on the surface, ostensibly, outwardly, to all appearances, to all intents and purposes

seemly *adjective* = fitting, appropriate, becoming, befitting, *comme il faut,* decent, decorous, fit, in good taste, meet *(archaic)*, nice, proper, suitable, the done thing

➤ **Antonyms**

improper, inappropriate, indecorous, in poor taste, out of keeping, out of place, unbecoming, unbefitting, unseemly, unsuitable

seep *verb* = ooze, bleed, exude, leach, leak, percolate, permeate, soak, trickle, well

seepage *noun* = leakage, exudation, leak, oozing, percolation

seer *noun* = prophet, augur, predictor, sibyl, soothsayer

seesaw *verb* = alternate, fluctuate, go from one extreme to the other, oscillate, pitch, swing, teeter

seethe *verb* **1** = be furious, be in a state *(informal)*, be incandescent, be incensed, be livid, be pissed (off) *(taboo slang)*, foam at the mouth, fume, get hot under the collar *(informal)*, go ballistic *(slang, chiefly U.S.)*, rage, see red *(informal)*, simmer, storm **2** = boil, bubble, churn, ferment, fizz, foam, froth

see-through *adjective* = transparent, diaphanous, filmy, fine, flimsy, gauzy, gossamer, sheer, thin, translucent

see through *verb* **1** = be undeceived by, be wise to *(informal)*, fathom, get to the bottom of, have (someone's) number *(informal)*, not fall for, penetrate, read (someone) like a book **2 see (something) through** = persevere (with), keep at, persist, see out, stay to the bitter end, stick out *(informal)* **3 see (someone) through**

= **help out**, stick by, support

see to verb = **take care of**, arrange, attend to, be responsible for, do, look after, manage, organize, sort out, take charge of

segment noun = **section**, bit, compartment, division, part, piece, portion, slice, wedge

segregate verb = **set apart**, discriminate against, dissociate, isolate, separate, single out
➤ Antonyms
amalgamate, desegregate, join together, mix, unify, unite

segregation noun = **separation**, apartheid, discrimination, isolation

seize verb 1 = **grab**, catch up, clutch, fasten, grasp, grip, lay hands on, snatch, take 2 = **confiscate**, appropriate, commandeer, impound, take possession of 3 = **take by storm**, abduct, annex, hijack 4 = **capture**, apprehend, arrest, catch, collar (informal), get, grasp, nab (informal), nail (informal), take captive
➤ Antonyms
≠**grab**: let go, loose ≠**confiscate**: hand back, relinquish ≠**capture**: free, release, set free, turn loose

seizure noun 1 = **attack**, convulsion, fit, paroxysm, spasm 2 = **capture**, abduction, apprehension, arrest 3 = **taking**, annexation, commandeering, confiscation, grabbing

seldom adverb = **rarely**, hardly ever, infrequently, not often, occasionally, once in a blue moon (informal), scarcely ever
➤ Antonyms
again and again, frequently, many a time, much, often, over and over again, time after time, time and again

select verb 1 = **choose**, cherry-pick, opt for, pick, prefer, single out, sort out ♦ adjective 2 = **choice**, excellent, first-class, first-rate, hand-picked, picked, prime, rare, selected, special, superior, top-notch (informal) 3 = **exclusive**, cliquish, elite, limited, privileged
➤ Antonyms
verb ≠**choose**: eliminate, reject, turn down ♦ adjective ≠**choice**: cheap, indifferent, inferior, ordinary, run-of-the-mill, second-rate, shoddy, substandard, unremarkable ≠**exclusive**: indiscriminate

selection noun 1 = **choice**, choosing, option, pick, preference 2 = **range**, anthology, assortment, choice, collection, line-up, medley, miscellany, mixed bag (informal), pick 'n' mix, potpourri, variety

selective adjective = **particular**, careful, discerning, discriminating, discriminatory, eclectic
➤ Antonyms
all-embracing, careless, desultory,

indiscriminate, unselective

self-assurance noun = **confidence**, assertiveness, nerve, poise, positiveness, self-confidence, self-possession

self-centred adjective = **selfish**, egotistic, inward looking, narcissistic, self-absorbed, self-seeking, wrapped up in oneself

self-confidence noun = **self-assurance**, aplomb, confidence, high morale, nerve, poise, self-reliance, self-respect

self-confident adjective = **self-assured**, assured, confident, fearless, poised, secure, self-reliant, sure of oneself

self-conscious adjective = **embarrassed**, affected, awkward, bashful, diffident, ill at ease, insecure, like a fish out of water, nervous, out of countenance, shamefaced, sheepish, uncomfortable

self-control noun = **willpower**, calmness, cool, coolness, restraint, self-discipline, self-mastery, self-restraint, strength of mind or will

self-denial noun = **abstemiousness**, asceticism, renunciation, self-abnegation, selflessness, self-sacrifice, unselfishness

self-esteem noun = **self-respect**, amour-propre, confidence, faith in oneself, pride, self-assurance, self-regard, vanity

self-evident adjective = **obvious**, axiomatic, clear, cut-and-dried (informal), incontrovertible, inescapable, manifestly or patently true, undeniable, written all over (something)

self-government noun = **autonomy**, democracy, devolution, home rule, independence, self-determination, self-rule, sovereignty

self-important adjective = **conceited**, arrogant, bigheaded, bumptious, cocky, full of oneself, overbearing, pompous, presumptuous, pushy (informal), strutting, swaggering, swollen-headed

self-indulgence noun = **intemperance**, dissipation, excess, extravagance, incontinence, self-gratification, sensualism

selfish adjective = **self-centred**, egoistic, egoistical, egotistic, egotistical, greedy, looking out for number one (informal), mean, mercenary, narrow, self-interested, self-seeking, ungenerous
➤ Antonyms
altruistic, benevolent, considerate, generous, magnanimous, philanthropic, self-denying, selfless, self-sacrificing, ungrudging, unselfish

selfless adjective = **unselfish**, altruistic, generous, magnanimous, self-denying, self-sacrificing, ungrudging

self-possessed adjective = **self-assured**, collected, confident, cool, cool as a cucumber (*informal*), poised, sure of oneself, together (*slang*), unruffled

self-possession *noun* = **self-assurance**, aplomb, composure, confidence, cool (*slang*), poise, sang-froid, self-command

self-reliant *adjective* = **Independent**, able to stand on one's own two feet (*informal*), capable, self-sufficient, self-supporting
➤ **Antonyms**
dependent, helpless, reliant, relying on

self-respect *noun* = **pride**, amour-propre, dignity, faith in oneself, morale, one's own image, self-esteem

self-restraint *noun* = **self-control**, abstemiousness, forbearance, patience, self-command, self-discipline, willpower

self-righteous *adjective* = **sanctimonious**, complacent, goody-goody (*informal*), holier-than-thou, hypocritical, pharisaic, pi (*Brit. slang*), pietistic, pious, priggish, self-satisfied, smug, superior, too good to be true

self-sacrifice *noun* = **selflessness**, altruism, generosity, self-abnegation, self-denial

self-satisfaction *noun* = **smugness**, complacency, contentment, ease of mind, flush of success, glow of achievement, pride, self-approbation, self-approval

self-satisfied *adjective* = **smug**, complacent, flushed with success, like a cat that has swallowed the canary, pleased with oneself, proud of oneself, puffed up, self-congratulatory, too big for one's boots *or* breeches, well-pleased

self-seeking *adjective* = **selfish**, acquisitive, calculating, careerist, fortune-hunting, gold-digging, looking out for number one (*informal*), mercenary, on the make (*slang*), opportunistic, out for what one can get, self-interested, self-serving

self-styled *adjective* = **so-called**, professed, quasi-, self-appointed, *soi-disant,* would-be

self-willed *adjective* = **stubborn**, headstrong, intractable, obstinate, opinionated, pig-headed, refractory, stiff-necked, stubborn as a mule, ungovernable, wilful

sell *verb* 1 = **trade**, barter, dispose of, exchange, put up for sale 2 = **deal in**, be in the business of, handle, hawk, market, merchandise, peddle, retail, stock, trade in, traffic in, vend 3 = **give up**, betray, deliver up, sell down the river (*informal*), sell out (*informal*), surrender 4 = **promote**, gain acceptance for, put across
➤ **Antonyms**
≠trade, deal in: acquire, buy, get, invest in, obtain, pay for, procure, purchase, shop for

seller *noun* = **dealer**, agent, merchant,

purveyor, rep, representative, retailer, salesman *or* saleswoman, shopkeeper, supplier, tradesman, traveller, vendor

selling *noun* 1 = **dealing**, business, commercial transactions, trading, traffic 2 = **marketing**, boosterism, merchandising, promotion, salesmanship

sell out *verb* 1 = **dispose of**, be out of stock of, get rid of, run out of, sell up 2 *Informal* = **betray**, break faith with, double-cross (*informal*), fail, give away, play false, rat on (*informal*), sell down the river (*informal*), stab in the back

semblance *noun* = **appearance**, air, aspect, bearing, façade, figure, form, front, guise, image, likeness, mask, mien, pretence, resemblance, show, similarity, veneer

semen *noun* = **sperm**, come *or* cum (*taboo*), seed (*archaic or dialect*), seminal fluid, spermatic fluid, spunk (*taboo*)

seminal *adjective* = **influential**, creative, formative, ground-breaking, imaginative, important, innovative, original, productive

seminary *noun* = **college**, academy, high school, institute, institution, school

send *verb* 1 = **dispatch**, communicate, consign, convey, direct, forward, remit, transmit 2 = **propel**, cast, deliver, fire, fling, hurl, let fly, shoot 3 *with* **off, out,** *etc.* = **emit**, broadcast, discharge, exude, give off, radiate 4 *Old-fashioned, slang* = **enrapture**, charm, delight, electrify, enthrall, excite, intoxicate, move, please, ravish, stir, thrill, titillate, turn (someone) on (*slang*)

send for *verb* = **summon**, call for, demand, order, request

sendoff *noun* = **farewell**, departure, going-away party, leave-taking, start, valediction

send-up *noun* = **imitation**, mockery, parody, satire, skit, spoof (*informal*), take-off (*informal*)

send up *verb* = **imitate**, burlesque, lampoon, make fun of, mimic, mock, parody, satirize, spoof (*informal*), take off (*informal*), take the mickey out of (*informal*), take the piss out of (*taboo slang*)

senile *adjective* = **doddering**, decrepit, doting, failing, gaga (*informal*), imbecile, in one's dotage, in one's second childhood

senility *noun* = **dotage**, Alzheimer's disease, caducity, decrepitude, infirmity, loss of one's faculties, second childhood, senescence, senile dementia

senior *adjective* 1 = **higher ranking**, superior 2 = **older**, elder, major (*Brit.*)
➤ **Antonyms**
≠higher ranking: inferior, junior, lesser,

lower, minor, subordinate ≠**older**: junior, younger

senior citizen noun = **pensioner**, elder, O.A.P., old age pensioner, old or elderly person, retired person

seniority noun = **superiority**, eldership, longer service, precedence, priority, rank

sensation noun 1 = **feeling**, awareness, consciousness, impression, perception, sense, tingle 2 = **excitement**, agitation, commotion, furore, scandal, stir, surprise, thrill, vibes (slang) 3 = **hit** (informal), crowd puller (informal), wow (slang, chiefly U.S.)

sensational adjective 1 = **exciting**, amazing, astounding, breathtaking, dramatic, electrifying, hair-raising, horrifying, lurid, melodramatic, revealing, scandalous, sensationalistic, shock-horror (facetious), shocking, spectacular, staggering, startling, thrilling 2 Informal = **excellent**, awesome (slang), boffo (slang), brill (informal), brilliant, chillin' (U.S. slang), cracking (Brit. informal), crucial (slang), def (slang), exceptional, fabulous (informal), first class, impressive, marvellous, mean (slang), mega (slang), mind-blowing (informal), out of this world (informal), smashing (informal), sovereign, superb
➤ Antonyms
≠**exciting**: boring, dull, humdrum, understated, undramatic, unexaggerated, unexciting ≠**excellent**: commonplace, mediocre, no great shakes (informal), ordinary, prosaic, run-of-the-mill, vanilla (informal)

sense noun 1 = **faculty**, feeling, sensation, sensibility 2 = **feeling**, appreciation, atmosphere, aura, awareness, consciousness, impression, intuition, perception, premonition, presentiment, sentiment 3 sometimes plural = **intelligence**, brains (informal), clear-headedness, cleverness, common sense, discernment, discrimination, gumption (Brit. informal), judgment, mother wit, nous (Brit. slang), quickness, reason, sagacity, sanity, sharpness, smarts (slang, chiefly U.S.), tact, understanding, wisdom, wit(s) 4 = **point**, advantage, good, logic, purpose, reason, use, value, worth 5 = **meaning**, definition, denotation, drift, gist, implication, import, interpretation, message, nuance, purport, significance, signification, substance ◆ verb 6 = **perceive**, appreciate, apprehend, be aware of, discern, divine, feel, get the impression, grasp, have a (funny) feeling (informal), have a hunch, just know, notice, observe, pick up, realize, suspect, understand
➤ Antonyms
noun ≠**intelligence**: folly, foolishness, idiocy, nonsense, silliness, stupidity ◆ verb

≠**perceive**: be unaware of, fail to grasp or notice, miss, misunderstand, overlook

senseless adjective 1 = **stupid**, absurd, asinine, crazy, daft (informal), dumb-ass (slang), fatuous, foolish, halfwitted, idiotic, illogical, imbecilic, inane, incongruous, inconsistent, irrational, ludicrous, mad, meaningless, mindless, moronic, nonsensical, pointless, ridiculous, silly, simple, unintelligent, unreasonable, unwise, without rhyme or reason 2 = **unconscious**, anaesthetized, cold, deadened, insensate, insensible, numb, numbed, out, out cold, stunned, unfeeling
➤ Antonyms
≠**stupid**: intelligent, meaningful, rational, reasonable, sensible, useful, valid, wise, worthwhile ≠**unconscious**: conscious, feeling, sensible

sensibility noun 1 = **awareness**, appreciation, delicacy, discernment, insight, intuition, perceptiveness, taste 2 often plural = **feelings**, emotions, moral sense, sentiments, susceptibilities 3 = **sensitivity**, responsiveness, sensitiveness, susceptibility
➤ Antonyms
≠**awareness**: insensibility, lack of awareness, unconsciousness, unperceptiveness ≠**sensitivity**: deadness, insensibility, insensitivity, numbness, unresponsiveness

sensible adjective 1 = **wise**, canny, discreet, discriminating, down-to-earth, far-sighted, intelligent, judicious, matter-of-fact, practical, prudent, rational, realistic, reasonable, sagacious, sage, sane, shrewd, sober, sound, well-reasoned, well-thought-out 2 = **perceptible**, appreciable, considerable, discernable, noticeable, palpable, significant, tangible, visible 3 Literary, usually with of = **aware**, acquainted with, alive to, conscious, convinced, mindful, observant, sensitive to, understanding
➤ Antonyms
≠**wise**: daft (informal), dumb-ass (slang), foolish, idiotic, ignorant, injudicious, irrational, senseless, silly, stupid, unreasonable, unwise ≠**aware**: blind, ignorant, insensible, insensitive, unaware, unmindful

sensitive adjective 1 = **easily hurt**, delicate, tender 2 = **susceptible**, delicate, easily affected, impressionable, reactive, responsive, sentient, touchy-feely (informal) 3 = **touchy**, easily offended, easily upset, irritable, temperamental, thin-skinned 4 = **precise**, acute, fine, keen, perceptive, responsive
➤ Antonyms
≠**easily hurt**: insensitive, tough ≠**susceptible, touchy**: callous, hard,

hardened, insensitive, thick-skinned, tough, uncaring, unfeeling ≠**precise**: approximate, imprecise, inexact, unperceptive

sensitivity *noun* = **sensitiveness**, delicacy, reactiveness, reactivity, receptiveness, responsiveness, susceptibility

sensual *adjective* **1** = **physical**, animal, bodily, carnal, epicurean, fleshly, luxurious, voluptuous **2** = **erotic**, lascivious, lecherous, lewd, libldinous, licentious, lustful, randy (*informal, chiefly Brit.*), raunchy (*slang*), sexual, sexy (*informal*), steamy (*informal*), unchaste

sensuality *noun* = **eroticism**, animalism, carnality, lasciviousness, lecherousness, lewdness, libidinousness, licentiousness, prurience, salaciousness, sexiness (*informal*), voluptuousness

sensuous *adjective* = **pleasurable**, bacchanalian, epicurean, gratifying, hedonistic, lush, rich, sensory, sumptuous, sybaritic
➤ **Antonyms**
abstemious, ascetic, celibate, plain, self-denying, Spartan

sentence *noun* **1** = **punishment**, condemnation, decision, decree, judgment, order, pronouncement, ruling, verdict
◆ *verb* **2** = **condemn**, doom, mete out justice to, pass judgment on, penalize

sententious *adjective* = **pompous**, canting, judgmental, moralistic, ponderous, preachifying (*informal*), sanctimonious

sentient *adjective* = **feeling**, conscious, live, living, reactive, sensitive

sentiment *noun* **1** = **emotion**, sensibility, soft-heartedness, tender feeling, tenderness **2** *often plural* = **feeling**, attitude, belief, idea, judgment, opinion, persuasion, saying, thought, view, way of thinking **3** = **sentimentality**, emotionalism, mawkishness, overemotionalism, romanticism, slush (*informal*)

sentimental *adjective* = **romantic**, corny (*slang*), dewy-eyed, emotional, gushy (*informal*), icky (*informal*), impressionable, maudlin, mawkish, mushy (*informal*), nostalgic, overemotional, schmaltzy (*slang*), sloppy (*informal*), slushy (*informal*), soft-hearted, tearful, tear-jerking (*informal*), tender, touching, weepy (*informal*)
➤ **Antonyms**
commonsensical, dispassionate, down-to-earth, earthy, hard-headed, practical, realistic, undemonstrative, unemotional, unfeeling, unromantic, unsentimental

sentimentality *noun* = **romanticism**, bathos, corniness (*slang*), emotionalism, gush (*informal*), mawkishness, mush

(*informal*), nostalgia, pathos, play on the emotions, schmaltz (*slang*), sloppiness (*informal*), slush (*informal*), sob stuff (*informal*), tenderness

sentinel *noun* = **guard**, lookout, picket, sentry, watch, watchman

separable *adjective* = **distinguishable**, detachable, divisible

separate *verb* **1** = **divide**, break off, cleave, come apart, come away, come between, detach, disconnect, disentangle, disjoin, keep apart, remove, sever, split, sunder, uncouple **2** = **part**, bifurcate, break up, disunite, diverge, divorce, estrange, go different ways, part company, set at variance *or* at odds, split up **3** = **isolate**, discriminate between, put on one side, segregate, single out, sort out ◆ *adjective* **4** = **unconnected**, detached, disconnected, discrete, disjointed, divided, divorced, isolated, unattached **5** = **individual**, alone, apart, autonomous, distinct, independent, particular, single, solitary
➤ **Antonyms**
verb ≠**divide**, **part**, **isolate**: amalgamate, combine, connect, join, link, merge, mix, unite ◆ *adjective* ≠**unconnected**, **individual**: affiliated, alike, connected, interdependent, joined, similar, unified, united

separated *adjective* = **disconnected**, apart, broken up, disassociated, disunited, divided, living apart, parted, put asunder, separate, split up, sundered

separately *adverb* = **individually**, alone, apart, independently, one at a time, one by one, personally, severally, singly
➤ **Antonyms**
as a group, as one, collectively, in a body, in concert, in unison, jointly, together

separation *noun* **1** = **division**, break, detachment, disconnection, disengagement, disjunction, dissociation, disunion, gap, segregation, severance **2** = **split-up**, break-up, divorce, estrangement, farewell, leave-taking, parting, rift, split

septic *adjective* = **infected**, festering, poisoned, pussy, putrefactive, putrefying, putrid, suppurating, toxic

sepulchral *adjective* = **gloomy**, cheerless, dismal, funereal, grave, lugubrious, melancholy, morbid, mournful, sad, sombre

sepulchre *noun* = **tomb**, burial place, grave, mausoleum, sarcophagus, vault

sequel *noun* **1** = **follow-up**, continuation, development **2** = **consequence**, conclusion, end, issue, outcome, payoff (*informal*), result, upshot

sequence *noun* = **succession**, arrangement, chain, course, cycle, order, procession, progression, series

sequestered *adjective* = **secluded**, cloistered, isolated, lonely, out-of-the-way, private, quiet, remote, retired, unfrequented

seraphic *adjective* = **angelic**, beatific, blissful, celestial, divine, heavenly, holy, pure, sublime

serene *adjective* **1** = **calm**, composed, imperturbable, peaceful, placid, sedate, tranquil, undisturbed, unruffled, untroubled **2** = **clear**, bright, cloudless, fair, halcyon, unclouded
➤ **Antonyms**
≠**calm**: agitated, anxious, disturbed, excitable, flustered, perturbed, troubled, uptight (*informal*)

serenity *noun* **1** = **calmness**, calm, composure, peace, peacefulness, peace of mind, placidity, quietness, quietude, stillness, tranquillity **2** = **clearness**, brightness, fairness

serf *noun* = **vassal**, bondsman, liegeman, servant, slave, villein

series *noun* = **sequence**, arrangement, chain, course, line, order, progression, run, set, string, succession, train

serious *adjective* **1** = **grave**, acute, alarming, critical, dangerous, severe **2** = **important**, crucial, deep, difficult, far-reaching, fateful, grim, momentous, no laughing matter, of moment *or* consequence, pressing, significant, urgent, weighty, worrying **3** = **solemn**, grave, humourless, long-faced, pensive, sedate, sober, stern, thoughtful, unsmiling **4** = **sincere**, deliberate, determined, earnest, genuine, honest, in earnest, resolute, resolved
➤ **Antonyms**
≠**important**: insignificant, minor, slight, trivial, unimportant ≠**solemn**: carefree, flippant, frivolous, jolly, joyful, light-hearted, smiling ≠**sincere**: capricious, flighty, flippant, frivolous, insincere, uncommitted, undecided

seriously *adverb* **1** = **gravely**, acutely, badly, critically, dangerously, distressingly, grievously, severely, sorely **2** = **sincerely**, all joking aside, earnestly, gravely, in all conscience, in earnest, no joking (*informal*), solemnly, thoughtfully, with a straight face

seriousness *noun* **1** = **importance**, danger, gravity, moment, significance, urgency, weight **2** = **solemnity**, earnestness, gravitas, gravity, humourlessness, sedateness, sobriety, staidness, sternness

sermon *noun* **1** = **homily**, address, exhortation **2** *Disparaging* = **lecture**, dressing-down (*informal*), harangue, talking-to (*informal*)

serpentine *adjective* = **twisting**, coiling,

sinuous, snaking, snaky, tortuous, twisty, winding

serrated *adjective* = **notched**, sawlike, sawtoothed, serrate, toothed

serried *adjective Literary* = **massed**, assembled, close, compact, dense, phalanxed

servant *noun* = **attendant**, domestic, drudge, help, helper, lackey, liegeman, maid, menial, retainer, skivvy (*chiefly Brit.*), slave, varlet (*archaic*), vassal

serve *verb* **1** = **work for**, aid, assist, attend to, be in the service of, be of assistance, be of use, help, minister to, oblige, wait on **2** = **perform**, act, attend, complete, discharge, do, fulfil, go through, observe, officiate, pass **3** = **provide**, arrange, deal, deliver, dish up, distribute, handle, present, purvey, set out, supply **4** = **be adequate**, answer, answer the purpose, be acceptable, be good enough, content, do, do duty as, do the work of, fill the bill (*informal*), function as, satisfy, suffice, suit

service *noun* **1** = **help**, advantage, assistance, avail, benefit, ministrations, supply, use, usefulness, utility **2** = **work**, business, duty, employ, employment, labour, office **3** = **overhaul**, check, maintenance, servicing **4** = **ceremony**, function, observance, rite, worship ◆ *verb* **5** = **overhaul**, check, fine tune, go over, maintain, recondition, repair, tune (up)

serviceable *adjective* = **useful**, advantageous, beneficial, convenient, dependable, durable, efficient, functional, hard-wearing, helpful, operative, practical, profitable, usable, utilitarian
➤ **Antonyms**
impractical, inefficient, unserviceable, unusable, useless, worn-out

servile *adjective* = **subservient**, abject, base, bootlicking (*informal*), craven, cringing, fawning, grovelling, humble, low, mean, menial, obsequious, slavish, submissive, sycophantic, toadying, toadyish, unctuous

servility *noun* = **subservience**, abjection, baseness, bootlicking (*informal*), fawning, grovelling, meanness, obsequiousness, self-abasement, slavishness, submissiveness, sycophancy, toadyism, unctuousness

serving *noun* = **portion**, helping, plateful

servitude *noun Formal* = **slavery**, bondage, bonds, chains, enslavement, obedience, serfdom, subjugation, thraldom, thrall

session *noun* = **meeting**, assembly, conference, congress, discussion, get-together (*informal*), hearing, period, seminar, sitting, term

set[1] *verb* **1** = **put**, aim, apply, deposit, direct, embed, fasten, fix, install, lay, locate, lodge, mount, park (*informal*), place, plant, plonk, plump, position, rest, seat, situate, station, stick, turn **2 = prepare**, arrange, lay, make ready, spread **3 = harden**, cake, condense, congeal, crystallize, gelatinize, jell, solidify, stiffen, thicken **4 = adjust**, coordinate, rectify, regulate, synchronize **5 = arrange**, agree upon, allocate, appoint, conclude, decide (upon), designate, determine, establish, fix, fix up, name, ordain, regulate, resolve, schedule, settle, specify **6 = assign**, allot, decree, impose, lay down, ordain, prescribe, specify **7 = go down**, decline, dip, disappear, sink, subside, vanish ♦ *noun* **8 = position**, attitude, bearing, carriage, fit, hang, posture, turn **9 = scenery**, *mise-en-scène*, scene, setting, stage set, stage setting ♦ *adjective* **10 = fixed**, agreed, appointed, arranged, customary, decided, definite, established, firm, prearranged, predetermined, prescribed, regular, scheduled, settled, usual **11 = inflexible**, entrenched, firm, hard and fast, hardened, hidebound, immovable, rigid, strict, stubborn **12 = conventional**, artificial, formal, hackneyed, rehearsed, routine, standard, stereotyped, stock, traditional, unspontaneous **13 set on** *or* **upon = determined**, bent, intent, resolute

➤ **Antonyms**
adjective ≠**inflexible:** flexible, free, open, open-minded, undecided

set² *noun* **1 = series**, assemblage, assortment, batch, collection, compendium, coordinated group, kit, outfit **2 = group**, band, circle, class, clique, company, coterie, crew (*informal*), crowd, faction, gang, outfit, posse (*informal*)

set about *verb* **1 = begin**, address oneself to, attack, get cracking (*informal*), get down to, get to work, make a start on, put one's shoulder to the wheel (*informal*), roll up one's sleeves, set to, start, tackle, take the first step **2 = assault**, assail, attack, belabour

set against *verb* **1 = balance**, compare, contrast, juxtapose, weigh **2 = alienate**, disunite, divide, drive a wedge between, estrange, make bad blood, make mischief, oppose, set at cross purposes, set at odds

set aside *verb* **1 = reserve**, earmark, keep, keep back, put on one side, save, select, separate, set apart, single out **2 = reject**, abrogate, annul, cancel, discard, dismiss, nullify, overrule, overturn, quash, render null and void, repudiate, reverse

setback *noun* **= hold-up**, blow, bummer (*slang*), check, defeat, disappointment, hitch, misfortune, rebuff, reverse, upset, whammy (*informal, chiefly U.S.*)

set back *verb* **= hold up**, delay, hinder, impede, retard, slow

set off *verb* **1 = leave**, depart, embark, sally forth, set out, start out **2 = detonate**, explode, ignite, kick-start, light, set in motion, touch off, trigger (off) **3 = enhance**, show off, throw into relief

set on *or* **upon** *verb* **= attack**, ambush, assail, assault, beat up, fall upon, fly at, go for, lay into (*informal*), let fly at, mug (*informal*), pitch into (*informal*), pounce on, put the boot in (*slang*), set about, turn on, work over (*slang*)

set out *verb* **1 = arrange**, array, display, dispose, exhibit, expose to view, lay out, present, set forth **2 = explain**, describe, detail, elaborate, elucidate **3 = embark**, begin, get under way, hit the road (*slang*), sally forth, set off, start out, take to the road

setting *noun* **= surroundings**, backdrop, background, context, frame, locale, location, *mise en scène*, perspective, scene, scenery, set, site, surround

settle *verb* **1 = put in order**, adjust, dispose, order, regulate, set to rights, straighten out, work out **2 = make oneself comfortable**, bed down **3 = land**, alight, come to rest, descend, light **4 = move to**, dwell, inhabit, live, make one's home, put down roots, reside, set up home, take up residence **5 = colonize**, found, people, pioneer, plant, populate **6 = calm**, allay, compose, lull, pacify, quell, quiet, quieten, reassure, relax, relieve, sedate, soothe, tranquillize **7 = subside**, decline, fall, sink **8 = pay**, acquit oneself of, clear, discharge, liquidate, square (up) **9 = resolve**, clear up, complete, conclude, decide, dispose of, put an end to, reconcile **10 often with on** *or* **upon = decide**, agree, appoint, arrange, choose, come to an agreement, confirm, determine, establish, fix

➤ **Antonyms**
≠**calm:** agitate, bother, discompose, disquieten, disturb, rattle, trouble, unsettle, upset

settlement *noun* **1 = agreement**, adjustment, arrangement, completion, conclusion, confirmation, establishment, resolution, working out **2 = payment**, clearance, clearing, defrayal, discharge, liquidation, satisfaction **3 = colony**, colonization, community, encampment, hamlet, outpost, peopling

settler *noun* **= colonist**, colonizer, frontiersman, immigrant, pioneer, planter

set-to *noun Informal* **= fight**, argument, argy-bargy (*Brit. informal*), barney (*informal*), brush, disagreement, dust-up (*informal*), fracas, quarrel, row, scrap (*informal*), slanging match (*Brit.*), spat, squabble, wrangle

setup *noun Informal* **= arrangement**,

circumstances, conditions, organization, regime, structure, system

set up *verb* 1 = **build**, assemble, construct, elevate, erect, put together, put up, raise 2 = **finance**, back, build up, establish, promote, subsidize 3 = **establish**, arrange, begin, compose, found, initiate, install, institute, make provision for, organize, prearrange, prepare

sever *verb* 1 = **cut**, bisect, cleave, cut in two, detach, disconnect, disjoin, disunite, divide, part, rend, separate, split, sunder 2 = **discontinue**, abandon, break off, dissociate, dissolve, put an end to, terminate
➤ **Antonyms**
≠**cut**: attach, connect, fix together, join, link, unite ≠**discontinue**: continue, maintain, uphold

several *adjective* 1 = **some**, assorted, different, disparate, diverse, manifold, many, sundry, various 2 *Formal* = **different**, distinct, individual, particular, respective, single

severe *adjective* 1 = **strict**, austere, cruel, Draconian, drastic, hard, harsh, inexorable, iron-handed, oppressive, pitiless, relentless, rigid, unbending, unrelenting 2 = **harsh**, astringent, biting, caustic, cutting, mordacious, mordant, satirical, scathing, unsparing, vitriolic 3 = **grim**, cold, disapproving, dour, forbidding, grave, serious, sober, stern, strait-laced, tight-lipped, unsmiling 4 = **plain**, ascetic, austere, chaste, classic, functional, restrained, simple, Spartan, unadorned, unembellished, unfussy 5 = **intense**, acute, bitter, critical, dangerous, distressing, extreme, fierce, violent 6 = **tough**, arduous, demanding, difficult, exacting, fierce, hard, punishing, rigorous, stringent, taxing, unrelenting
➤ **Antonyms**
≠**strict**: easy, lax, lenient, relaxed, tractable ≠**harsh**: compassionate, gentle, kind ≠**grim**: affable, genial ≠**plain**: embellished, fancy, ornamental, ornate, temperate ≠**intense**: gentle, mild, minor, moderate ≠**tough**: easy, manageable

severely *adverb* 1 = **strictly**, harshly, like a ton of bricks (*informal*), rigorously, sharply, sternly, with an iron hand, with a rod of iron 2 = **seriously**, acutely, badly, critically, dangerously, extremely, gravely, hard

severity *noun* = **strictness**, austerity, hardness, harshness, rigour, seriousness, severeness, sternness, stringency, toughness

sex *noun* 1 = **gender** 2 *Informal* = **(sexual) intercourse**, coition, coitus, copulation, fornication, fucking (*taboo slang*), going to bed (with someone), intimacy, legover (*slang*), lovemaking, nookie (*slang*), rumpy-pumpy (*slang*), screwing (*taboo*

slang*), sexual relations, shagging (*Brit. taboo slang*), the other (*informal*) 3 = **facts of life**, desire, libido, reproduction, sexuality, the birds and the bees (*informal*)

sex appeal *noun* = **desirability**, allure, attractiveness, glamour, magnetism, seductiveness, sensuality, sexiness (*informal*), voluptuousness

sexless *adjective* = **asexual**, androgynous, epicene, hermaphrodite, neuter, nonsexual

sexual *adjective* 1 = **carnal**, coital, erotic, intimate, of the flesh, sensual, sexy 2 = **reproductive**, genital, procreative, sex, venereal

sexual intercourse *noun* = **copulation**, bonking (*informal*), carnal knowledge, coition, coitus, congress, consummation, coupling, fucking (*taboo slang*), intimacy, legover (*slang*), mating, nookie (*slang*), penetration, rumpy-pumpy (*slang*), screwing (*taboo slang*), sex (*informal*), shagging (*Brit. taboo slang*), the other (*informal*), union

sexuality *noun* = **desire**, bodily appetites, carnality, eroticism, lust, sensuality, sexiness (*informal*), virility, voluptuousness

sexy *adjective* = **erotic**, arousing, come-hither (*informal*), flirtatious, inviting, naughty, provocative, provoking, seductive, sensual, sensuous, slinky, suggestive, titillating, voluptuous

shabby *adjective* 1 = **tatty**, dilapidated, down at heel, faded, frayed, having seen better days, mean, neglected, poor, ragged, run-down, scruffy, seedy, tattered, the worse for wear, threadbare, worn, worn-out 2 = **mean**, cheap, contemptible, despicable, dirty, dishonourable, ignoble, low, low-down (*informal*), rotten (*informal*), scurvy, shameful, shoddy, ungentlemanly, unworthy
➤ **Antonyms**
≠**tatty**: handsome, in mint condition, neat, new, smart, well-dressed, well-kept, well-to-do ≠**mean**: fair, generous, honourable, praiseworthy, worthy

shack *noun* = **hut**, cabin, dump (*informal*), hovel, lean-to, shanty

shackle *noun* 1 *often plural* = **fetter**, bond, chain, handcuff, hobble, iron, leg-iron, manacle, rope, tether ◆ *verb* 2 = **fetter**, bind, chain, handcuff, hobble, manacle, pinion, put in irons, secure, tether, tie, trammel 3 = **hamper**, constrain, embarrass, encumber, hamstring, impede, inhibit, limit, obstruct, restrain, restrict, tie (someone's) hands

shade *noun* 1 = **dimness**, coolness, dusk, gloom, gloominess, obscurity, screen, semidarkness, shadiness, shadow, shadows 2 = **screen**, blind, canopy, cover, covering, curtain, shield, veil **3** = **hue**, colour, stain, tinge, tint, tone **4** = **dash**, amount, degree, hint, nuance, suggestion, suspicion, trace **5** *Literary* = **ghost**, apparition, manes, phantom, shadow, spectre, spirit **6 put into the shade** = **outshine**, eclipse, make pale by comparison, outclass, overshadow ♦ *verb* **7** = **cover**, conceal, hide, mute, obscure, protect, screen, shield, veil **8** = **darken**, cast a shadow over, cloud, dim, shadow, shut out the light

shadow *noun* **1** = **dimness**, cover, darkness, dusk, gathering darkness, gloaming (*Scot. or poetic*), gloom, obscurity, protection, shade, shelter **2** = **trace**, hint, suggestion, suspicion **3** = **cloud**, blight, gloom, sadness ♦ *verb* **4** = **shade**, cast a shadow over, darken, overhang, screen, shield **5** = **follow**, dog, spy on, stalk, tail (*informal*), trail

shadowy *adjective* **1** = **dark**, dim, dusky, funereal, gloomy, indistinct, murky, obscure, shaded, shady, tenebrous **2** = **vague**, dim, dreamlike, faint, ghostly, illusory, imaginary, impalpable, intangible, nebulous, obscure, phantom, spectral, undefined, unreal, unsubstantial, wraithlike

shady *adjective* **1** = **shaded**, cool, dim, leafy, shadowy **2** *Informal* = **crooked**, disreputable, dodgy (*Brit., Austral., & N.Z. informal*), dubious, fishy (*informal*), questionable, shifty, slippery, suspect, suspicious, unethical, unscrupulous, untrustworthy
➤ **Antonyms**
≠**shaded**: bright, exposed, open, out in the open, sunlit, sunny, unshaded ≠**crooked**: above-board, ethical, honest, honourable, reputable, respectable, straight, trustworthy, upright

shaft *noun* **1** = **handle**, pole, rod, shank, stem, upright **2** *As in* **shaft of wit** *or* **humour** = **gibe**, barb, cut, dart, sting, thrust **3** = **ray**, beam, gleam, streak

shaggy *adjective* = **unkempt**, hairy, hirsute, long-haired, rough, tousled, unshorn
➤ **Antonyms**
close-cropped, crew-cut, cropped, neatly-trimmed, shorn, short-haired, smooth

shake *verb* **1** = **vibrate**, bump, fluctuate, jar, joggle, jolt, oscillate, quake, quiver, rock, shiver, shudder, sway, totter, tremble, waver, wobble **2** *often with* **up** = **agitate**, churn, convulse, rouse, stir **3** = **wave**, brandish, flourish **4** = **upset**, discompose, distress, disturb, frighten, intimidate, move, rattle (*informal*), shock, unnerve **5** = **undermine**, impair, weaken ♦ *noun* **6** = **vibration**, agitation, convulsion, disturbance, jar, jerk, jolt, jounce, pulsation, quaking, shiver, shock, shudder, trembling, tremor **7** *Informal* = **moment**, instant, jiffy (*informal*),

second, tick (*Brit. informal*), trice

shake off *verb* = **get rid of**, dislodge, elude, get away from, get shot of (*slang*), give the slip, leave behind, lose, rid oneself of, throw off

shake up *verb* **1** = **stir (up)**, agitate, churn (up), mix **2** = **reorganize**, overturn, turn upside down **3** *Informal* = **upset**, disturb, shock, unsettle

shaky *adjective* **1** = **unsteady**, faltering, insecure, precarious, quivery, rickety, tottering, trembling, tremulous, unstable, weak, wobbly **2** = **uncertain**, dubious, iffy (*informal*), questionable, suspect, undependable, unreliable, unsound, unsupported
➤ **Antonyms**
≠**unsteady**: firm, secure, stable, steady, strong ≠**uncertain**: dependable

shallow *adjective* **1** = **superficial**, empty, idle, meaningless, skin-deep, slight, surface, trivial **2** = **unintelligent**, flimsy, foolish, frivolous, ignorant, puerile, simple ♦ *noun* **3** *often plural* = **bank**, flat, sandbank, sand bar, shelf, shoal
➤ **Antonyms**
adjective ≠**superficial**: analytical, comprehensive, deep, in-depth, meaningful, penetrating, perceptive, profound, serious, weighty ≠**unintelligent**: serious, thoughtful

sham *noun* **1** = **phoney** *or* **phony** (*informal*), counterfeit, forgery, fraud, hoax, humbug, imitation, impostor, imposture, pretence, pretender, pseud (*informal*) ♦ *adjective* **2** = **false**, artificial, bogus, counterfeit, ersatz, feigned, imitation, mock, phoney *or* phony (*informal*), pretended, pseudo (*informal*), simulated, spurious, synthetic ♦ *verb* **3** = **fake**, affect, assume, counterfeit, feign, imitate, pretend, put on, simulate
➤ **Antonyms**
noun ≠**phoney** *or* **phony**: master, original, the genuine article, the real McCoy (*or* McKay), the real thing ♦ *adjective* ≠**false**: authentic, bona fide, genuine, legitimate, natural, real, sound, true, unfeigned, veritable

shambles *noun* = **chaos**, anarchy, confusion, disarray, disorder, disorganization, havoc, madhouse, mess, muddle

shambolic *adjective Informal* = **disorganized**, anarchic, at sixes and sevens, chaotic, confused, disordered, inefficient, in total disarray, muddled, topsy-turvy, unsystematic

shame *noun* **1** = **embarrassment**, abashment, chagrin, compunction, humiliation, ignominy, loss of face, mortification, shamefacedness **2** = **disgrace**, blot, contempt, degradation, derision,

discredit, dishonour, disrepute, ill repute,
infamy, obloquy, odium, opprobrium,
reproach, scandal, skeleton in the cupboard,
smear **3 put to shame = outdo**, disgrace,
eclipse, outclass, outstrip, show up, surpass
♦ *verb* **4 = embarrass**, abash, confound,
disconcert, disgrace, humble, humiliate,
mortify, reproach, ridicule, take (someone)
down a peg (*informal*) **5 = dishonour**, blot,
debase, defile, degrade, discredit, smear,
stain
➤ **Antonyms**
noun ≠**embarrassment**: brass neck (*Brit.
informal*), brazenness, cheek, shamelessness,
unabashedness ≠**disgrace**: credit,
distinction, esteem, glory, honour, pride,
renown, self-respect ♦ *verb* ≠**embarrass**: do
credit to, make proud ≠**dishonour**: acclaim,
credit, enhance the reputation of, honour
shamefaced *adjective* **= embarrassed**,
abashed, ashamed, chagrined,
conscience-stricken, contrite, discomfited,
humiliated, mortified, red-faced, remorseful,
sheepish
shameful *adjective* **1 = embarrassing**,
blush-making (*informal*), cringe-making
(*Brit. informal*), degrading, humiliating,
mortifying, shaming, toe-curling (*slang*) **2
= disgraceful**, atrocious, base, dastardly,
degrading, dishonourable, ignominious,
indecent, infamous, low, mean, outrageous,
reprehensible, scandalous, unbecoming,
unworthy, vile, wicked
➤ **Antonyms**
≠**disgraceful**: admirable, creditable,
estimable, exemplary, honourable, laudable,
right, worthy
shameless *adjective* **= brazen**, abandoned,
audacious, barefaced, brash, corrupt,
depraved, flagrant, hardened, immodest,
improper, impudent, incorrigible, indecent,
insolent, unabashed, unashamed,
unprincipled, wanton
shanty *noun* **= shack**, bothy (*Scot.*), cabin,
hovel, hut, lean-to, shed
shape *noun* **1 = form**, build, configuration,
contours, cut, figure, lines, make, outline,
profile, silhouette **2 = appearance**, aspect,
form, guise, likeness, semblance **3 = pattern**,
frame, model, mould **4 = condition**, fettle,
health, kilter, state, trim ♦ *verb* **5 = form**,
create, fashion, make, model, mould,
produce **6 = develop**, adapt, convert,
define, devise, frame, guide, modify, plan,
prepare
shapeless *adjective* **= formless**,
amorphous, asymmetrical, irregular,
misshapen, unstructured
➤ **Antonyms**
well-formed, well-proportioned, well-turned
shapely *adjective* **= well-formed**, comely,

curvaceous, elegant, graceful, neat, trim,
well-proportioned, well-turned
shape up *verb Informal* **= progress**, be
promising, come on, develop, look good,
proceed, turn out
share *noun* **1 = part**, allotment, allowance,
contribution, cut (*informal*), division, due,
lot, portion, proportion, quota, ration,
whack (*informal*) ♦ *verb* **2 = divide**,
apportion, assign, distribute, divvy up
(*informal*), parcel out, split **3 = go halves**,
go Dutch (*informal*), go fifty-fifty (*informal*)
4 = partake, participate, receive, use in
common
sharp *adjective* **1 = keen**, acute, cutting,
honed, jagged, knife-edged, knifelike,
pointed, razor-sharp, serrated, sharpened,
spiky **2 = sudden**, abrupt, distinct, extreme,
marked **3 = clear**, clear-cut, crisp, distinct,
well-defined **4 = quick-witted**, alert, apt,
astute, bright, clever, discerning, knowing,
observant, on the ball (*informal*),
penetrating, perceptive, quick, ready, subtle
5 = cunning, artful, crafty, dishonest, fly
(*slang*), shrewd, sly, smart, unscrupulous,
wily **6 = cutting**, acrimonious, barbed,
biting, bitter, caustic, harsh, hurtful,
sarcastic, sardonic, scathing, severe,
trenchant, vitriolic **7 = sour**, acerbic, acetic,
acid, acrid, burning, hot, piquant, pungent,
tart, vinegary **8 = acute**, distressing,
excruciating, fierce, gut-wrenching, intense,
painful, piercing, severe, shooting, sore,
stabbing, stinging, violent **9** *Informal*
= stylish, chic, classy (*slang*), dressy,
fashionable, natty (*informal*), smart, snappy,
trendy (*informal*) ♦ *adverb* **10 = promptly**,
exactly, on the dot, on time, precisely,
punctually
➤ **Antonyms**
adjective ≠**keen**: blunt, dull, rounded,
unsharpened ≠**sudden**: even, gentle,
gradual, moderate, progressive ≠**clear**:
blurred, fuzzy, ill-defined, indistinct, unclear
≠**quick-witted**: dim, dull-witted, dumb
(*informal*), slow, slow on the uptake, stupid
≠**cunning**: artless, guileless, ingenuous,
innocent, naive, simple, undesigning
≠**cutting**: amicable, courteous, friendly,
gentle, kindly, mild ≠**sour**: bland, mild,
tasteless ♦ *adverb* ≠**promptly**:
approximately, more or less, roughly, round
about, vaguely
sharpen *verb* **= whet**, edge, grind, hone,
put an edge on, strop
shatter *verb* **1 = smash**, break, burst, crack,
crush, demolish, explode, implode,
pulverize, shiver, split **2 = destroy**, blast,
blight, bring to nought, demolish, disable,
exhaust, impair, overturn, ruin, torpedo,
wreck **3 = upset**, break (someone's) heart,

crush, devastate

shattered *adjective Informal* **1**
= **exhausted**, all in (*slang*), dead beat
(*informal*), dead tired (*informal*), done in
(*informal*), drained, knackered (*slang*),
ready to drop, spent, tired out, weary, wiped
out (*informal*), worn out, zonked (*slang*) **2**
= **devastated**, crushed, gutted (*slang*)

shattering *adjective* = **devastating**,
crushing, overwhelming, paralysing, severe,
stunning

shave *verb* **1** = **trim**, crop, pare, plane, shear
2 = **brush**, graze, touch

shed[1] *noun* = **hut**, bothy (*chiefly Scot.*),
lean-to, lockup, outhouse, shack

shed[2] *verb* **1** = **give out**, afford, cast, diffuse,
drop, emit, give, pour forth, radiate, scatter,
shower, spill, throw **2** = **cast off**, discard,
moult, slough

sheen *noun* = **shine**, brightness, burnish,
gleam, gloss, lustre, patina, polish, shininess

sheepish *adjective* = **embarrassed**,
abashed, ashamed, chagrined, foolish,
mortified, self-conscious, shamefaced, silly,
uncomfortable
➤ **Antonyms**
assertive, audacious, bold, brash,
brass-necked (*Brit. informal*), brazen,
confident, unabashed, unapologetic,
unembarrassed

sheer *adjective* **1** = **total**, absolute, arrant,
complete, downright, out-and-out, pure,
rank, thoroughgoing, unadulterated,
unalloyed, unmitigated, unqualified, utter **2**
= **steep**, abrupt, headlong (*archaic*),
perpendicular, precipitous **3** = **fine**,
diaphanous, gauzy, gossamer, see-through,
thin, transparent
➤ **Antonyms**
≠**total**: moderate ≠**steep**: gentle, gradual,
horizontal, slanting, sloping ≠**fine**: coarse,
heavy, impenetrable, opaque, thick

sheet *noun* **1** = **coat**, film, lamina, layer, leaf,
membrane, overlay, stratum, surface, veneer
2 = **piece**, folio, pane, panel, plate, slab **3**
= **expanse**, area, blanket, covering, stretch,
sweep

shell *noun* **1** = **case**, carapace, husk, pod **2**
= **frame**, chassis, framework, hull, skeleton,
structure ♦ *verb* **3** = **husk 4** = **bomb**, attack,
barrage, blitz, bombard, strafe, strike

shell out *verb* = **pay out**, disburse, expend,
fork out (*slang*), give, hand over, lay out
(*informal*)

shelter *noun* **1** = **protection**, awning, cover,
covert, defence, guard, roof over one's head,
screen, umbrella **2** = **safety**, asylum, haven,
refuge, retreat, sanctuary, security ♦ *verb* **3**
= **take shelter**, hide, seek refuge **4**
= **protect**, cover, defend, guard, harbour,

hide, safeguard, shield, take in
➤ **Antonyms**
verb ≠**protect**: expose, lay open, leave
open, make vulnerable

sheltered *adjective* = **protected**, cloistered,
isolated, quiet, reclusive, retired, screened,
secluded, shaded, shielded, withdrawn
➤ **Antonyms**
exposed, laid bare, made public, open,
public, unconcealed, unprotected,
unsheltered

shelve *verb* = **postpone**, defer, dismiss,
freeze, hold in abeyance, hold over, lay
aside, mothball, put aside, put off, put on
ice, put on the back burner (*informal*),
suspend, take a rain check on (*U.S. &
Canad. informal*)

shepherd *noun* **1** = **herdsman**, drover,
grazier, stockman ♦ *verb* **2** = **guide**,
conduct, convoy, herd, marshal, steer, usher

shield *noun* **1** = **buckler**, escutcheon
(*Heraldry*) **2** = **protection**, aegis, bulwark,
cover, defence, guard, rampart, safeguard,
screen, shelter ♦ *verb* **3** = **protect**, cover,
defend, guard, safeguard, screen, shelter,
ward off

shift *verb* **1** = **move**, alter, budge, change,
displace, fluctuate, move around, rearrange,
relocate, remove, reposition, swerve, switch,
transfer, transpose, vary, veer ♦ *noun* **2**
= **move**, about-turn, alteration, change,
displacement, fluctuation, modification,
permutation, rearrangement, removal,
shifting, switch, transfer, veering **3**
= **scheme**, artifice, contrivance, craft, device,
dodge, expedient, move, resource, ruse,
stratagem, subterfuge, trick, wile

shiftless *adjective* = **lazy**, aimless,
good-for-nothing, idle, incompetent,
indolent, inefficient, inept, irresponsible,
lackadaisical, slothful, unambitious,
unenterprising

shifty *adjective* = **untrustworthy**, contriving,
crafty, deceitful, devious, duplicitous,
evasive, furtive, scheming, slippery, sly,
tricky, underhand, unprincipled, wily
➤ **Antonyms**
dependable, guileless, honest, honourable,
open, reliable, trustworthy, upright

shillyshally *verb Informal* = **be irresolute
or indecisive**, dilly-dally (*informal*), dither
(*chiefly Brit.*), falter, fluctuate, hem and haw
or hum and haw, hesitate, seesaw, swither
(*Scot.*), vacillate, waver

shimmer *verb* **1** = **gleam**, dance, glimmer,
glisten, scintillate, twinkle ♦ *noun* **2**
= **gleam**, diffused light, glimmer, glow,
incandescence, iridescence, lustre,
phosphorescence, unsteady light

shin *verb* **shin up** = **climb**, ascend, clamber,

scale, scramble, swarm

shine *verb* 1 = **gleam**, beam, emit light, flash, give off light, glare, glimmer, glisten, glitter, glow, radiate, scintillate, shimmer, sparkle, twinkle 2 = **polish**, brush, buff, burnish, rub up 3 = **be outstanding**, be conspicuous, be distinguished, be pre-eminent, excel, stand out, stand out in a crowd, star, steal the show ♦ *noun* 4 = **brightness**, glare, gleam, lambency, light, luminosity, radiance, shimmer, sparkle 5 = **polish**, glaze, gloss, lustre, patina, sheen

shining *adjective* 1 = **bright**, aglow, beaming, brilliant, effulgent, gleaming, glistening, glittering, luminous, radiant, shimmering, sparkling 2 = **outstanding**, brilliant, celebrated, conspicuous, distinguished, eminent, glorious, illustrious, leading, splendid

shiny *adjective* = **bright**, agleam, burnished, gleaming, glistening, glossy, lustrous, polished, satiny, sheeny

ship *noun* = **vessel**, boat, craft

shipshape *adjective* = **tidy**, Bristol fashion, businesslike, neat, orderly, spick-and-span, trig (*archaic or dialect*), trim, uncluttered, well-ordered, well-organized, well-regulated

shirk *verb* = **dodge**, avoid, body-swerve (*Scot.*), duck (out of) (*informal*), evade, get out of, shun, sidestep, skive (*Brit. slang*), slack

shirker *noun* = **slacker**, clock-watcher, dodger, idler, malingerer, quitter, shirk, skiver (*Brit. slang*)

shiver[1] *verb* 1 = **tremble**, palpitate, quake, quiver, shake, shudder ♦ *noun* 2 = **trembling**, flutter, *frisson,* quiver, shudder, thrill, tremble, tremor 3 **the shivers** = **the shakes** (*informal*), chattering teeth, chill, goose flesh, goose pimples

shiver[2] *verb* = **splinter**, break, crack, fragment, shatter, smash, smash to smithereens

shivery *adjective* = **shaking**, chilled, chilly, cold, quaking, quivery, shuddery, trembly

shoal *noun* 1 = **shallow** 2 = **sandbank**, sand bar, shelf

shock *verb* 1 = **horrify**, agitate, appal, disgust, disquiet, give (someone) a turn (*informal*), gross out (*U.S. slang*), nauseate, offend, outrage, raise eyebrows, revolt, scandalize, sicken, traumatize, unsettle 2 = **astound**, jar, jolt, numb, paralyse, shake, shake up (*informal*), stagger, stun, stupefy ♦ *noun* 3 = **impact**, blow, clash, collision, encounter, jarring, jolt 4 = **upset**, blow, bolt from the blue, bombshell, breakdown, collapse, consternation, distress, disturbance, prostration, rude awakening, state of shock, stupefaction, stupor, trauma, turn

(*informal*), whammy (*informal, chiefly U.S.*)

shocking *adjective* = **dreadful**, abominable, appalling, atrocious, detestable, disgraceful, disgusting, disquieting, distressing, foul, frightful, from hell (*informal*), ghastly, hellacious (*U.S. slang*), hideous, horrible, horrifying, loathsome, monstrous, nauseating, obscene, odious, offensive, outrageous, repulsive, revolting, scandalous, sickening, stupefying, unspeakable
➤ **Antonyms**
admirable, decent, delightful, excellent, fine, first-rate, gratifying, honourable, laudable, marvellous, pleasant, praiseworthy, satisfying, wonderful

shoddy *adjective* = **inferior**, cheap, cheapo (*informal*), junky (*informal*), low-rent (*informal, chiefly U.S.*), poor, rubbishy, second-rate, slipshod, tacky (*informal*), tatty, tawdry, trashy
➤ **Antonyms**
accurate, careful, craftsman-like, excellent, fine, first-rate, meticulous, quality, superlative, well-made

shoemaker *noun* = **cobbler**, bootmaker

shoot *verb* 1 = **hit**, bag, blast (*slang*), blow away (*slang, chiefly U.S.*), bring down, kill, open fire, pick off, plug (*slang*), pump full of lead (*slang*), zap (*slang*) 2 = **fire**, discharge, emit, fling, hurl, launch, let fly, project, propel 3 = **speed**, bolt, charge, dart, dash, flash, fly, hurtle, race, rush, scoot, spring, streak, tear, whisk, whizz (*informal*) 4 = **sprout**, bud, burgeon, germinate ♦ *noun* 5 = **sprout**, branch, bud, offshoot, slip, sprig, twig

shop *noun* = **store**, boutique, emporium, hypermarket, market, mart, supermarket

shore *noun* = **beach**, coast, lakeside, sands, seaboard (*chiefly U.S.*), seashore, strand (*poetic*), waterside

shore up *verb* = **support**, augment, brace, buttress, hold, prop, reinforce, strengthen, underpin

short *adjective* 1 = **concise**, abridged, brief, compressed, laconic, pithy, succinct, summary, terse 2 = **small**, diminutive, dumpy, knee high to a gnat, knee high to a grasshopper, little, low, petite, squat, wee 3 = **brief**, fleeting, momentary, short-lived, short-term 4 *often with* **of** *or* **on** = **lacking**, deficient, inadequate, in need of, insufficient, limited, low (on), meagre, missing, poor, scant, scanty, scarce, sparse, strapped (for) (*slang*), tight, wanting 5 = **abrupt**, blunt, brusque, curt, discourteous, gruff, impolite, offhand, sharp, terse, testy, uncivil 6 *Of pastry* = **crumbly**, brittle, crisp ♦ *adverb* 7 = **abruptly**, by surprise, suddenly, unaware, without warning 8 **short of** = **except**, apart

from, other than, unless ♦ *noun* **9 in short** = **briefly**, in a nutshell, in a word, in essence, to come to the point, to cut a long story short, to put it briefly
➤ **Antonyms**
adjective ≠**concise**: diffuse, lengthy, long, long-drawn-out, long-winded, prolonged, rambling, unabridged, verbose, wordy ≠**small**: big, high, lanky, lofty, tall ≠**brief**: extended, long, long-term ≠**lacking**: abundant, adequate, ample, bountiful, copious, inexhaustible, plentiful, sufficient, well-stocked ≠**abrupt**: civil, courteous, polite ♦ *adverb* ≠**abruptly**: bit by bit, gently, gradually, little by little, slowly

shortage *noun* = **deficiency**, dearth, deficit, failure, inadequacy, insufficiency, lack, leanness, paucity, poverty, scarcity, shortfall, want
➤ **Antonyms**
abundance, adequate amount, excess, overabundance, plethora, profusion, sufficiency, surfeit, surplus

shortcoming *noun* = **failing**, defect, drawback, fault, flaw, foible, frailty, imperfection, weakness, weak point

shorten *verb* = **cut**, abbreviate, abridge, curtail, cut back, cut down, decrease, diminish, dock, downsize, lessen, prune, reduce, trim, truncate, turn up
➤ **Antonyms**
draw out, elongate, expand, extend, increase, lengthen, make longer, prolong, protract, spin out, stretch

short-lived *adjective* = **brief**, ephemeral, fleeting, impermanent, passing, short, temporary, transient, transitory

shortly *adverb* **1** = **soon**, anon (*archaic*), any minute now, before long, in a little while, presently **2** = **curtly**, abruptly, sharply, tartly, tersely

short-sighted *adjective* **1** = **near-sighted**, blind as a bat, myopic **2** = **unthinking**, careless, ill-advised, ill-considered, impolitic, impractical, improvident, imprudent, injudicious, seeing no further than (the end of) one's nose

short-tempered *adjective* = **quick-tempered**, choleric, fiery, hot-tempered, impatient, irascible, peppery, ratty (*Brit. & N.Z. informal*), testy, touchy

shot¹ *noun* **1** = **throw**, discharge, lob, pot shot **2** = **pellet**, ball, bullet, lead, projectile, slug **3** = **marksman**, shooter **4** *Informal* = **attempt**, chance, crack (*informal*), effort, endeavour, essay, go (*informal*), opportunity, stab (*informal*), try, turn **5** *Informal* = **guess**, conjecture, surmise **6 like a shot** = **at once**, eagerly, immediately, like a bat out of hell (*slang*), like a flash, quickly,

unhesitatingly **7 shot in the arm** *Informal* = **boost**, encouragement, fillip, geeing-up, impetus, lift, stimulus

shot² *adjective* = **iridescent**, moiré, opalescent, watered

shoulder *noun* **1 put one's shoulder to the wheel** *Informal* = **work hard**, apply oneself, buckle down to (*informal*), exert oneself, get down to, make every effort, set to work, strive **2 rub shoulders with** *Informal* = **mix with**, associate with, consort with, fraternize with, hobnob with, socialize with **3 shoulder to shoulder: a** = **side by side b** = **together**, as one, in cooperation, in partnership, in unity, jointly, united ♦ *verb* **4** = **bear**, accept, assume, be responsible for, carry, take on, take upon oneself **5** = **push**, elbow, jostle, press, shove, thrust

shoulder blade *noun* = **scapula**

shout *noun* **1** = **cry**, bellow, call, roar, scream, yell ♦ *verb* **2** = **cry (out)**, bawl, bay, bellow, call (out), holler (*informal*), hollo, raise one's voice, roar, scream, yell

shout down *verb* = **silence**, drown, drown out, overwhelm

shove *verb* = **push**, crowd, drive, elbow, impel, jostle, press, propel, shoulder, thrust

shovel *verb* = **move**, convey, dredge, heap, ladle, load, scoop, shift, spoon, toss

shove off *verb Informal* = **go away**, bugger off (*taboo slang*), clear off (*informal*), depart, fuck off (*offensive taboo slang*), get on one's bike (*Brit. slang*), go to hell (*informal*), leave, push off (*informal*), scram (*informal*), sling one's hook (*Brit. slang*), slope off, take oneself off, vamoose (*slang, chiefly U.S.*)

show *verb* **1** = **be visible**, appear **2** = **present**, display, exhibit **3** = **prove**, assert, clarify, demonstrate, elucidate, evince, point out **4** = **instruct**, demonstrate, explain, teach **5** = **indicate**, demonstrate, disclose, display, divulge, evidence, evince, make known, manifest, register, reveal, testify to **6** = **act with**, accord, bestow, confer, grant **7** = **guide**, accompany, attend, conduct, escort, lead ♦ *noun* **8** = **entertainment**, presentation, production **9** = **exhibition**, array, demonstration, display, exposition, fair, manifestation, pageant, pageantry, parade, representation, sight, spectacle, view **10** = **pretence**, affectation, air, appearance, display, illusion, likeness, ostentation, parade, pose, pretext, profession, semblance
➤ **Antonyms**
verb ≠**be visible**: be invisible ≠**present**, **indicate**: conceal, hide, keep secret, mask, obscure, suppress, veil, withhold ≠**prove**: deny, disprove, gainsay (*archaic or literary*), refute

showdown noun Informal
= **confrontation**, breaking point, clash, climax, crisis, culmination, denouement, exposé, face-off (slang), moment of truth

shower noun 1 = **deluge**, barrage, downpour, fusillade, rain, stream, torrent, volley 2 Brit. slang = **rabble**, crew ♦ verb 3 = **inundate**, deluge, heap, lavish, load, pour, rain, spray, sprinkle

showing noun 1 = **display**, demonstration, exhibition, presentation, staging 2 = **performance**, account of oneself, appearance, demonstration, impression, show, track record

showman noun 1 = **performer**, entertainer 2 = **impresario**, publicist, stage manager

show-off noun Informal = **exhibitionist**, boaster, braggadocio, braggart, egotist, peacock, poseur, swaggerer

show off verb 1 = **exhibit**, advertise, demonstrate, display, flaunt, parade 2 Informal = **boast**, blow one's own trumpet, brag, make a spectacle of oneself, strut one's stuff (chiefly U.S.), swagger

show up verb 1 = **stand out**, appear, be conspicuous, be visible, catch the eye, leap to the eye 2 = **reveal**, expose, highlight, lay bare, pinpoint, put the spotlight on, unmask 3 Informal = **embarrass**, let down, mortify, put to shame, shame, show in a bad light 4 Informal = **arrive**, appear, come, make an appearance, put in an appearance, show one's face, turn up

showy adjective 1 = **ostentatious**, brash, flamboyant, flash (informal), flashy, over the top (informal), pompous, pretentious, splashy (informal) 2 = **gaudy**, garish, loud, tawdry, tinselly
➤ **Antonyms**
discreet, low-key, muted, quiet, restrained, subdued, tasteful, unobtrusive

shred noun 1 = **strip**, bit, fragment, piece, rag, ribbon, scrap, sliver, snippet, tatter 2 = **particle**, atom, grain, iota, jot, scrap, trace, whit

shrew noun = **nag**, ballbreaker (slang), dragon (informal), fury, harpy, harridan, scold, spitfire, virago, vixen

shrewd adjective = **clever**, acute, artful, astute, calculating, canny, crafty, cunning, discerning, discriminating, far-seeing, far-sighted, fly (slang), intelligent, keen, knowing, perceptive, perspicacious, sagacious, sharp, sly, smart, wily
➤ **Antonyms**
artless, dull, gullible, imprudent, ingenuous, innocent, naive, obtuse, slow-witted, stupid, trusting, undiscerning, unsophisticated, unworldly

shrewdly adverb = **cleverly**, artfully,

astutely, cannily, far-sightedly, knowingly, perceptively, perspicaciously, sagaciously, with all one's wits about one

shrewdness noun = **cleverness**, acumen, acuteness, astuteness, canniness, discernment, grasp, judgment, penetration, perspicacity, quick wits, sagacity, sharpness, smartness

shrewish adjective = **bad-tempered**, complaining, fault-finding, ill-humoured, ill-natured, ill-tempered, nagging, quarrelsome, scolding, sharp-tongued, vixenish

shriek verb, noun = **cry**, holler, howl, scream, screech, squeal, wail, whoop, yell

shrill adjective = **piercing**, acute, ear-piercing, ear-splitting, high, high-pitched, penetrating, piping, screeching, sharp
➤ **Antonyms**
deep, dulcet, mellifluous, silver-toned, soft, soothing, sweet-sounding, velvety, well-modulated

shrink verb 1 = **decrease**, contract, deflate, diminish, downsize, drop off, dwindle, fall off, grow smaller, lessen, narrow, shorten, shrivel, wither, wrinkle 2 = **recoil**, cower, cringe, draw back, flinch, hang back, quail, shy away, wince, withdraw
➤ **Antonyms**
≠decrease: balloon, dilate, distend, enlarge, expand, increase, inflate, mushroom, stretch, swell ≠recoil: confront, embrace, face, receive, welcome

shrivel verb 1 = **wither**, dehydrate, desiccate, dwindle, shrink, wilt, wizen, wrinkle 2 = **dry (up)**, burn, parch, scorch, sear

shrivelled adjective = **withered**, desiccated, dried up, dry, shrunken, wizened, wrinkled

shroud noun 1 = **winding sheet**, covering, grave clothes 2 = **covering**, cloud, mantle, pall, screen, veil ♦ verb 3 = **conceal**, blanket, cloak, cover, envelop, hide, screen, swathe, veil

shudder verb 1 = **shiver**, convulse, quake, quiver, shake, tremble ♦ noun 2 = **shiver**, convulsion, quiver, spasm, trembling, tremor

shuffle verb 1 = **scuffle**, drag, scrape, scuff, shamble 2 = **rearrange**, confuse, disarrange, disorder, intermix, jumble, mix, shift

shun verb = **avoid**, body-swerve (Scot.), cold-shoulder, elude, eschew, evade, fight shy of, give (someone or something) a wide berth, have no part in, keep away from, shy away from, steer clear of

shut verb 1 = **close**, bar, draw to, fasten, push to, seal, secure, slam 2 **shut in** = **confine**, cage, enclose, impound, imprison, pound, wall off or up 3 **shut out**

= **exclude**, keep out
➤ **Antonyms**
≠**close**: open, throw wide, unbar, unclose, undo, unfasten, unlock

shut down *verb* 1 = **stop**, cease operating, discontinue, halt, switch off 2 = **close**, shut up

shut out *verb* 1 = **exclude**, bar, black, blackball, debar, keep out, lock out, ostracize 2 = **conceal**, block out, cover, hide, mask, screen, veil

shuttle *verb* = **go back and forth**, alternate, commute, go to and fro, seesaw, shunt

shut up *verb* 1 *Informal* = **be quiet**, button one's lip (*slang*), fall silent, gag, hold one's tongue, hush, keep one's trap shut (*slang*), muzzle, pipe down (*slang*), put a sock in it (*Brit. slang*), silence 2 = **confine**, bottle up, box in, cage, coop up, immure, imprison, incarcerate, intern, keep in

shy[1] *adjective* 1 = **timid**, backward, bashful, coy, diffident, modest, mousy, nervous, reserved, reticent, retiring, self-conscious, self-effacing, shrinking 2 **shy of** = **cautious of**, chary of, distrustful of, hesitant about, suspicious of, wary of ♦ *verb* 3 *sometimes with* **off** *or* **away** = **recoil**, balk, buck, draw back, flinch, quail, rear, start, take fright, wince
➤ **Antonyms**
adjective ≠**timid**: assured, bold, brash, cheeky, confident, fearless, forward, pushy (*informal*), self-assured, self-confident ≠**cautious of**: rash, reckless, unsuspecting, unwary

shy[2] *verb* = **throw**, cast, chuck (*informal*), fling, hurl, lob (*informal*), pitch, propel, send, sling, toss

shyness *noun* = **timidness**, bashfulness, diffidence, lack of confidence, modesty, mousiness, nervousness, reticence, self-consciousness, timidity, timorousness

sibyl *noun* = **prophetess**, Cassandra, oracle, seer

sick *adjective* 1 = **nauseous**, green about the gills (*informal*), ill, nauseated, puking (*slang*), queasy 2 = **unwell**, ailing, diseased, feeble, indisposed, laid up (*informal*), poorly (*informal*), under par (*informal*), under the weather, weak 3 *Informal* = **morbid**, black, ghoulish, macabre, sadistic 4 **sick of** = **tired**, blasé, bored, fed up, jaded, satiated, weary
➤ **Antonyms**
≠**unwell**: able-bodied, fine, fit, fit and well, fit as a fiddle, hale and hearty, healthy, robust, up to par, well

sicken *verb* 1 = **disgust**, gross out (*U.S. slang*), make one's gorge rise, nauseate, repel, revolt, turn one's stomach 2 = **fall ill**, ail, be stricken by, contract, go down with,

show symptoms of, take sick

sickening *adjective* = **disgusting**, cringe-making (*Brit. informal*), distasteful, foul, gut-wrenching, loathsome, nauseating, nauseous, noisome, offensive, putrid, repulsive, revolting, stomach-turning (*informal*), vile, yucky *or* yukky (*slang*)
➤ **Antonyms**
delightful, inviting, marvellous, mouth-watering, pleasant, tempting, wholesome, wonderful

sickly *adjective* 1 = **unhealthy**, ailing, delicate, faint, feeble, indisposed, infirm, in poor health, lacklustre, languid, pallid, peaky, wan, weak 2 = **nauseating**, cloying, icky (*informal*), mawkish, revolting (*informal*)

sickness *noun* 1 = **illness**, affliction, ailment, bug (*informal*), complaint, disease, disorder, indisposition, infirmity, lurgy (*informal*), malady 2 = **nausea**, (the) collywobbles (*slang*), puking (*slang*), queasiness, vomiting

side *noun* 1 = **border**, boundary, division, edge, limit, margin, part, perimeter, periphery, rim, sector, verge 2 = **part**, aspect, face, facet, flank, hand, surface, view 3 = **party**, camp, cause, faction, sect, team 4 = **point of view**, angle, light, opinion, position, slant, stand, standpoint, viewpoint 5 *Brit. slang* = **conceit**, airs, arrogance, insolence, pretentiousness ♦ *adjective* 6 = **lateral**, flanking 7 = **subordinate**, ancillary, incidental, indirect, lesser, marginal, minor, oblique, roundabout, secondary, subsidiary ♦ *verb* 8 *usually with* **with** = **support**, ally with, associate oneself with, befriend, favour, go along with, join with, second, take the part of, team up with (*informal*)
➤ **Antonyms**
noun ≠**border**: centre, core, heart, middle ♦ *adjective* ≠**subordinate**: central, essential, focal, fundamental, key, main, middle, primary, principal ♦ *verb* ≠**support**: counter, oppose, stand against, withstand

sideline *noun* = **supplement**, subsidiary

sidelong *adjective* = **sideways**, covert, indirect, oblique

side-splitting *adjective* = **hilarious**, farcical, hysterical, rollicking, uproarious

sidestep *verb* = **avoid**, body-swerve (*Scot.*), bypass, circumvent, dodge, duck (*informal*), elude, evade, find a way round, skip, skirt

sidetrack *verb* = **distract**, deflect, divert, lead off the subject

sideways *adverb* 1 = **obliquely**, crabwise, edgeways, laterally, sidelong, sidewards, to the side ♦ *adjective* 2 = **oblique**, side, sidelong, slanted

sidle verb = edge, creep, inch, slink, sneak, steal

siesta noun = nap, catnap, doze, forty winks (informal), kip (Brit. slang), rest, sleep, snooze (informal), zizz (Brit. informal)

sieve noun 1 = strainer, colander, riddle, screen, sifter ♦ verb 2 = sift, bolt, remove, riddle, separate, strain

sift verb 1 = sieve, bolt, filter, pan, part, riddle, separate 2 = examine, analyse, go through, investigate, pore over, probe, research, screen, scrutinize, work over

sigh verb 1 = breathe, complain, grieve, lament, moan, sorrow 2 sigh for = long for, eat one's heart out over, languish over, mourn for, pine for, yearn for

sight noun 1 = vision, eye, eyes, eyesight, seeing 2 = view, appearance, apprehension, eyeshot, field of vision, ken, perception, range of vision, viewing, visibility 3 = spectacle, display, exhibition, pageant, scene, show, vista 4 Informal = eyesore, blot on the landscape (informal), fright (informal), mess, monstrosity, spectacle 5 catch sight of = spot, descry, espy, glimpse, recognize, view ♦ verb 6 = spot, behold, discern, distinguish, make out, observe, perceive, see

sign noun 1 = indication, clue, evidence, gesture, giveaway, hint, manifestation, mark, note, proof, signal, suggestion, symptom, token, trace, vestige 2 = notice, board, placard, warning 3 = symbol, badge, character, cipher, device, emblem, ensign, figure, logo, mark, representation 4 = omen, augury, auspice, foreboding, forewarning, portent, presage, warning ♦ verb 5 = autograph, endorse, initial, inscribe, set one's hand to, subscribe 6 = gesture, beckon, gesticulate, indicate, signal, use sign language, wave

signal noun 1 = sign, beacon, cue, gesture, go-ahead (informal), green light, indication, indicator, mark, token ♦ adjective 2 Formal = significant, conspicuous, exceptional, extraordinary, memorable, momentous, notable, noteworthy, outstanding, remarkable, serious (informal), striking ♦ verb 3 = gesture, beckon, communicate, gesticulate, give a sign to, indicate, motion, nod, sign, wave

sign away verb = give up, abandon, dispose of, forgo, lose, relinquish, renounce, surrender, transfer, waive

significance noun 1 = importance, consequence, consideration, impressiveness, matter, moment, relevance, weight 2 = meaning, force, implication(s), import, message, point, purport, sense, signification

significant adjective 1 = important,

critical, material, momentous, noteworthy, serious, vital, weighty 2 = meaningful, denoting, eloquent, expressing, expressive, indicative, knowing, meaning, pregnant, suggestive
➤ Antonyms
≠important: immaterial, inconsequential, insignificant, irrelevant, of no consequence, paltry, petty, trivial, unimportant, worthless ≠meaningful: meaningless

signify verb 1 = indicate, announce, be a sign of, betoken, communicate, connote, convey, denote, evidence, exhibit, express, imply, intimate, matter, mean, portend, proclaim, represent, show, stand for, suggest, symbolize 2 Informal = matter, be important, carry weight, count

sign up verb 1 = engage, employ, hire, put on the payroll, recruit, take into service, take on, take on board (informal) 2 = enlist, contract with, enrol, join, join up, register, volunteer

silence noun 1 = quiet, calm, hush, lull, noiselessness, peace, quiescence, stillness 2 = muteness, dumbness, reticence, speechlessness, taciturnity, uncommunicativeness ♦ verb 3 = quieten, cut off, cut short, deaden, extinguish, gag, muffle, quell, quiet, stifle, still, strike dumb, subdue, suppress
➤ Antonyms
noun ≠quiet: cacophony, din, noise, racket, sound, tumult, uproar ≠muteness: babble, chatter, garrulousness, hubbub, loquaciousness, prattle, speech, talk, talking, verbosity ♦ verb ≠quieten: amplify, broadcast, disseminate, encourage, foster, make louder, promote, promulgate, publicize, rouse, spread, support, ungag

silent adjective 1 = quiet, hushed, muted, noiseless, soundless, still, stilly (poetic) 2 = mute, dumb, nonvocal, not talkative, speechless, struck dumb, taciturn, tongue-tied, uncommunicative, unspeaking, voiceless, wordless 3 = unspoken, implicit, implied, tacit, understood, unexpressed, unpronounced

silently adjective = quietly, as quietly as a mouse (informal), dumbly, inaudibly, in silence, mutely, noiselessly, soundlessly, speechlessly, without a sound, wordlessly

silhouette noun 1 = outline, delineation, form, profile, shape ♦ verb 2 = outline, delineate, etch, stand out

silky adjective = smooth, silken, sleek, velvety

silly adjective 1 = foolish, absurd, asinine, brainless, childish, daft, dopy (slang), dozy (Brit. informal), dumb-ass (slang), fatuous, foolhardy, frivolous, giddy, idiotic, imprudent, inane, inappropriate,

irresponsible, meaningless, pointless,
preposterous, puerile, ridiculous, senseless,
stupid, unwise, witless **2** *Old-fashioned*
= dazed, benumbed, groggy (*informal*), in
a daze, muzzy, stunned, stupefied ◆ *noun* **3**
Informal **= fool**, clot (*Brit. informal*),
ignoramus, nerd *or* nurd (*slang*), ninny,
nitwit (*informal*), plonker (*slang*), prat
(*slang*), simpleton, twit (*informal*), wally
(*slang*)
➤ **Antonyms**
adjective ≠**foolish**: acute, aware, bright,
clever, intelligent, mature, perceptive,
profound, prudent, reasonable, sane,
sensible, serious, smart, thoughtful,
well-thought-out, wise

silt *noun* **1 = sediment**, alluvium, deposit,
ooze, residue, sludge ◆ *verb* **2 silt up**
= clog, choke, congest, dam

silver *noun* **1 = silverware**, silver plate
◆ *adjective* **2 = silvery**, argent (*poetic*),
pearly, silvered

similar *adjective* **= alike**, analogous, close,
comparable, congruous, corresponding,
homogeneous, homogenous, in agreement,
like, much the same, of a piece, resembling,
uniform
➤ **Antonyms**
antithetical, clashing, contradictory,
contrary, different, disparate, dissimilar,
diverse, heterogeneous, irreconcilable,
opposite, unalike, unrelated, various, varying

similarity *noun* **= resemblance**, affinity,
agreement, analogy, closeness,
comparability, concordance, congruence,
correspondence, likeness, point of
comparison, relation, sameness, similitude
➤ **Antonyms**
antithesis, contradictoriness, difference,
disagreement, discordance, discrepancy,
disparity, dissimilarity, diversity,
heterogeneity, incomparability,
irreconcilability, unalikeness, variation, variety

similarly *adverb* **= in the same way**, by the
same token, correspondingly, in like manner,
likewise

simmer *verb* **= fume**, be agitated, be angry,
be pissed (off) (*taboo slang*), be tense, be
uptight (*informal*), boil, burn, rage, see red
(*informal*), seethe, smart, smoulder

simmer down *verb Informal* **= calm down**,
collect oneself, contain oneself, control
oneself, cool off *or* down, grow quieter

simper *verb* **= smile coyly**, smile affectedly,
smile self-consciously, smirk

simpering *adjective* **= coy**, affected,
self-conscious

simple *adjective* **1 = uncomplicated**, clear,
easy, easy-peasy (*slang*), elementary,
intelligible, lucid, manageable, plain,

straightforward, understandable, uninvolved
2 = plain, classic, clean, natural, severe,
Spartan, unadorned, uncluttered,
unembellished, unfussy **3 = pure**,
elementary, single, unalloyed, unblended,
uncombined, undivided, unmixed **4**
= artless, childlike, frank, guileless,
ingenuous, innocent, naive, natural,
simplistic, sincere, unaffected, unpretentious,
unsophisticated **5 = honest**, bald, basic,
direct, frank, naked, plain, sincere, stark,
undeniable, unvarnished **6 = unpretentious**,
homely, humble, lowly, modest, rustic **7**
Informal **= feeble-minded**, brainless, dense,
dumb (*informal*), dumb-ass (*slang*), feeble,
foolish, half-witted, moronic, obtuse,
shallow, silly, slow, stupid, thick
➤ **Antonyms**
≠**uncomplicated**: advanced, complex,
complicated, convoluted, difficult, elaborate,
highly developed, intricate, involved, refined,
sophisticated ≠**plain**: contrived, elaborate,
fussy, intricate, ornate ≠**artless**: artful,
smart, sophisticated, worldly, worldly-wise
≠**unpretentious**: extravagant, fancy, flashy
≠**feeble-minded**: astute, bright, clever,
intelligent, knowing, on the ball, quick,
quick on the uptake, quick-witted, sharp,
smart, wise

simple-minded *adjective* **1**
= unsophisticated, artless, natural **2**
= feeble-minded, a bit lacking (*informal*),
addle-brained, backward, brainless,
dim-witted, foolish, idiot, idiotic, moronic,
retarded, simple, stupid

simpleton *noun* **= halfwit**, berk (*Brit.
slang*), blockhead, booby, charlie (*Brit.
informal*), chump, dickhead (*slang*), divvy
(*Brit. slang*), dolt, dope (*informal*), dork
(*slang*), dullard, dumb-ass (*slang*), dunce,
fathead (*informal*), fool, geek (*slang*),
gobshite (*Irish taboo slang*), gonzo (*slang*),
idiot, imbecile (*informal*), jackass, jerk
(*slang, chiefly U.S. & Canad.*), moron, nerd
or nurd (*slang*), nincompoop, ninny, nitwit
(*informal*), numpty (*Scot. informal*),
numskull *or* numbskull, oaf, plank (*Brit.
slang*), schmuck (*U.S. slang*), twerp *or*
twirp (*informal*), twit (*informal, chiefly
Brit.*), wally (*slang*)

simplicity *noun* **1 = ease**, absence of
complications, clarity, clearness, easiness,
elementariness, obviousness,
straightforwardness **2 = plainness**, clean
lines, lack of adornment, modesty,
naturalness, purity, restraint **3 = artlessness**,
candour, directness, guilelessness,
innocence, lack of sophistication, naivety,
openness
➤ **Antonyms**
≠**ease**: complexity, complicatedness,

difficulty, intricacy, lack of clarity
≠ **plainness**: decoration, elaborateness,
embellishment, fanciness, fussiness,
ornateness, ostentation ≠ **artlessness**:
brains, craftiness, cunning, deviousness,
guile, sharpness, slyness, smartness,
sophistication, worldliness

simplify *verb* = **make simpler**, abridge,
decipher, disentangle, dumb down,
facilitate, make intelligible, reduce to
essentials, streamline

simplistic *adjective* = **oversimplified**,
naive

simply *adverb* **1** = **plainly**, clearly, directly,
easily, intelligibly, modestly, naturally,
straightforwardly, unaffectedly,
unpretentiously, without any elaboration **2**
= **just**, merely, only, purely, solely **3**
= **totally**, absolutely, altogether, completely,
really, unreservedly, utterly, wholly

simulate *verb* = **pretend**, act, affect,
assume, counterfeit, fabricate, feign, imitate,
make believe, put on, reproduce, sham

simulated *adjective* **1** = **pretended**,
artificial, assumed, feigned, insincere,
make-believe, phoney *or* phony (*informal*),
put-on **2** = **synthetic**, artificial, fake,
imitation, man-made, mock, pseudo
(*informal*), sham, substitute

simultaneous *adjective* = **coinciding**, at
the same time, coincident, concurrent,
contemporaneous, synchronous

simultaneously *adverb* = **at the same
time**, all together, concurrently, in chorus, in
unison, together

sin *noun* **1** = **wrongdoing**, crime, damnation,
error, evil, guilt, iniquity, misdeed, offence,
sinfulness, transgression, trespass,
ungodliness, unrighteousness, wickedness,
wrong ♦ *verb* **2** = **transgress**, err, fall, fall
from grace, go astray, lapse, offend

sincere *adjective* = **honest**, artless, bona
fide, candid, earnest, frank, genuine,
guileless, heartfelt, natural, no-nonsense,
open, real, serious, straightforward, true,
unaffected, unfeigned, upfront (*informal*),
wholehearted
➤ **Antonyms**
affected, artful, artificial, deceitful, deceptive,
dishonest, false, feigned, hollow, insincere,
phoney *or* phony (*informal*), pretended, put
on, synthetic, token, two-faced

sincerely *adverb* = **honestly**, earnestly,
from the bottom of one's heart, genuinely,
in all sincerity, in earnest, in good faith,
really, seriously, truly, wholeheartedly

sincerity *noun* = **honesty**, artlessness,
candour, frankness, genuineness, good faith,
guilelessness, probity, seriousness,
straightforwardness, truth, wholeheartedness

sinecure *noun* = **cushy number** (*informal*),
gravy train (*slang*), money for jam *or* old
rope (*informal*), soft job (*informal*), soft
option

sinewy *adjective* = **muscular**, athletic,
brawny, lusty, powerful, robust, strong,
sturdy, vigorous, wiry

sinful *adjective* = **wicked**, bad, corrupt,
criminal, depraved, erring, guilty, immoral,
iniquitous, irreligious, morally wrong,
ungodly, unholy, unrighteous
➤ **Antonyms**
chaste, decent, free from sin, godly, holy,
honest, honourable, immaculate, moral,
pure, righteous, sinless, spotless,
squeaky-clean, unblemished, upright,
virtuous, without sin

sing *verb* **1** = **warble**, carol, chant, chirp,
croon, make melody, pipe, trill, vocalize,
yodel **2** = **hum**, buzz, purr, whine, whistle **3**
Slang, chiefly U.S. = **inform (on)**, betray,
blow the whistle (on) (*informal*), grass (*Brit.
slang*), rat (on) (*informal*), shop (*slang,
chiefly Brit.*), spill one's guts (*slang*), spill
the beans (*informal*), squeal (*slang*), tell all

singe *verb* = **burn**, char, scorch, sear

singer *noun* = **vocalist**, balladeer, cantor,
chanteuse (*fem.*), chorister, crooner,
minstrel, soloist, songster *or* songstress,
troubadour

single *adjective* **1** = **one**, distinct, individual,
lone, only, particular, separate, singular, sole,
solitary, unique **2** = **individual**, exclusive,
separate, undivided, unshared **3**
= **unmarried**, free, unattached, unwed **4**
= **simple**, unblended, uncompounded,
unmixed ♦ *verb* **5** *usually with* **out** = **pick**,
choose, distinguish, fix on, pick on *or* out,
put on one side, select, separate, set apart

single-handed *adverb* = **unaided**, alone,
by oneself, independently, on one's own,
solo, unassisted, under one's own steam,
without help

single-minded *adjective* = **determined**,
dedicated, dogged, fixed, hellbent
(*informal*), steadfast, stubborn, tireless,
undeviating, unswerving, unwavering

singly *adverb* = **one by one**, individually,
one at a time, separately

sing out *verb* = **call (out)**, cooee, cry (out),
halloo, holler (*informal*), make oneself
heard, shout, yell

singular *adjective* **1** = **single**, individual,
separate, sole **2** = **remarkable**, conspicuous,
eminent, exceptional, extraordinary, notable,
noteworthy, outstanding, prodigious, rare,
uncommon, unique, unparalleled **3**
= **unusual**, atypical, curious, eccentric,
extraordinary, odd, oddball (*informal*),
out-of-the-way, outré, peculiar, queer,

strange, wacko (*slang*)
➤ **Antonyms**
≠**remarkable, unusual:** common, common
or garden, commonplace, conventional,
everyday, familiar, normal, routine,
run-of-the-mill, unexceptional,
unremarkable, usual

singularity *noun* 1 = **oddness**,
abnormality, curiousness, extraordinariness,
irregularity, peculiarity, queerness,
strangeness 2 = **idiosyncrasy**, eccentricity,
oddity, particularity, peculiarity, quirk, twist

singularly *adverb* = **remarkably**,
conspicuously, especially, exceptionally,
extraordinarily, notably, outstandingly,
particularly, prodigiously, seriously
(*informal*), surprisingly, uncommonly,
unusually

sinister *adjective* = **threatening**, baleful,
bodeful, dire, disquieting, evil, forbidding,
injurious, malevolent, malign, malignant,
menacing, ominous
➤ **Antonyms**
auspicious, benevolent, benign, calming,
encouraging, good, heartening, heroic,
honourable, just, noble, promising,
propitious, reassuring, righteous, upright,
worthy

sink *verb* 1 = **descend**, cave in, decline, dip,
disappear, droop, drop, drown, ebb, fall,
founder, go down, go under, lower,
plummet, plunge, sag, slope, submerge,
subside 2 = **fall**, abate, collapse, drop, lapse,
relapse, retrogress, slip, slump, subside 3
= **stoop**, be reduced to, debase oneself,
lower oneself, succumb 4 = **decline**, decay,
decrease, degenerate, depreciate,
deteriorate, die, diminish, dwindle, fade, fail,
flag, go downhill (*informal*), lessen, weaken,
worsen 5 = **dig**, bore, drill, drive, excavate,
lay, put down
➤ **Antonyms**
≠**descend:** arise, ascend, climb, go up,
move up, rise, rise up ≠**decline:** go up,
grow, improve, increase, intensify, rise, rise
up, swell, wax

sink in *verb* = **be understood**, get through
to, make an impression, penetrate, register
(*informal*), take hold of

sinner *noun* = **wrongdoer**, evildoer,
malefactor, miscreant, offender, reprobate,
transgressor

sinuous *adjective Literary* = **curving**,
coiling, crooked, curvy, lithe, meandering,
serpentine, undulating, winding

sip *verb* 1 = **drink**, sample, sup, taste ♦ *noun*
2 = **swallow**, drop, taste, thimbleful

siren *noun* = **seductress**, charmer, Circe,
femme fatale, Lorelei, temptress, vamp
(*informal*), witch

sissy *or* **cissy** *noun* 1 = **wimp** (*informal*),
baby, coward, jessie (*Scot. slang*), milksop,
mummy's boy, namby-pamby, pansy, softie
(*informal*), weakling, wet (*Brit. informal*),
wuss (*slang*) ♦ *adjective* 2 = **wimpish** *or*
wimpy (*informal*), cowardly, effeminate,
feeble, namby-pamby, soft (*informal*),
unmanly, weak, wet (*Brit. informal*), wussy
(*slang*)

sit *verb* 1 = **rest**, be seated, perch, settle, take
a seat, take the weight off one's feet 2
= **convene**, assemble, be in session,
deliberate, meet, officiate, preside

site *noun* 1 = **location**, ground, place, plot,
position, setting, spot ♦ *verb* 2 = **locate**,
install, place, position, set, situate

sitting *noun* = **meeting**, congress,
consultation, get-together (*informal*),
hearing, period, session

situation *noun* 1 = **state of affairs**, ball
game (*informal*), case, circumstances,
condition, equation, kettle of fish (*informal*),
lie of the land, plight, scenario, state, status
quo, the picture (*informal*) 2 = **location**,
locale, locality, place, position, seat, setting,
site, spot 3 = **status**, rank, sphere, station 4
= **job**, berth (*informal*), employment, office,
place, position, post

sixth sense *noun* = **intuition**, clairvoyance,
second sight

sizable, sizeable *adjective* = **large**,
considerable, decent, decent-sized, goodly,
largish, respectable, substantial, tidy
(*informal*)

size *noun* = **dimensions**, amount, bigness,
bulk, extent, greatness, hugeness,
immensity, largeness, magnitude, mass,
measurement(s), proportions, range,
vastness, volume

size up *verb Informal* = **assess**, appraise,
evaluate, eye up, get (something) taped
(*Brit. informal*), get the measure of, take
stock of

sizzle *verb* = **hiss**, crackle, frizzle, fry, spit,
sputter

skedaddle *verb Informal* = **run away**,
abscond, beat a hasty retreat, bolt, decamp,
disappear, do a bunk (*Brit. slang*), flee, hop
it (*Brit. slang*), scarper (*Brit. slang*), scoot,
scram (*informal*)

skeletal *adjective* = **emaciated**, cadaverous,
fleshless, gaunt, hollow-cheeked,
lantern-jawed, skin-and-bone (*informal*),
wasted

skeleton *noun* = **framework**, bare bones,
bones, draft, frame, outline, sketch, structure

sketch *noun* 1 = **drawing**, delineation,
design, draft, outline, plan, skeleton ♦ *verb*
2 = **draw**, block out, delineate, depict, draft,

outline, paint, plot, portray, represent, rough out

sketchily *adverb* = **incompletely**, cursorily, hastily, imperfectly, patchily, perfunctorily, roughly

sketchy *adjective* = **incomplete**, cobbled together, crude, cursory, inadequate, perfunctory, rough, scrappy, skimpy, slight, superficial, unfinished, vague
➤ Antonyms
complete, detailed, full, thorough

skewwhiff *adjective Brit. informal* = **crooked**, askew, aslant, cockeyed (*informal*), out of true, squint (*informal*), tilted

skilful *adjective* = **expert**, able, accomplished, adept, adroit, apt, clever, competent, dexterous, experienced, handy, masterly, practised, professional, proficient, quick, ready, skilled, trained
➤ Antonyms
amateurish, awkward, bungling, cack-handed, clumsy, cowboy (*informal*), ham-fisted, incompetent, inept, inexperienced, inexpert, maladroit, slapdash, unaccomplished, unqualified, unskilful, unskilled

skill *noun* = **expertise**, ability, accomplishment, adroitness, aptitude, art, cleverness, competence, craft, dexterity, experience, expertness, facility, finesse, handiness, ingenuity, intelligence, knack, proficiency, quickness, readiness, skilfulness, talent, technique
➤ Antonyms
awkwardness, brute force, cack-handedness, clumsiness, gaucheness, ham-fistedness, inability, incompetence, ineptitude, inexperience, lack of finesse, maladroitness, unhandiness

skilled *adjective* = **expert**, able, accomplished, a dab hand at (*Brit. informal*), experienced, masterly, practised, professional, proficient, skilful, trained
➤ Antonyms
amateurish, cowboy (*informal*), inexperienced, inexpert, unprofessional, unqualified, unskilled, untalented, untrained

skim *verb* 1 = **separate**, cream 2 = **glide**, brush, coast, dart, float, fly, sail, soar 3 *usually with* **through** = **scan**, glance, run one's eye over, skip (*informal*), thumb *or* leaf through

skimp *verb* = **stint**, be mean with, be niggardly, be sparing with, cut corners, pinch, scamp, scant, scrimp, tighten one's belt
➤ Antonyms
act as if one had money to burn, be extravagant, be generous with, be prodigal,

blow (*slang*), fritter away, lavish, overspend, splurge, squander, throw money away

skimpy *adjective* = **inadequate**, exiguous, insufficient, meagre, miserly, niggardly, scant, scanty, short, sparse, thin, tight

skin *noun* 1 = **hide**, fell, integument, pelt 2 = **coating**, casing, crust, film, husk, membrane, outside, peel, rind 3 **by the skin of one's teeth** = **narrowly**, by a hair's-breadth, by a narrow margin, by a whisker (*informal*), only just 4 **get under one's skin** *Informal* = **annoy**, aggravate (*informal*), get in one's hair (*informal*), get on one's nerves (*informal*), grate on, irk, irritate, needle (*informal*), nettle, piss one off (*taboo slang*), rub up the wrong way ♦ *verb* 5 = **peel**, abrade, bark, excoriate, flay, graze, scrape

skin-deep *adjective* = **superficial**, artificial, external, meaningless, on the surface, shallow, surface

skinflint *noun* = **miser**, meanie *or* meany (*informal, chiefly Brit.*), niggard, penny-pincher (*informal*), Scrooge, tightwad (*U.S. & Canad. slang*)

skinny *adjective* = **thin**, emaciated, lean, scraggy, scrawny, skeletal, skin-and-bone (*informal*), undernourished
➤ Antonyms
beefy (*informal*), fat, fleshy, heavy, obese, plump, podgy, portly, stout, tubby

skip *verb* 1 = **hop**, bob, bounce, caper, cavort, dance, flit, frisk, gambol, prance, trip 2 = **pass over**, eschew, give (something) a miss, leave out, miss out, omit, skim over 3 *Informal* = **miss**, bunk off (*slang*), cut (*informal*), dog it *or* dog off (*dialect*), play truant from, wag (*dialect*)

skirmish *noun* 1 = **fight**, affair, affray (*Law*), battle, brush, clash, combat, conflict, contest, dust-up (*informal*), encounter, engagement, fracas, incident, scrap (*informal*), scrimmage, set-to (*informal*), spat, tussle ♦ *verb* 2 = **fight**, clash, collide, come to blows, scrap (*informal*), tussle

skirt *verb* 1 = **border**, edge, flank, lie alongside 2 *often with* **around** *or* **round** = **avoid**, body-swerve (*Scot.*), bypass, circumvent, detour, evade, steer clear of

skit *noun* = **parody**, burlesque, sketch, spoof (*informal*), takeoff (*informal*), travesty

skittish *adjective* = **lively**, antsy (*informal*), excitable, fickle, fidgety, frivolous, highly strung, jumpy, nervous, playful, restive
➤ Antonyms
calm, composed, demure, laid-back, placid, relaxed, sober, staid, steady, unexcitable, unfazed (*informal*), unflappable, unruffled

skive *verb Brit. informal* = **slack**, dodge, idle, malinger, shirk, skulk, swing the lead

skiver *noun Brit. informal* = **slacker**, dodger, idler, loafer, shirker

skulduggery *noun Informal* = **trickery**, double-dealing, duplicity, machinations, shenanigan(s) (*informal*), swindling, underhandedness, unscrupulousness

skulk *verb* **1** = **sneak**, creep, pad, prowl, slink **2** = **lurk**, lie in wait, loiter

sky *noun* **1** = **heavens**, firmament, upper atmosphere, vault of heaven **2 to the skies** = **fulsomely**, excessively, extravagantly, highly, immoderately, inordinately, profusely

slab *noun* = **piece**, chunk, hunk, lump, nugget, portion, slice, wedge, wodge (*Brit. informal*)

slack *adjective* **1** = **loose**, baggy, easy, flaccid, flexible, lax, limp, not taut, relaxed **2** = **negligent**, idle, inactive, inattentive, lax, lazy, neglectful, remiss, slapdash, slipshod, tardy **3** = **slow**, dull, inactive, quiet, slow-moving, sluggish ♦ *noun* **4** = **room**, excess, give (*informal*), leeway, looseness, play ♦ *verb* **5** = **shirk**, dodge, flag, idle, neglect, relax, skive (*Brit. slang*), slacken
➤ **Antonyms**
adjective ≠**loose**: inflexible, rigid, stiff, strained, stretched, taut, tight ≠**negligent**: concerned, diligent, exacting, hard, hard-working, meticulous, stern, strict ≠**slow**: active, bustling, busy, fast-moving, hectic

slacken *verb, often with* **off** = **lessen**, abate, decrease, diminish, drop off, ease (off), let up, loosen, moderate, reduce, relax, release, slack off, slow down

slacker *noun* = **layabout**, dodger, good-for-nothing, idler, loafer, passenger, shirker, skiver (*Brit. slang*)

slag *verb Slang, often with* **off** = **criticize**, abuse, berate, deride, insult, malign, mock, slam, slander, slang, slate

slake *verb* = **satisfy**, assuage, gratify, quench, sate, satiate

slam *verb* **1** = **bang**, crash, smash, thump **2** = **throw**, dash, fling, hurl **3** *Slang* = **criticize**, attack, blast, lambast(e), pan (*informal*), pillory, shoot down (*informal*), slate (*informal*), tear into (*informal*), vilify

slander *noun* **1** = **defamation**, aspersion, backbiting, calumny, libel, misrepresentation, muckraking, obloquy, scandal, smear ♦ *verb* **2** = **defame**, backbite, blacken (someone's) name, calumniate, disparage, libel, malign, muckrake, slur, smear, traduce, vilify
➤ **Antonyms**
noun ≠**defamation**: acclaim, acclamation, approval, praise, tribute ♦ *verb* ≠**defame**: acclaim, applaud, approve, compliment, eulogize, laud, praise, sing the praises of

slanderous *adjective* = **defamatory**, abusive, calumnious, damaging, libellous, malicious

slang *verb* = **insult**, abuse, berate, call names, hurl insults at, malign, revile, vilify, vituperate

slanging match *noun* = **quarrel**, altercation, argument, argy-bargy (*Brit. informal*), barney (*informal*), battle of words, row, set-to (*informal*), spat

slant *verb* **1** = **slope**, angle off, bend, bevel, cant, heel, incline, lean, list, shelve, skew, tilt **2** = **bias**, angle, colour, distort, twist, weight ♦ *noun* **3** = **slope**, camber, declination, diagonal, gradient, incline, pitch, rake, ramp, tilt **4** = **bias**, angle, attitude, emphasis, leaning, one-sidedness, point of view, prejudice, viewpoint

slanting *adjective* = **sloping**, angled, aslant, asymmetrical, at an angle, bent, diagonal, inclined, oblique, on the bias, sideways, slanted, slantwise, tilted, tilting

slap *noun* **1** = **smack**, bang, blow, chin (*slang*), clout (*informal*), cuff, spank, swipe, wallop (*informal*), whack **2 a slap in the face** = **insult**, affront, blow, humiliation, put-down, rebuff, rebuke, rejection, repulse, snub ♦ *verb* **3** = **smack**, bang, clap, clout (*informal*), cuff, hit, spank, strike, swipe, whack **4** *Informal, chiefly Brit.* = **plaster**, daub, plonk, spread ♦ *adverb* **5** *Informal* = **exactly**, bang, directly, plumb (*informal*), precisely, slap-bang (*informal*), smack (*informal*)

slapdash *adjective* = **careless**, clumsy, disorderly, haphazard, hasty, hurried, last-minute, messy, negligent, perfunctory, slipshod, sloppy (*informal*), slovenly, thoughtless, untidy
➤ **Antonyms**
careful, conscientious, fastidious, meticulous, ordered, orderly, painstaking, precise, punctilious, thoughtful, tidy

slaphappy *adjective* = **happy-go-lucky**, casual, haphazard, hit-or-miss (*informal*), irresponsible, nonchalant

slapstick *noun* = **knockabout comedy**, buffoonery, farce, horseplay

slap-up *adjective Brit. informal* = **luxurious**, elaborate, excellent, first-rate, lavish, magnificent, no-expense-spared, princely, splendid, sumptuous, superb

slash *verb* **1** = **cut**, gash, hack, lacerate, rend, rip, score, slit **2** = **reduce**, cut, drop, lower ♦ *noun* **3** = **cut**, gash, incision, laceration, rent, rip, slit

slate *verb Informal, chiefly Brit.* = **criticize**, berate, blame, blast, castigate, censure, haul over the coals (*informal*), lambast(e), lay into (*informal*), pan (*informal*), pitch into (*informal*), rap (someone's) knuckles, rebuke, roast (*informal*), scold, slam (*slang*), take to task, tear into (*informal*), tear (someone) off a strip (*informal*)

slattern *noun Old-fashioned* = **sloven**, drab (*archaic*), slut, trollop

slatternly *adjective Old-fashioned* = **slovenly**, bedraggled, dirty, sluttish, unclean, unkempt, untidy

slaughter *noun* **1** = **slaying**, blood bath, bloodshed, butchery, carnage, extermination, holocaust, killing, liquidation, massacre, murder ◆ *verb* **2** = **slay**, butcher, destroy, do to death, exterminate, kill, liquidate, massacre, murder, put to the sword **3** *Informal* = **defeat**, blow out of the water (*slang*), crush, hammer (*informal*), lick (*informal*), overwhelm, rout, tank (*slang*), thrash, trounce, vanquish, wipe the floor with (*informal*)

slaughterhouse *noun* = **abattoir**, butchery, shambles

slave *noun* **1** = **servant**, bondservant, bondsman, drudge, scullion (*archaic*), serf, skivvy (*chiefly Brit.*), slavey (*Brit. informal*), varlet (*archaic*), vassal, villein ◆ *verb* **2** = **toil**, drudge, grind (*informal*), slog, sweat, work one's fingers to the bone

slaver *verb* = **drool**, dribble, salivate, slobber

slavery *noun* = **enslavement**, bondage, captivity, serfdom, servitude, subjugation, thraldom, thrall, vassalage
➤ **Antonyms**
emancipation, freedom, liberty, manumission, release

slavish *adjective* **1** = **servile**, abject, base, cringing, despicable, fawning, grovelling, low, mean, menial, obsequious, submissive, sycophantic **2** = **imitative**, conventional, second-hand, unimaginative, uninspired, unoriginal
➤ **Antonyms**
≠**servile**: assertive, domineering, masterful, rebellious, self-willed, wilful ≠**imitative**: creative, imaginative, independent, inventive, original, radical, revolutionary

slay *verb Archaic or literary* = **kill**, annihilate, assassinate, butcher, destroy, dispatch, do away with, do in (*slang*), eliminate, exterminate, massacre, mow down, murder, slaughter

sleaze *noun Informal* = **corruption**, bribery, crookedness (*informal*), dishonesty, extortion, fiddling (*informal*), fraud, shady dealings (*informal*), unscrupulousness, venality

sleazy *adjective* = **sordid**, crummy, disreputable, low, run-down, seedy, squalid, tacky (*informal*)

sleek *adjective* = **glossy**, lustrous, shiny,

smooth, well-fed, well-groomed
➤ **Antonyms**
badly groomed, bedraggled, dishevelled, frowzy, ill-nourished, in poor condition, ratty (*Brit. & N.Z. informal*), rough, shaggy, sloppy, slovenly, unkempt

sleep *noun* **1** = **slumber(s)**, beauty sleep (*informal*), dormancy, doze, forty winks (*informal*), hibernation, kip (*Brit. slang*), nap, repose, rest, shuteye (*slang*), siesta, snooze (*informal*), zizz (*Brit. informal*) ◆ *verb* **2** = **slumber**, be in the land of Nod, catnap, doze, drop off (*informal*), drowse, go out like a light, hibernate, kip (*Brit. slang*), nod off (*informal*), snooze (*informal*), snore, take a nap, take forty winks (*informal*), zizz (*Brit. informal*)

sleepless *adjective* **1** = **wakeful**, disturbed, insomniac, restless, unsleeping **2** *Chiefly poetic* = **alert**, unsleeping, vigilant, watchful, wide awake

sleeplessness *noun* = **insomnia**, wakefulness

sleepwalker *noun* = **somnambulist**, noctambulist

sleepwalking *noun* = **somnambulism**, noctambulation, noctambulism, somnambulation

sleepy *adjective* **1** = **drowsy**, dull, heavy, inactive, lethargic, sluggish, somnolent, torpid **2** = **quiet**, dull, hypnotic, inactive, sleep-inducing, slow, somnolent, soporific
➤ **Antonyms**
≠**drowsy**: active, alert, animated, awake, boisterous, energetic, full of beans (*informal*), lively, wakeful, wide-awake ≠**quiet**: active, bustling, busy, lively, thriving

sleight of hand *noun* = **dexterity**, adroitness, legerdemain, manipulation, prestidigitation, skill

slender *adjective* **1** = **slim**, lean, narrow, slight, svelte, sylphlike, willowy **2** = **faint**, feeble, flimsy, fragile, poor, remote, slight, slim, tenuous, thin, weak **3** = **meagre**, inadequate, inconsiderable, insufficient, little, scant, scanty, small, spare
➤ **Antonyms**
≠**slim**: bulky, chubby, fat, heavy, large, podgy, stout, tubby, well-built ≠**faint**: good, solid, strong ≠**meagre**: ample, appreciable, considerable, generous, large, substantial

sleuth *noun Informal* = **detective**, dick (*slang, chiefly U.S.*), gumshoe (*U.S. slang*), private eye (*informal*), (private) investigator, sleuthhound (*informal*)

slice *noun* **1** = **piece**, cut, helping, portion, segment, share, sliver, wedge ◆ *verb* **2** = **cut**, carve, divide, sever

slick *adjective* **1** = **glib**, meretricious,

plausible, polished, smooth, sophistical, specious **2 = skilful**, adroit, deft, dexterous, dextrous, polished, professional, sharp ♦ *verb* **3 = smooth**, make glossy, plaster down, sleek, smarm down (*Brit. informal*)
➤ **Antonyms**
adjective ≠**skilful:** amateur, amateurish, clumsy, crude, inexpert, unaccomplished, unpolished, unprofessional, unskilful

slide *verb* **1 = slip**, coast, glide, skim, slither, toboggan, veer **2 let slide = neglect**, forget, gloss over, ignore, let ride, pass over, push to the back of one's mind, turn a blind eye to

slight *adjective* **1 = small**, feeble, inconsiderable, insignificant, insubstantial, meagre, measly, minor, modest, negligible, paltry, scanty, superficial, trifling, trivial, unimportant, weak **2 = slim**, delicate, feeble, fragile, lightly-built, small, spare ♦ *verb* **3 = snub**, affront, cold-shoulder, despise, disdain, disparage, give offence *or* umbrage to, ignore, insult, neglect, put down, scorn, show disrespect for, treat with contempt ♦ *noun* **4 = insult**, affront, discourtesy, disdain, disregard, disrespect, inattention, indifference, neglect, rebuff, slap in the face (*informal*), snub, (the) cold shoulder
➤ **Antonyms**
adjective ≠**small:** appreciable, considerable, great, heavy, important, large, noticeable, obvious, significant, substantial ≠**slim:** muscular, solid, strong, sturdy, well-built ♦ *verb* ≠**snub:** compliment, flatter, praise, speak well of, treat considerately ♦ *noun* ≠**insult:** compliment, flattery, praise

slightly *adverb* **= a little**, marginally, on a small scale, somewhat, to some extent *or* degree

slim *adjective* **1 = slender**, lean, narrow, slight, svelte, sylphlike, thin, trim **2 = slight**, faint, poor, remote, slender ♦ *verb* **3 = lose weight**, diet, reduce, slenderize (*chiefly U.S.*)
➤ **Antonyms**
adjective ≠**slender:** broad, bulky, chubby, fat, heavy, muscular, obese, overweight, sturdy, tubby, well-built, wide ≠**slight:** good, strong ♦ *verb* ≠**lose weight:** build oneself up, put on weight

slimy *adjective* **1 = viscous**, clammy, gloopy (*informal*), glutinous, miry, mucous, muddy, oozy **2** *Chiefly Brit.* **= obsequious**, creeping, grovelling, oily, servile, smarmy (*Brit. informal*), soapy (*slang*), sycophantic, toadying, unctuous

sling *verb* **1** *Informal* **= throw**, cast, chuck (*informal*), fling, heave, hurl, lob (*informal*), shy, toss **2 = hang**, dangle, suspend, swing

slink *verb* **= creep**, prowl, pussyfoot (*informal*), skulk, slip, sneak, steal

slinky *adjective* **= figure-hugging**, clinging, close-fitting, sinuous, skintight, sleek

slip[1] *verb* **1 = fall**, lose one's balance, miss *or* lose one's footing, skid, trip (over) **2 = slide**, glide, skate, slither **3 = sneak**, conceal, creep, hide, steal **4 = get away**, break away from, break free from, disappear, escape, get clear of **5** *sometimes with* **up = make a mistake**, blunder, boob (*Brit. slang*), drop a brick *or* clanger (*informal*), err, go wrong, miscalculate, misjudge, mistake **6 let slip = give away**, blurt out, come out with (*informal*), disclose, divulge, leak, let out (*informal*), let the cat out of the bag, reveal ♦ *noun* **7 = mistake**, bloomer (*Brit. informal*), blunder, boob (*Brit. slang*), error, failure, fault, faux pas, indiscretion, lapse, omission, oversight, slip of the tongue, slip-up (*informal*) **8 give (someone) the slip = escape from**, dodge, elude, evade, get away from, lose (someone), outwit, shake (someone) off

slip[2] *noun* **1 = strip**, piece, sliver **2 = cutting**, offshoot, runner, scion, shoot, sprig, sprout

slippery *adjective* **1 = smooth**, glassy, greasy, icy, perilous, slippy (*informal or dialect*), unsafe, unstable, unsteady **2 = untrustworthy**, crafty, cunning, devious, dishonest, duplicitous, evasive, false, foxy, shifty, sneaky, treacherous, tricky, two-faced, unpredictable, unreliable

slipshod *adjective* **= careless**, casual, loose, slapdash, sloppy (*informal*), slovenly, untidy

slit *noun* **1 = cut**, fissure, gash, incision, opening, rent, split, tear ♦ *verb* **2 = cut (open)**, gash, impale, knife, lance, pierce, rip, slash, split open

slither *verb* **= slide**, glide, skitter, slink, slip, snake, undulate

sliver *noun* **= shred**, flake, fragment, paring, shaving, slip, splinter

slob *noun* *Informal* **= layabout**, couch potato (*slang*), good-for-nothing, idler, loafer, lounger

slobber *verb* **= drool**, dribble, drivel, salivate, slaver, water at the mouth

slobbish *adjective* **= messy**, slatternly, sloppy (*informal*), slovenly, unclean, unkempt, untidy

slog *verb* **1 = work**, apply oneself to, keep one's nose to the grindstone, labour, persevere, plod, plough through, slave, toil, work one's fingers to the bone **2 = trudge**, tramp, trek **3 = hit**, hit for six, punch, slosh (*Brit. slang*), slug, sock (*slang*), strike, thump, wallop (*informal*) ♦ *noun* **4 = labour**, blood, sweat, and tears (*informal*), effort, exertion, struggle **5 = trudge**, hike, tramp, trek

slogan *noun* **= catch phrase**, catchword,

jingle, motto, rallying cry, tag-line

slop *verb* = **spill**, overflow, slosh (*informal*), spatter, splash, splatter

slope *noun* **1** = **inclination**, brae (*Scot.*), declination, declivity, descent, downgrade (*chiefly U.S.*), gradient, incline, ramp, rise, slant, tilt ♦ *verb* **2** = **slant**, drop away, fall, incline, lean, pitch, rise, tilt **3 slope off** or **away** *Informal* = **slink away**, creep away, make oneself scarce, skulk, slip away, steal

sloping *adjective* = **slanting**, atilt, bevelled, inclined, inclining, leaning, oblique

sloppy *adjective* **1** *Informal* = **careless**, amateurish, clumsy, hit-or-miss (*informal*), inattentive, messy, slipshod, slovenly, unkempt, untidy, weak **2** *Informal* = **sentimental**, gushing, icky (*informal*), mawkish, mushy (*informal*), overemotional, slushy (*informal*), soppy (*Brit. informal*) **3** = **wet**, sludgy, slushy, splashy, watery

slosh *verb Informal* **1** = **pour**, shower, slap, spray **2** = **splash**, flounder, slop, wade

slot *noun* **1** = **opening**, aperture, channel, groove, hole, slit, vent **2** *Informal* = **place**, niche, opening, position, space, time, vacancy ♦ *verb* **3** = **fit in**, adjust, assign, fit, insert, pigeonhole

sloth *noun* = **laziness**, idleness, inactivity, indolence, inertia, slackness, slothfulness, sluggishness, torpor

slothful *adjective Formal* = **lazy**, good-for-nothing, idle, inactive, indolent, inert, skiving (*Brit. slang*), slack, workshy

slouch *verb* = **slump**, droop, loll, stoop

slovenly *adjective* **1** = **untidy**, disorderly, slatternly, unkempt **2** = **careless**, heedless, loose, negligent, slack, slapdash, slipshod, sloppy (*informal*)
➤ **Antonyms**
≠**untidy**: clean, meticulous, neat, orderly, shipshape, smart, soigné or soignée, tidy, trim, well-groomed ≠**careless**: careful, conscientious, disciplined, methodical, meticulous, well-ordered

slow *adjective* **1** = **prolonged**, gradual, lingering, long-drawn-out, protracted, time-consuming **2** = **unhurried**, creeping, dawdling, deliberate, easy, lackadaisical, laggard, lagging, lazy, leaden, leisurely, loitering, measured, plodding, ponderous, slow-moving, sluggardly, sluggish **3** = **late**, backward, behind, behindhand, delayed, dilatory, long-delayed, tardy, unpunctual **4** = **stupid**, bovine, braindead (*informal*), dense, dim, dozy (*Brit. informal*), dull, dull-witted, dumb (*informal*), obtuse, retarded, slow on the uptake (*informal*), slow-witted, thick, unresponsive **5** = **dull**, boring, conservative, dead, dead-and-alive (*Brit.*), inactive, quiet, slack, sleepy, sluggish,

stagnant, tame, tedious, uneventful, uninteresting, unproductive, unprogressive **6 slow to** = **unwilling to**, averse to, disinclined to, hesitant to, indisposed to, loath to, reluctant to ♦ *verb* **7** *often with* **up** or **down** = **reduce speed**, brake, check, curb, decelerate, delay, detain, handicap, hold up, lag, rein in, relax, restrict, retard, slacken (off)
➤ **Antonyms**
adjective ≠**unhurried**: brisk, eager, fast, hectic, hurried, precipitate, prompt, quick, quickie (*informal*), quick-moving, sharp, speedy, swift ≠**stupid**: bright, clever, intelligent, perceptive, quick, quick-witted, sharp, smart ≠**dull**: action-packed, animated, exciting, interesting, lively, stimulating ♦ *verb* ≠**reduce speed**: accelerate, advance, aid, boost, help, pick up speed, quicken, speed up

slowly *adverb* = **gradually**, at a snail's pace, at one's leisure, by degrees, in one's own (good) time, leisurely, ploddingly, steadily, taking one's time, unhurriedly

sludge *noun* = **sediment**, dregs, gloop (*informal*), mire, muck, mud, ooze, residue, silt, slime, slop, slush

sluggish *adjective* = **inactive**, dull, heavy, indolent, inert, lethargic, lifeless, listless, slothful, slow, slow-moving, torpid, unresponsive
➤ **Antonyms**
alive and kicking, animated, brisk, dynamic, energetic, enthusiastic, fast, full of beans (*informal*), full of life, industrious, lively, swift, vigorous

sluggishness *noun* = **inactivity**, apathy, drowsiness, dullness, heaviness, indolence, inertia, languor, lassitude, lethargy, listlessness, slothfulness, somnolence, stagnation, torpor

sluice *verb* **1** = **drain**, flush **2** = **wash out**, cleanse, drench, irrigate, wash down

slum *noun* = **hovel**, ghetto

slumber *verb* = **sleep**, be inactive, doze, drowse, kip (*Brit. slang*), lie dormant, nap, repose, snooze (*informal*), zizz (*Brit. informal*)

slump *verb* **1** = **fall**, collapse, crash, decline, deteriorate, fall off, go downhill (*informal*), plummet, plunge, sink, slip **2** = **sag**, bend, droop, hunch, loll, slouch ♦ *noun* **3** = **fall**, collapse, crash, decline, depreciation, downturn, drop, failure, falling-off, lapse, low, reverse, stagnation, trough **4** = **recession**, depression
➤ **Antonyms**
verb ≠**fall**: advance, boom, develop, expand, flourish, grow, increase, prosper, thrive ♦ *noun* ≠**fall**: advance, boom, boost,

development, expansion, gain, growth,
improvement, increase, upsurge, upswing,
upturn

slur *noun* = **insult**, affront, aspersion,
calumny, discredit, disgrace, innuendo,
insinuation, reproach, smear, stain, stigma

slut *noun Offensive* = **tart**, drab (*archaic*),
scrubber (*Brit. & Austral. slang*), slag (*Brit.
slang*), slapper (*Brit. slang*), slattern, sloven,
trollop

sluttish *adjective* = **promiscuous**, coarse,
dissipated, immoral, tarty (*informal*),
trollopy, whorish

sly *adjective* **1** = **cunning**, artful, astute,
clever, conniving, covert, crafty, devious,
foxy, furtive, guileful, insidious, scheming,
secret, shifty, stealthy, subtle, underhand,
wily **2** = **roguish**, arch, impish, knowing,
mischievous ◆ *noun* **3 on the sly** = **secretly**,
behind (someone's) back, covertly, like a
thief in the night, on the q.t. (*informal*), on
the quiet, privately, surreptitiously,
underhandedly
➤ **Antonyms**
adjective ≠**cunning**: above-board, artless,
direct, frank, guileless, honest, ingenuous,
open, straightforward, trustworthy

smack *verb* **1** = **slap**, box, clap, cuff, hit,
pat, sock (*slang*), spank, strike, swipe, tap
◆ *noun* **2** = **slap**, blow, crack, swipe **3
smack in the eye** *Informal, chiefly Brit.*
= **snub**, rebuff, slap in the face ◆ *adverb* **4**
Informal = **directly**, exactly, plumb,
point-blank, precisely, right, slap (*informal*),
squarely, straight

smack of *verb* **1** = **smell of**, be redolent of,
reek of **2** = **be suggestive** *or* **indicative of**,
bear the stamp of, betoken, have all the
hallmarks of, suggest

small *adjective* **1** = **little**, diminutive,
immature, Lilliputian, mini, miniature,
minute, petite, pint-sized (*informal*),
pocket-sized, puny, pygmy *or* pigmy, slight,
teeny, teeny-weeny, tiny, undersized, wee,
young **2** = **meagre**, inadequate,
inconsiderable, insufficient, limited, measly,
scant, scanty **3** = **unimportant**, insignificant,
lesser, minor, negligible, paltry, petty,
trifling, trivial **4** = **petty**, base, grudging,
illiberal, mean, narrow **5** = **modest**, humble,
small-scale, unpretentious **6 make
(someone) feel small** = **humiliate**,
disconcert, humble, make (someone) look
foolish, mortify, put down (*slang*), show up
(*informal*), take down a peg or two
(*informal*)
➤ **Antonyms**
≠**little**: big, colossal, enormous, great, huge,
immense, massive, mega (*slang*), sizable *or*
sizeable, vast ≠**meagre**: ample,
considerable, generous, substantial

≠**unimportant**: appreciable, important,
major, powerful, serious, significant, urgent,
vital, weighty ≠**modest**: grand, large-scale

small-minded *adjective* = **petty**, bigoted,
grudging, intolerant, mean, narrow-minded,
ungenerous
➤ **Antonyms**
broad-minded, far-sighted, generous, liberal,
open, open-minded, tolerant, unbigoted

small-time *adjective* = **minor**, insignificant,
no-account (*U.S. informal*), of no account,
of no consequence, petty, piddling
(*informal*), unimportant

smarmy *adjective Informal* = **obsequious**,
bootlicking (*informal*), crawling, fawning,
fulsome, greasy, ingratiating, oily, servile,
slimy, smooth, soapy (*slang*), suave,
sycophantic, toadying, unctuous

smart *adjective* **1** = **chic**, elegant,
fashionable, fine, modish, natty (*informal*),
neat, snappy, spruce, stylish, trendy (*Brit.
informal*), trim, well turned-out **2** = **clever**,
acute, adept, agile, apt, astute, bright, brisk,
canny, ingenious, intelligent, keen, nimble,
quick, quick-witted, ready, sharp, shrewd **3**
= **impertinent**, nimble-witted, pointed,
ready, saucy, smart-alecky (*informal*), witty
4 = **brisk**, cracking (*informal*), jaunty, lively,
quick, spirited, vigorous **5** = **stinging**, hard,
keen, painful, piercing, resounding, sharp
◆ *verb* **6** = **sting**, burn, hurt, pain, throb,
tingle ◆ *noun* **7** = **sting**, burning sensation,
pain, pang, smarting, soreness
➤ **Antonyms**
adjective ≠**chic**: dowdy, dull, fogeyish, naff
(*Brit. slang*), old-fashioned, outmoded,
out-of-date, passé, scruffy, sloppy, uncool,
unfashionable, untrendy (*Brit. informal*)
≠**clever**: daft (*informal*), dense, dim-witted
(*informal*), dull, dumb (*informal*), dumb-ass
(*slang*), foolish, idiotic, moronic, slow,
stupid, thick, unintelligent

smart aleck *noun Informal* = **know-all**
(*informal*), clever-clogs (*informal*), clever
Dick (*informal*), smartarse (*slang*), smarty
boots (*informal*), smarty pants (*informal*),
wise guy (*informal*)

smarten *verb* = **tidy**, beautify, groom, put
in order, put to rights, spruce up

smash *verb* **1** = **break**, crush, demolish,
disintegrate, pulverize, shatter, shiver **2**
= **collide**, crash **3** = **destroy**, defeat, lay
waste, overthrow, ruin, total (*slang*), trash
(*slang*), wreck ◆ *noun* **4** = **destruction**,
collapse, defeat, disaster, downfall, failure,
ruin, shattering **5** = **collision**, accident,
crash, pile-up (*informal*), smash-up
(*informal*)

smashing *adjective Informal, chiefly Brit.*
= **excellent**, awesome (*slang*), boffo

(*slang*), brilliant (*informal*), cracking (*Brit. informal*), crucial (*slang*), def (*slang*), exhilarating, fabulous (*informal*), fantastic (*informal*), first-class, first-rate, great (*informal*), magnificent, marvellous, mean (*slang*), mega (*slang*), out of this world (*informal*), sensational (*informal*), sovereign, stupendous, super (*informal*), superb, superlative, terrific (*informal*), wonderful, world-class
➤ Antonyms
abysmal, appalling, average, awful, bad, boring, crap (*slang*), disappointing, disgraceful, disgusting, dreadful, dreary, dull, hideous, horrible, mediocre, no great shakes (*informal*), ordinary, rotten, run-of-the-mill, sickening, terrible, unexciting, uninspired, vile

smattering *noun* = **modicum**, bit, dash, elements, nodding acquaintance, passing acquaintance, rudiments, smatter, sprinkling

smear *verb* **1** = **spread over**, bedaub, coat, cover, daub, plaster, rub on **2** = **dirty**, bedim, besmirch, blur, smirch, smudge, soil, stain, sully **3** = **slander**, besmirch, blacken, calumniate, drag (someone's) name through the mud, malign, vilify ♦ *noun* **4** = **smudge**, blot, blotch, daub, smirch, splotch, streak **5** = **slander**, calumny, defamation, libel, mudslinging, vilification, whispering campaign

smell *verb* **1** = **sniff**, get a whiff of, nose, scent **2** = **stink**, be malodorous, hum (*slang*), pong (*Brit. informal*), reek, stink to high heaven (*informal*) ♦ *noun* **3** = **odour**, aroma, bouquet, fragrance, niff (*Brit. slang*), perfume, scent, whiff **4** = **stink**, fetor, malodour, niff (*Brit. slang*), pong (*Brit. informal*), stench

smelly *adjective* = **stinking**, evil-smelling, fetid, foul, foul-smelling, high, malodorous, niffy (*Brit. slang*), noisome, pongy (*Brit. informal*), putrid, reeking, stinky (*informal*), strong, strong-smelling, whiffy (*Brit. slang*)

smile *noun, verb* = **grin**, beam

smirk *noun* = **smug look**, grin, simper

smitten *adjective* **1** = **afflicted**, beset, laid low, plagued, struck **2** = **infatuated**, beguiled, bewitched, bowled over (*informal*), captivated, charmed, enamoured, swept off one's feet

smoky *adjective* = **black**, begrimed, grey, grimy, hazy, murky, smoke-darkened, sooty

smooth *adjective* **1** = **even**, flat, flush, horizontal, level, plain, plane, unwrinkled **2** = **sleek**, glassy, glossy, mirror-like, polished, shiny, silky, soft, velvety **3** = **easy**, effortless, untroubled, well-ordered **4** = **flowing**, fluent, regular, rhythmic, steady, uniform **5** = **mellow**, agreeable, bland, mild, pleasant, soothing **6** = **suave**, debonair, facile, glib,

ingratiating, persuasive, silky, slick, smarmy (*Brit. informal*), unctuous, urbane ♦ *verb* **7** = **flatten**, iron, level, plane, polish, press **8** = **ease**, allay, alleviate, appease, assuage, calm, extenuate, mitigate, mollify, palliate, soften, soothe **9** = **facilitate**, ease, iron out the difficulties of, pave the way
➤ Antonyms
adjective ≠**even**: bumpy, irregular, lumpy, rough, uneven ≠**sleek**: abrasive, coarse, jagged, rough, sharp ♦ *verb* ≠**ease**: aggravate, exacerbate, hamper, hinder, intensify, make worse, roughen

smother *verb* **1** = **extinguish**, snuff **2** = **suffocate**, choke, stifle, strangle **3** = **overwhelm**, cocoon, cover, envelop, heap, inundate, shower, surround **4** = **suppress**, conceal, hide, keep back, muffle, repress, stifle

smoulder *verb* = **seethe**, be resentful, boil, burn, fester, fume, rage, simmer

smudge *verb* **1** = **smear**, blacken, blur, daub, dirty, mark, smirch, soil ♦ *noun* **2** = **smear**, blemish, blot, blur, smut, smutch

smug *adjective* = **self-satisfied**, complacent, conceited, holier-than-thou, priggish, self-opinionated, self-righteous, superior

smuggler *noun* = **trafficker**, bootlegger, rum-runner, runner

smutty *adjective* = **obscene**, bawdy, blue, coarse, crude, dirty, filthy, improper, indecent, indelicate, lewd, off colour, pornographic, prurient, racy, raunchy (*U.S. slang*), risqué, salacious, suggestive, vulgar, X-rated (*informal*)

snack *noun* = **light meal**, bite, bite to eat, elevenses (*Brit. informal*), nibble, refreshment(s), titbit

snag *noun* **1** = **difficulty**, catch, complication, disadvantage, downside, drawback, hazard, hitch, inconvenience, obstacle, problem, stumbling block, the rub ♦ *verb* **2** = **catch**, hole, rip, tear

snaky *adjective* **1** = **twisting**, convoluted, serpentine, sinuous, tortuous, twisty **2** = **treacherous**, crafty, insidious, perfidious, sly, venomous

snap *verb* **1** = **break**, come apart, crack, give way, separate **2** = **crackle**, click, pop **3** = **bite at**, bite, catch, grip, nip, seize, snatch **4** = **speak sharply**, bark, fly off the handle at (*informal*), growl, jump down (someone's) throat (*informal*), lash out at, retort, snarl **5** **snap one's fingers at** *Informal* = **defy**, cock a snook at (*Brit.*), flout, pay no attention to, scorn **6** **snap out of it** *Informal* = **get over**, cheer up, get a grip on oneself, pull oneself together (*informal*), recover ♦ *noun* **7** = **crackle**, pop **8** = **bite**, grab, nip ♦ *adjective* **9** = **instant**, abrupt, immediate, spur-of-the-moment, sudden, unpremeditated

snappy *adjective* **1** = **smart**, chic, dapper, fashionable, modish, natty (*informal*), stylish, trendy (*Brit. informal*), up-to-the-minute, voguish **2** = **irritable**, apt to fly off the handle (*informal*), cross, edgy, impatient, like a bear with a sore head (*informal*), pissed (*taboo slang*), pissed off (*taboo slang*), quick-tempered, ratty (*Brit. & N.Z. informal*), snappish, testy, tetchy, touchy, waspish **3 make it snappy** = **hurry (up)**, be quick, buck up (*informal*), get a move on (*informal*), get one's skates on, look lively, make haste

snap up *verb* = **take advantage of**, avail oneself of, grab, grasp, nab (*informal*), pounce upon, seize, swoop down on

snare *noun* **1** = **trap**, catch, gin, net, noose, pitfall, wire ♦ *verb* **2** = **trap**, catch, entrap, net, seize, wire

snarl[1] *verb* = **growl**, show one's teeth (*of an animal*)

snarl[2] *verb, often with* **up** = **tangle**, complicate, confuse, embroil, enmesh, entangle, entwine, muddle, ravel

snarl-up *noun* = **tangle**, confusion, entanglement, muddle, (traffic) jam

snatch *verb* **1** = **seize**, catch up, clutch, grab, grasp, grip, pluck, pull, take, wrench, wrest ♦ *noun* **2** = **bit**, fragment, part, piece, smattering, snippet, spell

snazzy *adjective Informal* = **stylish**, attractive, dashing, flamboyant, flashy, jazzy (*informal*), showy, smart, sophisticated, swinging (*slang*), with it (*informal*)

sneak *verb* **1** = **slink**, cower, lurk, pad, sidle, skulk, slip, steal **2** = **slip**, smuggle, spirit **3** *Informal, chiefly Brit.* = **inform on**, grass on (*Brit. slang*), shop (*slang, chiefly Brit.*), sing (*slang, chiefly U.S.*), spill one's guts (*slang*), tell on (*informal*), tell tales ♦ *noun* **4** = **informer**, snake in the grass, telltale ♦ *adjective* **5** = **surprise**, clandestine, furtive, quick, secret, stealthy

sneaking *adjective* **1** = **nagging**, intuitive, niggling, persistent, uncomfortable, worrying **2** = **secret**, hidden, private, suppressed, unavowed, unconfessed, undivulged, unexpressed, unvoiced **3** = **underhand**, contemptible, furtive, mean, sly, sneaky, surreptitious, two-faced

sneaky *adjective* = **sly**, base, contemptible, cowardly, deceitful, devious, dishonest, double-dealing, furtive, low, mean, nasty, shifty, slippery, unreliable, unscrupulous, untrustworthy

sneer *noun* **1** = **scorn**, derision, disdain, gibe, jeer, mockery, ridicule ♦ *verb* **2** = **scorn**, deride, disdain, gibe, hold in

contempt, hold up to ridicule, jeer, laugh, look down on, mock, ridicule, scoff, sniff at, turn up one's nose (*informal*)

snide *or* **snidey** *adjective* = **nasty**, cynical, disparaging, hurtful, ill-natured, insinuating, malicious, mean, sarcastic, scornful, sneering, spiteful, unkind

sniff *verb* = **inhale**, breathe, smell, snuff, snuffle

snifty *adjective Informal* = **contemptuous**, condescending, disdainful, haughty, scornful, supercilious, superior

snigger *noun, verb* = **laugh**, giggle, smirk, sneer, snicker, titter

snip *verb* **1** = **cut**, clip, crop, dock, nick, nip off, shave, trim ♦ *noun* **2** *Informal, chiefly Brit.* = **bargain**, giveaway, good buy, steal (*informal*) **3** = **bit**, clipping, fragment, piece, scrap, shred, snippet

snipe *verb* = **criticize**, bitch, carp, denigrate, disparage, have a go (at) (*informal*), jeer, knock (*informal*), put down

snippet *noun* = **piece**, fragment, part, particle, scrap, shred, snatch

snivel *verb* = **whine**, blubber, cry, girn (*Scot. & Northern English dialect*), gripe (*informal*), grizzle (*informal, chiefly Brit.*), moan, sniffle, snuffle, weep, whimper, whinge (*informal*)

snob *noun* = **elitist**, highbrow, prig, social climber

snobbery *noun* = **arrogance**, airs, condescension, pretension, pride, side (*Brit. slang*), snobbishness, snootiness (*informal*), uppishness (*Brit. informal*)

snobbish *adjective* = **superior**, arrogant, condescending, high and mighty (*informal*), hoity-toity (*informal*), patronizing, pretentious, snooty (*informal*), stuck-up (*informal*), toffee-nosed (*slang, chiefly Brit.*), uppish (*Brit. informal*), uppity
➤ **Antonyms**
down to earth, humble, modest, natural, unassuming, unostentatious, unpretentious, without airs

snoop *verb* = **pry**, interfere, poke one's nose in (*informal*), spy

snooper *noun* = **nosy parker** (*informal*), busybody, meddler, pry, snoop (*informal*), stickybeak (*Austral. informal*)

snooty *adjective Informal* = **snobbish**, aloof, condescending, disdainful, haughty, high and mighty (*informal*), hoity-toity (*informal*), pretentious, proud, snotty, stuck-up (*informal*), supercilious, superior, toffee-nosed (*slang, chiefly Brit*), uppish (*Brit. informal*), uppity
➤ **Antonyms**
down to earth, humble, modest, natural,

unassuming, unpretentious, without airs

snooze *Informal* ♦ *verb* **1** = **doze**, catnap, drop off (*informal*), drowse, kip (*Brit. slang*), nap, nod off (*informal*), take forty winks (*informal*) ♦ *noun* **2** = **doze**, catnap, forty winks (*informal*), kip (*Brit. slang*), nap, siesta

snub *verb* **1** = **insult**, cold-shoulder, cut (*informal*), cut dead (*informal*), give (someone) the brush-off (*slang*), give (someone) the cold shoulder, humble, humiliate, kick in the teeth (*slang*), mortify, put down, rebuff, shame, slight ♦ *noun* **2** = **insult**, affront, brush-off (*slang*), humiliation, put-down, slap in the face

snug *adjective* **1** = **cosy**, comfortable, comfy (*informal*), homely, intimate, sheltered, warm **2** = **close**, compact, neat, trim

snuggle *verb* = **nestle**, cuddle, nuzzle

soak *verb* **1** = **wet**, bathe, damp, drench, immerse, infuse, marinate (*Cookery*), moisten, saturate, steep **2** = **penetrate**, permeate, seep **3 soak up** = **absorb**, assimilate, drink in, take in *or* up

soaking *adjective* = **soaked**, drenched, dripping, droukit *or* drookit (*Scot.*), like a drowned rat, saturated, soaked to the skin, sodden, sopping, streaming, waterlogged, wet through, wringing wet

soar *verb* **1** = **ascend**, fly, mount, rise, tower, wing **2** = **rise**, climb, escalate, rocket, shoot up
➤ **Antonyms**
descend, dive, drop, fall, nose-dive, plummet, plunge, swoop

sob *verb* = **cry**, bawl, blubber, greet (*Scot. or archaic*), howl, shed tears, snivel, weep

sober *adjective* **1** = **abstinent**, abstemious, moderate, on the wagon (*informal*), temperate **2** = **serious**, calm, clear-headed, composed, cool, dispassionate, grave, level-headed, lucid, practical, rational, realistic, reasonable, sedate, solemn, sound, staid, steady, unexcited, unruffled **3** = **plain**, dark, drab, quiet, severe, sombre, subdued ♦ *verb* **4** *usually with* **up** = **clear one's head**, come *or* bring to one's senses
➤ **Antonyms**
adjective ≠**abstinent**: bevvied (*dialect*), blitzed (*slang*), blotto (*slang*), bombed (*slang*), Brahms and Liszt (*slang*), drunk, flying (*slang*), fu' (*Scot.*), guttered (*slang*), having had one too many, inebriated, intoxicated, merry (*Brit. informal*), paralytic (*informal*), pie-eyed (*slang*), pissed (*taboo slang*), plastered, rat-arsed (*taboo slang*), sloshed (*slang*), smashed (*slang*), steamboats (*Scot. slang*), steaming (*slang*), tiddly (*slang, chiefly Brit.*), tight (*informal*), tipsy, tired and emotional (*euphemistic*),

wasted (*slang*), wrecked (*slang*), zonked (*slang*) ≠**serious**: excessive, frivolous, happy, immoderate, imprudent, injudicious, irrational, lighthearted, sensational, unrealistic ≠**plain**: bright, flamboyant, flashy, garish, gaudy, light ♦ *verb* ≠**clear one's head**: become intoxicated, get drunk

sobriety *noun* **1** = **abstinence**, abstemiousness, moderation, nonindulgence, self-restraint, soberness, temperance **2** = **seriousness**, calmness, composure, coolness, gravity, level-headedness, reasonableness, sedateness, solemnity, staidness, steadiness

so-called *adjective* = **alleged**, ostensible, pretended, professed, self-styled, soi-disant, supposed

sociability *noun* = **friendliness**, affability, companionability, congeniality, conviviality, cordiality, gregariousness, neighbourliness

sociable *adjective* = **friendly**, accessible, affable, approachable, companionable, convivial, cordial, familiar, genial, gregarious, neighbourly, outgoing, social, warm
➤ **Antonyms**
antisocial, businesslike, cold, distant, formal, introverted, reclusive, standoffish, stiff, tense, uncommunicative, unfriendly, unsociable, uptight (*informal*), withdrawn

social *adjective* **1** = **sociable**, companionable, friendly, gregarious, neighbourly **2** = **communal**, collective, common, community, general, group, organized, public, societal ♦ *noun* **3** = **get-together** (*informal*), do (*informal*), gathering, party

socialize *verb* = **mix**, be a good mixer, entertain, fraternize, get about *or* around, get together, go out

society *noun* **1** = **civilization**, culture, humanity, mankind, people, population, social order, the community, the general public, the public, the world at large **2** = **organization**, association, brotherhood *or* sisterhood, circle, club, corporation, fellowship, fraternity, group, guild, institute, league, order, union **3** = **upper classes**, beau monde, elite, gentry, high society, polite society, the country set, the nobs (*slang*), the smart set, the top drawer, upper crust (*informal*) **4** *Old-fashioned* = **companionship**, camaraderie, company, fellowship, friendship

sodden *adjective* = **soaked**, drenched, droukit *or* drookit (*Scot.*), marshy, miry, saturated, soggy, sopping, waterlogged

sodomy *noun* = **anal intercourse**, anal sex, buggery

sofa *noun* = **couch**, chaise longue, chesterfield, divan, ottoman, settee

soft *adjective* **1** = **pliable**, bendable, ductile (*of metals*), elastic, flexible, impressible, malleable, mouldable, plastic, supple, tensile **2** = **yielding**, cushioned, cushiony, doughy, elastic, gelatinous, pulpy, spongy, squashy **3** = **velvety**, downy, feathery, fleecy, furry, rounded, silky, smooth **4** = **quiet**, dulcet, gentle, low, mellifluous, mellow, melodious, murmured, muted, soft-toned, soothing, subdued, sweet, understated, whispered **5** = **pale**, bland, light, mellow, pastel, subdued **6** = **dim**, diffuse, dimmed, faint, restful **7** = **mild**, balmy, delicate, temperate **8** = **lenient**, easy-going, indulgent, lax, liberal, overindulgent, permissive, spineless, weak **9** *Informal* = **feeble-minded**, a bit lacking (*informal*), daft (*informal*), foolish, silly, simple, soft in the head (*informal*) **10** = **out of condition**, effeminate, flabby, flaccid, limp, namby-pamby, out of training, overindulged, pampered, podgy, weak **11** *Informal* = **easy**, comfortable, cushy (*informal*), easy-peasy (*slang*), undemanding **12** = **kind**, compassionate, gentle, pitying, sensitive, sentimental, sympathetic, tender, tenderhearted, touchy-feely (*informal*)
➤ **Antonyms**
≠**pliable, yielding:** firm, hard, inflexible, rigid, solid, stiff, tough, unyielding ≠**velvety:** abrasive, coarse, grating, hard, rough ≠**quiet:** harsh, loud, noisy, strident ≠**pale:** bright, garish, gaudy, glaring, harsh ≠**dim:** bright, glaring, harsh ≠**lenient:** austere, harsh, no-nonsense, stern, strict

soften *verb* = **lessen**, abate, allay, alleviate, appease, assuage, calm, cushion, diminish, ease, lighten, lower, melt, mitigate, moderate, modify, mollify, muffle, palliate, quell, relax, soothe, still, subdue, temper, tone down, turn down

softhearted *adjective* = **kind**, charitable, compassionate, generous, indulgent, sentimental, sympathetic, tender, tenderhearted, warm-hearted
➤ **Antonyms**
callous, cold, cruel, hard, hard-hearted, heartless, insensitive, uncaring, unkind, unsympathetic

soft-pedal *verb* = **play down**, tone down

soggy *adjective* = **sodden**, dripping, heavy, moist, mushy, pulpy, saturated, soaked, sopping, spongy, waterlogged

soil[1] *noun* **1** = **earth**, clay, dirt, dust, ground, loam **2** = **land**, country, region

soil[2] *verb* = **dirty**, befoul, begrime, besmirch, defile, foul, muddy, pollute, smear, smirch, spatter, spot, stain, sully, tarnish

sojourn *Literary* ◆ *noun* **1** = **stay**, rest, stop, stopover, visit ◆ *verb* **2** = **stay**, abide, dwell, lodge, reside, rest, stop, tarry

solace *noun* **1** = **comfort**, alleviation, assuagement, consolation, relief ◆ *verb* **2** = **comfort**, allay, alleviate, console, mitigate, soften, soothe

soldier *noun* = **fighter**, enlisted man (*U.S.*), GI (*U.S. informal*), man-at-arms, military man, redcoat, serviceman, squaddie *or* squaddy (*Brit. slang*), Tommy (*Brit. informal*), trooper, warrior

sold on *adjective Slang* = **convinced of**, converted to, hooked on, persuaded of, talked into, won over to

sole *adjective* = **only**, alone, exclusive, individual, one, one and only, single, singular, solitary

solecism *noun Formal* = **blunder**, bloomer (*Brit. informal*), breach of etiquette, faux pas, gaffe, gaucherie, impropriety, incongruity, lapse, mistake

solely *adverb* = **only**, alone, completely, entirely, exclusively, merely, single-handedly, singly

solemn *adjective* **1** = **formal**, august, awe-inspiring, ceremonial, ceremonious, dignified, grand, grave, imposing, impressive, majestic, momentous, stately **2** = **serious**, earnest, glum, grave, portentous, sedate, sober, staid, thoughtful
➤ **Antonyms**
≠**formal:** informal, relaxed, unceremonious ≠**serious:** bright, cheerful, chirpy (*informal*), frivolous, genial, happy, jovial, light-hearted, merry

solemnity *noun* **1** = **formality**, grandeur, gravitas, impressiveness, momentousness, portentousness **2** = **seriousness**, earnestness, gravity **3** *often plural* = **ritual**, celebration, ceremonial, ceremony, formalities, observance, proceedings, rite

solemnize *verb* = **celebrate**, commemorate, honour, keep, observe, perform

solicit *verb Formal* = **request**, ask, beg, beseech, canvass, crave, entreat, implore, importune, petition, plead for, pray, seek, supplicate

solicitous *adjective* **1** = **concerned**, anxious, apprehensive, attentive, careful, caring, earnest, troubled, uneasy, worried **2** = **eager**, zealous

solicitude *noun* = **concern**, anxiety, attentiveness, care, considerateness, consideration, regard, worry

solid *adjective* **1** = **firm**, compact, concrete, dense, hard, massed **2** = **strong**, stable, sturdy, substantial, unshakable **3** = **reliable**, decent, dependable, law-abiding, level-headed, sensible, serious, sober, trusty, upright, upstanding, worthy **4** = **continuous**, complete, unalloyed, unanimous, unbroken,

undivided, uninterrupted, united, unmixed **5**
= **sound**, genuine, good, pure, real, reliable
➤ **Antonyms**
≠**firm**: gaseous, hollow, liquid, permeable,
unsubstantial ≠**strong**: crumbling,
decaying, flimsy, precarious, shaky, unstable,
unsteady ≠**reliable**: flighty, irresponsible,
unreliable, unsound, unstable, unsteady
≠**sound**: impure, unreliable, unsound

solidarity noun = **unity**, accord,
camaraderie, cohesion, community of
interest, concordance, esprit de corps,
harmony, like-mindedness, singleness of
purpose, soundness, stability, team spirit,
unanimity, unification

solidify verb = **harden**, cake, coagulate,
cohere, congeal, jell, set

solitary adjective **1** = **unsociable**, cloistered,
isolated, reclusive, retired, unsocial **2**
= **single**, alone, lone, sole **3** = **lonely**,
companionless, friendless, lonesome **4**
= **isolated**, desolate, hidden, out-of-the-way,
remote, sequestered, unfrequented,
unvisited ◆ noun **5** = **hermit**, introvert, loner
(informal), lone wolf, recluse
➤ **Antonyms**
adjective ≠**unsociable**: companionable,
convivial, cordial, gregarious, outgoing,
sociable, social ≠**isolated**: bustling, busy,
frequented, public, well-frequented ◆ noun
≠**hermit**: extrovert, mixer, socialite

solitude noun = **isolation**, ivory tower,
loneliness, privacy, reclusiveness, retirement,
seclusion

solution noun **1** = **answer**, clarification,
elucidation, explanation, key, resolution,
result, solving, unfolding, unravelling **2**
Chemistry = **mixture**, blend, compound,
emulsion, mix, solvent, suspension **3**
= **dissolving**, disconnection, dissolution,
liquefaction, melting

solve verb = **answer**, clarify, clear up, crack,
decipher, disentangle, elucidate, explain, get
to the bottom of, interpret, resolve, suss
(out) (slang), unfold, unravel, work out

solvent adjective = **financially sound**, in the
black, solid, unindebted

sombre adjective **1** = **gloomy**, dismal,
doleful, funereal, grave, joyless, lugubrious,
melancholy, mournful, sad, sepulchral, sober
2 = **dark**, dim, drab, dull, dusky, gloomy,
obscure, shadowy, shady, sober
➤ **Antonyms**
≠**gloomy**: bright, cheerful, chirpy
(informal), effusive, full of beans, genial,
happy, lively, sunny, upbeat (informal)
≠**dark**: bright, colourful, dazzling, garish,
gaudy

somebody noun = **celebrity**, big hitter
(informal), big name, big noise (informal),

big shot (informal), celeb (informal),
dignitary, heavy hitter (informal),
heavyweight (informal), household name,
luminary, megastar (informal), name,
notable, personage, person of note, public
figure, star, superstar, V.I.P.
➤ **Antonyms**
also-ran, cipher, lightweight (informal),
menial, nobody, nonentity, nothing
(informal)

someday adverb = **eventually**, in the
fullness of time, one day, one of these (fine)
days, sooner or later, ultimately

somehow adverb = **one way or another**,
by fair means or foul, by hook or (by) crook,
by some means or other, come hell or high
water (informal), come what may

sometimes adverb = **occasionally**, at
times, every now and then, every so often,
from time to time, now and again, now and
then, off and on, once in a while, on
occasion
➤ **Antonyms**
always, consistently, constantly, continually,
eternally, ever, everlastingly, evermore,
forever, invariably, perpetually, unceasingly,
without exception

somnolent adjective Formal = **sleepy**,
comatose, dozy, drowsy, half-awake,
heavy-eyed, nodding off (informal),
soporific, torpid

song noun = **ballad**, air, anthem, canticle,
carol, chant, chorus, ditty, hymn, lay,
melody, number, pop song, psalm, shanty,
strain, tune

song and dance noun Brit. informal
= **fuss**, ado, commotion, flap (informal),
pantomime (informal), performance
(informal), stir, to-do

sonorous adjective **1** = **rich**, deep, full,
loud, resonant, resounding, ringing, rounded
2 = **grandiloquent**, high-flown,
high-sounding

soon adverb = **before long**, anon (archaic),
any minute now, in a little while, in a
minute, in a short time, in the near future,
shortly

soothe verb **1** = **calm**, allay, appease, calm
down, hush, lull, mitigate, mollify, pacify,
quiet, settle, smooth down, soften, still,
tranquillize **2** = **relieve**, alleviate, assuage,
ease
➤ **Antonyms**
≠**calm**: aggravate (informal), agitate, annoy,
disquiet, disturb, excite, get on one's nerves
(informal), hassle (informal), inflame,
irritate, rouse, upset, vex, worry ≠**relieve**:
exacerbate, increase, inflame, irritate,
stimulate

soothing adjective **1** = **calming**, relaxing,

restful **2** = **emollient**, easeful, lenitive, palliative

soothsayer *noun* = **prophet**, augur, diviner, fortune-teller, seer, sibyl

sophisticated *adjective* **1** = **cultured**, cosmopolitan, cultivated, jet-set, refined, urbane, worldly, worldly-wise **2** = **complex**, advanced, complicated, delicate, elaborate, highly-developed, intricate, refined, subtle
➤ **Antonyms**
≠**cultured**: naive, unrefined, unsophisticated, unworldly, wet behind the ears (*informal*) ≠**complex**: basic, old-fashioned, plain, primitive, simple, uncomplicated, unrefined, unsophisticated, unsubtle

sophistication *noun* = **savoir-faire**, finesse, poise, *savoir-vivre*, urbanity, worldliness, worldly wisdom

sophistry *noun* = **fallacy**, casuistry, quibble, sophism

soporific *adjective* **1** = **sleep-inducing**, hypnotic, sedative, sleepy, somnolent, tranquillizing ♦ *noun* **2** = **sedative**, anaesthetic, hypnotic, narcotic, opiate, tranquillizer

soppy *adjective Brit. informal*
= **sentimental**, corny (*slang*), gushy (*informal*), icky (*informal*), lovey-dovey, mawkish, overemotional, schmaltzy (*slang*), silly, slushy (*informal*), soft (*informal*), weepy (*informal*)

sorcerer *or* **sorceress** *noun* = **magician**, enchanter, mage (*archaic*), magus, necromancer, warlock, witch, wizard

sorcery *noun* = **black magic**, black art, charm, divination, enchantment, incantation, magic, necromancy, spell, witchcraft, witchery, wizardry

sordid *adjective* **1** = **dirty**, filthy, foul, mean, seamy, seedy, sleazy, slovenly, slummy, squalid, unclean, wretched **2** = **base**, debauched, degenerate, degraded, despicable, disreputable, low, shabby, shameful, vicious, vile **3** = **mercenary**, avaricious, covetous, grasping, selfish, self-seeking
➤ **Antonyms**
≠**dirty**: clean, fresh, pure, spotless, squeaky-clean, unblemished, undefiled, unsullied ≠**base**: blameless, decent, honourable, noble, pure, upright

sore *adjective* **1** = **painful**, angry, burning, chafed, inflamed, irritated, raw, reddened, sensitive, smarting, tender **2** = **annoying**, distressing, grievous, harrowing, severe, sharp, troublesome **3** = **annoyed**, aggrieved, angry, cross, grieved, hurt, irked, irritated, pained, peeved (*informal*), pissed (*taboo slang*), pissed (off) (*taboo slang*), resentful,

stung, upset, vexed **4** *Literary* = **urgent**, acute, critical, desperate, dire, extreme, pressing ♦ *noun* **5** = **abscess**, boil, chafe, gathering, inflammation, ulcer

sorrow *noun* **1** = **grief**, affliction, anguish, distress, heartache, heartbreak, misery, mourning, regret, sadness, unhappiness, woe **2** = **affliction**, blow, bummer (*slang*), hardship, misfortune, trial, tribulation, trouble, woe, worry ♦ *verb* **3** = **grieve**, agonize, bemoan, be sad, bewail, eat one's heart out, lament, moan, mourn, weep
➤ **Antonyms**
noun ≠**grief**: bliss, delight, elation, exaltation, exultation, gladness, happiness, joy, pleasure ≠**affliction**: good fortune, lucky break ♦ *verb* ≠**grieve**: celebrate, delight, exult, jump for joy, rejoice, revel

sorrowful *adjective* = **sad**, affecting, dejected, depressed, disconsolate, dismal, distressing, doleful, down in the dumps (*informal*), grieving, harrowing, heartbroken, heart-rending, heavy-hearted, lugubrious, melancholy, miserable, mournful, painful, piteous, rueful, sick at heart, sorry, tearful, unhappy, woebegone, woeful, wretched

sorry *adjective* **1** = **regretful**, apologetic, conscience-stricken, contrite, guilt-ridden, penitent, remorseful, repentant, self-reproachful, shamefaced **2** = **sympathetic**, commiserative, compassionate, full of pity, moved, pitying **3** = **sad**, disconsolate, distressed, grieved, melancholy, mournful, sorrowful, unhappy **4** = **wretched**, abject, base, deplorable, dismal, distressing, mean, miserable, paltry, pathetic, piteous, pitiable, pitiful, poor, sad, shabby, vile
➤ **Antonyms**
≠**regretful**: impenitent, not contrite, shameless, unapologetic, unashamed, unremorseful, unrepentant ≠**sympathetic**: heartless, indifferent, uncompassionate, unconcerned, unmoved, unpitying, unsympathetic ≠**sad**: cheerful, delighted, elated, happy, joyful

sort *noun* **1** = **kind**, brand, breed, category, character, class, denomination, description, family, genus, group, ilk, make, nature, order, quality, race, species, stamp, style, type, variety **2 out of sorts** = **in low spirits**, crotchety, down in the dumps (*informal*), down in the mouth (*informal*), grouchy (*informal*), not up to par, not up to snuff (*informal*), off colour, poorly (*informal*), under the weather (*informal*) **3 sort of** = **rather**, as it were, in part, moderately, reasonably, slightly, somewhat, to some extent ♦ *verb* **4** = **arrange**, catalogue, categorize, choose, class, classify, distribute, divide, file, grade, group, order, put in order, rank, select, separate, systematize, tabulate

sort out *verb* **1** = **resolve**, clarify, clear up, put *or* get straight **2** = **separate**, pick out, put on one side, segregate, select, sift **3** = **organize**, tidy up

so-so *adjective Informal* = **average**, adequate, fair, indifferent, middling, moderate, not bad (*informal*), O.K. *or* okay (*informal*), ordinary, passable, run-of-the-mill, tolerable, undistinguished

soul *noun* **1** = **spirit**, animating principle, essence, intellect, life, mind, psyche, reason, vital force **2** = **essence**, embodiment, epitome, incarnation, personification, quintessence, type **3** = **feeling**, animation, ardour, courage, energy, fervour, force, vitality, vivacity **4** = **person**, being, body, creature, individual, man *or* woman, mortal

soul-destroying *adjective* = **mind-numbing**, dreary, dull, humdrum, monotonous, tedious, tiresome, treadmill, unvarying, wearisome

soulful *adjective* = **expressive**, eloquent, heartfelt, meaningful, mournful, moving, profound, sensitive

soulless *adjective* **1** = **spiritless**, dead, lifeless, mechanical, soul-destroying, uninteresting **2** = **unfeeling**, callous, cold, cruel, harsh, inhuman, unkind, unsympathetic

sound[1] *noun* **1** = **noise**, din, report, resonance, reverberation, tone, voice **2** = **impression**, drift, idea, implication(s), look, tenor ♦ *verb* **3** = **resound**, echo, resonate, reverberate **4** = **seem**, appear, give the impression of, look, strike one as being **5** = **pronounce**, announce, articulate, declare, enunciate, express, signal, utter

sound[2] *adjective* **1** = **perfect**, complete, entire, firm, fit, hale, hale and hearty, healthy, intact, robust, solid, sturdy, substantial, undamaged, unhurt, unimpaired, uninjured, well-constructed, whole **2** = **safe**, established, proven, recognized, reliable, reputable, secure, solid, solvent, stable, tried-and-true **3** = **sensible**, correct, fair, just, level-headed, logical, proper, prudent, rational, reasonable, reliable, responsible, right, right-thinking, true, trustworthy, valid, well-founded, well-grounded, wise **4** = **deep**, peaceful, unbroken, undisturbed, untroubled
➤ **Antonyms**
≠**perfect**: ailing, damaged, frail, shaky, sketchy, superficial, unbalanced, unstable, weak ≠**safe**: unreliable, unsound, unstable ≠**sensible**: fallacious, faulty, flawed, irrational, irresponsible, specious ≠**deep**: broken, fitful, shallow, troubled

sound[3] *verb* **1** = **fathom**, plumb, probe **2** = **examine**, inspect, investigate, test

sound[4] *noun* = **channel**, passage, strait

sound out *verb* = **probe**, canvass, examine, pump, put out feelers to, question, see how the land lies, test the water

sour *adjective* **1** = **sharp**, acerb, acetic, acid, bitter, pungent, tart, unpleasant **2** = **gone off**, curdled, fermented, gone bad, rancid, turned, unsavoury, unwholesome **3** = **ill-natured**, acrimonious, churlish, cynical, disagreeable, discontented, embittered, grouchy (*informal*), grudging, ill-tempered, jaundiced, peevish, tart, ungenerous, waspish ♦ *verb* **4** = **embitter**, alienate, disenchant, exacerbate, turn off (*informal*)
➤ **Antonyms**
adjective ≠**sharp**: agreeable, bland, mild, pleasant, savoury, sugary, sweet ≠**gone off**: fresh, unimpaired, unspoiled ≠**ill-natured**: affable, amiable, congenial, friendly, genial, good-humoured, good-natured, good-tempered, pleasant, warm-hearted ♦ *verb* ≠**embitter**: enhance, improve, strengthen

source *noun* **1** = **origin**, author, beginning, cause, derivation, fount, fountainhead, originator, rise, spring, wellspring **2** = **informant**, authority

sourpuss *noun Informal* = **killjoy**, crosspatch (*informal*), grump (*informal*), misery (*Brit. informal*), prophet of doom

souse *verb* = **steep**, drench, dunk, immerse, marinate (*Cookery*), pickle, soak

souvenir *noun* = **keepsake**, memento, relic, reminder, token

sovereign *noun* **1** = **monarch**, chief, emperor *or* empress, king *or* queen, potentate, prince *or* princess, ruler, shah, supreme ruler, tsar *or* tsarina ♦ *adjective* **2** = **supreme**, absolute, chief, dominant, imperial, kingly *or* queenly, monarchal, paramount, predominant, principal, regal, royal, ruling, unlimited **3** = **excellent**, effectual, efficacious, efficient

sovereignty *noun* = **supreme power**, ascendancy, domination, kingship, primacy, supremacy, suzerainty, sway

sow *verb* = **scatter**, broadcast, disseminate, implant, inseminate, lodge, plant, seed

space *noun* **1** = **room**, amplitude, capacity, elbowroom, expanse, extension, extent, leeway, margin, play, scope, spaciousness, volume **2** = **gap**, blank, distance, interval, lacuna, omission **3** = **time**, duration, interval, period, span, while

spaceman *or* **spacewoman** *noun* = **astronaut**, cosmonaut

spacious *adjective* = **roomy**, ample, broad,

capacious, comfortable, commodious, expansive, extensive, huge, large, sizable or sizeable, uncrowded, vast
➤ **Antonyms**
close, confined, cramped, crowded, limited, narrow, poky, restricted, small

spadework noun = **preparation**, donkey-work, groundwork, labour

span noun 1 = **extent**, amount, distance, length, reach, spread, stretch 2 = **period**, duration, spell, term ◆ verb 3 = **extend across**, arch across, bridge, cover, cross, link, range over, traverse

spank verb = **smack**, belt (informal), cuff, give (someone) a hiding (informal), slap, slipper (informal), wallop (informal), whack

spanking adjective 1 Informal = **smart**, brand-new, fine, gleaming 2 = **fast**, brisk, energetic, lively, quick, smart, snappy, vigorous

spar verb = **argue**, bicker, dispute, fall out (informal), have a tiff, row, scrap (informal), squabble, wrangle

spare adjective 1 = **extra**, additional, emergency, free, in excess, in reserve, leftover, odd, over, superfluous, supernumerary, surplus, unoccupied, unused, unwanted 2 = **thin**, gaunt, lank, lean, meagre, slender, slight, slim, wiry 3 **go spare** Brit. slang = **become enraged**, become angry, become distraught, become mad (informal), become upset, be or get pissed (off) (taboo slang), blow one's top (informal), do one's nut (Brit. slang), go mental (slang), go up the wall (slang), have or throw a fit (informal) ◆ verb 4 = **have mercy on**, be merciful to, deal leniently with, go easy on (informal), leave, let off (informal), pardon, refrain from, release, relieve from, save from 5 = **afford**, allow, dispense with, do without, give, grant, let (someone) have, manage without, part with
➤ **Antonyms**
adjective ≠**extra**: allocated, designated, earmarked, in use, necessary, needed, set aside, spoken for ≠**thin**: corpulent, fat, flabby, fleshy, generous, heavy, large, plump ◆ verb ≠**have mercy on**: afflict, condemn, damn, destroy, hurt, punish, show no mercy to

spare time noun = **leisure**, free time, odd moments, time on one's hands, time to kill

sparing adjective = **economical**, careful, frugal, prudent, saving, thrifty
➤ **Antonyms**
extravagant, lavish, liberal, open-handed, prodigal, spendthrift

spark noun 1 = **flicker**, flare, flash, gleam, glint, scintillation, spit 2 = **trace**, atom, hint, jot, scintilla, scrap, vestige ◆ verb 3 often

with **off** = **start**, animate, excite, inspire, kick-start, kindle, precipitate, prod, provoke, rouse, set in motion, set off, stimulate, stir, touch off, trigger (off)

sparkle verb 1 = **glitter**, beam, dance, flash, gleam, glint, glisten, glow, scintillate, shimmer, shine, spark, twinkle, wink 2 = **fizz**, bubble, effervesce, fizzle ◆ noun 3 = **glitter**, brilliance, dazzle, flash, flicker, gleam, glint, radiance, spark, twinkle 4 = **vivacity**, animation, brio, dash, élan, gaiety, life, liveliness, panache, spirit, vim (slang), vitality, zip (informal)

sparse adjective = **scattered**, few and far between, meagre, scanty, scarce, sporadic
➤ **Antonyms**
crowded, dense, lavish, lush, luxuriant, numerous, plentiful, thick

spartan adjective = **austere**, abstemious, ascetic, bleak, disciplined, extreme, frugal, plain, rigorous, self-denying, severe, stern, strict, stringent

spasm noun 1 = **convulsion**, contraction, paroxysm, twitch 2 = **burst**, access, eruption, fit, frenzy, outburst, seizure

spasmodic adjective = **sporadic**, convulsive, erratic, fitful, intermittent, irregular, jerky

spat noun = **quarrel**, altercation, bicker, contention, controversy, dispute, squabble, tiff

spate noun = **flood**, deluge, flow, outpouring, rush, torrent

spatter verb = **splash**, bespatter, daub, dirty, scatter, soil, speckle, splodge, spray, sprinkle

speak verb 1 = **talk**, articulate, communicate, converse, discourse, enunciate, express, make known, pronounce, say, state, tell, utter, voice 2 = **lecture**, address, argue, declaim, deliver an address, descant, discourse, harangue, hold forth, plead, spout

speaker noun = **orator**, lecturer, public speaker, spokesman or spokeswoman, spokesperson

speak for verb = **represent**, act for or on behalf of, appear for

speak up or **out** verb 1 = **speak one's mind**, have one's say, make one's position plain, sound off, stand up and be counted 2 = **speak loudly**, make oneself heard, say it loud and clear

spearhead verb = **lead**, blaze the trail, head, initiate, launch, lead the way, pioneer, set in motion, set off

special adjective 1 = **exceptional**, distinguished, especial, extraordinary, important, memorable, momentous, out of

the ordinary, significant, uncommon, unique, unusual **2 = specific**, appropriate, certain, characteristic, distinctive, especial, individual, particular, peculiar, precise, specialized **3 = particular**, chief, main, major, primary
➤ **Antonyms**
≠**exceptional**: common, everyday, humdrum, mediocre, no great shakes (*informal*), normal, ordinary, routine, run-of-the-mill, undistinguished, unexceptional, usual ≠**specific**: general, multi-purpose, undistinctive, unspecialized

specialist *noun* = **expert**, authority, buff (*informal*), connoisseur, consultant, guru, hotshot (*informal*), master, professional, whizz (*informal*)

speciality *noun* = **forte**, bag (*slang*), claim to fame, distinctive *or* distinguishing feature, métier, *pièce de résistance*, special, specialty

species *noun* = **kind**, breed, category, class, collection, description, genus, group, sort, type, variety

specific *adjective* **1 = particular**, characteristic, definite, distinguishing, especial, peculiar, special **2 = precise**, clear-cut, definite, exact, explicit, express, limited, unambiguous, unequivocal
➤ **Antonyms**
≠**particular**: common, general ≠**precise**: approximate, general, hazy, imprecise, non-specific, uncertain, unclear, vague, woolly

specification *noun* = **requirement**, condition, detail, item, particular, qualification, stipulation

specify *verb* = **state**, be specific about, cite, define, designate, detail, enumerate, indicate, mention, name, spell out, stipulate

specimen *noun* = **sample**, embodiment, example, exemplar, exemplification, exhibit, individual, instance, model, pattern, proof, representative, type

specious *adjective* = **fallacious**, casuistic, deceptive, misleading, plausible, sophistic, sophistical, unsound

speck *noun* **1 = mark**, blemish, blot, defect, dot, fault, flaw, fleck, mote, speckle, spot, stain **2 = particle**, atom, bit, dot, grain, iota, jot, mite, modicum, shred, tittle, whit

speckled *adjective* = **flecked**, brindled, dappled, dotted, freckled, mottled, spotted, spotty, sprinkled, stippled

spectacle *noun* **1 = sight**, curiosity, laughing stock, marvel, phenomenon, scene, wonder **2 = show**, display, event, exhibition, extravaganza, pageant, parade, performance, sight

spectacular *adjective* **1 = impressive**, breathtaking, daring, dazzling, dramatic,

eye-catching, fantastic (*informal*), grand, magnificent, marked, remarkable, sensational, splendid, staggering, striking, stunning (*informal*) ◆ *noun* **2 = show**, display, extravaganza, spectacle
➤ **Antonyms**
adjective ≠**impressive**: everyday, modest, ordinary, plain, run-of-the-mill, simple, unimpressive, unostentatious, unspectacular

spectator *noun* = **onlooker**, beholder, bystander, eyewitness, looker-on, observer, viewer, watcher, witness
➤ **Antonyms**
contestant, contributor, partaker, participant, participator, party, player

spectral *adjective* = **ghostly**, insubstantial, phantom, shadowy, supernatural, wraithlike

spectre *noun* = **ghost**, apparition, phantom, presence, shade (*literary*), shadow, spirit, vision, wraith

speculate *verb* **1 = conjecture**, cogitate, consider, contemplate, deliberate, guess, hypothesize, meditate, muse, scheme, suppose, surmise, theorize, wonder **2 = gamble**, have a flutter (*informal*), hazard, play the market, risk, take a chance with, venture

speculation *noun* **1 = conjecture**, consideration, contemplation, deliberation, guess, guesswork, hypothesis, opinion, supposition, surmise, theory **2 = gamble**, gambling, hazard, risk

speculative *adjective* = **hypothetical**, abstract, academic, conjectural, notional, suppositional, tentative, theoretical

speech *noun* **1 = communication**, conversation, dialogue, discussion, intercourse, talk **2 = talk**, address, discourse, disquisition, harangue, homily, lecture, oration, spiel (*informal*) **3 = language**, articulation, dialect, diction, enunciation, idiom, jargon, lingo (*informal*), parlance, tongue, utterance, voice

speechless *adjective* **1 = mute**, dumb, inarticulate, lost for words, silent, tongue-tied, wordless **2 = astounded**, aghast, amazed, dazed, dumbfounded, dumbstruck, shocked, thunderstruck

speed *noun* **1 = swiftness**, acceleration, celerity, haste, hurry, momentum, pace, quickness, rapidity, rush, velocity ◆ *verb* **2 = race**, barrel (along) (*informal, chiefly U.S. & Canad.*), belt (along) (*slang*), bomb (along), burn rubber (*informal*), career, expedite, flash, gallop, go hell for leather (*informal*), go like a bat out of hell, go like a bomb (*Brit. & N.Z. informal*), go like the wind, hasten, hurry, lose no time, make haste, press on, quicken, rush, sprint, step on it (*informal*), tear, zoom **3 = help**,

advance, aid, assist, boost, expedite, facilitate, further, impel, promote
➤ Antonyms
noun ≠**swiftness**: delay, slowness, sluggishness, tardiness ◆ *verb* ≠**race**: crawl, creep, dawdle, delay, take one's time, tarry ≠**help**: delay, hamper, hinder, hold up, retard, slow

speed up *verb* = **accelerate**, gather momentum, get moving, get under way, increase, increase the tempo, put on speed
➤ Antonyms
brake, decelerate, reduce speed, rein in, slacken (off), slow down

speedy *adjective* = **quick**, express, fast, hasty, headlong, hurried, immediate, pdq (*slang*), precipitate, prompt, quickie (*informal*), rapid, swift, winged
➤ Antonyms
dead slow and stop, delayed, dilatory, late, leisurely, lingering, long-drawn-out, plodding, slow, sluggish, tardy, unhurried, unrushed

spell[1] *verb* = **indicate**, amount to, augur, herald, imply, mean, point to, portend, presage, promise, signify, suggest

spell[2] *noun* 1 = **incantation**, abracadabra, charm, conjuration, sorcery, witchery 2 = **enchantment**, allure, bewitchment, fascination, glamour, magic, trance

spell[3] *noun* = **period**, bout, course, interval, patch, season, stint, stretch, term, time, turn

spellbound *adjective* = **entranced**, bemused, bewitched, captivated, charmed, enthralled, fascinated, gripped, hooked, mesmerized, possessed, rapt, transfixed, transported, under a spell

spelling *noun* = **orthography**

spell out *verb* 1 = **make clear** *or* **plain**, clarify, elucidate, explicate, make explicit, specify 2 = **puzzle out**, discern, make out

spend *verb* 1 = **pay out**, disburse, expend, fork out (*slang*), lay out, shell out (*informal*), splash out (*Brit. informal*) 2 = **pass**, fill, occupy, while away 3 = **apply**, bestow, concentrate, devote, employ, exert, invest, lavish, put in, use 4 = **use up**, consume, deplete, dissipate, drain, empty, exhaust, fritter away, run through, squander, waste
➤ Antonyms
≠**pay out, use up**: hoard, invest, keep, put aside, put by, save, store

spendthrift *noun* 1 = **squanderer**, big spender, prodigal, profligate, spender, waster, wastrel ◆ *adjective* 2 = **wasteful**, extravagant, improvident, prodigal, profligate
➤ Antonyms
noun ≠**squanderer**: meanie *or* meany

(*informal, chiefly Brit.*), miser, penny-pincher (*informal*), Scrooge, skinflint, tight-arse (*taboo slang*), tight-ass (*U.S. taboo slang*), tightwad (*U.S. & Canad. slang*) ◆ *adjective* ≠**wasteful**: careful, economical, frugal, parsimonious, provident, prudent, sparing, thrifty

spent *adjective* 1 = **used up**, consumed, expended, finished, gone 2 = **exhausted**, all in (*slang*), burnt out, clapped out (*Austral. & N.Z. informal*), dead beat (*informal*), debilitated, done in *or* up (*informal*), drained, knackered (*slang*), played out (*informal*), prostrate, ready to drop (*informal*), shattered (*informal*), tired out, weakened, wearied, weary, whacked (*Brit. informal*), wiped out (*informal*), worn out, zonked (*informal*)

sperm *noun* 1 = **spermatozoon**, male gamete, reproductive cell 2 = **semen**, come *or* cum (*taboo*), seed (*archaic or dialect*), spermatozoa

spew *verb* = **vomit**, barf (*U.S. slang*), chuck (up) (*slang, chiefly U.S.*), chunder (*slang, chiefly Austral.*), disgorge, puke (*slang*), regurgitate, throw up (*informal*), upchuck (*U.S. slang*)

sphere *noun* 1 = **ball**, circle, globe, globule, orb 2 = **field**, capacity, department, domain, function, patch, province, range, realm, scope, territory, turf (*U.S. slang*), walk of life 3 = **rank**, station, stratum

spherical *adjective* = **round**, globe-shaped, globular, orbicular, rotund

spice *noun* 1 = **seasoning**, relish, savour 2 = **excitement**, colour, gusto, kick (*informal*), pep, piquancy, tang, zap (*slang*), zest, zing (*informal*), zip (*informal*)

spick-and-span *adjective* = **neat**, clean, immaculate, impeccable, shipshape, spotless, spruce, tidy, trim

spicy *adjective* 1 = **hot**, aromatic, flavoursome, piquant, pungent, savoury, seasoned, tangy 2 *Informal* = **scandalous**, hot (*informal*), improper, indecorous, indelicate, racy, ribald, risqué, sensational, suggestive, titillating

spiel *noun* = **patter**, pitch, recital, sales patter, sales talk, speech

spike *noun* 1 = **point**, barb, prong, spine ◆ *verb* 2 = **impale**, spear, spit, stick

spill *verb* 1 = **pour**, discharge, disgorge, overflow, scatter, shed, slop over, spill *or* run over, teem, throw off, upset 2 **spill the beans** *Informal* = **betray a secret**, blab, give the game away, grass (*Brit. slang*), inform, let the cat out of the bag, shop (*slang, chiefly Brit.*), sing (*slang, chiefly U.S.*), split (*slang*), squeal (*slang*), talk out of turn, tattle, tell all ◆ *noun* 3 *Informal* = **fall**, accident, cropper (*informal*), tumble

spin *verb* **1** = **revolve**, birl (*Scot.*), gyrate, pirouette, reel, rotate, turn, twirl, twist, wheel, whirl **2** *As in* **spin a yarn** = **tell**, concoct, develop, invent, narrate, recount, relate, unfold **3** = **reel**, be giddy, be in a whirl, grow dizzy, swim, whirl ♦ *noun* **4** = **revolution**, gyration, roll, twist, whirl **5** *Informal* = **drive**, hurl (*Scot.*), joy ride (*informal*), ride, turn, whirl

spindly *adjective* = **lanky**, attenuated, gangling, gangly, leggy, spidery, spindle-shanked

spine *noun* **1** = **backbone**, spinal column, vertebrae, vertebral column **2** = **barb**, needle, quill, ray, spike, spur

spine-chilling *adjective* = **frightening**, bloodcurdling, eerie, hair-raising, horrifying, scary (*informal*), spooky (*informal*), terrifying

spineless *adjective* = **weak**, boneless, chickenshit (*U.S. slang*), cowardly, faint-hearted, feeble, gutless (*informal*), inadequate, ineffective, irresolute, lily-livered, pathetic, soft, submissive, vacillating, weak-kneed (*informal*), weak-willed, without a will of one's own, yellow (*informal*)
➤ **Antonyms**
ballsy (*taboo slang*), bold, brave, courageous, gritty, strong, strong-willed

spin out *verb* = **prolong**, amplify, delay, drag out, draw out, extend, lengthen, pad out, protract

spiral *noun* **1** = **coil**, corkscrew, curlicue, helix, screw, whorl ♦ *adjective* **2** = **coiled**, circular, corkscrew, helical, scrolled, whorled, winding

spirit *noun* **1** = **life force**, air, breath, life, psyche, soul, vital spark **2** = **feeling**, atmosphere, gist, humour, tenor, tone **3** = **temperament**, attitude, character, complexion, disposition, essence, humour, outlook, quality, temper **4** = **liveliness**, animation, ardour, brio, earnestness, energy, enthusiasm, fire, force, life, mettle, resolution, sparkle, vigour, warmth, zest **5** = **courage**, backbone, balls (*taboo slang*), ballsiness (*taboo slang*), dauntlessness, gameness, grit, guts (*informal*), spunk (*informal*), stoutheartedness **6** = **will**, motivation, resolution, resolve, willpower **7** = **intention**, essence, intent, meaning, purport, purpose, sense, substance **8** = **ghost**, apparition, phantom, shade (*literary*), shadow, spectre, spook (*informal*), sprite, vision **9 spirits** = **mood**, feelings, frame of mind, humour, morale ♦ *verb* **10** *with* **away** *or* **off** = **remove**, abduct, abstract, carry, convey, make away with, purloin, seize, snaffle (*Brit. informal*), steal, whisk

spirited *adjective* = **lively**, active, animated, bold, courageous, energetic, feisty (*informal, chiefly U.S. & Canad.*), game, have-a-go (*informal*), high-spirited, mettlesome, plucky, sprightly, spunky (*informal*), vigorous, vivacious
➤ **Antonyms**
apathetic, bland, calm, dispirited, dull, feeble, half-hearted, lacklustre, lifeless, low-key, spiritless, timid, token, unenthusiastic, weary

spirits *noun* = **alcohol**, firewater, liquor, strong liquor, the hard stuff (*informal*)

spiritual *adjective* **1** = **nonmaterial**, immaterial, incorporeal **2** = **sacred**, devotional, divine, ethereal, holy, pure, religious
➤ **Antonyms**
≠**nonmaterial**: concrete, corporeal, material, nonspiritual, physical, substantial, tangible

spit *verb* **1** = **eject**, discharge, expectorate, hiss, spew, splutter, sputter, throw out ♦ *noun* **2** = **saliva**, dribble, drool, slaver, spittle

spite *noun* **1** = **malice**, animosity, bitchiness (*slang*), gall, hate, hatred, ill will, malevolence, malignity, rancour, spitefulness, spleen, venom **2 in spite of** = **despite**, (even) though, in defiance of, notwithstanding, regardless of ♦ *verb* **3** = **annoy**, gall, harm, hurt, injure, needle (*informal*), nettle, offend, pique, provoke, put out, put (someone's) nose out of joint (*informal*), vex
➤ **Antonyms**
noun ≠**malice**: benevolence, big-heartedness, charity, compassion, generosity of spirit, goodwill, kindliness, kindness, love, warm-heartedness ♦ *verb* ≠**annoy**: aid, benefit, help, please

spiteful *adjective* = **malicious**, barbed, bitchy (*informal*), catty (*informal*), cruel, ill-disposed, ill-natured, malevolent, malignant, nasty, snide, splenetic, venomous, vindictive

spitting image *noun* = **double**, clone, (dead) ringer (*slang*), likeness, living image, lookalike, picture, replica

splash *verb* **1** = **scatter**, bespatter, shower, slop, slosh (*informal*), spatter, splodge, spray, spread, sprinkle, squirt, strew, wet **2** = **dash**, batter, break, buffet, plop, smack, strike, surge, wash **3** = **publicize**, blazon, broadcast, flaunt, tout, trumpet ♦ *noun* **4** = **dash**, burst, patch, spattering, splodge, touch **5** *Informal* = **display**, effect, impact, sensation, splurge, stir **6 make a splash** *Informal* = **cause a stir**, be ostentatious, cut a dash, go overboard (*informal*), go to town, splurge

splash out *verb Informal* = **spend**, be extravagant, push the boat out (*Brit. informal*), spare no expense, splurge

spleen *noun* = **spite**, acrimony, anger, animosity, animus, bad temper, bile, bitterness, gall, hatred, hostility, ill humour, ill will, malevolence, malice, malignity, peevishness, pique, rancour, resentment, spitefulness, venom, vindictiveness, wrath

splendid *adjective* **1** = **excellent**, awesome (*slang*), boffo (*slang*), brill (*informal*), cracking (*Brit. informal*), crucial (*slang*), def (*slang*), fantastic (*informal*), fine, first-class, glorious, great (*informal*), marvellous, mean (*slang*), mega (*slang*), sovereign, wonderful **2** = **magnificent**, costly, dazzling, gorgeous, grand, imposing, impressive, lavish, luxurious, ornate, resplendent, rich, splendiferous (*facetious*), sumptuous, superb
➤ **Antonyms**
≠**excellent**: depressing, disgusting, lacklustre, mediocre, miserable, no great shakes (*informal*), ordinary, pathetic, poor, rotten, run-of-the-mill, tawdry, undistinguished, unexceptional ≠**magnificent**: beggarly, drab, dull, low, mean, plain, poor, poverty-stricken, sordid, squalid

splendour *noun* = **magnificence**, display, éclat, gorgeousness, grandeur, majesty, pomp, resplendence, richness, show, solemnity, spectacle, stateliness, sumptuousness
➤ **Antonyms**
lacklustreness, meanness, ordinariness, plainness, poverty, simplicity, squalor, tawdriness

splenetic *adjective Literary* = **irritable**, bad-tempered, choleric, crabby, cross, fretful, irascible, peevish, ratty (*Brit. & N.Z. informal*), testy, tetchy, touchy

splice *verb* = **join**, braid, entwine, graft, interlace, intertwine, intertwist, interweave, knit, marry, mesh, plait, unite, wed, yoke

splinter *noun* **1** = **sliver**, chip, flake, fragment, paring, shaving ♦ *verb* **2** = **shatter**, break into fragments, disintegrate, fracture, shiver, split

split *verb* **1** = **break**, break up, burst, come apart, come undone, crack, gape, give way, open, rend, rip, slash, slit, snap, splinter **2** = **separate**, bifurcate, branch, cleave, disband, disunite, diverge, fork, go separate ways, part, pull apart **3** = **share out**, allocate, allot, apportion, carve up, distribute, divide, divvy up (*informal*), dole out, halve, parcel out, partition, slice up **4 split on** *Slang* = **betray**, give away, grass (*Brit. slang*), inform on, shop (*slang, chiefly Brit.*), sing (*slang, chiefly U.S.*), squeal (*slang*) ♦ *noun* **5** = **crack**, breach, damage,

division, fissure, gap, rent, rip, separation, slash, slit, tear **6** = **division**, breach, break, break-up, difference, discord, disruption, dissension, disunion, divergence, estrangement, rift, rupture, schism
♦ *adjective* **7** = **divided**, ambivalent, bisected, broken, cleft, cracked, dual, fractured, ruptured

split up *verb* = **separate**, break up, disband, divorce, go separate ways, part, part company

spoil *verb* **1** = **ruin**, blemish, blow (*slang*), damage, deface, destroy, disfigure, harm, impair, injure, mar, mess up, put a damper on, scar, total (*slang*), trash (*slang*), undo, upset, wreck **2** = **overindulge**, coddle, cosset, indulge, kill with kindness, mollycoddle, pamper, spoon-feed **3** = **go bad**, addle, become tainted, curdle, decay, decompose, go off (*Brit. informal*), mildew, putrefy, rot, turn **4 spoiling for** = **eager for**, bent upon, desirous of, keen to, looking for, out to get (*informal*), raring to
➤ **Antonyms**
≠**ruin**: conserve, enhance, improve, keep, preserve, save ≠**overindulge**: be strict with, deprive, ignore, pay no attention to, treat harshly

spoils *plural noun* = **booty**, gain, loot, pickings, pillage, plunder, prey, prizes, swag (*slang*)

spoilsport *noun Informal* = **killjoy**, damper, dog in the manger, misery (*Brit. informal*), party-pooper (*U.S. slang*), wet blanket (*informal*)

spoken *adjective* = **said**, by word of mouth, expressed, oral, phonetic, put into words, told, unwritten, uttered, verbal, viva voce, voiced

spokesperson *noun* = **speaker**, mouthpiece, official, spin doctor (*informal*), spokesman *or* spokeswoman, voice

sponger *noun Informal* = **scrounger** (*informal*), bloodsucker (*informal*), cadge (*Brit.*), cadger, freeloader (*slang*), hanger-on, leech, parasite

spongy *adjective* = **porous**, absorbent, cushioned, cushiony, elastic, light, springy

sponsor *noun* **1** = **backer**, angel (*informal*), godparent, guarantor, patron, promoter ♦ *verb* **2** = **back**, finance, fund, guarantee, patronize, promote, put up the money for, subsidize

spontaneous *adjective* = **unplanned**, extempore, free, impromptu, impulsive, instinctive, natural, unbidden, uncompelled, unconstrained, unforced, unpremeditated, unprompted, voluntary, willing
➤ **Antonyms**
arranged, calculated, contrived, deliberate,

forced, mannered, orchestrated, planned, prearranged, premeditated, preplanned, stage-managed, studied

spontaneously *adverb* = **of one's own accord**, extempore, freely, impromptu, impulsively, instinctively, in the heat of the moment, off one's own bat, off the cuff (*informal*), on impulse, quite unprompted, voluntarily

spoof *noun Informal* 1 = **parody**, burlesque, caricature, lampoon, mockery, satire, send-up (*Brit. informal*), take-off (*informal*), travesty 2 = **trick**, bluff, deception, game, hoax, joke, leg-pull (*Brit. informal*), prank

spooky *adjective* = **eerie**, chilling, creepy (*informal*), frightening, ghostly, mysterious, scary (*informal*), spine-chilling, supernatural, uncanny, unearthly, weird

spoon-feed *verb* = **mollycoddle**, cosset, overindulge, overprotect, spoil, wrap up in cotton wool (*informal*)

sporadic *adjective* = **intermittent**, infrequent, irregular, isolated, occasional, on and off, random, scattered, spasmodic
➤ **Antonyms**
consistent, frequent, recurrent, regular, set, steady, systematic

sport *noun* 1 = **game**, amusement, diversion, entertainment, exercise, pastime, physical activity, play, recreation 2 = **fun**, badinage, banter, jest, joking, kidding (*informal*), merriment, mirth, raillery, ridicule, teasing ◆ *verb* 3 *Informal* = **wear**, display, exhibit, show off

sporting *adjective* = **fair**, game (*informal*), gentlemanly, sportsmanlike
➤ **Antonyms**
unfair, unsporting, unsportsmanlike

sportive *adjective* = **playful**, frisky, frolicsome, full of beans (*informal*), full of fun, gay, joyous, lively, merry, rollicking, skittish, sprightly

sporty *adjective* 1 = **athletic**, energetic, hearty, outdoor 2 = **casual**, jazzy (*informal*), snazzy (*informal*), stylish, trendy (*Brit. informal*)

spot *noun* 1 = **mark**, blemish, blot, blotch, daub, discoloration, flaw, scar, smudge, speck, speckle, stain, taint 2 = **place**, locality, location, point, position, scene, site, situation 3 = **pimple**, plook (*Scot.*), pustule, zit (*slang*) 4 *Informal, chiefly Brit.* = **bit**, little, morsel, splash 5 *Informal* = **predicament**, difficulty, hot water (*informal*), mess, plight, quandary, tight spot, trouble 6 **soft spot** = **fondness**, liking, partiality, weakness ◆ *verb* 7 = **see**, behold (*archaic or literary*), catch sight of, detect, discern, espy, identify, make out, observe, pick out, recognize, sight 8 = **mark**, besmirch, blot, dirty, dot, fleck,

mottle, scar, smirch, soil, spatter, speckle, splodge, splotch, stain, sully, taint, tarnish

spotless *adjective* 1 = **clean**, faultless, flawless, gleaming, immaculate, impeccable, pure, shining, snowy, unblemished, unstained, unsullied, untarnished, white 2 = **blameless**, above reproach, chaste, innocent, irreproachable, squeaky-clean, unimpeachable
➤ **Antonyms**
≠**clean**: besmirched, bespattered, blemished, defiled, dirty, filthy, flawed, impure, messy, soiled, spotted, stained, sullied, tainted, tarnished ≠**blameless**: notorious, reprehensible

spotlight *noun* 1 = **attention**, fame, interest, limelight, notoriety, public attention, public eye ◆ *verb* 2 = **highlight**, accentuate, draw attention to, feature, focus attention on, give prominence to, illuminate, point up, throw into relief

spot-on *adjective Informal* = **accurate**, correct, exact, precise, right, unerring

spotted *adjective* = **speckled**, dappled, dotted, flecked, mottled, pied, polka-dot, specked

spotty *adjective* 1 = **pimply**, blotchy, pimpled, plooky-faced (*Scot.*), poor-complexioned 2 = **inconsistent**, erratic, fluctuating, irregular, patchy, sporadic, uneven

spouse *noun* = **partner**, better half (*humorous*), companion, consort, helpmate, her indoors (*Brit. slang*), husband *or* wife, mate, significant other (*U.S. informal*)

spout *verb* 1 = **stream**, discharge, emit, erupt, gush, jet, shoot, spray, spurt, squirt, surge 2 *Informal* = **hold forth**, declaim, go on (*informal*), orate, pontificate, rabbit (on) (*Brit. informal*), ramble (on), rant, speechify, talk

sprawl *verb* 1 = **loll**, flop, lounge, slouch, slump 2 = **spread**, ramble, straggle, trail

spray[1] *noun* 1 = **droplets**, drizzle, fine mist, moisture, spindrift 2 = **aerosol**, atomizer, sprinkler ◆ *verb* 3 = **scatter**, atomize, diffuse, shower, sprinkle

spray[2] *noun* = **sprig**, bough, branch, corsage, floral arrangement, shoot

spread *verb* 1 = **open (out)**, be displayed, bloat, broaden, dilate, expand, extend, fan out, sprawl, stretch, swell, unfold, unfurl, unroll, widen 2 = **proliferate**, escalate, multiply, mushroom 3 = **circulate**, advertise, broadcast, cover, diffuse, disseminate, distribute, make known, make public, proclaim, promulgate, propagate, publicize, publish, radiate, scatter, strew, transmit ◆ *noun* 4 = **increase**, advance, advancement, development, diffusion,

dispersal, dissemination, escalation, expansion, proliferation, spreading, suffusion, transmission **5 = extent**, compass, period, reach, span, stretch, sweep, term **6** *Informal* **= feast**, array, banquet, repast
➤ **Antonyms**
verb ≠ **circulate**: contain, control, curb, hold back, hold in, repress, restrain, stifle

spree *noun* **= binge** (*informal*), bacchanalia, bender (*informal*), carousal, carouse, debauch, fling, orgy, revel, splurge

sprightly *adjective* **= lively**, active, agile, animated, brisk, cheerful, energetic, frolicsome, gay, jaunty, nimble, perky, playful, spirited, spry, vivacious
➤ **Antonyms**
dull, inactive, lethargic, sedentary, sluggish, torpid, unenergetic

spring *verb* **1 = jump**, bounce, bound, hop, leap, rebound, recoil, vault **2** *often with* **from = originate**, arise, be derived, be descended, come, derive, descend, emanate, emerge, grow, issue, proceed, start, stem **3** *often with* **up = appear**, burgeon, come into existence *or* being, develop, mushroom, shoot up ◆ *noun* **4 = jump**, bound, buck, hop, leap, vault **5 = source**, beginning, cause, fount, fountainhead, origin, root, well, wellspring **6 = elasticity**, bounce, bounciness, buoyancy, flexibility, give (*informal*), recoil, resilience, springiness ◆ *adjective* **7** *Of the season* **= vernal**, springlike

springy *adjective* **= elastic**, bouncy, buoyant, flexible, resilient, rubbery, spongy

sprinkle *verb* **= scatter**, dredge, dust, pepper, powder, shower, spray, strew

sprinkling *noun* **= scattering**, admixture, dash, dusting, few, handful, scatter, smattering, sprinkle

sprint *verb* **= race**, dart, dash, go at top speed, hare (*Brit. informal*), hotfoot, put on a burst of speed, scamper, shoot, tear, whizz (*informal*)

sprite *noun* **= spirit**, apparition, brownie, dryad, elf, fairy, goblin, imp, leprechaun, peri, pixie, sylph

sprout *verb* **= grow**, bud, develop, germinate, shoot, spring

spruce *adjective* **= smart**, dainty, dapper, elegant, natty (*informal*), neat, soigné *or* soignée, trig (*archaic or dialect*), trim, well-groomed, well turned out
➤ **Antonyms**
bedraggled, disarrayed, dishevelled, frowsy, messy, rumpled, uncombed, unkempt, untidy

spruce up *verb* **= smarten up**, groom, have a wash and brush-up (*Brit.*), tidy, titivate

spry *adjective* **= active**, agile, brisk, nimble, nippy (*Brit. informal*), quick, ready,

sprightly, supple
➤ **Antonyms**
awkward, decrepit, doddering, inactive, lethargic, slow, sluggish, stiff

spunk *noun Old fashioned, informal* **= courage**, backbone, balls (*taboo slang*), bottle (*Brit. slang*), gumption (*informal*), guts (*informal*), mettle, nerve, pluck, spirit

spur *noun* **1 = stimulus**, impetus, impulse, incentive, incitement, inducement, motive **2 = goad**, prick **3 on the spur of the moment = on impulse**, impetuously, impromptu, impulsively, on the spot, unpremeditatedly, unthinkingly, without planning, without thinking ◆ *verb* **4 = incite**, animate, drive, goad, impel, press, prick, prod, prompt, stimulate, urge

spurious *adjective* **= false**, artificial, bogus, contrived, counterfeit, deceitful, ersatz, fake, feigned, forged, imitation, mock, phoney *or* phony (*informal*), pretended, pseudo (*informal*), sham, simulated, specious, unauthentic
➤ **Antonyms**
authentic, bona fide, genuine, honest, kosher (*informal*), legitimate, real, sound, unfeigned, valid

spurn *verb* **= reject**, cold-shoulder, contemn, despise, disdain, disregard, kick in the teeth (*slang*), put down, rebuff, repulse, scorn, slight, snub, turn one's nose up at (*informal*)
➤ **Antonyms**
embrace, grasp, seize, take up, welcome

spurt *verb* **1 = gush**, burst, erupt, jet, shoot, spew, squirt, surge ◆ *noun* **2 = burst**, access, fit, rush, spate, surge

spy *noun* **1 = undercover agent**, double agent, fifth columnist, foreign agent, mole, nark (*Brit., Austral., & N.Z. slang*), secret agent, secret service agent ◆ *verb* **2** *usually with* **on = watch**, follow, keep under surveillance, keep watch on, shadow, tail (*informal*), trail **3 = catch sight of**, behold (*archaic or literary*), descry, espy, glimpse, notice, observe, set eyes on, spot

spying *noun* **= espionage**, secret service

squabble *verb* **1 = quarrel**, argue, bicker, brawl, clash, dispute, fall out (*informal*), fight, have words, row, scrap (*informal*), wrangle ◆ *noun* **2 = quarrel**, argument, barney (*informal*), difference of opinion, disagreement, dispute, fight, row, scrap (*informal*), set-to (*informal*), spat, tiff

squad *noun* **= team**, band, company, crew, force, gang, group, troop

squalid *adjective* **= dirty**, broken-down, decayed, disgusting, fetid, filthy, foul, low, nasty, poverty-stricken, repulsive, run-down, seedy, sleazy, slovenly, slummy, sordid,

unclean, yucky or yukky (*slang*)
➤ **Antonyms**
attractive, clean, hygienic, in good
condition, pleasant, salubrious,
spick-and-span, spotless, tidy, well-kempt,
well looked-after

squalor *noun* = **filth**, decay, foulness,
meanness, sleaziness, slumminess,
squalidness, wretchedness
➤ **Antonyms**
cleanliness, fine condition, luxury, neatness,
order, pleasantness, splendour

squander *verb* = **waste**, be prodigal with,
blow (*slang*), consume, dissipate, expend,
fritter away, lavish, misspend, misuse, run
through, scatter, spend, spend like water,
throw away
➤ **Antonyms**
be frugal, be thrifty, economize, keep, put
aside for a rainy day, save, store

square *noun* **1** *Informal* = **(old) fogey**,
conservative, die-hard, dinosaur,
fuddy-duddy (*informal*), stick-in-the-mud
(*informal*), traditionalist ♦ *adjective* **2**
= **honest**, above board, decent, equitable,
ethical, fair, fair and square, genuine, just,
kosher (*informal*), on the level (*informal*),
on the up and up, straight, straightforward,
upfront (*informal*), upright **3** *Informal*
= **old-fashioned**, behind the times,
conservative, conventional, dated, out of
date, out of the ark (*informal*), straight
(*slang*), strait-laced, stuffy ♦ *verb* **4** = **even
up**, accommodate, adapt, adjust, align, level,
regulate, suit, tailor, true (up) **5** *sometimes
with* **up** = **pay off**, balance, clear (up),
discharge, liquidate, make even, quit, satisfy,
settle **6** *often with* **with** = **agree**, accord,
conform, correspond, fit, harmonize, match,
reconcile, tally
➤ **Antonyms**
adjective ≠**old-fashioned**: fashionable, in
vogue, modern, modish, stylish, trendy (*Brit.
informal*), voguish

squash *verb* **1** = **crush**, compress, distort,
flatten, mash, pound, press, pulp, smash,
stamp on, trample down **2** = **suppress**,
annihilate, crush, humiliate, put down
(*slang*), put (someone) in his (*or* her) place,
quash, quell, silence

squashy *adjective* = **soft**, mushy, pappy,
pulpy, spongy, yielding

squawk *verb* **1** = **cry**, cackle, crow, hoot,
screech, yelp **2** *Informal* = **complain**, kick up
a fuss (*informal*), protest, raise Cain (*slang*)

squeak *verb* = **peep**, pipe, shrill, squeal,
whine, yelp

squeal *noun, verb* **1** = **scream**, screech,
shriek, wail, yell, yelp, yowl ♦ *verb* **2** *Slang*
= **inform on**, betray, blab, grass (*Brit.*

slang), rat on (*informal*), sell (someone)
down the river (*informal*), shop (*slang,
chiefly Brit.*), sing (*slang, chiefly U.S.*),
snitch (*slang*), tell all **3** *Informal, chiefly Brit.*
= **complain**, kick up a fuss (*informal*), moan,
protest, squawk (*informal*)

squeamish *adjective* **1** = **fastidious**,
delicate, finicky, nice (*rare*), particular, prissy
(*informal*), prudish, punctilious, scrupulous,
strait-laced **2** = **queasy**, nauseous, qualmish,
queer, sick, sickish
➤ **Antonyms**
≠**fastidious**: bold, brassy, brazen, coarse,
earthy, immodest, indifferent, tough,
wanton ≠**queasy**: strong-stomached

squeeze *verb* **1** = **press**, clutch, compress,
crush, grip, nip, pinch, squash, wring **2**
= **cram**, crowd, force, jam, jostle, pack,
press, ram, stuff, thrust, wedge **3** = **hug**,
clasp, cuddle, embrace, enfold, hold tight **4**
= **extort**, bring pressure to bear on, lean on
(*informal*), milk, oppress, pressurize, put the
screws on (*informal*), put the squeeze on
(*informal*), wrest ♦ *noun* **5** = **hug**, clasp,
embrace, handclasp, hold **6** = **crush**, squash
congestion, crowd, jam, press, squash

squint *adjective Informal* = **crooked**, askew,
aslant, awry, cockeyed, oblique, off-centre,
skew-whiff (*informal*)
➤ **Antonyms**
aligned, even, horizontal, in line, level,
perpendicular, plum, square, straight, true,
vertical

squire *verb Old-fashioned* = **escort**,
accompany, attend, companion

squirm *verb* = **wriggle**, fidget, flounder,
shift, twist, wiggle, writhe

stab *verb* **1** = **pierce**, bayonet, cut, gore,
impale, injure, jab, knife, puncture, run
through, spear, spill blood, stick, thrust,
transfix, wound **2** **stab in the back**
= **betray**, break faith with, deceive, do the
dirty on (*Brit. slang*), double-cross
(*informal*), let down, play false, sell, sell out
(*informal*) ♦ *noun* **3** = **wound**, gash,
incision, jab, puncture, rent, thrust **4**
= **twinge**, ache, pang, prick **5** *Informal*
= **attempt**, crack (*informal*), endeavour,
essay (*informal*), go, shot (*informal*), try

stability *noun* = **firmness**, constancy,
durability, permanence, solidity, soundness,
steadfastness, steadiness, strength
➤ **Antonyms**
changeableness, fickleness, fragility, frailty,
inconstancy, instability, unpredictability,
unreliability, unsteadiness

stable *adjective* **1** = **firm**, abiding, constant,
deep-rooted, durable, enduring, established,
fast, fixed, immovable, immutable,
invariable, lasting, permanent, secure,

sound, strong, sturdy, unalterable, unchangeable, unwavering, well-founded **2** = **steady**, reliable, staunch, steadfast, sure
➤ **Antonyms**
≠**firm:** changeable, erratic, inconstant, insecure, irresolute, mercurial, mutable, shaky, shifting, temperamental, uncertain, unpredictable, unreliable, unstable, variable, volatile, wavering ≠**steady:** unsteady, unsure

stack noun **1** = **pile**, heap, hoard, load, mass, mound, mountain ♦ verb **2** = **pile**, accumulate, amass, assemble, bank up, heap up, load, stockpile

staff noun **1** = **workers**, employees, lecturers, officers, organization, personnel, teachers, team, workforce **2** = **stick**, cane, crook, pole, prop, rod, sceptre, stave, wand

stage noun **1** = **step**, division, juncture, lap, leg, length, level, period, phase, point ♦ verb **2** = **present**, do, give, perform, play, produce, put on **3** = **organize**, arrange, engineer, lay on, mount, orchestrate

stagger verb **1** = **totter**, falter, lurch, reel, sway, teeter, waver, wobble **2** = **astound**, amaze, astonish, bowl over (informal), confound, dumbfound, flabbergast, give (someone) a shock, nonplus, overwhelm, shake, shock, strike (someone) dumb, stun, stupefy, surprise, take (someone) aback, take (someone's) breath away, throw off balance **3** = **alternate**, overlap, step

stagnant adjective = **stale**, brackish, motionless, quiet, sluggish, standing, still
➤ **Antonyms**
clear, flowing, fresh, moving, pure, running, unpolluted

stagnate verb = **vegetate**, decay, decline, deteriorate, fester, go to seed, idle, languish, lie fallow, rot, rust, stand still

staid adjective = **sedate**, calm, composed, decorous, demure, grave, quiet, self-restrained, serious, set in one's ways, sober, solemn, steady
➤ **Antonyms**
adventurous, capricious, demonstrative, exuberant, flighty, giddy, indecorous, lively, rowdy, sportive, wild

stain verb **1** = **mark**, blemish, blot, dirty, discolour, smirch, soil, spot, tarnish, tinge **2** = **dye**, colour, tint ♦ noun **3** = **mark**, blemish, blot, discoloration, smirch, spot **4** = **stigma**, blemish, disgrace, dishonour, infamy, shame, slur **5** = **dye**, colour, tint

stake[1] noun **1** = **pole**, pale, paling, palisade, picket, post, spike, stave, stick ♦ verb **2** often with **out** = **lay claim to**, define, delimit, demarcate, mark out, outline, reserve **3** = **support**, brace, prop, secure, tie up

stake[2] noun **1** = **bet**, ante, chance, hazard, peril, pledge, risk, venture, wager **2**

= **interest**, claim, concern, investment, involvement, share ♦ verb **3** = **bet**, chance, gamble, hazard, pledge, put on, risk, venture, wager

stale adjective **1** = **old**, decayed, dry, fetid, flat, fusty, hard, insipid, musty, sour, stagnant, tasteless **2** = **unoriginal**, antiquated, banal, cliché-ridden, common, commonplace, drab, flat, hackneyed, insipid, old hat, overused, repetitious, stereotyped, threadbare, trite, worn-out
➤ **Antonyms**
≠**old:** crisp, fresh ≠**unoriginal:** different, imaginative, innovative, lively, new, novel, original, refreshing

stalemate noun = **deadlock**, draw, impasse, standstill, tie

stalk verb **1** = **pursue**, creep up on, follow, haunt, hunt, shadow, tail (informal), track **2** = **strut**, flounce, march, pace, stride

stall verb = **play for time**, beat about the bush (informal), hedge, temporize

stalwart adjective **1** = **strong**, athletic, beefy (informal), brawny, hefty (informal), husky (informal), lusty, manly, muscular, robust, rugged, sinewy, stout, strapping, sturdy, vigorous **2** = **loyal**, dependable, reliable, staunch
➤ **Antonyms**
≠**strong:** feeble, frail, infirm, namby-pamby, puny, shilpit (Scot.), sickly, weak

stamina noun = **staying power**, endurance, energy, force, indefatigability, lustiness, power, power of endurance, resilience, resistance, strength, tenacity, vigour

stammer verb = **stutter**, falter, hem and haw, hesitate, pause, stumble

stamp noun **1** = **imprint**, brand, cast, earmark, hallmark, mark, mould, signature **2** = **type**, breed, cast, character, cut, description, fashion, form, kind, sort ♦ verb **3** = **trample**, beat, crush **4** = **identify**, brand, categorize, exhibit, label, mark, pronounce, reveal, show to be, typecast **5** = **imprint**, engrave, fix, impress, inscribe, mark, mould, print

stamp collecting noun = **philately**

stampede noun = **rush**, charge, flight, rout, scattering

stamp out verb = **eliminate**, crush, destroy, eradicate, extinguish, extirpate, put down, put out, quell, quench, scotch, suppress

stance noun **1** = **attitude**, position, stand, standpoint, viewpoint **2** = **posture**, bearing, carriage, deportment

stanch see STAUNCH[1]

stand verb **1** = **be upright**, be erect, be vertical, rise **2** = **put**, mount, place, position, rank, set **3** = **exist**, be in force, belong, be situated or located, be valid, continue, hold, obtain, prevail, remain, stay **4 = tolerate**, abide, allow, bear, brook, cope with, countenance, endure, experience, hack (slang), handle, put up with (informal), stomach, submit to, suffer, support, sustain, take, thole (dialect), undergo, withstand ♦ noun **5 = stall**, booth, table **6 = grandstand 7 = stop**, halt, rest, standstill, stay **8 = position**, attitude, determination, firm stand, opinion, stance, standpoint **9 = support**, base, bracket, dais, frame, place, platform, rack, rank, stage, tripod, trivet

standard noun **1 = level**, gauge, grade, measure **2 = criterion**, average, benchmark, example, guide, guideline, model, norm, par, pattern, sample, touchstone, yardstick **3** often plural **= principles**, canon, code of honour, ethics, ideals, moral principles, morals, rule **4 = flag**, banner, colours, ensign, pennant, pennon, streamer ♦ adjective **5 = usual**, average, basic, customary, normal, orthodox, popular, prevailing, regular, set, staple, stock, typical **6 = accepted**, approved, authoritative, classic, definitive, established, official, recognized
➤ **Antonyms**
adjective ≠**usual**: abnormal, atypical, exceptional, extraordinary, irregular, singular, strange, uncommon, unusual ≠**accepted**: unauthorised, unconventional, unofficial

standardize verb **= bring into line**, assimilate, institutionalize, mass-produce, regiment, stereotype

stand by verb **1 = be prepared**, wait, wait in the wings **2 = support**, back, befriend, be loyal to, champion, defend, stick up for (informal), take (someone's) part, uphold

stand for verb **1 = represent**, betoken, denote, exemplify, indicate, mean, signify, symbolize **2** Informal **= tolerate**, bear, brook, endure, put up with, suffer

stand-in noun **= substitute**, deputy, locum, replacement, reserve, stopgap, surrogate, understudy

stand in for verb **= be a substitute for**, cover for, deputize for, do duty for, replace, represent, take the place of, understudy

standing adjective **1 = permanent**, fixed, lasting, perpetual, regular, repeated **2 = upright**, erect, perpendicular, rampant (Heraldry), upended, vertical ♦ noun **3 = status**, eminence, estimation, footing, position, rank, reputation, repute, station **4 = duration**, continuance, existence, experience

standoffish adjective **= reserved**, aloof, cold, distant, haughty, remote,

unapproachable, unsociable
➤ **Antonyms**
affable, approachable, congenial, cordial, friendly, open, sociable, warm

stand out verb **= be conspicuous**, attract attention, be distinct, be highlighted, be obvious, be prominent, be striking, catch the eye, project, stare one in the face (informal), stick out a mile (informal), stick out like a sore thumb (informal)

standpoint noun **= point of view**, angle, position, stance, viewpoint

stand up for verb **= support**, champion, come to the defence of, defend, side with, stick up for (informal), uphold

stand up to verb **1 = resist**, brave, confront, defy, oppose, tackle **2 = withstand**, endure

staple adjective **= principal**, basic, chief, essential, fundamental, key, main, predominant, primary

star noun **1 = heavenly body 2 = celebrity**, big name, celeb (informal), idol, lead, leading man or lady, luminary, main attraction, megastar (informal), name ♦ adjective **3 = leading**, brilliant, celebrated, illustrious, major, paramount, principal, prominent, talented, well-known

starchy adjective **= formal**, conventional, precise, prim, punctilious, stiff, stuffy

stare verb **= gaze**, eyeball (slang), gape, gawk, gawp (Brit. slang), goggle, look, ogle, watch

stark adjective **1 = harsh**, austere, bare, barren, bleak, cold, depressing, desolate, dreary, grim, hard, plain, severe, unadorned **2 = absolute**, arrant, blunt, downright, entire, flagrant, out-and-out, palpable, patent, pure, sheer, simple, unalloyed, unmitigated, utter ♦ adverb **3 = absolutely**, altogether, clean, completely, entirely, quite, utterly, wholly

stark-naked adjective **= undressed**, buck naked (slang), in a state of nature, in one's birthday suit (informal), in the altogether (informal), in the buff (informal), naked, naked as the day one was born (informal), nude, stark, starkers (informal), stripped, unclad, without a stitch on (informal)

start verb **1 = begin**, appear, arise, come into being, come into existence, commence, get under way, go ahead, issue, originate **2 = set about**, embark upon, make a beginning, take the first step, take the plunge (informal) **3 = set in motion**, activate, engender, enter upon, get going, get (something) off the ground (informal), get or set or start the ball rolling, initiate, instigate, kick off (informal), kick-start, open, originate, trigger, turn on **4 = jump**, blench,

flinch, jerk, recoil, shy, twitch **5 = establish**, begin, create, father, found, inaugurate, initiate, institute, introduce, launch, pioneer, set up ♦ *noun* **6 = beginning**, birth, commencement, dawn, first step(s), foundation, inauguration, inception, initiation, kickoff (*informal*), onset, opening, outset **7 = advantage**, edge, head start, lead **8 = jump**, convulsion, jar, spasm, twitch **9 = opportunity**, backing, break (*informal*), chance, helping hand, introduction, opening, sponsorship
➤ **Antonyms**
verb ≠**begin**, set about, set in motion: abandon, bring to an end, call it a day (*informal*), cease, conclude, delay, desist, end, finish, give up, put aside, put off, quit, stop, switch off, terminate, turn off, wind up ♦ *noun* ≠**beginning**: cessation, conclusion, denouement, end, finale, finish, outcome, result, stop, termination, turning off, wind-up
startle *verb* **= surprise**, agitate, alarm, amaze, astonish, astound, frighten, give (someone) a turn (*informal*), make (someone) jump, scare, shock, take (someone) aback
startling *adjective* **= surprising**, alarming, astonishing, astounding, extraordinary, jaw-dropping, shocking, staggering, sudden, unexpected, unforeseen
starving *adjective* **= hungry**, famished, ravenous, ready to eat a horse (*informal*), sharp-set, starved
stash *verb Informal* **= store**, cache, hide, hoard, lay up, secrete, stockpile, stow
state *noun* **1 = condition**, case, category, circumstances, equation, mode, pass, plight, position, predicament, shape, situation, state of affairs **2 = frame of mind**, attitude, humour, mood, spirits **3 = country**, body politic, commonwealth, federation, government, kingdom, land, nation, republic, territory **4 = ceremony**, dignity, display, glory, grandeur, majesty, pomp, splendour, style **5 in a state** *Informal* **= distressed**, agitated, all steamed up (*slang*), anxious, disturbed, flustered, het up, panic-stricken, ruffled, upset, uptight (*informal*) ♦ *verb* **6 = express**, affirm, articulate, assert, aver, declare, explain, expound, present, propound, put, report, say, specify, utter, voice
stately *adjective* **= grand**, august, dignified, elegant, imperial, imposing, impressive, lofty, majestic, noble, regal, royal
➤ **Antonyms**
common, humble, lowly, modest, simple, undignified, undistinguished, unimpressive
statement *noun* **= account**, announcement, communication,

communiqué, declaration, explanation, proclamation, recital, relation, report, testimony, utterance
state-of-the-art *adjective* **= latest**, newest, up-to-date, up to-the-minute
➤ **Antonyms**
obsolescent, obsolete, old-fashioned, outdated, outmoded, out of date
static *adjective* **= stationary**, changeless, constant, fixed, immobile, inert, motionless, stagnant, still, stock-still, unmoving, unvarying
➤ **Antonyms**
active, dynamic, kinetic, lively, mobile, moving, travelling, varied
station *noun* **1 = headquarters**, base, depot **2 = position**, grade, post, rank, situation, sphere, standing, status **3 = occupation**, appointment, business, calling, employment **4 = place**, location, position, post, seat, situation ♦ *verb* **5 = assign**, establish, fix, garrison, install, locate, post, set
stationary *adjective* **= motionless**, at a standstill, fixed, inert, parked, standing, static, stock-still, unmoving
➤ **Antonyms**
changeable, changing, inconstant, mobile, moving, shifting, travelling, unstable, variable, varying, volatile
statuesque *adjective* **= well-proportioned**, dignified, imposing, Junoesque, majestic, regal, stately
stature *noun* **= importance**, consequence, eminence, high station, prestige, prominence, rank, size, standing
status *noun* **= position**, condition, consequence, degree, distinction, eminence, grade, prestige, rank, standing
statute *noun* **= law**, act, decree, edict, enactment, ordinance, regulation, rule
staunch[1], **stanch** *verb* **= stop**, arrest, check, dam, halt, plug, stay, stem
staunch[2] *adjective* **= loyal**, constant, dependable, faithful, firm, immovable, reliable, resolute, sound, stalwart, steadfast, stout, strong, sure, tried and true, true, true-blue, trustworthy, trusty
stave off *verb* **= hold off**, avert, evade, fend off, keep at arm's length, keep at bay, ward off
stay[1] *verb* **1 = remain**, abide, bide, continue, delay, establish oneself, halt, hang around (*informal*), hover, linger, loiter, pause, reside, settle, stand, stay put, stop, tarry, wait **2** *often with* **at = lodge**, be accommodated at, sojourn, visit ♦ *noun* **3 = visit**, holiday, sojourn, stop, stopover **4 = postponement**, deferment, delay, halt, pause, remission, reprieve, stopping, suspension

➤ **Antonyms**
verb ≠**remain:** abandon, depart, exit, go, leave, move on, pack one's bags (informal), pass through, quit, withdraw

stay[2] noun = **support**, brace, buttress, prop, reinforcement, stanchion

staying power noun = **endurance**, stamina, strength, toughness

steadfast adjective = **firm**, constant, dedicated, dependable, established, faithful, fast, fixed, immovable, intent, loyal, persevering, reliable, resolute, single-minded, stable, stalwart, staunch, steady, unfaltering, unflinching, unswerving, unwavering
➤ **Antonyms**
capricious, faint-hearted, faltering, fickle, flagging, half-hearted, inconstant, irresolute, uncommitted, undependable, unreliable, unstable, vacillating, wavering

steady adjective 1 = **firm**, fixed, immovable, on an even keel, safe, secure, stable, substantial, unchangeable, uniform 2 = **continuous**, ceaseless, confirmed, consistent, constant, even, habitual, incessant, nonstop, persistent, regular, rhythmic, unbroken, unfaltering, unfluctuating, uninterrupted, unremitting, unvarying, unwavering 3 = **dependable**, balanced, calm, equable, having both feet on the ground, imperturbable, level-headed, reliable, sensible, serious-minded, sober ♦ verb 4 = **stabilize**, balance, brace, secure, support
➤ **Antonyms**
adjective ≠**firm:** insecure, unsettled, unstable, unsteady ≠**continuous:** changeable, faltering, fluctuating, inconsistent, infrequent, intermittent, irregular, occasional, sporadic ≠**dependable:** careless, fickle, half-hearted, in two minds, uncommitted, unconscientious, undependable, unpredictable, unreliable, vacillating, wavering ♦ verb ≠**stabilize:** agitate, shake, tilt, upset

steal verb 1 = **take**, appropriate, be light-fingered, blag (slang), embezzle, filch, lift (informal), misappropriate, nick (slang, chiefly Brit.), pilfer, pinch (informal), pirate, plagiarize, poach, purloin, shoplift, swipe (slang), thieve, walk or make off with 2 = **sneak**, creep, flit, slink, slip, tiptoe

stealing noun = **theft**, embezzlement, larceny, misappropriation, pilfering, plagiarism, robbery, shoplifting, thieving

stealth noun = **secrecy**, furtiveness, slyness, sneakiness, stealthiness, surreptitiousness, unobtrusiveness

stealthy adjective = **secret**, clandestine, covert, furtive, secretive, skulking, sly, sneaking, sneaky, surreptitious, underhand

steamy adjective Informal = **erotic**, carnal, hot (slang), lascivious, lewd, raunchy (slang), sensual, sexy (informal), titillating

steel oneself verb = **brace oneself**, fortify oneself, grit one's teeth, harden oneself, make up one's mind

steep[1] adjective 1 = **sheer**, abrupt, headlong, precipitous 2 Informal = **high**, excessive, exorbitant, extortionate, extreme, overpriced, stiff, unreasonable
➤ **Antonyms**
≠**sheer:** easy, gentle, gradual, moderate, slight ≠**high:** fair, moderate, reasonable

steep[2] verb 1 = **soak**, damp, drench, immerse, marinate (Cookery), moisten, souse, submerge 2 = **saturate**, fill, imbue, infuse, permeate, pervade, suffuse

steer verb 1 = **drive**, control, direct, guide, handle, pilot 2 = **direct**, administer, conduct, control, govern 3 **steer clear of** = **avoid**, body-swerve (Scot.), circumvent, eschew, evade, give a wide berth to, shun

steersman noun = **pilot**, cox, coxswain, helmsman

stem[1] noun 1 = **stalk**, axis, branch, shoot, stock, trunk ♦ verb 2 **stem from** = **originate from**, arise from, be brought about by, be caused by, be generated by, derive from, develop from, emanate from, flow from

stem[2] verb = **stop**, bring to a standstill, check, contain, curb, dam, hold back, oppose, resist, restrain, stanch, staunch, withstand

stench noun = **stink**, foul smell, malodour, niff (Brit. slang), pong (Brit. informal), reek, whiff (Brit. slang)

stentorian adjective = **loud**, booming, carrying, powerful, ringing, strident, strong, thundering
➤ **Antonyms**
gentle, hushed, low, low-pitched, quiet, soft, subdued

step noun 1 = **footstep**, footfall, footprint, impression, pace, print, stride, trace, track 2 = **stage**, advance, advancement, move, phase, point, process, progression 3 = **action**, act, deed, expedient, manoeuvre, means, measure, move, procedure, proceeding 4 = **degree**, level, rank 5 = **gait**, walk 6 = **stair**, doorstep, rung, tread 7 **in step** Informal = **in agreement**, coinciding, conforming, in conformity, in harmony, in line, in unison 8 **out of step** Informal = **in disagreement**, erratic, incongruous, out of harmony, out of line, out of phase, pulling different ways 9 **take steps** = **take action**, act, intervene, move in, prepare, take measures, take the initiative 10 **watch one's step** Informal = **be careful**, be canny, be cautious, be discreet, be on one's guard, have one's wits about one, look out, mind how one goes, mind one's p's and q's, take care, take heed, tread carefully ♦ *verb* **11** = **walk**, move, pace, tread

step down *verb Informal* = **resign**, abdicate, bow out, give up, hand over, leave, pull out, quit, retire

step in *verb Informal* = **intervene**, become involved, chip in (*informal*), intercede, take action, take a hand

step up *verb Informal* = **increase**, accelerate, augment, boost, escalate, intensify, raise, speed up, up

stereotype *noun* **1** = **formula**, mould, pattern, received idea ♦ *verb* **2** = **categorize**, dub, pigeonhole, standardize, take to be, typecast

sterile *adjective* **1** = **germ-free**, antiseptic, aseptic, disinfected, sterilized **2** = **barren**, abortive, bare, dry, empty, fruitless, infecund, unfruitful, unproductive, unprofitable, unprolific
➤ **Antonyms**
≠ **germ-free**: contaminated, dirty, germ-ridden, infected, insanitary, unhygienic, unsterile ≠ **barren**: fecund, fertile, fruitful, productive, prolific

sterilize *verb* = **disinfect**, fumigate, purify

sterling *adjective* = **excellent**, authentic, fine, first-class, genuine, pure, real, sound, standard, substantial, superlative, true

stern *adjective* **1** = **strict**, austere, authoritarian, cruel, drastic, grim, hard, harsh, inflexible, relentless, rigid, rigorous, unrelenting **2** = **severe**, forbidding, frowning, serious
➤ **Antonyms**
≠ **strict**: compassionate, flexible, gentle, kind, lenient, liberal, permissive, soft, sympathetic, tolerant ≠ **severe**: approachable, friendly, warm

stew *noun* **1** = **hash**, goulash, ragout **2 in a stew** *Informal* = **troubled**, anxious, concerned, fretting, in a panic, worrying

stick[1] *noun* **1** = **cane**, baton, birch, crook, pole, rod, sceptre, staff, stake, switch, twig, wand **2** *Slang* = **abuse**, blame, criticism, flak (*informal*)

stick[2] *verb* **1** = **poke**, dig, gore, insert, jab, penetrate, pierce, pin, prod, puncture, spear, stab, thrust, transfix **2** = **fasten**, adhere, affix, attach, bind, bond, cement, cleave, cling, fix, fuse, glue, hold, hold on, join, paste, weld **3** *with* **out, up,** *etc.* = **protrude**, bulge, extend, jut, obtrude, poke, project, show **4** *Informal* = **put**, deposit, drop, fix, install, lay, place, plant, plonk, position, set, store, stuff **5** = **catch**, become immobilized, be embedded, clog, come to a standstill, jam, lodge, snag, stop **6** = **stay**, linger,

persist, remain **7** *Slang* = **tolerate**, abide, endure, hack (*slang*), stand, stomach, take

stick-in-the-mud *noun Informal* = **(old) fogey**, conservative, die-hard, dinosaur, fuddy-duddy (*informal*), reactionary

stickler *noun* = **fanatic**, fusspot (*Brit. informal*), maniac (*informal*), martinet, nut (*slang*), pedant, perfectionist, purist

stick out *verb Informal* = **endure**, bear, grin and bear it (*informal*), put up with (*informal*), see through, soldier on, take it (*informal*), weather

stick to *verb* = **remain faithful**, adhere to, cleave to, continue in, honour, keep, persevere in, remain loyal, remain true, stick at

stick up for *verb Informal* = **defend**, champion, stand up for, support, take the part *or* side of, uphold

sticky *adjective* **1** = **tacky**, adhesive, clinging, gluey, glutinous, gooey (*informal*), gummy, icky (*informal*), syrupy, viscid, viscous **2** *Informal* = **difficult**, awkward, delicate, discomforting, embarrassing, hairy (*slang*), nasty, painful, thorny, tricky, unpleasant **3** = **humid**, clammy, close, muggy, oppressive, sultry, sweltering

stiff *adjective* **1** = **inflexible**, brittle, firm, hard, hardened, inelastic, rigid, solid, solidified, taut, tense, tight, unbending, unyielding **2** = **unsupple**, arthritic, creaky (*informal*), rheumaticky **3** = **awkward**, clumsy, crude, graceless, inelegant, jerky (*informal*), ungainly, ungraceful **4** = **difficult**, arduous, exacting, fatiguing, formidable, hard, laborious, tough, trying, uphill **5** = **severe**, cruel, drastic, extreme, great, hard, harsh, heavy, oppressive, pitiless, rigorous, sharp, strict, stringent **6** = **unrelaxed**, artificial, chilly, cold, constrained, forced, formal, laboured, prim, standoffish, starchy (*informal*), stilted, uneasy, unnatural, wooden **7** = **powerful**, brisk, fresh, strong, vigorous
➤ **Antonyms**
≠ **inflexible**: bendable, ductile, elastic, flexible, pliable, pliant, yielding ≠ **unsupple**: flexible, limber, lissom(e), lithe, supple ≠ **unrelaxed**: casual, easy, informal, laid-back, natural, relaxed, spontaneous

stiffen *verb* **1** = **brace**, reinforce, starch, tauten, tense **2** = **set**, coagulate, congeal, crystallize, harden, jell, solidify, thicken

stiff-necked *adjective* = **stubborn**, obstinate, opinionated, uncompromising

stifle *verb* **1** = **suppress**, check, choke back, cover up, curb, extinguish, gag, hush, muffle, prevent, repress, restrain, silence, smother, stop **2** = **suffocate**, asphyxiate, choke, smother, strangle

stigma noun = **disgrace**, blot, brand, dishonour, mark, reproach, shame, slur, smirch, spot, stain

stigmatize verb = **brand**, cast a slur upon, defame, label, mark

still adjective 1 = **motionless**, at rest, calm, inert, lifeless, peaceful, placid, restful, serene, smooth, stationary, tranquil, undisturbed, unruffled, unstirring 2 = **silent**, hushed, noiseless, quiet ◆ noun 3 Poetic = **stillness**, hush, peace, quiet, silence, tranquillity ◆ verb 4 = **quieten**, allay, alleviate, appease, calm, hush, lull, pacify, quiet, settle, silence, smooth, smooth over, soothe, subdue, tranquillize ◆ conjunction 5 = **however**, but, for all that, nevertheless, notwithstanding, yet
➤ Antonyms
adjective ≠ **motionless**: active, agitated, astir, bustling, busy, humming, lively, moving, restless, turbulent ≠ **silent**: noisy ◆ noun ≠ **stillness**: bustle, clamour, hubbub, noise, uproar ◆ verb ≠ **quieten**: aggravate, agitate, exacerbate, increase, inflame, rouse, stir up

stilted adjective = **stiff**, artificial, arty-farty (informal), bombastic, constrained, forced, grandiloquent, high-flown, high-sounding, inflated, laboured, pedantic, pompous, pretentious, unnatural, wooden
➤ Antonyms
flowing, fluid, free, natural, spontaneous, unaffected, unpretentious

stimulant noun = **pick-me-up** (informal), bracer (informal), energizer, pep pill (informal), restorative, reviver, tonic, upper (slang)
➤ Antonyms
calmant, depressant, downer (slang), sedative, tranquilliser

stimulate verb = **encourage**, animate, arouse, fan, fire, foment, gee up, goad, impel, incite, inflame, inspire, instigate, prod, prompt, provoke, quicken, rouse, spur, turn on (slang), urge, whet

stimulating adjective = **exciting**, exhilarating, inspiring, intriguing, provocative, provoking, rousing, stirring, thought-provoking
➤ Antonyms
as dry as dust, boring, dull, mind-numbing, unexciting, unimaginative, uninspiring, uninteresting, unstimulating

stimulus noun = **incentive**, encouragement, fillip, geeing-up, goad, impetus, incitement, inducement, provocation, shot in the arm (informal), spur

sting verb 1 = **hurt**, burn, pain, smart, tingle, wound 2 = **anger**, gall, incense, inflame, infuriate, nettle, pique, provoke, rile 3

Informal = **cheat**, defraud, do (slang), fleece, overcharge, rip off (slang), skin (slang), swindle, take for a ride (informal)

stingy adjective = **mean**, avaricious, cheeseparing, close-fisted, illiberal, mingy (Brit. informal), miserly, near, niggardly, parsimonious, penny-pinching (informal), penurious, scrimping, snoep (S. African informal), tightfisted, ungenerous

stink noun 1 = **stench**, fetor, foulness, foul smell, malodour, pong (Brit. informal) 2 Slang As in **make, create** or **kick up a stink** = **fuss**, brouhaha, commotion, row, rumpus, scandal, stir, to-do, uproar ◆ verb 3 = **reek**, offend the nostrils, pong (Brit. informal), stink to high heaven (informal) 4 Slang = **be bad**, be abhorrent, be no good, be rotten

stinker noun Slang 1 = **scoundrel**, bounder (old-fashioned Brit. slang), cad (Brit. informal), cocksucker (taboo slang), cur, heel, nasty piece of work (informal), rotter (slang, chiefly Brit.), sod (slang), swine 2 = **problem**, beast, horror, poser, shocker

stinking adjective 1 = **foul-smelling**, fetid, ill-smelling, malodorous, noisome, pongy (Brit. informal), reeking, smelly, whiffy (Brit. slang) 2 Informal = **rotten**, contemptible, disgusting, low, low-down (informal), mean, shitty (taboo slang), unpleasant, vile, wretched

stint verb 1 = **be mean**, be frugal, begrudge, be mingy (Brit. informal), be parsimonious, be sparing, economize, hold back, save, scrimp, skimp on, withhold ◆ noun 2 = **share**, assignment, bit, period, quota, shift, spell, stretch, term, time, turn

stipulate verb = **specify**, agree, contract, covenant, insist upon, lay down, lay down or impose conditions, promise, require, settle

stipulation noun = **condition**, agreement, clause, contract, precondition, prerequisite, provision, proviso, qualification, requirement, restriction, rider, sine qua non, specification, term

stir verb 1 = **mix**, agitate, beat, disturb, flutter, move, quiver, rustle, shake, tremble 2 = **stimulate**, affect, animate, arouse, awaken, electrify, excite, fire, incite, inflame, inspire, instigate, kindle, move, prod, prompt, provoke, quicken, raise, rouse, spur, thrill, touch, urge 3 = **get moving**, bestir oneself, budge, exert oneself, get a move on (informal), hasten, look lively (informal), make an effort, move ◆ noun 4 = **commotion**, activity, ado, agitation, bustle, disorder, disturbance, excitement, ferment, flurry, fuss, movement, to-do, tumult, uproar
➤ Antonyms
verb ≠ **stimulate**: check, curb, dampen,

inhibit, restrain, stifle, suppress, throw cold water on (*informal*)

stirring *adjective* = **exciting**, dramatic, emotive, exhilarating, heady, impassioned, inspiring, intoxicating, lively, moving, rousing, spirited, stimulating, thrilling

stock *noun* 1 = **goods**, array, assortment, choice, commodities, merchandise, range, selection, variety, wares 2 = **supply**, fund, hoard, reserve, reservoir, stockpile, store 3 = **property**, assets, capital, funds, investment 4 = **livestock**, beasts, cattle, domestic animals 5 = **lineage**, ancestry, background, breed, descent, extraction, family, forebears, house, line, line of descent, parentage, pedigree, race, strain, type, variety 6 **take stock = review the situation**, appraise, estimate, see how the land lies, size up (*informal*), weigh up ◆ *adjective* 7 = **standard**, basic, commonplace, conventional, customary, formal, ordinary, regular, routine, run-of-the-mill, set, staple, traditional, usual 8 = **hackneyed**, banal, overused, stereotyped, trite, worn-out ◆ *verb* 9 = **sell**, deal in, handle, keep, supply, trade in 10 = **provide with**, equip, fill, fit out, furnish, kit out, provision, supply 11 **stock up = store (up)**, accumulate, amass, buy up, gather, hoard, lay in, put away, save, supply

stocky *adjective* = **thickset**, chunky, dumpy, solid, stubby, stumpy, sturdy

stodgy *adjective* 1 = **heavy**, filling, leaden, starchy, substantial 2 = **dull**, boring, dull as ditchwater, formal, fuddy-duddy (*informal*), heavy going, ho-hum, laboured, staid, stuffy, tedious, tiresome, turgid, unexciting, unimaginative, uninspired
➤ **Antonyms**
≠**heavy**: appetizing, fluffy, insubstantial, light ≠**dull**: animated, exciting, fresh, interesting, light, lively, stimulating, up-to-date

stoical *adjective* = **resigned**, calm, cool, dispassionate, impassive, imperturbable, indifferent, long-suffering, philosophic, phlegmatic, stoic, stolid

stoicism *noun* = **resignation**, acceptance, calmness, dispassion, fatalism, forbearance, fortitude, impassivity, imperturbability, indifference, long-suffering, patience, stolidity

stolid *adjective* = **apathetic**, bovine, doltish, dozy (*Brit. informal*), dull, heavy, lumpish, obtuse, slow, stupid, unemotional, wooden
➤ **Antonyms**
acute, animated, bright, emotional, energetic, excitable, intelligent, interested, lively, passionate, sharp, smart

stomach *noun* 1 = **belly**, abdomen, gut (*informal*), inside(s) (*informal*), paunch, pot, potbelly, spare tyre (*informal*), tummy

(*informal*) 2 = **inclination**, appetite, desire, mind, relish, taste ◆ *verb* 3 = **bear**, abide, endure, hack (*slang*), put up with (*informal*), suffer, swallow, take, tolerate

stony *adjective* = **cold**, adamant, blank, callous, chilly, expressionless, hard, harsh, heartless, hostile, icy, indifferent, merciless, obdurate, pitiless, unfeeling, unresponsive

stooge *noun* = **pawn**, butt, dupe, fall guy (*informal*), patsy (*slang, chiefly U.S. & Canad.*), puppet

stoop *verb* 1 = **bend**, be bowed *or* round-shouldered, bow, crouch, descend, duck, hunch, incline, kneel, lean, squat 2 **stoop to = lower oneself by**, condescend to, deign to, demean oneself by, descend to, resort to, sink to ◆ *noun* 3 = **slouch**, bad posture, droop, round-shoulderedness, sag, slump

stop *verb* 1 = **halt**, axe (*informal*), belay (*Nautical*), be over, break off, bring *or* come to a halt *or* standstill, call it a day (*informal*), cease, come to an end, conclude, cut out (*informal*), cut short, desist, discontinue, draw up, end, finish, leave off, pack in (*Brit. informal*), pause, peter out, pull up, put an end to, quit, refrain, run down, shut down, stall, terminate 2 = **prevent**, arrest, bar, break, check, close, forestall, frustrate, hinder, hold back, impede, intercept, interrupt, nip (something) in the bud, rein in, repress, restrain, suspend 3 = **plug**, block, bung, obstruct, seal, staunch, stem 4 = **stay**, break one's journey, lodge, rest, sojourn ◆ *noun* 5 = **end**, cessation, conclusion, discontinuation, finish, halt, standstill 6 = **stay**, break, rest, sojourn, stopover, visit 7 = **station**, depot, destination, halt, stage, termination, terminus 8 = **block**, bar, break, check, control, hindrance, impediment, plug, stoppage
➤ **Antonyms**
verb ≠**halt**: advance, begin, commence, continue, get going, get under way, give the go ahead, go, institute, keep going, keep on, kick off (*informal*), proceed, set in motion, set off, start ≠**prevent**: assist, boost, encourage, expedite, facilitate, further, gee up, hasten, promote, push ◆ *noun* ≠**end**: beginning, commencement, kick-off (*informal*), start ≠**block**: boost, encouragement, geeing-up, incitement

stopgap *noun* = **makeshift**, improvisation, resort, substitute, temporary expedient

stoppage *noun* 1 = **stopping**, abeyance, arrest, close, closure, cutoff, discontinuance, halt, hindrance, lay-off, shutdown, standstill 2 = **blockage**, check, curtailment, interruption, obstruction, occlusion, stopping up

store *verb* 1 = **put by**, accumulate, deposit,

garner, hoard, husband, keep, keep in reserve, lay by or in, lock away, put aside, put aside for a rainy day, put in storage, reserve, save, stash (*informal*), stock, stockpile ♦ *noun* **2** = **shop**, chain store, department store, emporium, hypermarket, market, mart, outlet, supermarket **3** = **supply**, accumulation, cache, fund, hoard, lot, mine, provision, quantity, reserve, reservoir, stock, stockpile **4** = **repository**, depository, depot, storehouse, storeroom, warehouse **5 set great store by** = **value**, appreciate, esteem, hold in high regard, prize, think highly of

storm *noun* **1** = **tempest**, blast, blizzard, cyclone, gale, gust, hurricane, squall, tornado, whirlwind **2** = **outburst**, agitation, anger, clamour, commotion, disturbance, furore, hubbub, outbreak, outcry, passion, roar, row, rumpus, stir, strife, tumult, turmoil, violence **3** = **attack**, assault, blitz, blitzkrieg, offensive, onset, onslaught, rush ♦ *verb* **4** = **attack**, assail, assault, beset, charge, rush, take by storm **5** = **rage**, bluster, fly off the handle (*informal*), fume, go ballistic (*slang, chiefly U.S.*), rant, rave, thunder **6** = **rush**, flounce, fly, stalk, stamp, stomp (*informal*)

stormy *adjective* = **wild**, blustering, blustery, foul, gusty, inclement, raging, rough, squally, tempestuous, turbulent, windy

story *noun* **1** = **tale**, account, anecdote, chronicle, fictional account, history, legend, narration, narrative, novel, recital, record, relation, romance, urban legend, urban myth, version, yarn **2** = **report**, article, feature, news, news item, scoop **3** *Informal* = **lie**, falsehood, fib, fiction, pork pie (*Brit. slang*), porky (*Brit. slang*), untruth, white lie

stout *adjective* **1** = **fat**, big, bulky, burly, corpulent, fleshy, heavy, obese, on the large or heavy side, overweight, plump, portly, rotund, substantial, tubby **2** = **strong**, able-bodied, athletic, beefy (*informal*), brawny, hardy, hulking, husky (*informal*), lusty, muscular, robust, stalwart, strapping, sturdy, substantial, thickset, tough, vigorous **3** = **brave**, bold, courageous, dauntless, doughty, fearless, gallant, indomitable, intrepid, lion-hearted, manly, plucky, resolute, valiant, valorous

➤ **Antonyms**

≠**fat**: insubstantial, lanky, lean, skin-and-bones (*informal*), skinny, slender, slight, slim ≠**strong**: feeble, flimsy, frail, insubstantial, puny ≠**brave**: cowardly, faint-hearted, fearful, irresolute, shrinking, soft, spineless, timid, weak

stouthearted *adjective* Old-fashioned = **brave**, bold, courageous, dauntless,

doughty, fearless, great-hearted, gutsy (*slang*), heroic, indomitable, intrepid, lion-hearted, plucky, spirited, stalwart, valiant, valorous

stow *verb* = **pack**, bundle, cram, deposit, jam, load, put away, secrete, stash (*informal*), store, stuff, tuck

straggle *verb* = **spread**, drift, ramble, range, roam, rove, stray, string out, wander

straight *adjective* **1** = **direct**, near, short, undeviating, unswerving **2** = **level**, aligned, even, horizontal, in line, right, smooth, square, true **3** = **upright**, erect, perpendicular, plumb, vertical **4** = **accurate**, authentic, fair, honest, reliable, trustworthy **5** = **frank**, blunt, bold, candid, downright, forthright, honest, outright, plain, point-blank, straightforward, unqualified, upfront (*informal*) **6** = **successive**, consecutive, continuous, nonstop, running, solid, sustained, uninterrupted, unrelieved **7** = **undiluted**, neat, pure, unadulterated, unmixed **8** = **orderly**, arranged, in order, neat, organized, put to rights, shipshape, sorted out, tidy **9** = **honest**, above board, decent, equitable, fair, fair and square, honourable, just, law-abiding, reliable, respectable, trustworthy, upright **10** *Slang* = **conventional**, bourgeois, conservative, orthodox, square (*informal*), traditional ♦ *adverb* **11** = **directly**, as the crow flies, at once, immediately, instantly **12** = **frankly**, candidly, honestly, in plain English, point-blank, pulling no punches (*informal*), with no holds barred

➤ **Antonyms**

adjective ≠**direct**: circuitous, indirect, roundabout, winding, zigzag ≠**level**: askew, bent, crooked, curved, skewwhiff (*Brit. informal*), twisted, uneven ≠**frank**: ambiguous, cryptic, equivocal, evasive, indirect, vague ≠**successive**: broken, discontinuous, interrupted, non-consecutive ≠**orderly**: confused, disorderly, disorganized, in disarray, messy, untidy ≠**honest**: bent (*slang*), crooked (*informal*), dishonest, dishonourable, shady (*informal*), unlawful ≠**conventional**: cool, fashionable, trendy (*Brit. informal*), voguish

straight away *adverb* = **immediately**, at once, directly, instantly, now, on the spot, right away, there and then, without any delay, without more ado

straighten *verb* = **neaten**, arrange, order, put in order, set or put to rights, smarten up, spruce up, tidy (up)

straighten out *verb* = **make clear**, clear up, correct, disentangle, put right, rectify, resolve, settle, sort out, work out

straightforward *adjective* **1** = **honest**, above board, candid, direct, forthright,

genuine, guileless, open, sincere, truthful, upfront (*informal*) **2** *Chiefly Brit.* = **simple**, clear-cut, easy, easy-peasy (*slang*), elementary, routine, uncomplicated, undemanding
➤ **Antonyms**
≠**honest**: devious, disingenuous, roundabout, shady, sharp, unscrupulous ≠**simple**: complex, complicated, confused, convoluted, unclear

strain[1] *noun* **1** = **stress**, anxiety, burden, pressure, tension **2** = **exertion**, effort, force, struggle **3** = **injury**, pull, sprain, tautness, tension, wrench **4 strains** = **tune**, air, melody, song, theme ◆ *verb* **5** = **strive**, bend over backwards (*informal*), break one's back *or* neck (*informal*), bust a gut (*informal*), do one's damnedest (*informal*), endeavour, give it one's all (*informal*), give it one's best shot (*informal*), go all out for (*informal*), go for broke (*slang*), go for it (*informal*), knock oneself out (*informal*), labour, make an all-out effort (*informal*), struggle **6** = **overexert**, drive, exert, fatigue, injure, overtax, overwork, pull, push to the limit, sprain, tax, tear, test, tire, twist, weaken, wrench **7** = **sieve**, filter, percolate, purify, screen, seep, separate, sift **8** = **stretch**, distend, draw tight, extend, tauten, tighten
➤ **Antonyms**
noun ≠**stress**, **exertion**: ease, effortlessness, lack of tension, relaxation ◆ *verb* ≠**strive**, **overexert**: idle, loose, pamper, relax, rest, slacken, take it easy, yield

strain[2] *noun* **1** = **breed**, ancestry, blood, descent, extraction, family, lineage, pedigree, race, stock **2** = **trace**, streak, suggestion, suspicion, tendency, trait

strained *adjective* **1** = **forced**, artificial, false, laboured, put on, unnatural **2** = **tense**, awkward, constrained, difficult, embarrassed, self-conscious, stiff, uncomfortable, uneasy, unrelaxed
➤ **Antonyms**
≠**forced**: natural ≠**tense**: comfortable, relaxed

strait *noun* **1** *often plural* = **channel**, narrows, sound **2 straits** = **difficulty**, crisis, dilemma, distress, emergency, extremity, hardship, hole (*slang*), mess, pass, plight, predicament, pretty *or* fine kettle of fish (*informal*)

strait-laced *or* **straight-laced** *adjective* = **puritanical**, moralistic, narrow, narrow-minded, old-maidish (*informal*), prim, proper, prudish, strict, Victorian
➤ **Antonyms**
broad-minded, earthy, immoral, loose, relaxed, uninhibited, unreserved

strand *noun* = **filament**, fibre, length, lock,

rope, string, thread, tress, twist, wisp

stranded *adjective* **1** = **beached**, aground, ashore, cast away, grounded, marooned, shipwrecked **2** = **helpless**, abandoned, high and dry, homeless, left in the lurch, penniless

strange *adjective* **1** = **odd**, abnormal, astonishing, bizarre, curious, eccentric, exceptional, extraordinary, fantastic, funny, irregular, left-field (*informal*), marvellous, mystifying, oddball (*informal*), off-the-wall (*slang*), out-of-the-way, outré, peculiar, perplexing, queer, rare, remarkable, rum (*Brit. slang*), singular, unaccountable, uncanny, uncommon, unheard-of, weird, wonderful **2** = **unfamiliar**, alien, exotic, foreign, new, novel, outside one's experience, unexplored, unknown, untried **3** = **out of place**, awkward, bewildered, disoriented, ill at ease, like a fish out of water, lost, uncomfortable **4 strange to** = **unaccustomed to**, a stranger to, ignorant of, inexperienced in, new to, unpractised in, unseasoned in, unused to, unversed in
➤ **Antonyms**
≠**odd**: accustomed, bog-standard (*Brit. & Irish slang*), common, commonplace, conventional, familiar, habitual, ordinary, regular, routine, run-of-the-mill, standard, typical, unexceptional, usual, well-known ≠**unfamiliar**: accustomed, familiar, habitual ≠**out of place**: at ease, at home, comfortable, relaxed

stranger *noun* = **newcomer**, alien, foreigner, guest, incomer, new arrival, outlander, unknown, visitor

strangle *verb* **1** = **throttle**, asphyxiate, choke, garrotte, smother, strangulate, suffocate **2** = **suppress**, gag, inhibit, repress, stifle

strap *noun* **1** = **belt**, leash, thong, tie ◆ *verb* **2** = **fasten**, bind, buckle, lash, secure, tie, truss

strapped *adjective* **strapped for** *Slang* = **short of**, financially embarrassed, in need of, straitened, stuck for

strapping *adjective* = **well-built**, beefy (*informal*), big, brawny, burly, hefty (*informal*), hulking, husky (*informal*), powerful, robust, stalwart, sturdy, well set-up

stratagem *noun* = **trick**, artifice, device, dodge, feint, intrigue, manoeuvre, plan, plot, ploy, ruse, scheme, subterfuge, wile

strategic *adjective* **1** = **tactical**, calculated, deliberate, diplomatic, planned, politic **2** = **crucial**, cardinal, critical, decisive, important, key, vital

strategy *noun* = **plan**, approach, grand design, planning, policy, procedure, programme, scheme

stratum *noun* **1** = **layer**, bed, level, lode,

seam, stratification, tier, vein **2 = class,** bracket, caste, category, estate, grade, group, level, rank, station

stray *verb* **1 = wander,** be abandoned *or* lost, drift, err, go astray, lose one's way, meander, range, roam, rove, straggle **2 = digress,** deviate, diverge, get off the point, get sidetracked, go off at a tangent, ramble ◆ *adjective* **3 = lost,** abandoned, homeless, roaming, vagrant **4 = random,** accidental, chance, erratic, freak, odd, scattered

streak *noun* **1 = band,** layer, line, slash, smear, strip, stripe, stroke, vein **2 = trace,** dash, element, strain, touch, vein ◆ *verb* **3 = band,** daub, fleck, slash, smear, striate, stripe **4 = speed,** barrel (along) (*informal, chiefly U.S. & Canad.*), dart, flash, fly, hurtle, sprint, sweep, tear, whizz (*informal*), zoom

stream *noun* **1 = river,** bayou, beck, brook, burn (*Scot.*), creek (*U.S.*), freshet, rill, rivulet, tributary **2 = flow,** course, current, drift, outpouring, run, rush, surge, tide, tideway, torrent ◆ *verb* **3 = flow,** cascade, course, emit, flood, glide, gush, issue, pour, run, shed, spill, spout

streamer *noun* **= banner,** colours, ensign, flag, pennant, pennon, ribbon, standard

streamlined *adjective* **= efficient,** modernized, organized, rationalized, sleek, slick, smooth, smooth-running, time-saving, well-run

street *noun* **1 = road,** avenue, boulevard, lane, roadway, row, terrace, thoroughfare **2 right up one's street** *Informal* **= to one's liking,** acceptable, compatible, congenial, familiar, one's cup of tea (*informal*), pleasing, suitable, to one's taste

strength *noun* **1 = might,** backbone, brawn, brawniness, courage, firmness, fortitude, health, lustiness, muscle, robustness, sinew, stamina, stoutness, sturdiness, toughness, wellness **2 = strong point,** advantage, asset, mainstay, tower of strength **3 = power,** concentration, effectiveness, efficacy, energy, force, intensity, potency, resolution, spirit, vehemence, vigour ➤ **Antonyms** ≠**might:** debility, feebleness, frailty, infirmity, powerlessness, weakness ≠**strong point:** Achilles heel, chink in one's armour, defect, failing, flaw, shortcoming, weakness ≠**power:** feebleness, impotence, powerlessness, weakness

strengthen *verb* **1 = fortify,** brace up, consolidate, encourage, gee up, give new energy to, harden, hearten, invigorate, rejuvenate, restore, stiffen, toughen **2 = reinforce,** augment, bolster, brace, build up, buttress, confirm, corroborate, enhance, establish, give a boost to, harden, heighten, increase, intensify, justify, steel, substantiate, support ➤ **Antonyms** crush, debilitate, destroy, dilute, enervate, render impotent, sap, subvert, undermine, weaken

strenuous *adjective* **1 = demanding,** arduous, exhausting, hard, Herculean, laborious, taxing, toilsome, tough, tough going, unrelaxing, uphill **2 = tireless,** active, bold, determined, eager, earnest, energetic, persistent, resolute, spirited, strong, vigorous, zealous ➤ **Antonyms** ≠**demanding:** easy, effortless, relaxing, undemanding, untaxing ≠**tireless:** relaxed, unenergetic

stress *noun* **1 = strain,** anxiety, burden, hassle (*informal*), nervous tension, pressure, tension, trauma, worry **2 = emphasis,** force, importance, significance, urgency, weight **3 = accent,** accentuation, beat, emphasis ◆ *verb* **4 = emphasize,** accentuate, belabour, dwell on, harp on, lay emphasis upon, point up, repeat, rub in, underline, underscore

stressful *adjective* **= worrying,** agitating, anxious, tense, traumatic

stretch *verb* **1 = extend,** cover, put forth, reach, spread, unfold, unroll **2 = pull,** distend, draw out, elongate, expand, inflate, lengthen, pull out of shape, rack, strain, swell, tighten ◆ *noun* **3 = expanse,** area, distance, extent, spread, sweep, tract **4 = period,** bit, run, space, spell, stint, term, time

strew *verb* **= scatter,** bestrew, disperse, litter, spread, sprinkle, toss

stricken *adjective* **= affected,** afflicted, hit, injured, laid low, smitten, struck, struck down

strict *adjective* **1 = severe,** austere, authoritarian, firm, harsh, no-nonsense, rigid, rigorous, stern, stringent **2 = exact,** accurate, close, faithful, meticulous, particular, precise, religious, scrupulous, true **3 = absolute,** complete, perfect, total, utter ➤ **Antonyms** ≠**severe:** easy-going, easy-oasy (*slang*), flexible, laid-back (*informal*), lax, mild, moderate, soft, tolerant

stricture *noun* *Formal* **= criticism,** animadversion, bad press, censure, flak (*informal*), stick (*slang*)

strident *adjective* **= harsh,** discordant, grating, jangling, jarring, rasping, raucous, screeching, shrill, unmusical ➤ **Antonyms** dulcet, gentle, harmonious, mellifluous, mellow, quiet, soft, soothing, sweet

strife *noun* = **conflict**, animosity, battle, bickering, clash, clashes, combat, contention, contest, controversy, discord, dissension, friction, quarrel, rivalry, row, squabbling, struggle, warfare, wrangling

strike *verb* 1 = **walk out**, down tools, mutiny, revolt 2 = **hit**, bang, beat, box, clobber (*slang*), clout (*informal*), cuff, deck (*slang*), hammer, knock, pound, punch, slap, smack, smite, sock (*slang*), swipe, thump, wallop (*informal*) 3 = **drive**, force, hit, impel, thrust 4 = **collide with**, be in collision with, bump into, clash, come into contact with, dash, hit, knock into, run into, smash into, touch 5 = **affect**, hit, make an impact on, reach, register (*informal*) 6 = **occur to**, come to, come to the mind of, dawn on *or* upon, hit, register (*informal*), seem 7 *sometimes with* **upon** = **discover**, come upon *or* across, encounter, find, happen *or* chance upon, hit upon, light upon, reach, stumble upon *or* across, turn up, uncover, unearth 8 = **reach**, achieve, arrange, arrive at, attain, effect 9 **strike at** = **attack**, affect, assail, assault, deal a blow to, devastate, fall upon, hit, invade, set upon, smite

strike out *verb* 1 *Also* **strike off, strike through** = **score out**, cancel, cross out, delete, efface, erase, excise, expunge, remove 2 = **begin**, get under way, set out, start out

striking *adjective* = **impressive**, astonishing, conspicuous, dazzling, dramatic, drop-dead (*slang*), extraordinary, jaw-dropping, memorable, noticeable, out of the ordinary, outstanding, stunning (*informal*), wonderful ➤ **Antonyms**
average, dull, indifferent, undistinguished, unexceptional, unextraordinary, unimpressive, uninteresting, vanilla (*informal*)

string *noun* 1 = **cord**, fibre, twine 2 = **series**, chain, file, line, procession, queue, row, sequence, strand, succession ◆ *verb* 3 = **hang**, festoon, link, loop, sling, stretch, suspend, thread 4 = **spread out**, disperse, extend, fan out, lengthen, protract, space out, straggle

string along *verb* 1 *often with* **with** = **accompany**, go along with 2 = **deceive**, bluff, dupe, fool, hoax, kid (*informal*), play fast and loose with (someone) (*informal*), play (someone) false, put one over on (someone) (*informal*), take (someone) for a ride (*informal*)

stringent *adjective* = **strict**, binding, demanding, exacting, inflexible, rigid, rigorous, severe, tight, tough ➤ **Antonyms**
flexible, lax, loose, relaxed, slack, unrigorous

strings *plural noun* = **conditions**, catches (*informal*), complications, obligations, prerequisites, provisos, qualifications, requirements, riders, stipulations

stringy *adjective* = **fibrous**, gristly, sinewy, tough, wiry

strip[1] *verb* 1 = **undress**, disrobe, unclothe, uncover 2 = **plunder**, bare, denude, deprive, despoil, dismantle, divest, empty, lay bare, loot, peel, pillage, ransack, rob, sack, skin, spoil

strip[2] *noun* = **piece**, band, belt, bit, fillet, ribbon, shred, slip, swathe

striped *adjective* = **banded**, barred, striated, stripy

stripling *noun* = **boy**, adolescent, lad, young fellow, youngster, youth

strive *verb* = **try**, attempt, bend over backwards (*informal*), break one's neck (*informal*), compete, contend, do all one can, do one's best, do one's damnedest (*informal*), do one's utmost, endeavour, exert oneself, fight, give it one's all (*informal*), give it one's best shot (*informal*), go all out (*informal*), go for broke (*slang*), go for it (*informal*), knock oneself out (*informal*), labour, make an all-out effort (*informal*), strain, struggle, toil, try hard

stroke *verb* 1 = **caress**, fondle, pat, pet, rub ◆ *noun* 2 = **apoplexy**, attack, collapse, fit, seizure, shock 3 = **blow**, hit, knock, pat, rap, swipe, thump 4 = **feat**, accomplishment, achievement, flourish, move, movement

stroll *verb* 1 = **walk**, amble, make one's way, mosey (*informal*), promenade, ramble, saunter, stretch one's legs, take a turn ◆ *noun* 2 = **walk**, airing, breath of air, constitutional, excursion, promenade, ramble, turn

strong *adjective* 1 = **powerful**, athletic, beefy (*informal*), brawny, burly, capable, fighting fit, fit, fit as a fiddle, hale, hardy, healthy, Herculean, lusty, muscular, robust, sinewy, sound, stalwart, stout, strapping, sturdy, tough 2 = **durable**, hard-wearing, heavy-duty, reinforced, sturdy, substantial, well-built 3 = **distinct**, clear, marked, overpowering, unmistakable 4 = **persuasive**, clear, clear-cut, cogent, compelling, convincing, effective, formidable, great, overpowering, potent, sound, telling, trenchant, weighty, well-established, well-founded 5 = **pungent**, biting, concentrated, heady, highly-flavoured, highly-seasoned, hot, intoxicating, piquant, powerful, pure, sharp, spicy, undiluted 6 = **self-confident**, aggressive, brave, courageous, determined, feisty (*informal, chiefly U.S. & Canad.*), forceful, hard as

nails, hard-nosed (*informal*), plucky, resilient, resolute, resourceful, self-assertive, steadfast, stouthearted, tenacious, tough, unyielding **7 = intense**, acute, dedicated, deep, deep-rooted, eager, fervent, fervid, fierce, firm, keen, severe, staunch, vehement, violent, zealous **8 = extreme**, Draconian, drastic, forceful, severe **9 = bright**, bold, brilliant, dazzling, glaring, loud, stark
➤ Antonyms
≠**powerful**: delicate, feeble, frail, ineffectual, namby-pamby, puny, weak ≠**distinct**: delicate, faint, slight ≠**pungent**: bland, mild, tasteless, vapid, weak ≠**self-confident**: characterless, faint-hearted, spineless, timid, unassertive ≠**bright**: dull, insipid, pale, pastel, washed-out

strong-arm *adjective Informal* = **bullying**, aggressive, coercive, forceful, high-pressure, terror, terrorizing, threatening, thuggish, violent

stronghold *noun* = **fortress**, bastion, bulwark, castle, citadel, fastness, fort, keep, refuge

strong-minded *adjective* = **determined**, firm, independent, iron-willed, resolute, strong-willed, unbending, uncompromising

strong point *noun* = **forte**, advantage, asset, métier, speciality, strength

stroppy *adjective Brit. informal* = **awkward**, bloody-minded (*Brit. informal*), cantankerous, difficult, obstreperous, perverse, quarrelsome, uncooperative, unhelpful

structure *noun* **1 = building**, construction, edifice, erection, pile **2 = arrangement**, configuration, conformation, construction, design, form, formation, make-up, organization ◆ *verb* **3 = arrange**, assemble, build up, design, organize, put together, shape

struggle *verb* **1 = strive**, bend over backwards (*informal*), break one's neck (*informal*), do one's damnedest (*informal*), exert oneself, give it one's all (*informal*), give it one's best shot (*informal*), go all out (*informal*), go for it (*informal*), knock oneself out (*informal*), labour, make an all-out effort (*informal*), make every effort, strain, toil, work **2 = fight**, battle, compete, contend, grapple, scuffle, wrestle ◆ *noun* **3 = effort**, exertion, grind (*informal*), labour, long haul, pains, scramble, toil, work **4 = fight**, battle, brush, clash, combat, conflict, contest, encounter, hostilities, skirmish, strife, tussle

strung up *adjective Informal* = **tense**, a bundle of nerves (*informal*), antsy (*informal*), edgy, jittery (*informal*), keyed up, nervous, on edge, on tenterhooks,

twitchy (*informal*), uptight (*informal*), wired (*slang*)

strut *verb* = **swagger**, parade, peacock, prance, stalk

stub *noun* **1 = butt**, dog-end (*informal*), end, fag end (*informal*), remnant, stump, tail, tail end **2 = counterfoil**

stubborn *adjective* = **obstinate**, bull-headed, dogged, fixed, headstrong, inflexible, intractable, mulish, obdurate, opinionated, persistent, pig-headed, recalcitrant, refractory, self-willed, stiff-necked, tenacious, unbending, unmanageable, unshakable, unyielding, wilful
➤ Antonyms
biddable, compliant, docile, flexible, half-hearted, irresolute, malleable, manageable, pliable, pliant, tractable, vacillating, wavering, yielding

stubby *adjective* = **stocky**, chunky, dumpy, short, squat, stumpy, thickset

stuck *adjective* **1 = fastened**, cemented, fast, firm, fixed, glued, joined **2** *Informal* = **baffled**, at a loss, at a standstill, at one's wits' end, beaten, nonplussed, stumped, up against a brick wall (*informal*) **3** *Slang* **stuck on = infatuated with**, crazy about, for, *or* over (*informal*), enthusiastic about, hung up on (*slang*), keen on, mad about, obsessed with, wild about (*informal*) **4 get stuck in** *Informal* = **set about**, get down to, make a start on, tackle, take the bit between one's teeth

stuck-up *adjective Informal* = **snobbish**, arrogant, bigheaded (*informal*), conceited, condescending, haughty, high and mighty (*informal*), hoity-toity (*informal*), patronizing, proud, snooty (*informal*), swollen-headed, toffee-nosed (*slang, chiefly Brit.*), uppish (*Brit. informal*), uppity (*informal*)

stud *verb* = **ornament**, bejewel, bespangle, dot, fleck, spangle, speckle, spot, sprinkle

student *noun* = **learner**, apprentice, disciple, pupil, scholar, trainee, undergraduate

studied *adjective* = **planned**, calculated, conscious, deliberate, intentional, premeditated, purposeful, well-considered, wilful
➤ Antonyms
impulsive, natural, spontaneous, spur-of-the-moment, unplanned, unpremeditated

studio *noun* = **workshop**, atelier

studious *adjective* **1 = scholarly**, academic, assiduous, bookish, diligent, eager, earnest, hard-working, intellectual, meditative, reflective, sedulous, serious, thoughtful **2**

= **careful**, attentive, deliberate, precise
➤ **Antonyms**
≠**scholarly**: frivolous, idle, lazy, loafing, unacademic, unintellectual, unscholarly
≠**careful**: careless, inattentive, indifferent, negligent

study verb 1 = **learn**, bone up on (informal), burn the midnight oil, cram (informal), mug up (Brit. slang), read up, swot (up) (Brit. informal) 2 = **contemplate**, apply oneself (to), consider, examine, go into, meditate, ponder, pore over, read 3 = **examine**, analyse, deliberate, investigate, look into, peruse, research, scrutinize, survey, work over ◆ noun 4 = **learning**, academic work, application, book work, cramming (informal), lessons, reading, research, school work, swotting (Brit. informal), thought 5 = **examination**, analysis, attention, cogitation, consideration, contemplation, inquiry, inspection, investigation, perusal, review, scrutiny, survey

stuff noun 1 = **substance**, essence, matter, pith, quintessence 2 = **things**, belongings, bits and pieces, clobber (Brit. slang), effects, equipment, gear, goods and chattels, impedimenta, junk, kit, luggage, materials, objects, paraphernalia, possessions, tackle, trappings 3 = **material**, cloth, fabric, raw material, textile ◆ verb 4 = **cram**, compress, crowd, fill, force, jam, load, pack, pad, push, ram, shove, squeeze, stow, wedge 5 **stuff oneself** or **one's face** = **gorge**, gobble, gormandize, guzzle, make a pig of oneself (informal), overindulge, pig out (slang)

stuffing noun 1 = **forcemeat** 2 = **filling**, kapok, packing, quilting, wadding

stuffy adjective 1 = **airless**, close, fetid, frowsty, heavy, muggy, oppressive, stale, stifling, suffocating, sultry, unventilated 2 Informal = **staid**, as dry as dust, conventional, deadly, dreary, dull, fusty, old-fashioned, old-fogeyish, pompous, priggish, prim, prim and proper, stilted, stodgy, strait-laced, uninteresting
➤ **Antonyms**
≠**airless**: airy, breezy, cool, draughty, fresh, gusty, pleasant, well-ventilated

stumble verb 1 = **trip**, blunder about, come a cropper (informal), fall, falter, flounder, lose one's balance, lurch, reel, slip, stagger 2 = **falter**, fluff (informal), hesitate, stammer, stutter 3 with **across**, **on** or **upon** = **discover**, blunder upon, chance upon, come across, encounter, find, happen upon, light upon, run across, turn up

stumbling block noun = **obstacle**, bar, barrier, difficulty, hazard, hindrance, hurdle, impediment, obstruction, snag

stump verb 1 = **baffle**, bewilder, bring (someone) up short, confound, confuse,

dumbfound, flummox, foil, mystify, nonplus, outwit, perplex, puzzle, snooker, stop, stymie 2 = **stamp**, clump, lumber, plod, stomp (informal), trudge

stump up verb Brit. informal = **pay**, chip in (informal), come across with (informal), contribute, cough up (informal), donate, fork out (slang), hand over, shell out (informal)

stumpy adjective = **stocky**, chunky, dumpy, heavy, short, squat, stubby, thick, thickset

stun verb 1 = **overcome**, amaze, astonish, astound, bewilder, confound, confuse, dumbfound, flabbergast (informal), overpower, shock, stagger, strike (someone) dumb, stupefy, take (someone's) breath away 2 = **knock out**, daze

stung adjective = **goaded**, angered, exasperated, hurt, incensed, nettled, piqued, roused, wounded

stunned adjective 1 = **staggered**, astounded, at a loss for words, bowled over (informal), devastated, dumbfounded, flabbergasted (informal), gobsmacked (Brit. slang), numb, shocked, struck dumb 2 = **knocked out**, dazed

stunner noun Informal = **beauty**, dazzler, humdinger (slang), knockout (informal), looker (informal, chiefly U.S.), lovely (slang), sensation, smasher (informal), wow (slang, chiefly U.S.)

stunning adjective Informal = **wonderful**, beautiful, brilliant, dazzling, devastating (informal), dramatic, drop-dead (slang), gorgeous, great (informal), heavenly, impressive, jaw-dropping, lovely, marvellous, out of this world (informal), ravishing, remarkable, sensational (informal), smashing (informal), spectacular, striking
➤ **Antonyms**
average, dreadful, horrible, mediocre, no great shakes (informal), ordinary, plain, poor, rotten, run-of-the-mill, ugly, unattractive, unimpressive, uninspiring, unremarkable

stunt noun = **feat**, act, deed, exploit, feature, trick

stunted adjective = **undersized**, diminutive, dwarfed, dwarfish, little, small, tiny

stupefy verb = **astound**, amaze, bewilder, confound, daze, dumbfound, knock senseless, numb, shock, stagger, stun

stupendous adjective 1 = **wonderful**, amazing, astounding, breathtaking, brilliant, fabulous (informal), fantastic (informal), jaw-dropping, marvellous, mind-blowing (informal), mind-boggling (informal), out of this world (informal), overwhelming, phenomenal, prodigious, sensational (informal), staggering, stunning (informal), superb, tremendous (*informal*), wondrous (*archaic or literary*) **2 = huge**, colossal, enormous, gigantic, mega (*slang*), vast

➤ **Antonyms**

≠**wonderful:** average, mediocre, modest, no great shakes (*informal*), ordinary, petty, unexciting, unimpressive, unremarkable, unsurprising ≠**huge:** diminutive, puny, tiny

stupid *adjective* **1 = unintelligent**, braindead (*informal*), brainless, crass, cretinous, dense, dim, doltish, dopey (*informal*), dozy (*Brit. informal*), dull, dumb (*informal*), dumb-ass (*slang*), gullible, half-witted, moronic, naive, obtuse, simple, simple-minded, slow, slow on the uptake (*informal*), slow-witted, sluggish, stolid, thick, thickheaded, witless, woodenheaded (*informal*) **2 = silly**, asinine, crackbrained, crackpot (*informal*), daft (*informal*), foolish, futile, half-baked (*informal*), idiotic, ill-advised, imbecilic, inane, irresponsible, laughable, ludicrous, meaningless, mindless, nonsensical, pointless, puerile, rash, senseless, short-sighted, trivial, unintelligent, unthinking **3 = dazed**, groggy, in a daze, insensate, punch-drunk, semiconscious, senseless, stunned, stupefied

➤ **Antonyms**

≠**unintelligent:** astute, brainy, bright, brilliant, clear-headed, clever, intelligent, lucid, on the ball (*informal*), quick, quick on the uptake, quick-witted, sensible, sharp, shrewd, smart, wise ≠**silly:** astute, prudent, realistic, reasonable, sensible, shrewd, thoughtful, well-thought-out, wise

stupidity *noun* **1 = lack of intelligence**, asininity, brainlessness, denseness, dimness, dopiness (*slang*), doziness (*Brit. informal*), dullness, dumbness (*informal*), feeble-mindedness, imbecility, naivety, obtuseness, simplicity, slowness, thickheadedness, thickness **2 = silliness**, absurdity, fatuousness, folly, foolhardiness, foolishness, futility, idiocy, impracticality, inanity, irresponsibility, ludicrousness, lunacy, madness, pointlessness, puerility, rashness, senselessness

stupor *noun* **= daze**, coma, inertia, insensibility, lethargy, numbness, stupefaction, torpor, trance, unconsciousness

sturdy *adjective* **1 = robust**, athletic, brawny, firm, hardy, hearty, lusty, muscular, powerful, stalwart, staunch, thickset, vigorous **2 = substantial**, built to last, durable, secure, solid, well-built, well-made

➤ **Antonyms**

≠**robust:** feeble, infirm, puny, skinny, weak ≠**substantial:** flimsy, frail, rickety, unsubstantial

stutter *verb* **= stammer**, falter, hesitate, speak haltingly, splutter, stumble

style *noun* **1 = design**, cut, form, manner **2 = manner**, approach, custom, method, mode, technique, way **3 = elegance**, chic, cosmopolitanism, dash, dressiness (*informal*), élan, fashionableness, flair, grace, panache, polish, refinement, savoir-faire, smartness, sophistication, stylishness, taste, urbanity **4 = type**, category, genre, kind, pattern, sort, spirit, strain, tenor, tone, variety **5 = fashion**, mode, rage, trend, vogue **6 = luxury**, affluence, comfort, ease, elegance, gracious living, grandeur **7 = mode of expression**, expression, phraseology, phrasing, turn of phrase, vein, wording ♦ *verb* **8 = design**, adapt, arrange, cut, dress, fashion, shape, tailor **9 = call**, address, christen, denominate, designate, dub, entitle, label, name, term

stylish *adjective* **= smart**, à la mode, chic, classy (*slang*), dapper, dressy (*informal*), fashionable, in fashion, in vogue, modish, natty (*informal*), polished, snappy, snazzy (*informal*), trendy (*Brit. informal*), urbane, voguish, well turned-out

➤ **Antonyms**

naff (*Brit. slang*), old-fashioned, outmoded, out-of-date, passé, scruffy, shabby, slovenly, tacky, tawdry, unfashionable, unstylish, untrendy (*Brit. informal*)

stymie *verb* **= frustrate**, balk, confound, defeat, flummox, foil, hinder, snooker, spike (someone's) guns, thwart

suave *adjective* **= smooth**, affable, agreeable, bland, charming, cool (*informal*), courteous, debonair, gracious, polite, smooth-tongued, sophisticated, svelte, urbane, worldly

subconscious *adjective* **= hidden**, inner, innermost, intuitive, latent, repressed, subliminal, suppressed

➤ **Antonyms**

aware, conscious, knowing, sensible, sentient

subdue *verb* **1 = overcome**, break, conquer, control, crush, defeat, get the better of, get the upper hand over, get under control, master, overpower, put down, quell, tame, trample, triumph over, vanquish **2 = moderate**, check, control, mellow, quieten down, repress, soften, suppress, tone down

➤ **Antonyms**

≠**moderate:** agitate, arouse, awaken, incite, provoke, stir up, waken, whip up

subdued *adjective* **1 = quiet**, chastened, crestfallen, dejected, downcast, down in the mouth, out of spirits, sad, sadder and wiser, serious, sobered **2 = soft**, dim, hushed, low-key, muted, quiet, shaded, sober, subtle, toned down, unobtrusive

➤ **Antonyms**

≠**quiet:** cheerful, enthusiastic, full of beans (*informal*), happy, lively, vivacious ≠**soft:**

bright, loud, strident

subject *noun* 1 = **topic**, affair, business, issue, matter, object, point, question, subject matter, substance, theme 2 = **participant**, case, client, guinea pig (*informal*), patient, victim 3 = **citizen**, dependant, liegeman, national, subordinate, vassal ♦ *adjective* 4 = **subordinate**, captive, dependent, enslaved, inferior, obedient, satellite, subjugated, submissive, subservient 5 **subject to: a = liable to**, disposed to, prone to **b = vulnerable to**, at the mercy of, exposed to, in danger of, open to, susceptible to **c = conditional on**, contingent on, dependent on ♦ *verb* 6 = **put through**, expose, lay open, make liable, submit, treat

subjective *adjective* = **personal**, biased, emotional, nonobjective, prejudiced
➤ **Antonyms**
detached, disinterested, dispassionate, impartial, impersonal, objective, open-minded, unbiased

subjugate *verb* = **conquer**, bring (someone) to his knees, crush, defeat, enslave, hold sway over, master, overcome, overpower, overthrow, put down, quell, subdue, suppress, tame, vanquish

sublimate *verb* = **channel**, divert, redirect, transfer, turn

sublime *adjective* = **noble**, elevated, eminent, exalted, glorious, grand, great, high, imposing, lofty, magnificent, majestic
➤ **Antonyms**
bad, commonplace, lowly, mundane, ordinary, poor, ridiculous

subliminal *adjective* = **subconscious**, unconscious

submerge *verb* = **immerse**, deluge, dip, drown, duck, dunk, engulf, flood, inundate, overflow, overwhelm, plunge, sink, swamp

submerged *adjective* = **immersed**, drowned, submarine, submersed, sunk, sunken, undersea, underwater

submission *noun* 1 = **surrender**, acquiescence, assent, capitulation, cave-in (*informal*), giving in, yielding 2 = **presentation**, entry, handing in, submitting, tendering 3 = **proposal**, argument, contention 4 = **meekness**, compliance, deference, docility, obedience, passivity, resignation, submissiveness, tractability, unassertiveness

submissive *adjective* = **meek**, abject, accommodating, acquiescent, amenable, biddable, compliant, deferential, docile, dutiful, humble, obedient, passive, pliant, resigned, tractable, uncomplaining, unresisting, yielding

➤ **Antonyms**
awkward, difficult, disobedient, headstrong, intractable, obstinate, stubborn, uncooperative, unyielding

submit *verb* 1 = **surrender**, accede, acquiesce, agree, bend, bow, capitulate, cave in (*informal*), comply, defer, endure, give in, knuckle under, put up with (*informal*), resign oneself, stoop, succumb, toe the line, tolerate, yield 2 = **present**, commit, hand in, proffer, put forward, refer, table, tender

subnormal *adjective* No longer in technical use = **retarded**, cretinous, feeble-minded, imbecilic, mentally defective, moronic, simple, slow

subordinate *adjective* 1 = **lesser**, dependent, inferior, junior, lower, minor, secondary, subject, subservient 2 = **supplementary**, ancillary, auxiliary, subsidiary ♦ *noun* 3 = **inferior**, aide, assistant, attendant, dependant, junior, second, subaltern, underling
➤ **Antonyms**
adjective ≠**lesser**: central, essential, greater, higher, key, main, necessary, predominant, senior, superior, vital ♦ *noun* ≠**inferior**: boss (*informal*), captain, chief, commander, head, leader, master, principal, senior, superior

subordination *noun* = **inferiority**, inferior or secondary status, servitude, subjection

subscribe *verb* 1 = **contribute**, chip in (*informal*), donate, give, offer, pledge, promise 2 = **support**, acquiesce, advocate, agree, consent, countenance, endorse

subscription *noun* 1 Chiefly Brit. = **membership fee**, annual payment, dues 2 = **contribution**, donation, gift, offering

subsequent *adjective* = **following**, after, consequent, ensuing, later, succeeding, successive
➤ **Antonyms**
antecedent, earlier, erstwhile, former, one-time, past, preceding, previous, prior

subsequently *adverb* = **later**, afterwards, at a later date, consequently, in the end

subservient *adjective* 1 = **servile**, abject, bootlicking (*informal*), deferential, inferior, obsequious, slavish, subject, submissive, sycophantic 2 = **subordinate**, ancillary, auxiliary, subsidiary
➤ **Antonyms**
≠**servile**: bolshie, bossy, disobedient, domineering, overbearing, overriding, rebellious, superior, wilful

subside *verb* 1 = **decrease**, abate, de-escalate, diminish, dwindle, ease, ebb, lessen, let up, level off, peter out, quieten, recede, slacken, wane 2 = **drop**, decline, descend, ebb, fall 3 = **collapse**, cave in,

drop, lower, settle, sink
> **Antonyms**
≠**decrease, drop:** escalate, grow, heighten, increase, inflate, intensify, mount, rise, soar, swell

subsidence *noun* **1** = **decrease**, abatement, de-escalation, diminution, easing off, lessening, slackening **2** = **drop**, decline, descent, ebb **3** = **sinking**, collapse, settlement, settling

subsidiary *adjective* = **lesser**, ancillary, assistant, auxiliary, contributory, minor, secondary, subordinate, subservient, supplemental, supplementary
> **Antonyms**
central, chief, head, key, leading, main, major, primary, principal, vital

subsidize *verb* = **fund**, finance, promote, put up the money for, sponsor, support, underwrite

subsidy *noun* = **aid**, allowance, assistance, contribution, financial aid, grant, help, stipend, support

subsist *verb* = **stay alive**, continue, exist, keep going, last, live, survive, sustain oneself

subsistence *noun* = **living**, existence, livelihood, maintenance, survival, upkeep

substance *noun* **1** = **material**, body, element, fabric, stuff, texture **2** = **meaning**, essence, gist, import, main point, matter, pith, significance, subject, theme **3** = **reality**, actuality, concreteness, entity, force **4** = **wealth**, affluence, assets, estate, means, property, resources

substandard *adjective* = **inferior**, damaged, imperfect, inadequate, second-rate, shoddy, unacceptable

substantial *adjective* **1** = **big**, ample, considerable, generous, goodly, important, large, significant, sizable *or* sizeable, tidy (*informal*) **2** = **solid**, bulky, firm, hefty, massive, sound, stout, strong, sturdy **3** *Formal* = **real**, actual, positive, true, valid, weighty
> **Antonyms**
≠**big:** inadequate, inconsiderable, insignificant, insubstantial, meagre, niggardly, pathetic, poor, skimpy, small ≠**solid:** feeble, frail, infirm, insubstantial, light-weight, rickety, weak ≠**real:** fictitious, imaginary, imagined, insubstantial, nonexistent, unreal

substantially *adverb* = **essentially**, in essence, in the main, largely, materially, to a large extent

substantiate *verb* = **support**, affirm, attest to, authenticate, bear out, confirm, corroborate, establish, prove, validate, verify
> **Antonyms**
confute, contradict, controvert, disprove,

expose, invalidate, make a nonsense of, negate, prove false, rebut, refute

substitute *verb* **1** = **replace**, change, commute, exchange, interchange, swap, switch **2 substitute for** = **stand in for**, act for, be in place of, cover for, deputize for, fill in for, take over from ♦ *noun* **3** = **replacement**, agent, deputy, locum, locum tenens, makeshift, proxy, representative, reserve, stand-by, stopgap, sub, surrogate ♦ *adjective* **4** = **replacement**, acting, alternative, fall-back, proxy, reserve, second, surrogate

substitution *noun* = **replacement**, change, exchange, interchange, swap, switch

subterfuge *noun* = **trick**, artifice, deception, dodge, duplicity, machination, manoeuvre, ploy, pretence, pretext, ruse, stratagem

subtle *adjective* **1** = **faint**, delicate, implied, indirect, slight, understated **2** = **crafty**, artful, astute, cunning, devious, ingenious, Machiavellian, scheming, shrewd, sly, wily **3** = **sophisticated**, delicate, discriminating, nice, refined
> **Antonyms**
≠**faint:** overwhelming, strong ≠**crafty:** artless, blunt, direct, downright, guileless, obvious, simple, straightforward ≠**sophisticated:** crass, heavy-handed, lacking finesse, tactless, unsophisticated, unsubtle

subtlety *noun* **1** = **fine point**, delicacy, discernment, intricacy, nicety, refinement, sophistication **2** = **cunning**, acumen, acuteness, artfulness, astuteness, cleverness, craftiness, deviousness, guile, ingenuity, sagacity, skill, slyness, wiliness **3** = **discrimination**, discernment, finesse

subtract *verb* = **take away**, deduct, detract, diminish, remove, take from, take off, withdraw
> **Antonyms**
add, add to, append, increase by, supplement

suburb *noun* = **residential area**, environs, neighbourhood, outskirts, suburbia

subversive *adjective* **1** = **seditious**, destructive, insurrectionary, overthrowing, riotous, treasonous, underground, undermining ♦ *noun* **2** = **dissident**, fifth columnist, insurrectionary, quisling, saboteur, seditionary, seditionist, terrorist, traitor

subvert *verb* = **overturn**, demolish, destroy, ruin, sabotage, undermine, upset, wreck

succeed *verb* **1** = **make it** (*informal*), be successful, bring home the bacon (*informal*), come off (*informal*), crack it (*informal*), cut it (*informal*), do the trick

(*informal*), do well, flourish, get to the top, hit the jackpot (*informal*), make good, make one's mark (*informal*), make the grade (*informal*), prosper, thrive, triumph, turn out well, work **2 = follow**, be subsequent, come next, ensue, result **3 = take over**, accede, assume the office of, come into, come into possession of, inherit, replace, step into (someone's) boots
➤ **Antonyms**
≠**make it**: be unsuccessful, collapse, come a cropper (*informal*), fail, fall by the wayside, fall flat, fall short, flop (*informal*), go belly up (*informal*), go by the board, not make the grade, not manage ≠**follow**: be a precursor of, come before, go ahead of, go before, pave the way, precede

succeeding *adjective* = **following**, ensuing, next, subsequent, successive
➤ **Antonyms**
antecedent, earlier, former, preceding, previous, prior

success *noun* **1 = favourable outcome**, ascendancy, eminence, fame, fortune, happiness, luck, prosperity, triumph **2 = hit** (*informal*), best seller, big name, celebrity, market leader, megastar (*informal*), sensation, smash (*informal*), smash hit (*informal*), somebody, star, V.I.P., winner, wow (*slang*)
➤ **Antonyms**
≠**favourable outcome**: collapse, disaster, downfall, failure, misfortune ≠**hit**: clunker (*informal*), dead duck (*slang*), fiasco, flop (*informal*), loser, nobody, no-hoper, washout

successful *adjective* **1 = thriving**, booming, favourable, flourishing, fortunate, fruitful, lucky, lucrative, moneymaking, on a roll, paying, profitable, rewarding, top, victorious **2 = prosperous**, wealthy
➤ **Antonyms**
≠**thriving**: defeated, failed, ineffective, losing, luckless, uneconomic, unprofitable, unsuccessful, useless

successfully *adverb* = **well**, famously (*informal*), favourably, in triumph, victoriously, with flying colours

succession *noun* **1 = series**, chain, continuation, course, cycle, flow, order, procession, progression, run, sequence, train **2 = taking over**, accession, assumption, elevation, entering upon, inheritance **3 in succession** = one after the other, consecutively, one behind the other, on the trot (*informal*), running, successively

successive *adjective* = **consecutive**, following, in a row, in succession, succeeding

succinct *adjective* = **brief**, compact, concise, condensed, gnomic, laconic, pithy, summary, terse, to the point

➤ **Antonyms**
circuitous, circumlocutory, diffuse, discursive, long-winded, prolix, rambling, verbose, wordy

succour *noun* **1 = help**, aid, assistance, comfort, relief, support ♦ *verb* **2 = help**, aid, assist, befriend, comfort, encourage, foster, minister to, nurse, relieve, render assistance to, support

succulent *adjective* = **juicy**, luscious, lush, moist, mouthwatering, rich

succumb *verb* **1 = surrender**, capitulate, cave in (*informal*), give in, give way, go under, knuckle under, submit, yield **2 = die**, fall, fall victim to
➤ **Antonyms**
≠**surrender**: beat, conquer, get the better of, master, overcome, rise above, surmount, triumph over

sucker *noun Slang* = **fool**, butt, cat's paw, dupe, easy game *or* mark (*informal*), mug (*Brit. slang*), nerd *or* nurd (*slang*), pushover (*slang*), sitting duck (*informal*), sitting target, victim

suck up to *verb Informal* = **ingratiate oneself with**, butter up, curry favour with, dance attendance on, fawn on, flatter, get on the right side of, keep in with (*informal*), pander to, play up to (*informal*), toady, truckle

sudden *adjective* = **quick**, abrupt, hasty, hurried, impulsive, rapid, rash, swift, unexpected, unforeseen, unusual
➤ **Antonyms**
anticipated, deliberate, expected, foreseen, gentle, gradual, slow, unhasty

suddenly *adverb* = **abruptly**, all at once, all of a sudden, on the spur of the moment, out of the blue (*informal*), unexpectedly, without warning

sue *verb Law* = **take (someone) to court**, bring an action against (someone), charge, indict, institute legal proceedings against (someone), prefer charges against (someone), prosecute, summon

suffer *verb* **1 = undergo**, bear, endure, experience, feel, go through, sustain **2 = be affected**, ache, agonize, be in pain, be racked, feel wretched, go through a lot (*informal*), have a bad time, hurt **3 = deteriorate**, be impaired, fall off **4 = tolerate**, put up with (*informal*) **5 = be shown to disadvantage**, appear in a poor light, be handicapped

suffering *noun* = **pain**, affliction, agony, anguish, discomfort, distress, hardship, misery, ordeal, torment, torture

suffice *verb* = **be enough**, answer, be adequate, be sufficient, do, fill the bill (*informal*), meet requirements, serve

sufficient *adjective* = **adequate**,

competent, enough, satisfactory
➤ **Antonyms**
deficient, inadequate, insufficient, meagre, not enough, poor, scant, short, sparse

suffocate *verb* = **choke**, asphyxiate, smother, stifle, strangle

suffrage *noun* = **right to vote**, ballot, franchise, voice, vote

suffuse *verb* = **spread through** *or* **over**, bathe, cover, flood, imbue, infuse, overspread, permeate, pervade, steep, transfuse

suggest *verb* 1 = **recommend**, advise, advocate, move, offer a suggestion, prescribe, propose, put forward 2 = **bring to mind**, evoke, put one in mind of 3 = **hint**, imply, indicate, insinuate, intimate, lead one to believe

suggestible *adjective* = **impressionable**, amenable, malleable, open, open-minded, pliant, receptive, susceptible
➤ **Antonyms**
firm, headstrong, impervious, obdurate, single-minded, unwavering

suggestion *noun* 1 = **recommendation**, motion, plan, proposal, proposition 2 = **hint**, breath, indication, insinuation, intimation, suspicion, trace, whisper

suggestive *adjective* 1 = **smutty**, bawdy, blue, immodest, improper, indecent, indelicate, off colour, provocative, prurient, racy, ribald, risqué, rude, spicy (*informal*), titillating, unseemly 2 **suggestive of** = **evocative of**, expressing, indicative of, redolent of, reminiscent of

suit *noun* 1 = **outfit**, clothing, costume, dress, ensemble, habit 2 = **lawsuit**, action, case, cause, industrial tribunal, proceeding, prosecution, trial 3 **follow suit** = **copy**, emulate ◆ *verb* 4 = **befit**, agree, agree with, become, be seemly, conform to, correspond, go with, harmonize, match, tally 5 = **be acceptable to**, answer, do, gratify, please, satisfy

suitability *noun* = **appropriateness**, aptness, fitness, opportuneness, rightness, timeliness

suitable *adjective* = **appropriate**, acceptable, applicable, apposite, apt, becoming, befitting, convenient, cut out for, due, fit, fitting, in character, in keeping, opportune, pertinent, proper, relevant, right, satisfactory, seemly, suited
➤ **Antonyms**
discordant, inapposite, inappropriate, incorrect, inopportune, jarring, out of character, out of keeping, unbecoming, unfitting, unseemly, unsuitable, unsuited

suite *noun* 1 = **rooms**, apartment 2 = **set**, collection, series 3 = **furniture**

suitor *noun Old-fashioned* = **admirer**, beau, follower (*obsolete*), swain (*archaic*), young man

sulk *verb* = **be sullen**, be in a huff, be put out, brood, have the hump (*Brit. informal*), pout

sulky *adjective* = **huffy**, cross, disgruntled, ill-humoured, in the sulks, moody, morose, petulant, put out, querulous, resentful, sullen

sullen *adjective* = **morose**, brooding, cross, dour, gloomy, glowering, moody, silent, sour, sulky, surly, unsociable
➤ **Antonyms**
amiable, bright, cheerful, cheery, chirpy (*informal*), genial, good-humoured, good-natured, pleasant, sociable, sunny, warm, warm-hearted

sullenness *noun* = **moroseness**, glumness, ill humour, moodiness, sourness, sulkiness, sulks

sully *verb* 1 = **dishonour**, besmirch, disgrace, ruin, smirch 2 = **defile**, befoul, blemish, contaminate, dirty, pollute, spoil, spot, stain, taint, tarnish

sultry *adjective* 1 = **humid**, close, hot, muggy, oppressive, sticky, stifling, stuffy, sweltering 2 = **seductive**, amorous, erotic, passionate, provocative, sensual, sexy (*informal*), voluptuous
➤ **Antonyms**
≠**humid**: cool, fresh, invigorating, refreshing

sum *noun* = **total**, aggregate, amount, entirety, quantity, reckoning, score, sum total, tally, totality, whole

summarily *adverb* = **immediately**, at short notice, forthwith, on the spot, peremptorily, promptly, speedily, swiftly, without delay

summarize *verb* = **sum up**, abridge, condense, encapsulate, epitomize, give a rundown of, give the main points of, outline, précis, put in a nutshell, recap, recapitulate, review

summary *noun* 1 = **synopsis**, abridgment, digest, outline, précis, recapitulation, résumé, review, rundown, summing-up ◆ *adjective* 2 = **hasty**, cursory, perfunctory

summit *noun* = **peak**, acme, apex, crest, crown, crowning point, culmination, head, height, pinnacle, top, zenith
➤ **Antonyms**
base, bottom, depths, foot, lowest point, nadir

summon *verb* 1 = **send for**, arouse, assemble, bid, call, call together, convene, convoke, invite, rally, rouse 2 *often with* **up** = **gather**, call into action, draw on, invoke, muster

sumptuous *adjective* = **luxurious**, costly, dear, de luxe, expensive, extravagant,

gorgeous, grand, lavish, magnificent, opulent, plush (*informal*), posh (*informal, chiefly Brit.*), rich, ritzy (*slang*), splendid, superb
➤ **Antonyms**
austere, basic, cheap, frugal, inexpensive, meagre, mean, miserly, plain, shabby, wretched

sum up *verb* 1 = **summarize**, close, conclude, put in a nutshell, recapitulate, review 2 = **form an opinion of**, estimate, get the measure of, size up (*informal*)

sun *noun* 1 = **Sol** (*Roman myth*), Helios (*Greek myth*), Phoebus (*Greek myth*), Phoebus Apollo (*Greek myth*) ◆ *verb* 2 **sun oneself** = **sunbathe**, bake, bask, tan

sunburnt *adjective* = **tanned**, bronzed, brown, brown as a berry, burnt, peeling, red, ruddy, scarlet

sundry *adjective* = **various**, assorted, different, miscellaneous, several, some, varied

sunken *adjective* 1 = **hollow**, concave, drawn, haggard, hollowed 2 = **lower**, at a lower level, below ground, buried, depressed, immersed, recessed, submerged

sunny *adjective* 1 = **bright**, brilliant, clear, fine, radiant, summery, sunlit, sunshiny, unclouded, without a cloud in the sky 2 = **cheerful**, beaming, blithe, buoyant, cheery, chirpy (*informal*), genial, happy, joyful, light-hearted, optimistic, pleasant, smiling
➤ **Antonyms**
≠**bright:** cloudy, depressing, dreary, dreich (*Scot.*), dull, gloomy, murky, overcast, rainy, shaded, shadowy, sunless, wet, wintry ≠**cheerful:** doleful, down in the dumps (*informal*), gloomy, miserable, morbid, unsmiling

sunrise *noun* = **dawn**, break of day, cockcrow, daybreak, daylight, sunup

sunset *noun* = **nightfall**, close of (the) day, dusk, eventide, gloaming (*Scot. or poetic*), sundown

super *adjective Informal* = **excellent**, awesome (*slang*), boffo (*slang*), brill (*informal*), cracking (*Brit. informal*), crucial (*slang*), def (*slang*), glorious, incomparable, magnificent, marvellous, matchless, mean (*slang*), mega (*slang*), out of this world (*informal*), outstanding, sensational (*informal*), smashing (*informal*), sovereign, superb, terrific (*informal*), top-notch (*informal*), wonderful

superannuated *adjective* 1 = **retired**, discharged, pensioned off, put out to grass (*informal*) 2 = **obsolete**, aged, antiquated, decrepit, old, past it (*informal*), senile, unfit

superb *adjective* = **splendid**, admirable, awesome (*slang*), boffo (*slang*),

breathtaking, brill (*informal*), choice, divine, excellent, exquisite, fine, first-rate, gorgeous, grand, magnificent, marvellous, mega (*slang*), superior, superlative, unrivalled, world-class
➤ **Antonyms**
abysmal, awful, bad, disappointing, dreadful, inferior, mediocre, no great shakes (*informal*), pathetic, poor quality, run-of-the-mill, terrible, third-rate, uninspired, woeful

supercilious *adjective* = **scornful**, arrogant, condescending, contemptuous, disdainful, haughty, high and mighty (*informal*), hoity-toity (*informal*), lofty, lordly, overbearing, patronizing, proud, snooty (*informal*), stuck-up (*informal*), toffee-nosed (*slang, chiefly Brit.*), uppish (*Brit. informal*)
➤ **Antonyms**
deferential, humble, meek, modest, obsequious, self-effacing, submissive, unassuming, unpretentious

superficial *adjective* 1 = **hasty**, casual, cursory, desultory, hurried, passing, perfunctory, sketchy, slapdash 2 = **outward**, apparent, evident, ostensible, seeming 3 = **shallow**, empty, empty-headed, frivolous, lightweight, silly, trivial 4 = **surface**, cosmetic, exterior, external, on the surface, skin-deep, slight
➤ **Antonyms**
≠**hasty:** complete, comprehensive, detailed, exhaustive, in depth, major, penetrating, probing, thorough ≠**shallow:** earnest, serious ≠**surface:** deep, profound

superficiality *noun* = **shallowness**, emptiness, lack of depth, lack of substance, triviality

superficially *adverb* = **at first glance**, apparently, at face value, externally, on the surface, ostensibly, to the casual eye

superfluity *noun* = **excess**, glut, plethora, superabundance, surfeit, surplus

superfluous *adjective* = **excess**, excessive, extra, in excess, left over, redundant, remaining, residuary, spare, superabundant, supernumerary, surplus, surplus to requirements, uncalled-for, unnecessary, unneeded, unrequired
➤ **Antonyms**
called for, essential, imperative, indispensable, necessary, needed, requisite, vital, wanted

superhuman *adjective* 1 = **heroic**, herculean, phenomenal, prodigious, stupendous 2 = **supernatural**, divine, paranormal, preternatural

superintend *verb* = **supervise**, administer, control, direct, handle, look after, manage, overlook, oversee, run

superintendence *noun* = **supervision**, care, charge, control, direction, government, guidance, management

superintendent *noun* = **supervisor**, administrator, chief, conductor, controller, director, governor, inspector, manager, overseer

superior *adjective* 1 = **better**, grander, greater, higher, more advanced, more expert, more skilful, paramount, predominant, prevailing, surpassing, unrivalled 2 = **supercilious**, condescending, disdainful, haughty, lofty, lordly, patronizing, pretentious, snobbish, stuck-up (*informal*) 3 = **first-class**, choice, de luxe, excellent, exceptional, exclusive, fine, first-rate, good, good quality, high calibre, high-class, of the first order, world-class ♦ *noun* 4 = **boss** (*informal*), chief, director, manager, principal, senior, supervisor
➤ **Antonyms**
adjective ≠**better**: inferior, less, lesser, lower, not as good, poorer, worse ≠**first-class**: average, inferior, mediocre, no great shakes (*informal*), ordinary, second-class, second-rate, substandard, unremarkable ♦ *noun* ≠**boss**: assistant, cohort (*chiefly U.S.*), dogsbody, inferior, junior, lackey, minion, subordinate, underling

superiority *noun* = **supremacy**, advantage, ascendancy, excellence, lead, predominance, pre-eminence, prevalence

superlative *adjective* = **supreme**, consummate, excellent, greatest, highest, matchless, of the highest order, outstanding, peerless, surpassing, unparalleled, unrivalled, unsurpassed
➤ **Antonyms**
abysmal, appalling, average, dreadful, easily outclassed, inferior, ordinary, poor, rotten, run-of-the-mill, undistinguished, unexceptional, uninspired, unspectacular

supernatural *adjective* = **paranormal**, ghostly, hidden, miraculous, mysterious, mystic, occult, phantom, preternatural, psychic, spectral, uncanny, unearthly, unnatural

supernumerary *adjective* = **extra**, excess, excessive, in excess, odd, redundant, spare, superfluous, surplus, unrequired

supersede *verb* = **replace**, displace, oust, remove, supplant, take over, take the place of, usurp

supervise *verb* = **oversee**, administer, be responsible for, conduct, control, direct, handle, have *or* be in charge of, inspect, keep an eye on, look after, manage, preside over, run, superintend

supervision *noun* = **superintendence**, administration, auspices, care, charge, control, direction, guidance, instruction, management, oversight, stewardship

supervisor *noun* = **boss** (*informal*), administrator, chief, foreman, gaffer (*informal, chiefly Brit.*), inspector, manager, overseer, steward, superintendent

supervisory *adjective* = **managerial**, administrative, executive, overseeing, superintendent

supine *adjective Formal* = **flat on one's back**, flat, horizontal, recumbent
➤ **Antonyms**
lying on one's face, prone, prostrate

supplant *verb* = **replace**, displace, oust, overthrow, remove, supersede, take over, take the place of, unseat

supple *adjective* 1 = **flexible**, limber, lissom(e), lithe, loose-limbed 2 = **pliant**, bending, elastic, plastic, pliable
➤ **Antonyms**
≠**flexible**: awkward, creaky (*informal*), graceless, inflexible, stiff, unsupple ≠**pliant**: firm, inflexible, rigid, stiff, taut, unbending, unyielding

supplement *noun* 1 = **addition**, added feature, addendum, add-on, appendix, codicil, complement, extra, insert, postscript, pull-out, sequel ♦ *verb* 2 = **add**, augment, complement, extend, fill out, reinforce, supply, top up

supplementary *adjective* = **additional**, accompanying, add-on, ancillary, auxiliary, complementary, extra, secondary, supplemental

supplicant *noun Formal* = **petitioner**, applicant, suitor

supplication *noun Formal* = **plea**, appeal, entreaty, petition, pleading, prayer, request, solicitation

supply *verb* 1 = **provide**, afford, cater to *or* for, contribute, endow, equip, furnish, give, grant, produce, purvey, stock, store, yield ♦ *noun* 2 = **store**, cache, fund, hoard, quantity, reserve, reservoir, source, stock, stockpile 3 **supplies** = **provisions**, equipment, food, foodstuff, items, materials, necessities, provender, rations, stores

support *verb* 1 = **bear**, bolster, brace, buttress, carry, hold, hold up, prop, reinforce, shore up, sustain, underpin, uphold 2 = **provide for**, finance, fund, keep, look after, maintain, subsidize, sustain, take care of 3 = **help**, aid, assist, back, be a source of strength to, boost (someone's) morale, buoy up, champion, defend, encourage, go along with, promote, second, side with, stand up for, stick up for (*informal*), strengthen, succour, take (someone's) part, uphold 4 = **bear out**,

attest to, authenticate, confirm, corroborate, endorse, lend credence to, substantiate, verify ◆ *noun* **5** = **help**, aid, approval, assistance, backing, blessing, encouragement, friendship, loyalty, moral support, patronage, protection, succour **6** = **prop**, abutment, back, brace, foundation, pillar, post, stanchion, stiffener, underpinning **7** = **supporter**, backbone, backer, mainstay, prop, second, tower of strength **8** = **upkeep**, keep, livelihood, maintenance, subsistence, sustenance
➤ **Antonyms**
verb ≠**provide for:** live off, sponge off ≠**help:** go against, hinder, hold out against, oppose, reject, stab in the back, turn one's back on, undermine, walk away from ≠**bear out:** challenge, contradict, deny, refute ◆ *noun* ≠**help:** burden, encumbrance, hindrance, impediment, opposition, undermining ≠**supporter:** antagonist

supporter *noun* = **follower**, adherent, advocate, ally, champion, defender, fan, friend, helper, henchman, patron, protagonist, sponsor, well-wisher
➤ **Antonyms**
adversary, antagonist, challenger, competitor, foe, opponent, rival

supportive *adjective* = **helpful**, caring, encouraging, reassuring, sympathetic, understanding

suppose *verb* **1** = **presume**, assume, calculate (*U.S. dialect*), conjecture, dare say, expect, guess (*informal, chiefly U.S. & Canad.*), imagine, infer, judge, opine, presuppose, surmise, take as read, take for granted, think **2** = **imagine**, believe, conceive, conclude, conjecture, consider, fancy, hypothesize, postulate, pretend

supposed *adjective* **1** = **presumed**, accepted, alleged, assumed, hypothetical, presupposed, professed, putative, reputed, rumoured **2** *usually with* **to** = **meant**, expected, obliged, required

supposedly *adverb* = **presumably**, allegedly, at a guess, avowedly, by all accounts, hypothetically, ostensibly, professedly, purportedly, theoretically
➤ **Antonyms**
absolutely, actually, certainly, in actuality, in fact, really, surely, truly, undoubtedly, without a doubt

supposition *noun* = **guess**, conjecture, doubt, guesswork, hypothesis, idea, notion, presumption, speculation, surmise, theory

suppress *verb* **1** = **stop**, check, clamp down on, conquer, crack down on, crush, extinguish, overpower, overthrow, put an end to, quash, quell, stamp out, subdue **2** = **restrain**, conceal, contain, cover up, curb, hold in *or* back, hold in check, keep secret, muffle, repress, silence, smother, stifle, withhold
➤ **Antonyms**
encourage, foster, further, gee up, incite, inflame, promote, rouse, spread, stimulate, stir up, whip up

suppression *noun* **1** = **elimination**, check, clampdown, crackdown, crushing, prohibition, quashing, termination **2** = **inhibition**, smothering

suppurate *verb Pathology* = **discharge**, fester, gather, ooze, weep

supremacy *noun* = **domination**, absolute rule, ascendancy, dominance, dominion, lordship, mastery, predominance, pre-eminence, primacy, sovereignty, supreme power, sway

supreme *adjective* = **highest**, cardinal, chief, crowning, culminating, extreme, final, first, foremost, greatest, head, incomparable, leading, matchless, mother of all (*informal*), paramount, peerless, predominant, pre-eminent, prevailing, prime, principal, sovereign, superlative, surpassing, top, ultimate, unsurpassed, utmost
➤ **Antonyms**
least, least successful, lowest, most inferior, most minor, most subordinate, most trivial, poorest, worst

supremo *noun Brit. informal* = **head**, boss (*informal*), commander, director, governor, leader, master, principal, ruler

sure *adjective* **1** = **certain**, assured, clear, confident, convinced, decided, definite, free from doubt, persuaded, positive, satisfied **2** = **reliable**, accurate, dependable, effective, foolproof, indisputable, infallible, never-failing, precise, sure-fire (*informal*), tried and true, trustworthy, trusty, undeniable, undoubted, unerring, unfailing **3** = **inevitable**, assured, bound, guaranteed, inescapable **4** = **secure**, fast, firm, fixed, safe, solid, stable, steady
➤ **Antonyms**
≠**certain:** distrustful, doubtful, dubious, sceptical, unassured, uncertain, unconvinced, uneasy, unsure ≠**reliable:** dodgy (*Brit., Austral., & N.Z. informal*), dubious, fallible, iffy (*informal*), undependable, unreliable, untrustworthy, vague ≠**inevitable:** touch-and-go, unsure ≠**secure:** insecure

surely *adverb* = **undoubtedly**, assuredly, beyond the shadow of a doubt, certainly, come what may, definitely, doubtlessly, for certain, indubitably, inevitably, unquestionably, without doubt, without fail

surety *noun* **1** = **guarantor**, bondsman, sponsor **2** = **security**, bond, deposit, guarantee, indemnity, insurance, pledge, warranty

surface noun 1 = outside, covering, exterior, façade, face, facet, plane, side, skin, top, veneer 2 on the surface = at first glance, apparently, ostensibly, outwardly, seemingly, superficially, to all appearances, to the casual eye ♦ verb 3 = appear, arise, come to light, come up, crop up (informal), emerge, materialize, transpire

surfeit noun = excess, glut, overindulgence, plethora, superabundance, superfluity
➤ Antonyms
dearth, deficiency, insufficiency, lack, scarcity, shortage, shortness, want

surge noun 1 = rush, flood, flow, gush, outpouring, uprush, upsurge 2 = wave, billow, breaker, roller, swell ♦ verb 3 = rush, gush, rise, swell, well forth 4 = roll, billow, eddy, heave, swirl, undulate

surly adjective = ill-tempered, brusque, churlish, cross, grouchy (informal), gruff, morose, sulky, sullen, testy, uncivil, ungracious
➤ Antonyms
agreeable, cheerful, cheery, genial, good-natured, happy, pleasant, sunny

surmise verb 1 = guess, come to the conclusion, conclude, conjecture, consider, deduce, fancy, hazard a guess, imagine, infer, opine, presume, speculate, suppose, suspect ♦ noun 2 = guess, assumption, conclusion, conjecture, deduction, hypothesis, idea, inference, notion, possibility, presumption, speculation, supposition, suspicion, thought

surmount verb = overcome, conquer, master, overpower, prevail over, surpass, triumph over, vanquish

surpass verb = outdo, beat, best, cap (informal), eclipse, exceed, excel, go one better than (informal), outshine, outstrip, override, overshadow, put in the shade, top, transcend

surpassing adjective = supreme, exceptional, extraordinary, incomparable, matchless, outstanding, phenomenal, rare, unrivalled

surplus noun 1 = excess, balance, remainder, residue, superabundance, superfluity, surfeit ♦ adjective 2 = extra, excess, in excess, left over, odd, remaining, spare, superfluous, unused
➤ Antonyms
noun ≠excess: dearth, deficiency, deficit, insufficiency, lack, paucity, shortage, shortfall ♦ adjective ≠extra: deficient, falling short, inadequate, insufficient, lacking, limited, scant, scanty, scarce

surprise noun 1 = shock, bolt from the blue, bombshell, eye-opener (informal), jolt, revelation, start (informal), turn-up for the books (informal) 2 = amazement, astonishment, bewilderment, incredulity, stupefaction, wonder ♦ verb 3 = amaze, astonish, astound, bewilder, bowl over (informal), confuse, disconcert, flabbergast (informal), nonplus, stagger, stun, take aback, take (someone's) breath away 4 = catch unawares or off-guard, burst in on, catch in the act or red-handed, catch on the hop (informal), discover, spring upon, startle

surprised adjective 1 = amazed, astonished, at a loss, disconcerted, incredulous, nonplussed, speechless, startled, taken aback, thunderstruck, unable to believe one's eyes 2 = taken by surprise, caught on the hop (Brit. informal)

surprising adjective = amazing, astonishing, astounding, bewildering, extraordinary, incredible, jaw-dropping, marvellous, remarkable, staggering, startling, unexpected, unlooked-for, unusual, wonderful

surrender verb 1 = give in, capitulate, cave in (informal), give oneself up, give way, quit, show the white flag, submit, succumb, throw in the towel, yield 2 = give up, abandon, cede, concede, deliver up, forego, part with, relinquish, renounce, waive, yield ♦ noun 3 = submission, capitulation, cave-in (informal), relinquishment, renunciation, resignation, yielding
➤ Antonyms
verb ≠give in: defy, fight (on), make a stand against, oppose, resist, stand up to, withstand

surreptitious adjective = secret, clandestine, covert, furtive, sly, sneaking, stealthy, underhand, veiled
➤ Antonyms
blatant, conspicuous, frank, honest, manifest, obvious, open, overt, unconcealed, undisguised

surrogate noun = substitute, deputy, proxy, representative, stand-in

surround verb = enclose, close in on, encircle, encompass, envelop, fence in, girdle, hem in, ring

surrounding adjective = nearby, neighbouring

surroundings plural noun = environment, background, environs, location, milieu, neighbourhood, setting

surveillance noun = observation, inspection, scrutiny, superintendence, supervision, watch

survey verb 1 = look over, contemplate, examine, eyeball (slang), eye up, inspect, observe, scrutinize, view 2 = estimate, appraise, assess, eye up, measure, plan, plot, prospect, size up, take stock of 3 = study, research, review ♦ *noun* 4 = **examination**, inspection, once-over (*informal*), overview, perusal, scrutiny 5 = **study**, inquiry, review

survive *verb* = **remain alive**, endure, exist, hold out, last, live, live on, outlast, outlive, pull through, subsist

susceptibility *noun* = **vulnerability**, liability, predisposition, proneness, propensity, responsiveness, sensitivity, suggestibility, weakness

susceptible *adjective* 1 *usually with* **to** = **liable**, disposed, given, inclined, open, predisposed, prone, subject, vulnerable 2 = **impressionable**, alive to, easily moved, receptive, responsive, sensitive, suggestible, tender
➤ **Antonyms**
≠**liable**: immune, insusceptible, invulnerable, resistant, unaffected by ≠**impressionable**: insensitive, unaffected by, unmoved by, unresponsive

suspect *verb* 1 = **believe**, conclude, conjecture, consider, fancy, feel, guess, hazard a guess, speculate, suppose, surmise, think probable 2 = **distrust**, doubt, have one's doubts about, mistrust ♦ *adjective* 3 = **dubious**, dodgy (*Brit., Austral., & N.Z. informal*), doubtful, fishy (*informal*), iffy (*informal*), open to suspicion, questionable
➤ **Antonyms**
verb ≠**believe**: accept, be certain, be confident of, believe, buy (*slang*), know, swallow (*informal*) ≠**distrust**: have faith in, think innocent, trust ♦ *adjective* ≠**dubious**: above suspicion, innocent, reliable, straightforward, trustworthy, trusty

suspend *verb* 1 = **hang**, append, attach, dangle, swing 2 = **postpone**, adjourn, arrest, cease, cut short, debar, defer, delay, discontinue, hold off, interrupt, lay aside, put off, shelve, stay, withhold
➤ **Antonyms**
≠**postpone**: carry on, continue, re-establish, reinstate, restore, resume, return

suspense *noun* = **uncertainty**, anticipation, anxiety, apprehension, doubt, expectancy, expectation, indecision, insecurity, irresolution, tension, wavering

suspension *noun* = **postponement**, abeyance, adjournment, break, breaking off, deferment, delay, discontinuation, interruption, remission, respite, stay

suspicion *noun* 1 = **distrust**, doubt, dubiety, funny feeling (*informal*), jealousy, misgiving, mistrust, qualm, scepticism, wariness 2 = **idea**, conjecture, guess, gut feeling (*informal*), hunch, impression, notion, supposition, surmise 3 = **trace**, glimmer, hint, shade, shadow, *soupçon*, strain, streak, suggestion, tinge, touch 4

above suspicion = **blameless**, above reproach, honourable, like Caesar's wife, pure, sinless, unimpeachable, virtuous

suspicious *adjective* 1 = **suspect**, dodgy (*Brit., Austral., & N.Z. informal*), doubtful, dubious, fishy (*informal*), funny, irregular, queer, questionable, shady (*informal*) 2 = **distrustful**, apprehensive, doubtful, jealous, mistrustful, sceptical, suspecting, unbelieving, wary
➤ **Antonyms**
≠**suspect**: above board, beyond suspicion, open, straight, straightforward, unquestionable ≠**distrustful**: believing, credulous, gullible, trustful, trusting, unsuspecting, unsuspicious

suss out *verb Brit. & NZ slang* = **work out**, figure out, find out, puzzle out, resolve, solve

sustain *verb* 1 = **maintain**, continue, keep alive, keep going, keep up, prolong, protract 2 = **keep alive**, aid, assist, comfort, foster, help, nourish, nurture, provide for 3 = **suffer**, bear, bear up under, endure, experience, feel, undergo, withstand 4 = **support**, bear, carry, keep from falling, keep up, uphold 5 = **uphold**, approve, confirm, endorse, ratify, validate, verify

sustained *adjective* = **continuous**, constant, nonstop, perpetual, prolonged, steady, unremitting
➤ **Antonyms**
broken, discontinuous, intermittent, irregular, periodic, spasmodic, sporadic

sustenance *noun* = **nourishment**, comestibles, daily bread, eatables, food, provender, provisions, rations, refreshments, victuals

svelte *adjective* = **slender**, graceful, lissom(e), lithe, slinky, sylphlike, willowy

swagger *verb* 1 = **show off** (*informal*), bluster, boast, brag, parade, prance, strut, swank (*informal*) ♦ *noun* 2 = **ostentation**, arrogance, bluster, braggadocio, display, pomposity, show, showing off (*informal*), swank (*informal*), swashbuckling

swallow *verb* 1 = **gulp**, absorb, consume, devour, down (*informal*), drink, eat, ingest, swig (*informal*), swill, wash down 2 *Informal* = **believe**, accept, buy (*slang*), fall for 3 = **hold in**, choke back, repress 4 be swallowed up = **be absorbed**, be assimilated, be consumed, be engulfed, be enveloped, be overrun, be overwhelmed

swamp *noun* 1 = **bog**, everglade(s) (*U.S.*), fen, marsh, mire, morass, quagmire, slough ♦ *verb* 2 *Naut.* = **flood**, capsize, drench, engulf, inundate, overwhelm, sink, submerge, swallow up, upset, wash over, waterlog 3 = **overwhelm**, beset, besiege, deluge, engulf, flood, inundate, overload, snow under, submerge

swampy *adjective* = **boggy**, fenny, marshy, miry, quaggy, waterlogged, wet

swank *Informal* ♦ *verb* **1** = **show off** (*informal*), give oneself airs, posture, put on side (*Brit. slang*), swagger ♦ *noun* **2** = **boastfulness**, display, ostentation, show, swagger

swanky *adjective Informal* = **ostentatious**, de luxe, exclusive, expensive, fancy, fashionable, flash, flashy, glamorous, glitzy (*slang*), gorgeous, grand, lavish, luxurious, plush (*informal*), posh (*informal, chiefly Brit.*), rich, ritzy (*slang*), showy, smart, stylish, sumptuous, swish (*informal, chiefly Brit.*)
➤ **Antonyms**
discreet, humble, inconspicuous, low-key, low-profile, modest, subdued, unassuming, unostentatious, unpretentious

swap, swop *verb* = **exchange**, bandy, barter, interchange, switch, trade, traffic

swarm *noun* **1** = **multitude**, army, bevy, crowd, drove, flock, herd, horde, host, mass, myriad, shoal, throng ♦ *verb* **2** = **crowd**, congregate, flock, mass, stream, throng **3** = **teem**, abound, be alive, be infested, be overrun, bristle, crawl

swarthy *adjective* = **dark-skinned**, black, brown, dark, dark-complexioned, dusky, tawny

swashbuckling *adjective* = **dashing**, bold, daredevil, flamboyant, gallant, spirited, swaggering

swastika *noun* = **crooked cross**, fylfot

swathe *verb* = **wrap**, bandage, bind, bundle up, cloak, drape, envelop, enwrap, fold, furl, lap, muffle up, sheathe, shroud, swaddle

sway *verb* **1** = **bend**, incline, lean, lurch, oscillate, rock, roll, swing, wave **2** = **influence**, affect, control, direct, dominate, govern, guide, induce, persuade, prevail on, win over ♦ *noun* **3** = **power**, ascendency, authority, clout (*informal*), command, control, dominion, government, influence, jurisdiction, predominance, rule, sovereignty **4 hold sway** = **prevail**, predominate, reign, rule, run

swear *verb* **1** = **curse**, be foul-mouthed, blaspheme, cuss (*informal*), take the Lord's name in vain, utter profanities **2** = **vow**, attest, avow, give one's word, pledge oneself, promise, state under oath, take an oath, testify, warrant **3** = **declare**, affirm, assert, asseverate **4 swear by** = **trust**, depend on, have confidence in, rely on

swearing *noun* = **bad language**, blasphemy, cursing, cussing (*informal*), foul language, imprecations, profanity

swearword *noun* = **oath**, curse, cuss (*informal*), expletive, four-letter word, obscenity, profanity

sweat *noun* **1** = **perspiration 2** *Slang* = **labour**, backbreaking task, chore, drudgery, effort, toil **3** *Informal* = **worry**, agitation, anxiety, distress, flap (*informal*), panic, strain ♦ *verb* **4** = **perspire**, break out in a sweat, exude moisture, glow **5** *Informal* = **worry**, agonize, be on pins and needles (*informal*), be on tenterhooks, fret, lose sleep over, suffer, torture oneself **6 sweat it out** *Informal* = **endure**, see (something) through, stay the course, stick it out (*informal*)

sweaty *adjective* = **perspiring**, bathed or drenched or soaked in perspiration, clammy, glowing, sticky, sweating

sweep *verb* **1** = **clear**, brush, clean, remove **2** = **sail**, flounce, fly, glide, hurtle, pass, scud, skim, tear, zoom ♦ *noun* **3** = **arc**, bend, curve, gesture, move, movement, stroke, swing **4** = **extent**, compass, range, scope, span, stretch, vista **5** = **lottery**, draw, raffle, sweepstake

sweeping *adjective* **1** = **wide-ranging**, all-embracing, all-inclusive, broad, comprehensive, extensive, global, overarching, radical, thoroughgoing, wide **2** = **indiscriminate**, across-the-board, blanket, exaggerated, overstated, unqualified, wholesale
➤ **Antonyms**
≠**wide-ranging**: constrained, limited, minor, narrow, restricted

sweet *adjective* **1** = **sugary**, cloying, honeyed, icky (*informal*), luscious, saccharine, sweetened, treacly **2** = **charming**, affectionate, agreeable, amiable, gentle, kind, sweet-tempered, tender, unselfish **3** = **delightful**, appealing, attractive, beautiful, cute, engaging, fair, likable or likeable, lovable, taking, winning, winsome **4** = **melodious**, dulcet, euphonious, harmonious, mellow, musical, silver-toned, silvery, soft, sweet-sounding, tuneful **5** = **fragrant**, aromatic, balmy, clean, fresh, new, perfumed, pure, sweet-smelling, wholesome **6 sweet on** = **in love with**, enamoured of, fond of, head over heels in love with, infatuated with, keen on, taken with, wild or mad about (*informal*) ♦ *noun* **7** *usually plural* = **confectionery**, bonbon, candy (*U.S.*), sweetie, sweetmeats **8** *Brit.* = **dessert**, afters (*Brit. informal*), pudding, sweet course
➤ **Antonyms**
adjective ≠**sugary**: acerbic, acetic, acid, bitter, savoury, sharp, sour, tart, vinegary ≠**charming**: bad-tempered, disagreeable, grouchy (*informal*), grumpy, ill-tempered,

nasty, obnoxious ≠**delightful**: hated, loathsome, nasty, objectionable, obnoxious, unappealing, unattractive, unlovable, unpleasant ≠**melodious**: cacophonous, discordant, grating, harsh, shrill, strident, unharmonious, unmusical, unpleasant ≠**fragrant**: fetid, foul, noisome, rank, stinking

sweeten verb **1** = **sugar**, honey, sugar-coat **2** = **mollify**, alleviate, appease, pacify, soften up, soothe, sugar the pill

sweetheart noun = **love**, admirer, beau, beloved, boyfriend or girlfriend, darling, dear, follower (obsolete), inamorata or inamorato, lover, steady (informal), suitor, swain (archaic), sweetie (informal), truelove, valentine

sweet-talk verb Informal = **flatter**, beguile, cajole, chat up, coax, dupe, entice, inveigle, manoeuvre, persuade, seduce, soft-soap (informal), tempt, wheedle

swell verb **1** = **expand**, balloon, become bloated or distended, become larger, be inflated, belly, billow, bloat, bulge, dilate, distend, enlarge, extend, fatten, grow, increase, protrude, puff up, rise, round out, well up **2** = **increase**, add to, augment, enhance, heighten, intensify, mount, surge ♦ noun **3** = **wave**, billow, rise, surge, undulation **4** Old-fashioned, informal = **dandy**, beau, cockscomb (informal), fashion plate, fop, nob (slang), toff (Brit. slang)
➤ Antonyms
verb ≠**expand**: become smaller, contract, deflate, shrink ≠**increase**: decrease, diminish, ebb, fall, go down, lessen, reduce, wane

swelling noun = **enlargement**, blister, bulge, bump, dilation, distension, inflammation, lump, protuberance, puffiness, tumescence

sweltering adjective = **hot**, airless, baking, boiling, burning, humid, oppressive, roasting, scorching, steaming, stifling, sultry, torrid

swerve verb = **veer**, bend, deflect, depart from, deviate, diverge, incline, sheer off, shift, stray, swing, turn, turn aside, wander, wind

swift adjective = **quick**, abrupt, express, fast, flying, hurried, pdq (slang), prompt, quickie (informal), rapid, ready, short, short-lived, speedy, sudden, winged
➤ Antonyms
lingering, plodding, ponderous, slow, sluggish, tardy, unhurried

swiftly adverb = **quickly**, apace, (at) full tilt, double-quick, fast, hell for leather, hotfoot, hurriedly, like greased lightning (informal), like lightning, like the clappers (Brit.

informal), posthaste, promptly, pronto (informal), rapidly, speedily, without losing time

swiftness noun = **speed**, celerity, fleetness, promptness, quickness, rapidity, speediness, velocity

swill verb **1** = **drink**, bevvy (dialect), consume, drain, gulp, guzzle, imbibe, quaff, swallow, swig (informal) **2** Chiefly Brit., often with **out** = **rinse**, drench, flush, sluice, wash down, wash out ♦ noun **3** = **waste**, mash, mush, pigswill, slops

swimmingly adverb = **successfully**, as planned, effortlessly, like a dream, like clockwork, smoothly, very well, with no trouble, without a hitch

swindle verb **1** = **cheat**, bamboozle (informal), bilk (of), con, deceive, defraud, diddle (informal), do (slang), dupe, fleece, hornswoggle (slang), rip (someone) off (slang), rook (slang), skin (slang), sting (informal), take (someone) for a ride (informal), take to the cleaners (informal), trick ♦ noun **2** = **fraud**, con trick (informal), deceit, deception, double-dealing, fiddle (Brit. informal), racket, rip-off (slang), scam (slang), sharp practice, sting (informal), swizz (Brit. informal), swizzle (Brit. informal), trickery

swindler noun = **cheat**, charlatan, chiseller (informal), confidence trickster, con man (informal), fraud, fraudster, grifter (slang, chiefly U.S. & Canad.), hustler (U.S. informal), mountebank, rascal, rogue, shark, sharper, trickster

swing verb **1** = **sway**, fluctuate, oscillate, rock, vary, veer, vibrate, wave **2** usually with **round** = **turn**, curve, pivot, rotate, swivel, turn on one's heel, wheel **3** = **hang**, be suspended, dangle, move back and forth, suspend ♦ noun **4** = **swaying**, fluctuation, oscillation, stroke, sway, vibration **5 in full swing** = **at its height**, lively, on the go (informal), under way

swingeing adjective Chiefly Brit. = **severe**, Draconian, drastic, excessive, harsh, heavy, huge, oppressive, punishing, stringent

swinging adjective = **trendy** (Brit. informal), fashionable, happening (informal), hip (slang), lively, up-to-date, up to the minute, with it (informal)

swipe verb **1** Informal = **hit**, clip (informal), deck (slang), fetch (someone) a blow, lash out at, slap, slosh (Brit. slang), sock (slang), strike, wallop (informal) **2** Slang = **steal**, appropriate, filch, lift (informal), make off with, nick (slang, chiefly Brit.), pilfer, pinch (informal), purloin, snaffle (Brit. informal) ♦ noun **3** = **blow**, clip (informal), clout (informal), clump (slang), cuff, slap, smack, thump, wallop (*informal*)

swirl *verb* = **whirl**, agitate, boil, churn, eddy, spin, surge, twirl, twist

swish *adjective Informal, chiefly Brit.* = **smart**, de luxe, elegant, exclusive, fashionable, grand, plush *or* plushy (*informal*), posh (*informal, chiefly Brit.*), ritzy (*slang*), sumptuous

switch *noun* **1** = **change**, about-turn, alteration, change of direction, reversal, shift **2** = **exchange**, substitution, swap ♦ *verb* **3** = **change**, change course, deflect, deviate, divert, shift, turn aside **4** = **exchange**, interchange, replace by, substitute, swap, trade

swivel *verb* = **turn**, pirouette, pivot, revolve, rotate, spin, swing round

swollen *adjective* = **enlarged**, bloated, distended, inflamed, puffed up, puffy, tumescent, tumid

swoop *verb* **1** = **pounce**, descend, dive, rush, stoop, sweep ♦ *noun* **2** = **pounce**, descent, drop, lunge, plunge, rush, stoop, sweep

swop *see* SWAP

sword *noun* **1** = **blade 2 the sword: a** = **military power**, aggression, arms, war **b** = **death**, butchery, massacre, murder, slaying, violence **3 cross swords** = **fight**, argue, come to blows, dispute, spar, wrangle

swot *verb Informal* = **study**, apply oneself to, bone up on (*informal*), cram (*informal*), mug up (*Brit. slang*), pore over, revise, toil over, work

sybarite *noun* = **hedonist**, epicure, epicurean, sensualist, voluptuary

sybaritic *adjective* = **pleasure-loving**, bacchanalian, epicurean, hedonistic, luxurious, luxury-loving, self-indulgent, sensual, voluptuous

sycophancy *noun* = **obsequiousness**, bootlicking (*informal*), fawning, flattery, grovelling, kowtowing, servility, toadyism, truckling

sycophant *noun* = **crawler**, ass-kisser (*U.S. & Canad. taboo slang*), bootlicker (*informal*), fawner, flatterer, hanger-on, parasite, toady, truckler, yes man

sycophantic *adjective* = **obsequious**, bootlicking (*informal*), crawling, fawning, flattering, grovelling, ingratiating, parasitical, servile, slimy, smarmy (*Brit. informal*), toadying, unctuous

syllabus *noun* = **course of study**, curriculum

sylphlike *adjective* = **slender**, graceful, lithe, svelte, willowy

symbol *noun* = **sign**, badge, emblem, figure, glyph, image, logo, mark, representation, token, type

symbolic *adjective* = **representative**, allegorical, emblematic, figurative, significant

symbolize *verb* = **represent**, betoken, connote, denote, exemplify, mean, personify, signify, stand for, typify

symmetrical *adjective* = **balanced**, in proportion, proportional, regular, well-proportioned
➤ **Antonyms**
asymmetrical, irregular, lopsided, unbalanced, unequal, unsymmetrical

symmetry *noun* = **balance**, agreement, correspondence, evenness, form, harmony, order, proportion, regularity

sympathetic *adjective* **1** = **caring**, affectionate, compassionate, concerned, feeling, interested, kind, kindly, pitying, responsive, supportive, tender, understanding, warm, warm-hearted **2** = **like-minded**, agreeable, companionable, compatible, congenial, friendly, responsive **3 sympathetic to** = **favourably disposed towards**, agreeable with, approving of, encouraging, friendly to, in sympathy with, pro, well-disposed towards
➤ **Antonyms**
≠**caring**: apathetic, callous, cold, cold-hearted, disinterested, indifferent, inhumane, insensitive, uncaring, uncompassionate, unfeeling, uninterested, unmoved, unsympathetic ≠**like-minded**: uncongenial, unresponsive

sympathetically *adverb* = **feelingly**, kindly, responsively, sensitively, warm-heartedly, warmly, with compassion, with feeling, with interest

sympathize *verb* **1** = **feel for**, commiserate, condole, empathize, have compassion, pity **2** = **agree**, be in accord, be in sympathy, go along with, identify with, side with, understand
➤ **Antonyms**
≠**feel for**: disdain, disregard, have no feelings for, mock, scorn ≠**agree**: disagree, fail to understand, misunderstand, oppose, reject

sympathizer *noun* = **supporter**, partisan, protagonist, well-wisher

sympathy *noun* **1** = **compassion**, commiseration, condolence(s), empathy, pity, tenderness, thoughtfulness, understanding **2** = **affinity**, agreement, congeniality, correspondence, fellow feeling, harmony, rapport, union, warmth
➤ **Antonyms**
≠**compassion**: callousness, coldness, disdain, hard-heartedness, indifference, insensitivity, lack of feeling *or* understanding *or* sympathy, pitilessness, scorn ≠**affinity**:

antagonism, disapproval, hostility, opposition, resistance, unfriendliness

symptom *noun* = **sign**, expression, indication, mark, note, syndrome, token, warning

symptomatic *adjective* = **indicative**, characteristic, suggestive

synonymous *adjective* = **equivalent**, equal, identical, identified, interchangeable, one and the same, similar, tantamount, the same

synopsis *noun* = **summary**, abridgment, abstract, digest, outline, précis, résumé, review, rundown

synthesis *noun* **1** = **combining**, amalgamation, coalescence, integration, unification, welding **2** = **combination**, amalgam, blend, composite, compound, fusion, meld, union

synthetic *adjective* = **artificial**, ersatz, fake, man-made, manufactured, mock, pseudo (*informal*), sham, simulated
➤ **Antonyms**
authentic, genuine, kosher (*informal*),

natural, pure, real

system *noun* **1** = **method**, fixed order, frame of reference, methodology, modus operandi, practice, procedure, routine, technique **2** = **orderliness**, definite plan, logical process, method, methodicalness, regularity, systematization **3** = **arrangement**, classification, combination, coordination, organization, scheme, setup (*informal*), structure

systematic *adjective* = **methodical**, businesslike, efficient, orderly, organized, precise, standardized, systematized, well-ordered
➤ **Antonyms**
arbitrary, disorderly, disorganized, haphazard, indiscriminate, random, slapdash, unbusinesslike, unmethodical, unsystematic

systematize *verb* = **arrange**, classify, methodize, organize, put in order, rationalize, regulate, schematize, sequence, standardize

T t

tab *noun* = **flap**, flag, label, marker, sticker, tag, ticket

tabby *adjective* = **striped**, banded, brindled, stripy

table *noun* **1** = **counter**, bench, board, slab, stand **2** = **list**, agenda, catalogue, chart, diagram, digest, graph, index, inventory, plan, record, register, roll, schedule, synopsis, tabulation **3** *Formal* = **food**, board, diet, fare, spread (*informal*), victuals ♦ *verb* **4** *Brit.* = **submit**, enter, move, propose, put forward, suggest

tableau *noun* = **picture**, representation, scene, spectacle

tableland *noun* = **plateau**, flat, flatland, mesa, plain, table

taboo *noun* **1** = **prohibition**, anathema, ban, disapproval, interdict, proscription, restriction ♦ *adjective* **2** = **forbidden**, anathema, banned, beyond the pale, disapproved of, frowned on, not allowed, not permitted, off limits, outlawed, prohibited, proscribed, ruled out, unacceptable, unmentionable, unthinkable
➤ Antonyms
adjective ≠**forbidden:** acceptable, allowed, permitted, sanctioned

tabulate *verb* = **arrange**, catalogue, categorize, chart, classify, codify, index, list, order, range, systematize

tacit *adjective* = **implied**, implicit, inferred, silent, taken for granted, undeclared, understood, unexpressed, unspoken, unstated, wordless
➤ Antonyms
explicit, express, spelled-out, spoken, stated

taciturn *adjective* = **uncommunicative**, mute, quiet, reserved, reticent, silent, tight-lipped, unforthcoming, withdrawn
➤ Antonyms
chatty, communicative, forthcoming, garrulous, loquacious, open, outgoing, sociable, talkative, verbose, voluble, wordy

tack[1] *noun* **1** = **nail**, drawing pin, pin, staple, thumbtack (*U.S.*), tintack ♦ *verb* **2** = **fasten**, affix, attach, fix, nail, pin, staple **3** *Brit.* = **stitch**, baste, sew **4 tack on** = **append**, add, annex, attach, tag

tack[2] *noun* = **course**, approach, bearing, direction, heading, line, method, path, plan, procedure, tactic, way

tackle *verb* **1** = **deal with**, apply oneself to, attempt, begin, come *or* get to grips with, embark upon, engage in, essay, get stuck into (*informal*), have a go *or* stab at (*informal*), set about, take on, try, turn one's hand to, undertake **2** = **confront**, block, challenge, grab, grasp, halt, intercept, seize, stop, take hold of ♦ *noun* **3** = **challenge**, block, stop **4** = **equipment**, accoutrements, apparatus, gear, implements, outfit, paraphernalia, rig, rigging, tools, trappings

tacky[1] *adjective* = **sticky**, adhesive, gluey, gummy, icky (*informal*), wet

tacky[2] *Informal adjective* **1** = **vulgar**, cheap, naff (*Brit. slang*), sleazy, tasteless **2** = **shabby**, seedy, shoddy, tatty

tact *noun* = **diplomacy**, adroitness, consideration, delicacy, discretion, finesse, judgment, perception, savoir-faire, sensitivity, skill, thoughtfulness, understanding
➤ Antonyms
awkwardness, clumsiness, gaucherie, heavy-handedness, indiscretion, insensitivity, lack of consideration, lack of discretion, tactlessness

tactful *adjective* = **diplomatic**, careful, considerate, delicate, discreet, judicious, perceptive, polished, polite, politic, prudent, sensitive, subtle, thoughtful, understanding
➤ Antonyms
awkward, clumsy, gauche, inconsiderate, indiscreet, insensitive, tactless, tasteless, thoughtless, undiplomatic, unsubtle, untoward

tactic *noun* **1** = **policy**, approach, course, device, line, manoeuvre, means, method, move, ploy, scheme, stratagem, tack, trick, way **2 tactics** = **strategy**, campaigning, generalship, manoeuvres, plans

tactical *adjective* = **strategic**, artful, clever, cunning, diplomatic, shrewd, skilful, smart
➤ Antonyms
blundering, clumsy, gauche, impolitic, inept

tactician *noun* = **strategist**, campaigner, coordinator, director, general, mastermind, planner, schemer

tactless *adjective* = **insensitive**, blundering, boorish, careless, clumsy, discourteous, gauche, impolite, impolitic, inconsiderate, indelicate, indiscreet, injudicious, rude, thoughtless, undiplomatic, unfeeling, tag 717 **take on**

unkind, unsubtle
➤ **Antonyms**
considerate, diplomatic, discreet, polite,
subtle, tactful

tag *noun* **1** = **label**, flap, identification, mark,
marker, note, slip, tab, ticket ◆ *verb* **2**
= **label**, earmark, flag, identify, mark, ticket **3**
with **along** *or* **on** = **accompany**, attend,
follow, shadow, tail (*informal*), trail **4** *with*
on = **add**, adjoin, affix, annex, append,
fasten, tack

tail *noun* **1** = **extremity**, appendage, end,
rear end, tailpiece, train **2 turn tail** = **run
away**, cut and run, escape, flee, make off,
retreat, run for it (*informal*), run off, scarper
(*Brit. slang*), skedaddle (*informal*), take off
(*informal*), take to one's heels ◆ *verb* **3**
Informal = **follow**, dog the footsteps of,
keep an eye on, shadow, stalk, track, trail

tail off *or* **away** *verb* = **decrease**, die out,
drop, dwindle, fade, fall away, peter out,
wane
➤ **Antonyms**
grow, increase, intensify, wax

tailor *noun* **1** = **outfitter**, clothier, costumier,
couturier, dressmaker, garment maker,
seamstress ◆ *verb* **2** = **adapt**, accommodate,
adjust, alter, convert, customize, cut,
fashion, fit, modify, mould, shape, style, suit

tailor-made *adjective* **1**
= **made-to-measure**, cut to fit, fitted, made
to order **2** = **perfect**, custom-made, ideal,
just right, right, suitable

taint *verb* **1** = **spoil**, besmirch, blemish,
blight, blot, contaminate, corrupt, damage,
defile, dirty, foul, infect, poison, pollute,
ruin, smear, smirch, soil, stain, sully, tarnish
◆ *noun* **2** = **stain**, black mark, blemish, blot,
defect, demerit, fault, flaw, smear, smirch,
spot **3** = **disgrace**, dishonour, shame, stigma
4 = **contamination**, contagion, infection,
pollution
➤ **Antonyms**
verb ≠**spoil**: clean, cleanse, decontaminate,
disinfect, purify

take *verb* **1** = **accompany**, bring, conduct,
convoy, escort, guide, lead, usher **2** = **carry**,
bear, bring, cart, convey, ferry, fetch, haul,
tote (*informal*), transport **3** = **obtain**,
acquire, carry off, catch, clutch, gain
possession of, get, get hold of, grasp, grip,
have, help oneself to, lay hold of, receive,
secure, seize, win **4** = **steal**, abstract,
appropriate, carry off, filch, misappropriate,
nick (*slang, chiefly Brit.*), pinch (*informal*),
pocket, purloin, run off with, swipe (*slang*),
walk off with **5** = **capture**, abduct, arrest,
seize **6** = **choose**, book, buy, engage, hire,
lease, pay for, pick, purchase, rent, reserve,
select **7** = **require**, call for, demand,
necessitate, need **8** = **consume**, drink, eat,

imbibe, ingest, inhale, swallow **9** = **perform**,
do, effect, execute, have, make **10** = **accept**,
adopt, assume, enter upon, undertake **11**
= **tolerate**, abide, bear, brave, brook,
endure, go through, put up with (*informal*),
stand, stomach, submit to, suffer, swallow,
thole (*Scot.*), undergo, withstand **12** = **have
room for**, accept, accommodate, contain,
hold **13** = **subtract**, deduct, eliminate,
remove **14** = **work**, do the trick (*informal*),
have effect, operate, succeed **15** = **assume**,
believe, consider, deem, hold, interpret as,
perceive, presume, receive, regard, see as,
think of as, understand
➤ **Antonyms**
≠**carry**: send ≠**steal**: give, give back, hand
over, restore, return, surrender, yield
≠**capture**: free, let go, release ≠**accept**:
decline, dismiss, eschew, ignore, refuse,
reject, scorn, spurn ≠**tolerate**: avoid,
dodge, give in, give way ≠**subtract**: add,
put ≠**work**: fail, flop (*informal*)

take back *verb* **1** = **retract**, disavow,
disclaim, recant, renege, renounce, unsay,
withdraw **2** = **regain**, get back, recapture,
reclaim, reconquer, repossess, retake **3**
= **give one a refund for**, exchange

take down *verb* **1** = **make a note of**,
minute, note, put on record, record, set
down, transcribe, write down **2** = **dismantle**,
demolish, disassemble, level, take apart, take
to pieces, tear down **3** = **remove**, depress,
drop, haul down, let down, lower, pull
down, take off **4** = **humble**, deflate,
humiliate, mortify, put down (*slang*)

take in *verb* **1** = **understand**, absorb,
assimilate, comprehend, digest, get the hang
of (*informal*), grasp **2** = **deceive**, bilk, cheat,
con (*informal*), do (*slang*), dupe, fool,
hoodwink, mislead, pull the wool over
(someone's) eyes (*informal*), swindle, trick **3**
= **include**, comprise, contain, cover,
encompass **4** = **let in**, accommodate, admit,
receive

takeoff *noun* **1** = **departure**, launch, liftoff **2**
Informal = **parody**, caricature, imitation,
lampoon, mocking, satire, send-up (*Brit.
informal*), spoof (*informal*), travesty

take off *verb* **1** = **remove**, discard, divest
oneself of, doff, drop, peel off, strip off **2**
= **lift off**, become airborne, leave the
ground, take to the air **3** *Informal* = **depart**,
abscond, beat it (*slang*), decamp, disappear,
go, hit the road (*slang*), leave, set out, slope
off, split (*slang*) **4** *Informal* = **parody**,
caricature, imitate, lampoon, mimic, mock,
satirize, send up (*Brit. informal*), spoof
(*informal*), take the piss (out of) (*taboo
slang*), travesty

take on *verb* **1** = **engage**, employ, enlist,
enrol, hire **2** = **acquire**, assume, come to

have **3 = accept**, agree to do, have a go at
(*informal*), tackle, undertake **4 = compete
against**, contend with, face, fight, oppose,
pit oneself against

takeover *noun* = **merger**, change of
leadership, coup, incorporation

take over *verb* = **gain control of**, assume
control of, become leader of, take command
of

take to *verb* **1** = **like**, become friendly with,
be taken with, get on with, warm to **2**
= **start**, have recourse to, make a habit of,
resort to

take up *verb* **1** = **occupy**, absorb, consume,
cover, extend over, fill, use up **2** = **start**,
adopt, assume, become involved in, engage
in

taking *adjective* = **charming**, attractive,
beguiling, captivating, cute, delightful,
enchanting, engaging, fascinating, fetching
(*informal*), likable *or* likeable, pleasing,
prepossessing, winning
➤ **Antonyms**
abhorrent, loathsome, offensive, repulsive,
unattractive, unpleasant

takings *plural noun* = **revenue**, earnings,
gain, gate, income, pickings, proceeds,
profits, receipts, returns, take, yield

tale *noun* **1** = **story**, account, anecdote,
fable, fiction, legend, narration, narrative,
novel, report, romance, saga, short story,
urban legend, urban myth, yarn (*informal*) **2**
= **lie**, cock-and-bull story (*informal*),
fabrication, falsehood, fib, gossip, rumour,
tall story (*informal*), untruth

talent *noun* = **ability**, aptitude, bent,
capacity, endowment, faculty, flair, forte,
genius, gift, knack, power

talented *adjective* = **gifted**, able, artistic,
brilliant

talisman *noun* = **charm**, amulet, fetish,
lucky charm, mascot

talk *verb* **1** = **speak**, articulate, chat, chatter,
communicate, converse, express oneself, gab
(*informal*), give voice to, gossip, natter,
prate, prattle, rap (*slang*), say, spout, utter,
verbalize, witter (*informal*) **2** = **discuss**,
confabulate, confer, have a confab
(*informal*), hold discussions, negotiate,
parley **3** = **inform**, blab, give the game
away, grass (*Brit. slang*), let the cat out of
the bag, reveal information, shop (*slang,
chiefly Brit.*), sing (*slang, chiefly U.S.*), spill
the beans (*informal*), squeal (*slang*), tell all
♦ *noun* **4** = **speech**, address, discourse,
disquisition, dissertation, lecture, oration,
sermon **5** = **discussion**, confab (*informal*),
confabulation, conference, consultation,
dialogue **6** = **conversation**, blether, chat,
chatter, chitchat, crack (*Scot. & Irish*), gab

(*informal*), natter, rap (*slang*) **7** = **gossip**,
hearsay, rumour, tittle-tattle **8** = **meeting**,
conclave, conference, congress, negotiation,
parley, seminar, symposium

talkative *adjective* = **loquacious**,
big-mouthed (*slang*), chatty, effusive, gabby
(*informal*), garrulous, gossipy, long-winded,
mouthy, verbose, voluble, wordy
➤ **Antonyms**
quiet, reserved, reticent, silent, taciturn,
tight-lipped, uncommunicative,
unforthcoming

talker *noun* = **speaker**, chatterbox,
conversationalist, lecturer, orator,
speechmaker

talking-to *noun Informal* = **reprimand**,
criticism, dressing-down (*informal*), lecture,
rap on the knuckles, rebuke, reproach,
reproof, row, scolding, telling-off (*informal*),
ticking-off (*informal*)
➤ **Antonyms**
commendation, encouragement, praise

talk into *verb* = **persuade**, bring round
(*informal*), convince, prevail on *or* upon,
sway, win over

tall *adjective* **1** = **high**, big, elevated, giant,
lanky, lofty, soaring, towering **2** *As in* **tall
story** *Informal* = **implausible**, absurd,
cock-and-bull (*informal*), exaggerated,
far-fetched, incredible, preposterous, steep
(*Brit. informal*), unbelievable **3** *As in* **tall
order** = **difficult**, demanding, hard,
unreasonable, well-nigh impossible
➤ **Antonyms**
≠**high**: short, small, squat, stumpy, tiny, wee
≠**implausible**: accurate, believable,
plausible, realistic, reasonable, true,
unexaggerated

tally *verb* **1** = **agree**, accord, coincide,
concur, conform, correspond, fit, harmonize,
match, parallel, square, suit **2** = **keep score**,
compute, count up, total ♦ *noun* **3**
= **record**, count, mark, reckoning, running
total, score, total
➤ **Antonyms**
verb ≠**agree**: clash, conflict, contradict,
differ, disagree

tame *adjective* **1** = **domesticated**,
amenable, broken, cultivated, disciplined,
docile, gentle, obedient, tractable **2**
= **unafraid**, fearless **3** = **submissive**,
compliant, docile, manageable, meek,
obedient, spiritless, subdued, unresisting **4**
= **unexciting**, bland, boring, dull, flat,
humdrum, insipid, lifeless, prosaic, tedious,
tiresome, uninspiring, uninteresting, vapid,
wearisome ♦ *verb* **5** = **domesticate**, break
in, house-train, make tame, pacify, train **6**
= **subdue**, break the spirit of, conquer, curb,
discipline, humble, master, repress,
subjugate, suppress

> ➤ **Antonyms**
> *adjective* ≠**domesticated**: aggressive, feral, ferocious, savage, undomesticated, untamed, wild ≠**submissive**: aggressive, argumentative, obdurate, strong-willed, stubborn, unmanageable ≠**unexciting**: exciting, frenzied, hot, interesting, lively, stimulating ◆ *verb* ≠**domesticate**: make fiercer ≠**subdue**: arouse, incite, intensify

tamper *verb* **1** = **interfere**, alter, fiddle (*informal*), fool about (*informal*), intrude, meddle, mess about, monkey around, muck about (*Brit. slang*), poke one's nose into (*informal*), tinker **2** = **influence**, bribe, corrupt, fix (*informal*), get at, manipulate, rig

tang *noun* **1** = **taste**, aroma, bite, flavour, odour, piquancy, savour, scent, smack, smell **2** = **trace**, hint, suggestion, tinge, touch, whiff

tangible *adjective* = **definite**, actual, concrete, corporeal, evident, manifest, material, objective, palpable, perceptible, physical, positive, real, solid, substantial, tactile, touchable
> ➤ **Antonyms**
> abstract, disembodied, ethereal, immaterial, impalpable, imperceptible, indiscernible, insubstantial, intangible, theoretical, unreal

tangle *noun* **1** = **knot**, coil, entanglement, jungle, mass, mat, mesh, snarl, twist, web **2** = **confusion**, complication, entanglement, fix (*informal*), imbroglio, jam, labyrinth, maze, mess, mix-up ◆ *verb* **3** = **twist**, coil, confuse, entangle, interlace, interlock, intertwist, interweave, jam, knot, mat, mesh, ravel, snarl **4** *often with* **with** = **come into conflict**, come up against, contend, contest, cross swords, dispute, lock horns **5** = **catch**, enmesh, ensnare, entangle, entrap
> ➤ **Antonyms**
> *verb* ≠**twist**: disentangle, extricate, free, straighten out, unravel, untangle

tangled *adjective* **1** = **twisted**, entangled, jumbled, knotted, knotty, matted, messy, snarled, tousled **2** = **complicated**, complex, confused, convoluted, involved, knotty, messy, mixed-up

tangy *adjective* = **sharp**, piquant, pungent, spicy, tart

tantalize *verb* = **torment**, entice, frustrate, keep (someone) hanging on, lead on, provoke, taunt, tease, titillate, torture

tantamount *adjective* **tantamount to** = **equivalent to**, as good as, commensurate with, equal to, synonymous with, the same as

tantrum *noun* = **outburst**, fit, flare-up, hysterics, ill humour, paddy (*Brit. informal*), paroxysm, storm, temper

tap[1] *verb* **1** = **knock**, beat, drum, pat, rap, strike, touch ◆ *noun* **2** = **knock**, beat, light blow, pat, rap, touch

tap[2] *noun* **1** = **valve**, faucet (*U.S.*), spigot, spout, stopcock **2** = **stopper**, bung, plug **3** = **bug** (*informal*), listening device **4** **on tap**: **a** *Informal* = **available**, at hand, in reserve, on hand, ready **b** = **on draught** ◆ *verb* **5** = **listen in on**, bug (*informal*), eavesdrop on **6** = **use**, draw on, exploit, make use of, milk, mine, put to use, turn to account, utilize **7** = **draw off**, bleed, broach, drain, open, siphon off

tape *noun* **1** = **strip**, band, ribbon ◆ *verb* **2** = **record**, tape-record, video **3** = **bind**, seal, secure, stick, wrap

taper *verb* **1** = **narrow**, come to a point, thin **2** **taper off** = **decrease**, die away, die out, dwindle, fade, lessen, reduce, subside, thin out, wane, weaken, wind down
> ➤ **Antonyms**
> ≠**decrease**: grow, increase, intensify, step up, strengthen, swell, widen

tardiness *noun* = **lateness**, belatedness, dilatoriness, slowness, unpunctuality

tardy *adjective* **1** = **late**, behindhand, belated, dilatory, overdue, unpunctual **2** = **slow**, backward, retarded

target *noun* **1** = **goal**, aim, ambition, end, Holy Grail (*informal*), intention, mark, object, objective **2** = **victim**, butt, scapegoat

tariff *noun* **1** = **tax**, assessment, duty, excise, impost, levy, rate, toll **2** = **price list**, bill of fare, charges, menu, schedule

tarnish *verb* **1** = **stain**, blemish, blot, darken, dim, discolour, dull, lose lustre *or* shine, rust, soil, spot **2** = **damage**, blacken, smirch, sully, taint ◆ *noun* **3** = **stain**, blemish, blot, discoloration, rust, spot, taint
> ➤ **Antonyms**
> *verb* ≠**stain**: brighten, enhance, polish up, shine ≠**damage**: enhance

tarry *verb* *Old-fashioned* **1** = **linger**, bide, dally, dawdle, delay, hang around (*informal*), loiter, pause, remain, take one's time, wait **2** = **stay**, abide, dwell, lodge, rest, sojourn
> ➤ **Antonyms**
> ≠**linger**: hasten, hurry, move on, rush, scoot, step on it (*informal*)

tart[1] *noun* = **pie**, pastry, tartlet

tart[2] *adjective* **1** = **sharp**, acid, acidulous, astringent, bitter, piquant, pungent, sour, tangy, vinegary **2** = **cutting**, acrimonious, barbed, biting, caustic, harsh, hurtful, nasty, scathing, sharp, short, trenchant, vitriolic, wounding
> ➤ **Antonyms**
> ≠**sharp**: honeyed, sugary, sweet, syrupy, toothsome ≠**cutting**: agreeable, delightful, gentle, kind, pleasant

tart[3] *noun* = **slut**, call girl, fallen woman, floozy (*slang*), harlot, hooker (*U.S. slang*), loose woman, prostitute, scrubber (*Brit. & Austral. slang*), slag (*Brit. slang*), streetwalker, strumpet, trollop, whore, woman of easy virtue

task *noun* **1** = **job**, assignment, business, charge, chore, duty, employment, enterprise, exercise, labour, mission, occupation, toil, undertaking, work **2 take to task** = **criticize**, bawl out (*informal*), blame, blast, censure, give a rocket (*Brit. & N.Z. informal*), lambast(e), lecture, read the riot act, rebuke, reprimand, reproach, reprove, scold, tear into (*informal*), tear (someone) off a strip (*Brit. informal*), tell off (*informal*), upbraid

taste *noun* **1** = **flavour**, relish, savour, smack, tang **2** = **bit**, bite, dash, drop, morsel, mouthful, nip, sample, sip, soupçon, spoonful, swallow, titbit, touch **3** = **liking**, appetite, bent, desire, fancy, fondness, inclination, leaning, partiality, penchant, predilection, preference, relish **4** = **refinement**, appreciation, cultivation, culture, discernment, discrimination, elegance, grace, judgment, perception, polish, sophistication, style **5** = **propriety**, correctness, decorum, delicacy, discretion, politeness, restraint, tact, tactfulness ♦ *verb* **6** = **distinguish**, differentiate, discern, perceive **7** = **sample**, nibble, savour, sip, test, try **8** = **have a flavour of**, savour of, smack of **9** = **experience**, come up against, encounter, feel, have knowledge of, know, meet with, partake of, undergo
➤ **Antonyms**
noun ≠**flavour**: blandness, insipidity, tastelessness ≠**liking**: disinclination, dislike, distaste, hatred, loathing ≠**refinement**: lack of discernment, lack of judgment, mawkishness, tackiness, tastelessness ≠**propriety**: bawdiness, coarseness, crudeness, impropriety, indelicacy, obscenity (*informal*), tactlessness, unsubtlety ♦ *verb* ≠**distinguish**: fail to discern ≠**experience**: fail to achieve, miss, remain ignorant of

tasteful *adjective* = **refined**, aesthetically pleasing, artistic, beautiful, charming, cultivated, cultured, delicate, discriminating, elegant, exquisite, fastidious, graceful, handsome, harmonious, in good taste, polished, restrained, smart, stylish, urbane
➤ **Antonyms**
brash, flashy, garish, gaudy, inelegant, loud, objectionable, offensive, showy, sick, tacky (*informal*), tasteless, tawdry, twee, uncultured, unrefined, vulgar

tasteless *adjective* **1** = **insipid**, bland, boring, dull, flat, flavourless, mild, stale, tame, thin, watered-down, weak **2** = **vulgar**, cheap, coarse, crass, crude, flashy, garish, gaudy, graceless, gross, impolite, improper,

indecorous, indelicate, indiscreet, inelegant, low, naff (*Brit. slang*), rude, tacky (*informal*), tactless, tawdry, uncouth, unseemly
➤ **Antonyms**
≠**insipid**: appetizing, delectable, delicious, flavoursome, savoury, scrumptious (*informal*), tasty ≠**vulgar**: elegant, graceful, refined, tasteful

tasty *adjective* = **delicious**, appetizing, delectable, flavourful, flavoursome, full-flavoured, luscious, palatable, savoury, scrumptious (*informal*), toothsome, yummy (*slang*)
➤ **Antonyms**
bland, flavourless, insipid, tasteless, unappetizing, unsavoury

tatters *plural noun* **1** = **rags**, bits, pieces, scraps, shreds ♦ *noun* **2 in tatters** = **ragged**, down at heel, in rags, in shreds, ripped, tattered, threadbare, torn

tattle *verb* **1** = **gossip**, babble, blab, chatter, jabber, prattle, spread rumours, tell tales, title-tattle ♦ *noun* **2** = **gossip**, babble, chatter, chitchat, hearsay, idle talk, jabber, prattle, small talk, title-tattle

tatty *adjective Chiefly Brit.* = **shabby**, bedraggled, dilapidated, down at heel, neglected, ragged, run-down, scruffy, the worse for wear, threadbare, unkempt, worn, worn out
➤ **Antonyms**
good, new, smart, well-preserved

taunt *verb* **1** = **jeer**, deride, insult, mock, provoke, ridicule, sneer, take the piss (out of) (*taboo slang*), tease, torment ♦ *noun* **2** = **jeer**, barb, derision, dig, gibe, insult, provocation, ridicule, sarcasm, teasing

taut *adjective* = **tight**, flexed, rigid, strained, stressed, stretched, tense
➤ **Antonyms**
loose, relaxed, slack

tautological *adjective* = **repetitive**, iterative, redundant, repetitious

tautology *noun* = **repetition**, iteration, redundancy, repetitiousness, repetitiveness

tavern *noun* = **inn**, alehouse (*archaic*), bar, boozer (*Brit., Austral., & N.Z. informal*), hostelry, pub (*informal, chiefly Brit.*), public house, taproom, watering hole (*facetious slang*)

tawdry *adjective* = **vulgar**, cheap, flashy, gaudy, gimcrack, naff (*Brit. slang*), plastic (*slang*), showy, tacky (*informal*), tasteless, tatty
➤ **Antonyms**
elegant, graceful, plain, refined, simple, stylish, tasteful, unflashy, unostentatious, well-tailored

tax *noun* **1** = **charge**, assessment,

contribution, customs, duty, excise, imposition, impost, levy, rate, tariff, tithe, toll, tribute ♦ *verb* 2 = **charge**, assess, demand, exact, impose, levy a tax on, rate 3 = **strain**, burden, drain, exhaust, load, make heavy demands on, overburden, push, put pressure on, sap, stretch, test, try, weaken, wear out, weary 4 = **accuse**, arraign, blame, charge, impeach, impugn, incriminate, lay at one's door
➤ Antonyms
verb ≠ **accuse**: acquit, clear, exculpate, exonerate, vindicate

taxing *adjective* = **demanding**, exacting, heavy, onerous, punishing, sapping, stressful, tiring, tough, trying, wearing, wearisome
➤ Antonyms
easy, easy-peasy (*slang*), effortless, light, unburdensome, undemanding

teach *verb* = **instruct**, advise, coach, demonstrate, direct, discipline, drill, edify, educate, enlighten, give lessons in, guide, impart, inform, instil, school, show, train, tutor

teacher *noun* = **instructor**, coach, don, educator, guide, guru, lecturer, master *or* mistress, mentor, pedagogue, professor, schoolmaster *or* schoolmistress, schoolteacher, trainer, tutor

team *noun* 1 = **group**, band, body, bunch, company, crew, gang, line-up, posse (*informal*), set, side, squad, troupe 2 = **pair**, span, yoke ♦ *verb* 3 *often with* **up** = **join**, band together, cooperate, couple, get together, link, unite, work together

teamwork *noun* = **cooperation**, collaboration, coordination, esprit de corps, fellowship, harmony, unity

tear *verb* 1 = **rip**, divide, rend, run, rupture, scratch, shred, split, sunder 2 = **pull apart**, claw, lacerate, mangle, mutilate, sever 3 = **rush**, bolt, career, charge, dart, dash, fly, gallop, hurry, race, run, shoot, speed, sprint, zoom 4 = **seize**, grab, pluck, pull, rip, snatch, wrench, wrest, yank ♦ *noun* 5 = **hole**, laceration, rent, rip, run, rupture, scratch, split

tearaway *noun Brit.* = **hooligan**, delinquent, good-for-nothing, rowdy, ruffian

tearful *adjective* = **weeping**, blubbering, crying, in tears, lachrymose, sobbing, weepy (*informal*), whimpering

tears *plural noun* 1 = **crying**, blubbering, distress, sobbing, wailing, weeping, whimpering 2 **in tears** = **weeping**, blubbering, crying, distressed, sobbing, whimpering

tease *verb* 1 = **mock**, aggravate (*informal*), annoy, badger, bait, bother, chaff, goad, needle (*informal*), pester, plague (*informal*), provoke, pull someone's leg (*informal*), take

the mickey (*informal*), take the piss (out of) (*taboo slang*), taunt, torment, vex, wind up (*Brit. slang*) 2 = **tantalize**, lead on

technical *adjective* = **scientific**, hi-tech *or* high-tech, skilled, specialist, specialized, technological

technique *noun* 1 = **method**, approach, course, fashion, manner, means, mode, modus operandi, procedure, style, system, way 2 = **skill**, adroitness, art, artistry, craft, craftsmanship, execution, facility, knack, know-how (*informal*), performance, proficiency, touch

tedious *adjective* = **boring**, banal, deadly dull, drab, dreary, dull, ho-hum (*informal*), humdrum, irksome, laborious, long-drawn-out, mind-numbing, monotonous, prosaic, soporific, tiresome, tiring, unexciting, uninteresting, vapid, wearisome
➤ Antonyms
enjoyable, enthralling, exciting, exhilarating, imaginative, inspiring, interesting, quickly finished, short, stimulating

tedium *noun* = **boredom**, banality, deadness, drabness, dreariness, dullness, ennui, monotony, routine, sameness, tediousness, the doldrums
➤ Antonyms
challenge, excitement, exhilaration, fascination, interest, liveliness, stimulation

teem[1] *verb* = **be full of**, abound, be abundant, bear, be crawling with, be prolific, brim, bristle, burst at the seams, overflow, produce, swarm

teem[2] *verb* = **pour**, bucket down (*informal*), lash, pelt (down), rain cats and dogs (*informal*), stream

teeming[1] *adjective* = **full**, abundant, alive, brimful, brimming, bristling, bursting, chock-a-block, chock-full, crawling, numerous, overflowing, packed, replete, swarming, thick
➤ Antonyms
deficient, lacking, short, wanting

teeming[2] *adjective* = **pouring**, bucketing down (*informal*), pelting, streaming

teenage *adjective* = **youthful**, adolescent, immature, juvenile

teenager *noun* = **youth**, adolescent, boy, girl, juvenile, minor

teeny *adjective Informal* = **tiny**, diminutive, microscopic, miniature, minuscule, minute, teeny-weeny, wee

teeter *verb* = **wobble**, rock, seesaw, stagger, sway, totter, waver

teetotaller *noun* = **abstainer**, nondrinker, Rechabite

telegram *noun* = **cable**, radiogram,

telegraph, telex, wire (*informal*)

telegraph *noun* **1** = **cable**, telegram, telex, wire (*informal*) ♦ *verb* **2** = **cable**, send, telex, transmit, wire (*informal*)

telepathy *noun* = **mind-reading**, sixth sense, thought transference

telephone *noun* **1** = **phone**, blower (*informal*), dog and bone (*slang*), handset, line, mobile (phone) ♦ *verb* **2** = **call**, buzz (*informal*), call up, dial, give (someone) a bell (*Brit. slang*), give (someone) a buzz (*informal*), give (someone) a call, give (someone) a ring (*informal, chiefly Brit.*), give someone a tinkle (*Brit. informal*), phone, ring (*chiefly Brit.*)

telescope *noun* **1** = **glass**, spyglass ♦ *verb* **2** = **shorten**, abbreviate, abridge, capsulize, compress, condense, consolidate, contract, curtail, cut, shrink, tighten, trim, truncate
➤ **Antonyms**
verb ≠**shorten**: amplify, draw out, elongate, extend, flesh out, lengthen, protract, spread out

television *noun* = **TV**, gogglebox (*Brit. slang*), idiot box (*slang*), receiver, small screen (*informal*), telly (*Brit. informal*), the box (*Brit. informal*), the tube (*slang*), TV set

tell *verb* **1** = **inform**, acquaint, announce, apprise, communicate, confess, disclose, divulge, express, get off one's chest (*informal*), impart, let know, make known, mention, notify, proclaim, reveal, say, speak, state, utter **2** = **instruct**, authorize, bid, call upon, command, direct, enjoin, order, require, summon **3** = **describe**, chronicle, depict, give an account of, narrate, portray, recount, relate, report **4** = **see**, comprehend, discern, discover, make out, understand **5** = **distinguish**, differentiate, discern, discriminate, identify **6** = **have** *or* **take effect**, carry weight, count, have force, make its presence felt, register, take its toll, weigh

telling *adjective* = **effective**, considerable, decisive, effectual, forceful, forcible, impressive, influential, marked, potent, powerful, significant, striking, trenchant, weighty
➤ **Antonyms**
easily ignored, inconsequential, indecisive, ineffectual, insignificant, lightweight, minor, negligible, slight, trivial, unimportant

telling-off *noun* = **reprimand**, censure, criticism, dressing-down (*informal*), lecture, rap on the knuckles, rebuke, reproach, reproof, row, scolding, slating (*informal*), talking-to, ticking-off (*informal*)

tell off *verb* = **reprimand**, bawl out (*informal*), berate, censure, chide, give (someone) a piece of one's mind, give (someone) a rocket (*Brit. & N.Z. informal*),

haul over the coals (*informal*), lecture, read the riot act, rebuke, reproach, reprove, scold, take to task, tear into (*informal*), tear (someone) off a strip (*Brit. informal*), tick off (*informal*), upbraid

temerity *noun* = **audacity**, boldness, brass neck (*Brit. informal*), cheek, chutzpah (*U.S. & Canad. informal*), effrontery, front, gall (*informal*), impudence, nerve (*informal*), rashness, recklessness

temper *noun* **1** = **rage**, bad mood, fit of pique, fury, gall, paddy (*Brit. informal*), passion, tantrum **2** = **irritability**, anger, annoyance, heat, hot-headedness, ill humour, irascibility, irritation, passion, peevishness, petulance, resentment, surliness **3** = **self-control**, calm, calmness, composure, cool (*slang*), coolness, equanimity, good humour, moderation **4** = **frame of mind**, attitude, character, constitution, disposition, humour, mind, mood, nature, temperament ♦ *verb* **5** = **moderate**, allay, assuage, calm, lessen, mitigate, mollify, palliate, restrain, soften, soft-pedal (*informal*), soothe, tone down **6** = **strengthen**, anneal, harden, toughen
➤ **Antonyms**
noun ≠**irritability**: contentment, goodwill ≠**self-control**: agitation, anger, bad mood, excitability, foul humour, fury, grumpiness, indignation, irascibility, irritation, pique, vexation, wrath ♦ *verb* ≠**moderate**: aggravate, arouse, excite, heighten, intensify, provoke, stir ≠**strengthen**: soften

temperament *noun* **1** = **nature**, bent, cast of mind, character, complexion, constitution, disposition, frame of mind, humour, make-up, mettle, outlook, personality, quality, soul, spirit, temper, tendencies, tendency **2** = **excitability**, anger, hot-headedness, impatience, moodiness, moods, petulance, volatility

temperamental *adjective* **1** = **moody**, capricious, easily upset, emotional, erratic, excitable, fiery, highly strung, hot-headed, hypersensitive, impatient, irritable, mercurial, neurotic, passionate, petulant, sensitive, touchy, volatile **2** *Informal* = **unreliable**, erratic, inconsistent, inconstant, undependable, unpredictable **3** = **natural**, congenital, constitutional, inborn, ingrained, inherent, innate
➤ **Antonyms**
≠**moody**: calm, cool-headed, easy-going, even-tempered, level-headed, phlegmatic, unexcitable, unflappable, unperturbable ≠**unreliable**: constant, dependable, reliable, stable, steady

temperance *noun* **1** = **moderation**, continence, discretion, forbearance, restraint, self-control, self-discipline, self-restraint **2**

= **teetotalism**, abstemiousness, abstinence, prohibition, sobriety
➤ **Antonyms**
≠**moderation**: excess, immoderation, intemperance, overindulgence, prodigality

temperate *adjective* **1** = **mild**, agreeable, balmy, calm, clement, cool, fair, gentle, moderate, pleasant, soft **2** = **moderate**, calm, composed, dispassionate, equable, even-tempered, mild, reasonable, self-controlled, self-restrained, sensible, stable
➤ **Antonyms**
≠**mild**: extreme, harsh, inclement, intemperate, severe, torrid ≠**moderate**: intemperate, uncontrolled, undisciplined, unreasonable, unrestrained, wild

tempest *noun Literary* = **storm**, cyclone, gale, hurricane, squall, tornado, typhoon

tempestuous *adjective* **1** = **stormy**, agitated, blustery, breezy, gusty, inclement, raging, squally, turbulent, windy **2** = **passionate**, boisterous, emotional, excited, furious, heated, impassioned, intense, stormy, turbulent, uncontrolled, violent, wild
➤ **Antonyms**
≠**passionate**: calm, peaceful, quiet, serene, still, tranquil, undisturbed, unruffled

temple *noun* = **shrine**, church, holy place, place of worship, sanctuary

tempo *noun* = **pace**, beat, cadence, measure (*Prosody*), metre, pulse, rate, rhythm, speed, time

temporal *adjective* **1** = **secular**, earthly, fleshly, lay, material, mundane, worldly **2** = **temporary**, evanescent, impermanent, momentary, passing, short-lived, transient, transitory

temporarily *adverb* = **briefly**, fleetingly, for a little while, for a moment, for a short time, for a short while, for the moment, for the time being, momentarily, pro tem

temporary *adjective* = **impermanent**, brief, ephemeral, evanescent, fleeting, here today and gone tomorrow, interim, momentary, passing, pro tem, *pro tempore*, provisional, short-lived, transient, transitory
➤ **Antonyms**
durable, enduring, eternal, everlasting, long-lasting, long-term, permanent

temporize *verb* = **play for time**, beat about the bush, be evasive, delay, hum and haw, procrastinate, stall

tempt *verb* **1** = **entice**, coax, decoy, inveigle, invite, lead on, lure, seduce, tantalize **2** = **attract**, allure, appeal to, draw
➤ **Antonyms**
≠**entice**: deter, discourage, dissuade, hinder, inhibit, put off

temptation *noun* **1** = **enticement**,

allurement, bait, coaxing, come-on (*informal*), decoy, inducement, invitation, lure, pull, seduction, snare, tantalization **2** = **appeal**, attraction, attractiveness, draw

tempting *adjective* = **Inviting**, alluring, appetizing, attractive, enticing, mouthwatering, seductive, tantalizing
➤ **Antonyms**
off-putting (*Brit. informal*), unappetizing, unattractive, undesirable, uninviting, untempting

tenable *adjective* = **sound**, arguable, believable, defendable, defensible, justifiable, maintainable, plausible, rational, reasonable, viable
➤ **Antonyms**
indefensible, insupportable, unjustifiable, untenable

tenacious *adjective* **1** = **firm**, clinging, fast, forceful, immovable, iron, strong, tight, unshakable **2** = **stubborn**, adamant, determined, dogged, firm, immovable, inflexible, intransigent, obdurate, obstinate, persistent, resolute, staunch, steadfast, stiff-necked, strong-willed, sure, unswerving, unyielding
➤ **Antonyms**
≠**stubborn**: changeable, flexible, irresolute, vacillating, wavering, yielding

tenacity *noun* **1** = **firmness**, fastness, force, forcefulness, power, strength **2** = **perseverance**, application, determination, diligence, doggedness, firmness, inflexibility, intransigence, obduracy, obstinacy, persistence, resoluteness, resolution, resolve, staunchness, steadfastness, strength of purpose, strength of will, stubbornness
➤ **Antonyms**
≠**firmness**: looseness, powerlessness, slackness, weakness

tenancy *noun* = **lease**, holding, occupancy, occupation, possession, renting, residence

tenant *noun* = **leaseholder**, holder, inhabitant, lessee, occupant, occupier, renter, resident

tend[1] *verb* **1** = **be inclined**, be apt, be biased, be disposed, be liable, be likely, gravitate, have a leaning, have an inclination, have a tendency, incline, lean, trend **2** = **go**, aim, bear, head, lead, make for, move, point

tend[2] *verb* = **take care of**, attend, care for, cater for, control, cultivate, feed, guard, keep, keep an eye on, look after, maintain, manage, minister to, nurse, nurture, protect, see to, serve, wait on, watch, watch over
➤ **Antonyms**
disregard, ignore, neglect, overlook, shirk

tendency *noun* **1** = **inclination**, bent, disposition, leaning, liability, partiality,

penchant, predilection, predisposition,
proclivity, proneness, propensity, readiness,
susceptibility **2 = course**, bearing, bias,
direction, drift, movement, tenor, trend

tender[1] *adjective* **1 = gentle**, affectionate,
amorous, benevolent, caring, compassionate,
considerate, fond, humane, kind, loving,
pitiful, sentimental, softhearted, sympathetic,
tenderhearted, warm, warm-hearted **2
= vulnerable**, immature, impressionable,
inexperienced, raw, sensitive, young,
youthful **3 = sensitive**, aching, acute,
bruised, inflamed, irritated, painful, raw,
smarting, sore
➤ **Antonyms**
≠**gentle**: brutal, cold-hearted, cruel, hard,
hard-hearted, inhuman, insensitive, pitiless,
tough, uncaring, unkind, unsympathetic
≠**vulnerable**: advanced, elderly,
experienced, grown-up, mature, seasoned,
sophisticated, worldly, worldly-wise

tender[2] *verb* **1 = offer**, extend, give, hand
in, present, proffer, propose, put forward,
submit, suggest, volunteer ◆ *noun* **2 = offer**,
bid, estimate, proffer, proposal, submission,
suggestion

tenderness *noun* **1 = gentleness**,
affection, amorousness, care, compassion,
consideration, devotion, fondness,
humaneness, humanity, kindness, liking,
love, mercy, pity, sentimentality,
softheartedness, sympathy,
tenderheartedness, warm-heartedness,
warmth **2 = vulnerability**, immaturity,
impressionableness, inexperience, sensitivity,
youth, youthfulness **3 = soreness**, ache,
aching, bruising, inflammation, irritation,
pain, painfulness, rawness, sensitiveness,
sensitivity, smart
➤ **Antonyms**
≠**gentleness**: cruelty, hardness, harshness,
indifference, insensitivity, unkindness

tenet *noun* **= principle**, article of faith,
belief, canon, conviction, creed, doctrine,
dogma, maxim, precept, rule, teaching, view

tenor *noun* **= direction**, course, drift,
meaning, purport, sense, substance,
tendency, theme, trend

tense *adjective* **1 = nervous**, antsy
(*informal*), anxious, apprehensive, edgy,
fidgety, jittery (*informal*), jumpy, keyed up,
on edge, on tenterhooks, overwrought,
restless, strained, twitchy (*informal*), under
pressure, uptight (*informal*), wired (*slang*),
wound up (*informal*) **2 = exciting**, moving,
nerve-racking, stressful, worrying **3 = tight**,
rigid, strained, stretched, taut ◆ *verb* **4
= tighten**, brace, flex, strain, stretch, tauten
➤ **Antonyms**
adjective ≠**nervous**: calm, collected,
cool-headed, easy-going, self-possessed,

serene, unconcerned, unruffled, unworried
≠**exciting**: boring, dull, uninteresting
≠**tight**: flaccid, flexible, limp, loose, pliant,
relaxed ◆ *verb* ≠**tighten**: loosen, relax,
slacken

tension *noun* **1 = strain**, anxiety,
apprehension, edginess, hostility,
nervousness, pressure, stress, suspense, the
jitters (*informal*), unease **2 = tightness**,
pressure, rigidity, stiffness, straining, stress,
stretching, tautness
➤ **Antonyms**
≠**strain**: calmness, peacefulness, relaxation,
restfulness, serenity, tranquillity

tentative *adjective* **1 = unconfirmed**,
conjectural, experimental, indefinite,
provisional, speculative, unsettled **2
= hesitant**, cautious, diffident, doubtful,
faltering, timid, uncertain, undecided, unsure
➤ **Antonyms**
≠**unconfirmed**: conclusive, confirmed,
decisive, definite, final, fixed, resolved,
settled ≠**hesitant**: assured, bold, certain,
confident, unhesitating

tenuous *adjective* **1 = slight**, doubtful,
dubious, flimsy, insignificant, insubstantial,
nebulous, questionable, shaky, sketchy, weak
2 = fine, attenuated, delicate, gossamer, slim
➤ **Antonyms**
≠**slight**: significant, solid, sound, strong,
substantial

tenure *noun* **= holding**, occupancy,
occupation, possession, residence, tenancy,
term, time

tepid *adjective* **1 = lukewarm**, slightly warm,
warmish **2 = half-hearted**, apathetic, cool,
indifferent, lukewarm, unenthusiastic
➤ **Antonyms**
≠**half-hearted**: animated, eager,
enthusiastic, excited, keen, passionate,
vibrant, zealous

tergiversate *verb Formal* **1 = prevaricate**,
beat about the bush, dodge, equivocate,
fence, hedge, pussyfoot (*informal*), vacillate
2 = change sides, defect, desert, go over to
the other side, renege, turn traitor

term *noun* **1 = word**, appellation,
denomination, designation, expression,
locution, name, phrase, title **2 = period**,
duration, interval, season, space, span, spell,
time, while **3 = session**, course ◆ *verb* **4
= call**, denominate, designate, dub, entitle,
label, name, style

terminal *adjective* **1 = fatal**, deadly,
incurable, killing, lethal, mortal **2 = final**,
bounding, concluding, extreme, last,
limiting, ultimate, utmost ◆ *noun* **3
= terminus**, depot, end of the line, station
➤ **Antonyms**
adjective ≠**final**: beginning, commencing,

first, initial, introductory, opening

terminate *verb* = **end**, abort, axe
(*informal*), bring *or* come to an end, cease,
close, complete, conclude, cut off,
discontinue, expire, finish, issue, lapse, put
an end to, stop, wind up
➤ **Antonyms**
begin, commence, inaugurate, initiate,
instigate, introduce, open, start

termination *noun* = **ending**, abortion,
cessation, close, completion, conclusion,
consequence, discontinuation, effect, end,
expiry, finish, wind-up
➤ **Antonyms**
beginning, commencement, inauguration,
initiation, opening, start

terminology *noun* = **language**, argot,
cant, jargon, lingo (*informal*), nomenclature,
patois, phraseology, terms, vocabulary

terminus *noun* = **end of the line**, depot,
garage, last stop, station

terms *plural noun* 1 = **language**, manner of
speaking, phraseology, terminology 2
= **conditions**, particulars, provisions,
provisos, qualifications, specifications,
stipulations 3 = **price**, charges, fee, payment,
rates 4 = **relationship**, footing, position,
relations, standing, status 5 **come to terms
with** = **learn to live with**, be reconciled to,
come to accept

terrain *noun* = **ground**, country, going,
land, landscape, topography

terrestrial *adjective* = **earthly**, global,
worldly

terrible *adjective* 1 = **serious**, bad,
dangerous, desperate, extreme, severe 2
Informal = **bad**, abhorrent, abysmal, awful,
beastly (*informal*), dire, dreadful, duff (*Brit.
informal*), foul, frightful, from hell
(*informal*), godawful (*slang*), hateful,
hideous, loathsome, obnoxious, obscene,
odious, offensive, poor, repulsive, revolting,
rotten (*informal*), unpleasant, vile 3
= **fearful**, appalling, awful, dread, dreaded,
dreadful, frightful, gruesome, harrowing,
hellacious (*U.S. slang*), horrendous, horrible,
horrid, horrifying, monstrous, shocking,
terrifying, unspeakable
➤ **Antonyms**
≠**serious**: harmless, insignificant, mild,
moderate, paltry, small ≠**bad**: admirable,
brilliant, delightful, excellent, fine, great,
magic, noteworthy, pleasant, remarkable,
super, superb, terrific, very good, wonderful
≠**fearful**: calming, comforting, encouraging,
reassuring, settling, soothing

terribly *adverb* = **extremely**, awfully
(*informal*), decidedly, desperately,
exceedingly, gravely, greatly, much,
seriously, thoroughly, very

terrific *adjective* 1 = **great**, awesome, awful,
dreadful, enormous, excessive, extreme,
fearful, fierce, gigantic, harsh, horrific, huge,
intense, monstrous, severe, terrible,
tremendous 2 *Informal* = **excellent**,
amazing, awesome (*slang*), boffo (*slang*),
breathtaking, brilliant, cracking (*Brit.
informal*), fabulous (*informal*), fantastic
(*informal*), fine, great (*informal*),
magnificent, marvellous, mean (*slang*),
outstanding, sensational (*informal*),
smashing (*informal*), stupendous, super
(*informal*), superb, very good, wonderful
➤ **Antonyms**
≠**great**: insignificant, mild, moderate, paltry
≠**excellent**: appalling, awful, bad, dreadful,
terrible

terrified *adjective* = **frightened**, alarmed,
appalled, frightened out of one's wits,
horrified, horror-struck, intimidated,
panic-stricken, petrified, scared, scared stiff,
scared to death, shocked, terror-stricken

terrify *verb* = **frighten**, alarm, appal, fill with
terror, frighten out of one's wits, horrify,
intimidate, make one's blood run cold, make
one's flesh creep, make one's hair stand on
end, petrify, scare, shock, terrorize

territory *noun* = **district**, area, country,
domain, land, patch, province, region,
sector, state, terrain, tract, turf (*U.S. slang*),
zone

terror *noun* 1 = **fear**, alarm, anxiety, awe,
consternation, dismay, dread, fright, horror,
intimidation, panic, shock 2 = **scourge**,
bogeyman, bugbear, devil, fiend, monster

terrorize *verb* 1 = **oppress**, browbeat, bully,
coerce, intimidate, menace, threaten 2
= **terrify**, alarm, appal, fill with terror,
frighten, frighten out of one's wits, horrify,
intimidate, make one's blood run cold, make
one's flesh creep, make one's hair stand on
end, petrify, scare, shock, strike terror into

terse *adjective* 1 = **concise**, aphoristic, brief,
clipped, compact, condensed, crisp,
elliptical, epigrammatic, gnomic, laconic,
monosyllabic, neat, pithy, short, succinct, to
the point 2 = **curt**, abrupt, brusque, short,
snappy
➤ **Antonyms**
≠**concise**: circumlocutory, confused,
discursive, lengthy, long-winded, rambling,
roundabout, vague, verbose, wordy ≠**curt**:
chatty, polite

test *verb* 1 = **check**, analyse, assay, assess,
examine, experiment, investigate, prove, put
to the test, research, try, try out, verify
◆ *noun* 2 = **examination**, acid test, analysis,
assessment, check, evaluation, investigation,
proof, research, trial

testament *noun* 1 = **proof**, attestation,

demonstration, evidence, testimony, tribute, witness **2** = **will**, last wishes

testicles *plural noun* = **balls** (*taboo slang*), bollocks *or* ballocks (*taboo slang*), nuts (*taboo slang*)

testify *verb* = **bear witness**, affirm, assert, attest, certify, corroborate, declare, give testimony, show, state, swear, vouch, witness
➤ **Antonyms**
belie, contradict, controvert, disprove, dispute, gainsay (*archaic or literary*), oppose

testimonial *noun* = **tribute**, certificate, character, commendation, credential, endorsement, recommendation, reference

testimony *noun* **1** = **evidence**, affidavit, affirmation, attestation, avowal, declaration, deposition, statement, submission **2** = **proof**, corroboration, demonstration, evidence, indication, manifestation, support, verification

testing *adjective* = **difficult**, arduous, challenging, demanding, exacting, rigorous, searching, strenuous, taxing, tough
➤ **Antonyms**
easy, friendly, gentle, simple, straightforward, undemanding

testy *adjective* = **irritable**, bad-tempered, cantankerous, cross, fretful, grumpy, impatient, irascible, peevish, quick-tempered, ratty (*Brit. & N.Z. informal*), short-tempered, snappish, snappy, tetchy, touchy

tetchy *adjective* = **irritable**, bad-tempered, cantankerous, cross, fretful, grumpy, impatient, irascible, peevish, quick-tempered, ratty (*Brit. & N.Z. informal*), short-tempered, snappish, snappy, testy, touchy

tête-à-tête *noun* **1** = **private conversation**, chat, confab (*informal*), cosy chat, private word, talk ♦ *adverb* **2** = **in private**, intimately, privately

tether *noun* **1** = **rope**, chain, fetter, halter, lead, leash, restraint **2 at the end of one's tether** = **exasperated**, at one's wits' end, exhausted ♦ *verb* **3** = **tie**, bind, chain, fasten, fetter, secure

text *noun* **1** = **contents**, body, main body, matter **2** = **words**, wording **3** = **passage**, paragraph, sentence, verse **4** = **reference book**, source, textbook

texture *noun* = **feel**, character, composition, consistency, constitution, fabric, grain, make, quality, structure, surface, tissue, weave

thank *verb* = **say thank you**, express gratitude, show gratitude, show one's appreciation

thankful *adjective* = **grateful**, appreciative, beholden, indebted, in (someone's) debt, obliged, pleased, relieved
➤ **Antonyms**
thankless, unappreciative, ungrateful

thankless *adjective* = **unrewarding**, fruitless, unappreciated, unprofitable, unrequited, useless
➤ **Antonyms**
fruitful, productive, profitable, rewarding, useful, worthwhile

thanks *plural noun* **1** = **gratitude**, acknowledgment, appreciation, credit, gratefulness, recognition, thanksgiving **2 thanks to** = **because of**, as a result of, by reason of, due to, owing to, through

thaw *verb* = **melt**, defrost, dissolve, liquefy, soften, unfreeze, warm
➤ **Antonyms**
chill, congeal, freeze, harden, solidify, stiffen

theatrical *adjective* **1** = **dramatic**, dramaturgic, Thespian **2** = **exaggerated**, actorly *or* actressy, affected, artificial, camp (*informal*), dramatic, histrionic, mannered, melodramatic, ostentatious, overdone, showy, stagy
➤ **Antonyms**
≠**exaggerated:** natural, plain, simple, straightforward, unaffected, unassuming, unexaggerated, unpretentious, unsophisticated

theft *noun* = **stealing**, embezzlement, fraud, larceny, pilfering, purloining, rip-off (*slang*), robbery, swindling, thievery, thieving

theme *noun* **1** = **subject**, argument, idea, keynote, matter, subject matter, text, thesis, topic **2** = **motif**, leitmotif, recurrent image, unifying idea **3** = **essay**, composition, dissertation, exercise, paper

theological *adjective* = **religious**, divine, doctrinal, ecclesiastical

theorem *noun* = **proposition**, formula, hypothesis, principle, rule, statement

theoretical *adjective* = **abstract**, academic, conjectural, hypothetical, ideal, impractical, notional, pure, speculative
➤ **Antonyms**
applied, experiential, factual, practical, realistic

theorize *verb* = **speculate**, conjecture, formulate, guess, hypothesize, project, propound, suppose

theory *noun* **1** = **hypothesis**, assumption, conjecture, guess, presumption, speculation, supposition, surmise, thesis **2** = **system**, philosophy, plan, proposal, scheme
➤ **Antonyms**
≠**hypothesis:** certainty, experience, fact, practice, reality

therapeutic *adjective* = **beneficial**, corrective, curative, good, healing, remedial, restorative, salutary

> ➤ **Antonyms**
adverse, damaging, destructive, detrimental, harmful

therapist *noun* = **healer**, physician

therapy *noun* = **remedy**, cure, healing, remedial treatment, treatment

therefore *adverb* = **consequently**, accordingly, as a result, ergo, for that reason, hence, so, then, thence, thus, whence

thesaurus *noun* = **wordbook**, dictionary, encyclopedia, wordfinder

thesis *noun* **1** = **dissertation**, composition, disquisition, essay, monograph, paper, treatise **2** = **proposition**, contention, hypothesis, idea, opinion, proposal, theory, view **3** *Logic* = **premise**, assumption, postulate, proposition, statement, supposition, surmise

thick *adjective* **1** = **wide**, broad, bulky, deep, fat, solid, substantial **2** = **dense**, close, clotted, coagulated, compact, concentrated, condensed, crowded, deep, heavy, impenetrable, opaque **3** = **full**, abundant, brimming, bristling, bursting, chock-a-block, chock-full, covered, crawling, numerous, packed, replete, swarming, teeming **4** *Informal* = **stupid**, brainless, dense, dim-witted (*informal*), dopey (*informal*), dozy (*Brit. informal*), dull, dumb-ass (*informal*), insensitive, moronic, obtuse, slow, slow-witted, thickheaded **5** = **strong**, broad, decided, distinct, marked, pronounced, rich **6** *As in* **thick as thieves** *Informal* = **friendly**, chummy (*informal*), close, devoted, familiar, inseparable, intimate, matey *or* maty (*Brit. informal*), on good terms, pally (*informal*) **7** *a bit thick* *Brit. informal* = **unreasonable**, excessive, over the score (*informal*), too much, unfair, unjust ◆ *noun* **8** = **middle**, centre, heart, midst
> ➤ **Antonyms**
adjective ≠**wide**: narrow, slight, slim, thin ≠**dense**: clear, diluted, runny, thin, watery, weak ≠**full**: bare, clear, devoid of, empty, free from, sparse, thin ≠**stupid**: articulate, brainy, bright, clever, intellectual, intelligent, quick-witted, sharp, smart ≠**strong**: faint, slight, vague, weak ≠**friendly**: antagonistic, distant, hostile, unfriendly

thicken *verb* = **set**, cake, clot, coagulate, condense, congeal, deepen, jell
> ➤ **Antonyms**
dilute, thin, water down, weaken

thicket *noun* = **wood**, brake, coppice, copse, covert, grove

thickhead *noun* *Slang* = **idiot**, berk (*Brit. slang*), blockhead, bonehead (*slang*), chump, dimwit (*informal*), divvy (*Brit.*

slang), dolt, dope (*informal*), dork (*slang*), dumb-ass (*slang*), dummy (*slang*), dunce, dunderhead, fool, imbecile, lamebrain (*informal*), moron, numbskull *or* numskull, numpty (*Scot. informal*), pillock (*Brit. slang*), plonker (*slang*), prat (*slang*), twit (*informal, chiefly Brit.*), wally (*slang*)

thickheaded *adjective* = **idiotic**, blockheaded, brainless, dense, dim-witted (*informal*), doltish, dopey (*informal*), dozy (*Brit. informal*), dumb-ass (*informal*), moronic, obtuse, slow, slow-witted, stupid, thick

thickset *adjective* **1** = **stocky**, beefy (*informal*), brawny, bulky, burly, heavy, muscular, powerfully built, strong, stubby, sturdy, well-built **2** = **dense**, closely packed, densely planted, solid, thick
> ➤ **Antonyms**
≠**stocky**: angular, bony, gangling, gaunt, lanky, rawboned, scraggy, scrawny, weedy (*informal*)

thick-skinned *adjective* = **insensitive**, callous, hardened, impervious, stolid, tough, unfeeling, unsusceptible
> ➤ **Antonyms**
concerned, feeling, sensitive, tender, thin-skinned, touchy

thief *noun* = **robber**, bandit, burglar, crook (*informal*), embezzler, housebreaker, larcenist, mugger (*informal*), pickpocket, pilferer, plunderer, shoplifter, stealer

thieve *verb* = **steal**, blag (*slang*), embezzle, filch, knock off (*slang*), lift (*informal*), misappropriate, nick (*slang, chiefly Brit.*), pilfer, pinch (*informal*), plunder, poach, purloin, rip off (*slang*), rob, run off with, swipe (*slang*)

thievish *adjective* = **thieving**, larcenous, light-fingered, rapacious

thin *adjective* **1** = **narrow**, attenuate, attenuated, fine **2** = **slim**, bony, emaciated, lank, lanky, lean, light, meagre, scraggy, scrawny, skeletal, skin and bone, skinny, slender, slight, spare, spindly, thin as a rake, undernourished, underweight **3** = **meagre**, deficient, scanty, scarce, scattered, skimpy, sparse, wispy **4** = **fine**, delicate, diaphanous, filmy, flimsy, gossamer, see-through, sheer, translucent, transparent, unsubstantial **5** = **watery**, diluted, runny, weak **6** = **unconvincing**, feeble, flimsy, inadequate, insufficient, lame, poor, scant, scanty, slight, superficial, unsubstantial, weak ◆ *verb* **7** = **reduce**, attenuate, cut back, dilute, diminish, prune, rarefy, refine, trim, water down, weaken, weed out
> ➤ **Antonyms**
adjective ≠**narrow**: heavy, thick ≠**slim**: bulky, corpulent, fat, heavy, obese, stout ≠**meagre**: abundant, adequate, plentiful,

profuse ≠**fine**: bulky, dense, heavy, strong, substantial, thick ≠**watery**: concentrated, dense, strong, thick, viscous ≠**unconvincing**: adequate, convincing, strong, substantial

thing noun 1 = **object**, affair, article, being, body, circumstance, entity, fact, matter, something, substance 2 = **factor**, aspect, detail, facet, feature, item, particular, point, statement 3 = **happening**, act, deed, event, eventuality, feat, incident, occurrence, phenomenon, proceeding 4 = **device**, apparatus, contrivance, gadget, implement, instrument, machine, means, mechanism, tool 5 Informal = **obsession**, attitude, bee in one's bonnet, fetish, fixation, hang-up (informal), mania, phobia, preoccupation, quirk 6 **things** = **possessions**, baggage, belongings, bits and pieces, clobber (Brit. slang), clothes, effects, equipment, gear, goods, impedimenta, luggage, odds and ends, paraphernalia, stuff

think verb 1 = **believe**, conceive, conclude, consider, deem, determine, esteem, estimate, guess (informal, chiefly U.S. & Canad.), hold, imagine, judge, reckon, regard, suppose, surmise 2 = **ponder**, brood, cerebrate, cogitate, consider, contemplate, deliberate, meditate, mull over, muse, obsess, rack one's brains, reason, reflect, revolve, ruminate, turn over in one's mind, weigh up 3 **think much** or **a lot of** = **have a high opinion of**, admire, attach importance to, esteem, hold in high regard, rate (slang), respect, set store by, think highly of, value ♦ noun 4 Informal = **consideration**, assessment, contemplation, deliberation, look, reflection

thinker noun = **philosopher**, brain (informal), intellect (informal), mastermind, sage, theorist, wise man

thinking noun 1 = **reasoning**, assessment, conclusions, conjecture, idea, judgment, opinion, outlook, philosophy, position, theory, thoughts, view ♦ adjective 2 = **thoughtful**, contemplative, intelligent, meditative, philosophical, rational, reasoning, reflective, sophisticated

think over verb = **consider**, consider the pros and cons of, contemplate, give thought to, mull over, ponder, weigh up

think up verb = **devise**, come up with, concoct, contrive, create, dream up, imagine, improvise, invent, manufacture, trump up, visualize

thin-skinned adjective = **easily hurt**, hypersensitive, quick to take offence, sensitive, susceptible, touchy, vulnerable
➤ **Antonyms**
callous, hard, heartless, insensitive, obdurate, stolid, thick-skinned, tough, unfeeling

third-rate adjective = **mediocre**, bad, indifferent, inferior, low-grade, no great shakes (informal), not much cop (informal), poor, poor-quality, ropey or ropy (Brit. informal), shoddy

thirst noun 1 = **thirstiness**, craving to drink, drought, dryness 2 = **craving**, ache, appetite, desire, eagerness, hankering, hunger, keenness, longing, lust, passion, yearning, yen (informal)
➤ **Antonyms**
≠**craving**: apathy, aversion, disinclination, dislike, distaste, loathing, revulsion

thirsty adjective 1 = **parched**, arid, dehydrated, dry 2 with **for** = **eager**, athirst, avid, burning, craving, desirous, dying, greedy, hankering, hungry, itching, longing, lusting, thirsting, yearning

thorn noun 1 = **prickle**, barb, spike, spine 2 **thorn in one's side** or **flesh** = **irritation**, affliction, annoyance, bane, bother, curse, hassle (informal), irritant, nuisance, pest, plague, scourge, torment, trouble

thorny adjective 1 = **prickly**, barbed, bristling with thorns, bristly, pointed, sharp, spiky, spiny 2 = **troublesome**, awkward, difficult, hard, irksome, problematic(al), sticky (informal), ticklish, tough, trying, unpleasant, worrying

thorough adjective 1 = **careful**, all-embracing, all-inclusive, assiduous, complete, comprehensive, conscientious, efficient, exhaustive, full, in-depth, intensive, leaving no stone unturned, meticulous, painstaking, scrupulous, sweeping 2 = **complete**, absolute, arrant, deep-dyed (usually derogatory), downright, entire, out-and-out, outright, perfect, pure, sheer, total, unmitigated, unqualified, utter
➤ **Antonyms**
≠**careful**: careless, cursory, half-hearted, haphazard, lackadaisical, sloppy ≠**complete**: imperfect, incomplete, partial, superficial

thoroughbred adjective = **purebred**, blood, full-blooded, of unmixed stock, pedigree, pure-blooded
➤ **Antonyms**
crossbred, crossed, half-breed, hybrid, mongrel, of mixed breed

thoroughfare noun = **road**, access, avenue, highway, passage, passageway, roadway, street, way

thoroughly adverb 1 = **carefully**, assiduously, completely, comprehensively, conscientiously, efficiently, exhaustively, from top to bottom, fully, inside out, intensively, leaving no stone unturned, meticulously, painstakingly, scrupulously, sweepingly, through and through, throughout 2 = **completely**, absolutely,

downright, entirely, perfectly, quite, totally, to the full, to the hilt, utterly, without reservation
➤ Antonyms
≠carefully: carelessly, cursorily, half-heartedly, haphazardly, lackadaisically, sloppily ≠ completely: imperfectly, incompletely, in part, partly, somewhat, superficially

though *conjunction* 1 = although, albeit, despite the fact that, even if, even supposing, even though, granted, notwithstanding, tho' (*U.S. or poetic*), while ♦ *adverb* 2 = nevertheless, all the same, for all that, however, nonetheless, notwithstanding, still, yet

thought *noun* 1 = thinking, brainwork, cogitation, consideration, contemplation, deliberation, introspection, meditation, musing, reflection, rumination 2 = idea, assessment, belief, concept, conception, conclusion, conjecture, conviction, estimation, judgment, notion, opinion, thinking, view 3 = consideration, attention, heed, regard, scrutiny, study 4 = intention, aim, design, idea, notion, object, plan, purpose 5 = expectation, anticipation, aspiration, dream, hope, prospect

thoughtful *adjective* 1 = considerate, attentive, caring, helpful, kind, kindly, solicitous, unselfish 2 = well-thought-out, astute, canny, careful, cautious, circumspect, deliberate, discreet, heedful, mindful, prudent 3 = reflective, contemplative, deliberative, in a brown study, introspective, lost in thought, meditative, musing, pensive, rapt, ruminative, serious, studious, thinking, wistful
➤ Antonyms
≠considerate: cold-hearted, impolite, inconsiderate, insensitive, neglectful, selfish, uncaring ≠well-thought-out: flippant, heedless, irresponsible, rash, thoughtless, unthinking ≠reflective: extrovert, shallow, superficial

thoughtless *adjective* = inconsiderate, impolite, indiscreet, insensitive, rude, selfish, tactless, uncaring, undiplomatic, unkind
➤ Antonyms
attentive, considerate, diplomatic, tactful, thoughtful, unselfish

thrall *noun* = slavery, bondage, enslavement, servitude, subjection, subjugation

thrash *verb* 1 = beat, belt (*informal*), birch, cane, flagellate, flog, give (someone) a (good) hiding (*informal*), horsewhip, leather, scourge, spank, tan (*slang*), whip 2 = defeat, beat, beat (someone) hollow (*Brit. informal*), blow out of the water (*slang*), clobber (*slang*), crush, drub, lick (*informal*),

make mincemeat of (*informal*), overwhelm, paste (*slang*), rout, run rings around (*informal*), slaughter (*informal*), stuff (*slang*), tank (*slang*), trounce, wipe the floor with (*informal*) 3 = thresh, flail, heave, jerk, plunge, squirm, toss, toss and turn, writhe

thrashing *noun* 1 = beating, belting (*informal*), caning, drubbing, flogging, hiding (*informal*), lashing, punishment, tanning (*slang*), whipping 2 = defeat, beating, drubbing, hammering (*informal*), hiding (*informal*), pasting (*slang*), rout, trouncing

thrash out *verb* = settle, argue out, debate, discuss, have out, resolve, solve, talk over

thread *noun* 1 = strand, cotton, fibre, filament, line, string, yarn 2 = theme, course, direction, drift, plot, story line, strain, train of thought ♦ *verb* 3 = string 4 = pass, ease, inch, meander, pick (one's way), squeeze through

threadbare *adjective* 1 = shabby, down at heel, frayed, old, ragged, scruffy, tattered, tatty, worn, worn-out 2 = hackneyed, clichéd, cliché-ridden, common, commonplace, conventional, corny (*slang*), familiar, overused, stale, stereotyped, stock, tired, trite, well-worn
➤ Antonyms
≠shabby: brand-new, good, new, smart, unused, well-preserved ≠hackneyed: different, fresh, new, novel, original, unconventional, unfamiliar, unusual

threat *noun* 1 = menace, intimidatory remark, threatening remark 2 = warning, foreboding, foreshadowing, omen, portent, presage, writing on the wall 3 = danger, hazard, menace, peril, risk

threaten *verb* 1 = intimidate, browbeat, bully, lean on (*slang*), make threats to, menace, pressurize, terrorize, warn 2 = endanger, imperil, jeopardize, put at risk, put in jeopardy, put on the line 3 = foreshadow, be imminent, be in the air, be in the offing, forebode, impend, portend, presage, warn
➤ Antonyms
≠intimidate, endanger: defend, guard, protect, safeguard, shelter, shield

threatening *adjective* 1 = menacing, bullying, intimidatory, terrorizing 2 = ominous, baleful, bodeful, forbidding, grim, inauspicious, sinister
➤ Antonyms
≠ominous: auspicious, bright, comforting, encouraging, favourable, promising, propitious, reassuring

threesome *noun* = trio, triad, trilogy,

trinity, triple, triplet, triptych, triumvirate

threnody *noun Formal* = **lament**, coronach (*Scot. & Irish*), dirge, elegy, funeral ode, keen, requiem

threshold *noun* **1** = **entrance**, door, doorstep, doorway **2** = **start**, beginning, brink, dawn, inception, opening, outset, starting point, verge **3** = **minimum**, lower limit
➤ **Antonyms**
≠ **start**: close, decline, end, finish, twilight

thrift *noun* = **economy**, carefulness, frugality, good husbandry, parsimony, prudence, saving, thriftiness
➤ **Antonyms**
carelessness, extravagance, prodigality, profligacy, recklessness, squandering, waste

thriftless *adjective* = **spendthrift**, extravagant, improvident, imprudent, lavish, prodigal, profligate, unthrifty, wasteful
➤ **Antonyms**
careful, economical, frugal, provident, prudent, sparing, thrifty

thrifty *adjective* = **economical**, careful, frugal, parsimonious, provident, prudent, saving, sparing
➤ **Antonyms**
extravagant, free-spending, generous, improvident, prodigal, spendthrift, wasteful

thrill *noun* **1** = **pleasure**, buzz (*slang*), charge (*slang*), flush of excitement, glow, kick (*informal*), sensation, stimulation, tingle, titillation **2** = **trembling**, flutter, fluttering, quiver, shudder, throb, tremor, vibration ◆ *verb* **3** = **excite**, arouse, electrify, flush, get a charge (*slang*), get a kick (*informal*), move, send (*slang*), stimulate, stir, tingle, titillate **4** = **tremble**, flutter, quake, quiver, shake, shudder, throb, vibrate
➤ **Antonyms**
noun ≠ **pleasure**: boredom, dreariness, dullness, ennui, monotony, tedium

thrilling *adjective* **1** = **exciting**, electrifying, gripping, hair-raising, riveting, rousing, sensational, sexy (*informal*), stimulating, stirring **2** = **trembling**, quaking, shaking, shivering, shuddering, vibrating
➤ **Antonyms**
≠ **exciting**: boring, dreary, dull, monotonous, quiet, staid, tedious, tiresome, uninteresting, unmoving

thrive *verb* = **prosper**, advance, bloom, boom, burgeon, develop, do well, flourish, get on, grow, grow rich, increase, succeed
➤ **Antonyms**
decline, droop, fail, languish, perish, shrivel, stagnate, wane, wilt, wither

thriving *adjective* = **successful**, blooming, booming, burgeoning, developing, doing well, flourishing, going strong, growing,

healthy, prosperous, well
➤ **Antonyms**
ailing, bankrupt, failing, impoverished, languishing, on the rocks, poverty-stricken, unsuccessful, withering

throaty *adjective* = **hoarse**, deep, gruff, guttural, husky, low, thick

throb *verb* **1** = **pulsate**, beat, palpitate, pound, pulse, thump, vibrate ◆ *noun* **2** = **pulse**, beat, palpitation, pounding, pulsating, thump, thumping, vibration

throes *plural noun* **1** = **pains**, convulsions, fit, pangs, paroxysm, spasms, stabs **2 in the throes of** = **struggling with**, in the midst of, in the pangs of, suffering from

throng *noun* **1** = **crowd**, assemblage, congregation, crush, horde, host, jam, mass, mob, multitude, pack, press, swarm ◆ *verb* **2** = **crowd**, congregate, converge, cram, fill, flock, herd, jam, mill around, pack, swarm around
➤ **Antonyms**
verb ≠ **crowd**: break up, disband, dispel, disperse, scatter, separate, spread out

throttle *verb* **1** = **strangle**, choke, garrotte, strangulate **2** = **suppress**, control, gag, inhibit, silence, stifle

through *preposition* **1** = **from one side to the other of**, between, by, from end to end of, in and out of, past **2** = **because of**, as a consequence *or* result of, by means of, by virtue of, by way of, using, via, with the help of **3** = **during**, in, in the middle of, throughout ◆ *adjective* **4** *with* **with** = **finished**, done, having had enough of **5** = **completed**, done, ended, finished, terminated ◆ *adverb* **6 through and through** = **completely**, altogether, entirely, fully, thoroughly, totally, to the core, unreservedly, utterly, wholly

throughout *preposition* **1** = **through the whole of**, all over, all through, during the whole of, everywhere in, for the duration of, right through ◆ *adverb* **2** = **from start to finish**, all the time, all through, from beginning to end, from the start, right through, the whole time

throw *verb* **1** = **hurl**, cast, chuck (*informal*), fling, heave, launch, lob (*informal*), pitch, project, propel, put, send, shy, sling, toss **2** = **bring down**, dislodge, fell, floor, hurl to the ground, overturn, unseat, upset **3** *Informal* = **confuse**, astonish, baffle, confound, disconcert, dumbfound, faze, put one off one's stroke, throw off, throw one off one's stride ◆ *noun* **4** = **toss**, cast, fling, heave, lob (*informal*), pitch, put, shy, sling

throwaway *adjective Chiefly Brit.* = **casual**, careless, offhand, passing, understated

throw away *verb* **1** = **discard**, bin

(*informal*), cast off, chuck (*informal*), dispense with, dispose of, ditch (*slang*), dump (*informal*), get rid of, jettison, junk (*informal*), reject, scrap, throw out **2** = **waste**, blow (*slang*), fail to make use of, fritter away, lose, squander
➤ **Antonyms**
≠**discard:** conserve, keep, preserve, rescue, retain, retrieve, salvage, save

throw off *verb Literary* = **free oneself of**, abandon, cast off, discard, drop, rid oneself of, shake off

throw out *verb* **1** = **discard**, bin (*informal*), cast off, chuck (*informal*), dispense with, ditch (*slang*), dump (*informal*), jettison, junk (*informal*), reject, scrap, throw away **2** = **expel**, dismiss, eject, evict, get rid of, kick out (*informal*), oust, show one the door, turf out (*Brit. informal*)

throw over *verb Old-fashioned* = **abandon**, break with, chuck (*informal*), desert, drop (*informal*), finish with, forsake, jilt, leave, split up with, walk out on (*informal*)

throw up *verb* **1** *Informal* = **vomit**, barf (*U.S. slang*), be sick, bring up, chuck (up) (*slang, chiefly U.S.*), chunder (*slang, chiefly Austral.*), heave, puke (*slang*), regurgitate, retch, spew **2** = **give up**, abandon, chuck (*informal*), jack in, leave, quit, relinquish, renounce, resign from, step down from (*informal*) **3** = **throw together**, jerry-build **4** = **produce**, bring forward, bring to light, bring to the surface, reveal

thrust *verb* **1** = **push**, butt, drive, force, impel, jam, plunge, poke, press, prod, propel, ram, shove, urge **2** = **stab**, jab, lunge, pierce, stick **3** = **shove**, elbow *or* shoulder one's way, push ♦ *noun* **4** = **push**, drive, lunge, poke, prod, shove, stab **5** = **momentum**, impetus, motive force, motive power, propulsive force

thud *noun, verb* = **thump**, clunk, crash, knock, smack, wallop (*informal*)

thug *noun* = **ruffian**, bruiser (*informal*), bully boy, gangster, heavy (*slang*), hooligan, mugger (*informal*), tough, tsotsi (*S. African*)

thumb *noun* **1** = **pollex 2 all thumbs** = **clumsy**, butterfingered (*informal*), cack-handed (*informal*), ham-fisted (*informal*), inept, maladroit **3 thumbs down** = **disapproval**, no, rebuff, refusal, rejection **4 thumbs up** = **approval**, acceptance, affirmation, encouragement, go-ahead (*informal*), green light, O.K. *or* okay (*informal*), yes ♦ *verb* **5** = **handle**, dog-ear, finger, mark **6** = **hitch** (*informal*), hitchhike **7 thumb one's nose at** = **show contempt for**, be contemptuous of, cock a snook at, flout, laugh in the face of, show disrespect

to **8 thumb through** = **flick through**, browse through, flip through, glance at, leaf through, riffle through, run one's eye over, scan the pages of, skim through, turn over

thumbnail *adjective* = **brief**, compact, concise, pithy, quick, short, succinct

thump *noun* **1** = **thud**, bang, clunk, crash, thwack **2** = **blow**, clout (*informal*), knock, punch, rap, smack, swipe, wallop (*informal*), whack ♦ *verb* **3** = **thud**, bang, crash, thwack **4** = **strike**, batter, beat, belabour, clobber (*slang*), clout (*informal*), hit, knock, pound, punch, rap, smack, swipe, thrash, wallop (*informal*), whack **5** = **throb**, beat

thumping *adjective Slang* = **huge**, colossal, enormous, excessive, gargantuan, gigantic, great, impressive, massive, monumental, terrific, titanic, tremendous, whopping (*informal*)
➤ **Antonyms**
inconsequential, insignificant, meagre, measly (*informal*), negligible, paltry, petty, piddling (*informal*), trifling, trivial

thunder *noun* **1** = **rumble**, boom, booming, cracking, crash, crashing, explosion, pealing, rumbling ♦ *verb* **2** = **rumble**, blast, boom, clap, crack, crash, explode, peal, resound, reverberate, roar **3** = **shout**, bark, bellow, roar, yell

thundering *adjective Old-fashioned slang* = **great**, enormous, excessive, monumental, remarkable, unmitigated, utter

thunderous *adjective* = **loud**, booming, deafening, ear-splitting, noisy, resounding, roaring, tumultuous

thunderstruck *adjective* = **amazed**, aghast, astonished, astounded, bowled over (*informal*), dazed, dumbfounded, flabbergasted (*informal*), floored (*informal*), flummoxed, gobsmacked (*Brit. slang*), knocked for six (*informal*), left speechless, nonplussed, open-mouthed, shocked, staggered, struck dumb, stunned, taken aback

thus *adverb* **1** = **therefore**, accordingly, consequently, ergo, for this reason, hence, on that account, so, then **2** = **in this way**, as follows, in this fashion, in this manner, like so, like this, so, to such a degree

thwack *verb* **1** = **smack**, bash (*informal*), beat, clout (*informal*), hit, swipe, thump, wallop (*informal*), whack ♦ *noun* **2** = **smack**, bash (*informal*), blow, clout (*informal*), swipe, thump, wallop (*informal*), whack

thwart *verb* = **frustrate**, balk, check, defeat, foil, hinder, impede, obstruct, oppose, outwit, prevent, put a spoke in someone's wheel (*informal*), snooker, stop, stymie
➤ **Antonyms**
aggravate, aid, assist, encourage, exacerbate,

facilitate, hasten, help, intensify, support

tic *noun* = **twitch**, jerk, spasm

tick[1] *noun* **1** = **mark**, dash, stroke **2** = **tapping**, clack, click, clicking, tap, ticktock **3** *Brit. informal* = **moment**, flash, instant, jiffy (*informal*), minute, sec (*informal*), second, shake (*informal*), split second, trice, twinkling ♦ *verb* **4** = **mark**, check off, choose, indicate, mark off, select **5** = **tap**, clack, click, ticktock **6 what makes someone tick** *Informal* = **motivation**, drive, motive, *raison d'être*

tick[2] *noun Brit. informal* = **credit**, account, deferred payment, the slate (*Brit. informal*)

ticket *noun* **1** = **voucher**, card, certificate, coupon, pass, slip, token **2** = **label**, card, docket, marker, slip, sticker, tab, tag

tickle *verb* = **amuse**, delight, divert, entertain, excite, gratify, please
➤ **Antonyms**
annoy, bore, bother, irritate, pester, trouble, vex, weary

ticklish *adjective* = **difficult**, awkward, critical, delicate, risky, sensitive, thorny, touchy, tricky

tick off *verb* **1** = **mark off**, check off, put a tick at **2** *Informal* = **scold**, bawl out (*informal*), berate, carpet (*informal*), censure, chide, haul over the coals (*informal*), lecture, read the riot act, rebuke, reprimand, reproach, reprove, take to task, tell off (*informal*), upbraid

tide *noun* **1** = **current**, course, ebb, flow, stream, tideway, undertow **2** = **tendency**, course, current, direction, drift, movement, trend

tide over *verb* = **keep one going**, aid, assist, help, keep one's head above water, see one through

tidings *plural noun* = **news**, bulletin, communication, gen (*Brit. informal*), information, intelligence, latest (*informal*), message, report, word

tidy *adjective* **1** = **neat**, businesslike, clean, in apple-pie order (*informal*), methodical, ordered, orderly, shipshape, spick-and-span, spruce, trim, well-groomed, well-kept, well-ordered **2** *Informal* = **considerable**, ample, fair, generous, good, goodly, handsome, healthy, large, largish, respectable, sizable *or* sizeable, substantial ♦ *verb* **3** = **neaten**, clean, groom, order, put in order, put to rights, spruce up, straighten
➤ **Antonyms**
adjective ≠**neat**: careless, dirty, dishevelled, disordered, disorderly, filthy, in disarray, messy, scruffy, sloppy, slovenly, unbusinesslike, unkempt, unmethodical, unsystematic, untidy ≠**considerable**:

inconsiderable, insignificant, little, small, tiny
♦ *verb* ≠**neaten**: dirty, dishevel, disorder, mess, mess up

tie *verb* **1** = **fasten**, attach, bind, connect, join, knot, lash, link, make fast, moor, rope, secure, tether, truss, unite **2** = **restrict**, bind, confine, hamper, hinder, hold, limit, restrain **3** = **draw**, be even, be neck and neck, equal, match ♦ *noun* **4** = **bond**, affiliation, affinity, allegiance, commitment, connection, duty, kinship, liaison, obligation, relationship **5** = **fastening**, band, bond, connection, cord, fetter, joint, knot, ligature, link, rope, string **6** *Brit.* = **match**, contest, fixture, game **7** = **draw**, dead heat, deadlock, stalemate **8** = **encumbrance**, hindrance, limitation, restraint, restriction
➤ **Antonyms**
verb ≠**fasten**: free, loose, release, separate, undo, unfasten, unhitch, unknot, untie ≠**restrict**: free, release

tie-in *noun* = **link**, association, connection, relation, relationship, tie-up

tie in *verb* = **link**, be relevant, connect, fit in, have bearing, relate

tier *noun* = **row**, bank, layer, level, line, order, rank, series, storey, stratum

tie-up *noun* = **link**, association, connection, linkup, relation, relationship, tie-in

tie up *verb* **1** = **bind**, attach, pinion, restrain, tether, truss **2** = **moor**, lash, make fast, rope, secure **3** = **occupy**, engage, engross, keep busy

tiff *noun* = **quarrel**, difference, disagreement, dispute, falling-out (*informal*), row, squabble

tight *adjective* **1** = **taut**, rigid, stiff, stretched, tense **2** = **close-fitting**, close, compact, constricted, cramped, narrow, snug **3** = **secure**, fast, firm, fixed **4** = **sealed**, impervious, proof, sound, watertight **5** = **strict**, harsh, inflexible, rigid, rigorous, severe, stern, stringent, tough, uncompromising, unyielding **6** = **difficult**, dangerous, hazardous, perilous, precarious, problematic, sticky (*informal*), ticklish, tough, tricky **7** *Informal* = **miserly**, close, grasping, mean, niggardly, parsimonious, penurious, sparing, stingy, tightfisted **8** = **close**, even, evenly-balanced, near, well-matched **9** *Informal* = **drunk**, bevvied (*dialect*), bladdered (*slang*), blitzed (*slang*), blotto (*slang*), half cut (*Brit. slang*), inebriated, intoxicated, legless (*informal*), out of it (*slang*), out to it (*Austral. & N.Z. slang*), paralytic (*informal*), pissed (*taboo slang*), plastered (*slang*), rat-arsed (*taboo slang*), smashed (*slang*), sozzled (*informal*), steamboats (*Scot. slang*), steaming (*slang*), stoned (*slang*), tiddly (*slang, chiefly Brit.*), tipsy, under the influence (*informal*),

wasted (*slang*), wrecked (*slang*)
➤ **Antonyms**
≠**taut**: relaxed, slack ≠**close-fitting**: loose,
spacious ≠**sealed**: loose, open, porous
≠**strict**: easy, easy-going, generous, lax,
lenient, liberal, relaxed, soft, undemanding
≠**difficult**: easy ≠**miserly**: abundant,
extravagant, generous, lavish, munificent,
open, prodigal, profuse, spendthrift ≠**close**:
easy, landslide, overwhelming, runaway,
uneven ≠**drunk**: sober

tighten *verb* 1 = **stretch**, stiffen, tauten,
tense 2 = **squeeze**, close, constrict, cramp,
narrow 3 = **fasten**, fix, screw, secure
➤ **Antonyms**
≠**stretch**: loosen, relax, slacken, weaken
≠**squeeze**: ease off, let out, slacken
≠**fasten**: unbind, unfasten, unscrew

tightfisted *adjective* = **miserly**, close,
close-fisted, grasping, mean, niggardly,
parsimonious, penurious, snoep (*S. African
informal*), stingy, tight

tight-lipped *adjective* = **secretive**,
close-lipped, close-mouthed, mum, quiet,
reticent, silent, taciturn, uncommunicative,
unforthcoming

till [1] *verb* = **cultivate**, dig, plough, turn over,
work

till [2] *noun* = **cash register**, cash box, cash
drawer

tilt *verb* 1 = **slant**, cant, heel, incline, lean,
list, slope, tip 2 = **joust**, clash, contend, duel,
encounter, fight ◆ *noun* 3 = **slope**, angle,
cant, inclination, incline, list, pitch, slant 4
Medieval history = **joust**, clash, combat,
duel, encounter, fight, lists, set-to
(*informal*), tournament 5 **(at) full tilt** = **full
speed**, for dear life, full force, headlong

timber *noun* 1 = **wood**, beams, boards,
logs, planks 2 = **trees**, forest

timbre *noun* = **tone**, colour, resonance, ring

time *noun* 1 = **period**, age, chronology,
date, duration, epoch, era, generation, hour,
interval, season, space, span, spell, stretch,
term, while 2 = **occasion**, instance, juncture,
point, stage 3 = **tempo**, beat, measure,
metre, rhythm 4 **at one time: a** = **once**, for
a while, formerly, hitherto, once upon a
time, previously **b** = **simultaneously**, all at
once, at the same time, together 5 **at times**
= **sometimes**, every now and then, every so
often, from time to time, now and then,
occasionally, once in a while, on occasion 6
for the time being = **for now**, for the
moment, for the present, in the meantime,
meantime, meanwhile, pro tem, temporarily
7 **from time to time** = **occasionally**, at
times, every now and then, every so often,
now and then, once in a while, on occasion,
sometimes 8 **in no time** = **quickly**, in a flash,

in a jiffy (*informal*), in a moment, in an
instant, in a trice, rapidly, speedily, swiftly 9
in time: a = **on time**, at the appointed time,
early, in good time, on schedule, with time
to spare **b** = **eventually**, by and by, in the
fullness of time, one day, someday, sooner
or later, ultimately 10 **on time** = **punctually**,
in good time, on the dot 11 **time and again**
= **frequently**, many times, often, on many
occasions, over and over again, repeatedly,
time after time ◆ *verb* 12 = **measure**, clock,
count, judge 13 = **schedule**, set

time-honoured *adjective*
= **long-established**, age-old, ancient,
conventional, customary, established, fixed,
old, traditional, usual

timeless *adjective* = **eternal**, abiding,
ageless, ceaseless, changeless, deathless,
endless, enduring, everlasting, immortal,
immutable, imperishable, indestructible,
lasting, permanent, persistent, undying
➤ **Antonyms**
ephemeral, evanescent, momentary, mortal,
passing, temporal, temporary, transitory

timely *adjective* = **opportune**, appropriate,
at the right time, convenient, judicious,
prompt, propitious, punctual, seasonable,
suitable, well-timed
➤ **Antonyms**
ill-timed, inconvenient, inopportune, late,
tardy, unseasonable, untimely

timeserver *noun* = **opportunist**, hypocrite,
self-seeker

timetable *noun* = **schedule**, agenda,
calendar, curriculum, diary, list, order of the
day, programme

timeworn *adjective* 1 = **decrepit**, aged,
ancient, broken-down, run-down, shabby,
the worse for wear, weathered, worn 2
= **hackneyed**, clichéd, dated, hoary, old hat,
out of date, outworn, passé, stale, stock,
threadbare, tired, trite, well-worn

timid *adjective* = **fearful**, afraid,
apprehensive, bashful, cowardly, coy,
diffident, faint-hearted, mousy, nervous,
pusillanimous, shrinking, shy, timorous
➤ **Antonyms**
aggressive, arrogant, ballsy (*taboo slang*),
bold, brave, confident, daring, fearless,
fierce, forceful, forward, presumptuous,
self-assured, self-confident, shameless,
unabashed

timorous *adjective* *Literary* = **timid**, afraid,
apprehensive, bashful, cowardly, coy,
diffident, faint-hearted, fearful, frightened,
mousy, nervous, pusillanimous, shrinking,
shy
➤ **Antonyms**
assertive, assured, audacious, bold,
confident, courageous, daring, fearless

tinge *noun* **1** = **tint**, cast, colour, dye, shade, stain, tincture, wash **2** = **bit**, dash, drop, pinch, smattering, *soupçon*, sprinkling, suggestion, touch, trace ◆ *verb* **3** = **tint**, colour, dye, imbue, shade, stain, suffuse

tingle *verb* **1** = **prickle**, have goose pimples, itch, sting, tickle ◆ *noun* **2** = **quiver**, goose pimples, itch, itching, pins and needles (*informal*), prickling, shiver, stinging, thrill

tinker *verb* = **meddle**, dabble, fiddle (*informal*), mess about, monkey, muck about (*Brit. slang*), play, potter, toy

tinpot *adjective Brit. informal* = **worthless**, inferior, Mickey Mouse (*slang*), paltry, pants (*slang*), second-class, second-rate, toytown (*slang*), two-bit (*U.S. & Canad. slang*), twopenny-halfpenny, unimportant

tinsel *adjective* = **showy**, cheap, flashy, gaudy, ostentatious, plastic (*slang*), sham, specious, superficial, tawdry, trashy

tint *noun* **1** = **shade**, cast, colour, hue, tone **2** = **dye**, rinse, stain, tincture, tinge, wash ◆ *verb* **3** = **dye**, colour, rinse, stain, tincture, tinge

tiny *adjective* = **small**, diminutive, dwarfish, infinitesimal, insignificant, Lilliputian, little, microscopic, mini, miniature, minute, negligible, petite, pint-sized (*informal*), puny, pygmy *or* pigmy, slight, teeny-weeny, trifling, wee
➤ **Antonyms**
colossal, enormous, extra-large, gargantuan, giant, gigantic, great, huge, immense, mammoth, massive, monstrous, titanic, vast

tip¹ *noun* **1** = **end**, apex, cap, crown, extremity, head, peak, pinnacle, point, summit, top ◆ *verb* **2** = **cap**, crown, finish, surmount, top

tip² *noun* **1** = **gratuity**, gift, perquisite **2** = **hint**, gen (*Brit. informal*), information, inside information, pointer, suggestion ◆ *verb* **3** = **reward**, remunerate **4** = **advise**, give a clue, give a hint, suggest, tip (someone) the wink (*Brit. informal*)

tip³ *verb* **1** = **tilt**, cant, capsize, incline, lean, list, overturn, slant, spill, topple over, upend, upset **2** *Brit.* = **dump**, ditch (*slang*), empty, pour out, unload ◆ *noun* **3** *Brit.* = **dump**, midden (*dialect*), refuse heap, rubbish heap

tip-off *noun* = **hint**, clue, gen (*Brit. informal*), information, inside information, pointer, suggestion, warning, word, word of advice

tip off *verb* = **advise**, caution, forewarn, give a clue, give a hint, suggest, tip (someone) the wink (*Brit. informal*), warn

tipple *verb* **1** = **drink**, bend the elbow (*informal*), bevvy (*dialect*), imbibe, indulge (*informal*), quaff, swig, take a drink, tope ◆ *noun* **2** = **alcohol**, booze (*informal*),

drink, liquor, poison (*informal*)

tippler *noun* = **drinker**, boozer (*informal*), drunk, drunkard, inebriate, soak (*slang*)

tipsy *adjective* = **tiddly** (*slang, chiefly Brit.*), babalas (*S. African*), fuddled, happy (*informal*), mellow, merry (*Brit. informal*), slightly drunk, woozy (*informal*)

tirade *noun* = **outburst**, abuse, denunciation, diatribe, fulmination, harangue, invective, lecture

tire *verb* **1** = **exhaust**, drain, enervate, fatigue, knacker (*slang*), take it out of (*informal*), wear down, wear out, weary **2** = **flag**, droop, fail **3** *usually passive* = **bore**, aggravate (*informal*), annoy, exasperate, get on one's nerves (*informal*), harass, hassle (*informal*), irk, irritate, weary
➤ **Antonyms**
≠**exhaust**: energize, enliven, exhilarate, invigorate, liven up, pep up, refresh, restore, revive

tired *adjective* **1** = **exhausted**, all in (*slang*), asleep *or* dead on one's feet (*informal*), clapped out (*Austral. & N.Z. informal*), dead beat (*informal*), dog-tired (*informal*), done in (*informal*), drained, drowsy, enervated, fatigued, flagging, knackered (*slang*), ready to drop, sleepy, spent, weary, whacked (*Brit. informal*), worn out, zonked (*slang*) **2** = **bored**, annoyed, exasperated, fed up, irked, irritated, sick, weary **3** = **hackneyed**, clichéd, conventional, corny (*slang*), familiar, old, outworn, stale, stock, threadbare, trite, well-worn
➤ **Antonyms**
≠**exhausted**: alive and kicking, energetic, fresh, full of beans (*informal*), lively, refreshed, rested, wide-awake ≠**bored**: enthusiastic about, fond of, keen on ≠**hackneyed**: innovative, original

tireless *adjective* = **energetic**, determined, indefatigable, industrious, resolute, unflagging, untiring, unwearied, vigorous
➤ **Antonyms**
drained, exhausted, fatigued, flagging, tired, weak, weary, worn out

tiresome *adjective* = **boring**, annoying, dull, exasperating, flat, irksome, irritating, laborious, monotonous, tedious, trying, uninteresting, vexatious, wearing, wearisome
➤ **Antonyms**
exhilarating, inspiring, interesting, refreshing, rousing, stimulating

tiring *adjective* = **exhausting**, arduous, demanding, enervative, exacting, fatiguing, laborious, strenuous, tough, wearing, wearying

tissue *noun* **1** = **fabric**, gauze, mesh, structure, stuff, texture, web **2** = **paper**, paper handkerchief, wrapping paper **3**

= series, accumulation, chain, collection, combination, mass, network, pack, web

titan *noun* = **giant**, colossus, leviathan

titanic *adjective* = **gigantic**, colossal, enormous, giant, herculean, huge, immense, massive, mighty, vast

titbit *noun* = **delicacy**, choice item, dainty, goody, juicy bit, morsel, scrap, snack, treat

tithe *noun* 1 = **tax**, assessment, duty, impost, levy, tariff, tenth, tribute ♦ *verb* 2 = **tax**, assess, charge, levy, rate 3 = **pay a tithe on**, give up, pay, render, surrender, turn over

titillate *verb* = **excite**, arouse, interest, provoke, stimulate, tantalize, tease, thrill, turn on (*slang*)

titillating *adjective* = **exciting**, arousing, interesting, lewd, lurid, provocative, sensational, stimulating, suggestive, teasing, thrilling

titivate *verb* = **smarten up**, doll up (*slang*), do up (*informal*), make up, preen, primp, tart up (*Brit. slang*), touch up

title *noun* 1 = **name**, appellation, denomination, designation, epithet, handle (*slang*), moniker *or* monicker (*slang*), nickname, nom de plume, pseudonym, sobriquet, term 2 = **heading**, caption, inscription, label, legend, name, style 3 *Sport* = **championship**, crown, laurels 4 *Law* = **ownership**, claim, entitlement, prerogative, privilege, right

titter *verb* = **snigger**, chortle (*informal*), chuckle, giggle, laugh, tee-hee

tittle *noun* = **bit**, atom, dash, drop, grain, iota, jot, mite, particle, scrap, shred, speck, whit

tittle-tattle *noun* 1 = **gossip**, blether, chatter, chitchat, dirt (*U.S. slang*), hearsay, idle chat, natter, rumour ♦ *verb* 2 = **gossip**, babble, blether, chat, chatter, chitchat, natter

titular *adjective* = **in name only**, honorary, nominal, putative, so-called, token
➤ **Antonyms**
actual, effective, functioning, real, true

toady *noun* 1 = **sycophant**, bootlicker (*informal*), crawler (*slang*), creep (*slang*), fawner, flatterer, flunkey, hanger-on, lackey, minion, parasite, yes man ♦ *verb* 2 = **fawn on**, be obsequious to, bow and scrape, butter up, crawl, creep, cringe, curry favour with, flatter, grovel, kowtow to, lick (someone's) boots, pander to, suck up to (*informal*)
➤ **Antonyms**
verb ≠ **fawn on**: confront, defy, oppose, rebel, resist, stand against, withstand

toast[1] *verb* 1 = **brown**, grill, roast 2 = **warm**, heat

toast[2] *noun* 1 = **tribute**, compliment, drink,

health, pledge, salutation, salute 2 = **favourite**, darling, hero *or* heroine ♦ *verb* 3 = **drink to**, drink (to) the health of, pledge, salute

to-do *noun* = **fuss**, agitation, bother, brouhaha, bustle, commotion, disturbance, excitement, furore, hue and cry, quarrel, ruction (*informal*), rumpus, stir, tumult, turmoil, upheaval, uproar

toe *noun* **tread on someone's toes** = **offend**, affront, annoy, disgruntle, get someone's back up, hurt, hurt someone's feelings, irk, vex

together *adverb* 1 = **collectively**, as a group, as one, cheek by jowl, closely, hand in glove, hand in hand, in a body, in concert, in cooperation, in unison, jointly, mutually, shoulder to shoulder, side by side 2 = **at the same time**, all at once, as one, at one fell swoop, concurrently, contemporaneously, en masse, in unison, simultaneously, with one accord 3 *Old-fashioned* = **in succession**, consecutively, continuously, in a row, one after the other, on end, successively, without a break, without interruption ♦ *adjective* 4 *Slang* = **self-possessed**, calm, composed, cool, stable, well-adjusted, well-balanced, well-organized
➤ **Antonyms**
adverb ≠ **collectively**: alone, apart, independently, individually, one at a time, one by one, separately, singly

toil *noun* 1 = **hard work**, application, blood, sweat, and tears (*informal*), donkey-work, drudgery, effort, elbow grease (*informal*), exertion, graft (*informal*), industry, labour, pains, slog, sweat, travail ♦ *verb* 2 = **labour**, bend over backwards (*informal*), break one's neck (*informal*), do one's damnedest (*informal*), drudge, give it one's all (*informal*), give it one's best shot (*informal*), graft (*informal*), grind (*informal*), knock oneself out (*informal*), make an all-out effort (*informal*), push oneself, slave, slog, strive, struggle, sweat (*informal*), work, work like a dog, work like a Trojan, work one's fingers to the bone
➤ **Antonyms**
noun ≠ **hard work**: idleness, inactivity, indolence, inertia, laziness, sloth, torpor

toilet *noun* 1 = **lavatory**, bathroom, bog (*slang*), can (*U.S. & Canad. slang*), closet, convenience, gents *or* ladies (*Brit. informal*), john (*slang, chiefly U.S. & Canad.*), khazi (*slang*), ladies' room, latrine, little boy's *or* little girl's room (*informal*), loo (*Brit. informal*), outhouse, powder room, privy, urinal, washroom, water closet, W.C. 2 *Old-fashioned* = **dressing**, ablutions, bathing, grooming, toilette

toilsome *adjective Literary* = **laborious**, arduous, backbreaking, difficult, fatiguing, hard, herculean, strenuous, taxing, tough

token *noun* **1** = **symbol**, badge, clue, demonstration, earnest, evidence, expression, indication, manifestation, mark, note, proof, representation, sign ♦ *adjective* **2** = **nominal**, hollow, minimal, perfunctory, superficial, symbolic

tolerable *adjective* **1** = **bearable**, acceptable, allowable, endurable, sufferable, supportable **2** *Informal* = **fair**, acceptable, adequate, all right, average, fairly good, fair to middling, good enough, indifferent, mediocre, middling, not bad (*informal*), O.K. *or* okay (*informal*), ordinary, passable, run-of-the-mill, so-so (*informal*), unexceptional
➤ **Antonyms**
≠**bearable**: insufferable, intolerable, unacceptable, unbearable, unendurable
≠**fair**: awful, bad, dreadful, rotten

tolerance *noun* **1** = **broad-mindedness**, forbearance, indulgence, magnanimity, open-mindedness, patience, permissiveness, sufferance **2** = **endurance**, fortitude, hardiness, hardness, resilience, resistance, stamina, staying power, toughness **3** = **variation**, fluctuation, play, swing
➤ **Antonyms**
≠**broad-mindedness**: bigotry, discrimination, intolerance, narrow-mindedness, prejudice, sectarianism

tolerant *adjective* = **broad-minded**, catholic, fair, forbearing, latitudinarian, liberal, long-suffering, magnanimous, open-minded, patient, unbigoted, understanding, unprejudiced
➤ **Antonyms**
biased, bigoted, dogmatic, illiberal, intolerant, narrow-minded, prejudiced, sectarian

tolerate *verb* **1** = **allow**, accept, admit, brook, condone, countenance, indulge, permit, put up with (*informal*), sanction, take **2** = **endure**, abide, bear, put up with (*informal*), stand, stomach, submit to, suffer, swallow, take, thole (*Scot.*)
➤ **Antonyms**
≠**allow**: ban, disallow, disapprove, forbid, outlaw, preclude, prohibit, veto

toleration *noun* = **acceptance**, allowance, endurance, indulgence, permissiveness, sanction, sufferance

toll¹ *verb* **1** = **ring**, chime, clang, knell, peal, sound, strike **2** = **announce**, call, signal, summon, warn ♦ *noun* **3** = **ringing**, chime, clang, knell, peal, ring, tolling

toll² *noun* **1** = **charge**, assessment, customs, demand, duty, fee, impost, levy, payment, rate, tariff, tax, tribute **2** = **damage**, cost, inroad, loss, penalty

tomb *noun* = **grave**, burial chamber, catacomb, crypt, mausoleum, sarcophagus, sepulchre, vault

tombstone *noun* = **gravestone**, headstone, marker, memorial, monument

tome *noun* = **book**, title, volume, work

tomfoolery *noun* = **foolishness**, buffoonery, childishness, clowning, fooling around (*informal*), horseplay, idiocy, messing around (*informal*), shenanigans (*informal*), silliness, skylarking (*informal*), stupidity
➤ **Antonyms**
demureness, gravity, heaviness, reserve, sedateness, seriousness, sobriety, solemnity, sternness

tone *noun* **1** = **pitch**, accent, emphasis, force, inflection, intonation, modulation, strength, stress, timbre, tonality, volume **2** = **character**, air, approach, aspect, attitude, drift, feel, manner, mood, note, quality, spirit, style, temper, vein **3** = **colour**, cast, hue, shade, tinge, tint ♦ *verb* **4** = **harmonize**, blend, go well with, match, suit

tone down *verb* = **moderate**, dampen, dim, mitigate, modulate, play down, reduce, restrain, soften, soft-pedal (*informal*), subdue, temper

tone up *verb* = **get into condition**, get in shape, shape up, trim, tune up

tongue *noun* = **language**, argot, dialect, idiom, lingo (*informal*), parlance, patois, speech, talk, vernacular

tongue-tied *adjective* = **speechless**, at a loss for words, dumb, dumbstruck, inarticulate, mute, struck dumb
➤ **Antonyms**
articulate, chatty, effusive, garrulous, loquacious, talkative, verbose, voluble, wordy

tonic *noun* = **stimulant**, boost, bracer (*informal*), fillip, livener, pick-me-up (*informal*), refresher, restorative, shot in the arm (*informal*)

too *adverb* **1** = **also**, as well, besides, further, in addition, into the bargain, likewise, moreover, to boot **2** = **excessively**, exorbitantly, extremely, immoderately, inordinately, over-, overly, unduly, unreasonably, very

tool *noun* **1** = **implement**, apparatus, appliance, contraption, contrivance, device, gadget, instrument, machine, utensil **2** = **puppet**, cat's-paw, creature, dupe, flunkey, hireling, lackey, minion, pawn, stooge (*slang*) **3** = **means**, agency, agent, intermediary, medium, vehicle, wherewithal ♦ *verb* **4** = **make**, chase, cut, decorate, ornament, shape, work

toothsome *adjective* = **appetizing**, dainty, delectable, delicious, luscious, mouthwatering, nice, palatable, savoury, scrumptious (*informal*), sweet, tasty, tempting, yummy (*slang*)

top *noun* 1 = **peak**, acme, apex, apogee, crest, crown, culmination, head, height, high point, meridian, pinnacle, summit, vertex, zenith 2 = **first place**, head, highest rank, lead 3 = **lid**, cap, cork, cover, stopper 4 **over the top** = **excessive**, a bit much (*informal*), going too far, immoderate, inordinate, over the limit, too much, uncalled-for ◆ *adjective* 5 = **leading**, best, chief, crack (*informal*), crowning, culminating, dominant, elite, finest, first, foremost, greatest, head, highest, lead, pre-eminent, prime, principal, ruling, sovereign, superior, topmost, upper, uppermost ◆ *verb* 6 = **cover**, cap, crown, finish, garnish, tip 7 = **reach the top of**, ascend, climb, crest, scale, surmount 8 = **lead**, be first, be in charge of, command, head, rule 9 = **surpass**, beat, best, better, eclipse, exceed, excel, go beyond, outdo, outshine, outstrip, transcend
➤ **Antonyms**
noun ≠ **peak**: base, bottom, foot, nadir, underneath, underside ◆ *adjective* ≠ **leading**: amateurish, bottom, incompetent, inept, inferior, least, lower, lowest, second-rate, unknown, unranked, worst ◆ *verb* ≠ **surpass**: fail to equal, fall short of, not be as good as

topic *noun* = **subject**, issue, matter, point, question, subject matter, text, theme, thesis

topical *adjective* = **current**, contemporary, newsworthy, popular, up-to-date, up-to-the-minute

topmost *adjective* = **highest**, dominant, foremost, leading, loftiest, paramount, principal, supreme, top, upper, uppermost
➤ **Antonyms**
base, basic, bottom, bottommost, last, lowest, undermost

topple *verb* 1 = **fall over**, capsize, collapse, fall, fall headlong, keel over, knock down, knock over, overbalance, overturn, tip over, totter, tumble, upset 2 = **overthrow**, bring down, bring low, oust, overturn, unseat

topsy-turvy *adjective* = **confused**, chaotic, disarranged, disorderly, disorganized, inside-out, jumbled, messy, mixed-up, untidy, upside-down
➤ **Antonyms**
neat, ordered, orderly, organized, shipshape, systematic, tidy

top up *verb* = **supplement**, add to, augment, boost, enhance, fill out *or* up

torment *verb* 1 = **torture**, afflict, agonize,

crucify, distress, excruciate, harrow, pain, rack 2 = **tease**, aggravate (*informal*), annoy, bedevil, bother, harass, harry, hassle (*informal*), hound, irritate, nag, persecute, pester, plague, provoke, trouble, vex, worry ◆ *noun* 3 = **suffering**, agony, anguish, distress, hell, misery, pain, torture 4 = **trouble**, affliction, annoyance, bane, bother, harassment, hassle (*informal*), irritation, nuisance, pain in the neck (*informal*), persecution, pest, plague, provocation, thorn in one's flesh *or* side, vexation, worry
➤ **Antonyms**
verb ≠ **torture**: comfort, delight, ease, encourage, make happy, put at ease, reassure, soothe ◆ *noun* ≠ **suffering**: bliss, comfort, ease, ecstasy, encouragement, happiness, joy, reassurance, rest

torn *adjective* 1 = **cut**, lacerated, ragged, rent, ripped, slit, split 2 = **undecided**, divided, in two minds (*informal*), irresolute, split, uncertain, unsure, vacillating, wavering

tornado *noun* = **whirlwind**, cyclone, gale, hurricane, squall, storm, tempest, twister (*U.S. informal*), typhoon

torpid *adjective* = **inactive**, dull, indolent, inert, lackadaisical, languid, languorous, lazy, lethargic, passive, slothful, slow, slow-moving, sluggish

torpor *noun* = **inactivity**, apathy, drowsiness, dullness, indolence, inertia, inertness, languor, laziness, lethargy, listlessness, numbness, passivity, sloth, sluggishness, stupor
➤ **Antonyms**
animation, energy, get-up-and-go (*informal*), go, liveliness, pep, vigour

torrent *noun* = **stream**, cascade, deluge, downpour, effusion, flood, flow, gush, outburst, rush, spate, tide

torrid *adjective* 1 = **hot**, blistering, boiling, broiling, burning, dry, flaming, parching, scorching, sizzling, stifling, sultry, sweltering, tropical 2 = **arid**, dried, parched, scorched 3 = **passionate**, ardent, fervent, intense, steamy (*informal*)

tortuous *adjective* 1 = **winding**, bent, circuitous, convoluted, crooked, curved, indirect, mazy, meandering, serpentine, sinuous, twisted, twisting, twisty, zigzag 2 = **complicated**, ambiguous, convoluted, cunning, deceptive, devious, indirect, involved, misleading, roundabout, tricky
➤ **Antonyms**
≠ **complicated**: candid, direct, honest, ingenuous, open, reliable, straightforward, upright

torture *verb* 1 = **torment**, afflict, agonize, crucify, distress, excruciate, harrow, martyr,

pain, persecute, put on the rack, rack
♦ *noun* 2 = **agony**, affliction, anguish,
distress, hell, martyrdom, misery, pain,
pang(s), persecution, rack, suffering, torment
➤ Antonyms
verb ≠**torment**: alleviate, comfort, console,
ease, mollify, relieve, salve, solace, soothe
♦ *noun* ≠**agony**: amusement, bliss, delight,
enjoyment, happiness, joy, pleasure,
well-being

toss *verb* 1 = **throw**, cast, chuck (*informal*),
fling, flip, hurl, launch, lob (*informal*), pitch,
project, propel, shy, sling 2 = **thrash**,
agitate, disturb, jiggle, joggle, jolt, rock, roll,
shake, tumble, wriggle, writhe 3 = **heave**,
labour, lurch, pitch, roll, wallow ♦ *noun* 4
= **throw**, cast, fling, lob (*informal*), pitch, shy

tot *noun* 1 = **infant**, ankle-biter (*Austral.
slang*), baby, child, little one, mite, rug rat
(*slang*), sprog (*slang*), toddler, wean (*Scot.*)
2 = **measure**, dram, finger, nip, shot
(*informal*), slug, snifter (*informal*)

total *noun* 1 = **whole**, aggregate, all,
amount, entirety, full amount, mass, sum,
totality ♦ *adjective* 2 = **complete**, absolute,
all-out, arrant, comprehensive, consummate,
deep-dyed (*usually derogatory*), downright,
entire, full, gross, out-and-out, outright,
overarching, sheer, sweeping, thorough,
thoroughgoing, unconditional, undivided,
unmitigated, unqualified, utter, whole
♦ *verb* 3 = **amount to**, come to, mount up
to, reach 4 = **add up**, reckon, sum up, tot
up
➤ Antonyms
noun ≠**whole**: individual amount, part,
subtotal ♦ *adjective* ≠**complete**: conditional,
fragmentary, incomplete, limited, mixed,
part, partial, qualified, restricted,
uncombined ♦ *verb* ≠**add up**: deduct,
subtract

totalitarian *adjective* = **dictatorial**,
authoritarian, despotic, one-party,
oppressive, tyrannous, undemocratic
➤ Antonyms
autonomous, democratic, egalitarian,
popular, self-governing

totality *noun* 1 = **whole**, aggregate, all,
entirety, everything, sum, total 2
= **completeness**, entireness, fullness,
wholeness

totally *adverb* = **completely**, absolutely,
comprehensively, consummately, entirely,
fully, one hundred per cent, perfectly, quite,
thoroughly, unconditionally, unmitigatedly,
utterly, wholeheartedly, wholly
➤ Antonyms
incompletely, in part, partially, partly,
somewhat, to a certain extent

totter *verb* = **stagger**, falter, lurch, reel, rock,
shake, stumble, sway, teeter, walk

unsteadily, waver, wobble

tot up *verb* = **add up**, calculate, count up,
reckon, sum (up), tally, total

touch *verb* 1 = **handle**, brush, caress,
contact, feel, finger, fondle, graze, lay a
finger on, palpate, stroke 2 = **tap**, pat, push
3 = **come into contact**, abut, adjoin, be in
contact, border, brush, come together,
contact, converge, graze, impinge upon,
meet 4 = **affect**, get through to, get to
(*informal*), have an effect on, impress,
influence, inspire, make an impression on,
mark, strike 5 = **move**, disturb, stir, upset 6
= **consume**, drink, eat, partake of 7
= **match**, be a match for, be in the same
league as, be on a par with, come near,
come up to, compare with, equal, hold a
candle to (*informal*), parallel, rival 8 **touch
on** = **refer to**, allude to, bring in, cover, deal
with, mention, speak of ♦ *noun* 9 = **feeling**,
feel, handling, palpation, physical contact 10
= **contact**, brush, caress, fondling, stroke 11
= **tap**, blow, hit, pat, push 12 = **bit**, dash,
detail, drop, hint, jot, pinch, smack, small
amount, smattering, *soupçon*, speck, spot,
suggestion, suspicion, taste, tinge, trace,
whiff 13 = **style**, approach, characteristic,
handiwork, manner, method, technique,
trademark, way

touch and go *adjective* = **risky**, close,
critical, near, nerve-racking, precarious

touched *adjective* 1 = **moved**, affected,
disturbed, impressed, softened, stirred,
swayed, upset 2 = **mad**, barmy (*slang*),
batty (*slang*), bonkers (*slang, chiefly Brit.*),
crazy, daft (*informal*), loopy (*informal*), not
all there, not right in the head, nuts (*slang*),
nutty (*slang*), nutty as a fruitcake (*slang*),
off one's rocker (*slang*), off one's trolley
(*slang*), out to lunch (*slang*), soft in the
head (*informal*)

touchiness *noun* = **irritability**, bad temper,
fretfulness, grouchiness (*informal*),
irascibility, peevishness, petulance, surliness,
testiness, tetchiness

touching *adjective* = **moving**, affecting,
emotive, heartbreaking, melting, pathetic,
piteous, pitiable, pitiful, poignant, sad,
stirring, tender

touch off *verb* = **trigger (off)**, arouse,
begin, cause, foment, give rise to, initiate,
provoke, set in motion, spark off

touchstone *noun* = **standard**, criterion,
gauge, measure, norm, par, yardstick

touch up *verb* 1 = **enhance**, brush up, give
a face-lift to, gloss over, improve, patch up,
polish up, renovate, retouch, revamp, titivate
2 = **finish off**, perfect, put the finishing
touches to, round off

touchy *adjective* = **oversensitive**,

bad-tempered, captious, cross, easily offended, grouchy (*informal*), grumpy, irascible, irritable, peevish, petulant, querulous, quick-tempered, ratty (*Brit. & N.Z. informal*), surly, testy, tetchy, thin-skinned
➤ **Antonyms**
affable, cheerful, easy-going, genial, good-humoured, imperious, indifferent, insensitive, light-hearted, pleasant, sunny, sweet, thick-skinned, unconcerned

tough *adjective* **1** = **resilient**, durable, firm, hard, inflexible, leathery, resistant, rigid, rugged, solid, stiff, strong, sturdy, tenacious **2** = **strong**, brawny, fit, hard as nails, hardened, hardy, resilient, seasoned, stalwart, stout, strapping, sturdy, vigorous **3** = **rough**, hard-bitten, pugnacious, ruthless, vicious, violent **4** = **strict**, exacting, firm, hard, inflexible, intractable, merciless, resolute, severe, stern, unbending, unforgiving, unyielding **5** = **difficult**, arduous, baffling, exacting, exhausting, hard, irksome, knotty, laborious, perplexing, puzzling, strenuous, thorny, troublesome, uphill **6** *As in* **tough luck!** *Informal* = **unlucky**, bad, lamentable, regrettable, too bad (*informal*), unfortunate ◆ *noun* **7** = **ruffian**, bruiser (*informal*), brute, bully, bully boy, heavy (*slang*), hooligan, rough (*informal*), roughneck (*slang*), rowdy, thug, tsotsi (*S. African*)
➤ **Antonyms**
adjective ≠**resilient**: delicate, flexible, flimsy, fragile, soft, tender, weak ≠**strong**: delicate, soft, weak ≠**rough**: civilized, gentle, humane, soft, tender ≠**strict**: accommodating, benign, compassionate, considerate, easy, flexible, gentle, humane, indulgent, kind, lenient, merciful, mild, soft, sympathetic, tender, unexacting ≠**difficult**: easy, easy-peasy (*slang*), unexacting

tour *noun* **1** = **journey**, excursion, expedition, jaunt, outing, progress, trip **2** = **course**, circuit, round ◆ *verb* **3** = **visit**, explore, go on the road, go round, holiday in, journey, sightsee, travel round, travel through

tourist *noun* = **traveller**, excursionist, globetrotter, holiday-maker, journeyer, sightseer, tripper, voyager

tournament *noun* **1** = **competition**, contest, event, match, meeting, series **2** *Medieval* = **joust**, the lists, tourney

tousle *verb* = **dishevel**, disarrange, disarray, disorder, mess up, ruffle, rumple, tangle

tout *verb* **1** = **solicit**, canvass, drum up **2** *Informal* = **recommend**, approve, commend, endorse, praise, promote, speak well of

tow *verb* = **drag**, draw, hale, haul, lug, pull,

trail, trawl, tug, yank

towards *preposition* **1** = **in the direction of**, en route for, for, on the road to, on the way to, to **2** = **regarding**, about, concerning, for, with regard to, with respect to **3** = **just before**, almost, close to, coming up to, getting on for, nearing, nearly, not quite, shortly before

tower *noun* **1** = **column**, belfry, obelisk, pillar, skyscraper, steeple, turret ◆ *verb* **2** *usually with* **over** = **rise**, ascend, be head and shoulders above, dominate, loom, mount, overlook, overtop, rear, soar, surpass, top, transcend

towering *adjective* **1** = **tall**, colossal, elevated, high, lofty, soaring **2** = **impressive**, extraordinary, imposing, magnificent, prodigious, striking, supreme, surpassing, transcendent **3** = **intense**, excessive, extreme, immoderate, inordinate, intemperate, mighty, passionate, vehement, violent

toxic *adjective* = **poisonous**, deadly, harmful, lethal, noxious, pernicious, pestilential, septic
➤ **Antonyms**
harmless, invigorating, non-poisonous, nontoxic, safe, salubrious

toy *noun* **1** = **plaything**, doll, game ◆ *verb* **toy with 2** = **play**, amuse oneself with, dally with, flirt with, fool (about *or* around) with, sport, trifle **3** = **fiddle** (*informal*), play

trace *verb* **1** = **find**, ascertain, detect, determine, discover, ferret out, follow, hunt down, pursue, search for, seek, shadow, stalk, track, unearth **2** = **copy 3** = **outline**, chart, delineate, depict, draw, map, mark out, show, sketch ◆ *noun* **4** = **track**, footmark, footprint, footstep, path, slot, spoor, trail **5** = **bit**, dash, drop, hint, iota, jot, shadow, *soupçon*, suggestion, suspicion, tinge, touch, whiff **6** = **remnant**, evidence, indication, mark, record, relic, remains, sign, survival, token, vestige

track *noun* **1** = **path**, course, flight path, line, orbit, pathway, road, trajectory, way **2** = **trail**, footmark, footprint, footstep, mark, path, scent, slipstream, spoor, trace, wake **3** = **line**, permanent way, rail, rails **4 keep track of** = **keep up with**, follow, keep an eye on, keep in sight, keep in touch with, keep up to date with, monitor, oversee, watch **5 lose track of** = **lose**, lose sight of, misplace ◆ *verb* **6** = **follow**, chase, dog, follow the trail of, hunt down, pursue, shadow, stalk, tail (*informal*), trace, trail

track down *verb* = **find**, apprehend, bring to light, capture, catch, dig up, discover, expose, ferret out, hunt down, run to earth *or* ground, sniff out, trace, unearth

tracks *plural noun* **1** = **trail**, footprints,

impressions, imprints, tyre marks, tyre prints, wheel marks **2 make tracks = leave**, beat it (*slang*), depart, get going, get moving, go, head off, hit the road (*slang*), set out, split (*slang*), take off (*informal*) **3 stop in one's tracks = bring to a standstill**, freeze, immobilize, petrify, stop dead, transfix

tract¹ *noun* **= area**, district, estate, expanse, extent, lot, plot, quarter, region, stretch, territory, zone

tract² *noun* **= treatise**, booklet, brochure, dissertation, essay, homily, leaflet, monograph, pamphlet

tractable *adjective Formal* **1 = manageable**, amenable, biddable, compliant, controllable, docile, governable, obedient, persuadable, submissive, tame, willing, yielding **2 = malleable**, ductile, fictile, plastic, pliable, pliant, tensile, tractile, workable
➤ **Antonyms**
≠**manageable**: defiant, headstrong, obstinate, refractory, stiff-necked, stubborn, unruly, wilful

traction *noun* **1 = pulling**, drag, draught, drawing, haulage, pull **2 = grip**, adhesion, friction, purchase, resistance

trade *noun* **1 = commerce**, barter, business, buying and selling, dealing, exchange, traffic, transactions, truck **2 = job**, avocation, business, calling, craft, employment, line, line of work, métier, occupation, profession, pursuit, skill ◆ *verb* **3 = deal**, bargain, barter, buy and sell, cut a deal, do business, exchange, have dealings, peddle, traffic, transact, truck **4 = exchange**, barter, swap, switch

trader *noun* **= dealer**, broker, buyer, marketer, merchandiser, merchant, purveyor, seller, supplier

tradesman *noun* **1 = craftsman**, artisan, journeyman, skilled worker, workman **2 = shopkeeper**, dealer, merchant, purveyor, retailer, seller, supplier, vendor

tradition *noun* **= custom**, convention, customs, established practice, folklore, habit, institution, lore, ritual, unwritten law, usage

traditional *adjective* **= customary**, accustomed, ancestral, conventional, established, fixed, historic, long-established, old, time-honoured, unwritten, usual
➤ **Antonyms**
avant-garde, contemporary, ground-breaking, innovative, modern, new, novel, off-the-wall (*slang*), original, revolutionary, unconventional, unusual

traduce *verb Formal* **= malign**, abuse, bad-mouth (*slang, chiefly U.S. & Canad.*), blacken, calumniate, decry, defame, denigrate, deprecate, depreciate, detract,

disparage, knock (*informal*), revile, rubbish (*informal*), run down, slag (off) (*slang*), slander, smear, speak ill of, vilify

traffic *noun* **1 = transport**, freight, movement, passengers, transportation, vehicles **2 = trade**, barter, business, buying and selling, commerce, dealing, dealings, doings, exchange, intercourse, peddling, relations, truck ◆ *verb* **3 = trade**, bargain, barter, buy and sell, cut a deal, deal, do business, exchange, have dealings, have transactions, market, peddle, truck

tragedy *noun* **= disaster**, adversity, affliction, bummer (*slang*), calamity, catastrophe, grievous blow, misfortune
➤ **Antonyms**
fortune, happiness, joy, prosperity, success

tragic *adjective* **1 = distressing**, appalling, awful, calamitous, catastrophic, deadly, dire, disastrous, dreadful, fatal, grievous, ill-fated, ill-starred, lamentable, ruinous, sad, shocking, unfortunate, woeful, wretched **2 = sad**, anguished, dismal, doleful, heartbreaking, heart-rending, miserable, mournful, pathetic, pitiable, sorrowful
➤ **Antonyms**
≠**distressing**: beneficial, fortunate, lucky, satisfying, worthwhile ≠**sad**: cheerful, comic, happy, joyful

trail *noun* **1 = path**, beaten track, footpath, road, route, track, way **2 = tracks**, footprints, footsteps, mark, marks, path, scent, slipstream, spoor, trace, wake **3 = stream**, appendage, tail, train ◆ *verb* **4 = drag**, dangle, draw, hang down, haul, pull, stream, tow **5 = follow**, chase, hunt, pursue, shadow, stalk, tail (*informal*), trace, track **6 = lag**, bring up the rear, dawdle, fall behind, follow, hang back, linger, loiter, straggle, traipse (*informal*)

trail away or **off** *verb* **= fade away** or **out**, decrease, die away, diminish, dwindle, fall away, grow faint, grow weak, lessen, peter out, shrink, sink, subside, tail off, taper off, weaken

train *verb* **1 = instruct**, coach, discipline, drill, educate, guide, improve, prepare, rehearse, school, teach, tutor **2 = exercise**, prepare, work out **3 = aim**, direct, focus, level, point ◆ *noun* **4 = sequence**, chain, concatenation, course, order, progression, series, set, string, succession **5 = tail**, appendage, trail

trainer *noun* **= coach**, handler

training *noun* **1 = instruction**, coaching, discipline, education, grounding, guidance, schooling, teaching, tuition, tutelage, upbringing **2 = exercise**, body building, practice, preparation, working out

traipse *Informal* ◆ *verb* **1 = trudge**, drag

oneself, footslog, slouch, trail, tramp ◆ *noun*
2 = **trudge**, long walk, slog, tramp, trek

trait *noun* = **characteristic**, attribute, feature,
idiosyncrasy, mannerism, peculiarity, quality,
quirk

traitor *noun* = **betrayer**, apostate,
back-stabber, deceiver, defector, deserter,
double-crosser (*informal*), fifth columnist,
informer, Judas, quisling, rebel, renegade,
turncoat
➤ **Antonyms**
defender, loyalist, patriot, supporter

traitorous *adjective* = **treacherous**,
apostate, disloyal, double-crossing
(*informal*), double-dealing, faithless, false,
perfidious, treasonable, unfaithful, untrue
➤ **Antonyms**
constant, faithful, loyal, patriotic, staunch,
steadfast, true, trusty

trajectory *noun* = **path**, course, flight,
flight path, line, route, track

trammel *verb* 1 = **hinder**, bar, block, check,
curb, fetter, hamper, handicap, impede,
restrain, restrict, snag, tie ◆ *noun* 2
trammels = **restrictions**, bars, blocks,
bonds, chains, checks, curbs, fetters,
handicaps, hindrances, impediments,
obstacles, reins, shackles, stumbling blocks
➤ **Antonyms**
verb ≠**hinder**: advance, assist, expedite,
facilitate, foster, further, promote, support

tramp *verb* 1 = **hike**, footslog, march,
ramble, range, roam, rove, slog, trek, walk 2
= **trudge**, march, plod, stamp, stump, toil,
traipse (*informal*), walk heavily ◆ *noun* 3
= **vagrant**, bag lady (*chiefly U.S.*), bum
(*informal*), derelict, dosser (*Brit. slang*),
down-and-out, drifter, hobo (*chiefly U.S.*),
vagabond 4 = **hike**, march, ramble, slog,
trek 5 = **tread**, footfall, footstep, stamp

trample *verb* 1 *often with* **on** = **crush**,
flatten, run over, squash, stamp, tread, walk
over 2 **trample on** = **show no
consideration for**, hurt, ride roughshod over

trance *noun* = **daze**, abstraction, dream,
ecstasy, hypnotic state, rapture, reverie,
spell, stupor, unconsciousness

tranquil *adjective* = **calm**, at peace,
composed, cool, peaceful, placid, quiet,
restful, sedate, serene, still, undisturbed,
unexcited, unperturbed, unruffled,
untroubled
➤ **Antonyms**
agitated, busy, confused, disturbed, excited,
hectic, restless, troubled

tranquillity *noun* = **calm**, calmness,
composure, coolness, equanimity, hush,
imperturbability, peace, peacefulness,
placidity, quiet, quietness, quietude, repose,
rest, restfulness, sedateness, serenity, stillness

➤ **Antonyms**
agitation, commotion, confusion,
disturbance, excitement, noise, restlessness,
turmoil, upset

tranquillize *verb* = **calm**, lull, pacify, quell,
quiet, relax, sedate, settle one's nerves,
soothe
➤ **Antonyms**
agitate, confuse, distress, disturb, harass,
perturb, ruffle, trouble, upset

tranquillizer *noun* = **sedative**, barbiturate,
bromide, downer (*slang*), opiate

transact *verb* = **carry out**, accomplish, carry
on, conclude, conduct, discharge, do, enact,
execute, handle, manage, negotiate,
perform, see to, settle, take care of

transaction *noun* 1 = **deal**, action, affair,
bargain, business, coup, deed, enterprise,
event, matter, negotiation, occurrence,
proceeding, undertaking 2 *plural* = **records**,
affairs, doings, goings-on (*informal*),
minutes, proceedings

transcend *verb* = **surpass**, eclipse, exceed,
excel, go above, go beyond, leave behind,
outdo, outshine, outstrip, rise above

transcendence *noun* = **greatness**,
excellence, incomparability, matchlessness,
pre-eminence, sublimity, superiority,
supremacy

transcendent *adjective* = **unparalleled**,
consummate, exceeding, extraordinary,
incomparable, matchless, peerless,
pre-eminent, second to none, sublime,
superior, transcendental, unequalled, unique,
unrivalled

transcribe *verb* 1 = **write out**, copy out,
note, reproduce, rewrite, set out, take down,
transfer 2 = **record**, tape, tape-record

transcript *noun* = **copy**, carbon, carbon
copy, duplicate, manuscript, note, notes,
record, reproduction, transcription,
translation, transliteration, version

transfer *verb* 1 = **move**, carry, change,
consign, convey, displace, hand over, pass
on, relocate, remove, shift, translate,
transmit, transplant, transport, transpose
◆ *noun* 2 = **move**, change, displacement,
handover, relocation, removal, shift,
transference, translation, transmission,
transposition

transfigure *verb* = **change**, alter, convert,
metamorphose, transform, transmute

transfix *verb* 1 = **stun**, engross, fascinate,
halt or stop in one's tracks, hold, hypnotize,
mesmerize, paralyse, petrify, rivet the
attention of, root to the spot, spellbind, stop
dead 2 = **pierce**, fix, impale, puncture, run
through, skewer, spear, spit
➤ **Antonyms**
≠**stun**: bore, fatigue, tire, weary

transform *verb* = **change**, alter, convert, make over, metamorphose, reconstruct, remodel, renew, revolutionize, transfigure, transmogrify (*jocular*), transmute

transformation *noun* = **change**, alteration, conversion, metamorphosis, radical change, renewal, revolution, revolutionary change, sea change, transfiguration, transmogrification (*jocular*), transmutation

transfuse *verb* *Literary* = **permeate**, instil, pervade, spread over, suffuse

transgress *verb* *Formal* **1** = **break**, be out of order, break the law, contravene, defy, disobey, do *or* go wrong, err, fall from grace, go astray, infringe, lapse, misbehave, offend, sin, trespass, violate **2** = **go beyond**, encroach, exceed, overstep

transgression *noun* = **crime**, breach, contravention, encroachment, error, fault, infraction, infringement, iniquity, lapse, misbehaviour, misdeed, misdemeanour, offence, peccadillo, sin, trespass, violation, wrong, wrongdoing

transgressor *noun* = **criminal**, culprit, delinquent, evildoer, felon, lawbreaker, malefactor, miscreant, offender, sinner, trespasser, villain, wrongdoer

transience *noun* = **briefness**, brevity, ephemerality, impermanence, shortness, transitoriness

transient *adjective* = **brief**, ephemeral, evanescent, fleeting, flying, here today and gone tomorrow, impermanent, momentary, passing, short, short-lived, short-term, temporary, transitory
> **Antonyms**
abiding, constant, durable, enduring, eternal, imperishable, long-lasting, long-term, permanent, perpetual, persistent, undying

transit *noun* **1** = **movement**, carriage, conveyance, crossing, motion, passage, shipment, transfer, transport, transportation, travel **2 in transit** = **en route**, on the journey, on the move, on the road, on the way, while travelling

transition *noun* = **change**, alteration, changeover, conversion, development, evolution, flux, metamorphosis, passage, passing, progression, shift, transit, transmutation, upheaval

transitional *adjective* = **changing**, developmental, fluid, intermediate, passing, provisional, temporary, transitionary, unsettled

transitory *adjective* = **short-lived**, brief, ephemeral, evanescent, fleeting, here today and gone tomorrow, impermanent, momentary, passing, short, short-term,

temporary, transient
> **Antonyms**
abiding, enduring, eternal, everlasting, lasting, long-lived, long-term, permanent, perpetual, persistent, undying

translate *verb* **1** = **interpret**, construe, convert, decipher, decode, paraphrase, render, transcribe, transliterate **2** = **convert**, alter, change, transform, transmute, turn

translation *noun* **1** = **interpretation**, decoding, gloss, paraphrase, rendering, rendition, transcription, transliteration, version **2** = **rephrasing**, elucidation, explanation, paraphrase, rewording, simplification **3** = **conversion**, alteration, change, transformation, transmutation

translator *noun* = **interpreter**, linguist

translucent *adjective* = **semitransparent**, clear, diaphanous, limpid, lucent, pellucid

transmigration *noun* = **reincarnation**, metempsychosis, migration, movement, passage, rebirth

transmission *noun* **1** = **transfer**, communication, conveyance, diffusion, dispatch, dissemination, sending, shipment, spread, transference, transport **2** = **broadcasting**, dissemination, putting out, relaying, sending, showing **3** = **programme**, broadcast, show

transmit *verb* **1** = **pass on**, bear, carry, communicate, convey, diffuse, dispatch, disseminate, forward, hand down, hand on, impart, send, spread, take, transfer, transport **2** = **broadcast**, disseminate, put on the air, radio, relay, send, send out

transmute *verb* = **transform**, alter, change, convert, metamorphose, remake, transfigure

transparency *noun* **1** = **clarity**, clearness, diaphanousness, filminess, gauziness, limpidity, limpidness, pellucidity, pellucidness, translucence, translucency, transparence **2** = **obviousness**, apparentness, distinctness, explicitness, patentness, plainness, unambiguousness **3** = **photograph**, slide
> **Antonyms**
≠**clarity:** cloudiness, murkiness, opacity, unclearness ≠**obviousness:** obscurity, unclearness, vagueness

transparent *adjective* **1** = **clear**, crystal clear, crystalline, diaphanous, filmy, gauzy, limpid, lucent, lucid, pellucid, see-through, sheer, translucent **2** = **obvious**, apparent, as plain as the nose on one's face (*informal*), bold, distinct, evident, explicit, manifest, patent, perspicuous, plain, recognizable, unambiguous, understandable, undisguised, visible
> **Antonyms**
≠**clear:** cloudy, muddy, opaque, thick,

turbid, unclear ≠**obvious**: hidden, mysterious, opaque, uncertain, unclear, vague

transpire *verb* 1 = **become known**, be disclosed, be discovered, be made public, come out, come to light, emerge 2 *not universally accepted* = **happen**, arise, befall, chance, come about, come to pass (*archaic*), occur, take place

transplant *verb* = **transfer**, displace, relocate, remove, resettle, shift, uproot

transport *verb* 1 = **convey**, bear, bring, carry, fetch, haul, move, remove, run, ship, take, transfer 2 *History* = **exile**, banish, deport, sentence to transportation 3 = **enrapture**, captivate, carry away, delight, electrify, enchant, entrance, move, ravish, spellbind ♦ *noun* 4 = **vehicle**, conveyance, transportation, wheels (*informal*) 5 = **transference**, carriage, conveyance, removal, shipment, shipping, transportation 6 = **ecstasy**, bliss, cloud nine (*informal*), delight, enchantment, euphoria, happiness, heaven, rapture, ravishment, seventh heaven
➤ **Antonyms**
noun ≠**ecstasy**: blues (*informal*), depression, despondency, doldrums, dumps (*informal*), melancholy

transpose *verb* = **interchange**, alter, change, exchange, move, rearrange, relocate, reorder, shift, substitute, swap, switch, transfer

transverse *adjective* = **crossways**, athwart, crosswise, diagonal, oblique

trap *noun* 1 = **snare**, ambush, gin, net, noose, pitfall, springe, toils 2 = **trick**, ambush, deception, device, ruse, stratagem, subterfuge, wile ♦ *verb* 3 = **catch**, corner, enmesh, ensnare, entrap, snare, take 4 = **trick**, ambush, beguile, deceive, dupe, ensnare, inveigle

trapped *adjective* 1 = **caught**, ambushed, at bay, cornered, cut off, ensnared, in a tight corner, in a tight spot, netted, snared, stuck (*informal*), surrounded 2 = **tricked**, beguiled, deceived, duped, inveigled

trappings *plural noun* = **accessories**, accoutrements, adornments, bells and whistles, decorations, dress, equipment, finery, fittings, fixtures, fripperies, furnishings, gear, livery, ornaments, panoply, paraphernalia, things, trimmings

trash *noun* 1 = **nonsense**, balderdash, balls (*taboo slang*), bilge (*informal*), bosh (*informal*), bull (*slang*), bullshit (*taboo slang*), bunkum *or* buncombe (*chiefly U.S.*), cobblers (*Brit. taboo slang*), crap (*slang*), drivel, foolish talk, garbage (*informal*), hogwash, hot air (*informal*), kak (*S. African taboo*), moonshine, pants (*slang*), piffle (*informal*), poppycock (*informal*), rot, rubbish, shit (*taboo slang*), tommyrot, tripe (*informal*), twaddle 2 *Chiefly U.S. & Canad.* = **litter**, dreck (*slang, chiefly U.S.*), dregs, dross, garbage, junk (*informal*), offscourings, refuse, rubbish, sweepings, waste
➤ **Antonyms**
≠**nonsense**: logic, reason, sense, significance

trashy *adjective* = **worthless**, cheap, cheap-jack (*informal*), crappy (*slang*), inferior, poxy (*slang*), rubbishy, shabby, shoddy, tawdry, tinsel
➤ **Antonyms**
A1 *or* A-one (*informal*), excellent, exceptional, first-class, first-rate, outstanding, superlative

trauma *noun* 1 = **shock**, anguish, ordeal, pain, strain, suffering, torture, upheaval, upset 2 = **injury**, agony, damage, hurt, wound

traumatic *adjective* 1 = **shocking**, disturbing, painful, scarring, upsetting 2 = **wounding**, agonizing, damaging, hurtful, injurious
➤ **Antonyms**
≠**shocking**: calming, relaxing, therapeutic ≠**wounding**: healing, helpful, therapeutic, wholesome

travail *noun Literary* = **toil**, drudgery, effort, exertion, grind (*informal*), hardship, hard work, labour, slog, strain, suffering, sweat

travel *verb* 1 = **go**, cross, journey, make a journey, make one's way, move, proceed, progress, ramble, roam, rove, take a trip, tour, traverse, trek, voyage, walk, wander, wend 2 = **be transmitted**, carry, get through, move ♦ *noun* 3 *usually plural* = **journey**, excursion, expedition, globetrotting, movement, passage, peregrination, ramble, tour, touring, trip, voyage, walk, wandering

traveller *noun* 1 = **voyager**, excursionist, explorer, globetrotter, gypsy, hiker, holiday-maker, journeyer, migrant, nomad, passenger, tourist, tripper, wanderer, wayfarer 2 = **travelling salesman**, agent, commercial traveller, rep, representative, salesman, sales rep

travelling *adjective* = **itinerant**, migrant, migratory, mobile, moving, nomadic, peripatetic, restless, roaming, roving, touring, unsettled, wandering, wayfaring

traverse *verb* = **cross**, bridge, cover, cut across, go across, go over, make one's way across, negotiate, pass over, range, roam, span, travel over, wander

travesty *noun* 1 = **mockery**, burlesque, caricature, distortion, lampoon, parody, perversion, send-up (*Brit. informal*), sham, spoof (*informal*), takeoff (*informal*) ♦ *verb* 2

= **mock**, burlesque, caricature, distort, lampoon, make a mockery of, make fun of, parody, pervert, ridicule, send up (*Brit. informal*), sham, spoof (*informal*), take off (*informal*)

treacherous *adjective* 1 = **disloyal**, deceitful, double-crossing (*informal*), double-dealing, duplicitous, faithless, false, perfidious, traitorous, treasonable, unfaithful, unreliable, untrue, untrustworthy 2 = **dangerous**, deceptive, hazardous, icy, perilous, precarious, risky, slippery, slippy (*informal or dialect*), tricky, unreliable, unsafe, unstable
➤ **Antonyms**
≠**disloyal:** dependable, faithful, loyal, reliable, true, trustworthy ≠**dangerous:** reliable, safe

treachery *noun* = **betrayal**, disloyalty, double-cross (*informal*), double-dealing, duplicity, faithlessness, infidelity, perfidiousness, perfidy, stab in the back, treason
➤ **Antonyms**
allegiance, dependability, faithfulness, fidelity, loyalty, reliability

tread *verb* 1 = **crush underfoot**, squash, trample 2 = **step**, hike, march, pace, plod, stamp, stride, tramp, trudge, walk ♦ *noun* 3 = **step**, footfall, footstep, gait, pace, stride, walk

treason *noun* = **disloyalty**, duplicity, lese-majesty, mutiny, perfidy, sedition, subversion, traitorousness, treachery
➤ **Antonyms**
allegiance, faithfulness, fidelity, loyalty, patriotism

treasonable *adjective* = **disloyal**, false, mutinous, perfidious, seditious, subversive, traitorous, treacherous, treasonous
➤ **Antonyms**
dependable, faithful, loyal, patriotic, reliable, trustworthy

treasure *noun* 1 = **riches**, cash, fortune, funds, gold, jewels, money, valuables, wealth 2 *Informal* = **darling**, apple of one's eye, gem, jewel, nonpareil, paragon, pearl, precious, pride and joy, prize ♦ *verb* 3 = **prize**, adore, cherish, dote upon, esteem, hold dear, idolize, love, revere, value, venerate, worship

treasury *noun* 1 = **storehouse**, bank, cache, hoard, repository, store, vault 2 = **funds**, assets, capital, coffers, exchequer, finances, money, resources, revenues

treat *verb* 1 = **behave towards**, act towards, consider, deal with, handle, look upon, manage, regard, use 2 = **take care of**, apply treatment to, attend to, care for, doctor, medicate, nurse 3 = **provide**, buy for,

entertain, foot or pay the bill, give, lay on, pay for, regale, stand (*informal*) 4 **treat of** = **deal with**, be concerned with, contain, discuss, go into, touch upon ♦ *noun* 5 = **entertainment**, banquet, celebration, feast, gift, party, refreshment 6 = **pleasure**, delight, enjoyment, fun, gratification, joy, satisfaction, surprise, thrill

treatise *noun* = **paper**, disquisition, dissertation, essay, exposition, monograph, pamphlet, study, thesis, tract, work, writing

treatment *noun* 1 = **care**, cure, healing, medication, medicine, remedy, surgery, therapy 2 = **handling**, action, behaviour, conduct, dealing, management, manipulation, reception, usage

treaty *noun* = **agreement**, alliance, bargain, bond, compact, concordat, contract, convention, covenant, entente, pact

trek *noun* 1 = **journey**, expedition, footslog, hike, long haul, march, odyssey, safari, slog, tramp ♦ *verb* 2 = **journey**, footslog, hike, march, plod, range, roam, rove, slog, traipse (*informal*), tramp, trudge

tremble *verb* 1 = **shake**, oscillate, quake, quiver, rock, shiver, shudder, teeter, totter, vibrate, wobble ♦ *noun* 2 = **shake**, oscillation, quake, quiver, shiver, shudder, tremor, vibration, wobble

tremendous *adjective* 1 = **huge**, awesome, colossal, enormous, formidable, gargantuan, gigantic, great, immense, monstrous, prodigious, stupendous, terrific, titanic, towering, vast, whopping (*informal*) 2 = **excellent**, amazing, awesome (*slang*), brilliant, cracking (*Brit. informal*), exceptional, extraordinary, fabulous (*informal*), fantastic (*informal*), great, incredible, marvellous, sensational (*informal*), super (*informal*), terrific (*informal*), wonderful
➤ **Antonyms**
≠**huge:** diminutive, little, minuscule, minute, small, tiny ≠**excellent:** abysmal, appalling, average, awful, dreadful, mediocre, no great shakes (*informal*), ordinary, rotten, run-of-the-mill, so-so, terrible

tremor *noun* 1 = **shake**, agitation, quaking, quaver, quiver, quivering, shaking, shiver, tremble, trembling, vibration, wobble 2 = **earthquake**, quake (*informal*), shock

tremulous *adjective Literary* = **trembling**, aflutter, agitated, antsy (*informal*), anxious, excited, fearful, frightened, jittery (*informal*), jumpy, nervous, quavering, quivering, scared, shaking, shivering, timid

trench *noun* = **ditch**, channel, cut, drain, earthwork, entrenchment, excavation, furrow, gutter, pit, trough, waterway

trenchant *adjective* 1 = **scathing**, acerbic,

acid, acute, biting, caustic, cutting, hurtful, incisive, keen, mordant, penetrating, piquant, pointed, pungent, sarcastic, severe, sharp, tart, vitriolic **2 = effective**, driving, effectual, emphatic, energetic, forceful, potent, powerful, strong, vigorous
➤ **Antonyms**
≠**scathing:** appeasing, kind, mollifying, soothing

trend noun **1 = tendency**, bias, course, current, direction, drift, flow, inclination, leaning **2 = fashion**, craze, fad (informal), look, mode, rage, style, thing, vogue ♦ verb **3 = tend**, bend, flow, head, incline, lean, run, stretch, swing, turn, veer

trendsetter noun **= leader of fashion**, arbiter of taste, pacesetter

trendy Brit. informal ♦ adjective **1 = fashionable**, in fashion, in vogue, modish, stylish, voguish, with it (informal) ♦ noun **2 = poser** (informal), pseud (informal)

trepidation noun Formal **= anxiety**, agitation, alarm, apprehension, butterflies (informal), cold feet (informal), cold sweat (informal), consternation, dismay, disquiet, disturbance, dread, fear, fright, jitters (informal), nervousness, palpitation, perturbation, quivering, shaking, trembling, uneasiness, worry
➤ **Antonyms**
aplomb, calm, composure, confidence, coolness, equanimity, self-assurance

trespass verb **1 = intrude**, encroach, infringe, invade, obtrude, poach ♦ noun **2 = intrusion**, encroachment, infringement, invasion, poaching, unlawful entry, wrongful entry **3** Old-fashioned **= sin**, breach, crime, error, evildoing, fault, infraction, iniquity, misbehaviour, misconduct, misdeed, misdemeanour, offence, transgression, wrongdoing

trespasser noun **1 = intruder**, infringer, interloper, invader, poacher, unwelcome visitor **2** Archaic **= sinner**, criminal, delinquent, evildoer, malefactor, offender, transgressor, wrongdoer

tresses plural noun **= hair**, locks

triad noun **= threesome**, trilogy, trinity, trio, triple, triplet, triptych, triumvirate, triune

trial noun **1** Law **= hearing**, industrial tribunal, judicial examination, litigation, tribunal **2 = test**, audition, check, dry run (informal), examination, experiment, probation, proof, testing, test-run **3 = attempt**, crack (informal), effort, endeavour, go (informal), shot (informal), stab (informal), try, venture **4 = hardship**, adversity, affliction, burden, cross to bear, distress, grief, hard times, load, misery, ordeal, pain, suffering, tribulation, trouble,

unhappiness, vexation, woe, wretchedness **5 = nuisance**, bane, bother, drag (informal), hassle (informal), irritation, pain in the neck (informal), pest, plague (informal), thorn in one's flesh or side, vexation ♦ adjective **6 = experimental**, exploratory, pilot, probationary, provisional, testing

tribe noun **= race**, blood, caste, clan, class, dynasty, ethnic group, family, house, people, seed (chiefly biblical), stock

tribulation noun **= trouble**, adversity, affliction, bummer (slang), burden, care, cross to bear, distress, grief, hardship, hassle (informal), heartache, misery, misfortune, ordeal, pain, sorrow, suffering, trial, unhappiness, woe, worry
➤ **Antonyms**
blessing, bliss, ease, good fortune, happiness, joy, pleasure, rest

tribunal noun **= hearing**, bar, bench, court, industrial tribunal, judgment seat, judicial examination, trial

tribute noun **1 = accolade**, acknowledgment, applause, commendation, compliment, eulogy, gift, gratitude, honour, panegyric, praise, recognition, respect, testimonial **2 = tax**, charge, contribution, customs, duty, excise, homage, offering, payment, ransom, subsidy, toll
➤ **Antonyms**
≠**accolade:** blame, complaint, condemnation, criticism, disapproval, reproach, reproof

trice noun As in **in a trice = moment**, flash, instant, jiffy (informal), minute, second, split second, tick (Brit. informal)

trick noun **1 = deception**, artifice, con (slang), deceit, dodge, fraud, hoax, manoeuvre, ploy, ruse, scam (slang), sting (informal), stratagem, subterfuge, swindle, trap, wile **2 = joke**, antic, caper, gag (informal), jape, leg-pull (Brit. informal), practical joke, prank, put-on (slang), stunt **3 = secret**, art, craft, expertise, hang (informal), knack, know-how (informal), skill, technique **4 = sleight of hand**, device, feat, legerdemain **5 = mannerism**, characteristic, foible, habit, idiosyncrasy, peculiarity, practice, quirk, trait **6 do the trick** Informal **= work**, be effective or effectual, have effect, produce the desired result ♦ verb **7 = deceive**, cheat, con (informal), defraud, delude, dupe, fool, have (someone) on, hoax, hoodwink, kid (informal), mislead, pull a fast one on (informal), pull the wool over (someone's) eyes, sting (informal), swindle, take in (informal), trap

trickery noun **= deception**, cheating, chicanery, con (informal), deceit, dishonesty, double-dealing, fraud, funny

business, guile, hanky-panky (*informal*),
hoax, jiggery-pokery (*informal, chiefly Brit.*),
monkey business (*informal*), skulduggery
(*informal*), swindling
➤ **Antonyms**
artlessness, candour, directness, frankness,
honesty, openness, straightforwardness,
uprightness

trickle *verb* **1** = **dribble**, crawl, creep, drip,
drop, exude, ooze, percolate, run, seep,
stream ♦ *noun* **2** = **dribble**, drip, seepage

trick out *verb* = **dress up**, adorn, array,
attire, bedeck, deck out, doll up (*slang*), do
up (*informal*), get up (*informal*)

trickster *noun* = **deceiver**, cheat, chiseller
(*informal*), con man (*informal*), fraud,
fraudster, hoaxer, hustler (*U.S. informal*),
joker, practical joker, swindler

tricky *adjective* **1** = **difficult**, complicated,
delicate, knotty, problematic, risky, sticky
(*informal*), thorny, ticklish, touch-and-go **2**
= **crafty**, artful, cunning, deceitful,
deceptive, devious, foxy, scheming, slippery,
sly, subtle, wily
➤ **Antonyms**
≠**difficult**: clear, easy, obvious, simple,
straightforward, uncomplicated ≠**crafty**:
above board, artless, direct, genuine, honest,
ingenuous, open, sincere, truthful

trifle¹ *noun* **1** = **knick-knack**, bagatelle,
bauble, child's play (*informal*), gewgaw,
nothing, plaything, toy, triviality **2** = **little**,
bit, dash, drop, jot, pinch, spot, touch, trace

trifle² *verb* = **toy**, amuse oneself, dally, flirt,
mess about, play, play fast and loose
(*informal*)

trifling *adjective* = **insignificant**, empty,
footling (*informal*), frivolous, inconsiderable,
measly, minuscule, negligible, paltry, petty,
piddling (*informal*), shallow, silly, slight,
small, tiny, trivial, unimportant, valueless,
worthless
➤ **Antonyms**
considerable, crucial, important, large,
major, serious, significant, vital, weighty

trigger *verb* = **set off**, activate, bring about,
cause, elicit, generate, give rise to, produce,
prompt, provoke, set in motion, spark off,
start
➤ **Antonyms**
bar, block, hinder, impede, inhibit, obstruct,
prevent, repress, stop

trim *adjective* **1** = **neat**, compact, dapper,
natty (*informal*), nice, orderly, shipshape,
smart, soigné *or* soignée, spick-and-span,
spruce, tidy, well-groomed, well turned-out
2 = **slender**, fit, shapely, sleek, slim,
streamlined, svelte, willowy ♦ *verb* **3** = **cut**,
barber, clip, crop, cut back, even up, lop,
pare, prune, shave, shear, tidy **4** = **decorate**,

adorn, array, beautify, bedeck, deck out,
dress, embellish, garnish, ornament **5**
= **adjust**, arrange, balance, distribute, order,
prepare, settle ♦ *noun* **6** = **decoration**,
adornment, border, edging, embellishment,
frill, fringe, garnish, ornamentation, piping,
trimming **7** = **condition**, fettle, fitness, form,
health, order, repair, shape (*informal*),
situation, state, wellness **8** = **cut**, clipping,
crop, pruning, shave, shearing, tidying up,
trimming
➤ **Antonyms**
adjective ≠**neat**: disarrayed, disorderly,
messy, scruffy, shabby, sloppy, ungroomed,
unkempt, untidy

trimming *noun* **1** = **decoration**,
adornment, border, braid, edging,
embellishment, festoon, frill, fringe, garnish,
ornamentation, piping **2** *trimmings*
= **extras**, accessories, accompaniments,
appurtenances, frills, garnish, ornaments,
paraphernalia, trappings

trinity *noun* = **threesome**, triad, trilogy, trio,
triple, triplet, triptych, triumvirate

trinket *noun* = **ornament**, bagatelle, bauble,
bibelot, gewgaw, gimcrack, knick-knack, toy,
trifle

trio *noun* = **threesome**, triad, trilogy, trinity,
triple, triplet, triptych, triumvirate

trip *noun* **1** = **journey**, errand, excursion,
expedition, foray, jaunt, outing, ramble, run,
tour, travel, voyage **2** = **stumble**, blunder,
fall, false move, false step, misstep, slip
♦ *verb* **3** = **stumble**, fall, lose one's balance,
lose one's footing, make a false move,
misstep, slip, tumble **4** = **catch out**, confuse,
disconcert, put off one's stride, throw off,
trap, unsettle **5** = **skip**, caper, dance, flit,
frisk, gambol, hop, spring, tread lightly **6**
Informal = **take drugs**, get high (*informal*),
get stoned (*slang*), turn on (*slang*)

tripe *noun Informal* = **nonsense**, balderdash,
balls (*taboo slang*), bilge (*informal*),
bollocks (*Brit. taboo slang*), bosh
(*informal*), bull (*slang*), bullshit (*taboo
slang*), claptrap (*informal*), cobblers (*Brit.
taboo slang*), crap (*slang*), drivel, foolish
talk, garbage (*informal*), hogwash, hot air
(*informal*), moonshine, pants (*slang*), piffle
(*informal*), poppycock (*informal*), rot,
rubbish, shit (*taboo slang*), tommyrot, tosh
(*slang, chiefly Brit.*), trash, twaddle

triple *adjective* **1** = **threefold**, three times as
much, three-way, tripartite ♦ *verb* **2**
= **treble**, increase threefold, triplicate
♦ *noun* **3** = **threesome**, triad, trilogy, trinity,
trio, triplet, triumvirate

triplet *noun* = **threesome**, triad, trilogy,
trinity, trio, triple, triumvirate

tripper *noun Chiefly Brit.* = **tourist**,

trite 747 **trouble**

excursionist, holiday-maker, sightseer, voyager

trite *adjective* = **unoriginal**, banal, clichéd, common, commonplace, corny (*slang*), dull, hack, hackneyed, ordinary, pedestrian, routine, run-of-the-mill, stale, stereotyped, stock, threadbare, tired, uninspired, worn
➤ Antonyms
exciting, fresh, interesting, new, novel, original, out-of-the-ordinary, uncommon, unexpected, unfamiliar

triumph *noun* 1 = **joy**, elation, exultation, happiness, jubilation, pride, rejoicing 2 = **success**, accomplishment, achievement, attainment, conquest, coup, feat, feather in one's cap, hit (*informal*), mastery, sensation, smash (*informal*), smash hit (*informal*), tour de force, victory, walkover (*informal*) ♦ *verb* 3 *often with* **over** = **succeed**, come out on top (*informal*), get the better of, overcome, overwhelm, prevail, prosper, vanquish, win 4 = **rejoice**, celebrate, crow, exult, gloat, glory, jubilate, revel
➤ Antonyms
noun ≠**success**: catastrophe, clunker (*informal*), defeat, disaster, failure, fiasco, flop (*informal*), washout (*informal*) ♦ *verb* ≠**succeed**: come a cropper (*informal*), fail, fall, flop (*informal*), lose

triumphant *adjective* 1 = **victorious**, boastful, cock-a-hoop, conquering, elated, exultant, glorious, proud, successful, swaggering, undefeated, winning 2 = **celebratory**, jubilant, rejoicing, triumphal
➤ Antonyms
≠**victorious**: beaten, defeated, embarrassed, humbled, humiliated, shamed, unsuccessful

trivia *noun* = **minutiae**, details, petty details, trifles, trivialities
➤ Antonyms
basics, brass tacks (*informal*), core, essentials, fundamentals, nitty-gritty (*informal*), rudiments

trivial *adjective* = **unimportant**, commonplace, everyday, frivolous, incidental, inconsequential, inconsiderable, insignificant, little, meaningless, minor, negligible, paltry, petty, puny, slight, small, trifling, valueless, worthless
➤ Antonyms
considerable, crucial, essential, important, profound, serious, significant, uncommon, unusual, vital, weighty, worthwhile

triviality *noun* 1 = **insignificance**, frivolity, inconsequentiality, littleness, meaninglessness, negligibility, paltriness, pettiness, slightness, smallness, unimportance, valuelessness, worthlessness 2 = **trifle**, detail, no big thing, no great matter, nothing, petty detail, technicality

➤ Antonyms
≠**insignificance**: consequence, importance, significance, value, worth ≠**trifle**: essential, rudiment

trivialize *verb* = **undervalue**, belittle, laugh off, make light of, minimize, play down, scoff at, underestimate, underplay

trollop *noun Derogatory* = **slut**, fallen woman, floozy (*slang*), harlot, hussy, loose woman, prostitute, scrubber (*Brit. & Austral. slang*), slag (*Brit. slang*), slattern, streetwalker, strumpet, tart (*informal*), wanton, whore

troop *noun* 1 = **group**, assemblage, band, bevy, body, bunch (*informal*), company, contingent, crew (*informal*), crowd, drove, flock, gang, gathering, herd, horde, multitude, pack, posse (*informal*), squad, swarm, team, throng, unit 2 **troops** = **soldiers**, armed forces, army, fighting men, men, military, servicemen, soldiery ♦ *verb* 3 = **flock**, crowd, march, parade, stream, swarm, throng, traipse (*informal*)

trophy *noun* = **prize**, award, bays, booty, cup, laurels, memento, souvenir, spoils

tropical *adjective* = **hot**, humid, steamy, stifling, sultry, sweltering, torrid
➤ Antonyms
arctic, chilly, cold, cool, freezing, frosty, frozen, parky (*Brit. informal*)

trot *verb* 1 = **run**, canter, go briskly, jog, lope, scamper ♦ *noun* 2 = **run**, brisk pace, canter, jog, lope 3 **on the trot** *Informal* = **one after the other**, consecutively, in a row, in succession, without break, without interruption

trot out *verb Informal* = **repeat**, bring forward, bring up, come out with, drag up, recite, reiterate

troubadour *noun* = **minstrel**, balladeer, poet, singer

trouble *noun* 1 = **distress**, agitation, annoyance, anxiety, bummer (*slang*), disquiet, grief, hardship, hassle (*informal*), heartache, irritation, misfortune, pain, sorrow, suffering, torment, tribulation, vexation, woe, worry 2 = **ailment**, complaint, defect, disability, disease, disorder, failure, illness, malfunction, upset 3 = **disorder**, agitation, bother (*informal*), commotion, discontent, discord, dissatisfaction, disturbance, hassle (*informal*), row, strife, tumult, unrest 4 = **effort**, attention, care, exertion, inconvenience, labour, pains, struggle, thought, work 5 = **difficulty**, bother, concern, danger, deep water (*informal*), dilemma, dire straits, hassle (*informal*), hot water (*informal*), mess, nuisance, pest, pickle (*informal*), predicament, problem, scrape (*informal*),

spot (*informal*), tight spot ◆ *verb* **6**
= **bother**, afflict, agitate, annoy, discompose,
disconcert, disquiet, distress, disturb, faze,
harass, hassle (*informal*), pain, perplex,
perturb, pester, plague, sadden, torment,
upset, vex, worry **7** = **take pains**, exert
oneself, go to the effort of, make an effort,
take the time **8** = **inconvenience**, bother,
burden, discommode, disturb, impose upon,
incommode, put out
➤ Antonyms
noun ≠**distress**: comfort, contentment,
good fortune, happiness, pleasure,
tranquillity ≠**disorder**: agreement,
contentment, harmony, peace, tranquillity,
unity ≠**effort**: convenience, ease, facility
◆ *verb* ≠**bother**: appease, calm, mollify,
please, relieve, soothe ≠**take pains**: avoid,
dodge ≠**inconvenience**: relieve

troublemaker *noun* = **mischief-maker**,
agent provocateur, agitator, bad apple (*U.S.
informal*), firebrand, incendiary, instigator,
meddler, rabble-rouser, rotten apple (*Brit.
informal*), stirrer (*informal*)
➤ Antonyms
appeaser, arbitrator, conciliator, pacifier,
peace-maker

troublesome *adjective* **1** = **bothersome**,
annoying, arduous, burdensome,
demanding, difficult, harassing, hard,
importunate, inconvenient, irksome,
irritating, laborious, taxing, tiresome, tricky,
trying, upsetting, vexatious, wearisome,
worrisome, worrying **2** = **disorderly**,
insubordinate, rebellious, recalcitrant,
refractory, rowdy, turbulent, uncooperative,
undisciplined, unruly, violent
➤ Antonyms
≠**bothersome**: agreeable, calming,
congenial, easy, pleasant, simple, soothing,
undemanding ≠**disorderly**: disciplined,
eager-to-please, obedient, well-behaved

trough *noun* **1** = **manger**, crib, water
trough **2** = **channel**, canal, depression, ditch,
duct, flume, furrow, gully, gutter, trench,
watercourse

trounce *verb* = **defeat heavily** *or* **utterly**,
beat, beat (someone) hollow (*Brit.
informal*), blow out of the water (*slang*),
clobber (*slang*), crush, drub, give a hiding
(*informal*), give a pasting (*slang*), hammer
(*informal*), lick (*informal*), overwhelm, rout,
run rings around (*informal*), slaughter
(*informal*), tank (*slang*), thrash, wipe the
floor with (*informal*)

troupe *noun* = **company**, band, cast

trouper *noun* = **performer**, actor, artiste,
entertainer, player, thespian

truancy *noun* = **absence**, absence without
leave, malingering, shirking, skiving (*Brit.
slang*)

truant *noun* **1** = **absentee**, delinquent,
deserter, dodger, malingerer, runaway,
shirker, skiver (*Brit. slang*) ◆ *adjective* **2**
= **absent**, absent without leave, A.W.O.L.,
missing, skiving (*Brit. slang*)

truce *noun* = **ceasefire**, armistice, break,
cessation, cessation of hostilities, let-up
(*informal*), lull, moratorium, peace, respite,
stay, treaty

truckle *verb* = **give in**, fawn, give way,
knuckle under, kowtow, lick (someone's)
boots, pander to, submit, toady, yield

truculent *adjective* = **hostile**, aggressive,
antagonistic, bad-tempered, bellicose,
belligerent, combative, contentious, cross,
defiant, fierce, ill-tempered, obstreperous,
pugnacious, sullen
➤ Antonyms
agreeable, amiable, civil, co-operative,
gentle, good-natured, peaceable, placid

trudge *verb* **1** = **plod**, clump, drag oneself,
footslog, hike, lumber, march, slog, stump,
traipse (*informal*), tramp, trek, walk heavily
◆ *noun* **2** = **tramp**, footslog, haul, hike,
march, slog, traipse (*informal*), trek

true *adjective* **1** = **correct**, accurate, actual,
authentic, bona fide, exact, factual, genuine,
legitimate, natural, precise, pure, real, right,
truthful, valid, veracious, veritable **2**
= **faithful**, constant, dedicated, devoted,
dutiful, fast, firm, loyal, reliable, sincere,
staunch, steady, true-blue, trustworthy,
trusty **3** = **exact**, accurate, correct, on target,
perfect, precise, proper, spot-on (*Brit.
informal*), unerring **4 come true** = **happen**,
become reality, be granted, be realized,
come to pass, occur ◆ *adverb* **5** = **truthfully**,
honestly, rightly, veraciously, veritably
➤ Antonyms
adjective ≠**correct**: abnormal, artificial,
atypical, bogus, counterfeit, erroneous, fake,
false, fictional, fictitious, illegitimate,
imaginary, inaccurate, incorrect, made-up,
make-believe, phoney *or* phony (*informal*),
pretended, self-styled, spurious, unofficial,
untrue, untruthful ≠**faithful**: deceitful,
disloyal, faithless, false, treacherous,
unreliable, untrue, untrustworthy ≠**exact**:
askew, awry, inaccurate, incorrect

true-blue *adjective* = **staunch**, confirmed,
constant, dedicated, devoted,
dyed-in-the-wool, faithful, loyal, trusty,
uncompromising, unwavering

truism *noun* = **cliché**, axiom, bromide,
commonplace, platitude, stock phrase, trite
saying

truly *adverb* **1** = **correctly**, accurately,
authentically, beyond doubt, beyond
question, exactly, factually, genuinely, in
actuality, in fact, in reality, in truth,

legitimately, precisely, really, rightly, truthfully, veraciously, veritably, without a doubt **2 = faithfully**, confirmedly, constantly, devotedly, dutifully, firmly, loyally, sincerely, staunchly, steadily, with all one's heart, with dedication, with devotion **3 = really**, exceptionally, extremely, greatly, indeed, of course, seriously (*informal*), to be sure, verily, very
➤ **Antonyms**
≠**correctly:** doubtfully, falsely, fraudulently, inaccurately, incorrectly, mistakenly

trump *noun, verb* **1 = ruff** ♦ *verb* **2 = outdo**, cap, excel, surpass, top

trumped up *adjective* **= invented**, concocted, contrived, cooked-up (*informal*), fabricated, fake, false, falsified, made-up, manufactured, phoney *or* phony (*informal*), untrue
➤ **Antonyms**
actual, authentic, bona fide, genuine, real, sound, true, veritable

trumpery *noun* **= trifle**, bagatelle, bauble, gewgaw, knick-knack, toy, trinket

trumpet *noun* **1 = horn**, bugle, clarion **2 = roar**, bay, bellow, call, cry **3 blow one's own trumpet = boast**, brag, crow, sing one's own praises ♦ *verb* **4 = proclaim**, advertise, announce, broadcast, crack up (*informal*), extol, publish, shout from the rooftops, tout (*informal*)
➤ **Antonyms**
verb ≠**proclaim:** conceal, hide, hush up, keep secret, make light of, play down, soft pedal (*informal*)

trump up *verb* **= invent**, concoct, contrive, cook up (*informal*), create, fabricate, fake, make up, manufacture

truncate *verb* **= shorten**, abbreviate, clip, crop, curtail, cut, cut short, dock, lop, pare, prune, trim
➤ **Antonyms**
drag out, draw out, extend, lengthen, prolong, protract, spin out, stretch

truncheon *noun Chiefly Brit.* **= club**, baton, cudgel, staff

trunk *noun* **1 = stem**, bole, stalk, stock **2 = chest**, bin, box, case, casket, coffer, crate, portmanteau **3 = body**, torso **4 = snout**, proboscis

truss *verb* **1 = tie**, bind, fasten, make fast, pack, secure, strap, tether ♦ *noun* **2** *Medical* **= support**, bandage **3 = joist**, beam, brace, buttress, prop, shore, stanchion, stay, strut, support

trust *verb* **1 = believe in**, bank on, count on, depend on, have faith in, lean on, pin one's faith on, place confidence in, place one's trust in, place reliance on, rely upon, swear by, take as gospel, take at face value **2 = entrust**, assign, command, commit, confide, consign, delegate, give, put into the hands of, sign over, turn over **3 = expect**, assume, believe, hope, presume, suppose, surmise, think likely ♦ *noun* **4 = confidence**, assurance, belief, certainty, certitude, conviction, credence, credit, expectation, faith, hope, reliance **5 = responsibility**, duty, obligation **6 = custody**, care, charge, guard, guardianship, protection, safekeeping, trusteeship
➤ **Antonyms**
verb ≠**believe in:** be sceptical of, beware, disbelieve, discredit, distrust, doubt, lack confidence in, lack faith in, mistrust, suspect ♦ *noun* ≠**confidence:** distrust, doubt, fear, incredulity, lack of faith, mistrust, scepticism, suspicion, uncertainty, wariness

trustful, trusting *adjective* **= unsuspecting**, confiding, credulous, gullible, innocent, naive, optimistic, simple, unguarded, unsuspicious, unwary
➤ **Antonyms**
cagey (*informal*), cautious, chary, distrustful, guarded, on one's guard, suspicious, wary

trustworthy *adjective* **= dependable**, ethical, honest, honourable, principled, reliable, reputable, responsible, staunch, steadfast, to be trusted, true, trusty, truthful, upright
➤ **Antonyms**
deceitful, dishonest, disloyal, irresponsible, treacherous, undependable, unethical, unprincipled, unreliable, untrustworthy

trusty *adjective* **= reliable**, dependable, faithful, solid, staunch, steady, strong, true, trustworthy
➤ **Antonyms**
dishonest, irresolute, irresponsible, undependable, unfaithful, unreliable

truth *noun* **1 = truthfulness**, accuracy, actuality, exactness, fact, factuality, factualness, genuineness, legitimacy, precision, reality, validity, veracity, verity **2 = fact**, axiom, certainty, law, maxim, proven principle, reality, truism, verity
➤ **Antonyms**
≠**truthfulness:** error, falsity, inaccuracy ≠**fact:** delusion, fabrication, falsehood, fiction, invention, legend, lie, make-believe, myth, old wives' tale, untruth

truthful *adjective* **1 = honest**, candid, faithful, forthright, frank, plain-spoken, reliable, sincere, straight, straightforward, true, trustworthy, upfront (*informal*), veracious **2 = true**, accurate, correct, exact, literal, naturalistic, precise, realistic, veritable
➤ **Antonyms**
≠**honest:** deceptive, dishonest, false, insincere, lying, untruthful ≠**true:** fabricated, false, fictional, fictitious,

inaccurate, incorrect, made-up, untrue, untruthful

try *verb* **1** = **attempt**, aim, bend over backwards (*informal*), break one's neck (*informal*), do one's best, do one's damnedest (*informal*), endeavour, essay, exert oneself, give it one's all (*informal*), give it one's best shot (*informal*), go for it (*informal*), have a crack (*informal*), have a go, have a shot (*informal*), have a stab (*informal*), have a whack (*informal*), knock oneself out (*informal*), make an all-out effort (*informal*), make an attempt, make an effort, move heaven and earth, seek, strive, struggle, undertake **2** = **test**, appraise, check out, evaluate, examine, experiment, inspect, investigate, prove, put to the test, sample, taste **3** = **strain**, afflict, annoy, irk, irritate, pain, plague, stress, tax, tire, trouble, upset, vex, weary **4** = **judge**, adjudge, adjudicate, examine, hear ◆ *noun* **5** = **attempt**, crack (*informal*), effort, endeavour, essay, go (*informal*), shot (*informal*), stab (*informal*), whack (*informal*)

trying *adjective* = **annoying**, aggravating (*informal*), arduous, bothersome, difficult, exasperating, hard, irksome, irritating, stressful, taxing, tiresome, tough, troublesome, upsetting, vexing, wearisome
➤ **Antonyms**
calming, easy, no bother, no trouble, painless, simple, straightforward, undemanding

try out *verb* = **test**, appraise, check out, evaluate, experiment with, inspect, put into practice, put to the test, sample, taste

tubby *adjective* = **fat**, chubby, corpulent, obese, overweight, plump, portly, stout

tuck *verb* **1** = **push**, fold, gather, insert ◆ *noun* **2** = **fold**, gather, pinch, pleat **3** *Brit. informal* = **food**, comestibles, eats (*slang*), grub (*slang*), nosh (*slang*), scoff (*slang*), tack (*informal*), victuals, vittles (*obsolete or dialect*)

tuck in *verb* **1** = **make snug**, bed down, enfold, fold under, put to bed, swaddle, wrap up **2** *Informal* = **eat up**, chow down (*slang*), eat heartily, fall to, get stuck in (*informal*)

tuft *noun* = **clump**, bunch, cluster, collection, knot, tussock

tug *verb* **1** = **pull**, drag, draw, haul, heave, jerk, lug, tow, wrench, yank ◆ *noun* **2** = **pull**, drag, haul, heave, jerk, tow, traction, wrench, yank

tuition *noun* = **training**, education, instruction, lessons, schooling, teaching, tutelage, tutoring

tumble *verb* **1** = **fall**, drop, fall headlong, flop, pitch, plummet, roll, stumble, topple,

toss, trip up ◆ *noun* **2** = **fall**, collapse, drop, flop, headlong fall, plunge, roll, spill, stumble, toss, trip

tumbledown *adjective* = **dilapidated**, crumbling, decrepit, disintegrating, falling to pieces, ramshackle, rickety, ruined, shaky, tottering
➤ **Antonyms**
durable, firm, solid, sound, stable, sturdy, substantial, well-kept

tumid *adjective* **1** = **swollen**, bloated, bulging, distended, enlarged, inflated, protuberant, puffed up, puffy, tumescent **2** = **pompous**, arty-farty (*informal*), bombastic, flowery, fulsome, grandiloquent, grandiose, high-flown, inflated, magniloquent, pretentious

tummy *noun Informal* = **stomach**, abdomen, belly, gut (*informal*), inside(s) (*informal*), paunch, pot, potbelly, spare tyre (*informal*), tum (*informal*)

tumour *noun* = **growth**, cancer, carcinoma (*Pathology*), lump, sarcoma (*Medical*), swelling

tumult *noun* = **commotion**, ado, affray (*Law*), agitation, altercation, bedlam, brawl, brouhaha, clamour, din, disorder, disturbance, excitement, fracas, hubbub, hullabaloo, outbreak, pandemonium, quarrel, racket, riot, row, ruction (*informal*), stir, stramash (*Scot.*), strife, turmoil, unrest, upheaval, uproar
➤ **Antonyms**
calm, hush, peace, quiet, repose, serenity, silence, stillness

tumultuous *adjective* **1** = **turbulent**, agitated, confused, disturbed, exciting, hectic, stormy **2** = **wild**, boisterous, clamorous, disorderly, excited, noisy, raging, riotous, rowdy, unrestrained, unruly, uproarious, violent
➤ **Antonyms**
calm, hushed, peaceful, quiet, restful, serene, still, tranquil

tune *noun* **1** = **melody**, air, melody line, motif, song, strain, theme **2** = **concord**, agreement, concert, consonance, euphony, harmony, pitch, unison **3 call the tune** = **be in control**, be in charge, be in command, call the shots (*slang*), command, dictate, govern, lead, rule **4 change one's tune** = **change one's attitude**, change one's mind, do an about-face, have a change of heart, reconsider, take a different tack, think again ◆ *verb* **5** = **adjust**, adapt, attune, bring into harmony, harmonize, pitch, regulate
➤ **Antonyms**
noun ≠**concord**: clashing, conflict, contention, disagreement, discord, discordance, disharmony, disunity, friction

tuneful *adjective* = **melodious**, catchy, easy on the ear (*informal*), euphonic, euphonious, harmonious, mellifluous, melodic, musical, pleasant
➤ **Antonyms**
cacophonous, clashing, discordant, dissonant, harsh, jangly, tuneless, unmelodious

tuneless *adjective* = **discordant**, atonal, cacophonous, clashing, dissonant, harsh, unmelodic, unmelodious, unmusical
➤ **Antonyms**
harmonious, melodious, musical, pleasing, sonorous, symphonic, tuneful

tunnel *noun* 1 = **passage**, burrow, channel, hole, passageway, shaft, subway, underpass
♦ *verb* 2 = **dig**, burrow, dig one's way, excavate, mine, penetrate, scoop out

turbid *adjective Literary* = **murky**, clouded, cloudy, dim, muddy, opaque, unclear, unsettled

turbulence *noun* = **confusion**, agitation, commotion, disorder, instability, pandemonium, roughness, storm, tumult, turmoil, unrest, upheaval
➤ **Antonyms**
calm, peace, quiet, repose, rest, stillness

turbulent *adjective* 1 = **wild**, anarchic, boisterous, disorderly, lawless, mutinous, rebellious, refractory, rowdy, undisciplined, ungovernable, unruly, uproarious, violent 2 = **agitated**, blustery, choppy, confused, disordered, foaming, furious, raging, rough, tempestuous, tumultuous, unsettled, unstable
➤ **Antonyms**
≠**agitated:** calm, glassy, peaceful, quiet, smooth, still, unruffled

turf *noun* 1 = **grass**, clod, divot, green, sod, sward 2 **the turf** = **horse-racing**, racecourse, racetrack, racing, the flat

turf out *verb Brit. informal* = **throw out**, banish, cast out, chuck out (*informal*), discharge, dismiss, dispossess, eject, evict, expel, fire (*informal*), fling out, kick out (*informal*), show one the door

turgid *adjective* = **pompous**, arty-farty (*informal*), bombastic, flowery, fulsome, grandiloquent, grandiose, high-flown, inflated, magniloquent, overblown, pretentious, windy

turmoil *noun* = **confusion**, agitation, bedlam, brouhaha, bustle, chaos, commotion, disarray, disorder, disturbance, ferment, flurry, hubbub, noise, pandemonium, row, stir, strife, trouble, tumult, turbulence, upheaval, uproar, violence
➤ **Antonyms**
calm, peace, quiet, repose, rest, serenity,

stillness, tranquillity

turn *verb* 1 = **change course**, change position, go back, move, return, reverse, shift, swerve, switch, veer, wheel 2 = **rotate**, circle, go round, gyrate, move in a circle, pivot, revolve, roll, spin, swivel, twirl, twist, wheel, whirl 3 = **go round**, arc, come round, corner, negotiate, pass, pass around, take a bend 4 = **change**, adapt, alter, become, convert, divert, fashion, fit, form, metamorphose, mould, mutate, remodel, shape, transfigure, transform, transmute 5 = **shape**, construct, execute, fashion, frame, make, mould, perform 6 = **go bad**, become rancid, curdle, go off (*Brit. informal*), go sour, make rancid, sour, spoil, taint 7 = **sicken**, nauseate, upset 8 **turn to** = **appeal**, apply, approach, go, have recourse, look, resort ♦ *noun* 9 = **rotation**, bend, change, circle, curve, cycle, gyration, pivot, reversal, revolution, spin, swing, turning, twist, whirl 10 = **change of direction**, bend, change of course, curve, departure, deviation, shift 11 = **opportunity**, chance, crack (*informal*), fling, go, period, round, shift, shot (*informal*), spell, stint, succession, time, try, whack (*informal*) 12 = **direction**, drift, heading, tendency, trend 13 = **excursion**, airing, constitutional, drive, jaunt, outing, promenade, ride, saunter, spin (*informal*), stroll, walk 14 = **inclination**, affinity, bent, bias, leaning, propensity 15 = **style**, cast, fashion, form, manner, mode, way 16 *As in* **good turn** = **act**, action, deed, favour, gesture, service 17 = **twist**, bend, distortion, warp 18 *Informal* = **shock**, fright, scare, start, surprise 19 **to a turn** *Informal* = **perfectly**, correctly, exactly, just right, precisely

turncoat *noun* = **traitor**, apostate, backslider, defector, deserter, renegade

turn down *verb* 1 = **lower**, diminish, lessen, muffle, mute, quieten, reduce the volume of, soften 2 = **refuse**, abstain from, decline, rebuff, reject, repudiate, say no to, spurn, throw out
➤ **Antonyms**
≠**lower:** amplify, augment, boost, increase, raise, strengthen, swell, turn up ≠**refuse:** accede, accept, acquiesce, agree, receive, take

turn in *verb Informal* 1 = **go to bed**, go to sleep, hit the hay (*slang*), hit the sack (*slang*), retire for the night 2 = **hand in**, deliver, give back, give up, hand over, return, submit, surrender, tender

turning *noun* = **turn-off**, bend, crossroads, curve, junction, side road, turn

turning point *noun* = **crossroads**, change, crisis, critical moment, crux, decisive moment, moment of decision, moment of truth, point of no return

turn-off *noun* = **turning**, branch, exit, side road, turn

turn off *verb* **1** = **branch off**, change direction, depart from, deviate, leave, quit, take another road, take a side road **2** = **stop**, cut out, put out, shut down, switch off, turn out, unplug **3** *Informal* = **put off**, alienate, bore, disenchant, disgust, gross out (*U.S. slang*), lose one's interest, nauseate, offend, repel, sicken

turn on *verb* **1** = **start**, activate, energize, ignite, kick-start, put on, set in motion, start up, switch on **2** = **attack**, assail, assault, fall on, round on **3** *Informal* = **arouse**, arouse one's desire, attract, excite, please, stimulate, thrill, titillate, work up **4** = **depend on**, balance on, be contingent on, be decided by, hang on, hinge on, pivot on, rest on
➤ **Antonyms**
≠**start**: cut out, put out, shut off, stop, switch off, turn off

turnout *noun* **1** = **attendance**, assemblage, assembly, audience, congregation, crowd, gate, number, throng **2** = **output**, amount produced, production, production quota, productivity, turnover, volume, yield

turn out *verb* **1** = **turn off**, put out, switch off, unplug **2** = **produce**, bring out, fabricate, finish, make, manufacture, process, put out **3** = **expel**, banish, cast out, deport, discharge, dismiss, dispossess, drive out, evict, fire (*informal*), give one the sack (*informal*), kick out (*informal*), oust, put out, relegate, sack (*informal*), show one the door, throw out, turf out (*Brit. informal*), unseat **4** = **empty**, clean out, clear, take out the contents of **5** = **prove to be**, come to light, crop up (*informal*), develop, emerge, happen **6** = **end up**, become, come about, come to be, eventuate, evolve, result, transpire (*informal*), work out **7** = **dress**, accoutre, attire, clothe, fit, outfit, rig out **8** = **come**, appear, assemble, attend, be present, gather, go, put in an appearance, show up (*informal*), turn up

turnover *noun* **1** = **output**, business, flow, production, productivity, volume, yield **2** = **movement**, change, coming and going, replacement

turn over *verb* **1** = **overturn**, capsize, flip over, keel over, reverse, tip over, upend, upset **2** = **consider**, contemplate, deliberate, give thought to, mull over, ponder, reflect on, revolve, ruminate about, think about, think over **3** = **hand over**, commend, commit, deliver, give over, give up, pass on, surrender, yield **4** = **start up**, activate, set going, set in motion, switch on, warm up

turn up *verb* **1** = **arrive**, appear, attend,

come, put in an appearance, show (*informal*), show one's face, show up (*informal*) **2** = **find**, bring to light, come up with, dig up, disclose, discover, expose, reveal, unearth **3** = **come to light**, appear, become known, be found, come to pass, crop up (*informal*), pop up, transpire **4** = **increase**, amplify, boost, enhance, increase the volume of, intensify, make louder, raise
➤ **Antonyms**
≠**find**: hide ≠**come to light**: disappear, evaporate, fade, vanish ≠**increase**: diminish, lessen, lower, reduce, soften, turn down

turpitude *noun Formal* = **wickedness**, badness, baseness, corruption, criminality, degeneracy, depravity, evil, immorality, iniquity, sinfulness

tussle *noun* **1** = **fight**, battle, bout, brawl, competition, conflict, contention, contest, fracas, fray, punch-up (*Brit. informal*), scrap (*informal*), scrimmage, scuffle, set-to (*informal*), shindig (*informal*), shindy (*informal*), struggle ◆ *verb* **2** = **fight**, battle, brawl, contend, grapple, scrap (*informal*), scuffle, struggle, vie, wrestle

tutelage *noun Formal* = **guidance**, care, charge, custody, education, guardianship, instruction, schooling, teaching, tuition

tutor *noun* **1** = **teacher**, coach, educator, guardian, guide, guru, instructor, lecturer, master *or* mistress, mentor, schoolmaster *or* schoolmistress ◆ *verb* **2** = **teach**, coach, direct, drill, educate, guide, instruct, lecture, school, train

tutorial *noun* **1** = **seminar**, individual instruction, lesson ◆ *adjective* **2** = **teaching**, coaching, guiding, instructional

TV *noun* = **television**, gogglebox (*Brit. slang*), small screen (*informal*), television set, telly (*Brit. informal*), the box (*Brit. informal*), the tube (*slang*), TV set

twaddle *noun* **1** = **nonsense**, balderdash, balls (*taboo slang*), bilge (*informal*), bosh (*informal*), bullshit (*taboo slang*), bunkum *or* buncombe (*chiefly U.S.*), claptrap (*informal*), cobblers (*Brit. taboo slang*), crap (*slang*), drivel, foolish talk, garbage (*informal*), gobbledegook (*informal*), guff (*slang*), hogwash, hot air (*informal*), moonshine, pants (*slang*), pap, piffle (*informal*), poppycock (*informal*), rot, rubbish, shit (*taboo slang*), tommyrot, tosh (*slang, chiefly Brit.*), trash, tripe (*informal*), verbiage, waffle (*informal, chiefly Brit.*)
◆ *verb* **2** = **talk nonsense**, gabble, prattle, rattle on, waffle (*informal, chiefly Brit.*)

tweak *verb, noun* = **twist**, jerk, nip, pinch, pull, squeeze, twitch

twee *adjective Informal* = **sweet**, bijou, cute, dainty, precious, pretty, quaint, sentimental

twiddle verb 1 = fiddle (informal), finger, jiggle, play with, twirl, wiggle 2 **twiddle one's thumbs** = be idle, be unoccupied, do nothing, have nothing to do, mark time, sit around

twig[1] noun = branch, offshoot, shoot, spray, sprig, stick

twig[2] verb Brit. informal = understand, catch on (informal), comprehend, fathom, find out, get, grasp, see, tumble to (informal)

twilight noun 1 = dusk, dimness, evening, gloaming (Scot. or poetic), gloom, half-light, sundown, sunset 2 = decline, ebb, last phase ◆ adjective 3 = evening, crepuscular, darkening, dim 4 = declining, dying, ebbing, final, last
➤ Antonyms
noun ≠dusk: dawn, daybreak, morning, sunrise, sunup ≠decline: climax, crowning moment, height, peak

twin noun 1 = double, clone, counterpart, duplicate, fellow, likeness, lookalike, match, mate, ringer (slang) ◆ verb 2 = pair, couple, join, link, match, yoke

twine noun 1 = string, cord, yarn ◆ verb 2 = twist together, braid, entwine, interlace, interweave, knit, plait, splice, twist, weave 3 = coil, bend, curl, encircle, loop, spiral, twist, wind, wrap, wreathe

twinge noun = pain, bite, pang, pinch, prick, sharp pain, spasm, stab, stitch, throb, twist

twinkle verb 1 = sparkle, blink, coruscate, flash, flicker, gleam, glint, glisten, glitter, scintillate, shimmer, shine, wink ◆ noun 2 = sparkle, blink, coruscation, flash, flicker, gleam, glimmer, glistening, glittering, light, scintillation, shimmer, shine, spark, wink

twinkling noun As in **in the twinkling of an eye** = moment, flash, instant, jiffy (informal), second, shake (informal), split second, tick (Brit. informal), trice, twinkle

twirl verb 1 = turn, gyrate, pirouette, pivot, revolve, rotate, spin, turn on one's heel, twiddle, twist, wheel, whirl, wind ◆ noun 2 = turn, gyration, pirouette, revolution, rotation, spin, twist, wheel, whirl

twist verb 1 = distort, contort, screw up 2 = wind, coil, corkscrew, curl, encircle, entwine, intertwine, screw, spin, swivel, twine, weave, wrap, wreathe, wring 3 = sprain, rick, turn, wrench 4 = misrepresent, alter, change, distort, falsify, garble, misquote, pervert, warp 5 **twist someone's arm** = force, bully, coerce, persuade, pressurize, talk into ◆ noun 6 = wind, coil, curl, spin, swivel, twine 7 = coil, braid, curl, hank, roll 8 = development, change, revelation, slant,

surprise, turn, variation 9 = curve, arc, bend, convolution, meander, turn, undulation, zigzag 10 = distortion, defect, deformation, flaw, imperfection, kink, warp 11 = jerk, pull, sprain, turn, wrench 12 **round the twist** Brit. slang = mad, barmy (slang), batty (slang), bonkers (slang, chiefly Brit.), crazy, cuckoo (informal), daft (informal), insane, loopy (informal), not all there, not right in the head, nuts (slang), nutty (slang), nutty as a fruitcake (slang), off one's rocker (slang), off one's trolley (slang), out to lunch (informal), up the pole (informal), wacko or whacko (informal)
➤ Antonyms
verb ≠distort: straighten, untwist ≠wind: straighten, uncoil, unravel, unroll, untwist, unwind

twister noun Brit. = swindler, cheat, chiseller (informal), con man (informal), crook (informal), deceiver, fraud, fraudster, grifter (slang, chiefly U.S. & Canad.), hustler (U.S. informal), rogue, trickster

twit[1] verb = make fun of, deride, jeer, poke fun at, scorn, taunt, tease

twit[2] noun Informal, chiefly Brit. = fool, airhead (slang), ass, berk (Brit. slang), blockhead, chump (informal), dickhead (slang), divvy (Brit. slang), dope (informal), dork (slang), dumb-ass (slang), dweeb (U.S. slang), geek (slang), gobshite (Irish taboo slang), halfwit, idiot, jerk (slang, chiefly U.S. & Canad.), nerd or nurd (slang), nincompoop, ninny, nitwit (informal), numbskull or numskull, numpty (Scot. informal), oaf, pillock (Brit. slang), plonker (slang), prat (slang), prick (slang), schmuck (U.S. slang), simpleton, twerp or twirp (informal), wally (slang)

twitch verb 1 = jerk, flutter, jump, squirm 2 = pull, pluck, snatch, tug, yank ◆ noun 3 = jerk, flutter, jump, spasm, tic, tremor, twinge

twitter verb 1 = chirrup, chatter, cheep, chirp, trill, tweet, warble, whistle 2 = chatter, prattle ◆ noun 3 = chirrup, call, chatter, cheep, chirp, cry, song, trill, tweet, warble, whistle 4 As in **in a twitter** = nervousness, agitation, anxiety, bustle, dither (chiefly Brit.), excitement, flurry, fluster, flutter, tizzy (informal), whirl

two-edged adjective = ambiguous, ambivalent, backhanded, double-edged, equivocal

two-faced adjective = hypocritical, deceitful, deceiving, dissembling, double-dealing, duplicitous, false, insincere, perfidious, treacherous, untrustworthy
➤ Antonyms
artless, candid, frank, genuine, honest, ingenuous, sincere, trustworthy

tycoon *noun* = **magnate**, baron, big cheese (*slang, old-fashioned*), big noise (*informal*), capitalist, captain of industry, fat cat (*slang, chiefly U.S.*), financier, industrialist, merchant prince, mogul, plutocrat, potentate, wealthy businessman

type *noun* **1** = **kind**, breed, category, class, classification, form, genre, group, ilk, order, sort, species, stamp, strain, style, subdivision, variety **2** = **print**, case, characters, face, font, fount, printing

typhoon *noun* = **storm**, cyclone, squall, tempest, tornado, tropical storm

typical *adjective* = **characteristic**, archetypal, average, bog-standard (*Brit. & Irish slang*), classic, conventional, essential, illustrative, in character, indicative, in keeping, model, normal, orthodox, representative, standard, stock, true to type, usual
➤ **Antonyms**
atypical, exceptional, out of keeping, out of the ordinary, singular, uncharacteristic, unconventional, unexpected, unique, unrepresentative, unusual

typify *verb* = **represent**, characterize, embody, epitomize, exemplify, illustrate, incarnate, personify, sum up, symbolize

tyrannical *adjective* = **oppressive**, absolute, arbitrary, authoritarian, autocratic, cruel, despotic, dictatorial, domineering, high-handed, imperious, overbearing, severe, tyrannous
➤ **Antonyms**
democratic, easy-going, lax, lenient, liberal, reasonable, tolerant, understanding

tyrannize *verb* = **oppress**, browbeat, bully, domineer, enslave, intimidate, subjugate, terrorize

tyranny *noun* = **oppression**, absolutism, authoritarianism, autocracy, cruelty, despotism, dictatorship, high-handedness, imperiousness
➤ **Antonyms**
democracy, liberality, tolerance

tyrant *noun* = **dictator**, absolutist, authoritarian, autocrat, bully, despot, Hitler, martinet, oppressor, slave-driver

tyro *noun* = **beginner**, apprentice, greenhorn (*informal*), initiate, learner, neophyte, novice, novitiate, pupil, student, trainee

U u

ubiquitous *adjective* = **everywhere**, all-over, ever-present, omnipresent, pervasive, universal

ugly *adjective* 1 = **unattractive**, homely (*chiefly U.S.*), ill-favoured, no oil painting (*informal*), not much to look at, plain, unlovely, unprepossessing, unsightly 2 = **unpleasant**, disagreeable, disgusting, distasteful, frightful, hideous, horrid, monstrous, objectionable, repugnant, repulsive, revolting, shocking, terrible, vile 3 = **ominous**, baleful, bodeful, dangerous, forbidding, menacing, sinister, threatening 4 = **bad-tempered**, angry, dark, evil, malevolent, nasty, spiteful, sullen, surly
➤ **Antonyms**
≠**unattractive**: attractive, beautiful, cute, good-looking, gorgeous, handsome, lovely, pretty ≠**unpleasant**: agreeable, pleasant ≠**ominous**: auspicious, promising ≠**bad-tempered**: good-humoured, good-natured

ulcer *noun* = **sore**, abscess, boil, fester, gathering, gumboil, peptic ulcer, pustule

ulcerous *adjective* = **festering**, cankerous, ulcerative

ulterior *adjective* = **hidden**, concealed, covert, personal, secondary, secret, selfish, undisclosed, unexpressed
➤ **Antonyms**
apparent, declared, manifest, obvious, overt, plain

ultimate *adjective* 1 = **final**, conclusive, decisive, end, eventual, extreme, furthest, last, terminal 2 = **supreme**, extreme, greatest, highest, maximum, most significant, paramount, superlative, topmost, utmost 3 = **fundamental**, basic, elemental, primary, radical ♦ *noun* 4 *As in* **the ultimate in** = epitome, culmination, extreme, greatest, height, mother of all (*informal*), peak, perfection, summit, the last word

ultimately *adverb* 1 = **finally**, after all, at last, at the end of the day, eventually, in due time, in the end, in the fullness of time, sooner or later 2 = **fundamentally**, basically

ultra- *prefix* = **extremely**, excessively, fanatically, immoderately, radically

ultramodern *adjective* = **advanced**, ahead of its time, avant-garde, futuristic, modernistic, progressive, way-out (*informal*)

ululate *verb* = **howl**, bawl, cry, keen, lament, wail, yowl

umbrage *noun* *As in* **take umbrage** = **offence**, anger, chagrin, displeasure, grudge, high dudgeon, huff, indignation, pique, resentment, sense of injury
➤ **Antonyms**
amity, cordiality, goodwill, harmony

umbrella *noun* 1 = **brolly** (*Brit. informal*), gamp (*Brit. informal*) 2 = **cover**, aegis, patronage, protection

umpire *noun* 1 = **referee**, adjudicator, arbiter, arbitrator, judge, ref (*informal*)
♦ *verb* 2 = **referee**, adjudicate, arbitrate, call (*Sport*), judge, mediate

umpteen *adjective Informal* = **very many**, a good many, considerable, countless, ever so many, millions, n, numerous

unabashed *adjective* = **unembarrassed**, blatant, bold, brazen, confident, unconcerned, undaunted, undismayed
➤ **Antonyms**
abashed, embarrassed, humbled, mortified, shamefaced, sheepish

unable *adjective* = **incapable**, impotent, inadequate, ineffectual, no good, not able, not equal to, not up to, powerless, unfit, unfitted, unqualified
➤ **Antonyms**
able, adept, adequate, capable, competent, effective, powerful

unabridged *adjective* = **uncut**, complete, full-length, uncondensed, unexpurgated, unshortened, whole

unacceptable *adjective* = **unsatisfactory**, beyond the pale, disagreeable, displeasing, distasteful, improper, inadmissible, insupportable, objectionable, offensive, unpleasant
➤ **Antonyms**
acceptable, agreeable, delightful, pleasant, pleasing

unaccompanied *adjective* 1 = **alone**, by oneself, lone, on one's own, solo, unescorted 2 *Music* = **a cappella**

unaccountable *adjective* 1 = **inexplicable**, baffling, incomprehensible, mysterious, odd, peculiar, puzzling, strange, unexplainable, unfathomable, unintelligible 2 = **not answerable**, clear, exempt, free, not responsible, unliable
➤ **Antonyms**
≠**inexplicable**: accountable,

comprehensible, explicable, intelligible, understandable

unaccounted-for *adjective* = **missing**, lost, not explained, unexplained

unaccustomed *adjective* 1 = **unfamiliar**, new, out of the ordinary, remarkable, special, strange, surprising, uncommon, unexpected, unprecedented, unusual, unwonted 2 **unaccustomed to** = **not used to**, a newcomer to, a novice at, inexperienced at, not given to, unfamiliar with, unpractised in, unused to, unversed in
➤ Antonyms
≠**unfamiliar**: accustomed, familiar, ordinary, regular, usual ≠**not used to**: experienced at, given to, practised in, used to, well-versed in

unadorned *adjective* = **plain**, restrained, severe, simple, stark, straightforward, unembellished, unfussy, unornamented

unadventurous *adjective* = **cautious**, cagey (*informal*), careful, chary, hesitant, prudent, safe, stay-at-home, tentative, timid, timorous, unenterprising, wary
➤ Antonyms
adventurous, audacious, bold, daredevil, daring, enterprising, intrepid

unaffected[1] *adjective* = **natural**, artless, genuine, honest, ingenuous, naive, plain, simple, sincere, straightforward, unassuming, unpretentious, unsophisticated, unspoilt, unstudied, without airs
➤ Antonyms
affected, assumed, designing, devious, insincere, mannered, pretentious, put-on, snobbish, sophisticated

unaffected[2] *adjective* = **impervious**, aloof, not influenced, proof, unaltered, unchanged, unimpressed, unmoved, unresponsive, untouched
➤ Antonyms
affected, changed, concerned, disrupted, hard-hit, influenced, interested, responsive, sympathetic, touched

unafraid *adjective* = **fearless**, confident, daring, dauntless, intrepid, unfearing, unshakable
➤ Antonyms
afraid, alarmed, anxious, fearful, frightened, scared

unalterable *adjective* = **unchangeable**, fixed, immovable, immutable, invariable, permanent, steadfast, unchanging
➤ Antonyms
alterable, changeable, changing, flexible, mutable, variable

unanimity *noun* = **agreement**, accord, assent, chorus, concert, concord, concurrence, consensus, harmony, like-mindedness, one mind, unison, unity

➤ Antonyms
difference, disagreement, discord, disunity, division, variance

unanimous *adjective* = **agreed**, agreeing, at one, common, concerted, concordant, harmonious, in agreement, in complete accord, like-minded, of one mind, united
➤ Antonyms
differing, discordant, dissident, disunited, divided, schismatic, split

unanimously *adverb* = **without exception**, by common consent, nem. con., unitedly, unopposed, with one accord, without opposition

unanswerable *adjective* 1 = **insoluble**, insolvable, unascertainable, unexplainable, unresolvable 2 = **conclusive**, absolute, incontestable, incontrovertible, indisputable, irrefutable, unarguable, undeniable

unanswered *adjective* = **unresolved**, disputed, in doubt, open, undecided, unsettled, up in the air

unappetizing *adjective* = **unpleasant**, disgusting, distasteful, insipid, off-putting (*Brit. informal*), repulsive, tasteless, unappealing, unattractive, uninteresting, uninviting, unpalatable, unsavoury
➤ Antonyms
agreeable, appealing, appetizing, attractive, delicious, interesting, inviting, mouthwatering, palatable, savoury, scrumptious (*informal*), succulent, tasty, tempting, toothsome

unapproachable *adjective* 1 = **unfriendly**, aloof, chilly, cool, distant, frigid, remote, reserved, standoffish, unsociable, withdrawn 2 = **inaccessible**, out of reach, out-of-the-way, remote, un-get-at-able (*informal*), unreachable
➤ Antonyms
≠**unfriendly**: affable, approachable, congenial, cordial, friendly, sociable

unarmed *adjective* = **defenceless**, assailable, exposed, helpless, open, open to attack, unarmoured, unprotected, weak, weaponless
➤ Antonyms
armed, equipped, fortified, protected, ready, strengthened

unasked *adverb* = **voluntarily**, off one's own bat, of one's own accord, without prompting

unassailable *adjective* = **impregnable**, invincible, invulnerable, secure, well-defended

unassuming *adjective* = **modest**, diffident, humble, meek, quiet, reserved, retiring, self-effacing, simple, unassertive, unobtrusive, unostentatious, unpretentious
➤ Antonyms
assuming, audacious, conceited,

ostentatious, overconfident, presumptuous, pretentious

unattached *adjective* 1 = **free**, autonomous, independent, nonaligned, unaffiliated, uncommitted 2 = **single**, a free agent, available, by oneself, footloose and fancy-free, left on the shelf, not spoken for, on one's own, unengaged, unmarried
➤ **Antonyms**
≠**free**: affiliated, aligned, attached, committed, dependent, implicated, involved

unattended *adjective* 1 = **abandoned**, disregarded, ignored, left alone, not cared for, unguarded, unwatched 2 = **alone**, on one's own, unaccompanied, unescorted

unauthorized *adjective* = **illegal**, off the record, unapproved, unconstitutional, under-the-table, unlawful, unofficial, unsanctioned, unwarranted
➤ **Antonyms**
authorized, constitutional, lawful, legal, official, sanctioned, warranted

unavoidable *adjective* = **inevitable**, bound to happen, certain, compulsory, fated, inescapable, inexorable, necessary, obligatory, sure

unaware *adjective* = **ignorant**, heedless, not in the loop (*informal*), oblivious, unconscious, unenlightened, uninformed, unknowing, unmindful, unsuspecting
➤ **Antonyms**
attentive, aware, conscious, informed, in the loop (*informal*), knowing, mindful

unawares *adverb* 1 = **by surprise**, aback, off guard, on the hop (*Brit. informal*), suddenly, unexpectedly, unprepared, without warning 2 = **unknowingly**, accidentally, by accident, by mistake, inadvertently, mistakenly, unconsciously, unintentionally, unwittingly
➤ **Antonyms**
≠**by surprise**: forewarned, on the lookout, prepared ≠**unknowingly**: deliberately, knowingly, on purpose, wittingly

unbalanced *adjective* 1 = **shaky**, asymmetrical, irregular, lopsided, not balanced, unequal, uneven, unstable, unsymmetrical, wobbly 2 = **biased**, inequitable, one-sided, partial, partisan, prejudiced, unfair, unjust 3 = **deranged**, barking mad (*slang*), crazy, demented, disturbed, eccentric, erratic, insane, irrational, loopy (*informal*), lunatic, mad, *non compos mentis*, not all there, not the full shilling (*informal*), off one's trolley (*slang*), out to lunch (*informal*), touched, unhinged, unsound, unstable, wacko *or* whacko (*informal*)
➤ **Antonyms**
≠**shaky**: balanced, equal, even, stable, symmetrical

unbearable *adjective* = **intolerable**, insufferable, insupportable, oppressive, too much (*informal*), unacceptable, unendurable
➤ **Antonyms**
acceptable, bearable, endurable, supportable, tolerable

unbeatable *adjective* = **invincible**, indomitable, unconquerable, unstoppable, unsurpassable

unbeaten *adjective* = **undefeated**, triumphant, unbowed, unsubdued, unsurpassed, unvanquished, victorious, winning

unbecoming *adjective* 1 = **unattractive**, ill-suited, inappropriate, unbefitting, unfit, unflattering, unsightly, unsuitable, unsuited 2 = **unseemly**, discreditable, improper, indecorous, indelicate, offensive, tasteless
➤ **Antonyms**
≠**unseemly**: becoming, decent, decorous, delicate, proper, seemly

unbelievable *adjective* 1 = **incredible**, astonishing, beyond belief, cock-and-bull (*informal*), far-fetched, implausible, impossible, improbable, inconceivable, jaw-dropping, outlandish, preposterous, staggering, unconvincing, unimaginable, unthinkable 2 = **wonderful**, awesome (*slang*), bad (*slang*), bodacious (*slang, chiefly U.S.*), boffo (*slang*), brill (*informal*), chillin' (*U.S. slang*), colossal, cracking (*Brit. informal*), crucial (*slang*), def (*slang*), divine (*informal*), excellent, fabulous (*informal*), fantastic (*informal*), glorious, great (*informal*), jim-dandy (*slang*), magnificent, mean (*slang*), mega (*slang*), sensational (*informal*), smashing (*informal*), sovereign, splendid, stupendous, super (*informal*), superb, terrific (*informal*), topping (*Brit. slang*), wicked (*informal*)
➤ **Antonyms**
≠**incredible**: authentic, believable, credible, likely, plausible, possible, probable, trustworthy ≠**wonderful**: awful, bad, terrible

unbeliever *noun* = **atheist**, agnostic, disbeliever, doubting Thomas, infidel, sceptic

unbend *verb* = **relax**, be informal, calm down, chill out (*slang, chiefly U.S.*), cool it (*slang*), ease up, let oneself go, lighten up (*slang*), loosen up, slacken, slow down, take it easy, unwind

unbending *adjective* = **inflexible**, firm, intractable, resolute, rigid, severe, strict, stubborn, tough, uncompromising, unyielding

unbiased *adjective* = **fair**, disinterested, dispassionate, equitable, even-handed, impartial, just, neutral, objective, open-minded, unprejudiced

➤ **Antonyms**
biased, bigoted, partial, prejudiced, slanted, swayed, unfair, unjust

unbidden *adjective* **1** = **uninvited**, unasked, unwanted, unwelcome **2** = **voluntary**, free, spontaneous, unforced, unprompted, willing

unbind *verb* = **free**, loosen, release, set free, unbridle, unchain, unclasp, undo, unfasten, unfetter, unloose, unshackle, unstrap, untie, unyoke
➤ **Antonyms**
bind, chain, fasten, fetter, restrain, shackle, tie, yoke

unblemished *adjective* = **spotless**, flawless, immaculate, impeccable, perfect, pure, unflawed, unspotted, unstained, unsullied, untarnished
➤ **Antonyms**
blemished, flawed, imperfect, impure, stained, sullied, tarnished

unblushing *adjective* = **shameless**, bold, brazen, forward, immodest, unabashed, unashamed, unembarrassed

unborn *adjective* = **expected**, awaited, embryonic, *in utero*

unbosom *verb* = **confide**, admit, confess, disclose, divulge, get (something) off one's chest (*informal*), get (something) out of one's system, let out, reveal, tell, unburden
➤ **Antonyms**
conceal, cover up, guard, hold back, suppress, withhold

unbounded *adjective* = **unlimited**, absolute, boundless, endless, immeasurable, infinite, limitless, unbridled, unchecked, unconstrained, uncontrolled, unrestrained, vast
➤ **Antonyms**
bounded, confined, constrained, curbed, limited, restricted

unbreakable *adjective* = **indestructible**, durable, lasting, nonbreakable, resistant, rugged, shatterproof, solid, strong, toughened
➤ **Antonyms**
breakable, brittle, delicate, flimsy, fragile

unbridled *adjective* = **unrestrained**, excessive, full-on (*informal*), intemperate, licentious, rampant, riotous, unchecked, unconstrained, uncontrolled, uncurbed, ungoverned, unruly, violent, wanton

unbroken *adjective* **1** = **intact**, complete, entire, solid, total, unimpaired, whole **2** = **continuous**, ceaseless, constant, endless, incessant, progressive, successive, uninterrupted, unremitting **3** = **undisturbed**, deep, fast, profound, sound, untroubled **4** = **untamed**, unsubdued
➤ **Antonyms**
≠**intact**: broken, cracked, damaged,

fragmented, in pieces, shattered
≠**continuous**: erratic, fitful, intermittent, interrupted, irregular, occasional, off-and-on, uneven

unburden *verb* = **confess**, come clean (*informal*), confide, disclose, get (something) off one's chest (*informal*), lay bare, make a clean breast of, reveal, tell all, unbosom

uncalled-for *adjective* = **unnecessary**, gratuitous, inappropriate, needless, undeserved, unjust, unjustified, unprovoked, unwarranted, unwelcome
➤ **Antonyms**
appropriate, deserved, just, justified, necessary, needed, provoked, warranted

uncanny *adjective* **1** = **weird**, creepy (*informal*), eerie, eldritch (*poetic*), mysterious, preternatural, queer, spooky (*informal*), strange, supernatural, unearthly, unnatural **2** = **extraordinary**, astonishing, astounding, exceptional, fantastic, incredible, miraculous, prodigious, remarkable, singular, unheard-of, unusual

uncaring *adjective* = **unconcerned**, indifferent, unfeeling, uninterested, unmoved, unresponsive, unsympathetic

unceasing *adjective* = **continual**, ceaseless, constant, continuing, continuous, endless, incessant, never-ending, nonstop, perpetual, persistent, unending, unfailing, unremitting
➤ **Antonyms**
fitful, intermittent, irregular, occasional, periodic, spasmodic, sporadic

uncertain *adjective* **1** = **unpredictable**, ambiguous, chancy, conjectural, doubtful, iffy (*informal*), incalculable, indefinite, indeterminate, indistinct, questionable, risky, speculative, undetermined, unforeseeable **2** = **unsure**, doubtful, dubious, hazy, in two minds, irresolute, unclear, unconfirmed, undecided, undetermined, unfixed, unresolved, unsettled, up in the air, vacillating, vague **3** = **changeable**, erratic, fitful, iffy (*informal*), inconstant, insecure, irregular, precarious, unpredictable, unreliable, variable
➤ **Antonyms**
≠**unpredictable**: certain, clear, clear-cut, decided, definite, firm, fixed, known, predictable, unambiguous ≠**unsure**: certain, positive, resolute, settled, sure, unhesitating ≠**changeable**: certain, reliable, unvarying

uncertainty *noun* **1** = **unpredictability**, ambiguity, inconclusiveness, state of suspense **2** = **doubt**, confusion, dilemma, dubiety, hesitancy, hesitation, indecision, irresolution, lack of confidence, misgiving, puzzlement, qualm, quandary, scepticism, vagueness
➤ **Antonyms**
≠**unpredictability**: conclusiveness,

predictability ≠**doubt**: assurance, certainty, confidence, decision, resolution, sureness, trust

unchangeable *adjective* = **unalterable**, changeless, constant, fixed, immovable, immutable, inevitable, invariable, irreversible, permanent, stable, steadfast, strong
➤ **Antonyms**
changeable, inconstant, irregular, mutable, shifting, unstable, variable, wavering

unchanging *adjective* = **constant**, abiding, changeless, continuing, enduring, eternal, immutable, imperishable, lasting, permanent, perpetual, unchanged, unvarying

uncharitable *adjective* = **unkind**, cruel, hardhearted, insensitive, merciless, unchristian, unfeeling, unforgiving, unfriendly, ungenerous, unsympathetic
➤ **Antonyms**
charitable, feeling, friendly, generous, kind, merciful, sensitive, sympathetic

uncharted *adjective* = **unexplored**, not mapped, strange, undiscovered, unfamiliar, unknown, unplumbed, virgin

uncivil *adjective* = **impolite**, bad-mannered, boorish, brusque, churlish, discourteous, disrespectful, ill-bred, ill-mannered, rude, surly, uncouth, unmannerly
➤ **Antonyms**
civil, courteous, mannerly, polite, refined, respectful, well-bred, well-mannered

uncivilized *adjective* **1** = **primitive**, barbarian, barbaric, barbarous, illiterate, savage, wild **2** = **uncouth**, beyond the pale, boorish, brutish, churlish, coarse, gross, philistine, uncultivated, uncultured, uneducated, unmannered, unpolished, unsophisticated, vulgar

unclean *adjective* = **dirty**, contaminated, corrupt, defiled, evil, filthy, foul, impure, polluted, soiled, spotted, stained, sullied, tainted
➤ **Antonyms**
clean, faultless, flawless, pure, spotless, unblemished, unstained, unsullied

unclear *adjective* **1** = **indistinct**, bleary, blurred, dim, faint, fuzzy, hazy, ill-defined, indiscernible, indistinguishable, misty, muffled, obscure, out of focus, shadowy, undefined, vague, weak **2** = **doubtful**, ambiguous, confused, indefinite, indeterminate, unintelligible, vague
➤ **Antonyms**
≠**indistinct**: clear, defined, discernible, distinct, distinguishable ≠**doubtful**: determinate, evident, intelligible

uncomfortable *adjective* **1** = **painful**, awkward, causing discomfort, cramped, disagreeable, hard, ill-fitting, incommodious, irritating, rough, troublesome **2** = **uneasy**, awkward, confused, discomfited, disquieted, distressed, disturbed, embarrassed, ill at ease, like a fish out of water, out of place, self-conscious, troubled
➤ **Antonyms**
≠**uneasy**: at ease, at home, comfortable, easy, relaxed, serene, untroubled

uncommitted *adjective* = **uninvolved**, floating, free, free-floating, neutral, nonaligned, nonpartisan, not involved, (sitting) on the fence, unattached

uncommon *adjective* **1** = **rare**, bizarre, curious, few and far between, infrequent, novel, odd, out of the ordinary, peculiar, queer, scarce, singular, strange, thin on the ground, unfamiliar, unusual **2** = **extraordinary**, distinctive, exceptional, incomparable, notable, noteworthy, outstanding, rare, remarkable, singular, special, superior, unparalleled, unprecedented
➤ **Antonyms**
≠**rare**: common, familiar, frequent, regular, routine, usual ≠**extraordinary**: average, banal, commonplace, everyday, humdrum, mundane, ordinary, run-of-the-mill

uncommonly *adverb* **1** = **rarely**, hardly ever, infrequently, not often, occasionally, only now and then, scarcely ever, seldom **2** = **exceptionally**, extremely, particularly, peculiarly, remarkably, seriously (*informal*), strangely, unusually, very

uncommunicative *adjective* = **reticent**, close, curt, guarded, reserved, retiring, secretive, short, shy, silent, taciturn, tight-lipped, unforthcoming, unresponsive, unsociable, withdrawn
➤ **Antonyms**
chatty, communicative, forthcoming, garrulous, loquacious, responsive, talkative, voluble

uncompromising *adjective* = **inflexible**, die-hard, firm, hardline, inexorable, intransigent, obdurate, obstinate, rigid, stiff-necked, strict, stubborn, tough, unbending, unyielding

uncondern *noun* = **indifference**, aloofness, apathy, detachment, insouciance, lack of interest, nonchalance, remoteness, uninterestedness

unconcerned *adjective* **1** = **indifferent**, aloof, apathetic, cool, detached, dispassionate, distant, incurious, oblivious, uninterested, uninvolved, unmoved, unsympathetic **2** = **untroubled**, blithe, carefree, careless, easy, insouciant, nonchalant, not bothered, not giving a toss (*informal*), relaxed, serene, unperturbed, unruffled, unworried
➤ **Antonyms**
≠**indifferent**: avid, curious, eager,

interested, involved ≠**untroubled:** agitated, anxious, concerned, distressed, perturbed, uneasy, worried

unconditional *adjective* = **absolute,** categorical, complete, downright, entire, full, out-and-out, outright, plenary, positive, thoroughgoing, total, unlimited, unqualified, unreserved, unrestricted, utter
➤ **Antonyms**
conditional, limited, partial, qualified, reserved, restricted

uncongenial *adjective* = **unfriendly,** antagonistic, antipathetic, disagreeable, displeasing, distasteful, incompatible, not one's cup of tea (*informal*), uninviting, unpleasant, unsuited, unsympathetic
➤ **Antonyms**
affable, agreeable, compatible, congenial, genial, pleasant, pleasing, sympathetic

unconnected *adjective* **1** = **separate,** detached, disconnected, divided, independent **2** = **incoherent,** disconnected, disjointed, illogical, irrelevant, meaningless, nonsensical, not related, unrelated
➤ **Antonyms**
≠**incoherent:** coherent, connected, intelligible, logical, meaningful, related, relevant

unconscionable *adjective* **1** = **unscrupulous,** amoral, criminal, unethical, unfair, unjust, unprincipled **2** = **excessive,** exorbitant, extravagant, extreme, immoderate, inordinate, outrageous, preposterous, unreasonable

unconscious *adjective* **1** = **senseless,** blacked out (*informal*), comatose, dead to the world (*informal*), insensible, knocked out, numb, out, out cold, out for the count (*Boxing*), stunned **2** = **unaware,** blind to, deaf to, heedless, ignorant, in ignorance, lost to, oblivious, unknowing, unmindful, unsuspecting **3** = **unintentional,** accidental, inadvertent, unintended, unpremeditated, unwitting **4** = **subconscious,** automatic, instinctive, involuntary, latent, reflex, repressed, subliminal, suppressed, unrealized
➤ **Antonyms**
≠**senseless:** awake, conscious, sensible
≠**unaware:** alert, aware, conscious
≠**unintentional:** calculated, conscious, deliberate, intentional, planned, studied, wilful

uncontrollable *adjective* = **wild,** beside oneself, carried away, frantic, furious, irrepressible, irresistible, like one possessed, mad, strong, ungovernable, unmanageable, unruly, violent

uncontrolled *adjective* = **unrestrained,** furious, lacking self-control, out of control, out of hand, rampant, riotous, unbridled, unchecked, uncurbed, undisciplined,

ungoverned, unruly, violent
➤ **Antonyms**
contained, controlled, disciplined, restrained, subdued

unconventional *adjective* = **unusual,** atypical, bizarre, bohemian, different, eccentric, far-out (*slang*), idiosyncratic, individual, individualistic, informal, irregular, left-field (*informal*), nonconformist, odd, oddball (*informal*), offbeat, off-the-wall (*slang*), original, out of the ordinary, outré, uncustomary, unorthodox, way-out (*informal*)
➤ **Antonyms**
conventional, normal, ordinary, orthodox, proper, regular, typical, usual

unconvincing *adjective* = **implausible,** cock-and-bull (*informal*), dubious, feeble, fishy (*informal*), flimsy, hard to believe, improbable, inconclusive, lame, questionable, specious, suspect, thin, unlikely, unpersuasive, weak
➤ **Antonyms**
believable, conclusive, convincing, credible, likely, persuasive, plausible, probable

uncooperative *adjective* = **unhelpful,** awkward, bloody-minded (*Brit. informal*), cussed (*informal*), difficult, disobliging, obstructive, unaccommodating, unresponsive, unsupportive
➤ **Antonyms**
accommodating, cooperative, helpful, obliging, responsive, supportive

uncoordinated *adjective* = **clumsy,** all thumbs, awkward, bumbling, bungling, butterfingered (*informal*), graceless, lumbering, maladroit, ungainly, ungraceful

uncouth *adjective* = **coarse,** awkward, barbaric, boorish, clumsy, crude, gawky, graceless, gross, ill-mannered, loutish, oafish, rough, rude, uncivilized, uncultivated, ungainly, unrefined, unseemly, vulgar
➤ **Antonyms**
civilized, courteous, cultivated, elegant, graceful, refined, seemly, well-mannered

uncover *verb* **1** = **open,** bare, lay open, lift the lid, show, strip, unwrap **2** = **reveal,** blow wide open (*slang*), bring to light, disclose, discover, divulge, expose, lay bare, make known, unearth, unmask
➤ **Antonyms**
≠**reveal:** conceal, cover, cover up, hide, keep under wraps, suppress

uncritical *adjective* = **undiscriminating,** easily pleased, indiscriminate, undiscerning, unexacting, unfussy, unperceptive, unselective, unthinking
➤ **Antonyms**
critical, discerning, discriminating, fastidious, fussy, perceptive, selective

unctuous *adjective* = **obsequious**, glib, gushing, ingratiating, insincere, oily, plausible, slick, smarmy (*Brit. informal*), smooth, suave, sycophantic

undaunted *adjective* = **undeterred**, bold, brave, courageous, dauntless, fearless, intrepid, not discouraged, nothing daunted, not put off, resolute, steadfast, undiscouraged, undismayed

undeceive *verb* = **enlighten**, correct, disabuse, disillusion, open (someone's) eyes (to), put (someone) right, set (someone) straight, shatter (someone's) illusions

undecided *adjective* **1** = **unsure**, ambivalent, dithering (*chiefly Brit.*), doubtful, dubious, hesitant, in two minds, irresolute, swithering (*Scot.*), torn, uncertain, uncommitted, wavering **2** = **unsettled**, debatable, iffy (*informal*), indefinite, in the balance, moot, open, pending, unconcluded, undetermined, up in the air, vague
➤ **Antonyms**
≠**unsure**: certain, committed, decided, resolute, sure ≠**unsettled**: decided, definite, determined, resolved, settled

undefined *adjective* **1** = **unspecified**, imprecise, indeterminate, inexact, unclear, unexplained **2** = **indistinct**, formless, hazy, indefinite, shadowy, tenuous, vague
➤ **Antonyms**
≠**unspecified**: clear, defined, determinate, exact, explicit, precise, specified
≠**indistinct**: clear, defined, definite

undemonstrative *adjective* = **reserved**, aloof, cold, contained, distant, formal, impassive, restrained, reticent, unaffectionate, uncommunicative, unemotional, unresponsive, withdrawn
➤ **Antonyms**
affectionate, demonstrative, emotional, expressive, friendly, outgoing, overemotional, unreserved, warm

undeniable *adjective* = **certain**, beyond (a) doubt, beyond question, clear, evident, incontestable, incontrovertible, indisputable, indubitable, irrefutable, manifest, obvious, patent, proven, sound, sure, unassailable, undoubted, unquestionable
➤ **Antonyms**
debatable, deniable, doubtful, dubious, questionable, uncertain, unproven

under *preposition* **1** = **below**, beneath, on the bottom of, underneath **2** = **subject to**, directed by, governed by, inferior to, junior to, reporting to, secondary to, subordinate to, subservient to **3** = **included in**, belonging to, comprised in ♦ *adverb* **4** = **below**, beneath, down, downward, lower, to the bottom
➤ **Antonyms**
preposition ≠**below**: above, over, up, upper,

upward ♦ *adverb* ≠**below**: above, over, up, upward

underclothes *plural noun* = **underwear**, lingerie, smalls (*informal*), underclothing, undergarments, underlinen, underthings, undies (*informal*), unmentionables (*humorous*)

undercover *adjective* = **secret**, clandestine, concealed, confidential, covert, hidden, hush-hush (*informal*), intelligence, private, spy, surreptitious, underground
➤ **Antonyms**
manifest, open, overt, plain, unconcealed, visible

undercurrent *noun* **1** = **undertow**, crosscurrent, rip, rip current, riptide, tideway, underflow **2** = **undertone**, atmosphere, aura, drift, feeling, flavour, hint, murmur, overtone, sense, suggestion, tendency, tinge, trend, vibes (*slang*), vibrations

undercut *verb* **1** = **underprice**, sell at a loss, sell cheaply, undercharge, undersell **2** = **cut away**, cut out, excavate, gouge out, hollow out, mine, undermine

underdog *noun* = **weaker party**, fall guy (*informal*), little fellow (*informal*), loser, outsider, victim

underestimate *verb* = **underrate**, belittle, hold cheap, minimize, miscalculate, misprize, not do justice to, set no store by, think too little of, undervalue
➤ **Antonyms**
exaggerate, inflate, overdo, overestimate, overrate, overstate

undergo *verb* = **experience**, bear, be subjected to, endure, go through, stand, submit to, suffer, sustain, weather, withstand

underground *adjective* **1** = **subterranean**, below ground, below the surface, buried, covered **2** = **secret**, clandestine, concealed, covert, hidden, surreptitious, undercover **3** = **avant-garde**, alternative, experimental, radical, revolutionary, subversive ♦ *noun* **4 the underground: a** = **the Resistance**, partisans, the Maquis **b** = **the tube** (*Brit.*), the metro, the subway

undergrowth *noun* = **scrub**, bracken, brambles, briars, brush, brushwood, underbrush, underwood

underhand *adjective* = **sly**, clandestine, crafty, crooked (*informal*), deceitful, deceptive, devious, dishonest, dishonourable, fraudulent, furtive, secret, secretive, sneaky, stealthy, surreptitious, treacherous, underhanded, unethical, unscrupulous
➤ **Antonyms**
above board, frank, honest, honourable,

legal, open, outright, principled, scrupulous

underline *verb* 1 = **underscore**, italicize, mark, rule a line under 2 = **emphasize**, accentuate, bring home, call *or* draw attention to, give emphasis to, highlight, point up, stress
➤ **Antonyms**
≠**emphasize**: gloss over, make light of, minimize, play down, soft-pedal (*informal*)

underling *noun Derogatory* = **subordinate**, cohort (*chiefly U.S.*), flunky, hireling, inferior, lackey, menial, minion, servant, slave

underlying *adjective* 1 = **hidden**, concealed, latent, lurking, veiled 2 = **fundamental**, basic, elementary, essential, intrinsic, primary, prime, radical, root

undermine *verb* 1 = **weaken**, debilitate, disable, impair, sabotage, sap, subvert, threaten 2 = **wear away**, dig out, eat away at, erode, excavate, mine, tunnel, undercut
➤ **Antonyms**
≠**weaken**: fortify, promote, reinforce, strengthen, sustain ≠**wear away**: fortify, reinforce, strengthen, sustain

underpinning *noun* = **support**, base, footing, foundation, groundwork, substructure

underprivileged *adjective* = **disadvantaged**, badly off, deprived, destitute, impoverished, in need, in want, needy, on the breadline, poor

underrate *verb* = **underestimate**, belittle, discount, disparage, fail to appreciate, misprize, not do justice to, set (too) little store by, undervalue
➤ **Antonyms**
exaggerate, overestimate, overrate, overvalue

undersell *verb* = **undercut**, cut, mark down, reduce, slash, undercharge

undersized *adjective* = **stunted**, dwarfish, miniature, pygmy *or* pigmy, runtish, small, squat, teeny-weeny, tiny, underdeveloped, underweight
➤ **Antonyms**
big, colossal, giant, huge, massive, oversized, overweight

understand *verb* 1 = **comprehend**, appreciate, apprehend, be aware, catch on (*informal*), conceive, cotton on (*informal*), discern, fathom, follow, get, get one's head round, get the hang of (*informal*), get to the bottom of, grasp, know, make head or tail of (*informal*), make out, penetrate, perceive, realize, recognize, see, see the light, take in, tumble to (*informal*), twig (*Brit. informal*) 2 = **believe**, assume, be informed, conclude, gather, hear, learn, presume, suppose, take it, think 3 = **sympathize with**, accept, appreciate, be able to see, commiserate, empathize with,

show compassion for

understandable *adjective* = **reasonable**, justifiable, legitimate, logical, natural, normal, to be expected

understanding *noun* 1 = **perception**, appreciation, awareness, comprehension, discernment, grasp, insight, intelligence, judgment, knowledge, penetration, sense 2 = **interpretation**, belief, conclusion, estimation, idea, judgment, notion, opinion, perception, view, viewpoint 3 = **agreement**, accord, common view, gentlemen's agreement, pact ♦ *adjective* 4 = **sympathetic**, compassionate, considerate, discerning, forbearing, forgiving, kind, kindly, patient, perceptive, responsive, sensitive, tolerant
➤ **Antonyms**
noun ≠**perception**: ignorance, incomprehension, insensitivity, misapprehension, misunderstanding, obtuseness ≠**agreement**: disagreement, dispute ♦ *adjective* ≠**sympathetic**: inconsiderate, insensitive, intolerant, strict, unfeeling, unsympathetic

understood *adjective* 1 = **implied**, implicit, inferred, tacit, unspoken, unstated 2 = **assumed**, accepted, axiomatic, presumed, taken for granted

understudy *noun* = **stand-in**, double, fill-in, replacement, reserve, sub, substitute

undertake *verb* 1 = **agree**, bargain, commit oneself, contract, covenant, engage, guarantee, pledge, promise, take upon oneself 2 = **take on**, attempt, begin, commence, embark on, endeavour, enter upon, set about, tackle, try

undertaker *noun* = **funeral director**, mortician (*U.S.*)

undertaking *noun* 1 = **task**, affair, attempt, business, effort, endeavour, enterprise, game, operation, project, venture 2 = **promise**, assurance, commitment, pledge, solemn word, vow, word, word of honour

undertone *noun* 1 = **murmur**, low tone, subdued voice, whisper 2 = **undercurrent**, atmosphere, feeling, flavour, hint, suggestion, tinge, touch, trace, vibes (*slang*)

undervalue *verb* = **underrate**, depreciate, hold cheap, look down on, make light of, minimize, misjudge, misprize, set no store by, underestimate
➤ **Antonyms**
exaggerate, overestimate, overrate, overvalue

underwater *adjective* = **submerged**, submarine, sunken, undersea

under way *adjective* = **in progress**, afoot, begun, going on, in business, in motion, in operation, started

underwear *noun* = **underclothes**, lingerie, smalls (*informal*), underclothing, undergarments, underlinen, underthings, undies (*informal*), unmentionables (*humorous*)

underweight *adjective* = **skinny**, emaciated, half-starved, puny, skin and bone (*informal*), undernourished, undersized

underworld *noun* **1** = **criminals**, criminal element, gangland (*informal*), gangsters, organized crime **2** = **nether world**, abode of the dead, Hades, hell, infernal region, nether regions, the inferno

underwrite *verb* **1** = **finance**, back, fund, guarantee, insure, provide security, sponsor, subsidize **2** = **sign**, countersign, endorse, initial, subscribe **3** = **support**, agree to, approve, consent, O.K. *or* okay (*informal*), sanction

undesirable *adjective* = **objectionable**, disagreeable, disliked, distasteful, obnoxious, offensive, out of place, repugnant, (to be) avoided, unacceptable, unattractive, unpleasing, unpopular, unsavoury, unsuitable, unwanted, unwelcome, unwished-for
➤ **Antonyms**
acceptable, agreeable, appealing, attractive, desirable, inviting, pleasing, popular, welcome

undeveloped *adjective* **1** = **immature**, embryonic, in embryo **2** = **potential**, inchoate, latent

undignified *adjective* = **unseemly**, beneath one, beneath one's dignity, improper, inappropriate, indecorous, inelegant, infra dig (*informal*), lacking dignity, unbecoming, ungentlemanly, unladylike, unsuitable
➤ **Antonyms**
appropriate, becoming, decorous, dignified, elegant, proper, seemly, suitable

undisciplined *adjective* = **uncontrolled**, disobedient, obstreperous, unpredictable, unreliable, unrestrained, unruly, unschooled, untrained, wayward, wild, wilful
➤ **Antonyms**
controlled, disciplined, obedient, predictable, reliable, restrained, trained

undisguised *adjective* = **obvious**, blatant, evident, explicit, manifest, open, overt, patent, transparent, unconcealed, unfeigned, unmistakable
➤ **Antonyms**
concealed, covert, disguised, feigned, hidden, secret

undisputed *adjective* = **acknowledged**, accepted, beyond question, certain, conclusive, incontestable, incontrovertible, indisputable, irrefutable, recognized, sure, unchallenged, uncontested, undeniable,

undoubted, unquestioned
➤ **Antonyms**
deniable, disputed, doubtful, dubious, inconclusive, questioned, uncertain

undistinguished *adjective* = **ordinary**, commonplace, everyday, indifferent, mediocre, no great shakes (*informal*), pedestrian, prosaic, run-of-the-mill, so-so (*informal*), unexceptional, unexciting, unimpressive, unremarkable, vanilla (*informal*)
➤ **Antonyms**
distinguished, exceptional, exciting, extraordinary, impressive, notable, outstanding, remarkable, striking

undisturbed *adjective* **1** = **quiet**, calm, peaceful, restful, sedate, serene, still, tranquil **2** = **calm**, collected, composed, equable, placid, sedate, serene, tranquil, unagitated, unbothered, unfazed (*informal*), unperturbed, unruffled, untroubled **3** = **uninterrupted**, without interruption **4** = **untouched**, not moved
➤ **Antonyms**
≠**calm**: agitated, antsy (*informal*), bothered, disturbed, excited, flustered, nervous, perturbed, troubled, upset ≠**uninterrupted**: interrupted ≠**untouched**: interfered with, moved

undivided *adjective* **1** = **complete**, concentrated, entire, exclusive, full, thorough, total, undistracted, whole, wholehearted **2** = **united**, concerted, entire, solid, unanimous, whole

undo *verb* **1** = **open**, disengage, disentangle, loose, loosen, unbutton, unclasp, unfasten, unlock, unstrap, untie, unwrap **2** = **reverse**, annul, cancel, invalidate, neutralize, nullify, offset, wipe out **3** = **ruin**, defeat, destroy, mar, overturn, quash, shatter, subvert, undermine, upset, wreck

undoing *noun* **1** = **ruin**, collapse, defeat, destruction, disgrace, downfall, humiliation, overthrow, overturn, reversal, ruination, shame **2** = **downfall**, affliction, blight, curse, fatal flaw, misfortune, the last straw, trial, trouble, weakness

undone[1] *adjective* = **unfinished**, incomplete, left, neglected, not completed, not done, omitted, outstanding, passed over, unattended to, unfulfilled, unperformed
➤ **Antonyms**
accomplished, attended to, complete, done, finished, fulfilled, performed

undone[2] *adjective* = **ruined**, destroyed, overcome

undoubted *adjective* = **certain**, acknowledged, definite, evident, incontrovertible, indisputable, indubitable, obvious, sure, undisputed, unquestionable, unquestioned

undoubtedly *adverb* = **certainly,** assuredly, beyond a shadow of (a) doubt, beyond question, definitely, doubtless, of course, surely, undeniably, unmistakably, unquestionably, without doubt

undreamed-of *or* **undreamt-of** *adjective* = **unimagined,** astonishing, inconceivable, incredible, miraculous, unexpected, unforeseen, unheard-of, unsuspected, unthought-of

undress *verb* **1** = **strip,** disrobe, divest oneself of, peel off (*slang*), shed, take off one's clothes ♦ *noun* **2** = **nakedness,** deshabille, disarray, nudity

undue *adjective* = **excessive,** disproportionate, extravagant, extreme, immoderate, improper, inappropriate, inordinate, intemperate, needless, overmuch, too great, too much, uncalled-for, undeserved, unjustified, unnecessary, unseemly, unsuitable, unwarranted
➤ **Antonyms**
appropriate, due, fitting, justified, necessary, proper, suitable

undulate *verb* = **wave,** billow, heave, ripple, rise and fall, roll, surge, swell

unduly *adverb* = **excessively,** disproportionately, extravagantly, immoderately, improperly, inordinately, out of all proportion, overly, overmuch, unjustifiably, unnecessarily, unreasonably
➤ **Antonyms**
duly, justifiably, moderately, ordinately, properly, proportionately, reasonably

undying *adjective* = **eternal,** constant, continuing, deathless, everlasting, infinite, perennial, permanent, perpetual, unending, unfading
➤ **Antonyms**
ephemeral, finite, fleeting, impermanent, inconstant, momentary, mortal, short-lived

unearth *verb* **1** = **discover,** bring to light, expose, ferret out, find, reveal, root up, turn up, uncover **2** = **dig up,** disinter, dredge up, excavate, exhume

unearthly *adjective* **1** = **eerie,** eldritch (*poetic*), ghostly, haunted, nightmarish, phantom, preternatural, spectral, spooky (*informal*), strange, supernatural, uncanny, weird **2** = **unreasonable,** abnormal, absurd, extraordinary, ridiculous, strange, ungodly (*informal*), unholy (*informal*)

uneasiness *noun* = **anxiety,** agitation, alarm, apprehension, apprehensiveness, disquiet, doubt, misgiving, nervousness, perturbation, qualms, suspicion, trepidation, worry

➤ **Antonyms**
calm, composure, cool, ease, peace, quiet, serenity

uneasy *adjective* **1** = **anxious,** agitated, antsy (*informal*), apprehensive, discomposed, disturbed, edgy, ill at ease, impatient, jittery (*informal*), nervous, on edge, perturbed, restive, restless, troubled, twitchy (*informal*), uncomfortable, unsettled, upset, wired (*slang*), worried **2** = **precarious,** awkward, constrained, insecure, shaky, strained, tense, uncomfortable, unstable **3** = **disturbing,** bothering, dismaying, disquieting, troubling, upsetting, worrying
➤ **Antonyms**
≠**anxious:** at ease, calm, comfortable, relaxed, tranquil, unfazed (*informal*), unflustered, unperturbed, unruffled

uneconomic *adjective* = **unprofitable,** loss-making, nonpaying, non-profit-making, nonviable
➤ **Antonyms**
economic, money-making, productive, profitable, remunerative, viable

uneducated *adjective* **1** = **ignorant,** illiterate, unlettered, unread, unschooled, untaught **2** = **lowbrow,** benighted, uncultivated, uncultured
➤ **Antonyms**
≠**ignorant:** educated, informed, instructed, literate, schooled, taught, tutored

unemotional *adjective* = **impassive,** apathetic, cold, cool, indifferent, listless, passionless, phlegmatic, reserved, undemonstrative, unexcitable, unfeeling, unimpressionable, unresponsive
➤ **Antonyms**
demonstrative, emotional, excitable, feeling, passionate, responsive, sensitive

unemployed *adjective* = **out of work,** idle, jobless, laid off, on the dole (*Brit. informal*), out of a job, redundant, resting (*of an actor*), workless

unending *adjective* = **perpetual,** ceaseless, constant, continual, endless, eternal, everlasting, incessant, interminable, never-ending, unceasing, unremitting

unendurable *adjective* = **unbearable,** insufferable, insupportable, intolerable, more than flesh and blood can stand
➤ **Antonyms**
bearable, endurable, sufferable, tolerable

unenthusiastic *adjective* = **indifferent,** apathetic, blasé, bored, half-hearted, lukewarm, neutral, nonchalant, unimpressed, uninterested, unmoved, unresponsive
➤ **Antonyms**
ardent, eager, enthusiastic, excited, interested, keen, passionate

unenviable *adjective* = **unpleasant**, disagreeable, painful, thankless, uncomfortable, undesirable
➤ **Antonyms**
agreeable, attractive, desirable, enviable, pleasant

unequal *adjective* **1** = **different**, differing, disparate, dissimilar, not uniform, unlike, unmatched, variable, varying **2** = **disproportionate**, asymmetrical, ill-matched, irregular, unbalanced, uneven **3** *with* **to** = **inadequate for**, found wanting, insufficient for, not up to
➤ **Antonyms**
≠**different**: equal, equivalent, identical, like, matched, similar, uniform

unequalled *adjective* = **incomparable**, beyond compare, inimitable, matchless, nonpareil, paramount, peerless, pre-eminent, second to none, supreme, unmatched, unparalleled, unrivalled, unsurpassed, without equal

unequivocal *adjective* = **clear**, absolute, black-and-white, certain, clear-cut, cut-and-dried (*informal*), decisive, definite, direct, evident, explicit, incontrovertible, indubitable, manifest, plain, positive, straight, unambiguous, uncontestable, unmistakable
➤ **Antonyms**
ambiguous, doubtful, equivocal, evasive, indecisive, noncommittal, vague

unerring *adjective* = **accurate**, certain, exact, faultless, impeccable, infallible, perfect, sure, unfailing

unethical *adjective* = **immoral**, dirty, dishonest, dishonourable, disreputable, illegal, improper, not cricket (*informal*), shady (*informal*), underhand, under-the-table, unfair, unprincipled, unprofessional, unscrupulous, wrong
➤ **Antonyms**
ethical, honest, honourable, legal, moral, proper, scrupulous, upright

uneven *adjective* **1** = **rough**, bumpy, not flat, not level, not smooth **2** = **variable**, broken, changeable, fitful, fluctuating, intermittent, irregular, jerky, patchy, spasmodic, unsteady **3** = **unbalanced**, asymmetrical, lopsided, not parallel, odd, out of true **4** = **unequal**, disparate, ill-matched, one-sided, unfair
➤ **Antonyms**
≠**rough**: even, flat, level, plane, smooth

uneventful *adjective* = **humdrum**, boring, dull, ho-hum (*informal*), monotonous, ordinary, quiet, routine, tedious, unexceptional, unexciting, uninteresting, unmemorable, unremarkable, unvaried
➤ **Antonyms**
eventful, exceptional, exciting, interesting,

memorable, momentous, remarkable

unexampled *adjective* = **unprecedented**, unequalled, unheard-of, unique, unmatched, unparalleled

unexceptional *adjective* = **ordinary**, bog-standard (*Brit. & Irish slang*), common or garden (*informal*), commonplace, conventional, insignificant, mediocre, no great shakes (*informal*), normal, pedestrian, run-of-the-mill, undistinguished, unimpressive, unremarkable, usual
➤ **Antonyms**
distinguished, exceptional, impressive, notable, noteworthy, outstanding, remarkable, significant, unusual

unexpected *adjective* = **unforeseen**, abrupt, accidental, astonishing, chance, fortuitous, not bargained for, out of the blue, startling, sudden, surprising, unanticipated, unlooked-for, unpredictable
➤ **Antonyms**
anticipated, awaited, expected, foreseen, normal, planned, predictable

unfailing *adjective* **1** = **continuous**, boundless, ceaseless, continual, endless, inexhaustible, never-failing, persistent, unflagging, unlimited **2** = **reliable**, certain, constant, dependable, faithful, infallible, loyal, staunch, steadfast, sure, tried and true, true
➤ **Antonyms**
≠**reliable**: disloyal, fallible, inconstant, uncertain, unfaithful, unreliable, unsure, untrustworthy

unfair *adjective* **1** = **biased**, arbitrary, bigoted, discriminatory, inequitable, one-sided, partial, partisan, prejudiced, unjust **2** = **unscrupulous**, crooked (*informal*), dishonest, dishonourable, uncalled-for, unethical, unprincipled, unsporting, unwarranted, wrongful
➤ **Antonyms**
≠**unscrupulous**: ethical, fair, honest, just, principled, scrupulous

unfaithful *adjective* **1** = **faithless**, adulterous, fickle, inconstant, two-timing (*informal*), unchaste, untrue **2** = **disloyal**, deceitful, faithless, false, false-hearted, perfidious, traitorous, treacherous, treasonable, unreliable, untrustworthy
➤ **Antonyms**
≠**faithless**: constant, faithful ≠**disloyal**: faithful, loyal, steadfast, true, trustworthy

unfamiliar *adjective* **1** = **strange**, alien, beyond one's ken, curious, different, little known, new, novel, out-of-the-way, unaccustomed, uncommon, unknown, unusual **2** **unfamiliar with** = **unacquainted with**, a stranger to, inexperienced in, unaccustomed to, unconversant with, uninformed about, uninitiated in,

unpractised in, unskilled at, unversed in
➤ **Antonyms**
≠ **strange:** accustomed, average, common, commonplace, everyday, familiar, normal, unexceptional, usual, well-known
≠ **unacquainted with:** accustomed to, acquainted with, conversant with, experienced in, familiar with, knowledgeable about, well-versed in

unfashionable *adjective* = **passé**, antiquated, behind the times, dated, obsolete, old-fashioned, old hat, out, outmoded, out of date, out of fashion, out of the ark (*informal*), square (*informal*), unpopular
➤ **Antonyms**
à la mode, fashionable, modern, popular, stylish, trendy (*Brit. informal*)

unfasten *verb* = **undo**, detach, disconnect, let go, loosen, open, separate, unclasp, uncouple, unlace, unlock, unstrap, untie

unfathomable *adjective* 1 = **baffling**, abstruse, deep, esoteric, impenetrable, incomprehensible, indecipherable, inexplicable, profound, unknowable 2 = **immeasurable**, bottomless, unmeasured, unplumbed, unsounded

unfavourable *adjective* 1 = **adverse**, bad, contrary, disadvantageous, ill-suited, inauspicious, infelicitous, inopportune, ominous, threatening, unfortunate, unlucky, unpromising, unpropitious, unseasonable, unsuited, untimely, untoward 2 = **hostile**, inimical, low, negative, poor, unfriendly
➤ **Antonyms**
≠ **hostile:** amicable, approving, favourable, friendly, positive, warm, well-disposed

unfeeling *adjective* 1 = **callous**, apathetic, cold, cruel, hardened, hardhearted, heartless, inhuman, insensitive, pitiless, stony, uncaring, unsympathetic 2 = **numb**, insensate, insensible, sensationless
➤ **Antonyms**
≠ **callous:** benevolent, caring, concerned, feeling, gentle, humane, kind, sensitive, sympathetic

unfettered *adjective* = **uncontrolled**, free, unbridled, unchecked, unconfined, unconstrained, unlimited, unrestrained, unshackled, untrammelled

unfinished *adjective* 1 = **incomplete**, deficient, half-done, imperfect, in the making, lacking, unaccomplished, uncompleted, undone, unfulfilled, wanting 2 = **rough**, bare, crude, natural, raw, sketchy, unpolished, unrefined
➤ **Antonyms**
≠ **rough:** finished, flawless, perfected, polished, refined, smooth

unfit *adjective* 1 = **incapable**, ill-equipped, inadequate, incompetent, ineligible, no good, not cut out for, not equal to, not up to, unprepared, unqualified, useless 2 = **unsuitable**, ill-adapted, inadequate, inappropriate, ineffective, not designed, not fit, unsuited, useless 3 = **out of shape**, debilitated, decrepit, feeble, flabby, in poor condition, out of trim, unhealthy
➤ **Antonyms**
≠ **incapable:** able, capable, competent, equipped, qualified, ready ≠ **unsuitable:** acceptable, adequate, appropriate, suitable ≠ **out of shape:** fit, healthy, in good condition, strong, sturdy, well

unflappable *adjective Informal* = **imperturbable**, calm, collected, composed, cool, impassive, level-headed, self-possessed, unfazed (*informal*), unruffled
➤ **Antonyms**
antsy (*informal*), excitable, flappable, hot-headed, nervous, temperamental, twitchy (*informal*), volatile

unflattering *adjective* 1 = **blunt**, candid, critical, honest, uncomplimentary 2 = **unattractive**, not shown in the best light, not shown to advantage, plain, unbecoming, unprepossessing

unfledged *adjective* = **inexperienced**, callow, green, immature, raw, undeveloped, untried, young

unflinching *adjective* = **determined**, bold, constant, firm, immovable, resolute, stalwart, staunch, steadfast, steady, unfaltering, unshaken, unshrinking, unswerving, unwavering
➤ **Antonyms**
cowed, faltering, scared, shaken, shrinking, wavering

unfold *verb* 1 = **open**, disentangle, expand, flatten, spread out, straighten, stretch out, undo, unfurl, unravel, unroll, unwrap 2 = **reveal**, clarify, describe, disclose, divulge, explain, illustrate, make known, present, show, uncover 3 = **develop**, bear fruit, blossom, evolve, expand, grow, mature

unforeseen *adjective* = **unexpected**, abrupt, accidental, out of the blue, startling, sudden, surprise, surprising, unanticipated, unenvisaged, unlooked-for, unpredicted
➤ **Antonyms**
anticipated, envisaged, expected, foreseen, predicted

unforgettable *adjective* = **memorable**, exceptional, extraordinary, fixed in the mind, impressive, never to be forgotten, notable, striking

unforgivable *adjective* = **inexcusable**, deplorable, disgraceful, indefensible, shameful, unjustifiable, unpardonable, unwarrantable

➤ **Antonyms**
allowable, excusable, forgivable, justifiable, pardonable, venial

unfortunate *adjective* 1 = **disastrous**, adverse, calamitous, ill-fated, ill-starred, infelicitous, inopportune, ruinous, unfavourable, untimely, untoward 2 = **unlucky**, cursed, doomed, hapless, hopeless, luckless, out of luck, poor, star-crossed, unhappy, unprosperous, unsuccessful, wretched 3 = **regrettable**, deplorable, ill-advised, inappropriate, lamentable, unbecoming, unsuitable
➤ **Antonyms**
≠**disastrous**: auspicious, felicitous, fortuitous, fortunate, opportune, timely ≠**unlucky**: fortunate, happy, lucky, successful ≠**regrettable**: appropriate, becoming, unsuitable

unfounded *adjective* = **groundless**, baseless, fabricated, false, idle, spurious, trumped up, unjustified, unproven, unsubstantiated, without basis, without foundation
➤ **Antonyms**
attested, confirmed, factual, justified, proven, substantiated, verified

unfrequented *adjective* = **isolated**, deserted, godforsaken, lone, lonely, off the beaten track, remote, sequestered, solitary, uninhabited, unvisited

unfriendly *adjective* 1 = **hostile**, aloof, antagonistic, chilly, cold, disagreeable, distant, ill-disposed, inhospitable, not on speaking terms, uncongenial, unneighbourly, unsociable 2 = **unfavourable**, alien, hostile, inauspicious, inhospitable, inimical, unpropitious
➤ **Antonyms**
≠**hostile**: affable, amiable, convivial, friendly, hospitable, sociable, warm ≠**unfavourable**: auspicious, congenial, hospitable, propitious

ungainly *adjective* = **awkward**, clumsy, gangling, gawky, inelegant, loutish, lubberly, lumbering, uncoordinated, ungraceful
➤ **Antonyms**
attractive, comely, elegant, graceful, pleasing

ungodly *adjective* 1 = **wicked**, blasphemous, corrupt, depraved, godless, immoral, impious, irreligious, profane, sinful, vile 2 *Informal* = **unreasonable**, dreadful, horrendous, intolerable, outrageous, unearthly, unholy (*informal*), unseemly

ungovernable *adjective* 1 = **uncontrollable**, unrestrainable, wild 2 = **unruly**, rebellious, refractory, unmanageable

ungracious *adjective* = **bad-mannered**, churlish, discourteous, ill-bred, impolite, offhand, rude, uncivil, unmannerly

➤ **Antonyms**
affable, civil, courteous, gracious, mannerly, polite, well-mannered

ungrateful *adjective* = **unappreciative**, selfish, thankless, unmindful, unthankful
➤ **Antonyms**
appreciative, aware, grateful, mindful, thankful

unguarded *adjective* 1 = **unprotected**, defenceless, open to attack, undefended, vulnerable 2 = **frank**, artless, candid, direct, guileless, open, straightforward 3 = **careless**, foolhardy, heedless, ill-considered, impolitic, imprudent, incautious, indiscreet, rash, thoughtless, uncircumspect, undiplomatic, unthinking, unwary
➤ **Antonyms**
≠**careless**: cagey (*informal*), careful, cautious, diplomatic, discreet, guarded, prudent, wary

unhallowed *adjective* 1 = **unconsecrated**, not sacred, unblessed, unholy, unsanctified 2 = **wicked**, evil, godless, irreverent, profane, sinful

unhappiness *noun* = **sadness**, blues, dejection, depression, despondency, discontent, dissatisfaction, gloom, heartache, low spirits, melancholy, misery, sorrow, wretchedness

unhappy *adjective* 1 = **sad**, blue, crestfallen, dejected, depressed, despondent, disconsolate, dispirited, down, downcast, down in the dumps (*informal*), gloomy, long-faced, low, melancholy, miserable, mournful, sorrowful 2 = **unlucky**, cursed, hapless, ill-fated, ill-omened, luckless, unfortunate, wretched
➤ **Antonyms**
≠**sad**: cheerful, chirpy (*informal*), content, exuberant, happy, joyful, light-hearted, overjoyed, over the moon (*informal*), satisfied ≠**unlucky**: fortunate, lucky

unharmed *adjective* = **unhurt**, in one piece (*informal*), intact, safe, safe and sound, sound, undamaged, uninjured, unscarred, unscathed, untouched, whole, without a scratch
➤ **Antonyms**
damaged, harmed, hurt, impaired, injured, scarred, scathed

unhealthy *adjective* 1 = **harmful**, deleterious, detrimental, insalubrious, insanitary, noisome, noxious, unwholesome 2 = **sick**, ailing, delicate, feeble, frail, infirm, in poor health, invalid, poorly (*informal*), sickly, unsound, unwell, weak 3 = **unwholesome**, bad, corrupt, corrupting, degrading, demoralizing, morbid, negative, undesirable
➤ **Antonyms**
≠**harmful**: beneficial, good, healthy,

salubrious, salutary, wholesome ≠**sick**: fit, healthy, robust, well ≠**unwholesome**: desirable, moral, positive

unheard-of *adjective* 1 = **unprecedented**, ground-breaking, inconceivable, never before encountered, new, novel, singular, unbelievable, undreamed of, unexampled, unique, unusual 2 = **shocking**, disgraceful, extreme, offensive, outrageous, preposterous, unacceptable, unthinkable 3 = **obscure**, little known, undiscovered, unfamiliar, unknown

unheeded *adjective* = **ignored**, disobeyed, disregarded, forgotten, neglected, overlooked
➤ **Antonyms**
heeded, noted, noticed, obeyed, observed, regarded, remembered

unheralded *adjective* = **unannounced**, out of the blue, surprise, unexpected, unforeseen, unproclaimed, unpublicized

unhesitating *adjective* 1 = **instant**, immediate, instantaneous, prompt, ready, without delay 2 = **wholehearted**, implicit, resolute, steadfast, unfaltering, unquestioning, unreserved, unswerving, unwavering
➤ **Antonyms**
≠**wholehearted**: diffident, hesitant, irresolute, questioning, tentative, uncertain, unsure, wavering

unhinge *verb* = **unbalance**, confound, confuse, craze, dement, derange, drive out of one's mind, madden, unsettle

unholy *adjective* 1 = **evil**, base, corrupt, depraved, dishonest, heinous, immoral, iniquitous, irreligious, profane, sinful, ungodly, vile, wicked 2 *Informal* = **outrageous**, appalling, awful, dreadful, horrendous, shocking, unearthly, ungodly (*informal*), unreasonable
➤ **Antonyms**
≠**evil**: devout, faithful, godly, holy, pious, religious, saintly, virtuous

unhurried *adjective* = **leisurely**, calm, deliberate, easy, easy-going, sedate, slow, slow and steady, slow-paced
➤ **Antonyms**
brief, cursory, hasty, hectic, hurried, quick, rushed, speedy, swift

unidentified *adjective* = **unnamed**, anonymous, mysterious, nameless, unclassified, unfamiliar, unknown, unmarked, unrecognized, unrevealed
➤ **Antonyms**
classified, familiar, identified, known, marked, named, recognized

unification *noun* = **union**, alliance, amalgamation, coalescence, coalition, combination, confederation, federation, fusion, merger, uniting

uniform *noun* 1 = **outfit**, costume, dress, garb, habit, livery, regalia, regimentals, suit
♦ *adjective* 2 = **unvarying**, consistent, constant, equable, even, regular, smooth, unbroken, unchanging, undeviating 3 = **alike**, equal, identical, like, same, selfsame, similar
➤ **Antonyms**
adjective ≠**unvarying**: changeable, changing, deviating, inconsistent, irregular, uneven, varying

uniformity *noun* 1 = **regularity**, constancy, evenness, homogeneity, invariability, sameness, similarity 2 = **monotony**, drabness, dullness, flatness, lack of diversity, sameness, tedium

unify *verb* = **unite**, amalgamate, bind, bring together, combine, confederate, consolidate, federate, fuse, join, merge
➤ **Antonyms**
alienate, disconnect, disjoin, disunite, divide, separate, sever, split

unimaginable *adjective* = **inconceivable**, beyond one's wildest dreams, fantastic, impossible, incredible, indescribable, ineffable, mind-boggling (*informal*), unbelievable, unheard-of, unthinkable

unimaginative *adjective* = **unoriginal**, banal, commonplace, derivative, dry, dull, hackneyed, lifeless, matter-of-fact, ordinary, pedestrian, predictable, prosaic, routine, tame, uncreative, uninspired, unromantic, usual, vanilla (*informal*)
➤ **Antonyms**
creative, different, exciting, fresh, ground-breaking, imaginative, innovative, inventive, original, unhackneyed, unusual

unimpeachable *adjective* = **beyond question**, above reproach, beyond criticism, blameless, faultless, impeccable, irreproachable, perfect, squeaky-clean, unassailable
➤ **Antonyms**
blameworthy, faulty, imperfect, reprehensible, reproachable, shameful

unimpeded *adjective* = **unhindered**, free, open, unblocked, unchecked, unconstrained, unhampered, unrestrained, untrammelled
➤ **Antonyms**
blocked, checked, constrained, hampered, hindered, impeded, restrained

unimportant *adjective* = **insignificant**, immaterial, inconsequential, irrelevant, low-ranking, minor, nickel-and-dime (*U.S. slang*), not worth mentioning, nugatory, of no account, of no consequence, of no moment, paltry, petty, slight, trifling, trivial, worthless
➤ **Antonyms**
essential, grave, important, major, significant, urgent, vital, weighty

uninhabited *adjective* = **deserted**, abandoned, barren, desert, desolate, empty, lonely, unoccupied, unpopulated, unsettled, untenanted, vacant, waste

uninhibited *adjective* **1** = **unselfconscious**, candid, frank, free, free and easy, informal, instinctive, liberated, natural, open, relaxed, spontaneous, unrepressed, unreserved **2** = **unrestrained**, free, unbridled, unchecked, unconstrained, uncontrolled, uncurbed, unrestricted
➤ **Antonyms**
≠**unselfconscious:** bashful, careful, demure, inhibited, modest, self-conscious, shy, uptight (*informal*) ≠**unrestrained:** checked, constrained, controlled, curbed, hampered, inhibited, restrained

uninspired *adjective* = **unexciting**, banal, commonplace, dull, humdrum, indifferent, ordinary, prosaic, stale, stock, unimaginative, uninspiring, uninteresting, unoriginal, vanilla (*informal*)
➤ **Antonyms**
brilliant, different, exciting, imaginative, inspired, interesting, original, outstanding

uninspiring *adjective* = **unexciting**, as dry as dust, boring, drab, dreary, dry, dull, flat, humdrum, insipid, mundane, pedestrian, plain, prosaic, spiritless, uninteresting
➤ **Antonyms**
exciting, inspiring, moving, rousing, stimulating, stirring, uplifting

unintelligent *adjective* = **stupid**, braindead (*informal*), brainless, dense, dozy (*Brit. informal*), dull, dumb-ass (*slang*), empty-headed, foolish, gormless (*Brit. informal*), obtuse, slow, thick, unreasoning, unthinking
➤ **Antonyms**
bright, clever, intelligent, sharp, smart, thinking

unintelligible *adjective* = **incomprehensible**, illegible, inarticulate, incoherent, indecipherable, indistinct, jumbled, meaningless, muddled
➤ **Antonyms**
clear, coherent, comprehensible, intelligible, legible, lucid, understandable

unintentional *adjective* = **accidental**, casual, fortuitous, inadvertent, involuntary, unconscious, undesigned, unintended, unpremeditated, unthinking, unwitting
➤ **Antonyms**
conscious, deliberate, designed, intended, intentional, premeditated, voluntary, wilful

uninterested *adjective* = **indifferent**, apathetic, blasé, bored, distant, impassive, incurious, listless, unconcerned
➤ **Antonyms**
alert, concerned, curious, enthusiastic, interested, keen

uninteresting *adjective* = **boring**, as dry as dust, commonplace, drab, dreary, dry, dull, flat, ho-hum (*informal*), humdrum, mind-numbing, monotonous, tedious, tiresome, unenjoyable, uneventful, unexciting, uninspiring, wearisome
➤ **Antonyms**
absorbing, compelling, enjoyable, exciting, gripping, inspiring, interesting, intriguing, stimulating

uninterrupted *adjective* = **continuous**, constant, continual, nonstop, steady, sustained, unbroken, undisturbed, unending

uninvited *adjective* = **unasked**, not asked, not invited, unbidden, unwanted, unwelcome

uninviting *adjective* = **unattractive**, disagreeable, offensive, off-putting (*Brit. informal*), repellent, repulsive, unappealing, unappetizing, undesirable, unpleasant, untempting, unwelcoming
➤ **Antonyms**
agreeable, appealing, appetizing, attractive, desirable, inviting, pleasant, tempting, welcoming

union *noun* **1** = **joining**, amalgam, amalgamation, blend, combination, conjunction, fusion, mixture, synthesis, uniting **2** = **alliance**, association, Bund, coalition, confederacy, confederation, federation, league **3** = **agreement**, accord, concord, concurrence, harmony, unanimity, unison, unity **4** = **intercourse**, coition, coitus, copulation, coupling, marriage, matrimony, wedlock

unique *adjective* **1** = **single**, lone, one and only, only, solitary **2** = **unparalleled**, incomparable, inimitable, matchless, nonpareil, peerless, unequalled, unexampled, unmatched, unrivalled, without equal

unison *noun* = **agreement**, accord, accordance, concert, concord, cooperation, harmony, unanimity, unity
➤ **Antonyms**
disagreement, discord, disharmony, dissension, dissidence, dissonance

unit *noun* **1** = **item**, entity, module, piece, portion, whole **2** = **part**, component, constituent, element, member, section, segment **3** = **section**, detachment, group **4** = **measure**, measurement, quantity **5** = **system**, assembly

unite *verb* **1** = **join**, amalgamate, blend, coalesce, combine, consolidate, couple, fuse, incorporate, link, marry, meld, merge, unify, wed **2** = **cooperate**, ally, associate, band, close ranks, club together, collaborate, confederate, join forces, join together, league, pool, pull together
➤ **Antonyms**
≠**join:** break, detach, disunite, divide, part,

separate, sever, split ≠**cooperate**: break,
divorce, part, separate, split
united adjective 1 = **combined**, affiliated,
allied, banded together, collective,
concerted, in partnership, leagued, pooled,
unified 2 = **in agreement**, agreed, in accord,
like-minded, of like mind, of one mind, of
the same opinion, one, unanimous
unity noun 1 = **wholeness**, entity, integrity,
oneness, singleness, undividedness,
unification, union 2 = **agreement**, accord,
assent, concord, concurrence, consensus,
harmony, peace, solidarity, unanimity,
unison
➤ **Antonyms**
≠**wholeness**: disunity, division,
heterogeneity, multiplicity, separation
≠**agreement**: disagreement, discord,
disunity, division, factionalism, ill will,
independence, individuality, in-fighting, strife
universal adjective = **widespread**,
all-embracing, catholic, common,
ecumenical, entire, general, omnipresent,
overarching, total, unlimited, whole,
worldwide
universality noun = **comprehensiveness**,
all-inclusiveness, completeness, entirety,
generality, generalization, totality, ubiquity
universally adverb = **everywhere**, across
the board, always, in all cases, in every
instance, invariably, uniformly, without
exception
universe noun = **cosmos**, creation,
everything, macrocosm, nature, the natural
world
unjust adjective = **unfair**, biased,
inequitable, one-sided, partial, partisan,
prejudiced, undeserved, unjustified,
unmerited, wrong, wrongful
➤ **Antonyms**
equitable, fair, impartial, just, justified, right,
unbiased
unjustifiable adjective = **inexcusable**,
indefensible, outrageous, unacceptable,
unforgivable, unjust, unpardonable,
unwarrantable, wrong
unkempt adjective 1 = **uncombed**, shaggy,
tousled 2 = **untidy**, bedraggled,
disarranged, disarrayed, dishevelled,
disordered, messy, rumpled, scruffy, shabby,
slatternly, sloppy (informal), slovenly,
sluttish, ungroomed
➤ **Antonyms**
≠**untidy**: neat, presentable, soigné or
soignée, spruce, tidy, trim, well-groomed
unkind adjective = **cruel**, hardhearted,
harsh, inconsiderate, inhuman, insensitive,
malicious, mean, nasty, spiteful, thoughtless,
uncaring, uncharitable, unchristian,
unfeeling, unfriendly, unsympathetic

➤ **Antonyms**
benevolent, caring, charitable, considerate,
generous, kind, soft-hearted, sympathetic,
thoughtful
unkindness noun = **cruelty**,
hardheartedness, harshness, ill will,
inhumanity, insensitivity, malevolence,
malice, maliciousness, meanness, spite,
spitefulness, unfeeling
➤ **Antonyms**
benevolence, charity, friendliness, generosity,
goodwill, kindness, sympathy,
thoughtfulness
unknown adjective 1 = **hidden**, concealed,
dark, mysterious, secret, unrecognized,
unrevealed, untold 2 = **strange**, alien, new 3
= **unidentified**, anonymous, beyond one's
ken, nameless, uncharted, undiscovered,
unexplored, unnamed 4 = **obscure**, humble,
little known, undistinguished, unfamiliar,
unheard-of, unrenowned, unsung
➤ **Antonyms**
≠**obscure**: celebrated, distinguished,
familiar, known, recognized, renowned,
well-known
unlawful adjective = **illegal**, actionable,
against the law, banned, criminal, forbidden,
illegitimate, illicit, outlawed, prohibited,
unauthorized, under-the-table, unlicensed
unleash verb = **release**, free, let go, let
loose, unbridle, unloose, untie
unlettered adjective = **uneducated**,
ignorant, illiterate, unlearned, unschooled,
untaught, untutored
➤ **Antonyms**
educated, learned, literate, schooled, taught,
tutored
unlike adjective = **different**, as different as
chalk and cheese (informal), contrasted,
dissimilar, distinct, divergent, diverse,
ill-matched, incompatible, not alike,
opposite, unequal, unrelated
➤ **Antonyms**
compatible, equal, like, matched, related,
similar
unlikely adjective 1 = **improbable**,
doubtful, faint, not likely, remote, slight,
unimaginable 2 = **unbelievable**,
cock-and-bull (informal), implausible,
incredible, questionable, unconvincing
unlimited adjective 1 = **infinite**, boundless,
countless, endless, extensive, great,
illimitable, immeasurable, immense,
incalculable, limitless, unbounded, vast 2
= **total**, absolute, all-encompassing,
complete, full, unconditional, unconstrained,
unfettered, unqualified, unrestricted
➤ **Antonyms**
≠**infinite**: bounded, confined, finite, limited
≠**total**: constrained, limited, restricted

unload *verb* = **empty**, discharge, dump, lighten, off-load, relieve, unburden, unpack

unlock *verb* = **open**, free, let loose, release, unbar, unbolt, undo, unfasten, unlatch

unlooked-for *adjective* = **unexpected**, chance, fortuitous, out of the blue, surprise, surprising, unanticipated, undreamed of, unforeseen, unhoped-for, unpredicted, unthought-of

unlovable *adjective* = **unattractive**, dislikable *or* dislikeable, obnoxious, odious, repellent, repulsive, unadorable, undesirable, unlovely, unpleasant
➤ **Antonyms**
adorable, attractive, cute, desirable, enchanting, engaging, likable *or* likeable, lovable, lovely

unloved *adjective* = **uncared-for**, disliked, forsaken, loveless, neglected, rejected, spurned, uncherished, unpopular, unwanted
➤ **Antonyms**
adored, beloved, cherished, liked, loved, popular, precious, wanted

unlucky *adjective* **1** = **unfortunate**, cursed, disastrous, hapless, luckless, miserable, unhappy, unsuccessful, wretched **2** = **ill-fated**, doomed, ill-omened, ill-starred, inauspicious, ominous, unfavourable, untimely
➤ **Antonyms**
≠**unfortunate:** blessed, favoured, fortunate, happy, lucky, prosperous

unman *verb* **1** = **unnerve**, daunt, demoralize, discourage, dispirit, intimidate, psych out (*informal*), weaken **2** = **emasculate**

unmanageable *adjective* **1** = **difficult to handle**, awkward, bulky, clunky (*informal*), cumbersome, inconvenient, unhandy, unwieldy **2** = **uncontrollable**, difficult, fractious, intractable, obstreperous, out of hand, refractory, stroppy (*Brit. slang*), unruly, wild
➤ **Antonyms**
≠**difficult to handle:** manageable, wieldy
≠**uncontrollable:** amenable, compliant, docile, easy, manageable, submissive, tractable

unmanly *adjective* **1** = **effeminate**, camp (*informal*), feeble, sissy, soft (*informal*), weak, womanish **2** = **cowardly**, abject, chicken-hearted, craven, dishonourable, ignoble, weak-kneed (*informal*), yellow (*informal*)

unmannerly *adjective* = **bad-mannered**, badly behaved, discourteous, disrespectful, ill-bred, ill-mannered, impolite, misbehaved, rude, uncivil, uncouth
➤ **Antonyms**
civil, courteous, mannerly, polite, respectful, well-behaved, well-bred, well-mannered

unmarried *adjective* = **single**, bachelor, celibate, maiden, on the shelf, unattached, unwed, unwedded, virgin

unmask *verb* = **reveal**, bare, bring to light, disclose, discover, expose, lay bare, show up, uncloak, uncover, unveil

unmatched *adjective* = **unequalled**, beyond compare, consummate, incomparable, matchless, paramount, peerless, second to none, supreme, unparalleled, unrivalled, unsurpassed

unmentionable *adjective* = **taboo**, disgraceful, disreputable, forbidden, frowned on, immodest, indecent, obscene, scandalous, shameful, shocking, unspeakable, unutterable, X-rated (*informal*)

unmerciful *adjective* = **merciless**, brutal, cruel, hard, heartless, implacable, inhumane, pitiless, relentless, remorseless, ruthless, uncaring, unfeeling, unsparing
➤ **Antonyms**
beneficent, caring, feeling, humane, merciful, pitying, sparing, tender-hearted

unmistakable *adjective* = **clear**, blatant, certain, conspicuous, decided, distinct, evident, glaring, indisputable, manifest, obvious, palpable, patent, plain, positive, pronounced, sure, unambiguous, unequivocal
➤ **Antonyms**
ambiguous, dim, doubtful, equivocal, hidden, mistakable, obscure, uncertain, unclear, unsure

unmitigated *adjective* **1** = **unrelieved**, grim, harsh, intense, oppressive, persistent, relentless, unabated, unalleviated, unbroken, undiminished, unmodified, unqualified, unredeemed **2** = **complete**, absolute, arrant, consummate, deep-dyed (*usually derogatory*), downright, out-and-out, outright, perfect, rank, sheer, thorough, thoroughgoing, utter

unmoved *adjective* = **unaffected**, cold, dry-eyed, impassive, indifferent, unconcerned, unfeeling, unimpressed, unresponsive, unstirred, untouched
➤ **Antonyms**
affected, concerned, impressed, moved, stirred, touched

unnatural *adjective* **1** = **strange**, bizarre, extraordinary, freakish, outlandish, queer, supernatural, unaccountable, uncanny **2** = **abnormal**, aberrant, anomalous, irregular, odd, perverse, perverted, unusual **3** = **false**, affected, artificial, assumed, contrived, feigned, forced, insincere, laboured, mannered, phoney *or* phony (*informal*), self-conscious, stagy, stiff, stilted, strained,

studied, theatrical **4** = **inhuman**, brutal, callous, cold-blooded, evil, fiendish, heartless, monstrous, ruthless, savage, unfeeling, wicked
➤ **Antonyms**
≠**strange, abnormal:** normal, ordinary, typical ≠**false:** genuine, honest, natural, sincere, unaffected, unfeigned, unpretentious ≠**inhuman:** caring, humane, loving, warm

unnecessary *adjective* = **needless**, dispensable, expendable, inessential, nonessential, redundant, superfluous, surplus to requirements, uncalled-for, unneeded, unrequired, useless
➤ **Antonyms**
essential, indispensable, necessary, needed, required, vital

unnerve *verb* = **intimidate**, confound, daunt, demoralize, disarm, disconcert, discourage, dishearten, dismay, dispirit, faze, fluster, frighten, psych out (*informal*), rattle (*informal*), shake, throw off balance, unhinge, unman, upset
➤ **Antonyms**
arm, brace, encourage, gee up, hearten, nerve, steel, strengthen, support

unnoticed *adjective* = **unobserved**, disregarded, ignored, neglected, overlooked, undiscovered, unheeded, unperceived, unrecognized, unremarked, unseen
➤ **Antonyms**
discovered, heeded, noted, noticed, observed, perceived, recognized, remarked

unobtrusive *adjective* = **inconspicuous**, humble, keeping a low profile, low-key, meek, modest, quiet, restrained, retiring, self-effacing, subdued, unassuming, unnoticeable, unostentatious, unpretentious
➤ **Antonyms**
blatant, bold, conspicuous, eye-catching, high-profile, noticeable, obtrusive, outgoing, prominent

unoccupied *adjective* **1** = **empty**, tenantless, uninhabited, untenanted, vacant **2** = **idle**, at a loose end, at leisure, disengaged, inactive, unemployed

unofficial *adjective* = **unauthorized**, informal, off the record, personal, private, unconfirmed, wildcat

unorthodox *adjective* = **unconventional**, abnormal, heterodox, irregular, off-the-wall (*slang*), uncustomary, unusual, unwonted
➤ **Antonyms**
conventional, customary, established, orthodox, sound, traditional, usual

unpaid *adjective* **1** = **voluntary**, honorary, unsalaried **2** = **owing**, due, not discharged, outstanding, overdue, payable, unsettled

unpalatable *adjective* = **unpleasant**, bitter, disagreeable, displeasing, distasteful, horrid,

offensive, repugnant, unappetizing, unattractive, uneatable, unsavoury
➤ **Antonyms**
agreeable, appetizing, attractive, eatable, palatable, pleasant, pleasing, savoury, tasty

unparalleled *adjective* = **unequalled**, beyond compare, consummate, exceptional, incomparable, matchless, peerless, rare, singular, superlative, unique, unmatched, unprecedented, unrivalled, unsurpassed, without equal

unpardonable *adjective* = **unforgivable**, deplorable, disgraceful, indefensible, inexcusable, outrageous, scandalous, shameful, unjustifiable

unperturbed *adjective* = **calm**, as cool as a cucumber, collected, composed, cool, placid, poised, self-possessed, tranquil, undismayed, unfazed (*informal*), unflustered, unruffled, untroubled, unworried
➤ **Antonyms**
anxious, dismayed, flustered, perturbed, ruffled, troubled, worried

unpleasant *adjective* = **nasty**, abhorrent, bad, disagreeable, displeasing, distasteful, horrid, ill-natured, irksome, objectionable, obnoxious, repulsive, troublesome, unattractive, unlikable *or* unlikeable, unlovely, unpalatable
➤ **Antonyms**
agreeable, good-natured, likable *or* likeable, lovely, nice, pleasant

unpleasantness *noun* **1** = **nastiness**, awfulness, disagreeableness, dreadfulness, grimness, horridness, ugliness **2** = **hostility**, animosity, antagonism, bad feeling, ill humour *or* will, malice, offensiveness, rudeness, unfriendliness
➤ **Antonyms**
≠**nastiness:** agreeableness, delight, enjoyment, pleasantness ≠**hostility:** friendliness, good humour *or* will, pleasantness

unpolished *adjective* **1** = **crude**, rough, rough and ready, rude, sketchy, unfinished **2** = **unrefined**, uncivilized, uncouth, uncultivated, uncultured, unsophisticated, vulgar

unpopular *adjective* = **disliked**, avoided, detested, not sought out, out in the cold, out of favour, rejected, shunned, unattractive, undesirable, unloved, unwanted, unwelcome
➤ **Antonyms**
desirable, favoured, liked, loved, popular, wanted, welcome

unprecedented *adjective*
= **extraordinary**, abnormal, exceptional, freakish, ground-breaking, new, novel,

original, remarkable, singular, unexampled, unheard-of, unparalleled, unrivalled, unusual

unpredictable *adjective* = **inconstant**, chance, changeable, doubtful, erratic, fickle, fluky (*informal*), hit-and-miss (*informal*), hit-or-miss (*informal*), iffy (*informal*), random, unforeseeable, unreliable, unstable, variable
➤ Antonyms
certain, constant, dependable, foreseeable, predictable, reliable, stable, steady, unchanging

unprejudiced *adjective* = **impartial**, balanced, even-handed, fair, fair-minded, just, nonpartisan, objective, open-minded, unbiased, uninfluenced
➤ Antonyms
biased, bigoted, influenced, narrow-minded, partial, prejudiced, unfair, unjust

unprepared *adjective* 1 = **taken off guard**, caught napping, caught on the hop (*Brit. informal*), surprised, taken aback, unaware, unready, unsuspecting 2 = **improvised**, ad-lib, extemporaneous, off the cuff (*informal*), spontaneous

unpretentious *adjective* = **modest**, homely, honest, humble, plain, simple, straightforward, unaffected, unassuming, unimposing, unobtrusive, unostentatious, unspoiled
➤ Antonyms
affected, arty-farty (*informal*), conceited, obtrusive, ostentatious, pretentious, showy

unprincipled *adjective* = **dishonest**, amoral, corrupt, crooked, deceitful, devious, dishonourable, immoral, tricky, unconscionable, underhand, unethical, unprofessional, unscrupulous
➤ Antonyms
decent, ethical, honest, honourable, moral, righteous, scrupulous, upright, virtuous

unproductive *adjective* 1 = **useless**, fruitless, futile, idle, ineffective, inefficacious, unavailing, unprofitable, unremunerative, unrewarding, vain, valueless, worthless 2 = **barren**, dry, fruitless, sterile, unprolific
➤ Antonyms
≠useless: effective, fruitful, profitable, remunerative, rewarding, useful, worthwhile
≠barren: abundant, fertile, fruitful, productive, prolific

unprofessional *adjective* 1 = **unethical**, improper, lax, negligent, unfitting, unprincipled, unseemly, unworthy 2 = **amateurish**, amateur, cowboy (*informal*), incompetent, inefficient, inexperienced, inexpert, slapdash, slipshod, untrained
➤ Antonyms
≠amateurish: adept, competent, efficient, experienced, expert, professional, skilful

unpromising *adjective* = **inauspicious**, adverse, discouraging, doubtful, gloomy, infelicitous, ominous, unfavourable, unpropitious

unprotected *adjective* = **vulnerable**, defenceless, exposed, helpless, naked, open, open to attack, unarmed, undefended, unguarded, unsheltered, unshielded
➤ Antonyms
defended, guarded, immune, protected, safe, secure, shielded

unqualified *adjective* 1 = **unfit**, ill-equipped, incapable, incompetent, ineligible, not equal to, not up to, unprepared 2 = **unconditional**, categorical, downright, outright, unmitigated, unreserved, unrestricted, without reservation 3 = **total**, absolute, complete, consummate, deep-dyed (*usually derogatory*), downright, out-and-out, outright, thorough, thoroughgoing, utter

unquestionable *adjective* = **certain**, absolute, beyond a shadow of doubt, clear, conclusive, definite, incontestable, incontrovertible, indisputable, indubitable, irrefutable, manifest, patent, self-evident, sure, undeniable, unequivocal, unmistakable
➤ Antonyms
ambiguous, doubtful, dubious, inconclusive, questionable, uncertain, unclear

unravel *verb* 1 = **undo**, disentangle, extricate, free, separate, straighten out, unknot, untangle, unwind 2 = **solve**, clear up, explain, figure out (*informal*), get straight, get to the bottom of, interpret, make out, puzzle out, resolve, suss (out) (*slang*), work out

unreadable *adjective* 1 = **illegible**, crabbed, undecipherable 2 = **turgid**, badly written, dry as dust, heavy going

unreal *adjective* 1 = **imaginary**, chimerical, dreamlike, fabulous, fanciful, fictitious, hypothetical, illusory, make-believe, mythical, phantasmagoric, storybook, visionary 2 = **insubstantial**, immaterial, impalpable, intangible, nebulous 3 = **fake**, artificial, false, insincere, mock, ostensible, pretended, seeming, sham
➤ Antonyms
≠fake: authentic, bona fide, genuine, real, realistic, sincere, true, veritable

unrealistic *adjective* 1 = **impractical**, half-baked (*informal*), impracticable, improbable, quixotic, romantic, starry-eyed, theoretical, unworkable 2 = **unauthentic**, non-naturalistic, unlifelike, unreal
➤ Antonyms
≠impractical: practical, pragmatic, probable, realistic, sensible, unromantic, workable

unreasonable *adjective* 1 = **excessive**,

absurd, exorbitant, extortionate, extravagant, far-fetched, immoderate, irrational, preposterous, steep (*informal*), too great, uncalled-for, undue, unfair, unjust, unwarranted **2 = biased**, arbitrary, blinkered, headstrong, illogical, opinionated
> Antonyms
≠**excessive**: fair, just, justified, moderate, reasonable, warranted ≠**biased**: fair-minded, flexible, open-minded

unregenerate *adjective* = **unrepentant**, hardened, intractable, obdurate, obstinate, recalcitrant, refractory, self-willed, stubborn, unconverted, unreformed
> Antonyms
converted, reformed, regenerate, repentant

unrelated *adjective* **1 = unconnected**, different, dissimilar, not kin, not kindred, not related, unlike **2 = irrelevant**, beside the point, extraneous, inapplicable, inappropriate, not germane, unassociated, unconnected

unrelenting *adjective* **1 = merciless**, cruel, implacable, intransigent, pitiless, relentless, remorseless, ruthless, stern, tough, unsparing **2 = steady**, ceaseless, constant, continual, continuous, endless, incessant, perpetual, unabated, unbroken, unremitting, unwavering

unreliable *adjective* **1 = undependable**, irresponsible, not conscientious, treacherous, unstable, untrustworthy **2 = uncertain**, deceptive, erroneous, fake, fallible, false, implausible, inaccurate, mistaken, specious, unconvincing, unsound
> Antonyms
≠**undependable**: conscientious, dependable, reliable, responsible, stable, trustworthy ≠**uncertain**: accurate, infallible

unremitting *adjective* = **constant**, continual, continuous, incessant, indefatigable, perpetual, relentless, remorseless, unabated, unbroken, unceasing, unwavering

unrepentant *adjective* = **impenitent**, abandoned, callous, hardened, incorrigible, not contrite, shameless, unregenerate, unremorseful, unrepenting
> Antonyms
ashamed, contrite, penitent, remorseful, repentant, rueful, sorry

unreserved *adjective* **1 = total**, absolute, complete, entire, full, unconditional, unlimited, unqualified, wholehearted, without reservation **2 = uninhibited**, demonstrative, extrovert, forthright, frank, free, open, open-hearted, outgoing, outspoken, unrestrained, unreticent
> Antonyms
≠**uninhibited**: demure, inhibited, reserved, restrained, reticent, shy, undemonstrative

unresolved *adjective* = **undecided**, doubtful, moot, open to question, pending, problematical, unanswered, undetermined, unsettled, unsolved, up in the air, vague, yet to be decided

unrest *noun* **1 = discontent**, agitation, disaffection, discord, dissatisfaction, dissension, protest, rebellion, sedition, strife, tumult, turmoil, upheaval **2 = uneasiness**, agitation, anxiety, disquiet, distress, perturbation, restlessness, trepidation, worry
> Antonyms
calm, contentment, peace, relaxation, rest, stillness, tranquillity

unrestrained *adjective* = **uncontrolled**, abandoned, free, immoderate, inordinate, intemperate, natural, unbounded, unbridled, unchecked, unconstrained, unhindered, uninhibited, unlimited, unrepressed
> Antonyms
checked, constrained, frustrated, hindered, inhibited, repressed, restrained

unrestricted *adjective* **1 = unlimited**, absolute, free, free-for-all (*informal*), open, unbounded, uncircumscribed, unhindered, unregulated **2 = open**, clear, public, unobstructed, unopposed

unrivalled *adjective* = **unparalleled**, beyond compare, incomparable, matchless, nonpareil, peerless, supreme, unequalled, unexcelled, unmatched, unsurpassed, without equal

unruffled *adjective* **1 = calm**, collected, composed, cool, peaceful, placid, sedate, serene, tranquil, undisturbed, unfazed (*informal*), unflustered, unmoved, unperturbed **2 = smooth**, even, flat, level, unbroken

unruly *adjective* = **uncontrollable**, disobedient, disorderly, fractious, headstrong, insubordinate, intractable, lawless, mutinous, obstreperous, rebellious, refractory, riotous, rowdy, turbulent, ungovernable, unmanageable, wayward, wild, wilful
> Antonyms
amenable, biddable, docile, governable, manageable, obedient, orderly, tractable

unsafe *adjective* = **dangerous**, hazardous, insecure, perilous, precarious, risky, threatening, treacherous, uncertain, unreliable, unsound, unstable
> Antonyms
harmless, reliable, safe, secure, sound

unsaid *adjective* = **unspoken**, left to the imagination, tacit, undeclared, unexpressed, unstated, unuttered, unvoiced

unsatisfactory *adjective* = **not good enough**, deficient, disappointing, displeasing, inadequate, insufficient,

mediocre, no great shakes (*informal*), not much cop (*Brit. slang*), not up to par, not up to scratch (*informal*), pathetic, poor, unacceptable, unsuitable, unworthy
➤ **Antonyms**
acceptable, adequate, passable, pleasing, satisfactory, sufficient, suitable

unsavoury *adjective* 1 = **unpleasant**, distasteful, nasty, objectionable, obnoxious, offensive, repellent, repugnant, repulsive, revolting 2 = **unappetizing**, disagreeable, distasteful, nauseating, sickening, unpalatable
➤ **Antonyms**
≠**unappetizing**: agreeable, appetizing, palatable, pleasant, savoury, tasteful, tasty, toothsome

unscathed *adjective* = **unharmed**, in one piece, safe, sound, unhurt, uninjured, unmarked, unscarred, unscratched, untouched, whole

unscrupulous *adjective* = **unprincipled**, corrupt, crooked (*informal*), dishonest, dishonourable, immoral, improper, ruthless, unethical
➤ **Antonyms**
ethical, honest, honourable, moral, principled, proper, scrupulous, upright

unseasonable *adjective* = **untimely**, ill-timed, inappropriate, inopportune, mistimed, out of keeping, unsuitable

unseat *verb* 1 = **throw**, unhorse, unsaddle 2 = **depose**, dethrone, discharge, dismiss, displace, oust, overthrow, remove

unseemly *adjective* = **improper**, discreditable, inappropriate, indecorous, indelicate, in poor taste, out of keeping, out of place, unbecoming, unbefitting, undignified, unsuitable
➤ **Antonyms**
acceptable, appropriate, becoming, decorous, fitting, proper, seemly, suitable

unseen *adjective* 1 = **hidden**, concealed, invisible, obscure, veiled 2 = **unobserved**, undetected, unnoticed, unobtrusive, unperceived

unselfish *adjective* = **generous**, altruistic, charitable, devoted, disinterested, humanitarian, kind, liberal, magnanimous, noble, self-denying, selfless, self-sacrificing

unsettle *verb* = **disturb**, agitate, bother, confuse, discompose, disconcert, disorder, faze, fluster, perturb, rattle (*informal*), ruffle, throw (*informal*), throw into confusion, throw off balance, trouble, unbalance, unnerve, upset

unsettled *adjective* 1 = **unstable**, disorderly, insecure, shaky, unsteady 2 = **restless**, agitated, anxious, confused, disturbed, flustered, on edge, perturbed,

restive, shaken, tense, troubled, uneasy, unnerved, wired (*slang*) 3 = **inconstant**, changeable, changing, uncertain, unpredictable, variable 4 = **unresolved**, debatable, doubtful, moot, open, undecided, undetermined, up in the air 5 = **owing**, due, in arrears, outstanding, payable, pending

unshakable *adjective* = **firm**, absolute, certain, constant, fixed, immovable, resolute, secure, staunch, steadfast, sure, unassailable, unswerving, unwavering, well-founded
➤ **Antonyms**
insecure, shaky, uncertain, unsure, wavering, wobbly

unshaken *adjective* = **unmoved**, calm, collected, composed, impassive, unaffected, unalarmed, undaunted, undismayed, undisturbed, unfazed (*informal*), unperturbed, unruffled

unsightly *adjective* = **ugly**, disagreeable, hideous, horrid, repulsive, revolting (*informal*), unattractive, unpleasant, unprepossessing
➤ **Antonyms**
agreeable, attractive, beautiful, comely, cute, handsome, pleasing, prepossessing, pretty

unskilled *adjective* = **unprofessional**, amateurish, cowboy (*informal*), inexperienced, uneducated, unqualified, untalented, untrained
➤ **Antonyms**
adept, expert, masterly, professional, qualified, skilled, talented

unsociable *adjective* = **unfriendly**, chilly, cold, convivial, distant, hostile, introverted, reclusive, retiring, standoffish, uncongenial, unforthcoming, unneighbourly, unsocial, withdrawn
➤ **Antonyms**
congenial, convivial, friendly, gregarious, neighbourly, outgoing, sociable

unsolicited *adjective* = **unasked for**, free-will, gratuitous, spontaneous, uncalled-for, unforced, uninvited, unrequested, unsought, unwelcome, voluntary, volunteered

unsophisticated *adjective* 1 = **natural**, artless, childlike, guileless, inexperienced, ingenuous, innocent, naive, unaffected, unworldly 2 = **simple**, plain, straightforward, uncomplex, uncomplicated, uninvolved, unrefined, unspecialized
➤ **Antonyms**
≠**simple**: advanced, complex, complicated, intricate, sophisticated

unsound *adjective* 1 = **unhealthy**, ailing, defective, delicate, deranged, diseased, frail, ill, in poor health, unbalanced, unhinged, unstable, unwell, weak 2 = **invalid**, defective, erroneous, fallacious, false, faulty, flawed,

ill-founded, illogical, shaky, specious, unreliable, weak **3 = unstable**, flimsy, insecure, not solid, rickety, shaky, tottering, unreliable, unsafe, unsteady, wobbly
➤ **Antonyms**
≠**unstable**: reliable, safe, solid, sound, stable, steady, strong, sturdy

unsparing *adjective* **1 = lavish**, abundant, bountiful, generous, liberal, munificent, open-handed, plenteous, prodigal, profuse, ungrudging, unstinting **2 = severe**, cold-blooded, hard, harsh, implacable, relentless, ruthless, stern, stringent, uncompromising, unforgiving, unmerciful

unspeakable *adjective* **1 = indescribable**, beyond description, beyond words, inconceivable, ineffable, inexpressible, overwhelming, unbelievable, unimaginable, unutterable, wonderful **2 = dreadful**, abominable, abysmal, appalling, awful, bad, evil, execrable, frightful, from hell (*informal*), heinous, hellacious (*U.S. slang*), horrible, loathsome, monstrous, odious, repellent, shocking, too horrible for words

unspoiled, unspoilt *adjective* **1** **= undamaged**, intact, perfect, preserved, unaffected, unblemished, unchanged, unharmed, unimpaired, untouched **2** **= natural**, artless, innocent, unaffected, unassuming, unstudied, wholesome
➤ **Antonyms**
≠**undamaged**: affected, blemished, changed, damaged, harmed, impaired, imperfect, spoilt, touched

unspoken *adjective* **1 = tacit**, assumed, implicit, implied, inferred, left to the imagination, not put into words, not spelt out, taken for granted, undeclared, understood, unexpressed, unstated **2** **= unsaid**, mute, silent, unuttered, voiceless, wordless
➤ **Antonyms**
≠**tacit**: clear, declared, explicit, expressed, spoken, stated

unstable *adjective* **1 = insecure**, not fixed, precarious, rickety, risky, shaky, tottering, unsettled, unsteady, wobbly **2** **= changeable**, fitful, fluctuating, inconstant, unpredictable, unsteady, variable, volatile **3** **= unpredictable**, capricious, changeable, erratic, inconsistent, irrational, temperamental, unreliable
➤ **Antonyms**
≠**changeable**: constant, predictable, stable, steady ≠**unpredictable**: consistent, level-headed, rational, reliable, stable

unsteady *adjective* **1 = unstable**, infirm, insecure, precarious, reeling, rickety, shaky, tottering, treacherous, unsafe, wobbly **2** **= erratic**, changeable, flickering, fluctuating, inconstant, irregular, temperamental,

unreliable, unsettled, variable, volatile, wavering

unsubstantial *adjective* **1 = flimsy**, airy, fragile, frail, inadequate, light, slight, thin **2** **= immaterial**, dreamlike, fanciful, illusory, imaginary, impalpable, visionary

unsubstantiated *adjective* **= unconfirmed**, open to question, unattested, uncorroborated, unestablished, unproven, unsupported
➤ **Antonyms**
attested, confirmed, corroborated, established, proven, substantiated, supported

unsuccessful *adjective* **1 = useless**, abortive, failed, fruitless, futile, ineffective, unavailing, unproductive, vain **2 = unlucky**, balked, defeated, foiled, frustrated, hapless, ill-starred, losing, luckless, unfortunate
➤ **Antonyms**
≠**useless**: flourishing, fruitful, productive, prosperous, remunerative, successful, thriving, useful, worthwhile ≠**unlucky**: fortunate, lucky, triumphant, victorious, winning

unsuitable *adjective* **= inappropriate**, improper, inapposite, inapt, incompatible, incongruous, ineligible, infelicitous, out of character, out of keeping, out of place, unacceptable, unbecoming, unbefitting, unfit, unfitting, unseasonable, unseemly, unsuited
➤ **Antonyms**
acceptable, apposite, appropriate, apt, compatible, eligible, fitting, proper, suitable

unsung *adjective* **= unacknowledged**, anonymous, disregarded, neglected, unacclaimed, unappreciated, uncelebrated, unhailed, unhonoured, unknown, unnamed, unrecognized

unsure *adjective* **1 = lacking in confidence**, insecure, unassured, unconfident **2** **= doubtful**, distrustful, dubious, hesitant, in a quandary, irresolute, mistrustful, sceptical, suspicious, unconvinced, undecided
➤ **Antonyms**
assured, certain, confident, convinced, decided, persuaded, resolute, sure

unsurpassed *adjective* **= supreme**, consummate, exceptional, incomparable, matchless, nonpareil, paramount, peerless, second to none, superlative, transcendent, unequalled, unexcelled, unparalleled, unrivalled, without an equal

unsuspecting *adjective* **= unconscious**, credulous, gullible, inexperienced, ingenuous, innocent, naive, off guard, trustful, trusting, unsuspicious, unwarned, unwary

unswerving *adjective* **= constant**, dedicated, devoted, direct, firm, resolute, single-minded, staunch, steadfast, steady, true, undeviating, unfaltering, unflagging, untiring, unwavering

unsympathetic *adjective* = **hard**, apathetic, callous, cold, cruel, harsh, heartless, indifferent, insensitive, soulless, stony-hearted, uncompassionate, unconcerned, unfeeling, unkind, unmoved, unpitying
➤ **Antonyms**
caring, compassionate, concerned, kind, pitying, sensitive, supportive, sympathetic, understanding

untamed *adjective* = **wild**, barbarous, feral, fierce, not broken in, savage, unbroken, uncontrollable, undomesticated, untameable

untangle *verb* 1 = **disentangle**, extricate, unravel, unsnarl 2 = **solve**, clear up, explain, straighten out
➤ **Antonyms**
≠**disentangle**: enmesh, entangle, jumble, muddle, snarl, tangle ≠**solve**: complicate, confuse, muddle, puzzle

untenable *adjective* = **unsustainable**, fallacious, flawed, groundless, illogical, indefensible, insupportable, shaky, unreasonable, unsound, weak
➤ **Antonyms**
defensible, justified, logical, rational, reasonable, sensible, sound, supportable, unarguable, uncontestable, valid, verifiable, well-grounded

unthinkable *adjective* 1 = **impossible**, absurd, illogical, improbable, not on (*informal*), out of the question, preposterous, unlikely, unreasonable 2 = **inconceivable**, beyond belief, beyond the bounds of possibility, implausible, incredible, insupportable, unbelievable, unimaginable

unthinking *adjective* 1 = **thoughtless**, blundering, inconsiderate, insensitive, rude, selfish, tactless, undiplomatic 2 = **unconscious**, careless, heedless, impulsive, inadvertent, instinctive, mechanical, negligent, oblivious, unmindful
➤ **Antonyms**
≠**unconscious**: careful, conscious, deliberate, heedful, mindful

untidy *adjective* = **messy**, bedraggled, chaotic, cluttered, disarrayed, disordered, higgledy-piggledy (*informal*), jumbled, littered, muddled, muddly, rumpled, shambolic, slatternly, slipshod, sloppy (*informal*), slovenly, topsy-turvy, unkempt
➤ **Antonyms**
methodical, neat, orderly, presentable, ship-shape, spruce, systematic, tidy, well-kept

untie *verb* = **undo**, free, loosen, release, unbind, unbridle, unclasp, unfasten, unknot, unlace, unstrap

untimely *adjective* 1 = **early**, premature, unseasonable 2 = **ill-timed**, awkward, badly timed, inappropriate, inconvenient, inopportune, mistimed, unfortunate, unsuitable
➤ **Antonyms**
≠**early**: seasonable, timely ≠**ill-timed**: appropriate, convenient, opportune, suitable, well-timed

untiring *adjective* = **tireless**, constant, determined, dogged, incessant, indefatigable, persevering, persistent, steady, unfaltering, unflagging, unremitting, unwearied

untold *adjective* 1 = **indescribable**, inexpressible, undreamed of, unimaginable, unspeakable, unthinkable, unutterable 2 = **countless**, incalculable, innumerable, measureless, myriad, numberless, uncountable, uncounted, unnumbered 3 = **undisclosed**, hidden, private, secret, unknown, unpublished, unrecounted, unrelated, unrevealed

untouched *adjective* 1 = **unharmed**, intact, safe and sound, undamaged, unhurt, uninjured, unscathed, without a scratch 2 = **unmoved**, indifferent, unaffected, unconcerned, unimpressed, unstirred
➤ **Antonyms**
≠**unmoved**: affected, concerned, impressed, moved, softened, stirred, touched

untoward *adjective* 1 = **troublesome**, annoying, awkward, disastrous, ill-timed, inconvenient, irritating, unfortunate, vexatious 2 = **unfavourable**, adverse, contrary, inauspicious, inopportune, unlucky, untimely

untrained *adjective* = **amateur**, green, inexperienced, raw, uneducated, unpractised, unqualified, unschooled, unskilled, untaught, untutored
➤ **Antonyms**
educated, experienced, expert, qualified, schooled, skilled, taught, trained

untried *adjective* = **untested**, in the experimental stage, new, novel, unattempted, unessayed, unproved

untroubled *adjective* = **undisturbed**, calm, composed, cool, peaceful, placid, sedate, serene, steady, tranquil, unagitated, unconcerned, unfazed (*informal*), unflappable (*informal*), unflustered, unperturbed, unruffled, unstirred, unworried
➤ **Antonyms**
agitated, anxious, concerned, disturbed, flustered, perturbed, ruffled, troubled, worried

untrue *adjective* 1 = **false**, deceptive, dishonest, erroneous, fallacious, inaccurate, incorrect, lying, misleading, mistaken, sham,

spurious, untruthful, wrong **2 = unfaithful,**
deceitful, disloyal, faithless, false, forsworn,
inconstant, perfidious, traitorous,
treacherous, two-faced, untrustworthy
➤ **Antonyms**
≠**false:** accurate, correct, factual, right, true
≠**unfaithful:** constant, dependable, faithful,
loyal

untrustworthy *adjective* **= unreliable,**
deceitful, devious, dishonest, disloyal,
fair-weather, faithless, false, fly-by-night
(*informal*), not to be depended on, slippery,
treacherous, tricky, two-faced,
undependable, unfaithful, untrue, untrusty
➤ **Antonyms**
dependable, faithful, honest, loyal, reliable,
steadfast, true, trustworthy, trusty

untruth *noun* **= lie,** deceit, fabrication,
falsehood, falsification, fib, fiction, pork pie
(*Brit. slang*), porky (*Brit. slang*),
prevarication, story, tale, whopper (*informal*)

untruthful *adjective* **= dishonest,** crooked
(*informal*), deceitful, deceptive, dissembling,
false, fibbing, hypocritical, lying, mendacious
➤ **Antonyms**
candid, honest, sincere, true, truthful,
veracious

untutored *adjective* **1 = uneducated,**
ignorant, illiterate, unlearned, unschooled,
untrained, unversed **2 = unsophisticated,**
artless, inexperienced, simple, unpractised,
unrefined

unused *adjective* **1 = unutilized,** available,
extra, left, leftover, remaining, unconsumed,
unexhausted **2 = new,** fresh, intact, pristine,
untouched **3** *with* **to = unaccustomed to,** a
stranger to, inexperienced in, new to,
unfamiliar with

unusual *adjective* **= extraordinary,**
abnormal, atypical, bizarre, curious,
different, exceptional, left-field (*informal*),
notable, odd, out of the ordinary,
phenomenal, queer, rare, remarkable,
singular, strange, surprising, uncommon,
unconventional, unexpected, unfamiliar,
unwonted
➤ **Antonyms**
average, banal, commonplace, conventional,
everyday, familiar, normal, routine,
traditional, typical, unremarkable, usual

unutterable *adjective* **= indescribable,**
beyond words, extreme, ineffable,
overwhelming, unimaginable, unspeakable

unvarnished *adjective* **= plain,** bare,
candid, frank, honest, naked, pure, pure and
simple, simple, sincere, stark,
straightforward, unadorned, unembellished

unveil *verb* **= reveal,** bare, bring to light,
disclose, divulge, expose, lay bare, lay open,
make known, make public, uncover

➤ **Antonyms**
cloak, conceal, cover, disguise, hide, mask,
obscure, veil

unwanted *adjective* **= undesired,** *de trop,*
going begging, outcast, rejected,
superfluous, surplus to requirements,
unasked, uninvited, unneeded, unsolicited,
unwelcome, useless
➤ **Antonyms**
desired, necessary, needed, useful, wanted,
welcome

unwarranted *adjective* **= unnecessary,**
gratuitous, groundless, indefensible,
inexcusable, uncalled-for, unjust, unjustified,
unprovoked, unreasonable, wrong

unwary *adjective* **= careless,** heedless,
imprudent, incautious, indiscreet, rash,
reckless, thoughtless, uncircumspect,
unguarded, unwatchful
➤ **Antonyms**
cautious, chary, circumspect, discreet,
guarded, prudent, wary, watchful

unwavering *adjective* **= steady,** consistent,
dedicated, determined, immovable, resolute,
single-minded, staunch, steadfast,
undeviating, unfaltering, unflagging,
unshakable, unshaken, unswerving, untiring

unwelcome *adjective* **1 = unwanted,**
excluded, rejected, unacceptable,
undesirable, uninvited, unpopular, unwished
for **2 = disagreeable,** displeasing, distasteful,
thankless, undesirable, unpleasant
➤ **Antonyms**
acceptable, agreeable, desirable, pleasant,
pleasing, popular, wanted, welcome

unwell *adjective* **= ill,** ailing, at death's door,
indisposed, in poor health, off colour, out of
sorts, poorly (*informal*), sick, sickly, under
the weather (*informal*), unhealthy
➤ **Antonyms**
fine, healthy, robust, sound, well

unwholesome *adjective* **1 = harmful,**
deleterious, insalubrious, insanitary, noxious,
poisonous, tainted, unhealthy, unnourishing
2 = wicked, bad, corrupting, degrading,
demoralizing, depraving, evil, immoral **3**
= sickly, anaemic, pale, pallid, pasty, wan
➤ **Antonyms**
≠**harmful:** beneficial, germ-free, healthy,
hygienic, salubrious, sanitary, wholesome
≠**wicked:** moral

unwieldy *adjective* **1 = awkward,**
burdensome, cumbersome, inconvenient,
unhandy, unmanageable **2 = bulky,** clumsy,
clunky (*informal*), hefty, massive,
ponderous, ungainly, weighty

unwilling *adjective* **= reluctant,** averse,
disinclined, grudging, indisposed, loath, not
in the mood, opposed, resistant,
unenthusiastic

➤ **Antonyms**
amenable, compliant, disposed, eager,
enthusiastic, inclined, voluntary, willing

unwind *verb* **1** = **unravel**, disentangle,
slacken, uncoil, undo, unreel, unroll,
untwine, untwist **2** = **relax**, calm down, let
oneself go, loosen up, mellow out
(*informal*), sit back, slow down, take a
break, take it easy, wind down

unwise *adjective* = **foolish**, asinine,
foolhardy, ill-advised, ill-considered,
ill-judged, impolitic, improvident, imprudent,
inadvisable, inane, indiscreet, injudicious,
irresponsible, rash, reckless, senseless,
short-sighted, silly, stupid
➤ **Antonyms**
discreet, judicious, politic, prudent,
responsible, sensible, shrewd, wise

unwitting *adjective* **1** = **unintentional**,
accidental, chance, inadvertent, involuntary,
undesigned, unintended, unmeant,
unplanned **2** = **unknowing**, ignorant,
innocent, unaware, unconscious,
unsuspecting
➤ **Antonyms**
≠**unintentional**: deliberate, designed,
intended, intentional, meant, planned
≠**unknowing**: conscious, deliberate,
knowing, witting

unwonted *adjective* = **unusual**, atypical,
extraordinary, infrequent, out of the
ordinary, peculiar, rare, singular,
unaccustomed, uncommon, uncustomary,
unexpected, unfamiliar

unworldly *adjective* **1** = **spiritual**, abstract,
celestial, metaphysical, nonmaterialistic,
religious, transcendental **2** = **naive**, as green
as grass, green, idealistic, inexperienced,
innocent, raw, trusting, unsophisticated, wet
behind the ears (*informal*) **3**
= **otherworldly**, ethereal, extraterrestrial,
unearthly

unworthy *adjective* **1** = **undeserving**,
ineligible, not deserving of, not fit for, not
good enough, not worth **2**
= **dishonourable**, base, contemptible,
degrading, discreditable, disgraceful,
disreputable, ignoble, shameful **3 unworthy
of** = **unbefitting**, beneath, improper,
inappropriate, out of character, out of place,
unbecoming, unfitting, unseemly, unsuitable
➤ **Antonyms**
≠**undeserving**: deserving, eligible, fit,
meritorious, worthy ≠**dishonourable**:
commendable, creditable, honourable

unwritten *adjective* **1** = **oral**, unrecorded,
vocal, word-of-mouth **2** = **customary**,
accepted, conventional, tacit, traditional,
understood

unyielding *adjective* = **firm**, adamant,

determined, hardline, immovable, inflexible,
intractable, obdurate, obstinate, relentless,
resolute, rigid, staunch, steadfast,
stiff-necked, stubborn, tough, unbending,
uncompromising, unwavering
➤ **Antonyms**
adaptable, compliant, compromising,
cooperative, flexible, movable, tractable,
yielding

up-and-coming *adjective* = **promising**,
ambitious, eager, go-getting (*informal*)

upbeat *adjective Informal* = **cheerful**,
buoyant, cheery, encouraging, favourable,
forward-looking, heartening, hopeful,
looking up, optimistic, positive

upbraid *verb* = **scold**, admonish, bawl out
(*informal*), berate, blame, castigate, censure,
chew out (*U.S. & Canad. informal*), chide,
condemn, dress down (*informal*), give
(someone) a rocket (*Brit. & N.Z. informal*),
lecture, rap (someone) over the knuckles,
read the riot act, rebuke, reprimand,
reproach, reprove, slap on the wrist, take to
task, tear into (*informal*), tear (someone) off
a strip (*Brit. informal*), tell off (*informal*),
tick off (*informal*)

upbringing *noun* = **education**, breeding,
bringing-up, care, cultivation, nurture,
raising, rearing, tending, training

update *verb* = **bring up to date**, amend,
modernize, rebrand, renew, revise

upgrade *verb* = **promote**, advance,
ameliorate, better, elevate, enhance,
improve, raise
➤ **Antonyms**
degrade, demote, downgrade, lower

upheaval *noun* = **disturbance**, cataclysm,
disorder, disruption, eruption, overthrow,
revolution, turmoil, violent change

uphill *adjective* **1** = **ascending**, climbing,
mounting, rising **2** = **arduous**, difficult,
exhausting, gruelling, hard, laborious,
punishing, strenuous, taxing, tough,
wearisome
➤ **Antonyms**
≠**ascending**: descending, downhill, lowering

uphold *verb* = **support**, advocate, aid, back,
champion, defend, encourage, endorse, hold
to, justify, maintain, promote, stand by, stick
up for (*informal*), sustain, vindicate

upkeep *noun* **1** = **maintenance**,
conservation, keep, preservation, repair,
running, subsistence, support, sustenance **2**
= **running costs**, expenditure, expenses,
operating costs, outlay, overheads

uplift *verb* **1** = **raise**, elevate, heave, hoist,
up **2** = **improve**, advance, ameliorate,
better, civilize, cultivate, edify, inspire, raise,
refine, upgrade ◆ *noun* **3** = **improvement**,
advancement, betterment, cultivation,

edification, enhancement, enlightenment,
enrichment, refinement

upper *adjective* **1** = **higher**, high, loftier,
superior, top, topmost **2** = **superior**,
elevated, eminent, greater, important
➤ **Antonyms**
≠**higher**: bottom, inferior, low, lower
≠**superior**: inferior, junior, low, lower

upper-class *adjective* = **aristocratic**,
blue-blooded, highborn, high-class, noble,
patrician, top-drawer, well-bred

upper hand *noun* = **control**, advantage,
ascendancy, dominion, edge, mastery,
superiority, supremacy, sway, whip hand

uppermost *adjective* **1** = **top**, highest,
loftiest, most elevated, topmost, upmost **2**
= **supreme**, chief, dominant, foremost,
greatest, leading, main, paramount,
predominant, pre-eminent, primary,
principal
➤ **Antonyms**
≠**top**: bottom, bottommost, lowermost,
lowest ≠**supreme**: humblest, least, lowliest,
slightest

uppish *adjective Brit. informal* = **conceited**,
affected, arrogant, cocky, high and mighty
(*informal*), hoity-toity (*informal*),
overweening, presumptuous, putting on airs,
self-important, snobbish, stuck-up
(*informal*), supercilious, toffee-nosed (*slang,
chiefly Brit.*), uppity (*informal*)
➤ **Antonyms**
diffident, humble, lowly, meek, obsequious,
servile, unaffected, unassertive

uppity *adjective Informal* = **conceited**,
bigheaded (*informal*), bumptious, cocky, full
of oneself, impertinent, on one's high horse
(*informal*), overweening, self-important, too
big for one's boots *or* breeches (*informal*),
uppish (*Brit. informal*)

upright *adjective* **1** = **vertical**, erect, on end,
perpendicular, straight **2** = **honest**, above
board, conscientious, ethical, faithful, good,
high-minded, honourable, incorruptible, just,
principled, righteous, straightforward, true,
trustworthy, unimpeachable, virtuous
➤ **Antonyms**
≠**vertical**: flat, horizontal, lying, prone,
prostrate, supine ≠**honest**: corrupt, devious,
dishonest, dishonourable, unethical, unjust,
untrustworthy, wicked

uprightness *noun* = **honesty**, fairness,
goodness, high-mindedness, incorruptibility,
integrity, justice, probity, rectitude,
righteousness, trustworthiness, virtue

uprising *noun* = **rebellion**, disturbance,
insurgence, insurrection, mutiny, outbreak,
putsch, revolt, revolution, rising, upheaval

uproar *noun* = **commotion**, bagarre, brawl,
brouhaha, clamour, confusion, din, furore,

hubbub, hullabaloo, hurly-burly, mayhem,
noise, outcry, pandemonium, racket, riot,
ruckus (*informal*), ruction (*informal*),
rumpus, turbulence, turmoil

uproarious *adjective* **1** = **hilarious**,
hysterical, killing (*informal*), rib-tickling,
rip-roaring (*informal*), screamingly funny,
side-splitting, very funny **2** = **boisterous**,
loud, rollicking, unrestrained
➤ **Antonyms**
≠**hilarious**: mournful, sad, serious, tragic
≠**boisterous**: peaceful, quiet

uproot *verb* **1** = **pull up**, dig up, pull out by
the roots, rip up, root out, weed out **2**
= **displace**, disorient, exile **3** = **destroy**, do
away with, eliminate, eradicate, extirpate,
remove, wipe out

ups and downs *plural noun*
= **fluctuations**, changes, ebb and flow,
moods, vicissitudes

upset *adjective* **1** = **distressed**, agitated,
bothered, confused, disconcerted, dismayed,
disquieted, disturbed, frantic, grieved,
hassled (*informal*), hurt, overwrought, put
out, ruffled, troubled, worried **2** = **sick**,
disordered, disturbed, ill, poorly (*informal*),
queasy **3** = **disordered**, at sixes and sevens,
chaotic, confused, disarrayed, in disarray, in
disorder, messed up, muddled, topsy-turvy **4**
= **overturned**, capsized, spilled, tipped over,
toppled, tumbled, upside down ♦ *verb* **5**
= **tip over**, capsize, knock over, overturn,
spill, topple over **6** = **mess up**, change,
disorder, disorganize, disturb, mix up, put
out of order, spoil, turn topsy-turvy **7**
= **distress**, agitate, bother, discompose,
disconcert, dismay, disquiet, disturb, faze,
fluster, grieve, hassle (*informal*), perturb,
ruffle, throw (someone) off balance, trouble,
unnerve ♦ *noun* **8** = **reversal**, defeat,
shake-up (*informal*), sudden change **9**
= **distress**, agitation, bother, discomposure,
disquiet, disturbance, hassle (*informal*),
shock, trouble, worry **10** = **illness**, bug
(*informal*), complaint, disorder, disturbance,
indisposition, malady, queasiness, sickness

upshot *noun* = **result**, conclusion,
consequence, culmination, end, end result,
event, finale, issue, outcome, payoff
(*informal*), sequel

upside down *adjective* **1** = **inverted**,
bottom up, on its head, overturned,
upturned, wrong side up **2** *Informal*
= **confused**, chaotic, disordered,
higgledy-piggledy (*informal*), in chaos, in
confusion, in disarray, in disorder, jumbled,
muddled, topsy-turvy

upstanding *adjective* **1** = **honest**, ethical,
good, honourable, incorruptible, moral,
principled, true, trustworthy, upright **2**
= **sturdy**, firm, hale and hearty, hardy,

healthy, robust, stalwart, strong, upright, vigorous
> **Antonyms**
≠**honest:** bad, corrupt, dishonest, false, immoral, unethical, unprincipled, untrustworthy ≠**sturdy:** delicate, feeble, frail, infirm, puny, unhealthy, weak

upstart *noun* = **social climber**, arriviste, nobody, *nouveau riche,* parvenu, status seeker

uptight *adjective Informal* = **tense**, anxious, edgy, nervy (*Brit. informal*), neurotic, on edge, uneasy, wired (*slang*)

up-to-date *adjective* = **modern**, all the rage, current, fashionable, happening (*informal*), in, in vogue, newest, now (*informal*), stylish, trendy (*Brit. informal*), up-to-the-minute, with it (*informal*)
> **Antonyms**
antiquated, dated, *démodé,* obsolete, old fashioned, outmoded, out of date, out of the ark (*informal*), passé

upturn *noun* = **rise**, advancement, boost, improvement, increase, recovery, revival, upsurge, upswing

urban *adjective* = **civic**, city, inner-city, metropolitan, municipal, town

urbane *adjective* = **sophisticated**, civil, civilized, cosmopolitan, courteous, cultivated, cultured, debonair, elegant, mannerly, polished, refined, smooth, suave, well-bred, well-mannered
> **Antonyms**
boorish, clownish, discourteous, gauche, impolite, rude, uncivilized, uncouth, uncultured

urbanity *noun* = **sophistication**, charm, civility, courtesy, culture, elegance, grace, mannerliness, polish, refinement, suavity, worldliness

urchin *noun* = **ragamuffin**, brat, gamin, guttersnipe, street Arab (*offensive*), waif

urge *noun* 1 = **impulse**, compulsion, desire, drive, fancy, itch, longing, thirst, wish, yearning, yen (*informal*) ♦ *verb* 2 = **beg**, appeal to, beseech, entreat, exhort, implore, plead, press, solicit 3 = **advocate**, advise, counsel, insist on, push for, recommend, support 4 = **drive**, compel, constrain, egg on, encourage, force, gee up, goad, hasten, impel, incite, induce, instigate, press, prompt, propel, push, spur, stimulate
> **Antonyms**
noun ≠**impulse:** aversion, disinclination, distaste, indisposition, reluctance, repugnance ♦ *verb* ≠**advocate, drive:** caution, deter, discourage, dissuade, warn

urgency *noun* = **importance**, extremity, gravity, hurry, imperativeness, necessity, need, pressure, seriousness, stress

urgent *adjective* 1 = **crucial**, compelling, critical, immediate, imperative, important, instant, not to be delayed, now or never, pressing, top-priority 2 = **insistent**, clamorous, earnest, importunate, intense, persistent, persuasive
> **Antonyms**
≠**crucial:** low-priority, minor, trivial, unimportant ≠**insistent:** apathetic, casual, feeble, half-hearted, lackadaisical, perfunctory, weak

urinate *verb* = **pee** (*slang*), make water, pass water, piddle (*informal*), piss (*taboo slang*), spend a penny (*Brit. informal*), tinkle (*Brit. informal*), wee (*informal*), wee-wee (*informal*)

usable *adjective* = **serviceable**, at one's disposal, available, current, fit for use, functional, in running order, practical, ready for use, utilizable, valid, working

usage *noun* 1 = **use**, control, employment, handling, management, operation, regulation, running, treatment 2 = **practice**, convention, custom, form, habit, matter of course, method, mode, procedure, regime, routine, rule, tradition, wont

use *verb* 1 = **employ**, apply, avail oneself of, bring into play, exercise, exert, find a use for, make use of, operate, ply, practise, put to use, turn to account, utilize, wield, work 2 = **take advantage of**, exploit, manipulate, misuse 3 = **consume**, exhaust, expend, run through, spend, waste ♦ *noun* 4 = **usage**, application, employment, exercise, handling, operation, practice, service, treatment 5 = **good**, advantage, application, avail, benefit, help, mileage (*informal*), point, profit, service, usefulness, utility, value, worth 6 = **purpose**, call, cause, end, necessity, need, object, occasion, point, reason

used *adjective* = **second-hand**, cast-off, hand-me-down (*informal*), nearly new, not new, reach-me-down (*informal*), shopsoiled, worn
> **Antonyms**
brand-new, fresh, new, pristine, unused

used to *adjective* = **accustomed to**, at home in, attuned to, familiar with, given to, habituated to, hardened to, in the habit of, inured to, wont to

useful *adjective* = **helpful**, advantageous, beneficial, effective, fruitful, of help, of service, of use, practical, profitable, serviceable, valuable, worthwhile
> **Antonyms**
inadequate, ineffective, pants (*slang*), unbeneficial, unhelpful, unproductive, useless, vain, worthless

usefulness *noun* = **helpfulness**, benefit,

convenience, effectiveness, efficacy, help, practicality, profit, service, use, utility, value, worth

useless *adjective* 1 = **worthless**, disadvantageous, fruitless, futile, hopeless, idle, impractical, ineffective, ineffectual, of no use, pants (*slang*), pointless, profitless, unavailing, unproductive, unworkable, vain, valueless 2 *Informal* = **inept**, hopeless, incompetent, ineffectual, no good, pants (*slang*), stupid, weak
➤ **Antonyms**
≠**worthless**: advantageous, effective, fruitful, practical, productive, profitable, useful, valuable, workable, worthwhile

use up *verb* = **consume**, absorb, burn up, deplete, devour, drain, exhaust, finish, fritter away, run through, squander, waste

usher *noun* 1 = **attendant**, doorkeeper, doorman, escort, guide, usherette ◆ *verb* 2 = **escort**, conduct, direct, guide, lead, show in *or* out, steer 3 *usually with* **in** = **introduce**, bring in, herald, inaugurate, initiate, launch, open the door to, pave the way for, precede

usual *adjective* = **normal**, accustomed, bog-standard (*Brit. & Irish slang*), common, customary, everyday, expected, familiar, general, habitual, ordinary, regular, routine, standard, stock, typical, wonted
➤ **Antonyms**
exceptional, extraordinary, new, novel, off-beat, out of the ordinary, peculiar, rare, singular, strange, uncommon, unexpected, unique, unorthodox, unusual

usually *adverb* = **normally**, as a rule, as is the custom, as is usual, by and large, commonly, for the most part, generally, habitually, in the main, mainly, mostly, most often, on the whole, ordinarily, regularly, routinely

usurp *verb* = **seize**, appropriate, assume, commandeer, lay hold of, take, take over, wrest

utility *noun* = **usefulness**, advantageousness, avail, benefit, convenience, efficacy, mileage (*informal*), point, practicality, profit, service, serviceableness, use

utilize *verb* = **use**, avail oneself of, employ, have recourse to, make the most of, make use of, profit by, put to use, resort to, take advantage of, turn to account

utmost *adjective* 1 = **greatest**, chief, extreme, highest, maximum, paramount, pre-eminent, supreme 2 = **farthest**, extreme, final, last, most distant, outermost, remotest, uttermost ◆ *noun* 3 = **greatest**, best, hardest, highest, most

Utopia *noun* = **paradise**, bliss, Eden, Garden of Eden, heaven, ideal life, perfect place, seventh heaven, Shangri-la

Utopian *adjective* 1 = **perfect**, dream, fanciful, fantasy, ideal, idealistic, illusory, imaginary, impractical, romantic, visionary ◆ *noun* 2 = **dreamer**, Don Quixote, idealist, romanticist, visionary

utter[1] *verb* = **express**, articulate, enunciate, pronounce, put into words, say, speak, verbalize, vocalize, voice

utter[2] *adjective* = **absolute**, arrant, complete, consummate, deep-dyed (*usually derogatory*), downright, entire, out-and-out, outright, perfect, sheer, stark, thorough, thoroughgoing, total, unmitigated, unqualified

utterance *noun* 1 = **speech**, announcement, declaration, expression, opinion, remark, statement, words 2 = **expression**, articulation, verbalization, vocalization, vociferation

utterly *adverb* = **totally**, absolutely, completely, entirely, extremely, fully, one hundred per cent, perfectly, thoroughly, to the core, to the nth degree, wholly

uttermost *adjective* = **farthest**, extreme, final, last, outermost, remotest, utmost

V v

vacancy *noun* **1** = **job**, opening,
opportunity, position, post, room, situation **2**
= **emptiness**, gap, space, vacuum, void

vacant *adjective* **1** = **unoccupied**, available,
disengaged, empty, free, idle, not in use, to
let, unemployed, unengaged, unfilled,
untenanted, void **2** = **blank**, absent-minded,
abstracted, ditzy *or* ditsy (*slang*), dreaming,
dreamy, expressionless, idle, inane,
thoughtless, unthinking, vacuous, vague
➤ **Antonyms**
≠**unoccupied**: busy, engaged, full,
inhabited, in use, occupied, taken ≠**blank**:
animated, engrossed, expressive, lively,
reflective, thoughtful

vacate *verb* = **leave**, evacuate, quit

vacillate *verb* = **keep changing one's
mind**, be irresolute *or* indecisive, blow hot
and cold (*informal*), chop and change,
dither (*chiefly Brit.*), shillyshally (*informal*),
swither (*Scot.*), waver

vacillating *adjective* = **irresolute**, in two
minds (*informal*), shillyshallying (*informal*),
uncertain, unresolved, wavering

vacillation *noun* = **indecisiveness**,
dithering (*chiefly Brit.*), fluctuation,
irresoluteness, irresolution, shillyshallying
(*informal*), wavering

vacuity *noun* = **unintelligence**, blankness,
emptiness, inanity, incognizance,
incomprehension, vacuousness

vacuous *adjective* = **unintelligent**, blank,
inane, stupid, uncomprehending, vacant

vacuum *noun* = **emptiness**, free space, gap,
nothingness, space, vacuity, void

vagabond *noun* = **vagrant**, bag lady
(*chiefly U.S.*), beggar, bum (*informal*),
down-and-out, hobo (*U.S.*), itinerant,
migrant, nomad, rover, tramp, wanderer,
wayfarer

vagary *noun* = **whim**, caprice, crotchet,
fancy, humour, notion, whimsy

vagina *noun* = **vulva**, beaver (*taboo slang*),
cunt (*taboo*), fanny (*Brit. taboo slang*),
muff (*taboo slang*), pussy (*taboo slang*),
snatch (*taboo slang*)

vagrant *noun* **1** = **tramp**, bag lady (*chiefly
U.S.*), beggar, bum (*informal*), drifter, hobo
(*U.S.*), itinerant, person of no fixed address,
rolling stone, wanderer ◆ *adjective* **2**
= **itinerant**, nomadic, roaming, rootless,
roving, unsettled, vagabond

➤ **Antonyms**
adjective ≠**itinerant**: established, fixed,
purposeful, rooted, settled

vague *adjective* **1** = **unclear**, doubtful,
generalized, hazy, imprecise, indefinite,
loose, uncertain, unspecified, woolly **2**
= **indistinct**, amorphous, blurred, dim, fuzzy,
hazy, ill-defined, indeterminate, nebulous,
obscure, shadowy, unclear, unknown
➤ **Antonyms**
≠**unclear**: clear, clear-cut, definite, distinct,
exact, explicit, precise, specific ≠**indistinct**:
clear, distinct, lucid, well-defined

vaguely *adverb* **1** = **imprecisely**, dimly,
evasively, in a general way, obscurely,
slightly **2** = **absent-mindedly**, vacantly

vagueness *noun* = **impreciseness**,
ambiguity, inexactitude, lack of preciseness,
looseness, obscurity, undecidedness,
woolliness
➤ **Antonyms**
clarity, clearness, definition, exactness,
obviousness, preciseness, precision

vain *adjective* **1** = **proud**, arrogant,
bigheaded (*informal*), cocky, conceited,
egotistical, inflated, narcissistic, ostentatious,
overweening, pleased with oneself,
self-important, stuck-up (*informal*),
swaggering, swollen-headed (*informal*) **2**
= **futile**, abortive, empty, fruitless, hollow,
idle, pointless, senseless, time-wasting,
trifling, trivial, unavailing, unimportant,
unproductive, unprofitable, useless,
worthless **3 be vain** = **have a high opinion
of oneself**, have a swelled head (*informal*),
think a lot of oneself, think oneself the cat's
whiskers *or* pyjamas (*slang*) ◆ *noun* **4 in
vain** = **to no avail**, fruitless(ly),
ineffectual(ly), to no purpose,
unsuccessful(ly), useless(ly), vain(ly), wasted,
without success
➤ **Antonyms**
adjective ≠**proud**: bashful, humble, meek,
modest, self-deprecating ≠**futile**: fruitful,
profitable, serious, successful, useful, valid,
worthwhile, worthy

valediction *noun* = **farewell**, adieu,
goodbye, leave-taking, sendoff (*informal*)

valedictory *adjective* = **farewell**, final,
parting

valiant *adjective* = **brave**, bold, courageous,
dauntless, doughty, fearless, gallant, heroic,
indomitable, intrepid, lion-hearted, plucky,

redoubtable, stouthearted, valorous
➤ **Antonyms**
cowardly, craven, fearful, shrinking,
spineless, timid, weak

valid *adjective* **1 = sound**, acceptable,
cogent, conclusive, convincing, good, just,
logical, powerful, sensible, substantial,
telling, weighty, well-founded,
well-grounded **2 = legal**, authentic, bona
fide, genuine, lawful, legally binding,
legitimate, official, signed and sealed
➤ **Antonyms**
≠**sound**: baseless, bogus, fallacious, false,
illogical, sham, spurious, unacceptable,
unfounded, unrealistic, unrecognized,
untrue, weak ≠**legal**: illegal, inoperative,
invalid, unlawful, unofficial

validate *verb* **1 = confirm**, certify,
corroborate, prove, substantiate **2
= authorize**, authenticate, endorse, ratify

validity *noun* **1 = soundness**, cogency,
force, foundation, grounds, point, power,
strength, substance, weight **2 = legality**,
authority, lawfulness, legitimacy, right

valley *noun* **= hollow**, coomb, cwm
(*Welsh*), dale, dell, depression, dingle, glen,
strath (*Scot.*), vale

valorous *adjective* **= brave**, bold,
courageous, dauntless, doughty, fearless,
gallant, heroic, intrepid, lion-hearted, plucky,
valiant

valour *noun* **= bravery**, boldness, courage,
doughtiness, fearlessness, gallantry, heroism,
intrepidity, lion-heartedness, spirit
➤ **Antonyms**
cowardice, dread, fear, timidity, trepidation,
weakness

valuable *adjective* **1 = precious**, costly,
dear, expensive, high-priced **2 = useful**,
beneficial, cherished, esteemed, estimable,
held dear, helpful, important, prized,
profitable, serviceable, treasured, valued,
worth one's *or* its weight in gold,
worthwhile, worthy ♦ *noun* **3 valuables**
= treasures, heirlooms
➤ **Antonyms**
adjective ≠**precious**: cheap, cheapo
(*informal*), chickenshit (*U.S. slang*), crappy
(*slang*), inexpensive, worthless ≠**useful**:
insignificant, pointless, silly, trifling, trivial,
unimportant, useless, worthless

value *noun* **1 = importance**, advantage,
benefit, desirability, help, merit, mileage
(*informal*), profit, serviceableness,
significance, use, usefulness, utility, worth **2
= cost**, equivalent, market price, monetary
worth, rate **3 values = principles**, code of
behaviour, ethics, (moral) standards ♦ *verb* **4
= evaluate**, account, appraise, assess,
compute, estimate, price, put a price on,

rate, set at, survey **5 = regard highly**,
appreciate, cherish, esteem, hold dear, hold
in high regard *or* esteem, prize, respect, set
store by, treasure
➤ **Antonyms**
noun ≠**importance**: insignificance,
unimportance, uselessness, worthlessness
♦ *verb* ≠**regard highly**: disregard, have no
time for, hold a low opinion of,
underestimate, undervalue

valued *adjective* **= highly regarded**,
cherished, dear, esteemed, loved, prized,
treasured

valueless *adjective* **= worthless**, no good,
of no value, useless

vamoose *Slang, chiefly U.S. verb* **= go
away**, bugger off (*taboo slang*), clear off
(*informal*), fuck off (*offensive taboo slang*),
make off, make oneself scarce (*informal*),
run away, scarper (*Brit. slang*), scram
(*informal*)

vandal *noun* **= hooligan**, delinquent, rowdy,
yob *or* yobbo (*Brit. slang*)

vanguard *noun* **= forefront**, advance
guard, cutting edge, forerunners, front, front
line, front rank, leaders, spearhead,
trailblazers, trendsetters, van
➤ **Antonyms**
back, rear, rearguard, stern, tail, tail end

vanish *verb* **= disappear**, become invisible,
be lost to sight, die out, disappear from
sight *or* from the face of the earth, dissolve,
evanesce, evaporate, fade (away), melt
(away), vanish off the face of the earth
➤ **Antonyms**
appear, arrive, become visible, come into
view, materialize, pop up

vanity *noun* **= pride**, affected ways, airs,
arrogance, bigheadedness (*informal*),
conceit, conceitedness, egotism, narcissism,
ostentation, pretension, self-admiration,
self-love, showing off (*informal*),
swollen-headedness (*informal*)
➤ **Antonyms**
humility, meekness, modesty,
self-abasement, self-deprecation

vanquish *verb Literary* **= defeat**, beat, blow
out of the water (*slang*), clobber (*slang*),
conquer, crush, lick (*informal*), master,
overcome, overpower, overwhelm, put
down, quell, rout, run rings around
(*informal*), triumph over, wipe the floor with
(*informal*)

vapid *adjective* **= dull**, bland, boring, flat,
insipid, tame, uninspiring, uninteresting,
weak, wishy-washy (*informal*)

vapour *noun* **= mist**, breath, dampness,
exhalation, fog, fumes, haze, miasma,
smoke, steam

variable *adjective* **= changeable**, capricious,

fitful, flexible, fluctuating, inconstant,
mercurial, mutable, shifting, temperamental,
uneven, unstable, unsteady, vacillating,
wavering
> **Antonyms**
constant, firm, fixed, settled, stable, steady,
unalterable, unchanging

variance *noun* **at variance = in
disagreement**, at loggerheads, at odds, at
sixes and sevens (*informal*), conflicting, in
opposition, out of harmony, out of line

variant *adjective* **1 = different**, alternative,
derived, divergent, exceptional, modified
♦ *noun* **2 = variation**, alternative, derived
form, development, modification, sport
(*Biology*)

variation *noun* **= difference**, alteration,
break in routine, change, departure,
departure from the norm, deviation,
discrepancy, diversification, diversity,
innovation, modification, novelty, variety
> **Antonyms**
dullness, monotony, sameness, tedium,
uniformity

varied *adjective* **= different**, assorted,
diverse, heterogeneous, manifold,
miscellaneous, mixed, motley, sundry,
various
> **Antonyms**
homogeneous, repetitive, similar,
standardized, uniform, unvarying

variegated *adjective* **= mottled**, diversified,
many-coloured, motley, parti-coloured, pied,
streaked, varicoloured

variety *noun* **1 = diversity**, change,
difference, discrepancy, diversification,
many-sidedness, multifariousness, variation **2
= range**, array, assortment, collection, cross
section, intermixture, medley, miscellany,
mixed bag (*informal*), mixture, multiplicity **3
= type**, brand, breed, category, class, kind,
make, order, sort, species, strain
> **Antonyms**
≠diversity: homogeneity, invariability,
monotony, similarity, similitude, uniformity

various *adjective* **= different**, assorted,
differing, disparate, distinct, diverse,
diversified, heterogeneous, manifold, many,
miscellaneous, several, sundry, varied
> **Antonyms**
alike, equivalent, matching, same, similar,
uniform

varnish *noun, verb* **1 = lacquer**, glaze,
gloss, japan, polish, shellac ♦ *verb* **2
= adorn**, decorate, embellish, gild

vary *verb* **1 = change**, alter, fluctuate,
transform **2 = differ**, be unlike, depart,
disagree, diverge **3 = alternate**, diversify,
permutate, reorder **4 = modify**

varying *adjective* **1 = changing**, fluctuating,

inconsistent **2 = different**, distinct,
distinguishable, diverse
> **Antonyms**
≠changing: consistent, fixed, monotonous,
regular, settled, unchanging, unvarying

vassal *noun* **= serf**, bondservant, bondsman,
liegeman, retainer, slave, subject

vassalage *noun* **= serfdom**, bondage,
dependence, servitude, slavery, subjection

vast *adjective* **= huge**, astronomical,
boundless, colossal, elephantine, enormous,
extensive, gigantic, great, illimitable,
immeasurable, immense, limitless,
mammoth, massive, measureless, mega
(*slang*), monstrous, monumental,
never-ending, prodigious, sweeping,
tremendous, unbounded, unlimited,
voluminous, wide
> **Antonyms**
bounded, limited, microscopic, narrow,
negligible, paltry, puny, small, tiny, trifling

vault[1] *noun* **1 = strongroom**, depository,
repository **2 = crypt**, catacomb, cellar,
charnel house, mausoleum, tomb, undercroft
3 = arch, ceiling, roof, span

vault[2] *verb* **= jump**, bound, clear, hurdle,
leap, spring

vaulted *adjective* **= arched**, cavernous,
domed

vaunt *verb* **= boast about**, brag about, exult
in, flaunt, give oneself airs about, make a
display of, make much of, parade, show off

veer *verb* **= change direction**, be deflected,
change, change course, sheer, shift, swerve,
tack, turn

vegetate *verb* **= stagnate**, be inert,
deteriorate, go to seed, idle, languish, loaf,
moulder, veg out (*slang, chiefly U.S.*)
> **Antonyms**
accomplish, develop, grow, participate,
perform, react, respond

vehemence *noun* **= forcefulness**, ardour,
eagerness, earnestness, emphasis, energy,
enthusiasm, fervency, fervour, fire, force,
heat, intensity, keenness, passion, verve,
vigour, violence, warmth, zeal
> **Antonyms**
apathy, coolness, indifference, inertia,
lethargy, listlessness, passivity, stoicism,
torpor

vehement *adjective* **= strong**, ablaze,
ardent, eager, earnest, emphatic,
enthusiastic, fervent, fervid, fierce, flaming,
forceful, forcible, impassioned, intense,
passionate, powerful, violent, zealous
> **Antonyms**
apathetic, calm, cool, dispassionate,
half-hearted, impassive, lukewarm, moderate

vehicle *noun* **1 = transport**, conveyance,
means of transport, transportation **2**

= **medium**, apparatus, channel, means, means of expression, mechanism, organ

veil noun 1 = **cover**, blind, cloak, curtain, disguise, film, mask, screen, shade, shroud
♦ verb 2 = **cover**, cloak, conceal, dim, disguise, hide, mantle, mask, obscure, screen, shield
➤ Antonyms
verb ≠ **cover**: disclose, display, divulge, expose, lay bare, reveal, uncover, unveil

veiled adjective = **disguised**, concealed, covert, hinted at, implied, masked, suppressed

vein noun 1 = **blood vessel** 2 = **seam**, course, current, lode, stratum, streak, stripe 3 = **trait**, dash, hint, strain, streak, thread 4 = **mood**, attitude, bent, character, faculty, humour, mode, note, style, temper, tenor, tone, turn

velocity noun = **speed**, pace, quickness, rapidity, swiftness

velvety adjective = **soft**, delicate, downy, smooth

venal adjective = **corrupt**, bent (slang), corruptible, crooked (informal), dishonourable, mercenary, unprincipled
➤ Antonyms
honest, honourable, incorruptible, law-abiding, principled, upright

vendetta noun = **feud**, bad blood, blood feud, quarrel

veneer noun 1 = **layer**, finish, gloss 2 = **mask**, appearance, façade, false front, front, guise, pretence, semblance, show

venerable adjective = **respected**, august, esteemed, honoured, revered, reverenced, sage, wise, worshipped
➤ Antonyms
discredited, disdained, disgraced, dishonourable, disreputable, ignominious, inglorious, scorned

venerate verb = **respect**, adore, esteem, hold in awe, honour, look up to, revere, reverence, worship
➤ Antonyms
deride, dishonour, disregard, execrate, mock, scorn, spurn

veneration noun = **respect**, adoration, awe, deference, esteem, reverence, worship

vengeance noun 1 = **revenge**, an eye for an eye, avenging, reprisal, requital, retaliation, retribution, settling of scores 2 **with a vengeance** = **to the utmost**, and no mistake, extremely, greatly, to the full, to the nth degree, with no holds barred
➤ Antonyms
≠ **revenge**: absolution, acquittal, exoneration, forbearance, forgiveness, mercy, pardon, remission

vengeful adjective = **unforgiving**, avenging, retaliatory, revengeful, thirsting for revenge

venial adjective = **forgivable**, allowable, excusable, insignificant, minor, pardonable, slight, trivial

venom noun 1 = **malice**, acidity, acrimony, bitterness, gall, grudge, hate, ill will, malevolence, maliciousness, rancour, spite, spitefulness, spleen, virulence 2 = **poison**, bane, toxin
➤ Antonyms
≠ **malice**: benevolence, charity, compassion, favour, goodwill, kindness, love, mercy

venomous adjective 1 = **malicious**, baleful, hostile, malignant, rancorous, savage, spiteful, vicious, vindictive 2 = **poisonous**, baneful (archaic), mephitic, noxious, poison, toxic, virulent
➤ Antonyms
≠ **malicious**: affectionate, benevolent, compassionate, forgiving, harmless, loving, magnanimous ≠ **poisonous**: harmless, nonpoisonous, nontoxic, nonvenomous

vent noun 1 = **outlet**, aperture, duct, hole, opening, orifice, split ♦ verb 2 = **express**, air, come out with, discharge, emit, empty, give expression to, give vent to, pour out, release, utter, voice
➤ Antonyms
verb ≠ **express**: bottle up, curb, hold back, inhibit, quash, quell, repress, stifle, subdue

ventilate verb = **discuss**, air, bring out into the open, broadcast, debate, make known, talk about

venture noun 1 = **undertaking**, adventure, chance, endeavour, enterprise, fling, gamble, hazard, jeopardy, project, risk, speculation
♦ verb 2 = **risk**, chance, endanger, hazard, imperil, jeopardize, put in jeopardy, speculate, stake, wager 3 = **go**, embark on, plunge into, set out 4 = **dare**, advance, dare say, hazard, make bold, presume, take the liberty, volunteer

venturesome adjective = **daring**, adventurous, bold, courageous, enterprising, fearless, intrepid, plucky, spirited

veracious adjective = **truthful**, ethical, frank, high-principled, honest, trustworthy

veracity noun 1 = **truthfulness**, candour, frankness, honesty, integrity, probity, rectitude, trustworthiness, uprightness 2 = **accuracy**, credibility, exactitude, precision, truth

verbal adjective = **spoken**, literal, oral, unwritten, verbatim, word-of-mouth

verbally adverb = **orally**, by word of mouth

verbatim adverb = **word for word**, exactly, precisely, to the letter

verbiage *noun* = **verbosity**, circumlocution, periphrasis, pleonasm, redundancy, repetition, tautology

verbose *adjective* = **long-winded**, circumlocutory, diffuse, garrulous, periphrastic, pleonastic, prolix, tautological, windy, wordy
➤ **Antonyms**
brief, brusque, concise, curt, quiet, reticent, short, succinct, terse, untalkative

verbosity *noun* = **long-windedness**, garrulity, loquaciousness, prolixity, rambling, verbiage, verboseness, windiness, wordiness

verdant *adjective Literary* = **green**, flourishing, fresh, grassy, leafy, lush

verdict *noun* = **decision**, adjudication, conclusion, finding, judgment, opinion, sentence

verge *noun* 1 = **border**, boundary, brim, brink, edge, extreme, limit, lip, margin, roadside, threshold ♦ *verb* 2 **verge on** = **come near to**, approach, border

verification *noun* = **proof**, authentication, confirmation, corroboration, substantiation, validation

verify *verb* 1 = **check** 2 = **prove**, attest, attest to, authenticate, bear out, confirm, corroborate, substantiate, support, validate
➤ **Antonyms**
≠**prove:** deny, discount, discredit, dispute, invalidate, nullify, undermine, weaken

verisimilitude *noun* = **realism**, credibility, plausibility, resemblance, semblance, show of

vernacular *noun* 1 = **dialect**, argot, cant, idiom, jargon, native language, parlance, patois, speech, vulgar tongue ♦ *adjective* 2 = **colloquial**, common, indigenous, informal, local, mother, native, popular, vulgar

versatile *adjective* = **adaptable**, adjustable, all-purpose, all-round, all-singing, all-dancing, flexible, functional, handy, many-sided, multifaceted, resourceful, variable
➤ **Antonyms**
fixed, inflexible, invariable, limited, one-sided, unadaptable

versed *adjective* = **knowledgeable**, accomplished, acquainted, competent, conversant, experienced, familiar, practised, proficient, qualified, seasoned, skilled, well informed, well up in (*informal*)
➤ **Antonyms**
callow, green, ignorant, inexperienced, new, raw, unacquainted, unfledged, unpractised, unschooled, unskilled, unversed

version *noun* 1 = **form**, design, kind, model, style, type, variant 2 = **account**, interpretation, side, take (*informal, chiefly U.S.*) 3 = **adaptation**, portrayal, reading, rendering, translation

vertex *noun* = **top**, acme, apex, apogee, crest, crown, culmination, extremity, height, pinnacle, summit, zenith

vertical *adjective* = **upright**, erect, on end, perpendicular
➤ **Antonyms**
flat, horizontal, level, plane, prone

vertigo *noun* = **dizziness**, giddiness, light-headedness, loss of equilibrium

verve *noun* = **enthusiasm**, animation, brio, dash, élan, energy, force, get-up-and-go (*informal*), gusto, life, liveliness, pep, punch (*informal*), sparkle, spirit, vigour, vim (*slang*), vitality, vivacity, zeal, zip (*informal*)
➤ **Antonyms**
apathy, disdain, half-heartedness, indifference, inertia, lack of enthusiasm, languor, lethargy, lifelessness, reluctance, torpor

very *adverb* 1 = **extremely**, absolutely, acutely, awfully (*informal*), decidedly, deeply, eminently, exceedingly, excessively, greatly, highly, jolly (*Brit.*), noticeably, particularly, profoundly, really, remarkably, seriously (*informal*), superlatively, surpassingly, terribly, truly, uncommonly, unusually, wonderfully ♦ *adjective* 2 = **exact**, actual, appropriate, express, identical, perfect, precise, real, same, selfsame, unqualified

vessel *noun* 1 = **ship**, barque (*poetic*), boat, craft 2 = **container**, pot, receptacle, utensil

vest *verb, with* **in** *or* **with** = **place**, authorize, be devolved upon, bestow, confer, consign, empower, endow, entrust, furnish, invest, lodge, put in the hands of, settle

vestibule *noun* = **hall**, anteroom, entrance hall, foyer, lobby, porch, portico

vestige *noun* = **trace**, evidence, glimmer, hint, indication, relic, remainder, remains, remnant, residue, scrap, sign, suspicion, token

vet *verb* = **check**, appraise, check out, examine, give (someone *or* something) the once-over (*informal*), investigate, look over, pass under review, review, scan, scrutinize, size up (*informal*)

veteran *noun* 1 = **old hand**, master, old stager, old-timer, past master, pro (*informal*), trouper, warhorse (*informal*) ♦ *adjective* 2 = **long-serving**, adept, battle-scarred, expert, old, proficient, seasoned
➤ **Antonyms**
noun ≠**old hand:** apprentice, beginner, freshman, initiate, neophyte, novice, recruit, tyro

veto *noun* 1 = **ban**, boycott, embargo, interdict, nonconsent, prohibition ♦ *verb* 2 = **ban**, boycott, disallow, forbid, give the

thumbs down to, interdict, prohibit, put the kibosh on (*slang*), refuse permission, reject, rule out, turn down
➤ Antonyms
noun ≠**ban**: approval, endorsement, go-ahead (*informal*), ratification ♦ *verb* ≠**ban**: approve, endorse, O.K. *or* okay (*informal*), pass, ratify

vex *verb* = **annoy**, aggravate (*informal*), agitate, bother, bug (*informal*), displease, distress, disturb, exasperate, gall, get one's back up, get on one's nerves (*informal*), grate on, harass, hassle (*informal*), irritate, nark (*Brit., Austral., & N.Z. slang*), needle (*informal*), nettle, offend, peeve (*informal*), pester, pique, plague, provoke, put one's back up, put out, rile, torment, trouble, upset, worry
➤ Antonyms
allay, appease, comfort, console, gratify, hush, mollify, please, quiet, soothe

vexation *noun* 1 = **annoyance**, aggravation (*informal*), chagrin, displeasure, dissatisfaction, exasperation, frustration, irritation, pique 2 = **problem**, bother, difficulty, hassle (*informal*), headache (*informal*), irritant, nuisance, thorn in one's flesh, trouble, upset, worry

vexatious *adjective* = **annoying**, aggravating (*informal*), bothersome, burdensome, disagreeable, distressing, exasperating, harassing, irksome, irritating, nagging, provoking, tormenting, troublesome, trying, unpleasant, upsetting, worrisome, worrying
➤ Antonyms
agreeable, balmy, calming, comforting, pleasant, reassuring, relaxing, soothing

vexed *adjective* 1 = **annoyed**, aggravated (*informal*), agitated, bothered, confused, displeased, distressed, disturbed, exasperated, fed up, hacked (off) (*U.S. slang*), harassed, irritated, miffed (*informal*), nettled, peeved (*informal*), pissed (*taboo slang*), pissed off (*taboo slang*), provoked, put out, riled, ruffled, tormented, troubled, upset, worried 2 = **controversial**, contested, disputed, moot, much debated

viable *adjective* = **workable**, applicable, feasible, operable, practicable, usable, within the bounds of possibility
➤ Antonyms
hopeless, impossible, impracticable, inconceivable, out of the question, unthinkable, unworkable

vibes *plural noun Informal* 1 = **feelings**, emotions, reaction, response 2 = **atmosphere**, aura, emanation, vibrations

vibrant *adjective* = **energetic**, alive, animated, colourful, dynamic, electrifying, full of pep (*informal*), sparkling, spirited,

storming, vigorous, vivacious, vivid

vibrate *verb* = **shake**, fluctuate, judder (*informal*), oscillate, pulsate, pulse, quiver, resonate, reverberate, shiver, sway, swing, throb, tremble, undulate

vibration *noun* = **shake**, judder (*informal*), oscillation, pulsation, pulse, quiver, resonance, reverberation, throb, throbbing, trembling, tremor

vicarious *adjective* 1 = **indirect**, at one remove 2 = **substituted**, surrogate 3 = **delegated**, deputed

vice *noun* 1 = **wickedness**, corruption, degeneracy, depravity, evil, evildoing, immorality, iniquity, profligacy, sin, turpitude, venality 2 = **fault**, blemish, defect, failing, imperfection, shortcoming, weakness
➤ Antonyms
≠**wickedness**: honour, morality, virtue
≠**fault**: gift, good point, strong point, talent

vice versa *adverb* = **conversely**, contrariwise, in reverse, the other way round

vicinity *noun* = **neighbourhood**, area, district, environs, locality, neck of the woods (*informal*), precincts, proximity, purlieus

vicious *adjective* 1 = **savage**, abhorrent, atrocious, bad, barbarous, cruel, diabolical, ferocious, fiendish, foul, heinous, monstrous, vile, violent 2 = **malicious**, backbiting, bitchy (*informal*), cruel, defamatory, mean, rancorous, slanderous, spiteful, venomous, vindictive
➤ Antonyms
≠**savage**: docile, friendly, gentle, good, honourable, kind, playful, tame, upright, virtuous ≠**malicious**: appreciative, complimentary, congratulatory

viciousness *noun* 1 = **savagery**, cruelty, ferocity 2 = **malice**, bitchiness (*slang*), rancour, spite, spitefulness, venom
➤ Antonyms
≠**malice**: gentleness, goodness, goodwill, graciousness, kindness, mercy, virtue

vicissitudes *plural noun* = **changes of fortune**, alterations, life's ups and downs (*informal*), shifts

victim *noun* 1 = **casualty**, fatality, injured party, martyr, sacrifice, scapegoat, sufferer 2 = **prey**, dupe, fall guy (*informal*), innocent, patsy (*slang, chiefly U.S. & Canad.*), sitting duck (*informal*), sitting target, sucker (*slang*)
➤ Antonyms
≠**casualty**: survivor ≠**prey**: assailant, attacker, culprit, guilty party, offender

victimize *verb* = **persecute**, discriminate against, have a down on (someone) (*informal*), have it in for (someone) (*informal*), pick on

victor *noun* = **winner**, champ (*informal*),

champion, conquering hero, conqueror, first, prizewinner, top dog (*informal*), vanquisher
➤ Antonyms
also-ran, dud (*informal*), failure, flop (*informal*), loser, vanquished

victorious *adjective* = **winning**, champion, conquering, first, prizewinning, successful, triumphant, vanquishing
➤ Antonyms
beaten, conquered, defeated, failed, losing, overcome, unsuccessful, vanquished

victory *noun* = **win**, conquest, laurels, mastery, success, superiority, the prize, triumph
➤ Antonyms
defeat, failure, loss

victuals *plural noun Old-fashioned* = **food**, comestibles, eatables, eats (*slang*), grub (*slang*), meat, nosh (*slang*), provisions, rations, stores, supplies, tack (*informal*), viands, vittles (*obsolete*)

vie *verb* = **compete**, contend, strive, struggle

view *noun* 1 *sometimes plural* = **opinion**, attitude, belief, conviction, feeling, impression, judgment, notion, point of view, sentiment, thought, way of thinking 2 = **scene**, aspect, landscape, outlook, panorama, perspective, picture, prospect, spectacle, vista 3 = **vision**, range or field of vision, sight 4 = **look**, contemplation, display, examination, inspection, recce (*slang*), scan, scrutiny, sight, survey, viewing 5 **with a view to** = **with the aim** or **intention of**, in order to, in the hope of, so as to ◆ *verb* 6 = **regard**, consider, deem, judge, look on, think about 7 = **look at**, behold, check, check out (*informal*), clock (*Brit. slang*), contemplate, examine, explore, eye, eyeball (*slang*), gaze at, get a load of (*informal*), inspect, observe, recce (*slang*), regard, scan, spectate, stare at, survey, take a dekko at (*Brit. slang*), watch, witness

viewer *noun* = **watcher**, observer, onlooker, spectator, TV watcher

viewpoint *noun* = **attitude**, angle, frame of reference, perspective, point of view, position, slant, stance, standpoint, vantage point, way of thinking

vigilance *noun* = **watchfulness**, alertness, attentiveness, carefulness, caution, circumspection, observance

vigilant *adjective* = **watchful**, alert, Argus-eyed, attentive, careful, cautious, circumspect, on one's guard, on one's toes, on the alert, on the lookout, on the qui vive, on the watch, unsleeping, wakeful, wide awake
➤ Antonyms
careless, inattentive, lax, neglectful, negligent, remiss, slack

vigorous *adjective* = **energetic**, active, alive and kicking, brisk, dynamic, effective, fighting fit, fit as a fiddle (*informal*), forceful, forcible, full of beans (*informal*), full of energy, hale, hale and hearty, hardy, healthy, intense, lively, lusty, powerful, red-blooded, robust, sound, spirited, strenuous, strong, vital
➤ Antonyms
apathetic, effete, enervated, feeble, frail, inactive, indolent, lethargic, lifeless, spiritless, torpid, weak, weedy (*informal*), wimpish or wimpy (*informal*), wishy-washy, wussy (*slang*)

vigorously *adverb* = **energetically**, eagerly, forcefully, hammer and tongs, hard, like mad (*slang*), lustily, strenuously, strongly, with a vengeance, with might and main

vigour *noun* = **energy**, activity, animation, brio, dash, dynamism, force, forcefulness, gusto, liveliness, might, oomph (*informal*), pep, power, punch (*informal*), robustness, spirit, strength, verve, vim (*slang*), vitality
➤ Antonyms
apathy, feebleness, fragility, frailty, impotence, inactivity, inertia, infirmity, lethargy, sluggishness, weakness

vile *adjective* 1 = **wicked**, abandoned, appalling, bad, base, contemptible, corrupt, debased, degenerate, depraved, despicable, disgraceful, evil, impure, loathsome, low, mean, nefarious, perverted, shocking, sinful, ugly, vicious, vulgar 2 = **disgusting**, foul, horrid, loathsome, nasty, nauseating, noxious, obscene, offensive, repellent, repugnant, repulsive, revolting, sickening, yucky or yukky (*slang*)
➤ Antonyms
≠**wicked**: chaste, cultured, genteel, honourable, noble, polite, pure, refined, righteous, upright, worthy ≠**disgusting**: agreeable, delicate, lovely, marvellous, pleasant, splendid, sublime

vileness *noun* 1 = **wickedness**, corruption, degeneracy, depravity, dreadfulness, enormity, evil, heinousness, turpitude, ugliness 2 = **foulness**, noxiousness, offensiveness

vilification *noun* = **denigration**, abuse, aspersion, calumniation, calumny, defamation, disparagement, invective, mudslinging, scurrility, vituperation

vilify *verb* = **malign**, abuse, asperse, bad-mouth (*slang, chiefly U.S. & Canad.*), berate, calumniate, decry, defame, denigrate, disparage, knock (*informal*), pull to pieces (*informal*), revile, rubbish (*informal*), run down, slag (off) (*slang*), slander, smear, speak ill of
➤ Antonyms
adore, commend, esteem, exalt, glorify,

honour, praise, revere, venerate

villain noun 1 = **evildoer**, blackguard, criminal, knave (archaic), malefactor, miscreant, rapscallion, reprobate, rogue, scoundrel, wretch 2 = **antihero**, baddy (informal)
➤ Antonyms
≠antihero: goody, hero, heroine

villainous adjective = **wicked**, bad, base, criminal, cruel, degenerate, depraved, detestable, diabolical, evil, fiendish, hateful, heinous, infamous, inhuman, nefarious, sinful, terrible, vicious, vile
➤ Antonyms
angelic, good, heroic, humane, moral, noble, righteous, saintly, virtuous

villainy noun = **wickedness**, baseness, crime, criminality, delinquency, depravity, devilry, iniquity, sin, turpitude, vice

vindicate verb 1 = **clear**, absolve, acquit, exculpate, exonerate, free from blame, rehabilitate 2 = **justify**, defend, excuse
➤ Antonyms
≠clear: accuse, blame, condemn, convict, incriminate, punish, reproach

vindication noun 1 = **exoneration**, exculpating, exculpation 2 = **justification**, defence, excuse

vindictive adjective = **vengeful**, implacable, malicious, malignant, rancorous, relentless, resentful, revengeful, spiteful, unforgiving, unrelenting, venomous
➤ Antonyms
forgiving, generous, magnanimous, merciful, relenting, unvindictive

vintage noun 1 = **harvest**, crop 2 = **era**, epoch, generation, time of origin, year ♦ adjective 3 = **best**, choice, classic, mature, prime, rare, ripe, select, superior

violate verb 1 = **break**, contravene, disobey, disregard, encroach upon, infract, infringe, transgress 2 = **desecrate**, abuse, befoul, defile, dishonour, invade, outrage, pollute, profane 3 = **rape**, abuse, assault, debauch, ravish
➤ Antonyms
≠break: honour, obey, respect, uphold
≠desecrate: defend, honour, protect, respect, revere, set on a pedestal

violation noun 1 = **infringement**, abuse, breach, contravention, encroachment, infraction, transgression, trespass 2 = **desecration**, defilement, profanation, sacrilege, spoliation

violence noun 1 = **force**, bloodshed, bloodthirstiness, brutality, brute force, cruelty, destructiveness, ferocity, fierceness, fighting, frenzy, fury, passion, savagery, strong-arm tactics (informal), terrorism, thuggery, vehemence, wildness 2

= **intensity**, abandon, acuteness, fervour, force, harshness, severity, sharpness, vehemence 3 = **power**, boisterousness, raging, roughness, storminess, tumult, turbulence, wildness

violent adjective 1 = **destructive**, bloodthirsty, brutal, cruel, fiery, flaming, forcible, furious, hot-headed, intemperate, murderous, passionate, powerful, raging, riotous, rough, savage, strong, tempestuous, uncontrollable, ungovernable, unrestrained, vehement, vicious, wild 2 = **intense**, acute, agonizing, biting, excruciating, extreme, inordinate, painful, severe, sharp 3 = **powerful**, boisterous, devastating, gale force, raging, storming, strong, tempestuous, tumultuous, turbulent, wild
➤ Antonyms
≠destructive: calm, composed, gentle, mild, peaceful, placid, quiet, rational, sane, serene, unruffled, well-behaved ≠powerful: calm, gentle, mild, placid, serene

V.I.P. noun = **celebrity**, big hitter (informal), big name, heavy hitter (informal), luminary, somebody, star

virago noun = **harridan**, ballbreaker (slang), battle-axe (informal), fury, scold, shrew

virgin noun 1 = **maiden** (archaic), damsel (archaic), girl, maid (archaic), vestal, virgo intacta ♦ adjective 2 = **pure**, chaste, immaculate, maidenly, modest, uncorrupted, undefiled, unsullied, vestal, virginal 3 = **fresh**, new, pristine, unsullied, untouched, unused
➤ Antonyms
adjective ≠pure: corrupted, defiled, impure ≠fresh: contaminated, dirty, impure, polluted, spoiled, used

virginal adjective 1 = **pure**, celibate, chaste, immaculate, maidenly, uncorrupted, undefiled, virgin 2 = **fresh**, immaculate, pristine, pure, snowy, spotless, undisturbed, untouched, white

virginity noun = **chastity**, maidenhood

virile adjective = **manly**, forceful, lusty, macho, male, manlike, masculine, potent, red-blooded, robust, strong, vigorous
➤ Antonyms
camp (informal), effeminate, emasculate, feminine, girlie, impotent, unmanly, weak, weedy (informal), wimpish or wimpy (informal), wussy (slang)

virility noun = **masculinity**, machismo, manhood, potency, vigour
➤ Antonyms
effeminacy, femininity, impotence, softness, unmanliness, weakness

virtual adjective = **practical**, essential, implicit, implied, in all but name, indirect, tacit, unacknowledged

virtually *adverb* = **practically**, almost, as good as, effectually, for all practical purposes, in all but name, in effect, in essence, nearly, to all intents and purposes

virtue *noun* 1 = **goodness**, high-mindedness, incorruptibility, integrity, justice, morality, probity, quality, rectitude, righteousness, uprightness, worth, worthiness 2 = **merit**, advantage, asset, attribute, credit, good point, good quality, plus (*informal*), strength 3 = **chastity**, honour, innocence, purity, virginity 4 **by virtue of** = **because of**, as a result of, by dint of, by reason of, in view of, on account of, owing to, thanks to
➤ **Antonyms**
≠**goodness:** corruption, debauchery, depravity, dishonesty, dishonour, evil, immorality, sin, sinfulness, turpitude, vice ≠**merit:** drawback, failing, frailty, shortcoming, weak point ≠**chastity:** promiscuity, unchastity

virtuosity *noun* = **mastery**, brilliance, craft, éclat, expertise, finish, flair, panache, polish, skill

virtuoso *noun* 1 = **master**, artist, genius, grandmaster, maestro, magician, master hand ♦ *adjective* 2 = **masterly**, bravura (*Music*), brilliant, dazzling

virtuous *adjective* 1 = **good**, blameless, ethical, excellent, exemplary, high-principled, honest, honourable, incorruptible, just, moral, praiseworthy, pure, righteous, squeaky-clean, upright, worthy 2 = **chaste**, celibate, clean-living, innocent, pure, spotless, virginal
➤ **Antonyms**
≠**good:** corrupt, debauched, depraved, dishonest, evil, immoral, sinful, unrighteous, vicious, wicked ≠**chaste:** impure, loose, promiscuous, unchaste

virulence *noun* 1 = **bitterness**, acrimony, antagonism, hatred, hostility, ill will, malevolence, malice, rancour, resentment, spite, spleen, venom, viciousness, vindictiveness 2 = **deadliness**, harmfulness, hurtfulness, infectiousness, injuriousness, malignancy, noxiousness, poisonousness, toxicity, virulency

virulent *adjective* 1 = **bitter**, acrimonious, envenomed, hostile, malevolent, malicious, rancorous, resentful, spiteful, splenetic, venomous, vicious, vindictive 2 = **deadly**, baneful (*archaic*), infective, injurious, lethal, malignant, pernicious, poisonous, septic, toxic, venomous
➤ **Antonyms**
≠**bitter:** amiable, benign, compassionate, kind, magnanimous, sympathetic, warm ≠**deadly:** harmless, innocuous, nonpoisonous, nontoxic

viscous *adjective* = **thick**, gelatinous, gluey, gluey, glutinous, gooey (*informal*), icky (*informal*), sticky, syrupy, viscid

visible *adjective* = **apparent**, bold, clear, conspicuous, detectable, discernible, discoverable, distinguishable, evident, in sight, in view, manifest, not hidden, noticeable, observable, obvious, palpable, patent, perceivable, perceptible, plain, to be seen, unconcealed, unmistakable
➤ **Antonyms**
concealed, hidden, imperceptible, invisible, obscured, unnoticeable, unseen

vision *noun* 1 = **sight**, eyes, eyesight, perception, seeing, view 2 = **image**, castle in the air, concept, conception, daydream, dream, fantasy, idea, ideal, mental picture, pipe dream 3 = **hallucination**, apparition, chimera, delusion, ghost, illusion, mirage, phantasm, phantom, revelation, spectre, wraith 4 = **foresight**, breadth of view, discernment, farsightedness, imagination, insight, intuition, penetration, prescience 5 = **picture**, dream, sight, sight for sore eyes, spectacle

visionary *adjective* 1 = **idealistic**, dreaming, dreamy, impractical, quixotic, romantic, speculative, starry-eyed, unrealistic, unworkable, utopian, with one's head in the clouds 2 = **prophetic**, mystical 3 = **imaginary**, chimerical, delusory, fanciful, fantastic, ideal, idealized, illusory, unreal ♦ *noun* 4 = **idealist**, daydreamer, Don Quixote, dreamer, romantic, theorist, utopian, zealot 5 = **prophet**, mystic, seer
➤ **Antonyms**
adjective ≠**idealistic:** pragmatic, realistic ≠**imaginary:** actual, mundane, real, unimaginary ♦ *noun* ≠**idealist:** cynic, pessimist, pragmatist, realist

visit *verb* 1 = **call on**, be the guest of, call in, drop in on (*informal*), go to see, inspect, look (someone) up, pay a call on, pop in (*informal*), stay at, stay with, stop by, take in (*informal*) 2 *Old-fashioned* = **afflict**, assail, attack, befall, descend upon, smite, trouble 3 *with* **on** *or* **upon** = **inflict**, bring down upon, execute, impose, wreak ♦ *noun* 4 = **call**, sojourn, stay, stop

visitation *noun* 1 = **inspection**, examination, visit 2 = **catastrophe**, bane, blight, calamity, cataclysm, disaster, infliction, ordeal, punishment, scourge, trial

visitor *noun* = **guest**, caller, company, visitant

vista *noun* = **view**, panorama, perspective, prospect

visual *adjective* 1 = **optical**, ocular, optic 2 = **observable**, discernible, perceptible, visible
➤ **Antonyms**
≠**observable:** imperceptible, indiscernible,

invisible, out of sight, unnoticeable, unperceivable

visualize *verb* = **picture**, conceive of, conjure up a mental picture of, envisage, imagine, see in the mind's eye

vital *adjective* **1** = **essential**, basic, cardinal, fundamental, imperative, indispensable, necessary, radical, requisite **2** = **important**, critical, crucial, decisive, key, life-or-death, significant, urgent **3** = **lively**, animated, dynamic, energetic, forceful, full of beans (*informal*), full of the joy of living, sparky, spirited, vibrant, vigorous, vivacious, zestful
➤ **Antonyms**
≠**essential**: dispensable, inessential, nonessential, unnecessary ≠**important**: minor, trivial, unimportant ≠**lively**: apathetic, lethargic, listless, uninvolved

vitality *noun* = **energy**, animation, brio, exuberance, go (*informal*), life, liveliness, lustiness, pep, robustness, sparkle, stamina, strength, vigour, vim (*slang*), vivaciousness, vivacity
➤ **Antonyms**
apathy, inertia, lethargy, listlessness, sluggishness, weakness

vitiate *verb* = **spoil**, harm, impair, injure, invalidate, mar, undermine, water down

vitiation *noun* = **spoiling**, deterioration, devaluation, dilution, impairment, marring, reduction, undermining

vitriolic *adjective* = **bitter**, acerbic, acid, bitchy (*informal*), caustic, envenomed, sardonic, scathing, venomous, virulent, withering

vituperation *noun* = **abuse**, blame, castigation, censure, fault-finding, flak (*informal*), invective, rebuke, reprimand, reproach, tongue-lashing, vilification
➤ **Antonyms**
acclaim, approval, commendation, eulogy, flattery, praise, tribute

vituperative *adjective* = **abusive**, belittling, calumniatory, censorious, defamatory, denunciatory, derogatory, harsh, insulting, opprobrious, scurrilous, withering

vivacious *adjective* = **lively**, animated, bubbling, cheerful, chirpy (*informal*), ebullient, effervescent, full of beans (*informal*), full of life, gay, high-spirited, jolly, light-hearted, merry, scintillating, sparkling, sparky, spirited, sprightly, upbeat (*informal*), vital
➤ **Antonyms**
boring, dull, languid, lifeless, listless, melancholy, spiritless, unenthusiastic

vivacity *noun* = **liveliness**, animation, brio, ebullience, effervescence, energy, gaiety, high spirits, life, pep, quickness, sparkle,

spirit, sprightliness
➤ **Antonyms**
apathy, ennui, fatigue, heaviness, inertia, languor, lethargy, listlessness, weariness

vivid *adjective* **1** = **bright**, brilliant, clear, colourful, glowing, highly-coloured, intense, rich **2** = **clear**, distinct, dramatic, graphic, lifelike, memorable, powerful, realistic, sharp, sharply-etched, stirring, strong, telling, true to life
➤ **Antonyms**
≠**bright**: colourless, cool, drab, dull, pale, pastel, sombre ≠**clear**: unclear, unmemorable, vague

vividness *noun* **1** = **brightness**, brilliancy, glow, radiance, resplendence **2** = **clarity**, distinctness, intensity, realism, sharpness, strength **3** = **liveliness**

vixen *noun* = **shrew**, ballbreaker (*slang*), fury, harpy, harridan, hellcat, scold, spitfire, termagant (*rare*), virago

viz. *adverb* = **namely**, that is to say, to wit, videlicet

vocabulary *noun* = **words**, dictionary, glossary, language, lexicon, wordbook, word stock

vocal *adjective* **1** = **spoken**, articulate, articulated, oral, put into words, said, uttered, voiced **2** = **outspoken**, articulate, blunt, eloquent, expressive, forthright, frank, free-spoken, noisy, plain-spoken, strident, vociferous
➤ **Antonyms**
≠**outspoken**: inarticulate, quiet, reserved, reticent, retiring, shy, silent, uncommunicative

vocation *noun* = **profession**, business, calling, career, employment, job, life's work, life work, métier, mission, office, post, pursuit, role, trade

vociferous *adjective* = **noisy**, clamorous, loud, loudmouthed (*informal*), obstreperous, outspoken, ranting, shouting, strident, uproarious, vehement, vocal
➤ **Antonyms**
hushed, muted, noiseless, quiet, silent, still

vogue *noun* **1** = **fashion**, craze, custom, dernier cri, last word, mode, style, the latest, the rage, the thing (*informal*), trend, way **2** *As in* **in vogue** = **popularity**, acceptance, currency, fashionableness, favour, prevalence, usage, use ◆ *adjective* **3** = **fashionable**, in, modish, now (*informal*), popular, prevalent, trendy (*Brit. informal*), up-to-the-minute, voguish, with it (*informal*)

voice *noun* **1** = **sound**, articulation, language, power of speech, tone, utterance, words **2** = **say**, decision, expression, part, view, vote, will, wish **3** = **instrument**, agency, medium, mouthpiece, organ, spokesman, spokesperson, spokeswoman, vehicle ◆ *verb* **4** = **express**, air, articulate, assert, come out with (*informal*), declare, divulge, enunciate, give expression *or* utterance to, put into words, say, utter

void *noun* **1** = **emptiness**, blank, blankness, gap, lack, opening, space, vacuity, vacuum, want ◆ *adjective* **2** = **invalid**, dead, ineffective, ineffectual, inoperative, nonviable, null and void, useless, vain, worthless **3** *Old-fashioned* = **empty**, bare, clear, drained, emptied, free, tenantless, unfilled, unoccupied, vacant **4** *with* of = **devoid**, destitute, lacking, without ◆ *verb* **5** = **invalidate**, abnegate, cancel, nullify, rescind **6** = **empty**, discharge, drain, eject, eliminate (*Physiology*), emit, evacuate
➤ **Antonyms**
adjective ≠**empty**: abounding, complete, filled, full, occupied, replete, tenanted

volatile *adjective* **1** = **changeable**, explosive, inconstant, unsettled, unstable, unsteady, variable **2** = **temperamental**, airy, erratic, fickle, flighty, inconstant, lively, mercurial, up and down (*informal*), whimsical
➤ **Antonyms**
≠**changeable**: constant, inert, settled, stable, steady ≠**temperamental**: calm, consistent, cool-headed, dependable, reliable, self-controlled, sober

volition *noun* = **free will**, choice, choosing, determination, discretion, option, preference, purpose, resolution, will

volley *noun* = **barrage**, blast, bombardment, burst, cannonade, discharge, explosion, fusillade, hail, salvo, shower

volubility *noun* = **talkativeness**, fluency, garrulity, gift of the gab, glibness, loquaciousness, loquacity

voluble *adjective* = **talkative**, articulate, blessed with the gift of the gab, fluent, forthcoming, glib, loquacious
➤ **Antonyms**
hesitant, inarticulate, reticent, succinct, taciturn, terse, tongue-tied, unforthcoming

volume *noun* **1** = **capacity**, compass, cubic content, dimensions **2** = **amount**, aggregate, body, bulk, mass, quantity, total **3** = **book**, publication, title, tome, treatise

voluminous *adjective* **1** = **large**, ample, big, billowing, bulky, capacious, cavernous, full, massive, roomy, vast **2** = **copious**, prolific
➤ **Antonyms**
≠**large**: skimpy, slight, small, tiny ≠**copious**: inadequate, insufficient, scanty

voluntarily *adverb* = **willingly**, by choice, freely, off one's own bat, of one's own accord, of one's own free will, without being asked, without prompting

voluntary *adjective* = **unforced**, discretional, discretionary, free, gratuitous, honorary, intended, intentional, optional, spontaneous, uncompelled, unconstrained, unpaid, volunteer, willing
➤ **Antonyms**
automatic, conscripted, forced, instinctive, involuntary, obligatory, unintentional

volunteer *verb* **1** = **offer**, offer one's services, present, proffer, propose, put oneself at (someone's) disposal, step forward **2** = **suggest**, advance, put forward, tender
➤ **Antonyms**
≠**offer**: begrudge, deny, keep, refuse, retain, withdraw, withhold

voluptuary *noun* = **sensualist**, *bon vivant*, epicurean, hedonist, luxury-lover, pleasure seeker, sybarite

voluptuous *adjective* **1** = **buxom**, ample, curvaceous (*informal*), enticing, erotic, full-bosomed, provocative, seductive, shapely **2** = **sensual**, epicurean, hedonistic, licentious, luxurious, pleasure-loving, self-indulgent, sybaritic
➤ **Antonyms**
≠**sensual**: abstemious, ascetic, celibate, rigorous, self-denying, Spartan

voluptuousness *noun* **1** = **curvaceousness** (*informal*), seductiveness, shapeliness **2** = **sensuality**, carnality, licentiousness, opulence

vomit *verb* = **be sick**, barf (*U.S. slang*), bring up, chuck (up) (*slang, chiefly U.S.*), chunder (*slang, chiefly Austral.*), disgorge, eject, emit, heave, puke (*slang*), regurgitate, retch, sick up (*informal*), spew out *or* up, throw up (*informal*)

voracious *adjective* **1** = **gluttonous**, devouring, greedy, hungry, insatiable, omnivorous, ravening, ravenous **2** = **avid**, hungry, insatiable, prodigious, rapacious, uncontrolled, unquenchable
➤ **Antonyms**
≠**avid**: moderate, sated, satisfied, self-controlled, temperate

voracity *noun* **1** = **greed**, hunger, ravenousness **2** = **avidity**, eagerness, hunger, rapacity

vortex *noun* = **whirlpool**, eddy, maelstrom

votary *noun* = **devotee**, adherent, aficionado, believer, disciple, follower

vote *noun* **1** = **poll**, ballot, franchise, plebiscite, referendum, show of hands **2** = **right to vote**, suffrage ◆ *verb* **3** = **cast one's vote**, ballot, elect, go to the polls, opt, return **4** *Informal* = **declare**, judge, pronounce, propose, recommend, suggest

voucher *noun* = **ticket**, coupon, token

vouch for *verb* **1** = **guarantee**, answer for, back, certify, give assurance of, go bail for, stand witness, swear to **2** = **confirm**, affirm, assert, attest to, support, uphold

vouchsafe *verb Old-fashioned* = **grant**, accord, condescend to give, confer, deign, favour (someone) with, yield

vow *noun* **1** = **promise**, oath, pledge, troth (*archaic*) ◆ *verb* **2** = **promise**, affirm, pledge, swear, undertake solemnly

voyage *noun* = **journey**, crossing, cruise, passage, travels, trip

vulgar *adjective* **1** = **crude**, blue, boorish, cheap and nasty, coarse, common, common as muck, dirty, flashy, gaudy, gross, ill-bred, impolite, improper, indecent, indecorous, indelicate, low, nasty, off colour, ribald, risqué, rude, suggestive, tasteless, tawdry, uncouth, unmannerly, unrefined **2** = **vernacular**, general, native, ordinary, unrefined
➤ **Antonyms**
≠**crude**: aristocratic, classical, decorous, elegant, genteel, high-brow, polite, refined, sophisticated, tasteful, upper-class, urbane, well-mannered

vulgarian *noun* = **upstart**, arriviste, boor, churl, *nouveau riche,* parvenu, philistine

vulgarity *noun* = **crudeness**, bad taste, coarseness, crudity, gaudiness, grossness, indecorum, indelicacy, lack of refinement, ribaldry, rudeness, suggestiveness, tastelessness, tawdriness
➤ **Antonyms**
decorum, gentility, good breeding, good manners, good taste, refinement, sensitivity, sophistication, tastefulness

vulnerable *adjective* **1** = **susceptible**, sensitive, tender, thin-skinned, weak **2** = **exposed**, accessible, assailable, defenceless, open to attack, unprotected, wide open
➤ **Antonyms**
≠**susceptible**: immune, impervious, insensitive, thick-skinned ≠**exposed**: guarded, invulnerable, unassailable, well-protected

W w

wad *noun* = **mass**, ball, block, bundle, chunk, hunk, lump, plug, roll

wadding *noun* = **padding**, filler, lining, packing, stuffing

waddle *verb* = **shuffle**, rock, sway, toddle, totter, wobble

wade *verb* **1** = **walk through**, ford, paddle, splash **2 wade in** *or* **into** = **launch oneself at**, assail, attack, get stuck in (*informal*), go for, light into (*informal*), set about, tackle, tear into (*informal*) **3 wade through** = **plough through**, drudge at, labour at, peg away at, toil at, work one's way through

waffle *verb* **1** = **prattle**, blather, jabber, prate, rabbit (on) (*Brit. informal*), verbalize, witter on (*informal*) ♦ *noun* **2** = **verbosity**, blather, jabber, padding, prating, prattle, prolixity, verbiage, wordiness

waft *verb* **1** = **carry**, bear, be carried, convey, drift, float, ride, transmit, transport ♦ *noun* **2** = **current**, breath, breeze, draught, puff, whiff

wag *verb* **1** = **wave**, bob, flutter, nod, oscillate, quiver, rock, shake, stir, vibrate, waggle, wiggle ♦ *noun* **2** = **wave**, bob, flutter, nod, oscillation, quiver, shake, toss, vibration, waggle, wiggle

wage *noun* **1** *Also* **wages** = **payment**, allowance, compensation, earnings, emolument, fee, hire, pay, recompense, remuneration, reward, stipend ♦ *verb* **2** = **engage in**, carry on, conduct, practise, proceed with, prosecute, pursue, undertake

wager *noun* **1** = **bet**, flutter (*Brit. informal*), gamble, pledge, punt (*chiefly Brit.*), stake, venture ♦ *verb* **2** = **bet**, chance, gamble, hazard, lay, pledge, punt (*chiefly Brit.*), put on, risk, speculate, stake, venture

waggle *verb* = **wag**, flutter, oscillate, shake, wave, wiggle, wobble

waif *noun* = **stray**, foundling, orphan

wail *verb* **1** = **cry**, bawl, bemoan, bewail, deplore, grieve, howl, keen, lament, ululate, weep, yowl ♦ *noun* **2** = **cry**, complaint, grief, howl, keen, lament, lamentation, moan, ululation, weeping, yowl

wait *verb* **1** = **remain**, abide, bide one's time, cool one's heels, dally, delay, hang fire, hold back, hold on (*informal*), kick one's heels, linger, mark time, pause, rest, stand by, stay, tarry ♦ *noun* **2** = **delay**, entr'acte, halt, hold-up, interval, pause, rest, stay

> **Antonyms**
verb ≠**remain**: depart, go, go away, leave, move off, quit, set off, take off (*informal*)

waiter, waitress *noun* = **attendant**, server, steward *or* stewardess

wait on *or* **upon** *verb* = **serve**, attend, minister to, tend

waive *verb* = **set aside**, abandon, defer, dispense with, forgo, give up, postpone, put off, refrain from, relinquish, remit, renounce, resign, surrender

> **Antonyms**
claim, demand, insist, maintain, press, profess, pursue, uphold

waiver *noun* = **renunciation**, abandonment, abdication, disclaimer, giving up, relinquishment, remission, resignation, setting aside, surrender

wake¹ *verb* **1** = **awaken**, arise, awake, bestir, come to, get up, rouse, rouse from sleep, stir **2** = **activate**, animate, arouse, awaken, enliven, excite, fire, galvanize, kindle, provoke, quicken, rouse, stimulate, stir up ♦ *noun* **3** = **vigil**, deathwatch, funeral, watch

> **Antonyms**
verb ≠**awaken**: catnap, doze, drop off (*informal*), hibernate, nod off (*informal*), sleep, snooze (*informal*), take a nap

wake² *noun* = **slipstream**, aftermath, backwash, path, track, trail, train, wash, waves

wakeful *adjective* **1** = **sleepless**, insomniac, restless, unsleeping **2** = **watchful**, alert, alive, attentive, heedful, observant, on guard, on the alert, on the lookout, on the qui vive, unsleeping, vigilant, wary

> **Antonyms**
≠**sleepless**: asleep, dormant, dozing ≠**watchful**: dreamy, drowsy, heedless, inattentive, off guard, sleepy

waken *verb* = **awaken**, activate, animate, arouse, awake, be roused, come awake, come to, enliven, fire, galvanize, get up, kindle, quicken, rouse, stimulate, stir

> **Antonyms**
be inactive, doze, lie dormant, nap, repose, sleep, slumber, snooze (*informal*)

walk *verb* **1** = **go**, advance, amble, foot it, go by shanks's pony (*informal*), go on foot, hike, hoof it (*slang*), march, move, pace, perambulate, promenade, saunter, step, stride, stroll, traipse (*informal*), tramp, travel on foot, tread, trek, trudge **2 = escort**, accompany, convoy, take ♦ *noun* **3 = stroll**, constitutional, hike, march, perambulation, promenade, ramble, saunter, traipse (*informal*), tramp, trek, trudge, turn **4 = gait**, carriage, manner of walking, pace, step, stride **5 = path**, aisle, alley, avenue, esplanade, footpath, lane, pathway, pavement, promenade, sidewalk, trail **6 walk of life = profession**, area, arena, calling, career, course, field, line, métier, sphere, trade, vocation

walker *noun* **= pedestrian**, footslogger, hiker, rambler, wayfarer

walkout *noun* **= strike**, industrial action, protest, stoppage

walk out *verb* **1 = leave suddenly**, flounce out, get up and go, storm out, take off (*informal*), vote with one's feet **2 = go on strike**, down tools, stop work, strike, take industrial action, withdraw one's labour **3 walk out on = abandon**, chuck (*informal*), desert, forsake, jilt, leave, leave in the lurch, pack in (*informal*), run away from, strand, throw over
➤ **Antonyms**
≠**abandon:** be loyal to, defend, remain, stand by, stay, stick with, support, uphold

walkover *noun* **= pushover** (*slang*), breeze (*U.S. & Canad. informal*), cakewalk (*informal*), child's play (*informal*), cinch (*slang*), doddle (*Brit. slang*), duck soup (*U.S. slang*), easy victory, picnic (*informal*), piece of cake (*informal*), snap (*informal*)
➤ **Antonyms**
effort, grind (*informal*), labour, ordeal, strain, struggle, trial

wall *noun* **1 = partition**, divider, enclosure, panel, screen **2 = barricade**, breastwork, bulwark, embankment, fortification, palisade, parapet, rampart, stockade **3 = barrier**, block, fence, hedge, impediment, obstacle, obstruction **4 go to the wall** *Informal* **= fail**, be ruined, collapse, fall, go bust (*informal*), go under **5 drive up the wall** *Slang* **= infuriate**, aggravate (*informal*), annoy, dement, derange, drive crazy (*informal*), drive insane, exasperate, get on one's nerves (*informal*), irritate, madden, piss one off (*taboo slang*), send one's head (*slang*), try

wallet *noun* **= holder**, case, notecase, pocketbook, pouch, purse

wallop *verb* **1 = hit**, batter, beat, clobber (*slang*), pound, pummel, strike, swipe, thrash, thump, whack ♦ *noun* **2 = blow**, bash, punch, slug, smack, swipe, thump, thwack, whack

wallow *verb* **1 = revel**, bask, delight, glory, indulge oneself, luxuriate, relish, take

pleasure **2 = roll about**, lie, splash around, tumble, welter
➤ **Antonyms**
≠**revel:** abstain, avoid, do without, eschew, forgo, give up, refrain

wan *adjective* **1 = pale**, anaemic, ashen, bloodless, cadaverous, colourless, discoloured, ghastly, like death warmed up (*informal*), livid, pallid, pasty, sickly, washed out, waxen, wheyfaced, white **2 = dim**, faint, feeble, pale, weak
➤ **Antonyms**
≠**pale:** blooming, bright, flourishing, glowing, healthy, roseate, rosy, rubicund, ruddy, vibrant

wand *noun* **= stick**, baton, rod, sprig, twig, withe, withy

wander *verb* **1 = roam**, cruise, drift, knock about *or* around, meander, mooch around (*slang*), peregrinate, ramble, range, rove, straggle, stravaig (*Scot. & Northern English dialect*), stray, stroll, traipse (*informal*) **2 = deviate**, depart, digress, divagate (*rare*), diverge, err, get lost, go astray, go off at a tangent, go off course, lapse, lose concentration, lose one's train of thought, lose one's way, swerve, veer **3 = rave**, babble, be delirious, be incoherent, ramble, speak incoherently, talk nonsense ♦ *noun* **4 = excursion**, cruise, meander, peregrination, ramble, traipse (*informal*)
➤ **Antonyms**
verb ≠**deviate:** comply, conform, fall in with, follow, run with the pack, toe the line

wanderer *noun* **= traveller**, bird of passage, drifter, gypsy, itinerant, nomad, rambler, ranger, rolling stone, rover, stroller, vagabond, vagrant, voyager

wandering *adjective* **= nomadic**, drifting, homeless, itinerant, migratory, peripatetic, rambling, rootless, roving, strolling, travelling, vagabond, vagrant, voyaging, wayfaring

wane *verb* **1 = decline**, abate, atrophy, decrease, die out, dim, diminish, draw to a close, drop, dwindle, ebb, fade, fade away, fail, lessen, sink, subside, taper off, weaken, wind down, wither ♦ *noun* **2 on the wane = declining**, at its lowest ebb, dropping, dwindling, dying out, ebbing, fading, lessening, obsolescent, on its last legs, on the decline, on the way out, subsiding, tapering off, weakening, withering
➤ **Antonyms**
verb ≠**decline:** blossom, brighten, develop, expand, grow, improve, increase, rise, strengthen, wax

wangle *verb* **= contrive**, arrange, engineer, fiddle (*informal*), fix (*informal*), manipulate, manoeuvre, pull off

want *verb* **1** = **desire**, covet, crave, eat one's heart out over, feel a need for, hanker after, have a fancy for, have a yen for (*informal*), hope for, hunger for, long for, pine for, set one's heart on, thirst for, wish, would give one's eyeteeth for, yearn for **2** = **need**, be able to do with, be deficient in, be short of, be without, call for, demand, fall short in, have need of, lack, miss, require, stand in need of ♦ *noun* **3** = **wish**, appetite, craving, demand, desire, fancy, hankering, hunger, longing, necessity, need, requirement, thirst, yearning, yen (*informal*) **4** = **lack**, absence, dearth, default, deficiency, famine, insufficiency, paucity, scantiness, scarcity, shortage **5** = **poverty**, destitution, indigence, need, neediness, pauperism, penury, privation
➤ **Antonyms**
verb ≠**desire**: detest, dislike, hate, loathe, reject, spurn ≠**need**: be sated, have, own, possess ♦ *noun* ≠**lack**: abundance, adequacy, excess, plenty, sufficiency, surfeit, surplus ≠**poverty**: comfort, ease, luxury, wealth

wanting *adjective* **1** = **lacking**, absent, incomplete, less, missing, short, shy **2** = **inadequate**, defective, deficient, disappointing, faulty, imperfect, inferior, leaving much to be desired, not good enough, not much cop (*Brit. slang*), not up to expectations, not up to par, patchy, pathetic, poor, sketchy, substandard, unsound
➤ **Antonyms**
≠**lacking**: complete, full, replete, saturated ≠**inadequate**: adequate, enough, satisfactory, sufficient

wanton *adjective* **1** = **unprovoked**, arbitrary, cruel, evil, gratuitous, groundless, malevolent, malicious, motiveless, needless, senseless, spiteful, uncalled-for, unjustifiable, unjustified, vicious, wicked, wilful **2** = **promiscuous**, abandoned, dissipated, dissolute, fast, immoral, lecherous, lewd, libertine, libidinous, licentious, loose, lustful, of easy virtue, rakish, shameless, unchaste **3** = **reckless**, careless, devil-may-care, extravagant, heedless, immoderate, intemperate, lavish, outrageous, rash, unrestrained, wild ♦ *noun* **4** = **slut**, harlot, loose woman, prostitute, scrubber (*Brit. & Austral. slang*), slag (*Brit. slang*), strumpet, swinger (*informal*), tart, trollop, whore, woman of easy virtue
➤ **Antonyms**
adjective ≠**unprovoked**: called-for, excusable, justified, legitimate, motivated, provoked, warranted ≠**promiscuous**: overmodest, priggish, prim, prudish, puritanical, rigid, strait-laced, stuffy, Victorian ≠**reckless**: cautious, circumspect, guarded,

inhibited, moderate, prudent, reserved, restrained, temperate

war *noun* **1** = **fighting**, armed conflict, battle, bloodshed, combat, conflict, contention, contest, enmity, hostilities, hostility, strife, struggle, warfare ♦ *verb* **2** = **fight**, battle, campaign against, carry on hostilities, clash, combat, conduct a war, contend, contest, make war, strive, struggle, take up arms, wage war
➤ **Antonyms**
noun ≠**fighting**: accord, armistice, ceasefire, co-existence, compliance, co-operation, harmony, peace, peace-time, treaty, truce ♦ *verb* ≠**fight**: call a ceasefire, co-exist, co-operate, make peace

warble *verb* = **sing**, chirp, trill, twitter

war cry *noun* = **battle cry**, rallying cry, slogan, war whoop

ward *noun* **1** = **room**, apartment, cubicle **2** = **district**, area, division, precinct, quarter, zone **3** = **dependant**, charge, minor, protégé, pupil

warden *noun* = **keeper**, administrator, caretaker, curator, custodian, guardian, janitor, ranger, steward, superintendent, warder, watchman

warder, wardress *noun* = **jailer**, custodian, guard, keeper, prison officer, screw (*slang*), turnkey (*archaic*)

ward off *verb* = **repel**, avert, avoid, beat off, block, deflect, fend off, forestall, keep at arm's length, keep at bay, parry, stave off, thwart, turn aside, turn away
➤ **Antonyms**
accept, admit, allow, embrace, permit, receive, take in, welcome

wardrobe *noun* **1** = **clothes cupboard**, closet, clothes-press **2** = **clothes**, apparel, attire, collection of clothes, outfit

warehouse *noun* = **store**, depository, depot, stockroom, storehouse

wares *plural noun* = **goods**, commodities, lines, manufactures, merchandise, produce, products, stock, stuff

warfare *noun* = **war**, armed conflict, armed struggle, arms, battle, blows, campaigning, clash of arms, combat, conflict, contest, discord, fighting, hostilities, passage of arms, strategy, strife, struggle
➤ **Antonyms**
accord, amity, armistice, ceasefire, cessation of hostilities, conciliation, harmony, peace, treaty, truce

warily *adverb* = **cautiously**, cagily (*informal*), carefully, charily, circumspectly, distrustfully, gingerly, guardedly, suspiciously, vigilantly, watchfully, with care
➤ **Antonyms**
carelessly, hastily, heedlessly, irresponsibly,

rashly, recklessly, thoughtlessly, unwarily

wariness *noun* = **caution**, alertness, attention, caginess (*informal*), care, carefulness, circumspection, discretion, distrust, foresight, heedfulness, mindfulness, prudence, suspicion, vigilance, watchfulness
➤ **Antonyms**
carelessness, heedlessness, inattention, mindlessness, negligence, oblivion, recklessness, thoughtlessness

warlike *adjective* = **belligerent**, aggressive, bellicose, bloodthirsty, combative, hawkish, hostile, inimical, jingoistic, martial, militaristic, military, pugnacious, sabre-rattling, unfriendly, warmongering
➤ **Antonyms**
amicable, conciliatory, friendly, nonbelligerent, pacific, peaceable, peaceful, placid, unwarlike

warlock *noun* = **magician**, conjuror, enchanter, sorcerer, wizard

warm *adjective* **1** = **heated**, balmy, lukewarm, moderately hot, pleasant, sunny, tepid, thermal **2** = **affectionate**, affable, amiable, amorous, cheerful, congenial, cordial, friendly, genial, happy, hearty, hospitable, kindly, likable *or* likeable, loving, pleasant, tender ◆ *verb* **3** = **heat**, heat up, melt, thaw, warm up **4** = **rouse**, animate, awaken, excite, get going, interest, make enthusiastic, put some life into, stimulate, stir, turn on (*slang*)
➤ **Antonyms**
adjective ≠**heated**: chilly, cold, cool, freezing, icy ≠**affectionate**: aloof, apathetic, cold, cool, distant, half-hearted, hostile, phlegmatic, remote, stand-offish, uncaring, unenthusiastic, unfriendly, unwelcoming ◆ *verb* ≠**heat**: chill, cool, cool down, freeze ≠**rouse**: alienate, depress, sadden

warm-blooded *adjective* = **passionate**, ardent, earnest, emotional, enthusiastic, excitable, fervent, impetuous, lively, rash, spirited, vivacious

warm-hearted *adjective* = **kindly**, affectionate, compassionate, cordial, generous, kind-hearted, loving, sympathetic, tender, tender-hearted
➤ **Antonyms**
callous, cold, cold-hearted, hard, hard-hearted, harsh, heartless, insensitive, mean, merciless, unfeeling, unsympathetic

warmonger *noun* = **hawk**, belligerent, jingo, militarist, sabre-rattler

warmth *noun* **1** = **heat**, hotness, warmness **2** = **affection**, affability, amorousness, cheerfulness, cordiality, happiness, heartiness, hospitableness, kindliness, love, tenderness
➤ **Antonyms**
≠**heat**: chill, chilliness, cold, coldness,

coolness, iciness ≠**affection**: aloofness, apathy, austerity, cold-heartedness, hard-heartedness, hostility, indifference, insincerity, lack of enthusiasm, remoteness, sternness

warn *verb* = **notify**, admonish, advise, alert, apprise, caution, forewarn, give fair warning, give notice, inform, make (someone) aware, put one on one's guard, summon, tip off

warning *noun* **1** = **caution**, admonition, advice, alarm, alert, augury, caveat, foretoken, hint, notice, notification, omen, premonition, presage, sign, signal, threat, tip, tip-off, token, word, word to the wise ◆ *adjective* **2** = **cautionary**, admonitory, bodeful, monitory, ominous, premonitory, threatening

warp *verb* **1** = **twist**, bend, contort, deform, distort ◆ *noun* **2** = **twist**, bend, contortion, distortion, kink

warrant *noun* **1** = **authorization**, assurance, authority, carte blanche, commission, guarantee, licence, permission, permit, pledge, sanction, security, warranty ◆ *verb* **2** = **call for**, approve, authorize, commission, demand, deserve, empower, entail, entitle, excuse, give ground for, justify, license, necessitate, permit, require, sanction **3** = **guarantee**, affirm, answer for, assure, attest, avouch, certify, declare, pledge, secure, stand behind, underwrite, uphold, vouch for

warrantable *adjective* = **justifiable**, accountable, allowable, defensible, lawful, necessary, permissible, proper, reasonable, right
➤ **Antonyms**
indefensible, uncalled-for, undue, unjustifiable, unnecessary, unreasonable, unwarrantable, wrong

warranty *noun* = **guarantee**, assurance, bond, certificate, contract, covenant, pledge

warrior *noun* = **soldier**, champion, combatant, fighter, fighting man, gladiator, man-at-arms

wary *adjective* = **cautious**, alert, attentive, cagey (*informal*), careful, chary, circumspect, distrustful, guarded, heedful, leery (*slang*), on one's guard, on the lookout, on the qui vive, prudent, suspicious, vigilant, watchful, wide-awake
➤ **Antonyms**
careless, foolhardy, imprudent, negligent, rash, reckless, remiss, unguarded, unsuspecting, unwary

wash *verb* **1** = **clean**, bath, bathe, cleanse, launder, moisten, rinse, scrub, shampoo, shower, wet **2** = **sweep away**, bear away, carry off, erode, move, wash off **3** *Informal* = **be plausible**, bear scrutiny, be convincing, carry weight, hold up, hold water, stand up, stick **4 wash one's hands of** = have **nothing to do with**, abandon, accept no responsibility for, give up on, leave to one's own devices ✦ *noun* **5** = **cleaning**, ablution, bath, bathe, cleansing, laundering, rinse, scrub, shampoo, shower, washing **6** = **coat**, coating, film, layer, overlay, screen, stain, suffusion **7** = **swell**, ebb and flow, flow, roll, surge, sweep, wave

washed-out *adjective* **1** = **exhausted**, all in (*slang*), clapped out (*Austral. & N.Z. informal*), dead on one's feet (*informal*), dog-tired (*informal*), done in (*informal*), drained, drawn, fatigued, haggard, knackered (*slang*), pale, spent, tired-out, wan, weary, wiped out (*informal*), worn-out, zonked (*slang*) **2** = **faded**, blanched, bleached, colourless, etiolated, flat, lacklustre, mat, pale
➤ **Antonyms**
≠**exhausted**: alert, chirpy, energetic, full of beans (*informal*), full of pep (*informal*), lively, perky, refreshed, sprightly, zippy (*informal*)

washout *noun* **1** = **failure**, clunker (*informal*), disappointment, disaster, dud (*informal*), fiasco, flop (*informal*), mess **2** = **loser**, failure, incompetent
➤ **Antonyms**
≠**failure**: conquest, feat, success, triumph, victory, winner

waspish *adjective* = **bad-tempered**, cantankerous, captious, crabbed, crabby, cross, crotchety (*informal*), fretful, grumpy, ill-tempered, irascible, irritable, liverish, peevish, peppery, pettish, petulant, ratty (*Brit. & N.Z. informal*), snappish, splenetic, testy, tetchy, touchy, waxy (*informal, chiefly Brit.*)
➤ **Antonyms**
affable, agreeable, cheerful, easy-going, genial, good-humoured, good-natured, jovial, pleasant

waste *verb* **1** = **squander**, blow (*slang*), dissipate, fritter away, frivol away (*informal*), lavish, misuse, run through, throw away **2 waste away** = **decline**, atrophy, consume, corrode, crumble, debilitate, decay, deplete, disable, drain, dwindle, eat away, ebb, emaciate, enfeeble, exhaust, fade, gnaw, perish, sap the strength of, sink, undermine, wane, wear out, wither ✦ *noun* **3** = **squandering**, dissipation, expenditure, extravagance, frittering away, loss, lost opportunity, misapplication, misuse, prodigality, unthriftiness, wastefulness **4** = **rubbish**, debris, dregs, dross, garbage, leavings, leftovers, litter, offal, offscourings, refuse, scrap, sweepings, trash **5 wastes** = **desert**, solitude, void, wasteland, wild,

wilderness ✦ *adjective* **6** = **unwanted**, leftover, superfluous, supernumerary, unused, useless, worthless **7** = **uncultivated**, bare, barren, desolate, devastated, dismal, dreary, empty, uninhabited, unproductive, wild **8 lay waste** = **devastate**, depredate (*rare*), despoil, destroy, pillage, rape, ravage, raze, ruin, sack, spoil, total (*slang*), trash (*slang*), undo, wreak havoc upon
➤ **Antonyms**
verb ≠**squander**: conserve, economize, husband, preserve, protect, save ≠**decline**: build, develop, increase, rally, strengthen ✦ *noun* ≠**squandering**: economy, frugality, good housekeeping, saving, thrift ✦ *adjective* ≠**unwanted**: necessary, needed, utilized ≠**uncultivated**: arable, developed, fruitful, habitable, in use, productive, verdant

wasteful *adjective* = **extravagant**, improvident, lavish, prodigal, profligate, ruinous, spendthrift, thriftless, uneconomical, unthrifty
➤ **Antonyms**
economical, frugal, money-saving, parsimonious, penny-wise, provident, sparing, thrifty

waster *noun* = **layabout**, good-for-nothing, idler, loafer, ne'er-do-well, shirker, skiver (*Brit. slang*), wastrel

wastrel *noun* **1** = **layabout**, drone, good-for-nothing, idler, loafer, loser, malingerer, ne'er-do-well, shirker, skiver (*Brit. slang*), waster **2** = **spendthrift**, prodigal, profligate, squanderer

watch *verb* **1** = **look at**, check, check out (*informal*), clock (*Brit. slang*), contemplate, eye, eyeball (*slang*), feast one's eyes on, gaze at, get a load of (*informal*), look, look on, mark, note, observe, pay attention, peer at, regard, see, stare at, take a dekko at (*Brit. slang*), view **2** = **guard**, keep, look after, mind, protect, superintend, take care of, tend **3** = **be vigilant**, attend, be on the alert, be on the lookout, be wary, be watchful, keep an eye open (*informal*), look out, take heed, wait ✦ *noun* **4** = **wristwatch**, chronometer, clock, pocket watch, timepiece **5** = **lookout**, alertness, attention, eye, heed, inspection, notice, observation, supervision, surveillance, vigil, vigilance, watchfulness

watchdog *noun* **1** = **guard dog 2** = **guardian**, custodian, inspector, monitor, protector, scrutineer

watcher *noun* = **viewer**, fly on the wall, looker-on, lookout, observer, onlooker, spectator, spy, witness

watchful *adjective* = **alert**, attentive, circumspect, guarded, heedful, observant, on one's guard, on one's toes, on the lookout, on the qui vive, on the watch, suspicious, vigilant, wary, wide awake

> ➤ **Antonyms**
careless, inattentive, reckless, thoughtless, unaware, unguarded, unmindful, unobservant, unwary

watchfulness *noun* = **vigilance**, alertness, attention, attentiveness, caution, cautiousness, circumspection, heedfulness, wariness
> ➤ **Antonyms**
carelessness, heedlessness, inattention, indiscretion, irresponsibility, neglect, recklessness, thoughtlessness

watchman *noun* = **guard**, caretaker, custodian, security guard, security man

watch out *verb* = **be careful**, be alert, be on one's guard, be on the alert, be on (the) watch, be vigilant, be watchful, have a care, keep a sharp lookout, keep a weather eye open, keep one's eyes open, keep one's eyes peeled *or* skinned (*informal*), look out, mind out, watch oneself

watch over *verb* **1** = **look after**, defend, guard, keep safe, preserve, protect, shelter, shield, stand guard over **2** = **superintend**, direct, keep an eye on, oversee, preside over

watchword *noun* **1** = **motto**, battle cry, byword, catch phrase, catchword, maxim, rallying cry, slogan, tag-line **2** = **password**, countersign, magic word, shibboleth

water *noun* **1** = **liquid**, Adam's ale *or* wine, aqua, H₂O **2 hold water** = **be sound**, bear examination *or* scrutiny, be credible, be logical, make sense, pass the test, ring true, work **3 of the first water** = **excellent**, of the best, of the best quality, of the finest quality, of the highest degree, of the highest grade ◆ *verb* **4** = **moisten**, damp, dampen, douse, drench, flood, hose, irrigate, soak, souse, spray, sprinkle **5** = **dilute**, add water to, adulterate, put water in, thin, water down, weaken

water down *verb* **1** = **dilute**, add water to, adulterate, put water in, thin, water, weaken **2** = **weaken**, adulterate, mitigate, qualify, soften, tone down
> ➤ **Antonyms**
≠dilute: fortify, purify, strengthen, thicken

waterfall *noun* = **cascade**, cataract, chute, fall, force (*Northern English dialect*), linn (*Scot.*)

waterlogged *adjective* = **soaked**, drenched, dripping, droukit *or* drookit (*Scot.*), saturated, sodden, sopping, streaming, wet through, wringing wet

watertight *adjective* **1** = **waterproof**, sound **2** = **foolproof**, airtight, firm, flawless, impregnable, incontrovertible, sound, unassailable
> ➤ **Antonyms**
≠waterproof: leaky ≠foolproof: defective,

flawed, questionable, shaky, tenuous, uncertain, unsound, weak

watery *adjective* **1** = **wet**, aqueous, damp, fluid, humid, liquid, marshy, moist, soggy, squelchy **2** = **tearful**, rheumy, tear-filled, weepy **3** = **diluted**, adulterated, dilute, flavourless, insipid, runny, tasteless, thin, washy, watered-down, waterish, weak, wishy-washy (*informal*)
> ➤ **Antonyms**
≠diluted: concentrated, condensed, dense, fortified, solid, strong, thick

wave *verb* **1** = **signal**, beckon, direct, gesticulate, gesture, indicate, sign **2** = **brandish**, flap, flourish, flutter, move to and fro, oscillate, quiver, ripple, shake, stir, sway, swing, undulate, wag, waver, wield ◆ *noun* **3** = **ripple**, billow, breaker, comber, ridge, roller, sea surf, swell, undulation, unevenness **4** = **outbreak**, current, drift, flood, ground swell, movement, rash, rush, stream, surge, sweep, tendency, trend, upsurge

waver *verb* **1** = **hesitate**, be indecisive, be irresolute, be unable to decide, be unable to make up one's mind, blow hot and cold (*informal*), dither (*chiefly Brit.*), falter, fluctuate, hum and haw, seesaw, shillyshally (*informal*), swither (*Scot.*), vacillate **2** = **tremble**, flicker, fluctuate, quiver, reel, shake, sway, totter, undulate, vary, wave, weave, wobble
> ➤ **Antonyms**
≠hesitate: be decisive, be determined, be of fixed opinion, be resolute, determine, resolve, stand firm

wax *verb* = **increase**, become fuller, become larger, develop, dilate, enlarge, expand, fill out, get bigger, grow, magnify, mount, rise, swell
> ➤ **Antonyms**
contract, decline, decrease, diminish, dwindle, fade, lessen, narrow, shrink, wane

way *noun* **1** = **method**, approach, course of action, fashion, manner, means, mode, plan, practice, procedure, process, scheme, system, technique **2** = **style**, characteristic, conduct, custom, habit, idiosyncrasy, manner, nature, personality, practice, trait, usage, wont **3** = **aspect**, detail, feature, particular, point, respect, sense **4** = **route**, access, avenue, channel, course, direction, highway, lane, path, pathway, road, street, thoroughfare, track, trail **5** = **journey**, advance, approach, march, passage, progress **6** = **distance**, journey, length, stretch, trail **7** = **room**, elbowroom, opening, space **8** *As in* **get one's own way** = **will**, aim, ambition, choice, demand, desire, goal, pleasure, wish **9** *As in* **in a bad way**

= **condition**, circumstance, fettle, shape (*informal*), situation, state, status **10 by the way** = **incidentally**, by the bye, en passant, in parenthesis, in passing **11 give way: a** = **collapse**, break down, cave in, crack, crumple, fall, fall to pieces, give, go to pieces, subside **b** = **concede**, accede, acknowledge defeat, acquiesce, back down, make concessions, withdraw, yield **12 under way** = **in progress**, afoot, begun, going, in motion, moving, on the go (*informal*), on the move, started

wayfarer *noun* = **traveller**, bird of passage, globetrotter, gypsy, itinerant, journeyer, nomad, rover, trekker, voyager, walker, wanderer

wayfaring *adjective* = **roving**, drifting, itinerant, journeying, nomadic, peripatetic, rambling, travelling, voyaging, walking, wandering

waylay *verb* = **attack**, accost, ambush, catch, hold up, intercept, lie in wait for, pounce on, set upon, surprise, swoop down on

wayward *adjective* = **erratic**, capricious, changeable, contrary, contumacious, cross-grained, disobedient, fickle, flighty, froward (*archaic*), headstrong, inconstant, incorrigible, insubordinate, intractable, mulish, obdurate, obstinate, perverse, rebellious, refractory, self-willed, stubborn, undependable, ungovernable, unmanageable, unpredictable, unruly, wilful
➤ **Antonyms**
complaisant, compliant, dependable, good-natured, malleable, manageable, obedient, obliging, predictable, reliable, submissive, tractable

weak *adjective* **1** = **feeble**, anaemic, debilitated, decrepit, delicate, effete, enervated, exhausted, faint, fragile, frail, infirm, languid, puny, shaky, sickly, spent, tender, unsound, unsteady, wasted, weakly **2** = **deficient**, faulty, inadequate, lacking, pathetic, poor, substandard, under-strength, wanting **3** = **unsafe**, defenceless, exposed, helpless, unguarded, unprotected, untenable, vulnerable, wide open **4** = **irresolute**, boneless, cowardly, impotent, indecisive, ineffectual, infirm, namby-pamby, pathetic, powerless, soft, spineless, timorous, weak-kneed (*informal*) **5** = **unconvincing**, feeble, flimsy, hollow, inconclusive, invalid, lame, pathetic, shallow, slight, unsatisfactory **6** = **faint**, distant, dull, imperceptible, low, muffled, poor, quiet, slight, small, soft **7** = **tasteless**, diluted, insipid, milk-and-water, runny, thin, under-strength, waterish, watery, wishy-washy (*informal*)
➤ **Antonyms**
≠**feeble**: energetic, hardy, healthy, hefty,

mighty, strong, tough ≠**deficient**: able, capable, effective ≠**unsafe**: invulnerable, safe, secure, well-defended ≠**irresolute**: firm, resolute ≠**unconvincing**: conclusive, convincing, forceful, incontrovertible, obvious, powerful, solid, trustworthy, valid ≠**tasteless**: flavoursome, intoxicating, potent, tasty

weaken *verb* **1** = **lessen**, abate, debilitate, depress, diminish, droop, dwindle, ease up, enervate, fade, fail, flag, give way, impair, invalidate, lower, mitigate, moderate, reduce, sap, sap the strength of, soften up, take the edge off, temper, tire, undermine, wane **2** = **dilute**, adulterate, cut, debase, thin, thin out, water down
➤ **Antonyms**
≠**lessen**: boost, enhance, grow, improve, increase, invigorate, revitalize, strengthen

weakling *noun* = **sissy**, coward, doormat (*slang*), drip (*informal*), jellyfish (*informal*), jessie (*Scot. slang*), milksop, mouse, wet (*Brit. informal*), wimp (*informal*), wuss (*slang*)

weakness *noun* **1** = **frailty**, debility, decrepitude, enervation, faintness, feebleness, fragility, impotence, infirmity, irresolution, powerlessness, vulnerability **2** = **failing**, Achilles heel, blemish, chink in one's armour, defect, deficiency, fault, flaw, imperfection, lack, shortcoming **3** = **liking**, fondness, inclination, partiality, passion, penchant, predilection, proclivity, proneness, soft spot
➤ **Antonyms**
≠**frailty**: hardiness, health, impregnability, potency, power, stamina, sturdiness, validity, vigour, virtue, vitality ≠**failing**: advantage, forte, strength, strong point ≠**liking**: aversion, dislike, hatred, loathing

wealth *noun* **1** = **riches**, affluence, assets, big bucks (*informal, chiefly U.S.*), big money, capital, cash, estate, fortune, funds, goods, lucre, means, megabucks (*U.S. & Canad. slang*), money, opulence, pelf, possessions, pretty penny (*informal*), property, prosperity, resources, substance, tidy sum (*informal*), wad (*U.S. & Canad. slang*) **2** = **plenty**, abundance, bounty, copiousness, cornucopia, fullness, plenitude, profusion, richness, store
➤ **Antonyms**
≠**riches**: deprivation, destitution, indigence, penury, poverty ≠**plenty**: dearth, lack, need, paucity, poverty, scarcity, shortage, want

wealthy *adjective* = **rich**, affluent, comfortable, filthy rich, flush (*informal*), in the money (*informal*), loaded (*slang*), made of money (*informal*), moneyed, on Easy Street (*informal*), opulent, prosperous, quids in (*slang*), rolling in it (*slang*), stinking rich (*slang*), well-heeled (*informal*), well-off, well-to-do

➤ **Antonyms**

broke (*informal*), deprived, destitute, dirt-poor (*informal*), down and out, down at heel, flat broke (*informal*), impoverished, indigent, needy, on the breadline, penniless, poor, poverty-stricken, short, skint (*Brit. slang*), without two pennies to rub together (*informal*)

wear *verb* 1 = **be dressed in**, bear, be clothed in, carry, clothe oneself, don, dress in, have on, put on, sport (*informal*) 2 = **show**, display, exhibit, fly 3 = **deteriorate**, abrade, consume, corrode, erode, fray, grind, impair, rub, use, wash away, waste 4 *Brit. informal* = **accept**, allow, brook, countenance, fall for, permit, put up with (*informal*), stand for, stomach, swallow (*informal*), take 5 **wear well** = **last**, bear up, be durable, endure, hold up, stand up ♦ *noun* 6 = **clothes**, apparel, attire, costume, dress, garb, garments, gear (*informal*), habit, outfit, things, threads (*slang*) 7 = **damage**, abrasion, attrition, corrosion, depreciation, deterioration, erosion, friction, use, wear and tear 8 = **usefulness**, employment, mileage (*informal*), service, use, utility

➤ **Antonyms**

noun ≠**damage**: conservation, maintenance, preservation, repair, upkeep

wear down *verb* 1 = **erode**, abrade, be consumed, consume, corrode, grind down, rub away 2 = **undermine**, chip away at (*informal*), fight a war of attrition against, overcome gradually, reduce

weariness *noun* = **tiredness**, drowsiness, enervation, exhaustion, fatigue, languor, lassitude, lethargy, listlessness, prostration

➤ **Antonyms**

drive, energy, freshness, get-up-and-go (*informal*), liveliness, stamina, vigour, vitality, zeal, zest

wearing *adjective* = **tiresome**, exasperating, exhausting, fatiguing, irksome, oppressive, taxing, tiring, trying, wearisome

➤ **Antonyms**

easy, effortless, light, no bother, painless, refreshing, stimulating, undemanding

wearisome *adjective* = **tedious**, annoying, boring, bothersome, burdensome, dull, exasperating, exhausting, fatiguing, humdrum, irksome, mind-numbing, monotonous, oppressive, pestilential, prosaic, tiresome, troublesome, trying, uninteresting, vexatious, wearing

➤ **Antonyms**

agreeable, delightful, enjoyable, exhilarating, interesting, invigorating, pleasurable,

refreshing, stimulating

wear off *verb* 1 = **subside**, abate, decrease, diminish, disappear, dwindle, ebb, fade, lose effect, lose strength, peter out, wane, weaken 2 = **rub away**, abrade, disappear, efface, fade

➤ **Antonyms**

≠**subside**: grow, increase, intensify, magnify, persist, step up, strengthen, wax

wear out *verb* 1 = **deteriorate**, become useless, become worn, consume, erode, fray, impair, use up, wear through 2 *Informal* = **exhaust**, enervate, fag out (*informal*), fatigue, frazzle (*informal*), knacker (*slang*), prostrate, sap, tire, weary

➤ **Antonyms**

≠**exhaust**: buck up (*informal*), energize, invigorate, pep up, perk up, refresh, revitalize, stimulate, strengthen

weary *adjective* 1 = **tired**, all in (*slang*), asleep *or* dead on one's feet (*informal*), clapped out (*Austral. & N.Z. informal*), dead beat (*informal*), dog-tired (*informal*), done in (*informal*), drained, drooping, drowsy, enervated, exhausted, fagged (*informal*), fatigued, flagging, jaded, knackered (*slang*), ready to drop, sleepy, spent, wearied, whacked (*Brit. informal*), worn out, zonked (*slang*) 2 = **fed up**, bored, browned-off (*informal*), discontented, impatient, indifferent, jaded, sick (*informal*), sick and tired (*informal*) 3 = **tiring**, arduous, enervative, irksome, laborious, taxing, tiresome, wearing, wearisome ♦ *verb* 4 = **tire**, burden, debilitate, drain, droop, enervate, fade, fag (*informal*), fail, fatigue, grow tired, sap, take it out of (*informal*), tax, tire out, wear out 5 = **bore**, annoy, become bored, exasperate, have had enough, irk, jade, make discontented, plague, sicken, try the patience of, vex

➤ **Antonyms**

adjective ≠**tired**: energetic, fresh, full of beans (*informal*), full of get-up-and-go (*informal*), invigorated, lively, refreshed, stimulated ≠**fed up**: amused, excited, forebearing, patient ≠**tiring**: exciting, invigorating, original, refreshing ♦ *verb* ≠**tire**: enliven, invigorate, refresh, revive, stimulate ≠**bore**: amuse, excite, interest

weather *noun* 1 = **climate**, conditions 2 **under the weather**: **a** = **ill**, ailing, below par, indisposed, nauseous, not well, off-colour, out of sorts, poorly (*informal*), seedy (*informal*), sick **b** = **hung over** (*informal*), crapulent, crapulous, drunk, groggy (*informal*), inebriated, intoxicated, one over the eight (*slang*), rat-arsed (*taboo slang*), the worse for drink, three sheets in the wind (*informal*), under the influence (*informal*) ♦ *verb* 3 = **toughen**, expose,

harden, season **4** = **withstand**, bear up against, brave, come through, endure, get through, live through, make it (*informal*), overcome, pull through, resist, ride out, rise above, stand, stick it out (*informal*), suffer, surmount, survive
➤ **Antonyms**
verb ≠ withstand: cave in, collapse, fail, fall, give in, go under, succumb, surrender, yield

weave *verb* **1** = **knit**, blend, braid, entwine, fuse, incorporate, interlace, intermingle, intertwine, introduce, mat, merge, plait, twist, unite **2** = **create**, build, construct, contrive, fabricate, make, make up, put together, spin **3** = **zigzag**, crisscross, move in and out, weave one's way, wind **4 get weaving** *Informal* = **start**, get a move on, get going, get one's finger out (*Brit. informal*), get under way, hurry, make a start, shake a leg (*slang*)

web *noun* **1** = **spider's web**, cobweb **2** = **network**, interlacing, lattice, mesh, net, netting, screen, tangle, toils, weave, webbing

wed *verb* **1** = **marry**, become man and wife, be married to, espouse, get hitched (*slang*), get married, join, make one, plight one's troth (*old-fashioned*), splice (*informal*), take as one's husband, take as one's wife, take the plunge (*informal*), take to wife, tie the knot (*informal*), unite **2** = **unite**, ally, blend, coalesce, combine, commingle, dedicate, fuse, interweave, join, link, marry, merge, unify, yoke
➤ **Antonyms**
≠ **unite:** break up, disunite, divide, divorce, part, separate, sever, split

wedding *noun* = **marriage**, espousals, marriage ceremony, nuptial rite, nuptials, wedlock

wedge *noun* **1** = **block**, chock, chunk, lump, wodge (*Brit. informal*) ◆ *verb* **2** = **squeeze**, block, cram, crowd, force, jam, lodge, pack, ram, split, stuff, thrust

wedlock *noun* = **marriage**, matrimony

weed out *verb* = **eliminate**, dispense with, eradicate, extirpate, get rid of, remove, root out, separate out, shed, uproot

weedy *adjective* = **weak**, feeble, frail, ineffectual, namby-pamby, puny, skinny, thin

weekly *adjective* **1** = **once a week**, hebdomadal, hebdomadary ◆ *adverb* **2** = **every week**, by the week, hebdomadally, once a week

weep *verb* = **cry**, bemoan, bewail, blub (*slang*), blubber, boohoo, complain, greet (*Scot. or archaic*), keen, lament, moan, mourn, shed tears, snivel, sob, ululate, whimper, whinge (*informal*)
➤ **Antonyms**
be glad, celebrate, delight, exult, make

merry, rejoice, revel, triumph

weigh *verb* **1** = **have a weight of**, measure the weight of, put on the scales, tip the scales at (*informal*) **2** = **measure**, apportion, deal out, dole out **3** = **consider**, contemplate, deliberate upon, evaluate, examine, eye up, give thought to, meditate upon, mull over, ponder, reflect upon, study, think over **4** = **matter**, be influential, carry weight, count, cut any ice (*informal*), have influence, impress, tell

weigh down *verb* = **burden**, bear down, depress, get down, oppress, overburden, overload, press down, trouble, weigh upon, worry
➤ **Antonyms**
alleviate, ease, hearten, help, lift, lighten, refresh, relieve, unburden

weigh on *verb* = **oppress**, bear down, burden, prey

weight *noun* **1** = **heaviness**, avoirdupois, burden, gravity, heft (*informal*), load, mass, poundage, pressure, tonnage **2** = **load**, ballast, heavy object, mass **3** = **preponderance**, greatest force, main force, onus **4** = **importance**, authority, bottom, clout (*informal*), consequence, consideration, efficacy, emphasis, impact, import, influence, moment, persuasiveness, power, significance, substance, value **5** = **burden**, albatross, load, millstone, oppression, pressure, strain ◆ *verb* **6** = **load**, add weight to, ballast, charge, freight, increase the load on, increase the weight of, make heavier **7** = **bias**, load, slant, unbalance **8** = **burden**, encumber, handicap, impede, oppress, overburden, weigh down

weighty *adjective* **1** = **important**, consequential, considerable, critical, crucial, forcible, grave, momentous, portentous, serious, significant, solemn, substantial **2** = **heavy**, burdensome, cumbersome, dense, hefty (*informal*), massive, ponderous **3** = **onerous**, backbreaking, burdensome, crushing, demanding, difficult, exacting, oppressive, taxing, worrisome, worrying
➤ **Antonyms**
≠ **important:** frivolous, immaterial, incidental, inconsequential, insignificant, minor, petty, trivial, unimportant

weird *adjective* = **strange**, bizarre, creepy (*informal*), eerie, eldritch (*poetic*), far-out (*slang*), freakish, ghostly, grotesque, mysterious, odd, outlandish, queer, spooky (*informal*), supernatural, uncanny, unearthly, unnatural
➤ **Antonyms**
common, mundane, natural, normal, ordinary, regular, typical, usual

welcome *verb* **1** = **greet**, accept gladly, bid welcome, embrace, hail, meet, offer

hospitality to, receive, receive with open arms, roll out the red carpet for, usher in ◆ *noun* 2 = **greeting**, acceptance, entertainment, hospitality, reception, salutation ◆ *adjective* 3 = **acceptable**, accepted, agreeable, appreciated, delightful, desirable, gladly received, gratifying, pleasant, pleasing, pleasurable, refreshing, wanted 4 = **free**, at home, invited, under no obligation
➤ Antonyms
verb ≠**greet**: exclude, rebuff, refuse, reject, slight, snub, spurn, turn away ◆ *noun* ≠**greeting**: cold shoulder, exclusion, ostracism, rebuff, rejection, slight, snub ◆ *adjective* ≠**acceptable**: disagreeable, excluded, rebuffed, rejected, unacceptable, undesirable, unpleasant, unwanted, unwelcome

weld *verb* = **join**, bind, bond, connect, fuse, link, solder, unite

welfare *noun* = **wellbeing**, advantage, benefit, good, happiness, health, interest, profit, prosperity, success

well[1] *adverb* 1 = **satisfactorily**, agreeably, capitally, famously (*informal*), happily, in a satisfactory manner, like nobody's business (*informal*), nicely, pleasantly, smoothly, splendidly, successfully 2 = **skilfully**, ably, adeptly, adequately, admirably, conscientiously, correctly, effectively, efficiently, expertly, proficiently, properly, with skill 3 = **carefully**, accurately, attentively, closely 4 = **prosperously**, comfortably, flourishingly 5 = **suitably**, correctly, easily, fairly, fittingly, in all fairness, justly, properly, readily, rightly 6 = **intimately**, closely, completely, deeply, fully, personally, profoundly, thoroughly 7 = **favourably**, approvingly, glowingly, graciously, highly, kindly, warmly 8 = **considerably**, abundantly, amply, completely, fully, greatly, heartily, highly, substantially, sufficiently, thoroughly, very much 9 **as well** = **also**, besides, in addition, into the bargain, to boot, too 10 **as well as** = **including**, along with, at the same time as, in addition to, over and above ◆ *adjective* 11 = **healthy**, able-bodied, alive and kicking, fighting fit (*informal*), fit, fit as a fiddle, hale, hearty, in fine fettle, in good health, robust, sound, strong, up to par 12 = **satisfactory**, advisable, agreeable, bright, fine, fitting, flourishing, fortunate, good, happy, lucky, pleasing, profitable, proper, prudent, right, thriving, useful
➤ Antonyms
adverb ≠**satisfactorily**: badly, inadequately, poorly, wrongly ≠**skilfully**: badly, ham-fistedly, incompetently, incorrectly, ineptly, inexpertly, sloppily, unskilfully

≠**suitably**: unfairly, unjustly, unsuitably ≠**intimately**: slightly, somewhat, vaguely ≠**favourably**: coldly, disapprovingly, gracelessly, unkindly, unsympathetically ◆ *adjective* ≠**healthy**: ailing, at death's door, below par, feeble, frail, green about the gills, ill, infirm, poorly, run-down, sick, sickly, under-the-weather, unwell, weak ≠**satisfactory**: going badly, improper, unfitting, unsatisfactory, unsuccessful, wrong

well[2] *noun* 1 = **hole**, bore, pit, shaft 2 = **waterhole**, fount, fountain, pool, source, spring 3 = **source**, fount, mine, repository, wellspring ◆ *verb* 4 = **flow**, exude, gush, jet, ooze, pour, rise, run, seep, spout, spring, spurt, stream, surge, trickle

well-balanced *adjective* 1 = **sensible**, judicious, level-headed, rational, reasonable, sane, sober, sound, together (*slang*), well-adjusted 2 = **well-proportioned**, graceful, harmonious, proportional, symmetrical
➤ Antonyms
≠**sensible**: erratic, insane, irrational, neurotic, unbalanced, unreasonable, unsound, unstable, volatile

well-bred *adjective* 1 = **polite**, civil, courteous, courtly, cultivated, cultured, gallant, genteel, gentlemanly, ladylike, mannerly, polished, refined, sophisticated, urbane, well-brought-up, well-mannered 2 = **aristocratic**, blue-blooded, gentle, highborn, noble, patrician, well-born
➤ Antonyms
≠**polite**: bad-mannered, base, coarse, discourteous, ill-bred, rude, uncivilized, uncouth, uncultured, vulgar

well-fed *adjective* 1 = **well-nourished**, healthy, in good condition 2 = **plump**, chubby, fat, fleshy, podgy, portly, rotund, rounded, stout

well-groomed *adjective* = **smart**, dapper, neat, soigné *or* soignée, spruce, tidy, trim, well-dressed, well turned out

well-known *adjective* = **famous**, celebrated, familiar, illustrious, notable, noted, on the map, popular, renowned, widely known

well-nigh *adverb* = **almost**, all but, just about, more or less, nearly, next to, practically, virtually

well-off *adjective* 1 = **rich**, affluent, comfortable, flush (*informal*), loaded (*slang*), moneyed, prosperous, wealthy, well-heeled (*informal*), well-to-do 2 = **fortunate**, comfortable, flourishing, lucky, successful, thriving
➤ Antonyms
≠**rich**: badly off, broke (*informal*), destitute, dirt-poor (*informal*), down and out, down at

heel, flat broke (*informal*), hard up (*informal*), impoverished, indigent, needy, on the breadline, on the rocks (*informal*), penniless, poor, poverty-stricken, short, without two pennies to rub together (*informal*)

well-thought-of *adjective* = **respected**, admired, esteemed, highly regarded, of good repute, reputable, revered, venerated
➤ **Antonyms**
abhorred, derided, despised, disdained, reviled, scorned, spurned

well-to-do *adjective* = **rich**, affluent, comfortable, flush (*informal*), loaded (*slang*), moneyed, prosperous, wealthy, well-heeled (*informal*), well-off
➤ **Antonyms**
bankrupt, broke (*informal*), destitute, down at heel, hard up (*informal*), indigent, insolvent, needy, on the breadline, poor, ruined

well-worn *adjective* = **stale**, banal, commonplace, hackneyed, overused, stereotyped, trite

welt *noun* = **mark**, contusion, streak, stripe, wale, weal

welter *noun* = **jumble**, confusion, hotchpotch, mess, muddle, tangle, web

wet *adjective* 1 = **damp**, aqueous, dank, drenched, dripping, humid, moist, moistened, saturated, soaked, soaking, sodden, soggy, sopping, waterlogged, watery, wringing wet 2 = **rainy**, clammy, dank, drizzling, humid, misty, pouring, raining, showery, teeming 3 *Informal* = **feeble**, boneless, effete, foolish, ineffectual, irresolute, namby-pamby, nerdy *or* nurdy (*slang*), silly, soft, spineless, timorous, weak, weedy (*informal*), wussy (*slang*) 4 **wet behind the ears** *Informal* = **naive**, as green as grass, born yesterday, callow, green, immature, inexperienced, innocent, new, raw ◆ *noun* 5 = **rain**, damp weather, drizzle, rains, rainy season, rainy weather 6 *Informal* = **weakling**, drip (*informal*), milksop, weed (*informal*), wimp (*informal*), wuss (*slang*) 7 = **moisture**, clamminess, condensation, damp, dampness, humidity, liquid, water, wetness ◆ *verb* 8 = **moisten**, damp, dampen, dip, douse, drench, humidify, irrigate, saturate, soak, splash, spray, sprinkle, steep, water
➤ **Antonyms**
adjective ≠**damp**: bone-dry, dried, dry, hardened, parched, set ≠**rainy**: arid, dry, fine, sunny ◆ *noun* ≠**rain**: dry weather, fine weather ≠**moisture**: dryness ◆ *verb* ≠**moisten**: dehydrate, desiccate, dry, parch

whack *verb* 1 = **strike**, bang, belt (*informal*), clobber (*slang*), hit, smack, swipe, thrash, thump, thwack, wallop

(*informal*) ◆ *noun* 2 = **blow**, bang, belt (*informal*), hit, smack, stroke, swipe, thump, thwack, wallop (*informal*) 3 *Informal* = **share**, bit, cut (*informal*), part, portion, quota 4 *As in* **have a whack** = **attempt**, bash (*informal*), crack (*informal*), go (*informal*), shot (*informal*), stab (*informal*), try, turn

wharf *noun* = **dock**, jetty, landing stage, pier, quay

wheedle *verb* = **coax**, butter up, cajole, charm, court, draw, entice, flatter, inveigle, persuade, talk into, worm

wheel *noun* 1 = **circle**, gyration, pivot, revolution, roll, rotation, spin, turn, twirl, whirl 2 **at the wheel** = **in control**, at the helm, driving, in charge, in command, in the driving seat, steering ◆ *verb* 3 = **turn**, circle, gyrate, orbit, pirouette, revolve, roll, rotate, spin, swing, swivel, twirl, whirl

wheeze *verb* 1 = **gasp**, breathe roughly, catch one's breath, cough, hiss, rasp, whistle ◆ *noun* 2 = **gasp**, cough, hiss, rasp, whistle 3 *Brit. slang* = **trick**, expedient, idea, plan, ploy, ruse, scheme, stunt, wrinkle (*informal*) 4 *Informal* = **joke**, anecdote, chestnut (*informal*), crack (*slang*), gag (*informal*), old joke, one-liner (*slang*), story

whereabouts *noun* = **position**, location, site, situation

wherewithal *noun* = **resources**, capital, equipment, essentials, funds, means, money, ready (*informal*), ready money, supplies

whet *verb* 1 *As in* **whet someone's appetite** = **stimulate**, animate, arouse, awaken, enhance, excite, incite, increase, kindle, pique, provoke, quicken, rouse, stir 2 = **sharpen**, edge, file, grind, hone, strop
➤ **Antonyms**
≠**stimulate**: blunt, dampen, deaden, depress, dull, numb, smother, stifle, subdue, suppress ≠**sharpen**: blunt, dull

whiff *noun* 1 = **smell**, aroma, blast, breath, draught, gust, hint, niff (*Brit. slang*), odour, puff, scent, sniff ◆ *verb* 2 *Brit. slang* = **stink**, hum (*slang*), malodour, niff (*Brit. slang*), pong (*Brit. informal*), reek

whim *noun* = **impulse**, caprice, conceit, craze, crotchet, fad (*informal*), fancy, freak, humour, notion, passing thought, quirk, sport, sudden notion, urge, vagary, whimsy

whimper *verb* 1 = **cry**, blub (*slang*), blubber, grizzle (*informal, chiefly Brit.*), mewl, moan, pule, snivel, sob, weep, whine, whinge (*informal*) ◆ *noun* 2 = **sob**, moan, snivel, whine

whimsical *adjective* = **fanciful**, capricious, chimerical, crotchety, curious, droll, eccentric, fantastic, fantastical, freakish, funny, mischievous, odd, peculiar, playful, quaint, queer, singular, unusual, waggish, weird

whine noun 1 = **cry**, moan, plaintive cry, sob, wail, whimper 2 = **complaint**, beef (slang), gripe (informal), grouch (informal), grouse, grumble, moan, whinge (informal) ◆ verb 3 = **cry**, moan, sniffle, snivel, sob, wail, whimper 4 = **complain**, beef (slang), bellyache (slang), bleat, carp, cry, gripe (informal), grizzle (informal, chiefly Brit.), grouch (informal), grouse, grumble, kvetch (U.S. slang), moan, sob, wail, whimper, whinge (informal)

whinge Informal ◆ verb 1 = **complain**, bleat, carp, gripe (informal), grouse, grumble, moan ◆ noun 2 = **complaint**, gripe (informal), grouch, grouse, grumble, moan, whine

whip noun 1 = **lash**, birch, bullwhip, cane, cat-o'-nine-tails, crop, horsewhip, knout, rawhide, riding crop, scourge, switch, thong ◆ verb 2 = **lash**, beat, birch, cane, castigate, flagellate, flog, give a hiding (informal), lambast(e), leather, lick (informal), punish, scourge, spank, strap, switch, tan (slang), thrash 3 Informal = **dash**, dart, dive, flit, flounce, fly, rush, shoot, tear, whisk 4 = **whisk**, beat 5 = **incite**, agitate, compel, drive, foment, goad, hound, instigate, prick, prod, provoke, push, spur, stir, urge, work up 6 Informal = **beat**, best, blow out of the water (slang), clobber (slang), conquer, defeat, drub, hammer (informal), lick (informal), make mincemeat out of (informal), outdo, overcome, overpower, overwhelm, rout, run rings around (informal), stuff (slang), take apart (slang), thrash, trounce, wipe the floor with (informal), worst

whip out verb = **pull out**, exhibit, flash, jerk, produce, remove, seize, show, snatch, whisk

whipping noun = **beating**, birching, caning, castigation, flagellation, flogging, hiding (informal), lashing, leathering, punishment, spanking, tanning (slang), the strap, thrashing

whirl verb 1 = **spin**, circle, gyrate, pirouette, pivot, reel, revolve, roll, rotate, swirl, turn, twirl, twist, wheel 2 = **feel dizzy**, reel, spin ◆ noun 3 = **revolution**, birl (Scot.), circle, gyration, pirouette, reel, roll, rotation, spin, swirl, turn, twirl, twist, wheel 4 = **bustle**, flurry, merry-go-round, round, series, succession 5 = **confusion**, agitation, commotion, daze, dither (chiefly Brit.), giddiness, hurly-burly, spin, stir, tumult 6 **give (something) a whirl** Informal = **attempt**, have a bash, have a crack (informal), have a go (informal), have a shot (informal), have a stab (informal), have

a whack (informal), try

whirlwind noun 1 = **tornado**, dust devil, waterspout ◆ adjective 2 = **rapid**, hasty, headlong, impetuous, impulsive, lightning, quick, quickie (informal), rash, short, speedy, swift
➤ **Antonyms**
adjective ≠**rapid**: calculated, cautious, considered, deliberate, measured, prudent, slow, unhurried

whisk verb 1 = **speed**, barrel (along) (informal, chiefly U.S. & Canad.), burn rubber (informal), dart, dash, fly, hasten, hurry, race, rush, shoot, sweep, tear 2 = **flick**, brush, sweep, whip, wipe 3 = **beat**, fluff up, whip ◆ noun 4 = **flick**, brush, sweep, whip, wipe 5 = **beater**

whisky noun = **Scotch**, barley-bree (Scot.), bourbon, firewater, John Barleycorn, malt, rye, usquebaugh (Gaelic)

whisper verb 1 = **murmur**, breathe, say softly, speak in hushed tones, utter under the breath 2 = **rustle**, hiss, murmur, sigh, sough, susurrate (literary), swish 3 = **gossip**, hint, insinuate, intimate, murmur, spread rumours ◆ noun 4 = **murmur**, hushed tone, low voice, soft voice, undertone 5 Informal = **rumour**, buzz, dirt (U.S. slang), gossip, innuendo, insinuation, report, scuttlebutt (U.S. slang), word 6 = **rustle**, hiss, murmur, sigh, sighing, soughing, susurration or susurrus (literary), swish 7 = **hint**, breath, fraction, shadow, suggestion, suspicion, tinge, trace, whiff
➤ **Antonyms**
verb ≠**murmur**: bawl, bellow, clamour, roar, shout, thunder, yell

white adjective 1 = **pale**, ashen, bloodless, ghastly, grey, like death warmed up (informal), pallid, pasty, wan, waxen, wheyfaced 2 Of hair = **silver**, grey, grizzled, hoary, snowy 3 **whiter than white** = **immaculate**, clean, impeccable, innocent, pure, spotless, squeaky-clean, stainless, unblemished, unsullied
➤ **Antonyms**
≠**pale**: black, dark

white-collar adjective = **clerical**, executive, nonmanual, office, professional, salaried

whiten verb = **pale**, blanch, bleach, blench, etiolate, fade, go white, turn pale
➤ **Antonyms**
blacken, colour, darken

whitewash noun 1 = **cover-up**, camouflage, concealment, deception, extenuation ◆ verb 2 = **cover up**, camouflage, conceal, extenuate, gloss over, make light of, suppress
➤ **Antonyms**
verb ≠**cover up**: disclose, expose, lay bare,

reveal, uncover, unmask, unveil

whittle *verb* **1** = **carve**, cut, hew, pare, shape, shave, trim **2 whittle down** *or* **away** = **reduce**, consume, destroy, eat away, erode, undermine, wear away

whole *adjective* **1** = **complete**, entire, full, in one piece, integral, total, unabridged, uncut, undivided **2** = **undamaged**, faultless, flawless, good, in one piece, intact, inviolate, mint, perfect, sound, unbroken, unharmed, unhurt, unimpaired, uninjured, unmutilated, unscathed, untouched **3** *Archaic* = **healthy**, able-bodied, better, cured, fit, hale, healed, in fine fettle, in good health, recovered, robust, sound, strong, well ◆ *adverb* **4** = **in one piece**, in one ◆ *noun* **5** = **total**, aggregate, all, everything, lot, sum total, the entire amount **6** = **totality**, ensemble, entirety, entity, fullness, piece, unit, unity **7 on the whole: a** = **all in all**, all things considered, by and large, taking everything into consideration **b** = **generally**, as a rule, for the most part, in general, in the main, mostly, predominantly
➤ **Antonyms**
adjective ≠**complete**: cut, divided, fragmented, incomplete, in pieces, partial ≠**undamaged**: broken, damaged ≠**healthy**: ailing, diseased, ill, sick, sickly, under-the-weather, unwell ◆ *noun* ≠**totality**: bit, component, constituent, division, element, fragment, part, piece, portion

wholehearted *adjective* = **sincere**, committed, complete, dedicated, determined, devoted, earnest, emphatic, enthusiastic, genuine, heartfelt, hearty, real, true, unfeigned, unqualified, unreserved, unstinting, warm, zealous
➤ **Antonyms**
cool, grudging, half-hearted, insincere, qualified, reserved, unreal

wholesale *adjective* **1** = **extensive**, all-inclusive, broad, comprehensive, far-reaching, indiscriminate, mass, sweeping, wide-ranging ◆ *adverb* **2** = **extensively**, all at once, comprehensively, indiscriminately, on a large scale, without exception
➤ **Antonyms**
adjective ≠**extensive**: confined, discriminate, limited, partial, restricted, selective

wholesome *adjective* **1** = **healthy**, beneficial, good, healthful, health-giving, helpful, hygienic, invigorating, nourishing, nutritious, salubrious, salutary, sanitary, strengthening **2** = **moral**, apple-pie (*informal*), clean, decent, edifying, ethical, exemplary, honourable, improving, innocent, nice, pure, respectable, righteous, squeaky-clean, uplifting, virtuous, worthy
➤ **Antonyms**
≠**healthy**: putrid, rotten, unhealthy,

unhygienic, unwholesome ≠**moral**: blue, corrupt, degrading, dirty, dishonest, evil, filthy, immoral, lewd, obscene, pernicious, pornographic, tasteless, trashy, unprincipled, unwholesome, X-rated (*informal*)

wholly *adverb* **1** = **completely**, all, altogether, comprehensively, entirely, fully, heart and soul, in every respect, one hundred per cent (*informal*), perfectly, thoroughly, totally, utterly **2** = **solely**, exclusively, only, without exception
➤ **Antonyms**
≠**completely**: incompletely, in part, moderately, partially, partly, relatively, slightly, somewhat

whoop *noun* = **cry**, cheer, halloo, holler (*informal*), hoot, hurrah, scream, shout, shriek, yell

whopper *noun* **1** = **giant**, colossus, crackerjack (*informal*), jumbo (*informal*), leviathan, mammoth, monster **2** = **big lie**, fabrication, falsehood, tall story (*informal*), untruth

whopping *adjective* = **gigantic**, big, enormous, giant, great, huge, mammoth, massive

whore *noun* **1** = **prostitute**, brass (*slang*), call girl, cocotte, courtesan, demimondaine, demirep (*rare*), fallen woman, *fille de joie*, harlot, hooker (*U.S. slang*), hustler (*U.S. & Canad. slang*), lady of the night, loose woman, scrubber (*Brit. & Austral. slang*), slag (*Brit. slang*), streetwalker, strumpet, tart (*informal*), trollop, woman of easy virtue, woman of ill repute, working girl (*facetious slang*) ◆ *verb* **2** = **prostitute oneself**, be on the game (*slang*), hustle (*U.S. & Canad. slang*), sell one's body, sell oneself, solicit, walk the streets **3** = **sleep around** (*informal*), fornicate, lech *or* letch (*informal*), wanton, wench (*archaic*), womanize

wicked *adjective* **1** = **bad**, abandoned, abominable, amoral, atrocious, black-hearted, corrupt, debased, depraved, devilish, dissolute, egregious, evil, fiendish, foul, guilty, heinous, immoral, impious, iniquitous, irreligious, maleficent, nefarious, scandalous, shameful, sinful, sink, unprincipled, unrighteous, vicious, vile, villainous, worthless **2** = **mischievous**, arch, impish, incorrigible, naughty, rascally, roguish **3** = **harmful**, acute, agonizing, awful, crashing, destructive, dreadful, fearful, fierce, gut-wrenching, injurious, intense, mighty, painful, severe, terrible **4** = **troublesome**, bothersome, difficult, distressing, galling, offensive, trying, unpleasant **5** *Slang* = **expert**, adept, adroit, deft, masterly, mighty, outstanding, powerful, skilful, strong

> **Antonyms**

≠**bad:** benevolent, ethical, good, honourable, moral, noble, principled, virtuous ≠**mischievous:** good, mannerly, obedient, well-behaved ≠**harmful:** harmless, innocuous, mild, pleasant, wholesome

wide *adjective* **1 = broad**, ample, catholic, comprehensive, distended, encyclopedic, expanded, expansive, extensive, far-reaching, general, immense, inclusive, large, overarching, sweeping, vast **2 = spacious**, ample, baggy, capacious, commodious, full, loose, roomy **3 = expanded**, dilated, distended, fully open, outspread, outstretched **4 = distant**, away, off, off course, off target, remote ♦ *adverb* **5 = fully**, as far as possible, completely, right out, to the furthest extent **6 = off target**, astray, nowhere near, off course, off the mark, out

> **Antonyms**

adjective ≠**broad:** narrow, strict, tight ≠**spacious:** confined, constricted, cramped, tight ≠**expanded:** closed, limited, restricted, shut ♦ *adverb* ≠**fully:** narrowly, partially, partly

wide-awake *adjective* **1 = conscious**, fully awake, roused, wakened **2 = alert**, aware, heedful, keen, observant, on one's toes, on the alert, on the ball (*informal*), on the qui vive, vigilant, wary, watchful

> **Antonyms**

≠**alert:** distracted, dreamy, heedless, inattentive, negligent, oblivious, preoccupied, unaware, unobservant

wide-eyed *adjective* **= naive**, as green as grass, credulous, green, impressionable, ingenuous, innocent, simple, trusting, unsophisticated, unsuspicious, wet behind the ears (*informal*)

widen *verb* **= broaden**, dilate, enlarge, expand, extend, open out *or* up, open wide, spread, stretch

> **Antonyms**

compress, constrict, contract, cramp, diminish, narrow, reduce, shrink, tighten

wide-open *adjective* **1 = outspread**, fully extended, fully open, gaping, outstretched, splayed, spread **2 = unprotected**, at risk, defenceless, exposed, in danger, in peril, open, susceptible, vulnerable **3 = uncertain**, anybody's guess (*informal*), indeterminate, unpredictable, unsettled, up for grabs (*informal*)

widespread *adjective* **= common**, broad, ̶̶̶̶̶mic, extensive, far-flung, far-reaching, ̶̶̶̶̶̶pervasive, popular, prevalent, rife, ̶̶̶̶̶̶universal, wholesale

̶̶̶̶̶̶̶̶s

̶̶̶̶̶̶usive, limited, local, narrow,

rare, sporadic, uncommon

width *noun* **= breadth**, compass, diameter, extent, girth, measure, range, reach, scope, span, thickness, wideness

wield *verb* **1 = brandish**, employ, flourish, handle, manage, manipulate, ply, swing, use **2** *As in* **wield power = exert**, apply, be possessed of, command, control, exercise, have, have at one's disposal, hold, maintain, make use of, manage, possess, put to use, utilize

wife *noun* **= spouse**, better half (*humorous*), bride, helpmate, helpmeet, her indoors (*Brit. slang*), little woman (*informal*), mate, old lady (*informal*), old woman (*informal*), partner, significant other (*U.S. informal*), (the) missis *or* missus (*informal*), vrou (*S. African*), woman (*informal*)

wiggle *verb, noun* **= jerk**, jiggle, shake, shimmy, squirm, twitch, wag, waggle, writhe

wild *adjective* **1 = untamed**, feral, ferocious, fierce, savage, unbroken, undomesticated **2 = uncultivated**, free, indigenous, native, natural **3 = desolate**, desert, deserted, empty, godforsaken, lonely, trackless, uncivilized, uncultivated, uninhabited, unpopulated, virgin **4 = uncivilized**, barbaric, barbarous, brutish, ferocious, fierce, primitive, rude, savage **5 = uncontrolled**, boisterous, chaotic, disorderly, impetuous, lawless, noisy, riotous, rough, rowdy, self-willed, turbulent, unbridled, undisciplined, unfettered, ungovernable, unmanageable, unrestrained, unruly, uproarious, violent, wayward **6 = stormy**, blustery, choppy, furious, howling, intense, raging, rough, tempestuous, violent **7 = excited**, agog, avid, crazy (*informal*), daft (*informal*), delirious, eager, enthusiastic, frantic, frenzied, hysterical, mad (*informal*), nuts (*slang*), potty (*Brit. informal*), raving **8 = outrageous**, extravagant, fantastic, flighty, foolhardy, foolish, giddy, ill-considered, impracticable, imprudent, madcap, preposterous, rash, reckless **9 = dishevelled**, disordered, straggly, tousled, unkempt, untidy, windblown ♦ *adverb* **10 run wild: a = grow unchecked**, ramble, spread, straggle **b = go on the rampage**, abandon all restraint, cut loose, kick over the traces, rampage, run free, run riot, stray ♦ *noun* **11 wilds = wilderness**, back of beyond (*informal*), desert, middle of nowhere (*informal*), uninhabited area, wasteland

> **Antonyms**

adjective ≠**untamed:** broken, domesticated, tame ≠**uncultivated:** cultivated, farmed, planted ≠**desolate:** civilized, inhabited, populated, urban ≠**uncivilized:** advanced, civilized ≠**uncontrolled:** calm, careful, controlled, disciplined, domesticated, friendly, genteel, gentle, lawful, mild, ordered, orderly, peaceful, polite, quiet, restrained, self-controlled, thoughtful, well-behaved ≠**excited**. unenthusiastic, uninterested ≠**outrageous**: logical, practical, realistic, well-thought-out

wilderness noun 1 = **desert**, jungle, waste, wasteland, wilds 2 = **tangle**, clutter, confused mass, confusion, congeries, jumble, maze, muddle, welter

wildlife noun = **flora and fauna**

wiles plural noun 1 = **trickery**, artfulness, artifice, cheating, chicanery, craft, craftiness, cunning, fraud, guile, slyness 2 = **ploys**, artifices, contrivances, devices, dodges, impositions, lures, manoeuvres, ruses, stratagems, subterfuges, tricks

wilful adjective 1 = **obstinate**, adamant, bull-headed, determined, dogged, froward (archaic), headstrong, inflexible, intractable, intransigent, mulish, obdurate, persistent, perverse, pig-headed, refractory, self-willed, stiff-necked, stubborn, uncompromising, unyielding 2 = **intentional**, conscious, deliberate, intended, purposeful, volitional, voluntary, willed
➤ **Antonyms**
≠**obstinate**: biddable, complaisant, compromising, docile, flexible, good-natured, obedient, pliant, tractable, yielding ≠**intentional**: accidental, involuntary, uncalculated, unconscious, unintentional, unplanned, unwitting

will noun 1 = **determination**, aim, intention, purpose, resolution, resolve, willpower 2 = **wish**, choice, decision, decree, desire, fancy, inclination, mind, option, pleasure, preference, volition 3 = **testament**, declaration, last wishes 4 **at will** = **as one pleases**, as one thinks fit, as one wishes, at one's desire, at one's discretion, at one's inclination, at one's pleasure, at one's whim, at one's wish ◆ verb 5 = **decree**, bid, bring about, cause, command, determine, direct, effect, ordain, order, resolve 6 = **wish**, choose, desire, elect, opt, prefer, see fit, want 7 = **bequeath**, confer, give, leave, pass on, transfer

willing adjective = **ready**, agreeable, amenable, compliant, consenting, content, desirous, disposed, eager, enthusiastic, favourable, game (informal), happy, inclined, in favour, in the mood, nothing loath, pleased, prepared, so-minded
➤ **Antonyms**
averse, disinclined, grudging, indisposed, loath, not keen, reluctant, unenthusiastic, unwilling

willingly adverb = **readily**, by choice, cheerfully, eagerly, freely, gladly, happily, lief

(rare), of one's own accord, of one's own free will, voluntarily, with all one's heart, without hesitation, with pleasure
➤ **Antonyms**
grudgingly, hesitantly, involuntarily, reluctantly, unwillingly

willingness noun = **inclination**, agreeableness, agreement, consent, desire, disposition, enthusiasm, favour, goodwill, volition, will, wish
➤ **Antonyms**
aversion, disagreement, disinclination, hesitation, loathing, reluctance, unwillingness

willowy adjective = **slender**, graceful, lithe, slim, supple, svelte, sylphlike

willpower noun = **self-control**, determination, drive, firmness of purpose or will, fixity of purpose, force or strength of will, grit, resolution, resolve, self-discipline, single-mindedness
➤ **Antonyms**
apathy, hesitancy, indecision, irresolution, languor, lethargy, shilly-shallying (informal), torpor, uncertainty, weakness

wilt verb 1 = **droop**, become limp or flaccid, sag, shrivel, wither 2 = **weaken**, diminish, dwindle, ebb, fade, fail, flag, languish, lose courage, melt away, sag, sink, wane, wither

wily adjective = **cunning**, arch, artful, astute, cagey (informal), crafty, crooked, deceitful, deceptive, designing, fly (slang), foxy, guileful, intriguing, scheming, sharp, shifty, shrewd, sly, tricky, underhand
➤ **Antonyms**
artless, candid, dull, guileless, honest, ingenuous, naive, simple, straightforward

wimp noun Informal = **weakling**, coward, drip (informal), mouse, sissy, softy or softie, wuss (slang)

win verb 1 = **triumph**, achieve first place, achieve mastery, be victorious, carry all before one, carry the day, come first, conquer, finish first, gain victory, overcome, prevail, succeed, sweep the board, take the prize 2 = **gain**, accomplish, achieve, acquire, attain, bag (informal), catch, collect, come away with, earn, get, land, net, obtain, pick up, procure, receive, secure ◆ noun 3 = **victory**, conquest, success, triumph
➤ **Antonyms**
verb ≠**triumph**: fail, fall, suffer defeat, suffer loss ≠**gain**: forfeit, lose, miss ◆ noun ≠**victory**: beating, defeat, downfall, failure, loss, washout (informal)

wince verb 1 = **flinch**, blench, cower, cringe, draw back, quail, recoil, shrink, start ◆ noun 2 = **flinch**, cringe, start

wind[1] noun 1 = **air**, air-current, blast, breath, breeze, current of air, draught, gust, zeph⸍ 2 = **breath**, puff, respiration 3 = fla⸍⸍

flatus, gas **4 = talk**, babble, blather, bluster, boasting, empty talk, gab (*informal*), hot air, humbug, idle talk, verbalizing **5** As in **get wind of = hint**, clue, inkling, intimation, notice, report, rumour, suggestion, tidings, warning, whisper **6 get** or **have the wind up** Informal **= be afraid**, be alarmed, be frightened, be scared, fear, take fright **7 in the wind = imminent**, about to happen, approaching, close at hand, coming, impending, in the offing, near, on the cards (*informal*), on the way **8 put the wind up** Informal **= scare**, alarm, discourage, frighten, frighten off, scare off

wind² verb **1 = coil**, curl, encircle, furl, loop, reel, roll, spiral, turn around, twine, twist, wreathe **2 = meander**, bend, curve, deviate, ramble, snake, turn, twist, zigzag ♦ noun **3 = twist**, bend, curve, meander, turn, zigzag

wind down verb **= subside**, cool off, decline, diminish, dwindle, lessen, reduce, relax, slacken, taper off, unwind
➤ **Antonyms**
accelerate, amplify, escalate, expand, heat up, increase, intensify, magnify, step up

winded adjective **= out of breath**, breathless, gasping for breath, out of puff, out of whack (*informal*), panting, puffed, puffed out

windfall noun **= godsend**, bonanza, find, jackpot, manna from heaven, pot of gold at the end of the rainbow, stroke of luck
➤ **Antonyms**
bad luck, disaster, infelicity, misadventure, mischance, misfortune, mishap

winding noun **1 = twist**, bend, convolution, curve, meander, turn, undulation ♦ adjective **2 = twisting**, anfractuous, bending, circuitous, convoluted, crooked, curving, flexuous, indirect, meandering, roundabout, serpentine, sinuous, spiral, tortuous, turning, twisty
➤ **Antonyms**
adjective ≠**twisting**: direct, even, level, plumb, smooth, straight, undeviating, unswerving

wind up verb **1 = end**, bring to a close, close, close down, conclude, finalize, finish, liquidate, settle, terminate, tie up the loose ends (*informal*), wrap up **2 = end up**, be left, end one's days, find oneself, finish up **3** Informal **= excite**, make nervous, make tense, put on edge, work up
➤ **Antonyms**
≠**end**: begin, commence, embark on, initiate, instigate, institute, open, start

wi__ adjective **1 = breezy**, blowy, __g, blustery, boisterous, gusty, __squally, stormy, tempestuous, __ept **2 = pompous**, boastful, __fuse, empty, garrulous,

long-winded, loquacious, meandering, prolix, rambling, turgid, verbose, wordy **3** Old-fashioned slang **= frightened**, afraid, antsy (*informal*), chicken (*slang*), chickenshit (*U.S. slang*), cowardly, fearful, nervous, nervy (*informal*), scared, timid
➤ **Antonyms**
≠**breezy**: becalmed, calm, motionless, smooth, still, windless ≠**pompous**: modest, quiet, reserved, restrained, reticent, shy, taciturn, unforthcoming ≠**frightened**: bold, brave, courageous, daring, fearless, gallant, unafraid, undaunted

wing noun **1 = organ of flight**, pennon (*poetic*), pinion (*poetic*) **2 = annexe**, adjunct, ell, extension **3 = faction**, arm, branch, cabal, circle, clique, coterie, group, grouping, schism, section, segment, set, side ♦ verb **4 = fly**, glide, soar **5 = fly**, fleet, hasten, hurry, race, speed, zoom **6 = wound**, clip, hit, nick

wink verb **1 = blink**, bat, flutter, nictate, nictitate **2 = twinkle**, flash, gleam, glimmer, sparkle ♦ noun **3 = blink**, flutter, nictation, nictitation **4 = twinkle**, flash, gleam, glimmering, sparkle **5 = moment**, instant, jiffy (*informal*), second, split second, twinkling

wink at verb **= condone**, allow, blink at, connive at, disregard, ignore, overlook, pretend not to notice, put up with (*informal*), shut one's eyes to, tolerate, turn a blind eye to

winkle out verb **= extract**, dig out, dislodge, draw out, extricate, force out, prise out, smoke out, worm out

winner noun **= victor**, champ (*informal*), champion, conquering hero, conqueror, first, master, vanquisher

winning adjective **1 = victorious**, conquering, successful, triumphant **2 = charming**, alluring, amiable, attractive, bewitching, captivating, cute, delectable, delightful, disarming, enchanting, endearing, engaging, fascinating, fetching, likable or likeable, lovely, pleasing, prepossessing, sweet, taking, winsome
➤ **Antonyms**
≠**charming**: disagreeable, irksome, offensive, repellent, tiresome, unappealing, unattractive, unpleasant

winnings plural noun **= spoils**, booty, gains, prize, proceeds, profits, takings

winnow verb **= separate**, comb, cull, divide, fan, part, screen, select, separate the wheat from the chaff, sift, sort out

win over verb **= convince**, allure, attract, bring or talk round, charm, convert, disarm, influence, persuade, prevail upon, sway

wintry adjective **1 = cold**, brumal, chilly,

freezing, frosty, frozen, harsh, hibernal, hiemal, icy, snowy **2 = bleak**, cheerless, cold, desolate, dismal
➤ **Antonyms**
balmy, bright, mild, pleasant, summery, sunny, warm

wipe *verb* **1 = clean**, brush, dry, dust, mop, rub, sponge, swab **2 = erase**, clean off, get rid of, remove, rub off, take away, take off ◆ *noun* **3 = rub**, brush, lick, swab

wipe out *verb* **= destroy**, annihilate, blot out, blow away (*slang, chiefly U.S.*), efface, eradicate, erase, expunge, exterminate, extirpate, kill to the last man, massacre, obliterate, take out (*slang*), wipe from the face of the earth

wiry *adjective* **1 = lean**, sinewy, strong, tough **2 = stiff**, bristly, kinky
➤ **Antonyms**
≠**lean**: fat, feeble, flabby, fleshy, frail, podgy, puny, spineless, weak

wisdom *noun* **= understanding**, astuteness, circumspection, comprehension, discernment, enlightenment, erudition, foresight, insight, intelligence, judgment, judiciousness, knowledge, learning, penetration, prudence, reason, sagacity, sapience, sense, smarts (*slang, chiefly U.S.*), sound judgment
➤ **Antonyms**
absurdity, daftness (*informal*), folly, foolishness, idiocy, injudiciousness, nonsense, senselessness, silliness, stupidity

wise *adjective* **1 = sensible**, aware, clever, clued-up (*informal*), discerning, enlightened, erudite, informed, intelligent, in the loop (*informal*), judicious, knowing, perceptive, politic, prudent, rational, reasonable, sagacious, sage, sapient, shrewd, sound, understanding, well-advised, well-informed **2 put wise** *Slang* **= inform**, alert, apprise, clue in *or* up (*informal*), let (someone) into the secret, notify, tell, tip off, warn
➤ **Antonyms**
≠**sensible**: daft (*informal*), foolish, injudicious, rash, silly, stupid, unintelligent, unwise

wisecrack *noun* **1 = joke**, barb, funny (*informal*), gag (*informal*), jest, jibe, pithy remark, quip, sally, sardonic remark, smart remark, witticism ◆ *verb* **2 = joke**, be facetious, jest, jibe, quip, tell jokes

wish *verb* **1 = want**, aspire, covet, crave, desiderate, desire, hanker, hope, hunger, long, need, set one's heart on, sigh for, thirst, yearn **2 = require**, ask, bid, command, desire, direct, instruct, order **3 = bid**, greet with ◆ *noun* **4 = desire**, aspiration, hankering, hope, hunger, inclination, intention, liking, longing, thirst, urge, want, whim, will, yearning **5 = request**, bidding,

command, desire, order, will
➤ **Antonyms**
noun ≠**desire**: aversion, disinclination, dislike, distaste, loathing, reluctance, repulsion, revulsion

wispy *adjective* **= thin**, attenuated, delicate, fine, flimsy, fragile, frail

wistful *adjective* **= melancholy**, contemplative, disconsolate, dreaming, dreamy, forlorn, longing, meditative, mournful, musing, pensive, reflective, sad, thoughtful, yearning

wit *noun* **1 = humour**, badinage, banter, drollery, facetiousness, fun, jocularity, levity, pleasantry, raillery, repartee, wordplay **2 = humorist**, card (*informal*), comedian, epigrammatist, *farceur*, joker, punster, wag **3 = cleverness**, acumen, brains, common sense, comprehension, discernment, ingenuity, insight, intellect, judgment, mind, nous (*Brit. slang*), perception, practical intelligence, reason, sense, smarts (*slang, chiefly U.S.*), understanding, wisdom
➤ **Antonyms**
≠**humour**: dullness, gravity, humourlessness, seriousness, sobriety, solemnity
≠**cleverness**: folly, foolishness, ignorance, lack of perception, obtuseness, silliness, stupidity

witch *noun* **= enchantress**, crone, hag, magician, necromancer, occultist, sorceress

witchcraft *noun* **= magic**, black magic, enchantment, incantation, necromancy, occultism, sorcery, sortilege, spell, the black art, the occult, voodoo, witchery, witching, wizardry

withdraw *verb* **1 = remove**, draw back, draw out, extract, pull, pull out, take away, take off **2 = retreat**, absent oneself, back off, back out, cop out (*slang*), depart, detach oneself, disengage, drop out, fall back, go, leave, make oneself scarce (*informal*), pull back, pull out, retire, secede **3 = retract**, abjure, disavow, disclaim, recall, recant, rescind, revoke, take back, unsay
➤ **Antonyms**
≠**retreat**: advance, forge ahead, go on, move forward, persist, press on, proceed, progress

withdrawal *noun* **1 = removal**, extraction **2 = retreat**, departure, disengagement, exit, exodus, retirement, secession **3 = retraction**, abjuration, disavowal, disclaimer, recall, recantation, repudiation, rescission, revocation

withdrawn *adjective* **1 = uncommunicative**, aloof, detached, distant, introverted, quiet, reserved, retiring, shrinking, shy, silent, taciturn, timorous, unforthcoming **2 = secluded**, hidden,

isolated, out-of-the-way, private, remote, solitary
➤ **Antonyms**
≠**uncommunicative:** extrovert, forward, friendly, gregarious, open, outgoing, sociable ≠**secluded:** easily accessible

wither *verb* 1 = **wilt**, atrophy, blast, blight, decay, decline, desiccate, disintegrate, droop, dry, fade, languish, perish, shrink, shrivel, wane, waste 2 = **humiliate**, abash, blast, mortify, put down, shame, snub
➤ **Antonyms**
≠**wilt:** bloom, blossom, develop, flourish, increase, prosper, succeed, thrive, wax

withering *adjective* 1 = **scornful**, blasting, blighting, devastating, humiliating, hurtful, mortifying, snubbing 2 = **destructive**, deadly, death-dealing, devastating, killing, murderous, slaughterous

withhold *verb* 1 = **keep back**, check, conceal, deduct, hide, hold back, keep, keep secret, refuse, repress, reserve, resist, restrain, retain, sit on (*informal*), suppress 2 *with* **from** = **refrain**, forbear, keep oneself, stop oneself
➤ **Antonyms**
≠**keep back:** accord, expose, get off one's chest (*informal*), give, grant, hand over, let go, release, relinquish, reveal

withstand *verb* = **resist**, bear, brave, combat, confront, cope with, defy, endure, face, grapple with, hold off, hold out against, oppose, put up with (*informal*), stand firm against, stand up to, suffer, take, take on, thwart, tolerate, weather
➤ **Antonyms**
capitulate, falter, give in, give way, relent, succumb, surrender, weaken, yield

witless *adjective* = **foolish**, dumb-ass (*slang*), halfwitted, idiotic, inane, moronic, senseless, silly, stupid

witness *noun* 1 = **observer**, beholder, bystander, eyewitness, looker-on, onlooker, spectator, viewer, watcher 2 = **testifier**, attestant, corroborator, deponent 3 **bear witness: a** = **give evidence**, depone, depose, give testimony, testify **b** = **confirm**, attest, bear out, be evidence of, be proof of, betoken, constitute proof of, corroborate, demonstrate, evince, prove, show, testify to, vouch for ♦ *verb* 4 = **see**, attend, behold (*archaic or literary*), be present at, look on, mark, note, notice, observe, perceive, view, watch 5 = **sign**, countersign, endorse 6 **witness to** = **testify**, attest, authenticate, bear out, bear witness, confirm, corroborate, depone, depose, give evidence, give testimony

wits *plural noun* 1 = **intelligence**, acumen, astuteness, brains (*informal*), cleverness, comprehension, faculties, ingenuity,

judgment, nous (*Brit. slang*), reason, sense, smarts (*slang, chiefly U.S.*), understanding 2 **at one's wits' end** = **in despair**, at a loss, at the end of one's tether, baffled, bewildered, lost, stuck (*informal*), stumped

witter *verb* = **chatter**, babble, blather, chat, gabble, jabber, prate, prattle, waffle (*informal, chiefly Brit.*)

witticism *noun* = **quip**, bon mot, clever remark, epigram, one-liner (*slang*), play on words, pleasantry, pun, repartee, riposte, sally, witty remark

witty *adjective* = **humorous**, amusing, brilliant, clever, droll, epigrammatic, facetious, fanciful, funny, gay, ingenious, jocular, lively, original, piquant, sparkling, waggish, whimsical
➤ **Antonyms**
boring, dull, humourless, stupid, tedious, tiresome, unamusing, uninteresting, witless

wizard *noun* 1 = **magician**, conjuror, enchanter, mage (*archaic*), magus, necromancer, occultist, shaman, sorcerer, thaumaturge (*rare*), warlock, witch 2 = **virtuoso**, ace (*informal*), adept, buff (*informal*), expert, genius, guru, hotshot (*informal*), maestro, master, maven (*U.S.*), prodigy, star, whizz (*informal*), whizz kid (*informal*), wiz (*informal*)

wizardry *noun* = **magic**, sorcery, voodoo, witchcraft

wizened *adjective* = **wrinkled**, dried up, gnarled, lined, sere (*archaic*), shrivelled, shrunken, withered, worn
➤ **Antonyms**
bloated, plump, rounded, smooth, swollen, turgid

wobble *verb* 1 = **shake**, quake, rock, seesaw, sway, teeter, totter, tremble, vibrate, waver 2 = **hesitate**, be unable to make up one's mind, be undecided, dither (*chiefly Brit.*), fluctuate, shillyshally (*informal*), swither (*Scot.*), vacillate, waver ♦ *noun* 3 = **unsteadiness**, quaking, shake, tremble, tremor, vibration

wobbly *adjective* = **unsteady**, rickety, shaky, teetering, tottering, uneven

woe *noun* = **grief**, adversity, affliction, agony, anguish, burden, curse, dejection, depression, disaster, distress, gloom, hardship, heartache, heartbreak, melancholy, misery, misfortune, pain, sadness, sorrow, suffering, trial, tribulation, trouble, unhappiness, wretchedness
➤ **Antonyms**
bliss, elation, felicity, fortune, happiness, joy, jubilation, pleasure, prosperity, rapture

woeful *adjective* 1 = **sad**, afflicted, agonized, anguished, calamitous, catastrophic, cruel, deplorable, disastrous,

disconsolate, dismal, distressing, doleful, dreadful, gloomy, grieving, grievous, harrowing, heartbreaking, heart-rending, lamentable, miserable, mournful, pathetic, piteous, pitiable, pitiful, plaintive, sorrowful, tragic, unhappy, wretched **2 = pitiful**, abysmal, appalling, awful, bad, deplorable, disappointing, disgraceful, dreadful, duff (*Brit. informal*), feeble, godawful (*slang*), hopeless, inadequate, lousy (*slang*), mean, miserable, not much cop (*Brit. slang*), paltry, pathetic, pitiable, poor, rotten (*informal*), shitty (*taboo slang*), shocking, sorry, terrible, wretched
➤ **Antonyms**
≠**sad**: carefree, cheerful, chirpy (*informal*), contented, delighted, glad, happy, jolly, joyful, jubilant, light-hearted ≠**pitiful**: abundant, ample, bountiful, enviable, extensive, generous, lavish, luxurious, profuse, prosperous

wolf *verb with* **down = devour**, bolt, cram, eat like a horse, gobble, gollop, gorge, gulp, pack away (*informal*), pig out (*slang*), scoff (*slang*), stuff
➤ **Antonyms**
bite, nibble, nip, peck, pick at

woman *noun* **1 = lady**, bird (*slang*), chick (*slang*), dame (*slang*), female, gal (*slang*), girl, ho (*U.S. derogatory slang*), lass, lassie (*informal*), maid (*archaic*), maiden (*archaic*), miss, she, wench (*facetious*) **2 = maid**, chambermaid, char (*informal*), charwoman, domestic, female servant, handmaiden, housekeeper, lady-in-waiting, maidservant **3** *Informal* **= girlfriend**, bride, girl, ladylove, mate, mistress, old lady (*informal*), partner, significant other (*U.S. informal*), spouse, sweetheart, wife
➤ **Antonyms**
≠**lady**: bloke (*Brit. informal*), boy, chap (*informal*), gentleman, guy (*informal*), lad, laddie, male, man

womanizer *noun* **= philanderer**, Casanova, Don Juan, lady-killer, lech *or* letch (*informal*), lecher, Lothario, seducer, wolf (*informal*)

womanly *adjective* **= feminine**, female, ladylike, matronly, motherly, tender, warm

wonder *verb* **1 = think**, ask oneself, be curious, be inquisitive, conjecture, cudgel one's brains (*informal*), doubt, inquire, meditate, ponder, puzzle, query, question, speculate **2 = be amazed**, be astonished, be awed, be dumbstruck, be flabbergasted (*informal*), boggle, gape, gawk, marvel, stand amazed, stare ♦ *noun* **3 = phenomenon**, curiosity, marvel, miracle, nonpareil, portent, prodigy, rarity, sight, spectacle, wonderment **4 = amazement**, admiration, astonishment, awe,

bewilderment, curiosity, fascination, stupefaction, surprise, wonderment

wonderful *adjective* **1 = excellent**, ace (*informal*), admirable, awesome (*slang*), bodacious (*slang, chiefly U.S.*), boffo (*slang*), brill (*informal*), brilliant, chillin' (*U.S. slang*), cracking (*Brit. informal*), fabulous (*informal*), fantastic (*informal*), great (*informal*), jim-dandy (*slang*), like a dream come true, magnificent, marvellous, mean (*slang*), out of this world (*informal*), outstanding, sensational (*informal*), smashing (*informal*), sovereign, stupendous, super (*informal*), superb, terrific, tiptop, topping (*Brit. slang*), tremendous **2 = remarkable**, amazing, astonishing, astounding, awe-inspiring, awesome, extraordinary, fantastic, incredible, jaw-dropping, marvellous, miraculous, odd, peculiar, phenomenal, staggering, startling, strange, surprising, unheard-of, wondrous (*archaic or literary*)
➤ **Antonyms**
≠**excellent**: abominable, abysmal, appalling, average, awful, bad, depressing, dire, dreadful, frightful, grim, hellacious (*U.S. slang*), indifferent, lousy (*slang*), mediocre, miserable, modest, no great shakes (*informal*), rotten, terrible, unpleasant, vile ≠**remarkable**: common, commonplace, ordinary, run-of-the-mill, uninteresting, unremarkable, usual

wonky *adjective* **= shaky**, unsteady, wobbly

wont *adjective* **1 = accustomed**, given, in the habit of, used ♦ *noun* **2 = habit**, custom, practice, rule, use, way

wonted *adjective* **1 = in the habit of**, accustomed, given, habituated, used **2 = customary**, accustomed, common, conventional, familiar, frequent, habitual, normal, regular, usual

woo *verb* **= court**, chase, cultivate, importune, pay court to, pay one's addresses to, pay suit to, press one's suit with, pursue, seek after, seek the hand of, seek to win, solicit the goodwill of, spark (*rare*)

wood *noun* **1 = timber**, planks **2** *Also* **woods = woodland**, coppice, copse, forest, grove, hurst (*archaic*), thicket, trees **3 out of the wood(s) = safe**, clear, home and dry (*Brit. slang*), in the clear, out of danger, safe and sound, secure

wooded *adjective* **= tree-covered**, forested, sylvan (*poetic*), timbered, tree-clad, woody

wooden *adjective* **1 = woody**, ligneous, made of wood, of wood, timber **2 = expressionless**, blank, colourless, deadpan, dull, emotionless, empty, glassy, lifeless, spiritless, unemotional, unresponsive, vacant **3 = awkward**, clumsy, gauche,

gawky, graceless, inelegant, maladroit, rigid, stiff, ungainly
➤ **Antonyms**
≠**awkward:** agile, comely, elegant, flexible, flowing, graceful, lissom(e), nimble, supple

wooden-headed *adjective* = **stupid,** dense, dim, dim-witted (*informal*), dozy (*Brit. informal*), dull, dull-witted, obtuse, slow, thick, witless

wool *noun* 1 = **fleece,** hair, yarn 2 **dyed in the wool** = **hardened,** confirmed, diehard, fixed, inflexible, inveterate, settled, unchangeable, uncompromising, unshakable 3 **pull the wool over someone's eyes** = **deceive,** bamboozle (*informal*), con (*slang*), delude, dupe, fool, hoodwink, kid (*informal*), lead (someone) up the garden path (*informal*), pull a fast one (on someone) (*informal*), put one over on (*slang*), take in (*informal*), trick

woolgathering *noun* = **daydreaming,** absent-mindedness, abstraction, building castles in the air, dreaming, inattention, musing, preoccupation, reverie
➤ **Antonyms**
alertness, attention, awareness, concentration, heed, observation, thoughtfulness, vigilance, watchfulness

woolly *adjective* 1 = **fleecy,** flocculent, hairy, made of wool, shaggy, woollen 2 = **vague,** blurred, clouded, confused, foggy, fuzzy, hazy, ill-defined, indefinite, indistinct, muddled, nebulous, unclear
➤ **Antonyms**
≠**vague:** clear, clear-cut, definite, distinct, exact, obvious, precise, sharp, well-defined

word *noun* 1 = **term,** expression, locution, name, vocable 2 = **chat,** brief conversation, chitchat, colloquy, confab (*informal*), confabulation, consultation, discussion, talk, tête-à-tête 3 = **remark,** brief statement, comment, declaration, expression, utterance 4 = **message,** account, advice, bulletin, communication, communiqué, dispatch, gen (*Brit. informal*), information, intelligence, intimation, latest (*informal*), news, notice, report, tidings 5 = **promise,** affirmation, assertion, assurance, guarantee, oath, parole, pledge, solemn oath, solemn word, undertaking, vow, word of honour 6 = **command,** bidding, commandment, decree, edict, go-ahead (*informal*), mandate, order, ukase (*rare*), will 7 **in a word** = **briefly,** concisely, in a nutshell, in short, succinctly, to put it briefly, to sum up 8 **last word: a** = **final say,** finis, summation, ultimatum **b** = **epitome,** best, cream, *crème de la crème,* crown, mother of all (*informal*), *ne plus ultra,* perfection, quintessence, ultimate **c** = **vogue,** *dernier cri,* fashion, latest, newest, rage ♦ *verb* 9 = **express,**

couch, phrase, put, say, state, utter

wording *noun* = **phraseology,** language, phrasing, terminology, words

wordplay *noun* = **puns,** punning, repartee, wit, witticisms

words *plural noun* 1 = **text,** lyrics 2 *As in* **have words** ♦ *noun* = **argument,** altercation, angry exchange, angry speech, barney (*informal*), bickering, disagreement, dispute, falling-out (*informal*), quarrel, row, run-in (*informal*), set-to (*informal*), squabble

wordy *adjective* = **long-winded,** diffuse, discursive, garrulous, loquacious, pleonastic, prolix, rambling, verbose, windy
➤ **Antonyms**
brief, concise, laconic, pithy, short, succinct, terse, to the point

work *noun* 1 = **effort,** drudgery, elbow grease (*facetious*), exertion, grind (*informal*), industry, labour, slog, sweat, toil, travail (*literary*) 2 = **employment,** bread and butter (*informal*), business, calling, craft, duty, job, line, livelihood, métier, occupation, office, profession, pursuit, trade 3 = **task,** assignment, chore, commission, duty, job, stint, undertaking 4 = **creation,** achievement, composition, handiwork, *oeuvre,* opus, performance, piece, production 5 **out of work** = **unemployed,** idle, jobless, on the dole (*Brit. informal*), on the street, out of a job ♦ *verb* 6 = **labour,** break one's back, drudge, exert oneself, peg away, slave, slog (away), sweat, toil 7 = **be employed,** be in work, do business, earn a living, have a job 8 = **operate,** act, control, direct, drive, handle, manage, manipulate, move, ply, use, wield 9 = **function,** go, operate, perform, run 10 = **cultivate,** dig, farm, till 11 = **manipulate,** fashion, form, handle, knead, make, mould, process, shape 12 = **progress,** force, make one's way, manoeuvre, move 13 *Informal* = **manipulate,** arrange, bring off, contrive, exploit, fiddle (*informal*), fix (*informal*), handle, pull off, swing (*informal*) 14 = **accomplish,** achieve, bring about, carry out, cause, contrive, create, effect, encompass, execute, implement 15 = **move,** be agitated, convulse, twitch, writhe
➤ **Antonyms**
noun ≠**effort:** ease, leisure, relaxation, rest ≠**employment:** entertainment, hobby, holiday, play, recreation, retirement, spare time, unemployment ♦ *verb* ≠**labour:** have fun, mark time, play, relax, skive (*Brit. slang*), take it easy ≠**function:** be broken, be out of order

workable *adjective* = **viable,** doable, feasible, possible, practicable, practical
➤ **Antonyms**
hopeless, impossible, impractical,

inconceivable, unattainable, unthinkable, unworkable, useless

workaday *adjective* = **ordinary**, bog-standard (*Brit. & Irish slang*), common, commonplace, everyday, familiar, humdrum, mundane, practical, prosaic, routine, run-of-the-mill
➤ **Antonyms**
atypical, different, exciting, extraordinary, rare, special, uncommon, unfamiliar, unusual

worker *noun* = **employee**, artisan, craftsman, hand, labourer, proletarian, tradesman, wage earner, working man *or* working woman, workman

working *adjective* **1** = **employed**, active, in a job, in work, labouring **2** = **functioning**, going, operative, running **3** = **effective**, practical, useful, viable ♦ *noun* **4** = **mine**, digging, excavation, pit, quarry, shaft **5 workings** = **operation**, action, functioning, manner, method, mode of operation, running

workman *noun* = **labourer**, artificer, artisan, craftsman, employee, hand, journeyman, mechanic, operative, tradesman, worker

workmanlike, workmanly *adjective* = **efficient**, adept, careful, expert, masterly, painstaking, professional, proficient, satisfactory, skilful, skilled, thorough
➤ **Antonyms**
amateurish, botchy, careless, clumsy, cowboy (*informal*), incompetent, slap-dash, slipshod, unprofessional, unskilful

workmanship *noun* = **skill**, art, artistry, craft, craftsmanship, execution, expertise, handicraft, handiwork, manufacture, technique, work

work out *verb* **1** = **solve**, calculate, clear up, figure out, find out, puzzle out, resolve, suss (out) (*slang*) **2** = **plan**, arrange, construct, contrive, develop, devise, elaborate, evolve, form, formulate, put together **3** = **happen**, come out, develop, evolve, go, pan out (*informal*), result, turn out **4** = **succeed**, be effective, flourish, go as planned, go well, prosper, prove satisfactory **5** = **exercise**, do exercises, drill, practise, train, warm up **6 work out at** = **amount to**, add up to, come to, reach, reach a total of

works *plural noun* **1** = **factory**, mill, plant, shop, workshop **2** = **writings**, canon, *oeuvre*, output, productions **3** = **deeds**, actions, acts, doings **4** = **mechanism**, action, guts (*informal*), innards (*informal*), insides (*informal*), machinery, movement, moving parts, parts, workings

workshop *noun* **1** = **studio**, atelier, factory, mill, plant, shop, workroom, works **2** = **seminar**, class, discussion group, masterclass, study group

work up *verb* = **excite**, agitate, animate, arouse, enkindle, foment, generate, get (someone) all steamed up (*slang*), incite, inflame, instigate, move, rouse, spur, stir up, wind up (*informal*)

world *noun* **1** = **earth**, earthly sphere, globe **2** = **mankind**, everybody, everyone, humanity, humankind, human race, man, men, the public, the race of man **3** = **universe**, cosmos, creation, existence, life, nature **4** = **planet**, heavenly body, star **5** = **sphere**, area, domain, environment, field, kingdom, province, realm, system **6** = **period**, age, days, epoch, era, times **7 for all the world** = **exactly**, in every respect, in every way, just as if, just like, precisely, to all intents and purposes **8 on top of the world** *Informal* = **overjoyed**, beside oneself with joy, cock-a-hoop, ecstatic, elated, exultant, happy, in raptures, on cloud nine (*informal*), over the moon (*informal*) **9 out of this world** *Informal* = **wonderful**, awesome (*slang*), bodacious (*slang, chiefly U.S.*), excellent, fabulous (*informal*), fantastic (*informal*), great (*informal*), incredible, indescribable, marvellous, superb, unbelievable

worldly *adjective* **1** = **earthly**, carnal, fleshly, lay, mundane, physical, profane, secular, sublunary, temporal, terrestrial **2** = **materialistic**, avaricious, covetous, grasping, greedy, selfish, worldly-minded **3** = **worldly-wise**, blasé, cosmopolitan, experienced, knowing, politic, sophisticated, urbane, well versed in the ways of the world
➤ **Antonyms**
≠**earthly**: divine, ethereal, heavenly, immaterial, noncorporeal, spiritual, transcendental, unworldly ≠**materialistic**: moral, nonmaterialistic, unworldly ≠**worldly-wise**: ingenuous, innocent, naive, unsophisticated, unworldly

worldwide *adjective* = **global**, general, international, omnipresent, pandemic, ubiquitous, universal
➤ **Antonyms**
confined, insular, limited, local, narrow, national, parochial, provincial, restricted

worn *adjective* **1** = **ragged**, frayed, shabby, shiny, tattered, tatty, the worse for wear, threadbare **2** = **haggard**, careworn, drawn, lined, pinched, wizened **3** = **exhausted**, fatigued, jaded, played-out (*informal*), spent, tired, tired out, wearied, weary, worn-out

worn-out *adjective* **1** = **run-down**, broken-down, clapped out (*Brit., Austral., & N.Z. informal*), decrepit, done, frayed, moth-eaten, on its last legs, ragged, shabby, tattered, tatty, threadbare, used, used-up,

useless, worn **2 = exhausted**, all in (*slang*), clapped out (*Austral. & N.Z. informal*), dead *or* out on one's feet (*informal*), dog-tired (*informal*), done in (*informal*), fatigued, fit to drop, jiggered (*dialect*), knackered (*slang*), played-out, prostrate, shagged out (*Brit. slang*), spent, tired, tired out, weary, wiped out (*informal*), zonked (*slang*)
➤ **Antonyms**
≠**exhausted**: fresh, refreshed, relaxed, renewed, rested, restored, revived, strengthened

worried *adjective* **= anxious**, afraid, antsy (*informal*), apprehensive, bothered, concerned, distracted, distraught, distressed, disturbed, fearful, fretful, frightened, hot and bothered, ill at ease, nervous, on edge, overwrought, perturbed, tense, tormented, troubled, uneasy, unquiet, upset, wired (*slang*)
➤ **Antonyms**
calm, fearless, peaceful, quiet, tranquil, unafraid, unconcerned, unfazed (*informal*), unworried

worry *verb* **1 = be anxious**, agonize, brood, feel uneasy, fret, obsess **2 = trouble**, annoy, badger, bother, disquiet, distress, disturb, harass, harry, hassle (*informal*), hector, importune, irritate, make anxious, perturb, pester, plague, tantalize, tease, torment, unsettle, upset, vex **3 = attack**, bite, gnaw at, go for, harass, harry, kill, lacerate, savage, tear ♦ *noun* **4 = anxiety**, annoyance, apprehension, care, concern, disturbance, fear, irritation, misery, misgiving, perplexity, torment, trepidation, trouble, unease, vexation, woe **5 = problem**, annoyance, bother, care, hassle (*informal*), irritation, pest, plague, torment, trial, trouble, vexation
➤ **Antonyms**
verb ≠**be anxious**: be apathetic, be unconcerned, be unperturbed ≠**trouble**: calm, comfort, console, solace, soothe ♦ *noun* ≠**anxiety**: calm, comfort, consolation, peace of mind, reassurance, serenity, solace, tranquillity

worsen *verb* **1 = aggravate**, damage, exacerbate **2 = deteriorate**, decay, decline, degenerate, get worse, go downhill (*informal*), go from bad to worse, retrogress, sink, take a turn for the worse
➤ **Antonyms**
≠**aggravate**: ameliorate, enhance, improve, mend, rectify, upgrade ≠**deteriorate**: be on the mend, improve, mend, recover

worship *verb* **1 = praise**, adore, adulate, deify, exalt, glorify, honour, laud, pray to, respect, revere, reverence, venerate **2 = love**, adore, idolize, put on a pedestal ♦ *noun* **3 = praise**, adoration, adulation, deification,

devotion, exaltation, glorification, glory, homage, honour, laudation, love, prayer(s), regard, respect, reverence
➤ **Antonyms**
verb ≠**praise**: blaspheme, deride, dishonour, flout, mock, revile, ridicule, scoff at ≠**love**: despise, disdain, spurn

worst *verb* **= beat**, best, blow out of the water (*slang*), clobber (*slang*), conquer, crush, defeat, gain the advantage over, get the better of, lick (*informal*), master, overcome, overpower, overthrow, run rings around (*informal*), subdue, subjugate, undo, vanquish, wipe the floor with (*informal*)

worth *noun* **1 = value**, cost, price, rate, valuation **2 = importance**, aid, assistance, avail, benefit, credit, desert(s), estimation, excellence, goodness, help, merit, quality, usefulness, utility, value, virtue, worthiness
➤ **Antonyms**
≠**importance**: futility, insignificance, paltriness, triviality, unworthiness, uselessness, worthlessness, wretchedness

worthless *adjective* **1 = useless**, a dime a dozen, chickenshit (*U.S. slang*), futile, ineffectual, insignificant, inutile, meaningless, measly, miserable, nickel-and-dime (*U.S. slang*), not much cop (*Brit.slang*), not worth a hill of beans (*chiefly U.S.*), no use, nugatory, paltry, pants (*slang*), pointless, poor, poxy (*slang*), rubbishy, trashy, trifling, trivial, two a penny (*informal*), unavailing, unimportant, unusable, valueless, wanky (*taboo slang*), wretched **2 = good-for-nothing**, abandoned, abject, base, contemptible, depraved, despicable, ignoble, useless, vile
➤ **Antonyms**
≠**useless**: consequential, effective, fruitful, important, precious, productive, profitable, significant, useful, valuable, worthwhile
≠**good-for-nothing**: decent, honourable, noble, upright, worthy

worthwhile *adjective* **= useful**, beneficial, constructive, expedient, gainful, good, helpful, justifiable, productive, profitable, valuable, worthy
➤ **Antonyms**
inconsequential, pointless, trivial, unimportant, unworthy, useless, vain, valueless, wasteful, worthless

worthy *adjective* **1 = praiseworthy**, admirable, commendable, creditable, decent, dependable, deserving, estimable, excellent, good, honest, honourable, laudable, meritorious, reliable, reputable, respectable, righteous, upright, valuable, virtuous, worthwhile ♦ *noun* **2 = dignitary**, big hitter (*informal*), big shot (*informal*), bigwig (*informal*), heavy hitter (*informal*), luminary, notable, personage

> ➤ Antonyms

adjective ≠ **praiseworthy**: demeaning, disreputable, dubious, ignoble, undeserving, unproductive, untrustworthy, unworthy, useless ♦ *noun ≠* **dignitary**. member of the rank and file, nobody, pleb, punter (*informal*)

would-be *adjective* = **budding**, self-appointed, self-styled, unfulfilled, wannabe (*informal*)

wound *noun* 1 = **injury**, cut, damage, gash, harm, hurt, laceration, lesion, slash, trauma (*Pathology*) 2 = **insult**, anguish, distress, grief, heartbreak, injury, offence, pain, pang, sense of loss, shock, slight, torment, torture, trauma ♦ *verb* 3 = **injure**, cut, damage, gash, harm, hit, hurt, irritate, lacerate, pierce, slash, wing 4 = **offend**, annoy, cut (someone) to the quick, distress, grieve, hurt, hurt the feelings of, mortify, pain, shock, sting, traumatize

wrangle *verb* 1 = **argue**, altercate, bicker, brawl, contend, disagree, dispute, fall out (*informal*), fight, have words, quarrel, row, scrap, spar, squabble ♦ *noun* 2 = **argument**, altercation, angry exchange, argy-bargy (*Brit. informal*), bagarre, barney (*informal*), bickering, brawl, clash, contest, controversy, dispute, falling-out (*informal*), quarrel, row, set-to (*informal*), slanging match (*Brit.*), squabble, tiff

wrap *verb* 1 = **cover**, absorb, bind, bundle up, cloak, encase, enclose, enfold, envelop, fold, immerse, muffle, pack, package, roll up, sheathe, shroud, surround, swathe, wind ♦ *noun* 2 = **cloak**, cape, mantle, shawl, stole
> ➤ Antonyms

verb ≠ **cover**: disclose, open, strip, uncover, unfold, unpack, unwind, unwrap

wrapper *noun* = **cover**, case, envelope, jacket, packaging, paper, sheath, sleeve, wrapping

wrap up *verb* 1 = **giftwrap**, bundle up, enclose, enwrap, pack, package 2 = **dress warmly**, muffle up, put warm clothes on, wear something warm 3 *Informal* = **end**, bring to a close, conclude, finish off, polish off, round off, terminate, tidy up, wind up 4 *Slang* = **be quiet**, be silent, button it (*slang*), button one's lip (*slang*), hold one's tongue, put a sock in it (*Brit. slang*), shut one's face (*Brit. slang*), shut one's mouth (*slang*), shut one's trap (*slang*), shut up

wrath *noun* = **anger**, choler, displeasure, exasperation, fury, indignation, ire, irritation, passion, rage, resentment, temper
> ➤ Antonyms

amusement, contentment, delight, enjoyment, gladness, gratification, happiness, joy, pleasure, satisfaction

wrathful *adjective* = **angry**, beside oneself with rage, choked, displeased, enraged, furious, incandescent, incensed, indignant, infuriated, irate, on the warpath (*informal*), pissed (*taboo slang*), pissed off (*taboo slang*), raging, wroth (*archaic*)
> ➤ Antonyms

amused, calm, contented, delighted, glad, gratified, happy, joyful, pleased, satisfied

wreath *noun* = **garland**, band, chaplet, coronet, crown, festoon, loop, ring

wreathe *verb* = **surround**, adorn, coil, crown, encircle, enfold, engarland, entwine, envelop, enwrap, festoon, intertwine, interweave, twine, twist, wind, wrap, writhe

wreck *verb* 1 = **destroy**, blow (*slang*), break, cock up (*Brit. slang*), dash to pieces, demolish, devastate, fuck up (*offensive taboo slang*), mar, play havoc with, ravage, ruin, screw up (*informal*), shatter, smash, spoil, total (*slang*), trash (*slang*), undo 2 = **go** *or* **run aground**, founder, run onto the rocks, shipwreck, strand ♦ *noun* 3 = **shipwreck**, derelict, hulk, sunken vessel 4 = **ruin**, desolation, destruction, devastation, disruption, mess, overthrow, undoing
> ➤ Antonyms

verb ≠ **destroy**: build, conserve, create, fulfil, make possible, preserve, reconstruct, salvage, save ♦ *noun ≠* **ruin**: conservation, creation, formation, fulfilment, preservation, restoration, salvage, saving

wreckage *noun* = **remains**, debris, fragments, hulk, pieces, rubble, ruin, wrack

wrench *verb* 1 = **twist**, force, jerk, pull, rip, tear, tug, wrest, wring 2 = **sprain**, distort, rick, strain ♦ *noun* 3 = **twist**, jerk, pull, rip, tug, yank 4 = **sprain**, strain, twist 5 = **blow**, ache, pain, pang, shock, upheaval, uprooting 6 = **spanner**, adjustable spanner, shifting spanner

wrest *verb* = **seize**, extract, force, take, win, wrench

wrestle *verb* = **fight**, battle, combat, contend, grapple, scuffle, strive, struggle, tussle

wretch *noun* 1 = **scoundrel**, asshole (*U.S. & Canad. taboo slang*), asswipe (*U.S. & Canad. taboo slang*), bad egg (*old-fashioned informal*), bastard (*offensive*), blackguard, bugger (*taboo slang*), cocksucker (*taboo slang*), cur, good-for-nothing, miscreant, mother (*taboo slang, chiefly U.S.*), motherfucker (*taboo slang, chiefly U.S.*), outcast, profligate, rascal, rat (*informal*), rogue, rotter (*slang, chiefly Brit.*), ruffian, scumbag (*slang*), shit (*taboo slang*), son-of-a-bitch (*slang, chiefly U.S. & Canad.*), swine, turd (*taboo slang*), vagabond, villain, worm 2 = **poor thing**, poor soul, unfortunate

wretched *adjective* 1 = **unhappy**, abject, brokenhearted, cheerless, comfortless, crestfallen, dejected, deplorable, depressed, disconsolate, dismal, distressed, doleful, downcast, down in the dumps (*informal*), forlorn, funereal, gloomy, hapless, hopeless, melancholy, miserable, pathetic, pitiable, pitiful, poor, sorry, unfortunate, woebegone, woeful, worthless 2 = **worthless**, calamitous, deplorable, inferior, miserable, paltry, pathetic, poor, sorry 3 = **shameful**, base, contemptible, crappy (*slang*), despicable, low, low-down (*informal*), mean, paltry, poxy (*slang*), scurvy, shabby, vile
➤ **Antonyms**
≠**unhappy**: carefree, cheerful, contented, happy, jovial, light-hearted, untroubled ≠**worthless**: excellent, flourishing, great, splendid, successful, thriving ≠**shameful**: admirable, decent, noble, worthy

wriggle *verb* 1 = **twist**, jerk, jiggle, squirm, turn, wag, waggle, wiggle, writhe 2 = **crawl**, slink, snake, twist and turn, worm, zigzag 3 *As in* **wriggle out of** = **manoeuvre**, crawl, dodge, extricate oneself, sneak, talk one's way out, worm ◆ *noun* 4 = **twist**, jerk, jiggle, squirm, turn, wag, waggle, wiggle

wring *verb* = **twist**, coerce, extort, extract, force, screw, squeeze, wrench, wrest

wrinkle[1] *noun* 1 = **crease**, corrugation, crinkle, crow's-foot, crumple, fold, furrow, gather, line, pucker, rumple ◆ *verb* 2 = **crease**, corrugate, crinkle, crumple, fold, furrow, gather, line, pucker, ruck, rumple
➤ **Antonyms**
verb ≠**crease**: even out, flatten, iron, level, press, smooth, straighten, unfold

wrinkle[2] *noun* = **trick**, device, dodge, gimmick, idea, plan, ploy, ruse, scheme, stunt, tip, wheeze (*Brit. slang*)

writ *noun* = **summons**, court order, decree, document

write *verb* = **record**, author (*nonstandard*), commit to paper, compose, copy, correspond, create, draft, draw up, indite, inscribe, jot down, pen, put down in black and white, put in writing, scribble, set down, take down, tell, transcribe

write off *verb* 1 = **cancel**, cross out, disregard, forget about, give up for lost, score out, shelve 2 *Informal* = **wreck**, crash, damage beyond repair, destroy, smash up, total (*slang*), trash (*slang*)

writer *noun* = **author**, columnist, essayist, hack, littérateur, man of letters, novelist, penman, penny-a-liner (*rare*), penpusher, scribbler, scribe, wordsmith

writhe *verb* = **squirm**, contort, convulse, distort, jerk, struggle, thrash, thresh, toss,
twist, wiggle, wriggle

writing *noun* 1 = **script**, calligraphy, chirography, hand, handwriting, penmanship, print, scrawl, scribble 2 = **document**, book, composition, letter, opus, publication, title, work 3 = **literature**, belles-lettres, letters

wrong *adjective* 1 = **incorrect**, erroneous, fallacious, false, faulty, inaccurate, in error, mistaken, off base (*U.S. & Canad. informal*), off beam (*informal*), off target, out, unsound, untrue, way off beam (*informal*), wide of the mark 2 = **bad**, blameworthy, criminal, crooked, dishonest, dishonourable, evil, felonious, illegal, illicit, immoral, iniquitous, not cricket (*informal*), reprehensible, sinful, under-the-table, unethical, unfair, unjust, unlawful, wicked, wrongful 3 = **inappropriate**, funny, improper, inapt, incongruous, incorrect, indecorous, infelicitous, malapropos, not done, unacceptable, unbecoming, unconventional, undesirable, unfitting, unhappy, unseemly, unsuitable 4 = **defective**, amiss, askew, awry, faulty, not working, out of commission, out of order 5 = **opposite**, inside, inverse, reverse ◆ *adverb* 6 = **incorrectly**, badly, erroneously, inaccurately, mistakenly, wrongly 7 = **amiss**, askew, astray, awry 8 **go wrong**: **a** = **fail**, come to grief (*informal*), come to nothing, fall through, flop (*informal*), go pear-shaped (*informal*), miscarry, misfire **b** = **make a mistake**, boob (*Brit. slang*), err, go astray, slip up (*informal*) **c** = **break down**, cease to function, conk out (*informal*), fail, go kaput (*informal*), go on the blink (*slang*), go phut (*informal*), malfunction, misfire **d** = **lapse**, err, fall from grace, go astray, go off the straight and narrow (*informal*), go to the bad, sin ◆ *noun* 9 = **offence**, abuse, bad *or* evil deed, crime, error, grievance, infraction, infringement, injury, injustice, misdeed, sin, transgression, trespass 10 = **wickedness**, immorality, inequity, iniquity, injustice, sinfulness, unfairness 11 **in the wrong** = **guilty**, at fault, blameworthy, in error, mistaken, off beam (*informal*), off course, off target, to be blamed ◆ *verb* 12 = **mistreat**, abuse, cheat, discredit, dishonour, dump on (*slang, chiefly U.S.*), harm, hurt, ill-treat, ill-use, impose upon, injure, malign, maltreat, misrepresent, oppress, shit on (*taboo slang*), take advantage of
➤ **Antonyms**
adjective ≠**incorrect**: accurate, correct, precise, right, true ≠**bad**: ethical, fair, fitting, godly, honest, honourable, just, lawful, legal, moral, righteous, rightful, square, upright, virtuous ≠**inappropriate**: appropriate, apt, becoming, commendable,

correct, fitting, laudable, praiseworthy, proper, seemly, sensible, suitable ♦ *adverb* ≠**incorrectly**: accurately, correctly, exactly, precisely, properly, squarely, truly ♦ *noun* ≠**offence**: favour, good deed, good turn ≠**wickedness**: decency, fairness, good, goodness, high-mindedness, honesty, lawfulness, legality, morality, propriety, virtue ♦ *verb* ≠**mistreat**: aid, do a favour, help, support, treat well

wrongdoer *noun* = **offender**, criminal, culprit, delinquent, evildoer, lawbreaker, malefactor, miscreant, sinner, transgressor, trespasser (*archaic*), villain

wrongful *adjective* = **improper**, blameworthy, criminal, dishonest, dishonourable, evil, felonious, illegal, illegitimate, illicit, immoral, reprehensible, under-the-table, unethical, unfair, unjust, unlawful, wicked

➤ **Antonyms**
ethical, fair, honest, honourable, just, lawful, legal, legitimate, moral, proper, rightful

wry *adjective* **1** = **ironic**, droll, dry, mocking, mordacious, pawky (*Scot.*), sarcastic, sardonic **2** = **contorted**, askew, aslant, awry, crooked, deformed, distorted, off the level, skewwhiff (*Brit. informal*), twisted, uneven, warped

➤ **Antonyms**
≠**contorted**: aligned, even, level, smooth, straight, unbent

Xx, Yy, Zz

Xmas *noun* = **Christmas**, Christmastide, festive season, Noel, Yule (*archaic*), Yuletide (*archaic*)

X-rays *plural noun* = **Röntgen rays** (*old name*)

yank *verb, noun* = **pull**, hitch, jerk, snatch, tug, wrench

yardstick *noun* = **standard**, benchmark, criterion, gauge, measure, par, touchstone

yarn *noun* 1 = **thread**, fibre 2 *Informal* = **story**, anecdote, cock-and-bull story (*informal*), fable, tale, tall story, urban legend, urban myth

yawning *adjective* = **gaping**, cavernous, chasmal, vast, wide, wide-open

yearly *adjective* 1 = **annual** ♦ *adverb* 2 = **annually**, every year, once a year, per annum

yearn *verb* = **long**, ache, covet, crave, desire, eat one's heart out over, hanker, have a yen for (*informal*), hunger, itch, languish, lust, pant, pine, set one's heart upon, suspire (*archaic or poetic*), would give one's eyeteeth for

yell *verb* 1 = **scream**, bawl, holler (*informal*), howl, screech, shout, shriek, squeal ♦ *noun* 2 = **scream**, cry, howl, screech, shriek, whoop
➤ **Antonyms**
verb, noun ≠**scream**: mumble, murmur, mutter, whisper

yelp *verb* = **cry**, yammer (*informal*), yap, yip (*chiefly U.S.*), yowl

yen *noun* = **longing**, ache, craving, desire, hankering, hunger, itch, passion, thirst, yearning

yes man *noun* = **sycophant**, ass-kisser (*U.S. & Canad. taboo slang*), bootlicker (*informal*), bosses' lackey, company man, crawler (*slang*), creature, minion, timeserver, toady

yet *conjunction* 1 = **nevertheless**, however, notwithstanding, still ♦ *adverb* 2 = **so far**, as yet, thus far, until now, up to now 3 = **still**, additionally, as well, besides, further, in addition, into the bargain, moreover, over and above, to boot 4 = **now**, already, just now, right now, so soon

yield *verb* 1 = **produce**, afford, bear, bring forth, bring in, earn, furnish, generate, give, net, pay, provide, return, supply 2 = **surrender**, abandon, abdicate, admit

defeat, bow, capitulate, cave in (*informal*), cede, cry quits, give in, give up the struggle, give way, knuckle under, lay down one's arms, lose, part with, raise the white flag, relinquish, resign, resign oneself, submit, succumb, throw in the towel 3 = **comply**, accede, agree, allow, bow, concede, consent, go along with, grant, permit ♦ *noun* 4 = **profit**, crop, earnings, harvest, income, output, produce, return, revenue, takings
➤ **Antonyms**
verb ≠**produce**: consume, use, use up ≠**surrender**: appropriate, commandeer, grab, hold on to, hold out, keep, maintain, reserve, retain, seize, struggle ≠**comply**: combat, counterattack, defy, oppose, resist ♦ *noun* ≠**profit**: consumption, input, loss

yielding *adjective* 1 = **submissive**, accommodating, acquiescent, biddable, compliant, docile, easy, flexible, obedient, pliant, tractable 2 = **soft**, elastic, pliable, quaggy, resilient, spongy, springy, supple, unresisting
➤ **Antonyms**
≠**submissive**: dogged, headstrong, mulish, obstinate, opinionated, perverse, stiff-necked, stubborn, tenacious, wilful

yob, yobbo *noun* = **thug**, hooligan, lout, roughneck (*slang*), ruffian

yoke *noun* 1 = **bond**, chain, coupling, ligament, link, tie 2 = **oppression**, bondage, burden, enslavement, helotry, serfdom, service, servility, servitude, slavery, thraldom, vassalage ♦ *verb* 3 = **link**, bracket, connect, couple, harness, hitch, join, tie, unite

yokel *noun* = **peasant**, boor, bucolic, clodhopper (*informal*), (country) bumpkin, country cousin, countryman, hayseed (*U.S. & Canad. informal*), hick (*informal, chiefly U.S. & Canad.*), hillbilly, hind (*obsolete*), rustic

young *adjective* 1 = **immature**, adolescent, callow, green, growing, infant, in the springtime of life, junior, juvenile, little, unfledged, youthful 2 = **new**, at an early stage, early, fledgling, newish, not far advanced, recent, undeveloped ♦ *plural noun* 3 = **offspring**, babies, brood, family, issue, litter, little ones, progeny
➤ **Antonyms**
adjective ≠**immature**: adult, aged, elderly, full-grown, grown-up, mature, old, senior

≠**new:** advanced, developed, old ♦ *plural noun* ≠**offspring:** adults, grown-ups, parents

youngster *noun* = **youth**, boy, cub, girl, juvenile, kid (*informal*), lad, lass, pup (*Informal, chiefly Brit.*), teenager, teenybopper (*slang*), urchin, young adult, young hopeful, young person, young shaver (*informal*), young 'un (*informal*)

youth *noun* **1** = **immaturity**, adolescence, boyhood *or* girlhood, early life, girlhood, juvenescence, salad days, young days **2** = **boy**, adolescent, kid (*informal*), lad, shaveling (*archaic*), stripling, teenager, young man, young shaver (*informal*), youngster **3** = **young people**, teenagers, the rising generation, the young, the younger generation
➤ **Antonyms**
≠**immaturity:** adulthood, age, later life, manhood *or* womanhood, maturity, old age ≠**boy:** adult, grown-up, OAP, pensioner, senior citizen ≠**young people:** the aged, the elderly, the old

youthful *adjective* **1** = **fresh**, active, spry, vigorous, young at heart, young looking **2** = **young**, boyish, childish, girlish, immature, inexperienced, juvenile, pubescent, puerile
➤ **Antonyms**
≠**fresh:** aged, ancient, decaying, decrepit, hoary, over the hill, tired, waning, weary ≠**young:** adult, aged, ageing, elderly, grown-up, mature, old, senile

zany *adjective* = **comical**, clownish, crazy, eccentric, goofy (*informal*), madcap, wacky (*slang*)

zeal *noun* = **enthusiasm**, ardour, devotion, eagerness, earnestness, fanaticism, fervency, fervour, fire, gusto, keenness, militancy, passion, spirit, verve, warmth, zest
➤ **Antonyms**
apathy, coolness, indifference, passivity, stoicism, torpor, unresponsiveness

zealot *noun* = **fanatic**, bigot, energumen, enthusiast, extremist, fiend (*informal*), maniac, militant

zealous *adjective* = **enthusiastic**, ablaze, afire, ardent, burning, devoted, eager, earnest, fanatical, fervent, fervid, impassioned, keen, militant, passionate, rabid, spirited
➤ **Antonyms**
apathetic, cold, cool, half-hearted, indifferent, lackadaisical, lacklustre,

languorous, listless, low-key, torpid, unenthusiastic, unimpassioned

zenith *noun* = **height**, acme, apex, apogee, climax, crest, high noon, high point, meridian, peak, pinnacle, summit, top, vertex
➤ **Antonyms**
base, bottom, depths, lowest point, nadir, rock bottom

zero *noun* **1** = **nothing**, cipher, naught, nil, nought **2** = **bottom**, lowest point *or* ebb, nadir, nothing, rock bottom

zero hour *noun* = **moment of truth**, appointed hour, crisis, moment of decision, turning point, vital moment

zest *noun* **1** = **enjoyment**, appetite, delectation, gusto, keenness, relish, zeal, zing (*informal*) **2** = **flavour**, charm, interest, kick (*informal*), piquancy, pungency, relish, savour, smack, spice, tang, taste
➤ **Antonyms**
≠**enjoyment:** abhorrence, apathy, aversion, disinclination, distaste, indifference, lack of enthusiasm, loathing, repugnance, weariness

zing *noun Informal* = **vitality**, animation, brio, dash, energy, go (*informal*), life, liveliness, oomph (*informal*), pep, pizzazz *or* pizazz (*informal*), spirit, vigour, zest, zip (*informal*)

zip *noun* **1** *Informal* = **energy**, brio, drive, get-up-and-go (*informal*), go (*informal*), gusto, life, liveliness, oomph (*informal*), pep, pizzazz *or* pizazz (*informal*), punch (*informal*), sparkle, spirit, verve, vigour, vim (*slang*), vitality, zest, zing (*informal*) ♦ *verb* **2** = **speed**, barrel (along) (*informal, chiefly U.S. & Canad.*), burn rubber (*informal*), dash, flash, fly, hurry, rush, shoot, tear, whizz (*informal*), zoom
➤ **Antonyms**
noun ≠**energy:** apathy, indifference, inertia, laziness, lethargy, listlessness, sloth, sluggishness

zone *noun* = **area**, belt, district, region, section, sector, sphere

zoom *verb* = **speed**, barrel (along) (*informal, chiefly U.S. & Canad.*), burn rubber (*informal*), buzz, dash, dive, flash, fly, hare (*Brit. informal*), hum (*slang*), hurtle, pelt, rip (*informal*), rush, shoot, streak, tear, whirl, whizz (*informal*), zip (*informal*)